Hoover's Handbook of Emerging Companies 2020

Austin, Texas

Hoover's Handbook of Emerging Companies 2020 is intended to provide readers with accurate and authoritative information about the enterprises covered in it. Hoover's researched all companies and organizations profiled, and in many cases contacted them directly so that companies represented could provide information. The information contained herein is as accurate as we could reasonably make it. In many cases we have relied on third-party material that we believe to be trustworthy, but were unable to independently verify. We do not warrant that the book is absolutely accurate or without error. Readers should not rely on any information contained herein in instances where such reliance might cause financial loss. The publisher, the editors, and their data suppliers specifically disclaim all warranties, including the implied warranties of merchantability and fitness for a specific purpose. This book is sold with the understanding that neither the publisher, the editors, nor any content contributors are engaged in providing investment, financial, accounting, legal, or other professional advice.

The financial data (Historical Financials sections) in this book are from a variety of sources. Mergent Inc., provided selected data for the Historical Financials sections of publicly traded companies. For private companies and for historical information on public companies prior to their becoming public, we obtained information directly from the companies or from trade sources deemed to be reliable. Hoover's, Inc., is solely responsible for the presentation of all data.

Many of the names of products and services mentioned in this book are the trademarks or service marks of the companies manufacturing or selling them and are subject to protection under US law. Space has not permitted us to indicate which names are subject to such protection, and readers are advised to consult with the owners of such marks regarding their use. Hoover's is a trademark of Hoover's, Inc.

Copyright © 2020 by Dun & Bradstreet. All rights reserved. No part of this book may be reproduced or transmitted in any form or by any means, electronic or mechanical, including by photocopying, facsimile transmission, recording, rekeying, or using any information storage and retrieval system, without permission in writing from Hoover's, except that brief passages may be quoted by a reviewer in a magazine, in a newspaper, online, or in a broadcast review.

10 9 8 7 6 5 4 3 2 1

Publishers Cataloging-in-Publication Data

Hoover's Handbook of Emerging Companies 2020

   Includes indexes.

   ISBN: 978-1-64141-563-7

   ISSN 1073-6433

   1. Business enterprises — Directories. 2. Corporations — Directories.

HF3010 338.7

U.S. AND WORLD BOOK SALES

Mergent Inc.

580 Kingsley Park Drive
Fort Mill, SC 29715
Phone: 704-5596961
e-mail: skardon@ftserussell.com
Web: www.mergentbusinesspress.com

Mergent Inc.

Executive Managing Director: John Pedernales

Publisher and Managing Director of Print Products : Thomas Wecera

Director of Print Products: Charlot Volny

Quality Assurance Editor: Wayne Arnold

Production Research Assistant: Davie Christna

Data Manager: Jason Horvat

MERGENT CUSTOMER SERVICE-PRINT
Support and Fulfillment Manager: Thomas Wecera 212-413-7726

ABOUT MERGENT INC.

For over 100 years, Mergent, Inc. has been a leading provider of business and financial information on public and private companies globally. Mergent is known to be a trusted partner to corporate and financial institutions, as well as to academic and public libraries. Today we continue to build on a century of experience by transforming data into knowledge and combining our expertise with the latest technology to create new global data and analytical solutions for our clients. With advanced data collection services, cloud-based applications, desktop analytics and print products, Mergent and its subsidiaries provide solutions from top down economic and demographic information, to detailed equity and debt fundamental analysis. We incorporate value added tools such as quantitative Smart Beta equity research and tools for portfolio building and measurement. Based in the U.S., Mergent maintains a strong global presence, with offices in New York, Charlotte, San Diego, London, Tokyo, Kuching and Melbourne. Mergent, Inc. is a member of the London Stock Exchange plc group of companies. The Mergent business forms part of LSEG's Information Services Division, which includes FTSE Russell, a global leader in indexes.

Abbreviations

AFL-CIO – American Federation of Labor and Congress of Industrial Organizations
AMA – American Medical Association
AMEX – American Stock Exchange
ARM – adjustable-rate mortgage
ASP – application services provider
ATM – asynchronous transfer mode
ATM – automated teller machine
CAD/CAM – computer-aided design/computer-aided manufacturing
CD-ROM – compact disc – read-only memory
CD-R – CD-recordable
CEO – chief executive officer
CFO – chief financial officer
CMOS – complementary metal oxide silicon
COO – chief operating officer
DAT – digital audiotape
DOD – Department of Defense
DOE – Department of Energy
DOS – disk operating system
DOT – Department of Transportation
DRAM – dynamic random-access memory
DSL – digital subscriber line
DVD – digital versatile disc/digital video disc
DVD-R – DVD-recordable
EPA – Environmental Protection Agency
EPS – earnings per share
ESOP – employee stock ownership plan
EU – European Union
EVP – executive vice president
FCC – Federal Communications Commission
FDA – Food and Drug Administration
FDIC – Federal Deposit Insurance Corporation
FTC – Federal Trade Commission
GATT – General Agreement on Tariffs and Trade
GDP – gross domestic product
HMO – health maintenance organization
HR – human resources
HTML – hypertext markup language
ICC – Interstate Commerce Commission
IPO – initial public offering
IRS – Internal Revenue Service
ISP – Internet service provider
kWh – kilowatt-hour
LAN – local-area network
LBO – leveraged buyout
LCD – liquid crystal display
LNG – liquefied natural gas
LP – limited partnership
Ltd. – limited
mips – millions of instructions per second
MW – megawatt
NAFTA – North American Free Trade Agreement
NASA – National Aeronautics and Space Administration
NASDAQ – National Association of Securities Dealers Automated Quotations
NATO – North Atlantic Treaty Organization
NYSE – New York Stock Exchange
OCR – optical character recognition
OECD – Organization for Economic Cooperation and Development
OEM – original equipment manufacturer
OPEC – Organization of Petroleum Exporting Countries
OS – operating system
OSHA – Occupational Safety and Health Administration
OTC – over-the-counter
PBX – private branch exchange
PCMCIA – Personal Computer Memory Card International Association
P/E – price to earnings ratio
RAID – redundant array of independent disks
RAM – random-access memory
R&D – research and development
RBOC – regional Bell operating company
RISC – reduced instruction set computer
REIT – real estate investment trust
ROA – return on assets
ROE – return on equity
ROI – return on investment
ROM – read-only memory
S&L – savings and loan
SEC – Securities and Exchange Commission
SEVP – senior executive vice president
SIC – Standard Industrial Classification
SOC – system on a chip
SVP – senior vice president
USB – universal serial bus
VAR – value-added reseller
VAT – value-added tax
VC – venture capitalist
VoIP – Voice over Internet Protocol
VP – vice president
WAN – wide-area network

Contents

Companies Profiled vi
About *Hoover's Handbook of Emerging Companies 2020* x
Using Hoover's Handbooks xi
A List-Lover's Compendium 1a
    The 300 Largest Companies by Sales in In *Mergents*
    Data Base for 2020 ....2a
    The 300 Largest Employers in In *Mergents*
    Data Base for 2020 ....4a
    Top 200 Companies by Net Income in In *Mergents*
    Data Base for 2020 ....6a
The Companies 1
The Indexes 455
    Index of Companies by Headquarters Location 457
    Index of Company Executives 483

Companies Profiled

1ST Constitution Bancorp 1
1st Source Corp. 1
ABIOMED, Inc. 2
ACM Research Inc 3
ACNB Corp 3
Addus HomeCare Corp. 3
Advanced Emissions Solutions Inc 4
AGNC Investment Corp 5
Agree Realty Corp. 5
Air Lease Corp 6
Air Transport Services Group, Inc. 7
Alarm.com Holdings Inc 8
Alerus Financial Corp 8
Alexandria Real Estate Equities Inc 8
Align Technology Inc 9
Allegiance Bancshares Inc 10
Allegiant Travel Company 10
Alpine Banks of Colorado 11
Altair Engineering Inc 11
Alteryx Inc 11
Altra Industrial Motion Corp 11
Ambac Financial Group, Inc. 12
Amedisys, Inc. 13
Amerant Bancorp Inc 15
America First Multifamily Investors LP ...15
American Business Bank (Los Angeles, CA) 15
American Express Credit Corp. 15
American Homes 4 Rent 16
American National Bankshares, Inc. (Danville, VA) 16
American Woodmark Corp. 18
Ameris Bancorp 19
AMN Healthcare Services Inc 20
ANI Pharmaceuticals Inc 21
Ansys Inc. 22
Antero Midstream Corp 23
Apogee Enterprises Inc 23
Apollo Medical Holdings Inc 24
AppFolio Inc 24
Apple Hospitality REIT Inc 24
Arbor Realty Trust Inc 24
Ares Management Corp 24
Arista Networks Inc. 25
Arrowhead Pharmaceuticals Inc. 25
Ashford Inc (Holding Co) 26
Associated Banc-Corp 26
AstroNova Inc 27
At Home Group Inc 28
Atlantic Capital Bancshares Inc 28
Atlantic Union Bankshares Corp 29
Axcelis Technologies Inc. 29
Axon Enterprise Inc 30
Axos Financial Inc 31
B Riley Financial Inc 32
B&G Foods Inc 32
BancFirst Corp. (Oklahoma City, Okla) ...33
Bandwidth Inc 35
Bank First Corp 35
Bank Of Commerce Holdings (CA) 35
Bank OZK 35
BankUnited Inc. 37
Bankwell Financial Group Inc 38

Banner Corp. 38
Bar Harbor Bankshares 39
Barrett Business Services, Inc. 40
BayCom Corp 41
BBX Capital Corp (New) 41
BCB Bancorp Inc 41
Beasley Broadcast Group Inc 42
BellRing Brands Inc 42
Berkshire Hills Bancorp Inc 42
Berry Petroleum Corp. 43
BG Staffing Inc 43
Biglari Holdings Inc (New) 43
Bio-Techne Corp 44
Biospecifics Technologies Corp. 45
BioTelemetry Inc. 46
Blackbaud, Inc. 47
Blackhawk Bancorp Inc 48
Blackstone Mortgage Trust Inc 48
BOK Financial Corp 48
Boot Barn Holdings Inc 49
Bridge Bancorp, Inc. (Bridgehampton, NY) 50
Bridgford Foods Corp. 50
Bright Horizons Family Solutions, Inc 51
Brookline Bancorp Inc (DE) 51
Brooks Automation Inc 52
BRT Apartments Corp 53
Bryn Mawr Bank Corp 54
Business First Bancshares Inc 55
Byline Bancorp Inc 55
Cabot Microelectronics Corp 55
Cactus Inc 56
Cadence Bancorporation 56
CAI International Inc 56
CalAmp Corp 57
Calavo Growers, Inc. 58
California Bancorp 59
Callaway Golf Co (DE) 59
Callon Petroleum Co. (DE) 60
Cambridge Bancorp 61
Camden National Corp. (ME) 61
Cantel Medical Corp 62
Capital Bancorp Inc (MD) 63
Capital Southwest Corp. 64
CapStar Financial Holdings Inc 64
Carbon Energy Corp (DE) 65
Care.com Inc 65
CareTrust REIT Inc 65
Carey Watermark Investors Inc 66
CarGurus Inc 66
Carolina Financial Corp (New) 66
Carrols Restaurant Group Inc 66
Cars.com Inc 67
Casa Systems Inc 67
Casella Waste Systems, Inc. 67
Cathay General Bancorp 68
Cavco Industries Inc (DE) 69
CB Financial Services Inc 69
CBB Bancorp Inc 69
CenterState Bank Corp 69
Central Garden & Pet Co 70
Central Valley Community Bancorp 73
Century Bancorp, Inc. 73

Century Communities Inc 74
Cerence Inc 74
Charles River Laboratories International Inc. 74
Chatham Lodging Trust 76
Chefs' Warehouse Inc (The) 76
Cherry Hill Mortgage Investment Corp ...77
Chesapeake Utilities Corp. 78
Chimera Investment Corp 79
Choice Hotels International, Inc. 79
Citizens Financial Services Inc 80
Civista Bancshares Inc 81
Clearway Energy Inc 81
CNB Community Bancorp Inc 82
CNB Financial Corp. (Clearfield, PA) 82
CNX Midstream Partners LP 83
Codorus Valley Bancorp, Inc. 83
Cogent Communications Holdings, Inc. .84
Cognex Corp 84
Coherent Inc 85
Cole Credit Property Trust IV Inc 86
Columbia Banking System Inc 86
Columbia Financial Inc 87
Columbus McKinnon Corp. (NY) 87
Comfort Systems USA Inc. 88
Communities First Financial Corp 89
Community Bank System Inc. 90
Community Financial Corp (The) 91
Community West Bancshares 91
Computer Programs & Systems Inc 92
Comtech Telecommunications Corp. 93
ConnectOne Bancorp Inc (New) 94
Consolidated-Tomoka Land Co. 94
Construction Partners Inc 95
Contura Energy Inc 95
Copart Inc 95
Corcept Therapeutics Inc 96
CorEnergy Infrastructure Trust Inc 97
CoreSite Realty Corp 97
Corporate Property Associates 18 Global Inc 98
CoStar Group, Inc. 98
County Bancorp, Inc. 99
Cousins Properties Inc 99
Cowen Inc 100
CRA International Inc 101
Credit Acceptance Corp (MI) 103
CubeSmart 103
Cullen/Frost Bankers, Inc. 104
Customers Bancorp Inc 106
CV Sciences Inc 108
CVB Financial Corp. 108
Cypress Semiconductor Corp. 109
Dave & Busters Entertainment Inc 110
Del Taco Restaurants Inc (New) 111
Diamond Hill Investment Group Inc. ...111
Diamondback Energy, Inc. 112
Diodes, Inc. 112
Diversified Gas & Oil PLC 113
DMC Global Inc 113
Douglas Dynamics, Inc. 114
Douglas Emmett Inc 114
Duluth Holdings Inc 115

Companies Profiled (continued)

Company	Page
Dunkin' Brands Group Inc	115
e.l.f. Beauty Inc	116
EACO Corp	116
Eagle Bancorp Inc (MD)	116
Eagle Bulk Shipping Inc	117
Eagle Pharmaceuticals, Inc.	118
Earthstone Energy Inc	119
East West Bancorp, Inc	119
Easterly Government Properties Inc	120
Eastern Co.	120
EastGroup Properties Inc	121
Ebix Inc	121
Echo Global Logistics Inc	123
Educational Development Corp	124
Eldorado Resorts Inc	124
Elevate Credit Inc	124
Ellington Financial Inc	124
Embassy Bancorp Inc	125
Emergent BioSolutions Inc	125
Energizer Holdings Inc (New)	126
Energy Recovery Inc	126
Enova International Inc	127
Ensign Group Inc	127
Entegris Inc	128
Enterprise Bancorp, Inc. (MA)	129
Enterprise Financial Services Corp	130
Envestnet Inc	130
Enviva Partners LP	132
Epam Systems, Inc.	132
EPR Properties	133
EQM Midstream Partners LP	134
Equitrans Midstream Corp	134
Equity Bancshares Inc	134
ESCO Technologies, Inc.	135
Esquire Financial Holdings Inc	135
Essex Property Trust Inc.	136
Etsy Inc	137
Evans Bancorp, Inc.	137
Evercore Inc	137
Evolution Petroleum Corp.	138
Exchange Bank (Santa Rosa, CA)	139
Exelixis Inc	139
ExlService Holdings Inc	140
Extra Space Storage Inc.	141
Extraction Oil & Gas Inc	142
F & M Bank Corp.	142
FactSet Research Systems Inc.	142
Fair Isaac Corp	144
Farmers & Merchants Bancorp (Lodi, CA)	144
Farmers National Banc Corp. (Canfield, OH)	144
Farmland Partners Inc.	145
FB Financial Corp	145
Federal Agricultural Mortgage Corp	145
Federal Home Loan Bank Boston	146
Federal Home Loan Bank Chicago	147
Federal Home Loan Bank Indianapolis	147
Federal Home Loan Bank Of Cincinnati	147
Federal Home Loan Bank Of Dallas	147
Federal Home Loan Bank of Pittsburgh	147
Federal Home Loan Bank Topeka	148
Federal Signal Corp.	148
FedNat Holding Co.	149
Fentura Financial Inc	150
Ferro Corp	150
Fidelity D&D Bancorp Inc	151
Financial Institutions Inc.	151
Finemark Holdings Inc	152
Finjan Holdings Inc	152
First Advantage Bancorp	153
First Bancorp (NC)	153
First Bancshares Inc (MS)	153
First Bank (Williamstown, NJ)	154
First Busey Corp.	154
First Business Financial Services, Inc.	155
First Capital Inc.	156
First Choice Bancorp	156
First Citizens BancShares Inc (NC)	156
First Commonwealth Financial Corp (Indiana, PA)	158
First Community Corp (SC)	159
First Defiance Financial Corp	159
First Financial Bancorp (OH)	160
First Financial Bankshares, Inc.	161
First Financial Northwest Inc	162
First Foundation Inc	162
First Guaranty Bancshares, Inc.	162
First Horizon National Corp	163
First Internet Bancorp	164
First Interstate BancSystem Inc	164
First Merchants Corp	165
First Mid Bancshares Inc	166
First Midwest Bancorp, Inc. (Naperville, IL)	167
First National Corp. (Strasburg, VA)	168
First Northern Community Bancorp	168
First Northwest Bancorp	169
First of Long Island Corp	169
First Savings Financial Group Inc	170
FirstCash Inc	170
Five Below Inc	171
Flagstar Bancorp, Inc.	172
FleetCor Technologies Inc	173
Floor & Decor Holdings Inc	175
FNB Corp	175
Forestar Group Inc (New)	176
FormFactor Inc	177
Fortinet Inc	178
Fortress Transportation & Infrastructure Investors LLC	179
Forward Air Corp	179
Four Corners Property Trust Inc	180
Fox Factory Holding Corp	180
Franklin Financial Network Inc	181
Frontdoor Inc	181
FS Bancorp (Indiana)	181
FS Bancorp Inc (Washington)	181
Funko Inc	182
FVCBankcorp Inc	182
Gaming & Leisure Properties, Inc.	182
Gannett Co Inc (New)	182
Gencor Industries Inc	183
Generac Holdings Inc	184
GEO Group Inc (The) (New)	184
German American Bancorp Inc	186
Getty Realty Corp.	187
Glacier Bancorp, Inc.	188
Gladstone Commercial Corp	188
Global Medical REIT Inc	189
Global Net Lease Inc	189
Globus Medical Inc.	190
Goldman Sachs BDC Inc	191
GrafTech International Ltd	191
Gray Television Inc	192
Great Western Bancorp Inc	192
Green Brick Partners Inc	193
Green Dot Corp	193
Green Plains Partners LP	194
Greene County Bancorp Inc	194
GreenSky Inc	195
GrubHub Inc	195
Guaranty Bancshares Inc	195
Guaranty Federal Bancshares Inc (Springfield, MO)	195
Guidewire Software Inc	196
Gulfport Energy Corp.	196
Hamilton Lane Inc	197
Hancock Whitney Corp	198
Hanmi Financial Corp	198
Hannon Armstrong Sustainable Infrastructure Capital Inc	199
HarborOne Bancorp Inc (New)	200
Harrow Health Inc	200
Hawkins Inc	201
HC2 Holdings Inc	201
Health Insurance Innovations Inc	202
Healthcare Services Group, Inc.	202
Healthcare Trust Of America Inc	203
HealthEquity Inc	204
Heartland BancCorp	204
Heartland Financial USA, Inc. (Dubuque, IA)	204
HEICO Corp	206
Heidrick & Struggles International, Inc.	207
Helios Technologies Inc	207
Heritage Commerce Corp	208
Heritage Financial Corp (WA)	208
Heritage Insurance Holdings Inc	209
Heska Corp.	209
Hi-Crush Inc	210
Hilton Grand Vacations Inc	210
Hingham Institution for Savings	211
HMN Financial Inc.	211
Holly Energy Partners LP	212
Home Bancorp Inc	212
Home BancShares Inc	213
HomeStreet Inc	214
HomeTrust Bancshares Inc.	215
Hooker Furniture Corp	215
Hope Bancorp Inc	216
Horizon Bancorp Inc	216
Houlihan Lokey Inc	217
Howard Hughes Corp.	217
Hudson Pacific Properties Inc	218
IBERIABANK Corp	219
Ichor Holdings Ltd	221
ICU Medical Inc	221
Idexx Laboratories, Inc.	222
IES Holdings Inc	223
II-VI Inc	224
Immersion Corp	225
Incyte Corporation	226
Independence Realty Trust Inc	227
Independent Bank Corp (MA)	227
Independent Bank Corporation (Ionia, MI)	228
Independent Bank Group Inc.	228
Innospec Inc	229
Innoviva Inc.	230
Inogen, Inc.	230
Installed Building Products Inc	231
Integer Holdings Corp	232
Integra LifeSciences Holdings Corp	233
Intelligent Systems Corp.	234
Interactive Brokers Group Inc	234
Invesco DB Commodity Index Tracking Fund	235
Investar Holding Corp	235
Investors Bancorp Inc (New)	236
Ionis Pharmaceuticals Inc	237
IPG Photonics Corp	237
iRadimed Corp	239
iRobot Corp	239
iShares S&P GSCI Commodity-Indexed Trust	240
J.Jill Inc	240
j2 Global Inc (New)	240
JBG SMITH Properties	241
John Bean Technologies Corp	241
John Marshall Bancorp Inc	242
Kadant Inc	242
Kearny Financial Corp (MD)	243
KEMET Corp.	243
Kennedy-Wilson Holdings Inc	244
Kentucky Bancshares Inc	245
Kilroy Realty Corp.	245
Kilroy Realty L.P.	246
Kimball Electronics Inc	246
Kinsale Capital Group Inc	246
KKR & Co Inc	246
KKR Real Estate Finance Trust Inc	247
KLX Energy Services Holdings Inc	247
Korn Ferry	247
Kraton Corp.	248
Ladder Capital Corp	249
Ladenburg Thalmann Financial Services Inc	249
Lakeland Bancorp, Inc.	250

Companies Profiled (continued)

Company	Page
Lakeland Financial Corp	251
Landmark Infrastructure Partners LP	252
Laredo Petroleum, Inc	252
LCI Industries	252
LeMaitre Vascular Inc	253
LendingTree Inc (New)	254
Level One Bancorp Inc	254
LGI Homes, Inc.	255
LHC Group Inc	255
Liberty Oilfield Services Inc	256
Life Storage Inc	256
Ligand Pharmaceuticals Inc	257
Littelfuse Inc	257
Live Oak Bancshares Inc	259
Live Ventures Inc	259
LogMeIn Inc	259
Lonestar Resources US Inc	260
LTC Properties, Inc.	260
Luminex Corp	261
Luna Innovations Inc	262
Luther Burbank Corp.	262
Lydall, Inc.	263
M/I Homes Inc	263
Macatawa Bank Corp.	265
Mackinac Financial Corp	265
Madison Square Garden Co (The) (New)	266
Majesco	266
Malibu Boats Inc	266
Malvern Bancorp Inc	266
Mammoth Energy Services Inc	266
Marcus & Millichap Inc	267
Marcus Corp. (The)	267
Marine Products Corp	268
MarineMax Inc.	269
MarketAxess Holdings Inc.	270
Marlin Business Services Corp	270
Masimo Corp.	271
Mastech Digital Inc	272
MasterCraft Boat Holdings Inc	272
Matador Resources Co	273
Match Group Inc	273
Maxus Realty Trust Inc	273
Medical Properties Trust Inc	273
Medifast Inc	274
Medpace Holdings Inc.	275
Mercantile Bank Corp.	275
Merchants Bancorp (Indiana)	276
Mercury Systems Inc	276
Meridian Bancorp Inc	277
Merit Medical Systems, Inc.	277
Meritage Hospitality Group Inc	279
Mesa Laboratories, Inc.	279
Mesabi Trust	280
Meta Financial Group Inc	280
MetroCity Bankshares Inc	281
Metropolitan Bank Holding Corp	281
Mid Penn Bancorp Inc	281
Mid-America Apartment Communities Inc	282
Middlefield Banc Corp.	282
Midland States Bancorp Inc	282
MidWestOne Financial Group, Inc.	283
Miller Industries Inc. (TN)	284
MKS Instruments Inc	285
Modine Manufacturing Co	286
Moelis & Co	287
Monmouth Real Estate Investment Corp.	287
Monolithic Power Systems Inc	288
Montage Resource Corp	289
Mountain Commerce Bancorp Inc	289
Mr Cooper Group Inc	289
MSCI Inc	290
MTS Systems Corp	291
MutualFirst Financial Inc	292
MVB Financial Corp	292
MYR Group Inc.	292
NASB Financial Inc	293
National Bank Holdings Corp	293
National Beverage Corp.	294
National Health Investors, Inc.	295
National Retail Properties Inc	296
National Storage Affiliates Trust	297
National Vision Holdings Inc.	297
Natural Alternatives International, Inc.	297
Natural Grocers By Vitamin Cottage Inc	298
Nautilus Inc	299
Nektar Therapeutics	299
Nelnet Inc	300
Neogen Corp	301
Network-1 Technologies, Inc.	302
New Residential Investment Corp	302
Newmark Group Inc.	303
NextEra Energy Partners LP	303
NexTier Oilfield Solutions Inc	303
NI Holdings Inc	303
Nicolet Bankshares Inc	303
NMI Holdings Inc	304
Nobility Homes, Inc.	304
Noble Midstream Partners LP	305
Northeast Bank (ME)	305
Northeast Community Bancorp Inc	305
Northfield Bancorp Inc (DE)	305
Northwest Indiana Bancorp	306
Norwood Financial Corp.	306
Novanta Inc	306
Novation Companies Inc	307
Nuvasive Inc	308
Nuvera Communications Inc	308
NV5 Global Inc	309
Oak Valley Bancorp (Oakdale, CA)	309
Oasis Midstream Partners LP	310
OceanFirst Financial Corp	310
Old National Bancorp (Evansville, IN)	311
Old Second Bancorp., Inc. (Aurora, Ill.)	312
Ollie's Bargain Outlet Holdings Inc	313
Omega Healthcare Investors, Inc.	313
Omnicell Inc	314
On Deck Capital Inc	315
Onto Innovation Inc.	315
OP Bancorp	316
Opus Bank (Irvine, CA)	316
OraSure Technologies Inc.	317
Orrstown Financial Services, Inc.	318
OTC Markets Group Inc	318
Pacific Mercantile Bancorp	318
Pacific Premier Bancorp Inc	319
PacWest Bancorp	319
Palatin Technologies Inc	320
Parade Technologies Ltd.	320
Paramount Group Inc	321
Parke Bancorp Inc.	321
Parsley Energy Inc	321
Patrick Industries Inc	321
Pattern Energy Group Inc	322
Paycom Software Inc	323
Paylocity Holding Corp.	323
PBF Logistics LP	323
PCB Bancorp	323
PCSB Financial Corp	323
Peapack-Gladstone Financial Corp.	324
Pebblebrook Hotel Trust	325
Pegasystems Inc	325
Pendrell Corp	326
Penn Virginia Corp (New)	327
PennyMac Financial Services Inc (New)	327
Penumbra Inc.	328
People's United Financial Inc	328
People's Utah Bancorp	330
Peoples Bancorp Inc (Marietta, OH)	331
PGT Innovations Inc	331
Phillips 66 Partners LP	332
Phillips Edison & Co Inc.	332
Physicians Realty Trust	333
Pinnacle Financial Partners Inc	333
PJT Partners Inc	335
Planet Fitness Inc	335
Plumas Bancorp Inc.	335
Polaris Infrastructure Inc	335
PotlatchDeltic Corp.	336
PQ Group Holdings Inc.	337
Preferred Apartment Communities Inc.	337
Preferred Bank (Los Angeles, CA)	338
Primerica Inc.	339
ProPetro Holding Corp	339
Proto Labs Inc	339
Provident Bancorp Inc (MD)	340
Prudential Bancorp Inc (New)	340
Pzena Investment Management Inc	340
QCR Holdings Inc	341
Qualys, Inc.	341
Quidel Corp.	342
QuinStreet, Inc.	343
Radiant Logistics, Inc.	344
Rand Worldwide Inc.	344
Rayonier Advanced Materials Inc	344
RBB Bancorp	344
RBC Bearings Inc	345
Ready Capital Corp	346
RealPage Inc	346
Realty Income Corp	347
Redwood Trust Inc	348
Regency Centers Corp	349
REGENXBIO Inc	349
Regional Management Corp	350
Reliant Bancorp Inc	350
Renasant Corp	351
Renewable Energy Group, Inc.	352
Repligen Corp.	353
Republic Bancorp, Inc. (KY)	353
Republic First Bancorp, Inc.	355
Retail Opportunity Investments Corp	356
Revere Bank (Laurel, MD)	356
Rexford Industrial Realty Inc.	356
Ring Energy Inc	357
River Financial Corp	357
Riverview Bancorp, Inc.	357
Riverview Financial Corp (New)	358
RLJ Lodging Trust	358
RMR Group Inc (The)	358
Rogers Corp.	358
Royal Gold Inc	359
S & T Bancorp Inc (Indiana, PA)	360
Sabra Health Care REIT Inc	362
Sachem Capital Corp	362
Safehold Inc	362
Salisbury Bancorp, Inc.	363
Sanchez Energy Corp	363
Sandy Spring Bancorp Inc	363
Santa Cruz County Bank (CA)	364
SB Financial Group Inc	365
SB One Bancorp	365
Scripps (EW) Company (The)	365
Seacoast Banking Corp. of Florida	367
Select Bancorp Inc (New)	368
Select Energy Services Inc	368
ServisFirst Bancshares Inc	368
Shake Shack Inc	369
Shell Midstream Partners LP	369
Shenandoah Telecommunications Co	370
Shutterstock Inc	370
Siebert Financial Corp	371
Sierra Bancorp	371
SIGA Technologies Inc.	372
Signature Bank (New York, NY)	372
Silvercrest Asset Management Group Inc	373
Simmons First National Corp.	373
Simpson Manufacturing Co., Inc. (DE)	375
Simulations Plus Inc	375
SiteOne Landscape Supply Inc	376
SLM Corp.	376
Smart Sand Inc	377
SmartFinancial Inc	377
Solaris Oilfield Infrastructure Inc	378
Somero Enterprises Inc	378
Sound Financial Bancorp Inc	378
South Jersey Industries Inc	378
South State Corp	379
Southeastern Banking Corp. (Darien, GA)	380
Southern First Bancshares, Inc.	381

Companies Profiled (continued)

Southern Missouri Bancorp, Inc. 381
Southern National Bancorp Of Virginia Inc 381
Southern Power Co 381
Southside Bancshares, Inc. 382
Spartan Motors, Inc. 383
SPS Commerce, Inc. 384
STAG Industrial Inc 384
Stamps.com Inc. 385
Standard AVB Financial Corp 386
Starwood Property Trust Inc. 386
Sterling Bancorp (DE) 387
Sterling Bancorp Inc (MI) 387
Sterling Construction Co Inc 387
Stitch Fix Inc 388
Stock Yards Bancorp Inc 388
STORE Capital Corp 389
Summit Financial Group Inc 389
Summit Hotel Properties Inc 390
Summit Materials Inc 390
Summit Midstream Partners LP 391
Summit State Bank (Santa Rosa, CA) 391
Sun Communities Inc 391
Suncrest Bank (Visalia, CA) 392
Sunrun Inc 392
Superior Group of Companies Inc 393
Superior Industries International, Inc. 393
Supernus Pharmaceuticals Inc 394
Surmodics Inc 395
SWK Holdings Corp 395
Synalloy Corp. 396
Synovus Financial Corp 396
Tactile Systems Technology Inc 397
Tallgrass Energy LP 397
Talos Energy Inc 398
TCF Financial Corp (New) 398
Tennant Co. 399
TerraForm Power Inc 400
Terreno Realty Corp 400
Tetra Tech Inc 401
Texas Capital Bancshares Inc 402
Texas Pacific Land Trust 403

Texas Roadhouse Inc 404
TGR Financial, Inc 404
The Bancorp Inc 405
The Trade Desk Inc 406
Thomasville Bancshares, Inc. 406
Tile Shop Holdings Inc 406
Timberland Bancorp, Inc. 406
Tiptree Inc 407
TopBuild Corp 407
TowneBank 407
TPG RE Finance Trust Inc 407
TPG Specialty Lending Inc 408
Transamerica Advisors Life Insurance Co 408
Transcontinental Realty Investors, Inc. 408
TransUnion 408
Trex Co Inc 409
TriCo Bancshares (Chico, CA) 410
TriState Capital Holdings Inc 410
Triumph Bancorp Inc 411
Turning Point Brands Inc 411
Turtle Beach Corp 411
Tyler Technologies, Inc. 412
U.S. Physical Therapy, Inc. 413
Ubiquiti Inc 414
UFP Technologies Inc. 414
Ultra Clean Holdings Inc 415
Union Bank (Greenville, NC) 415
United Bancshares Inc. (OH) 416
United Bankshares Inc 416
United Community Banks Inc (Blairsville, GA) 417
United Security Bancshares (CA) 418
Uniti Group Inc 419
Unity Bancorp, Inc. 419
Universal Insurance Holdings Inc 419
Univest Financial Corp 420
US Concrete Inc 421
USANA Health Sciences Inc 422
USD Partners LP 423
Vail Resorts Inc 423
Valley National Bancorp (NJ) 425
Valley Republic Bancorp 426

Vanda Pharmaceuticals Inc 426
Veeva Systems Inc 427
Verisk Analytics Inc 428
Veritex Holdings Inc 429
VICI Properties Inc 429
Victory Capital Holdings Inc (DE) 430
Viper Energy Partners LP 430
Virginia National Bankshares Corp 430
Virtusa Corp 430
VSE Corp. 431
Walker & Dunlop Inc 432
Warrior Met Coal Inc 434
Webster Financial Corp (Waterbury, Conn) 434
Wellesley Bancorp Inc 435
Wells Fargo Real Estate Investment Corp 435
WesBanco Inc 436
West Bancorporation, Inc. 437
Westbury Bancorp Inc 438
Western Alliance Bancorporation 438
Western Asset Mortgage Capital Corp 439
Western Midstream Partners LP 439
Western New England Bancorp Inc 439
Wex Inc 440
Whitestone REIT 440
Willdan Group Inc 441
Willis Lease Finance Corp 442
Wilson Bank Holding Co 442
Wingstop Inc 443
Winnebago Industries, Inc. 443
Wintrust Financial Corp (IL) 444
WisdomTree Investments, Inc. 446
World Wrestling Entertainment Inc 447
WSFS Financial Corp. 448
Wyndham Hotels & Resorts Inc 449
XPEL Inc 450
Yelp Inc 450
Yeti Holdings Inc 451
ZAGG Inc 451
Zix Corp 452
Zynex Inc 453

About Hoover's Handbook of Emerging Companies 2020

Hoover's Handbook of Emerging Companies enters its 26th year as one of America's premier sources of business information on younger, growth-oriented enterprises. Given our current economic realities, finding value in the marketplace becomes ever more difficult, and so we are particularly pleased to present this edition of Hoover's Handbook of Emerging Companies 2020 — the result of a search of our extensive database of business information for companies with demonstrated growth and the potential for future gains.

The 600 companies in this book were chosen from the universe of public US companies with sales between $10 million and $2.5 billion. Their selection was based primarily on sales growth and profitability, although in a few cases we made some rather subjective decisions about which companies we chose to include. They all have reported at least three years of sales and have sustained annualized sales growth of at least 7% during that time. Also, they are profitable (through year-end September 2016).

In addition to the companies featured in our handbooks, comprehensive coverage of more than 40,000 business enterprises is available in electronic format on our website, Hoover's Online (www.hoovers.com). Our goal is to provide one site that offers authoritative, updated intelligence on US and global companies, industries, and the people who shape them. Hoover's has partnered with other prestigious business information and service providers to bring you all the right business information, services, and links in one place.

Hoover's Handbook of Emerging Companies is one of our four-title series of handbooks that covers, literally, the world of business. The series is available as an indexed set, and also includes Hoover's Handbook of American Business, Hoover's Handbook of World Business, and Hoover's Handbook of Private Companies. This series brings you information on the biggest, fastest-growing, and most influential enterprises in the world.

We believe that anyone who buys from, sells to, invests in, lends to, competes with, interviews with, or works for a company should know as much as possible about that enterprise. Taken together, Hoover's Handbook of Emerging Companies 2016 and the other Hoover's products represent the most complete source of basic corporate information readily available to the general public.

How to use this book

This book has four sections:

1. "Using Hoover's Handbooks" describes the contents of our profiles.

2. "A List-Lover's Compendium" contains lists of the fastest-growing and most profitable companies. The lists are based on the information in our profiles, or compiled from well-known sources.

3. The company profiles section makes up the largest and most important part of the book — 600 profiles arranged alphabetically. Each profile features an overview of the company; some larger and more visible companies have an additional History section. All companies have up to five years of financial information, product information where available, and a list of company executives and key competitors.

4. At the end of this volume are the combined indexes from our 2020 editions of all Hoover's Handbooks. The information is organized into three separate sections. The first sorts companies by industry groups, the second by headquarters location. The third index is a list of all the executives found in the Executives section of each company profile. For a more thorough description of our indexing style, see page xii.

Using Hoover's Handbooks

ORGANIZATION

The profiles in this volume are presented in alphabetical order. This alphabetization is generally word by word, which means that Bridge Bancorp precedes Bridgepoint Education. You will find the commonly used name of the enterprise at the beginning of the profile; the full, legal name is found in the Locations section. If a company name starts with initials, such as BJ's Restaurants or U.S. Physical Therapy, look for it under the combined initials (in the above example, BJ or US, respectively).

Basic financial data is listed under the heading Historical Financials; also included is the exchange on which the company's stock is traded, the ticker symbol used by the stock exchange, and the company's fiscal year-end. The annual financial information contained in the profiles is current through fiscal year-ends occurring as late as January 2017. We have included certain nonfinancial developments, such as officer changes, through January 2020.

OVERVIEW

In the first section of the profile, we have tried to give a thumbnail description of the company and what it does. The description will usually include information on the company's strategy, reputation, and ownership. We recommend that you read this section first.

HISTORY

This extended section, which is available for some of the larger and more well-known companies, reflects our belief that every enterprise is the sum of its history and that you have to know where you came from in order to know where you are going. While some companies have limited historical awareness, we think the vast majority of the enterprises in this book have colorful backgrounds. We have tried to focus on the people who made the enterprises what they are today. We have found these histories to be full of twists and ironies; they make fascinating reading.

EXECUTIVES

Here we list the names of the people who run the company, insofar as space allows. In the case of public companies, we have shown the ages and pay of key officers. The published data is for the previous fiscal year, although the company may have announced promotions or retirements since year-end. The pay represents cash compensation, including bonuses, but excludes stock option programs.

Although companies are free to structure their management titles any way they please, most modern corporations follow standard practices. The ultimate power in any corporation lies with the shareholders, who elect a board of directors, usually including officers or "insiders," as well as individuals from outside the company. The chief officer, the person on whose desk the buck stops, is usually called the chief executive officer (CEO). Often, he or she is also the chairman of the board.

As corporate management has become more complex, it is common for the CEO to have a "right-hand person" who oversees the day-to-day operations of the company, allowing the CEO plenty of time to focus on strategy and long-term issues. This right-hand person is usually designated the chief operating officer (COO) and is often the president of the company. In other cases one person is both chairman and president.

A multitude of other titles exists, including chief financial officer (CFO), chief administrative officer, and vice chairman. We have always tried to include the CFO, the chief legal officer, and the chief human resources or personnel officer. Our best advice is that officers' pay levels are clear indicators of who the board of directors thinks are the most important members of the management team.

The people named in the Executives section are indexed at the back of the book.

The Executives section also includes the name of the company's auditing (accounting) firm, where available.

LOCATIONS

Here we include the company's full legal name and its headquarters, street address, telephone and fax numbers, and website, as available. The back of the book includes an index of companies by headquarters locations.

In some cases we have also included information on the geographic distribution of the company's business, including sales and profit data. Note that these profit numbers, like those in the Products/Operations section below, are usually operating or pretax profits rather than net profits. Operating profits are generally those before financing costs (interest income and payments) and before taxes, which are considered costs attributable to the whole company rather than to one division or part of the world. For this reason the net income figures (in the Historical Financials section) are usually much lower, since they are after interest and taxes. Pretax profits are after interest but before taxes.

PRODUCTS/OPERATIONS

This section lists as many of the company's products, services, brand names, divisions, subsidiaries, and joint ventures as we could fit. We have tried to include all its major lines and all familiar brand names. The nature of this section varies by company and the amount of information available. If the company publishes sales and profit information by type of business, we have included it.

COMPETITORS

In this section we have listed companies that compete with the profiled company. This feature is included as a quick way to locate similar companies and compare them. The universe of competitors includes all public companies and all private companies with sales in excess of $500 million. In a few instances we have identified smaller private companies as key competitors.

HISTORICAL FINANCIALS

Here we have tried to present as much data about each enterprise's financial performance as we could compile in the allocated space. Although the information varies somewhat from industry to industry, the following is generally present.

A five-year table, with relevant annualized compound growth rates, covers:

- Sales — fiscal year sales (year-end assets for most financial companies)
- Net income — fiscal year net income (before accounting changes)
- Net profit margin — fiscal year net income as a percent of sales (as a percent of assets for most financial firms)
- Employees — fiscal year-end or average number of employees
- Stock price — the fiscal year closing price
- P/E — high and low price/earnings ratio
- Earnings per share — fiscal year earnings per share (EPS)
- Dividends per share — fiscal year dividends per share
- Book value per share — fiscal year-end book value (common shareholders' equity per share)

The information on the number of employees is intended to aid the reader interested in knowing whether a company has a long-term trend of increasing or decreasing employment. As far as we know, we are the only company that publishes this information in print format.

The numbers on the left in each row of the Historical Financials section give the month and the year in which the company's fiscal year actually ends. Thus, a company with a September 30, 2020, year-end is shown as 9/18.

In addition, we have provided in graph form a stock price history for each company. The graphs, covering up to five years, show the range of trading between the high and the low price, as well as the closing price for each fiscal year.

Key year-end statistics in this section generally show the financial strength of the enterprise, including:

- Debt ratio (long-term debt as a percent of shareholders' equity)
- Return on equity (net income divided by the average of beginning and ending common shareholders' equity)
- Cash and cash equivalents
- Current ratio (ratio of current assets to current liabilities)
- Total long-term debt (including capital lease obligations)
- Number of shares of common stock outstanding
- Dividend yield (fiscal year dividends per share divided by the fiscal year-end closing stock price)
- Dividend payout (fiscal year dividends divided by fiscal year EPS)
- Market value at fiscal year-end (fiscal year-end closing stock price multiplied by fiscal year-end number of shares outstanding)

Per-share data has been adjusted for stock splits. The data for public companies has been provided to us by Morningstar, Inc. Other public company information was compiled by Hoover's, which takes full responsibility for the content of this section.

Hoover's Handbook of Emerging Companies

A List-Lover's Compendium

The 300 Largest Public Global Companies by Sales in Mergent's Database

Rank	Company	Sales ($mil)	Rank	Company	Sales ($mil)	Rank	Company	Sales $mil
1	Walmart Inc	$514,405	61	ITOCHU Corp (Japan)	$104,751	121	Disney (Walt) Co. (The)	$69,570
2	China Petroleum & Chemical C	$420,334	62	Nissan Motor Co., Ltd.	$104,514	122	Engie SA	$69,394
3	Royal Dutch Shell Plc	$396,556	63	Wells Fargo & Co (New)	$101,060	123	MetLife Inc	$67,941
4	PetroChina Co Ltd	$342,176	64	JXTG Holdings Inc	$100,499	124	AUDI AG	$67,851
5	BP PLC	$303,282	65	Citigroup Inc	$97,120	125	China Evergrande Group	$67,778
6	Exxon Mobil Corp	$290,212	66	Marathon Petroleum Corp.	$97,102	126	Procter & Gamble Co (The)	$67,684
7	Amazon.com Inc	$280,522	67	Petroleo Brasileiro SA	$95,584	127	JD.com, Inc.	$67,171
8	Toyota Motor Corp	$272,933	68	Siemens AG (Germany)	$94,741	128	Marubeni Corp.	$66,832
9	Volkswagen AG	$270,093	69	Bosch (Robert) GmbH (Germany)	$93,582	129	Roche Holding AG	$65,947
10	Cementos Bio-Bio S.A. (Chile)	$262,569	70	Nestle SA	$93,269	130	Renault S.A. (France)	$65,756
11	Apple Inc	$260,174	71	Anthem Inc	$92,105	131	Munich Re Group	$65,280
12	Berkshire Hathaway Inc	$247,837	72	Aedas Homes SAU	$91,413	132	Federal Reserve Bank Of N Y	$65,090
13	UnitedHealth Group Inc	$226,247	73	SK C&C Co Ltd	$91,042	133	PepsiCo Inc	$64,661
14	Glencore PLC	$219,754	74	Dell Technologies Inc	$90,621	134	Archer Daniels Midland Co.	$64,341
15	Samsung Electronics Co Ltd	$218,651	75	Uniper SE	$89,608	135	Prudential Financial Inc	$62,992
16	McKesson Corp	$214,319	76	Carrefour S.A.	$89,230	136	Mitsui & Co., Ltd.	$62,825
17	CVS Health Corp	$194,579	77	HSBC Holdings Plc	$88,667	137	Seven & i Holdings Co. Ltd.	$61,297
18	Daimler AG	$191,662	78	CITIC Ltd	$88,459	138	Toyota Tsusho Corp	$61,066
19	Total SA	$184,106	79	ENI S.p.A.	$88,109	139	Albertsons Companies Inc	$60,535
20	AmerisourceBergen Corp.	$179,589	80	Banco Santander SA	$87,740	140	Dai-ichi Life Holdings Inc	$60,237
21	Hon Hai Precision Industry C	$173,087	81	Hyundai Motor Co., Ltd.	$86,836	141	Centene Corp	$60,116
22	AT&T Inc	$170,756	82	SoftBank Group Corp	$86,707	142	Sysco Corp	$60,114
23	Industrial and Commercial Ba	$167,571	83	Enel SpA	$86,659	143	Lockheed Martin Corp	$59,812
24	Chevron Corporation	$166,339	84	Credit Agricole SA	$86,655	144	Rewe-Zentral AG (Ger, Fed	$59,300
25	Alphabet Inc	$161,857	85	Deutsche Telekom AG	$86,641	145	Alimentation Couche-Tard Inc	$59,118
26	Ford Motor Co. (DE)	$155,900	86	Hitachi, Ltd.	$85,608	146	HP Inc	$58,756
27	Costco Wholesale Corp	$152,703	87	Mexican Petroleum	$85,492	147	Unilever Plc (United Kingdom	$58,384
28	Ping An Insurance (Group) Co	$150,600	88	Reliance Industries Ltd	$85,217	148	Unilever N.V.	$58,384
29	China Construction Bank Corp	$145,666	89	Peugeot SA	$84,775	149	POSCO (South Korea)	$58,282
30	Cardinal Health, Inc.	$145,534	90	EDF Trading Ltd	$83,472	150	Repsol S.A.	$57,263
31	Mitsubishi Corp	$145,414	91	Electricite de France	$83,472	151	Tokyo Electric Power Co	$57,236
32	Honda Motor Co., Ltd.	$143,472	92	Tesco PLC	$83,156	152	Tumana, Inc.	$56,912
33	General Motors Co	$137,237	93	Assicurazioni Generali S.p.A	$83,137	153	Brookfield Asset Management	$56,771
34	Walgreens Boots Alliance Inc	$136,866	94	BNP Paribas (France)	$82,614	154	Societe Generale	$56,486
35	JPMorgan Chase & Co	$131,412	95	Johnson & Johnson	$81,581	155	Alibaba Group Holding Ltd	$56,136
36	SAIC Motor Corp Ltd	$131,165	96	Equinor ASA	$79,593	156	Nippon Steel Corp (New)	$55,786
37	Verizon Communications Inc	$130,863	97	International Business Machi	$79,591	157	Telefonica SA	$55,763
38	Agricultural Bank of China L	$127,091	98	Sony Corp	$78,250	158	Country Garden Holdings CL	$55,112
39	Fiat Chrysler Automobiles NV	$126,443	99	United Technologies Corp	$77,046	159	LG Electronics Inc	$55,020
40	Microsoft Corporation	$125,843	100	Aeon Co. Ltd. (Japan)	$76,885	160	Caterpillar Inc.	$54,722
41	General Electric Co	$121,615	101	Boeing Co.	$76,559	161	Deutsche Bahn AG	$54,655
42	Kroger Co (The)	$121,162	102	ArcelorMittal SA	$76,033	162	Anheuser Busch InBev SA/NV	$54,619
43	Fannie Mae	$120,101	103	Target Corp	$75,356	163	Korea Electric Power Corp KE	$54,380
44	PJSC Gazprom	$118,260	104	Deutscher Sparkassen-und	$74,762	164	Energy Transfer Operating LP	$54,087
45	Rosneft Oil Co OJSC (Moscow)	$118,200	105	Nippon Life Insurance Co.	$74,447	165	Energy Transfer LP	$54,087
46	Valero Energy Corp	$117,033	106	Freddie Mac	$73,598	166	CNP Assurances S.A.	$53,999
47	Federal Reserve System	$116,764	107	Airbus SE	$72,957	167	LVMH Moet Hennessy Louisi	$53,651
48	AXA SA	$115,360	108	Panasonic Corp	$72,263	168	Pfizer Inc	$53,647
49	Japan Post Holdings Co Ltd	$115,356	109	PTT Public Co Ltd	$72,216	169	Novartis AG Basel	$53,166
50	PJSC Lukoil	$115,300	110	Intel Corp	$71,965	170	America Movil SAB de CV	$52,797
51	Allianz SE	$114,506	111	United Parcel Service Inc	$71,861	171	Goldman Sachs Group Inc	$52,528
52	Phillips 66	$114,217	112	BASF SE	$71,775	172	Christian Dior SE	$52,345
53	Bayerische Motoren Werke AG	$111,634	113	Koninklijke Ahold Delhaize N	$71,600	173	Cisco Systems Inc	$51,904
54	Bank of America Corp	$110,584	114	China Communications Con	$71,365	174	China Pacific Insurance (Gro	$51,519
55	Comcast Corp	$108,942	115	Lowe's Companies Inc	$71,309	175	Royal Bank of Can (Montre	$51,310
56	Home Depot Inc	$108,203	116	Facebook Inc	$70,697	176	Lenovo Group Ltd	$51,038
57	China Railway Group Ltd	$107,648	117	Indian Oil Corp., Ltd. (Indi	$70,561	177	Vinci SA	$50,895
58	Nippon Telegraph & Telephone	$107,273	118	Deutsche Post AG	$70,487	178	Continental AG (Germ Fed	$50,852
59	China Mobile Limited	$107,122	119	Japan Post Insurance Co Ltd	$70,168	179	Shanghai Jinfeng Investm C	$50,700
60	China Railway Construction C	$106,149	120	FedEx Corp	$69,693	180	Itau Unibanco Holding S.A.	$50,422

SOURCE: MERGENT INC., DATABASE, FEBRUARY 2020

The 300 Largest Public Global Companies by Sales in Mergent's Database (continued)

Rank	Company	Sales ($ mil.)	Rank	Company	Sales ($ mil.)	Rank	Company	Sales ($ mil.)
181	Kia Motors Corp. (South Kore	$50,216	221	ZF Friedrichshafen AG (Germa	$43,687	261	NIKE Inc	$39,117
182	Morgan Stanley	$50,193	222	Volvo AB	$43,662	262	A.P. Moller - Maersk A/S	$39,019
183	Banco Bilbao Vizcaya Argenta	$49,391	223	American Express Co.	$43,281	263	LyondellBasell Industries NV	$39,004
184	Vodafone Group Plc	$49,039	224	China Vanke Co Ltd	$43,278	264	TJX Companies, Inc.	$38,973
185	Tianjin Tianhai Investment C	$48,918	225	Accenture plc	$43,215	265	Imperial Brands PLC	$38,896
186	SK Innovation Co Ltd	$48,800	226	Dow Inc	$42,951	266	ConocoPhillips	$38,727
187	MS&AD Insurance Group Ho	$48,722	227	Best Buy Inc	$42,899	267	Intesa Sanpaolo S.P.A.	$38,614
188	Tokio Marine Holdings Inc	$48,654	228	Casino Guichard PerrachS.	$42,528	268	Fresenius SE & Co KGaA	$38,398
189	Cigna Corp (New)	$48,650	229	Jardine Matheson Holdings	$42,527	269	China Shenhua Energy , Lt	$38,396
190	Denso Corp. (Japan)	$48,425	230	Tyson Foods Inc	$42,405	270	Talanx AG	$38,387
191	Mitsubishi UFJ Financial Gro	$48,360	231	Woolworths Group Ltd	$42,307	271	J.Sainsbury PLC	$37,921
192	Sumitomo Corp.	$48,212	232	Merck & Co Inc	$42,294	272	Centrica Plc	$37,902
193	Compagnie de Saint-Gobain	$47,874	233	China Unicom (Hong Kong)	$42400	273	Banco Bradesco SA	$37,545
194	State Bank Of India	$47,832	234	China United Network Coni	$42,289	274	Daiwa House Industry Co Ltd	$37,415
195	Orange	$47,393	235	Deutsche Bank AG	$42,277	275	Tech Data Corp.	$37,239
196	American International Group	$47,389	236	ACS Actividades de Construcc	$42,244	276	Brookfield Business Partners	$37,168
197	Zurich Insurance Group AG	$47,180	237	Metallurgical Corp China Ltd	$42,094	277	Swiss Re AG	$37,047
198	JBS S.A.	$46,811	238	Honeywell International Inc	$41,802	278	Mitsubishi Heavy Industries	$36,827
199	HCA Healthcare Inc	$46,677	239	Lufthansa AG (Germany, Fed.	$41,656	279	Barclays PLC	$36,730
200	Manufacturers Life Insurance	$46,621	240	United Airlines Holdings Inc	$41,303	280	Vale SA	$36,575
201	Rallye S.A. Neuilly-Sur-Sein	$46,313	241	Sanofi	$40,857	281	Enterprise Products Partners	$36,534
202	KDDI Corp	$45,875	242	Sumitomo Mitsui Financial Gr	$40,840	282	Aisin Seiki Co Ltd	$36,509
203	Toronto Dominion Bank	$45,798	243	Magna International Inc	$40,827	283	Publix Super Markets, Inc.	$36,396
204	Charter Communications Inc (	$45,764	244	Mitsubishi Electric Corp	$40,814	284	AIA Group Ltd.	$36,297
205	Bunge Ltd.	$45,743	245	Xiamen C & D Inc	$40,763	285	SK Hynix Inc	$36,277
206	Tencent Holdings Ltd.	$45,461	246	Rio Tinto Ltd	$40,522	286	Exelon Corp	$35,985
207	Bayer AG	$45,334	247	Rio Tinto Plc (United Kingdo	$40,522	287	Canon Inc	$35,937
208	Saudi Basic Industries Corp -	$45,101	248	ThyssenKrupp AG	$40,281	288	Meiji Yasuda Life Insurance	$35,810
209	T-Mobile US Inc	$44,998	249	Iberdrola SA	$40,169	289	Gazprom Neft PJSC	$35,717
210	American Airlines Group Inc	$44,541	250	innogy SE	$40,154	290	Fujitsu Ltd	$35,690
211	Wilmar International Ltd	$44,498	251	Idemitsu Kosan Co Ltd	$39,958	291	George Weston Ltd	$35,665
212	Delta Air Lines Inc (DE)	$44,438	252	Hongkong And ShangBankin	$39,831	292	Suning.com Co Ltd	$35,613
213	Baoshan Iron & Steel Co Ltd	$44,372	253	Sberbank Russia	$39,817	293	Power Corp. of Canada	$35,440
214	Tata Motors Ltd	$44,312	254	Allstate Corp	$39,815	294	Mitsubishi Chemical Holdings	$35,428
215	BHP Group Plc	$44,288	255	World Fuel Services Corp.	$39,750	295	Bank Nova Scotia Halifax	$35,409
216	BHP Group Ltd	$44,288	256	Bouygues S.A.	$39,624	296	CK Hutchison Holdings Ltd	$35,384
217	Pegatron Corp	$43,813	257	Oracle Corp	$39,506	297	JFE Holdings Inc	$34,979
218	UBS Group AG	$43,790	258	GlaxoSmithKline Plc	$39,351	298	Suzuki Motor Corp.	$34,959
219	Hanwha Corp	$43,717	259	General Dynamics Corp	$39,350	299	Loblaw Companies Ltd	$34,718
220	Zhejiang Material Industrial	$43,694	260	Deere & Co.	$39,258	300	Power Financial Corp	$34,601

The 300 Largest Public Global Companies by Employees in Mergent's Database

Rank	Company	Employees
1	Walmart Inc	2,200,000
2	Amazon.com Inc	798,000
3	Randstad NV	709,720
4	Volkswagen AG	664,496
5	Compass Group PLC (United Ki	596,452
6	G4S Plc	559,880
7	Deutsche Post AG	547,459
8	Kelly Services, Inc.	506,800
9	Agricultural Bank of China L	495,848
10	Accenture plc	492,000
11	United Parcel Service Inc	481,000
12	Sodexo	470,237
13	Jardine Matheson Holdings Lt	469,000
14	PJSC Gazprom	466,100
15	Tesco PLC	464,505
16	China Mobile Limited	459,152
17	Kroger Co (The)	453,000
18	Yum China Holdings Inc	450,000
19	Industrial and Commercial Ba	449,296
20	China Petroleum & Chemical C	423,543
21	Aeon Co. Ltd. (Japan)	419,912
22	Home Depot Inc	413,000
23	Japan Post Holdings Co Ltd	407,488
24	Bosch (Robert) GmbH (Germany	402,166
25	Tata Consultancy Services Lt	394,998
26	Berkshire Hathaway Inc	389,000
27	Siemens AG (Germany)	385,000
28	Ping An Insurance (Group) Co	376,900
29	Koninklijke Ahold Delhaize N	372,000
30	Toyota Motor Corp	370,870
31	Securitas AB	369,633
32	Nippon Telegraph & Telephone	366,156
33	Carrefour S.A.	363,862
34	Target Corp	360,000
35	International Business Machi	350,600
36	Yue Yuen Industrial (Holding	348,000
37	Starbucks Corp.	346,000
38	China Construction Bank Corp	345,971
39	Walgreens Boots Alliance Inc	342,000
40	Rosneft Oil Co OJSC (Moscow)	325,600
41	Sumitomo Electric Industries	312,930
42	Deutscher Sparkassen-und Giro	312,800
43	Deutsche Bahn AG	310,935
44	Nestle SA	308,000
45	Teleperformance SA	306,532
46	UnitedHealth Group Inc	300,000
47	Lowe's Companies Inc	300,000
48	CK Hutchison Holdings Ltd	300,000
49	Daimler AG	298,683
50	Fomento Economico Mexicano,	297,073
51	Hitachi, Ltd.	295,941
52	CVS Health Corp	295,000
53	Sberbank Russia	293,752
54	Aramark	283,500
55	General Electric Co	283,000
56	Cognizant Technology Solutio	281,600
57	X5 Retail Group NV	278,399
58	Fresenius SE & Co KGaA	276,750
59	CITIC Ltd	273,344
60	Panasonic Corp	271,869
61	TJX Companies, Inc.	270,000
62	AT&T Inc	268,000
63	PepsiCo Inc	267,000
64	Albertsons Companies Inc	267,000
65	HCA Healthcare Inc	262,000
66	China Unicom (Hong Kong) Ltd	260,964
67	Wells Fargo & Co (New)	259,000
68	State Bank Of India	257,252
69	JPMorgan Chase & Co	256,105
70	Costco Wholesale Corp	254,000
71	Jardine Cycle & Carriage Ltd	250,000
72	Engie SA	249,795
73	Continental AG (Germany, Fed	243,226
74	United Technologies Corp	243,200
75	Synnex Corp	240,900
76	FedEx Corp	239,000
77	HSBC Holdings Plc	235,217
78	Wal-Mart de Mexico S.A.B. de	234,431
79	Half Robert International In	231,600
80	Rallye S.A. Neuilly-Sur-Sein	231,544
81	JBS S.A.	230,000
82	Dairy Farm International Hol	230,000
83	P.T. Astra International TBK	226,140
84	Yamato Holdings Co., Ltd.	225,125
85	Rewe-Zentral AG (Germany, Fed	224,931
86	Disney (Walt) Co. (The)	223,000
87	Honda Motor Co., Ltd.	219,722
88	ONEX Corp (Canada)	217,000
89	Deutsche Telekom AG	215,675
90	Casino Guichard Perrachon S.	214,458
91	Capgemini SE	211,313
92	Vinci SA	211,233
93	Peugeot SA	211,013
94	McDonald's Corp	210,000
95	ArcelorMittal SA	208,583
96	Denso Corp. (Japan)	206,521
97	Infosys Ltd.	204,107
98	Bank of America Corp	204,000
99	Citigroup Inc	204,000
100	Banco Santander SA	202,713
101	BNP Paribas (France)	202,625
102	Woolworths Group Ltd	202,000
103	Publix Super Markets, Inc.	202,000
104	Flex Ltd	200,000
105	Jabil Inc	200,000
106	Fiat Chrysler Automobiles NV	198,545
107	George Weston Ltd	197,000
108	Loblaw Companies Ltd	197,000
109	Accor SA	196,020
110	Canon Inc	195,056
111	America Movil SAB de CV	194,431
112	ACS Actividades de Construcc	191,823
113	Ford Motor Co. (DE)	190,000
114	Comcast Corp	190,000
115	Darden Restaurants, Inc. (Un	184,514
116	Renault S.A. (France)	183,002
117	Dollar Tree Inc	182,100
118	Compagnie de Saint-Gobain	181,001
119	J.Sainsbury PLC	179,900
120	JD.com, Inc.	178,927
121	Marriott International, Inc.	176,000
122	Industria De Diseno Textil I	174,386
123	Anheuser Busch InBev SA/NV	172,603
124	Veolia Environnement	171,495
125	Hilton Worldwide Holdings In	169,000
126	Prosegur Compania De Segurid	167,987
127	Lear Corp.	164,100
128	General Motors Co	164,000
129	Royal Mail Plc	161,978
130	Boeing Co.	161,100
131	ThyssenKrupp AG	161,096
132	Nissan Motor Co., Ltd.	160,183
133	Wipro Ltd	160,000
134	ITOCHU Corp (Japan)	158,517
135	Glencore PLC	158,000
136	Dell Technologies Inc	157,000
137	LVMH Moet Hennessy Louis Vui	156,088
138	Schneider Electric SE	155,286
139	Unilever Plc (United Kingdom	155,000
140	Unilever N.V.	155,000
141	Atento SA	153,038
142	Metro AG (New)	152,426
143	Electricite de France	152,033
144	EDF Trading Ltd	151,073
145	Orange	150,711
146	Societe Generale	149,022
147	Aisin Seiki Co Ltd	148,359
148	Shoprite Holdings, Ltd.	147,268
149	ABB Ltd	146,600
150	ZF Friedrichshafen AG (Germa	146,148
151	Fujitsu Ltd	145,845
152	Mitsubishi Electric Corp	145,817
153	Mitsubishi UFJ Financial Gro	144,700
154	Seven & i Holdings Co. Ltd.	144,628
155	Verizon Communications Inc	144,500
156	Microsoft Corporation	144,000
157	Bridgestone Corp. (Japan)	143,509
158	Sun Art Retail Group Ltd.	143,143
159	Allianz SE	142,460
160	Tyson Foods Inc	141,000
161	Aptiv PLC	141,000
162	ABM Industries, Inc.	140,000
163	Grupo Bimbo SAB de CV (Mexic	138,432
164	Associated British Foods Plc	138,097
165	Nidec Corp	137,791
166	Fast Retailing Co., Ltd.	137,281
167	Apple Inc	137,000
168	Oracle Corp	136,000
169	Lufthansa AG (Germany, Fed.	135,534
170	Zug Estates Holding AG	135,400
171	Johnson & Johnson	135,100
172	Dollar General Corp	135,000
173	Gap Inc	135,000
174	Bayerische Motoren Werke AG	134,682
175	WPP Plc (New)	134,281
176	Cencosud SA	133,846
177	Airbus SE	133,671
178	Elior SCA	132,000
179	China Evergrande Group	131,694
180	Country Garden Holdings Co L	131,387
181	Macy's Inc	130,000
182	DXC Technology Co	130,000
183	Kohl's Corp.	129,000

SOURCE: HOOVER'S, INC., DATABASE, JANUARY 2020

The 300 Largest Public Global Companies by Employees in Mergent's Database (continued)

Rank	Company	Employees	Rank	Company	Employees	Rank	Company	Employees
184	American Airlines Group Inc	128,900	223	Volvo AB	105,175	262	Organizacion Soriana, S.A.B.	97,154
185	Toshiba Corp	128,697	224	Schlumberger Ltd	105,000	263	Procter & Gamble Co (The)	97,000
186	Christian Dior SE	128,637	225	Wesfarmers Ltd.	105,000	264	SAP SE	96,498
187	NTT Data Corp	126,953	226	TDK Corp	104,781	265	3M Co	96,163
188	Wendel	126,362	227	Total SA	104,460	266	AutoZone, Inc.	96,000
189	Nippon Steel Corp (New)	125,960	228	Sanofi	104,226	267	Nichii Gakkan Co. (Japan)	95,992
190	Banco Bilbao Vizcaya Argenta	125,627	229	Mitsubishi Corp	104,168	268	GlaxoSmithKline Plc	95,490
191	Novartis AG Basel	125,161	230	AXA SA	104,065	269	Ericsson	95,359
192	Best Buy Inc	125,000	231	Caterpillar Inc.	104,000	270	British American Tobacco Plc	95,239
193	Mexican Petroleum	124,818	232	Johnson Controls Internation	104,000	271	Charter Communications Inc (	95,100
194	Bidvest Group Ltd	123,841	233	Morrison (Wm.) Supermarkets	103,630	272	Penney (J.C.) Co.,Inc. (Hold	95,000
195	Hennes & Mauritz AB	123,283	234	Nokia Corp	103,083	273	Ferrovial SA	94,905
196	Barrett Business Services, I	122,958	235	Abbott Laboratories	103,000	274	Mitsubishi Heavy Industries	93,173
197	Poste Italiane SpA	122,665	236	General Dynamics Corp	102,900	275	Swire Pacific Ltd. (Hong Kon	93,000
198	Atos Origin	122,110	237	China Life Insurance Co Ltd	102,817	276	Bloomin' Brands Inc	93,000
199	Telefonica SA	120,138	238	Carnival Plc	102,000	277	SG Holdings Co Ltd	92,982
200	Bouygues S.A.	119,836	239	Alibaba Group Holding Ltd	101,958	278	Ricoh Co Ltd	92,663
201	Bertelsmann AG (Germany, Fed	119,089	240	Bank Nova Scotia Halifax	101,813	279	Safran	92,639
202	Alphabet Inc	118,899	241	Suzuki Motor Corp.	101,523	280	Koc Holdings AS	92,631
203	BASF SE	118,371	242	Telefonaktiebolaget LM Erics	100,735	281	Leoni AG	92,549
204	Cie Generale des Etablisseme	117,393	243	Itau Unibanco Holding S.A.	100,300	282	Pfizer Inc	92,400
205	Tenet Healthcare Corp.	115,500	244	China National Building Mate	100,218	283	Intesa Sanpaolo S.P.A.	92,117
206	Royal Philips NV	115,392	245	S.A.C.I. Falabella (Chile)	100,155	284	SoftBank Group Corp	92,069
207	Surgutneftegas PJSC	115,000	246	FirstGroup Plc	100,046	285	United Airlines Holdings Inc	92,000
208	Faurecia	114,693	247	Brookfield Asset Management	100,000	286	Whirlpool Corp	92,000
209	Sony Corp	114,400	248	XPO Logistics, Inc.	100,000	287	Carnival Corp	92,000
210	Honeywell International Inc	114,000	249	WPP AUNZ Ltd	100,000	288	Deutsche Bank AG	91,737
211	Valeo	113,600	250	Sumitomo Mitsui Financial Gr	99,800	289	AUDI AG	91,674
212	Fresenius Medical Care AG &	112,658	251	East Japan Railway Co.	99,034	290	Sumitomo Corp.	91,362
213	ICICI Bank Ltd (India)	112,360	252	Eaton Corp plc	99,000	291	Indofood Sukses Makmur TBK	91,217
214	WH Group Ltd	112,000	253	Vodafone Group Plc	98,996	292	Grupo Aval Acciones Y Valore	91,191
215	Bayer AG	110,838	254	Minebea Mitsumi Inc	98,741	293	Companhia Brasileira de Dist	91,106
216	Intel Corp	110,800	255	Banco Bradesco SA	98,605	294	Wilmar International Ltd	90,000
217	NEC Corp	110,595	256	En+ Group Plc	98,000	295	Northrop Grumman Corp	90,000
218	First Pacific Co. Ltd.	110,394	257	Unicredit SpA	97,775	296	Medtronic PLC	90,000
219	Lockheed Martin Corp	110,000	258	Roche Holding AG	97,735	297	CBRE Group Inc	90,000
220	Alimentation Couche-Tard Inc	109,000	259	FIH Mobile Ltd	97,484	298	Jones Lang LaSalle Inc	90,000
221	BT Group Plc	106,700	260	SGS SA	97,368	299	Metro Inc	90,000
222	Danone	105,783	261	Sime Darby Plantation Bhd	97,223	300	PT Bank Rakyat	89,943

The 300 Largest Public Global Companies by Net Income in Mergent's Database

Rank	Company	Net Income ($ mil.)	Rank	Company	Net Income ($ mil.)	Rank	Company	Net Income ($ mil.)
1	Apple Inc	$59,531	61	Total SA	$8,631	121	3M Co	$5,349
2	British American Tobacco Plc	$50,695	62	Home Depot Inc	$8,630	122	PNC Financial Services Group	$5,338
3	Berkshire Hathaway Inc	$44,940	63	Nippon Telegraph & Telephone	$8,567	123	HP Inc	$5,327
4	Industrial and Commercial Ba	$43,957	64	Toronto Dominion Bank	$8,414	124	AbbVie Inc	$5,309
5	Samsung Electronics Co Ltd	$38,781	65	Reckitt Benckiser Group Plc	$8,336	125	SAIC Motor Corp Ltd	$5,288
6	China Construction Bank Corp	$37,068	66	Allianz SE	$8,155	126	Mitsubishi Corp	$5,275
7	Alphabet Inc	$30,736	67	General Motors Co	$8,014	127	United Technologies Corp	$5,269
8	Verizon Communications Inc	$30,101	68	Anheuser Busch InBev SA/NV	$7,996	128	China Overseas Land & Invest	$5,216
9	AT&T Inc	$29,450	69	Tata Consultancy Services Lt	$7,947	129	McDonald's Corp	$5,192
10	Agricultural Bank of China	$28,946	70	Banco Santander SA	$7,935	130	Banco Bradesco SA	$5,159
11	JPMorgan Chase & Co	$24,441	71	Philip Morris International	$7,911	131	Abengoa, S.A.	$5,128
12	Cementos Bio-Bio S.A. (Chile)	$23,859	72	Prudential Financial Inc	$7,863	132	Phillips 66	$5,106
13	Toyota Motor Corp	$23,487	73	China Petroleum & Chemical C	$7,855	133	Lockheed Martin Corp	$5,046
14	Wells Fargo & Co (New)	$22,183	74	Novartis AG Basel	$7,703	134	Walgreens Boots Alliance Inc	$5,024
15	Facebook Inc	$22,112	75	Ford Motor Co. (DE)	$7,602	135	National Grid plc	$4,988
16	Pfizer Inc	$21,308	76	Toshiba Corp	$7,572	136	BlackRock Inc	$4,970
17	Intel Corp	$21,053	77	AXA SA	$7,443	137	China Life Insurance Co Ltd	$4,956
18	Exxon Mobil Corp	$19,710	78	Sprint Corp (New)	$7,389	138	Saudi Basic Industries Corp –	$4,915
19	Bank of America Corp	$18,232	79	Nestle SA	$7,360	139	United Parcel Service Inc	$4,910
20	China Mobile Limited	$17,561	80	BASF SE	$7,286	140	LyondellBasell Industries NV	$4,879
21	Svenska Cellulosa AB SCA	$17,287	81	Unilever Plc (United Kingdom	$7,256	141	PepsiCo Inc	$4,857
22	Microsoft Corporation	$16,571	82	Unilever N.V.	$7,256	142	SAP SE	$4,817
23	Micron Technology Inc.	$14,135	83	PJSC Lukoil	$7,244	143	E.ON SE	$4,705
24	Ping An Insurance (Group) Co	$13,690	84	Itau Unibanco Holding S.A.	$7,215	144	Hon Hai Precision Industry C	$4,679
25	Volkswagen AG	$13,611	85	Bank of Japan	$7,202	145	Lloyds Banking Group Plc	$4,669
26	Sberbank Russia	$12,980	86	Sumitomo Mitsui Financial Gr	$7,157	146	Gilead Sciences Inc	$4,628
27	Royal Dutch Shell Plc	$12,977	87	Nissan Motor Co., Ltd.	$7,034	147	Sony Corp	$4,622
28	Daimler AG	$12,617	88	NTT DoCoMo Inc	$7,012	148	Australia & New Zealand Bank	$4,616
29	Disney (Walt) Co. (The)	$12,598	89	Alecta pensionsforsakring, om	$6,979	149	AFLAC Inc.	$4,604
30	PJSC Gazprom	$12,355	90	China Shenhua Energy Co., Lt	$6,921	150	Equinor ASA	$4,590
31	Broadcom Inc (DE)	$12,259	91	Commonwealth Bank of Austral	$6,888	151	FedEx Corp	$4,572
32	Burlington Northern & Santa F	$12,119	92	Honeywell International Inc	$6,765	152	ArcelorMittal SA	$4,568
33	Comcast Corp	$11,731	93	Siemens AG (Germany)	$6,726	153	Enel SpA	$4,530
34	Taiwan Semiconductor Manufac	$11,571	94	CVS Health Corp	$6,622	154	Starbucks Corp.	$4,518
35	Mitsubishi UFJ Financial Gro	$11,566	95	Unicredit SpA	$6,561	155	CK Hutchison Holdings Ltd	$4,491
36	Naspers Ltd	$11,357	96	ING Groep NV	$6,550	156	21st Century Fox Inc	$4,464
37	Hongkong And Shanghai Bankin	$11,328	97	Bank Nova Scotia Halifax	$6,368	157	Biogen Inc	$4,431
38	Kraft Heinz Co (The)	$10,999	98	Sun Hung Kai Properties Ltd	$6,366	158	Gazprom Neft PJSC	$4,381
39	Tencent Holdings Ltd.	$10,989	99	U.S. Bancorp (DE)	$6,218	159	Canadian National Railway Co	$4,375
40	HSBC Holdings Plc	$10,798	100	LVMH Moet Hennessy Louis Vui	$6,148	160	Credit Agricole SA	$4,374
41	UnitedHealth Group Inc	$10,558	101	Novo-Nordisk AS	$6,140	161	Swire Properties Ltd.	$4,345
42	Boeing Co.	$10,460	102	Renault S.A. (France)	$6,130	162	Japan Post Holdings Co Ltd	$4,338
43	Bayerische Motoren Werke AG	$10,333	103	AIA Group Ltd.	$6,120	163	China Vanke Co Ltd	$4,311
44	Visa Inc	$10,301	104	Link Real Estate Investment	$6,113	164	L'Oreal S.A.	$4,293
45	Altria Group Inc	$10,222	105	Morgan Stanley	$6,111	165	Goldman Sachs Group Inc	$4,286
46	Alibaba Group Holding Ltd	$10,210	106	Union Pacific Corp	$5,966	166	AUDI AG	$4,262
47	Sanofi	$10,110	107	Westpac Banking Corp	$5,838	167	Banco Bilbao Vizcaya Argenta	$4,218
48	Amazon.com Inc	$10,073	108	Glencore PLC	$5,777	168	Industria De Diseno Textil I	$4,195
49	SK Hynix Inc	$9,982	109	International Business Machi	$5,753	169	Fiat Chrysler Automobiles NV	$4,185
50	Honda Motor Co., Ltd.	$9,976	110	Safran	$5,742	170	Singapore Telecommunications	$4,162
51	Walmart Inc	$9,862	111	Rolls Royce Holdings Plc	$5,682	171	Kweichow Moutai Co., Ltd.	$4,161
52	SoftBank Group Corp	$9,784	112	Freddie Mac	$5,625	172	Bank of Montreal (Quebec)	$4,151
53	Procter & Gamble Co (The)	$9,750	113	CITIC Ltd	$5,618	173	PTT Public Co Ltd	$4,149
54	Royal Bank of Canada (Montre	$9,444	114	Lloyds Bank plc	$5,591	174	Deutsche Telekom AG	$4,149
55	BNP Paribas (France)	$9,301	115	Hongkong Land Holdings Ltd	$5,585	175	National Australia Bank Ltd.	$4,142
56	Chevron Corporation	$9,195	116	Reliance Industries Ltd	$5,545	176	Jardine Strategic Holdings L	$4,119
57	Roche Holding AG	$8,846	117	Vale SA	$5,507	177	Bank of New York Mellon Corp	$4,090
58	Bayer AG	$8,794	118	Investor AB	$5,402	178	Valero Energy Corp	$4,065
59	Intesa Sanpaolo S.P.A.	$8,770	119	KDDI Corp	$5,392	179	CME Group Inc	$4,063
60	Rio Tinto Ltd	$8,762	120	NextEra Energy Inc	$5,378	180	Accenture plc	$4,060

SOURCE: MERGENT INC., FEBRUARY 2020

The 300 Largest Public Global Companies by Net Income in Mergent's Database (continued)

Rank	Company	Net Income ($ mil.)	Rank	Company	Net Income ($ mil.)	Rank	Company	Net Income ($ mil.)
181	ENI S.p.A.	$4,045	221	Dai-ichi Life Holdings Inc	$3,427	261	Henkel AG & Co KGAA	$3,020
182	Canadian Imperial Bank Of Co	$4,011	222	China Yangtze Power Co Ltd	$3,421	262	Denso Corp. (Japan)	$3,019
183	MetLife Inc	$4,010	223	Hitachi, Ltd.	$3,418	263	Ford Motor Credit Company LL	$3,007
184	Country Garden Holdings Co L	$4,005	224	Toyota Motor Credit Corp.	$3,410	264	Vodafone Group Plc	$3,007
185	Porsche Automobil Holding SE	$3,994	225	JXTG Holdings Inc	$3,408	265	Zurich Insurance Group AG	$3,004
186	Boc Hong Kong Holdings Ltd	$3,976	226	BP PLC	$3,389	266	AstraZeneca Plc	$3,001
187	Diageo Plc	$3,974	227	Mondelez International Inc	$3,381	267	Dominion Energy Inc (New)	$2,999
188	Mitsui & Co., Ltd.	$3,941	228	Norges Bank (Norway)	$3,373	268	Tokyo Electric Power Company	$2,995
189	Mastercard Inc	$3,915	229	Surgutneftegas PJSC	$3,367	269	Eaton Corp plc	$2,985
190	Henderson Land Development C	$3,894	230	Societe Generale	$3,364	270	New World Development Co. Ltd.	$2,974
191	Chubb Ltd	$3,861	231	Iberdrola SA	$3,361	271	AEGON NV	$2,960
192	CK Asset Holdings Ltd	$3,855	232	Japan Post Bank Co Ltd	$3,322	272	Orix Corp	$2,949
193	DowDuPont Inc	$3,844	233	Transneft	$3,321	273	Baoshan Iron & Steel Co Ltd	$2,946
194	Anthem Inc	$3,843	234	Applied Materials, Inc.	$3,313	274	China Resources Land Ltd	$2,945
195	Rosneft Oil Co OJSC (Moscow)	$3,840	235	CSX Corp	$3,309	275	Danone	$2,941
196	Oracle Corp	$3,825	236	Bosch (Robert) GmbH (Germany	$3,300	276	Celgene Corp	$2,940
197	EDF Trading Ltd	$3,804	237	Scentre Group	$3,298	277	Target Corp	$2,934
198	Electricite de France	$3,804	238	Vinci SA	$3,293	278	Unibail-Rodamco SE	$2,924
199	Cnooc Ltd.	$3,792	239	DBS Group Holdings Ltd.	$3,272	279	General Dynamics Corp	$2,912
200	Qatar National Bank	$3,788	240	Deutsche Post AG	$3,252	280	Sumitomo Corp.	$2,905
201	Jardine Matheson Holdings Lt	$3,785	241	Danske Bank A/S	$3,239	281	T-Mobile US Inc	$2,888
202	Hyundai Motor Co., Ltd.	$3,783	242	Danske Bank Plc	$3,239	282	BT Group Plc	$2,855
203	iTOCHU Corp (Japan)	$3,770	243	Northrop Grumman Corp	$3,229	283	Lufthansa AG (Germany, Fed.	$2,834
204	Telefonica SA	$3,754	244	Prudential Plc	$3,227	284	Baidu Inc	$2,812
205	China Evergrande Group	$3,745	245	Allstate Corp	$3,189	285	Las Vegas Sands Corp	$2,806
206	Central Japan Railway Co.	$3,725	246	Anglo American Plc (United K	$3,166	286	Enterprise Products Partners	$2,799
207	BHP Group Plc	$3,705	247	China Communications Constru	$3,163	287	Wharf (Holdings) Ltd (The)	$2,799
208	BHP Group Ltd	$3,705	248	Carnival Plc	$3,152	288	Deutscher Sparkassen-und Giro	$2,798
209	Texas Instruments, Inc.	$3,682	249	Carnival Corp	$3,152	289	National Westminster Bank Pl	$2,789
210	Nordea Bank ABp	$3,633	250	Costco Wholesale Corp	$3,134	290	RWE AG	$2,775
211	Continental AG (Germany, Fed	$3,578	251	Orsted A/S	$3,129	291	Newell Brands Inc	$2,749
212	Delta Air Lines Inc (DE)	$3,577	252	Merck KGaA (Germany)	$3,117	292	Shinhan Financial Group Co.	$2,737
213	Suncor Energy Inc	$3,556	253	KB Financial Group, Inc.	$3,106	293	American Express Co.	$2,736
214	Stryker Corp	$3,553	254	Medtronic PLC	$3,104	294	East Japan Railway Co.	$2,721
215	PetroChina Co Ltd	$3,503	255	Oversea-Chinese Banking Corp	$3,104	295	Novatek Joint Stock Co	$2,705
216	Japan Tobacco Inc.	$3,488	256	KBC Group NV	$3,087	296	Formosa Petrochemical Corp	$2,704
217	Lowe's Companies Inc	$3,447	257	Indian Oil Corp., Ltd. (Indi	$3,061	297	Saudi Telecom Co	$2,702
218	Airbus SE	$3,444	258	Duke Energy Corp	$3,059	298	Nippon Life Insurance Co.	$2,701
219	Gree Electric Appliances Inc	$3,442	259	NVIDIA Corp	$3,047	299	Exelon Generation Co LLC	$2,694
220	Marathon Petroleum Corp.	$3,432	260	Tyson Foods Inc	$3,024	300	Banco Santander Brasil SA	$2,694

Hoover's Handbook of Emerging Companies 2020

1ST Constitution Bancorp

EXECUTIVES
Vice President, Tom Berger
Senior Vice President Chief Accounting Officer, Naqi Naqvi
Vice President Commercial Loans, Steve Landau
Auditors: BDO USA, LLP

LOCATIONS
HQ: 1ST Constitution Bancorp
  2650 Route 130, P.O. Box 634, Cranbury, NJ 08512
Phone: 609 655-4500
Web: www.1stconstitution.com

COMPETITORS
Amboy Bancorp
Bank of America
Brunswick Bancorp
Hudson City Bancorp
OceanFirst Financial
PNC Financial
Provident Financial Services
Sovereign Bank
Sun Bancorp (NJ)
Wells Fargo

HISTORICAL FINANCIALS
Company Type: Public

Income Statement — FYE: December 31

	ASSETS ($ mil.)	NET INCOME ($ mil.)	INCOME AS % OF ASSETS	EMPLOYEES
12/18	1,177.8	12.0	1.0%	197
12/17	1,079.2	6.9	0.6%	185
12/16	1,038.2	9.2	0.9%	206
12/15	967.9	8.6	0.9%	183
12/14	956.7	4.3	0.5%	187
Annual Growth	5.3%	29.0%	—	1.3%

2018 Year-End Financials
Return on assets: 1.0%
Return on equity: 10.0%
Long-term debt ($ mil.): —
No. of shares (mil.): 8.6
Sales ($ mil): 59.3
Dividends
  Yield: 1.2%
  Payout: 23.3%
Market value ($ mil.): 172.0

	STOCK PRICE ($) FY Close	P/E High/Low	PER SHARE ($) Earnings	Dividends	Book Value
12/18	19.93	16 13	1.40	0.26	14.77
12/17	18.30	23 19	0.83	0.16	13.81
12/16	18.70	16 10	1.14	0.10	13.11
12/15	12.87	12 10	1.07	0.00	12.72
12/14	10.89	19 17	0.58	0.00	11.63
Annual Growth	16.3%	— —	24.6%	—	6.2%

1st Source Corp

Need a bank? Don't give it a 2nd thought. Contact 1st Source Corporation parent of 1st Source Bank which provides commercial and consumer banking services through some 80 branches in northern Indiana and southwestern Michigan. The bank offers deposit accounts; business agricultural and consumer loans; residential and commercial mortgages; credit cards; and trust services. Its specialty finance group provides financing for aircraft automobile fleets trucks and construction and environmental equipment through about two-dozen offices nationwide; such loans account for nearly half of 1st Source's portfolio.

Operations
1st Source Bank subsidiary Specialty Finance Group offers specialized financing for new and used private and cargo aircraft automobiles and light trucks for leasing and rental agencies medium and heavy duty trucks and construction and environmental equipment. Another subsidiary 1st Source Insurance provides commercial and retail property/casualty coverage and life and health coverage. 1st Source Corporation Investment Advisors serves trust and investment clients of 1st Source Bank as well as the investment advisor of Wasatch Mutual Funds.

Geographic Reach
Indiana-based 1st Source serves customers across around 20 counties in Michigan and its home state.

Sales and Marketing
1st Source offers commercial and agricultural loans and leases to the transportation construction and real estate sectors. It offers retail loans to individuals.

Financial Performance
1st Source Corporation's revenues have been climbing for the past five years. Similarly net income has been on an upward trajectory.

In 2017 revenue increased 10% to a record $284.3 million as both interest and non-interest income rose. Net interest income grew 9% while non-interest income (including equipment rentals trust and wealth advisory fees and gains on investment securities) grew 11%.

Thanks to the higher revenue net income rose 18% to $68.1 million in 2017.

The company ended 2017 with $78 million in cash and cash equivalents a 28% decline from what it had at the end of 2016. Operating activities provided some $113 million and financing activities provided another $315 million but investment activities used $462 million that year.

Strategy
1st Source has been investing in its technology to better serve its customers. It invested $1.3 million on a new customer relationship management system during 2017 and it expects to continue development and implementation of that project. It also spent $2.2 million on cyber security initiatives that year. Additionally the company is increasing the bandwidth at its branches.

When it believes it can serve a new customer base the bank adds new branches to its network. In 2018 it opened a location on the campus of Indiana University South Bend. However like all banking companies 1st Source has seen a decline in transactions at its branches as customers embrace mobile banking. During 2017 the company consolidated three locations.

To improve its mobile experience 1st Source offers live customer support via Facebook Messenger.

EXECUTIVES
Chairman and CEO, Christopher J. (Chris) Murphy, age 72, $726,923 total compensation
EVP Administration Secretary and General Counsel, John B. Griffith, age 61, $328,429 total compensation
EVP CFO and Treasurer, Andrea G. Short, age 56, $275,769 total compensation
President 1st Source Bank, James R. Seitz, age 66, $325,010 total compensation
SVP and Chief Credit Officer 1st Source Bank, Jeffrey L. Buhr, $226,565 total compensation
President 1st Source Insurance, John Ball
Vice President, Sean Brady
Vice President Of Sales Officer, Scott Carter
Assistant Vice President Construction Equipment Financing Sales, Robert Mater
Assistant Vice President, Amy Wagoner
Vice President, Rick Michalski
Vice President, John Lutz
Vice President, Luke Squires
Assistant Vice President, Adam Hamilton
Vice President, Dave Smedley
Senior Vice President Online Home Banking Division, Jim Seitz
Asstant Vice President Small Business Banking, Julie Herring
Assistant Vice President, Michele Miller
Assistant Vice President Manager Of Tale, Janet Hughes
Vice President andAmp; Controller Loan Accounting, Dave Crim
Vice President And Trust Officer, Alberta Barker
Vice President, David Silvers
Vice President, Denise Myers
Vice President Trust Tax Manager, Pam Stearns
Assistant Vice President, Bryan Byers
Vice President And Retirement Services Manager, Steven Perlewitz
Assistant Vice President Infrastructure And Networks, Steven Moore
Vice President And Trust Officer, Michael Evans
Vice President, Richard Curran
Assistant Vice President, Mark Taylor
Vice President, Robert Jamieson
Auditors: BKD LLP

LOCATIONS
HQ: 1st Source Corp
  100 North Michigan Street, South Bend, IN 46601
Phone: 574 235-2000
Web: www.1stsource.com

PRODUCTS/OPERATIONS

2017 Sales

	$ mil.	% of total
Interest		
Loans & leases	194.7	62
Taxable investment securities	13.7	4
Tax-exempt investment securities	2.6	1
Other	1.4	-
Interest expenses		
Non-interest		
Equipment rentals	30.4	10
Trust fees	21.0	7
Debit card income	11.8	4
Service charges on deposit accounts	9.6	3
Insurance commissions	5.9	2
Mortgage banking	4.8	2
Gains on investment securities available-for-sale	4.3	1
Other	10.9	4
Total	**284.3**	**100**

Selected Subsidiaries
1st Source Bank
  1st Source Capitol Corporation
  1st Source Corporation Investment Advisors Inc.
  1st Source Insurance Inc.
  1st Source Solar 1 LLC
  1st Source Specialty Finance Inc.
  Michigan Transportation Finance Corporation

SFG Aircraft Inc.
SFG Commercial Aircraft Leasing
SFG Equipment Leasing Corporation I
Washington and Michigan Insurance Inc.
1st Source Funding LLC
1st Source Intermediate Holding LLC
1st Source Master Trust
Trustcorp Mortgage Company

COMPETITORS

Bank of America
Fifth Third
Huntington Bancshares
JPMorgan Chase
KeyCorp
Old National Bancorp
PNC Financial
U.S. Bancorp
Wells Fargo

HISTORICAL FINANCIALS

Company Type: Public

Income Statement — FYE: December 31

	ASSETS ($ mil.)	NET INCOME ($ mil.)	INCOME AS % OF ASSETS	EMPLOYEES
12/18	6,293.7	82.4	1.3%	1,150
12/17	5,887.2	68.0	1.2%	1,125
12/16	5,486.2	57.7	1.1%	1,150
12/15	5,187.9	57.4	1.1%	1,150
12/14	4,829.9	58.0	1.2%	1,100
Annual Growth	6.8%	9.1%	—	1.1%

2018 Year-End Financials

Return on assets: 1.3%
Return on equity: 11.1%
Long-term debt ($ mil.): —
No. of shares (mil.): 25.7
Sales ($ mil): 354.3
Dividends
  Yield: 2.3%
  Payout: 31.8%
Market value ($ mil.): 1,040.0

	STOCK PRICE ($) FY Close	P/E High/Low	PER SHARE ($) Earnings	Dividends	Book Value
12/18	40.34	19 12	3.16	0.96	29.56
12/17	49.45	20 16	2.60	0.76	27.70
12/16	44.66	20 12	2.22	0.72	26.00
12/15	30.87	16 13	2.17	0.67	24.75
12/14	34.31	16 13	2.17	0.65	23.41
Annual Growth	4.1%	— —	9.8%	10.4%	6.0%

ABIOMED, Inc.

ABIOMED gives weary hearts a rest. The medical device maker has developed a range of cardiac assist devices and is developing a self-contained artificial heart. Its Impella micro heart pumps can temporarily take over blood circulation during surgery or catheterization. Its AB5000 ventricular assist device temporarily takes over the heart's pumping function and improves circulatory flow in patients with acute heart failure thus allowing their hearts to rest and recover. ABIOMED markets its products through both a direct sales force and distributors.

Operations

ABIOMED has also developed a battery-powered implantable replacement heart system called AbioCor which can be used to extend life for dying patients who aren't eligible for a heart transplant. ABIOMED developed the AbioCor system based on technology developed at Pennsylvania State University. However due to the limited number of patients that qualify for use of the AbioCor the company places little emphasis on marketing efforts for this product line.

Geographic Reach

While many of ABIOMED's products are approved for use in other countries international sales to Canada parts of Europe Asia South America and the Middle East only make up some 10% of its revenue. The company intends to improve its international results with more sales and support teams in Europe. It manufactures its Impella products at a facility in Germany while the rest of its products are made in Massachusetts.

In addition to its locations in Massachusetts and Aachen Germany the company has a sales and marketing office in Paris and another office in Tokyo where it is preparing for a commercial launch of products.

Financial Performance

After years of steady sales growth ABIOMED made its first profit in 2012. Sales have continued to rise and in fiscal 2015 (ended March) revenue rose 25% to $230.3 million on higher sales of the Impella system. This was largely due to disposable catheter sales in the US and growing business in Europe primarily Germany.

Net income jumped more than 1000% in fiscal 2015 to $113.7 million. That sharp increase was driven both by the higher revenues and changes in income tax benefit provisions. Operating cash flow increased 84% to $43.3 million that year.

Strategy

The company's research efforts are focused on developing new products for acute heart failure patients as well as next-generation versions and support systems for its existing products. The company has shifted more of its development and sales efforts onto the Impella product line in order to expand its uses and variations while gradually discontinuing its other products.

In addition to expanding its product portfolio and approvals the company also dedicates personnel and financial resources to raising awareness of its products in the medical community. ABIOMED also continuously evaluates opportunities for strategic acquisitions. To that end it acquired a German heart catheter pump maker in 2014 expanding its product line and German sales efforts.

Mergers and Acquisitions

In 2014 as part of its plan to expand it product line and its German sales force ABIOMED purchased Berlin-based ECP Entwicklungsgesellschaft for $14 million. ECP produces heart catheter pumps that use an external drive shaft to increase circulation.

HISTORY

David Lederman founded ABIOMED in 1981 to make products he had designed (such as artificial heart pumps and valves) as well as dental diagnostic products. ABIOMED went public in 1987. In 1988 it got about $1 million from the National Institutes of Health for heart replacement device (HRD) research and development. In 1990 it began working with Canada's World Heart on HRD technology. In 1992 ABIOMED launched BVS-5000.

In 1990 the company formed ABIODENT to consolidate its dental operations. It received FDA clearance to market the PerioTemp device in 1994. In 1996 it voluntarily recalled some of its BVS-5000 blood pumps citing component irregularities (it said no patients were affected).

To fund product development ABIOMED accepted government funding to finish testing its battery-powered HRD (1996) and to develop a laser-based tissue-welding system (1998). Biotech firm Genzyme invested about $15 million in ABIOMED that year acquiring 14% of the firm.

In 1998 ABIOMED again recalled some lots of BVS-5000 this time for electrical problems. The company attributed 1998's losses to an increase in self-funding on the HRD project as well as to red ink in its now-discontinued dental business.

ABIOMED received funding from the National Heart Lung and Blood Institutes in 2000 to support the testing of its AbioCor product an implantable heart replacement device. The following year AbioCor became the first artificial heart implanted in a patient.

The FDA approved the use of the artificial hearts in five patients in 2001 all of whom were considered too sick to receive heart transplants. The first patient died the same year but the cause of death was not attributed to AbioCor.

The fifth patient to receive the device died early in 2002. By late 2002 seven patients had been fitted with the device but only one was living. A moratorium on recruiting new patients was imposed. ABIOMED wanted patients that were healthy enough to live long past the time of implantation but only patients that were extremely ill would be considered candidates for the device.

By January of 2003 the moratorium had been lifted and three more patients had received implants by March. Because of the troubles with finding qualified recipients for its AbioCor product the company began focusing on other products to sustain revenues. It got good news on that front that same year when the FDA approved ABIOMED's AB5000 Circulatory Support System Console a device that temporarily pumps the patient's blood when the heart has failed.

EXECUTIVES

Chairman President and CEO, Michael R. Minogue, age 52, $519,663 total compensation
Chief Medical Officer, Karim Benali, age 53, $171,200 total compensation
VP Healthcare Solutions, Andrew J. Greenfield, age 47, $211,592 total compensation
CTO, Thorsten Siess
COO, David M. Weber, age 58, $341,844 total compensation
VP and General Manager Global Sales and Marketing, Michael G. Howley, age 55, $296,970 total compensation
VP and CFO, Michael Tomsicek, age 53
Vice President and Corporate Controller, Ian Mcleod
Vice President Human Resources, Franky Leblanc
VP Manufacturing, Matt Plano
Vp Human Resources, Kelley Boucher
Vice President Asia Pacific, Geoffrey Christanday
Auditors: DELOITTE & TOUCHE LLP

LOCATIONS

HQ: ABIOMED, Inc.
  22 Cherry Hill Drive, Danvers, MA 01923
Phone: 978 646-1400   **Fax:** 978 777-8411
Web: www.abiomed.com

PRODUCTS/OPERATIONS

2015 Revenues

	$ mil.	% of total
Impella products	212.7	92
Service & other revenue	13.8	6
Other products	3.5	2
Funded research & development	0.3	—
Total	**230.3**	**100**

COMPETITORS

CardiacAssist	St. Jude Medical
Edwards Lifesciences	Teleflex
Getinge	Terumo
HeartWare	Thoratec Corp
Medtronic	

HISTORICAL FINANCIALS
Company Type: Public

Income Statement — FYE: March 31

	REVENUE ($ mil.)	NET INCOME ($ mil.)	NET PROFIT MARGIN	EMPLOYEES
03/19	769.4	259.0	33.7%	1,371
03/18	593.7	112.1	18.9%	1,143
03/17	445.3	52.1	11.7%	908
03/16	329.5	38.1	11.6%	747
03/15	230.3	113.6	49.4%	589
Annual Growth	35.2%	22.9%	—	23.5%

2019 Year-End Financials

Debt ratio: —
Return on equity: 31.8%
Cash ($ mil.): 121.0
Current ratio: 6.39
Long-term debt ($ mil.): —
No. of shares (mil.): 45.1
Dividends
  Yield: —
  Payout: —
Market value ($ mil.): 12,887.0

	STOCK PRICE ($) FY Close	P/E High/Low	PER SHARE ($) Earnings	Dividends	Book Value
03/19	285.59	78 48	5.61	0.00	20.76
03/18	290.99	116 76	2.45	0.00	15.54
03/17	125.20	109 19	1.17	0.00	10.35
03/16	94.81	118 66	0.85	0.00	8.66
03/15	71.58	26 7	2.65	0.00	7.05
Annual Growth	41.3%	— —	20.6%	—	31.0%

ACM Research Inc

Auditors: BDO China Shu Lun Pan Certified Public Accountants LLP

LOCATIONS

HQ: ACM Research Inc
42307 Osgood Road, Suite I, Fremont, CA 94539
Phone: 510 445-3700
Web: www.acmrcsh.com

HISTORICAL FINANCIALS
Company Type: Public

Income Statement — FYE: December 31

	REVENUE ($ mil.)	NET INCOME ($ mil.)	NET PROFIT MARGIN	EMPLOYEES
12/18	74.6	6.5	8.8%	273
12/17	36.5	(0.3)	—	191
12/16	27.3	1.0	3.8%	187
12/15	31.2	5.3	17.2%	0
Annual Growth	33.7%	6.9%	—	—

2018 Year-End Financials

Debt ratio: 9.1%
Return on equity: 14.2%
Cash ($ mil.): 27.1
Current ratio: 2.08
Long-term debt ($ mil.): —
No. of shares (mil.): 16.0
Dividends
  Yield: —
  Payout: —
Market value ($ mil.): 174.0

	STOCK PRICE ($) FY Close	P/E High/Low	PER SHARE ($) Earnings	Dividends	Book Value
12/18	10.88	36 11	0.37	0.00	3.27
12/17	5.25	— —	(0.05)	0.00	2.60
12/16	0.00	— —	0.18	0.00	3.36
Annual Growth	—	— —	43.4%	—	(1.4%)

ACNB Corp

EXECUTIVES

Vice President Commercial Lending, Merle Zehr
Assistant Vice President Adams County National Bank, Kim Elmo
Senior Vice President Of Commercial Loan, John Kashner
Vice President Comml Lending, Scott Miller
Vice President, Dennis Hollinger
Vice President, James Showvaker
Vice President Mortgage Lending, Rhonda Winterstein
Executive Vice President and Chief Lending and Revenue Officer of ACNB Bank, Douglas Seibel
Vice President, Daniel Baer
Vice President, Thomas Holmes
Chief Governance Officer Secretary and Executive Vice President of the Corporation and the Bank, Lynda Glass
Auditors: BDO USA, LLP

LOCATIONS

HQ: ACNB Corp
16 Lincoln Square, Gettysburg, PA 17325
Phone: 717 334-3161
Web: www.acnb.com

COMPETITORS

First Commonwealth Financial	PNC Financial
Fulton Financial	Univest
M&T Bank	Wells Fargo

HISTORICAL FINANCIALS
Company Type: Public

Income Statement — FYE: December 31

	ASSETS ($ mil.)	NET INCOME ($ mil.)	INCOME AS % OF ASSETS	EMPLOYEES
12/18	1,647.7	21.7	1.3%	361
12/17	1,595.4	9.7	0.6%	358
12/16	1,206.3	10.8	0.9%	303
12/15	1,147.9	11.0	1.0%	296
12/14	1,089.8	10.2	0.9%	297
Annual Growth	10.9%	20.6%	—	5.0%

2018 Year-End Financials

Return on assets: 1.3%
Return on equity: 13.5%
Long-term debt ($ mil.): —
No. of shares (mil.): 7.0
Sales ($ mil): 80.4
Dividends
  Yield: 2.2%
  Payout: 28.8%
Market value ($ mil.): 277.0

	STOCK PRICE ($) FY Close	P/E High/Low	PER SHARE ($) Earnings	Dividends	Book Value
12/18	39.25	13 9	3.09	0.89	23.86
12/17	29.55	21 17	1.50	0.80	21.92
12/16	31.25	18 12	1.80	0.80	19.80
12/15	21.30	12 11	1.83	0.80	18.99
12/14	21.75	13 11	1.71	0.77	18.29
Annual Growth	15.9%	— —	15.9%	3.7%	6.9%

Addus HomeCare Corp

Addus HomeCare is there for those who need in-home personal and medical care services. Doing business through subsidiary Addus HealthCare it serves the elderly and disabled. Its home and community unit provides long-term non-medical social services such as bathing grooming housekeeping meal preparation and transportation. State and county government payors generate most of its revenues. Operating from more than 100 locations Addus provides its services in about 25 states primarily in the midwestern and western US with its largest markets in Illinois California Nevada and Washington.

Operations

The company employs home care aides to cover a range of patient needs. In its home and community segment it also operates a handful of community adult day care centers in Illinois that offer social activities transportation exercise and cognitive therapy in a group setting.

Sales and Marketing

Addus provides personal and home support services that are reimbursed by state and county elder care programs. The Illinois Department of Aging is its largest customer (40% of revenues). Medicare is its second-largest payer group (12% of revenues) with Addus providing services to Medicare-eligible patients recovering from acute medical conditions. Other payer clients include the Veterans Health Administration commercial insurers and private individuals.

Strategy

Addus' ability to keep its net revenues growing is dependent on maintaining current payer client relationships winning new payers and increasing its referrals through coordinated care. It is also dependent on state agencies continuing to authorize home health care services to consumers. The company is focused on serving dual eligibility customers (patients that qualify for elderly and disability Medicare/Medicaid benefits). Addus is working widen the breadth of its service offerings open new offices and make strategic acquisitions of smaller providers in existing and new markets.

Mergers and Acquisitions

Addus regularly buys small to midsized home care companies to expand its operations. With the aging US population it expects demand for its offerings will continue to grow. In 2017 it bought Options Home Care which provides home care services in New Mexico. The following year it acquired another New Mexico firm Ambercare Corporation for some $40 million.

EXECUTIVES

EVP and Chief Human Resources Officer, Brenda A. Belger, age 64
President CEO and Director, R. Dirk Allison, age 63
EVP and COO, W. Bradley Bickham, age 56
Chief Business Development and Strategy Officer, Darby Anderson, age 53, $293,170 total compensation
CIO, James G. (Zeke) Zoccoli
EVP and CFO, Brian W. Poff
Board Member, Jean Rush
Auditors: PricewaterhouseCoopers LLP

LOCATIONS

HQ: Addus HomeCare Corp
6801 Gaylord Parkway, Suite 110, Frisco, TX 75034
Phone: 469 535-8200
Web: www.addus.com

COMPETITORS

Active Day	Home Instead
Amedisys	LHC Group
American HomePatient	Lincare Holdings
Apria Healthcare	LivHOME
Critical Homecare Solutions	National Home Health Personal-Touch Home Care
Gentiva	Star Multi Care
Girling Health Care	
Guardian Home Care Holdings	

HISTORICAL FINANCIALS
Company Type: Public

Income Statement — FYE: December 31

	REVENUE ($ mil.)	NET INCOME ($ mil.)	NET PROFIT MARGIN	EMPLOYEES
12/18	518.1	17.5	3.4%	33,153
12/17	425.7	13.6	3.2%	26,097
12/16	400.6	12.0	3.0%	23,070
12/15	336.8	11.6	3.5%	21,395
12/14	312.9	12.2	3.9%	18,054
Annual Growth	13.4%	9.3%	—	16.4%

2018 Year-End Financials

Debt ratio: 4.8%
Return on equity: 7.7%
Cash ($ mil.): 70.4
Current ratio: 3.02
Long-term debt ($ mil.): 17.2
No. of shares (mil.): 13.1
Dividends
  Yield: —
  Payout: —
Market value ($ mil.): 891.0

	STOCK PRICE ($) FY Close	P/E High/Low	PER SHARE ($) Earnings	Dividends	Book Value
12/18	67.88	53 24	1.41	0.00	20.99
12/17	34.80	34 25	1.17	0.00	15.05
12/16	35.05	34 15	1.06	0.00	13.79
12/15	23.28	34 18	1.04	0.00	12.76
12/14	24.27	26 15	1.10	0.00	11.62
Annual Growth	29.3%	— —	6.4%	—	15.9%

Advanced Emissions Solutions Inc

Advanced Emissions Solutions wants to make "clean coal" more than just a marketing term. The company makes environmental technology systems and specialty chemicals to reduce emissions at coal-burning power plants. It offers integrated mercury control systems as well as flue gas conditioning and combustion aid chemicals. Advanced Emissions Solutions provides consulting and testing services and mercury measurement equipment. It also has a joint venture with NexGen Refined Coal to market technology that reduces emissions of nitrogen oxides and mercury from some treated coals. The company has three reportable segments: Refined Coal Emission Control and CO2 Capture.

Change in Company Type

Advanced Emissions Solutions took itself private in 2103.

Operations

The Refined Coal segment (92% of Advanced Emissions Solutions' 2012 revenues) includes revenues from coal facilities and sales.

The Emission Control segment includes revenues from the supply of emissions control systems including powdered activated carbon injection systems and dry sorbent injection systems to reduce emissions of pollutants (including particulate matter SO2 NOx mercury and acid gases) and from the licensing of technology and its consulting services.

The CO2 Capture segment generates revenues from the CO2 capture and control market including projects co-funded by the Department of Energy (DOE) and private industry.

Advanced Emissions Solutions' four subsidiaries are Advanced Emissions Solutions and ADA Intellectual Property LLC (neither of which had operations in 2012); BCSI; and ADA Environmental Solutions.

Advanced Emissions Solutions also holds 42.5% of Clean Coal Solutions a Colorado limited liability company. The joint venture's partners include an affiliate of NexGen Resources and an affiliate of Goldman Sachs.

Financial Performance

The company's revenues grew by almost 300% in 2012 primarily due to the increased rental income from leased Refined Coal facilities and higher Refined Coal sales from raw coal purchases that Clean Coal Solutions operated on its own account.

Emission Control revenues increased due to increased systems and equipment sales and flue gas chemicals and services. This was partially offset by lower consulting revenues as a result of potential clients deferring compliance work until 2013.

Advanced Emissions Solutions' net loss decreased by 34% in 2012 thanks to higher revenues a decrease in legal and settlement costs associated with its arbitration and litigation and higher net income from unconsolidated entities as a result of the relinquishment of its interest in ADA Carbon Solutions in late 2011. This was partially offset by the absence of a deferred income tax benefit.

Strategy

Advanced Emissions Solutions sees the activated carbon market growing rapidly as coal-fired power plants in 19 states and four Canadian provinces move to meet mercury mitigation regulations and as other governments promulgate new rules.

In 2012 it had several consulting R&D contracts funded by the DOE industry groups and Advanced Emissions Solutions aimed at controlling mercury emissions through dry sorbent injection systems providing CO2 capture and supporting other Refined Coal and Emission Control activities.

That year the Clean Coal Solutions joint venture finalized a contract for a fifth Refined Coal facility with a new investor with a value for Advanced Emissions Solutions of $10 million. The JV subsequently leased two additional Refined Coal facilities to an existing coal investor for $14 million.

Mergers and Acquisitions

In 2012 the company spent $2 million in cash and $3 million (in payouts over time) to acquire the assets of Bulk Conveyor Specialist a maker of systems coal-fired power plants use to reduce acid gas emissions. The acquisition includes a manufacturing facility and Bulk Conveyor Services which provides testing and related services. The purchase positions Advanced Emissions Solutions to take advantage of upcoming EPA mandates to reduce the level of acid gas emissions from coal-fired plants. The assets are held in a wholly-owned subsidiary BCSI.

The acquisition increases the company's market leading position in commercial acid gas control and allows the company to vertically-integrate its Emissions Control business operations including expanding its capacity to supply Activated Carbon Injection systems.

Auditors: Moss Adams LLP

LOCATIONS

HQ: Advanced Emissions Solutions Inc
640 Plaza Drive, Suite 270, Highlands Ranch, CO 80129
Phone: 720 598-3500
Web: www.advancedemissionssolutions.com

PRODUCTS/OPERATIONS

2012 Sales

	$ mil.	% of total
Refined Coal		
Coal sales	157.9	75
Rental income	36.9	17
Other	0.1	-
Emission Control		
Systems & equipment	9.6	5
Consulting & development	4.2	2
Chemicals	0.8	-
COS Capture 3.0	1	
Total	212.5	100

COMPETITORS

ALSTOM	Nalco
BWX Technologies	Wahlco
Calgon Carbon	Wheelabrator
Clyde Bergemann EEC	Woodward Governor
Donaldson Company	

HISTORICAL FINANCIALS
Company Type: Public

Income Statement — FYE: December 31

	REVENUE ($ mil.)	NET INCOME ($ mil.)	NET PROFIT MARGIN	EMPLOYEES
12/18	23.9	35.4	148.1%	128
12/17	35.6	27.8	78.1%	29
12/16	50.6	97.6	193.0%	25
12/15	62.7	(30.1)	—	69
12/14	16.9	1.3	8.2%	231
Annual Growth	9.1%	124.9%	—	(13.7%)

2018 Year-End Financials

Debt ratio: 46.4% No. of shares (mil.): 18.5
Return on equity: 50.1% Dividends
Cash ($ mil.): 18.5 Yield: 9.4%
Current ratio: 1.47 Payout: 56.8%
Long-term debt ($ mil.): 50.0 Market value ($ mil.): 196.0

	STOCK PRICE ($) FY Close	P/E High/Low	PER SHARE ($) Earnings	Dividends	Book Value
12/18	10.55	7 4	1.76	1.00	3.66
12/17	9.66	9 6	1.29	0.75	3.54
12/16	9.24	2 1	4.34	0.00	3.46
12/15	9.40	— —	(1.37)	0.00	(1.15)
12/14	22.79	930 302	0.06	0.00	(0.03)
Annual Growth	(17.5%)	—	—132.7%	—	—

AGNC Investment Corp

AGNC Investment (formerly American Capital Agency) is taking on the rocky real estate market. The real estate investment trust (REIT) was created in 2008 to invest in securities backed by single-family residential mortgages and collateralized mortgage obligations guaranteed by government agencies Fannie Mae Freddie Mac and Ginnie Mae. The Maryland-based REIT is externally managed and advised by American Capital AGNC Management a subsidiary of US publicly traded alternative asset manager American Capital which spun off American Capital Agency in 2008 but retained about a 33% stake in the REIT.

Operations
American Capital Agency generates income from investing in leveraged agency mortgage-backed securities (agency MBS) which consist of residential mortgage pass-through securities and collateralized mortgage obligations (CMOs) backed by federal agencies. About 97% of its total revenue came from interest income in 2014 while the remainder came from gains on agency securities sales. It may also collect gains on derivative instruments and other securities.

Its leverage was 5.3 times its stockholders' equity in 2014 (down from 7.3 times in 2013).

Financial Performance
American Capital Agency's revenue and profits had been trending higher over the past few years as the security valuations rose with the strengthening housing market leading to higher interest income.

The REIT's revenues and profits fell steeply in 2014 mostly as it lost $1.24 billion on derivative instruments and other securities (compared to a gain of $1.2 billion in 2013). Additionally its investment portfolio value declined by 29% after shifting its investments from MBS repo funded assets to TBA dollar roll funded assets which led to 33% less interest income.

American Capital Agency's operating cash levels fell by 35% to $1.62 billion in 2014 due to lower cash earnings.

Strategy
Set up as an investment vehicle American Capital Agency's chief goal is to preserve its net asset value (NAV) and generate risk-adjusted returns for shareholders through regular monthly dividends and net realized gains from its investments and hedging activities.

The REIT's investment strategy as it reiterated in 2015 is designed to: manage a portfolio of agency securities and similar assets with attractive risk-adjusted returns; take advantage of undervalued agency securities in the market; manage financing interest rate prepayment and extension risks; preserve its net book value; and continue providing regular monthly distributions to its shareholders as a REIT.

Company Background
American Capital Agency raised some $300 million from its 2008 IPO. The REIT used the proceeds from the offering to build and develop its investment portfolio.

EXECUTIVES

EVP and CFO; VP and Treasurer American Capital Agency Management, John R. Erickson, age 56
Chairman President and CEO; President American Capital Agency Management, Malon Wilkus, age 64
VP American Capital Agency Management, Thomas A. (Tom) McHale
EVP and Secretary; VP and Secretary American Capital Agency Management, Samuel A. Flax, age 59
SVP and Chief Investment Officer; SVP and Managing Director American Capital, Gary D. Kain, age 51
Senior Vice President Treasurer, Jeffrey S. Beyersdorfer
Senior Vice President General Counsel Secretary, Lowry Barfield
Senior Vice President - Agency Portfolio Investments, Christopher Kuehl
Senior Vice President; Chief Risk Officer, Peter Federico
Director, Larry K. Harvey, age 51
Director, Alvin N. Puryear, age 79
Director, Randy E. Dobbs, age 65
Director, Morris A. Davis, age 43
Independent Director, Robert Couch
Auditors: Ernst & Young LLP

LOCATIONS
HQ: AGNC Investment Corp
2 Bethesda Metro Center, 12th Floor, Bethesda, MD 20814
Phone: 301 968-9315   **Fax:** 301 968-9301
Web: www.agnc.com

COMPETITORS

ARMOUR Residential REIT	CIFC
Annaly Capital Management	Capstead Mortgage
	Chimera
Anworth Mortgage Asset	Hatteras Financial
Bimini Capital Management	JAVELIN Mortgage
	MFA Financial
	Redwood Trust

HISTORICAL FINANCIALS
Company Type: Public

Income Statement — FYE: December 31

	ASSETS ($ mil.)	NET INCOME ($ mil.)	INCOME AS % OF ASSETS	EMPLOYEES
12/18	109,241.0	129.0	0.1%	56
12/17	70,376.0	771.0	1.1%	56
12/16	56,880.0	623.0	1.1%	54
12/15	57,021.0	215.0	0.4%	3
12/14	67,766.0	(233.0)	—	0
Annual Growth	12.7%	—	—	—

2018 Year-End Financials

Return on assets: 0.1% Dividends
Return on equity: 1.3% Yield: 12.3%
Long-term debt ($ mil.): — Payout: 1,028.5%
No. of shares (mil.): 536.3 Market value ($ mil.): 9,407.0
Sales ($ mil): 1,402.0

	STOCK PRICE ($) FY Close	P/E High/Low	PER SHARE ($) Earnings	Dividends	Book Value
12/18	17.54	95 82	0.21	2.16	18.47
12/17	20.19	11 9	2.04	2.16	22.37
12/16	18.13	11 9	1.79	2.30	22.22
12/15	17.34	41 31	0.54	2.48	23.62
12/14	21.83	— —	(0.72)	2.61	26.72
Annual Growth	(5.3%)	—	—	(4.6%)	(8.8%)

Agree Realty Corp.

Shopping sprees really agree with Agree Realty. The self-managed real estate investment trust (REIT) owns develops and manages retail real estate primarily freestanding big-box properties. It owns around 280 retail properties spanning 5.5 million square feet of leasable space across 40-plus states. Most of its tenants are national retailers with its largest tenants being Wal-Mart Wawa and Walgreens. The REIT typically acquires either property portfolios or single-asset net lease retail properties (worth between $2 million and $30 million per asset) with creditworthy tenants. It was founded in 1979 by CEO Richard Agree.

Operations
The REIT's portfolio was made up of 278 properties in 41 states at the end of 2015 which spanned 5.2 million square feet of gross leasable space. All but three of these properties were net lease properties that contributed 97.6% to the REIT's rental income. The three others were community shopping centers.

Geographic Reach
While Agree Realty had properties in 41 US states during 2015 about 20% of its rental revenue came from properties in Michigan while another 20% came from properties based in Florida Ohio

and Texas. All other regions each accounted for less than 6% of its revenue.

Sales and Marketing

The REIT mostly leases properties to retailers such as pharmacies restaurants general merchandisers apparel retailers grocery stores warehouse clubs sporting goods stores health & fitness centers convenience stores and dollar stores among others.

Agree Realty's largest tenant by revenue continues to be Walgreens which leased 32 properties and contributed 17.2% to the REIT's total rental income during 2015. Its four next largest tenants that year were Wal-Mart (5.5% of rental income) Wawa (3.4%) CVS (3.4%) and Academy Sports (2.8%).

Financial Performance

Agree Realty's annual revenues have more than doubled since 2011 mostly as rent-boosting acquisitions have increased its gross leasable square footage by 46% while nearly tripling its property count from 87 to 278 at the end of 2015. The REIT's net income has nearly quadrupled over the period as it's managed to keep a lid on rising operating expenses.

The REIT's revenue climbed 31% to almost $70 million during 2015 mostly as its 150 property acquisitions made from 2014 through 2015 boosted minimum rental revenues. Its existing property rental income increased by 13% thanks to better tenant performance and higher rental rates.

Strong revenue growth combined with $12.1 million in property sale gains in 2015 caused Agree Realty's net income to more than double to $39 million for the year. The company's operating cash levels jumped 28% to $44.7 million in 2015 mostly thanks to a spike in cash-denominated earnings from higher rental income.

Strategy

The REIT typically acquires either property portfolios or single-asset net lease retail properties (worth between $2 million and $30 million per asset) with creditworthy tenants to diversify its portfolio of "industry-leading" retailers.

Agree Realty normally holds onto its properties for long-term investment which is why it prefers to establish long-term leases and invest in capital improvements. Indeed at the end of 2015 the REIT's property portfolio boasted a 99.5% occupancy rate and a weighted average remaining lease term of 11.4 years.

EXECUTIVES

Interim CFO, Kenneth R. Howe, age 71, $42,325 total compensation
President CEO and Director, Joey Agree, age 41, $414,064 total compensation
EVP and COO, Laith M. Hermiz, age 48, $269,259 total compensation
Vice President, Craig Willian
Vice President Construction, Jeff Konkle
Vice President Transactions, Philip Carbone
Chairman, Richard Agree, age 76
Board Member, Jerome Rossi
Auditors: Grant Thornton LLP

LOCATIONS

HQ: Agree Realty Corp.
 70 E. Long Lake Road, Bloomfield Hills, MI 48304
Phone: 248 737-4190 **Fax:** 248 737-9410
Web: www.agreerealty.com

PRODUCTS/OPERATIONS

2015 sales

	$ mil.	% of total
Minimum rents	64.3	92
operating cost reimbursement	5.3	8
Percentage rents	0.2	—
other income	0.2	—
Total	**70.0**	**100**

COMPETITORS

CBL & Associates Properties	Pennsylvania Real Estate
DDR	Ramco-Gershenson
GGP	Simon Property Group
Kimco Realty	Taubman Centers

HISTORICAL FINANCIALS

Company Type: Public

Income Statement   FYE: December 31

	REVENUE ($ mil.)	NET INCOME ($ mil.)	NET PROFIT MARGIN	EMPLOYEES
12/18	148.2	58.1	39.3%	36
12/17	116.5	58.1	49.9%	32
12/16	91.5	45.1	49.3%	24
12/15	69.9	39.0	55.8%	20
12/14	53.5	18.4	34.5%	14
Annual Growth	29.0%	33.2%	—	26.6%

2018 Year-End Financials

Debt ratio: 35.5%
Return on equity: 5.4%
Cash ($ mil.): 53.9
Current ratio: 1.87
Long-term debt ($ mil.): 720.4
No. of shares (mil.): 37.5
Dividends
 Yield: 3.6%
 Payout: 121.1%
Market value ($ mil.): 2,220.0

	STOCK PRICE ($) FY Close	P/E High/Low		PER SHARE ($) Earnings	Dividends	Book Value
12/18	59.12	35	25	1.78	2.16	32.92
12/17	51.44	25	21	2.08	2.03	29.31
12/16	46.05	26	16	1.97	1.92	26.10
12/15	33.99	16	13	2.16	1.85	21.86
12/14	31.09	26	22	1.24	1.74	20.16
Annual Growth	17.4%	—	—	9.5%	5.5%	13.0%

Air Lease Corp

Air Lease doesn't really lease air unless of course you include the air inside the cabins of its fleet of airplanes. An aircraft leasing company Air Lease buys new and used commercial aircraft from manufacturers and airlines and then leases to airline carriers in Europe the Asia-Pacific region and the Americas. It owns a fleet of almost 240 aircraft comprised of 181 single-aisle narrowbody jet aircraft 40 twin-aisle widebody jet aircraft and 19 turboprop aircraft. In addition to leasing Air Lease also offers fleet management services such as lease management and sales.

Geographic Reach

Air Lease is based in Los Angeles and has airline customers throughout the world. Europe accounted for 32% of its net sales in 2015. Other markets included China (22%); Asia excluding China (19%); Central America South America and Mexico (10%); the Middle East and Africa (8%); the US and Canada (5%); and the Pacific Australia and New Zealand (4%).

Sales and Marketing

Its customers have included Air Canada; Sunwing Airlines; WestJet; AeroMexico; Aeromar; Interjet; Volaris; Hawaiian Airlines; Southwest Airlines; Spirit Airlines; Sun Country; United Continental Holdings; Liat Airline; and Caribbean Airlines.

Financial Performance

Air Lease has experienced explosive growth over the years with revenues reaching a record-setting $1.22 billion in 2015. Profits also remained consistent hovering around the $255 million mark for both 2014 and 2015. The static profits for 2015 was attributed to about $72 million it paid in litigation settlement expenses. The company's cash from operating activities has gradually increased the last five years climbing by 9% from 2014 to 2015.

The historic growth for 2015 was fueled by an 18% spike in the rental of flight equipment. This was aided by the delivery of 51 additional aircraft all of which were leased at the time of delivery. Air Lease also enjoyed major growth in the key markets of the Middle East and Africa (89%); the Pacific Australia and New Zealand (52%) and China (21%).

Strategy

Although the largest portion of its fleet is leased to customers in Western Europe Air Lease is setting its sights on markets in the Asia-Pacific region Eastern Europe South America and the Middle East where it predicts the travel industry will grow the fastest in coming years. It has also targeted carriers in stable but slower-growing travel markets such as North America.

One way Air Lease has achieved impressive revenue growth over the years is by adding to its fleet size. In 2015 it purchased and took delivery of 51 aircraft and sold 24 aircraft ending the year with a total of 240 owned aircraft. During 2015 it increased its managed fleet by 12 aircraft ending the year with 29 aircraft in its managed fleet portfolio. (The company typically sells aircraft that are currently operated by an airline with multiple years of lease term remaining on the contract.)

Company Background

Air Lease went public in 2011. Udvar-Házy and other Air Lease used a significant portion of the proceeds raised to acquire additional aircraft and for general corporate purposes. With sufficient capital and financing already in place Air Lease has placed orders for some 150 new aircraft to be delivered by 2017. While most of its fleet will consist of Boeing and Airbus passenger airplanes the company has ordered similar aircraft manufactured by Embraer and turboprops from Avions de Transport Régional (ATR).

Udvar-Házy had co-founded ILFC now one of the largest aircraft leasing companies in the industry in the 1970s. He stayed on after AIG bought ILFC in the 1990s and continued to head the company until 2010 when he retired in the wake of the ongoing financial trouble that hit AIG in 2008. Udvar-Házy subsequently founded Air Lease with the help of institutional investors including some that were large shareholders prior to the IPO's filing (Ares Management which held an 11% stake; Leonard Green & Partners 11%; and Commonwealth Bank of Australia 10%). Udvar-Házy maintained a 7% stake in Air Lease in 2013.

EXECUTIVES

Executive Vice President, Jie Chen
Svp, Kishore Korde
Assistant Vice President, Matthew Stevens
Executive Vice President, Grant Levy
Executive Vice President, Marc Baer
Vice President Technical Asset Management, Pierce Chang
Vice President Technical Asset Management, Eric Hoogenkamp
Executive Vice President, Alex Khatibi
Assistant Vice President Information Technology, Pablo Chavez
Treasurer, AJ Abedin
Auditors: KPMG LLP

LOCATIONS

HQ: Air Lease Corp
2000 Avenue of the Stars, Suite 1000N, Los Angeles, CA 90067
Phone: 310 553-0555
Web: www.airleasecorp.com

PRODUCTS/OPERATIONS

2015 Sales

	$ mil.	% of total
Rental of flight equipment	1,174.5	96
Aircraft sales trading and other	48.3	4
Total	**1,222.8**	**100**

COMPETITORS

AerCap	Fly Leasing
Aircastle	GE Capital Aviation Services
Aviation Capital Group	ICON Capital
Boeing Capital	ILFC
CIT Transportation Finance	

HISTORICAL FINANCIALS

Company Type: Public

Income Statement — FYE: December 31

	REVENUE ($ mil.)	NET INCOME ($ mil.)	NET PROFIT MARGIN	EMPLOYEES
12/18	1,679.7	510.8	30.4%	97
12/17	1,516.3	756.1	49.9%	87
12/16	1,419.0	374.9	26.4%	76
12/15	1,222.8	253.3	20.7%	74
12/14	1,050.4	256.0	24.4%	65
Annual Growth	12.5%	18.9%	—	10.5%

2018 Year-End Financials

Debt ratio: 62.4%
Return on equity: 11.4%
Cash ($ mil.): 300.1
Current ratio: 1.55
Long-term debt ($ mil.): 11,538.9
No. of shares (mil.): 110.9
Dividends
 Yield: 1.4%
 Payout: 9.3%
Market value ($ mil.): 3,352.0

	STOCK PRICE ($) FY Close	P/E High/Low		PER SHARE ($) Earnings	Dividends	Book Value
12/18	30.21	10	6	4.60	0.43	43.32
12/17	48.09	7	5	6.82	0.33	39.83
12/16	34.33	10	6	3.44	0.23	32.89
12/15	33.48	16	12	2.34	0.17	29.44
12/14	34.31	17	12	2.38	0.13	27.07
Annual Growth	(3.1%)	—	—	17.9%	34.9%	12.5%

Air Transport Services Group, Inc.

Air Transport Services Group (ATSG) has a lease on (aircraft) life. Through its subsidiaries the company provides aircraft leases maintenance operations and other support services to the cargo transportation and package delivery industries. The company's largest segment ACMI Services provides aircraft crew maintenance and insurance operations to the company's largest customers DHL and the US military through airline subsidiaries Ohio-based ABX Air Inc. and Arkansas-based ATI. ATSG's Cargo Aircraft Management (CAM) subsidiary leases converted cargo Boeing 767 and 757 aircraft internally to ATSG airlines and to external customers through multiyear agreements.

Operations

Under its support services business ATSG provides aircraft maintenance repair and overhaul (MRO) through Airborne Maintenance and Engineering Services Inc.; flight crew training and flight simulator rental through ABX; aircraft parts and brokerage through AMES Material Services Inc.; facility maintenance and ground equipment rentals for aircraft support through LGSTX Services Inc.; and aircraft dispatch and flight tracking services through Global Flight Source. The support services business also operates five mail sorting centers for the US Postal Service through LGSTX Distribution Services Inc.

Sales and Marketing

Another subsidiary Airborne Global Solutions Inc. (AGS) provides sales leads to ATSG businesses and develops customized air cargo plans to meet customer needs. ATSG's largest customers DHL Network Operations (USA) and the US military accounted for 55% and 16% of revenue respectively in fiscal 2014.

Financial Performance

ATSG experienced revenue declines and a net loss of $20 million for 2013; however revenues improved marginally by 2% to reach $590 million in 2014. The slight growth was driven by a 4% bump in sales from its cargo aircraft management segment. The company also posted $30 million of positive net income in 2014 mostly due to the absence of impairment of goodwill charges that were present the previous year.

Strategy

To extend its European reach in 2014 ATSG acquired a 25% interest in West Atlantic AB of Gothenburg Sweden. West Atlantic AB through its two airlines — Atlantic Airlines Ltd. and West Air Sweden AB — operates a fleet of 40 aircraft and is Europe's largest regional cargo aircraft operator. West Atlantic AB operates its aircraft on behalf of European regional mail carriers and express logistics providers.

Mergers and Acquisitions

In 2018 Air Transport Services agreed to acquire Omni Air International LLC for $845 million. Omni Air provides passenger aircraft crew maintenance and insurance (ACMI) and charter services with significant sales to US and allied foreign governments and commercial customers. With the acquisition Air Transport anticipates expanding its customer base and increasing its presence in the growing government passenger charter services market.

Company Background

ATSG was formed as a holding company in late 2007 from the reorganization of ABX.

EXECUTIVES

Vice President Of Ground Operations, Brady Templeton
President CEO and Director, Joseph C. (Joe) Hete, age 65, $535,000 total compensation
CFO, Quint O. Turner, age 56, $302,500 total compensation
Chief Commercial Officer and President Cargo Aircraft Management, Richard F. (Rich) Corrado, age 59, $259,077 total compensation
Vice President of Flight Operations, Larry Gray
Vice President Human Resources, John Starkovich
Vice President, Rich Stout
Vice President Air Park Services, Gary Stover
Vice President General Counsel, George Golder
Chairman, James H. Carey, age 86
Board Member, Richard Baudouin
Auditors: DELOITTE & TOUCHE LLP

LOCATIONS

HQ: Air Transport Services Group, Inc.
145 Hunter Drive, Wilmington, OH 45177
Phone: 937 382-5591
Web: www.atsginc.com

PRODUCTS/OPERATIONS

2014 Sales

	$ mil.	% of total
ACMI Services	439.9	59
CAM	166.3	22
Other	142.3	19
Adjustments	(158.9)	-
Total	**589.6**	**100**
Services		
Aircraft leasing		
ACMI services		
Support services		

COMPETITORS

ASTAR USA	Atlas Air Worldwide
American Airlines Group	Delta Air Lines
	Evergreen Holdings
Amerijet	Kalitta Air
Arrow Air	United Continental

HISTORICAL FINANCIALS

Company Type: Public

Income Statement — FYE: December 31

	REVENUE ($ mil.)	NET INCOME ($ mil.)	NET PROFIT MARGIN	EMPLOYEES
12/18	892.3	69.2	7.8%	3,830
12/17	1,068.2	18.5	1.7%	3,010
12/16	768.8	23.4	3.1%	3,230
12/15	619.2	41.2	6.7%	2,170
12/14	589.5	29.8	5.1%	1,810
Annual Growth	10.9%	23.4%	—	20.6%

2018 Year-End Financials

Debt ratio: 56.7%
Return on equity: 16.6%
Cash ($ mil.): 59.3
Current ratio: 1.13
Long-term debt ($ mil.): 1,371.6
No. of shares (mil.): 59.1
Dividends
 Yield: —
 Payout: —
Market value ($ mil.): 1,349.0

	STOCK PRICE ($) FY Close	P/E High/Low	PER SHARE ($) Earnings	Dividends	Book Value
12/18	22.81	23 15	0.91	0.00	7.38
12/17	23.14	82 48	0.31	0.00	6.69
12/16	15.96	45 24	0.37	0.00	5.58
12/15	10.08	17 12	0.63	0.00	5.68
12/14	8.56	20 13	0.46	0.00	5.36
Annual Growth	27.8%	— —	18.6%	—	8.3%

Alarm.com Holdings Inc

Auditors: PricewaterhouseCoopers LLP

LOCATIONS

HQ: Alarm.com Holdings Inc
8281 Greensboro Drive, Suite 100, Tysons, VA 22102
Phone: 877 389-4033
Web: www.alarm.com

HISTORICAL FINANCIALS
Company Type: Public

Income Statement   FYE: December 31

	REVENUE ($ mil.)	NET INCOME ($ mil.)	NET PROFIT MARGIN	EMPLOYEES
12/18	420.4	21.5	5.1%	884
12/17	338.9	29.2	8.6%	784
12/16	261.1	10.1	3.9%	607
12/15	208.8	11.7	5.6%	507
12/14	167.3	13.5	8.1%	400
Annual Growth	25.9%	12.4%	—	21.9%

2018 Year-End Financials

Debt ratio: 15.1%
Return on equity: 8.4%
Cash ($ mil.): 146.0
Current ratio: 3.03
Long-term debt ($ mil.): 67.0
No. of shares (mil.): 48.1
Dividends
  Yield: —
  Payout: —
Market value ($ mil.): 2,495.0

	STOCK PRICE ($) FY Close	P/E High/Low	PER SHARE ($) Earnings	Dividends	Book Value
12/18	51.87	130 78	0.43	0.00	5.77
12/17	37.75	78 43	0.59	0.00	4.93
12/16	27.83	150 65	0.21	0.00	4.14
12/15	16.68	— —	(0.30)	0.00	3.74
Annual Growth	46.0%	— —	—	—	15.6%

Alerus Financial Corp

EXECUTIVES

President; Chief Executive Officer Chairman Director, Randy Newman
Regional President Twin Cities, Sara Ausman
Vice President Commercial Relationship Manager, Robert Hartzell
Auditors: CliftonLarsonAllen LLP

LOCATIONS

HQ: Alerus Financial Corp
401 Demers Avenue, Grand Forks, ND 58021
Phone: 701 795-3200   **Fax:** 701 795-3378
Web: www.alerusfinancial.com

HISTORICAL FINANCIALS
Company Type: Public

Income Statement   FYE: December 31

	ASSETS ($ mil.)	NET INCOME ($ mil.)	INCOME AS % OF ASSETS	EMPLOYEES
12/18	2,179.0	25.8	1.2%	0
12/17	2,137.0	15.4	0.7%	0
12/16	2,050.5	14.0	0.7%	0
12/15	1,744.8	16.5	0.9%	0
12/14	1,488.3	20.2	1.4%	0
Annual Growth	10.0%	6.3%	—	—

2018 Year-End Financials

Return on assets: 1.2%
Return on equity: 13.7%
Long-term debt ($ mil.): —
No. of shares (mil.): 13.7
Sales ($ mil): 190.4
Dividends
  Yield: 2.7%
  Payout: 28.8%
Market value ($ mil.): 265.0

	STOCK PRICE ($) FY Close	P/E High/Low	PER SHARE ($) Earnings	Dividends	Book Value
12/18	19.25	14 10	1.84	0.53	14.30
12/17	20.45	18 15	1.10	0.48	13.18
12/16	17.00	19 16	1.00	0.44	12.47
12/15	18.90	17 15	1.17	0.42	13.61
12/14	19.75	42 14	1.44	0.38	(0.00)
Annual Growth	(0.6%)	— —	6.3%	8.4%	—

Alexandria Real Estate Equities Inc

The pearl of the Mediterranean might be found in Egypt but the pearls of science are typically found in the lab. Alexandria Real Estate Equities owns develops and operates offices and labs to life science tenants including biotech and pharmaceutical companies universities research institutions medical office developers and government agencies. A real estate investment trust (REIT) Alexandria owns approximately 170 specialized properties with more than 15 million sq. ft. of rentable space in the US and Canada. Its portfolio is largely located in high-tech hotbeds such as Boston greater New York City the San Francisco Bay area San Diego Seattle and suburban Washington DC.

EXECUTIVES

Chairman and CEO, Joel S. Marcus, age 71, $895,000 total compensation
EVP CFO and Treasurer, Dean A. Shigenaga, age 52, $450,000 total compensation
EVP and Regional Market Director San Diego, Daniel J. Ryan, $375,000 total compensation
SVP and Regional Market Director Seattle, John J. Cox
SVP and Regional Market Director Maryland, Larry J. Diamond
EVP and Regional Market Director Greater Boston, Thomas J. Andrews, $475,000 total compensation
COO and Regional Market Director San Francisco Bay Area, Stephen A. Richardson, $450,000 total compensation
Chief Investment Officer, Peter M. Moglia, $450,000 total compensation
SVP and Regional Market Director New York City, John H. Cunningham
EVP; General Counsel and Corporate Secretary, Jennifer J. Banks
Vice President San Francisco Bay Area, Todd Miller
Vice President Risk Management, Vahe Simitian
Vice President, Daniel Tsang
Senior Vice President, Joseph Hakman
Assistant Vice President Life Sciences, Amanda Cashin
Assistant Vice President Accounting And Finance, Marc Binda
Vice President Corporate Counsel, Aaron Jacobson
Vice President Financial Reporting, Jonathan Dapeer
Vice President Strategic Operations, Hart Cole
Vice President Accounting, Andrew Houghton
Assistant Vice President, Jeffrey Mccomish
Assistant Vice President Design Construction, Mike Barbera
Vice President Design and Construction, Steve Pomerenke
Senior Vice President Construction Development, Greg Gehlen
Vice President, Naoya Matsuda
VICE PRESIDENT SAN FRANCISCO REGION, Jesse Nelson
Senior Vice President Regional Leasing and Asset Services, Bret Gossett
Assistant Vice President, Howard Yao
Vice President, Julie Trinh
Senior Vice President Chief Technology Officer, Mehran Khordodi
VICE PRESIDENT OPERATIONS, Natasha Moon
Vice President Information Security It Risk, Scot Hutton
Vice President Tax, Keith Downs
Assistant Vice President Strategic Programming, Margaret Dipp
Board Member, James Richardson
Auditors: Ernst & Young LLP

LOCATIONS

HQ: Alexandria Real Estate Equities Inc
26 North Euclid Avenue, Pasadena, CA 91101
Phone: 626 578-0777
Web: www.are.com

PRODUCTS/OPERATIONS

2015 Sales

	$ mil.	% of total
Rental	608.8	72
Tenant recoveries	209.1	25
Other	25.6	3
Total	**843.5**	**100**

2015 Client Tenant Mix by ABR

	% of total
Public Biotechnology	26
Multinational Pharmaceutical	22
Life Science Product Service and Device	22
Institutional	20
Private Biotechnology	7
Office & Tech Office	3
Total	**100**

Align Technology Inc

Brace-face begone! Align Technology produces and sells the Invisalign System which corrects malocclusion (aka crooked teeth) to orthodontists and dentists worldwide. Instead of using metal or ceramic mounts cemented on the teeth and connected by wires (traditional braces) the system uses custom manufactured clear plastic removable aligners to straighten teeth. Align also manufactures and markets the iTero orthodontic scanner used by dentists orthodontists periodontists and oral surgeons to capture various dental images (teeth width distance overbite measurements) and link them to patient records. Most of the company's revenues come from the US (52% of sales) the Netherlands (30%) and China (8%).

Operations

Align Technology operates through two segments: Clear Aligner and Scanners and Services (Scanner). Clear Aligner is the Invisalign product representing 86% of revenue. The Scanner segment accounts for 14%.

The Invisalign system uses the company's proprietary online ClinCheck application in its diagnosis and treatment planning process. The ClinCheck software simulates tooth movement in stages and details timing and placement of any features or attachments to be used during treatment.

Align has approximately 70000 active Invisalign trained doctors which the company defines as having submitted at least one case in the prior 12-month period. More than 6 million people worldwide have been treated with Invisalign. In 2018 Align trained more than 19600 new Invisalign doctors of which about 11800 were trained in the International region and 7900 were trained in the Americas region.

At the end of 2018 Align had about 450 active US patents some 425 active foreign patents and approximately 485 pending global patent applications.

Geographic Reach

San Jose California-based Align Technology has North American regional headquarters in Raleigh North Carolina; European regional headquarters in Amsterdam the Netherlands; and Asia/Pacific regional headquarters in Singapore.

Manufacturing facilities are located in Juarez Mexico and Ziyang China where it conducts aligner fabrication distributes and repairs scanners and performs CAD/CAM services; and in Or Yehuda Israel where it produces its handheld intra-oral scanner wand and performs the final assembly of its iTero scanner. Align also has a research and development facility in Moscow.

Invisalign digital treatment planning and interpretation for iTero restorative cases are conducted at facilities in China Costa Rica Germany and Spain.

More than half of sales come from the US but the company continues to focus on increasing sales to the Asia/Pacific (APAC) and Europe Middle East Africa (EMEA) markets.

Sales and Marketing

Align Technology's sales efforts are focused primarily on the Invisalign System which is sold primarily through a direct sales force in North America Asia/Pacific EMEA (Europe Middle East and Africa) and Latin America. The company also has distribution partners that sell Invisalign in smaller non-core international country markets.

For the iTero scanner it has a small team of direct sales representatives and a few distributors in North America who leverage leads generated by Invisalign sales including customer events and industry trade-shows.

The company sells the vast majority of its products directly to customers: orthodontists and general practitioner dentists as well as to restorative and aesthetic dentists including prosthodontists periodontists and oral surgeons. Because the teenage and younger market makes up 75% of the approximately 12 million total orthodontic case starts each year the company continues to target teenage and younger patients through sales and marketing programs.

Financial Performance

Throughout the five-year period ending in 2018 Align Technology reported year-over-year revenue growth as advancements in product and technology continued to strengthen doctors' clinical confidence in the use of Invisalign. During that same period profits also rose except for a slight dip from 2014 to 2015.

The company reported nearly $2.0 billion in revenue for fiscal 2018 up from $1.47 billion for the prior fiscal period. Align attributes the increase to Invisalign and scanner volume growth across all regions. It had some 1.2 million people start Invisalign treatment for the first time resulting in its 6 millionth Invisalign patient. The number of teenagers treated with Invisalign in 2018 grew 40%. The company also trained a record number of new Invisalign doctors more than half of which were international doctors.

Net income was $400.2 million in 2018 up from $231.4 million in 2017. Align attributed revenue gains and a lower tax rate as reasons for the jump. Its provision for income taxes was $57.7 million and $130.2 for 2018 and 2017 respectively representing effective tax rates of about 12% and 36% respectively.

Cash at the end of 2018 was $636.9 million. Cash from operations was $554.7 million while investing activities provided $6.9 million. Financing activities used $369.4 million.

Strategy

Align Technology is the largest company in the clear aligner orthodontics market in North America. The firm boosts sales by increasing the number of dentists and orthodontists that are committed to selling the products. It also increases brand awareness through consumer marketing programs.

Align needs to innovate to stay ahead of newcomers to the market especially as several of its patents expired in 2017 and 2018. As such the company develops new versions and variations of the Invisalign system as well as new tools that make it easier for dentists to adopt use of the system. In 2018 it launched Invisalign with Mandibular Advancement in the US. It also continues to make improvements to its Invisalign treatment software ClinCheck Pro.

Geographically the firm is looking to expand into new markets as well as building up business in existing markets. It is also investing in its infrastructure abroad to further grow operations. In 2018 it opened new treatment planning facilities in Madrid to support customers in this region and expanded facilities in Costa Rica to support growth.

In 2019 Align lost an arbitration case which resulted in the company's forced closure of its 12 Invisalign retail locations and a divestiture of its minority share in SmileDirectClub. Align was involved in a legal dispute with SmileDirectClub and an arbitrator determined Align broke a non-compete clause misused confidential SmileDirectClub information and violated its fiduciary duties toward SmileDirectClub.

Company Background

In 1997 five employees in a small duplex in Redwood City California founded Align Technology with a single concept in mind ? how to leverage technology to straighten teeth. In 1999 Align Technology introduced the Invisalign system and sub-launched a large US national advertising campaign. The company went public in 2001 at which point it had manufactured one million unique aligners and trained more than ten thousand doctors.

EXECUTIVES

VP Legal Affairs and General Counsel, Roger E. George, age 54, $382,368 total compensation
President and CEO, Joseph M. (Joe) Hogan, age 61, $548,077 total compensation
VP; Managing Director Americas, Lynn S. Pendergrass
VP Operations, Emory M. Wright, age 50, $349,543 total compensation
VP; Managing Director North America, Christopher C. Puco, age 58

COMPETITORS

Beacon Capital Partners
BioMed Realty
Boston Properties
Brandywine Realty
Equity Commonwealth
First Industrial Realty
Liberty Property Trust
PS Business Parks
Shorenstein

HISTORICAL FINANCIALS

Company Type: Public

Income Statement
FYE: December 31

	REVENUE ($ mil.)	NET INCOME ($ mil.)	NET PROFIT MARGIN	EMPLOYEES
12/19	1,531.3	363.1	23.7%	439
12/18	1,327.4	379.3	28.6%	386
12/17	1,128.1	169.0	15.0%	323
12/16	921.7	(65.9)	—	285
12/15	843.4	144.2	17.1%	278
Annual Growth	16.1%	26.0%	—	12.1%

2019 Year-End Financials

Debt ratio: 36.8%
Return on equity: 4.4%
Cash ($ mil.): 242.6
Current ratio: 0.18
Long-term debt ($ mil.): 6,777.4
No. of shares (mil.): 120.8
Dividends
Yield: 2.4%
Payout: 392.1%
Market value ($ mil.): 19,519.0

	STOCK PRICE ($) FY Close	P/E High/Low	PER SHARE ($) Earnings	Dividends	Book Value
12/19	161.58	52 36	3.12	4.00	73.39
12/18	115.24	37 31	3.52	3.73	66.14
12/17	130.59	84 68	1.58	3.45	59.63
12/16	111.13	— —	(1.99)	3.23	55.85
12/15	90.36	63 51	1.63	3.05	54.79
Annual Growth	15.6%	— —	17.6%	7.0%	7.6%

VP Research and Development, Zelko Relic, age 54, $366,231 total compensation
VP iTero Scanner and Services Chief Marketing Portfolio and Business Development Officer, Raphael S. Pascaud, age 47, $374,317 total compensation
VP; Managing Director EMEA, Simon Beard, age 52
VP; Managing Director Asia/Pacific, Julie Tay, age 52
VP; Managing Director Doctor-Directed Consumer Channel, Jennifer Olson-Wilk
CFO, John F. Morici
VP Information Technology, Sreelakshmi Kolli
Managing Director Latin America, Ritesh Sharma
Vice President, Scott Meggs
Vice President Product Innovation, Srini Kaza
Chairman, C. Raymond Larkin, age 70
Auditors: PricewaterhouseCoopers LLP

LOCATIONS

HQ: Align Technology Inc
2820 Orchard Parkway, San Jose, CA 95134
Phone: 408 470-1000
Web: www.aligntech.com

PRODUCTS/OPERATIONS

2017 Sales by Segment

	$ mil.	% of total
Clear Align	1,309.3	89
Scanner	164.1	11
Total	**1,473.4**	**100**

COMPETITORS

3M	Patterson Companies
Dentsply Sirona	Straumann
Henry Schein	Sybron Dental

HISTORICAL FINANCIALS

Company Type: Public

Income Statement — FYE: December 31

	REVENUE ($ mil.)	NET INCOME ($ mil.)	NET PROFIT MARGIN	EMPLOYEES
12/18	1,966.4	400.2	20.4%	11,660
12/17	1,473.4	231.4	15.7%	8,715
12/16	1,079.8	189.6	17.6%	6,060
12/15	845.4	144.0	17.0%	4,375
12/14	761.6	145.8	19.1%	3,580
Annual Growth	**26.8%**	**28.7%**	**—**	**34.3%**

2018 Year-End Financials

Debt ratio: —
Return on equity: 33.3%
Cash ($ mil.): 636.9
Current ratio: 1.88
Long-term debt ($ mil.): —
No. of shares (mil.): 79.7
Dividends
  Yield: —
  Payout: —
Market value ($ mil.): 16,708.0

	STOCK PRICE ($) FY Close	P/E High/Low		PER SHARE ($) Earnings	Dividends	Book Value
12/18	209.43	79	39	4.92	0.00	15.70
12/17	222.19	91	31	2.83	0.00	14.37
12/16	96.13	42	25	2.33	0.00	12.51
12/15	65.85	38	29	1.77	0.00	10.67
12/14	55.91	35	25	1.77	0.00	9.39
Annual Growth	**39.1%**		**—**	**29.1%**	**—**	**13.7%**

Allegiance Bancshares Inc

Auditors: Crowe LLP

LOCATIONS

HQ: Allegiance Bancshares Inc
8847 West Sam Houston Parkway N., Suite 200, Houston, TX 77040
Phone: 281 894-3200
Web: www.alliancebank.com

HISTORICAL FINANCIALS

Company Type: Public

Income Statement — FYE: December 31

	ASSETS ($ mil.)	NET INCOME ($ mil.)	INCOME AS % OF ASSETS	EMPLOYEES
12/18	4,655.2	37.3	0.8%	569
12/17	2,860.2	17.6	0.6%	375
12/16	2,450.9	22.8	0.9%	327
12/15	2,084.5	15.7	0.8%	310
12/14	1,280.0	9.0	0.7%	304
Annual Growth	**38.1%**	**42.7%**	**—**	**17.0%**

2018 Year-End Financials

Return on assets: 0.9%
Return on equity: 7.3%
Long-term debt ($ mil.): —
No. of shares (mil.): 21.9
Sales ($ mil): 165.9
Dividends
  Yield: —
  Payout: —
Market value ($ mil.): 710.0

	STOCK PRICE ($) FY Close	P/E High/Low		PER SHARE ($) Earnings	Dividends	Book Value
12/18	32.37	19	12	2.37	0.00	32.04
12/17	37.65	30	23	1.31	0.00	23.20
12/16	36.15	21	9	1.75	0.00	21.59
12/15	23.65	18	15	1.43	0.00	20.17
Annual Growth	**11.0%**		**—**	**18.3%**	**—**	**16.7%**

Allegiant Travel Company

Allegiant Travel pledges to serve the vacation needs of residents of more than 100 small US cities in 41 states. Through Allegiant Air the company provides nonstop service to tourist destinations such as Las Vegas Los Angeles and Orlando Florida from places such as Cedar Rapids Iowa; Fargo North Dakota; and Toledo Ohio. It maintains a fleet of about 50 MD-80 series aircraft. Besides scheduled service Allegiant Air offers charter flights for casino operators Caesars Entertainment (formerly Harrah's Entertainment) and MGM MIRAGE in addition to other customers. Sister company Allegiant Vacations works with partners to allow customers to book hotel rooms and rental cars along with their airline tickets.

Operations

Allegiant Travel's operating fleet consists of 51 MD-80 aircraft 26 A320 series aircraft and five Boeing 757-200 aircraft providing service on 294 routes to 104 cities. The company is also expecting that the services would expand to 322 routes and 111 cities by late 2016.

Geographic Reach

The company has a route network providing service on 294 routes between 87 cities and 17 leisure destinations. It serves 41 US states.

Financial Performance

Allegiant Travel has achieved extraordinary growth over the last five years with revenues surging 11% from $1.14 billion in 2014 to peak at $1.26 billion in 2015 a company milestone. Profits also more than doubled from $87 million in 2014 to reach a record-setting $220 million in 2015 mostly due to the lower price of fuel. Cash flow has also followed the same upward trend climbing by 35% in 2015.

The historic growth for 2015 was attributed to a spike in ancillary air-related revenue fueled by an increase in scheduled service passengers as well as continued revenue optimization efforts. In addition increased customer convenience fees and the effective yield management of other existing products drove an increase in its average ancillary air-related fare per passenger.

Strategy

Allegiant Travel's business strategy includes expanding its ancillary products and services and adding new destinations to its flight network. During 2015 the company added service to four leisure destinations commenced service on 69 new routes and discontinued service on under-performing routes. Based on its currently published schedule through August 2016 the company plans to increase total routes to 322 increase the number of leisure destinations served to 19 and increase the number of cities served to 92.

In 2016 the company entered into forward purchase agreements for 11 Airbus A320 series aircraft. It expects delivery of seven aircraft in 2016 and the remaining four in the first half of 2017.

EXECUTIVES

President, John T. Redmond, age 61
Chairman and CEO, Maurice J. (Maury) Gallagher, age 69
EVP and Chief Marketing Officer, M. Ponder Harrison, age 57, $185,000 total compensation
SVP and CIO, Scott M. Allard, age 51, $195,000 total compensation
SVP CFO and Interim COO, D. Scott Sheldon, age 41, $195,000 total compensation
VP and Principal Accounting Officer, Gregory C. Anderson, $147,500 total compensation
Executive Vice President and Chief Operations Officer Sunseeker Resorts, Micah Richins
Auditors: KPMG LLP

LOCATIONS

HQ: Allegiant Travel Company
1201 North Town Center Drive, Las Vegas, NV 89144
Phone: 702 851-7300
Web: www.allegiant.com

PRODUCTS/OPERATIONS

Selected Products and Services

Air-related ancillary products and services.
Fixed fee contract air transportation.
Scheduled service air transportation.
Third party ancillary products and services

2015 Sales

	$ mil.	% of total
Scheduled service	735.6	58
Ancillary revenues		
Air-related charges	434.3	34
Third party products	40.2	3
Fixed fee contract revenues	19.7	2
Other	32.4	3
Total	**1,262.2**	**100**

COMPETITORS

AirTran Airways	Frontier Airlines
Alaska Air	Horizon Air
American Airlines Group	JetBlue
Delta Air Lines	Southwest Airlines
	United Continental

HISTORICAL FINANCIALS
Company Type: Public

Income Statement   FYE: December 31

	REVENUE ($ mil.)	NET INCOME ($ mil.)	NET PROFIT MARGIN	EMPLOYEES
12/18	1,667.4	161.8	9.7%	4,159
12/17	1,503.7	194.9	13.0%	3,951
12/16	1,362.8	219.5	16.1%	3,589
12/15	1,262.1	220.3	17.5%	3,018
12/14	1,137.0	86.6	7.6%	2,564
Annual Growth	10.0%	16.9%	—	12.9%

2018 Year-End Financials

Debt ratio: 50.9%
Return on equity: 26.1%
Cash ($ mil.): 81.5
Current ratio: 0.96
Long-term debt ($ mil.): 1,119.4
No. of shares (mil.): 16.1
Dividends
  Yield: 2.7%
  Payout: 28.0%
Market value ($ mil.): 1,622.0

	STOCK PRICE ($) FY Close	P/E High/Low		PER SHARE ($) Earnings	Dividends	Book Value
12/18	100.22	18	10	10.00	2.80	42.66
12/17	154.75	15	10	11.93	2.80	34.11
12/16	166.40	14	9	13.21	2.40	28.47
12/15	167.83	18	11	12.94	2.75	20.83
12/14	150.33	30	18	4.86	2.50	16.82
Annual Growth	(9.6%)	—	—	19.8%	2.9%	26.2%

Alpine Banks of Colorado

Auditors: Dalby Wendland & Co., P.C.

LOCATIONS
HQ: Alpine Banks of Colorado
  2200 Grand Avenue, Glenwood Springs, CO 81601
Phone: 970 384-3257   **Fax:** 970 945-2214
Web: www.alpinebank.com

HISTORICAL FINANCIALS
Company Type: Public

Income Statement   FYE: December 31

	REVENUE ($ mil.)	NET INCOME ($ mil.)	NET PROFIT MARGIN	EMPLOYEES
12/18	188.1	54.8	29.2%	730
12/17	163.3	33.6	20.6%	0
12/16	144.1	33.4	23.2%	0
12/15	128.3	27.6	21.5%	0
Annual Growth	13.6%	25.7%	—	—

2018 Year-End Financials

Debt ratio: 1.8%
Return on equity: 19.7%
Cash ($ mil.): 367.7
Current ratio: 0.11
Long-term debt ($ mil.): 69.1
No. of shares (mil.): 0.1
Dividends
  Yield: —
  Payout: 20.8%
Market value ($ mil.): —

	STOCK PRICE ($) FY Close	P/E High/Low	PER SHARE ($) Earnings	Dividends	Book Value
12/18	0.00	— —	520.00	0.00	2,823.66
Annual Growth	—	— —	—	—	—

Altair Engineering Inc

Auditors: Ernst & Young LLP

LOCATIONS
HQ: Altair Engineering Inc
  1820 East Big Beaver Road, Troy, MI 48083
Phone: 248 614-2400
Web: www.altair.com

HISTORICAL FINANCIALS
Company Type: Public

Income Statement   FYE: December 31

	REVENUE ($ mil.)	NET INCOME ($ mil.)	NET PROFIT MARGIN	EMPLOYEES
12/18	396.3	13.7	3.5%	2,850
12/17	333.3	(99.4)	—	2,400
12/16	313.2	10.1	3.2%	1,600
12/15	294.1	10.9	3.7%	0
Annual Growth	10.5%	7.9%	—	—

2018 Year-End Financials

Debt ratio: 6.5%
Return on equity: 7.7%
Cash ($ mil.): 35.3
Current ratio: 1.21
Long-term debt ($ mil.): 31.4
No. of shares (mil.): 70.5
Dividends
  Yield: —
  Payout: —
Market value ($ mil.): 1,945.0

	STOCK PRICE ($) FY Close	P/E High/Low		PER SHARE ($) Earnings	Dividends	Book Value
12/18	27.58	217	121	0.18	0.00	4.10
12/17	23.92	—	—	(1.89)	0.00	1.00
12/16	0.00	—	—	0.18	0.00	(0.69)
Annual Growth	—	—	—	(0.0%)	—	—

Alteryx Inc

Auditors: DELOITTE & TOUCHE LLP

LOCATIONS
HQ: Alteryx Inc
  3345 Michelson Drive, Suite 400, Irvine, CA 92612
Phone: 888 836-4274
Web: www.alteryx.com

HISTORICAL FINANCIALS
Company Type: Public

Income Statement   FYE: December 31

	REVENUE ($ mil.)	NET INCOME ($ mil.)	NET PROFIT MARGIN	EMPLOYEES
12/18	253.5	28.0	11.1%	800
12/17	131.6	(17.5)	—	555
12/16	85.7	(24.2)	—	424
12/15	53.8	(21.4)	—	0
12/14	37.9	(20.3)	—	0
Annual Growth	60.7%	—	—	—

2018 Year-End Financials

Debt ratio: 28.0%
Return on equity: 12.3%
Cash ($ mil.): 89.9
Current ratio: 3.71
Long-term debt ($ mil.): 173.6
No. of shares (mil.): 61.5
Dividends
  Yield: —
  Payout: —
Market value ($ mil.): 3,662.0

	STOCK PRICE ($) FY Close	P/E High/Low		PER SHARE ($) Earnings	Dividends	Book Value
12/18	59.47	140	56	0.43	0.00	4.90
12/17	25.27	—	—	(0.37)	0.00	2.57
Annual Growth	135.3%	—	—	—	—	90.4%

Altra Industrial Motion Corp

Altra Industrial Motion likes to move things around. The company manufactures mechanical power transmission and motion control products for virtually any industrial application. It specializes in industrial clutches and brakes couplings and gear drives for diverse applications from elevator braking systems to lawnmowers. The company serves industries like energy general industrial metals mining transportation and turf and garden. Its products are marketed under multiple brands such as?TB Wood's?and Warner Electric and sold directly to OEMs and through a network of more than 3000 distributors. North America accounts for about 50% of sales. The company was founded in 2004 and went public in 2006.

Operations
Altra operates through three segments: Couplings Clutches and Brakes; Electromagnetic Clutches and Brakes; and Gearing.

Altra's Couplings Clutches and Brakes (CCB) segment is the largest segment accounting for half of total sales. The company manufactures these products in two categories: heavy duty and overrunning. Its line of heavy duty clutches and brakes are marketed under the Wichita Twiflex Svendborg and Stromag brand names. Overrunning clutches are used to prohibit a shaft's rotation in one direction while enabling its rotation in the opposite direction and are sold under the Formsprag Marland and Stieber brand names.

The Electromagnetic Clutches and Brakes (ECB) segment (nearly 30%) makes products used in industrial and commercial markets including agricultural machinery material handling motion control and turf and garden. These products use electromagnetic friction-type connections and sport brand names like Warner Electric Inertia Dynamics Matrix and Stromag.

Lastly the Gearing segment accounting for more than 20% of sales makes gears used primarily in industrial applications. Gearing also includes Altra's engineered bearing assemblies manufactured under the Kilian brand name.

Geographic Reach
In addition to its headquarters in Braintree MA Altra maintains 35 manufacturing facilities about half of which are in North America half in Europe and a handful in Asia. It sells its products in more than 70 countries worldwide. More than 50% of sales generated in North America about 40% in Europe and about 10% in Asia and other countries.

Sales and Marketing
Altra's global sales and marketing network includes more than 1000 direct OEM customers and over 3000 distributor outlets. Some 25% of its net sales are generated through independent industrial distributors such as Motion Industries?Applied Industrial Technologies?Kaman Industrial Technologies and?W.W. Grainger. Its largest distributor accounts for about 5% of total sales.

Financial Performance
After a two-year decline in net sales Altra's revenue rebounded to $876.7 million in 2017 a 24% increase from 2016. The increase was primarily due to the acquisition of Stromag strategic price increases and higher sales across the business.

Net income more than doubled to $51.4 million mainly as a result of higher net sales as well as lower restructuring costs and the absence of impairment charges compared with the previous year ($6.7 million in 2016).

Cash at the end of fiscal 2017 was $52.0 million a decrease of $17.1 million from the prior year. Cash from operations contributed $80.6 million to the coffers while investing activities used $26.7 million mainly for capital expenditures related to construction costs at three facilities. Financing activities used another $74.0 million which included $51.6 million in debt repayments.

Strategy
Altra is working to improve profits with facility consolidations pricing improvements and supply chain efficiencies. The recent acquisitions of Stromag and Fortive's Automation and Specialty (A&S) business are also paving the way for expansion into more industries.

Part of Altra's long-term business strategy includes global process automation and strategic pricing and supply chain management initiatives. The company uses its manufacturing centers of excellence to consolidate purchasing activities across geographies and business lines.

Its acquisition strategy is also benefiting Altra's top line. The integration of the Stromag business has increased efficiencies across Altra's manufacturing operations and supply chain. With the addition of Stromag's sales force Altra has realigned sales with a stronger focus on end markets versus products and has ventured into new markets such as marine cranes and hoists. The A&S platform acquired from Fortive adds electronic and software content in precision motion control that increases Altra's exposure to higher-margin business categories like the medical robotics factory automation and food and beverage industries.

Mergers and Acquisitions
In 2018 Altra acquired Fortive's Automation and Specialty (A&S) platform for $3 billion. Fortive's software for precision motion control including engineered servo-motors and direct drive and linear automation technologies allows Altra to branch out into higher-margin businesses such as robotics and factory automation.

In 2016 Altra acquired Germany-based Stromag from GKN plc for €186.4 million. Stromag makes engineered products including clutches and brakes flexible couplings limit switches and friction discs. The Stromag purchase extended the company's geographic reach into Europe China and India.

EXECUTIVES
VP and CFO, Christian Storch, age 59, $405,000 total compensation
Chairman and CEO, Carl R. Christenson, age 60, $650,000 total compensation
VP Legal and Human Resources General Counsel and Secretary, Glenn E. Deegan, age 52, $325,000 total compensation
Assistant Treasurer, Tracy Sorrell
Auditors: DELOITTE & TOUCHE LLP

LOCATIONS
HQ: Altra Industrial Motion Corp
300 Granite Street, Suite 201, Braintree, MA 02184
Phone: 781 917-0600
Web: www.altramotion.com

PRODUCTS/OPERATIONS
2017 sales

	% of total
Couplings Clutches & Brakes	50
Electromagnetic Clutches & Brakes	28
Gearing	22
Inter-segment eliminations	-
Total	**100**

Selected Products
Electric Clutches and Brakes
Heavy Duty Clutches and Brakes
Overrunning Clutches
Couplings
Gear Drives
Gear Motors
Belted Drives
Engineered Bearing Assemblies
Limit Switches
Linear Actuators and Controls

Selected Brands
Ameridrives
Bauer Gear Motor
Bibby Turboflex
Boston Gear
Delroyd Worm Gear
Formsprag Clutch
Guardian Couplings
Huco
Industrial Clutch
Inertia Dynamics
Kilian
Lamiflex Couplings
Marland Clutch
Matrix
Nuttall Gear
Stieber
Stromag
Svendborg Brakes
TB Wood's
Twiflex
Warner Electric
Warner Linear
Wichita Clutch

COMPETITORS
Baldor Electric
Danaher
Eaton
Emerson Electric
GE
Harbin Electric
Hitachi
IMI plc
OGURA CLUTCH CO. LTD.
Regal Beloit
Rexnord
Rockwell Automation
Siemens AG

HISTORICAL FINANCIALS
Company Type: Public

Income Statement   FYE: December 31

	REVENUE ($ mil.)	NET INCOME ($ mil.)	NET PROFIT MARGIN	EMPLOYEES
12/18	1,175.3	35.3	3.0%	9,300
12/17	876.7	51.4	5.9%	4,850
12/16	708.9	25.1	3.5%	4,564
12/15	746.6	35.4	4.7%	3,855
12/14	819.8	40.1	4.9%	3,957
Annual Growth	9.4%	(3.1%)	—	23.8%

2018 Year-End Financials
Debt ratio: 39.3%
Return on equity: 3.1%
Cash ($ mil.): 168.9
Current ratio: 2.09
Long-term debt ($ mil.): 1,690.9
No. of shares (mil.): 64.1
Dividends
  Yield: 2.7%
  Payout: 73.9%
Market value ($ mil.): 1,614.0

	STOCK PRICE ($) FY Close	P/E High/Low		PER SHARE ($) Earnings	Dividends	Book Value
12/18	25.15	57	26	0.92	0.68	28.79
12/17	50.40	28	20	1.77	0.66	13.65
12/16	36.90	41	22	0.97	0.60	10.41
12/15	25.08	22	17	1.36	0.57	9.41
12/14	28.39	25	18	1.47	0.46	9.82
Annual Growth	(3.0%)	—	—	(11.1%)	10.3%	30.9%

Ambac Financial Group, Inc.

Ambac has scaled back in a major way. Holding company Ambac Financial operates through subsidiaries including its flagship unit Ambac Assurance Everspan Financial Guarantee and Ambac Assurance UK. The businesses offered financial guarantees and related services to customers around the world. Ambac Assurance guaranteed public finance and structured finance obligations but it has stopped offering new business and placed its existing business in run-off (meaning it still accepts premium payments due on existing policies and pays out claims as it can).

Operations
In addition to its core financial guarantee offerings in better days Ambac also insured infrastructure and utility finance deals internationally. Its Ambac Financial Services unit offered interest rate swaps credit swaps and investment management primarily to states and municipal authorities tied to their bond financing. These operations are also in run-off through means including transaction terminations settlements and scheduled contract amortizations.

How did a once-solid municipal bond insurer fall so hard? Along with other US bond insurers including FGIC and MBIA the US subprime mortgage meltdown knocked the wind out of Ambac. Its financial guarantee business fizzled and the company began to post heavy losses. Meanwhile Ambac's portfolio bulged with collateralized debt obligations (CDOs) of asset-backed securities — the financial equivalent of a sack of rotten potatoes once the credit markets turned sour.

Geographic Reach

Ambac's run-off operations primarily bring in revenues from the US market which accounts for three-fourths of revenues. The company also has international operations (also in runoff) in markets including the UK (some 20% of revenues) Australia Austria Germany and Italy.

Financial Performance

Ambac's run-off (existing account) insurance operations brought in some $644 million in revenues in 2015 nearly doubling that of 2014. Those improved earnings marked a turnaround after a couple of years of declining revenues; they were a result of increased premiums earned lower losses on derivatives and a gain on extinguishment of debt.

Net income has remained relatively flat for the past few years and in 2015 rose a modest 2% to $492 million. That was thanks to the higher revenue but partially offset by goodwill impairment charges incurred in 2014.

After reporting an operating cash outflow of $971 million in 2014 Ambac had an inflow of operating cash totaling $87.5 million in 2015 as it has lower losses and loss expenses.

Strategy

Ambac is hoping to diversify its business and has its sights set on either buying or developing new operations. It is interested in such activities as advisory services asset management and even insurance. In late 2015 the group launched a residential property investment program.

HISTORY

Mortgage Guaranty Insurance Corporation (MGIC) in 1971 founded American Municipal Bond Assurance Corporation (Ambac Indemnity) in Milwaukee. That year Ambac wrote the very first municipal bond insurance policy — for a bond to fund a medical building and a sewage treatment facility in Juneau Alaska. New York City's 1975 moratorium on debt payments helped make the new product more attractive. The company wrote the first insurance policies for mutual funds (1977) and secondary market municipal bonds (1983). In 1981 Ambac moved to New York; four years later it became a Citibank subsidiary. It went public in 1991.

In 1995 Ambac and rival MBIA allied to offer bond insurance overseas. Two years later the company formed a UK subsidiary to serve Europe. In recognition of the growing market the joint venture was amended in 2000 to provide for individual operations by the two partners in Europe though they continued to reinsure each other there and to work jointly in Japan. Ambac went on a buying spree in 1996 and 1997 buying the investment advisory and broker dealer operations of Cadre and Construction Loan Insurance (renamed Connie Lee Holdings) a guarantor of college bonds and hospital infrastructure bonds.

In 1998 as Ambac lost share in the US municipal bond market because it declined to cut premiums the company began concentrating on asset-backed securities and international bonds. Two years later Ambac entered the Japanese market through a joint venture with Yasuda Fire & Marine.

In late 2010 after missing a scheduled interest payment and failing to reach an agreement for a prepackaged bankruptcy proceeding with its creditors the company voluntarily filed for Chapter 11 bankruptcy protection. Through the filing Ambac hoped to restructure more than $1.6 billion in outstanding debt. The company also haggled with the IRS over $700 million in allegedly improper tax refunds received between 2003 and 2008.

The bankruptcy court approved a plan of reorganization for Ambac in 2012 and the plan went into effect the following year.

EXECUTIVES

Senior Managing Director Chief Accounting Officer and Controller, Robert B. Eisman, age 51, $500,000 total compensation
President and CEO Ambac Financial Group and Ambac Assurance Corporation, Claude L. LeBlanc, age 54
Senior Managing Director CFO and Treasurer, David Trick, age 48, $770,000 total compensation
President CEO and Director, Nader Tavakoli, age 60, $1,800,000 total compensation
Senior Managing Director and General Counsel, Stephen M. Ksenak, age 53, $525,000 total compensation
Senior Managing Director Restructuring and Corporate Development, David Barranco, age 48
Senior Managing Director CIO and Chief Administrative Office, Michael Reilly, age 62
Assistant Vice President Business Applications and Support, Sarbah Arthur
Vice President Automation Support, Alexandre Duarte
Assistant Vice President and Closing Coordinator, Yolanda Ortiz
Vice President, Valerie Anderson
First Vice President Structured Real Estate, Gregory Mayer
Vice President, Gary Stein
First Vice President, Sunil Rao
Vice President Technology, Scott Brown
Senior Vice President Internal Auditing, Dean Rogers
Assistant Vice President Risk Operations, Pranay Nadkarni
Assistant Vice President Finance, Chris Dudonis
Vice President Of Technology, Charu Kanbur
Avp In Technology, Venka Korsapati
Assistant Vice President Payroll, Yanira Vergara
First Vice President Housing Group, Kelly Wimmer
First Vice President Credit Risk Management, Robert Bose
Vice President Of Finance, David Harris
Vice President, Linda Ebrahim
First Vice President, Sulexan Chery
Vice President, Alice Wong
First Vice President, Roza Dimitrova
Vice President, Veronica Prasad
Chairman, Jeffrey S. Stein
Board Member, Ian Haft
Member Board of Directors, Alexander Greene
Auditors: KPMG LLP

LOCATIONS

HQ: Ambac Financial Group, Inc.
One State Street Plaza, New York, NY 10004
Phone: 212 658-7470   **Fax:** 212 208 3414
Web: www.ambac.com

PRODUCTS/OPERATIONS

2015 Net Premiums

	% of total
Accelerated earnings	44
Public Finance	31
International Finance	14
Structured Finance	11
Total	**100**

2015 Sales

	% of total
Net premiums earned	44
Total	37
Net realized investment gains	8
Net change in fair value of credit derivatives	6
Income (loss) on variable interest entities	4
Other income	1
Net other-than-temporary impairment losses recognized in earnings	-
Derivative products	-
Total	**100**

Selected Services

Adversely Classified Credit
Amendment Waiver and Consen
Credit Risk Management (CRM)
International Finance Insured Portfolio
U.S. Public Finance Insured Portfolio
U.S. Structured Finance

COMPETITORS

Assured Guaranty   MBIA
FGIC

HISTORICAL FINANCIALS

Company Type: Public

Income Statement FYE: December 31

	ASSETS ($ mil.)	NET INCOME ($ mil.)	INCOME AS % OF ASSETS	EMPLOYEES
12/18	14,588.7	267.4	1.8%	113
12/17	23,192.3	(328.7)	—	124
12/16	22,635.7	74.8	0.3%	154
12/15	23,728.0	493.4	2.1%	171
12/14	25,159.8	484.0	1.9%	188
Annual Growth	(12.7%)	(13.8%)	—	(11.9%)

2018 Year-End Financials

Return on assets: 1.4%   Dividends
Return on equity: 17.9%   Yield: —
Long-term debt ($ mil.): —   Payout: —
No. of shares (mil.): 45.3   Market value ($ mil.): 782.0
Sales ($ mil): 510.6

	STOCK PRICE ($) FY Close	P/E High/Low		PER SHARE ($) Earnings	Dividends	Book Value
12/18	17.24	5	3	3.99	0.00	35.12
12/17	15.98	—	—	(7.25)	0.00	30.52
12/16	22.50	16	7	1.64	0.00	37.94
12/15	14.09	3	1	10.72	0.00	37.41
12/14	24.50	3	2	10.31	0.00	31.09
Annual Growth	(8.4%)	—	—	(21.1%)	—	3.1%

Amedisys, Inc.

Because the last thing you want to do when you're ailing is drive to a doctor's office Amedisys brings health care home. Through more than 320 home health care agencies located throughout the

US the company provides skilled nursing and home health services primarily to geriatric patients covered by Medicare. It is also a post-acute care partner to some 3000 hospitals and 59000 physicians across the country. Its range of services includes disease-specific programs that help patients recovering from stroke as well as assistance for those coping with emphysema or diabetes. In addition to home health services Amedisys owns or manages about 140 hospice centers that offer palliative care to terminally ill patients.

Operations

Amedisys provides home health hospice care and personal care services to about 370000 patients annually. Home health operations account for more than 70% of annual revenues; the hospice segment accounts for nearly another quarter of revenue and the personal care business brings in the remainder.

The company owns and operates around 320 Medicare-certified home health centers more than 80 Medicare-certified hospice care centers and 15 personal care centers. Due to the demographics of its patient base its services are primarily paid by Medicare.

Geographic Reach

Amedisys operates in more than 35 states with the heaviest concentration of home health and hospice operations in the Southeast (Georgia Massachusetts South Carolina and Alabama are its largest markets). Over the years the company has moved into new markets through acquisitions and organic growth measures.

Sales and Marketing

Because Amedisys serves predominantly older patients some three-fourths of its revenue is derived from Medicare. The company promotes its products and services through direct contact with customers and through promotional materials. Advertising expense for 2017 was some $6.5 million versus $7.8 million in 2016 and $6.9 million in 2015.

Financial Performance

Amedisys' revenue has been generally climbing since 2014 but net income has been a bit more volatile: The company even lost money in 2015 and 2013.

In 2017 revenue increased 7% to $1.5 billion. Volume at its home health care and hospice segments increased that year. Additionally non-Medicare payments for home health offerings rose which helped offset a decline in Medicare rate cuts. The acquisitions of three home health two hospice care and two personal care businesses that year also boosted revenue.

Net income fell 19% to $30.3 million. Income tax expenses more than doubled in 2017 cutting into the company's bottom line.

Amedisys ended 2017 with $86.4 million in net cash some $56 million more than it had at the end of 2016. Operating activities provided $105.7 million in cash investing activities used $44 million and financing activities used $5.5 million.

Strategy

Amedisys is intent on building its business in home health care hospice and personal care. It is open to acquisitions large and small as well as opening new facilities where there is strong demand. It is focused on growing new contracts with managed care providers as well as maintaining the contracts it already has in place. The company is also dedicating efforts to improving the quality of care it provides which is evidenced in the numerous 4-star and 5-star ratings it has recently received.

In addition to periodic acquisitions of home health and hospice agencies in target markets Amedisys also strives to grow organically adding patients by expanding its service offerings maintaining referral relationships with doctors and hospitals and recruiting qualified home health nurses and aids. It also adds service centers to stretch its coverage area in existing markets. The company is counting on the growing population of older Americans to keep the need for home health and hospice services on the rise.

However Amedisys is heavily reliant on Medicare payments which leaves it vulnerable to system reform under debate. A reduction in Medicare expenditures would significantly impact the company.

Mergers and Acquisitions

In a move to become even larger in the hospice sector Amedisys acquired New Jersey-based Compassionate Care Hospice for $340 million in early 2019. That deal was the largest the firm has made in a decade and it expanded its hospice presence from 22 states to 34 states.

In 2018 subsidiary Associated Home Care acquired Massachusetts-based personal care provider Bring Care Home. This was the latest in a series of deals to expand in Massachusetts which has become a core market. In 2017 the company acquired Home Staff which provides home-based nursing personal care transportation and other services for $4 million. It also acquired Intercity Home Care in Massachusetts for $9.6 million.

The company also purchased five home health and hospice care centers from Tenet Healthcare for $20.5 million. In addition to Massachusetts the centers are located in Arizona Illinois and Texas — other key markets for Amedisys.

EXECUTIVES

President and CEO, Paul B. Kusserow, age 57, $905,289 total compensation
CFO, Gary D. Willis, age 54
CIO, Michael North
Chief Human Resources Officer, Lawrence R. (Larry) Pernosky, age 66, $258,173 total compensation
COO, Christopher Gerard
Area Vice President, Tiffany Jones
Senior Vice President Hospice Clinical Operations, Regarner Thompson
Vice President, Kelly Mckedy
Vice President of Operations, Cheryl Lacey
Area Vice President of Operations, Cami Oravetz
Area Vice President Of Business Development, Carolyn Erskine
Area Vice President of Business Development, Andrea Stevens
Senior Vice President Marketing And Communications, Jacqueline Valencia
Area Vice President Of Operations, Brenda Dile
Area Vice President of Business Development, David Brumitt
Vice President Enterprise Support, Valerie Gill
Area Vice President Business Development, Jonathan Richey
Vice President Business Development, Michael Elrod
Area Vice President Operations, Gwen Klutsch
Senior Vice President Payer Relations And Network Innovation, Christy Vitulli
Medical Director, Christopher Standley
Vice President Of Business Development, Nathan Degodt
Vice President, Lisa Newell
Vice President Talent Acquisition, Candy Lindsay
Vice Chairman, Ronald A. LaBorde, age 62
Chairman, Donald A. (Don) Washburn, age 74
Auditors: KPMG LLP

LOCATIONS

HQ: Amedisys, Inc.
3854 American Way, Suite A, Baton Rouge, LA 70816
Phone: 225 292-2031
Web: www.amedisys.com

PRODUCTS/OPERATIONS

2017 Sales by Segment

	$ mil.	% of total
Home Health	1,101.8	72
Hospice	371.0	24
Personal Care	60.9	4
Total	**1,533.7**	**100**

2017 Centers

	No.
Georgia	68
Alabama	37
Massachusetts	29
South Carolina	26
Florida	21
Kentucky	17
West Virginia	17
Louisiana	14
North Carolina	14
Virginia	14
Pennsylvania	13
Maryland	10
Mississippi	9
Indiana	6
Maine	6
Missouri	6
New Hampshire	6
Oklahoma	6
Arkansas	5
Connecticut	5
New York	5
Arizona	4
California	4
Oregon	4
Illinois	3
New Jersey	3
Ohio	3
Rhode Island	3
Delaware	2
Kansas	2
Texas	2
Washington	1
Wisconsin	1
Washington DC	1
Total	**421**

COMPETITORS

Addus HomeCare	Golden Horizons
American HomePatient	Home Instead
Apria Healthcare	Hospice of Michigan
Coram	LHC Group
Critical Homecare Solutions	Life Care Centers
	Lincare Holdings
Five Star Senior Living	NHC
	National Home Health
Genesis Healthcare	Star Multi Care
Gentiva	VITAS Healthcare
Girling Health Care	

Amerant Bancorp Inc

Auditors: PricewaterhouseCoopers LLP

LOCATIONS
HQ: Amerant Bancorp Inc
220 Alhambra Circle, Coral Gables, FL 33134
Phone: 305 460-4038
Web: www.mercantilbank.com

HISTORICAL FINANCIALS
Company Type: Public

Income Statement — FYE: December 31

	ASSETS ($ mil.)	NET INCOME ($ mil.)	INCOME AS % OF ASSETS	EMPLOYEES
12/18	8,124.3	45.8	0.6%	911
12/17	8,436.7	43.0	0.5%	939
12/16	8,434.2	23.5	0.3%	0
12/15	0.0	15.0	***********%	0
Annual Growth	—	45.0%	—	—

2018 Year-End Financials
Return on assets: 0.5%
Return on equity: 6.1%
Long-term debt ($ mil.): —
No. of shares (mil.): 44.6
Sales ($ mil): 363.2
Dividends
  Yield: 0.0%
  Payout: 87.0%
Market value ($ mil.): 580.0

	STOCK PRICE ($) FY Close	P/E High/Low	PER SHARE ($) Earnings	Dividends	Book Value
12/18	13.01	54 6	1.08	0.94	16.76
12/17	0.00	— —	1.02	0.00	17.73
Annual Growth	—	— —	5.9%	—	(5.5%)

America First Multifamily Investors LP

Auditors: PricewaterhouseCoopers LLP

LOCATIONS
HQ: America First Multifamily Investors LP
1004 Farnam Street, Suite 400, Omaha, NE 68102
Phone: 402 444-1630
Web: www.ataxfund.com

HISTORICAL FINANCIALS
Company Type: Public

Income Statement — FYE: December 31

	ASSETS ($ mil.)	NET INCOME ($ mil.)	INCOME AS % OF ASSETS	EMPLOYEES
12/18	982.7	41.1	4.2%	0
12/17	1,069.7	30.5	2.9%	0
12/16	944.1	23.7	2.5%	0
12/15	872.5	26.6	3.0%	0
12/14	744.2	15.0	2.0%	0
Annual Growth	7.2%	28.6%	—	—

	STOCK PRICE ($) FY Close	P/E High/Low	PER SHARE ($) Earnings	Dividends	Book Value
12/18	5.62	11 9	0.60	0.50	6.57
12/17	6.05	14 12	0.44	0.50	6.76
12/16	5.40	18 13	0.34	0.50	5.33
12/15	5.06	17 15	0.34	0.50	5.20
12/14	5.26	26 21	0.25	0.50	5.14
Annual Growth	1.7%	— —	24.5%	(0.0%)	6.3%

American Business Bank (Los Angeles, CA)

Auditors: Grant Thorton LLP

LOCATIONS
HQ: American Business Bank (Los Angeles, CA)
523 W. 6th Street, Suite 900, Los Angeles, CA 90014
Phone: 213 430-4000
Web: www.americanbusinessbank.com

HISTORICAL FINANCIALS
Company Type: Public

Income Statement — FYE: December 31

	REVENUE ($ mil.)	NET INCOME ($ mil.)	NET PROFIT MARGIN	EMPLOYEES
12/18	1,662.5	119.3	7.2%	21,000
12/17	1,533.6	30.3	2.0%	17,900
12/16	1,437.4	37.2	2.6%	16,000
12/15	1,280.5	(3.0)	—	16,100
12/14	1,204.5	12.7	1.1%	13,200
Annual Growth	8.4%	74.8%	—	12.3%

2018 Year-End Financials
Debt ratio: 1.0%
Return on equity: 23.9%
Cash ($ mil.): 20.2
Current ratio: 1.01
Long-term debt ($ mil.): 5.7
No. of shares (mil.): 31.9
Dividends
  Yield: —
  Payout: —
Market value ($ mil.): 3,744.0

	STOCK PRICE ($) FY Close	P/E High/Low	PER SHARE ($) Earnings	Dividends	Book Value
12/18	117.11	39 14	3.55	0.00	15.06
12/17	52.71	73 47	0.88	0.00	15.17
12/16	42.63	49 28	1.10	0.00	13.70
12/15	39.32	— —	(0.09)	0.00	12.19
12/14	29.35	77 34	0.39	0.00	11.82
Annual Growth	41.3%	— —	73.7%	—	6.2%

American Express Credit Corp.

EXECUTIVES
Ceo, David L Yowan
Auditors: PricewaterhouseCoopers LLP

LOCATIONS
HQ: American Express Credit Corp.
200 Vesey Street, New York, NY 10285
Phone: 212 640-2000

HISTORICAL FINANCIALS
Company Type: Public

Income Statement — FYE: December 31

	ASSETS ($ mil.)	NET INCOME ($ mil.)	INCOME AS % OF ASSETS	EMPLOYEES
12/18	2,157.4	16.3	0.8%	0
12/17	1,873.5	8.3	0.4%	0
12/16	1,843.1	12.7	0.7%	0
12/15	1,671.2	12.1	0.7%	0
12/14	1,535.5	11.4	0.7%	27
Annual Growth	8.9%	9.4%	—	—

2018 Year-End Financials
Return on assets: —
Return on equity: —
Long-term debt ($ mil.): —
No. of shares (mil.): 7.7
Sales ($ mil): 74.0
Dividends
  Yield: —
  Payout: —
Market value ($ mil.): 243.0

	STOCK PRICE ($) FY Close	P/E High/Low	PER SHARE ($) Earnings	Dividends	Book Value
12/18	31.55	20 15	2.09	0.00	21.42
12/17	39.40	39 32	1.07	0.00	20.27
12/16	34.95	20 16	1.72	0.00	18.26
12/15	32.25	19 16	1.67	0.00	18.06
12/14	27.76	20 18	1.54	0.00	(0.00)
Annual Growth	3.3%	— —	8.0%	—	—

Income Statement — FYE: December 31

	REVENUE ($ mil.)	NET INCOME ($ mil.)	NET PROFIT MARGIN	EMPLOYEES
12/18	1,461.0	387.0	26.5%	5
12/17	1,087.0	(603.0)	—	6
12/16	718.0	197.0	27.4%	6
12/15	755.0	214.0	28.3%	6
12/14	929.0	353.0	38.0%	8
Annual Growth	12.0%	2.3%	—	(11.1%)

2018 Year-End Financials
Debt ratio: 71.9%
Return on equity: 19.0%
Cash ($ mil.): 102.0
Current ratio: 2.56
Long-term debt ($ mil.): 27,970.0
No. of shares (mil.): 1.5
Dividends
  Yield: —
  Payout: —
Market value ($ mil.): —

American Homes 4 Rent

Auditors: Ernst & Young LLP

LOCATIONS

HQ: American Homes 4 Rent
30601 Agoura Road, Suite 200, Agoura Hills, CA 91301
Phone: 805 413-5300
Web: www.americanhomes4rent.com

HISTORICAL FINANCIALS

Company Type: Public

Income Statement — FYE: December 31

	REVENUE ($ mil.)	NET INCOME ($ mil.)	NET PROFIT MARGIN	EMPLOYEES
12/18	1,072.8	108.2	10.1%	1,234
12/17	960.4	81.0	8.4%	1,135
12/16	878.8	6.7	0.8%	953
12/15	630.5	(62.3)	—	781
12/14	398.8	(48.0)	—	752
Annual Growth	28.1%	—	—	13.2%

2018 Year-End Financials

Debt ratio: 31.1%
Return on equity: 2.0%
Cash ($ mil.): 30.2
Current ratio: 0.31
Long-term debt ($ mil.): 2,454.3
No. of shares (mil.): 296.6
Dividends
Yield: 1.0%
Payout: 250.0%
Market value ($ mil.): 5,888.0

	STOCK PRICE ($) FY Close	P/E High/Low	PER SHARE ($) Earnings	Dividends	Book Value
12/18	19.85	29 12	0.08	0.20	17.70
12/17	21.84	— —	(0.08)	0.20	17.96
12/16	20.98	— —	(0.14)	0.20	17.23
12/15	16.66	— —	(0.40)	0.20	15.68
12/14	17.03	— —	(0.34)	0.20	16.31
Annual Growth	3.9%	— —	—	(0.0%)	2.1%

American National Bankshares, Inc. (Danville, VA)

American National Bankshares with total assets of around $2.5 billion is the holding company for American National Bank and Trust. Founded in 1909 the bank operates some 30 branches that serve southern and central Virginia and north central North Carolina. Operating through two segments — Community Banking and Trust and Investment Services — it offers checking and savings accounts CDs IRAs and insurance. Lending activities primarily consist of real estate loans: Commercial mortgages account for about 40% of its loan portfolio while residential mortgages bring in another 20%. American National Bankshares' trust and investment services division manages nearly $610 million in assets.

Operations

American National Bankshares operates through two segments: Community Banking which accounts for more than 80% of the company's total revenue and offers deposit accounts and loans to individuals and small and middle-market businesses; and Trust and Investment Services which provides estate planning trust account administration investment management and retail brokerage services.

The bank makes more than 80% of its revenue from interest income. About 68% of its total revenue came from loan interest during 2015 while another 13% came from interest income on investment securities. The rest of its revenue came from trust fees (6% of revenue) deposit account service charges (3%) mortgage banking income (2%) brokerage fees (1%) and other miscellaneous income sources.

Geographic Reach

Danville Virginia-based American National Bankshares has 25 branches mostly in southern Virginia and in North Carolina (including in Alamance and Guilford Counties). It also has two loan production offices in Roanoke Virginia and Raleigh North Carolina.

Sales and Marketing

American National Bankshares has been cutting back on its advertising and marketing spend in recent years. It spent $356000 on advertising and marketing in 2015 up from $453000 and $607000 in 2014 and 2013 respectively.

Financial Performance

The bank group has struggled to consistently grow its revenues and profits over the past several years despite steadily increasing loan business mostly due to shrinking interest margins on loans stemming from the low-interest environment.

American National had a breakthrough year in 2015 however as its revenue jumped 17% to $68.46 million almost entirely thanks to its acquisition of MainStreet BankShares which boosted its loan and other interest-earning assets by double digits and increased its non-interest income by 19% with newly acquired deposit and other fee related income.

Double-digit revenue growth in 2015 drove the group's net income up 18% to $15.04 million. The bank's operating cash levels climbed 16% to $19.26 million for the year thanks to the boost in cash-denominated earnings.

Strategy

American National Bankshares grows its branch reach as well as its loan and deposit business by opening new branch locations or by buying other branches or banks.

The bank continues to have the largest deposit market share in the Dannville Virginia metro area boasting a 32.8% market share in the region as of mid-2015. It also had the second-largest market share in Pittsylvania County Virginia with a 21.1% share.

Mergers and Acquisitions

In 2019 American National Bankshares acquired Roanoke Virginia-based Hometown Bankshares for about $85 million. The acquisition expands American National's network to around 30 branches. The combined company has about $2.5 billion in assets.

Company Background

In 2011 American National acquired bank holding company MidCarolina Financial expanding its presence in North Carolina specifically in both Alamance and Guilford counties.

EXECUTIVES

EVP and CFO, William W. Traynham, age 62, $211,232 total compensation
President and CEO, Jeffrey V. Haley, age 58, $240,000 total compensation
EVP; EVP and Chief Administrative Officer American National Bank and Trust, Dabney T. P. (Dexter) Gilliam, age 63, $124,544 total compensation
EVP; EVP and Chief Credit Officer American National Bank and Trust, R. Helm Dobbins, age 67, $139,570 total compensation
Executive Vice President President - Alamance Region, Charles T. Canaday, age 58
EVP; EVP and Chief Banking Officer American National Bank and Trust, H. Gregg Strader
Senior Vice President, Debra Carlson
Sr Vice President, Troy Woodard
Vice President, Lee Burris
Assistant Vice President, Terri Claar
Assistant Vice President, Derwin Hall
Vice President, Bill Via
Executive Vice President, Edward Martin
Executive Vice President, Kevin Meade
Senior Vice President, Gray Goldsmith
Senior Vice President, Andy Agee
Senior Vice President, Allen Clark
Vice President Commercial Relationship Manager, Mike Gee
Assistant Vice President Mortgage Loan Officer, Amy Lowman
Chairman, Charles H. (Charlie) Majors, age 73
Board Member, Rhonda Owen
Board Of Directors, Michael Haley
Board Member, Joel Shepherd
Auditors: Yount, Hyde & Barbour, P.C.

LOCATIONS

HQ: American National Bankshares, Inc. (Danville, VA)
628 Main Street, Danville, VA 24541
Phone: 434 792-5111
Web: www.amnb.com

PRODUCTS/OPERATIONS

2015 Sales

	$ mil.	% of total
Interest and Dividend Income		
Interest and fees on loans	46.9	69
Taxable	4.2	6
Tax-exempt	3.9	5
Other	0.1	1
Non-interest income		
Trust fees	3.9	7
Service charges on deposit accounts	2.1	3
Other fees and commissions	2.4	3
Other	4.9	6
Total	68.4	100

Selected Subsidiaries

American National Bank and Trust Company
AMNB Statutory Trust I A Delaware Statutory Trust
MidCarolina Trust I A Delaware Statutory Trust
MidCarolina Trust II A Delaware Statutory Trust

Selected Services
Business Banking
  Cash Management
  Checking
  Loans
  Savings
Personal Banking
  Checking
  Loans
  Savings
Insurance
  Business
  Personal

COMPETITORS

BB&T
Bank of America
First Century Bankshares
First Citizens BancShares
NewBridge Bancorp

HISTORICAL FINANCIALS
Company Type: Public

Income Statement
FYE: December 31

	ASSETS ($ mil.)	NET INCOME ($ mil.)	INCOME AS % OF ASSETS	EMPLOYEES
12/18	1,862.8	22.5	1.2%	305
12/17	1,816.0	15.2	0.8%	328
12/16	1,678.6	16.3	1.0%	320
12/15	1,547.6	15.0	1.0%	303
12/14	1,346.4	12.7	0.9%	284
Annual Growth	8.5%	15.4%	—	1.8%

2018 Year-End Financials

Return on assets: 1.2%
Return on equity: 10.4%
Long-term debt ($ mil.): —
No. of shares (mil.): 8.7
Sales ($ mil): 82.0
Dividends
  Yield: 3.4%
  Payout: 38.6%
Market value ($ mil.): 256.0

	STOCK PRICE ($) FY Close	P/E High/Low		PER SHARE ($) Earnings	Dividends	Book Value
12/18	29.31	16	11	2.59	1.00	25.52
12/17	38.30	24	20	1.76	0.97	24.13
12/16	34.80	19	12	1.89	0.96	23.37
12/15	25.61	15	12	1.73	0.93	22.95
12/14	24.81	16	13	1.62	0.92	22.07
Annual Growth	4.3%	—	—	12.4%	2.1%	3.7%

American Realty Investors, Inc.

EXECUTIVES

EVP and CFO, Gene S. Bertcher, age 64
EVP General Counsel Tax Counsel and Secretary, Louis J. Corna, age 65
Chairman, Henry A. Butler, age 63
EVP Residential Construction, Alfred Crozier, age 60
President and COO, Daniel J. (Danny) Moos, age 63
Treasurer, Daecho Kim, age 36
Director; VP Project Development Prime, RL S. Lemke, age 57

Director, Ted R. Munselle, age 56
Independent Director, Sharon Hunt, age 73
Director, Robert A. Jakuszewski, age 51
Director, Martha C. Stephens, age 67
Director; VP Project Development Prime, RL S. Lemke, age 57
Auditors: Farmer, Fuqua & Huff, P.C.

LOCATIONS

HQ: American Realty Investors, Inc.
  1603 Lyndon B. Johnson Freeway, Suite 800, Dallas, TX 75234
Phone: 469 522-4200 **Fax:** 469 522-4299
Web: www.amrealtytrust.com

COMPETITORS

Apartment Investment and Management
AvalonBay
Cousins Properties
Equity Residential
Kimco Realty
Milestone Management

HISTORICAL FINANCIALS
Company Type: Public

Income Statement
FYE: December 31

	REVENUE ($ mil.)	NET INCOME ($ mil.)	NET PROFIT MARGIN	EMPLOYEES
12/18	120.9	173.7	143.6%	0
12/17	126.2	(8.4)	—	0
12/16	119.6	(2.7)	—	0
12/15	104.1	(1.9)	—	0
12/14	79.4	30.8	38.9%	0
Annual Growth	11.1%	54.0%	—	—

2018 Year-End Financials

Debt ratio: 53.9%
Return on equity: 93.7%
Cash ($ mil.): 36.4
Current ratio: 3.91
Long-term debt ($ mil.): 445.5
No. of shares (mil.): 16.0
Dividends
  Yield: —
  Payout: —
Market value ($ mil.): 193.0

	STOCK PRICE ($) FY Close	P/E High/Low		PER SHARE ($) Earnings	Dividends	Book Value
12/18	12.07	2	1	10.81	0.00	16.15
12/17	12.85	—	—	(0.61)	0.00	7.22
12/16	5.17	—	—	(0.25)	0.00	7.86
12/15	5.62	—	—	(0.21)	0.00	7.93
12/14	5.46	5	2	2.28	0.00	8.86
Annual Growth	21.9%	—	—	47.6%	—	16.2%

American Vanguard Corp.

American Vanguard Corporation wants to be your vanguard against pestilence. This California based specialty chemical manufacturer sells products to protect crops turf and ornamental plants as well as human and animal health. Products include insecticides fungicides herbicides molluscicides growth regulators and soil fumigants. Through its subsidiary AMVAC Chemical Corporation the company pursues new product acquisitions and licensing for US domestic sales and worldwide product distribution. Its products are sold across the US and more than 60 countries around the world.

Geographic Reach

In the US American Vanguard has presence across the country including California Texas Idaho and Alabama. Internationally it operates in Mexico Costa Rica the Netherlands China and the Asia Pacific region. The US accounts for 70% of annual sales.

Sales and Marketing

American Vanguard sells products in two categories: crop and non-crop.

Crop products include insecticides its leading product ($132 million in 2017) followed by herbicides soil fumigants & fungicides ($121 million) and plant growth regulators ($48 million). Though non-crop sales account for only 15% of total company sales this segment has seen a YOY growth of more than 30%.

Products reach more than 60 countries worldwide.

The company delivers its products through "closed delivery systems" like SmartBox Lock 'n Load and EZ Load systems and is developing a precision application technology known as SIMPAS which will allow multiple delivery in a single pass.

The company's advanced delivery system allows for controlled and regular dissemination of crop protection products and multiple crop protection options thereby not allowing insects to develop resistance to any one pesticide.

Domestic customers include distribution companies buying groups or co-operatives. International sales are handled through AMVAC BV with sales offices in Mexico and Costa Rica.

Financial Performance

Although American Vanguard's revenue has gone up for the last three years annual sales were still short of a peak $381 million posted in 2013. In 2017 revenue grew some 15% to $355 million. The increase came from product line growth primarily domestic cotton (increased acreage and pest pressure) as well as hike in sales from heightened hurricane activity. Four new acquisitions in 2017 also increased volumes sold.

The company's net income has gone up steadily for the last four years. In 2017 it posted $20 million in profits a 58% increase YOY mostly from continued improvement in factory performance factory cost recovery and higher margins in raw material purchasing. However the company faced competitive pricing pressure in the Midwest herbicide market and a larger volume of lower-margin sales due to new acquisitions.

Strategy

American Vanguard continues to show great growth potential thanks to an aggressive acquisition strategy as well as licensing of new product lines targeted at market niches around the world. Both revenue and profit margins are on the upswing despite a depressed commodities and oil market.

Through skillful marketing diligent product registration quality manufacturing American Vanguard has positioned itself as one of the leading product suppliers of the market. AMVAC has a very active licensing department as well as trademark protection to guard its impressive portfolio. Its plant regulators have seen a YOY sales growth of 62%.

Mergers and Acquisitions

The year 2017 was a busy year of acquisitions for American Vanguard with five acquisitions.

In October 2017 AMVAC BV completed the purchase of AgriCenter a Costa Rican distributor of end-use chemicals for crop applications. The acquired assets included product registration trade names and trademarks.

The same month AMVAC acquired most assets of OHP a US-based distribution company specializing in the greenhouse and nursery production markets.

In August AMVAC BV acquired specific herbicides & Syngenta in Mexico used to protect crops like sugarcane tomatoes potatoes and hot peppers.

Earlier in June AMVAC also acquired herbicides fungicides and insecticides assets from Adama Agricultural Solutions and related groups.

At the very beginning of the year the company acquired certain proprietary formulation assets from The Andersons Inc.

In 2016 AMVAC BV purchased 15% interest in BiPA NV/SA a Belgian company specializing in the development and early commercialization of biological products for use in agriculture.

EXECUTIVES

Chairman and CEO, Eric G. Wintemute, age 63, $605,000 total compensation
CFO, David T. Johnson, age 62, $318,500 total compensation
COO and EVP AMVAC Chemical Corporation, Ulrich (Bob) Trogele, age 61, $354,462 total compensation
Vice President Sales, Jim Lehman
Chief Sales Officer, Todd Hollingsworth
Board Member, John Killmer
Board Member, Morton Erlich
Board Member, Scott Baskin
Board Director, Larry Clark
Auditors: BDO USA, LLP

LOCATIONS

HQ: American Vanguard Corp.
4695 MacArthur Court, Newport Beach, CA 92660
Phone: 949 260-1200
Web: www.american-vanguard.com

PRODUCTS/OPERATIONS

2016 Sales

	$ mil.	% of total
Crops		
Insecticides	119.2	38
Herbicides	123.6	40
Other	29.4	9
Non-crop	39.9	13
Total	**312.1**	**100**

COMPETITORS

Bayer CropScience
Dow AgroSciences
DuPont Agriculture
FMC
KMG Chemicals

HISTORICAL FINANCIALS

Company Type: Public

Income Statement   FYE: December 31

	REVENUE ($ mil.)	NET INCOME ($ mil.)	NET PROFIT MARGIN	EMPLOYEES
12/18	454.2	24.2	5.3%	624
12/17	355.0	20.2	5.7%	605
12/16	312.1	12.7	4.1%	395
12/15	289.3	6.5	2.3%	347
12/14	298.6	4.8	1.6%	382
Annual Growth	11.1%	49.5%	—	13.1%

2018 Year-End Financials

Debt ratio: 16.2%   No. of shares (mil.): 29.8
Return on equity: 7.6%   Dividends
Cash ($ mil.): 6.1   Yield: 0.5%
Current ratio: 2.13   Payout: 9.8%
Long-term debt ($ mil.): 96.6   Market value ($ mil.): 453.0

	STOCK PRICE ($) FY Close	P/E High/Low		PER SHARE ($) Earnings	Dividends	Book Value
12/18	15.19	29	17	0.81	0.08	11.03
12/17	19.65	34	22	0.68	0.06	10.24
12/16	19.15	45	23	0.44	0.03	9.61
12/15	14.01	69	43	0.23	0.09	9.20
12/14	11.62	144	56	0.17	0.17	8.99
Annual Growth	6.9%	—	—	47.7%	(17.2%)	5.2%

American Woodmark Corp.

American Woodmark has more cabinet selections than the prime minister of Russia. A top maker of home cabinets in the US the company makes and distributes about 500 styles of low- to mid-priced kitchen cabinets and vanities. Styles vary by finish (oak cherry hickory maple as well as laminate) and door design. Brands include American Woodmark Shenandoah Cabinetry Timberlake and Waypoint. Targeting the remodeling and new home construction markets American Woodmark sells its lineup through home centers and independent dealers and distributors; it also sells directly to major builders. American Woodmark was established through a leveraged buyout of Boise Cascade's cabinet division.

Operations

Business is divided between two markets — remodeling and new home construction. Products are distributed through four assembly plants and a third-party logistics network.

Through its seven service centers nationwide American Woodmark offers complete turnkey installation services to its direct builder customers.

The company keeps in stock about 85 door designs in more than 20 colors.

Geographic Reach

Virginia-based American Woodmark operates nine manufacturing facilities in Arizona Georgia Indiana Kentucky Maryland Tennessee Virginia and West Virginia. Its coast-to-coast service centers expand its customer reach beyond the Sun Belt construction market.

Sales and Marketing

Together Lowe's and The Home Depot accounted for 45% of the company's fiscal 2015 (ended April) sales.

Through three primary channels — home centers builders and independent dealers and distributors — American Woodmark services the remodeling and new home construction markets. Its brand names include American Woodmark Timberlake (sold to major home builders) Shenandoah Cabinetry (Lowe's) Potomac (Lowe's) and Waypoint Living Spaces.

In fiscal 2015 advertising expenses totaled $34.3 million up from $30.4 million in fiscal 2014 but down from $36.5 million in fiscal 2013.

Financial Performance

American Woodmark has enjoyed rising revenue since 2009. In fiscal 2014 (ended April) the cabinet maker reported sales of $825.5 million a 14% increase versus the prior year. The double-digit growth was largely driven by increased sales in the new construction market as well as higher per-unit revenue.

After experiencing losses in 2011 and 2012 the company's profits have rebounded. Higher revenues helped net income rise 73% to $35.5 million in fiscal 2015 (although increased income tax expense partially offset those gains). Cash flow from operations also rose growing 45% to $58.7 million that year.

HISTORY

Alvin Goldhush in 1951 started cabinet company Form Laminates which lumber giant Boise Cascade acquired two decades later. Four senior managers of Boise Cascade's cabinet division — William Brandt Jeff Holcomb Al Graber and Donald Mathias — engineered an LBO of the unit in 1980 and named it American Woodmark after a popular line of cabinets. The company started selling cabinets nationwide through distribution centers and went public in 1986.

American Woodmark spent the first half of the 1990s diversifying its product and brands. In 1990 it introduced Timberlake a cabinet line for the construction industry. Other brands including Coventry and Case Crestwood and Scots Pine were added and quintupled its product line.

President and COO Jake Gosa became CEO in 1996. The sales cupboard was rather bare that year from a downturn in the closely linked home centers industry. The market surged in 1997 causing American Woodmark's profits to nearly triple and new equipment and manufacturing techniques boosted output. In 1998 the company began offering hickory cabinets (its first new wood species in a decade) kitchen accessories and high-quality ready-to-assemble framed cabinets (Flat Pack).

In 1999 American Woodmark expanded its hickory cabinet offerings (adding the Newport and Charleston brands). The company began operations at its new assembly facility in Gas City Indiana in 2000. To both preserve and increase market share in a slow-growth economy in 2001 American Woodmark initiated plans to expand two plants and open two more in Kentucky and Oklahoma.

EXECUTIVES

SVP and General Manager New Construction, R. Perry Campbell, age 53, $240,623 total compensation

President and CEO, S. Cary Dunston, age 53, $396,218 total compensation
SVP Remodel Sales and Marketing, Bradley S. (Brad) Boyer, age 59, $267,984 total compensation
CFO, M. Scott Culbreth, age 47
National Account Manager, Jason Bryan
Vice President of Field Sales Home Depot, Barry Rudolph
Vice President Logistics, Mike Mills
Vice President and Chief Human Resources Officer, Heather Banks
Vice President Lowes Account, Matt Majher
National Account Manager, Derek Cook
Chairman, Kent B. Guichard, age 62
Assistant Treasurer, Dunnigan Kevin
Auditors: KPMG LLP

LOCATIONS

HQ: American Woodmark Corp.
561 Shady Elm Road, Winchester, VA 22602
Phone: 540 665-9100
Web: www.americanwoodmark.com

PRODUCTS/OPERATIONS

Selected Brands
American Woodmark
Potomac
Shenandoah Cabinetry
Timberlake
Waypoint Living Spaces

COMPETITORS

Armstrong World Industries
Elkay Manufacturing
Masco
MasterBrand Cabinets
Norcraft Companies Inc.
US Home Systems

HISTORICAL FINANCIALS

Company Type: Public

Income Statement FYE: April 30

	REVENUE ($ mil.)	NET INCOME ($ mil.)	NET PROFIT MARGIN	EMPLOYEES
04/19	1,645.3	83.6	5.1%	9,300
04/18	1,250.2	63.1	5.1%	9,400
04/17	1,030.2	71.2	6.9%	5,808
04/16	947.0	58.7	6.2%	5,600
04/15	825.4	35.5	4.3%	5,070
Annual Growth	18.8%	23.9%	—	16.4%

2019 Year-End Financials
Debt ratio: 45.2%
Return on equity: 13.9%
Cash ($ mil.): 59.1
Current ratio: 2.05
Long-term debt ($ mil.): 689.2
No. of shares (mil.): 16.8
Dividends
Yield: —
Payout: —
Market value ($ mil.): 1,515.0

	STOCK PRICE ($) FY Close	P/E High/Low	PER SHARE ($) Earnings	Dividends	Book Value
04/19	89.93	22 11	4.83	0.00	36.82
04/18	82.20	37 21	3.77	0.00	33.23
04/17	91.90	21 14	4.34	0.00	21.71
04/16	72.84	25 13	3.57	0.00	17.28
04/15	50.70	25 12	2.21	0.00	14.29
Annual Growth	15.4%	—	21.6%	—	26.7%

Ameris Bancorp

Ameris Bancorp enjoys the financial climate of the Deep South. It is the holding company of Ameris Bank which holds roughly $3.6 billion in assets and serves retail and consumer customers through more than 75 full-service and mortgage branches in Alabama Georgia South Carolina and northern Florida. In addition to its standard banking products and services the bank also provides treasury services mortgage and refinancing solutions and investment services through an agreement with Raymond James Financial. Loans secured by commercial real estate accounted for approximately 45% of the company's loan portfolio while 1-4 family residential and construction & land development mortgages accounted for nearly a quarter and about 10% respectively.

Operations
Like most banks Ameris earns the vast majority of its recurring revenue (71.5%) from interest income from loans. Nearly 80% of these loans are made up of commercial real estate 1-4 family residential and construction & land development loans. The remaining 20% are from a mix of commercial multi-family residential and consumer loans (home improvement home equity personal lines of credit auto loans and student loans). Traditional banking products (deposit accounts) and services along with investment products and services (which primarily earn income from fees and commissions) made up about 28% of the bank's annual sales in fiscal 2013.

Sales and Marketing
Through an acquisition-oriented growth strategy Ameris seeks to grow its brand and presence in the markets it currently serves in Georgia Alabama Florida and South Carolina as well as in neighboring communities. In addition the bank expects its community-oriented philosophy will help strengthen existing customer relations and attract new customers.

The company spent $1.62 million on advertising and public relations in Fiscal Year 2013 just under the $1.622 million it spent in 2012 and more than double the $722000 it spent in 2011. The company increased its advertising spending by $900000 during 2012 to support its revenue and growth- strategies during the year.

Financial Performance
Ameris carried $3.67 billion in total assets as of December 31 2013. Loans made up $2.5 billion (approximately 68.9% of total assets). The bank also reported carrying $3 billion in deposits.

Ameris' net revenue dipped in fiscal 2013 declining 5% to $163 million from its high of $172 million in 2012 mostly from an $11.3 million dip in non-interest revenue. But this dip in non-interest revenue is primarily because the bank recorded a large gain of $20 million from acquisitions in 2012. When excluding this acquisition gain from 2012's revenues and thanks to $6.1 million revenue increase in mortgage banking activity management reports that total non-interest income actually increased $8.7 million in 2013 compared to 2012. A decline in interest-earning loan assets from $2.47 billion in 2013 compared to $2.5 billion in 2012 also played a role in the dip in net revenues.

Thanks to aggressive acquisitions and despite revenue decreasing net income jumped a whopping 43% to $20 million in 2013 from $14 million in 2012. This is only slightly below the bank's net income high of $21 million in 2011. It's most notable acquisition of Prosperity Bank increased Ameris' total assets by $744.9 million and added $449.7 million in loans to its interest-earning loan portfolio. Adding to the extra income from new loans Ameris collected higher net interest margins on all of its loans which increased to 4.74% in 2013 from 4.60% in 2012.

Strategy
Ameris plans to continue using its community banking philosophy to lessen its risk and identify prime local lending markets. Management reports that by encouraging a personalized service experience and building deeper customer relationships the bank has already grown a "substantial" base of low-cost core deposits (which pad the bank's reserves and lessen financial risk). And between its bench of experienced decision makers and lenders operating in a "decentralized" structure (which differentiates Ameris from mega banks) and its deep familiarity with local markets management believes the bank can better identify prime growth markets (for lending and bank services) with managed risk in the years ahead.

Mergers and Acquisitions
Integral to the bank's growth strategy Ameris has aggressively acquired banks to broaden its reach into its primary southern markets.

In 2019 the company's shareholders voted to acquire Fidelity Southern the holding company for Fidelity Bank. The combined company will have $16.2 billion in assets. Following the transaction Ameris will have more than 70 branches and some $4.7 billion in deposits in the Atlanta metropolitan area and about 25 branches and roughly $1.8 billion in deposits in the Jacksonville metropolitan area.

Ameris Bancorp purchased Jacksonville Bancorp and its eight branches more than doubling its branch network in Jacksonville Illinois to 14 branches.

Company Background
In addition to acquiring several troubled and failing banks with help from the FDIC Ameris merged with Prosperity Bank in 2013 which broadened its reach into Florida through Prosperity's branches in St. Augustine Jacksonville Panama City Lynn Haven Palatka and Ormand Beach.

Georgia's economy was one of the hardest hit in the US during the recession and Ameris has taken advantage of the plethora of banks seized by regulators in the state. Since 2009 the company has acquired about 10 failed banks in Georgia though FDIC-assisted transactions adding some 20 branches to its network. Ameris also snagged the failed First Bank of Jacksonville in Florida which had two locations.

EXECUTIVES

Chief Banking Executive Ameris Bancorp and Ameris Bank, Andrew B. (Andy) Cheney, age 69, $400,000 total compensation
EVP and Chief Credit Officer, Jon S. Edwards, age 57, $260,000 total compensation
EVP Chief Administrative Officer and Corporate Secretary, Cindi H. Lewis, age 65, $90,333 total compensation
President and CEO, Edwin W. (Ed) Hortman, age 65, $625,000 total compensation

EVP and Banking Group President Ameris Bancorp and President Ameris Bank, Lawton E. Bassett
EVP CFO and COO, Dennis J. Zember, age 49, $320,000 total compensation
EVP and Chief Risk Officer, Stephen A. Melton, $275,000 total compensation
EVP and Chief Banking Officer, James A. LaHaise
Exec V Pres-cio, Thomas Limerick
Assistant Vice President, Ann Dunn
Vice President Branch Manager, Colleen Cline
Vice President, Thomas Luther
Senior Vice President, Rob Kowkabany
Vice President Special Assets Division, Leo Story
Vice President Residential Mortgage, Greg Seabaugh
Senior Vice President Division President Construction, Chap Bennett
Vice President Commercial Lender, Greg Marini
Senior Vice President, Karen Cross
Assistant Vice President Commercial Banker, Jason Glas
Senior Vice President, Jw Dukes
Vice President Senior Treasury Services Advisor, Lori Putnam
Vice President, Connie Romay
Vice President Mortgage Sales Manager, Marlene Buhler
Senior Vice President, Jayson Griffin
Vice President Treasury Services Product And Risk Management, Debbie Dennis
Vice President Business Banker, Robbie Nichols
Senior Vice President Commercial Banking, Gerald Lockhart
Senior Vice President, Frank Cox
Senior Vice President Commercial Lending, Jennifer Ccim
Chairman, Daniel B. Jeter, age 67
Board Member, William Bowen
Auditors: Crowe LLP

LOCATIONS

HQ: Ameris Bancorp
3490 Piedmont Rd NE, Suite 1550., Atlanta, GA 30305
Phone: 404 639-6500
Web: www.amerisbank.com

PRODUCTS/OPERATIONS

2016 sales chart

	$ mil.	% of total
Interest income:		
Interest and fees on loans	218.7	64
Interest on taxable securities	17.9	5
Interest on nontaxable securities	1.8	-
Interest on deposits in other banks	0.9	-
Interest on federal funds sold	-	-
Non Interest income:		
Service charges on deposit accounts	42.8	13
Mortgage banking activity	48.2	14
Other service charges commissions and fees	3.5	1
Net gains on sales of securities	-	-
Gain on sale of SBA loans	3.9	1
Other noninterest income	7.1	2
Total	**344.8**	**100**

2016 sales chart

	% of total
Banking Division	91
Retail Mortgage Division	5
Warehouse Lending Division	3
SBA Division	1
Total	**100**

Selected Acquisitions
American United Bank
Central Bank of Georgia
Darby Bank & Trust
First Bank of Jacksonville
High Trust Bank
Montgomery Bank & Trust
One Georgia Bank
Satilla Community Bank
Tifton Banking Company
United Security Bank

COMPETITORS

BBVA Compass Bancshares
Bank of America
Capital City Bank
Colony Bankcorp
Community Capital Bancshares
First South Bancorp (NC)
Regions Financial
Southwest Georgia Financial
SunTrust
Thomasville Bancshares

HISTORICAL FINANCIALS

Company Type: Public

Income Statement — FYE: December 31

	ASSETS ($ mil.)	NET INCOME ($ mil.)	INCOME AS % OF ASSETS	EMPLOYEES
12/18	11,443.5	121.0	1.1%	1,804
12/17	7,856.2	73.5	0.9%	1,460
12/16	6,892.0	72.1	1.0%	1,298
12/15	5,588.9	40.8	0.7%	1,304
12/14	4,037.0	38.7	1.0%	1,027
Annual Growth	29.8%	33.0%	—	15.1%

2018 Year-End Financials

Return on assets: 1.2%
Return on equity: 10.7%
Long-term debt ($ mil.): —
No. of shares (mil.): 47.5
Sales ($ mil): 531.7
Dividends Yield: 0.0%
Payout: 14.2%
Market value ($ mil.): 1,504.0

	STOCK PRICE ($) FY Close	P/E High/Low	PER SHARE ($) Earnings	Dividends	Book Value
12/18	31.67	21 11	2.80	0.40	30.66
12/17	48.20	26 21	1.98	0.40	21.59
12/16	43.60	23 12	2.08	0.30	18.51
12/15	33.99	27 18	1.27	0.20	15.98
12/14	25.64	18 13	1.46	0.15	13.67
Annual Growth	5.4%	— —	17.7%	27.8%	22.4%

AMN Healthcare Services Inc

Operating under such brands as American Mobile Healthcare NurseChoice NursesRx Med Travelers Staff Care and O'Grady-Peyton International AMN HEalthcare Services is one of the leading temporary health care staffing companies in the world. It places nurses technicians and therapists for 13-week stints at hospitals clinics and schools across the US. With professionals recruited from Australia Canada South Africa the UK and the US AMN provides travel reimbursement and housing for its nurse and health care workers on assignment. The majority of temporary assignments for its clients are at acute-care hospitals.

Operations

AMN Healthcare Services operates through three primary segments: nurse and allied solutions locum tenens (physician staffing) solutions and other workforce solutions.

The nurse and allied solutions segment is AMN's largest bringing in some 60% of total revenue. It consists of the firm's nursing allied local and labor disruption/rapid response operations.

The locum tenens segment provides physicians advanced practice clinicians and dentists on a temporary basis to health care organizations around the nation. It brings in some 20% of total revenue.

The other workforce solutions segment provides permanent physician placement interim leadership staffing and executive search services vendor management systems and other specialized offerings. Through MedPartners and Peak Health Solutions the group offers remote medical coding clinical documentation improvement case management and auditing and advisory services. The segment accounts for another 20% of total revenue.

Geographic Reach

AMN Healthcare Services has offices in California Illinois North Carolina Oregon Colorado Pennsylvania Massachusetts New Mexico Georgia Maryland New York Tennessee Hawaii Minnesota Ohio Texas Iowa Missouri and Oklahoma. The company also operates an international nurse staffing office in the UK.

All of its revenue comes from the US. Its three largest markets are California Virginia and New York.

Sales and Marketing

AMN Healthcare Services provides staffing for acute-care hospitals health care facilities physician groups dialysis clinics pharmacies ambulatory surgery centers rehabilitation centers and home health services providers. Its customers include Kaiser Foundation Hospitals (which accounts for around 15% of total revenue) Catholic Health Initiatives MedStar Health and LifePoint Health.

Financial Performance

AMN Healthcare's revenue has been steadily climbing for the past five years which can partly be attributed to high levels of health care job vacancies in the US. As a result net income has also been on the rise.

In 2018 revenue increased 7% to $2.1 billion. The largest segment nurse and allied solutions rose 5% while the other workforce solutions segment increased 37% due to acquisitions made that year. Those gains were partially offset by a 9% decline in the locum tenens segment which had lower placement numbers.

Net income rose 7% to $141.7 million that year.

The company ended 2018 with $84.3 million in net cash about $15 million less than it had at the end of 2017. Operating activities provided $227 million in net cash (representing a 41% increase over the prior year) and financing activities provided another $37.5 million while investing activities used $279.3 million.

Strategy

Demand for the types of services AMN Healthcare offers has grown due to the nation's aging population which has increased the need for health care services while creating shortages in the health care workforce. Additionally as the health care system becomes increasingly complex and more reliant on technology the company's strategic workforce solutions are in higher demand. However AMN could lose business if the Affordable Care Act is repealed and demand for health care services falls.

AMN's growth strategy consists of increasing its network of temporary health care workers and making strategic acquisitions that complement its core offerings. For example it has expanded its other growing other workforce solutions segment organically and through acquisitions including the purchase of MedPartners (2018). The segment's managed services vendor management systems workforce optimization and other technology-enabled services typically operate at higher margins than temporary staffing; they have given AMN added sources of recurring revenue.

The company is also focused on turning around its locum tenens segment which has lagged behind the other operations. It is investing in building up the unit's sales force.

AMN's typical client contract is non-exclusive which makes the company vulnerable to losing job placements with existing customers to competitors including group purchasing organizations or other staffing firms.

Mergers and Acquisitions

AMN Healthcare Services acquired Silversheet in early 2019. Silversheet provides cloud-based credentialing and privileging software and services and at the time of the purchase it served more than 500 facilities nationwide.

In 2018 AMN acquired MedPartners a Florida-based provider of mid-revenue cycle workforce solutions for $195 million.

Also in 2018 the company acquired two Boston-based brands — Phillips DiPisa and Leaders for Today — for $30 million. That purchase boosted its executive search operations.

Company Background

American Mobile Nurses (AMN) was established in Las Vegas in 1985. The company moved to San Diego California two years later. It created American Mobile Therapist in the early 1990s and the two units merged to create American Mobile Healthcare.

In 1998 AMN Healthcare was launched. The company went public in 2001.

EXECUTIVES

CEO President and Director, Susan R. Salka, age 55, $788,077 total compensation
Chief Clinical Officer and SVP Operations, Marcia R. Faller
President Healthcare Staffing, Ralph S. Henderson, age 58, $448,846 total compensation
President of Physician Permanent Placement at AMN Healthcare Services Inc. and President of Merritt Hawkins & Associates, Mark Smith
CFO Chief Accounting Officer and Treasurer, Brian M. Scott, age 49, $448,846 total compensation
Division President Travel Nursing, Landry Seedig
CIO, Jeanette Sanchez
President Locums Tenens Division, Jeff Decker
SVP Candidate Sourcing and Digital Marketing, Brian McCloskey
President Strategic Workforce Solutions, Dan White
Vice President Government and Community Relations, Steve Wehn
Chairman, Douglas D. (Doug) Wheat, age 68
Member Board Of Directors, Paul Weaver
Auditors: KPMG LLP

LOCATIONS

HQ: AMN Healthcare Services Inc
12400 High Bluff Drive, Suite 100, San Diego, CA 92130
Phone: 866 871-8519
Web: www.amnhealthcare.com

PRODUCTS/OPERATIONS

2018 Sales by Segment

	$ mil.	% of total
Nurse & allied solutions	1,306.5	61
Locum tenens solutions	393.4	18
Other workforce solutions	436.2	21
Total	**2,136.1**	**100**

COMPETITORS

ATC Healthcare	Jackson Healthcare
C&A Industries	Kelly Services
CHG Healthcare	Maxim Healthcare Services Inc.
Cross Country Healthcare	On Assignment
EmCare	TeamStaff

HISTORICAL FINANCIALS

Company Type: Public

Income Statement   FYE: December 31

	REVENUE ($ mil.)	NET INCOME ($ mil.)	NET PROFIT MARGIN	EMPLOYEES
12/18	2,136.0	141.7	6.6%	2,920
12/17	1,988.4	132.5	6.7%	2,980
12/16	1,902.2	105.8	5.6%	2,990
12/15	1,463.0	81.8	5.6%	2,550
12/14	1,036.0	33.2	3.2%	1,800
Annual Growth	19.8%	43.7%	—	12.9%

2018 Year-End Financials

Debt ratio: 29.5% No. of shares (mil.): 46.6
Return on equity: 23.5% Dividends
Cash ($ mil.): 13.8 Yield: —
Current ratio: 1.57 Payout: —
Long-term debt ($ mil.): 440.6 Market value ($ mil.): 2,643.0

	STOCK PRICE ($) FY Close	P/E High/Low		PER SHARE ($) Earnings	Dividends	Book Value
12/18	56.66	23	16	2.91	0.00	13.70
12/17	49.25	18	13	2.68	0.00	11.85
12/16	38.45	20	10	2.15	0.00	9.44
12/15	31.05	22	11	1.68	0.00	7.29
12/14	19.60	28	15	0.69	0.00	5.50
Annual Growth	30.4%	—	—	43.3%	—	25.6%

ANI Pharmaceuticals Inc

ANI Pharmaceuticals wants to stabilize hormonal ups and downs. The firm is developing topical hormone therapy gels to deliver supplemental estrogen progestogen and testosterone. It focuses on areas including narcotics anti-cancers hormones and steroids and complex products with extended release or combination formulations. More than half of the company's earnings come from its menopause treatment Esterified Estrogen with Methyltestosterone (EEMT); other products include Hydrocortisone Enema (for ulcerative colitis) Methazolamide (for ocular conditions) and Opium Tincture (diarrhea). The firm is also developing potential cancer vaccine therapies. ANI also performs contract manufacturing.

Operations

Generic products account for nearly three-fourths of ANI's revenues while branded products bring in some 15%. Contract services and manufacturing represent the rest of the firm's earnings.

Geographic Reach

ANI Pharmaceuticals operates in the US. It has two manufacturing facilities (totaling some 173000 sq. ft.) in Baudette Minnesota.

Sales and Marketing

ANI Pharmaceuticals markets and distributes its products through wholesalers such as McKesson and AmerisourceBergen and through retail outfits including Walgreen and Wal-Mart. It also uses distributors such as ExpressScripts and Omnicare as well as group purchasing organizations (MedAssets etc.). Wholesalers McKesson Cardinal Health and AmerisourceBergen bring in more than 60% of ANI's net revenues.

Financial Performance

Revenues have been on the rise for the past three years. In 2015 ANI's revenue rose 36% to $76 million thanks largely to a 54% jump in generics sales. This was attributed to an increase in the sales price of EEMT as well as the recent launches of Methazolamide Etodolac Propafenone and Vancomycin. Branded product sales remained steady and contract manufacturing operations slowed down but contract services and royalty income rose that year.

Net income which had been rising significantly declined 47% to $15 million in 2015 due to higher selling general and administrative expenses. Cash flow from operations has followed net income's suit: In 2015 it fell 22% to $17 million on the lower profits as well as changes in income taxes and accounts payable.

Strategy

ANI Pharmaceuticals is actively launching new products to grow its prescription drug sales. In 2015 it received abbreviated new drug applications (ANDAs) for more than 20 generic products. The company will buy portfolios of existing drugs to boost its portfolio. It also partners with other firms to introduce products to the US market. For example it entered a distribution agreement with IDT Australia in 2015 through which it will market a number of products.

Mergers and Acquisitions

In 2018 ANI Pharmaceuticals acquired a portfolio of six generic drugs from Amneal Pharmaceuticals and Impax Laboratories. The deal included related manufacturing and supply agreements as well as equipment and technical information.

EXECUTIVES

SVP Finance CFO and Secretary, Phillip B. Donenberg, age 59, $285,552 total compensation
VP Operations, Bill Milling
President and CEO, Arthur S. Przybyl
Vice President Operations, James Marken
Senior Vice President of New Business Development and Specialty Sales, Robert Schrepfer
Chairman, Louis W. Sullivan, age 84
Auditors: EisnerAmper LLP

LOCATIONS

HQ: ANI Pharmaceuticals Inc
210 Main Street West, Baudette, MN 56623
Phone: 218 634-3500
Web: www.anipharmaceuticals.com

PRODUCTS/OPERATIONS

2015

	% of total
Generic pharmaceutical products	72
Branded pharmaceutical products	15
Contract manufacturing	6
Contract services and other income	7
Total	100

Selected Brands
Cortenema
Lithobid
Reglan
Vancocin

Selected Products and Candidates
Hormone therapy products and candidates
  Bio-T-Gel (transdermal testosterone supplement for men with Teva)
  Elestrin (transdermal estrogen supplement)
  LibiGel (transdermal testosterone supplement for women)
  Pill Plus (birth control with androgen)
Cancer vaccine candidates

COMPETITORS

Abbott Labs
Agenus
Allergan plc
Boehringer Ingelheim
GlaxoSmithKline
Lumara
Noven Pharmaceuticals
Pfizer
Upsher-Smith

HISTORICAL FINANCIALS

Company Type: Public

Income Statement
FYE: December 31

	REVENUE ($ mil.)	NET INCOME ($ mil.)	NET PROFIT MARGIN	EMPLOYEES
12/18	201.5	15.4	7.7%	299
12/17	176.8	(1.0)	—	173
12/16	128.6	3.9	3.1%	143
12/15	76.3	15.3	20.1%	108
12/14	55.9	28.7	51.4%	92
Annual Growth	37.8%	(14.3%)	—	34.3%

2018 Year-End Financials

Debt ratio: 42.5%
Return on equity: 8.3%
Cash ($ mil.): 43.0
Current ratio: 0.92
Long-term debt ($ mil.): 67.3
No. of shares (mil.): 11.8
Dividends
  Yield: —
  Payout: —
Market value ($ mil.): 534.0

	STOCK PRICE ($) FY Close	P/E High/Low	PER SHARE ($) Earnings	Dividends	Book Value
12/18	45.02	55 31	1.30	0.00	16.63
12/17	64.45	— —	(0.09)	0.00	14.99
12/16	60.62	206 83	0.34	0.00	14.63
12/15	45.13	54 28	1.32	0.00	13.91
12/14	56.39	23 7	2.59	0.00	12.26
Annual Growth	(5.5%)	— —	(15.8%)	—	7.9%

Ansys Inc.

It's good to look before you leap - and even before you make. That's why ANSYS helps designers and engineers see how their ideas play out even before a prototype is built by simulating designs on a computer. The company's software analyzes the models for their response to combinations of such physical variables as stress pressure impact temperature and velocity. Ranging from small consulting firms to multinational enterprises its customers come from a broad range of industries and have included Delphi Airbus Invensys and Plexus. ANSYS generates about 60% of revenue from outside the US with Japan and Germany among its leading international markets.

Operations
ANSYS makes money by licensing its software to customers and by maintaining and servicing those accounts. About 60% of the company's revenue comes from licensing and the rest comes from maintenance and service.

The company's products include ANSYS Workbench a framework that ties together the entire simulation process guiding the user through multiphysics analyses. Other products are geared toward more specific uses and industries. They include Structures Fluids Electronics Semiconductors Embedded Software Systems High-Performance Computing 3-D Design and Customization.

Geographic Reach
ANSYS has more than 75 sales offices around the world. The US accounts for about 40% revenue and Japan and Germany each account for about 12% of revenue each. Other European countries supply about 20% of revenue.

Sales and Marketing
ANSYS sells its products directly and through channel partners worldwide. It uses distribution partners in more than 40 countries. Indirect sales account for about one-fourth of ANSYS' revenue. ANSYS also partners with hardware suppliers — including AMD Dell Cray Intel Microsoft and Hewlett-Packard among others — to ensure that its products are compatible with technology upgrades. In addition it collaborates with CAD and electronic design automation (EDA) system providers such as Autodesk and Cadence to provide links between between design packages and ANSYS' simulation portfolio. These strategic alliances provide additional marketing opportunities for the company.

Financial Performance
ANSYS has posted consistently rising revenue for the past five years but net income has had a more up-and-down ride.

The company's revenue rose 10% to a company record $1.1 billion in 2017 from 2016. Revenue increased in software licenses and service and maintenance as well as in geographic areas. Driving the increase were sales to aerospace and defense electronics and automotive companies.

Net income slipped 2% to $259 million in 2017 from 2016 as ANSYS had higher operating expenses for personnel workforce realignment and stock-based compensation. The company also had a significantly higher tax rate in 2017 because of charges associated with the enactment of the U.S. Tax Cuts and Jobs Act.

ANSYS had $881 million in cash in 2017 an increase from $822 million in 2016.

Strategy
A key to ANSYS maintaining steady revenue and net income growth is delivering timely updates to its product line through in-house R&D and acquisitions. The company relies more on R&D spending about 18% of revenue ($200 million in 2017) on in-house initiatives. Its acquisitions have cost an average of just $42 million over the past three years.

The company has introduced the ANSYS 18 which has new topology optimization technology and the RedHawk-SC for the semiconductor industry. The ANSYS Discovery Live system provides instant simulation with direct geometry modeling. Like updating a spreadsheet with the touch of a key design engineers using Discovery Live can manipulate geometry materials and physics and see 3-D results right away.

ANSYS has made acquisitions to extend its product line. With CLK Design Automation the company can provide semiconductor customers with better accuracy in chip design. The purchase of Computational Engineering International boosted visualization capabilities. The deal of 3DSIM provides ANSYS with a simulation product for additive manufacturing.

Mergers and Acquisitions
ANSYS's makes acquisitions to extend product lines and fill in product holes.

In 2017 ANSYS bought three companies that extend its capabilities in automation visualization and simulation. The total paid for the three deals was $67 million. The acquired firms were CLK Design Automation which provides semiconductor customers with better accuracy as they develop next-generation chips; Computational Engineering International which develops visualization tools; and 3DSIM which brings a simulation product for additive manufacturing.

EXECUTIVES

VP Finance and Administration and CFO, Maria T. Shields, age 54, $345,333 total compensation
Chief Product Officer, Walid Abu-Hadba, age 53, $347,500 total compensation
VP and CIO, Manish Sinha
President and CEO, Ajei S. Gopal
VP Marketing, Mark Hindsbo, age 47, $151,667 total compensation
Sales Training Vice President, John Gilmore
Vice President And Gm Electronics Fluids And Mechanical Business Units, Shane Emswiler
Vice President, Justin Nescott
Vice President, Paolo Colombo
Vice President Customer Support At Asg Inc, Vinay Carpenter
Senior Vice President And General Manager Rtl Power Business, Vic Kulkarni
VICE PRESIDENT, Norman Chang
Vice President And General Manager, Eric Bantegnie
Vp Business Development and Corporate Marketing, Matthew Zack
Vice President Worldwide Customer Excellence, Renee Demay
Vp Of It, Jihong Wang
Chairman, James E. (Jim) Cashman, age 65
Board Member, Guy Dubois
Auditors: DELOITTE & TOUCHE LLP

LOCATIONS

HQ: Ansys Inc.
  2600 ANSYS Drive, Canonsburg, PA 15317
Phone: 844 462-6797
Web: www.ansys.com

PRODUCTS/OPERATIONS

2017 Sales

	$ mil.	% of total
Software licenses:		
Lease licenses	376,886.0	34
Perpetual licenses	248,078.0	23
Maintenance & service:		
Maintenance	440,428.0	40
Service	29,858.0	3
Total	1,095,250.0	100

Selected Acquisitions

FY 2017
CLK Design Automation (automation software for semiconductors)
Computational Engineering International (visualization tools)
3DSIM (simulation software for metal additive manufacturing)
FY 2015
Newmerical Technologies (simulation software for aircraft)
FY 2014
Reaction Design (California chemistry simulation software)
FY 2013
Evolutionary Engineering AG (Switzerland composite analysis)
FY 2012
Esterel Technologies (France critical systems simulation software)
FY 2011
Apache Design Solutions (semiconductor simulation software)
FY 2008
Ansoft (electronic design automation software)
FY 2006
Aavid Thermal Technologies
FY 2005
Century Dynamics

COMPETITORS

Altair Engineering	Kubotek USA
Autodesk	MSC Software
Bentley Systems	MathWorks
Cadence Design	Mentor Graphics
Dassault	PTC
Delcam	Siemens PLM Software

HISTORICAL FINANCIALS

Company Type: Public

Income Statement
FYE: December 31

	REVENUE ($ mil.)	NET INCOME ($ mil.)	NET PROFIT MARGIN	EMPLOYEES
12/18	1,293.6	419.3	32.4%	3,400
12/17	1,095.2	259.2	23.7%	2,900
12/16	988.4	265.6	26.9%	2,800
12/15	942.7	252.5	26.8%	2,800
12/14	936.0	254.6	27.2%	2,700
Annual Growth	8.4%	13.3%	—	5.9%

2018 Year-End Financials

Debt ratio: —
Return on equity: 17.1%
Cash ($ mil.): 777.1
Current ratio: 2.50
Long-term debt ($ mil.): —
No. of shares (mil.): 83.6
Dividends
  Yield: —
  Payout: —
Market value ($ mil.): 11,955.0

	STOCK PRICE ($) FY Close	P/E High/Low	PER SHARE ($) Earnings	Dividends	Book Value
12/18	142.94	38 27	4.88	0.00	31.68
12/17	147.59	50 31	2.98	0.00	26.68
12/16	92.49	32 27	2.99	0.00	25.77
12/15	92.50	35 28	2.76	0.00	24.90
12/14	82.00	31 26	2.70	0.00	24.43
Annual Growth	14.9%	— —	15.9%	—	6.7%

Antero Midstream Corp

Auditors: KPMG LLP

LOCATIONS

HQ: Antero Midstream Corp
  1615 Wynkoop Street, Denver, CO 80202
Phone: 303 357-7310
Web: www.anteromidstreamgp.com

HISTORICAL FINANCIALS

Company Type: Public

Income Statement
FYE: December 31

	REVENUE ($ mil.)	NET INCOME ($ mil.)	NET PROFIT MARGIN	EMPLOYEES
12/18	142.9	66.6	46.6%	0
12/17	69.7	2.3	3.3%	0
12/16	16.9	9.7	57.3%	0
12/15	1.2	0.7	61.8%	0
Annual Growth	383.5%	340.2%	—	—

2018 Year-End Financials

Debt ratio: —
Return on equity: —
Cash ($ mil.): 2.8
Current ratio: 0.17
Long-term debt ($ mil.): —
No. of shares (mil.): 186.2
Dividends
  Yield: 0.0%
  Payout: 163.9%
Market value ($ mil.): 2,082.0

	STOCK PRICE ($) FY Close	P/E High/Low	PER SHARE ($) Earnings	Dividends	Book Value
12/18	11.18	67 32	0.33	0.54	0.17
12/17	19.72	752 559	0.03	0.00	0.08
12/16	0.00	— —	(0.00)	0.00	(0.00)
Annual Growth	—	— —	—	—	—

Apogee Enterprises Inc

EXECUTIVES

SVP Technology and Strategy, Donald C. Pyatt
General Counsel; Secretary, Patricia A. Beithon, age 62, $277,070 total compensation
CFO, James S. Porter, age 55, $334,750 total compensation
President CEO and Director, Russell Huffer, age 65, $700,000 total compensation
VP Human Resources, Warren Planitzer
Chairman, Bernard P. (Bernie) Aldrich, age 66
VP and Treasurer, Gary R. Johnson, age 54, $192,679 total compensation
President, Rick A. Marshall
Director Investor Relations, Mary Ann Jackson
President Tru Vue, Jane Boyce
Senior Vice President Operations and Supply Chain Management, John A. Klein
President; Chief Executive Officer; Director, Joseph Puishys
Vice President - Finance; Corporate Controller, Mark Augdahl
President CEO and Director, Russell Huffer, age 65
Director, Jerome L. Davis Sr., age 61
Director, John T. (Terry) Manning, age 67
Director, Robert J. Marzec, age 71
Director, David E. Weiss, age 72
Director, Stephen C. Mitchell, age 72
Director, Sara L. Hays, age 51
Director, Richard V. Reynolds, age 67
Auditors: Deloitte & Touche LLP

LOCATIONS

HQ: Apogee Enterprises Inc
  4400 West 78th Street - Suite 520, Minneapolis, MN 55435
Phone: 952 835-1874
Web: www.apog.com

COMPETITORS

AGC North America	Pilkington Group
Asahi Glass	Pilkington North America
Cardinal Glass	Saint-Gobain
Guardian Glass	Schott Corporation
Nippon Sheet Glass	Vitro
PPG Industries	

HISTORICAL FINANCIALS

Company Type: Public

Income Statement
FYE: March 2

	REVENUE ($ mil.)	NET INCOME ($ mil.)	NET PROFIT MARGIN	EMPLOYEES
03/19	1,402.6	45.6	3.3%	7,000
03/18	1,326.1	79.4	6.0%	6,700
03/17*	1,114.5	85.7	7.7%	5,511
02/16	981.1	65.3	6.7%	4,614
02/15	933.9	50.5	5.4%	4,802
Annual Growth	10.7%	(2.5%)	—	9.9%

*Fiscal year change

2019 Year-End Financials

Debt ratio: 23.0%
Return on equity: 9.0%
Cash ($ mil.): 17.0
Current ratio: 1.63
Long-term debt ($ mil.): 245.7
No. of shares (mil.): 27.0
Dividends
  Yield: 0.0%
  Payout: 39.7%
Market value ($ mil.): 973.0

	STOCK PRICE ($) FY Close	P/E High/Low	PER SHARE ($) Earnings	Dividends	Book Value
03/19	36.03	31 16	1.63	0.65	18.37
03/18	43.97	21 15	2.76	0.58	18.16
03/17*	58.19	20 13	2.97	0.52	16.41
02/16	39.41	27 15	2.22	0.46	14.16
02/15	45.85	27 16	1.72	0.41	13.17
Annual Growth	(5.8%)	—	(1.3%)	12.1%	8.7%

*Fiscal year change

Apollo Medical Holdings Inc

EXECUTIVES

Chb, Edward Schreck
Vice President Operations Corporate Secretary, Nidia Flores
Vp Operational Finance Integration, Shawn Zhou
Auditors: BDO USA, LLP

LOCATIONS

HQ: Apollo Medical Holdings Inc
1668 S. Garfield Avenue, 2nd Floor, Alhambra, CA 91801
Phone: 626 282-0288
Web: www.apollomed.net

HISTORICAL FINANCIALS
Company Type: Public

Income Statement — FYE: December 31

	REVENUE ($ mil.)	NET INCOME ($ mil.)	NET PROFIT MARGIN	EMPLOYEES
12/18	519.9	10.8	2.1%	575
12/17*	367.7	26.8	7.2%	613
03/17	57.4	(8.9)	—	1,149
03/16	44.0	(9.3)	—	1,235
03/15	32.9	(1.8)	—	1,190
Annual Growth	99.2%	—	—	(16.6%)

*Fiscal year change

2018 Year-End Financials

Debt ratio: 2.6%
Return on equity: 6.3%
Cash ($ mil.): 106.8
Current ratio: 2.40
Long-term debt ($ mil.): 13.5
No. of shares (mil.): 34.5
Dividends
 Yield: —
 Payout: —
Market value ($ mil.): 686.0

	STOCK PRICE ($) FY Close	P/E High/Low		PER SHARE ($) Earnings	Dividends	Book Value
12/18	19.85	91	40	0.29	0.00	5.22
12/17*	24.00	24	6	0.90	0.00	4.95
03/17	9.00	—	—	(1.49)	0.00	(0.06)
03/16	5.93	—	—	(1.79)	0.00	0.99
03/15	0.50	—	—	(0.37)	0.00	(0.58)
Annual Growth	151.0%			—	—	—

*Fiscal year change

AppFolio Inc

Auditors: PricewaterhouseCoopers LLP

LOCATIONS

HQ: AppFolio Inc
50 Castilian Drive, Santa Barbara, CA 93117
Phone: 805 364-6093

HISTORICAL FINANCIALS
Company Type: Public

Income Statement — FYE: December 31

	REVENUE ($ mil.)	NET INCOME ($ mil.)	NET PROFIT MARGIN	EMPLOYEES
12/18	190.0	19.9	10.5%	916
12/17	143.8	9.7	6.8%	672
12/16	105.5	(8.2)	—	626
12/15	74.9	(15.6)	—	573
12/14	47.6	(8.6)	—	430
Annual Growth	41.3%	—	—	20.8%

2018 Year-End Financials

Debt ratio: 28.3%
Return on equity: 22.5%
Cash ($ mil.): 74.0
Current ratio: 3.83
Long-term debt ($ mil.): 48.6
No. of shares (mil.): 33.9
Dividends
 Yield: —
 Payout: —
Market value ($ mil.): 2,007.0

	STOCK PRICE ($) FY Close	P/E High/Low		PER SHARE ($) Earnings	Dividends	Book Value
12/18	59.22	154	66	0.56	0.00	2.71
12/17	41.50	178	76	0.28	0.00	2.50
12/16	23.85	—	—	(0.25)	0.00	2.07
12/15	14.60	—	—	(0.73)	0.00	2.17
Annual Growth	59.5%			—	—	7.7%

Apple Hospitality REIT Inc

Auditors: Ernst & Young LLP

LOCATIONS

HQ: Apple Hospitality REIT Inc
814 East Main Street, Richmond, VA 23219
Phone: 804 344-8121
Web: www.applehospitalityreit.com

HISTORICAL FINANCIALS
Company Type: Public

Income Statement — FYE: December 31

	REVENUE ($ mil.)	NET INCOME ($ mil.)	NET PROFIT MARGIN	EMPLOYEES
12/18	1,270.5	206.0	16.2%	62
12/17	1,238.6	182.4	14.7%	56
12/16	1,041.0	144.6	13.9%	56
12/15	898.3	117.2	13.1%	54
12/14	803.9	6.8	0.9%	51
Annual Growth	12.1%	134.3%	—	5.0%

2018 Year-End Financials

Debt ratio: 28.6%
Return on equity: 5.9%
Cash ($ mil.): 33.6
Current ratio: 0.31
Long-term debt ($ mil.): 1,412.2
No. of shares (mil.): 224.0
Dividends
 Yield: 8.4%
 Payout: 133.3%
Market value ($ mil.): 3,194.0

	STOCK PRICE ($) FY Close	P/E High/Low		PER SHARE ($) Earnings	Dividends	Book Value
12/18	14.26	22	15	0.90	1.20	15.22
12/17	19.61	25	21	0.82	1.10	15.53
12/16	19.98	27	23	0.76	1.20	15.78
12/15	19.97	32	25	0.65	0.80	15.18
Annual Growth	(10.6%)			11.5%	14.5%	0.1%

Arbor Realty Trust Inc

EXECUTIVES

Vice President Quality Control, Victor Bove
Vice President, Stephen York
Vice President, Joan Gredys
Executive Vice President And Treasurer, John Natalone
Auditors: Ernst & Young LLP

LOCATIONS

HQ: Arbor Realty Trust Inc
333 Earle Ovington Boulevard, Suite 900, Uniondale, NY 11553
Phone: 516 506-4200
Web: www.arbor.com

COMPETITORS

Annaly Capital Management	Institutional Financial Markets
Anworth Mortgage Asset	RAIT Financial Trust
Capital Trust	Redwood Trust
Drive Shack	Starwood Property
Impac Mortgage Holdings	iStar Financial Inc

HISTORICAL FINANCIALS
Company Type: Public

Income Statement — FYE: December 31

	REVENUE ($ mil.)	NET INCOME ($ mil.)	NET PROFIT MARGIN	EMPLOYEES
12/18	484.9	180.2	37.2%	468
12/17	346.6	121.6	35.1%	445
12/16	213.2	74.6	35.0%	288
12/15	142.5	53.4	37.5%	39
12/14	141.0	93.0	66.0%	37
Annual Growth	36.2%	18.0%	—	88.6%

2018 Year-End Financials

Debt ratio: 71.8%
Return on equity: 22.6%
Cash ($ mil.): 160.0
Current ratio: 0.28
Long-term debt ($ mil.): 2,179.2
No. of shares (mil.): 83.9
Dividends
 Yield: 11.2%
 Payout: 75.3%
Market value ($ mil.): 846.0

	STOCK PRICE ($) FY Close	P/E High/Low		PER SHARE ($) Earnings	Dividends	Book Value
12/18	10.07	8	5	1.50	1.13	10.66
12/17	8.64	8	6	1.12	0.72	11.27
12/16	7.46	10	7	0.83	0.62	11.42
12/15	7.15	8	7	0.90	0.58	11.09
12/14	6.77	4	4	1.70	0.52	10.61
Annual Growth	10.4%			(3.1%)	21.4%	0.1%

Ares Management Corp

Auditors: Ernst & Young LLP

LOCATIONS

HQ: Ares Management Corp
2000 Avenue of the Stars, 12th Floor, Los Angeles, CA 90067
Phone: 310 201-4100
Web: www.aresmgmt.com

HISTORICAL FINANCIALS
Company Type: Public

Income Statement   FYE: December 31

	REVENUE ($ mil.)	NET INCOME ($ mil.)	NET PROFIT MARGIN	EMPLOYEES
12/18	958.4	57.0	5.9%	1,100
12/17	1,415.5	76.1	5.4%	1,000
12/16	1,199.2	111.8	9.3%	925
12/15	814.4	19.3	2.4%	870
12/14	603.8	34.9	5.8%	800
Annual Growth	12.2%	13.0%		8.3%

2018 Year-End Financials
Debt ratio: 72.5%
Return on equity: 12.8%
Cash ($ mil.): 494.8
Current ratio: 7.06
Long-term debt ($ mil.): 7,368.3
No. of shares (mil.): 101.6
Dividends
  Yield: 7.5%
  Payout: 444.4%
Market value ($ mil.): 1,806.0

	STOCK PRICE ($) FY Close	P/E High/Low	Earnings	Dividends	Book Value
12/18	17.78	84 56	0.30	1.33	5.79
12/17	20.00	38 28	0.62	1.13	6.97
12/16	19.20	16 9	1.20	0.83	7.32
12/15	12.93	90 54	0.23	0.88	3.35
12/14	17.14	46 36	0.43	0.42	16.67
Annual Growth	0.9% (23.2%)	— —	(8.6%)	33.5%	

Arista Networks Inc

Auditors: Ernst & Young LLP

LOCATIONS
HQ: Arista Networks Inc
5453 Great America Parkway, Santa Clara, CA 95054
Phone: 408 547-5500
Web: www.arista.com

HISTORICAL FINANCIALS
Company Type: Public

Income Statement   FYE: December 31

	REVENUE ($ mil.)	NET INCOME ($ mil.)	NET PROFIT MARGIN	EMPLOYEES
12/18	2,151.3	328.1	15.3%	2,300
12/17	1,646.1	423.2	25.7%	1,800
12/16	1,129.1	184.1	16.3%	1,500
12/15	837.5	121.1	14.5%	1,200
12/14	584.1	86.8	14.9%	1,000
Annual Growth	38.5%	39.4%	—	23.1%

2018 Year-End Financials
Debt ratio: 1.1%
Return on equity: 17.2%
Cash ($ mil.): 649.9
Current ratio: 4.48
Long-term debt ($ mil.): 35.4
No. of shares (mil.): 75.6
Dividends
  Yield: —
  Payout: —
Market value ($ mil.): 15,943.0

	STOCK PRICE ($) FY Close	P/E High/Low	Earnings	Dividends	Book Value
12/18	210.70	70 43	4.06	0.00	28.33
12/17	235.58	42 15	5.35	0.00	22.55
12/16	96.77	37 20	2.50	0.00	15.64
12/15	77.84	48 31	1.67	0.00	11.57
12/14	60.76	66 39	1.29	0.00	8.48
Annual Growth	36.5%	— —	33.2%	—	35.2%

Arrowhead Pharmaceuticals Inc

Arrowhead Pharmaceuticals develops drugs that silence disease-causing genes in the body. Its RNA interference (RNAi) platform named Targeted RNAi Molecule or TRiM reduces the messenger RNA in charge of producing proteins tied to diseases. The company's ARO-HBV drug is in clinical trials for the treatment of hepatitis B. Arrowhead has other RNA assets that are being explored to work in combination with ARO-HBV to treat various diseases. In late 2016 the company stopped developing its intravenously delivered dynamic polyconjugate delivery vehicle programs in order to focus on its TRiM technology.

Operations
Arrowhead's focus is on genetic diseases that involve the overproduction of one or more proteins. Its pipeline includes ARO-AAT (liver disease) AMG 890 (cardiovascular disease not related to cholesterol levels) and ARO-HBV (hepatitis B).

The company has a partnership with Amgen which holds the exclusive license to develop and commercialize AMG 890. In 2018 Arrowhead entered into a collaboration with Janssen Pharmaceuticals through which Janssen gained the worldwide license for ARO-HBV.

Geographic Reach
Arrowhead is headquartered in Pasadena California but most of its employees work at its R&D facility in Madison Wisconsin.

Financial Performance
Arrowhead had yet to top $1 million until 2017 when it recorded $31.4 million in licensing revenue. However as a development-stage pharmaceutical with no product sales to date the company continues to operate at a loss. At the end of fiscal 2017 (ended September) Arrowhead had an accumulated deficit of $432.8 million.

In fiscal 2017 Arrowhead recognized upfront payments from Amgen related to its licensing deal for AMG 890 and ARO-AMG1. That revenue helped lower the company's net loss 58% to $34.4 million.

The company ended fiscal 2017 with $24.8 million in cash about 71% less than it started with. In mid-2016 it placed an equity offering which provided some $43.2 million in net cash. Net cash used in operating activities and investing activities totaled $72.6 million.

Strategy
Arrowhead has focused its business development efforts on securing partnerships with pharmaceutical and biotech companies. It scored a major collaboration with Janssen Pharmaceuticals in 2018; through the licensing deal Arrowhead received some $250 million and is eligible to gain as much as $3.7 billion in milestone payments.

In late 2016 the company halted further development of its three clinical programs including its lead candidate for the treatment of hepatitis B. It is instead focused on its TRiM pipeline. As part of the restructuring Arrowhead laid off 30% of its workforce.

EXECUTIVES
President CEO and Director, Christopher (Chris) Anzalone, age 50, $394,485 total compensation
CFO, Kenneth (Ken) Myszkowski, age 53
Chief Operating Officer, Brendan P. Rae
Vice President Program Management, Thomas Schluep
Vice President Head of Regulatory Affairs QA Compliance, Susan Boynton
Vice President Strategic Business Initiatives, Peter Leone
Chairman, R. Bruce Stewart, age 83
Board Member, William Waddill
Auditors: Rose, Snyder & Jacobs LLP

LOCATIONS
HQ: Arrowhead Pharmaceuticals Inc
177 E. Colorado Blvd, Suite 700, Pasadena, CA 91105
Phone: 626 304-3400
Web: www.arrowheadpharmaceuticals.com

PRODUCTS/OPERATIONS

Selected Pipeline Products
ARO-AAT
ARO-HBV
ARO-APOC3
ARO-ANG3
ARO-ENaC
ARO-HIF2
AMG 890
ARO-AMG1

COMPETITORS
GenVec
Lexicon Pharmaceuticals
Oxford BioMedica
PharmaMar
Progen Pharmaceuticals
Quark Pharmaceuticals
Silence Therapeutics
bluebird bio

HISTORICAL FINANCIALS
Company Type: Public

Income Statement   FYE: September 30

	REVENUE ($ mil.)	NET INCOME ($ mil.)	NET PROFIT MARGIN	EMPLOYEES
09/19	168.8	67.9	40.3%	109
09/18	16.1	(54.4)	—	95
09/17	31.4	(34.3)	—	93
09/16	0.1	(81.7)	—	113
09/15	0.3	(91.9)	—	104
Annual Growth	358.5%	—	—	1.2%

2019 Year-End Financials
Debt ratio: —
Return on equity: 39.9%
Cash ($ mil.): 221.8
Current ratio: 2.73
Long-term debt ($ mil.): —
No. of shares (mil.): 95.5
Dividends
  Yield: —
  Payout: —
Market value ($ mil.): 2,691.0

	STOCK PRICE ($) FY Close	P/E High/Low	Earnings	Dividends	Book Value
09/19	28.18	48 15	0.69	0.00	2.56
09/18	19.17	— —	(0.65)	0.00	1.08
09/17	4.33	— —	(0.47)	0.00	1.09
09/16	7.35	— —	(1.34)	0.00	1.37
09/15	5.76	— —	(1.60)	0.00	1.85
Annual Growth	48.7%	—	—	—	8.5%

Ashford Inc (Holding Co)

Auditors: BDO USA, LLP

LOCATIONS
HQ: Ashford Inc (Holding Co)
14185 Dallas Parkway, Suite 1100, Dallas, TX 75254
Phone: 972 490-9600
Web: www.ashfordinc.com

HISTORICAL FINANCIALS
Company Type: Public

Income Statement			FYE: December 31
	REVENUE ($ mil.)	NET INCOME ($ mil.)	NET PROFIT MARGIN	EMPLOYEES
12/18	195.5	10.1	5.2%	700
12/17	81.5	(18.3)	—	402
12/16	67.6	(2.4)	—	103
12/15	58.9	(1.1)	—	108
12/14	17.2	(46.4)	—	92
Annual Growth	83.4%	—	—	66.1%

2018 Year-End Financials
Debt ratio: 4.6%
Return on equity: 6.8%
Cash ($ mil.): 51.5
Current ratio: 2.01
Long-term debt ($ mil.): 15.1
No. of shares (mil.): 2.3
Dividends
  Yield: —
  Payout: —
Market value ($ mil.): 124.0

	STOCK PRICE ($) FY Close	P/E High/Low	PER SHARE ($) Earnings	Dividends	Book Value
12/18	51.90	44 22	(2.11)	0.00	111.35
12/17	93.00	— —	(9.59)	0.00	14.42
12/16	43.14	— —	(2.56)	0.00	18.54
12/15	53.25	— —	(4.45)	0.00	16.00
12/14	94.00	— —	(23.43)	0.00	7.54
Annual Growth	(13.8%)	— —	—	—	96.0%

Associated Banc-Corp

A lot of Midwesterners are associated with Associated Banc-Corp the holding company for Associated Bank. One of the largest banks based in Wisconsin the bank operates about 200 branches in that state as well as in Illinois and Minnesota. Catering to consumers and local businesses it offers deposit accounts loans mortgage banking credit and debit cards and leasing. The bank's wealth management division offers investments trust services brokerage insurance and employee group benefits plans. Commercial loans including agricultural construction and real estate loans make up more than 60% of bank's loan portfolio. The bank also writes residential mortgages consumer loans and home equity loans.

Operations
Associated Banc-Corp boasts total assets of more than $27 billion making it one of the 50 largest publicly traded US bank holding companies. More than 70% of revenue comes from interest income mostly from loans. Roughly 60% of Associated Banc-Corp's $18 billion loan portfolio consists of commercial and industrial real estate construction commercial real estate loans and lease financing.

Nearly 30% of the company's income is from non-interest sources including: trust service fees service charges insurance commissions brokerage and annuity commissions and mortgage banking income among others. It also offers benefits consulting services through its Associated Financial Group subsidiary.

Geographic Reach
The company offers a full range of financial products and services in more than 200 banking locations serving more than 100 communities throughout Wisconsin Illinois and Minnesota and commercial financial services in Indiana Michigan Missouri Ohio and Texas.

Sales and Marketing
Associated Banc-Corp spent $26.1 million on business development and advertising in 2014 compared to $23.3 million in 2013 and $21.3 million in 2012.

Financial Performance
Associated Banc-Corp's revenue has remained flat for the past several years at just above $1 billion. Revenue in 2014 inched up by less than 1% to $1.03 billion mostly thanks to higher interest income as loan assets grew by 11% and as interest and dividends on investment securities also grew by double digits. Offsetting much of this growth the company's net mortgage banking income shrunk by $28 million (56%) driven by lower gains on sales and related income as secondary mortgage production declined.

Profit levels have been steadily rising over the past several years since losses in 2009 and 2010 with net income in 2014 rising by 1% to $190.51 million. Higher revenue combined with lower interest expenses on deposits and lower personnel costs all helped to boost the company's bottom line.

Despite higher earnings cash from operations fell 56% to $212.74 million primarily as the company made fewer net proceeds from the sale of its mortgage loans held for sale. The company's total loans grew by 11% to $17.6 billion in 2014 while total deposits rose by 9% to $18.77 billion.

Strategy
The company intends to continue pursuing a profitable growth strategy by carefully screening its prospective customers in light of the risks expenses and difficulties frequently encountered by companies in significant growth stages of development. Associated Banc-Corp hopes to keep its momentum going via organic growth including increasing its fee income and commercial deposits among other measures. It is also remodeling or relocating many of its branches.

Associated Banc-Corp also plans to continue strong loan business growth. For 2015 the company expects high single-digit annual average loan growth after posting loan double-digit loan growth across most categories in 2014.

Mergers and Acquisitions
Associated purchased BankMutual a Wisconsin-based bank in 2018.

In early 2015 subsidiary Associated Financial Group agreed to buy Minnesota-based Ahmann & Martin Co a risk and benefits consulting firm to gain new clients and expand its financial risk and insurance product and service lines.

Company Background
Hampered by one of the worst economic environments in recent history the bank saw an increase in nonperforming loans (particularly business- and housing-related loans) and more than tripled its provision for loan losses from 2008 to 2009. The company cut its losses in 2010 and nearly turned a profit as it concentrated on improving its credit quality. It moved away from construction lending and its nonperforming loans and its provisions for loan losses decreased. Even though 2011 revenues were down Associated Banc-Corp returned to profitability as credit quality continued to improve.

EXECUTIVES
EVP and Chief Risk Officer, Arthur G. (Art) Heise, age 61
President and CEO, Philip B. (Phil) Flynn, age 61, $1,250,000 total compensation
EVP General Counsel and Corporate Secretary, Randall J. Erickson, age 60, $406,667 total compensation
EVP and Head Retail Banking, David L. Stein, age 55, $545,849 total compensation
EVP and Chief Human Resources Officer, Judith M. Docter, age 58
EVP and Chief Credit Officer, Scott S. Hickey, age 63, $644,531 total compensation
EVP and Chief Strategy Officer, Oliver Buechse, age 50
EVP and Head Commercial Real Estate, Breck F. Hanson
EVP and Head Corporate Banking, Donna N. Smith
EVP and Head Specialized Industries and Commercial Financial Services, John A. Utz, $348,417 total compensation
EVP and Head Community Markets, Timothy J. Lau
EVP and CFO, Christopher J. Del Moral-Niles, $477,500 total compensation
EVP and Chief Audit Executive, Patrick J. Derpinghaus
EVP CIO and COO, James Yee, $458,333 total compensation
EVP and Head Private Client and Institutional Services, William M. Bohn
President Southern Illinois, Phillip Hickman
Senior Vice President Investme, Sara Walker
Vice President Information Security Engineer, Patrick Pirwitz
Assistant Vice President Insured Risk Manager, Jean Ehren
Assistant Vice President Residential Mortgage Lender, Brandon Strayer
Vice President Customer Care Program And Operations Manager, Wendy Kumm
Senior Vice President Specialized Financial Services Insurance Industry, Peter Bulandr
Vice President Commercial Lending, Jon Hein
Vice President of Call Centre, Michael Fumelle
Vice President, Ed Parada
Vice President Atm Channel Manager, Deanna Helminiak
Senior Vice President Commer, Julian LaMue
Vice President Treasury Management Officer, Shelly Lapoint
Vice President Foreign Exchange, Jessie Bushmaker
Assistant Vice President Senior Bank Manager, Kim Klinkner
Executive Vice President, Diana Paltz
Vice President, Brett Stone
Assistant Vice President Residential Loan Officer, Kim Anders

Senior Vice President, Diane Gantner
Executive Vice President and Director Human Resources, Judy Docter
Assistant Vice President Senior Branch Manager, Ernesto Guillen
Sr. Branch Manager Avp, Jake Nyen
Avp Digital Solutions Sr Analyst, John Krueger
Vp Business Analyst Manager, Brad Abts
Vice President Field Exams, Jeff Kohr
Vice President International Banking, Paul Eversman
Senior Vice President Regional Manager, Gregory T Warsek
Vice President Public Relations Senior Manager, Jennifer Kaminski
Svp Standardized Services Manager Commercial Support Services, Jason Wilson
Vice President Of Operation Management, Caryn Levey
Svp and Business Solutions Director It Shared Services, Bob Kapla
Vice President Senior Client Advisor, Chad Heath
Vice President Commercial Banking Relationship Manager, Scott Hoerth
Vice President Investments, Brad Hanna
Porfolio Manager Vice President, Mark Buechler
Vice President Senior Contract Management, Jeremy Allen
ASSISTANT VICE PRESIDENT ADMINISTRATIVE ANALYST PROJECT ADMINISTRATOR, Nata Nash
Vice President And Portfolio Manager, Liliana Huerta
Vice President, Ryun Van Cuyk
SENIOR VICE PRESIDENT, Jessica Brandom
Senior Vice President Group Manager, Michael Sedivy
Vice President, John Adams
Vice President Design and Construction Services, Anthony Ferro
Senior Vice President Senior Manager Interactive Consumer Marketing, Jennifer Ott
VICE PRESIDENT SENIOR SYSTEMS ANALYST, Steven Weber
Executive Vice President Chief Credit Officer, John Hankerd
Vice President Market Manager, Chris Davis
Senior Vice President, Farhan Iqbal
Vice President, Adam Demont
Vice President Senior Project Manager, Melissa Birling
Svp Texas Market Manager, Dean Rosencrans
Vice President, Dave Bolwerk
Vice President Relationship Manager Government Banking, Joseph Hockers
Vice President Relationship Manager, Gary Krenke
VICE PRESIDENT, David Brookfield
Vice President Portfolio Manager, John Lotzer
Avp Talent Acquisition Consultant, Ashley Koepke
VICE PRESIDENT EXPERIENTIAL MARKETING MANAGER, Jenny Strachota
Vice President and Multicultural and Affordable Sales Integration Manager, LaDonna Reed
Vice President Process Architect, Mary Thornton
Assistant Vice President, Michael Corbett
Senior Vice President Special Loan Group Team Lead, Mike Waltz
Vice President Senior Program Manager, Marck Simson
Vice President Human Resource Business Partner, Lynn Smits
Assistant Vice President, Kimberly Mccann
Senior Vice President Market Manager Commercial Real Estate, Jim Vitt
Vice President Of Private Banking, Welter Douglas
Svp Private Banking Credit Manager, Daniel Bishop
Vice President Private Banker, Gene Williams
Vp Sr Project Manager Commercial Banking, Kristi Hatcher
Vice President Telecommunications Services Lead, Don Cross
Avp and Senior Records Management Analyst, Adam Mcvey
Vice President Private Banking Manager, Tracy Stansbury
Vice President Operations Senior Unit Manager, Teriann Van Sistine
Senior Vice President, Kathy Bozek
Vice President Business Intelligence, Amit Padgilwar
Senior Vice President, Daniel Holzhauer
Vp Risk and Controls Manager Operations and Technology, Kevin Ress
Vice President Information Technology, Kathleen Wenzel
Vice President Portfolio Management, John Shaw
Vice President Senior Benefits Consultant, Dustin Rossow
Vice President Leadership Development Program Manager, Heidi Smith
Vp and Sr Relationship Manager Retirement Plan Services, Scott Hoene
Vice President Special Loans Group, Michael Stevens
Assistant Vice President Business Banking Officer, Chelsea Horton
Vice President, Barb Pahnke
Vice President Portfolio Manager, Steven Berglund
Vice President, Judith Wood
Senior Vice President, Anthony Pecora
Assistant Vice President, Jim Larchrid
Vice President Foreign Exchange, Angie Kappel
Avp International Trade Capital Markets, Sonia Ott
Vice President, Lisa Sawczuk
Vice President, Jon Gluckman
Vice President Portfolio Manager, Laurie Johnson
Assistant Vice President, Jeffrey Schaefer
Assistant Vice President Residential Loan Officer, Tammy Niemann
Bank Manager Assistant Vice President, Lynn Lusch
Assistant Vice President Bank Manager, Boyd Schenck
Vice President and Senior Relationship Manager Trust Officer, Chad Borns
Senior Vice President, Karen Dunevant
Vice President, Sonia Schneider
Chairman, William R. Hutchinson, age 76
Treasurer, Tim Watson
Auditors: KPMG LLP

LOCATIONS

HQ: Associated Banc-Corp
433 Main Street, Green Bay, WI 54301
Phone: 920 491-7500
Web: www.associatedbank.com

PRODUCTS/OPERATIONS

2016 Sales

	$ mil.	% of total
Interest		
Loans including fees	659.5	58
Investment securities including dividends and Interest	127.2	11
Other	4.8	0
Noninterest		
Insurance Commissions	80.8	7
Service charges on deposit accounts	66.6	6
Card-based & other nondeposit fees	50.1	4
Trust Service fees	46.9	4
Other	108.6	10
Total	**1,144.5**	**100**

2016 Sales

	% of total
Community Consumer and Business	59
Corporate and Commercial Specialty	36
Risk Management and Shared Services	5
Total	**100**

COMPETITORS

Bank Mutual	Northern Trust
Harris	TCF Financial
KeyCorp	U.S. Bancorp

HISTORICAL FINANCIALS

Company Type: Public

Income Statement — FYE: December 31

	ASSETS ($ mil.)	NET INCOME ($ mil.)	INCOME AS % OF ASSETS	EMPLOYEES
12/18	33,647.8	333.5	1.0%	4,655
12/17	30,483.5	229.2	0.8%	4,388
12/16	29,139.3	200.2	0.7%	4,441
12/15	27,715.0	188.3	0.7%	4,383
12/14	26,821.7	190.5	0.7%	4,300
Annual Growth	5.8%	15.0%		2.0%

2018 Year-End Financials

Return on assets: 1.0%
Return on equity: 9.5%
Long-term debt ($ mil.): —
No. of shares (mil.): 164.4
Sales ($ mil): 1,509.7
Dividends Yield: 3.1%
Payout: 32.8%
Market value ($ mil.): 3,254.0

	STOCK PRICE ($) FY Close	P/E High/Low		PER SHARE ($) Earnings	Dividends	Book Value
12/18	19.79	15	10	1.89	0.62	22.99
12/17	25.40	18	15	1.42	0.50	21.18
12/16	24.70	20	12	1.26	0.45	20.32
12/15	18.75	17	14	1.19	0.41	19.42
12/14	18.63	17	13	1.16	0.37	18.48
Annual Growth	1.5%	—	—	13.0%	13.8%	5.6%

AstroNova Inc

The sky's the limit for AstroNova. The company makes data recorders and ruggedized printers used on commercial airplanes. Its Test & Measurement (T&M) division (29% of sales) makes products that record and monitor data for customers in the aerospace automotive metal mill power and telecommunications industries. Its QuickLabel Systems (71% of sales) makes digital color label printers bar code printers automatic labelers and printer consumables. Following the divestment of its former medical devices unit Grass Technologies in 2013 the company in 2015 changed its name to AstroNova from Astro-Med.

Geographic Reach

AstroNova has manufacturing plants in Canada Germany and the US (Rhode Island). Sales and service offices are in Canada France Germany Mexico the UK and the US.

The company generates 72% of its sales from customers in the US. Its biggest overseas market is Europe which accounts for 18% of sales.

Sales and Marketing
AstroNova uses a direct sales force in its major markets (Canada China France Germany the UK and the US) as well as a network of about 90 independent dealers and representatives for all other countries.

Target markets for its hardware and software products include aerospace apparel automotive avionics chemicals computer peripherals communications distribution food and beverage general manufacturing packaging and transportation.

Financial Performance
Year-over-year sales rose about 7% to $86 million in 2016 (year-end January). By segment QuickLabel surged 12% while T&M sales decreased 4%. QuickLabel did well behind strong demand for printers especially the new Kiaro! product line and label and tag products. T&M slipped on reduced demand for aerospace printers as those customers deferred purchases.

AstroNova's profit fell 3% to $4.5 million in 2016 from 2015 on higher costs which were mainly related to stock-based compensation. The company also has expenses related to its name change and branding initiatives.

Strategy
AstroNova shareholders approved the new name in May 2016 as a signal that the company is committed to its data visualization products. It intends to develop new products internally and acquire others through strategic purchases. The company introduced the DDX100 Smartcorder a high-speed portable data acquisition system.

Mergers and Acquisitions
In 2015 AstroNova completed its acquisition of the aerospace printer product line for civil and commercial aircraft from Rugged Information Technology Equipment Corporation (RITEC) for $7.3 million. The products include aerospace printers for use in commercial aircraft and is a part of the Test & Measurement (T&M) segment.

In early 2014 AstroNova paid $6.7 million in cash for the ruggedized printer product line from Miltope Corporation. The printers are used in commercial and military aircraft and will strengthens AstroNova's global geographic footprint through the addition of a number of airline contracts.

EXECUTIVES
VP Operations, Stephen M. Petrarca, age 57
VP International Branches, Michael M. Morawetz, age 60, $179,084 total compensation
VP and General Manager AstroNova Aerospace, Thomas W. Carll
VP and General Manager QuickLabel Systems, Eric E. Pizzuti, age 52
President and CEO, Gregory A. Woods, age 60, $342,346 total compensation
VP and CTO, Michael J. Natalizia, age 55, $148,923 total compensation
Interim CFO and Principal Accounting Officer, Joseph P. OÂ'Connell
Vp Of Treasurer And Cfo, David Smith
Chairman, Hermann Viets, age 76
Board Member, Harold Schofield
Auditors: Wolf & Company, P.C.

LOCATIONS
HQ: AstroNova Inc
600 East Greenwich Avenue, West Warwick, RI 02893
Phone: 401 828-4000
Web: www.astronovainc.com

PRODUCTS/OPERATIONS

2016 Sales

	$ mil.	% of total
QuickLabel	67.1	71
Test & measurement	27.5	29
Total	94.6	100

Selected Products
QuickLabel Systems
  Automatic labelers
  Digital color label printers
  Labeling software
  Labels
  Label and tag substrates
  Monochrome thermal-transfer bar code label printers
  Print and apply systems
  Printing inks
  Ribbon
  Tags
  Thermal transfer ribbon
  Toner
Test and Measurement
  Paperless data recorders
  Portable data recorders
  Real-time data acquisition recorders and workstations
  Ruggedized data recorders printers and supplies
  Ruggedized Ethernet switches
  Telemetry recorders

COMPETITORS

Ampex
Canon
DRS Technologies
Datamax-O'Neil
Epson
HP
Printronix
Ricoh Company
Source Technologies
TPG IPB
Toshiba
Xerox
Zebra Technologies

HISTORICAL FINANCIALS
Company Type: Public

Income Statement
FYE: January 31

	REVENUE ($ mil.)	NET INCOME ($ mil.)	NET PROFIT MARGIN	EMPLOYEES
01/19	136.6	5.7	4.2%	374
01/18	113.4	3.2	2.9%	352
01/17	98.4	4.2	4.3%	312
01/16	94.6	4.5	4.8%	329
01/15	88.3	4.6	5.3%	340
Annual Growth	11.5%	5.3%	—	2.4%

2019 Year-End Financials
Debt ratio: 16.4%
Return on equity: 8.5%
Cash ($ mil.): 7.5
Current ratio: 2.54
Long-term debt ($ mil.): 12.8
No. of shares (mil.): 6.9
Dividends
  Yield: 1.4%
  Payout: 48.2%
Market value ($ mil.): 139.0

	STOCK PRICE ($) FY Close	P/E High/Low	PER SHARE ($) Earnings	Dividends	Book Value
01/19	19.98	28 15	0.81	0.28	10.03
01/18	13.50	32 25	0.47	0.28	9.40
01/17	13.86	29 22	0.56	0.28	9.46
01/16	15.69	25 20	0.61	0.28	9.18
01/15	14.95	27 19	0.60	0.28	8.76
Annual Growth	7.5%	—	7.8%	(0.0%)	3.4%

At Home Group Inc

Auditors: Ernst & Young LLP

LOCATIONS
HQ: At Home Group Inc
1600 East Plano Parkway, Plano, TX 75074
Phone: 972 265-6227
Web: www.athome.com

HISTORICAL FINANCIALS
Company Type: Public

Income Statement
FYE: January 26

	REVENUE ($ mil.)	NET INCOME ($ mil.)	NET PROFIT MARGIN	EMPLOYEES
01/19	1,165.9	49.0	4.2%	5,364
01/18	950.5	31.8	3.3%	4,400
01/17	765.6	27.0	3.5%	3,172
01/16	622.1	3.5	0.6%	2,941
01/15	497.7	(0.4)	—	0
Annual Growth	23.7%	—	—	—

2019 Year-End Financials
Debt ratio: 34.5%
Return on equity: 7.5%
Cash ($ mil.): 10.9
Current ratio: 0.88
Long-term debt ($ mil.): 371.4
No. of shares (mil.): 63.6
Dividends
  Yield: —
  Payout: —
Market value ($ mil.): 1,427.0

	STOCK PRICE ($) FY Close	P/E High/Low	PER SHARE ($) Earnings	Dividends	Book Value
01/19	22.43	52 21	0.74	0.00	11.18
01/18	33.73	64 27	0.50	0.00	9.62
01/17	15.14	33 21	0.48	0.00	8.86
Annual Growth	21.7%	—	24.2%	—	12.3%

Atlantic Capital Bancshares Inc

Auditors: Ernst & Young LLP

LOCATIONS
HQ: Atlantic Capital Bancshares Inc
945 East Paces Ferry Road N.E., Suite 1600, Atlanta, GA 30326
Phone: 404 995-6050
Web: www.atlanticcapitalbank.com

HISTORICAL FINANCIALS
Company Type: Public

Income Statement
FYE: December 31

	ASSETS ($ mil.)	NET INCOME ($ mil.)	INCOME AS % OF ASSETS	EMPLOYEES
12/18	2,955.4	28.5	1.0%	340
12/17	2,891.4	(3.7)	—	353
12/16	2,727.5	13.4	0.5%	347
12/15	2,638.7	(1.3)	—	361
12/14	1,314.8	7.5	0.6%	106
Annual Growth	22.4%	39.6%	—	33.8%

Atlantic Union Bankshares Corp

Union Bankshares (formerly Union First Market Bankshares) is the holding company for Union Bank & Trust which operates approximately 100 branches in central northern and coastal portions of Virginia. The bank offers standard services such as checking and savings accounts credit cards and certificates of deposit. Union Bank & Trust maintains a loan portfolio heavily weighted towards real estate: Commercial real estate loans make up more than 30% while one- to four-family residential mortgages and construction loans account for approximately 15% and 20% respectively. The bank also originates personal and business loans.

EXECUTIVES

EVP and Director of Mortgage and Wealth Management, Jeffrey W. Farrar, age 58
EVP Union Bankshares and Chief Retail Officer Union Bank & Trust, Elizabeth M. Bentley, age 58, $268,491 total compensation
EVP and Chief Risk Officer, David G. (Dave) Bilko, age 59
President and CEO Union Bankshares Corporation and CEO Union Bank & Trust, John C. Asbury, age 54
EVP and CFO, Robert M. (Rob) Gorman, age 60, $351,167 total compensation
EVP Union Bankshares and Chief Banking Officer Union Bank & Trust, D. Anthony (Tony) Peay, age 59, $348,997 total compensation
EVP and CIO, M. Dean Brown, age 54, $259,625 total compensation
SVP and Chief Marketing Officer, L. Duane Smith, age 52
EVP and Chief Human Resource Officer, Loreen A. LaGatta, age 50
EVP and President Union Bank & Trust, John G. Stallings, age 52
Vice President Commercial Lender, Greg Gruner
Vice President Business Banking Relationship Manager, Ann Hillsman
Senior Vice President And Trust Advisor Union Wealth Management, Jack Catlett
Senior Vice President, Michael Horan
Vice President And Trust Advisor Union Wealth Management, Sharon Barcalow
Assistant Vice President Commercial Real Estate, Diana Allen
Vice President and Senior Branch Manager, Sherry Cillo
Vice President and Senior Branch Manager, Terri Hirst
Assistant Vice President Branch Manager, Jody Hardy
Senior Vice President Private Banking Services and Client Advisor RJFS, Norfleet Stallings
Senior Vice President, Mike Walsh
Vice President Uis Financial Advisor, Chris Rinehart
Vice President And Senior Market Manager, Cheryl Kirby
Evp And President Union Bank and Trust, Maria P Tedesco
Senior Vice President Union Bank and Trust Company, Jay Baldwin
Vice President And Trust Advisor, Barbara Dickinson
Vice President Private Banking Services And Client Advisor Rjfs, Brian Adams
Vice President Uis And Financial Advisor Rjfs, John Faith
Vice President Uis And Financial Advisor Rjfs, Mason Garner
Vice President Uis And Financial Advisor Rjfs, Michael Johnson
Vice President Uis And Financial Advisor Rjfs, Preston Wall
Vice President Uis And Financial Advisor Rjfs, John Tekavec
Vice President And Portfolio Manager Union Wealth Management, Michael Snow
Senior Vice President Private Banking Services And Client Advisor Rjfs, Ben Mason
Svp, Michael D'aiutolo
Vp Director Digital Marketing, Valerie Wiederhorn
Vp Director Community Engagement, Kat Costello
Vp Svp Portfolio Manager, Chris O'brien
Vice Chairman Union Bankshares Corporation and Union Bank & Trust, G. William (Billy) Beale, age 69
Chairman, Raymond D. (Ray) Smoot, age 72
Auditors: Ernst & Young LLP

LOCATIONS

HQ: Atlantic Union Bankshares Corp
1051 East Cary Street, Suite 1200, Richmond, VA 23219
Phone: 804 633-5031
Web: www.bankatunion.com

PRODUCTS/OPERATIONS

2015 Sales

	$ mil.	% of total
Interest		
Loans including fees	247.5	72
Other	29.3	9
Noninterest		
Other service charges commission and fees	15.6	5
Service charges on deposit accounts	18.9	5
others	30.8	9
Adjustments	(0.3)	-
Total	**341.8**	**100**

Selected Subsidiaries
Union First Market Bank
Union Insurance Group LLC
Union Investment Services Inc.
Union Mortgage Group Inc.

COMPETITORS

BB&T	PNC Financial
Bank of America	Regions Financial
C&F Financial	SunTrust
Eastern Virginia Bankshares	TowneBank
JPMorgan Chase	Wells Fargo

HISTORICAL FINANCIALS
Company Type: Public

Income Statement
FYE: December 31

	ASSETS ($ mil.)	NET INCOME ($ mil.)	INCOME AS % OF ASSETS	EMPLOYEES
12/18	13,765.6	146.2	1.1%	1,609
12/17	9,315.1	72.9	0.8%	1,149
12/16	8,426.7	77.4	0.9%	1,416
12/15	7,693.2	67.0	0.9%	1,422
12/14	7,359.1	52.5	0.7%	1,471
Annual Growth	16.9%	29.1%	—	2.3%

2018 Year-End Financials
Return on assets: 1.2%
Return on equity: 9.8%
Long-term debt ($ mil.): —
No. of shares (mil.): 65.9
Sales ($ mil): 633.0
Dividends
Yield: 3.1%
Payout: 39.6%
Market value ($ mil.): 1,863.0

	STOCK PRICE ($) FY Close	P/E High/Low		PER SHARE ($) Earnings	Dividends	Book Value
12/18	28.23	19	12	2.22	0.88	29.17
12/17	36.17	23	18	1.67	0.81	23.92
12/16	35.74	21	12	1.77	0.77	22.95
12/15	25.24	18	13	1.49	0.68	22.23
12/14	24.08	23	19	1.14	0.58	21.66
Annual Growth	4.1%	—	—	18.1%	11.0%	7.7%

2018 Year-End Financials (Atlantic Union)
Return on assets: 0.9%
Return on equity: 9.0%
Long-term debt ($ mil.): —
No. of shares (mil.): 25.2
Sales ($ mil): 104.8
Dividends
Yield: —
Payout: —
Market value ($ mil.): 414.0

	STOCK PRICE ($) FY Close	P/E High/Low		PER SHARE ($) Earnings	Dividends	Book Value
12/18	16.37	19	13	1.09	0.00	12.80
12/17	17.60	—	—	(0.15)	0.00	11.99
12/16	19.00	35	22	0.53	0.00	12.10
12/15	14.98	—	—	(0.09)	0.00	11.79
Annual Growth	3.0%	—	—	—	—	2.8%

Axcelis Technologies Inc

Ions are iconic at Axcelis Technologies. The company develops and makes ion implanters that semiconductor manufacturers use to insert ions into silicon wafers to change their conductive properties. Axcelis Technologies manufactures its ion implantation devices in house at its plant in Beverly Massachusetts. In addition to equipment it offers aftermarket service and support including spare parts equipment upgrades maintenance and training. While the company sells its products around the world the US accounts for about two-thirds of sales.

Operations

Ion implantation devices (sold under the Purion brand name) and services and royalties surrounding them account for 90% of Axcelis Technologies' revenue. The other 10% comes from its legacy processing systems. The company works with customers and industry experts to design applications and processes at its Advanced Technology Center in Beverly Massachusetts.

Geographic Reach

The company has 30 field offices serving customers in a dozen countries. Its primary operations are in China France Germany Italy Japan Korea Malaysia Singapore Taiwan and the US.

Sales and Marketing

Axcelis Technologies sells equipment and services through a direct sales force from offices in China Germany Italy Singapore South Korea and Taiwan. The US is its largest market while sales to customers in Asia make up 23% of revenues and Europe accounts for about 14%.

The company also has a limited customer base; two customers accounted for 17% of revenue and its top 10 customers accounted for about 70% of revenue.

Financial Performance

After two years of declining revenue Axcelis Technologies recorded a 4% increase in 2014 to reach to $203.1 million. The increase came from better product sales as chip makers loosened their purse strings to buy new systems spare parts product upgrades and used systems from Axcelis Technologies.

The company recorded a net loss for the third straight in 2014 but the loss was less. The 2014 loss was $11.2 million compared to $17 million in 2013 and $35 million in 2012. The company spent less in 2014 to reduce the loss.

The company had a negative cash flow of $16 million in 2014 compared to a negative $15 million in 2013.

Strategy

To address the challenges facing the semiconductor equipment industry the company restructures its operations just about every year. For the past two years restructuring has cost about $5 million overall. In 2015 the company sold its corporate headquarters facility to Beverly Property Owner LLC an affiliate of Middleton Partners a real estate investment firm for about $50 million in a sale-leaseback arrangement.

Axcelis Technologies aims to push its sales of its Purion systems into the Korean semiconductor market. The common Purion platform combines a high-speed state-of-the-art single wafer end station that has throughput of 500 wafers per hour.

EXECUTIVES

Chairman and CEO, Mary G. Puma, age 61, $400,481 total compensation
EVP Engineering and Marketing, William (Bill) Bintz, age 62, $271,385 total compensation
EVP Corporate Marketing and Strategy, Douglas A. (Doug) Lawson, age 59
EVP Human Resources Legal and General Counsel, Lynnette C. Fallon, age 59, $301,538 total compensation
EVP Customer Operations, John E. Aldeborgh, age 63, $271,154 total compensation
EVP and CFO, Kevin J. Brewer, age 60, $310,962 total compensation
Auditors: Ernst & Young LLP

LOCATIONS

HQ: Axcelis Technologies Inc
108 Cherry Hill Drive, Beverly, MA 01915
Phone: 978 787-4000 **Fax:** 978 787-3000
Web: www.axcelis.com

PRODUCTS/OPERATIONS

2014 Sales

	$ mil.	% of total
Ion implantation systems services & royalties	183.2	90
Other products services & royalties	19.9	10
Total	203.1	100

2014 Sales

	% of total
Product	88
Services	12
Total	100

COMPETITORS

Applied Materials
BTU International
Mattson Technology
Nissin Electric
Sumitomo Heavy Industries
Tokyo Electron
ULVAC
USHIO
Ultratech

HISTORICAL FINANCIALS

Company Type: Public

Income Statement FYE: December 31

	REVENUE ($ mil.)	NET INCOME ($ mil.)	NET PROFIT MARGIN	EMPLOYEES
12/18	442.5	45.8	10.4%	1,079
12/17	410.5	126.9	30.9%	985
12/16	266.9	11.0	4.1%	845
12/15	301.5	14.6	4.9%	808
12/14	203.0	(11.2)	—	765
Annual Growth	21.5%	—	—	9.0%

2018 Year-End Financials

Debt ratio: 8.7%
Return on equity: 12.0%
Cash ($ mil.): 177.9
Current ratio: 4.67
Long-term debt ($ mil.): 47.7
No. of shares (mil.): 32.5
Dividends
  Yield: —
  Payout: —
Market value ($ mil.): 580.0

	STOCK PRICE ($) FY Close	P/E High/Low		PER SHARE ($) Earnings	Dividends	Book Value
12/18	17.80	22	11	1.35	0.00	12.54
12/17	28.70	9	3	3.80	0.00	11.03
12/16	14.55	38	6	0.36	0.00	6.82
12/15	2.59	7	5	0.48	0.00	6.56
12/14	2.56	—	—	(0.40)	0.00	5.97
Annual Growth	62.4%	—	—	—	—	20.4%

Axon Enterprise Inc

Axon Enterprise's weapons aim to take perps down but not out. The company formerly known as TASER International is well known for designing and manufacturing various non-lethal TASER lines of stun guns including its best-selling TASER X26. These electronic control devices (ECDs) are geared at the law enforcement corrections military and private security markets as well as consumers. The company also offers AXON wearable video cameras for officers and a hosted product called Evidence.com that allows digital evidence to be viewed shared and managed from a Web browser. Products are sold worldwide through a direct sales force distribution partners and online store and third-party resellers.

Operations

Axon's most popular product is the TASER X26 with shaped pulse technology which is geared toward the law enforcement corrections military and private security markets. It generates about 40% of the company's total sales. On the consumer side its primary product is the TASER C2 a compact device that provides the same NMI effectiveness as the market-leading TASER X26 law enforcement version. Private citizens who buy the C2 for their own personal defense must undergo identification verification before the device is activated.

Geographic Reach

Worldwide more than 17000 law enforcement agencies in more than 150 countries have purchased TASER brand products for testing or deployment. More than a dozen US state correctional agencies from Oregon to Tennessee also use TASER devices. On the military side Axon develops products for both the US (including the US Department of Defense) and certain foreign allies through contracts. The US generates 80% of its sales.

Financial Performance

Axon has achieved unprecedented growth over the years with revenues peaking at a record-setting $165 million in 2014. Profits also reached almost $20 million in 2014 another company milestone. In addition its operating cash flow has skyrocketed the last five years soaring from only $732 thousand in 2010 to $35 million in 2014.

The historic growth for 2014 was driven by the introduction of its new TASER X26P smart weapon and significant growth from its AXON product line. It also was helped by the absence of litigation expenses for the year.

Strategy

In addition to product line extensions Axon is putting significant R&D time and money into technology-based products an area that it views as likely to sustain the most growth. Its TASER Cam is a video recording device that captures both video and audio of TASER use incidents.

The company also developed its officer video and digital evidence management system consisting of the AXON tactical computer (an earpiece with imager speaker and microphone built in) and Evidence.com hosted site (from which agencies and legal professionals can quickly and securely access key evidence data). The company is poised for explosive growth within these segments as a growing number of police departments across the US place orders for body cameras that officers can wear to document their interactions with the public.

Geographically the company is heavily dependent on the US market for sales. However it is working to diversify that base by increasing marketing of its products in such places as Australia New Zealand Brazil and various parts of Europe. It has recently created a wholly owned subsidiary that is established to facilitate sales and provide customer service to European customers.

Adhering to this strategy in 2015 the company purchased Tactical Safety Responses Limited (TSR) a licensed distributor of smart weapons and body cameras in the UK.

EXECUTIVES

Vice President, George Fenton
CEO and Director, Patrick W. (Rick) Smith, age 48, $265,000 total compensation
EVP Software and Services, Marcus Womack
President, Luke Larson
EVP Global Sales, Josh Isner
CIO, Kathy Trontell
EVP Axon Devices, Todd Basche
VP Marketing Training and Communications, Darren Steele

CFO, Jawad Ahsan
Vp Manufacturing, Bill Denzer
Senior Vice President Global Operations, Joshua Goldman
Auditors: Grant Thornton LLP

LOCATIONS

HQ: Axon Enterprise Inc
17800 North 85th Street, Scottsdale, AZ 85255
Phone: 480 991-0797
Web: www.axon.com

PRODUCTS/OPERATIONS

2014 Sales by Product

	$ mil.	% of total
ECD Segment		
TASER X26P	43.5	26
Single cartridges	38.5	23
TASER X2	28.8	18
TASER X26	18.7	11
Extended Warranties icluding TAP	6.0	4
TASER XREP	2.6	2
TASER C2	2.1	1
TASER M26	0.7	1
Other	4.7	3
AXON Segment		
AXON Solutions	9.0	5
AXON/EVIDENCE.com	4.0	2
TASER Cam	4.7	3
Other	1.2	1
Total	**164.5**	**100**

COMPETITORS

Applied Energetics	Mace Security
Colt Defense	Metal Storm
Digital Ally	PepperBall
Glock	Technologies

HISTORICAL FINANCIALS

Company Type: Public

Income Statement — FYE: December 31

	REVENUE ($ mil.)	NET INCOME ($ mil.)	NET PROFIT MARGIN	EMPLOYEES
12/18	420.0	29.2	7.0%	1,386
12/17	343.8	5.2	1.5%	1,095
12/16	268.2	17.3	6.4%	901
12/15	197.8	19.9	10.1%	670
12/14	164.5	19.9	12.1%	567
Annual Growth	26.4%	10.0%	—	25.0%

2018 Year-End Financials

Debt ratio: —
Return on equity: 9.2%
Cash ($ mil.): 349.4
Current ratio: 3.36
Long-term debt ($ mil.): —
No. of shares (mil.): 58.8
Dividends
Yield: —
Payout: —
Market value ($ mil.): 2,573.0

	STOCK PRICE ($) FY Close	P/E High/Low	PER SHARE ($) Earnings	Dividends	Book Value
12/18	43.75	144 48	0.50	0.00	7.95
12/17	26.50	273 211	0.10	0.00	3.16
12/16	24.24	89 44	0.32	0.00	2.88
12/15	17.29	95 44	0.36	0.00	2.92
12/14	26.48	71 28	0.37	0.00	2.44
Annual Growth	13.4%	— —	7.8%	—	34.4%

Axos Financial Inc

Formerly BofI Holding Axos Financial is the holding company for Axos Bank which provides consumers and businesses a variety of deposit and loan products via the internet. It conducts its business without any physical bank branches supporting its customers through a comprehensive online banking platform and the occasional physical retail locations of its partners. Most of its business originates in its home state of California though its operations attract customers from every US state. Founded in 2000 the company holds some $10.9 billion in assets more than $8.6 billion in deposits and a total portfolio of net loans and leases of about $9.1 billion.

Operations

Axos Financial operates through two segments: Banking Business and Securities Business.

The holding company's Banking Business division provides nearly all its revenue houses its online and concierge banking prepaid card mortgage vehicle and unsecured lending services. The Banking Business addresses consumers and small businesses through its online platform and over the phone. The segment also offers software products and consulting services for Chapter 7 bankruptcy and non-Chapter 7 trustees and fiduciaries cash management and commercial and industrial real estate loans.

Axos' Securities Business accounts for about 2% of revenue and provides broker-dealer and registered investment advisor services to its own clients and Banking Business clients.

More than 80% of Axos' revenue is generated by net interest income; non-interest income is derived mostly from banking and service fees. The bank's net loan and lease portfolio is dominated by single-family real estate: nearly 50% of its value is represented by mortgages; almost 10% comprises commercial specialty lender finance and construction loans secured by single-family real estate and warehouses. Some 20% is secured by multi-family real estate and another roughly 15% is made up of commercial and real estate loans.

Geographic Reach

San Diego California-based Axos Financial holds deposits from customers in every US state with large sources of balances in Florida and the Mid-Atlantic states. Around 70% of its mortgage portfolio is secured by real estate in California. Its next largest geographic segments by loan principal are New York and Florida each of which comprises less than 10%.

Sales and Marketing

Because the bank is branchless the traditional means of attracting customers?such as local advertising a physical bank presence community charity sponsorship?are not used. Rather the bank creates brand awareness through direct mail email digital marketing personal sales and print advertising. It also garners deposits through financial advisory companies and affinity partnerships.

Financial Performance

In recent years Axos Financial has experienced strong annual increases in revenue and in net income: each has added more than 170% since fiscal 2014. Net interest income?the company's greatest source of income?was boosted by its growing loan and lease portfolio particularly in residential real estate.

Axos posted revenue of $439.4 million in 2018 a 15% increase from 2017. A rise in the bank's net interest margin and a larger loan portfolio accounted for most of the gain. Banking and service fees pushed up non-interest income marginally. Net income rose 13% to $152.4 million on the strength of revenue.

The holding company depleted $20.6 million of its cash to end the year with $622.9 million. Operations generated $167.9 million and financing activities added $837.4 million entirely due to increased deposits. Axos used $1 Billion on investments?principally loans held for investment.

Strategy

Axos Financial's strategy is simply to grow its loan portfolio?and therefore its interest income?through new products expanded distribution channels leveraged data mining and acquisitions.

In 2018 the bank introduced two new products: factoring?in which a company sells its accounts receivable at a discount often to meet short term cash requirements?and its Universal Digital Bank online banking platform. The platform expands the bank's analytics and personalization capabilities enabling greater product cross-selling. It also facilitates development of in-house and third-party apps.

Axos is also growing through a spate of recent acquisitions. In 2019 the company received regulatory approval to acquire about $170 million in deposits from MWABank. That year the company also acquired financial advisor WiseBanyan Holdings gaining its digital wealth management platform and about $150 million in assets under management. Furthermore it expanded its service offerings and added about $35 million in yearly fee income through its purchase of clearing firm COR Clearing. In 2018 it bought Nationwide Building Society's banking and lending business?including $0.7 billion in checking savings and money market accounts and $1.7 billion in time deposit accounts. It also acquired the trustee and fiduciary services business of Epiq Systems which encompasses its software and consulting services for Chapter 7 and non-Chapter 7 trustees and fiduciaries.

Mergers and Acquisitions

In 2019 Axos Financial took a step toward growing its deposit base when it received regulatory approval to acquire about $170 million in deposits from MWABank. That year the company also acquired financial advisor WiseBanyan Holdings gaining its digital wealth management platform and about $150 million in assets under management. Furthermore it expanded its service offerings and added about $35 million in yearly fee income through its purchase of clearing firm COR Clearing.

Axos bought Nationwide Building Society's banking and lending business?including $0.7 billion in checking savings and money market accounts and $1.7 billion in time deposit accounts?in 2018. It also acquired the trustee and fiduciary services business of Epiq Systems encompassing its software and consulting services for Chapter 7 and non-Chapter 7 trustees and fiduciaries.

Company Background

Axos Financial launched in 2000 as Bank of Internet USA as a digital bank offering checking accounts. The company went public in 2005 as BofI Holding. In 2018 after launching its Universal Digital Bank Platform BofI changed its name to Axos Financial in tandem with a listing on the NYSE.

EXECUTIVES

EVP and CFO BofI Holding Inc. and BofI Federal Bank, Andrew J. Micheletti, age 62, $231,000 total compensation
President and CEO BofI Holding Inc. and BofI Federal Bank, Gregory Garrabrants, age 48, $375,000 total compensation
EVP Specialty Finance and Chief Legal Officer BofI Federal Bank, Eshel Bar-Adon, age 64, $250,000 total compensation
EVP and Chief Credit Officer BofI Federal Bank, Thomas Constantine, age 57, $235,000 total compensation
EVP and Chief Lending Officer BofI Federal Bank, Brian Swanson, age 39, $235,000 total compensation
EVP Chief of Staff and Chief Performance Officer BofI Federal Bank, Jan Durrans
EVP Chief Deposit Officer and Chief Marketing Officer BofI Federal Bank, Eduardo Urdapilleta
Senior Vice President, Jason Kenoyer
Vice President Director Of Financial Reporting, Pete Bauer
First Vice President And Compliance Management, Sandy Hill
Senior Vice President Warehouse Lending And Loan Operations, Darin Sullivan
Vice President Construction Loan Manager, David Thomas
Assistant Vice President Product Delivery, Bryan Iv Hugh
Senior Vice President Risk, Justin Liang
Executive Vice President Director Of Deposits Development, Lane Elliott
Vice President Marketing, Dana Berry
Executive Vice President Human Resources, Mary Ciafardini
Chairman, Paul J. Grinberg, age 58
Vice Chairman, Nicholas A. Mosich
Board Member, James Court
Board Member, Edward Ratinoff
Board Member, James Argalas
Auditors: BDO USA, LLP

LOCATIONS

HQ: Axos Financial Inc
9205 West Russell Road, STE 400, Las Vegas, NV 89148
Phone: 858 649-2218
Web: www.bofiholding.com

PRODUCTS/OPERATIONS

2018 Sales

	$ mil.	% of total
Interest and dividend income:		
Loans and leases including fees	447.0	79
Investments	28.1	5
Interest expense	(106.6)	-
Non-interest income:		
Banking and service fees	47.8	11
Mortgage banking income	13.7	3
Gain on sale - other	5.7	1
Prepayment penalty fee income	3.9	1
Gain (loss) on sale of securities	(0.2)	-
Total	**455.3**	**100**

COMPETITORS

Ally Bank	ISN Bank
California Bank & Trust	MUFG Americas Holdings
Discover	PacWest Bancorp
	San Diego County
E*TRADE Bank	Credit Union
First IB	Scottrade
HSBC USA	

HISTORICAL FINANCIALS
Company Type: Public

Income Statement — FYE: June 30

	ASSETS ($ mil.)	NET INCOME ($ mil.)	INCOME AS % OF ASSETS	EMPLOYEES
06/19	11,220.2	155.1	1.4%	1,007
06/18	9,539.5	152.4	1.6%	801
06/17	8,501.6	134.7	1.6%	681
06/16	7,601.3	119.2	1.6%	647
06/15	5,823.7	82.6	1.4%	467
Annual Growth	17.8%	17.0%	—	21.2%

2019 Year-End Financials
Return on assets: 1.4%
Return on equity: 15.2%
Long-term debt ($ mil.): —
No. of shares (mil.): 61.1
Sales ($ mil): 647.6
Dividends
  Yield: —
  Payout: —
Market value ($ mil.): 1,666.0

	STOCK PRICE ($) FY Close	P/E High/Low	PER SHARE ($) Earnings	Dividends	Book Value
06/19	27.25	17 10	2.48	0.00	17.55
06/18	40.91	19 10	2.37	0.00	15.32
06/17	23.72	16 7	2.07	0.00	13.13
06/16	17.71	77 7	1.85	0.00	10.81
06/15	105.71	79 49	1.34	0.00	8.59
Annual Growth	(28.7%)	—	16.6%	—	19.5%

B Riley Financial Inc

EXECUTIVES

Chb-ceo, Andy Gumaer
Senior Vice President, Bill Soncini
Vice President Investment Banking, Erik Bullock
Western Region Vice President, Jennie Kim
Vice President, Ryan Mulcunry
Auditors: Marcum LLP

LOCATIONS

HQ: B Riley Financial Inc
21255 Burbank Boulevard, Suite 400, Woodland Hills, CA 91367
Phone: 818 884-3737
Web: www.brileyfin.com

HISTORICAL FINANCIALS
Company Type: Public

Income Statement — FYE: December 31

	REVENUE ($ mil.)	NET INCOME ($ mil.)	NET PROFIT MARGIN	EMPLOYEES
12/18	422.9	15.5	3.7%	1,071
12/17	322.1	11.5	3.6%	833
12/16	190.3	21.5	11.3%	388
12/15	112.5	11.8	10.5%	220
12/14	77.1	(5.8)	—	225
Annual Growth	53.0%	—	—	47.7%

2018 Year-End Financials
Debt ratio: 75.1%
Return on equity: 5.9%
Cash ($ mil.): 179.4
Current ratio: 1.39
Long-term debt ($ mil.): 538.9
No. of shares (mil.): 26.6
Dividends
  Yield: 4.6%
  Payout: 117.4%
Market value ($ mil.): 378.0

	STOCK PRICE ($) FY Close	P/E High/Low	PER SHARE ($) Earnings	Dividends	Book Value
12/18	14.20	38 24	0.58	0.74	9.70
12/17	18.10	43 27	0.48	0.67	10.01
12/16	18.45	16 7	1.17	0.28	7.80
12/15	9.90	19 13	0.73	0.32	6.65
12/14	9.90	— —	(0.60)	0.03	6.08
Annual Growth	9.4%	—	—	122.9%	12.4%

B&G Foods Inc

Peter Piper picks more than a peck of peppers from B&G Foods. The company makes markets and distributes a wide variety of shelf-stable foods frozen foods and household goods. Many of B&G's products are regional or national best-sellers including B&M and B&G (beans condiments) Clabber Girl (baking) Green Giant (frozen and canned foods) Spice Islands (seasonings) McCann's (oatmeal) Ortega (Mexican foods) Grandma's and Brer Rabbit (molasses) Snackwell's (snacks) and Underwood (meat spread). They're sold through B&G's subsidiaries to supermarkets mass merchants warehouse clubs and drug store chains as well as institutional and food service operators in the US Canada and Puerto Rico.

Financial Performance

B&G Foods has seen its sales rise during the past five years. Overall sales have doubled since fiscal 2014.

In fiscal 2018 the company saw revenue increase 3% to $1.7 billion from the prior year in part due to an increase in unit volume and net pricing as well as the acquisition of McCann's oatmeal.

Net income in fiscal 2018 fell 20% to $172.4 million. Selling general and administrative expenses dropped by $16 million to $167.4 million for fiscal 2018 in part because of a decrease in acquisition-and-divestiture-related and non-recurring expenses.

Cash from operations contributed $209.4 million to the coffers while investing activities provided $568.1 million mainly as a result of the sale of the company's Pirate Brands. Financing activities used $753.3 million for debt payments and stock repurchases.

Strategy

Acquisitions have been key to B&G's growth as it extends its reach throughout the grocery store. In recent years it acquired Clabber Girl baking goods (2019) McCann's oatmeal (2018) and Snackwell and Back to Nature Foods snack foods (2017).

The company is expanding its growing Green Giant product line into new categories such as pizza and frozen entrees. New products have included Green Giant Cauliflower Pizza Crusts Green Giant Protein Bowls and Little Green Sprout's Organics.

Deciding to reduce its snack footprint B&G sold its Pirate Brands business — which includes Pirate's Booty cheese puffs — to Hershey for $420 million in 2018. B&G used the proceeds to pay down debt.

To combat rising freight and input costs the company is embarking on a cost-savings program to cut expenses across nearly all areas of business including logistics procurement manufacturing administrative and packaging.

Mergers and Acquisitions

In 2019 B&G Foods acquired Clabber Girl baking products and in 2018 the company bought McCann's oatmeal.

In 2017 B&G Foods acquired the Snackwell cookie and Back to Nature granola bars businesses from Brynwood Partners and Mondelez International for more than $162 million in cash. The deal gives B&G a stronger lineup to approach natural food grocery chains like Whole Foods Markets and Sprouts. Back to Nature's products include cookies crackers nuts and trail mixes granola juices soups and cereal. B&G expects the acquisition to add about $80 million in revenue.

In line with its growth goals in 2016 the company acquired ACH Food Companies' spice and seasonings business for $365 million in cash. Through the deal the company added Spice Islands Tone's Durkee and Weber brands to its product line up. The acquisition significantly expands the company's existing flavor enhancing products which include Ms. Dash Ac'cent and Emeril's seasonings.

EXECUTIVES

EVP Finance and CFO, Thomas P. Crimmins, age 50, $307,692 total compensation
President and CEO, Robert C. (Bob) Cantwell, age 62, $700,000 total compensation
EVP General Counsel Secretary and Chief Compliance Officer, Scott E. Lerner, age 46, $412,000 total compensation
EVP Sales and Marketing, Vanessa E. Maskal, age 62, $400,000 total compensation
EVP Operations, William F. (Bill) Herbes, age 64, $291,500 total compensation
EVP Quality Assurance and Research and Development, William H. (Bill) Wright, age 74
EVP Human Resources and Chief Human Resources Officer, Eric H. Hart, age 52
Vice President Sales, Steve Fortunato
Vice President Trade Marketing, Anthony Pacelli
Vice President, Bill Wright
Executive Vice President of Operations, Bill Herbes
Vice President Marketing Advertising and Brand Management, Jordan Greenberg
Vice President General Manager, Marc Simon
VICE PRESIDENT, Clay Wiedemann
Executive Vice President And Chief Customer Officer, Ellen Schum
Chairman, Stephen C. Sherrill, age 66
Board Member, David Wenner
Auditors: KPMG LLP

LOCATIONS

HQ: B&G Foods Inc
Four Gatehall Drive, Parsippany, NJ 07054
Phone: 973 401-6500
Web: www.bgfoods.com

PRODUCTS/OPERATIONS

2016 Sales

	$ mil.	% of total
Green Giant	506.7	36
Ortega	142.0	10
Pirate Brands	84.9	6
Maple Grove Farms of Vermont	72.8	5
Cream of Wheat	62.2	4
Mrs. Dash	60.6	4
Bear Creek Country Kitchens	52.9	4
Las Palmas	39.1	3
Mama Mary's	35.8	2
Polaner	34.3	2
New York Style	33.1	2
Spices & Seasonings	28.2	2
All other brands	238.6	17
Total	**1,391.3**	**100**

Selected Products
Bagel chips
Canned meats and beans
Dry soups
Frozen and canned vegetables
Fruit spreads
Hot cereals
Hot sauces
Maple syrup
Mexican-style sauces
Molasses
Nut clusters
Peppers
Pickles
Pizza crusts
Puffed corn
Rice snacks
Salad dressings
Salsas
Seasonings
Spices
Taco shells and kits
Wine vinegar

Selected Brands
Ac'cent
B&G
B&M
Baker's Joy
Brer Rabbit
Cream of Rice
Cream of Wheat
Devonsheer
Don Pepino
Emeril's (licensed)
Grandma's Molasses
JJ Flats
Joan of Arc
Kleen Guard (sells and distributes)
Las Palmas
Maple Grove Farms of Vermont
Molly McButter
Mrs. Dash
New York Style
Old London
Ortega
Polaner
Red Devil
Regina
Sa-son
Sclafani
Static Guard (sells and distributes)
Sugar Twin
Trappey's
TrueNorth
Underwood
Vermont Maid
Wright's

COMPETITORS

ACH Food Companies
Adams Extract & Spice
Best Maid Products
Big Heart Pet Brands
Bolner's Fiesta Products
Bruce Foods
Bush Brothers
Campbell Soup
ConAgra
Frito-Lay
General Mills
Goya
Heinz
Herdez
Homestat Farm
Hormel
Kikkoman
Kraft Heinz
La Flor
MOM Brands
McCormick & Company
McIlhenny
MegaMex Foods
Mondelez International
Nestlé
PepsiCo
Pinnacle Foods
Renée's Gourmet Foods
Smucker
Snyder's-Lance
Spectrum Organic Products

HISTORICAL FINANCIALS

Company Type: Public

Income Statement
FYE: December 29

	REVENUE ($ mil.)	NET INCOME ($ mil.)	NET PROFIT MARGIN	EMPLOYEES
12/18	1,700.7	172.4	10.1%	2,675
12/17	1,668.0	217.4	13.0%	2,680
12/16*	1,391.2	109.4	7.9%	2,590
01/16	966.3	69.0	7.1%	2,003
01/15	848.0	40.9	4.8%	956
Annual Growth	19.0%	43.2%	—	29.3%

*Fiscal year change

2018 Year-End Financials

Debt ratio: 53.5%
Return on equity: 19.4%
Cash ($ mil.): 11.6
Current ratio: 2.27
Long-term debt ($ mil.): 1,635.8
No. of shares (mil.): 65.6
Dividends
  Yield: 0.0%
  Payout: 72.6%
Market value ($ mil.): 1,967.0

	STOCK PRICE ($) FY Close	P/E High/Low		Earnings	PER SHARE ($) Dividends	Book Value
12/18	29.96	14	8	2.60	1.89	13.71
12/17	35.15	15	9	3.26	1.86	13.25
12/16*	43.80	30	19	1.73	1.73	11.83
01/16	35.02	31	23	1.22	1.38	7.89
01/15	29.68	46	36	0.76	1.36	6.30
Annual Growth	0.2%	—	—	36.0%	8.6%	21.5%

*Fiscal year change

BancFirst Corp. (Oklahoma City, Okla)

This Oklahoma bank wants to be more than OK. It wants to be super. BancFirst Corporation is the holding company for BancFirst a super-community bank that emphasizes decentralized management and centralized support. BancFirst operates more than 100 branches in more than 50 Oklahoma communities. It serves individuals and small to midsized businesses offering traditional deposit products such as checking and savings accounts CDs and IRAs. Commercial real estate lending (including farmland and multifamily residential loans) makes up more than a third of the bank's loan portfolio while one-to-four family residential mortgages represent about 20%. The bank also issues business construction and consumer loans.

Operations

The company operates three core units: metropolitan banks community banks and other financial service. Metropolitan and community banks offer traditional banking products such as commercial and retail lending and a full line of deposit accounts in the metropolitan Oklahoma City and Tulsa areas. Community banks consist of banking locations in communities throughout Oklahoma. Other financial services are specialty product business units including guaranteed small business lending residential mortgage lending trust services securities brokerage electronic banking and insurance.

The company's BancFirst Insurance Services arm sells property/casualty coverage while the bank's trust and investment management division oversees some $1.21 billion of assets on behalf of clients. Bank subsidiaries Council Oak Investment Corporation and Council Oak Real Estate focus on small business and property investments respectively.

Like other retail banks BancFirst makes the bulk of its money from interest income. More than 60% of its total revenue came from loan interest (including fees) during 2015 while another 2% came from interest on taxable securities. The rest of its revenue came from service charges on deposits (19% of revenue) insurance commissions (5%) trust revenue (3%) securities transactions (3%) and loan sales (1%).

Geographic Reach
BancFirst has 95 banking locations serving more than 52 communities across Oklahoma.

Sales and Marketing
The bank customers are generally small to medium-sized businesses engaged in light manufacturing local wholesale and retail trade commercial and residential real estate development and construction services agriculture and the energy industry.

BancFirst spent about $6.9 million for advertising and promotion during 2015 compared to $6.6 million in each of 2014 and 2013.

Financial Performance
BancFirst's annual revenues have risen 20% since 2011 thanks to continued loan asset and deposit growth (partly thanks to branch expansion). The company's annual profits have grown more than 40% over the same period as it's kept a lid on operating expenses and loan loss provisions.

BancFirst's revenue climbed 6% to $306.85 million during 2015 thanks to a combination of loan asset growth and gains on the sales of some of its securities.

Revenue growth in 2015 drove the company's net income up nearly 4% to $66.17 million. The bank's operating cash levels increased by almost 2% to $78.1 million with the rise in cash-based earnings.

Strategy
BancFirst's strategy focuses on providing a full range of commercial banking services to retail customers and small to medium-sized businesses in both the non-metropolitan trade centers and cities in the metropolitan statistical areas of Oklahoma. It operates as a 'super community bank' managing its community banking offices on a decentralized basis which permits them to be responsive to local customer needs. Underwriting funding customer service and pricing decisions are made by presidents in each market within the company's strategic parameters.

Mergers and Acquisitions
In October 2015 BancFirst purchased $196 million-asset CSB Banchsares and its Bank of Commerce branches in Yukon Mustang and El Reno in Oklahoma. The deal also added $148 million in new loan business and $170 million in deposits.

Company Background
The company has been buying smaller banks to expand in Oklahoma. In 2011 it acquired FBC Financial Corporation and its subsidiary bank 1st Bank Oklahoma with about five branches throughout the state. In 2010 BancFirst acquired Union Bank of Chandler Okemah National Bank and Exchange National Bank of Moore adding about another five branches. It acquired First State Bank Jones in 2009 to expand in eastern Oklahoma.

President and CEO David Rainbolt owns some 40% of BancFirst.

EXECUTIVES

EVP Investments BancFirst, Robert M. Neville, age 63
EVP Financial Services BancFirst, D. Jay Hannah, age 63
EVP Interim CFO and Chief Risk Officer, Randy P. Foraker, age 63, $174,423 total compensation
EVP Human Resources BancFirst, J. Michael Rogers, age 75
EVP and CIO BancFirst, Scott Copeland, age 54
SEVP and Chairman Executive Committee, Dennis L. Brand, age 71, $525,000 total compensation
Vice Chairman and CEO Council Oak Investment Corporation and Council Oak Real Estate Inc., William O. Johnstone, age 71, $200,000 total compensation
EVP and Chief Credit Officer BancFirst, Roy C. Ferguson, age 72
Regional Executive BancFirst, Karen James, age 63
President and CEO BancFirst, Darryl Schmidt, age 57, $350,000 total compensation
Regional Executive BancFirst, David M. Seat, age 68
EVP and CTO BancFirst, David Westman, age 63
CEO, David R. Harlow, age 56, $325,000 total compensation
Regional Executive BancFirst, Harvey G. Robinson, age 60
EVP CFO and Treasurer, Kevin Lawrence, age 40, $214,231 total compensation
President BancFirst Frederick, Jason McQueen
EVP and Chief Internal Auditor, Paul Fleming, age 68
Regional Executive BancFirst, John Anderson, age 63
Senior Vice President Technologist, Stephen Florea
Executive Vice President, Debbie Kuykendall
Vice President, Tyler Smith
Senior Vice President, Patrick A Lippmann
Senior Vice President General Manager, Michael Kernan
Assistant Vice President Branch Manager, Desiree Raburn
Senior Vice President, Blane Allen
Senior Vice President Chief In, Scott Lewis
Senior Vice President Treasury Sales Director, Ashlea Briggs
Senior Vice President, Denise Duffle
Senior Vice President, Brian Renz
Vice President Lockbox Manager, Jennifer Seargent
Assistant Vice President, Tamara Reed
Vice President Financial Reporting, Chesney Whetstone
Assistant Vice President Network Services, Dian Joysizemore
Vice President, JON PENNINGTON
Vice President Marketing, Ben Harrington
Vice President, Matt Harp
Executive Vice President, Sean Shadid
Vice President consumer lending, Shirley Myers
Senior Vice President Investments, Bob Neville
Senior Vice President, David Vinall
EXECUTIVE VICE PRESIDENT, Janet W Gotwals
SENIOR VICE PRESIDENT, Kevin J Calabrese
Executive Vice President, Bob Winchester
Vice President, Delynn Rains
Assistant Vice President, Scott Hofmann
Assistant Vice President Commercial Loan Officer, Mary Johnston
Senior Vice President Corporate Banking, Matt Crew
Senior Vice President, Mark C Demos
Senior Vice President, Trent Cronk
Vice Chairman, James R. Daniel, age 79
Vice Chairman, K. Gordon Greer, age 82
Chairman, David E. Rainbolt, age 63
Auditors: BKD, LLP

LOCATIONS
HQ: BancFirst Corp. (Oklahoma City, Okla)
101 N. Broadway, Oklahoma City, OK 73102-8405
Phone: 405 270-1086   **Fax:** 405 270-1089
Web: www.bancfirst.com

PRODUCTS/OPERATIONS

2015 Sales

	$ mil.	% of total
Interest		
Loans including fees	190.3	63
Securities	6.5	2
Interest-bearing deposit	4.2	1
Noninterest		
Service charges on deposits	57.7	18
Insurance commissions	14.8	5
Security transactions	9.3	3
Trust revenue	9.1	3
Income from sale of loans	2.0	1
Cash management	7.5	2
Other	5.5	2
Total	**306.9**	**100**

Selected Subsidiaries
BancFirst
  BancFirst Agency Inc. (credit life insurance)
  BancFirst Community Development Corporation
  Council Oak Investment Corporation (small business investments)
  Council Oak Real Estate Inc. (real estate investments)
Council Oak Partners LLC
BancFirst Insurance Services Inc.

COMPETITORS

Arvest Bank	Midland Financial
BOK Financial	Southwest Bancorp
Bank of America	UMB Financial
International Bancshares	Wells Fargo

HISTORICAL FINANCIALS
Company Type: Public

Income Statement   FYE: December 31

	ASSETS ($ mil.)	NET INCOME ($ mil.)	INCOME AS % OF ASSETS	EMPLOYEES
12/18	7,574.2	125.8	1.7%	1,906
12/17	7,253.1	86.4	1.2%	1,782
12/16	7,018.9	70.6	1.0%	1,773
12/15	6,692.8	66.1	1.0%	1,744
12/14	6,574.9	63.8	1.0%	1,688
Annual Growth	3.6%	18.5%	—	3.1%

Bandwidth Inc

Auditors: Ernst & Young LLP

LOCATIONS
HQ: Bandwidth Inc
900 Main Campus Drive, Raleigh, NC 27606
Phone: 800 808-5150
Web: www.bandwidth.com

HISTORICAL FINANCIALS
Company Type: Public

Income Statement — FYE: December 31

	REVENUE ($ mil.)	NET INCOME ($ mil.)	NET PROFIT MARGIN	EMPLOYEES
12/18	204.1	17.9	8.8%	611
12/17	162.9	5.9	3.7%	378
12/16	152.1	22.3	14.7%	338
12/15	137.8	(6.7)	—	0
Annual Growth	14.0%			

2018 Year-End Financials
Debt ratio: —
Return on equity: 19.3%
Cash ($ mil.): 41.2
Current ratio: 2.79
Long-term debt ($ mil.): —
No. of shares (mil.): 19.4
Dividends
Yield: —
Payout: —
Market value ($ mil.): 792.0

	STOCK PRICE ($) FY Close	P/E High/Low		PER SHARE ($) Earnings	Dividends	Book Value
12/18	40.75	58	21	0.85	0.00	5.60
12/17	23.12	58	43	0.37	0.00	4.35
12/16	0.00	—	—	1.51	0.00	(0.05)
Annual Growth	—		—	(25.0%)	—	—

Bank First Corp

EXECUTIVES
Chb, Robert S Weinert
Vice President, Bill Bradley
Vice President Of Business Banking, Brandon Suemnicht
Vice President Retail Market Manager North Region, Bill Rehn
Vice President Business Banking Manager, Dennis Tienor
Vice President Business Banking, Christopher Stream
Senior Vice President Business Banking, Aaron Faulkner
Vp Of Agricultural Lending, Brad Rahmlow
Auditors: Dixon Hughes Goodman, LLP

LOCATIONS
HQ: Bank First Corp
402 North Eighth Street, P.O. Box 10, Manitowoc, WI 54220-0010
Phone: 920 652-3100   **Fax:** 920 652-3182
Web: www.bankfirstnational.com

HISTORICAL FINANCIALS
Company Type: Public

Income Statement — FYE: December 31

	ASSETS ($ mil.)	NET INCOME ($ mil.)	INCOME AS % OF ASSETS	EMPLOYEES
12/18	1,793.1	25.4	1.4%	253
12/17	1,753.4	15.3	0.9%	249
12/16	1,316.0	14.9	1.1%	173
12/15	1,237.6	13.4	1.1%	0
12/14	1,105.0	12.6	1.1%	0
Annual Growth	12.9%	19.2%	—	—

2018 Year-End Financials
Return on assets: 1.4%
Return on equity: 15.1%
Long-term debt ($ mil.): —
No. of shares (mil.): 6.6
Sales ($ mil): 89.4
Dividends
Yield: 1.4%
Payout: 17.8%
Market value ($ mil.): 308.0

	STOCK PRICE ($) FY Close	P/E High/Low		PER SHARE ($) Earnings	Dividends	Book Value
12/18	46.60	15	11	3.81	0.68	26.37
12/17	44.70	18	14	2.44	0.64	23.76
12/16	33.33	14	11	2.40	0.59	20.53
12/15	28.25	13	10	2.13	0.51	18.97
12/14	22.65	12	9	1.99	0.34	17.42
Annual Growth	19.8%	—	—	17.6%	18.9%	10.9%

(From previous page — 2018 Year-End Financials)
Return on assets: 1.7%
Return on equity: 14.9%
Long-term debt ($ mil.): —
No. of shares (mil.): 32.6
Sales ($ mil): 428.4
Dividends
Yield: 2.0%
Payout: 30.2%
Market value ($ mil.): 1,627.0

	STOCK PRICE ($) FY Close	P/E High/Low		PER SHARE ($) Earnings	Dividends	Book Value
12/18	49.90	17	13	3.76	1.02	27.69
12/17	51.15	40	18	2.65	0.80	24.32
12/16	93.05	42	23	2.22	0.74	22.49
12/15	58.62	32	26	2.09	0.70	21.01
12/14	63.39	33	25	2.02	0.65	19.65
Annual Growth	(5.8%)	—	—	16.8%	11.9%	9.0%

Bank Of Commerce Holdings (CA)

EXECUTIVES
Assistant Vice President and Operation Bank of Commerce Roseville, Cathy Smallhouse
Assistant Vice President Credit Administration Officer, Kendra Nelson
Vice President Information Security Officer, Rob Mcqueen
Senior Vice President, Scott Holthaus
Senior Vice President, Robert O'neil
Auditors: Moss Adams LLP

LOCATIONS
HQ: Bank Of Commerce Holdings (CA)
555 Capitol Mall, Suite 1255, Sacramento, CA 95814
Phone: 800 421-2575
Web: www.bankofcommerceholdings.com

COMPETITORS
American River Bankshares
Bank of America
North Valley Bancorp
Plumas Bancorp
PremierWest
U.S. Bancorp
Wells Fargo

HISTORICAL FINANCIALS
Company Type: Public

Income Statement — FYE: December 31

	ASSETS ($ mil.)	NET INCOME ($ mil.)	INCOME AS % OF ASSETS	EMPLOYEES
12/18	1,307.1	15.7	1.2%	197
12/17	1,269.4	7.3	0.6%	189
12/16	1,140.9	5.2	0.5%	191
12/15	1,015.4	8.5	0.8%	168
12/14	997.1	5.7	0.6%	157
Annual Growth	7.0%	28.7%	—	5.8%

2018 Year-End Financials
Return on assets: 1.2%
Return on equity: 11.8%
Long-term debt ($ mil.): —
No. of shares (mil.): 16.3
Sales ($ mil): 56.7
Dividends
Yield: 1.3%
Payout: 22.7%
Market value ($ mil.): 179.0

	STOCK PRICE ($) FY Close	P/E High/Low		PER SHARE ($) Earnings	Dividends	Book Value
12/18	10.96	14	11	0.96	0.15	8.47
12/17	11.50	26	19	0.48	0.12	7.82
12/16	9.50	24	14	0.39	0.12	7.00
12/15	6.68	12	9	0.62	0.12	6.76
12/14	5.96	17	14	0.41	0.12	7.79
Annual Growth	16.5%	—	—	23.7%	5.7%	2.1%

Bank OZK

Bank of the Ozarks is the holding company for the bank of the same name which has about 260 branches in Alabama Arkansas California the Carolinas Florida Georgia New York and Texas. Focusing on individuals and small to midsized businesses the $12-billion bank offers traditional deposit and loan services in addition to personal and commercial trust services retirement and financial planning and investment management. Commercial real estate and construction and land development loans make up the largest portion of Bank of the Ozarks' loan portfolio followed by residential mortgage business and agricultural loans. Bank of the Ozarks grows its loan and deposit business by acquiring smaller banks and opening branches across the US.

Operations
The bank makes three-fourths of its total revenue from interest income while the rest comes from fee-based sources. About 43% of Bank of the Ozark's total revenue came from non-purchased loan interest in 2014 while another 26%

came from interest on purchased loans and a further 8% came from interest on its investment securities. The rest of its revenue came from service charges on deposit accounts (8% of revenue) mortgage lending income (1%) trust income (1%) and other non-recurring sources.

Geographic Reach

Bank of the Ozarks had 174 branches in eight states at the end of 2014 with 81 of them in Alabama and another 75 branches split among Georgia North Carolina and Texas. It has two loan offices in Houston and Manhattan that serve as an extension of the bank's Dallas-based Real Estate Specialties Group.

Sales and Marketing

The bank spent $3.03 million on advertising and public relations expenses in 2014 compared to $2.2 million and $4.09 million in 2013 and 2012 respectively.

Financial Performance

Bank of the Ozarks' annual revenues and profits have doubled since 2010 mostly as its loan assets have doubled from recent bank acquisitions spawning higher interest income.

The bank's revenue jumped 31% to $376 million during 2014 mostly thanks to strong purchased and non-purchased loan asset growth during the year from recent bank acquisitions. Its non-interest income grew 12% thanks to a 20% increase in deposit account service charges stemming from newly acquired deposit customers.

Strong revenue growth in 2014 boosted Bank of the Ozarks' net income by 30% to $119 million for the year. Its operating cash levels jumped 22% to $61 million during the year mostly thanks to higher cash earnings.

Strategy

Bank of the Ozarks continues its strategy of loan and deposit volume growth by acquiring smaller banks in new and existing geographic markets. It has also opened new branches and loan offices sparingly. During 2014 for example the bank opened retail branches in Bradenton Florida; Cornelius North Carolina; and Hilton Head Island South Carolina along with a new loan production office in Asheville North Carolina.

Mergers and Acquisitions

In July 2016 Bank of the Ozarks acquired Georgia-based Community & Southern Holdings and its Community & Southern Bank subsidiary. Adding some 45 branch locations in Georgia plus another in Florida it was the company's largest acquisition to-date.

Also in July 2016 the bank purchased C1 Financial along with its 32 C1 Bank branches on the west coast of Florida and in Miami-Dade and Orange Counties. The deal added $1.7 billion in total assets $1.4 billion in loans and $1.3 billion in deposits. This transaction was the bank's fifteenth acquisition in the past six years.

In August 2015 the bank purchased Bank of the Carolinas Corporation (BCAR) — and its eight Bank of the Carolinas branches in North Carolina $345 million in total assets $277 million in loans and $296 million in deposits — for a total price of $65.4 million.

In February 2015 Bank of the Ozarks bought Intervest Bancshares Corporation and its seven Intervest National Bank branches in (five in Clearwater Florida and two more in New York City and Pasadena Florida) for $238.5 million. The deal added $1.5 billion in assets including $1.1 billion in loans and $1.2 billion in deposits.

In May 2014 it bought Arkansas-based Summit Bancorp Inc. and its 23 Summit Bank branches across Arkansas for $42.5 million though it closed more than a handful of them later in the year.

In March 2014 the company acquired Houston-based Bancshares Inc. and its subsidiary Omnibank N.A. for $21.5 million adding three branches in Houston Texas and a branch each in Austin Cedar Park Lockhart and San Antonio.

Company Background

The expansion strategy of Bank of the Ozarks - which had a mere five branches in Arkansas 20 years ago — centered on opening new locations in smaller communities in Arkansas. But with the financial crash the bank was able to expand to more states through a series of FDIC-assisted transactions to take over failed banks. It bought Chestatee State Bank First Choice Community Bank Horizon Bank Oglethorpe Bank Park Avenue Bank Unity National and Woodlands Bank.

Chairman and CEO George Gleason initially bought the bank more than three decades ago at age 25.

EXECUTIVES

Chief Credit Officer Bank of the Ozarks, Darrel Russell, age 65, $252,308 total compensation
Chairman; Chief Executive Officer of the Company and the Bank, George G. Gleason, age 65, $1,730,769 total compensation
President Leasing Division Bank of the Ozarks, Scott Hastings, age 61, $181,925 total compensation
President Mortgage Division Bank of the Ozarks, Gene Holman, age 71, $150,042 total compensation
President Trust and Wealth Management Division Bank of the Ozarks, Rex Kyle, age 62, $241,674 total compensation
Vice Chairman; President Real Estate Specialties Group and Chief Lending Officer Bank of the Ozarks, Dan Thomas, age 56, $1,242,308 total compensation
CFO and Chief Accounting Officer Bank of the Ozarks Inc. and Bank of the Ozarks, Greg McKinney, age 51, $368,077 total compensation
Chief Operating Officer and Chief Banking Officer of the Company and the Bank, Tyler Vance, age 44, $366,923 total compensation
President Western Division, Don Keesee
Senior Vice President Market Leader, Russell Hewatt
Senior Vice President of Information Systems, Malcolm Hicks
Vice President Payment Systems, Paula Shaw
Senior Vice President, Chris Bragg
Senior Vice President Retail Banking Manager, Bob Moore
Vice President Regional Manager, Lisa Amato
Vice President Commercial Loan Officer, Austin Simpson
Vice President Lending, Erik Larson
Assistant Vice President Community Development Officer, Kimberly L Marshall
Vice President Marketing, Mark Greenhaw
Senior Vice President Treasury Management, Steve Woodruff
Assistant Vice President Branch Operations Manager, Fabian Garantiva
Senior Vice President Commercial Lender, Jeni Chokron
Vice President, Eric Teague
Senior Vice President, Ryan Tanner
Assistant Vice President Branch Manager, Pam Toney
Assistant Vice President Branch Manager, Derek Labrosse
Assistant Vice President Community Development Officer, Joann Smith
Executive Vice President, David Sarner
Executive Vice President, Martin Ball
Senior Vice President, Aram Zakian
Vice President Loan Officer, Dawn Speas
Vice President Treasury Management Wire Manager, Mona Kalchik
Auditors: PricewaterhouseCoopers LLP

LOCATIONS

HQ: Bank OZK
17901 Chenal Parkway, Little Rock, AR 72223
Phone: 501 978-2265 **Fax:** 501 978-2224
Web: www.bankozarks.com

PRODUCTS/OPERATIONS

2014 Sales

	$ mil.	% of total
Interest income		
Non-purchased loans and leases	162.5	43
Purchased loans	98.2	26
Investment securities	30.7	8
Non-interest income		
Service charges on deposit accounts	26.6	8
Other income from purchased loans net	14.8	4
Others	43.5	11
Total	**376.3**	**100**

Selected Services

Personal Banking
Apple PayChecking AccountsCredit CardsFree Bill PayFREE Debit CardsCustom Debit CardsEMV Chip CardsMobile BankingMortgage LoansMy Change KeeperOnline BankingOverdraft ProtectionPersonal LoansReloadable Spending CardsRetirement PlanningReorder ChecksSafe
Business Banking
Business ProductsApple Pay for BusinessDebit CardEMV Chip CardsBusiness Credit CardsChecking & Money MarketCommercial LoansExpress DepositMerchant ProcessingOnline BankingOverdraft ProtectionReorder ChecksTreasury Management Services
Online & Mobile Banking
Online BankingMobile BankingMobile DepositOnline Bill Pay
Wealth Management Services
Investment ProgramsFinancial PlanningCustomer Service

COMPETITORS

Arvest Bank	IBERIABANK
BOK Financial	JPMorgan Chase
BancorpSouth	Regions Financial
Bank of America	Simmons First
Bear State Financial	SunTrust
Cullen/Frost Bankers	Wells Fargo
Home BancShares	

HISTORICAL FINANCIALS

Company Type: Public

Income Statement FYE: December 31

	ASSETS ($ mil.)	NET INCOME ($ mil.)	INCOME AS % OF ASSETS	EMPLOYEES
12/18	22,388.0	417.1	1.9%	2,563
12/17	21,275.6	421.8	2.0%	2,400
12/16	18,890.1	269.9	1.4%	2,315
12/15	9,879.4	182.2	1.8%	1,642
12/14	6,766.5	118.6	1.8%	1,479
Annual Growth	34.9%	36.9%	—	14.7%

2018 Year-End Financials

Return on assets: 1.9%
Return on equity: 11.5%
Long-term debt ($ mil.): —
No. of shares (mil.): 128.6
Sales ($ mil): 1,208.6
Dividends
Yield: 3.4%
Payout: 22.7%
Market value ($ mil.): 2,936.0

	STOCK PRICE ($) FY Close	P/E High/Low		PER SHARE ($) Earnings	Dividends	Book Value
12/18	22.83	16	7	3.24	0.80	29.32
12/17	48.45	17	12	3.35	0.37	26.98
12/16	52.59	21	13	2.58	0.63	23.02
12/15	49.46	26	15	2.09	0.55	16.19
12/14	37.92	46	20	1.52	0.47	11.37
Annual Growth	(11.9%)	—	—	20.8%	14.0%	26.7%

BankUnited Inc.

BankUnited is uniting the north and south again. It's the bank holding company for BankUnited N.A. which provides standard banking services to individuals and businesses through nearly 90 banking centers in about 15 Florida counties and five banking centers in the New York metro area. Deposit offerings include checking and savings accounts treasury management services and certificates of deposit. Commercial loans including multi-family residential mortgages account for some 80% of the bank's lending portfolio. In 2018 the company launched BankUnitedDirect an online division offering money market and CD accounts nationwide. BankUnited does not offer investment banking or wealth management services.

Sales and Marketing
BankUnited serves individuals growing companies and established middle-market companies. It markets its products through local television and radio ads digital and print ads and direct mail campaigns.

Financial Performance
BankUnited's revenue has been growing steadily for the last five years. Profits were relatively static until 2017 when they more than doubled. Cash flow has been somewhat volatile.

In 2017 revenue increased 14% to $1.1 billion as both interest and non-interest income grew. Interest on loans and securities rose while gains of sales of loans boosted non-interest income.

Net income rose 172% to $591 million that year. Part of that gain was due to a $327.9 million income tax benefit received.

The company ended 2017 with some $195 million in cash versus $448 million held at the end of 2016. Financing activities provided $1.9 billion in cash and operating activities provided $319 million. Investing activities used $2.5 billion in 2017 (the fifth straight year investments have used more than $2 billion).

Strategy
BankUnited has placed its bets on two large and growing markets — the Miami metro area and the Tri-State area of New York New Jersey and Connecticut. Because those geographic markets are so attractive though competition is fierce.

The company is also open to making strategic acquisitions of other financial firms or companies in complementary businesses.

Company Background
BankUnited was formed in 2009 following the demise of the former BankUnited FSB which collapsed under the weight of bad mortgages. A team of private investors bought BankUnited from the FDIC injected $900 million in fresh capital and in 2011 took the company public via an initial public offering (IPO); it was the first IPO of a rescued bank during the economic crisis.

In February 2012 BankUnited acquired Herald National Bank for $65 million in cash and stock. At the time of the purchase BankUnited converted to a bank holding company. It also converted the charter of subsidiary BankUnited from a thrift to a national commercial bank. Herald National was merged into BankUnited in mid-2012.

EXECUTIVES

President New York Region, Joseph (Joe) Roberto, age 62, $300,000 total compensation
Chief Risk Officer, Mark P. Bagnoli, age 67
President and CEO, Rajinder P. (Raj) Singh, age 48, $500,000 total compensation
CFO, Leslie N. Lunak, age 62, $400,000 total compensation
COO, Thomas M. Cornish, age 61, $500,000 total compensation
CIO, Julio Jogaib
Vice President Information Technology, William Hynes
Senior Vice President Commercial Real Estate, Robert Hummel
Assistant Vice President Portfolio Manager, Tracey Snow
Senior Vice President, Steven Hart
Vice President, Kenneth Lipke
Senior Vice President Commercial Private Banking, Corey Prinz
Executive Vice President, Cristina Di Mauro
Vice President, Laura Lowy
Vice President, Bill Williams
Vice President, Peter Dumelle
Senior Vice President, Elizabeth Claisse
Assistant Vice President, Pedro Garcia
Vice President, Susan Kay
Vice President Project Management Office, Janet Marotta
Senior Vice President Associate General Counsel, Alina Pastiu
Vice President Credit Officer, Patrick Rigney
Vice President Community Development Outreach, Naima Oyo
Vice President Treasury Management Relationship Manager Treasury Management, Mark Stevens
Vice President, Carol Hammond
Assistant Vice President Design and Development, Sonya Moro
Vice President, Sabine Bouchereau
Senior Vice President Corporate Finance, Cristina Frias
Senior Vice President Community Development Officer, Claire Raley
Vice President Banking Center Assistant Manager, Theresa Schuman
Vice President Electronic Banking, Juliana Tancrati
Vice President Commercial Banker, Jaime Fimiani
Vice President Accounting Department, Dorrett Boothe
Vice President Portfolio Analytics Manager, Matthew Crawford
Senior Vice President Bsa Officer, Scott Nathan
Senior Vice President Enterprise Stress Testing, Filippo Ghia
Senior Vice President Marketing and Public Relations, Mary Harris
Vice President Financial Center Manager, John Hernandez
Senior Vice President Corporate Banking, Joseph Disanti
Vice President Corporate Banking, Justin Allbright
Vice President And Business Banking, Jose Alonso
Vice President Relationship Manager, Patricia Lubian
Vice President Human Resources And Employee Relations, Ellen Gioia
Vice President Senior Relationship Manager, Daniel Vaccaro
Vice President Business Banking, Jason Costello
Vice President Commercial Banking, Ted Kunkel
Assistant Vice President Corporate Real Estate, Kristin Maresca
Vice President Banking Center Manager, Paige Homan
Vice President Commercial Real Estate, Jeremy Romine
Vice President Business Development Officer, Amy Rice
Senior Vice President Corporate Lending, Gerry Mcpartland
Senior Vice President, Michael Del Rocco
Vice President, Oleg Kochanov
Vice President, Wendy Spears
Senior Vice President Senior Credit Officer Commercial Real Estate, John Kenyon
Vice President Underwriter, Alexandra Tovar
Assistant Vice President, Gloria Persaud
Vice President Commercial And Consumer Loan Servic, Rebecca Thrasher
Vice President Corporate Portfolio Manager, Jeff Landroche
Vice President Business Banker, Timothy Byrnes
Senior Vice President Environmental Risk Manager, Michael Tartanella
Senior Vice President Business Banking Sales Manager, Gregory Milford
Vice President Banking Center Manager, Pat Kelly
Vice President Branch Sales Leader, Milton Price
Vice President, Monica Antongeorgi
Vice President Corporate Portfolio Manager, Thomas Mcgregor
Vice President Corporate Banking Division, Milciades Herrera
Senior Vice President, Tyson Carballo
Svp Commercial Real Estate Lender, Ellen Hoey
Executive Vice President, Gardner Semet
Senior Vice President Corporate Team Lead, Arthur Rhatigan
Vice President Corporate Portfolio Manager, Bradley Hendren
Senior Vice President, Larry Crowley
Vice President Operations Manager, Jose Alvarado
Vice President Corporate Banking, Jennifer Garcia-Barbon
Vice President Commercial Private Banker, Mike Smith
Vice President Business Development Officer, Marissa Ames
Vice President Private Client Team Lead, Thomas Pla
Vp, Tatiana Eyzaguirre
Vice President Commercial Underwriter Bankunited, Gregory O'Brien
Vice President Business Banking Lead Underwriter, Alexanders Saenz
Senior Vice President Corporate Team Leader, Christine Gerula
Assistant Vice President Project Administrator and Executive Assistant, Natalia Valenti
Assistant Vice President Financial Reporting, Niurka Hiott

Vice President, Guillermo Doria
Vp Corporate Portfolio Manager, Jasmine Varghese
Assistant Vice President, Shannie DeFreitas
Executive Vice President Mortgage Services, Ray Barbone
Vice President Doral Branch Sales Leader, Ralph Vasallo
Vice President Branch Sales Leader, Monica Ribeiro
Vice President Business Development Officer, Stephen Speer
Senior Vice President Team Leader, Thomas Riele
Senior Executive Vice President, Nick Bustle
Vice President, Dianne Brodie
Vice President; Business Banking, Jairo Cardona
Vice President Market Manager, Jeff Fusco
Senior Vice President, Brett Shulick
Vice President Business Banking Relationship Manager, Marshall Fulton
AVP SBA Loan Closer, Leslie Giannantoni
Executive Vice President Director Of Business Banking, Brian Clay
SVP Credit Review Group Manager, Nancy Lanzoni
VP Credit Review Examination Manager, David Young
Vice President Retail And Small Business Banking, Sean Chaderton
Senior Vice President Senior CRE Credit Officer Florida Region, Raul Llanes
Vice President Business Banking Lead Underwriter, Larry Candelario
Senior Vice President Commercial Private Banking, Kelly Sleece
Vice President Relationship Manager, Larry Marchini
Assistant Vice President Branch Manager, Darlene Curti
Vice President Business Development Officer, Alan Hice
Senior Vice President, Benjamin Fisher
Senior Vice President Corporate Banking, Jackson Young
Vice President Business Banking, Richard Rippy
Vice President Business Development Officer, Jared Johnson
Senior Vice President Corporate Finance, Jorge Ray
Senior Vice President, Luis Garcia
Vice President Branch Sales Manager, Kathy Nemeth
Assistant Vice President Mortgage Warehouse Lending, Rosemarie Loparrino
Vice President Sba Underwriter, Scott Meckes
Executive Vice President New York, Ben Stacks
Vice President Sba Underwriter, Amy Luce
Vice President Senior Analyst Business Development Officer, Will Tinsley
Vice President, Lon Gopie
Vice President, Peter Hughes
Senior Vice President Of Government Institutional Banking Gib Team Leader For Private Client Svc, Emsley Hylton
Vice President Branch Manager, Sebastian Cannata
Senior Vice President, Steven Markowski
Vice President, Kevin Karstens
Svp Commercial Private Banking, Theonie Golden
VICE PRESIDENT PORTFOLIO MANAGER, Noel Lassise
Vice President Credit Officer, Ward Burns
Executive Vice President, Michael Wilcox
Assistant Vice President Sba Loan Closer, Pannah Hem
Assistant Vice President Senior Servicing Portfolio Officer, Michael Castle
Chairman, John A. Kanas, age 72
Assistant Treasurer, Robert Treadwell

Vice Chairman Credit Risk Management, Jack Leonard
Board Member, Sanjiv Sobti
Board Member, Lynne Wines
Auditors: KPMG LLP

LOCATIONS

HQ: BankUnited Inc.
14817 Oak Lane, Miami Lakes, FL 33016
Phone: 305 569-2000
Web: www.bankunited.com

COMPETITORS

BB&T	Ocean Bankshares
Bank of America	PNC Financial
Capital One	Regions Financial
Citibank	Signature Bank
Great Florida Bank	SunTrust
JPMorgan Chase	TD Bank USA
M&T Bank	Valley National Bancorp
New York Community Bancorp	Wells Fargo

HISTORICAL FINANCIALS

Company Type: Public

Income Statement   FYE: December 31

	ASSETS ($ mil.)	NET INCOME ($ mil.)	INCOME AS % OF ASSETS	EMPLOYEES
12/18	32,164.3	324.8	1.0%	1,790
12/17	30,346.9	614.2	2.0%	1,763
12/16	27,880.1	225.7	0.8%	1,706
12/15	23,883.4	251.6	1.1%	1,741
12/14	19,210.5	204.2	1.1%	1,647
Annual Growth	13.8%	12.3%	—	2.1%

2018 Year-End Financials

Return on assets: 1.0%   Dividends
Return on equity: 10.9%   Yield: 2.8%
Long-term debt ($ mil.): —   Payout: 28.0%
No. of shares (mil.): 99.1   Market value ($ mil.): 2,968.0
Sales ($ mil): 1,581.1

	STOCK PRICE ($) FY Close	P/E High/Low	PER SHARE ($) Earnings	Dividends	Book Value
12/18	29.94	15 9	2.99	0.84	29.49
12/17	40.72	7 5	5.58	0.84	28.32
12/16	37.69	18 13	2.09	0.84	23.22
12/15	36.06	17 11	2.35	0.84	21.65
12/14	28.97	18 14	1.95	0.84	20.19
Annual Growth	0.8%	— —	11.3%	(0.0%)	9.9%

Bankwell Financial Group Inc

Auditors: RSM US LLP

LOCATIONS

HQ: Bankwell Financial Group Inc
220 Elm Street, New Canaan, CT 06840
Phone: 203 652-0166
Web: www.mybankwell.com

HISTORICAL FINANCIALS

Company Type: Public

Income Statement   FYE: December 31

	ASSETS ($ mil.)	NET INCOME ($ mil.)	INCOME AS % OF ASSETS	EMPLOYEES
12/18	1,873.6	17.4	0.9%	144
12/17	1,796.6	13.8	0.8%	141
12/16	1,628.9	12.3	0.8%	127
12/15	1,330.3	9.0	0.7%	125
12/14	1,099.5	4.5	0.4%	130
Annual Growth	14.3%	39.8%	—	2.6%

2018 Year-End Financials

Return on assets: 0.9%   Dividends
Return on equity: 10.4%   Yield: 1.6%
Long-term debt ($ mil.): —   Payout: 31.1%
No. of shares (mil.): 7.8   Market value ($ mil.): 225.0
Sales ($ mil): 83.9

	STOCK PRICE ($) FY Close	P/E High/Low	PER SHARE ($) Earnings	Dividends	Book Value
12/18	28.71	16 12	2.21	0.48	22.21
12/17	34.34	21 16	1.78	0.28	20.77
12/16	32.50	21 12	1.62	0.22	19.14
12/15	19.85	17 14	1.21	0.05	17.53
12/14	21.00	28 21	0.78	0.00	17.98
Annual Growth	8.1%	— —	29.7%	—	5.4%

Banner Corp.

Flagging bank accounts? See Banner Corporation. Banner is the holding company for Banner Bank which serves the Pacific Northwest through about 100 branches and 10 loan production offices in Washington Oregon and Idaho. The company also owns Islanders Bank which operates three branches in Washington's San Juan Islands. The banks offer standard products such as deposit accounts credit cards and business and consumer loans. Commercial loans including business agriculture construction and multifamily mortgage loans account for about 90% of the company's portfolio. Bank subsidiary Community Financial writes residential mortgage and construction loans.

Geographic Reach

Washington-based Banner Bank is focused on five primary markets in the Northwest: the Puget Sound region of Washington; the greater Portland Oregon market; Boise Idaho; and Spokane Washington. The fifth is the bank's historical base in the agricultural communities in the Columbia Basin region of Washington and Oregon.

Sales and Marketing

Banner Corp. reported advertising and marketing expenses of $6.9 million in 2013 versus $7.2 million in 2012. Banner Bank launched a redesigned website and new ad campaign in Boise Seattle and Portland and on social media in fall 2014.

Financial Performance

The regional bank holding company reported revenue of $223 million in 2013 an increase of 4% versus 2012. The rise in revenue was due to increased operating income as a result of gains on the sale of securities and a fee received from the termination of the bank's proposed acquisition of Home Federal Bancorp. The bank's growing customer base led to increased income from deposit fees and other service charges of $1.3 billion (5%) in 2013 versus the prior year. Net income declined 28% in 2013 versus 2012 to $46.6 million primarily due to higher provision for income tax expenses. After three consecutive years of losses (2008 thru 2010) the bank returned to profitability in 2011 and has remained profitable.

Banner Corp. has total consolidated assets of about $4.5 billion.

Strategy

Historically Banner Corp. has grown by acquisition. Since going public (in 1995) Banner has acquired about 10 commercial banks. Islanders Bank was acquired in 2007 the same year Banner acquired F&M Bank and NCW Community Bank of Wenatchee both also based in Washington. After the spate of acquisitions the company focused on opening branches. The company continues to look for acquisition opportunities with an eye on banks shut down by regulators.

In 2013 however a plan to merge with Home Federal Bancorp was terminated when that bank received a better offer from Cascade Bancorp. Also the company abandoned plans to buy Idaho Banking Company out of bankruptcy after being outbid.

Mergers and Acquisitions

In August 2014 Banner Bank acquired Siuslaw Financial Group the holding company for Siuslaw Bank the operator of 10 branches along the coast of Oregon. In June 2014 Banner Bank purchased six branches in Oregon from Sterling Savings Bank.

EXECUTIVES

EVP and CFO Banner Corporation, Lloyd W. Baker, age 70, $260,724 total compensation
EVP Retail Banking and Administration, Cynthia D. (Cindy) Purcell, age 61, $289,038 total compensation
EVP and Chief Lending Officer Banner Corporation and Banner Bank, Richard B. Barton, age 75, $264,895 total compensation
President and CEO, Mark J. Grescovich, age 54, $716,415 total compensation
EVP and Real Estate Lending Manager Banner Bank, Douglas M. Bennett, age 66, $236,174 total compensation
EVP and CIO, Steven W. (Steve) Rust, age 71
EVP Retail Products and Services, Gary W. Wagers, age 58
EVP and Commercial Executive East Region, M. Kirk Quillin, age 56
EVP and Commercial Executive West Region, James T. (Jim) Reed, age 56
EVP and CFO Banner Bank, Peter J. Conner, age 53
EVP Human Resources, Kayleen Kohler
EVP and Mortgage Banking Director, Kenneth A. (Ken) Larsen, age 49
EVP and General Counsel Banner Bank, Craig Miller
EVP and Chief Risk Officer Banner Bank, Judy Steiner
EVP and Commercial Executive (South Region), Keith A. Western, age 63
Senior Vice President And Sba Manager, Walter Mclaughlin
Vice President Sr. Commercial Relationship Manager, Jeanne Walker
Assistant Vice President Training Manager, Terri Anderson
Vice President Credit Risk Manager, Heidi Collins
Vice Chairman Banner Corporation and Banner Bank, Jesse G. Foster, age 81
Chairman Banner Corporation and Banner Bank, Gary L. Sirmon, age 76
Auditors: Moss Adams LLP

LOCATIONS

HQ: Banner Corp.
   10 South First Avenue, Walla Walla, WA 99362
Phone: 509 527-3636
Web: www.bannerbank.com

PRODUCTS/OPERATIONS

2016 Sales

	% of total
INTEREST INCOME:	
Loans receivable	75
Mortgage-backed securities	4
Securities and cash equivalents	3
NON-INTEREST INCOME:	
Deposit fees and other service charges	10
Mortgage banking operations	6
BOLI	1
Miscellaneous	1
Total	**100**

COMPETITORS

Bank of America	Sound Financial
Cascade Bancorp	U.S. Bancorp
Columbia Banking	Umpqua Holdings
FCA	Washington Federal
Glacier Bancorp	Wells Fargo
KeyCorp	

HISTORICAL FINANCIALS

Company Type: Public

Income Statement
FYE: December 31

	ASSETS ($ mil.)	NET INCOME ($ mil.)	INCOME AS % OF ASSETS	EMPLOYEES
12/18	11,871.3	136.5	1.2%	2,187
12/17	9,763.2	60.7	0.6%	2,128
12/16	9,793.6	85.3	0.9%	2,137
12/15	9,796.3	45.2	0.5%	2,143
12/14	4,723.9	54.1	1.1%	1,193
Annual Growth	25.9%	26.0%	—	16.4%

2018 Year-End Financials

Return on assets: 1.2%
Return on equity: 9.9%
Long-term debt ($ mil.): —
No. of shares (mil.): 35.1
Sales ($ mil): 565.5
Dividends
  Yield: 3.4%
  Payout: 69.0%
Market value ($ mil.): 1,882.0

	STOCK PRICE ($) FY Close	P/E High/Low		PER SHARE ($) Earnings	Dividends	Book Value
12/18	53.48	16	12	4.15	1.83	42.03
12/17	55.12	34	28	1.84	1.98	38.89
12/16	55.81	22	15	2.52	0.65	39.34
12/15	45.86	28	21	1.89	0.72	37.97
12/14	43.02	16	13	2.79	0.72	29.82
Annual Growth	5.6%	—	—	10.4%	26.3%	9.0%

Bar Harbor Bankshares

Bar Harbor Bankshares which holds Bar Harbor Bank & Trust is a Maine-stay. Boasting $1.6 billion in assets the bank offers traditional deposit and retirement products trust services and a variety of loans to individuals and businesses through 15 branches in the state's Hancock Knox and Washington counties. Commercial real estate and residential mortgages loans make up nearly 80% of the bank's loan portfolio though it also originates business construction agricultural home equity and other consumer loans. About 10% of its loans are to the tourist industry which is associated with nearby Acadia National Park. Subsidiary Bar Harbor Trust Services offers trust and estate planning services.

Operations

Around 80% of the bank's loan assets are tied to real estate. About 41% of its loan portfolio was made up of residential real estate mortgages at the end of 2015 while another 37% was made up of commercial real estate mortgages. The rest of the portfolio was tied to commercial and industrial loans (8% of loan assets) home equity loans (5%) agricultural and farming loans (3%) commercial construction (3%) and other consumer loans (1%).

More than 80% of Bar Harbor's revenue comes from interest income. About 61% of its total revenue came from loan interest (including fees) during 2015 while another 25% came from interest income on investment securities. The remainder of its revenue came from trust and other financial services (6% of revenue) debit card service charges and fees (3%) deposit account service charges (1%) and other miscellaneous income sources.

Geographic Reach

The Bar Harbor Maine-based group operates 15 branches across the downeast midcoast and central regions of Maine more specifically in Bar Harbor Northeast Harbor Southwest Harbor Somesville Deer Isle Blue Hill Ellsworth Rockland Topsham South China Augusta Winter Harbor Milbridge Machias and Lubec.

Sales and Marketing

Bar Harbor serves individuals and retirees nonprofits municipalities as well as businesses that are vital to Maine's coastal economy including retailers restaurants seasonal lodging bio research laboratories.

Financial Performance

The group's annual revenues have risen more than 10% since 2011 as its loan assets have swelled over 35% to $990 million. Its profits have grown more than 30% over the same period as Bar Harbor has kept a lid on rising operating costs and as it's enjoyed low interest rates.

Bar Harbor's revenue climbed 4% to $64.2 million during 2015 mostly as its loan and other interest earning assets grew by more than 7%.

Revenue growth in 2015 drove the bank's net income up 4% to $15.15 million. Bar Harbor's operating cash levels spiked 31% to $20.33 million for the year mainly thanks to favorable working capital changes related to changes in other assets.

Strategy

Bar Harbor Bankshares looks to grow its loan and deposit business organically and through strategic bank acquisitions targeting the downeast midcoast and central Maine markets. It also continued in 2016 to focus on managing its operating expenses building upon its strong efficient ratio of 56.3% in 2015.

EXECUTIVES

EVP Business Banking Bar Harbor Bank & Trust, Gregory W. Dalton, age 59, $203,000 total compensation
EVP Retail Banking, Stephen M. Leackfeldt, age 62, $225,000 total compensation
EVP and Chief Risk Officer, Richard B. Maltz, $255,000 total compensation
EVP CFO and Treasurer, Josephine Iannelli, age 47
President and CEO Bar Harbor Bankshares and Bar Harbor Bank & Trust, Curtis C. Simard, age 48, $438,000 total compensation
Senior Vice President, Steve Gurin
Senior Vice President Internal Audit, Johanne Lapointe
Executive Vice President Regional President Of Nh Vt Of Bhbt, William Mciver
Chairman, David B. Woodside, age 67
Board Member, David Colter
Auditors: RSM US LLP

LOCATIONS

HQ: Bar Harbor Bankshares
P.O. Box 400, 82 Main Street, Bar Harbor, ME 04609-0400
Phone: 207 288-3314
Web: www.bhbt.com

PRODUCTS/OPERATIONS

2015 sales

	$ mil.	% of total
Interest and dividend income		
Interest and fees on loans	39.3	61
Interest on securities	15.3	24
Dividends on FHLB stock	0.6	1
Non-interest income		
Trust and other financial services	3.9	6
Debit card service charges and fees	1.7	3
Net securities gains	1.3	2
Other operating income	1.2	2
Service charges on deposit accounts	0.9	1
Total	**64.2**	**100**

Selected Services
Retail Products and Services
Retail Brokerage Services
Electronic Banking Services
Commercial Products and Services

COMPETITORS

Bangor Savings Bank	TD Bank USA
Bank of America	The First Bancorp
Camden National	
People's United Financial	

HISTORICAL FINANCIALS
Company Type: Public

Income Statement   FYE: December 31

	ASSETS ($ mil.)	NET INCOME ($ mil.)	INCOME AS % OF ASSETS	EMPLOYEES
12/18	3,608.4	32.9	0.9%	445
12/17	3,565.1	25.9	0.7%	423
12/16	1,755.3	14.9	0.9%	186
12/15	1,580.0	15.1	1.0%	221
12/14	1,459.3	14.6	1.0%	223
Annual Growth	25.4%	22.5%	—	18.9%

2018 Year-End Financials
Return on assets: 0.9%
Return on equity: 9.0%
Long-term debt ($ mil.): —
No. of shares (mil.): 15.5
Sales ($ mil): 155.3
Dividends
Yield: 3.5%
Payout: 37.1%
Market value ($ mil.): 348.0

	STOCK PRICE ($) FY Close	P/E High/Low		PER SHARE ($) Earnings	Dividends	Book Value
12/18	22.43	14	10	2.12	0.79	23.87
12/17	27.01	28	15	1.70	0.75	22.96
12/16	47.33	30	18	1.63	0.73	17.19
12/15	34.42	22	18	1.67	0.67	17.10
12/14	32.00	24	15	1.63	0.60	16.40
Annual Growth	(8.5%)	—	—	6.7%	6.9%	9.8%

Barrett Business Services, Inc.

Barrett Business Services (BBSI) is employed in helping businesses. BBSI offers professional employment organization (PEO) services to some 6400 small and mid-sized businesses and their nearly 200000 employees. Its PEO services business provides outsourced human resource services such as payroll management benefits administration risk management recruiting and placement. The company also offers temporary and long-term staffing services such as on-demand or short-term staffing on-site management contract staffing master-vendor programs. Established in 1965 BBSI operates through more than 60 branch offices across 10 US states. About 80% of revenue comes from clients in California.

Operations
BBSI operates through two categories of services: Professional Employer Services (PEO) and Staffing.

Accounting for nearly 85% of company revenue the company's PEO services provide employee payroll payroll taxes workers? compensation coverage and certain other administrative functions to small and mid-sized businesses.

Staffing services bringing in about 15% of revenue includes on-demand or short-term staffing assignments contract staffing direct placement and long-term or indefinite-term on-site management.

Geographic Reach
BBSI operates through about 60 branch offices a dozen states many of which are located throughout California and Oregon as well as Utah and Washington. The company supports clients' employees in two dozen states but does 80% of its business in California which leaves the company's financial performance largely dependent on a single state's economy.

Sales and Marketing
BBSI relies on referrals from existing clients as well as B2B sales initiatives managed by area managers and a referral network to growth its client base. It serves small to mid-sized businesses operating in an array of industries including electronics manufacturers agriculture companies transportation and shipping enterprises telecommunications companies public utilities construction contractors and professional services firms.

Financial Performance
BBSI's revenue has been trending upwards in recent years growing nearly 50% between 2014 and 2018. During the same five-year span net income fluctuated between a loss of $25 million and profits of $38 million but has failed to pace the company's revenue trend.

In 2018 BBSI reported $940.6 million in revenue a 2% increase from the previous year. The mild increase was driven by a 5% uptick in its PEO services business which was offset by a 9% decrease in its smaller Staffing business. That year the company's new client numbers outpaced its contractual losses resulting in its PEO business serving 6400 clients in 2018 up from 5600 clients in 2017. The company attributed declines in its staffing business in 2018 to a tight labor market.

Net income rose to $38.1 million from $25.1 million in 2017 the increase driven by higher investment income earned than in the prior year.

Cash on hand at the end of the year was $140.7 million an increase of $20.4 million from 2017 total cash. Cash from operations contributed $69.8 million consisting of net income and increased workers? compensation claims liabilities. Investing activities used $39.3 million and financing activities used $10 million mostly for dividend payments and stock repurchases.

Strategy
BBSI's growth strategy centers on building its client numbers through organic means. It relies on existing client referrals sales mangers recruiting clients through direct B2B sales and a sales referral network. Its referral network is composed of business professionals like lawyers financial advisors and insurance brokers that refer their small- to mid-sized business clients to BBSI in exchange for a fee.

The company also looks for opportunities to expand geographically within and outside of its core California market. BBSI will either expand its staff at existing locations to facilitate client number increases or when necessary open a new branch office to reach clients in a new geographic area.

EXECUTIVES

VP and COO Corporate Operations, Gregory R. (Greg) Vaughn, age 63, $400,000 total compensation
President and CEO, Michael L. (Mike) Elich, age 54, $650,000 total compensation
VP and COO Field Operations, Gerald R. Blotz, age 49, $400,000 total compensation
CFO, Gary Kramer, age 39
Chairman, Anthony Meeker, age 80
Board Member, Jon Justesen
Auditors: DELOITTE & TOUCHE LLP

LOCATIONS

HQ: Barrett Business Services, Inc.
8100 NE Parkway Drive, Suite 200, Vancouver, WA 98662
Phone: 360 828-0700   Fax: 360 828-0701
Web: www.barrettbusiness.com

PRODUCTS/OPERATIONS

2018 Sales

	$ mil.	% of total
Professional employer service fees	793.4	84
Staffing services	147.3	16
Total	940.7	100

Selected Services
PEO services
  Employee benefits
  Health insurance
  Human resource administration
  Drug testing
  Hiring
  Interviewing
  Placement
  Recruiting
  Regulatory compliance
  Payroll
  Workers' compensation coverage
  Workplace safety programs
Staffing services
  Contract
  Long-term
  Short-term

COMPETITORS

ADP TotalSource   Paychex
Adecco   Robert Half
Insperity   TeamStaff
Kelly Services   TriNet Group
ManpowerGroup

HISTORICAL FINANCIALS

Company Type: Public

Income Statement   FYE: December 31

	REVENUE ($ mil.)	NET INCOME ($ mil.)	NET PROFIT MARGIN	EMPLOYEES
12/18	940.7	38.0	4.0%	122,958
12/17	920.4	25.1	2.7%	124,212
12/16	840.5	18.8	2.2%	115,746
12/15	740.8	25.4	3.4%	103,250
12/14	636.1	(27.0)	—	93,040
Annual Growth	10.3%	—	—	7.2%

2018 Year-End Financials

Debt ratio: 0.5%
Return on equity: 36.6%
Cash ($ mil.): 35.3
Current ratio: 0.98
Long-term debt ($ mil.): 3.9
No. of shares (mil.): 7.4
Dividends
  Yield: 1.7%
  Payout: 24.4%
Market value ($ mil.): 423.0

	STOCK PRICE ($) FY Close	P/E High/Low		PER SHARE ($) Earnings	Dividends	Book Value
12/18	57.25	19	10	4.98	1.00	16.10
12/17	64.49	20	14	3.33	1.00	12.17
12/16	64.10	25	9	2.55	0.88	9.62
12/15	43.54	15	7	3.47	0.88	7.57
12/14	27.40	—	—	(3.78)	0.76	5.42
Annual Growth	20.2%			—	7.1%	31.2%

BayCom Corp

Auditors: Moss Adams LLP

LOCATIONS

HQ: BayCom Corp
500 Ygnacio Valley Road, Walnut Creek, CA 94596
Phone: 925 476-1880
Web: www.unitedbusinessbank.com

HISTORICAL FINANCIALS

Company Type: Public

Income Statement   FYE: December 31

	ASSETS ($ mil.)	NET INCOME ($ mil.)	INCOME AS % OF ASSETS	EMPLOYEES
12/18	1,478.4	14.4	1.0%	214
12/17	1,245.7	5.2	0.4%	0
12/16	675.3	5.9	0.9%	0
12/15	623.3	7.4	1.2%	0
12/14	504.3	5.1	1.0%	0
Annual Growth	30.8%	29.3%	—	—

2018 Year-End Financials

Return on assets: 1.0%
Return on equity: 9.0%
Long-term debt ($ mil.): —
No. of shares (mil.): 10.8
Sales ($ mil): 63.9
Dividends
  Yield: —
  Payout: —
Market value ($ mil.): 251.0

	STOCK PRICE ($) FY Close	P/E High/Low		PER SHARE ($) Earnings	Dividends	Book Value
12/18	23.09	18	13	1.50	0.00	18.47
12/17	19.45	24	18	0.81	0.00	15.82
12/16	14.86	14	11	1.09	0.00	14.26
12/15	13.25	10	8	1.36	0.00	13.18
12/14	11.90	11	9	1.08	0.00	11.93
Annual Growth	18.0%	—	—	8.6%	—	11.5%

BBX Capital Corp (New)

EXECUTIVES

Managing Director Investor Relations, Leo Hinkley
Vice Chairman, John Abdo
Board Member, Jade Coldren
Auditors: Grant Thornton LLP

LOCATIONS

HQ: BBX Capital Corp (New)
401 East Las Olas Boulevard, Suite 800, Fort Lauderdale, FL 33301
Phone: 954 940-4900
Web: www.bbxcapital.com

COMPETITORS

BKF Capital Group   Huizenga Holdings
Bank of America   St. Joe
H.I.G. Capital   Sun Capital

BCB Bancorp Inc

HISTORICAL FINANCIALS

Company Type: Public

Income Statement   FYE: December 31

	REVENUE ($ mil.)	NET INCOME ($ mil.)	NET PROFIT MARGIN	EMPLOYEES
12/18	947.5	35.1	3.7%	7,307
12/17	815.7	82.2	10.1%	6,914
12/16	764.0	28.3	3.7%	6,141
12/15	740.2	122.4	16.5%	6,108
12/14	672.1	13.8	2.1%	5,364
Annual Growth	9.0%	26.2%	—	8.0%

2018 Year-End Financials

Debt ratio: 46.7%
Return on equity: 6.2%
Cash ($ mil.): 366.3
Current ratio: 23.45
Long-term debt ($ mil.): 796.2
No. of shares (mil.): 93.2
Dividends
  Yield: 0.7%
  Payout: 11.1%
Market value ($ mil.): 534.0

	STOCK PRICE ($) FY Close	P/E High/Low		PER SHARE ($) Earnings	Dividends	Book Value
12/18	5.73	27	14	0.36	0.04	5.90
12/17	7.97	11	6	0.79	0.03	5.75
12/16	4.88	15	8	0.32	0.02	4.64
12/15	3.39	3	2	1.40	0.00	4.46
12/14	3.20	26	17	0.16	0.00	3.03
Annual Growth	15.7%	—	—	22.5%	—	18.1%

EXECUTIVES

COO and Director; COO and CFO BCB Community Bank, Thomas M. Coughlin, age 56, $128,544 total compensation
Chairman, Mark D. Hogan, age 50
Director; Senior Lending Officer BCB Community Bank, James E. Collins, age 67, $131,222 total compensation
VP Commercial Lending BCB Community Bank, Amer Saleem, age 61, $94,500 total compensation
Independent Vice Chairman of the Board, Joseph Brogan, age 77
Chief Financial Officer of BCB Community Bank and BCB Bancorp, Kenneth Walter
COO and Director; COO and CFO BCB Community Bank, Thomas M. Coughlin, age 56
Director; Senior Lending Officer BCB Community Bank, James E. Collins, age 67
Independent Director, Robert Ballance, age 57
Independent Director, Judith Q. Bielan, age 51
Independent Director, Alexander Pasiechnik, age 54
Independent Director, Joseph Lyga, age 56
Independent Director, Gary Stetz
Independent Director, Robert Hughes
Independent Director, Spencer Robbins
Auditors: Wolf & Company, P.C.

LOCATIONS

HQ: BCB Bancorp Inc
104-110 Avenue C, Bayonne, NJ 07002
Phone: 201 823-0700
Web: www.bcb.bank

COMPETITORS

Bank of America
City National Bancshares
Hudson City Bancorp
Meridian Capital Group
New York Community Bancorp
PNC Financial
Provident Financial Services
Sterling Bank
Stewardship Financial

HISTORICAL FINANCIALS
Company Type: Public

Income Statement — FYE: December 31

	ASSETS ($ mil.)	NET INCOME ($ mil.)	NET INCOME AS % OF ASSETS	EMPLOYEES
12/18	2,674.7	16.7	0.6%	365
12/17	1,942.8	9.9	0.5%	314
12/16	1,708.2	8.0	0.5%	353
12/15	1,618.4	7.0	0.4%	331
12/14	1,301.9	7.5	0.6%	327
Annual Growth	19.7%	21.9%	—	2.8%

2018 Year-End Financials

Return on assets: 0.7%
Return on equity: 8.9%
Long-term debt ($ mil.): —
No. of shares (mil.): 15.8
Sales ($ mil.): 113.0
Dividends
Yield: 5.3%
Payout: 75.6%
Market value ($ mil.): 166.0

	STOCK PRICE ($) FY Close	P/E High/Low		PER SHARE ($) Earnings	Dividends	Book Value
12/18	10.47	16	10	1.01	0.56	12.60
12/17	14.50	22	16	0.75	0.56	11.73
12/16	13.00	21	16	0.63	0.56	11.63
12/15	10.40	18	14	0.69	0.56	11.91
12/14	11.73	17	14	0.81	0.54	12.18
Annual Growth	(2.8%)	—	—	5.7%	0.9%	0.8%

Beasley Broadcast Group Inc

Beasley Broadcast Group is a leading radio broadcaster with some 52 stations operating in about a dozen large and mid-sized markets in seven states primarily Florida Georgia and North Carolina. The company's stations (serving 7.7 million listeners per week) broadcast a variety of formats including news sports and talk radio as well as Top 40 Urban Oldies and other music formats. Most of its stations operate as part of a cluster within a specific market allowing the company to combine certain business functions between those stations and achieve greater operating efficiencies. Beasley Broadcast Group was founded by George Beasley in 1961.

Geographic Reach

The company's market include Atlanta and Augusta GA; Boston MA; Fayetteville and Greenville-New Bern-Jacksonville NC; Fort Myers-Naples Miami-Fort Lauderdale and West Palm Beach-Boca Raton FL; Las Vegas NV; Philadelphia PA; and Wilmington DE.

Financial Performance

Beasley reported revenue of about $105 million in 2013 up 5% from the prior year as it saw significant increases in advertising revenue in the Philadelphia and Las Vegas markets. Net income which has been rising every year since 2009 was also up 5% to $11.5 million.

Cash from operations has been following a similar trajectory as net income although it was down slightly in 2013 to $19.9 million on increases in cash paid for station operating expenses income tax payments and cash receipts from the sale of advertising airtime.

EXECUTIVES

National Sales Manager, Anthony Maisano
Vice President Of Strategic Planning, Kathryn Cook
National Sales Manager, Matthew Cowper
Auditors: Crowe LLP

LOCATIONS

HQ: Beasley Broadcast Group Inc
 3033 Riviera Drive, Suite 200, Naples, FL 34103
Phone: 239 263-5000   **Fax:** 239 263-8191
Web: www.bbgi.com

COMPETITORS

CBS Radio
Cox Radio
Cumulus Media
Entravision
Lincoln Financial Media
Radio One Inc.
SIRIUS XM
Univision Radio
iHeartCommunications

HISTORICAL FINANCIALS
Company Type: Public

Income Statement — FYE: December 31

	REVENUE ($ mil.)	NET INCOME ($ mil.)	NET PROFIT MARGIN	EMPLOYEES
12/18	257.4	6.4	2.5%	1,488
12/17	232.1	87.1	37.5%	1,484
12/16	136.6	47.4	34.7%	1,406
12/15	105.9	6.3	6.0%	809
12/14	58.7	40.0	68.1%	807
Annual Growth	44.7%	(36.6%)	—	16.5%

2018 Year-End Financials

Debt ratio: 35.7%
Return on equity: 2.3%
Cash ($ mil.): 13.4
Current ratio: 2.46
Long-term debt ($ mil.): 243.2
No. of shares (mil.): 27.5
Dividends
Yield: 5.3%
Payout: 7.4%
Market value ($ mil.): 103.0

	STOCK PRICE ($) FY Close	P/E High/Low		PER SHARE ($) Earnings	Dividends	Book Value
12/18	3.75	58	14	0.24	0.20	9.98
12/17	13.40	5	2	3.14	0.18	9.92
12/16	6.15	4	2	1.98	0.18	7.02
12/15	3.59	20	11	0.28	0.18	5.75
12/14	5.11	5	3	1.74	0.18	5.65
Annual Growth	(7.4%)	—	—	(39.1%)	2.7%	15.3%

BellRing Brands Inc

Auditors: PricewaterhouseCoopers LLP

LOCATIONS

HQ: BellRing Brands Inc
 2503 S. Hanley Road, St. Louis, MO 63144
Phone: 314 644-7600
Web: www.bellring.com

HISTORICAL FINANCIALS
Company Type: Public

Income Statement — FYE: September 30

	REVENUE ($ mil.)	NET INCOME ($ mil.)	NET PROFIT MARGIN	EMPLOYEES
09/19	854.4	123.1	14.4%	400
09/18	827.5	96.1	11.6%	380
09/17	713.2	35.2	4.9%	0
09/16	574.7	19.9	3.5%	0
Annual Growth	14.1%	83.6%	—	—

2019 Year-End Financials

Debt ratio: —
Return on equity: 26.2%
Cash ($ mil.): 5.5
Current ratio: 2.37
Long-term debt ($ mil.): —
No. of shares (mil.): 39.4
Dividends
Yield: —
Payout: —
Market value ($ mil.): —

	STOCK PRICE ($) FY Close	P/E High/Low		PER SHARE ($) Earnings	Dividends	Book Value
09/19	0.00	—	—	(0.00)	0.00	12.34
Annual Growth		—	—	—	—	—

Berkshire Hills Bancorp Inc

EXECUTIVES

President Chief Executive Officer, Michael P. Daly, age 54, $450,000 total compensation
Chairman, Lawrence A. (Larry) Bossidy, age 81
Executive Vice President of Human Resources, Linda A. Johnston
SVP Commercial Lending, Michael J. Ferry
EVP, Michael J. (Mike) Oleksak, age 57, $225,000 total compensation
Executive Vice President of Retail Banking, Sean A. Gray
Executive Vice President Chief Financial Officer Treasurer, Kevin P. Riley, age 56, $250,000 total compensation
Executive Vice President Chief Risk Officer, Richard M. Marotta
Chief Compliance Officer and Anti Money Laundering Officer, Brian Kindelan
Chief Investment Officer, Charles N. Leach
Executive Vice President of Commercial Banking and Wealth Management, Patrick Sullivan
Vice President Manager, Paul Lesukoski
Vice President Personal Lines, James Herrick
Director, Rodney C. Dimock, age 69
Director, Cornelius D. Mahoney, age 70

President CEO and Director Berkshire Hills Bancorp and Berkshire Bank, Michael P. Daly, age 54
Director, Catherine B. Miller, age 73
Director, Corydon L. Thurston, age 62
Director, D. Jeffrey Templeton, age 74
Director, David E. Phelps, age 63
Director, Robert M. Curley
Director, John B. Davis, age 66
Director, Wallace W. Altes, age 73
Director, Susan M. Hill, age 66
Independent Director, John Davies
Independent Director, Williar Dunlaevy
Auditors: Crowe LLP

LOCATIONS

HQ: Berkshire Hills Bancorp Inc
  60 State Street, Boston, MA 02109
Phone: 800 773-5601
Web: www.berkshirebank.com

COMPETITORS

Bank of America	RBS Citizens Financial Group
Hudson City Bancorp	Sovereign Bank
KeyCorp	TD Bank USA
Pathfinder Bancorp	

HISTORICAL FINANCIALS
Company Type: Public

Income Statement   FYE: December 31

	ASSETS ($ mil.)	NET INCOME ($ mil.)	INCOME AS % OF ASSETS	EMPLOYEES
12/18	12,212.2	105.7	0.9%	1,917
12/17	11,570.7	55.2	0.5%	1,992
12/16	9,162.5	58.6	0.6%	1,731
12/15	7,831.9	49.5	0.6%	1,221
12/14	6,502.0	33.7	0.5%	1,091
Annual Growth	17.1%	33.1%	—	15.1%

2018 Year-End Financials
Return on assets: 0.8%
Return on equity: 6.9%
Long-term debt ($ mil.): —
No. of shares (mil.): 45.4
Sales ($ mil): 581.0
Dividends
  Yield: 3.2%
  Payout: 38.4%
Market value ($ mil.): 1,225.0

	STOCK PRICE ($) FY Close	P/E High/Low	PER SHARE ($) Earnings	Dividends	Book Value
12/18	26.97	19 11	2.29	0.88	34.19
12/17	36.60	28 24	1.39	0.84	33.04
12/16	36.85	20 13	1.88	0.80	30.65
12/15	29.11	17 14	1.73	0.76	28.64
12/14	26.66	20 16	1.36	0.72	28.17
Annual Growth	0.3%	— —	13.9%	5.1%	5.0%

Berry Petroleum Corp

Auditors: KPMG LLP

LOCATIONS

HQ: Berry Petroleum Corp
  16000 Dallas Parkway, Suite 500, Dallas, TX 75248
Phone: 661 616-3900
Web: www.berrypetroleum.com

HISTORICAL FINANCIALS
Company Type: Public

Income Statement   FYE: December 31

	REVENUE ($ mil.)	NET INCOME ($ mil.)	NET PROFIT MARGIN	EMPLOYEES
12/18	586.5	147.1	25.1%	322
12/17*	319.6	(21.0)	—	278
02/17	92.7	(502.9)	—	0
12/16	410.9	(1,283.2)	—	0
Annual Growth	12.6%	—	—	—

*Fiscal year change

2018 Year-End Financials
Debt ratio: 23.1%
Return on equity: 15.7%
Cash ($ mil.): 68.6
Current ratio: 1.59
Long-term debt ($ mil.): 391.7
No. of shares (mil.): 81.2
Dividends
  Yield: 2.4%
  Payout: 24.7%
Market value ($ mil.): 711.0

	STOCK PRICE ($) FY Close	P/E High/Low	PER SHARE ($) Earnings	Dividends	Book Value
12/18	8.75	21 9	0.85	0.21	12.39
12/17*	8.90	— —	(0.98)	0.00	26.10
02/17	0.00	— —	(0.00)	0.00	(0.00)
Annual Growth	—	— —	—	—	—

*Fiscal year change

BG Staffing Inc

Auditors: Whitley Penn LLP

LOCATIONS

HQ: BG Staffing Inc
  5850 Granite Parkway, Suite 730, Plano, TX 75024
Phone: 972 692-2400
Web: www.bgstaffing.com

HISTORICAL FINANCIALS
Company Type: Public

Income Statement   FYE: December 30

	REVENUE ($ mil.)	NET INCOME ($ mil.)	NET PROFIT MARGIN	EMPLOYEES
12/18	286.8	17.5	6.1%	30,349
12/17	272.6	5.8	2.1%	29,349
12/16	253.8	6.8	2.7%	29,291
12/15	217.5	5.3	2.5%	26,840
12/14	172.8	(0.4)	—	24,170
Annual Growth	13.5%	—	—	5.9%

2018 Year-End Financials
Debt ratio: 20.0%
Return on equity: 33.5%
Cash ($ mil.): —
Current ratio: 2.14
Long-term debt ($ mil.): 15.8
No. of shares (mil.): 10.2
Dividends
  Yield: 0.0%
  Payout: 64.2%
Market value ($ mil.): 207.0

	STOCK PRICE ($) FY Close	P/E High/Low	PER SHARE ($) Earnings	Dividends	Book Value
12/18	20.23	16 8	1.79	1.15	6.42
12/17	15.94	28 19	0.65	1.00	4.47
12/16	15.55	25 14	0.82	1.00	4.67
12/15	13.72	19 14	0.73	0.90	3.51
12/14	11.99	— —	(0.08)	0.15	2.48
Annual Growth	14.0%	— —	—	66.4%	26.9%

Biglari Holdings Inc (New)

Beef and ice cream is an unbeatable combination for this restaurant company. Formerly The Steak n Shake Company Biglari Holdings is a multi-concept dining operator with two chains operating under the names Steak n Shake and Western Sizzlin. Its flagship concept encompasses about 680 company-owned and franchised family dining spots in more than 25 states mostly in the Midwest and Southeast. The diners open 24-hours a day are popular for their Steakburger sandwiches and milkshakes as well as breakfast items and other dishes. About 415 of the units are company-owned while the rest are franchised. Western Sizzlin meanwhile oversees about 60 franchised steak buffet restaurants in about 15 states. The company also has operations in insurance and media.

Operations
Biglari is a holding company with businesses in media property and casualty insurance and restaurants (its biggest business by far).

The company's restaurants are Steak n Shake Inc. and Western Sizzlin Corp.

Steak n Shake owns operates and franchises restaurants whose popular offerings are burgers chili mac and milkshakes. It operates some 415 company-operated restaurants and about 200 franchised units. Steak n Shake generates about 95% of the company's revenue.

Western Sizzlin restaurants offer steaks as well as other American fare. Other restaurant concepts are the Great American Steak & Buffet and Wood Grill Buffet which offer buffet-style dining. It operates about five company restaurants and franchises about 60 franchised units. It brings less than 5% of the revenue.

The operates First Guard Insurance Co. and its agency. First Guard is a direct underwriter of commercial trucking insurance selling physical damage and nontrucking liability insurance to truckers. Its media business products and services are marketed under Maxim.

Geographic Reach
Steak n Shake has built a popular following in the midsection of the US. Its restaurants are primarily in the Midwest and Southeast including Florida Illinois Indiana Ohio and Missouri (which together represent about 55% of locations). It also operates in France (more than half of international locations) as well as England Italy Portugal Qatar Saudi Arabia and Spain.

Western Sizzlin operates in about 10 US states with Arkansas Oklahoma and North Carolina its largest markets.

Financial Performance
Biglari's revenue slipped to about $840 million in 2017 from $850 million in 2016. Steak n Shake's same-store sales fell about 2% although customer traffic was down 4%.

Cost of revenue increased as food prices rose cutting net income in about half $50 million in 2017 compared to 2016.

The company's cash on hand dropped to $67 million in 2017 from $76 million in 2016.

Strategy
The family dining industry has been under pressure from the downturn in the economy forcing Steak n Shake to focus on cutting costs. Part of the effort has included closing a handful of underperforming locations. The company has also sold some of its corporate-run locations to franchise operators. During 2017 Steak n Shake opened 40 franchised units and closed 13. The company closed Six Western franchise units in 2017 and didn't open any.

Bilgari's attempts at diversification into insurance and media are in the early stages and have yet to produce significant revenue.

Mergers and Acquisitions
In 2017 Biglari acquired Pacific Specialty and its affiliated agency McGraw Insurance Inc. for a shade less than $300 million. The deal expanded Biglari's insurance business to motorcycle personal watercraft and residential property insurance.

EXECUTIVES

Chairman CEO and Director, Sardar Biglari, age 42, $900,000 total compensation
Vice Chairman, Philip L (Phil) Cooley, age 75
Auditors: DELOITTE & TOUCHE LLP

LOCATIONS

HQ: Biglari Holdings Inc (New)
 17802 IH 10 West, Suite 400, San Antonio, TX 78257
Phone: 210 344-3400   **Fax:** 317 633-4105
Web: www.biglariholdings.com

PRODUCTS/OPERATIONS

2017 Sales

	% of total
Restaurant operations	96
Media advertising and other	1
Insurance premiums and other	3
Total	**100**

2017 Sales

	% of total
Steak n Shake	94
Western	2
Maxim	1
First Guard	3
Total	**100**

COMPETITORS

American Blue Ribbon Holdings	Huddle House
Big Boy Restaurants	Max & Erma's Restaurants
Brinker	OSI Restaurant Partners
Carlson Restaurants	Perkins & Marie Callender's
Cheesecake Factory	
Cracker Barrel	Red Robin
Culver's	Ruby Tuesday
Darden	Skyline Chili
Denny's	
DineEquity	Sonic Corp.
Frisch's	Waffle House
Golden Corral	White Castle
Homestyle Dining	

HISTORICAL FINANCIALS
Company Type: Public

Income Statement   FYE: December 31

	REVENUE ($ mil.)	NET INCOME ($ mil.)	NET PROFIT MARGIN	EMPLOYEES
12/18	809.8	19.3	2.4%	18,684
12/17	839.8	50.0	6.0%	20,732
12/16	850.0	99.4	11.7%	21,519
12/15	861.4	(15.8)	—	22,958
12/14	224.4	91.0	40.6%	23,851
Annual Growth	37.8%	(32.1%)	—	(5.9%)

2018 Year-End Financials
Debt ratio: 23.8%   No. of shares (mil.): 2.2
Return on equity: 3.4%   Dividends
Cash ($ mil.): 48.5   Yield: —
Current ratio: 0.93   Payout: —
Long-term debt ($ mil.): 240.0   Market value ($ mil.): 258.0

	STOCK PRICE ($) FY Close	P/E High/Low		PER SHARE ($) Earnings	Dividends	Book Value
12/18	113.58	7	2	66.85	0.00	250.69
12/17	414.40	12	7	40.77	0.00	276.32
12/16	473.20	6	4	81.28	0.00	257.32
12/15	325.82	—	—	(10.18)	0.00	218.40
12/14	399.51	8	7	48.45	0.00	351.26
Annual Growth	(27.0%)	—	—	8.4%	—	(8.1%)

Bio-Techne Corp

Bio-Techne is a biotechnology research specialist. Through subsidiaries including Research and Diagnostic Systems (R&D Systems) Boston Biochem BiosPacific and Tocris the firm makes and distributes biological research supplies used by researchers around the globe to study cellular and immune system responses. Bio-Techne's products include cytokines (purified proteins that affect cell behavior) and diagnostic reagents (including antibodies and enzymes) as well as its Quantikine assay kits that determine the amount of cytokine in a given sample. R&D Systems also makes hematology controls and calibrators for blood analysis systems and sells them to equipment makers.

Operations
Bio-Techne operates through three reportable segments: Biotechnology Clinical Controls and Protein Platforms.

Bio-Techne's Biotechnology segment which makes products used by laboratories for both drug discovery research and clinical diagnostic purposes accounts for more than 70% of sales. Cytokines are a key product offering as commercial and institutional researchers are increasingly using the proteins as a swift and effective means of impacting the processes of cells and tissues. Subsidiary R&D Systems and its BiosPacific Boston Biochem and R&D Systems China as well as the R&D Systems Europe (UK) unit and its Tocris and R&D Systems (Germany) units are all included in the Biotechnology segment.

The newest segment established in 2014 is Protein Platforms (15% of sales). It develops and commercializes systems for protein analysis. The smallest Clinical Controls segment (13% of sales) develops and manufactures controls and calibrators for the global clinical market.

Altogether Bio-Techne sells more than 275000 products under such brands as Novus Biologicals Tocris Bioscience ProteinSimple R&D Systems BiosPacific CLINIQA and RNA Medical.

Geographic Reach
The US market accounts for more than half of Bio-Techne's annual revenues. Europe is the second-largest region accounting for about 30% of sales; the firm also conducts sales in Asia and other regions.

The company has operations in the US Europe and China.

Sales and Marketing
Bio-Techne sells its products through subsidiaries and third-party distributors worldwide. Its R&D Systems Europe and Tocris subsidiaries handle distribution efforts abroad and have a direct presence in France Germany and the UK. The company is growing its Asian distribution network which includes the R&D Systems China subsidiary. Thermo Fisher Scientific distributes Bio-Techne's R&D Systems Tocris and Boston Biochem products in the US and Canada.

Customers of the Biotechnology segment include researchers employed by pharma and biotech drug companies as well as universities and government agencies.

Bio-Techne has been increasing its advertising expenditures which totaled $4.1 million in fiscal 2015 (ended June). It spent $3.4 million in fiscal 2014 and $3.2 million in fiscal 2013.

Financial Performance
Bio-Techne's revenue which has been trending upward over the past five years increased 26% to $452.2 million in fiscal 2015 (ended June). Both the Biotechnology and Clinical Controls segment saw growth that year thanks to the recent acquisitions of Novus Biologicals and Bionostics as well as through continuing organic growth. (The newly formed Protein Platforms segment was no slouch either contributing 15% of the company's total earnings that year.)

After years of remaining relatively flat net income slipped a marginal 3% to $107.7 million in fiscal 2015. Despite the revenue growth higher operating expenses related to acquisitions as well as investments in resources and infrastructure ended up cutting into profits.

Cash flow from operations rose 2% to $139.4 million that year as cash inflows from accounts payable more than offset the decline in net income.

Strategy
Bio-Techne works to expand its product offerings through internal R&D efforts. The firm develops hundreds of new biological proteins antibodies and immunoassays each year. It also develops new hematology control technologies to keep up with changing technologies and markets as well as to provide efficient and high-quality offerings. In addition Bio-Techne grows its offerings through acquisitions partnerships and joint ventures.

The company has expanded the scope of its operations over the years by building up a collection of minority stakes in a number of drug developers and biotech companies working in complementary areas. It owns about 15% of drug developer ChemoCentryx which is researching chemokines a type of cytokine involved in immune response. Other investments have included blood filtration technology firm Hemerus Medical diagnostics developer Nephromics and biotechnology firm ACTGen.

In 2015 the company launched its first Simple Plex platform member Ella through its new Proteins Platform segment. It rebranded the CyPlex immunoassay platform acquired from CyVek under the name ProteinSimple.

Mergers and Acquisitions

In early 2018 Bio-Techne acquired Atlanta Biologicals and its Scientific Ventures affiliate. Atlanta Biologicals supplies cell culture cera media and reagents for life science research customers. The purchase helped Bio-Techne expand its cell culture and tissue regeneration capabilities.

Later that year the company bought Massachusetts-based Exosome Diagnostics which makes non-invasive liquid biopsy tests. The $250 million deal positions Bio-Techne for growth in that market as it expands its offerings for scientific researchers.

HISTORY

David Mundschenk founded biological products maker Research and Diagnostics Systems in 1976. In 1983 Mundschenk made a disastrous move buying heavily indebted French hematology instrument maker Hycel. R&D System's disgruntled board named Thomas Oland (at the time a consultant) CEO.

Enter TECHNE. Founded in 1981 by George Kline and Peter Peterson to pursue profitable acquisitions it went public in 1983 and in 1985 bought R&D Systems (which became an operating subsidiary of TECHNE) a sign of their confidence in Oland. TECHNE formed a biotechnology division in 1986 to produce and market human cytokines. In 1988 Kline resigned following a failed acquisition attempt by medical test kit maker Incstar.

In 1991 TECHNE bought Amgen's research reagent and diagnostic assay kit business and began selling Quantikine cytokine diagnostic kits. In 1993 it acquired what would become the company's R&D Europe unit.

In 1995 the company debuted 10 new Quantikine immunoassay kits. TECHNE restructured its European research operation in 1997 pulling underperforming molecular biology products from the market and refocusing on TECHNE's core cytokine-related products. The next year TECHNE bought Genzyme's research products business (antibodies proteins and research kits) for about $65 million.

As drug and biotechnology research became growth markets in the late 1990s and early 21st century TECHNE expanded through purchases. In 1999 it bought the reagent business and immunoassay patents of partner Cistron. The next year the firm increased its ownership in drug developer ChemoCentryx to almost 50% (reduced in 2001 to about 25% and then again in 2004 to 20%). TECHNE also acquired research and diagnostic market rights to all products developed by the firm. A similar deal was made in 2001 with functional genomics firm Discovery Genomics; that investment was not realized to TECHNE's satisfaction so it wrote off the investment in 2004.

It didn't wait long to fill the gap when it acquired the operations of Fortron Bio Science and Biospacific in 2005. The makers of antibodies and reagents had been partners since 1992 before they were integrated into TECHNE's R&D Systems division.

In 2007 the company set up a sales and distribution subsidiary in Shanghai to capitalize on the growing Chinese market. In 2007 TECHNE acquired minority stakes in two additional companies: diagnostics developer Nephromics and biotechnology firm ACTGen.

EXECUTIVES

SVP Clinical Controls, Marcel Veronneau, age 65, $210,000 total compensation
CFO and Vice President - Finance and Treasurer, Gregory J. (Greg) Melsen, age 68, $384,375 total compensation
President and CEO, Charles R. (Chuck) Kummeth, age 59
CIO, Fernando Bazan
Vice President Human Resources, Struan Robertson
Vice Chairman, Roger C. Lucas, age 76
Chairman, Robert V. Baumgartner, age 63
Auditors: KPMG LLP

LOCATIONS

HQ: Bio-Techne Corp
614 McKinley Place N.E., Minneapolis, MN 55413
Phone: 612 379-8854
Web: www.bio-techne.com

PRODUCTS/OPERATIONS

2015 Sales by Segment

	$ mil.	% of total
Biotechnology	325.9	72
Protein Platforms	66.2	15
Clinical Controls	60.4	13
Adjustments	(0.3)	-
Total	**452.2**	**100**

Selected Products and Services

R&D Systems
 Activity assays and reagents
 Antibodies
 Biomarker testing service
 ELISAs
 ELISpot kits & FluoroSpot kits
 Flow cytometry and cell selection/detection
 General laboratory reagents
 Multiplex assays/arrays
 Proteins
 Stem cell and cell culture products
Tocris
 Caged compounds
 Controlled substances
 Fluorescent probes
 Ligand sets
 Peptides
 Screening libraries
 Small molecules
 Toxins
Boston Biochem
 Affinity matrices/proteins
 Antibodies
 Buffers solutions and standards
 Fractions
 Inhibitors
 Kits
 Proteasome
 Substrate Proteins
 Ubiquitin

COMPETITORS

ABCAM PLC
Abbott Labs
BD Biosciences
Beckman Coulter
Bio-Rad Labs
Enzo Biochem
GE Healthcare Medical Diagnostics
Life Technologies Corporation
Marker Gene Technologies
Merck KGaA
Ortho-Clinical Diagnostics
Santa Cruz Biotechnology
Sigma-Aldrich
Streck
Thermo Fisher Scientific

HISTORICAL FINANCIALS

Company Type: Public

Income Statement — FYE: June 30

	REVENUE ($ mil.)	NET INCOME ($ mil.)	NET PROFIT MARGIN	EMPLOYEES
06/19	714.0	96.0	13.5%	2,250
06/18	642.9	126.1	19.6%	2,000
06/17	563.0	76.0	13.5%	1,800
06/16	499.0	104.4	20.9%	1,560
06/15	452.2	107.7	23.8%	1,356
Annual Growth	12.1%	(2.8%)	—	13.5%

2019 Year-End Financials

Debt ratio: 26.8%
Return on equity: 8.5%
Cash ($ mil.): 100.8
Current ratio: 4.05
Long-term debt ($ mil.): 492.6
No. of shares (mil.): 37.9
Dividends
 Yield: 0.0%
 Payout: 51.8%
Market value ($ mil.): 7,909.0

	STOCK PRICE ($) FY Close	P/E High/Low		PER SHARE ($) Earnings	Dividends	Book Value
06/19	208.49	85	52	2.47	1.28	30.73
06/18	147.95	49	34	3.31	1.28	28.69
06/17	117.50	58	48	2.03	1.28	25.42
06/16	112.77	41	29	2.80	1.28	23.60
06/15	98.47	35	30	2.89	1.27	22.80
Annual Growth	20.6%	—	—	(3.8%)	0.2%	7.7%

Biospecifics Technologies Corp.

BioSpecifics Technologies specifically uses collagenase (an enzyme that breaks the bonds of collagen) to treat a variety of skin-thickening diseases and conditions. Its current product named Xiaflex (Xiapex in Europe) is an injectable collagenase that treats Dupuytren's disease and Peyronie's disease. It partners with Endo International to market Xiaflex in the US and with Swedish Orphan Biovitrum to market Xiapex in Europe and Eurasia. BioSpecifics is also testing collagenase treatments for human and canine lipoma (benign fatty tumor) frozen shoulder cellulite plantar fibromatosis and lateral hip fat.

Operations

Most of BioSpecific's revenues come from royalties and other payments it receives related to the development manufacturing and commercialization of its drug candidate.

Sales and Marketing

BioSpecifics partners with Endo International to sell Xiaflex in the US and Canada. Endo partners with Swedish Orphan Biovitrum to market Xiapex in the European Union; it partners with Asahi Kasei Pharma to sell Xiaflex in Japan and with Actelion Pharmaceuticals to commercialize the drug in Australia and New Zealand.

Financial Performance

BioSpecifics' revenue has been rising over the past few years. That revenue comes primarily from the company's licensing agreement with Endo International which markets Xiaflex in various markets around the world. Its net income has generally been on the rise as well.

In 2017 revenue increased 4% to $17.7 million. Royalties increased that year thanks to higher product sales and a slight price increase but that was partially offset by the absence of licensing fees and milestone payments.

Net income slipped 1% to $11.3 million in 2017. Primary factors of that decline were an increase in general and administrative expenses and a $7 million income tax provision made.

The company ended 2017 with $7.3 million in net cash $2.6 million more than it had at the end of 2016. Operating activities provided the company with $13.2 million in cash while investing activities used $10.4 million and financing activities used $0.2 million.

Strategy

BioSpecifics will continue to develop Xiaflex for Peyronie's disease frozen shoulder cellulite and lipomas while looking for additional indications where the drug would be useful. It sees potential for double-digit growth in Xiaflex sales as the vast majority of patients with Peyronie's disease and Dupuytren's contracture are currently not being treated. To reach those potential customers it has awareness educational and advertising campaigns in place.

BioSpecifics also sees promise in its drug to treat uterine fibroids which could help cut the number of hysterectomies performed.

The company relies heavily on the activities of Endo International which holds the right to develop manufacture market and sell its products worldwide. If Endo is not successful in these activities or if it decides to terminate the companies' agreement that would have a dramatic impact on BioSpecifics' revenue. Additionally Endo has faced some struggles lately and it cut its workforce by 18% in 2017.

EXECUTIVES

President, Thomas L. Wegman, age 64, $350,000 total compensation
Auditors: EisnerAmper LLP

LOCATIONS

HQ: Biospecifics Technologies Corp.
35 Wilbur Street, Lynbrook, NY 11563
Phone: 516 593-7000
Web: www.biospecifics.com

COMPETITORS

Cynosure
Genzyme
Pfizer

HISTORICAL FINANCIALS
Company Type: Public

Income Statement — FYE: December 31

	REVENUE ($ mil.)	NET INCOME ($ mil.)	NET PROFIT MARGIN	EMPLOYEES
12/18	32.9	20.0	60.8%	5
12/17	27.4	11.3	41.3%	5
12/16	26.2	11.3	43.3%	5
12/15	22.7	9.6	42.3%	5
12/14	14.0	4.6	33.0%	5
Annual Growth	23.7%	44.1%	—	0.0%

2018 Year-End Financials

Debt ratio: —
Return on equity: 24.2%
Cash ($ mil.): 13.1
Current ratio: 39.24
Long-term debt ($ mil.): —
No. of shares (mil.): 7.2
Dividends
 Yield: —
 Payout: —
Market value ($ mil.): 441.0

	STOCK PRICE ($) FY Close	P/E High/Low	PER SHARE ($) Earnings	Dividends	Book Value
12/18	60.60	23 14	2.73	0.00	13.41
12/17	43.33	37 27	1.55	0.00	9.39
12/16	55.70	35 19	1.56	0.00	7.86
12/15	42.97	49 26	1.32	0.00	6.48
12/14	38.62	57 29	0.66	0.00	4.50
Annual Growth	11.9%	— —	42.6%	—	31.4%

BioTelemetry Inc

BioTelemetry knows how to keep a beat. The company provides real-time outpatient cardiac rhythm monitoring and telemetry services for patients throughout the US. Its core product Mobile Cardiac Outpatient Telemetry (MCOT) helps physicians diagnose and monitor heart arrhythmia in patients by providing continuous heartbeat monitoring and transmitting a complete picture of the heart's functions to physicians. The system which uses real-time two-way wireless communication accommodates patient mobility and remote physician adjustment. BioTelemetry also manufactures and sells traditional cardiac event and Holter monitors that record patient heart rhythm data but cannot transmit the data in real time.

Operations

BioTelemetry's CardioNet MCOT services rely on the system's FDA-approved monitoring equipment wireless transmission network proprietary software and a 24-hour monitoring center. The MCOT system automatically detects rhythm irregularities and transmits the corresponding ECG (electrocardiogram) data to the monitoring center.

The company operates through three segments: patient services which provides diagnosis and monitoring services to physicians; product which manufactures and services its heart monitoring devices; and research services which provides consulting heart monitoring and data management services to companies conducting medical trials.

Sales and Marketing

BioTelemetry's CardioNet System is marketed directly to doctors and patients throughout the US and has been used with more than 500000 patients. While Medicare reimbursements account for a more than a third of the company's revenues it also has contracts with more than 400 commercial payers. Part of BioTelemetry's strategy is to increase the number of (more lucrative) commercial payer contracts it has as compared to its government contracts.

Strategy

BioTelemetry has plans to use its technology to create instant telemetry beds (which allow patients to be continually monitored by technology) in rural hospitals step-down units or skilled nursing facilities to help cope with acute nursing shortages by reducing the number of nurses needed to oversee ECG monitoring and reduce capital equipment costs. The company also leverages acquisitions to expand its products services and geographic range.

Mergers and Acquisitions

Acquisitions have helped BioTelemetry with its expansion of products services and geographic range. The company intends to move beyond arrhythmia monitoring into new market areas such as disease management for congestive heart failure diabetes and other diseases that require outpatient or ambulatory monitoring and management.

In 2019 BioTelemetry acquired Geneva healthcare which provides remote monitoring of implantable cardiac devices.

In 2017 the company bought Swiss digital health systems provider LifeWatch whose offerings allow physicians to improve care by determining the most appropriate course of treatment. LifeWatch's subsidiaries include the US-based LifeWatch Services (cardiac monitoring services) Israel-based LifeWatch Technologies (digital health products) and Turkey-based LifeWatch Saglik Hizmetlerine (mobile cardiac telemetry services).

EXECUTIVES

President and CEO, Joseph H. (Joe) Capper, age 55
SVP Sales and Marketing, Andy Broadway
CFO, Heather C. Getz, age 44
Vice President Of Sales U.S, Ken Nelson
Vp Biotelemetry, Liz Watts
Vice President Quality And Regulatory Affairs, Kent Sayler
Vice President Strategic Accounts, Sarah Somrak
Senior Vice President Technical Operations, Dan Wisniewski
Vp Human Resources, Tim Raher
Auditors: Ernst & Young LLP

LOCATIONS

HQ: BioTelemetry Inc
1000 Cedar Hollow Road #102, Malvern, PA 19355
Phone: 610 729-7000

PRODUCTS/OPERATIONS

Selected Acquisitions
ECG Scanning & Medical Services (2012 $6 million patient monitoring services)
Biotel (2010 $11 million wireless monitoring technology & data management services)
PDSHeart (2007 $52 million monitoring services)

COMPETITORS

Criticare
Diagnostic Health
GE Healthcare
LifeWatch
Philips Healthcare
Philips Remote Cardiac Services
Spacelabs Healthcare
United Therapeutics
Welch Allyn
eResearchTechnology

HISTORICAL FINANCIALS
Company Type: Public

Income Statement
FYE: December 31

	REVENUE ($ mil.)	NET INCOME ($ mil.)	NET PROFIT MARGIN	EMPLOYEES
12/18	399.4	42.8	10.7%	1,500
12/17	286.7	(15.9)	—	1,600
12/16	208.3	53.4	25.6%	1,087
12/15	178.5	7.4	4.2%	938
12/14	166.5	(9.7)	—	922
Annual Growth	24.4%	—	—	12.9%

2018 Year-End Financials
Debt ratio: 34.1%
Return on equity: 15.2%
Cash ($ mil.): 80.8
Current ratio: 2.96
Long-term debt ($ mil.): 193.5
No. of shares (mil.): 33.4
Dividends
Yield: —
Payout: —
Market value ($ mil.): 1,995.0

	STOCK PRICE ($) FY Close	P/E High	P/E Low	PER SHARE ($) Earnings	Dividends	Book Value
12/18	59.72	56	23	1.20	0.00	9.29
12/17	29.90	—	—	(0.53)	0.00	7.72
12/16	22.35	12	5	1.75	0.00	4.92
12/15	11.68	62	30	0.26	0.00	2.78
12/14	10.03	—	—	(0.37)	0.00	2.39
Annual Growth	56.2%	—	—	—	—	40.5%

Blackbaud, Inc.

Blackbaud wants to make it easy to give. The company provides financial fundraising and administrative software for not-for-profit organizations and educational institutions. Software offerings include The Raiser's Edge for fundraising management Blackbaud Enterprise CRM for customer relationship management The Financial Edge for accounting and The Education Edge for managing school admissions registration and billing. Blackbaud has about 35000 customers in more than 60 countries including colleges environmental groups health and human services providers churches and animal welfare groups. The company generates most of its sales in the US.

Operations
Blackbaud generates 52% of its revenue from subscriptions to its cloud-based services to which the company has transitioned over the past few years. Maintenance and services revenue account for 24% and 21% respectively. Licensing and fee revenue for its on-premise software packages generated just 3% of revenue in 2015 and that was down 23% from 2014.

Geographic Reach
The US is its largest market accounting for 89% of sales. Canada and Europe each account for 4% of sales while the Australia generates 3%. Blackbaud has roughly 10 offices spanning the US and a handful of international offices in Australia Canada the Netherlands New Zealand and the UK.

Sales and Marketing
Blackbaud sells into three markets. The General Markets Business is the biggest generating 49% of revenue. It focuses on marketing sales delivery and support to emerging and mid-sized prospects and customers in North America.

The Enterprise Customer Business unit sells to and works wit large and strategic prospects and customers in North America. It accounts for 44% of sales.

The self-explanatory International Business unit delivered 7% of sales.

Financial Performance
Blackbaud has experienced strong revenue growth over the past decade with 2015 sales up 13% to reach $638 million. Subscriptions for its cloud-based software offerings rose 26%. The company also had double digit growth in its general markets and enterprise businesses. International sales fell 11%.

Increased spending on sales and marketing reduced profit 9% to $25.6 million in 2015 from 2014. It was the second straight year of declining profit as Blackbaud invests in sales and marketing to drive customers to its cloud products and increase market share.

Cash flow from operations rose to $114 million in 2015 from $102 million in 2014.

Strategy
Blackbaud is looking to expand its product offerings for the Internet. Online donations account for a growing percentage of charitable donations and marketing membership newsletters event management and volunteer recruitment can often be done over the Internet at a lower cost and a higher success rate. Its Sphere eMarketing Suite which facilitates online giving can be integrated into its most popular product The Raiser's Edge.

The latest product Blackbaud SKY is part of the company's cloud strategy. It combines infrastructure processes and integrated services (payments analytics email and online donations) to help customers achieve their goals.

The company's strategy also includes expanding geographically. Over the years it has established a Hong Kong office and a Mexico City office which joined other international offices in Canada the UK and Australia.

Mergers and Acquisitions
In 2017 Blackbaud acquired YourCause a developer of software for corporate philanthropy corporate social responsibility and employee engagement for about $157 million. The deal expands Blackbaud's offerings to software that helps companies address social causes. YourCause's customers include Fortune 500 companies and small businesses.

Blackbaud acquired JustGiving a crowd-source funding provider for charities for £95 million in 2017. The acquisition added a peer-to-peer fundraising source to Blackbaud's offerings. Peer-to-peer fundraising is a growing force in social and mobile arenas. Blackbaud rolled out a personal crowdfunding capability in the US. UK-based JustGiving also expanded Blackbaud's reach in that market.

EXECUTIVES

Senior Vice President New Business Development, Charlie Cumbaa
EVP and President General Markets, Kevin W. Mooney, age 61, $433,914 total compensation
EVP Human Resources, John J. Mistretta, age 64, $310,277 total compensation
CTO, Mary Beth Westmoreland
SVP and Chief Scientist, Charles L. (Chuck) Longfield, age 62, $226,667 total compensation
EVP Finance and Administration and CFO, Anthony W. (Tony) Boor, age 56, $447,615 total compensation
President and CEO, Michael P. (Mike) Gianoni, age 58, $679,526 total compensation
President and General Manager everydayhero, Jerry Needel
EVP and President Enterprise Business, Brian E. Boruff, age 59, $419,241 total compensation
EVP and Chief Products Officer, Kevin McDearis
President Higher Education Solutions Group, Tim Hill
President Healthcare Solutions Group, Russ Cobb
CIO, Todd Lant
SVP and President International Markets Group, Jerome Moisan
VICE PRESIDENT OF CUSTOMER SUCCESS, Kevin Knight
Vice President of Customer Support, Marty North
Vice President Of Strategic Accounts, Chris Krackeler
Senior Vp Technical Consultant IV, Kevin Yanzetich
Vice President of Product Development, Mary Westmoreland
Vp Of Sales, Patrick Hodges
Vice President, Ben Brownlee
Senior Vice President Products and Ser, Charles T Cumbaa
Vice President Ndash Professional Services, Autumn Vaupel
Senior Vp Vp Staff Technical Writer, Nikki Tremann
Vice President Engineering, David Respass
Senior Vp Technical Consultant, Donald Clark
Vice President of Enterprise Sales, Robert Flaherty
Vice President Distinguished Engineer, Michael Andrews
Vice President Corporate Communications and Branding, Amy Lucia
Senior Vice President Smart Tuition, Ben Heroux
Vp Total Rewards, Kyle Crager
National Sales Manager, Greg Taylor
Vice President Product Operations, Mike Rabanal
Chairman, Andrew M. Leitch, age 75
Board Member, Joyce Nelson
Board Member, Seth Kight
Board Member, Peter Kight
Board Member, Wilson Nash
Auditors: PricewaterhouseCoopers LLP

LOCATIONS
HQ: Blackbaud, Inc.
65 Fairchild Street, Charleston, SC 29492
Phone: 843 216-6200 **Fax:** 843 216-6100
Web: www.blackbaud.com

PRODUCTS/OPERATIONS

2015 Sales
	$ mil.	% of total
General Markets Business Unit (GMBU)	313.9	49
Enterprise Customer Business Unit (ECBU)	279.9	44
International Business Unit (IBU)	42.0	7
Other	2.1	-
Total	637.9	100

2015 Sales
	$ mil.	% of total
Subscriptions	331.8	52
Maintenance	153.8	24
Services	132.9	21
Licenses	19.4	3
Total	637.9	100

Selected Products
Accounting software
  Blackbaud Forms (wealth identification)
  The Financial Edge (not-for-profit accounting)
Analytical services
  Prospect Management (prospect management and research)
  Wealth & Affluence Indicators (wealth identification and information)
Business intelligence software
  Altru (general admissions management)
  The Patron Edge (ticketing management for admissions)
Customer relationship management
  Blackbaud Enterprise CRM
  eTapestry
Education administration software
  The Education Edge (admissions registrar business office and development office software)
  Small Colleges (suite for colleges under 300 students)
  Student Billing
  Total Campus Solution (suite for colleges under 2000 students)
Fundraising management software
  The Raiser's Edge (fundraising management system)

COMPETITORS

Acorn Systems	Microsoft
Advanced Solutions	Oracle
Auctionpay	Sage Software
Campus Management Corp	SunGard
Intuit	salesforce.com
MicroEdge	

HISTORICAL FINANCIALS
Company Type: Public

Income Statement — FYE: December 31

	REVENUE ($ mil.)	NET INCOME ($ mil.)	NET PROFIT MARGIN	EMPLOYEES
12/18	848.6	44.8	5.3%	3,353
12/17	788.3	65.9	8.4%	3,182
12/16	730.8	41.5	5.7%	3,156
12/15	637.9	25.6	4.0%	3,095
12/14	564.4	28.2	5.0%	3,033
Annual Growth	10.7%	12.2%	—	2.5%

2018 Year-End Financials

Debt ratio: 23.9%
Return on equity: 13.1%
Cash ($ mil.): 30.8
Current ratio: 0.74
Long-term debt ($ mil.): 379.6
No. of shares (mil.): 48.5
Dividends
  Yield: 0.7%
  Payout: 34.7%
Market value ($ mil.): 3,055.0

	STOCK PRICE ($) FY Close	P/E High/Low	PER SHARE ($) Earnings	Dividends	Book Value
12/18	62.90	125 62	0.93	0.48	7.70
12/17	94.49	74 44	1.38	0.48	6.38
12/16	64.00	79 57	0.88	0.48	5.21
12/15	65.86	121 75	0.55	0.48	4.48
12/14	43.26	72 47	0.62	0.48	4.01
Annual Growth	9.8%	— —	10.7%	(0.0%)	17.7%

Blackhawk Bancorp Inc

EXECUTIVES

Vice President of Information Technology, Phyllis Oldenburg
Assistant Vice President Relationship Manager Associate, Shelly Kuhl
Vice President, Sherrin Mulae
Senior Vice President Consumer Banking, Dale Reeves
Senior Vice President, Todd L Larson
Vice President Retail Sales Manager, Mathew Reynolds
Senior Vice President Business Banking, Cliff Kieser
Executive Vice President Chief Financial, James Todd
Avp Marketing Manager, Jan Barth
Vp Cash Management, Kimberly Lantta
Vice President Business Banking, Jack Walden
Auditors: Plante & Moran, PLLC

LOCATIONS

HQ: Blackhawk Bancorp Inc
400 Broad Street, Beloit, WI 53511
Phone: 608 364-8911   **Fax:** 608 363-6186
Web: www.blackhawkbank.com

COMPETITORS

Associated Banc-Corp	Harris
Bank of America	JPMorgan Chase

HISTORICAL FINANCIALS
Company Type: Public

Income Statement — FYE: December 31

	ASSETS ($ mil.)	NET INCOME ($ mil.)	INCOME AS % OF ASSETS	EMPLOYEES
12/18	817.2	8.1	1.0%	0
12/17	720.6	6.2	0.9%	0
12/16	665.7	5.9	0.9%	0
12/15	602.5	3.9	0.7%	165
12/14	581.4	2.2	0.4%	0
Annual Growth	8.9%	37.9%	—	—

2018 Year-End Financials

Return on assets: 1.0%
Return on equity: 10.0%
Long-term debt ($ mil.): —
No. of shares (mil.): 3.2
Sales ($ mil): 43.6
Dividends
  Yield: 0.0%
  Payout: 15.3%
Market value ($ mil.): 87.0

	STOCK PRICE ($) FY Close	P/E High/Low	PER SHARE ($) Earnings	Dividends	Book Value
12/18	26.60	12 11	2.47	0.38	25.76
12/17	27.05	13 11	2.01	0.28	24.02
12/16	23.00	9 7	2.59	0.16	21.68
12/15	17.85	10 8	1.73	0.12	20.17
12/14	15.25	19 12	0.92	0.06	18.84
Annual Growth	14.9%	— —	28.0%	58.6%	8.1%

Blackstone Mortgage Trust Inc

EXECUTIVES

Executive Vice President Capital Markets and Treasurer, Douglas Armer
Managing Director and Head of Asset Management, Thomas Ruffing
Auditors: DELOITTE & TOUCHE LLP

LOCATIONS

HQ: Blackstone Mortgage Trust Inc
345 Park Avenue, 42nd Floor, New York, NY 10154
Phone: 212 655-0220

COMPETITORS

Annaly Capital Management	MFA Financial
Arbor Realty Trust	RAIT Financial Trust
Drive Shack	Redwood Trust
Institutional Financial Markets	iStar Financial Inc

HISTORICAL FINANCIALS
Company Type: Public

Income Statement — FYE: December 31

	REVENUE ($ mil.)	NET INCOME ($ mil.)	NET PROFIT MARGIN	EMPLOYEES
12/18	756.1	285.0	37.7%	0
12/17	537.9	217.6	40.5%	0
12/16	497.9	238.3	47.9%	0
12/15	410.6	196.8	47.9%	0
12/14	184.7	90.0	48.7%	0
Annual Growth	42.2%	33.4%	—	—

2018 Year-End Financials

Debt ratio: 75.1%
Return on equity: 9.0%
Cash ($ mil.): 105.6
Current ratio: 1.27
Long-term debt ($ mil.): 10,870.1
No. of shares (mil.): 123.4
Dividends
  Yield: 7.7%
  Payout: 99.2%
Market value ($ mil.): 3,933.0

	STOCK PRICE ($) FY Close	P/E High/Low	PER SHARE ($) Earnings	Dividends	Book Value
12/18	31.86	14 12	2.50	2.48	27.25
12/17	32.18	14 13	2.27	2.48	26.98
12/16	30.07	12 9	2.53	2.48	26.38
12/15	26.76	13 11	2.41	2.28	26.60
12/14	29.14	16 14	1.86	1.98	25.15
Annual Growth	2.3%	— —	7.7%	5.8%	2.0%

BOK Financial Corp

With seven principal banking divisions in eight midwestern and southwestern states multi-bank holding company BOK offers a range of financial services to consumers and regional businesses. In addition to traditional deposit lending and trust services its banks provide investment management wealth advisory and mineral and real estate management services through a network of branches in Arizona Arkansas Colorado Kansas Missouri New Mexico Oklahoma and Texas. Brokerage subsidiary BOSC underwrites public private and municipal securities. BOK also owns electronic funds network TransFund and institutional asset manager Cavanal Hill.

Operations

BOK Financial operates through three primary segments: Commercial Banking Consumer Banking and Wealth Management. The Commercial Banking segment brings in more than 75% of BOK's total revenue with offerings including lending treasury and cash management and risk management products for small midsized and large companies. The Consumer Banking segment which brings in about 15% of total revenue is the retail arm providing lending and deposit services and all mortgage activities. The Wealth Management segment provides private bank and investment advisory services across all markets and it has more than $16 billion in assets under management. The segment is also engaged in trading and it underwrites state and municipal securities.

Geographic Reach

Most of Tulsa-based BOK Financial's locations are located in and around Tulsa; Oklahoma City; Dallas/Fort Worth; Houston; Albuquerque New Mexico; Denver; Phoenix; and Kansas City in Kansas and Missouri. The company's primary operations facilities lare in Tulsa; Oklahoma City; Dallas; and Albuquerque New Mexico.

Sales and Marketing

In 2017 BOK Financials spent $28.9 million on promotional costs versus $26.6 million in 2016 and $27.9 million in 2015.

Financial Performance

Thanks largely to the improving US economy BOK's revenues have been trending upward for the past five years. Net income has been somewhat more volatile but reached a peak in 2017.

Revenue increased 9% to $1.5 billion in 2017 as interest income increased 17%. Loan trading securities and interest-bearing cash and cash equivalents revenues saw significant growth that year. Asset management income also rose gaining some 20%. These increases were partially offset by a decline in mortgage banking revenue.

With the higher revenue plus certain lower operating expenses (including mortgage banking costs and insurance expenses) net income rose 44% to $331.1 million in 2017.

The company ended 2017 with $2.3 billion in net cash some $220 million less than it had at the end of 2016. Operating activities provided $214.9 million and investing activities provided $739.6 million. Financing activities used $1.2 billion.

Strategy

BOK emphasizes local decision-making at its flagship subsidiary Bank of Oklahoma and its operating divisions Bank of Albuquerque Bank of Arizona Bank of Arkansas Bank of Texas Colorado State Bank and Trust and Mobank. Commercial loans primarily to the energy services health care and wholesale and retail industries make up the majority of the company's loan portfolio. Commercial real estate residential mortgage car and consumer loans round out its lending activities.

The company is also focused on diversifying its revenue stream by growing its mortgage banking brokerage and wealth management operations.

With banking operations in several major oil- and natural gas-producing states more than 15% of the group's lending portfolio is in the energy sector. Because the energy industry has been challenged with low commodity prices BOK's energy-related charge-offs have grown significantly. In Q2 of 2018 net charge-offs reached $10.5 million — more than half of which was attributed to a single energy customer.

Mergers and Acquisitions

In October 2018 BOK Financial acquired financial services company CoBiz Financial which provides commercial banking and other financial services to businesses in Arizona and Colorado through its Colorado Business Bank and Bank of Arizona subsidiaries. The deal valued at $1 billion more than doubled BOK Financial's deposit market share in the two states.

EXECUTIVES

President and CEO, Steven G. (Steve) Bradshaw, age 59, $484,275 total compensation
EVP and CFO, Steven E. Nell, age 57, $439,354 total compensation
EVP Corporate Banking, Stacy C. Kymes, age 48
Chief Credit Officer, Marc C. Maun, age 61
Chairman and CEO Bank of Texas, Norman P. Bagwell, age 56, $403,054 total compensation
EVP and Chief Human Resources Officer, Stephen D. Grossi
EVP and CIO, Donald T. Parker
EVP Consumer Banking, Patrick E. Piper
EVP Wealth Management and CEO BOSC. Inc., Scott B. Grauer
CEO Oklahoma City Market, John Higginbotham
Assistant Vice President Process Consultant, Diana Pruitt
Assistant Vice President Finance And Administration, Lanny L Randolph
Senior Vice President Perf. Reporting and Analysis, Kent Rugeley
Vice President Credit Administration, Becky Keesling
Vice President Perf. Reporting and Analysis, Tamara Cobb
Senior Vice President And Chief Marketing Officer, Alan Nykiel
Senior Vice President, Guy Evangelista
Vice President Help Desk, Blu Bean
Vice President Production, Kathy Davis
Senior Vice President, Michael Bickel
Senior Vice President Information Technology, Jane Romine
Vice President, Alice Worthington
Vice President Middle Office Manager, John Williamson
Senior Vice President Credit Administration, Carol Cable
Senior Vice President, Lee Allen
Vice President Business Performance Measurement, Richard Hubbard
Vice President, Debi Briscoe
Senior Vice President Director Of Contact Center Operations, John Holt
Vice President, Lisa Albers
Vice President Marketing, Margot McKoy
Vice President, Candice Williams
Senior Vice President, Jill Hall
Senior Vice President, Jeff Sanders
Vice President, Mary Campbell
Vice President and TRUST Officer, Claudia Cepeda
Vice President and Portfolio Manager, Tim Hopkins
Senior Vice President Director of Business Banking, John Anderson
Vice President Risk Management, Don Mallory
Vice President Accounting Control Reporting, Ed Disney
Assistant Vice President Information Technology Project Manager, Lisa Porter Lisa Porter
Vice President Trust Officer III, Mary Thomason
Chairman, George B. Kaiser, age 76
Board Member, Kimberley Henry
Auditors: Ernst & Young LLP

LOCATIONS

HQ: BOK Financial Corp
Bank of Oklahoma Tower, Boston Avenue at Second Street, Tulsa, OK 74192
Phone: 918 588-6000
Web: www.bokf.com

PRODUCTS/OPERATIONS

2017 Sales

	% of total
Commercial Banking	76
Consumer Banking	7
Wealth Management	17
Total	**100**

Selected Banking Subsidiaries

Bank of Albuquerque National Association
Bank of Arizona National Association
Bank of Arkansas National Association
Bank of Oklahoma National Association
Bank of Texas National Association
Colorado State Bank & Trust
Mobank

COMPETITORS

BBVA Compass Bancshares	JPMorgan Chase
Bank of America	Regions Financial
Bank of the West	UMB Financial
Comerica	Wells Fargo
Commerce Bancshares	Zions Bancorporation
First National of Nebraska	

HISTORICAL FINANCIALS

Company Type: Public

Income Statement   FYE: December 31

	ASSETS ($ mil.)	NET INCOME ($ mil.)	INCOME AS % OF ASSETS	EMPLOYEES
12/18	38,020.5	445.6	1.2%	5,313
12/17	32,272.1	334.6	1.0%	4,930
12/16	32,772.2	232.6	0.7%	4,884
12/15	31,476.1	288.5	0.9%	4,789
12/14	29,089.7	292.4	1.0%	4,743
Annual Growth	6.9%	11.1%	—	2.9%

2018 Year-End Financials

Return on assets: 1.2%
Return on equity: 11.2%
Long-term debt ($ mil.): —
No. of shares (mil.): 72.1
Sales ($ mil): 1,845.2
Dividends
Yield: 2.5%
Payout: 30.3%
Market value ($ mil.): 5,289.0

	STOCK PRICE ($) FY Close	P/E High/Low	PER SHARE ($) Earnings	Dividends	Book Value
12/18	73.33	16 11	6.63	1.90	61.45
12/17	92.32	18 15	5.11	1.77	53.45
12/16	83.04	24 13	3.53	1.73	50.12
12/15	59.79	17 13	4.21	1.69	49.03
12/14	60.04	17 14	4.22	1.62	47.78
Annual Growth	5.1%	— —	12.0%	4.1%	6.5%

Boot Barn Holdings Inc

Auditors: DELOITTE & TOUCHE LLP

LOCATIONS

HQ: Boot Barn Holdings Inc
15345 Barranca Pkwy, Irvine, CA 92618
Phone: 949 453-4400
Web: www.bootbarn.com

HISTORICAL FINANCIALS
Company Type: Public

Income Statement — FYE: March 30

	REVENUE ($ mil.)	NET INCOME ($ mil.)	NET PROFIT MARGIN	EMPLOYEES
03/19	776.8	39.0	5.0%	4,000
03/18*	677.9	28.8	4.3%	3,500
04/17	629.8	14.2	2.3%	3,000
03/16	569.0	9.8	1.7%	2,900
03/15	402.6	13.7	3.4%	1,700
Annual Growth	17.9%	29.8%	—	23.9%

*Fiscal year change

2019 Year-End Financials

Debt ratio: 29.1%
Return on equity: 16.3%
Cash ($ mil.): 16.6
Current ratio: 1.83
Long-term debt ($ mil.): 184.9
No. of shares (mil.): 28.3
Dividends
  Yield: —
  Payout: —
Market value ($ mil.): 835.0

	STOCK PRICE ($) FY Close	P/E High/Low		PER SHARE ($) Earnings	Dividends	Book Value
03/19	29.44	23	11	1.35	0.00	9.32
03/18*	17.73	18	6	1.05	0.00	7.86
04/17	9.89	31	11	0.53	0.00	6.77
03/16	9.34	89	15	0.37	0.00	6.13
03/15	23.21	46	30	0.54	0.00	5.51
Annual Growth	6.1%	—	—	25.7%	—	14.0%

*Fiscal year change

Bridge Bancorp, Inc. (Bridgehampton, NY)

Bridge Bancorp wants you to cross over to its subsidiary The Bridgehampton National Bank which operates about 25 branches on eastern Long Island New York. Founded in 1910 the bank offers traditional deposit services to area individuals small businesses and municipalities including checking savings and money market accounts and CDs. Deposits are invested primarily in mortgages which account for some 80% of the bank's loan portfolio. Title insurance services are available through bank subsidiary Bridge Abstract; wealth management services include financial planning estate administration and trustee services. Bridge Bancorp bought Hamptons State Bank in 2011 to fortify its presence on Long Island.

Geographic Reach
Bridgehampton New York-based Bridge Bancorp's market area is Suffolk County in eastern Long Island. The bank serves customers in the towns of East Hampton Southampton Southold and Riverhead. It also has branches in Brookhaven Babylon and Islip.

Financial Performance
The bank reported net income of $13.1 million in 2013 versus $12.8 million in 2012. Revenue increased 3% to $67.3 million on rising net interest income. Bridge Bancorp had total assets of $1.9 billion in 2013 an increase of 17% versus the prior year. Total deposits rose 9% in 2013 versus 2012 to $1.5 billion.

Mergers and Acquisitions
In February 2014 Bridge Bancorp acquired FNBNY Bancorp and its wholly-owned subsidiary the First National Bank of New York and converted its three branches to Bridgehampton National Bank (BNB) branches. The purchase expanded BNB's reach into Nassau County. Following the acquisition Bridge Bancorp's assets totaled approximately $2.1 billion with loans of approximately $1.1 billion and deposits of $1.7 billion with 26 branches throughout Long Island and one loan production office in Manhattan.

EXECUTIVES

President and CEO, Kevin M. O'Connor, age 56, $300,000 total compensation
EVP and Chief Lending Officer, Kevin L. Santacroce, $180,000 total compensation
SVP and CIO, Thomas H. Simson, $175,000 total compensation
President CEO and Director, Kevin OConnor
Chief Financial Officer, Adam Hall
EVP and Chief Retail Banking Officer, James J. Manseau, $235,000 total compensation
Senior Vice President and Regional Manager, Ralph Meyer
Vice Chairman, Dennis A. Suskind, age 76
Chairman, Marcia Z. Hefter, age 75
Board Member, Albert Mccoy
Board Member, Rudolph Santoro
Chief Financial Officer Executive Vice President Treasurer, John Mccaffery
Auditors: Crowe LLP

LOCATIONS

HQ: Bridge Bancorp, Inc. (Bridgehampton, NY)
2200 Montauk Highway, Bridgehampton, NY 11932
Phone: 631 537-1000
Web: www.bridgenb.com

COMPETITORS

Bank of America
Bank of New York Mellon
JPMorgan Chase
Suffolk Bancorp

HISTORICAL FINANCIALS
Company Type: Public

Income Statement — FYE: December 31

	ASSETS ($ mil.)	NET INCOME ($ mil.)	INCOME AS % OF ASSETS	EMPLOYEES
12/18	4,700.7	39.2	0.8%	473
12/17	4,430.0	20.5	0.5%	480
12/16	4,054.5	35.4	0.9%	477
12/15	3,781.9	21.1	0.6%	433
12/14	2,288.6	13.7	0.6%	348
Annual Growth	19.7%	29.9%	—	8.0%

2018 Year-End Financials

Return on assets: 0.8%
Return on equity: 8.8%
Long-term debt ($ mil.): —
No. of shares (mil.): 19.7
Sales ($ mil): 180.5
Dividends
  Yield: 3.6%
  Payout: 98.9%
Market value ($ mil.): 504.0

	STOCK PRICE ($) FY Close	P/E High/Low		PER SHARE ($) Earnings	Dividends	Book Value
12/18	25.49	19	12	1.97	0.92	22.93
12/17	35.00	37	29	1.04	0.92	21.78
12/16	37.90	19	13	2.00	0.92	21.36
12/15	30.43	22	17	1.43	0.92	19.62
12/14	26.75	23	20	1.18	0.92	15.03
Annual Growth	(1.2%)	—	—	13.7%	(0.0%)	11.1%

Bridgford Foods Corp.

Too many cooks might spoil Bridgford Foods' business. The company manufactures markets and distributes a slew of frozen refrigerated and snack foods. Its lineup ranges from biscuits and bread dough to deli meats dry sausage and beef jerky. (It's one of the nation's largest sellers of jerky and other meat snacks). Bridgford adds to its offerings by buying for resale some snack and refrigerated foods made by other processors. The company sells to food service (restaurants and institutions) and retailers (supermarkets mass merchandise and convenience stores) in the US and Canada largely through distributors brokers and a direct store delivery network. Wal-Mart generates about 20% of Bridgford's sales.

Geographic Reach
California-based Bridgford Foods manufactures products in Anaheim and Modesto California; Statesville North Carolina and in Chicago and Dallas. Its products are sold in all 50 US states Canada and several markets overseas.

Sales and Marketing
Bridgford counts Wal-Mart and Dollar General among its largest customers. In fiscal 2013 (ended October) Wal-Mart accounted for 20% of the company sales while Dollar General represented 10%. The company sells its food products through wholesalers cooperatives and distributors. Products made by the company's Frozen Food Products business are generally supplied to food service and retail distributors.

Financial Performance
Bridgford rang up $129 million in sales in fiscal 2013 (ended October) a 1% increase versus the prior year. Net income fell 20% over the same period to $2.9 million. Driving the modest sales gain was a 7% increase at its Frozen Food Products business due to price increases in mid-2013 partially offset by an 8% decline in revenue by its Refrigerated and Snack Food Products unit. The decline in profitability was due to higher expenses and depreciation primarily related to the replacement of delivery fleet vehicles.

Strategy
Bridgford's focus on convenience foods is unwavering; it has not pursued acquisitions nor significantly diversified its product portfolio during the last five years. It managed to stay profitable in 2010 despite higher prices for grains meats and petroleum and a slip in year-over-year sales which remain relatively flat.

The company has however made a strategic shift in operations. The record cost of key commodities and a decision to make a significant adjustment to its provision for taxes drove deepening losses. Price increases and the elimination of under-performing products and operations failed to counter the financial toll. Its hard choices were rewarded in 2009 and along with lower commodity costs helped the company rebound and mark its fourth earnings high.

Among its choices Bridgford has increased its push of products made by the company coupled with supplementing its own direct store delivery network and distributor partnerships. In 2010 it inked a deal with Golden Flake Snack Foods (owned by Golden Enterprises) to sell Bridgford's dry sausage and meat snacks. Bridgford has also continued to tweak its offerings. During the year it developed a single-serve version of its popular monkey bread launched a handful of new beef jerky items and refined its self-stable sandwich and bakery products with an investment in new packaging technology. The company's frozen food business also added several new varieties of bread dough. Such moves enable the company to sell through a greater variety of retail and on-line outlets.

Bridgford's focus is heavily influenced by the founding Bridgford family. The family owns more than 80% of the company. Moreover three members are actively involved in its management and serve on the board of directors.

EXECUTIVES

EVP CFO Treasurer and Member Executive Committee, Raymond F. Lancy, age 66, $244,482 total compensation
President, John V. Simmons, age 64, $244,482 total compensation
President Bridgford Marketing of California, Bruce H. Bridgford
VP Information Technologies, Bob Delong
President Bridgford Processing CompanyIllinois and Bridgford Foods Illinois, R.H. Bridgford
President Dallas Superior Foods Division, Blaine K. Bridgford
VP Dallas Frozen-Rite Division, Joseph deAlcuaz
Bakery Manager Anaheim Bread Division, Jeffrey D. Robinson
VP; Member Executive Committee, Allan L. Bridgford, $146,689 total compensation
VP Manufacturing, Joe deAlcuaz
Chairman Executive Committee, Hugh William Bridgford, age 87
Chairman, William L. (Bill) Bridgford, age 65
Auditors: SQUAR MILNER LLP

LOCATIONS

HQ: Bridgford Foods Corp.
1308 North Patt Street, Anaheim, CA 92801
Phone: 714 526-5533
Web: www.bridgford.com

PRODUCTS/OPERATIONS

Company-Made Products
Beef jerky
Biscuits
Bread dough items
Cheeses
Dry sausage products
Luncheon meats
Roll dough items
Sandwiches
Products Purchased for Resale
Cheeses
Delicatessen type food products
Jerky
Mexican foods
Nuts
Party dips
Salads

COMPETITORS

AdvancePierre	Hillshire Brands
Boar's Head	Hormel
Carl Buddig	Interbake Foods
ConAgra	Maple Leaf Foods
Eby-Brown	Mondelez International
Frito-Lay	Oberto Sausage Company
General Mills	Snyder's-Lance

HISTORICAL FINANCIALS
Company Type: Public

Income Statement — FYE: November 1

	REVENUE ($ mil.)	NET INCOME ($ mil.)	NET PROFIT MARGIN	EMPLOYEES
11/19	188.7	6.4	3.4%	564
11/18	174.2	6.5	3.7%	544
11/17*	167.2	8.8	5.3%	544
10/16	140.0	7.7	5.5%	508
10/15	130.4	15.4	11.8%	507
Annual Growth	9.7%	(19.5%)	—	2.7%

*Fiscal year change

2019 Year-End Financials
Debt ratio: 11.5%
Return on equity: 9.8%
Cash ($ mil.): 3.4
Current ratio: 2.65
Long-term debt ($ mil.): 12.1
No. of shares (mil.): 9.7
Dividends
  Yield: —
  Payout: —
Market value ($ mil.): 245.0

	STOCK PRICE ($) FY Close	P/E High/Low	Earnings	Dividends	Book Value
11/19	25.20	52 25	0.71	0.00	6.85
11/18	17.30	30 17	0.72	0.00	7.24
11/17*	13.10	17 11	0.97	0.00	6.17
10/16	11.80	18 10	0.86	0.00	4.29
10/15	9.10	6 4	1.70	0.00	3.93
Annual Growth	29.0%	—	(19.6%)	—	14.9%

*Fiscal year change

Bright Horizons Family Solutions, Inc

EXECUTIVES

Senior Vice President of Business Operations, Dave Shaby
Chief Executive Officer Director; Executive Chairman, Roger H Brown
Divisional Vice President, Peggy Gerety
Division Vice President Of Operations, Leslie Spanier
Vice President Client Relations, Yvonne Lynch
Division Vice President Of Operations, Cynthia Hartzel
Vice President, Alan Robins
Senior Vice President Back Up Care Services, Mandy Berman
Senior Vice President Client Relations, Patrick Donovan
Division Vice President of Operations, Tammy Chuprevich
Vice President Client Solutions Back up Centers, Kevin Brown
Division Vice President, Patti Eickhoff
Division Vice President, Linda Bartleson
Svp Marketing And Client Relations, Gary Oneil
Vice President Application Development, David Brand
Vice President, Deborah Koshansky
Division Vice President, Sheila Niehaus
Vice President, Joanne Urso
Auditors: DELOITTE & TOUCHE LLP

LOCATIONS

HQ: Bright Horizons Family Solutions, Inc
200 Talcott Avenue, Watertown, MA 02472
Phone: 617 673-8000
Web: www.brighthorizons.com

HISTORICAL FINANCIALS
Company Type: Public

Income Statement — FYE: December 31

	REVENUE ($ mil.)	NET INCOME ($ mil.)	NET PROFIT MARGIN	EMPLOYEES
12/18	1,903.1	157.9	8.3%	33,350
12/17	1,740.9	156.9	9.0%	31,600
12/16	1,569.8	94.7	6.0%	31,200
12/15	1,458.4	93.9	6.4%	26,000
12/14	1,353.0	72.0	5.3%	25,400
Annual Growth	8.9%	21.7%	—	7.0%

2018 Year-End Financials
Debt ratio: 46.1%
Return on equity: 20.6%
Cash ($ mil.): 15.4
Current ratio: 0.40
Long-term debt ($ mil.): 1,036.8
No. of shares (mil.): 57.4
Dividends
  Yield: —
  Payout: —
Market value ($ mil.): 6,408.0

	STOCK PRICE ($) FY Close	P/E High/Low	Earnings	Dividends	Book Value
12/18	111.45	45 34	2.66	0.00	13.56
12/17	94.00	36 26	2.59	0.00	12.91
12/16	70.02	45 38	1.55	0.00	11.68
12/15	66.80	45 29	1.50	0.00	12.13
12/14	47.01	43 33	1.07	0.00	12.20
Annual Growth	24.1%	—	25.6%	—	2.7%

Brookline Bancorp Inc (DE)

Boston-based Brookline Bancorp is the holding company for Brookline Bank Bank Rhode Island (BankRI) and First Ipswich Bank which together operate more than 50 full-service branches in eastern Massachusetts and Rhode Island. Commercial and multifamily mortgages backed by real estate such as apartments condominiums and office buildings account for the largest portion of the company's loan portfolio followed by indirect auto loans commercial loans and consumer loans. Established in 1997 as Brookline Savings Bank the bank went public five years later and changed its name to Brookline Bank in 2003.

Operations

Brookline Bancorp focuses its services and products to commercial enterprises. It offers commercial business and retail banking services such as cash management products on-line banking services consumer and residential loans and investment services. The holding company provides equipment financing through its Eastern Funding and Macrolease Corporation subsidiaries. Eastern Funding holds loans with higher-than-normal credit risk (and higher yields) due to the limited capital of its typical customers: coin-operated laundries dry cleaning businesses and convenience stores in the New York City metropolitan area.

Geographic Reach
Boston-based Brookline Bancorp operates primarily in Boston MA and Providence Rhode Island.

Financial Performance
Brookline Bancorp generated $263 million in interest & dividend income and another $32 million of non-interest income. Combined the $295 million of 2017 annual revenue exceeded the previous year's result by 12% aided heavily by the bank's one-time gain of $11 million on the sale of investment securities. Its loan portfolio grew 6% to $5.7 billion in 2017.

Despite the healthy improvement in revenue net income fell 4% to $50.5 million due in large part to an unusually high income tax bill triggered by the passing of the US Federal Tax Reform bill in late 2017.

Strategy
Brookline has grown from a sleepy suburban community savings bank to a publicly-traded commercial lender with loan volumes that put it among Massachusetts' top banks. Its operational approach of a holding company with local largely independent banks gives it certain advantages. The local banks are empowered to address local market needs whether in the form of products services or even interest rates on loans. This gives each bank the opportunity to build its own brand along with strong long-term relationships with commercial customers while leaving the corporate functions (IT risk management etc.) to the centralized holding company.

Mergers and Acquisitions
In 2018 the bank purchased for $264 million First Commons Bank N.A. to extend its reach into the western suburbs of Boston MA.

EXECUTIVES

President and CEO, Paul A. Perrault, age 68, $715,000 total compensation
COO, James M. Cosman, age 68, $265,000 total compensation
President and CEO Bank Rhode Island, Mark J. Meiklejohn, age 55, $330,000 total compensation
Chief Risk Officer General Counsel and Secretary, Michael W. McCurdy, age 50
Chief Credit Officer, M. Robert Rose, age 67, $288,000 total compensation
President and CEO The First National Bank of Ipswich, Russell G. Cole, age 61
CFO, Carl M. Carlson, age 55, $335,000 total compensation
Senior Vice President, Bill Mackenzie
Vice President Regional Manager, Cathy Pierce
Vice President, Tony Glazier
Vice President Of Commercial Lending, Tim Steiner
Vice President Underwriting And Operations, Gretchen Annese
Vice President, James Vallone
Vice President, Maryanne Bland
Vp Benefits and Payroll, Edgar Oteiza
Chairman, Joseph J. Slotnik, age 83
Treasurer, Reed H Whitman
Auditors: KPMG LLP

LOCATIONS
HQ: Brookline Bancorp Inc (DE)
131 Clarendon Street, Boston, MA 02116
Phone: 617 425-4600
Web: www.brooklinebancorp.com

PRODUCTS/OPERATIONS
2017 sales

	$ mil.	% of total
Interest and dividend income:		
Loans and leases	247.0	84
Debt securities	12.5	4
Marketable and restricted equity securities	3.1	1
Short-term investments	.4	-
Non-interest income:		
Deposit fees	10.1	3
Loan fees	1.1	—
Loan level derivative income net	2.2	1
Gain on sales of investment securities	11.4	4
Gain on sales of loans and leases held-for-sale	2.6	1
Other	4.8	2
Total	**295.3**	**100**

Selected Services
Personal
Checking
Savings
Borrowing
Investment Services
Business
Signature Business Banking
Business Checking Accounts
Business Savings
Business Lending
Business Online Banking
Cash Management
Service Center
Branch Locations
ATM Locations
Online Banking
Mobile Banking
Telephone Services
Mail Services
Order Checks
Order Foreign Currency
Overdraft Privilege Service

COMPETITORS
Bank of America
Berkshire Hills Bancorp
Boston Private
Central Bancorp
Century Bancorp (MA)
Citizens Financial Group
Eastern Bank
Sovereign Bank
TD Bank USA

HISTORICAL FINANCIALS
Company Type: Public

Income Statement   FYE: December 31

	ASSETS ($ mil.)	NET INCOME ($ mil.)	INCOME AS % OF ASSETS	EMPLOYEES
12/18	7,392.8	83.0	1.1%	791
12/17	6,780.2	50.5	0.7%	765
12/16	6,438.1	52.3	0.8%	743
12/15	6,042.3	49.7	0.8%	718
12/14	5,799.8	42.7	0.7%	725
Annual Growth	6.3%	18.1%	—	2.2%

2018 Year-End Financials
Return on assets: 1.1%
Return on equity: 9.7%
Long-term debt ($ mil.): —
No. of shares (mil.): 80.1
Sales ($ mil): 339.1
Dividends
  Yield: 2.8%
  Payout: 45.4%
Market value ($ mil.): 1,108.0

	STOCK PRICE ($) FY Close	P/E High/Low	PER SHARE ($) Earnings	Dividends	Book Value
12/18	13.82	19 12	1.04	0.40	11.23
12/17	15.70	25 20	0.68	0.36	10.42
12/16	16.40	22 14	0.74	0.36	9.82
12/15	11.50	17 13	0.71	0.36	9.45
12/14	10.03	17 14	0.61	0.34	9.09
Annual Growth	8.3%	— —	14.3%	3.8%	5.4%

Brooks Automation Inc

Brooks Automation supplies a steady stream of production tools and factory automation products for the semiconductor industry. It makes tool automation products such as vacuum robots and cluster assemblies used by semiconductor manufacturers. Brooks' wafer handling systems include vacuum cassette elevator loadlocks transfer robots and thermal conditioning modules and aligners. It also makes vacuum equipment for makers of flat-panel displays and data storage devices. The company also works in life science providing sample storage and handling systems. Brooks' semiconductor customers include Applied Materials Samsung and Micron. Among its life science customers are AstraZeneca Biomarin and Abbvie.

Operations
Brooks Automation operates in two segments. The semiconductor unit supplies about 80% of the company's revenue. It makes a range of equipment critical for the manufacture of semiconductor production machines. Brooks Automation semiconductor products include atmospheric and vacuum tool automation systems atmospheric and vacuum robots and robotic modules thermal management products and cryogenic pumping assemblies.

The company's life sciences segment about 20% of revenue was formed from acquisitions it made several years ago. The unit's products include sample storage management systems blood fractionation equipment sample preparation and handling equipment parts consumables and support services for the biotechnology laboratory pharmaceutical and research industry sectors.

Geographic Reach
Brooks operates manufacturing plants in the US (California Colorado and Massachusetts) as well as in China Germany Japan Singapore South Korea and the UK. Overall the company has operations in about a dozen countries and customers in some 50 countries.

Customers in Asia account for more than 45% of revenue followed by US customers with about 35% and UK customers with more than 10%.

Sales and Marketing
Brooks sells its products and services in North America Asia Europe and the Middle East through a direct sales force. Sales in Japan are made through Yaskawa Brooks Automation a joint venture with Yaskawa Electric Corporation. Its sales cycle is lengthy (up to 18 months) and generally involves several employees from sales marketing engineering and senior management.

Brooks Automation's top 10 customers account for about 40% of revenue.

Financial Performance
Brooks Automation's revenue increased about 7% a year from 2013-2016 but it jumped 24% in 2017 thanks to strong results in its semiconductor and life sciences segments. Revenue hit about $693 million in 2017 (ended September) up $132 million from 2016. Sales in 2017 were propelled by a 20% increase in the semiconductor group which sold more contamination control systems cryogenic pump products and robotic automation products. The life sciences group's sales rose nearly 40% from organic growth in sample storage services automated storage systems including the BioStore III Cryo and consumables and instruments as well as contributions from acquisitions.

Brooks reported a $132 million turnaround on its bottom line that took it from a $69 million loss to a profit of about $63 million in 2017. The profit was produced by operating income of about $60 million and a lower income tax provision of about $64 million.

The company had cash and cash equivalents of about $104 million in 2017 and about $91 million in 2016. The increase came from about $96 million generated from operations partially offset by cash payments related to acquisitions dividend payments to shareholders and capital expenditures.

Strategy

Brooks Automation is well-positioned with its semiconductor and life sciences groups. The markets the company serves are growing and the company maintains that its products neatly fit those markets. Its semiconductor products it says are key to the manufacturing process of computer chips and its products for high-growth markets comprise more than half of its semiconductor revenue. The company's life sciences revenue increased about 40% from organic and acquisition-related sales in 2017. Its automated cryogenic sample store reached $5 million in sales for the year.

Brooks also makes acquisitions to build out its product portfolio in the semiconductor and life sciences groups. In 2017 the company secured funding for acquisitions with a loan of about $200 million. The money was to be used for general corporate purchases including acquisitions.

The company sold its cryogenics business in 2019 to Atlas Copco for about $675 million. Brooks applied $495 million cash from the proceeds to reduce debt resulting in about $50 million gross debt and no net debt on its balance sheet.

Half of Brooks' revenue originates in the Asia/Pacific region putting the company at risk should trade tensions rise around the world. The US and China have signaled that higher tariffs and other trade sanctions are possible. Brooks' products could be affected by higher prices and controls on imports and exports.

Mergers and Acquisitions

In 2018 Brooks acquired BioSpeciMan Corp. a Canadian provider of storage services for biological sample materials for $5 million. The acquisition expanded its customer relationships and geographic reach within growing sample management storage business of Life Sciences unit.

In 2017 in another life sciences deal Brooks bought 4titude Ltd a manufacturer of scientific consumables for biological sample materials for $65 million. Also in 2017 it acquired Pacific Bio-Material Management a provider of storage and cold-chain logistics for biological sample materials for $33 million.

For the semiconductor group Brooks bought Tec-Sem Group AG a provider of semiconductor manufacturing automation equipment for $16 million. Tec-Sem's products focus on reticle management.

EXECUTIVES

President and CEO, Stephen S. Schwartz, age 59, $625,000 total compensation
EVP and CFO, Lindon G. Robertson, age 57, $425,000 total compensation
SVP Semiconductor Automation, David E. Jarznyka, $319,192 total compensation
President Life Science Systems, Maurice H. (Dusty) Tenney, $425,000 total compensation
SVP Chief Strategy and New Business Officer, David C. Gray, $350,000 total compensation
Vice President of Supply Chain, Lori Ciano
Vice President, David Jarznyka
Senior Vice President Engineering and NPI, Rob Woodward
Vice President Corporate Development, John OBrien
Vice President Sales And Marketing, Drew Mitchell
Vice President, Roark Daniel
Chairman, Joseph R. Martin, age 71
Board Member, Larry Heath
Senior Vice President General Counsel Secretary, Jason Joseph
Board Member, Fritz Allen
Auditors: PricewaterhouseCoopers LLP

LOCATIONS

HQ: Brooks Automation Inc
15 Elizabeth Drive, Chelmsford, MA 01824
Phone: 978 262-2400
Web: www.brooks.com

PRODUCTS/OPERATIONS

2017 Sales

	$ mil.	% of total
Brooks Semiconductor Solutions	544.2	79
Brooks Life Science Systems	148.7	21
Total	692.9	100

Selected Products and Services

Air flow control
Alignment and calibration tools
Atmospheric tools
Consumables
Cryopumping
Factory automation systems
Field service
Life science instruments and devices
Life science software (Sprint 6)
Load port modules
Material handling systems
Productivity services
RFID and tracking products
Repair
Robots and modules
Spare parts
Vacuum pumps and gauges
Wafer handling systems
Waterpump and chillers

COMPETITORS

Cohu
Covance
DAIHEN CORPORATION
Daifuku
Daw Tech
Entegris
Fortrend Engineering
HIRATA CORPORATION
INFICON
Kawasaki Heavy Industries
LabCorp
MKS Instruments
RORZE CORPORATION
SINFONIA TECHNOLOGY CO. LTD.
Sumitomo Heavy Industries
TDK
Thermo Fisher Scientific

HISTORICAL FINANCIALS
Company Type: Public

Income Statement
FYE: September 30

	REVENUE ($ mil.)	NET INCOME ($ mil.)	NET PROFIT MARGIN	EMPLOYEES
09/19	780.8	437.4	56.0%	2,984
09/18	631.5	116.5	18.5%	1,548
09/17	692.8	62.6	9.0%	1,661
09/16	560.3	(69.4)	—	1,310
09/15	552.7	14.2	2.6%	1,426
Annual Growth	9.0%	135.5%	—	20.3%

2019 Year-End Financials

Debt ratio: 3.3%
Return on equity: 47.1%
Cash ($ mil.): 301.6
Current ratio: 2.38
Long-term debt ($ mil.): 50.3
No. of shares (mil.): 72.3
Dividends
 Yield: 1.0%
 Payout: 81.6%
Market value ($ mil.): 2,677.0

	STOCK PRICE ($) FY Close	P/E High/Low		PER SHARE ($) Earnings	Dividends	Book Value
09/19	37.03	7	4	6.04	0.40	15.75
09/18	35.03	24	14	1.64	0.40	10.15
09/17	30.36	34	14	0.89	0.40	8.70
09/16	13.61	—	—	(1.01)	0.40	8.05
09/15	11.71	64	46	0.21	0.40	9.35
Annual Growth	33.4%	—	—	131.6%	(0.0%)	13.9%

BRT Apartments Corp

EXECUTIVES

SVP, Israel Rosenzweig, age 64
SVP, Matthew J. Gould, age 52
VP and CFO, George E. Zweier, age 46, $175,134 total compensation
SVP and General Counsel, Mark H. Lundy, age 49, $181,020 total compensation
SVP and Secretary, Simeon Brinberg, age 75, $133,934 total compensation
President CEO and Trustee, Jeffrey A. Gould, age 46, $442,890 total compensation
Chairman, Fredric H. Gould, age 76
SVP Finance, David W. Kalish, age 69
EVP, Mitchell K. Gould, $247,360 total compensation
Director Marketing, Dana Canavan
Senior Underwriter, William O'Hagen
VP, Lonnie Halpern
President CEO and Trustee, Jeffrey A. Gould, age 46
Trustee, Kenneth F. Bernstein, age 50
Trustee, Jeffrey G. Rubin, age 44
Trustee, Gary Hurand, age 65
Trustee, Louis C. (Lou) Grassi, age 56
Trustee, Alan H. Ginsburg, age 73
Trustee, Jonathan H. (Jon) Simon, age 46
Trustee, Elie Weiss, age 39
Auditors: BDO USA LLP

LOCATIONS

HQ: BRT Apartments Corp
60 Cutter Mill Road, Great Neck, NY 11021
Phone: 516 466-3100
Web: www.brtrealty.com

COMPETITORS
CIFC
CapLease
Capital Trust
Drive Shack
RAIT Financial Trust
iStar Financial Inc

HISTORICAL FINANCIALS
Company Type: Public

Income Statement — FYE: September 30

	REVENUE ($ mil.)	NET INCOME ($ mil.)	NET PROFIT MARGIN	EMPLOYEES
09/18	119.6	23.7	19.9%	13
09/17	105.7	13.6	12.9%	12
09/16	94.2	31.2	33.2%	12
09/15	82.5	(2.3)	—	13
09/14	66.4	(9.4)	—	0
Annual Growth	15.9%	—	—	—

2018 Year-End Financials
Debt ratio: 71.9%
Return on equity: 13.0%
Cash ($ mil.): 27.3
Current ratio: 2.13
Long-term debt ($ mil.): 829.4
No. of shares (mil.): 15.0
Dividends
Yield: 0.0%
Payout: 48.4%
Market value ($ mil.): 181.0

	STOCK PRICE ($) FY Close	P/E High/Low		PER SHARE ($) Earnings	Dividends	Book Value
09/18	12.04	9	6	1.61	0.78	13.16
09/17	10.72	11	8	0.97	0.18	12.45
09/16	8.00	4	2	2.23	0.00	11.43
09/15	7.09	—	—	(0.17)	0.00	9.13
09/14	7.50	—	—	(0.66)	0.00	9.53
Annual Growth	12.6%	—	—	—	—	8.4%

Bryn Mawr Bank Corp

Bryn Mawr Bank Corporation stands atop a "big hill" in Pennsylvania. Bryn Mawr (which in Welsh translates as "big hill") is the bank holding company for Bryn Mawr Trust operates some 20 offices in Pennsylvania and Delaware. The bank offers traditional services as checking and savings accounts CDs mortgages and business and consumer loans in addition to insurance products equipment leasing investment management retirement planning tax planning and preparation and trust services. Founded in 1889 Bryn Mawr boasts more than $5 billion of assets under administration and management.

Operations
Bryn Mawr operates two business segments. Its Banking segment which makes up two-thirds of overall business provides commercial and retail banking services. The Wealth Management division which includes the Bryn Mawr Trust of Delaware and Lau Associates businesses makes up about one-third of the bank's overall revenue and provides a variety of custody investment management tax and brokerage services.

Broadly speaking the company generated 60% of its total revenue from interest and fees on loans and leases in 2014 while another 30% of its total revenue came from fees for wealth management services.

Bryn Mawr operated 19 full-service branches seven Life Care Community Offices five wealth offices and a full-service insurance agency in 2014.

Geographic Reach
The bank corporation has branches and offices across Montgomery Delaware Chester and Dauphin counties in Pennsylvania and New Castle county in Delaware.

Financial Performance
Bryn Mawr has enjoyed rising revenues and profits over the past several years reflecting strong growth in its loan business and wealth management business.

The bank's revenue rose by 4% to a record $131.23 million in 2014 mostly thanks to higher interest income from loans as it grew its loan assets by $153.9 million during the year. The company's Wealth Management services fees also grew by 5% thanks to new business acquisitions and solid market appreciation during the year which resulted in higher assets under management.

Higher revenue and a strong grip on costs in 2014 also boosted Bryn Mawr's net income by 14% to a record $27.84 million. Despite higher earnings the bank's operating cash declined by 6% to $37.68 million for the year as it made less in net proceeds from the sales of its loans held for resale.

Strategy
Bryn Mawr Bank Corporation continued to push its acquisition strategy in 2015 designed to broaden its service offerings boost its loan and deposit business and expand its branch network. The bank looks to strategically acquire smaller insurance businesses small to mid-sized banks and community banks wealth management companies and advisory and planning services firm that complement its existing businesses.

Besides acquisitions the company has been growing its wealth management business through marketing campaigns to raise brand awareness.

Mergers and Acquisitions
In April 2015 to grow its wealth management business the bank purchased Robert J. McAllister Agency which provides insurance and risk management solutions to individuals and businesses in the Philadelphia region.

In January 2015 Bryn Mawr acquired the Continental Bank Holdings and its Plymouth Meeting-based flagship Continental Bank adding some $433 million in loans and $480 million in deposits along with 10 full-service branches located in key markets in Montgomery Chester and Philadelphia counties.

In October 2014 Bryn Mawr bought the Rosemont Pennsylvania-based insurance agency Powers Craft Parker & Beard Inc. (PCPB) for $7 million to enhance its own insurance business among individuals and commercial clients.

In 2012 as part of a strategy to build its wealth management division the company acquired Davidson Trust adding some $1 billion in assets under management.

Company Background
In 2011 the company bought the private wealth management business of Hershey Trust Company for more than $14.5 million; that deal brought in approximately $1 billion of assets under management. In 2010 the company purchased First Keystone Financial adding about 10 bank branches in Pennsylvania and some $2.7 billion in trust and investment assets.

EXECUTIVES

EVP and COO, Alison E. Gers, age 61, $250,000 total compensation
EVP and Chief Lending Officer Bryn Mawr Trust, Joseph G. (Joe) Keefer, age 60, $238,500 total compensation
President and CEO, Francis J. Leto, age 59, $310,000 total compensation
EVP Secretary and Chief Risk Officer, Geoffrey L. Halberstadt
CFO and Treasurer Bryn Mawr Bank Corporation; EVP CFO and Treasurer Bryn Mawr Bank, Michael W. (Mike) Harrington, age 56
EVP Wealth Management Division, Harry R. Madeira
Senior Vice President of Wealth Management Division, Rande Whitham
Senior Vice President Wealth Management, Barbara Pettit
Sr Vice President Market Leader, Tony Poluch
Assistant Vice President And Trust Advisor, Yvonne Lalime
VICE PRESIDENT OPERATIONS MANAGER RETAIL CREDIT CENTER DIVISION, Mandy Payne
Senior Vice President Commercial Lending, Mike Bunn
Senior Vice President Operations, Mame Skelly
Vice President Wealth Management Division, J Keefer-Hugill
Assistant Vice President Trust Tax Advisor, John Fotiou
Vice President; Executive Vice President and Chief Administrative Officer of the Bank, Alison Eichert
Vice President, Cheryl Howard
Vice President Small Business Account Lending Division, Douglas Whalen
VICE PRESIDENT, Sally Worrell
Vice President, Drew Smith
Vice President Relationship Manager, Shawn Williams
Vice President Director Of Investment Services, Bryan Andersen
Vice President Mortgage Division, Anne Stulpin
VICE PRESIDENT COMPTROLLERS AND FINANCE, Maral Kaloustian
Senior Vice President Managing Partner, Robert McLaughlin
Assistant Vice President And Senior Fiduciary Tax Acct, Amanda Decaria
VICE PRESIDENT, John Tucker
Svp And Relationship Manager, Joseph J Dimaio
Vice President And Trust Tax Advisor, Lisa Miles
Vice President Small Business Portfolio Manager, Kirsten Althoff
Assistant Vice President Service Manager Chadds Ford Branch, Leslie Paynter
Avp Recruitment Manager, Maria Delimitros
Svp And Chief Credit Officer, Liam Brickley
Senior Vice President Relationship Manager Bmt Wealth Management, Joanne Shallcross
VICE PRESIDENT SENIOR MORTGAGE LOAN OFFICER, Patt Mcgowan
Senior Vice President And Director Of Facilities, Emanuel Ball
Senior Vice President Director Of Capital Markets, Mark Henderson
Senior Vice President Head Of Commercial And Industrial Banking, Jim Donovan
Senior Vice President Chief Investment Officer, Ernest E Cecilia
Senior Vice President Commercial, Dennis B Levasseur
Senior Vice President, Albert B Murphy
Senior Vice President, Ned Lee
Chairman, Britton H. Murdoch

Assistant Treasurer, Linda McLaughlin
Board Member, Michael Clement
Auditors: KPMG LLP

LOCATIONS
HQ: Bryn Mawr Bank Corp
  801 Lancaster Avenue, Bryn Mawr, PA 19010
Phone: 610 525-1700
Web: www.bmtc.com

PRODUCTS/OPERATIONS

2014 Sales

	$ mil.	% of total
Interest		
Interest & fees on loans & leases	78.5	60
Investment securities	4.2	3
Cash & cash equivalents	0.2	.
Noninterest		
Fees for wealth management services	36.7	30
Service charges on deposits	2.6	2
Net gain on sale of residential mortgages	1.8	1
Loan Servicing and other fees	1.8	1
Other	5.4	3
Total	**131.2**	**100**

Selected Subsidiaries
Bryn Mawr Advisors Inc.
Bryn Mawr Asset Management Inc.
Bryn Mawr Brokerage Co. Inc.
Bryn Mawr Financial Services Inc.
Bryn Mawr Trust Company of Delaware
Joseph W. Roskos Co. Inc.
Lau Associates LLC
The Bryn Mawr Trust Company
  BMT Leasing Inc.
  BMT Mortgage Services Inc.
  BMT Settlement Services Inc.
  Insurance Counsellors of Bryn Mawr Inc.

COMPETITORS

Alliance Bancorp of Pennsylvania	Royal Bancshares
Firstrust Savings Bank	Sovereign Bank
PNC Financial	Wells Fargo

HISTORICAL FINANCIALS
Company Type: Public

Income Statement
FYE: December 31

	ASSETS ($ mil.)	NET INCOME ($ mil.)	INCOME AS % OF ASSETS	EMPLOYEES
12/18	4,652.4	63.7	1.4%	696
12/17	4,449.7	23.0	0.5%	680
12/16	3,421.5	36.0	1.1%	544
12/15	3,031.0	16.7	0.6%	530
12/14	2,246.5	27.8	1.2%	444
Annual Growth	20.0%	23.0%	—	11.9%

2018 Year-End Financials
Return on assets: 1.4%
Return on equity: 11.6%
Long-term debt ($ mil.): —
No. of shares (mil.): 20.1
Sales ($ mil): 257.0
Dividends
  Yield: 2.7%
  Payout: 48.9%
Market value ($ mil.): 694.0

	STOCK PRICE ($) FY Close	P/E High/Low	PER SHARE ($) Earnings	Dividends	Book Value
12/18	34.40	16 11	3.13	0.94	28.04
12/17	44.20	34 28	1.32	0.86	26.23
12/16	42.15	20 11	2.12	0.82	22.50
12/15	28.72	33 29	0.94	0.78	21.42
12/14	31.20	15 13	2.01	0.74	17.83
Annual Growth	2.4%	—	11.7%	6.2%	12.0%

Business First Bancshares Inc

Auditors: Hannis T. Bourgeois, LLP

LOCATIONS
HQ: Business First Bancshares Inc
  500 Laurel Street, Suite 101, Baton Rouge, LA 70801
Phone: 225 248-7600
Web: www.b1bank.com

HISTORICAL FINANCIALS
Company Type: Public

Income Statement
FYE: December 31

	ASSETS ($ mil.)	NET INCOME ($ mil.)	INCOME AS % OF ASSETS	EMPLOYEES
12/18	2,094.9	14.0	0.7%	333
12/17	1,321.2	4.8	0.4%	219
12/16	1,105.8	5.1	0.5%	208
12/15	1,076.0	4.1	0.4%	184
12/14	684.5	4.0	0.6%	0
Annual Growth	32.3%	36.7%	—	—

2018 Year-End Financials
Return on assets: 0.8%
Return on equity: 6.4%
Long-term debt ($ mil.): —
No. of shares (mil.): 13.2
Sales ($ mil): 83.9
Dividends
  Yield: 0.9%
  Payout: 30.7%
Market value ($ mil.): 320.0

	STOCK PRICE ($) FY Close	P/E High/Low	PER SHARE ($) Earnings	Dividends	Book Value
12/18	24.23	23 17	1.22	0.24	19.68
Annual Growth	—	—	—	—	—

Byline Bancorp Inc

Auditors: Moss Adams LLP

LOCATIONS
HQ: Byline Bancorp Inc
  180 North LaSalle Street, Suite 300, Chicago, IL 60601
Phone: 773 244-7000
Web: www.bylinebancorp.com

HISTORICAL FINANCIALS
Company Type: Public

Income Statement
FYE: December 31

	ASSETS ($ mil.)	NET INCOME ($ mil.)	INCOME AS % OF ASSETS	EMPLOYEES
12/18	4,942.5	41.1	0.8%	943
12/17	3,366.1	21.7	0.6%	844
12/16	3,295.8	66.7	2.0%	791
12/15	2,479.8	(14.9)	—	0
Annual Growth	25.8%	—	—	—

2018 Year-End Financials
Return on assets: 0.9%
Return on equity: 7.4%
Long-term debt ($ mil.): —
No. of shares (mil.): 36.3
Sales ($ mil): 258.5
Dividends
  Yield: —
  Payout: 1.9%
Market value ($ mil.): 605.0

	STOCK PRICE ($) FY Close	P/E High/Low	PER SHARE ($) Earnings	Dividends	Book Value
12/18	16.66	20 13	1.18	0.00	17.90
12/17	22.97	59 50	0.38	0.00	15.64
12/16	0.00	— —	3.27	0.00	15.54
Annual Growth	—	—	(39.9%)	—	7.3%

Cabot Microelectronics Corp

Cabot Microelectronics sits atop a mountain of slurry. The company is a top maker of slurries (consumables) used in chemical mechanical planarization (CMP). CMP is a wafer polishing process that enables semiconductor manufacturers to produce smaller faster and more complex devices. Cabot Micro's CMP slurries consist of liquids containing abrasives and chemicals that aid in the CMP process. The company is also a leading provider of polishing pads for CMP and it makes slurries used to polish the substrates and magnetic heads of hard-disk drives. TSMC United Microelectronics Samsung and Intel are among its largest customers.

Operations
Sales of various slurries (tungsten dielectric copper and data storage slurries) and polishing pads account for more than 85% of Cabot Micro's revenues.

In addition the company's Engineered Surface Finishes (ESF) business (5% of sales) develops new polishing techniques and processes that are focused on production efficiency improvements and applications in industries outside of semiconductors. Within the ESF division Cabot Micro's QED Technologies subsidiary makes precision polishing and metrology systems used to shape and surface optical components including lenses mirrors and prisms. Its automated polishing systems use magnetic fluids to polish an array of shapes and finishes. Its metrology systems are based on Subaperture Stitching Interferometer (SSI) which measures non-spherical surfaces.

Geographic Reach
Cabot Micro has five manufacturing plants in Japan Singapore South Korea Taiwan and the US (in Illinois). It has regional sales customer service and technical support offices in Europe Asia and the US. About 80% of sales come from the Asia/Pacific region.

Sales and Marketing
Cabot Micro serves customers that make or provide logic IC (integrated circuit) devices memory IC devices or IC foundry services. Its five largest customers make up more than half of sales. Its top two customers are TSMC and Samsung which respectively account for 18% and 15% of annual sales.

The company primarily uses a direct sales force and depends on independent distributors in some regional markets.

Financial Performance

Sales slid 2.4% in 2015 to $414 million from $424.6 million in 2014. The company had lower sales volumes and was hit by currency exchange rates particularly in Japan and South Korea.

Net income on the other hand rose 10% to $56.5 million in 2015 from $50.7 million in 2014. The company cut some costs including in sales and marketing to achieve the profit gain.

Cash flow from operations was $98 million in 2015 compared to $67 million in 2014.

Strategy

To improve product performance quality and consistency Cabot also works to streamline processes and reduce product variation levels. Some product improvement efforts are conducted in collaboration with customers and strategic partners. In addition to R&D efforts on core lines of slurries and pads for CMP processes the ESF business develops new polishing techniques and processes for applications in industries outside of semiconductors such as precision optics and electronic substrates. These efforts aim to reduce Cabot Micro's dependence on one product for most of its sales which increases its vulnerability to competition.

Mergers and Acquisitions

In 2018 Cabot agreed to buy KMG Chemicals Inc. for $1.2 billion in cash and stock. The deal would strengthen Cabot's position as a supplier to the semiconductor industry by adding KMG's high-purity chemicals to its product portfolio. The transaction was expected to close by the end of 2018.

EXECUTIVES

EVP and CFO, William S. (Bill) Johnson, age 62, $370,000 total compensation
President and CEO, David H. Li, age 46, $496,500 total compensation
VP Japan and Asia Operations, Yumiko Damashek, age 63
VP and CTO, Ananth Naman, $338,400 total compensation
VP Secretary and General Counsel, H. Carol Bernstein, $337,800 total compensation
Vice President Corporate Development, Brian O'leary
Auditors: PricewaterhouseCoopers LLP

LOCATIONS

HQ: Cabot Microelectronics Corp
870 North Commons Drive, Aurora, IL 60504
Phone: 630 375-6631
Web: www.cabotcmp.com

PRODUCTS/OPERATIONS

2015 Sales

	$ mil.	% of total
Tungsten slurries	178.8	44
Dielectric slurries	96.4	23
Other Metals slurries	71.6	17
Polishing pads	32.0	8
Engineered surface finishes	21.5	5
Data storage slurries	13.7	3
Total	**414.0**	**100**

Selected Products
CMP Polishing Pads
Polished Surface Finishes
Slurries

Barrier
Copper
Data Storage
Dielectric
Emerging Applications
Silicon Carbide Wafer
Silicon Wafer
TSV
Tungsten

COMPETITORS

3M
ATMI
Air Products
Fujimi Corp.
Hitachi Chemical
Praxair
Saint-Gobain Abrasives

HISTORICAL FINANCIALS

Company Type: Public

Income Statement FYE: September 30

	REVENUE ($ mil.)	NET INCOME ($ mil.)	NET PROFIT MARGIN	EMPLOYEES
09/19	1,037.7	39.2	3.8%	2,047
09/18	590.1	110.0	18.6%	1,219
09/17	507.1	86.9	17.1%	1,179
09/16	430.4	59.8	13.9%	1,145
09/15	414.1	56.1	13.6%	1,111
Annual Growth	25.8%	(8.6%)	—	16.5%

2019 Year-End Financials

Debt ratio: 41.6%
Return on equity: 4.7%
Cash ($ mil.): 188.5
Current ratio: 2.97
Long-term debt ($ mil.): 928.4
No. of shares (mil.): 29.1
Dividends
  Yield: 1.1%
  Payout: 42.2%
Market value ($ mil.): 4,109.0

	STOCK PRICE ($) FY Close	P/E High/Low	PER SHARE ($) Earnings	Dividends	Book Value
09/19	141.21	106 61	1.35	1.64	33.69
09/18	103.17	29 19	4.19	1.00	26.14
09/17	79.93	23 15	3.40	0.78	23.54
09/16	52.91	22 14	2.43	0.54	20.30
09/15	38.74	23 16	2.26	0.00	17.55
Annual Growth	38.2%	—	(12.1%)	—	17.7%

Cactus Inc

Auditors: PricewaterhouseCoopers LLP

LOCATIONS

HQ: Cactus Inc
920 Memorial City Way, Suite 300, Houston, TX 77024
Phone: 713 626-8800
Web: www.CactusWHD.com

HISTORICAL FINANCIALS

Company Type: Public

Income Statement FYE: December 31

	REVENUE ($ mil.)	NET INCOME ($ mil.)	NET PROFIT MARGIN	EMPLOYEES
12/18	544.1	51.6	9.5%	1,200
12/17	341.1	66.5	19.5%	880
12/16	155.0	(8.1)	—	880
12/15	221.4	21.2	9.6%	0
Annual Growth	35.0%	34.5%	—	—

2018 Year-End Financials

Debt ratio: 2.7%
Return on equity: 73.0%
Cash ($ mil.): 70.8
Current ratio: 3.68
Long-term debt ($ mil.): 8.7
No. of shares (mil.): 74.8
Dividends
  Yield: —
  Payout: —
Market value ($ mil.): 2,053.0

	STOCK PRICE ($) FY Close	P/E High/Low	PER SHARE ($) Earnings	Dividends	Book Value
12/18	27.41	25 13	1.58	0.00	2.37
12/17	0.00	—	—1,258.36	0.00	(0.79)
Annual Growth	—	—	(99.9%)	—	—

Cadence Bancorporation

Auditors: Ernst & Young LLP

LOCATIONS

HQ: Cadence Bancorporation
2800 Post Oak Boulevard, Suite 3800, Houston, TX 77056
Phone: 713 871-4000
Web: www.cadencebank.com

HISTORICAL FINANCIALS

Company Type: Public

Income Statement FYE: December 31

	ASSETS ($ mil.)	NET INCOME ($ mil.)	INCOME AS % OF ASSETS	EMPLOYEES
12/18	12,730.2	166.2	1.3%	1,811
12/17	10,948.9	102.3	0.9%	1,206
12/16	9,530.8	65.7	0.7%	1,193
12/15	8,811.5	39.2	0.4%	0
12/14	0.0	44.8	************%	0
Annual Growth	—	38.8%	—	—

2018 Year-End Financials

Return on assets: 1.4%
Return on equity: 11.8%
Long-term debt ($ mil.): —
No. of shares (mil.): 82.5
Sales ($ mil): 607.3
Dividends
  Yield: 3.2%
  Payout: 27.9%
Market value ($ mil.): 1,384.0

	STOCK PRICE ($) FY Close	P/E High/Low	PER SHARE ($) Earnings	Dividends	Book Value
12/18	16.78	16 8	1.97	0.55	17.43
12/17	27.12	22 16	1.25	0.00	16.25
Annual Growth	(38.1%)	—	57.6%	—	7.3%

CAI International Inc

Is it bigger than a breadbox? CAI International can pack it. The company leases large steel boxes to ship freight by plane train or truck around the world. More than 65% of its container fleet is owned by CAI and the balance owned by container investors is managed by CAI. The leasing segment offers 280-plus shipping companies short-term and long-term leases with some leases giving the lessees the option to purchase the container. The container management segment provides container investors with the ability to lease re-lease and dispose of their container portfolio; services also include container repair relocation and storage.

Geographic Reach
CAI caters to 280 customers from 16 offices spanning 13 countries. CAI purchases the majority of its containers in China and operates from offices in Belgium Hong Kong Japan Korea Singapore Taiwan the UK and the US among others.

Sales and Marketing
The top ten largest lessees account for about 60% of its total leasing segment sales (approximately 55% of total sales). Its largest customer CMA CGM generates 11% of sales.

Financial Performance
CAI has enjoyed four straight years of unprecedented growth. Revenues climbed 7% from $212 million in 2013 to reach a historic high of $228 million in 2014. Profits however fell 6% from $64 million in 2013 to $60 million in 2014 due to increased storage handling and other expenses.

The growth for 2014 was driven by a 8% spike in rental revenue due to an increase in the average number of owned containers on lease. The company was also helped by a 11% bump in finance lease sales. This growth was offset by a 17% decrease in management fee revenue.

Company Background
Founded by Hiromitsu Ogawa in 1989 CAI has evolved from solely an intermodal leasing concern to a more ambitious manager of containers owned by investors.

EXECUTIVES

President and CEO, Victor M. Garcia, age 51, $323,833 total compensation
VP Operations, Camille G. Cutino, age 60, $164,800 total compensation
CFO, Timothy Page
Vice President Technical Services, Mike Hohndorf
Senior Vice President CAI Rail, James Magee
Vice President Marketing Europe, John Pacey
Vice President Marketing, Geoff Hopkins
Vice President Marketing Cai Rail, Mike Macmahon
Vice President Operations, Freddy Fernandez
Vice President Of Marketing Based In Hong Kong, Paul Bevan
Vice President Marketing South America West, Iris Vicencio
Vice President, Brian Akers
Senior Vice President, Jason Miller
Vice President Cai Logistics International Logistics, George Meyer
Board Member, Gary Sawka
Assistant Treasurer, Sean Nakahara
Board Member, John Williford
Auditors: KPMG LLP

LOCATIONS
HQ: CAI International Inc
Steuart Tower, 1 Market Plaza, Suite 2400, San Francisco, CA 94105
Phone: 415 788-0100
Web: www.capps.com

PRODUCTS/OPERATIONS
2014 Sales

	% of total
Rental revenue	93
Management fee revenue	3
Finance lease income	4
Gain on sale of container portfolios	0
Total	**100**

Selected Operations
Container leasing
  Container owned by CAI
  Full benefits of ownership
  Placed on long- and short-term leases to shipping lines
Container management
  Container sold to investors
  Generate cash flow through management fee revenue and trading income
  Managed by CAI over expected life of asset

COMPETITORS
COSCO Group   Seaco
SeaCube Container   Touax
Seacastle   XTRA Corp.

HISTORICAL FINANCIALS
Company Type: Public

Income Statement   FYE: December 31

	REVENUE ($ mil.)	NET INCOME ($ mil.)	NET PROFIT MARGIN	EMPLOYEES
12/18	432.1	78.6	18.2%	261
12/17	348.3	72.0	20.7%	215
12/16	294.3	6.0	2.0%	212
12/15	249.6	26.8	10.7%	128
12/14	227.5	60.2	26.5%	101
Annual Growth	17.4%	6.9%	—	26.8%

2018 Year-End Financials
Debt ratio: 71.6%   No. of shares (mil.): 18.7
Return on equity: 12.4%   Dividends
Cash ($ mil.): 45.3   Yield: —
Current ratio: 0.52   Payout: —
Long-term debt ($ mil.): 1,847.6   Market value ($ mil.): 436.0

	STOCK PRICE ($) FY Close	P/E High/Low		Earnings	Dividends	Book Value
12/18	23.23	8	5	3.71	0.00	37.36
12/17	28.32	10	3	3.68	0.00	27.65
12/16	8.67	33	16	0.31	0.00	24.01
12/15	10.08	20	7	1.28	0.00	22.87
12/14	23.20	9	6	2.85	0.00	21.27
Annual Growth	0.0%	—	—	6.8%	—	15.1%

CalAmp Corp

When machines talk CalAmp helps you listen. The former military supplier makes hardware and software to track trucks planes and industrial equipment and to keep them communicating. It provides asset tracking devices mobile telemetry units fixed and mobile wireless gateways and wireless router transmission for machine resource management (MRM) and machine-to-machine (M2M) communication. CalAmp keeps track of it all through cloud-based telematics and applications offered through as-a-service models. The company's customers are in the energy government heavy equipment transportation and automotive markets. CalAmp discontinued its satellite business when EchoStar its only customer consolidated suppliers.

Operations
CalAmp's operations have been segmented into Wireless Datacom and Satellite units.
Some 86% of CalAmp's 2016 (ended February) revenue came from the Wireless Datacom line with the rest generated by Satellite services.
Most of the company's manufacturing and assembly is handled by contractors.

Geographic Reach
Based in Oxnard California the company also operates wireless datacom locations in Virginia and Minnesota in the US and in Quebec Canada and Auckland New Zealand.
About 83% of sales are to customers in the US with international customers supplying the other 17%.

Sales and Marketing
CalAmp offers its wireless datacom through direct and indirect sales force in US and through sales personnel in Latin America Israel and the UK.
Its Satellite segment has sold its products primarily to EchoStar an affiliate of DISH Network which has accounted for a diminishing portion of revenue. It was 14% in 2016 (ended January) 15% in 2015 and 21% in 2014.

Financial Performance
In 2016 (ended January) CalAmp reported revenue growth of 12% to about $281 million driven by higher wireless datacom revenues (up 13%) due to increased sales of MRM products into the fleet management and non-vehicle asset tracking markets. The company also had a boost from an order from a heavy equipment manufacturer.
Net income increased 2.6% in 2016 to about $17 million from 2015. Higher sales combined with a tax benefit to produce a profit.
Cash provided by operations strengthened to $47 million in 2016 from $28.6 million in 2015.

Strategy
CalAmp is not looking back wistfully at its satellite business. With the loss of EchoStar as a customer CalAmp discontinued that part of its operations in its 2017 fiscal year ended February. It is moving deeper into wireless data communications and expects no negative impact from cutting its Satellite business.
A major way CalAmp is expanding its wireless operations is through acquisitions that add technology for MRM and M2M products and services to its lineup.

Mergers and Acquisitions
In 2018 CalAmp spent $50 million to buy Synovia to expand its software subscription services. Synovia specializes in telematics software for K-12 school buses and other fleets operated by state and local government agencies. The deal expands CalAmp's fleet management and vehicle safety services portfolio to serve another 125000 vehicles and increases its consumer reach to an average of 300000 student and parent users of Synovia's Here Comes The Bus smartphone application.
The buy adds more than 125000 vehicles to CalAmp's service base and some 300000 students and parents who use Synovia's Here Comes The Bus app which features real-time alerts on bus location for pick-ups and drop-offs.

a provider of In 2016 CalAmp spent about $131 million to buy LoJack Corp. a provider of vehicle theft recovery systems and advanced fleet management technologies. The acquisition should accelerate CalAmp's progress into the automotive telematics business.

In 2015 CalAmp Corp. made a similar acquisition with privately held Crashboxx an early stage company focused on insurance telematics applications. The price was $1.5 million.

CalAmp invested in another telematics startup SmartDriverClub Ltd. which develops connected car services and applications aimed at consumers and auto dealers in the UK.

EXECUTIVES

SVP and General Manager Satellite Products, Robert Hannah, $215,000 total compensation
EVP CFO and Secretary, Richard K. (Rick) Vitelle, age 65, $330,000 total compensation
President and CEO, Michael J. Burdiek, age 59, $440,000 total compensation
SVP Operations, John J. Warwick
SVP and General Manager Wireless Networks, Michael P. (Mike) Zachan, age 70
SVP Marketing and Business Development, Justin Schmid
SVP and General Manager MRM/M2M, Greg Gower
Senior Vice President, Richard Rose
Senior Vice President Global Sales, Carl Burrow
Vice President Business Development Insurance Telematics, Peter Byrne
Svp Product Management, Paul Washicko
Vice President Information Technology, Pete Girgis
Vice President Corporate Marketing, Nadine Traboulsi
Vice President Professional Services, Brian Burda
Chairman, A.J. (Bert) Moyer
Auditors: DELOITTE & TOUCHE LLP

LOCATIONS

HQ: CalAmp Corp
15635 Alton Parkway, Suite 250, Irvine, CA 92618
Phone: 949 600-5600
Web: www.calamp.com

PRODUCTS/OPERATIONS

2016 Sales

	$ mil.	% of total
Wireless DataCom	241.4	86
Satellite	39.3	14
Total	**280.7**	**100**

2016 Sales

	$ mil	% of total
Products		85
Application subscriptions and other services		15
Total		**100**

Selected Products

Satellite components
  Amplifiers
  Downconverters
  Feedhorns
Wireless access equipment
  Antennas
  Broadband analog scrambling/decoding systems (MultiCipher)
  Transceivers (passive planar stand-alone)

COMPETITORS

AML Communications
Broadcast Microwave Services
COM DEV
Cohu
Enfora
Filtronic
Kratos Defense & Security Solutions
Motorola Solutions
Novatel Wireless
STC Microwave Systems
Sharp Corp.
Sierra Wireless
Trimble
WebTech
Wistron NeWeb

HISTORICAL FINANCIALS

Company Type: Public

Income Statement
FYE: February 28

	REVENUE ($ mil.)	NET INCOME ($ mil.)	NET PROFIT MARGIN	EMPLOYEES
02/19	363.8	18.4	5.1%	931
02/18	365.9	16.6	4.5%	900
02/17	351.1	(7.9)	—	970
02/16	280.7	16.9	6.0%	490
02/15	250.6	16.5	6.6%	530
Annual Growth	9.8%	2.7%	—	15.1%

2019 Year-End Financials

Debt ratio: 45.7%
Return on equity: 9.1%
Cash ($ mil.): 256.5
Current ratio: 4.83
Long-term debt ($ mil.): 275.9
No. of shares (mil.): 33.5
Dividends
  Yield: —
  Payout: —
Market value ($ mil.): 466.0

	STOCK PRICE ($) FY Close	P/E High/Low		PER SHARE ($) Earnings	Dividends	Book Value
02/19	13.90	47	22	0.52	0.00	6.13
02/18	23.40	53	33	0.46	0.00	5.57
02/17	16.21	—	—	(0.22)	0.00	4.62
02/16	17.71	47	33	0.46	0.00	5.17
02/15	19.15	75	33	0.45	0.00	4.18
Annual Growth	(7.7%)	—	—	3.7%	—	10.0%

Calavo Growers, Inc.

Calavo (a combination of "California" and "avocado") began as a growers' marketing cooperative founded in 1924 in order to transform the exotic hobby crop avocados into a culinary staple. Mission accomplished. Since the avocado has become if not a staple a regular in US supermarket shopping carts. Calavo procures and processes avocados papaya pineapple tomatoes and other fresh fruits grown mainly in California but the company also uses fruit from Chile Peru and Mexico. The products are then distributed to retail food outlets food service operators and produce wholesalers throughout the world.

Operations

Calavo operates its business through three segments: Fresh Products (59% of sales in 2015) Calavo Foods (7%) and Renaissance Food Group (RFG 34%).

Some 1900 growers deliver their crops to Calavo for processing. In addition to whole avocados the company manufactures avocado pulp and frozen peeled avocado halves through its Fresh business unit. Meanwhile its Calavo Foods business unit sells guacamole and the Salsa Lisa line of fresh salsas hummus and tortilla chips. RFG produces markets and distributes healthy high-quality products (fresh-cut fruit and vegetables grab-and-go salads snacks and sandwiches) for consumers nationwide through retailers.

FreshRealm is the company's technology firm that's focused on building a platform for those who are in the fresh food business.

Geographic Reach

Calavo operates a number of facilities throughout the US including packaging houses in California and operating and distribution centers in California Arizona Florida Hawaii Minnesota New Jersey and Texas. It also has facilities in Michoacán and Jalisco Mexico.

Sales and Marketing

The company distributes its goods to food service industry and retail customers. It develops various store packaging and displays to entice buyers particularly impulse buyers in the produce section.

The Fresh Products segment's five largest customers accounted for a combined 18% of its consolidated revenues; RFG's top five customers accounted for 23% of its consolidated revenues.

Calavo logged $200000 in advertising expenses in fiscal 2015 and 2014 up from $100000 in 2013.

Financial Performance

Revenues have been on a steady rise for the past five years. In fiscal 2015 revenue increased 9% to $856.8 million largely due to growth in the RFG segment (although the Fresh Products and Calavo Foods segments also saw sales increases). RFG's growth was attributed to a rise in sales of cut fruits and vegetables and deli products.

After taking a net loss of $97000 in 2014 the company returned to the black in 2015 when net income jumped to $27.2 million. That turnaround was partly due to higher sales but also due to the absence of contingent considerations related to the 2011 acquisition of RFG. Cash flow from operations rose 52% to $37.2 million that year.

Strategy

The Calavo Foods and RFG segments represent the company's move beyond fresh avocados and commodity produce into the market for fresh refrigerated packaged foods. It has expanded such holdings through acquisitions.

In the Fresh Products segment Calavo still seeks to expand its presence in the avocado market but also considers the distribution of other promising crops. In order to grow its business the company pursues partnerships with major food services companies.

In 2015 Calavo added a second packinghouse in Mexico in the prime growing region of Jalisco.

EXECUTIVES

Chairman President and CEO, Lecil E. (Lee) Cole, age 80, $635,133 total compensation
VP Sales and Fresh Marketing, Robert J. (Rob) Wedin, age 70, $309,356 total compensation
Director Operations Calavo de México, Dionisio Ortiz
VP Fresh Operations, Michael A. (Mike) Browne, age 61, $309,356 total compensation
CFO and Secretary, B. John Lindeman, $325,000 total compensation
VP Foods Division Sales and Operations, Ron Araiza
Board Member, John Hunt
Board Member, Marc Brown

Board Member, Egidio Carbone
Board Member, Scott Van Der Kar
Board Member, Harold Edwards
Auditors: DELOITTE & TOUCHE LLP

LOCATIONS

HQ: Calavo Growers, Inc.
1141-A Cummings Road, Santa Paula, CA 93060
Phone: 805 525-1245   **Fax:** 805 921-3223
Web: www.calavo.com

PRODUCTS/OPERATIONS

2015 Sales

	$ mil.	% of total
Fresh Products	500.7	59
RFG (Renaissance Food Group)	293.9	34
Calavo Foods	62.2	7
Total	**856.8**	**100**

Selected Products

Fresh
  Whole avocado
  Avocado halves
  Avocado pulp
  Papaya
  Pineapple
  Tomato
Calavo Foods
  Guacamole
  Salsa Lisa
  Tortilla chips

Selected Services

Growing
Ripening
Packing
Sales
Warehousing
Shipping & distribution

COMPETITORS

Azteca Foods	Gentile Bros.
BC Hot House Foods	Giumarra Companies
Brooks Tropicals	Goya
Caribe Food	Gruma Corporation
Chiquita Brands	Grupo Bimbo
Coast Citrus	H. J. Heinz Limited
Distributors	Hain Celestial
ConAgra	Index Fresh
Dole Food	Interfresh
Don Miguel Mexican	JR Simplot
Foods	La Tortilla Factory
Eastern Fresh Growers	Oceanside Produce
Inc.	Pacific Tomato Growers
Fresh Del Monte	Pinos Produce
Produce	Rancho Mission Viejo
FreshPoint	Shamrock Foods

HISTORICAL FINANCIALS

Company Type: Public

Income Statement   FYE: October 31

	REVENUE ($ mil.)	NET INCOME ($ mil.)	NET PROFIT MARGIN	EMPLOYEES
10/19	1,195.7	36.6	3.1%	3,657
10/18	1,088.7	32.2	3.0%	2,979
10/17	1,075.5	37.2	3.5%	2,516
10/16	935.6	38.0	4.1%	2,096
10/15	856.8	27.2	3.2%	2,064
Annual Growth	8.7%	7.7%	—	15.4%

2019 Year-End Financials

Debt ratio: 1.5%   No. of shares (mil.): 17.6
Return on equity: 13.3%   Dividends
Cash ($ mil.): 7.9   Yield: 0.0%
Current ratio: 1.41   Payout: 48.0%
Long-term debt ($ mil.): 5.4   Market value ($ mil.): 1,526.0

	STOCK PRICE ($) FY Close	P/E High/Low	Earnings	Dividends	Book Value
10/19	86.73	48 34	2.08	1.00	16.15
10/18	97.00	58 37	1.84	0.95	14.98
10/17	73.70	36 24	2.13	0.90	13.87
10/16	59.15	32 22	2.18	0.80	12.28
10/15	51.41	39 25	1.57	0.75	10.64
Annual Growth	14.0%	— —	7.3%	7.5%	11.0%

California Bancorp

Auditors: Crowe LLP

LOCATIONS

HQ: California Bancorp
1300 Clay Street, Suite 500, Oakland, CA 94612
Phone: 510 457-3751
Web: www.californiabankofcommerce.com

HISTORICAL FINANCIALS

Company Type: Public

Income Statement   FYE: December 31

	REVENUE ($ mil.)	NET INCOME ($ mil.)	NET PROFIT MARGIN	EMPLOYEES
12/18	44.6	8.7	19.5%	0
12/17	37.7	5.6	14.9%	0
12/16	32.3	5.1	16.1%	99
12/15	20.9	2.2	10.8%	0
Annual Growth	28.6%	56.6%	—	—

2018 Year-End Financials

Debt ratio: 0.4%   No. of shares (mil.): 7.9
Return on equity: 8.4%   Dividends
Cash ($ mil.): 78.7   Yield: —
Current ratio: 0.09   Payout: —
Long-term debt ($ mil.): 4.9   Market value ($ mil.): 139.0

	STOCK PRICE ($) FY Close	P/E High/Low	Earnings	Dividends	Book Value
12/18	17.45	20 14	1.19	0.00	15.15
12/17	21.75	24 21	0.85	0.00	13.21
12/16	0.00	— —	0.80	0.00	12.42
Annual Growth	—	— —	22.0%	—	10.4%

Callaway Golf Co (DE)

EXECUTIVES

SEVP and Chief Administrative Officer, Steven C. (Steve) McCracken, age 65, $550,000 total compensation
President CEO and Director, Oliver G. (Chip) Brewer III, age 52
SEVP and CFO, Bradley J. (Brad) Holiday, age 62, $500,000 total compensation
Chairman, Ronald S. Beard, age 77
SVP and General Counsel, Mike Rider
VP Business Innovation, Mike Yagley
Managing Director Europe Middle East and Africa, Neil Howie
SVP International, Thomas T. Yang, age 63, $385,000 total compensation
VP Public Relations, Michele Szynal
SVP Operations, David A. Laverty, age 58, $360,000 total compensation
SVP Global Brand and Product, Jeffrey M. (Jeff) Colton, age 43
Director European Marketing, Jeff Dodds
VP Finance and Investor Relations, Eric Struik
Contact, Tim Buckman
Director Callaway Golf KK; President Asia, Alex M. Boezeman
Managing Director Southeast Asia South Pacific and India, Leighton Richards
Senior Vice President Of Marketing, Harry Arnett
Director, John C. Cushman III, age 75
Director, John F. Lundgren, age 64
Director, Samuel H. Armacost, age 77
Director, Yotaro Kobayashi, age 83
Director, Richard L. (Rick) Rosenfield, age 70
President CEO and Director, Oliver G. (Chip) Brewer III, age 52
Director, Anthony S. (Tony) Thornley, age 70
Director, Adebayo O. (Bayo) Ogunlesi, age 63
Auditors: DELOITTE & TOUCHE LLP

LOCATIONS

HQ: Callaway Golf Co (DE)
2180 Rutherford Road, Carlsbad, CA 92008
Phone: 760 931-1771
Web: www.callawaygolf.com

COMPETITORS

Acushnet	McHenry Metals Golf
Adams Golf	Mitsushiba
Amer Sports	International
Bridgestone	Mizuno
Cleveland Golf	NIKE
Dick's Sporting Goods	PUMA SE
Eaton	Sumitomo Rubber
Garmin	TaylorMade-adidas Golf
Karsten	Yamaha

HISTORICAL FINANCIALS

Company Type: Public

Income Statement   FYE: December 31

	REVENUE ($ mil.)	NET INCOME ($ mil.)	NET PROFIT MARGIN	EMPLOYEES
12/18	1,242.8	104.7	8.4%	2,400
12/17	1,048.7	40.8	3.9%	2,100
12/16	871.1	189.9	21.8%	1,700
12/15	843.7	14.5	1.7%	1,700
12/14	886.9	16.0	1.8%	1,700
Annual Growth	8.8%	59.9%	—	9.0%

Callon Petroleum Co. (DE)

Callon Petroleum can call on new technologies to find old petroleum resources employing computer-aided techniques such as enhanced 3-D surveys and horizontal drilling to explore and develop oil and gas properties. It also focuses on acquiring properties. Once a major offshore player the firm's holdings are now primarily onshore in Texas. In 2012 Callon's estimated proved reserves stood at 14.1 million barrels of oil equivalent. About 68% of Callon's oil and gas reserves are located onshore in the Permian Basin; 77% of its proved reserve volumes are in the form of crude oil which also accounts for the bulk of its the company's revenues.

Operations
Callon produced nearly 1.6 million barrels of oil equivalent of natural gas and NGLs and crude oil in 2012.

That year the company derived about 87% of its revenues from crude oil sales; the remaining came from natural gas and NGL sales.

Sales and Marketing
Callon's production is sold generally on month-to-month contracts at prevailing prices. Shell Trading Company and Enterprise Crude Oil accounted for 39% and 32% of its 2012 net sales respectively.

Financial Performance
The company's revenues declined by 13% in 2012 due to lower sales of crude oil natural gas and NGLs.

In 2012 Callon's crude oil sales decreased due to lower commodity prices and a drop in production volumes as the result of down-time at the Habanero and Medusa fields and the normal declines from its other offshore properties. These production declines were offset by new production from its Permian wells (22 vertical and two horizontal) which began production that year.

Natural gas revenues also declined in 2012 due to lower production driven by down time at its Haynesville well (which was shut-in for 70 days) and at its East Cameron 257 well (which was suspended due to a natural gas leak in an upstream section of the Stingray Pipeline that transports production volumes from the field). The average realized price for natural gas also decreased by 25% in 2012 although the value of the NGLs in its natural gas stream (from its Permian basin and deepwater production) kept Callon's natural gas sales prices above NYMEX prices.

The company's net income decreased by 97% in 2012 due to lower revenues and higher income tax expenses.

Strategy
To secure better long term returns Callon is shifting its asset base from primarily offshore to primarily onshore. It is focused on bringing its existing Permian acreage position to production and on making opportunistic producing property and leasehold acquisitions. The company is developing an established production base from vertical Wolfberry wells. It is also drilling an inventory of horizontal locations identified in the southern Midland basin and is conducting exploration activities on its acreage in the northern Midland basin.

To pay down debt in 2013 Callon sold its interests in the Medusa field Medusa Spar LLC and all of its Gulf of Mexico shelf assets for $88 million.

The company's estimated proved reserves decreased by 12% in fiscal 2012 due to the sale of its stake in the Habanero field and the downward revision of its Haynesville Shale undeveloped reserves (reduced due to low natural gas pricing assumptions). These decreases were partially offset by the company's development of a portion of its Permian Basin on which it added seven proved developed producing and 19 proved undeveloped reserve wells during 2012.

To increase its financial flexibility in 2012 it sold its 11.25% working interest in the Habanero field (Garden Banks Block 341) to a Royal Dutch Shell unit for $39 million.

Mergers and Acquisitions
In 2016 Callon agreed to buy certain undeveloped acreage and producing oil and gas assets in the Southern Delaware Basin for $615 million.

Company Background
In 2012 Callon spent about $32 million to acquire 16233 gross (14653 net) acres in Borden county Texas (in the northern Midland basin) an additional 8095 gross acres (6964 net) in this area and 2319 gross (1762 net) acres in southern Reagan county Texas

In light of a weak economy the company's strategy (reported in 2009) was to reduce its oil and gas exploration in the Gulf of Mexico focus on longer-lived lower risk onshore US properties (such as its Haynesville Shale development) and to seek partnerships in order to finance its future property acquisitions.

Boosting its onshore assets in 2009 Callon acquired stakes in 22 producing wells in Crockett Ector Midland and Upton counties (in West Texas) for $16.3 million. In 2010 the company received a cash injection of $44.7 million when the federal Bureau of Ocean Energy Management Regulation and Enforcement reimbursed it for overpayment of royalties at its Medusa asset in the Gulf of Mexico.

To raise cash to pay down debt in 2008 it sold a 50% stake in the Entrada Field in the Gulf of Mexico (it acquired an 80% stake a year earlier) to CIECO for $175 million. In 2007 the company sold non-operated onshore royalty and mineral interests for $61.5 million to Indigo Minerals LLC.

Callon was formed in 1994 through the consolidation of a publicly traded limited partnership an independent energy company owned by some members of current Callon management and a joint venture with a consortium of European entities.

EXECUTIVES

Controller Callon Petroleum Company and Callon Petroleum Operating Company, Mitzi P. Conn, age 49, $198,370 total compensation
SVP and COO, Gary A. Newberry, age 64, $367,308 total compensation
President CEO and CFO, Joseph C. Gatto, age 48, $367,308 total compensation
VP Land, Jerry A. Weant, age 60, $250,000 total compensation
VP Permian Operations, Michael O'Connor
Chairman, L. Richard Flury, age 72
Board of Directors, Tony Nocchiero
Auditors: Grant Thornton LLP

LOCATIONS

HQ: Callon Petroleum Co. (DE)
One Briarlake Plaza, 2000 W. Sam Houston Parkway S., Suite 2000, Houston, TX 77042
Phone: 281 589-5200
Web: www.callon.com

PRODUCTS/OPERATIONS

2015 Sales

	$ mil.	% of total
Oil sales	125.2	91
Natural gas sales	12.3	9
Total	**137.5**	**100**

COMPETITORS

Abraxas Petroleum	Parallel Petroleum
Apache	Pioneer Natural
BP	Resources
Carrizo Oil & Gas	Range Resources
Devon Energy	SM Energy
Exxon Mobil	TOTAL
Occidental Oil and Gas	

HISTORICAL FINANCIALS

Company Type: Public

Income Statement
FYE: December 31

	REVENUE ($ mil.)	NET INCOME ($ mil.)	NET PROFIT MARGIN	EMPLOYEES
12/18	587.6	300.3	51.1%	218
12/17	366.4	120.4	32.9%	169
12/16	200.8	(91.8)	—	121
12/15	137.5	(240.1)	—	93
12/14	151.8	37.7	24.9%	109
Annual Growth	40.3%	67.9%	—	18.9%

2018 Year-End Financials

Debt ratio: 29.8%
Return on equity: 13.9%
Cash ($ mil.): 16.0
Current ratio: 0.71
Long-term debt ($ mil.): 1,189.4
No. of shares (mil.): 227.5
Dividends
  Yield: —
  Payout: —
Market value ($ mil.): 1,477.0

	STOCK PRICE ($) FY Close	P/E High/Low		PER SHARE ($) Earnings	Dividends	Book Value
12/18	6.49	11	4	1.35	0.00	10.74
12/17	12.15	29	17	0.56	0.00	9.20
12/16	15.37	—	—	(0.78)	0.00	8.62
12/15	8.34	—	—	(3.77)	0.00	4.53
12/14	5.45	18	6	0.65	0.00	7.85
Annual Growth	4.5%		—	20.0%	—	8.1%

2018 Year-End Financials

Debt ratio: 4.7%
Return on equity: 15.2%
Cash ($ mil.): 63.9
Current ratio: 1.73
Long-term debt ($ mil.): 7.2
No. of shares (mil.): 94.5
Dividends
  Yield: 0.2%
  Payout: 3.7%
Market value ($ mil.): 1,446.0

	STOCK PRICE ($) FY Close	P/E High/Low		PER SHARE ($) Earnings	Dividends	Book Value
12/18	15.30	22	12	1.08	0.04	7.67
12/17	13.93	36	23	0.42	0.04	6.86
12/16	10.96	6	4	1.98	0.04	6.36
12/15	9.42	57	42	0.17	0.04	4.40
12/14	7.70	49	33	0.20	0.04	3.76
Annual Growth	18.7%		—	52.4%	(0.0%)	19.5%

Cambridge Bancorp

Cambridge Bancorp is the nearly $2 billion-asset holding company for Cambridge Trust Company a community bank serving Cambridge and the Greater Boston area through about a dozen branch locations in Massachusetts. It offers standard retail products and services including checking and savings accounts CDs IRAs and credit cards. Residential mortgages including home equity loans account for about 50% of the company's loan portfolio while commercial real estate loans make up more than 40%. The company also offers commercial industrial and consumer loans. Established in 1892 the bank also offers trust and investment management services.

Operations
The commercial bank operates a traditional retail banking line focused on lending as well as its Wealth Management Group which investment management and trust business. The bank had $1.8 billion in total assets and $2.4 billion in client assets under management at the end of 2015.

As with other retail banks Cambridge Bancorp makes the bulk of its revenue from interest income. About 58% of its total revenue came from loan interest during 2015 while another 10% came from interest on taxable and tax-exempt investment securities. The rest of its revenue came from wealth management income (24% of revenue) deposit account fees (3%) ATM/Debit card income (1%) and other non-interest income sources.

Geographic Reach
Cambridge Bancorp has 12 branches in Massachusetts in Cambridge Boston Belmont Concord Lexington Lincoln and Weston. It also has wealth management offices in Boston as well as in New Hampshire in Concord Manchester and Portsmouth.

Sales and Marketing
The company spent $2.38 million on marketing during 2015 up from $2.12 million in 2014.

Financial Performance
Cambridge's annual revenues and profits have been steadily rising over the past several years thanks to continued commercial real estate mortgage growth and as its Wealth Management business has nearly doubled its managed assets since 2011 spurring higher fee revenue.

The bank's revenue climbed 7% to $80.2 million during 2015 on 10% loan growth mostly driven by commercial real estate loans which spurred higher interest income. The company's wealth management business income grew 7% as its client assets continued to grow with new investor inflows.

Revenue growth in 2015 drove Cambridge Bancorp's net income up 5% to $15.7 million. The bank's operating cash levels rose 24% to $20 million for the year with an increase in cash-based earnings and favorable changes in working capital mostly related to a change in accrued interest receivable deferred taxes and other assets and liabilities.

Strategy
Cambridge Bancorp continued in 2016 to lean on the success of its commercial mortgage business though it plans to pivot more to commercial and industrial lending to diversify its commercial lending portfolio.

To better prepare for rising interest rates Cambridge Bancorp in 2015 and 2016 modified its commercial loan strategy from long-term fixed-rate loans (which are vulnerable to interest rate risk) to a new interest rate derivative product to offer an alternative long-term financing for its customers while helping the bank earn a variable rate of interest on its loans. For its consumer banking unit the bank in 2015 began a plan to sell the majority of its long-term residential mortgage production including secondary loans to the secondary market.

EXECUTIVES
Chairman President and CEO, Denis K. Sheahan, age 53
SVP and Chief Investment Officer, James F. Spencer
SVP Commercial Real Estate Cambridge Trust, Martin B. Millane
EVP and CIO Cambridge Trust, Lynne M. Burrow
EVP and Head of Wealth Management Cambridge Trust, Michael A. Duca
EVP and Consumer Banking Director Cambridge Trust, Thomas A. Johnson
CFO, Michael Carotenuto
SVP and President Cambridge Trust Company of New Hampshire, Susan Martore-Baker
SVP and Marketing Director, Robert N. Siegrist
Vp Finance, Patricia Hartnett
Vice President, Laura Mcgregor
Assistant Vice President And Tax Manager, Theresa Giglio
Assistant Vp Private Banking, Scott Mcgill
Avp Compliance Officer, Philip Pace
Assistant Vice President And Branch Manager, Fenton Martin
Vice President And Manager Of Community Business Development, Dina Scianna
Avp Hr Business Partner And Recruiter, Ashley Thomas
Auditors: KPMG LLP

LOCATIONS
HQ: Cambridge Bancorp
1336 Massachusetts Avenue, Cambridge, MA 02138
Phone: 617 876-5500
Web: www.cambridgetrust.com

PRODUCTS/OPERATIONS

2015 Sales

	% of total
Interest Income	
Interest on loans	58
Interest on taxable investment securities	7
Interest on tax exempt investment securities	3
Non-Interest Income	
Wealth Management Income	24
Deposits accounts fee	3
ATM/Debit card income	1
Bank Owned life insurance income	1
Gain on disposition on investment securities	1
Gain on loans held of sale	1
Other income	1
Loan related derivative income	—
Total	**100**

Products/Services
Personal Banking
Checking
Savings CDs & IRAs
Online Banking
Mobile Banking
Mortgages
Home Equity
Credit Cards
Personal Loans
More Services
Business Banking
Checking & Savings
Commercial Lending
Commercial Real Estate
Cash Management
Remote Deposit Capture
Online Banking
Mobile Banking
Professional Services Program
More Services
Wealth Management
Investment Process
Investment Management
Fiduciary & Planning Services
Estate Settlement
Wealth Management Personnel
Forums
Online Access

COMPETITORS
Bank of America
Cambridge Financial
Central Bancorp
Century Bancorp (MA)
Citizens Financial Group
Eastern Bank
Middlesex Savings
Peoples Federal Bancshares Inc.

HISTORICAL FINANCIALS
Company Type: Public

Income Statement — FYE: December 31

	ASSETS ($ mil.)	NET INCOME ($ mil.)	INCOME AS % OF ASSETS	EMPLOYEES
12/18	2,101.3	23.8	1.1%	262
12/17	1,949.9	14.8	0.8%	247
12/16	1,849.0	16.9	0.9%	0
12/15	1,706.2	15.6	0.9%	0
12/14	1,573.6	14.9	0.9%	0
Annual Growth	7.5%	12.4%	—	—

2018 Year-End Financials
Return on assets: 1.1%
Return on equity: 15.1%
Long-term debt ($ mil.): —
No. of shares (mil.): 4.1
Sales ($ mil): 102.0
Dividends
Yield: 2.3%
Payout: 41.3%
Market value ($ mil.): 342.0

	STOCK PRICE ($) FY Close	P/E High/Low	PER SHARE ($) Earnings	Dividends	Book Value
12/18	83.25	16 13	5.77	1.96	40.67
12/17	79.80	24 17	3.61	1.86	36.24
12/16	62.29	15 11	4.15	1.84	33.36
12/15	47.40	13 11	3.93	1.80	31.26
12/14	46.50	13 10	3.78	1.68	29.50
Annual Growth	15.7%	— —	11.2%	3.9%	8.4%

Camden National Corp. (ME)

Camden National Corporation is the holding company for Camden National Bank which boasts nearly 45 branches in about a dozen Maine counties and provides standard deposit products such as checking and savings accounts CDs and IRAs. Commercial mortgages and loans make up 50%

of its loan portfolio while residential mortgages make up another 40% and consumer loans constitute the remainder. Subsidiary Acadia Trust provides trust fiduciary investment management and retirement plan administration services while Camden Financial Consultants offers brokerage and insurance services. The largest bank headquartered in Maine Camden National Bank was founded in 1875 and once issued its own US currency.

Operations

About 63% of Camden National's total revenue came from loan interest (including fees) in 2014 while another 15% came from interest on its US government and sponsored enterprise obligations (investment securities). The rest of its revenue came from deposit account service charges (5%) other service charges and fees (5%) income from fiduciary services (4%) brokerage and insurance commissions (2%) and other miscellaneous income sources. The bank had a staff of 471 employees at the end of 2014.

Geographic Reach

Camden National has around 45 branches in 12 counties throughout Maine with one commercial loan office in Manchester New Hampshire. Its primary markets are in the counties of Androscoggin Cumberland Hancock Kennebec Knox Lincoln Penobscot Piscataquis Somerset Waldo Washington and York.

Sales and Marketing

The company offers deposit and loan services to consumers institutions municipalities non-profits and commercial customers.

Financial Performance

The company has struggled to consistently grow its revenues and profits in recent years mostly due to shrinking interest margins on loans amidst the low-interest environment.

Camden National's revenue dipped by 3% to $112.8 million in 2014 mostly because the bank in 2013 had collected a non-recurring $2.7 million gain from the sale of its five Franklin County branches and because its mortgage banking income fell by $1.1 million as it decided to retain most of its 30-year fixed rate residential mortgage production in 2014.

Despite revenue declines in 2014 the bank's net income jumped by 8% to $24.6 million mostly because in 2013 it had recorded a non-recurring $2.8 million goodwill impairment charge related to its financial services reporting unit. Camden's operating cash levels rose by 1% to $29.9 million for the year on higher cash earnings.

Strategy

The bank competes with larger financial institutions by emphasizing customer service to build customer loyalty and long-term relationships. It also sometimes pursues acquisitions of banks and branches in its target markets in Maine to grow its loan and deposit business.

Camden may also be expanding its franchise beyond Maine in future years. In 2014 it opened a commercial loan office in Manchester New Hampshire enabling it to serve more customers across northern New England.

Mergers and Acquisitions

In March 2015 Camden National Corporation agreed to purchase SBM Financial along with its subsidiary The Bank of Maine subsidiary. The deal expected to be completed in late 2015 would add $813 million in assets and make Camden National Bank Maine's largest community bank.

In late 2012 the bank acquired 15 full-service branches from Bank of America for $12 million.

EXECUTIVES

Vice President risk Management, Steve Matteo
EVP COO and CFO, Deborah A. Jordan, age 53, $223,327 total compensation
EVP Retail Banking, June B. Parent, age 55, $189,248 total compensation
EVP Risk Management, Joanne T. Campbell, age 56, $124,585 total compensation
President and CEO, Gregory A. (Greg) Dufour, age 58, $398,077 total compensation
SVP Information Technology, Scott Buckheit
EVP Commercial Lending, Timothy P. Nightingale, age 61, $213,846 total compensation
Vice President, Richard Nickerson
Vice President Compliance Manager, Jennifer Mazurek
Vice President, Cynthia Bergin
Vice President Information Security Manager, Anthony Mazzeo
Vice President Credit Risk Officer, Susan Weber
Vice President Loan Servicing, Mark Richards
Vice President of Mortgage Operations, Paul Palmer
Senior Vice President Director of Corporate Services, Susan Giffard
Vice President Commercial Portfolio Manager, Matthew Gilbert
Senior Vice President Commercial Lending Officer, Stephen Lawrence
Vice President Senior Trust Officer, Lauren Epstein
Chairman Camden National Corporation and Camden National Bank, Karen W. Stanley, age 73
Secretary, Diane Marion
Auditors: RSM US LLP

LOCATIONS

HQ: Camden National Corp. (ME)
2 Elm Street, Camden, ME 04843
Phone: 207 236-8821 **Fax:** 207 236-6256
Web: www.CamdenNational.com/healthprofunding

PRODUCTS/OPERATIONS

2014 Sales

	$ mil.	% of total
Interest		
Loans including fees	70.7	63
US government & agency securities	17.4	14
Other investments	0.4	1
Noninterest		
Service charges on deposit accounts & others	12.4	11
Income from fiduciary services	5.0	4
Brokerage and insurance commission	1.7	2
Other	5.2	5
Total	**112.8**	**100**

COMPETITORS

Bangor Savings Bank	People's United Financial
Bar Harbor Bankshares	TD Bank USA
KeyCorp	The First Bancorp
Northeast Bancorp	
Norway Bancorp	

HISTORICAL FINANCIALS

Company Type: Public

Income Statement FYE: December 31

	ASSETS ($ mil.)	NET INCOME ($ mil.)	INCOME AS % OF ASSETS	EMPLOYEES
12/18	4,297.4	53.0	1.2%	634
12/17	4,065.4	28.4	0.7%	636
12/16	3,864.2	40.0	1.0%	631
12/15	3,709.8	20.9	0.6%	652
12/14	2,789.8	24.5	0.9%	471
Annual Growth	11.4%	21.2%	—	7.7%

2018 Year-End Financials

Return on assets: 1.2% Dividends
Return on equity: 12.6% Yield: 3.0%
Long-term debt ($ mil.): — Payout: 47.8%
No. of shares (mil.): 15.5 Market value ($ mil.): 561.0
Sales ($ mil): 189.5

	STOCK PRICE ($) FY Close	P/E High/Low		PER SHARE ($) Earnings	Dividends	Book Value
12/18	35.97	14	10	3.39	1.10	27.95
12/17	42.13	26	20	1.82	0.92	25.99
12/16	44.45	19	11	2.57	0.80	25.30
12/15	44.09	26	21	1.73	0.80	23.69
12/14	39.84	19	16	2.19	0.72	22.00
Annual Growth	(2.5%)	—	—	11.6%	11.2%	6.2%

Cantel Medical Corp

Just ask Cantel Medical — cleanliness is second to nothing when it comes to medical and scientific equipment. Through its subsidiaries the firm sells infection prevention and control products to hospitals dentists drug makers researchers and others in the US and abroad in the field of health care. Its diverse offerings include medical device reprocessing systems and disinfectants for dialyzers and endoscopes water purification equipment masks and bibs used in dental offices and therapeutic filtration systems. Fast-growing Cantel Medical employs an active acquisition strategy.

Operations

Cantel Medical's major subsidiaries include: Mar Con Purification (water filtration and purification); Medivators (disposables disinfection sterilization); Crosstex (infection control and prevention); and Saf-T-Pak (packaging medical shipping systems). International units include Cantel Medical (UK) Cantel Medical Asia/Pacific Cantel Medical Devices (China) Biolab Equipment Medivators and Cantel Medical (Italy).

The company operates through four segments: Endoscopy Water Purification and Filtration Healthcare Disposables and Dialysis.

Endoscopy products include medical device reprocessing systems disinfectants detergents and other supplies for disinfection. The segment also provides technical maintenance services. Endoscopy is Cantel Medical's largest segment accounting for more than half of its total revenue.

Water Purification and Filtration offerings include filtration and separation products disinfectants and sterilization and decontamination products for the medical biotech pharmaceutical beverage and commercial industrial industries. That segment accounts for about a quarter of total sales.

Meanwhile Healthcare Disposable offers single-use products such as face masks sterilization pouches towels and bibs tray covers saliva ejectors wipes and disinfectants as well as products for maintaining safe dental unit waterlines. Healthcare Disposables contributes about 15% of Cantel's total sales.

The smallest segment Dialysis (about 5% of sales) provides medical device reprocessing systems sterilants and disinfectants dialysate concentrates and other supplies used in renal dialysis.

Geographic Reach
Cantel Medical rings up about 80% of its sales in the US. Foreign markets include Canada Europe Africa the Middle East South America and the Asia/Pacific region.

Sales and Marketing
Cantel's customers include diagnostic clinical and university laboratories; pharma and biotech companies; US and Canadian government agencies; hospitals; and medical research facilities.

In the US the company uses its own sales force to market its products; in international markets it employs independent distribution companies

In fiscal 2016 (ended July) Cantel Medical spent $3.3 million on advertising in line with what it spent in 2015 and up from the $2.7 million it spent in 2014.

Financial Performance
Cantel Medical's revenues and net income have been steadily rising for the past five years. In fiscal 2016 (ended July) revenue rose 18% to $664.8 million as organic product sales and service income increased. Growing demand in the endoscopy market was a primary driver of the higher sales; additionally in the health care disposables business the company's profits increased as Cantel sold more higher margin product and demand for its products grew in response to the Ebola virus. Overall net income rose 25% to $60 million thanks to the higher revenue but partially offset by higher cost of sales and operating expenses (including growth initiatives).

Strategy
Cantel Medical intends to double its sales and profits within the next five years. It has seen strong growth in its endoscopy and health care disposables businesses thanks partly to acquisitions of other firms that have added to its product portfolio.

The company has grown and diversified by employing an active acquisition strategy. It targets companies in the infection prevention and control market health care disposable products and water purification and filtration markets among others. More recently Cantel has focused on endoscopy its largest segment. It supplements acquisitions with occasional product launches such as the recently introduced SECURE FIT earloop face mask.

In 2015 the company sold its specialty packaging business a non-core operation.

Mergers and Acquisitions
In early 2019 Cantel Medical acquired Vista Research Group which makes water treatment purification and management products for the dental industry. The $10.5 million purchase expanded Cantel's dental water purification portfolio.

The company acquired Belgium-based Aexis Medical for $24.8 million in 2018. Aexis specializes in data analytics particularly around the area of infection prevention.

In mid-2017 Cantel acquired Germany's BHT Group for $60.8 million. BHT holds a portfolio of automatic endoscope reprocessors and endoscope drying and storage cabinets. With the purchase Cantel expanded its international endoscopy business.

EXECUTIVES

President Asia Pacific and Emerging Markets, David Rosen
EVP General Counsel and Secretary, Eric W. Nodiff, age 62, $361,875 total compensation
CEO, Jorgen B. Hansen, age 53, $453,529 total compensation
EVP and CFO, Peter G. Clifford, age 50, $128,077 total compensation
President Medivators Division, David C. Hemink
President Americas Sales and Global Service, Michael G. Spicer
Vice President Global Research and Development, Suranjan Roychowdhury
Vice President Deputy General Counsel, Jeff Mann
Vice Chairman, George L. Fotiades, age 66
Chairman, Charles M. Diker, age 84
Auditors: DELOITTE & TOUCHE LLP

LOCATIONS

HQ: Cantel Medical Corp
150 Clove Road, Little Falls, NJ 07424
Phone: 973 890-7220   **Fax:** 973 890-7270
Web: www.cantelmedical.com

PRODUCTS/OPERATIONS

2016 Sales

	$ mil.	% of total
Endoscopy	341.7	51
Water purification & filtration	177.6	27
Healthcare Disposables	112.6	17
Dialysis	32.8	5
Total	**664.7**	**100**

Selected Acquisitions
FY2014
  PuriCore International Limited ($27 million; Somerset UK; endoscope products)
FY2013
  Jet Prep Ltd ($5 million; Herzliya Israel; developer of JET PREP Flushing device)
FY2012
  Byrne Medical Inc. ($100 million; Houston TX; infection control products)
FY2011
  ConFirm Monitoring Systems Inc. ($7.5 million; Denver Colorado; sterilization monitoring products)
  Gambro Medical Water Systems ($23.7 million; Colorado; production of medical grade water)

Selected Subsidiaries
Biolab Equipment Ltd.
Carsen Group Inc. (Canada)
Crosstex International Inc.
Medivators Inc.
Medivators Japan K.K.
Saf-T-Pak Inc. (Canada)
Strong Dental Products Inc.

COMPETITORS

3M Health Care	Getinge
CONMED Corporation	Johnson & Johnson
Danaher	Kimberly-Clark Health
Dentsply Sirona	Olympus
Ecolab	STERIS
Fresenius	Siemens AG
GE Water and Process	TIDI Products
Technologies	

HISTORICAL FINANCIALS
Company Type: Public

Income Statement
FYE: July 31

	REVENUE ($ mil.)	NET INCOME ($ mil.)	NET PROFIT MARGIN	EMPLOYEES
07/19	918.1	55.0	6.0%	2,775
07/18	871.9	91.0	10.4%	2,693
07/17	770.1	71.3	9.3%	2,337
07/16	664.7	59.9	9.0%	2,000
07/15	565.0	47.9	8.5%	1,680
Annual Growth	12.9%	3.5%	—	13.4%

2019 Year-End Financials
Debt ratio: 21.5%
Return on equity: 8.6%
Cash ($ mil.): 44.5
Current ratio: 2.32
Long-term debt ($ mil.): 220.8
No. of shares (mil.): 41.7
Dividends
  Yield: 0.2%
  Payout: 15.1%
Market value ($ mil.): 3,855.0

	STOCK PRICE ($) FY Close	P/E High/Low		PER SHARE ($) Earnings	Dividends	Book Value
07/19	92.28	74	49	1.32	0.20	15.84
07/18	92.71	60	34	2.18	0.17	14.60
07/17	74.20	50	40	1.71	0.14	12.56
07/16	66.95	51	34	1.44	0.12	10.89
07/15	54.88	48	29	1.15	0.10	9.77
Annual Growth	13.9%	—	—	3.5%	18.9%	12.8%

Capital Bancorp Inc (MD)

Auditors: Elliott Davis, PLLC

LOCATIONS

HQ: Capital Bancorp Inc (MD)
2275 Research Boulevard, Suite 600, Rockville, MD 20850
Phone: 301 468-8848
Web: www.capitalbankmd.com

HISTORICAL FINANCIALS
Company Type: Public

Income Statement
FYE: December 31

	ASSETS ($ mil.)	NET INCOME ($ mil.)	INCOME AS % OF ASSETS	EMPLOYEES
12/18	1,105.0	12.7	1.2%	204
12/17	1,026.0	7.1	0.7%	195
12/16	905.6	9.4	1.0%	0
12/15	743.4	7.4	1.0%	0
Annual Growth	14.1%	19.4%	—	—

2018 Year-End Financials
Return on assets: 1.2%
Return on equity: 13.1%
Long-term debt ($ mil.): —
No. of shares (mil.): 13.6
Sales ($ mil): 85.2
Dividends
  Yield: —
  Payout: —
Market value ($ mil.): 156.0

	STOCK PRICE ($) FY Close	P/E High/Low	PER SHARE ($) Earnings	Dividends	Book Value
12/18	11.41	13 11	1.02	0.00	8.38
12/17	0.00	— —	0.62	0.00	6.94
Annual Growth	—	— —	64.5%	—	20.7%

Capital Southwest Corp.

A private equity firm Capital Southwest owns significant minority stakes in around 30 companies many of them in Texas. The business development company (BDC) offers growth capital recapitalization and acquisition financing and funding for management buyouts to companies in a variety of industries. It typically invests between $5 million to $15 million per transaction in target firms which do not include troubled companies startups real estate developments or other less-than-stable ventures. The company is also focused on investments in the US especially firms located in the Southwest Southeast Midwest and Mountain regions.

Operations
Its 12 largest holdings including Alamo Group The RectorSeal corporation Trax Holdings and The Whitmore Manufacturing Company account for more than 95% of the value of its investment portfolio. An active investor Capital Southwest is usually represented on its portfolio companies' boards and provides strategic and financial advice in addition to capital. The company claims to have the flexibility to hold onto its investments indefinitely; indeed its average holding period is around 20 years.

Sales and Marketing
Capital Southwest focuses on investing in the energy services industrial technologies and specialty chemicals sectors.

Financial Performance
Capital Southwest has enjoyed a steady rise in revenues over the last three years. Revenues climbed 16% from $9.3 million in 2012 to $10.8 million in 2013 due to increased dividend and interest income. Profits surged 16% from $92 million to $107 million as the company made about $88 million on selling several investments during 2013.

Strategy
Like all private equity firms the company generates additional cash by net realized gain on investments. In 2013 it sold 2774250 shares of common stock in Encore Wire Corporation generating a capital gain of $66 million. It also sold all its ownership in Extreme International generating net cash proceeds of nearly $11 million. In addition it sold all its investment ownership in Heelys and earned cash proceeds of roughly $21 million.

EXECUTIVES

Vice President Interactive Systems, Melvin McArthur
Vice President Treasurer, Mike Viola
Assistant Vice President Compliance Privacy, Anne Wolfe
Vice President Information Technology Network Planning, Andre Fuetsch
Vice President of Data Products, Bob Bickerstaff
Vice President, John Goetz
Regional Vice President General Manager, Jeff Goldstein
Assistant Vice President Global Business Operations and Sourcing, Sean Van Ausdall
Senior Vice President Corporate Development, Rick Moore
Vice President Information Technology Engineering, Ray Johnson
Area Vice President Sales, Marcus Cathey
Assistant Vice President network Contracting, Roland Tunez
Vice President, Linda A Rogers
Assistant Vice President Life Cycle Management, Andy Staple
Sales Vice President, Dan Roche
Assistant Vice President Federal Relations, Allen Chew
Vice President of Restaurant Operations, Daniel Kaepernik
Vice President and Associate General Counsel Legal, Jack Zinman
Auditors: RSM US LLP

LOCATIONS

HQ: Capital Southwest Corp.
5400 Lyndon B. Johnson Freeway, Suite 1300, Dallas, TX 75240
Phone: 214 238-5700
Web: www.capitalsouthwest.com

PRODUCTS/OPERATIONS

Selected Holdings
Alamo Group Inc. (22% tractor-mounted mowing and agricultural equipment)
Atlantic Capital Bancshares Inc. (2%)
Balco Inc. (91% specialty building products)
Boxx Technologies Inc. (15% graphics workstations)
Cinatra Clean Technologies Inc. (69% environmentally safe storage tank cleaning)
Encore Wire Corporation (17% electrical wire and cable)
iMemories Inc. (27% video and photo storage)
KBI Biopharma Inc. (17% drug development)
Palletone Inc. (8% pallets and pressure-treated wood products)
Palm Harbor Homes Inc. (30% manufactured homes)
The RectorSeal Corporation (specialty chemicals)
Texas Capital Bancshares Inc. (2%)
TitanLiner (30% spill containment system)
Trax Holdings Inc. (31% freight audit and logistics services)
Wellogix Inc. (19% supply chain management software for the oil and gas industry)
The Whitmore Manufacturing Company (80% specialty lubricants)

COMPETITORS

American Capital	Fifth Street Finance
Apollo Investment	Gladstone Capital
Ares Capital	MCG Capital
BlackRock	MVC Capital
CapEx	

HISTORICAL FINANCIALS
Company Type: Public

Income Statement FYE: March 31

	ASSETS ($ mil.)	NET INCOME ($ mil.)	INCOME AS % OF ASSETS	EMPLOYEES
03/19	551.8	23.7	4.3%	22
03/18	417.4	16.2	3.9%	19
03/17	325.7	7.8	2.4%	17
03/16	284.4	(10.6)	—	15
03/15	776.8	(2.4)	—	17
Annual Growth	(8.2%)	—	—	6.7%

	STOCK PRICE ($) FY Close	P/E High/Low	PER SHARE ($) Earnings	Dividends	Book Value
03/19	21.04	16 12	1.42	2.27	18.62
03/18	17.02	18 15	1.01	0.99	19.08
03/17	16.91	33 27	0.50	0.79	17.80
03/16	13.87	— —	(0.68)	0.14	17.34
03/15	46.42	— —	(0.16)	0.20	49.30
Annual Growth	(17.9%)		(21.6%)	83.5%	—

CapStar Financial Holdings Inc

Auditors: Elliott Davis, LLC

LOCATIONS

HQ: CapStar Financial Holdings Inc
1201 Demonbreun Street, Suite 700, Nashville, TN 37203
Phone: 615 732-6400
Web: www.capstarbank.com

HISTORICAL FINANCIALS
Company Type: Public

Income Statement FYE: December 31

	ASSETS ($ mil.)	NET INCOME ($ mil.)	INCOME AS % OF ASSETS	EMPLOYEES
12/18	1,963.8	9.6	0.5%	295
12/17	1,344.4	1.5	0.1%	175
12/16	1,333.6	9.1	0.7%	170
12/15	1,206.8	7.5	0.6%	166
12/14	1,128.4	4.9	0.4%	0
Annual Growth	14.9%	17.9%	—	—

2018 Year-End Financials
Return on assets: 0.5%
Return on equity: 4.8%
Long-term debt ($ mil.): —
No. of shares (mil.): 17.7
Sales ($ mil): 83.2
Dividends
  Yield: 0.5%
  Payout: 9.8%
Market value ($ mil.): 261.0

	STOCK PRICE ($) FY Close	P/E High/Low	PER SHARE ($) Earnings	Dividends	Book Value
12/18	14.73	30 19	0.67	0.08	14.35
12/17	20.77	169 125	0.12	0.00	12.69
12/16	21.96	22 16	0.81	0.00	12.42
Annual Growth	(18.1%)	— —	(9.1%)	—	7.5%

Carbon Energy Corp (DE)

EXECUTIVES

Ceo, Patrick R McDonald
Auditors: Plante & Moran, PLLC

LOCATIONS

HQ: Carbon Energy Corp (DE)
  1700 Broadway, Suite 1170, Denver, CO 80290
Phone: 720 407-7030
Web: www.carbonenergycorp.com

HISTORICAL FINANCIALS

Company Type: Public

Income Statement — FYE: December 31

	REVENUE ($ mil.)	NET INCOME ($ mil.)	NET PROFIT MARGIN	EMPLOYEES
12/18	53.0	8.4	15.8%	222
12/17	22.4	6.3	28.1%	168
12/16	8.2	(12.4)	—	55
12/15	11.6	(8.3)	—	30
12/14	24.0	6.9	28.8%	30
Annual Growth	21.8%	4.9%	—	64.9%

2018 Year-End Financials

Debt ratio: 51.1%
Return on equity: 26.9%
Cash ($ mil.): 5.7
Current ratio: 0.83
Long-term debt ($ mil.): 159.0
No. of shares (mil.): 7.6
Dividends
  Yield: —
  Payout: —
Market value ($ mil.): 71.0

	STOCK PRICE ($) FY Close	P/E High/Low	PER SHARE ($) Earnings	Dividends	Book Value
12/18	9.25	14 7	0.87	0.00	6.24
12/17	11.00	12 0	0.49	0.00	2.44
12/16	0.45	— —	(2.27)	0.00	1.30
12/15	0.70	— —	(1.60)	0.00	3.22
12/14	0.64	1 1	1.20	0.00	4.57
Annual Growth	95.0%	— —	(7.7%)	—	8.1%

Care.com Inc

Care.com lets families shop for child care senior care special needs care pet care tutoring and housekeeping services via web and mobile platforms. The site has more than 14 million members including more than 7.5 million families and more than 6 million caregivers who use Care.com to market their services and find employment. The service which is actively used in more than 15 countries (primarily the US but also Canada the UK and other parts of Western Europe) averages about 6.5 million unique visitors each month including about 4 million visitors per month from mobile devices. Care.com also offers household payroll management (HomePay) and other services. In early 2014 Care.com went public.

IPO
Care.com raised $90 million through its IPO. The company will use the proceeds for working capital and other general corporate purposes including potential acquisitions.

Operations
The majority of the site's listings are for part-time assistance. About 60% of all job postings are for part-time care services with the remaining 40% of postings seeking full-time care.
Care.com's HomePay consumer payments solution which is similar to PayPal lets families electronically pay a caregiver and subscribe to tax preparation services.

Geographic Reach
A little more than 90% of the company's revenue comes from the US though the percentage as been falling slowly as the company expands overseas. It operates in more than 15 countries.

Sales and Marketing
Care.com allows caregivers to create personal profiles listing their skills experience and any other information they would like to include to stand out.
In 2014 Care.com spent about $30.5 million on advertising up from $22.3 million in 2013. The company primarily targets women since they make up the largest percentage of both care-seekers and care-givers.

Financial Performance
The company has enjoyed tremendous growth in its revenue and members. Its revenue grew from $12.9 million in fiscal 2010 to $116.7 million in 2014 which was a 43% increase over the previous year. The bump was due to an increase in paying members and higher revenue per member as well as contributions from an acquisition. However despite the years of revenue growth Care.com has seen increasing net losses culminating in a loss of $80.3 million in 2014 largely due to high operating expenses and acquisition-related goodwill impairment. The losses have lead to a nearly continuous increase is cash used in operations from $12.66 in 2013 to $24.28 million in 2014.

Strategy
Though Care.com has seen years of increasing revenue without being profitable its strategy focuses purely on increasing memberships and revenues expanding internationally and pursuing acquisitions.

Mergers and Acquisitions
In 2013 Care.com acquired certain assets of BigTent an online forum for parenting groups for $700000.
The following year it effectively bought all the employees of Consmr Inc. the developer of a mobile review app for $600000. Its biggest purchase to date is the 2014 $31 million acquisition of Citrus Lane a consumer-product subscription service aimed at moms.

EXECUTIVES

Founder Chairwoman and CEO, Sheila Lirio Marcelo, age 49, $269,167 total compensation
General Counsel and Corporate Secretary, Diane Musi
Co-Founder & Chief Technology Officer, Dave Krupinski, age 53, $209,167 total compensation
Co-Founder & VP Policy and CSR, Donna Levin
VP & GM Operations Sales & B2B, Michael Marty
Co-Founder VP & GM US Consumer Subscriptions, Zenobia Moochhala
Interim CFO, Steve Boulanger
Vice President of Care Management, Jody Gastfriend
Auditors: Ernst & Young LLP

LOCATIONS

HQ: Care.com Inc
  77 Fourth Avenue, Fifth Floor, Waltham, MA 02451
Phone: 781 642-5900
Web: www.care.com

COMPETITORS

Bright Horizons Family Solutions
Facebook
Google
Monster Worldwide
PayPal
Yahoo!
craigslist

HISTORICAL FINANCIALS

Company Type: Public

Income Statement — FYE: December 29

	REVENUE ($ mil.)	NET INCOME ($ mil.)	NET PROFIT MARGIN	EMPLOYEES
12/18	192.2	52.8	27.5%	2,376
12/17	174.0	10.6	6.1%	891
12/16	161.7	7.0	4.4%	787
12/15	138.6	(35.0)	—	799
12/14	116.7	(80.2)	—	853
Annual Growth	13.3%	—	—	29.2%

2018 Year-End Financials

Debt ratio: —
Return on equity: 29.8%
Cash ($ mil.): 92.4
Current ratio: 3.20
Long-term debt ($ mil.): —
No. of shares (mil.): 32.0
Dividends
  Yield: —
  Payout: —
Market value ($ mil.): 631.0

	STOCK PRICE ($) FY Close	P/E High/Low	PER SHARE ($) Earnings	Dividends	Book Value
12/18	19.67	16 11	1.29	0.00	6.71
12/17	18.04	90 36	0.22	0.00	4.60
12/16	8.57	117 50	0.10	0.00	3.95
12/15	7.27	— —	(1.09)	0.00	2.73
12/14	8.33	— —	(2.77)	0.00	3.73
Annual Growth	24.0%	— —	—	—	15.8%

CareTrust REIT Inc

Auditors: DELOITTE & TOUCHE LLP

LOCATIONS

HQ: CareTrust REIT Inc
  905 Calle Amanecer, Suite 300, San Clemente, CA 92673
Phone: 949 542-3130
Web: www.caretrustreit.com

HISTORICAL FINANCIALS

Company Type: Public

Income Statement — FYE: December 31

	REVENUE ($ mil.)	NET INCOME ($ mil.)	NET PROFIT MARGIN	EMPLOYEES
12/18	156.9	57.9	36.9%	57
12/17	132.9	25.8	19.5%	50
12/16	104.6	29.3	28.0%	50
12/15	74.9	10.0	13.4%	46
12/14	58.9	(8.1)	—	43
Annual Growth	27.8%	—	—	7.3%

2018 Year-End Financials

Debt ratio: 37.9%
Return on equity: 8.5%
Cash ($ mil.): 36.7
Current ratio: 1.43
Long-term debt ($ mil.): 489.7
No. of shares (mil.): 85.8
Dividends
  Yield: 4.4%
  Payout: 146.4%
Market value ($ mil.): 1,585.0

	STOCK PRICE ($) FY Close	P/E High/Low		PER SHARE ($) Earnings	Dividends	Book Value
12/18	18.46	28	18	0.72	0.82	8.95
12/17	16.76	56	42	0.35	0.74	7.88
12/16	15.32	30	19	0.52	0.68	6.98
12/15	10.95	57	40	0.26	0.64	5.50
12/14	12.33	—	—	(0.36)	6.01	3.63
Annual Growth	10.6%			—	(39.2%)	25.3%

Carey Watermark Investors Inc

Auditors: PricewaterhouseCoopers LLP

LOCATIONS

HQ: Carey Watermark Investors Inc
  50 Rockefeller Plaza, New York, NY 10020
Phone: 212 492-1100
Web: www.careywatermark.com

HISTORICAL FINANCIALS

Company Type: Public

Income Statement   FYE: December 31

	REVENUE ($ mil.)	NET INCOME ($ mil.)	NET PROFIT MARGIN	EMPLOYEES
12/18	613.8	8.0	1.3%	0
12/17	629.1	4.9	0.8%	0
12/16	651.1	(8.7)	—	0
12/15	542.1	(25.7)	—	0
12/14	348.0	(32.7)	—	0
Annual Growth	15.2%	—	—	—

2018 Year-End Financials

Debt ratio: 59.9%
Return on equity: 1.1%
Cash ($ mil.): 66.5
Current ratio: 1.02
Long-term debt ($ mil.): 1,367.6
No. of shares (mil.): 139.6
Dividends
  Yield: —
  Payout: 950.0%
Market value ($ mil.): —

	STOCK PRICE ($) FY Close	P/E High/Low		PER SHARE ($) Earnings	Dividends	Book Value
12/18	0.00	—	—	0.06	0.57	5.04
12/17	0.00	—	—	0.04	0.57	5.47
Annual Growth	—			—	50.0%	(0.0%) (7.8%)

CarGurus Inc

Auditors: Ernst & Young LLP

LOCATIONS

HQ: CarGurus Inc
  2 Canal Park, 4th Floor, Cambridge, MA 02141
Phone: 617 354-0068
Web: www.cargurus.com

HISTORICAL FINANCIALS

Company Type: Public

Income Statement   FYE: December 31

	REVENUE ($ mil.)	NET INCOME ($ mil.)	NET PROFIT MARGIN	EMPLOYEES
12/18	454.0	65.1	14.4%	732
12/17	316.8	13.2	4.2%	549
12/16	198.1	6.5	3.3%	514
12/15	98.5	(1.6)	—	0
Annual Growth	66.4%	—	—	—

2018 Year-End Financials

Debt ratio: —
Return on equity: 40.5%
Cash ($ mil.): 34.8
Current ratio: 3.07
Long-term debt ($ mil.): —
No. of shares (mil.): 110.4
Dividends
  Yield: —
  Payout: —
Market value ($ mil.): 3,725.0

	STOCK PRICE ($) FY Close	P/E High/Low		PER SHARE ($) Earnings	Dividends	Book Value
12/18	33.73	93	49	0.57	0.00	1.76
12/17	29.98	251	212	0.12	0.00	1.20
12/16	0.00	—	—	(0.58)	0.00	1.54
Annual Growth	—			—	—	6.9%

Carolina Financial Corp (New)

Auditors: Elliott Davis, LLC

LOCATIONS

HQ: Carolina Financial Corp (New)
  288 Meeting Street, Charleston, SC 29401
Phone: 843 723-7700

HISTORICAL FINANCIALS

Company Type: Public

Income Statement   FYE: December 31

	ASSETS ($ mil.)	NET INCOME ($ mil.)	INCOME AS % OF ASSETS	EMPLOYEES
12/18	3,790.7	49.6	1.3%	773
12/17	3,519.0	28.5	0.8%	770
12/16	1,683.7	17.5	1.0%	441
12/15	1,409.6	14.4	1.0%	421
12/14	1,199.0	8.3	0.7%	394
Annual Growth	33.3%	56.4%	—	18.4%

2018 Year-End Financials

Return on assets: 1.3%
Return on equity: 9.4%
Long-term debt ($ mil.): —
No. of shares (mil.): 22.3
Sales ($ mil): 196.1
Dividends
  Yield: 0.8%
  Payout: 11.0%
Market value ($ mil.): 662.0

	STOCK PRICE ($) FY Close	P/E High/Low		PER SHARE ($) Earnings	Dividends	Book Value
12/18	29.59	20	12	2.26	0.25	25.70
12/17	37.15	22	16	1.73	0.17	22.61
12/16	30.79	21	11	1.42	0.13	13.00
12/15	18.00	12	9	1.48	0.11	11.63
12/14	13.99	48	15	0.88	0.09	9.64
Annual Growth	20.6%			— 26.8%	30.0%	27.8%

Carrols Restaurant Group Inc

This company has some fast food royalty in its blood. Carrols Restaurant Group is a leading quick-service restaurant operator and the world's #1 Burger King franchisee with about 660 locations in the US. Like other franchise operators Carrols pays Burger King Worldwide royalties in order to use the BK banner and other intellectual property for its restaurants. Prior to the July 2012 spin-off of wholly-owned subsidiary Fiesta Restaurant Group Carrols also operated quick-service chains Taco Cabana and Pollo Tropical. The company has Burger King locations in 15 states.

Geographic Reach

The company's Burger King locations are concentrated in the Midwest the Northeast and the Southeast.

Sales and Marketing

Burger King restaurants rely heavily on national television radio newspaper and magazine marketing campaigns (supplemented by local advertising) and new menu additions to drive guest traffic. Carrols' annual advertising expense is normally about 5% of restaurant sales.

Financial Performance

Carrols reported revenue of $692.7 million in fiscal 2014. That was an increase of more than $29 million compared to the company's fiscal 2013 revenue. Despite the spike in revenue Carrols slumped to a new loss of $38.1 million in fiscal 2014. That was an increase of more than $25 million compared to the loss the company suffered in fiscal 2013.

Carrols ended fiscal 2014 with $14.7 million in cash on hand. That was a decrease of $6.8 million compared to the company's prior fiscal period's cash levels.

Strategy

The company's strategy is focused on remodeling its current restaurants according to the Burger King's 20/20 restaurant image which has improved the customer experience increased traffic and led to a higher average check size.

Carrols remodeled more than 300 of its restaurants in fiscal 2014 and the company plans to remodel another 150 locations by 2017.

The company also plans to acquire select Burger King Restaurants across its service area.

EXECUTIVES

VP; CFO and Treasurer, Paul R. Flanders, age 62, $263,268 total compensation
Chairman; CEO; President and Director, Daniel T. Accordino, age 68, $533,032 total compensation
Vice President Of Real Estate, Richard Cross
Vice President Operations, Joseph Hoffman
Auditors: DELOITTE & TOUCHE LLP

LOCATIONS

HQ: Carrols Restaurant Group Inc
  968 James Street, Syracuse, NY 13203
Phone: 315 424-0513
Web: www.carrols.com

COMPETITORS

Akwen   Jack in the Box

American Dairy Queen
Austaco
Biglari Holdings
Boddie-Noell
Bojangles'
Boston Market
Carolina Restaurant
 Group
Chick-fil-A
Chipotle
Church's Chicken
Einstein Noah
 Restaurant Group
Hardee's
McDonald's
Morgan's Foods
Panera Bread
Popeyes
Quiznos
R&L Foods
Sonic Corp.
Subway
Taco Bueno
V & J Holding
Wendy's
Whataburger
White Castle
YUM!

HISTORICAL FINANCIALS
Company Type: Public

Income Statement — FYE: December 30

	REVENUE ($ mil.)	NET INCOME ($ mil.)	NET PROFIT MARGIN	EMPLOYEES
12/18	1,179.3	10.1	0.9%	24,500
12/17*	1,088.5	7.1	0.7%	23,500
01/17	943.5	45.4	4.8%	21,500
01/16	859.0	0.0	0.0%	20,350
12/14	692.7	(38.1)	—	20,400
Annual Growth	14.2%	—	—	4.7%

*Fiscal year change

2018 Year-End Financials
Debt ratio: 46.6%
Return on equity: 5.7%
Cash ($ mil.): 4.0
Current ratio: 0.42
Long-term debt ($ mil.): 278.0
No. of shares (mil.): 35.7
Dividends
 Yield: —
 Payout: —
Market value ($ mil.): 335.0

	STOCK PRICE ($) FY Close	P/E High	P/E Low	PER SHARE ($) Earnings	PER SHARE ($) Dividends	PER SHARE ($) Book Value
12/18	9.38	74	42	0.22	0.00	5.19
12/17*	12.15	105	63	0.16	0.00	4.77
01/17	15.25	15	11	1.01	0.00	4.39
01/16	11.74	—	—	(0.00)	0.00	3.08
12/14	7.71	—	—	(1.23)	0.00	3.06
Annual Growth	5.0%	—	—	—	—	14.1%

*Fiscal year change

Cars.com Inc

Auditors: Ernst & Young LLP

LOCATIONS
HQ: Cars.com Inc
 300 S. Riverside Plaza, Suite 1000, Chicago, IL 60606
Phone: 312 601-5000
Web: www.cars.com

HISTORICAL FINANCIALS
Company Type: Public

Income Statement — FYE: December 31

	REVENUE ($ mil.)	NET INCOME ($ mil.)	NET PROFIT MARGIN	EMPLOYEES
12/18	662.1	38.8	5.9%	1,400
12/17	626.2	224.4	35.8%	1,100
12/16	633.1	176.3	27.9%	1,275
12/15	596.5	157.8	26.5%	0
12/14	145.9	16.2	11.1%	0
Annual Growth	45.9%	24.4%	—	—

2018 Year-End Financials
Debt ratio: 26.6%
Return on equity: 2.3%
Cash ($ mil.): 25.4
Current ratio: 1.39
Long-term debt ($ mil.): 665.3
No. of shares (mil.): 68.2
Dividends
 Yield: —
 Payout: —
Market value ($ mil.): 1,468.0

	STOCK PRICE ($) FY Close	P/E High	P/E Low	PER SHARE ($) Earnings	PER SHARE ($) Dividends	PER SHARE ($) Book Value
12/18	21.50	59	37	0.55	0.00	23.83
12/17	28.84	10	7	3.13	0.00	23.44
Annual Growth	(25.5%)	—	—	(82.4%)	—	1.7%

Casa Systems Inc

Auditors: PricewaterhouseCoopers LLP

LOCATIONS
HQ: Casa Systems Inc
 100 Old River Road, Andover, MA 01810
Phone: 978 688-6706
Web: www.casa-systems.com

HISTORICAL FINANCIALS
Company Type: Public

Income Statement — FYE: December 31

	REVENUE ($ mil.)	NET INCOME ($ mil.)	NET PROFIT MARGIN	EMPLOYEES
12/18	297.1	73.0	24.6%	743
12/17	351.5	88.5	25.2%	680
12/16	316.1	88.6	28.0%	604
12/15	272.4	67.9	24.9%	0
12/14	211.2	59.7	28.3%	352
Annual Growth	8.9%	5.2%	—	20.5%

2018 Year-End Financials
Debt ratio: 62.2%
Return on equity: 116.8%
Cash ($ mil.): 280.5
Current ratio: 4.69
Long-term debt ($ mil.): 293.2
No. of shares (mil.): 82.9
Dividends
 Yield: —
 Payout: —
Market value ($ mil.): 1,089.0

	STOCK PRICE ($) FY Close	P/E High	P/E Low	PER SHARE ($) Earnings	PER SHARE ($) Dividends	PER SHARE ($) Book Value
12/18	13.13	39	14	0.79	0.00	0.90
12/17	17.76	52	42	0.26	1.76	0.62
Annual Growth	(26.1%)	—	—	203.8%	—	45.8%

Casella Waste Systems, Inc.

The wasteful habits of Americans are big business for Casella Waste Systems which operates regional waste-hauling businesses mainly in the northeastern US. The company serves residential commercial industrial and municipal customers. In 2016 it owned and/or operated 34 solid waste collection operations 44 transfer stations 18 recycling facilities nine Subtitle D landfills four landfill gas-to-energy facilities and one landfill permitted to accept construction and demolition materials. With a strategy focused on increasing waste volumes at its land fills Casella Waste Systems added 0.8 million tons in 2015.

Operations
Casella Waste Systems' broad portfolio of waste service assets includes solid waste collection businesses disposal facilities recycling plants transfer stations and gas-to-energy and waste-to-energy facilities.

The company's operations comprise a full range of non-hazardous solid waste services including collections transfer stations Material Recovery Facilities (MRFs) and disposal facilities. In 2015 it generated 44% of its total revenues from its collection business and 29% from its disposal activities.

Geographic Reach
Casella Waste Systems conducts its operation on a geographic basis through two regional operating segments: the Eastern and Western regions; and a third operating segment Recycling which comprises larger-scale recycling operations and commodity brokerage operations.

The company provides integrated solid waste services in six states: Vermont New Hampshire New York Massachusetts Maine and Pennsylvania.

Sales and Marketing
The waste services company serves commercial industrial municipal and residential customers.

Financial Performance
Casella Waste System's revenues grew by 48% in 2015 (to $546.5 million) largely as the result of a rise in solid waste revenues driven by higher volumes and favorable collection and disposal pricing. Customer Solutions revenues increased by 0.2% ($1.2 million) due to organic business growth partially offset by the pass-through impact of unfavorable commodity prices.

Gains were also partially offset by a 0.4% ($2 million) drop in Recycling revenues due to unfavorable commodity prices.

Organics net sales dropped by $0.7 million as the result of lower volumes and a decline in the floating rate fuel and oil recovery fee in response to lower diesel fuel index prices on which the surcharge was based.

Casella Waste System's net loss ballooned from $5.8 million in 2014 to $11.8 million in 2015 mainly due to a 58% jump in interest expense and a 92% increase in the provision for income taxes.

Net cash provided by operating activities increased from $38.3 million in 2014 to $70.5 million in 2015 due to favorable cash flow impacts associated with prepaid expenses inventories and other assets and accrued expenses and other liabilities due to lower final capping and closure and post-closure payments. These were partially offset by unfavorable cash flow impacts associated with accounts payable and accounts receivable.

Strategy
Over the last few years the company has simplified its business structure improved cash flows and reduced risk exposure by divesting and closing underperforming operations. Its strategy for improving financial performance includes increasing landfill returns; driving additional profitability at

collection operations; and creating incremental value through offering a range of resource services (including materials processing industrial recycling clean energy and organics).

With a goal of increasing waste volumes by 0.5 million tons annually at its landfills by the end of 2015 the company exceeded this goal with overall landfill volumes for 2015 up by 0.8 million tons.

Company Background

The company was founded in 1975 with one truck.

EXECUTIVES

SVP and General Counsel, David L. Schmitt, age 68, $256,113 total compensation
Chairman CEO and Secretary, John W. Casella, age 68, $402,016 total compensation
President and COO, Edwin D. (Ed) Johnson, age 62, $351,375 total compensation
Director Investor Relations, Edmond R. (Ned) Coletta, $258,905 total compensation
VP Finance and Chief Accounting Officer, Christopher B Heald, $165,733 total compensation
Auditors: RSM US LLP

LOCATIONS

HQ: Casella Waste Systems, Inc.
25 Greens Hill Lane, Rutland, VT 05701
Phone: 802 775-0325
Web: www.casella.com

PRODUCTS/OPERATIONS

2015 Sales

	$ mil.	% of total
Solid Waste Operations		
Collection	238.3	44
Disposal	156.5	29
Power generation	6.8	1
Processing	6.1	1
Customer Solutions	53.3	10
Recycling	46.3	8
Organics	39.1	7
Total	**546.4**	**100**

COMPETITORS

CertainTeed	Waste Connections
Johns Manville	Waste Connections US
Republic Services	Waste Industries USA
Rumpke	Waste Management

HISTORICAL FINANCIALS

Company Type: Public

Income Statement — FYE: December 31

	REVENUE ($ mil.)	NET INCOME ($ mil.)	NET PROFIT MARGIN	EMPLOYEES
12/18	660.6	6.4	1.0%	2,300
12/17	599.3	(21.8)	—	2,000
12/16	565.0	(6.8)	—	2,000
12/15	546.5	(12.9)	—	1,900
12/14	368.3	(6.0)	—	1,900
Annual Growth	15.7%	—	—	4.9%

2018 Year-End Financials

Debt ratio: 74.3%
Return on equity: —
Cash ($ mil.): 4.0
Current ratio: 0.87
Long-term debt ($ mil.): 542.0
No. of shares (mil.): 42.9
Dividends
 Yield: —
 Payout: —
Market value ($ mil.): 1,223.0

	STOCK PRICE ($) FY Close	P/E High/Low	PER SHARE ($) Earnings	Dividends	Book Value
12/18	28.49	225 149	0.15	0.00	(0.37)
12/17	23.02	— —	(0.52)	0.00	(0.90)
12/16	12.41	— —	(0.17)	0.00	(0.59)
12/15	5.98	— —	(0.32)	0.00	(0.52)
12/14	4.04	— —	(0.15)	0.00	(0.30)
Annual Growth	63.0%	— —	—	—	—

Cathay General Bancorp

Cathay General Bancorp is the holding company for Cathay Bank which mainly serves Chinese and Vietnamese communities from some 30 branches in California and about 20 more in Illinois New Jersey New York Massachusetts Washington and Texas. It also has a branch in Hong Kong and offices in Shanghai and Taipei. Catering to small to medium-sized businesses and individual consumers the bank offers standard deposit services and loans. Commercial mortgage loans account for more than half of the bank's portfolio; business loans comprise nearly 25%. The bank's Cathay Wealth Management unit offers online stock trading mutual funds and other investment products and services through an agreement with PrimeVest.

Geographic Reach

California state-chartered Cathay Bank has branches in California Illinois Massachusetts New Jersey New York Texas and Washington. Overseas it has a branch in Hong Kong and offices in Shanghai and Taipei.

Financial Performance

The bank's revenue is on a downward trend. In 2012 revenue declined more than 5% vs. 2011 after posting a 3% decline in the previous annual comparison. Indeed between 2008 and 2012 revenue dipped by about 17% on lower interest income and dividend income. However the bank's profit picture is improving with net income up in 2012 for the third consecutive year.

Strategy

With 60% of its branches in California — a state hard hit by the downturn in the housing market — Cathay Bank's real estate secured loan portfolio has suffered as the value of the underlying collateral plummeted. In 2010 the company entered into a memorandum of understanding with the FDIC to reduce its concentration of commercial real estate loans improve its capital ratios reduce overall risk and strengthen asset quality. The moves have helped the company to cut its losses. The bank has also been successful growing deposits.

Mergers and Acquisitions

In 2016 Cathay Bank agreed to buy SinoPac Bancorp from Taiwan's Bank SinoPac for $340 million. SinoPac's Far East National Bank operates nine branches including five in Los Angeles. After the deal closes Cathay plans to close a number of branches. The transaction will help boost the company's balance sheet.

EXECUTIVES

SEVP and COO, Irwin Wong, age 70, $339,777 total compensation
EVP and Chief Credit Officer Cathay Bank, Donald S. Chow, age 68, $312,615 total compensation
EVP CFO and Treasurer, Heng W. Chen, age 67, $416,542 total compensation
EVP and General Manager East and Midwest Region Cathay Bank, Pin Tai, $424,900 total compensation
EVP and Chief Risk Officer Cathy Bank, Kim R. Bingham, age 62
Assistant Vice President Marketing, Chris Lu
Auditors: KPMG LLP

LOCATIONS

HQ: Cathay General Bancorp
777 North Broadway, Los Angeles, CA 90012
Phone: 213 625-4700
Web: www.cathaybank.com

PRODUCTS/OPERATIONS

2015 sales

	$ mil.	% of total
Interest and Dividend income		
Loan receivable	427.6	88
Investment securities- taxable	21.5	4
Federal Home Loan Bank stock	3.2	1
Deposits with banks	1.4	-
Non-Interest income		
Securities losses net	(3.3)	-
Letters of credit commissions	5.6	1
Depository service fees	5.3	1
Other operating income	25.1	5
Total	**486.4**	**100**

Products/Services

Personal
Accounts
 Checking Accounts
 Savings Accounts
 CDs
 IRA CD
Debit Cards
Loans
 Mortgage Loan
 Home Equity Financing
 Auto Loan
 Credit Cards
Cathay Online Banking
Mobile Banking
Business/Commercial
Business Accounts
 Business Checking Account
 Business Savings Account
 CDs
 Cash Management Services
 Merchant Deposit Capture
 Zero Balance Account
 Lockbox Service
 Merchant Bankard Services
 Courier Deposit Service
 Armored Transport Services
 Cash Vault Services
 Business Online Banking
Loans
 Commercial Financing
 Real Estate & Construction Financing
 International Banking & Financing
 Smart Capital Line
 SBA Guaranteed Loan Program
 Credit Cards

COMPETITORS

Bank of America	Grandpoint
Citibank	Hanmi Financial
East West Bancorp	Hope Bancorp
Far East National Bank	U.S. Bancorp

HISTORICAL FINANCIALS
Company Type: Public

Income Statement   FYE: December 31

	ASSETS ($ mil.)	NET INCOME ($ mil.)	INCOME AS % OF ASSETS	EMPLOYEES
12/18	16,784.7	271.8	1.6%	1,277
12/17	15,640.1	176.0	1.1%	1,271
12/16	14,520.7	175.1	1.2%	1,129
12/15	13,254.1	161.1	1.2%	1,122
12/14	11,516.8	137.8	1.2%	1,074
Annual Growth	9.9%	18.5%	—	4.4%

2018 Year-End Financials
Return on assets: 1.6%
Return on equity: 13.2%
Long-term debt ($ mil.): —
No. of shares (mil.): 80.5
Sales ($ mil): 719.6
Dividends
  Yield: 3.0%
  Payout: 36.2%
Market value ($ mil.): 2,699.0

	STOCK PRICE ($) FY Close	P/E High/Low		PER SHARE ($) Earnings	Dividends	Book Value
12/18	33.53	13	10	3.33	1.03	26.36
12/17	42.17	20	16	2.17	0.87	24.39
12/16	38.03	17	12	2.19	0.75	22.97
12/15	31.33	17	12	1.98	0.56	21.63
12/14	25.59	16	13	1.72	0.29	20.08
Annual Growth	7.0%	—	—	18.0%	37.3%	7.0%

Cavco Industries Inc (DE)

EXECUTIVES
Chairman President Chief Executive Officer, Steven G. Bunger, age 55
Chairman of the Board; President; Chief Executive Officer, Joseph H. (Joe) Stegmayer, age 65, $236,250 total compensation
Senior Vice President Global Ferroalloys, William C. (Bill) Boor, age 50
VP CFO and Treasurer, Daniel L. Urness, age 47, $175,000 total compensation
VP and General Manager Cavco Park Homes and Cabins, Timothy M. Gage
General Counsel and Secretary, James P. Glew
President of Fleetwood Homes; Inc, Charles Lott
President of Palm Harbor Homes; Inc., Larry Keener
Director, Steven G. Bunger, age 55
Director, William C. (Bill) Boor, age 50
Director, David A. Greenblatt, age 54
Director, Jack Hanna, age 69
Auditors: RSM US LLP

LOCATIONS
HQ: Cavco Industries Inc (DE)
3636 North Central Avenue, Suite 1200, Phoenix, AZ 85012
Phone: 602 256-6263
Web: www.cavco.com

COMPETITORS
All American Group	Fairmont Homes
American Homestar	Liberty Homes
Cavalier Homes	PulteGroup
Champion Home Builders	Skyline
Clayton Homes	Sunshine Homes

HISTORICAL FINANCIALS
Company Type: Public

Income Statement   FYE: March 30

	REVENUE ($ mil.)	NET INCOME ($ mil.)	NET PROFIT MARGIN	EMPLOYEES
03/19	962.7	68.6	7.1%	4,650
03/18*	871.2	61.5	7.1%	4,500
04/17	773.8	37.9	4.9%	4,300
04/16	712.3	28.5	4.0%	3,750
03/15	566.6	23.8	4.2%	3,700
Annual Growth	14.2%	30.3%	—	5.9%

*Fiscal year change

2019 Year-End Financials
Debt ratio: 4.8%
Return on equity: 13.9%
Cash ($ mil.): 187.3
Current ratio: 2.66
Long-term debt ($ mil.): 14.6
No. of shares (mil.): 9.1
Dividends
  Yield: —
  Payout: —
Market value ($ mil.): 1,069.0

	STOCK PRICE ($) FY Close	P/E High/Low		PER SHARE ($) Earnings	Dividends	Book Value
03/19	117.53	34	15	7.40	0.00	58.21
03/18*	173.75	26	16	6.68	0.00	50.54
04/17	116.40	28	20	4.17	0.00	43.85
04/16	93.20	31	20	3.15	0.00	39.56
03/15	75.03	32	24	2.64	0.00	36.14
Annual Growth	11.9%	—	—	29.4%	—	12.7%

*Fiscal year change

CB Financial Services Inc

Auditors: Baker Tilly Virchow Krause, LLP

LOCATIONS
HQ: CB Financial Services Inc
100 North Market Street, Carmichaels, PA 15320
Phone: 724 966-5041
Web: www.communitybank.tv

HISTORICAL FINANCIALS
Company Type: Public

Income Statement   FYE: December 31

	ASSETS ($ mil.)	NET INCOME ($ mil.)	INCOME AS % OF ASSETS	EMPLOYEES
12/18	1,281.3	7.0	0.6%	269
12/17	934.4	6.9	0.7%	201
12/16	846.0	7.5	0.9%	200
12/15	830.6	8.4	1.0%	198
12/14	846.3	4.2	0.5%	193
Annual Growth	10.9%	13.2%	—	8.7%

2018 Year-End Financials
Return on assets: 0.6%
Return on equity: 6.1%
Long-term debt ($ mil.): —
No. of shares (mil.): 5.4
Sales ($ mil): 51.9
Dividends
  Yield: 3.5%
  Payout: 70.0%
Market value ($ mil.): 135.0

	STOCK PRICE ($) FY Close	P/E High/Low		PER SHARE ($) Earnings	Dividends	Book Value
12/18	24.78	25	16	1.40	0.89	25.33
12/17	30.00	18	15	1.69	0.88	22.77
12/16	25.85	14	10	1.86	0.88	21.89
12/15	22.92	11	9	2.07	0.85	21.29
12/14	19.90	13	12	1.63	0.84	20.12
Annual Growth	5.6%	—	—	(3.7%)	1.5%	5.9%

CBB Bancorp Inc

Auditors: Crowe LLP

LOCATIONS
HQ: CBB Bancorp Inc
3435 Wilshire Blvd., Suite 700, Los Angeles, CA 90010
Phone: 323 988-3000   **Fax:** 323 988-3001
Web: www.cbb-bank.com

HISTORICAL FINANCIALS
Company Type: Public

Income Statement   FYE: December 31

	REVENUE ($ mil.)	NET INCOME ($ mil.)	NET PROFIT MARGIN	EMPLOYEES
12/18	69.6	16.6	23.9%	0
12/17	60.2	12.0	20.0%	0
12/16	51.1	11.4	22.4%	0
12/15	44.6	11.2	25.2%	0
Annual Growth	16.0%	13.9%	—	—

2018 Year-End Financials
Debt ratio: 0.8%
Return on equity: 13.4%
Cash ($ mil.): 14.2
Current ratio: 0.02
Long-term debt ($ mil.): 10.0
No. of shares (mil.): 10.1
Dividends
  Yield: —
  Payout: —
Market value ($ mil.): 130.0

	STOCK PRICE ($) FY Close	P/E High/Low		PER SHARE ($) Earnings	Dividends	Book Value
12/18	12.90	12	8	1.60	0.00	13.06
12/17	19.00	16	11	1.15	0.00	11.48
12/16	12.70	11	9	1.13	0.00	10.20
12/15	11.78	20	10	1.12	0.00	10.09
/0.00	—	—	—	(0.00)	0.00	(0.00)
Annual Growth	—	—	—	—	—	—

CenterState Bank Corp

CenterState Banks is the holding company for CenterState Bank of Florida which serves the Sunshine State through about 60 branches. The bank offers standard deposit products such as checking and savings accounts money market accounts and

CDs. Real estate loans primarily residential and commercial mortgages make up 85% of the company's loan portfolio while the rest is made up of business loans and consumer loans. The bank's correspondent division provides bond securities accounting and loans to small and mid-sized banks across the Southeast and Texas. It also sells mutual funds annuities and other investment products.

Operations
About 65% of CenterState Banks' total revenue came from loan interest in 2014 while another 10% came from interest on its investment securities. The rest of the bank's revenue came form correspondent banking capital markets revenue and related revenue (11%) deposit account service charges (5%) debit/ATM and merchant card fees (3%) wealth management fees (2%) and other miscellaneous income sources. The company had a staff of 785 employees by the end of 2014.

Geographic Reach
CenterState has nearly 60 branches across 20 counties in central southeast and northeast Florida. Its loan production offices are in Tampa Gainesville Crystal River and Ft. Meyers.

Sales and Marketing
CenterState offers consumer and commercial banking services to individuals businesses and industries across Florida.

Financial Performance
The company has struggled to consistently grow its revenues in recent years due to shrinking interest margins on loans amidst the low-interest environment. Its profits however have been rising thanks to declining loan loss provisions as its loan portfolio's credit quality has improved with higher property valuations in the strengthened economy.

CenterState had a breakout year in 2014 however with its revenue jumping 22% to $164.5 million thanks to higher interest income stemming from new loan business from its acquisitions of First Southern Bancorp and Gulfstream Bancshares during the year.

Higher revenue and stable costs in 2014 also drove the bank's net income higher by 6% to a record $12.96 million. CenterState's operating cash levels plummeted by 90% to $1.4 million after adjusting its earnings for non-cash items mostly related to the net proceeds from its trading securities sales.

Strategy
CenterState Banks continues to seek out additional acquisition opportunities to boost its loan and deposit business and expand into more markets across Florida. To this end the bank's 2014 acquisitions extended its reach into Broward Palm Beach and Martin counties for the first time while adding more than $1.3 billion in new deposits and over $600 million in new loan business to its books.

Struggling to grow its revenues the bank has also worked to become more efficient and profitable through selective branch closures. During 2014 the company closed seven smaller branches and a standalone drive-thru facility to free up resources for more profitable bank acquisitions.

Mergers and Acquisitions
CenterState is buying Platinum Bank Holding Company parent company of Platinum Bank for approximately $83.9 million. The acquisition will add seven banking branches in the Tampa-St. Petersburg-Clearwater and Lakeland-Winter Haven areas. It will also add some $584 million in assets.

In June 2014 CenterState purchased First Southern Bancorp which expanded its market reach into Broward County after adding a net of seven new branches. The deal also added some $600 million in new loan assets and $853 million in deposits.

In January 2014 the company expanded into Palm Beach and Martin counties after buying Gulfstream Bancshares and its four branches with $479 million in deposits.

EXECUTIVES
Senior Vice President Corporate Auditor, Wayne Stewart
SVP and CFO, James J. Antal, age 68, $312,750 total compensation
President CEO and Director CenterState Banks Inc. and Centerstate Bank of Florida, John Corbett, age 50, $420,250 total compensation
Corporate Chief Risk Officer, Daniel E. Bockhorst, $217,500 total compensation
Treasurer, Stephen Young, $278,333 total compensation
First Vice President Business Development, Chris Wright
Assistant Vice President Marketing And Business Development, Dana Townsend
Vice President, Todd Patrick
Vice President Commercial Lending, Dan Jackson
Senior Vice President And Commercial Lending Officer, Bill Daniels
Assistant Vice President Merchant Services Divison, Deborah Joyce
Assistant Vice President Business Analyst Ii, Chante Carlson
First Vice President, Stacey A Dunn
Senior Vice President and Director of Operations, Darlene Bennett
Vice President, Stacy Byrd
Vice President Retail Market Manager, Bretta Christakos
Senior Vice President, Mark Tucker
Assistant Vice President Project Manager, Lexie Williams
Vice President Commercial Relationship Manager, Luis Gonzalez
First Vice President, Richard Skopick
Vice President Commercial Lender, Winn Keeton
Senior Vice President Commercial Banking, Garry Lubi
Senior Vice President Community President, Mark Stevens
First Vice President Prepaid Cards Division, Bruce Davidson
First Vice President, Doug Elmore
Senior Vice President, Scott Clemmons
Assistant Vice President Branch Manager, Denise Tarafa
Vice President Special Assets Team Lead, Idania Kestel
Vice President, Jim Hagerty
Vice President Commercial Relationship Manager, Ben Malik
Chairman, Ernest S. (Ernie) Pinner, age 71
Auditors: Crowe LLP

LOCATIONS
HQ: CenterState Bank Corp
1101 First Street South, Suite 202, Winter Haven, FL 33880
Phone: 863 293-4710
Web: www.centerstatebanks.com

PRODUCTS/OPERATIONS
2011 Sales

	$ mil.	% of total
Interest		
Loans	65.9	36
Investment securities available for sale	15.7	9
Other	0.6	—
Noninterest		
Bargain purchase gain	57.0	31
Correspondent banking & bond sales	24.9	13
Service charges on deposit accounts	6.3	3
Net gain on sale of securities	3.5	2
Other	10.3	6
Total	**184.2**	**100**

COMPETITORS
BB&T	Regions Financial
BBX Capital	Seacoast Banking
Bank of America	SunTrust
Fifth Third	Wells Fargo
JPMorgan Chase	

HISTORICAL FINANCIALS
Company Type: Public

Income Statement   FYE: December 31

	ASSETS ($ mil.)	NET INCOME ($ mil.)	INCOME AS % OF ASSETS	EMPLOYEES
12/18	12,337.5	156.4	1.3%	2,113
12/17	7,123.9	55.8	0.8%	1,200
12/16	5,078.5	42.3	0.8%	952
12/15	4,022.7	39.3	1.0%	784
12/14	3,776.8	12.9	0.3%	785
Annual Growth	34.4%	86.4%	—	28.1%

2018 Year-End Financials
Return on assets: 1.6%
Return on equity: 10.8%
Long-term debt ($ mil.): —
No. of shares (mil.): 95.6
Sales ($ mil): 565.7
Dividends
  Yield: 1.9%
  Payout: 22.7%
Market value ($ mil.): 2,013.0

	STOCK PRICE ($) FY Close	P/E High/Low	PER SHARE ($) Earnings	Dividends	Book Value
12/18	21.04	18 11	1.76	0.40	20.60
12/17	25.73	29 23	0.95	0.24	15.04
12/16	25.17	29 15	0.88	0.16	11.47
12/15	15.65	19 13	0.85	0.07	10.79
12/14	11.91	37 31	0.31	0.04	9.98
Annual Growth	15.3%	— —	54.4%	77.8%	19.9%

Central Garden & Pet Co

Central Garden & Pet tends to all things pets and pests. It is among the largest US producers and distributors of lawn garden and pet supplies providing its products to retailers home improvement centers nurseries and mass merchandisers among them Wal-Mart. The company operates some 35 manufacturing plants and about 20 distribution centers throughout the US. Central Garden & Pet's sells private label and also branded lines such as AMDRO fire ant bait Four Paws animal products Kaytee bird seed Nylabone dog chews and TFH pet books.

Operations

The company operates two businesses Pet and Garden. The Pet segment generates a little more than 60% of revenue by producing distributing marketing and selling a wide variety of pet-related products for the US. The company mainly targets the pet supplies market which includes edible bones chew toys rawhide pet beds and carriers grooming supplies animal health products aquariums water conditioners and other items. Recognizable brands include Four Paws Coralife Kaytee Breeder's Choice and Life Sciences. The US pet market is highly fragmented with about 1400 manufacturers. Central Garden & Pet has a competitive advantage in that it operates its own sales and logistics network.

The Garden segment accounts for a little less than 40% of total revenue. It markets and produces grass seed wild bird feed insect control products lawn and garden care items fertilizers and outdoor patio products. Notable brands include Pennington Seed AMDRO Lilly Miller the Pottery Group and Gulfstream.

About 10% of the products sold by Central Garden & Pet are made in China making it susceptible to tariffs placed on Chinese-made goods in the ongoing tensions between the US and China over trade.

Geographic Reach

Walnut Creek California-headquartered Central Garden & Pet operates 35 manufacturing facilities totaling approximately 5.5 million square feet and 60 sales and logistics facilities totaling approximately 4.4 million square feet. Most sales and logistics centers are comprised of office and warehouse space and several large bays for loading and unloading. Each sales and logistics center provides warehouse distribution sales and support functions for its geographic area.

Although most operations and facilities are in the US the company has a presence in Canada China Mexico and the UK.

Sales and Marketing

Central Garden & Pet relies heavily on just a few national retail chains for much of its sales. The company's largest customer Wal-Mart accounts for about 15% of total sales and about 30% of sales for the company's Garden segment. The Home Depot Lowe's Costco PetSmart along with Wal-Mart generate about half of overall revenue. PETCO is also a big customer.

The company relies on a domestic sales network to promote its proprietary brands to thousands of independent specialty stores.

Financial Performance

Central Garden & Pet runs a steady financial organization. For over a decade its revenue remained in a tight range between $1.6 billion and $1.8 billion before breaking the $2 billion mark in 2017 and 2018 (ended September). Net income followed with large gains in the past two years.

In 2018 Central Garden & Pet's built on the previous year's 12% sales increase. Revenue rose 8% to $2.2 billion on 8% increases in sales of pet and garden products. Acquisitions helped the pet segment to the tune of $56 million as well as the garden segment with $84 million.

Net income for the year leaped 58% higher to $123.6 million in 2018 beating the company high established the year before. Costs associated with acquisitions were higher in 2018 but the US Tax Cuts and Jobs Act lowered Central Garden & Pet's income taxes some $43 million.

Cash at the end of 2018 was $482 million up $450 million from the prior year. Cash from operations was stable at $114 million year-to-year while investing activities used $139 million primarily to acquire businesses. Financing activities however provided about $475 million due to about $300 million in debt issued in 2018. In 2017 financing activities used about $10 million mainly for stock buybacks.

Strategy

Central Garden & Pet focuses on building leading brand names by introducing innovative products and packaging extending existing product lines and entering new product categories. It also continues to make selected strategic acquisitions of companies that complement existing brands and product offerings.

Central Garden & Pet is no stranger to acquisitions having purchased more than 40 companies over its lifespan. In 2018 it bought General Pet Supply based in Milwaukee Wisconsin and Bell Nursery which operates in the mid-Atlantic region.

Because a significant portion of its revenue comes from a handful of retailers the company views customer relationships as a key performance indicator. In 2018 it received awards from Lowe's Petco and Pet Valu for products and service.

The company is streamlining and improving its technologies to enhance efficiency. It has reduced the number of enterprise resource systems from 37 (accumulated through acquisitions) to fewer than 10.

Mergers and Acquisitions

In 2018 Central Garden & Pet purchased General Pet Supply a Midwestern pet food and supplies purveyor for $24 million. The acquisition was expected to expand the company's pet food and supply distribution footprint and provide access to the veterinary channel.

Also in 2018 the company acquired Bell Nursery a distributor in the mid-Atlantic region for $61 million.

In 2017 Central Garden & Pet purchased K&H Manufacturing a producer of premium pet supplies and the largest marketer of heated pet products in the US for $48 million.

Company Background

Central Garden & Pet Company's roots go back to 1955 when it was founded as a small California distributor of lawn and garden supplies. After nearly three decades of unremarkable growth it was purchased in 1980 by William Brown a former VP of finance at camera maker Vivitar. The company acquired small distributors but let them operate autonomously. By 1987 Central had sales of $25 million with distribution in California.

The company's first major acquisition was the result of a restructuring of forestry giant Weyerhaeuser which had diversified into insurance home building and diapers among other products but was selling noncore divisions to focus solely on timber. It sold Weyerhaeuser Garden Supply to Central in 1990 for $32 million.

Overnight Central became a national powerhouse with 25 distribution centers serving 38 states. In 1991 sales reached $280 million of which acquired operations accounted for nearly 70%. The purchase also gave Central 10 high-volume retail customers — including Costco Kmart and Wal-Mart — which accounted for half of its business. That year the company also acquired a pet distributor its first move into pet supplies.

To pay down debt associated with the Weyerhaeuser acquisition the company (then officially known as Central Garden & Pet Company) went public in 1993 (a 1992 IPO was withdrawn when a warehouse fire damaged inventory). With the capital for growth Central continued to acquire other distributors (from early 1993 to early 1994 it acquired six distributors with about $70 million in sales).

In 1994 the company's largest supplier Solaris (then a unit of Monsanto and maker of Ortho and Roundup products) decided to bypass Central as its distributor and sell products directly. Solaris products accounted for nearly 40% of the company's sales and revenues dipped in 1995. However that year Solaris decided that self-distribution was too difficult and made Central its exclusive distributor. Total sales increased about 65% in 1996.

Broadening its pet supply distribution network in 1996 Central paid $33 million for Kenlin Pet Supply the East Coast's largest pet distributor and Longhorn Pet Supply in Texas. The following year the company bought Four Paws Products and Sandoz Agro.

In 1997 Central paid $132 million for TFH Publications one of the nation's largest producers of pet books and maker of Nylabone dog snacks and Kaytee Products a maker of bird seed. It added Pennington Seed a maker of grass and bird seed in 1998.

The company broadened its scope in 1999 with the purchase of Norcal Pottery Products. It also tried to buy Solaris but that year Monsanto sold its Solaris unit to grass firm The Scotts Co. (now Scotts Miracle-Gro). In a familiar refrain for Central Scotts then decided to shift partially toward self-distribution costing Central between $200 million and $250 million in annual sales; Scotts would completely sever distribution ties with Central the following year leading to countering lawsuits.

Central said in early 2000 it would spin off its lawn and garden distribution business to shareholders but the company abandoned the plan less than a year later. In March 2000 the company acquired AMDRO fire ant killer and IMAGE a weed herbicide from American Home Products (now Wyeth) for $28 million. Later that year Central purchased All-Glass Aquarium Company a manufacturer and marketer of aquariums and related products.

HISTORY

Central Garden & Pet Company's roots go back to 1955 when it was founded as a small California distributor of lawn and garden supplies. After nearly three decades of unremarkable growth it was purchased in 1980 by William Brown a former VP of finance at camera maker Vivitar. The company acquired small distributors but let them operate autonomously. By 1987 Central had sales of $25 million with distribution in California.

The company's first major acquisition was the result of a restructuring of forestry giant Weyerhaeuser which had diversified into insurance home building and diapers among other products but was selling noncore divisions to focus solely on timber. It sold Weyerhaeuser Garden Supply to Central in 1990 for $32 million.

Overnight Central became a national powerhouse with 25 distribution centers serving 38 states. In 1991 sales reached $280 million of which acquired operations accounted for nearly 70%. The purchase also gave Central 10 high-volume retail customers — including Costco Kmart and Wal-Mart — which accounted for half of its business. That year the company also acquired a pet distributor its first move into pet supplies.

To pay down debt associated with the Weyerhaeuser acquisition the company (then officially known as Central Garden & Pet Company) went public in 1993 (a 1992 IPO was withdrawn when a warehouse fire damaged inventory). With the capital for growth Central continued to acquire other distributors (from early 1993 to early 1994 it acquired six distributors with about $70 million in sales).

In 1994 the company's largest supplier Solaris (then a unit of Monsanto and maker of Ortho and Roundup products) decided to bypass Central as its distributor and sell products directly. Solaris products accounted for nearly 40% of the company's sales and revenues dipped in 1995. However that year Solaris decided that self-distribution was too difficult and made Central its exclusive distributor. Total sales increased about 65% in 1996.

Broadening its pet supply distribution network in 1996 Central paid $33 million for Kenlin Pet Supply the East Coast's largest pet distributor and Longhorn Pet Supply in Texas. The following year the company bought Four Paws Products and Sandoz Agro.

In 1997 Central paid $132 million for TFH Publications one of the nation's largest producers of pet books and maker of Nylabone dog snacks and Kaytee Products a maker of bird seed. It added Pennington Seed a maker of grass and bird seed in 1998.

The company broadened its scope in 1999 with the purchase of Norcal Pottery Products. It also tried to buy Solaris but that year Monsanto sold its Solaris unit to grass firm The Scotts Company (now Scotts Miracle-Gro). In a familiar refrain for Central Scotts then decided to shift partially toward self-distribution costing Central between $200 million and $250 million in annual sales; Scotts would completely sever distribution ties with Central the following year leading to countering lawsuits.

Central said in early 2000 it would spin off its lawn and garden distribution business to shareholders but the company abandoned the plan less than a year later. In March 2000 the company acquired AMDRO fire ant killer and IMAGE a weed herbicide from American Home Products (now Wyeth) for $28 million. Later that year Central purchased All-Glass Aquarium Company a manufacturer and marketer of aquariums and related products.

As a result of no longer being the distributor of Scotts products Central closed 13 of its distribution centers in 2001. Central announced the next year that it would restate its financial results for 1998 through 2002. The company said the changes would improve fiscal 2001 net results by $2 million but decrease net results by $1.7 million in 2000 $0.3 million in 1999 and $0.1 million in 1998. Also that year Mars' Kal Kan Division and Arch Chemicals stopped using Central as a distributor.

In 2003 Central acquired a 49% stake in E. M. Matson a lawn and garden manufacturer in the western US.

In 2004 the company completed a menagerie's worth of acquisitions: Kent Marine an aquarium supplements maker; New England Pottery which sells decorative pottery and Christmas items (from Heritage Partners); Lawrence plc's pet products division Interpet; KRB Seed which does business as Budd Seed (Rebel and Palmer's Pride grass-seed brands); and Energy Savers Unlimited which distributes aquarium lighting systems and related environmental controls and conditioners.

It continued along the same path throughout the rest of the decade acquiring Gulfstream Home & Garden (garden products) Pets International (small animal and specialty pet supplies) Farnam Companies (animal health products) and the assets of family-owned pet food maker Breeder's Choice. The firm also increased its stakes in insect control products supplier Tech Pac (from 20% to 80%) and garden controls manufacturer Matson (from 50% to full ownership).

EXECUTIVES

President and CEO, George C. Roeth, age 58, $232,500 total compensation
EVP, Michael A. Reed, age 71, $480,808 total compensation
General Counsel and Corporate Secretary, George A. Yuhas, age 66, $459,438 total compensation
CFO, Nicholas (Niko) Lahanas
Vice President, Carl Peterson
Vice President Retail Sales and Services, Roger Mosshart
Senior Vice President Marketing, Todd Regan
Vice President of Marketing, Kameshia Watkins
Vice President Marketing, Darren Horst
Vice President Planning and Procurement, Dave Norman
Vice President Legal Affairs, Barry Harrison
Senior Vice President General Manager Central Pet Home Essentials, Cristina Weekes
Vice President of Operations, Scott Peterson
Vice President Of Marketing, Clare Schueren
Vice President, Gary Sparks
Vice President Sales, Wendy Melin
Vice President of Distribution, Jordan Downs
Vice President, Jim Stewart
Senior Vice President of Human Resources, Marilyn Leahy
Vice President of Sales, Patricia Owens
Regional Vice President Distribution, Johnny Laturell
Executive Vice President Pennington Seed, Dan Pennington
National Account Manager, Eric Spiegler
Vice President Total Rewards, Derek Hess
Senior Vice President Marketing, David Carrillo
National Account Manager, Mike Flynn
Vice President, James Mathews
Svp Operations, William Lynch
Vice President Grocery Sales, David Kofsky
Senior Vice President and General Manager Central Life Sciences, Trevor Thorley
Senior Vice President Operations, Bill Lynch
NATIONAL SALES MANAGER SPECIALTY PRODUCTS, Richard Alford
Vice President Marketing, Kevin Tompkins
Vice President Global Supply Chain, Brice Beehler
Senior Vice President General Manager, Scott Lazarczyk
Chairman, William E. (Bill) Brown, age 78
Board Member, Kip Edwards
Board Member, Andrew Woeber
Auditors: DELOITTE & TOUCHE LLP

LOCATIONS

HQ: Central Garden & Pet Co
1340 Treat Blvd., Suite 600, Walnut Creek, CA 94597
Phone: 925 948-4000
Web: www.central.com

PRODUCTS/OPERATIONS

2018 Sales

	$ mil.	% of total
Pet Products		
Dog and cat products	444.4	20
Other pet products	896.5	40
Garden Products		
Garden controls and fertilizer products	345.7	16
Other garden supplies	528.8	24
Total	**2,215.4**	**100**

Selected Products and Brands

Pet products
  Aquatics
  All-Glass Aquarium
  Kent Marine
  Bird and small animal
  Kaytee
  Dog and cat
  Four Paws
  Interpet
  Nylabone
  Pet Select
  TFH
  Insect control and animal health
  Strike
  Zodiac
Garden products
  Garden decor and pottery
  New England Pottery
  Grass seed
  Lofts Seed
  Pennington
  Rebel
  Weed insect and pest control
  AMDRO
  IMAGE
  Lilly Miller
  Over'n Out
  Sevin
  Wild bird
  Kaytee
  Pennington

COMPETITORS

A.C. Graham
Boss Holdings
Doskocil Manufacturing Company
Dow AgroSciences
Hartz Mountain
Meda Pharmaceuticals
Rollins Inc.
Scotts Miracle-Gro
Spectrum Brands
Virbac Corporation

HISTORICAL FINANCIALS

Company Type: Public

Income Statement
FYE: September 28

	REVENUE ($ mil.)	NET INCOME ($ mil.)	NET PROFIT MARGIN	EMPLOYEES
09/19	2,383.0	92.7	3.9%	5,800
09/18	2,215.3	123.5	5.6%	5,400
09/17	2,054.4	78.8	3.8%	4,100
09/16	1,829.0	44.5	2.4%	3,600
09/15	1,650.7	31.9	1.9%	3,300
Annual Growth	9.6%	30.5%	—	15.1%

2019 Year-End Financials

Debt ratio: 34.2%
Return on equity: 9.5%
Cash ($ mil.): 510.7
Current ratio: 4.69
Long-term debt ($ mil.): 693.0
No. of shares (mil.): 56.1
Dividends
  Yield: —
  Payout: —
Market value ($ mil.): 1,570.0

	STOCK PRICE ($) FY Close	P/E High/Low	PER SHARE ($) Earnings	Dividends	Book Value
09/19	27.95	22 13	1.61	0.00	17.73
09/18	33.14	17 14	2.32	0.00	16.49
09/17	37.19	24 14	1.52	0.00	12.26
09/16	24.39	28 13	0.87	0.00	10.83
09/15	16.78	26 11	0.64	0.00	10.10
Annual Growth	13.6%	— —	25.9%	—	15.1%

Central Valley Community Bancorp

EXECUTIVES

Vice President Cash Management Manager, Cathy Chatoian
Executive Vice President Chief Administrative Officer, Teresa Gilio
Senior Vice President, Steve Romeo
Senior Vice President Director Of Client Relationships, Karen Smith
Vice President and Compliance Officer, Denise Jereb
Senior Vice President Real Estate Team Leader, Jeff Pace
Vice President Sales, Shannon Reinard
Vice President Assistant Credit Admin, Steve Freeland
Vice President, Jean Ornelas
Senior Vice President, Mark Smith
Vice President Commercial Loan, Robert Walker
Vice President Controller Central Valley Community Bank, Dawn Crusinberry
Vice President Commercial Loan Officer, Chad Bringe
Vice President Manager, Ramina Ushana
Senior Vice President Loan Servicing, Renee Savage
Vice President Commercial Banking, Brad Wible
Vice President Commercial Relationship Officer, Elaine Pasch
Senior Vice President Chief Credit Officer, Tom Sommer
Senior Vice President Agribusiness Team Leader, Rick Shaeffer
Vice President Commercial Relationship Manager, Becki Roberts
Assistant Vice President And Customer Service Manager, Suzi Lewis
Vice President: Commercial Relationship Officer, Bruce Lofgren
Vice President Commercial Loan, Thomas Crawley
Senior Vice President Sba Manager, Dorothy Thomas
Senior Vice President Director Of Information Technology, Dan Demmers
Senior Vice President, Stefani Woods
Senior Vice President Human Resources, Dawn Cagle
Senior Vice President Senior Credit Officer, Chris Clark
Executive Vice President Market Executive Of The Bank, Blaine Lauhon
Vice Chairman, Daniel N Cunningham
Board Member, Karen Musson
Auditors: Crowe LLP

LOCATIONS
HQ: Central Valley Community Bancorp
7100 N. Financial Dr., Suite 101, Fresno, CA 93720
Phone: 559 298-1775
Web: www.cvcb.com

COMPETITORS
American River Bankshares
Bank of America
Comerica
MUFG Americas Holdings
RCB Corp.
Sierra Bancorp
TriCo Bancshares
United Security Bancshares
Westamerica

HISTORICAL FINANCIALS
Company Type: Public

Income Statement				FYE: December 31
	ASSETS ($ mil.)	NET INCOME ($ mil.)	INCOME AS % OF ASSETS	EMPLOYEES
12/18	1,537.8	21.2	1.4%	290
12/17	1,661.6	14.0	0.8%	316
12/16	1,443.3	15.1	1.1%	287
12/15	1,276.7	10.9	0.9%	282
12/14	1,192.1	5.2	0.4%	290
Annual Growth	6.6%	41.6%	—	0.0%

2018 Year-End Financials
Return on assets: 1.3%
Return on equity: 9.9%
Long-term debt ($ mil.): —
No. of shares (mil.): 13.7
Sales ($ mil): 74.5
Dividends
Yield: 1.6%
Payout: 26.9%
Market value ($ mil.): 260.0

	STOCK PRICE ($) FY Close	P/E High/Low	PER SHARE ($) Earnings	Dividends	Book Value
12/18	18.87	14 11	1.54	0.31	15.98
12/17	20.18	21 16	1.10	0.24	15.30
12/16	19.96	15 8	1.33	0.24	13.51
12/15	12.03	13 10	1.00	0.23	12.67
12/14	11.08	28 22	0.48	0.20	11.93
Annual Growth	14.2%	— —	33.8%	11.6%	7.6%

Century Bancorp, Inc.

Century Bancorp is the holding company for Century Bank and Trust which serves Boston and surrounding parts of northeastern Massachusetts from more than 25 branches. Boasting some $3.6 billion in total assets the bank offers standard deposit products including checking savings and money market accounts; CDs; and IRAs. Nearly two-thirds of its loan portfolio is comprised of commercial and commercial real estate loans. while residential mortgages and home equity loans make up around 30%. The bank also writes construction and land development loans business loans and personal loans. It offers brokerage services through an agreement with third-party provider LPL Financial.

Operations
Century Bank also provides cash management short-term financing and transaction processing services to municipalities in Massachusetts and Rhode Island. It offers automated lockbox collection services to its municipal customers as well as commercial clients. The bank also continues to open new branches in its traditional market area in metropolitan Boston.

The bank gets more than 80% of its revenue in the form of interest income (mostly from loans). It generated 32% of its total revenue from taxable loans in 2014 while another 18% came from non-taxable loans and 35% came from interest income on the bank's investment securities. On the non-interest side the bank made 8% of its overall revenue from service charges on deposit accounts 3% from lockbox fees and a negligible amount on brokerage commissions and gains on sales of securities or mortgage loans.

Geographic Reach
The bank operates more than 25 branches in 20 cities and towns across Massachusetts ranging from Braintree in the South to Andover in the northern part of the state.

Sales and Marketing
Most of Century Bank's business comes from small and medium-sized businesses needing commercial loans though the bank also serves retail customers as well as local governments and other institutions throughout Massachusetts.

The bank spent $1.79 million on advertising in 2014 compared to $1.75 million and $1.85 million in 2013 and 2012 respectively.

Financial Performance
Century Bancorp's revenues and profits have been steadily rising over the past few years thanks to increased loan business and declining loan loss provisions as its loan portfolio's credit quality has been improving in the strengthening economy.

The bank's revenue rose by more than 2% to a record $100.64 million in 2014 mostly as it collected more interest income from long-term securities and non-taxable loans during the year. The bank's earning securities assets grew by 8.5% during the year while the size of its loan business swelled by double-digits with increased tax-exempt lending and residential second mortgage lending; all of which boosted interest income during the year.

Higher revenue lower interest expenses on deposits and a continued dip in loan loss provisions in 2014 pushed Century's net income higher by 9% to a record $21.86 million. The bank's operating cash also grew by 7% to $22.39 million thanks to higher cash earnings.

Strategy
Century Bancorp has been growing organically through new branch openings and digital bank product launches in recent years. In 2014 for example the bank opened its new branch in Woburn Massachusetts and launched its all-new Century Bank Mobile App which boosted customer convenience and allowed the bank to better compete with larger banks with more expansive branch networks.

Showcasing its strong financial capitalization the bank received an "A" rating from the Standard and Poor's credit ratings agency in 2015 making Century Bank the only regional bank in the state to receive such a rating.

EXECUTIVES

Senior Vice President, Susan Delahunt
EVP Century Bank and Trust Company, Paul A. Evangelista, age 55, $337,614 total compensation
EVP Century Bank and Trust Company, David B. Woonton, age 63, $337,614 total compensation

President CEO and Director, Barry R. Sloane, age 64, $569,207 total compensation
CFO and Treasurer, William P. Hornby, age 52, $294,708 total compensation
EVP Century Bank and Trust Company, Linda Sloane Kay, age 57, $294,708 total compensation
EVP Century Bank and Trust, Brian J. Feeney, age 58, $294,708 total compensation
Vice President, Jim Smith
Senior Vice President, James Flynn
Vice President, Anna Gorska
VICE PRESIDENT, Nancy M Marsh
Senior Vice President, Brad Buckley
Senior Vice President Director Of Underwriting And Loan Review, Thomas Piemontese
Vice President, Bradford J Buckley
Senior Vice President, Deb Rush
Chairman, Marshall M. Sloane, age 92
Auditors: KPMG LLP

LOCATIONS
HQ: Century Bancorp, Inc.
  400 Mystic Avenue, Medford, MA 02155
Phone: 781 391-4000
Web: www.centurybank.com

PRODUCTS/OPERATIONS

2014 Sales

	$ mil.	% of total
Interest		
Loans	50.1	50
Securities	2.9	3
Other	32.4	32
Noninterest		
Service charges on deposit accounts	8.1	8
Lockbox fees	3.1	3
Gains on sales of Mortgage loans	2.5	3
Other	1.5	1
Total	**100.6**	**100**

COMPETITORS

Boston Private	Eastern Bank
Brookline Bancorp	Middlesex Savings
Cambridge Financial	Peoples Federal
Capital Crossing	Bancshares Inc.
Central Bancorp	Sovereign Bank
Citizens Financial Group	

HISTORICAL FINANCIALS
Company Type: Public

Income Statement — FYE: December 31

	ASSETS ($ mil.)	NET INCOME ($ mil.)	INCOME AS % OF ASSETS	EMPLOYEES
12/18	5,163.9	36.2	0.7%	460
12/17	4,785.5	22.3	0.5%	447
12/16	4,462.6	24.5	0.5%	438
12/15	3,947.4	23.0	0.6%	438
12/14	3,624.0	21.8	0.6%	440
Annual Growth	9.3%	13.4%	—	1.1%

2018 Year-End Financials
Return on assets: 0.7%
Return on equity: 12.9%
Long-term debt ($ mil.): —
No. of shares (mil.): 5.5
Sales ($ mil): 153.3
Dividends
  Yield: 0.7%
  Payout: 10.1%
Market value ($ mil.): 377.0

	STOCK PRICE ($) FY Close	P/E High/Low	PER SHARE ($) Earnings	Dividends	Book Value
12/18	67.73	11 8	6.50	0.48	53.96
12/17	78.25	18 12	4.01	0.48	46.75
12/16	60.00	12 7	4.41	0.48	43.11
12/15	43.46	9 8	4.13	0.48	38.53
12/14	40.06	8 7	3.93	0.48	34.57
Annual Growth	14.0%	— —	13.4%	(0.0%)	11.8%

Century Communities Inc

Auditors: Ernst & Young LLP

LOCATIONS
HQ: Century Communities Inc
  8390 East Crescent Parkway, Suite 650, Greenwood Village, CO 80111
Phone: 303 770-8300

HISTORICAL FINANCIALS
Company Type: Public

Income Statement — FYE: December 31

	REVENUE ($ mil.)	NET INCOME ($ mil.)	NET PROFIT MARGIN	EMPLOYEES
12/18	2,147.4	96.4	4.5%	1,389
12/17	1,423.8	50.3	3.5%	1,011
12/16	994.4	49.5	5.0%	565
12/15	734.4	39.8	5.4%	510
12/14	362.3	20.0	5.5%	397
Annual Growth	56.0%	48.2%	—	36.8%

2018 Year-End Financials
Debt ratio: 48.4%
Return on equity: 12.1%
Cash ($ mil.): 57.2
Current ratio: 6.79
Long-term debt ($ mil.): 1,091.8
No. of shares (mil.): 30.1
Dividends
  Yield: —
  Payout: —
Market value ($ mil.): 520.0

	STOCK PRICE ($) FY Close	P/E High/Low	PER SHARE ($) Earnings	Dividends	Book Value
12/18	17.26	11 5	3.17	0.00	28.50
12/17	31.10	15 10	2.03	0.00	24.92
12/16	21.00	9 6	2.33	0.00	21.91
12/15	17.71	12 8	1.88	0.00	19.22
12/14	17.28	22 15	1.03	0.00	17.49
Annual Growth	(0.0%)	— —	32.5%	—	13.0%

Cerence Inc

Auditors: BDO USA, LLP

LOCATIONS
HQ: Cerence Inc
  15 Wayside Road, Burlington, MA 01803
Phone: 857 362-7300
Web: www.cerence.com

HISTORICAL FINANCIALS
Company Type: Public

Income Statement — FYE: September 30

	REVENUE ($ mil.)	NET INCOME ($ mil.)	NET PROFIT MARGIN	EMPLOYEES
09/19	303.3	100.2	33.1%	1,400
09/18	276.9	5.8	2.1%	1,300
09/17	244.7	47.2	19.3%	0
09/16	211.1	34.9	16.5%	0
Annual Growth	12.8%	42.1%	—	—

2019 Year-End Financials
Debt ratio: —
Return on equity: 9.7%
Cash ($ mil.): —
Current ratio: 0.72
Long-term debt ($ mil.): —
No. of shares (mil.): 36.4
Dividends
  Yield: —
  Payout: —
Market value ($ mil.): —

	STOCK PRICE ($) FY Close	P/E High/Low	PER SHARE ($) Earnings	Dividends	Book Value
09/19	0.00	— —	2.76	0.00	29.35
Annual Growth	—	— —	—	—	—

Charles River Laboratories International Inc.

Charles River Laboratories International provides early-stage contract research organization (CRO) services to pharmaceutical firms and other manufacturers and institutions. The company provides contract drug discovery services including target identification and toxicology through its Discovery and Safety Assessment segment. Its Research Models and Services (RMS) segment is a leading global provider of research models (lab rats and mice) bred specifically for use in medical testing. The Manufacturing Support unit offers biologics testing and chicken eggs for vaccines. Charles River has operations in about 20 countries but generates more than half of sales in the US.

Operations

Charles River operates through three reportable segments: Discovery and Safety Assessment (DSA) Research Models and Services (RMS) and Manufacturing Support.

The DSA segment which accounts for nearly 60% of revenue provides outsourced services required to take a drug through early development stages in a range of disease categories including oncology cardiovascular care neurology and immunology. The Discovery Services business provides target identification and validation services including in vitro and in vivo biology medicinal chemistry and biomarker development. The Safety Assessment unit provides bioanalysis pharmacology pharmacokinetics toxicology pathology and other non-clinical drug safety testing services.

The RMS segment accounts for about 25% of sales. Its Research Models business provides small and large research models (purpose-bred rats and mice) and related services. The Genetically Engineered Model Services unit provides models for biomedical research while the Research Animal Diagnostic Services unit provides model health monitoring services. Insourcing Solutions (IS) provides colony management of clients' research operations including recruitment training and management services.

The Manufacturing Support segment accounting for about 20% of revenue includes the Microbial Solutions business which provides in vitro laboratory quality control testing for drugs and consumer goods. It also includes Biologics Testing Solutions which provides testing of biologics and Avian Vaccine Services which supplies specific-pathogen-free (SPF) fertile chicken eggs and chickens used in vaccine production. The Accugenix subsidiary provides contract microbial identification and genetic sequence testing.

Geographic Reach

Based in Wilmington Massachusetts Charles River has about 80 locations in 20 countries. While sales in the US account for more than half of its annual revenue the company is growing its operations in other key markets including Europe (about 30% of sales) Canada (nearly 10%) and the Asia/Pacific region (about 5%).

Sales and Marketing

Charles River provides its products and services directly to customers around the globe. Clients include small midsized and large pharmaceutical biotechnology agricultural chemical and life science companies as well as educational health care and government institutions. It also supplies research models to other CROs.

The company primarily sells its products and services through a direct sales force and business development professionals in North America Europe and the Asia/Pacific region. In some markets sales are assisted by international distributors and agents. Marketing efforts include organizing scientific conferences publishing scientific papers conducting webinars and presenting at trade shows. It also participates in online and direct mail marketing.

Charles River spent $1.9 million on advertising costs for 2018 up from $1.6 million in 2017.

Financial Performance

Charles River's revenue has climbed steadily higher in recent years rising 75% between 2014 and 2018. Net income remained in the $125 to $150 million range between 2014 and 2017 and then rose above $200 million in 2018.

The company reported a sales increase of 22% in 2018 to nearly $2.3 billion due to strong increases in customer demand in the DSA and Manufacturing Services segments as well as increased demand in the RMS segment (primarily in China). Acquisitions also contributed to growth that year primarily in the DSA segment.

Net income rose 84% to some $226.4 million in 2018 due to higher revenue and lower tax expenses (related to the US Tax Act) despite higher operating and acquisition costs.

The company ended 2018 with $197.3 million in cash up $31 million from 2017. Operating activities contributed $441.1 million while investing activities used $955 million (mostly on acquisitions) and financing activities contributed $558.1 million via an expanded credit line.

Strategy

Charles River's services aim to help clients bring new therapies to market quickly cost-effectively and safely. As drug and biotech companies look to outsource more R&D processes Charles River is working to deliver a one-stop full-service CRO solution for companies looking to outsource early-stage drug discovery and development efforts. Towards that end the company has worked to improve efficiencies within its organization to better support clients. In 2018 it combined its Discovery and Safety Assessment units into one segment to provide more integrated services.

Forming new long-term relationships and expanding service contracts with large global drugmakers government agencies and research institutions is core to the company's expansion strategy. It also works to provide highly flexible solutions to small biotech companies.

The firm has made several acquisitions in recent years to expand its Discovery and Safety Assessment segment. The company also partners with other research firms; it teamed up with Distributed Bio to begin offering antibody platform services in 2018 and with Atomwise to provide AI-driven drug discovery services in 2019.

The company grows organically by launching new product offerings. In 2018 it expanded its early discovery services when it began offering high-speed pharmacokinetics screening to help firms identify small-molecule candidates.

As a CRO the company is dependent on its clients' research budgets. Any market downturn in spending on drug R&D could negatively impact its finances.

Mergers and Acquisitions

Charles River Laboratories has been on a buying spree as of late. In 2019 it acquired non-clinical CRO Citoxlab for some $510 million. Citoxlab specializes in regulated safety assessment services non-regulated discovery services and medical device testing with operations in North America and Europe.

The company bought early-stage CRO MPI Research for some $800 million in 2018 to expand its safety assessment operations. MPI has a roster of small and midsized biotech customers which Charles River Laboratories sees as a fast-growing market. That purchase also expanded the company's toxicology testing abilities.

To expand its in vivo discovery service offerings in early 2018 the company acquired CRO KWS BioTest which provides in vitro and in vivo discovery testing services for areas including immuno-oncology and inflammatory and infectious diseases in a deal worth up to $24 million. It also purchased Australian microbial identification firm Microgenetix that year.

Company Background

The company was founded in 1947 as Charles River Breeding Laboratories in Boston Massachusetts by Dr. Henry Foster. It began commercial pathogen-free rodent production in 1955 at its new headquarters in Wilmington Massachusetts. In 1966 it expanded overseas by opening an animal production facility in France.

The company was acquired by Bausch & Lomb in 1984. In 1997 Jim Foster purchased Charles River back from Bausch & Lomb. The company went public on the NYSE in 2000.

Acquisitions over the years included Argenta BioFocus Agilux Labs and Brains On-Line.

EXECUTIVES

Corporate EVP Human Resources Chief Administrative Officer General Counsel and Secretary, David P. Johst, age 57, $567,496 total compensation
Senior Financial Advisor, Thomas F. Ackerman, age 65, $512,245 total compensation
Chairman President and CEO, James C. Foster, age 68, $1,069,089 total compensation
Corporate SVP; President European Preclinical Services, Brian Bathgate, age 59
Corporate EVP and Chief Scientific Officer, Nancy A. Gillett, age 63, $500,523 total compensation
VP Charles River Europe, J ¶rg M. Geller, age 64, $400,520 total compensation
Corporate EVP and President Global Research Models & Services and Preclinical Services Operations, Davide Molho, $450,853 total compensation
Corporate SVP Global Sales and Marketing, William D. Barbo
SVP Information Technology and CIO, Arthur C. Hubbs
Corporate SVP and General Manager Research Models & Services Europe and Asia, Colin Dunn
EVP and CFO, David R. Smith
Corporate Senior Vice President North American Safety Assessment, Glenn Washer
Senior Vice President Information Technology and Chief Officer, Shanna Cotti
Corporate Vice President, Greg Beattie
Board Member, George Massaro
Board Member, Stephen Chubb
Board Member, Martin Mackay
Auditors: PricewaterhouseCoopers LLP

LOCATIONS

HQ: Charles River Laboratories International Inc. 251 Ballardvale Street, Wilmington, MA 01887
Phone: 781 222-6000
Web: www.criver.com

PRODUCTS/OPERATIONS

2016 Sales

	$ mil.	% of total
Discovery and safety assessment	836.6	50
Research Models & Services	494.0	29
Manufacturing support	350.8	21
Total	**1,681.4**	**100**

Selected Services

Agrochemical & veterinary services
Antibody production services
Avian products & services
Biopharmaceutical services
Clinical trial services
Consulting & staffing services
Discovery & imaging services
Endotoxin & microbial detection
Equipment & instrumentation
Facilities design & management services
Genetic testing services
Genetically engineered models & services
In Vitro services
Pathology associates
Preclinical services
Program management
Regulatory navigator services
Research animal diagnostic services
Research animal models
Surgical model services

COMPETITORS

Albany Molecular Research	Jackson Laboratory
BioReliance	MPI Research
Bioanalytical Systems	Nordion
Covance	PAREXEL
Deltagen	PRA Health Sciences
Harlan Laboratories	PharmaNet Development Group
ICON	Taconic
IQVIA	WuXi PharmaTech

HISTORICAL FINANCIALS
Company Type: Public

Income Statement — FYE: December 29

	REVENUE ($ mil.)	NET INCOME ($ mil.)	NET PROFIT MARGIN	EMPLOYEES
12/18	2,266.1	226.3	10.0%	14,700
12/17	1,857.6	123.3	6.6%	11,800
12/16	1,681.4	154.7	9.2%	11,000
12/15	1,363.3	149.3	11.0%	8,600
12/14	1,297.6	126.7	9.8%	7,900
Annual Growth	15.0%	15.6%	—	16.8%

2018 Year-End Financials
Debt ratio: 43.2%
Return on equity: 19.2%
Cash ($ mil.): 195.4
Current ratio: 1.61
Long-term debt ($ mil.): 1,636.6
No. of shares (mil.): 48.2
Dividends
Yield: —
Payout: —
Market value ($ mil.): 5,386.0

	STOCK PRICE ($) FY Close	P/E High/Low	PER SHARE ($) Earnings	Dividends	Book Value
12/18	111.72	29 21	4.62	0.00	27.33
12/17	109.45	45 29	2.54	0.00	22.05
12/16	76.19	27 20	3.23	0.00	17.67
12/15	80.08	26 19	3.13	0.00	15.70
12/14	64.29	24 19	2.66	0.00	14.20
Annual Growth	14.8%	— —	14.8%	—	17.8%

Chatham Lodging Trust

Self-advised real estate investment trust (REIT) Chatham Lodging acquires upscale extended-stay hotels including Residence Inn by Marriott Homewood Suites by Hilton and Hyatt House locations To a lesser extent the firm will also buy select-service and full-service hotels such as Courtyard by Marriott Hampton Inn and Hilton Garden Inn. Chatham Lodging owns nearly 40 hotels with almost 5700 rooms across 15 US states. Through two joint ventures it also has minority interests in 95 other hotels with 12500 rooms/suites. When assembling its portfolio the REIT seeks properties being sold at a discount particularly in large US metropolitan markets including Dallas Denver and Pittsburgh.

Operations
Chatham Lodging operates mainly select service or limited service hotels and as such does not book significant revenue from food and beverages or group conference facilities. Indeed room revenue accounted for 94% of the REIT's total revenue during 2014.

Geographic Reach
Palm Beach-based Chatham Lodging has properties in 16 states: California Colorado Connecticut Florida Georgia Kentucky Maine Massachusetts Minnesota New Hampshire New York Pennsylvania Tennessee Texas Virginia Washington and Washington DC.

Sales and Marketing
The REIT has been boosting its advertising spend in recent years to support sales growth. It spent $3.7 million on advertising during 2014 up from $2.8 million and $2.3 million in 2013 and 2012 respectively.

Financial Performance
Chatham Lodging's revenue has grown more than eight-fold since 2010 as it has expanded its property portfolio through acquisitions and has charged higher rental rates as the real estate market has strengthened. It's also been climbing back from years of losses as it's kept a lid on operating costs and interest expenses on its long-term debt.

The REIT's revenue spiked 56% to $197.22 million during 2014 mostly thanks to added room revenue stemming from six hotel acquisitions in 2013 and nine hotel acquisitions in 2014.

Strong revenue growth in 2014 drove Chatham Lodging's net income sharply up to $67.1 million (compared to $3 million in 2013). The REIT's operating cash levels jumped 56% to $49.3 million for the year as cash earnings rose.

Strategy
Chatham reiterated in 2016 that it looked to acquire upscale extended-stay hotels and premium branded select-service hotel properties in the 25 largest metro areas in the US that are priced below replacement costs in their markets. Indeed through acquisitions made between 2010 and 2014 the REIT has more than quintupled its hotel property investments from $208 million to nearly $1.1 billion.

While Chatham also takes minority interests in other hotels through joint ventures it also sells off properties that could yield big profits. In 2014 for example the REIT reached an agreement to sell the hotels owned by its joint venture with Cerberus Capital Management (acquired in 2011) to Northstar Realty Finance with Chatham netting a gain of $80 million on the $1.3 billion sale.

EXECUTIVES
Chairman President and CEO, Jeffrey H. Fisher, age 64, $209,589 total compensation
EVP and COO, Dennis M. Craven, age 47, $88,233 total compensation
EVP and Chief Investment Officer, Peter M. Willis, age 52, $199,110 total compensation
CFO, Jeremy Wegner
Vice President Of Financial Analysis, Rick Fenton
Auditors: PricewaterhouseCoopers LLP

LOCATIONS
HQ: Chatham Lodging Trust
222 Lakeview Avenue, Suite 200, West Palm Beach, FL 33401
Phone: 561 802-4477
Web: www.chathamlodgingtrust.com

PRODUCTS/OPERATIONS

2014 sales

	% of total
Room	94
Food and Beverage	1
Cost reimbursements	1
Others	4
Total	100

COMPETITORS

Ashford Hospitality Trust	Hersha Hospitality
Chesapeake Lodging	Host Hotels & Resorts
DiamondRock Hospitality	Innkeepers USA
FelCor	Sunstone Hotel Investors

HISTORICAL FINANCIALS
Company Type: Public

Income Statement — FYE: December 31

	REVENUE ($ mil.)	NET INCOME ($ mil.)	NET PROFIT MARGIN	EMPLOYEES
12/18	324.2	30.6	9.5%	40
12/17	298.8	29.4	9.9%	45
12/16	293.8	31.4	10.7%	45
12/15	276.9	32.9	11.9%	47
12/14	197.2	66.8	33.9%	45
Annual Growth	13.2%	(17.7%)	—	(2.9%)

2018 Year-End Financials
Debt ratio: 40.5%
Return on equity: 3.8%
Cash ($ mil.): 7.1
Current ratio: 0.75
Long-term debt ($ mil.): 583.2
No. of shares (mil.): 46.5
Dividends
Yield: 7.4%
Payout: 200.0%
Market value ($ mil.): 823.0

	STOCK PRICE ($) FY Close	P/E High/Low	PER SHARE ($) Earnings	Dividends	Book Value
12/18	17.68	35 26	0.66	1.32	17.14
12/17	22.76	33 26	0.73	1.32	17.70
12/16	20.55	30 20	0.81	1.38	17.64
12/15	20.48	36 23	0.86	1.20	18.09
12/14	28.97	13 9	2.30	0.93	17.22
Annual Growth	(11.6%)	— —	(26.8%)	9.1%	(0.1%)

Chefs' Warehouse Inc (The)

A distributor of specialty food products Chefs' Warehouse sells such gourmet food items as artisan charcuterie specialty cheeses hormone-free protein truffles caviar and chocolates as well as basic food ingredients like cooking oils flour butter milk and eggs. The company provides more than 55000 items sourced from 2200 suppliers to a core customer base comprising chefs from independent restaurants fine dining establishments culinary schools hotels and country clubs. Its Allen Brothers subsidiary sells prime cuts direct to consumers via mail and online. Chefs' Warehouse typically focuses on culinary hotbeds such as New York City San Francisco Los Angeles and Washington DC. Tracing its roots back to 1985 Chefs' Warehouse went public in 2011.

Financial Performance
Chefs' Warehouse's revenue has been tracking upward consistently over the last ten years mostly due to acquisitions.

In fiscal 2018 (ended December 28) the company's sales grew 11% to $1.4 billion due to a mixture of organic growth and contributions from newly acquired companies. Chefs' Warehouses' specialty category grew 6% and its center-of-the-plate (prime meat cuts) category grew 3%. Sales in 2018 were boosted by the first full-year contribution of Fells Point a specialty protein manufacturer acquired in mid-2017.

Net income grew 42% to $20.4 million thanks to higher sales and margin growth in the center-of-the-plate category partially offset by a percentage increase in operating expenses.

Chefs' Warehouse's cash on hand grew slightly during 2018 ending the year $906000 higher at $42.4 million. The company's operations generated $45.1 million while its investing activities used $33.7 million and its financing used $10.4 million. Chef's Warehouse's main cash uses in 2018 were capital expenditures ($19.8 million) acquisitions ($13.9 million) and debt repayments while it also took on new borrowing.

Strategy

Chefs' Warehouse's growth strategy rests on acquiring new food distributors and increasing sales to new and existing customers. It is focused on expanding the depth and breadth of its product offering providing exceptional customer service increasing the use of technology across its operations and consolidating the fragmented specialty foodservice industry. Chefs' Warehouse has completed eight acquisitions since the start of 2015 (at a cost of $188.3 million) helping the company penetrate new markets and expand its product lines. Acquisitions have been funding by borrowing and proceeds from stock offerings.

Mergers and Acquisitions

Going forward Chefs' Warehouse's growth strategy continues to include acquisitions of small food distributors that beef up its entree offerings. In 2013 the company purchased Qzina Specialty Foods North America a Florida-based supplier of gourmet chocolate dessert and pastry products that serves pastry chefs in a deal worth some $32.7 million. In 2012 it bought out Michael's Finer Meats a Midwest distributor of meat and seafood for approximately $54.3 million. The deal was one of several; earlier in the year Chefs' Warehouse purchased Praml International a specialty foods importer and foodservice distributor founded in 1987. The acquisition extended the company's reach to some 500 locations in Las Vegas and Reno. Chefs' Warehouse expanded its operations into south Florida after acquiring Monique & Me Inc. (dba Culinaire Specialty Foods) for $3.7 million in 2010. The previous year it bought the San Francisco division of European Imports for $3.8 million. The transaction bolstered its California operations.

Company Background

The Pappas family originally founded the company in 1985 as Dairyland USA a specialty dairy product distributor that served chefs in the New York metropolitan area. The company later expanded into other large US markets through acquisitions of small specialty food products distributors.

EXECUTIVES

Chief Information Officer, Frank ODowd
CFO, John D. Austin
Executive Vice President West Coast and Canada, Bruce Luong
Regional Vice President, Rodney Aguirre
Vice President Finance, Lori Snowden
Vice President Finance, Brad Lavaty
Vice President of Sales, John Groendyke
Regional Vice President Sales Del Monte Meat Company, Vince Licata
Vice President Of Business Development West, Tara Brennan
Vice President Of Marketing, David Vogel
Vp It, Matthew Wyman
Vice President Sales, Colby Morse
Vice President Of Purchasing, Matthew Harris
Vice Chairman, John Pappas, age 55
Board Member, Alan Guarino
Board Member, Dominick Cerbone
Auditors: BDO USA, LLP

LOCATIONS

HQ: Chefs' Warehouse Inc (The)
  100 East Ridge Road, Ridgefield, CT 06877
Phone: 203 894-1345
Web: www.chefswarehouse.com

PRODUCTS/OPERATIONS

2018 Products sales

	% of total
Center of plate	44
Dry Goods	18
Pastries	14
Cheeses and Charcuterie	10
Dairy and Eggs	7
Oils and Vinegars	5
Kitchen supplies	2
Total	**100**

Selected Products

Baking
Beverages
Caviar
Cheese & dairy
Chocolate
Coffee & tea
Condiments
Dry goods
Foie gras & pate
Fruits & nuts
Gluten-free
Molecular gastronomy
Oil & vinegar
Organic
Pasta
Specialty meats
Specialty seafood
Spices
Regional

COMPETITORS

American Milk Products	Economy Foods
Cheney Brothers	European Imports
DPI Specialty Foods	World Finer Foods
Dole & Bailey Inc.	atalanta

HISTORICAL FINANCIALS
Company Type: Public

Income Statement
FYE: December 28

	REVENUE ($ mil.)	NET INCOME ($ mil.)	NET PROFIT MARGIN	EMPLOYEES
12/18	1,444.6	20.4	1.4%	2,316
12/17	1,301.5	14.3	1.1%	1,994
12/16	1,192.8	3.0	0.3%	1,948
12/15	1,059.0	16.2	1.5%	1,693
12/14	836.6	14.2	1.7%	1,281
Annual Growth	14.6%	9.5%	—	16.0%

2018 Year-End Financials

Debt ratio: 37.9%
Return on equity: 7.3%
Cash ($ mil.): 42.4
Current ratio: 2.62
Long-term debt ($ mil.): 278.1
No. of shares (mil.): 29.9
Dividends
  Yield: —
  Payout: —
Market value ($ mil.): 939.0

	STOCK PRICE ($) FY Close	P/E High/Low	PER SHARE ($) Earnings	Dividends	Book Value
12/18	31.33	55 27	0.70	0.00	10.30
12/17	20.50	39 22	0.54	0.00	8.74
12/16	15.80	170 87	0.12	0.00	7.37
12/15	17.37	37 21	0.63	0.00	7.15
12/14	22.03	51 27	0.57	0.00	5.86
Annual Growth	9.2%	— —	5.3%	—	15.1%

Cherry Hill Mortgage Investment Corp

Cherry Hill Mortgage Investment is interested in real estate assets that lie far beyond Cherry Hill New Jersey. Formed in 2012 Cherry Hill is a real estate investment trust or REIT that looks to acquire invest in and manage real estate assets across the US. It plans to build a portfolio that comprises excess mortgage servicing rights (excess MSRs are servicing fees that exceed basic MSR servicing fees) agency residential mortgage-backed securities (secured by the government agencies like Fannie Mae and Freddie Mac) and other residential mortgage assets. The REIT is externally managed by Cherry Hill Mortgage Management an affiliate of Freedom Mortgage. It went public in 2013.

IPO

Cherry Hill Mortgage intends to use a portion of its $130 million in proceeds to invest in its initial portfolio of excess MSRs and agency RMBS.

Operations

Cherry Hill Mortgage capitalized a taxable REIT subsidiary Cherry Hill TRS LLC at the end of 2013 to obtain mortgage servicing licenses.

Financial Performance

Cherry Hill Mortgage attributes its $6 million in fiscal 2013 operating cash outflow to becoming a public company and executing its initial investment strategy.

Strategy

Cherry Hill Mortgage plans to leverage funds raised through its IPO and other investors to establish its portfolio of excess MSRs and agency RMBS. The REIT also intends to grow the portfolio through subsequent investments in other types of real estate-backed assets including prime jumbo mortgage loans.

The firm looks to leverage its relationship with Freedom Mortgage to continue to acquire Excess MSRs on a flow and bulk basis. It also co-invests in Excess MSRs with Freedom Mortgage.
Auditors: Ernst & Young LLP

LOCATIONS

HQ: Cherry Hill Mortgage Investment Corp
1451 Route 34, Suite 303, Farmingdale, NJ 07727
Phone: 877 870-7005
Web: www.chmireit.com

PRODUCTS/OPERATIONS

Selected Investment Types
Agency Residential Mortgage Backed Securities
Excess Mortgage Servicing Rights

COMPETITORS

ARMOUR Residential REIT
American Capital Agency Corp.
Annaly Capital Management
Capstead Mortgage
Invesco Mortgage Capital
MFA Financial
Redwood Trust

HISTORICAL FINANCIALS

Company Type: Public

Income Statement — FYE: December 31

	REVENUE ($ mil.)	NET INCOME ($ mil.)	NET PROFIT MARGIN	EMPLOYEES
12/18	94.1	37.2	39.6%	4
12/17	82.4	47.3	57.4%	4
12/16	42.3	24.8	58.7%	4
12/15	25.6	13.2	51.6%	3
12/14	7.8	2.3	30.1%	0
Annual Growth	86.3%	99.5%	—	—

2018 Year-End Financials

Debt ratio: 7.4%
Return on equity: 10.9%
Cash ($ mil.): 31.8
Current ratio: 0.03
Long-term debt ($ mil.): 159.5
No. of shares (mil.): 16.6
Dividends
Yield: 11.1%
Payout: 96.7%
Market value ($ mil.): 292.0

	STOCK PRICE ($) FY Close	P/E High/Low		PER SHARE ($) Earnings	Dividends	Book Value
12/18	17.54	9	7	2.18	2.11	21.66
12/17	17.99	5	4	3.98	1.96	25.15
12/16	18.19	6	4	3.30	2.11	20.50
12/15	13.00	11	7	1.76	1.98	20.13
12/14	18.49	66	57	0.31	2.03	21.28
Annual Growth	(1.3%)	—	—	62.8%	1.0%	0.4%

Chesapeake Utilities Corp.

Chesapeake Utilities gasses up the Chesapeake Bay and then some. Chesapeake's regulated natural gas distribution divisions serve customers in the Northeast and Florida. Another unit distributes electricity to more than 30000 customers in Florida. On the unregulated side the company also serves retail propane customers in Delaware Florida Maryland and Virginia. In addition Chesapeake has interstate gas pipeline and gas marketing operations.

Operations

The utility operates through three divisions: regulated energy unregulated energy and other. Regulated the largest consists of electricity and natural gas distribution and transmission. Unregulated includes propane distribution wholesaling and storage (some 4 million gallons of it) as well as natural gas marketing gathering and processing electricity and steam generation and energy-related services. The segment "Other" covers payment processor SkipJack and Eastern Shore Real Estate.

Geographic Reach

Chesapeake Utilities provides its goods and services in Delaware Virginia Maryland Pennsylvania Ohio and Florida.

Sales and Marketing

Chesapeake Utilities serves more than 235000 customers. The company primarily distributes gas to some 150000 customers in Delaware Maryland and Florida as well as electricity to about 32000 customers in Florida. Additionally through subsidiary Eastern Shore Natural Gas the company engages in gas transmission in the Delmarva Peninsula and Florida.

On the unregulated side Chesapeake manages propane distribution in Delaware Maryland Pennsylvania and Florida serving an additional 55000 customers.

Lastly the company also provides marketing of propane crude oil and natural gas in Delmarva Peninsula Florida and Ohio as well as natural gas supplygathering and processing in Ohio and electricity & steam generation through the Eight Flags co-generation gas plant in Florida.

Financial Performance

Revenue jumped up some 24% in 2017 to some $618 million up from $499 million in 2016. Most of the growth came from a 60% hike in revenue from the unregulated energy businesses of Chesapeake accounting for $325 million. Regulated energy also saw a modest 6% annual sales gain. The revenue boost came from new customers being served and natural gas service expansion in Florida.

Net income soared about 30% to $58 million year-over-year mostly due to a $115 million gain in operating income compared to 2016.

Cash holdings at the end of 2017 stood at $5.6 million. Operations generated $111 million offset by $187 million used by operations. Financing activities contributed $78 million in cash inflows.

Strategy

Chesapeake is actively expanding energy distribution and transmission businesses for the last several years. Its success at both regulated and unregulated energy markets have been striking.

The company's midstream and downstream investment focus especially in Florida is proving successful. Chesapeake made three strategic acquisitions in 2017 all in Florida.

The regulated segment is pursuing two major expansion projects at Eastern Shore Natural Gas (ESNG)/Florida natural gas and at Peninsula Pipeline. The Peninsula project consists of two pipeline constructions one each in Escambia and Palm Beach that will interconnect with the FGT. Chesapeake's unregulated segment grew an impressive 60% thanks to a flourishing propane businesses at Sharp Energy and Flo-gas.

Customer base climbed impressively in Delmarva and Florida and with continued acquisitions the company is slated to grow impressively in the near term.

Mergers and Acquisitions

In December 2018 Chesapeake's subsidiary Sharp Energy purchased the propane assets of R.F. Ohl Fuel Oil for an undisclosed sum with an aim to further expand its Pennsylvania footprint. The acquired company already serves 2500 customers in the Carbon Monroe Northampton Lehigh and Schuylkill counties bringing up Sharp's customers served to 6000.

Chesapeake acquired three companies in year prior. Through Flo-gas it acquired some assets of Central Gas a propane distributor with some 325 residential and commercial customers in Florida. Flo-gas also acquired specific Chipola Propane Gas assets broadening Chesapeake's reach in the Marianna region of the sunshine state. The last acquisition was through its PESCO subsidiary which acquired natural gas marketing assets of ARM for $6.8 million complementing its regional footprint and retail demand.

Company Background

The company was founded in 1859 as the Dover Gas Light Company. It became Chesapeake Utilities Corporation in 1947. In 2003 Chesapeake began to exit the water services business selling six of its seven dealerships. The company sold the remaining water dealership in 2004. Chesapeake Utilities expanded into Florida through the acquisition of Florida Public Utilities Company in 2009 where it is expanding more recently.

EXECUTIVES

SVP CFO and Corporate Secretary, Beth W. Cooper, age 52, $300,625 total compensation
SVP; President and COO Eastern Shore Natural Gas Company and Sandpiper Energy, Stephen C. (Steve) Thompson, age 58, $333,750 total compensation
President CEO and Director, Michael P. (Mike) McMasters, age 61, $531,250 total compensation
President Sharp Energy, S. Robert (Bob) Zola, age 68, $143,750 total compensation
SVP Strategic Development, Elaine B. Bittner, age 50, $271,250 total compensation
President Florida Public Utilities and Peninsula Pipeline Company, Jeffry M. Householder, $291,500 total compensation
President Xeron, Richard G. Garcia
Vice President Of Business Development, John J Lewnard
Assistant Vice President Finance, James Moore
Vice President and Corporate Controller, Naimul Islam
Vice President And Controller, Joseph D Steinmetz
Assistant Vp Chesapeake Utilities, Shane E Breakie
Vice President, Aleida Socarras
Vice President Aspire Energy, Douglas M Ward
Assistant Vice President Of Corporate Governance, Stacie L Roberts
Vice President And Chief Human Resources Officer, Louis J Anatrella
Chairman, John R. Schimkaitis, age 72
Board Member, Thomas Hill
Auditors: Baker Tilly Virchow Krause, LLP

LOCATIONS

HQ: Chesapeake Utilities Corp.
909 Silver Lake Boulevard, Dover, DE 19904
Phone: 302 734-6799
Web: www.chpk.com

PRODUCTS/OPERATIONS

2016 Sales

	$ mil.	% of total
Regulated energy	305.7	60
Unregulated energy	203.8	40
Other	(10.6)	-
Total	**498.9**	**100**

Selected Subsidiaries
Chesapeake Service Company
  BravePoint Inc. (formerly United Systems Inc. information technology)
  Chesapeake Investment Company (real estate investments)
  Eastern Shore Real Estate Inc. (office building leases)
  Skipjack Inc. (office building leases)
Eastern Shore Natural Gas Company (transmission)
Florida Public Utilities Company (gas power and propane distribution)
  Flo-Gas Corporation
Peninsula Energy Services Company Inc
Peninsula Pipeline Company Inc.
Sharp Energy Inc. (propane distribution)
  Sharpgas Inc.
Xeron Inc. (propane marketing)

COMPETITORS

Constellation Energy Group	JEA
Delmarva Power	New Jersey Resources
Energy Transfer	NextEra Energy
Ferrellgas Partners	Suburban Propane
	UGI

HISTORICAL FINANCIALS
Company Type: Public

Income Statement   FYE: December 31

	REVENUE ($ mil.)	NET INCOME ($ mil.)	NET PROFIT MARGIN	EMPLOYEES
12/18	717.4	56.5	7.9%	983
12/17	617.5	58.1	9.4%	945
12/16	498.8	44.6	9.0%	903
12/15	459.2	41.1	9.0%	832
12/14	498.8	36.0	7.2%	753
Annual Growth	9.5%	11.9%	—	6.9%

2018 Year-End Financials

Debt ratio: 36.7%
Return on equity: 11.2%
Cash ($ mil.): 6.0
Current ratio: 0.36
Long-term debt ($ mil.): 316.0
No. of shares (mil.): 16.3
Dividends
  Yield: 1.7%
  Payout: 41.5%
Market value ($ mil.): 1,332.0

	STOCK PRICE ($) FY Close	P/E High/Low		PER SHARE ($) Earnings	Dividends	Book Value
12/18	81.30	27	19	3.45	1.44	31.65
12/17	78.55	24	18	3.55	1.28	29.75
12/16	66.95	24	19	2.86	1.20	27.36
12/15	56.75	22	17	2.72	1.13	23.45
12/14	49.66	29	16	2.47	1.07	20.59
Annual Growth	13.1%	—	—	8.7%	7.7%	11.4%

Chimera Investment Corp

EXECUTIVES

CFO and Secretary, A. Alexandra Denahan, age 45
Managing Director; Head - Business Development, Matthew Lambiase, age 49
Head of Investments, Christian J. Woschenko, age 55
Head of Underwriting, William B. Dyer, age 69
Chairman, Paul Donlin, age 54
Director, Jeremy Diamond, age 52
Director, Mark Abrams, age 67
Director, Gerard (Gerry) Creagh, age 57
Managing Director; Head - Business Development, Matthew Lambiase, age 49
Director, Paul A. Keenan, age 49
Director, Dennis Mahoney
Independent Director, John Reilly
Auditors: Ernst & Young LLP

LOCATIONS

HQ: Chimera Investment Corp
520 Madison Avenue, 32nd Floor, New York, NY 10022
Phone: 212 626-2300
Web: www.chimerareit.com

COMPETITORS

Annaly Capital Management	MFA Financial
Capstead Mortgage	Walter Investment Management
Impac Mortgage Holdings	

HISTORICAL FINANCIALS
Company Type: Public

Income Statement   FYE: December 31

	ASSETS ($ mil.)	NET INCOME ($ mil.)	INCOME AS % OF ASSETS	EMPLOYEES
12/18	27,708.6	411.6	1.5%	38
12/17	21,222.0	524.6	2.5%	38
12/16	16,684.9	551.9	3.3%	38
12/15	15,344.6	250.3	1.6%	32
12/14	19,155.0	589.2	3.1%	0
Annual Growth	9.7%	(8.6%)	—	—

2018 Year-End Financials

Return on assets: 1.6%
Return on equity: 11.2%
Long-term debt ($ mil.): —
No. of shares (mil.): 187.0
Sales ($ mil): 1,199.0
Dividends
  Yield: 11.2%
  Payout: 102.0%
Market value ($ mil.): 3,333.0

	STOCK PRICE ($) FY Close	P/E High/Low		PER SHARE ($) Earnings	Dividends	Book Value
12/18	17.82	10	8	1.96	2.00	19.80
12/17	18.48	8	7	2.61	2.00	19.35
12/16	17.02	6	4	2.92	2.44	16.64
12/15	13.64	13	2	1.25	1.44	15.70
12/14	3.18	1	1	2.85	1.80	17.55
Annual Growth	53.9%	—	—	(8.9%)	2.7%	3.1%

Choice Hotels International, Inc.

This company offers a lot of hospitality choices. Choice Hotels is a leading hotel franchisor with more than 7000 locations and nearly 570000 rooms throughout the US and more than 40 other countries. Flagship brands include Comfort Inn one of the largest limited-service brands with more than 2000 properties (including Comfort Suites) and Quality Inn a midscale brand with another 2000 locations. Its Econo Lodge chain offers lodging primarily for budget-minded travelers. Among its nearly a dozen other brands include Ascend Hotel Collection (boutique) Cambria Hotel (upscale) and Rodeway Inn (economy). It also operates extended stay hotels such as MainStay Suites and WoodSpring Suites.

Operations
Choice Hotels' brands compete at various price points including economy mid-scale upper mid-scale and upscale. The company collects marketing and reservation system fees from its franchisors (more than 50% of revenue). It also earns revenue from initial re-licensing and continuing royalty fees from franchisors (about 40% of revenue). Re-licensing fees include fees charged to new owners of a franchised property whenever an ownership change occurs and the property remains in the franchise system.

Procurement services (about 5% of revenue) involve implementing new brand programs and conducting business with qualified vendors and strategic alliance partners. Remaining revenue sources include fees for non-compliance contract termination and other franchising services as well as non-hotel franchising activities.

The firm gives hotel investors the opportunity to develop new builds as well as the opportunity to convert independent brands and non-Choice affiliated hotels. New build brands include Cambria Hotels Comfort Sleep Inn and WoodSpring while conversion brands include Quality Ascend Hotel Collection and Econo Lodge.

Geographic Reach
Rockville Maryland-based Choice Hotels has offices in Dallas Texas; Phoenix Arizona; and Chevy Chase Maryland. Outside the US the company has offices in Australia Canada Germany Italy France the Netherlands India Mexico and the UK.

Despite having "international" in its moniker the firm does most of its business in the US. Choice Hotels has nearly 1200 international properties representing about 15% of its portfolio.

Sales and Marketing
Choice Hotels advertises on national television radio digital and print media; uses telemarketing and personal sales calls; and participates in promotional events with qualified vendors and corporate partners.

Its Choice Privileges loyalty program rewards travelers with points towards free hotel nights airline miles and gift certificates at participating retailers.

Advertising expenses totaled $141.8 million $114.1 million and $102.7 million in 2018 2017 and 2016 respectively.

Financial Performance

Choice Hotels has recorded strong consistent growth over the last five years as it expands its hotel- and room-count.

In 2018 the company?s revenue reached $1.0 billion up from $941 million in 2017. The acquisition of hotel franchisor WoodSpring Suites in 2018 increased domestic royalties for the year. The purchase added some 240 hotels and more than 28000 rooms to Choice Hotels' portfolio.

Choice Hotel?s net income rose to $216.4 million in 2018 up from $122.3 million in 2017 on higher revenue. The company also benefited from a lower income tax rate. (Income tax rates were about 20% and more than 50% for 2018 and 2017 respectively.)

Cash at the end of 2018 was $26.6 million. Cash from operations was $242.9 million while investing activities used $321.3 million. Financing activities used $129.4 million.

Strategy

Choice Hotels continues to expand its hotel portfolio growing its total number of domestic properties from 5500 in 2017 to more than 5800 in 2018 while adding about 30 properties to international portfolio during the same time frame. At the end of 2018 it had more than 1000 properties approved for development.

The company also continues to upgrade its technology in order to meet increasing customer demand for personalization and convenience. As part of these efforts it launched its cloud-based global reservation system ChoiceEDGE in 2018. ChoiceEDGE manages all distribution for the company by optimizing rate inventory and booking for its website mobile apps and third-party distribution partners.

Mergers and Acquisitions

In 2018 Choice Hotels acquired WoodSpring Suites a hotel franchisor serving the economy extended-stay market with 240 hotels in 35 states for $231 million. The acquisition of WoodSpring resulted in about 75 new construction franchise agreements in 2018.

Company Background

Choice Hotels started as Quality Courts United a marketing cooperative founded by several Florida motor court owners in 1941 to combat the poor image of roadside lodgings as dens of undesirable drifters. By 1963 Quality Courts had established a strong brand and began to sell franchises. In 1990 Quality was renamed Choice Hotels International.

EXECUTIVES

Chief Development Officer, David A. Pepper, age 52, $488,154 total compensation
SVP General Counsel and Corporate Secretary and External Affairs, Simone Wu, age 54, $422,308 total compensation
SVP Upscale Brands, Janis Cannon
President and CEO, Patrick S. Pacious, age 53, $662,531 total compensation
CIO, Todd Davis, age 56
Chief Commercial Officer, Robert McDowell
CFO, Dominic E. Dragisich
Regional Vice President Franchise Sales, Thomas Bernardo
Senior Vice President Strategy And Services, John Bonds
Vice President Of Engineering, Tony Pallas
SENIOR VICE PRESIDENT PERFORMANCE ANALYTICS, Bill Carlson
Regional Vp, Pat Mandas
Vice President International Operations, Carl Oldsberg
Regional Vice President San Antonio Texas Area, Jared Meabon
Vice President External Communications and Public Relations, Lorri Christou
Vp Strategic Finance, Raul Ramirez
Vice President Internal Audit, David Scott
Vice President Franchise Development and Upscale Brands, Mark Shalala
Regional Vice President Franchise Development, Sonia Egyhazy
National Account Manager, Louis Massato
Vice President Real Estate Investment and Asset Management, Justin Roberts
National Account Manager, Ted Scales
Vp Global Sales, Chad Fletcher
Regional Vp, Lisa Adams
Vp Marketing And Customer Acquisition, Brent Bouldin
Regional Vp Franchise Development Woodspring Suites, Keith Jones
Vp Of Franchise Services, Curtis Osekowsky
Vice President Treasurer, Maria Uy
Vice President Sales and Marketing, Pally Singh
Vp Engineering, Jason Simpson
Vp Revenue Management, Douglas Lisi
National Account Manager, Kyle Nelson
Chairman, Stewart Bainum, age 73
Board Member, Monte Koch
Auditors: Ernst & Young LLP

LOCATIONS

HQ: Choice Hotels International, Inc.
1 Choice Hotels Circle, Suite 400, Rockville, MD 20850
Phone: 301 592-5000
Web: www.choicehotels.com

PRODUCTS/OPERATIONS

2017 Sales

	$ mil.	% of total
Marketing and reservation	567.1	56
Royalty fees	345.3	34
Procurement services	34.7	4
Initial franchise and re-licensing fees	26.3	2
Other	34.0	4
Total	1,007.4	100

2017 Sales

	$ mil.	% of total
Franchising	996.5	99
SkyTouch Technology	3.1	—
Corporate & Other	7.8	1
Total	1,007.4	100

Selected Brands
Ascend Collection
Cambria Suites
Clarion
Comfort Inn
Comfort Suites
Econo Lodge
MainStay Suites
Quality
Rodeway Inn
Sleep Inn
Suburban Extended Stay Hotel
WoodSpring Suites

COMPETITORS

Accor North America
Best Western
Carlson Hotels
Drury Inns
Extended Stay America Inc.
Hilton Worldwide
InterContinental Hotels
La Quinta
Marriott
Wyndham Destinations

HISTORICAL FINANCIALS

Company Type: Public

Income Statement
FYE: December 31

	REVENUE ($ mil.)	NET INCOME ($ mil.)	NET PROFIT MARGIN	EMPLOYEES
12/18	1,041.3	216.3	20.8%	1,882
12/17	1,007.3	114.8	11.4%	1,987
12/16	924.6	139.3	15.1%	1,789
12/15	859.8	128.0	14.9%	1,462
12/14	757.9	123.1	16.2%	1,331
Annual Growth	8.3%	15.1%	—	9.0%

2018 Year-End Financials

Debt ratio: 66.2%
Return on equity: —
Cash ($ mil.): 26.6
Current ratio: 0.77
Long-term debt ($ mil.): 753.5
No. of shares (mil.): 55.6
Dividends
Yield: 1.2%
Payout: 22.6%
Market value ($ mil.): 3,986.0

	STOCK PRICE ($) FY Close	P/E High/Low		PER SHARE ($)		
				Earnings	Dividends	Book Value
12/18	71.58	22	17	3.80	0.86	(3.30)
12/17	77.60	39	26	2.02	0.86	(3.74)
12/16	56.05	23	17	2.46	0.83	(5.53)
12/15	50.41	29	21	2.22	0.79	(7.03)
12/14	56.02	27	21	2.10	0.75	(7.48)
Annual Growth	6.3%	—	—	16.0%	3.5%	—

Citizens Financial Services Inc

EXECUTIVES

EVP and Secretary Citizens Financial Services and First Citizens National Bank, Terry B. Osborne, age 62, $165,000 total compensation
President CEO and Director Citizens Financial Services and First Citizens National Bank, Randall E. (Randy) Black, age 49, $210,000 total compensation
SVP and Director Marketing and Training First Citizens National Bank, Kathleen M. Campbell, age 55, $92,100 total compensation
VP and Branch Administrator First Citizens National Bank, Patty Vlajic
VP and Business Development Officer First Citizens National Bank, Rob Fitzgerald
VP and Senior Business Development Officer First Citizens National Bank, Chris Landis
VP and Wealth Management Division Manager First Citizens National Bank, Robert B. Mosso, age 45
VP Technology and Operations, Gregory J. Anna, age 54
VP and Western Regional Manager First Citizens National Bank, Rob Carleton
VP and Eastern Regional Manager First Citizens National Bank, Jeff Carr
VP and Business Development Officer First Citizens National Bank, Brian Dygert
VP and Central Regional Manager First Citizens National Bank, Mark Griffis
VP and Professional Development Officer First Citizens National Bank, Carol Strong

Business Development Officer First Citizens
National Bank, Dave Morris
Assistant VP and Wellsville Office Manager First
 Citizens National Bank, Abbie Pritchard
Assistant VP and Towanda Office Manager First
 Citizens National Bank, Lorraine Brown
Assistant VP and LeRaysville Office Manager
 First Citizens National Bank, Deb Donnelly
Assistant VP and Millerton Office Manager First
 Citizens National Bank, Kathy Webster
Assistant VP and Weis and Wal-Mart Sales
 Manager First Citizens National Bank, Dick Pino
Assistant VP and Canton Office Manager First
 Citizens National Bank, Janet Holmes
Assistant VP and Gillett Office Manager First
 Citizens National Bank, Cassy Dygert
Assistant VP and Wellsboro Office Manager First
 Citizens National Bank, Marsha Jones
Assistant VP and Sayre Lockhart Office Manager
 First Citizens National Bank, Cathy Pientka
Customer Service Manager First Citizens National
 Bank, Alaina Knisely
Assistant VP and Ulysses Office Manager First
 Citizens National Bank, Phil Vaughn
Assistant VP and Blossburg Office Manager First
 Citizens National Bank, Beth Weiskopff
Assistant VP and Mansfield Office Manager First
 Citizens National Bank, Kevin Green
Assistant VP and Executive Administrator First
 Citizens National Bank, Gina Boor
Assistant VP CFMP and Marketing Officer First
 Citizens National Bank, Wendy Southard
Assistant VP and Credit Administration Officer
 First Citizens National Bank, Valerie Stickler
Assistant VP and Deposit Operations Manager
 First Citizens National Bank, Joanne Marvin
Assistant VP and Loan Operations Manager First
 Citizens National Bank, Michele Litzelman
Assistant VP and Controller First Citizens
 National Bank, Ryan Allen
Assistant VP and Financial Consultant First
 Citizens National Bank, Matt Geer
VP and Credit Administration Manager First
 Citizens National Bank, Allan Reed
Assistant VP and Tioga County Mortgage Manager
 First Citizens National Bank, Shari Johnson
Assistant VP and Trust Officer First Citizens
 National Bank, Jean Knapp
Vice President, Bob Williams
President CEO and Director Citizens Financial
 Services and First Citizens National Bank,
 Randall E. (Randy) Black, age 49
Director, Mark L. Dalton, age 61
Director, Roger C. Graham Jr., age 60
Director, Rudolph J. van der Hiel, age 76
Director, Robert W. Chappell, age 49
Director, Thomas E. Freeman, age 56
Independent Director, Rudolph Hiel
Auditors: S.R. Snodgrass, P.C.

LOCATIONS

HQ: Citizens Financial Services Inc
 15 South Main Street, Mansfield, PA 16933
Phone: 570 662-2121
Web: www.firstcitizensbank.com

COMPETITORS

CCFNB Bancorp   Northwest Bancshares
Citizens & Northern   Norwood Financial
Elmira Savings Bank   Penns Woods Bancorp
Fidelity D & D   Penseco Financial
First Keystone   Services
First National   Peoples Financial
 Community Bancorp   Services

HISTORICAL FINANCIALS
Company Type: Public

Income Statement
FYE: December 31

	ASSETS ($ mil.)	NET INCOME ($ mil.)	INCOME AS % OF ASSETS	EMPLOYEES
12/18	1,430.7	18.0	1.3%	274
12/17	1,361.8	13.0	1.0%	273
12/16	1,223.0	12.6	1.0%	270
12/15	1,162.9	11.6	1.0%	280
12/14	925.0	13.3	1.4%	206
Annual Growth	11.5%	7.7%	—	7.4%

2018 Year-End Financials
Return on assets: 1.2% Dividends
Return on equity: 13.4% Yield: 3.1%
Long-term debt ($ mil.): — Payout: 34.2%
No. of shares (mil.): 3.5 Market value ($ mil.): 197.0
Sales ($ mil): 64.4

	STOCK PRICE ($) FY Close	P/E High/Low		PER SHARE ($) Earnings	Dividends	Book Value
12/18	55.55	13	11	5.09	1.74	39.33
12/17	63.00	17	14	3.67	1.64	36.27
12/16	53.00	15	13	3.53	1.55	34.67
12/15	49.00	15	13	3.54	1.60	33.19
12/14	53.65	14	12	4.07	2.02	30.58
Annual Growth	0.9%	—	—	5.8%	(3.6%)	6.5%

Civista Bancshares Inc

EXECUTIVES

Vice President And Commercial Lender, John
 Desanto
Auditors: S. R. Snodgrass, P.C.

LOCATIONS

HQ: Civista Bancshares Inc
 100 East Water Street, Sandusky, OH 44870
Phone: 419 625-4121

COMPETITORS

Fifth Third   PNC Financial
Huntington Bancshares   U.S. Bancorp
KeyCorp

HISTORICAL FINANCIALS
Company Type: Public

Income Statement
FYE: December 31

	ASSETS ($ mil.)	NET INCOME ($ mil.)	INCOME AS % OF ASSETS	EMPLOYEES
12/18	2,138.9	14.1	0.7%	432
12/17	1,525.8	15.8	1.0%	350
12/16	1,377.2	17.2	1.3%	337
12/15	1,315.0	12.7	1.0%	326
12/14	1,213.1	9.5	0.8%	303
Annual Growth	15.2%	10.4%	—	9.3%

2018 Year-End Financials
Return on assets: 0.7% Dividends
Return on equity: 5.8% Yield: 1.8%
Long-term debt ($ mil.): — Payout: 40.5%
No. of shares (mil.): 15.6 Market value ($ mil.): 272.0
Sales ($ mil): 91.8

	STOCK PRICE ($) FY Close	P/E High/Low		PER SHARE ($) Earnings	Dividends	Book Value
12/18	17.42	23	15	1.02	0.32	19.16
12/17	22.00	16	13	1.28	0.25	18.09
12/16	19.43	10	5	1.57	0.22	16.49
12/15	12.83	8	7	1.17	0.20	15.96
12/14	10.28	11	7	0.85	0.19	15.04
Annual Growth	14.1%	—	—	4.7%	13.9%	6.2%

Clearway Energy Inc

EXECUTIVES

President and CEO, Christopher S. (Chris) Sotos,
 age 48
EVP and CFO, Kirkland B. Andrews, age 52
EVP and General Counsel, David R. Hill, age 56
Vice President and Chief Accounting Officer,
 Mary-lee Stillwell
Chairman, Mauricio Gutierrez, age 49
Auditors: KPMG LLP

LOCATIONS

HQ: Clearway Energy Inc
 300 Carnegie Center, Suite 300, Princeton, NJ 08540
Phone: 609 608-1525
Web: www.nrgyield.com

PRODUCTS/OPERATIONS

2016 Sales

	$ mil.	% of total
Energy	575.0	53
Capacity	345.0	32
Other	169.0	15
Contract Amortization	(68)	-
Total	**1,021.0**	**100**

Selected Properties
Natural Gas
 Marsh Landing (California)
Natural Gas/Oil
 GenConn-Devon (Connecticut)
 GenConn-Middletown (Connecticut)
Solar
 Alpine (California)
 Avenal (California)
 Avra Valley (California)
 Blythe (California)
 Borrego (California)
 California Valley Solar Ranch
 Roadrunner (New Mexico)
Thermal
 NRG Energy Center Dover (Delaware)
 NRG Energy Center Harrisburg (Pennsylvania)
 NRG Energy Center Minneapolis
 NRG Energy Center Phoenix
 NRG Energy Center Pittsburgh
 NRG Energy Center Princeton (New Jersey)
 NRG Energy Center San Diego
 NRG Energy Center San Francisco
Wind
 South Trent (Texas)

COMPETITORS

AEP
AES
Berkshire Hathaway
 Energy
Calpine
Direct Energy
Duke Energy
Edison International
Entergy
FirstEnergy
PG&E Corporation

HISTORICAL FINANCIALS
Company Type: Public

Income Statement FYE: December 31

	REVENUE ($ mil.)	NET INCOME ($ mil.)	NET PROFIT MARGIN	EMPLOYEES
12/18	1,053.0	52.0	4.9%	269
12/17	1,009.0	(8.0)	—	0
12/16	1,021.0	67.0	6.6%	0
12/15	869.0	13.0	1.5%	0
12/14	583.0	33.0	5.7%	0
Annual Growth	15.9%	12.0%	—	—

2018 Year-End Financials
Debt ratio: 70.3%
Return on equity: 2.9%
Cash ($ mil.): 407.0
Current ratio: 1.07
Long-term debt ($ mil.): 5,447.0
No. of shares (mil.): 193.2
Dividends
 Yield: 7.2%
 Payout: 273.4%
Market value ($ mil.): 3,334.0

	STOCK PRICE ($) FY Close	P/E High/Low		PER SHARE ($) Earnings	Dividends	Book Value
12/18	17.25	45	34	0.46	1.26	9.43
12/17	18.90	—	—	(0.16)	1.10	9.45
12/16	15.80	32	19	0.58	0.95	10.12
12/15	14.76	68	29	0.40	0.63	10.07
Annual Growth	5.3%	—	—	4.8%	26.3%	(2.2%)

CNB Community Bancorp Inc

Auditors: Rehmann Robson LLC

LOCATIONS

HQ: CNB Community Bancorp Inc
One South Howell Street, Hillsdale, MI 49242
Phone: 517 439-0401 **Fax:** 517 439-0403
Web: www.countynationalbank.com

HISTORICAL FINANCIALS
Company Type: Public

Income Statement FYE: December 31

	REVENUE ($ mil.)	NET INCOME ($ mil.)	NET PROFIT MARGIN	EMPLOYEES
12/18	34.8	8.4	24.3%	0
12/17	31.1	6.0	19.4%	3
12/16	28.7	4.7	16.5%	0
12/15	25.3	4.2	16.5%	0
12/14	23.7	3.9	16.7%	0
Annual Growth	10.1%	20.9%	—	—

2018 Year-End Financials
Debt ratio: 3.6%
Return on equity: 15.9%
Cash ($ mil.): 54.4
Current ratio: 0.10
Long-term debt ($ mil.): 23.8
No. of shares (mil.): 2.1
Dividends
 Yield: 3.4%
 Payout: 27.3%
Market value ($ mil.): 68.0

	STOCK PRICE ($) FY Close	P/E High/Low		PER SHARE ($) Earnings	Dividends	Book Value
12/18	32.00	9	6	4.06	1.11	26.61
12/17	23.60	8	8	2.93	0.40	23.81
12/16	19.50	—	—	2.32	0.90	21.88
12/15	19.50	—	—	2.06	0.88	20.51
12/14	19.50	—	—	1.95	0.86	19.37
Annual Growth	13.2%	—	—	20.1%	6.6%	8.3%

CNB Financial Corp. (Clearfield, PA)

CNB Financial is the holding company for CNB Bank ERIEBANK and FCBank. The banks and subsidiaries provide traditional deposit and loan services as well as wealth management merchant credit card processing and life insurance through nearly 30 CNB Bank- and ERIEBANK-branded branches in Pennsylvania and nine FCBank branches in central Ohio. Commercial industrial and agricultural loans make up more than one-third of the bank's loan portfolio while commercial mortgages make up another one-third. It also makes residential mortgages consumer and credit card loans. The company's non-bank subsidiaries include CNB Securities Corporation Holiday Financial Services Corporation and CNB Insurance Agency.

Operations
Commercial industrial and agricultural loans made up 36% of the bank's $16.74 billion loan portfolio at the end of 2015 while commercial mortgages made up another 33%. The rest of the portfolio was made up of residential mortgages (15% of loan assets) consumer (14%) overdrafts (less than 1%) and credit card loans (less than 1%).

The group makes more than 80% of its revenue from interest income. About 70% of its revenue came from loan interest during 2015 while another 15% came from interest income from taxable and tax-exempt securities. The remainder of its revenue came from deposit account service charges (4% of revenue) wealth and asset management fees (3%) and other miscellaneous income sources.

Geographic Reach
Clearfield Pennsylvania-based CNB Financial serves clients in its home state as well as in Ohio. CNB Financial serves a specific market area such as the Pennsylvania counties of Cambria Cameron Centre Clearfield Crawford Elk Erie Indiana Jefferson McKean and Warren.

Sales and Marketing
The group serves individuals businesses government and institutional customers.

CNB Financial has been increasing its advertising spend in recent years. It spent $1.6 million during 2015 up from $1.5 million and $1 million in 2014 and 2013 respectively.

Financial Performance
CNB Financial's revenues have risen more than 30% since 2011 as its loan assets have nearly doubled to $1.58 billion. The firm's profits have grown nearly 50% over the same period as low-interest rates and declining loan loss provisions have lowered operating costs.

The group's revenue climbed 1% to $102 million during 2015 thanks to a modest rise in interest income stemming mostly from 16% loan asset growth.

Despite revenue growth in 2015 CNB Financial's net income dipped 4% to $22.2 million mostly due to nearly 10% rise in salary and employee benefit costs from new hires and more expensive benefits. The group's operating cash levels jumped 16% to $34 million for the year thanks to favorable working capital changes related to accrued interest payables and other liabilities.

Strategy
CNB Financial has been acquiring other banks and opening branches in new geographic markets in recent years to boost its loan and deposit business. As a sign of success the bank noted that its assets have nearly doubled in size since 2009 from $1.16 billion to $2.29 billion at the end of 2015.

Toward its branch expansion plans the group's ERIEBANK brand entered Ohio by opening a loan production office there in 2014 with plans to open another by the end of 2016. After opening an FCBank branch in Dublin Ohio in 2014 the group in 2016 also continued to push its FCBank brand which has been enjoying double-digit loan and deposit business growth in the Columbus and Lancaster regions in Ohio. It plans to open a new FCBank branch in Worthington Ohio by the end of 2016.

Mergers and Acquisitions
In 2016 CNB looked expanded into Northeast Ohio after buying Mentor Ohio-based Lake National Bank — and its $152 million in assets — for nearly $25 million. Lake National Bank's operations were folded into ERIEBANK's operations when the transaction closed.

In 2013 extending its reach in Ohio CNB Financial acquired FC Banc Corp. for $41.6 million. The deal gave CNB Financial Farmers Citizens Bank which serves the northern Ohio communities of Bucyrus Cardington Fredericktown Mount Hope and Shiloh as well as the greater Columbus Ohio area.

Company Background
In 2012 CNB Financial acquired an Ebensburg Pennsylvania-based consumer discount company which brought with it a loan portfolio valued at about $1 million.

EXECUTIVES

EVP Human Resources, Mary Ann Conaway
SEVP and Chief Credit Officer CNB Bank, Mark D. Breakey, age 60, $211,000 total compensation
President and CEO, Joseph B. Bower, age 55, $458,000 total compensation
SEVP and COO CNB Bank, Richard L Greslick, age 43, $221,000 total compensation
EVP CFO and Treasurer CNB Bank and Treasurer Principal Financial Officer and Principal Accounting Officer CNB Financial Corporation, Brian W. Wingard, age 45, $210,000 total compensation

EVP and Chief Commercial Banking Officer CNB Bank, Joseph E. Dell, age 63, $211,000 total compensation
EVP Customer Experience, Leanne D. Kassab
Assistant Vice President of Mortgage Lending, Eileen Ryan
Avp Human Resources, Shannon Irwin
Vice Presidents Commercial Banking, Joseph Yaros
Assistant Vice President Compliance, Kylie Ogden
Vice President, Andrew Roman
Senior Vice President Chief Lending Officer, Jeffrey Alabran
Executive Vice President Coo, Rich Greslick
Senior Vice President Of Operations, Vincent C Turiano
Vice President Information Technology, Bonnie Garito
Chairman, Peter F. Smith, age 64
Board Member, Jeffrey Powell
Board Member, Robert Montler
Board Member, Deborah Pontzer
Auditors: Crowe LLP

LOCATIONS
HQ: CNB Financial Corp. (Clearfield, PA)
1 South Second Street, P.O. Box 42, Clearfield, PA 16830
Phone: 814 765-9621
Web: www.cnbbank.bank

PRODUCTS/OPERATIONS

2015 Sales

	% of total
Interest and Dividend Income	
Loans including fees	70
Securities	
Taxable	10
Tax-exempt	4
Dividends	1
Non-Interest Income	
Wealth and asset management fees	3
Service charges on deposit accounts	4
Other service charges and fees	3
Other revenues	5
Total	**100**

Selected Services
Checking
Credit cards
Loans
Savings

COMPETITORS

AmeriServ Financial	M&T Bank
CBT Financial	Northwest Bancshares
Citizens Financial Group	PNC Financial
First Commonwealth Financial	S&T Bancorp

HISTORICAL FINANCIALS
Company Type: Public

Income Statement
FYE: December 31

	ASSETS ($ mil.)	NET INCOME ($ mil.)	INCOME AS % OF ASSETS	EMPLOYEES
12/18	3,221.5	33.7	1.0%	556
12/17	2,768.7	23.8	0.9%	528
12/16	2,573.8	20.5	0.8%	507
12/15	2,285.1	22.2	1.0%	454
12/14	2,189.2	23.0	1.1%	426
Annual Growth	10.1%	9.9%	—	6.9%

2018 Year-End Financials
Return on assets: 1.1%
Return on equity: 13.3%
Long-term debt ($ mil.): —
No. of shares (mil.): 15.2
Sales ($ mil): 152.5
Dividends
Yield: 2.9%
Payout: 36.4%
Market value ($ mil.): 349.0

	STOCK PRICE ($) FY Close	P/E High/Low	Earnings	Dividends	Book Value
12/18	22.95	15 10	2.21	0.67	17.28
12/17	26.24	19 13	1.57	0.66	15.98
12/16	26.74	20 12	1.42	0.66	14.64
12/15	18.03	12 11	1.54	0.66	14.01
12/14	18.50	12 10	1.60	0.66	13.09
Annual Growth	5.5%	— —	8.4%	0.4%	7.2%

CNX Midstream Partners LP

Auditors: Ernst & Young LLP

LOCATIONS
HQ: CNX Midstream Partners LP
1000 CONSOL Energy Drive, Canonsburg, PA 15317-6506
Phone: 724 485-4000
Web: www.cnxmidstream.com

HISTORICAL FINANCIALS
Company Type: Public

Income Statement
FYE: December 31

	REVENUE ($ mil.)	NET INCOME ($ mil.)	NET PROFIT MARGIN	EMPLOYEES
12/18	256.6	134.0	52.2%	110
12/17	233.8	114.9	49.2%	100
12/16	239.2	96.4	40.3%	100
12/15	203.4	71.2	35.0%	95
12/14	130.1	56.9	43.8%	90
Annual Growth	18.5%	23.9%	—	5.1%

2018 Year-End Financials
Debt ratio: 51.5%
Return on equity: —
Cash ($ mil.): 3.9
Current ratio: 0.62
Long-term debt ($ mil.): 477.2
No. of shares (mil.): 63.6
Dividends
Yield: 8.1%
Payout: 69.9%
Market value ($ mil.): 1,036.0

	STOCK PRICE ($) FY Close	P/E High/Low	Earnings	Dividends	Book Value
12/18	16.28	11 8	1.89	1.32	5.21
12/17	16.77	14 9	1.72	1.15	6.19
12/16	23.55	15 5	1.58	1.00	5.51
12/15	9.85	21 7	1.20	0.88	5.37
12/14	24.12	— —	(0.00)	0.00	5.03
Annual Growth	(9.4%)	— —	—	—	0.9%

Codorus Valley Bancorp, Inc.

EXECUTIVES

Vp Director Of Marketing and Client Experience, Kristen Heisey
Vp Client Care Center Manager, Susan Cerifko
Board Member, Brian Brunner
Treasurer, Larry Pickett
Auditors: BDO USA, LLP

LOCATIONS
HQ: Codorus Valley Bancorp, Inc.
105 Leader Heights Road, P.O. Box 2887, York, PA 17405
Phone: 717 747-1519

COMPETITORS

Citizens Financial Group	M&T Bank
Fulton Financial	Northwest Bancshares

HISTORICAL FINANCIALS
Company Type: Public

Income Statement
FYE: December 31

	ASSETS ($ mil.)	NET INCOME ($ mil.)	INCOME AS % OF ASSETS	EMPLOYEES
12/18	1,807.4	19.5	1.1%	348
12/17	1,709.2	12.0	0.7%	339
12/16	1,611.5	13.1	0.8%	304
12/15	1,456.3	11.1	0.8%	292
12/14	1,213.8	11.7	1.0%	258
Annual Growth	10.5%	13.5%	—	7.8%

2018 Year-End Financials
Return on assets: 1.1%
Return on equity: 11.4%
Long-term debt ($ mil.): —
No. of shares (mil.): 9.9
Sales ($ mil): 93.6
Dividends
Yield: 2.9%
Payout: 30.1%
Market value ($ mil.): 211.0

	STOCK PRICE ($) FY Close	P/E High/Low	Earnings	Dividends	Book Value
12/18	21.25	17 10	1.96	0.59	18.01
12/17	27.53	28 20	1.22	0.47	16.72
12/16	28.60	22 15	1.34	0.43	15.88
12/15	20.34	15 13	1.44	0.42	16.45
12/14	19.68	14 12	1.59	0.38	15.92
Annual Growth	1.9%	— —	5.4%	11.4%	3.1%

Cogent Communications Holdings, Inc.

Cogent Communications offers a compelling sales pitch: data at the speed of light. The company operates a fiber-optic data network that serves customers in North America Europe and Asia. It offers dedicated Internet access and data transport services to businesses through Ethernet connections that link its 51 data center facilities directly to customer office buildings. Clients include financial services companies law firms ad agencies and other professional services businesses. Cogent also sells access to its network and provides colocation management services to ISPs hosting companies and other high-volume bandwidth users.

Operations
Cogent does business in 191 metropolitan markets in 41 countries serving almost 2250 connected office buildings most of which are multi-tenant. Its network is made up of in-building riser facilities metropolitan optical fiber networks metropolitan traffic aggregation points and inter-city transport facilities.

The company has more than 56000 route miles of intercity fiber and more than 28100 metro fiber miles.

Geographic Reach
Cogent has offices data centers colocation facilities and points-of-presence across North America and Europe. North America (mostly the US) represents more than 80% of sales with the rest in Europe.

Sales and Marketing
Cogent employs a direct sales approach that includes telemarketing.

Financial Performance
The company generates most of its revenues from customers connected directly to its network (on-net customers) while clients served through other carriers' facilities (off-net customers) account for a quarter of revenues.

Cogent has enjoyed steady revenue growth over the past decade; overall sales increased 6% in 2015 to $404 million as its customer base grew from almost 46000 to 53000. Profits have been less consistent as its business is capital-intensive. Profits jumped 514% higher to $4.9 million in 2015 on higher revenue and in comparison to 2014 when tax provisions were incurred.

Cash flow from operations rose to about $84 million in 2015 compared to $73 million in 2014.

Strategy
The company has said that it is focusing on expanding its on-net customers; with multi-tenant office buildings the customer base is built in. It has also expanded its sales force to address a broader range of clients. Cogent is also investing in its network infrastructure to reach more clients in areas that represent significant concentrations of Internet traffic.

In 2015 Cogent entered into an interconnection agreements with CenturyLink AT&T and Verizon to expand its public IP networks.

EXECUTIVES
Chairman President and CEO, David (Dave) Schaeffer, age 62, $332,623 total compensation
CFO and Treasurer, Thaddeus G. (Tad) Weed, age 58, $257,262 total compensation
Vice President of Tax, Hunter Payne
Senior Vice President;Portfolio Director, Brian Shearrow
National Account Manager, Christopher Castro
Vp, Tim Oneill
Auditors: Ernst & Young LLP

LOCATIONS
HQ: Cogent Communications Holdings, Inc.
2450 N Street N.W., Washington, DC 20037
Phone: 202 295-4200
Web: www.cogentco.com

PRODUCTS/OPERATIONS

2015 Sales
	% of total
On-net	73
Off-net	27
Total	**100**

COMPETITORS
AT&T
Covad Communications Group
EarthLink
Everest Interlink Broadband
Verio Inc
Verizon
XO Holdings

HISTORICAL FINANCIALS
Company Type: Public

Income Statement
FYE: December 31

	REVENUE ($ mil.)	NET INCOME ($ mil.)	NET PROFIT MARGIN	EMPLOYEES
12/18	520.1	28.6	5.5%	978
12/17	485.1	5.8	1.2%	928
12/16	446.9	14.9	3.3%	897
12/15	404.2	4.9	1.2%	836
12/14	380.0	0.8	0.2%	772
Annual Growth	8.2%	144.9%	—	6.1%

2018 Year-End Financials
Debt ratio: 107.4%
Return on equity: —
Cash ($ mil.): 276.0
Current ratio: 4.65
Long-term debt ($ mil.): 788.1
No. of shares (mil.): 46.3
Dividends
Yield: 4.6%
Payout: 642.4%
Market value ($ mil.): 2,095.0

	STOCK PRICE ($) FY Close	P/E High/Low	PER SHARE ($) Earnings	Dividends	Book Value
12/18	45.21	89 66	0.63	2.12	(3.22)
12/17	45.30	415293	0.13	1.80	(2.23)
12/16	41.35	132 92	0.33	1.51	(1.17)
12/15	34.69	363238	0.11	1.46	(0.27)
12/14	35.39	21541488	0.02	0.61	1.81
Annual Growth	6.3%	—	—136.9%	36.5%	—

Cognex Corp

Machines might not possess big picture vision but Cognex machines have excellent vision when it comes to detail. The company is one of the world's largest producers of systems that linked to a video camera serve as eyes where human vision is insufficient. Manufacturers of consumer electronics and vehicles as well as logistics companies use the company's machine vision and industrial identification systems to position and identify products gauge sizes and locate defects. Cognex's big market is factory automation and it also offers consulting and educational services and tech support for its products. Sales to customers based outside the US account for about three-quarters of sales.

Operations
Cognex offers several types of machine vision products. Its Vision software provides users the general-purpose library of Cognex vision tools with cameras frame grabbers and peripheral equipment. Vision Systems combine camera processor and vision software into a rugged package with a flexible user interface for configuring applications. Vision Sensors are designed to deliver simple and reliable tools for a limited number of common vision applications such as checking the presence and size of parts. The company's ID Products business which includes the DataMan line offers bar code readers for use in automotive pharmaceutical aircraft component and medical device manufacturing.

Geographic Reach
Customers in Europe account for 45% of Cognex's sales while US customers supply about 25% and customers in China generate about 15% of sales. The company's products are assembled by a contract manufacturer in Indonesia. Testing and shipping is done from its Natick Massachusetts facility for US customers and from its Ireland facility for customers outside the US.

Sales and Marketing
Cognex sells through a worldwide direct sales force and via a global network of integration and distribution partners.

The company's customers are in the consumer electronics automotive consumer products food and beverage medical devices and pharmaceutical industries. About 40% of revenue is from consumer electronics 25% each from automotive and logistics and the rest from other customers.

Cognex has a lot of eggs in the Apple basket with the iPhone and MacBook maker directly and indirectly accounting for about a fifth of Cognex's revenue.

Financial Performance
It doesn't take a Cognex product to recognize the company's sales growth. The company's top line number has increased an annual average of nearly 30% over five years. Sales grew even faster in 2017 from 2016 rising 44% to $748 million. Sales rose more than 60% in Asia 40% in Europe and 33% in the US. Strong sales to logistics customers drove sales in the US and demand from consumer electronics customers boosted results in Europe and Asia.

Net income rose 18% to about $177 million in 2017 from 2016 lifted by higher revenue.

Cash on hand rose to about $106 million in 2017 from about $80 million the year before.

Strategy

Cognex focuses on factory automation as its best bet for continued growth. Its business has grown significantly in China and other parts of Asia where consumer electronics manufacturing is concentrated. Asia and China in particular have been targets of US trade sanctions which include higher tariffs on products made outside the US.

Cognex spends about an eighth of its revenue on research and development (nearly $100 million in 2017). The company continued to expand its 2D vision systems which include the DataMan 70 series of barcode readers that offer better read rates for factories and distribution centers. In 3D systems the company has increased its offerings with the help of six acquisitions since 2016 adding capabilities that allow distribution center robots to process objects of different shapes and sizes. The systems generate about 5% of Cognex's revenue but sales have grown at a fast pace (50% in 2017).

Mergers and Acquisitions

Cognex has built out its 3D vision capabilities with the help of acquisitions. In 2017 the company Cognex acquired ViDi Systems which develops deep learning artificial intelligence software for industrial applications for about $23 million. In another 2017 deal it bought GVi Ventures a maker of preconfigured vision tools for common automotive applications for more than $5 million.

HISTORY

Robert Shillman and two MIT colleagues Marilyn Matz and William Silver started Cognex (short for "cognition experts") in 1981 to create vision replacement machines for factories. Competition and inadequate technology forced the firm to reevaluate its distribution strategy in 1986. Cognex began supplying machine vision technology to original equipment manufacturers. The company introduced the first custom vision chip in 1988 and went public the next year.

Cognex found success where human vision fails — in the high-speed detailed repetitive processes required in making semiconductors. The company expanded by purchasing Acumen a developer of machine vision systems for semiconductor wafer identification (1995); Isys Controls a maker of quality control systems (1996); and Mayan Automation a maker of surface inspection systems (1997).

Low demand for semiconductor and printed circuit board manufacturing equipment in Asia hurt sales in 1998. Nonetheless the company boosted R&D by 10% and acquired some of Rockwell Automation's machine vision operations also becoming the preferred global supplier to Rockwell's plants. Orders picked up in early 1999 and Cognex invested $1 million in upstart Avalon Imaging (machine vision for the plastics industry) its first investment in such a company.

A series of acquisitions and in-house innovations enabled Cognex to expand into factory automation inspection which accounts for more than 90% of its business.

EXECUTIVES

President CEO and Director, Robert Willett, age 51, $377,942 total compensation
SVP and CFO, John J. Curran, age 54
Vice President Global Operations, Rocco Volpe
Senior Vice President ww Sales and Marketing, Didier Lacroix
Vice President Operations, Herb Lade
Vice President Sales and Service Asia, Patrice Denizard
Vice President Regional Information Systems, Dan O'Donnell
Chairman and Chief Culture Officer, Robert J. (Bob) Shillman, age 72
Board Member, Jeff Miller
Secretary, Anthony J Medaglia
Board Member, Jerry Schneider
Auditors: Grant Thornton LLP

LOCATIONS

HQ: Cognex Corp
   One Vision Drive, Natick, MA 01760-2059
Phone: 508 650-3000
Web: www.cognex.com

PRODUCTS/OPERATIONS

Selected Products In-Sight 8000 Series In-Sight 7000 Series In-Sight Laser Profiler 3D Vision Systems VisionPro Cognex Designer

COMPETITORS

Adept Technology	KLA-Tencor
Camtek	Keyence
Clemex	National Instruments
CyberOptics	OMRON
Data Translation	Orbotech
Elbit Vision	PPT VISION
Electro Scientific Industries	Perceptron
	RoboGroup T.E.K.
Image Sensing Systems	SICK
Integral Vision	Scanner Technologies

HISTORICAL FINANCIALS

Company Type: Public

Income Statement   FYE: December 31

	REVENUE ($ mil.)	NET INCOME ($ mil.)	NET PROFIT MARGIN	EMPLOYEES
12/18	806.3	219.2	27.2%	2,124
12/17	747.9	177.1	23.7%	1,771
12/16	520.7	149.5	28.7%	1,421
12/15	450.5	187.0	41.5%	1,305
12/14	486.2	121.4	25.0%	1,322
Annual Growth	13.5%	15.9%	—	12.6%

2018 Year-End Financials

Debt ratio: —   No. of shares (mil.): 170.8
Return on equity: 19.6%   Dividends
Cash ($ mil.): 108.2   Yield: 0.4%
Current ratio: 8.54   Payout: 22.2%
Long-term debt ($ mil.): —   Market value ($ mil.): 6,606.0

	STOCK PRICE ($) FY Close	P/E High/Low		PER SHARE ($) Earnings	Dividends	Book Value
12/18	38.67	55	28	1.24	0.19	6.65
12/17	61.16	142	60	0.99	0.17	6.31
12/16	63.62	74	33	0.86	0.15	5.60
12/15	33.77	48	31	1.07	0.11	4.87
12/14	41.33	63	46	0.68	0.00	4.25
Annual Growth	(1.6%)	—	—	16.2%	—	11.8%

Coherent Inc

Coherent is a leading maker of lasers for commercial industrial and scientific applications. The company's lasers and laser technologies are used in microelectronics manufacturing medical diagnostics therapeutic medical applications and scientific research. Its products also are used to make vehicles machine tools consumer goods and medical devices. Coherent's biggest market is the semiconductor industry. The company handles most of its own manufacturing with sites in the US and around the world. Coherent based in Santa Clara California gets more than 80% of its revenue from international customers. The company has been turning out laser technology since it was founded in 1966.

Financial Performance

Coherent's sales more than doubled from 2016 to 2017 driven by acquisitions. The company's net income also has jumped significantly.

In 2018 (ended September) sales rose 10% to $1.9 billion up about $180 million from 2017. The increase was fueled by a 16% advance in the microelectronics market and smaller increases in the OEM components and instrumentation scientific and government programs and materials processing markets. Also contributing were sales from Rofin acquired in the 2017 fiscal year and OR Laser acquired in fiscal 2018.

Coherent's net income climbed to $247.4 million in 2018 about $40 million better than 2017 lifted by higher year-over-year sales.

Coherent had about $324 million in cash in 2018 compared to $457 million in 2017. Operations generated $236 million in 2018 while investing activities used about $68 million and financing activities used $299 million.

The company took on about $740 million in debt to finance the Rofin acquisition. The debt reduces Coherent's flexibility to respond to changing business and economic conditions and increases its borrowing costs.

Strategy

Coherent's acquisition of Rofin in 2016 helped the company strengthen its presence in the semiconductor automotive machine-tool and solar sectors as well as others. It also boosted Coherent's sales significantly. The deal also has had its challenges. A problem integrating Rofin into Coherent's enterprise resource planning software delayed shipments resulting in lower quarterly revenue. Coherent also took on significant debt to make the purchase.

Providing tools to make flat-panel displays have helped Coherent's revenue growth. From large screens to mobile phone displays the business has been a boon for Coherent especially as more mobile phone makers such as Apple adopt OLED technology. Coherent relies on a flat-panel customer Advanced Process Systems Corp. for more than 10% of its revenue. Loss of that business could affect Coherent's top line.

The trade war between the US and China has weighed on Coherent's sales. Customers in China accounted for about 12% of revenue in 2018 and the company expected that to decline in 2019 because of the tariffs the US and China have placed on each other's products.

Mergers and Acquisitions

In late 2016 Coherent acquired ROFIN-SINAR Technologies Inc. a developer and manufacturer of high-performance industrial laser sources and laser-based components for $942 million.

In 2015 Coherent bought Raydiance Inc. for $5 million and the Tinsley Optics business from L-3 Communications Corp. for approximately $4.3 million.

EXECUTIVES

President CEO and Director, John R. Ambroseo, age 58, $625,019 total compensation
EVP and General Manager Specialty Laser Systems Business Group, Mark Sobey, age 58, $375,992 total compensation
EVP and CTO, Luis Spinelli, age 72, $256,006 total compensation
EVP Worldwide Sales Service and Marketing, Paul W. Sechrist, age 59, $355,663 total compensation
EVP and CFO, Kevin S. Palatnik, age 62
EVP General Counsel and Corporate Secretary, Bret M. DiMarco, age 51, $341,876 total compensation
Vice President Corporate Controller, Dan Hunter
Vice President of Finance, Joseph Zambataro
Vice President Of Finance, John Thomas
Vice President European Field Operations, Richard Gleeson
Vice President Finance, Celentano Paul
Executive Vice President And General Manager Industrial Lasers and Systems, Thomas Merk
Chairman, Garry W. Rogerson, age 67
Board Member, Jay Flatley
Board Member, Sandeep Vij
Board Member, Susan James
Board Member, Stephen Skaggs
Board Member, Pamela Fletcher
Board Member, L William Krause
Auditors: DELOITTE & TOUCHE LLP

LOCATIONS

HQ: Coherent Inc
5100 Patrick Henry Drive, Santa Clara, CA 95054
Phone: 408 764-4000
Web: www.coherent.com

PRODUCTS/OPERATIONS

2018 Sales

	$ mil.	% of total
OEM Laser Sources	1,259.5	66
Industrial Lasers and Systems	643.1	34
Total	**1,902.6**	**100**

2018 Sales by Market

	$ mil.	% of total
Microelectronics	1,036.4	54
Materials Processing	520.9	27
OEM Components and Instrumentation	220.8	12
Scientific and Government Programs	124.5	7
Total	**1,902.6**	**100**

COMPETITORS

Cymer	Novanta
Gemfire	Princeton Lightwave
IPG Photonics	Roper Technologies
Jenoptik	Spectris
Komatsu	TRUMPF
Lumentum	USHIO
MKS Inc.	Viavi Solutions
Newport Corp.	

HISTORICAL FINANCIALS
Company Type: Public

Income Statement — FYE: September 28

	REVENUE ($ mil.)	NET INCOME ($ mil.)	NET PROFIT MARGIN	EMPLOYEES
09/19	1,430.6	53.8	3.8%	5,184
09/18	1,902.5	247.3	13.0%	5,418
09/17*	1,723.3	207.1	12.0%	5,218
10/16	857.3	87.5	10.2%	2,787
10/15	802.4	76.4	9.5%	2,586
Annual Growth	15.6%	(8.4%)	—	19.0%

*Fiscal year change

2019 Year-End Financials

Debt ratio: 19.5%
Return on equity: 4.1%
Cash ($ mil.): 305.8
Current ratio: 4.56
Long-term debt ($ mil.): 392.2
No. of shares (mil.): 23.9
Dividends
 Yield: —
 Payout: —
Market value ($ mil.): 3,634.0

	STOCK PRICE ($) FY Close	P/E High/Low	Earnings	Dividends	Book Value
09/19	151.54	80 42	2.22	0.00	53.57
09/18	172.19	32 15	9.95	0.00	54.10
09/17*	235.17	33 12	8.36	0.00	47.23
10/16	110.54	31 14	3.58	0.00	37.45
10/15	54.68	22 17	3.06	0.00	33.23
Annual Growth	29.0%	— —	(7.7%)	—	12.7%

*Fiscal year change

Cole Credit Property Trust IV Inc

Auditors: DELOITTE & TOUCHE LLP

LOCATIONS

HQ: Cole Credit Property Trust IV Inc
2398 East Camelback Road, 4th Floor, Phoenix, AZ 85016
Phone: 602 778-8700
Web: www.colecapital.com

HISTORICAL FINANCIALS
Company Type: Public

Income Statement — FYE: December 31

	REVENUE ($ mil.)	NET INCOME ($ mil.)	NET PROFIT MARGIN	EMPLOYEES
12/18	431.2	37.2	8.6%	0
12/17	424.1	79.4	18.7%	0
12/16	407.4	71.8	17.6%	0
12/15	367.7	64.7	17.6%	0
12/14	256.2	11.1	4.4%	0
Annual Growth	13.9%	35.1%	—	—

2018 Year-End Financials

Debt ratio: 54.5%
Return on equity: 1.7%
Cash ($ mil.): 10.5
Current ratio: 1.22
Long-term debt ($ mil.): 2,516.9
No. of shares (mil.): 311.3
Dividends
 Yield: —
 Payout: 520.8%
Market value ($ mil.): —

	STOCK PRICE ($) FY Close	P/E High/Low	Earnings	Dividends	Book Value
12/18	0.00	— —	0.12	0.63	6.43
12/17	0.00	28 28	0.25	0.63	6.92
12/16	8.62	37 0	0.23	0.63	7.27
Annual Growth	—	— —	(27.8%)	(0.0%)	(6.0%)

Columbia Banking System Inc

Columbia Banking System (CBS) is the roughly $13 billion-asset holding company for Columbia Bank. The regional community bank has about 150 branches in Washington from Puget Sound to the timber country in the southwestern part of the state as well as in northern Oregon and Idaho. Targeting retail and small to medium-sized business customers the bank offers standard retail services such as checking and savings accounts CDs IRAs credit cards loans and mortgages. Commercial and multifamily residential real estate loans make up about 45% of the company's loan portfolio while business loans make up another 40%.

Financial Performance

Bolstered by consistent growth in its loan and securities portfolio caused by acquisitions and organic growth Columbia Banking System (CBS) has seen rising revenue each of the last five years to yield an overall expansion of more than 50%; net income fared even better?more than doubling in that time as the bank consolidated physical branches.

The holding company increased its revenue 22% to $565.9 million in 2018 on a large increase in CBS's loan and securities portfolios following its 2017 acquisition of Pacific Continental the parent company of Pacific Continental Bank?which had $2.9 billion in assets.

CBS's net income rose 53% to $172.9 million on the strength of its revenue gains and a lower income tax provision caused by US tax reform.

The company used $64.9 million of its cash in 2018 to end the year with $277.6 million. Operations provided $237.2 million and financing activities?primarily Federal Home Loan Bank advances?generated $203.9 million. CBS used $506 million on investments which mainly comprised purchases of debt securities available for sale.

Strategy

Columbia Banking System (CBS) has grown its loan and securities base recently through a major acquisition while reducing its costs by consolidating physical branches and adopting digital banking technologies.

In 2017 CBS acquired Pacific Continental for $644.8 million. Pacific Continental is the holding company for Pacific Continental Bank which had 14 branches in Oregon and Washington. The purchase gave CBS $2.9 billion in assets (including $1.9 billion in loans) and $2.1 billion in deposits.

Amid the rising popularity of digital banking CBS consolidated one branch in 2017 and seven branches in 2018. It has plans to consolidate a further three branches in 3Q19. The company's

2018 digital banking initiatives include programs to enable digital commercial business and healthcare banking; use data to drive its workforce; upgrade its digital enterprise workflows; and expand its base of employees with expertise in the digital environment. CBS's Columbia Connect platform allows retail customers to deposit checks pay bills transfer funds or locate physical branches or ATMs via internet-connected devices.

Company Background

Columbia Banking System took advantage of the rash of bank failures in past years to increase its presence in the Pacific Northwest region. It added more than 30 branches in 2010 when it acquired most of the deposits and assets of failed banks Columbia River Bank and American Marine Bank a week apart. In similar transactions in 2011 it acquired most of the operations of the failed institutions Summit Bank First Heritage Bank and Bank of Whitman. Those deals added more than a dozen branches in Washington.

EXECUTIVES

EVP and Chief Credit Officer, Andrew L. (Andy) McDonald, age 60, $298,000 total compensation
EVP and CFO, Clint E. Stein, age 48, $345,000 total compensation
CEO, Hadley S. Robbins, age 62, $369,827 total compensation
EVP and General Counsel, Kumi Yamamoto Baruffi, age 49
EVP and Chief Human Resources Officer, David C. (Dave) Lawson, age 61, $247,500 total compensation
Vice President, Michael Drake
Vice President Fiduciary Officer, Barbara Root
Senior Vice President and Manager, Kathy Peterman
Senior Vice President Team Leader, Chris Gruenfeld
Vice President, Chris Bohl
Vice President Appraisal Review, Michael Munson
Vice President Senior Financial Advisor with CB Financial, John Brunk
Vice President Operations, Avery Johnson
Vice President Professional Banking Officer, Chris Frankovich
Vice President, Thomas Poole
Vice President Commercial Banking Officer, Antoine White
Vice President, Harold Boucher
Vice President Private Banking Relationship Manager, Donna Himpler
AVP Wealth Advisor, Ron Polluconi
Vice President Branch Manager, Deb Wilding
Vice President Branch Manager, Rob Stewart
Vice President District Manager, Ryan Munsey
Vice President, Melissa Case
Assistant Vice President Residential Loan Officer, Alan Day
Vice President, Stephen Maffett
Vice President, Windy Rudd
Vice President, Cameron Moorehead
Vice President Private Banking Officer, Amy Mullins
Senior Vice President, Jan Furey
Vice President Lakewood Branch Mangaer, Melissa Missall
Vice President, Tom Kirkwood
Vice President, Kai Neizman
Senior Vice President Cash Management Manager, Janice Phillips
Vice President Branch Manager, Amy Hart
CFP Assistant Vice President Private Banking Officer, Nori Roman
Assistant Vice President Senior Residential Loan Officer, Lorry Gilbreath
Senior Vice President Private Banking Officer, Vince Martinez
Assistant Vice President Senior Residential Loan Officer, Wanda Hemenway
Vice President Manager, Debbie Patterson
Senior Vice President Real Estate Group Manager, Kevin Conklin
Assistant Vice President Marketing Creative Manager Marketing, Bryan Habeck
Vice President Professional Banking Officer, Debbie Woodrich
Vice President and Treasury Management Sales Officer, Janis Watford
Senior Vice President Chief Accounting Officer, Brock Lakely
Svp, Michael Evans
Vice President Branch Manager III, Alfredo Aguilar
VICE PRESIDENT, Chris Skandalis
Vice President Market Manager, Suzanne Vanamburgh
As Vice President Business Development Officer, Derek Rawnsley
Chairman, William T. Weyerhaeuser, age 76
Board Member, David Dietzler
Board Member, Ford Elsaesser
Board Member, John Folsom
Board Member, Thomas Hulbert
Board Member, Mark Finkelstein
Board Member, Elizabeth Seaton
Auditors: DELOITTE & TOUCHE LLP

LOCATIONS

HQ: Columbia Banking System Inc
1301 A Street, Tacoma, WA 98402-2156
Phone: 253 305-1900
Web: www.columbiabank.com

PRODUCTS/OPERATIONS

2018 Revenue

	% of total
Net Interest Income	
Loans	73
Taxable securities	10
Tax-exempt securities	2
Non-interest Income	15
Total	**100**

COMPETITORS

BECU	JPMorgan Chase
Bank of America	KeyCorp
Banner Corp	U.S. Bancorp
Heritage Financial	Washington Federal
HomeStreet	Wells Fargo

HISTORICAL FINANCIALS
Company Type: Public

Income Statement				FYE: December 31
	ASSETS ($ mil.)	NET INCOME ($ mil.)	INCOME AS % OF ASSETS	EMPLOYEES
12/18	13,095.1	172.8	1.3%	2,137
12/17	12,716.8	112.8	0.9%	2,120
12/16	9,509.6	104.8	1.1%	1,819
12/15	8,951.7	98.8	1.1%	1,868
12/14	8,578.8	81.5	1.0%	1,844
Annual Growth	11.2%	20.7%	—	3.8%

2018 Year-End Financials

Return on assets: 1.3% Dividends
Return on equity: 8.6% Yield: 2.7%
Long-term debt ($ mil.): — Payout: 58.7%
No. of shares (mil.): 73.2 Market value ($ mil.): 2,658.0
Sales ($ mil): 585.3

	STOCK PRICE ($) FY Close	P/E High/Low	PER SHARE ($) Earnings	Dividends	Book Value
12/18	36.29	20 14	2.36	1.14	27.76
12/17	43.44	25 19	1.86	0.88	26.70
12/16	44.68	25 15	1.81	1.53	21.55
12/15	32.51	21 15	1.71	1.34	21.52
12/14	27.61	19 16	1.52	0.94	21.38
Annual Growth	7.1%	— —	11.6%	4.9%	6.7%

Columbia Financial Inc

Auditors: KPMG LLP

LOCATIONS

HQ: Columbia Financial Inc
19-01 Route 208 North, Fair Lawn, NJ 07410
Phone: 800 522-4167
Web: www.columbiabankonline.com

HISTORICAL FINANCIALS
Company Type: Public

Income Statement				FYE: December 31
	ASSETS ($ mil.)	NET INCOME ($ mil.)	INCOME AS % OF ASSETS	EMPLOYEES
12/18	6,691.6	22.7	0.3%	663
12/17*	5,766.5	3.6	0.1%	0
09/17	5,429.3	31.0	0.6%	679
09/16	5,037.4	32.9	0.7%	0
Annual Growth	9.9%	(11.6%)	—	—

*Fiscal year change

2018 Year-End Financials

Return on assets: 0.3% Dividends
Return on equity: 3.1% Yield: —
Long-term debt ($ mil.): — Payout: —
No. of shares (mil.): 115.8 Market value ($ mil.): 1,772.0
Sales ($ mil): 247.9

	STOCK PRICE ($) FY Close	P/E High/Low	PER SHARE ($) Earnings	Dividends	Book Value
12/18	15.29	88 74	0.20	0.00	8.39
12/17*	0.00	— —	(0.00)	0.00	
	47,207,000.00				
Annual Growth	(100.0%)	— —	—	—	—

*Fiscal year change

Columbus McKinnon Corp. (NY)

Columbus McKinnon's machinery products can be extremely uplifting — literally. Founded in 1875 the company is one of North America's largest producers of equipment for lifting positioning or securing all kinds of large materials. Columbus McKinnon's hoists cranes actuators and steel lifting and rigging tools are used in construction general manufacturing and industrial machinery forestry mining and even wind energy. Well known in the marketplace its brand names include Coffing Duff-Norton Shaw-Box and Yale (made by NACCO). Hoists are the company's biggest seller generating almost 60% sales. In addition to OEMs the company sells to hardware distributors and rental outlets.

Operations
Hoists account for 59% of the company's total revenue while chain and rigging tools account for 13%. Other products include industrial cranes (5%) actuators and rotary unions (11%) digital power control and delivery systems (8%) elevator application drive systems (2%) and other products (2%).

Geographic Reach
New York-based Columbus McKinnon operates 19 principal manufacturing facilities in China France Germany Hungary Mexico the UK and the US. It has a network of roughly 38 sales and service offices in 23 countries and nine warehouse facilities spanning five countries. The US accounts for about 64% of sales followed by Europe with 25%.

Sales and Marketing
The company sells its products via a sales force of more than 165 sales people and independent sales representatives worldwide. The products are sold to over 15500 general and specialty distributors end users and OEMs globally.

Financial Performance
The company's sales increased 3% in fiscal 2015 (ended March) versus the prior year to $597 million. The growth was fueled by a 15% bump in industrial cranes sales particularly within the US. Columbus McKinnon's net income however fell 28% from 2014 to 2015 to $20 million. This was attributed to additional costs associated with acquisitions and losses affiliated with unfavorable foreign currency translations.

Strategy
Columbus McKinnon's sights are set on South America and China where industrial opportunities are expected to be strong. Its direction is supported by a number of product introductions relevant to developing economies including lightweight high-speed industrial air hoists forged lifting attachments and hand hoists and lever tools made at lower-cost facilities in China.

Mergers and Acquisitions
In 2016 Columbus McKinnon agreed to acquire Konecranes' Germany business Stahl for around $240 million.

In 2015 the company paid almost $183 million to acquire Magnetek a designer and manufacturer of digital power and motion control systems for material handling elevators and mining applications. The transaction enhanced Columbus McKinnon's development of "smart" and integrated technology into its own portfolio of hoisting systems.

In February 2014 Columbus McKinnon acquired Michigan-based Unified Industries a privately-owned company with annual sales of about $13 million. Unified Industries designs makes and sells overhead aluminum light rail workstations that are primarily used in automotive and other industrial applications.

EXECUTIVES
President Magnetek, Peter M. (Pete) McCormick, age 60
President CEO and Director, Mark D. Morelli, age 56
VP Solutions Group, Gene P. Buer, age 67, $300,998 total compensation
VP Europe Middle East Africa (EMEA), Ivo Celi, age 57, $289,176 total compensation
VP and CFO, Gregory P. Rustowicz, age 59, $337,653 total compensation
VP Americas, Kurt F. Wozniak, age 55, $288,200 total compensation
VP Information Services, Mark Paradowski, age 49
VP Asia Pacific (APAC), Benjamin AuYeung, age 55
Executive Director and Chief Procurement Officer, Lawrence Gavin
Vice President Human Resources, Randy Biggs
Chairman, Ernest R. (Ernie) Verebelyi, age 71
Auditors: Ernst & Young LLP

LOCATIONS
HQ: Columbus McKinnon Corp. (NY)
205 Crosspoint Parkway, Getzville, NY 14068
Phone: 716 689-5400
Web: www.cmworks.com

PRODUCTS/OPERATIONS
2016 sales

	$ mil.	% of total
Hoists	352.0	59
Actuators and rotary unions	63.9	11
Chain & forged attachments	75.4	13
Digital power control and delivery system	50.4	8
Industrial cranes	30.5	5
Other	24.9	4
Total	597.1	100

Selected Products
Hoists
  Electrification (cable/cable reels conductor bar festoon)
  Load chain (disc grade/manual star grade/electric)
  Manual (hand chain lever)
  Powered (air chain air wire rope electric chain electric wire rope)
  Trolleys (manual powered)
Rigging
  Below the hook (pallet lifters coil lifters lifting beams sheet lifters bartender rack)
  Carbon chain and attachments (cold shuts rings chain links)
  CM rigging (hoist rings clamps wire rope clips/thimbles shackles hooks rigging accessories/turnbuckles)
  Dixie forestry (hookaroons handled product tongs)
  Farm hardware and fence tools (pins clevis)
  Heavy duty truck (binders tire chain tire chain hooks binder chain assemblies towing/trucking heavy duty components)
  Overhead lifting (attachments hooks chain slings)
  Towing (bridle assemblies tow chain assemblies)
Cranes
  Components (rotating axle fixed axle top/under running channel type high-cap single girder)
  Enclosed track (freestanding ceiling mounted jib cranes components)
  Jib cranes (base mounted pillar wall mounted)

Selected Brands
Abell Howe
Alltec
Budgit Hoists
Cady Lifters
CES (Crane Equipment & Service Inc.)
Chester Hoist
Coffing Hoists
CM (Columbus McKinnon)
Duff Norton
Little Mule
LodeRail
Pfaff Silberblau
Shaw-Box
WECO (Washington Equipment Co.)
Yale

COMPETITORS
Aluminum Ladder
Bridon Group
CLARK Material Handling
Cascade Corp.
Deublin
JLG Industries
Kito
Konecranes
Linamar Corp.
Nook Industries
Parker-Hannifin
Taylor Group
Terex
Terex MHPS
Toyota Material Handling
Werner Co.

HISTORICAL FINANCIALS
Company Type: Public

Income Statement   FYE: March 31

	REVENUE ($ mil.)	NET INCOME ($ mil.)	NET PROFIT MARGIN	EMPLOYEES
03/19	876.2	42.5	4.9%	3,128
03/18	839.4	22.0	2.6%	3,328
03/17	637.1	8.9	1.4%	3,107
03/16	597.1	19.5	3.3%	2,896
03/15	579.6	27.1	4.7%	2,747
Annual Growth	10.9%	11.9%	—	3.3%

2019 Year-End Financials
Debt ratio: 28.2%
Return on equity: 10.1%
Cash ($ mil.): 71.0
Current ratio: 1.72
Long-term debt ($ mil.): 235.3
No. of shares (mil.): 23.3
Dividends
  Yield: 0.0%
  Payout: 11.1%
Market value ($ mil.): 803.0

	STOCK PRICE ($) FY Close	P/E High/Low		PER SHARE ($) Earnings	Dividends	Book Value
03/19	34.35	24	15	1.80	0.20	18.43
03/18	35.84	46	24	0.95	0.16	17.71
03/17	24.82	65	32	0.43	0.16	15.13
03/16	15.76	28	14	0.96	0.16	14.24
03/15	26.94	22	15	1.34	0.16	13.44
Annual Growth	6.3%	—	—	7.7%	5.7%	8.2%

Comfort Systems USA Inc

Comfort Systems USA alters ambient air automatically. The company sells and services commercial HVAC (heating ventilation and air conditioning) systems in apartments health care facilities office buildings manufacturing plants retail centers and schools. Some company locations also offer fire protection and electrical services. A small share of revenue comes from designing building automation control systems that integrate monitor and operate HVAC lighting and access control systems. Comfort Systems was established in 1997.

Geographic Reach
Houston-based Comfort Systems operates through more than 125 locations spanning nearly 30 states throughout the US.

Sales and Marketing
Comfort Systems' customers include building owners and developers and property managers as well as general contractors architects and consulting engineers. Major customers come from categories including industrial (nearly 30% of revenue) education (nearly 20%) healthcare (15%) and office buildings (slightly less than 15%).

Financial Performance
Throughout the five-year period ending in 2018 Comfort Systems reported year-over-year revenue growth. During that same period profits also rose except for a dip in 2017.

The company reported $2.2 billion in revenue for fiscal 2018 up 22% from $1.8 billion in 2017. The increase included a 5.1% increase related to two acquisitions and a 17.0% increase in revenue related to same?store activity. The same?store revenue growth was due to an increase in business in North Carolina Virginia and Wisconsin.

Net income was $112.9 million in 2018 up from $55.3 billion the prior year on higher revenue and a lower tax rate.

Cash at the end of 2018 was $46 million. Cash from operations was $147.2 million while investing activities used $95.7 million. Financing activities used $42.4 million.

Strategy
Comfort Systems has identified six core competencies that it believes are critical to attracting and retaining customers increasing operating income and cash flow and maximizing productivity. These include safety customer service design and build expertise effective pre-construction processes job and cost tracking and service excellence.

Most revenue — approximately 85% — is earned on a project basis for the installation of HVAC systems in newly constructed facilities or for replacement of HVAC systems in existing facilities. As part of the negotiation and bidding process to obtain installation contracts Comfort Systems estimates contract costs which include all materials labor tools and depreciation costs. Variations from estimated project costs could have a significant impact on operating results.

To diversify its revenues Comfort Systems is investing in initiatives to expand the proportion of its revenue that is service-based and is concentrating its existing managerial resources on training and hiring experienced employees to procure and perform service work. In some locations it has added service capability and it believes its investments and efforts will stimulate growth in all aspects of the commercial HVAC and service and repair business.

Comfort Systems believes it can increase its cash flow and operating income by continuing to enter new markets or service lines through acquisitions. It continues to seek opportunities to acquire businesses that have strong assembled workforces attractive market positions and desirable locations.

Mergers and Acquisitions
In 2019 Comfort Systems announced acquired Walker TX Holding Company and its related subsidiaries headquartered in Irving Texas. Walker is a family-owned business that provides commercial electrical and related services in Texas with has offices and operations in the Dallas/Fort Worth area Houston San Antonio and Austin. Comfort Systems made the purchase to enhance its electrical contracting business stating that Walker TX complements and strengthens its existing mechanical plumbing controls fire suppression and electrical lines of business across the US.

The company had previously expanded its geographic footprint in 2018 when it acquired an operating location in Indiana.

Company Background
Comfort Systems went public in June 1997 with the intention of becoming a nationwide provider of building systems installation and maintenance.

Its growth came from successfully expanding services to existing customers and attracting companies into its network of subsidiary companies. Many of them have been operating for 60 years or more.

EXECUTIVES
EVP and CFO, William George, age 55, $370,800 total compensation
SVP and Chief Accounting Officer, Julie S. Shaeff, age 54, $247,200 total compensation
President and CEO, Brian E. Lane, age 62, $515,000 total compensation
SVP and General Counsel, Trent T. McKenna, age 47, $293,550 total compensation
SVP Service, James Mylett, $300,000 total compensation
Vice President Service Region 4, Joe Lang
Senior Vice President Of Service, Terrence Young
Chairman, Franklin Myers, age 66
Board Member, Alan P Krusi
Board Member, James H Schultz
Board Member, Constance Skidmore
Board Member, Vance Tang
Auditors: Ernst & Young LLP

LOCATIONS
HQ: Comfort Systems USA Inc
675 Bering Drive, Suite 400, Houston, TX 77057
Phone: 713 830-9600   **Fax:** 713 830-9696
Web: www.comfortsystemsusa.com

PRODUCTS/OPERATIONS
2015 Sales
	% of total
HVAC	77
Plumbing	14
Building automation control systems	5
Other	4
Total	100

2015 Sales
	% of total customers
Manufacturing	21
Education	15
Health care	11
Office buildings	13
Government	10
Retail & restaurants	7
Multi-family	5
Lodging & entertainment	5
Distribution	2
Technology	7
Religious/non-profit	1
Residential	1
Other	2
Total	100

SOLUTIONS & SERVICES
Construction Services
Retrofit & Replacement
Building Automation Systems
Energy Services

COMPETITORS
ACCO	Honeywell
Aegion	International
Athena Engineering	Koch Air LLC
Barnes Group	Layne Christensen
Cubic Corp.	Lennox
Cupertino Electric	MYR Group
Dycom	MasTec
EMCOR	Pike Corporation
Encore Wire	Primoris
GATX	TDIndustries
Granite Construction	Trane Inc.
Great Lakes Dredge & Dock	University Mechanical & Engineering
Greenbrier Companies	Wabash National

HISTORICAL FINANCIALS
Company Type: Public

Income Statement
FYE: December 31

	REVENUE ($ mil.)	NET INCOME ($ mil.)	NET PROFIT MARGIN	EMPLOYEES
12/18	2,182.8	112.9	5.2%	9,900
12/17	1,787.9	55.2	3.1%	8,700
12/16	1,634.3	64.9	4.0%	7,700
12/15	1,580.5	49.3	3.1%	7,301
12/14	1,410.8	23.0	1.6%	7,077
Annual Growth	11.5%	48.7%	—	8.8%

2018 Year-End Financials
Debt ratio: 7.2%   No. of shares (mil.): 36.8
Return on equity: 24.6%   Dividends
Cash ($ mil.): 45.6   Yield: 0.7%
Current ratio: 1.31   Payout: 11.0%
Long-term debt ($ mil.): 73.6   Market value ($ mil.): 1,612.0

	STOCK PRICE ($) FY Close	P/E High/Low		PER SHARE ($) Earnings	Dividends	Book Value
12/18	43.68	20	13	3.00	0.33	13.50
12/17	43.65	30	22	1.47	0.30	11.24
12/16	33.30	20	14	1.72	0.28	10.12
12/15	28.42	26	12	1.30	0.25	9.26
12/14	17.12	32	21	0.61	0.23	8.22
Annual Growth	26.4%	—	—	48.9%	10.0%	13.2%

Communities First Financial Corp

Auditors: Crowe, LLP

LOCATIONS
HQ: Communities First Financial Corp
7690 N.Palm Avenue, Suite 101, Fresno, CA 93711
Phone: 559 439 0200
Web: www.fresnofirstbank.com

HISTORICAL FINANCIALS
Company Type: Public

Income Statement
FYE: December 31

	ASSETS ($ mil.)	NET INCOME ($ mil.)	INCOME AS % OF ASSETS	EMPLOYEES
12/18	467.2	6.2	1.3%	0
12/17	407.4	3.6	0.9%	0
12/16	363.5	3.0	0.8%	0
12/15	296.0	2.5	0.9%	0
12/14	253.3	2.1	0.8%	0
Annual Growth	16.5%	31.1%	—	—

Community Bank System Inc

Community Bank System is right up front about what it is. The holding company owns Community Bank which operates about 195 branches across upstate New York and northeastern Pennsylvania where it operates as First Liberty Bank and Trust. Focusing on small underserved towns and non-urban markets the bank offers standard products and services such as checking and savings accounts certificates of deposit and loans and mortgages to consumer business and government clients. Boasting over $11.0 billion in assets the bank's loan portfolio consists of mostly business loans residential mortgages and consumer loans. Community Bank System's subsidiaries offer employee benefit services wealth management and insurance products and services.

Operations
Community Bank System operates three business segments. The Banking segment which made up 83% of the company's total revenue during 2015 provides lending and deposit services to individuals businesses and municipalities. Employee Benefit Services (12% of revenue) offers trust investment fund retirement plan actuarial healthcare consulting and other administrative services through Benefit Plan Administrative Services (BPAS). The All Other segment (5% of revenue) includes its Wealth Management (operating through Community Investment Services) and Insurance businesses (operating through CBNA Insurance Agency).

Nearly 70% of the company's revenue comes from interest income. About 49% of its revenue came from loan interest during 2015 while another 19% came from interest on taxable and nontaxable investments. The rest of its revenue came from deposit service fees (14% of revenue) employee benefit services (12%) wealth management and insurance services (5%) and other banking revenues (1%).

Geographic Reach
Community Bank System operated 194 branches and six back-office operating facilities in 36 counties in upstate New York and six counties in northeastern Pennsylvania at the end of 2015.

Sales and Marketing
The bank has been ramping up its advertising spend in recent years. It spent $3.6 million on advertising during 2015 up from $3.2 million and $3.0 million in 2014 and 2013 respectively.

Financial Performance
Community Bank System's annual revenues have been slowly trending higher since 2013 despite a decline in loan interest mostly as it's been building its non-interest related business lines. Meanwhile its net income has risen more than 15% as it's had to pay less in interest expenses on deposits amidst the low interest environment.

The bank's revenue grew 2% to $382.92 million during 2015 thanks to a combination of employee benefit services business growth from new customers and expanding business relationships with existing customers as well as from new service offerings; higher interest income from loans and taxable investments as such interest-earning asset balances grew modestly; and a 13% jump in wealth management and insurance services revenue stemming from the acquisition of OneGroup from the Oneida Financial Group acquisition.

Despite revenue growth in 2015 Community's net income dipped less than 1% to $91.23 million for the year due to costs related to the Oneida acquisition. The company's operating cash levels shrank 5% to $116.46 million mostly due to unfavorable working capital changes related to deferred income tax provisions and changes in other assets and liabilities.

Strategy
Community Bank System looks to continue building its loan and deposit business as well as its non-interest service lines organically and through strategic acquisitions of other banks and financial companies. The financial company in 2015 began exploring expansion opportunities into neighboring markets in eastern Ohio upper New England and New Jersey and in 2017 acquired Northeast Retirement Services (NRS) for around $146 million. NRS provides institutional transfer agency master recordkeeping services custom target date fund administration trust product administration and customized reporting services to institutional clients.

Mergers and Acquisitions
Community Bank System acquired Kinderhook Bank in 2019 for $93.4 million. Kinderhook has 11 offices in five New York counties (including in the Capital District of upstate New York) and holds nearly $640 million in assets and about $560 million in deposits. The deal extends Community Bank's reach into the Capital District markets.

In spring 2017 Community Bank acquired Vermont-based Merchants Bancshares. Merchants operates nearly 35 branches and has assets in excess of $1.8 billion; the acquisition will expand Community Bank's operations into Vermont and western Massachusetts.

Company Background
In mid-2012 the bank purchased about 20 branches in upstate New York from HSBC. The deal which was made to satisfy antitrust concerns regarding First Niagara's purchase of 195 branches in New York from HSBC strengthened Community Bank Systems' geographic footprint.

In 2011 the company bought bank holding company The Wilber Corporation adding about 20 locations in the Catskills Mountains region of central New York.

In 2011 expanding its trust and benefits administration business it bought retirement plan administrator CAI Benefits which has offices in New York and Northern New Jersey.

EXECUTIVES

EVP and CFO, Scott A. Kingsley, age 54, $422,500 total compensation
President CEO and Director, Mark E. Tryniski, age 58, $725,000 total compensation
EVP and Chief Banking Officer, Brian D. Donahue, age 63, $350,000 total compensation
CTO, J. Michael Wilson, age 48
SVP Retail Banking Sales and Marketing, Harold M. (Harry) Wentworth, age 54
SVP and Chief Investment Officer, Joseph J. Lemchak, age 57
President Pennsylvania Banking, Robert P. Matley, age 67
SVP Municipal Banking Director, Joseph E. Sutaris, age 51
SVP and Senior Commercial Lending Officer Northern New York, Nicholas S. (Nick) Russell, age 51
SVP and Chief Credit Administrator, Stephen G. Hardy, age 64
EVP and General Counsel, George J. Getman, age 62, $375,000 total compensation
SVP and Chief Risk Officer, Paul J. Ward
SVP and Chief Credit Officer, Joseph Serbun, $248,107 total compensation
Assistant Vice President Marketing an, Mary K Barnette
Executive Vice President Marketing, Aaron Kurtz
Senior Vice President Commercial Banking, Joe Tomko
Executive Vice President Marketing, Deborah Fitch
Vice President Marketing, Art Gentry
Executive Vice President Marketing, Barbara Call
Vice President and Manager Financial Analysis, Robert Frost
Vice President Director Mortgage Lending, George J Burke
Vice President and Information Technology Manager, James Wilson
Senior Vice President, Marlene Walker
Vice President Administration, Eric Wollman
Finance Senior Vice President, Richard Heidrick
Vice President Commercial, Dave Unberger
Vice President Of Human Resources, Denise Cooper
Vice President Information Technology, Brian Montalbano
Vice President And Marketing Director, Blake Boyer
Vice President Commercial Banker, Allison Mosher
Assistant Vice President Cash Management Sales Officer, Lindsay Horn
Vice President Commercial Banking, Craig Stevens
Assistant Vice President, Melissa Peryea
Vice President Farm Loan Manager, Edward Ward
Vice President Commercial Relationship Officer, Michael Moore
Vp Commercial Banking Officer, Edward Michalek
Vp Commercial Loan Officer, Christopher Humphrey
Vp Br Manager, Diane Easton
Vp Commercial Banking Officer, Richard Ferrari
Vp, Russell Williamson
Senior Vice President, Richard Kazmerick
Senior Vice President, Edward Nork
Vice President Client Service, Kevin Wade
Assistant Vice President Loan Ptflo Ofc Assistant, William Giglio

2018 Year-End Financials

Return on assets: 1.4%
Return on equity: 16.6%
Long-term debt ($ mil.): —
No. of shares (mil.): 2.8
Sales ($ mil): 21.2
Dividends Yield: —
Payout: —
Market value ($ mil.): 57.0

	STOCK PRICE ($) FY Close	P/E High/Low		Earnings	PER SHARE ($) Dividends	Book Value
12/18	19.80	12	9	2.14	0.00	14.24
12/17	19.55	17	9	1.28	0.00	12.19
12/16	11.50	10	9	1.12	0.00	10.96
12/15	10.16	11	10	0.93	0.00	10.00
12/14	10.75	12	10	0.79	0.00	12.57
Annual Growth	16.5%	—	—	28.3%	—	3.2%

Svp Regional Executive, Jeffrey Levy
Vice President For Finance, Richard Halberg
Chair, Sally A. Steele, age 63
Board Member, Eric Stickels
Board Member, Raymond Pecor
Auditors: PricewaterhouseCoopers LLP

LOCATIONS

HQ: Community Bank System Inc
 5790 Widewaters Parkway, DeWitt, NY 13214-1883
Phone: 315 445-2282
Web: www.communitybankna.com

PRODUCTS/OPERATIONS

2015 Sales

	$ mil.	% of total
Interest Income:		
Interest and fees on loans	187.7	49
Taxable investments	52.9	14
Nontaxable investments	19.0	5
Noninterest		
Deposit service fees	52.7	14
Employee benefit services	45.4	12
Wealth management	20.2	5
Other	5.0	1
Total	**382.9**	**100**

Selected Subsidiaries & Affiliates

Benefit Plans Administrative Services Inc.
Benefit Plans Administrative Services LLC
Brilie Corporation
CBNA Insurance Agency Inc.
CBNA Preferred Funding Corp.
CBNA Treasury Management Corporation
Community Bank N.A. (also dba First Liberty Bank & Trust)
Community Investment Services Inc.
First of Jermyn Realty Company
First Liberty Service Corporation
Flex Corporation
Hand Benefit & Trust Company
Hand Securities Inc.
Harbridge Consulting Group LLP
Nottingham Advisors Inc.
Town & Country Agency LLC
Western Catskill Realty Inc.

COMPETITORS

Arrow Financial	Financial Institutions
Bank of America	HSBC USA
Canandaigua National	JPMorgan Chase
Chemung Financial	KeyCorp
Citizens Financial Group	M&T Bank
	NBT Bancorp
Elmira Savings Bank	

HISTORICAL FINANCIALS

Company Type: Public

Income Statement
FYE: December 31

	ASSETS ($ mil.)	NET INCOME ($ mil.)	INCOME AS % OF ASSETS	EMPLOYEES
12/18	10,607.3	168.6	1.6%	2,933
12/17	10,746.2	150.7	1.4%	2,874
12/16	8,666.4	103.8	1.2%	2,499
12/15	8,552.6	91.2	1.1%	2,490
12/14	7,489.4	91.3	1.2%	2,182
Annual Growth	9.1%	16.6%	—	7.7%

2018 Year-End Financials

Return on assets: 1.5%
Return on equity: 10.0%
Long-term debt ($ mil.): —
No. of shares (mil.): 51.2
Sales ($ mil.): 586.7
Dividends
 Yield: 2.4%
 Payout: 44.4%
Market value ($ mil.): 2,988.0

	STOCK PRICE ($) FY Close	P/E High/Low	PER SHARE ($) Earnings	Dividends	Book Value
12/18	58.30	20 16	3.24	1.44	33.43
12/17	53.75	20 16	3.03	1.32	32.26
12/16	61.79	27 15	2.32	1.26	26.96
12/15	39.94	20 15	2.19	1.22	26.06
12/14	38.13	18 15	2.22	1.16	24.24
Annual Growth	11.2%	— —	9.9%	5.6%	8.4%

Community Financial Corp (The)

EXECUTIVES

Assistant Vice President, Donna Goldey
Executive Vice President, Greg Cockerham
Assistant Vice President, Cathy Thompson
Board Member, Mary Peterson
Board Member, Kathryn Zabriskie
Board Member, Mohammad Javaid
Auditors: Dixon Hughes Goodman LLP

LOCATIONS

HQ: Community Financial Corp (The)
 3035 Leonardtown Road, Waldorf, MD 20601
Phone: 301 645-5601
Web: www.cbtc.com

COMPETITORS

American Bank Holdings	M&T Bank
BB&T	Old Line Bancshares
Burke & Herbert Bank	WSB Holdings
Independence Federal	

HISTORICAL FINANCIALS

Company Type: Public

Income Statement
FYE: December 31

	ASSETS ($ mil.)	NET INCOME ($ mil.)	INCOME AS % OF ASSETS	EMPLOYEES
12/18	1,689.2	11.2	0.7%	189
12/17	1,405.9	7.2	0.5%	165
12/16	1,334.2	7.3	0.5%	162
12/15	1,143.3	6.3	0.6%	171
12/14	1,082.8	6.4	0.6%	172
Annual Growth	11.8%	14.7%	—	2.4%

2018 Year-End Financials

Return on assets: 0.7%
Return on equity: 8.4%
Long-term debt ($ mil.): —
No. of shares (mil.): 5.5
Sales ($ mil): 69.2
Dividends
 Yield: 1.3%
 Payout: 32.0%
Market value ($ mil.): 163.0

	STOCK PRICE ($) FY Close	P/E High/Low	PER SHARE ($) Earnings	Dividends	Book Value
12/18	29.24	19 13	2.02	0.40	27.70
12/17	38.30	26 18	1.56	0.40	23.65
12/16	29.00	19 12	1.59	0.40	22.54
12/15	20.96	18 14	1.35	0.40	21.48
12/14	20.07	18 15	1.35	0.40	24.79
Annual Growth	9.9%	— —	10.6%	(0.0%)	2.8%

Community West Bancshares

EXECUTIVES

Vice President Underwriting Manager, Seth Harvey
Vice President Community Banking Manager, Julie Richardson
Vice President Human Resources Manager, Jennifer Ofner
Auditors: RSM US LLP

LOCATIONS

HQ: Community West Bancshares
 445 Pine Avenue, Goleta, CA 93117
Phone: 805 692-5821   **Fax:** 805 692-5835
Web: www.communitywest.com

PRODUCTS/OPERATIONS

2008 Sales

	$ mil.	% of total
Interest		
Loans	43.0	85
Investment securities	2.2	4
Other	0.3	1
Non-interest		
Loan fees	2.1	4
Loan sales	1.0	2
Other fees	1.7	3
Other	0.3	1
Total	**50.6**	**100**

COMPETITORS

Bank of America	Rabobank America
PacWest Bancorp	Wells Fargo

HISTORICAL FINANCIALS

Company Type: Public

Income Statement
FYE: December 31

	ASSETS ($ mil.)	NET INCOME ($ mil.)	INCOME AS % OF ASSETS	EMPLOYEES
12/18	877.2	7.4	0.8%	139
12/17	833.3	4.9	0.6%	128
12/16	710.5	5.2	0.7%	120
12/15	621.2	2.8	0.5%	107
12/14	557.3	7.0	1.3%	116
Annual Growth	12.0%	1.3%	—	4.6%

2018 Year-End Financials

Return on assets: 0.8%
Return on equity: 10.1%
Long-term debt ($ mil.): —
No. of shares (mil.): 8.5
Sales ($ mil): 45.2
Dividends
 Yield: 1.8%
 Payout: 25.6%
Market value ($ mil.): 86.0

	STOCK PRICE ($) FY Close	P/E High/Low	PER SHARE ($) Earnings	Dividends	Book Value
12/18	10.03	14 11	0.88	0.19	8.92
12/17	10.65	18 15	0.57	0.16	8.55
12/16	9.24	15 11	0.62	0.14	8.07
12/15	6.97	23 21	0.30	0.11	7.55
12/14	6.56	10 8	0.75	0.04	8.17
Annual Growth	11.2%	— —	4.1%	47.6%	2.2%

Computer Programs & Systems Inc

Computer Programs and Systems sounds like an intro to computers. But what you get at Computer Programs and Systems Inc. (CPSI) is administrative software and hardware systems and outsourcing services for acute care community hospitals. CPSI develops and supports electronic health records (EHR) as well as financial and clinical information management software and IT systems for small and midsized hospitals in the US. The company boasts a client base of more than 1000 healthcare facilities hospitals across 49 states. CPSI's software enables users to manage their patients staff finances and facilities. Subsidiary TruBridge offers managed IT services and business office outsourcing services.

Operations
CPSI products form an integrated data management system so the company markets its various applications as a single system. Among the various functions its electronic health record (EHR) system covers the basic necessary system includes patient management and financial accounting along with the hardware needed to run those programs. The other applications available to customers are patient care clinical record keeping and reporting and enterprise applications. Enterprise applications include such functions as system backups integrated fax document scanning and more. In 2015 CPSI formed Evident a subsidiary that offers EHR services to rural and community hospitals.

About 37% of the company's revenue comes from system sales 36% is from support and maintenance while business management consulting and managed IT services (Trubridge) generate 27%.

Geographic Reach
CPSI extended its reach beyond the US when it installed a system on St. Maarten in the Caribbean in 2014.

Sales and Marketing
Nearly all of CPSI's customers are organizations with 100 or fewer acute care beds but its target market includes hospitals with up to 300 such beds. The company serves less than 15% of the estimated size of its larger target market and less than one-quarter of its core market giving it room to continue the growth it has enjoyed so far.

For the most part CPSI lands new customers through referrals from existing customers. It also attracts potential customers with presentations at industry seminars and tradeshows and advertisements in publications for the healthcare industry. The company's typical sales cycle can be anywhere from six to 18 months.

Financial Performance
Revenue and net income inched up for CPSI in 2014.

The company reported $204.7 million in revenue for the year a 2% gain from 2013. It eked out a 0.54% increase in net income of $32.9 million in 2014 from $32.7 million.

System sales were off 6% in 2014 but support and maintenance increased 3% while Trubridge's business management consulting and managed IT services posted a robust 13% increase; the unit accounts for 27% of the company's revenue. The company blamed lower system sales on the quick pace of EHRs by hospitals leaving fewer potential customers.

Strategy
CPSI named its outsourcing division TruBridge in early 2013. TruBridge offers include network management and monitoring server and storage management hosted email firewall management malware protection data center services and help desk support and more. Business management services include electronic billing patient statement processing payroll processing website hosting and others.

With the Evident subsidiary CPSI offers EHR services previously sold under the corporate banner as well as additional services. The company will use Evident to distinguish itself in the market and to expand beyond its core offerings with rural and community healthcare facilities.

CPSI dipped its toe in international waters with the installation of a system on St. Maarten which produced about $1 million in revenue in 2014. The company also is looking to the north for expansion. It eyes a ready market in Canada which is about five years behind the US in adoption of EHR.

Mergers and Acquisitions
In 2019 CPSI agreed to buy Get Real Health which develops software to improve patient outcomes and engagement strategies for care providers for $11 million. With the deal CPSI intends to strengthen its position in community healthcare by offering Get Real Health's patient engagement and empowerment tools. The transaction is to close in the 2019 second quarter.

EXECUTIVES

President CEO and Director, J. Boyd Douglas, age 52, $521,154 total compensation
EVP Corporate and Business Development, Victor S. Schneider, age 60, $442,454 total compensation
SVP Software Services, Robert D. Hinckle, age 49
SVP Product Development Services, Michael K. Muscat, age 45
President TruBridge, Christopher L. Fowler, age 43
VP Information Technology Services, J. Scott Littrell, age 44
Vice President Information Technology, Immel Patrick
Senior Vice President of Sales, Troy Rosser
Vice President Sales, Dawn Severance
Chairman of the Board; Chief Financial Officer; Treasurer; Secretary, David A. Dye, age 49
Auditors: Grant Thornton LLP

LOCATIONS

HQ: Computer Programs & Systems Inc
6600 Wall Street, Mobile, AL 36695
Phone: 251 639-8100
Web: www.cpsi.com

PRODUCTS/OPERATIONS

2014 Sales

	$ mil.	% of total
System sales	75.1	37
Support & maintenance	73.5	36
Business management services	56.1	27
Total	**204.7**	**100**

Selected Products
Clinical information systems
  Anatomic pathology
  Cardiopulmonary
  Laboratory information systems
  Blood inventory
  Microbology
  Quality control
  Laboratory instrument interfaces
  Medical image management systems
  Pharmacy
  Physical therapy
  Radiology information systems
Enterprise applications
Financial accounting applications
  Accounts payable applications
  Budgeting
  Electronic direct deposit
  Executive information
  Fixed asset information
  General ledger applications
  Human resources
  Payroll and personnel
  Time and attendance applications
Home health
Patient care
  Care plans
  Core measures system
  Medication management
  Order entry/results reporting
  Patient activity
Patient management applications
  Contract management
  Electronic file management
  Health information management
  Patient accounting
  Quality improvement applications
  Registration systems

Selected Services
Application services
Internet services
Outsourcing services
  Business office management
  Electronic billing
  Statement processing
Support
System implementation and conversion
Training

COMPETITORS

Cerner	QuadraMed
Epic Systems	Quality Systems
MEDHOST	Siemens Healthcare
MEDITECH	Streamline Health
McKesson	Solutions

HISTORICAL FINANCIALS

Company Type: Public

Income Statement
FYE: December 31

	REVENUE ($ mil.)	NET INCOME ($ mil.)	NET PROFIT MARGIN	EMPLOYEES
12/18	280.4	17.6	6.3%	2,000
12/17	276.9	(17.4)	—	2,000
12/16	267.2	3.9	1.5%	2,000
12/15	182.1	18.3	10.1%	1,500
12/14	204.7	32.9	16.1%	1,379
Annual Growth	8.2%	(14.5%)	—	9.7%

2018 Year-End Financials
Debt ratio: 39.9%
Return on equity: 11.9%
Cash ($ mil.): 5.7
Current ratio: 1.82
Long-term debt ($ mil.): 124.5
No. of shares (mil.): 14.0
Dividends
  Yield: 1.5%
  Payout: 31.7%
Market value ($ mil.): 353.0

STOCK PRICE ($)	P/E	PER SHARE ($)		
FY Close	High/Low	Earnings	Dividends	Book Value
12/18 25.10	27 19	1.26	0.40	11.35
12/17 30.05	— —	(1.27)	0.85	9.89
12/16 23.60	199 78	0.29	1.86	11.67
12/15 49.75	39 23	1.62	2.56	6.67
12/14 60.75	24 19	2.94	2.28	7.21
Annual Growth 12.0%	(19.8%)	— —	(19.1%)	(35.3%)

Comtech Telecommunications Corp.

Comtech means contact. Through its subsidiaries Comtech Telecommunications operates in three divisions: mobile data communications telecommunications transmission and radio-frequency (RF) microwave amplifiers. Comtech makes equipment used largely by the US government and related defense contractors. Other customers include satellite systems integrators communications service providers and oil companies. Its transmission equipment includes modems frequency converters very-small-aperture terminal (VSAT) satellite transceivers and antennas and microwave radios. Comtech's RF amplifiers enable wireless instrumentation and medical systems and provide satellite-based messaging services and location tracking.

Operations
Comtech's biggest segment with 67% of revenue is Telecommunications Transmission which provides equipment and systems that enhance satellite transmission efficiency and that enable wireless communications in environments where terrestrial communications are unavailable or impractical. The RF Microwave Amplifiers segment contributes 25% of sales from satellite earth station traveling wave tube amplifiers and solid-state high-power narrow and broadband amplifiers. About 8% of revenue is from Mobile Data Communications which provides customers with integrated systems for global satellite-based communications when mobile real-time secure transmission is required.

Geographic Reach
Headquartered in Melville New York Comtech makes its products in Santa Clara California and Germantown Maryland. Its telecommunications transmission segment also has offices in Brazil Canada China India North Africa Singapore and the UK. Its sales to international customers jumped to 59% of revenue in 2014 (ended July) from 50% in 2013.

Sales and Marketing
Comtech sells through its sales staff and through independent sales companies and value-added resellers. Customers include AT&T Inc. China Mobile Limited Raytheon Company and Varian Medical Systems. The company sales to US government entities were 28% of total revenue in 2014 off from about 35% in 2013.

Financial Performance
While revenue in 2014 (ended July) rose 8% from 2013 it was still less than the $747 million in revenue its posted in 2010. Sales declined in the following years with fewer orders from the US Army which has been Comtech's biggest customer. In 2014 revenue was $347 million compared to about $320 million the year before. Sales were boosted from a contract with a North African government to design and supply in a communication network. A decrease in mobile data communications revenue was attributed to lower funding and the timing of work performed related to BFT-1 sustainment services for the US Army.

Comtech's net income jumped 41% to $25 million in 2014 from 2013's $17.8 million with the higher revenue and a drop in interest expense as the result of the settlement of $200 million principal of 3% convertible senior notes.

The company's cash flow from operations dropped by about $3 million in 2014 to $34.6 million because of high capital requirements and the timing of billings and commission payments on contracts for over-the-horizon microwave system contracts.

Strategy
Comtech plans to stretch its international sales beyond the 59% it now has by expanding international marketing efforts with more independent sales reps distributors and value-added resellers. It also intends to set up more foreign sales offices.

For it RF Microwave Amplifiers segment Comtech plans to set itself up as one-stop shop approach for RF microwave amplifiers; to =handle more amplifier production outsourced by other companies; and exploit its traveling wave tube amplifier in the direct-to-home market. The company's mobile data communications unit seeks opportunities with the US Army including blue force tracking (BFT) 2.5 and seek expansion into foreign military markets.

The BFT efforts paid off in 2014 when Comtech won two new contracts for BFT-1 sustainment totaling more than $68 million.

EXECUTIVES
SVP and President Comtech Systems Inc., Richard L. Burt, age 78, $380,000 total compensation
Chairman President and CEO, Fred V. Kornberg, age 83, $760,000 total compensation
SVP and CFO, Michael D. Porcelain, age 50, $395,000 total compensation
President Enterprise Technologies, Jay F. Whitehurst, age 59
SVP and President Comtech EF Data Corp. and Xicom Technology Inc., John Branscum
President Comtech PST Corp., Michael Hrybenko
COO, Michael Galletti
President Safety and Security Technologies, Lynne Houserman
President Command and Control Technologies, Michael Atcheson
Vice President Finance And Business Oper, Frank Roden
Group Vice President and General Manager, Kent Hellebust
Auditors: DELOITTE & TOUCHE LLP

LOCATIONS
HQ: Comtech Telecommunications Corp.
68 South Service Road, Suite 230, Melville, NY 11747
Phone: 631 962-7000   Fax: 631 962-7001
Web: www.comtechtel.com

PRODUCTS/OPERATIONS
2016 Sales
	$ mil.	% of total
Commercial Solutions	249.0	61
Government Solutions	162.0	39
Total	411.0	100

Selected Products
Mobile data communications services
  Location tracking
  Two-way messaging
Telecommunications transmission equipment
  Error-correction and compression chips
  Over-the-horizon microwave communications products
  Satellite earth station equipment (modems frequency converters amplifiers transceivers)
Radio-frequency microwave amplifiers

COMPETITORS
Advantech	Northrop Grumman
CPI International	QUALCOMM
Ericsson	Raytheon
General Dynamics	Surrey Satellite Technology
Gilat Satellite	
Harmonic	Teledyne Technologies
Harris Corp.	VT iDirect
Lockheed Martin	ViaSat

HISTORICAL FINANCIALS
Company Type: Public

Income Statement   FYE: July 31

	REVENUE ($ mil.)	NET INCOME ($ mil.)	NET PROFIT MARGIN	EMPLOYEES
07/19	671.8	25.0	3.7%	2,013
07/18	570.5	29.7	5.2%	1,852
07/17	550.3	15.8	2.9%	1,813
07/16	411.0	(7.7)	—	2,031
07/15	307.2	23.2	7.6%	978
Annual Growth	21.6%	1.9%	—	19.8%

2019 Year-End Financials
Debt ratio: 18.6%   No. of shares (mil.): 24.2
Return on equity: 4.8%   Dividends
Cash ($ mil.): 45.5   Yield: 1.3%
Current ratio: 1.93   Payout: 37.0%
Long-term debt ($ mil.): 165.0   Market value ($ mil.): 721.0

	STOCK PRICE ($)	P/E	PER SHARE ($)		
	FY Close	High/Low	Earnings	Dividends	Book Value
07/19	29.76	35 20	1.03	0.40	22.07
07/18	33.60	28 14	1.24	0.40	21.22
07/17	18.00	29 14	0.68	0.60	20.36
07/16	13.07	— —	(0.46)	1.20	20.16
07/15	28.81	28 19	1.42	1.20	24.88
Annual Growth (3.0%)	0.8%	— —	(7.7%)	(24.0%)	

ConnectOne Bancorp Inc (New)

ConnectOne Bancorp (formerly Center Bancorp) is the holding company for ConnectOne Bank which operates some two dozen branches across New Jersey. Serving individuals and local businesses the bank offers such deposit products as checking savings and money market accounts; CDs; and IRAs. It also performs trust services. Commercial loans account for about 60% of the bank's loan portfolio; residential mortgages account for most of the remainder. It also has a subsidiary that sells annuities and property/casualty life and health coverage. The former Center Bancorp acquired rival community bank ConnectOne Bancorp in 2014 and took that name.

Geographic Reach
ConnectOne has 24 branches in Bergen Essex Hudson Manhattan Mercer Monmouth Morris and Union Counties in New Jersey.

Mergers and Acquisitions
In 2019 ConnectOne Bancorp agreed to acquire online business lending marketplace company BoeFly. BoeFly connects franchisors and small business owners with lenders and loan brokers in the US and has facilitated more than $5 billion in financing transactions. BoeFly's online platform and client network will enhance and expand ConnectOne's Small Business Adminstration (SBA) line of business.

EXECUTIVES
VICE PRESIDENT, Lisa Wagner
Vice President, William Tierney
Auditors: Crowe LLP

LOCATIONS
HQ: ConnectOne Bancorp Inc (New)
  301 Sylvan Avenue, Englewood Cliffs, NJ 07632
Phone: 201 816-8900
Web: www.centerbancorp.com

COMPETITORS

BCB Bancorp	New York Community Bancorp
Bank of America	
Citizens Financial Corp.	Oritani Financial
	PNC Financial
Fulton Financial	Provident Financial Services
Hudson City Bancorp	
Investors Bancorp	Sovereign Bank
JPMorgan Chase	Valley National Bancorp
Kearny Financial	
Lakeland Bancorp	Westamerica

HISTORICAL FINANCIALS
Company Type: Public

Income Statement — FYE: December 31

	ASSETS ($ mil.)	NET INCOME ($ mil.)	INCOME AS % OF ASSETS	EMPLOYEES
12/18	5,462.0	60.3	1.1%	0
12/17	5,108.4	43.2	0.8%	0
12/16	4,426.3	31.0	0.7%	0
12/15	4,016.7	41.3	1.0%	0
12/14	3,448.5	18.5	0.5%	0
Annual Growth	12.2%	34.3%	—	—

2018 Year-End Financials
Return on assets: 1.1%
Return on equity: 10.2%
Long-term debt ($ mil.): —
No. of shares (mil.): 32.3
Sales ($ mil): 221.8
Dividends
  Yield: 1.6%
  Payout: 16.1%
Market value ($ mil.): 597.0

	STOCK PRICE ($) FY Close	P/E High/Low		PER SHARE ($) Earnings	Dividends	Book Value
12/18	18.47	17	9	1.86	0.30	18.99
12/17	25.75	21	16	1.34	0.30	17.63
12/16	25.95	26	15	1.01	0.30	16.62
12/15	18.69	16	13	1.36	0.30	15.87
12/14	19.00	25	21	0.79	0.30	15.03
Annual Growth	(0.7%)	—	—	23.9%	(0.0%)	6.0%

Consolidated-Tomoka Land Co.

From golf courses and retail centers to timber and hay farms land developer Consolidated-Tomoka owns a chunk of the Southeast. The company focuses on Florida but also has holdings in other neighboring states. Its portfolio includes retail properties (tenants include Bank of America CVS Walgreens a couple of golf courses (including the national headquarters of the LPGA) and some 10000 acres of agricultural land that the company is converting into other income properties. Through its subsidiaries it also holds subsurface oil gas and mineral interests on land throughout Florida and properties in North Carolina and Georgia. Consolidated-Tomoka was founded in 1902.

Operations
The company divides its operations across four segments: real estate operations income property golf and investment in a commercial mortgage loan collateralized by a hotel property in Atlanta.

Its income properties are the biggest moneymaker accounting for about half of overall sales. It owns 35 single-tenant income properties in seven states that are triple or double net leases and ground leases where the tenant pays for all real estate taxes insurance utilities maintenance and capital expenditures.

Geographic Reach
Consolidated-Tomoka is headquartered in Florida. The majority of its real estate is located there but other properties are in Arizona California Colorado Georgia Illinois and North Carolina.

Financial Performance
Overall sales grew almost 50% in 2013 to $25 million after the company recognized rents from nine properties bought in 2013 and a full year of results for six properties bought in late 2012. In addition Consolidated-Tomoka bought a mortgage loan in 2013 and began adding the accrued interest to its revenue mix. Profits grew 514% from $600000 in 2013 to $3 million in 2013.

Mergers and Acquisitions
As part of its strategy of investing in income-producing properties in 2013 Consolidated-Tomoka bought nine income properties for a combined $39 million including four buildings leased to Bank of America in Southern California and two office complexes leased to Hilton in Florida. At the same time it sold five properties for $18.6 million.

EXECUTIVES
SVP General Counsel and Corporate Secretary, Daniel E. Smith, $185,000 total compensation
President and CEO, John P. Albright, $500,000 total compensation
SVP and CFO, Mark E. Patten, $220,500 total compensation
SVP Investments, Steven R. Greathouse
Vice Chairman, A. Chester Skinner
Chairman, Thomas P. Warlow
Auditors: Grant Thornton LLP

LOCATIONS
HQ: Consolidated-Tomoka Land Co.
  1140 N. Williamson Blvd., Suite 140, Daytona Beach, FL 32114
Phone: 386 274-2202   **Fax:** 386 274-1223
Web: www.ctlc.com

PRODUCTS/OPERATIONS
2015 Sales

	% of total
Income Properties	44
Real Estate Operations	37
Golf Operations	12
Interest Income from Commercial Loan Investments	7
Agriculture and Other income	-
Total	100

COMPETITORS

AV Homes	Rayonier
Alico Inc.	St. Joe
Anthony Forest Products	Stiles
	Stratus Properties
Echelon Development	Tejon Ranch
Forestar	Turnberry Associates

HISTORICAL FINANCIALS
Company Type: Public

Income Statement — FYE: December 31

	REVENUE ($ mil.)	NET INCOME ($ mil.)	NET PROFIT MARGIN	EMPLOYEES
12/18	86.6	37.1	42.9%	14
12/17	91.4	41.7	45.6%	14
12/16	71.0	16.2	22.9%	14
12/15	43.0	8.3	19.4%	14
12/14	35.5	6.3	18.0%	14
Annual Growth	25.0%	55.3%	—	0.0%

2018 Year-End Financials
Debt ratio: 44.5%
Return on equity: 18.7%
Cash ($ mil.): 2.3
Current ratio: 0.72
Long-term debt ($ mil.): 247.6
No. of shares (mil.): 5.4
Dividends
  Yield: 0.5%
  Payout: 4.0%
Market value ($ mil.): 285.0

	STOCK PRICE ($) FY Close	P/E High/Low		PER SHARE ($) Earnings	Dividends	Book Value
12/18	52.50	10	7	6.72	0.27	38.95
12/17	63.50	8	7	7.48	0.18	32.98
12/16	53.42	19	15	2.85	0.12	25.97
12/15	52.71	44	34	1.43	0.08	22.81
12/14	55.80	54	30	1.10	0.07	21.83
Annual Growth	(1.5%)	—	—	57.2%	40.1%	15.6%

Construction Partners Inc

Auditors: RSM US LLP

LOCATIONS

HQ: Construction Partners Inc
290 Healthwest Drive, Suite 2, Dothan, AL 36303
Phone: 334 673-9763
Web: www.constructionpartners.net

HISTORICAL FINANCIALS
Company Type: Public

Income Statement — FYE: September 30

	REVENUE ($ mil.)	NET INCOME ($ mil.)	NET PROFIT MARGIN	EMPLOYEES
09/19	783.2	43.1	5.5%	2,289
09/18	680.1	50.7	7.5%	2,154
09/17	568.2	26.0	4.6%	1,856
09/16	542.3	22.0	4.1%	0
Annual Growth	13.0%	25.1%	—	—

2019 Year-End Financials
Debt ratio: 9.4%
Return on equity: 13.4%
Cash ($ mil.): 80.6
Current ratio: 2.18
Long-term debt ($ mil.): 42.4
No. of shares (mil.): 51.7
Dividends
Yield: —
Payout: —
Market value ($ mil.): 807.0

	STOCK PRICE ($) FY Close	P/E High	P/E Low	Earnings	Dividends	Book Value
09/19	15.58	20	10	0.84	0.00	6.63
09/18	12.10	13	10	1.11	0.00	5.82
09/17	0.00	—	—	0.63	0.00	3.65
Annual Growth	—			15.5%	—	34.8%

Contura Energy Inc

Auditors: KPMG LLP

LOCATIONS

HQ: Contura Energy Inc
340 Martin Luther King Jr. Blvd., Bristol, TN 37620
Phone: 423 573-0300
Web: www.conturaenergy.com

HISTORICAL FINANCIALS
Company Type: Public

Income Statement — FYE: December 31

	REVENUE ($ mil.)	NET INCOME ($ mil.)	NET PROFIT MARGIN	EMPLOYEES
12/18	2,031.2	299.1	14.7%	4,420
12/17	1,649.9	154.5	9.4%	0
12/16*	506.3	(10.9)	—	0
07/16	411.1	(67.2)	—	0
12/15	926.0	(417.5)	—	0
Annual Growth	21.7%			

*Fiscal year change

2018 Year-End Financials
Debt ratio: 21.4%
Return on equity: 51.4%
Cash ($ mil.): 233.6
Current ratio: 2.34
Long-term debt ($ mil.): 545.2
No. of shares (mil.): 19.1
Dividends
Yield: —
Payout: —
Market value ($ mil.): 1,256.0

	STOCK PRICE ($) FY Close	P/E High	P/E Low	Earnings	Dividends	Book Value
12/18	65.74	3	2	25.54	0.00	56.08
12/17	59.38	5	4	14.35	9.00	9.34
12/16*	71.00	—	—	(1.06)	0.00	3.61
Annual Growth	(3.8%) 293.9%			—	—	—

*Fiscal year change

Copart Inc

What happens to cars totaled in wrecks or natural disasters or stolen cars recovered after the insurance settlement? Copart takes those vehicles and auctions them for insurers as well as auto dealers fleet operations charities and banks. The buyers are mostly rebuilders licensed dismantlers and used-car dealers and exporters. The company has replaced live auctions with Internet auctions using a platform known as Virtual Bidding Third Generation (VB3 for short). It also provides services such as towing and storage to buyers and other salvage companies. Copart serves customers throughout North America Europe the Middle East and Brazil although the US accounts for about 85% of sales.

Financial Performance
With dozens of new facilities opened Copart has seen strong growth in sales and profits over the past several years. Revenue is up 55% and net income up 134% since fiscal 2014.

In fiscal 2018 (ended July) the company's revenue jumped 25% to $1.8 billion. The growth was powered primarily by increased volumes and higher auction selling prices in the US. Hurricane Harvey which hit southern Texas in August 2017 boosted volume as it resulted in a huge number of flood-damaged vehicles.

Net income that year was up 6% to $417.9 million. Higher revenue boosted the bottom line but growth was offset somewhat by a larger income tax expense compared to 2017.

Cash at the end of fiscal 2018 was $274.5 million an increase of $64.4 million from the prior year. Cash from operations contributed $535.1 million to the coffers while investing activities used $288.5 million mainly for capital expenditures. Financing activities used another $182 million primarily for loan repayments.

Strategy
Copart's growth strategy includes developing or acquiring facilities in new regions as well as regions already served by the company. In the three years through fiscal 2018 it opened or purchased some 30 facilities including multiple facilities in Europe in 2018. Germany and by extension the rest of Western Europe is a key geographic target. The company has opened some half a dozen physical yards in Germany and conducts weekly auctions at two of those sites.

Technology is another important investment area for Copart which bills itself as a "technology company." Current investments include advanced machine learning such as that used in its ProQuote engine a pricing estimator used by customers to value salvage vehicles and powered by machines that learn from every additional transaction. The company's vehicle recommendation engine uses similar technology as do some of its online auction tools.

HISTORY
Copart was co-founded in 1982 by Willis Johnson who had owned and operated an auto dismantling business for more than 10 years. After buying out his partner in 1986 he became CEO and used his own money to expand the company into a network of four California salvage yards by 1991. In the next two years Copart nearly tripled the number of salvage operations it owned by acquiring companies throughout the US. HPB Associates a private investor group came on board in 1993 buying 26% of the firm for $10 million and the company went public the next year.

Copart doubled its total facilities in 1995 with the acquisition of NER Auction Systems the largest privately held salvage auction company in the US. The firm acquired or opened more than 30 facilities between 1995 and 1997. In 1998 the company started an online auction site; expanded through acquisitions into Alabama Iowa Michigan and South Carolina; and opened new locations in California and Minnesota. The next year rival Insurance Auto Auctions spurned its merger overtures.

In 2000 Copart opened three new salvage vehicle auction facilities and acquired eight more. That year the company also signed an agreement to sell Keystone Automotive Industries' parts through its Web site. In 2001 and 2002 the company acquired or opened 13 new locations. Continuing its acquisition strategy the company opened or acquired five more facilities in 2004.

In 2005 the company made two acquisitions for about $4.5 million: Kentucky Auto Salvage Pool a 25-acre salvage facility in Lexington Kentucky; and Insurance Auctions of Missouri. In November Copart acquired the salvage pool assets of Central Penn Sales a vehicle salvage disposal company with four sites in Pennsylvania and Maryland totaling 255 acres. In December the company opened a second salvage facility in Michigan.

In June 2007 Copart acquired Universal Salvage the operator of about 10 salvage yards in the UK and a vehicle remarketer to the insurance and automotive industries for about $120 million. Adding to its UK holdings in August Copart purchased Century Salvage Sales Limited which has three salvage yards and AG Watson which has four salvage yards in England and Scotland.

During 2008 the company launched CopartDirect. The service allows Copart to sell cars to the general public using its VB 2 application so that individuals can avoid the inconvenience of selling a vehicle themselves.

In February 2010 Willis Johnson relinquished the CEO's title to A. Jayson Adair who formerly served as president of Copart. Johnson continued as chairman of the company.

In 2011 Copart acquired the Indiana-based auto auction firm Barodge Auto Pool expanding its presence in Indiana and surrounding states. The company also broadened its existing range of farming equipment in the UK when it acquired Hewitt

International an auctioneer of agricultural vehicles and equipment based in central England in 2011.

In 2012 the company made several acquisitions in international markets including Brazil Canada Germany and Dubai UAE. That year Copart expanded into Germany (the world's fourth largest auto market) with the purchase of WOM Wreck Online Marketing a leading European salvage vehicle auction platform there. Earlier in the year it bought Canada's Diamond Auto Bids and Disposals a privately-held automotive auction that gives Copart a foothold in Western Canada specifically Calgary and Edmonton. It also extended the reach of its business into South America through its purchase of Central de Leiloes LTDA based in Sao Paulo Brazil.

EXECUTIVES

CEO, A. Jayson Adair, age 49
EVP, William E. Franklin, age 63, $363,423 total compensation
President, Vincent W. Mitz, age 56, $265,000 total compensation
SVP and CFO, Jeffrey Liaw, age 43
National Account Manager, Daren Meis
National Sales Manager, Susan Gordon
Vice President Product Development, Vinay Kudithipudi
National Sales Manager, Jim Miller
National Account Manager, Daniel Smith
Vice President Information Technology Infrastructure and Operations, Sam Selby
Vice President, Richard Kruse
Vice President Of Operations, Steve Powers
Auditors: Ernst & Young LLP

LOCATIONS

HQ: Copart Inc
14185 Dallas Parkway, Suite 300, Dallas, TX 75254
Phone: 972 391-5000
Web: www.copart.com

PRODUCTS/OPERATIONS

2018 Sales

	$ mil.	% of total
Services	1,578.5	86
Vehicles	227.2	14
Total	1,805.7	100

Selected Services

Copart Access (online vehicle information retrieval)
Copart Dealer Services (online trade-in vehicle sales)
Copart Direct (online used car sales)
CoPartfinder (online used-parts search engine)
DMV processing (title document processing)
Monthly reporting (summary of all vehicles processed by company for suppliers)
Online bidding (online auctions)
Salvage brokerage network (coordination of vehicle disposal outside areas of current operation)
Salvage Lynk (software providing online information on vehicles being processed)
Transportation services (fleet of transport trucks)
Vehicle inspection stations (central locations for insurance companies to inspect vehicles)
Vehicle preparation and merchandising (cleaning and weather protection direct mailings to buyers)

COMPETITORS

Advance Auto Parts	KAR Auction Services
Columbus Fair Auto Auction	LKQ
Cox Automotive	Pittsburgh Independent Auto Auction
Cox Enterprises	

HISTORICAL FINANCIALS
Company Type: Public

Income Statement
FYE: July 31

	REVENUE ($ mil.)	NET INCOME ($ mil.)	NET PROFIT MARGIN	EMPLOYEES
07/19	2,041.9	591.6	29.0%	7,327
07/18	1,805.7	417.8	23.1%	6,026
07/17	1,447.9	394.2	27.2%	5,323
07/16	1,268.4	270.3	21.3%	4,844
07/15	1,146.0	219.7	19.2%	4,267
Annual Growth	15.5%	28.1%	—	14.5%

2019 Year-End Financials

Debt ratio: 15.7%
Return on equity: 35.2%
Cash ($ mil.): 186.3
Current ratio: 2.44
Long-term debt ($ mil.): 400.0
No. of shares (mil.): 229.7
Dividends
 Yield: —
 Payout: —
Market value ($ mil.): 17,816.0

	STOCK PRICE ($) FY Close	P/E High/Low		PER SHARE ($) Earnings	Dividends	Book Value
07/19	77.53	31	17	2.46	0.00	7.74
07/18	57.39	33	17	1.73	0.00	6.76
07/17	31.49	36	17	1.66	0.00	4.76
07/16	50.44	43	28	1.11	0.00	3.52
07/15	36.03	44	35	0.84	0.00	4.01
Annual Growth	21.1%	—	—	31.0%	—	17.8%

Corcept Therapeutics Inc

Corcept Therapeutics wants to help people who are beyond blue. The biotechnology firm is exploring treatments that regulate the presence of cortisol a steroid hormone associated with some psychiatric and metabolic disorders. Its sole commercial product Korlym is a version of the compound mifepristone (commonly known as RU-486 or the "abortion pill") used to regulate release patterns of cortisol. The drug is approved in the US for use in patients with Cushing's Syndrome a metabolic disorder caused by high levels of cortisol in the blood. The company is also developing mifepristone for treatment of patients with psychotic depression.

Operations

Corcept is investigating three additional proprietary selective cortisol modulators for the treatment of Cushing syndrome and of solid-tumor cancers. In certain cancers cortisol activity promotes the growth of tumors; Corcept is studying the idea that adding a cortisol modulator to a patient's treatment will activate the body's immune system.

The company does not manufacture Korlym or its drug candidates but rather relies on contract manufacturers Produits Chimiques Auxiliaires et de Synthese and Alcami Corporation.

Geographic Reach

Corcept sells Korlym in the US. It does not have immediate plans to market the drug in other markets.

Sales and Marketing

Corcept markets Korlym in the US through direct sales representatives health care providers and via medical science liaisons. The company has significantly increased the size of its sales force in recent years.

Financial Performance

Corcept's revenues have been rising rapidly over the past five years thanks to higher sales volumes and price increases. In 2016 revenue increased 62% to $81.3 million. With the higher revenue the company became profitable that year netting $8.1 million (versus losses of $6.4 million in 2015 and $31.4 million in 2014).

Cash flow from operations has also been steadily increasing. In 2016 it totaled $18.4 million more than quadruple the $3.1 million it totaled in 2015.

Strategy

Corcept typically allots about 30% of its operating expenses to research and development. In fiscal 2016 the company spent $23.8 million on R&D up from $15.4 million in 2015 and $18.4 million in 2014. It expects these expenses to rise as its clinical studies activities ramp up and it hires additional clinical staff.

Right now the company is reliant on Korlym for its growth as its other candidates won't be commercialized for years. Although sales of Korlym have been on the rise the drug faces competition from Novartis' Signifor which is also approved to treat adults with Cushing's disease (which the majority of patients with Cushing's syndrome have).

EXECUTIVES

President and CEO, Joseph K. Belanoff, age 61, $597,670 total compensation
CFO, G. Charles Robb, age 56, $363,472 total compensation
SVP Commercial, Sean Maduck
Chief Medical Officer, Robert S. Fishman, age 57, $104,956 total compensation
VP Regulatory Affairs, Susan Rinne
Vice President Marketing And Training, Rob Adamoski
MEDICAL DIRECTOR, Andreas Moraitis
VICE PRESIDENT ONCOLOGY, Stacie Shepherd
Vice President, Alan Arroyo
Vice President, Behn Sarafpour
Vice President Manufacturing, Yip-fong Chia
Chairman, James N. Wilson
Auditors: Ernst & Young LLP

LOCATIONS

HQ: Corcept Therapeutics Inc
149 Commonwealth Drive, Menlo Park, CA 94025
Phone: 650 327-3270
Web: www.corcept.com

COMPETITORS

AstraZeneca	Janssen Pharmaceuticals
Bayer HealthCare Pharmaceuticals	Merck
Bristol-Myers Squibb	Mylan
Eli Lilly	Novartis
GlaxoSmithKline	Pfizer

HISTORICAL FINANCIALS

Company Type: Public

Income Statement — FYE: December 31

	REVENUE ($ mil.)	NET INCOME ($ mil.)	NET PROFIT MARGIN	EMPLOYEES
12/18	251.2	75.4	30.0%	166
12/17	159.2	129.1	81.1%	136
12/16	81.3	8.1	10.0%	103
12/15	50.2	(6.4)	—	96
12/14	26.5	(31.3)	—	92
Annual Growth	75.4%			15.9%

2018 Year-End Financials

Debt ratio: —
Return on equity: 32.3%
Cash ($ mil.): 41.6
Current ratio: 6.66
Long-term debt ($ mil.): —
No. of shares (mil.): 115.0
Dividends
Yield: —
Payout: —
Market value ($ mil.): 1,537.0

	STOCK PRICE ($) FY Close	P/E High/Low	PER SHARE ($) Earnings	Dividends	Book Value
12/18	13.36	39 17	0.60	0.00	2.40
12/17	18.06	18 6	1.04	0.00	1.66
12/16	7.26	139 47	0.07	0.00	0.37
12/15	4.98	— —	(0.06)	0.00	0.17
12/14	3.00	— —	(0.31)	0.00	(0.03)
Annual Growth	45.3%				

CorEnergy Infrastructure Trust Inc

EXECUTIVES

President CEO and Director, David J. Schulte, age 58
Chief Accounting Officer Treasurer and Secretary, Rebecca Sandring
Senior Vice President, Jeff Fulmer
Vice President Finance, Jeff Teeven
Auditors: Ernst & Young LLP

LOCATIONS

HQ: CorEnergy Infrastructure Trust Inc
1100 Walnut, Ste. 3350, Kansas City, MO 64106
Phone: 816 875-3705
Web: www.investors.corenergy.reit

PRODUCTS/OPERATIONS

2015 Sales

	% of total
Lease	68
Transportation	20
Sales	10
Financing	2
Total	100

COMPETITORS

Adams Express
FMR
First Reserve
OHA Investment
Petroleum & Resources Corporation
Prospect Capital
The Vanguard Group

HISTORICAL FINANCIALS

Company Type: Public

Income Statement — FYE: December 31

	REVENUE ($ mil.)	NET INCOME ($ mil.)	NET PROFIT MARGIN	EMPLOYEES
12/18	89.2	43.7	49.0%	22
12/17	88.7	32.6	36.7%	20
12/16	89.2	29.6	33.2%	22
12/15	71.2	12.3	17.3%	22
12/14	40.3	7.0	17.4%	21
Annual Growth	22.0%	58.0%		1.2%

2018 Year-End Financials

Debt ratio: 24.0%
Return on equity: 9.5%
Cash ($ mil.): 69.2
Current ratio: 19.77
Long-term debt ($ mil.): 150.0
No. of shares (mil.): 11.9
Dividends
Yield: 9.0%
Payout: 107.5%
Market value ($ mil.): 396.0

	STOCK PRICE ($) FY Close	P/E High/Low	PER SHARE ($) Earnings	Dividends	Book Value
12/18	33.08	14 11	2.79	3.00	38.04
12/17	38.20	19 15	2.07	3.00	38.75
12/16	34.88	17 5	2.14	3.00	34.20
12/15	14.84	30 5	0.79	2.75	35.01
12/14	6.48	8 6	1.05	2.57	33.31
Annual Growth	50.3%		27.7%	3.9%	3.4%

CoreSite Realty Corp

CoreSite Realty leases data center space to those with data center needs. The real estate investment trust (REIT) owns develops and operates these specialized facilities which require enough power security and network interconnection to handle often complex IT operations. Its property portfolio includes more than 15 operating data center facilities with additional space under development. These properties comprise around 3 million rentable sq. ft. and are located in major US tech hubs including Silicon Valley. Tenants include enterprise organizations communications service providers media and content companies government agencies and schools. The REIT has grown along with demand for data center space.

Operations

Unlike most REITs which earn virtually all of their revenue from lease income CoreSite also makes money from the power and cross connections it supplies to its tenants. About 56% of its total revenue came from rental income during 2015 while about 27% came from power revenue and 13% came from interconnection revenue.

Geographic Reach

Denver-based CoreSite Realty operates 17 data center campuses in nine North American markets. Almost 75% of the REIT's rental income came from its properties in Los Angeles San Francisco Bay and Northern Virginia during 2015 while another nearly 25% came from its properties in Chicago Boston and New York. The rest came from its Miami- and Denver-based properties.

Sales and Marketing

The REIT boasts a global customer base of more than 900 tenants (as of early 2016) including ISPs (Internet Service Providers) and telecommunications carriers (including AT&T Verizon Comcast Time Warner China Mobile and Tata Communications) content and media entertainment providers (such as Facebook Google Microsoft and DreamWorks Animation) cloud providers (Amazon Computer Science Corp. Hewlett-Packard) as well as enterprise financial educational institutions and government agencies.

CoreSite's 10 largest tenants made up 35.6% of its annualized rent during 2015 reflecting a diversified tenant base.

Financial Performance

CoreSite Realty's annual revenues have nearly doubled since 2011 as new property acquisitions and demand for data center space has driven higher rental income. The REIT's profits have skyrocketed as it has managed to keep a lid on the growth of operating costs.

The REIT's revenue jumped 22% to a record $333.29 million during 2015 as new and expansion leases increased its occupied space by 20% to 1.49 million net rental square feet (NRSF) boosting rental and power income sources. Interconnection revenue also rose 25% as new and existing customers added 2226 new cross connections.

Strong revenue growth in 2015 drove CoreSite's net income up 52% to a record $34.71 million. The company's operating cash levels spiked 43% to $142.6 million for the year as its cash-based rental power and interconnection revenues increased.

Strategy

The properties in CoreSite's portfolio are strategically located in major metropolitan cities known for being high-tech hotbeds such as Boston Chicago Los Angeles New York City and the San Francisco Bay and Northern Virginia areas. Data centers especially outsourced ones (which are cheaper than in-house ones) are growing in these cities and others because they meet specific technology needs with specialized infrastructures that supply multiple network connectivity uninterruptible power backup generators cooling equipment fire suppression systems and physical security.

The company hopes to capitalize on demand that is outpacing supply for outsourced data centers in these markets. Supply of new data center facilities has been hampered in part by industry consolidation and lack of capital to develop additional space. CoreSite intends to market its existing portfolio — coupled with its development capabilities and the network interconnection services it offers — to attract more quality tenants.

Company Background

The company's first data center was purchased in 2000. Acquisitions of these properties throughout its history have been funded and held through real estate funds affiliated with global private equity firm The Carlyle Group.

CoreSite Realty Corp. started in 2001 as CRG West a portfolio company of The Carlyle Group. CoreSite Realty went public in September 2010 with an offering worth $270.4 million. CoreSite used the proceeds of its IPO to develop and redevelop additional data centers and to retire debt.

EXECUTIVES

President and CEO, Paul E. Szurek, age 59
CFO, Jeffrey S. (Jeff) Finnin, age 55, $382,308 total compensation

SVP Field Operations and Network Engineering, Dominic M. Tobin, age 65, $203,750 total compensation
SVP General Counsel and Secretary, Derek S. McCandless, age 48, $291,635 total compensation
SVP Product and Marketing, Brian P. Warren, age 49, $225,961 total compensation
SVP Sales and Sales Operations, Steven J. Smith, age 54, $310,961 total compensation
Senior Management (Senior Vice President General Manager Director), Matt Gleason
Vice President Sales Va, Juan Font
Vice President, Gerry Fassig
Vice President Of Human Resources, Geoff Danheiser
Vice President of Facilities, Anthony Hatzenbuehler
Vice President Of Sales Network And Mobility, Ben Green
Vice President Of Design And Construction, Robert Dean
Vice President Sales Channel, Dave Biermann
Auditors: KPMG LLP

LOCATIONS

HQ: CoreSite Realty Corp
1001 17th Street, Suite 500, Denver, CO 80202
Phone: 866 777-2673
Web: www.coresite.com

PRODUCTS/OPERATIONS

2015 Sales

	$ mil.	% of total
Data Center:		
Rental	183.3	56
Power	89.4	27
Interconnection	44.2	13
Tenant reimbursement & other	8.3	2
Office light-industrial & other	8.0	2
Total	**333.2**	**100**

COMPETITORS

AT&T	Internap
CenturyLink	QTS Realty Trust Inc.
CyrusOne	SAVVIS
Digital Realty	Telx Group
DuPont Fabros	Terremark Worldwide
Equinix	Zayo Group

HISTORICAL FINANCIALS

Company Type: Public

Income Statement — FYE: December 31

	REVENUE ($ mil.)	NET INCOME ($ mil.)	NET PROFIT MARGIN	EMPLOYEES
12/18	544.3	77.9	14.3%	454
12/17	481.8	74.8	15.5%	465
12/16	400.3	58.7	14.7%	422
12/15	333.2	34.7	10.4%	391
12/14	272.4	22.7	8.4%	354
Annual Growth	18.9%	36.0%	—	6.4%

2018 Year-End Financials

Debt ratio: 71.9%
Return on equity: 29.7%
Cash ($ mil.): 2.6
Current ratio: 0.15
Long-term debt ($ mil.): 1,333.5
No. of shares (mil.): 36.7
Dividends
  Yield: 4.7%
  Payout: 186.4%
Market value ($ mil.): 3,202.0

Stock Price ($) / **P/E** / **Per Share ($)**

	STOCK PRICE ($) FY Close	P/E High/Low	Earnings	Dividends	Book Value
12/18	87.23	53 37	2.22	4.14	6.61
12/17	113.90	65 44	1.84	3.58	8.21
12/16	79.37	59 35	1.54	2.39	12.85
12/15	56.72	57 37	1.03	1.79	13.58
12/14	39.05	58 44	0.66	1.47	14.83
Annual Growth 22.3% (18.3%)		—	—	35.4%	29.5%

Corporate Property Associates 18 Global Inc

Auditors: PricewaterhouseCoopers LLP

LOCATIONS

HQ: Corporate Property Associates 18 Global Inc
50 Rockefeller Plaza, New York, NY 10020
Phone: 212 492-1100
Web: www.cpa18global.com

HISTORICAL FINANCIALS

Company Type: Public

Income Statement — FYE: December 31

	REVENUE ($ mil.)	NET INCOME ($ mil.)	NET PROFIT MARGIN	EMPLOYEES
12/18	216.7	96.7	44.6%	0
12/17	205.6	26.5	12.9%	0
12/16	184.3	(30.0)	—	0
12/15	135.9	(57.7)	—	0
12/14	54.3	(55.8)	—	0
Annual Growth	41.3%	—	—	—

2018 Year-End Financials

Debt ratio: 54.0%
Return on equity: 11.8%
Cash ($ mil.): 170.9
Current ratio: 3.87
Long-term debt ($ mil.): 1,246.1
No. of shares (mil.): 146.2
Dividends
  Yield: —
  Payout: 175.4%
Market value ($ mil.): —

CoStar Group, Inc.

CoStar has all the dirt on the commercial real estate industry. A provider of commercial real estate information CoStar has a proprietary database of some 4 million properties in the US the UK and France. The database contains information on more than 10 billion square feet of sale and lease listings. It also has more than 12 million digital images of buildings floor plans and maps. Its hundreds of data fields include location ownership and tenant names. CoStar additionally offers marketing and analytic services. Clients include government agencies real estate brokerages real estate investment trusts (REITs) and property owners and managers. Most of CoStar's sales come from subscription fees.

Operations

The company employs a team of more than 1000 research professionals and contractors who collect and analyze commercial real estate information. Its subscription-based services consist primarily of CoStar Property Professional (comprehensive inventory) CoStar Tenant (tenant information) CoStar COMPS Professional (comparable sales information) FOCUS (data on UK market) and Propex (UK market info for professional investors). It does business in England through CoStar UK.

Geographic Reach

The company's sales teams are located in 30 field sales offices throughout the US and in offices located in London England; Manchester England; Glasgow Scotland and Paris France. Sales in the US accounted for about 95% of total revenues in fiscal 2012.

Sales and Marketing

The company draws its customers from commercial real estate and related business community. Commercial real estate brokers have traditionally formed the largest portion of CoStar clients. The company also provides services to owners landlords financial institutions retailers vendors appraisers investment banks governmental agencies and other parties involved in commercial real estate.

CoStar sells its products and services through a direct sales force located in field sales offices. Its E-commerce advertising expenses were approximately $3 million in fiscal 2012.

Financial Performance

CoStar's revenue has spiked nearly 40% in fiscal 2012 compared to the previous year. The company brought in almost $350 million in revenue during fiscal 2012 after reporting about $251.7 million in fiscal 2011 and $226.3 million back in fiscal 2010.

The increase in revenues during fiscal 2012 was primarily attributable to additional revenue from the acquisition of LoopNet the penetration of the subscription-based information services and successful cross-selling of the company's services to its customers in existing markets combined with continued high renewal rates.

Net income decreased in fiscal 2012 mainly due to the increase in income tax expense and the impact of costs related to the LoopNet acquisition that are not deductible for tax purposes.

Mergers and Acquisitions

In 2012 the company significantly expanded its holdings with the $860 million purchase of LoopNet a complementary provider of online commercial real estate information. The deal doubled the size of CoStar's paid subscriber base to some 160000. The previous year CoStar enhanced its real estate brokerage offerings when it obtained Virtual Premise a provider of real estate management software and lease abstraction services. Each month Virtual Premise manages over $1 billion in rent payments for its customers.

EXECUTIVES

President CEO and Director, Andrew C. Florance, age 55, $561,267 total compensation
CTO and SVP Information Technology Loopnet, Wayne B. Warthen, age 56
CIO, Frank Simuro, age 52

EVP, Brian J. Radecki, age 48, $357,031 total compensation
EVP Sales, Max Linnington
President LoopNet, Curtis M. Kroeker, age 48
EVP Operations, Francis (Frank) Carchedi, $287,273 total compensation
President Apartments.com, Brad Long
CEO Resolve Technology, Eric C. Forman, age 59
Managing Director CoStar UK Limited, Giles R. Newman
Managing Director PPR, Hans G. Nordby, age 52
President Virtual Premise, M. Andrew Thomas, age 56
CFO, Scott Wheeler
Vice President Major Accounts, Gerry Perrine
Vice President Research, Simon Law
Vp Of Research, Dean Violagis
Vice President Sales, Jason Walpert
Vp Human Resources, Donna Tanenbaum
Vice President Software Development, Jason Butler
Regional Vice President Sales, Jeffrey Reesing
Vice President Sales Operations, Lonnie Lucas
Regional Vice President West, Jamie Jump
VICE PRESIDENT MULTIFAMILY MARKETING NATIONAL ACCOUNTS, Karen Blue
Vice President, David Sambrook
Regional Vice President, Marc Swartz
Vice President Consulting, Jimmy Dykes
Regional Vice President Multifamily, Mike Follis
Regional Vice President Of Sales, Mindi Woodson
Vice President Shared Services, Cameron Blakely
Vice President Business Development, Martin Johnson
Chairman, Michael R. Klein, age 77
Board Member, Marc Kaplan
Auditors: Ernst & Young LLP

LOCATIONS

HQ: CoStar Group, Inc.
1331 L Street, N.W., Washington, DC 20005
Phone: 202 346-6500   **Fax:** 877 739-0486
Web: www.costargroup.com

PRODUCTS/OPERATIONS

Selected Subscription Products
CoStar COMPS Professional (comparable sales information)
CoStar Property Professional (flagship real estate database)
CoStar Tenant (tenant information)
FOCUS (UK real estate information)

Selected Data
Building characteristics
Contact information
Demographic information
For-sale information
Historical trends
Income and expense histories
Lease expirations
Mortgage and deed information
Number of retail stores
Ownership
Retail sales per square foot
Sales and lease comparables
Site and zoning information
Space availability
Tax assessments
Tenant names

COMPETITORS

First American	Reed Business Information
Market Leader	
Move Inc.	Reis
PropertyInfo	Zillow

HISTORICAL FINANCIALS
Company Type: Public

Income Statement   FYE: December 31

	REVENUE ($ mil.)	NET INCOME ($ mil.)	NET PROFIT MARGIN	EMPLOYEES
12/18	1,191.8	238.3	20.0%	3,705
12/17	965.2	122.7	12.7%	3,711
12/16	837.6	85.0	10.2%	3,064
12/15	711.7	(3.4)	—	2,631
12/14	575.9	44.8	7.8%	2,444
Annual Growth	19.9%	51.8%		11.0%

2018 Year-End Financials
Debt ratio: —
Return on equity: 8.4%
Cash ($ mil.): 1,100.4
Current ratio: 7.87
Long-term debt ($ mil.): —
No. of shares (mil.): 36.4
Dividends
  Yield: —
  Payout: —
Market value ($ mil.): 12,295.0

	STOCK PRICE ($) FY Close	P/E High/Low		Earnings	Dividends	Book Value
12/18	337.34	68	45	6.54	0.00	82.92
12/17	296.95	84	50	3.66	0.00	73.43
12/16	188.49	85	56	2.62	0.00	50.73
12/15	206.69	—	—	(0.11)	0.00	47.49
12/14	183.63	145	93	1.46	0.00	46.83
Annual Growth	16.4%			45.5%	—	15.4%

County Bancorp, Inc.

Auditors: Plante & Moran, PLLC

LOCATIONS

HQ: County Bancorp, Inc.
2400 South 44th Street, Manitowoc, WI 54221
Phone: 920 686-9998
Web: www.investorscommunitybank.com

HISTORICAL FINANCIALS
Company Type: Public

Income Statement   FYE: December 31

	ASSETS ($ mil.)	NET INCOME ($ mil.)	INCOME AS % OF ASSETS	EMPLOYEES
12/18	1,521.0	14.2	0.9%	166
12/17	1,397.0	10.4	0.7%	156
12/16	1,242.6	10.6	0.9%	150
12/15	884.8	10.9	1.2%	111
12/14	771.7	8.2	1.1%	103
Annual Growth	18.5%	14.8%	—	12.7%

2018 Year-End Financials
Return on assets: 0.9%
Return on equity: 9.7%
Long-term debt ($ mil.): —
No. of shares (mil.): 6.7
Sales ($ mil): 73.0
Dividends
  Yield: 1.6%
  Payout: 14.5%
Market value ($ mil.): 117.0

	STOCK PRICE ($) FY Close	P/E High/Low		Earnings	Dividends	Book Value
12/18	17.37	16	9	2.04	0.28	22.70
12/17	29.76	23	15	1.49	0.24	21.13
12/16	26.97	16	11	1.61	0.20	19.93
12/15	19.50	13	9	1.82	0.16	21.14
Annual Growth	(3.8%)	—	—	3.9%	20.5%	2.4%

Cousins Properties Inc

Cousins Properties only wants the best office properties in the Deep South. The real estate investment trust (REIT) buys develops and manages Class-A office properties mainly in high-growth markets in the Sunbelt region of the US. Its portfolio includes around 41 office properties with almost 20 million sq. ft. of space in Atlanta Austin Houston and Charlotte. While the REIT also owns a handful of retail centers and apartment complexes in Atlanta it's been winding those down to focus on prime office properties. Cousins Properties also provides property and construction management services and develops properties for third parties.

Operations
Cousins Properties' highest-grossing office rental properties include the Greenway Plaza (which made up 33% of its net operating income in 2015) and the Post Oak Central (12%) properties in Houston; and the Northpark Town Center property in Atlanta (10%).

Geographic Reach
The Atlanta-based REIT owns properties in its Atlanta; Austin Texas; Houston and Charlotte. About 40% of the company's net operating income came from its office properties in Houston during 2015 while another 39% came from its office properties in Atlanta. The rest came from its properties in Austin (8% of net operating income) and Charlotte (6%).

Sales and Marketing
Reflecting a broad tenant base the REIT's top 20 tenants made up 41% of its annualized base rental income during 2015 with no single tenant accounting for more than 8% of its rental income. More than 20% of its rental base comes from tenants in the energy sector.

Some of the REIT's tenants include the American Cancer Society and Fifth Third Bank. Past tenants have included Bank of America and Dimensional Fund Advisors.

Financial Performance
The REIT's annual revenues have more than tripled since 2011 as property acquisitions in new markets have spurred additional rental income. Its profits have also skyrocketed over the same period thanks to property sale gains and tight operating cost controls.

Cousins Properties' revenue climbed 6% to $381.6 million during 2015 mostly thanks to added rental income stemming from its newly-operational Colorado Tower property and its 2014 property acquisitions. Its same-property rental revenue increased by 0.2%.

Revenue growth in 2015 combined with higher property sale gains from its North Point Center

East The Points at Waterview and 2100 Ross dispositions more than doubled the REIT's net income to $125.5 million. Cousins Properties' operating cash levels rose 7% to $151.6 million for the year thanks to a rise in cash-based earnings.

Strategy

Cousins Properties acquires develops and manages Class-A office properties in high-growth Sunbelt markets though it also may buy mixed-use commercial buildings if the right opportunity arises. To diversify its revenue streams it continues to to acquire properties outside of Atlanta moving into the Houston and Austin markets in Texas and also into Charlotte North Carolina in recent years.

Some of its more recent acquisitions include the proposed $1.95 billion acquisition of Parkway Properties and its 41 properties in the Southeast in 2016; the $27 million-purchase of 4.2 acres of land in Atlanta to build NCR's corporate headquarters in 2015 and the $348 million-acquisition of the 1.5 million sq. ft. Northpark Town Center in Atlanta in 2014; and the 2014 purchase of the almost 700000 sq. ft. Fifth Third Center in Charlotte for $215 million.

Mergers and Acquisitions

In October 2016 Cousins Properties acquired Orlando-based Parkway Properties for $1.95 billion in stock. The deal expanded Cousins' presence to 41 properties in the Southeast.

The combined group immediately spun off its Houston-based assets creating a new public REIT named Parkway.

Company Background

Cousins Properties experienced challenges from the depressed economy and the downturn in the real estate markets following the financial crisis. The REIT responded by restructuring reducing headcount selling non-core assets and curtailing new development projects. It sold all of its industrial properties to focus on Class-A office properties. It also continues to wind down its multifamily residential portfolio.

Institutional investors own about a third of Cousins Properties' stock. Morgan Stanley holds the largest stake at more than 11% followed by BlackRock Inc. and The Vanguard Group. Chairman Emeritus Thomas G. Cousins owns about 11% of the firm's shares.

EXECUTIVES

Senior Vice President and Director of Leasing, Darryl Bonner
Vice President Information Systems, Dennis A Granger
EVP and CFO, Gregg D. Adzema, age 54, $390,000 total compensation
Chairman and CEO The Cousins Foundation Inc., Lillian C. Giornelli, age 58
EVP, John S. McColl, age 57, $341,453 total compensation
Chairman and CEO, Lawrence L. Gellerstedt, age 63, $600,000 total compensation
SVP, J. Thad Ellis, $294,175 total compensation
President and COO, M. Colin Connolly, age 43, $250,000 total compensation
Vice President Human Resources, Marva Lewis
Vice President, Chip Andrews
Vice President Internal Audit, Timothy A O'Connell
Vice President Treasurer, Mary Caneer
Executive Vice President And Director Of Development Retail Division, William Bassett
Vice President SEC Reporting, Patricia Grimes
Senior Vice President and Managing Director, Matt Mooney
Vice President Financial Reporting, Matt Ams
ASSISTANT TREASURER, Nsharra Gross
Auditors: DELOITTE & TOUCHE LLP

LOCATIONS

HQ: Cousins Properties Inc
3344 Peachtree Road NE, Suite 1800, Atlanta, GA 30326-4802
Phone: 404 407-1000
Web: www.cousins.com

PRODUCTS/OPERATIONS

2011 Sales

	$ mil.	% of total
Rental property	135.6	76
Third-party management & leasing	19.4	11
Fee income	13.8	8
Multifamily residential unit sales	4.7	3
Residential & outparcel	3.0	2
Other	2.0	-
Total	178.5	100

COMPETITORS

American Realty Investors	Highwoods Properties
Chelsea Property	Macerich
DDR	Poag & McEwen Lifestyle Centers
Duke Realty	Simon Property Group
Equity Office	Trammell Crow
GGP	Residential

HISTORICAL FINANCIALS

Company Type: Public

Income Statement — FYE: December 31

	REVENUE ($ mil.)	NET INCOME ($ mil.)	NET PROFIT MARGIN	EMPLOYEES
12/19	657.5	150.4	22.9%	331
12/18	475.2	79.1	16.7%	257
12/17	466.1	216.2	46.4%	261
12/16	259.2	79.1	30.5%	279
12/15	381.6	125.5	32.9%	257
Annual Growth	14.6%	4.6%	—	6.5%

2019 Year-End Financials

Debt ratio: 31.0%
Return on equity: 4.2%
Cash ($ mil.): 15.6
Current ratio: 0.55
Long-term debt ($ mil.): 2,222.9
No. of shares (mil.): 146.7
Dividends
Yield: 1.4%
Payout: 126.0%
Market value ($ mil.): 6,047.0

	STOCK PRICE ($) FY Close	P/E High/Low		PER SHARE ($) Earnings	Dividends	Book Value
12/19	41.20	35	7	1.17	0.58	29.70
12/18	7.90	13	10	0.76	1.04	26.32
12/17	9.25	5	4	2.08	1.20	26.40
12/16	8.51	9	6	1.24	0.96	24.97
12/15	9.43	5	4	2.32	0.00	31.84
Annual Growth	44.6%	—	—	(15.7%)	—	(1.7%)

Cowen Inc

The Cowen Group aims to herd its clients' investments in the right direction. The firm along with its subsidiaries offers alternative investment management research investment banking and sales and trading services. Its Ramius arm with some $12.5 billion of assets under management handles alternative investments while another subsidiary Cowen and Company represents the firm's investment banking and brokerage practice which mainly entails strategic advisory and corporate finance services for small to midsized companies. Cowen Group offers expanded trading operations through LaBranche & Co. a market maker for options exchange-traded funds and futures.

Operations

Cowen operates two main business segments: Broker-Dealer and Alternative Investment.

The firm's broker-dealer business Cowen and Company provides investment banking services to growth-oriented companies. Its services include advisory global capital markets origination and research services as well as a sales and trading platform for institutional investors. Its research team covers nearly 800 companies mostly across the health care technology energy capital goods and industrial basic materials consumer and real estate sectors.

The smaller alternative investment segment includes hedge funds mutual funds managed futures funds fund of funds real estate and healthcare royalty funds among other types of strategies. Cowen Group generated roughly 40% of its total revenue from its investment banking services in 2014 with an additional 33% of revenues coming from its brokerage services. Management fees made up another 9% of total revenues while interest and dividends on the company's investments made up another 11%.

Geographic Reach

Based in New York Cowen Group operates globally through US offices in New York Georgia Massachusetts Illinois Ohio and California as well through international offices in Hong Kong London and Luxembourg. It serves China through Cowen and Company (Asia) Limited and Europe through UK broker-dealer Cowen International Limited (CIL).

Sales and Marketing

Cowen Group's institutional investors include pension funds insurance companies banks foundations and endowments wealth management organizations and family offices.

Its broker-dealer businesses include research brokerage and investment banking services to companies and institutional investor clients primarily in the healthcare technology media and telecommunications consumer aerospace and defense industrials REITs and clean technology sectors. Its research and brokerage businesses serve more than 1000 domestic and international clients.

Financial Performance

As the financial markets have been strongly appreciating over the last few years so have Cowen Group's revenues and profits. The firm's revenue jumped by 31% to $427.78 million in 2014 which was mostly driven by 62% growth in its investment banking revenue on higher underwriting transaction and strategic advisory transactions. Cowen's brokerage income also rose by 22% thanks to higher commission revenue on higher customer trading volumes in cash equities options and electronic trades. The company's management fees also increased by 9% thanks to higher fee income from healthcare funds.

The firm's net income skyrocketed to $167.22 million in 2014 mostly thanks to higher revenues combined with a $125 million income tax benefit as the company in a prior year deferred more in federal and state taxes than was required.

Cowen's cash levels declined in 2014 with operations using $66.72 million (compared to operations providing $150.58 in 2013) after adjusting its earnings for non-cash items mostly relating to its sales proceeds on its securities.

Strategy

Cowen Group has been selectively expanding its alternative management business Ramius in recent years cutting its underperforming investment strategy teams while partnering with other firms to expand its better performing strategies.

In 2014 for example its Ramius subsidiary sold its interests in its global long/short credit investment strategy manager Orchard Square Partners. Meanwhile that year it partnered with Quadratic Capital to launch its options-based global macro strategy complete with low volatility and defined risk. The deal expanded Ramius' unique product offerings essential to attracting investor capital while also allowing Quadratic to take advantage of Ramius' brand strength to make it a more competitive emerging fund.

After assessing the most efficient uses of its capital Cowen Group in 2014 decided to wind down its securities lending business.

Mergers and Acquisitions

Cowen Group has focused on acquisitions that expand its business in multiple sectors.

Its 2013 purchase of Dahlman Rose & Company a privately-held investment bank specializing in the energy metals and mining transportation chemicals and agriculture sectors. The deal gave Cowen Group additional sectors such as energy transportation metals and mining chemicals and agriculture.

In November 2012 the company completed the acquisition of KDC Securities LP (KDC) a securities lending business. KDC was the broker-dealer subsidiary of Kellner Capital LLC an alternative investment manager. KDC was renamed Cowen Equity Finance LP (Cowen Equity Finance) following the acquisition.

Also in 2012 Cowen bought multi-asset class trading business Algorithmic Trading Management.

EXECUTIVES

Chairman and CEO, Peter A. Cohen, age 73, $950,000 total compensation
CFO, Stephen A. Lasota, $450,000 total compensation
President; CEO Cowen and Company, Jeffrey M. Solomon, $950,000 total compensation
Vice Chairman; Chairman Ramius, Thomas W. Strauss
Chief Administrative Officer, John Holmes, $450,000 total compensation
CEO Ramius, Michael Singer
General Counsel, Owen Littman, $450,000 total compensation
CIO, Ann Neidenbach
Head Marketing and Client Services, Kelly Weigel
Executive Vice President, Karen Cowen
Vice President Metals and Mining, Novid Rassouli
Vice President Equity Research, Matt Elkott
Vice President Corporate Development, Ctibor Cemper
Vice President, Gail Rosenblum
Vice President Institutional Equity Sales, Ally Hanna
Vice President Investment Banking, Zachary Stern
Cfa Vice President Industrials Aerospace Defense Electronics, Lucy Guo
Vice President, Kyle Rasbach
Vice President, Patrick Overholser
Vice President Sales, Carl Mano
Senior Vice President, Giancarlo Battaglia
Senior Vice President Head of Financial Technology and Process, Charles Diana
Senior Vice President, Shari Grant
Vice Chairman, Fred S. Fraenkel
Auditors: KPMG LLP

LOCATIONS

HQ: Cowen Inc
599 Lexington Avenue, New York, NY 10022
Phone: 646 562-1000
Web: www.cowen.com

PRODUCTS/OPERATIONS

2014 Sales

	$ mil.	% of total
Investment Banking	170.5	40
Brokerage	140.1	33
Interest and dividend income	48.9	11
Management fees	40.6	9
Reimbursement from affiliates	12.5	3
Incentive income	2.8	1
Other revenues	9.5	2
Consolidated Funds revenues	2.9	1
Total	427.8	100

Selected Subsidiaries

Cowen Alternative Investments LLC
Cowen Asia Limited (Hong Kong)
Cowen Capital LLC
Cowen Capital Partners II LLC
Cowen and Company LLC
Cowen and Company (Asia) Limited (Hong Kong)
Cowen Financial Technology LLC
Cowen Healthcare Royalty Management LLC
Cowen Holdings Inc.
Cowen International Limited (UK)
Cowen International Trading Limited (UK)
Cowen Latitude Capital Group LLC
Cowen Latitude China Holdings Limited
Cowen Latitude Investment Consulting Co. Ltd. (China)
Cowen Overseas Investment LP
Cowen Services Company LLC
Cowen Structured Holdings Inc.
Cowen Structured Holdings LLC (Hong Kong)
Cowen Structured Products Specialists LLC
October LLC
Ramius Advisors LLC
Ramius Alternative Solutions LLC
Ramius Asia LLC
Raimus Enterprise Master Fund Ltd (Cayman Islands)
Ramius Japan Ltd.
Ramius LLC
Ramius Optimum Investments LLC
Ramius Securities LLC
Ramius Structured Credit Group LLC

COMPETITORS

Citadel
Citigroup Global Markets
Credit Suisse (USA)
D. E. Shaw
Deutsche Bank
Fortress Investment Group
Goldman Sachs
Jefferies Group
Macquarie Group
Merrill Lynch
Morgan Stanley
Robert W. Baird & Co.

HISTORICAL FINANCIALS

Company Type: Public

Income Statement FYE: December 31

	REVENUE ($ mil.)	NET INCOME ($ mil.)	NET PROFIT MARGIN	EMPLOYEES
12/18	966.9	42.8	4.4%	1,212
12/17	658.7	(60.8)	—	1,124
12/16	471.5	(19.2)	—	843
12/15	464.5	43.7	9.4%	769
12/14	427.7	167.2	39.1%	664
Annual Growth	22.6%	(28.9%)	—	16.2%

2018 Year-End Financials

Debt ratio: 24.2%
Return on equity: 5.5%
Cash ($ mil.): 473.9
Current ratio: 0.66
Long-term debt ($ mil.): 134.4
No. of shares (mil.): 28.4
Dividends
 Yield: 0.0%
 Payout: 84.6%
Market value ($ mil.): 379.0

	STOCK PRICE ($) FY Close	P/E High/Low		PER SHARE ($) Earnings	Dividends	Book Value
12/18	13.34	14	10	1.17	0.99	27.93
12/17	13.65	—	—	(2.29)	0.00	25.24
12/16	15.50	—	—	(0.97)	0.00	28.90
12/15	3.83	5	3	1.36	0.00	29.92
12/14	4.80	1	1	5.60	0.00	24.27
Annual Growth	29.1%	—	—	(32.4%)	—	3.6%

CRA International Inc

CRA International doing business as Charles River Associates employs nearly 700 consultants offering economic financial and management counsel to corporate clients attorneys government agencies and other clients. Practices are organized into two areas. Litigation Regulatory and Financial Consulting advises on topics such as antitrust and competition damages valuation financial accounting and insurance economics. Management Consulting focus areas include auctions and competitive bidding business strategy and enterprise risk management. Charles River Associates has about 20 offices mainly in North America but also in Europe. Most business is conducted in the US. The firm was founded in 1965.

Operations

Charles River Associates' litigation regulatory and financial consulting arm typically works with law firms working for companies involved in antitrust damages or labor disputes. Its consultants help to develop theory and prepare testimony of expert witnesses. They also provide general litigation support such as legal brief reviews and appeals support.

The management consulting arm provides expertise of its own to companies seeking organizational operational and/or strategic changes. Its specialties include transaction advisory services organization and performance improvement enterprise risk management and corporate strategy.

Geographic Reach

Headquartered in Boston Massachusetts Charles River Associates has some 20 offices throughout North America and Europe including in New York

San Francisco Chicago and London. The US accounts for some 80% of revenue.

Sales and Marketing
Charles River Associates' clients include domestic and foreign corporations; federal state and local domestic government agencies; governments of foreign countries; public and private utilities; accounting firms; and national and international trade associations. Frequently it works with major law firms on behalf of their clients.

The company relies on its employee consultants particularly vice presidents and principals to market its services. Existing clients are an important source of repeat business and referrals. Charles River Associates supplements referrals with direct marketing to new clients through conferences seminars publications presentations and direct solicitations.

Charles River Associates derived approximately 23% 25% and 17% of its revenue from fixed-price contracts in fiscal 2018 fiscal 2017 and fiscal 2016 respectively.

Financial Performance
Charles River Associates' revenues have been steadily climbing upward for the past few years. Net income has been more sporadic; profits have ranged from a low of less than $10 million to a high of more than $20 million within the last five fiscal years.

In 2018 revenue increased 13% to $417.6 million up from $370.1 million in 2017. Consultant headcount and billable hours increased as did utilization of consultants. (The company calculates utilization — a key indicator for measuring operating performance — by dividing the total hours consultants worked by the total number of hours that consultants were available to work.)

Net income rose $22.5 million in 2018 versus $7.7 million the prior year on higher revenue and a lower income tax rate.

The company ended 2018 with $38.0 million in net cash a decrease of $16 million from the prior year primarily because of higher bonus payouts the repurchase and retirement of shares of stock throughout the year under the firm's share repurchase program payments of dividends loan payments and build-out costs at its New York San Francisco Chicago and London offices. Operating activities provided $36.2 million investing activities used $15.4 million and financing activities used $35.7 million.

Strategy
Charles River Associates prefers to expand through organic measures including recruitment efforts to boost headcount and opening new office locations but it does make acquisitions from time to time. The company attributes its competitive advantage to consultants many of whom are recognized nationally and internationally as experts in their respective fields. It complements its staff by maintaining close working relationships with a select group of academic and industry experts.

Company Background
Charles River Associates was founded in 1965 and filed an initial public offering in 1998. The company has expanded through organic growth and strategic acquisitions. Its purchase of Marakon Associates in 2009 significantly strengthened the company's management consulting capabilities.

EXECUTIVES

Vice President, Gerben Weistra
VP and General Counsel, Jonathan D. Yellin
President CEO and Director, Paul A. Maleh, age 55, $660,000 total compensation
EVP CFO and Treasurer, Chad Holmes, $350,000 total compensation
Vice President, Rhett Johnson
Vice President Competition Practice, Geoff Edwards
Vice President Marakon Value Management, Andrew Macpherson
Vice President, Jim Mctaggart
Vice President London, Brian Burwell
Vice President, Randy Degeer
Vice President, Michelle Burtis
Vice President, Gregory Bell
Vice President In The Competition Practice, John Hayes
Vice President, Robert Maness
Vice President, Charles Trabandt
Vice President, Peter Rankin
Vice President, Tim Wilsdon
Vice President New York, Mason Kissell
Vice President, Peter Boberg
Vice President, Janice Halpern
Vice President, Sean Durkin
Vice President, Steven Tenn
Vice President Life Sciences, Jeffrey Aroy
Vice President, Michael Kim
Vice President, Renee McMahon
Vice President, Nicholas Weir
Vice President, Anne Layne-farrar
Vice President, Daniel Brand
Vice President, Dan Chai
Vice President, Guler A Wiefling
Vice President, Joanne Mccollum
Vice President, Ron Langford
Vice President, Sean May
Vice President, Timothy Snail
Vice President, Jeffery Stec
Vice President, Matthew Bennett
Vice President, Keith Bockus
Vice President, David Persampeiri
Vice President, Bob Lee
Vice President, James Mcmahon
Vice President Cyber Response Leader, Bill Hardin
Vice President and Practice Leader Forensic Services, Kristofer Swanson
Executive Vice President, Arnie Lowenstein
Vice President, Simon Chisholm
Vice President, Andrew Parece
Vice President Forensic Services, Andy Obuchowski
Vice President, Ryan Bilbrey
Vice President, Kevin Brubacher
Vice President, Reto Kohler
VICE PRESIDENT, Elizabeth Rountree
Vice President, Robert Broadnax
CFF CFE Vice President Forensic Services, Peter Resnick
Vp Forensic Services Practice, Geoff Fisher
Vice President, Josh Hass
Vp and Head Of Auctions and Ecommerce Practice, Bradley Miller
Vice President, Stephen Oneil
Vice President, Dan Donath
Vice President, Gopal Das Varma
Vice President, Rob Brunner
Vice President, Peter Nolan
Vice President, Mike Tate
Vice President, Scott Solomon
Chairman, Rowland T. (Row) Moriarty, age 72
Board Member, Robert Holthausen
Board Member, Robert Whitman
Auditors: Ernst & Young LLP

LOCATIONS
HQ: CRA International Inc
200 Clarendon Street, Boston, MA 02116-5092
Phone: 617 425-3000   **Fax:** 617 425-3132
Web: www.crai.com

PRODUCTS/OPERATIONS

Selected Practice Areas
Litigation regulatory and financial consulting
  Antitrust and competition
  Damages and valuation
  Financial accounting and valuation
  Financial economics
  Forensic and cyber investigations
  Insurance economics
  Intellectual property
  International arbitration
  Labor and employment
  Mergers and acquisitions
  Regulatory economics and compliance
  Securities and financial markets
  Transfer pricing
Management consulting
  Auctions and competitive bidding
  Corporate and business strategy
  Enterprise risk management
  Environmental and energy strategy
  Intellectual property and technology management
  Organization and performance improvement
  Transaction advisory services

Selected Industries Served
Agriculture
Banking and capital markets
Chemicals
Communications and media
Consumer products
Energy
Entertainment
Financial services
Health care
Insurance
Life sciences
Manufacturing
Metals mining and materials
Oil and gas
Real estateRetail
Sports
Telecommunications
Transportation
Technology

COMPETITORS

Accenture
Bain & Company
Booz Allen
Boston Consulting
Capgemini
Cornerstone Research
Deloitte Consulting
Exponent
FTI Consulting
Huron Consulting
McKinsey & Company
Navigant Consulting
PA Consulting

HISTORICAL FINANCIALS
Company Type: Public

Income Statement   FYE: December 29

	REVENUE ($ mil.)	NET INCOME ($ mil.)	NET PROFIT MARGIN	EMPLOYEES
12/18	417.6	22.4	5.4%	687
12/17	370.0	7.6	2.1%	631
12/16*	324.7	12.8	4.0%	540
01/16	303.5	7.6	2.5%	511
01/15	306.3	13.6	4.5%	451
Annual Growth	8.1%	13.3%	—	11.1%

*Fiscal year change

Credit Acceptance Corp (MI)

In the world of Credit Acceptance Corporation (CAC) to purchase a car is not an impossible dream for problem borrowers. CAC makes the effort a reality. Working with more than 55000 independent and franchised automobile dealers in the US CAC provides capital for auto loans to people with substandard credit. The company also provides other services to dealers including payment servicing receivables management marketing and service contracts. CAC which concentrates its operations in a handful of US states typically funds about 1.5 million auto loans per year.

Operations
CAC steps in to help finance auto purchases for those whose credit histories aren't ideal. Auto dealers in turn benefit from the vehicle sales and from repeat and referral sales generated by these customers.

Geographic Reach
Michigan-based CAC serves consumers nationwide. Its largest markets include New York Texas Ohio and Pennsylvania.

Sales and Marketing
CAC caters to and partners with some 56000 independent and franchised automobile dealers throughout the US.

Financial Performance
The company's revenue has been growing for several years. In fiscal 2013 CAC posted 12% increases in revenue to $682.1 million as compared to 2012's $609.2 million. CAC points to a 10% boost in finance charges due to an increase in the average net loans receivable balance for the 2013 gains. These were offset however by a drop in the average yield on loan portfolio. Thanks to a new profit-sharing arrangement CAC entered in 2012 with third party providers (TPPs) other income jumped some 68% during the reporting period. Helping other income was an increase in GPS-SID fee income due to rising fee earned per unit purchased primarily resulting from new the new profit-sharing agreement. CAC's net income has been on the same trajectory. In 2013 net income rose some 15% to $253.1 million vs. 2012's $219.7 million bolstered by the company's higher revenue offset in part by an increased provision for income tax. Cash flow from operations also rose in 2013 — from $308.6 million in 2012 to $325.7 million in 2013 — attributable to higher net income a decrease in the provision for credit losses and a change in working capital.

Strategy
The company funds loans in two ways: It advances money to its dealer-partners in exchange for the servicing rights to the underlying loan or it purchases loans directly from dealers. CAC earns most of its revenues from finance charges servicing fees and monthly program fees it charges its dealer partners. Indeed finance charges in 2013 accounted for 87% of revenue.

EXECUTIVES
CEO, Brett A. Roberts, age 52, $1,025,000 total compensation
President, Steven M. Jones, age 55, $625,000 total compensation
CFO, Kenneth S. Booth, age 51, $414,792 total compensation
CIO, John S. Soave, age 54
Vice President Information Technology, Brian Uptain
Vice President Of Sales, Jeffrey Brock
Senior Vice President Accounting And Financial Reporting, Jay Martin
Vice President Business Information Services, Noah Kotch
Chief Sales Officer, Dan Ulatowski
Vice President, Wayne Mancini
Vice President Underwriting, Nathan Wray
Vice President Of Collections, Dianne Pulles
Chairman, Donald A. Foss, age 74
Assistant Treasurer, Jeff Soutar
Auditors: Grant Thornton LLP

LOCATIONS
HQ: Credit Acceptance Corp (MI)
25505 West Twelve Mile Road, Southfield, MI 48034-8339
Phone: 248 353-2700

PRODUCTS/OPERATIONS

2016 Sales

	$ mil.	% of total
Finance charges	874.3	90
Premiums earned	43.0	5
Other	51.9	5
Total	**969.2**	**100**

Selected Subsidiaries
Buyers Vehicle Protection Plan Inc.
CAC Leasing Inc.
CAC Reinsurance Ltd.
CAC Warehouse Funding Corp. II III IV
Credit Acceptance Wholesale Buyers Club Inc.
Vehicle Remarketing Services Inc.
VSC Re Company

COMPETITORS
Ally Financial
American Honda Finance
Bank of America
Capital One Auto Finance
First Investors Financial Services
Ford Motor Credit
GM Financial
Mercedes-Benz Credit
Mercedes-Benz Financial Services USA
Toyota Motor Credit
Volkswagen Financial Services

2018 Year-End Financials
Debt ratio: —
Return on equity: 11.1%
Cash ($ mil.): 38.0
Current ratio: 1.27
Long-term debt ($ mil.): —
No. of shares (mil.): 8.0
Dividends
Yield: 0.0%
Payout: 27.2%
Market value ($ mil.): 328.0

	STOCK PRICE ($) FY Close	P/E High/Low	PER SHARE ($) Earnings	Dividends	Book Value
12/18	40.92	21 15	2.61	0.71	24.53
12/17	44.95	52 36	0.89	0.59	24.94
12/16*	36.60	25 11	1.49	0.14	24.86
01/16	18.65	38 21	0.83	0.00	23.90
01/15	30.36	23 13	1.38	0.00	23.20
Annual Growth	7.7%	— —	17.3%	—	1.4%

*Fiscal year change

CubeSmart

CubeSmart (formerly U-Store-It Trust) is a real estate investment trust (REIT) that owns more than 420 self-storage facilities with nearly 30 million sq. ft. of rentable space in about 25 states and Washington DC. The company also manages manages more than 100 self-storage facilities for third parties. Amenities at its properties include security systems and wider aisles for larger vehicles as well as climate-controlled units and outdoor storage for vehicles and boats at selected sites. The REIT also sells storage-related items such as packing supplies and locks to tenants who typically rent units on a month-to-month basis.

Operations
Operating through partnership CubeSmart L.P the company generates just under 90% of its revenue from rental income from leasing out its storage units. About 10% of revenue comes from other property-related income including administrative charges late fees tenant insurance commissions and sales of storage supplies. The rest of CubeSmart's revenue comes from property management fee income (primarily from its third-party management business).

Geographic Reach
CubeSmart owns or manages facilities in more than 20 states across the US with facilities in New York Florida Texas and California producing over 50% of total revenues. Another 15% of the company's revenue comes from New Jersey Illinois and Connecticut. Cubesmart also owns or manages facilities in Puerto Rico.

HISTORICAL FINANCIALS
Company Type: Public

Income Statement
FYE: December 31

	REVENUE ($ mil.)	NET INCOME ($ mil.)	NET PROFIT MARGIN	EMPLOYEES
12/18	1,285.8	574.0	44.6%	2,040
12/17	1,110.0	470.2	42.4%	1,817
12/16	969.2	332.8	34.3%	1,609
12/15	825.3	299.7	36.3%	1,425
12/14	723.5	266.2	36.8%	1,303
Annual Growth	15.5%	21.2%	—	11.9%

2018 Year-End Financials
Debt ratio: 61.2%
Return on equity: 32.5%
Cash ($ mil.): 25.7
Current ratio: 2.10
Long-term debt ($ mil.): 3,820.9
No. of shares (mil.): 18.9
Dividends
Yield: —
Payout: —
Market value ($ mil.): 7,243.0

	STOCK PRICE ($) FY Close	P/E High/Low	PER SHARE ($) Earnings	Dividends	Book Value
12/18	381.76	16 10	29.39	0.00	104.94
12/17	323.48	14 8	24.04	0.00	79.53
12/16	217.51	13 10	16.31	0.00	59.05
12/15	214.02	19 9	14.28	0.00	46.10
12/14	136.41	14 9	11.92	0.00	34.09
Annual Growth	29.3%	— —	25.3%	—	32.5%

Sales and Marketing
The company spent $7.7 million on advertising and marketing in 2014 compared to $7.6 million and $8.1 million in 2013 and 2012 respectively.

Financial Performance
CubeSmart's revenues and profits have trended sharply higher over the past several years as the REIT has enjoyed more rental income from acquisitions and rental rate increases buoyed by the strengthened US economy.

The REIT's revenue jumped by 18% to $377 million in 2014 mostly thanks to higher rental income from 2014 and 2013 property acquisitions but also thanks to higher net rental rates and higher average occupancy rates on existing properties. CubeSmart's property management fee income also rose by 26% for the year as its third-party management business grew which further helped the REIT's top line.

Despite higher revenue in 2014 CubeSmart's net income dove 36% to $26.4 million mostly as the REIT made $27.4 million in property sale gains in 2013 compared to no comparable gains during 2014. CubeSmart's operating cash levels grew by 16% to $166 million however mostly as it generated more cash income from new property acquisitions.

Strategy
CubeSmart's strategy is to grow through acquisitions mainly in high-growth areas such as the Northeastern and Middle Atlantic regions in the US along with Georgia Florida Texas Illinois and California. The company hopes to gradually increase rental income by selectively acquiring properties in markets with high barriers to entry strong demographic fundamentals and high demand. In addition more locations offer higher economies of scale and greater operating efficiencies for higher operating margins.

Indeed from 2011 through late 2014 management had announced more than 100 facility acquisitions totaling roughly $1.3 billion. During 2014 alone CubeSmart acquired 53 self-storage facilities for a total price of $568.2 million including a $223 million purchase of 26 facilities across six states from Harrison Street Real Estate Capital in late 2014.

The company also plans to continue selling facilities in slower growing low barrier-to-entry locations and using proceeds to purchase new facilities in target markets. In 2013 for example it sold 35 locations mostly in California Indiana Tennessee and Texas for approximately $126.4 million. In 2012 it sold 26 locations (including 14 from New Mexico and Ohio) for $60 million.

Besides expansion CubeSmart plans to maximize rental revenues from existing facilities by raising rent increasing occupancy levels (which are around 90% up from 80% in 2011) controlling operating expenses and expanding and enhancing the facilities themselves. As a final step for growth CubeSmart will utilize relationships with third-party owners to help source future acquisitions and expand through these existing relationships.

Company Background
As part of a rebranding initiative CubeSmart changed its name from U-Store-It in 2011.

EXECUTIVES
CEO, Christopher P. (Chris) Marr, age 54, $600,000 total compensation
CFO, Timothy M. (Tim) Martin, age 48, $390,000 total compensation
SVP and CIO, Ajai Nair
SVP and Chief Investment Officer, Jonathan Perry
Vice President Third Party Management, Guy Middlebrooks
Vice President, Doug Tyrell
Divisional Vice President, Joe Fitzgerald
Chairman, William M. Diefenderfer, age 74
Auditors: KPMG LLP

LOCATIONS
HQ: CubeSmart
5 Old Lancaster Road, Malvern, PA 19355
Phone: 610 535-5000
Web: www.cubesmart.com

PRODUCTS/OPERATIONS
2015 Sales

	$ mil.	% of total
Rental income	392.4	88
Property management fees	7.0	10
Other property-related income	45.1	2
Total	**444.5**	**100**

COMPETITORS
AMERCO	Mobile Mini
Extra Space	PODS Enterprises
Life Storage	Public Storage

HISTORICAL FINANCIALS
Company Type: Public

Income Statement — FYE: December 31

	REVENUE ($ mil.)	NET INCOME ($ mil.)	NET PROFIT MARGIN	EMPLOYEES
12/18	597.9	163.8	27.4%	2,815
12/17	558.9	134.2	24.0%	2,508
12/16	510.0	87.9	17.2%	2,136
12/15	444.5	77.7	17.5%	1,837
12/14	376.9	26.3	7.0%	1,640
Annual Growth	12.2%	57.9%	—	14.5%

2018 Year-End Financials
Debt ratio: 46.5%
Return on equity: 9.8%
Cash ($ mil.): 3.7
Current ratio: 0.18
Long-term debt ($ mil.): 1,747.0
No. of shares (mil.): 187.1
Dividends
Yield: 4.2%
Payout: 138.6%
Market value ($ mil.): 5,369.0

	STOCK PRICE ($) FY Close	P/E High/Low	PER SHARE ($) Earnings	Dividends	Book Value
12/18	28.69	37 28	0.88	1.22	9.14
12/17	28.92	40 31	0.74	1.11	8.94
12/16	26.77	74 53	0.45	0.90	9.19
12/15	30.62	73 51	0.42	0.69	9.41
12/14	22.07	164 112	0.14	0.55	8.83
Annual Growth	6.8%	— —	58.3%	22.0%	0.8%

Cullen/Frost Bankers, Inc.

One of the largest independent bank holding companies in Texas Cullen/Frost Bankers owns Frost Bank and other financial subsidiaries through a second-tier holding company The New Galveston Company. The community-oriented bank serves individuals and local businesses as well as clients in neighboring parts of Mexico through 120-plus branches in Texas metropolitan areas. It offers commercial and consumer deposit products and loans trust and investment management services mutual funds insurance brokerage and leasing. Subsidiaries include Frost Insurance Agency Frost Brokerage Services Frost Investment Advisors and investment banking arm Frost Securities. Cullen/Frost has total assets of $26.5 billion.

Geographic Reach
San Antonio-based Cullen/Frost Bankers has branches throughout Texas including the Austin Corpus Christi Dallas Fort Worth Houston Permian Basin the Rio Grande Valley and San Antonio regions.

Financial Performance
Cullen/Frost reported revenue of $945.3 million in 2013 an increase of 3% versus 2012 on increased interest income on loans and deposits and an increase in trust and investment management fees. Net income was $237.9 a flat comparison with the prior year. 2013 marked the third consecutive year of rising revenue following a dip in 2010. The bank's fortunes are rising along with the thriving energy and technology sectors in Texas.

Strategy
Cullen/Frost has built its insurance business through acquisitions in recent years; since 2009 it has bought agencies in Dallas Houston San Antonio and San Marcos that provide group employee benefit plans. The company continues to seek out acquisition opportunities while it also looks for ways to expand and diversify within its existing markets. To reduce its reliance on interest rate spreads Cullen/Frost wants to grow its income from fees such as insurance commissions trust investment fees and service charges on deposit accounts.

Mergers and Acquisitions
In June 2014 Frost Bank acquired Odessa Texas-based Western National Bank (WNB) increasing its presence in the oil-rich Permian Basin Midland and Odessa markets in West Texas. Seven of WNB's eight branches were converted to the Frost name (an office in San Antonio was closed) increasing the number of Frost branches statewide to more than 120. The acquisition of WNB added $1.8 billion in assets $1.6 billion in deposits and $668 million in total loans to Cullen/Frost. The purchase of WNB was the first time in nearly seven years that Frost acquired another bank.

EXECUTIVES
Chairman and CEO, Phillip D. Green, age 64, $565,000 total compensation
President Frost Bank; EVP Frost Wealth Advisors, Patrick B. (Pat) Frost, age 59, $485,000 total compensation

President, Paul H. Bracher, age 62, $500,000 total compensation
EVP and CFO, Jerry Salinas, $400,000 total compensation
Vice President, Stephanie Conti
Vice President of Marketing, Bobby Jacob
Vice President of Marketing, Linda Hopkins
Vice President of Marketing, Howard Kasanoff
Senior Vice President It, Harvey Gutierrez
Vice President And Senior Real Property Appraiser, Michael L Cleary
Senior Executive Vice Presiden, William Sirakos
Senior Vice President Director Of Investor Relatio, Greg Parker
Vice President of Finance, Vicki Ball
Senior Vice President, David Hamilton
Executive Vice President, Mark Freeman
Senior Vice President Treasury Management, Darlene Selsor
Executive Vice President, John Robb
Vice President, Hilary Stull
Senior Vice President, John Hind
Vice President of Operation, Cliff McCauley
Vice President of Finance, Gregory Dreier
Senior Vice President, Dan Taaffe
Vice President, Oscar Molina
Senior Vice President, Cliff Perez
Senior Vice President, Cathy Garison
Senior Vice President, Vennesa Starr
Vice President, Jonathan Pursch
Senior Vice President, Clay Cary
Senior Vice President, Casey Maxfield
Vice President Executive Benni, Darleen Schauer
Senior Vice President, Jill Stacy
Vice President Sales, Talal Tay
Vice President, Julius Eccell
Vice President of Marketing, Wendy Erickson
Vice President of Finance, Wayne Baker
Vice President Marketing, Ericka Pullin
Senior Vice President, Michael S Cain
Senior Vice President, Mark Seeberger
Senior Vice President, Edward Porras
Senior Vice President, James Valdez
Senior Vice President, Scott Tellkamp
Assistant Vice President, Kelly Shanteau
Senior Vice President, David Seitze
Vice President of Operation, Erica Noriega
Senior Vice President Capital Markets, Mark Brell
Senior Vice President, Tara Menchaca
Senior Vice President, Roger Lind
Vice President Administration, Gary Roney
Vice President, Teresa Woods
Vice President, Clay Jones
Vice President of Information technology, Diane Madalin
Senior Vice President Project Manager, Terrie Ramirez
Senior Vice President, Leigh Olejer
Vice President Collections, Alan McCabe
Vice President, Floyd Wilson
Senior Vice President, Michael Nutter
Senior Vice President, Mike Davis
Vice President of Employee Benefits, Tony Zavala
Vice President Of Finance, Andrea Knight
Senior Vice President, Carl Mclaughlin
Vice President, Maro Rodriguez
Vice President, Susan Carruthers
Regional Vice President, Lorraine Neff
Senior Vice President, Olga Harrison
Executive Vice President, Gary Mcknight
Assistant Vice President, Austin Burns
Assistant Vice President, Hope S Molina
Vice President, Matt Badders
Senior Vice President Institutional Trust Administration, Steven A Klein
Senior Vice President, Terry Frank
Senior Vice President, Letty Dominguez

Vice President Of Finance, Mark Cranmer
Senior Vice President Community Leader, Jeff Fuller
Vice President Technology Infrastructure, Robert Jacobs
Senior Vice President Wealth Advisor Private Trust, John Sands
Vice President Mineral Asset Management Frost Banking Investments, Robert Turnbull
Senior Vice President Compliance, Jan Robertson
Senior Vice President Corporate Banki, Susie Howell
Senior Vice President Capital Markets, Victor Quiroga
Vice President of Marketing, Daryl Hoffmann
Executive Vice President, Sue Turnage
Senior Vice President Workout Officer, Jennifer Crabtree
Senior Vice President of Investment Division, Jeanne Glorioso
Senior Vice President North Texas Sales Manager Public Finance, Shirley Cox
Assistant Vice President of Network Engineering, Danny Leal
Senior Vice President Application Support, Jeff Sanders
Senior Vice President, Shannon Watt
Assistant Vice President, Elsie Boone
Senior Vice President Investments, Linnie Phebus
EXECUTIVE VICE PRESIDENT MARKETING, Debbie Danmeter
Vice President, Ben Kavanagh
Senior Vice President, Carol Lampier
Assistant Vice President, Beth Pence
Assistant Vice President Employee Benefits, Brenda Smith
Senior Vice President, Gina Prill
Executive Vice President, Richard Foster
Assistant Vice President, Rene Ramirez
Senior Vice President, Melissa Adams
Vice President Of Finance, Vance Arnold
Vice President Energy Finance, Alex Zemkoski
Vice President, Duncan Morrow
Senior Vice President Special Assets, Betsy Gleiser
Executive Vice President, Roderick Washington
Vice President Finance, Charles Stockton
Vice President Of Marketing, John Greenwood
Executive Vice President Compliance Manager, Cindy Reeves
Senior Vice President Compliance, Verna Fletcher
Senior Executive Vice President, James Allen
Executive Vice President, Louis Barton
Senior Vice President, Stacy L Flores
Senior Vice President Of Private Trust Services, Debbie Eippert
Senior Vice President, Mark Ritter
Assistant Vice President, Mariela Hernandez
Vice President, Ken Orsburn
Assistant Vice President, Patricio Perez
Assistant Vice President, Lauren Urban
Assistant Vice President Commercial Banking, Jennifer Grimes
Assistant Vice President, Yolanda Gonzales
Vice President, Michael Aubuchon
Vice President, Van C Carter
Vice President, Anna Sanchez
Senior Vice President, Brent Bike
Vice President, Anabell Rodriguez
Vice President Corporate Banking Frost Banking Investments, Luke Healy
Vice President Equipment Leasing And Finance, Laura Eckhardt
Vice President, Sallie Newman
Vice President, Margaret Velasquez
Vice President, Gwen Dominic
Assistant Vice President, Justin Steinbach

Assistant Vice President, Samuel Lopez
Vice President, Laura Pinto
Senior Vice President, Carole Kilpatrick
Assistant Vice President, Karla Riley
Vice President Intl Private Banking, Elvia Daley
Assistant Vice President, Trey McCord
Senior Vice President, Anthony White
Vice President Sales, Linda Wileman
Vice President SBA Loan Coordinator, Kathy Raia
Senior Vice President Trust Internal Audit, Deanna Rankin
Vice President, Allison Byers
Senior Vice President, Lou Kissling
Sr. Vice Pres., Barbara Kelly
Vice President In Human Resources Department, Janet Lane
Vice President, Albert Shannon
Executive Vice President And General Counsel, Stanley McCormick
Executive Vice President, Chas Mella
Senior Vice President, James Winton
Vice President, Sherry Mcgillicuddy
Senior Vice President, Kaye Carpenter
Vice President, Ileana Payne
Vice President Business Services, Gloria Kopycinski
Principal Vice President, Christy Bachmeyer
Vice President, Susan Essex
Senior Vice President, Phil Rosenfeld
Vice President, Adrian Cadena
Assistant Vice President Assistant Controller, Cindy Jacobs
Vice President Business Banking, Marie Sanchez
Executive Vice President, Keith Donahoe
Vice President Research and Strategy Marketing Department RB7, Tammy Herrera
Vice President, Kim Franks
Assistant Vice President of Commercial Lending, Daniel Nash
Senior Vice President, Richard Murray
Senior Vice President, Tim Mccormick
Vice President Relationship Manager, Carlos Gutierrez
Vice President, Tracy Broughton
Vice President, Alan Croley
Senior Vice President Securities Lending, Paul Grimm
Senior Vice President Director of Investor Relations, Gregory Parker
Assistant Vice President Commercial Lending, Alison Boyd
Senior Vice President, David Rathke
Vice President, Art Canales
Senior Vice President, Joe Rodriguez
Senior Vice President, Chris White
Assistant Vice President, David Moor
Senior Vice President, Gregg Chinn
Evp, Jim Crosby
Vice President Trust Real Estate, Will Steubing
VICE PRESIDENT COMMERCIAL BANKING SALES AND MARKETING, Leonard Calderon
Vice President, Vivian Kotara
Senior Vice President and Trust Officer, Ralph Ruske
Assistant Vice President, Reid Wendell
Vice President Of Financial Systems, Austin Kroll
Assistant Vice President, Roman Cooper
Senior Vice President, DAVID HAGEMANN
Vice President Treasury Management Marketing Officer, Christina Stowe
Assistant Vice President Commercial Banking, Josephus Howard
Vice President, Tricia Richardson
Vice President, Julianne H Shively
Vice President Treasury Management, Kim Duncan
Assistant Vice President, Hayley Vaughan

Assistant Vice President Software Development, Santhosh Mathew
Vice President Wealth Management, Carleen Pirro
Vice President Of Commercial Banking, Kristin Edgeller
Vice President Relationship Manager Commercial Banking, Vanessa Johnson
Assistant Vice President Frost Wealth Advisors Frost Banking Investments, Stephanie Allen
Vice President Appraisal Services Frost Banking Investments, Charles Nolen
Assistant Vice President, Turner Vaught
Assistant Vice President, Micah Salinas
Senior Vice President, Randy Silva
Avp Private Banking Officer, Meloni Davis
Senior Vice President, Todd Breeding
Vice President, Robert Malina
Assistant Vice President, Krista Corkill
Vice President, Ken Gates
Assistant Vice President, Karen Sheppard
Vice President Private Banking Officer, Beverly Hankinso
Assistant Vice President, Mike Benso
Senior Vice President, Laurie Wieters
SENIOR VICE PRESIDENT AND CHIEF APPRAISER, Tina Reyes
EXECUTIVE VICE PRESIDENT, Jose Oscos
Vice President Business Banking Services, Audrey Vanburen
Vice President, Jose Opengo
VICE PRESIDENT PUBLIC AFFAIRS AND COMMUNICATIONS, Erica Hurtak
Relationship Manager Assistant Vice President, Scott Odom
Vice President, Garrett Gomez
Assistant Vice President, Nelda Stade
Vice President North Texas Region, Randy Hale
Senior Vice President Mineral Asset Management Frost Banking Investments, Stacey West
Assistant Vice President, Jacob Cavazos
Vice President, Julia Saldana
Assistant Vice President, Mary Walter
Sr Vp Private Banking Manager, Jerry Liesman
Executive Vice President Of Ecommerce, Bobby Berman
Vice President, Rene Deases
Assistant Vice President of Corporate Banking Northwest Hills Financial Center, Ryan Meyer
Senior Vice President, Steve Spears
Assistant Vice President, Karen Cecalek
Vice President, Jeff Mcbride
Vice President Treasury Management Sales, Karen Green
Vice President, Stacey Czaja
Senior Vice President, Elizabeth Torres
Assistant Vice President, Cheryl Lewis
Assistant Vice President, Vicki Lassere
Assistant Vice President, Carlos De Lachica
Vice President Of Finance, Norman Witcher
SvpFinancial Management Services, Adam Suhr
Senior Vice President Commercial Real Estate, Sheffie Hilliard
Senior Vice President, Bill Conner
Vice President, J R Manatt
Board Member, Horace Wilkins
Board Member, Charles Matthews
Board Member, Crawford Edwards
Treasurer, Heather Hurd
Board Member, Ida Steen
Treasurer Senior Vice President, Ashley Threlkeld
Board Member, James A Eckel
Board Member, Denny Alexander
Board Member, Chris Avery
Board Member, Noel Byrne
Auditors: Ernst & Young LLP

LOCATIONS
HQ: Cullen/Frost Bankers, Inc.
111 W. Houston Street, San Antonio, TX 78205
Phone: 210 220-4011 Fax: 210 220-5578
Web: www.frostbank.com

PRODUCTS/OPERATIONS

2016 Sales

	% of total
Interest	
Loans including fees	40
Securities	28
Interest-bearing deposits	1
Federal funds sold and resell agreements	-
Non-interest	
Trust and investment management fees	9
Service charges on deposit accounts	7
Insurance commissions & fees	4
Interchange and debit card transaction fees	2
Other charges commissions and fees	4
Net gain (loss) on securities transactions	1
Other	4
Total	100

2016 Sales

	% of total
Banking	88
Frost Wealth Advisors	12
Total	100

Selected Subsidiaries
Carton Service Corporation
Cullen BLP Inc.
Cullen/Frost Capital Trust II
Frost Bank
Frost Brokerage Services Inc.
Frost Insurance Agency Inc.
Frost Investment Advisors Inc.
Main Plaza Corporation
Tri-Frost Corporation

COMPETITORS

BBVA Compass Bancshares
Bank of America
Broadway Bancshares
Capital One
Comerica
Extraco
First Financial Bankshares
International Bancshares
JPMorgan Chase
Lone Star Bank
PlainsCapital
Prosperity Bancshares
Texas Capital Bancshares
Wells Fargo
Woodforest Financial

HISTORICAL FINANCIALS
Company Type: Public

Income Statement FYE: December 31

	ASSETS ($ mil.)	NET INCOME ($ mil.)	INCOME AS % OF ASSETS	EMPLOYEES
12/19	34,027.4	443.6	1.3%	4,659
12/18	32,292.9	454.9	1.4%	4,370
12/17	31,747.8	364.1	1.1%	4,270
12/16	30,196.3	304.2	1.0%	4,217
12/15	28,567.1	279.3	1.0%	4,211
Annual Growth	4.5%	12.3%	—	2.6%

2019 Year-End Financials
Return on assets: 1.3%
Return on equity: 12.1%
Long-term debt ($ mil.): —
No. of shares (mil.): 62.6
Sales ($ mil): 1,497.6
Dividends
Yield: 2.8%
Payout: 39.6%
Market value ($ mil.): 6,128.0

	STOCK PRICE ($) FY Close	P/E High/Low	PER SHARE ($)		
			Earnings	Dividends	Book Value
12/19	97.78	15 12	6.84	2.80	62.42
12/18	87.94	17 12	6.90	2.58	53.49
12/17	94.65	18 15	5.51	2.25	51.95
12/16	88.23	19 9	4.70	2.15	47.30
12/15	60.00	19 14	4.28	2.10	46.63
Annual Growth	13.0%	— —	12.4%	7.5%	7.6%

Customers Bancorp Inc

Customers Bancorp makes it pretty clear who they want to serve. Boasting some $8.5 billion in assets the bank holding company operates about 15 branches mostly in southeastern Pennsylvania but also in New York and New Jersey. It offers personal and business checking savings and money market accounts as well as loans certificates of deposit credit cards and concierge or appointment banking (they come to you seven days a week). Around 95% of the bank's loan portfolio is made up of commercial loans while the rest consists of consumer loans. It was formed in 2010 as a holding company for Customers Bank which was created in 1994 as New Century Bank.

Operations
Customers Bancorp operates two main business lines: Commercial Lending and Consumer Lending. Its Commercial Lending business provides commercial and industrial loans small and middle-market business banking and small business administration (SBA) loans multi-family and commercial real estate loans and commercial loans to mortgage originators. Its Consumer Lending division mostly makes local market mortgage loans and home equity loans. More than 95% of the bank's loan portfolio was made up of commercial loans at the end of 2015 while the rest consisted of consumer loans.

Broadly speaking the bank makes roughly 90% of its revenue from interest income. About 66% of its revenue came from loan interest during 2015 while another 19% came from interest loans held for sale and 4% came from interest on investment securities. The remainder of its revenue came from mortgage warehouse transactional fees (4%) and other miscellaneous and non-recurring sources.

Geographic Reach
The bank had 14 branches at the end of 2015 including nine in Philadelphia and Southeastern Pennsylvania; four in Berks County Pennsylvania; one in Westchester County New York; and one in Mercer County New Jersey. It also had a handful of additional offices in Boston; New York City; Portsmouth New Hampshire; Providence Rhode Island; and Suffolk County New York.

Sales and Marketing
Customers Bancorp's customers include private businesses business customers non-profits and consumers. Its commercial lending division typically makes loans to companies with revenues between $1 million to $50 million needing between $0.5 million to $10 million in credit.

The bank has been ramping up its advertising spend in recent years. It spent $1.48 million on advertising in 2015 up from $1.33 million and $1.27 million in 2014 and 2013 respectively.

Financial Performance

The bank's annual revenues have nearly quadrupled since 2011 as its loan assets have more than tripled (its loan assets reached $5.45 billion by of the end of 2015). Meanwhile growing revenues strong cost controls and low interest rates have pushed the bank's annual profits up almost 15-fold over the same period.

Customers Bancorp's revenue jumped 29% to $277.5 million during 2015 mostly as its average balance of interest-earning loan and securities assets rose by 31% to $6.7 billion for the year.

Revenue growth in 2015 drove the bank's net income up 36% to $58.5 million. Customer Bancorp's operating cash levels declined sharply to $356.6 million for the year as the bank originated more loans held for sale than it actually sold.

Strategy

With its eye on becoming the leading regional bank holding company Customers Bancorp continued in 2016 to focus on expanding its market share with its high-touch personalized Concierge Banking services and its "high-tech" BankMobile offerings which include remote account opening remote deposit capture and mobile banking. The BankMobile and online banking channels allow Customers Bancorp to slow expensive branch-expansion plans and cut operating costs significantly while giving customers faster access to banking services.

But even with digital banking the bank occasionally opens new branches (and selectively acquire others) to grow its loan and deposit business. In January 2016 it opened and replaced an existing branch in Hamilton New Jersey onto Route 33 in the same city. In June 2015 Customers opened a new Long Island location in Mellville New York to expand its private and commercial banking services to local clients there.

Mergers and Acquisitions

In December 2015 Customers Bank expanded its deposit business and added 2 million new student customers after buying the One Account Student Checking and Refund Management Disbursement Services business from higher education refund disbursement provider Higher One Inc for $42 million.

Company Background

In late 2011 Customers purchased Berkshire Bancorp and picked up five branches in Berks County Pennsylvania for about $11.3 million.

EXECUTIVES

Chairman and CEO, Jay S. Sidhu, age 67, $300,000 total compensation
President and COO, Richard A. Ehst, age 73, $225,000 total compensation
Executive Vice President President of Community Banking, Warren Taylor, age 61, $190,000 total compensation
EVP and Chief Credit Officer, Thomas Jastrem
EVP and Chief Administrative Officer, Jim Collins
EVP and Chief Lending Officer, Timothy D. Romig
EVP and President Special Assets Group, Robert A. White
EVP and CFO, James D. Hogan
EVP and Director Multi-Family and Investment CRE Lending, Kenneth A. Keiser
Senior Vice President, Randy Hanks
Vice President, Michael Mccarrie
VICE PRESIDENT, John Gerhart

Assistant Vice President And Appraisal Review Officer, Richard Nagy
Senior Vice President, Mary Moffitt
Vice President, Margaret Donovan
Senior Vice President Credit O, Barbara Bergman
Senior Vice President, William Hirst
Vice President of Operations, Richard Kirk
Vice President Government Guaranteed Lending, Lisa Kennedy
Vice President Government Guaranteed Lending, Michele Vervlied
Assistant Vice President Capital Markets, Dana Galvin
Vice President, Scott Gates
Assistant Vice President And Assistant Branch Manager, Lisa Gearheart
Assistant Vice President Sox Internal Control Manager, Frank Bommentre
Senior Vice President, Kevin Cornwall
Assistant Vice President, Terry Meehan
Assistant Vice President And Portfolio Manager, Christopher Haley
Senior Vice President Facilities And Security, James Zardecki
Vice President Commercial Lending, John Camero
Manager Deposit Operations Vice President, Natasha Alexander
Senior Vice President NE Director of Pla, Paula Pais
Vice President And Government Guaranteed Lender, Jennifer Mason
Senior Vice President Commercial Finance Group, Sam Smith
Vice President Sales And Industrial Group, Kurt Kolesha
Vice President Government Guaranteed Lending Sba And Usda, Mario Campbell
Vice President And Government Guaranteed Lender, Jennifer Mckay
Vice President, Joanne Jolin
Vice President, Laura Simon
Senior Vice President Commercial Real Estate Lending, Stephen King
Senior Vice President Regional Chief Lending Officer, Robert Fischer
Vice President Small Business Lending, Martin Hernandez
Assistant Vice President Collateral Manager, Donna Abel
Vice President, Kimberly Miller
Business Development Officer Vice President, Sunita Raina
Senior Vice President, Veder Reddick
VICE PRESIDENT COMMERCIAL LENDING, Brett V Long
VICE PRESIDENT INSURANCE RISK MANAGEMENT, Antonette Tumminello
Senior Vice President Senior Credit Officer, Clifford Gaysunas
Senior Vice President, Samuel H Smith
SENIOR VICE PRESIDENT AUDIT DIRECTOR, Brion Watson
VICE PRESIDENT LEAD CORPORATE COUNSEL, Michael Detommaso
Vice President Special Assets Financial Reporting, Doan Dang
Assistant Vice President And Lead Information Technology Auditor, Patrick Direnzo
Executive Vice President And Deputy Credit Officer, Andrew Bowman
Vice President Special Assets Group, Kathy Hansen
Vice President, Kimberly Stack
Senior Vice President Director Of Mortgage Servicing, Debra Hutchinson
Assistant Vice President, John Chung
Vice President, Diane Billman

Vice President, Keith Munley
Vice President Consumer Lending Compliance, Matt Kachurka
Vice President And Senior Analyst, Joann Zerbo
Avp Portfolio Manager, Chris Lacroix
Vice President, Lucia Deangelo
Senior Vice President Commercial Deposit Services Manager, Lary Snow
Auditors: DELOITTE & TOUCHE LLP

LOCATIONS

HQ: Customers Bancorp Inc
1015 Penn Avenue, Suite 103, Wyomissing, PA 19610
Phone: 610 933-2000
Web: www.customersbank.com

PRODUCTS/OPERATIONS

2015

	% of total
Interest income	
Loans receivable including fees	66
Loans held for sale	19
Investment securities	4
Other	2
Non interest income	
Mortgage warehouse transnational fees	4
Bank-owned life insurance	3
Gains on sales of loans	1
Deposit fees	0
Mortgage loan and banking income	0
Gain (loss) on sale of investment securities)	0
Other	1
Total	**100**

Products include
Equipment Loans
Mortgage Warehouse Loans
Multi-Family And Commercial Real Estate Loans
Residential Mortgage Loans
Small Business Loans

COMPETITORS

Bank of America	Huntington Bancshares
Capital One	JPMorgan Chase
Citigroup	KeyCorp
Comerica	PNC Financial
Fifth Third	U.S. Bancorp
HSBC	Wells Fargo

HISTORICAL FINANCIALS

Company Type: Public

Income Statement FYE: December 31

	ASSETS ($ mil.)	NET INCOME ($ mil.)	INCOME AS % OF ASSETS	EMPLOYEES
12/18	9,833.4	71.7	0.7%	827
12/17	9,839.5	78.8	0.8%	765
12/16	9,382.7	78.7	0.8%	739
12/15	8,401.3	58.5	0.7%	517
12/14	6,825.3	43.2	0.6%	426
Annual Growth	9.6%	13.5%	—	18.0%

2018 Year-End Financials
Return on assets: 0.7%
Return on equity: 7.6%
Long-term debt ($ mil.): —
No. of shares (mil.): 31.0
Sales ($ mil): 476.9
Dividends
Yield: —
Payout: —
Market value ($ mil.): 564.0

	STOCK PRICE ($) FY Close	P/E High/Low		PER SHARE ($) Earnings	Dividends	Book Value
12/18	18.20	18	9	1.78	0.00	30.86
12/17	25.99	17	12	1.97	0.00	29.35
12/16	35.82	15	9	2.31	0.00	28.26
12/15	27.22	15	9	1.96	0.00	20.59
12/14	19.46	14	11	1.55	0.00	16.57
Annual Growth	(1.7%)	—	—	3.5%	—	16.8%

CV Sciences Inc

EXECUTIVES

Pres-sec-treas, Michael Mona
Vice President Human Nutrition, Stuart Tomc
Auditors: DELOITTE & TOUCHE LLP

LOCATIONS

HQ: CV Sciences Inc
10070 Barnes Canyon Road, San Diego, CA 92121
Phone: 866 290-2157

HISTORICAL FINANCIALS
Company Type: Public

Income Statement   FYE: December 31

	REVENUE ($ mil.)	NET INCOME ($ mil.)	NET PROFIT MARGIN	EMPLOYEES
12/18	48.2	10.0	20.7%	81
12/17	20.6	(4.9)	—	52
12/16	11.0	(14.1)	—	39
12/15	11.5	(12.2)	—	45
12/14	10.1	(1.3)	—	36
Annual Growth	47.5%	—	—	22.5%

2018 Year-End Financials

Debt ratio: 1.2%
Return on equity: 43.0%
Cash ($ mil.): 12.6
Current ratio: 5.80
Long-term debt ($ mil.): —
No. of shares (mil.): 94.9
Dividends
  Yield: —
  Payout: —
Market value ($ mil.): 409.0

	STOCK PRICE ($) FY Close	P/E High/Low		PER SHARE ($) Earnings	Dividends	Book Value
12/18	4.31	65	3	0.09	0.00	0.32
12/17	0.62	—	—	(0.06)	0.00	0.18
12/16	0.43	—	—	(0.27)	0.00	0.23
12/15	0.24	—	—	(0.35)	0.00	0.51
12/14	2.36	—	—	(0.04)	0.00	0.63
Annual Growth	16.2% (15.8%)	—	—	—	—	—

CVB Financial Corp

CVB Financial is into the California Vibe Baby. The holding company's Citizens Business Bank offers community banking services to primarily small and midsized businesses but also to consumers through nearly 50 branch and office locations across central and southern California. Boasting more than $7 billion in assets the bank offers checking money market CDs and savings accounts trust and investment services and a variety of loans. Commercial real estate loans account for about two-thirds of the bank's loan portfolio which is rounded out by business consumer and construction loans; residential mortgages; dairy and livestock loans; and municipal lease financing.

Operations

In addition to its 40 business financial centers CVB operates seven Commercial Banking Centers (CBCs). The CBCs operate primarily as sales offices and focus on business clients professionals and high-net-worth individuals. The bank also has three trust offices.

Citizens Business Bank provides auto and equipment leasing and brokers mortgage loans through its Citizens Financial Services Division; CitizensTrust offers trust and investment services.

Overall the bank made 63% of its total revenue from interest income on loans and leases in 2014 with another 24% of total revenue coming from interest income on the bank's investment securities. About 5% of total revenue came from service charges on deposit accounts and 3% came from trust and investment services income.

Geographic Reach

CVB Financial has 40 Business Financial Centers located in the Inland Empire Los Angeles County Orange County San Diego County and the Central Valley regions in California.

Sales and Marketing

CVB Financial provides services to companies from a variety of industries including: industrial and manufacturing dairy and livestock agriculture education nonprofit entertainment medical professional services title and escrow government and property management.

Financial Performance

CVB's revenue has been in decline in recent years due to shrinking interest margins on loans amidst the low-interest environment. The firm's profits however have been rising thanks to declining loan loss provisions as its loan portfolio's credit quality has been improving in the strengthening economy.

CVB enjoyed a breakout year in 2014 with revenue rebounding by 12% to $289.32 million mostly thanks to higher interest income as the bank grew its loan and lease assets by 7% during the year and grew its investment security assets by 18%. Most of its loan growth came from commercial real estate loans while SFR mortgage loans consumer loans and construction loans also helped boost the company's top line. The bank's non-interest income also jumped by 44% during the year thanks to a $6 million gain on loans held-for-sale and a net $3.6 million decrease in its FDIC loss sharing asset.

Higher revenue and a $16.1 million loan loss provision recapture in 2014 also drove the bank's net income higher by 9% to $104.02 million.

Despite higher earnings for the year CVB's operating cash levels shrank by 22% to $87.70 million as the bank used more cash toward employee payments and income taxes.

Strategy

CVB Financial continues to seek out acquisitions of smaller banking trust and investment companies to grow its loan and deposit business as well as its geographic reach in key markets in (mostly Southern) California. With its 2014 acquisition of American Security Bank for example CVB boosted its assets by 6% to over $7 billion while adding branches in more than a handful of key markets in Southern California.

Remaining profitable throughout the economic downturn CVB Financial credits its success in part to its strict loan underwriting standards. The bank targets family-owned or other privately held businesses with annual revenues of up to $200 million with the goal of maintaining its client relationships for decades.

Mergers and Acquisitions

In March 2014 CVB Financial through its Citizens Business Bank (CBB) subsidiary purchased Southern California-based American Security Bank (the flagship subsidiary of American Bancshares) for a total of $57 million. The deal would add American Security Bank's $431 million in assets and boost CBB's branch presence across key markets in Newport Beach Corona Laguna Niguel Lancastar Victorville and Apple Valley.

In 2016 CVB Financial agreed to buy the $416 million-asset Valley Commerce Bancorp the holding company for Valley Business Bank. Valley Business has four banking locations in California's Visalia Tulare Fresno and Woodlake.

Company Background

In 2009 CVB Financial healthier than most California banks acquired the failed San Joaquin Bank after the FDIC took it over. The deal added five branches banking centers in the Bakersfield area.

EXECUTIVES

EVP and General Counsel CVB Financial Corporation and Citizens Business Bank, Richard H. Wohl, age 60
President and CEO CVB Financial and Citizens Business Bank, Christopher D. (Chris) Myers, age 56, $800,000 total compensation
EVP and CFO, E. Allen Nicholson, age 52
EVP and CIO, Elsa I. Zavala
EVP and Dairy and Livestock Industries Group Manager Citizens Business Bank, G. Larry Zivelonghi
SVP and Regional Manager Citizens Business Bank, Ted J. Dondanville
SVP and Regional Manager Citizens Business Bank, David A. Brager, $300,000 total compensation
EVP and COO Citizens Business Bank, David C. Harvey, $300,000 total compensation
EVP; Head CitizensTrust, R. Daniel Banis
EVP and Chief Risk Officer Citizens Business Bank, Yamynn De Angelis
EVP Ventura/Santa Barbara, Donald R. Toussaint
Executive Vice President, Daniel Banis
Vice President Relationship Manager, Nadine Ortega
Senior Vice President, Michael D Stain
Vice President Relationship Manager, Jason Gould
Vice President Senior Product Manager, John Outwater
Vice President Administration, Joe Pacis
Senior Vice President, Robert Peccini
Senior Vice President, John Stenz
Vice President And Relationship Manager, Maria Padilla
Evp Of Cfo, Allen Nicholson
Vice President Specialty Service Officer Commercial Banking Group, Martha Ponce
Vice President Special Assets Portfolio Manager, Bruce Adams

Vp And Special Assets Portfolio Manager, Verona Chion
VICE PRESIDENT CENTER MANAGER, Pamela Gaspar
Vice President Credit Officer, Frank Yu
Vice Chairman, George A. Borba, age 86
Chairman, Raymond V. OÂ'Brien
Auditors: KPMG LLP

LOCATIONS

HQ: CVB Financial Corp
701 North Haven Ave., Suite 350, Ontario, CA 91764
Phone: 909 980-4030
Web: www.cbbank.com

PRODUCTS/OPERATIONS

2014 Sales

	$ mil.	% of total
Interest		
Loans including fees	181.6	62
Investment securities	68.4	24
Other	2.9	1
Noninterest		
Service charges on deposit accounts	15.8	5
Trust & investment services	8.1	3
Bankcard services	3.4	1
BOLI income	2.4	1
Other	10.3	3
Adjustments	(3.6)	-
Total	**289.3**	**100**

COMPETITORS

Bank of America	Popular Inc.
Bank of the West	Provident Financial
City National	Holdings
Comerica	U.S. Bancorp
JPMorgan Chase	Wells Fargo
MUFG Americas Holdings	

HISTORICAL FINANCIALS

Company Type: Public

Income Statement
FYE: December 31

	ASSETS ($ mil.)	NET INCOME ($ mil.)	INCOME AS % OF ASSETS	EMPLOYEES
12/18	11,529.1	152.0	1.3%	0
12/17	8,270.5	104.4	1.3%	0
12/16	8,073.7	101.4	1.3%	0
12/15	7,671.2	99.1	1.3%	0
12/14	7,377.9	104.0	1.4%	0
Annual Growth	11.8%	9.9%	—	—

2018 Year-End Financials

Return on assets: 1.5%
Return on equity: 10.4%
Long-term debt ($ mil.): —
No. of shares (mil.): 140.0
Sales ($ mil): 405.3
Dividends
Yield: 2.7%
Payout: 50.9%
Market value ($ mil.): 2,832.0

	STOCK PRICE ($) FY Close	P/E High/Low	PER SHARE ($) Earnings	Dividends	Book Value
12/18	20.23	20 15	1.24	0.56	13.22
12/17	23.56	26 21	0.95	0.52	9.70
12/16	22.93	25 15	0.94	0.36	9.15
12/15	16.92	20 16	0.93	0.48	8.68
12/14	16.02	17 14	0.98	0.40	8.29
Annual Growth	6.0%	— —	6.1%	8.8%	12.4%

Cypress Semiconductor Corp.

Cypress Semiconductor makes an array of embedded and memory processors for automotive industrial and consumer machines and devices. Its microcontroller devices which generate most of the company's revenue are embedded in products that range from Audi and Subaru autos to Samsung and Under Armour wearable fitness devices as well as smart TVs and smartphones. Cypress memory products are used in automated driver assist systems networking modems medical instruments and other devices. The company makes significant sales through distributors such as Fujitsu Electronics and Arrow Electronics. In 2019 Cypress agreed to be bought by Germany-based Infineon Technologies for $10.1 billion (?9 billion).

Change in Company Type

Cypress Semiconductor agreed in 2019 to become a part of Infineon Technologies in an equity and cash transaction valued at $10.1 billion (?9 billion). The combined company would be the eighth-biggest chip company by revenue and the top supplier of semiconductors for automotive applications. Together the companies would have a broader reach in chips for industrial uses and the Internet of Things the network of connected sensors and other devices. Geographically Germany-based Infineon would expand its presence in the US market. In the face of other semiconductor consolidations the deal bolsters Infineon and Cypress to compete against bigger rivals. The deal was expected to close by early 2020.

Operations

Cypress's microcontroller and connectivity products generate about 60% of its revenue. The unit's offerings include the Traveo CapSense Wi-Fi Bluetooth and EZ-PD products.

Memory products supply the other 40% of revenue from products that include NOR flash memories SRAM (static RAM) F-RAM (Ferroelectric RAM) and programmable system-on-chip devices.

More than 70% of Cypress's products are made by about a dozen contract manufacturers with input from Cypress's own manufacturing facility. The arrangement allows Cypress to manage its supply chain to meet demand while limiting capital expenses. The company also has test-and-assembly operations.

Geographic Reach

About 40% of Cypress's sales are to customers in China Taiwan and Hong Kong while customers in Japan account for about 25% of revenue and customers in Europe and the US generate 15% and 10% of sales respectively.

Cypress's reliance on Asian markets makes it subject to fallout from the uneasy trade relations between the US and China. Tariffs have generated uncertainty in the market making customers more cautious in making buying decisions.

The company operates design and software development centers in the US Europe India Japan and China. The company's test-and-assembly operations are in the Philippines Thailand and Malaysia.

Sales and Marketing

Cypress Semiconductor sells directly to original equipment manufacturers (OEMs) as well as through a network of distributors. More than a third of the company's sales go through just two distributors: Fujitsu Electronics 20% of sales a year and Arrow Electronics about 15%.

In terms of markets Cypress's sales are spread among automotive applications about 35% of revenue consumer applications about 30% and industrial and enterprise applications about 20% each. Ford Bosch Toyota Visteon Medtronic Roku and BMW are among Cypress's customers.

Financial Performance

Cypress's revenue has climbed higher for the past five years as its microcontroller business has bloomed in the automotive sector and acquisitions added sales. Profit has been a trickier proposition with the company posting losses in four of the past six years.

Sales rose about 7% in 2018 to about $2.5 billion up $156 million from 2017 fueled by increases in both segments. The Memory Products segment's sales advanced about 10% from stronger performances in NOR and NAND products. The Microcontroller and Connectivity Products segment's sales gained about 5% from customers ramping up new products. Automotive-related revenue which includes sales from both segments rose 13% year-over-year.

Cypress halted three straight years of losses in 2018 with a hefty $354 million profit made possible by a $315.6 million tax benefit. Operating income before taxes of $164.4 million in 2018 was higher than 2017 when it was $78 million.

Cypress had $285.7 million in cash and equivalents in 2018 compared to $151.6 million the year before. In 2018 cash from operations was $471.7 million while investing and financing activities used $49.7 million and $287.9 million respectively.

Strategy

Although Cypress bolstered its product portfolio through acquisitions and expanded its automotive business the company remained subject to volatile markets and competition from bigger companies. Cypress addressed those issues by agreeing in 2019 to be acquired by Infineon Technologies a larger chip maker (sales of $9 billion in 2018) for about $10.1 billion (?9 million). The companies said the complementary nature of their product lineups as well as their unified size would enable the combined firm to better compete against rivals. It would be the eighth-biggest chip company by revenue and the top automotive chip supplier.

Besides its automotive products Cypress brings to the deal products that target the Internet of Things. The company has developed low power technologies such as Bluetooth Low Energy devices that consume little power compared to previous generations. The company also is investing in the USB market with the Type C standard (USB-C) as well as combo devices that offer Bluetooth and USB-C. Cypress shipped its two-billionth USB device in 2018.

In 2019 Cypress moved to limit its exposure to the volatile commodity memory market by forming a joint venture with SK hynix systems ic. Called SkyHigh Memory Ltd. the venture will make NAND memory chips for the consumer networking industrial and automotive markets. SK hynix system ic owns 60% and Cypress owns the rest of the Hong Kong-based venture.

Cypress reconfigured its costs and revenue in 2018 by consolidating two factories to one introducing products in line with its gross margin goals and restructuring its memory business to focus on more stable and predictable specialty storage products for the automotive industrial and enterprise end markets and leaving lower-margin markets.

EXECUTIVES

EVP Marketing, Paul D. Keswick, age 61, $329,077 total compensation
Vice President and Treasurer, Neil Weiss
EVP Human Resources, Carmine Renzulli
EVP Quality, Sabbas A. Daniel, age 56
VP Synchronous SRAM Memory and Imaging, Dana C. Nazarian, age 52, $279,968 total compensation
EVP and CTO, J. Augusto de Oliveira
President and CEO, Hassane El-Khoury, age 39, $401,964 total compensation
EVP Finance and Administration and CFO, Thad Trent, age 51, $350,000 total compensation
EVP Worldwide Sales and Applications, Michael Balow
SVP Memory Products, Sam Geha
SVP Programmable Systems, Sudhir Gopalswamy
EVP Manufacturing, Joseph (Joe) Rauschmayer, $345,213 total compensation
Vp Engineering, Andy Hawkins
Vp Flash Business Unit, Rainer Hoehler
Vice President Engineering, Dennis Keesling
Vice President Business Unit, Ajay Srikrishna
Vice President Sales And Marketing, Rick Reifer
Vice President Technology Development, Ravi Kapre
Vice President of Engineering, Jay Kilby
Executive Vice President Sales And Applications, Jdaniel McCranie
Vice President Product Engineer, Kevin Huey
Vice President Biometrics, Jeff Lee
Vice President, James Nulty
Executive Vice President Chief Legal and Human Resource Officer and Corporate Secretary, Pamela Tondreau
Vp Engineering, Vikram Gupta
Vp Product Line Marketing, John Dacosta
Vice President Corporate Strategy, Lalitha Suryanarayana
Vp Design Engineering, Brad Hoskins
Svp Engineering, Dina Mckinney
Vice President Corporate Communications, Ann Minooka
Executive Vice President Ww Manufacturing, Wei-chung Wang
Chairman, W. Steve Albrecht, age 72
Sr. Assistant Treasurer, Eugene Spevakov
Auditors: PricewaterhouseCoopers LLP

LOCATIONS

HQ: Cypress Semiconductor Corp.
  198 Champion Court, San Jose, CA 95134
Phone: 408 943-2600
Web: www.cypress.com

PRODUCTS/OPERATIONS

2018 Sales

	$ mil.	% of total
Microcontroller and Connectivity Products	1,474.4	59
Memory Products	1,009.4	41
Total	2,483.8	100

2018 Sales

	% of total
Automotive	33
Consumer	29
Industrial	19
Enterprise	19
Total	100

Selected Products

Clocks and buffers
  Application-specific clocks
  Programmable clock buffers (RoboClock)
  Programmable clocks
Framer and mapper chips
Memory
  Dual-port memories
  First in-first out (FIFO) specialty memories
  Programmable read-only memories (PROMs)
  Static random-access memories (SRAMs)
Physical layer (PHY) devices
Programmable logic devices (PLDs)
Programmable system-on-chip (PSoC) microcontrollers
Universal Serial Bus (USB) microcontrollers

COMPETITORS

EverSpin Technologies
Fujitsu Semiconductor
Integrated Device Technology
Integrated Silicon Solution
Marvell Technology
MediaTek
Microchip Technology
Micron Technology
NXP Semiconductors
Renesas Electronics
SK Hynix
STMicroelectronics
Silicon Labs
Synaptics
Texas Instruments

HISTORICAL FINANCIALS

Company Type: Public

Income Statement   FYE: December 30

	REVENUE ($ mil.)	NET INCOME ($ mil.)	NET PROFIT MARGIN	EMPLOYEES
12/18	2,483.8	354.5	14.3%	5,846
12/17*	2,327.7	(80.9)	—	6,099
01/17	1,923.1	(686.2)	—	6,546
01/16	1,607.8	(378.8)	—	6,279
12/14	725.5	17.9	2.5%	3,350
Annual Growth	36.0%	110.9%	—	14.9%

*Fiscal year change

2018 Year-End Financials

Debt ratio: 23.8%
Return on equity: 18.0%
Cash ($ mil.): 285.7
Current ratio: 1.64
Long-term debt ($ mil.): 874.2
No. of shares (mil.): 361.4
Dividends
  Yield: 0.0%
  Payout: 46.3%
Market value ($ mil.): 4,572.0

	STOCK PRICE ($) FY Close	P/E High/Low		PER SHARE ($) Earnings	Dividends	Book Value
12/18	12.65	19	12	0.95	0.44	5.85
12/17*	15.24	—	—	(0.24)	0.44	5.16
01/17	11.44	—	—	(2.15)	0.44	5.85
01/16	9.81	—	—	(1.25)	0.44	8.19
12/14	14.60	133	75	0.11	0.44	1.27
Annual Growth	(3.5%)	—	—	71.4%	(0.0%)	46.4%

*Fiscal year change

Dave & Busters Entertainment Inc

Fun and games collide with food and drink at these nightspots. Dave & Buster's Entertainment owns and operates more than 85 entertainment complexes that offer casual dining full bar service and a cavernous game room. The adult fun centers feature the latest in video games and motion simulators as well as games of skill played for prizes. For dining Dave & Buster's offers a menu that features traditional American fare such as burgers seafood and steak. Partners David Corriveau and James "Buster" Corley opened the first Dave & Buster's in 1982. It went public in late 2014.

Operations

Slightly less than 50% of sales come from food and beverages while the remaining sales come from amusements such as air hockey skee-ball and video games.

Geographic Reach

Dave & Buster's owns and operates locations in 33 states and Canada. About 27 of the company's 87 entertainment complexes are concentrated within the three states of California New York and Texas.

Sales and Marketing

Dave & Buster's is concentrating on increased sales and marketing efforts to reinvigorate its brand and grow the special events portion of its business. The chain helped pioneer a new segment in casual dining but few adult fun arcade chains have followed and flourished. One notable exception is Champps a chain of suburban nightspots popular for live music games and karaoke. Dave & Buster's also faces stiff competition in the general food and drink category from such franchises as Applebee's Buffalo Wild Wings and Hooters.

Financial Performance

The company reported revenue of $866.98 million for fiscal 2016 which was an increase of $120.23 million (or 16%) compared to its fiscal 2015 revenue. The primary reason for the spike was increased revenues from comparable store sales driven by a continued focus on sports viewing new game launches and new menu offerings.

Dave & Buster's net income was $59.61 million in fiscal 2016 which was an increase of $51.98 million compared to its fiscal 2015 net income.

The company ended fiscal 2016 with $186.98 million in cash flow from operations. That was an increase of a little more than $100 million compared to Dave & Buster's cash on hand at the end of fiscal 2015.

Strategy

The chain's recent expansion efforts have slanted towards opening new units that are a smaller format store the company developed out of the need to reduce construction and operating costs. The company is focused on its growth through geographic expansion.

HISTORY

Late in the 1970s David Corriveau and James "Buster" Corley were running two businesses located next to each other in Little Rock Arkansas. Corriveau operated a billiards and game parlor called Slick Willie's and Corley ran Buster's a restaurant that Corriveau helped finance. The two noticed a large amount of traffic between the two locales and the idea of Dave & Buster's was formed. The first site opened in a converted Dallas warehouse in 1982; the second opened six years later. Eager for expansion Corriveau and Corley sold an 80% stake in the business to Dallas retailer Edison Brothers in 1990. Edison grew weary of the cash drain however and divested its stake in 1995. The company went public that year.

The company picked up its expansion pace in 1996 opening three more locations. The next year the first West Coast Dave & Buster's opened in

Ontario California and brewer Bass (later Six Continents) opened the first international site in the UK. (A second UK location opened the following year.) In 1998 Dave & Buster's signed a franchise agreement with TaiMall Development to open seven locations across the Pacific Rim (the first of which opened that year in Taiwan) and an agreement with SVAG Development to open several stores in Germany Switzerland and Austria.

New stores opened in Texas and Florida the following year. Dave & Buster's also inked an agreement with Funtime Hospitality to open 10 locations in Canada. (The company opened a single location in Toronto in 2000; it acquired Funtime's assets and terminated its development rights in 2003.) Results during 1999 were disappointing however causing the company to slow its expansion plans in 2000. That year Bass terminated its license agreement and closed the UK locations. SVAG cancelled its development deal the next year. Also in 2001 the company signed an agreement to develop five locations in South Korea.

A group led by management and backed by Investcorp agreed to buy the company and take it private for $255 million in 2002. Unable to get financing however the deal was called off late that year prompting public complaints from investors. With the founders at the helm for years Dave & Buster's separated the offices of chairman and CEO in 2003. Former co-chairs and co-CEOs Corriveau and Corley gained new titles (president and CEO respectively) and director Peter Edison was named non-executive chairman.

The company opened no new stores in 2003 and only one in 2004. However in 2004 the company purchased nine Jillian's locations and the Jillian's trade name for $47 million $20 million more than the original proposal. Most of the entertainment night spots were converted to Dave & Buster's locations.

Wellspring Capital Management took Dave & Buster's private in 2006 for $375 million. Corley stepped down as CEO following the deal and turned the reins over to Stephen King formerly head of international operations for Carlson Restaurants (T.G.I. Friday's). Corriveau was replaced the following year by Starlette Johnson.

In 2008 Dave & Buster's announced plans to go public again through an IPO but that deal was later shelved due to the deteriorating economy. Wellspring sold the restaurant business to private-equity firm Oak Hill Capital for $570 million in 2010. Dave & Buster's eventually filed its IPO in 2011 only to cancel those plans in 2012.

EXECUTIVES

SVP and CFO, Brian A. Jenkins, age 57, $316,731 total compensation
SVP Purchasing and International Operations, J. Michael (Mike) Plunkett, age 68, $194,615 total compensation
CEO, Stephen M. King, age 61, $600,000 total compensation
President and COO, Dolf Berle, age 56
SVP Entertainment and Games Strategy, Kevin Bachus
Assistant Vice President Finance, Joe Deprospero
Chairman, Alan J. Lacy
Auditors: KPMG LLP

LOCATIONS

HQ: Dave & Busters Entertainment Inc
2481 Manana Drive, Dallas, TX 75220
Phone: 214 357-9588
Web: www.daveandbusters.com

PRODUCTS/OPERATIONS

2017 Sales

	$ mil.	% of total
Amusement and other revenues	553.0	55
Food and beverage revenues	452.2	45
Total	1,005.2	100

COMPETITORS

AMF Bowling	Carlson Restaurants
Applebee's	Damon's
International	Hooters
Brinker	Houlihan's
Brunswick Corp.	Rock Bottom
Buffalo Wild Wings	Restaurants

HISTORICAL FINANCIALS

Company Type: Public

Income Statement FYE: February 3

	REVENUE ($ mil.)	NET INCOME ($ mil.)	NET PROFIT MARGIN	EMPLOYEES
02/19	1,265.3	117.2	9.3%	16,098
02/18*	1,139.7	120.9	10.6%	14,840
01/17	1,005.1	90.8	9.0%	13,983
01/16	866.9	59.6	6.9%	12,495
02/15	746.7	7.6	1.0%	10,930
Annual Growth	14.1%	97.9%	—	10.2%

*Fiscal year change

2019 Year-End Financials

Debt ratio: 30.9%
Return on equity: 29.0%
Cash ($ mil.): 21.5
Current ratio: 0.37
Long-term debt ($ mil.): 378.4
No. of shares (mil.): 37.5
Dividends
 Yield: 0.0%
 Payout: 10.2%
Market value ($ mil.): 1,926.0

	STOCK PRICE ($) FY Close	P/E High/Low	PER SHARE ($) Earnings	Dividends	Book Value
02/19	51.34	22 13	2.93	0.30	10.34
02/18*	47.70	25 15	2.84	0.00	10.51
01/17	54.80	27 14	2.10	0.00	10.41
01/16	36.27	29 19	1.39	0.00	8.32
02/15	28.74	140 78	0.21	0.00	6.47
Annual Growth	15.6%	— —	93.3%	—	12.4%

*Fiscal year change

Del Taco Restaurants Inc (New)

EXECUTIVES

Chb-ceo, Levy F Lawrence
Vice President of Human Resources, Jeanne Graves
Senior Vice President Oprs, David A Pear
Vice President of Finance, Pete Honer
Auditors: Ernst & Young LLP

LOCATIONS

HQ: Del Taco Restaurants Inc (New)
25521 Commercentre Drive, Lake Forest, CA 92630
Phone: 949 462-9300

HISTORICAL FINANCIALS

Company Type: Public

Income Statement FYE: January 1

	REVENUE ($ mil.)	NET INCOME ($ mil.)	NET PROFIT MARGIN	EMPLOYEES
01/19	505.4	18.9	3.8%	7,544
01/18	471.4	49.8	10.6%	7,656
01/17*	452.0	20.9	4.6%	7,368
12/15	215.4	2.6	1.2%	6,690
06/15	208.5	2.1	1.0%	0
Annual Growth	24.8%	73.3%	—	—

*Fiscal year change

2019 Year-End Financials

Debt ratio: 23.6%
Return on equity: 4.5%
Cash ($ mil.): 7.1
Current ratio: 0.59
Long-term debt ($ mil.): 178.6
No. of shares (mil.): 37.3
Dividends
 Yield: —
 Payout: —
Market value ($ mil.): 373.0

	STOCK PRICE ($) FY Close	P/E High/Low	PER SHARE ($) Earnings	Dividends	Book Value
01/19	9.99	29 19	0.49	0.00	11.32
01/18	12.11	12 9	1.25	0.00	10.83
01/17*	14.32	28 16	0.53	0.00	9.64
12/15	10.70	234 142	0.07	0.00	9.49
06/15	15.22	45 26	0.37	0.00	(0.00)
Annual Growth	(10.0%)	— —	7.3%	—	—

*Fiscal year change

Diamond Hill Investment Group Inc.

Diamond Hill Investment Group takes a shine to investment management. Operating through flagship subsidiary Diamond Hill Capital Management the firm oversees some $11.5 billion in assets most of it invested in mutual funds. Serving institutional and individual clients the company administers several mutual funds and sells them mainly through independent investment advisers broker-dealers financial planners investment consultants and third-party marketing firms. The firm hews to a value-based investment philosophy and takes a long-term perspective to investing. Formed in 1990 Diamond Hill Investment Group also manages separate accounts and hedge funds.

Operations

Diamond Hill Investment Group operates through its subsidiaries: Diamond Hill Capital Management; and Beacon Hill Fund Services and BHIL Distributors collectively known as Beacon Hill. Beacon Hill provides fund administration and statutory underwriting services to various clients including Diamond Hill Funds.

Financial Performance

Diamond Hill Investment Group's revenue rose 4% in 2012 versus 2011 to $66.6 million. The increase was due to a 13% rise in fees from mutual fund administration while investment advisory fees rose a more modest 3%. Net income rose 18% over the same period to $16.9 million. Assets under management at the end of 2012 exceeded $9.4 billion an increase of nearly 9% over the prior year. The firm's revenue and profits have increased steadily since 2008 after taking a hit during the financial crisis as investors retreated from the market.

EXECUTIVES

Co-Chief Investment Officer, Christopher A. (Chris) Welch
COO, Lisa M. Wesolek, age 56
Managing Director Investments and Portfolio Manager, Chuck Bath
President CEO and Portfolio Manager, Christopher (Chris) Bingaman, age 54
CFO, Thomas E. (Tom) Line, age 53
Co-Chief Investment Officer and Portfolio Manager, Austin Hawley
Chairman, Roderick H. (Ric) Dillon, age 62
Auditors: KPMG LLP

LOCATIONS

HQ: Diamond Hill Investment Group Inc.
325 John H. McConnell Blvd., Suite 200, Columbus, OH 43215
Phone: 614 255-3333
Web: www.diamond-hill.com

PRODUCTS/OPERATIONS

2015 Sales

	$ mil.	% of total
Investment advisory	107.9	87
Mutual fund administration	16.5	13
Total	**124.4**	**100**

Selected Products
Diamond Hill Small Cap Fund
Diamond Hill Small-Mid Cap Fund
Diamond Hill Large Cap Fund
Diamond Hill Select Fund Fund
Diamond Hill Long-Short Fund
Diamond Hill Strategic Income Fund

COMPETITORS

AllianceBernstein
American Century
Calamos Asset Management
Cohen & Steers
Columbia Management
Davis Advisers
Duncan-Hurst
Eaton Vance
Edelman Financial
Edward Jones
Epoch
FMR
Franklin Templeton
GAMCO Investors
Legg Mason
MFS
Putnam
Pzena Investment Management
Raymond James Financial
SEI Investments
T. Rowe Price
The Vanguard Group
Waddell & Reed
Westwood Holdings

HISTORICAL FINANCIALS
Company Type: Public

Income Statement
FYE: December 31

	REVENUE ($ mil.)	NET INCOME ($ mil.)	NET PROFIT MARGIN	EMPLOYEES
12/18	145.6	47.3	32.5%	125
12/17	145.2	49.9	34.4%	118
12/16	136.1	46.0	33.8%	112
12/15	124.4	37.0	29.8%	126
12/14	104.5	31.5	30.2%	107
Annual Growth	**8.6%**	**10.7%**	**—**	**4.0%**

2018 Year-End Financials
Debt ratio: —
Return on equity: 25.7%
Cash ($ mil.): 84.4
Current ratio: 2.32
Long-term debt ($ mil.): —
No. of shares (mil.): 3.5
Dividends
  Yield: 5.3%
  Payout: 51.4%
Market value ($ mil.): 523.0

	STOCK PRICE ($) FY Close	P/E High/Low	PER SHARE ($) Earnings	Dividends	Book Value
12/18	149.45	16 10	13.48	8.00	55.89
12/17	206.66	15 13	14.48	7.00	49.69
12/16	210.38	16 11	13.49	6.00	40.81
12/15	189.00	20 11	11.03	5.00	30.84
12/14	138.04	14 11	9.67	4.00	22.40
Annual Growth	**2.0%**	**—**	**8.7%**	**18.9%**	**25.7%**

Diamondback Energy, Inc.

EXECUTIVES

Vice President Drilling, Yong Cho
Auditors: Grant Thornton LLP

LOCATIONS

HQ: Diamondback Energy, Inc.
500 West Texas, Suite 1200, Midland, TX 79701
Phone: 432 221-7400
Web: www.diamondbackenergy.com

COMPETITORS

3ROC
BJ Services
Berry Petroleum
Clayton Williams Energy
Concho
ConocoPhillips
Laredo Petroleum Holdings
Linn Energy
Occidental Permian
SandRidge Energy
Whiting Petroleum

HISTORICAL FINANCIALS
Company Type: Public

Income Statement
FYE: December 31

	REVENUE ($ mil.)	NET INCOME ($ mil.)	NET PROFIT MARGIN	EMPLOYEES
12/18	2,176.2	845.6	38.9%	711
12/17	1,205.1	482.2	40.0%	251
12/16	527.1	(165.0)	—	158
12/15	446.7	(550.6)	—	141
12/14	495.7	193.7	39.1%	114
Annual Growth	**44.8%**	**44.5%**	**—**	**58.0%**

2018 Year-End Financials
Debt ratio: 20.6%
Return on equity: 8.9%
Cash ($ mil.): 214.5
Current ratio: 0.91
Long-term debt ($ mil.): 4,464.3
No. of shares (mil.): 164.2
Dividends
  Yield: 0.4%
  Payout: 4.6%
Market value ($ mil.): 15,228.0

	STOCK PRICE ($) FY Close	P/E High/Low	PER SHARE ($) Earnings	Dividends	Book Value
12/18	92.70	17 11	8.06	0.38	83.39
12/17	126.25	26 17	4.94	0.00	53.53
12/16	101.06	— —	(2.20)	0.00	41.02
12/15	66.90	— —	(8.74)	0.00	28.08
12/14	59.78	25 12	3.64	0.00	30.78
Annual Growth	**11.6%**	**—**	**22.0%**	**—**	**28.3%**

Diodes, Inc.

Diodes Incorporated knows how important it is to be discrete in business. The company makes discrete semiconductors — fixed-function devices that are much less complex than integrated circuits. Diodes' products include diodes transistors and rectifiers; they are used by computer and consumer electronics manufacturers in products such as notebooks LCD monitors smartphones and game consoles. Other applications include power supplies climate control systems GPS devices and networking gear. Cisco LG Electronics Samsung Flextronics and Hon Hai are among its more than 250 OEM and contract manufacturing customers. The company's products are sold throughout Asia Europe and North America.

Operations
The semiconductor manufacturer operates design marketing and engineering centers in the US the UK Germany and Taiwan as well as a joint venture manufacturing plants in China and other manufacturing facilities in Neuhaus Germany and Taiwan.

Geographic Reach
Asia is the Texas-based company's largest market accounting for 79% of its annual sales. China is its single largest market contributing 60% of sales. Taiwan Germany and the US account for single digit percentages of sales.

Sales and Marketing
The company markets and sells its products worldwide through direct sales and marketing personnel independent sales representatives and distributors in the US Europe and Asia. Customers include some 250 leading OEMs as well as major electronic manufacturing service (EMS) providers. Additionally Diodes has about 65 distributor customers including Arrow Electronics and Avnet through which it indirectly serves more than 10000 customers worldwide.

End users for the company's semiconductors include the: consumer electronics (32% of sales); communications (24% of sales) industrial (21% of sales); and automotive industries (5% of sales).

Financial Performance
In 2015 Diodes' revenue slipped 5% to $849 million down from $891 million in 2014 due to weaker demand across several key end markets and geographies and lower average selling prices.

The company's net income tumbled 62% to $24 million from $64 million in 2014. Diodes had higher costs for selling general and administrative purpose and an increase in its research and development budget. Some of the higher costs were related to its Pericom acquisition.

Cash flow from operations was $118 million in 2015 down from $134 million in 2014.

Strategy

Diodes is under continuous pressure from customers and competitors to reduce the prices of its products which can result in lower sales and profits for the company. The company has countered by expanding into higher-margin proprietary product lines such as high-density arrays and ultra-miniature switching diodes used in mobile applications. It also continues to become more vertically integrated which brings down cost and increases efficiency of operations. Diodes is looking to expand manufacturing capacity R&D capabilities product development and its sales and marketing organization in part through acquisitions. It's also looking to reduce its gold consumption.

Mergers and Acquisitions

Diodes completed the Pericom Semiconductor acquisition in 2015. The $413 million deal broadened Diodes' analog footprint and adds a mixed-signal connectivity offering. Pericom also brought an extensive timing product line complementary to Diodes' standard product portfolio.

In 2013 the company acquired BCD Semiconductor Manufacturing Limited for about $151 million in an effort to broaden its reach in Asia particularly China where BCD is strong. Previously Diodes purchased Power Analog Microelectronics a provider of advanced analog and high-voltage power ICs for $16 million in 2012. The purchase strengthened its position in analog products.

EXECUTIVES

Vice President Of Corporate Operations, Edmund Tang
President CEO and Director, Keh-Shew Lu, age 72, $539,250 total compensation
SVP Operations, Joseph Liu, age 77, $294,167 total compensation
SVP Sales and Marketing, Mark A. King, age 60, $327,292 total compensation
VP Worldwide Discrete Products, Francis Tang, age 65, $286,417 total compensation
CFO Secretary and Treasurer, Richard D. White, age 71, $327,292 total compensation
VP Worldwide Analog Products, Julie Holland, age 57
VP Corporate Supply Chain/Planning Outsourcing and Quality, Clemente (Clay) Beltran
Executive Vice President Investor Relations, Leanne Sievers
Chairman, Raymond Soong, age 77
Vice Chairman, C. H. Chen, age 76
Board Member, Peter Menard
Auditors: Moss Adams LLP

LOCATIONS

HQ: Diodes, Inc.
4949 Hedgcoxe Road, Suite 200, Plano, TX 75024
Phone: 972 987-3900
Web: www.diodes.com

PRODUCTS/OPERATIONS

2015 Sales by Market

	% of total
Consumer electronics	32
Computing	18
Industrial	21
Communications	24
Automotive	5
Total	**100**

Selected Products

Diodes
 Schottky diodes
 Switching diodes
 Zener diodes
High-density arrays
Metal oxide semiconductor field-effect transistors (MOSFETs)
Rectifiers
 Bridge rectifiers
 Schottky rectifiers
 Standard fast superfast and ultrafast recovery rectifiers
Transient voltage suppressors
 Thyristor surge protection devices
 Zener transient-voltage suppressors
Transistors
 Bipolar transistors
 Darlington transistors
 Prebiased transistors

COMPETITORS

Advanced Photonix	ROHM
BCD Semiconductor	STMicroelectronics
Fairchild	Sanken Electric
Semiconductor	Shindengen Electric
IXYS	Manufacturing
Infineon Technologies	Siliconix
Microsemi	Toshiba Semiconductor
NXP Semiconductors	& Storage Products
ON Semiconductor	Vishay Intertechnology

HISTORICAL FINANCIALS

Company Type: Public

Income Statement				FYE: December 31
	REVENUE ($ mil.)	NET INCOME ($ mil.)	NET PROFIT MARGIN	EMPLOYEES
12/18	1,213.9	104.0	8.6%	7,710
12/17	1,054.2	(1.8)	—	8,586
12/16	942.1	15.9	1.7%	7,693
12/15	848.9	24.2	2.9%	7,695
12/14	890.6	63.6	7.1%	6,794
Annual Growth	8.1%	13.1%	—	3.2%

2018 Year-End Financials

Debt ratio: 14.6%
Return on equity: 11.8%
Cash ($ mil.): 241.0
Current ratio: 2.89
Long-term debt ($ mil.): 186.1
No. of shares (mil.): 50.2
Dividends
 Yield: —
 Payout: —
Market value ($ mil.): 1,620.0

	STOCK PRICE ($) FY Close	P/E High/Low		PER SHARE ($) Earnings	Dividends	Book Value
12/18	32.26	19	13	2.04	0.00	18.55
12/17	28.67	—	—	(0.04)	0.00	16.92
12/16	25.67	82	51	0.32	0.00	16.09
12/15	22.98	61	38	0.49	0.00	16.52
12/14	27.57	22	15	1.31	0.00	16.14
Annual Growth	4.0%			11.7%	—	3.5%

Diversified Gas & Oil PLC

Auditors: Crowe UK LLP

LOCATIONS

HQ: Diversified Gas & Oil PLC
1100 Corporate Drive, Birmingham, AL 35242
Phone:
Web: www.dgoc.com

HISTORICAL FINANCIALS

Company Type: Public

Income Statement				FYE: December 31
	REVENUE ($ mil.)	NET INCOME ($ mil.)	NET PROFIT MARGIN	EMPLOYEES
12/18	289.7	201.1	69.4%	600
12/17	41.7	8.8	21.2%	162
12/16	18.2	17.6	96.7%	74
12/15	6.3	(0.4)	—	39
12/14	7.3	(0.2)	—	32
Annual Growth	150.5%	—	—	108.1%

2018 Year-End Financials

Debt ratio: 31.2%
Return on equity: 47.9%
Cash ($ mil.): 1.3
Current ratio: 1.74
Long-term debt ($ mil.): 485.0
No. of shares (mil.): 542.6
Dividends
 Yield: —
 Payout: 21.5%
Market value ($ mil.): —

DMC Global Inc

Dynamic Materials Corporation (DMC) has an explosive personality when it comes to working with metal. Formerly Explosive Fabricators the company uses explosives to metallurgically bond or "clad" metal plates; the process usually joins a corrosion-resistant alloy with carbon steel — metals that do not bond easily. Its clad metal plates are central to making heavy-duty pressure vessels and heat exchangers used in such industries as alternative energy and shipbuilding. Its Oilfield Products segment (operating as DYNAenergetics) makes explosive devices used to knock open oil and gas wells. Its AMK Welding unit machines and welds parts for commercial and military aircraft engines and power-generation turbines.

EXECUTIVES

Vice President Operations, Gary Burke
Vice President Strategic Initiatives and Chief Information Officer, Jeff Fithian
Board Member, David Aldous
Board Member, Richard Graff
Auditors: Ernst & Young LLP

LOCATIONS

HQ: DMC Global Inc
11800 Ridge Parkway, Suite 300, Broomfield, CO 80021
Phone: 303 665-5700
Web: www.dmcglobal.com

PRODUCTS/OPERATIONS

2015 Sales

	$ mil.	% of total
NobelClad	90.0	54
DynaEnergetics	76.9	46
Total	**166.9**	**100**

COMPETITORS

AMETEK	Halliburton
American Commerce	Japan Steel Works
Solutions	Metal Fabricators and
Asahi Kasei	Welding
Eagle-Picher	Schlumberger
Engineered Materials	Technical Materials
Solutions	
HITCO Carbon	
Composites	

HISTORICAL FINANCIALS
Company Type: Public

Income Statement — FYE: December 31

	REVENUE ($ mil.)	NET INCOME ($ mil.)	NET PROFIT MARGIN	EMPLOYEES
12/18	326.4	30.4	9.3%	665
12/17	192.8	(18.8)	—	536
12/16	158.5	(6.5)	—	428
12/15	166.9	(23.9)	—	424
12/14	202.5	2.5	1.3%	503
Annual Growth	12.7%	85.6%	—	7.2%

2018 Year-End Financials
Debt ratio: 17.2%
Return on equity: 25.3%
Cash ($ mil.): 13.3
Current ratio: 2.05
Long-term debt ($ mil.): 38.2
No. of shares (mil.): 14.9
Dividends
 Yield: 0.2%
 Payout: 8.9%
Market value ($ mil.): 523.0

	STOCK PRICE ($) FY Close	P/E High/Low		PER SHARE ($) Earnings	Dividends	Book Value
12/18	35.12	25	10	2.04	0.08	9.01
12/17	25.05	—	—	(1.31)	0.08	7.16
12/16	15.85	—	—	(0.46)	0.08	7.75
12/15	6.99	—	—	(1.72)	0.14	8.33
12/14	16.02	133	85	0.18	0.16	11.07
Annual Growth	21.7%			83.5%	(15.9%)	(5.0%)

Douglas Dynamics, Inc.

EXECUTIVES
Chairman President and CEO, James L. Janik, $490,348 total compensation
EVP and CFO, Robert McCormick, $310,724 total compensation
SVP Sales and Marketing, Mark Adamson, age 62, $237,461 total compensation
SVP Operations, Keith Hagelin, age 59, $227,660 total compensation
Auditors: Ernst & Young LLP

LOCATIONS
HQ: Douglas Dynamics, Inc.
7777 North 73rd Street, Milwaukee, WI 53223
Phone: 414 354-2310
Web: www.douglasdynamics.com

PRODUCTS/OPERATIONS

2015 Sales

	$ mil.	% of total
Equipment	349.4	87
Parts & accessories	51.0	13
Total	400.4	100

Selected Brands
Blizzard
Fisher
Snowex
Sweepex
Turfex
Western

COMPETITORS
Dana
Tenneco
Visteon
ZF Friedrichshafen

HISTORICAL FINANCIALS
Company Type: Public

Income Statement — FYE: December 31

	REVENUE ($ mil.)	NET INCOME ($ mil.)	NET PROFIT MARGIN	EMPLOYEES
12/18	524.0	43.9	8.4%	1,663
12/17	474.9	55.3	11.6%	1,664
12/16	416.2	39.0	9.4%	1,633
12/15	400.4	44.1	11.0%	1,104
12/14	303.5	39.9	13.2%	993
Annual Growth	14.6%	2.4%	—	13.8%

2018 Year-End Financials
Debt ratio: 40.7%
Return on equity: 16.2%
Cash ($ mil.): 27.8
Current ratio: 2.52
Long-term debt ($ mil.): 242.9
No. of shares (mil.): 22.7
Dividends
 Yield: 2.9%
 Payout: 56.0%
Market value ($ mil.): 815.0

	STOCK PRICE ($) FY Close	P/E High/Low		PER SHARE ($) Earnings	Dividends	Book Value
12/18	35.89	26	18	1.89	1.06	12.46
12/17	37.80	18	12	2.40	0.96	11.36
12/16	33.65	20	10	1.70	0.94	9.80
12/15	21.07	12	10	1.94	0.89	8.96
12/14	21.43	14	8	1.77	0.87	7.78
Annual Growth	13.8%			1.7%	5.1%	12.5%

Douglas Emmett Inc

Office Space is more than the name of a cult movie to Douglas Emmett. The self-administered and self-managed real estate investment trust (REIT) invests in commercial real estate in Southern California and Hawaii. It owns about 50 Class A office properties (totaling 13.3 million sq. ft.) mostly in the heart of Hollywood and surrounding areas. Its office holdings account for about 85% of its total revenues. The REIT also owns nearly 2900 apartment units in tony neighborhoods of West Los Angeles and Honolulu. Douglas Emmett's portfolio includes some of the most notable addresses on the West Coast including the famed Sherman Oaks Galleria Burbank's Studio Plaza and office tower 100 Wilshire.

Geographic Reach

The Santa Monica-based firm's portfolio includes properties in California and Hawaii. Submarkets include Los Angeles County (Brentwood Olympic Corridor Century City Santa Monica Beverly Hills Westwood Sherman Oaks/Encino Warner Center/Woodland Hills and Burbank) and Honolulu. Douglas Emmett has a growing presence in Honolulu where it controls about 35% of the office market.

Financial Performance

The REIT reported $591.5 million in revenue in 2013 a 2% gain versus 2012. Net income rose 98% to $45.3 million over the same period. Indeed 2013 marked the third consecutive year of rising revenue and profit — as well as rising average office rental rates — for the firm after the economic recession caused some tenants to downsize or default on rents in 2009 and 2010. Revenue from the REIT's multifamily properties increased by about 4% year over year while office rental revenue was up less than by nearly 1%.

Strategy

Douglas Emmett which targets tenants in the health care legal entertainment and technology industries operates in markets where high barriers to entry such as environmental restrictions or steep property values limit new competition. Its properties are often located in communities with high-end lifestyle amenities and a diverse economic base. The company is a relatively conservative investor maintaining its portfolio while slowly making new acquisitions and considering new markets.

Focusing on its core submarkets the REIT is working on two multifamily projects one in Brentwood in Los Angeles and the other in Honolulu. It expects to break ground on another 452 apartments at its Moanalua Hillside Apartments in Honolulu by mid-2014. It's also seeking to build a highrise apartment project in Los Angeles although construction isn't expected to begin before at least mid-2015.

Mergers and Acquisitions

In August 2013 the REIT purchased a 191000-square-foot Class A office building on Ventura Blvd. for $61 million. In May Douglas Emmett bought a 225000-square-foot Class A office building at 8484 Wilshire Blvd. in Beverly Hills for $89 million.

In 2010 the REIT acquired Bishop Square the largest office project in Hawaii.

EXECUTIVES
Chief Investment Officer, Kevin A. Crummy, $600,000 total compensation
President and CEO, Jordan L. Kaplan, age 58, $1,000,000 total compensation
COO, Kenneth M. (Ken) Panzer, age 59, $1,000,000 total compensation
CFO, Mona Gisler, age 47
Senior Vice President, Kevin Kuritani
Senior Vice President Commercial Leasing, Andrew Goodman
Senior Vice President, Michele Aronson
Chairman, Dan A. Emmett, age 79
Board Member, Thomas O'hern
Board Member, Christopher Anderson
Board Member, William Simon
Board Member, Virginia Mcferran
Auditors: Ernst & Young LLP

LOCATIONS
HQ: Douglas Emmett Inc
1299 Ocean Avenue, Suite 1000, Santa Monica, CA 90401
Phone: 310 255-7700
Web: www.douglasemmett.com

PRODUCTS/OPERATIONS

2015 Sales

	$ mil.	% of total
Office rental		
Rental revenues	412.5	65
Parking and other income	85.4	13
Tenant recoveries	43.1	7
Multifamily rental		
Rental revenues	87.9	14
Parking and other income	6.9	1
Total	635.8	100

COMPETITORS

Apartment Investment and Management	Hudson Pacific
C.J. Segerstrom & Sons	Intergroup
Castle & Cooke	Irvine Company
Equity Residential	Kilroy Realty
Essex Property Trust	Majestic Realty
Gables Residential Services	UDR
	Vestar Development

HISTORICAL FINANCIALS

Company Type: Public

Income Statement — FYE: December 31

	REVENUE ($ mil.)	NET INCOME ($ mil.)	NET PROFIT MARGIN	EMPLOYEES
12/18	881.3	116.0	13.2%	670
12/17	812.0	94.4	11.6%	600
12/16	742.5	85.4	11.5%	600
12/15	635.7	58.3	9.2%	600
12/14	599.5	44.6	7.4%	560
Annual Growth	10.1%	27.0%	—	4.6%

2018 Year-End Financials

Debt ratio: 50.0%
Return on equity: 4.8%
Cash ($ mil.): 146.2
Current ratio: 1.02
Long-term debt ($ mil.): 4,134.0
No. of shares (mil.): 170.2
Dividends
  Yield: 2.9%
  Payout: 148.5%
Market value ($ mil.): 5,809.0

	STOCK PRICE ($) FY Close	P/E High/Low	Earnings	Dividends	Book Value
12/18	34.13	60 48	0.68	1.01	14.11
12/17	41.06	71 63	0.58	0.94	14.38
12/16	36.56	68 44	0.55	0.89	12.68
12/15	31.18	80 67	0.39	0.85	13.11
12/14	28.40	95 75	0.30	0.81	13.42
Annual Growth	4.7%	— —	22.7%	5.7%	1.3%

Duluth Holdings Inc

Auditors: Grant Thornton LLP

LOCATIONS

HQ: Duluth Holdings Inc
201 East Front Street, Mount Horeb, WI 53572
Phone: 608 424-1544
Web: www.duluthtrading.com

HISTORICAL FINANCIALS

Company Type: Public

Income Statement — FYE: February 3

	REVENUE ($ mil.)	NET INCOME ($ mil.)	NET PROFIT MARGIN	EMPLOYEES
02/19*	568.1	23.1	4.1%	2,794
01/18	471.4	23.3	5.0%	2,172
01/17	376.1	21.3	5.7%	1,627
01/16	304.1	27.4	9.0%	1,187
02/15	231.8	23.6	10.2%	1,316
Annual Growth	25.1%	(0.5%)	—	20.7%

*Fiscal year change

2019 Year-End Financials

Debt ratio: 23.5%
Return on equity: 15.3%
Cash ($ mil.): 0.7
Current ratio: 2.25
Long-term debt ($ mil.): 69.3
No. of shares (mil.): 32.5
Dividends
  Yield: —
  Payout: —
Market value ($ mil.): 765.0

	STOCK PRICE ($) FY Close	P/E High/Low	Earnings	Dividends	Book Value
02/19*	23.48	48 23	0.72	0.00	4.92
01/18	18.68	32 21	0.72	0.00	4.19
01/17	22.97	55 21	0.66	0.00	3.43
01/16	16.51	16 13	1.06	0.00	2.75
Annual Growth	12.5%	— —	(12.1%)	—	21.4%

*Fiscal year change

Dunkin' Brands Group Inc

Dunkin' Brands Group is a leading quick service restaurant franchisor operating both the Dunkin' and Baskin-Robbins chains with more than 20900 locations in about 60 countries. Dunkin' is the world's leading donut chain boasting nearly 13000 units in about 45 countries (including approximately 3500 in the US). Baskin-Robbins is a top ice cream and frozen snacks outlet with more than 8000 locations in about 55 countries (some 2600 in the US). Having divested all its company-operated restaurants Dunkin' Brands counts royalty income and franchise fees as a key revenue source. The company ropped the "Donuts" from its name in 2019. It was founded in 1950.

Financial Performance

Over the five-year period from 2014 to 2018 the company reported year-over-year revenue growth thanks to strong performance in the espresso iced coffee and other beverage categories. It posted a particularly significant spike in 2016 when it benefited from transitioning its stores to franchisee-operated locations. Net income was more choppy falling and rising to hit a high in 2017.

Dunkin Brands generated $1.32 billion in revenue in 2018 a 3.61% increase from 2017. Much of the growth was attributed to sales increases at Dunkin' stores in the Middle East Europe Latin America and South Korea. In the US Dunkin's growth was driven primarily by beverage sales including iced coffee frozen and espresso drinks and breakfast sandwich sales. Ice cream sales at Baskin-Robbins' US stores declined in 2018. However Baskin-Robbins' International comparable store sales increased 3.8% due to growth in South Korea and Japan.

Net income in 2018 dropped to $229.9 million versus $271.2 million in 2017 driven by an increase in income tax expense. It also reported an increase in net interest expense due to borrowings incurred during a refinancing transaction completed during 2017.

Net cash was $517.6 million for the year. Net cash provided by operating activities was $269.0 million. Cash used in investing activities was $51.8 million and cash for financing activities $732.4 million.

Strategy

The company claims its franchise business model offers strategic and financial benefits. Because it doesn't own or operate restaurants it can focus on menu innovation marketing and franchisee support. Financially the franchise model allows it to expand globally with limited investment in construction and operating expenses. The business model also lets Dunkin' Brands control how franchisees operate their shops helping ensure consistency in quality and service.

In 2018 approximately 44% of revenue was derived from royalty income and franchise fees. The company also receives fees from franchisees for providing advertising services (37% of revenues). Advertising fees are paid on a weekly basis based on a percentage of franchisee gross sales. Other revenue comes from rental income from franchisees that lease their properties from the firm and sales of ice cream and other products to franchisees in certain international markets.

As part of a rebranding effort in 2019 Dunkin' dropped the "Donuts" from its restaurant name as it continues its focus on selling coffee and other drinks. Beverages especially coffee make up 60% of Dunkin's US sales. At the same time the restaurant chain is overhauling its stores modernizing the designs with digital kiosks mobile order drive-through lanes and an expanded Grab & Go section. It is also introducing cold nitro brew coffee and other new drinks.

EXECUTIVES

SVP and Chief Communications Officer, Karen Raskopf, age 64
SVP and Chief Brand Officer Baskin-Robbins U.S. and Canada, William M. (Bill) Mitchell, age 53, $504,808 total compensation
SVP Baskin-Robbins U.S. and Canada, Weldon Spangler, age 53
Chief Information and Strategy Officer, Jack Clare, age 48
Chairman and CEO, Nigel Travis, age 69, $1,019,231 total compensation
President DunkinÂ' Donuts U.S. and Canada, David L. (Dave) Hoffmann, age 51, $175,000 total compensation
CFO, Kate Jaspon
Senior Vice President Chief Supply Officer, Scott Murphy
Regional Vice President Midwest, Jean Grossman
Regional Vice President Philadelphia Baltimore Washington And Puerto Rico, Lou Beccarelli
Vice President Infrastructure Information Securi, Santhosh Kumar
Senior Vice President And Chief Information Officer, Kim Cairns
Board Member, Linda Boff
Board Member, Roland Smith
Auditors: KPMG LLP

LOCATIONS

HQ: Dunkin' Brands Group Inc
130 Royall Street, Canton, MA 02021
Phone: 781 737-3000
Web: www.dunkinbrands.com

PRODUCTS/OPERATIONS

2015 Sales

	$ mil.	% of total
Franchise fees and royalty income	513.2	63
Sales of ice cream products	115.2	14
Rental Income	100.4	12
Sale of company-owned restaurants	28.3	3
Other	53.6	8
Total	**810.9**	**100**

2015 Sales

	% of total
Dunkin' Donuts	
US	73
International	3
Baskin Robbins	
International	15
US	6
Other	4
Total	**100**

Selected Menu Items
Dunkin' Donuts
  Coffee
  Donuts
  Other bakery products
  Muffins
  Bagels
  Breakfast sandwiches
Baskin-Robbins
  Beverages
  Frozen coffee drinks
  Shakes
  Smoothies
  Cakes
  Ice cream
  Soft serve
  Sundaes

COMPETITORS

Auntie Anne's	Krispy Kreme
Bruegger's	McDonald's
Burger King	Mrs. Fields
Dairy Queen	Peet's Coffee & Tea
Daylight Donuts	Starbucks
Einstein Noah Restaurant Group	Subway
FOCUS Brands	Tim Hortons
Fresh «ns	Wendy's
Kahala	YUM!

HISTORICAL FINANCIALS
Company Type: Public

Income Statement FYE: December 29

	REVENUE ($ mil.)	NET INCOME ($ mil.)	NET PROFIT MARGIN	EMPLOYEES
12/18	1,321.6	229.9	17.4%	1,107
12/17	860.5	350.9	40.8%	1,148
12/16	828.8	195.5	23.6%	1,163
12/15	810.9	105.2	13.0%	1,145
12/14	748.7	176.3	23.6%	1,134
Annual Growth	15.3%	6.9%	—	(0.6%)

2018 Year-End Financials
Debt ratio: 88.2%
Return on equity: —
Cash ($ mil.): 517.5
Current ratio: 1.51
Long-term debt ($ mil.): 3,017.6
No. of shares (mil.): 82.5
Dividends
  Yield: 0.0%
  Payout: 51.2%
Market value ($ mil.): 5,236.0

	STOCK PRICE ($) FY Close	P/E High/Low		Earnings	PER SHARE ($) Dividends	Book Value
12/18	63.42	28	21	2.71	1.39	(8.63)
12/17	64.47	17	13	3.80	1.29	0.09
12/16	52.44	26	18	2.11	1.20	(1.79)
12/15	42.36	51	36	1.08	1.06	(2.39)
12/14	42.37	32	25	1.65	0.92	3.52
Annual Growth	10.6%	—	—	13.2%	10.9%	

e.l.f. Beauty Inc

Auditors: DELOITTE & TOUCHE LLP

LOCATIONS
HQ: e.l.f. Beauty Inc
  570 10th Street, Oakland, CA 94607
Phone: 510 778-7787
Web: www.elfcosmetics.com

HISTORICAL FINANCIALS
Company Type: Public

Income Statement FYE: December 31

	REVENUE ($ mil.)	NET INCOME ($ mil.)	NET PROFIT MARGIN	EMPLOYEES
12/18	267.4	15.5	5.8%	414
12/17	269.8	33.4	12.4%	413
12/16	229.5	5.3	2.3%	351
12/15	191.4	4.3	2.3%	231
12/14	135.1	(9.2)	—	0
Annual Growth	18.6%	—	—	—

2018 Year-End Financials
Debt ratio: 34.5%
Return on equity: 7.3%
Cash ($ mil.): 51.2
Current ratio: 3.30
Long-term debt ($ mil.): 140.5
No. of shares (mil.): 48.7
Dividends
  Yield: —
  Payout: —
Market value ($ mil.): 422.0

	STOCK PRICE ($) FY Close	P/E High/Low		Earnings	PER SHARE ($) Dividends	Book Value
12/18	8.66	68	24	0.32	0.00	4.71
12/17	22.31	40	26	0.68	0.00	4.16
12/16	28.94	—	—	(39.47)	0.00	3.11
Annual Growth	(45.3%)	—	—	—	—	23.0%

EACO Corp

EXECUTIVES
Chairman and CEO; CEO Bisco, Glen F. Ceiley, age 67
Director; VP Technology Bisco, William L. Means, age 69
President and COO Bisco, Donald S. (Don) Wagner, age 51
Controller, Michael Bains
Auditors: SQUAR MILNER LLP

LOCATIONS
HQ: EACO Corp
  1500 North Lakeview Loop, Anaheim, CA 92807
Phone: 714 876-2490
Web: www.eacocorp.com

COMPETITORS

Allied Electronics	Newark Corporation
Digi-Key	Realty Income
GE Franchise Finance	

HISTORICAL FINANCIALS
Company Type: Public

Income Statement FYE: August 31

	REVENUE ($ mil.)	NET INCOME ($ mil.)	NET PROFIT MARGIN	EMPLOYEES
08/19	221.2	9.4	4.3%	489
08/18	193.2	6.9	3.6%	464
08/17	156.9	4.0	2.6%	407
08/16	148.5	4.1	2.8%	414
08/15	140.2	3.7	2.7%	424
Annual Growth	12.1%	26.0%	—	3.6%

2019 Year-End Financials
Debt ratio: 12.4%
Return on equity: 20.2%
Cash ($ mil.): 4.6
Current ratio: 2.26
Long-term debt ($ mil.): 6.1
No. of shares (mil.): 4.8
Dividends
  Yield: —
  Payout: —
Market value ($ mil.): 95.0

	STOCK PRICE ($) FY Close	P/E High/Low		Earnings	PER SHARE ($) Dividends	Book Value
08/19	19.55	10	6	1.92	0.00	10.53
08/18	14.00	10	4	1.41	0.00	8.62
08/17	6.32	11	7	0.82	0.00	7.16
08/16	5.96	7	6	0.83	0.00	6.34
08/15	5.20	25	6	0.75	0.00	5.54
Annual Growth	39.2%	—	—	26.5%	—	17.4%

Eagle Bancorp Inc (MD)

For those nest eggs that need a little help hatching holding company Eagle Bancorp would recommend its community-oriented EagleBank subsidiary. The bank serves businesses and individuals through more than 20 branches in Maryland Virginia and Washington DC and its suburbs. Deposit products include checking savings and money market accounts; certificates of deposit; and IRAs. Commercial real estate loans represent more than 70% of its loan portfolio while construction loans make up another more than 20%. The bank which has significant expertise as a Small Business Administration lender also writes business consumer and home equity loans. EagleBank offers insurance products through an agreement with The Meltzer Group.

Operations

Like other retail banks Eagle Bancorp makes the bulk of its money from loan interest. About 86% of its total revenue came from loan interest (including fees) during 2015 while another 4% came from interest on investment securities. The rest of its revenue came from deposit account service charges (2% of revenue) and non-recurring income sources.

The bank has two direct subsidiaries: Bethesda Leasing LLC which holds the bank's foreclosed real estate (owned and acquired); and Eagle Insurance Services LLC which provides commercial and retail insurance products through a referral arrangement with insurance broker The Meltzer Group.

Geographic Reach
The Bethesda Maryland-based bank operates 21 branches in Maryland Virginia and Washington DC (as of mid-2016) including nine in Northern Virginia seven in Montgomery County and five in the District of Columbia.

Sales and Marketing
Eagle Bancorp serves local businesses professional clients individuals sole proprietors small and medium-sized businesses non-profits and investors. Other clients are from the healthcare accountant and attorney markets.

The bank spent $2.7 million on marketing and advertising during 2015 up 38% from the $2 million it spent in 2014 mostly due to higher digital and print advertising and sponsorship costs.

Financial Performance
Eagle Bancorp's annual revenue has more than doubled since 2011 mostly thanks to strong loan growth with the addition of new branches. Meanwhile its net income has more than tripled as the bank has kept a lid on credit loss provisions and overhead costs.

The bank's revenue jumped 33% to $279.8 million during 2015 largely thanks to a rise in interest income as its loan assets grew 16%.

Strong revenue growth in 2015 coupled with an absence of merger expenses drove Eagle Bancorp's net income up 55% to $84.1 million. The bank's operating cash levels spiked 66% to $98.5 million for the year thanks to a strong rise in cash-based earnings.

Strategy
The company has been focused on growing within its existing markets. Its strategy for further growth includes continuing to seek opportunities to open or acquire new banking locations while waiting out record low interest rates. Eagle's strict loan underwriting standards — it didn't write subprime residential mortgages and didn't buy securities backed by subprime mortgages — has helped it have fewer problem loans the downfall for many banks.

Beyond its core lending and deposit businesses Eagle Bancorp continues to expand its other product offerings as well. In 2015 it introduced a Full Service Equipment Leasing program which provided alternative and convenient financing for all types of business equipment for customers.

Mergers and Acquisitions
In November 2014 Eagle Bancorp significantly expanded its presence in Northern Virginia after it purchased Fairfax County-based Virginia Heritage. The deal added six Virginia Heritage Bank branches (renamed as EagleBank) in northern Virginia along with $917.4 million in assets — including $715 million in loans and $737 million in deposits.

EXECUTIVES

EVP; SEVP and COO EagleBank, Susan G. Riel, age 70, $478,806 total compensation
Chairman President and CEO; Chairman and CEO EagleBank; President Ronald D. Paul Cos., Ronald D. Paul, age 64, $863,565 total compensation
EVP; EVP and Chief Credit Officer EagleBank, Janice L. Williams, age 62, $391,758 total compensation
EVP and General Counsel Eagle Bancorp and EagleBank, Laurence E. Bensignor, age 63
EVP; EVP and Chief Lending Officer Commercial Real Estate EagleBank, Antonio F. Marquez, age 61, $368,256 total compensation
EVP; EVP and Chief Lending Officer Commercial and Industrial EagleBank, Lindsey S. Rheaume, age 59
EVP and CFO, Charles D. Levingston, age 39
Vice President, Joan Grant
Vice President Special Assets, Jodee Lichtenstein
Senior Vice President Commercial Banking Team Leader, Derek Whitwer
Vice President, Linda Dawkins
Vice President Facilities Operations Manager, Shawn Cox
Vice Chairman Of The Board Of Company And Bank, Norman Pozez
Vice President Treasurer, Scott Clark
Auditors: Dixon Hughes Goodman LLP

LOCATIONS
HQ: Eagle Bancorp Inc (MD)
7830 Old Georgetown Road, Third Floor, Bethesda, MD 20814
Phone: 301 986-1800
Web: www.eaglebankcorp.com

PRODUCTS/OPERATIONS
Selected Subsidiaries
EagleBank
  Bethesda Leasing LLC
  Eagle Insurance Services LLC
  Fidelity Mortgage Inc.
Eagle Commercial Ventures LLC

COMPETITORS
BB&T
Bank of America
Capital One
M&T Bank
OBA Financial Services
PNC Financial
Sandy Spring Bancorp
SunTrust

HISTORICAL FINANCIALS
Company Type: Public

Income Statement
FYE: December 31

	ASSETS ($ mil.)	NET INCOME ($ mil.)	INCOME AS % OF ASSETS	EMPLOYEES
12/18	8,389.1	152.2	1.8%	470
12/17	7,479.0	100.2	1.3%	466
12/16	6,890.1	97.7	1.4%	469
12/15	6,076.6	84.1	1.4%	434
12/14	5,247.8	54.2	1.0%	427
Annual Growth	12.4%	29.4%	—	2.4%

2018 Year-End Financials
Return on assets: 1.9%
Return on equity: 14.7%
Long-term debt ($ mil.): —
No. of shares (mil.): 34.3
Sales ($ mil): 415.8
Dividends
  Yield: —
  Payout: —
Market value ($ mil.): 1,675.0

	STOCK PRICE ($) FY Close	P/E High/Low	PER SHARE ($) Earnings	Dividends	Book Value
12/18	48.71	15 10	4.42	0.00	32.25
12/17	57.90	23 17	2.92	0.00	27.80
12/16	60.95	22 15	2.86	0.00	24.77
12/15	50.47	22 13	2.50	0.00	22.07
12/14	35.52	18 15	1.95	0.00	20.60
Annual Growth	8.2%	— —	22.7%	—	11.9%

Eagle Bulk Shipping Inc

Some eagles soar through the skies but Eagle Bulk Shipping rides the waves. The company owns a fleet of 45 Handymax dry bulk carriers that it charters to customers typically on one- to three-year contracts. Most of its vessels are classified as Supramaxes and range in capacity from 50000 to 60000 deadweight tons (DWT). Overall the company's fleet has a carrying capacity of more than 1.1 million DWT. Cargo carried by charterers of Eagle Bulk Shipping's vessels includes cement coal fertilizer grain and iron ore. In mid-2014 Eagle Bulk Shipping filed for Chapter 11 bankruptcy protection and emerged in October of the same year.

Financial Performance
In 2011 Eagle's revenues reached historic levels. It generated $313 million in total sales an 18% increase from the $265 million it posted in 2010. The increase in revenue was due to the company's expanded fleet size and ability to transport more goods and freight and serve additional customers. However the other side of that coin was that it suffered a net loss of almost $15 million as a result of the expenses paid to add eight vessels to its fleet. The 2011 net loss represented Eagle's first period of unprofitability in six years.

Strategy
Eagle is focused on utilizing its newly enhanced fleet size to achieve growth. After adding several ships in 2010 the company's operating days (the number of days vessels actually generate revenues) increased nearly 50%. The company added eight additional vessels by the end of 2011 and increased its potential DWT by more than 450000. The company also began utilizing chartered in (ships leased for a specified period of time) in late 2010 to meet shipping demands.

EXECUTIVES

Chairman and CEO, Sophocles N. Zoullas, age 49, $875,000 total compensation
CFO and Secretary, Alan S. Ginsberg, age 56, $275,282 total compensation
COO Eagle Shipping International (USA), Claude G. Thouret Jr.
Director; President Eagle Shipping International, Alexis P. Zoullas, age 44
Chief Financial Officer; Principal Financial Officer and Principal Accounting Officer, Adir Katzav
Director, Thomas B. Winmill, age 54
Director, Joseph M. Cianciolo, age 76
Director, David B. Hiley, age 76
Director, Forrest E. Wylie, age 51

Director, Douglas P. Haensel, age 52
Director, Jon Tomasson, age 56
Director; President Eagle Shipping International, Alexis P. Zoullas, age 44
Auditors: DELOITTE & TOUCHE LLP

LOCATIONS

HQ: Eagle Bulk Shipping Inc
300 First Stamford Place, 5th Floor, Stamford, CT 06902
Phone: 203 276-8100
Web: www.eagleships.com

PRODUCTS/OPERATIONS

Selected Vessels

Avocet
Bittern
Canary
Cardinal
Condor
Crane
Crested Ea
Crowned
Egret Bulk
Falcon
Gannet Bul
Golden Eag
Goldeneye
Grebe Bulk
Harrier
Hawk I
Ibis Bulke
Imperial E
Jaeger0
Jay
Kestrel I
Kingfisher
Kite
Kittiwake
Martin
Merlin
NightHawk
Oriole
Osprey I(
Owl
Peregrine
Petrel Bul
Puffin Bul
Redwing
Roadrunner
Sandpiper
Shrike0
Skua
Sparrow
Stellar Ea
Tern
Thrasher(
Thrush
Woodstar(
Wren

COMPETITORS

A.P. M_ller - M_rsk
DryShips Inc.
Excel Maritime Carriers
Genco Shipping and Trading
Hanjin Shipping
Kawasaki Kisen
Mitsui O.S.K. Lines
Overseas Shipholding Group
Pacific Basin Shipping
Star Bulk

HISTORICAL FINANCIALS
Company Type: Public

Income Statement — FYE: December 31

	REVENUE ($ mil.)	NET INCOME ($ mil.)	NET PROFIT MARGIN	EMPLOYEES
12/18	310.0	12.5	4.1%	912
12/17	236.7	(43.8)	—	941
12/16	124.4	(223.5)	—	820
12/15	103.8	(148.3)	—	0
12/14	31.0	(11.5)	—	0
Annual Growth	77.7%	—	—	—

2018 Year-End Financials

Debt ratio: 39.0%
Return on equity: 2.6%
Cash ($ mil.): 67.2
Current ratio: 1.88
Long-term debt ($ mil.): 301.5
No. of shares (mil.): 71.0
Dividends
  Yield: —
  Payout: —
Market value ($ mil.): —

Eagle Pharmaceuticals, Inc.

Like the talons of its namesake Eagle Pharmaceuticals specializes in sharps. The firm develops and commercializes injectable treatments primarily to address unmet needs in oncology and critical care. The company has five FDA-approved products — blood thinner Argatroban malignant hyperthermia treatment Ryanodex anti-inflammatory drug diclofenac-misoprostol cancer drug Non-Alcohol Docetaxel Injection and leukemia and non-Hodgkin lymphoma treatment Bendeka. Eagle Pharmaceuticals also has a handful of candidates under development. Commercial and development partners include Cephalon Albany Molecular Research Sandoz and The Medicines Company.

Operations
Eagle Pharmaceuticals has four candidates either in late-stage development or under FDA review.

Sales and Marketing
Going forward Eagle plans to keep its US sales and marketing efforts in-house while using partners and third-parties for European distribution.

Financial Performance
In 2014 Eagle changed its fiscal year end from September to December. When combining the revenue for the entire year the company made $24.7 million in 2014. The following year revenue rose 168% to $66.2 million. This was primarily due to $45 million in licensing and other revenue but also largely due to an increase in product sales and a doubling of royalty earnings. The company recognizes licensing revenue from Teva subsidiary Cephalon related to sales of Bendeka.

After years of losing money and thanks to the increased revenue Eagle entered the black in 2015 with $2.6 million in net income (compared to a loss of $23.5 million in 2014).

Strategy
A big part of Eagle's strategy for success is to be ready when the patent expires on a popular drug and release its "new and improved" version no later than the first generic. It feels it can offer a price point and efficacy improvement over the name brand while offering something closer to a brand than the generics. The company intends to leverage its knowledge of the approval process to line up improved drugs for launch. It will partner for European sales and handle domestic sales and marketing itself while continuing to expand its intellectual property portfolio.

Mergers and Acquisitions
In late 2016 Eagle agreed to buy Arsia Therapeutics for some $30 million plus up to an additional $48 million in milestone payments. That deal will mark the company's entry into the biosimilar market.

EXECUTIVES

President CEO and Director, Scott L. Tarriff, age 59, $645,590 total compensation
EVP Research and Development, Peter E. Grebow, age 72
CFO, David E. Riggs, age 67, $390,913 total compensation
EVP and Chief Scientific Officer, Steven L. Krill, age 59, $390,913 total compensation
EVP and Chief Medical Officer, Adrian Hepner, age 57, $311,766 total compensation
EVP and General Counsel, John LaRocca
SVP Sales and Marketing, Sherry Korczynski
Vice President Of Portfolio and Project Management, Linda Dell
Vice President Finance, Brian Cahill
Chairman, Michael (Mike) Graves, age 56
Auditors: BDO USA, LLP

LOCATIONS

HQ: Eagle Pharmaceuticals, Inc.
50 Tice Boulevard, Suite 315, Woodcliff Lake, NJ 07677
Phone: 201 326-5300
Web: www.eagleus.com

PRODUCTS/OPERATIONS

2016 Sales

	$ mil.	% of total
Product sales	13.0	20
Royalty income	8.2	12
License and other income	45.0	68
Total	**66.2**	**100**

COMPETITORS

Abbott Labs
Allergan plc
AstraZeneca
Bayer HealthCare Pharmaceuticals Inc.
Biogen
Bristol-Myers Squibb
GlaxoSmithKline
Johnson & Johnson
Merck
Mylan
Novartis
Pfizer
Sandoz International GmbH
Sanofi
Teva

HISTORICAL FINANCIALS
Company Type: Public

Income Statement — FYE: December 31

	REVENUE ($ mil.)	NET INCOME ($ mil.)	NET PROFIT MARGIN	EMPLOYEES
12/18	213.3	31.9	15.0%	96
12/17	236.7	51.9	21.9%	108
12/16	189.4	81.4	43.0%	77
12/15	66.2	2.5	3.9%	41
12/14	5.6	(5.5)	—	0
Annual Growth	148.4%	—	—	—

Earthstone Energy Inc

2018 Year-End Financials

Debt ratio: 18.6%
Return on equity: 18.7%
Cash ($ mil.): 78.7
Current ratio: 4.13
Long-term debt ($ mil.): 38.1
No. of shares (mil.): 13.9
Dividends
  Yield: —
  Payout: —
Market value ($ mil.): 561.0

	STOCK PRICE ($) FY Close	P/E High/Low		Earnings	Dividends	Book Value
12/18	40.29	39	17	2.09	0.00	11.55
12/17	53.42	28	14	3.27	0.00	12.07
12/16	79.34	17	6	4.96	0.00	9.87
12/15	88.67	592	90	0.16	0.00	5.78
12/14	15.50	—	—	(0.39)	0.00	1.99
Annual Growth	27.0%			—	—	55.3%

EXECUTIVES

EVP Drilling and Development, Francis M. Mury, age 67
President and CEO, Frank A. Lodzinski, age 70
EVP Northern Region, Ray Singleton, age 68, $183,574 total compensation
EVP Accounting and Administration, Tony Oviedo
EVP Corporate Development and Engineering, Robert J. Anderson, age 57
EVP and CFO, Mark Lumpkin
EVP Land and Marketing, Christopher E. Cottrell
EVP Completions and Operations, Steven C. Collins
EVP Geology and Geophysics, Timothy D. Merrifield
Vice President, Bill Wiederkehr
Auditors: Moss Adams, LLP

LOCATIONS

HQ: Earthstone Energy Inc
1400 Woodloch Forest Drive, Suite 300, The Woodlands, TX 77380
Phone: 281 298-4246
Web: www.earthstoneenergy.com

COMPETITORS

Canadian Natural
Chesapeake Energy
ConocoPhillips
PDC Energy
Pioneer Natural Resources
SM Energy
SRC Energy
Statoil
TransGlobe Energy
Williams Companies

HISTORICAL FINANCIALS

Company Type: Public

Income Statement   FYE: December 31

	REVENUE ($ mil.)	NET INCOME ($ mil.)	NET PROFIT MARGIN	EMPLOYEES
12/18	165.3	42.3	25.6%	65
12/17	108.0	(12.5)	—	58
12/16	42.2	(54.5)	—	49
12/15	49.3	(116.5)	—	51
12/14	47.9	(28.8)	—	52
Annual Growth	36.2%	—	—	5.7%

East West Bancorp, Inc

2018 Year-End Financials

Debt ratio: 7.8%
Return on equity: 13.7%
Cash ($ mil.): 0.3
Current ratio: 0.78
Long-term debt ($ mil.): 78.8
No. of shares (mil.): 64.1
Dividends
  Yield: —
  Payout: —
Market value ($ mil.): 290.0

	STOCK PRICE ($) FY Close	P/E High/Low		Earnings	Dividends	Book Value
12/18	4.52	8	3	1.50	0.00	5.22
12/17	10.63	—	—	(0.53)	0.00	4.39
12/16	13.74	—	—	(2.92)	0.00	10.84
12/15	13.31	—	—	(8.43)	0.00	14.46
12/14	23.50	—	—	(3.11)	0.00	22.90
Annual Growth	(33.8%) (30.9%)			—	—	—

East West Bancorp banks in both hemispheres of the world. It's the holding company for East West Bank which provides standard banking services and loans through more than 130 branches in major US metropolitan areas and about 10 offices across in China Hong Kong and Taiwan. Boasting $29 billion in assets East West Bank focuses on making commercial and industrial real estate loans which account for the majority of the company's loan portfolio. Catering to the Asian-American community it also provides international banking and trade financing to importers/exporters doing business in the Asia/Pacific region. East West Bank offers multilingual service in English Cantonese Mandarin Vietnamese and Spanish.

Operations
East West Bancorp operates two business segments. The commercial banking segment (which generated 62% of its total revenue in 2014) includes commercial industrial and commercial real estate primarily generates commercial and industrial real estate loans and offers a wide variety of international finance and trade services and products. The retail banking segment (33% of total revenue) focuses primarily on retail operations through the East West Bank's branch network. The bank also offers insurance products through East West Insurance.

Broadly speaking the bank made 93% of its revenue from loan interest (including fees) in 2014 and another 7% from interest on investment securities investment in Federal Home Loan Bank and Federal Reserve Bank Stock and short-term investments. It had a staff of roughly 2700 employees at the end of 2014.

Geographic Reach
East West's bank network in the US is mainly in California (in and around Los Angeles the San Francisco Bay area Orange County and Silicon Valley) and in the Atlanta Boston Houston New York and Seattle metropolitan areas. Internationally the bank has five branches in Hong Kong and Greater China (Shanghai Shantou and Shenzhen) and five representative offices in Beijing Chongqing Guangzhou Xiamen and Taiwan.

Sales and Marketing
East West Bancorp caters its banking and loan business to companies in the manufacturing wholesale trade and service sectors.

Financial Performance
The bank has struggled to consistently grow its revenues in recent years due to shrinking interest margins on loans amidst the low-interest environment. Its profits however have been rising thanks to declining loan loss provisions as its loan portfolio's credit quality has improved with higher property valuations in the strengthened economy.

East West had a breakout year in 2014 as its revenue climbed by 17% to $1.14 billion mostly thanks to an increase in non-covered loan volumes. Higher revenue in 2014 drove East West Bancorp's net income higher by 16% to $342.5 million. Lower income tax provisions resulting from additional purchases of affordable housing partnerships and tax-credited investments also help pad the bank's bottom line.

The bank's operating cash levels dipped by 8% to $392.9 million mostly due to unfavorable working capital changes related to accrued interest receivables and other asset balances.

Strategy
East West Bancorp's long-term vision reiterated in 2015 is to "serve as the financial bridge between the United States and Greater China" by reaching more customers with its cross-border products and capabilities. Its full-service branches in Greater China offer traditional letters of credit and trade finance between businesses while also providing the bank a way to serve existing clients and establish new business relationships.

Toward its international expansion plans the company opened two new branches in Greater China's Shenzhen and Shanghai Pilot Free Trade Zone during 2014 which would better position it to help its customers and facilitate their financial needs between Greater China and the US.

The bank may also occasionally pursue acquisitions of other banks to broaden its market reach and grow its loan and deposit business.

Mergers and Acquisitions
In 2014 East West Bancorp expanded its presence in Texas and California after it purchased Metrocorp along with its 19 MetroBank and Metro United Bank branches in the Houston Dallas and San Diego markets. The deal also added $1.7 billion in assets and $1.4 billion in new loan assets.

Company Background
East West Bancorp was founded in 1998.

In 2009 the company acquired more than 60 branches and most of the banking operations of larger rival United Commercial Bank which had been seized by regulators. The deal gave East West Bank about 40 more California branches plus some 20 additional US locations beyond the state.

EXECUTIVES

EVP Chief Risk Officer General Counsel and Secretary East West Bancorp and East West Bank, Douglas P. Krause, age 63, $403,090 total compensation
Chairman and CEO East West Bancorp and East West Bank, Dominic Ng, age 60, $1,000,000 total compensation
Vice Chairman East West Bancorp and East West Bank, John M. Lee, age 87
EVP and Head of International and Commercial Banking, Andy Yen, age 61, $370,977 total compensation

EVP and CFO East West Bancorp and East West Bank, Irene H. Oh, age 41, $403,090 total compensation
EVP and Chief Credit Officer East West Bank, Albert Sun, age 64
President and COO East West Bancorp and East West Bank, Gregory L. Guyett, age 55
EVP Head of U.S. Eastern and Texas Regions and Head of Consumer and Business Banking, Wendy Cai-Lee
First Vice President and Customer Communications Manager, Manni Liu
Senior Vice President Industry Manager, Victor Owens
Senior Vice President, Frances Ng
Senior Vice President, Bennett Chui
Vice President, Samsonz Lam
First Vice President Relationship Manager, Steve Reichmuth
Vice President Assistant Branch Manager El Monte, Fiona Yao
Vice President Bm, Betty Liaw
Vice President Business Development Officer, Ellen Chiang
Senior Vice President, Mary Wei
Avp Loan Portfolio Manager, Sheng-ta Tsai
Avp Loan Documentation And Funding, Jacquelynn Forte
Assistant Vice President Credit Analyst, Joseph Au
Senior Vice President Head Of Special Assets, Stuart Bonomo
Vice President Portfolio Manager Commercial Real Estate Eastern Region, Akmar Wallace
Vice President Tms Sales Consultant II, Stacy So
First Vice President, Johnny Cheng
First Vice President Head of Information Technology Operations, Bill Likes
First Vice President Loan Support Manager, Peggy Donovan
First Vice President Interest Rates And Foreign Exchange, Supat Tipayamongkol
Vice President Commercial Banking, Ricky Lam
Senior Vice President, Andrew Stein
Avp Tax Supervisor, Sophia Xie
Vice President Financial Planning Manager, Nia Chen
Senior Vice President, Al Cheng
Assistant Vice President, Elvira Valenzuela
Abm, Sophia Lam
Auditors: KPMG LLP

LOCATIONS

HQ: East West Bancorp, Inc
  135 North Los Robles Ave., 7th Floor, Pasadena, CA 91101
Phone: 626 768-6000
Web: www.eastwestbank.com

PRODUCTS/OPERATIONS

2011 Sales

	$ mil.	% of total
Commercial lending	619.8	57
Retail banking	358.8	33
Other & adjustments	112.8	10
Total	**1,091.4**	**100**

COMPETITORS

Bank of America	Hanmi Financial
Bank of East Asia	Hope Bancorp
Cathay General Bancorp	JPMorgan Chase
Citibank	U.S. Bancorp
City National	Wells Fargo
Comerica	

HISTORICAL FINANCIALS
Company Type: Public

Income Statement   FYE: December 31

	ASSETS ($ mil.)	NET INCOME ($ mil.)	INCOME AS % OF ASSETS	EMPLOYEES
12/18	41,042.3	703.7	1.7%	3,200
12/17	37,150.2	505.6	1.4%	3,000
12/16	34,788.8	431.6	1.2%	2,873
12/15	32,350.9	384.6	1.2%	2,833
12/14	28,738.0	342.4	1.2%	2,709
Annual Growth	9.3%	19.7%		4.3%

2018 Year-End Financials
Return on assets: 1.8%
Return on equity: 17.0%
Long-term debt ($ mil.): —
No. of shares (mil.): 144.9
Sales ($ mil.): 1,862.6
Dividends
  Yield: 1.9%
  Payout: 20.3%
Market value ($ mil.): 6,310.0

	STOCK PRICE ($) FY Close	P/E High/Low		PER SHARE ($) Earnings	Dividends	Book Value
12/18	43.53	15	8	4.81	0.86	30.52
12/17	60.83	18	14	3.47	0.80	26.58
12/16	50.83	17	9	2.97	0.80	23.78
12/15	41.56	17	13	2.66	0.80	21.70
12/14	38.71	16	13	2.38	0.72	19.85
Annual Growth	3.0%	—	—	19.2%	4.5%	11.3%

Easterly Government Properties Inc

Auditors: PricewaterhouseCoopers LLP

LOCATIONS

HQ: Easterly Government Properties Inc
  2101 L Street N.W., Suite 650, Washington, DC 20037
Phone: 202 595-9500
Web: www.easterlyreit.com

HISTORICAL FINANCIALS
Company Type: Public

Income Statement   FYE: December 31

	REVENUE ($ mil.)	NET INCOME ($ mil.)	NET PROFIT MARGIN	EMPLOYEES
12/18	160.5	5.7	3.6%	32
12/17	130.6	4.4	3.4%	30
12/16	104.6	3.4	3.3%	27
12/15	71.3	(1.6)	—	25
12/14	6.3	(3.6)	—	25
Annual Growth	124.5%	—	—	6.4%

2018 Year-End Financials
Debt ratio: 41.1%
Return on equity: 0.7%
Cash ($ mil.): 6.8
Current ratio: 1.12
Long-term debt ($ mil.): 766.3
No. of shares (mil.): 60.8
Dividends
  Yield: 6.6%
  Payout: 1,300.0%
Market value ($ mil.): 954.0

	STOCK PRICE ($) FY Close	P/E High/Low	PER SHARE ($) Earnings	Dividends	Book Value
12/18	15.68	238 170	0.08	1.04	14.69
12/17	21.34	201 175	0.10	1.00	14.91
12/16	20.02	187 150	0.10	0.92	15.17
12/15	17.18	— —	(0.08)	0.54	15.61
Annual Growth	(3.0%)	— —	—	24.4%	(2.0%)

Eastern Co.

The Eastern Company has latched on to the security industry. The company's security products group makes coin acceptors used in laundry facilities smart card payment systems and keyless locks sold under such brands as Big Tag Duo Warlock Searchalert Sesamee Prestolock and Huski. It also manufactures industrial hardware including latches locks and hinges used by the transportation industry. Eastern owns a foundry that makes metal anchoring devices to support underground mine roofs clamps for construction and railroad brake system components. The company sells mainly to manufacturers distributors and locksmiths through its operations in North America China Mexico and Taiwan.

EXECUTIVES

Vice President Programming, Carmen Mitcho
Board Member, Charles W Henry
Secretary, Teri Dews
Auditors: Fiondella, Milone & LaSaracina LLP

LOCATIONS

HQ: Eastern Co.
  112 Bridge Street, Naugatuck, CT 06770
Phone: 203 729-2255
Web: www.easterncompany.com

PRODUCTS/OPERATIONS

Selected Products
Industrial Hardware
  Cam-type vehicular locks
  Fasteners
  Handles
  Hinges
  Passenger restraint locks
  Slam draw & deadbolt latches
  Sleeper boxes
  Tool box locks
Security Products
  Access control units
  Cabinet locks
  Coin chutes
  Combination padlocks
  Drop meters
  Electric switch locks
  Meter cases
  Money boxes
  Oven door latches
  Smart cards & smart card readers
  Timers
  Tubular key locks
  Value transfer stations
Metal Products
  Adjustable clamps for construction
  Anchors for underground mine roof support
  Couplers for railroad braking systems
  Fittings for electrical installations

COMPETITORS

ASSA ABLOY
CompX International
DOM Security
Ingersoll-Rand Security Technologies
Kwikset Corporation
Master Lock
NL Industries
SARGENT Manufacturing
STRATTEC
Stanley Black and Decker

HISTORICAL FINANCIALS
Company Type: Public

Income Statement — FYE: December 29

	REVENUE ($ mil.)	NET INCOME ($ mil.)	NET PROFIT MARGIN	EMPLOYEES
12/18	234.2	14.5	6.2%	1,327
12/17	204.2	5.0	2.5%	1,189
12/16*	137.6	7.7	5.7%	862
01/16	144.5	5.7	4.0%	911
01/15	140.8	7.6	5.4%	942
Annual Growth	13.6%	17.3%	—	8.9%

*Fiscal year change

2018 Year-End Financials
Debt ratio: 15.8% No. of shares (mil.): 6.2
Return on equity: 15.8% Dividends
Cash ($ mil.): 13.9 Yield: 0.0%
Current ratio: 3.36 Payout: 19.0%
Long-term debt ($ mil.): 26.3 Market value ($ mil.): 152.0

	STOCK PRICE ($) FY Close	P/E High/Low		PER SHARE ($) Earnings	Dividends	Book Value
12/18	24.34	13	10	2.31	0.44	15.55
12/17	26.15	39	24	0.80	0.44	13.88
12/16*	20.90	17	12	1.25	0.44	13.18
01/16	18.80	22	17	0.92	0.45	12.71
01/15	18.49	15	12	1.23	0.48	12.01
Annual Growth	7.1%	—	—	17.1%	(2.2%)	6.7%

*Fiscal year change

EastGroup Properties Inc

EastGroup Properties points its compass all across the Sunbelt. The self-administered real estate investment trust (REIT) invests in develops and manages industrial properties with a particular emphasis on Florida Texas Arizona and California. EastGroup specializes in operating multitenant distribution and bulk distribution facilities from 5000 to 50000 sq. ft. in size located near major transportation hubs. Its portfolio includes some 300 industrial properties and an office building totaling more than 34 million sq. ft. of leasable space. The REIT has developed build-to-suit projects for clients including United Stationers Supply Company and Dal-Tile Corporation.

Geographic Reach
Jackson Mississippi-based EastGroup Properties has regional offices in Orlando Houston and Phoenix. Although its portfolio is focused on the Sun Belt (Arizona California Florida North Carolina and Texas) the REIT also owns properties in Colorado Louisiana Mississippi Nevada and Oklahoma.

Financial Performance
The REIT reported revenue of $202.2 million in 2013 an increase of 9% versus 2012 on increased rental income from its real estate operations due to the acquisition and development of new properties. Rising occupancy rates in 2013 compared to 2012 also helped boost revenue. Net income was flat (up less than 1%) over the same period. EastGroup's revenue has increased over the past decade with growth accelerating over the past two year as its portfolio of industrial properties has grown.

Strategy
EastGroup focuses its property portfolio on premier business distribution facilities clustered near major transportation hubs. In 2013 the REIT acquired two operating properties (nine buildings totaling 837000 square feet) in Dallas and Charlotte for $724 million as well as about 50 acres of development land in Charlotte and San Antonio for $6.6 million. Also during 2013 EastGroup began construction of 13 development projects containing nearly 1.2 million sq. ft. in Charlotte Denver Houston Orlando Phoenix and San Antonio.

Although the economic downturn impacted the REIT with decreased occupancies EastGroup has continued to invest in new properties and developments. Its growth strategy includes identifying and carving out new core markets. One of most promising new markets has been Charlotte North Carolina which has experienced both job and population growth and is located near major transportation corridors. The company eventually plans to branch out into the Greensboro and Research Triangle regions.

EXECUTIVES

EVP CFO Secretary and Treasurer, N. Keith McKey, age 68, $371,000 total compensation
SVP and Head of Western Regional Office Phoenix, William D. Petsas, age 61, $350,000 total compensation
President and CEO, Marshall A. Loeb, age 56, $416,667 total compensation
SVP Florida Regional Office Orlando, John F. Coleman, age 59, $361,000 total compensation
VP Property Management, William D. (Bill) Gray
VP Information Technology, Brian Laird
VP Operations Dallas and San Antonio, David Y. Hicks
Chairman, David H. Hoster, age 74
Auditors: KPMG LLP

LOCATIONS

HQ: EastGroup Properties Inc
400 W Parkway Place, Suite 100, Ridgeland, MS 39157
Phone: 601 354-3555
Web: www.eastgroup.net

PRODUCTS/OPERATIONS

2016 Sales

	$ mil.	% of total
Income from Real estate operations	252.2	100
Other	0.8	-
Total	**253.0**	**100**

COMPETITORS

Brandywine Realty
DCT Industrial Trust
Duke Realty
First Industrial Realty
Highwoods Properties
Kilroy Realty
Lexington Realty Trust
Liberty Property Trust
PS Business Parks
Prologis

HISTORICAL FINANCIALS
Company Type: Public

Income Statement — FYE: December 31

	REVENUE ($ mil.)	NET INCOME ($ mil.)	NET PROFIT MARGIN	EMPLOYEES
12/18	300.3	88.5	29.5%	75
12/17	274.1	83.1	30.3%	71
12/16	253.0	95.5	37.7%	71
12/15	235.0	47.8	20.4%	73
12/14	219.8	47.9	21.8%	71
Annual Growth	8.1%	16.6%	—	1.4%

2018 Year-End Financials
Debt ratio: 51.8% No. of shares (mil.): 36.5
Return on equity: 10.7% Dividends
Cash ($ mil.): 0.3 Yield: 2.9%
Current ratio: 0.48 Payout: 109.2%
Long-term debt ($ mil.): 1,105.7 Market value ($ mil.): 3,348.0

	STOCK PRICE ($) FY Close	P/E High/Low		PER SHARE ($) Earnings	Dividends	Book Value
12/18	91.73	41	31	2.49	2.72	24.74
12/17	88.38	39	28	2.44	2.52	21.56
12/16	73.84	26	17	2.93	2.44	19.13
12/15	55.61	45	35	1.49	2.34	17.11
12/14	63.32	45	37	1.52	2.22	17.72
Annual Growth	9.7%	—	—	13.1%	5.2%	8.7%

Ebix Inc

Ebix Inc. helps the worlds of several information-dependent industries go 'round. The company supplies on-demand software and ecommerce services for insurance financial and healthcare. Its Ebix-Exchange service acts as an online auction house where buyers and carriers can exchange bids for auto home health life and other types of insurance while paying Ebix a fee on each transaction. Ebix also provides agency management software that includes workflow and customer relationship management (CRM) capabilities as well as other back-office functions for insurance brokers and insurance carriers. Ebix also offers money transfer services in India and Asia.

Operations
Ebix operates through four channels: Exchanges Broker P&C (property and casualty) Systems Risk Compliance Solutions (RCS) and Carrier P&C Systems.

Exchanges which generate about 70% of the company's revenue are data exchanges for finance travel life insurance annuities employee health benefits risk management workers compensation insurance underwriting and property and casualty. The exchanges connect multiple entities in financial and insurance markets enabling the participant to carry and process data from one end to another.

The focus of Broker P&C Systems 4% revenue is outside the US. Ebix operates three back-end systems: eGlobal which targets multinational P&C insurance brokers; WinBeat which targets P&C brokers in Australia and New Zealand; and Ebix-ASP which is a system for the P&C insurance brokers in the US.

Through RCS about a quarter of revenue Ebix provides business process outsourcing services that include domain intensive project management time and material-based consulting the creation and tracking of certificates of insurance issued in the US and Australia the provision of claims adjudication and settlement call center and back office support.

Ebix has reduced emphasis on Carrier P&C Systems about 1% of revenue in favor of its other businesses. The unit designs and deploys on-demand back-end systems for P&C insurance companies.

Geographic Reach
Atlanta-based Ebix's #1 market is the US accounting for nearly 60% of its sales with India and Australia accounting for about 20% and 9% respectively. The firm's international operations are managed from Dubai. The company has more than 50 offices across the Australia Brazil New Zealand Singapore the UK Canada and India.

Financial Performance
Ebix Inc.'s revenue and profit have grown fortified by the several acquisitions the company makes each year. Revenue has risen for the past decade while profit has been on a steady rise higher for the past four years.

In 2017 the company's revenue increased 22% to about $364 million from 2016 pushed by the latest round of acquisitions. The Exchange division's revenues jumped 26% with help from the acquisitions of ItzCash YouFirst Wall Street Paul Merchants and Via. The Risk Compliance Solutions division's revenue rose 17% on new e-governance sales from operations in India and consulting service sales from the Wdev acquisition. A 4% increase in Broker P&C Systems revenue was aided by the effects of currency exchange rates. Carrier P&C Systems division revenues fell 16% with the end of some large projects.

Higher revenue drove net income to more than $100 million in 2017 a 7% increase from 2016.

Ebix had about $64 million in cash and cash equivalents at the end of 2017 down from about $114 million in 2016. The company spent about $200 million on acquisitions in 2017 about $190 million than it spent on acquisitions in 2016.

Strategy
Ebix finds companies that add to or fill in its portfolio of products and services buys them and integrates them into its framework. The plan has built revenue from about $75 million in 2008 to about $364 million in 2017.

With this strategy Ebix has expanded beyond insurance and into financials and healthcare markets as well as geographic markets. Geographically India has become an important market for Ebix. The company's revenue from India grew to more than $61 million in 2017 from less than $4 million in 2015 making the country its second-biggest market. In India and other southeast Asia countries Ebix through its EbixCash Financial Exchange offerings provides domestic and international money remittance travel pre-paid and gift cards utility payments and more.

Mergers and Acquisitions
The Ebix mergers and acquisitions team had to be one of the busiest such units making several acquisitions some of which boosted its business in India.

In 2019 Ebix made a $340 million unsolicited bid to buy Yatra an online travel portal in India. If accepted the deal would further build out the travel portion of Ebix's offerings.

In 2019 Ebix acquired 80% of Zillious an on-demand software-as-a-service (SaaS) travel technology provider with a strong position in corporate travel in India. The Zillious Exchange processes more than eight million travel bookings a year. Ebix intends to operate Zillious as a non-aligned technology platform and expand it to the Middle East the US and Asia.

Previously Ebix entered into a joint venture with the India-based Essel Group to acquire an 80% stake in ItzCash India's leading payment exchange for about $120 million.

Other acquisitions Ebix made to build its India operations have included:

— Via an online travel and assisted ecommerce exchange in India. Ebix paid about $80 million.

— The Money Transfer Service Scheme (MTSS) Business of Paul Merchants the largest international remittance service provider in India. Ebix paid about $37 million.

— The MTSS Business of YouFirst another international remittance service provider in India. The cost was about $10 million.

— The MTSS Business of Wall Street an international remittance service provider in India and its subsidiary Goldman Securities Limited. The price was about $7 million.

— The assets of beBetter a technology-enabled corporate wellness provider of tools and programs such as health screening coaching tobacco cessation weight and stress management health information and others. Ebix paid about $1 million.

EXECUTIVES

Chairman President and CEO, Robin Raina, age 50, $1,300,000 total compensation
EVP and Corporate Officer of Mergers & Acquisitions and Special Projects, Robert F. (Bob) Kerris, age 65, $225,000 total compensation
SVP Agency Systems, Graham Prior, age 62, $154,126 total compensation
SVP Ebix Health, James (Jim) Senge, age 58, $225,000 total compensation
Managing Director Ebix Australia Group, Leon d'Apice, age 62, $164,250 total compensation
Managing Director Ebix New Zealand, Tony Wisniewski
Head of Enterprise Solutions EbixExchange, Ash Sawhney
CFO, Sean T. Donaghy, age 54
Vice President Of Operations, Ashley Franco
Senior Vice President, Dan Delity
Assistant Vice President Professional Services, Albert Golbasarians
Vice President Sales, David Greiff
Vice President, Alex Mattelaer
Vice President Of Operations, Bill Fallert
Vice President Software Development Rcs, Bhoga Pappu
Vp Operations Ebix Exchange, Tom Lebleu
Vice President Solution Architecture and Implementation, Andy Labrot
Vice President Business Development, Venkat Vaddadi
Vice President Of Annuity Sales, Chad Ross
Board Member, Hans Keller
Auditors: T R Chadha & Co LLP

LOCATIONS

HQ: Ebix Inc
1 Ebix Way, Johns Creek, GA 30097
Phone: 678 281-2020
Web: www.ebix.com

PRODUCTS/OPERATIONS

2017 Sales

	$ mil.	% of total
Exchanges	259,470.0	71
Risk Compliance Solutions	86,832.0	24
Broker systems	14,672.0	4
Carrier systems	2,995.0	1
Total	**363,971.0**	**100**

COMPETITORS

Answer Financial	InsWeb
Applied Systems	Intuit
BenefitMall	Life Quotes
CCC Information	SunGard
Computer Sciences Corp.	The Hartford
	TriZetto
Cover-All	Ultimate Software
Crawford & Company	Vertafore
Datamonitor	salesforce.com
Guidewire Software	

HISTORICAL FINANCIALS

Company Type: Public

Income Statement   FYE: December 31

	REVENUE ($ mil.)	NET INCOME ($ mil.)	NET PROFIT MARGIN	EMPLOYEES
12/18	497.8	93.1	18.7%	9,263
12/17	363.9	100.6	27.6%	4,515
12/16	298.2	93.8	31.5%	2,988
12/15	265.4	79.5	30.0%	2,707
12/14	214.3	63.5	29.7%	2,343
Annual Growth	23.5%	10.0%	—	41.0%

2018 Year-End Financials

Debt ratio: 44.5%   No. of shares (mil.): 30.5
Return on equity: 19.2%   Dividends
Cash ($ mil.): 147.7   Yield: 0.7%
Current ratio: 1.35   Payout: 8.5%
Long-term debt ($ mil.): 699.2   Market value ($ mil.): 1,301.0

	STOCK PRICE ($) FY Close	P/E High/Low		PER SHARE ($) Earnings	Dividends	Book Value
12/18	42.56	29	14	2.95	0.30	15.64
12/17	79.25	26	17	3.19	0.30	15.62
12/16	57.05	22	10	2.86	0.30	13.30
12/15	32.79	17	7	2.28	0.30	12.24
12/14	16.99	11	7	0.30	0.30	11.94
Annual Growth	25.8%	—	—	77.1%	(0.0%)	7.0%

Echo Global Logistics Inc

By land air or sea Echo Global Logistics delivers the goods. The company provides a wide range of transportation and supply chain management services using a proprietary technology platform for truckload quoting and transit times. Its main business is arranging transportation by truckload (TL) and less than truckload (LTL) carriers. It also offers intermodal services—a combination of truck and rail delivery—and some air and ocean delivery services. Its logistics solutions encompass services such as rate negotiation shipment tracking and freight management and reporting.

Operations
About 40000 transportation providers make up Echo Global's carrier network which consists of small and midsized fleets trucking companies and single-truck owners.

Echo Global offers mode-specific transportation services as well as logistics services on a shipment-to-shipment basis (transactional) or via long-term contracts (managed transportation). Its truckload (TL) shipping service generates close to 70% of net sales and includes dry van temperature-controlled and flatbed trucks. TL services utilizes its Truckload Quoting Tool technology which uses predictive pricing algorithms and capacity data to provide the best rates for its customers. Echo's less than truckload business (LTL) accounts for more than 25% of net sales. LTL services uses its RateIQ 2.0 technology to get real-time price and transit times for all LTL shipments.

The company also provides intermodal transportation services (a combination of truck and rail) small parcel shipping domestic air shipments and international ocean freight services. These account for about 5% of revenue.

As part of its shipping business the company offers logistics services including customized freight management solutions such as rate negotiation procurement shipment tracking and reporting freight bill payment and audit and integration of shipping applications into customers' e-commerce sites.

Geographic Reach
Echo is stationed in Chicago and has about 30 sales offices located across the US as well as two data centers.

Sales and Marketing
The company caters to a wide range of industries including manufacturing construction food and beverage consumer products and retail. Its customers are divided into two types: transactional (services provided on a shipment-by-shipment basis) and managed transportation (under multi-year contracts). Transactional clients represent about 80% of total revenue with 20% generated by managed transportation clients.

Financial Performance
Echo Global Logistics has experienced double-digit growth over the last five years. Net sales increased to $1.9 billion in 2017 a $227 million increase (or 13%) from 2016. The increase is attributed to higher shipment volume and revenue per shipment driven by an increase in truckload rates.

The company reported net income of $12.6 million in 2017 compared with $1.6 million the previous year primarily due to an $8.3 million tax benefit and an increase in net revenue. Negatively affecting Echo Global's bottom line were an increase in transportation costs driven by higher carrier rates. Transportation costs as a percentage of revenue increased by more than 1%.

Cash at the end of fiscal 2017 was $23.5 million an increase of $6.9 million from the prior year. Cash from operations contributed $48.7 million to the coffers while investing activities used $20.7 million mainly for purchases of property and equipment. Financing activities used another $21.1 million for the company's stock repurchase program.

Strategy
Echo Global Logistics plans to continue to grow through investments in technology and through acquisitions.

Echo Global's proprietary technology platforms are driving revenue growth. With logistics being one of the fastest growing industries Echo continues to leverage its expertise in technology-based logistics solutions and plans to hire more than 70 technology professionals in 2018. With a focus on its client portal EchoShip and its carrier portal and mobile platform EchoDrive the company aims to continue to develop tools to further automate and digitize data such as capacity rates shipment status and settlement documents. It has also invested in productivity tools for its sales force.

Echo Global is also focused on acquisitions to further growth. Its 2018 acquisition of Freight Management Plus (FMP) adds approximately $15 million in annual revenue experienced LTL sales talent and expands its reach to small and middle-market shippers.

Mergers and Acquisitions
In 2018 Echo acquired Freight Management Plus Inc. (FMP) a third-party logistics company headquartered in Allison Park PA. FMP specializes in LTL managed transportation solutions. With the purchase of FMP Echo hopes to expand its portfolio of small to middle-market shippers.

EXECUTIVES

President and COO, David B. (Dave) Menzel, age 57, $546,000 total compensation
Chairman and CEO, Douglas R. (Doug) Waggoner, age 60, $760,000 total compensation
CIO, Tim Kutz
CFO, Kyle L. Sauers, age 48, $425,000 total compensation
SVP Marketing, Christopher N. Clemmensen
Senior Vice President of Talent, Cheryl Johnson
National Account Manager, Brian Godla
Vice President Of Sales, Jamie Petrzelka
National Account Manager, Jared Rames
National Account Manager, Joseph Amici
National Account Manager, Mark Baginski
National Account Manager, Drew Evans
National Account Manager, Fred Pettey
Vice President Truckload Solutions, Baraka Nevels
Executive Vice President, Andy Arquette
National Account Manager, Kevin Holtrup
National Account Manager, Brandon Gardner
National Account Manager, Ben Boelter
National Account Manager, Jason Agostino
National Account Manager, Dustin Williams
National Account Manager, Natalie Benedettini
National Account Manager, Alex Fitzpatrick
Vice President Of Specialized Services, Milburn Miranda
National Account Manager, Chris Silungan
National Account Manager, Erik Liscinsky
National Account Manager, Dean DeWilder
National Account Manager, Lyndsey Whelan
National Account Manager, Jon Lisek
National Account Manager, Trinidad Burks
National Account Manager, Kevin Jamsa
National Account Manager, Teresa Unkovich
Regional Vice President, Steve Brown
Senior Vice President Of Business Development, Sean Burke
National Account Manager, Brandon Scott
Vice President Of Business Development, Mike Dupre
Regional Vice President, Paul Warren
Regional Vice President, Darrell Lubenow
Regional Vice President, Sam Freni
National Account Manager, Lisa Dean
National Account Manager, Thomas Tebben
National Account Manager, Becky Jones
National Accounts Manager, Brandon Hubbard
National Accounts Manager, Erika Klatte
Vp Of Strategic Analytics, Scott Friesen
National Account Manager, John Mercer
Regional Vice President, Daniel Despain
NATIONAL ACCOUNT MANAGER, James Masi
National Account Manager, Kevin Tracy
National Account Manager, Vadim Vaytsman
Division Vice President, Andrew Kimelman
Regional Vice President, Jerry Mcconnell
Auditors: Ernst & Young LLP

LOCATIONS

HQ: Echo Global Logistics Inc
600 West Chicago Avenue, Suite 725, Chicago, IL 60654
Phone: 800 354-7993
Web: www.echo.com

PRODUCTS/OPERATIONS

2017 Sales

	% of total
Truckload (TL)	68
Less Than Truckload (LTL)	27
Intermodal	3
Transportation	2
Total	**100**

Selected Services
Truckload services (TL)
Less than Truckload services (LTL)
Intermodal services
Domestic air and expedited services
International air and ocean transportation services
Small Parcel services
EchoTrak
EchoIQ
RateIQ 2.0
FastLane
Truckload Quoting Tool
EchoDrive carrier portal
EchoShip client portal

COMPETITORS

ABF Freight System
C.H. Robinson Worldwide
Expeditors
FedEx
Hub Group
J.B. Hunt
MIQ Logistics
Ozburn-Hessey Logistics
Roadrunner Transportation Systems
Ryder System
Schneider Logistics
Total Quality Logistics
Transplace
UPS
XPO logistics

HISTORICAL FINANCIALS
Company Type: Public

Income Statement				FYE: December 31
	REVENUE ($ mil.)	NET INCOME ($ mil.)	NET PROFIT MARGIN	EMPLOYEES
12/18	2,439.7	28.7	1.2%	2,595
12/17	1,943.0	12.6	0.6%	2,453
12/16	1,716.1	1.5	0.1%	2,350
12/15	1,512.3	7.8	0.5%	2,335
12/14	1,173.3	16.7	1.4%	1,734
Annual Growth	20.1%	14.4%	—	10.6%

2018 Year-End Financials
Debt ratio: 20.9%
Return on equity: 7.6%
Cash ($ mil.): 40.2
Current ratio: 1.48
Long-term debt ($ mil.): 183.8
No. of shares (mil.): 27.4
Dividends
  Yield: —
  Payout: —
Market value ($ mil.): 557.0

	STOCK PRICE ($) FY Close	P/E High/Low	PER SHARE ($) Earnings	Dividends	Book Value
12/18	20.33	35 18	1.03	0.00	14.23
12/17	28.00	62 29	0.45	0.00	13.17
12/16	25.05	475 317	0.05	0.00	12.73
12/15	20.39	118 59	0.28	0.00	13.30
12/14	29.20	41 22	0.71	0.00	7.84
Annual Growth	(8.7%)	—	9.7%	—	16.1%

Educational Development Corp.

EXECUTIVES
Chairman President CEO and Treasurer, Randall W. White, age 71, $150,000 total compensation
VP Information Systems, Craig M. White, age 45
Controller and Secretary, Marilyn R. Welborn
Director, James F. Lewis, age 71
Director, John A. Clerico, age 71
Director, Ronald T. (Ron) McDaniel, age 75
Independent Director, Kara Neal
Auditors: HoganTaylor LLP

LOCATIONS
HQ: Educational Development Corp.
  5402 South 122nd East Avenue, Tulsa, OK 74146
Phone: 918 622-4522
Web: www.edcpub.com

COMPETITORS
Amazon.com
American Girl
Barnes & Noble
Media Source
Pearson plc
S&P Global
Scholastic
Simon & Schuster

HISTORICAL FINANCIALS
Company Type: Public

Income Statement				FYE: February 28
	REVENUE ($ mil.)	NET INCOME ($ mil.)	NET PROFIT MARGIN	EMPLOYEES
02/19	118.8	6.6	5.6%	178
02/18	111.9	5.2	4.7%	193
02/17	106.6	2.8	2.7%	202
02/16	63.6	2.1	3.3%	150
02/15	32.5	0.8	2.6%	83
Annual Growth	38.2%	67.0%	—	21.0%

2019 Year-End Financials
Debt ratio: 28.5%
Return on equity: 28.8%
Cash ($ mil.): 3.2
Current ratio: 1.76
Long-term debt ($ mil.): 18.8
No. of shares (mil.): 8.2
Dividends
  Yield: 2.4%
  Payout: 23.8%
Market value ($ mil.): 66.0

	STOCK PRICE ($) FY Close	P/E High/Low	PER SHARE ($) Earnings	Dividends	Book Value
02/19	8.05	33 9	0.81	0.20	3.16
02/18	19.35	36 11	0.64	0.05	2.49
02/17	9.55	42 20	0.35	0.18	1.86
02/16	11.34	65 15	0.26	0.17	1.63
02/15	4.31	55 34	0.11	0.16	1.53
Annual Growth	16.9%	—	66.7%	5.7%	19.9%

Eldorado Resorts Inc

Auditors: Ernst & Young LLP

LOCATIONS
HQ: Eldorado Resorts Inc
  100 West Liberty Street, Suite 1150, Reno, NV 89501
Phone: 775 328-0100
Web: www.eldoradoresorts.com

HISTORICAL FINANCIALS
Company Type: Public

Income Statement				FYE: December 31
	REVENUE ($ mil.)	NET INCOME ($ mil.)	NET PROFIT MARGIN	EMPLOYEES
12/18	2,056.0	95.2	4.6%	18,700
12/17	1,473.5	73.9	5.0%	12,500
12/16	892.9	24.8	2.8%	7,400
12/15	719.7	114.1	15.9%	7,800
12/14	361.8	(14.4)	—	7,100
Annual Growth	54.4%	—	—	27.4%

2018 Year-End Financials
Debt ratio: 71.4%
Return on equity: 9.6%
Cash ($ mil.): 247.7
Current ratio: 1.43
Long-term debt ($ mil.): 4,221.1
No. of shares (mil.): 77.4
Dividends
  Yield: —
  Payout: —
Market value ($ mil.): 2,804.0

	STOCK PRICE ($) FY Close	P/E High/Low	PER SHARE ($) Earnings	Dividends	Book Value
12/18	36.21	40 25	1.22	0.00	13.29
12/17	33.15	31 14	1.09	0.00	12.30
12/16	16.95	32 17	0.52	0.00	6.34
12/15	11.00	5 2	2.43	0.00	5.78
12/14	4.05	— —	(0.48)	0.00	3.26
Annual Growth	72.9%	—	—	—	42.1%

Elevate Credit Inc

Auditors: Grant Thornton LLP

LOCATIONS
HQ: Elevate Credit Inc
  4150 International Plaza, Suite 300, Fort Worth, TX 76109
Phone: 817 928-1500
Web: www.elevate.com

HISTORICAL FINANCIALS
Company Type: Public

Income Statement				FYE: December 31
	REVENUE ($ mil.)	NET INCOME ($ mil.)	NET PROFIT MARGIN	EMPLOYEES
12/18	786.6	12.5	1.6%	685
12/17	673.1	(6.9)	—	615
12/16	580.4	(22.3)	—	540
12/15	434.0	(19.9)	—	0
Annual Growth	21.9%	—	—	—

2018 Year-End Financials
Debt ratio: 74.6%
Return on equity: 11.7%
Cash ($ mil.): 58.3
Current ratio: 1.63
Long-term debt ($ mil.): 562.5
No. of shares (mil.): 43.3
Dividends
  Yield: —
  Payout: —
Market value ($ mil.): 194.0

	STOCK PRICE ($) FY Close	P/E High/Low	PER SHARE ($) Earnings	Dividends	Book Value
12/18	4.48	38 13	0.28	0.00	2.70
12/17	7.53	— —	(0.20)	0.00	2.28
12/16	0.00	— —	(1.74)	0.00	1.04
Annual Growth	—	—	—	—	60.7%

Ellington Financial Inc

EXECUTIVES
Director, Edward (Ed) Resendez, age 59
Chairman and Co-Chief Investment Officer, Michael W. Vranos, age 54
President CEO and Director, Laurence E. Penn
Co-Chief Investment Officer, Mark Tecotzky
Chief Financial Officer, Lisa Mumford
Director, Ronald I. Simon, age 78
Director, Thomas F. Robards, age 69
Director, Edward (Ed) Resendez, age 59
President CEO and Director, Laurence E. Penn
Auditors: PricewaterhouseCoopers LLP

LOCATIONS

HQ: Ellington Financial Inc
53 Forest Avenue, Old Greenwich, CT 06870
Phone: 203 698-1200
Web: www.ellingtonfinancial.com

COMPETITORS

Annaly Capital Management	MFA Financial
Chimera	MFResidential
Galiot Capital	Sutherland
	Western Asset Mortgage

HISTORICAL FINANCIALS
Company Type: Public

Income Statement
FYE: December 31

	REVENUE ($ mil.)	NET INCOME ($ mil.)	NET PROFIT MARGIN	EMPLOYEES
12/18	135.0	43.1	31.9%	150
12/17	93.9	35.1	37.4%	160
12/16	80.1	35.7	44.6%	160
12/15	104.6	66.1	63.3%	160
12/14	93.8	58.7	62.6%	150
Annual Growth	9.5%	(7.4%)	—	0.0%

2018 Year-End Financials

Debt ratio: 12.5%
Return on equity: 7.4%
Cash ($ mil.): 44.6
Current ratio: 0.32
Long-term debt ($ mil.): 497.0
No. of shares (mil.): 29.8
Dividends
 Yield: —
 Payout: —
Market value ($ mil.): 457.0

	STOCK PRICE ($) FY Close	P/E High/Low		PER SHARE ($) Earnings	Dividends	Book Value
12/18	15.33	12	10	1.42	0.00	18.92
12/17	14.51	15	13	1.10	0.00	19.15
12/16	15.52	17	14	1.09	0.00	19.75
12/15	16.78	11	8	1.98	0.00	22.10
12/14	19.96	12	9	2.10	0.00	23.38
Annual Growth	(6.4%)	—	—	(9.3%)	—	(5.2%)

Embassy Bancorp Inc

EXECUTIVES

Prin, David M Lobach
Vice President, Bryce Ruggieri
Auditors: Baker Tilly Virchow Krause, LLP

LOCATIONS

HQ: Embassy Bancorp Inc
One Hundred Gateway Drive, Suite 100, Bethlehem, PA 18017
Phone: 610 882-8800
Web: www.embassybank.com

HISTORICAL FINANCIALS
Company Type: Public

Income Statement
FYE: December 31

	ASSETS ($ mil.)	NET INCOME ($ mil.)	INCOME AS % OF ASSETS	EMPLOYEES
12/18	1,099.3	10.0	0.9%	91
12/17	996.9	7.3	0.7%	84
12/16	924.2	7.1	0.8%	83
12/15	804.0	7.4	0.9%	76
12/14	719.0	6.4	0.9%	69
Annual Growth	11.2%	12.0%	—	7.2%

2018 Year-End Financials

Return on assets: 0.9%
Return on equity: 12.0%
Long-term debt ($ mil.): —
No. of shares (mil.): 7.4
Sales ($ mil): 40.4
Dividends
 Yield: 1.1%
 Payout: 14.9%
Market value ($ mil.): 112.0

	STOCK PRICE ($) FY Close	P/E High/Low		PER SHARE ($) Earnings	Dividends	Book Value
12/18	14.95	13	10	1.34	0.17	11.69
12/17	16.00	16	13	0.97	0.14	10.71
12/16	13.00	14	11	0.96	0.13	9.84
12/15	10.91	11	10	1.00	0.10	9.19
12/14	10.30	12	9	0.87	0.06	8.34
Annual Growth	9.8%	—	—	11.4%	29.7%	8.8%

Emergent BioSolutions Inc

Emergent BioSolutions specializes in therapies that treat or protect against public health threats. It offers vaccines and medicines to address bioagents infectious diseases travel-related diseases and opioid-related ailments. Primary product BioThrax is the only FDA-approved anthrax vaccine. Most BioThrax revenue comes from direct sales to US federal agencies including the Department of Defense (DOD) and the Department of Health and Human Services (HHS). Other offerings include vaccines ACAM2000 (smallpox) Vivotif (typhoid fever) and Vaxchora (cholera); opioid overdose drug Narcan; and inhaled anthrax treatment raxibacumab. Emergent also has contract manufacturing and research operations.

Financial Performance

Emergent BioSolutions' revenue has increased steadily over the past few years as the company has expanded through acquisitions and research programs. Sales nearly doubled between 2014 and 2018 with revenue growth reported each year except 2016 (the year the company spun-off its biosciences division).

The company reported revenue of $782.4 million in 2018 up 39% from 2017. Most of the growth came from increased product sales related to the 2017 and 2018 acquisitions of ACAM2000 raxibacumab NARCAN Vivotif and Vaxchora. BioThrax sales declined slightly due to lower volume requirements from the US government. Revenue from contract manufacturing contracts and grants also contributed to growth.

Net income declined 24% to $62.7 million due to higher operating expenses (manufacturing sales and R&D costs partly related to acquisitions). The drop was somewhat offset by lower income tax provisions from the 2017 Tax Act.

Emergent ended 2018 with $112.4 million in cash down $66.9 million from 2017. Operating activities contributed $41.8 million while investing activities used $897.2 million (mostly on acquisitions) and financing activities contributed $788.7 million via an expanded credit line.

Strategy

While Emergent BioSolutions dominates the anthrax vaccine niche its over-reliance on a single product (BioThrax accounts for nearly half of sales) leaves it vulnerable to fluctuations in demand from a narrow customer base (namely US federal agencies).

To reduce its dependence on BioThrax the company has expanded its product offerings through aggressive acquisitions in recent years focusing on both government-procured products and more widespread commercial opportunities. Purchases have helped Emergent move beyond biothreat and infectious disease medicines into travelers' disease and opioid abuse treatments.

The company has also expanded its R&D pipeline through acquisitions and partnerships. It particularly pursues research projects with potential funding from government agencies and other health organizations. Vaccine candidates target anthrax Ebola adenovirus chikungunya Lassa fever and hemorrhagic fever. Drug candidates (antibody therapies and device-combination treatments) target influenza Zika infections cyanide poisoning opioid overdose and nerve agent treatment.

Emergent wants to increase its presence in international markets via foreign approvals of existing products and acquisitions of new products.

Mergers and Acquisitions

In 2018 Emergent BioSolutions acquired private firm Adapt Pharma which makes Narcan the only needle-free drug that treats opioid overdose. The deal was valued at up to $735 million including an upfront payment of $635 million.

Later that year the company acquired specialty vaccines firm PaxVax for $270 million. That deal brought Emergent two marketed vaccines — Vivotif (for typhoid fever) and Vaxchora (for cholera).

Company Background

Emergent BioSolutions was founded in 1998 in Michigan and was reorganized as Delaware corporation in 2004.

In 2014 Emergent acquired Cangene gaining treatments BAT (botulism) Anthrasil (anthrax infection) and VIGIV (adverse vaccine reactions).

In 2016 the firm spun off its biosciences division which worked on therapies for leukemia and lymphoma and vaccines for such infectious diseases as influenza as the new public company Aptevo Therapeutics.

In 2017 Emergent acquired smallpox vaccine ACAM2000 from Sanofi. It also purchased raxibacumab an antibody product for treatment of inhalated anthrax from Human Genome Sciences GlaxoSmithKline.

EXECUTIVES

SVP and Chief Scientific Officer, W. James Jackson, age 59
President and CEO, Daniel J. Abdun-Nabi, age 64, $589,695 total compensation

Director; President and CEO BioPort, Robert G. (Bob) Kramer, age 62, $428,560 total compensation
EVP and President Corporate Affairs Division, Allen Shofe
EVP and President BioDefense Division, Adam R. Havey, age 48, $332,648 total compensation
EVP and General Counsel, A.B. Cruz
Vp Regulatory Affairs, David Wonnacott
Vp Research and Development, Richard Welch
Vice President, Robert Burrows
Senior Vice President Corporate Development, Yasmine Gibellini
Vice President And Chief Security Officer, Jeff Hauk
Vice President Commercial Markets, Jeff Hackman
Svp Sales And Marketing, Darren Buchwald
Svp Global Government Affairs, Christopher W Frech
Svp Chief Ethics And Compliance Officer, Laura K Kennedy
Svp And Cio, Sharon Solomon
Svp External Development And Government Contracting, Barbara Solow
Vice President Internal Audit, David Lacroix
Chairman, Fuad El-Hibri, age 61
Board Member, George Joulwan
Auditors: Ernst & Young LLP

LOCATIONS

HQ: Emergent BioSolutions Inc
  400 Professional Drive, Suite 400, Gaithersburg, MD 20879
Phone: 240 631-3200
Web: www.emergentbiosolutions.com

PRODUCTS/OPERATIONS

2014 Sales

	$ mil.	% of total
Products	308.3	68
Contracts & grants	110.9	25
Contract manufacturing	30.9	7
Total	**450.1**	**100**

2014 Sales

	% of total
Biodefense	82
Biosciences	18
Total	**100**

Selected Acquisitions and Ventures

COMPETITORS

Altimmune	Human Genome Sciences
Amgen	Pfenex
Biogen	Pfizer
Elusys Therapeutics	Roche Holding
Genentech	Soligenix

HISTORICAL FINANCIALS
Company Type: Public

Income Statement — FYE: December 31

	REVENUE ($ mil.)	NET INCOME ($ mil.)	NET PROFIT MARGIN	EMPLOYEES
12/18	782.4	62.7	8.0%	1,705
12/17	560.8	82.5	14.7%	1,256
12/16	488.7	51.7	10.6%	1,098
12/15	522.7	62.8	12.0%	1,292
12/14	450.1	36.7	8.2%	1,280
Annual Growth	14.8%	14.3%	—	7.4%

2018 Year-End Financials
Debt ratio: 35.6%
Return on equity: 6.5%
Cash ($ mil.): 112.2
Current ratio: 3.10
Long-term debt ($ mil.): 784.5
No. of shares (mil.): 51.2
Dividends
  Yield: —
  Payout: —
Market value ($ mil.): 3,035.0

	STOCK PRICE ($) FY Close	P/E High/Low	PER SHARE ($) Earnings	PER SHARE ($) Dividends	PER SHARE ($) Book Value
12/18	59.28	59 36	1.22	0.00	19.74
12/17	46.47	24 14	1.71	0.00	18.47
12/16	32.84	34 19	1.13	0.00	14.69
12/15	40.01	25 16	1.41	0.00	16.75
12/14	27.23	29 20	0.88	0.00	14.67
Annual Growth	21.5%	— —	8.5%	—	7.7%

Energizer Holdings Inc (New)

Auditors: PricewaterhouseCoopers LLP

LOCATIONS

HQ: Energizer Holdings Inc (New)
  533 Maryville University Drive, St. Louis, MO 63141
Phone: 314 985-2000
Web: www.energizerholdings.com

HISTORICAL FINANCIALS
Company Type: Public

Income Statement — FYE: September 30

	REVENUE ($ mil.)	NET INCOME ($ mil.)	NET PROFIT MARGIN	EMPLOYEES
09/19	2,494.5	51.1	2.0%	7,500
09/18	1,797.7	93.5	5.2%	4,000
09/17	1,755.7	201.5	11.5%	4,400
09/16	1,634.2	127.7	7.8%	4,800
09/15	1,631.6	(4.0)	—	5,100
Annual Growth	11.2%	—	—	10.1%

2019 Year-End Financials
Debt ratio: 64.1%
Return on equity: 17.9%
Cash ($ mil.): 258.5
Current ratio: 1.91
Long-term debt ($ mil.): 3,461.6
No. of shares (mil.): 68.9
Dividends
  Yield: 2.7%
  Payout: 1,500.0%
Market value ($ mil.): 3,003.0

	STOCK PRICE ($) FY Close	P/E High/Low	PER SHARE ($) Earnings	PER SHARE ($) Dividends	PER SHARE ($) Book Value
09/19	43.58	104 57	0.58	1.20	7.89
09/18	58.65	42 27	1.52	1.16	0.41
09/17	46.05	18 13	3.22	1.10	1.40
09/16	49.96	25 15	2.04	1.00	(0.49)
09/15	38.71	— —	(0.06)	0.25	(0.97)
Annual Growth	3.0%	— —	—	48.0%	—

Energy Recovery Inc

Desalination makes seawater potable; Energy Recovery (ERI) makes desalination practical. The company designs develops and manufactures energy recovery devices used in sea water reverse osmosis (SWRO) desalination plants. The SWRO process is energy intensive using high pressure to drive salt water through membranes to produce fresh water. The company's main product the PX Pressure Exchanger helps recapture and recycle up to 98% of the energy available in the high-pressure reject stream a by-product of the SWRO process. The PX can reduce the energy consumption of a desalination plant by up to 60% compared with a plant lacking an energy recovery device. Subsidiary Pump Engineering also makes high pressure pumps.

Geographic Reach
ERI has its headquarters and main manufacturing center located in California. Other offices reside in Shanghai and Dubai.

Sales and Marketing
Primary customers for ERI consist of international engineering procurement and construction firms that build large desalination plants. Energy Recovery also sells its products and services to OEMs of pumps and other water-related equipment for small to mid-size plants used in hotels cruise ships farm operations and power plants. Major customers have included IDE Technologies Ltd Thiess Degremont J.V. Hydrochem Acciona Agua and UTE Mostaganem.

Financial Performance
ERI's revenues decreased 29% from 2013 to 2014. The decrease was primarily due to significantly lower mega-project (MPD) shipments as well as lower OEM shipments. The decreases in MPD and OEM sales were offset by higher aftermarket shipments and revenue attributable to an oil and gas operating lease and lease buy-out.

ERI has suffered five straight years of net losses. Its $19 million net loss in 2014 was fueled by higher sales and marketing expenses coupled with the lower net revenue. Research and development expenses also spiked during 2014.

Strategy
Going forward ERI intends to benefit from a significant presence in Spain and other countries. Energy Recovery's lineup for example supports most of Spain's desalination plants. ERI also plans to enter into the material science and manufacturing of ceramics — a key component of its PX devices. The strategy aims to boost device production cut costs and improve product quality.

EXECUTIVES

Vice President, Nocair Bensalah
Vp Of Corporate Strategy, Eric Siebert
Auditors: DELOITTE & TOUCHE LLP

LOCATIONS

HQ: Energy Recovery Inc
  1717 Doolittle Drive, San Leandro, CA 94577
Phone: 510 483-7370
Web: www.energyrecovery.com

PRODUCTS/OPERATIONS

2014 Sales

	$ mil.	% of total
PX devices & related products & services	20.9	69
Turbochargers & pumps	8.7	29
Oil and gas product operating lease	0.8	2
Total	**30.4**	**100**

PRODUCTS
VorTeq
IsoBoost
IsoGen
IsoBoost for Syngas & Ammonia
PX Pressure Exchanger
Turbochargers
Pumping Systems

Selected Products
Energy recovery devices
  PX pressure exchanger devices (PX-300 the 65 series the 4S series and brackish PX devices)
  Turbochargers (HTCAT series the HALO line and the LPT series for brackish water desalination)
High pressure and circulation pumps (AquaBold series the AquaSpire series and a line of small circulation pumps)
Technical support and replacement parts

COMPETITORS

Flowserve
GE Water and Process Technologies
KSB AG
Seprotech
Siemens Water Technologies
Sulzer

HISTORICAL FINANCIALS
Company Type: Public

Income Statement   FYE: December 31

	REVENUE ($ mil.)	NET INCOME ($ mil.)	NET PROFIT MARGIN	EMPLOYEES
12/18	74.5	22.0	29.6%	143
12/17	63.1	12.3	19.6%	133
12/16	54.7	1.0	1.9%	120
12/15	44.7	(11.6)	—	114
12/14	30.4	(18.7)	—	124
Annual Growth	25.1%	—	—	3.6%

2018 Year-End Financials

Debt ratio: —
Return on equity: 22.5%
Cash ($ mil.): 21.9
Current ratio: 4.41
Long-term debt ($ mil.): —
No. of shares (mil.): 53.9
Dividends
  Yield: —
  Payout: —
Market value ($ mil.): 363.0

	STOCK PRICE ($) FY Close	P/E High/Low		PER SHARE ($) Earnings	Dividends	Book Value
12/18	6.73	24	16	0.40	0.00	2.10
12/17	8.75	49	27	0.22	0.00	1.53
12/16	10.35	818	268	0.02	0.00	1.23
12/15	7.07	—	—	(0.22)	0.00	1.21
12/14	5.27	—	—	(0.36)	0.00	1.35
Annual Growth	6.3%	—	—	—	—	11.8%

Enova International Inc

Auditors: PricewaterhouseCoopers LLP

LOCATIONS

HQ: Enova International Inc
175 West Jackson Blvd., Chicago, IL 60604
Phone: 312 568-4200
Web: www.enova.com

HISTORICAL FINANCIALS
Company Type: Public

Income Statement   FYE: December 31

	REVENUE ($ mil.)	NET INCOME ($ mil.)	NET PROFIT MARGIN	EMPLOYEES
12/18	1,114.0	70.1	6.3%	1,218
12/17	843.7	29.2	3.5%	1,109
12/16	745.5	34.6	4.6%	1,099
12/15	652.6	43.9	6.7%	1,132
12/14	809.8	111.6	13.8%	1,151
Annual Growth	8.3%	(11.0%)	—	1.4%

2018 Year-End Financials

Debt ratio: 64.5%
Return on equity: 22.2%
Cash ($ mil.): 77.2
Current ratio: 11.15
Long-term debt ($ mil.): 857.9
No. of shares (mil.): 33.5
Dividends
  Yield: —
  Payout: —
Market value ($ mil.): 654.0

	STOCK PRICE ($) FY Close	P/E High/Low		PER SHARE ($) Earnings	Dividends	Book Value
12/18	19.46	19	8	1.99	0.00	10.35
12/17	15.20	19	13	0.86	0.00	8.41
12/16	12.55	13	5	1.03	0.00	7.26
12/15	6.61	18	5	1.33	0.00	6.22
12/14	22.26	9	6	3.38	3.71	4.67
Annual Growth	(3.3%)	—	—	(12.4%)	—	22.1%

Ensign Group Inc

The Ensign Group hangs its insignia at more than 200 senior living facilities. Most of its facilities are skilled nursing homes but it also operates a number of assisted-living and independent-living facilities as well as combination nursing assisted and independent-living centers. Some locations also offer rehabilitation hospice and physical therapy services. Ensign's facilities are either owned by the company or operated under lease agreements. The health care provider operates some 120 long-term care centers with a capacity of some 13200 beds in about a dozen states in the southwestern and western US. Ensign also operates home health and hospice agencies.

Operations
Ensign is a holding company that counts among its operations more than 240 facilities 25 hospice companies and about 20 home health businesses. The company has a decentralized operating structure with its portfolio of homes organized into five regional operating companies. Each home operates under local — and largely independent — management. As part of its business the company relies on reimbursement from government and commercial health insurance plans as well as sales to private pay customers. It generates about three-fourths of its revenues from Medicaid and Medicare programs.

Geographic Reach
California-based Ensign has facilities in California Arizona Texas Washington Utah Idaho Colorado Nevada Iowa Nebraska Oregon South Carolina and Wisconsin. California and Texas are the company's largest markets home to more than 50% of its beds.

Strategy
Ensign's growth strategy — and a growing population of increasingly infirm patients — has resulted in a decade of steady and significant revenue growth. Ensign primarily expands its operations by snapping up underperforming nursing homes in existing or new territories and turning them around both in terms of operating performance and clinical quality. In addition to acquiring new facilities and establishing local leadership teams the company works to boost patient occupancy at its existing facilities especially those facing financial troubles and extremely low occupancy rates. It does this by developing quality staff and clinical processes and through facility upgrades as well as by adding services such as outpatient therapy services. It is also focused on attracting more high-acuity patients who require higher levels of medical and rehabilitative care and for whom the company is generally reimbursed at higher rates.

Mergers and Acquisitions
Ensign regularly boosts its facility portfolio through purchases of both struggling and well-performing businesses. In 2019 it acquired South Texas-based firm All County Home Care and Hospice. It continues to seek acquisition opportunities.

EXECUTIVES

President CEO and Director, Christopher R. Christensen, age 51, $462,327 total compensation
COO Ensign Services Inc., Barry R. Port, age 45, $326,227 total compensation
President Bandera Healthcare, John P. Albrechtsen, age 42, $164,687 total compensation
CFO, Suzanne D. Snapper, age 45, $307,500 total compensation
VP and General Counsel, Beverly B. Wittekind, age 54, $410,612 total compensation
President Cornerstone Healthcare, Daniel H. (Danny) Walker
President Bridgestone Living, John Guerreri
President Milestone Healthcare, Jorge Rojas
EVP and Secretary, Chad A. Keetch, age 41, $280,833 total compensation
President Pennant Healthcare, Spencer Burton
President Keystone Healthcare, Kevin Reese
Director Of Nursing Services, Traishon Lockett
Director Of Nursing Services, Kay Gudgell
Director of Nursing, Janice Diez
Vice President, Ryan Jones
Director of Clinical Services, Mira Jensen
Director of Nursing, Linda Kolpin
Senior Business Intelligence Developer, Semir Taletovic
Director Of Nursing Services, Megan Rolfing
Executive Vice President Of Construction And Development, Aaron Dunyon
Chairman, Roy E. Christensen, age 86
Board Member, Barry Smith
Auditors: Deloitte & Touche LLP

LOCATIONS

HQ: Ensign Group Inc
29222 Rancho Viejo Road, Suite 127, San Juan Capistrano, CA 92675
Phone: 949 487-9500
Web: www.ensigngroup.net

PRODUCTS/OPERATIONS

2016 Sales

	$ mil.	% of total
Medicaid	558.0	34
Medicare	477.0	29
Private & other	266.9	16
Managed care	265.5	16
Medicaid - skilled	87.5	5
Total	**1,654.9**	**100**

2016 Sales

	$ mil.	% of total
Transitional and Skilled Services	1,377.7	83
Assisted and Independent Living Services	123.7	7
Home Health and Hospice Services	115.8	7
All Other	42.8	3
Elimination	-5.1	-
Total	**1,341.8**	**100**

COMPETITORS

Amedisys	Enlivant
American Baptist Homes of the West	Five Star Senior Living
Apria Healthcare	Genesis Healthcare
Brookdale Senior Living	Golden Horizons
	Kindred Healthcare
Covenant Care	Life Care Centers
Dignity Health	RehabCare
Diversicare Healthcare Services	SavaSeniorCare
	Sunrise Senior Living
Encompass Health	

HISTORICAL FINANCIALS

Company Type: Public

Income Statement
FYE: December 31

	REVENUE ($ mil.)	NET INCOME ($ mil.)	NET PROFIT MARGIN	EMPLOYEES
12/19	2,036.5	110.5	5.4%	24,500
12/18	2,040.6	92.3	4.5%	23,463
12/17	1,849.3	40.4	2.2%	21,301
12/16	1,654.8	49.9	3.0%	19,482
12/15	1,341.8	55.4	4.1%	16,494
Annual Growth	11.0%	18.8%	—	10.4%

2019 Year-End Financials

Debt ratio: 13.8%
Return on equity: 17.7%
Cash ($ mil.): 59.1
Current ratio: 1.20
Long-term debt ($ mil.): 325.2
No. of shares (mil.): 53.4
Dividends
  Yield: 0.4%
  Payout: 11.0%
Market value ($ mil.): 2,427.0

	STOCK PRICE ($) FY Close	P/E High/Low		PER SHARE ($) Earnings	Dividends	Book Value
12/19	45.37	29	18	1.97	0.19	12.23
12/18	38.79	27	13	1.70	0.18	11.24
12/17	22.20	31	22	0.77	0.17	9.59
12/16	22.21	24	18	0.96	0.16	8.98
12/15	22.63	49	20	1.06	0.15	8.32
Annual Growth	19.0%	—	—	16.8%	6.0%	10.1%

Entegris Inc

Entegris makes products integral to the manufacture of semiconductors and computer disk drives. The company makes some 20000 standard and custom products used to transport and protect semiconductor and disk drive materials during processing. Its semiconductor products include wafer carriers storage boxes and chip trays as well as chemical delivery products such as pipes fittings and valves. Its disk drive offerings include shippers stamper cases and transport trays. Top customers include Applied Materials ASML MEMC Siltronic Tokyo Electron and Taiwan Semiconductor Manufacturing. In 2019 Entegris and Versum Materials agreed to merge in an all-stock deal valued at about $4 billion.

Operations
Entegris identifies its products as capital-driven (dependent on capital spending to expand manufacturing capacity) and unit-driven and consumable (products that are used or consumed in the manufacturing process). Unit-driven products which make up nearly four-fifths of sales include liquid filters specialized graphite components and wafers shippers. They provide some protection against industry cycles by providing a recurring source of revenue. Capital-driven products 20% of revenue include wafer process carriers and gas microcontamination control systems. Those products give the company access to more capital when chip makers retrofit or expand production facilities.

Geographic Reach
Entegris has manufacturing and research and development facilities in France German Israel Singapore China Japan Malaysia South Korea Taiwan and the US. It also has sales and service offices throughout Asia and Europe.

The US and Taiwan each account for 23% of the company's revenue followed by South Korea with 14% and Japan with 12%. Combined customers in Asia account for more than 60% of its revenue.

Sales and Marketing
The company sells its products through a direct sales force and strategic distributors serving a range of markets including Semiconductor Flat Panel Display Manufacturing Compound Semiconductor Disk Data Storage Aerospace Solar/Clean Energy Life Sciences Emerging Technologies and Water Treatment industries.

In 2015 sales to the company's 10 biggest customers accounted for 44% of revenue. It sold products to 2400 companies.

Financial Performance
Entegris posted a 12% gain in revenue to reach $1.08 billion in 2015. The company realized $105.3 million in revenue from the ATMI acquisition. The company said the strong US dollar cost it almost $7 million in 2015.

The company's profit jumped sharply — more than 900% -to $80 million in 2015 from just about $8 million in 2014. A gain related to the sale of an equity investment and lack of ATMI merger costs as well as reduced integration expenditures boosted net income.

Entegris had about $121 million in cash flow in 2015 compared to $126.42 million in 2014. The company carried higher inventories in 2015.

Strategy
In order to counter the cycles of the semiconductor industry Entegris has expanded into adjacent and ancillary markets including applications in solar flat-panel displays and high-purity chemicals. Non-semiconductor industries include the aerospace biomedical glass container and electrical discharge machining markets. Its focus includes strategic acquisitions and partnerships and related transactions that enable it to complement its product markets and broaden its technological capabilities and product offerings.

It expanded its operations in Taiwan to provide manufacturing capabilities to support important customers in the region and also established sales and service offices in China in anticipation of a growing semiconductor manufacturing base in that region and expanded its presence in Singapore to enhance its global and regional management of supply chain and manufacturing processes.

The company expanded engineering research and development operations in South Korea and Taiwan in late 2015 and early 2016. Entegris said the operations are to enhance collaboration between its engineers and its customers in designing and manufacturing products.

Mergers and Acquisitions
In 2019 Entegris and Versum Materials based in Tempe Arizona agreed to merge in a $4 billion all-stock deal that would give Entegris shareholders 52.5% ownership while Versum shareholders would own the rest. The combined company would have annual revenue of about $3 billion based on each firm's 2018 revenue. The companies said that combined operations would lead to $75 million in cost reductions. The companies said that their complementary products and operations would broaden the new entity's reach as the semiconductor industry adopts new manufacturing materials and methods in the coming years. The deal is expected to close in the second half of 2019.

EXECUTIVES

EVP and Chief Administrative Officer, Bertrand Loy, age 53, $625,000 total compensation
EVP and CFO, Gregory B. (Greg) Graves, age 58, $321,826 total compensation
SVP and COO, Todd Edlund, age 56, $291,577 total compensation
Vice President Of Marketing, Wenge Yang
Senior Vice President, Clint Haris
Vice President Director Of Information Technology Risk Management, Mark Puttock
Chairman, Paul L. H. Olson, age 68
Auditors: KPMG LLP

LOCATIONS

HQ: Entegris Inc
129 Concord Road, Billerica, MA 01821
Phone: 978 436-6500

PRODUCTS/OPERATIONS

2015 Sales

	$ mil.	% of total
Critical Materials Handling	671.3	62
Electronic Materials	409.8	38
Total	**1,081.1**	**100**

COMPETITORS

3M	Pall Corporation
Air Products	Parker-Hannifin
Brooks Automation	Peak International
Donaldson Company	SAES Getters
Illinois Tool Works	Saint-Gobain
L'Air Liquide	Schweiter Technologies
MKS Instruments	Shin-Etsu Chemical
Mersen Group	Tokai Carbon
Mirae	

HISTORICAL FINANCIALS
Company Type: Public

Income Statement
FYE: December 31

	REVENUE ($ mil.)	NET INCOME ($ mil.)	NET PROFIT MARGIN	EMPLOYEES
12/18	1,550.5	240.7	15.5%	4,900
12/17	1,342.5	85.0	6.3%	3,900
12/16	1,175.2	97.1	8.3%	3,727
12/15	1,081.1	80.3	7.4%	3,557
12/14	962.0	7.8	0.8%	3,528
Annual Growth	12.7%	135.1%	—	8.6%

2018 Year-End Financials

Debt ratio: 40.5%
Return on equity: 24.0%
Cash ($ mil.): 482.0
Current ratio: 3.82
Long-term debt ($ mil.): 934.8
No. of shares (mil.): 135.9
Dividends
  Yield: 1.0%
  Payout: 16.5%
Market value ($ mil.): 3,793.0

	STOCK PRICE ($) FY Close	P/E High/Low		PER SHARE ($)		
			Earnings	Dividends	Book Value	
12/18	27.90	23 14	1.69	0.28	7.44	
12/17	30.45	55 30	0.59	0.07	7.03	
12/16	17.90	27 15	0.68	0.00	6.36	
12/15	13.27	26 21	0.57	0.00	5.71	
12/14	13.21	234 171	0.06	0.00	5.35	
Annual Growth	20.5%	—	130.4%	—	8.6%	

Enterprise Bancorp, Inc. (MA)

Enterprise Bancorp caters to more customers than just entrepreneurs. The holding company owns Enterprise Bank and Trust which operates more than 20 branches in north-central Massachusetts and southern New Hampshire. The $2 billion-asset bank offers traditional deposit and loan products specializing in lending to businesses professionals high-net-worth individuals and not-for-profits. About half of its loan portfolio is tied to commercial real estate while another one-third is tied to commercial and industrial and commercial construction loans. Subsidiaries Enterprise Investment Services and Enterprise Insurance Services provide investments and insurance geared to the bank's target business customers.

Operations
More than 50% of Enterprise Bancorp's $1.86 billion loan portfolio was tied to commercial real estate loans at the end of 2015 while commercial and industrial and commercial construction loans made up another 25% and 11% of the bank's loan assets. The rest of the bank's portfolio was tied to residential mortgages (9% of loan assets) home equity loans and lines of credit (4%) and consumer loans (less than 1%).

Nearly 80% of the bank's total revenue comes from loan interest while investment advisory fees and deposit and interchange fees each make up another 5%.

Geographic Reach
The Lowell Massachusetts-based bank operated 23 branches mostly located in the greater Merrimack Valley and North Central regions of Massachusetts and Southern New Hampshire at the end of 2015.

Sales and Marketing
Enterprise spent $2.7 million on advertising and public relations during 2015 down from $2.9 million in 2014.

Financial Performance
The bank's annual revenues have risen more than 40% since 2011 as its loan assets have swelled by 50% to $1.86 billion. Meanwhile its net income has grown more than 50% as it's kept a lid on loan loss provisions and operating costs.

Enterprise Bancorp's revenue climbed 8% to $98.4 million during 2015 thanks to 11% loan asset growth driven by a "seasoned" lending team a sales and service culture and geographic market expansion. Commercial construction loans grew the fastest rate during the year though all loans grew albeit at a slightly slower rate.

Revenue growth in 2015 drove the bank's net income up 10% to $16.1 million despite higher salary and employee benefit expenses. Enterprise Bancorp's operating cash levels nearly doubled to $25.7 million for the year largely thanks to positive changes in working capital mainly related to prepaid expenses and other assets.

Strategy
Enterprise Bancorp has traditionally expanded its loan and deposit business by opening new branches rather than by acquiring other banks. Enterprise hopes to take advantage of the trend to switch from larger banks to smaller community-oriented institutions. The company has also invested in upgrading its branches and operations systems.

EXECUTIVES

EVP and CFO Enterprise Bancorp and Enterprise Bank and Trust, James A. (Jim) Marcotte, age 61, $194,806 total compensation
CEO Enterprise Bancorp and Enterprise Bank and Trust, John P. (Jack) Clancy, age 61, $400,000 total compensation
President Enterprise Bancorp and Enterprise Bank and Trust, Richard W. (Dick) Main, age 71, $258,918 total compensation
EVP and COO Enterprise Bank and Trust, Stephen J. Irish, age 64, $194,804 total compensation
SVP and Chief Commercial Lender, Brian H. Bullock, age 61
SVP and Chief Commercial Real Estate Lender, Steven R. Larochelle, age 55
SVP and Sales Manager, Chester J. (Chet) Szablak, age 61
Vice President, Paul Rousseau
Vice Chairman Enterprise Bancorp and Enterprise Bank and Trust, Arnold S. Lerner, age 89
Chairman Enterprise Bancorp and Enterprise Bank and Trust, George L. Duncan, age 78
Auditors: RSM US LLP

LOCATIONS
HQ: Enterprise Bancorp, Inc. (MA)
222 Merrimack Street, Lowell, MA 01852
Phone: 978 459-9000

PRODUCTS/OPERATIONS

2015 Sales

	$ mil.	% of total
Interest and dividend income:		
Loans and loans held for sale	77.9	79
Investment securities	5.3	5
Other interest-earning assets	0.2	-
Non-interest income:		
Investment advisory fees	4.8	5
Deposit and interchange fees	4.9	5
Net gains on sales of investment securities	1.8	2
Income on bank-owned life insurance net	0.5	1
Gains on sales of loans	0.5	1
Other income	2.5	3
Total	98.4	100

Products and Services
Lending Products:
Residential Loans
Home Equity Loans and Lines of Credit
Consumer Loans
Credit Risk and Allowance for Loan Losses
Deposit Products:
Cash Management Services
Product Delivery Channels
Investment Services
Insurance Services

COMPETITORS

Bank of America	Peoples Federal
Citizens Financial	Bancshares Inc.
Group	Sovereign Bank
Eastern Bank	TD Bank USA

HISTORICAL FINANCIALS
Company Type: Public

Income Statement
FYE: December 31

	ASSETS ($ mil.)	NET INCOME ($ mil.)	INCOME AS % OF ASSETS	EMPLOYEES
12/18	2,964.3	28.8	1.0%	508
12/17	2,817.5	19.3	0.7%	482
12/16	2,526.2	18.7	0.7%	468
12/15	2,285.5	16.1	0.7%	426
12/14	2,022.2	14.6	0.7%	412
Annual Growth	10.0%	18.5%	—	5.4%

2018 Year-End Financials

Return on assets: 1.0%
Return on equity: 11.8%
Long-term debt ($ mil.): —
No. of shares (mil.): 11.7
Sales ($ mil): 134.8
Dividends
  Yield: 1.8%
  Payout: 27.2%
Market value ($ mil.): 377.0

	STOCK PRICE ($) FY Close	P/E High/Low	Earnings	Dividends	Book Value
12/18	32.16	17 12	2.46	0.58	21.80
12/17	34.05	23 18	1.66	0.54	19.97
12/16	37.56	22 12	1.70	0.52	18.72
12/15	22.85	16 13	1.55	0.50	17.38
12/14	25.25	18 12	1.44	0.48	16.35
Annual Growth	6.2%	—	14.3%	4.8%	7.5%

Enterprise Financial Services Corp

Enterprise Financial Services wants you to boldly bank where many have banked before. It's the holding company for Enterprise Bank & Trust which mostly targets closely-held businesses and their owners but also serves individuals in the St. Louis Kansas City and Phoenix metropolitan areas. Boasting $3.8 billion in assets and 16 branches Enterprise offers standard products such as checking savings and money market accounts and CDs. Commercial and industrial loans make up over half of the company's lending activities while real estate loans make up another 45%. The bank also writes consumer and residential mortgage loans. Bank subsidiary Enterprise Trust offers wealth management services.

Operations
Enterprise Trust the company's wealth management unit targets business owners wealthy individuals and institutional investors providing financial planning business succession planning and related services. The unit also invests in Missouri state tax credits from funds for affordable housing development which it then sells to clients and others.

About 82% of Enterprise Financial's total revenue came from loan interest (including fees) in 2014 while another 7% came from interest on its taxable and tax-exempt investment securities. The rest of its revenue came from wealth management income (4%) service fees (3%) gains on state tax credits (1%) and other miscellaneous income sources. The bank had a staff of 452 full-time employees at the end of 2014.

Geographic Reach
Enterprise Bank & Trust operates eight banking locations in or around Kansas City six banking locations and a support center in the St. Louis area and two banking locations in the Phoenix metro area.

Financial Performance
The company has struggled to consistently grow its revenues in recent years mostly due to shrinking interest margins on its loans amidst the low-interest environment. Its profits however have mostly trended higher thanks to declining loan loss provisions as its loan portfolio's credit quality has improved with higher property valuations in the strengthened economy.

Enterprise Financials' revenue fell by 9% to $148.4 million in 2014 mostly due to double-digit declines in interest income as its purchased credit-impaired (PCI) loan balances and accelerated payments declined and as interest margins on its loans continued to shrink. The bank's portfolio loan balances increased however helping to offset some of its interest income decline.

Lower revenue and higher loan loss provisions (it received a loan loss benefit of $642 thousand in 2013) in 2014 caused the bank's net income to dive 18% to $27.2 million. Enterprise Financial's operating cash levels rose by 7% to $31.5 million despite lower earnings for the year mostly thanks to favorable changes in its working capital related to a $12-million change in other asset balances.

Strategy
Enterprise Financial Services planned in 2015 to continue its long-term strategy of keeping a "relationship-oriented distribution and sales approach"; growing its fee income and niche businesses; practicing "prudent" credit and interest rate risk management; and using advanced technology and controlled-expense growth. The company added that it planned on "operating branches with larger average deposits and employing experienced staff who are compensated on the basis of performance and customer service."

Though it just had two branches in Phoenix in 2015 the bank believes the fast-growing Phoenix market offers long-term growth opportunities for the company with its underlying demographic and geographic factors. Indeed at the end of 2014 the market had over 90000 privately-held businesses and 80000-plus households each with investable assets of more than $1 million.

Mergers and Acquisitions
In 2017 Enterprise Financial Services completed the acquisition of Jefferson County Bancshares the holding company of Eagle Bank and Trust Company in Missouri. The deal added 13 branches in metropolitan St. Louis and Perry County Missouri. The acquisition expanded EFS's assets to nearly $5 billion.

Company Background
In a restructuring move Enterprise Financial Services sold life insurance arm Millennium Brokerage in 2010 five years after investing in the company.

EXECUTIVES
President Enterprise Bank and Trust, Scott R. Goodman, age 55, $318,150 total compensation
EVP and CFO, Keene S. Turner, age 39, $333,125 total compensation
CEO, James B. Lally, age 51, $331,342 total compensation
Chief Credit Officer Enterprise Bank & Trust, Douglas N. Bauche, age 50, $253,270 total compensation
Senior Vice President Trust Officer, Steven Ray
Senior Vice President Relationship Manager, Tim Barringhaus
Senior Vice President Treasury Management, Rhonda Harrelson
Vice President Operations, Colleen Shea
Senior Vice President Treasury Management, Mark Lawson
Vice President Treasury Management, Shirley Jacobs
Senior Vice President, Debbie Barstow
Vice President Relationship Manager, Brian Bonfanti
Vice President Treasury Management, Beth Selanders
Senior Vice President, Tim Kelley
Executive Vice President Wholesale, Greg Willert
Vice President Finance, Matt Eusterbrock
Chairman, John S. Eulich, age 68
Auditors: Deloitte and Touche LLP

LOCATIONS
HQ: Enterprise Financial Services Corp
150 North Meramec, Clayton, MO 63105
Phone: 314 725-5500
Web: www.enterprisebank.com

PRODUCTS/OPERATIONS
2011 Sales

	$ mil.	% of total
Interest		
Loans including fees	130.1	79
Securities	11.8	7
Other	0.9	1
Noninterest		
Wealth management	6.8	4
Service charges on deposit accounts	5.1	3
Gain on state tax credits net	3.7	2
Other service charges and fee income	1.7	1
Other	4.7	3
Adjustments	(3.5)	-
Total	**161.3**	**100**

Selected Acquisitions

COMPETITORS
BOK Financial
Bank of America
Commerce Bancshares
First Clover Leaf Financial
Midwest BankCentre
Pulaski Financial
U.S. Bancorp
Wells Fargo

HISTORICAL FINANCIALS
Company Type: Public

Income Statement
FYE: December 31

	ASSETS ($ mil.)	NET INCOME ($ mil.)	INCOME AS % OF ASSETS	EMPLOYEES
12/18	5,645.6	89.2	1.6%	650
12/17	5,289.2	48.1	0.9%	635
12/16	4,081.3	48.8	1.2%	479
12/15	3,608.4	38.4	1.1%	459
12/14	3,277.0	27.1	0.8%	452
Annual Growth	14.6%	34.6%	—	9.5%

2018 Year-End Financials
Return on assets: 1.6%
Return on equity: 15.4%
Long-term debt ($ mil.): —
No. of shares (mil.): 22.8
Sales ($ mil): 276.1
Dividends
Yield: 1.2%
Payout: 12.2%
Market value ($ mil.): 858.0

	STOCK PRICE ($) FY Close	P/E High/Low	PER SHARE ($) Earnings	Dividends	Book Value
12/18	37.63	15 10	3.83	0.47	26.47
12/17	45.15	22 18	2.07	0.44	23.76
12/16	43.00	18 10	2.41	0.41	19.31
12/15	28.35	16 10	1.89	0.26	17.53
12/14	19.73	15 12	1.35	0.21	15.94
Annual Growth	17.5%	— —	29.8%	22.3%	13.5%

Envestnet Inc

Envestnet provides managed account services for around 50000 financial institutions and investment advisers. The company's online financial planning programs assist brokers banks insurance companies and registered investment advisers with portfolio construction and analysis generating proposals and managing client accounts. Subsidiary Portfolio Management Consultants (Envestnet | PMC) provides consulting services to financial advisors and affords them access to managed accounts mutual funds exchange-traded funds and alternative investments. Founded in 1999 Envestnet supports approximately $851 billion in assets across some 3.5 million investor accounts.

Operations

In addition to its AdvisorSuite software and Envestnet | PMC services the company operates Envestnet Reporting Solutions (Envestnet | Vantage) which provides investment advisors with a detailed picture of their clients' holdings. Altogether Envestnet's capabilities allow advisors to select from a wide range of investments and services that best match their client's needs.

Envestnet operates two segments: Envestnet which generated 97% of the company's total revenue in 2015 and provides wealth management software and services to support financial advisors and institutions; and Envestnet | Yodlee which began in 2015 and is a data aggregation and data analytics platform for digital financial services.

Envestnet earns most of its money by charging fees based on a percentage of assets managed or administered on its platform by its financial advisor clients (the majority of its revenue) and by licensing its its technology. It generated 79% of its total revenue from assets under management or administration during 2015. The remainder of its revenue came from subscription and licensing fees (18% of revenue) for its platforms and professional services and other income (3% of revenue).

Geographic Reach

Chicago-based Envestnet has offices in nine US cities including Boston New York and Seattle and an office in Trivandrum India. The firm generated 92% of its revenue from business in the US during 2015 while the rest came from overseas.

Sales and Marketing

The company's major clients include FMR LLC Northwestern Mutual National Financial Partners and National Planning Holdings. Financial services giant FMR accounted for 18% of Envestnet's total revenue in 2015. More than 950 companies were using the firm's Envestnet | Yodlee platform as of early 2016 including 12 of the 20 largest US banks and hundreds of Internet services companies.

Envestnet markets its products and services through paid print and online advertisements e-blast campaigns and sponsored webinars for financial advisors. It also partners with independent broker-dealers to create direct mail campaigns to target financial advisors. The firm's sales teams are organized by sales channel and product offering with its enterprise sales team focusing on enterprise clients its advisory sales teams serving financial advisors of broker-dealer and RIA firms and a direct sales and pre-sales team to serve leading global financial institutions.

Altogether the company spent $645000 on advertising during 2015 down from $675000 and $1.03 million in 2014 and 2013 respectively.

Financial Performance

Rising financial markets and new customer business from acquisitions have helped Envestnet's assets under management and administration swell over the years causing revenue to more than triple since 2012. Meanwhile its annual profits have risen more than ten-fold as the firm has kept a lid on overhead costs.

The company's revenue jumped 21% to $420.92 million during 2015 mostly thanks to 13% growth in assets under management or administration income as its platform AUM/A swelled by 20% to $851.44 billion. Subscription and licensing income spiked 31% as demand for its Envestnet | Tamarac professional services grew.

Despite strong revenue growth in 2015 Envestnet's net income plummeted more than two-thirds to $4.44 million during the year mostly as a string of recent acquisitions led to higher headcounts systems development costs professional and legal fees and other associated costs. The company's operating cash levels fell more than 55% to $24.43 million in 2015 mostly due to the sharp fall in cash earnings.

Strategy

Envestnet maintains a growth strategy centered around making acquisitions that bolster the attractiveness of its technology platforms hoping to expand its client base and grow its assets under management. To build its business organically the firm which entered a new business market after acquiring data aggregator and analysis company Yodlee in late 2015 intends to cross-sell its new Envestnet | Yodlee product to existing customers.

With its eye on the long-term trend Envestnet has been catering to the growing number of independent and boutique investment advisers a market which may not have the technological resources and tools of larger firms. The company sees a promising trend of advisors leaving larger firms to start their own practices or move to boutiques.

Mergers and Acquisitions

In 2019 Envestnet agreed to acquire PIEtech for about $500 million. PIEtech owns the MoneyGuide family of financial planning software for financial advisors. The MoneyGuide app complements Envestnet's Logix and Apprise financial planning programs.

EXECUTIVES

Group President Envestnet | Tamarac, Stuart DePina
Chairman and CEO, Judson (Jud) Bergman, age 62, $422 total compensation
Group President Advisory Services, William (Bill) Crager, age 55, $335,000 total compensation
CIO Portfolio Management Consultants, Brandon Thomas, $259,167 total compensation
EVP, James W. Lumberg, age 53
CTO, Scott Grinis, age 57, $245,000 total compensation
EVP Strategic Development, Viggy Mokkarala, age 59
Group President Envestnet Retirement Solutions, Babu Sivadasan, age 46
EVP Advisor Managed Programs, James Patrick
EVP and Managing Director, Ajit K
EVP and Senior Managing Director Engineering Prof. Services Envestnet India, Anilal Ravi
COO, Josh Mayer
CFO, Peter (Pete) D'Arrigo, $287,500 total compensation
EVP and Managing Director Advisor Suite, Mike Apker
EVP Envestnet | WMS, Kevin B. Osborn
Executive Vice President Envestnet | Placemark, Ron Pruitt
Vice President Business Development, Bryan Watson
Assistant Vice President Relationship Manager, Kathleen Sullivan
Senior Vice President, David Robinson
Vice President Director, Eric Wilcher
Vice President Investment Specialist, Russell Colburn
Senior Vice President Relationship Management, John Fitzpatrick
Assistant Vice President Head Trader, Rodney Succes
Assistant Vice President Senior Regional Consultant, Jesse Nichols
Vice President Trading, James Dean
Assistant Vice President, Christina Riley
Senior Vice President Operations, Rene Johnston
Assistant Vice President Specialist, Regan Ryan
Vice President Wealth Consultant, Charles Gaudreau
Senior Vice President Advisory Services, John Phoenix
Vice President Regional Director, Jeff Delcorse
Associate Vice President Senior Regional Consultant, Frederic Diaz
Assistant Vice President Regional Consultant, Brian Dumonte
Vice President, Rob Chateauneuf
Assistant Vice President Institutional Client Services, Robert Auclair
Vice President Data Conversion Management, Cheng Yeh
Vice President, Libby Chase
Assistant Vice President Relationship Manager, Kristin Allard
Associate Vice President, James Mcglynn
Assistant Vice President Super, Kimberly Mendoza
Vice President Technical Support, John Mcgarry
Senior Vice President, Linda Bready
Vice President Regional Director, Kipp Cormier
Assistant Vice President Supervisor, Christen Brown
Vice President Product Management, Jeff Wingo
Senior Vice President, Michelle Garrett
Associate Vice President, Edmund Kelly
Senior Vice President Director Of Internal Sales and Con, Scott Opper
Vice President Controller Of Financial Operations, Jill Darnill
Associate Vice President, Fred Diaz
Vice President, Ryan Darr
Senior Vice President Finance, Chris Tarrach
Vice President, Frank Wei
Vice President Regional Sales Director, Brion Valashinas
Assistant Vice President Project Manager, Emily Vaughan
Vice President, Cynthia Crandall
Vice President Midwest Regional Director, Matt Erickson
Vice President Marketing, Kaili Xu
Senior Vice President, Noah Krieger
Assistant Vice President, Patrick Schumacher
Assistant Vice President Director of Operations, Karen Pless
Senior Vice President, Janet Mariconti
Associate Vice President Product Management, Steve Misheikis
Assistant Vice President, Donna Castellano
Vice President Application Manager, Lenny Shohet
Vice President Systems, Greg Grintsvayg
Senior Vice President Relationship Management, Gino Cipriano
Executive Vice President, Richard Dion
Vice President, Stephanie Sledjeski
Vice President Wealth Consultant, Michael Saldutti
Vice President Of Software Architecture, Biju Babu
Vice President Information Security, Nicholas Fahrney
Vice President Relationship Manager, Karle McLaughlin
Vice President Director of Technology, Jeremy Lowery

Vice President Advisor Launch Coordinator, Robert Vines
Senior Vice President Program Management, Brett Rainey
Assistant Vice President, James Byrns
Vice President Operations, Babu Sunod
Assistant Vice President Wealth Management, James Nestor
Vp Enterprise Consulting, Dawn Riggleman
Assistant Vice President Institutional Client Services, Lisa Seery
Associate Vice President Account Management, Stephen Vacanti
Assistant Vice President Insti, Bob Auclair
Vice President Senior Compliance Officer, Lacey Kassirer
Vp Director Of Development, Kenan Avdic
Vice President Senior Compliance Officer, David Hein
Vice President, Marianne Quinn
Assistant Vice President Implementation Manager (Pas), Stefan Daniels
Senior Vice President Finance And Treasurer, Laura Dunne
Vice President Enterprise Consulting, Yasemin Green
Vice President, Marianna Prontnicki
SENIOR VICE PRESIDENT CLIENT RELATIONS, Andina Anderson
Svp Strategic Development, Kent Bonniwell
ASSISTANT VICE PRESIDENT ADVISOR SERVICES MANAGER, Ryan Bamert
Vice President, Christina Eaves
Vice President and Asset Manager Relationship Management, Sharon Hughes
Senior Vice President Manager Services, Estee Jimerson
Vice President Portfolio Strategy Consultant, Brett Wayman
Vice President Business Solutions, Jim Kelly
Assistant Vice President Attorney, Alicia Malik
Avp Business Development Consultant, Mark Marcellino
Vp Business Solutions Strategic Business Development, Anuj Gupta
Avp Institutional Liaison, Morgan Manchester
Vice President Portfolio Administration Services, Kimberly Troy
Vp Sales Emea, Matt Cockayne
VICE PRESIDENT, Sean Lawlor
Vp Ux Design, Christo Claassens
Vice President Portfolio Administration Services, Stephanie Bream
Vp Sr. Compliance Officer, Lacey Zavelovich
Vice President Business Solutions Group, John Clifford
Vp Business Solutions, Tim Fisk
Vice President Of Quality Assurance, Mona Manchanda
Vice President Operations And Portfolio Management, Bryant Cal
Vice President Software Architect, Kavitha Venkatachalam
Vp Enterprise Consulting, Allan Avena
Vp and Assistant Corporate Secretary, Phinesia Johnson
Vice President Product Management, Stephen Mennella
ASSISTANT VICE PRESIDENT ADVISOR SERVICES, Luis Mendoza
Assistant Vice President Conversion Consultant, George Lew
Vice President Advisor Services, Darren Abbott
Vice Chairman, Anil Arora
Auditors: KPMG LLP

LOCATIONS
HQ: Envestnet Inc
35 East Wacker Drive, Suite 2400, Chicago, IL 60601
Phone: 312 827-2800   **Fax:** 312 827-2801
Web: www.envestnet.com

PRODUCTS/OPERATIONS
2015 Sales

	$ mil.	% of total
Assets under management or administration	333.7	79
Subscription and licensing	75.3	18
Professional services and other	11.9	3
Total	**420.9**	**100**

2015 Sales

	$ mil.	% of total
Envestnet	406.8	97
Envestnet | Yodlee	14.1	3
Total	**420.9**	**100**

Envestnet Segment solutions
Advisor Suite
Finance Logix
PMC
Retirement Solutions (ERS)
Tamarac
Vantage

COMPETITORS
Advent Software   Fiserv
Ameriprise   Genworth Financial
Bank of New York Mellon   Intuit
Cetera   LPL Financial
Charles Schwab   SEI Investments
Fidelity National Information Services   State Street
    Unified Financial Services

HISTORICAL FINANCIALS
Company Type: Public

Income Statement   FYE: December 31

	REVENUE ($ mil.)	NET INCOME ($ mil.)	NET PROFIT MARGIN	EMPLOYEES
12/18	812.3	5.7	0.7%	3,920
12/17	683.6	(3.2)	—	3,516
12/16	578.1	(55.5)	—	3,197
12/15	420.9	4.4	1.1%	2,665
12/14	348.7	14.1	4.1%	1,257
Annual Growth	23.5%	(20.2%)	—	32.9%

2018 Year-End Financials
Debt ratio: 35.0%   No. of shares (mil.): 48.1
Return on equity: 1.0%   Dividends
Cash ($ mil.): 289.3   Yield: —
Current ratio: 1.11   Payout: —
Long-term debt ($ mil.): 294.7   Market value ($ mil.): 2,367.0

	STOCK PRICE ($) FY Close	P/E High/Low	PER SHARE ($) Earnings	Dividends	Book Value
12/18	49.19	491 359	0.12	0.00	13.17
12/17	49.85	— —	(0.08)	0.00	9.78
12/16	35.25	— —	(1.30)	0.00	9.57
12/15	29.85	478 237	0.12	0.00	10.49
12/14	49.14	133 83	0.38	0.00	5.87
Annual Growth	0.0%	—	(25.0%)	—	22.4%

Enviva Partners LP

Auditors: Ernst & Young LLP

LOCATIONS
HQ: Enviva Partners LP
7200 Wisconsin Ave., Suite 1000, Bethesda, MD 20814
Phone: 301 657-5560
Web: www.envivabiomass.com

HISTORICAL FINANCIALS
Company Type: Public

Income Statement   FYE: December 31

	REVENUE ($ mil.)	NET INCOME ($ mil.)	NET PROFIT MARGIN	EMPLOYEES
12/18	573.7	6.9	1.2%	0
12/17	543.2	17.5	3.2%	0
12/16	464.2	21.3	4.6%	0
12/15	457.3	23.1	5.1%	0
12/14	290.1	0.2	0.1%	338
Annual Growth	18.6%	126.5%	—	—

2018 Year-End Financials
Debt ratio: 57.7%   No. of shares (mil.): 26.4
Return on equity: —   Dividends
Cash ($ mil.): 2.4   Yield: 9.0%
Current ratio: 0.58   Payout: 6,275.0%
Long-term debt ($ mil.): 429.9   Market value ($ mil.): 735.0

	STOCK PRICE ($) FY Close	P/E High/Low	PER SHARE ($) Earnings	Dividends	Book Value
12/18	27.75	825 628	0.04	2.51	5.54
12/17	27.65	48 38	0.61	2.28	7.99
12/16	26.80	30 15	0.91	2.03	11.90
12/15	18.15	14 7	1.58	0.70	13.05
Annual Growth	15.2%	—	(70.6%)	52.8%	(24.8%)

Epam Systems, Inc.

EPAM provides software development and other IT services to US and European customers primarily from development centers in Russia Belarus Hungary Ukraine Kazakhstan and Poland. In addition to software product development the company offers services in such areas as e-commerce support data warehousing customer relationship management and application integration. EPAM also offers its own hosted and stand-alone enterprise software for sales force automation content management order management and other business processes. Half of sales come from North America.

Operations
EPAM generates 69% of its revenue from software development. Another 19% comes from testing applications with application maintenance accounting for 8%.

Geographic Reach
North America is EPAM's biggest market accounting for 50% of revenue. European customers provide 39%. Russia and former members of the Soviet Union account for 15% of revenue.

The company has expanded geographically by adding client management offices in locations that are close to customers — including the US UK Germany Sweden Switzerland Russia and Kazakhstan — and by adding new development centers. In certain cases (such as Russia and Kazakhstan) EPAM has both development centers and client management offices in the same country.

Financial Performance
EPAM has posted steady growth in revenue and net income over the past several years. Revenue increased 31% in 2014 to $730 million. The company broadened its sales to existing customers and found new ones to drive up revenue. Sales jumped 30% in North America in 2014.

Net income rose 12% in 2014 to $69.6 million. Cash flow from operations also rose in 2014 reaching $104 million compared to $58 million in 2013.

Strategy
EPAM is looking to extend its expertise in targeted industry verticals which include independent software vendors banking and financial services business information and media hospitality and travel and retail and consumer. To do this EPAM continues to recruit IT professionals with specific industry knowledge and to pursue acquisitions that add to its service portfolio and customer base. Another part of EPAM's growth strategy is to make acquisitions of companies that have a significant presence in China Latin America and other emerging markets.

Mergers and Acquisitions
In 2019 EPAM acquired Competentum an educational content services company and its learning platform ShareKnowledge. The addition of Competentum helps EPAM extend its digital services in the media publishing and EdTech industries. Competentum develops educational programs digital learning platforms and services for schools (for learning science technology engineering and math) healthcare and Governance Risk Management and Compliance (GRC).

EXECUTIVES
President and CEO, Arkadiy Dobkin, age 59, $437,500 total compensation
SVP and CFO, Jason Peterson
SVP and Co-Head of Global Business, Balazs Fejes, age 44, $292,326 total compensation
Head of Global Operations, Yuriy Goliyad
Co-Head of Global Business, Boris Shnayder, age 53, $257,500 total compensation
Co-Head Global Delivery, Sergey Yezhkov
Co-Head Global Delivery, Victor Dvorkin
Senior Vice President Head of Global Business Development, Robert Corace
Vice President Compensation And Benefits, Scott Haverlock
Vice President, Daniel Lloyd
Vp Enterprise Products, Jitin Agarwal
Auditors: DELOITTE & TOUCHE LLP

LOCATIONS
HQ: Epam Systems, Inc.
41 University Drive, Suite 202, Newtown, PA 18940
Phone: 267 759-9000
Web: www.epam.com

PRODUCTS/OPERATIONS
2014 Sales
	$ mil.	% of total
Software development	504.6	69
Application testing services	140.4	19
Application maintenance & support	58.8	8
Infrastructure services	14.2	2
Licensing	3.6	1
Reimbursable expenses & other revenues	8.4	1
Total	**730.0**	**100**

2014 Sales by Industry
	$ mil.	% of total
Banking & financial services	215.4	29
Independent software vendors & technology	157.9	22
Travel & hospitality	157.8	22
Business information & media	91.7	13
Other verticals	98.8	13
Reimbursable expenses & other revenues	8.4	1
Total	**730.0**	**100**

Selected Services
Application development
Application maintenance and support
Application testing
Business intelligence
Business process management
Content management
Customer Relationship Management (CRM)
Data warehousing and business intelligence
E-commerce
Enterprise application integration
Enterprise resource planning
Infrastructure and hosting
Knowledge management
Localization
Offshore software development
Quality assurance consulting and testing strategy transformation
Server and network management

COMPETITORS
Accenture
Atos
Camelot Information
Capgemini
Cognizant Tech Solutions
Computer Sciences Corp.
GlobalLogic
HCL Technologies
IBM Global Services
Infosys
MindTree
Pactera
Sapient
Symphony Technology Group LLC
Tata Consultancy
VanceInfo
Wipro
iSoftStone

HISTORICAL FINANCIALS
Company Type: Public

Income Statement
FYE: December 31

	REVENUE ($ mil.)	NET INCOME ($ mil.)	NET PROFIT MARGIN	EMPLOYEES
12/18	1,842.9	240.2	13.0%	30,156
12/17	1,450.4	72.7	5.0%	25,962
12/16	1,160.1	99.2	8.6%	22,383
12/15	914.1	84.4	9.2%	18,354
12/14	730.0	69.6	9.5%	14,109
Annual Growth	26.0%	36.3%	—	20.9%

2018 Year-End Financials
Debt ratio: 1.5%
Return on equity: 21.4%
Cash ($ mil.): 770.5
Current ratio: 4.56
Long-term debt ($ mil.): 25.0
No. of shares (mil.): 54.0
Dividends
 Yield: —
 Payout: —
Market value ($ mil.): 6,274.0

	STOCK PRICE ($) FY Close	P/E High/Low	PER SHARE ($) Earnings	Dividends	Book Value
12/18	116.01	32 23	4.24	0.00	23.35
12/17	107.43	78 45	1.32	0.00	18.40
12/16	64.31	40 29	1.87	0.00	15.29
12/15	78.62	48 26	1.62	0.00	12.22
12/14	47.75	35 20	1.40	0.00	9.61
Annual Growth	24.8%	— —	31.9%	—	24.9%

EPR Properties

EPR Properties (formerly Entertainment Properties Trust) invests in places to play and learn. The self-administered real estate investment trust (REIT) owns around 140 movie megaplex theaters and theater-anchored entertainment retail centers around the US and Canada. The REIT buys properties from theater operators and leases them back to the original owners. Many of its theaters are leased to AMC Entertainment. EPR also owns ski resorts (for clients including Camelback Mountain Resorts) golf resorts (for operator TopGolf) waterparks (including Schlitterbahn parks) public charter schools early education centers and private schools.

Operations
The REIT owns three main types of properties: Entertainment Education and Recreation. Its Entertainment properties which generated 63% of its total revenue during 2015 in the form of rental income include multiplex theaters entertainment retail centers and family entertainment centers. Its Education properties (19% of revenue) consists of 70 public charter school properties 18 early childhood centers and three private schools.

Its Recreation properties (17% of revenue) consist of ski areas waterparks and golf courses. Its Metro Daily Ski business consists of 14 ski properties located close to metropolitan areas including: Camelback Mountain Resort in Pennsylvania; Vermont's Mt. Snow; and a dozen other properties in Ohio and nine other mostly eastern states. EPR's waterpark properties are leased to Schlitterbahn. Its four Texas golf properties are operated by TopGolf.

Geographic Reach
The Kansas City Missouri-based REITs five largest markets are in Texas (13% of 2015 revenues) Ontario (10%) California (9%) Arizona (7%) and Illinois (6%).

Sales and Marketing
The REIT has more than 250 tenants and about 99% of its properties are currently leased. Its largest tenant is theater operator AMC which accounted for about 20% of its annual revenue during 2015. Other tenants include Schlitterbahn Regal Studio Movie Grill Altitude Trampoline Park TopGolf and Carolina Cinemas.

Financial Performance
EPR Properties' annual revenues have risen 40% since 2011 as new property acquisitions have spurred additional rental income. Its annual profits have grown nearly 70% over the same period as the REIT has kept a lid on rising operating and overhead costs.

The REIT's revenue climbed 9% to $421 million during 2015 as property acquisitions (mostly movie theaters) and build-to-suite projects added to its rental revenue.

Strong revenue growth and gains from property sales in 2015 boosted EPR's net income by 8% to $194.5 million for the year. The REIT's operating cash levels rose 11% to $278.5 million thanks to the rise in cash-denominated earnings.

Strategy

EPR Properties remains focused on its core movie theater business as Americans continue to flock to the movies even in uncertain markets. In April 2014 the company invested $118 million on 11 theater properties in seven states continuing to build its massive collection.

Although megaplexes account for the majority of its holdings the company continues to look for opportunities to diversify its real estate holdings.

EXECUTIVES

President and CEO, Gregory K. (Greg) Silvers, age 55, $484,500 total compensation
SVP and Chief Investment Officer, Morgan G. (Jerry) Earnest, age 63, $392,700 total compensation
SVP CFO and Treasurer, Mark A. Peterson, age 55, $346,500 total compensation
SVP Secretary and General Counsel, Neil E. Sprague, age 63, $300,000 total compensation
Vice President, Tom Hudak
Vice President Corporate Communications, Brian Moriarty
Vice President And Associate General Counsel, Rebecca Beal
V Pres Strategic Planning, Michael L Hirons
Vice President Finance, James Lee
Vice President And Controller, April Jenkins
Vice President, Tonya Mater
Vice President, Aaron Linn
Vice President And Associate General Counsel, Paul Turvey
Executive Vice President And Chief Investment Officer, Gregory E Zimmerman
Vice President Human Resources And Administration, Liz Grace
Chairman, Robert J. Druten, age 72
Auditors: KPMG LLP

LOCATIONS

HQ: EPR Properties
909 Walnut Street, Suite 200, Kansas City, MO 64106
Phone: 816 472-1700   **Fax:** 816 472-5794
Web: www.eprkc.com

PRODUCTS/OPERATIONS

2015 Sales

	$ mil.	% of total
Rental Revenue	330.9	78
Mortgage and other financing income	70.2	17
Tenant reimbursements	16.3	4
Other income	3.6	1
Total	421.0	100

2015 Sales

	$ mil.	% of total
Entertainment	262.9	63
Education	82.1	19
Recreation	72.6	17
Corporate	3.0	1
Other	0.4	—
Total	421.0	100

COMPETITORS

Acadia Realty Trust
Cousins Properties
Lexington Realty Trust
National Retail Properties
One Liberty Properties
Reading International
Realty Income
Regal Entertainment
Simon Property Group
Tanger Factory Outlet
Taubman Centers
Vornado Realty

HISTORICAL FINANCIALS

Company Type: Public

Income Statement   FYE: December 31

	REVENUE ($ mil.)	NET INCOME ($ mil.)	NET PROFIT MARGIN	EMPLOYEES
12/18	700.7	266.9	38.1%	64
12/17	575.9	262.9	45.7%	63
12/16	493.2	224.9	45.6%	57
12/15	421.0	194.5	46.2%	49
12/14	385.0	179.6	46.7%	40
Annual Growth	16.1%	10.4%	—	12.5%

2018 Year-End Financials

Debt ratio: 48.7%
Return on equity: 9.2%
Cash ($ mil.): 5.8
Current ratio: 0.42
Long-term debt ($ mil.): 2,986.0
No. of shares (mil.): 74.3
Dividends
  Yield: 6.7%
  Payout: 128.5%
Market value ($ mil.): 4,760.0

	STOCK PRICE ($) FY Close	P/E High/Low	PER SHARE ($) Earnings	Dividends	Book Value
12/18	64.03	22 16	3.27	4.32	38.54
12/17	65.46	24 19	3.29	4.08	39.49
12/16	71.77	27 17	3.17	3.84	34.34
12/15	58.45	22 17	2.93	3.63	34.10
12/14	57.63	21 17	2.86	3.42	33.72
Annual Growth	2.7%	— —	3.4%	6.0%	3.4%

EQM Midstream Partners LP

Auditors: Ernst & Young, LLP

LOCATIONS

HQ: EQM Midstream Partners LP
625 Liberty Avenue, Suite 2000, Pittsburgh, PA 15222
Phone: 412 395-2688
Web: www.eqtmidstreampartners.com

HISTORICAL FINANCIALS

Company Type: Public

Income Statement   FYE: December 31

	REVENUE ($ mil.)	NET INCOME ($ mil.)	NET PROFIT MARGIN	EMPLOYEES
12/18	1,495.1	668.0	44.7%	0
12/17	834.1	571.9	68.6%	0
12/16	735.6	537.9	73.1%	0
12/15	614.1	393.4	64.1%	0
12/14	392.9	232.7	59.2%	0
Annual Growth	39.7%	30.2%	—	—

2018 Year-End Financials

Debt ratio: 43.1%
Return on equity: —
Cash ($ mil.): 17.5
Current ratio: 0.55
Long-term debt ($ mil.): 4,081.6
No. of shares (mil.): 121.9
Dividends
  Yield: 9.9%
  Payout: 176.7%
Market value ($ mil.): 5,272.0

	STOCK PRICE ($) FY Close	P/E High/Low	PER SHARE ($) Earnings	Dividends	Book Value
12/18	43.25	32 16	2.43	4.30	39.49
12/17	73.10	16 13	5.19	3.66	26.20
12/16	76.68	15 11	5.21	3.05	24.30
12/15	75.46	19 13	4.70	2.51	19.85
12/14	88.00	28 17	3.52	2.02	11.16
Annual Growth	(16.3%)	— —	(8.8%)	20.8%	37.2%

Equitrans Midstream Corp

Auditors: Ernst & Young, LLP

LOCATIONS

HQ: Equitrans Midstream Corp
625 Liberty Avenue, Suite 2000, Pittsburgh, PA 15222
Phone: 724 271-7600
Web: www.equitransmidstream.com

HISTORICAL FINANCIALS

Company Type: Public

Income Statement   FYE: December 31

	REVENUE ($ mil.)	NET INCOME ($ mil.)	NET PROFIT MARGIN	EMPLOYEES
12/18	1,495.1	218.4	14.6%	0
12/17	895.5	(27.1)	—	0
12/16	732.2	65.1	8.9%	0
12/15	632.9	174.3	27.5%	0
Annual Growth	33.2%	7.8%	—	—

2018 Year-End Financials

Debt ratio: 44.3%
Return on equity: 27.2%
Cash ($ mil.): 294.1
Current ratio: 1.04
Long-term debt ($ mil.): 4,660.2
No. of shares (mil.): 254.2
Dividends
  Yield: 0.0%
  Payout: 47.6%
Market value ($ mil.): 5,091.0

	STOCK PRICE ($) FY Close	P/E High/Low	PER SHARE ($) Earnings	Dividends	Book Value
12/18	20.02	27 22	0.86	0.41	1.80
12/17	0.00	— —	(0.59)	0.00	(0.00)
Annual Growth	—	— —	—	—	—

Equity Bancshares Inc

Auditors: Crowe LLP

LOCATIONS

HQ: Equity Bancshares Inc
7701 East Kellogg Drive, Suite 300, Wichita, KS 67207
Phone: 316 612-6000
Web: www.equitybank.com

ESCO Technologies, Inc.

ESCO Technologies is a diversified manufacturer that addresses several markets. The company's meter-reading technology and video surveillance systems are used to monitor industrial applications. The company's filters are used in industrial applications fuel systems medical applications and appliances. Test products include electromagnetic compatibility equipment such as antennas probes turntables and calibration equipment as well as radio-frequency shielding products. ESCO's customers are in the commercial and military aerospace space healthcare wireless consumer electronics electric utility and renewable energy industries Subsidiaries include PTI Doble VACCO and ETS-Lindgren. About 70% of sales are to customers in the US.

Financial Performance
ESCO's sales velocity picked up in 2017 and 2018 fueled by acquisitions. Net income followed suit especially in 2018.

In 2018 (ended September) sales rose about 12% to about $772 million up about $86 million from 2017. All segments posted higher sales led by a 30% increase in USG on the strength of the NRG Morgan Schaffer and Vanguard Instruments acquisitions. Filtration accounted for more than 35% of revenue followed by USG about 35% Test about 25% and Technical Packaging about 10%.

ESCO's profit jumped to $92 million in 2018 from about $54 million in 2017 on higher sales and a tax benefit.

The company's coffers held $30.5 million in cash in 2018 compared to $40.5 million in 2017. Operations generated $93 million in 2018 while investing and financing activities used $41.6 and $66.4 respectively.

Strategy
ESCO in 2018 moved to run more efficiently and improve its cost competitiveness shutting down or consolidating some facilities and reducing headcount in the USG segment sharing production lines in Oxnard California between the VACCO and PTI businesses and moving aircraft parts to the PTI segment. In Europe the company shrank its footprint in 2019 closing its headquarters in the UK and relocating manufacturing activities to two plants one in the UK and the other in Poland.

In the US ESCO sold its Doble facility in Watertown New York and moved it to Marlborough Massachusetts. The company pocketed money from the sale and intends to improve employee recruiting and retention because of lower costs in Massachusetts while providing a more accessible place to customers to visit.

ESCO also invests in automation another efficiency move and in research and development to create new products. The company spends about $13 million a year on R&D.

While emphasizing organic growth ESCO remains on the lookout for acquisitions. In 2019 it bought Global Composite Solutions a supplier of materials for US Navy submarines. The Global Composite brought a number of multi-year contracts to supply stealth components on the growing fleet of US submarines. It was made part of ESCO's Filtration segment.

ESCO makes significant sales to the US government and its prime contractors that account for up to 20% of revenue a year. A shift or reduction in defense spending could affect the company's revenue.

Mergers and Acquisitions
ESCO through its subsidiary NRG systems acquired a portfolio of advanced Lidar technology developed by Pentalum in 2018.

EXECUTIVES
EVP and CFO, Gary E. Muenster, age 57, $526,000 total compensation
SVP Secretary and General Counsel, Alyson S. Barclay, age 58, $312,000 total compensation
Chairman President and CEO, Victor L. (Vic) Richey, age 62, $790,000 total compensation
Vice President Human Resources, Deborah Hanlon
Vice President And Controller, G Muenster
Board Member, Leon Olivier
Board Member, Vinod Khilnani
Board Member, Robert Phillippy
Auditors: KPMG LLP

LOCATIONS
HQ: ESCO Technologies, Inc.
9900A Clayton Road, St. Louis, MO 63124-1186
Phone: 314 213-7200
Web: www.escotechnologies.com

PRODUCTS/OPERATIONS

2018 Sales
	$ mil.	% of total
Filtration	286.8	37
USG	214.0	28
Test	182.9	24
Technical Packaging	87.9	11
Total	**771.6**	**100**

Selected Operating Units
Utility Solutions
  Comtrak Technologies L.L.C.
  Distribution Control Systems Caribe Inc.
  Distribution Control Systems Inc. (DCSI)
  Doble Engineering Company
  Hexagram Inc.
  Nexus Energy Software Inc.
Filtration
  Crissair Inc.
  PTI Technologies Inc.
  Thermoform Engineered Quality LLC
  VACCO Industries
Test
  Beijing Lindgren ElectronMagnetic Technology Co. Ltd.
  EMV Elektronische Messgeräte Vertriebs-GmbH
  ETS-Lindgren Japan Inc.
  ETS-Lindgren L.P.
  Lindgren RF Enclosures Inc.

COMPETITORS
3M Purification
Atos
CLARCOR
Comverge
Itron
Moog
Pall Corporation
Parker-Hannifin
Rohde & Schwarz

HISTORICAL FINANCIALS
Company Type: Public

Income Statement   FYE: December 31

	ASSETS ($ mil.)	NET INCOME ($ mil.)	INCOME AS % OF ASSETS	EMPLOYEES
12/18	4,061.7	35.8	0.9%	627
12/17	3,170.5	20.6	0.7%	526
12/16	2,192.1	9.3	0.4%	415
12/15	1,585.7	10.3	0.6%	297
12/14	1,175.3	8.9	0.8%	262
Annual Growth	36.3%	41.3%	—	24.4%

2018 Year-End Financials
Return on assets: 0.9%
Return on equity: 8.6%
Long-term debt ($ mil.): —
No. of shares (mil.): 15.7
Sales ($ mil): 181.2
Dividends
  Yield: —
  Payout: —
Market value ($ mil.): 557.0

	STOCK PRICE ($) FY Close	P/E High/Low	PER SHARE ($) Earnings	Dividends	Book Value
12/18	35.25	19 14	2.28	0.00	28.87
12/17	35.41	22 18	1.62	0.00	25.62
12/16	33.64	34 19	1.07	0.00	22.09
12/15	23.39	16 15	1.54	0.00	20.37
Annual Growth	14.7%	—	14.0%	—	12.3%

Esquire Financial Holdings Inc

Auditors: Crowe LLP

LOCATIONS
HQ: Esquire Financial Holdings Inc
100 Jericho Quadrangle, Suite 100, Jericho, NY 11753
Phone: 516 535-2002
Web: www.esquirebank.com

HISTORICAL FINANCIALS
Company Type: Public

Income Statement   FYE: September 30

	REVENUE ($ mil.)	NET INCOME ($ mil.)	NET PROFIT MARGIN	EMPLOYEES
09/19	812.9	81.0	10.0%	3,239
09/18	771.5	92.1	11.9%	3,117
09/17	685.7	53.7	7.8%	3,254
09/16	571.4	45.8	8.0%	2,643
09/15	537.2	42.5	7.9%	2,323
Annual Growth	10.9%	17.5%	—	8.7%

2019 Year-End Financials
Debt ratio: 19.5%
Return on equity: 10.2%
Cash ($ mil.): 61.8
Current ratio: 1.97
Long-term debt ($ mil.): 265.0
No. of shares (mil.): 25.9
Dividends
  Yield: 0.4%
  Payout: 9.8%
Market value ($ mil.): 2,067.0

	STOCK PRICE ($) FY Close	P/E High/Low	PER SHARE ($) Earnings	Dividends	Book Value
09/19	79.56	27 19	3.10	0.32	31.80
09/18	68.05	20 16	3.54	0.32	29.31
09/17	59.95	30 21	2.07	0.24	26.01
09/16	46.42	26 18	1.77	0.32	23.92
09/15	35.90	24 20	1.62	0.32	22.63
Annual Growth	22.0%	—	17.6%	(0.0%)	8.9%

HISTORICAL FINANCIALS
Company Type: Public

Income Statement   FYE: December 31

	ASSETS ($ mil.)	NET INCOME ($ mil.)	INCOME AS % OF ASSETS	EMPLOYEES
12/18	663.9	8.7	1.3%	74
12/17	533.6	3.6	0.7%	61
12/16	424.8	2.8	0.7%	52
12/15	352.6	1.1	0.3%	43
Annual Growth	23.5%	95.3%		19.8%

2018 Year-End Financials
Return on assets: 1.4%
Return on equity: 9.9%
Long-term debt ($ mil.): —
No. of shares (mil.): 7.5
Sales ($ mil): 36.8
Dividends
Yield: —
Payout: —
Market value ($ mil.): 163.0

	STOCK PRICE ($) FY Close	P/E High/Low	PER SHARE ($) Earnings	Dividends	Book Value
12/18	21.70	23 16	1.13	0.00	12.32
12/17	19.74	36 25	0.58	0.00	11.38
12/16	0.00	— —	0.55	0.00	10.43
Annual Growth	—	— —	43.3%	—	8.7%

Essex Property Trust Inc

Essex Property Trust acquires develops redevelops and manages apartment communities focusing on the metropolitan areas of Los Angeles San Diego San Francisco and Seattle. The self-managed and self-administered real estate investment trust (REIT) owns more than 240 apartment communities — mostly in Southern California — and eight community properties under development. Essex also owns a handful of office buildings in its home state and has partial stakes in several apartment communities through joint ventures. The REIT adds to its portfolio through acquisitions and through the development and renovation of properties. Essex significantly expanded its property base after its 2014 acquisition of BRE Properties in a $4.3 billion deal.

Operations
Essex Property had interests in 246 communities (mostly garden-style but some mid-rise and high-rise) spanning 59160 apartment homes on the West Coast at the end of 2015. It also had stakes in four commercial buildings spanning over 319000 sq. ft. and eight active development projects with nearly 2450 apartment homes in various stages of development. Its property occupancy rates exceeded 96%.

Rent from the apartment communities generated more than 99% of the company's total revenue in 2015.

Geographic Reach
Palo Alto-based Essex Property's generated 44% of its revenue from properties in Southern California (in Los Angeles Orange San Diego and Ventura counties) during 2015; about 35% of its revenue from properties in Northern California (in the San Francisco Bay area); and 17% of its revenue from properties in the Seattle metro area. The REIT has offices in Woodland Hills Irvine San Jose and San Diego California; and in Bellevue Washington.

Financial Performance
Essex Property's annual revenues have more than doubled while its profits have grown nearly five-fold since 2011 thanks to rent-boosting property acquisitions and rising rental rates stemming from the strengthened economy.

The REIT's revenue jumped 23% to $1.19 billion during 2015 mostly as newly acquired properties from the BRE merger and 10 other communities boosted rental revenues. Same-property revenues also increased thanks to an 8.1% rise in average rental rates (which reached $1741 per apartment home) as housing demand continued to strengthen.

Strong revenue growth in 2015 allowed Essex Property's net income to nearly double to $232.12 million for the year. Its operating cash levels climbed 25% to $617.4 million on rising cash earnings.

Strategy
When making acquisitions Essex usually targets multifamily properties with more than 100 units and spends from $300 million to $500 million per transaction. It likes to be active in supply-constrained markets with populations of at least one million and drives rent growth through high occupancy rates (approximately 96% at year-end 2015).

The REIT continually monitors its existing markets and isn't afraid to exit if the housing supply increases too much. The company sells off assets if they no longer fit into its strategy and often uses the money raised to buy newer communities and parcels of land.

Mergers and Acquisitions
During 2015 Essex bought interests in seven communities spanning 1722 apartment homes for $638 million which included the 8th & New Hope The Huxley The Dylan Reveal Avant Avant II and Enso community properties.

In April 2014 Essex Property Trust acquired California-based BRE Properties forming a combined company in which former Essex shareholders hold about 63% of the combined company's stock and former BRE shareholders hold 37%. (The combined company retained the name Essex Property Trust.) The deal valued at about $4.3 billion greatly bolstered the REIT's presence in the multifamily market on the West Coast.

In 2013 Essex acquired ownership interests in eight communities comprising 1472 units for $462.5 million. The acquired apartment complexes are in San Francisco (2) Los Angeles Mountain View and San Diego California and in Kirkland and Seattle (2) Washington.

EXECUTIVES

Vice President, Bruce A Knoblock
Group Vice President, Bryan Meyer
EVP Acquisitions, Craig K. Zimmerman, age 68, $325,000 total compensation
EVP Development, John D. Eudy, age 64, $325,000 total compensation
President and CEO, Michael J. (Mike) Schall, age 61, $450,000 total compensation
Executive Vice President Asset Management, John F. Burkart, $275,000 total compensation
Executive Vice President And Chief Financial Officer, Angela Kleiman
Vice President Development, Bob Linder
Vice Chairman, Keith R. Guericke, age 70
Chairman, George M. Marcus, age 78
Board Member, Janice Sears
Board Member, Byron Scordelis
Board Member, Irving Lyons
Board Member, Thomas Robinson
Auditors: KPMG LLP

LOCATIONS
HQ: Essex Property Trust Inc
1100 Park Place Suite 200, San Mateo, CA 94403
Phone: 650 655-7800
Web: www.essex.com

PRODUCTS/OPERATIONS

2015 Sales

	$ mil.	% of total
Rental & other property revenues		
Southern California	529.4	44
Northern California	416.3	35
Seattle Metro	201.4	17
Other real estate assets	38.3	3
Management & other fees from affiliates	9.0	1
Total	1,194.4	100

COMPETITORS

Apartment Investment and Management
AvalonBay
Camden Property
Equity Residential
Fairfield Residential
Irvine Apartment Communities
UDR

HISTORICAL FINANCIALS
Company Type: Public

Income Statement   FYE: December 31

	REVENUE ($ mil.)	NET INCOME ($ mil.)	NET PROFIT MARGIN	EMPLOYEES
12/18	1,400.0	390.1	27.9%	1,826
12/17	1,363.9	433.0	31.8%	1,835
12/16	1,294.0	414.9	32.1%	1,799
12/15	1,194.4	232.1	19.4%	1,806
12/14	969.3	122.1	12.6%	1,725
Annual Growth	9.6%	33.7%	—	1.4%

2018 Year-End Financials
Debt ratio: 45.2%
Return on equity: 6.2%
Cash ($ mil.): 151.4
Current ratio: 1.37
Long-term debt ($ mil.): 5,605.9
No. of shares (mil.): 65.8
Dividends
Yield: 3.0%
Payout: 126.1%
Market value ($ mil.): 16,157.0

	STOCK PRICE ($) FY Close	P/E High/Low	PER SHARE ($) Earnings	Dividends	Book Value
12/18	245.21	45 37	5.90	7.44	95.11
12/17	241.37	41 34	6.57	7.00	95.03
12/16	232.50	38 31	6.27	6.40	94.50
12/15	239.41	70 59	3.49	5.76	95.41
12/14	206.60	103 69	2.06	5.11	94.57
Annual Growth	4.4%	— —	30.1%	9.8%	0.1%

Etsy Inc

Auditors: PricewaterhouseCoopers LLP

LOCATIONS

HQ: Etsy Inc
117 Adams Street, Brooklyn, NY 11201
Phone: 718 880-3660
Web: www.etsy.com

HISTORICAL FINANCIALS
Company Type: Public

Income Statement — FYE: December 31

	REVENUE ($ mil.)	NET INCOME ($ mil.)	NET PROFIT MARGIN	EMPLOYEES
12/18	603.6	77.4	12.8%	874
12/17	441.2	81.8	18.5%	744
12/16	364.9	(29.9)	—	1,043
12/15	273.5	(54.0)	—	819
12/14	195.5	(15.2)	—	685
Annual Growth	32.5%	—	—	6.3%

2018 Year-End Financials
Debt ratio: 37.9%
Return on equity: 19.4%
Cash ($ mil.): 366.9
Current ratio: 6.07
Long-term debt ($ mil.): 338.5
No. of shares (mil.): 119.7
Dividends
  Yield: —
  Payout: —
Market value ($ mil.): 5,698.0

	STOCK PRICE ($) FY Close	P/E High/Low	PER SHARE ($) Earnings	Dividends	Book Value
12/18	47.57	90 28	0.61	0.00	3.35
12/17	20.45	32 14	0.68	0.00	3.26
12/16	11.78	— —	(0.26)	0.00	2.97
12/15	8.26	— —	(0.59)	0.00	2.94
Annual Growth	79.2%	— —	—	—	4.5%

Evans Bancorp, Inc.

EXECUTIVES

Vice President Operations Manager, Mary Palmer
Vice President Commercial Lines Manager, Mark St George
Auditors: KPMG LLP

LOCATIONS

HQ: Evans Bancorp, Inc.
One Grimsby Drive, Hamburg, NY 14075
Phone: 716 926-2000
Web: www.evansbancorp.com

COMPETITORS

HSBC USA	M&T Bank
KeyCorp	Northwest Bancshares

HISTORICAL FINANCIALS
Company Type: Public

Income Statement — FYE: December 31

	ASSETS ($ mil.)	NET INCOME ($ mil.)	INCOME AS % OF ASSETS	EMPLOYEES
12/18	1,388.2	16.3	1.2%	237
12/17	1,295.6	10.4	0.8%	271
12/16	1,100.7	8.2	0.8%	254
12/15	939.1	7.8	0.8%	258
12/14	846.8	8.1	1.0%	251
Annual Growth	13.2%	18.9%	—	(1.4%)

2018 Year-End Financials
Return on assets: 1.2%
Return on equity: 13.0%
Long-term debt ($ mil.): —
No. of shares (mil.): 4.8
Sales ($ mil): 72.8
Dividends
  Yield: 2.8%
  Payout: 27.7%
Market value ($ mil.): 158.0

	STOCK PRICE ($) FY Close	P/E High/Low	PER SHARE ($) Earnings	Dividends	Book Value
12/18	32.51	14 9	3.32	0.92	27.13
12/17	41.90	20 15	2.16	0.80	24.74
12/16	31.55	19 12	1.90	0.76	22.50
12/15	25.72	14 12	1.82	0.72	21.44
12/14	24.31	13 11	1.95	0.65	20.41
Annual Growth	7.5%	— —	14.2%	9.1%	7.4%

Evercore Inc

Evercore Partners makes Investment Banking advisory its core business. It provides advisory services on mergers and acquisitions restructurings divestitures and financing to corporate clients. Boasting some $14 billion in assets under management the firm's investment management business principally manages and invests capital for clients including institutional investors such as corporate and public pension funds endowments insurance companies and high net-worth individuals. Evercore also makes private equity investments. Beyond the US the company operates globally through subsidiaries such as Evercore Europe in London. Evercore also has offices in Brazil Hong Kong and Singapore.

Operations
The firm's Investment Banking advisory segment is its core business accounting for 88% of its revenue in 2014. Evercore's Institutional Equities services offering equity research and securities trading for institutional clients resides under the Investment banking umbrella.

Its Investment Management segment (12% of revenue) focuses on asset management for institutions wealthy individuals and private equity clients. The segment had $14 million in assets under management at the end of 2014 with $8.1 million of that attributable to Institutional Asset Management $5.7 billion attributable to Wealth Management and $0.3 billion attributable to Private Equity Clients. As part of this segment Evercore Trust provides investment management and trustee services to employee benefits plans.

Geographic Reach
While Evercore Partners operates globally the US accounted for about 65% of the firm's revenue in 2014. Latin America accounted for 7% while Europe and other countries made up 27%. Evercore's offices are in the US the UK Brazil Hong Kong and Singapore. It also has strategic alliances with leading firms in China Japan India Korea and Argentina.

Sales and Marketing
Evercore Partners had a staff of 1300 employees worldwide at the end of 2014.

Financial Performance
Evercore Partner's rising revenues and profits over the last several years have been fueled by higher demand for its advisory services amidst a surge of merger and acquisition activity as the financial markets in the US and UK have become increasingly more attractive to investors.

The firm's annual revenue jumped 20% to $915.8 million in 2014 mostly as its Investment Banking revenue rose from increased advisory fees from US- and UK-based businesses partially stemming from its late-2014 acquisition of ISI. The Investment Banking segment served some 418 clients during the year with 173 fees valued in excess of $1 million. The firm's investment advisory and management fees grew by 4% year-over-year as its assets under management in its Wealth Management unit continued to grow.

Higher revenue and an absence of loss from discontinued operations in 2014 pushed Evercore's net income higher by 63% to $86.9 million while the firm's operating cash levels rose by 9% to $216 million on higher cash earnings.

Strategy
Evercore continues to grow by acquiring financial advisory firms that enhance its capabilities and by bolstering its Investment Banking business through expanding the number of sectors it serves. In 2014 Evercore continued to expand the scope of its core Advisory business by hiring experienced talent to bolster its proficiency in the fast-growing Technology Media and Telecommunications sector as well as the technology healthcare telecom and oil & gas sectors in the US and Europe. Its

The firm also continues to move into new geographic markets that are receptive to its Investment Banking business model. In recent years Evercore has expanded into Canada and Singapore while forming advisory affiliates and alliances in Brazil Argentina Japan China South Korea and India as well as in Australia in early 2015.

As an independent investment banking firm that isn't involved in commercial banking or proprietary trading Evercore has avoided the controversy swirling around competitors such as Goldman Sachs that results from the conflicts of interest that may occur at larger firms that both underwrite and invest in their clients.

Mergers and Acquisitions
In May 2015 Evercore expanded its reach into Germany and enhanced its sector expertise after buying the Frankfurt-based investment banking advisory boutique Kuna & Co. KG which specialized in real estate in Germany.

In November 2014 the firm purchased ISI International Strategy & Investment bolstering its Investment Banking business' position as a scaled provider of non-proprietary capital markets advice and execution. The acquired company which was renamed Evercore ISI would start by providing macro research and fundamental coverage of more than 600 companies across 12 industries (60% of the S&P 500's market capitalization value).

Company Background

Some of Evercore's past high-profile transactions include the 2012 breakup of Kraft Foods (now Mondelez International) the recapitalizations of GM and CIT Group and the acquisition of Lubrizol by Berkshire Hathaway.

Evercore was launched in 1996 (it went public 10 years later) by Roger Altman who formerly led investment banking and merger advisory practices at Lehman Brothers and The Blackstone Group. Altman resigned as CEO in 2009 and was succeeded by Ralph Schlosstein co-founder of asset management giant BlackRock; Altman remained executive chairman.

EXECUTIVES

President and CEO, Ralph L. Schlosstein, age 68, $500,000 total compensation
Senior Managing Director and General Counsel, Adam B. Frankel, age 51
Senior Managing Director and CEO Evercore Partners Mexico and Evercore Partners Mexico S. de R.L., Augusto Arellano, age 44
Senior Managing Director and CFO, Robert B. Walsh, age 63, $500,000 total compensation
Senior Managing Director; Vice Chairman and CEO Europe Investment Banking, Andrew Sibbald, age 52, $400,000 total compensation
Chairman Evercore ISI and Head Economic Research Team, Edward S. (Ed) Hyman, age 74
Co-Chair Evercore Partners Asia, Keith Magnus
Vice President, Paulo Coelho
Vice President, Meredith Bourne
Vice President Corporate Advisory, Doug Rogers
Vice President, Tejwantie Niranjan
Vice President, Fausto Borotto
Vice President Information Technology, Lizandro Perez
Vice President Information Technology, Joseph Sterling
Vice President, Drew Braucht
Vice President, Yohan Minaya
Vice President, Michael Catts
Vice President, Michael Gugino
Vice President And Litigation Counsel, Brogiin Keeton
Vice President, Jake Stuiver
Vice President, Javier Valenti
Vice President, Katherine Rossolimo
Vice President, Brian Chung
Vice President, Jon Whitt
Vice President, Rahul Dutta
Vice President, Christian Vonmassenbach
Vice President, Nate Littlefield
Vice President And Financial Advisor, Carly Mckeeman
Vice President, Ben Charon
Vice President, Pranav Gupta
Vice President, Linda Slevin
Vice President Corporate Strategy, Noah Sakimura
Vice President, Dan Gelfand
Vice President, Tim Ott
Vice President, Elena Perceleanu
Vice President, Jin Mook Choi
Vice President Operations, John Maloney
Vice President, David Burton
Vice President Product Development And Range Mana, Sheree Sabin
Vice President Technology M And A, Buzz Black
Founder and Senior Chairman, Roger C. Altman, age 74
Chairman, John S. Weinberg, age 62
Auditors: Deloitte & Touche LLP

LOCATIONS

HQ: Evercore Inc
55 East 52nd Street, New York, NY 10055
Phone: 212 857-3100 **Fax:** 212 857-3101
Web: www.evercore.com

PRODUCTS/OPERATIONS

2011 Sales

	$ mil.	% of total
Investment banking	430.6	80
Investment management	99.2	18
Other	13.9	2
Total	**543.7**	**100**

COMPETITORS

Allen & Company	Greenhill
Atalanta Sosnoff	JPMorgan Chase
Bank of America	Lazard
Barclays Capital	Merrill Lynch
Blackstone Group	Moelis & Company
Citigroup Global Markets	Morgan Stanley
Credit Suisse	Rothschild North America
Deutsche Bank	UBS Investment Bank
Goldman Sachs	

HISTORICAL FINANCIALS

Company Type: Public

Income Statement FYE: December 31

	REVENUE ($ mil.)	NET INCOME ($ mil.)	NET PROFIT MARGIN	EMPLOYEES
12/18	2,064.7	377.2	18.3%	1,700
12/17	1,704.3	125.4	7.4%	1,600
12/16	1,440.0	107.5	7.5%	1,475
12/15	1,223.2	42.8	3.5%	1,400
12/14	915.8	86.8	9.5%	1,300
Annual Growth	22.5%	44.4%	—	6.9%

2018 Year-End Financials

Debt ratio: 7.9%   No. of shares (mil.): 39.7
Return on equity: 57.9%   Dividends
Cash ($ mil.): 793.2   Yield: 2.6%
Current ratio: 1.98   Payout: 22.8%
Long-term debt ($ mil.): 168.6   Market value ($ mil.): 2,844.0

	STOCK PRICE ($) FY Close	P/E High/Low		PER SHARE ($) Earnings	Dividends	Book Value
12/18	71.56	12	7	8.33	1.90	19.07
12/17	90.00	29	21	2.80	1.42	13.91
12/16	68.70	26	15	2.43	1.27	13.45
12/15	54.07	51	41	0.98	1.15	12.73
12/14	52.37	26	19	2.08	1.03	15.21
Annual Growth	8.1%	—	—	41.5%	16.5%	5.8%

Evolution Petroleum Corp

Just as petroleum and natural gas evolves from old living forms Evolution Petroleum has evolved by producing these ancient hydrocarbons. The company operates oil and gas producing fields in Louisiana Oklahoma and Texas. Its strategy is to acquire already-established properties and redevelop them making the fields more profitable. One method it uses is gas flooding which uses carbon dioxide to free up trapped oil deposits. Assets include a CO2-project in Louisiana's Delhi Field and patented artificial lift technology to extend the life and ultimate recoveries of wells with oil or associated water production. It reported 10.8 million barrels of oil equivalent proved reserves in fiscal 2016.

Operations

Evolution Petroleum is engaged in the acquisition exploitation and development of properties for the production of crude oil and natural gas. It five major projects are Delhi Field Enhanced Oil Recovery(EOR)-Northeast Louisiana (which has produced 192 million barrels of crude oil and substantial amounts of natural gas to date); Mississippi Lime-North Central Oklahoma Kay County (a limestone formation that horizontal drilling combined with multistage hydraulic fracturing has opened up to redevelopment); GARP (Gas Assisted Rod Pump artificial lift technology being commercialized through subsidiary NGS Technologies; and Giddings Field-Central Texas (2180 net developed acres); and Lopez Field-South Texas (782 net acres).

Geographic Reach

The company has operations in Northeast Louisiana Southeast Oklahoma South Texas Central Texas and North Central Oklahoma.

Sales and Marketing

The company markets its production to third parties. It sells its crude oil under the Delhi Field operator's agreement with Plains Marketing LP for the delivery and pricing.

Financial Performance

Evolution Petroleum's revenues decreased by 5.4% to $26.35 million in fiscal 2016 (June year end) due to a 55% slump in realized prices which more than offset a 45% increase in production volumes.

The company's net income increased by 394% in fiscal 2016 to $24.7 million due to litigation settlement proceeds insurance proceeds and realized hedging gains offset in part by increased DD&A expenses litigation expenses and higher income tax expense. The company settled outstanding litigation with the operator of Delhi field during the year. In the settlement Evolution Petroleum received $27.5 million in cash.

In fiscal 2016 cash flows provided by operating activities of $30.7 million reflected $28.9 million provided by operations and $1.8 million provided by other working capital changes. Of the $28.9 million provided before working capital changes some $24.7 million came from net income and $4.2 million from non-cash expenses and gains.

Strategy

Evolution Petroleum acquires known underdeveloped oil and natural gas resources and exploit them through the application of capital sound engineering and modern technology to increase production ultimate recoveries or both.

It strategy is intended to generate scalable low unit cost development and re-development opportunities that minimize or eliminate exploration risks. These opportunities involve the application of modern technology its own proprietary technology and its specific expertise in overlooked areas of the United States where it may or may not choose to be the operator. The assets it exploits currently fit into three types of project opportunities: EOR Bypassed Primary Resources and Unconventional Development using its staff expertise in horizontal drilling.

Company Background
In 2013 to raise cash the company sold all of its non-GARP producing wells and drilling locations in its Giddings assets.

In 2008 in order to raise cash Evolution Petroleum sold its working interests in some oil fields in LaSalle and Winn Parishes Louisiana to a private buyer for $4.6 million.

The company was formed in 2003.

EXECUTIVES
President and CEO, Randall D. Keys, age 59, $295,500 total compensation
SVP and CFO, David Joe, age 54, $205,000 total compensation
Chairman, Robert S. Herlin, age 64
Auditors: Moss Adams LLP

LOCATIONS
HQ: Evolution Petroleum Corp
1155 Dairy Ashford Road, Suite 425, Houston, TX 77079
Phone: 713 935-0122   **Fax:** 713 935-0199
Web: www.evolutionpetroleum.com

PRODUCTS/OPERATIONS

2016 Sales

	% of total
Crude oil	99
Artificial lift technology services	1
Total	**100**

Selected Operations
CO2-based enhanced oil recovery
Low-permeablitiy reservoir development
Technology-based redevelopment of old oil and gas fields

COMPETITORS

Abraxas Petroleum	Chesapeake Energy
Anadarko Petroleum	EOG
Callon Petroleum	Midstates Petroleum
Carrizo Oil & Gas	Saratoga Resources

HISTORICAL FINANCIALS
Company Type: Public

Income Statement   FYE: June 30

	REVENUE ($ mil.)	NET INCOME ($ mil.)	NET PROFIT MARGIN	EMPLOYEES
06/19	43.2	15.3	35.6%	4
06/18	41.2	19.6	47.5%	4
06/17	34.4	8.0	23.3%	5
06/16	26.3	24.6	93.6%	6
06/15	27.8	4.9	17.9%	10
Annual Growth	11.6%	32.5%	—	(20.5%)

2019 Year-End Financials

Debt ratio: —
Return on equity: 19.5%
Cash ($ mil.): 31.5
Current ratio: 12.78
Long-term debt ($ mil.): —
No. of shares (mil.): 33.1
Dividends
 Yield: 0.0%
 Payout: 86.9%
Market value ($ mil.): 237.0

	STOCK PRICE ($) FY Close	P/E High/Low	PER SHARE ($) Earnings	Dividends	Book Value
06/19	7.15	27 13	0.46	0.40	2.41
06/18	9.85	17 11	0.59	0.35	2.34
06/17	8.10	48 25	0.21	0.26	2.07
06/16	5.47	10 5	0.73	0.20	2.32
06/15	6.59	85 44	0.13	0.30	1.48
Annual Growth	2.1%	— —	37.2%	7.5%	13.0%

Exchange Bank (Santa Rosa, CA)

Exchange Bank serves personal and business customers from some 20 branch offices throughout Sonoma County California. It also has a branch in nearby Placer County. The bank provides standard products including checking and savings accounts Visa credit cards online banking and a variety of real estate business and consumer loans. It also offers investment services such as wealth management personal trust administration employee benefits plans and individual retirement accounts. Effective early 2014 Exchange Bank is on its eighth president since its inception in 1890. The Doyle Trust which was established by co-founder Frank Doyle owns a majority of the bank.

Operations
Exchange Bank's lending activity is concentrated in Sonoma County. Commercial real estate loans represent more than half of its loan portfolio. Exchange Bank believes it will continue to benefit from growth in the local technology and biomedical industries and lower unemployment increased tourism and a decline in commercial real estate vacancies in Sonoma County.

Geographic Reach
Based in Santa Rosa California Exchange Bank operates primarily in Sonoma County but also in Placer and Contra counties.

Sales and Marketing
Exchange Bank counts some 25000 customers among its clients serving them through about 20 branch offices. It caters to customers online as well through its website which in fiscal 2013 earned 1.5 million customer visits.

Financial Performance
Revenue dropped 4% in fiscal 2013 to $85.9 million as compared to $89.1 million in 2012. Exchange Bank attributes the decrease to lower interest income resulting from a decline in interest received on term loans offset in part by increased interest on securities. From $12.26 million in 2012 the firm's net income grew some 28% to $15.73 million. Exchange Bank points to noteworthy drops in the provision for loan and lease losses and a decrease in interest and non-interest income for the net income gains.

EXECUTIVES
Vice President, Jason Hinde
Auditors: KPMG LLP

LOCATIONS
HQ: Exchange Bank (Santa Rosa, CA)
545 Fourth Street, Santa Rosa, CA 95401
Phone: 707 524-3301
Web: www.exchangebank.com

COMPETITORS

Bank of America	U.S. Bancorp
First Northern	Wells Fargo
JPMorgan Chase	Westamerica
MUFG Americas Holdings	

HISTORICAL FINANCIALS
Company Type: Public

Income Statement   FYE: December 31

	ASSETS ($ mil.)	NET INCOME ($ mil.)	INCOME AS % OF ASSETS	EMPLOYEES
12/18	2,653.9	38.5	1.5%	0
12/17	2,584.0	19.5	0.8%	0
12/16	2,179.4	21.5	1.0%	0
12/15	2,062.5	21.0	1.0%	0
12/14	1,887.6	17.7	0.9%	0
Annual Growth	8.9%	21.4%		

2018 Year-End Financials

Return on assets: 1.4%
Return on equity: 17.7%
Long-term debt ($ mil.): —
No. of shares (mil.): 1.7
Sales ($ mil): 121.7
Dividends
 Yield: 2.3%
 Payout: 22.5%
Market value ($ mil.): 283.0

	STOCK PRICE ($) FY Close	P/E High/Low	PER SHARE ($) Earnings	Dividends	Book Value
12/18	165.00	9 7	22.46	3.85	135.08
12/17	152.00	14 11	11.38	3.40	118.53
12/16	125.00	11 6	12.54	2.80	110.35
12/15	89.00	7 6	12.27	2.20	100.98
12/14	84.00	8 7	10.25	1.55	93.37
Annual Growth	18.4%	— —	21.7%	25.5%	9.7%

Exelixis Inc

We've come a long way baby but we still have a lot in common with the fruit fly. Exelixis a pharmaceutical research and development firm got its start analyzing genetic data from fruit flies and other organisms as a means to speed the development of drugs and other products. Its early genomic work has yielded a pipeline of drug candidates primarily in the area of cancer therapies as well as some potential treatments for metabolic and cardiovascular diseases. Lead candidate Cometriq gained FDA approval for treatment of thyroid cancer in late 2012 and was launched in the US in early 2013. Exelixis takes its name from the Greek word for evolution.

Operations
Exelixis has built upon its past in genomics research to become a full-fledged drug development company focusing increasingly on its pharmaceuticals pipeline. Exelixis has historically relied on licensing and co-development partnerships to fund its operations. In fact most of its development-stage candidates are licensed out to third parties

though the company retains some marketing rights on select candidates (including Cometriq). Development and licensing partners include Bristol-Myers Squibb Merck Daiichi Sankyo Genentech and Sanofi. The company expects sales of Cometriq to further support its R&D efforts.

The Exelixis-discovered cobimetinib compound a selective inhibitor of mitogen-activated protein kinase (MEK) is being studied by Roche and Genentech in collaboration with Exelixis. Roche has completed a Market Authorization Application (MAA) for the compound to be used in combination with vemurafenib in Europe; in the US the FDA has granted the compound's New Drug Application. Another compound XL888 is an HSP90 inhibitor under investigation.

Other pipeline products include METEOR (a phase III pivotal trial in second-line metastatic renal carcinoma) and CELESTIAL (a phase III pivotal trial in second-line hepatocellular cancer).

Geographic Reach
The company leases 367773 sq. ft. of office and lab space in San Francisco.

Sales and Marketing
In 2014 Diplomat Specialty Pharmacy accounted for 99% of the company's revenues. Commerical product Cometriq is distributed by Diplomat Specialty Pharmacy in the US market and is warehoused and shipped by a third-party logistics firm.

Exelixis contracts with third parties to manufacture the active pharmaceutical ingredients (APIs) and finished drug products for use in clinical studies.

Financial Performance
As a development-stage company Exelixis has struggled to turn a profit. It did manage to grow its revenues each year for several years by entering new partnerships and licensing agreements and by achieving milestone payouts on existing contracts including a 55% increase to $289.6 million in 2011. However the rise in revenue and was due primarily to accelerated payouts from discontinued licensing agreements and therefore revenues dropped 84% the following year. Revenues have declined since then; in 2014 it decreased 20% to $25 million on lower license and contract revenues.

Net loss increased by 10% in 2014 to $268 million on higher R&D costs related to an increase in clinical trial activity as well as on charges related to a corporate restructuring initiated that year. Exelixis has lost money every year since its founding with the exception of fiscal 2011. At the end of 2014 it has accumulated debt of $1.8 billion.

Operating cash outflow increased 18% to $235 million in 2014 due to factors such as a decline in cash provided by clinical trial liability and changes in accounts payable.

Strategy
Exelixis is focused on development of proprietary partnered and licensed candidates for cancer cardiovascular and metabolic candidates. In addition it is focused on promoting Cometriq as well as other candidates once they gain approval. Exelixis also seeks out new development and licensing partners to fuel its research programs.

Cometriq (cabozantinib) was the company's main research focus prior to approval; in addition to the approved application for thyroid cancer the company is developing Cometriq for treatment of prostate breast renal and other cancers. In 2014 the drug was approved in Europe for the treatment of adults with progressive unresectable medullary thyroid cancer. In 2015 the firm extended its agreement with Swedish Orphan Biovitrum to support the distribution and commercialization of Cometriq in certain European markets.

After cabozantinib failed in one of its phase III pivotal trials in 2014 Exelixis initiated a corporate restructuring reducing its workforce. It recorded some $6 million in aggregate restructuring charges of which approximately 95% was recorded that year. (The rest is expected to be recorded in 2015.) The company is changing its focus to other phase III pivotal trials of cabozantinib.

Also in 2014 GlaxoSmithKline (GSK) terminated the development of foretinib returning it to Exelixis for development and commercialization; GSK remains entitled to a 3% royalty on net sales of any product with cabozantinib (including Cometriq) and a 4% royalty on net sales of any product containing foretinib.

EXECUTIVES

President Product Development and Medical Affairs; Chief Medical Officer, Gisela M. Schwab, age 62, $513,906 total compensation
President and CEO, Michael M. Morrissey, age 58, $755,192 total compensation
EVP Scientific Strategy and Chief Scientific Officer, Peter Lamb, age 58, $407,042 total compensation
EVP and CFO, Christopher J. (Chris) Senner
EVP and General Counsel, Jeffrey J. Hesseikiel, age 49, $380,769 total compensation
SVP Medical Affairs, William Berg
VP Marketing, Gregg Bernier
Chairman, Stelios Papadopoulos, age 71
Auditors: Ernst & Young LLP

LOCATIONS

HQ: Exelixis Inc
 1851 Harbor Bay Parkway, Alameda, CA 94502
Phone: 650 837-7000
Web: www.exelixis.com

COMPETITORS

Amgen	Keryx
ArQule	Biopharmaceuticals
Array BioPharma	Madrigal
AstraZeneca	Pharmaceuticals
Bayer HealthCare	Millennium: The Takeda
Pharmaceuticals Inc.	Oncology Company
Biogen	Novartis
Bristol-Myers Squibb	OSI Pharmaceuticals
Eli Lilly	Onyx Pharmaceuticals
Genentech	Pfizer
Genmab	Sanofi
Genzyme	Semafore
GlaxoSmithKline	Pharmaceuticals

HISTORICAL FINANCIALS
Company Type: Public

Income Statement
FYE: December 28

	REVENUE ($ mil.)	NET INCOME ($ mil.)	NET PROFIT MARGIN	EMPLOYEES
12/18	853.8	690.0	80.8%	484
12/17	452.4	154.2	34.1%	372
12/16	191.4	(70.2)	—	287
12/15	37.1	(169.7)	—	115
12/14	25.1	(268.5)	—	98
Annual Growth	141.5%	—	—	49.1%

2018 Year-End Financials
Debt ratio: —   No. of shares (mil.): 299.8
Return on equity: 88.0%   Dividends
Cash ($ mil.): 314.7   Yield: —
Current ratio: 8.50   Payout: —
Long-term debt ($ mil.): —   Market value ($ mil.): 5,830.0

	STOCK PRICE ($) FY Close	P/E High/Low		PER SHARE ($) Earnings	Dividends	Book Value
12/18	19.44	14	6	2.21	0.00	4.29
12/17	30.40	59	28	0.49	0.00	0.96
12/16	14.91	—	—	(0.28)	0.00	0.31
12/15	5.64	—	—	(0.81)	0.00	(0.46)
12/14	1.44	—	—	(1.38)	0.00	(0.59)
Annual Growth	91.7%			—	—	—

ExlService Holdings Inc

Have an extra-large task you'd rather not take on? Outsource it to ExlService Holdings. The company known as EXL offers business process outsourcing (BPO) research and analytics and consulting services. EXL's BPO offerings which generate most of its sales include claims processing collections customer support and finance and accounting. Customers come mainly from the banking financial services and insurance industries as well as from the utilities and telecommunications sectors. EXL operates offices around the world including the US and countries in Eastern Europe and Asia. The company was established in 1999.

Geographic Reach
EXL operates through six offices in the US 19 offices in India as well as through a half-a-dozen locations in the Czech Republic Bulgaria Romania Malaysia and the Philippines. The company also has a sales office in the UK and networking and telecommunications centers in California New Jersey and New York.

Sales and Marketing
EXL earned revenue from more than 600 clients in 2014 with its top three clients generating 22% of its revenue.

Financial Performance
The company's revenue was $499 million in fiscal 2014. That was an increase of more than $20 million compared to the prior fiscal period. EXL's net income was $32.4 million in fiscal 2014 which was a decrease of $15.7 million compared to its fiscal 2013 net income. The company's cash flow from operations decreased by more than $16 million during fiscal 2014 compared to the prior fiscal period but the company still ended the year with $66.7 million in cash on hand.

EXECUTIVES

Vice Chairman and CEO, Rohit Kapoor, age 54, $600,000 total compensation
President and COO, Pavan Bagai, age 57, $242,590 total compensation
EVP and Business Head Insurance, Vikas Bhalla, age 47
EVP and Business Head Health Care, Rembert de Villa, age 62, $382,534 total compensation
EVP and CFO, Vishal Chhibbar, age 51, $251,341 total compensation

EVP General Counsel and Corporate Secretary, Nancy Saltzman, age 53
CTO, Mike Toma
EVP and Chief Human Resource Officer, Nalin Miglani, age 58, $400,000 total compensation
Assistant Vice President Consulting, Rohit Saini
Executive Vice President Chief Growth Officer, Nagaraja Srivatsan
Vp Of It, Martin Thomas
Global Head Analytics Products and Vice President, Nagendra Shishodia
Chairman, Garen K. Staglin, age 74
Board Member, Clyde Ostler
Auditors: DELOITTE & TOUCHE LLP

LOCATIONS

HQ: ExlService Holdings Inc
320 Park Avenue, 29th Floor, New York, NY 10022
Phone: 212 277-7100
Web: www.exlservice.com

PRODUCTS/OPERATIONS

2014 Sales

	$ mil.	% of total
Operations Management	388.7	78
Analytics and Business Transformation	110.6	22
Total	**499.3**	**100**

COMPETITORS

Accenture	Infosys
Genpact	Tata Consultancy
HP Enterprise Services	WNS (Holdings)
IBM Global Services	Wipro

HISTORICAL FINANCIALS
Company Type: Public

Income Statement
FYE: December 31

	REVENUE ($ mil.)	NET INCOME ($ mil.)	NET PROFIT MARGIN	EMPLOYEES
12/18	883.1	56.7	6.4%	29,100
12/17	762.3	48.8	6.4%	27,800
12/16	685.9	61.7	9.0%	26,000
12/15	628.4	51.5	8.2%	24,100
12/14	499.2	32.4	6.5%	22,800
Annual Growth	15.3%	15.0%	—	6.3%

2018 Year-End Financials

Debt ratio: 26.8%
Return on equity: 9.3%
Cash ($ mil.): 280.3
Current ratio: 3.22
Long-term debt ($ mil.): 263.5
No. of shares (mil.): 34.2
Dividends
  Yield: —
  Payout: —
Market value ($ mil.): 1,801.0

	STOCK PRICE ($) FY Close	P/E High/Low	PER SHARE ($) Earnings	Dividends	Book Value
12/18	52.62	40 30	1.62	0.00	18.06
12/17	60.35	43 31	1.39	0.00	17.70
12/16	50.44	29 23	1.79	0.00	15.82
12/15	44.93	31 18	1.51	0.00	14.07
12/14	28.71	31 25	0.96	0.00	12.74
Annual Growth	16.4%	— —	14.0%	—	9.1%

Extra Space Storage Inc

When closets are bursting at the seams and garages are overflowing Extra Space Storage gives its customers room to breathe. One of the largest operators and managers of self-storage properties in the US the self-administered self-managed real estate investment trust (REIT) wholly-owns owns in joint-venture partnerships or operates for third parties about 1030 facilities with some 680000 units totaling nearly 76 million sq. ft. of rentable space. Active in metropolitan areas in nearly 35 states and Washington DC the company also offers business boat and RV storage and leases to nearly 600000 tenants nationwide.

Operations

Extra Space Storage operates through three segments: rental operations; tenant reinsurance; and property management acquisition and development.

The rental operations segment focuses on rentals of the self-storage facilities it owns. Tenant reinsurance covers the reinsurance of risks relating to the loss of goods stored by tenants in the company's self-storage facilities. Its last segment — property management acquisition and development — manages acquires develops and sells self-storage facilities.

Geographic Reach

Utah-based Extra Space Storage operates its business throughout the US in 35 states Puerto Rico and Washington DC.

Financial Performance

The storage company's revenue rose some $111.22 million in fiscal 2013 or 27% to $520.6 million continuing several years of incremental growth. It attributes the increases to a boost in property rental and tenant reinsurance revenue. Property rental revenue rose thanks to its purchase of 78 properties during 2013 and 91 properties during 2012.

Extra Space Storage logged $172.1 million in net income in fiscal 2013 representing a $54.78 million increase or a 47% jump overall. Higher revenues a gain on the sale of real estate assets and the purchase of a joint venture partners' interest all contributed to the spike.

Cash flow from operations also increased — by $55.38 million in 2013 — to $271.26 million from higher net income and the net change in working capital.

Strategy

The REIT has relied on acquisitions in growing markets to expand its business. In 2014 Extra Space Storage acquired a self-storage portfolio of 17 assets located in Virginia for about $200 million. The deal gave the company 1.5 million sq. ft. of net rentable space across 14000 units. The company also has another five properties under contract for an approximate purchase price of $58 million. In 2012 Extra Space Storage added to its holdings with the acquisition of 21 properties in about a dozen states from a joint venture partner. It acquired a noteworthy 55 properties in 2011.

Extra Space Storage is also looking to expand Extra Space Management its third-party property management subsidiary.

EXECUTIVES

CEO and Director, Joseph D. (Joe) Margolis, age 58, $290,000 total compensation
EVP and CFO, P. Scott Stubbs, $437,750 total compensation
SVP Marketing and Corporate Communications, James Overturf
VP Revenue Management, Samrat Sondhi
EVP and Chief Legal Officer, Gwyn McNeal
Vice President, Stephen Blake
Svp Operations West, Matthew Herrington
Vice President And Corporate Controller, Grace Kunde
Vice President, Bron McCall
Vice President Asset Management, Matthias Kellmer
Chairman, Kenneth M. Woolley, age 72
Board Member, Spencer Kirk
Auditors: Ernst & Young LLP

LOCATIONS

HQ: Extra Space Storage Inc
2795 East Cottonwood Parkway, Suite 300, Salt Lake City, UT 84121
Phone: 801 365-4600
Web: www.extraspace.com

PRODUCTS/OPERATIONS

2015 Sales

	$ mil.	% of total
Property rental	676.1	87
Tenant reinsurance	72.0	9
Management & franchise fees	34.2	4
Total	**782.3**	**100**

COMPETITORS

AMERCO	Mobile Mini
CubeSmart	PODS Enterprises
Life Storage	Public Storage

HISTORICAL FINANCIALS
Company Type: Public

Income Statement
FYE: December 31

	REVENUE ($ mil.)	NET INCOME ($ mil.)	NET PROFIT MARGIN	EMPLOYEES
12/18	1,196.6	415.2	34.7%	3,624
12/17	1,105.0	479.0	43.3%	3,380
12/16	991.8	366.1	36.9%	3,287
12/15	782.2	189.4	24.2%	3,209
12/14	647.1	178.3	27.6%	2,643
Annual Growth	16.6%	23.5%	—	8.2%

2018 Year-End Financials

Debt ratio: 61.3%
Return on equity: 17.4%
Cash ($ mil.): 57.5
Current ratio: 0.40
Long-term debt ($ mil.): 4,730.5
No. of shares (mil.): 127.1
Dividends
  Yield: 3.7%
  Payout: 102.7%
Market value ($ mil.): 11,500.0

	STOCK PRICE ($) FY Close	P/E High/Low	PER SHARE ($) Earnings	Dividends	Book Value
12/18	90.48	31 24	3.27	3.36	18.99
12/17	87.45	23 19	3.76	3.12	18.66
12/16	77.24	32 24	2.91	2.93	17.83
12/15	88.21	57 37	1.56	2.24	16.83
12/14	58.64	39 27	1.53	1.81	14.93
Annual Growth	11.5%	— —	20.9%	16.7%	6.2%

Extraction Oil & Gas Inc

Auditors: PricewaterhouseCoopers LLP

LOCATIONS

HQ: Extraction Oil & Gas Inc
  370 17th Street, Suite 5300, Denver, CO 80202
Phone: 720 557-8300
Web: www.extractionog.com

HISTORICAL FINANCIALS
Company Type: Public

Income Statement — FYE: December 31

	REVENUE ($ mil.)	NET INCOME ($ mil.)	NET PROFIT MARGIN	EMPLOYEES
12/18	1,060.7	114.5	10.8%	279
12/17	604.3	(44.4)	—	227
12/16	278.0	(456.0)	—	161
12/15	197.7	(47.2)	—	120
12/14	92.8	49.8	53.7%	0
Annual Growth	83.9%	23.1%	—	—

2018 Year-End Financials

Debt ratio: 34.0%
Return on equity: 6.2%
Cash ($ mil.): 234.9
Current ratio: 1.15
Long-term debt ($ mil.): 1,417.6
No. of shares (mil.): 171.6
Dividends
  Yield: —
  Payout: —
Market value ($ mil.): 736.0

	STOCK PRICE ($) FY Close	P/E High/Low		PER SHARE ($) Earnings	Dividends	Book Value
12/18	4.29	31	7	0.56	0.00	11.13
12/17	14.31	—	—	(0.35)	0.00	10.32
12/16	20.04	—	—	(1.54)	0.00	10.30
Annual Growth	(53.7%)	—	—	—	—	4.0%

F & M Bank Corp.

EXECUTIVES

Assistant Vice President Branch Manager, Natalie Strickler
Vice President And Operations Manager, Karen Rose
Auditors: Yount, Hyde & Barbour, P.C.

LOCATIONS

HQ: F & M Bank Corp.
  P.O. Box 1111, Timberville, VA 22853
Phone: 540 896-8941
Web: www.FMBankVA.com

COMPETITORS

Ames National
BB&T
Bank of America
Community Financial (VA)
Fauquier Bankshares
First National
First United
Highlands Bankshares Inc.
Pioneer Bankshares
Summit Financial (WV)
SunTrust
Village Bank & Trust

HISTORICAL FINANCIALS
Company Type: Public

Income Statement — FYE: December 31

	ASSETS ($ mil.)	NET INCOME ($ mil.)	INCOME AS % OF ASSETS	EMPLOYEES
12/18	780.2	9.0	1.2%	172
12/17	753.2	9.0	1.2%	178
12/16	744.8	9.5	1.3%	173
12/15	665.3	8.4	1.3%	168
12/14	605.3	5.8	1.0%	156
Annual Growth	6.6%	11.9%	—	2.5%

2018 Year-End Financials

Return on assets: 1.1%
Return on equity: 9.9%
Long-term debt ($ mil.): —
No. of shares (mil.): 3.2
Sales ($ mil): 44.7
Dividends
  Yield: 4.0%
  Payout: 54.3%
Market value ($ mil.): 96.0

	STOCK PRICE ($) FY Close	P/E High/Low		PER SHARE ($) Earnings	Dividends	Book Value
12/18	30.00	15	11	2.53	1.20	28.43
12/17	33.10	13	10	2.48	0.91	27.86
12/16	26.05	10	8	2.57	0.80	26.29
12/15	22.70	10	8	2.25	0.73	25.07
12/14	19.50	11	9	1.80	0.68	23.50
Annual Growth	11.4%	—	—	8.9%	15.3%	4.9%

FactSet Research Systems Inc.

Analysts portfolio managers and investment bankers know FactSet Research Systems has the facts down pat. The company offers global financial and economic information for investment analysis. FactSet also offers software for use in downloading and manipulating the data. (Its products can be fully integrated with Microsoft applications such as Excel and PowerPoint.) Among the company's applications are tools for presentations data warehousing portfolio analysis and report writing. Revenues are derived from month-to-month subscriptions to services databases and financial applications. More than 80% of revenue comes from investment managers; investment banking clients account for the rest.

Geographic Reach

About 30% of the company's revenues come from outside the US. Recent geographic growth efforts include the build out of new space in Paris and New York as well as the continued expansion of offices in India and the Philippines. It opened its 24th office located in Dubai in 2011. In addition to those locations FactSet has international offices in Australia Germany Italy Japan Hong Kong and the Netherlands.

Strategy

The company's success is in part due to its focus on growing its proprietary content collection efforts as well as investing in products and applications. Concurrent with the growth of its products and services the company has gained new clients and users both in the US and internationally.

HISTORY

Howard Wille and Charles Snyder founded FactSet in 1978. Both had previously worked for Wall Street investment firm Faulkner Dawkins & Sullivan (acquired by Shearson Hayden Stone in 1977). The company spent the 1980s building its client base and developing software that allowed clients to manipulate data on their own PCs.

FactSet opened an office in London in 1993 and one in Tokyo the next year. In 1994 the company added Morgan Stanley Capital International and EDGAR SEC filings to its database offerings. It added World Bank subsidiary International Finance Corp. in 1995 and the Russell U.S. Equity Profile report and Toyo Keizai a Japanese company database the next year. FactSet went public in 1996. Market Guide's information on US firms and ADRs (American depositary receipts) as well as the economic and financial databases of DRI/McGraw-Hill were added in 1997.

Snyder retired in 1999 but remained vice chairman. The following year Wille retired and Philip Hadley became chairman and CEO. The company made its first acquisition in 2000 when it bought Innovative Systems Techniques (Insyte) a maker of database management and decision support systems.

The company then began acquiring several content businesses. Its 2003 purchase of Mergerstat gave the company a database of global merger and acquisition and related information. In 2004 the company purchased JCF Group a provider of broker estimates and other financial data to institutional investors and CallStreet a provider of quarterly earnings call transcripts to the investment community. The following year the company purchased TrueCourse a provider of corporate competitive intelligence.

FactSet continued its acquisition spree with the 2005 purchase of Derivative Solutions (DSI) which offers fixed income analytics portfolio management and risk management services to financial institutions and the 2006 purchase of AlphaMetrics which provides institutional clients with software for capturing measuring and ranking financial information.

FactSet in 2007 released its ExcelConnect offering which enables data and analytics to be compatible with Microsoft Excel. Also that year the company enhanced its wireless capabilities giving users access to market company and portfolio information via PDAs and other wireless devices.

In 2008 FactSet expanded with the acquisition of the Thomson Fundamentals business which includes a global financial database with coverage of more than 43000 companies. The company also purchased investment banking workflow tool DealMaven reflecting its strategy of developing tools to make client workflows more efficient.

The company expanded in 2010 with the purchase of Market Metrics a US-based market research firm focused on advisor-sold investments and insurance products. FactSet used the acquisition to increase its global sales leveraging its own international network to sell Market Metrics products outside the US.

In 2011 FactSet expanded its presence in the Middle East when it opened an office in Dubai.

EXECUTIVES

Senior Vice President Director of Learning and Development, Laura Ruhe

Senior Vice President Director of Product Development Research And Market Data, Goran Skoko
SVP and CFO, Maurizio Nicolelli, age 51, $225,000 total compensation
SVP Strategic Resources and General Counsel, Rachel R. Stern
President CEO and Director, F. Philip Snow, age 54, $290,000 total compensation
EVP Chief Technology and Product Officer, Gene Fernandez
EVP and Global Head of Sales and Client Solutions, John W. Wiseman
SVP and CHRO, Edward Baker-Greene
Vp Director Of Information Systems, Lucy Tancredi
Vice President Portfolio Analytic Sales, Lata Prabhakar
Vice President Information Technology, Sharon Dipre
The Executive Vice President Head Of Analytics And Trading Analytics Solutions, Robert Robie
Vice President Director Content Development, Joseph Clair
Vice President Business Analyst, Amanda Harchuck
Vice President Finance Manager, Neil Ivler
Vp Sr Product Manager, Mark Hedley
Vice President Finance, Jaime Beckel
Senior Vice President Director Content Integration Engineering, Mark Thomford
Vice President Associate Director Databa, Sara Potter
Vice President Strategic Partnerships and Alliances, Erik Abbott
Vice President Sales Manager Research Management Solutions Americas, Jeswin Thomas
Vice President Of Sales, David Sheldon
Vice President, Lisa Knoll
Senior Vice President, Laura C Ruhe
Vice President Global Account Manager, Terence Yarde
Vice President Associate Director, Ken Ambrosio
Vice President Information Systems, Jonathan Shea
Senior Vice President Director Global Sales Operations, Jason Baroni
Vice President Product Marketing Manager, Alison J Stewart
Vice President Global Account Manager, Brian Paul
Senior Vice President and Director of Content Development, Ken Zockoll
Vice President Principal Software Engineer, Joseph Adam
Vice President Associate Director, Michael Cheng
Assistant Vice President Key Accounts, Jordan Kamps
Vice President Institutional Sales Executive, Julie Zimmerman
Vice President, Prasanna Venkatesh
Vice President, Rick Barrett
Senior Vice President Director Core Technologies, Jason Dennis
Vice President, David Werkheiser
Vice President Principal Software Engineer, Owen McCabe
Vice President Senior Sales Manager Americas Institutional Asset Management, Sean Savage
Vice President, Stacey Geller
Assistant Vice President, Varun Bhushan
Vice President Sales Manager, Yumi Tanaka
Vice President Brand Management, John Sanders
SENIOR VICE PRESIDENT, Anthony Jetnil
Vice President Institutional Sales, Stefanie Tavolato

Vice President Director of Wealth Management Americas, Michael Medvinsky
Vice President Director Americas Client Consult, Michael Giordano
Vice President Senior Human Resources Manager, Leonard F Johnson
Vice President Principal Software Engineer, John Hennessy
VICE PRESIDENT PRODUCT MANAGER, Julie Kinney
Vice President Associate Director Content Integration Engineering, Jon Loach
Vice President Institutional Sales, Meredith Schiffer
Vice President Investor Relations, Rima Hyder
VICE PRESIDENT MULTI ASSET CLASS RISK SOLUTIONS, Shamin Parikh
Vice President Human Resources Global Product Content And Technology, Katherine Parente
EXECUTIVE VICE PRESIDENT GLOBAL DIRECTOR OF SALES, Scott G Miller
Vice President Principal Software Engineer, Dave DeFonce
W M Assistant Vice President Key Account, Parker Taylor
VICE PRESIDENT INSTITUTIONAL SALES REPRESENTATIVE, Akw Vizag
VICE PRESIDENT SALES MANAGER, Andrea Williams
SENIOR VICE PRESIDENT, Gregory Jones
VICE PRESIDENT SALES MANAGER, Michael Schiffer
VICE PRESIDENT HEAD OF IMPLEMENTATION, Robert Long
Senior Vice President Finance And Interim Principal Accounting Officer, Brian G Daly
Vice President Associate Director, Anant Singh
Vp Fixed Income Analytics, Sangeeta Reddy
Chairman, Philip A. Hadley, age 57
Board Member, James Mcgonigle
Board Member, Laurie Siegel
Board Member, Sheila Jordan
Board Member, Malcolm Frank
Auditors: Ernst & Young LLP

LOCATIONS

HQ: FactSet Research Systems Inc.
45 Glover Avenue, Norwalk, CT 06850
Phone: 203 810-1000   Fax: 203 810-1001
Web: www.investor.factset.com

PRODUCTS/OPERATIONS

2015 Sales

	% of total
US	67
Europe	25
Asia/Pacific	8
Total	100

Selected Applications
Company Analysis
Data Warehousing
Economic Analysis
Fixed Income Analysis
Pitchbook Building
Portfolio Analysis
Quantitative Analysis
Real-time Market Data

Selected Content Providers
Dow Jones & Company
Global Insight
Interactive Data Corporation
Merrill Lynch
Morningstar
Standard and Poor's
Thomson Reuters

Selected Product and Service Offerings:
Investment Managers
Equity Analysis
Quant and Risk Analysis
Portfolio Analysis
Markets and Economics
Fixed Income Analysis
Data Integration
Charting
Wireless Connectivity
Global Banking & Brokerage Professionals
Models and Presentations
Company and Industry Analytics
Deal Analytics
Idea Screening
People Intelligence
Accountability
Corporate Governance
Wireless Connectivity
Other Global Professionals
Hedge Funds
Private Equity and Venture Capital
Sell-Side Research
Equity Sales
Trading and Managing Market Data
Consultants and Advisors
Investor Relations and Corporate Strategy
Legal Accounting Management Consulting and Other Professionals
Academia - Professors and Students

COMPETITORS

Avention	MSCI
Bloomberg L.P.	Pearson plc
CME	Telvent DTN
Capital IQ	Thomson Reuters
Dealogic	Track Data
Hoover's Inc.	thinkorswim
LexisNexis	

HISTORICAL FINANCIALS

Company Type: Public

Income Statement   FYE: August 31

	REVENUE ($ mil.)	NET INCOME ($ mil.)	NET PROFIT MARGIN	EMPLOYEES
08/19	1,435.3	352.7	24.6%	9,681
08/18	1,350.1	267.0	19.8%	9,571
08/17	1,221.1	258.2	21.1%	9,074
08/16	1,127.0	338.8	30.1%	8,375
08/15	1,006.7	241.0	23.9%	7,360
Annual Growth	9.3%	10.0%	—	7.1%

2019 Year-End Financials

Debt ratio: 36.8%   No. of shares (mil.): 38.1
Return on equity: 58.8%   Dividends
Cash ($ mil.): 359.8   Yield: 0.0%
Current ratio: 2.67   Payout: 29.9%
Long-term debt ($ mil.): 574.1   Market value ($ mil.): 10,371.0

	STOCK PRICE ($) FY Close	P/E High/Low	PER SHARE ($) Earnings	Dividends	Book Value
08/19	272.09	33 20	9.08	2.72	17.64
08/18	229.39	33 23	6.78	2.40	13.77
08/17	157.18	28 23	6.51	2.12	14.34
08/16	178.03	22 16	8.19	1.88	12.92
08/15	157.92	30 20	5.71	1.66	12.87
Annual Growth	14.6%	— —	12.3%	13.1%	8.2%

Fair Isaac Corp

EXECUTIVES

Chief Executive Officer; Director, William J. (Will) Lansing, age 57
Executive Vice-President Scores, James M. Wehmann
Analytic Research Fellow, Larry E. Rosenberger, age 69, $353,077 total compensation
SVP and Chief Human Resources Officer, Richard S. Deal, age 48, $290,000 total compensation
Chairman, A. George (Skip) Battle, age 72
Executive Vice President Chief Product and Technology Officer, Stuart C. Wells
Executive Vice President General Counsel and Corporate Secretary, Mark R. Scadina, age 46, $352,885 total compensation
EVP Sales Services and Marketing, Charles L. (Charlie) III, age 61, $317,308 total compensation
Executive Vice President Chief Financial Officer and Investor Relations, Michael J. (Mike) Pung, age 52
Assistant Corporate Secretary, Nancy E. Fraser
Senior Manager Strategic Marketing, Lynn Johnson
SVP and Chief Analytics Officer, Andrew N. Jennings, age 60
VP Corporate Strategy, John Nash
SVP Professional Services, Richard A. (Dick) Stewart, age 63
VP Corporate Communications, Stephen Astle
VP Sales Americas, Debora Schmidt
Executive Vice President Sales Services and Marketing, Michael (Mike) Gordon
Treasurer, Sheila Colgan
Senior Manager Public Relations, Craig Watts
VP Product Management, David Lightfoot
Vice President and Managing Director FICO Asia Pacific, Daniel McConaghy
Chief Accounting Officer; Vice President, Michael Leonard
Vice President Application Development and Deployment Research, Stephen Hendrick
Vice President Managing Director for FICO in Europe, Hayley Kershaw
CEO, William J. (Will) Lansing, age 57
Director, James D. (Jim) Kirsner, age 72
Director, Duane E. White, age 60
Director, Rahul N. Merchant, age 59
Director, Nicholas F. (Nick) Graziano, age 44
Independent Director, David Rey
Auditors: DELOITTE & TOUCHE LLP

LOCATIONS

HQ: Fair Isaac Corp
181 Metro Drive, Suite 700, San Jose, CA 95110-1346
Phone: 408 535-1500
Web: www.fico.com

COMPETITORS

Acxiom	Gallagher
Advantage Credit	Hewlett-Packard
Angoss Software	ISO
CGI Group	Intersections Inc.
Epsilon Data	LexisNexis
Equifax	Neural Technologies
Experian Americas	S&P
Fidelity National Information Services	SAS Institute
Fiserv	TransUnion

HISTORICAL FINANCIALS
Company Type: Public

Income Statement — FYE: September 30

	REVENUE ($ mil.)	NET INCOME ($ mil.)	NET PROFIT MARGIN	EMPLOYEES
09/19	1,160.0	192.1	16.6%	4,009
09/18	1,032.4	142.4	13.8%	3,668
09/17	932.1	128.2	13.8%	3,299
09/16	881.3	109.4	12.4%	3,088
09/15	838.7	86.5	10.3%	2,803
Annual Growth	8.4%	22.1%	—	9.4%

2019 Year-End Financials

Debt ratio: 57.5%
Return on equity: 69.4%
Cash ($ mil.): 106.4
Current ratio: 0.93
Long-term debt ($ mil.): 606.7
No. of shares (mil.): 28.9
Dividends
Yield: —
Payout: —
Market value ($ mil.): 8,785.0

	STOCK PRICE ($) FY Close	P/E High/Low	PER SHARE ($) Earnings	Dividends	Book Value
09/19	303.52	56 26	6.34	0.00	10.01
09/18	228.55	50 30	4.57	0.00	9.09
09/17	140.50	35 27	3.98	0.04	14.10
09/16	124.59	38 23	3.39	0.08	14.44
09/15	84.50	35 20	2.65	0.08	13.97
Annual Growth	37.7%	—	24.4%	—	(8.0%)

Farmers & Merchants Bancorp (Lodi, CA)

EXECUTIVES

Chb-pres-ceo, Kent A Steinwert
Vice President, Chris Winek
Vice President And Chief Appraiser, Jon Schrader
VICE PRESIDENT, Pam Mcglynn
VICE PRESIDENT RETAIL CREDIT SALES MANAGER, Gary Spears
ASSISTANT VICE PRESIDENT RETAIL ADMINISTRATION, Jackie Phillips
Vice President Commercial Loan Officer, Claire Forsythe
VICE PRESIDENT RELATIONSHIP MANAGER, Corinne Santos
VICE PRESIDENT TREASURY RELATIONSHIP MANAGER, Mike Caselli
VICE PRESIDENT DIRECTOR OF TREASURY OPERATIONS, Patty Ducato
VICE PRESIDENT TREASURY MANAGEMENT SPECIALIST LL, Patricia Preston
SENIOR VICE PRESIDENT, Carol Murray
Assistant Vice President Operations Supervisor, Carrie Henshaw
Vice President Commercial Account Officer, Jesse Pataria
Auditors: Moss Adams LLP

LOCATIONS

HQ: Farmers & Merchants Bancorp (Lodi, CA)
111 W. Pine Street, Lodi, CA 95240
Phone: 209 367-2300
Web: www.fmbonline.com

HISTORICAL FINANCIALS
Company Type: Public

Income Statement — FYE: December 31

	ASSETS ($ mil.)	NET INCOME ($ mil.)	INCOME AS % OF ASSETS	EMPLOYEES
12/18	3,434.2	45.5	1.3%	376
12/17	3,075.4	28.3	0.9%	330
12/16	2,922.1	29.7	1.0%	339
12/15	2,615.3	27.3	1.0%	316
12/14	2,360.5	25.4	1.1%	310
Annual Growth	9.8%	15.7%	—	4.9%

2018 Year-End Financials

Return on assets: 1.4%
Return on equity: 14.9%
Long-term debt ($ mil.): —
No. of shares (mil.): 0.7
Sales ($ mil): 148.6
Dividends
Yield: 1.9%
Payout: 30.9%
Market value ($ mil.): 549.0

	STOCK PRICE ($) FY Close	P/E High/Low	PER SHARE ($) Earnings	Dividends	Book Value
12/18	700.00	13 11	56.82	13.90	397.10
12/17	676.00	20 17	35.03	13.55	368.90
12/16	640.00	17 13	37.44	13.10	346.80
12/15	540.00	17 13	34.82	12.90	318.46
12/14	463.00	14 13	32.64	12.70	297.39
Annual Growth	10.9%	—	14.9%	2.3%	7.5%

Farmers National Banc Corp. (Canfield, OH)

Farmers National Banc is willing to help even nonfarmers grow their seed income into thriving bounties of wealth. The bank provides commercial and personal banking from nearly 20 branches in Ohio. Founded in 1887 Farmers National Banc offers checking and savings accounts credit cards and loans and mortgages. Farmers' lending portfolio is composed of real estate mortgages consumer loans and commercial loans. The company also includes Farmers National Insurance and Farmers Trust Company a non-depository trust bank that offers wealth management and trust services.

Geographic Reach

Farmers National Banc operates 19 branches located throughout Mahoning Trumbull Columbiana Stark and Cuyahoga Counties. Farmers Trust Company operates two offices located in Boardman and Howland Ohio.

Financial Performance

The company's revenues have ranged from $40 million to $60 million in the past decade. In 2013 overall sales fell 1% to $54 million; the slight dip was due to lessened interest income on loans and taxable securities. (Financial institutions make their money on interest income from loans and non-interest income from fees.) Its non-interest income experienced growth from service charges insurance agency commissions and consulting fees for retirement planning.

Profits decreased by 22% to $8 million in 2013 due to increase in a provision for loan losses and non-interest expenses such as salary and employee benefits.

Mergers and Acquisitions
In 2013 the bank added retirement planning services to their portfolio with the acquisition of Cleveland-based National Associates Inc. for $4.4 million. The acquisition was part of its plan to boost noninterest income and complement its existing retirement services.

EXECUTIVES

Vice President, Jon Schmied
Vice President Retail Operations Manager, Jim Swift
Vice President, David Simko
Assistant Vice President, Anita Jarvis
Vice President Commercial Lending Relationship Manager, Darrell Smucker
Senior Vice President Commercial Lending Team Leader, Thomas Stocksdale
Vp Commercial Lending Relationship Manager, David Benavides
Assistant Vice President Branch Manager Downtown Massillon, Katherine Shultz
Senior Vice President, Michael Oberhaus
Board Member, Anne Crawford
Board Member, Ralph Macali
Board Member, David Paull
Board Member, Gregory Bestic
Vice Chairman Of The Board, James Smail
Board Member, Terry Moore
Board Member, Edward Muransky
Auditors: CliftonLarsonAllen, LLP

LOCATIONS

HQ: Farmers National Banc Corp. (Canfield,OH)
20 South Broad Street, Canfield, OH 44406
Phone: 330 533-3341
Web: www.farmersbankgroup.com

PRODUCTS/OPERATIONS

Selected Products
Personal
Certificate of DepositChecking AccountsChildren's AccountsConsumer LoansHome Equity Loans & LinesMortgage LoansOnline BankingPersonal Credit CardPersonal Debit CardPhone BankingRetirementSavings Accounts
Business
Business Credit CardBusiness Debit CardBusiness DepositsBusiness LoansCash ManagementRemote Deposit Capture
Wealth Management and Insurance
Farmers Trust CompanyFarmers National InvestmentsFarmers National Insurance
On-line banking

COMPETITORS

CSB Bancorp	JPMorgan Chase
Central Federal	Killbuck Bancshares
Consumers Bancorp	National Bancshares
Cortland Bancorp	Ohio Legacy
FFD Financial	Tri-State 1st Banc
Fifth Third	United Community Financial
First Financial Bancorp	Wayne Savings Bancshares
First Niles Financial	
Home Loan Financial	

HISTORICAL FINANCIALS
Company Type: Public

Income Statement FYE: December 31

	ASSETS ($ mil.)	NET INCOME ($ mil.)	INCOME AS % OF ASSETS	EMPLOYEES
12/18	2,328.8	32.5	1.4%	453
12/17	2,159.0	22.7	1.1%	445
12/16	1,966.1	20.5	1.0%	441
12/15	1,869.9	8.0	0.4%	432
12/14	1,136.9	8.9	0.8%	327
Annual Growth	19.6%	38.1%	—	8.5%

2018 Year-End Financials
Return on assets: 1.4%
Return on equity: 12.9%
Long-term debt ($ mil.): —
No. of shares (mil.): 27.7
Sales ($ mil): 117.2
Dividends
 Yield: 2.3%
 Payout: 28.8%
Market value ($ mil.): 354.0

	STOCK PRICE ($) FY Close	P/E High/Low		PER SHARE ($) Earnings	Dividends	Book Value
12/18	12.74	14	10	1.16	0.30	9.44
12/17	14.75	19	15	0.82	0.22	8.79
12/16	14.20	20	11	0.76	0.16	7.88
12/15	8.60	24	20	0.36	0.12	7.35
12/14	8.35	18	14	0.48	0.12	6.71
Annual Growth	11.1%	—	—	24.7%	25.7%	8.9%

Farmland Partners Inc

Auditors: Plante & Moran LLP

LOCATIONS

HQ: Farmland Partners Inc
4600 South Syracuse Street, Suite 1450, Denver, CO 80237
Phone: 720 452-3100
Web: www.farmlandpartners.com

HISTORICAL FINANCIALS
Company Type: Public

Income Statement FYE: December 31

	REVENUE ($ mil.)	NET INCOME ($ mil.)	NET PROFIT MARGIN	EMPLOYEES
12/18	56.0	12.2	21.9%	13
12/17	46.2	7.9	17.1%	16
12/16	31.0	4.3	13.9%	18
12/15	13.7	1.2	8.9%	13
12/14	4.2	(0.5)	—	7
Annual Growth	90.9%	—	—	16.7%

2018 Year-End Financials
Debt ratio: 45.9%
Return on equity: 2.7%
Cash ($ mil.): 16.8
Current ratio: 1.90
Long-term debt ($ mil.): 523.6
No. of shares (mil.): 30.5
Dividends
 Yield: 7.8%
 Payout: —
Market value ($ mil.): 139.0

FB Financial Corp

Auditors: Crowe LLP

LOCATIONS

HQ: FB Financial Corp
211 Commerce Street, Suite 300, Nashville, TN 37201
Phone: 615 564-1212
Web: www.firstbankonline.com

HISTORICAL FINANCIALS
Company Type: Public

Income Statement FYE: December 31

	ASSETS ($ mil.)	NET INCOME ($ mil.)	INCOME AS % OF ASSETS	EMPLOYEES
12/18	5,136.7	80.2	1.6%	1,356
12/17	4,727.7	52.4	1.1%	1,386
12/16	3,276.8	40.5	1.2%	1,108
12/15	2,899.4	47.8	1.7%	1,038
12/14	2,428.1	32.4	1.3%	0
Annual Growth	20.6%	25.4%	—	—

2018 Year-End Financials
Return on assets: 1.6%
Return on equity: 12.6%
Long-term debt ($ mil.): —
No. of shares (mil.): 30.7
Sales ($ mil): 370.2
Dividends
 Yield: 0.5%
 Payout: 7.8%
Market value ($ mil.): 1,076.0

	STOCK PRICE ($) FY Close	P/E High/Low		PER SHARE ($) Earnings	Dividends	Book Value
12/18	35.02	17	13	2.55	0.20	21.87
12/17	41.99	23	13	1.86	0.00	19.54
12/16	25.95	12	9	2.10	4.03	13.71
Annual Growth	16.2%	—	—	10.2%	(77.7%)	26.3%

	STOCK PRICE ($) FY Close	P/E High/Low		PER SHARE ($) Earnings	Dividends	Book Value
12/18	4.54	—	—	(0.01)	0.36	14.33
12/17	8.68	38	1274	0.03	0.51	14.06
12/16	11.16	133	111	0.09	0.51	9.33
12/15	10.97	155	123	0.08	0.50	9.05
12/14	10.41	—	—	(0.15)	0.33	8.58
Annual Growth	(18.7%)	—	—	—	2.2%	13.7%

Federal Agricultural Mortgage Corp

Farmer Mac (Federal Agricultural Mortgage Corporation) is Fannie Mae and Freddie Mac's country cousin. Like its city-slicker kin it provides liquidity in its markets (agricultural real estate and rural housing mortgages) by buying loans from lenders and then securitizing the loans into Farmer Mac Guaranteed Securities. Farmer Mac buys both conventional loans and those guaranteed by the US Department of Agriculture. Farmer Mac was created by Congress in 1987 to establish a secondary market for agricultural mortgage and rural utilities loans. It is a stockholder-owned publicly-traded corporation based in Washington DC with an underwriting office in Iowa.

Operations

Farmer Mac operates four segments: Farm & Ranch which accounted for 39% of revenue during 2015 purchases mortgage loans secured by first liens on agricultural real estate including part-time farms and rural housing; Institutional Credit (28% of revenue) which buys or guarantees general lender obligations secured by eligible pools of loans; the USDA Guarantees segment (18%) which buys USDA-backed agricultural rural development business and industry and community facilities loans; and Rural Utilities (10%) which buys mortgages tied to eligible rural utilities loans. The organization generates more than 90% of its revenue from interest income stemming from a roughly even mix of loans and backed loan securities. About 47% of its revenue came from interest on Farmer Mac Guaranteed or USDA securities during 2015 while another 41% came from interest on loans. The rest came from interest on other investments (5% of revenue) guarantee and commitment fees (5%) and gains on financial derivatives and hedging activities (1%).

Geographic Reach

The Washington DC-based group serves the US from satellite operations in Ames Iowa; Boise Idaho; Canton Michigan; Fresno California; Johnston Iowa; and Scottsdale Arizona.

Sales and Marketing

Farmer Mac markets its services personally and directly to agricultural lenders by participating regularly in events such as state and national banking conferences. It also has alliances with the American Bankers Association and the Independent Community Bankers of Alliances and has a business relationship with the members of the Farm Credit System.

Financial Performance

Farmer Mac's annual revenues have risen more than 25% since 2011 thanks to a stronger agricultural economy as well as product developments which have driven customer and overall loan asset growth over the years. Its annual profits have also trended higher but have fluctuated more due to the volatility of the gains it's made from financial derivatives hedging activities and other trading securities.

The group's revenue climbed 4% to $284 million during 2015 mostly thanks to double-digit interest income growth as its loan assets grew 12% to $3.96 billion and as its Farm & Ranch loans USDA Securities and AgVantage securities balances grew as well. Farmer Mac's non-interest income shrank 39% as it collected $37.4 million less in trading securities gains as it did in 2014.

Revenue growth and a decline in interest expenses in 2015 drove Farmer Mac's net income up 43% to $68.7 million. The lender's operating cash levels jumped 19% to $184 million as its cash-based earnings rose and as working capital increased with changes in other assets.

Strategy

Farmer Mac seeks to improve the availability of long-term credit at stable interest rates to rural communities. To this end its primary strategy for managing interest rate risk is to fund asset purchases with liabilities that have similar duration and cash flow characteristics so that they will perform similarly as interest rates change.

EXECUTIVES

President and CEO, Timothy L. (Tim) Buzby, age 50, $643,750 total compensation
EVP CFO and Treasurer, R. Dale Lynch, age 52, $375,950 total compensation
SVP Agricultural Finance, J. Curtis Covington, age 63
SVP General Counsel and Secretary, Stephen P. Mullery, age 52, $340,930 total compensation
Vice President Corporate Affairs, Chris Bohanon
Senior Vice President Business Strategy and Financial Research, Brian Brinch
Chairman, Lowell L. Junkins, age 75
Vice Chairman, Myles J. Watts, age 68
Auditors: PricewaterhouseCoopers LLP

LOCATIONS

HQ: Federal Agricultural Mortgage Corp
1999 K Street, N.W., 4th Floor, Washington, DC 20006
Phone: 202 872-7700

PRODUCTS/OPERATIONS

2015 Sales

	% of total
Interest income	
Farmer Mac Guaranteed Securities and USDA Securities	47
Loans	41
Investments and cash equivalents	5
Noninterest income	
Guarantee and commitment fees	5
Gains on financial derivatives and hedging activities	1
Other	1
Total	**100**

2015 Sales

	% of total
Farm & Ranch	39
USDA Guarantees	28
Rural Utilities	18
Institutional Credit	10
Corporate	4
Reconciling Adjustments	1
Total	**100**

Selected Operations
Farm & Ranch (Farmer Mac I)
USDA Guarantees (Farmer Mac II)
Rural Utilities

COMPETITORS

AgFirst	Fannie Mae
AgStar	Farm Credit Services
AgriBank	of Mid-America
Bank of America	Freddie Mac
Citigroup	

HISTORICAL FINANCIALS

Company Type: Public

Income Statement — FYE: December 31

	ASSETS ($ mil.)	NET INCOME ($ mil.)	INCOME AS % OF ASSETS	EMPLOYEES
12/18	18,694.3	108.0	0.6%	103
12/17	17,792.2	84.4	0.5%	88
12/16	15,606.0	77.3	0.5%	81
12/15	15,540.3	68.7	0.4%	71
12/14	14,287.8	48.0	0.3%	71
Annual Growth	7.0%	22.4%	—	9.7%

2018 Year-End Financials

Return on assets: 0.5%
Return on equity: 14.8%
Long-term debt ($ mil.): —
No. of shares (mil.): 10.6
Sales ($ mil): 556.0
Dividends
Yield: 3.8%
Payout: 26.2%
Market value ($ mil.): 645.0

	STOCK PRICE ($) FY Close	P/E High/Low		PER SHARE ($) Earnings	Dividends	Book Value
12/18	60.44	11	6	8.83	2.32	70.54
12/17	78.24	12	8	6.60	1.44	66.69
12/16	57.27	10	4	5.97	1.04	61.05
12/15	31.57	8	5	4.19	0.64	51.79
12/14	30.34	10	8	3.37	0.56	49.90
Annual Growth	18.8%			27.2%	42.7%	9.0%

Federal Home Loan Bank Boston

Federal Home Loan Bank of Boston (FHLB Boston) is banking on the continued support of other banks. The government-supported enterprise provides funds for residential mortgages and community development loans to its members which consist of more than 440 financial institutions across New England including banks thrifts credit unions and insurance companies. The bank also lends to nonmember institutions the likes of state housing finance agencies primarily to promote the funding of low to moderate income housing in the region. FHLB Boston is one of 12 regional wholesale banks in the Federal Home Loan Bank System. Its region includes Connecticut Maine Massachusetts New Hampshire Rhode Island and Vermont.

Operations

FHLB Boston provides its members with loans or advances and other services to promote community development. As a government-sponsored enterprise the bank enjoys favorable interest rates on its own borrowings. It is overseen by the Federal Housing Finance Agency.

Financial Performance

FHLB Boston logged its highest annual net income in its history in fiscal 2013 posting $212.3 million — a $5.2 million increase from 2012's $207.1 million. It attributes this to $53.3 million in litigation settlements related to certain investments in private-label mortgage-backed securities.

Strategy

The bank's performance is closely tied with the economy including the current low-interest rate environment and the value of its investments in private-label mortgage-backed securities. Ongoing factors contributing to the health (or non-health) of those securities are high unemployment widespread foreclosures and the number of borrowers who are underwater on their homes. While the stormy financial climate has had and will continue to have a negative impact on the bank net income has been rising.

EXECUTIVES

Vice President and Director of Financial Strategies Research and Membership Applications, Jason Hwang
Vice President Deputy Director Housing A, Mary Jutras
Vice President, Patrick Green
Vice President And Corporate And Finance Counsel, Keith Walsh
Assistant Vice President, George Maroun
Assistant Vice President Technical Research and De, William Evans
Senior Vice President Executive Director Human Resources, Barry Gale
Vice President Transaction Management, Kathy Judge
Vice President Director Of Bank Operatio, Newton Thompson
Assistant Vice President Relationship Manager, Maria Nichols
Vice President Director, Joanne Sullivan
Vice President Operations, Rachele McDonough
Vice President Director Of Internal Audit, Brian Chase
AVP Payments and Safekeeping, Theresa Mahoney
Vice President Assistant General Counsel, Jane Harper
Vice President and Director Marketing Strategy and Communications, Adam Coldwell
Auditors: Boston, Massachusetts

LOCATIONS

HQ: Federal Home Loan Bank Boston
800 Boylston Street, Boston, MA 02199
Phone: 617 292-9600
Web: www.fhlbboston.com

HISTORICAL FINANCIALS
Company Type: Public

Income Statement — FYE: December 31

	REVENUE ($ mil.)	NET INCOME ($ mil.)	NET PROFIT MARGIN	EMPLOYEES
12/18	1,447.4	216.7	15.0%	200
12/17	959.8	190.2	19.8%	203
12/16	737.4	173.2	23.5%	202
12/15	756.9	289.3	38.2%	206
12/14	578.4	149.7	25.9%	200
Annual Growth	25.8%	9.7%	—	0.0%

2018 Year-End Financials
Debt ratio: 92.7%
Return on equity: 6.3%
Cash ($ mil.): 8,602.6
Current ratio: 0.26
Long-term debt ($ mil.): 25,912.6
No. of shares (mil.): 25.2
Dividends
  Yield: —
  Payout: 60.0%
Market value ($ mil.): —

Federal Home Loan Bank Indianapolis

Auditors: PricewaterhouseCoopers LLP

LOCATIONS

HQ: Federal Home Loan Bank Indianapolis
8250 Woodfield Crossing Boulevard, Indianapolis, IN 46240
Phone: 317 465-0200
Web: www.fhlbi.com

HISTORICAL FINANCIALS
Company Type: Public

Income Statement — FYE: December 31

	REVENUE ($ mil.)	NET INCOME ($ mil.)	NET PROFIT MARGIN	EMPLOYEES
12/18	1,565.0	194.7	12.4%	249
12/17	1,016.6	156.4	15.4%	241
12/16	694.8	113.0	16.3%	218
12/15	543.7	120.9	22.2%	216
12/14	495.2	116.6	23.5%	215
Annual Growth	33.3%	13.7%	—	3.7%

2018 Year-End Financials
Debt ratio: 93.5%
Return on equity: 6.5%
Cash ($ mil.): 7,609.1
Current ratio: 0.36
Long-term debt ($ mil.): 40,265.4
No. of shares (mil.): 19.3
Dividends
  Yield: —
  Payout: 47.8%
Market value ($ mil.): —

HISTORICAL FINANCIALS
Company Type: Public

Income Statement — FYE: December 31

	ASSETS ($ mil.)	NET INCOME ($ mil.)	INCOME AS % OF ASSETS	EMPLOYEES
12/18	99,202.5	339.1	0.3%	229
12/17	106,895.2	313.5	0.3%	226
12/16	104,635.2	268.1	0.3%	211
12/15	118,796.7	248.7	0.2%	203
12/14	106,640.4	244.2	0.2%	204
Annual Growth	(1.8%)	8.6%	—	2.9%

2018 Year-End Financials
Return on assets: 0.3%
Return on equity: 6.4%
Long-term debt ($ mil.): —
No. of shares (mil.): 43.2
Sales ($ mil): 2,391.4
Dividends
  Yield: —
  Payout: 75.6%
Market value ($ mil.): —

Federal Home Loan Bank Of Dallas

Auditors: PricewaterhouseCoopers LLP

LOCATIONS

HQ: Federal Home Loan Bank Of Dallas
8500 Freeport Parkway South, Suite 600, Irving, TX 75063-2547
Phone: 214 441-8500
Web: www.fhlb.com

HISTORICAL FINANCIALS
Company Type: Public

Income Statement — FYE: December 31

	ASSETS ($ mil.)	NET INCOME ($ mil.)	INCOME AS % OF ASSETS	EMPLOYEES
12/18	72,773.2	198.7	0.3%	197
12/17	68,524.3	150.2	0.2%	205
12/16	58,212.0	79.4	0.1%	218
12/15	42,083.2	67.1	0.2%	207
12/14	38,045.8	48.5	0.1%	192
Annual Growth	17.6%	42.3%	—	0.6%

2018 Year-End Financials
Return on assets: 0.2%
Return on equity: 5.4%
Long-term debt ($ mil.): —
No. of shares (mil.): 25.5
Sales ($ mil): 1,548.7
Dividends
  Yield: —
  Payout: 29.7%
Market value ($ mil.): —

Federal Home Loan Bank Chicago

Auditors: PricewaterhouseCoopers LLP

LOCATIONS

HQ: Federal Home Loan Bank Chicago
200 East Randolph Drive, Chicago, IL 60601
Phone: 312 565-5700
Web: www.fhlbc.com

Federal Home Loan Bank Of Cincinnati

Auditors: PricewaterhouseCoopers LLP (PwC)

LOCATIONS

HQ: Federal Home Loan Bank Of Cincinnati
600 Atrium Two, P.O Box 598, Cincinnati, OH 45201-0598
Phone: 513 852-7500
Web: www.fhlbcin.com

Federal Home Loan Bank of Pittsburgh

The Federal Home Loan Bank of Pittsburgh helps revitalize neighborhoods and fund low-income housing in the City of Champions and beyond. One of a dozen banks in the Federal Home

Loan Bank System the government-sponsored entity (FHLB Pittsburgh for short) uses private capital and public sponsorships to provide low-cost funding for residential mortgages and community and economic development loans in Delaware Pennsylvania and West Virginia. It is cooperatively owned by about 300 member banks thrifts credit unions and insurance companies in its three-state district. The bank also offers member banks correspondent banking services such as depository funds transfer settlement and safekeeping services.

Financial Performance
FHLB Pittsburgh which boasts $71 billion in assets logged net income of $147.8 million in fiscal 2013 up $18.1 million from 2012's $129.7 million. The institution attributes the boost to higher net gains on derivatives and hedging activities lower net other-than-temporary-impairment (OTTI) credit losses and net gains on the early extinguishment of debt. These gains however were partially offset by lower net interest income and higher other expenses.

Strategy
The wholesale bank has been shying away from higher-yielding assets including private label mortgage-backed securities and replacing those with less risky agency securities. While demand for advances remains low the bank plans to prudently manage its capital position and continue enhancing its risk management practices.

While FHLB Pittsburgh earns the largest portion of its revenue from investments in securities such as US Treasurys and mortgage-backed securities about a third comes from accrued interest on loan advances to other financial institutions. Its five largest customers — Ally Bank PNC Bank Sovereign Bank Susquehanna Bank and TD Bank— account for more than 70% of its credit products and own around 45% of its stock.

The Federal Housing Finance Agency oversees the twelve Federal Home Loan Banks. FHLB Pittsburgh members include any eligible institution in Delaware Pennsylvania or West Virginia.

Company Background
As a mortgage lender for other banks the Federal Home Loan Bank of Pittsburgh suffered during the mortgage crisis. The Pittsburgh bank experienced its first-ever net loss in 2009 and was unable to set aside the usual 10% for the FDIC's Affordable Housing Program. In 2010 bank executives began reducing its use of derivatives improving processes and systems and employing outside experts on risk management. The moves helped FHLB Pittsburgh to return to profitability. Also that year as part of the Housing and Economic Recovery Act Community Development Financial Institutions including community development loan funds venture capital firms and state-chartered credit unions without federal deposit insurance became eligible to become members of a Federal Home Loan Bank.

EXECUTIVES

Vice President and Relationship Manager, Vincent Moye
Vice President Relationship Manager, John Foff
Vice President and Relationship Manager, Fred Duncan
Vice President, Francis Vargas
Vice President Coo, Russell W Huxtable
Vice President, Susie Salisbury
Auditors: PricewaterhouseCoopers LLP

LOCATIONS
HQ: Federal Home Loan Bank of Pittsburgh
601 Grant Street, Pittsburgh, PA 15219
Phone: 412 288-3400
Web: www.fhlb-pgh.com

HISTORICAL FINANCIALS
Company Type: Public

Income Statement — FYE: December 31

	REVENUE ($ mil.)	NET INCOME ($ mil.)	NET PROFIT MARGIN	EMPLOYEES
12/18	2,272.3	347.1	15.3%	224
12/17	1,485.9	339.6	22.9%	215
12/16	1,010.5	260.0	25.7%	214
12/15	740.0	256.5	34.7%	215
12/14	701.7	255.7	36.4%	219
Annual Growth	34.1%	7.9%	—	0.6%

2018 Year-End Financials
Debt ratio: 94.1%
Return on equity: 6.7%
Cash ($ mil.): 7,934.5
Current ratio: 13.25
Long-term debt ($ mil.): 101,195.2
No. of shares (mil.): 40.2
Dividends
  Yield: —
  Payout: 66.0%
Market value ($ mil.): —

Federal Home Loan Bank Topeka

EXECUTIVES

Vice President And Director Marketing And Communications, Julie M Devader
Vice President of Network Services, Kathleen Grote
Vice President Director Of Member Services, Julia Burghart
Vice President and Portfolio Manager, Gregory Mclaren
Vice President Regional Account Manager, Don Cushing
Assistant Vice President and Director of Planning, Martin L Schlossman
Vice President Director Of Institutional Sales, David Harris
Senior Vice President Member Products, Sonia Betsworth
Vice President Risk Management, Michael Surface
Chief Accounting Officer Senior Vice President, Denise Cauthon
Vice President, Greg Mclaren
First Vice President Internal Audit, Tom Millburn
Assistant Vice President And Regional Account Manager, Donald Cushing
Vice President Government Relations Officer, Ryan Gilliland
Board Member, Jenifer Whitehead
Secretary, Pat Doran
Auditors: PricewaterhouseCoopers LLP

LOCATIONS
HQ: Federal Home Loan Bank Topeka
500 SW Wanamaker Road, Topeka, KS 66606
Phone: 785 233-0507
Web: www.fhlbtopeka.com

HISTORICAL FINANCIALS
Company Type: Public

Income Statement — FYE: December 31

	REVENUE ($ mil.)	NET INCOME ($ mil.)	NET PROFIT MARGIN	EMPLOYEES
12/18	1,257.0	170.2	13.5%	234
12/17	831.9	197.2	23.7%	233
12/16	580.4	161.7	27.9%	238
12/15	465.4	93.3	20.1%	218
12/14	428.3	106.0	24.7%	217
Annual Growth	30.9%	12.6%	—	1.9%

2018 Year-End Financials
Debt ratio: 93.4%
Return on equity: 6.8%
Cash ($ mil.): 10,320.4
Current ratio: 18.57
Long-term debt ($ mil.): 44,574.7
No. of shares (mil.): 15.2
Dividends
  Yield: —
  Payout: —
Market value ($ mil.): —

Federal Signal Corp.

Federal Signal likes to believe it keeps people property and the environment safe. Through segments that include environmental solutions and safety and security systems the company designs and manufactures products for municipal governmental industrial and commercial customers. Offerings include street sweepers vacuum trucks and water blasters for environmental cleanup; emergency communications and public warning systems for public safety. Federal Signal caters primarily to the US market. It sold its Fire Rescue Group segment throughout late 2015 and early 2016.

Operations
Federal Signal divides its operations across two segments. Environmental solutions accounts for 70% of revenue and distributes through dealer networks and a direct sales staff. The environmental solutions dealer channel serves the municipal market while the direct sales channel addresses the industrial utility and construction markets.

The safety & security systems segment 30% of revenue sells to industrial customers municipal and governmental customers through wholesalers and distributors.

Geographic Reach
The majority of the company's sales (75%) are made in the US where its sells such market-leading brands as Elgin street sweepers and Jetstream water blasters.

Financial Performance
Federal Signal's net sales rose declined 16% from from 2014 to 2015 mainly due to the divestiture of its Fire Rescue Group operations. The company also experienced declines in safety & security systems sales due to reduced orders for outdoor warning systems. Also environmental solutions revenue decreased in 2015 due to reductions in orders for vacuum trucks street sweepers and sewer cleaners.

Strategy
To focus on its remaining two segments Federal Signal sold its Fire Rescue Group business throughout late 2015 and 2016. The segment served such customers as fire departments indus-

trial fire services electric utilities and maintenance rental companies.

Mergers and Acquisitions
In 2019 Federal Signal purchased US-based Mark Rite Lines Equipment Company for about $55 million. Mark Rite is a manufacturer of truck-mounted and ride-on road-marking equipment. The deal bolsters Federal Signal's stable of specialty vehicle offerings.

EXECUTIVES

President and CEO, Jennifer L. Sherman, age 54, $650,000 total compensation
VP Corporate Controller and Interim CFO, Ian A. Hudson, age 42, $259,713 total compensation
SVP Environmental Solutions Group, Samuel E. Miceli, age 52, $287,163 total compensation
COO, David G. Martin
Vice President and General Manager Integrated Systems Division, Ray White
Information Technology Management: Executive Vice President Senior Vice President, Jim Dickson
Vice President Business Development and Innovation, Scott Rohrbaugh
Vice President of Industrial Sales and Jetstream Assembly, Tony Fuller
Chairman, Dennis J. Martin, age 68
Vice President Treasurer And Corporate Development, Svetlana Vinokur
Auditors: DELOITTE & TOUCHE LLP

LOCATIONS

HQ: Federal Signal Corp.
1415 West 22nd Street, Oak Brook, IL 60523
Phone: 630 954-2000 **Fax:** 630 954-2030
Web: www.federalsignal.com

PRODUCTS/OPERATIONS

2015 Sales

	$ mil.	% of total
Environmental Solutions	534.1	70
Safety and Security Systems	233.9	30
Total	**768.0**	**100**

Selected Products
Alerting systems
Hydro-excavators
Industrial vacuum loaders
Mining systems
Parking systems
Sewer cleaners
Sirens
Street sweepers
Truck-mounted aerial platforms
Water blasters

COMPETITORS

Bosch
Collins Industries
Flow International
Manitowoc
Napco Security

R.P.M. Tech
TYMCO
Tennant
TransCore

HISTORICAL FINANCIALS
Company Type: Public

Income Statement
FYE: December 31

	REVENUE ($ mil.)	NET INCOME ($ mil.)	NET PROFIT MARGIN	EMPLOYEES
12/18	1,089.5	94.0	8.6%	3,300
12/17	898.5	61.6	6.9%	3,100
12/16	707.9	43.8	6.2%	2,200
12/15	768.0	63.5	8.3%	2,200
12/14	779.1	63.7	8.2%	2,700
Annual Growth	8.7%	10.2%	—	5.1%

2018 Year-End Financials
Debt ratio: 20.5%
Return on equity: 19.0%
Cash ($ mil.): 37.4
Current ratio: 2.07
Long-term debt ($ mil.): 209.9
No. of shares (mil.): 60.2
Dividends
  Yield: 1.5%
  Payout: 20.1%
Market value ($ mil.): 1,198.0

	STOCK PRICE ($) FY Close	P/E High/Low	PER SHARE ($) Earnings	Dividends	Book Value
12/18	19.90	18 12	1.54	0.31	8.81
12/17	20.09	22 13	1.02	0.28	7.62
12/16	15.61	23 16	0.71	0.28	6.61
12/15	15.85	17 13	1.00	0.25	6.52
12/14	15.44	16 12	1.00	0.09	5.95
Annual Growth	6.5%	— —	11.4%	36.2%	10.3%

FedNat Holding Co

Trashed trailer crashed car damaged dwelling? Federated National Holding Company has a policy to cover that. Through Federated National Insurance Company and other subsidiaries it underwrites a variety of personal property/casualty insurance lines in Florida. Products include homeowners flood liability and nonstandard automobile coverage. Recently formed property insurance unit Monarch National (established in 2015) offers a complete homeowners policy special form (HO-3) multi-peril insurance product for Florida homeowners (and plans to introduce a similar product for condominiums). The firm distributes its products through independent agents and its Insure-Link agency.

Operations
Federated National underwrites homeowners commercial general liability federal flood personal auto and other lines of insurance. It is licensed as an admitted carrier for more than 300 classes of commercial general liability coverage in Alabama Georgia Louisiana and Texas. The company's affiliates are also able to market and underwrite other carriers' lines of business and process and adjust claims for third-party carriers.

The firm's independent agency Insure-Link distributes all of the company's products. Such vertical integration is unusual for small regional insurers but is part of Federated National's strategy to control all aspects of the insurance underwriting distribution and claims process.

Homeowners accounted for more than 90% of the firm's net premiums earned in fiscal 2014.

Geographic Reach
Federated National operates in the US Europe and Asia. In the US it primarily operates in the Southeast: Alabama Florida Georgia Louisiana Mississippi Missouri Nevada South Carolina and Texas.

Sales and Marketing
The company markets and distributes its and other carriers' products and services through its Insure-Link network of independent agents and through general agents.

Financial Performance
Federated National's revenues have spiked over the past couple of years on increases in homeowners' net premiums earned (thanks to more policies being sold) and higher commissions. In 2014 revenue increased 65% to $201 million; also contributing to the rise was higher investment earnings. Net income has followed revenue and in 2014 it rose 192% to $37 million.

However cash flow from operations fell 21% to $63 million as more cash was used in prepaid reinsurance premiums and for other expenses.

Strategy
Federated National is working on expanding its product offerings and underwriting additional profitable types of coverage. It also plans on introducing its wares in more states building on its Florida base. In 2015 its formed Monarch Insurance a new property/casualty insurance provider in Florida offering homeowners' policies.

EXECUTIVES

Vice President Accounting And Financial Reporting, Donald Braun
President and CEO, Michael H. Braun, age 51, $229,824 total compensation
CFO, Ronald Jordan, age 51
Vice President Marketing, Marty Kramer
Vice President Of Human Resources, Tracy Wiggan
Vice President Of Risk Management, Gordan Jennings
Assistant Vice President, Gordon Baker
Vice President Operations, Steve Young
Chairman, Bruce F. Simberg, age 70
Board Member, Thomas Rogers
Board Member, Roberta Young
Auditors: Ernst & Young LLP

LOCATIONS

HQ: FedNat Holding Co
14050 N.W. 14th Street, Suite 180, Sunrise, FL 33323
Phone: 800 293-2532
Web: www.FedNat.com

PRODUCTS/OPERATIONS

2014 Premiums

	% of total
Homeowners	92
Commercial general liability	6
Automobile	2
Total	**100**

2014 Revenue

	$ mil.	% of total
Net premiums earned	170.9	86
Direct written policy fees	8.7	4
Net investment income	5.4	3
Commission income	4.5	2
Net realized investment gains	4.4	2
Finance revenue	1.5	1
Quota share profit sharing	2.8	1
Other income	2.5	1
Total	**200.7**	**100**

COMPETITORS

Allstate
AssuranceAmerica
Bankers Financial
GEICO
Main Street America
Progressive Corporation
Safeco
Safeway Insurance
State Farm
Universal Insurance Holdings

HISTORICAL FINANCIALS
Company Type: Public

Income Statement				FYE: December 31
	ASSETS ($ mil.)	NET INCOME ($ mil.)	INCOME AS % OF ASSETS	EMPLOYEES
12/18	925.3	14.9	1.6%	318
12/17	904.8	7.9	0.9%	419
12/16	813.1	(0.2)	—	381
12/15	638.3	40.8	6.4%	297
12/14	503.6	37.2	7.4%	219
Annual Growth	16.4%	(20.4%)	—	9.8%

2018 Year-End Financials
Return on assets: 1.6%
Return on equity: 6.9%
Long-term debt ($ mil.): —
No. of shares (mil.): 12.7
Sales ($ mil): 396.0
Dividends
  Yield: 1.6%
  Payout: 13.8%
Market value ($ mil.): 255.0

	STOCK PRICE ($) FY Close	P/E High/Low		PER SHARE ($) Earnings	Dividends	Book Value
12/18	19.92	23	12	1.16	0.32	16.84
12/17	16.57	34	17	0.61	0.32	16.29
12/16	18.69	—	—	(0.01)	0.25	16.26
12/15	29.56	11	7	2.92	0.17	16.86
12/14	24.16	11	4	2.99	0.12	14.13
Annual Growth	(4.7%)	—	—	(21.1%)	27.8%	4.5%

Fentura Financial Inc

EXECUTIVES

President CEO and Director Fentura Financial and The State Bank, Donald L. Grill, age 68, $235,434 total compensation
SVP and Secretary; President and CEO West Michigan Community Bank, Ronald L. Justice, age 51, $139,646 total compensation
Independent Vice Chairman of the Board, Brian P. Petty, age 58
Vice Chairman, Thomas P. McKenney, age 64
SVP The State Bank, Dennis E. Leyder, age 62, $145,000 total compensation
SVP; President Davison State Bank, Holly J. Pingatore, age 58, $104,181 total compensation
Chief Financial Officer, James W. Distelrath
President CEO and Director Fentura Financial and The State Bank, Donald L. Grill, age 68
Vice Chairman, Thomas P. McKenney, age 63
Independent Director, William Dery
Independent Director, Frederick Dillingham
Independent Director, Joanne Shaw
Independent Director, Ronald Rybar
Independent Director, Randy Hicks
Auditors: Rehmann Robson LLC

LOCATIONS

HQ: Fentura Financial Inc
P.O. Box 725, Fenton, MI 48430-0725
Phone: 810 629-2263
Web: www.fentura.com

COMPETITORS

Clarkston Financial
FNBH Bancorp
Fifth Third
First Federal of Northern Michigan Bancorp
Flagstar Bancorp
Oxford Bank

HISTORICAL FINANCIALS
Company Type: Public

Income Statement				FYE: December 31
	ASSETS ($ mil.)	NET INCOME ($ mil.)	INCOME AS % OF ASSETS	EMPLOYEES
12/18	926.4	10.1	1.1%	0
12/17	781.4	8.6	1.1%	0
12/16	703.3	4.4	0.6%	0
12/15	446.4	4.6	1.1%	0
12/14	393.5	3.3	0.9%	0
Annual Growth	23.9%	31.7%	—	—

2018 Year-End Financials
Return on assets: 1.1%
Return on equity: 13.5%
Long-term debt ($ mil.): —
No. of shares (mil.): 4.6
Sales ($ mil): 44.6
Dividends
  Yield: 1.1%
  Payout: 9.0%
Market value ($ mil.): 97.0

	STOCK PRICE ($) FY Close	P/E High/Low		PER SHARE ($) Earnings	Dividends	Book Value
12/18	21.00	8	7	2.65	0.24	19.31
12/17	18.88	8	6	2.39	0.20	16.37
12/16	16.00	9	8	1.70	0.40	14.00
12/15	13.86	8	5	1.87	0.12	12.90
12/14	9.90	10	5	1.35	0.09	11.24
Annual Growth	20.7%	—	—	18.4%	27.8%	14.5%

Ferro Corp

Ferro holds a colorful portfolio of products. The specialty materials and chemicals producer makes various colorants including ceramic glazes pigments and porcelain enamels. It also produces electronics color and glass materials (such as conductive metals and pastes used in solar cells) and polymer and ceramic engineered materials. Its products are used in construction and by makers of appliances autos ceramic tile electronics and household furnishings. With more than 50 manufacturing plants worldwide Ferro is a global leader in producing glass porcelain enamels and ceramic glaze coatings.

Operations

Ferro operates through three segments. Performance coatings account for about two-fifth of total sales Performance color and glass about 30% and color solutions around 25%.

The company is a supplier of technology-based performance materials including glass-based coatings pigments and colors and polishing materials. It makes Performance Materials -Frits porcelain and other glass enamels glazes stains decorating colors pigments inks polishing materials specialty dielectrics electronic glasses and other specialty coatings; and Performance Chemicals - engineered plastic compounds and pigment dispersion.

Geographic Reach

Ferro owns manufacturing plants located in US (Ohio and New York) Spain Germany Belgium Colombia and the Mexico. The US is the single largest market accounting for about 25% of total sales and Spain accounts for 15%.

Sales and Marketing

Ferro sells to the building and construction automotive appliances electronics household furnishings and industrial products markets. It primarily sells its products directly to customers but also uses indirect sales channels such as agents and distributors.

Financial Performance

In 2017 Ferro's net sales increased 22% to driven by higher sales in Color Solutions ($111 million) Performance Colors ($73 million) and Glass and Performance Coatings ($67 million). Results improved primarily due to increases in organic growth new acquisitions and operational efficiency gains.

Net income was $58 million compared with net loss of $120 million in 2016 primarily due to an absence of $64.5 million in discontinued operations.

Cash holdings increased to $64 million by the end of 2017. Operations provided $85 million and finances contributed $108 million more. This was offset by $179 million in investments.

Strategy

Ferro's growth strategy includes continual investment in its core businesses to drive efficiencies and enhance operations; continual improvements to its lines of products and services; and expanding either organically or through acquisition into profitable markets.

The company is investing in product development customer technical support and lean manufacturing processes to reduce costs and improve its competitive position. Ferro has spent $36 million in 2017 in R&D focused on product and application technology as well as customer technical support.

It also acquired several companies in the 2016-17 period to increase its portfolio of high-end products especially in materials packaging pigments and ceramics tile businesses.

Mergers and Acquisitions

To increase its portfolio of high-end products Ferro acquired Endeka in 2017 which gives it access to high-end products for the ceramic tile market. The deal was worth €72.7 million.The company followed this with a complementary acquisition in Israel's Dip-Tech a leading provider of ceramic digital glass solutions for $76 million. Ferro plans to take advantage of the fast-growing digital glass printing business.

The previous year was all about paints and coatings by contrast. The company dished out €50.5 million to buy Capelle Pigments a leader in specialty high-performance inorganic and organic pigments . Another €15 million acquisition of Spain-based Pinturas Benicarló added new waterborne coatings technology to the company's repertoire.

Ferro also invested $75 million in the electronic packaging materials space by acquiring Electro-Science Laboratories.

Company Background
Ferro Corporation was incorporated in Ohio in 1919 as an enameling company. It eventually transformed into a producer of specialty materials for a broad range of manufacturers serving the end-use markets.

EXECUTIVES
Chairman President and CEO, Peter T. Thomas, age 64, $890,950 total compensation
Vice President - Human Resources, Ann E. Killian, age 64, $378,700 total compensation
VP and CFO, Benjamin Schlater
VP Global Sourcing and Supply Chain, Lori Saviers
Board Member, Marran Ogilvie
Auditors: DELOITTE & TOUCHE LLP

LOCATIONS
HQ: Ferro Corp
6060 Parkland Boulevard, Suite 250, Mayfield Heights, OH 44124
Phone: 216 875-5600 **Fax:** 216 875-5627
Web: www.ferro.com

PRODUCTS/OPERATIONS

2017 Sales
	$ mil.	% of total
Performance Coatings	594.0	42
Performance Colors and Glass	444.6	32
Color Solution	358.1	26
Total	**1,396.7**	**100**

PRODUCTS
PERFORMANCE COATINGS
Fine Ceramics
Porcelain Enamel
Structural Ceramics
Tile Coatings
Vetriceramici
PERFORMANCE COLORS AND GLASS
Automotive
Decoration
Electronic
Industrial
PIGMENTS POWDERS & OXIDES
Liquid Colors & Dispersions
Metal Powders
Nubiola
Pigments
Surface Technologies

COMPETITORS
AMETEK
Akzo Nobel
Axiall
BASF SE
Chemtura
PPG Industries
PolyOne
RPM International
Rockwood Holdings
SI Group
Saint-Gobain Ceramics & Plastics
Sherwin-Williams
Teknor Apex

HISTORICAL FINANCIALS
Company Type: Public

Income Statement
FYE: December 31

	REVENUE ($ mil.)	NET INCOME ($ mil.)	NET PROFIT MARGIN	EMPLOYEES
12/18	1,612.4	80.0	5.0%	6,059
12/17	1,396.7	57.0	4.1%	5,682
12/16	1,145.2	(20.8)	—	5,125
12/15	1,075.3	64.1	6.0%	4,846
12/14	1,111.6	86.0	7.7%	3,979
Annual Growth	9.7%	(1.8%)		11.1%

2018 Year-End Financials
Debt ratio: 45.3%
Return on equity: 22.2%
Cash ($ mil.): 104.3
Current ratio: 2.30
Long-term debt ($ mil.): 811.1
No. of shares (mil.): 83.0
Dividends
  Yield: —
  Payout: —
Market value ($ mil.): 1,301.0

	STOCK PRICE ($) FY Close	P/E High/Low	PER SHARE ($) Earnings	Dividends	Book Value
12/18	15.68	26 16	0.94	0.00	4.54
12/17	23.59	37 20	0.67	0.00	4.10
12/16	14.33	— —	(0.25)	0.00	2.96
12/15	11.12	23 14	0.72	0.00	3.77
12/14	12.96	15 12	0.99	0.00	3.73
Annual Growth	4.9%	— —	(1.3%)	—	5.0%

Fidelity D&D Bancorp Inc

EXECUTIVES
Senior Vice President And Investment Advisor, Bill Mcandrew
Auditors: RSM US LLP

LOCATIONS
HQ: Fidelity D&D Bancorp Inc
Blakely & Drinker Streets, Dunmore, PA 18512
Phone: 570 342-8281
Web: www.bankatfidelity.com

COMPETITORS
Citizens Financial Group
Citizens Financial Services
Community Bank System
First National Community Bancorp
NBT Bancorp
PNC Financial
Penseco Financial Services
Peoples Financial Services
Sovereign Bank

HISTORICAL FINANCIALS
Company Type: Public

Income Statement
FYE: December 31

	ASSETS ($ mil.)	NET INCOME ($ mil.)	INCOME AS % OF ASSETS	EMPLOYEES
12/18	981.1	11.0	1.1%	181
12/17	863.6	8.7	1.0%	175
12/16	792.9	7.6	1.0%	167
12/15	729.3	7.1	1.0%	164
12/14	676.4	6.3	0.9%	159
Annual Growth	9.7%	14.7%	—	3.3%

2018 Year-End Financials
Return on assets: 1.1%
Return on equity: 12.1%
Long-term debt ($ mil.): —
No. of shares (mil.): 3.7
Sales ($ mil): 44.5
Dividends
  Yield: 1.5%
  Payout: 35.5%
Market value ($ mil.): 241.0

	STOCK PRICE ($) FY Close	P/E High/Low	PER SHARE ($) Earnings	Dividends	Book Value
12/18	64.18	25 15	2.90	0.98	24.89
12/17	41.30	25 14	2.33	0.88	23.40
12/16	36.10	18 15	2.09	0.83	21.91
12/15	34.50	20 16	1.93	0.77	20.83
12/14	33.00	20 15	1.75	0.73	19.83
Annual Growth	18.1%	— —	13.5%	7.5%	5.8%

Financial Institutions Inc.

Financial Institutions may not have a luxurious name but they specialize in five star service. The holding company owns Five Star Bank which provides standard deposit products such as checking and savings accounts CDs and IRAs to retail and business customers through some 50 branches across western and central New York. Indirect consumer loans originated through agreements with area franchised car dealers account for the largest percentage of the company's loan portfolio (35%) followed by commercial mortgages. The company also sells insurance while its Five Star Investment Services subsidiary offers brokerage and financial planning services.

Operations
Financial Institutions operates through two business segments: banking which includes the bank's retail and commercial banking operations; and insurance which sells insurance to both personal and business clients through its Scott Danahy Naylon Co (SDN) subsidiary.

About 65% of the company's total revenue came from loan interest (including fees) in 2014 while another 15% came from interest on its investment securities. The rest of its revenue came from deposit account service charges (7%) ATM and debit card fees (4%) insurance income (2%) investment advisory (2%) and other miscellaneous income sources.

Geographic Reach
Five Star Bank boasts 50 branches and an ATM network across Western and Central New York in the counties of Allegany Cattaraugus Cayuga Chautauqua Chemung Erie Genesee Livingston Monroe Ontario Orleans Schuyler Seneca Steuben Wyoming and Yates.

Sales and Marketing
The company offers financial and banking services to individuals municipalities and businesses in Western and Central New York.

Financial Performance
Financial Institution's revenues and profits have been rising over the past few years thanks to growing loan business (organically and from 2012 acquisitions) lower interest expenses and rising fee-based revenue.

The company's revenue rose by 2% to $126.4 million in 2014 mostly thanks to the addition of insurance income from stemming from the bank's acquisition of SDN. Financial's loan interest grew by 1% on organic loan business growth while interest on investment securities grew by 7% as it purchased more interest-earning assets.

Higher revenue and a decline in loan loss provisions from a more credit-worthy loan portfolio in 2014 drove Financial Institution's net income higher by 15% to a record $29.4 million. The company's operating cash levels dipped by 5% to $35.2 million during the year due to unfavorable changes in working capital related to its contributions to its defined benefit pension plan.

Strategy

Financial Institutions' long-term strategy reiterated in 2015 has been to "maintain a community bank philosophy which consists of focusing on and understanding the individualized banking needs of individuals municipalities and businesses of the local communities surrounding their primary service area." The firm believes this focus will enable it to better respond to customer needs and provide a higher level of personalized services giving it a competitive advantage over larger competitors.

The company has also pursued acquisitions to bolster its service lines to grow its non-interest business. Its 2014 acquisition of a New-York based full-service insurance agency for example launched it beyond banking into the insurance business.

Mergers and Acquisitions

In January 2015 Financial Institutions bolstered its investment service business after acquiring Courier Capital which offers customized investment management investment consulting and retirement plan services to some 1100 individuals businesses and institutions.

In 2014 Financial Institutions expanded its services into the insurance business after acquiring Buffalo-based Scott Danahy Naylon Co. (SDN) a full-service insurance agency for a total of $16.9 million plus a promise of $3.4 million in future payments contingent on SDN meeting revenue performance goal targets through 2017.

Company Background

In 2012 Five Star Bank acquired four retail branches owned by HSBC Bank and four owned by First Niagara Bank in upstate New York.

Five Star Bank was formed in 2005 when the company consolidated its four banking subsidiaries (First Tier Bank & Trust National Bank of Geneva Wyoming County Bank and Bath National Bank) into a single entity. First Tier Bank & Trust absorbed the other three banks and changed its name to Five Star Bank.

EXECUTIVES

Vice President Customer Service, David Macintyre
EVP CFO and Treasurer, Kevin B. Klotzbach, age 66, $230,000 total compensation
President and CEO, Martin K. Birmingham, $420,000 total compensation
EVP Commercial Executive and Regional President, Jeffrey P. Kenefick, $209,100 total compensation
SVP and Director of Human Resources and Enterprise Planning, Paula D. Dolan, $140,000 total compensation
EVP and Chief Risk Officer, Kenneth V. Winn
Executive Vice President, Basar Ordukaya

Vice President of Commercial Lending, Robert McFadden
Senior Vice President And Treasurer, Marc Swanson
Vice President, Richard Simpson
Senior Vice President And Manager Work, Steven Ambrose
Vice President Information Technology Operations, Chip Shepard
Senior Vice President, Darren Haugen
Vice Presidenti Information Technology, R McLaughlin
Senior Vice President Chief Commercial Credit Officer Of The Bank, David Case
Senior Vice President CandI Lending Executive And Buffalo Regional President Of The Bank, Edward Oexle
Senior Vice President Consumer Lending Manager, Jonathan Chase
Senior Vice President and Administrator Loan Revie, David Squire
Senior Vice President Business Banking Executive, Vito Caraccio
Senior Vice President Commercial Real Estate Executive Of The Bank, Craig Burton
Board Member, Samuel M Gullo
Chairman, Robert N. Latella, age 76
Treasurer, Kevin Kotzbach
Board Member, Susan Holliday
Auditors: RSM US LLP

LOCATIONS

HQ: Financial Institutions Inc.
220 Liberty Street, Warsaw, NY 14569
Phone: 585 786-1100
Web: www.fiiwarsaw.com

PRODUCTS/OPERATIONS

2013 Sales

	$ mil.	% of total
Interest income		
Loans including fees	81.5	66
Investment securities	17.5	14
Noninterest income		
Service charges on deposits	9.9	9
ATM & debit card	5.1	4
Investment advisory	2.4	2
Other	7.4	5
Total	123.7	100

COMPETITORS

Astoria Financial	HSBC USA
Citibank	KeyCorp
Community Bank System	M&T Bank
ESL Federal Credit Union	

HISTORICAL FINANCIALS

Company Type: Public

Income Statement   FYE: December 31

	ASSETS ($ mil.)	NET INCOME ($ mil.)	INCOME AS % OF ASSETS	EMPLOYEES
12/18	4,311.7	39.5	0.9%	725
12/17	4,105.2	33.5	0.8%	656
12/16	3,710.3	31.9	0.9%	654
12/15	3,381.0	28.3	0.8%	691
12/14	3,089.5	29.3	1.0%	645
Annual Growth	8.7%	7.7%	—	3.0%

2018 Year-End Financials

Return on assets: 0.9%   Dividends
Return on equity: 10.1%   Yield: 3.7%
Long-term debt ($ mil.): — Payout: 40.1%
No. of shares (mil.): 15.9 Market value ($ mil.): 409.0
Sales ($ mil): 189.2

	STOCK PRICE ($) FY Close	P/E High/Low	PER SHARE ($) Earnings	Dividends	Book Value
12/18	25.70	14 10	2.39	0.96	24.88
12/17	31.10	17 12	2.13	0.85	23.94
12/16	34.20	16 12	2.10	0.81	22.02
12/15	28.00	15 12	1.90	0.80	20.71
12/14	25.15	13 10	2.00	0.77	19.80
Annual Growth	0.5%	— —	4.6%	5.7%	5.9%

Finemark Holdings Inc

Auditors: Hacker, Johnson & Smith P.A.

LOCATIONS

HQ: Finemark Holdings Inc
12681 Creekside Lane, Fort Myers, FL 33919
Phone: 239 461-5900   **Fax:** 239 461-5902
Web: www.finemarkbank.com

HISTORICAL FINANCIALS

Company Type: Public

Income Statement   FYE: December 31

	REVENUE ($ mil.)	NET INCOME ($ mil.)	NET PROFIT MARGIN	EMPLOYEES
12/18	81.4	15.1	18.6%	0
12/17	65.4	9.6	14.7%	178
12/16	54.5	7.9	14.6%	0
12/15	45.0	6.1	13.6%	0
Annual Growth	21.8%	35.0%	—	—

2018 Year-End Financials

Debt ratio: 12.4%   No. of shares (mil.): 8.8
Return on equity: 10.0%   Dividends
Cash ($ mil.): 33.6   Yield: —
Current ratio: 0.04   Payout: —
Long-term debt ($ mil.): 226.0   Market value ($ mil.): —

	STOCK PRICE ($) FY Close	P/E High/Low	PER SHARE ($) Earnings	Dividends	Book Value
12/18	0.00	— —	1.70	0.00	18.02
Annual Growth	—	—	—	—	—

Finjan Holdings Inc

EXECUTIVES

Chairman President and CEO, Edward J. (Ed) Gildea, age 62, $222,879 total compensation
EVP Administration and CFO, David R. (Dave) Allen, age 59, $152,376 total compensation
VP Waste Management, John A. (Jack) Walsdorf, age 66, $104,230 total compensation

Director Product Research and Development,
William A. (Bill) Torello, age 63
Director Finance and Accounting, Ellen P. O'Neil
VP Marketing, David A. Flannery
Director Sales, Gerard H. (Gerry) Gould
General Manager President of Industrial Waste Water Division, Kristen Brandt
Auditors: Marcum LLP

LOCATIONS
HQ: Finjan Holdings Inc
2000 University Avenue, Suite 600, East Palo Alto, CA 94303
Phone: 650 282-3228
Web: www.finjan.com

COMPETITORS
CF Industries
Koch Industries Inc.
The Mosaic Company
Yara North America

HISTORICAL FINANCIALS
Company Type: Public

Income Statement — FYE: December 31

	REVENUE ($ mil.)	NET INCOME ($ mil.)	NET PROFIT MARGIN	EMPLOYEES
12/18	82.3	20.7	25.2%	10
12/17	50.4	22.8	45.2%	10
12/16	18.3	0.3	1.9%	12
12/15	4.6	(12.6)	—	14
12/14	5.0	(10.4)	—	14
Annual Growth	101.4%	—	—	(8.1%)

2018 Year-End Financials
Debt ratio: —
Return on equity: 40.6%
Cash ($ mil.): 32.0
Current ratio: 8.13
Long-term debt ($ mil.): —
No. of shares (mil.): 27.5
Dividends
 Yield: —
 Payout: —
Market value ($ mil.): 69.0

	STOCK PRICE ($) FY Close	P/E High/Low	PER SHARE ($) Earnings	Dividends	Book Value
12/18	2.51	7 2	0.70	0.00	1.98
12/17	2.16	5 2	0.68	0.00	1.71
12/16	1.13	— —	(0.28)	0.00	0.62
12/15	1.15	— —	(0.56)	0.00	0.28
12/14	2.70	— —	(0.47)	0.00	0.81
Annual Growth	(1.8%)	—	—	—	25.2%

First Advantage Bancorp

EXECUTIVES
Senior Vice President, Joe Corlew
Senior Vice President Operations, Daniel Walker
Auditors: Horne LLP

LOCATIONS
HQ: First Advantage Bancorp
1430 Madison Street, Clarksville, TN 37040
Phone: 931 552-6176
Web: www.firstadvantagebanking.com

COMPETITORS
Bank of America
First Horizon
Regions Financial
SunTrust

HISTORICAL FINANCIALS
Company Type: Public

Income Statement — FYE: December 31

	ASSETS ($ mil.)	NET INCOME ($ mil.)	INCOME AS % OF ASSETS	EMPLOYEES
12/18	664.3	7.3	1.1%	0
12/17	571.5	4.3	0.8%	0
12/16	528.4	2.8	0.5%	0
12/15	487.3	3.3	0.7%	0
12/14	442.5	3.2	0.7%	0
Annual Growth	10.7%	22.7%	—	—

2018 Year-End Financials
Return on assets: 1.1%
Return on equity: 10.0%
Long-term debt ($ mil.): —
No. of shares (mil.): 3.9
Sales ($ mil): 35.3
Dividends
 Yield: 2.1%
 Payout: 33.7%
Market value ($ mil.): 96.0

	STOCK PRICE ($) FY Close	P/E High/Low	PER SHARE ($) Earnings	Dividends	Book Value
12/18	24.50	14 12	1.79	0.52	19.77
12/17	23.50	20 15	1.06	0.40	19.48
12/16	18.00	23 19	0.73	0.40	18.48
12/15	16.40	18 15	0.85	0.40	18.24
12/14	13.95	16 15	0.80	0.28	17.78
Annual Growth	15.1%	—	22.3%	16.7%	2.7%

First Bancorp (NC)

EXECUTIVES
EVP and CFO First Bancorp and First Bank, Eric P. Credle, age 50, $325,000 total compensation
President and Director First Bancorp and President and CEO First Bank, Michael G. Mayer, age 59, $425,000 total compensation
President CEO and Director, Richard H. Moore, age 58, $525,000 total compensation
Senior Vice President Retail Market Manager, Carol Clagett
Senior Vice President Legal Division, Kirsten Foyles
Vice President, Jason Williams
Assistant Vice President, Laurie Byrd
Mortgage Loan Originator Assistant Vice President, Patrick Blackburn
Vice President Branch Manager, Sheldon Moser
Chairman First Bancorp and First Bank, James C. Crawford, age 62
Board Member, Dennis Wicker
Board Member, John Gould
Auditors: BDO USA, LLP

LOCATIONS
HQ: First Bancorp (NC)
300 S.W. Broad St., Southern Pines, NC 28387
Phone: 910 246-2500
Web: www.localFirstbank.com

PRODUCTS/OPERATIONS
2016 Sales

	$ mil.	% of total
Interest Income	130.9	84
Non-interest Income	25.6	16
Total	**156.5**	**100**

COMPETITORS
BB&T
BNC Bancorp
Bank of America
CommunityOne Bancorp
First Citizens BancShares
NewBridge Bancorp
PNC Financial
South Street Financial
SunTrust
Wells Fargo

HISTORICAL FINANCIALS
Company Type: Public

Income Statement — FYE: December 31

	ASSETS ($ mil.)	NET INCOME ($ mil.)	INCOME AS % OF ASSETS	EMPLOYEES
12/18	5,864.1	89.2	1.5%	1,098
12/17	5,547.0	45.9	0.8%	1,166
12/16	3,614.8	27.5	0.8%	861
12/15	3,362.0	27.0	0.8%	840
12/14	3,218.3	25.0	0.8%	825
Annual Growth	16.2%	37.5%	—	7.4%

2018 Year-End Financials
Return on assets: 1.5%
Return on equity: 12.2%
Long-term debt ($ mil.): —
No. of shares (mil.): 29.7
Sales ($ mil): 293.0
Dividends
 Yield: 1.2%
 Payout: 14.8%
Market value ($ mil.): 971.0

	STOCK PRICE ($) FY Close	P/E High/Low	PER SHARE ($) Earnings	Dividends	Book Value
12/18	32.66	14 10	3.01	0.40	25.71
12/17	35.31	21 15	1.82	0.32	23.38
12/16	27.14	21 13	1.33	0.32	17.66
12/15	18.74	15 12	1.30	0.32	17.33
12/14	18.47	16 13	1.19	0.32	19.67
Annual Growth	15.3%	—	26.1%	5.7%	6.9%

First Bancshares Inc (MS)

EXECUTIVES
Vice President, Kevin Miller
Vp Appraisal Analyst, Lindsey Smith
Board Member, David Bomboy
Board Member, Fred Mcmurry
Board Member, Ted Parker
Auditors: Crowe LLP

LOCATIONS
HQ: First Bancshares Inc (MS)
6480 U.S. Highway 98 West, Suite A, Hattiesburg, MS 39402
Phone: 601 268-8998
Web: www.thefirstbank.com

COMPETITORS

BancorpSouth
Community Bancshares of Mississippi
Hancock Holding
Peoples Financial
Renasant
Trustmark

HISTORICAL FINANCIALS
Company Type: Public

Income Statement   FYE: December 31

	ASSETS ($ mil.)	NET INCOME ($ mil.)	INCOME AS % OF ASSETS	EMPLOYEES
12/18	3,003.9	21.2	0.7%	641
12/17	1,813.2	10.6	0.6%	487
12/16	1,277.3	10.1	0.8%	315
12/15	1,145.1	8.8	0.8%	305
12/14	1,093.7	6.6	0.6%	278
Annual Growth	28.7%	33.8%	—	23.2%

2018 Year-End Financials
Return on assets: 0.8% Dividends
Return on equity: 7.2% Yield: 0.6%
Long-term debt ($ mil.): — Payout: 14.8%
No. of shares (mil.): 14.8 Market value ($ mil.): 449.0
Sales ($ mil): 120.5

	STOCK PRICE ($) FY Close	P/E High/Low	PER SHARE ($) Earnings	Dividends	Book Value
12/18	30.25	25 17	1.62	0.20	24.49
12/17	34.20	31 24	1.11	0.15	19.92
12/16	27.50	15 8	1.64	0.15	17.19
12/15	18.34	11 8	1.62	0.15	19.24
12/14	14.51	12 11	1.25	0.15	18.10
Annual Growth	20.2%	— —	6.7%	7.5%	7.9%

First Bank (Williamstown, NJ)

EXECUTIVES

Coo, Ryan K Manville
Senior Vice President Market Executive, Marianne Desimone
Svp Controller, Donald Theobald
Vp Business Development Officer, Frank Puleio
Vp Internal Auditor, Maria Mayshura
Evp Chief Financial Officer, Stephen Carman
Evp Chief Deposits Officer, Emilio Cooper
Vp Credit Officer, Thao Nguyen
Auditors: RSM US LLP

LOCATIONS

HQ: First Bank (Williamstown, NJ)
2465 Kuser Road, Hamilton, NJ 08690
Phone: 609 643-4211
Web: www.firstbanknj.com

HISTORICAL FINANCIALS
Company Type: Public

Income Statement   FYE: December 31

	ASSETS ($ mil.)	NET INCOME ($ mil.)	INCOME AS % OF ASSETS	EMPLOYEES
12/18	1,711.1	17.5	1.0%	188
12/17	1,452.3	6.9	0.5%	153
12/16	1,073.2	6.4	0.6%	110
12/15	855.5	3.8	0.5%	101
12/14	677.4	5.8	0.9%	96
Annual Growth	26.1%	31.8%	—	18.3%

2018 Year-End Financials
Return on assets: 1.1% Dividends
Return on equity: 9.8% Yield: 0.9%
Long-term debt ($ mil.): — Payout: 16.0%
No. of shares (mil.): 18.6 Market value ($ mil.): 226.0
Sales ($ mil): 76.1

	STOCK PRICE ($) FY Close	P/E High/Low	PER SHARE ($) Earnings	Dividends	Book Value
12/18	12.12	15 12	0.95	0.12	10.43
12/17	13.85	30 23	0.48	0.08	9.36
12/16	11.60	20 10	0.61	0.00	7.78
12/15	6.61	17 14	0.41	0.00	7.26
12/14	6.24	11 9	0.63	0.00	6.88
Annual Growth	18.1%	— —	10.8%	—	11.0%

First Busey Corp

First Busey Corporation keeps itself busy taking care of deposits and making loans. It's the holding company for Busey Bank which boasts $4 billion in assets and 40 branches across Illinois Florida and Indiana. The bank offers standard deposit products and services using funds from deposits to originate primarily real estate loans and mortgages. Subsidiary Busey Wealth Management which manages $5 billion in assets provides asset management trust brokerage and related services to individuals businesses and foundations while FirsTech provides retail payment processing services. Most of Busey Bank's branches are located in downstate Illinois.

Operations
First Busey Corporation operates three business segments Busey Bank which generated more than 99% of its total revenue in 2014 and serves retail and corporate customers; FirsTech which provides remittance processing for online bill payments lock box and walk-in payments; and Busey Wealth Management which provides asset management tax preparation philanthropic advisory services and investment and fiduciary services to individuals businesses and foundations.

Real estate loans including commercial and residential mortgages accounted for 70% of the bank's loan portfolio in 2014 while commercial loans (25%) construction loans (4%) and consumer installments and other loans (0.5%) comprised the rest.

About 55% of First Busey's total revenue came from loan interest (including fees) while another 10% came from interest income on taxable and non-taxable investment securities. The rest of its revenue came from trust fees (11%) deposit account service charges (7%) remittance processing fees (6%) commissions and brokers' fees (2%) and various types of gains on securities and loan sales.

Geographic Reach
Busey Bank has nearly 30 branches in Illinois seven locations in southwest Florida and another office in Indianapolis. Its FirsTech subsidiary accepts payments from its 3000 agent locations across 36 US states.

Sales and Marketing
The bank which staffed 801 employees at the end of 2014 serves individuals businesses and foundations.

Financial Performance
First Busey's revenues have declined in recent years due to shrinking interest margins on loans amidst the low-interest environment. Its profits however have been rising thanks to lower interest expenses on deposits and declining loan loss provisions as its loan portfolio's credit quality has improved with higher property valuations in the strengthened economy.

The bank's revenue dipped by 2% to $167 million mostly as it collected smaller gains from loan sales due to lower refinancing volumes as interest rates began to rise. The bank's loan interest income also continued to decline with lower yields on loan and security assets in the low-interest environment.

Despite generating less revenue in 2014 First Busey's net income jumped by 14% to $32.8 million thanks to continued declines in interest expenses on deposits and lower loan loss provisions. The company's operating cash levels fell by 31% to $68.1 million after adjusting its earnings for non-cash items related to its net proceeds from its loans held-for-sale.

Strategy
First Busey sometimes strategically acquires smaller banks in its target markets to boost its market share broaden its service offerings and boost its loan and deposit business.

Mergers and Acquisitions
In 2019 First Busey agreed to acquire Fort Myers Florida-based wealth advisory firm Investors' Security Trust which will be integrated into the wealth management division of Busey Bank. The combined entity will have assets under management of more than $9.2 billion.

EXECUTIVES

EVP and Chief Risk Officer, Barbara J. Harrington, age 59
President CEO and Director, Van A. Dukeman, age 60, $537,308 total compensation
EVP; President and CEO Busey Bank N.A., Robert F. (Bob) Plecki, age 58, $268,654 total compensation
CIO and President and CEO FirsTech Inc., Howard F. Mooney, age 54, $240,216 total compensation
EVP and Regional President Busey Bank, Christopher M. (Chris) Shroyer, age 53, $268,654 total compensation
EVP and General Counsel, John J. Powers
COO and CFO, Robin N. Elliott, $256,731 total compensation
Vice President Senior Retirement Plan Services Advisor, Charlee Seaton
Senior Vice President Commercial Real Estate, Kent Poli

Senior Vice President Loan Operations, Michael Stevenson
Vice President, Kelly Dennemann
Senior Vice President Managing Director Fixed Income, Zach Hillard
Assistant Vice President Special Assets, Shana Reed-harper
Executive Vice President, Robert Ballsrud
Assistant Vice President, Emerson Schoonover
Vice President Retail Market Manager, Tami Crouch
Vice President, Brenda Carlson
Senior Vice President, Janice Wolters
Assistant Vice President Risk Management Analyst, Annie Feleccia
Vice President Senior Loan Officer, Brian Church
Assistant Vice President Wealth Advisor Assistant, Monya Russell
Vice President Retail Market Manager, Linda Smith
Vice President Commercial Credit Manager, Thomas Richlak
Vice President Mortgage Operations Manager, Kevin Hoogeveen
Vice President; Senior Mortgage Loan Originator, Erin Trescott
Assistant Vice President Wire Services Manager, Karen Aulph
Assistant Vice President, Anthony Baima
Assistant Vice President, Valerie Garrett
Senior Vice President, Harry Mcsteen
Senior Vice President, Ed Paine
Chairman, Gregory B. (Greg) Lykins, age 71
Vice Chairman, Ed Scharlau
Auditors: RSM US LLP

LOCATIONS

HQ: First Busey Corp
  100 W. University Ave., Champaign, IL 61820
Phone: 217 365-4544

PRODUCTS/OPERATIONS

2014 Sales

	$ mil.	% of total
Interest		
Loans including fees	92.4	55
Interest & dividends on securities	15.7	10
Noninterest		
Trust fees	19.6	11
Service charges on deposit accounts	12.0	7
Remittance processing	9.4	6
Gain on sales of loans	4.7	3
Commissions and broker's fees net	2.7	2
Other	10.5	6
Total	**167.0**	**100**

COMPETITORS

Bank of America
CIB Marine Bancshares
Fifth Third
First Mid-Illinois Bancshares
First Midwest Bancorp
JPMorgan Chase
Mercantile Bancorp
PNC Financial
Wintrust Financial

HISTORICAL FINANCIALS

Company Type: Public

Income Statement FYE: December 31

	ASSETS ($ mil.)	NET INCOME ($ mil.)	INCOME AS % OF ASSETS	EMPLOYEES
12/18	7,702.3	98.9	1.3%	1,270
12/17	7,860.6	62.7	0.8%	1,347
12/16	5,425.1	49.6	0.9%	1,295
12/15	3,998.9	39.0	1.0%	795
12/14	3,665.6	32.7	0.9%	801
Annual Growth	20.4%	31.8%	—	12.2%

2018 Year-End Financials

Return on assets: 1.2%
Return on equity: 10.2%
Long-term debt ($ mil.): —
No. of shares (mil.): 48.8
Sales ($ mil): 376.0
Dividends
  Yield: 3.2%
  Payout: 46.2%
Market value ($ mil.): 1,199.0

	STOCK PRICE ($) FY Close	P/E High/Low		PER SHARE ($) Earnings	Dividends	Book Value
12/18	24.54	16	12	2.01	0.80	20.36
12/17	29.94	22	19	1.45	0.72	19.21
12/16	30.78	22	13	1.40	0.68	15.54
12/15	20.63	17	5	1.32	0.17	13.01
12/14	6.51	6	5	1.11	0.57	14.98
Annual Growth	39.3%	—	—	16.0%	8.8%	8.0%

First Business Financial Services, Inc.

Business comes first at First Business Financial Services which serves small and midsized companies entrepreneurs professionals and high-networth individuals through First Business Bank and First Business Bank - Milwaukee. The banks offer deposits loans cash management and trust services from a handful of offices in Wisconsin and Kansas. Over 60% of the company's loan portfolio is made up of commercial real estate loans. Subsidiary First Business Capital specializes in asset-based lending while First Business Equipment Finance provides commercial equipment financing. First Business Trust & Investments offers investment management and retirement services.

Operations

First Business Financial Services backs its subsidiaries with low-cost corporate services such as human resources finance IT and marketing. First Business Credit Cards provides revolving lines of credit and term loans for financial and strategic acquisitions capital expenditures working capital used to support rapid growth bank debt refinancing debt restructuring and other corporate financing needs.

The company generated 80% of its total revenue from interest on loans and leases in 2014 and another 5% from interest on its securities. About 7% of revenue came from trust and investment services fee income while service charges on deposits and loan fees made up 4% and 2% of revenue respectively.

Geographic Reach

The company's primary market areas are in Wisconsin Kansas and Missouri. First Business's loan production offices are in Wisconsin in Oshkosh Green Bay Appleton and Kenosha while its two Kansas offices are in Leawood and Overland Park. In Wisconsin it targets Madison Milwaukee Appleton Green Bay Oshkosh and their surrounding communities.

Sales and Marketing

Beyond individual customers the bank generally targets businesses with annual sales between $2 million and $75 million.

Financial Performance

The company has struggled to consistently grow its revenues in recent years due to shrinking interest margins on loans amidst the low-interest environment. Its profits however have been rising thanks to declining loan loss provisions as its loan portfolio's credit quality has improved with higher property valuations in a strengthened economy.

First Business had a breakout year in 2014 however as its revenue rose 9% to $67.8 million on higher loan interest as its commercial and industrial loans comercial real estate and other mortgage loans and direct financing leases businesses all enjoyed "favorable volume variances." The bank's non-interest income also jumped by 20% which was mostly driven by growth in trust and investment services fee income on higher assets under management.

Higher revenue and lower interest expenses on deposits in 2014 pushed the company's net income up by 3% to $14.1 million. First Business' operating cash levels fell by 25% to $11.9 million due to unfavorable changes in working capital related to an increase in accrued interest payable and other liabilities.

Strategy

First Business Financial Services continued in 2015 to focus on maintaining its loan asset quality while organically growing its loan and lease portfolio in addition to growing its customer account based to increase its fee-based revenues on its variety of treasury management trust and investment services and SBA loans. It also planned to boost its investment in utilizing technology to support these initiatives while staying efficient as the business grows.

The company occasionally opens new offices or strategically acquires other banks and financial companies to extend its reach into its target markets and to grow its loan and deposit business. In 2014 its FBB-Milwaukee bank subisidiary expanded more into the southeastern area of Wisconsin after opening a loan production office in Kenosha; while its acquisition of Aslin Group and Alterra Bank furthered its exposure to new markets and loan and deposit business in Kansas.

Mergers and Acquisitions

In November 2014 First Business Financial Services expanded its Midwest market and extended its reach into Kansas after its acquisition of Leawood-based Aslin Group including its Alterra Bank subsidiary. The deal added $223 million in total assets including $182 million in new loan assets and $192 million in new deposits.

EXECUTIVES

President and CEO, Corey A. Chambas, age 56, $416,000 total compensation
SVP and Chief Credit Officer, Michael J. Losenegger, age 61, $221,950 total compensation

President and CEO First Business Capital, Charles H. (Chuck) Batson, age 65, $242,927 total compensation
President and CEO First Business Bank - Madison, Mark J. Meloy, age 57, $201,800 total compensation
President First Business Trust & Investments, Joan A. Burke, age 67
President and CEO First Business Bank - Milwaukee, David J. (Dave) Vetta, age 64
CFO, Edward G. (Ed) Sloane, age 58
President Kenosha Region, Wesley Ricchio
SVP and COO First Business Capital Corp., Peter Lowney
COO and Interim President and CEO Alterra Bank, David R. Seiler
CIO, Daniel S. Ovokaitys, age 45
First Vice President Equipment And Finance, Tom Rude
Senior Vice President Compliance and Risk Management, Theresa Wiese
Vice President Treasury Management, Charlene Breunig
Vice President, Josh Hoesch
Senior Vice President First Business Bank Madison, Beth Korth
Assistant Vice President Business Development Officer, Jerimiah Janssen
Senior Vice President Commercial Banking, Kelly Foster
Assistant Vice President Treasury Management, Wade Hanna
Vice President Consumer Loans, Penny Byrne
Vice President Business Development, Greg Lherault
Vice President, Mark Buchert
Vice President Private Wealth Management, Monica Schlicht
VICE PRESIDENT COMMERCIAL REAL ESTATE, Ryan Hughes
VICE PRESIDENT BUSINESS DEVELOPMENT OFFICER, Chris Mckernan
Vice President Internal Loan Review, Gretchen Griffin
Vice President Talent Development Manager, Bonnie Van
Assistant Vice President Treasury Management, Laura Shoemaker
Vice President Commercial Banking, Jessica Meier
Vice President, Cymbre Vanfossen
Vice President Business Development Officer, Anne Roslin
Chairman, Jerome R. (Jerry) Smith, age 68
Auditors: Crowe LLP

LOCATIONS

HQ: First Business Financial Services, Inc.
401 Charmany Drive, Madison, WI 53719
Phone: 608 238-8008
Web: www.firstbusiness.com

COMPETITORS

Associated Banc-Corp
Bank Mutual
Harris
TCF Financial
U.S. Bancorp

HISTORICAL FINANCIALS
Company Type: Public

Income Statement — FYE: December 31

	ASSETS ($ mil.)	NET INCOME ($ mil.)	INCOME AS % OF ASSETS	EMPLOYEES
12/18	1,966.4	16.3	0.8%	289
12/17	1,794.0	11.9	0.7%	264
12/16	1,780.7	14.9	0.8%	272
12/15	1,782.8	16.5	0.9%	258
12/14	1,629.3	14.1	0.9%	231
Annual Growth	4.8%	3.6%	—	5.8%

2018 Year-End Financials
Return on assets: 0.8%
Return on equity: 9.3%
Long-term debt ($ mil.): —
No. of shares (mil.): 8.7
Sales ($ mil): 109.4
Dividends
Yield: 2.8%
Payout: 30.1%
Market value ($ mil.): 171.0

	STOCK PRICE ($) FY Close	P/E High/Low	PER SHARE ($) Earnings	Dividends	Book Value
12/18	19.51	14 10	1.86	0.56	20.57
12/17	22.12	21 15	1.36	0.52	19.32
12/16	23.72	15 11	1.71	0.48	18.55
12/15	25.01	25 12	1.90	0.44	17.34
12/14	47.91	28 21	1.76	0.42	15.88
Annual Growth	(20.1%)	— —	1.5%	7.5%	6.7%

First Capital Inc.

EXECUTIVES

Board Member, William Orwick
Board Member, Mark D Shireman
Auditors: Monroe Shine & Co., Inc.

LOCATIONS

HQ: First Capital Inc.
220 Federal Drive NW, Corydon, IN 47112
Phone: 812 738-2198
Web: www.firstharrison.com

COMPETITORS

First Savings Financial
JPMorgan Chase
PNC Financial
Regions Financial
Stock Yards Bancorp
U.S. Bancorp

HISTORICAL FINANCIALS
Company Type: Public

Income Statement — FYE: December 31

	ASSETS ($ mil.)	NET INCOME ($ mil.)	INCOME AS % OF ASSETS	EMPLOYEES
12/18	794.1	9.2	1.2%	210
12/17	758.9	7.4	1.0%	206
12/16	743.6	6.8	0.9%	204
12/15	715.8	5.2	0.7%	191
12/14	472.7	5.5	1.2%	150
Annual Growth	13.8%	13.4%	—	8.8%

2018 Year-End Financials
Return on assets: 1.1%
Return on equity: 11.1%
Long-term debt ($ mil.): —
No. of shares (mil.): 3.3
Sales ($ mil): 35.0
Dividends
Yield: 2.1%
Payout: 36.8%
Market value ($ mil.): 143.0

	STOCK PRICE ($) FY Close	P/E High/Low	PER SHARE ($) Earnings	Dividends	Book Value
12/18	42.48	17 13	2.77	0.92	25.59
12/17	36.74	17 13	2.23	0.86	24.25
12/16	32.42	17 12	2.05	0.84	22.69
12/15	26.10	15 12	1.87	0.84	22.28
12/14	24.34	12 10	2.03	0.84	20.84
Annual Growth	14.9%	— —	8.1%	2.3%	5.3%

First Choice Bancorp

Auditors: Eide Bailly LLP

LOCATIONS

HQ: First Choice Bancorp
17785 Center Court Drive N, Suite 750, Cerritos, CA 90703
Phone: 562 345-9092
Web: www.firstchoicebankca.com

HISTORICAL FINANCIALS
Company Type: Public

Income Statement — FYE: December 31

	ASSETS ($ mil.)	NET INCOME ($ mil.)	INCOME AS % OF ASSETS	EMPLOYEES
12/18	1,622.5	15.1	0.9%	177
12/17	903.8	7.3	0.8%	0
12/16	863.4	8.2	1.0%	0
12/15	811.9	5.3	0.7%	0
12/14	626.4	4.0	0.6%	0
Annual Growth	26.9%	38.8%	—	—

2018 Year-End Financials
Return on assets: 1.2%
Return on equity: 8.5%
Long-term debt ($ mil.): —
No. of shares (mil.): 11.7
Sales ($ mil): 67.9
Dividends
Yield: 3.5%
Payout: 67.2%
Market value ($ mil.): 265.0

	STOCK PRICE ($) FY Close	P/E High/Low	PER SHARE ($) Earnings	Dividends	Book Value
12/18	22.60	19 13	1.64	0.80	21.16
Annual Growth	—	— —	—	—	—

First Citizens BancShares Inc (NC)

First Citizens BancShares owns First-Citizens Bank which operates more than 550 branches in 20 states mainly in the southeastern and western US and urban areas scattered nationwide. The $32 billion-asset bank provides standard services such as deposits loans mortgages and trust services in addition to processing and operational support to other banks. Real estate loans including commercial residential and revolving mortgages and construction and land development loans comprise most of its loan portfolio. Subsidiaries First Citizens Investor Services First Citizens Securities Corporation and First Citizens Asset Management offers investment and discount brokerage services to bank clients.

Operations
The company provides consumer business and commercial banking wealth investments and insurance through a network of branch offices internet banking mobile banking telephone banking and ATMs.

More than 60% of the bank's total revenue came from loan and lease interest during 2015 while another 6% came from interest income on investment securities. The rest of its revenue came from merchant services (6% of revenue) service charges on deposit accounts (6%) wealth management services (6%) cardholder services (4%) mortgage income (1%) insurance commissions (1%) and other miscellaneous income sources.

Geographic Reach
First Citizens BancShares has nearly 560 branches in almost 20 states (Arizona California Colorado Florida Georgia Kansas Maryland Missouri New Mexico North Carolina Oklahoma Oregon South Carolina Tennessee Texas Virginia Washington and West Virginia) and Washington DC.

Sales and Marketing
First Citizens BancShares serves both individuals and commercial entities operating in the healthcare dental practices legal services property management agribusiness nonprofit and trade association markets.

The bank has been ramping up its advertising spend in recent years. It spent $12.4 million in 2015 up from $11.4 million and $8.2 million in 2014 and 2013 respectively.

Financial Performance
First Citizens BancShares' annual revenues have risen more than 35% since 2013 thanks to growth in its variety of non-banking business. Its profits have also been trending higher thanks to declining loan loss provisions as its loan portfolio's credit quality has improved with higher property valuations in the strengthened economy.

The bank's revenue jumped 30% to $1.44 billion during 2015 mostly thanks to higher loan and lease interest income stemming from added loan business from the acquisition of First Citizens Bancorporation. Its non-interest income sources grew 36% during the year as well.

Strong revenue growth in 2015 drove First Citizen's net income up 52% to $210.3 million. The bank's operating cash levels rose 28% to $233 million with the rise in cash-based earnings.

Strategy
FCB has expanded its branch network into new markets while bolstering its loan and deposit business by acquiring small community banks in new territory.

Mergers and Acquisitions
In 2019 First Citizens Bancshares acquired Spartanburg South Carolina-based First South Bancorp the holding company for First South Bank. First South had $236 million in assets $206 million in deposits and $183 million in gross loans.

The deal expanded First Citizens' geographic reach in South Carolina.

Company Background
First Citizens BancShares has been fortifying its presence along the West Coast by snapping up failed financial institutions. Since 2009 it has acquired most of the banking operations of Temecula Valley Bank Washington-based Venture Bank and First Regional Bank in Southern California. It also acquired the failed Florida-based bank Sun American and entered Colorado through the acquisitions of United Western Bank and Colorado Capital Bank. All were FDIC-assisted transactions and each acquired institution became branches of First-Citizens Bank. The deals added about 50 branches to the bank's network. First Citizens BancShares continues to seek out acquisitions of other seized institutions.

Though the company has been able to grow geographically thanks to the economic downturn its IronStone Bank division which focused on business customers suffered from weakened markets in Florida and Georgia. (First Citizens Bancshares merged IronStone into First-Citizens Bank in 2011 to increase efficiency and unify the company's brand.) It has remained profitable thanks in part to its acquisitions which include loss-sharing agreements with the FDIC but has had to increase its provisions for loan losses each of the last five years.

The Holding family which occupies several positions in the company's board room and executive suite controls First Citizens BancShares.

EXECUTIVES
COO BancShares and First-Citizens Bank & Trust Company, Edward L. (Ed) Willingham, age 64, $585,125 total compensation
President and Corporate Sales Executive of BancShares and First-Citizens Bank & Trust Company, Peter M. Bristow, age 53
Chairman and CEO First Citizens BancShares First-Citizens Bank & Trust and IronStone Bank, Frank B. Holding, age 58, $902,875 total compensation
EVP Finance and CFO, Craig L. Nix, age 47
Vice Chairman and Vice Chairman EVP and Business Banking Segment Manager First-Citizens Bank and Trust and President IronStone Bank, Hope Holding Connell, age 56, $563,750 total compensation
EVP and Chief Human Resources Officer First-Citizens Bank & Trust, Lou J. Davis, age 66
EVP and Chief Credit Officer First-Citizens Bank & Trust; Group VP and Chief Credit Officer IronStone, Ricky T. Holland, age 65
Executive Vice President and General Auditor of FCB, Donald Preskenis
Senior Vice President Commercial Banking, Stephanie Logan
Vice President, Rhonda Chapman
Vice President Marketing, Christine Thompson
Vice President, Scott German
Vice President Business Banking, Jessica Chisholm
VICE PRESIDENT SBA LOAN OFFICER, Alan Black
Vice President Commercial Banking, Drew Schiavone
Senior Vice President, Virginia Lee
Svp Branch Development and Project Management, Peter Watson
Vice President Senior Business Analyst Loan Officer, Joanna Warrick

Senior Vice President Commercial Banking, Tiffani Tedder
Vp Of Sba Lending Central Region, Brett Stacey
Vice President Business Banker, Laura Mccombs
Auditors: Dixon Hughes Goodman LLP

LOCATIONS
HQ: First Citizens BancShares Inc (NC)
4300 Six Forks Road, Raleigh, NC 27609
Phone: 919 716-7000
Web: www.firstcitizens.com

PRODUCTS/OPERATIONS
2013 Sales

	$ mil.	% of total
Interest		
Loans & leases	757.2	72
Investment securities including dividends	36.9	3
Overnight investments	2.7	-
Noninterest		
Service charges on deposit accounts	60.7	5
Wealth management services	59.6	5
Merchant services	56.0	4
Cardholder services	48.4	4
Fees from processing services	22.7	1
Other service charges and fees	15.7	1
Adjustments	(72.3)	-
Other	72.8	5
Total	1,060.4	100

COMPETITORS
BB&T	JPMorgan Chase
BBVA Compass Bancshares	PNC Financial Regions Financial
Bank of America	SunTrust
Capital One	Synovus
Citibank	Wachovia Corp
First Horizon	Wells Fargo

HISTORICAL FINANCIALS
Company Type: Public

Income Statement				FYE: December 31
	ASSETS ($ mil.)	NET INCOME ($ mil.)	INCOME AS % OF ASSETS	EMPLOYEES
12/18	35,408.6	400.3	1.1%	6,683
12/17	34,527.5	323.7	0.9%	6,799
12/16	32,990.8	225.4	0.7%	6,296
12/15	31,475.9	210.3	0.7%	6,232
12/14	30,075.1	138.5	0.5%	6,440
Annual Growth	4.2%	30.4%	—	0.9%

2018 Year-End Financials
Return on assets: 1.1%
Return on equity: 11.7%
Long-term debt ($ mil.): —
No. of shares (mil.): 11.6
Sales ($ mil): 1,645.9
Dividends
Yield: 0.3%
Payout: 4.3%
Market value ($ mil.): 4,384.0

	STOCK PRICE ($) FY Close	P/E High/Low		PER SHARE ($)		
				Earnings	Dividends	Book Value
12/18	377.05	14	11	33.53	1.45	300.04
12/17	403.00	16	12	26.96	1.25	277.60
12/16	355.00	19	12	18.77	1.20	250.82
12/15	258.17	15	12	17.52	1.20	239.14
12/14	252.79	20	16	13.56	1.20	223.77
Annual Growth	10.5%	—	—	25.4%	4.8%	7.6%

First Commonwealth Financial Corp (Indiana, PA)

First Commonwealth Financial is the holding company for First Commonwealth Bank which provides consumer and commercial banking services from nearly 115 branches across 15 central and western Pennsylvania counties as well as in Columbus Ohio. The bank's loan portfolio mostly consists of commercial and industrial loans including real estate operating agricultural and construction loans. It also issues consumer loans such as education automobile and home equity loans and offers wealth management insurance financial planning retail brokerage and trust services. The company has total assets of some $6.7 billion with deposits of roughly $4.5 billion.

Operations
The bank made 65% of its total revenue from interest and fees on loans in 2014 while another 12% came from interest and dividends on its investments. Another 6% of First Commonwealth's revenue came from service charges on deposit accounts while trust income and insurance and retail brokerage commissions each made up 2% of the bank's total revenue.

Geographic Reach
The bank boasts nearly 115 branch offices in western and central Pennsylvania and Columbus Ohio. It also has loan production offices in downtown Pittsburgh Pennsylvania and Cleveland Ohio.

Sales and Marketing
First Commonwealth Financial spent $2.95 million on advertising in 2014 compared to $3.13 million and $4.16 million in 2013 and 2012 respectively.

Financial Performance
First Commonwealth's revenues have been slowly decline over the past few years due to shrinking interest margins on loans amidst the low-interest environment. The firm's profits however have been rising thanks to declining loan loss provisions as its loan portfolio's credit quality has been improving in the strengthening economy.

The bank's revenue dipped by more than 1% to $263.04 million in 2014 mostly as interest margins on loans continued to decline as it issued new loans with lower rates in the low-interest environment.

Despite lower revenue in 2014 the bank's net income jumped by 7% to $44.45 million for the year mostly thanks to further decreases in loan loss provisions with a strengthening credit portfolio and lower interest expenses on deposits. First Commonwealth's operating cash fell by 4% to $82.14 million despite higher earnings mostly as the bank collected less in cash proceeds from the sales of its mortgage loans held for sale.

Strategy
First Commonwealth Financial has historically expanded its branch reach through the acquisition smaller banks and thrifts in its market area. However in recent years the company has also been adding non-banking businesses such as insurance firms to bolster its existing non-banking service lines.

Mergers and Acquisitions
First Commonwealth Bank acquired 13 branches in Canton and Ashtabula Ohio from FirstMerit Bank in 2016. The acquisition related to FirstMerit's acquisition by Huntington Bancshares added some $735 million in deposits and some 34000 customers. It is also buying Ohio's DCB Financial parent company of Delaware County Bank & Trust for some $106 million. That deal will add nine full-service branches in central Ohio.

In 2014 First Commonwealth Bank entered the Columbus Ohio market for the first time with its purchase of the Ohio-based First Community Bank for $14.75 million cash.

Also in 2014 the bank bolstered its insurance business through its acquisition of Thompson/McLay Insurance Associates which boasted long-term client relationships in the home auto commercial and specialty insurance lines. The deal added the insurance firm's experienced sales and account management personnel as well as the popular Thompson/McLay Insurance Associates brand which it would keep as a division of its own insurance agency.

EXECUTIVES

EVP and Chief Revenue Officer, Jane Grebenc, $355,833 total compensation
EVP and Chief Credit Officer, I. Robert (Bob) Emmerich, $274,500 total compensation
President and CEO, Thomas Michael (Mike) Price, age 56, $435,567 total compensation
EVP CFO and Treasurer, James R. Reske, $237,372 total compensation
EVP Business Integration, Norman J. Montgomery, $261,792 total compensation
EVP Chief Risk Officer General Counsel and Secretary, Matthew C. (Matt) Tomb
EVP Human Resources, Carrie Riggle
Vice President Administration, Wendy Reynolds
Vice President of Networking Security, Sheila Hoover
Vice President, Terry Lingenfelter
Vice President, Kevin Cribbs
ASSISTANT VICE PRESIDENT AND HRIS MANAGER, Karen Livermore
Vice President, Stephen Orban
Vice President and Office Manager of Murrysville and Export Offices, John Mango
Vice President And Commercial Real Estate, Brian Pukylo
Assistant Vice President Operations, Mona Straw
Vice President And Staffing Manager, Vicki Fox
Vice President Office Manager II, David Louis
Vice President Bank Secrecy Act Officer First Commonwealth Bank, David Mcgreevy
Executive Vice President First Commonwealth Advisors, David Buckiso
Senior Vice President Relationship Manager, David McGowan
Assistant Vice President Benefits Administration, Natalie Felix
Investment Commercial Real Estate Vp, Megan Dellapina
Senior Vice President Relationship Manager, Douglas Sako
Vice President Business Banker, Dan Poirier
Assistant Vice President Corporate Loan Officer, Ronald DiBiase
Senior Vice President Internal Audit, Steven Melletz
Business Banker Vice President, Susan Henigin
Vice President Sec And Regulatory Reporting, Morgan Cypher
Vice President Secured Credit, Joe Innocenti
Senior Vice President Financial Solutions Market Leader, Scott Vidovich
Executive Vice President and Chief Credit Officer of First Commonwealth Bank, Brian Karrip
Assistant Vice President, Bradley Wojnar
Vice President Special Assets Administration, Brenda Wainwright
Vice President Senior Corporate Banker First Commonwealth Bank, Matthew Zuro
Assistant Vice President Financial Solutions Center Manager, Melissa Bartolomeo
Vice President Senior Treasury Officer, Tricia Baker
Senior Vice President Commercial Banking, Mary Patton
Assistant Vice President and Foreclosure OREO Officer, Mark Oresick
Assistant Vice President Assistant Business Continuity Manager, Hann Candi Beltowsk
SENIOR VICE PRESIDENT, Regis Scanlon
Assistant Vice President Financial Solutions Center Manager, Mikey Boyer
Vice President Finance, Kristin Robertucci
Assistant Vice President Community Engagement Manager, Elizabeth Saraceno
Vice President Treasury Management Sales Officer, Amy Holbrook
Senior Vice President Private Banking, Walters Barbara
Vice President, Charles Bennett
Senior Vice President Corporate Banking, Huey Bartolini
Vice President Senior Analyst Business Development Officer, Richard Robinson
Senior Vice President Managing Director, Antonio Benton
Assistant Vice President Mortgage Loan Originator, Nancy Garrabrant
Evp Chief Audit Executive, Len Lombardi
Executive Vice President, Joe Culos
Chairman, David S. (Dave) Dahlmann, age 69
Auditors: KPMG LLP

LOCATIONS

HQ: First Commonwealth Financial Corp (Indiana, PA)
601 Philadelphia Street, Indiana, PA 15701
Phone: 724 349-7220
Web: www.fcbanking.com

PRODUCTS/OPERATIONS

2014 Sales

	$ mil.	% of total
Interest		
Loans including fees	171.2	65
Taxable investments	31.0	12
Noninterest		
Service charges on deposit accounts	15.7	7
Insurance & retail brokerage commissions	6.5	2
Trust income	6.0	2
Others	32.6	12
Total	**263.0**	**100**

Selected Subsidiaries
First Commonwealth Bank
    First Commonwealth Insurance Agency
    First Commonwealth Home Mortgage LLC (49.9%)
First Commonwealth Financial Advisors Incorporated

COMPETITORS

Allegheny Valley Bancorp	F.N.B. (PA)
AmeriServ Financial	Fidelity Bancorp (PA)
Citizens Financial Group	Northwest Bancshares
Dollar Bank	PNC Financial
	S&T Bancorp

HISTORICAL FINANCIALS

Company Type: Public

Income Statement — FYE: December 31

	ASSETS ($ mil.)	NET INCOME ($ mil.)	INCOME AS % OF ASSETS	EMPLOYEES
12/18	7,828.2	107.5	1.4%	1,512
12/17	7,308.5	55.1	0.8%	1,476
12/16	6,684.0	59.5	0.9%	1,376
12/15	6,566.8	50.1	0.8%	1,311
12/14	6,360.2	44.4	0.7%	1,363
Annual Growth	5.3%	24.7%	—	2.6%

2018 Year-End Financials

Return on assets: 1.4%
Return on equity: 11.5%
Long-term debt ($ mil.): —
No. of shares (mil.): 98.5
Sales ($ mil): 380.8
Dividends
Yield: 2.9%
Payout: 32.4%
Market value ($ mil.): 1,190.0

	STOCK PRICE ($) FY Close	P/E High/Low		PER SHARE ($) Earnings	Dividends	Book Value
12/18	12.08	16	10	1.08	0.35	9.90
12/17	14.32	26	21	0.58	0.32	9.11
12/16	14.18	21	12	0.67	0.28	8.43
12/15	9.07	18	14	0.56	0.28	8.09
12/14	9.22	20	16	0.48	0.28	7.81
Annual Growth	7.0%	—	—	22.5%	5.7%	6.1%

First Community Corp (SC)

EXECUTIVES

Assistant Vice President Business Services the Local Bank For Local Business, Patricia Junqueira
Vice President Mortgage Origination, Charlie Branham
SENIOR VICE PRESIDENT AND CHIEF COMPLIANCE OFFICER, Ann Robertson
Auditors: Elliott Davis, LLC

LOCATIONS

HQ: First Community Corp (SC)
5455 Sunset Boulevard, Lexington, SC 29072
Phone: 803 951-2265

COMPETITORS

BB&T	Regions Financial
Bank of America	Security Federal
First Citizens Bancorporation	Synovus

HISTORICAL FINANCIALS

Company Type: Public

Income Statement — FYE: December 31

	ASSETS ($ mil.)	NET INCOME ($ mil.)	INCOME AS % OF ASSETS	EMPLOYEES
12/18	1,091.6	11.2	1.0%	226
12/17	1,050.7	5.8	0.6%	224
12/16	914.7	6.6	0.7%	202
12/15	862.7	6.1	0.7%	186
12/14	812.3	5.1	0.6%	185
Annual Growth	7.7%	21.7%	—	5.1%

2018 Year-End Financials

Return on assets: 1.0%
Return on equity: 10.2%
Long-term debt ($ mil.): —
No. of shares (mil.): 7.6
Sales ($ mil): 50.3
Dividends
Yield: 2.0%
Payout: 34.4%
Market value ($ mil.): 148.0

	STOCK PRICE ($) FY Close	P/E High/Low		PER SHARE ($) Earnings	Dividends	Book Value
12/18	19.43	18	13	1.45	0.40	14.73
12/17	22.60	29	21	0.83	0.36	13.93
12/16	18.05	19	13	0.98	0.32	12.20
12/15	14.92	16	12	0.91	0.28	11.81
12/14	11.31	15	13	0.78	0.24	11.18
Annual Growth	14.5%	—	—	16.8%	13.6%	7.1%

First Defiance Financial Corp

Named for its hometown not its attitude First Defiance Financial is the holding company for First Federal Bank of the Midwest which operates more than 30 branches serving northwestern Ohio western Indiana and southern Michigan. The thrift offers standard deposit products including checking savings and money market accounts and CDs. Commercial real estate loans account for more than half of the bank's loan portfolio; commercial loans make up another quarter of all loans. The company's insurance agency subsidiary First Insurance Group of the Midwest which accounts for some 7% of the company's revenues provides life insurance property/casualty coverage and investments. In 2019 First Defiance Financial agreed to merge with Ohio-based United Community Financial (the holding company for Home Savings Bank and HSB Insurance) in a deal valued at $473 million.

Strategy

First Defiance Financial has boosted its non-banking product lines via acquisitions. It bought the employee benefits insurance business of another local agency Andres O'Neil & Lowe in 2010; and property/casualty agency Payak-Dubbs Insurance Agency in 2011. Both additions became part of First Insurance Group of the Midwest (formerly named First Insurance & Investments).

In 2016 the company agreed to buy another bank serving northwest Ohio Commercial Bancshares. The deal is valued at some $63 million and adds seven branches and $342 million in assets.

Mergers and Acquisitions

In 2019 First Defiance Financial agreed to merge with Ohio-based United Community Financial (the holding company for Home Savings Bank and HSB Insurance) in a deal valued at $473 million. United Community's Home Savings Bank subsidiary will merge into First Federal to create a bank with more than $6 billion in assets. First Defiance shareholders will have a 52.5% stake in the new company.

EXECUTIVES

EVP Business Banking First Federal Bank, Dennis E. Rose, age 50, $144,077 total compensation
President and CEO First Defiance Financial and First Federal Bank, Donald P. Hileman, age 66, $400,000 total compensation
EVP General Counsel and Chief Risk Officer First Defiance Financial Corp and First Federal Bank, John R. Reisner, age 63, $180,147 total compensation
EVP and Community Banking President Â– First Federal Bank, Gregory R. Allen, age 55, $200,000 total compensation
EVP and President Western Market Area First Federal Bank, James R. Williams, age 51
EVP and President Eastern Market Area First Federal Bank, Timothy K. (Tim) Harris, age 60
EVP and Chief Credit Officer First Federal Bank, Michael D. Mulford, age 54, $149,387 total compensation
EVP and President Northern Market Area First Federal Bank, Marybeth Shunck, age 49
EVP and CFO First Defiance Financial Corp. and First Federal Bank, Kent T. Thompson, age 65, $218,360 total compensation
EVP and Director Human Resources First Defiance Financial Corp. and First Federal Bank, Sharon L. Davis, age 37
EVP and President Southern Market Area First Federal Bank, Amy L. Hackenberg, age 48
Assistant Vice President Human Resources, Diane Beam
Assistant Vice President, Julie Harris
Senior Vice President, Lisa R Christy
Avp Information Security Analyst, Chad Kaup
Senior Vice President Information Technology, Kathy Miller
Vice President Senior Accountant, Steve Giesige
Chairman, William J. (Bill) Small, age 68
Vice Chairman, Stephen L. Boomer, age 68
Auditors: Crowe LLP

LOCATIONS

HQ: First Defiance Financial Corp
601 Clinton Street, Defiance, OH 43512
Phone: 419 782-5015
Web: www.fdef.com

PRODUCTS/OPERATIONS

2016 Sales

	$ mil.	% of total
Interest		
Loans	80.2	66
Investment securities		
Taxable	3.2	3
Tax-exempt	3.0	2
Interest-bearing deposits	0.4	-
FHLB stock dividends	0.6	1
Non-interest		
Service fees & other charges	10.9	9
Insurance commissions	10.4	9
Mortgage banking income	7.3	6
Trust income	1.7	1
Gain on sale of non-mortgage loans	0.8	1
Income from bank owned life insurance	0.9	1
Gain on sale or call of securities	0.5	-
Other	1.5	1
Total	121.4	100

COMPETITORS

Farmers National	Huntington Bancshares
Fifth Third	KeyCorp
First Citizens Banc Corp	PNC Financial
First Financial Bancorp	SB Financial Group

HISTORICAL FINANCIALS
Company Type: Public

Income Statement   FYE: December 31

	ASSETS ($ mil.)	NET INCOME ($ mil.)	INCOME AS % OF ASSETS	EMPLOYEES
12/18	3,181.7	46.2	1.5%	696
12/17	2,993.4	32.2	1.1%	674
12/16	2,477.6	28.8	1.2%	581
12/15	2,297.6	26.4	1.2%	586
12/14	2,178.9	24.2	1.1%	555
Annual Growth	9.9%	17.5%	—	5.8%

2018 Year-End Financials

Return on assets: 1.5%
Return on equity: 11.9%
Long-term debt ($ mil.): —
No. of shares (mil.): 20.1
Sales ($ mil): 163.9
Dividends
Yield: 2.6%
Payout: 28.3%
Market value ($ mil.): 494.0

	STOCK PRICE ($) FY Close	P/E High/Low	PER SHARE ($) Earnings	Dividends	Book Value
12/18	24.51	30 10	2.26	0.64	19.81
12/17	51.97	35 29	1.61	0.50	18.38
12/16	50.74	32 22	1.60	0.44	16.31
12/15	37.78	29 21	1.41	0.39	15.39
12/14	34.06	27 19	1.22	0.31	15.13
Annual Growth	(7.9%)	— —	16.7%	19.6%	7.0%

First Financial Bancorp (OH)

First Financial Bancorp spreads itself thick. The holding company's flagship subsidiary First Financial Bank operates nearly 110 branches in Ohio Indiana and Kentucky. Founded in 1863 the bank offers checking and savings accounts money market accounts CDs credit cards private banking and wealth management services through its First Financial Wealth Management subsidiary. Commercial loans including real estate and construction loans make up more than 50% of First Financial's total loan portfolio; the bank also offers residential mortgage and consumer loans. First Financial Bancorp boasts more than $7 billion in assets including nearly $5 billion in loans.

Operations
The company's private banking business First Financial Wealth Management had $2.4 billion in assets under management in early 2015.

Sales and Marketing
First Financial spent $3.60 million on marketing in 2014 compared to $4.27 million and $5.55 million in 2013 and 2012 respectively.

Financial Performance
First Financial's revenue has been in decline in recent years due to shrinking interest margins on loans amidst the low-interest environment. The company has also struggled to grow its profits much past the $65 million-mark though profit levels are more than twice as high as they were prior to 2009.

The company's revenue dipped by 2% to $311.82 million in 2014 mostly as its loan interest income declined by nearly 4% as interest margins continued to shrink in the low-interest environment. First Financial's non-interest income fell by double-digits mostly due to lower FDIC loss sharing income lower income from the accelerated discount on prepaid covered loans and smaller gains on investment securities sales.

Despite lower revenue in 2014 First Financial's net income rebounded by 34% to $65 million for the year mostly thanks to an 80% reduction in loan and lease loss provisions as the bank's loan portfolio's credit quality improved with the strengthening economy. The company's non-interest expenses also declined by double-digits mostly because the bank in 2013 incurred a non-recurring $22.4 million FDIC indemnification valuation adjustment.

First Financial's operating cash declined by 66% to $56.65 million after adjusting its earnings for non-cash items related to the indemnification asset decrease and net sales proceeds on its loans held for sale.

Strategy
First Financial has been focusing on branch expansion (on its own or through acquisitions) in three core metropolitan markets: Cincinnati Dayton and Indianapolis. In 2014 for example First Financial acquired three Ohio-based banks and their branches in 2014 expanding its branch network in Central Ohio while adding new loan and deposit business at the same time.

Mergers and Acquisitions
In 2017 First Financial agreed to acquire MainSource Financial Group with an expected deal completion in 2Q 2018. The purchase extends its reach in Indiana (80 branches) Ohio Illinois and Kentucky.

In 2014 to expand further into key markets in Columbus and Central Ohio First Financial purchased The First Bexley Bank which served commercial and consumer bank clients from its one branch location in Bexley Ohio. Similarly that year it purchased Insight Bank operated a branch in Worthington Ohio and a mortgage origination office in Newark Ohio; and bought Worthington-based Guernsey Bancorp and its three branches in Central Ohio.

Company Background
In the past the bank acquired 16 branches in western Ohio from Liberty Savings Bank and bought 22 Indianapolis-area branches from Flagstar Bank in 2011. Together the two acquisitions furthered the bank's growth strategy for the key markets of Dayton and Indianapolis.

EXECUTIVES

President Western Markets Commercial Banking and Wealth Management, C. Douglas (Doug) Lefferson
President and CEO, Claude E. Davis
President and COO, Anthony M. (Tony) Stollings
Chief Credit Officer, Richard S. Barbercheck
SVP and CFO, John Gavigan
President Mortgage Banking, Jill A. Stanton
EVP and Chief Compliance Officer, Holly M. Foster
President Corporate Banking, Brad Ringwald
Vice President Commercial Underwriter, Brian Englert
Assistant Vice President Sales Center Manager III, Cooley Andrew
Vice President Of Mortgage Lending, Wade Spain
Senior Vice President, Robert Mason
Vice President Network, Brad Stroeh
Vice President, Stephen Vegh
First Vice President Director Of Corporate Facilities, Jeffrey Weingartner
Vice President Commercial Real Estate, Steve Tanner
First Financial Center Banking Center Manager Assistant Vice President, Julie Estep
Vice President Digital Sales Channel Manager, Brano Tomic
Assistant Vice President Business Banking Branch Manager, Kimberly Stitt
Assistant Vice President, Mark Gregg
Senior Vice President Chief Talent Officer, Mary Findley
Vice President And Fiduciary Manager, Paul Schwarz
Vice President, Jim Osmon
Vice President, Josh Riley
Assistant Vice President Mortgage Sales Manager, Mark Spangler
Vice President Commercial Banking First Financial Bank, Jason King
Vice President And Senior Trust Officer, Linda Glass
Assistant Vice President, Teresa Peyton
Vice President Business Development Officer, Kevin Stewart
Vice President Credit Risk Review, Mike Hurley
Vice President, Jimmy Chandler
Chairman, Murph Knapke
Vice Chairman, J. Wickliffe Ach
Board Member, J Ach
Auditors: Crowe LLP

LOCATIONS

HQ: First Financial Bancorp (OH)
255 East Fifth Street, Suite 800, Cincinnati, OH 45202
Phone: 877 322-9530
Web: www.bankatfirst.com

PRODUCTS/OPERATIONS

2014 Sales

	$ mil.	% of total
Interest		
Loans including fees	208.8	66
Investment securities	44.5	14
(Adjustment)	(5.5)	-
Noninterest		
Service charges on deposit accounts	20.3	7
Trust and wealth management fees	13.6	5
Bankcard income	10.7	3
Net gains from sales on loans	4.4	1
Accelerated discount on covered/formerly covered loans	4.2	1
Others	10.8	3
Total	311.8	100

COMPETITORS

AMB Financial
Commercial Bancshares
Farmers National
Fifth Third
First Defiance Financial
First Franklin
LCNB
Liberty Capital
Logansport Financial
MutualFirst Financial
PNC Financial
Peoples Community Bancorp
Peoples-Sidney
SB Financial Group
U.S. Bancorp

HISTORICAL FINANCIALS
Company Type: Public

Income Statement
FYE: December 31

	ASSETS ($ mil.)	NET INCOME ($ mil.)	INCOME AS % OF ASSETS	EMPLOYEES
12/18	13,986.6	172.6	1.2%	2,131
12/17	8,896.9	96.7	1.1%	1,366
12/16	8,437.9	88.5	1.0%	1,521
12/15	8,147.4	75.0	0.9%	1,471
12/14	7,217.8	65.0	0.9%	1,442
Annual Growth	18.0%	27.7%	—	10.3%

2018 Year-End Financials
Return on assets: 1.5%
Return on equity: 11.4%
Long-term debt ($ mil.): —
No. of shares (mil.): 97.8
Sales ($ mil): 643.7
Dividends
Yield: 3.2%
Payout: 44.0%
Market value ($ mil.): 2,322.0

	STOCK PRICE ($) FY Close	P/E High/Low	PER SHARE ($) Earnings	Dividends	Book Value
12/18	23.72	17 11	1.93	0.78	21.23
12/17	26.35	19 15	1.56	0.68	14.99
12/16	28.45	20 10	1.43	0.64	13.96
12/15	18.07	17 13	1.21	0.64	13.13
12/14	18.59	17 14	1.09	0.61	12.76
Annual Growth	6.3%	—	15.4%	6.3%	13.6%

First Financial Bankshares, Inc.

Texas hold 'em? Well sort of. First Financial Bankshares is the holding company for eleven banks consolidated under the First Financial brand all of which are located in small and midsized markets in Texas. Together they have about 50 locations. The company maintains a decentralized management structure with each of the subsidiary banks having their own local leadership and decision-making authority. Its First Financial Trust & Asset Management subsidiary administers retirement and employee benefit plans in addition to providing trust services. First Financial Bankshares also owns an insurance agency.

EXECUTIVES
Chairman President and CEO; Chairman First Financial Bank N.A., F. Scott Dueser, age 66, $754,167 total compensation
EVP and CFO, J. Bruce Hildebrand, age 64, $445,000 total compensation
EVP and Chief Administrative Officer, Ronald D. (Ron) Butler, age 58, $405,000 total compensation
EVP Lending, Marna Yerigan
EVP Lending, T. Luke Longhofer
EVP and CIO, Thomas S. (Stan) Limerick
EVP and Lending Officer, Gary S.Gragg, age 59, $325,000 total compensation
EVP Retail and Training, Monica Houston
EVP Chief Risk Officer, Randy Roewe
Executive Vice President, Rodney Foster
Senior Vice President, Kay Berry
Vice President, Wade Spain
Vice President Branch Manager N.A, Shay Minor
Vice President, Isabel Montoya
Senior Vice President Mortgage Lending, Janet O'Dell
Vice President of Human Resources, Jennifer Harper
Vice President Of Information Technology, Kim Tatom
Senior Vice President, Joe Love
Vice President, Sara Burnside
Vice President Fair Lending And Responsible Banking, Jane Parsons
Senior Vice President Mortgage Lending, Wes Masters
Vice President Mortgage Lending, Jayden Slentz
Senior Vice President, Will Christoferson
Vice President Information Technology, Reid Sharp
Vice President, Robert Charles
Board Member, Kade Matthews
Board Member, Ron Giddiens
Board Member, Tim Lancaster
Auditors: Ernst & Young LLP

LOCATIONS
HQ: First Financial Bankshares, Inc.
400 Pine Street, Abilene, TX 79601
Phone: 325 627-7155
Web: www.ffin.com

PRODUCTS/OPERATIONS

2015 sales

	$ mil.	% of total
Interest Income		
Interest and fees on loans	151.7	51
Interest on investment securities	69.7	24
Interest on federal funds sold and interest-bearing deposits in banks		0.2
Non-Interest Income		
ATM interchange and credit card fees	21.9	7
Trust fees	19.2	6
Service charges on deposit accounts	17.2	6
Real estate mortgage operations	10.4	4
Net gain on sale of available-for-sale securities	0.5	-
Net gain on sale of foreclosed assets	0.5	-
Net loss on sale of assets	(0.8)	-
Other	4.6	2
Total	295.1	100

Products/ServicesPersonal
Learn
Online Banking
Mobile Banking
Consumer Education
FAQS
Privacy & Security Information
Resources
Testimonials
Tools
Bank
Checking
Savings
Invest
CDS & IRAS
Broker Services
Borrow
Mortgage Loans
Mortgage Lenders
Auto Loans
Recreational Loans
Home Equity Loans
Personal Line of Credit
CD Secured Loans
Banking with First Financial
Mobile Banking
Online Banking
Pay Bills
Get Cash
Make Deposit
Move Money
Keep Track
Business
Learn
Online Banking
Mobile Banking
Business Education
Starting your Business
Growing your Business
Tools
Business Banking Services
Manage Cash
Send Payments
Receive Payments
Manage Fraud and Risk
Other Services
Trust & Wealth Management
Investment Management
Trust Management
Estate Management
Oil & Gas Management
Real Estate and Property Management
Company Retirement Plans

Selected Subsidiaries
First Financial Bank National Association Abilene Texas.
First Technology Services Inc. Abilene Texas (wholly owned subsidiary of First Financial Bank National Association Abilene Texas).
First Financial Trust & Asset Management Company National Association Abilene Texas.
First Financial Insurance Agency Inc. Abilene Texas.
First Financial Investments Inc. Abilene Texas.

COMPETITORS
BBVA Compass Bancshares
Bank of America
Cullen/Frost Bankers
JPMorgan Chase
Wells Fargo
Woodforest Financial

HISTORICAL FINANCIALS
Company Type: Public

Income Statement
FYE: December 31

	ASSETS ($ mil.)	NET INCOME ($ mil.)	INCOME AS % OF ASSETS	EMPLOYEES
12/18	7,731.8	150.6	1.9%	1,350
12/17	7,254.7	120.3	1.7%	1,300
12/16	6,809.9	104.7	1.5%	1,300
12/15	6,665.0	100.3	1.5%	1,270
12/14	5,848.2	89.5	1.5%	1,140
Annual Growth	7.2%	13.9%	—	4.3%

2018 Year-End Financials
Return on assets: 2.0%
Return on equity: 15.2%
Long-term debt ($ mil.): —
No. of shares (mil.): 134.5
Sales ($ mil): 393.4
Dividends
Yield: 2.8%
Payout: 73.8%
Market value ($ mil.): 7,763.0

	STOCK PRICE ($) FY Close	P/E High/Low	PER SHARE ($) Earnings	Dividends	Book Value
12/18	57.69	60 40	1.11	0.82	7.83
12/17	45.05	53 41	0.91	0.38	7.02
12/16	45.20	58 31	0.80	0.35	6.39
12/15	30.17	47 32	0.77	0.62	6.15
12/14	29.88	95 39	0.70	0.55	5.36
Annual Growth	17.9%	—	12.4%	10.5%	9.9%

First Financial Northwest Inc

Searching for green in The Evergreen State First Financial Northwest is the holding company for First Financial Northwest Bank (formerly First Savings Bank Northwest). The small community bank offers deposit services like checking and savings accounts and a variety of lending services to customers in western Washington. Almost 40% of First Savings Bank's loan portfolio consists of one-to four-family residential loans while commercial real estate loans made up another 35%. Because the bank focuses almost exclusively on real estate loans it writes very few unsecured consumer and commercial loans.

Operations
About 17% of First Financial Northwest Bank's loan portfolio was comprised of multi-family mortgage loans while construction/land development loans made up 7%. Less than 2% of the bank's portfolio was made up of business and consumer loans.

The bank generated 93% of its total revenue from loan interest (including fees) in 2014 and another 6% came from interest on its investments available-for-sale.

Geographic Reach
Renton-based First Financial Northwest Bank's one branch office primarily serves King county as well as Pierce Snohomish and Kitsap counties (to a lesser extent) in the western part of Washington State.

Financial Performance
First Financial Northwest's revenues have been in decline in recent years due to shrinking interest margins on loans amidst the low-interest environment. The firm's profits however have trended thanks to declining loan loss provisions as its loan portfolio's credit quality has improved with the strengthened housing market and overall economy.

The company's revenue remained mostly flat around $39.2 million in 2014 with slightly higher interest income as it grew its loan business but with slightly lower non-interest income as it had sold an investment property for a $325000 gain in 2013.

First Financial's net income plummeted by 56% to $10.7 million despite stable revenue in 2014 mostly because it had collected a (non-recurring) $13.5 million tax benefit in 2013 (compared to a tax expense of $5.9 million in 2014) after a reversal of its deferred tax asset valuation allowance. Not counting this event the company's before-tax profit grew by more than 50% as its operational expenses fell and its loan loss provisions continued to decline. First Financial's operating levels rose by 22% to $18.6 million thanks to higher cash earnings.

Strategy
First Financial Northwest's long-term business strategy is to grow First Financial Northwest Bank "as a well-capitalized and profitable community bank" with continued focus on one-to-four family residential loans and commercial real estate loans. It also planned in 2015 to promote its "diversified array" of deposit loan and other products and services to individuals and businesses highlighting its locality in its target Puget Sound regional market.

To ensure low-cost funding sources the bank in 2015 planned to continue using wholesale funding sources from Federal Home Loan Bank advances and acquired deposits in the national brokered certificate of deposit market. To minimize risk it would continue to diversify its loan types and manage its loss-invoking credit risk and diminish interest rate risk to keep its interest margins up.

The bank in 2015 also expected to improve profitability through "disciplined pricing expense control and balance sheet management while continuing to provide excellent customer service."

Company Background
First Financial Northwest changed the name of its subsidiary bank to First Financial Northwest Bank from First Savings Bank Northwest in July 2015 to reflect that it was "more than just a savings bank" according to the company's CEO.

EXECUTIVES

Vice President Marketing, Carol Janssen
Vice President Cyber And Information Security, Boelling Don
Assistant Vice President, Randi Haela
Auditors: Moss Adams LLP

LOCATIONS

HQ: First Financial Northwest Inc
  201 Wells Avenue South, Renton, WA 98057
Phone: 425 255-4400

PRODUCTS/OPERATIONS

2014 Sales

	% of total
Interest income	
Loans(including fees)	93
Investments available-for-sale	6
Interest-earning deposits with banks	
Non-interest income	1
Total	**100**

COMPETITORS

Bank of America
Banner Corp
Columbia Banking

JPMorgan Chase
U.S. Bancorp

HISTORICAL FINANCIALS
Company Type: Public

Income Statement
FYE: December 31

	ASSETS ($ mil.)	NET INCOME ($ mil.)	INCOME AS % OF ASSETS	EMPLOYEES
12/18	1,252.4	14.9	1.2%	156
12/17	1,210.2	8.4	0.7%	145
12/16	1,037.5	8.8	0.9%	121
12/15	979.9	9.1	0.9%	107
12/14	937.0	10.6	1.1%	101
Annual Growth	7.5%	8.7%	—	11.5%

2018 Year-End Financials
Return on assets: 1.2%
Return on equity: 10.0%
Long-term debt ($ mil.): —
No. of shares (mil.): 10.7
Sales ($ mil): 58.7
Dividends
  Yield: 2.0%
  Payout: 21.2%
Market value ($ mil.): 166.0

	STOCK PRICE ($) FY Close	P/E High/Low	PER SHARE ($) Earnings	Dividends	Book Value
12/18	15.47	14 10	1.43	0.31	14.35
12/17	15.51	26 18	0.81	0.27	13.27
12/16	19.74	27 17	0.74	0.24	12.63
12/15	13.96	21 17	0.67	0.24	12.40
12/14	12.04	17 14	0.71	0.20	11.96
Annual Growth	6.5%	— —	19.1%	11.6%	4.7%

First Foundation Inc

Auditors: Eide Bailly LLP

LOCATIONS

HQ: First Foundation Inc
  18101 Von Karman Avenue, Suite 700, Irvine, CA 92612
Phone: 949 202-4160
Web: www.ff-inc.com

HISTORICAL FINANCIALS
Company Type: Public

Income Statement
FYE: December 31

	ASSETS ($ mil.)	NET INCOME ($ mil.)	INCOME AS % OF ASSETS	EMPLOYEES
12/18	5,840.4	42.9	0.7%	482
12/17	4,541.1	27.5	0.6%	394
12/16	3,975.4	23.3	0.6%	335
12/15	2,592.5	13.3	0.5%	295
12/14	1,355.4	8.3	0.6%	207
Annual Growth	44.1%	50.4%	—	23.5%

2018 Year-End Financials
Return on assets: 0.8%
Return on equity: 9.0%
Long-term debt ($ mil.): —
No. of shares (mil.): 44.5
Sales ($ mil.): 243.0
Dividends
  Yield: —
  Payout: —
Market value ($ mil.): 572.0

	STOCK PRICE ($) FY Close	P/E High/Low	PER SHARE ($) Earnings	Dividends	Book Value
12/18	12.86	20 12	1.01	0.00	12.57
12/17	18.54	36 17	0.78	0.00	10.34
12/16	28.50	41 28	0.70	0.00	8.69
12/15	23.59	41 29	0.58	0.00	8.13
12/14	18.14	37 33	0.52	0.00	6.34
Annual Growth	(8.2%)	— —	18.3%	—	18.6%

First Guaranty Bancshares, Inc.

Auditors: Castaing, Hussey & Lolan, LLC

LOCATIONS

HQ: First Guaranty Bancshares, Inc.
  400 East Thomas Street, Hammond, LA 70401
Phone: 985 345-7685
Web: www.eguaranty.com

HISTORICAL FINANCIALS
Company Type: Public

Income Statement — FYE: December 31

	ASSETS ($ mil.)	NET INCOME ($ mil.)	INCOME AS % OF ASSETS	EMPLOYEES
12/18	1,817.2	14.2	0.8%	373
12/17	1,750.4	11.7	0.7%	349
12/16	1,500.9	14.0	0.9%	304
12/15	1,459.7	14.5	1.0%	289
12/14	1,518.8	11.2	0.7%	272
Annual Growth	4.6%	6.1%	—	8.2%

2018 Year-End Financials
Return on assets: 0.8%
Return on equity: 9.7%
Long-term debt ($ mil.): —
No. of shares (mil.): 9.6
Sales ($ mil): 83.6

Dividends
Yield: 3.0%
Payout: 43.7%
Market value ($ mil.): 225.0

	STOCK PRICE ($) FY Close	P/E High/Low	PER SHARE ($) Earnings	Dividends	Book Value
12/18	23.21	19 13	1.46	0.64	15.20
12/17	25.00	24 18	1.25	0.60	14.86
12/16	23.93	16 10	1.53	0.58	13.51
12/15	18.75	13 10	1.66	0.54	12.84
12/14	19.00	15 11	1.29	0.53	16.67
Annual Growth	5.1%	— —	3.2%	4.9%	(2.3%)

First Horizon National Corp

First Horizon National would like to be on banking consumers' horizons in the Volunteer State and beyond. The bank holding company operates more than 170 First Tennessee Bank branches in its home state and neighboring markets. Boasting roughly $26 billion in total assets it offers traditional banking services like loans deposit accounts and credit cards as well as trust asset management financial advisory and investment services. Subsidiary FTN Financial performs securities sales and trading fixed-income underwriting and other investment banking services through more than 25 offices in more than 15 states as well as in Hong Kong.

Operations
First Horizon operates two core business segments: Regional Banking and Capital Markets.

Regional Banking is the company's largest division (it generated 73% of the bank's total revenue in 2014) and provides traditional banking products and services to retail and commercial customers mostly in Tennessee but also in neighboring markets. The division also provides investments financial panning trust services and asset management as well as correspondent banking services such as credit depository and other banking related services for financial institutions.

The Capital Markets segment which contributed 18% to total revenues in 2014 serves mainly institutional clients in the US and overseas. Its services consist of fixed-income sales trading loan sales portfolio advisory and derivative sales.

First Horizon's two non-core segments include a Corporate division which collects gains and losses related to the bank's debt and investment activities; and the non-strategic segment (11% of total revenues in 2014) which consists of the wind down of the company's national consumer lending activities its legacy mortgage banking elements including service fees its trust preferred loan portfolio and exited businesses.

The company has diversified revenue streams generating about 56% of its total revenue from interest income (mostly from loans) in 2014 16% from capital markets-related fees nearly 10% from deposit transactions and cash management fees about 6% from its Mortgage Banking business and 6% from a combination of brokerage fees and trust services and management fees.

Geographic Reach
First Horizon National boasts more than 180 branch locations across seven US states. More than 90% of the branches are in Tennessee while just over a dozen are in the states of Georgia (northwestern) Mississippi (northwestern) North Carolina Virginia South Carolina and Florida. It also has more than 25 financial offices in 16 states across the US plus a financial office in Hong Kong.

Sales and Marketing
The company spent $18.68 million on advertising and public relations in 2014 up from $18.24 million and $17.44 million in 2013 and 2012 respectively.

Financial Performance
First Horizon's revenue has been in decline in recent years due to shrinking interest margins on loans amidst the low-interest environment. The firm's profits however have been rising thanks to declining loan loss provisions as its loan portfolio's credit quality has been improving in the strengthening economy.

The company's revenue fell by 4% to $1.26 billion in 2014 mostly as the Capital Markets business shrank by 26% as fixed-income markets suffered from low rates low market volatility and uncertainty around the Federal Reserve's monetary policy. The bank's interest income also fell by 3% despite rising commercial loan business mostly due to a combination of continued run-off of non-strategic loan portfolios lower-yielding commercial loans and lower strategic loan balances. Offsetting some of the top-line decline First Horizon's mortgage banking revenue more than doubled for the year mostly thanks to a nearly $40 million gain on the sale of its mortgage loans held-for-sale.

Despite revenue declines in 2014 First Horizon's net income skyrocket nearly seven-fold to $219.52 million thanks to a combination of lower interest and non-interest expenses and a significant decline in loan loss provisions as its loan portfolio's credit condition improved.

The company's operating cash also jumped by 63% to $704.7 million during the year as cash earnings rose and as net cash proceeds from the bank's mortgage loans held-for-sale increased.

Strategy
First Horizon National's flagship First Tennessee Bank has been expanding its geographic reach in recent years through both branch openings and strategic acquisitions of smaller banks and branches in target markets. In 2014 the bank opened its first office in Florida (in Jacksonville) as it continued its plans for growth in the Mid-Atlantic region which includes North Carolina South Carolina Virginia and northern parts of Florida. Also that year the bank agreed to purchase 13 bank branches located in the Middle and East Tennessee for a total of nearly $438 million which would add some $437 million worth of new deposits and expand its reach in its home state.

Mergers and Acquisitions
In 2014 First Horizon agreed to purchase TrustAtlantic Financial Corporation along with its five TrustAtlantic Bank branches in North Carolina (mostly in the Raleigh-Cary metro area). The deal matched First Horizon's objectives to expand in North Carolina's fast-growing Research Triangle region of the state.

In mid-2013 First Tennessee bank acquired Mountain National Bank from the FDIC adding 12 new branch locations in Sevier and Blount counties in Eastern Tennessee as well as $249 million in loan assets and $362 million in deposits.

In 2012 the company added to FTN Financial with the purchase of Las Vegas-based Main Street Capital Advisors which provides investment management and consulting services mainly to state and local municipalities.

Company Background
At the start of the recession First Horizon began selling non-core assets and refocused growth closer to home. First Horizon exited the Baltimore-Washington DC and Atlanta markets. The company also sold some 230 First Horizon Home Loan offices as well as the unit's loan origination and servicing operations outside of Tennessee to MetLife. After the sale First Horizon Financial outsourced some its mortgage origination processing and servicing operations within Tennessee to PHH Mortgage.

In 2008 the bank discontinued its specialty construction and consumer lending activities beyond Tennessee. It exited the institutional equity research business in 2010 and sold its First Horizon Insurance unit to Brown & Brown the following year. Also in 2011 First Horizon sold a subsidiary that provided administrative services for health savings accounts.

EXECUTIVES

EVP and Chief Human Resources Officer, John M. Daniel, age 64
EVP Regional Banking; COO First Tennessee Bank, David T. Popwell, age 58, $450,000 total compensation
Chairman President and CEO, D. Bryan Jordan, age 57, $815,000 total compensation
EVP and General Counsel, Charles T. Tuggle, age 70, $475,000 total compensation
EVP Corporate Communications, Kimberley C. (Kim) Cherry
EVP Technology and Operations and CIO, Bruce A. Livesay
EVP and CFO, William C. (BJ) Losch, age 48, $425,000 total compensation
EVP and Chief Risk Officer, Yousef A. Valine, age 59, $362,692 total compensation
President FTN Financial, Michael E. Kisber, age 59, $600,000 total compensation
EVP and Chief Credit Officer, Susan L. Springfield, age 54
EVP and Chief Operating and Financial Officer FTN Financial, Michael K. Waddell
EVP Consumer Banking First Tennessee Bank, David W. Miller
EVP Corporate Banking, Steve J. Hawkins
President First Tennessee Bank Mid-Atlantic Region, Billy Frank, age 48

President First Tennessee Bank Mid-Atlantic region, John Fox, age 66
Regional President First Tennessee Bank Tennessee Banking Group, Richard Shaffer, age 54
EVP and Chief Audit Executive, Vernon H. Stafford
Senior Vice President Facilities Management, Stephen Bieber
Vice President Risk Management, Kathleen Mooney
Vice President Business Process Services, Nancy Bradley
Senior Vice President and Chief Investment.., Karen Kruse
Senior Vice President and Counsel (2004), John Arthur Niemoeller
Senior Vice President, Christine Bland
Vice President, David Ward
Svp Small Business Administration, Adrienne Sipe
Svp And Credit Risk Manager, Darin Johnson
Vice President, Jack Yokley
Board Member, Luke Yancy
Board Member, Scott Niswonger
Board Member, Colin Reed
Board Member, Cecelia Stewart
Board Member, Rajesh Subramaniam
Auditors: KPMG LLP

LOCATIONS

HQ: First Horizon National Corp
165 Madison Avenue, Memphis, TN 38103
Phone: 901 523-4444
Web: www.firsthorizon.com

PRODUCTS/OPERATIONS

2014 Sales

	$ mil.	% of total
Interest		
Loans including fees	571.8	45
Investment securities	93.2	7
Trading securities	32.0	3
Loans held for sale	11.2	1
Other	1.1	-
Noninterest		
Capital markets	200.5	16
Deposit transactions & cash management	112.0	9
Mortagage banking	71.3	6
Brokerage management fees & commissions	49.1	4
Trust services and investment management	27.7	2
Bankcard income	23.7	2
Bank owned life insurance	16.4	1
Other	49.3	4
Total	**1,259.3**	**100**

COMPETITORS

Athens Federal Community Bank	JPMorgan Chase
BB&T	Regions Financial
Bank of America	SunTrust
Citigroup	Trustmark
	Wells Fargo

HISTORICAL FINANCIALS
Company Type: Public

Income Statement — FYE: December 31

	ASSETS ($ mil.)	NET INCOME ($ mil.)	INCOME AS % OF ASSETS	EMPLOYEES
12/18	40,832.2	545.0	1.3%	5,577
12/17	41,423.3	165.5	0.4%	5,984
12/16	28,555.2	227.0	0.8%	4,288
12/15	26,195.1	85.8	0.3%	4,293
12/14	25,672.8	219.5	0.9%	4,310
Annual Growth	12.3%	25.5%	—	6.7%

2018 Year-End Financials
Return on assets: 1.3%
Return on equity: 12.4%
Long-term debt ($ mil.): —
No. of shares (mil.): 318.5
Sales ($ mil): 2,268.8
Dividends
Yield: 3.6%
Payout: 29.0%
Market value ($ mil.): 4,192.0

	STOCK PRICE ($) FY Close	P/E High/Low		PER SHARE ($) Earnings	Dividends	Book Value
12/18	13.16	12	7	1.65	0.48	14.09
12/17	19.99	31	24	0.65	0.36	13.11
12/16	20.01	22	12	0.94	0.28	10.31
12/15	14.52	48	36	0.34	0.24	9.83
12/14	13.58	15	12	0.91	0.20	9.80
Annual Growth	(0.8%)	—	—	16.0%	24.5%	9.5%

First Internet Bancorp

EXECUTIVES

Vice President, Tom Natale
Vice President Asset Quality, Gregg Feigh
Vice President Of Commercial Loan Servicing, David Sewell
Vice President Commercial Lender, Carl Osberg
Vice President Commercial Lending, Jim Laine
Vice President Commercial Lending, Kevin Lynch
Vice President Of Commercial Banking Group, Christy Smith
Vice President Commercial Banking, Suzy Sottong
Vp Human Resources, Angie Redmon
Auditors: BKD, LLP

LOCATIONS

HQ: First Internet Bancorp
11201 USA Parkway, Fishers, IN 46037
Phone: 317 532-7900
Web: www.firstinternetbancorp.com

COMPETITORS

Bank of America	Citibank
BofI	E*TRADE Bank

HISTORICAL FINANCIALS
Company Type: Public

Income Statement — FYE: December 31

	ASSETS ($ mil.)	NET INCOME ($ mil.)	INCOME AS % OF ASSETS	EMPLOYEES
12/18	3,541.6	21.9	0.6%	201
12/17	2,767.6	15.2	0.6%	206
12/16	1,854.3	12.0	0.7%	192
12/15	1,269.8	8.9	0.7%	152
12/14	970.5	4.3	0.4%	143
Annual Growth	38.2%	50.0%	—	8.9%

2018 Year-End Financials
Return on assets: 0.6%
Return on equity: 8.5%
Long-term debt ($ mil.): —
No. of shares (mil.): 10.1
Sales ($ mil): 124.2
Dividends
Yield: 1.1%
Payout: 10.1%
Market value ($ mil.): 208.0

	STOCK PRICE ($) FY Close	P/E High/Low		PER SHARE ($) Earnings	Dividends	Book Value
12/18	20.44	18	8	2.30	0.24	28.39
12/17	38.15	19	12	2.13	0.24	26.65
12/16	32.00	14	10	2.30	0.24	23.76
12/15	28.69	18	7	1.96	0.24	23.28
12/14	16.74	26	16	0.96	0.24	21.80
Annual Growth	5.1%	—	—	24.4%	(0.0%)	6.8%

First Interstate BancSystem Inc

This Treasure State bank wants to be your treasury. First Interstate BancSystem is the holding company for First Interstate Bank which has about 80 branches in Montana western South Dakota and Wyoming. Serving area consumers businesses and municipalities the bank provides traditional services including deposit accounts wealth management and loans. Commercial loans including mortgages make up more than half of the bank's loan portfolio; residential real estate agricultural and construction loans round out its lending activities. On the wealth management side the bank has more than $8 billion in trust assets held in a fiduciary or agent capacity.

Financial Performance
The company's revenue decreased in fiscal 2013 compared to the previous period. It reported $369.3 million in revenue for fiscal 2013 down from $388.8 million in fiscal 2012. However despite the decreased annual revenue the company's net income increased in fiscal 2013 to $86 million up from a net income of $58 million the prior fiscal year. Cash flow increased by about $15 million in fiscal 2013 compared to 2012 levels.

Strategy
The company is always looking for opportunities for expansion including organic growth as well as growth through acquisitions. It expanded into the northwest growth market with the acquisition of Cascade Bancorp for around $589 million.

EXECUTIVES

SVP and CIO, Kevin J. Guenthner, age 55, $205,385 total compensation
President and CEO, Kevin P. Riley, age 59, $307,270 total compensation
EVP and Chief Banking Officer, Bill Gottwals
EVP and CFO, Marcy D. Mutch, age 59
Executive Vice President and Chief Banking Officer, Michael Huston
ASSISTANT VICE PRESIDENT AND PERSONAL BANKING OFFICER, Julie Mazza
Vice Chairman, James R. Scott, age 69
SECRETARY, Jana Garza
Auditors: RSM US LLP

LOCATIONS

HQ: First Interstate BancSystem Inc
401 North 31st Street, Billings, MT 59116-0918
Phone: 406 255-5390
Web: www.fibk.com

PRODUCTS/OPERATIONS

Selected ServicesBanking
Checking Accounts
Credit Cards
Debit Cards
Escrow Services
Foreign Currency
Overdraft Protection
Personal Resources
Prepaid Cards
Savings Accounts
Borrowing
AdvanceLine
Auto & Recreation
Debt Consolidation
Home Equity
Home Mortgage
Personal Loans
Create & Build Wealth
Long-Term Planning
Planning for the Unexpected
Saving for College
Saving for Retirement
Wealth Resources
Protect & Preserve Wealth
Asset Management
Employee Exit Strategies
Health Concerns
Investment Services
Retirement Plan Services
Sales 2015

Interest income	282.4	70
Non-interest income	121.0	30
Total	**403.4**	**100**

COMPETITORS

Bank of the West
Crazy Woman Creek
Eagle Bancorp
Glacier Bancorp
Great Western Bancorp
U.S. Bancorp
Wells Fargo

HISTORICAL FINANCIALS

Company Type: Public

Income Statement   FYE: December 31

	ASSETS ($ mil.)	NET INCOME ($ mil.)	INCOME AS % OF ASSETS	EMPLOYEES
12/18	13,300.2	160.2	1.2%	2,330
12/17	12,213.2	106.5	0.9%	2,207
12/16	9,063.9	95.6	1.1%	1,721
12/15	8,728.2	86.8	1.0%	1,742
12/14	8,609.9	84.2	1.0%	1,705
Annual Growth	11.5%	17.4%	—	8.1%

2018 Year-End Financials

Return on assets: 1.2%
Return on equity: 10.2%
Long-term debt ($ mil.): —
No. of shares (mil.): 60.6
Sales ($ mil): 616.7
Dividends Yield: 3.0%
Payout: 40.7%
Market value ($ mil.): 2,216.0

	STOCK PRICE ($) FY Close	P/E High/Low		PER SHARE ($)		
			Earnings	Dividends	Book Value	
12/18	36.56	17	13	2.75	1.12	27.94
12/17	40.05	22	16	2.05	0.96	25.28
12/16	42.55	20	12	2.13	0.88	21.87
12/15	29.07	16	12	1.90	0.80	20.92
12/14	27.82	16	13	1.87	0.64	19.85
Annual Growth	7.1%	—	—	10.1%	15.0%	8.9%

First Merchants Corp

First Merchants is the holding company that owns First Merchants Bank which operates some 120 branches in Indiana Illinois and western Ohio. Through its Lafayette Bank & Trust and First Merchants Private Wealth Advisors divisions the bank provides standard consumer and commercial banking services including checking and savings accounts CDs check cards and consumer commercial agricultural and real estate mortgage loans. First Merchants also provides trust and asset management services. Founded in 1982 First Merchants has nearly $9.4 billion worth of consolidated assets.

Operations
Real estate loans made up about 70% of First Merchants's loan portfolio while commercial and industrial agricultural and consumer loans account for the remainder of the bank's lending activity.

Geographic Reach
Muncie Indiana-based First Merchants's 120-plus bank branches are located across Indiana and in two counties each in Illinois and Ohio.

Sales and Marketing
First Merchants's marketing expense was $3.73 million in 2017 $3 million (2016) and $3.5 million (2015).

Financial Performance
Revenue jumped by 19% to $348.2 million in 2017 driven by higher interest income from more organic and inorganic loan business and more investment security income following the bank's recent acquisitions. The bank also collected significantly more non-interest income from deposit account service charges electronic card fees and insurance-related gains as it grew its customer base through acquisitions. Higher revenue drove the bank's net income up 18% to $96 million.

Total cash on hand at the end of fiscal 2017 stood at $154.9 million which was $27 million higher than cash at the start of the year. Cash from operations contributed $126 million and cash generated through financing activities added $535.8 while investments in securities and other uses used $635.3 million.

Strategy
A key part of the First Merchants's growth strategy is to expand geographically through acquisitions of small community banks operating in its key Indiana Illinois and western Ohio markets.

In 2017 and 2018 First Merchants added more nearly 3 dozen branches to its banking network after acquiring Michigan-based Monroe Bank & Trust Ohio-based Arlington Bank and Independent Alliance Banks located in Indiana. The bank has in recent years acquired 1-2 community banks operating in these states each year often adding a handful of branches as well as loans and other assets through each transaction.

Mergers and Acquisitions
In 2018 First Merchants acquired MBT Financial Corporation the holding company for Monroe Bank & Trust and its 20 branches serving Monroe Michigan and the southeastern Michigan area.

In 2017 First Merchants bought Columbus Ohio-based Arlington Bank. for $82.6 million. The same year it spent $238.8 million to acquire a majority stake in Independent Alliance Banks and IAB's 16 banking centers located in and around Fort Wayne Indiana.

EXECUTIVES

First Vice President Corporate Controller, Jeff Lorentson
EVP and CFO, Mark K. Hardwick, age 48, $317,347 total compensation
CTO, Stephan H. Fluhler, $205,268 total compensation
President and CEO, Michael C. (Mike) Rechin, age 60, $502,181 total compensation
EVP and Chief Banking Officer, Michael J. (Mike) Stewart, age 53, $310,077 total compensation
EVP and Chief Credit Officer, John J. Martin, age 52, $249,193 total compensation
SVP and Chief Risk Officer, Jeffery B. Lorentson
Vice President oF marketing, Deanne Beard
Vice President, Tom Dunson
Vice President of Loans, Christopher Allen
Vice President Marketing Manager, Dana Talaga
Vice President Cash Management, Jennifer Wehrly
Vice President Commercial Lending, Greg Lanter
Vice President, Lentz Gregory
Executive Vice President Mortgage Operations, Debra Rynearson
Senior Vice President Human RE, Leslie Holland
Vice President and Purchasing Director, Lisa Brothers
Vice President, Joseph Keyler
Vice President, Alex Jones
Assistant Vice President Relationship Manager, Michael Kahne
Vice President, Margaret Hoke
Senior Vice President, John Ditmars
Vice President Manager Small Business Credit, Robert Spencer
Assistant Vice President Banking Center Manager, Veronica Avila
Senior Vice President Chief Sales Officer Lakeshore Region, Dale Clapp
Senior Vice President and Director of Human Resources, Kim A Ellington
Vice President Retail Market L, Roberta Salway
Vice President Structured Finance, Dave Decraene
Vice President, Daniel J Gick
Vice President Retail Lending Leader, Jill Engerer
Vice President, Candy Shumard
Vice President, James F Zimmerman
Assistant Vice President, Tammy Hall
First Vice President, Mark Stevenson
Vice President, Jeffrey Lorentson
Vice President, Josh McKenney
Vice President, Adam Treibic
Assistant Vice President Merchant Services, Brad Garrison

Vice President Manager Mortgage Sales, Elizabeth Chenore
Vice President Senior Product Manager, LuAnne Whewell
Vice President Relationship Manager III, Kevin Wagner
Assistant Vice President Business Banking Officer, Duane Kamminga
Senior Vice President And Director Of Finance, Michele Kawiecki
Assistant Vice President, Rob Garrett
Vice President Information Systems Director, Kevin Scharnowske
Assistant Vice President, Derek Rogers
Assistant Vice President Banking Center Manager, Sally Conyers
VICE PRESIDENT AND CLIENT ADVISOR, Rita K Smith
VICE PRESIDENT, Benjamin J Hartings
ASSISTANT VICE PRESIDENT MANAGER FACILITIES PROJECTS AND PLANNING, Lindsay S Sweet
VICE PRESIDENT RELATIONSHIP MANAGER III, Kevin M Orourke
VICE PRESIDENT RETIREMENT PLAN ADVISOR, Kristopher Feldmeyer
Vice President, Bill Robertson
Vice President Manager Commercial Lending, Scott Casbon
Senior Vice President, Brian Emmons
Vp Mortgage Operations Merchant Bank, Toni Nisbit
Assistant Vice President Executive Assistant To The Chief Operating Officer Chief Financial Officer, Nicole Weaver
VICE PRESIDENT, Paul Orner
VICE PRESIDENT MANAGER COMMERCIAL BANKING, John Novosel
Senior Vice President, Joseph Peterson
VICE PRESIDENT RELATIONSHIP MANAGER III, Kevin Orourke
Vice President Commercial Lending, Clark Scott
Vice President Account Executive, Lehman Gary
First Vice President Director Talent Development, Sharissa Ulrey
Svp Cash Management, Patty Hudson
Senior Vice President Director Of Human Resources, Steven Harris
Board Member, Terry Walker
Chairman, Charles E. Schalliol, age 72
Board Member, Patrick Sherman
Board Member, Robert R Halderman
Auditors: BKD, LLP

LOCATIONS

HQ: First Merchants Corp
  200 East Jackson Street, Muncie, IN 47305-2814
Phone: 765 747-1500
Web: www.firstmerchants.com

PRODUCTS/OPERATIONS

2017 Sales

	$ mil.	% of total
Interest		
Loans	274.4	71
Investment Securities	38.9	10
Federal Reserve and Federal Home Loan Bank stock	.9	-
Interest Expense/Other	(36.9)	-
Non-interest		
Service charges on deposits	18.7	5
Fiduciary activities	11.6	3
Other customer fees	20.9	5
Earnings on cash surrender value of life insurance	3.9	1
Net gains and fees on sales of loans	7.6	2
Net realized gains on sales of available for sale securities	2.6	1
Others	5.7	2
Total	**348.3**	**100**

COMPETITORS

Ameriana Bancorp
Bank of America
Citigroup
Harris
JPMorgan Chase
MutualFirst Financial
NorthWest Indiana Bancorp
Old National Bancorp
STAR Financial Group
U.S. Bancorp

HISTORICAL FINANCIALS

Company Type: Public

Income Statement				FYE: December 31
	ASSETS ($ mil.)	NET INCOME ($ mil.)	INCOME AS % OF ASSETS	EMPLOYEES
12/18	9,884.7	159.1	1.6%	1,702
12/17	9,367.4	96.0	1.0%	1,684
12/16	7,211.6	81.0	1.1%	1,449
12/15	6,761.0	65.3	1.0%	1,529
12/14	5,824.1	60.1	1.0%	1,415
Annual Growth	14.1%	27.5%	—	4.7%

2018 Year-End Financials

Return on assets: 1.6%
Return on equity: 11.7%
Long-term debt ($ mil.): —
No. of shares (mil.): 49.3
Sales ($ mil): 484.4
Dividends
  Yield: 2.4%
  Payout: 26.0%
Market value ($ mil.): 1,691.0

	STOCK PRICE ($) FY Close	P/E High/Low	PER SHARE ($) Earnings	Dividends	Book Value
12/18	34.27	15 10	3.22	0.84	28.54
12/17	42.06	21 17	2.12	0.69	26.52
12/16	37.65	19 11	1.98	0.54	22.04
12/15	25.42	16 13	1.72	0.41	20.92
12/14	22.75	14 12	1.65	0.29	19.29
Annual Growth	10.8%	—	18.2%	30.5%	10.3%

First Mid Bancshares Inc

EXECUTIVES

Vice President Branch Operations And Cashier, Rhonda Rawlings
Vice President Marketing, Rodney Morris
Executive Vice President, Clay Dean
Assistant Vice President, Jaci Manzella
Vice President, Darlene Johnson
Assistant Vice President, Dena Clifton
Senior Management (Senior Vice President General Manager Director), Jason Tucker
Assistant Vice President Mortgage Lending, Mary White
Senior Vice President, Robert Weber
Senior Vice President Risk Management, Christopher Slabach
Vice President, Theresa Mangieri
SENIOR VICE PRESIDENT, Andrew Zavarella
Assistant Vice President Mortgage Loan Administration, Sue Radloff
Vice Presidents, Nancy Zike
Vice President Regional Lending Manager, Dave Garrett
Vice President Director of Marketing, Laura Zuhone
Sr V Pres, Rhonda Gatons
Vice President, Jack Franklin
Board Member, Holly Bailey
Board Member, Gary Melvin
Board Member, Mary Westerhold
Board Member, Robert Cook
Board Member, James Zimmer
Auditors: BKD, LLP

LOCATIONS

HQ: First Mid Bancshares Inc
  1421 Charleston Avenue, Mattoon, IL 61938
Phone: 217 234-7454   **Fax:** 217 258-0485
Web: www.firstmid.com

PRODUCTS/OPERATIONS

Selected Subsidiaries

The Checkley Agency Inc. (dba First Mid Insurance Group)
First Mid-Illinois Bank & Trust N.A.
First Mid-Illinois Statutory Trust I II
Mid-Illinois Data Services Inc.

COMPETITORS

Bank of America
Fifth Third
First BancTrust
First Busey
Northern Trust
PNC Financial
U.S. Bancorp

HISTORICAL FINANCIALS

Company Type: Public

Income Statement				FYE: December 31
	ASSETS ($ mil.)	NET INCOME ($ mil.)	INCOME AS % OF ASSETS	EMPLOYEES
12/18	3,839.7	36.6	1.0%	818
12/17	2,841.5	26.6	0.9%	592
12/16	2,884.5	21.8	0.8%	598
12/15	2,114.5	16.5	0.8%	513
12/14	1,607.1	15.4	1.0%	400
Annual Growth	24.3%	24.0%	—	19.6%

2018 Year-End Financials

Return on assets: 1.1%
Return on equity: 9.3%
Long-term debt ($ mil.): —
No. of shares (mil.): 16.6
Sales ($ mil): 159.9
Dividends
  Yield: 3.2%
  Payout: 45.4%
Market value ($ mil.): 531.0

	STOCK PRICE ($) FY Close	P/E High/Low	PER SHARE ($) Earnings	Dividends	Book Value
12/18	31.92	17 12	2.52	1.04	28.59
12/17	38.54	20 14	2.13	0.66	24.32
12/16	34.00	17 11	2.05	0.62	22.51
12/15	26.00	14 10	1.81	0.59	24.25
12/14	18.55	13 9	1.85	0.55	23.45
Annual Growth	14.5%	—	8.0%	17.3%	5.1%

First Midwest Bancorp, Inc. (Naperville, IL)

There's a lot of cabbage in corn country. Just ask First Midwest Bancorp the holding company for First Midwest Bank. Through nearly 110 branches the bank mainly serves suburban Chicago though its market extends into central and western Illinois and neighboring portions of Iowa and Indiana. Focusing on area small to mid-sized businesses it offers deposit products loans trust services wealth management insurance and retirement plan services; it has $7.2 billion of client trust and investment assets under management. Commercial real estate loans account for more than half of the company's portfolio.

Operations
More than 85% of the company's loan portfolio consists of corporate loans (the majority of which are secured by commercial real estate) while the remainder of the portfolio consists of consumer loans (which include home equity loans lines of credit and 1-4 family mortgages). Illustrative of its commitment to business lending First Midwest does not originate sub-prime lending or investment banking activities.

The bank's subsidiaries include: equipment leasing and commercial financier First Midwest Equipment Finance Co.; investment security managers First Midwest Securities Management LLC and First Midwest Holdings Inc.; Section 8 housing venture investor LIH Holdings; and Synergy Property Holdings LLC which manages the bank's OREO properties.

Geographic Reach
The company operates 109 banking offices largely located in various communities throughout the suburban metropolitan Chicago market as well as central and western Illinois and eastern Iowa. It owns 145 automated teller machines most of which are housed at banking locations. First Midwest and Allpoint together provide access to more than 50000 free ATMs worldwide.

Sales and Marketing
The company serves different industry segments including manufacturing health care pharmaceutical higher education wholesale and retail trade service and agricultural. First Midwest spent about $8.2 million on advertising and promotions in 2014 up from $7.8 million in 2013 and $5.1 million in 2012.

Financial Performance
Following a modest rebound in 2013 First Midwest's revenue in 2014 dipped by less than 1% to $426.48 million mostly because of a 76% drop in net securities gains as the bank in 2013 was able to collect a non-recurring equity investment sale gain of $34 million. Lower mortgage banking income resulting from lower market pricing also contributed to the modest dip in revenue. The bank did however report higher interest income as its loan business grew higher wealth management fees with growth in assets under management and higher service charge fees as deposit accounts grew.

After healthy profit growth in 2013 net income fell by nearly 13% to $69.31 million in 2014 mostly as the bank incurred higher costs associated with the acquisition and integration of Popular and Great Lakes and because the bank had higher loan loss provision expenses. In 2013 First Midwest had posted a large jump in net income thanks to higher revenue a decrease in the provision for loan and covered loan losses and lower interest and non-interest expenses.

Continuing its annual cash declines the bank's operations provided $122.93 million (or 10% less cash than in 2013) mostly due to lower earnings.

Mergers and Acquisitions
First Midwest Bancorp acquired Bridgeview Bank in 2019. Bridgeview has about $1.1 billion in assets $755 million in loans and $1 billion in deposits.

In early 2017 the company completed the acquisition of another Chicago-area bank Standard Bancshares. The deal will add 35 branches $2.3 billion in assets $2.1 billion in deposits and $1.9 million in loans.

Company Background
First Midwest capitalized on the rash of bank failures that have occurred in the Chicago area amid the recessionary economy. Its relative financial soundness put it in a position to acquire three failed Illinois banks through separate FDIC-facilitated transactions in 2009 and 2010: First DuPage Bank Peotone Bank and Trust and Palos Bank and Trust. The deals which included loss-sharing agreements with the regulator added a total of nearly 10 branches. In 2012 the company acquired the deposits and loans of Waukegan Savings Bank in another FDIC-assisted deal that added two more branches to its network. First Midwest will continue to consider acquisitions of failed banks in the Chicago area.

EXECUTIVES

President CEO and Director; Chairman and CEO First Midwest Bank, Michael L. Scudder, age 58, $750,000 total compensation
EVP CIO and COO First Midwest Bank, Kent S. Belasco, age 68, $224,000 total compensation
EVP and CFO First Midwest Bancorp Inc. & First Midwest Bank, Paul F. Clemens, age 67, $376,000 total compensation
SEVP and COO; Vice Chairman and President First Midwest Bank, Mark G. Sander, age 60, $545,000 total compensation
EVP and Treasurer First Midwest Bancorp Inc. & First Midwest Bank, James P. Hotchkiss, age 62
EVP and Chief Risk Officer First Midwest Bancorp Inc. & First Midwest Bank, Kevin L. Moffitt
EVP Corporate Secretary and General Counsel, Nicholas J. Chulos
Senior Vice President, Heidi Smithson
Avp Loan Operations System Administrator, Kwicha Nettles
Vice President Field, Phillip Tan
Vice President, Juan Cortez
Executive Vice President and Director Commercial Banking First Midwest Bank, Victor Carapella
Senior Vice President, Jim Schramm
Vice President Compliance Review Manager, Beth Uhlir
First Vice President, Ed Garner
Vice President, Marianne Coneset
Senior Vice President, Rob Schultz
Vice President Administration, Cheri Rubocki
Vice President Administration, Connie Steinke
Executive Vice President Chief Administrative Officer, Dean Glassberg
Vice President, Mike Trunck
Vice President, Martha Sandoval
Vice President, Sue Barreto
Vice President, Jodie Speers
Senior Vice President Director Applic, John Hudak
Assistant Vice President, Justin Luppino
Senior Vice President Financial Planning, Rich Padula
Assistant Vice President Regional Recruitment Manager, Michael Gossen
Vice President Area Sales Manager, Evan Klee
Senior Vice President, Matthew Burns
Vice President Public Funds, Susan Wade
Vice President And Assistant General Counsel, Steve Babinski
Senior Vice President BusinessBanking Group Manager, Chris Esposito
Vice President Treasury Management, Ala Swais
Senior Vice President Wealth Management, Chris Ksoll
Senior Vice President, John Gaughan
Assistant Vice President, Megan Miller
Business Banking Relationship Manager III And Assistant Vice President, Michelle Payla
Vice President, Nick Yerkes
Vice President Business Banking, Dave Kurow
Vice President, Chad Lyons
Vice President, Gia Ormond
Vice President Commercial Banking, Abdullah Tadros
Vice President, Angela Hart
Senior Vice President Total Rewards, Steven Kull
Svp Head Structured Finance, Joseph Angel
Senior Vice President Commercial Banking, James Schramm
Executive Vice President And Chief Risk Officer, Jeff Newcom
Vice President Commercial Banking Officer, Sheela Prahlad
Assistant Vice President, Andrew Trasatt
Vice President Business Banking, Tony Martino
Senior Vice President, Steve Clingen
Vice President Sales Regional Sales Manager, Joe Creamons
Vice President Middle Market Banking, Chris Hannon
Vice President Commercial Banking Officer, Tim Meyer
Vice President ABL Relationship Manager Business Credit, Thomas Brennan
Vice President Trust Relationship Manager, Michael Lambert
Vice President Senior Talent Acquisition Manager, Jeff Boulos
Senior Vice President Structured Finance, Aaron Markos
Vice President CRA Manager, Mary Morstadt
Vice President Franchise Banking Group, Kara Symeonides
Vice President, Robert Rodie
Senior Vice President Manager Business Banking, Brian Burke
Senior Vice President, Matthew Brennan
Vice President, Rick Lang
Vice President Group Sales Manager, Joseph Palazzolo
Senior Vice President, Jim Ringer
Vice President Senior Human Resources Consultant, Anita Dwyer
Vice President, Dana Pike
Vice President Centralized Credit Underwriting, Jesse Newkirk
Senior Vice President Audit Services Director, Ted Roknich
Vice President Colleague Communications, Bridget Glavaz

Vice President First Midwest Bank, Nancy Henningfield
Vice President Regional Recruitment Manager, Linda Cleveland
Senior Vice President, Neil Prendergast
Vice President Mortgage Underwriting Manager, Erin Wehman
AVP HR Consultant (Business Partner), Amy Crabbe
Senior Vice President Healthcare Banking Coverage Group, James Goody
Vice President, Terrence Duffy
Svp And Director Corporate Communications, Maurissa Kanter
Executive Vice President And Chief Human Resources Officer, Doug Rose
Executive Vice President And Chief Credit Officer, Kevin Geoghegan
Vice President, Constance Simms
Senior Vice President, William Almond
Senior Vice President Healthcare Finance, Michael Mason
Chairman, Robert P. (Bob) O'Meara, age 81
Board Member, Barbara Boigegrain
Auditors: Ernst & Young LLP

LOCATIONS

HQ: First Midwest Bancorp, Inc. (Naperville, IL)
 8750 West Bryn Mawr Avenue, Suite 1300, Chicago, IL 60631-3655
Phone: 703 831-7483
Web: www.firstmidwest.com

PRODUCTS/OPERATIONS

2016

	$ mil.	% of total
Interest Income		
Loans	338.0	63
Investment securities - taxable	28.7	5
Investment securities - tax-exempt	8.7	2
Other short-term investments	2.9	0
Noninterest Income		
Service charges on deposit accounts	40.7	8
Wealth management fees	33.1	6
Card-based fees	29.1	5
Merchant servicing fees	12.5	2
Mortgage banking income	10.1	2
Capital market products income	10.0	2
Other service charges commissions and fees	9.6	2
Net gain on sale-leaseback transaction	5.5	1
BOLI income	3.7	1
Net securities gains	1.4	0
Other income	3.6	1
Total	**537.6**	**100**

COMPETITORS

Bank of America
BankFinancial
Cummins-Allison
Fifth Third
First Busey
Harris
JPMorgan Chase
Meta Financial Group
Northern Trust
PrivateBank
QCR Holdings
West Suburban Bancorp
Wintrust Financial

HISTORICAL FINANCIALS
Company Type: Public

Income Statement FYE: December 31

	ASSETS ($ mil.)	NET INCOME ($ mil.)	INCOME AS % OF ASSETS	EMPLOYEES
12/18	15,505.6	157.8	1.0%	2,046
12/17	14,077.0	98.3	0.7%	2,152
12/16	11,422.5	92.3	0.8%	1,882
12/15	9,732.6	82.0	0.8%	1,790
12/14	9,445.1	69.3	0.7%	1,788
Annual Growth	13.2%	22.9%	—	3.4%

2018 Year-End Financials

Return on assets: 1.0%
Return on equity: 8.0%
Long-term debt ($ mil.): —
No. of shares (mil.): 106.3
Sales ($ mil): 727.0
Dividends
 Yield: 2.2%
 Payout: 38.7%
Market value ($ mil.): 2,107.0

	STOCK PRICE ($) FY Close	P/E High/Low		PER SHARE ($) Earnings	Dividends	Book Value
12/18	19.81	18	12	1.52	0.45	19.32
12/17	24.01	27	22	0.96	0.39	18.16
12/16	25.23	22	14	1.14	0.36	15.46
12/15	18.43	19	15	1.05	0.36	14.70
12/14	17.11	19	17	0.92	0.31	14.17
Annual Growth	3.7%	—	—	13.4%	9.8%	8.1%

First National Corp. (Strasburg, VA)

EXECUTIVES

Senior Vice President, Lisa Ghost
Vice President Sales And Marketing, Laura Allen
Executive Vice President and Chief Financial Officer of the Company and the Bank, Shane Bell
Senior Vice President, Susan M Ralls
Vice President, Kevin Nixon
Vice President, Darcus Breneman
Board Member, Elizabeth H Cottrell
Member Board Of Directors, Emily Beck
Board Member, Michael Funk
Board Member, Gerald Smith
Auditors: Yount, Hyde & Barbour, P.C.

LOCATIONS

HQ: First National Corp. (Strasburg, VA)
 112 West King Street, Strasburg, VA 22657
Phone: 540 465-9121
Web: www.fbvirginia.com

COMPETITORS

BB&T
Bank of America
Bank of the James
F & M Bank
Fauquier Bankshares
Pioneer Bankshares

HISTORICAL FINANCIALS
Company Type: Public

Income Statement FYE: December 31

	ASSETS ($ mil.)	NET INCOME ($ mil.)	INCOME AS % OF ASSETS	EMPLOYEES
12/18	752.9	10.1	1.3%	160
12/17	739.1	6.4	0.9%	160
12/16	716.0	5.9	0.8%	153
12/15	692.3	2.6	0.4%	187
12/14	518.1	7.6	1.5%	156
Annual Growth	9.8%	7.4%	—	0.6%

2018 Year-End Financials

Return on assets: 1.3%
Return on equity: 16.2%
Long-term debt ($ mil.): —
No. of shares (mil.): 4.9
Sales ($ mil): 40.3
Dividends
 Yield: 1.0%
 Payout: 9.8%
Market value ($ mil.): 96.0

	STOCK PRICE ($) FY Close	P/E High/Low		PER SHARE ($) Earnings	Dividends	Book Value
12/18	19.40	11	9	2.04	0.20	13.45
12/17	18.00	14	10	1.30	0.14	11.76
12/16	12.85	11	7	1.20	0.12	10.58
12/15	8.95	32	26	0.31	0.10	9.35
12/14	8.65	7	4	1.32	0.08	12.14
Annual Growth	22.4%	—	—	11.5%	27.8%	2.6%

First Northern Community Bancorp

EXECUTIVES

Senior Vice President, Steve Mccurley
Vice President, Patricia Armlin
Vice President Loan Officer, Joan Schindel
Avp Commercial Loan Officer, Lydia Looknanan
Vice President, Juanita Holmes
Vice President Community Relations Officer, Carol Garcia
Auditors: Moss Adams LLP

LOCATIONS

HQ: First Northern Community Bancorp
 195 N. First Street, Dixon, CA 95620
Phone: 707 678-3041
Web: www.thatsmybank.com

COMPETITORS

Bank of America
Bank of the West
Citibank
MUFG Americas Holdings
RCB Corp.
U.S. Bancorp
Westamerica

HISTORICAL FINANCIALS

Company Type: Public

Income Statement FYE: December 31

	ASSETS ($ mil.)	NET INCOME ($ mil.)	INCOME AS % OF ASSETS	EMPLOYEES
12/18	1,249.8	12.5	1.0%	201
12/17	1,217.6	8.7	0.7%	191
12/16	1,166.7	8.0	0.7%	185
12/15	1,044.6	6.9	0.7%	212
12/14	957.8	5.8	0.6%	209
Annual Growth	6.9%	20.9%	—	(1.0%)

2018 Year-End Financials

Return on assets: 1.0%
Return on equity: 11.8%
Long-term debt ($ mil.): —
No. of shares (mil.): 12.2
Sales ($ mil): 52.8
Dividends
Yield: —
Payout: —
Market value ($ mil.): 137.0

	STOCK PRICE ($) FY Close	P/E High/Low	PER SHARE ($) Earnings	Dividends	Book Value
12/18	11.14	14 11	1.04	0.00	9.18
12/17	13.30	18 13	0.72	0.00	8.19
12/16	9.60	15 11	0.67	0.00	7.58
12/15	8.19	15 13	0.56	0.00	7.08
12/14	7.92	18 15	0.48	0.00	7.64
Annual Growth	8.9%	— —	21.2%	—	4.7%

First Northwest Bancorp

Auditors: Moss Adams LLP

LOCATIONS

HQ: First Northwest Bancorp
105 West 8th Street, Port Angeles, WA 98362
Phone: 360 457-0461
Web: www.ourfirstfed.com

HISTORICAL FINANCIALS

Company Type: Public

Income Statement FYE: December 31

	ASSETS ($ mil.)	NET INCOME ($ mil.)	INCOME AS % OF ASSETS	EMPLOYEES
12/18	1,258.7	7.1	0.6%	210
12/17*	1,215.6	1.6	0.1%	204
06/17	1,087.6	5.1	0.5%	204
06/16	1,010.1	3.9	0.4%	178
06/15	936.8	(5.0)	—	157
Annual Growth	7.7%	—	—	7.5%

*Fiscal year change

2018 Year-End Financials

Return on assets: 0.5%
Return on equity: 4.0%
Long-term debt ($ mil.): —
No. of shares (mil.): 11.1
Sales ($ mil): 51.7
Dividends
Yield: 0.2%
Payout: 5.3%
Market value ($ mil.): 166.0

	STOCK PRICE ($) FY Close	P/E High/Low	PER SHARE ($) Earnings	Dividends	Book Value
12/18	14.83	26 20	0.68	0.03	15.42
12/17*	16.30	114 95	0.16	0.00	15.02
06/17	15.77	37 28	0.46	0.00	14.93
06/16	12.74	43 36	0.33	0.00	14.97
06/15	12.47	— —	(0.42)	0.00	14.56
Annual Growth	4.4%	— —	—	—	1.5%

*Fiscal year change

First of Long Island Corp

When it comes to banking The First of Long Island wants to be the first thing on Long Islanders' minds. The company owns The First National Bank of Long Island which offers a variety of lending investment and deposit services through around 45 commercial and retail branches on New York's Long Island and the boroughs of Manhattan and Queens. Residential and Commercial Mortgages (particularly tied to multifamily properties) make up more than 90% of the bank's loan portfolio though the bank also writes revolving home equity business and consumer loans. Its two bank subsidiaries include insurance agency The First of Long Island Agency and investment firm FNY Service.

Operations
The First National Bank of Long Island also operates an investment management division that offers trust and investment management estate and custody services.

The bank makes more than 90% of its revenue from interest income. About 70% of its total revenue came from loan interest during 2015 while another 21% came from interest income on taxable and non-taxable investment securities. The rest of its revenue came from deposit account service charges (3% of revenue) investment management division income (2%) gains on securities sales (1%) and other income sources.

Geographic Reach
The New York City-based bank operated 45 branches at the end of 2015 including 41 in Long Island and two each in Manhattan and Queens.

Sales and Marketing
First serves individuals professionals corporations institutions and governmental clients through its branches.

The bank markets its services through customer service personnel tele-sales lending relationships referral sources and advertisements. It spent $877000 on marketing during 2015 compared to $927000 and $670000 in 2014 and 2013 respectively.

Financial Performance
The First of Long Island's annual revenues have risen more than 20% since 2011 as its loan assets have more than doubled to $2.25 billion. Meanwhile the bank's profits have swelled more than 30% thanks to revenue growth and low interest expenses.

First's revenue jumped 13% to $101 million during 2015 mostly thanks to higher interest income as its average loan balances grew 26% and as its non-taxable security assets rose by 6%. The bulk of the loan asset growth was tied to residential mortgages while most of the rest came from multi-family commercial mortgage growth.

Double-digit revenue growth drove the bank's net income up 12% to $25.9 million. First's operating cash levels dipped 1% to $35 million despite the rise in earnings due to unfavorable working capital changes mostly related to a decrease in accrued expenses and other liabilities.

Strategy
The bank has been opening new branches utilizing "effective relationship management" using targeted solicitation efforts and expanding its product and service offerings to boost its loan and deposit business in recent years.

In early 2016 the company planned to open between eight and 12 more The First National Bank of Long Island branches in Queens after opening two branches there in Howard Beach and Whitestone in 2015. It also planned to open branches in Brooklyn. Expanding its branch network on Long Island the bank in 2015 launched new branches in Patchogue and Melville.

EXECUTIVES

SVP and EVP and Senior Lending Officer Commercial Lending The First National Bank Long Island, Donald L. Manfredonia, age 67, $222,500 total compensation
SVP, Richard Kick, age 61, $230,100 total compensation
SVP and Treasurer; EVP CFO and Cashier The First National Bank of Long Island, Mark D. Curtis, age 64, $242,700 total compensation
President and CEO The First of Long Island Corporation and The First National Bank of Long Island, Michael N. Vittorio, age 66, $468,000 total compensation
SVP and Secretary; SEVP The First National Bank of Long Island, Sallyanne K. Ballweg, age 63, $264,000 total compensation
EVP and Chief Risk Officer First National Bank of Long Island, Christopher Becker
Vice President, Jane Reed
Assistant Vice President, Giuseppe Sparacino
Vice President, Robert Eisen
Vice President And Trust Officer, Sharon Pazienza
Vice President Director Of Human Resources, Sue Hempton
Vice President Director Of Marketing, Laura Ierulli
Avp Branch Administration, Kalpa Ved
Senior Vice President And Chief Investment Officer, Jay Mcconie
Executive Vice President, Christopher Hilton
Chairman The First of Long Island Corporation and The First National Bank of Long Island, Walter C. Teagle, age 69
Auditors: Crowe LLP

LOCATIONS

HQ: First of Long Island Corp
10 Glen Head Road, Glen Head, NY 11545
Phone: 516 671-4900
Web: www.fnbli.com

First Savings Financial Group Inc

PRODUCTS/OPERATIONS

2015 Sales

	$ mil.	% of total
Interest and dividend income:		
Loans	70.6	70
Investment securities		
Taxable	8.0	8
Nontaxable	13.6	13
Noninterest income		
Investment Management Division income	2.0	2
Service charges on deposit accounts	2.6	3
Net gains on sales of securities	1.3	1
Other	2.8	3
Total	**100.9**	**100**

Selected Services:
Checking
Savings
Saving for Retirement & Education
Online Banking & Bill Pay
FirstLink Online Banking
Quicken/Quickbooks
FirstPay Bill PayPop
MoneyAccount to Account Transfers

COMPETITORS

Astoria Financial
Bank of America
Citibank
Dime Community Bancshares
Flushing Financial
JPMorgan Chase
New York Community Bancorp
Ridgewood Savings Bank
Suffolk Bancorp

HISTORICAL FINANCIALS
Company Type: Public

Income Statement FYE: December 31

	ASSETS ($ mil.)	NET INCOME ($ mil.)	INCOME AS % OF ASSETS	EMPLOYEES
12/18	4,241.0	41.5	1.0%	344
12/17	3,894.7	35.1	0.9%	333
12/16	3,510.3	30.8	0.9%	314
12/15	3,130.3	25.8	0.8%	302
12/14	2,721.4	23.0	0.8%	284
Annual Growth	11.7%	15.9%	—	4.9%

2018 Year-End Financials

Return on assets: 1.0%
Return on equity: 11.2%
Long-term debt ($ mil.): —
No. of shares (mil.): 25.4
Sales ($ mil): 140.5
Dividends
Yield: 3.1%
Payout: 40.5%
Market value ($ mil.): 507.0

	STOCK PRICE ($) FY Close	P/E High/Low		PER SHARE ($) Earnings	Dividends	Book Value
12/18	19.95	18	12	1.63	0.62	15.27
12/17	28.50	22	18	1.43	0.58	14.37
12/16	28.55	30	19	1.34	0.55	12.90
12/15	30.00	26	19	1.22	0.52	11.85
12/14	28.37	39	21	1.10	0.47	11.20
Annual Growth	(8.4%)	—	—	10.3%	7.1%	8.1%

First Savings Financial Group Inc

EXECUTIVES

Vice President Commercial Real Estate, Sean Keane
Assistant Vice President Credit Administration, Kyle Whittinghill
Senior Vice President, Douglas E Pearson
Risk Officer Vice President, Michelle Sloan
Auditors: Monroe Shine & Co., Inc.

LOCATIONS

HQ: First Savings Financial Group Inc
501 East Lewis & Clark Parkway, Clarksville, IN 47129
Phone: 812 283-0724
Web: www.fsbbank.net

COMPETITORS

First Capital
JPMorgan Chase
PNC Financial
Regions Financial
River Valley Bancorp

HISTORICAL FINANCIALS
Company Type: Public

Income Statement FYE: September 30

	ASSETS ($ mil.)	NET INCOME ($ mil.)	INCOME AS % OF ASSETS	EMPLOYEES
09/19	1,222.5	16.1	1.3%	473
09/18	1,034.4	10.9	1.1%	364
09/17	891.1	9.3	1.0%	201
09/16	796.5	7.9	1.0%	178
09/15	749.9	6.7	0.9%	170
Annual Growth	13.0%	24.4%	—	29.2%

2019 Year-End Financials

Return on assets: 1.4%
Return on equity: 14.7%
Long-term debt ($ mil.): —
No. of shares (mil.): 2.3
Sales ($ mil): 94.8
Dividends
Yield: 1.0%
Payout: 10.3%
Market value ($ mil.): 149.0

	STOCK PRICE ($) FY Close	P/E High/Low		PER SHARE ($) Earnings	Dividends	Book Value
09/19	63.22	10	6	6.82	0.63	51.51
09/18	68.28	15	11	4.60	0.59	43.11
09/17	53.40	13	8	3.97	0.55	41.52
09/16	36.16	10	9	3.41	0.51	39.27
09/15	34.00	11	8	2.93	0.47	43.21
Annual Growth	16.8%	—	—	23.5%	7.6%	4.5%

FirstCash Inc

FirstCash operates more than 2000 pawnshops and cash advance stores in the US Mexico El Salvador and Guatemala. The company lends money secured by such personal property as jewelry electronics tools sporting goods musical equipment and firearms (in select markets). Its First Cash Pawn and Famous Pawn shops sell merchandise forfeited by borrowers. The company's Fast Cash Advance locations offer short-term and payday loans. The company exited the check cashing business in late 2014 when it discontinued its Cash & Go joint venture. The company then named First Cash Financial Services merged with US pawn rival Cash America International in September 2016.

Change in Company Type

In 2016 First Cash Financial Services and Cash America International completed a $2.4 billion "merger of equals" deal to form a new company FirstCash. The merger combined First Cash Financial's large store count in Mexico and presence in Guatemala and El Salvador with Cash America's large store count in the US creating one of the largest pawn store networks in the US and Latin America with more than 2000 stores across four countries.

Operations

Prior to the merger First Cash Financial Services made most of its money from merchandise sales. About 63% of its total revenue came from retail merchandise sales of collateral forfeitures and over-the-counter store purchases during 2015 while another 28% of revenue came from pawn loan fees. The rest of its income came from wholesale scrap jewelry revenue (5% of revenue) and consumer loan and credit services fees (4%).

Geographic Reach

In 2015 Texas-based First Cash Financial Services operated 705 stores in 29 states in Mexico another 338 shops in 14 US states (with its largest markets being in Texas Colorado Maryland and the Carolinas) and 32 stores in Guatemala. The company generated 52% of its revenue from its shops in the Latin American countries during 2015 with most of that coming from Mexico.

Sales and Marketing

The company has been cutting back on its advertising spend in recent years. It spent $679000 on advertising during 2015 down from $1.33 million and $2.24 million in 2014 and 2013 respectively.

Financial Performance

Fueled by rapid store expansion and growing merchandise sales annual revenues and profits have been trending higher over the past few years.

The company's revenue dipped 1% to $704.6 million during 2015 however mostly due to a decline in wholesale scrap jewelry sales as it sold less gold and as gold prices fell from $1268 per ounce to just $1145 per ounce for the year. Its consumer loan income shrank 24% as it continued to wind down its Cash & Go business and due to increased competition and regulation.

Revenue declines in 2015 combined with an uptick in interest expenses and store operating expenses from newly acquired or opened stores made net income plunge 29% to $60.7 million for the year. Operating cash levels tumbled 5% to $92.7 million in 2015 as cash-based earnings declined.

Strategy

FirstCash continues to expand its store network (either organically or by acquiring existing store fronts) especially in Mexico and broader Latin America to boost its business. Mexico has been a ripe market for years as the country's 6000 to 8000 competing pawn stores are mostly jewelry-focused businesses. The company also continues grow in the US by opening new shops or buying individual pawn shops.

As part of its store expansion strategy the company made its largest move into Latin America to date in early 2016 after buying 211 full-service pawn stores mostly in Mexico but also in the new markets of Guatemala and El Salvador. It also bought 33 US pawn stores in six US states during 2015.

To reduce its risk to new regulations associated with payday lending First Cash began winding down its short term loan and credit business in the US in 2014 through the discontinuation of Cash & Go which operated 37 check cashing and financial services kiosks located inside convenience stores in Texas.

Mergers and Acquisitions

In September 2016 First Cash Financial Services merged with US rival Cash America International to form FirstCash.

In January 2016 the company expanded into Mexico and entered two new Latin American markets after buying 211 full-service pawn stores in the region including 166 pawn shops in Mexico 32 pawn locations in Guatemala (via its $10.45 million-acquisition of Maxi Prenda Guatemala S.A.) and 13 pawn locations in El Salvador.

In June 2015 First Cash bought 24 large-format pawn shops in North Carolina along with less than a handful of additional locations in Virginia and Kentucky.

In October 2014 First Cash acquired a chain of 15 large-format pawn stores located in Kentucky Missouri Tennessee and South Carolina. The purchase came on the heels of its purchase of 47 pawn shops in Mexico Colorado and Texas in August.

In 2012 First Cash announced a larger US deal with the acquisition of a 24-store chain of pawn stores operating under the Mister Money brand. The $25.5 million transaction expanded First Cash's geographic footprint in Colorado Kentucky Wyoming and Nebraska. The company later arranged to purchase 16 pawn stores operating as Fast Cash Pawn in the Denver area. That deal carried an approximately $46 million price tag.

Company Background

The company first expanded its presence into Mexico in 2008 with the acquisition of Presta Max a chain of 16 pawn shops in southern Mexico.

HISTORY

First Cash grew from a single pawnshop in Dallas. John Payne traded some land in Colorado for the store after selling his Dallas bank in 1979. He and his wife ran the shop until 1985 when they sold it and built a new shop in the suburbs aiming to achieve the ambience of a video store.

It was an opportune moment: The Texas economy particularly the banking industry was just beginning its slide. Payne (who later left the company) incorporated First Cash in 1988 and brought in professional management under former banker Rick Powell in 1990.

Eight-store First Cash went public in 1991. Acquisitions and expansions included the 1994 purchase of a Baltimore/Washington DC area chain. The next year First Cash upgraded its computers to improve inventory control and loan valuations and became the first major pawn chain to stop selling or making loans on handguns.

In 1996 and 1997 First Cash added stores in Maryland and Texas. The next year it bought 10-store chain JB Pawn (from a brother of First Cash director Richard Burke) and about 20 individual shops. First Cash also moved into check-cashing buying 11-store Miraglia.

To reflect the diversification the company changed its name to First Cash Financial Services in early 1999. That year First Cash joined other pawnbrokers and short-term lenders in moving into Mexico. In 2000 First Cash partnered with Pawnbroker.com to provide online financial and support services to pawn shops.

First Cash discontinued its auto loan operations in 2008 two years after purchasing dealer and lender Auto Master. In the midst of a worldwide credit crunch First Cash sold Auto Master to Minneapolis-based Interstate Auto Group (dba CarHop).

The company first expanded its presence into Mexico in 2008 with the acquisition of Presta Max a chain of 16 pawn shops in southern Mexico.

EXECUTIVES

Vice President Human Resources and Administration, Jan Hartz
Chairman President and CEO, Rick L. Wessel, age 60, $963,040 total compensation
EVP CFO Secretary and Treasurer, R. Douglas (Doug) Orr, age 58, $454,480 total compensation
General Counsel, Peter H. Watson, age 69, $386,250 total compensation
SVP Latin American Operations, Raul R. Ramos, age 52, $322,537 total compensation
SVP Store Development and Facilities, Sean D. Moore, age 41, $286,038 total compensation
Vice President Facility maintenance, Rick Work
VP Finance And Treasurer, Austin Nettle
Auditors: RSM US LLP

LOCATIONS

HQ: FirstCash Inc
1600 West 7th Street, Fort Worth, TX 76102
Phone: 817 335-1100
Web: www.firstcash.com

PRODUCTS/OPERATIONS

2015 Sales

	$ mil.	% of total
Retail merchandise	449.3	63
Pawn loan fees	195.4	28
Wholesale Scrap jewelry	32.0	5
Consumer loan and credit services fees	27.9	4
Total	704.6	100

Selected Subsidiaries

All Access Special Events LLC
American Loan Employee Services S.A. de C.V. (Mexico)
Cardplus Inc.
College Park Jewelers Inc.
Famous Pawn Inc.
FCFS MO Inc.
FCFS OK Inc.
FCFS SC Inc.
First Cash Corp.
First Cash Credit Ltd.
First Cash Inc.
First Cash Credit Management LLC
First Cash Ltd.
First Cash Management LLC
First Cash S.A. de C.V. (Mexico)
King Pawn Inc.
King Pawn II Inc.
Maryland Precious Metals Inc.
SHAC LLC
T.J. Unlimited LLC

COMPETITORS

ACE Cash Express
EZCORP
World Acceptance
Xponential

HISTORICAL FINANCIALS

Company Type: Public

Income Statement — FYE: December 31

	REVENUE ($ mil.)	NET INCOME ($ mil.)	NET PROFIT MARGIN	EMPLOYEES
12/19	1,864.4	164.6	8.8%	21,000
12/18	1,780.8	153.2	8.6%	19,000
12/17	1,779.8	143.8	8.1%	17,000
12/16	1,088.3	60.1	5.5%	16,200
12/15	704.6	60.7	8.6%	8,600
Annual Growth	27.5%	28.3%	—	25.0%

2019 Year-End Financials

Debt ratio: 25.8%
Return on equity: 12.3%
Cash ($ mil.): 46.5
Current ratio: 3.65
Long-term debt ($ mil.): 631.5
No. of shares (mil.): 42.3
Dividends
 Yield: 1.2%
 Payout: 28.1%
Market value ($ mil.): 3,413.0

	STOCK PRICE ($) FY Close	P/E High/Low		PER SHARE ($)		
				Earnings	Dividends	Book Value
12/19	80.63	28	18	3.81	1.02	31.89
12/18	72.35	28	20	3.41	0.91	30.23
12/17	67.45	23	14	3.00	0.77	31.45
12/16	47.00	31	18	1.72	0.57	29.89
12/15	37.43	26	17	2.14	0.00	15.28
Annual Growth	21.1%	—	—	15.5%	—	20.2%

Five Below Inc

Five Below may be growing as quickly as its youthful clientele. Operating a fast-growing chain of specialty retail stores it sells a broad range of trend-right products all priced under $5. The company which targets teen and pre-teen girls and boys operates some 750 stores in shopping centers in 30-plus US states; it also operates an e-commerce site. Core merchandise includes fun but inexpensive items meant to entice teens such as jewelry and accessories novelty T-shirts casual footwear sports gear decor and crafts and mobile phone accessories. Five Below was founded in 2002.

Operations

Five Below has three categories of youth-oriented merchandise: leisure fashion and home and party and snack. Leisure is the largest segment accounting for about 50% of revenue and includes games electronics accessories and sporting goods among other products. Fashion and home (more than 30%) includes T-shirts personal accessories and beauty offerings while party and snack (nearly 20%) includes candy and beverages greeting cards and party goods.

Working with a large number of vendors allows the chain to switch products quickly as it tries to capitalize on the popular items of the moment. Its stores measure about 8000 square feet.

Geographic Reach

From its base in the Northeast (the company is headquartered in Philadelphia) Five Below has aggressively expanded into the Southeast and Midwest. With additional moves into Texas and California the company has stores in about 35 states across all regions of the country. Texas Pennsylvania and New York are its largest markets.

The company has distribution centers in Pedricktown New Jersey and Olive Branch Mississippi. It is building a new distribution center in Monroe County Georgia (just south of Atlanta).

Sales and Marketing

Five Below's marketing strategy includes traditional advertising in newspapers and on television as well as digital advertising and a growing social media presence. New store openings which are grouped by market to leverage the company's efforts generally include contests giveaways and signature events such as "Five Cent" hot dogs.

As its geography and store count has increased so has Five Below's spending on advertising. It spent $31 million $27 million and $22 million in fiscal years 2017 2016 and 2015 respectively.

Financial Performance

Amid a rapidly expanding network of stores Five Below has seen strong growth over the past five years. Revenue has more than doubled since fiscal 2014 (ended January 2015) and net income has more than tripled.

In fiscal 2017 (ended January 2018) the company reported revenue of $1.3 billion up more than 25% from the prior year. The results were driven primarily by new store openings (some 100 that year) but same-store sales were also up 6.5%.

Primarily as a result of the strong revenue growth net income was also up in fiscal 2017. It jumped more than 40% to $103 million.

Cash at the end of fiscal 2017 was $113 million an increase of $37 million from the prior year. Cash from operations contributed $167 million to the coffers while investing activities used $139 million mainly for purchases of investment securities. Financing activities added another $8 million from proceeds of exercise of stock options and vesting of restricted stock units.

Strategy

Like many deep-discount retailers Five Below is expanding its store base at a rapid clip. Indeed it added more than 100 new locations in fiscal 2017 (ended January 2018) with plans for 125 more in 2018. The company expects it can eventually build a store network across the US of some 2500 locations.

In addition to new store growth merchandising is also key to Five Below's strategy. It is very focused on its teen and pre-teen customer base stocking what it considers to be fun exciting and dynamic products at prices those customers can afford. The company works with hundreds of different vendors so it can monitor trends and quickly respond when products move into the mainstream. This pricing and selection strategy has helped Five Below withstand the Amazon effect by undercutting the online behemoth in price while creating a "treasure hunt" vibe (you never know what you might find) that attracts young shoppers to its stores.

E-commerce is not as important for Five Below as it is for some other retailers but the company is working to establish an online presence. It got a bit of late start as it didn't begin selling through its fivebelow.com site until August 2016 and is still developing its online capabilities and determining how to maintain the $5 and below price point.

Company Background

Five Below was founded in 2002 as Cheap Holdings by former CEO Thomas Vellios and David Schlessinger. The company changed its name to Five Below later in 2002 and went public in 2012.

EXECUTIVES

Chief Administrative Officer, Eric M. Specter, age 61, $500,000 total compensation
CFO Secretary and Treasurer, Kenneth R. Bull, age 56, $400,000 total compensation
President CEO and Director, Joel D. Anderson, age 54, $700,000 total compensation
EVP Merchandising, Michael F. Romanko, age 53, $450,000 total compensation
EVP Retail Operations, George Hill
Vice President Information Technology, Chris DeMeester
Executive Vice President Real Estate, Linda Moser
Senior Vice President Human Resources, Bill Clark
Vice President Of Human Resources, Jim Gorenc
Vice President Investor Relations, Christiane Pelz
Vice President Claims Manager Claims Corporate Solutions, Bill Ashton
Senior Vice President and Corporate Treasurer, Tony Cossetti
Senior Vice President Director of Marketing and Creative Services, Jennifer Shockley
Vice President Senior Commercial Lender, Janet Helms
ASSISTANT VICE PRESIDENT AND RELATIONSHIP MANAGER, Kelly Zane
Vice President Operations, Robert Maines
Assistant Vice President, Jonathan Wetzel
Vice President Real Estate Division Head, Sean Finnegan
Executive Vice President And Chief Experience Officer, Judy Werthauser
Senior Vice President, James Bonner
Vice President and Budgeting and Planning Manager, Amy Hall
Vice President, Paul Johnson
Senior Vice President, Lori Ross
Vice President Commercial Lending, Jim Amon
Vice President, Mark Digiovanni
Assistant Vice President Quality Assurance Officer, Dana Baldorossi
VICE PRESIDENT COMMERCIAL BANKING, Anthony Murphy
Vice President, Lynn Nolan
Vice President Market Director, Jennifer Macmullen
Vice President Creative Services Manager, Kerry Sczepkowski
Vice President Compensation Manager, Joy Ross
Senior Vice President, Rocco Perate
Vice President Human Resources, Karin Durham
Senior Vice President, Deborah M Fretz
Chairman, Thomas G. (Tom) Vellios, age 64
Assistant Treasurer, Tom Barnes
Auditors: KPMG LLP

LOCATIONS

HQ: Five Below Inc
 701 Market Street, Suite 300, Philadelphia, PA 19106
Phone: 215 546-7909
Web: www.fivebelow.com

PRODUCTS/OPERATIONS

2017 Sales

	% of total
Leisure	51
Fashion & home	32
Party & snack	18
Total	**100**

COMPETITORS

Big Lots	Hot Topic
CVS	Kmart
Claire's Stores	Rite Aid
Dollar General	TJX Companies
Dollar Tree	Target Corporation
Family Dollar Stores	Wal-Mart
Forever 21	Walgreen

HISTORICAL FINANCIALS

Company Type: Public

Income Statement — FYE: February 2

	REVENUE ($ mil.)	NET INCOME ($ mil.)	NET PROFIT MARGIN	EMPLOYEES
02/19	1,559.5	149.6	9.6%	13,900
02/18*	1,278.2	102.4	8.0%	12,100
01/17	1,000.4	71.8	7.2%	9,500
01/16	831.9	57.6	6.9%	7,600
01/15	680.2	48.0	7.1%	6,700
Annual Growth	23.1%	32.9%	—	20.0%

*Fiscal year change

2019 Year-End Financials

Debt ratio: —
Return on equity: 27.9%
Cash ($ mil.): 251.7
Current ratio: 2.54
Long-term debt ($ mil.): —
No. of shares (mil.): 55.7
Dividends
 Yield: —
 Payout: —
Market value ($ mil.): 6,955.0

	STOCK PRICE ($) FY Close	P/E High/Low	PER SHARE ($) Earnings	Dividends	Book Value
02/19	124.73	50 23	2.66	0.00	11.03
02/18*	62.94	39 20	1.84	0.00	8.27
01/17	37.60	40 25	1.30	0.00	6.04
01/16	35.23	38 26	1.05	0.00	4.48
01/15	33.32	52 37	0.88	0.00	3.20
Annual Growth 39.1%		— —	31.9%	—	36.2%

*Fiscal year change

Flagstar Bancorp, Inc.

Flagstar Bancorp is the holding company for Flagstar Bank which operates around 110 branches (including 10 in retail stores) mostly in Michigan. Beyond offering traditional deposit and loan products Michigan's largest bank specializes in originating purchasing and servicing one-to-four family residential mortgage loans across all 50 states through a network of brokers and correspondents. Around 70% of the Flagstar's revenue is linked to mortgage origination and servicing while another 25% comes from its community banking business. Boasting $14 billion in assets Flagstar is one of the nation's 10 largest savings banks.

Operations

Flagstar Bancorp operates four business segments: Mortgage Originations which made up 58% of its total revenue during 2015 and acquires and sells one-to-four family residential mortgage loans; Mortgage Servicing (12% of revenue) which charges a fee to service and sub-service mortgage loans for its own community bank and other parties; and Community Banking (24%) which provides deposit and loan products (including warehouse lending) to businesses individuals government entities and held-for-investment portfolio groups.

Unlike traditional banks which focus on interest income Flagstar makes most of its revenue from its mortgage banking business. Only about 43% of its revenue came from interest during 2015 (mostly from loans) while most of the rest came from gains on mortgage loan sales (36% of revenue) loan fees and charges (8%) and other mortgage-banking related fees (10%).

Geographic Reach

The Troy Michigan-based company had 99 branches in Michigan and another 10 locations in retail locations in nine highly-populous states. Its mortgage banking business does business in all 50 states.

Sales and Marketing

Flagstar spent $9 million on advertising in 2015 compared to $10 million and $9 million in 2014 and 2013 respectively.

Financial Performance

As with other mortgage bankers Flagstar has struggled to grow its revenues over the past few years as many borrowers have already refinanced their loans to take advantage of low interest rates. The lender has also been in and out of the red in recent years suffering losses in 2014 and 2011.

Flagstar Bancorp's revenue rebounded 28% to $825 million during 2015 however thanks to a combination of higher interest income and mortgage sales. On the mortgage side a 40% jump in loan sale gains were driven by higher fallout-adjusted lock volumes improved margins and lower representation and warranty provisions. The company's interest income grew 24% as it continued to build its average loans held-for-sale loans held-for-investment and investment security assets.

Strong revenue growth in 2015 and a sharp decline in loan loss provisions on an improving quality credit portfolio drove the company's net income up 28% to $158 million (compared to a $70 million loss in 2014). Despite earnings growth Flagstar's operations used $9.55 billion in cash or about 17% more than in 2014 mostly as it used more cash to originate mortgage loans.

Strategy

While home mortgage lending remains key to Flagstar the company hopes to diversify its revenue streams so the business eventually accounts for about a third of sales. Over the past few years the company has been transforming its branches into full-service community banks and moving toward cross-selling an expanded suite of retail commercial and government banking services.

In February 2016 the company expanded and diversified more into commercial lending after launching its national homebuilder lending platform designed to offer financing to residential developers and homebuilders across the US. In past years it introduced a line of consumer loans such as credit cards and home equity lines of credit and added services for small and midsized businesses like treasury management and specialty lending.

Company Background

In 2011 to raise capital after suffering the effects of the housing bust the company sold 27 bank branches in the suburbs north of Atlanta along with their deposits to PNC. The company also sold its 22 Indiana branches to First Financial Bancorp later that year. In addition to bringing in some cash the divestitures help Flagstar focus on its Michigan operations.

MP Thrift an affiliate of private equity firm MatlinPatterson Global Advisors assumed a controlling stake of Flagstar in 2009. Today it owns 64% of the company.

EXECUTIVES

EVP and Director Performing Servicing, Mark Landschulz, age 54
President Mortgage Banking, Leonard (Len) Israel
President CEO and Director, Alessandro P. DiNello, age 64
EVP and Senior Deputy General Counsel, Paul D. Borja, age 58, $749,982 total compensation
EVP and Treasurer, Brian D.J. Boike, age 42
EVP and COO, Lee M. Smith
EVP and CFO, James K. Ciroli
EVP and Chief Risk Officer, Steve Figliuolo
EVP and Director MIS and Analytics, William D. Belekewicz
EVP and CIO, Tony Buttrick
EVP Secondary Marketing, Palmer T. Heenan
EVP and Director Mortgage Fulfillment, Donna M. Krall
EVP and Chief Lending Officer Commercial Banking, Thomas R. Kuslits
EVP and Chief Human Resources Officer, Cynthia M. Myers
EVP and Chief Credit Officer, Joseph M. Redoutey
EVP and Chief Compliance Officer, Karen A. Sabatowski
Chairman, John D. Lewis
Auditors: PricewaterhouseCoopers LLP

LOCATIONS

HQ: Flagstar Bancorp, Inc.
5151 Corporate Drive, Troy, MI 48098-2639
Phone: 248 312-2000
Web: www.flagstar.com

PRODUCTS/OPERATIONS

2015 Sales

	$ mil.	% of total
Interest income		
Loans	295.0	36
Investment securities	59.0	7
Interest-earning deposits and other	1.0	-
Non interest income		
Net gain on loan sales	288.0	36
Loan fees & charges	67.0	8
Deposit fees and charges	25.0	3
Loan administration income	26.0	3
Net return on mortgage serving assets	28.0	3
Net (loss) gain on sale of assets	(1)	-
Representation and warranty benefit (provision)	19.0	2
Other non-interest income	18.0	2
Total	825.0	100

2015 Sales

	% of total
Mortgage origination	58
Community Banking	24
Mortgage Servicing	12
Others	6
Total	100

Selected Products/Services

Personal Banking
Banking
Checking Accounts
Checking
Savings Accounts
Savings Accounts: Personal
Banking Goals
View All Rates
Online Banking Login: Personal Accounts
Mobile Banking
Detroit Red Wings Partnership
Foreign Currency
Loans
Home Loans
Refinance
Home Equity Solutions
Credit Cards
Money Market
Investment Accounts: Personal

COMPETITORS

Bank of America	JPMorgan Chase
Comerica	KeyCorp
Fifth Third	Northern Trust
Harris	PNC Financial
Huntington Bancshares	

HISTORICAL FINANCIALS

Company Type: Public

Income Statement
FYE: December 31

	ASSETS ($ mil.)	NET INCOME ($ mil.)	INCOME AS % OF ASSETS	EMPLOYEES
12/18	18,531.0	187.0	1.0%	3,938
12/17	16,912.0	63.0	0.4%	3,525
12/16	14,053.0	171.0	1.2%	2,886
12/15	13,715.0	158.0	1.2%	2,713
12/14	9,839.8	(69.4)	—	2,739
Annual Growth	17.1%	—	—	9.5%

2018 Year-End Financials

Return on assets: 1.0%
Return on equity: 12.6%
Long-term debt ($ mil.): —
No. of shares (mil.): 57.7
Sales ($ mil): 1,122.0
Dividends
 Yield: —
 Payout: —
Market value ($ mil.): 1,525.0

	STOCK PRICE ($) FY Close	P/E High/Low		PER SHARE ($) Earnings	Dividends	Book Value
12/18	26.40	12	8	3.21	0.00	27.19
12/17	37.42	35	23	1.09	0.00	24.41
12/16	26.94	11	6	2.66	0.00	23.51
12/15	23.11	11	6	2.24	0.00	27.07
12/14	15.73	—	—	(1.72)	0.00	24.37
Annual Growth	13.8%	—	—	—	—	2.8%

FleetCor Technologies Inc

Helping companies manage motor fleets is at the core of FLEETCOR's mission. The company is a leading provider of fleet cards and payment processing services aimed at commercial and government fleets. Its cards carry the names Fuelman CFN Keyfuels CCS and Fuelcard. The fleet cards function like typical charge cards and can be used to purchase fuel and lodging. FLEETCOR tracks purchases to help manage employee spending. The company serves more than 500000 accounts and has millions of cards active in the US the UK and Brazil as well as 50 other countries around the world. Major customers include oil giants BP Shell and Speedway. The company fuels growth through acquisitions.

Operations
FLEETCOR makes the majority of its sales from fuel card payments corporate payments and toll products as well as gift and lodging cards. It also offers fleet-related and workforce payment services such as fleet maintenance management and employee benefit payments.

The company processes around 3 billion transactions each year. It makes its money from transaction fees card fees and network fees and charges which can be fixed fees cost-plus-mark-up or percentage based. It also charges late payment fees based on customer credit risk.

By product category fuel cards account for some 50% of revenue; tolls generate about 15% corporate payments and gift cards supply about 10% each and lodging accounts for about 5%.

It operates its own "closed-loop" networks — under the brands Fuelman Comdata Commercial fueling Network and Pacific Pride — where possible but also makes use of third-party networks to broaden its card acceptance and use. These include MasterCard and Carnet in Mexico.

Geographic Reach
North America accounts for around 65% of Norcross Georgia-based FLEETCOR's sales. Brazil generates about 20% and the UK supplies more than 10%. Beyond those three the company does business in more than 55 other countries across Africa Europe (including Russia) Latin America and Australasia.

Sales and Marketing
FLEETCOR offers its commercial payment services to retailers commercial fleets major oil companies petroleum marketers and government entities in a variety of industries such as retail healthcare construction and hospitality. The company has relationships with 800 such partners.

Financial Performance
Fueled by smaller fleet service and portfolio acquisitions FLEETCOR's annual revenues have tripled and its profits doubled since 2011 (the company went public in 2010).

In 2017 sales grew 22% to $2.2 billion as total transactions increased 33% to 2.9 billion boosted by a 122% increase in international transactions due to acquisitions.

Net income jumped more than 60% in 2017 to $740 million from $452 million in 2016 driven by the strong revenue growth. The company recorded a $44 million impairment loss from its Masternaut investment.

Cash in FLEETCOR's coffers totaled $913 million in 2017 compared to $475 million in 2016.

Strategy
FLEETCOR's primary means of growth is through acquisitions: it has made more than 70 since 2002. It targets smaller and regional fleet service providers in markets it currently serves and in new markets overseas. It also looks to buy commercial account portfolios technologies services and products.

Its acquisition activity has taken FLEETCOR international. The company has snapped up companies in growing markets in Europe Asia and Latin America. It expanded in Brazil when it bought San Paulo-based electronic toll payment company STP in mid-2016.

FLEETCOR sold its NexTraq telematics business to Michelin in 2017. FLEETCOR divested the business because it did not fit with the company's core payments business. Terms were not disclosed. The company bought NexTraq in 2013.

Mergers and Acquisitions
In 2017 FLEETCOR acquired Creative Lodging Solutions a provider of long-term stay lodging for businesses.

In another 2017 acquisition FLEETCOR bought Cambridge Global Payments an international payments provider for about $690 million. The deal puts FLEETCOR in the business-to-business cross-border payments market. In August 2016 FLEETCOR paid $1.2 billion to acquire San Paulo-based electronic toll payment company Servicos e Tecnologia de Pagamentos S.A (STP). The firm collects some $2.5 billion in toll parking and fuel payments from 4.5 million active users annually and provided cardless fuel payments at Shell sites throughout Brazil.

Company Background
Founded in 2000 FleetCor went public in December 2010 via an initial public offering that raised about $290 million. The proceeds went to FleetCor's private equity shareholders Advent International Bain Capital and Summit Partners.

EXECUTIVES
President Global Fuel Cards, Steve Greene
Chairman and CEO, Ronald F. (Ron) Clarke, age 63, $1,000,000 total compensation
CFO, Eric R. Dey, age 59, $373,077 total compensation
President North American Partners, David D. Maxsimic, age 59
President International Corporate Development, Andrew R. Blazye, age 60, $340,137 total compensation
President North America Fuel Cards, Todd W. House, age 47, $398,077 total compensation
EVP Global Sales, Charles R. Freund, age 46, $343,077 total compensation
EVP Global Corporate Development, John S. Coughlin, age 51, $398,077 total compensation
CIO, John A. Reed, age 64
President Brazil, Armando L. Netto, age 50, $280,048 total compensation
President Comdata Corporate Payments, Kurt P. Adams, age 49
President Continental Europe, Alexey Gavrilenya, age 42
President UK Australia and New Zealand, Alan King, age 42
President North American Trucking, Greg L. Secord, age 56
Vice President of Sales, Chet Panhans
Vice President Process Excellence and Program Management, Ed Thomas
Vp Technology, Todd Hemphill
Vice President Global Sales Planning and Analysis, Jason Cole
Vice President Information Security, Bruce R Evans, age 62
Executive Vice President Business Development, John Couglin
Vice President US Sales Operations, Steve Casper
Senior Vice President Information Technology, Tom Pierce
Senior Vice President of Financial Planning and Analysis, Chad Richardson
Senior Vice President Inside Sales, Christopher Alff
Vice President and GM North American Partners, Kelly Fifarek
Senior Vice President Product and Growth, Mary Rachide
Vice President Digital Analytics and Optimization, Joby Moore
Vp Strategic Portfolio Sales, Monica Fallo
Senior Vice President and Chief Information Security Officer CISO, James Edgar
Svp It and Global Enterprise Systems, Pamela Rendine-cook
Svp Inside Sales, Donald Wilczynski
VICE PRESIDENT RELATIONSHIP MANAGEMENT, Justin Boothby
Board Member, Jeffrey Sloan
Board Member, Michael Buckman
Board Member, Thomas Hagerty
Auditors: Ernst & Young LLP

LOCATIONS
HQ: FleetCor Technologies Inc
 5445 Triangle Parkway, Peachtree Corners, GA 30092
Phone: 770 449-0479
Web: www.fleetcor.com

PRODUCTS/OPERATIONS
2017 Sales

	% of total
Fuel	49
Tolls	14
Corporate Payments	12
Gift	9
Lodging	5
Other	11
Total	**100**

Selected Brands and Subsidiaries
CCS
CFN Holding Co.
CLC Group
Corporate Lodging Consultants Inc.
FleetCards
FleetNet
Fuelman
The Fuelcard Company
Fuel Vend Limited
Keyfuels
Mannatec Inc.
Transit Card

COMPETITORS
American Express
Arval
Edenred
Multi Service
Retail Decisions
Sodexo USA
U.S. Bancorp
WEX
World Fuel Services

HISTORICAL FINANCIALS
Company Type: Public

Income Statement   FYE: December 31

	REVENUE ($ mil.)	NET INCOME ($ mil.)	NET PROFIT MARGIN	EMPLOYEES
12/18	2,433.4	811.4	33.3%	7,580
12/17	2,249.5	740.2	32.9%	7,890
12/16	1,831.5	452.3	24.7%	7,100
12/15	1,702.8	362.4	21.3%	5,330
12/14	1,199.3	368.7	30.7%	4,780
Annual Growth	19.3%	21.8%	—	12.2%

2018 Year-End Financials
Debt ratio: 35.1%
Return on equity: 23.1%
Cash ($ mil.): 1,031.1
Current ratio: 0.86
Long-term debt ($ mil.): 2,748.4
No. of shares (mil.): 85.8
Dividends
  Yield: —
  Payout: —
Market value ($ mil.): 15,943.0

	STOCK PRICE ($) FY Close	P/E High/Low	PER SHARE ($) Earnings	Dividends	Book Value
12/18	185.72	25 19	8.81	0.00	38.91
12/17	192.43	24 16	7.91	0.00	40.94
12/16	141.52	36 23	4.75	0.00	33.58
12/15	142.93	42 35	3.85	0.00	30.64
12/14	148.71	36 23	4.24	0.00	30.04
Annual Growth	5.7%	— —	20.1%	—	6.7%

Floor & Decor Holdings Inc

Auditors: Ernst & Young LLP

LOCATIONS

HQ: Floor & Decor Holdings Inc
2500 Windy Ridge Parkway SE, Atlanta, GA 30339
Phone: 404 471-1634
Web: www.FloorandDecor.com

HISTORICAL FINANCIALS

Company Type: Public

Income Statement   FYE: December 27

	REVENUE ($ mil.)	NET INCOME ($ mil.)	NET PROFIT MARGIN	EMPLOYEES
12/18	1,709.8	116.1	6.8%	6,566
12/17	1,384.7	102.7	7.4%	5,534
12/16	1,050.7	43.0	4.1%	4,391
12/15	784.0	26.8	3.4%	0
12/14	584.5	15.1	2.6%	0
Annual Growth	30.8%	66.6%	—	—

2018 Year-End Financials
Debt ratio: 11.7%
Return on equity: 22.6%
Cash ($ mil.): 0.6
Current ratio: 1.38
Long-term debt ($ mil.): 141.8
No. of shares (mil.): 97.5
Dividends
  Yield: —
  Payout: —
Market value ($ mil.): 2,538.0

	STOCK PRICE ($) FY Close	P/E High/Low	PER SHARE ($) Earnings	Dividends	Book Value
12/18	26.01	48 20	1.11	0.00	5.99
12/17	49.59	43 28	1.03	0.00	4.64
Annual Growth	(47.5%)	— —	7.8%	—	29.1%

FNB Corp

F.N.B. Corporation is the holding company for First National Bank of Pennsylvania which serves consumers and small to midsized businesses though almost 290 bank branches in Pennsylvania northeastern Ohio and Maryland. The company also has more than 70 consumer finance offices operating as Regency Finance in those states as well as Tennessee and Kentucky. In addition to community banking and consumer finance F.N.B. also has segments devoted to insurance and wealth management. It also offers leasing and merchant banking services. F.N.B. has extended its reach in its target states through acquisitions of banks including Metro Bancorp Annapolis Bancorp and PVF Capital Corp.

Operations

F.N.B operates four segments. The Community Banking segment which made up almost 90% of the company's total revenue during 2015 provides commercial and consumer banking services including corporate banking small business banking investment real estate financing asset-based lending capital markets services and lease financing as well as traditional consumer banking products.

The company's Wealth Management segment (5% of revenue) offers trust and other fiduciary services while the Insurance segment (2% of revenue) offers commercial and personal insurance through major carriers. F.N.B.'s Consumer Finance segment (6% of revenue) which operates through subsidiary Regency Finance Company provides installment loans to individuals and buys installment loans from retail merchants.

Like other retail banks F.N.B. makes the bulk of its money from interest income. Nearly 70% of the bank's total revenue came from loan and lease interest (including fees) during 2015 while 9% came from interest on taxable and non-taxable securities. The rest of money came from service charges (10% of revenue) trust income (3%) insurance commissions and fees (2%) securities commissions and fees (2%) mortgage banking (1%) and other non-interest income sources.

Geographic Reach

Most of the Pittsburgh-based company's branches are concentrated in Pennsylvania with the next largest markets being in Ohio Maryland and West Virginia. Its consumer finance offices are mostly in Pennsylvania and Tennessee with others in Kentucky and Ohio.

Sales and Marketing

F.N.B. boosted its advertising and promotional spend by 7% to $8.4 million during 2015 mostly because of higher expenses associated with the bank's recent acquisitions as it worked to get the name out in new territories such as in Cleveland Ohio and Baltimore.

Financial Performance

F.N.B. Corporation's annual revenues have risen nearly 40% since 2011 as its loan assets have nearly doubled with new branch openings and acquisitions. Its profits have doubled as well over the period as the company has kept a lid on growing costs.

The bank's revenue climbed 6% to $709.21 million during 2015 thanks to continued loan business growth stemming from recent bank acquisitions.

Revenue growth in 2015 drove F.N.B.'s net income up 11% to $159.65 million. The company's operating cash levels plunged 50% to $223.48 million for the year due to unfavorable changes in working capital related to securities classified as trading in business combination and sold.

Strategy

F.N.B. Corporation grows its loan and deposit business while expanding into new markets by acquiring smaller banks and select bank branches. In 2016 it agreed to buy North Carolina-based Yadkin Financial for $1.4 billion. That deal will add around 100 banking locations in the Carolinas and some $7.5 billion in assets. The combined bank will have some 400 branches across the Mid-Atlantic and Southeast US.

Mergers and Acquisitions

In April 2016 the company bought 17 branch locations in the Pittsburgh area from Fifth Third Bank as well as $100000 in loans and over $300000 in deposits.

In February 2016 F.N.B. Corporation purchased Metro Bancorp along with its $3 billion in assets and more than 30 Metro Bank branches in south-central Pennsylvania. The deal effectively merged Metro Bank into F.N.B.'s First National Bank of Pennsylvania subsidiary.

In September 2015 the bank purchased five branches in southeastern Pennsylvania from Bank of America along with almost $155000 in associated deposits.

In October 2013 F.N.B. moved to expand its presence in the greater Cleveland area by purchasing PVF Capital Corp. which owned Park View Federal Savings Bank with some 20 offices in Cleveland and northeastern Ohio.

In April 2013 F.N.B. purchased Annapolis Bancorp the parent company of BankAnnapolis in an all-stock transaction valued at about $51 million. The deal expanded F.N.B.'s reach into Maryland.

Company Background

F.N.B. which moved its headquarters from Pennsylvania to Florida in 2001 spun off First National Bankshares of Florida at the start of 2004 and returned to the Pittsburgh area. F.N.B. still operates two loan offices in Florida but these primarily manage the company's legacy loan portfolio there.

The bank is again rooted firmly in the Keystone State and bordering markets. After returning it expanded via several acquisitions prior to the Parkvale deal including bank holding companies NSD Bancorp Slippery Rock Financial North East Bancshares Omega Financial and Iron and Glass Bancorp. In 2011 F.N.B. expanded in northeastern Pennsylvania through the acquisition of Comm Bancorp. The deal valued at some $70 million brought in 15 branches.

EXECUTIVES

SVP and Corporate Controller, Timothy G. Rubritz, age 66, $215,016 total compensation
Chief Legal Officer, James G. Orie, age 60, $165,000 total compensation
CFO, Vincent J. Calabrese, age 56, $385,008 total compensation
Chief Credit Officer, Gary Guerrieri, age 58, $350,016 total compensation
President and CEO; CEO First National Bank, Vincent J. (Vince) Delie, age 54, $770,016 total compensation
President First National Bank, John C. Williams, $385,008 total compensation
President Charlotte Region, Gregory L. (Greg) Heaton
Vice President Of IT Network Services, Brian Diegan
Vice President Business Development Officer, Leslie Harrison
Senior Vice President, Paul Puleo
Vice President, Mark Renzini
Vice President Commercial Banking First National Bank Maryland Region, Joseph Zajdel

Assistant Vice President Business Development Officer, Donnie Rhodes
Credit Support Senior Vice President Credit Officer First National Bank, Ron Scarton
Senior Vice President, Craig Muthler
Vice President, Michael Griffo
Vice President Private Banking, Donna Logan
Vice President, Colleen Ensinger
Vice President Commercial Loan Officer, Shane Moser
Vice President, Mike DeRosa
Vice President Financial Advisor, Daniel Richardson
Assistant Vice President Germantown Branch Merchant Services First National Bank, Jean Carpinone
Vice President Wealth Advisor Maryland Region, Nick Ey
Public Square Assistant Vice President Relationship Manager Investment Real Estate, Dean Razek
Vice President Business Development Officer, Sean Laurin
SENIOR VICE PRESIDENT MANAGING DIRECTOR, Nick Bellino
Svp Regional Manager Of Commercial Banking, Douglas Brown
Svp Market Executive, Craig Caplan
Vice President and Relationship Advisor, Keith Nazak
Vp Business Banking, Philip Persons
Senior Vice President, Mike Hendricks
Evp Capital Markets And Specialty Finance Businesses, D Bryant Mitchell
Vice President Regional Underwriting Manager, Amar Grover
Assistant Vice President Branch Manager, Amanda Escobar
Vice President, Shari Furbee
Vice President, Cindy Davidson
Chairman, Stephen J. (Steve) Gurgovits, age 75
Board Member, Stephen Martz
Board Member, Sheila Stewart
Auditors: Ernst & Young LLP

LOCATIONS

HQ: FNB Corp
One North Shore Center, 12 Federal Street, Pittsburgh, PA 15212
Phone: 800 555-5455
Web: www.fnb-online.com

PRODUCTS/OPERATIONS

2015 Sales by Segment

	$ mil.	% of total
Community banking	616.2	87
Consumer finance	42.8	6
Wealth management	35.2	5
Insurance	13.1	2
parent & other	1.8	-
Total	709.1	100

2015 Sales

	$ mil.	% of total
Interest		
Loans including fees	482.1	68
Securities including dividends	64.6	9
Other	0.1	-
Non-interest		
Service charges	70.7	10
Trust Services	20.8	3
Insurance commissions & fees	16.3	2
Securities commissions & fees	13.6	2
Other	40.9	6
Total	709.1	100

Selected Subsidiaries

F.N.B. Capital Corporation (merchant banking)
First National Bank of Pennsylvania
  Bank Capital Services LLC (also dba F.N.B. Commercial Leasing)
  First National Trust Company
  F.N.B. Investment Advisors
  First National Investment Services Company
First National Insurance Agency LLC
Regency Finance Company
  Citizens Financial Services Inc.
  F.N.B. Consumer Discount Company
  Finance and Mortgage Acceptance Corporation

COMPETITORS

Bank of America
Citizens Financial Group
Dollar Bank
Fifth Third
First Commonwealth Financial
Fulton Financial
Glen Burnie Bancorp
Huntington Bancshares
M&T Bank
Northwest Bancshares
PNC Financial
S&T Bancorp
Sandy Spring Bancorp
Sovereign Bank
United Community Financial

HISTORICAL FINANCIALS

Company Type: Public

Income Statement
FYE: December 31

	ASSETS ($ mil.)	NET INCOME ($ mil.)	INCOME AS % OF ASSETS	EMPLOYEES
12/18	33,102.0	373.0	1.1%	4,420
12/17	31,417.6	199.2	0.6%	4,748
12/16	21,844.8	170.8	0.8%	3,821
12/15	17,557.6	159.6	0.9%	3,205
12/14	16,127.0	144.0	0.9%	3,145
Annual Growth	19.7%	26.9%	—	8.9%

2018 Year-End Financials

Return on assets: 1.1%
Return on equity: 8.2%
Long-term debt ($ mil.): —
No. of shares (mil.): 324.3
Sales ($ mil.): 1,446.0
Dividends
  Yield: 4.8%
  Payout: 42.8%
Market value ($ mil.): 3,191.0

	STOCK PRICE ($) FY Close	P/E High/Low	PER SHARE ($) Earnings	Dividends	Book Value
12/18	9.84	13 8	1.12	0.48	14.21
12/17	13.82	26 19	0.63	0.48	13.63
12/16	16.03	21 14	0.78	0.48	12.18
12/15	13.34	17 14	0.86	0.48	11.95
12/14	13.32	17 14	0.80	0.48	11.62
Annual Growth	(7.3%)	— —	8.8%	(0.0%)	5.2%

Forestar Group Inc (New)

A majority-owned subsidiary of D.R. Horton?which is one of the largest homebuilders in the US?residential lot development company Forestar Group owns or controls over 20000 residential lots. Most of those are under contract are either under contract to sell to D.R. Horton or are assigned to D.R. Horton for right of first offer. The company owns around 1600 developed lots. Forestar operates in about 35 markets across more than 15 states and while it sometimes develops land for commercial properties?including apartments retail centers and offices?Forestar primarily sells lots to homebuilders and developers for single-family homes.

Change in Company Type

In 2017 Forestar Group became a majority-owned subsidiary of hombuilding giant D.R. Horton which paid more than $550 million for a 75% stake in the company. The deal improved the lot developer's overhead leverage and provided it far greater access to land sourcing experienced development teams and low-cost capital. Under a Master Supply Agreement both companies identify opportunities for land development which Forestar then develops for sale to D.R. Horton or other homebuilders.

Operations

Forestar Group operates two segments: Real estate and Other. Effectively all of the company's revenue comes from its Real estate business. Forestar acquires its land outright or gains control through option contracts. It then obtains entitlements and develops single-family residential community infrastructure. Forestar generates most of its revenue?about 95%—from sales of residential single-family finished lots. More than 5500 of the 20000 lots it owns or controls are under contract to sell to D.R. Horton. D.R. Horton also has the right of first offer on almost another 8100 of the majority-owned subsidiaries lots. Additionally Forestar makes short-term investments in finished lots and undeveloped land which it then sells to D.R. Horton. Forestar owns around 1600 developed lots.

Geographic Reach

Austin Texas-based Forestar Group operates in about 35 markets across more than 15 US states. The company leases office space in Atlanta Georgia; Dallas Texas; and Houston Texas.

Sales and Marketing

Beyond its relationship with D.R. Horton Forestar group targets its lot sales to local regional and national homebuilders.

Financial Performance

With limited access to high-cost capital Forestar Group saw its revenue decline each year since 2014 as it struggled to use its excess cash to identify attractive projects expand its geographic footprint or deepen its presence in established markets. The company's fortunes may be reversing following its 2017 majority acquisition by D.R. Horton which improved the lot developer's overhead leverage and provided it far greater access to land sourcing experienced development teams and low-cost capital. Despite a massive loss in 2015 caused by impairment charges on its former oil and gas segment spurred by low prices and price projections Forestar's net income clawed back in 2016 and 2018 to post five-year growth of more than 300%. The company also managed to pay down some three-quarters of its debt between 2014 and 2018 while growing its cash stores by nearly 90%.

Despite increased sales volume driven by sales to D.R. Horton in the nine months ended Sept. 30 2018 compared with the 12 months ended Dec. 31 2017 (Forestar moved back its fiscal year following its majority acquisition) Forestar's revenue fell 31% to $78.3 million due lower average selling prices.

Disposal of its oil and gas business in 2016 and 2017 and greatly reduced operating general and administrative expenses?thanks to its majority parent?helped drive up the company's net income which added 37% in 2018 to end the year at $68.8 million.

Forestar's cash increased by $3.3 million in 2018. Operations used $283 million mostly for net expenditures on real estate development and acquisitions. Asset sales accounted for nearly all proceeds from investment activities which totaled $259 million. Changes in restricted cash drove gains from financing of $19.8 million.

Strategy

Forestar Group established its key strategic relationship through the sale of a 75% to homebuilding giant D.R. Horton in 2017. Under its Master Supply Agreement both companies identify opportunities for land development which Forestar then develops for sale to D.R. Horton or other homebuilders. In 2018 the company had more than 20000 residential lots which it owned or controlled through option purchase contracts. Forestar is under contract to sell greater than 5500 of those to D.R. Horton and D.R. Horton has the right of first offer on nearly 8100.

All told the transaction far improved the lot developer's overhead leverage and provided it greater access to land sourcing experienced development teams and low-cost capital.

In conjunction with that scheme Forestar has sold off nearly all of its non-core and underperforming assets. The company divested its oil and gas business in 2016 and 2017 and is reducing its holdings in land for commercial real estate. In 2018 it sold off 24 legacy projects including about 750 developed and under-development lots; 4000 future undeveloped lots; 730 unentitled acres in California; and its interests in a multifamily property and a multifamily development location. In 2018 its revenue from commercial real estate fell by 85% to $2 million?representing less than 3% of total sales.

EXECUTIVES

Chief Real Estate Officer, Bruce F. Dickson, age 66, $370,833 total compensation
EVP Real Estate Acquisitions, John Pierret
EVP Real Estate West Region, Tom Burleson
EVP Chief Administrative Officer General Counsel and Secretary, David M. Grimm, age 59, $290,000 total compensation
CFO, Charles D. (Chuck) Jehl, age 51
President Community Development, Michael Quinley
President Multifamily, Charles T. (Tom) Etheredge, age 57, $225,000 total compensation
CEO, Phillip J. (Phil) Weber, $310,000 total compensation
Senior Vice President Water Resources, Brent Covert
Vice President Multifamily Construction, Greg S Schmittou
Vice President Of Engineering And Development, Randy McCuistion
Chairman, James A. (Jim) Rubright, age 72
Board Member, Daniel Silvers
Auditors: Ernst & Young LLP

LOCATIONS

HQ: Forestar Group Inc (New)
  2221 E. Lamar Blvd., Suite 790, Arlington, TX 76006
Phone: 817 769-1860
Web: www.forestargroup.com

PRODUCTS/OPERATIONS

2018 Sales

	$ mil.	% of total
Real estate	75.6	96
Commercial real estate	2.0	3
Other	0.7	1
Total	**78.3**	**100**

COMPETITORS

Belz	Lennar
Cencor Realty	Michael Crews Development
Cornerstone Communities	PulteGroup
Davidson Communities	Schlosser Development
Hillwood	Shea Homes
Hines	Toll Brothers
LGI Development	William Lyon Homes

HISTORICAL FINANCIALS

Company Type: Public

Income Statement   FYE: September 30

	REVENUE ($ mil.)	NET INCOME ($ mil.)	NET PROFIT MARGIN	EMPLOYEES
09/19	428.3	33.0	7.7%	78
09/18*	78.3	68.8	87.9%	41
12/17	114.3	50.2	44.0%	34
12/16	197.3	58.6	29.7%	59
12/15	262.4	(213.0)	—	106
Annual Growth	**13.0%**	**—**	**—**	**(7.4%)**

*Fiscal year change

2019 Year-End Financials

Debt ratio: 31.6%   No. of shares (mil.): 48.0
Return on equity: 4.4%   Dividends
Cash ($ mil.): 382.8   Yield: —
Current ratio: 2.12   Payout: —
Long-term debt ($ mil.): 460.5 Market value ($ mil.): 877.0

	STOCK PRICE ($) FY Close	P/E High/Low		PER SHARE ($) Earnings	Dividends	Book Value
09/19	18.28	27	16	0.79	0.00	16.84
09/18*	21.20	16	12	1.64	0.00	16.06
12/17	22.00	19	11	1.19	0.00	14.41
12/16	13.30	10	6	1.38	0.00	13.47
12/15	10.94	—	—	(6.22)	0.00	14.87
Annual Growth	**13.7%**			**—**	**—**	**3.2%**

*Fiscal year change

FormFactor Inc

Why test each microchip one by one when you can test them all in one place? That's the question FormFactor answers with its interconnect technology called MicroSpring. The companyy makes wafer probe cards that test semiconductor circuits (especially memory chips) while they are still part of semiconductor wafers — before the wafers are cut into individual chips. FormFactor touts the process for its cost-effectiveness since it allows testing of many chips at once across a range of scales and temperatures. While the most of the company's products are made in the US the majority of sales are to customers in the Asia/Pacific region.

Geographic Reach

FormFactor primarily manufactures its products in California but it also has smaller manufacturing facilities in China and Japan. It also has sales and services offices in China Germany Japan Singapore South Korea and Taiwan. South Korea is the biggest market for FormFactor products accounting for 20% of revenue followed by Taiwan with 18%. About 28% of sales come from customers in North America.

Sales and Marketing

Sales to its largest customer Intel accounted for about 20% of 2014 sales up from about 18% in 2013. Another top customer SK Hynix accounted for about 15% of sales in 2014. Micron's business was about 15% of revenue in 2014 up from 11% in 2013.

Financial Performance

Sales jumped 16% higher in 2014 to $268.5 million boosted by increases in the System-on-a-Chip (SOC) and DRAM markets. Flash memory revenue were down 34%. SOC sales were driven by demand from the mobile PC and automotive microcontroller markets. FormFactor cut its loss to $19 million in 2014 from $57.6 million in 2013. Stronger revenue and lower operating costs combined to reduce the loss. Cash flow improved $17 million in 2014 from a negative $5.8 million in 2013.

Strategy

The company responds to changes in the global semiconductor market by restructuring including several rounds of minor workforce reductions. Following workforce reductions in 2011 2012 and 2013 the company cut about 50 jobs in 2014.

Looking to improve its business in the flash memory market FormFactor introduced a new product for testing NAND flash devices in 2014. Gaining a foothold in the growing flash storage sector is important for the company's growth.

Like all semiconductor equipment manufacturers FormFactor makes substantial investments in R&D in order to develop next-generation process architecture and testing products. The company is focused on new product development for the SoC market which is less volatile than the memory market. It also invests in technology through acquisitions.

EXECUTIVES

VP of Finance Controller and Chief Accounting Officer, Michael M. Ludwig, age 57, $282,692 total compensation
SVP General Counsel and Secretary, Stuart L. Merkadeau, age 57, $273,269 total compensation
CEO and Director, Michael (Mikie) Slessor, age 51, $300,000 total compensation
CTO and SVP Engineering & Product Development, Jarek (January) Kister
VP Marketing, Amy Leong
CIO Senior Vice President New Business Initiatives, Benjamin Eldridge
Vice President Of Administrative Services, Prahlad Moharir
Vice President Strategic And Product Management, Tim Eichenseer
Senior Vice President, Richard Freeman
Vice President Strategic Sales, Todd Martin
Chairman, Thomas (Tom) St. Dennis, age 66
Auditors: KPMG LLP

LOCATIONS

HQ: FormFactor Inc
7005 Southfront Road, Livermore, CA 94551
Phone: 925 290-4000
Web: www.formfactor.com

PRODUCTS/OPERATIONS

2014 Sales by Market

	$ mil.	% of total
System-on-a-Chip (SoC)	142.3	53
DRAM	110.8	41
Flash memory devices	15.4	6
Total	**268.5**	**100**

Selected Products

DRAM
  Harmony eXP
  PH150XP and PH Series
Flash
  Harmony OneTouch
Known good die (KGD)
  HFTAP (K1 K3 K5)
Logic/SoC
  BladeRunner 175
  TrueScale PP40
MicroSpring interconnect technology
Probe cards
Probe heads (PH50 PH75 PH100 PH150 models)
Special Products
  Parametric
  Takumi Pico
  Takumi Femto
TRE test technology

COMPETITORS

ASE Test
Advantest
Aehr Test Systems
Cascade Microtech
EG Systems
Everett Charles Technologies
Interconnect Devices
JAPAN ELECTRONIC MATERIALS CORPORATION
MICRONICS JAPAN CO. LTD.
Mirae
QualiTau
Synopsys
Teradyne
Tokyo Electron
Xcerra

HISTORICAL FINANCIALS

Company Type: Public

Income Statement

FYE: December 29

	REVENUE ($ mil.)	NET INCOME ($ mil.)	NET PROFIT MARGIN	EMPLOYEES
12/18	529.6	104.0	19.6%	1,676
12/17	548.4	40.9	7.5%	1,685
12/16	383.8	(6.5)	—	1,571
12/15	282.3	(1.5)	—	958
12/14	268.5	(19.1)	—	907
Annual Growth	18.5%	—	—	16.6%

2018 Year-End Financials

Debt ratio: 8.9%
Return on equity: 20.0%
Cash ($ mil.): 98.4
Current ratio: 3.30
Long-term debt ($ mil.): 34.9
No. of shares (mil.): 74.1
Dividends
  Yield: —
  Payout: —
Market value ($ mil.): 1,039.0

Stock History

	STOCK PRICE ($) FY Close	P/E High/Low		PER SHARE ($) Earnings	Dividends	Book Value
12/18	14.01	12	8	1.38	0.00	7.83
12/17	15.65	32	19	0.55	0.00	6.32
12/16	11.20	—	—	(0.10)	0.00	5.66
12/15	9.11	—	—	(0.03)	0.00	5.07
12/14	8.65	—	—	(0.34)	0.00	5.12
Annual Growth	12.8%	—	—	—	—	11.2%

Fortinet Inc

Fortinet provides computer and network security through hardware and software products. The company makes network security appliances (sold under its FortiGate line) and software that integrate antivirus firewall content filtering intrusion prevention systems (IPS) and anti-spam functions to protect against computer viruses worms and inappropriate web content. Its FortiGuard subscription services offer continuous updates on all new threats to provide real-time network protection. Fortinet also makes its own specialized security computer processors. The company also offers complementary products that include its FortiManager security management and FortiAnalyzer event analysis systems.

Operations

Fortinet's four area of businesses are Network Security which sells the FortiGate line of network security appliances; the Fortinet Security Fabric platform which protects the network core endpoints applications data centers and cloud environments; Cloud Security which helps customers connect securely to cloud environments; and the Internet of Things and Operational Technology which tracks the flow of data across multiple devices.

The company's services account for 65% of sales while its products supply about 35% of sales.

The company's Fortinet outsources the manufacturing of its appliance products to contract manufacturers and original design manufacturers. The company's manufacturers include Micro-Star International Co. Ltd. IBASE Technology Adlink Technology Inc. Wistron Senao Networks Inc. and several Taiwan-based manufacturers.

Geographic Reach

Fortinet's sales are well spread geographically. The US accounts for about a third of revenue followed by the Europe Middle East and Africa region about 40% and the Asia/Pacific region about 20%. Latin America and Canada combine to provide about 10% of revenue.

The company operates sales and service offices in about 30 countries worldwide.

Sales and Marketing

Fortinet sells through channel partners to end-customers that range from small businesses to large enterprises and industries that include government telecommunications technology government financial services education retail manufacturing and health care. The company gets 40% of revenue from just two customers Exclusive Networks Group 30% of revenue and Ingram Micro Inc. 10%.

Financial Performance

Fortinet has security in its revenue growth. From 2014 through 2018 its sales jumped more than 130% — an annual rate of about 26%.

In 2018 sales rose 20% to $1.8 billion up $306 million from 2017 on higher sales in all geographic regions — led by the EMEA region. Product and service revenue advanced 17% and 23% respectively year-over-year. FortiGate unit shipments increased in 2018 compared to 2017 while sales of non-FortiGate products such as the Fortinet Security Fabric hardware and software products also grew significantly.

Fortinet's net income leaped some $300 million to $332 million in 2018 from 2017 driven by higher sales and an income tax benefit.

The company's coffers held $1.1 billion in cash and equivalents in 2018 compared to $811 million in 2017. Fortinet's operations generated $639 million in 2018 while investing and financing activities used $135 million and $202 million respectively.

Strategy

Fortinet sells its products to distributors and resellers who have significant purchasing power and deployment capabilities while at the same time strengthening its customer support network in high-growth regions.

Fortinet invests about 14% of its revenue in research and development efforts to create new software and hardware offerings for customers. The company has R&D employees in Canada China and the US.

The company benefits from releases of new products. In 2018 it was the E-series of high-performance firewalls which delivered higher performance security.

Fortinet takes a pragmatic approach to providing cloud security with its software-defined wide-area network (SD-Wan) products for hybrid cloud environments. That approach matches customers' reluctance to commit to cloud-only preferring to keep some of their data and operations running on their own systems.

A place where Fortinet strikes out on its own is with its specialized security computer chip which it calls the SPU as in security processing unit. The chips are designed for running intensive security-related tasks that including policy enforcement threat detection and encryption.

Mergers and Acquisitions

In 2018 Fortinet bought ZoneFox Ltd. a private cloud-based insider threat detection-and-response company for about $16 million. The addition of ZoneFox's technology strengthen's Fortinet's Security Fabric.

Also in 2018 Fortinet acquired Bradford Networks a provider of network access control security products and services for about $7 million. The deal extends the Fortinet Security Fabric to include network access control.

EXECUTIVES

Chairman and CEO, Ken Xie, age 56, $406,372 total compensation
VP Engineering and CTO, Michael Xie, age 50, $360,490 total compensation
SVP International Sales and Support, Patrice Perche
CFO, Andrew (Drew) Del Matto, $381,401 total compensation
VP Corporate Development and Strategic Alliances and General Counsel, John Whittle, $332,695 total compensation

Vice President Marketing At Fortinet Inc, Tamir Hardof
Vice President Americas Channels and Enhanced Technologies, Joe Sykora
Vice President Product Engineering, Guansong Zhang
Vice President Southeast, Mike Sims
Vice President Cloud Services, Chad Whalen
Vice President Support And Services, Dave Monery
National Account Manager, Jeffrey Laniewski
National Account Manager, Bahman Sharifian
Vice President Product Engineering, David Wang
Vice President Corporate Communications And Investor Relations, Michelle Spolver
Vice President Strategic Accounts, John DiFerdinando
VP Finance, Christiane Ohlgart
Vice President of Strategic Programs, Jonathan Nguyen-Duy
Vice President Europe, Yann Pradelle
Svp Usa And Canada, Andy Travers
Vice President, Xj Zhong
Vice President Sales Central US, Jim Overbeck
National Account Manager, Carrie Sinnott
Vice President Investor Relations, Peter Salkowski
Vice President Federal Sector, Bob Fortna
Board Member, Iosef Cohen
Auditors: DELOITTE & TOUCHE LLP

LOCATIONS

HQ: Fortinet Inc
899 Kifer Road, Sunnyvale, CA 94086
Phone: 408 235-7700   **Fax:** 408 235-7737
Web: www.fortinet.com

PRODUCTS/OPERATIONS

2018 Sales

	$ mil.	% of total
Security Subscription	606.1	34
Technical Support and Other	520.7	29
Products	674.4	37
	1801.2	100

Selected Products

Database security appliance (FortiDB)
E-mail antispam (FortiMail)
Endpoint security software (FortiClient)
Endpoint vulnerability management appliance (FortiScan)
Network event correlation and content archiving (FortiAnalyzer)
Network security appliances (FortiGate)
Secure wireless access product (FortiAP)
Security management (FortiManager)
Spam and virus control subscription (FortiGuard)
Support (FortiCare)
Web application firewall appliance (FortiWeb)

COMPETITORS

CA Inc.	McAfee
Check Point Software	Microsoft
Cisco Systems	Palo Alto Networks
F5 Networks	Proofpoint
Infoblox	Symantec
Juniper Networks	VeriSign

HISTORICAL FINANCIALS
Company Type: Public

Income Statement — FYE: December 31

	REVENUE ($ mil.)	NET INCOME ($ mil.)	NET PROFIT MARGIN	EMPLOYEES
12/18	1,801.2	332.2	18.4%	5,845
12/17	1,494.9	31.4	2.1%	5,066
12/16	1,275.4	32.1	2.5%	4,665
12/15	1,009.2	7.9	0.8%	4,018
12/14	770.3	25.3	3.3%	2,854
Annual Growth	23.7%	90.3%	—	19.6%

2018 Year-End Financials

Debt ratio: —
Return on equity: 41.5%
Cash ($ mil.): 1,112.4
Current ratio: 1.77
Long-term debt ($ mil.): —
No. of shares (mil.): 169.8
Dividends
  Yield: —
  Payout: —
Market value ($ mil.): 11,959.0

	STOCK PRICE ($) FY Close	P/E High/Low		PER SHARE ($) Earnings	Dividends	Book Value
12/18	70.43	47	22	1.91	0.00	5.95
12/17	43.69	251	167	0.18	0.00	3.51
12/16	30.12	196	125	0.18	0.00	4.84
12/15	31.17	977	584	0.05	0.00	4.41
12/14	30.66	209	127	0.15	0.00	4.06
Annual Growth	23.1%	—	—	88.9%	—	10.0%

Fortress Transportation & Infrastructure Investors LLC

Auditors: Ernst & Young LLP

LOCATIONS

HQ: Fortress Transportation & Infrastructure Investors LLC
1345 Avenue of the Americas, 45th Floor, New York, NY 10105
Phone: 212 798-6100
Web: www.ftandi.com

HISTORICAL FINANCIALS
Company Type: Public

Income Statement — FYE: December 31

	REVENUE ($ mil.)	NET INCOME ($ mil.)	NET PROFIT MARGIN	EMPLOYEES
12/18	379.8	5.8	1.5%	0
12/17	217.6	0.1	0.1%	0
12/16	148.7	(20.0)	—	0
12/15	136.5	(11.8)	—	0
12/14	57.9	7.7	13.4%	0
Annual Growth	60.0%	(6.8%)	—	—

2018 Year-End Financials

Debt ratio: 46.8%
Return on equity: 0.6%
Cash ($ mil.): 99.6
Current ratio: 0.57
Long-term debt ($ mil.): 1,237.3
No. of shares (mil.): 84.0
Dividends
  Yield: 9.2%
  Payout: 1,885.7%
Market value ($ mil.): 1,205.0

	STOCK PRICE ($) FY Close	P/E High/Low		PER SHARE ($) Earnings	Dividends	Book Value
12/18	14.34	286	185	0.07	1.32	11.87
12/17	19.93	—	—	(0.00)	1.32	12.50
12/16	13.30	—	—	(0.26)	1.32	13.91
12/15	11.26	—	—	(0.18)	0.48	15.40
Annual Growth	8.4%	—	—	—	40.1%	(8.3%)

Forward Air Corp

When it's time to haul freight Forward Air never looks back. The company transports deferred airfreight by truck — cargo that requires specific-time delivery but is less time-sensitive than airfreight. Forward Air typically receives freight that has been transported by plane sends it to a sorting facility then dispatches it by truck to a terminal near its destination. The company has nearly 3777 trailers and more than 570 owned and 100 leased tractors and straight trucks in its fleet. It operates from about 85 terminals at or near airports in the US and Canada including about a dozen regional hubs. It also provides services such as warehousing and local pick-up and delivery.

Operations

The company markets its services to airfreight forwarders air cargo carriers and airlines rather than directly to shippers. Although Forward Air does facilitate overnight delivery of freight the company doesn't compete in the parcel delivery market because it handles larger shipments.

Besides its expedited transportation business the company offers pool distribution services through a second business segment Forward Air Solutions. (Pool distribution involves combining goods from multiple shippers into loads headed to the same location.) Forward Air Solutions maintains about 30 terminals near airport in major cities. Because the segment's customers tend to be retailers located in malls and outlet-based chains revenues are dependent upon the health of the retail industry.

As with its competitors Forward Air uses a fuel surcharge as a way to compensate for fluctuating fuel prices. The rates are based upon the national average price of diesel per gallon and tonnage delivered.

Geographic Reach

Forward Air operates regional hubs in Atlanta; Charlotte North Carolina; Chicago Dallas/Ft. Worth; Denver Kansas City; Los Angeles; New Orleans; Newark New Jersey; Newburgh New York; Orlando Florida; and Sacramento California. Its airport-to-airport network consists of terminals located in 87 cities.

In addition the company leases and maintains 76 additional terminals including its pool distribution terminals located in major cities throughout the US and Canada.

Mergers and Acquisitions

In 2019 Forward Air agreed to acquire final mile provider FSA Logistix for $27 million. FSA has offices in Florida and Texas and specializes in last mile delivery for American national retailers manufacturers e-tailers and third-party logistics companies. The acquisition expands Forward Air's delivery services directly to consumers' homes.

EXECUTIVES

Senior Vice President Sales, Craig Drum
Chairman President and CEO, Bruce A. Campbell, age 68, $620,999 total compensation
EVP Operations, Chris C. Ruble, age 57, $414,072 total compensation
EVP Intermodal Services and Chief Strategy Officer, Matthew J. Jewell, age 53, $413,240 total compensation
SVP Chief Legal Officer and Secretary, Michael L. Hance, age 47, $334,200 total compensation
SVP CFO and Treasurer, Michael J. Morris, age 51
Vice President Of Systems And Process Engineering, Kelly Brown
Vice President Fleet Maintenance, Dave Kreigh
Svp Of Hr, Mithchin Kyle
Vp Operations Southeast Region, John Miller
Board Member, Ana Amicarella
Board Member, Craig Carlock
Auditors: Ernst & Young LLP

LOCATIONS

HQ: Forward Air Corp
1915 Snapps Ferry Road, Building N, Greeneville, TN 37745
Phone: 423 636-7000
Web: www.forwardair.com

PRODUCTS/OPERATIONS

2014 Sales

	$ mil.	% of total
Forward Air	608.1	78
Forward Air Solutions	124.4	16
TQI	48.5	6
Total	**7,801.0**	**100**

Services
Expedited Linehaul Service
Forward Air Complete
Canadian Transborder Service
Airline Logistics Services
Freight Management Services
Container Freight Stations
Truckload Services

COMPETITORS

Alliance Air	Old Dominion Freight
CRST Expedited	Panther Expedited
CRST International	Services
Daylight Transport	Schneider National
FedEx Freight	Towne Air Freight
New Penn Motor Express	XPO logistics

HISTORICAL FINANCIALS

Company Type: Public

Income Statement — FYE: December 31

	REVENUE ($ mil.)	NET INCOME ($ mil.)	NET PROFIT MARGIN	EMPLOYEES
12/18	1,320.8	92.0	7.0%	5,369
12/17	1,100.8	87.3	7.9%	4,898
12/16	982.5	27.6	2.8%	4,868
12/15	959.1	55.5	5.8%	4,536
12/14	780.9	61.1	7.8%	3,902
Annual Growth	14.0%	10.8%	—	8.3%

2018 Year-End Financials

Debt ratio: 6.2%
Return on equity: 16.9%
Cash ($ mil.): 25.6
Current ratio: 2.69
Long-term debt ($ mil.): 47.3
No. of shares (mil.): 28.5
Dividends
  Yield: 1.1%
  Payout: 18.7%
Market value ($ mil.): 1,565.0

	STOCK PRICE ($) FY Close	P/E High/Low	PER SHARE ($) Earnings	Dividends	Book Value
12/18	54.85	23 16	3.12	0.63	19.39
12/17	57.44	20 16	2.89	0.60	18.11
12/16	47.38	55 40	0.90	0.51	16.59
12/15	43.01	32 23	1.78	0.48	16.70
12/14	50.37	25 21	1.96	0.48	15.32
Annual Growth	2.2%	— —	12.3%	7.0%	6.1%

Four Corners Property Trust Inc

Auditors: KPMG LLP

LOCATIONS

HQ: Four Corners Property Trust Inc
591 Redwood Highway, Suite 1150, Mill Valley, CA 94941
Phone: 415 965-8030
Web: www.fcpt.com

HISTORICAL FINANCIALS

Company Type: Public

Income Statement — FYE: December 31

	REVENUE ($ mil.)	NET INCOME ($ mil.)	NET PROFIT MARGIN	EMPLOYEES
12/18	143.6	82.4	57.4%	361
12/17	133.2	71.3	53.6%	342
12/16	124.0	156.8	126.4%	324
12/15	33.4	5.7	17.0%	334
12/14	17.7	0.0	0.2%	350
Annual Growth	68.8%	612.3%	—	0.8%

2018 Year-End Financials

Debt ratio: 45.8%
Return on equity: 13.6%
Cash ($ mil.): 92.0
Current ratio: 19.29
Long-term debt ($ mil.): 615.8
No. of shares (mil.): 68.2
Dividends
  Yield: 4.2%
  Payout: 85.9%
Market value ($ mil.): 1,787.0

	STOCK PRICE ($) FY Close	P/E High/Low	PER SHARE ($) Earnings	Dividends	Book Value
12/18	26.20	22 17	1.28	1.10	10.13
12/17	25.70	23 17	1.18	1.00	8.39
12/16	20.52	9 5	2.63	9.29	7.76
12/15	24.16	26 19	0.91	0.00	10.33
Annual Growth	2.7%	— —	12.0%	—	(0.6%)

Fox Factory Holding Corp

Talk about shock value. Fox Factory makes suspension products — i.e. shocks — for high-performance mountain bikes and other powered vehicles that give riders a smooth ride over rough terrain. Some two-thirds of sales are for shocks for bicycles but the other third of revenue comes from shocks for ATVs motorcycles snowmobiles and off-road vehicles and trucks. Fox Factory sells its shocks to original equipment manufacturers (OEMs) such as Specialized and Trek (bikes) and Ford and Polaris (powered vehicles). It also sells branded apparel such as T-shirts sweatshirts and hats. Fox Factory went public in 2013.

Geographic Reach

Sales outside the US account for about two-thirds of revenue because Fox Factory sells directly to OEMs that have primary manufacturing operations in Asia. The majority of its own manufacturing operations are in California but Fox Factory does have a plant in Taiwan. The company is shifting all of its manufacturing to Taiwan by 2016.

Sales and Marketing

Fox Factory sells its suspension products to more than 150 OEMs and distributes its products to more than 2300 retail dealers and distributors worldwide. In 2012 80% of sales were to OEM customers and 20% were to dealers and distributors for resale in the aftermarket channel.

Financial Performance

The company has experienced steady growth over the years. Sales increased about 20% in 2012 due to increased demand from both OEMs and aftermarket customers. Fox Factory has also been consistently profitable.

Company Background

Fox Factory was founded in 1974 by Robert Fox who built a racing suspension shock in his friend's garage. The company was bought by Compass Diversified Holdings in 2008. In 2013 Fox Factory went public and Compass held onto a majority share; Compass subsequently divested shares in Fox Factory but still maintains a minority ownership stake.

EXECUTIVES

CEO, Larry L. Enterline, age 66, $702,821 total compensation
CFO, Zvi Glasman, age 55, $270,100 total compensation
President, Mario Galasso, age 53, $295,654 total compensation
SVP Global Operations, William H. (Bill) Katherman
Vice President, Wesley Allinger
Vice President General Counsel, David Haugen
Chairman, Elias J. Sabo, age 48
Board Member, Ted Waitman
Board Member, Elizabeth Fetter
Auditors: Grant Thornton LLP

LOCATIONS

HQ: Fox Factory Holding Corp
6634 Hwy 53, Braselton, GA 30517
Phone: 831 274-6500
Web: www.ridefox.com

PRODUCTS/OPERATIONS

2015 Sales

	$ mil.	% of total
Bikes	211.7	58
Power vehicles	155.1	42
Total	**366.8**	**100**

COMPETITORS

Giant Manufacturing	Tenneco
KAYABA INDUSTRY CO. LTD.	Truck-Lite
SRAM	ZF Group NAO

HISTORICAL FINANCIALS
Company Type: Public

Income Statement — FYE: December 28

	REVENUE ($ mil.)	NET INCOME ($ mil.)	NET PROFIT MARGIN	EMPLOYEES
12/18	619.2	84.0	13.6%	2,240
12/17	475.6	43.1	9.1%	1,800
12/16	403.0	35.6	8.9%	1,700
12/15	366.8	24.9	6.8%	1,500
12/14	306.7	27.6	9.0%	1,000
Annual Growth	19.2%	32.0%	—	22.3%

2018 Year-End Financials

Debt ratio: 12.2%
Return on equity: 30.3%
Cash ($ mil.): 27.9
Current ratio: 2.40
Long-term debt ($ mil.): 52.5
No. of shares (mil.): 37.9
Dividends
  Yield: —
  Payout: —
Market value ($ mil.): 2,277.0

	STOCK PRICE ($) FY Close	P/E High/Low	PER SHARE ($) Earnings	Dividends	Book Value
12/18	59.93	34 15	2.16	0.00	8.45
12/17	38.85	38 22	1.11	0.00	6.24
12/16	27.75	29 15	0.94	0.00	5.01
12/15	16.53	29 22	0.66	0.00	4.11
12/14	16.23	25 18	0.73	0.00	3.47
Annual Growth	38.6%	—	31.2%	—	24.9%

Franklin Financial Network Inc

Auditors: Crowe LLP

LOCATIONS

HQ: Franklin Financial Network Inc
722 Columbia Avenue, Franklin, TN 37064
Phone: 615 236-2265
Web: www.franklinsynergybank.com

HISTORICAL FINANCIALS
Company Type: Public

Income Statement — FYE: December 31

	ASSETS ($ mil.)	NET INCOME ($ mil.)	INCOME AS % OF ASSETS	EMPLOYEES
12/18	4,249.4	34.5	0.8%	338
12/17	3,843.5	28.0	0.7%	281
12/16	2,943.1	28.0	1.0%	268
12/15	2,167.7	16.0	0.7%	226
12/14	1,355.8	8.4	0.6%	220
Annual Growth	33.1%	42.3%	—	11.3%

2018 Year-End Financials

Return on assets: 0.8%
Return on equity: 10.1%
Long-term debt ($ mil.): —
No. of shares (mil.): 14.5
Sales ($ mil): 180.6
Dividends
  Yield: —
  Payout: —
Market value ($ mil.): 383.0

	STOCK PRICE ($) FY Close	P/E High/Low	PER SHARE ($) Earnings	Dividends	Book Value
12/18	26.37	17 10	2.34	0.00	25.64
12/17	34.10	20 14	2.04	0.00	23.01
12/16	41.85	17 10	2.42	0.00	20.73
12/15	31.38	20 11	1.54	0.00	17.86
12/14	17.30	17 13	1.27	0.00	15.70
Annual Growth	11.1%	—	16.5%	—	13.0%

Frontdoor Inc

Auditors: Deloitte & Touche LLP

LOCATIONS

HQ: Frontdoor Inc
150 Peabody Place, Memphis, TN 38103
Phone: 901 701-5002
Web: www.frontdoorhome.com

HISTORICAL FINANCIALS
Company Type: Public

Income Statement — FYE: December 31

	REVENUE ($ mil.)	NET INCOME ($ mil.)	NET PROFIT MARGIN	EMPLOYEES
12/18	1,258.0	125.0	9.9%	2,200
12/17	1,157.0	160.0	13.8%	2,700
12/16	1,020.0	124.0	12.2%	0
12/15	917.0	120.0	13.1%	0
Annual Growth	11.1%	1.4%	—	—

2018 Year-End Financials

Debt ratio: 94.5%
Return on equity: 78.8%
Cash ($ mil.): 305.0
Current ratio: 0.96
Long-term debt ($ mil.): 977.0
No. of shares (mil.): 84.5
Dividends
  Yield: —
  Payout: —
Market value ($ mil.): 2,250.0

	STOCK PRICE ($) FY Close	P/E High/Low	PER SHARE ($) Earnings	Dividends	Book Value
12/18	26.61	33 14	1.47	0.00	(4.07)
12/17	0.00	— —	(0.00)	0.00	(0.00)
Annual Growth	—	—	—	—	—

FS Bancorp (Indiana)

Auditors: Crowe Horwath LLP

LOCATIONS

HQ: FS Bancorp (Indiana)
220 South Detroit Street, La Grange, IN 46761
Phone: 260 463-7111   **Fax:** 260 463-7341
Web: www.farmersstatebank.com

HISTORICAL FINANCIALS
Company Type: Public

Income Statement — FYE: December 31

	ASSETS ($ mil.)	NET INCOME ($ mil.)	INCOME AS % OF ASSETS	EMPLOYEES
12/18	760.5	9.3	1.2%	0
12/17	734.0	7.5	1.0%	0
12/16	680.4	7.4	1.1%	0
12/15	603.8	6.1	1.0%	172
12/14	570.6	6.2	1.1%	0
Annual Growth	7.4%	10.7%	—	—

2018 Year-End Financials

Return on assets: 1.2%
Return on equity: 13.6%
Long-term debt ($ mil.): —
No. of shares (mil.): 2.1
Sales ($ mil): 35.5
Dividends
  Yield: 1.8%
  Payout: 34.1%
Market value ($ mil.): 175.0

	STOCK PRICE ($) FY Close	P/E High/Low	PER SHARE ($) Earnings	Dividends	Book Value
12/18	79.90	28 13	4.22	1.44	32.53
12/17	92.00	27 20	3.36	1.23	30.09
12/16	68.25	24 18	3.33	1.17	28.09
12/15	60.00	23 21	2.73	1.03	26.43
12/14	57.00	21 16	2.79	1.00	24.63
Annual Growth	8.8%	—	10.9%	9.5%	7.2%

FS Bancorp Inc (Washington)

EXECUTIVES

Vice President Indirect Sales Manager, Craig Brown
Senior Vice President Compliance, May-Ling Sowell
Vice President Manager, Robert Jorgenson
Vice President Of Finance and Treasurer, David Tun
Auditors: Moss Adams LLP

LOCATIONS

HQ: FS Bancorp Inc (Washington)
6920 220th Street SW, Mountlake Terrace, WA 98043
Phone: 425 771-5299
Web: www.fsbwa.com

COMPETITORS

Bank of America	KeyCorp
Banner Corp	Washington Banking
Columbia Banking	Washington Federal
Heritage Financial	Wells Fargo

HISTORICAL FINANCIALS
Company Type: Public

Income Statement — FYE: December 31

	ASSETS ($ mil.)	NET INCOME ($ mil.)	INCOME AS % OF ASSETS	EMPLOYEES
12/18	1,621.6	24.3	1.5%	424
12/17	981.7	14.0	1.4%	326
12/16	827.9	10.5	1.3%	306
12/15	677.5	8.8	1.3%	241
12/14	509.7	4.5	0.9%	210
Annual Growth	33.6%	52.2%	—	19.2%

2018 Year-End Financials
Return on assets: 1.8%
Return on equity: 16.1%
Long-term debt ($ mil.): —
No. of shares (mil.): 4.4
Sales ($ mil): 89.2
Dividends
  Yield: 1.2%
  Payout: 12.2%
Market value ($ mil.): 193.0

	STOCK PRICE ($) FY Close	P/E High/Low		PER SHARE ($) Earnings	Dividends	Book Value
12/18	42.88	10	6	6.29	0.53	40.08
12/17	54.57	13	8	4.28	0.43	33.15
12/16	35.95	10	6	3.51	0.37	26.49
12/15	26.00	9	6	2.93	0.27	23.24
12/14	18.25	12	11	1.52	0.23	20.35
Annual Growth	23.8%	—		42.6%	23.2%	18.5%

Funko Inc

Auditors: Ernst & Young LLP

LOCATIONS
HQ: Funko Inc
2802 Wetmore Avenue, Everett, WA 98201
Phone: 425 783-3616
Web: www.funko.com

HISTORICAL FINANCIALS
Company Type: Public

Income Statement   FYE: December 31

	REVENUE ($ mil.)	NET INCOME ($ mil.)	NET PROFIT MARGIN	EMPLOYEES
12/18	686.0	9.3	1.4%	702
12/17	516.0	3.7	0.7%	588
12/16	426.7	26.8	6.3%	472
12/15*	56.5	(15.5)	—	0
10/15	217.4	27.5	12.6%	0
Annual Growth	33.3%	(23.6%)	—	—

*Fiscal year change

2018 Year-End Financials
Debt ratio: 37.3%
Return on equity: 6.5%
Cash ($ mil.): 13.4
Current ratio: 1.89
Long-term debt ($ mil.): 216.7
No. of shares (mil.): 48.5
Dividends
  Yield: —
  Payout: —
Market value ($ mil.): 638.0

	STOCK PRICE ($) FY Close	P/E High/Low		PER SHARE ($) Earnings	Dividends	Book Value
12/18	13.15	80	16	0.37	0.00	3.23
12/17	6.65	243	150	0.04	0.00	2.71
Annual Growth	97.7%	—		—825.0%	—	18.9%

FVCBankcorp Inc

Auditors: Yount, Hyde & Barbour, P.C.

LOCATIONS
HQ: FVCBankcorp Inc
11325 Random Hills Road, Suite 240, Fairfax, VA 22030
Phone: 703 436-3800
Web: www.fvcbank.com

HISTORICAL FINANCIALS
Company Type: Public

Income Statement   FYE: December 31

	ASSETS ($ mil.)	NET INCOME ($ mil.)	INCOME AS % OF ASSETS	EMPLOYEES
12/18	1,351.5	10.8	0.8%	128
12/17	1,053.2	7.6	0.7%	0
12/16	909.3	6.9	0.8%	0
12/15	736.8	5.4	0.7%	0
12/14	604.7	4.1	0.7%	0
Annual Growth	22.3%	27.3%	—	—

2018 Year-End Financials
Return on assets: 0.9%
Return on equity: 8.4%
Long-term debt ($ mil.): —
No. of shares (mil.): 13.7
Sales ($ mil): 53.5
Dividends
  Yield: —
  Payout: —
Market value ($ mil.): 241.0

	STOCK PRICE ($) FY Close	P/E High/Low		PER SHARE ($) Earnings	Dividends	Book Value
12/18	17.61	22	17	0.85	0.00	11.55
12/17	17.52	28	23	0.67	0.00	9.04
12/16	16.80	29	23	0.63	0.00	7.84
12/15	17.25	45	25	0.51	0.00	7.17
12/14	15.50	44	37	0.40	0.00	6.59
Annual Growth	3.2%	—		20.4%	—	15.0%

Gaming & Leisure Properties, Inc

Auditors: DELOITTE & TOUCHE LLP

LOCATIONS
HQ: Gaming & Leisure Properties, Inc
845 Berkshire Blvd., Suite 200, Wyomissing, PA 19610
Phone: 610 401-2900
Web: www.glpropinc.com

HISTORICAL FINANCIALS
Company Type: Public

Income Statement   FYE: December 31

	REVENUE ($ mil.)	NET INCOME ($ mil.)	NET PROFIT MARGIN	EMPLOYEES
12/18	1,055.7	339.5	32.2%	644
12/17	971.3	380.6	39.2%	714
12/16	828.2	289.3	34.9%	751
12/15	575.0	128.1	22.3%	792
12/14	635.9	185.3	29.2%	807
Annual Growth	13.5%	16.3%	—	(5.5%)

2018 Year-End Financials
Debt ratio: 68.2%
Return on equity: 14.3%
Cash ($ mil.): 25.7
Current ratio: 0.41
Long-term debt ($ mil.): 5,853.5
No. of shares (mil.): 214.2
Dividends
  Yield: 7.9%
  Payout: 141.9%
Market value ($ mil.): 6,921.0

	STOCK PRICE ($) FY Close	P/E High/Low		PER SHARE ($) Earnings	Dividends	Book Value
12/18	32.31	23	20	1.58	2.57	10.58
12/17	37.00	22	17	1.79	2.50	11.56
12/16	30.62	22	15	1.60	2.32	11.72
12/15	27.80	34	23	1.08	2.18	(2.19)
12/14	29.34	31	17	1.58	14.32	(1.10)
Annual Growth	2.4%	—		(0.0%)	(34.9%)	—

Gannett Co Inc (New)

New Media Investment Group (formerly GateHouse Media) lets the local news flow freely. The company is a leading community-newspaper publisher with more than 400 publications. Its portfolio includes roughly 80 daily newspapers along with many more weeklies and shoppers that reach about 10 million readers. New Media Investment generates revenue primarily through advertising; its papers serve ads from almost 300000 business advertisers. In conjunction with its print publications the company operates more than 600 websites. New Media Investment also produces a halfdozen yellow page directories and offers commercial printing services.

Operations
The company has three operating segments: advertising circulations and commercial printing. Advertising accounted for almost 70% of revenue in fiscal 2012.

Geographic Reach
New Media Investment operates newspapers and websites in about 20 states.

Sales and Marketing
New Media Investment itself reported total advertising expenses of $3.4 million in fiscal 2012.

Financial Performance
The company's revenue decreased 6% and its net loss increased 38% in fiscal 2012 compared with the previous year. The decrease in revenue was attributed to decreases in advertising revenue and circulation revenue partially offset by an increase in commercial printing and other revenue. New Media's net loss increased primarily due to the decrease in total revenue not because of increased operating expenses.

Strategy
The downturn in the economy and the decline of the newspaper industry have forced the company to concentrate mostly on cutting costs streamlining operations and converting to a more multimedia company. The company has tried to improve the productivity of its labor force. New Media Investment also relies on the loyalty of readers interested in local news as about 85% of its newspapers have been around for more than 100 years.

Company Background
New Media Investment was formed in 1997 as Liberty Group Publishing to buy about 160 publications from newspaper giant Hollinger International (later Sun-Times Media Group). It went public in 2006 changing its name in the process.

EXECUTIVES

CFO and Chief Accounting Officer, Gregory W. (Greg) Freiberg, age 51
COO and CEO GateHouse Media, Kirk A. Davis, age 58, $494,785 total compensation
CEO and Director, Michael E. (Mike) Reed, age 53, $500,000 total compensation
CIO GateHouse Media, Paul Ameden
Evp Brand Agency Leader, Gail Hollander
Vice President Executive Producer, Tim Legallo
Evp Executive Creative Director, David Corr
Vice President Executive Producer, Sharon Petro
Chairman, Wesley R. (Wes) Edens, age 57
Board Member, Kevin Sheehan
Auditors: Ernst & Young LLP

LOCATIONS

HQ: Gannett Co Inc (New)
1345 Avenue of the Americas, 45th floor, New York, NY 10105
Phone: 212 479-3160
Web: www.newmediainv.com

PRODUCTS/OPERATIONS

Selected Daily Newspapers
Daily Messenger (Canandaigua NY)
The Enterprise (Brockton MA)
Evening Tribune (Hornell NY)
The Holland Sentinel (Michigan)
The Independent (Massillon OH)
Journal Star (Peoria IL)
The Leavenworth Times (Kansas)
The Leader (Corning NY)
MetroWest Daily News (Framingham MA)
The Patriot Ledger (Quincy MA)
The Repository (Canton OH)
Rockford Register Star (Illinois)
The State Journal-Register (Springfield IL)
The Times-Reporter (New Philadelphia OH)
Wellsville Daily Reporter (New York)

COMPETITORS

Advance Publications
Community Newspaper Holdings
Lee Enterprises
McClatchy Company
New York Times
Schurz Communications
Star Tribune
Sun-Times Media Holdings
TEGNA
Tribune Media

HISTORICAL FINANCIALS

Company Type: Public

Income Statement — FYE: December 30

	REVENUE ($ mil.)	NET INCOME ($ mil.)	NET PROFIT MARGIN	EMPLOYEES
12/18	1,526.0	18.2	1.2%	10,638
12/17	1,342.0	(0.9)	—	10,516
12/16	1,255.3	31.6	2.5%	10,092
12/15	1,195.8	67.6	5.7%	9,509
12/14	652.3	(3.2)	—	6,133
Annual Growth	23.7%	—	—	14.8%

2018 Year-End Financials
Debt ratio: 30.5%
Return on equity: 2.6%
Cash ($ mil.): 48.6
Current ratio: 1.20
Long-term debt ($ mil.): 428.1
No. of shares (mil.): 60.3
Dividends
  Yield: 0.0%
  Payout: 480.6%
Market value ($ mil.): 692.0

	STOCK PRICE ($) FY Close	P/E High/Low		PER SHARE ($) Earnings	Dividends	Book Value
12/18	11.47	61	36	0.31	1.49	11.89
12/17	16.78	—	—	(0.02)	1.42	12.67
12/16	15.96	29	20	0.70	1.34	14.11
12/15	19.73	17	9	1.52	1.29	14.47
12/14	24.09	—	—	(0.10)	0.54	12.92
Annual Growth	(16.9%)			—	28.9%	(2.1%)

Gencor Industries Inc

Gencor Industries is a US manufacturer of heavy machinery used in the production of highway construction materials synthetic fuels and environmental control equipment. Subsidiary Bituma designs and manufactures hot-mix asphalt batch plants used in the production of asphalt paving materials. Subsidiary General Combustion engineers combustion systems namely large burners that can transform almost any fuel into energy or burn multiple fuels simultaneously and fluid heat transfer systems under the Hy-Way and Beverley brands. With two manufacturing facilities in the US it sells products through its own sales force and independent dealers and agents located throughout the world.

Operations
Gencor's operations are comprised of Hetherington and Berner (H&B) Hy-Way Heat Bituma Corporation Thermotech Systems and General Combustion.

H&B is a manufacturer of asphalt batch mixing plants while Hy-Way produces thermal fluid process equipment and targets the industrial and asphalt markets. Bituma builds hot mix storage silo systems and Thermotech Systems offers a portable patented thermal absorption process used for processing contaminated soil. General Combustion specializes in advanced combustion technology.

Geographic Reach
Gencor is stationed in Orlando Florida and has two manufacturing facilities in Iowa and Florida. It serves North America Europe the Middle East and Asia. All of its revenue comes from the US.

Sales and Marketing
Gencor's products are sold through sales representatives and independent dealers and agents located throughout the world. It primarily targets the highway construction industry.

Financial Performance
After experiencing two straight years of growth Gencor saw its revenues decrease 23% from $63 million in 2012 to $49 million in 2013. Its profits however surged by 50% from $4.5 million to $6.7 million.

The revenue decline for 2013 was the result of the completion of a large asphalt plant delivered in 2012 and continued weak domestic road construction activity. In addition its Canadian sales declined as various Canadian government's infrastructure spend programs neared completion.

The surge in profits was fueled by continued improvements in production lower purchasing costs reduced product engineering and development expenses and tight controls on selling general and administrative expenses.

Strategy
In response to lower demand for its products and services Gencor is focused on conserving cash and streamlining its operations and cost structure. These actions included adjustments to its workforce reduced purchases of raw materials and reductions in selling general and administrative expenses. In addition it reviews its internal processes to identify inefficiencies and cost reduction opportunities.

EXECUTIVES

Secretary, Jeanne M. Lyons
President and Director, Marc G. Elliott, $384,000 total compensation
Chairman of the Board; Chief Executive Officer, E. J. (Mike) Elliott, $600,000 total compensation
VP and Controller, Lawrence C. Maingot, age 55
SVP Sales and Marketing, Dennis B. Hunt, $250,000 total compensation
CFO, Eric E. Mellen
VP Product Support, Larry K. Miles
Controller, Allen Bradley
President and Director, Marc G. Elliott
Director, Randolph H. Fields
Director, David A. Air
Director, Cort J. Dondero
Director, James P. Sharp
Auditors: Moore Stephens Lovelace, P.A.

LOCATIONS

HQ: Gencor Industries Inc
5201 North Orange Blossom Trail, Orlando, FL 32810
Phone: 407 290-6000
Web: www.gencor.com

PRODUCTS/OPERATIONS

Selected Products and Services
Asphalt Storage Tanks
Baghouse Filtration
Batch Plants
Burners and Combustion Systems
Cold Feed Systems
Gencor Control Automation
Drag Slat Conveyors
Drum Mix Plants
Heat Thermal Fluid Systems
Hot Mix Silos
Mineral Additive Systems
(RAP) Recycle Systems
Soil Remediation Plants
Used Equipment

COMPETITORS

Astec Industries
CMI Terex
Caterpillar
Cleaver-Brooks
Coen Company
Forney Corporation
Paul Mueller

HISTORICAL FINANCIALS

Company Type: Public

Income Statement — FYE: September 30

	REVENUE ($ mil.)	NET INCOME ($ mil.)	NET PROFIT MARGIN	EMPLOYEES
09/19	81.3	10.2	12.5%	334
09/18	98.6	12.5	12.7%	372
09/17	80.6	8.4	10.4%	335
09/16	69.9	7.0	10.1%	273
09/15	39.2	(1.8)	—	216
Annual Growth	20.0%	—	—	11.5%

2019 Year-End Financials

Debt ratio: —
Return on equity: 6.8%
Cash ($ mil.): 10.3
Current ratio: 24.20
Long-term debt ($ mil.): —
No. of shares (mil.): 14.5
Dividends
Yield: —
Payout: —
Market value ($ mil.): 169.0

	STOCK PRICE ($) FY Close	P/E High/Low		PER SHARE ($) Earnings	Dividends	Book Value
09/19	11.61	21	15	0.69	0.00	10.66
09/18	12.05	21	14	0.85	0.00	9.78
09/17	17.65	31	19	0.57	0.00	8.94
09/16	11.98	37	18	0.49	0.00	8.36
09/15	9.04	—	—	(0.13)	0.00	7.88
Annual Growth	6.5%	—	—	—	—	7.9%

Generac Holdings Inc

Financial Performance
Except for a dip in 2015 Generac's revenue has seen steady growth the last five years rising 38% between 2014 and 2018. US residential product growth has been driven by increased shipments of home generators amid rising awareness about the need for residential back-up power. Higher demand from equipment rental telecom healthcare and energy markets boosted sales of Generac's commercial and industrial generators.

Sales in 2018 increased 20% to $2 billion compared to $1.7 billion in 2017. Growth in 2018 was fueled by continued demand for residential generators amid higher awareness of power outages. Sales in both the residential and commercial and industrial segments grew 20% over 2017; the other products segment saw sales rise 29%.

Net income rose 51% to $238.3 million in 2018 compared to 2017 primarily due to higher income from operations on increased sales volumes.

Cash at the end of 2018 was $224.5 million an increase of $86 million from the prior year. Cash from operations contributed $247.2 million to the coffers while investing activities used $108.9 million mainly for capital expenditures and an acquisition. Financing activities used $52 million primarily for repayments of long-term debt.

Strategy
Generac is focused on fortifying its lead in the North American home standby generator market while growing internationally and developing products that are greener and offer greater connectivity.

The company holds more than 75% of the North American home standby generator market but fewer than 5% of US households own a standby generator. Amid this low level of market penetration Generac plans to grow by leveraging increasing consumer awareness about the benefits of standby power. The company continually builds out its dealer network so its sales installation and service capabilities keep pace with rising demand. Markets outside the US are also a target area for growth; Generac's international sales rose 18% in 2018 compared to the prior year.

As the world looks to clean energy Generac has developed products that are greener and made key acquisitions that make energy consumption more efficient. The company has expanded its line of standby generators that operate on natural gas and in 2019 Generac acquired Pika Energy a Maine-based manufacturer of battery storage systems used to capture and store solar or grid power for homes and businesses.

Also in 2019 Generac purchased Neurio Technology a Canadian energy data company that offers electrical metering technology and analytics that optimize energy use. The deal compliments Generac's Wi-Fi-enabled Mobil Link technology that home standby generator owners can use to monitor their generator and energy use remotely using a computer or mobile device. Mobile Link also provides Generac with a wealth of data from the company's installed base of equipment which it aims to leverage in the development of future products and services that modernize how home energy is generated stored and used.

EXECUTIVES

EVP North America, Russell S. (Russ) Minick, $371,279 total compensation
Chairman President and CEO, Aaron Jagdfeld, age 47, $731,134 total compensation
CFO, York A. Ragen, age 48, $362,668 total compensation
EVP Global Engineering, Allen D Gillette, age 63, $180,009 total compensation
EVP Strategic Global Sourcing, Roger F. Pascavis, age 59, $227,740 total compensation
Vice President Operational Excellence, Dan Waschow
National Account Manager, Todd Dufur
Vice President Retail Sales, Jason Hall
Vice President Service Operations, Paul Cannestra
National Account Manager, Josh Langenfeld
Senior Vice President New Business Development, Steve Goran
National Accounts Manager, Paul Ross
National Account Manager, Brian Essenmacher
Vice President Of Global Sourcing Supply Chain andamp; Logistics, Fabian Ciavaglia
Executive Vice President Global Engineering, Patrick Forsythe
VICE PRESIDENT RETAIL SALES, Tom Lewis
Vice President Of Sales, Ryan Jeske
Vice President Global Product Engineering, Joe Moses
NATIONAL ACCOUNT MANAGER, Austin Partida
Vice President New Product Sourcing, Rob Moody
Vice President Global IT, Daniel Bourquin
Board Member, David Ramon
Board Member, John Bowlin
Board Member, Andrew Lampereur
Board Member, Bennett Morgan
Auditors: DELOITTE & TOUCHE LLP

LOCATIONS
HQ: Generac Holdings Inc
S45 W29290 Hwy. 59, Waukesha, WI 53189
Phone: 262 544-4811
Web: www.generac.com

PRODUCTS/OPERATIONS

2015 Sales
	$ mil.	% of total
Residential power products	673.8	51
Commercial & Industrial products	548.4	42
Other	95.1	7
Total	**1,317.3**	**100**

Selected Products and Brands
Generators
 Commercial (QuietSource)
 Industrial (gaseous diesel bi-fuel modular power systems (MPS) Gemini)
 Portable (GP XG XP iX)
 Recreational vehicle (gasoline propane diesel)
 Residential (QuietSource Guardian)

Selected Markets
Agricultural/mining
Business office
Commercial/retail
Data center
Education
Healthcare
Manufacturing
Municipal
Research
Residential
Telecom

COMPETITORS

Aggreko
Atlas Copco USA Holdings
Briggs & Stratton Power Products
Caterpillar
Cummins Power Generation
Doosan Corp
Honda
Kohler
Multiquip
Taylor Group
Techtronic
Terex
Westerbeke Corp.

HISTORICAL FINANCIALS
Company Type: Public

Income Statement
FYE: December 31

	REVENUE ($ mil.)	NET INCOME ($ mil.)	NET PROFIT MARGIN	EMPLOYEES
12/18	2,023.4	238.2	11.8%	5,664
12/17	1,672.4	159.3	9.5%	4,556
12/16	1,444.4	98.7	6.8%	4,202
12/15	1,317.3	77.7	5.9%	3,156
12/14	1,460.9	174.6	12.0%	3,587
Annual Growth	8.5%	8.1%	—	12.1%

2018 Year-End Financials

Debt ratio: 38.0%
Return on equity: 36.1%
Cash ($ mil.): 224.4
Current ratio: 2.00
Long-term debt ($ mil.): 876.4
No. of shares (mil.): 62.1
Dividends
Yield: —
Payout: —
Market value ($ mil.): 3,088.0

	STOCK PRICE ($) FY Close	P/E High/Low		PER SHARE ($) Earnings	Dividends	Book Value
12/18	49.70	17	12	3.54	0.00	12.24
12/17	49.52	20	13	2.56	0.00	8.97
12/16	40.74	29	18	1.50	0.00	6.40
12/15	29.77	44	24	1.12	0.00	7.06
12/14	46.76	24	15	2.49	0.00	7.11
Annual Growth	1.5%	—	—	9.2%	—	14.6%

GEO Group Inc (The) (New)

The GEO Group sticks to its convictions and it relies on them to generate business. The real estate investment trust (REIT) is one of the largest correctional systems in the US with operations in more than 30 states and electronic monitoring services in every state. Its worldwide operations include some 135 maximum- medium- and mini-mum-security correctional detention (including immigrant detention) and mental health facilities with roughly 96000 beds. It also conducts community supervision of more than 210000 offenders and pretrial defendants. Furthermore GEO runs educational rehabilitative and vocational training programs at its facilities. Its GEO Care unit provides mental health and residential treatment services for parolees probationers and pretrial defendants. About 90% of GEO's revenue derives from the US.

HISTORY

The company that became The Geo Group began as part of the Wackenhut Corporation (now known as G4S Secure Solutions (USA)) which was founded in 1954 as an investigation firm and moved into the security guard business the next year. When the prison population began to grow in the late 1970s and early 1980s (because of tougher sentences and new federal drug laws) Wackenhut established its Wackenhut Corrections division in 1984 to focus on prison management.

In 1986 the division won its first contract to construct a Colorado facility for the Immigration and Naturalization Service. Two years later Wackenhut Corrections became a full-fledged subsidiary of its parent. Wackenhut Corrections ventured overseas in 1992 when it began operating a prison in Australia and formed a joint venture Premier Prison Services with Serco Group to provide prison management services in the UK.

The company's next step was to go public which it did in 1994 when Wackenhut Corporation sold a minority stake. Also that year Premier Prison Services won its first contract to operate a prison in the town of Doncaster in the UK. The joint venture won another deal in 1997 to manage a 500-bed prison in Kilmarnock Scotland. However Wackenhut Corrections was forced to change policies after violence at some of its foreign prisons. To solve the problem the company replaced American guards with native hires and began paying more attention to troublesome inmates.

Wackenhut Corrections moved beyond prisons in 1997 buying an 86-bed psychiatric hospital in Fort Lauderdale Florida. The next year Wackenhut Corrections spun off a real estate investment trust (REIT) Correctional Properties Trust to buy and build prison facilities and lease them back to the company. (The REIT was later renamed CentraCore Properties Trust.)

Wackenhut Corrections stumbled in 1999 when the state of Texas took over control of a Wackenhut-operated prison in Austin after allegations that guards had had sex with female inmates. In addition a riot at a New Mexico prison sparked bad publicity. But business continued to roll in and the company gained contracts to run a prison in New Zealand and a hospital in Florida.

After its closure in 2000 Wackenhut's juvenile facility in Jena Louisiana was named in a lawsuit brought by the US Justice Department against Louisiana prisons. The company shifted focus to its international operations in 2001 — it expanded existing prisons in Australia and opened prisons in South Africa and the UK.

Danish security firm Group 4 Falck gained control of Wackenhut Corrections in 2002 when it acquired Wackenhut Corporation. Late in the year Wackenhut Corrections acquired four additional facilities in Michigan New Mexico North Carolina and Texas.

In an effort to raise capital needed to expand its prison systems Wackenhut Corrections sold its 50% stake in Premier Custodial Group to Serco in 2003. Also that year Wackenhut Corrections bought back the 57% stake that Group 4 Falck held in the company. As a condition of the purchase the company changed its name to The GEO Group and abandoned its connection to the Wackenhut trademark and name.

GEO expanded in 2005 by buying smaller US rival Correctional Services Corporation. GEO paid about $62 million in cash for Correctional Services and assumed about $124 million of the company's debt. Upon the deal's closing GEO sold Correctional Services' juvenile operations to Correctional Services CEO James Slattery. Correctional Services' adult operations — 16 facilities with an overall capacity of about 8000 beds — were absorbed into those of GEO.

In 2006 the company sold its mental health subsidiary Atlantic Shores Healthcare (ASH) which included a 72-bed mental health hospital for approximately $11.5 million. Also that year GEO renewed its contract (for an additional five years) with the US Department of State and the US Department of Homeland Security to operate the Migrant Operations Center (MOC) at Guantanamo Bay. The MOC a separate facility from the controversial GITMO detention center is intended for immigrants caught at sea without US entry documents.

In 2009 GEO opened a new $62 million Florida Civil Commitment Center (FCCC) in Arcadia Florida. The facility has a capacity of 720 residents and provides treatment services to sexually violent predators. FCCC is operated by GEO Care under a management contract with the Florida Department of Children and Families. Also that year GEO purchased Just Care a provider of medical and mental health services to detainees primarily in Georgia and South Carolina for about $40 million.

Events in 2010 included the company's $730 million acquisition of rival Cornell Companies a private provider of educational treatment and correctional services. Cornell's business which comprises outsourced-contracts with federal state and local governmental agencies is included in GEO's US Detention & Corrections and GEO Care segments which due to the Cornell acquisition generated sales of about $85 and $66 million respectively. The Cornell investment came subsequent to GEO's

GEO also wrapped up a number of projects in 2010 including the completion of the Aurora ICE Processing Center (Colorado) Blackwater River Correctional Facility (Florida) and Harmondsworth Immigration Removal Centre (London). Additionally it landed a new management contract with the D. Ray James Correctional Facility (Georgia).

EXECUTIVES

Vice President Programs, Gary Templeton
Vice President Of Administrative Services, George Gintoli
Chairman and CEO, George C. Zoley, age 69, $1,179,350 total compensation
SVP; President GEO Corrections and Detention, John M. Hurley, age 71, $515,000 total compensation
SVP and CFO, Brian R. Evans, age 51, $515,000 total compensation
SVP; President GEO Community Services, Ann M. Schlarb
Vice President Of Transportation, Ed Stubbs
Vp Finance And Treasurer, Shayn P March, age 55
Divisional Vice President Finance, Larry Sherman
Vice President Pricing, Matt Denadel
Vice President Construction Services, Gregor Heinrich
Vice President, Amber Martin
Vice President Of Finance And Treasurer, Shayn March
Vice President, Louis Carrillo
Vice President Construction Services, Rick Zahner
Vice President, Jackie Santiago
Executive Vice President Cont, Patricia Persante
Senior Vice President Business Development, David Venturella
Divisional Vice President Community, Loren Grayer
Divisional Vice President Continuum of Care, John Thurston
Eastern Region Vice President, Blake Davis
Executive Vice President, Ernesto Alvarez
Executive Vice President, Adam Hasner
Vice President Health Services, Juan Castillo
Clinical Director, Thomas Selby
Board Member, Anne Foreman
Unit Secretary, Jacqueline Reid
Board Member, Julie Wood
Auditors: Grant Thornton LLP

LOCATIONS

HQ: GEO Group Inc (The) (New)
4955 Technology Way, Boca Raton, FL 33431
Phone: 561 893-0101
Web: www.geogroup.com

PRODUCTS/OPERATIONS

2018 Revenue by Segment

	$ mil.	% of total
US Corrections & Detention	1,493.0	64
GEO Care	580.3	25
International Services	253.9	11
Facility Construction & Design	4.2	-
Total	**2,331.4**	**100**

Selected Products and Services

Adult inmate management
Behavioral health and residential treatment services for youthful offenders
Community-based residential re-entry services
Construction management
Correctional health care services
Electronic monitoring devices
Facility design
Facility maintenance
Facility management
Facility operation
Infrastructure financing
Pre-trial and immigration custody services
Residential mental health / special needs services
Secure prisoner escort

Selected Facilities

Arizona State Prison - Phoenix West (Phoenix Arizona)
Aurora ICE Processing Center (Aurora Colorado)
Blackwater River Correctional Facility (Milton Florida)
Bronx Community Re-Entry Center (Bronx New York)
Broward Transition Center (Deerfield Beach Florida)
D. Ray James Correctional Facility (Folkston Georgia)
Harmondsworth Immigration Removal Centre (London England)
Lawrenceville Correctional Center (Lawrenceville Virginia)
South Bay Correctional Facility (South Bay Florida)

COMPETITORS

3M
Avalon Correctional Services
Corizon
Corrections Corporation of America
G4S
MHM Services
Management & Training
Res-Care
Sodexo

HISTORICAL FINANCIALS
Company Type: Public

Income Statement FYE: December 31

	REVENUE ($ mil.)	NET INCOME ($ mil.)	NET PROFIT MARGIN	EMPLOYEES
12/18	2,331.3	145.0	6.2%	22,000
12/17	2,263.4	146.2	6.5%	18,512
12/16	2,179.4	148.7	6.8%	19,370
12/15	1,843.3	139.4	7.6%	15,806
12/14	1,691.6	143.9	8.5%	17,479
Annual Growth	8.3%	0.2%	—	5.9%

2018 Year-End Financials
Debt ratio: 64.7%
Return on equity: 12.9%
Cash ($ mil.): 31.2
Current ratio: 0.85
Long-term debt ($ mil.): 2,416.8
No. of shares (mil.): 120.5
Dividends
 Yield: 9.5%
 Payout: 156.6%
Market value ($ mil.): 2,376.0

	STOCK PRICE ($) FY Close	P/E High/Low	PER SHARE ($) Earnings	Dividends	Book Value
12/18	19.70	23 16	1.20	1.88	8.63
12/17	23.60	40 19	1.21	1.88	9.67
12/16	35.93	27 15	1.33	1.73	8.66
12/15	28.91	36 21	1.25	1.67	8.99
12/14	40.36	31 23	1.32	0.41	9.40
Annual Growth	(16.4%)	—	(2.4%)	46.0%	(2.1%)

German American Bancorp Inc

German American Bancorp is the holding company for German American Bank which operates some 65 branches in southern Indiana and Kentucky. Founded in 1910 the bank offers such standard retail products as checking and savings accounts certificates of deposit and IRAs. It also provides trust services while sister company German American Investment Services provides trust investment advisory and brokerage services. German American Bancorp also owns German American Insurance which offers corporate and personal insurance products. The group's core banking operations provide more than 90% of its total sales.

Geographic Reach
German American is headquartered in Jasper Indiana. Its subsidiaries operate from more than 60 locations in southern Indiana and Kentucky.

Sales and Marketing
German American Bancorp spent $3.5 million on advertising in 2017. Advertising expenses totaled $2.7 million in 2016 and $3.7 million in 2015.

Financial Performance
German American's revenue has been climbing steadily for the past five years thanks to the company's acquisitions of other area banks. Similarly net income has also been on the rise. In 2017 the company marked its eighth consecutive year of record earnings.

In 2017 revenue increased 4% to $131.8 million. That increase was partially due to the addition of River Valley Financial Bank which German American acquired in 2016. Growth in the company's loan portfolio also boosted net interest income. This was slightly offset by a 1% decline in non-interest income. Although trust and insurance operations rose other operating income declined $1.1 million (29%).

Net income rose 16% to $35.2 million in 2017; in addition to having higher revenue the company recognized a benefit related to the reduced corporate tax rate that year.

German American ended 2017 with $70.4 million in net cash $5.5 million more than it had at the end of 2016. Operating activities provided $54.9 million in cash and financing activities provided $139.9 million. Investing activities used $189.3 million.

Strategy
German American Bancorp has grown recently through a number of acquisitions including bank branches an insurance office and other bank holding companies. These acquisitions have also helped the company grow into new geographic markets including locations in Kentucky.

Growth by acquisition can be somewhat risky though. The company could unknowingly acquire problem assets or have difficulties integrating other banks it purchases. These issues could bring down its financial performance.

German American operates in a relatively small region which leaves it vulnerable to economic downturns in that area. If economic conditions in its market decline German American faces the risk of increased delinquencies and charge-offs. The company's larger more widespread competitors would be less impacted in such a case.

Mergers and Acquisitions
German American Bancorp agreed to acquire Citizens First in early 2019 in a cash-and-stock transaction valued at about $70 million. German American will gain Citizens' branch offices in the Barren Hart Simpson and Warren counties of Kentucky. Citizens has about $475 million in assets loans of some $375 million and deposits of around $390 million.

In October 2018 German American Bancorp acquired Kentucky's First Security Bank for $101 million. With that deal the company expanded into Kentucky's Owensboro Bowling Green and Lexington markets.

EXECUTIVES

Vice President, Lisa Matheis
General technical; Senior Vice President, Floyd Alsman
Chairman and CEO, Mark A. Schroeder, age 66, $342,500 total compensation
President, Clay W. Ewing, age 64, $250,000 total compensation
EVP CFO and Senior Administrative Officer, Bradley M. Rust, age 53, $210,000 total compensation
SVP and Chief Credit Officer, Keith A. Leinenbach, age 60, $180,000 total compensation
SVP and Head of Retail Banking, Randall L. Braun, age 59, $180,000 total compensation
Vice President Deposit Services Secruity, Dale Altstadt
Senior Vice President of Technology and Operations, Clay Barrett
Vice President Commercial Banking, Dan Collignon
Senior Vice President Commercial Banking, Joe Hauersperger
Regional Senior Vice President, Jim Thomas
Vice President, Christina Lebeau
Vice President Private Banking, Sherri Alley
Vice President, Ashley McCreary
Regional Vice President Commercial Lending, Doug Bell
REGION SENIOR VICE PRESIDENT, Tony Loudermilk
Svp Senior Retail Officer, Jenny Darnold
Vice President Commercial Banking, Rob Bingham
Vice President Commercial Banking, John Newcomer
Vice President, Eric Kehl
Senior Vice President Retail Banking, Brock Goggins
Senior Vice President Senior Wealth Advisor, Alan VanCleef
REGIONAL VICE PRESIDENT TREASURY MANAGEMENT, Alicia Berry
Board Member, Chris Ramsey
Auditors: Crowe LLP

LOCATIONS
HQ: German American Bancorp Inc
711 Main Street, Jasper, IN 47546
Phone: 812 482-1314
Web: www.germanamerican.com

PRODUCTS/OPERATIONS

2017 Sales

	$ mil.	% of total
Interest		
Loans including fees	91.7	64
Securities including dividends	19.2	13
Short-term investments	0.1	-
Non-interest		
Insurance	8.0	6
Service charges on deposit accounts	6.2	4
Trust & investment product fees	5.3	4
Other	12.4	9
Adjustments	(11.1)	-
Total	131.8	100

COMPETITORS

Fidelity Federal	Home Financial Bancorp
Fifth Third	Old National Bancorp
First Bancorp of Indiana	Porter Bancorp
First Capital	SVB&T

HISTORICAL FINANCIALS
Company Type: Public

Income Statement FYE: December 31

	ASSETS ($ mil.)	NET INCOME ($ mil.)	INCOME AS % OF ASSETS	EMPLOYEES
12/18	3,929.0	46.5	1.2%	738
12/17	3,144.3	40.6	1.3%	614
12/16	2,955.9	35.1	1.2%	597
12/15	2,373.7	30.0	1.3%	596
12/14	2,237.1	28.3	1.3%	484
Annual Growth	15.1%	13.2%	—	11.1%

2018 Year-End Financials

Return on assets: 1.3%
Return on equity: 11.3%
Long-term debt ($ mil.): —
No. of shares (mil.): 24.9
Sales ($ mil): 170.8
Dividends
Yield: 2.1%
Payout: 30.1%
Market value ($ mil.): 693.0

	STOCK PRICE ($) FY Close	P/E High/Low	PER SHARE ($) Earnings	Dividends	Book Value
12/18	27.77	19 13	1.99	0.60	18.37
12/17	35.33	30 17	1.77	0.52	15.90
12/16	52.61	34 19	1.57	0.48	14.43
12/15	33.32	23 18	1.51	0.45	12.67
12/14	30.52	22 17	1.43	0.43	11.54
Annual Growth	(2.3%)	— —	8.7%	8.9%	12.3%

Getty Realty Corp.

Getty Realty a self-administered real estate investment trust (REIT) owns or leases about 940 gas service stations adjacent convenience stores and petroleum distribution terminals in around 30 US states and Washington DC. Most of its properties are company-owned and located in the Northeast (about a third in New York). Major gas brands distributed at Getty properties include BP Citgo Conoco Exxon Getty Shell and Valero. The company's three most significant tenants by revenue — which together occupy about one-third of its properties — are petroleum distributors and gas station operators Global Partners Apro and Chestnut Petroleum.

Operations
Getty Realty owns leases and finances retail gas stations convenience stores and petroleum distribution terminals. The REIT owns some 860 of its properties and leases about 80. Income from rental properties comprises some 85% of Getty's revenue stream. Tenant reimbursements make up nearly 15% of revenue.

Geographic Reach
Getty Realty (headquartered in Jericho New York) owns or leases properties in about 30 US states and Washington DC. After New York which is home to nearly 30% of the REIT's properties Massachusetts and Connecticut are the firm's two largest operating centers together comprising about 20% of its locations. In addition to its Northeast base Getty Realty has properties across the country.

Sales and Marketing
Getty Realty's three biggest tenants by revenue contribution are petroleum distributors and gas station operators Global Partners (about 20% of total) Apro (some 15%) and Chestnut Petroleum (nearly 15%).

Financial Performance
Amid an expansion of its property portfolio via acquisition Getty Realty has seen moderate growth over the past five years with revenue increasing about 15% since 2013. The company's net income has risen strongly as least since 2014 when it fell more than 60% from the prior year when earnings were inflated by proceeds from the sale of real estate.

In 2017 the company reported revenue of $120.1 million which is up 4% from the prior year. The top line was boosted by increased rent revenue following Getty's simultaneous acquisition and leasing of 87 properties that year from and to gas station/convenience store operators Petroleum Partners LLC and Applegreen PLC.

The REIT's net income increased 23% to $47.2 million in 2017 attributable primarily to increases in legal settlements and judgments which jumped $5.9 million.

Cash at the end of fiscal 2017 was $20.8 million an increase of $7.6 million from the prior year. Cash from operations contributed $56.7 million to the coffers while investing activities used $206.2 million mainly for property acquisitions. Financing activities added another $157.1 million due mostly to proceeds from borrowings and stock issuances.

Strategy
Getty Realty's strategy is to acquire new convenience stores and gas stations that increase its geographic and tenant diversity. The company is also redeveloping some of its properties for new convenience or gasoline use or as single-tenant retail businesses such as quick service restaurants car parts and service stores specialty retail stores and bank branches.

Acquisitions in 2017 and 2018 added some 150 properties to Getty's portfolio strengthening its position in existing markets and expanding its reach into new territories. One transaction broadened the REIT's network in southwestern US states including Arizona New Mexico and Texas. Another marked its entrance into the southeastern US market and diversified its tenant base with the addition of several stand-alone Burger King restaurants.

In 2017 the company completed two redevelopment projects including a new convenience store and gas station leased to Sheetz in central Pennsylvania. Getty is actively redeveloping nine other properties and has signed leases on four additional redevelopment properties.

Mergers and Acquisitions
In 2018 Getty purchased and leased 30 gas station/convenience store properties from and to convenience store chain E-Z Mart Stores for $52 million. The stores are in metropolitan areas in Arkansas Louisiana Oklahoma and Texas. The company also acquired six additional Columbia metropolitan area stores from Applegreen for $17 million that year.

The prior year Getty Realty acquired 103 new properties for a total of $214 million including 49 properties from wholesale fuel distributor Empire Petroleum Partners LLC for $123 million and 38 properties from convenience and gas operator Applegreen PLC for $68 million.

The Empire transaction broadened the REIT's network in southwestern US states including Arizona New Mexico and Texas. The Applegreen deal which marked Getty's entrance into the southeastern US market included five standalone Burger King restaurants and 33 convenience stores (many of which also house Burger King Subway or Blimpie restaurants). All the properties Getty bought from Applegreen are in the greater Columbia South Carolina metropolitan area.

Company Background
Getty was founded in 1955 with a single gas service station in New York City and conducted its IPO in 1971 as Power Test Corp. The company acquired the assets and trademark of northeast US petroleum distributor Getty Oil Company from Texaco in 1985.

EXECUTIVES

EVP and COO, Mark J. Olear, age 55, $195,000 total compensation
SVP General Counsel and Secretary, Joshua Dicker, age 59, $276,538 total compensation
President CEO and Director, Christopher J. Constant, age 40, $236,538 total compensation
VP CFO and Treasurer, Danion Fielding
Vice President Of Real Estate And Asset Management, Jim Craig
Chairman, Leo Liebowitz, age 91
Board Member, Richard Montag
Auditors: PricewaterhouseCoopers LLP

LOCATIONS

HQ: Getty Realty Corp.
Two Jericho Plaza, Suite 110, Jericho, NY 11753-1681
Phone: 516 478-5400   **Fax:** 516 478-5476
Web: www.gettyrealty.com

PRODUCTS/OPERATIONS

2017 Sales

	$ mil.	% of total
Rental properties	101.3	84
Tenant reimbursements	15.8	13
Interest on notes & mortgages receivable	3.0	3
Total	**120.1**	**100**

Selected Property Brands
76
BP
Citgo
Conoco
Exxon
Getty
Gulf
Mobil
Shell
Sunoco
Valero

COMPETITORS

7-Eleven
Cumberland Farms
GE Franchise Finance
Motiva Enterprises
Realty Income
Sheetz
TravelCenters of America
Warren Equities
Wawa Inc.

HISTORICAL FINANCIALS

Company Type: Public

Income Statement — FYE: December 31

	REVENUE ($ mil.)	NET INCOME ($ mil.)	NET PROFIT MARGIN	EMPLOYEES
12/18	136.1	47.7	35.1%	29
12/17	120.1	47.1	39.3%	30
12/16	115.2	38.4	33.3%	31
12/15	110.7	37.4	33.8%	32
12/14	99.8	23.4	23.4%	32
Annual Growth	8.0%	19.5%	—	(2.4%)

2018 Year-End Financials

Debt ratio: 38.1%
Return on equity: 8.4%
Cash ($ mil.): 46.8
Current ratio: 1.61
Long-term debt ($ mil.): 441.6
No. of shares (mil.): 40.8
Dividends
Yield: 4.4%
Payout: 111.9%
Market value ($ mil.): 1,202.0

| | STOCK PRICE ($) | P/E | PER SHARE ($) | | |
	FY Close	High/Low	Earnings	Dividends	Book Value
12/18	29.41	27 19	1.17	1.31	14.23
12/17	27.16	24 18	1.26	1.16	13.95
12/16	25.49	23 15	1.12	1.03	12.53
12/15	17.15	17 14	1.11	1.15	12.16
12/14	18.21	29 25	0.69	0.96	12.18
Annual Growth	12.7%	—	14.1%	8.1%	4.0%

Glacier Bancorp, Inc.

Glacier Bancorp is on a Rocky Mountain high. The holding company owns about a dozen community bank divisions with about 100 locations in Montana Idaho Utah Washington Arizona Colorado and Wyoming. Serving individuals small to midsized businesses not-for-profits and public entities the banks offer traditional deposit products and credit cards in addition to retail brokerage and investment services through agreements with third-party providers. Its lending activities consist of commercial real estate loans (about half of the company's loan portfolio) as well as residential mortgages business loans and consumer loans.

Financial Performance
Glacier's financial results are on a steady upward swing since 2012 with yearly increases in interest income and near-annual improvement in non-interest income and net income.

In 2017 the company generated $375 million in interest income and $112 million in non-interest income for total revenue of $487 million. Its loan portfolio grew by $601 million or 11% in the year bringing the size of its loan portfolio to just less than $6.5 billion.

Net income for the year was $116 million 4% more than 2016 due to the higher revenue partially offset by an increase in loan loss provisions employee compensation and income tax expense.

Glacier Bancorp ended 2017 with $200 million in cash an increase of nearly $50 million over the previous year. Financing activities used $230 million for loan repayments stock dividends and a decrease in deposits. Investing activities added $24 million to the coffers and operating activities contributed $255 million mostly from net income a deferred tax expense and proceeds from selling some of its loan portfolio.

Strategy
Glacier Bancorp hopes to capitalize on additional acquisition opportunities that it expects to arise as small banks deal with new industry regulations. To this end it has been on a buying spree in recent years. In early 2018 it acquired Inter-Mountain Bancorp (Montana) Columbine Capital Corporation (Colorado); in 2017 it purchased TFB Bancorp (Arizona); in 2016 it bought Treasure State Bank (Montana) and in 2015 Glacier acquired Canon Bank Corporation (Colorado) and Montana Community Banks (Montana). In total these purchases cost $377 million.

The company is also banking on organic growth with the populations of the states in its market area growing faster than the national average thanks to an influx of retiring Baby Boomers and an increase in energy- and natural resource-related jobs.

EXECUTIVES

EVP and CFO, Ron J. Copher, $352,651 total compensation
EVP and Chief Administrative Officer, Don J. Cherry, $299,950 total compensation
President and CEO, Randall M. (Randy) Chesler, age 61, $153,846 total compensation
Vice President And Cra And Compliance Officer, Lanette Marcum
Senior Vice President, Robert Taylor
Vice President Internal Auditor, Judy Overcast
Vice President Compliance, April Kelso
Vice President, Ryan T Screnar
Senior Vice President Business Developme, Steve Lloyd
Senior Vice President Consumer Lending, Greg Wilcox
Vice President Finance, Mike Romm
Vice President Internal Auditor, Jessica Rice
Vice President Of Human Resources, Roger Bamford
Vice President of Human Resources, Christopher Murphy
Vp, Preston Romm
Vice President, Melody Pieri
Senior Vice President Corporate Re Manager, Paul Peterson
Vice President Corporate BSA Officer, Mary Strozzi
Senior Vice President Enterprise wide Risk Manager, T Frickle
Vice President, Don McCarthy
Vice President Risk Management, T J Frickle
Senior Vice President, Lynn Riley
Board Member, Craig A Langel
Chairman, Dallas I. Herron, age 74
Board Member, Annie Goodwin
Board Member, Douglas Mcbride
Board Member, James English
Board Member, Mark Semmens
Auditors: BKD, LLP

LOCATIONS

HQ: Glacier Bancorp, Inc.
49 Commons Loop, Kalispell, MT 59901
Phone: 406 756-4200
Web: www.glacierbank.com

PRODUCTS/OPERATIONS

2016 Sales

	% of total
Interest income	
Commercial loans	47
Investment securities	17
Residential real estate loans	7
Consumer and other loans	7
Non-interest income	
Service charges and other fees	14
Gain on sale of loans	6
Miscellaneous loan fees and charges	1
(Loss) gain on sale of investments	
Other income	2
Total	100

Selected Services
Commercial loan
Consumer loan
Deposits
Mortgage origination services
Real estate loan
Retail brokerage services
Transaction and savings

Selected Bank Divisions
1st Bank (Wyoming)
Bank of the San Juans (Colorado)
Big Sky Western Bank (Montana)
Citizens Community Bank (Idaho)
Collegiate Peaks Bank
First Bank of Montana
First Bank of Wyoming
First Security Bank (Montana)
First State Bank (Wyoming)
Foothills Bank
Glacier Bank (Montana)
Mountain West Bank (Idaho)
North Cascades Bank (Washington)
Valley Bank of Helena (Montana)
Western Security Bank (Montana)

COMPETITORS

Eagle Bancorp
First Citizens Banc Corp
First Interstate
U.S. Bancorp
Wells Fargo
Zions Bancorporation

HISTORICAL FINANCIALS
Company Type: Public

Income Statement   FYE: December 31

	ASSETS ($ mil.)	NET INCOME ($ mil.)	INCOME AS % OF ASSETS	EMPLOYEES
12/18	12,115.4	181.8	1.5%	2,723
12/17	9,706.3	116.3	1.2%	2,354
12/16	9,450.6	121.1	1.3%	2,291
12/15	9,089.2	116.1	1.3%	2,245
12/14	8,306.5	112.7	1.4%	2,030
Annual Growth	9.9%	12.7%	—	7.6%

2018 Year-End Financials
Return on assets: 1.6%
Return on equity: 13.4%
Long-term debt ($ mil.): —
No. of shares (mil.): 84.5
Sales ($ mil): 587.8
Dividends
Yield: 2.5%
Payout: 57.0%
Market value ($ mil.): 3,349.0

	STOCK PRICE ($) FY Close	P/E High/Low	PER SHARE ($) Earnings	Dividends	Book Value
12/18	39.62	22 17	2.17	1.01	17.93
12/17	39.39	27 21	1.50	1.44	15.37
12/16	36.23	24 14	1.59	1.10	14.59
12/15	26.53	20 14	1.54	1.05	14.15
12/14	27.77	20 16	1.51	0.68	13.70
Annual Growth	9.3%	—	9.5%	10.4%	7.0%

Gladstone Commercial Corp

Gladstone Commercial a real estate investment trust (REIT) invests in and owns office and industrial real estate properties. The company owns about 100 properties in around 25 states with assets that include office buildings medical office buildings warehouses retail stores and manufacturing facilities. Gladstone generally provides net leases with terms between seven and 15 years for small to very large private and public companies. Tenants include General Motors Morgan Stanley and T-Mobile. The business is managed by its external adviser Gladstone Management which is also headed by chairman and CEO David Gladstone.

Operations

Gladstone Commercial owns about 100 properties totaling nearly 12 million sq. ft. — including office buildings medical office buildings warehouses retail stores and manufacturing facilities — in around 25 states. Virtually all of the REIT's revenue comes from rental income from tenants most of whom sign net leases which require them to pay most or all of a property's operating maintenance repair and insurance costs and real estate taxes.

Geographic Reach

Headquartered in McLean Virginia Gladstone Commercial owns properties in about 25 states. Texas accounts for the most rental revenue with more than 15% followed by Pennsylvania (more than 10%) and Ohio (about 10%). Other large markets include Florida North Carolina Georgia and South Carolina.

Sales and Marketing

Gladstone derives at least 10% of its rental revenue from tenants in each of the telecommunications healthcare automobile and diversified/conglomerate services industries. Its five largest tenants account for nearly 20% of rental revenue.

Financial Performance

Since 2013 Gladstone Commercial's net income has skyrocketed nearly 300% alongside substantial revenue expansion of over 50%. The REIT's growth has accelerated as office and industrial properties in the US see vacancy rates fall and rental rates rise both of which have contributed to an increase in construction in many markets.

In 2017 the company reported revenue of $94.8 million which is up 10% from the prior year. The top line was boosted by increased rent revenue following Gladstone's acquisition of seven properties that year.

The REIT's net income increased 50% to $5.9 million in 2017 owing to increased rental revenue and a gain from the sale of four properties.

Cash at the end of fiscal 2017 was $6.7 million an increase of 43% from the prior year. Cash from operations contributed $46.8 while investing activities used $99.2 million mainly for property acquisitions. Financing activities added another $54.4 million.

Strategy

Gladstone Commercial seeks to assemble a diversified property portfolio both geographically and by tenant and industry type. The REIT's tenants span about 20 different industries including telecommunications healthcare and automobiles from small businesses to very large public and private companies. Geographically its target markets include Washington Oregon Nevada Arizona Tennessee and Kentucky.

The company is working to increase acquisitions of industrial properties. As of late 2018 the company had a potential acquisition pipeline of nearly 20 properties about half of them industrial. Gladstone is seeking fully developed industrial parks with areas of 50000 to 300000 square feet in size and warehouse clear heights of 24 to 28 feet and trailer parking that are occupied by middle-market non-rated tenants.

The company is conducting a capital recycling program wherein it sells properties outside of its core markets to fund acquisitions in target secondary growth markets or repay debt. In 2017 the company sold four non-core properties totaling about 590000 square feet and used the proceeds to pay down some debt and fund the acquisition of seven new properties. The strategy continued in 2018 when Gladstone divested a property in Texas.

Mergers and Acquisitions

In 2017 Gladstone Commercial a REIT purchased seven new properties including buildings leased to Jacobs Engineering Group the National Archives and Records Administration federal records center Automatic Data Processing and Morgan Stanley. It continued adding properties to its portfolio in 2018 including industrial properties in Alabama Michigan and Ohio.

Company Background

The REIT Gladstone Commercial is part of the Gladstone Companies which include the three affiliated public entities Gladstone Capital Gladstone Investment and Gladstone Land. Gladstone Capital and Gladstone Investment invest in small and medium sized private businesses while Gladstone Land invests in farmland.

EXECUTIVES

Chairman and CEO, David J. Gladstone, age 77, $68,833 total compensation
Managing Director, Matt Tucker
Vice Chairman and COO, Terry Lee Brubaker
President, Robert G. Cutlip
Senior Managing Director, Buzz Cooper
Managing Director, Andrew White
CFO, Michael Sodo
Board Member, Paul Adelgren
Auditors: PricewaterhouseCoopers LLP

LOCATIONS

HQ: Gladstone Commercial Corp
1521 Westbranch Drive, Suite 100, McLean, VA 22102
Phone: 703 287-5800   **Fax:** 703 287-5801
Web: www.GladstoneCommercial.com

PRODUCTS/OPERATIONS

2017 Sales

	$ mil.	% of total
Rental	92.8	98
Tenant recovery	2.0	2
Total	**94.8**	**100**

COMPETITORS

Colony Northstar	Monmouth Real Estate
Equity Commonwealth	One Liberty Properties
Mack-Cali	PS Business Parks
Meredith Enterprises	iStar Financial Inc

HISTORICAL FINANCIALS
Company Type: Public

Income Statement				FYE: December 31
	REVENUE ($ mil.)	NET INCOME ($ mil.)	NET PROFIT MARGIN	EMPLOYEES
12/18	106.8	12.3	11.5%	0
12/17	94.8	5.9	6.3%	0
12/16	86.3	3.9	4.6%	0
12/15	83.7	3.6	4.3%	66
12/14	73.7	(5.9)	—	0
Annual Growth	9.7%	—	—	—

2018 Year-End Financials

Debt ratio: 60.3%
Return on equity: 3.5%
Cash ($ mil.): 6.5
Current ratio: 2.89
Long-term debt ($ mil.): 566.0
No. of shares (mil.): 30.1
Dividends
  Yield: 8.3%
  Payout: 5,000.0%
Market value ($ mil.): 540.0

	STOCK PRICE ($) FY Close	P/E High/Low	PER SHARE ($) Earnings	Dividends	Book Value
12/18	17.92	694561	0.03	1.50	11.13
12/17	21.06	— —	(0.19)	1.50	11.96
12/16	20.10	— —	(0.16)	1.50	12.02
12/15	14.59	— —	(0.07)	1.50	9.97
12/14	17.17	— —	(0.61)	1.50	10.67
Annual Growth	1.1%	— —	—	(0.0%)	1.1%

Global Medical REIT Inc

Auditors: MaloneBailey, LLP

LOCATIONS

HQ: Global Medical REIT Inc
2 Bethesda Metro Center, Suite 440, Bethesda, MD 20814
Phone: 202 524-6851
Web: www.globalmedicalreit.com

HISTORICAL FINANCIALS
Company Type: Public

Income Statement				FYE: December 31
	REVENUE ($ mil.)	NET INCOME ($ mil.)	NET PROFIT MARGIN	EMPLOYEES
12/18	53.1	13.4	25.4%	0
12/17	30.3	(0.0)	—	0
12/16	8.2	(6.3)	—	0
12/15	2.0	(1.6)	—	0
12/14	0.6	(0.4)	—	0
Annual Growth	207.3%	—	—	—

2018 Year-End Financials

Debt ratio: 49.5%
Return on equity: 5.2%
Cash ($ mil.): 4.8
Current ratio: 0.57
Long-term debt ($ mil.): 315.0
No. of shares (mil.): 25.9
Dividends
  Yield: 9.0%
  Payout: 228.5%
Market value ($ mil.): 231.0

	STOCK PRICE ($) FY Close	P/E High/Low	PER SHARE ($) Earnings	Dividends	Book Value
12/18	8.89	28 19	0.35	0.80	10.38
12/17	8.20	— —	(0.09)	0.80	11.39
12/16	8.92	— —	(0.68)	0.74	8.81
12/15	0.15	— —	(6.44)	1.02	(0.55)
12/14	0.15	— —	(1.64)	0.09	6.90
Annual Growth	177.5%	— —	—	74.9%	10.7%

Global Net Lease Inc

Auditors: PricewaterhouseCoopers LLP

LOCATIONS

HQ: Global Net Lease Inc
405 Park Ave., 3rd Floor, New York, NY 10022
Phone: 212 415-6500

Globus Medical Inc

HISTORICAL FINANCIALS
Company Type: Public

Income Statement
FYE: December 31

	REVENUE ($ mil.)	NET INCOME ($ mil.)	NET PROFIT MARGIN	EMPLOYEES
12/18	282.2	10.9	3.9%	1
12/17	259.3	23.5	9.1%	1
12/16	214.1	47.1	22.0%	1
12/15	205.3	(2.0)	—	0
12/14	93.3	(53.5)	—	0
Annual Growth	31.8%	—	—	—

2018 Year-End Financials
Debt ratio: 53.5%
Return on equity: 0.7%
Cash ($ mil.): 100.3
Current ratio: 4.29
Long-term debt ($ mil.): 1,772.4
No. of shares (mil.): 76.0
Dividends
Yield: 12.0%
Payout: 21,300.0%
Market value ($ mil.): 1,341.0

	STOCK PRICE ($) FY Close	P/E High/Low	PER SHARE ($) Earnings	Dividends	Book Value
12/18	17.62	2222 1564	0.01	2.13	18.74
12/17	20.58	83 25	0.30	1.78	21.00
12/16	7.83	11 8	0.81	0.00	20.34
12/15	7.95	— —	(0.03)	2.13	21.41
Annual Growth	30.4%	— —	—	(0.0%)	(4.3%)

Globus Medical makes procedural and therapeutic medical devices used during spinal surgery. Offerings range from screws and plates to disc replacement systems and biomaterials for bone grafts. The company has two product segments: Musculoskeletal Solutions (implantable devices biologics surgical instruments and accessories) and Enabling Technologies (imaging navigation and robotic-assisted surgery systems). Globus Medical has about 200 spinal devices on the market in the US where it earns most of its revenue; its products are also sold in more than 50 countries worldwide.

Financial Performance
Globus Medical increased its revenue each year over the past five years reporting an overall 50% sales increase between 2014 and 2018. Net income remained steady in the $100 million to $150 million range. New product launches and acquisitions drove the company's expansion.

The firm reported a 12% revenue increase in 2018 to some $713 million. Growth was even across the US and international segments fueled by increased sales from spinal products and robotic systems in the US Japan and other established markets. The Musculoskeletal Solutions segment which accounts for more than 90% of Globus Medical's sales increased by 7% while the Enabling Technologies segment tripled its revenue figure.

Net income increased to $156.5 million in 2018 up 46% from 2017 results due to lower income tax provisions (related to the 2017 Tax Act) and higher revenue despite a rise in operating expenses.

The company ended 2018 with $139.7 million in cash up $20.9 million from 2017. Operating activities contributed $181.6 million while investing activities used $193 million (mostly on purchases of marketable securities property and equipment) and financing activities contributed $ 32.6 million via stock option proceeds.

Strategy
Putting new products on the market is crucial in the medical device industry. Globus Medical is pursuing R&D projects in both the Musculoskeletal Solutions and Enabling Technologies segments. In addition to new product development the firm works to improve existing products. It actively works with surgeons to develop more efficient and effective offerings.

Globus Medical introduced 10 new products during 2018 and had about 30 new products in the development pipeline as of 2019. To expand beyond its spinal products in 2018 the Musculoskeletal Solutions segment launched a line of orthopedic trauma solutions addressing extremity and hip conditions.

R&D processes are costly especially if a product fails to gain approval and companies must convince health providers and payers to adopt new technologies once they're approved by regulatory agencies. Companies are also vulnerable to product recall and liability issues.

Other means of growth include pursuit of acquisitions or strategic alliances increasing international market penetration growing the US and international sales forces and hiring and retaining personnel with market experience.

Mergers and Acquisitions
Globus Medical acquired privately held firm Nemaris in 2018. Nemaris developed the Surgimap surgical planning software platform for the spinal surgery market.

Company Background
Globus Medical was founded in 2003 by CEO David Paul a former product development director at medical device maker Synthes. Globus Medical relied on venture capital funding prior to its 2012 IPO.

In 2016 Globus Medical acquired the international business of medical device firm Alphatec for $80 million. The deal included international distribution operations in Japan Brazil the UK Italy and other nations.

In 2017 Globus Medical acquired KB Medical a Swiss robotics developer. That transaction underscored the firm's commitment to producing robotic technology for surgeries.

EXECUTIVES
CEO, David M. (Dave) Demski, age 61, $337,765 total compensation
Group President Commercial Operations, A. Brett Murphy, age 55, $309,309 total compensation
SVP Operations, David D. Davidar, age 53, $234,738 total compensation
SVP and CFO, Daniel T. Scavilla, age 54
Vice President of Business Development, Brian Kearns
National Sales Manager, Shawn Bowers
Vice President Business Development, Rick Kreppel
Vice President Sales Central Zone, Greg Cavaleri
Vice President US Sales West Zone, David Hole
Vp Sales Orthopedic Trauma, Daniel Gregoris
Chairman, David C. Paul, age 52
Auditors: Deloitte & Touche LLP

LOCATIONS
HQ: Globus Medical Inc
2560 General Armistead Avenue, Audubon, PA 19403
Phone: 610 930-1800   **Fax:** 302 636-5454
Web: www.globusmedical.com

PRODUCTS/OPERATIONS
2015 Sales

	$ mil.	% of total
Innovative fusion	288.1	53
Disruptive technologies	256.7	47
Total	544.8	100

Selected Products
Innovative Fusion Products:
Cervical
ASSURE (anterior cervical plate system)
ELLIPSE (posterior occipital cervical thoracic stabilization system)
PROVIDENCE (anterior cervical plate system)
VIP (anterior cervical plate system)
XTEND (anterior cervical plate system)
Thoracolumbar:
BEACON Posted Screw (posted pedicle screw system)
REVERE Degen (comprehensive pedicle screw and rod system)
SI-LOK (sacroiliac joint fixation system)
Interbody/Corpectomy
COALITION (anterior cervical stand-alone fusion device)
COLONIAL (anterior cervical interbody fusion device)
FORTIFY (self-locking expandable corpectomy device)
INDEPENDENCE (anterior lumbar stand-alone fusion device)
SUSTAIN (spacers for partial or complete vertebrectomy)
XPAND (expandable corpectomy spacer)
Deformity Tumor and Trauma
REVERE Anterior (pedicle screw and rod deformity system)
REVERE Deformity (comprehensive pedicle screw hook and rod deformity system)
TRUSS (lateral compressible thoracolumbar plate system)
Minimally Invasive Surgery Products:
CALIBER (expandable posterior lumbar interbody fusion device)
CALIBER-L (expandable lateral lumbar interbody fusion device)
INTERCONTINENTAL (lateral lumbar interbody fusion device)
MARS 3V (three-blade retractor system)
REVOLVE (minimally invasive pedicle screw and rod system)
SIGNATURE (articulating transforaminal interbody fusion device)
TRANSCONTINENTAL (lateral lumbar interbody fusion device)
Motion Preservation:
FLEXUS (minimally invasive unilateral PEEK interspinous process spacer)
ORBIT-R (anterior lumbar disc replacement)
SECURE-CR (articulating cervical disc replacement device)
SP-FIX (interspinous process fusion device)
TRANSITION (stabilization system)
TRIUMPH (transforaminal lumbar disc replacement device)
ZYFLEX (stabilization system)

COMPETITORS
Alphatec Spine
DePuy Spine
Integra LifeSciences
Medtronic
Medtronic Sofamor Danek
NuVasive
Orthofix
Stryker
Synthes
Zimmer Biomet

Goldman Sachs BDC Inc

Auditors: PricewaterhouseCoopers LLP

LOCATIONS

HQ: Goldman Sachs BDC Inc
  200 West Street, New York, NY 10282
Phone: 212 902-0300
Web: www.goldmansachsbdc.com

HISTORICAL FINANCIALS
Company Type: Public

Income Statement — FYE: December 31

	REVENUE ($ mil.)	NET INCOME ($ mil.)	NET PROFIT MARGIN	EMPLOYEES
12/18	146.7	82.8	56.5%	0
12/17	136.7	79.9	58.5%	0
12/16	125.1	76.2	60.9%	0
12/15	118.4	74.5	63.0%	0
12/14	73.2	52.7	72.0%	0
Annual Growth	19.0%	11.9%	—	—

2018 Year-End Financials

Debt ratio: 47.1%
Return on equity: 11.5%
Cash ($ mil.): 6.1
Current ratio: 0.66
Long-term debt ($ mil.): 659.1
No. of shares (mil.): 40.2
Dividends
  Yield: 9.7%
  Payout: 100.0%
Market value ($ mil.): 739.0

	STOCK PRICE ($) FY Close	P/E High/Low	PER SHARE ($) Earnings	Dividends	Book Value
12/18	18.38	17 14	1.34	1.80	17.65
12/17	22.18	20 17	1.28	1.80	18.09
12/16	23.52	21 16	1.12	1.80	18.31
12/15	19.00	12 8	2.14	1.80	18.97
Annual Growth	(1.1%)	— —	(14.4%)	(0.0%)	(2.4%)

GrafTech International Ltd

GrafTech International is a leading maker in the US of graphite electrodes which are essential to the production of electric arc furnaces steel and various other ferrous and nonferrous metals. GrafTech also manufactures advanced carbon materials flexible graphite products flow field plates gas diffusion layers and carbon electrodes and refractories for the aeronautics construction energy fire protection marine and transportation industries. Customers have included such notable names as Arcelor Mittal BaoSteel Elkem and Griffin Wheel (railroad wheels). In 2015 GrafTech was acquired by Brookfield Asset Management an investment firm.

Operations

GrafTech has two reportable segments: Industrial Materials and Engineered Solutions. The products are marketed under brand names such as GRAFOAM SPREADERSHIELD eGRAF GRAFOIL and GrafPower among others. Industrial Materials comprises graphite electrodes and refractory products. Graphite electrodes act as conductors of electricity and are used primarily in steel manufacturing to generate sufficient heat to scrap metal in electric arc furnaces. Refractory products include carbon and graphite refractory bricks which are used for their high thermal conductivity.

Engineered Solutions comprises advanced graphite materials and natural graphite products. Advanced graphite materials include primary products which are sold to customers for further processing (such as steel railroad car wheels). Natural graphite products consist of flexible graphite and electronic thermal management solutions used in electronics power generation automotive petrochemical and transportation industries.

Geographic Reach

The company services customers in about 70 countries through its 15 manufacturing facilities located on four continents. It currently has the capacity to manufacture approximately 195000 metric tons of graphite electrodes annually. GrafTech gets about 75% of its total sales from outside the US.

Sales and Marketing

The company sells its products primarily through a direct sales force independent sales representatives and distributors to a range of sectors including aerospace defense electrochemical processes glass and ceramics semiconductor manufacture and oil and gas exploration.

Strategy

GrafTech is dependent on the health of the steel minimill transportation semiconductor solar petrochemical and other metal industries. The company strives to keep costs low so it can ride out the cycles of the market. It has also grown its product portfolio and augmented its technology through acquisitions.

EXECUTIVES

President CEO and Director, David J. Rintoul
VP Finance and Treasurer, Quinn J. Coburn, $310,667 total compensation
Chairman, Denis A. Turcotte
Auditors: DELOITTE & TOUCHE LLP

LOCATIONS

HQ: GrafTech International Ltd
  982 Keynote Circle, Brooklyn Heights, OH 44131
Phone: 216 676-2000
Web: www.graftech.com

PRODUCTS/OPERATIONS

Selected Products
Carbon and graphite cathodes (conductors of electricity in aluminum smelters)
Carbon electrodes (used to produce silicon metal ferronickel and thermal phosphorus)
Flexible graphite (used in gaskets and other sealing applications)
Graphite electrodes (used to generate heat for melting steel in steel minimills)
Refractory products (carbon and graphite used to protect walls of blast furnaces)

COMPETITORS

Asbury Carbons	Nippon Carbon
Baosteel	PetroChina
Indian Oil	Phillips 66
JXTG Holdings	SGL CARBON
Mersen Group	Showa Denko
Mitsubishi Chemical Holdings	Superior Graphite
	Tokai Carbon

HISTORICAL FINANCIALS
Company Type: Public

Income Statement — FYE: December 31

	REVENUE ($ mil.)	NET INCOME ($ mil.)	NET PROFIT MARGIN	EMPLOYEES
12/18	1,895.9	854.2	45.1%	1,387
12/17	550.7	7.9	1.4%	1,310
12/16	437.9	(235.8)	—	1,244
12/15*	248.7	(33.5)	—	1,921
08/15	437.9	(120.6)	—	0
Annual Growth	44.2%	—	—	—

*Fiscal year change

2018 Year-End Financials

Debt ratio: 143.2%
Return on equity: —
Cash ($ mil.): 49.8
Current ratio: 1.95
Long-term debt ($ mil.): 2,050.3
No. of shares (mil.): 290.5
Dividends
  Yield: 8.1%
  Payout: 32.5%
Market value ($ mil.): 3,324.0

	STOCK PRICE ($) FY Close	P/E High/Low	PER SHARE ($) Earnings	Dividends	Book Value
12/18	11.44	8 4	2.87	0.93	(3.71)
Annual Growth	—	— —	—	—	—

(Preceding entry, top of page)

HISTORICAL FINANCIALS
Company Type: Public

Income Statement — FYE: December 31

	REVENUE ($ mil.)	NET INCOME ($ mil.)	NET PROFIT MARGIN	EMPLOYEES
12/18	712.9	156.4	21.9%	1,800
12/17	635.9	107.3	16.9%	1,500
12/16	563.9	104.3	18.5%	1,400
12/15	544.7	112.7	20.7%	1,200
12/14	474.3	92.4	19.5%	900
Annual Growth	10.7%	14.0%	—	18.9%

2018 Year-End Financials

Debt ratio: —
Return on equity: 14.5%
Cash ($ mil.): 139.7
Current ratio: 6.56
Long-term debt ($ mil.): —
No. of shares (mil.): 98.5
Dividends
  Yield: —
  Payout: —
Market value ($ mil.): 4,266.0

	STOCK PRICE ($) FY Close	P/E High/Low	PER SHARE ($) Earnings	Dividends	Book Value
12/18	43.28	36 26	1.54	0.00	12.03
12/17	41.10	37 22	1.10	0.00	10.01
12/16	24.81	26 19	1.08	0.00	8.67
12/15	27.82	24 17	1.17	0.00	7.50
12/14	23.77	28 19	0.97	0.00	6.18
Annual Growth	16.2%	— —	12.3%	—	18.1%

Gray Television Inc

Gray Television is one of the largest independent operators of TV stations in the US. It owns and operates local TV stations in 91 markets including some 150 affiliates of ABC NBC CBS and FOX. Its station portfolio reaches approximately 24% of total US TV households. The company also owns video production marketing and digital businesses including Raycom Sports Tupelo-Raycom and RTM Studios. Revenue comes primarily from broadcast and internet ads and from retransmission consent fees. In 2019 Gray expanded significantly with the $3.6 billion acquisition of Raycom Media. Former CEO J. Mack Robinson and his family control nearly 40% of the company.

Financial Performance

Revenues between 2014 and 2018 grew steadily year-over-year reaching a high in 2018. Local and national ad revenue increased as a result of special broadcasts on its NBC-affiliated stations in 2018 such as the Super Bowl and the Winter Olympic Games. Over the same five-year-period net income grew every year except 2018 when profits slipped from $262.0 million to $210.8 million.

For 2018 revenue was $1.1 billion a 23% increase over 2017. Political advertising revenue increased approximately $138.6 million due to 2018 being the on-year of the two-year election cycle. Retransmission consent revenue increased by approximately $78.8 million or 28% to $355.4 million primarily due to higher retransmission consent rates.

Net income dropped in 2018 due to increased income tax expense relative to the income tax benefit that occurred in 2017. Corporate and administrative expenses also increased jumping 30% from 2017 to 2018. The increase was due primarily to increases of $7.3 million in legal and other professional fees associated with acquisition activity in 2018.

Cash at the end of 2018 was $667.0 million. Cash from operations was $323.3 million while investing activities used $47.4 million. Financing activities contributed $680.6 million.

Strategy

Gray Television's 2019 acquisition of Raycom completed its transformation from a small regional broadcaster to a leading media company with nationwide scale. With the purchase Gray gained stations in 34 markets including eight stations in designated market areas (DMAs) larger than the top 50 television markets. (The US has 210 DMAs or geographic regions in which Nielsen measures TV viewing.)

Most revenue comes from CBS-affiliated channels (36% of revenues) followed by NBC affiliates (33%) ABC affiliates (18%) and FOX affiliates (4%). In 2018 the company's largest market by revenue was Springfield Missouri which contributed approximately 5% of revenue. The company's top 10 markets contributed approximately 32% of revenue that year.

A key component of the company's strategy is to create high-quality and locally-driven content. The company's affiliates place an emphasis on strong local news and information programming to win viewers. Gray seeks to operate in markets that it believes can earn significant political advertising revenue during election seasons. It stands to gain from the local state and national political advertising spots for a range of campaigns that are expected to flood markets ahead of the US elections in 2020. Outside political sources the company derives approximately 25% of total broadcast advertising revenue from customers in the automotive industry.

Mergers and Acquisitions

In 2019 Gray Television acquired Raycom Media for $3.6 billion making it the #3 TV station in the US. It financed the deal through a combination of cash stock fixed rate debt and an amended term loan facility.

EXECUTIVES

EVP and CFO, James C. (Jim) Ryan, age 58, $500,000 total compensation
Vice Chairman, Hilton H. Howell, age 56, $850,000 total compensation
EVP and Co-COO, Bob Smith, age 56
EVP and Co-COO, Nick Waller, age 65
EVP and Chief Digital and Technology Officer, Jason Effinger
EVP and Chief Legal and Development Officer, Kevin P. Latek, age 48, $550,000 total compensation
Vice President General Manager, Michael King
Auditors: RSM US LLP

LOCATIONS

HQ: Gray Television Inc
4370 Peachtree Road N.E., Atlanta, GA 30319
Phone: 404 504-9828
Web: www.gray.tv

PRODUCTS/OPERATIONS

2016 sales

	% of total
Local	50
National	12
Political	11
Retransmission consent	25
Other	2
Total	100

Selected Television Stations
KAKE (ABC; Wichita-Hutchinson KS)
KBTX (CBS; Bryan TX)
KCRG (ABC MY ANT; Cedar Rapids IA)
KCWY (NBC; Casper WY)
KGIN (CBS; Grand Island NE)
KGWN (CBS NBC CW; Cheyenne WY)
KKCO (NBC; Grand Junction CO)
KKTV (CBS; Colorado Springs CO)
KLBY (ABC; Colby KS)
KMVT (CBS CW Twin Falls ID)
KNOE (CBS CW ABC; Monroe-El Dorado LA)
KOLN (CBS; Lincoln-Hastings-Kearney NE)
KOLO (ABC; Reno NV)
KOSA (CBS MY; Odessa - Midland TX)
KSNB (NBC MY; Lincoln - Hastings - Kearney NE)
KSTB (CBS CW; Scottsbluff NE)
KSVT (FOX MY; Twin Falls ID)
KUPK (ABC; Garden City KS)
KWTX (CBS; Waco-Temple-Bryan TX)
KXII (CBS; Sherman TX)
WAGM (FOX CBS; Presque Isle ME)
WAHU (FOX; Charlottesville VA)
WBKO (ABC; Bowling Green KY)
WCAV (CBS; Charlottesville VA)
WCTV (CBS; Tallahassee FL)
WEAU (NBC La Crosse-Eau Claire WI)
WHSV (ABC; Harrisonburg VA)
WIBW (CBS; Topeka KS)
WIFR (CBS; Rockford IL)
WILX (NBC; Lansing MI)
WITN (NBC; Greenville NC)
WJHG (NBC; Panama City FL)
WKYT (CBS; Lexington KY)
WMTV (NBC; Madison WI)
WNDU (NBC; South Bend IN)
WOWT (NBC; Omaha NE)
WRDW (CBS; Augusta GA)
WSAW (CBS; Wausau-Rhinelander WI)
WSAZ (NBC; Charleston WV)
WSWG (CBS; Albany GA)
WTAP (NBC; Parkersburg WV)
WTOK (ABC; Meridian MS)
WTVY (CBS; Dothan AL)
WVAW (ABC; Charlottesville VA)
WVLT (CBS; Knoxville TN)
WYMT (CBS; Hazard KY)

COMPETITORS

ACME Communications
Barrington Broadcasting
Evening Post
Hoak Media
Journal Broadcast Group
Media General
Morris Multimedia
New Young Broadcasting
Nexstar Broadcasting
Quincy Newspapers
Raycom Media
Schurz Communications
Sinclair Broadcast Group

HISTORICAL FINANCIALS
Company Type: Public

Income Statement
FYE: December 31

	REVENUE ($ mil.)	NET INCOME ($ mil.)	NET PROFIT MARGIN	EMPLOYEES
12/18	1,084.1	210.8	19.4%	8,523
12/17	882.7	261.9	29.7%	3,938
12/16	812.4	62.2	7.7%	3,996
12/15	597.3	39.3	6.6%	3,819
12/14	508.1	48.0	9.5%	2,937
Annual Growth	20.9%	44.7%	—	30.5%

2018 Year-End Financials
Debt ratio: 60.5%
Return on equity: 19.3%
Cash ($ mil.): 666.9
Current ratio: 5.80
Long-term debt ($ mil.): 2,549.2
No. of shares (mil.): 88.7
Dividends
Yield: —
Payout: —
Market value ($ mil.): 1,308.0

	STOCK PRICE ($) FY Close	P/E High/Low		PER SHARE ($) Earnings	Dividends	Book Value
12/18	14.74	8	4	2.37	0.00	13.38
12/17	16.75	5	3	3.55	0.00	11.05
12/16	10.85	19	8	0.86	0.00	6.80
12/15	16.30	31	16	0.57	0.00	5.93
12/14	11.20	18	9	0.82	0.00	3.70
Annual Growth	7.1%	—	—	30.4%	—	37.9%

Great Western Bancorp Inc

Auditors: Ernst & Young LLP

LOCATIONS

HQ: Great Western Bancorp Inc
225 South Main Avenue, Sioux Falls, SD 57104
Phone: 605 334-2548
Web: www.greatwesternbank.com

HISTORICAL FINANCIALS
Company Type: Public

Income Statement   FYE: September 30

	ASSETS ($ mil.)	NET INCOME ($ mil.)	INCOME AS % OF ASSETS	EMPLOYEES
09/19	12,788.3	167.3	1.3%	1,666
09/18	12,116.8	157.9	1.3%	1,664
09/17	11,690.0	144.7	1.2%	1,689
09/16	11,531.1	121.2	1.1%	1,649
09/15	9,798.6	109.0	1.1%	1,475
Annual Growth	6.9%	11.3%	—	3.1%

2019 Year-End Financials

Return on assets: 1.3%
Return on equity: 8.9%
Long-term debt ($ mil.): —
No. of shares (mil.): 56.2
Sales ($ mil): 603.6
Dividends
Yield: 3.3%
Payout: 40.0%
Market value ($ mil.): 1,857.0

	STOCK PRICE ($) FY Close	P/E High/Low	PER SHARE ($) Earnings	Dividends	Book Value
09/19	33.00	15 10	2.92	1.10	33.76
09/18	42.19	17 14	2.67	0.90	31.24
09/17	41.28	18 13	2.45	0.74	29.83
09/16	33.32	16 11	2.14	0.56	28.34
09/15	25.37	14 9	1.90	0.36	26.43
Annual Growth	6.8%	— —	11.3%	32.2%	6.3%

Green Brick Partners Inc

Green Brick Partners (formerly BioFuel Energy) climbed aboard the ethanol bandwagon but found that bandwagon be on traveling down an uncertain course. The company's two plants (sold 2013) had the combined capacity to produce 220 million gallons of ethanol annually as well as 720000 tons of distillers grains. It sold all of its production to agribusiness giant Cargill which in turn gave it reliable corn supplies an established logistics/transportation network and marketing expertise. BioFuel Energy went public in 2007 using the proceeds to repay outstanding debts as well as to fund construction of its ethanol facilities. The name change to Green Brick Partners occurred in late 2014.

Operations
Cargill supplied all of the corn that was needed by Green Brick about 41 million bushels per year at each of its two plants (Wood River Nebraska and Fairmont Minnesota). The company believed that its plants' proximity to corn supplies natural gas and rail transportation positioned it to compete favorably in the ethanol industry.

Corn oil produced at its two plants was nonfood grade used primarily as a feedstock for the production of biodiesel and as an animal feed ingredient. Distillers grain was sold by the ton and based upon the amount of moisture retained in the product was either sold 'wet' or 'dry.'

In 2013 facing financial difficulties the company agreed to sell its two ethanol plants.

Sales and Marketing
Green Brick marketed the corn oil produced in the Wood River facility although a portion was often sold to the same third-party marketer that purchased its dried distillers grain from that facility. Most of the corn oil produced in Fairmont was sold to a biodiesel producer under an off-take agreement.

Financial Performance
Green Brick got most of its revenues from ethanol sales. However due to the divestment of its ethanol distillers grain and corn oil assets in 2013 the company did not report revenues that year. Its revenues had decreased $165 million primarily due to lower sales volumes (the Fairmont plant was idle for all of 2013) partially offset by an increase in prices received for both its ethanol and co-products.

Its net income decreased by 2% in fiscal 2013 due to a decreased loss from discontinued operations offset by an increased loss on its disposal of its plants.

Cash flow from operations increased by $12 million in 2013 due to a decrease in net loss offset by working capital sources and noncash charges (depreciation and amortization and loss on disposal of plants).

Strategy
Facing heavy debts and a difficult market in 2013 Green Brick engaged Piper Jaffray & Co to act as its financial adviser to help explore strategic alternatives including a potential sale of one or both of its plants.

That year a definitive agreement was entered into for the lenders to sell Green Brick's ethanol plants plus working capital to Green Plains Renewable Energy. Through the deal the lenders agreed to pay the company $3 million in full satisfaction of any obligations of the lenders amd extinguish all of the amounts due under Green Brick's credit facility ($177 million in principal and interest).

Prior to this deal hedge fund firms Greenlight Capital and Third Point controlled more than 50% of the company. Cargill owned another 10%.

Company Background
Cargill which had owned 5% of the company's stock since 2007 gained another 5% from Green Brick's rights offering in February 2011 which satisfied the company's debt to Cargill.

Despite favorable tax credits for renewable fuels Green Brick has been struggling since a slump in the ethanol market began in 2009. Several ethanol plants were shuttered after the economic downturn and high gasoline prices caused people to drive less. The prices of corn the company's main ingredient had increased in June 2008. Green Brick experienced hedging losses on corn and subsequently restructured its debt with Cargill.

EXECUTIVES
CEO, James R. Brickman
COO, John Jason Corley
Head Land Acquisition and Development, Jed Dolson
CFO, Richard A. Costello
Auditors: RSM US LLP

LOCATIONS
HQ: Green Brick Partners Inc
2805 Dallas Parkway, Suite 400, Plano, TX 75093
Phone: 469 573-6755
Web: www.greenbrickpartners.com

COMPETITORS
ADM
Abengoa Bioenergy
Cargill
Encore Energy Systems
GreenField Ethanol
Hawkeye Energy Holdings
Valero Energy

HISTORICAL FINANCIALS
Company Type: Public

Income Statement   FYE: December 31

	REVENUE ($ mil.)	NET INCOME ($ mil.)	NET PROFIT MARGIN	EMPLOYEES
12/18	623.6	51.6	8.3%	390
12/17	454.3	14.9	3.3%	260
12/16	380.3	23.7	6.2%	220
12/15	291.1	15.3	5.3%	200
12/14	246.1	50.0	20.3%	150
Annual Growth	26.2%	0.8%	—	27.0%

2018 Year-End Financials
Debt ratio: 25.5%
Return on equity: 11.5%
Cash ($ mil.): 38.3
Current ratio: 8.20
Long-term debt ($ mil.): 200.3
No. of shares (mil.): 50.5
Dividends
Yield: —
Payout: —
Market value ($ mil.): 366.0

	STOCK PRICE ($) FY Close	P/E High/Low	PER SHARE ($) Earnings	Dividends	Book Value
12/18	7.24	12 7	1.02	0.00	9.43
12/17	11.30	40 30	0.30	0.00	8.23
12/16	10.05	21 10	0.49	0.00	7.86
12/15	7.20	38 17	0.38	0.00	7.36
12/14	8.20	4 1	3.40	0.00	5.48
Annual Growth	(3.1%)	—	(26.0%)	—	14.5%

Green Dot Corp

Bank holding company Green Dot offers prepaid debit cards through more than 100000 retail locations in the US under brand names including Green Dot GoBank MoneyPak AccountNow RushCard and RapidPay. The MasterCard- and Visa-branded reloadable cards function like credit cards for purchases and cash withdrawals. The company's Green Dot Bank subsidiary provides issuing settlement and capital management services and garners interest from capital investments and deposits. Green Dot's products are designed for people who aren't able or choose not to utilize traditional credit card and banking services. The company makes most of its money from new card monthly maintenance and ATM fees.

Financial Performance
Green Dot has enjoyed rising revenue over the past several years as consumers warm up to prepaid cards. The company has grown by about 75% since 2014; its net income has also risen precipitously?by about 175%.

Green Dot's revenue broke $1 billion in 2018 increasing 17% from the previous year. The gains were driven by greater active accounts and engagement with new products. Gross dollar and purchase volumes and ATM transactions all rose. Furthermore cash transfers tax refund processing and Simply Paid disbursements increased.

Net income added 38% to $119 million that year primarily on the strength of the company's revenue. Income tax expense also fell significantly.

Green Dot added $85.1 million to its cash in 2018 to end the year with $1.1 billion. Operations generated $251.1 million. Investments and financing activities used $115 million and $51 million respectively. Property equipment and available-for-sale investment securities purchases drove investment spend. Financing activities were dominated by taxes paid related to net share settlement of equity awards.

Strategy

Green Dot aims to attract new customers and diversify its revenue by expanding its line of financial products through internal development and acquisitions.

In 2018 the company launched its TaxSlayer Prepaid Visa Card via its Banking as a Service (BaaS) platform through which it also offers portfolio and program management. In 2018 family-owned company TaxSlayer conducted 10 million state and federal e-files and issued refunds of $12 billion. Users of Green Dot's TaxSlayer have access to early direct deposit feeless bill pay a feeless ATM network and no overdraft or penalty fees.

The previous year Green Dot acquired online prepaid card company UniRush. UniRush's products include RushCard a general purpose reloadable card and Rapid! PayCard a corporate payroll card. That deal represented the fifth step (seek strategic synergistic and accretive acquisitions) in the company's "Six Step Plan" announced in 2017. Other elements of that plan which it completed in 2017 included adjusting acquisition and retention approaches to return to active card growth achieve savings through UniRush integration and complete share buy-backs.

Company Background

The company's July 2010 initial public offering exceeded its own expectations raising nearly $165 million. Although the IPO of secondary shares raised a significant amount Green Dot did not keep any of the money for itself. Instead the money was distributed to existing shareholders the most prominent being Wal-Mart. Prior to the IPO the retail giant took a minority stake in Green Dot — a move that cemented the pair's partnership.

EXECUTIVES

Chairman President CEO and Acting CFO, Steven W. Streit, age 58, $666,000 total compensation
SVP Corporate Strategy and Mergers and Acquisitions and Acting CFO, Mark Shifke, age 60, $450,000 total compensation
COO, Kuan Archer, age 47, $440,000 total compensation
CEO Green Dot Bank, Mary J. Dent
Senior Vice President Customer Operations, Madeline Fernandez
Vice President Green Dot Network, Taylor Driggs
Senior Vice President Information Technology Governance and Shared Services, Christopher Strader
Vice President Banking Operations, Kathy Clark
Vice President Product, Michael Panzarella
Vice President Product Marketing Interac, Sarah Howell
Vice President Corporate Procurement, Frank Parraz
Senior Vice President Technology and International Development Center, James Lo
Senior Vice President, Mark Lauderdale
VICE PRESIDENT PRODUCT MANAGEMENT, William Coats
Senior Vice President Product Development, David Banta
Chairman, William I. Jacobs, age 78
Treasurer, Matt Kohler
Auditors: Ernst & Young LLP

LOCATIONS

HQ: Green Dot Corp
3465 E. Foothill Blvd., Pasadena, CA 91107
Phone: 626 765-2000
Web: www.greendot.com

PRODUCTS/OPERATIONS

2018 Revenue

	$ mil.	% of total
Card revenues and other fees	482.9	46
Processing and settlement service revenues	248.0	24
Interchange revenues	310.9	30
Total	**1,041.8**	**100**

COMPETITORS

American Express	MoneyGram
Blackhawk Network	International
DFC Global	NetSpend
FSV Payment Systems	PreCash
First Data	U.S. Bancorp
H&R Block	Visa Inc
JPMorgan Chase	Western Union
Jackson Hewitt	nFinanSe

HISTORICAL FINANCIALS

Company Type: Public

Income Statement   FYE: December 31

	REVENUE ($ mil.)	NET INCOME ($ mil.)	NET PROFIT MARGIN	EMPLOYEES
12/18	1,041.7	118.7	11.4%	1,100
12/17	890.1	85.8	9.6%	1,152
12/16	718.7	41.6	5.8%	974
12/15	694.7	38.4	5.5%	1,012
12/14	601.5	42.6	7.1%	857
Annual Growth	14.7%	29.1%	—	6.4%

2018 Year-End Financials

Debt ratio: —	No. of shares (mil.): 52.9
Return on equity: 14.1%	Dividends
Cash ($ mil.): 1,094.7	Yield: —
Current ratio: 1.03	Payout: —
Long-term debt ($ mil.): —	Market value ($ mil.): 4,208.0

	STOCK PRICE ($) FY Close	P/E High/Low		PER SHARE ($)		
				Earnings	Dividends	Book Value
12/18	79.52	41	25	2.18	0.00	17.19
12/17	60.26	38	14	1.61	0.00	14.95
12/16	23.55	31	19	0.80	0.00	13.54
12/15	16.42	29	19	0.72	0.00	13.13
12/14	20.49	29	18	0.90	0.00	12.30
Annual Growth	40.4%	—	—	24.8%	—	8.7%

Green Plains Partners LP

Auditors: KPMG LLP

LOCATIONS

HQ: Green Plains Partners LP
1811 Aksarben Drive, Omaha, NE 68106
Phone: 402 884-8700
Web: www.greenplainspartners.com

HISTORICAL FINANCIALS

Company Type: Public

Income Statement   FYE: December 31

	REVENUE ($ mil.)	NET INCOME ($ mil.)	NET PROFIT MARGIN	EMPLOYEES
12/18	100.7	55.6	55.3%	40
12/17	106.9	58.8	55.0%	45
12/16	103.7	56.8	54.7%	0
12/15	50.9	16.3	32.2%	0
12/14	12.8	2.1	16.6%	0
Annual Growth	67.4%	126.0%	—	—

2018 Year-End Financials

Debt ratio: 175.0%	No. of shares (mil.): 23.1
Return on equity: —	Dividends
Cash ($ mil.): 0.5	Yield: 13.9%
Current ratio: 2.03	Payout: 107.0%
Long-term debt ($ mil.): 142.0	Market value ($ mil.): 314.0

	STOCK PRICE ($) FY Close	P/E High/Low		PER SHARE ($)		
				Earnings	Dividends	Book Value
12/18	13.57	10	7	1.81	1.90	(3.13)
12/17	18.70	12	10	1.81	1.78	(1.98)
12/16	19.80	12	7	1.75	1.64	(2.02)
12/15	16.25	23	18	0.71	0.40	2.06
Annual Growth	(5.8%)	—	—	36.6%	68.0%	—

Greene County Bancorp Inc

EXECUTIVES

Vice President, Trisha M Lamb
Board Member, Charles Schaefer
Auditors: Bonadio & Co., LLP

LOCATIONS

HQ: Greene County Bancorp Inc
302 Main Street, Catskill, NY 12414
Phone: 518 943-2600
Web: www.tbogc.com

COMPETITORS

HSBC USA	M&T Bank
KeyCorp	TrustCo Bank Corp NY

HISTORICAL FINANCIALS
Company Type: Public

Income Statement — FYE: June 30

	ASSETS ($ mil.)	NET INCOME ($ mil.)	INCOME AS % OF ASSETS	EMPLOYEES
06/19	1,269.4	17.4	1.4%	172
06/18	1,151.4	14.4	1.3%	164
06/17	982.2	11.1	1.1%	146
06/16	868.7	8.9	1.0%	140
06/15	738.6	7.1	1.0%	136
Annual Growth	14.5%	24.9%	—	6.0%

2019 Year-End Financials
Return on assets: 1.4%
Return on equity: 16.7%
Long-term debt ($ mil.): —
No. of shares (mil.): 8.5
Sales ($ mil): 54.6
Dividends
  Yield: 0.0%
  Payout: 19.5%
Market value ($ mil.): 251.0

	STOCK PRICE ($) FY Close	P/E High/Low	PER SHARE ($) Earnings	Dividends	Book Value
06/19	29.42	17 14	2.05	0.40	13.16
06/18	33.90	22 13	1.69	0.39	11.27
06/17	27.20	21 12	1.31	0.38	9.82
06/16	16.27	40 15	1.06	0.37	8.77
06/15	28.49	36 30	0.85	0.36	7.92
Annual Growth	0.8%	—	24.8%	2.7%	13.5%

GreenSky Inc

Auditors: PricewaterhouseCoopers LLP

LOCATIONS
HQ: GreenSky Inc
5565 Glenridge Connector, Suite 700, Atlanta, GA 30342
Phone: 678 264-6105
Web: www.greensky.com

HISTORICAL FINANCIALS
Company Type: Public

Income Statement — FYE: December 31

	REVENUE ($ mil.)	NET INCOME ($ mil.)	NET PROFIT MARGIN	EMPLOYEES
12/18	414.6	24.2	5.8%	1,088
12/17	325.8	103.2	31.7%	949
12/16	263.8	99.2	37.6%	0
12/15	173.4	76.2	43.9%	0
Annual Growth	33.7%	(31.7%)	—	—

2018 Year-End Financials
Debt ratio: 48.1%
Return on equity: —
Cash ($ mil.): 303.3
Current ratio: 3.11
Long-term debt ($ mil.): 386.8
No. of shares (mil.): 183.0
Dividends
  Yield: —
  Payout: —
Market value ($ mil.): 1,752.0

	STOCK PRICE ($) FY Close	P/E High/Low	PER SHARE ($) Earnings	Dividends	Book Value
12/18	9.57	62 20	0.41	0.00	0.14
12/17	0.00	— —	7.49	0.00	(1.95)
Annual Growth	—	—	(94.5%)	—	—

GrubHub Inc

Auditors: Crowe LLP

LOCATIONS
HQ: GrubHub Inc
111 W. Washington Street, Suite 2100, Chicago, IL 60602
Phone: 877 585-7878
Web: www.grubhub.com

HISTORICAL FINANCIALS
Company Type: Public

Income Statement — FYE: December 31

	REVENUE ($ mil.)	NET INCOME ($ mil.)	NET PROFIT MARGIN	EMPLOYEES
12/18	1,007.2	78.4	7.8%	2,722
12/17	683.0	98.9	14.5%	2,125
12/16	493.3	49.5	10.0%	1,518
12/15	361.8	38.0	10.5%	1,105
12/14	253.8	24.2	9.6%	1,090
Annual Growth	41.1%	34.1%	—	25.7%

2018 Year-End Financials
Debt ratio: 16.5%
Return on equity: 6.1%
Cash ($ mil.): 211.2
Current ratio: 1.63
Long-term debt ($ mil.): 335.5
No. of shares (mil.): 90.7
Dividends
  Yield: —
  Payout: —
Market value ($ mil.): 6,971.0

	STOCK PRICE ($) FY Close	P/E High/Low	PER SHARE ($) Earnings	Dividends	Book Value
12/18	76.81	167 76	0.85	0.00	15.89
12/17	71.80	64 29	1.12	0.00	12.88
12/16	37.62	76 32	0.58	0.00	11.34
12/15	24.20	105 51	0.44	0.00	10.33
12/14	36.32	137 91	0.30	0.00	9.41
Annual Growth	20.6%	— —	29.7%	—	14.0%

Guaranty Bancshares Inc

EXECUTIVES
Senior Vice President, Terry Todd
Senior Vice President, Steve Bledsoe
Executive Vice President General Counsel, Randall Kucera
Auditors: Whitley Penn LLP

LOCATIONS
HQ: Guaranty Bancshares Inc
16475 Dallas Parkway, Suite 600, Addison, TX 75001
Phone: 888 572-9881
Web: www.gnty.com

PRODUCTS/OPERATIONS

2008 Sales
	$ mil.	% of total
Interest		
Loans including fees	31.2	70
Securities	6.3	13
Other	1.1	2
Noninterest		
Service charges	4.2	8
Other	3.3	7
Total	**46.1**	**100**

COMPETITORS
BancorpSouth — Southside Bancshares
Bank of America — Wells Fargo
Capital One — Woodforest Financial
Cullen/Frost Bankers

HISTORICAL FINANCIALS
Company Type: Public

Income Statement — FYE: December 31

	ASSETS ($ mil.)	NET INCOME ($ mil.)	INCOME AS % OF ASSETS	EMPLOYEES
12/18	2,266.9	20.6	0.9%	454
12/17	1,962.6	14.4	0.7%	407
12/16	1,828.3	12.1	0.7%	397
12/15	1,682.6	10.1	0.6%	0
12/14	1,334.0	9.7	0.7%	0
Annual Growth	14.2%	20.7%	—	—

2018 Year-End Financials
Return on assets: 0.9%
Return on equity: 9.1%
Long-term debt ($ mil.): —
No. of shares (mil.): 11.8
Sales ($ mil): 101.5
Dividends
  Yield: 2.0%
  Payout: 41.1%
Market value ($ mil.): 353.0

	STOCK PRICE ($) FY Close	P/E High/Low	PER SHARE ($) Earnings	Dividends	Book Value
12/18	29.82	20 16	1.77	0.60	20.68
12/17	30.65	25 20	1.40	0.40	18.75
12/16	26.50	— —	1.35	0.52	16.22
12/15	26.50	— —	1.15	0.50	15.47
12/14	26.50	— —	1.25	1.50	14.01
Annual Growth	3.0%	— —	9.1%	(20.5%)	10.2%

Guaranty Federal Bancshares Inc (Springfield, MO)

Auditors: BKD, LLP

LOCATIONS
HQ: Guaranty Federal Bancshares Inc (Springfield, MO)
2144 E Republic Rd, Suite F200, Springfield, MO 65804
Phone: 833 875-2492
Web: www.gbankmo.com

Guidewire Software Inc

Guidewire Software develops software for the insurance industry. The company's InsuranceSuite offers applications to property and casualty insurers for underwriting policy administration (PolicyCenter) claims management (ClaimsCenter) and billing (BillingCenter). Its software is intended to replace paper-based processes and legacy systems built around outdated programming languages. Its products can run on-premise or from the cloud. Guidewire counts some 210 customers in two dozen countries. It customers include Tokio Marine Nationwide Mutual and Zurich Financial Services.

Operations
Licensing of the company's software brings in about 47% of revenue while service accounts for another 40%. Maintenance rounds out the revenue pie with a 13% slice.

Guidewire's software is generally licensed over a five-year contract and is priced according to the number of the insurance provider's written premiums. It charges customers in advance for both term license and maintenance fees.

Geographic Reach
Guidewire's corporate headquarters is in Foster City California. It also leases facilities for distributed sales and international operations in Dublin Ireland; Edina Minnesota; London United Kingdom; Mississauga Ontario Canada; Munich Germany; Paris France; Sydney Australia; and Tokyo Japan.

In 2015 the US accounted for 55% of Guidewire's revenues. The UK supplies 12% of revenue and Canada's share is 10%.

Sales and Marketing
The company has more than 230 employees in a sales and marketing capacity including 41 direct sales representatives organized by geographic region across Australia Canada France Germany Hong Kong Japan the UK and the US. Guidewire's 10 largest customers accounted for 31% of revenue in 2015 a bit lower than the 35% of 2014.

Financial Performance
Guidewire's revenue increased 8% to $380.5 million in 2015 (ended July) driven by continued adoption of the company's InsuranceSuite package. A growing customer based led to a 19% increase in maintenance fees. Geographically the company had strong growth in Europe and Asia-Pacific but saw reduced revenue from Canada and other countries in the Americas other than the US where sales increased 2%.

Net income decreased 33% in 2015 due to an increase in operating expenses such as an increase in research and development expenses and taxes. Profit has declined since it peaked at $35.5 million in 2011.

Strategy
The company has extensive relationships with system integration consulting and industry partners. It encourages partners to co-market pursue joint sales initiatives and drive broader adoption of their technology. Its leading system integrator partners include Capgemini Ernst & Young IBM Global Services and PricewaterhouseCoopers.

Guidewire is intent on expanding its insurance software footprint internationally. It established a Regional Development Centre in Krakow to help the company further expand its global operations. It is Guidewire's sixth global development center joining teams in California Dublin Pennsylvania Tokyo and Toronto.

The company also expanded its Ireland operations by the leasing of additional office space to handle its growing team. It anticipates hiring 60-80 new staff in 2015-2016.

Company Background
Guidewire was founded in 2001 by CEO Marcus Ryu Product Strategy Director Kenneth Branson and four others who are no longer with the company. Its ClaimCenter product launched in 2003 PolicyCenter in 2004 and BillingCenter in 2006.

Guidewire filed a $100 million initial public offering in September 2011 and began trading on the NYSE in 2012.

EXECUTIVES
President and CEO, Marcus S. Ryu, age 45, $418,750 total compensation
SVP Corporate Development and Chief Administrative Officer, Priscilla Hung, $252,800 total compensation
Chief Business Officer, Scott Roza, $232,500 total compensation
CFO, Richard Hart, $140,673 total compensation
Chief Delivery Officer, Mike Polelle, $80,827 total compensation
Chief Product Officer, Ali Kheirolomoom, $220,346 total compensation
Managing Director Europe Middle East and Africa, Keith Stonell
Vice President Strategy, Neil Betteridge
Vice President Product Management, Amy Mollin
Vice President of Sales and Marketing, Rick Wong
Vice President Professional Services, Daniel Wang
Vp Engineering Cyence Risk Analytics, Akin Dirik
Chairman, Craig A. Conway, age 64
Auditors: KPMG LLP

LOCATIONS
HQ: Guidewire Software Inc
2850 S. Delaware St., Suite 400, San Mateo, CA 94403
Phone: 650 357-9100   **Fax:** 650 357-9101
Web: www.guidewire.com

PRODUCTS/OPERATIONS
2014 Sales

	$ mil.	% of total
Licenses	179.2	47
Services	151.3	40
Maintenance	50.0	13
Total	**380.5**	**100**

COMPETITORS
Accenture
Applied Systems
CCC Information
Computer Sciences Corp.
Cover-All
Duck Creek
Ebix
Oracle
Pegasystems
SAP
Sapiens
StoneRiver
SunGard Financial Systems
Tata Consultancy
Vertafore

HISTORICAL FINANCIALS
Company Type: Public

Income Statement   FYE: July 31

	REVENUE ($ mil.)	NET INCOME ($ mil.)	NET PROFIT MARGIN	EMPLOYEES
07/19	719.5	20.7	2.9%	2,355
07/18	661.0	(19.6)	—	2,292
07/17	514.2	21.2	4.1%	1,893
07/16	424.4	14.9	3.5%	1,536
07/15	380.5	9.8	2.6%	1,341
Annual Growth	17.3%	20.3%	—	15.1%

2019 Year-End Financials
Debt ratio: 14.6%
Return on equity: 1.3%
Cash ($ mil.): 254.1
Current ratio: 5.75
Long-term debt ($ mil.): 317.3
No. of shares (mil.): 82.1
Dividends
  Yield: —
  Payout: —
Market value ($ mil.): 8,385.0

	STOCK PRICE ($) FY Close	P/E High/Low		PER SHARE ($) Earnings	Dividends	Book Value
07/19	102.08	434	298	0.25	0.00	19.16
07/18	86.20	—	—	(0.25)	0.00	17.66
07/17	72.16	251	170	0.28	0.00	11.91
07/16	61.47	304	205	0.20	0.00	10.73
07/15	59.05	429	284	0.14	0.00	9.71
Annual Growth	14.7%	—	—	15.6%	—	18.5%

HISTORICAL FINANCIALS
Company Type: Public

Income Statement   FYE: December 31

	ASSETS ($ mil.)	NET INCOME ($ mil.)	INCOME AS % OF ASSETS	EMPLOYEES
12/18	965.1	7.3	0.8%	226
12/17	794.4	5.1	0.6%	173
12/16	687.9	5.5	0.8%	172
12/15	652.8	5.7	0.9%	170
12/14	628.4	5.7	0.9%	165
Annual Growth	11.3%	6.1%	—	8.2%

2018 Year-End Financials
Return on assets: 0.8%
Return on equity: 9.4%
Long-term debt ($ mil.): —
No. of shares (mil.): 4.4
Sales ($ mil): 49.8
Dividends
  Yield: 2.2%
  Payout: 40.3%
Market value ($ mil.): 97.0

	STOCK PRICE ($) FY Close	P/E High	P/E Low	PER SHARE ($) Earnings	Dividends	Book Value
12/18	21.84	15	12	1.64	0.48	18.05
12/17	22.45	19	16	1.16	0.30	16.93
12/16	21.18	17	12	1.27	0.34	15.87
12/15	15.25	12	10	1.30	0.23	15.12
12/14	13.17	10	8	1.33	0.15	14.20
Annual Growth	13.5%	—	—	5.4%	33.7%	6.2%

Gulfport Energy Corp.

Gulfport Energy put its energy into exploring for hydrocarbons near the Gulf of Mexico and elsewhere. The oil and gas exploration and production company' main producing properties are located along the Louisiana Gulf Coast in the Permian basin in West Texas in the Niobrara Shale Formation in western Colorado and in the Utica Shale in eastern Ohio. Additionally Gulfport Energy holds a sizeable acreage position in the Alberta oil sands in Canada through its interest in Grizzly Oil Sands ULC and it has interests in entities that operate in the Phu Horm gas field in northern Thailand. In 2015 the company reported proved reserves of 6.4 million barrels of oil and 1.5 trillion cu. ft. of natural gas.

Operations
Gulfport Energy's average daily net production from its Utica Shale in 205 was 586.9 barrels of oil equivalent 59% of which was from natural gas.

In 2015 it drilled 49 gross (38.4 net) wells participated in an additional 25 gross (7.3 net) wells that were drilled by other operators on Utica Shale acreage and recompleted 72 gross and net wells. Of 49 new wells drilled ten were completed as producing wells and at year end 36 were in various stages of completion and three were drilling. That year it recompleted 35 existing wells. In the Hackberry Field Gulfport Energy recompleted 37 existing wells.

During the year gas accounted for 72% of revenues; oil and condensate 20%; and natural gas liquids 8%.

Geographic Reach
The company's principal operating area includes Louisiana's West Cote Blanche Bay field East Hackberry field (in the Permian Basin) Utica shale in Ohio the Niobrara Shale in Colorado Canadian oil sands in Alberta and the Phu Horm gas field in Thailand.

Sales and Marketing
In 2015 Gulfport Energy sold 90% and 10% of its oil production to Shell and Marathon Oil respectively; 76% and 24% of its natural gas liquids production to MarkWest and Antero Resources respectively; and 79% 14% and 5% of its natural gas production to BP DTE Energy and Hess respectively.

In Ohio the company entered into firm transportation contracts to deliver 725000 MMBtu to 775000 MMBtu per day for 2016.

For 2017 it entered into firm transportation contracts to deliver 775000 MMBtu to 1125000 MMBtu per day. For 2018 through 2020 the company had firm transportation contracts to deliver 1125000 MMBtu per day.

Financial Performance
In 2015 Gulfport Energy's net revenues increased by 6% due to a 128% increase in net production partially offset by a 54% decrease in realized Mcfe prices as the result of a decline in commodity prices and a shift in the company's production mix toward natural gas and NGLs in 2015.

The company incurred a huge net loss of $1.22 billion (and overall decrease of 595% compared to net income in 2014). This loss was mainly due to impairment of oil and gas properties of $1.4 billion.

In 2015 cash from operating activities declined by 21% due to impairment charges.

Strategy
The company sells some assets to pay down debt. It is also focused on building up its lucrative Utica shale assets. Gulfport Energy's strategy includes well development reserve acquisitions midstream infrastructure and other activities.

A key part of our strategy involves using some of the latest available horizontal drilling and completion techniques.

It spud 49 gross (38.4 net) wells on Utica Shale acreage and in 2016 (through February 10 2016) they had spud four gross (2.2 net) wells. As of February 2016 one well was waiting on completion and three were still being drilled.

In 2016 the company planned to drill 29 to 32 gross (19 to 21 net) horizontal wells and commence sales from 44 to 48 gross (28 to 30 net) horizontal wells on Utica Shale acreage for an estimated aggregate cost of $219 million to $247. It anticipated 17 to 19 gross (two to three net) horizontal wells will be drilled and sales commenced from 30 to 34 gross (eight to nine net) horizontal wells by other operators on our Utica Shale acreage during 2016 for an estimated net cost to us of $90 million to $100 million.

In 2014 Gulfport Energy sold Blackhawk Midstream's (50% owned by Gulfport) equity interest in two entities Ohio Gathering Company LLC and Ohio Condensate Company LLC to Summit Midstream Partners for $190 million.

Mergers and Acquisitions
In 2016 Gulfport Energy agreed to buy 12600 net undeveloped acres in northern Monroe County Ohio in the core of the dry gas window of the Utica Shale for $87 million.

In 2015 the company acquired Paloma for $301.9 million. Paloma holds approximately 24000 net nonproducing acres in the Utica Shale of Ohio. It also bought 6198 gross and net acres located in Belmont and Jefferson Counties Ohio from AEU for $68.2 million.

Gulfport Energy also bought 38965 gross (27228 net) acres located in Monroe County Ohio 14.6 MMcf per day of average net production 18 gross (11.3 net) drilled but uncompleted wells an 11 mile gas gathering system and a four well pad location from AEU for a total purchase price of approximately $319.0 million

Company Background
In 2013 Gulfport Energy acquired 22000 net acres in the Utica Shale from Windsor Ohio LLC an affiliate of Wexford Capital for $220 million; with an expectation of net production to be about 22200 barrels of oil equivalent per day.

In 2012 the company purchased 37000 net acres in the Utica Shale for about $372 million boosting its leasehold interests in the shale play to 137000 gross (106000 net) acres.

In 2012 the company completed its contribution of its oil and gas interests in the Permian Basin to Diamondback prior to the closing of the Diamondback IPO. In 2013 the company received an additional payment from Diamondback of $19 million.

EXECUTIVES

CEO; Director, Michael G. (Mike) Moore, age 62, $460,000 total compensation
VP Geological and Geophysical, Stuart A. Maier, age 66, $400,000 total compensation
VP Reservoir Engineering, Steve R. Baldwin, age 66
CFO, Keri Crowell, age 45, $250,000 total compensation
VP Land, Lester Zitkus
VP Operations, Mark Malone
VP Drilling, Rob Jones
Managing Director Midstream Operations, Ty Peck
Chairman, David L. Houston, age 66
Board Member, Craig Groeschel
Board Member, Charles Johnson
Auditors: Grant Thornton LLP

LOCATIONS
HQ: Gulfport Energy Corp.
3001 Quail Springs Parkway, Oklahoma City, OK 73134
Phone: 405 252-4600
Web: www.gulfportenergy.com

PRODUCTS/OPERATIONS

2015 Sales

	$ mil.	% of total
Gas	507.7	72
Oil & condensate	142.0	20
Natural gas liquids	59.4	8
Other	0.4	—
Total	709.5	100

COMPETITORS

Abraxas Petroleum	EOG
Apache	Exxon Mobil
Bill Barrett	FieldPoint Petroleum
BreitBurn	MarkWest Energy
Cabot Oil & Gas	Partners
Chesapeake Energy	XTO Energy
Devon Energy	

HISTORICAL FINANCIALS
Company Type: Public

Income Statement — FYE: December 31

	REVENUE ($ mil.)	NET INCOME ($ mil.)	NET PROFIT MARGIN	EMPLOYEES
12/18	1,355.0	430.5	31.8%	350
12/17	1,320.3	435.1	33.0%	331
12/16	385.9	(979.7)	—	241
12/15	709.4	(1,224.8)	—	230
12/14	671.2	247.4	36.9%	203
Annual Growth	19.2%	14.9%	—	14.6%

2018 Year-End Financials
Debt ratio: 34.5%
Return on equity: 13.3%
Cash ($ mil.): 52.3
Current ratio: 0.59
Long-term debt ($ mil.): 2,086.7
No. of shares (mil.): 162.9
Dividends
 Yield: —
 Payout: —
Market value ($ mil.): 1,068.0

	STOCK PRICE ($) FY Close	P/E High/Low		PER SHARE ($) Earnings	Dividends	Book Value
12/18	6.55	5	3	2.45	0.00	20.42
12/17	12.76	9	5	2.41	0.00	16.94
12/16	21.64	—	—	(7.97)	0.00	13.75
12/15	24.57	—	—	(12.27)	0.00	18.82
12/14	41.74	26	13	2.88	0.00	26.81
Annual Growth	(37.1%)	—	—	(4.0%)	—	(6.6%)

Hamilton Lane Inc

Auditors: Ernst & Young LLP

LOCATIONS
HQ: Hamilton Lane Inc
One Presidential Blvd., 4th Floor, Bala Cynwyd, PA 19004
Phone: 610 934-2222
Web: www.hamiltonlane.com

HISTORICAL FINANCIALS
Company Type: Public

Income Statement   FYE: March 31

	REVENUE ($ mil.)	NET INCOME ($ mil.)	NET PROFIT MARGIN	EMPLOYEES
03/19	252.1	33.5	13.3%	370
03/18	244.0	17.3	7.1%	340
03/17	179.8	0.6	0.3%	290
03/16	180.8	57.1	31.6%	290
03/15	155.3	69.2	44.6%	0
Annual Growth	12.9%	(16.6%)	—	—

2019 Year-End Financials
Debt ratio: 19.6%
Return on equity: 35.5%
Cash ($ mil.): 49.3
Current ratio: 0.71
Long-term debt ($ mil.): 70.9
No. of shares (mil.): 50.8
Dividends
 Yield: 0.0%
 Payout: 60.7%
Market value ($ mil.): 2,218.0

	STOCK PRICE ($) FY Close	P/E High/Low	PER SHARE ($) Earnings	Dividends	Book Value
03/19	43.58	37 23	1.40	0.85	2.17
03/18	37.23	42 19	0.93	0.70	1.61
03/17	18.67	642 601	0.03	0.00	1.28
Annual Growth	52.8%	—	−583.1%	—	30.2%

Hancock Whitney Corp

EXECUTIVES
President CEO and Director, John M. Hairston, age 56, $707,000 total compensation
COO, D. Shane Loper, age 53, $400,000 total compensation
CFO, Michael M. Achary, age 58, $400,000 total compensation
President Whitney Bank, Joseph S. Exnicios, age 63, $375,000 total compensation
Chief Credit Officer Whitney Bank, Suzanne C. Thomas, age 64
Chief Credit Risk Officer, Samuel B. Kendricks, age 59
Chief Investment Officer, David J. Lundgren
Executive Vice President General Counsel Corporate Secretary, Joy Phillips
Vice President And Private Banker, Larry Cuervo
Senior Vice President Financial And Estate Planner, Emile Koury
Assistant Vice President, Kim Gibson
Assistant Vice President, Jimmy Campbell
Assistant Vice President Technology, Roland Pittman
Vice President Project Manager Enterprise Project Office, Heather Argent
Vice President Senior Business Banker, Kai Sonnenschein
Assistant Vice President Merchant Services Sales Specialist, Lisa Parks
Assistant Vice President And Trust Officer, Kevin Peyton
Vice President, Rachel Nunez
Vice President Retirement Plan Services, Amy Grace
Assistant Vice President, Katie Widdows
Vice President Social Media And Public Relations, Janel Evans
Vice President And Business Banker, Mike Cadden
Vice President Relationship Manager, Mark Menard
Chairman, James B. Estabrook, age 75
Auditors: PricewaterhouseCoopers LLP

LOCATIONS
HQ: Hancock Whitney Corp
 Hancock Whitney Plaza,, 2510 14th Street, Gulfport, MS 39501
Phone: 228 868-4000
Web: www.hancockbank.com

PRODUCTS/OPERATIONS

2017 Sales

	$ mil.	% of total
Interest income		
Loans including fees	772.0	66
Securities	124.2	11
Other	4.3	—
Interest expense	(108.3)	—
Non interest income		
Service charges on deposit accounts	83.2	7
Bank card and ATM fees	53.8	5
Trust fees	44.5	4
Investment and annuity fees	20.5	2
Secondary mortgage market operations	15.2	1
Insurance commissions and fees	3.2	—
Other	49.9	4
Total	1,062.5	100

Selected Services
Banking
Checking
Credit Cards
Currency Exchange
Home Equity Loans and Lines
Investment Services
Investments
Loans & Credit
Mobile Banking
Mortgage
Online & Mobile Banking
Online Banking
Personal Loans and Lines
Savings

COMPETITORS
BancorpSouth
Capital One
First Horizon
IBERIABANK
Investar
MidSouth Bancorp
Regions Financial
Renasant
Trustmark

HISTORICAL FINANCIALS
Company Type: Public

Income Statement   FYE: December 31

	ASSETS ($ mil.)	NET INCOME ($ mil.)	INCOME AS % OF ASSETS	EMPLOYEES
12/18	28,235.9	323.7	1.1%	3,933
12/17	27,336.0	215.6	0.8%	3,887
12/16	23,975.3	149.3	0.6%	3,724
12/15	22,839.4	131.4	0.6%	3,921
12/14	20,747.2	175.7	0.8%	3,794
Annual Growth	8.0%	16.5%	—	0.9%

2018 Year-End Financials
Return on assets: 1.1%
Return on equity: 10.8%
Long-term debt ($ mil.): —
No. of shares (mil.): 85.6
Sales ($ mil): 1,313.4
Dividends
 Yield: 2.9%
 Payout: 31.4%
Market value ($ mil.): 2,968.0

	STOCK PRICE ($) FY Close	P/E High/Low	PER SHARE ($) Earnings	Dividends	Book Value
12/18	34.65	15 9	3.72	1.02	35.98
12/17	49.50	21 17	2.48	0.96	33.86
12/16	43.10	24 11	1.87	0.96	32.29
12/15	25.17	20 15	1.64	0.96	31.14
12/14	30.70	18 14	2.10	0.96	30.74
Annual Growth	3.1%	—	15.4%	1.5%	4.0%

Hanmi Financial Corp.

Hanmi Financial owns Hanmi Bank which serves Korean-American and other ethnic communities in California Colorado Georgia Illinois New Jersey New York Texas Virginia and Washington. The company which holds $5.5 billion in assets offers traditional banking services to small and midsized businesses from about 40 branches and eight loan offices. Real estate loans — including for retail hospitality mixed-use apartment office industrial gas station faith-based facility and warehouse properties — account for about 80% of its loan portfolio; commercial and industrial loans and leases receivable make up most of the rest.

Operations
Hanmi Financial originates real estate loans (including commercial construction and residential property) commercial and industrial loans (including commercial term commercial lines of credit and international) equipment lease financing consumer loans and Small Business Administration (SBA) loans. The bank also offers traditional deposit products including checking savings negotiable order of withdrawal (NOW) and money market accounts and CDs.

Hanmi's $4.6 billion loan portfolio is made up mostly of real estate loans — particularly commercial property loans including retail (about 20% of total portfolio) hospitality (20%) and other loans (30%). Other loans include loans for mixed-use apartment office industrial gas station faith-based facility and warehouse properties. Residential property loans comprise around 10%.

Commercial and industrial loans and leases receivable together make up about 15% of the bank's portfolio.

Geographic Reach
Headquartered in a penthouse suite on Los Angeles' Wilshire Boulevard Hanmi Financial has one bank branch in each of New Jersey New York and Virginia; some five branches in Illinois; about 10 branches in Texas; and around 25 branches in California. The majority of its loan and deposit concentration is in Southern California.

Sales and Marketing
Hanmi Financial's lending is concentrated in real estate loans commercial loans and leases and Small Business Administration (SBA) loans for small and middle market businesses in California Texas Illinois and New York — primarily among Korean-American and other multi-ethnic communities.

Financial Performance
Since 2013 Hanmi Financial has grown its revenue and net income by about 60% and 40% respectively thanks to increasing net interest income.

But the company also depleted its cash stores by about 15% and more than doubled its long-term debt in that time mostly due to Federal Home Loan Bank advances in 2016.

The bank's revenue increased 9% in 2017 compared with 2016 reaching $210.2 million. Higher interest and fees on loans and leases drove the improvement which was partially offset by higher expense for interest on deposits. Average loans and leases and the percentage of loans and leases in Hanmi's mix of interest-earning assets both increased in 2017.

Net income slipped 3% to $54.7 million owing mostly to an increase in the bank's income tax provision which included a $3.9 million charge for a one-time revaluation adjustment connected with the Tax Cuts and Jobs Act (TCJA).

Hanmi added $6.6 million to its cash stores in 2017 for a total of $153.8 million. Operations and financings provided $79.9 million and $445.1 million respectively. Investment activity used $518.4 million.

Strategy

Hanmi Financial is working to diversify its loan portfolio to reduce its reliance on commercial real estate and increase its composition of leases and commercial industrial and residential real estate loans. Since 2014 the company has increased the proportion of its portfolio made up of leases and residential real estate while maintaining the proportion of commercial and industrial loans.

After a review of its cost structure and operating efficiency in 2018 the company is moderating its growth expectations lowering its non-interest expenses and consolidating about 10% of its branches.

Hanmi also hired a Chief Technology officer in 2018 to implement a strategy to improve the company's use of technology including using it to increase efficiency of regulatory compliance activities (for which the company heavily relies on human capital).

Mergers and Acquisitions

In its first foray outside of California in late 2013 Hanmi agreed to acquire Central Bancorp Inc. the parent of Texas-based United Central Bank. United Central Bank serves multi-ethnic communities in Texas Illinois Virginia California New York and New Jersey through some two dozen branches. Once the acquisition is complete Hanmi will have about 50 branches and two loan production offices serving a broad range of ethnic communities in California Texas Illinois New York New Jersey Virginia and Georgia.

Company Background

Hanmi Financial was founded in 1982.

EXECUTIVES

SEVP and COO, Bonita I. (Bonnie) Lee, age 56
Chief Compliance and BSA Officer, Jean Lim
EVP and CFO, Michael W. McCall
President CEO and Director, Chong Guk (C. G.) Kum
EVP and Chief Credit Officer, Randall G. Ewig
EVP and Chief Administrative Officer, Greg D. Kim
EVP and Chief Banking Officer, Peter Yang
EVP and Chief Lending Officer, Anthony Kim
Assistant Vice President, Sue Kim
Assistant Vice President Compliance Officer, Michael Santiago
Assistant Vice President Treasury Management, Debby Sassoon
Vice President, Maheboob Kurani
Assistant Vice President andamp; Credit Analyst, Daniel Park
First Vice President And Branch Manager, Annie Chung
Vice President Human Resources Officer, Ashley Sowa
Avp And Sba Closing Officer, Liz Choe
SENIOR VICE PRESIDENT AND OPERATIONS ADMINISTRATOR, Nancy Lee
Vp Hr Business Partner, Kathy Kim
Vice President Human Resources Officer, Lan Nguyen
Vice President And Business Development Officer, Yusin Lee
Chairman, Joseph K. Rho, age 78
Board Member, Anna Chung
Board Member, David Yang
Auditors: Crowe LLP

LOCATIONS

HQ: Hanmi Financial Corp.
3660 Wilshire Boulevard, Penthouse Suite A, Los Angeles, CA 90010
Phone: 213 382-2200
Web: www.hanmi.com

PRODUCTS/OPERATIONS

2017 Sales

	$ mil.	% of total
Net interest income	176.8	84
Non-interest income	33.4	16
Total	210.2	100

COMPETITORS

Bank of America	Far East National Bank
Broadway Financial	Hope Bancorp
Cathay General Bancorp	JPMorgan Chase
East West Bancorp	Woori

HISTORICAL FINANCIALS

Company Type: Public

Income Statement — FYE: December 31

	ASSETS ($ mil.)	NET INCOME ($ mil.)	INCOME AS % OF ASSETS	EMPLOYEES
12/18	5,502.2	57.8	1.1%	635
12/17	5,210.4	54.6	1.0%	642
12/16	4,701.3	56.4	1.2%	638
12/15	4,234.5	53.8	1.3%	622
12/14	4,232.4	49.7	1.2%	699
Annual Growth	6.8%	3.8%	—	(2.4%)

2018 Year-End Financials

Return on assets: 1.0%
Return on equity: 10.3%
Long-term debt ($ mil.): —
No. of shares (mil.): 30.9
Sales ($ mil): 258.9
Dividends
Yield: 4.8%
Payout: 53.3%
Market value ($ mil.): 609.0

	STOCK PRICE ($) FY Close	P/E High/Low	PER SHARE ($) Earnings	Dividends	Book Value
12/18	19.70	18 10	1.79	0.96	17.87
12/17	30.35	21 15	1.69	0.80	17.34
12/16	34.90	20 11	1.75	0.66	16.42
12/15	23.72	16 12	1.68	0.47	15.45
12/14	21.81	16 12	1.56	0.28	14.21
Annual Growth	(2.5%)	—	—	3.5%	36.1%	5.9%

Hannon Armstrong Sustainable Infrastructure Capital Inc

Hannon Armstrong Sustainable Infrastructure Capital has its hands in both kinds of green. The REIT provides securitized funding for environmentally friendly infrastructure projects. It is a key provider of financing for the US government's energy efficiency projects. Hannon Armstrong focuses on energy efficiency clean energy (solar and wind) and other sustainable projects including water and communications that improve energy consumption and the use of natural resources. The company manages some $5 billion in assets and operates mostly in the US.

Operations

Hannon Armstrong manages about $5 billion in assets across more than 175 investments in projects to improve energy efficiency and develop renewable energy sources and sustainable infrastructure. About 45% of the REIT's projects are focused on solar energy; wind nearly 30%; energy efficiency more than 20%; and sustainable infrastructure (which includes water and seismic retrofit projects) about 5%.

Nearly 55% of the company's revenue is derived from interest income on receivables. Almost 20% each comes from rental income and gain on sale of receivables and investments.

When making investment decisions Hannon Armstrong calculates the estimated metric tons of carbon emissions or equivalent avoided a calculation it calls CarbonCount. The company's 2017 CarbonCount calculation estimates its investments will reduce carbon emissions by about 530000 metric tons.

Geographic Reach

Based in Annapolis Maryland Hannon Armstrong operates primarily in the US.

Sales and Marketing

Hannon Armstrong provides securitized funding for environmentally friendly infrastructure projects by US federal state and local governments and high credit quality institutions.

Financial Performance

Thanks to growing popularity and falling costs of efficient and renewable energy Hannon Armstrong has seen more than a 325% expansion of revenue in the last five years accompanying a jump in net income to more than $30 million in 2017 compared with a loss of more than $10 million in 2013. Meanwhile the company bolstered its cash stores by about 270% while long-term debt climbed around 325%.

In 2017 the REIT reported revenue of $105.6 million up 30% from the prior year. Interest income on receivables and rental income each account for more than 30% of that growth; around 15% each came from gain on sale of receivables and investments and interest income on investments.

Hannon Armstrong's net income in 2017 ballooned 111% to $30.9 million thanks to improvements in revenue and income from investments.

Cash at the end of fiscal 2017 was $118.1 million double that of the prior year. Cash from operations provided $11.7 million while investing activities used $297.9 million due mostly to equity method investments and purchases of real estate. Financing activities added another $345.2 million primarily from proceeds from non-recourse debt.

Strategy

Hannon Armstrong intends to continue investing in clean energy technologies that it believes benefit society and that generally are tied to long-term utility contracts.

In November 2018 SunStong Capital Holdings a joint venture between the REIT and solar energy company SunPower completed a $400 million asset-backed securitization to refinance the JV's residential lease portfolio debt.

In October 2018 Hannon Armstrong Sustainable Real Estate (HASRE) a collaboration between Hannon Armstrong and Counterpoint Sustainable Real Estate completed a 25-year $10.5 million Commercial Property Assessed Clean Energy (C-PACE) financing for energy efficiency standards and seismic retrofitting of a Hyatt hotel in Sacramento California. Through C-PACE property owners can access inexpensive long-term financing for conservation renewable energy and hazard reduction projects.

In March 2017 Hannon Armstrong closed an $84 million offering of sustainable yield bonds to fund energy efficiency and solar energy projects for more than 90 public schools and 20 local governments.

In February 2017 the company paid $144 million for more than 4000 acres of land leased to 20 solar energy projects under long-term contracts.

Company Background

Formed in 2012 to be a REIT the company went public in 2013 though it traces its roots to the 1980s and Hannon Armstrong Capital LLC.

EXECUTIVES

EVP and CFO, J. Brendan Herron, age 58, $295,000 total compensation
Chairman President and CEO, Jeffrey W. Eckel, age 60, $495,000 total compensation
EVP and General Counsel, Steven L. (Steve) Chuslo, age 61, $300,000 total compensation
EVP Origination, M. Rhem Wooten, age 59, $285,000 total compensation
EVP and COO, Nathaniel J. Rose, age 41, $275,000 total compensation
EVP, Daniel K. McMahon, age 47
Auditors: Ernst & Young LLP

LOCATIONS

HQ: Hannon Armstrong Sustainable Infrastructure Capital Inc
1906 Towne Centre Blvd, Suite 370, Annapolis, MD 21401
Phone: 410 571-9860

PRODUCTS/OPERATIONS

2017 Sales

	$ mil.	% of total
Interest income financing receivables	56.7	53
Rental income	19.8	19
Gain on sale of receivables and investments	21.0	20
Interest income investments	5.1	5
Fee income	3.0	3
Total	**105.6**	**100**

Selected Project Types
Clean Energy
Energy Efficiency
Other Sustainable Infrastructure

COMPETITORS
Bank of America
Goldman Sachs
JPMorgan Chase
Wells Fargo

HISTORICAL FINANCIALS
Company Type: Public

Income Statement   FYE: December 31

	REVENUE ($ mil.)	NET INCOME ($ mil.)	NET PROFIT MARGIN	EMPLOYEES
12/18	137.8	41.5	30.2%	49
12/17	105.5	30.8	29.2%	47
12/16	81.2	14.6	18.0%	40
12/15	32.2	7.9	24.6%	32
12/14	28.6	9.6	33.6%	28
Annual Growth	48.1%	44.2%	—	15.0%

2018 Year-End Financials
Debt ratio: 57.6%
Return on equity: 5.7%
Cash ($ mil.): 21.4
Current ratio: 3.27
Long-term debt ($ mil.): 983.1
No. of shares (mil.): 60.5
Dividends
  Yield: 6.9%
  Payout: 176.0%
Market value ($ mil.): 1,153.0

	STOCK PRICE ($) FY Close	P/E High/Low	PER SHARE ($) Earnings	Dividends	Book Value
12/18	19.05	32 23	0.75	1.32	13.24
12/17	24.06	44 32	0.57	1.32	12.37
12/16	18.99	78 52	0.32	1.23	12.27
12/15	18.92	102 65	0.21	1.08	11.57
12/14	14.23	35 30	0.43	0.92	10.21
Annual Growth	7.6%	— —	14.9%	9.4%	6.7%

HarborOne Bancorp Inc (New)

Auditors: Wolf & Company, P.C.

LOCATIONS

HQ: HarborOne Bancorp Inc (New)
770 Oak Street, Brockton, MA 02301
Phone: 508 895-1000
Web: www.harborone.com

HISTORICAL FINANCIALS
Company Type: Public

Income Statement   FYE: December 31

	ASSETS ($ mil.)	NET INCOME ($ mil.)	INCOME AS % OF ASSETS	EMPLOYEES
12/18	3,653.1	11.3	0.3%	658
12/17	2,684.9	10.3	0.4%	581
12/16	2,448.3	5.9	0.2%	614
12/15	2,163.1	5.7	0.3%	387
12/14	2,041.8	2.5	0.1%	0
Annual Growth	15.7%	45.1%	—	—

2018 Year-End Financials
Return on assets: 0.3%
Return on equity: 3.2%
Long-term debt ($ mil.): —
No. of shares (mil.): 32.5
Sales ($ mil): 164.9
Dividends
  Yield: —
  Payout: —
Market value ($ mil.): 517.0

	STOCK PRICE ($) FY Close	P/E High/Low	PER SHARE ($) Earnings	Dividends	Book Value
12/18	15.89	56 42	0.36	0.00	10.98
12/17	19.16	67 49	0.33	0.00	10.52
12/16	19.34	— —	(0.00)	0.00	10.25
Annual Growth	(9.4%)	—	—	—	3.5%

Harrow Health Inc

EXECUTIVES

Chb-ceo, Mark L Baum
Vice President Quality, Pramod Sharma
Auditors: KMJ Corbin & Company LLP

LOCATIONS

HQ: Harrow Health Inc
102 Woodmont Blvd., Suite 610, Nashville, TN 37205
Phone: 858 704-4040
Web: www.imprimispharma.com

HISTORICAL FINANCIALS
Company Type: Public

Income Statement   FYE: December 31

	REVENUE ($ mil.)	NET INCOME ($ mil.)	NET PROFIT MARGIN	EMPLOYEES
12/18	41.3	14.6	35.4%	134
12/17	26.7	(11.9)	—	128
12/16	19.9	(19.0)	—	144
12/15	9.7	(15.9)	—	112
12/14	1.6	(10.1)	—	64
Annual Growth	123.4%	—	—	20.3%

2018 Year-End Financials
Debt ratio: 30.8%
Return on equity: 106.8%
Cash ($ mil.): 6.8
Current ratio: 2.76
Long-term debt ($ mil.): 12.0
No. of shares (mil.): 24.3
Dividends
  Yield: —
  Payout: —
Market value ($ mil.): 138.0

	STOCK PRICE ($) FY Close	P/E High/Low	PER SHARE ($) Earnings	Dividends	Book Value
12/18	5.69	9 2	0.61	0.00	1.02
12/17	1.70	— —	(0.60)	0.00	0.13
12/16	2.50	— —	(1.50)	0.00	0.35
12/15	6.93	— —	(1.66)	0.00	(0.14)
12/14	7.50	— —	(1.11)	0.00	0.88
Annual Growth	(6.7%)	—	—	—	3.7%

Hawkins Inc

Hawkins wants its customers to bulk up — on chemicals that is. The company processes and distributes bulk specialty chemicals. Its Industrial Chemicals segment stores and distributes caustic soda phosphoric acid and aqua ammonia among others. The segment also makes bleach (sodium hypochlorite) repackages liquid chlorine and custom blends other chemicals. Hawkins' Water Treatment group distributes products and equipment used to treat drinking water municipal and industrial wastewater and swimming pools. It also distributes laboratory-grade chemicals for the pharmaceutical industry. The company operates 29 facilities and has a fleet of trucks and tankers to serve customers throughout the Midwest US.

Operations
Hawkins operates in two segments: Industrial (68% of net sales) and Water Treatment (32%).

The Industrial Group specializes in providing industrial chemicals products and services to industries such as agriculture energy electronics food chemical processing pharmaceutical medical device and plating. Its main products are acids alkalis and industrial and food-grade salts and segment conducts its business primarily through distribution centers and terminal operations.

The Water Treatment Group specializes in providing chemicals equipment and services for potable water municipal and industrial wastewater industrial process water and non-residential swimming pool water.

Geographic Reach
The company has 39 facilities spanning 17 states.

Sales and Marketing
The company's Industrial sales are concentrated in Illinois Iowa Minnesota Missouri North Dakota South Dakota Tennessee and Wisconsin while the group's food-grade products are sold across the US.

The Water Treatment segment operates out of warehouses in 20 cities supplying products and services to customers in Arkansas Illinois Indiana Iowa Kansas Kentucky Minnesota Missouri Montana Nebraska North Dakota Oklahoma Ohio South Dakota Wisconsin and Wyoming.

Financial Performance
Hawkins achieved a revenue milestone in 2015 posting a record-setting $364 million. The historic growth for 2015 was fueled by a 11% spike in Water Treatment sales and a 2% rise in Industrial sales. Water Treatment sales increased due to newly acquired Florida and Oklahoma locations plus growth in newer branches and increased sales of specialty chemicals.

The company's net income increased 6% from 2014 to 2015 mainly due to the additional revenue coupled with favorable changes in interest income. After several years of growth the company's operating cash flow plummeted by 40% in 2015 primarily due to changes in working capital as a result of the timing of inventory purchases mainly increased inventory levels which included purchases of large quantities of bulk chemicals.

Strategy
The company has traditionally operated as a distributor of bulk chemicals but over time increased its sales of repackaged blended and manufactured specialty chemical products. More recently Hawkins' strategy has been to focus on its sales of higher-margin blended and manufactured products.

Expanding its geographic coverage Hawkins opened one new warehouse in each of fiscal 2014 2013 and 2012 and it plans to continue to invest in existing and new branches. To increase its manufacturing capability and flexibility Hawkins opened a new Rosemount Minnesota facility in 2013 that has more space for rail operations and increased bulk storage capacity for key raw materials and finished products.

Mergers and Acquisitions
In late 2015 the company purchased Stauber Performance Ingredients from ICV Partners II L.P. for $157 million. The deal gave Hawkins access to a new customer base and established a new business segment entitled Specialty Ingredients.

Company Background
The company was founded in 1938 and incorporated in Minnesota in 1955. It became a publicly-traded company in 1972.

EXECUTIVES

VP Industrial Group, John R. Sevenich, age 61, $256,134 total compensation
President and CEO, Patrick H. Hawkins, age 48, $386,885 total compensation
VP Water Treatment Group, Thomas J. Keller, age 59, $248,269 total compensation
VP CFO and Treasurer, Jeffrey P. Oldenkamp, age 46
VP Operations, Steven D. Matthews
President Stauber Performance Ingredients, Oliver A. Guiot, age 43
National Account Manager, Gina King
National Accounts Manager, Bob Ganassin
Chairman, John S. (Jack) McKeon, age 74
Auditors: KPMG LLP

LOCATIONS

HQ: Hawkins Inc
2381 Rosegate, Roseville, MN 55113
Phone: 612 331-6910
Web: www.hawkinsinc.com

PRODUCTS/OPERATIONS

2015 Sales

	$ mil.	% of total
Industrial	249.1	68
Water Treatment	114.9	32
Total	364.0	100

Selected Products
Industrial chemicals
Manufactured chemicals
Manufactured food ingredients
Specialty chemicals
Surface finishing chemicals
Water treatment and waste treatment products

COMPETITORS

Brenntag North America
Harcros Chemicals
JCI Jones Chemicals
K.A. Steel Chemicals
Kemira Water Solutions
Univar USA

HISTORICAL FINANCIALS
Company Type: Public

Income Statement
FYE: March 31

	REVENUE ($ mil.)	NET INCOME ($ mil.)	NET PROFIT MARGIN	EMPLOYEES
03/19*	556.3	24.4	4.4%	657
04/18	504.1	(9.1)	—	653
04/17	483.5	22.5	4.7%	659
04/16	413.9	18.1	4.4%	636
03/15	364.0	19.2	5.3%	419
Annual Growth	11.2%	6.2%	—	11.9%

*Fiscal year change

2019 Year-End Financials
Debt ratio: 21.9%
Return on equity: 11.6%
Cash ($ mil.): 9.2
Current ratio: 2.52
Long-term debt ($ mil.): 74.6
No. of shares (mil.): 10.5
Dividends
  Yield: 0.0%
  Payout: 29.8%
Market value ($ mil.): 390.0

	STOCK PRICE ($) FY Close	P/E High/Low		PER SHARE ($) Earnings	Dividends	Book Value
03/19*	36.83	19	14	2.28	0.68	20.57
04/18	35.15	—	—	(0.86)	0.88	19.02
04/17	49.00	26	17	2.13	0.84	20.58
04/16	37.15	25	18	1.72	0.80	19.12
03/15	37.90	24	18	1.81	0.76	18.36
Annual Growth	(0.7%)		—	5.9%	(2.7%)	2.9%

*Fiscal year change

HC2 Holdings Inc

Holding company HC2 Holdings owns a diverse set of companies in several industries. Under HC2's umbrella are DBM a structural and steel construction company; Continental Insurance Group which sells life and long-term care insurance; Global Marine a provider of engineering and underwater services (undersea cables); American Natural Gas a retailer of compressed natural gas; Pansend a life sciences company; PTGi an international telecommunications carrier; and HC2 Broadcasting which owns about 180 broadcast TV stations in the US. About 90% of HC2's revenue comes from its companies based in the US. The companies' customers include Apple and Target (DBM) and AT&T and SingTel (Global Marine).

Operations
Of HC2's seven businesses PTGi is the biggest accounting for about 40% of revenue. The business provides voice and data call termination to the telecom industry worldwide. It offers transmission and termination of telephone calls through its own global network of Internet Protocol soft switches and media gateways.

DBM is the second biggest accounting for about 35% of revenue. The company offers integrated steel construction services and professional services which include design-assist design-build engineering building information modeling (BIM) project management and others. It builds commercial buildings healthcare structures convention centers stadiums gaming and hospitality projects bridges and international projects.

Continental Insurance about 10% of revenue offers life and long-term care insurance and annuities.

Marine Global also about 10% of revenue lays undersea cables for telecommunications and oil and gas companies. It also provides services to offshore wind farms and handles maintenance and repair.

HC2 Broadcasting 2% of revenue owns and operates about 15 full-power TV stations about 60 Class A stations and more than 100 low-power stations in 130 US markets.

American Natural Gas 1% of revenue designs builds owns and operates compressed natural gas commercial fueling stations. It has about 40 stations throughout the US.

Pansend which provides a negligible percentage of revenue does work in monitoring kidney function dermatology knee replacements and medical devices.

Geographic Reach

HC2 is based in New York City and six of its companies are based in the US. Global Marine is headquartered in London. The US companies supply about 90% of HC2's revenue.

Financial Performance

HC2's revenue has grown as the company has assembled its holdings rising an average of about 20% a year from 2015-2018.

In 2018 revenue was $1.9 billion up about $342 million from 2017 driven by the construction telecommunications insurance and broadcasting segments. The construction segment's rose about 24% on busier activity in large commercial projects in the west region while telecommunications revenue rose about 13% due to changes in the customer mix and fluctuations in wholesale traffic volumes. The acquisition of KIC drove insurance revenue more than 40% higher. The broadcasting segment's sales advanced on network advertising and distribution revenue from acquisitions.

HC2 reported net income of about $180 million in 2018 compared to a loss of about $50 million in 2017. The profit the first in several years resulted from a bargain purchase gain gains on the recapture of certain reinsurance treaties and the sale of BeneVir from the life sciences business.

The company had about $330 million in cash in 2018 compared to about $99 million in 2017. Operations produced about $341 million in 2018 while investing activities used $224 million and financing activities provided $115 million.

HC2 has a significant amount of debt about $743 million which carries risks such the inability to repay the debt if cash flow slows increased vulnerability to adverse economic and industry conditions and the impact of possible higher interest rates.

Strategy

HC2 has gathered an eclectic group of companies that have little in common. That's OK with HC2. In fact that's the idea: Provide investors with a diverse group of assets in one investment. Each company operates on its own with input from HC2's executives.

HC2 looks for more companies to add to its holdings and for companies to add to those it owns. In 2018 the DBM construction business bought Gray Wolf Industrial which added specialty maintenance repair and installation services to DBM's offerings. HC2 Broadcasting also has expanded adding stations to its nationwide portfolio.

HC2 not only adds it subtracts. The company sold BeneVir which was part of the Pansend life sciences business in 2018 for more than $100 million.

EXECUTIVES

EVP Business Development, Robert M. Pons, age 63
President and CEO Schuff International and Schuff Steel Company, Rustin Roach
Chairman President and CEO, Philip Falcone
COO, Keith Hladek
CFO Corporate Controller Treasurer and Chief Compliance Officer, Mesfin Demise
Managing Director Investments, Ian Estus
Vice President Of Customer Service, Scott Reskey
Auditors: BDO USA, LLP

LOCATIONS

HQ: HC2 Holdings Inc
450 Park Avenue, 30th Floor, New York, NY 10022
Phone: 212 235-2690
Web: www.hc2.com

PRODUCTS/OPERATIONS

2018 Sales

	% of total
Telecommunications	40
Construction	36
Insurance	11
Marine Services	10
Broadcasting	2
Energy	1
Other	-
Eliminations	-
Total	**100**

COMPETITORS

AT&T	Quebecor
Allstream	Rogers Communications
BCE	Shaw Communications
BT	Sprint Nextel
COGECO	TELUS
COLT Group	Telecom Corporation of
Cable & Wireless	New Zealand
Carphone Warehouse	Telstra
EarthLink	Verizon
Optus	Virgin Media

HISTORICAL FINANCIALS

Company Type: Public

Income Statement — FYE: December 31

	REVENUE ($ mil.)	NET INCOME ($ mil.)	NET PROFIT MARGIN	EMPLOYEES
12/18	1,976.7	162.0	8.2%	4,119
12/17	1,634.1	(46.9)	—	3,358
12/16	1,558.1	(94.5)	—	2,744
12/15	1,120.8	(35.5)	—	1,970
12/14	543.2	(12.1)	—	1,886
Annual Growth	38.1%	—	—	21.6%

2018 Year-End Financials

Debt ratio: 11.4%
Return on equity: 155.8%
Cash ($ mil.): 325.0
Current ratio: 0.13
Long-term debt ($ mil.): 743.9
No. of shares (mil.): 44.9
Dividends
  Yield: —
  Payout: —
Market value ($ mil.): 119.0

	STOCK PRICE ($) FY Close	P/E High/Low		PER SHARE ($) Earnings	Dividends	Book Value
12/18	2.64	2	1	2.90	0.00	2.41
12/17	5.95	—	—	(1.16)	0.00	2.25
12/16	5.93	—	—	(2.83)	0.00	1.76
12/15	5.29	—	—	(1.50)	0.00	4.16
12/14	8.43	—	—	(0.72)	0.00	5.44
Annual Growth (18.4%)	(25.2%)	—		—	—	—

Health Insurance Innovations Inc

Auditors: Grant Thornton LLP

LOCATIONS

HQ: Health Insurance Innovations Inc
15438 North Florida Avenue, Suite 201, Tampa, FL 33613
Phone: 813 397-1187
Web: www.hiiquote.com

HISTORICAL FINANCIALS

Company Type: Public

Income Statement — FYE: December 31

	REVENUE ($ mil.)	NET INCOME ($ mil.)	NET PROFIT MARGIN	EMPLOYEES
12/18	351.1	12.9	3.7%	222
12/17	250.4	17.8	7.1%	199
12/16	184.5	4.5	2.4%	174
12/15	104.7	0.6	0.6%	192
12/14	88.7	(0.3)	—	285
Annual Growth	41.0%	—	—	(6.1%)

2018 Year-End Financials

Debt ratio: 3.4%
Return on equity: 13.5%
Cash ($ mil.): 9.3
Current ratio: 1.37
Long-term debt ($ mil.): 15.0
No. of shares (mil.): 14.9
Dividends
  Yield: —
  Payout: —
Market value ($ mil.): 399.0

	STOCK PRICE ($) FY Close	P/E High/Low		PER SHARE ($) Earnings	Dividends	Book Value
12/18	26.73	58	21	0.97	0.00	7.22
12/17	24.95	22	9	1.50	0.00	5.20
12/16	17.85	32	7	0.57	0.00	3.24
12/15	6.70	117	52	0.08	0.00	2.74
12/14	7.16	—	—	(0.06)	0.00	2.63
Annual Growth	39.0%	—		—	—	28.8%

Healthcare Services Group, Inc.

Healthcare Services Group provides food housekeeping laundry and linen and maintenance services to hospitals nursing homes rehabilitation centers and retirement facilities throughout the US. The company's dietary services purchases food and prepares meals for residents and monitors nutritional needs in more than 1500 facilities. Healthcare Services Group also tidies up around 3500 facilities mostly primarily providers of long-term care many of which rely on Medicare Medicaid and third-party payors? reimbursement funds. The Pennsylvania-based company operates in nearly all 50 states. Healthcare Services Group was established in 1976.

Operations
Healthcare Services Group's operations are divided in two business units: Dietary and Housekeeping. Dietary services generate some 52% of revenue while Housekeeping contributes about 48%.

The company's Dietary unit manages food purchasing meal preparation and dietary consulting. Consulting services including creating meal plans based on individual patient's dietary needs.

Its Housekeeping unit manages clients' housekeeping departments which are responsible for the cleaning disinfecting and sanitizing patient rooms and common areas of clients' facilities. The business unit also offers laundering and processing of patient clothing.

Geographic Reach
Healthcare Services Group based in Bensalem Pennsylvania operates in 48 states. The company manages operations regionally through offices in Pennsylvania Colorado South Carolina Connecticut Georgia California and New Jersey.

Sales and Marketing
Sales and marketing activities at Healthcare Services Group include referrals and in-person solicitation of target facilities. The company regularly industry trade shows health care trade associations and healthcare support service seminars.

Healthcare Services Group's largest customer Genesis Healthcare accounts for nearly 20% of total revenue.

Financial Performance
Revenue at Healthcare Services Group have trended upwards over the past decade. The market for the company's services particularly in long-term and post-acute care is expected to continue to grow as the US population ages.

In 2018 revenue grew about 8% rising to $2.0 billion. The increase came from growth at the company's Dietary business which provided services to a greater number of existing Housekeeping clients.

Net income dropped slightly in 2018 to $83.5 million down from $88.2 million in 2017. Healthcare Services recorded a charge related to two of its customers to account for the possibility that it might not receive payment. The two customers reported corporate restructurings during 2018 with one filing for Chapter 11 bankruptcy protection.

Total cash flow at the end of fiscal 2018 was $26 million and cash from operations contributed $80.0 million. The company used $19.6 million in investing activities and $54.0 million in financing activities. The primary uses of cash for financing activities is to pay dividends to shareholders funded through cash from operations. In 2018 Healthcare Services Group paid quarterly cash dividends totaling more than $14 million per quarter.

Strategy
Healthcare Services Group's growth strategy centers on renewing and extending contracts with existing clients. Much of the company's recent financial success is driven by aggressive cross-selling of its Dietary service to its existing Housekeeping services clients.

Healthcare Services Group is focused on transitioning customers to what it calls an "accelerated payment model" in order to strengthen customer payment terms and conditions. The model increases customer payment frequency from monthly to semimonthly or weekly. In 2018 the company successfully transitioned over 40% of its customers to an accelerated payment model and expects to further this trend going forward.

EXECUTIVES

Vice President Northeastern Division, Joseph Mccartney
EVP, Michael E. McBryan, $102,492 total compensation
EVP, Bryan D. McCartney, $102,492 total compensation
President and CEO, Theodore Wahl, age 45, $996,255 total compensation
CFO, John Shea, $389,039 total compensation
Regional Vice President, Josh Dubler
Vice President, Jim Keeley
Divisional Vice President, Stephen Foresman
Executive Vice President and Chief Administrative Officer, Andrew Kush
Vice President Of Information Technology, Jason Osbeck
Regional Vice President, Jim Bleming
Divisional Vice President, Jason Lecroy
Divisional Vice President, Bryan Foy
Vice President of Financial Services, Patrick Orr
Divisional Vice President, Donnie Warren
Regional Vice President, Ryan Magee
Regional Vice President, Tim Hubka
Vice President, John Bullock
Regional Vice President, John Fenstermacher
Regional Vp, Steve Newns
Chairman, Daniel P. McCartney, age 67
Board Member, Robbie Moss
Auditors: Grant Thornton LLP

LOCATIONS
HQ: Healthcare Services Group, Inc.
3220 Tillman Drive, Suite 300, Bensalem, PA 19020
Phone: 215 639-4274   **Fax:** 215 639-2152
Web: www.hcsgcorp.com

PRODUCTS/OPERATIONS

2017 Sales

	$ mil.	% of total
Housekeeping services	979.6	52
Dietary services	886.5	48
Total	**1,866.1**	**100**

Selected Services
Senior living housekeeping & laundry services
Senior living dining & nutrition services
Hospital environmental services
Hospital dining & nutrition services

COMPETITORS
ABM Industries
ARAMARK
Alsco
Angelica Corporation
Crothall Healthcare
Ecolab
G&K Services
Sodexo USA
SureQuest Systems

HISTORICAL FINANCIALS
Company Type: Public

Income Statement — FYE: December 31

	REVENUE ($ mil.)	NET INCOME ($ mil.)	NET PROFIT MARGIN	EMPLOYEES
12/18	2,008.8	83.5	4.2%	55,000
12/17	1,866.1	88.2	4.7%	55,000
12/16	1,562.6	77.4	5.0%	48,900
12/15	1,436.8	58.0	4.0%	8,600
12/14	1,293.1	21.8	1.7%	8,600
Annual Growth	11.6%	39.8%	—	59.0%

2018 Year-End Financials

Debt ratio: 4.3%   No. of shares (mil.): 73.8
Return on equity: 19.8%   Dividends
Cash ($ mil.): 26.0   Yield: 1.9%
Current ratio: 3.11   Payout: 79.6%
Long-term debt ($ mil.): —   Market value ($ mil.): 2,968.0

	STOCK PRICE ($) FY Close	P/E High/Low		PER SHARE ($) Earnings	Dividends	Book Value
12/18	40.18	50	32	1.12	0.77	5.97
12/17	52.72	46	32	1.19	0.75	5.45
12/16	39.17	40	31	1.05	0.73	4.67
12/15	34.87	47	37	0.80	0.71	4.12
12/14	30.93	103	83	0.31	0.69	3.88
Annual Growth	6.8%	—	—	37.9%	2.8%	11.3%

Healthcare Trust Of America Inc

EXECUTIVES
Chb-pres-ceo, Scott D Peters
Vice President Operations, Judy Romero
Senior Vice President Leasing, Jaime Northam
Vice President Of Operations Southeast, Henry Torre
Vice President Development, Jeff Spiller
Board Of Directors, Gary Wescombe
Auditors: Deloitte & Touche LLP

LOCATIONS
HQ: Healthcare Trust Of America Inc
16435 N. Scottsdale Road, Suite 320, Scottsdale, AZ 85254
Phone: 480 998-3478   **Fax:** 480 991-0755
Web: www.htareit.com

HISTORICAL FINANCIALS
Company Type: Public

Income Statement — FYE: December 31

	REVENUE ($ mil.)	NET INCOME ($ mil.)	NET PROFIT MARGIN	EMPLOYEES
12/18	696.4	213.4	30.7%	282
12/17	613.9	63.9	10.4%	270
12/16	460.9	45.9	10.0%	214
12/15	403.8	32.9	8.2%	181
12/14	371.5	45.3	12.2%	170
Annual Growth	17.0%	47.3%	—	13.5%

2018 Year-End Financials

Debt ratio: 41.0%
Return on equity: 6.5%
Cash ($ mil.): 133.5
Current ratio: 0.72
Long-term debt ($ mil.): 2,541.2
No. of shares (mil.): 205.2
Dividends
 Yield: 4.8%
 Payout: 120.5%
Market value ($ mil.): 5,195.0

	STOCK PRICE ($) FY Close	P/E High/Low		PER SHARE ($) Earnings	Dividends	Book Value
12/18	25.31	29	23	1.02	1.23	15.86
12/17	30.04	94	82	0.34	1.21	16.00
12/16	29.11	102	77	0.33	1.19	11.91
12/15	26.97	115	87	0.26	1.17	10.86
12/14	26.94	72	26	0.37	0.29	11.57
Annual Growth	(1.5%)	—	—	28.9%	43.5%	8.2%

HealthEquity Inc

Auditors: PricewaterhouseCoopers LLP

LOCATIONS

HQ: HealthEquity Inc
 15 West Scenic Pointe Drive, Suite 100, Draper, UT 84020
Phone: 801 727-1000
Web: www.healthequity.com

HISTORICAL FINANCIALS
Company Type: Public

Income Statement   FYE: January 31

	REVENUE ($ mil.)	NET INCOME ($ mil.)	NET PROFIT MARGIN	EMPLOYEES
01/19	287.2	73.9	25.7%	1,141
01/18	229.5	47.3	20.6%	1,027
01/17	178.3	26.3	14.8%	875
01/16	126.7	16.6	13.1%	636
01/15	87.8	10.1	11.6%	455
Annual Growth	34.5%	64.2%	—	25.8%

2019 Year-End Financials

Debt ratio: —
Return on equity: 17.9%
Cash ($ mil.): 361.4
Current ratio: 13.58
Long-term debt ($ mil.): —
No. of shares (mil.): 62.4
Dividends
 Yield: —
 Payout: —
Market value ($ mil.): 3,893.0

	STOCK PRICE ($) FY Close	P/E High/Low		PER SHARE ($) Earnings	Dividends	Book Value
01/19	62.34	84	42	1.17	0.00	7.64
01/18	50.62	69	50	0.77	0.00	5.69
01/17	46.25	108	35	0.44	0.00	4.40
01/16	21.55	121	65	0.28	0.00	3.52
01/15	20.77	66	43	0.21	0.00	2.63
Annual Growth	31.6%	—	—	53.6%	—	30.6%

Heartland BancCorp

EXECUTIVES

Chb-ceo, Scott G McComb
Agribusiness Banker Avp, Bennett Musselman
Assistant Vice President, Seth Middleton
Svp And General Counsel, Molly Z Brown

LOCATIONS

HQ: Heartland BancCorp
 430 North Hamilton Road, Gahanna, OH 43213
Phone: 614 337-4600
Web: www.heartlandbank.com

HISTORICAL FINANCIALS
Company Type: Public

Income Statement   FYE: December 31

	ASSETS ($ mil.)	NET INCOME ($ mil.)	INCOME AS % OF ASSETS	EMPLOYEES
12/18	1,047.0	11.4	1.1%	0
12/17	900.9	8.8	1.0%	0
12/16	781.3	7.9	1.0%	0
12/15	729.5	8.1	1.1%	0
12/14	649.6	6.0	0.9%	0
Annual Growth	12.7%	17.1%	—	—

2018 Year-End Financials

Return on assets: 1.1%
Return on equity: 11.7%
Long-term debt ($ mil.): —
No. of shares (mil.): 2.0
Sales ($ mil): 48.8
Dividends
 Yield: 2.3%
 Payout: 28.3%
Market value ($ mil.): 163.0

	STOCK PRICE ($) FY Close	P/E High/Low		PER SHARE ($) Earnings	Dividends	Book Value
12/18	81.00	15	12	6.68	1.89	57.08
12/17	82.60	15	12	5.40	1.72	48.77
12/16	64.01	14	9	4.97	1.55	45.10
12/15	45.00	10	8	5.13	1.47	42.61
12/14	40.00	11	8	3.87	1.42	39.05
Annual Growth	19.3%	—	—	14.6%	7.5%	10.0%

Heartland Financial USA, Inc. (Dubuque, IA)

Heartland Financial USA is an $11.3 billion multi-bank holding company that owns flagship subsidiary Dubuque Bank and Trust (Iowa) and ten other banks that together operate more than 120 branches in about a dozen states primarily in the West and Midwest. In addition to standard deposit loan and mortgage services the banks also offer retirement wealth management trust insurance and investment services. Heartland also owns consumer lender Citizens Finance which has about a dozen offices in Illinois Iowa and Wisconsin.

Operations

Heartland Financial USA operates two main segments: community and other banking and retail mortgage banking services which account for about 90% and 10% of revenue respectively. The community banking business generates revenue from interest earned on loans and investment securities and fees from deposit services. Its retail mortgage banking services division collects revenue from interest from mortgage loans held for sale gains on sales of loans on the secondary market the servicing of mortgage loans for investors and loan origination fee income.

About three-quarters of Heartland's loan portfolio comes from commercial and commercial real estate loans but — in keeping with the bank's Midwestern identity — it also makes agricultural residential mortgage and consumer loans.

Heartland's subsidiaries include: Citywide Banks (approximately $1.9 billion total deposits) New Mexico Bank & Trust ($1.2 billion) Dubuque Bank and Trust Company ($1.1 billion) Wisconsin Bank & Trust ($890 million) First Bank & Trust ($820 million) Premier Valley Bank ($710 million) Illinois Bank & Trust ($690 million) Morrill & Janes Bank and Trust ($560 million) Arizona Bank & Trust ($520 million) Rocky Mountain Bank ($420 million) and Minnesota Bank & Trust ($180 million).

Geographic Reach

Dubuque Iowa-based Heartland Financial USA operates through about 145 locations (including branches and loan production offices) in local communities in Iowa Illinois Wisconsin New Mexico Arizona Montana Colorado Minnesota Kansas Missouri Texas and California. The company's three largest bank subsidiaries by number of locations are Colorado's Citywide Banks with about 25 and Wisconsin Bank & Trust and New Mexico Bank & Trust with about 20 each.

Sales and Marketing

Heartland Financial USA offers its banking services to businesses public sector and non-profit entities and individuals.

The company's Commercial Card team works with its commercial clients to help cut manual processes and costs from employee travel entertainment spending and vendor payments.

Financial Performance

As it grows its assets and loan portfolio via acquisitions Heartland Financial USA had positive overall performance in the last five years increasing revenue by some 70% and net income by more than 100% — all while expanding its cash by about 55% and reducing long-term debt by nearly 20%.

Revenue ticked up 6% to $432.3 million in 2017 on increased interest income mostly from interest and fees on a larger loan portfolio following the company's acquisitions of Citywide Banks and Founders Bancorp.

Net income trended down 6% to $75.3 million owing to higher income taxes salaries employee benefits and professional fees.

Heartland added $37.3 million to its cash stores in 2017 to end the year with $196 million. Operations and investments brought in $155.9 million and $27.3 million respectively. Financing activities used up $145.9 million due to a net decrease from savings accounts and repayments of short term Federal Home Loan Bank advances.

Strategy

Heartland Financial USA's strategy for the past two decades is centered on expanding through acquisitions in its existing and adjacent markets while balancing growth in newer western markets with the stability of its established midwestern markets. The company's goal is to have at least $1 billion in assets in each state where it operates.

Mergers and Acquisitions

In 2019 Heartland Financial USA acquired Overland Park Kansas-based Blue Valley Ban the holding company for Bank of Blue Valley. Blue Valley has $712 million in assets $564 million in gross loans outstanding and $587 million in deposits. The acquisition expands Heartland's presence in the Kansas City and Johnson County markets.

Heartland added its eleventh subsidiary in May 2018 through its acquisition of Lubbock Texas-based First Bank Lubbock Bancshares for $189.9 million. Operating under the name First Bank & Trust (which Heartland retained) the bank held $681.1 million in gross loans held to maturity and deposits of $893.8 million. First Bank & Trust has eight branches in West Texas and eight mortgage lending services offices throughout Texas.

In February 2018 the company acquired Minnetonka Minnesota-based Signature Bancshares for $61.4 million and incorporated it into its Minnesota Bank & Trust subsidiary. Signature had two branches in the Twin Cities metropolitan area with $324.5 million in gross loans held to maturity and deposits of $357.3 million.

Heartland acquired Citywide Banks (headquartered in Aurora Colorado) in July 2017 for $211.2 million. At the time of purchase Citywide had $985.4 million in net loans outstanding and $1.2 billion in deposits. Following incorporation of Citywide into its Centennial Bank and Trust subsidiary (which then adopted Citywide's name) Heartland had more than 25 branches in Colorado.

In February 2017 Heartland Financial USA acquired San Luis Obispo California-based Founders Bancorp which it incorporated into its Premier Valley Bank subsidiary for $31 million. The company's Founders Community Bank held loans totaling $96.4 million and the purchase increased Heartland's total number of branches in California from five to nine.

Company Background

Heartland Financial USA was founded in 1981 although it traces its roots back to the 1935 establishment of Dubuque Bank and Trust. It made its first bank acquisition in in 1989 - Key City Bank - and has continued acquiring community banks since.

EXECUTIVES

Vice President Marketing, Dawn Oelke
President and CEO Minnesota Bank & Trust, Catherine T. (Kate) Kelly
Chairman President and CEO Heartland Financial USA Inc.; Vice Chairman Dubuque Bank & Trust Wisconsin Bank & Trust New Mexico Bank & Trust Arizona Bank & Trust Rocky Mountain Bank Centennial Bank and Trust(1) Minnesota Bank & Trust and Premier Valley Bank, Lynn B. Fuller, age 69, $486,388 total compensation
EVP Lending, Douglas J. Horstmann, age 65, $275,156 total compensation
President and CEO New Mexico Bank & Trust, R. Greg Leyendecker
President and CEO Wisconsin Bank & Trust, Kevin S. Tenpas
President of Heartland Director Rocky Mountain Bank and President Heartland Financial USA Inc. Insurance Services, Bruce K. Lee, age 58, $383,519 total compensation
EVP Human Resources and Organizational Development, Mark G. Murtha, age 57
SVP Chief Accounting Officer, Janet M. Quick
President and CEO Riverside Community Bank, Steven E. Ward
EVP Wealth Management, Bruce C. Rehmke
EVP Commercial Sales, Frank E. Walter, age 72
EVP Senior General Counsel and Corporate Secretary, Michael J. Coyle, age 73
EVP Operations, Brian J. Fox, age 70, $190,000 total compensation
EVP and Chief Risk Officer, Rodney L. Sloan, age 59
EVP and CFO Heartland Financial USA Treasurer Citizens Finance Parent Co.. and Director Heartland Financial USA Inc. Insurance Services, Bryan R. McKeag, age 58, $305,625 total compensation
EVP Finance and Corporate Strategy, David L. Horstmann, age 69
President and CEO Arizona Bank & Trust, Jerry L. Schwallier
President and CEO Rocky Mountain Bank, Curtis Chrystal
President and CEO Morrill & Janes Bank and Trust Co., Kurt M. Saylor
EVP Private Client Services, Kelly J. Johnson, age 57
President and CEO Illinois Bank and Trust, Jeff Hultman
Chief Investment Officer, Nancy Tengler
EVP and Chief Credit Officer, Drew Townsend
EVP and Private Wealth Management Director, Rick O. Terry
President and CEO Heartland Mortgage, Paul Johnstun
CEO Centennial Bank and Trust, Jim Basey
President Heartland Mortgage, Jack Lloyd
Vice President Finance, Sandra Wild
Vice President, Kate Barth
Vice President, Jean Harkey
Vice President of Retirement Plan Services, Lisan Adams
Vice President Electronic Banking and Fraud, Linda Maas
Vice President Corporate Training Director, Bonnie Bollin
Assistant Vice President Commercial Services, Lynn Stoffregen
Vice President, Rachel Steiner
Vice President Information Technology, Les Oelke
Vice President Credit Administration, Ted Kraft
Senior Vice President Teller Operations Officer, Julie Shanahan
Senior Vice President Special Assets REO, John Hawkins
Vice President, Troy Steger
Vice President, Craig Sciara
Vice President Credit Administration, Tom Steinhaus
Senior Vice President Credit Administration Officer, Joe Davis
Assistant Vice President, Michelle Schoen
Assistant Vice President Information Services, Brent Wilke
Tm Wire Transfer Manager Avp, Cori Freihoefer
Vp Engineering, Mary Burns
VICE PRESIDENT DIRECTOR FINANCIAL PLANNING AND PERFORMANCE MANAGEMENT, Michael G Flood
CREDIT ADMIN OFFICER IV SENIOR VICE PRESIDENT, Ralph Atkinson
CREDIT ADMIN OFFICER IV SENIOR VICE PRESIDENT, Jeffery Viviano
PCS DIRECTOR OF FINANCIAL PLANNING VICE PRESIDENT, Chrisanna Elser
Executive Vice President and Chief Human Resources Officer, Deborah Deters
Vice President Director Financial Planning And Performance Management, Michael Flood
Vice President Sales, Brian Jackson
Vice President, Linda A Bessey
Vice Chairman of the Board of Heartland Financial USA Inc.; Chairman and Director of Dubuque Bank and Trust, Mark C. Falb, age 71
Vice Chairman of the Board of Heartland Financial USA Inc.; Director and Vice Chairman of the Board of Dubuque Bank and Trust, Thomas L. Flynn, age 63
Board Member, Duane White
Auditors: KPMG LLP

LOCATIONS

HQ: Heartland Financial USA, Inc. (Dubuque, IA)
1398 Central Avenue, Dubuque, IA 52001
Phone: 563 589-2100 **Fax:** 563 589-2011
Web: www.htlf.com

PRODUCTS/OPERATIONS

2017 Sales

	$ mil.	% of total
Interest		
Loans & leases including fees	304.0	65
Securities	58.1	13
Other	1.6	-
Interest expense	(33.3)	-
Noninterest		
Gains on sales of loans	22.2	5
Service charges and fees	39.2	8
Trust fees	15.8	3
Loan serving income	5.6	1
Brokerage & insurance commissions	4.0	1
Security gains	7.0	2
Other	8.1	2
Total	**432.3**	**100**

Selected Subsidiaries

Arizona Bank & Trust
Citywide Banks (Colorado)
Dubuque Bank and Trust Company (Iowa)
  DB&T Community Development Corp.
  DB&T Insurance
Illinois Bank & Trust
Minnesota Bank & Trust
Morrill & Janes Bank and Trust Company (Kansas)
New Mexico Bank & Trust
Premier Valley Bank (California)
Rocky Mountain Bank (Montana)
Wisconsin Bank & Trust

COMPETITORS

Associated Banc-Corp
BBVA Compass Bancshares
Bank of America
Bank of the West
First Banks
U.S. Bancorp
Wells Fargo
Zions Bancorporation

HISTORICAL FINANCIALS

Company Type: Public

Income Statement — FYE: December 31

	ASSETS ($ mil.)	NET INCOME ($ mil.)	INCOME AS % OF ASSETS	EMPLOYEES
12/18	11,408.0	117.0	1.0%	2,045
12/17	9,810.7	75.2	0.8%	2,008
12/16	8,247.0	80.3	1.0%	1,864
12/15	7,694.7	60.0	0.8%	1,799
12/14	6,052.3	41.9	0.7%	1,631
Annual Growth	17.2%	29.3%	—	5.8%

2018 Year-End Financials

Return on assets: 1.1%
Return on equity: 10.1%
Long-term debt ($ mil.): —
No. of shares (mil.): 34.4
Sales ($ mil): 574.9
Dividends
Yield: 1.3%
Payout: 16.7%
Market value ($ mil.): 1,515.0

	STOCK PRICE ($) FY Close	P/E High/Low	PER SHARE ($) Earnings	Dividends	Book Value
12/18	43.95	17 12	3.52	0.59	38.44
12/17	53.65	20 16	2.65	0.51	33.10
12/16	48.00	15 8	3.22	0.50	28.37
12/15	31.36	14 9	2.83	0.45	29.56
12/14	27.10	13 10	2.19	0.40	26.81
Annual Growth	12.8%	— —	12.6%	10.2%	9.4%

HEICO Corp

HEICO Corporation helps jets get airborne. Its Flight Support Group consisting of HEICO Aerospace and its subsidiaries makes FAA-approved replacement parts for jet engines that can be substituted for original parts including airfoils bearings and fuel pump gears. Flight Support also repairs overhauls and distributes jet engine parts as well as avionics and instruments for commercial air carriers. HEICO's second segment Electronic Technologies Group makes a variety of electronic equipment for the aerospace/defense electronic medical and telecommunications industries.

Operations
HEICO's business is comprised of two operating segments the Flight Support Group (FSG; about 65% of net sales) and the Electronic Technologies Group (ETG; 35%).

FSG competes with industry leading OEMs and to a lesser extent with smaller independent parts distributors. Historically the three main jet engine OEMs General Electric Pratt & Whitney and Rolls Royce have been the source of substantially all jet engine replacement parts for their own jet engines. HEICO is seeking to capture some of that market by adding new products at a rate of 300 to 500 manufacturer-approved parts (also called PMAs) per year.

Geographic Reach
HEICO has its operations and facilities in China India Singapore Canada France Korea Laos the Netherlands the UK and the US. The company markets its products and services in approximately 100 countries with the US counting for more than 65% of its net sales.

Sales and Marketing
HEICO sells its products through in-house personnel and independent manufacturers' representatives. It targets a broad customer base consisting of domestic and foreign commercial and cargo airlines repair and overhaul facilities other aftermarket suppliers of aircraft engine and airframe materials OEMs domestic and foreign military units electronic manufacturing services companies US and foreign governments manufacturers for the defense industry as well as medical telecommunications scientific and industrial companies. Net sales to its five largest customers account for around 20% of net sales each year.

Financial Performance
HEICO has achieved unprecedented growth over the years with revenues jumping 16% from $1.19 billion in 2015 to peak at a record-setting $1.38 billion in 2016. Profits also surged 17% from $134 million in 2015 to $156 million in 2016 another company milestone. In 2016 cash flow from operating activities increased due to a $37 million decrease in working capital a $23 million increase in net income from consolidated operations and a $12 million increase in depreciation and amortization expense (a non-cash item).

The historic growth for 2016 was fueled by increases in both of its segments. FSG jumped by 8% due to organic growth as well as additional net sales from a previous acquisition. The organic growth reflected new product offerings and favorable market conditions resulting in net sales within the aftermarket replacement parts and repair and overhaul services product lines.

ETG revenue soared by 31% due to additional net sales from a previous acquisition as well as organic growth of approximately 4%. The organic growth reflected an increase in demand for certain space and aerospace products.

Mergers and Acquisitions
HEICO uses acquisitions to build out a diverse product and service portfolio in order to reduce exposure to cyclical swings in any single market. Its current set of offerings have broad-range applications in aircraft missiles ships surveillance systems computer and networking devices telecom equipment surgical equipment CT scanners and X-ray systems.

In 2016 the company's ETG division acquired Arizona-based Robertson Fuel Systems for $255 million. Robertson has expertise in the design and production of mission-extending crashworthy and ballistically self-sealing auxiliary fuel systems for military rotorcraft. The acquisition will enhance the company's fuel systems product portfolio.

In 2015 the company's FSG division purchased Astroseal Products Manufacturing Corp. Astroseal makes expanded foil mesh that is integrated into composite aerospace structures for lightning strike protection in fixed and rotary wing aircraft. The deal expanded the group's offerings of aerospace composite products.

HISTORY

Founded in 1957 as Heinicke Instruments to make laboratory products the company moved into jet engine parts in 1974 with the acquisition of Jet Avion. The company changed its name to HEICO (a shortened version of its previous name) in 1985. After a faulty combustion chamber erupted in flames that year the FAA ordered all combustion chambers on US jets to be inspected and if necessary replaced. HEICO's sales skyrocketed but descended back to earth after airlines found they had overstocked.

EXECUTIVES

Co-President and Director; President and CEO HEICO Electronic Technologies, Victor H. Mendelson, age 51, $519,178 total compensation
Co-President and Director; President and CEO HEICO Aerospace Holdings, Eric A. Mendelson, age 54, $519,178 total compensation
Senior Executive Vice President, Thomas S. Irwin, age 73, $238,299 total compensation
Chairman and CEO, Laurans A. Mendelson, age 81, $973,425 total compensation
EVP CFO and Treasurer, Carlos L. Macau, $553,014 total compensation
Senior Vice President Development, Val Shelley
Vice President Sales And Customer Service, Brandi Dague
Vice President Acquisitions, Adam Bentkover
Vice President Sales (HPG) Latin America, Mike Garcia
Vice President, Pat Markham
Executive Vice President Operations, John Hunter
Vice President Sales And Business Development, Jim Osullivan
Auditors: DELOITTE & TOUCHE LLP

LOCATIONS

HQ: HEICO Corp
3000 Taft Street, Hollywood, FL 33021
Phone: 954 987-4000
Web: www.heico.com

PRODUCTS/OPERATIONS

2016 Sales
	$ mil.	% of total
Flight Support Group	875.9	63
Electronic Technologies Group	511.3	37
Intersegment sales	(10.9)	-
Total	**1,376.3**	**100**

Selected Products
Flight Support Group
  Cockpit/avionics parts
  Electro-mechanical components
  Engine parts
  Fuselage/interior parts
  Wing parts
Electronic Technologies Group
  Aircraft power supplies and batteries
  Circuit board shielding
  Electro-optical infrared simulation and test equipment
  Electro-optical laser products
  High-voltage interconnect and cable assembly devices
  Medical power supplies and power generators

COMPETITORS

AAR Corp.	Kellstrom Industries
ATI Ladish	LMI Aerospace
BBA Aviation	Pratt & Whitney
Barnes Group	Rolls-Royce
CIC International	SAFRAN
Doncasters	SIFCO
GE Aviation	TIMCO Aviation
Honeywell Aerospace	Triumph Group

HISTORICAL FINANCIALS
Company Type: Public

Income Statement
FYE: October 31

	REVENUE ($ mil.)	NET INCOME ($ mil.)	NET PROFIT MARGIN	EMPLOYEES
10/19	2,055.6	327.9	16.0%	5,900
10/18	1,777.7	259.2	14.6%	5,400
10/17	1,524.8	185.9	12.2%	5,100
10/16	1,376.2	156.1	11.3%	4,700
10/15	1,188.6	133.3	11.2%	4,600
Annual Growth	14.7%	25.2%	—	6.4%

2019 Year-End Financials
Debt ratio: 18.9%
Return on equity: 21.4%
Cash ($ mil.): 57.0
Current ratio: 2.81
Long-term debt ($ mil.): 561.0
No. of shares (mil.): 134.5
Dividends
  Yield: 0.1%
  Payout: 6.1%
Market value ($ mil.): 16,589.0

	STOCK PRICE ($) FY Close	P/E High/Low	PER SHARE ($) Earnings	Dividends	Book Value
10/19	123.34	60 29	2.39	0.14	12.39
10/18	83.83	50 37	1.90	0.12	10.52
10/17	90.68	65 47	1.37	0.10	8.80
10/16	67.56	62 41	1.17	0.08	7.33
10/15	50.44	61 46	1.01	0.07	6.20
Annual Growth	25.0%	— —	24.1%	18.2%	18.9%

Heidrick & Struggles International, Inc.

Finding top dogs for clients in many industries Heidrick & Struggles International is one of the largest global recruiting firms. The company has more than 300 headhunters spanning 50 offices in 25 countries filling CEO CFO director and other high-level positions for companies that range from start-up ventures to established FORTUNE 500 firms. It's divided into search groups that specialize by industry such as financial services and industrial which together account for half of sales. The company's fees are generally equal to one-third of a hired executive's first-year compensation. Heidrick & Struggles also provides temporary placement management assessment and professional development services.

Geographic Reach

Heidrick & Struggles has a global presence Africa Asia Pacific Europe Latin America the Middle East and North Africa and North America. Its worldwide network includes affiliate relationships in Finland South Africa Turkey and Portugal. During fiscal 2014 Americas contributed more than 50% of revenue with Europe accounting for about 20% and Asia Pacific bringing in about 17% of total revenue.

Financial Performance

In fiscal 2014 the firm's revenue was $513.2 million which was an increased of 7% compared to fiscal 2013. Heidrick & Struggles' net income was $6.8 million in fiscal 2014 which was also an increase of 7% compared to the previous period. Cash from operating activities was $56.8 million in fiscal 2014 an increase of 29% compared to fiscal 2013 levels.

Strategy

Heidrick & Struggles has to work hard to stand out from its competitors. The firm faces intense competition from other companies in the executive search industry such as Egon Zehnder International Korn/Ferry International and Russell Reynolds Associates. The firm also faces competition from Internet-based firms and smaller boutiques that specialize in certain regional markets or industry segments.

HISTORY

Founded in Chicago in 1953 by Gardner Heidrick and John Struggles Heidrick & Struggles began as a hometown operation recruiting professionals in the manufacturing and industrial fields throughout the 1950s and 1960s. In 1968 it opened its first international office in London. The next decade the company added practice groups (an innovation attributed to rival Korn/Ferry) each focusing on different industries.

In 1984 Heidrick & Struggles spun off its European operations as Heidrick & Struggles International to some of its European partners while retaining a sizable stake for itself. Meanwhile it added to its practice groups launching its aviation/aerospace/transportation energy and chemicals and physician executive groups over the next 15 years.

The company grew through acquisitions in the 1990s including the 1997 purchase of Germany's largest search firm Mulder & Partner and the 1998 purchase of Fenwick Partners an East Coast firm. It filed to go public in July 1998 but delayed the offer two months later because of a depressed IPO market. The company then remerged with Heidrick & Struggles International in early 1999 before going public in April of that year. Patrick Pittard became CEO of the merged firm. Later in 1999 the company bought Sullivan & Co. a headhunting firm specializing in the financial services market and unveiled online recruiting service LeadersOnline. The following year Heidrick & Struggles cancelled plans to take LeadersOnline public.

Piers Marmion took over as CEO of the company following the resignation of Pittard in 2001. Heidrick & Struggles also cut about 1000 jobs in 2001 and 2002. Marmion resigned and the company named Thomas Friel CEO in 2003.

Friel stepped down as CEO in mid-2006 but remained chairman. L. Kevin Kelly the former president of the firm's Europe Middle East Africa and Asia Pacific regions became CEO in September 2006. Friel eventually left the company in 2007 and board member Richard I. Beattie became chairman.

In late 2006 Heidrick & Struggles bought the assets of retained executive search firm Highland Partners a unit of Hudson Highland Group. Highland Partners which posted sales of more than $60 million in 2005 strengthened Heidrick & Struggles' operations in the financial services and life sciences industries.

EXECUTIVES

EVP and CFO, Richard W. (Rich) Pehlke, age 66, $400,000 total compensation
President CEO and Director, Krishnan Rajagopalan, age 59, $650,000 total compensation
EVP General Counsel and Chief Administrative Officer, Stephen W. Beard, age 47, $375,000 total compensation
EVP and Managing Partner Leadership Consulting, Colin Price, age 60, $387,435 total compensation
EVP and Chief Human Resources Officer, Richard W. Greene, age 55
Managing Partner Heidrick Consulting and Regional Leader Americas, Andrew LeSueur
Director IT CRM and Digital Applications, Anthony Bertoni
Vp Business Operations, Catherine Baderman
Vice President Strategy and Corporate Development, Evan Trent
Vice President, Stephen Bondi
Vp, Jeff Cesario
Vice President, Praveen Sharma
Chairman, Tracy R. Wolstencroft, age 60
Vice Chairman Managing Partner Of Global Chief Ex, John Wood
Assistant Treasurer, Jiehua Song
Treasurer, Maureen Resac
Auditors: RSM US LLP

LOCATIONS

HQ: Heidrick & Struggles International, Inc.
233 South Wacker Drive, Suite 4900, Chicago, IL 60606-6303
Phone: 312 496-1200
Web: www.heidrick.com

PRODUCTS/OPERATIONS

2014 Sales

	% of total
Financial Services	26
Industrial	23
Global technology & Services	21
Consumer markets	17
Healthcare & life science	9
Education nonprofit & Social enterprise	4
Total	**100**

COMPETITORS

A.T. Kearney	Korn/Ferry
Adecco	Monster Worldwide
Boyden World	PageGroup
CTPartners	Russell Reynolds
Diversified Search	Solomon Page
Egon Zehnder	Spencer Stuart
Handler & Associates	WJM Associates

HISTORICAL FINANCIALS

Company Type: Public

Income Statement
FYE: December 31

	REVENUE ($ mil.)	NET INCOME ($ mil.)	NET PROFIT MARGIN	EMPLOYEES
12/18	735.6	49.3	6.7%	1,611
12/17	640.0	(48.6)	—	1,635
12/16	600.9	15.4	2.6%	1,716
12/15	548.3	17.1	3.1%	1,659
12/14	513.2	6.8	1.3%	1,483
Annual Growth	9.4%	64.1%	—	2.1%

2018 Year-End Financials

Debt ratio: —	No. of shares (mil.): 18.9
Return on equity: 20.5%	Dividends
Cash ($ mil.): 279.9	Yield: 1.6%
Current ratio: 1.41	Payout: 20.6%
Long-term debt ($ mil.): —	Market value ($ mil.): 591.0

	STOCK PRICE ($) FY Close	P/E High/Low	PER SHARE ($) Earnings	Dividends	Book Value
12/18	31.19	17 9	2.52	0.52	14.09
12/17	24.55	— —	(2.60)	0.52	11.33
12/16	24.15	33 20	0.81	0.52	13.92
12/15	27.22	32 21	0.92	0.52	13.86
12/14	23.05	64 43	0.37	0.52	13.41
Annual Growth	7.9%	— —	61.5%	(0.0%)	1.2%

Helios Technologies Inc

It's not solar power that Sun Hydraulics delivers but fluid power. The company makes screw-in hydraulic cartridge valves and custom manifolds used to control speed force and motion in fluid power systems. Cartridge valves offer a general purpose floating design that is unique in pressure capacity reliability reduced size and installation. Sun Hydraulics' valves and manifolds are used in myriad industrial and mobile products including construction agricultural and utility equipment and to a lesser extent in machine tools and material handling equipment. The company operates through subsidiaries and distributors in the US UK Germany Korea China and India. The Americas represents almost 50% of sales.

Geographic Reach
Its products' worldwide manufacture and availability fuels the Floridian company's performance. Approximately 60% of sales are to customers outside of the US. About 20% of sales are buoyed by customers in the Asia/Pacific region.

Sales and Marketing
Sun's products are sold globally through a combination of wholly-owned companies representative sales offices and independent and authorized distributors. In addition to distributors the company sells directly to other companies within the hydraulics industry including competitors which incorporate its products into their hydraulic products or systems.

The company currently has 87 distributors 56 of which are located outside the US. In 2015 sales to Sun's largest distributor represented less than 6% of net sales.

Financial Performance
After achieving a milestone revenue total of $228 million in 2014 Sun saw its revenues drop 12% to $201 million in 2015. Profits also plunged from $44 million in 2014 to $33 million in 2015. The declines for 2015 were attributed to decreased sales across all its geographical segments including the Americas (13%) Europe (11%) and the Asia/Pacific (9%). This was fueled by lower demand for capital goods equipment coupled with unfavorable foreign exchange rates for the year.

Strategy
The company maintains a strategy of selectively expanding its core product two-thirds of which are sold for breadth of mobile equipment applications and the remainder for fixed-in-place or automation machinery applications. Emerging end markets include nontraditional sectors such as animatronics wind power solar power and amusement park rides.

EXECUTIVES
CFO, Tricia L. Fulton, age 52, $247,692 total compensation
Officer, Tim A. Twitty, age 52, $249,692 total compensation
Officer, Steven Hancox, age 58, $209,323 total compensation
Officer, Mark B. Bokorney, age 54, $176,539 total compensation
President and CEO, Wolfgang H. Dangel
Chairman, Philippe J. Lemaitre, age 69
Auditors: Grant Thornton LLP

LOCATIONS
HQ: Helios Technologies Inc
1500 West University Parkway, Sarasota, FL 34243
Phone: 941 362-1200
Web: www.sunhydraulics.com

PRODUCTS/OPERATIONS
Selected Products
Integrated packages (using custom designed manifolds)
Screw-in hydraulic cartridge valves (electrically actuated and non-electrically actuated)
Standard manifolds

COMPETITORS
Actuant
Bosch Rexroth Corp.
Dayco Products
Jet Research Development
Koch Enterprises
Parker-Hannifin
Sauer-Danfoss
Servotronics
Textron

HISTORICAL FINANCIALS
Company Type: Public

Income Statement — FYE: December 29

	REVENUE ($ mil.)	NET INCOME ($ mil.)	NET PROFIT MARGIN	EMPLOYEES
12/18	508.0	46.7	9.2%	2,065
12/17	342.8	31.5	9.2%	1,150
12/16*	196.9	23.3	11.8%	1,100
01/16	200.7	33.1	16.5%	680
12/14	227.6	43.7	19.2%	719
Annual Growth	22.2%	1.6%	—	30.2%

*Fiscal year change

2018 Year-End Financials
Debt ratio: 33.8%
Return on equity: 11.6%
Cash ($ mil.): 23.4
Current ratio: 2.12
Long-term debt ($ mil.): 347.4
No. of shares (mil.): 31.9
Dividends
  Yield: 0.0%
  Payout: 24.1%
Market value ($ mil.): 1,066.0

	STOCK PRICE ($) FY Close	P/E High/Low		PER SHARE ($) Earnings	Dividends	Book Value
12/18	33.36	47	21	1.49	0.36	16.60
12/17	64.69	56	29	1.17	0.29	10.07
12/16*	39.97	48	28	0.87	0.40	8.78
01/16	31.73	34	22	1.24	0.45	8.29
12/14	39.64	27	21	1.65	1.36	7.46
Annual Growth	(4.2%) 22.1%	—	—	(2.5%)	(28.3%)	

*Fiscal year change

Heritage Commerce Corp

EXECUTIVES
EVP and CFO, Lawrence D. McGovern, age 64, $260,753 total compensation
President and CEO, Walter T. (Walt) Kaczmarek, age 67, $368,509 total compensation
EVP and Director Business Development, Robert P. (Bob) Gionfriddo, age 73
EVP Banking Division, Michael E. Benito, $244,826 total compensation
COO, Keith A. Wilton, $243,025 total compensation
EVP and Chief Credit Officer, David E. Porter, $260,738 total compensation
EVP and Corporate Secretary, Deborah K. (Debbie) Reuter
EVP HOA and Deposit Services, Teresa Powell
Vice President, Nancy Landy
Vice President Business Development Officer, David Beronio
Senior Vice President, Mike Hansen
Vice President And Financial Planning And Analysis, Minny Sue
Vice President Account Manager, Greg Ketell
Vice President Audit, Michael Egbujor
Chairman, Jack W. Conner, age 79
Auditors: Crowe LLP

LOCATIONS
HQ: Heritage Commerce Corp
150 Almaden Boulevard, San Jose, CA 95113
Phone: 408 947-6900
Web: www.heritagecommercecorp.com

PRODUCTS/OPERATIONS
2017 Sales

	$ mil.	% of total
Interest		
Loans including fees	86.4	74
Taxable securities	13.7	12
Other	6.8	6
Interest expense	(5.4)	—
Noninterest		
Service charges & fees on deposit accounts	3.2	3
Increase in cash surrender value of life insurance	1.7	1
Gain on sales of SBA loans	1.1	1
Servicing income	1.0	1
Other	2.6	2
Total	**111.1**	**100**

COMPETITORS
Bank of America
Bank of the West
Citibank
Comerica
First Republic (CA)
JPMorgan Chase
MUFG Americas Holdings
SVB Financial
U.S. Bancorp
Wells Fargo

HISTORICAL FINANCIALS
Company Type: Public

Income Statement — FYE: December 31

	ASSETS ($ mil.)	NET INCOME ($ mil.)	INCOME AS % OF ASSETS	EMPLOYEES
12/18	3,096.5	35.3	1.1%	302
12/17	2,843.4	23.8	0.8%	278
12/16	2,570.8	27.3	1.1%	263
12/15	2,361.5	16.5	0.7%	260
12/14	1,617.1	13.4	0.8%	242
Annual Growth	17.6%	27.4%	—	5.7%

2018 Year-End Financials
Return on assets: 1.1%
Return on equity: 11.0%
Long-term debt ($ mil.): —
No. of shares (mil.): 43.2
Sales ($ mil): 139.4
Dividends
  Yield: 3.8%
  Payout: 78.5%
Market value ($ mil.): 491.0

	STOCK PRICE ($) FY Close	P/E High/Low		PER SHARE ($) Earnings	Dividends	Book Value
12/18	11.34	21	13	0.84	0.44	8.49
12/17	15.32	26	21	0.62	0.40	7.10
12/16	14.43	20	13	0.72	0.36	6.85
12/15	11.96	26	17	0.48	0.32	7.64
12/14	8.83	21	19	0.42	0.18	6.96
Annual Growth	6.5%	—	—	18.9%	25.0%	5.1%

Heritage Financial Corp (WA)

Heritage Financial is ready to answer the call of Pacific Northwesterners seeking to preserve their heritage. Heritage Financial is the holding company for Heritage Bank which operates more than 65 branches throughout Washington and Oregon.

Boasting nearly $4 billion in assets the bank offers a range of deposit products to consumers and businesses such as CDs IRAs and checking savings NOW and money market accounts. Commercial and industrial loans account for over 50% of Heritage Financial's loan portfolio while mortgages secured by multi-family real estate comprise about 5%. The bank also originates single-family mortgages land development construction loans and consumer loans.

Operations
The bank also does business under the Central Valley Bank name in the Yakima and Kittitas counties of Washington and under the Whidbey Island Bank name on Whidbey Island.

About 79% of Heritage Financial's total revenue came from loan interest (including fees) in 2014 while another 7% came from interest on its investment securities. The rest of its revenue came from service charges and other fees (8%) Merchant Visa income (1%) and other miscellaneous fees. The company had a staff of 748 employees at the end of that year.

Geographic Reach
The Olympia-based bank operates more than 65 branches across Washington and the greater Portland area. It has additional offices in eastern Washington mostly in Yakima county.

Sales and Marketing
Heritage targets small and medium-sized businesses along with their owners as well as individuals.

Financial Performance
Fueled by loan and deposit growth from a series of bank acquisitions Heritage Financial's revenues and profits have been on the rise in recent years.

The company's revenue jumped 70% to a record $137.6 million in 2014 mostly thanks to new loan business stemming from its acquisition of Washington Banking Company. Deposit service charge income also increased thanks to new deposit business from the acquisition.

Higher revenue in 2014 allowed Heritage Financial's net income to more than double to a record $21 million while its operating cash levels rose 66% to $51.3 million on higher cash earnings and net proceeds from the sale of its loans.

Strategy
The bank reiterated in 2015 that it would continue to pursue strategic acquisitions of community banks to grow market share across the Pacific Northwest (its region of expertise) expand its business lines and grow its loan and deposit business.

With its focus on business and commercial lending the bank also in 2015 emphasized the importance of seeking high asset quality loans lending to familiar markets that have a historical record of success. Recruiting and retaining "highly competent personnel" to execute its strategies was also key to its long-term agenda.

Mergers and Acquisitions
In May 2014 Heritage acquired Washington Banking Company and its Whidbey Island Bank subsidiary for $265 million which "significantly expanded and enhanced" its product offerings across its core geographic market.

In July 2013 the bank acquired Puyallup Washington-based Valley Community Bancshares and its eight Valley Bank branches for $44 million.

In January 2013 the company purchased Lakewood Washington-based Northwest Commercial Bank along with its two branch locations in Washington state for $5 million.

EXECUTIVES
President CEO and Director Heritage Financial and CEO Heritage Bank, Brian L. Vance, age 64, $494,316 total compensation
EVP and CFO Heritage Financial and Heritage Bank, Donald J. Hinson, age 58, $255,084 total compensation
EVP and Chief Credit Officer Heritage Bank, David A. Spurling, age 66, $237,342 total compensation
EVP Heritage Financial and President and COO Heritage Bank, Jeffrey J. (Jeff) Deuel, $291,516 total compensation
EVP and Chief Lending Officer Heritage Bank, Bryan D. McDonald, age 47, $261,374 total compensation
Vp Marketing Manager, Shaun Carson
Vice President And Financial Reporting Manager, Patrice Hernandez
Chairman, Brian S. Charneski, age 57
Board Member, Stephen Dennis
Auditors: Crowe LLP

LOCATIONS
HQ: Heritage Financial Corp (WA)
201 Fifth Avenue S.W., Olympia, WA 98501
Phone: 360 943-1500
Web: www.HF-WA.com

PRODUCTS/OPERATIONS
2014 Sales

	$ mil.	% of total
Interest income		
Interest and fees on loans	110.4	79
Investment securities	10.2	7
Others	0.5	-
Non-interest income		
Service charges and others	11.1	8
Merchant Visa income	1.1	1
Others	4.3	5
Total	**137.6**	**100**

COMPETITORS
Bank of America
Columbia Banking
FS Bancorp
KeyCorp
U.S. Bancorp
Washington Federal
Wells Fargo

HISTORICAL FINANCIALS
Company Type: Public

Income Statement
FYE: December 31

	ASSETS ($ mil.)	NET INCOME ($ mil.)	INCOME AS % OF ASSETS	EMPLOYEES
12/18	5,316.9	53.0	1.0%	859
12/17	4,113.2	41.7	1.0%	735
12/16	3,878.9	38.9	1.0%	760
12/15	3,650.7	37.4	1.0%	717
12/14	3,457.7	21.0	0.6%	748
Annual Growth	11.4%	26.1%	—	3.5%

2018 Year-End Financials
Return on assets: 1.1%
Return on equity: 8.3%
Long-term debt ($ mil.): —
No. of shares (mil.): 36.8
Sales ($ mil): 231.0
Dividends
  Yield: 2.0%
  Payout: 52.5%
Market value ($ mil.): 1,096.0

	STOCK PRICE ($) FY Close	P/E High/Low	PER SHARE ($) Earnings	Dividends	Book Value
12/18	29.72	25 19	1.49	0.72	20.63
12/17	30.80	23 16	1.39	0.61	16.98
12/16	25.75	20 13	1.30	0.72	16.08
12/15	18.84	16 12	1.25	0.69	15.68
12/14	17.55	23 19	0.82	0.50	15.02
Annual Growth	14.1%	— —	16.1%	9.5%	8.3%

Heritage Insurance Holdings Inc

Auditors: Plante & Moran, PLLC

LOCATIONS
HQ: Heritage Insurance Holdings Inc
2600 McCormick Drive, Suite 300, Clearwater, FL 33759
Phone: 727 362-7200
Web: www.heritagepci.com

HISTORICAL FINANCIALS
Company Type: Public

Income Statement
FYE: December 31

	ASSETS ($ mil.)	NET INCOME ($ mil.)	INCOME AS % OF ASSETS	EMPLOYEES
12/18	1,768.7	27.1	1.5%	447
12/17	1,771.2	(1.1)	—	431
12/16	1,033.2	33.8	3.3%	311
12/15	837.4	92.5	11.0%	247
12/14	615.0	47.1	7.7%	133
Annual Growth	30.2%	(12.9%)	—	35.4%

2018 Year-End Financials
Return on assets: 1.5%
Return on equity: 6.7%
Long-term debt ($ mil.): —
No. of shares (mil.): 29.4
Sales ($ mil): 480.1
Dividends
  Yield: 1.6%
  Payout: 23.0%
Market value ($ mil.): 434.0

	STOCK PRICE ($) FY Close	P/E High/Low	PER SHARE ($) Earnings	Dividends	Book Value
12/18	14.72	18 12	1.04	0.24	14.43
12/17	18.02	— —	(0.04)	0.24	14.67
12/16	15.67	19 10	1.14	0.23	12.41
12/15	21.82	9 6	3.05	0.05	11.71
12/14	19.43	10 6	1.82	0.00	8.56
Annual Growth	(6.7%)	— —	(13.1%)	—	13.9%

Heska Corp.

If you lie down with dogs Heska makes sure you don't get up with fleas. The company makes diagnostic products vaccines and pharmaceuticals for domestic animals primarily cats and dogs. Its products — both on the market and in development — include diagnostics and treatments for allergies arthritis cancer fleas heartworms skin problems thyroid problems and viral infections. As part of its business Heska also operates a diagnostic lab and manufactures veterinary diagnostic and monitoring devices. The company develops vaccines for cattle small mammals and fish as well. Products are sold worldwide through direct sales representatives and independent distributors.

Sales and Marketing

The company markets its animal health products in the US to veterinarians through an outside sales force of 40 individuals an inside sales force of 20 and a few independent distributors. Internationally Heska markets its products to veterinarians primarily through third-party veterinary diagnostic laboratories independent distributors and through a collaboration with Novartis Japan. Novartis Japan exclusively markets and distributes SOLO STEP CH and Heska's line of ERD HEALTHSCREEN urine test products in Japan.

Financial Performance

Net revenue for Heska rose some 7% in 2011 vs. 2010 boosted across its core business segments: core companion animal health and other vaccines pharmaceuticals and products. Sales of cattle vaccine helped this latter OVP segment's revenue rise thanks in part to its fruitful contract with AgriLabs and sales of other cattle vaccines. Revenue increases were offset however by slower sales of its bulk bovine biological product.

Heska has been vulnerable to the economic problems that have plagued the US in recent years as families put off vet visits and subsequently vets themselves delay making major purchases. Additionally the loss of a key supplier of Heska's handheld blood analyzer equipment had an adverse effect during both 2009 and 2010 on its core companion animal health business which brings in roughly 82% of Heska's income. This macroeconomic drag on Heska's business in recent years puts into perspective the positive push the AgriLabs agreement has made to level out its revenue.

Strategy

Some of Heska's top products include the SOLO STEP line of heartworm diagnostic tests for cats and dogs HEMATRUE Hematology Analyzer to measure a variety of blood parameters including white and red blood cell counts and hemoglobin levels and the DRI-CHEM 7000 which has the capacity to run more than 20 tests with a single blood sample.

The DRI-CHEM 7000 is a next-generation version of the DRI-CHEM 4000 and an example of how Heska grows its product lines by revamping best-sellers with additional features and capabilities. In 2012 Heska's wholly owned subsidiary Diamond Animal Health began to manufacture Pet-Trust Plus a heartworm preventative product that's based on an existing FDA-approved product. Once its products are sold Heska continues to garner income on many of them through the sale of adjunct supplies and services.

Heska is focused on developing external licensing deals and creating new collaborations to expand its product lines in both the CCA and its Other Vaccines Pharmaceuticals and Products (OVP) divisions. As part of this effort Heska in 2011 expanded its products portfolio of in-clinic blood analyzers by launching a lactate meter analyzer.

In the OVP segment Heska is keenly focused on marketing and growing its line of bovine vaccines licensed by the USDA. Heska also has a long-term non-exclusive agreement with Agri Laboratories to market and sell some of Heska's bovine vaccines — sold primarily under the Titanium and MasterGuard brands. The partnership generates a significant portion of OVP's revenue. OVP also produces vaccines and pharmaceuticals for other third parties.

EXECUTIVES

COO and Chief Strategist, Jason A. Napolitano, age 50, $316,775 total compensation
EVP Diagnostic Operations and Product Development, Nancy Wisnewski, age 56, $260,104 total compensation
EVP Companion Animal Health Sales, Rodney A. Lippincott, age 45, $175,000 total compensation
President and CEO, Kevin S. Wilson, age 47, $275,000 total compensation
EVP Companion Animal Health Sales, Steven M. Asakowicz, age 53, $175,000 total compensation
EVP Global Sales and Marketing, Steven M. (Steve) Eyl, age 53, $261,458 total compensation
CFO, John McMahon, age 54
Executive Vice President, Steve Eyl
Evp Of International Diagnostics, Jason Aroesty
Chair, Sharon L. Riley, age 58
Board Member, Scott Humphrey
Auditors: Plante & Moran, PLLC

LOCATIONS

HQ: Heska Corp.
 3760 Rocky Mountain Avenue, Loveland, CO 80538
Phone: 970 493-7272
Web: www.heska.com

COMPETITORS

Abaxis
American Animal Health
Bayer AG
Bayer Animal Health
Drs. Foster & Smith
ECO Animal Health
Eli Lilly
Farnam Companies
IDEXX Labs
Merck
Merck Animal Health
Merial
Neogen
Novartis
Pfizer
Sanofi-Aventis U.S
Skystar
Virbac

HISTORICAL FINANCIALS

Company Type: Public

Income Statement — FYE: December 31

	REVENUE ($ mil.)	NET INCOME ($ mil.)	NET PROFIT MARGIN	EMPLOYEES
12/18	127.4	5.8	4.6%	347
12/17	129.3	9.9	7.7%	345
12/16	130.0	10.5	8.1%	327
12/15	104.6	5.2	5.0%	310
12/14	89.8	2.6	2.9%	301
Annual Growth	9.1%	22.4%	—	3.6%

2018 Year-End Financials
Debt ratio: 3.8%
Return on equity: 5.2%
Cash ($ mil.): 13.3
Current ratio: 3.06
Long-term debt ($ mil.): 6.0
No. of shares (mil.): 7.6
Dividends
 Yield: —
 Payout: —
Market value ($ mil.): 661.0

	STOCK PRICE ($) FY Close	P/E High/Low	PER SHARE ($) Earnings	Dividends	Book Value
12/18	86.10	140 72	0.74	0.00	15.95
12/17	80.21	78 50	1.30	0.00	13.75
12/16	71.60	47 17	1.43	0.00	12.38
12/15	38.68	50 20	0.74	0.00	9.59
12/14	18.13	41 20	0.41	0.00	8.38
Annual Growth	47.6%	— —	15.9%	—	17.5%

Hi-Crush Inc

Auditors: DELOITTE & TOUCHE LLP

LOCATIONS

HQ: Hi-Crush Inc
 1330 Post Oak Blvd, Suite 600, Houston, TX 77056
Phone: 713 980-6200 **Fax:** 713 963-0088
Web: www.hicrushpartners.com

HISTORICAL FINANCIALS

Company Type: Public

Income Statement — FYE: December 31

	REVENUE ($ mil.)	NET INCOME ($ mil.)	NET PROFIT MARGIN	EMPLOYEES
12/18	842.8	137.6	16.3%	720
12/17	602.6	82.5	13.7%	0
12/16	204.0	(81.0)	—	0
12/15	339.6	28.2	8.3%	0
12/14	386.5	123.0	31.8%	0
Annual Growth	21.5%	2.8%	—	—

2018 Year-End Financials
Debt ratio: 31.0%
Return on equity: —
Cash ($ mil.): 114.2
Current ratio: 1.85
Long-term debt ($ mil.): 443.2
No. of shares (mil.): 100.8
Dividends
 Yield: 0.1%
 Payout: 84.5%
Market value ($ mil.): 361.0

	STOCK PRICE ($) FY Close	P/E High/Low	PER SHARE ($) Earnings	Dividends	Book Value
12/18	3.58	11 2	1.42	1.20	8.00
12/17	10.70	23 8	0.96	0.35	8.94
12/16	19.80	— —	(1.64)	0.00	4.56
12/15	5.92	54 7	0.73	0.00	3.70
12/14	31.03	22 10	3.00	0.00	4.76
Annual Growth	(41.7%)	— —	(17.1%)	—	13.9%

Hilton Grand Vacations Inc

Auditors: Ernst & Young LLP

LOCATIONS

HQ: Hilton Grand Vacations Inc
 6355 MetroWest Boulevard, Suite 180, Orlando, FL 32835
Phone: 407 613-3100
Web: www.hiltongrandvacations.com

HISTORICAL FINANCIALS

Company Type: Public

Income Statement   FYE: December 31

	REVENUE ($ mil.)	NET INCOME ($ mil.)	NET PROFIT MARGIN	EMPLOYEES
12/18	1,999.0	298.0	14.9%	8,600
12/17	1,711.0	327.0	19.1%	8,000
12/16	1,583.0	168.0	10.6%	7,750
12/15	1,475.0	174.0	11.8%	6,650
12/14	1,317.0	167.0	12.7%	0
Annual Growth	11.0%	15.6%	—	—

2018 Year-End Financials

Debt ratio: 49.5%
Return on equity: 52.5%
Cash ($ mil.): 108.0
Current ratio: 4.66
Long-term debt ($ mil.): 1,363.0
No. of shares (mil.): 94.5
Dividends
  Yield: —
  Payout: —
Market value ($ mil.): 2,495.0

	STOCK PRICE ($) FY Close	P/E High/Low		PER SHARE ($) Earnings	Dividends	Book Value
12/18	26.39	15	8	3.05	0.00	6.51
12/17	41.95	13	8	3.28	0.00	5.23
Annual Growth	(37.1%)	—	—	(7.0%)	—	24.7%

Hingham Institution for Savings

The Hingham Institution for Savings serves businesses and retail customers in Boston's south shore communities operating more than 10 branches in Massachusetts in Boston Cohasset Hingham Hull Norwell Scituate South Hingham and South Weymouth. Founded in 1834 the bank offers traditional deposit products such as checking and savings accounts IRAs and certificates of deposit. More than 90% of its loan portfolio is split between commercial mortgages and residential mortgages (including home equity loans) though the bank also originates construction business and consumer loans. More than 95% of the company's revenue comes from loan interest.

Operations

The Hingham Institution for Savings made 96% of its total revenue from loan interest during 2015 while about 2% came from interest in equities CODs and other investments. The rest of its revenue mostly came from service fees on deposit accounts.

Of its $1.4 billion loan portfolio (at the end of 2015) about 48% was made up of commercial real estate mortgages (including multi-family housing) while 45% was tied to residential mortgages (including home equity). The remainder of the portfolio was made up of residential and commercial construction loans (7% of loan assets) and commercial business loans and consumer loans (1%).

Subsidiary Hingham Unpledged Securities Corporation holds title to certain securities available for sale.

Geographic Reach

The company mostly serves clients in Boston the South Shore and the island of Nantucket. Its branches are in Boston Cohasset Hingham Hull Nantucket Norwell Scituate South Hingham and South Weymouth Massachusetts.

Sales and Marketing

The Hingham Institution for Savings serves both individuals and small businesses in its three target markets in Massachusetts. Some of its clients (as of mid-2016) include Lyons Associates The Hub TCR Development SYA+FH Steven Young Architect + Fine Home Builder and Park Drive Inc.

The bank spent $489000 on marketing expenses during 2015 down from $557000 in each of 2014 and 2013.

Financial Performance

The bank's annual revenues have slowly trended higher over the past several years as the promising Boston real estate market has fueled its commercial real estate and residential loan business growth.

Hingham's revenue dipped 1% to $64.34 million during 2015 despite 13% mortgage loan growth mostly because in 2014 it earned a gains on life insurance distributions. The bank also continued to lose fee income as it has eliminated many fees on its deposit products to simplify offerings and attract customer deposits.

Revenue declines and higher income tax provisions in 2015 (in 2014 it earned non-taxed death benefit proceeds) caused the bank's net income to fall 13% to $19.34 million. Hingham's operating cash levels rose 11% to $20.2 million for the year thanks to a jump in cash-based earnings.

Strategy

The Hingham Institution for Savings continued in 2016 to focus on originating commercial multi-family and single-family mortgage loans in its target markets of Boston the South Shore and the island of Nantucket in Massachusetts especially as the healthy real estate market in and around Boston has provided a tailwind for its lending business.

EXECUTIVES

Chief Executive Officer; President; Director, Robert H. Gaughen, $319,615 total compensation
Vice President Of Retail Banking, Andrew Vebber
Assistant Vice President Retail Lending, Patricia Talbot
Auditors: Wolf & Company, P.C.

LOCATIONS

HQ: Hingham Institution for Savings
55 Main Street, Hingham, MA 02043
Phone: 781 749-2200   **Fax:** 781 740-4889
Web: www.hinghamsavings.com

COMPETITORS

Bank of America
Citizens Financial Group
Eastern Bank
Independent Bank (MA)
Peoples Federal Bancshares Inc.
Sovereign Bank

HISTORICAL FINANCIALS

Company Type: Public

Income Statement   FYE: December 31

	ASSETS ($ mil.)	NET INCOME ($ mil.)	INCOME AS % OF ASSETS	EMPLOYEES
12/18	2,408.5	30.4	1.3%	96
12/17	2,284.6	25.7	1.1%	101
12/16	2,014.6	23.4	1.2%	103
12/15	1,768.5	19.3	1.1%	111
12/14	1,552.2	22.2	1.4%	121
Annual Growth	11.6%	8.1%	—	(5.6%)

2018 Year-End Financials

Return on assets: 1.3%
Return on equity: 15.2%
Long-term debt ($ mil.): —
No. of shares (mil.): 2.1
Sales ($ mil): 92.4
Dividends
  Yield: 0.8%
  Payout: 11.6%
Market value ($ mil.): 422.0

	STOCK PRICE ($) FY Close	P/E High/Low		PER SHARE ($) Earnings	Dividends	Book Value
12/18	197.74	16	14	13.90	1.73	99.67
12/17	207.00	19	14	11.81	1.62	87.29
12/16	196.78	18	11	10.89	1.52	75.50
12/15	119.80	15	9	9.02	2.14	64.83
12/14	87.01	9	7	10.44	1.37	57.08
Annual Growth	22.8%	—	—	7.4%	6.0%	15.0%

HMN Financial Inc.

EXECUTIVES

Executive Vice President Chief Financial Officer, Jon J. Eberle, age 51, $142,000 total compensation
SVP Technology Facilities and Compliance HMN Financial and Home Federal Savings Bank, Dwain C. Jorgensen, age 68, $112,300 total compensation
Director; SVP Home Federal Savings Bank, Susan K. Kolling, age 65, $119,300 total compensation
President and Director; President Home Federal Savings Bank, Bradley C. Krehbiel, age 58, $160,700 total compensation
Chief Credit Officer; Senior Vice President of the Bank, Lawrence McGraw
Director, Mahlon C. Schneider, age 77
Director; SVP Home Federal Savings Bank, Susan K. Kolling, age 65
Director, Hugh C. Smith, age 76
Director, Michael J. Fogarty, age 78
Director, Malcolm W. McDonald, age 80
Director, Karen L. Himle, age 61
President and Director; President Home Federal Savings Bank, Bradley C. Krehbiel, age 57
Independent Director, Allen Berning
Independent Director, Bernard Nigon
Auditors: CliftonLarsonAllen LLP

LOCATIONS

HQ: HMN Financial Inc.
1016 Civic Center Drive Northwest, Rochester, MN 55901
Phone: 507 535-1200
Web: www.hmnf.com

COMPETITORS

TCF Financial Wells Financial
U.S. Bancorp

HISTORICAL FINANCIALS
Company Type: Public

Income Statement FYE: December 31

	ASSETS ($ mil.)	NET INCOME ($ mil.)	INCOME AS % OF ASSETS	EMPLOYEES
12/18	712.3	8.2	1.2%	194
12/17	722.6	4.4	0.6%	196
12/16	682.0	6.3	0.9%	209
12/15	643.1	2.9	0.5%	194
12/14	577.4	7.3	1.3%	189
Annual Growth	5.4%	2.8%	—	0.7%

2018 Year-End Financials
Return on assets: 1.1%
Return on equity: 10.0%
Long-term debt ($ mil.): —
No. of shares (mil.): 4.8
Sales ($ mil): 38.1
Dividends
Yield: —
Payout: —
Market value ($ mil.): 95.0

	STOCK PRICE ($) FY Close	P/E High/Low	PER SHARE ($) Earnings	Dividends	Book Value
12/18	19.62	11 10	1.71	0.00	17.19
12/17	19.10	19 16	0.90	0.00	17.97
12/16	17.50	12 7	1.34	0.00	16.91
12/15	11.55	18 16	0.61	0.00	15.54
12/14	12.40	10 6	1.23	0.00	17.00
Annual Growth	12.2%	— —	8.6%	—	0.3%

Holly Energy Partners LP

Holly Energy Partners pipes petroleum products and crude oil from refineries. It operates petroleum product and crude gathering pipelines (in New Mexico Oklahoma Texas and Utah) distribution terminals (in Arizona Idaho New Mexico Oklahoma Texas Utah and Washington) and refinery tankage in New Mexico and Utah. It operates 1330 miles of refined petroleum pipelines (340 miles leased) 960 miles of crude oil trunk lines 10 refined product terminals one jet fuel terminal and two truck-loading facilities. It also has three 65-mile pipelines that ship feedstocks and crude oil. HollyFrontier holds a 41% stake in Holly Energy Partners.

EXECUTIVES

Vice President Engineering, Bruce Shaw
Vice President of Human Resources, Nancy Hartmann
Vice President and Treasurer, Stephen Wise
Vice President of Operations, Leland Griffin
Auditors: Ernst & Young LLP

LOCATIONS

HQ: Holly Energy Partners LP
2828 N. Harwood, Suite 1300, Dallas, TX 75201
Phone: 214 871-3555
Web: www.hollyenergy.com

COMPETITORS

ExxonMobil Pipeline Shell Pipeline
Magellan Midstream Wolverine Pipe Line Company
NuStar Energy

HISTORICAL FINANCIALS
Company Type: Public

Income Statement FYE: December 31

	REVENUE ($ mil.)	NET INCOME ($ mil.)	NET PROFIT MARGIN	EMPLOYEES
12/18	506.2	178.8	35.3%	283
12/17	454.3	195.0	42.9%	269
12/16	402.0	147.5	36.7%	249
12/15	358.8	137.2	38.2%	245
12/14	332.5	105.5	31.7%	273
Annual Growth	11.1%	14.1%	—	0.9%

2018 Year-End Financials
Debt ratio: 67.4%
Return on equity: —
Cash ($ mil.): 3.0
Current ratio: 1.15
Long-term debt ($ mil.): 1,418.9
No. of shares (mil.): 105.4
Dividends
Yield: 9.2%
Payout: 154.7%
Market value ($ mil.): 3,011.0

	STOCK PRICE ($) FY Close	P/E High/Low	PER SHARE ($) Earnings	Dividends	Book Value
12/18	28.56	20 16	1.70	2.63	4.05
12/17	32.49	17 13	2.28	2.51	3.88
12/16	32.06	22 13	1.69	2.32	6.02
12/15	31.14	23 17	1.60	2.17	4.92
12/14	29.91	31 24	1.20	2.05	5.46
Annual Growth	(1.1%)	— —	9.1%	6.5%	(7.2%)

Home Bancorp Inc

Making its home in Cajun Country Home Bancorp is the holding company for Home Bank a community bank which offers deposit and loan services to consumers and small to midsized businesses in southern Louisiana. Through about two dozen branches the bank offers standard savings and checking accounts as well as lending services such as mortgages consumer loans and credit cards. Its loan portfolio includes commercial real estate commercial and industrial loans as well as construction and land loans. Home Bancorp also operates about half a dozen bank branches in west Mississippi which were formerly part of Britton & Koontz Bank.

Geographic Reach
Home Bancorp serves the Louisiana areas of Greater Lafayette Baton Rouge Greater New Orleans and Northshore (of Lake Pontchartrain). Its markets in Mississippi include Vicksburg and Natchez.

Financial Performance
Although the company saw assets and loans grow in 2013 net income fell 20% that year to $7.3 million on lower operating income.

Mergers and Acquisitions
In early 2014 Home Bancorp spent about $35 million on Britton & Koontz Capital Corporation the holding company of Britton & Koontz Bank; the deal added five branches in west Mississippi to Home Bancorp's operations.

EXECUTIVES

Chief Operations Officers and Executive Vice President of the Bank, Scott T. Sutton, age 63
President; Chief Executive Officer; Director, John W. Bordelon, age 60, $215,000 total compensation
Executive Vice President; Chief Lending Officer of the Bank, Darren E. Guidry, age 53, $137,000 total compensation
Chief Financial Officer & Executive Vice President of the Bank, Joseph B. Zanco, age 46, $99,018 total compensation
Director and Secretary, Henry William Busch Jr., age 75, $30,300 total compensation
President CEO and Director Home Bancorp and Home Bank, John W. Bordelon, age 60
Director, Michael P. Maraist, age 68
Director, Paul J. Blanchet III, age 61
Director, Richard J. Bourgeois, age 69
Director and Secretary, Henry William Busch Jr., age 75
Director, John A. Hendry, age 66
Director, Marc W. Judice, age 69
Auditors: Wipfli LLP

LOCATIONS

HQ: Home Bancorp Inc
503 Kaliste Saloom Road, Lafayette, LA 70508
Phone: 337 237-1960 **Fax:** 337 264-9280
Web: www.home24bank.com

COMPETITORS

Capital One MidSouth Bancorp
IBERIABANK Regions Financial
JPMorgan Chase Teche Holding
Louisiana Bancorp

HISTORICAL FINANCIALS
Company Type: Public

Income Statement FYE: December 31

	ASSETS ($ mil.)	NET INCOME ($ mil.)	INCOME AS % OF ASSETS	EMPLOYEES
12/18	2,153.6	31.5	1.5%	0
12/17	2,228.1	16.8	0.8%	0
12/16	1,556.7	16.0	1.0%	0
12/15	1,551.9	12.5	0.8%	0
12/14	1,221.4	9.8	0.8%	0
Annual Growth	15.2%	33.7%	—	—

2018 Year-End Financials
Return on assets: 1.4%
Return on equity: 10.8%
Long-term debt ($ mil.): —
No. of shares (mil.): 9.4
Sales ($ mil): 115.7
Dividends
Yield: 2.0%
Payout: 24.1%
Market value ($ mil.): 335.0

	STOCK PRICE ($) FY Close	P/E High/Low	PER SHARE ($) Earnings	Dividends	Book Value
12/18	35.40	14 10	3.40	0.71	32.14
12/17	43.22	19 14	2.28	0.55	29.57
12/16	38.61	17 10	2.25	0.41	24.47
12/15	25.98	14 11	1.79	0.37	22.80
12/14	22.94	15 12	1.42	0.07	21.64
Annual Growth	11.5%	— —	24.4%	78.5%	10.4%

Home BancShares Inc

Home BancShares is the holding company for Centennial Bank which operates some 160 branches in Arkansas Florida and Alabama with an additional branch in each of New York City and Los Angeles (through which the company is building out a national lending platform). With $14.9 billion in assets the bank offers traditional services such as checking savings and money market accounts and CDs. About 60% of its lending portfolio is focused on commercial real estate loans — including non-farm and non-residential and construction and land development. The bank also writes residential mortgages and business and consumer loans. Through a subsidiary Home BancShares offers insurance services.

Operations
About 80% of Home Bancshares' $10.8 billion loan portfolio comprises real estate loans including non-farm and non-residential commercial loans which make up more than 40% of the total. Residential one-to-four-family loans and commercial construction and land development loans contribute about 20% and 15% respectively. Commercial and industrial loans make up around 10%.

The holding company has built a $6.3 billion portfolio of non-farm and non-residential commercial real estate loans primarily secured by commercial real estate. Around 50% 30% and 15% of the company's commercial real estate loan portfolio is in Florida Arkansas and with its Centennial Finance Group (CFG). Home Bancshares established the group in 2015 to manage loans acquired in the company's acquisition of the Florida Panhandle business of Banco Popular and to originate new loans (with a focus on commercial real estate and commercial and industrial loans) via a national lending platform.

About 30% and 60% of the company's $2.6 billion residential real estate loan portfolio are for one-to-four-family properties and non-owner occupied one-to-four family properties respectively.

The company's commercial and industrial loans account for about $1.3 billion of the portfolio; Arkansas Florida and Centennial CFG house about 40% 35% and 25% of that segment respectively.

Geographic Reach
Conway Arkansas-based Home Bancshares' holding company's Centennial Bank operates about 90 branches in Florida more than 75 in Arkansas around five in Southern Alabama and one in each of New York City and Los Angeles.

Sales and Marketing
Home Bancshares' non-farm and non-residential lending (comprising about 40% of the total) is made up of loans for shopping and retail centers hotels and motels offices industrial warehouses churches marinas and nursing homes.

Residential one-to-four-family residential mortgages for individuals make up some 20% of the company's portfolio. About 30% and 60% of its residential mortgage loans are for one-to-four-family owner-occupied and non-owner-occupied properties respectively.

The holding company also lends heavily to residential and commercial developers to construct commercial properties and develop land. Construction and land development loans make up about 15% of its portfolio.

Around 10% of the value of Home Bancshares' loans go to commercial and industrial clients.

Financial Performance
Home Bancshares reported revenue of $555.5 million in 2017 up 174% from 2013 and net income of $135.1 million up 103% over the same period. The company's cash stores and long-term debt both about tripled during that time to $635.9 million and $1.7 billion respectively.

The holding company's revenue increased 13% in 2017 compared with 2016 owing to increased interest income from loans.

Home Bancshares' net income fell 24% due mostly to an increase in income tax expense related to the passage of the Tax Cuts and Jobs Act.

The company's $419.3 million to its cash in 2017. Operating activities provided $176.9 million down from the previous year based on decreased net income and increased charges from indemnification and other assets and accrued interest payable on other liabilities. Investments used $355.5 million while financings added $597.8 million driven mostly by proceeds from issuance of subordinated debentures.

Strategy
Home Bancshares' strategy is focused on expanding in its core Florida market through the purchase of local managed community banks including four in 2017 and 2018.

In addition to growing its geographic footprint Home Bancshares is also diversifying its product offerings through acquisitions. In 2018 the company bought the Shore Premier Finance division of Union Bankshares. Shore originated direct consumer loans for high-end sail and power boats in southeast Florida.

Mergers and Acquisitions
Home Bancshares acquired Giant Holdings The Bank of Commerce and Stonegate Bank in 2017 as well as former Union Bankshares subsidiary Shore Premier Finance in 2018.

The holding company purchased Giant Holdings for $96 million. Giant operated six branches in the Ft. Lauderdale Florida area and had $398.1 million in total assets $327.8 million in loans and $304 million in deposits.

Home Bancshares acquired The Bank of Commerce from Bank of Commerce Holdings as part of that company's bankruptcy for $4.2 million. Bank of Commerce - which had $182.5 million in assets $127.5 million in loans and $141.7 million in deposits - operated three branches in the Sarasota Florida area.

Home Bancshares bought Stonegate Bank for $820 million adding the company's $3.1 billion in total assets $2.4 billion in loans and $2.6 billion in deposits to its books. Stonegate had 24 offices in Florida markets including Broward and Sarasota counties.

In 2018 the company acquired the Shore Premier Finance division of Union Bankshares for $374.5 million in cash and 1.3 million shares. Shore originates direct consumer loans for high-end sail and power boats at 16 locations in southeast Florida. At the deal's close Shore had $384.2 million in assets including $383.4 million in total loans.

Company Background
Home Bancshares formed in 1998 as First State Bank.

EXECUTIVES

CFO and Treasurer and Director, Randy E. Mayor, age 54, $300,000 total compensation
President and CEO, C. Randall (Randy) Sims, age 64, $390,000 total compensation
Regional President Centennial Bank, Robert F. Birch, age 69, $290,000 total compensation
President and CEO Centennial Bank, Tracy M. French, age 57, $290,000 total compensation
Chief Lending Officer, Kevin D. Hester, age 55
COO Home BancShares Inc. and Centennial Bank, John (Stephen) Tipton
Vice President Security, Jenni Holbrook
Vice President, Brian Jackson
Chairman, John W. Allison, age 72
Vice Chairman, Robert H. Adcock, age 70
Board Member, James Hinkle
Board Member, Thomas Longe
Board Member, Mike Beebe
Auditors: BKD, LLP

LOCATIONS

HQ: Home BancShares Inc
719 Harkrider, Suite 100, Conway, AR 72032
Phone: 501 339-2929
Web: www.homebancshares.com

COMPETITORS

Arvest Bank	Bear State Financial
BB&T	Regions Financial
BBX Capital	Simmons First
Bank of America	Woodforest Financial
Bank of the Ozarks	

HISTORICAL FINANCIALS
Company Type: Public

Income Statement
FYE: December 31

	ASSETS ($ mil.)	NET INCOME ($ mil.)	INCOME AS % OF ASSETS	EMPLOYEES
12/18	15,302.4	300.4	2.0%	1,815
12/17	14,449.7	135.0	0.9%	1,744
12/16	9,808.4	177.1	1.8%	1,503
12/15	9,289.1	138.2	1.5%	1,424
12/14	7,403.2	113.0	1.5%	1,376
Annual Growth	19.9%	27.7%	—	7.2%

2018 Year-End Financials
Return on assets: 2.0%
Return on equity: 13.1%
Long-term debt ($ mil.): —
No. of shares (mil.): 170.7
Sales ($ mil): 788.2
Dividends
 Yield: 2.8%
 Payout: 32.1%
Market value ($ mil.): 2,790.0

	STOCK PRICE ($)	P/E	PER SHARE ($)		
	FY Close	High/Low	Earnings	Dividends	Book Value
12/18	16.34	15 9	1.73	0.46	13.76
12/17	23.25	33 24	0.89	0.40	12.70
12/16	27.77	35 15	1.26	0.34	9.45
12/15	40.52	46 28	1.01	0.28	8.55
12/14	32.16	44 33	0.85	0.18	7.51
Annual Growth	(15.6%)	— —	19.4%	27.3%	16.3%

HomeStreet Inc

HomeStreet aims to offer home and business mortgages to all in the Pacific Northwest and Hawaii. Its subsidiary HomeStreet Bank offers traditional consumer banking accounts as well as commercial and private banking investment and insurance products and services through 45 branches and 65 loan offices in the Pacific Northwest California and Hawaii. Specializing in residential and commercial mortgages the bank and fellow subsidiary Homestreet Capital Corp originate home loans both directly and through a joint venture Windermere Real Estate which operates about 40 offices in Washington and Oregon. HomeStreet also provides specialty financing for income-producing properties.

Operations
HomeStreet operates two lines of business: Commercial and Consumer Banking and Mortgage Banking which originates residential mortgage loans for wale in the secondary markets to be securitized by GSAs. Its primary subsidiaries are HomeStreet Bank and HomeStreet Capital Corp. (HCC). HCC sells and services multifamily mortgage loans in conjunction with HomeStreet Bank.

HomeStreet gets most of its business from mortgage originations and sales. About 53% of the company's revenue came from its mortgage banking business (origination and sales) during 2015 while another 6% came from mortgage servicing income. Another 34% of its revenue came from loan interest.

Geographic Reach
Seattle-based HomeStreet operates bank branches in Arizona California Colorado Hawaii Idaho Oregon Utah and Washington.

Sales and Marketing
HomeStreet provides financial services for small- and middle-market businesses as well as consumers.

Financial Performance
HomeStreet's annual revenues and profits have more than doubled since 2011 thanks to strong mortgage banking and loan business growth driven by a strengthening housing market.

The company's revenue spiked 50% to $446.35 million during 2015 mostly thanks to a 64% increase in gains on mortgage loan origination sales resulting from a rise in single family mortgage interest rate lock commitments.

Strong revenue growth in 2015 caused HomeStreet's net income to nearly double to $41.32 million. The company's operating cash levels spiked to $8.31 million for the year (operations had used $348.6 million in 2014) mostly because it collected more in cash-denominated proceeds from its mortgage loan sales than it did in 2014.

Strategy
HomeStreet has been moving more toward commercial mortgage and SBA originations in recent years launching its HomeStreet commercial capital business in Orange County California in 2015. It also continues to acquire other small community banks in its region to grow its loan and deposit business and expand into new geographic markets.

Additionally it's been expanding its retail operations its own opening two new branches in San Diego's Mission Gorge and Kearny Mesa markets in March 2016. To boost profitability HomeStreet looked in 2016 to enhance productivity and cut costs by streamlining operations.

Mergers and Acquisitions
The company plans to buy two Southern California banks from Boston Private Bank & Trust. Through that acquisition HomeStreet will gain some $110 million in deposit accounts. It will then have a dozen retail branches in Southern California.

In February 2016 the company purchased Orange County Business Bank for $55 million extending its reach into "one of the premier commercial and consumer banking markets in the country" according to HomeStreet CEO and chairman Mark Mason.

In March 2015 HomeStreet expanded into Southern California's retail banking market after acquiring Simplicity Bancorp and its seven Simply Bank retail deposit branches in the greater Los Angeles area. Beyond geographic expansion the deal added valuable retail deposit and loan assets.

In November 2013 HomeStreet acquired Fortune Bank a community bank with two branches in Seattle and Bellevue for about $27 million. Concurrently it purchased YNB Financial Services Corp. the parent company of Yakima National Bank which operates four branches in Yakima Selah Sunnyside and Kennewick for about $10.3 million. The twin purchases along with the acquisition of two branches from AmericanWest Bank increased the number of retail deposit branches operates by HomeStreet to 29.

Company Background
HomeStreet went public in February 2012 with an offering worth $55 million. The company sold 1.6 million shares priced at $44 each. HomeStreet had postponed two previous attempts to go public in 2011 that had planned to sell many more shares. Proceeds from the 2012 IPO were used to meet capital-ratio requirements required by regulators in the wake of allegations that the bank engaged in unsafe practices.

HomeStreet was hit hard by the economic downturn and slowdown in the housing market. Trouble in its core mortgage lending business led to losses in 2009 and 2010 and the bank entered into agreements with regulators to improve its capital position earnings and management. It brought in a new management team and launched a turnaround plan to stabilize the business which included tightening its lending standards restructuring troubled loans when necessary and the sale of real estate backed by nonperforming loans. The measures helped HomeStreet return to profitability in 2011 and remain in the black for several years thereafter.

EXECUTIVES

Chairman President and CEO HomeStreet Inc. and HomeStreet Bank, Mark K. Mason, age 59, $537,500 total compensation
EVP Chief Administrative Officer General Counsel and Corporate Secretary Homestreet Inc. and Homestreet Bank, Godfrey B. Evans, age 65, $247,200 total compensation
SEVP Commercial Banking HomeStreet Bank, David H. Straus, age 72
EVP HomeStreet Inc. and EVP Residential Construction and Affiliated Businesses HomeStreet Bank, Richard W. H. (Rich) Bennion, age 69, $203,000 total compensation
EVP and Retail Banking Director HomeStreet Bank, Paulette Lemon, age 62
EVP and Human Resources Director Homestreet Bank, Pamela J. (Pam) Taylor, age 67
EVP Chief Risk Officer and Chief Credit Officer HomeStreet Inc. and Homestreet Bank, Jay C. Iseman, age 59, $200,000 total compensation
SEVP Mortgage Lending Director, Rose Marie David, age 55, $200,000 total compensation
EVP Commercial Real Estate and Commercial Capital President HomeStreet Bank, William D. Endresen, age 64
EVP and Residential Construction Lending Director HomeStreet Bank, Jeff Todhunter
EVP Chief Investment Officer and Treasurer HomeStreet Inc. and HomeStreet Bank, Darrell S. van Amen, age 53
Vice President Commercial Lending Manager, George Brace
Vice President Loan Officer, Carmen Esteban
Auditors: DELOITTE & TOUCHE LLP

LOCATIONS

HQ: HomeStreet Inc
601 Union Street, Suite 2000, Seattle, WA 98101
Phone: 206 623-3050
Web: www.homestreet.com

PRODUCTS/OPERATIONS

2015 Sales

	$ mil.	% of total
Interest		
Loans	152.6	34
Investment securities available for sale	11.6	3
Other	0.9	-
Non-interest		
Net gains on mortgage origination & sales activities	236.4	53
Mortgage servicing	24.4	6
Depositor & other retail banking fees	5.9	1
Gain on sale of investment securities available for sale	2.4	1
Bargain purchase gain	7.7	2
Insurance agency commission Income from WMS Series LLC and other		4.4
Total	**446.3**	**100**

Selected Services
Personal Banking
Home LoansInvestmentInsurancePrivate Bank
Commercial Banking
Builder Financing/Residential ConstructionCommercial LendingCommercial Real EstatePartnership Programs

COMPETITORS

American Savings Bank	KeyCorp
Bank of America	Sound Financial
Bank of Hawaii	U.S. Bancorp
Banner Corp	Umpqua Holdings
First Hawaiian	Washington Federal
JPMorgan Chase	Wells Fargo

HISTORICAL FINANCIALS
Company Type: Public

Income Statement FYE: December 31

	ASSETS ($ mil.)	NET INCOME ($ mil.)	INCOME AS % OF ASSETS	EMPLOYEES
12/18	7,042.2	40.0	0.6%	2,036
12/17	6,742.0	68.9	1.0%	2,419
12/16	6,243.7	58.1	0.9%	2,552
12/15	4,894.5	41.3	0.8%	2,139
12/14	3,535.0	22.2	0.6%	1,611
Annual Growth	18.8%	15.8%	—	6.0%

2018 Year-End Financials
Return on assets: 0.5%
Return on equity: 5.5%
Long-term debt ($ mil.): —
No. of shares (mil.): 27.0
Sales ($ mil.): 507.6
Dividends
 Yield: —
 Payout: —
Market value ($ mil.): 573.0

	STOCK PRICE ($) FY Close	P/E High/Low		PER SHARE ($) Earnings	Dividends	Book Value
12/18	21.23	22	14	1.47	0.00	27.39
12/17	28.95	13	9	2.54	0.00	26.20
12/16	31.60	14	8	2.34	0.00	23.48
12/15	21.71	12	9	1.96	0.00	21.08
12/14	17.41	14	11	1.49	0.44	20.34
Annual Growth	5.1%	—	—	(0.3%)	—	7.7%

HomeTrust Bancshares Inc.

Auditors: Dixon Hughes Goodman LLP

LOCATIONS
HQ: HomeTrust Bancshares Inc.
10 Woodfin Street, Asheville, NC 28801
Phone: 828 259-3939
Web: www.hometrustbancshares.com

HISTORICAL FINANCIALS
Company Type: Public

Income Statement FYE: June 30

	ASSETS ($ mil.)	NET INCOME ($ mil.)	INCOME AS % OF ASSETS	EMPLOYEES
06/19	3,476.1	27.1	0.8%	582
06/18	3,304.1	8.2	0.2%	520
06/17	3,206.5	11.8	0.4%	486
06/16	2,717.6	11.4	0.4%	465
06/15	2,783.1	8.0	0.3%	505
Annual Growth	5.7%	35.6%	—	3.6%

2019 Year-End Financials
Return on assets: 0.8%
Return on equity: 6.6%
Long-term debt ($ mil.): —
No. of shares (mil.): 17.9
Sales ($ mil.): 160.1
Dividends
 Yield: 0.0%
 Payout: 12.3%
Market value ($ mil.): 452.0

	STOCK PRICE ($) FY Close	P/E High/Low		PER SHARE ($) Earnings	Dividends	Book Value
06/19	25.14	20	16	1.46	0.18	22.74
06/18	28.15	65	50	0.44	0.00	21.49
06/17	24.40	41	27	0.65	0.00	20.96
06/16	18.50	32	26	0.65	0.00	20.00
06/15	16.76	40	35	0.42	0.00	19.04
Annual Growth	10.7%	—	—	36.5%	—	4.5%

Hooker Furniture Corp

Hooker Furniture wants to sell you the pieces that will turn your house into a home. The company offers hardwood and metal furniture including wall units home office items home theater cabinets living and dining room tables bedroom furniture and accent pieces. Its youth furniture is sold under the Opus Designs by Hooker label. Hooker Furniture's popular Bradington-Young line of residential upholstered furniture features leather reclining chairs and sofas. The furniture manufacturer's Sam Moore unit makes high-end chairs. Hooker Furniture's products are sold through specialty shops (Star Furniture Nebraska Furniture Mart) and department stores (Dillard's). Hooker Furniture was founded in 1924.

Operations
Hooker's operating segments casegoods (wood and metal furniture) and upholstery account for roughly two-thirds and a third of sales respectively. The upholstery segment includes the company's leather seating business Bradington-Young and chair settee and sectionals maker Sam Moore furniture. It also houses Opus Designs Hooker's youth bedroom lines division.

The company imports all of its wood furniture primarily purchased from China Guatemala Honduras Indonesia the Philippines Mexico and Vietnam. The furniture is sent to market through the company's half-dozen distribution centers located in the US and China. Hooker also operates one furniture showroom in High Point North Carolina.

Geographic Reach
Virginia-based Hooker Furniture generates more than 95% of its sales domestically. The company employs about 800 people in Virginia and North Carolina. In addition to factories in Bedford Virginia and Hickory North Carolina the company imports wood and some leather furniture from factories in Asia (China Indonesia Vietnam) Mexico and Central America.

Financial Performance
After a rough patch during the Great Recession and housing crisis Hooker Furniture is showing signs of life. The company reported sales of $228.3 million in fiscal 2014 (ended January) an increase of nearly $10 million or 4.5% versus the prior year. The increase in sales was primarily due to higher average selling prices on both casegoods and upholstered furniture partially offset by higher discounting and returns and allowances in the casegoods business. Net income declined 8% year over year to $7.9 million due primarily to start-up costs for Hooker's two new businesses: H Contract which furnishes upscale senior living facilities; and Homeware a direct-to-consumer e-commerce operation. Despite the positive news that Hooker's sales have risen in three of the past four years the $228.3 million the company rang up in fiscal 2014 is well below Hooker's record high of $350 million achieved in 2006.

Cash flow from operations has been erratic — posting large swings — over the past four years. In fiscal 2014 (ended January) cash generated from operations totaled $5.7 million compared with negative cash flow of $3.3 million in fiscal 2013.

Strategy
Optimistic about the health of the broader economy (housing job growth and the stock market) growing consumer confidence and improving retail conditions Hooker is planning for growth by expanding its domestic upholstery capacity warehousing and distribution in both the US and Asia and capital spending on information systems. The company sees potential for its two new businesses — H Contract and Homeware — targeting Millennials and Baby Boomers seeking senior living options.

The new H Contract product line supplies upholstered seating and casegoods to upscale senior living facilities while the Homeware product line offers direct-to-consumer customer-assembled modular upholstered and casegoods products designed for younger and more mobile furniture customers (think IKEA).

Hooker Furniture continues to focus on expanding the number of brand names and product categories it offers furniture retailers. To cater to a younger more frugal customer the company makes Envision furniture. Its youth design category was expanded through its purchase of kids furniture manufacturer Opus Designs in a deal valued at more than $5 million and builds on its acquisition of upholstered seating firm Bradington-Young. From its purchase of La-Z-Boy's Sam Moore Furniture business Hooker Furniture offers customized chairs.

Mergers and Acquisitions
In February 2016 Hooker Furniture made its largest ever acquisition in buying Home Meridian International (HMI). The $100 million-acquisition more than doubled Hooker's sales volume making it one of the top five furniture suppliers in the US furniture market. The combined companies annual revenues would be in excess of $550 million.

EXECUTIVES
Chairman and CEO, Paul B. Toms, age 65, $370,000 total compensation
President Sam Moore, Frank Richardson
COO, George Revington, age 72
President Bradington-Young, Craig Young
SVP Finance and Accounting and CFO, Paul A. Huckfeldt, age 62, $214,500 total compensation
President, Michael W. Delgatti, age 65, $300,000 total compensation
CIO, Charlene Bowling
President Hooker Casegoods, Steve Lush
President Hooker Upholstery, Jeremy Hoff
Auditors: KPMG LLP

LOCATIONS
HQ: Hooker Furniture Corp
440 East Commonwealth Boulevard, Martinsville, VA 24112
Phone: 276 632-2133
Web: www.hookerfurniture.com

PRODUCTS/OPERATIONS

FY017 Sales by Segment

	% of total
Home Meridian	60
Hooker Casegoods	25
Upholstery	14
All other	1
Total	100

Selected Brands and Collections
Bradington-Young
H Contract
Homeware
Prime Resources
Pulaski Furniture
Right 2 Home
Sanctuary
Sam Moore
Samuel Lawrence Hospitality
Waverly Place

COMPETITORS

Ashley Furniture
Bassett Furniture
Broyhill
Bush Industries
DMI Furniture
Drexel Heritage
Ethan Allen
Heritage Home Group
Herman Miller
Klaussner Furniture
La-Z-Boy
Sauder Woodworking
Stanley Furniture
Vaughan-Bassett Furniture
Williams-Sonoma

HISTORICAL FINANCIALS
Company Type: Public

Income Statement — FYE: February 3

	REVENUE ($ mil.)	NET INCOME ($ mil.)	NET PROFIT MARGIN	EMPLOYEES
02/19*	683.5	39.8	5.8%	1,263
01/18	620.6	28.2	4.6%	1,216
01/17	577.2	25.2	4.4%	952
01/16	247.0	16.1	6.6%	645
02/15	244.3	12.5	5.1%	674
Annual Growth	29.3%	33.4%	—	17.0%

*Fiscal year change

2019 Year-End Financials
Debt ratio: 9.5%
Return on equity: 15.9%
Cash ($ mil.): 11.4
Current ratio: 3.65
Long-term debt ($ mil.): 29.6
No. of shares (mil.): 11.7
Dividends
  Yield: 0.0%
  Payout: 16.8%
Market value ($ mil.): 344.0

	STOCK PRICE ($) FY Close	P/E High/Low		PER SHARE ($) Earnings	Dividends	Book Value
02/19*	29.20	15	8	3.38	0.57	22.33
01/18	39.55	21	12	2.42	0.50	19.51
01/17	33.95	18	10	2.18	0.42	17.12
01/16	28.71	20	12	1.49	0.40	14.43
02/15	18.04	16	12	1.16	0.40	13.26
Annual Growth	12.8%	—	—	30.7%	9.3%	13.9%

*Fiscal year change

Hope Bancorp Inc

EXECUTIVES

Senior Executive Vice President Regional President Eastern Region, Kyu Kim
Vice President And Systems Support Manager, Joshua Chu
Senior Vice President and Chief Credit Officer, Peter Koh
Senior Vice President and Manager Loan Center III We Are Now Bank of Hope, Christie Yoo
Vice President Information Technology Procurement Manager, Karina Moran
Vice President and Business Development Officer Commercial Lending Center I, Brian Chung
Assistant Vice President and Loan Servicing Officer Northern California Commercial Lending Center Bank of Hope, Aekyung Park
Assistant Vice President and Loan Officer, Hyelim Choe
Executive Vice President Managing Director Of The Corporate Banking Group Of Bank Of Hope, Steven Canup
First Vice President And Portfolio Manager Commercial Lending Center I Bank Of Hope, Kay Kim
Senior Vice President 8c Branch Manager, Cindy Chi
Senior Vice President Vendor Risk Management, Bradley Martin
AAP Senior Vice President TMS Operations Manager, Rachel Lim
Vice President and Operational Risk Management Assistant, Katelyn Kang
Vice President International Operations, Lisa Lee
Vp and Loan Officer III, Chris Kim
Avp Loan Officer, Gina Choi
Fvp And Branch Manager, Sang Ahn
Senior Vice President And Sba Manager, Sylvester Kim
Senior Vice President Branch Manager, Eric Lee
Senior Vice President International Operations Manager, Linda Kim
First Vice President, Alex Cho
Senior Vice President and Marketing Manager Senior Business Analyst Loan Department, Gene Pak
Assistant Vice President And Service Officer II, Gloria Wang
Vice President and Sba Loan Officer, Ellie Park
Svp Head Of Business Solutions, Ajay Guntupalli
Managing Director Middle Market Lending, Mark Smith
Vice President Project Manager, David Son
Senior Vice President Chief Corporate Banking Officer, Alex Kim
Auditors: Crowe LLP

LOCATIONS
HQ: Hope Bancorp Inc
3200 Wilshire Boulevard, Suite 1400, Los Angeles, CA 90010
Phone: 213 639-1700   **Fax:** 213 235-3033
Web: www.bankofhope.com

PRODUCTS/OPERATIONS

2015 Sales

	$ mil.	% of total
Interest income	313.7	88
Non-interest income	43.7	12
Total	357.4	100

COMPETITORS
Bank of America
Broadway Financial
Cathay General Bancorp
East West Bancorp
Far East National Bank
Grandpoint
Hanmi Financial
U.S. Bancorp
Wells Fargo
Woori

HISTORICAL FINANCIALS
Company Type: Public

Income Statement — FYE: December 31

	ASSETS ($ mil.)	NET INCOME ($ mil.)	INCOME AS % OF ASSETS	EMPLOYEES
12/18	15,305.9	189.5	1.2%	1,494
12/17	14,206.7	139.4	1.0%	1,470
12/16	13,441.4	113.7	0.8%	1,372
12/15	7,912.6	92.2	1.2%	938
12/14	7,140.3	88.6	1.2%	915
Annual Growth	21.0%	20.9%	—	13.0%

2018 Year-End Financials
Return on assets: 1.2%
Return on equity: 9.9%
Long-term debt ($ mil.): —
No. of shares (mil.): 126.6
Sales ($ mil): 710.3
Dividends
  Yield: 4.5%
  Payout: 43.9%
Market value ($ mil.): 1,502.0

	STOCK PRICE ($) FY Close	P/E High/Low		PER SHARE ($) Earnings	Dividends	Book Value
12/18	11.86	13	8	1.44	0.54	15.03
12/17	18.25	22	15	1.03	0.50	14.23
12/16	21.89	20	13	1.10	0.45	13.72
12/15	17.22	17	11	1.16	0.42	11.79
12/14	14.38	16	12	1.11	0.35	11.10
Annual Growth	(4.7%)	—	—	6.7%	11.5%	7.9%

Horizon Bancorp Inc

For those in Indiana and Michigan Horizon Bancorp stretches as far as the eye can see. The company is the holding company for Horizon Bank (and its Heartland Community Bank division) which provides checking and savings accounts IRAs CDs and credit cards to customers through more than 50 branches in north and central Indiana and southwest and central Michigan. Commercial financial and agricultural loans make up the largest segment of its loan portfolio which also includes mortgage warehouse loans (loans earmarked for sale into the secondary market) consumer loans and residential mortgages. Through subsidiaries the bank offers trust and investment management services; life health and property/casualty insurance; and annuities.

Operations
Horizon boasted more than $2.08 billion in total assets and $1.48 billion in deposits in 2014. Commercial loans made up 49% of the bank's total loan portfolio. The bank employed nearly 450 full and part time employees that year.

Horizon's subsidiaries include: Horizon Investments which manages the bank's investment portfolio; Horizon Properties which manages the real estate investment trust; Horizon Insurance Services which sells through the company's Wealth Management; and Horizon Grantor Trust which holds title to certain company-owned life insurance policies.

The bank generated 61% of its revenue from interest income on loans in 2014 while another 13% came from interest on its taxable and tax-exempt investments. About 8% of revenues came from gains on its mortgage sales while the remainder of revenues were mostly generated by a mix of service charges on deposit accounts interchange fees and fiduciary activities fees.

Geographic Reach
The bank's more than 30 branches serve customers in north and central Indiana and southwest and central Michigan. Its mortgage-banking services are offered across the Midwest.

Financial Performance
Horizon Bancorp's revenues and profits have been trending higher over the past few years mostly as it's continued to grow its loan business and deposit customer base through acquisitions.

The bank's revenue rose by 2% to $102.5 million in 2014 mostly as the bank increased its interest-earning assets during the year. Its non-interest income also increased thanks to higher service charges on deposits and interchange fee income resulting from the growth in transactional deposit accounts and volume.

Despite higher revenue in 2014 the company's net income fell by 9% to $18.1 million for the year on higher provisions for loan losses due to loan growth and a write off of a commercial account coupled with an increase in transaction costs related to its Summit acquisition and an increase in salaries and employee benefits due to growth. Horizon's operating cash levels fell by 62% to $17.7 million after adjusting its earnings for non-cash items related to its net proceeds on the sale of its held-for-sale loans.

Strategy
Horizon Bancorp continues to expand its geographic reach and loan business through acquisitions and new branches. It acquired several banks and opened new branches throughout 2016 and 2017.

Mergers and Acquisitions
In 2017 Horizon Bancorp agreed to buy Wolverine Bancorp for $92 million and Lafayette Community Bancorp for $32 million

In 2016 Horizon Bancorp bought LaPorte Bancorp for $98.9 million boosting its total assets by 20% to more than $3.24 billion while expanding its branch reach into the LaPorte area of Indiana. It also agreed to buy CNB Bancorp which operates Central National Bank & Trust in Attica Indiana.

In 2015 Horizon Bancorp agreed to buy Peoples Bancorp and subsidiary Peoples Federal Savings Bank of DeKalb County.

In April 2014 the company purchased SCP Bancorp including subsidiary Summit Community Bank and its two branches.

EXECUTIVES

President CEO Chief Administrative Officer and Director; Chairman and CEO Horizon Bank, Craig M. Dwight, age 62, $300,000 total compensation
EVP; President and COO Horizon Bank, Thomas H. Edwards, age 66, $187,000 total compensation
CFO, Mark E. Secor, age 53, $131,921 total compensation
President LaPorte County Indiana Horizon Bank, Steven C. Kring
President Southwest Michigan Horizon Bank, Donald E. (Don) Radde, age 66, $166,000 total compensation
President Porter County Indiana Horizon Bank, David G. Rose
Executive Vice President and Senior Bank Operations Officer, Kathie A Deruiter

Svp and Sr Auditor and Chief Enterprise Risk Officer, Nancy Wrzalinski
Chairman, Robert C. Dabagia, age 80
Board Member, Larry Middleton
Board Member, Peter Pairitz
Board Member, Spero Valavanis
Board Member, Susan Aaron
Board Member, Lawrence Burnell
Board Member, James Dworkin
Board Member, Daniel Hopp
Board Member, Michele Magnuson
Board Member, Steven Reed
Board Member, Eric Blackhurst
Auditors: BKD, LLP

LOCATIONS

HQ: Horizon Bancorp Inc
515 Franklin Street, Michigan City, IN 46360
Phone: 219 879-0211
Web: www.horizonbank.com

PRODUCTS/OPERATIONS

Selected Subsidiaries
Horizon Bank National Association
  Horizon Insurance Services Inc.
  Horizon Investments Inc.
  Horizon Trust & Investment Management N.A.

COMPETITORS

1st Source Corporation	Farmers Mutual of NE
American United Mutual	Fifth Third
Bank of America	First Merchants
Brotherhood Mutual	Indiana Farmers Mutual

HISTORICAL FINANCIALS
Company Type: Public

Income Statement　　　　　　　　　　　FYE: December 31

	ASSETS ($ mil.)	NET INCOME ($ mil.)	INCOME AS % OF ASSETS	EMPLOYEES
12/18	4,246.6	53.1	1.3%	716
12/17	3,964.3	33.1	0.8%	701
12/16	3,141.1	23.9	0.8%	665
12/15	2,652.4	20.5	0.8%	558
12/14	2,076.9	18.1	0.9%	448
Annual Growth	19.6%	30.9%	—	12.4%

2018 Year-End Financials
Return on assets: 1.2%　　　Dividends
Return on equity: 11.1%　　　Yield: 2.4%
Long-term debt ($ mil.): —　　Payout: 31.1%
No. of shares (mil.): 38.3　　Market value ($ mil.): 606.0
Sales ($ mil): 200.5

	STOCK PRICE ($) FY Close	P/E High/Low	PER SHARE ($) Earnings	Dividends	Book Value
12/18	15.78	24 11	1.38	0.39	12.82
12/17	27.80	30 26	0.95	0.32	11.94
12/16	28.00	40 26	0.79	0.27	10.25
12/15	27.96	33 26	0.84	0.25	9.93
12/14	26.14	30 22	0.84	0.23	9.38
Annual Growth	(11.9%)	— —	13.1%	14.3%	8.1%

Houlihan Lokey Inc

Auditors: KPMG LLP

LOCATIONS

HQ: Houlihan Lokey Inc
10250 Constellation Blvd., 5th Floor, Los Angeles, CA 90067
Phone: 310 788-5200
Web: www.hl.com

HISTORICAL FINANCIALS
Company Type: Public

Income Statement　　　　　　　　　　　FYE: March 31

	REVENUE ($ mil.)	NET INCOME ($ mil.)	NET PROFIT MARGIN	EMPLOYEES
03/19	1,084.3	159.1	14.7%	1,354
03/18	963.3	172.2	17.9%	1,228
03/17	872.0	108.3	12.4%	1,171
03/16	693.7	69.7	10.1%	1,171
03/15	680.8	79.8	11.7%	981
Annual Growth	12.3%	18.8%	—	8.4%

2019 Year-End Financials
Debt ratio: 0.6%　　　　　No. of shares (mil.): 65.4
Return on equity: 18.2%　　Dividends
Cash ($ mil.): 411.0　　　　Yield: 0.0%
Current ratio: 1.12　　　　　Payout: 44.6%
Long-term debt ($ mil.): 8.6　Market value ($ mil.): 2,999.0

	STOCK PRICE ($) FY Close	P/E High/Low	PER SHARE ($) Earnings	Dividends	Book Value
03/19	45.85	21 14	2.42	1.08	13.63
03/18	44.60	19 12	2.60	0.80	12.96
03/17	34.45	19 12	1.63	0.71	11.01
03/16	24.90	22 18	1.10	0.30	9.97
Annual Growth	22.6%	— —	30.1%	53.3%	11.0%

Howard Hughes Corp

The Howard Hughes Corporation (THHC) is involved in neither planes movies or medical research but one of the 20th century entrepreneur's later interests real estate. The company arose from the bankruptcy restructuring of shopping mall developer General Growth Properties (GGP) to oversee much of GGP's non-retail assets. THHC owns GGP's former portfolio of four master planned communities outside Columbia Maryland; Houston Texas; and Summerlin Nevada; as well as about two dozen other as-yet undeveloped sites and commercial properties in 16 states from New York to Hawaii including GGP's own headquarters building in downtown Chicago. Unlike GGP THHC does not operate as a REIT.

Operations
THHC owns manages and develops commercial residential and mixed-use real estate throughout the US. It organizes its business into three segments: master planned communities; operating assets; and strategic developments. THHC's holdings include eight mixed-use and retail properties nine office properties an apartment building a resort

and conference center a 36-hole golf course and country club three equity investments and four other revenue-generating assets.

The firm's 22500-acre flagship property outside Las Vegas Summerlin is home to about 100000 people and has another 7000 acres for sale and redevelopment. Its other three communities in Texas and Maryland have a combined 7000 acres for sale and redevelopment. Beyond that other holdings include nine mixed-use development projects four mall developments and seven distressed mall properties slated for redevelopment.

Geographic Reach
Dallas-based THHC has offices at select properties and in New York City and Los Angeles. The firm operates master planned communities in Houston and The Woodlands Texas; Howard and Price George's counties in Maryland; and in Las Vegas.

Financial Performance
THHC has logged substantial revenue growth in recent years. Indeed in 2013 the firm reported $474.6 million in revenue a 26% increase versus 2012. Driving the double-digit gain was growth in master planned communities due to higher demand for its residential superpad sites in Summerlin (Las Vegas) and finished lots in The Woodlands and $33 million in revenue generated from the sale of condominium rights in Hawaii to a 50:50 joint venture. Despite the revenue gain THHC posted a loss of nearly $73.8 million in 2013 versus a deeper loss in 2012. Indeed the firm has posted losses in four of the last five years.

Strategy
After taking a pounding at the hands of Superstorm Sandy in 2013 which resulted in damage and lost revenue THHC is doubling down on its investment in the South Street Seaport District in lower Manhattan with the proposed acquisition of 80 South Street. The firm is rebuilding pier 17 and is working with the community on a proposal for a mixed-use project that increased a hotel and residential units a new marina restoration of the Tin Building an extension of the East River Esplanade a food market and a plan to ensure the long-term future of the financially troubled Seaport Museum. Its plans for a 50-story hotel/condo tower on the site of the former historic Fulton Fish Market is meeting resistance from the community.

Mergers and Acquisitions
In 2011 THHC acquired the remainder of The Woodlands master planned community in Houston that it already didn't own from Morgan Stanley Real Estate Investing. The $117.5 million deal gave the company complete control over the The Woodlands brand. In addition to its residential properties Howard Hughes plans to focus on developing commercial properties within The Woodlands.

Company Background
The Summerlin name is also the company's tie to Howard Hughes. In the 1950s Mr. Hughes bought 25000 acres outside Las Vegas and named it Summerlin his maternal grandmother's maiden name. Three years before he died in 1973 Mr. Hughes created Summa Corporation which became Summerlin's new owner. Hughes' heirs sold Summa to The Rouse Company in 1996 for about $500 million. GGP bought The Rouse Company in 2004. During the bankruptcy GGP paid Hughes' heirs $230 million to settle Summerlin and in return named the new company after him.

EXECUTIVES
Senior Vice President Development, Mark Bulmash
Senior Vice President Development, Adam Meister
Vice President Asset Management, Ken Bendalin
Vice President Of Specialty Leasing, Joyce Roberts
Senior Vice President Development, John Dewolf
Vice President Finance, Robert Carroll
Vice President Strategic Partnerships, Peter Helfer
Vice President Innovation, Michael Caplovitz
Managing Director Events and Entertainment, Alan Kashian
Senior Vice President, Randy Kostroske
Vice President Tenant Coordination Design, Boun Somphanh
Vice President Capital Markets, Andrew Davis
Vice President Design And Construction Management, William Rowe
Vice President Of Marketing, Bill Weeshoff
Vice President, Karen Cherry
Vice President Of Hospitality, Scott Spann
Assistant Treasurer, Robert McDonald
Auditors: Ernst & Young LLP

LOCATIONS
HQ: Howard Hughes Corp
13355 Noel Road, 22nd Floor, Dallas, TX 75240
Phone: 214 741-7744   **Fax:** 214 741-3021
Web: www.howardhughes.com

PRODUCTS/OPERATIONS

Selected Propeties
American City Building (office building in Columbia MD)
Bridgeland (master-planned community in Houston)
Century Plaza (future development in Birmingham AL)
Columbia (master-planned community in Maryland)
Kendall Town Center (future mixed-use development near Miami FL)
Landmark Mall (mall in Alexandria VA)
Ridgley Building (office building in Columbia MD)
Riverwalk Marketplace (mall in New Orleans LA)
South Street Seaport (retail site in Manhattan NY)
Summerlin (master-planned community near Las Vegas)
The Woodlands (master-planned community in Houston)

COMPETITORS
Bresler & Reiner
CBL & Associates Properties
Deltona
Hillwood
Hines
Macerich
Newhall Land Related
Taubman Centers
Washington Real Estate
Weingarten Realty

HISTORICAL FINANCIALS
Company Type: Public

Income Statement — FYE: December 31

	REVENUE ($ mil.)	NET INCOME ($ mil.)	NET PROFIT MARGIN	EMPLOYEES
12/18	1,064.5	57.0	5.4%	1,400
12/17	1,100.1	168.4	15.3%	1,100
12/16	1,035.0	202.3	19.5%	1,100
12/15	797.0	126.7	15.9%	1,000
12/14	634.5	(23.5)	—	1,100
Annual Growth	13.8%	—	—	6.2%

2018 Year-End Financials
Debt ratio: 43.2%
Return on equity: 1.8%
Cash ($ mil.): 499.6
Current ratio: 1.03
Long-term debt ($ mil.): 3,181.2
No. of shares (mil.): 42.9
Dividends
  Yield: —
  Payout: —
Market value ($ mil.): 4,197.0

	STOCK PRICE ($) FY Close	P/E High/Low	Earnings	Dividends	Book Value
12/18	97.62	108 68	1.32	0.00	72.86
12/17	131.27	32 26	3.91	0.00	73.56
12/16	114.10	24 16	4.73	0.00	64.53
12/15	113.16	50 34	1.60	0.00	59.43
12/14	130.42	— —	(0.60)	0.00	56.10
Annual Growth	(7.0%)	— —	—	—	6.8%

Hudson Pacific Properties Inc

Hudson Pacific Properties wants to be the landlord to the stars. One of Hollywood's biggest landlords the real estate investment trust (REIT) buys and manages primarily office buildings but also and media and entertainment properties in California and the Pacific Northwest in cities such as Los Angeles Orange County San Diego San Francisco and Seattle. It owns more than 55 properties totaling some 15 million sq. ft. including two production studios on Hollywood's Sunset Boulevard. Its largest tenants range from tech giants such as Google Cisco Systems Uber to Hollywood producers including Warner Bros. Entertainment and Warner Music Group.

Operations
Hudson Pacific's portfolio consisted of 54 office properties spanning 14 million square feet and two Hollywood-based media and entertainment properties (the Sunset Gower property and Sunset Bronson property) with 0.9 million sq. ft. of space at the end of 2015.

Rental income from its office properties made up 93% of its total revenue that year while the media and entertainment properties accounted for the remainder.

Geographic Reach
The Los Angeles-based REIT's properties are mostly in Northern and Southern California and the Pacific Northwest (mainly in Seattle). Its target markets include Los Angeles Orange County San Diego San Francisco Seattle Silicon Valley the East Bay and the Pacific Northwest.

Sales and Marketing
The REIT's largest tenants during 2015 were Google Inc. and Weil Gotshal & Manges LLP which together made up 8% of its annualized base rent. Other major tenants included Riot Games Cisco Systems Uber Technologies Square Salesforce Warner Bros. Entertainment Warner Music Group. and EMC Corp.

Financial Performance
Hudson Pacific's annual revenues have more than quadrupled since 2011 thanks to rent-boosting property acquisitions and as rental rates have risen with increased demand for office properties in its target markets.

The REIT's revenue more than doubled to $520.8 million during 2015 on added rental income mostly stemming from its April 2015 acquisition of office properties from Blackstone which doubled the size of its portfolio. Same-store office property revenues rose 4.5% as the REIT signed new leases for Uber and Square at its 1455 Market property and a new lease for Sales Force at its Rincon Center property. Same-store media and entertainment property revenue dipped 1% as the REIT had to take certain buildings and stages offline to allow developers to work on its Sunset Bronson property.

Despite exceptional revenue growth and stable operating income in 2015 Hudson Pacific suffered a $16.08 million loss for the year due to a combination of interest expenses on long-term debt and acquisition-related expenses. The REIT's operating cash nearly tripled to $174.86 million during 2015 as it generated more in cash-based rental income.

Strategy
Hudson Pacific continued in 2016 to focus on acquiring office and media and entertainment properties situated in high barrier-to-entry submarkets in North and South California and in the Pacific Northwest. It also searches out distressed commercial properties in densely populated urban areas in these top markets where property is always in high demand.

In one of its most significant property acquisitions to date Hudson in April 2015 doubled its property holdings and reached further into the hot Silicon Valley real estate market through its $3.5 billion cash and stock purchase of 26 Bay Area office properties spanning 8.2 million sq. ft. from Blackstone Group. In mid-2015 the REIT also purchased the three-story 121000 sq.ft. "4th and Traction" manufacturing facility in Los Angeles's for $49 million; and a three-building 83200-sq. ft. redevelopment project in downtown Los Angeles' Arts District for $40 million.

Hudson also continues to expand in the fast-growing Seattle market. In February 2014 the REIT acquired an office building in Santa Monica California for $18.5 million and an office and retail property in downtown Seattle for $57.7 million. In July 2013 the company bought an 848001 square-foot office portfolio in Seattle from Spear Street Capital for approximately $368.4 million. The purchase included a two-building waterfront property in downtown Seattle occupied by tenants including Capital One and EMC Corp. and an office building occupied by Internet giant Amazon.com under a 10-year lease that commenced in late 2013.

Company Background
Hudson Pacific went public in June 2010 with an initial public offering worth $217.6 million. The firm used the proceeds from its IPO to pay off mortgage-related debt and acquire new properties.

Hudson Pacific Properties was founded by CEO Victor J. Coleman and President Howard S. Stern two former executives at another Los Angeles-based REIT Arden Realty. Arden Realty was sold to GE Real Estate in 2006.

EXECUTIVES

Chairman President and CEO, Victor J. Coleman, age 58, $600,000 total compensation
COO CFO and Treasurer, Mark T. Lammas, age 53, $450,000 total compensation
EVP Operations and Development, Christopher J. Barton, age 54, $375,000 total compensation
EVP Finance, Dale Shimoda, age 51, $300,000 total compensation
Chief Investment Officer, Alexander (Alex) Vouvalides, age 40, $310,000 total compensation
EVP General Counsel and Secretary, Kay L. Tidwell
SVP Northern California, Drew B. Gordon
SVP Southern California, Gary Hansel
SVP Pacific Northwest, David Tye
Vice President of Engineering, Jim Soutter
Vice President Head Of Investor Relations, Laura Campbell
Executive Vice President Operations, Josh Hatfield
Svp Leasing, Derric Dubourdieu
Vice President Portfolio Management, Anne Mehrtens
Vice President of IT, Jeff Ballard
Executive Vice President, Art Suazo
Sr V Pres, Andy Wattula
VICE PRESIDENT LEASING, Jeffrey Lasky
Board Member, Richard Fried
Treasurer, Latoya Ross
Auditors: Ernst & Young LLP

LOCATIONS

HQ: Hudson Pacific Properties Inc
11601 Wilshire Blvd., Ninth Floor, Los Angeles, CA 90025
Phone: 310 445-5700

PRODUCTS/OPERATIONS

2015 sales

	% of total
Non-Same-Store	57
Same-Store	43
Total	100

HUDSON PACIFIC MEDIA SERVICES
Catering
Control Room Rentals
Entertainment & Sports VIP Client Service
HD Camera Rentals
Lighting & Grip Rentals
Office / Facility Management
Production Office Space Rentals
Real Estate Professional Services
Recording Studio Rentals
Sound Stage Rentals

2015 Sales

	% of total
Office	
Rental	76
Tenant recoveries	13
Parking and other	4
Media & entertainment	
Rental	4
Tenant recoveries	0
Other property-related revenue	3
Others	0
Total	100

COMPETITORS

Douglas Emmett
EVOQ Properties
Irvine Company
J. H. Snyder
Kilroy Realty
Majestic Realty
Meredith Enterprises
Newhall Land
Pacific Office Properties Trust
Watson Land Co.

HISTORICAL FINANCIALS
Company Type: Public

Income Statement — FYE: December 31

	REVENUE ($ mil.)	NET INCOME ($ mil.)	NET PROFIT MARGIN	EMPLOYEES
12/18	728.4	98.7	13.6%	311
12/17	728.1	68.5	9.4%	293
12/16	639.6	27.9	4.4%	257
12/15	520.8	(16.4)	—	234
12/14	253.4	9.9	3.9%	151
Annual Growth	30.2%	77.5%	—	19.8%

2018 Year-End Financials

Debt ratio: 40.0%
Return on equity: 2.7%
Cash ($ mil.): 68.1
Current ratio: 0.78
Long-term debt ($ mil.): 2,828.1
No. of shares (mil.): 154.3
Dividends
  Yield: 3.4%
  Payout: 158.7%
Market value ($ mil.): 4,486.0

	STOCK PRICE ($) FY Close	P/E High/Low		PER SHARE ($)		
				Earnings	Dividends	Book Value
12/18	29.06	57	44	0.63	1.00	23.75
12/17	34.25	83	72	0.44	1.00	23.44
12/16	34.78	136	88	0.25	0.80	22.81
12/15	28.14	—	—	(0.19)	0.58	18.80
12/14	30.06	202	143	0.15	0.50	17.81
Annual Growth	(0.8%)	—	—	43.2%	18.9%	7.5%

IBERIABANK Corp

Holding company IBERIABANK Corporation through its flagship bank subsidiary IBERIABANK operates some 230 branches in Louisiana and about 10 other states. It also has about 30 title insurance offices in Louisiana Arkansas and Tennessee in addition to some 90 mortgage loan offices in a dozen states and about 20 wealth management offices in four states. Offering deposit products such as checking and savings accounts CDs and IRAs the bank uses funds gathered mainly to make loans. Commercial loans and leases make up around two-thirds of the company's $22.3 billion loan portfolio which also includes consumer loans and residential mortgages. IBERIABANK Corp. has $30.1 billion in assets.

Operations
IBERIABANK operates through its IBERIABANK mortgage and LTC segments.

The IBERIABANK segment — which includes commercial and retail banking wealth management capital markets and other corporate functions — accounts for about 90% of revenue. Net interest income comprises about 85% of the segment's revenue. Commercial loans provide about 70% of the holding company's loan interest income; consumer and other loans generate about 20% of its loan interest income.

The mortgage segment accounts for nearly 10% of revenue. Through that business IBERIABANK originates funds and sells one-to-four family residential mortgages. Such loans accounts for about 10% of the company's loan interest income.

IBERIABANK offers title insurance and loan closing services through its LTC segment.

Geographic Reach

IBERIABANK operates about 330 combined offices including around 230 bank branch offices and two loan production offices in Louisiana Arkansas Tennessee Alabama Texas Florida Georgia South Carolina New York and North Carolina; about 30 title insurance offices in Arkansas Tennessee and Louisiana; and mortgage representatives at some 90 locations in 12 US states.

Some 40% 20% and 10% of the company's loans are in Florida Louisiana and Texas respectively.

Financial Performance

IBERIABANK has seen strong revenue and net income growth from 2013 to 2017 adding 82% and 119% respectively. Cash stores increased 60% to $625.7 million while long-term debt ballooned by 433% to $1.5 billion.

The holding company's revenue trended up 15% to $1 billion in 2017 compared with 2016 thanks to increased interest and fees from loans caused by improvements in loan yields and average earning assets. The growth was offset slightly by a decline in non-interest income primarily from the residential mortgage business.

Net income however fell 24% to $142.4 million in that time owing to non-interest expenses related to IBERIABANK's acquisition of southeastern Florida bank chain Sabadell United Bank and a $51 million increase in income tax expense caused by the 2017 Tax Cuts and Jobs Act.

The bank's cash stores were depleted by $736.4 million in 2017. Operations added $263.6 million and investments used $1.9 billion including $490.4 million for acquisitions. Financings added another $908.5 million from proceeds from long-term debt and common stock issuances.

Strategy

IBERIABANK announced its 2020 strategic goals in April 2018 which include improving operating efficiency using a “branch-lite” approach that involves digitalization of client services and back-office processes. Since 2012 the company has increased the proportion of its alternative transactions — including via online digital and smart device delivery systems — by 10 percentage points. The bank opened 28 offices and closed 11 branches in 2017 and scheduled more than 20 branch closures or consolidations for 2018.

In 2018 IBERIABANK also launched a mobile banking app introduced robotic process automation back offices created a mortgage self-fulfillment application and announced plans to update its internet banking website.

IBERIABANK is working to increase its presence in Miami Florida which holds $226 billion in total market deposits. IBERIABANK acquired Southeast Florida-based Sabadell United Bank in July 2017. The deal gave IBERIABANK 25 offices serving the Miami metropolitan area and three offices in Naples Sarasota and Tampa. In March 2018 the bank acquired Gibraltar Private Bank & Trust another Florida bank with seven offices in the Miami Key West and Naples metropolitan areas and one in New York City.

The bank owns around 90 branches in Florida with about $9 billion total deposits. The company has significantly increased its presence in Florida; since 2014 it has grown the share of its portfolio comprising loans and deposits in that state by 13 and 22 percentage points respectively. Other growth markets for the company include Dallas and Houston as well as Atlanta Orlando and Tampa.

Mergers and Acquisitions

Since 2008 IBERIABANK has made more than 20 acquisitions of live and failing banks branches and wealth management and title insurance companies.

IBERIABANK acquired Gibraltar Private Bank & Trust another Florida bank in March 2018 for about $214.7 million. Gibraltar had seven offices in the Miami Key West and Naples metropolitan areas and one in New York City prior to the acquisition. The agreement conferred $1.5 billion in loans and $1.1 billion in deposits to IBERIABANK's portfolio.

The bank acquired SolomonParks Title & Escrow in January 2018 for $3.3 million thereby gaining eight title offices in the Nashville Tennessee area.

In July 2017 IBERIABANK acquired Southeast Florida-based Sabadell United Bank for $809.2 million in cash and 2.6 million IBERIABANK shares. The deal gave IBERIABANK $4 billion in loans and $4.4 billion in deposits as well as 25 offices serving the Miami metropolitan area and three offices in Naples Sarasota and Tampa.

Company Background

IBERIABANK was founded in 1887 in New Iberia Louisiana. It operated in just two states - Louisiana and Arkansas - until 2008 when it began spreading across the Southeast.

EXECUTIVES

President and CEO, Daryl G. Byrd, age 64, $1,015,000 total compensation
SEVP Mergers and Acquisitions Finance and Investor Relations; Director Financial Strategy and Mortgage, John R. Davis, age 58, $456,154 total compensation
Vice Chairman and Managing Director of Brokerage Trust and Wealth Management, Jefferson G. (Jeff) Parker, age 66, $480,192 total compensation
SEVP and Director Communications Facilities and Human Resources, Elizabeth A. (Beth) Ardoin, age 50
SEVP and CFO, Anthony J. Restel, age 49, $480,385 total compensation
Vice Chairman; SEVP and COO, Michael J. (Mike) Brown, age 55, $598,269 total compensation
President and CEO IberiaBank Mortgage, Bill Edwards
EVP and Director Retail Small Business and Mortgage, Robert M. (Bob) Kottler, age 60
EVP and Executive Credit Officer, H. Spurgeon Mackie, age 68
EVP and Chief Risk Officer, J. Randolph Bryan, age 51
EVP Corporate Secretary and General Counsel, Robert B. Worley, age 59
President and CEO Lender's Title Company, David B. Erb
Senior Vice President Training Manager, Tracey Hirsch
Assistant Vice President Retail Support Specialist, Sheila Montgomery
Vice President and Business Banking Relationship Manager, Daniel Maurin
Senior Vice President Director of Compliance BSA Officer, Donna Davidek
Senior Vice President, Steve Krueger
Assistant Vice President, Dolores Hernandez
Vice President, Tom Chelewski
Vice President Bcs Ore Officer, Neel Stacy
Vice President Support Services, Jerry Prejean
Vice President, Debbie Pasierb
Vice President Commercial Lending, Jeremy Young
Vice President, Mary Rice
Senior Vice President Network Support Manager, Chris Berthaut
Senior Vice President Retail Market Manager, Trich Worthington
Senior Vice President Retail Market Manager, Donnie Dobbins
Senior Vice President, Greg Mendez
Senior Vice President, William Albanese
Exec Vice President, Cleland Powell
Senior Vice President, Eric Movassaghi
Vice President ORE Property Manager, Brian Buczko
Senior Vice President Corporate Banking, C Mizelle
Vice President, Michael Hallmark
Vice President, Mark Pharr
Vice President, Carrie Curet
Senior Vice President Director Of Corporate Compensati, Andrew Wilson
Vice President Branch Manager Business Development Officer, Pedro Diaz
Vice President Business Credit Services Officer, Michael Schaefer
Vice President Public Relations Director, Judi Lejeune
Vice President Of Services, Timothy Wilson
Vice President Infrastructure Engineering, Kevin Plaisance
Senior Vice President Treasury Management Sales, Ted Graphos
Assistant Vice President, Patti Oufnac
Vice President, Howard Mary
Vice President Branch Manager, Cindy Winter
Vice President Senior Loan Review Officer, Geoffrey Houlditch
Svp Private Banking and Retail Market Manager, Ginger Harper
Senior Vice President Commercial Banking, Holly Popham
Vice President Human Resources And Employee Development And Training, Mike Pelletier
Vice President Controller, Angela Robert
Assistant Vice President Branch Manager, Melissa Krackenberger
Vice President Business Banking Relationship Manager, Jason Kern
Vice President Business Credit Services, David Krage
Assistant Vice President Marketing, Jessica Porter
Vice President, Keith Dameron
Vice President, Paul Cotoni
Senior Executive Vice President and Director of Communications Facilities and Human Resources, Beth Ardoin
Senior Vice President, Richard Perdue
Vice President Commercial Lending, Jamie Vaught
Vice President Business Banking, Eugene Castrejon
Assistant Vice President Commercial Portfolio Manager, Jennifer Bordelon
Executive Vice President, Norman Vascocu
Vice President Commercial Banking, William Biossat
Vice President, Sean Friend
Assistant Vice President, Cathleen Caldwell
Senior Vice President And Business And Retail Market Manger, Maurice Butler
Vice President, Kimberly Williams
Executive Vice President, Mark Tipton
Vice President Branch Manager, Samantha McDermott
Vice President Mortgage Executive, Mark Young

Evp Director Treasury Management Services, Donna Kasmiersky
Assistant Vice President, Felesha Finch
Assistant Vice President Treasury Management Sales Officer, Ansley Oliver Cooper
Vice President Corporate Accounting, Robert Robertson
Vice President Central Retail Administration, Donna Pye
Vice President of Asset Based Lending, Michael Jennings
Vice President, Blake Norris
Vice President Commercial Banking, Luke Spaulding
Vice President, ToniRae Hurley
Assistant Vice President Branch Manager, Adam Golden
Vice President, Linda Rodriguez
Vice President Private Banking Relationship Manager, Carrie Standlee
Vice President Business Banking, Tim Finn
Vice President, Cody Walker
Senior Vice President, Kevin Hagan
Vice President, Matthew Rink
Vice President Deposit Operations, Felicia Weeks
Vice President Quality Control, Cheryl Terry
Senior Vice President Relationship Manager Energy Banking, Tyler Thoem
Assistant Vice President Branch Manager, Kirstin Wicker
Senior Vice President Commercial Relationship Manager Assistant Rebecca Oberg, Kelly Gegerson
Vice President, Karen Hardy
Vice President Manager Commercial Cash Vault, Anna Taylor
Business Intelligence Analyst Assistant Vice President, Kevin Cagle
Senior Vice President Manager, Jill Merkt
Assistant Vice President Business Banking Relationship Manager, Deborah Sefcik
Vice President Construction Lending Manager, Lisa Bott
Vice President Commercial Lending, Jesse Erickson
Assistant Vice President Retail Support Specialist, Heather Wade
Assistant Vice President, Christie Bell
Asst. Vice President Branch Manager, Tamela Leger
Vice President Retail Support Lead Florida, Sherri Kinsey
Vp Treasury Management Operations Manager, Kevin Northcutt
Assistant Vice President, Erica Murphy
Vice President Private Banking, Casey Lawhead
Vice President Business Analyst III, Ron Zimmerman
Vice President Retail Support Lead, Terri Bridges
Executive Vice President and Commercial Group Manager, John Reingardt
Senior Vice President Compliance Manager Central Florida CRA Liaison, Susan DeFreese
Vice President, Kim Leech
Vice President Treasury Management Implementations Manager, Megan Alesci
Senior Vice President Commercial Banking Relationship Manager, Amanda Smith
Assistant Vice President Construction, Carmalynn May
Vice President Consumer Lending Manager, Todd Ezell
Vice President Commercial Relationship Manager, Tanner Livingston
Senior Vice President, Bob Burnside
Vice President Manager, Bill Roche

Vice President Senior Business Analyst Development Officer, Martin Chapman
Assistant Vice President Branch Manager, Heather Ross
Assistant Vice President Lending Services Supervisor, Heidi Tyra
Vice President Private Banking Relationship Manager, Jennifer Esler
Vice President Commercial Relationship Manager, Karen Shawdee
Vice President, Bob Ferguson
Vice President Relationship Manager, Amy Moore
Senior Vice President Commercial Manager Collin County, Shannon Bettis
Executive Vice President Dallas Region, Tony Kruse
Vice President Commercial Relationship Manager, Madalyn Allen
Senior Vice President Audit Manager, Emily Sebourn
Vice President Corporate Strategy, Oliver Greening
Assistant Vice President Branch Manager, Carolanne Parks
Vice President Director Boca And Delray Branches, Shane Sweet
Vice President Senior Underwriter, Daniel Scheuermann
Vice President Real Estate Appraisal Analyst, Matthew Reid
Vice President Senior Relationship Manager, Mitch Wilson
Vice President Private Mortgage Banker, Matthew Westervelt
Vice President Private Banking Relationship Manager, Peter Mihopoulos
Senior Vice President Corporate Banking, Brian Hanley
Vp Mortgage Branch Manager, Donna Frost
Vice President Marketing, Laura Sillars
Vice President, Sheila Cooley
Vice President, Don Lucas
Assistant Vice President Mortgage Loan Officer, Ginger Holton
Chairman, William H. Fenstermaker, age 70
Vice Chairman, E. Stewart Shea, age 67
Board Member, Angus Cooper
Auditors: Ernst & Young LLP

LOCATIONS

HQ: IBERIABANK Corp
200 West Congress Street, Lafayette, LA 70501
Phone: 337 521-4003
Web: www.iberiabank.com

COMPETITORS

BancorpSouth
Bank of America
Bank of the Ozarks
Capital One
Hancock Holding
Home Banc
Investar
JPMorgan Chase
Louisiana Bancorp
MidSouth Bancorp
Regions Financial
Teche Holding

HISTORICAL FINANCIALS
Company Type: Public

Income Statement				FYE: December 31
	ASSETS ($ mil.)	NET INCOME ($ mil.)	INCOME AS % OF ASSETS	EMPLOYEES
12/18	30,833.0	370.2	1.2%	3,441
12/17	27,904.1	142.4	0.5%	3,604
12/16	21,659.1	186.7	0.9%	3,155
12/15	19,504.0	142.8	0.7%	3,216
12/14	15,758.6	105.4	0.7%	2,825
Annual Growth	18.3%	36.9%	—	5.1%

2018 Year-End Financials

Return on assets: 1.2%
Return on equity: 9.5%
Long-term debt ($ mil.): —
No. of shares (mil.): 54.8
Sales ($ mil): 1,374.1
Dividends
Yield: 2.4%
Payout: 36.5%
Market value ($ mil.): 3,522.0

	STOCK PRICE ($) FY Close	P/E High/Low		PER SHARE ($) Earnings	Dividends	Book Value
12/18	64.28	13	9	6.46	1.56	74.02
12/17	77.50	33	27	2.59	1.46	68.62
12/16	83.75	21	10	4.30	1.40	65.62
12/15	55.07	19	15	3.68	1.36	60.74
12/14	64.85	22	18	3.30	1.36	55.39
Annual Growth	(0.2%)	—	—	18.3%	3.5%	7.5%

Ichor Holdings Ltd

Auditors: KPMG LLP

LOCATIONS

HQ: Ichor Holdings Ltd
3185 Laurelview Court, Fremont, CA 94538
Phone: 510 897-5200
Web: www.ichorsystems.com

HISTORICAL FINANCIALS
Company Type: Public

Income Statement				FYE: December 28
	REVENUE ($ mil.)	NET INCOME ($ mil.)	NET PROFIT MARGIN	EMPLOYEES
12/18	823.6	57.8	7.0%	1,490
12/17	655.8	56.4	8.6%	1,760
12/16	405.7	16.6	4.1%	787
12/15	290.6	5.6	1.9%	671
12/14	249.0	6.1	2.5%	0
Annual Growth	34.8%	75.0%	—	—

2018 Year-End Financials

Debt ratio: 41.3%
Return on equity: 27.9%
Cash ($ mil.): 43.8
Current ratio: 2.41
Long-term debt ($ mil.): 192.1
No. of shares (mil.): 22.2
Dividends
Yield: —
Payout: —
Market value ($ mil.): —

ICU Medical Inc

ICU Medical sees the future of infection prevention. The company's devices protect health care workers and patients from the spread of diseases such as HIV and hepatitis. Its primary products are intravenous (IV) connection devices called Clave needleless connectors that reduce the risk of needle sticks and disconnections. The firm also makes custom IV sets many of which use Clave connectors and other ICU products for third parties. Additionally ICU Medical makes critical care equipment such as angiography kits and heart monitors. ICU Medical sells its products to other equipment makers and distributors throughout the US and internationally.

Operations
ICU Medical develops makes and sells innovative medical devices used in vascular therapy oncology and critical care applications. Its products improve patient outcomes by helping prevent bloodstream infections and protecting health care workers from exposure to infectious diseases or hazardous drugs. The company's products include custom IV systems closed delivery systems for hazardous drugs needlefree IV connectors catheters and cardiac monitoring systems. About 70% of total revenue comes from infusion therapy services while critical care accounts about 20%; the remainder comes from oncology and other services.

Geographic Reach
The company sells its products to more than 60 countries in Europe the Middle East Africa the Asia/Pacific region Latin America and North America. Its administrative office are in San Clemente California; Vrable Slovakia; Roncanova Italy; Utrecht Netherlands; Bella Vista Australia; and Ludenscheid Germany. Customers in Europe are served by facilities in Slovakia and Germany. Customers elsewhere are served from facilities in the US and Mexico. ICU Medical operates a plant in Mexico with about 1350 workers in Ensenada; it has another plant in Vrable Slovakia (with about 240 employees). The company also maintains a plant in Salt Lake City Utah.

The US accounted for about 70% of total revenue in 2014.

Sales and Marketing
On the sales side the company is increasingly directing its marketing efforts toward securing long-term contracts with large buying organizations. ICU Medical is reacting to an increasingly consolidated health care provider marketplace because the providers have more buying power as they get larger. Long-term contracts help the company lock in prices even as the market changes around them.

Medical device maker Hospira is ICU Medical's biggest customer - it accounts for around 35% of revenue annually.

The company also sells to independent distributors and to end users through a direct sales force.

In 2014 advertising expenses totaled $0.1 million down from $0.3 million in 2013 and $0.2 million in 2012.

Financial Performance
After several years of increasing revenue in 2013 ICU Medical reported a 10% decrease from $316.9 million to $313.7 million due to lower infusion therapy sales to key American customer Hospira. Revenue fell a marginal 1% to $309 million in 2014 for the same reason. Higher international and critical care revenue helped offset the decline.

Net income has been falling the last few years and 2014 delivered a 35% drop to $26 million on lower sales and higher operating expenses (including R&D and restructuring costs). Cash flow from operations has also been on a slow decline: In 2014 it fell 8% to $61 million due to the decrease in net income and a change in inventories.

Strategy
ICU Medical has a long-standing relationship with Hospira. Way back in 2005 ICU Medical purchased Hospira's Salt Lake City manufacturing plant which produces catheters angiography kits and cardiac monitors among other devices. At that time the two companies entered a 20-year agreement under which ICU Medical will manufacture the products and Hospira will purchase them. Then in 2009 ICU Medical purchased the commercial rights and physical assets from Hospira's critical care product line giving ICU Medical complete control of manufacturing and marketing rights of the critical care line.

Through yet another agreement with Hospira ICU Medical makes and co-promotes custom IV systems under the name SetSource. That agreement is set to last through 2018. All told sales to Hospira account for about 35% of ICU Medical's yearly income.

Aside from bringing home the bacon ICU Medical's dealings with Hospira provide ICU Medical access to the IV set market in the US in which Hospira has a significant share. The company expects Hospira will be important to growing its CLAVE line custom infusion sets and its other products worldwide.

Outside of its dealings with Hospira ICU Medical's growth strategy hinges upon its ability to continue to develop and introduce new products to its customers particularly in the face of upcoming patent expirations on some of its products. Much like pharmaceutical companies medical device manufacturers enjoy a certain amount of market exclusivity on their patented products but once those patents expire competitors are free to introduce their own versions of the devices.

ICU Medical is preparing for patent expirations by diversifying its product line internally developing products and systems and by acquiring product lines. These products include the TEGO for use in dialysis the Orbit 90 diabetes set and a line of oncology products including the Spiros male luer connector device the Genie vial access device custom IV sets and ancillary products specifically designed for chemotherapy. The company is busy working on a new hemodynamic monitor part of its Critical Care business.

Mergers and Acquisitions
In 2015 ICU Medical acquired the New Jersey-based Excelsior Medical Corporation a medical device maker also focused on infection prevention for $59.5 million.

In early 2017 the company acquired Pfizer's global infusion therapy business Hospira Infusion Systems for $1 billion. The deal creates a company with a complete IV therapy product portfolio.

EXECUTIVES

Chairman President and CEO, George A. Lopez, age 72, $690,100 total compensation
VP Operations, Steven C. (Steve) Riggs, age 61, $339,900 total compensation
CEO, Vivek Jain, age 58
CFO Secretary and Treasurer, Scott E. Lamb, age 57, $378,448 total compensation
President Europe, Gabriele Giovanelli
Corporate Vice President Marketing and Communications and General Manager Critical Care, Tom McCall
Vice President International Sales and Marketing, Gregory P Pratt
Vice President Quality and Regulatory Affairs, Krishna Uppugonduri
Vice President General Counsel, Virginia Sanzone
Medical Director, JW Beard
Vp Operations Plant Manager, Rick Owens
Vice President Strategic Business Solutions, Paula Bowman
Vp Strategic Business Solutions, Jeff Chatfield
Corporate Vice President Gm, Dan Woolson
Vp Solutions Business, Dante Tisci
Vice President Global Services, Michael Aviotti
Vice President And General Manager Infusion Solutions, Voigtlander Christian
Vice President Marketing Infusion Systems, Chad Jansen
Vice President Strategic Business Solutions, Tammy Taylor
Auditors: Deloitte & Touche LLP

LOCATIONS
HQ: ICU Medical Inc
 951 Calle Amanecer, San Clemente, CA 92673
Phone: 949 366-2183
Web: www.icumed.com

PRODUCTS/OPERATIONS

2014 Sales

	% of total
Infusion Therapy	70
Critical Care	18
Oncology	12
Other	-
Total	**100**

COMPETITORS

B. Braun Melsungen	Edwards Lifesciences
Baxter International	Fresenius
Becton Dickinson	Merit Medical Systems
Cardinal Health	Navilyst Medical
CareFusion	

HISTORICAL FINANCIALS
Company Type: Public

Income Statement — FYE: December 31

	REVENUE ($ mil.)	NET INCOME ($ mil.)	NET PROFIT MARGIN	EMPLOYEES
12/18	1,400.0	28.7	2.1%	8,100
12/17	1,292.6	68.6	5.3%	6,802
12/16	379.3	63.0	16.6%	2,803
12/15	341.6	44.9	13.2%	2,446
12/14	309.2	26.3	8.5%	2,280
Annual Growth	45.9%	2.3%	—	37.3%

2018 Year-End Financials
Debt ratio: — No. of shares (mil.): 20.4
Return on equity: 2.3% Dividends
Cash ($ mil.): 382.1 Yield: —
Current ratio: 3.72 Payout: —
Long-term debt ($ mil.): — Market value ($ mil.): 4,705.0

	STOCK PRICE ($) FY Close	P/E High/Low	PER SHARE ($) Earnings	Dividends	Book Value
12/18	229.63	220 151	1.33	0.00	61.67
12/17	216.00	63 38	3.29	0.00	59.29
12/16	147.35	39 22	3.66	0.00	40.41
12/15	112.78	43 28	2.73	0.00	36.05
12/14	81.90	50 32	1.68	0.00	32.59
Annual Growth	29.4%	— —	(5.7%)	—	17.3%

Idexx Laboratories, Inc.

IDEXX can identify what's wrong with Fluffy Fido Flossie or Flicka. A leading animal health care company IDEXX develops manufactures and distributes products for pets livestock dairy and poultry markets. Veterinarians use the company's VetTest analyzers for blood and urine chemistry and its SNAP in-office test kits to detect heartworms feline leukemia and other diseases. The company also provides lab testing services and practice management software. In addition IDEXX makes products to test for contaminants in water. The company sells its products worldwide but the Americas account for more than half of its total revenue.

Operations
IDEXX operates through three primary segments: Companion Animal Group (CAG) Water Quality Products (Water) and Livestock Poultry and Dairy (LPD).

Products and services for companion animals (aka: pets) account for more than 80% of IDEXX's sales. Most of that revenue comes from diagnostic products and services including chemistry analyzers rapid test kits and laboratory services. The company operates a network of laboratories to which vets can send patient samples for analysis.

The LPD segment (horses cows pigs and chickens) is the second-largest business bringing in about 10% of total revenue. The segment sells diagnostic tests services and related instrumentation. Its products can test for Bovine Spongiform Encephalopathy (BSE or "mad cow" disease) as well as porcine illnesses and poultry diseases. Equine products make up a smaller portion of the company's sales.

The Water segment (about 5% of sales) makes tests which detect coliforms and E. coli in water. Water utilities and government laboratories are the primary customers for these products.

The company also makes and distributes diagnostics for the human market but those are not a substantial part of its business

Geographic Reach
More than half of IDEXX's sales are made in the US but it also maintains sales offices outside the US in Africa the Asia/Pacific region Europe the Middle East North America and Latin America. Many of its products and materials are manufactured by third parties but the company also maintains manufacturing and assembly facilities in Georgia and Maine and in Bern Switzerland and Montpellier France.

Sales and Marketing
IDEXX distributes its products through its own marketing and sales force and through independent distributors and resellers. In the US it solely relies on internal sales representatives to sell its companion animal diagnostics products.

Financial Performance
IDEXX's revenue has been growing for the past five years and in 2017 it rose 11% to $2 billion. This was due to increases in both product and sales revenues. In the CAG segment growth was driven by higher demand for lab diagnostics services and VetLab consumables as well as higher prices for certain products. Higher prices also boosted returns for the Water segment as did higher sales of the Colilert line of E. coli tests in the Asia/Pacific region and North America. The LPD segment had higher sales of swine tests in China as well as pregnancy tests in Europe and North America.

Thanks to the increasing revenues net income has also been on the rise. It increased 19% to $263.1 million in 2017. Similarly operating cash flow rose 10% to $373.3 million.

Strategy
IDEXX continues to grow by focusing on launching new products and consumables for its instruments and test kits. For example in 2017 it installed some 4000 new chemistry analyzers more than half of which were sold to new customers. These installations are a good sign of recurring revenue for the company as customers will then typically buy related consumables. New products include the SediVue DX urine sediment analyzer designed for use in veterinary clinics and the Catalyst SDMA Test to test for kidney disease.

The company enhances its offerings with companion software for veterinarians.

EXECUTIVES

Vice President Of Purchasing, Rick Cotta
Chairman President and CEO, Jonathan W. (Jon) Ayers, age 62, $800,000 total compensation
EVP CFO and Treasurer, Brian P. McKeon, age 57, $496,153 total compensation
EVP, Johnny D. Powers, age 57, $416,923 total compensation
EVP, Michael J. Williams, age 51, $416,923 total compensation
EVP, Jay Mazelsky, $416,923 total compensation
Vice President Cag Customer Support, Donalee Santoro
Division Vice President, John Rogers
Vice President Human Resource, Sue Rochon
Vice President General Manager, Scott Hamilton
Facilities Maintenance Senior Vice President Senior, Michael Flaherty
Corporate Vice President, Mike Lane
Vice President of Information Technology, Alexander Peterson
Senior Vice President and Chief Inform, Joe Beery
Vice President, Daniel Meyaard
Vice President, Kathy Turner
Corporate Vice President Research and Development, Jeffrey Thomas
Vice President of Information Technology, Arin Brost
Vice President Chief Marketing Officer, Patricia Venters
Corporate Vice President General Counsel And Corporate Secretary, Sharon Underberg
Board Member, Thomas Craig
Board Member, Christine Lane
Board Member, Daniel Junius
Board Member, Sophie Vandebroek
Board Member, Lawrence Kingsley
Auditors: PricewaterhouseCoopers LLP

LOCATIONS
HQ: Idexx Laboratories, Inc.
One IDEXX Drive, Westbrook, ME 04092
Phone: 207 556-0300 **Fax:** 207 856-0346
Web: www.idexx.com

PRODUCTS/OPERATIONS

2016 Sales

	$ mil.	% of total
CAG	1,522.7	86
Water	103.6	6
LPD	126.5	7
Other	22.6	1
Total	**1,775.4**	**100**

2016 Sales

	$ mil.	% of total
Product	1,071.0	60
Service	704.4	40
Total	**1,775.4**	**100**

COMPETITORS
Abaxis
Abbott Labs
Henry Schein
Heska
Instrumentation Laboratory Company
Neogen
Sdix
VCA
Zoetis

HISTORICAL FINANCIALS
Company Type: Public

Income Statement
FYE: December 31

	REVENUE ($ mil.)	NET INCOME ($ mil.)	NET PROFIT MARGIN	EMPLOYEES
12/18	2,213.2	377.0	17.0%	8,377
12/17	1,969.0	263.1	13.4%	7,600
12/16	1,775.4	222.0	12.5%	7,365
12/15	1,601.8	192.0	12.0%	6,800
12/14	1,485.8	181.9	12.2%	6,400
Annual Growth	10.5%	20.0%	—	7.0%

2018 Year-End Financials
Debt ratio: 65.0%
Return on equity: —
Cash ($ mil.): 123.7
Current ratio: 0.85
Long-term debt ($ mil.): 601.3
No. of shares (mil.): 86.1
Dividends
  Yield: —
  Payout: —
Market value ($ mil.): 16,016.0

	STOCK PRICE ($) FY Close	P/E High/Low		PER SHARE ($) Earnings	Dividends	Book Value
12/18	186.02	59	36	4.26	0.00	(0.11)
12/17	156.38	57	39	2.94	0.00	(0.62)
12/16	117.27	49	26	2.44	0.00	(1.23)
12/15	72.92	81	30	2.05	0.00	(0.93)
12/14	148.27	84	58	1.79	0.00	1.24
Annual Growth	5.8%	—	—	24.2%	—	—

IES Holdings Inc

IES installs and maintains electrical and communications systems for residential commercial and industrial customers. Work on commercial buildings and homes includes custom design construction and maintenance on electrical and mechanical systems such as intrusion and fire alarms audio/video and data network systems. IES performs electrical and mechanical systems construction and installation for industrial properties including office buildings manufacturing facilities data centers chemical plants municipal infrastructure and health care facilities. It has a network of about 80 locations serving the US. Banking investor Jeffrey Gendell through Tontine Capital Partners owns about 60% of IES.

Operations
IES operates its business through four segments — Commercial and Industrial Residential Infrastructure Solutions and Communications. They account for about 30% 30% 25% and 10% of the company's revenue respectively.

The residential segment provides electrical and solar power installation services to single-family housing and multi-family apartment complexes. Its communications segment provides infrastructure for corporate data centers as well as design building and maintenance of data network systems for audio/visual telephone fire and alarm systems.

IES's commercial and industrial segment provides electrical and mechanical design construction and maintenance services for projects including power plants data centers chemical plants wind farms solar facilities and office buildings. The company's infrastructure solutions segment provides maintenance and repair services for the steel rail marine petrochemical pulp and paper energy mining and automotive industries.

Geographic Reach

Houston Texas-based IES maintains about 80 locations in the US. The company has about 30 locations that house its residential business activities (in Texas and the Sunbelt Western and Mid-Atlantic regions) more than 20 locations for its commercial and industrial unit (in Texas Nebraska Oregon Wisconsin and the Southeast and Mid-Atlantic regions) about 15 locations for its Tempe Arizona-based communications division and around 10 locations for its infrastructure operations (covering Alabama Georgia Illinois Indiana Ohio West Virginia and California).

Sales and Marketing

IES' commercial and industrial and communications segments rely significantly on long-term repeat business which the company continues to cultivate. The majority of its customers for infrastructure services are located within a 200-mile radius of its facilities allowing the company to quickly respond to repair requests. For the company's residential services most of its single-family sales come from Texas while most of its multifamily sales come from the Mid-Atlantic and Western states.

Financial Performance

IES has seen strong revenue growth of about 70% over its last five fiscal years thanks to increased demand for services in in Commercial and Industrial Residential (owing to growing housing markets primarily in Texas) and Communications (which grew as the company expanded into new markets and service offerings). Concurrently the company has had major fluctuations in net income from about $5.3 million in 2014 to a high of around $120.8 million in 2016 caused by a tax benefit from a valuation allowance on deferred tax assets to a loss of some $14.2 million in 2018 due to Tax Cuts and Jobs Act-related expenses.

The company's revenue rose 8% to $876.8 million in 2018 bolstered by income from a full year of operations of businesses the company acquired in fiscal 2017. Those purchases mainly boosted the company's Commercial and Industrial segment which increased revenue about 20% and accounted for most of the company's overall revenue improvement.

IES's net income plummeted to a loss in fiscal 2018 from $13.4 million the previous year owing to a sevenfold increase in the company's provision for income taxes. The company incurred an income tax charge of $31.3 million in fiscal 2018 to remeasure its deferred tax assets and liabilities following changes in US income tax laws in December 2017.

IES had cash stores of $26.2 million at the end of fiscal 2018 down $2 million from the previous year. Operations provided $12.2 million and investments used $11.9 million for purchases of property and equipment and acquisitions. The company used $2.4 million in its financing activities primarily related to stock buyback.

Strategy

IES acquires stand-alone platform companies or companies that complement its existing business segments to widen its geographic footprint and diversify its revenue streams. The company targets businesses with low technological and/or product obsolescence risk established market positions and strong cash flows. The company does not have a fixed investment time horizon.

Mergers and Acquisitions

IES acquired Portland Oregon-based Azimuth Communications in fiscal 2018 extending the reach of its communications segment to the Pacific Northwest. Azimuth provides design and integration services for cabling physical security access control systems distributed antenna systems wireless access and audio/visual systems.

That year IES also purchased Electrical Contractors North an electrical contractor for multifamily residences and hotels in Utah.

In fiscal 2017 IES spent a total of $21 million to acquire Virginia-based mechanical maintenance services company Technical Services Ohio-based generator enclosure manufacturer Freeman Enclosure Systems and an 80% stake in Wisconsin-based electrical contractor NEXT Electric.

Company Background

Between its 1997 IPO and its 2011 transition to a holding company model IES comprised a group of electrical contractors. Member companies included South Texas-based Bexar Electric (which became a founding subsidiary of IES) South Carolina-based Davis Electrical Constructors Virginia-based ARC Electric Texas-based Houston-Stafford Electric Nebraska-based Kayton Electric and Arizona-based Federal Communication Group.

EXECUTIVES

President, Robert W. Lewey, $277,500 total compensation
President IES Residential, Dwayne Collier
President IES Commercial & Industrial, Thomas E. Santoni
President IES Communications, Donald Fishstein
SVP CFO and Treasurer, Tracy A. McLauchlin, age 48
President Infrastructure Solutions, Michael Rice
Vice President Supply Chain Management, Christopher Haas
Vice President Of Finance, James Valentine
Senior Vice President Chief Financial Officer, Terry Freeman
Vice President And Controller, Cindy Holder
Non Executive Chairman, David B Gendell
Board Member, Joe Koshkin
Board Member, Joseph Dowling
Auditors: Ernst & Young LLP

LOCATIONS

HQ: IES Holdings Inc
5433 Westheimer Road, Suite 500, Houston, TX 77056
Phone: 713 860-1500
Web: www.ies-corporate.com

PRODUCTS/OPERATIONS

2018 Sales

	$ mil.	% of total
Residential	285.7	33
Commercial & Industrial	274.3	31
Communications	219.6	25
Infrastructure Solutions	97.2	11
Total	**876.8**	**100**

Selected Services

Alarm & safety systems
Construction services
Design/build
Engineering services
Home standby generators
Solar installation
Structured cabling
Support services
Training resources

COMPETITORS

Bergelectric	Kelso-Burnett
Comfort Systems USA	MDU Construction
Cupertino Electric	Services
Dycom	MYR Group
EMCOR	Mass Electric
Enterprise Electric	Pike Corporation
Forest Electric	Quanta Services
Industrial Specialty	Rosendin Electric
Contractors	SASCO

HISTORICAL FINANCIALS

Company Type: Public

Income Statement			FYE: September 30	
	REVENUE ($ mil.)	NET INCOME ($ mil.)	NET PROFIT MARGIN	EMPLOYEES
09/19	1,077.0	33.2	3.1%	5,389
09/18	876.8	(14.1)	—	4,564
09/17	810.7	13.4	1.7%	3,532
09/16	695.9	120.7	17.4%	4,063
09/15	573.8	16.5	2.9%	3,106
Annual Growth	17.0%	19.0%	—	14.8%

2019 Year-End Financials

Debt ratio: 0.0%
Return on equity: 14.2%
Cash ($ mil.): 18.9
Current ratio: 1.53
Long-term debt ($ mil.): 0.3
No. of shares (mil.): 21.1
Dividends
 Yield: —
 Payout: —
Market value ($ mil.): 436.0

	STOCK PRICE ($) FY Close	P/E High/Low		PER SHARE ($)		
			Earnings	Dividends	Book Value
09/19	20.59	13	10	1.55	0.00	11.63
09/18	19.50	—	—	(0.67)	0.00	10.39
09/17	17.30	36	23	0.62	0.00	11.09
09/16	17.79	3	1	5.62	0.00	10.41
09/15	7.72	12	8	0.77	0.00	4.72
Annual Growth	27.8%	—	—	19.1%	—	25.3%

II-VI Inc

EXECUTIVES

VP Military and Materials Businesses, James Martinelli, age 58, $194,000 total compensation
President and CEO, Francis J. Kramer, age 67, $433,000 total compensation
Chairman, Carl J. Johnson, age 74, $212,000 total compensation
CFO and Treasurer, Craig A. Creaturo, age 46, $227,125 total compensation
EVP, Vincent D. (Chuck) Mattera Jr., age 60, $208,500 total compensation
Secretary, Robert D. German
Director, Marc Y. E. Pelaez, age 70
Director, Joseph J. (Joe) Corasanti, age 52

President CEO and Director, Francis J. Kramer, age 66
Director, Wendy F. DiCicco, age 49
Director, Peter W. Sognefest, age 75
Director, Thomas E. Mistler, age 74
Independent Director, Howard Xia
Auditors: Ernst & Young LLP

LOCATIONS

HQ: II-VI Inc
375 Saxonburg Boulevard, Saxonburg, PA 16056
Phone: 724 352-4455
Web: www.ii-vi.com

COMPETITORS

AXSUN Technologies
CVI Laser
Coherent Inc.
CoorsTek
Cree
Cymer
DRS Technologies
Dow Corning
Ferrotec
Goodrich Corp.
Jenoptik
Komatsu
Laird Technologies
LightPath
Newport Corp.
Nippon Steel & Sumitomo Metal Corporation
Northrop Grumman
Oplink Communications
Orbotech
ROFIN-SINAR
Raytheon
Saint-Gobain
Spectra-Physics
Sumitomo Electric
Umicore
Zygo

HISTORICAL FINANCIALS
Company Type: Public

Income Statement — FYE: June 30

	REVENUE ($ mil.)	NET INCOME ($ mil.)	NET PROFIT MARGIN	EMPLOYEES
06/19	1,362.5	107.5	7.9%	12,487
06/18	1,158.7	88.0	7.6%	11,443
06/17	972.0	95.2	9.8%	10,349
06/16	827.2	65.4	7.9%	8,927
06/15	741.9	65.9	8.9%	8,490
Annual Growth	16.4%	13.0%	—	10.1%

2019 Year-End Financials
Debt ratio: 23.9%
Return on equity: 9.9%
Cash ($ mil.): 204.8
Current ratio: 3.00
Long-term debt ($ mil.): 443.1
No. of shares (mil.): 63.7
Dividends
Yield: —
Payout: —
Market value ($ mil.): 2,329.0

	STOCK PRICE ($) FY Close	P/E High/Low		PER SHARE ($) Earnings	Dividends	Book Value
06/19	36.56	30	18	1.63	0.00	17.79
06/18	43.45	38	24	1.35	0.00	16.18
06/17	34.30	26	12	1.48	0.00	14.26
06/16	18.76	22	14	1.04	0.00	12.64
06/15	18.98	18	10	1.05	0.00	11.91
Annual Growth	17.8%	—	—	11.6%	—	10.5%

Immersion Corp

Immersion wants to immerse people in digital experiences with its haptics technology. The company develops touch feedback technology called haptics that simulates tactile experiences — such as the feel of an object or the jolt of an explosion during a video game — in order to improve how people interact with digital devices. Immersion licenses its TouchSense technology to companies such as Motorola and Samsung for use in mobile phones and to Logitech and Microsoft which use TouchSense in joysticks mice steering wheels and other peripherals. Its technology backed by more than 2000 issued and pending patents is also used in automotive consumer electronics and medical products.

Operations
Immersion's products for the mobile wearables and consumer market generate 60% of its revenue. Gaming devices bring in 27% with medical and automotive accounting for 8% and 5% respectively.

Geographic Reach
Headquartered in California the company operates offices in Canada China Japan South Korea and Taiwan. In 2014 South Korea (home to its largest customer Samsung) accounted for more than 50% of sales followed by the US more than 25%. The remainder came from Japan and other countries.

Sales and Marketing
Immersion uses a direct sales force in Asia Europe and the US to license its software and patents as well as partnerships and licensing agreements with component suppliers and system integrators. Samsung is its largest customer accounting for about 40% of all sales in 2014.

Financial Performance
Immersion followed a 48% revenue gain in 2013 with a 11.5% increase in 2014 to about $53 million. The company recorded higher royalty and licensing revenues from gaming licenses and the sale of gaming console products including the Sony PlayStation 4. A new contract with a European automaker boosted automotive revenue.

Immersion's net income dropped a whopping 89% in 2014 to $4 million. Still it was the company's third profit in the past decade. The company increased spending on sales and marketing and research and development.

The drop in net income helped reduce Immersion's cash flow from operations to $291000 in 2014 from $21 million in 2013. Cash flow was also affected by non-cash charges of $5.9 million including $5.3 million of non-cash stock-based compensation and $567000 in depreciation and amortization.

Strategy
Immersion doesn't face a lot of competition in the market for licensing haptics IP except from the customers themselves who may choose to develop their own haptics technology. Still it owns so many of the patents for the technology that Immersion has had to take some users to court.

The company focuses on market penetration through working with hardware component suppliers as well as the ecosystem of designers and content creators. It also wants to extend its technologies into newer markets such as wearables and networked devices as well as new form factors.

The company intends to continue to expand its international activities including continued investment in Asia.

In 2014 the company extended existing licenses and secured new licenses with mobile OEMs including LG in Korea Huawei in China and HTC in Taiwan.

The company also focuses on product portfolio expansion. In 2015 the company launched the TouchSense Engage software for mobile games. The software provides tools plus creative design support and services to adding custom tactile effects to products.

EXECUTIVES

President CEO and Interim CFO, Victor (Vic) Viegas, age 61, $351,346 total compensation
VP Engineering, Rob Lacroix
Vice President North America And Europe, Daniel Brongiel
Vice President Marketing, Todd Whitaker
Vice President Marketing, Hossam Bahlool
Chairman, Carl P. Schlachte, age 56
Auditors: DELOITTE & TOUCHE LLP

LOCATIONS

HQ: Immersion Corp
50 Rio Robles, San Jose, CA 95134
Phone: 408 467-1900
Web: www.immersion.com

PRODUCTS/OPERATIONS

2014 Sales

	$ mil.	% of total
Royalty & license	51.8	98
Development contracts & other	1.1	3
Total	52.9	100

2014 Sales by Market

	% of total
Mobile wearables and consumer	60
Gaming	27
Medical	8
Automotive	5
Total	100

Selected Products
TouchSense Engage Software Solution
TouchSenseTactile Feedback
Integrator for OEMs
Haptic SDK for Developers
TouchSense Force Feedback

COMPETITORS

Interlink Electronics	Nokia
LG Electronics	Panasonic Corp
Logitech	Philips Electronics
Microsoft	Samsung Group
Moog	Sony

HISTORICAL FINANCIALS
Company Type: Public

Income Statement — FYE: December 31

	REVENUE ($ mil.)	NET INCOME ($ mil.)	NET PROFIT MARGIN	EMPLOYEES
12/18	110.9	54.3	49.0%	64
12/17	35.0	(45.2)	—	81
12/16	57.0	(39.3)	—	132
12/15	63.3	2.8	4.5%	156
12/14	52.9	4.1	7.8%	141
Annual Growth	20.3%	90.5%	—	(17.9%)

Incyte Corporation

Incyte is focused on developing and selling drugs that inhibit specific enzymes associated with cancer and other diseases. The company's lead program is its JAK (Janus associated kinase) inhibitor program. Its first commercial product Jakafi is approved for treatment of polycythemia vera and myelofibrosis (two rare blood cancers) and graft-versus-host-disease in the US; partner Novartis markets the drug internationally. Another inhibitor drug Iclusig is marketed for certain forms of leukemia in Europe. Incyte has a number of product candidates in research and clinical development stages partially through partnerships with other drugmakers for various cancers inflammatory ailments and other conditions.

Financial Performance

Incyte has reported steadily increasing revenue over the past five years with sales tripling between 2014 and 2018. Net income has fluctuated in recent years rising into the black in 2015 2016 and 2018 but dropping to a net loss in 2014 and 2017 due to high R&D costs.

The company reported a 23% revenue increase in 2018 to some $1.9 billion due to increased revenue from sales of Jakafi and Iclusig as well as higher product royalty and milestone payments from partners.

Net income rose to $109.5 million in 2018 a vast improvement over a net loss of $313.1 million in 2017 as the company reported stronger sales and reigned in R&D expenses.

The company ended 2018 with $1.2 billion in cash up $264.6 million from 2017. Operating activities contributed $336.2 million while investing activities used $86.4 million (mostly capital expenditures) and financing activities contributed $14.7 million via proceeds from common stock issuance.

Strategy

In recent years Incyte has been focused on expanding sales of Jakafi in the US and Iclusig in Europe in targeted populations. It also continues to put extensive resources into its R&D programs to gain approval for new compounds and additional indications for Jakafi. The FDA approved Jakafi which accounts for most of annual sales for the treatment of graft-versus-host-disease in 2019.

Incyte is pursuing new commercialization partnerships for other pipeline drugs. In addition to Jakafi Incyte partners with Novartis to develop other cancer treatments. The company also has a collaboration with Eli Lilly to develop drugs for inflammatory disorders; Incyte receives royalty payments from Lilly on sales of one drug Olumiant outside the US. Other partners include Agenus Takeda (which markets Iclusig in the US) and MacroGenics; the company entered new partnerships with Syros Pharmaceuticals and Innovent Biologics in 2018.

Incyte spends a significant amount of its revenue on R&D programs leaving it vulnerable to adverse financial impacts if drugs fail to meet development goals or gain regulatory approval. In 2018 the company suffered a setback when its melanoma combination study involving candidate epacadostat and Merck's Keytruda failed.

EXECUTIVES

EVP and CFO, David W. (Dave) Gryska, age 63
EVP Human Resources, Paula J. Swain, $354,029 total compensation
EVP Chief Drug Development, Richard S. Levy, $373,423 total compensation
EVP and General Counsel, Eric H. Siegel
EVP and Chief Scientific Officer, Reid M. Huber
EVP Discovery Medicinal and Process Chemistry, Wenqing Yao
EVP and Chief Commercial Officer, James M. (Jim) Daly, $506,635 total compensation
EVP Business Development and Strategic Planning, Barry P. Flannelly
SVP and Chief Medical Officer, Steven H. Stein
President, David C. Hoak
CEO, Don Larsen
CIO, Steven Lerner
President and CEO and Director, Herve Hoppenot
VICE PRESIDENT REGULATORY AFFAIRS, Ron Falcone
Vice President Exploratory Development, William Williams
Vice President Global Phamacovigilance Operations, Katherine Roberts
Vice President Drug Safety, Robert Livingston
Vice President, Lance Leopold
Vice President, Jayant Shukla
Group Vice President of clinic Development, Victor Sandor
VP Operations, Keith Mikkelson
Vice President Pre Clinical Development, Swamy Yeleswaram
Vice President Of Sales, Eric Vogel
Vice President, Kevin Harris
Vice President Marketing, Bhavnish Parikh
Vice President of Development Operations, Michele Sample
Vice President Medical Affairs, Joe Cordaro
Executive Medical Director, Ahmad Naim
NATIONAL ACCOUNT MANAGER, Christopher Busch
Vice President Business Development, Erin Hugger
Vice President And Controller, Paul Trower
Vice President Exploratory Development, Bill Williams
Vice President Project Management, Kim Solomon
Group Vice President, Kris Vaddi
Vice President, Richard Wynn
VICE PRESIDENT ASSISTANT GENERAL COUNSEL, Michael Purvis
MEDICAL DIRECTOR GLOBAL PV AND SAFETY SURVEILLANCE, Alex Qiu
SENIOR MEDICAL DIRECTOR GLOBAL PV AND SAFETY SURVEILLANCE, Ronald Monroe
Group Vice President Us Medical Affairs, Margaret Squier
EXECUTIVE MEDICAL DIRECTOR ADVANCED MED GROUP, Michal Kuligowski
Group Vice President Us Medical Affairs, Peg Squier
Vice President Biostatistics And Programming, Lothar Tremmel
Vice President Clinical Development, Kiran Patel
Board Member, Wendy Dixon
Chairman, Richard U. De Schutter
Board Member, Paul A Brooke
Board Member, Paul Clancy
Assistant Treasurer, Scott Niemann
Board Member, Jean-jacques Bienaime
Board Member, Jacqualyn Fouse
Auditors: Ernst & Young LLP

LOCATIONS

HQ: Incyte Corporation
1801 Augustine Cut-Off, Wilmington, DE 19803
Phone: 302 498-6700
Web: www.incyte.com

PRODUCTS/OPERATIONS

2016 Sales

	$ mil.	% of total
Product revenues net	882.4	80
Product royalty revenues	110.7	10
Contract revenues	112.6	10
Other revenues	0.0	-
Total	1,105.7	100

COMPETITORS

Abbott Labs	Human Genome Sciences
Amgen	Janssen Biotech
Array BioPharma	Lexicon
Biogen	Pharmaceuticals
Bristol-Myers Squibb	Myriad Genetics
CTI BioPharma	PDL BioPharma
Celgene	Roche Holding
CuraGen	TargeGen
GlaxoSmithKline	Xencor

HISTORICAL FINANCIALS

Company Type: Public

Income Statement
FYE: December 31

	REVENUE ($ mil.)	NET INCOME ($ mil.)	NET PROFIT MARGIN	EMPLOYEES
12/18	1,881.8	109.4	5.8%	1,367
12/17	1,536.2	(313.1)	—	1,208
12/16	1,105.7	104.2	9.4%	980
12/15	753.7	6.5	0.9%	692
12/14	511.5	(48.4)	—	588
Annual Growth	38.5%	—	—	23.5%

2018 Year-End Financials

Debt ratio: 0.6%
Return on equity: 6.1%
Cash ($ mil.): 1,163.9
Current ratio: 4.31
Long-term debt ($ mil.): 17.4
No. of shares (mil.): 213.2
Dividends
Yield: —
Payout: —
Market value ($ mil.): 13,562.0

	STOCK PRICE ($) FY Close	P/E High/Low	PER SHARE ($) Earnings	Dividends	Book Value
12/18	63.59	194 113	0.51	0.00	9.03
12/17	94.71	— —	(1.53)	0.00	7.72
12/16	100.27	197 115	0.54	0.00	2.22
12/15	108.45	3287 1787	0.03	0.00	0.92
12/14	73.11	— —	(0.29)	0.00	(0.48)
Annual Growth	(3.4%)	— —	—	—	—

2018 Year-End Financials

Debt ratio: —
Return on equity: 99.4%
Cash ($ mil.): 110.9
Current ratio: 8.85
Long-term debt ($ mil.): —
No. of shares (mil.): 30.8
Dividends
Yield: —
Payout: —
Market value ($ mil.): 276.0

	STOCK PRICE ($) FY Close	P/E High/Low	PER SHARE ($) Earnings	Dividends	Book Value
12/18	8.96	10 4	1.73	0.00	3.23
12/17	7.06	— —	(1.55)	0.00	0.33
12/16	10.63	— —	(1.37)	0.00	1.91
12/15	11.66	139 78	0.10	0.00	3.06
12/14	9.47	96 50	0.14	0.00	2.76
Annual Growth	(1.4%)	— —	87.5%	—	4.0%

Independence Realty Trust Inc

Auditors: KPMG LLP

LOCATIONS
HQ: Independence Realty Trust Inc
1835 Market Street, Suite 2601, Philadelphia, PA
19103
Phone: 267 270-4800
Web: www.irtliving.com

HISTORICAL FINANCIALS
Company Type: Public

Income Statement   FYE: December 31

	REVENUE ($ mil.)	NET INCOME ($ mil.)	NET PROFIT MARGIN	EMPLOYEES
12/18	191.2	26.2	13.7%	455
12/17	161.2	30.2	18.7%	421
12/16	153.3	(9.8)	—	395
12/15	109.5	28.2	25.8%	0
12/14	49.2	2.9	6.0%	0
Annual Growth	40.4%	72.9%	—	—

2018 Year-End Financials
Debt ratio: 59.3%
Return on equity: 4.2%
Cash ($ mil.): 9.3
Current ratio: 0.84
Long-term debt ($ mil.): 985.4
No. of shares (mil.): 89.1
Dividends
  Yield: 7.8%
  Payout: 360.0%
Market value ($ mil.): 819.0

	STOCK PRICE ($) FY Close	P/E High/Low		PER SHARE ($)		
			Earnings	Dividends	Book Value
12/18	9.18	35 28	0.30	0.72	6.99
12/17	10.09	26 21	0.41	0.72	7.37
12/16	8.92	— —	(0.19)	0.72	7.35
12/15	7.51	13 9	0.78	0.72	7.74
12/14	9.31	76 59	0.14	0.72	7.90
Annual Growth	(0.4%)	— —	21.0%	(0.0%)	(3.0%)

Independent Bank Corp (MA)

Independent Bank wants to rock the northeast. Its banking subsidiary Rockland Trust operates almost 75 retail branches as well as investment and lending offices in Eastern Massachusetts and Rhode Island. Serving area individuals and small to midsized businesses the bank offers standard services such as checking and savings accounts CDs and credit cards in addition to insurance products financial planning trust services. Commercial loans including industrial construction and small business loans make up more than 70% of Rockland Trust's loan portfolio. Incorporated in 1985 the bank boasts total assets of some $7.5 billion.

Operations
About 28% of Independent Bank's loan portfolio is made up of consumer real estate loans which include residential mortgages and home equity loans and lines; while personal loans and auto loans make up around 1% of the portfolio. Through an agreement with LPL Investment Holdings Rockland Trust offers investment products such as securities and insurance.

Independent Bank generated 70% of its total revenue from interest and fee income on loans in 2014 and another 6% from interest and dividends on investment securities. Investment management fees made up 6% of total revenue for the year while deposit account fees and interchange and ATM fees combined made up 11%.

Geographic Reach
Rockland Trust boasts nearly 75 retail branches and three limited-services branches located in Eastern Massachusetts in the counties of Barnstable Bristol Middlesex Norfolk Plymouth and Worcester.

Sales and Marketing
The company's borrowers include consumers and small-to-medium sized businesses with credit needs up to $250000 and revenues of less than $2.5 million. Independent Bank spent $3.86 million on advertising in 2014 compared to $4.28 million and $3.95 million in 2013 and 2012 respectively.

Financial Performance
Independent Bank Corp's revenues and profits have trended higher in recent years thanks to continued loan business growth from both acquisitions and through organic expansion higher deposit account and ATM fee income from customer base growth and thanks to a decline in loan loss provisions as the credit quality of its loan portfolio has improved with the strengthened economy.

The bank's revenue rose by 5% to $286.40 million in 2014 mostly thanks to higher interest income as its loan business growth continued to outpace the margin-eating impacts of low interest rates. Independent's non-interest income also rose by 3% thanks to a combination of higher interchange and ATM fees and investment management fees.

Higher revenue and lower interest expenses on deposits in 2014 drove Independent Bank Corp's net income up by 19% to $59.85 million. Despite higher earnings the company's operating cash dove sharply primarily because of working capital changes related to its loans held for sale and changes in other assets.

Strategy
Independent Bank planned in 2015 to grow its loans organically between 4-6% for the year while growing its deposits between 3% and 4%. The company has also been expanding its fee-based revenue business especially in its investment management segment with expectations of growing the business by another 3% to 4% in 2015.

In addition to organic growth in other financial services areas Independent Bank has expanded via acquisitions.

Mergers and Acquisitions
In 2019 Independent Bank acquired Hyde Park Massachusetts-based Blue Hills Bancorp—the holding company for The Blue Hills Bank—for about $170 million. The acquisition furthers Independent's strategy of acquiring banks in overlapping and adjacent markets.

Company Background
In past years Independent Bank launched institutional asset managers Bright Rock Capital Management (2010) and Compass Exchange Advisors (2006) and formed a handful of mutual funds.

EXECUTIVES
Executive Vice President Director of Retail Delivery Business Banking & Home Equity Lending, Jane L. Lundquist, age 62, $262,981 total compensation
President CEO and Director Independent Bank Corp. and Rockland Trust, Christopher (Chris) Oddleifson, age 60, $589,616 total compensation
CFO, Robert D. Cozzone
Executive Vice President Commercial Banking, Gerard F. Nadeau, age 61, $322,308 total compensation
Chief Information Officer, Barry Jensen
Chairman, Donna L. Abelli
Auditors: Ernst & Young LLP

LOCATIONS
HQ: Independent Bank Corp (MA)
2036 Washington Street, Hanover, MA 02339
Phone: 781 878-6100
Web: www.RocklandTrust.com

PRODUCTS/OPERATIONS

2012 Sales

	$ mil.	% of total
Interest		
Loans	178.3	69
Taxable securities including dividends	16.7	6
Other	1.0	-
Noninterest		
Service charges on deposit accounts	16.0	6
Wealth management	14.8	6
Interchange & ATM fees	9.8	4
Other	21.7	9
Adjustments	(0.1)	-
Total	**258.2**	**100**

COMPETITORS
Bank of America
Citizens Financial Group
Eastern Bank
Hingham Institution for Savings
Sovereign Bank
TD Bank USA

HISTORICAL FINANCIALS
Company Type: Public

Income Statement   FYE: December 31

	ASSETS ($ mil.)	NET INCOME ($ mil.)	INCOME AS % OF ASSETS	EMPLOYEES
12/18	8,851.5	121.6	1.4%	1,188
12/17	8,082.0	87.2	1.1%	1,108
12/16	7,709.3	76.6	1.0%	1,103
12/15	7,210.0	64.9	0.9%	1,051
12/14	6,364.9	59.8	0.9%	980
Annual Growth	8.6%	19.4%	—	4.9%

2018 Year-End Financials
Return on assets: 1.4%
Return on equity: 12.0%
Long-term debt ($ mil.): —
No. of shares (mil.): 28.0
Sales ($ mil): 412.2
Dividends
  Yield: 2.1%
  Payout: 34.5%
Market value ($ mil.): 1,974.0

	STOCK PRICE ($) FY Close	P/E High/Low	Earnings	Dividends	Book Value
12/18	70.31	21 15	4.40	1.52	38.23
12/17	69.85	24 19	3.19	1.28	34.38
12/16	70.45	24 14	2.90	1.16	32.02
12/15	46.52	21 15	2.50	1.04	29.40
12/14	42.81	17 14	2.49	0.96	26.69
Annual Growth	13.2%	— —	15.3%	12.2%	9.4%

Independent Bank Corporation (Ionia, MI)

Independent Bank Corporation is the holding company for Independent Bank which serves rural and suburban communities of Michigan's Lower Peninsula from more than 100 branches. The bank offers traditional deposit products including checking and savings accounts and CDs. Loans to businesses account for about 40% of the bank's portfolio; real estate mortgages are more than a third. Independent Bank also offers additional products and services like title insurance through subsidiary Independent Title Services and investments through agreement with third-party provider PrimeVest.

Operations
The company also owns Mepco Finance which acquires and services payment plans for extended automobile warranties.

Financial Performance
The company's revenue has been trending down year-over-year. However its net income and cash on hand have both been spiking up across recent fiscal years.

Strategy
As Michigan's economy has exhibited signs of stabilizing and the company's results have relatively improved as well. Independent Bank has reduced its number of high-risk loans non-performing loans and delinquency rates.

EXECUTIVES
Vice President, Patrick Dunn
Assistant Vice President Senior Business Analyst, Phil Hamlin
Vice President Team Leader Commercial Loans, Stephen Hale
Assistant Vice President Bank Manager, Chelsee Warman
Senior Vice President, Hank B Risley
Executive Vice President And General Cou, Mark Collins
Auditors: Crowe LLP

LOCATIONS
HQ: Independent Bank Corporation (Ionia, MI)
4200 East Beltline, Grand Rapids, MI 49525
Phone: 616 527-5820
Web: www.independentbank.com

COMPETITORS
Bank of America
Chemical Financial
Fifth Third
Firstbank
Flagstar Bancorp
Huntington Bancshares
JPMorgan Chase
Mercantile Bank

HISTORICAL FINANCIALS
Company Type: Public

Income Statement — FYE: December 31

	ASSETS ($ mil.)	NET INCOME ($ mil.)	INCOME AS % OF ASSETS	EMPLOYEES
12/18	3,353.2	39.8	1.2%	976
12/17	2,789.3	20.4	0.7%	911
12/16	2,548.9	22.7	0.9%	885
12/15	2,409.0	20.0	0.8%	831
12/14	2,248.7	18.0	0.8%	876
Annual Growth	10.5%	21.9%	—	2.7%

2018 Year-End Financials
Return on assets: 1.3%
Return on equity: 13.1%
Long-term debt ($ mil.): —
No. of shares (mil.): 23.5
Sales ($ mil): 175.5
Dividends
Yield: 2.8%
Payout: 44.4%
Market value ($ mil.): 496.0

	STOCK PRICE ($) FY Close	P/E High/Low	PER SHARE ($) Earnings	Dividends	Book Value
12/18	21.02	16 12	1.68	0.60	14.38
12/17	22.35	24 20	0.95	0.42	12.42
12/16	21.70	21 13	1.05	0.34	11.71
12/15	15.23	18 14	0.86	0.26	11.28
12/14	13.05	18 15	0.77	0.18	10.91
Annual Growth	12.7%	— —	21.5%	35.1%	7.2%

Independent Bank Group Inc.

It makes sense that a company that calls itself Independent Bank Group (IBG) would do business in a state that was once its own country. The bank holding company does business through subsidiary Independent Bank which operates about 40 banking offices and 70 branches in North and Central Texas Houston and Colorado. The banks offer standard personal and business accounts and services including some focused on small business owners. IBG has total assets of nearly $8.9 billion and loans of about $6.4 billion. The company traces its roots back 100 years but took its current shape in 2002.

Operations
In addition to its banking activities Independent Bank Group (IBG)also owns IBG Adriatica a mixed use development in the Dallas-Fort Worth area. The company does not intend to move into real estate but purchased the development where one of its branches is located to help maintain business in the area. It had also made commercial loans to several tenants of the development and saw the purchase as a way to protect its investments rather than have the entire property go into foreclosure.

Financial Performance
Independent Bank Group has shown increasing net income for several years and in fiscal 2016 grew revenue a further 20% to $210.0 million. Net income has likewise been consistently growing reaching $53.5 million up 39%. Cash from operations increased 85% to $80.3 million.

Strategy
Independent Bank Group's strategy is all about growth. It seeks organic growth in loans and deposits in existing locations by developing customer relationships while maintaining the quality of its loan portfolio. It also makes acquisitions: since 2010 it has made nine acquisitions most recently of Carlile Bancshares and its subsidiary Northstar Bank and Grand Bank in Dallas.

Mergers and Acquisitions
Independent Bank Group acquired Carlile Bancshares and its subsidiary Northstar Bank for around $434 million in 2017.

EXECUTIVES
Chairman President and CEO, David R. Brooks, age 61, $650,000 total compensation
EVP and COO, James C. (Jim) White, age 54
Vice Chairman and Chief Lending Officer and President Independent Bank Central Texas, Brian E. Hobart, age 54, $350,000 total compensation
Executive Vice President and Chief Financial Officer, Michelle S. Hickox, age 52, $265,000 total compensation
EVP and Secretary and EVP and Senior Operations Officer Independent Bank, Jan C. Webb, age 61
Senior Vice President, Amy Feagin
Assistant Vice President, Mallory Smith
Vice President Commercial Lending, Richard Berman
Vice President Market Manager, Tisha Reyes
Senior Vice President Director Of Financial Reporting, Leslie Beseda
Vice President Commercial Lending, Ozzie Martinez
SVP HR Director Texas, Pam Murray
Vice President, Montgomery Brenda
Senior Vice President Director Of Human Resources, Murray Pam
Senior Vice President, Julie Crump
Senior Vice President, Noorani Feroz
Senior Vice President Commercial Relationship Manager, Charlie Cartwright
Vp. Treasury Management Operations Manager, Brian Oathout
Svp Commercial Lending, Tom Doonan
Assistant Vice President Senior Financial Analyst, Lesli Gilbert
Vice President, Lynda Dean
Vice President, Paul Langdale
Vice President Commercial Lending, Robin Thomas
Vice Chairman and Chief Risk Officer, Daniel W. Brooks, age 59
Auditors: RSM US LLP

LOCATIONS
HQ: Independent Bank Group Inc.
7777 Henneman Way, McKinney, TX 75070-1711
Phone: 972 562-9004
Web: www.ibtx.com

PRODUCTS/OPERATIONS

2012 Loan Portfolio

	% of total
Real estate	
Commercial	47
Residential	23
Construction land & land development	7
Single-family interim construction	5
Commercial	12
Agricultural	3
Consumer	3
Total	100

Selected Acquisition
Town Center Bank (2010 North Texas)
Farmersville Bancshares Inc. (2010 North Texas)
I Bank Holding Company Inc. (2012 Austin/Central Texas)
The Community Group Inc. (2012 Dallas/North Texas)

COMPETITORS
BBVA Compass Bancshares
Bank of America
Broadway Bancshares
Capital One
HSBC
International Bancshares
JPMorgan Chase
Lone Star Bank

Citigroup
Comerica
Cullen/Frost Bankers
Extraco
First Financial Bankshares
PlainsCapital
Prosperity Bancshares
Texas Capital Bancshares
Wells Fargo
Woodforest Financial

HISTORICAL FINANCIALS
Company Type: Public

Income Statement FYE: December 31

	ASSETS ($ mil.)	NET INCOME ($ mil.)	INCOME AS % OF ASSETS	EMPLOYEES
12/18	9,849.9	128.2	1.3%	1,087
12/17	8,684.4	76.5	0.9%	924
12/16	5,852.8	53.5	0.9%	577
12/15	5,055.0	38.7	0.8%	587
12/14	4,132.6	28.9	0.7%	511
Annual Growth	24.3%	45.0%	—	20.8%

2018 Year-End Financials
Return on assets: 1.3%
Return on equity: 8.7%
Long-term debt ($ mil.): —
No. of shares (mil.): 30.6
Sales ($ mil): 449.5
Dividends
Yield: 1.1%
Payout: 13.9%
Market value ($ mil.): 1,401.0

	STOCK PRICE ($) FY Close	P/E High/Low	PER SHARE ($) Earnings	Dividends	Book Value
12/18	45.77	18 10	4.33	0.54	52.50
12/17	67.60	24 18	2.97	0.40	47.28
12/16	62.40	22 9	2.88	0.34	35.63
12/15	32.00	21 13	2.21	0.32	34.09
12/14	39.06	33 21	1.85	0.24	31.75
Annual Growth	4.0%	— —	23.7%	22.5%	13.4%

Innospec Inc

Innospec has concluded that the company's future lies in applying innovative ideas to its specialty chemicals businesses by developing fuel additives and niche performance chemicals. Innospec's Fuel Specialties segment makes chemical additives that enhance fuel efficiency and engine performance and its Performance Chemicals unit makes several products used in the personal care home care agrochemical and mining. Meanwhile the oilfield services provide drilling and production chemical. It is also the sole producer of TEL (tetra ethyl lead) product an anti-knock gas additive sold to oil refineries worldwide.

Operations
Innospec operated through Fuel Specialties Performance Chemicals Oilfield Services and Octane Additives.

The company's Fuel Specialties segment accounts for 40% its total sales. It produces a range of specialty chemical products used as additives to help improve fuel efficiency boost engine performance and reduce harmful emissions. They are used to support the efficient operation of automotive marine and aviation engines power plant generators and heating oil.

Its Performance Chemicals segment (about 30%) provides technology-based solutions for customers' processes in the personal care home care agrochemical and mining markets.

Its Octane Additives segment (5%) sells TEL for use in automotive gasoline and trading provides services as part of the company's environmental remediation business.

Its Oilfield Services accounts for roughly 25% of revenue and develops and sells products to drilling operations chemical solutions stimulations and completion operations and products for oil and gas production.

Geographic Reach
Innospec operates in Belgium Brazil China France Germany Italy Singapore Switzerland the UK and the US. The US accounts for 40% of its sales.

Sales and Marketing
The company's products are sold primarily to oil and gas exploration and production companies oil refineries personal care and home care companies formulators of agrochemical and mining preparations and other chemical and industrial companies throughout the world.

Financial Performance
IIn 2017 revenue soared almost 50% to $1.3 billion up from $883 million the year before thanks to a sales increases from performance chemicals (due to Huntsman acquisition) and oilfield services due to higher demand triggered by oil price increases.

Net income for the year decreased to $62 million from $81 million in 2016 mostly due to a $40 million YOY increase in income tax expense.

Cash from operating activities was $83 million in 2017 compared to $106 million in 2016 mostly due to the $28 million used for the Huntsman acquisition.

Strategy
Innospec performed well in 2017 thanks to recovering oil prices and successful acquisition leading to better results in performance chemicals. The company had strong cash flows despite acquisition costs While the company is banking on fuel specialties and performance chemicals to deliver growth oilfield services to remain stable due to recovered oil prices a major concern is the future of its octane additives business which is struggling with its recent contract failure. However recent investments in specialty surfactants for its Iselux business as well as a new subsidiary in China to cater to growing demand for specialty chemicals should secure positive momentum.

Mergers and Acquisitions
In 2017 Innospec completed the acquisition of Huntsman's European Differentiated Surfactants business valued at about $200 million. The acquisition provides a small presence in new markets to Innospec including Agriculture Mining and Construction.

EXECUTIVES

COO, Philip J. (Phil) Boon, age 60, $322,590 total compensation
SVP and CTO, Ian M. McRobbie, age 70, $279,453 total compensation
President and CEO, Patrick S. Williams, age 54, $910,340 total compensation
EVP and CFO, Ian P. Cleminson, age 53, $352,064 total compensation
VP Strategic Planning and Regulatory Affairs, Brian R. Watt, age 60, $277,415 total compensation
Vice President Operations Support, Roger Mabee
Senior Vice President Business Development, Butch Gothard
Senior Vice President Human Resources, Cathy Hessner
Senior Vice President Production Chemical, Jake Hammond
Executive Vice President, Don Logan
Senior Vice President Operations, Clark Emrich
Senior Vice President Operations Ofs, Darren Garrett
Chairman, Milton C. (Bud) Blackmore, age 71
Board Member, Hugh Aldous
Board Member, Larry Padfield
Board Member, David Landless
Auditors: PricewaterhouseCoopers LLP

LOCATIONS
HQ: Innospec Inc
8310 South Valley Highway, Suite 350, Englewood, CO 80112
Phone: 303 792-5554
Web: www.innospecinc.com

PRODUCTS/OPERATIONS

2015 sales

	$ mil.	% of total
Fuel Specialties	758.3	75
Performance chemical	194.5	19
Octane Additives	59.5	6
Total	**1,012.3**	**100**

COMPETITORS

BASF SE	Infineum
Clean Diesel	KMG Chemicals
Detrex	Lubrizol
Dow Chemical	NewMarket
Ethyl Corporation	TPC Group

HISTORICAL FINANCIALS
Company Type: Public

Income Statement FYE: December 31

	REVENUE ($ mil.)	NET INCOME ($ mil.)	NET PROFIT MARGIN	EMPLOYEES
12/18	1,476.9	85.0	5.8%	2,000
12/17	1,306.8	61.8	4.7%	1,900
12/16	883.4	81.3	9.2%	1,800
12/15	1,012.3	119.5	11.8%	1,300
12/14	960.9	84.1	8.8%	1,300
Annual Growth	11.3%	0.3%		11.4%

2018 Year-End Financials
Debt ratio: 14.3%
Return on equity: 10.5%
Cash ($ mil.): 123.1
Current ratio: 2.24
Long-term debt ($ mil.): 187.7
No. of shares (mil.): 24.4
Dividends
Yield: 1.4%
Payout: 36.4%
Market value ($ mil.): 1,509.0

	STOCK PRICE ($) FY Close	P/E High/Low	PER SHARE ($) Earnings	Dividends	Book Value
12/18	61.76	24 17	3.45	0.89	33.76
12/17	70.60	29 21	2.52	0.77	32.60
12/16	68.50	21 13	3.33	0.67	27.15
12/15	54.31	12 8	4.86	0.61	25.10
12/14	42.70	13 10	3.38	0.55	21.24
Annual Growth	9.7%	— —	0.5%	12.8%	12.3%

Innoviva Inc

Innoviva (formerly Theravance) figures there's no sense in re-inventing the wheel. The biotech takes aim at already proven biological targets taking advantage of existing research to create next-generation treatments. The firm is focused on the discovery development and commercialization of small molecule medicines across a number of therapeutic areas including respiratory disease bacterial infections and central nervous system pain. Its VIBATIV product (an injectable antibiotic approved to treat skin infections and hospital-acquired pneumonia) was successfully developed and commercialized with partner Astellas. It also develops chronic obstructive pulmonary disease (COPD) products with GlaxoSmithKline (GSK).

Operations
VIBATIV is approved in the US and Europe for the treatment of certain difficult-to-treat infections. Other products include TD-4208 which is being investigated for the treatment of COPD; and Axelopran (TD-1211) a potential treatment for opioid-induced constipation. Earlier-stage assets are being tested for the treatment of diseases of the lung and gastrointestinal tract and infectious diseases.

Collaboration partner GSK has launched RELVAR/BREO ELLIPTA in a number of markets including the US Canada Japan the UK and Germany. GSK is also responsible for the commercialization of ANORO ELLIPTA.

Theravance Biopharma a subsidiary established in 2014 handles the company's R&D development operations. The unit was created when then-named Theravance split its R&D operations from its late-stage partnered respiratory assets.

Geographic Reach
Innoviva sells its products in the US Japan and Canada and in Western Europe.

Financial Performance
The company's revenues grew by a whopping 454% to $135.8 million in 2012 thanks to the recognition of deferred income from its collaboration with Astellas for VIBATIV which achieved commercialization in early 2012 (the agreement has since been dissolved). Revenues dropped back down in 2013 but rose 86% to $8.4 million in 2014 on royalties from the sale of RELVAR/BREO ELLIPTA and ANORO ELLIPTA (launched that year).

Innoviva has reported net losses every year since its inception. In 2014 its net loss decreased 1% to $168 million due to a decline in losses from discontinued operations. At the end of 2015 its accumulated deficit totaled approximately $1.7 billion.

Operating cash outflow increased 1% to $130 million in 2014.

Strategy
Innoviva actively seeks partnerships with global pharmaceutical companies to allow for faster development and marketing of its pipeline candidates.

Through an exclusive alliance with minority shareholder GSK Innoviva is developing a next-generation version of GSK's asthma medication Advair and other products. The company's collaboration with GSK is focused on its Advair-replacement candidate RELVAR/BREO ELLIPTA to treat asthma and COPD that was launched in the US Japan and Europe. The companies have additional collaborative respiratory treatments (MABA and LAMA) under development. GSK also has the option to exclusively license other Innoviva pipeline products in areas including gastrointestinal ailments and pain. In mid-2014 the partners submitted a supplemental New Drug Application to the FDA for an asthma treatment in patients aged 12 years and older.

Other projects in the pipeline include treatments for gastrointestinal motility disorders such as chronic constipation. It also has candidates in the works to treat infection chronic pain and Alzheimer's disease. The company plans to continue to add new therapeutic candidates and enhance its R&D capabilities. It also hopes to find development partners for all of its programs especially as they get closer to commercialization stages where teaming up with a larger company with an established sales and marketing organization would be beneficial.

Company Background
Innoviva began operating in 1997 under the name Advanced Medicine.

EXECUTIVES

President and CEO, Michael W. Aguiar, age 52, $441,726 total compensation
Head - Business Development, David L. Brinkley, age 61, $301,102 total compensation
VP and Research and Development Program Leader, Edmund J. Moran, age 57
SVP Research and Early Clinical Development, Mathai Mammen, age 52, $411,925 total compensation
VP Clinical and Medical Affairs, Steve Barriere
VP Pharmacology, Sharath S. Hegde
VP Medicinal Chemistry, Dan Marquess
VP Drug Metabolism and Pharmacokinetics, Philip Worboys
Vice President Molecular and Cellular Biology, Jeffrey T. Finer
Vice President Clinical Development, Daniel M. Canafax
SVP Operations, Frank Pasqualone
SVP and CFO, Eric d'Esparbes
Chairman, Rick E. Winningham, age 59
Auditors: Grant Thornton LLP

LOCATIONS

HQ: Innoviva Inc
1350 Old Bayshore Highway Suite 400, Burlingame, CA 94010
Phone: 650 238-9600
Web: www.inva.com

PRODUCTS/OPERATIONS

2014 Sales

	% of total
Royalty revenue	87
MABA program license	13
Total	**100**

Selected Development Products
Bacterial Infections
  TD-1792 (antibiotic for staph infections)
  VIBATIV (telavancin for complicated skin and skin structure infections or cSSSI including staph infections)
Central Nervous System/Pain
  TD-1211 (opioid-induced constipation)
  TD-9855 (chronic pain)
Cognitive Disorders
  TD-5108 (Alzheimer's disease)
Gastrointestinal
  TD-5108 (for severe constipation and irritable bowel syndrome)
  TD-8954 (motility)
Respiratory
  LAMA/LABA (or GSK573719/Vilanterol for chronic obstructive pulmonary disease or COPD with GlaxoSmithKline)
  MABA (or GSK961081 for COPD with GlaxoSmithKline)
  RELOVAIR (for asthma with GlaxoSmithKline)

COMPETITORS

Abbott Labs	NovaBay
Achillion	Novartis
AstraZeneca	Pfizer
Boehringer Ingelheim	Progenics
Cubist Pharmaceuticals	Pharmaceuticals
Eli Lilly	SkyePharma
Johnson & Johnson	Sucampo
Merck	Sunovion

HISTORICAL FINANCIALS
Company Type: Public

Income Statement
FYE: December 31

	REVENUE ($ mil.)	NET INCOME ($ mil.)	NET PROFIT MARGIN	EMPLOYEES
12/18	261.0	395.0	151.4%	6
12/17	217.2	134.1	61.8%	12
12/16	133.5	59.5	44.6%	14
12/15	53.9	(18.7)	—	13
12/14	8.4	(168.4)	—	10
Annual Growth	135.9%	—	—	(12.0%)

2018 Year-End Financials

Debt ratio: 69.8%	No. of shares (mil.): 101.1
Return on equity: —	Dividends
Cash ($ mil.): 62.4	Yield: —
Current ratio: 34.92	Payout: —
Long-term debt ($ mil.): 382.8	Market value ($ mil.): 1,764.0

	STOCK PRICE ($) FY Close	P/E High/Low		PER SHARE ($) Earnings	Dividends	Book Value
12/18	17.45	5	3	3.53	0.00	1.52
12/17	14.19	12	8	1.17	0.00	(2.38)
12/16	10.70	26	15	0.53	0.00	(3.26)
12/15	10.54	—	—	(0.16)	1.00	(2.99)
12/14	14.15	—	—	(1.50)	0.50	(1.92)
Annual Growth	5.4%	—	—	—	—	—

Inogen, Inc

Combine innovation with oxygen and you've got Inogen. The company makes portable oxygen-concentrators that provide supplemental oxygen by people with chronic respiratory conditions. Oxygen concentrators pull nitrogen from ambient air to supply an oxygen-rich mix through a breathing tube. Its 4.8- and 7-pound models are meant to replace both large in-home concentrators as well as portable tank systems which also eliminates the need for home delivery of oxygen tanks. Unlike most suppliers in the market Inogen sells and rents directly to patients. International customers account for about a third of revenue. Inogen was formed in 2001 and went public in early 2014.
IPO

The company plans to use its $70.6 million in IPO proceeds to increase its rental-unit capacity to improve and expand its manufacturing facilities to expand its sales and marketing force and for R&D.

Operations
The majority of Inogen's revenue comes from consumer-direct supplies but it does operate though oxygen supply companies as well mostly in international markets. A growing portion of its revenues come from equipment rental which it prefers doing to the predictable and recurring nature of rental income. The company develops and manufacturers its products.

Geographic Reach
Inogen sells to more than 40 countries mostly in Europe and believes its product is poised to do well internationally for several reasons. Some countries including the UK and France have insurance or other payors that reimburse better for portable oxygen concentrators than the US while other countries have infrastructure (or a lack thereof) that makes a self-sustaining portable option best. And in some countries including Australia insurance doesn't pay for portable oxygen at all making light-weight mobility and low-cost key factors for customers who have to foot the bill themselves.

Sales and Marketing
In the US about 70% of sales Inogen primarily markets directly to consumers while it uses mostly large oxygen supply distributors and gas companies overseas.

The company believes its system gives it an advantage in the marketplace since traditional systems require a delivery network for regular replacement of oxygen tanks making supply in rural areas difficult and costly. It markets directly to consumers to avoid the traditional model which is geared toward delivering oxygen tanks or supplying large home concentrators.

Financial Performance
Inogen recognizes revenue from sales rentals Medicare reimbursements sales of used equipment and from warranties service contracts and shipping markups (categorized as 'other'). In 2012 the company reported a 59% increase in total revenue as it sold and rented more units for higher prices. Accordingly it went from a net loss of about 2 million to a modest gain of .6 million and cash flow improved about 5% as operating and financing activities both improved.

Strategy
Going forward Inogen plans to leverage its direct relationship with costumers to improve existing products and develop new ones. It also intends to expand its sales and marketing efforts and sign contracts with private insurance and Medicaid.

EXECUTIVES

President and CEO, Scott Wilkinson, age 53, $278,000 total compensation
EVP Finance and CFO, Alison Bauerlein, age 37, $293,461 total compensation
EVP Operations, Matt Scribner, age 51
EVP Engineering, Brenton Taylor, age 37
EVP Sales and Marketing, Byron Myers, age 39
Executive Vice President Operations, Bart Sanford
Chairman, Heath Lukatch, age 51
Auditors: DELOITTE & TOUCHE LLP

LOCATIONS
HQ: Inogen, Inc
326 Bollay Drive, Goleta, CA 93117
Phone: 805 562-0500
Web: www.inogen.com

PRODUCTS/OPERATIONS

2014 Sales
	$ mil.	% of total
Sales	73.1	65
Rentals	39.4	35
Total	112.5	100

Selected Products
G2 Systems & Accessories
G3 Systems & Accessories
Inogen At Home Oxygen Concentrator
Inogen Freedom Bundle
Inogen Oxygen Accessories
Inogen Oxygen Concentrators for Sale

COMPETITORS
American HomePatient
Apria Healthcare
Chart Industries
DeVilbiss
Invacare
Lincare Holdings
Philips Electronics
Praxair
Rotech Healthcare

HISTORICAL FINANCIALS
Company Type: Public

Income Statement
FYE: December 31

	REVENUE ($ mil.)	NET INCOME ($ mil.)	NET PROFIT MARGIN	EMPLOYEES
12/18	358.1	51.8	14.5%	285
12/17	249.4	21.0	8.4%	770
12/16	202.8	20.5	10.1%	602
12/15	159.0	11.5	7.3%	547
12/14	112.5	6.8	6.1%	411
Annual Growth	33.6%	66.0%	—	(8.7%)

2018 Year-End Financials
Debt ratio: —
Return on equity: 19.2%
Cash ($ mil.): 240.3
Current ratio: 6.75
Long-term debt ($ mil.): —
No. of shares (mil.): 21.7
Dividends
 Yield: —
 Payout: —
Market value ($ mil.): 2,704.0

	STOCK PRICE ($) FY Close	P/E High/Low	PER SHARE ($) Earnings	Dividends	Book Value
12/18	124.17	116 46	2.30	0.00	14.25
12/17	119.08	126 62	0.96	0.00	10.82
12/16	67.17	67 29	0.97	0.00	8.93
12/15	40.09	91 50	0.56	0.00	6.77
12/14	31.37	95 42	0.30	0.00	6.20
Annual Growth	41.1%	—	66.4%	—	23.1%

Installed Building Products Inc

Installed Building Products (IBP) wants to insulate its customers from the elements. The company is a leading new residential insulation installer with more than 135 branches in all continental US states and Washington DC. IBP manages all aspects of the installation process for its customers including direct purchases of materials from national manufacturers delivery and installation. In addition to insulation IBP waterproofs and fireproofs homes and installs garage doors rain gutters shower doors shelving and mirrors.

Operations
Installed Building Products (IBP) operates through a single reporting segment. Residential new construction and repair and remodel comprise about 80% of its revenues while commercial construction accounts for the remainder.

Two-thirds of its sales are for insulation with fiberglass and cellulose insulation accounting for about 85% of that and spray foam insulation generating the rest. Waterproofing; shower doors shelving and mirrors; garage doors; rain gutters; and other building products each contribute anywhere from about 5% to 10% of revenue.

Geographic Reach
Columbus Ohio-based Installed Building Products (IBP) has more than 135 branches serving all continental US states and Washington DC. The company's geographic footprint covers 70% of all US residential permits.

It also has warehouse and office space in about 40 states with Ohio Texas and Indiana representing the most square footage.

Sales and Marketing
Installed Building Products' (IBP) sales force is made up of about 550 employees who on average have been with the company for nearly ten years. The company focuses on cross-selling services to existing customers and identifying customers who may need multiple services.

Its customers include homebuilders construction firms contractors and individuals. The top 10 customers which includes both national and regional builders account for about 15% of revenue.

Financial Performance
In large part due to its acquisitions of smaller local competitors Installed Building Products (IBP) has seen massive growth in the last five years with revenue net income and cash ballooning by 162% 581% and 1438% respectively. However the company's long-term debt has also increased more than tenfold in that time.?

In 2017 the company reported revenue of $1.1 billion up 31% from the prior year. Its acquisition of Alpha Insulation and Waterproofing accounted for 43% of that $269.9 million jump. Growth in completed job volume contributed 18% and factors such as customer and product mix market price variations and building code changes represented 13%.?

IBP's net income in 2017 remained relatively stable ticking up 7% to $41.1 million.

Cash at the end of fiscal 2017 was $62.5 million a 332% jump from the prior year. Cash from operations provided $68.8 million while investing activities used $200.4 million owing to its acquisitions. Financing activities added another $179.7 million.

Strategy
Installed Building Products (IBP) has adopted an aggressive acquisition strategy to build its geographic presence in the US completing more than 125 acquisitions since 1999. The company which has branches in every continental US state has made about 20 acquisitions in 2017 and 2018.

IBP is also focused on diversifying its product mix with the help of those acquisitions. The percentage of its sales derived from insulation dropped 10% to 67% in 2017 compared with 2016 while waterproofing services quadrupled as a percent of sales; shower doors shelving and mirrors and other building products also ticked up in 2017.

Mergers and Acquisitions

Installed Building Products' (IBP) strategy centers around aggressively acquiring smaller local competitors to diversify its geographic reach. The company has made more than 125 acquisitions since the late 1990s including 10 in 2017 and another 10 through late 2018. The company's biggest acquisitions by purchase price have included Custom Door & Gate Alpha Insulation and Waterproofing Columbia Shelving & Mirror and Astro Insulation.

Its largest acquisition to date is Alpha Insulation and Waterproofing purchased in January 2017 for $116.7 million. That purchase expanded IBP's presence in Georgia North Carolina Tennessee Florida and Texas and strengthened its complementary offerings such as fireproofing and waterproofing.

Purchases in 2018 have included Ohio's Advanced Fiber Technology Florida-based Water-Tite Solution and Cutting Edge Glass based in Colorado.

Company Background

Installed Building Products (IBP) was founded as Edwards Insulation in 1977. It had one location in Columbus Ohio. In the late 1990s it established a national presence with an aggressive acquisition strategy.

EXECUTIVES

Chairman President and CEO, Jeffrey w. Edwards, age 55, $83,077 total compensation
EVP CFO and Director, Michael T. Miller, age 54, $194,900 total compensation
COO, Jay P. Elliott, age 57, $194,900 total compensation
President External Affairs, W. Jeffrey Hire, age 67
Regional President, R. Scott Jenkins, age 63
Regional President, Matthew J. Momper, age 58
Regional President, Warren W. Pearce, age 60
Regional President, Randall S. Williamson, age 56
Vice President, Bill Jenkins
Auditors: DELOITTE & TOUCHE LLP

LOCATIONS

HQ: Installed Building Products Inc
495 South High Street, Suite 50, Columbus, OH 43215
Phone: 614 221-3399
Web: www.installedbuildingproducts.com

PRODUCTS/OPERATIONS

2017 Sales

	% of total
Residential new construction and repair and remodel	83
Commercial construction	17
Total	100

2017 Sales

	% of total
Insulation	67
Waterproofing	8
Shower doors shelving & mirrors	7
Garage doors	5
Rain gutters	4
Other	9
Total	100

COMPETITORS

ABC Supply   HD Supply

HISTORICAL FINANCIALS

Company Type: Public

Income Statement   FYE: December 31

	REVENUE ($ mil.)	NET INCOME ($ mil.)	NET PROFIT MARGIN	EMPLOYEES
12/18	1,336.4	54.7	4.1%	7,700
12/17	1,132.9	41.1	3.6%	6,900
12/16	862.9	38.4	4.5%	5,292
12/15	662.7	26.5	4.0%	4,510
12/14	518.0	13.9	2.7%	3,600
Annual Growth	26.7%	40.8%		20.9%

2018 Year-End Financials

Debt ratio: 55.5%   No. of shares (mil.): 29.9
Return on equity: 27.8%   Dividends
Cash ($ mil.): 100.5   Yield: —
Current ratio: 2.27   Payout: —
Long-term debt ($ mil.): 436.0   Market value ($ mil.): 1,008.0

	STOCK PRICE ($) FY Close	P/E High/Low		PER SHARE ($) Earnings	Dividends	Book Value
12/18	33.69	44	17	1.75	0.00	6.10
12/17	75.95	60	31	1.30	0.00	6.61
12/16	41.30	36	15	1.23	0.00	4.89
12/15	24.83	35	20	0.85	0.00	3.65
12/14	17.82	—	—	(0.20)	0.00	2.91
Annual Growth	17.3%			—	—	20.3%

Integer Holdings Corp

Integer Holdings is one of the world's largest medical device outsource (MDO) manufacturing companies and serves the cardiac neuromodulation orthopedics vascular and advanced surgical and portable medical markets. Its medical division makes batteries used in implantable medical devices such as pacemakers and cardioverter defibrillators (ICDs) as well as surgical guidewires catheters and stents. Integer's non-medical division comprises the Electrochem product line ? high-end batteries for demanding applications in the energy military and environmental sectors. The business gets more than 55% of its sales from the US. Its medical customers include large multi-national medical device OEMs such as Abbott Laboratories Biotronik Boehringer Ingelheim and Boston Scientific. Some of its Electrochem customers are Halliburton Teledyne Technologies and Weatherford International. The company operates through some 20 facilities in the US Europe Mexico South America and Southeast Asia.

Financial Performance

Integer Holdings' revenue has been on the rise for the last several years.

Sales in 2018 reached $1.2 billion a 7% increase compared with $1.1 billion the previous year driven by market growth and new business wins.

The company posted net income of $138.0 million in 2018 compared with $66.7 million in 2017. The majority of the increase was due to the sale of its Advanced Surgical and Orthopedic (AS&O) product lines.

Cash at the end of fiscal 2018 was $25.6 million a decrease of $18.5 million from the prior year. Cash from operations contributed $167.3 million to the coffers while investing activities provided $536.7 million mainly from the sale of AS&O. Financing activities used $725.1 million primarily to pay back long-term debt.

Strategy

After merging with rival LRM in 2015 and integrating the two entities' operations Integer Holdings set out in 2017 to focus its investments on research and development activities improving manufacturing operations and business processes and redirecting investments away from projects without significant market potential.

To improve efficiency in its operations Integer has established a new enterprise-wide manufacturing structure known as the Integer Production System (IPS) which comprises more standardized systems and processes.

In 2018 the company divested its Advanced Surgical & Orthopedics product line and intends to invest in its Cardio & Vascular Neuromodulation and Electrochem where it sees the potential for growth. It also plans to protect its Cardiac Rhythm Management product line while shoring up profitability in its orthopedics advanced surgical and power solutions businesses.

EXECUTIVES

President and COO, Thomas J. Hook, age 56, $719,192 total compensation
EVP and COO, Jeremy A. Friedman
EVP Quality and Regulatory Affairs, Joseph F. (Joe) Flanagan
EVP and Chief Human Resources Officer, Kristin E. Trecker
President Advanced Surgical and Orthopaedics, Declan Smyth
President Cardiac Rhythm Management (CRM) and Neuromodulation, Tony Gonzalez
President Electrochem, Jennifer Bolt
EVP and CFO, Gary Haire
Interim President Cardio and Vascular, John Harris
Executive Vice President Global Sales and Marketing, Thomas Hickman
Vice President and Chief Audit Executive, Dave Bolton
Senior Vice President and Chief Technology Officer, George Cintra
Vice President Of Research and Development, Dominick Frustaci
Vp Research and Development Marketing and Product Solutions Sales, Andrew Senn
Chairman, William R. (Bill) Sanford, age 74
Board Member, Filippo Passerini
Board Member, Jean Hobby
Auditors: DELOITTE & TOUCHE LLP

LOCATIONS

HQ: Integer Holdings Corp
5830 Granite Parkway, Suite 1150, Plano, TX 75024
Phone: 214 618-5243
Web: www.integer.net

Integra LifeSciences Holdings Corp

PRODUCTS/OPERATIONS

2018 Sales

	$ mil.	% of total
Cardio & Vascular	585.5	48
Advanced Surgical Orthopedics & Portable Medical	443.3	37
Cardio & Neuromodulation	133.2	11
Non-medical	53.0	4
Total	1,215.0	100

Selected Operations
MedicalCardio & Vascular
Introducers
Steerable Sheaths
Guidewires
Catheters and Stimulation Therapy Components
Subassemblies and Finished Device Cardiac & Neuromodulation
Batteries
Capacitors
Filtered and Unfiltered Feed-Throughs
Engineered Com

COMPETITORS

AVX
CONMED Corporation
Cardinal Health
Edwards Lifesciences
Integra LifeSciences
Invacare
Medtronic
Merit Medical Systems
Morgan Advanced Materials
Orthofix
Philips Healthcare
Stryker
Teleflex
West Pharmaceutical Services
Zimmer Biomet

HISTORICAL FINANCIALS
Company Type: Public

Income Statement
FYE: December 28

	REVENUE ($ mil.)	NET INCOME ($ mil.)	NET PROFIT MARGIN	EMPLOYEES
12/18	1,215.0	167.9	13.8%	8,250
12/17	1,461.9	66.6	4.6%	9,700
12/16*	1,386.7	5.9	0.4%	9,400
01/16	800.4	(7.5)	—	9,559
01/15	687.7	55.4	8.1%	3,690
Annual Growth	15.3%	31.9%	—	22.3%

*Fiscal year change

2018 Year-End Financials

Debt ratio: 39.7%
Return on equity: 17.2%
Cash ($ mil.): 25.5
Current ratio: 2.53
Long-term debt ($ mil.): 888.0
No. of shares (mil.): 32.4
Dividends
Yield: —
Payout: —
Market value ($ mil.): 2,469.0

	STOCK PRICE ($) FY Close	P/E High/Low		PER SHARE ($) Earnings	Dividends	Book Value
12/18	76.03	17	8	5.15	0.00	32.66
12/17	45.30	26	14	2.09	0.00	28.03
12/16*	29.45	284	96	0.19	0.00	23.45
01/16	52.50	—	—	(0.29)	0.00	27.80
01/15	48.66	23	18	2.14	0.00	24.47
Annual Growth	11.8%	—	—	24.6%	—	7.5%

*Fiscal year change

Integra LifeSciences a regenerative medicine specialist develops medical equipment for use in cranial procedures small bone and joint reconstruction and the repair and reconstruction of soft tissue. Integra makes surgical equipment including bone fixation devices spinal fixation systems tissue ablation equipment and drainage catheters used in neurosurgery and orthopedic reconstruction as well as basic surgical instruments. Its products are marketed worldwide through direct sales and distributors. Integra operates in two segments: Specialty Surgical Solutions (the larger segment it brings in some two-thirds of revenues) and Orthopedics and Tissue Technologies.

Operations
The Specialty Surgical Solutions segment makes products in the area of dural repair tissue ablation precision tools and neuro critical care. Meanwhile the Orthopedics and Tissue Technologies segments offers small bone repair and joint replacement hardware products for extremities as well as private-label regenerative medicine technologies.

The company's products are intended mainly for niche markets not targeted by larger medical device firms. Most of Integra's orthopedic products for instance are designed for orthopedic reconstruction of the extremities such as the feet and ankles (rather than the hip and knee replacement products offered by the likes of Zimmer and DePuy). However the company has reached those larger and more diverse markets through a select number of original equipment manufacturer deals with firms such as Medtronic and Zimmer.

Geographic Reach
The company's principal manufacturing and research facilities are located in the US (Massachusetts New Jersey Ohio and Pennsylvania) and in France Germany Ireland Mexico and Puerto Rico. Its distribution centers are in the US (Nevada Ohio and Pennsylvania) Australia Belgium Canada and France.

Integra also has repair centers in the US (California Massachusetts and Ohio) Australia and Germany.

The US accounts for more than three-fourths of total revenue; Europe accounts for 12%.

Sales and Marketing
The group sells its products through an internal sales force and through distributors and wholesalers. It also markets some products domestically through strategic partnerships.

Financial Performance
Integra's revenue had been on the rise until 2015 when revenue fell 5% to $883 million. That drop was due to the spin-off of SeaSpine Holdings; both segments actually had higher sales that year thanks largely to a number of acquisitions.

Net income which has been fluctuating for the past five years dropped in 2015. The company lost a net $4 million that year as selling general and administrative spending increased (again largely due to acquisition activity as well as the spin-off of the spine business). Cash flow from operations has been rising; it increased 19% to $94 million due to decline in inventories and changes in liabilities.

Strategy
Integra has expanded its operations over the years through acquisitions geographic expansion and product R&D efforts. It has expanded both its product lines and geographic reach through some 45 acquisitions since its formation including recent additions of direct distribution assets in Australia and the UK.

As a result of its growth efforts and string of acquisitions the company has implemented a number of cost-cutting measures. It has consolidated manufacturing and distribution facilities. In 2015 Integra separated its orthobiologics and spinal fusion hardware business SeaSpine Holdings which became a public company. The split will help both surviving entities operate in their respective arenas more effectively.

Additionally it has nearly completed the integration of a common enterprise resource planning (ERP) system.

Integra plans to launch its Omnigraft product for the treatment of diabetic foot ulcers.

Mergers and Acquisitions
Integra reached an agreement to acquire Derma Sciences a tissue regeneration company focused on advanced wound and burn care for around $204 million in early 2017. Also that year it bought Johnson & Johnson's Codman neurosurgery business which provides devices for areas including hydrocephaly neurocritical care and operative neurosurgery for $1.05 billion.

In 2015 the company acquired TEI Biosciences and TEI Medical for $312 million. That purchase boosted its offerings in regenerative wound care and tissue repair. Integra also purchased a line of lower extremity implants from Metasurg that year as well as the US rights to Tornier's Talari and Talaris XT ankle replacement products and its Futura toe replacement products. Finally it acquired Italian distribution arm Tekmed Instruments.

Integra gets a majority of its sales from its orthopedic segment and its neurosciences segment each accounting for about 40% of sales; nearly one-third of those segment revenues come from regenerative medicine supplies. Traditional medical instruments such as surgical forceps scopes lights and retractors account for about 20% of revenues.

EXECUTIVES

VP; President International, Dan Reuvers
CEO President and Director, Peter J. Arduini, age 54, $787,115 total compensation
President Instruments, Debbie Leonetti, age 63
VP; President Advanced Wound Care, Robert D. Paltridge, age 61, $215,000 total compensation
VP and CFO, Glenn Coleman, age 51
VP Global Operations and Supply Chain, John Mooradian
VP; President Neurosurgery, Robert T. Davis, $335,115 total compensation
Vice President Product Development, Jerry Klawitter
Vice President Marketing And R And D, William Weber
Vice President Product Development, Christopher Fedele
Vice President Global Total Rewards, Barbara Vietor
Vice President Regenerative Sales, Matthew Chiminski
Vice President Reimbursement and Market Access, Joseph Rolley
Vice President Sales And Marketing Neurosurgery Emea, Thierry Bordenave

Area Vice President Mid West BioDOptix Biodlogics, Mark Kennedy
Vice President Of Sales Neurosurgery, Tim Mccarthy
Senior Vice President Marketing, Deborah Leonetti
Marketing Vice President, Tarca Thomas
Vice President, Thomas Harrison
Chairman, Stuart M. Essig, age 57
Auditors: PricewaterhouseCoopers LLP

LOCATIONS
HQ: Integra LifeSciences Holdings Corp
311 Enterprise Drive, Plainsboro, NJ 08536
Phone: 609 275-0500
Web: www.integralife.com

PRODUCTS/OPERATIONS

2015 Sales

	$ mil.	% of total
Specialty Surgical Solutions	586.9	66
Orthopedics and Tissue Technologies	295.8	34
Total	**882.7**	**100**

Selected Acquisitions

COMPETITORS

Accuray	Organogenesis
Alphatec Spine	Orthofix
B. Braun Medical (UK)	RTI Surgical
CareFusion	Smith & Nephew
Genzyme Biosurgery	Stryker
Globus Medical	Synovis Life
Johnson & Johnson	Technologies
Medtronic	Synthes
NuVasive	Zimmer Biomet

HISTORICAL FINANCIALS
Company Type: Public

Income Statement — FYE: December 31

	REVENUE ($ mil.)	NET INCOME ($ mil.)	NET PROFIT MARGIN	EMPLOYEES
12/18	1,472.4	60.8	4.1%	4,500
12/17	1,188.2	64.7	5.4%	4,400
12/16	992.0	74.5	7.5%	3,700
12/15	882.7	(3.5)	—	3,500
12/14	928.3	34.0	3.7%	3,400
Annual Growth	12.2%	15.6%	—	7.3%

2018 Year-End Financials

Debt ratio: 43.5% No. of shares (mil.): 85.1
Return on equity: 5.2% Dividends
Cash ($ mil.): 138.8 Yield: —
Current ratio: 2.95 Payout: —
Long-term debt ($ mil.): 1,331.7 Market value ($ mil.): 3,841.0

	STOCK PRICE ($) FY Close	P/E High/Low	PER SHARE ($) Earnings	Dividends	Book Value
12/18	45.10	92 58	0.72	0.00	16.15
12/17	47.86	101 49	0.82	0.00	12.28
12/16	85.79	87 55	0.94	0.00	11.24
12/15	67.78	— —	(0.05)	0.00	10.17
12/14	54.23	104 84	0.52	0.00	10.76
Annual Growth	(4.5%)	— —	8.7%	—	10.7%

Intelligent Systems Corp.

EXECUTIVES
VP CFO and Secretary, Bonnie L. Herron, age 68, $154,403 total compensation
VP, J. William (Bill) Goodhew III, age 78
VP; President ChemFree, Francis A. (Frank) Marks Jr., age 82, $149,135 total compensation
Chairman President and CEO, J. Leland Strange, age 74, $273,942 total compensation
Director, James V. Napier, age 79
Director, Parker H. (Pete) Petit, age 76
Director, John B. Peatman, age 81
Auditors: Nichols, Cauley and Associates, LLC

LOCATIONS
HQ: Intelligent Systems Corp.
4355 Shackleford Road, Norcross, GA 30093
Phone: 770 381-2900
Web: www.intelsys.com

PRODUCTS/OPERATIONS

Selected Portfolio Companies
Alliance Technology Ventures
ChemFree Corporation
CoreCard Software Inc.
NKD Enterprises LLC (dba CoreXpand 26%)

COMPETITORS
Safeguard Scientifics

HISTORICAL FINANCIALS
Company Type: Public

Income Statement — FYE: December 31

	REVENUE ($ mil.)	NET INCOME ($ mil.)	NET PROFIT MARGIN	EMPLOYEES
12/18	20.1	6.2	31.1%	430
12/17	9.3	0.4	5.1%	350
12/16	8.1	(1.1)	—	286
12/15	4.7	18.0	376.8%	252
12/14	14.5	(0.0)	—	263
Annual Growth	8.3%	—	—	13.1%

2018 Year-End Financials

Debt ratio: — No. of shares (mil.): 8.8
Return on equity: 27.5% Dividends
Cash ($ mil.): 18.9 Yield: —
Current ratio: 7.57 Payout: —
Long-term debt ($ mil.): — Market value ($ mil.): 114.0

	STOCK PRICE ($) FY Close	P/E High/Low	PER SHARE ($) Earnings	Dividends	Book Value
12/18	12.92	21 6	0.70	0.00	2.94
12/17	4.56	95 70	0.05	0.00	2.22
12/16	4.24	— —	(0.13)	0.35	2.51
12/15	3.23	2 1	2.02	0.00	2.98
12/14	1.61	— —	(0.00)	0.00	0.98
Annual Growth	68.3%	—	—	—	31.6%

Interactive Brokers Group Inc

Global electronic broker Interactive Brokers Group performs low-cost trade order management execution and portfolio management services through its Interactive Brokers subsidiaries. Catering to institutional and experienced individual investors the company offers access to more than 120 electronic exchanges and trading centers worldwide executing around 850000 trades per day in stocks options futures foreign exchange instruments bonds and mutual funds. The company also licenses its trading interface to large banks and brokerages through white branding agreements. Interactive Brokers operates worldwide but generates about 80% of its revenue in the US. In 2017 the company announced plans to wind down its market making business.

Operations
Interactive Brokers Group operates through a pair of business segments. Electronic Brokerage accounts for more than 95% of the company's revenue. Its Market Making business provides the remainder; in 2017 the company announced plans to dispose of the segment.

Through its Interactive Brokers subsidiaries the company's Electronic Brokerage unit offers electronic execution and clearing services to institutional and individual clients. Interactive Brokers offers some of the lowest execution commission and financing rates in the US; automated real-time margin requirement monitoring; and analytics tools. The group also lends out its trading interface to large financial advisors and broker-dealers through white branding agreements wherein those clients provide Interactive Brokers' platform to their customers without referencing Interactive Brokers' name. Furthermore the firm markets securities financing services a block trade desk model portfolios and asset management.

Interactive Brokers Group garners about half of its revenue from net interest income while roughly 40% comes from commissions.

Geographic Reach
Greenwich Connecticut-based Interactive Brokers Group's customers span more than 200 countries and territories. It has US offices in cities including Boston Chicago San Francisco West Palm Beach and Washington DC. The company's overseas offices are in Switzerland the UK Estonia Luxembourg Russia Liechtenstein Hungary India Hong Kong China Japan and Australia. The US generates about 80% the group's revenue.

Sales and Marketing
Interactive Brokers Group serves about 600000 institutional and individual brokerage customers. It categorizes its clients into the two groups of cleared customers and non-cleared customers (or trade execution customers). Cleared customers include small group and individual market makers institutional and individual traders introducing brokers financial advisors and hedge funds. Non-cleared customers who clear with another prime broker or custodian bank encompass online brokers and commercial bank customer trading units.

Financial Performance
A continued decline in trading gains have caused headwinds for Interactive Brokers Group's

revenue and profits over the past several years. However rising commission fees and interest income more recently have led the company to growth. In the last five years it has posted about an 80% increase in revenue and a 275% increase in net income.

Interactive Brokers' revenue jumped 12% to $1.9 billion in 2018 as greater market volatility caused by geopolitical and economic uncertainty drove customer trading. The company's client account and asset bases both grew and higher benchmark interest rates pushed up net interest income.

Strong revenue growth and a large income tax expense reduction in 2018 drove the firm's net income up 122% to $169 million.

Interactive Brokers added $1.8 billion to its cash to end the year with stores of $10.1 billion. Operations provided $2.4 billion. The company used $399 million in its financing activities primarily distributions to non-controlling interests and spent $57 million on investment. Investments included purchases of property equipment intangible assets and other investments. Capital expenditures comprised software engineering staff compensation; computer network and communications hardware; and lease improvements.

Strategy

Interactive Brokers Group develops proprietary technologies to stay competitive and weather market fluctuations diversifying its equity currencies and focusing its operations through strategic business exits.

In 2019 the firm introduced online portfolio analysis product Portfolio Checkup within its PortfolioAnalyst portfolio performance reporting tool. The new feature generates a single page that presents performance measures against 230 industry benchmarks along risk metrics including max drawdown peak-to-valley and Sharpe ratio. The previous year Interactive Brokers made PortfolioAnalyst available to the public for free. In 2017 it began offering bitcoin futures trading and an Interactive Brokers Debit Mastercard to its customers. The card allows clients to spend and borrow against their brokerage accounts and invest in stocks bonds options futures and foreign exchange instruments from a single account.

As it is exposed to foreign exchange rate fluctuations the firm is working to diversify its equity currencies under its GLOBALs strategy. About 30% of its equity is held in non-US currencies.

The unpredictable nature of earnings from market making and increased competition from high frequency traders in recent years drove Interactive Brokers to start exiting that business in 2017. That year it sold its US options market making operations to Two Sigma Securities and terminated most of its international market making activities.

Company Background

Founder chairman and CEO Thomas Peterffy controls Interactive Brokers Group. Peterffy started the company in 1978 as T.P. & Co. It was the first market making firm to use daily-printed computer-generated fair value sheets.

EXECUTIVES

Chairman and CEO, Thomas Peterffy, age 74, $1,350,000 total compensation
CFO Treasurer Secretary and Director, Paul J. Brody, age 58, $380,000 total compensation
Executive Vice President; Chief Information Officer, Thomas A. J. Frank, $380,000 total compensation
EVP Marketing and Product Development, Steve Sanders
President and Director, Milan Galik, age 52, $380,000 total compensation
Vice Chairman, Earl H. Nemser, age 72
Auditors: DELOITTE & TOUCHE LLP

LOCATIONS

HQ: Interactive Brokers Group Inc
One Pickwick Plaza, Greenwich, CT 06830
Phone: 203 618-5800
Web: www.interactivebrokers.com

PRODUCTS/OPERATIONS

Trading Services
Account Management
Employee Track Management
Funding Reference
Investors' Marketplace
IRA Information
New Features Poll
Securities Financing

2018 Revenue

	$ mil.	% of total
Commissions	777.0	32
Interest income	1,392.0	59
Trading gains	39.0	2
Other	158.0	7
Interest expense	(463)	-
Total	**1,903.0**	**100**

2018 Revenue

	$ mil.	% of total
Electronic brokerage	1,842.0	96
Market making	76.0	4
Corporate	(15)	-
Total	**1,903.0**	**100**

COMPETITORS

Charles Schwab
Citigroup Global Markets Limited
E*TRADE Financial
GSEC
KCG Holdings
Merrill Lynch
Morgan Stanley
PEAK6 Investments
Susquehanna International Group LLP
TD Ameritrade
UBS

HISTORICAL FINANCIALS

Company Type: Public

Income Statement FYE: December 31

	REVENUE ($ mil.)	NET INCOME ($ mil.)	NET PROFIT MARGIN	EMPLOYEES
12/18	1,903.0	169.0	8.9%	1,413
12/17	1,702.0	76.0	4.5%	1,228
12/16	1,396.0	84.0	6.0%	1,204
12/15	1,189.0	49.0	4.1%	1,087
12/14	1,043.2	44.5	4.3%	960
Annual Growth	16.2%	39.6%	—	10.1%

2018 Year-End Financials

Debt ratio: 6.7%
Return on equity: 14.2%
Cash ($ mil.): 11,342.0
Current ratio: 1.07
Long-term debt ($ mil.): —
No. of shares (mil.): 75.1
Dividends
 Yield: 0.7%
 Payout: 25.0%
Market value ($ mil.): 4,189.0

	STOCK PRICE ($) FY Close	P/E High/Low		PER SHARE ($) Earnings	Dividends	Book Value
12/18	55.78	35	24	2.28	0.40	17.07
12/17	59.21	57	31	1.07	0.40	15.25
12/16	36.51	34	24	1.25	0.40	14.33
12/15	43.60	57	35	0.78	0.40	13.49
12/14	29.16	37	26	0.77	0.40	13.11
Annual Growth	17.6%	—	—	31.2%	(0.0%)	6.8%

Invesco DB Commodity Index Tracking Fund

Auditors: PricewaterhouseCoopers LLP

LOCATIONS

HQ: Invesco DB Commodity Index Tracking Fund
c/o Invesco Capital Management LLC, 3500 Lacey Road, Suite 700, Downers Grove, IL 60515
Phone: 800 983-0903
Web: www.invescopowershares.com

HISTORICAL FINANCIALS

Company Type: Public

Income Statement FYE: December 31

	ASSETS ($ mil.)	NET INCOME ($ mil.)	INCOME AS % OF ASSETS	EMPLOYEES
12/18	2,009.8	25.0	1.2%	0
12/17	2,263.9	(1.4)	—	0
12/16	2,559.2	(13.5)	—	0
12/15	2,011.2	(25.5)	—	0
12/14	4,948.2	(45.2)	—	0
Annual Growth	(20.2%)	—	—	—

	STOCK PRICE ($) FY Close	P/E High/Low		PER SHARE ($) Earnings	Dividends	Book Value
12/18	14.49	116	90	0.16	0.19	14.44
12/17	16.61	—	—	(0.01)	0.00	16.63
12/16	15.84	—	—	(0.09)	0.00	15.83
12/15	13.36	—	—	(0.15)	0.00	13.35
12/14	18.45	—	—	(0.21)	0.00	18.40
Annual Growth	(5.9%)	—	—	—	—	(5.9%)

Investar Holding Corp

Auditors: Ernst & Young LLP

LOCATIONS

HQ: Investar Holding Corp
10500 Coursey Boulevard, Baton Rouge, LA 70808
Phone: 225 227-2222

HISTORICAL FINANCIALS
Company Type: Public

Income Statement FYE: December 31

	ASSETS ($ mil.)	NET INCOME ($ mil.)	INCOME AS % OF ASSETS	EMPLOYEES
12/18	1,786.4	13.6	0.8%	255
12/17	1,622.7	8.2	0.5%	258
12/16	1,158.9	7.8	0.7%	152
12/15	1,031.5	7.0	0.7%	951
12/14	879.3	5.4	0.6%	179
Annual Growth	19.4%	26.0%	—	9.3%

2018 Year-End Financials
Return on assets: 0.8%
Return on equity: 7.6%
Long-term debt ($ mil.): —
No. of shares (mil.): 9.4
Sales ($ mil): 78.2
Dividends
Yield: 0.6%
Payout: 13.0%
Market value ($ mil.): 235.0

	STOCK PRICE ($) FY Close	P/E High/Low	PER SHARE ($) Earnings	Dividends	Book Value
12/18	24.80	21 15	1.39	0.17	19.22
12/17	24.10	26 20	0.96	0.07	18.15
12/16	18.65	18 12	1.10	0.04	15.88
12/15	17.60	18 14	0.97	0.03	15.05
12/14	13.85	15 13	0.93	0.01	14.24
Annual Growth	15.7%	— —	10.6%	87.3%	7.8%

Investors Bancorp Inc (New)

Investors Bancorp is the holding company for Investors Savings Bank which serves New Jersey and New York from more than 130 branch offices. Founded in 1926 the bank offers such standard deposit products as savings and checking accounts CDs money market accounts and IRAs. Nearly 40% of the bank's loan portfolio is made up of residential mortgages while multi-family loans and commercial real estate loans make up more than 50% combined. The bank also originates business industrial and consumer loans. Founded in 1926 Investors Bancorp's assets now exceed $20 billion.

Operations
About 86% of Investors Bancorp's revenue came from interest income from loans and loans held-for sale in 2014 while another 8% came from interest income on the bank's mortgage-backed securities municipal bonds and other debt. The remainder of its revenue came from fees and service charges (3%) and other miscellaneous income sources. Investors Bancorp boasted a staff of more than 1700 at the end of 2014.

Geographic Reach
Based in Short Hills New Jersey Investors Bancorp has more than 130 branches across New Jersey and New York. It also has lending offices in New York City Short Hills Spring Lake Newark Astoria and Brooklyn. Its operation center is in Iselin New Jersey.

Sales and Marketing
The company offers retail and commercial banking services to individuals professional service firms municipalities small and middle-market companies commercial and industrial firms and other businesses.

Financial Performance
Investors Bancorp's revenues and profits have been rising thanks to strong loan growth from bank acquisitions falling interest expenses on deposits and declining loan loss provisions as its loan portfolio's credit quality has improved with higher property valuations in the strengthened economy.

The bank's revenue jumped by 21% to a record $702.7 million in 2014 mostly thanks to loan asset growth stemming from the bank's 2014 acquisition of Gateway Community Financial.

Higher revenue and a continued decline in loan loss provisions in 2014 drove the bank's net income higher by 18% to a record $131.7 million. Investor Bancorp's operating cash levels spiked by 58% to $277.4 million for the year on higher cash earnings and favorable changes in its working capital.

Strategy
Investors Bancorp continues to expand its geographic reach in its core New Jersey and New York markets and boost its loan and deposit business mainly through select bank and branch acquisitions. Indeed the bank noted in 2015 that it had made eight bank or branch acquisitions since 2008 adding that they have counted for "a significant portion" of the bank's historic growth.

The company's 2014 and 2013 bank acquisitions bolstered its expansion in New Jersey into the suburbs of Philadelphia the boroughs of New York City the Nassau and Suffolk Counties on Long Island and historic markets throughout New Jersey.

Mergers and Acquisitions
In May 2016 Investors Bancorp agreed to purchase the $1 billion-asset The Bank of Princeton along with its 13 branches in the greater Princeton New Jersey and Philadelphia Pennsylvania areas. The added locations would grow Investors Bancorp's branch network by almost 10% to 156 branches in the Philadelphia to New York City corridor.

In January 2014 Investors Bancorp purchased Gateway Community Financial Corp along with its four branches in Gloucester County New Jersey. The deal added nearly $255 million in customer deposits and $195 million in new loan business to its books.

In December 2013 the company bought Roma Financial Corporation and its 26 branches in Burlington Ocean Mercer Camden and Middlesex counties in New Jersey. The deal added $1.34 billion in deposits and $991 million in loan assets while expanding the company's reach into the Philadelphia suburbs of New Jersey.

Company Background
In late 2012 the company acquired Marathon Banking Corporation (a subsidiary of Greece-based Piraeus Bank) for $135 million adding 13 branches in the New York metro area and more than doubling its branches in New York. The deal also would mark Investors Bancorp's entry into Manhattan and Staten Island.

EXECUTIVES
SEVP and COO, Domenick A. Cama, age 63, $621,000 total compensation
President and CEO, Kevin Cummings, age 64, $935,000 total compensation
EVP and Chief Lending Officer, Richard S. Spengler, age 57, $400,000 total compensation
EVP and Chief Retail Banking Officer, Paul Kalamaras, $375,000 total compensation
SVP and CFO, Sean Burke
Senior Vice President, Jawad Chaudhry
Vice President Information Security Officer
Director of Information Security, David Van
Vice President Systems, Charles Little
Chairman, Robert M. Cashill, age 76
Auditors: KPMG LLP

LOCATIONS
HQ: Investors Bancorp Inc (New)
101 JFK Parkway, Short Hills, NJ 07078
Phone: 973 924-5100
Web: www.myinvestorsbank.com

PRODUCTS/OPERATIONS
2014 Sales

	$ mil.	% of total
Interest		
Loans receivable and held-for-sale	603.4	86
Mortgage-backed securities	44.2	6
Federal Home Loan Bank stock	6.9	1
Municipal bonds & other debt	5.7	1
Other	0.7	-
Non-interest		
Fees & service charges	19.3	3
Gain on loan transaction	5.3	2
Others	17.2	1
Total	702.7	100

COMPETITORS
Bank of America	M&T Bank
Bank of New York Mellon	New York Community Bancorp
Citigroup	OceanFirst Financial
ConnectOne Bancorp	PNC Financial
Fulton Financial	

HISTORICAL FINANCIALS
Company Type: Public

Income Statement FYE: December 31

	ASSETS ($ mil.)	NET INCOME ($ mil.)	INCOME AS % OF ASSETS	EMPLOYEES
12/18	26,229.0	202.5	0.8%	1,962
12/17	25,129.2	126.7	0.5%	1,959
12/16	23,174.6	192.1	0.8%	1,829
12/15	20,888.6	181.5	0.9%	1,768
12/14	18,773.6	131.7	0.7%	1,708
Annual Growth	8.7%	11.4%	—	3.5%

2018 Year-End Financials
Return on assets: 0.7%
Return on equity: 6.6%
Long-term debt ($ mil.): —
No. of shares (mil.): 286.2
Sales ($ mil): 978.5
Dividends
Yield: 3.6%
Payout: 66.6%
Market value ($ mil.): 2,977.0

	STOCK PRICE ($) FY Close	P/E High/Low	PER SHARE ($) Earnings	Dividends	Book Value
12/18	10.40	20 14	0.72	0.38	10.50
12/17	13.88	34 29	0.43	0.33	10.21
12/16	13.95	22 16	0.64	0.26	10.09
12/15	12.44	24 19	0.55	0.25	9.89
12/14	11.23	74 26	0.38	0.08	9.99
Annual Growth	(1.9%)	— —	17.3%	47.6%	1.2%

Ionis Pharmaceuticals Inc

Ionis Pharmaceuticals develops biotech drugs to target neurological disorders and other conditions. Products are based on its antisense technology in which drugs attach themselves to strands of RNA to prevent them from producing disease-causing proteins; the hoped-for result is a therapy that fights disease without harming healthy cells. Commercial medicines approved in major global markets include SPINRAZA for spinal muscular atrophy and TEGSEDI for polyneuropathy caused by hereditary TTR amyloidosis (marketed by Biogen and majority-owned affiliate Akcea respectively). Ionis has more than 40 pipeline drugs under development in areas including neurological cardiovascular metabolic and rare diseases.

Financial Performance

Ionis Pharmaceuticals is working to establish a steady royalty stream from products successfully commercialized by its partners but its revenue thus far has been largely dependent on development milestone and licensing fee payments (which come at irregular intervals). The company has increased its revenue each year over the past five years with total sales nearly tripling between 2014 and 2018. Ionis reported net losses from 2014 through 2016 but brought its profits into the black in 2017 and 2018.

Revenue increased 17% in 2018 to some $599.7 million. The increase was largely due to a sizable bump in royalty payments on sales of SPINRAZA (from commercialization partner Biogen) despite a dip in R&D payments.

Net income attributable to stockholders rose to $273.7 million in 2018 a sharp increase from 2017 earnings of $300000. The rise was due to strong income tax benefits related to the 2017 Tax Act which outweighed high operating expenses and a loss related to Ionis' stake in Akcea.

The company ended 2018 with $278.8 million in cash up $149.2 million from 2017. Operating activities contributed $602.9 million while investing activities used $929.6 million (mostly on purchases of short-term investments) and financing activities contributed $475.9 million via proceeds on common stock issued to Biogen.

Strategy

Ionis Pharmaceuticals' strategy is to partner with other pharmaceutical companies to help secure development funding for promising drug candidates and then license the drug and receive royalty payments once the drug is commercialized. That way Ionis avoids footing all of the R&D and marketing expenses which can be weighty for a development-stage firm.

The company is focused on bringing its partnered drug candidates to commercialization stages as well as on forming additional collaborative agreements on early stage candidates. Partners include Biogen Roche Novartis AstraZeneca Bayer GlaxoSmithKline and majority-owned subsidiary Akcea.

R&D revenue makes up nearly 60% of sales while commercial products bring in the remainder. The largest portion of commercial revenue comes from Biogen which markets SPINRAZA in global markets. The company started receiving some revenue from Akcea in 2018 on sales of TEGSEDI which was approved and launched that year in the US Canada and the EU. While Ionis and Akcea suffered a setback when the FDA rejected rare disease drug WAYLIVRA for US sales in 2018 the companies are pursuing approval of the drug in the EU and other markets. Ionis also gets some payments from partner PTC Therapeutics which signed on to sell TEGSEDI and WAYLIVRA in Latin America in 2018.

In addition the company often licenses out development work on non-core candidates to biotech partners. For instance it collaborates with Alnylam Pharmaceuticals on RNAi therapeutics and with Regulus Therapeutics on microRNA-targeted therapeutics.

Company Background

Ionis was formed in 1989. The company's first antisense product came with the 1998 FDA approval of Vitravene an ophthalmic drug it discovered and licensed to Novartis. Novartis marketed the drug worldwide as a treatment for CMV retinitis a common eye infection in AIDS patients. However following the emergence of newer anti-HIV drugs and a decline in secondary infections including CMV Novartis halted its marketing efforts for the drug.

In 2014 the company formed Akcea Therapeutics to develop and commercialize drugs from its lipid franchise. Three years later Ionis spun off 25% of Akcea through an IPO as the subsidiary planned to file for FDA approval of volanesorsen (WAYLIVRA). However the FDA rejected the drug in 2018.

The company changed its name from Isis Pharmaceuticals to Ionis Pharmaceuticals in 2015.

Ionis sold rights to cholesterol-lowering drug Kynamro which Ionis had previously licensed to Genzyme to Kastle Therapeutics in 2016. Kynamro was marketed in the US and other countries.

EXECUTIVES

Vice President Human Resources, Shannon Devers
SVP Research, C. Frank Bennett, $397,077 total compensation
COO, B. Lynne Parshall, $641,574 total compensation
Chairman and CEO, Stanley T. Crooke, $735,169 total compensation
SVP Finance and CFO, Elizabeth L. Hougen, $365,496 total compensation
SVP Antisense Drug Discovery, Brett P. Monia, $381,288 total compensation
SVP Development, Richard S. Geary, $398,444 total compensation
President and CEO Akcea Therapeutics, Paula Soteropoulos
VICE PRESIDENT BIOMETRICS, John Su
Vice President Of Information Technology, Patrick Keivens
Vice President Metabolics Translational Medicine, Sanjay Bhanot
Vice President, Jeff Engelhardt
VICE PRESIDENT AND HEAD OF DRUG SAFETY, Charles Asare
Vice President Business Development, Joseph Baroldi
Vice President, Brian Lemay
Board Member, Joseph Wender
Auditors: Ernst & Young LLP

LOCATIONS

HQ: Ionis Pharmaceuticals Inc
2855 Gazelle Court, Carlsbad, CA 92010
Phone: 760 931-9200
Web: www.ionispharma.com

PRODUCTS/OPERATIONS

2016 Sales

	% of total
Research & development	94
Licensing & royalty	6
Total	**100**

Selected Products
KYNAMRO (treats homozygous FH)

COMPETITORS

Aegerion	Metabolex
AstraZeneca	Novartis
Enzo Biochem	Novo Nordisk
Gilead Sciences	Pfizer
Hemispherx BioPharma	RXi Pharmaceuticals
Idera	Rosetta Genomics
Lorus Therapeutics	Sarepta Therapeutics
Merck	

HISTORICAL FINANCIALS

Company Type: Public

Income Statement — FYE: December 31

	REVENUE ($ mil.)	NET INCOME ($ mil.)	NET PROFIT MARGIN	EMPLOYEES
12/18	599.6	273.7	45.6%	737
12/17	507.6	(5.9)	—	547
12/16	346.6	(86.5)	—	435
12/15	283.7	(88.2)	—	428
12/14	214.1	(38.9)	—	390
Annual Growth	29.4%	—	—	17.2%

2018 Year-End Financials

Debt ratio: 24.2%
Return on equity: 39.7%
Cash ($ mil.): 278.8
Current ratio: 7.88
Long-term debt ($ mil.): 632.9
No. of shares (mil.): 137.9
Dividends
 Yield: —
 Payout: —
Market value ($ mil.): 7,456.0

	STOCK PRICE ($) FY Close	P/E High/Low	PER SHARE ($) Earnings	Dividends	Book Value
12/18	54.06	28 19	2.07	0.00	7.60
12/17	50.30	805 474	0.08	0.00	2.65
12/16	47.83	— —	(0.72)	0.00	0.82
12/15	61.93	— —	(0.74)	0.00	1.67
12/14	61.74	— —	(0.33)	0.00	2.18
Annual Growth	(3.3%)	— —	—	—	36.7%

IPG Photonics Corp

IPG Photonics has a laser focus on spreading the use of lasers. The company makes fiber lasers and amplifiers and diode lasers which are primarily used in materials processing applications (nearly 90% of sales) such as welding cutting marking and engraving. Its fiber lasers are used in 3D printing and telecommunications. IPG Photonics is moving into automotive manufacturing applications and the developing market for medical uses. The company's customers have included BAE SYSTEMS Mitsubishi Heavy Industries and Nippon Steel. Deriving about 85% of its sales outside North America IPG Photonics operates sales offices in more than a dozen countries in Asia and Europe.

Operations
The vertically integrated manufacturer designs and makes most of the components used in its finished products (which can cost hundreds of thousands of dollars) from semiconductor diodes to optical fiber preforms finished fiber lasers and amplifiers. It also manufactures other products used in its lasers including optical delivery cables fiber couplers beam switches optical heads and chillers. By not outsourcing its manufacturing to third-party companies IPG Photonics is able to better control its proprietary processes and technologies as well as the supply of its materials.

The company's biggest market is in materials processing which accounts for 94% of revenue.

Geographic Reach
The company conducts R&D in the same city as its headquarters as well as in New Hampshire and overseas in the German city of Burbach (near Frankfurt) and in Fryazino Russia (outside Moscow).

It has four manufacturing facilities for lasers amplifiers and components one in each of its R&D cities and the fourth one in Cerro Maggiore Italy outside Milan. Manufacturing facilities for optical components are in India and China.

In terms of geographic markets China is the company's biggest accounting for 35% of revenue. The next biggest single country is the US generating 15% followed by Germany with 10% and Japan with 8%.

Sales and Marketing
IPG Photonics primarily uses a direct sales force. It has a diverse customer base - its five-largest customers only account for about 25% of sales. Its biggest customer is in China and accounts for 13% of sales. In 2015 the company shipped nearly 33000 units to moire than 3000 customers worldwide.

It has sales offices at each of its manufacturing facilities as well as in Michigan and California in the US. International sales offices are located in China Czech Republic France India Italy South Korea Spain Singapore Turkey and the UK.

Financial Performance
IPG Photonics is beaming after a 17% revenue increase in 2015. The company's sales reach $901 million for the year from $770 million in 2014. Materials processing of course provided most of the increase rising 16% with higher sales of quasi-continuous wave (QCW) pulsed lasers for welding and cutting. The company's smaller segments also grew in 2015 with the medical segment rising 100% for the year.

The rising sales at IPG Photonics drove profit 21% higher in 2015 to $242 million. Cash from operating activities also rose in 2015 from 2014.

Strategy
IPG remains focused on fiber lasers as an alternative to conventional lasers such as gas or crystal. Its strategy is to exploit the advantages that fiber lasers offer such as superiority in electrical efficiency beam quality and control maintenance costs longevity flexibility and usability. Traditional laser technologies have advantages that make them more suitable for some applications but fiber lasers continue to gain ground. Crystal lasers generate higher peak power pulses fiber lasers don't achieve the deep ultraviolet light needed for some semiconductor applications and carbon dioxide lasers are better for non-metallic applications such as plastics. Fiber lasers however have made improvements in power output that has opened them up to new markets and IPG believes the technology can reach additional nascent applications such as natural resource extraction.

IPG released a threebeam fiber laser system for brazing zinc-coated steel a process used in the automobile industry. The company is positioning fiber laser products for the auto industry and the trend toward the lighter weight metals such as high strength steel and aluminum. We are also encouraged by the potential for increased volumes of our laser seam stepper that welds auto bodies.

In 2015 some makers of consumer electronics adopted the company's QCW lasers for making their products and multi-hundred volume orders.

IPG formed a separate company IPG Medical in 2015 to focus on medical applications. The company is developing its Thulium fiber laser to break up kidney stones faster and and more simply than current technologies.

Mergers and Acquisitions
Increasing demand has led IPG to pursue operational expansion in Russia Germany and the US. In 2012 the company paid $55.4 million to acquire the 22.5% of Russia-based subsidiary NTO IRE-Polus that it did not already own to extend its control over R&D sales and manufacturing infrastructure in the country.

Also in 2012 IPG bought privately held J.P. Sercel Associates (JPSA) a New Hampshire-based supplier of UV excimer and diode-pumped solid-state industrial laser micromachining systems used in high-volume biomedical industrial automation LED microelectromechanical systems (MEMS) microfluidics thin-film solar panel and semiconductor manufacturing applications. The purchase expands IPG's custom laser system offerings to include fine processing precision cutting drilling and micromachining of ceramics glass and semiconductors. The company further enhanced its UV laser development with the purchase the following year of California-based Mobius Photonics.

EXECUTIVES
CEO and Chairman, Valentin P. Gapontsev, age 81, $687,981 total compensation
COO, Eugene Scherbakov, age 71, $450,449 total compensation
SVP and CFO, Timothy P. V. Mammen, age 50, $440,067 total compensation
Director of Research and Development IPG Laser, Igor Samartsev, age 57
SVP Components, Alexander (Alex) Ovtchinnikov, age 58, $400,579 total compensation
SVP U.S. Operations, Felix Stukalin, age 57
Vice President Strategic Marketing, Yuri Erokhin
Vice President Sales Marketing And Industrial Ma, Bill Shiner
Vice President Systems Development, Randy Hill
Vice President Advanced Industrial Applications, Leonid Lev
Auditors: DELOITTE & TOUCHE LLP

LOCATIONS
HQ: IPG Photonics Corp
50 Old Webster Road, Oxford, MA 01540
Phone: 508 373-1100
Web: www.ipgphotonics.com

PRODUCTS/OPERATIONS

2015 Sales by Market
	$ mil.	% of total
Materials processing	849.3	94
Advanced applications	28.9	3
Communications	14.4	2
Medical	8.6	1
Total	**901.2**	**100**

Selected Products
Broadband light sources
Continuous wave lasers
Diode laser systems
Diode-pumped solid-state laser systems
Erbium lasers
Fiber amplifiers
Fiber lasers
Fiber-coupled direct diode laser systems
Pulsed fiber lasers
Raman pump lasers
Thulium lasers
UV excimer laser systems
Ytterbium lasers

COMPETITORS
Cisco Systems	Newport Corp.
Coherent Inc.	Novanta
EMCORE	Oclaro
FANUC	Presstek
Furukawa Electric	Swatch
Huawei Technologies	TRUMPF
Mitsubishi Materials	Viavi Solutions

HISTORICAL FINANCIALS
Company Type: Public

Income Statement				FYE: December 31
	REVENUE ($ mil.)	NET INCOME ($ mil.)	NET PROFIT MARGIN	EMPLOYEES
12/18	1,459.8	404.0	27.7%	6,465
12/17	1,408.8	347.6	24.7%	5,390
12/16	1,006.1	260.7	25.9%	4,510
12/15	901.2	242.1	26.9%	4,020
12/14	769.8	200.4	26.0%	3,370
Annual Growth	17.3%	19.2%	—	17.7%

2018 Year-End Financials
Debt ratio: 1.7%
Return on equity: 19.1%
Cash ($ mil.): 544.3
Current ratio: 7.35
Long-term debt ($ mil.): 41.7
No. of shares (mil.): 52.9
Dividends
  Yield: —
  Payout: —
Market value ($ mil.): 5,998.0

	STOCK PRICE ($)	P/E	PER SHARE ($)		
	FY Close	High/Low	Earnings	Dividends	Book Value
12/18	113.29	35 14	7.38	0.00	41.66
12/17	214.13	38 15	6.36	0.00	37.71
12/16	98.71	21 15	4.85	0.00	29.25
12/15	89.16	22 15	4.53	0.00	23.82
12/14	74.92	20 16	3.79	0.00	19.98
Annual Growth	10.9%	— —	18.1%	—	20.2%

iRadimed Corp

Auditors: RSM US LLP

LOCATIONS

HQ: iRadimed Corp
  1025 Willa Springs Drive, Winter Springs, FL 32708
Phone: 407 677-8022 Fax: 407 677-5037
Web: www.iradimed.com

HISTORICAL FINANCIALS

Company Type: Public

Income Statement   FYE: December 31

	REVENUE ($ mil.)	NET INCOME ($ mil.)	NET PROFIT MARGIN	EMPLOYEES
12/18	30.4	6.3	20.7%	95
12/17	23.0	0.5	2.2%	83
12/16	32.5	7.2	22.2%	80
12/15	31.5	7.5	23.8%	68
12/14	15.6	2.0	13.1%	54
Annual Growth	18.1%	32.4%	—	15.2%

2018 Year-End Financials

Debt ratio: — No. of shares (mil.): 10.9
Return on equity: 16.8% Dividends
Cash ($ mil.): 28.0 Yield: —
Current ratio: 9.50 Payout: —
Long-term debt ($ mil.): — Market value ($ mil.): 269.0

	STOCK PRICE ($) FY Close	P/E High/Low	PER SHARE ($) Earnings	Dividends	Book Value
12/18	24.46	63 22	0.52	0.00	3.82
12/17	15.15	314 158	0.04	0.00	3.11
12/16	11.10	42 14	0.60	0.00	2.97
12/15	28.03	48 19	0.60	0.00	2.86
12/14	12.90	56 29	0.20	0.00	1.93
Annual Growth	17.3%	— —	27.0%	—	18.6%

---

iRobot Corp

If you want a glimpse of the robot future cast your eyes to the floor. That's where iRobot's Roomba vacuums scurry to and fro sweeping up dirt and dust bunnies. Models range from basic sweepers to higher end devices that can be programmed for specific houses. iRobot has offices in the US UK China and Hong Kong and sells its home products worldwide through retailers and distributors. Just more than half of its annual sales are in the US. Since its founding in 1990 by engineers from the Massachusetts Institute of Technology iRobot has sold more than 20 million robots.

Operations

iRobot sells consumer products that are designed for both indoor and outdoor cleaning applications. It offers Roomba floor vacuuming robots at prices ranging from $299 to $899. The company also offers the Braava family of mopping robots. In association with Aquatron Inc. iRobot sells the Mirra Pool Cleaning Robot for cleaning residential pools.

In 2016 iRobot sold its defense and security business unit and exited the remote presence market to focus on the consumer market.

Geographic Reach

Bedford Massachusetts-based iRobot has offices in the US the UK China Austria Belgium France Germany Netherlands Portugal Spain Japan and Hong Kong. Its research and development facilities are in Bedford and Pasadena California. Sales to customers outside the US account for nearly half of the company's revenue.

The company contracts manufacturing to third parties in China. Strained trade relations between the US and China that involve higher tariffs could have a negative impact on iRobot's sales.

Sales and Marketing

iRobot sells through distributors and retailers as well as online. Its biggest customer is Amazon.com which accounts for about 15% of revenue. About 60% of the company's revenue comes from 15 customers who are distributors or retailers.

The company markets its products through national advertising consumer and industry trade shows and direct marketing. The company increased its ad spending by about a third to about $92 million in 2017.

Financial Performance

iRobot has enjoyed rising sales and profit over the past few years thanks to its home robot line. Revenue rose about 33% to $883 million in 2017 from 2016 on a 25% increase in units shipped and an 11% increase in average selling price. US consumer revenue rose about 42% in 2017 which the company attributed to its investments in advertising and promotions and adoption of its Roomba 900 and Roomba 600 series robots. International consumer revenue rose about 28% in 2017 from 2016. The company shipped about 3.7 million robots in 2017 compared to about 2.9 million the year before.

The company's profit rose 21% to $51 million in 2017 from 2016 as it reduced cost of revenue and general and administrative expenses as a percentage of sales. Those savings were somewhat offset by higher expenses for research and development and sales and marketing.

Cash holdings at iRobot stood at about $128 million at the end of 2017 compared to about $214 million in 2016. The company spent about $150 million in 2017 to acquire distributors SODC and Robopolis. It also invested $23 million in property and equipment including machinery and tooling for new products.

Strategy

iRobot has locked in on the consumer market after selling off its defense-related business and getting out of the remote presence for medical applications business. The company has developed new products with a software that enables iRobot products to better understand the homes in which they operate.

The company's recent models extend mapping visual navigation and cloud connectivity to a wider range of customers. The iRobot HOME App allows users them to choose the appropriate cleaning options for their home. iRobot uses Amazon Web Services cloud to increase the number of connected robots it supports globally and provide more smart home capabilities.

The connectivity capabilities thrust iRobot into the news in 2017 over fears that the vacuums were spying on customers and that the company would sell customer information to third parties. iRobot officials said connectivity was necessary to communicate with customers' smart phones that most data would be kept in the vacuum's memory and that the company would not sell data.

iRobot invested in driving international sales with the acquisitions of key distributors in Europe (Robopolis) and Japan (Sales On Demand Corp. (SODC)) for about $150 million total. The acquisitions provide iRobot with greater control of the sales and marketing of its products in key overseas markets.

Mergers and Acquisitions

In 2017 iRobot acquired Robopolis SAS a French company to expand its enhance distribution network provide consistent branding and improved service for European customers.

Also in 2017 iRobot bought Sales On Demand Corp. (SODC) in Japan for the same reasons it acquired Robopolis.

EXECUTIVES

EVP Human Resources and Corporate Communications, Russell J. (Russ) Campanello, age 63, $51,923 total compensation
Chairman and CEO, Colin M. Angle, age 51, $463,897 total compensation
EVP and Chief Legal Counsel, Glen D. Weinstein, age 48, $290,353 total compensation
EVP and CFO, Alison Dean, age 54, $228,654 total compensation
COO, Christian Cerda
Svp Sales, Steven Rogers
Vice President and Assistant General Counsel, Tonya Drake
Senior Vice President Technology, Mario Munich
Vice President Advanced Development, Mark Chiappetta
Vice President Of Human Resources, Charu Manocha
Board Member, Deborah Ellinger
Member Board Of Directors, Mohamad Ali
Board Member, Michelle Stacy
Board Member, Michael Bell
Auditors: PricewaterhouseCoopers LLP

LOCATIONS

HQ: iRobot Corp
  8 Crosby Drive, Bedford, MA 01730
Phone: 781 430-3000
Web: www.irobot.com

COMPETITORS

AM General	General Dynamics
Allen-Vanguard Corporation	LG Electronics
	Lockheed Martin
BAE SYSTEMS	Miele
BISSELL	QinetiQ
Electrolux	Samsung Electronics
GE Appliances & Lighting	Whirlpool

HISTORICAL FINANCIALS
Company Type: Public

Income Statement FYE: December 29

	REVENUE ($ mil.)	NET INCOME ($ mil.)	NET PROFIT MARGIN	EMPLOYEES
12/18	1,092.5	87.9	8.1%	1,032
12/17	883.9	50.9	5.8%	920
12/16*	660.6	41.9	6.3%	607
01/16	616.7	44.1	7.2%	622
12/14	556.8	37.8	6.8%	572
Annual Growth	18.4%	23.5%	—	15.9%

*Fiscal year change

2018 Year-End Financials
Debt ratio: —
Return on equity: 17.5%
Cash ($ mil.): 130.3
Current ratio: 2.41
Long-term debt ($ mil.): —
No. of shares (mil.): 27.7
Dividends
Yield: —
Payout: —
Market value ($ mil.): 2,260.0

	STOCK PRICE ($) FY Close	P/E High/Low		PER SHARE ($) Earnings	Dividends	Book Value
12/18	81.32	37	18	3.07	0.00	19.26
12/17	76.70	58	29	1.77	0.00	16.83
12/16*	58.45	40	19	1.48	0.00	14.28
01/16	35.40	25	19	1.47	0.00	14.35
12/14	34.81	36	24	1.25	0.00	13.17
Annual Growth	23.6%	—	—	25.2%	—	10.0%

*Fiscal year change

iShares S&P GSCI Commodity-Indexed Trust

Auditors: PricewaterhouseCoopers LLP

LOCATIONS
HQ: iShares S&P GSCI Commodity-Indexed Trust
c/o iShares Delaware Trust Sponsor LLC, 400 Howard Street, San Francisco, CA 94105
Phone: 415 670-2000
Web: www.ishares.com

HISTORICAL FINANCIALS
Company Type: Public

Income Statement FYE: December 31

	REVENUE ($ mil.)	NET INCOME ($ mil.)	NET PROFIT MARGIN	EMPLOYEES
12/18	24.5	12.5	51.3%	0
12/17	9.7	(0.1)	—	0
12/16	2.2	(5.1)	—	0
12/15	0.2	(6.3)	—	0
12/14	0.5	(8.0)	—	0
Annual Growth	162.4%	—	—	—

2018 Year-End Financials
Debt ratio: —
Return on equity: —
Cash ($ mil.): 10.0
Current ratio: 1,487.35
Long-term debt ($ mil.): —
No. of shares (mil.): 86.5
Dividends
Yield: —
Payout: —
Market value ($ mil.): 1,213.0

	STOCK PRICE ($) FY Close	P/E High/Low		PER SHARE ($) Earnings	Dividends	Book Value
12/18	14.02	125	92	0.15	0.00	13.99
12/17	16.28	—	—	(0.00)	0.00	16.32
12/16	15.67	—	—	(0.09)	0.00	15.62
12/15	14.23	—	—	(0.15)	0.00	14.21
12/14	21.58	—	—	(0.24)	0.00	21.36
Annual Growth	(10.2%)	—	—	(10.0%)	—	—

J.Jill Inc

Auditors: PricewaterhouseCoopers LLP

LOCATIONS
HQ: J.Jill Inc
4 Batterymarch Park, Quincy, MA 02169
Phone: 617 376-4300
Web: www.jjill.com

HISTORICAL FINANCIALS
Company Type: Public

Income Statement FYE: February 2

	REVENUE ($ mil.)	NET INCOME ($ mil.)	NET PROFIT MARGIN	EMPLOYEES
02/19	706.2	30.5	4.3%	3,970
02/18*	698.1	55.3	7.9%	3,755
01/17	639.0	24.0	3.8%	3,801
01/16	420.0	4.3	1.0%	3,801
05/15	141.9	(1.9)	—	0
Annual Growth	49.4%	—	—	—

*Fiscal year change

2019 Year-End Financials
Debt ratio: 38.3%
Return on equity: 15.5%
Cash ($ mil.): 66.2
Current ratio: 1.70
Long-term debt ($ mil.): 237.4
No. of shares (mil.): 43.6
Dividends
Yield: —
Payout: —
Market value ($ mil.): 255.0

	STOCK PRICE ($) FY Close	P/E High/Low		PER SHARE ($) Earnings	Dividends	Book Value
02/19	5.84	13	6	0.69	0.00	4.90
02/18*	8.18	11	4	1.27	0.00	4.10
Annual Growth	(28.6%)	—	—	(45.7%)	—	19.4%

*Fiscal year change

j2 Global Inc (New)

EXECUTIVES
VP Engineering, Vincent P. (Vince) Niedzielski
VP Human Resources, Patty Brunton
EVP Corporate Strategy, Zohar Loshitzer, age 58
CEO, Nehemia (Hemi) Zucker, age 59, $459,000 total compensation
Chairman, Richard S. Ressler, age 58, $144,000 total compensation
CFO, Kathleen M. (Kathy) Griggs, age 62, $270,000 total compensation
President, R. Scott Turicchi, age 53, $375,000 total compensation
VP Products, Michael W. Harris, age 53
VP General Counsel and Secretary, Jeffrey D. (Jeff) Adelman, age 49, $270,000 total compensation
Vice President Marketing, Mike Pugh
VP Corporate Development, Ken Truesdale
VP Network Operations, Alan Alters
Vice President International, Tim McLean
VP and General Manager Europe, Paul Kinsella
Manager of Operations, Warner Bros
Vice President General Counsel Secretary, Jeff Adelman
Vice President Engineering, Vince Niedzielski
Chief Accounting Officer, Steve Dunn
Director, William B. (Brian) Kretzmer, age 61
Director, Douglas Y. Bech, age 71
Director, Robert J. Cresci, age 72
Director, John F. Rieley, age 73
Director, Michael P. Schulhof, age 74
Director, Stephen Ross, age 67
Auditors: BDO USA, LLP

LOCATIONS
HQ: j2 Global Inc (New)
6922 Hollywood Boulevard, Suite 500, Los Angeles, CA 90028
Phone: 323 860-9200
Web: www.j2.com

COMPETITORS
CommTouch Software	Notify Technology
Deltathree	Open Text
EasyLink	Satellink
FuzeBox	

HISTORICAL FINANCIALS
Company Type: Public

Income Statement FYE: December 31

	REVENUE ($ mil.)	NET INCOME ($ mil.)	NET PROFIT MARGIN	EMPLOYEES
12/18	1,207.3	128.6	10.7%	2,587
12/17	1,117.8	139.4	12.5%	2,487
12/16	874.2	152.4	17.4%	2,426
12/15	720.8	133.6	18.5%	1,608
12/14	599.0	124.3	20.8%	1,410
Annual Growth	19.1%	0.9%	—	16.4%

2018 Year-End Financials
Debt ratio: 39.5%
Return on equity: 12.5%
Cash ($ mil.): 209.4
Current ratio: 1.50
Long-term debt ($ mil.): 1,013.1
No. of shares (mil.): 47.4
Dividends
Yield: 2.4%
Payout: 65.1%
Market value ($ mil.): 3,294.0

	STOCK PRICE ($) FY Close	P/E High/Low		PER SHARE ($) Earnings	Dividends	Book Value
12/18	69.38	34	25	2.59	1.68	21.81
12/17	75.03	32	25	2.83	1.52	21.32
12/16	81.80	26	18	3.13	1.36	19.28
12/15	82.32	30	21	2.73	1.22	18.57
12/14	62.00	24	17	2.58	0.56	17.30
Annual Growth	2.9%	—	—	0.1%	31.5%	6.0%

JBG SMITH Properties

Auditors: DELOITTE & TOUCHE LLP

LOCATIONS
HQ: JBG SMITH Properties
4445 Willard Avenue, Suite 400, Chevy Chase, MD 20815
Phone: 240 333-3600
Web: www.jbgsmith.com

HISTORICAL FINANCIALS
Company Type: Public

Income Statement FYE: December 31

	REVENUE ($ mil.)	NET INCOME ($ mil.)	NET PROFIT MARGIN	EMPLOYEES
12/18	644.1	39.9	6.2%	914
12/17	543.0	(71.7)	—	1,020
12/16	478.5	61.9	13.0%	1,100
12/15	470.6	49.6	10.5%	0
12/14	472.9	81.3	17.2%	0
Annual Growth	8.0%	(16.3%)	—	—

2018 Year-End Financials
Debt ratio: 35.6%
Return on equity: 1.3%
Cash ($ mil.): 260.5
Current ratio: 3.41
Long-term debt ($ mil.): 2,135.5
No. of shares (mil.): 120.9
Dividends
 Yield: 2.5%
 Payout: 322.5%
Market value ($ mil.): 4,210.0

	STOCK PRICE ($) FY Close	P/E High/Low	PER SHARE ($) Earnings	Dividends	Book Value
12/18	34.81	131 100	0.31	1.00	24.70
12/17	34.73	— —	(0.70)	0.45	25.18
Annual Growth	0.2%	— —	—	122.2%	(1.9%)

John Bean Technologies Corp

John Bean Technologies Corporation (JBT) keeps food cold and jets in the air. JBT manufactures industrial equipment for the food processing and air transportation industries. Its JBT FoodTech segment makes commercial-grade refrigeration systems freezers ovens canning equipment and food processing systems for fruit meats seafood and ready-to-eat meals. JBT AeroTech manufactures and services ground support equipment (plane deicers aircraft tow vehicles and cargo loading systems) airport gate equipment (its Jetway brand) and military equipment. More than half of JBT's revenue is generated in the US.

Operations
JBT operates through two segments: FoodTech and AeroTech.

The FoodTech business (contributing more than 70% of total revenue) includes protein technology such as systems for chilling mixing grinding portioning and packaging meats; liquid foods solutions for extracting concentrating and preserving fruit juices; and automated systems including robotic vehicle systems for material handling in manufacturing and warehouse facilities.

Its AeroTech segment (close to 30%) provides airport ground support and services for airport authorities airlines airfreight companies military forces and defense contractors. Products include mobile equipment such as its Commander and Ranger cargo loaders and aircraft towing and deicing equipment; fixed equipment (its Jetway gate equipment for passenger boarding); and airport services such as maintenance for airport equipment systems and facilities.

Geographic Reach
JBT owns production facilities located in seven US states and six European countries as well as in South America South Africa and China. It also has several technical centers and sales and service offices located worldwide.

The company sells its products to more than 100 countries. The US accounts for more than half its sales.

Sales and Marketing
JBT sells and markets its products and services primarily through a direct sales force supplemented with independent distributors and sales representatives. It also educates its customers about products through newsletters websites seminars trade shows user groups and conferences.

Financial Performance
JBT's revenue increased 21% to $1.6 billion in 2017 compared with 2016. The increase in revenue was driven by sales from acquisitions in 2017.

Operating expenses for both products and services as well as research and development costs have increased significantly for JBT. Net income however has risen dramatically over the past three years with an increase of 19% to $80.5 million in 2017 and a 21% jump to $67.6 million in 2016. The increase in 2017 was mainly due to higher revenue as well as a $10.6 million decrease in restructuring expenses and a $15.5 million tax benefit due to the Tax Cuts and Jobs Act.

Cash at the end of fiscal 2017 was $34.0 million an increase of $800000 from the prior year. Cash from operations contributed $104.6 million to the coffers while investing activities used $139.9 million mainly for acquisitions. Financing activities used another $34.7 million for dividends to stockholders and the company's stock repurchase program.

Strategy
JBT is in the midst of its "Elevate" strategy launched in 2017 which encompasses four key priorities: new product development recurring revenue organic growth and efficiency and acquisitions.

New products include JBT's advanced DSI system which uses vision technology and software along with high-velocity water streams to cut poultry and other proteins into specific portions. The company also introduced its iOPS technology which uses data collection and advanced algorithms to monitor its customers' JBT equipment. iOPS provides automatic fault alerts reducing equipment down time. JBT is also tailoring its products to the exploding Asian market and has established a technology center in Kunshan China. In addition it's expanding the functionality of its automated guided vehicles (AGVs) for tasks such as repetitive forklift work and introducing new food equipment technology that automates manual tasks in food production facilities.

Acquisitions continue to be one of the company's key growth drivers. JBT has made more than six acquisitions in the past three years adding to its products and capabilities and expanding its geographic reach.

Mergers and Acquisitions
In 2018 JBT acquired Netherlands-based FTNON a provider of equipment and solutions for the fresh produce ready meals and pet food industries for €32 million. FTNON offers robotic technology for cutting coring and peeling fruits and vegetables allowing JBT to penetrate the fresh cut equipment market and leveraging the increasing demand for ready-to-eat fresh produce.

JBT made three acquisitions in 2017 aimed at bolstering revenue and adding to its portfolio of businesses. The company acquired Europe-based PLF International a provider of powder filling systems (for flour spices baby formula etc.) for the global food and beverage markets for £28 million. PLF adds complementary products and expertise to JBT's operations expands its business geographically and strengthens its aftermarket opportunities. In the same year it purchased Avure Technologies for $57 million. Avure makes high pressure processing (HPP) systems a cold pasteurization technology that ensures food safety and freshness without heat or preservatives. Avure will benefit from JBT's global sales force service support and extensive customer relationships.

Also in 2017 the company bought Aircraft Maintenance Support Services (AMSS) a privately held manufacturer of military aviation equipment based in the UK for £10 million. AMSS enhances JBT's AeroTech segment with military offerings and expanded access to foreign military organizations.

Company Background
John Bean Technologies was spun off from FMC Technologies in 2008. JBT Corporation takes its name from John Bean a California inventor who founded Bean Spray Pump Company in 1884 the company which eventually became Food Machinery Corporation (FMC) through a series of mergers and acquisitions in the 20th century. (The original Bean Spray Pump technology was adapted to make a plane deicer in the 1960s.)

EXECUTIVES
EVP and President JBT AeroTech, David C. Burdakin, age 64, $365,000 total compensation
Chairman President and CEO, Thomas W. Giacomini, age 54, $733,333 total compensation
EVP Human Resources, Mark K. Montague, $342,539 total compensation
EVP CFO and Treasurer, Brian A. Deck, $334,583 total compensation
EVP and President JBT FoodTech, Steven R. (Steve) Smith, $367,449 total compensation
EVP General Counsel and Secretary, James L. Marvin
Treasurer, Greg Packard
Auditors: KPMG LLP

LOCATIONS
HQ: John Bean Technologies Corp
70 West Madison Street, Suite 4400, Chicago, IL 60602
Phone: 312 861-5900
Web: www.jbtcorporation.com

PRODUCTS/OPERATIONS

2017 Sales

	$ mil.	% of total
JBT FoodTech	1,171.9	72
JBT AeroTech	463.0	28
Other revenue and eliminations	0.2	-
Total	**1,635.1**	**100**

2017 Sales

	$ mil.	% of total
Product revenue	1,376.8	84
Service revenue	258.3	16
Total	**1,635.1**	**100**

Selected Products & Services

JBT FoodTech
  Blow-Molders
  Brine Preparation
  Choppers Corers Cutters Emulsifiers & Peelers
  High Pressure Processors (HPP)
  Injection Equipment
  Installation Services
  Juicers Finishers & Extractors
  Laboratory Devices
  Liquid Process Engineering/Design & Build
  Lubricants
  Massagers (Polar)
  Ovens & Cookers
  Pasteurizers & Sterilizers
  Portioners & Slicers
  Product Labeling
  Tanks & ASME Pressure Vessels
  Tenderizers Macerators & Presses
  Washers Loaders Sizers & Conveyors
AeroTech
  Cargo Loaders
  Tempest Deicers
  Conventional Tow Bar Tractors
  Expediter Towbarless Tractors
  Jetaire Pre-Conditioned Air
  Jetpower Mobile GPUs
  Passenger Steps
  Belt Loaders
  Ambulift
  Fuel Tank Repair Trolley

COMPETITORS

Air T	Heat and Control
Alarko	Hobart Corp.
Barry-Wehmiller	Illinois Tool Works
Carlisle FoodService	Manitowoc
Duke Manufacturing	Middleby
GEA Group	ThyssenKrupp Elevator

HISTORICAL FINANCIALS

Company Type: Public

Income Statement
FYE: December 31

	REVENUE ($ mil.)	NET INCOME ($ mil.)	NET PROFIT MARGIN	EMPLOYEES
12/18	1,919.7	104.1	5.4%	5,800
12/17	1,635.1	80.5	4.9%	5,800
12/16	1,350.5	67.6	5.0%	5,000
12/15	1,107.3	55.9	5.0%	4,200
12/14	984.2	30.8	3.1%	3,500
Annual Growth	18.2%	35.6%	—	13.5%

2018 Year-End Financials

Debt ratio: 26.8%	No. of shares (mil.): 31.5
Return on equity: 23.1%	Dividends
Cash ($ mil.): 43.0	Yield: 0.5%
Current ratio: 1.27	Payout: 12.3%
Long-term debt ($ mil.): 387.1	Market value ($ mil.): 2,264.0

	STOCK PRICE ($) FY Close	P/E High/Low	PER SHARE ($) Earnings	Dividends	Book Value
12/18	71.81	38 21	3.23	0.40	14.49
12/17	110.80	47 32	2.53	0.40	13.99
12/16	85.95	40 18	2.27	0.40	6.17
12/15	49.83	27 16	1.88	0.37	4.45
12/14	32.86	33 25	1.03	0.36	4.10
Annual Growth	21.6%	—	33.1%	2.7%	37.1%

John Marshall Bancorp Inc

Auditors: Yount, Hyde & Barbour, P.C.

LOCATIONS

HQ: John Marshall Bancorp Inc
1943 Isaac Newton Square E., Suite 100, Reston, VA 20190
Phone: 703 584-0840   **Fax:** 703 584-0859

HISTORICAL FINANCIALS

Company Type: Public

Income Statement
FYE: December 31

	REVENUE ($ mil.)	NET INCOME ($ mil.)	NET PROFIT MARGIN	EMPLOYEES
12/18	59.1	12.1	20.6%	0
12/17	50.5	8.9	17.8%	0
12/16	43.3	8.3	19.1%	0
12/15	39.4	8.8	22.5%	0
Annual Growth	14.4%	11.1%	—	—

2018 Year-End Financials

Debt ratio: 6.6%	No. of shares (mil.): 12.8
Return on equity: 8.9%	Dividends
Cash ($ mil.): 101.7	Yield: —
Current ratio: 0.18	Payout: —
Long-term debt ($ mil.): 93.0	Market value ($ mil.): 192.0

	STOCK PRICE ($) FY Close	P/E High/Low	PER SHARE ($) Earnings	Dividends	Book Value
12/18	14.95	20 16	0.89	0.00	11.08
12/17	17.80	33 25	0.66	0.00	10.12
12/16	20.75	32 24	0.63	0.00	9.38
12/15	16.75	26 20	0.68	0.00	8.73
/0.00	—	—(0.00)	0.00	(0.00)	
Annual Growth	—	—	—	—	—

Kadant Inc

Kadant wants to hear the ka-ching of profits being made from its papermaking equipment. The company's papermaking machinery and components which Kadant develops and manufactures can be found in most of the world's pulp and paper mills. Its products include stock preparation; doctoring cleaning and filtration (for cleaning of paper rolls); and fluid handling (mainly drying). Its wood processing offerings include stranders debarkers chippers and logging machinery. It also recycles papermaking byproducts into biodegradable fiber-based granules for oil and grease absorption and lawn and garden applications. Kadant has operations in North America South America Europe and Asia. Most of Kadant's revenues are generated outside the US.

Operations

Kadant generates its revenue through its three segments: Papermaking Systems (close to 80% of revenue) Wood Processing Systems (nearly 20%) and Fiber-based Products (less than 5%).

The Papermaking Systems segment develops and manufactures equipment for the global papermaking recycling waste management and other process industries. Its principal products include stock-preparation systems for wastepaper conversion into recycled paper and balers for processing recycled materials; fluid-handling systems and equipment used in industrial piping systems to transfer fluid power and data; doctoring systems and equipment for paper machines; and filtration and cleaning systems for draining purifying and recycling water and for cleaning fabrics belts and rolls.

Through its Wood Processing Systems segment Kadant makes market stranders debarkers chippers and logging machinery used in the harvesting and production of lumber and OSB (oriented strand board). This segment also refurbishes and repairs pulping equipment for the pulp and paper industry.

The Fiber-based Products business sells biodegradable absorbent granules made from papermaking by-products that are used in agricultural for home and professional lawn and garden applications and for oil and grease absorption.

Geographic Reach

Kadant has 21 manufacturing facilities in 11 countries in Europe North and South America and Asia. Approximately 65% of its sales are to customers outside the US principally in Canada Europe and China.

Sales and Marketing

Kadant sells its products services and systems using a combination of direct sales independent sales agents and distributors. Technical service personnel product specialists and independent sales agents and distributors are utilized in certain markets and for certain product lines.

Financial Performance

Kadant has seen a general upward trend in revenue since 2013 with a significant increase of 24% to record sales of $515.0 million in 2017 (sales were also up a 43% in 2016 compared with 2015). The increase in 2017 is attributed to sales generated by acquisitions and favorable foreign currency translation.

Net income however slumped 3% in 2017 to $31.0 million (2016 net income was also down 7% from 2015). An increase in selling general and administrative (SG&A) expenses a higher provision for income taxes and increased R&D costs ate into Kadant's profits for 2017.

Cash at the end of fiscal 2017 was $75.4 million an increase of $3.9 million from the prior year. Cash from operations contributed $65.2 million to the coffers while investing activities used $221.9 million mainly for acquisitions. Financing activities provided $151.4 primarily from borrowings.

Strategy

Kadant's strategic growth initiatives involve increasing its penetration into emerging markets and expand its parts and consumables revenue by leveraging its low-cost manufacturing operations. It also continues to acquire well-positioned companies that offer differentiated products for process industries. The company recently agreed to purchase material handling equipment maker Syntron which has opened up new markets in the mining food processing and packaging industries. The acquisition of expansion joint maker Unaflex has increased sales in Kadant's parts and consumables business.

Mergers and Acquisitions

Kadant has seen its revenues soar with major strategic acquisitions in recent years. In 2019 the company acquired Syntron Material Handling Group for approximately $179 million. Syntron makes material handling equipment and systems such as conveying and vibratory equipment at its facilities in Tupelo MS and Changshu China under the Link-Belt and Syntron brands. The acquisition extends Kadant's footprint into new process industries such as mining aggregates food processing and packaging.

In 2017 Kadant acquired NII FPG Company's forest products business for approximately $170.8 million. Kadant aims to bolster its aftermarket business with NII FPG's products including equipment for sawmills veneer mills and other manufacturers in the forest products industry. Later that year it also acquired certain assets of Unaflex a maker of expansion joints and related products for process industries for $31.3 million. With Unaflex's business made up of primarliy parts and consumables the acquisition is aligned with Kadant's strategy to grow its aftermarket business.

EXECUTIVES

VP General Counsel and Secretary, Sandra L. Lambert, age 63, $290,000 total compensation
President and CEO, Jonathan W. (Jon) Painter, age 60, $586,000 total compensation
SVP and CFO, Michael J. McKenney, age 57, $253,000 total compensation
EVP and COO, Eric T. Langevin, age 56, $376,000 total compensation
EVP, Jeffrey L. Powell, age 60, $360,000 total compensation
CTO, Bilal Mehmood
Vice President, Dara Mitchell
Vice President, Michael Colwell
Vice President Marketing, Wes Martz
Treasurer, Daniel Walsh
Chairman, William A. (Bill) Rainville, age 77
Board Member, John Albertine
Board Member, William Tully
Board Member, Thomas Leonard
Auditors: KPMG LLP

LOCATIONS

HQ: Kadant Inc
 One Technology Park Drive, Westford, MA 01886
Phone: 978 776-2000
Web: www.kadant.com

PRODUCTS/OPERATIONS

2017 Sales

	$ mil.	% of total
Papermaking Systems		
Stock Preparation	193.8	38
Doctoring Cleaning & Filtration	109.6	21
Fluid Handling	104.1	20
Wood Processing Systems	95.1	19
Fiber-based Products	12.4	2
Total	**515.0**	**100**

Selected Products
Doctoring Cleaning and Filtration
 Doctoring
 Cleaning
 Filtration
 Forming
Fluid Handling
 Rotary joints and unions
 Expansion joints and flexible connectors
 Jet devices
 Condensate pumps
 Steam systems
 Accessories
Fiber Processing
 OCC recycled stock and pulp preparation
 Chemical pulping
Recycling Machinery
 Balers for recyclable materials
 Balers for waste RDF alfalfa
 Conveyors
Wood Processing
 Engineered wood (OSB)
 Chipping/screening
 Debarking
 Granules

COMPETITORS

Andritz AG	Lorentzen & Wettre
AstenJohnson	Metso
Barco	Ovivo
Columbus McKinnon	Sandusky International
Deublin	Voith

HISTORICAL FINANCIALS
Company Type: Public

Income Statement   FYE: December 29

	REVENUE ($ mil.)	NET INCOME ($ mil.)	NET PROFIT MARGIN	EMPLOYEES
12/18	633.7	60.4	9.5%	2,500
12/17	515.0	31.0	6.0%	2,400
12/16*	414.1	32.0	7.7%	2,000
01/16	390.1	34.3	8.8%	1,800
01/15	402.1	28.6	7.1%	1,800
Annual Growth	**12.0%**	**20.5%**	—	**8.6%**

*Fiscal year change

2018 Year-End Financials

Debt ratio: 24.2% No. of shares (mil.): 11.1
Return on equity: 17.2% Dividends
Cash ($ mil.): 45.8   Yield: 0.0%
Current ratio: 1.96   Payout: 16.4%
Long-term debt ($ mil.): 174.1 Market value ($ mil.): 901.0

	STOCK PRICE ($) FY Close	P/E High/Low		PER SHARE ($) Earnings	Dividends	Book Value
12/18	81.12	20	14	5.30	0.87	33.57
12/17	100.40	40	20	2.75	0.82	30.06
12/16*	61.20	22	12	2.88	0.74	25.84
01/16	40.61	18	12	3.10	0.66	24.75
01/15	42.38	17	13	2.56	0.58	24.33
Annual Growth	**17.6%**	—	—	**20.0%**	**10.9%**	**8.4%**

*Fiscal year change

Kearny Financial Corp (MD)

Auditors: Crowe LLP

LOCATIONS

HQ: Kearny Financial Corp (MD)
 120 Passaic Avenue, Fairfield, NJ 07004
Phone: 973 244-4500
Web: www.kearnybank.com

HISTORICAL FINANCIALS
Company Type: Public

Income Statement   FYE: June 30

	ASSETS ($ mil.)	NET INCOME ($ mil.)	INCOME AS % OF ASSETS	EMPLOYEES
06/19	6,634.8	42.1	0.6%	565
06/18	6,579.8	19.6	0.3%	565
06/17	4,818.1	18.6	0.4%	466
06/16	4,500.0	15.8	0.4%	459
06/15	4,237.1	5.6	0.1%	491
Annual Growth	**11.9%**	**65.4%**	—	**3.6%**

2019 Year-End Financials

Return on assets: 0.6% Dividends
Return on equity: 3.5%   Yield: 0.0%
Long-term debt ($ mil.): — Payout: 80.4%
No. of shares (mil.): 89.1 Market value ($ mil.): 1,184.0
Sales ($ mil): 250.8

	STOCK PRICE ($) FY Close	P/E High/Low		PER SHARE ($) Earnings	Dividends	Book Value
06/19	13.29	31	26	0.46	0.37	12.65
06/18	13.45	65	54	0.24	0.25	12.74
06/17	14.85	73	57	0.22	0.10	12.53
06/16	12.58	74	62	0.18	0.08	12.50
06/15	11.16	191	179	0.06	0.00	12.48
Annual Growth	**4.5%**	—	—	**66.4%**	—	**0.3%**

KEMET Corp.

KEMET is one of the world's largest makers of tantalum and multilayer ceramic capacitors — devices that store filter and regulate electrical energy and that are used in virtually all electronic devices. KEMET makes about 35 billion capacitors a year; its focus is on surface-mount capacitors including specialized units for aerospace automotive communications systems computers and military equipment. The company also makes solid aluminum capacitors for high-frequency applications. More than 70% of its sales come from outside the US.

Operations

KEMET makes about three quarters of its revenue from its solid capacitors group which produces tantalum aluminum polymer and ceramic capacitors with the rest coming from film and electrolytic which produces film paper and wet aluminum electrolytic capacitors.

Geographic Reach
Based in South Carolina KEMET operates 21 production facilities in Mexico China Italy the U.K. Portugal Finland Sweden Indonesia Germany Bulgaria and Macedonia. It has two specialty electronics companies — FELCO in Illinois and Dectron in Sweden.

Sales and Marketing
KEMET sells its vast array of products (it has nearly 250000 distinct part configurations) primarily to manufacturers such as Alcatel-Lucent Cisco Dell Hewlett-Packard IBM and Intel. Electronics accounted for 45% of sales 2015 with 10% of sales going to one distributor.

Financial Performance
Since revenue peaked at more than $1 billion in 2011 KEMET's revenue has declined year-to-year. It ended 2015 (ended March) with $823 million in revenue a 1.24% drop from 2014. Sales in its biggest segment solid capacitors were down 1%. Foreign exchange rates and fewer sales of lower margin products cut tantalum product sales.

KEMET trimmed its loss for the second straight year reporting a $14 million loss in 2015 compared to a loss of $68 million in 2014. In 2015 proceeds from the sale of its machinery division and lower operating costs contributed to reduce the loss.

The company reported positive cash flow of $24.4 million in 2015 compared to outflow of $6.7 million in 2014.

Strategy
KEMET is making changes through a program it calls the One KEMET campaign. The company has implemented standard practices and procedures throughout its businesses by working through programs such as Oracle 11iEBS and Lean and Six Sigma initiatives.

As part of its campaign to sharpen its corporate focus KEMET sold its machinery division in 2014 to Manz AG. KEMET had acquired the business as part of its purchase of Arcotronics Italia in 2007. The deal will help KEMET focus on designing producing and distributing electronic components as well as strategic initiatives such as its joint venture with NEC TOKIN in which KEMET has 34% economic interest and 51% voting interest.

Among KEMET's new products in the past year are tantalum capacitors for the automotive industry which buys an increasing amount of electronic components. The new line of tantalum capacitors help automotive electronics handle the demands placed on systems such as driver assistance energy recovery and infotainment.

Mergers and Acquisitions
KEMET bought IntelliData Inc. a developer of digital technologies for discovery decision support and the sales and marketing of electronic components. The company has been a KEMET vendor since 2000.

EXECUTIVES

Vice President and Chief Information Officer, Brian Burch

EVP and CFO, William M. Lowe, age 66, $492,500 total compensation

Senior Vice President Chief Technology and Marketing Officer, Philip M. (Phil) Lessner, age 60

Executive Vice President Solid Capacitor Business Group, Charles C. (Chuck) Meeks, age 58, $313,314 total compensation

Executive Vice President Tantalum Business Group, Conrado Hinojosa, age 54, $302,500 total compensation

Executive Vice President Ceramic Film and Electrolytics Business Group, Chuck Meeks

Vice President Ceramic Business Group, John Powers

Vice President Film and Electrolytic Business Group, Bob Willoughby

SVP Global Sales and Marketing, Claudio Lollini

CEO, Per-Olof Loof

Chairman, Frank G. Brandenberg, age 72

Auditors: Ernst & Young LLP

LOCATIONS

HQ: KEMET Corp.
KEMET Tower, One East Broward Blvd, Fort Lauderdale, FL 33301
Phone: 954 766-2800
Web: www.kemet.com

PRODUCTS/OPERATIONS

2015 Sales

	$ mil.	% of total
Solid Capacitors	621.3	75
Film & electrolytic	201.9	25
Total	823.2	100

Selected Products
Capacitors
 Aluminum (wet electrolytic and solid polymer)
 Multilayer ceramic
 Film
 Paper
 Tantalum

COMPETITORS

AVX	Panasonic Corp
Anhui Tongfeng Electronics	ROHM
	SANYO Semiconductor
Dover Corp.	Samsung Electronics
EPCOS	TDK
Man Yue	Taiyo Yuden
Maxwell Technologies	Vishay Intertechnology
Murata Manufacturing	

HISTORICAL FINANCIALS
Company Type: Public

Income Statement — FYE: March 31

	REVENUE ($ mil.)	NET INCOME ($ mil.)	NET PROFIT MARGIN	EMPLOYEES
03/19	1,382.8	206.5	14.9%	14,350
03/18	1,199.9	254.5	21.2%	14,850
03/17	757.7	47.9	6.3%	9,100
03/16	734.8	(53.6)	—	8,800
03/15	823.1	(14.1)	—	9,225
Annual Growth	13.8%	—	—	11.7%

2019 Year-End Financials
Debt ratio: 22.3%
Return on equity: 37.4%
Cash ($ mil.): 207.9
Current ratio: 2.31
Long-term debt ($ mil.): 266.0
No. of shares (mil.): 57.8
Dividends
 Yield: 0.0%
 Payout: 2.8%
Market value ($ mil.): 981.0

	STOCK PRICE ($) FY Close	P/E High	P/E Low	PER SHARE ($) Earnings	PER SHARE ($) Dividends	PER SHARE ($) Book Value
03/19	16.97	8	4	3.50	0.10	11.06
03/18	18.13	6	2	4.34	0.00	8.17
03/17	12.00	12	2	0.87	0.00	3.31
03/16	1.93	—	—	(1.17)	0.00	2.45
03/15	4.14	—	—	(0.31)	0.00	3.62
Annual Growth	42.3%	—	—	—	—	32.2%

Kennedy-Wilson Holdings Inc

International real estate company Kennedy-Wilson Holdings invests in and leases mostly commercial properties in the US UK Ireland Spain Italy and Japan. In addition to office space the company's KW Investments unit acquires and manages portfolios of multifamily residences loans secured by real estate retail space offices condos and industrial properties. With about $16 billion in assets under management its KW Investment Management and Real Estate Services (IMRES) division provides property and investment management auction and residential sales and brokerage services to financial institutions institutional investors insurance companies government entities and builders. Kennedy-Wilson has ownership interests more than 50 million sq. ft. of property.

Financial Performance
Kennedy-Wilson Holdings' revenue has nearly doubled in the last five years as new property acquisitions have spurred additional rental income. The company's net earnings have varied wildly in that time — from a low of $59 million in 2015 (when it realized low acquisition-related gains and incurred high investment interest expense) to a five-year peak of $212.1 million in 2018.

Despite increased rental and hotel income Kennedy-Wilson's revenue dipped 4% to $773.5 million in 2018 on lower gains on sale of real estate compared with the previous year when the company sold a building on its Capital Dock campus — one of the largest mixed-use developments in Ireland?to JPMorgan Chase.

Net income rose 54% in 2018 due to the deconsolidation of a joint venture with AXA Investment Managers for three multifamily assets in Dublin and the sale of two other multifamily assets in Dublin and one in Cork.

The company added $136.7 million to its total cash in 2018 to end the year with $488 million. Operations provided $93.1 million. Investments generated $593.2 million — primarily due to net proceeds from sale of real estate (related to the AXA deconsolidation); financing activities used $528.8 million — mainly for repayment of lines of credit term loans and mortgage debt; common stock repurchases; distributions to noncontrolling interests; and dividends paid.

Strategy
Unlike real estate investment trusts that strictly focus on investments Kennedy-Wilson Holdings' unique advantage over competitors is that it can offer a full array of real estate services to the properties and tenants that it manages. As is the case with many real estate companies Kennedy-Wilson relies on bargain-priced property acquisitions to boost its rental revenue over time. The firm focuses on acquiring properties in the geographic areas where it has expertise and has experienced the greatest success — particularly Ireland.

In 2019 Kennedy-Wilson increased its stake in Dublin mixed-use campus Capital Dock from 42.5% to 50%. Capital Dock is one of the largest single-phase developments in Ireland. It houses two class A office buildings with a total of nearly 400000 sq. ft.; 190 residential units; 1.5 acres of public space including a park; and 26000 sq. ft. in retail and restaurant properties. The previous year it purchased The Elysian in Cork. The property has 206 rental units and 67600 sq. ft. of retail space.

Kennedy-Wilson made a move to shore up its operations and focus on its core property acquisition and investment management functions with its 2018 sale of Meyers Research. Meyers provides residential real estate and new home development data through its Zonda mobile platform.

EXECUTIVES

Chief Administrative Officer, Barry S. Schlesinger, $600,000 total compensation
Chairman and CEO, William J. McMorrow, $950,000 total compensation
President and CEO Kennedy Wilson Europe, Mary L. Ricks, $750,000 total compensation
EVP and President Capital Markets Group, Donald J. Herrema
President Properties Group, James A. (Jim) Rosten
President Auction Group, Richard Rhett Winchell
President Commercial Investment Group, John C. Prabhu
President Residential Investment Group, Stuart Cramer
President Multifamily Management Group, Kurt Zech
EVP, Matt Windisch, $340,000 total compensation
CFO, Justin Enbody, $277,000 total compensation
President of Commercial Investments and Fund Management, Nicholas Colonna
Senior Vice President Finance, Ken Smotrys
Vice President, Omar Macedo
Auditors: KPMG LLP

LOCATIONS

HQ: Kennedy-Wilson Holdings Inc
151 S El Camino Drive, Beverly Hills, CA 90212
Phone: 310 887-6400
Web: www.kennedywilson.com

COMPETITORS

Baird & Warner
Brookfield Office Properties
CBRE Group
Colliers International
Cushman & Wakefield
Gale Company
Jones Lang LaSalle
Lincoln Property
Newmark Knight Frank

HISTORICAL FINANCIALS
Company Type: Public

Income Statement				FYE: December 31
	REVENUE ($ mil.)	NET INCOME ($ mil.)	NET PROFIT MARGIN	EMPLOYEES
12/18	773.5	150.0	19.4%	375
12/17	810.6	100.5	12.4%	498
12/16	703.4	5.6	0.8%	500
12/15	603.7	74.7	12.4%	495
12/14	398.6	21.9	5.5%	450
Annual Growth	18.0%	61.8%	—	(4.5%)

2018 Year-End Financials
Debt ratio: 73.5%
Return on equity: 11.4%
Cash ($ mil.): 488.0
Current ratio: 1.06
Long-term debt ($ mil.): 5,412.8
No. of shares (mil.): 143.2
Dividends
  Yield: 4.2%
  Payout: 75.0%
Market value ($ mil.): 2,602.0

	STOCK PRICE ($) FY Close	P/E High/Low	PER SHARE ($) Earnings	Dividends	Book Value
12/18	18.17	21 16	1.04	0.78	8.71
12/17	17.35	27 21	0.83	0.70	9.01
12/16	20.50	2408 1584	0.01	0.56	9.05
12/15	24.08	43 34	0.66	0.48	9.90
12/14	25.30	199 149	0.14	0.36	9.38
Annual Growth	(7.9%)	— —	65.1%	21.3%	(1.8%)

Kentucky Bancshares Inc

EXECUTIVES

Chb, Buckner Woodford
Auditors: Crowe LLP

LOCATIONS

HQ: Kentucky Bancshares Inc
P.O. Box 157, Paris, KY 40362-0157
Phone: 859 987-1795
Web: www.kybank.com

HISTORICAL FINANCIALS
Company Type: Public

Income Statement				FYE: December 31
	ASSETS ($ mil.)	NET INCOME ($ mil.)	INCOME AS % OF ASSETS	EMPLOYEES
12/18	1,086.0	12.4	1.1%	232
12/17	1,053.1	10.7	1.0%	233
12/16	1,028.4	8.5	0.8%	241
12/15	974.6	6.8	0.7%	243
12/14	855.2	7.0	0.8%	215
Annual Growth	6.2%	15.1%	—	1.9%

2018 Year-End Financials
Return on assets: 1.1%
Return on equity: 12.0%
Long-term debt ($ mil.): —
No. of shares (mil.): 5.9
Sales ($ mil): 55.6
Dividends
  Yield: 2.7%
  Payout: 30.7%
Market value ($ mil.): 135.0

	STOCK PRICE ($) FY Close	P/E High/Low	PER SHARE ($) Earnings	Dividends	Book Value
12/18	22.70	25 11	2.09	0.63	17.93
12/17	46.05	26 18	1.81	0.58	16.88
12/16	32.50	23 18	1.44	0.54	15.63
12/15	29.65	28 23	1.20	0.52	14.96
12/14	27.35	22 18	1.30	0.50	14.33
Annual Growth	(4.6%)	— —	12.6%	5.7%	5.8%

Kilroy Realty Corp

Kilroy is still here especially if you're referring to the West Coast. A self-administered real estate investment trust (REIT) Kilroy Realty owns manages and develops Class A office space mostly in suburban Southern California's Orange County San Diego and Los Angeles but it has since expanded to the San Francisco Bay and greater Seattle area to woo technology companies as tenants. Its portfolio includes about 115 office properties encompassing more than 13 million square feet of leasable space. A majority of Kilroy Realty's 500-plus tenants are involved in technology media financial services and real estate.

Geographic Reach
Besides 10 office buildings in Washington all of the REIT's property is located in California.

Sales and Marketing
Its 15 largest tenants accounted for 34% of the REIT's base rental revenue in 2012; these include DIRECTV Intuit and Bridgepoint Education. Its properties are 92% occupied.

Financial Performance
Overall sales grew 10% to $405 million in 2012. Profits jumped more than 300% to $270 million after the trust recorded gains on properties it sold.

As a REIT Kilroy Realty is exempt from paying federal income tax as long as it distributes quarterly dividends to shareholders.

Strategy
Kilroy Realty has moved away from owning industrial properties in order to focus on office buildings which generally earn more in rental income. In late 2012 it sold its entire portfolio of 44 industrial properties in California to two unnamed buyers for $355 million. The industrial properties totaled almost 4 million-sq.-ft. of space.

At the same time the trust boosted its portfolio of office buildings in San Francisco and Seattle home to many of the nation's wealthy tech companies. In 2012 it paid $330 million for three properties totaling 837000 square feet in Seattle $162 million for a 374000-sq.-ft. office park in Silicon Valley and it paid $52 million for a building in downtown San Francisco that it will spend another $200 million redeveloping into a 27-story glass office tower for new tenant salesforce.com. In addition the trust is spending $315 million to develop a 587000-sq.-ft. office complex for LinkedIn in Sunnyvale California.

Not missing a beat in 2013 the trust boosted its Bay Area construction pipeline to more than 1.8 million square feet with new developments in Redwood City and downtown San Francisco (most of the space is pre-leased).

In addition Kilroy Realty has approximately 110 acres of undeveloped land in San Diego with the capacity for more than 2 million sq. ft. of rentable office space.

EXECUTIVES

EVP and CFO, Tyler H. Rose, age 59, $500,000 total compensation
EVP and COO, Jeffrey C. Hawken, age 61, $675,000 total compensation
Chairman President and CEO, John B. Kilroy, age 71, $1,225,000 total compensation
SVP Asset Management, John T. Fucci
EVP Development and Construction Services, Justin W. Smart, $500,000 total compensation
EVP Chief Accounting Officer and Controller, Heidi R. Roth
EVP Southern California, David Simon
EVP Leasing and Business Development, A. Robert Paratte
EVP Northern California, Mike L. Sanford
Vice President Of Tax, Mike Stauffer

Vice President Coporate Finance And Corporate Counsel, Joseph Magri
Senior Vice President San Diego, Nelson Ackerly
Senior Vice President Investments, Jonathan Praw
SENIOR VICE PRESIDENT, Robert Swartz
Treasurer, Michelle Ngo
Auditors: DELOITTE & TOUCHE LLP

LOCATIONS

HQ: Kilroy Realty Corp
  12200 W. Olympic Boulevard, Suite 200, Los Angeles, CA 90064
Phone: 310 481-8400
Web: www.kilroyrealty.com

PRODUCTS/OPERATIONS

2015 Sales

	% of total
Rental income	91
Tenant reimbursements	9
Other property income	-
Total	**100**

COMPETITORS

BioMed Realty	Irvine Company
Brandywine Realty	Majestic Realty
Digital Realty	PS Business Parks
Douglas Emmett	Prologis
Equity Commonwealth	Shorenstein
Equity Office	The Koll Company
Hudson Pacific	Trammell Crow Company

HISTORICAL FINANCIALS
Company Type: Public

Income Statement — FYE: December 31

	REVENUE ($ mil.)	NET INCOME ($ mil.)	NET PROFIT MARGIN	EMPLOYEES
12/18	747.3	258.4	34.6%	276
12/17	719.0	164.6	22.9%	251
12/16	642.5	293.7	45.7%	245
12/15	581.2	234.0	40.3%	232
12/14	521.7	180.2	34.5%	226
Annual Growth	9.4%	9.4%	—	5.1%

2018 Year-End Financials

Debt ratio: 37.7%
Return on equity: 6.7%
Cash ($ mil.): 51.6
Current ratio: 1.14
Long-term debt ($ mil.): 2,932.6
No. of shares (mil.): 100.7
Dividends
  Yield: 2.8%
  Payout: 70.2%
Market value ($ mil.): 6,335.0

	STOCK PRICE ($) FY Close	P/E High/Low	PER SHARE ($) Earnings	Dividends	Book Value
12/18	62.88	30 23	2.55	1.79	39.01
12/17	74.65	51 44	1.51	1.65	37.53
12/16	73.22	26 16	2.97	3.38	38.01
12/15	63.28	32 26	2.42	1.40	34.37
12/14	69.07	36 25	1.95	1.40	30.91
Annual Growth	(2.3%)	— —	6.9%	6.3%	6.0%

Kilroy Realty L.P.

Auditors: DELOITTE & TOUCHE LLP

LOCATIONS

HQ: Kilroy Realty L.P.
  12200 W. Olympic Boulevard, Suite 200, Los Angeles, CA 90064
Phone: 310 481-8400

HISTORICAL FINANCIALS
Company Type: Public

Income Statement — FYE: December 31

	REVENUE ($ mil.)	NET INCOME ($ mil.)	NET PROFIT MARGIN	EMPLOYEES
12/18	747.3	263.2	35.2%	276
12/17	719.0	167.4	23.3%	251
12/16	642.5	300.0	46.7%	245
12/15	581.2	238.1	41.0%	232
12/14	521.7	183.5	35.2%	226
Annual Growth	9.4%	9.4%	—	5.1%

2018 Year-End Financials

Debt ratio: 37.7%
Return on equity: —
Cash ($ mil.): 51.6
Current ratio: 0.44
Long-term debt ($ mil.): 2,932.6
No. of shares (mil.): 102.7
Dividends
  Yield: —
  Payout: 70.2%
Market value ($ mil.): —

Kimball Electronics Inc

Auditors: DELOITTE & TOUCHE LLP

LOCATIONS

HQ: Kimball Electronics Inc
  1205 Kimball Boulevard, Jasper, IN 47546
Phone: 812 634-4000
Web: www.kimballelectronics.com

HISTORICAL FINANCIALS
Company Type: Public

Income Statement — FYE: June 30

	REVENUE ($ mil.)	NET INCOME ($ mil.)	NET PROFIT MARGIN	EMPLOYEES
06/19	1,181.8	31.5	2.7%	6,300
06/18	1,072.0	16.7	1.6%	5,700
06/17	930.9	34.1	3.7%	5,400
06/16	842.0	22.2	2.6%	4,500
06/15	819.3	26.2	3.2%	4,300
Annual Growth	9.6%	4.8%	—	10.0%

2019 Year-End Financials

Debt ratio: 16.5%
Return on equity: 8.7%
Cash ($ mil.): 49.2
Current ratio: 2.02
Long-term debt ($ mil.): 91.5
No. of shares (mil.): 25.4
Dividends
  Yield: —
  Payout: —
Market value ($ mil.): 413.0

	STOCK PRICE ($) FY Close	P/E High/Low	PER SHARE ($) Earnings	Dividends	Book Value
06/19	16.24	17 12	1.21	0.00	14.55
06/18	18.30	35 25	0.62	0.00	13.40
06/17	18.05	15 10	1.24	0.00	12.75
06/16	12.45	19 12	0.76	0.00	11.49
06/15	14.59	18 8	0.89	0.00	10.71
Annual Growth	2.7%	— —	8.0%	—	8.0%

Kinsale Capital Group Inc

Auditors: KPMG LLP

LOCATIONS

HQ: Kinsale Capital Group Inc
  2221 Edward Holland Drive, Suite 600, Richmond, VA 23230
Phone: 804 289-1300 **Fax:** 804 673-5697
Web: www.kinsalecapitalgroup.com

HISTORICAL FINANCIALS
Company Type: Public

Income Statement — FYE: December 31

	ASSETS ($ mil.)	NET INCOME ($ mil.)	INCOME AS % OF ASSETS	EMPLOYEES
12/18	773.0	33.7	4.4%	190
12/17	667.8	24.9	3.7%	164
12/16	614.3	26.1	4.3%	145
12/15	545.2	22.2	4.1%	145
12/14	437.6	12.9	3.0%	0
Annual Growth	15.3%	27.0%	—	—

2018 Year-End Financials

Return on assets: 4.6%
Return on equity: 13.4%
Long-term debt ($ mil.): —
No. of shares (mil.): 21.2
Sales ($ mil): 222.1
Dividends
  Yield: 0.5%
  Payout: 17.0%
Market value ($ mil.): 1,180.0

	STOCK PRICE ($) FY Close	P/E High/Low	PER SHARE ($) Earnings	Dividends	Book Value
12/18	55.56	40 27	1.56	0.28	12.43
12/17	45.00	38 24	1.16	0.24	11.32
12/16	34.01	61 32	0.56	0.10	10.03
Annual Growth	27.8%	— —	66.9%	67.3%	11.3%

KKR & Co Inc

Auditors: DELOITTE & TOUCHE LLP

LOCATIONS

HQ: KKR & Co Inc
  9 West 57th Street, Suite 4200, New York, NY 10019
Phone: 212 750-8300
Web: www.kkr.com

HISTORICAL FINANCIALS
Company Type: Public

Income Statement   FYE: December 31

	REVENUE ($ mil.)	NET INCOME ($ mil.)	NET PROFIT MARGIN	EMPLOYEES
12/18	2,395.8	1,131.0	47.2%	1,301
12/17	3,282.2	1,018.3	31.0%	1,184
12/16	1,908.0	309.3	16.2%	1,200
12/15	1,043.7	488.4	46.8%	1,196
12/14	1,110.0	477.6	43.0%	1,209
Annual Growth	21.2%	24.1%	—	1.9%

2018 Year-End Financials
Debt ratio: 44.1%
Return on equity: —
Cash ($ mil.): 2,445.1
Current ratio: 1.35
Long-term debt ($ mil.): 22,341.1
No. of shares (mil.): 833.9
Dividends
  Yield: 1.5%
  Payout: 14.3%
Market value ($ mil.): 16,370.0

	STOCK PRICE ($) FY Close	P/E High	P/E Low	PER SHARE ($) Earnings	PER SHARE ($) Dividends	PER SHARE ($) Book Value
12/18	19.63	13	9	2.06	0.30	10.37
12/17	21.06	10	8	1.95	0.00	14.78
12/16	15.39	27	17	0.59	0.00	13.13
12/15	15.59	23	13	1.01	0.00	12.12
12/14	23.21	21	16	1.16	0.00	12.46
Annual Growth	(4.1%)	—	—	15.4%	—	(4.5%)

KKR Real Estate Finance Trust Inc

Auditors: DELOITTE & TOUCHE LLP

LOCATIONS
HQ: KKR Real Estate Finance Trust Inc
9 West 57th Street, Suite 4200, New York, NY 10019
Phone: 212 750-8300
Web: www.kkrreit.com

HISTORICAL FINANCIALS
Company Type: Public

Income Statement   FYE: December 31

	REVENUE ($ mil.)	NET INCOME ($ mil.)	NET PROFIT MARGIN	EMPLOYEES
12/18	203.6	89.7	44.1%	0
12/17	100.8	59.0	58.6%	0
12/16	48.6	31.1	64.1%	0
12/15	22.8	16.7	73.3%	0
Annual Growth	107.3%	74.9%	—	—

2018 Year-End Financials
Debt ratio: 77.5%
Return on equity: 8.1%
Cash ($ mil.): 86.5
Current ratio: 2.75
Long-term debt ($ mil.): 4,059.3
No. of shares (mil.): 57.6
Dividends
  Yield: 8.8%
  Payout: 107.6%
Market value ($ mil.): 1,103.0

	STOCK PRICE ($) FY Close	P/E High	P/E Low	PER SHARE ($) Earnings	PER SHARE ($) Dividends	PER SHARE ($) Book Value
12/18	19.15	13	12	1.58	1.69	19.71
12/17	20.01	18	15	1.30	0.99	19.75
12/16	0.00	—	—	1.61	1.22	20.60
Annual Growth	—	—	—	(0.9%)	17.7%	(2.2%)

KLX Energy Services Holdings Inc

Auditors: Deloitte & Touche LLP

LOCATIONS
HQ: KLX Energy Services Holdings Inc
1300 Corporate Center Way, Wellington, FL 33414
Phone: 561 383-5100
Web: www.klxenergy.com

HISTORICAL FINANCIALS
Company Type: Public

Income Statement   FYE: January 31

	REVENUE ($ mil.)	NET INCOME ($ mil.)	NET PROFIT MARGIN	EMPLOYEES
01/19	495.3	14.4	2.9%	1,400
01/18	320.5	(24.1)	—	1,000
01/17	152.2	(89.6)	—	0
01/16	251.2	(750.4)	—	0
Annual Growth	25.4%	—	—	—

2019 Year-End Financials
Debt ratio: 36.0%
Return on equity: —
Cash ($ mil.): 163.8
Current ratio: 3.62
Long-term debt ($ mil.): 242.2
No. of shares (mil.): 22.6
Dividends
  Yield: —
  Payout: —
Market value ($ mil.): 589.0

	STOCK PRICE ($) FY Close	P/E High	P/E Low	PER SHARE ($) Earnings	PER SHARE ($) Dividends	PER SHARE ($) Book Value
01/19	26.06	48	28	0.71	0.00	15.08
01/18	0.00	—	—	(0.00)	0.00	(0.00)
Annual Growth						

Korn Ferry

Korn Ferry is a talent management firm helping private public and not-for-profit clients organize their strategies for talent acquisition (primarily at the executive level) talent assessment leadership development and rewards and benefits. It collects data on assessments candidates and rewards through its Data Hub and conducts research and analytics on HR trends through its Korn Ferry Institute. The company also serves consumers through Korn Ferry Advance which helps people looking to make their next career move and provides career services to employees within organizations. Korn Ferry operates in more than 100 offices in some 50 countries and was founded in 1969.

Financial Performance
Over the past five years revenue has increased steadily. Net income has been more sporadic growing most years but dropping in 2016 and 2019 as it incurred substantial costs including expenses related to hiring and retaining professional employees. Profitability largely depends on the adequate utilization and billing rates of its consultants.

Fee revenue was $1.926 billion during fiscal 2019 an increase of $158.8 million or 9% compared to fiscal 2018. The increase in fee revenue was attributable to organic growth in all solution areas. It reported a 6% increase in the number of executive search engagements billed and a 5% increase in the weighted-average fees billed per engagement.

Net income decreased during fiscal 2019 to $102.7 million down from $133.8 million in fiscal 2018. The decrease was due to a write-off of trade names related to re-branding efforts an increase in legal and other professional expenses and higher marketing and business development expenses. It also had higher compensation and benefits expenses related to a hiring spree. It made a 10% increase in average headcount.

Cash and cash equivalents increased to $626.4 million in 2019 compared to $520.8 million in 2018. Net cash from operating activities was $258.8 million. Net cash used in investing activities was $69.5 million while net cash used in financing activities was $64.6 million.

Strategy
In 2018 the company approved a plan to go to market under a single master brand and simplify its organizational structure. As part of this plan it eliminated and/or consolidated certain entities and sunset sub-brands including Futurestep Hay Group and Lominger. It renamed Hay Group which became Advisory and its Futurestep segment became RPO & Professional Search.

The firm is working to transform away from a fee-for-service executive search model and toward more recurring consulting revenue. Korn Ferry has more than 1400 consultants who are primarily responsible for originating client services. The company is focused on growing revenue from marquee accounts which include its multi-million-dollar clients that use multiple lines of the company's business. Executive search fees account for about 40% of total fee revenues and about 70% of the executive searches Korn Ferry performs are for board level chief executive and other senior executive and general management positions.

While most revenues come from service fees the company is working to grow revenue through product sales which include online subscription services and licenses to data files that support human resource processes for pay talent and engagement and assessments. Products also include books covering topics such as performance management team effectiveness and coaching and development.

Mergers and Acquisitions
Korn Ferry agreed to acquire three leadership development companies from TwentyEighty in 2019. The three companies Miller Heiman Group AchieveForum and Strategy Execution will be part of a newly branded Korn Ferry Digital segment and improve Korn Ferry's offerings in the corporate training and education market.

EXECUTIVES

President Global Productized Services, Andrew Huddart, age 51
President Asia Pacific Executive Search, Charles Tseng
President Global Industrial Market Executive Search, Yannick Binvel
EVP CFO and Chief Corporate Officer, Robert P. Rozek, age 58, $516,667 total compensation
President CEO and Director, Gary D. Burnison, age 58, $910,000 total compensation
President Financial Executive Search, Michael Franzino, age 69
CEO Futurestep, Byrne K. Mulrooney, age 58, $450,000 total compensation
SVP Chief Marketing Officer and President Korn Ferry Institute, Michael Distefano
President Asia Pacific Futurestep, Chong Ng
President Life Sciences Executive Search, Jay Kizer
CEO Korn Ferry Hay Group, Stephen Kaye, $187,500 total compensation
Managing Director Zurich and Senior Client Partner Consumer, Dominique Virchaux
President Technology Executive Search, Werner Penk
EVP Global Human Resources, Linda Hyman
President Europe Middle East and Africa (EMEA) and Chair Global Industrial and Consumer Markets Executive Search, Bernard S. Zen-Ruffinen
President Americas Executive Search, Doug Charles
SVP and CIO, Bryan Ackermann
Svp Corporate Development, Brian Suh
Senior Vice President Finance Treasury Tax Investor Relations, Gregg Kvochak
Vp Global Hr Korn Ferry Futurestep Chicago, Caroline C Werner
Vp Global Accounts And Strategic Development Korn Ferry Futurestep Philadelphia, George Vollmer
Chairman, George T. Shaheen, age 74
Auditors: Ernst & Young LLP

LOCATIONS

HQ: Korn Ferry
  1900 Avenue of the Stars, Suite 2600, Los Angeles, CA 90067
Phone: 310 552-1834
Web: www.kornferry.com

PRODUCTS/OPERATIONS

2016 Sales

	$ mil.	% of total
Executive Search		
North America	371.3	28
EMEA	144.3	11
Asia Pacific	80.5	6
Latin America	26.7	2
Hay Group	471.2	35
Futurestep	198.1	15
Reimbursed out-of-pocket engagement expense	54.6	3
Total	**1,346.7**	**100**

Solutions
Assessment & Succession
Board & CEO Services
Employer Branding
Executive Search
Leadership Development
Professional Search
Recruitment Process Outsourcing
Rewards & Benefits
Strategy Execution & Organization Design
Talent Strategy & Organizational Alignment
Workforce performance Inclusion & Diversity

COMPETITORS

A.T. Kearney
CCL
CTPartners
Development Dimensions International
Diversified Search
Egon Zehnder
Gap International
Handler & Associates
Heidrick & Struggles
PageGroup
Russell Reynolds
Solomon Page
Spencer Stuart

HISTORICAL FINANCIALS
Company Type: Public

Income Statement FYE: April 30

	REVENUE ($ mil.)	NET INCOME ($ mil.)	NET PROFIT MARGIN	EMPLOYEES
04/19	1,973.8	102.6	5.2%	8,678
04/18	1,819.5	133.7	7.4%	7,643
04/17	1,621.6	84.1	5.2%	7,232
04/16	1,346.7	30.9	2.3%	6,947
04/15	1,066.0	88.3	8.3%	3,687
Annual Growth	16.6%	3.8%	—	23.9%

2019 Year-End Financials
Debt ratio: 9.5%
Return on equity: 8.3%
Cash ($ mil.): 626.3
Current ratio: 2.06
Long-term debt ($ mil.): 222.8
No. of shares (mil.): 56.4
Dividends
  Yield: 0.8%
  Payout: 22.1%
Market value ($ mil.): 2,653.0

	STOCK PRICE ($) FY Close	P/E High/Low	PER SHARE ($) Earnings	Dividends	Book Value
04/19	47.02	37 21	1.81	0.40	21.99
04/18	53.46	23 13	2.35	0.40	21.53
04/17	32.40	22 13	1.47	0.40	19.03
04/16	27.14	66 44	0.58	0.40	18.25
04/15	31.53	19 14	1.76	0.10	16.12
Annual Growth	10.5%	— —	0.7%	41.4%	8.1%

Kraton Corp

Through Kraton Polymers Kraton Corporation makes hydrogenated and unhydrogenated styrenic block copolymers (SBCs). SBCs are used in a wide range of products including adhesives coatings consumer and personal care products sealants lubricants medical packaging automotive paving and roofing and footwear products and other applications. They impart qualities such as temperature cracking and impact resistance; water dispersion; soft-feel; and stretchiness. Industries served include automotive medical and personal care products. Under its Cariflex brand it sells non-SBC isoprene rubber latex products such as medical gloves and condoms. A chemicals segment makes products derived from pine wood pulping co-products. SBCs were invented and commercialized by Kraton more than 50 years ago.

Operations
Kraton operates through a Polymer segment and a Chemical segment.

The Polymer segment accounts for about 60% of total revenue and consists of three product categories performance products specialty polymers and Cariflex. Performance products includes styrenic block copolymers used in a wide range of application including adhesives coatings consumer and personal care products sealants lubricants medical packaging automotive paving roofing and footware products. The high-margin specialty unit makes difficult to produce SBCs that provide improve flow for sealants and lubricant; soft-feel grip for razor handles power tools etc; impact resistance; wire flexibility; stretchiness; ultraviolet light resistance; viscosity; and temperature resistance. Cariflex makes non-SBC rubber alternatives used in medical products paints coatings and footwear.

Chemical segment (40% of sales) sells pine wood pulping co-products and feedstocks like crude tall oil and crude sulfate turpentine. Products are made for the adhesive roads and construction and automotive industries.

Geographic Reach
Houston Texas-based Kraton has operations across North America South America Europe and Asia. The US generates about 35% of revenues and Germany is the next-biggest at around 10%. Other sales come from Europe the Middle East and the Asia/Pacific region. All told Kraton has around 800 customers in 70 countries.

Kraton produces products for its polymers segment at six facilities in Ohio Germany France Brazil Japan and Taiwan while the chemicals segment has eight facilities across the US Finland France Sweden and Germany.

Financial Performance
Acquisitions have helped Kraton's revenue double between 2015 and 2018. Profit growth has been less dynamic however and the company operates on relatively fine margins.

In 2018 the company's sales growth slowed to 3% reaching $2.0 billion. The increase was split fairly evenly between the polymer and chemicals segments. The polymer segment was boosted by pass-through effects of higher raw materials costs with gains focused in the specialty polymer and Cariflex units. The performance polymers unit witness a 7% decline in volumes due to lower paving sales outside North America and Europe. Growth in the chemicals segment arose from higher prices and a slight increase in volumes.

Net income fell 24% to $70.5 million mainly due to a large income tax benefit recorded in the prior year relating to the 2017 US Tax Cuts and Jobs Act. Excluding tax operating income was up 22% due to lower general expenses and stable R&D and depreciation and amortization costs.

Kraton's cash on hand fell $3.2 million to $85.9 million during 2018. The company's operations generated $246.6 million while investing activities used $111.1 million and financing used $136.7 million. The company's main cash uses were debt repayments and capital expenditures.

Mergers and Acquisitions
In 2016 Kraton completed the acquisition of Arizona Chemical Holdings Corporation the largest global provider of pine-based specialty chemicals for $1.3 million. Through the business combination the company expanded its offerings of polymers and specialty chemicals.

EXECUTIVES

EVP and CFO, Stephen E. Tremblay, age 60, $450,000 total compensation
President and CEO, Kevin M. Fogarty, age 54, $875,000 total compensation
SVP and CTO, Lothar P. Freund, age 59, $350,000 total compensation
SVP and Chief Commercial Officer, Holger R. Jung, age 56, $375,000 total compensation

VP and Chief Human Resources Officer, Melinda S. Conley, age 53, $311,875 total compensation
Vice President Sales and Marketing, Tony Speller
Vice President Global Distribution, Jim Smith
Chairman, Dan F. Smith, age 72
Secretary Partner, Karen Imfree
Board Member, Dominique Fournier
Auditors: KPMG LLP

LOCATIONS

HQ: Kraton Corp
15710 John F. Kennedy Blvd., Suite 300, Houston, TX 77032
Phone: 281 504-4700
Web: www.kraton.com

PRODUCTS/OPERATIONS

2018 Sales

	% of total
Polymers	61
Chemicals	39
Total	**100**

COMPETITORS

Kumho Petrochemical	Polimeri Europa
Kuraray	Sinopec Corp.
LG Chem	Zeon

HISTORICAL FINANCIALS

Company Type: Public

Income Statement — FYE: December 31

	REVENUE ($ mil.)	NET INCOME ($ mil.)	NET PROFIT MARGIN	EMPLOYEES
12/18	2,011.6	67.0	3.3%	1,918
12/17	1,960.3	97.5	5.0%	1,931
12/16	1,744.1	107.3	6.2%	1,971
12/15	1,034.6	(10.5)	—	917
12/14	1,230.4	2.4	0.2%	934
Annual Growth	13.1%	129.4%	—	19.7%

2018 Year-End Financials

Debt ratio: 52.9%
Return on equity: 9.9%
Cash ($ mil.): 85.8
Current ratio: 2.19
Long-term debt ($ mil.): 1,487.3
No. of shares (mil.): 31.9
Dividends
 Yield: —
 Payout: —
Market value ($ mil.): 697.0

	STOCK PRICE ($) FY Close	P/E High/Low		PER SHARE ($) Earnings	Dividends	Book Value
12/18	21.84	25	9	2.08	0.00	22.41
12/17	48.17	16	8	3.07	0.00	20.14
12/16	28.48	11	4	3.43	0.00	14.79
12/15	16.61	—	—	(0.34)	0.00	11.74
12/14	20.79	404	223	0.07	0.00	13.52
Annual Growth	1.2%		—	133.5%	—	13.5%

Ladder Capital Corp

This specialty finance firm is looking to climb to the top of the commercial real-estate lending business. Ladder Capital Corp. is a non-bank operating company engaged in three major lines of business: commercial mortgage lending mortgage backed securities and real-estate assets. Its loans typically range from $5 million to $100 million. More than 50% of its loans originate in the Northeast. Hotel retail and office properties account for about three-quarters of Ladder's loan portfolio. Since its founding in 2008 the commercial real estate finance firm has originated $5.4 billion in conduit loans. Ladder Capital went public in 2014 with an offering valued at $225 million.

IPO

The company's February 2014 IPO raised $225 million by offering 13.3 million shares at $17 the midpoint of the $16 to $18 range. Ladder Capital intends to use the IPO proceeds to grow its loan origination and related commercial real estate business lines and for general corporate purposes.

Geographic Reach

Ladder Capital is headquartered in New York City and has branches in Los Angeles and Boca Raton Florida.

EXECUTIVES

CFO, Marc A. Fox, age 59
CEO, Brian R. Harris, age 58, $1,000,000 total compensation
Head Asset Management, Robert M. Perelman, age 56
Head Merchant Banking and Capital Markets, Thomas Harney, age 57, $400,000 total compensation
President, Pamela McCormack, age 48, $600,000 total compensation
Chairman, Alan H. Fishman, age 73
Board Member, Michael Mazzei
Auditors: PricewaterhouseCoopers LLP

LOCATIONS

HQ: Ladder Capital Corp
345 Park Avenue, New York, NY 10154
Phone: 212 715-3170
Web: www.laddercapital.com

PRODUCTS/OPERATIONS

2013 Loans by Type

	% of total
Hotel	34
Retail	22
Office	20
Multifamily	15
Condo	7
Mixed use	2
Total	**100**

COMPETITORS

CIT Group	Citigroup

HISTORICAL FINANCIALS

Company Type: Public

Income Statement — FYE: December 31

	ASSETS ($ mil.)	NET INCOME ($ mil.)	INCOME AS % OF ASSETS	EMPLOYEES
12/18	6,272.8	180.0	2.9%	74
12/17	6,025.6	95.2	1.6%	72
12/16	5,578.3	66.7	1.2%	69
12/15	5,895.2	73.8	1.3%	73
12/14	5,823.6	44.1	0.8%	66
Annual Growth	1.9%	42.1%	—	2.9%

2018 Year-End Financials

Return on assets: 2.9%
Return on equity: 13.4%
Long-term debt ($ mil.): —
No. of shares (mil.): 117.0
Sales ($ mil): 595.1
Dividends
 Yield: 8.4%
 Payout: 83.4%
Market value ($ mil.): 1,811.0

	STOCK PRICE ($) FY Close	P/E High/Low		PER SHARE ($) Earnings	Dividends	Book Value
12/18	15.47	10	7	1.84	1.54	12.35
12/17	13.63	13	11	1.13	1.22	11.10
12/16	13.72	14	9	1.06	1.29	8.86
12/15	12.42	14	8	1.42	2.23	8.34
12/14	19.61	23	18	0.86	0.00	7.93
Annual Growth	(5.8%)	—	—	20.9%	—	11.7%

Ladenburg Thalmann Financial Services Inc

Ladenburg Thalmann Financial Services provides brokerage asset management and investment research banking and wholesale life insurance services to corporate institutional and individual clients throughout the US. The company serves primarily retail clients through independent broker-dealer subsidiaries which together have some 4300 financial advisors and manage about $160 billion in assets. The company's investment bank provides investment research on small- to mid-cap companies and finance and strategic advisory services to middle-market companies. Its asset management unit offers mutual funds alternative investments and investment counseling. Ladenburg's insurance subsidiaries provide support services to life insurance advisors and institutions.

Operations

The clear majority of Ladenburg Thalmann's revenue (about 90%) is generated by its independent advisory and brokerage services business. Through five subsidiaries employing about 4300 representatives Ladenburg provides financial advice primarily to retail investors especially individuals and households with $100000 to $1.5 million in net investible assets.

Ladenburg's investment banking practice which it calls its Ladenburg segment generates about 5% of revenue and includes Ladenburg Thalmann & Co. and Ladenburg Thalmann Asset Management (LTAM). The investment bank mostly finances companies with market caps below $500 million through underwritten public registered direct and at-the-market offerings and private placements. LTAM manages about $2.5 billion in assets for more than 14500 clients.

Ladenburg's insurance brokerage business also contributes about 5% of revenue. The company's Highland Capital Brokerage subsidiary provides life insurance and fixed and equity indexed annuities to investment and insurance providers. Highland and the Ladenburg Thalmann Annuity Insurance division provide services including risk underwriting back office processing advanced planning marketing strategy and point of sale support.

Geographic Reach
Ladenburg Thalmann is stationed in Miami. Its branch offices are in Naples and Boca Raton Florida; Melville Westhampton Beach and New York New York; Boston Massachusetts; Dallas Texas; and Calabasas and Irvine California. Substantially all of the company's revenue comes from the US where all of its long-lived assets are located.

Sales and Marketing
Ladenburg Thalmann's independent advisory and brokerage services business provides financial advice primarily to retail investors especially what the company calls “mass affluent” customers — individuals and households with $100000 to $1.5 million in net investible assets.

Financial Performance
Ladenburg Thalmann's revenue and cash have grown impressively in the last five years (63% and 242% respectively) while 2017 saw the company's net income regain some ground following huge losses in 2016 and 2015.

The company reported revenue of $1.3 billion in 2017 up 15% from the previous year driven primarily by a $96.8 million jump in fees from its independent advisory and brokerage subsidiaries as a result of improved market conditions. Commissions investment banking revenue and interest and dividends also rose.

The firm's net income increased by $7.7 million in 2017 a stark contrast to 2016 and 2015 when the company lost $22.3 million and $11.2 million respectively. The bounce-back was fueled by accelerating revenues and a $16.5 million cut in income tax expense which followed a $10 million tax expense increase in 2016 caused by the company's tax valuation allowance.

Cash at the end of fiscal 2017 was $172.1 million an increase of $73.2 million from the prior year. Cash from operations contributed $16.2 million while investing activities used $9.8 million — mainly for furniture and equipment purchases and leasehold improvements. Financing activities provided another $66.8 million due to several stock issuances.

Strategy
Key to Ladenburg Thalmann's strategy is expanding its network of independent advisors and equipping them with technologies and tools to grow their businesses. The company added about 300 advisors to its roster in 2017. Ladenburg gives all advisors access to its products and services including its wealth management division capital markets products investment banking services and investment research. The company also provides advisors with business coaching services and applications such as its Succession Continuity & Acquisitions (SCA) program; Retirement Plan Consulting Platform; and Behavioral Financial Advice Training Program.

Company Background
Founded in 1876 Ladenburg Thalmann boasts of having had Albert Einstein as a client. The company is the sixth oldest member on record as a New York Stock Exchange member.

EXECUTIVES
President CEO and Director, Richard J. (Dick) Lampen, age 65, $200,000 total compensation
EVP and Director, Mark Zeitchick, age 53, $375,000 total compensation
SVP and CIO, Doreen Griffith
SVP Wealth Management, Paul Lofties
SVP and CFO, Brett H. Kaufman, age 47, $325,000 total compensation
EVP and COO, Adam Malamed, age 47, $350,000 total compensation
Chief Risk Officer, Craig Timm
Senior Vice President Corporate And Regulatory Affairs, Joseph Giovanniello
Senior Vice President Enterprise Initiatives, Carly Maher
Vice President Sales, Herb Simon
Vice President Head Of Sponsor Relations, Oksana Poznak
Vice President Investment Banking, Jeffrey Caliva
Vice President Equity Research Telecom Media and Technology, Glenn G Mattson
Vice President Retirement And Fiduciary Services, Doug Baxley
Executive Vice President Equity Research Yield Oriented Equities, Christopher Nolan
Chairman, Phillip Frost, age 83
Vice Chairman, Howard M. Lorber, age 70
Board Member, Saul Gilinski
Board Member, Richard Krasno
Auditors: EisnerAmper LLP

LOCATIONS
HQ: Ladenburg Thalmann Financial Services Inc
4400 Biscayne Boulevard, 12th Floor, Miami, FL 33137
Phone: 305 572-4100
Web: www.ladenburg.com

PRODUCTS/OPERATIONS

2017 Sales
	$ mil.	% of total
Commissions	536.0	42
Advisory fees	560.9	44
Investment banking	46.5	4
Interest & dividends	25.0	2
Principal transactions	0.9	-
Service fees & other	98.9	8
Total	**1,268.2**	**100**

2017 Sales
	$ mil.	% of total
Independent Advisory & Brokerage	1,140.4	90
Ladenburg	66.7	5
Insurance Brokerage	57.1	5
Corporate	4.0	-
Total	**1,268.2**	**100**

COMPETITORS
Citigroup Global Markets
Detwiler Fenton
Investors Capital Holdings
JPMorgan Chase
LPL Financial
Morgan Stanley
National Holdings
Sage Advisory Services
UBS Financial Services

HISTORICAL FINANCIALS
Company Type: Public

Income Statement FYE: December 31

	REVENUE ($ mil.)	NET INCOME ($ mil.)	NET PROFIT MARGIN	EMPLOYEES
12/18	1,391.1	33.7	2.4%	1,512
12/17	1,268.1	7.7	0.6%	1,379
12/16	1,106.9	(22.2)	—	1,299
12/15	1,152.1	(11.1)	—	1,307
12/14	921.2	33.4	3.6%	1,109
Annual Growth	10.9%	0.2%	—	8.1%

2018 Year-End Financials
Debt ratio: 34.2% No. of shares (mil.): 146.5
Return on equity: 10.8% Dividends
Cash ($ mil.): 182.6 Yield: 1.9%
Current ratio: 1.10 Payout: —
Long-term debt ($ mil.): 254.0 Market value ($ mil.): 341.0

	STOCK PRICE ($) FY Close	P/E High/Low		PER SHARE ($) Earnings	Dividends	Book Value
12/18	2.33	—	—	(0.00)	0.05	1.73
12/17	3.16	—	—	(0.13)	0.02	1.87
12/16	2.44	—	—	(0.29)	0.00	1.87
12/15	2.76	—	—	(0.21)	0.00	2.06
12/14	3.95	49	26	0.08	0.00	1.82
Annual Growth	(12.4%)	—	—	—	—	(1.3%)

Lakeland Bancorp, Inc.

Lakeland Bancorp is the holding company for Lakeland Bank which serves northern and central New Jersey from around 50 branch offices. Targeting individuals and small to midsized businesses the bank offers standard retail products such as checking and savings accounts money market and NOW accounts and CDs. It also offers financial planning and advisory services for consumers. The bank's lending activities primarily consist of commercial loans and mortgages (around three-quarters of the company's loan portfolio) and residential mortgages. Lakeland also offers commercial lease financing for commercial equipment.

Operations
Lakeland Bancorp operates through a single business segment. Around 70% of its $4.3 billion loan portfolio is made up of commercial mortgages. Industrial commercial loans residential mortgages real estate construction loans and home equity and consumer loans each represent between 5%-10% of the company's lending activity. The company holds $5.5 billion in assets and $4.4 billion in deposits.

Geographic Reach
Headquartered in Oak Ridge New Jersey Lakeland Bancorp boasts about 50 banking offices across the New Jersey counties of Bergen Essex Morris Ocean Passaic Somerset Sussex Union and Warren. The company also has a branch in Highland Mills New York; six New Jersey regional commercial lending centers in Bernardsville Jackson Montville Newton Teaneck and Waldwick; and two commercial loan production offices serving Middlesex and Monmouth counties in New Jersey and the Hudson Valley region of New York.

Sales and Marketing
Lakeland Bancorp serves a variety of customers from individuals to businesses to municipalities.
One-fifth of Lakeland's commercial loan segment - the largest in its portfolio - is made up of owner-occupied real estate loans. Multifamily and retail loans make up about 15% each and industrial and office loans each comprise around 10%.

Financial Performance
Lakeland Bancorp has seen major five-year growth expanding revenue by 53% to $190.7 million net income by 111% to $52.6 million and cash by 39% to $142.9 million between 2013 and 2017.

However the company's debt has risen 85% to $296.9 million in that time.

The holding company's revenue increased 14% in 2017 owing primarily to increased net interest income from growing average earning assets. Net income added 27% on the strength of those gains.

Lakeland's cash dipped $32.9 million in 2017. Operations and financings contributed $67.5 million and investments used $355.1 million. Financings provided $254.8 million down nearly $200 million from the previous year following an increase in net deposits federal funds purchased and securities sold under repurchase agreements.

Strategy
Lakeland Bancorp is focused on growth through acquisitions. The company has acquired at least eight community banks since its inception including Highlands Bancorp. which operates in northern New Jersey. The company also offers internet banking mobile banking and cash management services.

Mergers and Acquisitions
In January 2019 Lakeland Bancorp acquired Vernon New Jersey-based Highlands Bancorp in a deal valued at $56.7 million. The holding company - which operated branches in the New Jersey municipalities of Sparta Totowa and Denville - had consolidated total assets of $5.53 billion.

Company Background
Lakeland Bancorp was founded in 1969. It organized into a bank holding company in 1989.

EXECUTIVES

President and CEO Lakeland Bancorp and Lakeland Bank, Thomas J. Shara, age 61, $650,000 total compensation
SEVP and COO, Ronald E. (Ron) Schwarz, age 62, $266,769 total compensation
SEVP and Regional President, Robert A. Vandenbergh, age 67, $360,212 total compensation
EVP and Senior Government Banking and Financial Services Officer, Jeffrey J. Buonforte, age 67, $205,075 total compensation
EVP and Chief Credit Officer, James R. Noonan, age 67
EVP and Chief Risk Officer, James M. Nigro
CFO, Thomas F. Splaine, age 54
First SVP and Chief Technology and Information Security Officer, Mary Kaye Nardone
EVP and Chief Retail Officer, Ellen Lalwani
EVP and Chief Lending Officer, David S. Yanagisawa, $220,000 total compensation
EVP Chief Administrative Officer General Counsel and Corporate Secretary, Timothy J. Matteson, age 49
EVP and Regional President, Michael A. Schutzer
Vice President Asset Based Lending, Steven Breeman
Vice President Commercial Lending, Bruce Bready
Vice President, Scott Heiman
Vice President Area Manager, Hafeza Mohammed
Executive Vice President And Chief Lending Officer Of The Company And The Bank, John Rath
Chairman Lakeland Bancorp and Lakeland Bank, Mary Ann Deacon, age 67
Board Member, Brian M Flynn
Board Member, Lawrence Inserra
Auditors: KPMG LLP

LOCATIONS
HQ: Lakeland Bancorp, Inc.
250 Oak Ridge Road, Oak Ridge, NJ 07438
Phone: 973 697-2000
Web: www.lakelandbank.com

PRODUCTS/OPERATIONS

2017 Sales

	$ mil.	% of total
Interest		
Loans & fees	172.3	80
Investment securities and other	17.9	8
Interest expense	(25.0)	-
Non-interest		
Service charges on deposit accounts	10.7	5
Commissions & fees	4.9	2
Income on bank owned life insurance	2.4	1
Other	7.5	4
Total	**190.7**	**100**

Selected Services
401K and IRA Rollovers
Certificates of deposit & individual retirement accounts
Checking accounts
Consumer loans
Home loans
Insurance
Investment management
Online services
Retirement income planning
Savings and money market accounts

COMPETITORS

Bank of America	PNC Financial
Bank of New York Mellon	Sovereign Bank
	Sussex Bancorp
Capital One	TD Bank USA
Clifton Bancorp	Valley National Bancorp
Hudson City Bancorp	
Investors Bancorp	Wells Fargo
JPMorgan Chase	
New York Community Bancorp	

HISTORICAL FINANCIALS
Company Type: Public

Income Statement FYE: December 31

	ASSETS ($ mil.)	NET INCOME ($ mil.)	INCOME AS % OF ASSETS	EMPLOYEES
12/18	5,806.0	63.4	1.1%	652
12/17	5,405.6	52.5	1.0%	621
12/16	5,093.1	41.5	0.8%	592
12/15	3,869.5	32.4	0.8%	551
12/14	3,538.3	31.1	0.9%	566
Annual Growth	13.2%	19.5%	—	3.6%

2018 Year-End Financials
Return on assets: 1.1%
Return on equity: 10.5%
Long-term debt ($ mil.): —
No. of shares (mil.): 47.4
Sales ($ mil): 235.4
Dividends
Yield: 3.0%
Payout: 35.0%
Market value ($ mil.): 703.0

	STOCK PRICE ($) FY Close	P/E High/Low	PER SHARE ($) Earnings	Dividends	Book Value
12/18	14.81	16 11	1.32	0.45	13.14
12/17	19.25	20 16	1.09	0.40	12.31
12/16	19.50	21 10	0.95	0.37	11.65
12/15	11.79	15 12	0.85	0.33	10.57
12/14	11.70	15 12	0.82	0.29	10.01
Annual Growth	6.1%	—	12.6%	11.0%	7.0%

Lakeland Financial Corp

EXECUTIVES

EVP and Retail Banking Manager, Kevin L. Deardorff, age 58, $217,963 total compensation
President and CEO Lakeland Financial and Lake City Bank, David M. Findlay, age 57, $493,360 total compensation
SVP Commercial Lake City Bank, Michael E. Gavin
EVP and CFO, Lisa M. O'Neill, age 51, $206,286 total compensation
SVP and General Counsel, Kristin L. Pruitt, age 47
SVP Wealth Advisory, Eric H. Ottinger, $218,263 total compensation
Vice President And Trust Officer, Patricia Culp
Vice President, Mark Rensner
VICE PRESIDENT COMMERCIAL BANKING OFFICER, Mike Ryan
Chairman Lakeland Financial and Lake City Bank, Michael L. Kubacki, age 67
Auditors: Crowe LLP

LOCATIONS
HQ: Lakeland Financial Corp
202 East Center Street, P.O. Box 1387, Warsaw, IN 46580
Phone: 574 267-6144
Web: www.lakecitybank.com

PRODUCTS/OPERATIONS

2017 Sales

	$ mil.	% of total
Interest		
Loans	151.0	75
Securities	14.3	7
Other	0.3	-
Interest expense	(29.8)	-
Noninteresst		
Service charges on deposit accounts	13.7	7
Loan and service fees	7.9	4
Wealth advisory fees	5.5	3
Investment brokerage fees	1.3	-
Other	7.7	4
Total	**171.9**	**100**

COMPETITORS

1st Source Corporation	PNC Financial
KeyCorp	Peoples Bancorp (IN)
Northeast Indiana Bancorp	

HISTORICAL FINANCIALS
Company Type: Public

Income Statement FYE: December 31

	ASSETS ($ mil.)	NET INCOME ($ mil.)	INCOME AS % OF ASSETS	EMPLOYEES
12/18	4,875.2	80.4	1.6%	553
12/17	4,682.9	57.3	1.2%	539
12/16	4,290.0	52.0	1.2%	524
12/15	3,766.2	46.3	1.2%	518
12/14	3,443.2	43.8	1.3%	496
Annual Growth	9.1%	16.4%	—	2.8%

2018 Year-End Financials

Return on assets: 1.6%
Return on equity: 16.2%
Long-term debt ($ mil.): —
No. of shares (mil.): 25.1
Sales ($ mil): 239.0
Dividends
Yield: 2.4%
Payout: 36.5%
Market value ($ mil.): 1,009.0

	STOCK PRICE ($) FY Close	P/E High/Low		PER SHARE ($) Earnings	Dividends	Book Value
12/18	40.16	16	12	3.13	1.00	20.76
12/17	48.49	23	18	2.23	0.63	18.72
12/16	47.36	26	16	2.05	0.73	17.12
12/15	46.62	26	20	1.83	0.63	15.83
12/14	43.47	25	20	1.74	0.55	14.63
Annual Growth	(2.0%)	—	—	15.8%	16.3%	9.1%

Landmark Infrastructure Partners LP

Auditors: Ernst & Young LLP

LOCATIONS

HQ: Landmark Infrastructure Partners LP
400 Continental Blvd, Suite 500, P.O. Box 3429, El Segundo, CA 90245
Phone: 310 598-3173
Web: www.landmarkmlp.com

HISTORICAL FINANCIALS

Company Type: Public

Income Statement — FYE: December 31

	REVENUE ($ mil.)	NET INCOME ($ mil.)	NET PROFIT MARGIN	EMPLOYEES
12/18	64.7	115.7	178.8%	35
12/17	52.6	19.2	36.6%	30
12/16	42.4	9.9	23.4%	30
12/15	27.7	(0.4)	—	20
12/14	14.2	0.5	3.8%	20
Annual Growth	46.1%	281.7%	—	15.0%

2018 Year-End Financials

Debt ratio: 48.1%
Return on equity: —
Cash ($ mil.): 4.1
Current ratio: 1.81
Long-term debt ($ mil.): 378.6
No. of shares (mil.): 25.3
Dividends
Yield: 12.7%
Payout: 33.9%
Market value ($ mil.): 292.0

	STOCK PRICE ($) FY Close	P/E High/Low		PER SHARE ($) Earnings	Dividends	Book Value
12/18	11.53	4	2	3.97	1.47	15.19
12/17	18.10	34	27	0.53	1.42	10.92
12/16	15.25	40	27	0.41	1.33	10.82
12/15	14.64	116	82	0.07	1.06	8.92
12/14	16.92	—	—	(0.34)	0.00	13.32
Annual Growth	(9.1%)	—	—	—	—	3.3%

Laredo Petroleum, Inc

Auditors: Grant Thornton LLP

LOCATIONS

HQ: Laredo Petroleum, Inc
15 W. Sixth Street, Suite 900, Tulsa, OK 74119
Phone: 918 513-4570
Web: www.laredopetro.com

HISTORICAL FINANCIALS

Company Type: Public

Income Statement — FYE: December 31

	REVENUE ($ mil.)	NET INCOME ($ mil.)	NET PROFIT MARGIN	EMPLOYEES
12/18	1,105.7	324.6	29.4%	360
12/17	822.1	548.9	66.8%	390
12/16	597.3	(260.7)	—	353
12/15	606.6	(2,209.9)	—	362
12/14	793.8	265.5	33.5%	491
Annual Growth	8.6%	5.1%	—	(7.5%)

2018 Year-End Financials

Debt ratio: 40.6%
Return on equity: 33.4%
Cash ($ mil.): 45.1
Current ratio: 0.96
Long-term debt ($ mil.): 983.6
No. of shares (mil.): 233.9
Dividends
Yield: —
Payout: —
Market value ($ mil.): 847.0

	STOCK PRICE ($) FY Close	P/E High/Low		PER SHARE ($) Earnings	Dividends	Book Value
12/18	3.62	8	2	1.39	0.00	5.02
12/17	10.61	7	4	2.29	0.00	3.16
12/16	14.14	—	—	(1.16)	0.00	0.75
12/15	7.99	—	—	(11.10)	0.00	0.61
12/14	10.35	16	4	1.85	0.00	10.88
Annual Growth	(23.1%) (17.6%)	—	—	(6.9%)	—	—

LCI Industries

LCI Industries (formerly Drew Industries) makes components for recreational vehicle (RVs) and other original equipment manufacturers. Through its primary operating subsidiary Lippert Components the company makes windows and doors chassis furniture and slide-out walls for travel trailers and fifth-wheel RVs (some 65% of sales). The company also serves adjacent markets including manufactured housing buses trailers boats and trains. LCI's aftermarket segment sells to RV and trailer dealers distributors and service centers. RV manufacturer Thor Industries accounts for more than 30% of sales. Through its Forest River and Clayton Homes subsidiaries Berkshire Hathaway accounts for nearly 25% of LCI's revenue.

Financial Performance

With the painful effects of the recession firmly behind it LCI has enjoyed unprecedented growth over the last five years. Revenues jumped 18% to peak at $1.4 billion in 2015. Profits also surged 19% to reach $74 million in 2015. (Both these totals represented historic milestones for the company.)

The historic growth for 2015 was driven by a 20% rise in RV sales thanks to an increase in industry-wide wholesale shipments of travel trailer and fifth-wheel RVs the company's primary RV market. Drew also experienced a bump in MH revenue as industry-wide wholesale shipments of manufactured homes increased as well as sales of components for new manufactured homes.

Mergers and Acquisitions

In 2019 through subsidiary Lippert Components LCI bought Rodan Enterprises maker of Sure-Shade retractable sun shade systems. LCI expects the addition of SureShade to compliment the company's line of sun shade product offerings to boat and RV OEMs as well as the recreational aftermarket.

EXECUTIVES

CEO, Jason D. Lippert, age 47, $856,800 total compensation
President and COO, Scott T. Mereness, age 47, $589,050 total compensation
CFO, Brian M. Hall, age 44, $225,727 total compensation
Vice President Chief Legal Officer Secretary, Andrew Namenye
Chairman, James F. Gero, age 75
Member Board Of Directors, Brendan Deely
Board Member, Kieran O'sullivan
Auditors: KPMG LLP

LOCATIONS

HQ: LCI Industries
3501 County Road 6 East, Elkhart, IN 46514
Phone: 574 535-1125
Web: www.lci1.com

PRODUCTS/OPERATIONS

2013 Sales

	$ mil.	% of total
Recreational vehicles	893.7	88
Manufactured housing	121.9	12
Total	**1,015.6**	**100**

Selected Products

Manufactured housing (MH) products
  Aluminum and vinyl patio doors
  Axles
  Entry doors
  Steel and fiberglass entry doors
  Steel chassis
  Steel chassis parts
  Replacement windows doors thermoformed bath products
  Thermoformed bath and kitchen products
  Vinyl and aluminum windows and screens
Recreational vehicle (RV) products (travel trailers and fifth-wheel RVs)
  Aluminum windows and screens
  Chassis components
  Entry and baggage doors
  Entry steps
  Furniture and mattresses
  Manual electric and hydraulic stabilizer and lifting systems
  Patio doors
  Slide-out mechanisms
  Specialty trailers for hauling boats personal watercraft snowmobiles and equipment
  Thermoformed bath kitchen and other products
  Towable axles and suspensions
  Towable steel chassis
  Toy hauler ramp doors

COMPETITORS

Atwood Mobile	Meritor
Coast Distribution	Patrick Industries
Elixir Industries	Quality Trailer
Euramax	Products
Featherlite	Tuthill
LaSalle Bristol	Wozniak Industries

HISTORICAL FINANCIALS
Company Type: Public

Income Statement — FYE: December 31

	REVENUE ($ mil.)	NET INCOME ($ mil.)	NET PROFIT MARGIN	EMPLOYEES
12/18	2,475.8	148.5	6.0%	10,260
12/17	2,147.7	132.8	6.2%	9,852
12/16	1,678.9	129.6	7.7%	7,654
12/15	1,403.0	74.3	5.3%	6,576
12/14	1,190.7	62.2	5.2%	5,845
Annual Growth	20.1%	24.3%	—	15.1%

2018 Year-End Financials
Debt ratio: 23.6%
Return on equity: 21.8%
Cash ($ mil.): 14.9
Current ratio: 2.97
Long-term debt ($ mil.): 293.5
No. of shares (mil.): 24.8
Dividends
  Yield: 3.5%
  Payout: 40.3%
Market value ($ mil.): 1,661.0

	STOCK PRICE ($) FY Close	P/E High/Low	PER SHARE ($) Earnings	Dividends	Book Value
12/18	66.80	22 10	5.83	2.35	28.41
12/17	130.00	25 17	5.24	2.05	26.12
12/16	107.75	21 10	5.20	1.40	22.23
12/15	60.89	21 16	3.02	2.00	18.01
12/14	51.07	21 16	2.56	0.00	16.56
Annual Growth	6.9%	— —	22.8%	—	14.4%

LeMaitre Vascular Inc

LeMaitre Vascular makes the veins run on time. The company makes both disposable and implanted surgical vascular devices including catheters and stents under such brands as AnastoClip EndoFit and Pruitt-Inahara. Originally founded by a vascular surgeon to develop a valvulotome to prepare veins for arterial bypass surgery the company has since expanded its offerings to include a device to create dialysis access sites and another to treat aortic aneurysms. Le Maitre sells 12 product lines most of which are used in open vascular surgery and some of which are used in endovascular procedures. Its products are sold to hospitals in North America Europe and Japan through a direct sales force.

Geographic Reach
LeMaitre manufactures most of its products in a single facility in Massachusetts.

In an effort to tap into the world's third-largest medical device market LaMaitre opened its first office in China in mid-2014.

Sales and Marketing
LeMaitre sells its products through a direct sales force but also relies on a few distributors in several countries. The company however is expanding its sales force to reach its customers more directly.

Strategy
LeMaitre has grown by competing in niche markets expanding its worldwide direct sales force and acquiring and developing complementary vascular devices. LeMaitre also intends to grow by pursuing regulatory approval of its products in new markets.

Along with acquisitions product enhancements and developments are at the heart of the firm's growth strategy. As new products are acquired or launched the company also cleans out its closet and discontinues or divests products it no longer considers complementary.

Mergers and Acquisitions
LeMaitre acquired the assets of Cardial a Becton Dickinson subsidiary for $2.3 million in 2018. Cardial makes knitted and woven vascular grafts valvulotomes and surgical glue. Earlier that year the company paid $14.2 million for the vascular clot business including a number of catheter products of Applied Medical Resources.

In 2016 LeMaitre acquired Restore Flow Allografts for $14 million plus potential performance payments. Restore Flow processes and cryopreserves vascular veins and arteries which LeMaitre will use as it expands its range of biologic products. Other recent acquisitions for the company include OmniFlow II and ProCol.

Company Background
LeMaitre was founded in 1983 by vascular surgeon George D. LeMaitre to develop a valvulotome to prepare veins for arterial bypass surgery.

In 2006 LeMaitre Vascular raised more than $30 million from its initial public offering. The company spent part of the proceeds to pay off debt; it also used proceeds toward its goals of increasing research and development efforts hiring new sales representatives and acquiring complementary products or businesses.

EXECUTIVES
Chairman and CEO, George W. LeMaitre, age 54, $315,580 total compensation
President, David B. (Dave) Roberts, age 55, $333,174 total compensation
President International Operations, Peter R. Gebauer, age 65, $295,149 total compensation
SVP Operations, Trent G. Kamke, age 48, $162,500 total compensation
CFO, Joseph P. Pellegrino, age 54, $247,236 total compensation
VP Central Europe and Sales, Maik D. Helmers, age 45
VP Information Technology, Jonathan W. Ngau, age 45
Country Manager Japan, Nobuhiro Okabe, age 66
VP Research and Development, Ryan H. Connelly, age 41
SVP Clinical Regulatory & Quality Affairs, Andrew Hodgkinson, age 43
Country Manager Italy, Giovannella Deiure
General Counsel, Laurie A. Churchill
Vice President Marketing, Kim Cieslak
Board Member, John Roush
Auditors: Grant Thornton LLP

LOCATIONS
HQ: LeMaitre Vascular Inc
  63 Second Avenue, Burlington, MA 01803
Phone: 781 221-2266
Web: www.lemaitre.com

PRODUCTS/OPERATIONS

Selected Products
Vascular
  Balloon catheters (for removing blood clots; occlusion and facilitation of blood flow)
  Carotid shunts (facilitation of blood flow to brain during carotid plaque removal)
  Remote endarterectomy devices (for removing blockages in major arteries in the leg)
  Valvulotomes (destroys vein valves to create vein bypass grafts)
  Vascular grafts (synthetic vessels used in bypass and replacement procedures)
  Vascular patches (synthetic and biological patches used in closing incisions in a blood vessel)
  Vein strippers (single-incision removal of varicose veins)
  Vessel closure systems (attachment of blood vessels mainly for dialysis access)
Endovascular
  Aortic stent grafts (endovascular repair of abdominal and thoracic aortic aneurysms and thoracic dissections; in clinical studies)
  Manual contrast injectors (contrast media injection into blood vessels)
  Modeling catheters (for improved sealing of aortic stent grafts; application submitted)
  Radiopaque tape (for improved precision of vascular and endovascular procedures)
General surgery
  Laparoscopic cholecystectomy devices (for introducing dye into the cystic duct and related uses)

COMPETITORS

Bard	Getinge
Cardiovascular Systems	Medtronic
Cook Group	Terumo
Edwards Lifesciences	W.L. Gore

HISTORICAL FINANCIALS
Company Type: Public

Income Statement — FYE: December 31

	REVENUE ($ mil.)	NET INCOME ($ mil.)	NET PROFIT MARGIN	EMPLOYEES
12/18	105.5	22.9	21.7%	483
12/17	100.8	17.1	17.0%	423
12/16	89.1	10.5	11.9%	397
12/15	78.3	7.7	9.9%	356
12/14	71.1	3.9	5.5%	341
Annual Growth	10.4%	55.6%	—	9.1%

2018 Year-End Financials
Debt ratio: —
Return on equity: 19.1%
Cash ($ mil.): 26.3
Current ratio: 4.76
Long-term debt ($ mil.): —
No. of shares (mil.): 19.6
Dividends
  Yield: 1.1%
  Payout: 26.9%
Market value ($ mil.): 464.0

	STOCK PRICE ($) FY Close	P/E High/Low	PER SHARE ($) Earnings	Dividends	Book Value
12/18	23.64	35 19	1.13	0.28	6.64
12/17	31.84	43 24	0.86	0.22	5.70
12/16	25.34	45 22	0.55	0.18	4.71
12/15	17.25	40 17	0.42	0.16	4.25
12/14	7.65	35 28	0.23	0.14	3.93
Annual Growth	32.6%	— —	48.9%	18.9%	14.0%

LendingTree Inc (New)

LendingTree (formerly Tree.com) helps consumers cut through a forest of options in financing education insurance home services and more. The company allows users to comparison shop for home loans through its most prominent branch LendingTree which helps match home buyers with lenders. Its lending network includes over 350 banks and other lenders. Other subsidiaries help consumers choose between colleges and home service providers. LendingTree also markets auto loans and credit cards. Services are free to consumers as the firm collects fees from the companies to which it refers business.

Operations
LendingTree operates four main business segments: Lending for consumers seeking home mortgage loans lines of credit reverse mortgages and personal loans; Auto which includes its auto refinance and purchase loan products; Education which includes a student enrollment product and student loan products; and Home Services which helps consumers research and find home improvement professional services through its marketplace of local and national contractors.

Overall 80% of the company's total revenue in 2014 came from mortgage products while non-mortgage lending products (such as personal loans home equity reverse mortgages and credit cards) made up another 12%.

Sales and Marketing
The online company has been ramping up its advertising in recent years. It spent $102.2 million on advertising in 2014 up from $80.7 million and $40.8 million in 2013 and 2012 respectively.

Financial Performance
LendingTree's revenues have more than tripled since 2011 thanks to a strengthened housing market which has driven more demand for its mortgage loan marketplace services. Its profits have also trended higher with business growth. (Note: The company's profit spiked in 2012 thanks to significant gains from the $56 million sale of its LendingTree Loans business to Discover.)

The firm's revenue jumped 20% to $167.4 million in 2014 mostly thanks to strong growth in its nonmortgage lending products stemming from its 2013 introduction of its reverse mortgage credit card and personal loan products. Mortgage lending product revenue also rose by 9% on notable increases in its purchase product supported by growth of its rate table offering launched in early 2013. The number of consumers matched on its lending marketplace spiked by 64% during the year though its average revenue earned from marketplace lenders per matched customer fell by 26% as more users went for lower-margin non-mortgage lending products.

Higher revenue in 2014 allowed the company's net income to more than double to $9.4 million. LendingTree's operating cash levels fell by 11% to $9.1 million due to unfavorable changes in working capital related mostly to its accounts payable accrued expenses and other current liabilities balances.

Strategy
LendingTree regularly introduces new products across new markets to keep consumers interested. In mid-2015 expanding beyond its mortgage-related wheelhouse LendingTree launched its new personal loan rates product which allowed consumers to shop among multiple lenders for personal loans. In 2014 the company introduced its new Small Business Loan marketplace (which included peer-to-peer lenders) and an online marketplace for car shoppers (via autos.lendingtree.com) to shop more than 2.5 million new and used cars and find auto financing through its marketplace services.

The company also releases new tools to keep visitors coming back to its website. In 2014 the company relaunched its My LendingTree platform that offered personalized loan comparison shopping free credit scores credit score analysis and an in-depth review of a consumer's credit profile.

Mergers and Acquisitions
LendingTree agreed in 2018 to acquire Value Holding the parent company of personal finance website ValuePenguin.com for $105 million in cash. The site provides financial analysis to consumers for products including insurance and credit cards. LendingTree believes the purchase will drive acquisition of insurance customers. The deal is expected to close in the first quarter of 2019.

In 2017 LendingTree acquired financial advice website MoneyTree.com for around $30 million.

Company Background
The company's roots formed with LendingTree which was founded by CEO Doug Lebda in 1996 and acquired by IAC/InterActiveCorp (IAC) in 2003. Five years later IAC spun off LendingTree and three other subsidiaries: ILG Ticketmaster and HSN. As part of the spinoff Tree.com was formed to operate LendingTree along with its other lending and real estate businesses as a separate publicly traded company.

EXECUTIVES

Chairman and CEO, Douglas R. (Doug) Lebda, age 49, $600,000 total compensation
President, Neil Salvage, age 46, $391,538 total compensation
Chief Product and Strategy Officer, Nikul Patel, age 46, $318,615 total compensation
SVP Chief Accounting Officer and Treasurer, Carla Shumate, $236,538 total compensation
Chief Sales Officer and Head of Mortgage, Sam Mischner
CFO, J.D. Moriarty, age 47
Auditors: PricewaterhouseCoopers LLP

LOCATIONS

HQ: LendingTree Inc (New)
11115 Rushmore Drive, Charlotte, NC 28277
Phone: 704 541-5351
Web: www.lendingtree.com

PRODUCTS/OPERATIONS

2014 Sales

	$ mil.	% of total
Lending		
Mortgage Products	134.2	80
Non-mortgage Products	20.4	12
Others	12.8	8
Total	**167.4**	**100**

Selected Brands
DegreeTree.com
DoneRight.com
GetSmart.com
HealthTree.com
InsuranceTree.com
LendingTreeAutos.com
LendingTree.com
ServiceTree.com

COMPETITORS

Bankrate
Internet Brands
XO Group
ditech

HISTORICAL FINANCIALS
Company Type: Public

Income Statement — FYE: December 31

	REVENUE ($ mil.)	NET INCOME ($ mil.)	NET PROFIT MARGIN	EMPLOYEES
12/18	764.8	96.5	12.6%	909
12/17	617.7	15.5	2.5%	535
12/16	384.4	27.4	7.2%	399
12/15	254.2	48.0	18.9%	312
12/14	167.3	9.3	5.6%	218
Annual Growth	46.2%	79.2%	—	42.9%

2018 Year-End Financials
Debt ratio: 41.9%
Return on equity: 30.1%
Cash ($ mil.): 105.1
Current ratio: 0.89
Long-term debt ($ mil.): 250.9
No. of shares (mil.): 12.8
Dividends
 Yield: —
 Payout: —
Market value ($ mil.): 2,813.0

	STOCK PRICE ($) FY Close	P/E High/Low		PER SHARE ($) Earnings	Dividends	Book Value
12/18	219.57	52	24	6.85	0.00	27.03
12/17	340.45	271	76	1.14	0.00	24.57
12/16	101.35	48	24	2.15	0.00	19.63
12/15	89.28	33	10	3.83	0.00	19.46
12/14	48.34	57	28	0.84	0.00	8.46
Annual Growth	46.0%	—	—	69.0%	—	33.7%

Level One Bancorp Inc

Auditors: Crowe LLP

LOCATIONS

HQ: Level One Bancorp Inc
32991 Hamilton Court, Farmington Hills, MI 48334
Phone: 248 737-0300
Web: www.levelonebank.com

HISTORICAL FINANCIALS
Company Type: Public

Income Statement — FYE: December 31

	ASSETS ($ mil.)	NET INCOME ($ mil.)	INCOME AS % OF ASSETS	EMPLOYEES
12/18	1,416.2	14.3	1.0%	251
12/17	1,301.2	9.8	0.8%	235
12/16	1,127.5	11.0	1.0%	0
12/15	0.0	12.5	***************%	0
Annual Growth	—	4.7%		

2018 Year-End Financials
Return on assets: 1.0%
Return on equity: 11.0%
Long-term debt ($ mil.): —
No. of shares (mil.): 7.7
Sales ($ mil): 70.8
Dividends
 Yield: 0.4%
 Payout: 5.8%
Market value ($ mil.): 174.0

	STOCK PRICE ($) FY Close	P/E High/Low		PER SHARE ($) Earnings	Dividends	Book Value
12/18	22.43	15	11	1.91	0.09	19.58
12/17	0.00	—	—	1.49	0.00	16.78
Annual Growth	—	—	—	28.2%	—	16.7%

LGI Homes, Inc.

LGI Homes wants everyone to stop wasting money on rent. Targeting first-time homebuyers the residential builder develops homes that appeal to renters looking to buy an affordable home in Texas Florida the Southwest the Southeast or the Northwest. During 2015 its homes were priced between $110000 and $475000 and ranged from 1100 to 4000 sq. ft. with each home selling for an average price of $185100. The builder's higher-quality Terrata Homes started at $350000 for a 2500 sq. ft. home. LGI Homes has sold more than 12000 homes since its founding in 2003. It went public in 2013.

Operations
The builder operates five segments organized by region: Texas Florida the Southwest (Arizona Colorado New Mexico) the Southeast (Florida Georgia North Carolina South Carolina) the Northwest (Washington).

Geographic Reach
The Woodlands Texas-based LGI Homes builds in 20 states with its largest state market being in Texas (particularly around the major cities) where it made 56% of its total sales during 2015. Its next largest market was Florida (especially in Tampa and Orlando) which accounted for 12% of sales. The rest of its sales came from states in the Southwest (17% of sales) Southeast (15%) and the Northwest (less than 1%).

Sales and Marketing
The homebuilder targets mostly home and apartment renters and markets products through print and digital advertising including direct mail newspaper ads social media and interactive online media as well as via directional signage and billboards.

It's been ramping up its advertising and direct mail spend in recent years to support sales growth. The builder spent $9.3 million on advertising and direct mail during 2015 up from $8.6 million and $3.3 million in 2014 and 2013 respectively.

Financial Performance
LGI's annual sales and profits have swelled more than ten-fold since 2011 as it's expanded into more states and as the housing market has heated up with higher home prices and more demand.

The homebuilder's sales spiked 64% to a record $630.24 million during 2015 mostly thanks to a 45% rise in home closings (which totaled 3404 home deliveries for the year) but also because its average home sale prices increased by 13.8% to $185146 per home thanks to product mix changes higher price points in new markets and a more favorable environment for growing home prices. Its Oakmont acquisition which led to 269 more home closing during the year also helped boost total sales.

Strong revenue growth in 2015 drove LGI Homes' net income up 87% to a record $53 million. While the homebuilder's operations used $89 million in cash for the year toward building its land inventory to support future home sales it spent about half as much cash as in 2014 as it eased up on inventory purchases.

Strategy
LGI Homes continued in 2016 to focus on acquiring land lots and building in its core markets which include Houston San Antonio Dallas/Fort Worth Austin Phoenix Tucson Tampa Orlando Atlanta Albuquerque Charlotte and Denver. The homebuilder hopes record-high rental rates especially in these markets will entice more potential first-time homebuyers to look at its homes.

Mergers and Acquisitions
In October 2014 LGI entered the Charlotte North Carolina market after acquiring Oakmont Home Builders as well as its 150 homes under construction and 1000 owned and controlled lots for a total price of $17.3 million.

Company Background
LGI Homes went public in 2013 raising $99 million which it used to buy back stock from investment firm GTIS Partners as well as to buy land develop lots and build more homes.

EXECUTIVES
Chairman and CEO, Eric Lipar, age 49
President and COO, Michael Snider, age 48
CFO, Charles Merdian, age 50
EVP Acquisitions, Jack Lipar, age 51
EVP and Chief Marketing Officer, Rachel Eaton, age 38
Auditors: Ernst & Young LLP

LOCATIONS
HQ: LGI Homes, Inc.
1450 Lake Robbins Drive, Suite 430, The Woodlands, TX 77380
Phone: 281 362-8998
Web: www.lgihomes.com

COMPETITORS
AV Homes	M.D.C.
Beazer Homes	M/I Homes
CalAtlantic	Meritage Homes
D.R. Horton	NVR
Drees Homes	PulteGroup
KB Home	Taylor Morrison
Lennar	Toll Brothers

HISTORICAL FINANCIALS
Company Type: Public

Income Statement — FYE: December 31

	REVENUE ($ mil.)	NET INCOME ($ mil.)	NET PROFIT MARGIN	EMPLOYEES
12/18	1,504.4	155.2	10.3%	857
12/17	1,257.9	113.3	9.0%	726
12/16	838.3	75.0	9.0%	591
12/15	630.2	52.8	8.4%	489
12/14	383.2	28.2	7.4%	390
Annual Growth	40.8%	53.2%	—	21.8%

2018 Year-End Financials
Debt ratio: 46.8%
Return on equity: 27.1%
Cash ($ mil.): 46.6
Current ratio: 15.89
Long-term debt ($ mil.): 653.7
No. of shares (mil.): 22.7
Dividends
 Yield: —
 Payout: —
Market value ($ mil.): 1,027.0

	STOCK PRICE ($) FY Close	P/E High	P/E Low	PER SHARE ($) Earnings	PER SHARE ($) Dividends	PER SHARE ($) Book Value
12/18	45.22	11	5	6.24	0.00	28.89
12/17	75.03	15	5	4.73	0.00	22.42
12/16	28.73	11	5	3.41	0.00	16.67
12/15	24.33	13	5	2.44	0.00	12.20
12/14	14.92	15	10	1.33	0.00	9.19
Annual Growth	31.9%			47.2%	—	33.1%

LHC Group Inc

LHC Group administers post-acute health care services through more than 760 home nursing agencies hospices and long-term acute care hospitals (LTACH). The company operates in rural areas in about three dozen US states. LHC's home health nursing agencies provide care to Medicare beneficiaries offering such services as private duty nursing physical therapy and medically-oriented social services. Its hospices provide palliative care for terminal patients while its LTACHs serve patients who no longer need intensive care but still require complex care in a hospital setting. In 2018 LHC Group acquired Almost Family a provider of home health care services; the combined entity became the #2 home health provider in the US.

Financial Performance
Bolstered by acquisitions and joint ventures LHC Group has seen strong growth over the past five years with revenue and net income both up well over 100% since 2014. The acquisitions have also resulted in growth of long-term debt however which has grown nearly 300% since 2014 to $236 million.

In 2018 the company reported revenue of $1.8 billion up 70% from the prior year primarily because of its purchase of competitor Almost Family. LHC ended the year with some 220 more facilities that it had at the end of 2017.

Net income was also up that year jumping 27% to $63.6 million on the increase in revenue.

Cash at the end of 2018 was $49.4 million an increase of $46.5 million from the prior year. Cash from operations contributed $108.6 million to the coffers while investing activities used $25.3 million mainly for capital expenditures. Financing activities used another $36.8 million for payments on line of credit and noncontrolling interest distributions.

Strategy
Home health care long-term care and nursing services are expected to see a surge in demand with the aging US population. LHC Group's strategy to benefit from that demand is to drive internal growth in its existing markets and expand into new markets often aided by acquisitions and joint ventures. The company doubled its size in 2018 with the acquisition of competitor Almost Family. It continues to add facilities to its portfolio with 2019 acquisitions and joint ventures in Alabama Maryland Missouri New Jersey and Ohio among other states.

EXECUTIVES
Vice President of Operations, Morris Sanford
Chairman and CEO, Keith G. Myers, age 60, $542,303 total compensation
President and COO, Donald D. (Don) Stelly, age 51, $395,816 total compensation
EVP and Chief Administrative Officer, Marcus D. Macip
SVP and CIO, Rajesh (Raj) Shetye
EVP CFO and Treasurer, Joshua L. Proffitt
Director Of Nursing, Toya Brown
Director of HIM, Suzonne Borque
Senior Vice President Investor Relations, Eric Elliott
Senior Vice President, Carla Hengst
Medical Director, Robert Ewing
Director Of Nursing, Marsha Smith
Director Of Medical Records, Ann Faile

Director Of Nursing, Barbara Jones
CAE Vice President Governmental Affairs, Sarah Myers
Division Vice President Of Sales, Rob Little
Division Vice President Of Market Development, Shelley Mckee
Interim Vice President Revenue Strategy, Gwen Guillotte
Director Of Nursing, Trina Brockett
Executive Vice President Chief Strategy and Innovation Officer, Bruce Greenstein
Director Of Health Information Management, Debra Hebert-myrick
Vice President Business Development, Gary Thietten
Board Director, Monica Azare
Auditors: KPMG LLP

LOCATIONS

HQ: LHC Group Inc
901 Hugh Wallis Road South, Lafayette, LA 70508
Phone: 337 233-1307   Fax: 337 235-8037
Web: www.lhcgroup.com

PRODUCTS/OPERATIONS

2018 Sales

	$ mil.	% of total
Home health	1,291.5	71
Hospice	199.1	11
Home and community-based	172.5	10
Facility-based	113.8	6
Healthcare innovations	33.1	2
Total	1,810.0	100

COMPETITORS

Amedisys
American HomePatient
Apria Healthcare
Consulate Health Care
Critical Homecare Solutions
Ensign Group
Gentiva
Girling Health Care
Guardian Home Care Holdings
Health First
Home Instead
Kindred Healthcare
NHC
National Home Health
Personal-Touch Home Care
RehabCare
VITAS Healthcare

HISTORICAL FINANCIALS

Company Type: Public

Income Statement — FYE: December 31

	REVENUE ($ mil.)	NET INCOME ($ mil.)	NET PROFIT MARGIN	EMPLOYEES
12/18	1,809.9	63.5	3.5%	30,985
12/17	1,072.0	50.1	4.7%	14,554
12/16	914.8	36.5	4.0%	11,598
12/15	816.3	32.3	4.0%	10,922
12/14	733.6	21.8	3.0%	10,767
Annual Growth	25.3%	30.6%	—	30.2%

2018 Year-End Financials

Debt ratio: 12.6%
Return on equity: 7.2%
Cash ($ mil.): 49.3
Current ratio: 1.78
Long-term debt ($ mil.): 235.9
No. of shares (mil.): 30.6
Dividends
  Yield: —
  Payout: —
Market value ($ mil.): 2,880.0

	STOCK PRICE ($) FY Close	P/E High/Low		PER SHARE ($) Earnings	Dividends	Book Value
12/18	93.88	45	26	2.29	0.00	42.93
12/17	61.25	25	16	2.79	0.00	25.29
12/16	45.70	22	16	2.07	0.00	22.45
12/15	45.29	27	16	1.84	0.00	20.32
12/14	31.18	25	16	1.26	0.00	18.44
Annual Growth	31.7%	—	—	16.1%	—	23.5%

Liberty Oilfield Services Inc

Auditors: DELOITTE & TOUCHE LLP

LOCATIONS

HQ: Liberty Oilfield Services Inc
950 17th Street, Suite 2400, Denver, CO 80202
Phone: 303 515-2800

HISTORICAL FINANCIALS

Company Type: Public

Income Statement — FYE: December 31

	REVENUE ($ mil.)	NET INCOME ($ mil.)	NET PROFIT MARGIN	EMPLOYEES
12/18	2,155.1	126.3	5.9%	2,437
12/17	1,489.8	168.5	11.3%	2,032
12/16	374.7	(60.5)	—	1,859
12/15	455.4	(9.0)	—	0
Annual Growth	67.9%	—	—	—

2018 Year-End Financials

Debt ratio: 9.5%
Return on equity: 29.1%
Cash ($ mil.): 103.3
Current ratio: 2.10
Long-term debt ($ mil.): 106.1
No. of shares (mil.): 113.5
Dividends
  Yield: 0.7%
  Payout: 5.5%
Market value ($ mil.): 1,471.0

	STOCK PRICE ($) FY Close	P/E High/Low		PER SHARE ($) Earnings	Dividends	Book Value
12/18	12.95	13	7	1.81	0.10	3.81
12/17	0.00	—	—	(0.00)	0.00	3.68
Annual Growth	—	—	—	—	—	3.5%

Life Storage Inc

A self-administered real estate investment trust (REIT) Life Storage operates some 700 facilities with more than 50 million sq. ft. of storage space. Its properties usually offer features such as humidity-controlled spaces; outdoor storage for cars boats and RVs; and the use of a free truck to help clients haul their stuff. Serving both individual and business customers the company owns properties in about 30 states. In mid-2016 it effected its corporate name change and began transitioning the name of its facilities from Uncle Bob's Self Storage to Life Storage.

Geographic Reach
Life Storage based in Buffalo New York owns about 700 self-storage properties in some 30 states. Its largest markets are Texas (22% of properties and revenue) and Florida (13% of properties and revenue).

Sales and Marketing
Life Storage uses internet marketing and its fleet of trucks to create brand awareness.

Financial Performance
Life Storage has reported steadily increasing revenue over the past five years. In 2017 sales rose 13% to about $530 million in 2016 on higher rents and more units rented. Same-store sales (430 core properties) were up about 1.6% for the year.

Net income increased about $11 million to $96 million in 2017 from 2016 boosted by higher revenue.

Cash and cash equivalents fell to about $9 million in 2017 from about $24 million in 2016.

Strategy
Life Storage pursues growth by purchasing self-storage facilities in a largely fragmented industry dominated by independent operators. The REIT concentrates its acquisition efforts in metropolitan areas of the South and Southeast; occasionally it acquires multiple facilities in new markets.

In 2017 the company integrated with LifeStorage an operator of 84 self-storage facilities acquired in 2016 for $1.3 billion. The combined company changed its name to Life Storage and has run branding campaigns centered around the name. The transaction slotted the company into Sacramento California and Las Vegas.

Life Storage introduced a way to book a storage space completely online in 2018. The Rent Now platform allows renters to book space select the specific space and gain access to it. The platform was to roll out to Life Storage's markets in 2018 and 2019.

EXECUTIVES

Vp Revenue Management, David Paolini
CEO, David L. Rogers, age 63, $484,000 total compensation
President and Director, Kenneth F. Myszka, age 70, $484,000 total compensation
CFO, Andrew J. Gregoire, $250,000 total compensation
EVP Sales and Operations, Edward F. Killeen, $250,000 total compensation
Regional VP, Jeffrey Myszka
Chief Investment Officer, Paul T. Powell, $250,000 total compensation
Regional VP, Randy Hillman
Regional VP, Christopher Runckel
Regional VP, Jim Kwitchoff
Director Information Technologies, Jeffrey O'Donnell
Regional VP, Philip Wilfong
Vice President Marketing, Chris Laczi
Regional Vp, Don Herzog
Vice President Store Operations, Jeff Myszka
Chairman, Robert J. Attea, age 77
Auditors: Ernst & Young LLP

LOCATIONS

HQ: Life Storage Inc
6467 Main Street, Williamsville, NY 14221
Phone: 716 633-1850   Fax: 716 633-1860
Web: www.unclebobs.com

PRODUCTS/OPERATIONS

2017 Sales

	$ mil.	% of total
Rental income	485.3	92
Other	44.4	8
Total	**529.7**	**100**

Selected Services
Storage
Truck Rental
Moving Boxes
Vehicle Storage
Commercial Storage

COMPETITORS

AMERCO	PODS Enterprises
CubeSmart	Public Storage
Extra Space	Smart Move
Mobile Mini	

HISTORICAL FINANCIALS
Company Type: Public

Income Statement				FYE: December 31
	REVENUE ($ mil.)	NET INCOME ($ mil.)	NET PROFIT MARGIN	EMPLOYEES
12/18	550.8	206.5	37.5%	1,953
12/17	529.7	96.3	18.2%	1,792
12/16	462.6	85.2	18.4%	1,537
12/15	366.6	112.5	30.7%	1,429
12/14	326.0	88.5	27.2%	1,378
Annual Growth	14.0%	23.6%	—	9.1%

2018 Year-End Financials

Debt ratio: 44.0% No. of shares (mil.): 46.6
Return on equity: 10.1% Dividends
Cash ($ mil.): 13.5 Yield: 4.3%
Current ratio: 0.31 Payout: 90.2%
Long-term debt ($ mil.): 1,714.1 Market value ($ mil.): 4,335.0

	STOCK PRICE ($) FY Close	P/E High/Low		PER SHARE ($) Earnings	Dividends	Book Value
12/18	92.99	23	17	4.43	4.00	44.14
12/17	89.07	44	34	2.07	3.95	43.57
12/16	85.26	60	40	1.96	3.70	44.96
12/15	107.31	35	27	3.16	3.20	32.75
12/14	87.22	33	24	2.67	2.72	28.61
Annual Growth	1.6%	—	—	13.5%	10.1%	11.4%

Ligand Pharmaceuticals Inc

Biopharmaceutical firm Ligand Pharmaceuticals seeks to discover disease-curing molecules. The drug development company works with gene transcription technology to address assorted illnesses. Its research and development projects include treatments for thrombocytopenia (low blood platelet count) osteoporosis cardiovascular disease cancer and diabetes. Ligand conducts many of its programs through partnerships with other drug makers including CyDex Pharmaceuticals Pfizer and Lilly. The company is focused on expanding its development pipeline through additional partnerships and technology licensing agreements as well as via acquisitions.

Operations

Ligand makes its money in three ways: from royalties from commercialized products (around two-thirds of revenue) from license and milestone payments (some 20% of revenue) and the development and commercialization of drugs using Captisol technology by CyDex Pharmaceuticals (around 15% of revenue).

Captisol is a formulation technology that has led to a number of FDA-approved products including Amgen's Spectrium. It is also being developed through clinical-stage partner programs.

The company's pipeline products include a receptor antagonist a selective androgen receptor modulator and Captisol-enabled Clopidogrel.

Strategy

Ligand's growth strategy is focused around increasing licensing milestone and royalty fees from its partners. The company has a vast portfolio of current and development-stage programs most of which are being developed through partnerships with other drug makers.

The company relies heavily on revenues from the sales of Promacta and Kyprolis for which it receives royalties from Novartis and Amgen respectively. Any slowdown in sales of those products — from causes such as the introduction of generics manufacturing issues or lower demand — would significantly impact Ligand's financial performance.

Mergers and Acquisitions

In 2018 Ligand acquired UK-based biotech firm Vernalis for some $42.3 million. The purchase brought the company programs in respiratory oncology and central nervous system therapies.

In 2017 the company purchased Crystal Bioscience along with its OmniChicken antibody discovery platform for $25 million. That deal boosted Ligand's work in developing antibodies for challenging targets.

EXECUTIVES

President and CEO, John L. Higgins, $500,331 total compensation
Vice President; General Counsel; Secretary, Charles S. Berkman, age 50, $283,351 total compensation
VP Biology, Keith Marschke
VP Chemistry and Pharmaceutical Sciences, Lin Zhi
EVP and COO, Matthew W. Foehr, $368,101 total compensation
CFO and Vice President Finance and Strategy, Nishan Silva
Chairman, John W. Kozarich
Auditors: Ernst & Young LLP

LOCATIONS

HQ: Ligand Pharmaceuticals Inc
3911 Sorrento Valley Boulevard, Suite 110, San Diego, CA 92121
Phone: 858 550-7500
Web: www.ligand.com

PRODUCTS/OPERATIONS

2017 Sales

	$ mil.	% of total
Royalties	88.7	63
Material sales (Captisol)	22.1	16
License fees milestones & other	30.3	21
Total	**141.1**	**100**

COMPETITORS

Adherex Technologies	GTx
Amgen	Merck
AstraZeneca	NPS Pharmaceuticals
Bayer HealthCare Pharmaceuticals	Protalex
	Roche Holding
Biogen	Sanofi
Chugai	Sunovion
Cytokinetics	Valeant
Eli Lilly	Vertex Pharmaceuticals
Evotec	Xencor

HISTORICAL FINANCIALS
Company Type: Public

Income Statement				FYE: December 31
	REVENUE ($ mil.)	NET INCOME ($ mil.)	NET PROFIT MARGIN	EMPLOYEES
12/18	251.4	143.3	57.0%	116
12/17	141.1	12.5	8.9%	39
12/16	108.9	(1.6)	—	22
12/15	71.9	257.3	357.8%	21
12/14	64.5	12.0	18.6%	19
Annual Growth	40.5%	85.8%	—	57.2%

2018 Year-End Financials

Debt ratio: 50.4% No. of shares (mil.): 20.7
Return on equity: 29.2% Dividends
Cash ($ mil.): 117.1 Yield: —
Current ratio: 10.58 Payout: —
Long-term debt ($ mil.): 609.8 Market value ($ mil.): 2,818.0

	STOCK PRICE ($) FY Close	P/E High/Low		PER SHARE ($) Earnings	Dividends	Book Value
12/18	135.70	41	19	5.96	0.00	27.01
12/17	136.93	245	167	0.53	0.00	19.80
12/16	101.61	—	—	(0.08)	0.00	17.74
12/15	108.42	9	4	12.12	0.00	15.26
12/14	53.21	135	72	0.56	0.00	1.34
Annual Growth	26.4%	—	—	80.6%	—	111.7%

Littelfuse Inc

Littelfuse is big on circuit protection. The company is one of the world's largest fuse makers. In addition to its fuses Littelfuse's other circuit protection devices include positive temperature coefficient devices that limit current when too much is being supplied and electrostatic discharge suppressors that redirect transient high voltage. The company's thyristors protect telecommunications circuits from transient voltage caused by lightning strikes. It also supplies fuses for HVAC systems elevators and machine tools. Littelfuse's 5800 customers include electronics manufacturers (Hewlett-Packard and Samsung) automakers (Ford and GM) and the automotive aftermarket (O'Reilly Automotive and Pep Boys).

Operations

The company operates through three business unit segments. Electronics includes circuit protection products for wireless telephones consumer electronics computers modems and telecommunications equipment and markets the products under brand names PICO and NANO. Considering the average car contains 30 to 100 fuses the automotive segment stays busy making fuses for gas and electric automobiles trucks and buses and to protect electrical power to operate lights heating air conditioning radios windows and other controls.

Some automotive brand names include ATO MasterFuse JCASE and CablePro. In addition to fuses electrical makes ground-fault and protection relays to safeguard personnel and equipment from electrical shock hazards in industrial environments and underground mining or water treatment applications. Brand names include POWR-GARD.

Geographic Reach
The company operates in three geographic territories — the Americas Europe and Asia/Pacific — and has 30 manufacturing and distribution facilities in about 15 countries. The company gets about 40% of its sales outside the US. China is another large market representing 22% of sales.

Sales and Marketing
Littlefuse markets its products indirectly through a worldwide organization of 60 manufacturers' representatives and distributes through a network of electronics automotive and electrical distributors. Its domestic sales and marketing staff of over 100 people maintains relationships with major OEMs and distributors.

Financial Performance
Littelfuse enjoyed unprecedented growth in 2015 as sales peaked at a record-setting $868 million. Profits however decreased by 17% due to additional pension settlement charges and expenses related with acquisitions. Littelfuse's operating cash flow has trended upward over the last four years and surged by 8% in 2015.

The historic growth for 2015 was fueled by an uptick in automotive sales and strong growth for automotive sensor products as a result of continued strength in the heavy truck market. This growth was offset by a general market slowdown within the construction agriculture and global mining industries.

Strategy
Littlefuse operates in a highly competitive industry matching up against much larger manufacturers by focusing on brand name price quality and service. The automotive industry witnessed a rash of bankruptcies before and during the recession and the electronics industry reeled from the economic downturn as well. The company's dependence on customers in the automotive communications and consumer electronics industries leaves Littelfuse vulnerable to cyclicality in those industries.

One important element of Littelfuse's strategy is product development which has resulted in about 200 patents in North America some 85 in the European Union and more than 60 in other foreign countries. After consulting with customers sales and marketing staff often suggest new products which then undergo a development process that can last from a few months to up to 18 months.

Mergers and Acquisitions
In 2017 Littelfuse acquired IXYS a maker of power semiconductors and integrated circuits for about $750 million in cash and stock. IXYS focuses on medium to high voltage power control chips for industrial communications consumer and medical markets. Littelfuse was to use IXYS technologies to expand in the industrial and automotive markets. The deal was Littelfuse's biggest.

In 2015 the company acquired TE Connectivity's circuit protection business (CPD) which has expertise in polymer-based resettable circuit protection devices. The business was acquired for $350 million and has operations in Menlo Park California and manufacturing facilities in Tsukuba Japan; and Shanghai and Kunshan China. The acquisition expanded the company's capabilities in the battery and automotive market and increased its presence in Japan.

Company Background
Littelfuse was formed in 1927 to make the first small fast-acting fuse able to protect test meters. In 1968 military electronics firm Tracor (later part of the UK's General Electric Company now telent) bought the company. Littelfuse entered the power (industrial) fuse market in 1983. Tracor ran into financial troubles with the end of the Cold War and filed for bankruptcy protection in 1991. As a result of Tracor's reorganization Littelfuse became an independent company in 1992.

EXECUTIVES

VP; General Manager Custom Products, Dal Ferbert, age 65, $232,662 total compensation
President CEO and Director, David W. Heinzmann, age 55, $477,532 total compensation
EVP and Chief Legal and Human Resources Officer, Ryan K. Stafford, age 52, $387,320 total compensation
SVP; General Manager Automotive, Dieter Roeder, age 62
SVP; General Manager Industrial, Matthew J. Cole
SVP; General Manager Electronics, Deepak Nayar
SVP and CTO; General Manager Semiconductor Products, Ian Highley
SVP Global Operations, Michael P. Rutz, $353,273 total compensation
EVP and CFO, Meenal A. Sethna, age 49
Chairman, Gordon B. Hunter, age 68
Board Member, Cary Fu
Board Member, Ronald L Schubel
Board Member, William P Noglows
Board Member, Anthony Grillo
Board Member, John Major
Auditors: Grant Thornton LLP

LOCATIONS

HQ: Littelfuse Inc
   8755 West Higgins Road, Suite 500, Chicago, IL 60631
Phone: 773 628-1000
Web: www.littelfuse.com

PRODUCTS/OPERATIONS

2015 Sales

	$ mil.	% of total
Electronics	405.5	47
Automotive	340.0	39
Electrical	122.4	14
Total	**867.9**	**100**

Selected Brands
ATO
JCASE Fuse
MAXI
MEGA
MIDI
MINI
NANO2
OMNI-BLOK
PICO II
POWR-GARD
PulseGuard

Selected Products
Automotive Sensors
Battery Management
Custom-Engineered Electrical Equipment
DC Power Distribution Modules
DC Solenoids and Relays
Fuse Blocks Fuse Holders and Fuse Accessories
Fuses
Fusible Switches and Panels
Gas Discharge Tubes
Magnetic Sensors and Reed Switches
Other Products and Accessories
Power Semiconductors
Protection Relays and Controls
Polymer ESD Suppressors
Resettable PTC Fuses
Semiconductors
Shock-Block GFCI
Surge Protection Module
Switches
Varistors

Selected Services
Custom Circuit Protection Solutions
Custom Power Centers and Electrical Equipment
Electrical Safety Services
MROplus Industrial Fuse Consolidation
Testing Services

COMPETITORS

AVX	ON Semiconductor
Bel Fuse	S&C Electric
Bourns	STMicroelectronics
EPCOS	TE Connectivity
Mersen Group	

HISTORICAL FINANCIALS
Company Type: Public

Income Statement — FYE: December 29

	REVENUE ($ mil.)	NET INCOME ($ mil.)	NET PROFIT MARGIN	EMPLOYEES
12/18	1,718.4	164.5	9.6%	12,300
12/17	1,221.5	119.5	9.8%	10,700
12/16*	1,056.1	104.4	9.9%	10,300
01/16	867.8	82.4	9.5%	8,800
12/14	852.0	99.4	11.7%	7,900
Annual Growth	19.2%	13.4%	—	11.7%

*Fiscal year change

2018 Year-End Financials

Debt ratio: 26.5% No. of shares (mil.): 24.7
Return on equity: 13.7% Dividends
Cash ($ mil.): 489.7 Yield: 0.0%
Current ratio: 3.50 Payout: 24.5%
Long-term debt ($ mil.): 684.7 Market value ($ mil.): 4,163.0

	STOCK PRICE ($) FY Close	P/E High/Low	PER SHARE ($) Earnings	Dividends	Book Value
12/18	168.03	35 23	6.52	1.60	59.67
12/17	197.82	40 28	5.21	1.40	41.64
12/16*	151.77	34 20	4.60	1.24	36.67
01/16	107.01	31 23	3.63	1.08	33.73
12/14	98.76	23 18	4.37	0.94	32.21
Annual Growth	14.2%	— —	10.5%	14.2%	16.7%

*Fiscal year change

Live Oak Bancshares Inc

Auditors: Dixon Hughes Goodman LLP

LOCATIONS

HQ: Live Oak Bancshares Inc
1741 Tiburon Drive, Wilmington, NC 28403
Phone: 910 790-5867
Web: www.liveoakbank.com

HISTORICAL FINANCIALS
Company Type: Public

Income Statement — FYE: December 31

	ASSETS ($ mil.)	NET INCOME ($ mil.)	INCOME AS % OF ASSETS	EMPLOYEES
12/18	3,670.4	51.4	1.4%	506
12/17	2,758.4	100.5	3.6%	528
12/16	1,755.2	13.7	0.8%	425
12/15	1,052.6	20.6	2.0%	366
12/14	673.3	10.0	1.5%	263
Annual Growth	52.8%	50.4%		17.8%

2018 Year-End Financials
Return on assets: 1.6%
Return on equity: 11.0%
Long-term debt ($ mil.): —
No. of shares (mil.): 40.1
Sales ($ mil): 266.4
Dividends
  Yield: 0.8%
  Payout: 4.2%
Market value ($ mil.): 595.0

	STOCK PRICE ($) FY Close	P/E High/Low		Earnings	PER SHARE ($) Dividends	Book Value
12/18	14.81	25	11	1.24	0.12	12.29
12/17	23.85	9	7	2.65	0.10	10.95
12/16	18.50	50	30	0.39	0.07	6.51
12/15	14.20	31	20	0.65	0.02	5.84
Annual Growth	1.4%	—	—	24.0%	81.7%	28.2%

Live Ventures Inc

EXECUTIVES

President; Chief Executive Officer; Director, Jon Isaac
Director, Thomas J. (Tom) Clarke Jr., age 60
Director, Greg A. LeClaire, age 47
Director, Richard D. Butler Jr., age 67
Independent Director, Dennis Gao
Auditors: WSRP, LLC

LOCATIONS

HQ: Live Ventures Inc
325 E Warm Springs Road, Suite 102, Las Vegas, NV 89119
Phone: 702 997-5968
Web: www.liveventures.com

COMPETITORS

Amazon.com	The Berry Company
Blucora	YPM
Buy.com	Yahoo!
Dex Media	Yellowbook
Google	craigslist
Infogroup	eBay
Overstock.com	

HISTORICAL FINANCIALS
Company Type: Public

Income Statement — FYE: September 30

	REVENUE ($ mil.)	NET INCOME ($ mil.)	NET PROFIT MARGIN	EMPLOYEES
09/18	199.6	5.9	3.0%	1,155
09/17	152.0	6.5	4.3%	1,211
09/16	78.9	17.8	22.6%	277
09/15	33.3	(14.6)	—	302
09/14	7.2	(4.6)	—	112
Annual Growth	129.0%	—		79.2%

2018 Year-End Financials
Debt ratio: 55.2%
Return on equity: 16.2%
Cash ($ mil.): 1.9
Current ratio: 1.76
Long-term debt ($ mil.): 64.2
No. of shares (mil.): 1.9
Dividends
  Yield: —
  Payout: —
Market value ($ mil.): 18.0

	STOCK PRICE ($) FY Close	P/E High/Low		Earnings	PER SHARE ($) Dividends	Book Value
09/18	9.00	7	3	1.58	0.00	20.28
09/17	12.40	9	1	1.61	0.00	16.86
09/16	1.91	0	0	5.40	0.00	8.67
09/15	1.68	—	—	(5.58)	0.00	2.24
09/14	2.98	—	—	(2.10)	0.00	5.50
Annual Growth	31.8%	—	—	—	—	38.6%

LogMeIn Inc

LogMeIn wants to help you stay productive even on the go. The company provides Web-based remote access software and services to consumers small and midsized businesses and IT service providers. Its user access and remote collaboration offerings serve consumers and business users while businesses and IT service providers use LogMeIn's technology to provide remote management and support. LogMeIn offers both free and subscription-based services. Its paid services add advanced features such as file transfer remote printing and drive mapping. Corporate customers include 3M AMD and IBM. About two-thirds of LogMeIn's sales come from US clients.In 2017 LogMeIn merged with GoToBusiness in a $1.8 billion transaction.

Change in Company Type
In 2017 LogMeIn merged with GoToBusiness which was spun out of Citrix Systems. The merged company is owned by Citrix (50.1%) and LogMeIn (48.9%) shareholders. The transaction was valued at about $1.8 billion. Adding GoTo products to its portfolio increases LogMeIn's presence in the small and medium business markets. The products are GoToAssist GoToMeeting GoToMyPC GoToTraining GoToWebinar Grasshopper and OpenVoice. The combined company expects annual revenue of about $1 billion.

Operations
Other advanced features of LogMeIn's paid services include high-definition remote control and content streaming remote sound and file sharing and syncing.

Services used by internal IT departments and customer care teams include device management disaster recovery and software update automation.

Geographic Reach
The company's services are available in 12 languages and are used in more than 240 countries. It has international sales offices in Australia Europe (Dublin and London) and India as well as two offshore IT offices in Hungary.

Sales and Marketing
LogMeIn uses free trials of its services to woo users and turn them into paying customers. Some of its funded marketing efforts include both online and offline advertising such as trade magazines newspapers and radio as well as tradeshows and events. With its extensive global presence and most sales still coming from the US the company plans to increase its spending on international sales and marketing. It also invests in expanding its range of connectivity services whether through internal development or strategic acquisitions. The company increased its advertising in 2014 spending $36.8 million up from $27.8 million in 2013.

Financial Performance
LogMeIn continued to generate revenue growth in 2014 raising its top line 34% to about $222 million. Much of that came from new customers as the number of subscribers to its premium join.me pro collaboration service grew. The company discontinued LogMeIn Free a free remote access service to focus on faster growing free services including join.me. The company reversed a $7 loss in 2013 (due in part to a legal settlement) to post a $7 million profit in 2014.

Strategy
LogMeIn is aiming to leverage its capabilities of connecting remote devices to become a player in the Internet of Things (the networking of sensors and other devices). Its Xively platform helps customers managed their connected devices and analyze the information collected by the devices. The 2014 acquisition of Ionia Corporation is part of LogMeIn's Internet of Things push.

Mergers and Acquisitions
LogMeIn acquired BBA Inc. known as Meldium for $10.6 million. Meldium provides single sign-on password management software and it expands LogMeIn's popular portfolio.

In an effort to capitalize on opportunities provided by the Internet of Things (allowing common objects to be connected to the network to send and receive data) LogMeIn purchased Ionia Corporation in 2014; Ionia is a systems integrator focused on connected solutions.

EXECUTIVES

Senior Vice President General Counsel Secretary, Michael Donahue
SVP and Chief Marketing Officer, W. Sean Ford, age 50, $299,653 total compensation
President and CEO, William R. Wagner, age 52, $410,000 total compensation
CFO, Edward K. (Ed) Herdiech, age 52, $228,000 total compensation
CTO, Sandor Palfy
Vice President CD, Paul Schauder
Vice President Of Channel Developer, Ted Roller
Vice President Network Operations, Joel Peterson

Svp Chief Of Staff, Tara Haas
Vice President Product Development, Kevin Bardos
Vice President Customer Support, Andrew Thompson
Senior Vice President Global Sales, Larry D'Angelo
Senior Vice President Corporate Strategy, Rob Lawrence
Senior Vice President Products, Andrew Burton
Vice President Customer Care, Bryce Cote
Senior Vice President Chief Marketing Officer, W Ford
Vice President Corporate Marketing, Alison Durant
Vice President Sales, Michelle Benfer
Senior Vice President of Sales, Lawrence D'Angelo
Vice President Corporate Development, Jeremy Segal
Vp Marketing Collaboration, Jim Somers
Senior Vice President General Manager, Chris Manton-jones
Vice President Sales Operations, Sharon Gould
Vice President, David Kubick
Vice President Real Estate And Facilities, Steve Nicholson
Senior Vice President, Scott Romesser
Vp Marketing Operations And Analytics, Kaylin Mckenney
Vice President Finance, Michael D'errico
Vp Lastpass Sales, Cid Ferrara
Chairman, Michael K. Simon, age 54
Auditors: DELOITTE & TOUCHE LLP

LOCATIONS

HQ: LogMeIn Inc
320 Summer Street, Boston, MA 02210
Phone: 781 638-9050   Fax: 781 437-1803
Web: www.LogMeIn.com

PRODUCTS/OPERATIONS

Selected Products
AppGuru
BoldChat
Cubby
join.me
LogMeIn Backup
LogMeIn Central
LogMeIn Hamachi
LogMeIn Pro
LogMeIn Rescue
Meldium
RemotelyAnywhere
Xively

COMPETITORS

Adobe Systems	LivePerson
Apple Inc.	Microsoft
Box Inc.	NetSuite
Cisco Systems	Oracle
Citrix Systems	Symantec
Google	

HISTORICAL FINANCIALS
Company Type: Public

Income Statement — FYE: December 31

	REVENUE ($ mil.)	NET INCOME ($ mil.)	NET PROFIT MARGIN	EMPLOYEES
12/18	1,203.9	74.3	6.2%	3,515
12/17	989.7	99.5	10.1%	2,760
12/16	336.0	2.6	0.8%	1,124
12/15	271.6	14.5	5.4%	1,006
12/14	221.9	7.9	3.6%	804
Annual Growth	52.6%	74.9%	—	44.6%

2018 Year-End Financials
Debt ratio: 5.0%   No. of shares (mil.): 50.6
Return on equity: 2.4% Dividends
Cash ($ mil.): 148.6   Yield: 1.4%
Current ratio: 0.63   Payout: 43.9%
Long-term debt ($ mil.): 200.0 Market value ($ mil.): 4,135.0

	STOCK PRICE ($) FY Close	P/E High/Low		PER SHARE ($) Earnings	Dividends	Book Value
12/18	81.57	93	53	1.42	1.20	58.68
12/17	114.50	64	47	1.93	1.25	60.19
12/16	96.55	1089	432	0.10	1.00	7.68
12/15	67.10	125	78	0.56	0.00	8.27
12/14	49.34	160	95	0.31	0.00	7.12
Annual Growth	13.4%	—	—	46.3%	—	69.4%

Lonestar Resources US Inc

Auditors: BDO USA, LLP

LOCATIONS

HQ: Lonestar Resources US Inc
111 Boland Street, Suite 301, Fort Worth, TX 76107
Phone: 817 921-1889
Web: www.lonestarresources.com

HISTORICAL FINANCIALS
Company Type: Public

Income Statement — FYE: December 31

	REVENUE ($ mil.)	NET INCOME ($ mil.)	NET PROFIT MARGIN	EMPLOYEES
12/18	201.1	19.3	9.6%	74
12/17	94.0	(38.6)	—	50
12/16	57.9	(94.3)	—	44
12/15	79.4	(27.3)	—	53
12/14	115.6	36.4	31.5%	0
Annual Growth	14.8%	(14.7%)	—	—

2018 Year-End Financials
Debt ratio: 58.7%   No. of shares (mil.): 24.6
Return on equity: 8.8% Dividends
Cash ($ mil.): 5.3   Yield: —
Current ratio: 0.72   Payout: —
Long-term debt ($ mil.): 436.8 Market value ($ mil.): 90.0

	STOCK PRICE ($) FY Close	P/E High/Low		PER SHARE ($) Earnings	Dividends	Book Value
12/18	3.65	38	12	0.28	0.00	9.03
12/17	3.97	—	—	(1.92)	0.00	8.79
12/16	8.54	—	—	(11.64)	0.00	7.62
12/15	4.51	—	—	(3.64)	0.00	24.32
12/14	0.18	0	0	4.84	0.00	28.33
Annual Growth	111.9% (24.9%)	—	—	(51.0%)	—	—

LTC Properties, Inc.

Specializing in TLC LTC Properties sees long-term care real estate as a healthy investment. The self-administered real estate investment trust (REIT) mostly invests in health care and long-term care facilities. Its portfolio includes more than 220 assisted living skilled-nursing and other healthcare properties with nearly 15000 living units across 30 states with its largest markets being in Texas Florida Colorado and Arizona. Its top tenant operators include Brookdale Senior Living Prestige Healthcare Senior Care Centers and Senior Lifestyle Corporation which in aggregate contribute around 45% to its total rental income. The REIT also invests in mortgage loans tied to long-term care properties.

Operations

The REIT's portfolio consisted of 224 properties at the end of 2015 including 104 assisted living centers (homes for elderly residents not requiring constant supervision) 100 skilled nursing facilities (which provide rehabilitative and restorative nursing care) seven other health care properties (such as independent living behavioral or memory care) a school and 11 land parcels. The assisted living and skilled nursing properties made up more than 90% of the REIT's rental income.

As with most leasing REITs LTC Properties makes most of its revenue from rental income from tenants/operators. About 83% of its total revenue came from rental income during 2015 while interest income from mortgage loans made up another 16%.

Geographic Reach

LTC's properties are located in 30 states. Texas Florida Colorado and Arizona are its largest markets.

Sales and Marketing

LTC Property's top tenant operators in 2015 included: Prestige Healthcare (which contributed 15% to the REIT's rental income) Brookdale Senior Living (11%) Senior Care Centers (9%) and Senior Lifestyle Corporation (9%) which in aggregate contributed around 45% to its total rental income.

Financial Performance

The REIT's annual revenues have risen more than 60% since 2011 thanks to regular rental rate increases and some rent-boosting property acquisitions. Its net income has nearly doubled over the same period on property sale gains and as it's managed to keep its operating and overhead costs in check.

LTC Property's revenue jumped 14% to $136.2 million during 2015 mostly thanks to rental rate increases associated with renewals though a two new skilled-nursing property acquisitions also helped increase its rental income. The REIT's interest income from its mortgage loans grew 34% as the company acquired more interest-earning loan assets.

Despite strong revenue growth in 2015 the REIT's net income dipped less than 1% to $73.08 million mostly as it didn't earn as much from property sale gains. Its operating cash levels climbed 7% to $102.34 million as it collected more in cash-denominated earnings.

Strategy

LTC Properties mostly invests in assisted living and skilled nursing facilities though it also invests in related healthcare facilities and even mortgages tied to such properties. To diversify its portfolio the REIT likes to buy properties in new geographic locations with new tenant operators.

EXECUTIVES

Vice Chairman and CFO, Wendy L. Simpson, age 69, $610,500 total compensation
EVP CFO and Secretary, Pamela J. (Pam) Shelley-Kessler, age 53, $365,833 total compensation
EVP and Chief Investment Officer, Clint B. Malin, age 47, $365,833 total compensation
SVP Controller and Treasurer, Caroline L. (Cece) Chikhale, age 42, $163,327 total compensation
SVP Investment and Portfolio Management, Brent P. Chappell, age 54, $245,833 total compensation
Auditors: Ernst & Young LLP

LOCATIONS

HQ: LTC Properties, Inc.
2829 Townsgate Road, Suite 350, Westlake Village, CA 91361
Phone: 805 981-8655
Web: www.ltcreit.com

PRODUCTS/OPERATIONS

2015 Sales

	$ mil.	% of total
Rental income	113.1	83
Interest income from mortgage loans	22.1	16
Interest & other income	1.0	1
Total	**136.2**	**100**

COMPETITORS

Chartwell Seniors Housing	Omega Healthcare Investors
HCP	Sabra Health Care
Healthcare Realty Trust	Senior Housing Properties
Legacy Healthcare	Tiptree
NHC	Ventas
National Health Investors	Welltower
NorthStar Healthcare Investors	

HISTORICAL FINANCIALS

Company Type: Public

Income Statement   FYE: December 31

	REVENUE ($ mil.)	NET INCOME ($ mil.)	NET PROFIT MARGIN	EMPLOYEES
12/18	168.6	154.9	91.9%	21
12/17	168.0	87.3	52.0%	20
12/16	161.5	85.1	52.7%	24
12/15	136.2	73.0	53.7%	22
12/14	118.9	73.4	61.7%	19
Annual Growth	9.1%	20.5%	—	2.5%

2018 Year-End Financials

Debt ratio: 42.6%
Return on equity: 19.6%
Cash ($ mil.): 2.6
Current ratio: 0.86
Long-term debt ($ mil.): 533.0
No. of shares (mil.): 39.6
Dividends
  Yield: 5.4%
  Payout: 58.6%
Market value ($ mil.): 1,653.0

	STOCK PRICE ($) FY Close	P/E High/Low	PER SHARE ($) Earnings	Dividends	Book Value
12/18	41.68	12 9	3.89	2.28	20.82
12/17	43.55	24 20	2.20	2.28	19.08
12/16	46.98	25 19	2.21	2.19	18.87
12/15	43.14	25 20	1.94	2.07	17.56
12/14	43.17	22 18	1.99	2.04	18.61
Annual Growth	(0.9%)	— —	18.2%	2.8%	2.8%

Luminex Corp

William Blake could "see a world in a grain of sand" and Luminex can reveal hundreds of secrets in a drop of fluid. Its xMAP (Multi-Analyte Profiling) technology allows simultaneous analysis of up to 500 bioassays or tests from a single drop of fluid. xMAP consists of instruments software and disposable microspheres (microscopic polystyrene beads on which tests are performed). Luminex also uses MultiCode real-time polymerase chain reaction and xTAG technology. Luminex's systems are used by clinical and research laboratories and are distributed through strategic partnerships with other life sciences firms. Luminex also develops testing assays and disposable testing supplies for the clinical diagnostics market.

Operations

The company's xMAP technology is being used in various segments of the life sciences industry including drug discovery and development clinical diagnostics genetic analysis bio-defense food safety and biomedical research. The MultiCode assay chemistry provides real-time polymerase chain reaction (PCR) and multiplex PCR-based applications.

Geographic Reach

More than 80% of Luminex's sales are made in the US. It also sells to customers in other countries in North America Europe and the Asia/Pacific region. Luminex has facilities in Australia Canada China Japan the Netherlands and the US.

Sales and Marketing

The company's technology is available commercially around the world; it is used by major pharmaceutical diagnostic biotechnology and life science companies. Luminex's largest customers include Laboratory Corporation of America (21% of revenue in 2014) Thermo Fisher Scientific (17% of revenue) and Bio-Rad Laboratories (7%).

Advertising expenses including trade show and convention activities were some $2.3 million in 2014 down from $2.6 million in in 2013 and $2.4 million in 2012.

Financial Performance

Revenue has grown over the past five years. It rose 6% to $227 million in 2014 on an increase in assay revenue and royalty earnings. Net income which had fallen for two years spiked 450% to $39 million that year as operating expenses declined.

Cash flow from operations also rose increasing 83% to $49 million in 2014.

Strategy

The technology-based firm has implemented a strategy to transform itself into a market-driven customer-focused company. To achieve this goal Luminex is focusing on key markets including life sciences research molecular infectious disease genetic disease pharmacogenetic testing bio-defense testing and immunodiagnostics. In addition it aims to develop next-generation systems to bring efficient portable testing solutions to market as well as market-leading assays in the human molecular diagnostic testing market. It is also working to develop strategic partnerships in its key markets and to pursue acquisitions that could hasten its goals.

Luminex is largely focused on the final development of its ARIES system; it hopes to improve the simplicity and ease of use of its multiplex products through the development of a new version of its multiplex PCR technology. In the area of molecular diagnostics the company is working to grow both its cleared Cytochrome P450 assays and the pharmacogenetic lab-developed test portfolios of its clinical customers.

The FDA cleared three new targets to the company's xTAG Gastrointestinal Pathogen Panel (GPP) in 2014; it also cleared xTAG GPP for use with specimens in Cary-Blair medium a common transport medium for the collection and preservation of microbiological specimens. The following year Luminex received Health Canada Class 3 Device License approval for its xTAG CYP2D6 Kit v. 3 comprehensive genotyping assay.

During 2014 Luminex's 46 partners who have commercialized xMAP-based assay products accounted for two-thirds of total revenue while all of its strategic partners represented some 70% of revenue.

Luminex closed its manufacturing facility in Brisbane Australia in 2014.

Mergers and Acquisitions

In 2016 Luminex bought molecular microbiology and diagnostics firm Nanosphere in a $58 million transaction. The purchase adds Nanosphere's Verigene technology which complements Luminex's existing infectious disease portfolio.

Company Background

Luminex takes its name from the special laser beams that each microsphere passes through during the bioassay screening process. The lasers excite dyes inside and on the surface of the microspheres and the resulting fluorescence is measured in real time and analyzed by the system's software.

EXECUTIVES

President and Chief Executive Officer; Director, Patrick J. Balthrop, age 63, $513,674 total compensation
Senior Vice President Research and Development, Jeremy Bridge-Cook, age 50, $355,048 total compensation
Senior Vice President Corporate Development and Global Marketing, Russell W. Bradley, age 56, $282,705 total compensation
Vice President Manufacturing and Quality Surveillance, Steve Back
Senior Vice President Operations, Michael F. Pintek, age 50, $325,297 total compensation
Vice President Luminex Molecular Diagnostics, Nancy Krunic
Vice President Biodefense, Amy L. Altman
President and CEO and Director, Nachum Shamir
Sr V Pres Hr, Nancy Fairchild
Global Vice President Of Sales, Andy Tao
Vice President Global Marketing, Eric Shapiro
Senior Vice President Of Global Manufacturing And Quality, Randy Myers
Chairman, G. Walter Loewenbaum, age 74
Board Member, Kevin McNamara

Board Member, Edward Ogunro
Auditors: Ernst & Young LLP

LOCATIONS
HQ: Luminex Corp
   12212 Technology Blvd., Austin, TX 78727
Phone: 512 219-8020
Web: www.luminexcorp.com

PRODUCTS/OPERATIONS

2014 Revenues

	$ mil.	% of total
Assay revenue	87.6	39
Consumable sales	48.3	21
Royalty revenue	39.4	17
System sales	29.2	13
Service revenue	9.4	6
Other	13.1	4
Total	**227.0**	**100**

Selected Products
Assay Development Tools
Calibration and Control Microspheres
Clinical Diagnostic Assays
FLEXMAP 3D
Life Science Research Assays
Luminex LX 100/200 (LX Systems)
MagPlex Microspheres
MicroPlex Microspheres
SeroMAP Microspheres
xPONENT
xTAG Microspheres

Selected Acquisitions

COMPETITORS
Abbott Labs
Affymetrix
Beckman Coulter
Becton Dickinson
Celera
Cepheid
GE Healthcare
Gen-Probe
GenMark
Hologic
Illumina
Johnson & Johnson
Life Technologies Corporation
Orchid Cellmark
QIAGEN
Roche Diagnostics
Sequenom
Siemens Healthcare

HISTORICAL FINANCIALS
Company Type: Public

Income Statement
FYE: December 31

	REVENUE ($ mil.)	NET INCOME ($ mil.)	NET PROFIT MARGIN	EMPLOYEES
12/18	315.8	18.5	5.9%	988
12/17	306.5	29.4	9.6%	896
12/16	270.6	13.8	5.1%	936
12/15	237.7	36.8	15.5%	797
12/14	226.9	39.0	17.2%	745
Annual Growth	8.6%	(17.0%)	—	7.3%

2018 Year-End Financials
Debt ratio: —
Return on equity: 4.0%
Cash ($ mil.): 76.4
Current ratio: 3.95
Long-term debt ($ mil.): —
No. of shares (mil.): 43.9
Dividends
  Yield: 1.0%
  Payout: 60.0%
Market value ($ mil.): 1,015.0

	STOCK PRICE ($) FY Close	P/E High/Low		PER SHARE ($) Earnings	Dividends	Book Value
12/18	23.11	83	45	0.41	0.24	10.65
12/17	19.70	33	27	0.67	0.24	10.09
12/16	20.23	73	55	0.32	0.00	9.43
12/15	21.39	26	17	0.86	0.00	8.71
12/14	18.76	22	17	0.93	0.00	7.65
Annual Growth	5.4%			(18.5%)	—	8.6%

Luna Innovations Inc

EXECUTIVES
Chairman, Richard W. (Rich) Roedel, age 66
Media Contact, Karin Clark
Interim CFO and Chief Commercialization Officer, Scott A. Graeff, age 49, $185,000 total compensation
CTO, Mark Froggatt, age 46, $158,750 total compensation
VP General Counsel and Secretary, Talfourd H. Kemper Jr., age 47
Vice President of Marketing, Geoffrey McCarty
President; Chief Executive Officer; Director, My Chung
Director, John B. Williamson III, age 61
Director, Edward G. Murphy, age 60
Director, N. Leigh Anderson, age 66
Director, Jonathan M. Cool, age 57
Director, Warner Dalhouse
Independent Director, Michael Wise
Auditors: Grant Thornton LLP

LOCATIONS
HQ: Luna Innovations Inc
   301 First Street S.W., Suite 200, Roanoke, VA 24011
Phone: 540 769-8400
Web: www.lunainc.com

PRODUCTS/OPERATIONS

2015 Sales

	% of total
Products and licensing	69
Technology development	31
Total	**100**

Selected Products
Applied research & development
Fiber optic sensing
Fiber optic test & measurement
High speed optical components
Optoelectronic solutions
Terahertz solutions

COMPETITORS
3M
Agilent Technologies
Bayer HealthCare Pharmaceuticals Inc.
Dow Chemical
General Dynamics
Leidos
Lockheed Martin
Robert Bosch
Viavi Solutions

HISTORICAL FINANCIALS
Company Type: Public

Income Statement
FYE: December 31

	REVENUE ($ mil.)	NET INCOME ($ mil.)	NET PROFIT MARGIN	EMPLOYEES
12/18	42.9	11.0	25.6%	196
12/17	46.2	14.6	31.6%	198
12/16	59.2	(2.3)	—	245
12/15	44.0	2.3	5.3%	243
12/14	21.2	5.9	28.2%	113
Annual Growth	19.2%	16.4%	—	14.8%

2018 Year-End Financials
Debt ratio: 0.9%
Return on equity: 19.6%
Cash ($ mil.): 42.4
Current ratio: 5.62
Long-term debt ($ mil.): 0.0
No. of shares (mil.): 27.9
Dividends
  Yield: —
  Payout: —
Market value ($ mil.): 94.0

	STOCK PRICE ($) FY Close	P/E High/Low		PER SHARE ($) Earnings	Dividends	Book Value
12/18	3.35	11	5	0.33	0.00	2.23
12/17	2.43	5	2	0.52	0.00	1.82
12/16	1.47	—	—	(0.09)	0.00	1.27
12/15	1.08	17	9	0.10	0.00	1.34
12/14	1.42	6	3	0.40	0.00	1.26
Annual Growth	23.9%			(4.7%)	—	15.4%

Luther Burbank Corp

Auditors: Crowe LLP

LOCATIONS
HQ: Luther Burbank Corp
   520 Third Street, Fourth Floor, Santa Rosa, CA 95401
Phone: 844 446-8201
Web: www.lutherburbanksavings.com

HISTORICAL FINANCIALS
Company Type: Public

Income Statement
FYE: December 31

	ASSETS ($ mil.)	NET INCOME ($ mil.)	INCOME AS % OF ASSETS	EMPLOYEES
12/18	6,937.2	45.0	0.6%	278
12/17	5,704.3	69.3	1.2%	266
12/16	5,064.5	52.1	1.0%	274
12/15	4,362.8	35.3	0.8%	0
Annual Growth	16.7%	8.4%	—	—

2018 Year-End Financials
Return on assets: 0.7%
Return on equity: 7.9%
Long-term debt ($ mil.): —
No. of shares (mil.): 56.3
Sales ($ mil): 230.1
Dividends
  Yield: 2.0%
  Payout: 17.6%
Market value ($ mil.): 509.0

	STOCK PRICE ($) FY Close	P/E High/Low		PER SHARE ($) Earnings	Dividends	Book Value
12/18	9.02	17	10	0.79	0.19	10.31
12/17	12.04	8	7	1.62	1.58	9.74
12/16	0.00	—	—	1.24	0.40	9.63
Annual Growth	—			(20.2%)	(31.5%)	3.5%

Lydall, Inc.

Lydall's products help to beat the heat nix the noise and filter the rest. The company makes thermal and acoustical barriers automotive heat shields and insulation products that offer protection in extreme temperatures. Lydall's thermal and acoustical products are used by the appliance and automotive industries and in industrial kilns and furnaces. The company rounds out its offerings with industrial and commercial air and liquid filtration products in addition to energy storage close-out panels and felt manufacturing services and products. Export sales represent about 35% of the company's annual net sales.

Operations
Lydall's segments include Thermal/Acoustical Metals and Fibers (nearly 60% of sales) which produces noise and heat abatement products for automotive applications and Performance Materials (12%) which encompasses its filtration and industrial thermal insulation businesses. Its Industrial Filtration segment offers industrial non-woven felt media and filter bags.

Geographic Reach
The company has operations in Europe Asia and the US which accounted for about 70% of its revenue in 2015.

Sales and Marketing
Lydall's products are primarily sold directly to customers through an internal sales force and external sales representatives and distributed via common carrier. The majority of products are sold to original equipment manufacturers and tier-one suppliers. Sales to Ford Motor Company accounted for almost 20% of net sales in 2015.

Financial Performance
After revenues peaked at a record-setting $536 million in 2014 Lydall saw its revenues fall 2% to $525 million in 2015. The company's profits however more than doubled from $22 million in 2014 to $46 million in 2015 mainly due to a gain on sale of its Life Sciences Vital Fluids business and a decrease in selling product development and administrative expenses.

The revenue dip for 2015 was fueled by lower sales from its Performance Materials segment and due to the divestiture of its Life Sciences Vital Fluids business. Performance Materials segment sales also decreased due to lower demand for air filtration products and thermal insulation products particularly in Asia and North America. It also experienced lower demand for its water purification and life protection application products and for cryogenic insulation products serving the liquid natural gas market.

Strategy
For its growth strategy Lydall focuses on new product development geographic expansion into Asia and Europe acquisitions and the application of Lean Six Sigma initiatives. A major focus for the company in 2014 is the integration of its acquired companies and the introduction of Lean Six Sigma principles to the acquired businesses.

In early 2014 the company acquired the industrial filtration business from Andrew Industries Limited for $83 million. The acquisition enhanced Lydall's already strong position in the filtration and engineered materials markets.

EXECUTIVES
EVP CFO and President Lydall Thermal/Acoustical Solutions, Scott M. Deakin, age 53
President and CEO, Dale G. Barnhart, age 66, $522,600 total compensation
President Lydall Performance Materials, Paul Marold, age 58
CIO, Joseph M. (Joe) Tait
SVP General Counsel and Chief Administration Officer, Chad A. McDaniel, $238,135 total compensation
Vice President Corporate Development and Investor Relations, David Glenn
Vice President Human Resources, William Lachenmeyer
Vice President Research And Development, Arvind Purushothaman
Evp And Cfo, Randall B Gonzales
Vp Global Sales And Engineering, Michael Panczyk
Vice President Global Sales, Greg Parlee
Vice President Operations, Brian Fields
Chairman, W. Leslie Duffy, age 79
Board Member, William Gurley
Auditors: PricewaterhouseCoopers LLP

LOCATIONS
HQ: Lydall, Inc.
One Colonial Road, Manchester, CT 06042
Phone: 860 646-1233   **Fax:** 860 646-4917
Web: www.lydall.com

PRODUCTS/OPERATIONS

2015 Sales

	$ mil.	% of total
Performance Materials Segment		
Filtration	62.7	11
Thermal Insulation	28.3	5
Life Sciences Filtration	10.5	2
Industrial Filtration Segment		
Industrial Filtration	139.1	26
Thermal/Acoustical Metals Segment		
Metal parts	141.1	26
Tooling	19.8	4
Thermal/Acoustical Fibers Segment		
Fiber parts	135.6	25
Tooling	3.2	1
Other Products and Services		
Life Sciences Vital Fluids	1.7	-
Eliminations and Other	(17.5)	-
Total	**524.5**	**100**

Selected Products
Performance Materials
Air Filtration
Liquid Filtration
High Temp. Insulation
Low Temp. Insulation
Energy Storage
Arioso for Gas Turbine
Solupor Venting Grade
HD ASHRAE
Industrial Filtration
Checkstatic
Felt Design & Specifying
Felt Manufacturing
Mate

COMPETITORS
CTA Acoustics
Dana
Donaldson Company
Johns Manville
Kaydon
Magna International
Morgan Advanced Materials
Pall Corporation
Specialty Products & Insulation
Tower International
Unifrax

HISTORICAL FINANCIALS
Company Type: Public

Income Statement
FYE: December 31

	REVENUE ($ mil.)	NET INCOME ($ mil.)	NET PROFIT MARGIN	EMPLOYEES
12/18	785.9	34.9	4.4%	3,300
12/17	698.4	49.3	7.1%	2,600
12/16	566.8	37.1	6.6%	2,700
12/15	524.5	46.2	8.8%	2,100
12/14	535.8	21.8	4.1%	2,100
Annual Growth	10.0%	12.5%	—	12.0%

2018 Year-End Financials
Debt ratio: 37.2%
Return on equity: 9.6%
Cash ($ mil.): 49.2
Current ratio: 2.61
Long-term debt ($ mil.): 314.6
No. of shares (mil.): 17.5
Dividends
Yield: —
Payout: —
Market value ($ mil.): 357.0

	STOCK PRICE ($) FY Close	P/E High/Low		PER SHARE ($) Earnings	Dividends	Book Value
12/18	20.31	25	9	2.02	0.00	21.03
12/17	50.75	22	16	2.85	0.00	20.38
12/16	61.85	29	12	2.16	0.00	15.87
12/15	35.48	14	9	2.71	0.00	14.31
12/14	32.82	25	13	1.28	0.00	12.28
Annual Growth	(11.3%)	—	—	12.1%	—	14.4%

M/I Homes Inc

M/I Homes sells single-family detached homes under the M/I Homes and Showcase Collection brands and to a lesser extent the Hans Hagen and Pinnacle Homes brands. It delivers more than 5800 homes a year to first-time move-up empty-nest and luxury buyers at prices ranging from about $180000 to $1.1 million (averaging $384000) and sizes ranging from 1400 to 5500 sq. ft. M/I Homes also builds attached townhomes in select markets. It caters to 16 markets throughout the Midwest Mid-Atlantic and South. Its M/I Financial mortgage banking subsidiary provides title and mortgage services.

Operations
M/I Homes' homebuilding operations comprise the most significant portion of its business accounting for almost all of the company's revenue. It currently offers over 750 different floor plans across all of its divisions.

Its Showcase collection is designed for move-up and luxury homebuyers and offers more design options larger floor plans and a higher-end product line of homes in upscale communities. Other plans include Smart Series (entry-level and move-down buyers) and City Collection (upscale urban lifestyle). The company also currently develops new floor plans and communities specifically for the growing empty-nester market.

Complementing its homebuilding activities the company provides mortgage banking and title services through its wholly owned subsidiary M/I Financial Corp.

In addition to home sales its homebuilding operations also generate revenue from the sale of land and lots.

Geographic Reach
M/I Homes is based in Columbus Ohio. Its biggest market is the Midwest (more than 40% of sales) followed by the Southern region including Texas (about 40%). The Mid-Atlantic region accounts for more than 15% of sales.

Sales and Marketing
M/I Homes focuses its marketing efforts on first-time and move-up homebuyers including home designs targeted to first-time millennial and empty-nester homebuyers. It primarily constructs homes in planned development communities and mixed-use communities.

The company markets its homes using traditional media such as newspapers direct mail billboards radio and television. It also uses enhanced search engine optimization search engine marketing and display advertising to increase the reach of its website. It maintains a presence on referral sites such as Zillow.com and NewHomeSource.com to drive sales leads to online sales associates.

M/I Homes also uses email marketing to maintain communication with existing prospects and customers. It uses its social media presence to communicate to potential homebuyers the experiences of customers who have purchased its homes and to provide content about its homes and design features.

Financial Performance
M/I Homes has experienced solid growth in recent years with revenue growth of more than 80% between fiscal years 2014 and 2018.

In fiscal year 2018 the company's revenue increased 17% to $2.2 billion a record high for the company. Revenue from homes delivered grew by 18% and revenue from the financial services segment increased by 5% year over year. The company's land sales fell by nearly $17 million in 2018 due to fewer land sales in the Mid-Atlantic region. The average sales price of homes delivered in 2018 grew by 4% to $384000.

Net income grew to $107.6 million in fiscal year 2018 up 48% from $72 million the previous year.

Cash at the end of fiscal 2018 was $21.5 million a decrease of $130.2 million over the previous year. The company used $2.6 million of cash in operating activities while investing activities used $134 million primarily due to the acquisition of Pinnacle Homes. Cash provided by financing activities totaled $6.4 million.

Strategy
M/I Homes has seen solid sales growth in the last five years. The company's strategy includes expanding its presence in existing markets by opening new communities offering more of its budget-friendly Smart Series homes and seeking new markets for expansion.

The company experienced record levels of new contracts homes delivered revenue and net income in 2018 thanks to a very strong selling environment in the first half of 2018. The second half of 2018 saw a softening in demand as a result of the affordability challenges for buyers created by higher mortgage interest rates and higher home prices.

The company's financial services business has also been doing well achieving record revenue and a record number of loans in 2018.

Mergers and Acquisitions
In early 2018 M/I Homes completed its acquisition of the residential homebuilding assets and operations of Pinnacle Homes a homebuilder in the Detroit Michigan market.

Company Background
M/I Homes was founded in 1976 in Ohio by Melvin and Irving Schottenstein. The company expanded into new markets in the 1980s including Florida Indiana and North Carolina. The company established M/I Financial in 1983.

The company went public in 1993. It continued to grow its market reach in upcoming years to include Illinois Maryland Minnesota Texas and Virginia.

EXECUTIVES

EVP and CFO, Phillip G. Creek, age 66, $600,000 total compensation
Chairman President and CEO, Robert H. Schottenstein, age 66, $900,000 total compensation
EVP Chief Legal Officer and Secretary, J. Thomas (Tom) Mason, age 61, $450,000 total compensation
Region President Charlotte Cincinnati Columbus Orlando Raleigh Tampa and Washington D.C. Divisions, Fred J. Sikorski, age 64
Region President Austin Dallas Houston and San Antonio Divisions, Thomas W. Jacobs, age 53
Region President Chicago Indianapolis and Minneapolis/St. Paul Divisions, Ronald H. Martin, age 50
Vice President Of Sales, Greg Jones
Vice President, David Parker
Vice President Of Construction, Brent Holsinger
Region Manager Vice President Mifc, Todd Miller
Vice President Of Land Development, Michael George
Vice President Of Land Acquisition, George Young
Executive Vice President Chief Legal Officer Secretary and Director, Thomas Mason
Vice President Of Land Development, Bob Wiggins
Vice President of Purchasing, Kelly Cunningham
Vice President Finance, Angie Alexander
Vice President of Purchasing, Kevin D Stewart
Vice President of Purchasing, Brian Potvin
Senior Vice President, Patrick Begg
Vice President Sales and Marketing, Desiree Davis
Vice President Operations, David Gipe
Vice President of Information Technology and Supply Chain, Peter Batchelder
Vice President Of Land Acquisition, Mark Connor
Vice President Of Operations, Gary Rae
Division Vice President, Paul Stern
Executive Vice President Chief Legal Officer and Secretary, J T Mason
Vice President of Purchasing, Rick Muravski
Vice President Land, Rob Romo
Vice President Secondary Marketing, Greg Otto
Vice President of Land Acquisition, Scott Herr
Vice President Of Land, John Rask
Vice President Sales and Marketing, Van Nguyen
Vice President Land Development, Scott Griffith
VICE PRESIDENT OPERATIONS, Chad Tschetter
Vice President Of Purchasing, Kevin Stark
Vice President and Assistant General Counsel, Maria Gargrave
Vice President Sales And Marketing, Jaci Calhoun
Vice President of Sales and Marketing, April Shumway
Vice President Of Construction, Curtis Ramey
Vice President Chief Estimator, Alan Morris
Vice President Of Land, Daniel Kaiser
Vice President of Land, Kevin Dym
Vice President National Accounts, Larry Sekely
Vice President Of Construction, Joseph Lucado
Vice President Land Development, Robert Schoen
Vice President Of Purchasing, Keith Blum
Auditors: DELOITTE & TOUCHE LLP

LOCATIONS
HQ: M/I Homes Inc
3 Easton Oval, Suite 500, Columbus, OH 43219
Phone: 614 418-8000   **Fax:** 614 418-8080
Web: www.mihomes.com

PRODUCTS/OPERATIONS

2015 Sales

	$ mil.	% of total
Southern Homebuilding	514.7	36
Midwest homebuilding	500.9	35
Mid-Atlantic homebuilding	366.8	26
Financial services	36.0	3
Total	**1,418.4**	**100**

Selected Markets
Charlotte NC
Chicago IL
Cincinnati OH
Columbus OH
Dayton OH
Houston TX
Indianapolis IN
Maryland
Orlando FL
Raleigh NC
San Antonio TX
Tampa FL
Virginia

COMPETITORS

Beazer Homes	Lennar
CalAtlantic	M.D.C.
Comstock Holding	NVR
D.R. Horton	Orleans Homebuilders
David Weekley Homes	PulteGroup
Dominion Homes	Rottlund
Drees Homes	Toll Brothers
Hovnanian Enterprises	WCI Communities
John Wieland Homes	Woodbridge Holdings
KB Home	

HISTORICAL FINANCIALS
Company Type: Public

Income Statement   FYE: December 31

	REVENUE ($ mil.)	NET INCOME ($ mil.)	NET PROFIT MARGIN	EMPLOYEES
12/18	2,286.2	107.6	4.7%	1,359
12/17	1,961.9	72.0	3.7%	1,238
12/16	1,691.3	56.6	3.3%	1,138
12/15	1,418.4	51.7	3.6%	1,008
12/14	1,215.1	50.7	4.2%	905
Annual Growth	17.1%	20.7%	—	10.7%

2018 Year-End Financials
Debt ratio: 40.6%
Return on equity: 13.4%
Cash ($ mil.): 21.5
Current ratio: 10.37
Long-term debt ($ mil.): 820.9
No. of shares (mil.): 27.5
Dividends
Yield: —
Payout: —
Market value ($ mil.): 578.0

	STOCK PRICE ($) FY Close	P/E High/Low		PER SHARE ($) Earnings	Dividends	Book Value
12/18	21.02	10	5	3.70	0.00	31.08
12/17	34.40	14	9	2.26	0.00	26.83
12/16	25.18	13	7	1.84	0.00	26.51
12/15	21.92	14	10	1.68	0.00	24.20
12/14	22.96	14	10	1.65	0.00	22.20
Annual Growth	(2.2%)	—	—	22.4%	—	8.8%

Macatawa Bank Corp.

Macatawa Bank Corporation is the holding company for Macatawa Bank. Since its 1997 founding the company has grown into a network of more than 25 branches serving western Michigan's Allegan Kent and Ottawa counties. The bank provides standard services including checking and savings accounts CDs safe deposit boxes and ATM cards. It also offers investment services and products through an agreement with a third-party provider. With deposit funds the bank primarily originates commercial and industrial loans and mortgages which account for nearly 75% of its loan book. Macatawa Bank also originates residential mortgages and consumer loans.

Operations
The bank carries total assets of $1.58 billion total loans of $1.12 billion and total deposits of $1.31 billion.

Through its Infinex affiliate the bank provides various brokerage services (including discount brokerage) personal financial planning and consultation regarding mutual funds.

The firm's Trust Department manages assets of approximately $648 million and offers retirement plan and personal trust services. Its personal trust services include financial planning investment management services trust and estate administration and custodial services.

Geographic Reach
Macatawa Bank operates more than 25 branches along with a lending and operation service facility in its primary market in western Michigan which includes the counties of Ottawa Kent and northern Allegan.

Sales and Marketing
Macatawa Bank targets small businesses mission-driven (non-profit) organizations builders manufacturers and service industry companies. Some of its clients include associations businesses churches financial institutions government authorities individuals and non-profit organizations.

Financial Performance
Macatawa's revenue has been declining ever since its peak in 2007. Revenue in fiscal 2014 fell by 2% to $63 million as the bank collected lower interest margins on its commercial residential and consumer loan portfolios amidst customer refinancing in the low interest-rate environment. The bank also generated less income from its short-term investments which hindered top line growth further.

Despite falling revenue the bank enjoyed its highest profit since 2007 as net income jumped by 10% to $10.47 million in 2014. This was thanks to a combination of lower interest expense on deposits and an improving real estate market which led to fewer losses from non-performing assets and fewer provisions for credit losses as real estate values improved.

Operations provided $16.62 million or 2% more cash than in 2013 thanks to higher earnings and because the bank wrote off more in non-cash accrued expenses and other liabilities.

EXECUTIVES

Assistant Vice President, Ron Buit
Vice President Commercial Lending, Frederick Lake
Vice President, Jason Coney
Vice President, Jason ME Coney
Vice President Mortgage Loan Officer, Bob Martin
Vice President Senior Audit Manager, Rick Wesolek
Vice President Treasury Management Sales, Kristin Timmer
Vice President Macatawa Bank, Linda Clatch
Vice President Retail Banking, Krista Geyer
Vice President Wealth Advisor, John Simonds
Vice President Team Lead Retail Banking Grand Rapids, Sandy Siedlecki
Commercial Banker Vice President, Mike Vanommen
Vice President Branch Manager Senior, Ben Overway
Vice President Private Banking Manager, Kirsen Doolittle
Branch Manager Senior Vice President, Eric Swensson
Auditors: BDO USA, LLP

LOCATIONS

HQ: Macatawa Bank Corp.
10753 Macatawa Drive, Holland, MI 49424
Phone: 616 820-1444
Web: www.macatawabank.com

PRODUCTS/OPERATIONS

2014 Sales

	$ mil.	% of total
Interest		
Loans including fees	42.9	67
Securities	3.2	5
Other	0.9	2
Noninterest		
ATM and debit card fees	4.7	8
Service charges & fees	4.3	7
Trust fees	2.7	4
Gain on sales of loans	2.0	3
Other	2.5	4
Total	**63.2**	**100**

COMPETITORS

Comerica	Huntington Bancshares
Fifth Third	PNC Financial
Flagstar Bancorp	

HISTORICAL FINANCIALS
Company Type: Public

Income Statement — FYE: December 31

	ASSETS ($ mil.)	NET INCOME ($ mil.)	INCOME AS % OF ASSETS	EMPLOYEES
12/18	1,975.1	26.3	1.3%	371
12/17	1,890.2	16.2	0.9%	368
12/16	1,741.0	15.9	0.9%	374
12/15	1,729.6	12.7	0.7%	385
12/14	1,583.8	10.4	0.7%	389
Annual Growth	5.7%	26.0%	—	(1.2%)

2018 Year-End Financials

Return on assets: 1.3%
Return on equity: 14.5%
Long-term debt ($ mil.): —
No. of shares (mil.): 34.0
Sales ($ mil): 86.5
Dividends
 Yield: 2.6%
 Payout: 39.6%
Market value ($ mil.): 328.0

	STOCK PRICE ($) FY Close	P/E High/Low		PER SHARE ($) Earnings	Dividends	Book Value
12/18	9.62	16	12	0.78	0.25	5.61
12/17	10.00	22	19	0.48	0.18	5.09
12/16	10.41	22	12	0.47	0.12	4.78
12/15	6.05	16	13	0.38	0.11	4.48
12/14	5.44	18	15	0.31	0.08	4.21
Annual Growth	15.3%	—	—	25.9%	33.0%	7.4%

Mackinac Financial Corp

EXECUTIVES

Vice President And Controller, Jennifer Stempki
Vice President, Laura Garvin
Executive Vice President Cco, Tammy McDowell
Vice President, Michael Caruso
Board Member, Robert Mahaney
Auditors: Plante & Moran, PLLC

LOCATIONS

HQ: Mackinac Financial Corp
130 South Cedar Street, Manistique, MI 49854
Phone: 888 343-8147

COMPETITORS

Baylake	Fifth Third
CNB Corp. (MI)	Huntington Bancshares
Community Shores Bank	

HISTORICAL FINANCIALS
Company Type: Public

Income Statement — FYE: December 31

	ASSETS ($ mil.)	NET INCOME ($ mil.)	INCOME AS % OF ASSETS	EMPLOYEES
12/18	1,318.0	8.3	0.6%	294
12/17	985.3	5.4	0.6%	221
12/16	983.5	4.4	0.5%	222
12/15	739.2	5.6	0.8%	173
12/14	743.7	1.7	0.2%	171
Annual Growth	15.4%	48.9%	—	14.5%

2018 Year-End Financials

Return on assets: 0.7%
Return on equity: 7.1%
Long-term debt ($ mil.): —
No. of shares (mil.): 10.7
Sales ($ mil): 59.6
Dividends
 Yield: 3.5%
 Payout: 82.7%
Market value ($ mil.): 146.0

	STOCK PRICE ($) FY Close	P/E High/Low		PER SHARE ($) Earnings	Dividends	Book Value
12/18	13.65	19	14	0.94	0.48	14.20
12/17	15.90	19	15	0.87	0.48	12.93
12/16	13.47	20	14	0.72	0.40	12.32
12/15	11.49	14	11	0.89	0.35	12.32
12/14	11.85	46	33	0.30	0.23	11.81
Annual Growth	3.6%	—	—	33.0%	20.9%	4.7%

Madison Square Garden Co (The) (New)

Auditors: KPMG LLP

LOCATIONS
HQ: Madison Square Garden Co (The) (New)
  Two Penn Plaza, New York, NY 10121
Phone: 212 465-6000
Web: www.themadisonsquaregardencompany.com

HISTORICAL FINANCIALS
Company Type: Public

Income Statement — FYE: June 30

	REVENUE ($ mil.)	NET INCOME ($ mil.)	NET PROFIT MARGIN	EMPLOYEES
06/19	1,631.0	11.4	0.7%	13,000
06/18	1,559.1	141.5	9.1%	11,700
06/17	1,318.4	(72.7)	—	13,000
06/16	1,115.3	(77.2)	—	8,900
06/15	1,071.5	(40.6)	—	8,364
Annual Growth	11.1%	—	—	11.7%

2019 Year-End Financials
Debt ratio: 1.4%
Return on equity: 0.4%
Cash ($ mil.): 1,086.3
Current ratio: 1.86
Long-term debt ($ mil.): 48.5
No. of shares (mil.): 23.7
Dividends
  Yield: —
  Payout: —
Market value ($ mil.): 6,651.0

	STOCK PRICE ($) FY Close	P/E High/Low	PER SHARE ($) Earnings	Dividends	Book Value
06/19	279.94	682 505	0.48	0.00	110.30
06/18	310.19	52 32	5.94	0.00	107.18
06/17	196.90	— —	(3.05)	0.00	102.28
06/16	172.51	— —	(3.12)	0.00	106.41
Annual Growth	17.5%	— —	—	—	1.2%

Majesco

Auditors: BDO USA, LLP

LOCATIONS
HQ: Majesco
  412 Mount Kemble Ave., Suite 110C, Morristown, NJ 07960
Phone: 973 461-5200
Web: www.majesco.com

HISTORICAL FINANCIALS
Company Type: Public

Income Statement — FYE: March 31

	REVENUE ($ mil.)	NET INCOME ($ mil.)	NET PROFIT MARGIN	EMPLOYEES
03/19	139.8	6.9	5.0%	2,682
03/18	122.9	(5.0)	—	2,248
03/17	121.7	(0.9)	—	2,054
03/16	113.3	(3.5)	—	2,134
03/15	79.2	(0.6)	—	1,781
Annual Growth	15.2%	—	—	10.8%

2019 Year-End Financials
Debt ratio: 0.3%
Return on equity: 9.6%
Cash ($ mil.): 11.3
Current ratio: 2.01
Long-term debt ($ mil.): 0.1
No. of shares (mil.): 42.8
Dividends
  Yield: —
Market value ($ mil.): 302.0

	STOCK PRICE ($) FY Close	P/E High/Low	PER SHARE ($) Earnings	Dividends	Book Value
03/19	7.05	47 26	0.18	0.00	2.29
03/18	5.06	— —	(0.14)	0.00	1.23
03/17	5.16	— —	(0.02)	0.00	1.26
03/16	6.09	— —	(0.10)	0.00	1.25
Annual Growth	5.0%	—	—	—	22.3%

Malibu Boats Inc

Auditors: KPMG LLP

LOCATIONS
HQ: Malibu Boats Inc
  5075 Kimberly Way, Loudon, TN 37774
Phone: 865 458-5478
Web: www.maliboats.com

HISTORICAL FINANCIALS
Company Type: Public

Income Statement — FYE: June 30

	REVENUE ($ mil.)	NET INCOME ($ mil.)	NET PROFIT MARGIN	EMPLOYEES
06/19	684.0	66.0	9.7%	1,835
06/18	497.0	27.6	5.6%	1,345
06/17	281.9	28.3	10.1%	586
06/16	252.9	18.0	7.1%	540
06/15	228.6	14.6	6.4%	509
Annual Growth	31.5%	45.7%	—	37.8%

2019 Year-End Financials
Debt ratio: 25.1%
Return on equity: 39.0%
Cash ($ mil.): 27.3
Current ratio: 1.69
Long-term debt ($ mil.): 113.6
No. of shares (mil.): 20.8
Dividends
  Yield: —
  Payout: —
Market value ($ mil.): 810.0

	STOCK PRICE ($) FY Close	P/E High/Low	PER SHARE ($) Earnings	Dividends	Book Value
06/19	38.85	18 10	3.15	0.00	9.79
06/18	41.94	33 18	1.36	0.00	6.54
06/17	25.87	16 8	1.58	0.00	2.74
06/16	12.08	21 11	1.00	0.00	0.77
06/15	20.09	26 18	0.93	0.00	(1.50)
Annual Growth	17.9%	—	35.7%	—	—

Malvern Bancorp Inc

EXECUTIVES
Vice Chairman Malvern Bancorp And Malvern Federal Savings Bank, John B Yerkes
Auditors: Baker Tilly Virchow Krause, LLP

LOCATIONS
HQ: Malvern Bancorp Inc
  42 E. Lancaster Avenue, Paoli, PA 19301
Phone: 610 644-9400

HISTORICAL FINANCIALS
Company Type: Public

Income Statement — FYE: September 30

	ASSETS ($ mil.)	NET INCOME ($ mil.)	INCOME AS % OF ASSETS	EMPLOYEES
09/19	1,265.2	9.3	0.7%	82
09/18	1,033.9	7.3	0.7%	85
09/17	1,046.0	5.8	0.6%	81
09/16	821.2	11.9	1.5%	83
09/15	655.6	3.7	0.6%	71
Annual Growth	17.9%	26.0%	—	3.7%

2019 Year-End Financials
Return on assets: 0.8%
Return on equity: 7.3%
Long-term debt ($ mil.): —
No. of shares (mil.): 7.7
Sales ($ mil.): 50.2
Dividends
  Yield: —
  Payout: —
Market value ($ mil.): 170.0

	STOCK PRICE ($) FY Close	P/E High/Low	PER SHARE ($) Earnings	Dividends	Book Value
09/19	21.83	18 15	1.22	0.00	18.35
09/18	23.95	25 19	1.13	0.00	16.84
09/17	26.75	30 19	0.90	0.00	15.60
09/16	16.40	10 8	1.86	0.00	14.42
09/15	15.65	27 19	0.58	0.00	12.41
Annual Growth	8.7%	—	20.4%	—	10.3%

Mammoth Energy Services Inc

Auditors: Grant Thornton LLP

LOCATIONS
HQ: Mammoth Energy Services Inc
  14201 Caliber Drive, Suite 300, Oklahoma City, OK 73134
Phone: 405 608-6007
Web: www.mammothenergy.com

Marcus & Millichap Inc

HISTORICAL FINANCIALS
Company Type: Public

Income Statement — FYE: December 31

	REVENUE ($ mil.)	NET INCOME ($ mil.)	NET PROFIT MARGIN	EMPLOYEES
12/18	1,690.0	235.9	14.0%	2,285
12/17	691.5	58.9	8.5%	1,846
12/16	231.0	(88.4)	—	520
12/15	359.9	(27.2)	—	500
12/14	259.5	(2.0)	—	0
Annual Growth	59.7%			

2018 Year-End Financials
Debt ratio: 0.2%
Return on equity: 37.4%
Cash ($ mil.): 67.6
Current ratio: 1.92
Long-term debt ($ mil.): 2.7
No. of shares (mil.): 44.8
Dividends
  Yield: 1.3%
  Payout: 4.7%
Market value ($ mil.): 807.0

	STOCK PRICE ($) FY Close	P/E High	P/E Low	PER SHARE ($) Earnings	Dividends	Book Value
12/18	17.98	8	3	5.24	0.25	16.80
12/17	19.63	16	8	1.42	0.00	11.39
12/16	15.20	—	—	(2.81)	0.00	9.09
Annual Growth	8.8%			—	—	35.9%

EXECUTIVES
First Vice President Investments, David Lincoln
Senior Vice President Investment, Jack Hopkins
Senior Vice President, Martin Cohan
Executive Managing Director Investments, Jeff Louks
Senior Vice President Investments, Steve Bogoyevac
Senior Vice President Investments, Barry Gordon
Senior Vice President Capital Markets, Farhan Kabani
Vice President Investments, Cliff David
Vice President Capital Markets, Danny Abergel
Senior Vice President Investments, Kevin King
Senior Vice President Investment, Gregory Mills
Senior Vice President, Robert Narchi
Svp And National Director Retail, Scott M Holmes
Vp Investment Denver, Skyler Cooper
Vp Investment Denver, Brian C Smith
Senior Vice President Division Manager, John Vorsheck
First Vice President General Counsel, Tyler Theobald
Senior Vice President National Director, Jeffery J Daniels
Vice President National Director, Adam A Lewis
Co Chairman, George A Marcus
Auditors: Ernst & Young LLP

LOCATIONS
HQ: Marcus & Millichap Inc
23975 Park Sorrento, Suite 400, Calabasas, CA 91302
Phone: 818 212-2250
Web: www.marcusmillichap.com

PRODUCTS/OPERATIONS

2015 Sales

	$ mil.	% of total
Real estate brokerage commissions	632.6	92
Financing fees	42.6	6
Other	13.9	2
Total	689.1	100

Selected Specializations
Health care
Hospitality and golf
Land
Manufactured housing
Multi-family
Net-leased
Office and industrial
Retail
Self-storage
Seniors housing
Student housing
Special assets

COMPETITORS
Baird & Warner
CBRE Group
Cassidy Turley
Coldwell Banker
Colliers International
Corky McMillin
Cushman & Wakefield
Grandbridge
Inland Group
Johnson Capital
Jones Lang LaSalle
Lee & Associates
NorthMarq Capital
ONCOR
Sperry Van Ness
Trammell Crow Company

Marcus Corp. (The)

With this company it's either showtime or bedtime. The Marcus Corporation operates movie theaters and hotels primarily in the Midwest. It owns or operates more than 55 theaters boasting some 680 screens in Iowa Illinois Minnesota Nebraska North Dakota Ohio and Wisconsin. Its Marcus Hotels subsidiary owns and operates more than 10 hotels and resorts in Illinois Missouri Oklahoma and Wisconsin; it also manages 10 hotels for third parties in a handful of US states. Other holdings also include Funset Boulevard a family entertainment center adjacent to one of its Wisconsin theatres. Chairman Stephen Marcus and his sister Diane Marcus Gershowitz together control more than 75% of the firm.

Operations
The Marcus Corporation owns and/or manages more than 5200 hotel rooms. Properties include the Pfister Hotel in downtown Milwaukee Wisconsin; the Four Points by Sheraton Chicago Downtown/Magnificent Mile; and the Hotel Phillips in Kansas City Missouri.

The company offers digital 3D systems at more than 35 of its movie theater properties. About three-fourths of its theater portfolio are megaplex theaters (12 or more screens). Marcus Corporation also offers its Big Screen Bistro in-theater dining concept at two locations.

In fiscal 2015 the company's Theatres segment generated 55% of revenue while the other 45% was generated by its Hotels/Resorts segment.

Geographic Reach
The theater division has operations in Wisconsin Illinois Ohio Minnesota Iowa North Dakota and Nebraska and a family entertainment center in Wisconsin. The hotels and resorts business has owned and operated hotels and resorts in Wisconsin Missouri Illinois and Oklahoma. It manages properties for third parties in Wisconsin Minnesota Ohio Texas Missouri Nevada and California.

Financial Performance
The company's revenue increased by $40 million in fiscal 2015 compared to the prior fiscal period. It reported about $488 million in revenue for fiscal 2015. Despite the increased revenue the company's net income decreased by $1 million in fiscal 2015 compared to fiscal 2014. The Marcus Corporation did claim a profit of $23.9 million in fiscal 2015 and net cash provided by operating activities increased by $14 million compared to fiscal 2014 levels.

Strategy
Marcus is working on upgrades at its theater facilities. It is adding special 70-foot-wide screens (called UltraScreens) to some locations and rolling out digital 3D cinema technology at its theaters. It is also introducing new food and beverage offerings at its theaters.

HISTORICAL FINANCIALS
Company Type: Public

Income Statement — FYE: December 31

	REVENUE ($ mil.)	NET INCOME ($ mil.)	NET PROFIT MARGIN	EMPLOYEES
12/18	814.8	87.2	10.7%	2,808
12/17	719.7	51.5	7.2%	2,593
12/16	717.4	64.6	9.0%	2,390
12/15	689.0	66.3	9.6%	2,243
12/14	572.1	49.5	8.7%	2,105
Annual Growth	9.2%	15.2%	—	7.5%

2018 Year-End Financials
Debt ratio: 1.3%
Return on equity: 24.0%
Cash ($ mil.): 214.6
Current ratio: 4.00
Long-term debt ($ mil.): 6.5
No. of shares (mil.): 38.8
Dividends
  Yield: —
  Payout: —
Market value ($ mil.): 1,333.0

	STOCK PRICE ($) FY Close	P/E High	P/E Low	PER SHARE ($) Earnings	Dividends	Book Value
12/18	34.33	18	13	2.22	0.00	10.55
12/17	32.61	25	18	1.32	0.00	8.21
12/16	26.72	18	11	1.66	0.00	6.83
12/15	29.14	31	17	1.69	0.00	5.05
12/14	33.25	27	11	1.27	0.00	3.16
Annual Growth	0.8%			—	15.0%	— 35.1%

EXECUTIVES
CFO and Treasurer, Douglas A. Neis, age 60, $318,923 total compensation
President CEO and Director, Gregory S. Marcus, age 54, $522,307 total compensation
Senior Managing Director MCS Capital LLC, William H. Reynolds, age 69
EVP and President and CEO Marcus Theatres Corporation, Rolando B. Rodriguez, age 59
President Marcus Hotels and Resorts, Joseph S. Khairallah
CIO and VP Technology Marcus Theatres Corporation, Kim M. Lueck
Executive Vice President Tech Corporat, Lee Dreyfus
Vice President of Revenue Strategy and Distribution, Linda Gulrajani

Vice President Of Human Resources, Fred Delmenhorst
Vice President Of Selling Support Services, Ken Day
Vice President Of Sales, Michael Lindley
Vice President Real Estate, Katie Falvey
Vice President, Marie McSzkowski
Senior Vice President Purchasing Officer, Dawn Dubinksi
Vice President, Tom Kissinger
Senior Vice President Development Marcus Hotels and Resorts, Andrea Foster
Vice President of Human Resources, John E Murray
Vice President Marketing Marcus Hotels And Resorts, Erin Levzow
Vice President Human Resources, Kurt Thomas
Chairman, Stephen H. Marcus, age 84
Board Member, Diane Gershowitz
Board Member, Philip Milstein
Board Member, Bruce J Olson
Auditors: DELOITTE & TOUCHE LLP

LOCATIONS

HQ: Marcus Corp. (The)
100 East Wisconsin Avenue, Suite 1900, Milwaukee, WI 53202-4125
Phone: 414 905-1000   **Fax:** 414 905-2879
Web: www.marcuscorp.com

PRODUCTS/OPERATIONS

Selected Hotels
Beverly Garland's Holiday Inn (North Hollywood California)
Crowne Plaza-Northstar Hotel (Minneapolis)
Four Points by Sheraton Chicago Downtown
The Grand Geneva Resort & Spa (Lake Geneva Wisconsin)
Hilton Garden Inn Houston
Hilton Madison at Monona Terrace (Wisconsin)
The Hilton Milwaukee City Center (Wisconsin)
Hotel Mead (Wisconsin Rapids Wisconsin)
Hotel Phillips (Kansas City)
The Pfister Hotel (Milwaukee)
Timber Ridge Lodge (Lake Geneva Wisconsin)

Selected Movie Theaters
Century Cinema Fargo (North Dakota)
Chicago Heights Cinema (Illinois)
Duluth Cinema (Minnesota)
Eastgate Cinema Madison (Wisconsin)
Lincoln Grand Cinema (Nebraska)
Northtown Cinema Milwaukee (Wisconsin)
Orland Park Cinema (Illinois)

COMPETITORS

AMC Entertainment
Carmike Cinemas
Cinemark
Heart of America Restaurants & Inns
Hilton Worldwide
Hostmark Hospitality
Hyatt
IMAX
InterContinental Hotels
Kerasotes ShowPlace
Kohler
Marriott
Nath Companies
Radisson Hotels
Ramada
Regal Entertainment
Starwood Hotels & Resorts
Wyndham Destinations

HISTORICAL FINANCIALS
Company Type: Public

Income Statement   FYE: December 27

	REVENUE ($ mil.)	NET INCOME ($ mil.)	NET PROFIT MARGIN	EMPLOYEES
12/18	707.1	53.3	7.6%	8,000
12/17	622.7	65.0	10.4%	7,800
12/16	543.8	37.9	7.0%	7,900
12/15*	324.2	23.5	7.3%	7,000
05/15	488.0	24.0	4.9%	7,100
Annual Growth	9.7%	22.1%	—	3.0%

*Fiscal year change

2018 Year-End Financials
Debt ratio: 26.9%
Return on equity: 11.4%
Cash ($ mil.): 17.1
Current ratio: 0.46
Long-term debt ($ mil.): 251.0
No. of shares (mil.): 28.3
Dividends
  Yield: 1.5%
  Payout: 18.2%
Market value ($ mil.): 1,092.0

	STOCK PRICE ($) FY Close	P/E High/Low		PER SHARE ($)		
				Earnings	Dividends	Book Value
12/18	38.51	23	12	1.86	0.60	17.28
12/17	27.20	14	10	2.29	0.50	15.98
12/16	31.55	23	13	1.36	0.45	14.10
12/15*	18.97	24	21	0.84	0.41	13.13
05/15	19.65	25	16	0.87	0.39	12.48
Annual Growth	18.3%	—	—	20.9%	11.4%	8.5%

*Fiscal year change

Marine Products Corp

A day on the water for you is a day at the office for Marine Products. The company builds recreational powerboats mainly though its Chaparral subsidiary. Its lineup includes fiberglass sterndrive and inboard deckboats cruisers and sport yachts ranging from 18 feet to 42 feet. Marine Products also makes a line of freshwater/saltwater sport fishing boats known for their "unsinkable hull" through subsidiary Robalo. Boats are sold to a network of about 230 independent dealers who then sell the lines to retail customers. The US generates the majority of the company's sales.

Geographic Reach
Headquartered at Atlanta the company sells its products to clients in Europe South America Asia Russia the Middle East and the US. Sales outside of the US accounted for 11% of its sales in 2015.

Sales and Marketing
Marine Products leverages a network of roughly 60 Chaparral dealers 25 Robalo dealers and 64 dealers selling both brands throughout the US. Oversees its boats are sold through some 85 international dealers.

Financial Performance
As the economy has gradually recovered Marine Products has achieved explosive growth over the years. Its total sales increased 21% from $171 million in 2014 to $207 million in 2015. Profits also surged 60% from $9 million in 2014 to $14 million in 2015. (Both these totals represented its highest amounts in at least eight years.)

The growth for 2015 was primarily due to a 23% increase in the number of boats sold. Unit sales increased due to higher sales of its Robalo outboard sport fishing boats as well as increased unit sales of its Chaparral Vortex jet boats and Suncoast outboards.

In addition to its trending revenue and net income Marine Products' operating cash flow surged by 51% from 2014 to 2015.

Strategy
With a health level of cash from operations and increasing production the company anticipates replenishing dealer inventories now normalizing from their historic low levels. Simultaneously it aims to enhance dealer offerings and spur retail purchases by manufacturing more models with standard features and fewer options.

Marine Products has recently launched new Chaparral and Robalo models: the Chaparral H2O Sport and Fish & Ski Boats and the Robalo R180 and R200. The new models are more affordable with a small number of standard features. They adhere to the company's strategy to produce lower-priced entry level models appealing to a value-conscious consumer.

EXECUTIVES

Vp Human Resources, Shannon Pope
President CEO and Director, Richard A. Hubbell, age 75, $350,000 total compensation
EVP and President Chaparral Boats, James A. Lane, age 76, $250,000 total compensation
VP CFO and Treasurer, Ben M. Palmer, age 58, $175,000 total compensation
Vice President of Loyalty Marketing, Holly Mendelson
Executive Vice President Sales and Marketing, Amy McPherson
Vice President Sales Strategy And Marketing Hotels, Frank Feruson
Regional Vice President Sales and Marketing, Jon Moore
Chairman, R. Randall Rollins, age 88
Board Member, Larry Prince
Board Member, Henry B Tippie
Board Member, Pamela Rollins
Board Member, Timothy Rollins
Secretary Vice President, William Pegg
Auditors: Grant Thornton LLP

LOCATIONS

HQ: Marine Products Corp
2801 Buford Highway, Suite 300, Atlanta, GA 30329
Phone: 404 321-7910
Web: www.marineproductscorp.com

PRODUCTS/OPERATIONS

Selected Products
Chaparral (family recreational cruiser and sport yachts)
  Premiere sport yachts (fiberglass sport yachts)
  Signature cruisers (fiberglass cruisers)
  SSi sportboats (fiberglass closed deck runabouts)
  SSX sportdecks (fiberglass bowrider crossover sportboats)
  Sunesta Xtreme tow boats (fiberglass pleasure boats)
Robalo (outboard sport fishing boats)

COMPETITORS

Bombardier
Brunswick Corp.
Bénéteau
Cigarette Racing Team
Correct Craft
Duckworth Boat Works
Fountain Powerboat
Sea Fox Boats
Sea Ray Boats
Sunseeker
Taylor Made Group
Viking Yacht
Yamaha Motor

MarineMax Inc

MarineMax aims to float your boat. The nation's largest recreational boat dealer has about 60 locations in around 16 states. Dealerships sell new and used pleasure boats fishing boats motor yachts ski boats and high-performance boats. Sales of new boats made by Brunswick including Sea Ray and Boston Whaler boats account for more than 40% of revenue. The company also sells boat engines trailers parts and accessories; arranges for financing and insurance; provides repair and maintenance; and offers boat brokerage and storage services. MarineMax is the exclusive dealer of Sea Ray in almost all the areas where it operates. Since its founding in 1998 MarineMax has acquired about 35 boat dealers.

Operations
MarineMax gets more than 70% of its revenue from the sale of brand new boats (average price: $195000). Used boat sales account for about 15% with the remainder provider by its repair finance and insurance and brokerage sales.

Within the new boat category sales of Sea Ray and Boston Whaler craft (made by Brunswick) account for about 25% and about 15% of revenue respectively. New Azimut boats and yachts supply about 10% of the company's revenue.

Geographic Reach
MarineMax is based in Florida (Clearwater) and the state accounts for more than half of its sales. The other 15 states in which it has retail locations are Alabama California Connecticut Florida Georgia Maryland Massachusetts Minnesota Missouri New Jersey New York North Carolina Ohio Oklahoma Rhode Island South Carolina and Texas. The company is also in the British Virgin Islands.

Sales and Marketing
MarineMax knows that nothing becomes a boat more than water and that's why many of its retail spots on waterfronts in popular destinations. To help get people to those locations the company uses its website email marketing and social media. It's also a constant presence at boat shows throughout the country.

Financial Performance
A rising economic tide has helped MarineMax's revenue increase 80% from 2014 through 2017. The company's sales plunged during the Great Recession but have rebounded in the years since.

In 2017 the company's sales rose 11% to just over $1 billion from 2016. Same store sales were up 5% in 2017 from incremental increases in new boat sales and increases in its other revenue sources such as brokerage sales storage services finance and insurance products and charter rentals pushed along by better economic conditions.

Net income rose about 4% to $23.5 million in 2017 from 2016. MarineMax held the line on most expenses but losses from Hurricane Irma forced sales general and administrative costs higher.

The company had about $42 million in cash at the end of 2017 up from about $39 million in 2016.

Strategy
Not to feel sorry for a business that sells yachts but the boating industry took a beating during the Great Recession. Annual sales averaged 309000 boats from 1990-2006 but slowed significantly after 2007 and 2008. (MarineMax closed 29 stores in 2009 alone). In 2016 about 188000 boats were sold industrywide but the trend line is rising.

Borrowing a page from the playbook of retailers like Home Depot MarineMax is trying to consolidate what has been a fragmented market dominated by local boat sellers. MarineMax has expanded through acquisitions making about 35 deals in its 20-year history.

The company also does more than sell boats. It trains the buyers on how to use them services them insures them and lends buyers money to buy them. It also charters boats to people who don't own one. MarineMax has extended the brands it carries to more of its markets to provide more choice for customers.

Mergers and Acquisitions
MarineMax acquired Island Marine Center which serves the southern New Jersey market in 2017. Island Marine has locations in Ocean View and Somers Point New Jersey.

In another 2017 deal MarineMax acquired Hall Marine Group which had six locations in North Carolina South Carolina and Georgia.

In 2016 MarineMax bought Russo Marine a boat dealer with three locations in Massachusetts and Rhode Island.

EXECUTIVES
EVP CFO and Secretary, Michael H. (Mike) McLamb, age 54, $315,000 total compensation
Chairman President and CEO, William H. McGill, age 76, $550,000 total compensation
EVP Chief Legal Officer and Assistant Secretary, Paulee C. Day, age 50, $260,000 total compensation
EVP and Chief Revenue Officer, Charles A. (Chuck) Cashman, age 56, $200,000 total compensation
EVP and COO, William Brett McGill, age 50, $200,000 total compensation
Vice President European Transaction Services, Lars Krosby
Board Member, Charles Oglesby
Board Member, Clint Moore
Auditors: KPMG LLP

LOCATIONS
HQ: MarineMax Inc
2600 McCormick Drive, Suite 200, Clearwater, FL 33759
Phone: 727 531-1700
Web: www.MarineMax.com

PRODUCTS/OPERATIONS

2017 Sales

	$ mil.	% of total
New boat sales	747.0	70
Used boat sales	157.0	15
Maintenance repair & storage services	60.0	6
Marine Engines Related Marine Equipment and Boating Parts and Accessories	38.0	2
F&I Products	25.0	4
Brokerage Sales	20.0	2
Total	**1,052.0**	**100**

Selected Products & Trade Names
Motor Yachts
  Azimut
  Hatteras Motor Yachts
Convertibles
  Cabo
  Hatteras Convertibles
Pleasure Boats
  Meridian
  Sea Ray
Fishing Boats
  Boston Whaler
  Grady White
Ski Boats
  Axis
  Malibu

COMPETITORS
Bass Pro Shops   Lenco Marine
Coast Distribution   Wal-Mart
Defender Industries   West Marine
L.L. Bean

HISTORICAL FINANCIALS
Company Type: Public

Income Statement   FYE: September 30

	REVENUE ($ mil.)	NET INCOME ($ mil.)	NET PROFIT MARGIN	EMPLOYEES
09/19	1,237.1	35.9	2.9%	1,754
09/18	1,177.3	39.3	3.3%	1,573
09/17	1,052.3	23.5	2.2%	1,516
09/16	942.0	22.5	2.4%	1,422
09/15	751.3	48.2	6.4%	1,289
Annual Growth	13.3%	(7.1%)	—	8.0%

2019 Year-End Financials
Debt ratio: 39.8%   No. of shares (mil.): 21.3
Return on equity: 9.9%   Dividends
Cash ($ mil.): 38.5   Yield: —
Current ratio: 1.38   Payout: —
Long-term debt ($ mil.): —   Market value ($ mil.): 330.0

HISTORICAL FINANCIALS
Company Type: Public

Income Statement   FYE: December 31

	REVENUE ($ mil.)	NET INCOME ($ mil.)	NET PROFIT MARGIN	EMPLOYEES
12/18	298.6	28.4	9.5%	976
12/17	267.3	19.3	7.2%	891
12/16	241.3	16.7	6.9%	823
12/15	207.0	14.3	6.9%	767
12/14	171.0	8.9	5.2%	605
Annual Growth	14.9%	33.7%	—	12.7%

2018 Year-End Financials
Debt ratio: —   No. of shares (mil.): 34.3
Return on equity: 39.3%   Dividends
Cash ($ mil.): 8.7   Yield: 2.3%
Current ratio: 3.56   Payout: 60.2%
Long-term debt ($ mil.): —   Market value ($ mil.): 580.0

	STOCK PRICE ($) FY Close	P/E High/Low		PER SHARE ($) Earnings	Dividends	Book Value
12/18	16.91	29	15	0.83	0.50	2.19
12/17	12.74	31	18	0.55	0.33	2.01
12/16	13.87	33	12	0.44	0.24	1.88
12/15	6.04	23	14	0.39	0.20	2.37
12/14	8.44	42	25	0.24	0.16	2.19
Annual Growth	19.0%	—	—	36.4%	33.0%	0.0%

MarketAxess Holdings Inc.

	STOCK PRICE ($) FY Close	P/E High/Low		PER SHARE ($) Earnings	Dividends	Book Value
09/19	15.48	16	9	1.57	0.00	17.30
09/18	21.25	14	9	1.71	0.00	15.57
09/17	16.55	24	14	0.95	0.00	13.81
09/16	20.95	23	15	0.91	0.00	12.87
09/15	14.13	14	7	1.92	0.00	11.72
Annual Growth	2.3%	—	—	(4.9%)	—	10.2%

A little creative spelling never got in the way of a good bond trade. MarketAxess offers an electronic multi-dealer platform for institutional traders buying and selling US corporate high-yield and emerging market bonds as well as Eurobonds. Participating broker-dealers include some of the world's largest such as BNP Paribas Citigroup Deutsche Bank Goldman Sachs and Merrill Lynch. In all MarketAxess serves more than 1000 investment firms mutual funds insurance companies pension funds and other institutional investors. The company also provides real-time corporate bond price information through its Corporate BondTicker service.

Operations
Nearly 85% of the company's revenue comes from monthly distribution fees and commissions for transactions executed on its platform between institutional investor and broker-dealer clients. About 10% of its revenue comes from its information and post-trade services from its Trax division (the trading name under Xtrakter Ltd.) which provides trade matching regulatory transaction reporting and market and reference data across a range of fixed income products. Less than 5% of its revenue comes from its technology products and services. MarketAxess had a staff of 303 employees at the end of 2014 with 187 of them based in teh US and the others mostly in the UK.

Geographic Reach
MarketAxess generates 85% of its revenue from the US while nearly all of the remainder comes from the UK. The company has office locations in the US UK Brazil and Singapore.

Sales and Marketing
To boost awareness of its brand and electronic trading platform MarketAxess uses advertising direct marketing promotional mailings and participates in industry conferences and media engagement. As an example it worked with The Wall Street Journal to make its Corporate BondTicker service the source of WSJ's information for its daily corporate bond and high-yield tables.

In the US high-grade corporate bond market more than 600 active institutional investors and 68 broker-dealers used MarketAxess' platform in 2014 including all of the top 20 broker-dealers as ranked by 2014 US corporate bond new-issue underwriting volume. The company's broker-dealer clients made up 96% of all underwriting activity for newly-issued corporate bonds in 2014.

Overall the firm spent $5.8 million on advertising in 2014 up 25% from $4.6 million spent in 2013.

Financial Performance
MarketAxess' revenues and profits have risen at a healthy clip over the past several years largely as the bond market has become more attractive to investors which has led to growth in both MarketAxess' commission income and information and post-trade services income.

The firm's revenue rose by 10% to $262.8 million in 2014 mostly thanks to commission income growth as trading activity in the bond market remained strong. Its revenue from its information and post-trade services also grew thanks to its 2013 acquisition of Xtrackter while favorable foreign currency exchange rates also added to the company's top-line growth.

Despite generating higher revenue in 2014 MarketAxess' net income dipped by 2% to $74.8 million for the year mostly because in 2013 it had enjoyed a $7.6 million (non-recurring) gain from its since-discontinued Greenline subsidiary. MarketAxess' operating cash levels jumped 21% to nearly $110 million in 2014 mostly as it generated higher cash earnings compared to the prior year.

Strategy
MarketAxess focuses on technology investments to expand its connectivity offerings for electronic transactions. Its main objective reiterated in 2015 is to "provide the leading global electronic trading platform for fixed-income securities connecting broker-dealers and institutional investors more easily and efficiently while offering a broad array of information trading and technology services to market participants across the trading cycle."

The strategy's key elements include: innovating and introducing new product offerings to the MarketAxess platform; leverage its existing client network to increase the number of potential counterparties and boost liquidity; continue to build on its existing service offerings to ensure that its platform is more full integrated into the workflow of its client base; and add new content and analytical capabilities to its Corporate BondTicker service.

The firm also fosters growth by entering strategic alliances or acquiring smaller marketplace firms to expand its service capabilities extend its market reach or bolsters its existing service expertise.

Mergers and Acquisitions
In February 2013 MarketAxess expanded its capacity when it acquired Xtrakter Limited a leading provider of regulatory transaction reporting financial market data and trade matching services to the European securities markets. The acquired company became MarketAxess' Trax division.

EXECUTIVES
Chairman President and CEO, Richard M. (Rick) McVey, age 60, $400,000 total compensation
CFO, Antonio L. (Tony) DeLise, age 57, $200,000 total compensation
CIO, Nicholas Themelis, age 56, $250,000 total compensation
Investor Relations, James N.B. (Jim) Rucker, $200,000 total compensation
Head of Marketing and Communications, Florencia Panizza
Head of US Sales, Kevin McPherson
Head Europe and Asia, Robert H. Urtheil
Vice President, Bill Barnett
Auditors: PricewaterhouseCoopers LLP

LOCATIONS
HQ: MarketAxess Holdings Inc.
55 Hudson Yards, 15th Floor, New York, NY 10001
Phone: 212 813-6000 **Fax:** 212 813-6390
Web: www.marketaxess.com

PRODUCTS/OPERATIONS
2014 Sales

	$ mil.	% of total
Commissions	221.1	84
Information and post-trade services	31.5	12
Technology products and services	6.9	3
Investment income	0.5	-
Others	2.8	1
Total	262.8	100

Selected Mergers and Acquisitions
FY2012
Xtrakter Limited (undisclosed price; London UK; provider of regulatory transaction reporting)

COMPETITORS
BGC Partners NEX
BondsOnline TRADEBOOK
Cantor Fitzgerald Tradeweb
GFI Group Weeden
Interactive Brokers
Intercontinental Exchange

HISTORICAL FINANCIALS
Company Type: Public

Income Statement — FYE: December 31

	REVENUE ($ mil.)	NET INCOME ($ mil.)	NET PROFIT MARGIN	EMPLOYEES
12/18	435.5	172.8	39.7%	454
12/17	397.4	148.0	37.3%	429
12/16	369.9	126.1	34.1%	383
12/15	303.1	96.0	31.7%	342
12/14	262.7	74.8	28.5%	303
Annual Growth	13.5%	23.3%	—	10.6%

2018 Year-End Financials
Debt ratio: —
Return on equity: 30.7%
Cash ($ mil.): 246.3
Current ratio: 6.21
Long-term debt ($ mil.): —
No. of shares (mil.): 37.6
Dividends
 Yield: 0.8%
 Payout: 39.6%
Market value ($ mil.): 7,954.0

	STOCK PRICE ($) FY Close	P/E High/Low		PER SHARE ($) Earnings	Dividends	Book Value
12/18	211.31	49	37	4.57	1.68	16.15
12/17	201.75	52	37	3.89	1.32	13.68
12/16	146.92	51	30	3.34	1.04	12.47
12/15	111.59	44	26	2.55	0.80	10.44
12/14	71.71	36	23	2.03	0.64	8.96
Annual Growth	31.0%	—	—	22.5%	27.3%	15.9%

Marlin Business Services Corp

Marlin is hooked on equipment leasing. Marlin Business Services leases more than 100 categories of commercial equipment to about 68000 small and mid-sized businesses — and it provides the financing for the deals in part through its Marlin Business Bank subsidiary. The market is known in the equipment leasing field as the "small-ticket" segment. Copiers makes up about 30% of Marlin's lease portfolio but its customers also can get products as diverse as computer hardware and software security systems telecom equipment dental implant systems water filtration systems and restaurant equipment. The company primarily operates through its main subsidiary Marlin Leasing.

Operations
The "small-ticket" segment covers the leasing of equipment up to $250000 although Marlin's average equipment lease is about $14000 and runs 50 months (leases usually range from 36 to 60 months). Customers can opt to buy equipment at the end of the initial contracts. More than 95% of the company's transactions originate through almost 12000 independent commercial equipment dealers; Marlin also uses direct communications with customers and lease brokers. Financing is increasingly offered through Marlin Business Bank; in addition it has a close relationship with Wells Fargo's Capital Finance.

About three quarters of Marlin's revenue comes from interest it charges on equipment financing. Fee income accounts for 17% of revenue with insurance at 7%.

Geographic Reach
Although Marlin Leasing has customers in across the US its business follows population trends with California and Texas as its largest markets each accounting for between 9% and 13% of lease payments.

In addition it has offices in Colorado Georgia New Jersey New Hampshire Pennsylvania and Utah.

Sales and Marketing
Marlin uses both telephone direct sales and for strategic larger accounts a team of about 140 outside sales executives.

Financial Performance
Marlin's revenue ticked 1% higher to about $90 million in 2015 from 2014. In the low interest environment the company's interst income was flat while fee and insurance income revenues were higher.

The company's net income of about $16 million in 2015 was 17% lower than 2014's figure. The company had higher expenses to deal with the exits of the chief executive and financial officers while also paying for additional workers overall.

Cash flow from operations in 2015 slipped to about $27 million a 19% drop from 2014.

Strategy
In 2015 Marlin opened several new business channels added sales people and offered a working capital loan product. It also initiated a product called Funding Stream a flexible loan program of Marlin Business Bank.

Marlin prides itself on having a diverse portfolio while working to effectively manage credit risk. It has a centralized collections department that assigns more experienced collectors to late-stage delinquent accounts and specialist collectors who focus on late fees property taxes bankruptcies and large balance accounts. While Marlin Business Bank is its primary funding source the company does have access to multiple funding sources.

EXECUTIVES
COO, Edward J. (Ed) Siciliano, age 57, $313,500 total compensation
SVP and CFO, W. Taylor Kamp, age 58, $111,919 total compensation
SVP Administration General Counsel and Secretary, Edward R. Dietz, age 44, $275,000 total compensation
CEO, Jeffrey A. Hilzinger
SVP and Chief Marketing Officer, Aswin Rajappa
Senior Vice President and Chief Sales Officer, Mark Scardigli
Assistant Vice President National Accounts, Greg Dietrich
Chairman, Lawrence J. (Larry) DeAngelo, age 52
Auditors: DELOITTE & TOUCHE LLP

LOCATIONS
HQ: Marlin Business Services Corp
300 Fellowship Road, Mount Laurel, NJ 08054
Phone: 888 479-9111
Web: www.marlincorp.com

PRODUCTS/OPERATIONS
2015 sales

	$ mil.	% of total
Interest	66.7	74
Fees	15.3	17
Insurance	5.9	7
Other	1.9	2
Total	**89.8**	**100**

COMPETITORS
American Express	KeyCorp
CalFirst	National Funding Inc
Citibank	Presidio Technology Capital
Comerica	
Deutsche Bank	Rabobank Group
HP Financial Services	Ricoh USA
IBM Global Financing	Wells Fargo
JPMorgan Chase	

HISTORICAL FINANCIALS
Company Type: Public

Income Statement — FYE: December 31

	REVENUE ($ mil.)	NET INCOME ($ mil.)	NET PROFIT MARGIN	EMPLOYEES
12/18	134.3	24.9	18.6%	341
12/17	119.0	25.2	21.2%	330
12/16	100.0	17.2	17.3%	318
12/15	89.7	15.9	17.8%	314
12/14	88.7	19.3	21.8%	285
Annual Growth	10.9%	6.6%	—	4.6%

2018 Year-End Financials

Debt ratio: 12.8%
Return on equity: 13.2%
Cash ($ mil.): 97.1
Current ratio: 0.17
Long-term debt ($ mil.): 150.0
No. of shares (mil.): 12.3
Dividends
Yield: 2.5%
Payout: 20.3%
Market value ($ mil.): 276.0

	STOCK PRICE ($) FY Close	P/E High/Low	PER SHARE ($) Earnings	Dividends	Book Value
12/18	22.33	15 10	2.00	0.56	16.05
12/17	22.40	15 10	2.01	0.56	14.43
12/16	20.90	16 10	1.38	0.56	12.91
12/15	16.06	17 10	1.25	2.53	12.10
12/14	20.53	19 11	1.49	0.47	13.55
Annual Growth	2.1%	— —	7.6%	4.5%	4.3%

Masimo Corp.

As important as the blood running through your veins is the oxygen it carries. Masimo knows that and makes tools that monitor arterial blood-oxygen saturation levels and pulse rates in patients. The company's product range which is based on Signal Extraction Technology (SET) offers pulse oximeters in both handheld and stand-alone (bedside) form. Product benefits include the provision of real-time information and elimination of signal interference such as patient movements. In addition to general product sales Masimo licenses SET-based products to dozens of medical equipment manufacturers including Philips Atom Mindray North America GE Medical Medtronic Spacelabs and Zoll.

Operations
Masimo's primary products include patient monitoring solutions sensor products and other devices and accessories such as adapter cables. The company also makes revenue on royalties.

Geographic Reach
While the US accounts for about two-thirds of its product sales Masimo is working to grow its operations in Africa Asia Australia Europe and the Middle East.

The company has locations in Switzerland Canada and Japan as well as two manufacturing facilities in Mexico.

Sales and Marketing
Masimo markets its products globally through direct sales representatives and distributors. Customers include hospitals alternative care entities and wholesalers. Two distributors Owens & Minor and Cardinal Health each account for more than 10% of annual sales.

The company has partnerships with several group purchasing organizations (GPOs) to facilitate increased direct sales of pulse oximetry products to hospitals.

Advertising costs for fiscal 2017 totaled $12.8 million compared to around $11 million in 2016.

Financial Performance
Masimo's revenues have been rising steadily for the past five years as product sales have grown. However net income has been more volatile rising significantly in 2016 due to a $270000 settlement award but falling back down the following year.

In 2017 revenue increased 15% to $798.1 million. Both product sales across all geographic segments and royalty income rose that year. The company's base of installed circuit boards and pulse oximeters nearly reached 1.6 million units a 6% increase for 2017. With that higher base sales of consumable and reusable sensor products also increased.

Net income fell 56% to $131.6 million in 2017 as the company had higher costs of sales and operating expenses (primarily increased R&D expenses) related to its growing business.

The company ended 2017 with $315.5 million in net cash $7.3 million more than it had at the end of 2016. This was largely due to the decrease in net income. Operating activities provided $56.1 million in cash while investing activities used $47.9 million and financing activities used $4.1 million.

Strategy
Masimo's strategies for growth include expanding its presence in the pulse oximetry market getting its products into more types of patient care

settings and selling more of its rainbow SET products and Root patient-monitoring products to hospitals and other care settings. The company's R&D efforts focus on novel products as well as improvement to existing products. It is expanding the applications of its rainbow products which measure multiple blood components at once; it is also adding products that reduce the invasiveness of testing and that provide remote monitoring and alarm capabilities.

To branch out beyond its traditionally targeted emergency and critical care setting markets Masimo is promoting existing products (and adding new products) to meet the general treatment needs of hospitals and non-hospital environments. For example the company is promoting its SET technology as ideal for use by home care agencies post-acute care hospitals and sleep diagnostic centers. It has also launched new handheld products that allow for fast and simple measurement of perimeters in a variety of care settings. The company expects moves such as these to greatly expand its presence in non-critical care markets.

Masimo also expands by entering new OEM licensing agreements; by widening agreements with wholesale distributors; and by making occasional acquisitions.

However the company is somewhat slow to breaking into new niches which has made it lose a bit of its market share to new competitors.

EXECUTIVES

Chairman and CEO, Joe E. Kiani, age 55, $883,518 total compensation
EVP and CIO, Yongsam Lee, age 55, $340,704 total compensation
President Worldwide OEM Business and Blood Management, Rick Fishel, age 61, $357,574 total compensation
EVP Business Development, Paul R. Jansen, age 48
COO, Anand Sampath, age 53, $369,277 total compensation
EVP Finance and CFO, Mark P. de Raad, age 59, $363,034 total compensation
EVP General Counsel and Corporate Secretary, Tom McClenahan, age 46
President Masimo Worldwide Sales Professional Services and Medical Affairs, Jon Coleman, age 55, $354,103 total compensation
VP Quality, Glenn Pohly
Regional Vice President, Michelle Hahn
Vice President Human Resources, Tracy Miller
Global Vice President Of Sales, Brad Snow
Senior Vice President, Dan Brothman
Executive Vice President, Raul Bennis
Vice President Oem Business, Nikolai Marinow
Vice President Design, Nicholas Barker
Vice President Global Government Affairs, Jim Bialick
Regional Vice President Of Sales, Kelsey Engel
Vice President Algorithm Development, Walter Weber
Regional Vice President, Ryan Abel
Executive Vice President Business Development, Tao Levy
Senior Vice President Of Finance, Todd Koning
Vice President, Terry Meehan
Auditors: Grant Thornton LLP

LOCATIONS

HQ: Masimo Corp.
52 Discovery, Irvine, CA 92618
Phone: 949 297-7000
Web: www.masimo.com

PRODUCTS/OPERATIONS

2017 Sales

	$ mil.	% of total
Products	741.3	93
Royalties	56.8	7
Total	798.1	100

COMPETITORS

Bio-logic   GE Healthcare
CAS Medical   Medtronic
Criticare

HISTORICAL FINANCIALS

Company Type: Public

Income Statement   FYE: December 29

	REVENUE ($ mil.)	NET INCOME ($ mil.)	NET PROFIT MARGIN	EMPLOYEES
12/18	858.2	193.5	22.5%	4,500
12/17	798.1	131.6	16.5%	4,600
12/16*	694.6	300.6	43.3%	4,293
01/16	630.1	83.3	13.2%	3,700
01/15	586.6	72.5	12.4%	3,600
Annual Growth	10.0%	27.8%	—	5.7%

*Fiscal year change

2018 Year-End Financials

Debt ratio: —   No. of shares (mil.): 53.0
Return on equity: 23.1%   Dividends
Cash ($ mil.): 552.4   Yield: —
Current ratio: 5.32   Payout: —
Long-term debt ($ mil.): —   Market value ($ mil.): 5,604.0

	STOCK PRICE ($) FY Close	P/E High/Low	PER SHARE ($) Earnings	Dividends	Book Value
12/18	105.56	34 22	3.45	0.00	18.25
12/17	84.80	41 26	2.36	0.00	13.69
12/16*	67.40	11 6	5.65	0.00	11.16
01/16	41.51	27 16	1.55	0.00	5.52
01/15	25.88	24 16	1.30	0.00	5.82
Annual Growth	42.1%	—	27.6%	—	33.1%

*Fiscal year change

Mastech Digital Inc

EXECUTIVES

National Managing Director, Jeremy Pigott
National Account Manager, Paul Rossmont
Senior Vice President Of Human Resources, Vishwanath Shetty
Vice President East Central, Jim Pagliero
Auditors: UHY LLP

LOCATIONS

HQ: Mastech Digital Inc
1305 Cherrington Parkway, Building 210, Suite 400, Moon Township, PA 15108
Phone: 412 787-2100
Web: www.mastechdigital.com

COMPETITORS

Adecco   Modis
CDI   NTT Data
COMFORCE   On Assignment
Computer Task Group Pomeroy IT
Hudson Global   Resources Global
Kelly Services   Professionals
Kforce   Volt Information

HISTORICAL FINANCIALS

Company Type: Public

Income Statement   FYE: December 31

	REVENUE ($ mil.)	NET INCOME ($ mil.)	NET PROFIT MARGIN	EMPLOYEES
12/18	177.1	6.6	3.8%	1,680
12/17	147.8	1.6	1.1%	1,530
12/16	132.0	2.5	1.9%	1,125
12/15	123.4	2.7	2.2%	970
12/14	113.5	3.4	3.0%	900
Annual Growth	11.8%	18.2%	—	16.9%

2018 Year-End Financials

Debt ratio: 41.8%   No. of shares (mil.): 10.9
Return on equity: 21.7%   Dividends
Cash ($ mil.): 1.2   Yield: —
Current ratio: 2.27   Payout: —
Long-term debt ($ mil.): 34.1   Market value ($ mil.): 69.0

	STOCK PRICE ($) FY Close	P/E High/Low	PER SHARE ($) Earnings	Dividends	Book Value
12/18	6.30	35 10	0.60	0.00	3.12
12/17	10.06	80 37	0.17	0.00	2.49
12/16	6.81	29 22	0.28	0.00	2.12
12/15	7.31	36 22	0.31	0.00	1.82
12/14	10.62	44 21	0.39	0.00	1.49
Annual Growth	(12.2%)	—	11.7%	—	20.2%

MasterCraft Boat Holdings Inc

Auditors: DELOITTE & TOUCHE LLP

LOCATIONS

HQ: MasterCraft Boat Holdings Inc
100 Cherokee Cove Drive, Vonore, TN 37885
Phone: 423 884-2221
Web: www.mastercraft.com

HISTORICAL FINANCIALS

Company Type: Public

Income Statement   FYE: June 30

	REVENUE ($ mil.)	NET INCOME ($ mil.)	NET PROFIT MARGIN	EMPLOYEES
06/19	466.3	21.3	4.6%	1,195
06/18	332.7	39.6	11.9%	882
06/17	228.6	19.5	8.6%	490
06/16	221.6	10.2	4.6%	510
06/15	214.3	5.5	2.6%	470
Annual Growth	21.4%	40.2%	—	26.3%

2019 Year-End Financials

Debt ratio: 45.7%
Return on equity: 34.2%
Cash ($ mil.): 5.8
Current ratio: 0.79
Long-term debt ($ mil.): 105.0
No. of shares (mil.): 18.7
Dividends
  Yield: —
  Payout: —
Market value ($ mil.): 368.0

	STOCK PRICE ($) FY Close	P/E High/Low	PER SHARE ($) Earnings	Dividends	Book Value
06/19	19.59	33 16	1.14	0.00	3.85
06/18	28.95	15 8	2.12	0.00	2.81
06/17	19.55	19 10	1.05	0.00	0.63
06/16	11.05	28 18	0.56	4.30	(0.45)
Annual Growth	21.0%	— —	26.7%		

Matador Resources Co

Auditors: KPMG LLP

LOCATIONS

HQ: Matador Resources Co
  5400 LBJ Freeway, Suite 1500, Dallas, TX 75240
Phone: 972 371-5200
Web: www.matadorresources.com

HISTORICAL FINANCIALS
Company Type: Public

Income Statement   FYE: December 31

	REVENUE ($ mil.)	NET INCOME ($ mil.)	NET PROFIT MARGIN	EMPLOYEES
12/18	899.6	274.2	30.5%	264
12/17	544.2	125.8	23.1%	217
12/16	264.4	(97.4)	—	165
12/15	316.1	(679.7)	—	151
12/14	431.0	110.7	25.7%	99
Annual Growth	20.2%	25.4%		27.8%

2018 Year-End Financials

Debt ratio: 37.5%
Return on equity: 19.2%
Cash ($ mil.): 83.9
Current ratio: 0.93
Long-term debt ($ mil.): 1,297.8
No. of shares (mil.): 116.3
Dividends
  Yield: —
  Payout: —
Market value ($ mil.): 1,807.0

	STOCK PRICE ($) FY Close	P/E High/Low	PER SHARE ($) Earnings	Dividends	Book Value
12/18	15.53	14 6	2.41	0.00	14.52
12/17	31.13	25 17	1.23	0.00	10.66
12/16	25.76	— —	(1.07)	0.00	6.94
12/15	19.77	— —	(8.34)	0.00	5.70
12/14	20.23	19 9	1.56	0.00	11.81
Annual Growth	(6.4%)	— —	11.5%		5.3%

Match Group Inc

Auditors: Ernst & Young LLP

LOCATIONS

HQ: Match Group Inc
  8750 North Central Expressway, Suite 1400, Dallas, TX 75231
Phone: 214 576-9352
Web: www.matchgroupinc.com

HISTORICAL FINANCIALS
Company Type: Public

Income Statement   FYE: December 31

	REVENUE ($ mil.)	NET INCOME ($ mil.)	NET PROFIT MARGIN	EMPLOYEES
12/18	1,729.8	477.9	27.6%	1,500
12/17	1,330.6	350.1	26.3%	1,400
12/16	1,222.5	171.4	14.0%	5,100
12/15	1,020.4	120.3	11.8%	4,800
12/14	888.2	147.7	16.6%	4,800
Annual Growth	18.1%	34.1%	—	(25.2%)

2018 Year-End Financials

Debt ratio: 73.8%
Return on equity: 152.4%
Cash ($ mil.): 186.9
Current ratio: 0.97
Long-term debt ($ mil.): 1,515.9
No. of shares (mil.): 278.3
Dividends
  Yield: 4.6%
  Payout: 168.0%
Market value ($ mil.): 11,906.0

	STOCK PRICE ($) FY Close	P/E High/Low	PER SHARE ($) Earnings	Dividends	Book Value
12/18	42.77	34 18	1.61	2.00	0.45
12/17	31.31	24 12	1.18	0.00	1.83
12/16	17.10	29 13	0.64	0.00	1.94
12/15	13.55	22 19	0.65	0.00	1.12
Annual Growth	46.7%	— —	35.3%		(26.2%)

Maxus Realty Trust Inc

Auditors: Mayer Hoffman McCann P.C.

LOCATIONS

HQ: Maxus Realty Trust Inc
  104 Armour Road, P.O. Box 34279, North Kansas City, MO 64116
Phone: 816 303-4500   Fax: 816 221-1829
Web: www.mrti.com

COMPETITORS

AMLI Residential
Apartment Investment and Management
Camden Property
CenterPoint Properties
Duke Realty
Equity Office
Equity Residential
Investors Real Estate Trust
Paragon Real Estate Trust

HISTORICAL FINANCIALS
Company Type: Public

Income Statement   FYE: December 31

	REVENUE ($ mil.)	NET INCOME ($ mil.)	NET PROFIT MARGIN	EMPLOYEES
12/18	113.7	6.4	5.6%	0
12/17	89.1	13.9	15.7%	0
12/16	74.3	14.6	19.7%	0
12/15	60.5	4.5	7.5%	0
12/14	55.5	13.4	24.1%	0
Annual Growth	19.6%	(16.8%)	—	—

2018 Year-End Financials

Debt ratio: 82.3%
Return on equity: 14.7%
Cash ($ mil.): 16.4
Current ratio: 0.42
Long-term debt ($ mil.): 693.2
No. of shares (mil.): 1.1
Dividends
  Yield: 0.0%
  Payout: 144.7%
Market value ($ mil.): 132.0

	STOCK PRICE ($) FY Close	P/E High/Low	PER SHARE ($) Earnings	Dividends	Book Value
12/18	112.00	26 17	4.63	6.70	35.88
12/17	100.00	10 5	10.44	5.00	38.31
12/16	75.00	7 4	11.34	3.55	30.51
12/15	49.00	15 7	3.33	1.50	20.83
12/14	32.00	3 2	10.26	0.00	18.70
Annual Growth	36.8%	— —	(18.0%)	—	17.7%

Medical Properties Trust Inc

Hospitals trust Medical Properties to provide the leases under which their facilities operate. The self-advised real estate investment trust (REIT) invests in and owns more than 120 health care facilities including acute care hospitals inpatient rehabilitation hospitals and wellness centers in 25 US states and Germany. California and Texas combined account for nearly 50% of the REIT's annual revenue. It leases the facilities to more than 25 hospital operating companies under long-term triple-net leases where the tenant bears most of the operating costs. Prime Healthcare Services and Ernest Health are among the REIT's largest clients. Medical Properties Trust entered the European health care market in 2013.

Geographic Reach

Alabama-based Medical Properties Trust (MPT) has properties in 25 US states and Germany. The REIT has 32 properties in Texas and 14 in California representing about 24% and 26% of its revenue respectively. New Jersey is another important market for the firm accounting for about 7% of annual revenue.

Financial Performance

MPT reported $242.5 million in revenue in 2013 an increase of 20% versus 2012. Net income increased by 8% over the same period to $97 million. The REIT has experienced rapid revenue and profit growth in recent years as it portfolio of properties has grown and rents and other income increased. Annual escalation provisions in its leases have contributed to the growth of rental revenue. Cash flow increased by $73 million in 2013 over 2013 due to an increase in cash from financing activities. MPT has more than $3 billion in assets.

Strategy

The REIT is focused on expanding and diversifying its tenant roster both in terms of the types of hospitals it owns and location. To that end Medical Properties Trust entered the European market in late 2013 with the purchase of 11 rehabilitation facilities in Germany from RHM Klinik-und Altenheimbetriebe GmbH & Co. for ?184 million ($254.3 million) The REIT which is looking to expand in other markets beyond the US was attracted by Germany's strong economic position and the health care environment. Back home in the US the REIT has been investing heavily in acquisitions and other related investments in 2013 and 2012 amounting to about $655 million and $621.5 million respectively. Purchases included three general acute-care hospitals from IASIS

Healthcare LLC as well as two acute-care hospitals in Kansas.

The firm owns a variety of health care related properties including acute care hospitals inpatient rehabilitation hospitals long-term acute care hospitals wellness centers medical office buildings and surgical facilities.

Mergers and Acquisitions

In 2016 MPT bought the real estate assets of nine hospitals operated by Steward Health Care in a $1.25 billion transaction; the deal included a $50 million investment in Steward as well a right of first refusal to buy future Steward facilities. The following year the REIT acquired 11 hospitals from IASIS Healthcare (which was then acquired by Steward) for $1.4 billion.

EXECUTIVES

EVP CFO and Director, R. Steven Hamner, age 62, $575,000 total compensation
Chairman President and CEO, Edward K. Aldag, age 55, $950,000 total compensation
EVP COO Treasurer and Secretary, Emmett E. McLean, age 63, $525,000 total compensation
Vice Chairman, William G. McKenzie, age 60
Auditors: PricewaterhouseCoopers LLP

LOCATIONS

HQ: Medical Properties Trust Inc
1000 Urban Center Drive, Suite 501, Birmingham, AL 35242
Phone: 205 969-3755   **Fax:** 205 969-3756
Web: www.medicalpropertiestrust.com

PRODUCTS/OPERATIONS

2015 Sales by Property Type

	% of total
General acute care hospitals	58
Rehabilitation hospitals	30
Long-term acute care hospitals	12
Wellness centers	—
Total	100

COMPETITORS

Extendicare	Omega Healthcare
HCP	Investors
Healthcare Realty	Physicians Realty
Trust	Universal Health
LTC Properties	Realty
National Health	Ventas
Investors	Welltower

HISTORICAL FINANCIALS

Company Type: Public

Income Statement   FYE: December 31

	REVENUE ($ mil.)	NET INCOME ($ mil.)	NET PROFIT MARGIN	EMPLOYEES
12/18	784.5	1,016.6	129.6%	77
12/17	704.7	289.7	41.1%	66
12/16	541.1	225.0	41.6%	54
12/15	441.8	139.6	31.6%	50
12/14	312.5	50.5	16.2%	45
Annual Growth	25.9%	111.8%	—	14.4%

2018 Year-End Financials

Debt ratio: 45.6%
Return on equity: 24.3%
Cash ($ mil.): 820.8
Current ratio: 4.90
Long-term debt ($ mil.): 4,037.3
No. of shares (mil.): 370.6
Dividends
  Yield: 6.2%
  Payout: 36.2%
Market value ($ mil.): 5,960.0

	STOCK PRICE ($) FY Close	P/E High/Low	PER SHARE ($) Earnings	Dividends	Book Value
12/18	16.08	6 4	2.76	1.00	12.27
12/17	13.78	17 15	0.82	0.96	10.48
12/16	12.30	18 11	0.86	0.91	10.13
12/15	11.51	24 17	0.63	0.88	8.88
12/14	13.78	49 42	0.29	0.84	8.00
Annual Growth	3.9%	— —	75.6%	4.5%	11.3%

Medifast Inc

Medifast tries to help people slim down and shape up... fast. The company develops and sells Medifast brand health and diet products including food and beverages (meal replacement shakes bars) as well as disease management products for diabetics. Until 2018 Medifast operated through two segments Medifast and Franchise Medifast Weight Control Centers (MWCC) and Wholesale. The Medifast segment included Direct (customers order Medifast products online) and OPTAVIA (formerly Take Shape For Life personal coaching division with independent contractor "health coaches") operations. MWCC and Wholesale covers franchised brick-and-mortar walk-in clinics.

Operations

Medifast operates through multiple distribution channels. Its OPTAVIA personal coaching division accounts for about 85% of total sales. Medifast Direct the online and call center sales division brings in another 10% of sales. Weight control support centers provide fee-based consultation services and branded products. Medifast Wholesale sold products through physicians' offices until 2018 when the company discontinued the practice.

Subsidiary Jason Pharmaceuticals makes some of the company's products.

Geographic Reach

Medifast operates a manufacturing plant in Owings Mills Maryland. It has distribution facilities in Ridgley Maryland and Dallas. The firm has a raw materials warehouse in Arbutus Maryland.

MWCC has more than 15 franchised support centers in Arizona California Louisiana Minnesota and Wisconsin. It has some 20 re-seller locations in California Maryland and Pennsylvania.

Sales and Marketing

Medifast uses multiple marketing strategies to reach its target audiences. It uses word-of-mouth communications digital marketing public relations events direct mail and social media channels. Advertising costs totaled $7.7 million in 2017 versus $9.4 million in 2016 and $15.3 million in 2015.

Financial Performance

After years of declines Medifast's revenues have been back on the rise. Net income has been somewhat volatile but annual cash flow has risen significantly.

Revenue increased 10% to $301.6 million in 2017 thanks to 15% growth in the OPTAVIA division which the company sees as key to its future growth. Medifast had an increased number of coaches and higher revenue per coach largely due to a 2016 price increase. That growth was partially offset by declining sales in the other businesses. Direct sales declined as the company continued to cut back on advertising. MWCC sales declined because fewer franchise centers were in operation — that number was cut by more than half during the year and the remaining centers had a slowdown in activity. Wholesale revenue also declined as the company enforced compliance requirements of distributors resulting in the loss of certain accounts.

Thanks to growth in the OPTAVIA division and the higher revenue as well as higher interest and other income net income jumped 56% to $27.7 million that year.

The company ended 2017 with $75.1 million in cash $22.7 more than it had at the beginning of the year. Operating activities provided $43.3 million in cash but financing activities (payments of dividends) used $17.4 million and investing activities used $3.2 million.

Strategy

While the ranks of the overweight are growing Medifast is also working to tailor its products to the rapidly growing population of diabetics. It maintains an in-house call center and support staff with registered dieticians on hand to assist customers.

At the beginning of 2018 the company discontinued the sales of products through physicians thus reducing the complexity of its product distribution. Even its OPTAVIA coaches simply direct customers to the website or call centers and receive commissions for orders placed there. Medifast is focused on growing the OPTAVIA business by adding new coaches; by the end of 2017 it had some 15000 coaches.

Medifast has faced an influx of competitors to the market which has led to a decline in its market presence. It has been slow to introduce new products thereby slipping in competitiveness. Additionally the company has had problems with having too much inventory on hand including older Medifast-branded items.

The company plans to expand into Hong Kong and Singapore in early 2019 citing growing demand for its lifestyle products in those markets.

Company Background

Medifast's promotion and distribution model has changed over time. When it was founded in 1993 the company primarily sold its products through doctor's offices. Customers received supervision from their family physician who in turn received commissions on any products sold. However as physicians had increasingly less time to spend with patients the method grew less effective. At the beginning of 2018 the company discontinued the sales of products through physicians thus reducing the complexity of its product distribution.

The company also exited the corporate support center model in 2014. It sold 41 centers to franchise partners and closed its remaining 34 corporate centers.

EXECUTIVES

CEO, Daniel R. (Dan) Chard, age 54, $172,268 total compensation
EVP and General Counsel, Jason L. Groves, age 48
CFO, Timothy G. Robinson, age 56, $331,206 total compensation
President Take Shape For Life, Mehrnaz M. Ameli, age 48, $301,488 total compensation
EVP Human Resources, Jeanne M. City, age 60, $232,727 total compensation
Corporate Vice President Of Infrastructure and Development, Richard Law

Vice President and Corporate Controller, Joe Kelleman
Vice President of Product Development, Douglas Zimmermann
Vice President Ecommerce And Digital Marketing, Ali Landow
Vice President, Doug Zimmermann
Executive Vice President Coach Success and Market President Optavia Usa, Nicholas Johnson
Chairman, Michael C. MacDonald, age 66
Board Of Directors, Donald Reilly
Auditors: RSM US LLP

LOCATIONS

HQ: Medifast Inc
100 International Drive, Baltimore, MD 21202
Phone: 410 581-8042
Web: www.medifastnow.com

PRODUCTS/OPERATIONS

2017 Sales

	$ mil.	% of total
OPTAVIA	256.6	85
Medifast Direct	31.9	11
MWCC	12.2	4
Medifast Wholesale	1.0	-
Total	**301.7**	**100**

Selected Subsidiaries
Jason Enterprises Inc.
Jason Pharmaceuticals Inc.
Jason Properties LLC
Medifast Franchise Systems Inc.
Medifast Nutrition Inc.
OPTAVIA LLC
Seven Crondall Associates LLC

COMPETITORS

Atkins Nutritionals
Herbalife Ltd.
Jenny Craig
NBTY
Nutrisystem
Reliv' International
Slim-Fast
USANA Health Sciences
Weight Watchers International
eDiets.com

HISTORICAL FINANCIALS
Company Type: Public

Income Statement
FYE: December 31

	REVENUE ($ mil.)	NET INCOME ($ mil.)	NET PROFIT MARGIN	EMPLOYEES
12/18	501.0	55.7	11.1%	420
12/17	301.5	27.7	9.2%	399
12/16	274.5	17.8	6.5%	422
12/15	272.7	20.0	7.4%	425
12/14	285.2	13.1	4.6%	579
Annual Growth	15.1%	43.4%	—	(7.7%)

2018 Year-End Financials
Debt ratio: —
Return on equity: 51.2%
Cash ($ mil.): 81.3
Current ratio: 2.41
Long-term debt ($ mil.): —
No. of shares (mil.): 11.8
Dividends
  Yield: 1.7%
  Payout: 47.4%
Market value ($ mil.): 1,484.0

	STOCK PRICE ($) FY Close	P/E High/Low		PER SHARE ($) Earnings	Dividends	Book Value
12/18	125.02	55	14	4.62	2.19	9.19
12/17	69.81	32	17	2.29	1.44	9.07
12/16	41.63	28	18	1.49	1.07	8.09
12/15	30.38	20	16	1.66	0.25	7.51
12/14	33.55	34	23	1.03	0.00	6.66
Annual Growth	38.9%	—	—	45.5%	—	8.4%

Medpace Holdings Inc

Auditors: DELOITTE & TOUCHE LLP

LOCATIONS

HQ: Medpace Holdings Inc
5375 Medpace Way, Cincinnati, OH 45227
Phone: 513 579-9911
Web: www.medpace.com

HISTORICAL FINANCIALS
Company Type: Public

Income Statement
FYE: December 31

	REVENUE ($ mil.)	NET INCOME ($ mil.)	NET PROFIT MARGIN	EMPLOYEES
12/18	704.5	73.1	10.4%	2,900
12/17	436.1	39.1	9.0%	2,500
12/16	421.5	13.4	3.2%	2,500
12/15	359.0	(8.6)	—	2,300
12/14	248.5	(14.3)	—	1,700
Annual Growth	29.8%	—	—	14.3%

2018 Year-End Financials
Debt ratio: 8.2%
Return on equity: 13.3%
Cash ($ mil.): 23.2
Current ratio: 0.69
Long-term debt ($ mil.): 79.7
No. of shares (mil.): 35.6
Dividends
  Yield: —
  Payout: —
Market value ($ mil.): 1,888.0

	STOCK PRICE ($) FY Close	P/E High/Low		PER SHARE ($) Earnings	Dividends	Book Value
12/18	52.93	31	16	1.97	0.00	16.53
12/17	36.26	38	22	0.98	0.00	14.20
12/16	36.07	100	71	0.37	0.00	15.02
Annual Growth	21.1%	—	—	—130.7%	—	4.9%

Mercantile Bank Corp.

Mercantile Bank Corporation is the holding company for Mercantile Bank of Michigan (formerly Mercantile Bank of West Michigan) which boasts assets of nearly $3 billion and operates more than 50 branches in central and western Michigan around Grand Rapids Holland and Lansing. The bank targets local consumers and businesses offering standard deposit services such as checking and savings accounts CDs IRAs and health savings accounts. Commercial loans make up more than three-fourths of the bank's loan portfolio. Outside of banking subsidiary Mercantile Insurance Center sells insurance products.

Operations
Mercantile Bank Corp. generated 82% of its total revenue from loan interest (including fees) in 2014 with securities interest contributing another 8% to total revenue. Service charges on deposit and sweep accounts and credit and debit card fees made up another 5% of Mercantile's total revenue while its mortgage banking income generated another 2%.

Sales and Marketing
Mercantile provides its banking services to businesses individuals and government organizations. Its commercial banking services mostly cater to small- to medium-sized businesses.

The company spent $1.315 million on advertising in 2014 compared to $1.113 million and $1.167 million in 2013 and 2012 respectively.

Financial Performance
Mercantile Bank Corp's revenues had been declining for a number of years as its loan business withered while profits have remained mostly flat.

The company had a breakout year in 2014 however after its historic acquisition of FirstBank Corp. The bank's revenue skyrocketed by 53% to $99.15 million (the highest level since 2009) mostly as the acquisition nearly doubled its loan assets and boosted its interest income on loans and securities by significant amounts. The bank's non-interest income also grew by 46% thanks to higher fee income across the board also resulting from the recent acquisition.

Higher revenue and a $3.2 million reduction in loan loss provisions with a stronger credit portfolio in 2014 also pushed the company's net income up by 2% to $17.33 million for the year. Mercantile's operating cash declined by 50% to $14.41 million due to changes in accrued interest and other liabilities during the year.

Strategy
Mercantile Bank Corporation has been growing its loan business and branch network reach through strategic acquisitions of smaller banks and bank branches. Its mid-2014 acquisition of Firstbank Corporation was perhaps the most effective to date as the purchase doubled its assets and boosted the size of its branch network nearly seven-fold from seven branches to a whopping 53.

Mergers and Acquisitions
In June 2014 Mercantile Bank Corp. purchased Firstbank Corp of Alma Michigan for a total purchase price of $173 million adding 46 branches and $1.3 billion in assets. The deal which made Mercantile the third-largest bank based in the state also expanded the bank's service offerings diversified its loan portfolio boosted its loan origination capacity and significantly extended its geographic footprint into Michigan's lower peninsula.

EXECUTIVES

SVP CFO and Treasurer Mercantile Bank Corporation and SVP and CFO Mercantile Bank of Michigan, Charles E. (Chuck) Christmas, age 53, $263,000 total compensation
President and CEO, Robert B. Kaminski, age 57, $315,000 total compensation
EVP Corporate Finance and Strategic Planning Mercantile Bank Corporation and Mercantile Bank of Michigan, Samuel G. Stone, age 74, $159,833 total compensation
Vice President Treasury Sales, John Byl
Vice President Electronic Banking, Shannon Tramontin
Vice President Security, Paul Wegener
Assistant Vice President Human Resources Specialist, Tina Van Valkenburg
Assistant Vice President, Amy Ervin
Senior Vice President Business Development Officer, Brian Talbot
Vice President Commercial Loan Officer, Jeff Hicks
Branch Manager Vice President, Andrea Spagnuolo
Vice President, Teresa Rupert
Assistant Vice President, Jennifer Harris
Senior Vice President, Mike Siminski
Senior Vice President Corporate Banking, Matt Zimmerman

Mortgage Operations Manager Vice President, Lori Schafer
VICE PRESIDENT COMMERCIAL LENDER, Andrew Miedema
Assistant Vice President Human Resources Administrator, Kate Glover
Assistant Vice President Assistant Controller, Peggy Coutchie
Senior Vice President Information Systems Manager, Allen Smith
Assistant Vice President Commercial Loan Officer, Justin Horn
Vice President, Martin Smith
Vice President Corporate Banking, Bob Klimczak
Assistant Vice President Mortgage Operations Manager, Sarah Smith
Senior Vice President General Counsel Chief Operating Officer and Secretary of the Company and Ban, Bob Worthington
Vice President Treasury Sales Officer, Tim Ladd
Vice President, Holly Williams
Vice President Commercial Loan Risk Assets, Traci Courter
Vice President, Betsy Mccue
Vice President Risk Asset Management, Danna Mathiesen
Assistant Vice President Leonard Branch Manager, Daniel Zink
Senior Vice President, Michael Erfourth
Vice President, Jim Kloostra
Vice President, Cindy Carter
Assistant Vice President Mortgage Lender, Debra Fuller
Senior Vice President Commercial Lending, Michael Stapleton
Chairman, Michael H. Price, age 62
Auditors: BDO USA, LLP

LOCATIONS

HQ: Mercantile Bank Corp.
310 Leonard Street N.W., Grand Rapids, MI 49504
Phone: 616 406-3000
Web: www.mercbank.com

PRODUCTS/OPERATIONS

2014 Sales

	$ mil.	% of total
Interest income		
Loans and leases including fees	80.8	82
Securities taxable	6.4	6
Securities tax-exempt	1.6	2
Other	0.2	-
Noninterest income		
Service charges on accounts	2.6	3
Credit and debit card fees	2.5	2
Mortgage banking activities	1.7	2
Other	3.3	3
Total	**99.1**	**100**

COMPETITORS

Chemical Financial	Flagstar Bancorp
ChoiceOne Financial Services	Huntington Bancshares
Comerica	Independent Bank (MI)
Fifth Third	Macatawa Bank

HISTORICAL FINANCIALS
Company Type: Public

Income Statement
FYE: December 31

	ASSETS ($ mil.)	NET INCOME ($ mil.)	INCOME AS % OF ASSETS	EMPLOYEES
12/18	3,363.9	42.0	1.2%	693
12/17	3,286.7	31.2	1.0%	701
12/16	3,082.5	31.9	1.0%	682
12/15	2,903.5	27.0	0.9%	701
12/14	2,893.3	17.3	0.6%	731
Annual Growth	3.8%	24.8%	—	(1.3%)

2018 Year-End Financials
Return on assets: 1.2%
Return on equity: 11.3%
Long-term debt ($ mil.): —
No. of shares (mil.): 16.5
Sales ($ mil): 160.9
Dividends
Yield: 3.2%
Payout: 72.1%
Market value ($ mil.): 467.0

	STOCK PRICE ($) FY Close	P/E High/Low	PER SHARE ($) Earnings	Dividends	Book Value
12/18	28.26	15 11	2.53	1.68	22.70
12/17	35.37	20 15	1.90	0.74	22.05
12/16	37.70	19 11	1.96	1.16	20.76
12/15	24.54	16 12	1.62	0.58	20.41
12/14	21.02	19 15	1.28	2.48	19.33
Annual Growth	7.7%	— —	18.6%	(9.3%)	4.1%

Merchants Bancorp (Indiana)

Auditors: BKD, LLP

LOCATIONS

HQ: Merchants Bancorp (Indiana)
410 Monon Blvd., Carmel, IN 46032
Phone: 317 569-7420
Web: www.merchantsbankofindiana.com

HISTORICAL FINANCIALS
Company Type: Public

Income Statement
FYE: December 31

	ASSETS ($ mil.)	NET INCOME ($ mil.)	INCOME AS % OF ASSETS	EMPLOYEES
12/18	3,884.1	62.8	1.6%	259
12/17	3,393.1	54.6	1.6%	194
12/16	2,718.5	33.1	1.2%	157
12/15	2,269.4	28.3	1.3%	0
Annual Growth	19.6%	30.4%	—	—

2018 Year-End Financials
Return on assets: 1.7%
Return on equity: 15.9%
Long-term debt ($ mil.): —
No. of shares (mil.): 28.6
Sales ($ mil): 190.1
Dividends
Yield: 1.2%
Payout: 10.2%
Market value ($ mil.): 573.0

	STOCK PRICE ($) FY Close	P/E High/Low	PER SHARE ($) Earnings	Dividends	Book Value
12/18	19.96	14 9	2.07	0.24	14.68
12/17	19.68	9 7	2.28	0.05	12.81
12/16	0.00	— —	1.47	0.20	9.77
Annual Growth	—	— —	18.7%	9.5%	22.6%

Mercury Systems Inc

Mercury Systems (formerly Mercury Computer Systems) delivers digital signals faster than a wing-footed messenger. The company makes real-time digital signal processing (DSP) systems for the homeland security military and aerospace and telecommunications markets. Its military systems process radar sonar and other signals. It also makes specialized electronics used in semiconductor wafer inspection and airport baggage screeners. Mercury Systems acts as a subcontractor to prime contractors such as Northrop Grumman and Raytheon.

Operations

Mercury Systems operates in two business segments: Mercury Commercial Electronics (MCE) 88% of revenue and Mercury Defense Systems (MDS) 12% of revenue. MCE provides specialized processing subsystems for defense and intelligence applications. Technologies and capabilities include embedded processing modules and subsystems RF and microwave multi-function assemblies and RF and microwave components.

MDS provides capabilities for systems used in electronic warfare (EW) electronic attack and electronic counter measure subsystems signal intelligence and radar environment test and simulation systems.

Geographic Reach

Mercury Systems has research and development centers and other facilities in the US (Alabama California Massachusetts New Hampshire New Jersey and Virginia) Japan and the UK. It generates more than 98% of sales from the US; Europe and the Asia-Pacific region each account for about 1%.

Sales and Marketing

Together Raytheon Northrop Grumman and Lockheed Martin account for more than 60% of revenue.

Financial Performance

Revenue jumped 12.5% in 2015 (ended June) to $234.8 million. In the previous two years revenue was stuck at about $208 million. Revenue in the MCE unit increased 18% in 2015 from projects such as the F-35 jet Patriot missile and the Surface Electronic Warfare Improvement Program (SEWIP).

Mercury posted a profit in 2014 $10.3 million for the first time in three years. Better sales combined with lower operating costs to produce the profit.

Strategy

After a series of acquisitions Mercury restructured some operations as part of integrating new units into the company. It cut about 70 jobs and closed four facilities relocating activities to its Advanced Microelectronics Center in Hudson New Hampshire. It also completed the first phase of the

Chelmsford Massachusetts headquarters consolidation in 2014.

Mercury closed the sale of its Mercury Intelligence Systems in 2015. It sold the unit because it didn't fit into its core business.

As part of its investment in research and development the company opened the second of four planned innovation centers. The new center is at Mercury's Chelmsford headquarters.

Mergers and Acquisitions

Mercury Systems uses acquisitions to add products services and technical capabilities.

In 2019 Mercury agreed to acquire American Panel Corp. which develops large area display technology for about $100 million. The company's capabilities are used in the US Army's Apache attack helicopter and M1A2 Abrams battle tank as well as the F-35 F-15 F-16 and F-18 fighter jets.

In 2017 the company acquired Richland Technologies which develops safety-critical and high integrity systems software and hardware and safety-certification services for mission-critical applications. Richland also develops safety-certifiable embedded graphics software for commercial and military aerospace applications.

The Richland acquisition complements Mercury's 2016 purchase of Creative Electronic Systems which also develops technology for mission critical technology for aviation and aerospace applications. The deals set up Mercury as a provider of secure and safety-critical subsystems for aerospace and defense.

EXECUTIVES

President Mercury Commercial Electronics, Didier M.C. Thibaud, age 58, $324,198 total compensation
EVP CFO and Treasurer, Gerald M. (Gerry) Haines, age 56, $316,796 total compensation
President and CEO, Mark Aslett, age 51, $510,962 total compensation
VP Controller and Chief Accounting Officer, Charles A. Speicher, age 60, $219,750 total compensation
Chairman, Vincent Vitto, age 78
Auditors: KPMG LLP

LOCATIONS

HQ: Mercury Systems Inc
50 Minuteman Road, Andover, MA 01810
Phone: 978 256-1300
Web: www.mrcy.com

PRODUCTS/OPERATIONS

2015 Sales

	$ mil.	% of total
Mercury Commercial Electronics	207.1	88
Mercury Defense Systems	27.4	12
Eliminations	0.3	-
Total	**234.8**	**100**

COMPETITORS

ADLINK Technology	GE Intelligent
Analog Devices	Platforms
Analogic	Kontron
Applied Signal	Pentek
CSP	RadiSys
Concurrent Computer	Spectrum Signal
DRS Technologies	Processing
Dedicated Computing	

HISTORICAL FINANCIALS
Company Type: Public

Income Statement FYE: June 30

	REVENUE ($ mil.)	NET INCOME ($ mil.)	NET PROFIT MARGIN	EMPLOYEES
06/19	654.7	46.7	7.1%	1,661
06/18	493.1	40.8	8.3%	1,320
06/17	408.5	24.8	6.1%	1,159
06/16	270.1	19.7	7.3%	965
06/15	234.8	10.3	4.4%	629
Annual Growth	29.2%	45.7%	—	27.5%

2019 Year-End Financials

Debt ratio: — No. of shares (mil.): 54.2
Return on equity: 4.5% Dividends
Cash ($ mil.): 257.9 Yield: —
Current ratio: 5.94 Payout: —
Long-term debt ($ mil.): — Market value ($ mil.): 3,816.0

	STOCK PRICE ($) FY Close	P/E High/Low	PER SHARE ($) Earnings	Dividends	Book Value
06/19	70.35	77 39	0.96	0.00	23.68
06/18	38.06	61 36	0.86	0.00	16.45
06/17	42.09	71 37	0.58	0.00	15.67
06/16	24.86	42 24	0.56	0.00	12.23
06/15	14.64	55 33	0.31	0.00	10.75
Annual Growth	48.1%	— —	32.7%	—	21.8%

Meridian Bancorp Inc

EXECUTIVES

CFO and Treasurer, Mark L. Abbate, age 64
SVP Consumer and Business Banking, Keith D. Armstrong
Chairman President and CEO Meridian Interstate Bancorp and East Boston Savings Bank, Richard J. Gavegnano, age 71, $311,400 total compensation
EVP Corporate Banking, Frank Romano
EVP Lending, John Migliozzi
EVP and COO, John A. Carroll
SVP Electronic Banking, Mary Hagen
SVP Retail Banking, James Morgan
SVP Residential Lending, Joseph Nash
Vice President, Michael Raftery
Auditors: Wolf & Company, P.C.

LOCATIONS

HQ: Meridian Bancorp Inc
67 Prospect Street, Peabody, MA 01960
Phone: 617 567-1500

PRODUCTS/OPERATIONS

2015 Sales

	$ mil.	% of total
Interest & dividend income		
Interest & fees on loans	118.6	87
Interest on debt securities	1.8	1
Dividends on equity securities	1.6	1
Others	1.3	1
Non-interest income		
Customer service fees	8.0	6
Gain on sales of securities net	2.4	2
Income from bank-owned life insurance	1.2	1
Loan fees	1.0	1
Mortgage banking gains & other income	0.5	-
Total	**136.4**	**100**

Selected Products & Services

Personal
  Deposit Rates
  Investments
  Personal Checking
  Personal Lending
  Personal Online Banking
  Retirement Services
  Savings & CDs
Business
  Business Checking
  Business Lending
  Business Online Banking
  Business Retirement Services
  Business Savings
  Deposit Rates
  Institutional Banking
  Merchant Services
Commercial
  Cash Management
  Commercial Lending
  Corporate Banking
  Deposit Rates

COMPETITORS

Bank of America	Middlesex Savings
Cambridge Financial	Peoples Federal
Citizens Financial	Bancshares Inc.
Group	Sovereign Bank
Eastern Bank	TD Bank USA

HISTORICAL FINANCIALS
Company Type: Public

Income Statement FYE: December 31

	ASSETS ($ mil.)	NET INCOME ($ mil.)	INCOME AS % OF ASSETS	EMPLOYEES
12/18	6,178.6	55.7	0.9%	549
12/17	5,299.4	42.9	0.8%	538
12/16	4,436.0	34.1	0.8%	500
12/15	3,524.5	24.6	0.7%	488
12/14	3,278.5	22.3	0.7%	466
Annual Growth	17.2%	25.7%	—	4.2%

2018 Year-End Financials

Return on assets: 0.9% Dividends
Return on equity: 8.4% Yield: 1.5%
Long-term debt ($ mil.): — Payout: 22.0%
No. of shares (mil.): 53.5 Market value ($ mil.): 767.0
Sales ($ mil): 236.6

	STOCK PRICE ($) FY Close	P/E High/Low	PER SHARE ($) Earnings	Dividends	Book Value
12/18	14.32	20 13	1.06	0.22	12.60
12/17	20.60	25 19	0.82	0.17	11.96
12/16	18.90	29 19	0.65	0.12	11.33
12/15	14.10	31 24	0.46	0.06	10.72
12/14	11.22	27 24	0.42	0.00	10.56
Annual Growth	6.3%	— —	26.0%	—	4.5%

Merit Medical Systems, Inc.

When it comes to medical devices this company believes its merits speak for themselves. Merit Medical Systems makes disposable medical products used during interventional and diagnostic cardiology radiology gastroenterology and pulmonary procedures. The company's products include catheters guide wires needles and tubing used in heart stent procedures pacemaker placement and angioplasties as well as products for endoscopy dialysis and other procedures. Merit Medical sells its products as stand-alone items or in custom-made kits to hospitals and other health care providers as well as to custom packagers and equipment makers worldwide.

Operations
Merit's largest operating segment — accounting for more than 95% of sales — is its cardiovascular division which makes cardiology and radiology devices for the diagnosis of arterial and vascular disease among other conditions. Offerings include stand-alone devices (which account for some 45% of revenues) custom procedure trays and kits inflation devices and catheters. It also includes embolotherapy products which use bioengineered microspheres to create targeted vascular occlusion (the blockage of blood vessels) and drug delivery.

Merit Medical's much smaller endoscopy segment makes devices for gastroenterology and pulmonary treatments including minimally invasive treatment of throat and biliary constriction from malignant tumors. The endoscopy operations are conducted through Merit Medical's Endotek subsidiary.

The company also conducts selected manufacturing of custom medical kits and components for third parties through its OEM division.

Geographic Reach
The US accounts for roughly 60% of Merit's total sales. China is the company's second-largest market bringing in another 10% of sales.

Merit Medical has manufacturing facilities in Ireland the US Mexico the Netherlands France Brazil Australia and Singapore. It has distribution centers in New Zealand India China the US Brazil the Netherlands Australia Canada Russia South Korea Mexico and Japan. The company has R&D facilities in the US Ireland France Singapore and the Netherlands. It has four sales offices in China and Hong Kong.

Sales and Marketing
Merit's marketing and sales efforts in the US and abroad are conducted through a direct sales force as well as through independent distributors and manufacturers. Products are marketed to hospital and clinic-based medical professionals in fields including cardiology radiology gastroenterology pulmonary medicine vascular surgery pain management and thoracic surgery.

The company also has direct or modified sales teams in Canada Europe Australia Brazil Russia Japan China Malaysia South Korea India and the United Arab Emirates.

Financial Performance
Merit Medical's revenues have been growing steadily for the past five years. Net income has generally been trending upward over the same period as the company works to balance costs with earnings. The firm is building up its international business which requires capital but it expects to increase profits because of those activities.

In 2017 revenue increased 21% to $727.9 million. Stand-alone cardiovascular product sales rose 44% that year while catheter sales rose 13% and endoscopy device sales grew 15%. Sales in China increased 22% driving up international sales.

Net income rose 37% to $27.5 million in 2017 thanks to the higher revenue but that gain was partially offset by higher expenses related to Merit's international expansion increased headcount and acquisitions.

The company ended 2017 with $32.3 million in net cash 68% more than it had at then end of 2016. Financing activities contributed $96.5 million in cash and operating activities contributed another $62.7 million. Investing activities primarily business acquisitions used $146.8 million.

Strategy
Though a sizable part of Merit Medical's strategy is growth by acquisition the company also invests about 7% of its annual income in R&D efforts. These activities help it develop new products but Merit is also focused on introducing existing products into new geographic markets.

The company has been transitioning much of its business model in international markets switching from outside distributors to direct sales operations.

Mergers and Acquisitions
Merit Medical acquired Cianna Medical in a deal valued at up to $200 million in 2018. Cianna Medical makes SAVI SCOUT the first US-approved wire-free radar breast tumor localization system for long-term implant capabilities. The system is awaiting approval in Europe.

Also in 2018 the company acquired the Achieve and other branded soft tissue core needle biopsy products from Becton Dickinson for $100 million. It then acquired most of the assets (including the ClariVein specialty infusion and occlusion catheter systems) of Massachusetts-based Vascular Insights for $40 million.

In 2017 Merit bought a custom procedure pack business in Australia from ITL Healthcare for $11.3 million. Also that year it purchased Osseon's vertebral augmentation product line for $6.8 million.

In early 2016 Merit Medical acquired the HeRO Graft product line for end-stage renal disease from CryoLife for $18.5 million. The HeRO Graft is a hemodialysis access graft used in patients who have catheter-dependent because of vein blockage.

EXECUTIVES

Vice President Global Human Resources, Louise Bott
Chairman President and CEO, Fred P. Lampropoulos, age 70, $1,108,654 total compensation
President Merit Endotek, Darla R. Gill
President Merit Technology Group, Joseph (Joe) Wright
EVP Global OEM and Europe the Middle East and Africa, Justin Lampropoulos
CIO, Joseph Pierce
CFO, Bernard Birkett
COO, Ronald A. Frost, age 57, $317,500 total compensation
Vp Benefits And Risk, Brent Bowen
Vice President Engineering, Neil Peterson
Vice President Business Development, George Frioux
Vice President Research and Development, Mark Ferguson
Vice President Regulatory Affairs, Glenn Norton
Vice President Advanced Products Group, Zeke Eller
Senior Vice President Chief Technology Officer, Jason Treft
Vice President Us Sales, Conor Nolan
Vice President Research And Development, Chris Heine
Vice President of Market Development, Monroe May
Vice President Government Affairs, Erin Barry
Executive Vice President Global Intelligence And Security, Nico Walker
Board Member, Gregg Stanger
Auditors: Deloitte & Touche LLP

LOCATIONS
HQ: Merit Medical Systems, Inc.
 1600 West Merit Parkway, South Jordan, UT 84095
Phone: 801 253-1600
Web: www.merit.com

PRODUCTS/OPERATIONS

2017 Sales by Segment

	$ mil.	% of total
Cardiovascular		
Stand-alone devices	275.4	38
Catheters	127.8	17
Custom kits & procedure trays	126.1	17
Inflation devices	79.9	11
Embolization devices	48.5	7
CRM/EP	41.9	6
Endoscopy	27.2	4
Total	**727.9**	**100**

Selected Products
Backstop (waste handling system)
BasixCOMPAK (inflation devices)
Blue Diamond (inflation devices)
Fountain (thrombolytic infusion catheters)
Medallion (specialty syringes)
Merit Disposal Depot (waste handling system)
Meritrans (disposable blood pressure transducer)
Monarch (inflation devices)
Prelude (sheath introducers)
ProGuide (chronic dialysis catheter)

COMPETITORS

3M	Cordis
Abbott Labs	Edwards Lifesciences
AngioDynamics	ICU Medical
B. Braun Medical	Medtronic
Becton Dickinson	Stryker
Boston Scientific	Teleflex
CONMED Corporation	Terumo
Cook Incorporated	

HISTORICAL FINANCIALS
Company Type: Public

Income Statement
FYE: December 31

	REVENUE ($ mil.)	NET INCOME ($ mil.)	NET PROFIT MARGIN	EMPLOYEES
12/18	882.7	42.0	4.8%	5,783
12/17	727.8	27.5	3.8%	4,876
12/16	603.8	20.1	3.3%	4,150
12/15	542.1	23.8	4.4%	3,754
12/14	509.6	22.9	4.5%	3,105
Annual Growth	14.7%	16.3%	—	16.8%

2018 Year-End Financials
Debt ratio: 24.3%
Return on equity: 5.2%
Cash ($ mil.): 67.3
Current ratio: 2.45
Long-term debt ($ mil.): 373.1
No. of shares (mil.): 54.8
Dividends
 Yield: —
 Payout: —
Market value ($ mil.): 3,064.0

	STOCK PRICE ($)	P/E	PER SHARE ($)		
	FY Close	High/Low	Earnings	Dividends	Book Value
12/18	55.81	82 53	0.78	0.00	16.99
12/17	43.20	81 44	0.55	0.00	13.46
12/16	26.50	59 35	0.45	0.00	11.16
12/15	18.59	47 28	0.53	0.00	10.53
12/14	17.33	33 22	0.53	0.00	9.98
Annual Growth	34.0%	— —	10.1%	—	14.2%

Meritage Hospitality Group Inc

EXECUTIVES
Vice President Facility Maintenance, Robert Potts
Auditors: Plante & Moran, PLLC

LOCATIONS
HQ: Meritage Hospitality Group Inc
45 Ottawa Ave SW, Suite 600, Grand Rapids, MI 49503
Phone: 616 776-2600   **Fax:** 616 776-2776
Web: www.meritagehospitality.com

COMPETITORS
American Dairy Queen	McDonald's
B.R. Associates	Quality Dining
Burger King	Subway
Carrols	Tubby's
Hardee's	YUM!
Interfoods	

HISTORICAL FINANCIALS
Company Type: Public

Income Statement   FYE: December 30

	REVENUE ($ mil.)	NET INCOME ($ mil.)	NET PROFIT MARGIN	EMPLOYEES
12/18	435.3	13.0	3.0%	10,000
12/17*	312.5	8.9	2.9%	6,800
01/17	235.7	6.4	2.7%	5,700
01/16	210.0	7.0	3.3%	5,100
12/14	160.2	2.7	1.7%	4,000
Annual Growth	28.4%	47.4%	—	25.7%

*Fiscal year change

2018 Year-End Financials
Debt ratio: 60.6%
Return on equity: 27.2%
Cash ($ mil.): 13.3
Current ratio: 0.32
Long-term debt ($ mil.): 156.1
No. of shares (mil.): 6.2
Dividends
  Yield: 0.0%
  Payout: —
Market value ($ mil.): 110.0

	STOCK PRICE ($)	P/E	PER SHARE ($)		
	FY Close	High/Low	Earnings	Dividends	Book Value
12/18	17.50	— —	(0.00)	0.15	9.17
12/17*	20.00	— —	(0.00)	0.10	6.25
01/17	11.15	— —	(0.00)	0.07	4.37
01/16	11.25	— —	(0.00)	0.06	3.63
12/14	4.97	— —	(0.00)	0.03	2.32
Annual Growth	37.0%		—	49.5%	40.9%

*Fiscal year change

Mesa Laboratories, Inc.

Mesa Laboratories measures its progress by the sales of its measurement devices. And so far it hasn't plateaued. The company makes niche-market electronic measurement testing and recording instruments for medical food processing electronics and aerospace applications. Mesa's products include sensors that record temperature humidity and pressure levels; flow meters for water treatment polymerization and chemical processing applications; and sonic concentration analyzers. The company also makes kidney dialysis treatment products including metering equipment and machines that clean dialyzers (or filters) for reuse. It also provides repair recalibration and certification services.

Operations
The company is organized into four segments - instruments 42% of revenue; biological indicators 40% of revenue; continuous monitoring 13% of revenue and cold chain 5%.

The instruments division includes the DataTrace (data loggers) Bios Torqo (bottle cap test systems) DialyGuard DryCal SureTorque BGI and Nusonics (ultrasonic fluid measurement systems) brands. Biological indicators sold under the Mesa PCD and Apex brands are used by dental offices hospitals and manufacturers of medical devices and pharmaceuticals for quality control testing in sterilization processes.

Continuous monitoring created in 2013 through acquisitions provides temperature control to laboratories that require stable environments such as hospitals blood banks pharmacies and medical device manufacturers. Brands include CheckPoint and AmegaView. The cold chain segment is Mesa's newest also formed through acquisitions. It provides parameter (primarily temperature) monitoring of products consulting services such as compliance monitoring packaging development and validation or mapping of transport and storage containers and thermal packaging products such as coolers boxes insulation materials and phase-change products to control temperature during transport.

Geographic Reach
Mesa Laboratories has manufacturing plants in Lakewood Colorado; Butler New Jersey; Bozeman Montana; and Omaha Nebraska. The new continuous monitoring division operates from Marlton New Jersey; and Emeryville California. The company's sales are split about two-thirds and one-third between the US and international markets.

Sales and Marketing
The company uses a direct sales force as well as distributors in the US. Overseas the company relies on about 270 distributors to gets its products to customers.

Financial Performance
Overall sales grew 19% in 2016 (ended March) to $84 million. Revenue from biological indicators jumped 23% with the help of a series of acquisitions and 2% rise in organic growth from new customers new markets and price increases. Instruments revenue rose 8% as a 55% increase in service revenue more than balanced a 3% drop in product sales. The BGI acquisition also aided revenue growth. Continuous monitoring revenue was off 1%. The cold chain segment reported $4.5 million revenue in its first year.

Mesa posted a 17% increase in profit to just more than $11 million in 2016 compared to the year before. Expenses were about a $1 million higher in 2016 than 2015. The company also paid about $1.7 million in a legal settlement but benefited by $860000 by adopting a different standard for stock compensation. Cash flow from operations increased to $17 million in 2016 from about $11 million in 2015. The company had gains in depreciation and amortization stock-based compensation and accrued liabilities and payments.

Strategy
Mesa's strategy is to provide products that serve niche markets and carry high margins. The lure of niche markets is that they are too small for big competitors leaving the field for Mesa to exploit. The company accomplishes some of it goals through develop its own products — organic growth is a healthy 6% a year. But it revs up its growth rate through acquisitions that complement and add to its portfolio. The company is building a product range that serves the supply chain in certain medical testing and control markets.

Mergers and Acquisitions
Mesa has stepped up its pace of acquisitions to build its offerings. In fiscal 2016 (ended March) the company made 10 deals and added several others in the 2016 calendar year. Deals made the year before totaled six.

The company jumped in to the cold chain business with its July 2015 acquisition of Infitrak Inc. a provider of monitoring instruments packaging products and consulting services to the cold chain markets in Canada and the US. Mesa followed up with the purchase of another cold chain business FreshLoc Technologies Inc. in November 2015. The new business segment added about $4.5 million to Mesa's sales — 5% of the total — in 2016.

Other acquisitions focused on Mesa's dental business and included a deal for North Bay Bioscience. North Bay provides sterilizer testing services for dental offices in Canada. The acquisition marks Mesa's entry into mail-in testing services. Mesa built on that with the purchase of mail-in rights from Mydent International Corp. Mydent's mail-in business involves the testing of small tabletop sterilizers in the US.

EXECUTIVES
VP and Chief Sales and Marketing Officer, Glenn E. Adriance, age 65, $240,153 total compensation
CFO, John V. Sakys, age 50, $235,995 total compensation
President CEO and Director, Gary M. Owens, age 51
Vice President of Corporate Development and Strategy, Pete Jung
Chairman, John J. Sullivan, age 67
Auditors: Plante & Moran, PLLC

LOCATIONS
HQ: Mesa Laboratories, Inc.
12100 West Sixth Avenue, Lakewood, CO 80228
Phone: 303 987-8000
Web: www.mesalabs.com

PRODUCTS/OPERATIONS

2016 Sales
	$ mil.	% of total
Product	66,085.0	78
Services	18,574.0	22
Total	84,659.0	100

2016 Sales

	$ mil.	% of total
Instruments	35,692.0	42
Biological indicators	33,649.0	40
Continuous Monitoring	10,792.0	13
Cold Chain	4,526.0	5
Total	**84,659.0**	**100**

Selected Products
Biological and chemical indicators (Raven Biological Laboratories)
Electronic thermal sensors
  DATATRACE
  DATATRACE Micropack Tracers
  ELOGG
  Flatpack Tracers
  FRB Tracers
Hemodialysis products (Automata)
  Database management software (Reuse Data Management System)
  Dialyzer reprocessors (ECHO MM-1000)
  Meters (Western Meters)
Sonic fluid measurement products (NuSonics)
  Sonic concentration analyzers
  Sonic flowmeters

COMPETITORS
3M Health Care	Rockwell Medical
Badger Meter	STERIS
Cantel Medical	Siemens Corp.
Coperion K-Tron	Siemens Water Technologies
Danaher	Teledyne Isco
Emerson Electric	Thermo Fisher Scientific
Euro Tech	Velocys
GE	
Gambro AB	
MEDIVATORS	

HISTORICAL FINANCIALS
Company Type: Public

Income Statement — FYE: March 31

	REVENUE ($ mil.)	NET INCOME ($ mil.)	NET PROFIT MARGIN	EMPLOYEES
03/19	103.1	7.4	7.3%	347
03/18	96.1	(2.9)	—	366
03/17	93.6	11.1	11.9%	381
03/16	84.6	11.1	13.2%	367
03/15	71.3	9.5	13.4%	276
Annual Growth	9.7%	(6.0%)	—	5.9%

2019 Year-End Financials

Debt ratio: 14.5%
Return on equity: 7.1%
Cash ($ mil.): 10.1
Current ratio: 1.42
Long-term debt ($ mil.): 20.6
No. of shares (mil.): 3.8
Dividends
  Yield: 0.0%
  Payout: 34.4%
Market value ($ mil.): 897.0

	STOCK PRICE ($) FY Close	P/E High/Low		Earnings	Dividends	Book Value
03/19	230.50	123	73	1.86	0.64	28.61
03/18	148.44	—	—	(0.79)	0.64	26.14
03/17	122.70	45	31	2.91	0.64	26.24
03/16	96.35	39	22	2.97	0.64	23.28
03/15	72.20	33	20	2.63	0.62	20.63
Annual Growth 33.7%		—	—	(8.3%)	0.8%	8.5%

Mesabi Trust

EXECUTIVES
Individual Trustee, Norman F. Sprague III, age 67
Individual Trustee, Richard G. Lareau, age 86
Individual Trustee, Robert C Berglund, age 68
Individual Trustee, James A. Ehrenberg, age 72
VP; Deutsche Bank Trust Company Americas, Kenneth R. Ring
Auditors: Baker Tilly Virchow Krause, LLP

LOCATIONS
HQ: Mesabi Trust
c/o Deutsche Bank Trust Company Americas, Trust & Agency Services, 60 Wall Street, 24th Floor, New York, NY 10005
Phone: 904 271-2520
Web: www.mesabi-trust.com

COMPETITORS
BHP Billiton	Rio Tinto Limited
Great Northern Iron Ore	

HISTORICAL FINANCIALS
Company Type: Public

Income Statement — FYE: January 31

	REVENUE ($ mil.)	NET INCOME ($ mil.)	NET PROFIT MARGIN	EMPLOYEES
01/19	47.2	45.5	96.3%	0
01/18	34.5	33.5	96.9%	0
01/17	10.7	9.6	89.5%	0
01/16	9.7	8.5	88.0%	0
01/15	26.0	24.7	95.0%	0
Annual Growth	16.0%	16.5%	—	—

2019 Year-End Financials

Debt ratio: —
Return on equity: 333.6%
Cash ($ mil.): 0.8
Current ratio: 1.90
Long-term debt ($ mil.): —
No. of shares (mil.): 13.1
Dividends
  Yield: 10.9%
  Payout: 86.4%
Market value ($ mil.): 360.0

	STOCK PRICE ($) FY Close	P/E High/Low		Earnings	Dividends	Book Value
01/19	27.44	9	6	3.47	3.00	1.28
01/18	24.80	12	5	2.55	2.53	0.80
01/17	13.70	19	5	0.73	0.64	0.78
01/16	4.40	27	5	0.65	0.09	0.69
01/15	17.08	12	9	1.89	1.84	0.12
Annual Growth 12.6%		—	—	16.5%	13.0%	79.7%

Meta Financial Group Inc

Delivering financial products and services to Iowa and South Dakota is the calling of Meta Financial Group. The group's biggest component is MetaBank a 10-branch operation that offers standard banking solutions such as deposit accounts CDs home mortgages and student loans. Other subsidiaries provide prepaid card services insurance and a variety of tax related solutions. It holds a loan portfolio that exceeds $1 billion and deposits that surpass $3 billion.

Operations
Meta Financial Group operates two customer-facing business segments Banking and Payments and a supporting segment that includes corporate services and other sources of revenue. The Banking segment generates the majority of interest income and a small amount of non-interest income. The Payments unit is the opposite where non-interest income accounts for 90% of its overall revenue and interest income is less than 10% of its business.

The Banking unit doing business as MetaBank operates 10 branches in four key geographic markets: Central Iowa Storm Lake Iowa Brookings South Dakota and Sioux Falls South Dakota. It offers standard deposit products and services including checking and savings accounts. Its lending and investment activities are weighted towards real estate and real estate-related assets; commercial and multifamily residential mortgages comprise more than half of the bank's loan portfolio. It also writes single-family residential mortgages and business loans.

Meta Financial's bread and butter however is the bank's Meta Payment Systems (MPS) division which provides prepaid cards consumer credit and ATM sponsorship services nationwide under operating names of MPS Refund Advantage EPS Financial and SCS. The segment has grown primarily through acquisitions.

Geographic Reach
The MetaBank subsidiary of Sioux Falls SD-based Meta Financial Group operates mainly in Iowa and South Dakota. Its Payment segment includes subsidiaries that run business out of Dallas TX Newport Beach CA Louisville KY Easton PA and Hurst TX.

Financial Performance
Non-interest income from the Payments business grew more than 70% in the year to $166 million. Interest income from the Bank segment rose 37% to $52 million. Total revenue for 2017 was $265 million. The stellar growth is the result of acquisitions and organic growth ? the Bank unit acquired $134 million of private student loans in late 2016 and a further $73 million portfolio in late 2017. The Payment business grew its tax refund business 13-fold underwriting and originating $1.3 billion of refund advance loans for the 2017 tax season.

Net income in 2017 rose 33% to $45 million thanks to the significant upswing in Payments revenue including big growth in its tax business along with improvements in card fee income.

Strategy
Meta Financial Group is looking to boost is non-interest income business endeavors in the Payments division. It feels constrained in its banking business by the need to raise more capital before it can lend out more money from which it would generate interest income. Without the ability to raise more capital (or to raise it at an advantageous cost) the Group believes its efforts are better directed at growth that is not hindered by insufficient capital.

EXECUTIVES

Chairman and CEO Meta Financial Group and MetaBank, J. Tyler Haahr, age 56, $550,000 total compensation
EVP Sales and Operations MetaBank and Director Meta Financial Group (MFG) and MetaBank, Troy Moore, age 51, $252,350 total compensation
EVP Secretary Treasurer and CFO, David W. Leedom, age 65, $215,000 total compensation
President Meta Financial Group Inc. (MFG) and MetaBank and Division President Meta Payment System, Bradley C. (Brad) Hanson, age 55, $550,000 total compensation
EVP Meta Payment Systems, Scott Galit, age 49, $235,000 total compensation
EVP and CFO Meta Financial Group (MFG) and MetaBank, Glen W. Herrick, age 56, $255,000 total compensation
Vice Chairman Meta Financial Group (MFG) and MetaBank, Frederick V. (Fred) Moore, age 63
Auditors: Crowe LLP

LOCATIONS

HQ: Meta Financial Group Inc
5501 South Broadband Lane, Sioux Falls, SD 57108
Phone: 605 782-1767
Web: www.metabank.com

COMPETITORS

Blackhawk Network
BofI
Citi Prepaid Services
First National of Nebraska
Great Western Bancorp
Green Dot
HF Financial
West Bancorporation

HISTORICAL FINANCIALS
Company Type: Public

Income Statement   FYE: September 30

	ASSETS ($ mil.)	NET INCOME ($ mil.)	INCOME AS % OF ASSETS	EMPLOYEES
09/19	6,182.8	97.0	1.6%	1,186
09/18	5,835.0	51.6	0.9%	1,219
09/17	5,228.3	44.9	0.9%	827
09/16	4,006.4	33.2	0.8%	672
09/15	2,529.7	18.0	0.7%	638
Annual Growth	25.0%	52.2%	—	16.8%

2019 Year-End Financials
Return on assets: 1.6%
Return on equity: 12.2%
Long-term debt ($ mil.): —
No. of shares (mil.): 37.8
Sales ($ mil): 548.2
Dividends
 Yield: 0.6%
 Payout: 9.3%
Market value ($ mil.): 1,233.0

	STOCK PRICE ($) FY Close	P/E High/Low	Earnings	Dividends	Book Value
09/19	32.61	33 7	2.49	0.20	22.22
09/18	82.65	70 46	1.67	0.18	19.00
09/17	78.40	66 39	1.61	0.17	15.05
09/16	60.61	47 28	1.31	0.17	13.10
09/15	41.77	59 36	0.89	0.17	11.08
Annual Growth	(6.0%)	— —	29.5%	3.6%	19.0%

MetroCity Bankshares Inc

Auditors: Crowe LLP

LOCATIONS

HQ: MetroCity Bankshares Inc
5114 Buford Highway, Doraville, GA 30340
Phone: 770 455-4989
Web: www.metrocitybank.com

HISTORICAL FINANCIALS
Company Type: Public

Income Statement   FYE: December 31

	ASSETS ($ mil.)	NET INCOME ($ mil.)	INCOME AS % OF ASSETS	EMPLOYEES
12/18	1,432.6	41.3	2.9%	0
12/17	1,288.9	31.9	2.5%	0
12/16	1,100.0	20.2	1.8%	0
12/15	671.0	16.6	2.5%	0
12/14	582.5	12.5	2.1%	0
Annual Growth	25.2%	34.9%	—	—

2018 Year-End Financials
Return on assets: 3.0%
Return on equity: 27.2%
Long-term debt ($ mil.): —
No. of shares (mil.): 24.2
Sales ($ mil): 110.4
Dividends
 Yield: 0.0%
 Payout: 22.4%
Market value ($ mil.): 801.0

	STOCK PRICE ($) FY Close	P/E High/Low	Earnings	Dividends	Book Value
12/18	33.00	19 11	1.69	0.38	6.95
12/17	19.90	— —	(0.00)	0.23	5.61
Annual Growth	65.8%	— —	—	68.9%	23.8%

Metropolitan Bank Holding Corp

Auditors: Crowe LLP

LOCATIONS

HQ: Metropolitan Bank Holding Corp
99 Park Avenue, New York, NY 10016
Phone: 212 659-0600
Web: www.metropolitanbankny.com

HISTORICAL FINANCIALS
Company Type: Public

Income Statement   FYE: December 31

	ASSETS ($ mil.)	NET INCOME ($ mil.)	INCOME AS % OF ASSETS	EMPLOYEES
12/18	2,182.6	25.5	1.2%	153
12/17	1,759.8	12.3	0.7%	129
12/16	1,220.3	5.0	0.4%	118
12/15	964.7	4.2	0.4%	0
Annual Growth	31.3%	81.6%	—	—

2018 Year-End Financials
Return on assets: 1.3%
Return on equity: 10.1%
Long-term debt ($ mil.): —
No. of shares (mil.): 8.2
Sales ($ mil): 96.1
Dividends
 Yield: —
 Payout: —
Market value ($ mil.): 254.0

	STOCK PRICE ($) FY Close	P/E High/Low	Earnings	Dividends	Book Value
12/18	30.85	18 10	3.06	0.00	32.19
12/17	42.10	21 15	2.34	0.00	28.90
12/16	0.00	— —	0.43	0.00	22.45
Annual Growth	—	— —	166.8%	—	19.7%

Mid Penn Bancorp Inc

EXECUTIVES

SVP and Senior Credit Officer Mid Penn Bank, Randall L. Klinger, age 67
Secretary; VP and Corporate Secretary Mid Penn Bank, Cindy L. Wetzel, age 54
VP and Treasurer; SEVP and Northern Region President and COO Mid Penn Bank, Kevin W. Laudenslager, age 52, $108,983 total compensation
President CEO and Director Mid Penn Bancorp and Mid Penn Bank, Rory G. Ritrievi, age 52
Vice Chairman, William A. Specht III, age 54
Chairman, Robert C. Grubic, age 64
SVP and CFO Mid Penn Bank, Edward P. Williams
Senior Vice President and Chief Lending Officer of the Bank, Scott Micklewright
President CEO and Director Mid Penn Bancorp and Mid Penn Bank, Rory G. Ritrievi, age 52
Vice Chairman, William A. Specht III, age 54
Independent Director, Robert Abel
Independent Director, Steven Boyer
Auditors: BDO USA, LLP

LOCATIONS

HQ: Mid Penn Bancorp Inc
349 Union Street, Millersburg, PA 17061
Phone: 866 642-7736
Web: www.midpennbank.com

COMPETITORS

Fulton Financial
PNC Financial
Pennsylvania State Employees Credit Union

HISTORICAL FINANCIALS
Company Type: Public

Income Statement   FYE: December 31

	ASSETS ($ mil.)	NET INCOME ($ mil.)	INCOME AS % OF ASSETS	EMPLOYEES
12/18	2,077.9	10.6	0.5%	406
12/17	1,170.3	7.0	0.6%	277
12/16	1,032.6	7.8	0.8%	257
12/15	931.7	6.5	0.7%	252
12/14	755.6	5.7	0.8%	203
Annual Growth	28.8%	16.8%	—	18.9%

Mid-America Apartment Communities Inc

2018 Year-End Financials
Return on assets: 0.6%
Return on equity: 7.0%
Long-term debt ($ mil.): —
No. of shares (mil.): 8.4
Sales ($ mil): 76.1
Dividends
Yield: 3.0%
Payout: 69.3%
Market value ($ mil.): 195.0

	STOCK PRICE ($) FY Close	P/E High/Low	PER SHARE ($) Earnings	Dividends	Book Value
12/18	23.02	25 15	1.48	0.70	26.38
12/17	33.10	21 14	1.67	0.77	17.85
12/16	23.83	13 8	1.85	0.68	16.65
12/15	16.10	12 10	1.47	0.54	16.58
12/14	15.55	11 9	1.53	0.45	16.90
Annual Growth	10.3%	— —	(0.8%)	11.7%	11.8%

EXECUTIVES

Senior Vice President Director Physical Assets, Kevin Perkins
Vice President Director Risk Management, Doug Clark
Chairman President and CEO, H. Eric Bolton, age 62, $404,133 total compensation
Executive VP Chief Operating Officer, Thomas L. (Tom) Grimes, $168,928 total compensation
EVP and CFO, Albert M. (Al) Campbell, age 52, $158,223 total compensation
SVP Management Information Systems, Shelton Barron
Executive Vice President For Development, Don Aldridge
Assistant Vice President Director of Advertising, Carol Murphy
Senior Vice President Treasurer, Andrew Schaeffer
VP Director Property Accounting, Peg Wahl
Regional Vice President, Gayle Mackovic
Senior Vp, Melanie Carpenter
Senior Vice President Controller, Micah Holton
Senior Vice President Director Of Intenral Audit, Larry Davis
Regional Vice President, Jon King
Evp Director Of Multifamily Investing, Brad Hill
Regional Vice President, Kristine Kee
Vice President Human Resources, Melanie Carter
Senior Vice President Marketing, Tilea Terry
Regional Vice President, Anna Lister
Vice President Operations Coastal Region, Bob Donnelly
Senior Vice President Director of Tax Management, Stephen Woo
VICE PRESIDENT CONSTRUCTION, Kelly C Carter
Vice President Construction, Robert Scheller
Svp Commercial, Dianne Slotnick
Senior Vice President Investments, Matt Smith
Vice President Legal, Joe Bartlett
Vice President Construction, Indrid Agaj
Board Member, Joe Fracchia
Auditors: Ernst & Young LLP

LOCATIONS

HQ: Mid-America Apartment Communities Inc
6815 Poplar Avenue, Suite 500, Germantown, TN 38138
Phone: 901 682-6600   **Fax:** 901 682-6667
Web: www.maac.com

PRODUCTS/OPERATIONS

2015 sales

	$ mil.	% of total
Rental	952.2	91
Other property	90.6	9
Total	**1,042.8**	**100**

COMPETITORS

AMLI Residential
Apartment Investment and Management
Berkshire Income Realty
Camden Property
Equity Residential
Milestone Management
Southern Management
UDR

HISTORICAL FINANCIALS
Company Type: Public

Income Statement   FYE: December 31

	REVENUE ($ mil.)	NET INCOME ($ mil.)	NET PROFIT MARGIN	EMPLOYEES
12/18	1,571.3	222.9	14.2%	2,552
12/17	1,528.9	328.3	21.5%	2,464
12/16	1,125.3	212.2	18.9%	2,528
12/15	1,042.7	332.2	31.9%	1,989
12/14	989.3	147.9	15.0%	2,090
Annual Growth	12.3%	10.8%	—	5.1%

2018 Year-End Financials
Debt ratio: 39.9%
Return on equity: 3.5%
Cash ($ mil.): 34.2
Current ratio: —
Long-term debt ($ mil.): 4,528.3
No. of shares (mil.): 113.8
Dividends
Yield: 3.8%
Payout: 191.1%
Market value ($ mil.): 10,895.0

	STOCK PRICE ($) FY Close	P/E High/Low	PER SHARE ($) Earnings	Dividends	Book Value
12/18	95.70	54 44	1.93	3.69	54.10
12/17	100.56	39 33	2.86	3.48	55.88
12/16	97.92	41 31	2.69	3.28	56.50
12/15	90.81	21 16	4.41	3.08	39.79
12/14	74.68	39 31	1.97	2.92	38.48
Annual Growth	6.4%	— —	(0.5%)	6.0%	8.9%

Middlefield Banc Corp.

EXECUTIVES

Evp And Chief Credit And Risk Officer, John D Lane
Auditors: S.R. Snodgrass, P.C.

LOCATIONS

HQ: Middlefield Banc Corp.
15985 East High Street, Middlefield, OH 44062-0035
Phone: 440 632-1666

COMPETITORS

Cortland Bancorp
Huntington Bancshares
PNC Financial
PVF Capital
U.S. Bancorp

HISTORICAL FINANCIALS
Company Type: Public

Income Statement   FYE: December 31

	ASSETS ($ mil.)	NET INCOME ($ mil.)	INCOME AS % OF ASSETS	EMPLOYEES
12/18	1,248.4	12.4	1.0%	200
12/17	1,106.3	9.4	0.9%	190
12/16	787.8	6.4	0.8%	139
12/15	735.1	6.8	0.9%	143
12/14	677.5	7.1	1.1%	139
Annual Growth	16.5%	14.7%	—	9.5%

2018 Year-End Financials
Return on assets: 1.0%
Return on equity: 10.0%
Long-term debt ($ mil.): —
No. of shares (mil.): 6.4
Sales ($ mil): 54.0
Dividends
Yield: 2.7%
Payout: 30.5%
Market value ($ mil.): 275.0

	STOCK PRICE ($) FY Close	P/E High/Low	PER SHARE ($) Earnings	Dividends	Book Value
12/18	42.43	28 21	1.92	0.59	19.77
12/17	48.20	35 25	1.55	0.54	18.63
12/16	38.70	26 21	1.52	0.54	17.00
12/15	32.40	20 17	1.70	0.54	16.59
12/14	33.61	20 15	1.75	0.52	15.56
Annual Growth	6.0%	— —	2.3%	3.0%	6.2%

Midland States Bancorp Inc

Born in rural Illinois Midland States Bancorp is now discovering banking life in new states. It is the $3 billion-asset holding company for Midland States Bank a community bank that operates more than 35 branches in central and northern Illinois and around 15 branches in the St. Louis metropolitan area. The bank offers traditional consumer and commercial banking products and services as well as merchant card services insurance and financial planning. Subsidiary Midland Wealth Management which boasts $1.2 billion-plus in assets under administration provides wealth management services while Heartland Business Credit offers commercial equipment leasing services. Midland States Bancorp went public in 2016.

IPO

The bank holding company raised $80.1 million in its initial public offering. It plans to contribute some $25 million to Midland States Bank and use the rest for general corporate purposes including possible acquisitions.

Operations

About 57% of Midland States Bancorp's total revenue came from loan interest during 2014 while another 17% came from interest income from investment securities. The rest came from wealth management fees (8% of revenue) deposit account service charges (3%) ATM and interchange revenue (3%) mortgage banking revenue (3%) merchant services revenue (1%) and nonrecurring gains on the sales of assets (around 8%).

Subsidiary Love Funding provides multifamily and healthcare facility FHA financing.

Geographic Reach

Midland has more than 80 branches and offices across the US with around 50 in Illinois and around the St. Louis metro area and the rest in California Colorado Florida Massachusetts North Carolina Ohio Tennessee and Texas.

Financial Performance

Midland States Bancorp's revenue climbed 3% to $93 million despite a decline in loan interest income during 2014 mostly thanks to profitable asset sales and other income.

Despite modest revenue growth in 2014 the bank's net income dove 67% to $3.2 billion as acquisition and integration expenses stemming from its late 2014 acquisition of Heartland ate up any revenue gains it had made. Excluding these non-recurring items the bank's net income grew modestly.

Strategy

Midland States Bancorp has been pursuing an acquisition and branch expansion growth strategy since 2007 after it replaced its executive management and laid out a plan to expand Midland States Bank's presence in Illinois. Midland States Bank continues to focus on moving into suburban areas and other markets in Illinois and Missouri that have growing populations. During 2015 it opened a new branches in the St. Louis region (in Jennings) downtown Joliet and downtown Effingham areas as well as a wealth management office in downtown Decatur.

The company also planned in 2016 to continue building its fast-growing wealth management business which now makes up nearly 10% of its total revenue. Thanks to Midland's efforts the business' wealth management assets under administration have skyrocketed twelve-fold since 2008 growing from $95 million then to $1.19 billion at the end of 2014.

Mergers and Acquisitions

Midland States Bancorp agreed to acquire HomeStar Financial Group in 2019 in a transaction valued at about $10 million. HomeStar's Manteno Illinois-based HomeStar Bank and Financial Services has about $375 million in assets $220 million in loans and $330 million in deposits. HomeStar has five locations in northern Illinois. The deal expands Midland's presence in the Kankakee Illinois metropolitan area.

In 2017 CEO Leon Holschbach signed a $175 million deal with rival Centrue Bank to merge. The two banks had been treading on each others' toes in Princeton Illinois.

Company Background

Between 2008 and 2010 the bank's branch locations grew from just a half-dozen in central Illinois and St. Louis to nearly 30 around the state and in the St. Louis metropolitan area. During that time the bank acquired the assets of Waterloo Bancshares and WestBridge in St. Louis AMCORE in northern Illinois and Strategic Capital in central Illinois. It also opened new locations in some of its faster-growing markets. As a result of its efforts Midland States Bancorp has watched its revenue and profits trend upward significantly from 2007 levels.

EXECUTIVES

Vice Chairman President and CEO, Leon J. Holschbach, age 66, $529,389 total compensation
EVP Midland States Bancorp and President Midland States Bank, Jeffrey G. Ludwig, age 47, $367,500 total compensation
EVP Banking, Jeffrey S. Medford
CFO Midland States Bancorp and Midland States Bank, Kevin L. Thompson
Vice President Commercial Banking, Jan Woodward
Senior Vice President and Corporate Counsel of the Company and the Bank, Douglas Tucker
Vice President, Deanna Haught
Vice President Mortgage Banking, Mark Widdicombe
Senior Vice President, Sharon Schaubert
Svp, James Thompson
Chairman, John M. Schultz, age 67
Board Member, Robert Schultz
Board Member, Deborah Golden
Board Member, Jeffrey Mcdonnell
Board Member, Dwight Miller
Board Member, Richard Ramos
Auditors: Crowe LLP

LOCATIONS

HQ: Midland States Bancorp Inc
1201 Network Centre Drive, Effingham, IL 62401
Phone: 217 342-7321
Web: www.midlandsb.com

PRODUCTS/OPERATIONS

2014 Sales

	% of total
Interest income	
Loans	57
Investment Securities & others	17
Noninterest income	
Wealth management revenue	8
Service charges on deposit accounts	3
Mortgage banking revenue	3
Gain on sale of other assets	3
ATM and interchange revenue	3
Impairments	-
Other	6
Total	**100**

Selected Services
Bank By Phone
Bill Paying
Checking
Debit Card
Online Banking
Savings & CDs

COMPETITORS

Bank of America
Edward D. Jones
Fifth Third
First Mid-Illinois Bancshares
Harris
Mercantile Bancorp
PNC Financial
U.S. Bancorp

HISTORICAL FINANCIALS
Company Type: Public

Income Statement FYE: December 31

	ASSETS ($ mil.)	NET INCOME ($ mil.)	INCOME AS % OF ASSETS	EMPLOYEES
12/18	5,637.6	39.4	0.7%	1,100
12/17	4,412.7	16.0	0.4%	840
12/16	3,233.7	31.5	1.0%	715
12/15	2,884.8	24.3	0.8%	700
12/14	2,676.6	10.8	0.4%	0
Annual Growth	20.5%	38.2%	—	—

2018 Year-End Financials
Return on assets: 0.7%
Return on equity: 7.4%
Long-term debt ($ mil.): —
No. of shares (mil.): 23.7
Sales ($ mil): 295.1
Dividends
Yield: 3.9%
Payout: 84.6%
Market value ($ mil.): 531.0

	STOCK PRICE ($) FY Close	P/E High/Low	PER SHARE ($) Earnings	Dividends	Book Value
12/18	22.34	21 12	1.66	0.88	25.62
12/17	32.48	40 33	0.87	0.80	23.51
12/16	36.18	17 9	2.17	0.36	20.78
Annual Growth	(21.4%)	— —	(12.5%)	56.3%	11.0%

MidWestOne Financial Group, Inc.

MidWestOne Financial Group is the holding company for MidWestOne Bank which operates about two dozen branches throughout central and east-central Iowa. The bank offers standard deposit products such as checking and savings accounts CDs and IRAs in addition to trust services credit cards insurance and brokerage and investment services. About two-thirds of MidWestOne Financial's loan portfolio consists of real estate loans including residential and commercial mortgages and farmland and construction loans. Founded in 1983 MidWestOne has total assets of $1.8 billion.

Geographic Reach

Headquartered in Iowa City MidWestOne Financial Group's MidWestOne Bank has branches and loan production offices in 15 counties in central and east-central Iowa.

Financial Performance

MidWestOne Financial Group reported net income of $18.6 million in 2013 a 13% increase over 2012. Earnings have been rising steadily while the bank's revenue has been trending downward. Indeed 2013's $80.8 million in revenue was 10% below 2012. Assets declined slightly over the same period as did deposits. (The bank is facing stiff competition for deposits from aggressive credit unions offering above market deposit rates.) However loans increased 5% year over year and the growth in loans combined with stable net interest margins of about 3.5% resulted in a modest uptick in net interest income. Non-interest income got a boost from the bank's wealth management division which posted a 7% revenue gain in 2013 versus 2012.

EXECUTIVES

President and CEO, Charles N. Funk, age 65, $422,000 total compensation
EVP and Chief Credit Officer, Kent L. Jehle, age 59, $271,000 total compensation
VP and Chief Risk Officer, James M. Cantrell, $205,000 total compensation
COO, Kevin Kramer
SVP and CFO, Katie A. Lorenson, age 39, $206,231 total compensation
Senior Regional President, Mitchell W. Cook, age 55, $204,400 total compensation

Vice President Information Technology Managing Officer, Allen Schneider
Senior Vice President Loan Sales, Jason Swestka
Vice President Lpl Financial Advisor Located, John Evans
Vice President and Program Manager, Daniel Bailey
SENIOR VICE PRESIDENT TREASURY MANAGEMENT, Kevin Pleasant
VICE PRESIDENT MORTGAGE LOAN OPERATIONS, Linda Nelson
Vice President And Trust Officer, Lia Lovelace
VICE PRESIDENT MORTGAGE LOAN OPERATIONS, Linda A Nelson
SECOND VICE PRESIDENT MORTGAGE BANKER, Niki Gysbers
SENIOR VICE PRESIDENT SMALL BUSINESS ADMINISTRATION, John Kimball
VICE PRESIDENT COMMERCIAL BANKING, Jeff Schebler
VICE PRESIDENT COMMERCIAL LENDING, Andrew L Brust
VICE PRESIDENT HUMAN RESOURCE MANAGER, Cathi Weber
Senior Vice President Retail Banking, David Lindstrom
Vice President Commercial Banking, Nick Raffensperger
Chairman, Kevin W. Monson, age 67
Board Member, Michael Hatch
Board Member, Nate Kaeding
Auditors: RSM US LLP

LOCATIONS

HQ: MidWestOne Financial Group, Inc.
102 South Clinton Street, Iowa City, IA 52240
Phone: 319 356-5800
Web: www.midwestone.com

PRODUCTS/OPERATIONS

2015 Sales

	$ mil.	% of total
Interest Income		
Interest and fees on loans	86.5	71
Interest on investment securities	13.3	11
Other	0.9	1
Non-Interest Income		
Trust investment and insurance fees	6.0	5
Other service charges commissions and fees	5.7	5
Service charges and fees on deposit accounts	4.4	3
Mortgage origination and loan servicing fees	2.8	2
Other	2.3	2
Total	121.9	100

Selected Subsidiaries
MidWestOne Bank
MidWestOne Insurance Services Inc.
MidWestOne Statutory Trust II

COMPETITORS

Bank of the West	U.S. Bancorp
Hills Bancorporation	Wells Fargo
QCR Holdings	West Bancorporation

HISTORICAL FINANCIALS
Company Type: Public

Income Statement FYE: December 31

	ASSETS ($ mil.)	NET INCOME ($ mil.)	INCOME AS % OF ASSETS	EMPLOYEES
12/18	3,291.4	30.3	0.9%	597
12/17	3,212.2	18.7	0.6%	610
12/16	3,079.5	20.3	0.7%	587
12/15	2,979.9	25.1	0.8%	648
12/14	1,800.3	18.5	1.0%	374
Annual Growth	16.3%	13.1%	—	12.4%

2018 Year-End Financials
Return on assets: 0.9%
Return on equity: 8.7%
Long-term debt ($ mil.): —
No. of shares (mil.): 12.1
Sales ($ mil): 151.6
Dividends
Yield: 3.1%
Payout: 45.3%
Market value ($ mil.): 302.0

	STOCK PRICE ($) FY Close	P/E High/Low		PER SHARE ($) Earnings	Dividends	Book Value
12/18	24.83	14	10	2.48	0.78	29.32
12/17	33.53	25	21	1.55	0.67	27.85
12/16	37.60	22	14	1.78	0.64	26.71
12/15	30.41	14	12	2.42	0.60	25.96
12/14	28.81	13	10	2.19	0.58	23.07
Annual Growth	(3.6%)	—	—	3.2%	7.7%	6.2%

Miller Industries Inc. (TN)

This body builder wants to pump up your chassis. Miller Industries makes bodies for light- and heavy-duty wreckers along with car carriers and multi-vehicle trailers. It serves as the official recovery team at some of the NASCAR races (including Talladega) as well as the Indy 500 races. Miller makes its recovery and towing vehicles at plants in the US and Europe. Its multi-vehicle transport trailers can carry as many as eight vehicles and loads up to 75 tons. Miller Industries' US brand names include Century Challenger Champion Chevron Eagle Holmes Titan and Vulcan. The company's European brands are Jige (France) and Boniface (UK). Miller and rival Jerr-Dan dominate the US market for wrecker bodies.

Operations
Professional wrecker operators repossession and salvage companies comprise the light-duty wrecker market. Commercial vehicle operators and professional wreckers are served by the company's heavy-duty vehicles.

The company creates vehicles by bending steel and aluminum and welding the parts together to create a frame; hydraulic cylinders pumps winches and valves are attached to complete the carrier or wrecker body. The bodies are then attached to truck chassis made by third-party manufacturers such as Kenworth (a brand belonging to PACCAR) which is Miller's primary provider of truck chassis.

Miller has developed a wrecker that allows for damage-free towing of newer aerodynamic vehicles that are made of composite or lighter weight materials. The company boasts innovative technology which includes underlift parallel linkage and L-arms and the Vulcan "scoop" — these systems offer better lift-and-carry options that also protect cargo.

Geographic Reach
The company has six manufacturing facilities in France the UK and the US. These facilities reside in Ooltewah (Chattanooga) Tennessee; Hermitage Pennsylvania; Mercer Pennsylvania; and Greeneville Tennessee. It also has manufacturing operations at two facilities located in the Lorraine region of France and manufacturing operations in Norfolk England. North America accounted for 86% of Miller's revenue in 2015.

Sales and Marketing
Its products primarily are sold through independent distributors consisting of approximately 80 distributors in North America that serve all 50 states Canada and Mexico and other foreign markets.

Financial Performance
Miller experienced historic revenue growth in 2015 when revenues peaked at a record-setting $541 million. Profits also spiked by 7% to reach $16 million in 2015 and cash flow from operations skyrocketed by 102% during the year. The unprecedented growth for 2015 was fueled by a 17% rise in North American sales due to higher production levels based on the continued recovery of economic conditions and improving consumer sentiment.

Strategy
The company's involvement with professional racing increases the exposure of Miller's products and supports sales and marketing efforts. Additionally the company focuses on domestic and international trade shows where it partners with its independent distributors in promotions.

Miller grows its operations by enhancing its production capacity. It continues to expand its Pennsylvania manufacturing facility and it began to enhance the facilities at its Ooltewah Tennessee; and Greeneville Tennessee plants during 2016 and beyond.

Company Background
Headed by William Miller the Miller Group (which owned Challenger Wrecker and Holmes International) acquired the wrecking operations of Century Holdings in 1990 and formed the basis for Miller Industries. However Miller Industries wasn't officially created until 1994 when the Miller Group placed all of its wrecking and towing businesses under that nameplate. The company went public in 1995.

EXECUTIVES

EVP CFO and Treasurer, J. Vincent Mish, age 68, $225,009 total compensation
EVP Secretary and General Counsel, Frank Madonia, age 70, $225,009 total compensation
Co-CEO, Jeffrey I. (Jeff) Badgley, age 67, $450,017 total compensation
President and Co-CEO, William G. Miller, $175,007 total compensation
Vp Sales, Vincent Tiano
Vice President Of Heavy duty Sales, John Hawkins
Vice President Sales, Weldon Wright
Vice President, Bruce L Niemeyer
Vice President, Jeanette L Ourada
Vice President, David Payne
Auditors: Elliott Davis, LLC

LOCATIONS

HQ: Miller Industries Inc. (TN)
8503 Hilltop Drive, Ooltewah, TN 37363
Phone: 423 238-4171   Fax: 423 238-5371
Web: www.millerind.com

PRODUCTS/OPERATIONS

Selected Products and Brands

Boniface (heavy-duty wreckers for the European market)
Century (wreckers car carriers)
Challenger (wreckers car carriers)
Champion (car carriers)
Chevron (wreckers car carriers towing and recovery equipment)
Eagle (light-duty wreckers)
Holmes (mid-priced wreckers and car carriers)
Jige (light- and heavy-duty wreckers and car carriers for the European market)
Miller (parts and accessories catalog)
SP Series (medium-duty wreckers & carriers)
Titan (multi-vehicle transport trailers)
Trailers (Titan T Series)
Vulcan (wreckers car carriers towing and recovery equipment)

COMPETITORS

Daimler Trucks North America
Jerr-Dan
Mitsubishi Fuso
Penske Truck Leasing
United Rentals

HISTORICAL FINANCIALS

Company Type: Public

Income Statement   FYE: December 31

	REVENUE ($ mil.)	NET INCOME ($ mil.)	NET PROFIT MARGIN	EMPLOYEES
12/18	711.7	33.7	4.7%	1,240
12/17	615.1	23.0	3.7%	1,120
12/16	601.1	19.9	3.3%	1,103
12/15	540.9	15.9	3.0%	990
12/14	492.7	14.9	3.0%	890
Annual Growth	9.6%	22.7%	—	8.6%

2018 Year-End Financials

Debt ratio: 4.3%
Return on equity: 15.6%
Cash ($ mil.): 27.0
Current ratio: 2.21
Long-term debt ($ mil.): 15.5
No. of shares (mil.): 11.3
Dividends
  Yield: 2.6%
  Payout: 24.3%
Market value ($ mil.): 308.0

	STOCK PRICE ($) FY Close	P/E High/Low	PER SHARE ($) Earnings	Dividends	Book Value
12/18	27.00	10 8	2.96	0.72	19.97
12/17	25.80	14 12	2.02	0.72	17.85
12/16	26.45	16 11	1.75	0.68	16.27
12/15	21.78	18 12	1.41	0.64	15.33
12/14	20.79	16 13	1.31	0.60	14.90
Annual Growth	6.8%	— —	22.6%	4.7%	7.6%

MKS Instruments Inc

MKS Instruments makes systems that analyze and control gases during semiconductor manufacturing and other thin film industrial processes such as those used to make flat panel displays LEDs solar cells and data storage media. Top customers include chip equipment heavyweights Applied Materials and Lam Research. Other applications include medical equipment pharmaceutical manufacturing energy generation and environmental monitoring. MKS Instruments generates more than half its revenue from customers in the US. In 2019 the company acquired Electro Scientific Industries for about $1 billion.

Financial Performance

MKS' sales have grown over five years rising an average of about 33% a year. The rate of revenue growth was outpaced by the company's profit which rose an average of 50% a year over the past five years.

In 2018 revenue advanced a relatively lackluster 8% to $2 billion up about $160 million from 2017. The total increase reflected an 8% increase in product sales which were spurred by the Vacuum & Analysis and the Light & Motion segments on volume increases from industrial technologies customers. Service revenue was 11% higher lifted by semiconductor customers. Customers in China Germany and Japan accounted for a significant portion of higher international sales.

MKS posted a profit of about $393 million in 2018 compared to $339 million in 2017 on higher revenue.

The company held $644 million in cash in 2018 compared to about $334 million the year before. In 2018 operations generated $414 million and investing activities provided about $73 million while investing activities used $178 million.

MKS has about $998 million in total outstanding debt which means higher interest expense. The money spent to service principal and interest could reduce funds available to respond to changing business and economic conditions. The company does have a revolving credit facility that provides senior secured financing of up to $100 million.

Strategy

In the past five years MKS has acted mainly through acquisitions to strengthen its semiconductor business and to expand into other areas such industrial technologies life and health sciences research and defense to develop diverse sources of revenue.

In 2019 MKS closed its acquisition of Electro Scientific Industries (ESI) which expanded its addressable market by about $2.2 billion. The addition of ESI bolsters the company's expertise in the lasers photonics and optics markets. Further ESI's capabilities in complex printed circuit board processing systems should help MKS improve the performance of its laser motion and photonics portfolio.

MKS anticipates the implementation of new 5G technology which will require upgraded wireless infrastructure and new mobile devices. The need for new semiconductor equipment should generate work for MKS' semiconductor and laser diode testing businesses as well as for ESI.

The company relies on its 10 biggest customers for more than 40% of its revenue. Applied Materials and Lam Research each account for more than 10% of sales.

Mergers and Acquisitions

A large part of MKS' strategy involves acquisitions.

In 2019 MKS acquired Electro Scientific Industries (ESI) for $1 billion. The amount surpasses the $980 million MKS paid for Newport Cop. in 2016. MKS expects the deal to strengthen its offerings in the photonics and optics markets. ESI has worked with MKS in the printed circuit board market and expects continued collaboration.

The addition of Newport's laser business in 2016 provided MKS an entry into research health and life sciences markets.

EXECUTIVES

President CEO and Director, Gerald G. Colella, age 62, $673,077 total compensation
VP CFO and Treasurer, Seth H. Bagshaw, age 59, $424,038 total compensation
SVP and COO, John T. C. Lee, age 56, $424,038 total compensation
SVP Global Operations, Brian C. Quirk, $339,423 total compensation
Vice President Corporate Development, John Ippolito
Vice President Global Applications Engineering, John Doherty
Senior Vice President Global Sales, John Abrams
Senior Vice President, Jack Abrams
Vice President and Corporate Controller, Derek Dantilio
Vice President Technology, Javier Morales
Senior Vice President Business Units, Dennis Werth
Vice President US Sales, Steven Kirsch
Assistant Vice President Global Human Resources, Sally Bouley
Vice President Strategic Accounts, Nate Armstrong
Chairman President and CEO, John R. Bertucci, age 79
Auditors: PricewaterhouseCoopers LLP

LOCATIONS

HQ: MKS Instruments Inc
2 Tech Drive, Suite 201, Andover, MA 01810
Phone: 978 645-5500
Web: www.mksinst.com

PRODUCTS/OPERATIONS

2018 Sales by Products

	% of total
Vacuum Solutions Products	26
Power Plasma and Reactive Gas Solutions Products	29
Analytical and Control Solutions Products	6
Laser Products	13
Optics Products	11
Photonics Products	15
Total	100

2018 Sales

	% of total
Vacuum and Analysis	61
Light and Motion	39
Total	100

Selected Products

Instruments and Control Systems
  Pressure Measurement and Control Products
  Baratron®; Pressure Measurement Products
  Automatic Pressure and Vacuum Control Products
  Materials Delivery Products
  Flow Measurement and Control Products
  Gas Composition Analysis Products
  Mass Spectrometry-Based Gas Composition Analysis Instruments
  Fourier Transform Infra-Red (FTIR) Based Gas Composition Analysis Products
  Control and Information Technology Products
  Control Products
  Information Technology Products
Power and Reactive Gas Products
  Power Delivery Products
  Reactive Gas Generation Products
  Processing Thin Films

Equipment Cleaning
Vacuum Products
    Vacuum Gauging Products
    Vacuum Valves Stainless Steel Components Process
    Solutions and Custom Stainless Steel Hardware
    Custom Manufactured Components

COMPETITORS

Advanced Energy Industries
Brooks Automation
CVD Equipment
Ebara
Entegris
HORIBA
Hitachi High-Technologies
INFICON
KLA-Tencor
L'Air Liquide
Nova Measuring
Veeco Instruments

HISTORICAL FINANCIALS
Company Type: Public

Income Statement — FYE: December 31

	REVENUE ($ mil.)	NET INCOME ($ mil.)	NET PROFIT MARGIN	EMPLOYEES
12/18	2,075.1	392.9	18.9%	4,851
12/17	1,915.9	339.1	17.7%	4,923
12/16	1,295.3	104.8	8.1%	4,667
12/15	813.5	122.3	15.0%	2,181
12/14	780.8	115.7	14.8%	2,371
Annual Growth	27.7%	35.7%	—	19.6%

2018 Year-End Financials
Debt ratio: 13.3%
Return on equity: 22.7%
Cash ($ mil.): 644.3
Current ratio: 5.56
Long-term debt ($ mil.): 343.8
No. of shares (mil.): 54.0
Dividends
  Yield: 1.2%
  Payout: 10.7%
Market value ($ mil.): 3,491.0

	STOCK PRICE ($) FY Close	P/E High/Low		PER SHARE ($) Earnings	Dividends	Book Value
12/18	64.61	17	8	7.14	0.78	34.66
12/17	94.50	17	10	6.16	0.71	29.23
12/16	59.40	31	16	1.94	0.68	23.14
12/15	36.00	17	14	2.28	0.68	21.82
12/14	36.60	17	12	2.16	0.66	20.35
Annual Growth	15.3%	—	—	34.8%	4.5%	14.2%

Modine Manufacturing Co

Modine Manufacturing designs and manufactures highly engineered heat transfer systems and components for a range of customers worldwide: automotive OEMs agricultural and construction machinery OEMs heating and cooling equipment OEMs construction contractors and wholesalers of plumbing and heating equipment. Products include heat transfer modules coils fuel and oil coolers radiators condensers and charge air coolers. With manufacturing operations in some 15 countries and technical centers in the US Germany and Italy more than half of Modine's revenues are generated outside of the US. The company was founded in 1916. In early 2019 Modine announced it was looking for strategic alternatives for its automotive business including a possible sale.

Operations
Modine's business is organized into three segments. Vehicular Thermal Solutions accounts for 59% of sales. Products include powertrain cooling components such as radiators and engine cooling assemblies as well as on-engine cooling systems and battery thermal management systems.

The Commercial and Industrial Solutions division makes coils coolers and protective coatings for HVAC and refrigeration applications and accounts for 32% of annual sales. Modine's Building HVAC segment makes up 9% of sales. Offerings include heaters duct furnaces rooftop ventilation units and air conditioning units for data centers.

Geographic Reach
Modine maintains a manufacturing presence in Austria Brazil China Germany Hungary India Italy Mexico the Netherlands Serbia South Korea Spain Sweden the UK and the US. After the US (46% of total sales) other major markets include Italy (10%) China (8%) and Hungary (7%).

Sales and Marketing
Modine serves 10 main customers that generate half of its total revenue. These include such big names as Carrier Caterpillar Daimler Deere & Company Navistar and Volkswagen. In fiscal 2019 and 2018 Daimler and Volkswagen were the only customers that accounted for 10% or more of total sales.

Financial Performance
Apart from a slight dip in 2016 Modine has had steady growth in each of its last five fiscal years amid rising demand in both mature and emerging markets. Revenue rose more than 45% from $1.5 billion in fiscal 2015 to $2.2 billion in fiscal 2019.

Sales in fiscal 2019 increased more than 5% to $2.2 billion compared to $2.1 billion in fiscal 2018. Growth in 2019 was fueled by sales volume increases across all its segments: Vehicular Thermal Systems (5% increase over 2018) Commercial and Industrial Solutions (4%) and Building HVAC (10%).

Net income increased 260% from $23.8 million in fiscal 2018 to $85.9 million in fiscal 2019 primarily due to more favorable tax rates under the Tax Cuts and Jobs Act and reduced restructuring costs.

Cash at the end of fiscal 2019 was $41.7 million an increase of $2.5 million from the prior year. Cash from operations contributed $103.3 million to the coffers while investing activities used $72.8 billion mainly for capital expenditures. Financing activities used $25.9 primarily for repayment of debt.

Strategy
Modine has announced it's evaluating strategic alternatives for the automotive operations of its Vehicular Thermal Solutions division (VTS) including a possible sale. The automotive business has high capital investment requirements and the company feels there are better strategic and growth opportunities in its commercial vehicle and off-highway markets.

In the company's Commercial and Industrial (CIS) segment Modine expects to benefit from rising demand in emerging markets as well as from more stringent energy and environmental regulations which should spur investments in the company's coil and cooler products. Similar trends should also drive demand for the Modine's lineup of building HVAC offerings.

Company Background
Modine was founded in 1916 by Arthur B. Modine. The company's "Turbotube" radiators were standard equipment on the Ford Motor Company's Model T. Upon his death at age 95 Arthur Modine had accumulated more than 120 US patents for the heat transfer products he developed.

EXECUTIVES

Regional VP Asia, Scott L. Bowser, age 55, $293,400 total compensation
President and CEO, Thomas A. (Tom) Burke, age 62, $740,000 total compensation
EVP and COO, Thomas F. (Tom) Marry, age 58, $350,000 total compensation
Regional Vice President - North America, Scott D. Wollenberg
VP Finance and CFO, Michael B. Lucareli, $322,000 total compensation
Regional Vice President - Europe, Holger Schwab
VP and CTO, Ralf Beck, age 58
VP Human Resources, Brian Agen
Vp Treasurer Investor Relations, Kathleen Powers
Vice President Corporate Controller and Tax, Mark Hudson
VICE PRESIDENT COMM AND INDUST SOLUTIONS, Dennis P Appel
VICE PRESIDENT COMM AND INDUST SOLUTIONS, Dennis Appel
Vice President General Counsel And Corporate Secretary, Sylvia Stein
Vice President, C Langer
Vp Of Information Technology, Steve Langer
Vice President Information Security, Denny Mueller
Board Member, Larry Moore
Chairman, Gary L. Neale, age 80
Board Member, Suresh Garimella
Board Member, Marsha C Williams
Auditors: PricewaterhouseCoopers LLP

LOCATIONS

HQ: Modine Manufacturing Co
1500 DeKoven Avenue, Racine, WI 53403
Phone: 262 636-1200 **Fax:** 262 636-1424
Web: www.modine.com

PRODUCTS/OPERATIONS

2015 Sales

	$ mil.	% of total
Original equipment		
Original equipment - Europe	578.2	38
Original equipment - North America	573.5	38
Original equipment - Asia	81.2	6
South America	93.9	6
Building HVAC	186.3	12
Adjustments	(16.7)	-
Total	**1,496.4**	**100**

2015 Sales by Product

	$ mil.	% of total
Modules/assemblies	367.5	25
Oil coolers	233.0	16
EGR coolers	183.5	12
Building HVAC	199.6	13
Charge-air coolers	148.9	10
Condensers	140.0	9
Radiators	124.8	8
Other	99.1	7
Total	**1,496.4**	**100**

2014 Sales by Product

	$ mil.	% of total
Modules/packages	379.9	25
Oil coolers	215.4	14
EGR coolers	172.5	12
Building HVAC	159.5	12
Charge-air coolers	157.0	11
Condensers	129.2	9
Radiators	129.0	8
Other	135.1	9
Total	**1,477.6**	**100**

COMPETITORS

Bergstrom Inc.	Greenheck
Blissfield Manufacturing	Honeywell International
C P Auto Products	Lennox
CalsonicKansei North America	Luvata
	Mestek
DENSO	Mobile Climate Control
Daikin	Red Dot Corporation
Dana	ThermaSys
Delphi Automotive Systems	Thomas & Betts
	Valeo
Emerson Electric	Visteon

HISTORICAL FINANCIALS
Company Type: Public

Income Statement — FYE: March 31

	REVENUE ($ mil.)	NET INCOME ($ mil.)	NET PROFIT MARGIN	EMPLOYEES
03/19	2,212.7	84.8	3.8%	12,200
03/18	2,103.1	22.2	1.1%	11,700
03/17	1,503.0	14.2	0.9%	11,200
03/16	1,352.5	(1.6)	—	7,100
03/15	1,496.4	21.8	1.5%	6,900
Annual Growth	10.3%	40.4%	—	15.3%

2019 Year-End Financials

Debt ratio: 29.2%
Return on equity: 16.5%
Cash ($ mil.): 41.7
Current ratio: 1.25
Long-term debt ($ mil.): 335.1
No. of shares (mil.): 50.7
Dividends
Yield: —
Payout: —
Market value ($ mil.): 703.0

	STOCK PRICE ($) FY Close	P/E High/Low		PER SHARE ($) Earnings	Dividends	Book Value
03/19	13.87	13	6	1.65	0.00	10.53
03/18	21.15	57	23	0.43	0.00	9.70
03/17	12.20	56	29	0.29	0.00	8.26
03/16	11.01	—	—	(0.03)	0.00	7.94
03/15	13.47	37	25	0.45	0.00	7.43
Annual Growth	0.7%			38.4%	—	9.1%

Moelis & Co

Auditors: DELOITTE & TOUCHE LLP

LOCATIONS
HQ: Moelis & Co
399 Park Avenue, 5th Floor, New York, NY 10022
Phone: 212 883-3800
Web: www.moelis.com

HISTORICAL FINANCIALS
Company Type: Public

Income Statement — FYE: December 31

	REVENUE ($ mil.)	NET INCOME ($ mil.)	NET PROFIT MARGIN	EMPLOYEES
12/18	885.8	140.6	15.9%	845
12/17	684.6	29.4	4.3%	749
12/16	613.3	38.3	6.3%	645
12/15	551.8	33.1	6.0%	660
12/14	518.7	(3.0)	—	550
Annual Growth	14.3%	—	—	11.3%

2018 Year-End Financials

Debt ratio: —
Return on equity: 38.5%
Cash ($ mil.): 261.1
Current ratio: 0.62
Long-term debt ($ mil.): —
No. of shares (mil.): 56.1
Dividends
Yield: 14.1%
Payout: 175.5%
Market value ($ mil.): 1,929.0

	STOCK PRICE ($) FY Close	P/E High/Low		PER SHARE ($) Earnings	Dividends	Book Value
12/18	34.38	21	10	2.78	4.88	7.21
12/17	48.50	52	35	0.78	2.48	6.09
12/16	33.90	19	12	1.58	3.29	4.10
12/15	29.18	21	16	1.55	1.00	3.27
12/14	34.93	—	—	(0.19)	1.40	2.21
Annual Growth	(0.4%)			—	36.6%	34.4%

Monmouth Real Estate Investment Corp

Monmouth specializes in mammoth industrial properties particularly warehouses and distribution centers. The real estate investment trust (REIT) owns about 80 industrial buildings and a single New Jersey shopping center comprising some 10.7 million sq. ft. in more than 25 states mostly in the East and Midwest. Most are net-leased (in which tenants pay insurance taxes and maintenance costs) under long-term leases. The REIT's two largest tenants FedEx and Milwaukee Electric Tool together account for half of its revenue. The firm also invests in REIT securities. Founded in 1968 Monmouth is one of the oldest public equity REITs in the nation.

Geographic Reach
New Jersey-based Monmouth's properties are located in 27 states including Arizona Connecticut Florida Illinois Michigan New Jersey New York Ohio Pennsylvania Tennessee Texas and Wisconsin.

Sales and Marketing
FedEx is the REIT's single largest customer accounting for 44% of its leasable space.

Financial Performance
The industrial REIT's revenue increased 5% in fiscal 2013 (ended September) versus the prior year to $66.3 million due to an increase in rental and reimbursement revenues generated by its larger portfolio of properties. Net income grew 15% over the same period to $21 million. The firm's revenue and profits have increased steadily over the past four years as its portfolio increased in size.

Strategy
The REIT specializes in net-leased industrial properties subject to long-term leases primarily to investment grade tenants. It derives its income primarily from real estate rental operations. Monmouth owns all of its properties with the exception of two in New Jersey in which it holds a majority interest.

In 2013 the REIT acquired five industrial properties totaling approximately 1.1 million square feet with net-leased terms ranging from 10 to 20 years of which about 237000 square feet (or 21%) is leased to FedEx Ground Package System. The REIT paid about $73.9 million for the five sites which are located in Kansas Kentucky Oklahoma Pennsylvania and Texas. The firm intends to continue increasing its real estate investments in fiscal 2014 through acquisitions and the expansion of select properties.

EXECUTIVES
CFO, Kevin S. Miller, age 49, $239,663 total compensation
President and CEO, Michael P. Landy, age 58, $525,000 total compensation
General Counsel, Allison Nagelberg, age 55, $312,656 total compensation
Chairman, Eugene W. Landy, age 86
Auditors: PKF O'Connor Davies, LLP

LOCATIONS
HQ: Monmouth Real Estate Investment Corp
101 Crawfords Corner Road, Suite 1405, Holmdel, NJ 07733
Phone: 732 577-9996
Web: www.mreic.reit

PRODUCTS/OPERATIONS

2016 Sales

	$ mil.	% of total
Rental	81.6	86
Reimbursement	13.3	14
Total	**94.9**	**100**

COMPETITORS

Brandywine Realty	Mack-Cali
CenterPoint Properties	One Liberty Properties
First Industrial Realty	PS Business Parks
	Prologis
First Potomac Realty	

HISTORICAL FINANCIALS
Company Type: Public

Income Statement — FYE: September 30

	REVENUE ($ mil.)	NET INCOME ($ mil.)	NET PROFIT MARGIN	EMPLOYEES
09/19	158.5	29.8	18.8%	17
09/18	139.3	56.0	40.2%	15
09/17	113.5	40.2	35.5%	15
09/16	94.9	32.4	34.2%	14
09/15	78.0	25.6	32.8%	15
Annual Growth	19.4%	3.9%	—	3.2%

2019 Year-End Financials

Debt ratio: 44.8%
Return on equity: 3.2%
Cash ($ mil.): 20.1
Current ratio: 11.04
Long-term debt ($ mil.): 839.9
No. of shares (mil.): 96.4
Dividends
  Yield: 4.7%
  Payout: 566.6%
Market value ($ mil.): 1,389.0

	STOCK PRICE ($) FY Close	P/E High/Low	PER SHARE ($) Earnings	Dividends	Book Value
09/19	14.41	137 100	0.12	0.68	10.49
09/18	16.72	37 28	0.49	0.68	9.79
09/17	16.19	29 23	0.56	0.64	9.43
09/16	14.27	30 20	0.50	0.64	8.67
09/15	9.75	28 21	0.43	0.60	7.18
Annual Growth	10.3%	— —	(27.3%)	3.2%	9.9%

Monolithic Power Systems Inc

Monolithic Power Systems (MPS) sends out mixed signals and that's a good thing. The fabless semiconductor company offers mixed-signal and analog microchips — especially DC-to-DC converters for powering flat-panel TVs wireless communications equipment notebook computers set-top boxes and other consumer electronic devices. MPS outsources production of its chips to three silicon foundries in China. The company's products are incorporated into electronic gear from tech heavyweights such as Dell Hewlett-Packard Samsung Electronics and Sony. The company was founded in 1997.

Operations
MPS has two main business segments. Its DC-to-DC products convert and control voltages in electronics from cell phones to TVs to medical equipment. The DC-to-DC chips are monolithic in that they accounted for 90% of the company's sales in 2015. MPS's lighting control products are used to backlight LCD and LED screens. The segment was 10% of sales in 2015.

Geographic Reach
MPS is headquartered in San Jose California but most of its activities are in Asia. Production assembly and packaging and testing are done at facilities in China and Malaysia. The finished products don't have far to go since 90% of sales are in Asia; China is the company's biggest market with 64% of sales. MPS has sales offices in the US Europe Singapore Taiwan China Korea and Japan.

Sales and Marketing
The company sells through distributors value-added resellers and directly to original equipment manufacturers (OEMs) original design manufacturers (ODMs) and electronic manufacturing service (EMS) companies. Sales to its largest distributor accounted for about 24% of revenue in 2015 and another distributor accounted for 10% of revenue in 2015. The MPS sales process includes working with customers in the design and use of MPS chips in their products.

Financial Performance
MPS's revenue grew at a healthy rate in 2015 while net income was flat.

Sales rose 18% in the company's DC to DC segment leading to an 18% growth rate from 2014 to 2015. It combined more unit sales with higher average sale prices to reach $333 million in revenue in 2015 compared to $282 in 2014.

Net income however slipped about 1% to $35.1 million from $35.5 million. MPS increased research and development spending in 2015 and paid more taxes compared to 2014.

Cash flow from operations dipped to $69.7 million in 2015 from $74 million in 2014.

Strategy
MPS is working to diversify its customers moving away from consumer-dependent products and to industrial automotive and lighting markets. It also is developing new products aimed at those markets and has signed distributor agreements. One such product is a DC-to-DC conversion technology QSMod that improves system efficiency which was introduced in 2013.

MPS spends about 20% of revenue on R&D each year.

Mergers and Acquisitions
In 2014 MPS acquired Sensima Technology a developer of magnetic sensor technologies which will be combined with MPS technologies for automotive industrial and cloud computing. The purchase price includes an initial cash payment of about $12 million and a subsequent cash earn-out payment of up to $9 million based on meeting performance goals.

EXECUTIVES

Chairman President and CEO, Michael R. Hsing, age 59, $448,000 total compensation
President - MPS Asia Operations, Deming Xiao, age 56, $340,000 total compensation
VP Strategic Corporate Development General Counsel and Secretary, Saria Tseng, age 48, $300,000 total compensation
SVP Worldwide Sales and Marketing, Maurice Sciammas, age 59, $300,000 total compensation
CFO, Bernie Blegen
Auditors: Ernst & Young LLP

LOCATIONS

HQ: Monolithic Power Systems Inc
4040 Lake Washington Blvd. NE, Suite 201, Kirkland, WA 98033
Phone: 425 296-9956
Web: www.monolithicpower.com

PRODUCTS/OPERATIONS

2011 Sales

	$ mil.	% of total
DC-to-DC converters	165.6	85
LCD backlight inverters	26.5	13
Audio amplifiers	4.4	2
Total	**196.5**	**100**

Selected Products
AC/DC Offline
  Bridge rectifier
  Controllers and regulators
  Synchronous rectifiers
Audio amplifiers
Backlighting solutions
  EL drivers
  White LED drivers (inductors and charge pumps)
Automotive
Battery chargers
  Cradle chargers
  Linear chargers
  Protection
  Switching chargers
Full-bridge and half-bridge power drivers
Isolated and transformer-based power supplies
Lighting and illumination
Low dropout (LDO) linear regulators
Motor drivers
  Brushless DC motor drivers
  Stepper DC motor drivers
Photo-flash chargers and drivers
Power Over Ethernet powered device (PD) solutions
  PD controllers
  PD identity
Precision analog
  Analog switches
  High-side current sense amplifiers
  Operational amplifiers
  Voltage reference
Supervisory circuits and voltage supervisors
Switching power supply regulators
  DC-DC (step-down)
    Controller
    Intelli-Phase (monolithic driver + MOSFET)
    Non-synchronous switcher
    Synchronous switcher
  DC-DC (step-up)
    Controller
    Energy storage and release management
    LNB power supply
    Non-synchronous switcher
    Synchronous switcher
USB and current-limit load switches

COMPETITORS

Analog Devices
Fairchild Semiconductor
Intersil
Maxim Integrated Products
Microchip Technology
Microsemi
O2Micro
ON Semiconductor
Power Integrations
ROHM
Richtek Technology Corp.
STMicroelectronics
Semtech
Texas Instruments

HISTORICAL FINANCIALS

Company Type: Public

Income Statement
FYE: December 31

	REVENUE ($ mil.)	NET INCOME ($ mil.)	NET PROFIT MARGIN	EMPLOYEES
12/18	582.3	105.2	18.1%	1,737
12/17	470.9	65.2	13.8%	1,534
12/16	388.6	52.7	13.6%	1,417
12/15	333.0	35.1	10.6%	1,260
12/14	282.5	35.5	12.6%	1,178
Annual Growth	19.8%	31.2%	—	10.2%

2018 Year-End Financials

Debt ratio: —
Return on equity: 18.1%
Cash ($ mil.): 172.7
Current ratio: 7.22
Long-term debt ($ mil.): —
No. of shares (mil.): 42.5
Dividends
  Yield: 1.0%
  Payout: 58.5%
Market value ($ mil.): 4,941.0

	STOCK PRICE ($) FY Close	P/E High/Low	PER SHARE ($) Earnings	Dividends	Book Value
12/18	116.25	61 42	2.36	1.20	15.06
12/17	112.36	80 52	1.50	0.80	12.54
12/16	81.93	66 43	1.26	0.80	10.57
12/15	63.71	77 51	0.86	0.80	9.29
12/14	49.74	55 34	0.89	0.45	8.92
Annual Growth	23.6%	— —	27.6%	27.8%	14.0%

Montage Resource Corp

Looking to eclipse its oil and gas rivals Eclipse Resources is an independent exploration and production company active in the Appalachian Basin. It has 227230 net acres in Eastern Ohio including 96240 net acres in the most prolific and economic area of the Utica Shale fairway (Utica Core Area) with 25740 net acres targeted as a highly liquids-rich area in the Marcellus Shale in Eastern Ohio (Marcellus Project Area). Eclipse operates 81% of its net acreage within the Utica Core and Marcellus Project areas. In 2014 the company reported estimated proved reserves of 109.6 billion cu. ft. equivalent and 18.3 million barrels of oil equivalent. It went public in June of that year.

IPO

The company plans to use its IPO proceeds of $818.1 million to pay down debt and fund its capital expenditure plan. Following the public offering Eclipse Resource Holdings L.P. held 81% of the company.

Operations

In 2014 Eclipse had identified 668 net horizontal drilling locations in the Utica Core and 195 locations in the Marcellus Project. That year the company and/or its operating partners had commenced drilling 72 gross wells within the Utica Core and 3 gross wells within the Marcellus Project.

Strategy

Eclipse intends to focus on developing its substantial inventory of horizontal drilling locations and will continue to add to this acreage position by acquiring acreage at attractive prices.

EXECUTIVES

EVP and COO, Thomas S. Liberatore, age 63, $261,038 total compensation
Chairman President and CEO, Benjamin W. Hulburt, age 45, $585,225 total compensation
EVP Secretary General Counsel and Director, Christopher K. Hulburt, age 48, $327,116 total compensation
EVP and CFO, Matthew R. DeNezza, age 48, $329,244 total compensation
Auditors: Grant Thornton LLP

LOCATIONS

HQ: Montage Resource Corp
122 West John Carpenter Freeway, Suite 300, Irving, TX 75039
Phone: 469 444-1647
Web: www.montageresources.com

PRODUCTS/OPERATIONS

2015 Sales

	$ mil.	% of total
Natural gas sales	69.5	51
Oil sales	47.3	34
NGLs sales		15
Total	137.8	100

COMPETITORS

Avenue Group
Carrizo Oil & Gas
Chesapeake Energy
Penn Virginia
Stone Energy
XTO Energy

HISTORICAL FINANCIALS

Company Type: Public

Income Statement — FYE: December 31

	REVENUE ($ mil.)	NET INCOME ($ mil.)	NET PROFIT MARGIN	EMPLOYEES
12/18	515.1	18.8	3.7%	159
12/17	383.6	8.5	2.2%	171
12/16	235.0	(203.8)	—	138
12/15	255.3	(971.4)	—	210
12/14	137.8	(183.1)	—	227
Annual Growth	39.0%	—	—	(8.5%)

2018 Year-End Financials

Debt ratio: 36.9%
Return on equity: 2.9%
Cash ($ mil.): 5.9
Current ratio: 0.64
Long-term debt ($ mil.): 530.2
No. of shares (mil.): 20.1
Dividends
 Yield: —
 Payout: —
Market value ($ mil.): 21.0

	STOCK PRICE ($) FY Close	P/E High	P/E Low	PER SHARE ($) Earnings	PER SHARE ($) Dividends	PER SHARE ($) Book Value
12/18	1.05	3	1	0.94	0.00	34.09
12/17	2.40	7	4	0.45	0.00	32.68
12/16	2.67	—	—	(12.60)	0.00	31.47
12/15	1.82	—	—	(66.90)	0.00	41.80
12/14	7.03	—	—	(19.05)	0.00	108.05
Annual Growth	(37.8%)			(25.1%)	—	—

Mountain Commerce Bancorp Inc

Auditors: Dixon Hughes Goodman LLP

LOCATIONS

HQ: Mountain Commerce Bancorp Inc
6101 Kingston Pike, P.O. Box 52942, Knoxville, TN 37919
Phone:
Web: www.mcb.com

HISTORICAL FINANCIALS

Company Type: Public

Income Statement — FYE: December 31

	REVENUE ($ mil.)	NET INCOME ($ mil.)	NET PROFIT MARGIN	EMPLOYEES
12/18	37.5	10.1	27.1%	0
12/17	30.2	5.4	18.1%	0
12/16	25.1	4.2	16.8%	0
12/15	20.6	3.0	14.8%	0
Annual Growth	22.0%	49.1%	—	—

2018 Year-End Financials

Debt ratio: 6.3%
Return on equity: 14.2%
Cash ($ mil.): 19.4
Current ratio: 0.16
Long-term debt ($ mil.): 53.9
No. of shares (mil.): 6.1
Dividends
 Yield: —
 Payout: —
Market value ($ mil.): 109.0

	STOCK PRICE ($) FY Close	P/E High	P/E Low	PER SHARE ($) Earnings	PER SHARE ($) Dividends	PER SHARE ($) Book Value
12/18	17.72	13	11	1.63	0.00	12.45
12/17	17.50	21	14	0.89	0.00	11.04
12/16	0.00	—	—	1.03	0.00	10.11
Annual Growth	—	—	—	25.8%	—	11.0%

Mr Cooper Group Inc

EXECUTIVES

Chm, Michael Willingham
Vice President Information Security Officer, Todd Bailey
Auditors: Ernst & Young LLP

LOCATIONS

HQ: Mr Cooper Group Inc
8950 Cypress Waters Blvd., Coppell, TX 75019
Phone: 469 549-2000
Web: www.mrcoopergroup.com

HISTORICAL FINANCIALS

Company Type: Public

Income Statement — FYE: December 31

	ASSETS ($ mil.)	NET INCOME ($ mil.)	INCOME AS % OF ASSETS	EMPLOYEES
12/18*	16,973.0	884.0	5.2%	8,500
07/18	0.0	154.0	**********%	0
12/17	614.1	25.8	4.2%	6
12/16	736.1	201.7	27.4%	6
12/15	685.0	(61.8)	—	6
Annual Growth	123.1%	—	—	513.5%

*Fiscal year change

2018 Year-End Financials

Return on assets: 23.9%
Return on equity: 166.1%
Long-term debt ($ mil.): —
No. of shares (mil.): 90.8
Sales ($ mil): 594.0
Dividends
 Yield: —
 Payout: —
Market value ($ mil.): 1,060.0

	STOCK PRICE ($) FY Close	P/E High	P/E Low	PER SHARE ($) Earnings	PER SHARE ($) Dividends	PER SHARE ($) Book Value
12/18*	11.67	2	0	9.54	0.00	21.39
07/18	1.36	1	0	1.55	0.00	(0.00)
12/17	0.85	13	5	0.12	0.00	34.67
12/16	1.55	1	0	3.60	0.00	40.49
12/15	2.59	—	—	(4.68)	0.00	29.80
Annual Growth	45.7%	—	—	—	—	(8.0%)

*Fiscal year change

MSCI Inc

MSCI formerly Morgan Stanley Capital International manages more than 145000 daily equity fixed income and hedge fund indices for use by large asset management firms. MSCI is organized through two business segments. Its Performance and Risk business provides equity indices portfolio risk and performance analytics credit analytics and environmental social and governance (ESG) products under brands such as MSCI RiskMetrics and Barra. Its Governance business provides corporate governance and specialized financial research and analysis. MSCI has about 7500 clients across more than 80 countries.

Operations
The company's indices act as benchmarks that measure the performance of global funds. Institutional investors use the indices as research tools and as the basis for their various investment vehicles. MSCI's Performance and Risk segment is by far its largest accounting for 87% of the company's revenue in 2012 while the company's Governance segment brought in the remaining 13%. MSCI makes the majority of its revenues (more than 75%) from annual recurring subscriptions to its products.

Geographic Reach
Nearly half of the company's revenues come from outside the Americas. MSCI has more than 38 offices in 22 countries worldwide including headquarters in New York and offices in San Francisco Chicago and S o Paulo Brazil. As part of its global expansion efforts in the last few years MSCI has opened international offices in Budapest Dubai Monterrey Mumbai and Shanghai.

Strategy
The company has consistently achieved revenue growth and positive earnings by continually expanding its relationships with investment institutions and regularly developing and enhancing its products. It has also made key acquisitions in order to complement or expand its client base and offerings.

EXECUTIVES

Chairman and CEO, Henry A. Fernandez, age 60, $950,000 total compensation
Chief Client Officer, Laurent Seyer, age 54, $481,597 total compensation
Head of Analytics, Jorge Mina, age 44
Managing Director and COO, C. D. Baer Pettit, age 54, $454,762 total compensation
CFO, Kathleen A. Winters, age 51, $350,000 total compensation
Managing Director and Global Head of Research and Product Development, Peter J. Zangari, age 51, $525,000 total compensation
Managing Director and Head of Equity Index Products, Diana H. Tidd, age 49, $425,000 total compensation
Managing Director and Global Head of Research, Remy Briand, age 53
Managing Director and General Counsel, Rick Bogdan
Managing Director and CTO, Tom Gwydir
Vice President Application Management, Terry King
Vice President, Troy Daley
Vice President, Francesco Faiola
Vice President Portfolio Management Analytics, Ting Fang
Vice President Product Management, Jean-michel Huet
Vice President, Kelly Taylor
Vice President Human Resources Generalist, Michelle Davidson
Vice President Systems Engineer, David Geller
Vice President Human Resources Projects And Processes (Recruitment Talent Management And Operations), Theresa Bowman
Vice President, Anil Rao
Vice President, Wei Yuan
Vice President, Andy Deutsch
Vice President, Michael Falag-ey
Vice President Product Manager, Samprabhu Rubandhas
Vice President of Finance, Weera Aroonratskul
Vice President, Bryan Murphy
Information Technology Vice President, Avi Vichniac
Vice President Quality Assurance, Matt Baxter
Vice President Finance, Yilin Lee
Vice President Information Technology Operations, Mike Bowman
Vice President Esg Consultant Client Coverage, Puja Modi
Vice President, Susan Yuann
Vice President Technology, Shane Fry
Vice President, Michael Salvatico
Vice President, Pravin Joshi
Vice President, Gergely Szalka
Vice President Risk Management Analytics, Alan Grabenstein
Vice President Corporate Services, Anil Thomas
Vice President, Beth Byington
Vice President Financial Planning And Analysis, Nitin Lad
Vice President, Hector Jimenez
Vice President, April Cody
Vice President And Head Of Esg Impact And Screening Research, Meggin Eastman
Vice President, Janos Szlatenyi
Vice President, Sarah Greenberg
Vice President Technology, Daoping Zhang
Vice President Head of Product Management, Blake McLaughlin
Vice President Application Development, Dylan McClung
Vice President Implementation Services, Chris Brady
Vice President, Sujit Kumar
Vice President, Abhijit Narvekar
Vice President, Zoltan Deme
Vice President, Istvan Varga-Haszonits
Vice President, Patrick Lee
Vice President, Roman Kouzmenko
Vice President, Collin Mcclain
Vice President, Santosh Kumar
Vice President Data Operations And Technology, Bala Amuthan
Vice President, Jerry Lettieri
Vice President Tax Reporting And Compliance, Savilla Kaltner
Vp Client Services, Sana Stephens
Vice President Finance, Anil Venherkar
Vice President Index Research, Pavlo Taranenko
Vice President Senior Technical Architect Technical Lead, Javier Perez
Vice President Investment Risk, Kelvin Chinyamutangira
Vice President Index Sales, Joseph Perri
Vice President Index Sales, Samir Sampat
Vice President Index Sales, Colin Miller
Vice President Department of Operations and Technology, Jason Handscombe
Vice President Human Resources, Shara Seeyave
Vice President, Jaroslav Lajos
Vice President Applied Research, Raina Oberoi
Vice President, Manish Shakdwipee
Vice President, Alia Karrazzi
Vice President, Alex Johnson
Vice President, Chandrashekhar Singh
Vice President, Sandesh Dsouza
Vice President, Chuck Nguyen
Vice President, Maxim Kuperman
VICE PRESIDENT OF SALES AND MARKETING, Isabel Stuart
Vice President Managed Service Operations, Cristina Garcia
VICE PRESIDENT RELATIONSHIP MANAGEMENT TEAM, Lee Grimmer
Vice President IPD, Glenn Corney
VICE PRESIDENT IN ANALYTICS RESEARCH, Jay Yao
Vice President Manila Client Services Analytics Team, Tiara Fontanilla
Vice President Client Coverage, Maria Lilli
Vice President, Silvia Zhao
Vice President Infrastructure Engineering, Jason Haibi
Vp Finance, Haro Bahadourian
Vice President, Amol Nayak
Vice President, Kirk Oldford
Vice President, Marco Vaccaro
Vice President Wealth Advisory Channel, Paul Riccardella
Vice President, Janet Green
Secretary, Ester Godinho
Board Member, Marcus Smith
Auditors: PricewaterhouseCoopers LLP

LOCATIONS

HQ: MSCI Inc
7 World Trade Center, 250 Greenwich Street, 49th Floor, New York, NY 10007
Phone: 212 804-3900
Web: www.msci.com

PRODUCTS/OPERATIONS

2014 Sales

	$ mil.	% of total
Index real estate and ESG	582.6	59
Risk management analytics	309.7	31
Portfolio management analytics	104.4	10
Total	**996.7**	**100**

Selected Offerings
Barra (equity and multi-asset class portfolio analytics product)
CFRA (forensic accounting risk research legal/regulatory risk assessment due-diligence and educational services)
FEA (entergy and commodity asset valuation analytics)
ISS (governance research and outsourced proxy voting and reporting services)
MSCI Indices (flagship global equity indices)
RiskMetrics (risk and wealth management products)

COMPETITORS

Algorithmics
Deutsche B ¶rse
Dow Jones
FTSE Group
FactSet
Liquid Holdings
Nomura Securities
Russell
S&P

MTS Systems Corp

In this world nothing is certain but death and taxes — and those things tested by MTS Systems. The company produces testing systems that simulate repeated or harsh conditions to determine mechanical behavior of materials products and structures. Its systems are used worldwide in infrastructure markets from inspecting steel to locomotive rails. MTS caters to auto makers with road simulators while in aerospace its equipment tests aircraft fatigue. Services include maintenance and training. MTS also supplies industrial sensors to increase machine efficiency and safety. International customers generate more than two-thirds of the company's revenue.

Operations
MTS's test segment primarily offers products for the testing of ground vehicles (accounting for about 50% of the segment's revenue) and products for testing materials in industries that include power generation aerospace vehicles and bio-medicine (25% of the segment's revenue). Structure-testing products for aerospace wind energy structural engineering petroleum and other industries account for the remainder of the test segment's revenue.

The company's sensors which account for about 35% of sales are used in construction agriculture mining and manufacturing (35% of the segment's revenue) and industrial sensors (about 20% of the segment's revenue) are used in heavy industrial markets and energy and power generation. Systems sensors (accounting for 10% of the segment's revenue) consist of dynamic test measurement and sensing systems used to test model and monitor the behavior of structures and processes.

Geographic Reach
MTS based in Eden Prairie Minnesota has manufacturing plants in China Germany and the US (in Minnesota New York Utah Michigan and North Carolina). Other offices are located across Asia Europe and the Americas. The US generates about a third of sales Europe about 25% China 20% and Asia (excluding China) about 20%.

Sales and Marketing
MTS's test segment has sales staff in the US and sales and service subsidiaries in Canada China France Germany Italy India Japan Russia South Korea Spain Sweden and the UK. The sensor segment has direct field sales and service representatives throughout US and sales subsidiaries in Italy the UK France Germany China Japan Canada and Belgium. The company also sells through distributors.

Financial Performance
MTS followed two years of declining revenue with two years of rising revenue including a 21% jump in 2017 (ended October) from 2016. The leap to $788 million in revenue for 2017 came courtesy of the acquisition of PCB which boosted Sensor revenue more than 100%. The company highlighted strong demand for positional sensors particularly in the heavy industrial markets. Test revenue fell about 2% from year-to-year.

Net income slipped to about $25 million in 2017 from $27.5 million in 2016 because of higher operating expenses some related to the PCB deal and increased interest expense.

Cash and cash equivalents rose to about $109 million in 2017 from about $85 million in 2016 driven by about $35 million in depreciation and amortization $25 million of net income an increase in working capital of about $11 million and other factors.

Strategy
MTS Systems' acquisition of PCB Group helped position the company take advantage of the growing market for sensors. Just in 2017 (ended October) the acquisition more than doubled MTS's sensor sales. The increasing number of sensors used in automotive applications for electric and self-driving vehicle technologies is an opportunity for MTS. The company also sees growth in sensors for industrial hydraulics and in equipment ordered by the US Department of Defense.

Mergers and Acquisitions
In 2016 MTS acquired PCB Group a manufacturer of piezoelectric sensors and components used for vibration pressure and force measurement for $580 million. The acquisition of PCB expanded MTS's market position in sensors.

EXECUTIVES

President and CEO, Jeffrey A. (Jeff) Graves, age 57, $647,500 total compensation
SVP and CIO, Mark D. Losee
President Material Test Systems, William C. Becker, age 65
President Vehicles and Structures Test Systems, Steven B. Harrison, age 53
SVP and CFO, Brian T. Ross, age 43
President MTS Sensors, David T. Hore, age 53, $125,000 total compensation
Senior Vice President Test, William E Bachrach
Vice President Sales, Kevin McQuillan
Vice President Customer Service And Support, J E Egerdal
Vice President Of Information Technology, Duane Fox
Senior Vice President Operational Excellence, David Saylor
Vice President Operations, Joe Zuiker
Chairman, David J. (Dave) Anderson, age 72
Board Member, David Johnson
Auditors: DELOITTE & TOUCHE LLP

LOCATIONS
HQ: MTS Systems Corp
14000 Technology Drive, Eden Prairie, MN 55344
Phone: 952 937-4000
Web: www.mts.com

PRODUCTS/OPERATIONS

2017 Sales

	$ mil.	% of total
Test	504.1	64
Sensors	283.8	36
Total	**787.9**	**100**

2017 Sales

	$ mil.	% of total
Product	691.4	88
Service	96.5	12
Total	**787.9**	**100**

COMPETITORS

ACS Motion Control	Mechanical Technology
AMETEK	Moog
Aero Systems Engineering	OYO
GE	Pepperl+Fuchs
HORIBA	PerkinElmer
Illinois Tool Works	Pure Technologies
Instron	Schmitt Industries
JT3	Tech/Ops Sevcon

HISTORICAL FINANCIALS
Company Type: Public

Income Statement
FYE: December 31

	REVENUE ($ mil.)	NET INCOME ($ mil.)	NET PROFIT MARGIN	EMPLOYEES
12/18	1,433.9	507.8	35.4%	3,112
12/17	1,274.1	303.9	23.9%	3,038
12/16	1,150.6	260.8	22.7%	2,862
12/15	1,075.0	223.6	20.8%	2,926
12/14	996.6	284.1	28.5%	2,926
Annual Growth	9.5%	15.6%	—	1.6%

2018 Year-End Financials
Debt ratio: 76.0%
Return on equity: 433.1%
Cash ($ mil.): 904.1
Current ratio: 1.77
Long-term debt ($ mil.): 2,575.5
No. of shares (mil.): 84.1
Dividends
  Yield: 1.3%
  Payout: 33.9%
Market value ($ mil.): 12,410.0

	STOCK PRICE ($) FY Close	P/E High/Low	PER SHARE ($) Earnings	Dividends	Book Value
12/18	147.43	31 22	5.66	1.92	(1.98)
12/17	126.54	38 23	3.31	1.32	4.45
12/16	78.78	33 23	2.70	1.00	3.48
12/15	72.13	36 23	2.03	0.80	8.92
12/14	47.44	20 16	2.43	0.18	12.78
Annual Growth	32.8%	— —	23.5%	80.7%	—

HISTORICAL FINANCIALS
Company Type: Public

Income Statement
FYE: September 28

	REVENUE ($ mil.)	NET INCOME ($ mil.)	NET PROFIT MARGIN	EMPLOYEES
09/19	892.5	43.0	4.8%	3,500
09/18	778.0	61.3	7.9%	3,400
09/17*	787.9	25.0	3.2%	3,500
10/16	650.1	27.4	4.2%	3,500
10/15	563.9	45.4	8.1%	2,400
Annual Growth	12.2%	(1.3%)	—	9.9%

*Fiscal year change

2019 Year-End Financials
Debt ratio: 39.4%
Return on equity: 8.9%
Cash ($ mil.): 57.9
Current ratio: 1.79
Long-term debt ($ mil.): 484.6
No. of shares (mil.): 19.1
Dividends
  Yield: 0.0%
  Payout: 54.3%
Market value ($ mil.): 1,057.0

	STOCK PRICE ($) FY Close	P/E High/Low	PER SHARE ($) Earnings	Dividends	Book Value
09/19	55.27	27 17	2.21	1.20	25.31
09/18	54.75	18 14	3.18	1.20	26.77
09/17*	53.45	45 32	1.31	1.20	24.14
10/16	46.03	40 25	1.70	1.20	24.33
10/15	57.73	25 18	3.00	1.20	17.29
Annual Growth	(1.1%)	— —	(7.4%)	(0.0%)	10.0%

*Fiscal year change

MutualFirst Financial Inc

EXECUTIVES

Senior Vice President Business Banking of MutualBank, Christopher Caldwell
Vice President Mutual Federal Savings Bank, Shayne Nagy
Assistant Vice President, Susan Smith
Assistant Vice President, Stephanie Salyer
Assistant Vice President, Preston Tollett
Senior Vice President Risk Management, Sharon Ferguson
Vice President, Kathy Balser
Vice President Client Relationship Manager Elkhart County, Vince Turner
Vice President Mutual Federal Savings Bank, Kathy Sears
Vice President Compliance Wealth Management, Martha Oprea
Vice President Mutual Federal Savings Bank, Dorothy Douglass
Vice President And Trust Investment Officer, David Riggs
Assistant Vice President Client Relationship Manager, Michele Banes
Auditors: BKD, LLP

LOCATIONS

HQ: MutualFirst Financial Inc
110 E. Charles Street, Muncie, IN 47305-2419
Phone: 765 747-2800

COMPETITORS

Ameriana Bancorp
Fifth Third
First Financial Bancorp
First Merchants
German American Bancorp
Huntington Bancshares
Old National Bancorp
PNC Financial
STAR Financial Group

HISTORICAL FINANCIALS
Company Type: Public

Income Statement
FYE: December 31

	ASSETS ($ mil.)	NET INCOME ($ mil.)	INCOME AS % OF ASSETS	EMPLOYEES
12/18	2,049.3	18.8	0.9%	528
12/17	1,588.9	12.3	0.8%	422
12/16	1,553.1	13.2	0.9%	442
12/15	1,478.2	12.2	0.8%	445
12/14	1,424.2	10.8	0.8%	438
Annual Growth	9.5%	14.9%	—	4.8%

2018 Year-End Financials

Return on assets: 1.0%
Return on equity: 10.7%
Long-term debt ($ mil.): —
No. of shares (mil.): 8.6
Sales ($ mil): 99.2
Dividends
Yield: 2.7%
Payout: 41.3%
Market value ($ mil.): 229.0

	STOCK PRICE ($) FY Close	P/E High/Low		PER SHARE ($) Earnings	Dividends	Book Value
12/18	26.57	18	11	2.21	0.74	23.52
12/17	38.55	24	18	1.64	0.66	20.34
12/16	33.10	19	13	1.76	0.58	19.12
12/15	24.80	15	12	1.62	0.48	18.46
12/14	21.88	15	11	1.46	0.32	17.63
Annual Growth	5.0%	—		10.9%	23.3%	7.5%

MVB Financial Corp

EXECUTIVES

Chief Executive Officer; President, Larry Nazza
Vice President Small Business Development Officer, Kevin Corey
Senior Vice President Audit Mv, Jim Potasky
Svp Fintech Compliance, Donna Rakes
Auditors: Dixon Hughes Goodman LLP

LOCATIONS

HQ: MVB Financial Corp
301 Virginia Avenue, Fairmont, WV 26554
Phone: 304 363-4800
Web: www.mvbbanking.com

HISTORICAL FINANCIALS
Company Type: Public

Income Statement
FYE: December 31

	ASSETS ($ mil.)	NET INCOME ($ mil.)	INCOME AS % OF ASSETS	EMPLOYEES
12/18	1,750.9	12.0	0.7%	0
12/17	1,534.3	7.5	0.5%	0
12/16	1,418.8	12.9	0.9%	382
12/15	1,384.4	6.8	0.5%	371
12/14	1,110.4	2.0	0.2%	324
Annual Growth	12.1%	55.0%	—	—

2018 Year-End Financials

Return on assets: 0.7%
Return on equity: 7.3%
Long-term debt ($ mil.): —
No. of shares (mil.): 11.6
Sales ($ mil): 108.4
Dividends
Yield: 0.6%
Payout: 12.3%
Market value ($ mil.): 209.0

	STOCK PRICE ($) FY Close	P/E High/Low		PER SHARE ($) Earnings	Dividends	Book Value
12/18	18.04	19	16	1.00	0.11	15.23
12/17	20.10	29	18	0.68	0.10	14.38
12/16	12.80	10	7	1.31	0.08	14.57
12/15	13.10	20	16	0.76	0.08	14.23
12/14	14.99	164	65	0.22	0.08	13.71
Annual Growth	4.7%	—		46.0%	8.3%	2.7%

MYR Group Inc

MYR Group's work can be electrifying. The specialty contractor builds and maintains electric delivery infrastructure systems for utilities and commercial clients. MYR Group constructs transmission and distribution lines for the oil and gas power and telecommunications industries. The company also installs and maintains electrical wiring in commercial and industrial facilities and traffic and rail systems. The group operates nationwide through subsidiaries including The L.E. Myers Co. Harlan Electric Hawkeye Construction Sturgeon Electric MYR Transmission Services and Great Southwestern Construction. MYR's transmission and distribution segment accounts for about three-fourths of the group's revenues.

Operations

The company's Transmission & Distribution customers generated 74% of MYR Group's revenue in 2014. Its Commercial & Industrial segment brought in 26% of revenue in 2014.

Completed projects include the Cross Texas Transmission 345kV Transmission Line Project Spearville to Axtell 345kV Transmission Line (also known as the KETA Project) the Meadowbrook to Loudoun 500kV Transmission Line and Carson Substation to Suffolk Substation 500kV Transmission Lines.

Sales and Marketing

Transmission & Distribution customers include electric utilities private developers cooperatives and municipalities. Its Commercial & Industrial segment provides electrical contracting services to property owners and general contractors in the Western US.

Its top 10 customers accounted for nearly 50% of revenues in fiscal 2014; no single customer accounted for more than 10% of sales.

MYR Group has logged between $400000 and $500000 each year since 2010 on selling general and administrative expenses (which include advertising expenses).

Financial Performance

With the exception of a slight dip in 2013 revenue has been on the rise for the past five years. In 2014 it increased 5% to $944 million largely on growth in the Commercial & Industrial segment. That segment's services were generally in higher demand; improving economic conditions in its core markets of Colorado and Arizona also helped boost business.

Net income has risen for the past five years and in 2014 it increased 5% to $36.6 million thanks both to MYR's higher revenue and increased interest earnings. Cash flow from operations fell 42% to $44 million that year as more cash was used for accounts payable.

Strategy

MYR Group looks to grow organically or through strategic acquisitions and joint ventures. It aims to improve its competitive position in existing markets while also expanding into new geographic markets. The company has also dog-eared funds to invest in additional properties and equipment to support its strategy.

The Transmission & Distribution segment counts some 125 cooperatives electric utilities and municipalities as customers. The business stands to benefit from a continued emphasis on improving and upgrading the country's power supply and the increasing market for alternative energy. As wind and solar farm developments grow there is an increasing demand to link the farms to large power grids. MYR Group works on numerous wind farm projects each year. The company expects increased activity in that sector.

The company's Commercial & Industrial segment has a regional focus in Colorado and Arizona.

MYR Group maintains one of the largest fleets of vehicles in the US (some 5000 units) that can be mobilized for transmission and distribution work around the country. Because of this asset MYR Group often is called to restore power in the aftermath of hurricanes floods ice storms and other natural disasters. This is a relatively small part of the company's business though.

The group's strategy to take advantage of the growing need for infrastructure work includes seeking out possible acquisition targets or joint venture partners as well as expanding into new markets. It will also add to its fleet as it deems beneficial and has been spending tens of millions of dollars on new specialty equipment and tooling.

Company Background

MYR was founded in 1891 by Lewis Edward Myers who briefly worked as a salesman with Thomas Edison.

EXECUTIVES

Vice President Information Technology, Brian Smolinski
SVP, William H. Green, age 75, $346,000 total compensation
President and CEO, Richard S. (Rick) Swartz, age 55, $376,500 total compensation
SVP CFO and Treasurer, Betty R. Johnson, age 60
SVP East and President L.E. Myers Co., Tod Cooper
Vice President Safety, Steve Cavanaugh
Vice President Assistant General Counsel, Michael Orndahl
Vice President Large Projects, Rick Pieper
Vice President Contract Performance, Marco Martinez
Vice President Information Technology, Jean Luber
Vice President Of Human Resources, Doreen Keller
VICE PRESIDENT, Kelley Lange
President and CEO, William A. (Bill) Koertner, age 69
Board Member, Gary Johnson
Auditors: Crowe LLP

LOCATIONS

HQ: MYR Group Inc
1701 Golf Road, Suite 3-1012, Rolling Meadows, IL 60008
Phone: 847 290-1891
Web: www.myrgroup.com

PRODUCTS/OPERATIONS

2014 Sales by Segment

	% of total
Transmission & Distribution	74
Commercial & Industrial	26
Total	100

Selected Services

Electrical
  Commercial/Industrial Construction
  Design-build services
  Directional boring
  Emergency storm response
  Fiber optics
  Foundations & caissons
  Gas distribution
  Highway lighting
  Overhead distribution
  PCS/Cellular towers
  Preconstruction services
  Substation
  Telecommunications
  Traffic signals
  Transmission
  Underground distribution
Mechanical
  Boiler construction and maintenance
  Erection of piping systems
  General contracting
  In-house fabrication
  Instrumentation
  Maintenance
  Preconstruction services
  Retrofit to existing systems

Selected Subsidiaries

ComTel Technology Inc.
Great Southwestern Construction Inc.
Harlan Electric Company
Hawkeye Construction Inc.
Meyers International Inc.
MYR Transmission Services Inc.
MYRpower Inc.
The L.E. Myers Co.
Sturgeon Electric Company Inc.

COMPETITORS

Austin Industries	MDU Resources
Cupertino Electric	MasTec
Dycom	Mass Electric
EEI	Pike Corporation
EMCOR	Quanta Services
Goldfield	Siemens AG
Henkels & McCoy	Vario Construction Company
IES Holdings	
Kelso-Burnett	

HISTORICAL FINANCIALS

Company Type: Public

Income Statement   FYE: December 31

	REVENUE ($ mil.)	NET INCOME ($ mil.)	NET PROFIT MARGIN	EMPLOYEES
12/18	1,531.1	31.0	2.0%	5,500
12/17	1,403.3	21.1	1.5%	5,275
12/16	1,142.4	21.4	1.9%	4,600
12/15	1,061.6	27.3	2.6%	4,075
12/14	943.9	36.5	3.9%	3,650
Annual Growth	12.9%	(4.0%)	—	10.8%

2018 Year-End Financials

Debt ratio: 12.3%
Return on equity: 10.1%
Cash ($ mil.): 7.5
Current ratio: 1.68
Long-term debt ($ mil.): 87.6
No. of shares (mil.): 16.5
Dividends
  Yield: —
  Payout: —
Market value ($ mil.): 467.0

	STOCK PRICE ($) FY Close	P/E High/Low	PER SHARE ($) Earnings	Dividends	Book Value
12/18	28.17	21 14	1.87	0.00	19.50
12/17	35.73	33 18	1.28	0.00	17.43
12/16	37.68	32 15	1.23	0.00	16.11
12/15	20.61	24 14	1.30	0.00	16.52
12/14	27.40	16 13	1.69	0.00	15.51
Annual Growth	0.7%	— —	2.6%	—	5.9%

NASB Financial Inc

EXECUTIVES

Vice President, Lori West
Vice President Human Resources, Christine M Schaben
Vice President, Ron Stafford
Vice President Construction and Development Lending, Christopher Vick
Assistant Vice President, Carmen Cunningham
Auditors: BKD, LLP

LOCATIONS

HQ: NASB Financial Inc
12498 South 71 Highway, Grandview, MO 64030
Phone: 816 765-2200
Web: www.nasb.com

COMPETITORS

Bank of America	Guaranty Federal
Commerce Bancshares	U.S. Bancorp
Dickinson Financial	UMB Financial

HISTORICAL FINANCIALS

Company Type: Public

Income Statement   FYE: September 30

	ASSETS ($ mil.)	NET INCOME ($ mil.)	INCOME AS % OF ASSETS	EMPLOYEES
09/19	2,605.2	43.1	1.7%	0
09/18	2,060.3	29.1	1.4%	0
09/17	2,062.3	29.4	1.4%	0
09/16	1,949.6	22.3	1.1%	0
09/15	1,530.6	21.5	1.4%	0
Annual Growth	14.2%	19.0%	—	—

2019 Year-End Financials

Return on assets: 1.8%
Return on equity: 17.4%
Long-term debt ($ mil.): —
No. of shares (mil.): 7.3
Sales ($ mil): 177.0
Dividends
  Yield: 4.5%
  Payout: 46.4%
Market value ($ mil.): 326.0

	STOCK PRICE ($) FY Close	P/E High/Low	PER SHARE ($) Earnings	Dividends	Book Value
09/19	44.20	8 6	5.85	2.00	35.56
09/18	40.60	11 9	3.94	3.82	31.37
09/17	36.11	10 8	3.98	1.22	31.55
09/16	33.75	11 9	3.02	0.98	28.92
09/15	29.00	11 8	2.90	2.80	26.66
Annual Growth	11.1%	— —	19.2%	(8.1%)	7.5%

National Bank Holdings Corp

National Bank Holdings is the holding company for NBH Bank which operates nearly 100 branches in four south and central US states under various brands including: Bank Midwest in Kansas and

Missouri Community Banks of Colorado in Colorado and Hillcrest Bank in Texas. Targeting small to medium-sized businesses and consumers the banks offer traditional checking and savings accounts as well as commercial and residential mortgages agricultural loans and commercial loans. The bank boasted $4.7 billion in assets at the end of 2015 including $2.6 billion in loans and $3.8 billion in deposits. Over 80% of its total revenue is made up of interest income.

Operations
About 63% of the bank's total revenue came from loan interest (including fees) during 2015 while another 19% came from interest on its investment securities. The rest of its revenue came from service charges (7%) bank card fees (5%) and other miscellaneous income sources.

Geographic Reach
National Bank Holdings had a network of 97 banking centers in four states at the end of 2015 with more than half of those in Colorado a third in Missouri nearly a dozen branches in Kansas and two branches in Texas.

Sales and Marketing
The bank serves small- to medium-sized businesses and consumers via its network of banking locations and through online and mobile banking products. It spent $4.3 million on advertising during 2015 down from $4.6 million and $5.3 million in 2014 and 2013 respectively.

Financial Performance
The group's annual revenues and profits have been trending downward over the past few years as it has been selling off branches and loan business to concentrate on the geographic markets and loan types where it carries the most expertise.

National Bank Holdings' revenue rebounded 5% to $192.86 million during 2015 mostly as it earned $21 million in FDIC-related income related to lower indemnification amortization increased FDIC loss-share income and a $5 million gain on an FDIC loss-share agreement termination.

Despite revenue growth in 2015 the group's net income plummeted 47% to $4.9 million mostly on higher loan loss provisions which climbed more than $6.2 million during the year as it increased its specific reserves on non 310-30 loans. National Bank Holdings' operations used $37.65 million compared to just $2.76 million in cash during 2014 mostly after adjusting its earnings for non-cash items mostly related to a decrease in net amounts due to the FDIC.

Strategy
National Bank Holdings has been trimming its branch count in recent years to focus on serving clients through full-service banking centers across its four chief markets of Colorado Kansas Missouri and Texas as well as through online and mobile banking channels. Toward this end in 2013 the bank began integrating its limited-service retirement center locations into its full-service banking centers while also exiting its limited presence in California (its banks there had operated under the Community Banks of California banner).

Meanwhile the regional community bank continues to selectively acquire smaller banks and complementary financial companies that serve small- and medium-sized businesses to grow its loan and deposit business.

Mergers and Acquisitions
In August 2015 National Bank Holdings bought $142 million-asset Pine River Bank in Colorado along with its $64 million in loans and $130 million in deposits for $9.5 million in cash.

Company Background
Formed in 2009 National Bank Holdings went public in 2012. Prior to its filing National Bank Holdings was minority-owned by a number of private shareholders and corporate entities including Taconic Capital Advisors Wellington Management and Paulson & Co.

EXECUTIVES

Chairman President and CEO, G. Timothy (Tim) Laney, age 59, $500,000 total compensation
Chief of Enterprise Technology & Integration and NBH Bank N.A. Midwest/ Texas Division President, Thomas M. (Tom) Metzger, $300,000 total compensation
Chief Financial Officer, Brian F. Lilly, age 60, $295,705 total compensation
Chief Risk Officer, Richard U. Newfield, age 58, $300,000 total compensation
Board Member, Burney Warren
Board Member, Robert Dean
Board Member, Arthur Zeile
Auditors: KPMG LLP

LOCATIONS

HQ: National Bank Holdings Corp
7800 East Orchard Road, Suite 300, Greenwood Village, CO 80111
Phone: 303 892-8715
Web: www.nationalbankholdings.com

PRODUCTS/OPERATIONS

2015 Sales

	% of total
Interest and dividend income:	
Interest and fees on loans	63
Interest and dividends on investment securities	18
Dividends on non-marketable securities	1
Interest on interest-bearing bank deposits	
Total	82
Non-interest income:	
Service charges	7
Bank card fees	5
Gain on sales of mortgages net	1
Bank-owned life insurance income	1
Other non-interest income	2
Bargain purchase gain	1
Gain on previously charged-off acquired loans	-
OREO related write-ups and other income	1
FDIC indemnification asset amortization net of gain on termination	-
FDIC loss sharing income (expense)	-
Total Non-Interest Income	18
Total	**100**

COMPETITORS

BBVA Compass Bancshares	FirstBank Holding Company
Bank of America	JPMorgan Chase
Bank of the West	KeyCorp
Capitol Federal Financial	U.S. Bancorp
	UMB Financial
Central Bancompany	Wells Fargo
Commerce Bancshares	Zions Bancorporation
Enterprise Financial Services	

HISTORICAL FINANCIALS
Company Type: Public

Income Statement   FYE: December 31

	ASSETS ($ mil.)	NET INCOME ($ mil.)	INCOME AS % OF ASSETS	EMPLOYEES
12/18	5,676.6	61.4	1.1%	1,332
12/17	4,843.4	14.5	0.3%	926
12/16	4,573.0	23.0	0.5%	1,004
12/15	4,683.9	4.8	0.1%	1,042
12/14	4,819.6	9.1	0.2%	1,056
Annual Growth	4.2%	60.9%		6.0%

2018 Year-End Financials
Return on assets: 1.1%   Dividends
Return on equity: 10.0%   Yield: 1.7%
Long-term debt ($ mil.): —   Payout: 27.6%
No. of shares (mil.): 30.7   Market value ($ mil.): 950.0
Sales ($ mil): 292.1

	STOCK PRICE ($) FY Close	P/E High/Low		PER SHARE ($) Earnings	Dividends	Book Value
12/18	30.87	21	15	1.95	0.54	22.59
12/17	32.43	68	56	0.53	0.34	19.81
12/16	31.89	40	23	0.79	0.22	20.32
12/15	21.37	166	127	0.14	0.20	20.34
12/14	19.41	97	84	0.22	0.20	20.43
Annual Growth	12.3%	—	—	72.5%	28.2%	2.5%

National Beverage Corp.

National Beverage makes and distributes the popular LaCroix sparkling water brand including a variety flavors. National Beverage also makes the Shasta and Faygo brands of flavored soft drinks (both of which were launched more than a century ago) the ClearFruit flavored waters Everfresh and Mr. Pure juice and juice-added drinks Rip It energy drink and Ohana lemonades and teas. Customers include national and regional grocers convenience stores and foodservice distributors. National Beverage operates a dozen facilities located in ten US states. Founded in 1985 chairman and CEO Nick Caporella owns 74% of the business.

Financial Performance
National Beverage had been ticking along steadily for decades until its LaCroix brand suddenly became immensely popular among millennials in 2015 and sales rocketed. Since then the brand lost its fizz as consumers discovered it lacked distinguishing features compared to copycat products made by bigger companies that popped up soon after.

In fiscal 2019 (ended April 27) the company's sales still grew 4% to $1.0 billion although this represented a sharp slowdown on growth rates seen over the last five years.

Net income fell 6% to $140.9 million the first fall in profit in five years. Higher cost of sales and general expenses weighed on margins although taxes decreased.

National Beverage's cash balance weakened during 2018 ending the year $33.7 million lower at $156.2 million. The company's operations generated $139.4 million while its investing activities used $38.3 million and its financing used $134.8 million. By National Beverage's biggest cash use in 2018 was a massive dividend of $134.8 million nearly its entire net income. The company also recorded capex of $38.3 million.

Strategy
National Beverage its fair to say got lucky in the mid-2010s when its LaCroix brand which has been around for decades suddenly exploded in popularity. The company's eccentric octogenarian CEO and chairman Nick Caporella is trying to keep the company's sales from going flat while paying massive dividends (mainly to himself). In 2017 for instance the company paid a whopping 98% dividend and 96% dividend in 2019. The company's main strategy is to position its products towards the "crossover consumers" demographic which desires healthier alternatives to artificially or sugar-sweetened drinks and provided the demand for LaCroix's great success.

EXECUTIVES

EVP Finance, George R. Bracken, age 76
SVP Operational Guidance, Dean A. McCoy, age 63, $225,000 total compensation
President and Director, Joseph G. (Joe) Caporella, age 60, $650,000 total compensation
Chairman and CEO, Nick A. Caporella, age 84
EVP BevCo Sales, Dennis L. Thompson, $200,000 total compensation
Executive Vice President Strategic Sourcing, James Bolton
Senior Vice President Sales, Anthony Kibbey
Executive Vice President Foodservice Shasta Sales, Charles Maier
Auditors: RSM US LLP

LOCATIONS

HQ: National Beverage Corp.
  8100 SW Tenth Street, Suite 4000, Fort Lauderdale, FL 33324
Phone: 954 581-0922
Web: www.nationalbeverage.com

PRODUCTS/OPERATIONS

SELECTED BRANDS
LaCroix
Shasta Sparkling
Everfresh and Mr. Pure
Rip It

SELECTED SUBSIDIARIES
BevCo Sales Inc.
Big Shot Beverages Inc.
Everfresh Beverages Inc.
Faygo Beverages Inc.
National Beverage Vending Company
NewBevCo Inc.
NutraFizz Products Corp.
Shasta Beverages Inc.
Sundance Beverage Company

COMPETITORS

Big Red	Mondelez International
Chiquita Brands	Monster Beverage
Citrus World	Mountain Valley
Clearly Canadian	Naked Juice
Coca-Cola	National Grape
Cott	Cooperative
Crystal Rock Holdings	Nestlé Waters North
Danone Water	America
Dole Food	Ocean Spray
Dr Pepper Snapple Group	Odwalla
	PepsiCo
Eldorado Artesian Springs	Red Bull
	South Beach Beverage
Energy Brands	Sunkist
Fiji Water	Sunny Delight
Gatorade	Tropicana
Hornell Brewing	Welch's
Impulse Energy USA	Wet Planet Beverages
Jones Soda	

HISTORICAL FINANCIALS
Company Type: Public

Income Statement — FYE: April 27

	REVENUE ($ mil.)	NET INCOME ($ mil.)	NET PROFIT MARGIN	EMPLOYEES
04/19	1,014.1	140.8	13.9%	1,640
04/18	975.7	149.7	15.3%	1,500
04/17	826.9	107.0	12.9%	1,300
04/16*	704.7	61.2	8.7%	1,200
05/15	645.8	49.3	7.6%	1,200
Annual Growth	11.9%	30.0%	—	8.1%

*Fiscal year change

2019 Year-End Financials

Debt ratio: —
Return on equity: 42.6%
Cash ($ mil.): 156.2
Current ratio: 3.31
Long-term debt ($ mil.): —
No. of shares (mil.): 46.6
Dividends
 Yield: 0.0%
 Payout: 96.6%
Market value ($ mil.): 2,682.0

	STOCK PRICE ($) FY Close	P/E High/Low		PER SHARE ($) Earnings	Dividends	Book Value
04/19	57.50	41	18	3.00	2.90	7.11
04/18	89.78	39	26	3.19	1.50	7.11
04/17	88.59	40	19	2.29	1.50	5.27
04/16*	46.74	37	16	1.31	0.00	4.43
05/15	22.42	25	16	1.05	0.00	3.19
Annual Growth	26.5%			30.0%	—	22.2%

*Fiscal year change

National Health Investors, Inc.

National Health Investors has a financial investment in the nation's health. The real estate investment trust (REIT) owns or makes mortgage investments in health care properties primarily long-term care facilities. With more than 180 properties in over 30 states its holdings also include residences for people with developmental disabilities assisted-living complexes medical office buildings retirement centers and an acute care hospital. About one-third of National Health Investors' properties are leased to its largest tenant National HealthCare Corporation; half are leased to regional health care providers. A majority of the REIT's facilities are located in Florida Texas and Tennessee.

Operations
The company owned 183 facilities in 31 states in 2014 including 106 senior housing communities 71 skilled nursing facilities four hospitals and two medical office buildings.

As a REIT National Health generates nearly 95% of its business from rental income with the remainder of its revenue coming from investment income and interest income on mortgage or other notes. About 40% of the REIT's total revenue came from rental income from regional operators in 2014 while rental income from publicly-owned operators and privately-owned national chains contributed 26% and 29% to the REIT's total revenue. Smaller operators contributed the remainder.

Geographic Reach
Tennessee-based National Health Investors has most of its properties in the states of Florida Texas and Tennessee.

Sales and Marketing
National Health's three main operators (tenants) include: an affiliate of Holiday Retirement National HealthCare Corporation and Bickford Senior Living; each of which contributed more than 10% of the REIT's total revenue during 2014. Senior Living Communities began making lease payments on eight retirement communities during 2015 which would amount to more than 17% of National Health's total revenue during the year.

Some of National Health's other top tenants include: Brookdale Senior Living Fundamental Health Services Management and Legend Healthcare.

Financial Performance
National Health Investors' revenues and profits have been on the rise in recent years thanks to aggressive expansion from property acquisitions. The REIT's revenue spiked by 51% to a record $177.51 million in 2014 mostly thanks to a 57% increase in rental income stemming from nearly $749 million worth of new real estate investment properties.

Despite higher revenue in 2014 National's net income dipped by 4% to $103.05 million as depreciating expenses rose with new property acquisitions and due to higher interest expenses from the company's credit borrowings during the year.

The REIT's operating cash levels rose by 21% to $21.95 million after adjusting its earnings for (non-cash) depreciation and amortization expenses.

Strategy
National Health Investments typically expands its property portfolio — and therefore rental income — through strategic property acquisitions of senior housing communities and assisted living properties from real estate investors mortgage loans or in operations through structures allowed by RIDEA. The REIT typically takes a purchase-leaseback approach in which it acquires properties and leases them back to their previous operators. It also may provide mortgage and construction loans to operators who agree to lease the property once built.

The REIT on occasion also makes divestitures of under-performing rental properties to free up resources for further investments in higher-potential properties. In 2014 for example National Health sold three of its decades-old skilled nursing facilities in Texas which averaged 41 years in age and housed some 484 beds to an affiliate of Fundamental Long Term Care Holdings for a total of $18.49 million.

Mergers and Acquisitions
In 2014 NHI purchased eight senior housing communities for $476 million which would be leased to Senior Living Communities (SLC) and

would continue to be managed by an SLC affiliate. Also that year it spent $42 million toward acquiring an 105-unit assisted living community in Idaho as well as three skilled nursing facilities in Oregon with plans for a sale-leaseback arrangement from Prestige Senior Living; and another $18.1 million toward the purchase of a 101-unit assisted living and memory care community in Middleton Ohio through its joint venture with Bickford Senior Living.

In late 2013 the company purchased 25 independent-living properties which boasted 2841 units from Holiday Acquisition Holdings for a total of $491 million.

In April 2013 the REIT acquired a pair of skilled nursing facilities in Canton and Corinth Texas for $26.3 million. The purchase added a total of 254 beds to the REIT's portfolio.

In 2012 NHI acquired a 181-unit senior living campus in Loma Linda California for $12 million from Chancellor Health Care (CHC) thereby establishing a presence in Southern California. CHC would lease and continue to operate the facility.

EXECUTIVES

Chief Credit Officer, Kristin S. Gaines, age 48, $155,167 total compensation
EVP Investments and Chief Investment Officer, Kevin C. Pascoe, age 39, $150,000 total compensation
Chief Accounting Officer, Roger R. Hopkins, age 58, $286,841 total compensation
President CEO and Director, D. Eric Mendelsohn, age 57, $198,000 total compensation
EVP Finance, John L. Spaid, age 60
Chairman, W. Andrew (Andy) Adams, age 74
Auditors: BDO USA, LLP

LOCATIONS

HQ: National Health Investors, Inc.
222 Robert Rose Drive, Murfreesboro, TN 37129
Phone: 615 890-9100
Web: www.nhireit.com

PRODUCTS/OPERATIONS

2014 Sales

	$ mil.	% of total
Rental income	166.3	94
Interest income from mortgage and others	7.0	4
Investment income and other	4.2	2
Total	177.5	100

2014 Portfolio by Operations

	% of total
Regional	40
National Chain (Privately Owned)	28
Public	27
Small	5
Total	100

COMPETITORS

Cousins Properties
HCP
Healthcare Realty Trust
LTC Properties
Medical Properties Trust
Omega Healthcare Investors
Senior Housing Properties
Ventas
Welltower

HISTORICAL FINANCIALS
Company Type: Public

Income Statement FYE: December 31

	REVENUE ($ mil.)	NET INCOME ($ mil.)	NET PROFIT MARGIN	EMPLOYEES
12/18	294.6	154.3	52.4%	16
12/17	278.6	159.3	57.2%	16
12/16	248.5	151.5	61.0%	15
12/15	228.9	148.8	65.0%	12
12/14	177.5	101.6	57.2%	12
Annual Growth	13.5%	11.0%	—	7.5%

2018 Year-End Financials

Debt ratio: 46.6%
Return on equity: 11.3%
Cash ($ mil.): 4.6
Current ratio: 1.95
Long-term debt ($ mil.): 1,281.6
No. of shares (mil.): 42.7
Dividends
 Yield: 5.3%
 Payout: 108.9%
Market value ($ mil.): 3,226.0

	STOCK PRICE ($) FY Close	P/E High/Low	PER SHARE ($) Earnings	Dividends	Book Value
12/18	75.54	22 17	3.67	4.00	32.55
12/17	75.38	21 18	3.87	3.80	31.83
12/16	74.17	21 14	3.87	3.60	30.36
12/15	60.87	19 14	3.95	3.40	29.52
12/14	69.96	23 18	3.04	3.08	27.74
Annual Growth	1.9%	— —	4.8%	6.8%	4.1%

National Retail Properties Inc

For National Retail Properties good things come in big boxes. The self-administered real estate investment trust (REIT) acquires develops and manages freestanding retail properties in heavily traveled commercial and residential areas. Its portfolio includes more than 2250 properties with some 25 million sq. ft. of leasable space in almost all 50 states concentrated in Texas the Southeast and the Midwest. National Retail Properties also invests in mortgages operates some of its retail properties and develops properties to sell them later for a profit. More than 30% of its rental income comes from convenience store and restaurant operators with its top clients being Sunoco Mister Car Wash LA Fitness The Pantry and Camping World.

Operations
While some retail REITs own entire strip malls or shopping malls National Retail Properties keeps it simple with freestanding retail properties. National Retail Properties typically signs triple-net leases with initial terms of 15 to 20 years in which tenants are responsible for expenses such as taxes utilities repairs and maintenance.

Geographic Reach
National Retail Properties' largest markets are in Texas (20% of rental income in 2015) and Florida (9%). Other large markets include Ohio North Carolina Illinois Georgia Virginia Indiana Alabama and Tennessee which combined made up around one-third of its rental income during 2015.

Sales and Marketing
The trust's retail tenants include convenience stores and gas stations full-service and limited-service restaurants and other retailers. Its five largest tenants by rental base during 2015 included Sunoco (5.9% of rental income) Mister Car Wash (4.4%) LA Fitness (3.7%) The Pantry (3.6%) and Camping World (3.6%).

Other tenants include Stripes (Susser Holdings) 7-Eleven; restuarant tenants Applebee's Chili's Denny's Logan's Roadhouse Taco Bell and Wendys; and retailers Best Buy CarQuest and Pep Boys.

Financial Performance
National Retail Properties' annual revenues and profits have more than doubled since 2010 mainly as new property acquisitions have spurred higher rental income.

The REIT's revenue jumped 11% to $482.91 million during 2015 mostly as its rental income increased with the acquisition of 221 new properties spanning 2.42 million square feet.

Strong revenue growth in 2015 drove National Retail Properties' net income up 4% to $197.84 million. The REIT's operating cash levels climbed 15% to $341.09 million for the year as it collected more in cash-based rental income.

Strategy
Keeping a diversified tenant base in mind National Retail Properties mostly targets single-building retail real estate property located near local markets where its retail tenants trade. During 2015 it acquired 221 of such properties expanding its portfolio by more than 10% while selling just 19 properties with six more up for sale.

EXECUTIVES

EVP CFO and Treasurer, Kevin B. Habicht, age 59, $450,000 total compensation
President and CEO, Julian E. (Jay) Whitehurst, age 61, $525,000 total compensation
EVP and Chief Investment Officer, Paul E. Bayer, age 57, $365,000 total compensation
EVP and General Counsel, Christopher P. (Chris) Tessitore, age 51, $355,000 total compensation
EVP and Chief Acquisition Officer, Stephen A. Horn, age 47, $325,000 total compensation
Vice President Information Technology, Craig Roy
Vice President Of Acquisitions, Josh Lewis
Vice President Underwriting, Matthew Sunderland
Senior Vice President Asset Management, Kristin Furniss
Legal Secretary, Ivette Cordero
Senior Vice President Tax, Michael Iannone
Chairman, Robert C. Legler, age 75
Auditors: Ernst & Young LLP

LOCATIONS

HQ: National Retail Properties Inc
450 South Orange Avenue, Suite 900, Orlando, FL 32801
Phone: 407 265-7348   **Fax:** 407 423-2894
Web: www.nnnreit.com

COMPETITORS

Acadia Realty Trust
Brixmor
DDR
Federal Realty Investment
Kimco Realty
One Liberty Properties
Realty Income
Regency Centers

HISTORICAL FINANCIALS
Company Type: Public

Income Statement   FYE: December 31

	REVENUE ($ mil.)	NET INCOME ($ mil.)	NET PROFIT MARGIN	EMPLOYEES
12/18	622.6	292.4	47.0%	68
12/17	584.9	264.9	45.3%	66
12/16	533.6	239.5	44.9%	65
12/15	482.9	197.8	41.0%	62
12/14	434.8	190.6	43.8%	64
Annual Growth	9.4%	11.3%		1.5%

2018 Year-End Financials
Debt ratio: 40.1%
Return on equity: 7.3%
Cash ($ mil.): 114.2
Current ratio: 7.35
Long-term debt ($ mil.): 2,851.4
No. of shares (mil.): 161.5
Dividends
  Yield: 4.0%
  Payout: 102.0%
Market value ($ mil.): 7,835.0

	STOCK PRICE ($) FY Close	P/E High/Low	PER SHARE ($) Earnings	Dividends	Book Value
12/18	48.51	31 22	1.65	1.95	25.72
12/17	43.13	32 25	1.45	1.86	25.01
12/16	44.20	38 28	1.38	1.78	26.62
12/15	40.05	37 28	1.20	1.71	23.70
12/14	39.37	33 24	1.24	1.65	23.35
Annual Growth	5.4%	— —	7.4%	4.3%	2.4%

National Storage Affiliates Trust

Auditors: KPMG LLP

LOCATIONS
HQ: National Storage Affiliates Trust
8400 East Prentice Avenue, 9th Floor, Greenwood Village, CO 80111
Phone: 720 630-2600
Web: www.nationalstorageaffiliates.com

HISTORICAL FINANCIALS
Company Type: Public

Income Statement   FYE: December 31

	REVENUE ($ mil.)	NET INCOME ($ mil.)	NET PROFIT MARGIN	EMPLOYEES
12/18	330.9	14.1	4.3%	1,100
12/17	268.1	2.9	1.1%	1,211
12/16	199.0	17.9	9.0%	995
12/15	133.9	12.4	9.3%	8
12/14	76.9	0.0	—	13
Annual Growth	44.0%	—	—	203.3%

2018 Year-End Financials
Debt ratio: 46.8%
Return on equity: 1.6%
Cash ($ mil.): 13.1
Current ratio: 1.56
Long-term debt ($ mil.): 1,278.1
No. of shares (mil.): 56.6
Dividends
  Yield: 4.3%
  Payout: 1,657.1%
Market value ($ mil.): 1,499.0

	STOCK PRICE ($) FY Close	P/E High/Low	PER SHARE ($) Earnings	Dividends	Book Value
12/18	26.46	45 7331	0.07	1.16	16.18
12/17	27.26	2759 2124	0.01	1.04	16.73
12/16	22.07	38 27	0.31	0.88	13.39
12/15	17.13	21 15	0.17	0.54	10.28
Annual Growth	15.6%	— —	(25.6%)	29.0%	16.3%

National Vision Holdings Inc

Auditors: DELOITTE & TOUCHE LLP

LOCATIONS
HQ: National Vision Holdings Inc
2435 Commerce Avenue, Building 2200, Duluth, GA 30096
Phone: 770 822-3600
Web: www.nationalvision.com

HISTORICAL FINANCIALS
Company Type: Public

Income Statement   FYE: December 29

	REVENUE ($ mil.)	NET INCOME ($ mil.)	NET PROFIT MARGIN	EMPLOYEES
12/18	1,536.8	23.6	1.5%	10,668
12/17	1,375.3	45.8	3.3%	10,902
12/16*	1,196.2	14.7	1.2%	10,360
01/16	1,062.5	3.6	0.3%	0
01/15	735.6	(27.0)	—	0
Annual Growth	20.2%			

*Fiscal year change

2018 Year-End Financials
Debt ratio: 34.8%
Return on equity: 3.3%
Cash ($ mil.): 17.1
Current ratio: 1.01
Long-term debt ($ mil.): 570.5
No. of shares (mil.): 78.1
Dividends
  Yield: —
  Payout: —
Market value ($ mil.): 2,265.0

	STOCK PRICE ($) FY Close	P/E High/Low	PER SHARE ($) Earnings	Dividends	Book Value
12/18	28.98	147 85	0.30	0.00	9.51
12/17	40.61	53 36	0.74	0.00	8.84
Annual Growth	(28.6%)	— —	(59.5%)	—	7.6%

Natural Alternatives International, Inc.

Natural Alternatives International (NAI) is a natural alternative for nutritional supplement marketers who want to outsource manufacturing. The company provides private-label manufacturing of vitamins minerals herbs and other customized nutritional supplements. Its main customers are direct sellers such as Mannatech and NSA International for whom it makes JuicePlus+ chewables capsules and powdered products. NAI also makes some branded products for sale in the US: the Pathway to Healing brand of nutritional supplements promoted by doctor and evangelist Reginald B. Cherry.

Operations
Natural Alternatives International (NAI) operates through three business segments. Private-label contract manufacturing is by far the largest representing more than 85% of sales. Its Branded Products business (just 2% of sales) markets and distributes branded nutritional supplements through direct-to-consumer marketing programs. NAI's Patent and Trademark licensing business segment is engaged in the sale and licensing of beta-alanine (an amino acid used by bodybuilders) under the CarnoSyn trade name.

NSA International and Mannatech are the company's biggest clients accounting for about 45% and 20% respectively of the company's sales. In addition to manufacturing products for its private-label clients NAI offers a range of complementary services such as regulatory assistance and packaging design.

Geographic Reach
The company has manufacturing and distribution facilities in California and in Switzerland. It also has sales support operations in Japan in order to assist clients operating in the Pacific Rim. The US accounts for 60% of NAI's sales. Outside the US NAI's primary market is Europe.

Financial Performance
The company's net sales grew a robust 30% in fiscal 2012 (ends June) vs. the prior year while net income fell by about 18% over the same period. Revenue from NAI's patent and trademark licensing business surged more than 350% in fiscal 2012 vs. 2011 driven by the increase in popularity of CarnoSyn as a sports nutrition supplement and expanded distribution of the product. The Private-label contract manufacturing segment saw its sales rise more than 20% due to increased sales to its two largest customers NSA International and Mannatech. Branded products was the laggard posting a 14% drop off in sales for the year which NAI blamed on soft sales of the Pathway to Healing product line.

Strategy
A key element of NAI's growth strategy is the commercialization of its beta-alanine patent through contract manufacturing royalty and licensing agreements and the protection of its proprietary rights (by legal means where necessary). Indeed the 350% surge in fiscal 2012 sales in the company's licensing business was credited to the CarnoSyn brand. To that end NAI in 2011 expanded its beta-alanine licensing programs through a supply agreement with Nestle Nutrition and a license and supply agreement with Abbott Laboratories. While the Nestle agreement expired in mid-2012 and was not renewed the agreement granting Abbott exclusive license for the use of beta-alanine in certain medical foods and medical nutritionals continues. Also NAI is looking to growth the CarnoSyn beta-alanine business through accretive acquisitions.

The company is also focusing on developing and growing its own line of branded products primarily through direct-to-consumer sales and distribution channels. To bolster is faltering Pathway to Healing line of branded products NAI relaunched the product line and increased its marketing and advertising activities to support future sales.

EXECUTIVES

Vice President Of Sales, Gene Quast
Vice President Operations, James Gause
Auditors: Haskell & White LLP

LOCATIONS

HQ: Natural Alternatives International, Inc.
1535 Faraday Ave, Carlsbad, CA 92008
Phone: 760 744-7700
Web: www.nai-online.com

COMPETITORS

Atrium Innovations	Nexgen
Botanical Laboratories	Perrigo
GNC	PureTek
Integrated BioPharma	Schiff Nutrition
NBTY	International
NNC	Soft Gel Technologies
Nature's Sunshine	USANA Health Sciences

HISTORICAL FINANCIALS

Company Type: Public

Income Statement — FYE: June 30

	REVENUE ($ mil.)	NET INCOME ($ mil.)	NET PROFIT MARGIN	EMPLOYEES
06/19	138.2	6.5	4.7%	312
06/18	132.4	5.0	3.8%	266
06/17	121.9	7.2	5.9%	227
06/16	114.2	9.5	8.4%	285
06/15	79.5	3.3	4.2%	167
Annual Growth	14.8%	18.2%	—	16.9%

2019 Year-End Financials

Debt ratio: —
Return on equity: 9.0%
Cash ($ mil.): 25.0
Current ratio: 5.01
Long-term debt ($ mil.): —
No. of shares (mil.): 7.2
Dividends
Yield: —
Payout: —
Market value ($ mil.): 84.0

	STOCK PRICE ($) FY Close	P/E High/Low	PER SHARE ($) Earnings	Dividends	Book Value
06/19	11.66	15 10	0.92	0.00	10.53
06/18	10.15	16 12	0.73	0.00	9.03
06/17	9.95	13 8	1.09	0.00	8.81
06/16	11.04	10 4	1.44	0.00	7.82
06/15	5.67	13 10	0.49	0.00	6.50
Annual Growth	19.8%	— —	17.1%	—	12.8%

Natural Grocers By Vitamin Cottage Inc

Natural Grocers by Vitamin Cottage is riding the wave of increased consumer interest in wellness and nutrition. The fast-growing company (both in sales and store count) operates about 140 stores in some 20 US states that sell natural and organic food including fresh produce meat frozen food and non-perishable bulk food; vitamins and dietary supplements; personal care products; pet care products; and books. The company uses United Natural Foods as its primary supplier and it also runs a bulk food repackaging facility and distribution center in its home state of Colorado. Founded by Margaret and Philip Isely in 1958 Natural Grocers by Vitamin Cottage is run by members of the Isely family.

Operations

The company's stores range in size from 5000 sq. ft. to 16000 sq. ft. (A typical new store averages 11000 sq. ft.) Each store offers about 21000 different natural and organic products and 6500 different dietary supplements.

Natural Grocers by Vitamin Cottage generates about two-thirds of its revenue from groceries with dietary supplements accounting for more than 20% and the remainder coming from body care pet care books and general merchandise.

Geographic Reach

Colorado is the company's home state and also its largest market with about a quarter of its stores. Other major markets for the company include Texas (home to about 15% of stores) as well as Arizona Oregon and Kansas. It operates a bulk food repackaging facility and distribution center in Colorado.

Sales and Marketing

Like other grocery retailers Natural Grocers by Vitamin Cottage advertises its weekly circular by mail and in local newspapers. The company plans to attract new customers through targeted marketing efforts such as distributing health-related newsletters and sponsoring health fairs and community wellness events. The chain devotes considerable marketing resources to educating customers on the benefits of natural and organic grocery products and dietary supplements. The company also occasionally relies on TV ads that are produced locally and primarily feature members of the founding Isely family.

Natural Grocers by Vitamin Cottage reported total advertising and marketing expenses for fiscal 2017 (ended September) of $10.7 million compared with $10.8 million the prior year.

Financial Performance

Natural Grocers has shown strong sales growth over the past five years as American consumers continue to focus on more natural healthy organic foods. Powered by new store openings the company's revenue has jumped some 75% since 2013. Increased competition however has put pressure on margins resulting in reduced net income.

In fiscal 2017 (ended September) Natural Grocers reported revenue of $769 million up 9% from the prior year. New store openings (about 15 that year) led the growth and was more than enough to offset a less than 1% decline in comparable-store sales.

Amid Natural Grocers' consistent store growth salaries supplies and other store-level expenses have been rising more rapidly than revenue in recent years. The company's operating margin fell more than a point in 2017 from 2.9% to 1.8% leading to net income of less than $7 million a 40% drop.

Cash at the end of 2017 was $6.5 million an increase of $2.5 million from the prior year. Cash from operations contributed $41 million to the coffers while investing activities used $38 million mainly for property and equipment used in the buildout of new stores. Financing activities added about $150000 as Natural Grocers borrowed and repaid about the same amount in debt (some $290 million).

Strategy

As part of its growth strategy Natural Grocers by Vitamin Cottage plans to continue expanding its store base although at a slower pace. After adding 23 and 14 new stores in fiscal years 2016 and 2017 respectively another 8-10 are planned in fiscal 2018. The stores are slated for Colorado Iowa Missouri Oregon Texas and Utah.

As it slows down new store openings the company plans to focus on improving same-store sales and other operating metrics. Amid an extremely competitive environment highlighted by Amazon's acquisition of Whole Foods Natural Grocers by Vitamin Cottage is hoping to distinguish itself with superior product standards while maintaining affordable prices. It also plans a new private label launch in 2018.

EXECUTIVES

CFO, Sandra M. Buffa, age 66, $320,000 total compensation
Chairman and Co-President, Kemper Isely, age 57, $607,800 total compensation
Co-President and Director, Zephyr Isely, age 70, $576,000 total compensation
EVP Corporate Secretary and Director, Heather Isely, age 53, $528,000 total compensation
EVP and Director, Elizabeth Isely, age 64, $480,000 total compensation
Auditors: KPMG LLP

LOCATIONS

HQ: Natural Grocers By Vitamin Cottage Inc
12612 West Alameda Parkway, Lakewood, CO 80228
Phone: 303 986-4600
Web: www.naturalgrocers.com

PRODUCTS/OPERATIONS

2017 Sales

	% of total
Grocery	67
Dietary supplements	22
Body care pet care and other	11
Total	100

COMPETITORS

ALDI	Sprouts
Blue Apron	Target Corporation
Costco Wholesale	Trader Joe's
Fresh Market	Vitacost
GNC	Vitamin Shoppe
H-E-B	Vitamin World
Kroger	Wal-Mart
Lidl	Whole Foods
Safeway	

Nautilus Inc

HISTORICAL FINANCIALS
Company Type: Public

Income Statement
FYE: September 30

	REVENUE ($ mil.)	NET INCOME ($ mil.)	NET PROFIT MARGIN	EMPLOYEES
09/19	903.5	9.4	1.0%	3,681
09/18	849.0	12.6	1.5%	3,598
09/17	769.0	6.8	0.9%	3,270
09/16	705.5	11.4	1.6%	3,074
09/15	624.6	16.2	2.6%	2,830
Annual Growth	9.7%	(12.7%)	—	6.8%

2019 Year-End Financials
Debt ratio: 17.8%
Return on equity: 6.2%
Cash ($ mil.): 6.2
Current ratio: 1.38
Long-term debt ($ mil.): 57.1
No. of shares (mil.): 22.4
Dividends
Yield: —
Payout: —
Market value ($ mil.): 224.0

	STOCK PRICE ($) FY Close	P/E High/Low	PER SHARE ($) Earnings	Dividends	Book Value
09/19	9.99	54 20	0.42	0.00	6.99
09/18	16.89	34 8	0.56	0.00	6.56
09/17	5.58	44 18	0.31	0.00	5.96
09/16	11.16	50 21	0.51	0.00	5.64
09/15	22.69	44 22	0.72	0.00	5.13
Annual Growth	(18.5%)	—	(12.6%)	—	8.0%

Nautilus wants to pump you up. The company makes and markets cardio and strength-building fitness equipment for home use. Its products include home gyms free weights and benches treadmills exercise bikes and elliptical machines that are sold under the popular brand names Bowflex Nautilus Schwinn Fitness and Universal. Nautilus sells its fitness equipment directly to consumers through its variety of brand websites and catalogs as well as through TV commercials. The company also markets its gear through specialty retailers in the US and Canada. Nautilus exited the commercial fitness category in recent years so that it could focus entirely on providing gear that consumers can use at home.

Operations
The company operates its fitness equipment business through a pair of reportable segments. Its Direct segment (64% of revenue) sells products directly to consumers through TV advertising the Internet and catalogs. As part of its Retail segment (34%) Nautilus sells products through a network of third-party retailers that operate websites and stores located in the US and internationally.

Geographic Reach
Nautilus operates in the US and Canada with warehouse and distribution facilities located in Oregon and Ohio in the US and in Manitoba in Canada.

The US accounts for about 85% of revenue.

Sales and Marketing
Nautilus sells its products to fitness enthusiasts and to those who want to work out regularly. It sells through two sales channels: direct and retail. In 2014 it spent about $42.6 million on advertising and expenses.

Financial Performance
Revenue which has been on a steady upward trajectory for five years rose 25% to $274 million in 2014 on the strength of new products. But net income which has fluctuated over the years was hit by spending on selling and marketing and plummeted 61% to $18.8 million

Strategy
Mostly because it had been largely unprofitable Nautilus opted to exit its commercial fitness business to focus on its core consumer fitness segment and the direct marketing model which have been key to its growth. The deep recession in the US had urged consumers to redirect spending to mostly essential goods and pushed commercial customers to cut back on equipment purchases.

EXECUTIVES
CEO and Director, Bruce M. Cazenave, age 64, $375,000 total compensation
COO, William B. McMahon, age 54, $250,000 total compensation
CFO, Sid Nayar
Vice President General Manager Direct, Robert O. (Rob) Murdock, $180,000 total compensation
Chairman, M. Carl Johnson
Auditors: DELOITTE & TOUCHE LLP

LOCATIONS
HQ: Nautilus Inc
17750 S.E. 6th Way, Vancouver, WA 98683
Phone: 360 859-2900
Web: www.nautilusinc.com

PRODUCTS/OPERATIONS

2014 Sales
	% of total
Direct	64
Retail	34
Royalty income	2
Total	100

Selected Brands
Bowflex
Nautilus
Schwinn Fitness
Universal

COMPETITORS
Amer Sports	ICON Health
Beachbody	Life Fitness
Cybex International	Precor
Dorel Industries	adidas
Escalade	

HISTORICAL FINANCIALS
Company Type: Public

Income Statement
FYE: December 31

	REVENUE ($ mil.)	NET INCOME ($ mil.)	NET PROFIT MARGIN	EMPLOYEES
12/18	396.7	14.6	3.7%	460
12/17	406.1	26.2	6.5%	491
12/16	406.0	34.1	8.4%	469
12/15	335.7	26.6	7.9%	470
12/14	274.4	18.8	6.8%	340
Annual Growth	9.7%	(6.0%)	—	7.8%

2018 Year-End Financials
Debt ratio: 9.6%
Return on equity: 8.1%
Cash ($ mil.): 63.5
Current ratio: 1.67
Long-term debt ($ mil.): 15.9
No. of shares (mil.): 29.5
Dividends
Yield: —
Payout: —
Market value ($ mil.): 322.0

	STOCK PRICE ($) FY Close	P/E High/Low	PER SHARE ($) Earnings	Dividends	Book Value
12/18	10.90	34 21	0.48	0.00	6.18
12/17	13.35	23 14	0.85	0.00	5.91
12/16	18.50	23 14	1.09	0.00	5.22
12/15	16.72	27 17	0.84	0.00	4.10
12/14	15.18	25 13	0.59	0.00	3.54
Annual Growth	(7.9%)	—	(5.0%)	—	14.9%

Nektar Therapeutics

Nektar Therapeutics has pegged its fortunes to making drugs more effective. The clinical-stage drug development firm uses its PEGylation technology (based upon polyethylene glycol) to improve the delivery and efficacy of existing drugs. Nektar's pipeline includes about 20 drugs focused on anti-infectives and anti-virals immunology oncology and pain treatments. Its lead candidates are NKTR-118 for opioid-induced constipation and NKTR-102 to treat breast cancer. Nektar receives royalties on about a dozen approved products including Neulasta Somavert and Macugen as well as its surgical and imaging technology. The company's development partners include Roche AstraZeneca Amgen and Pfizer.

Operations
Nektar's NKTR-102 candidate is in three separate clinical trials for breast colorectal and ovarian cancers. As the drug advances into late-stage clinical trials the company intends to find a collaborative partner to help shepherd it through regulatory filings and commercialization.

Geographic Reach
Nektar sells its products in the US and Europe with the latter contributing a bit more than half of revenues. It has production facilities in the US (California) and in India.

Sales and Marketing
The company has no sales force of its own but relies on its development partners and other third parties to get its products to market. UCB and Roche together account for more than 50% of Nektar's revenue.

Financial Performance
Nektar's revenue increased 14% in 2012 on the strength of higher demand among its partners. US revenue dropped slightly but was offset by an increase in Europe on strong demand. Royalty revenue also decreased as the company sold off its futures payments on Cimzia and Mircera for a lump sum. Net loss increased 28% as the company continues to pour money into R&D and pay for clinical trials but prudent investments kept the company's cash flow in the black.

Strategy
Collaborations are a key part of Nektar's business strategy and it routinely enters into partnerships with major pharmaceutical companies to help finance the development of new products. The

company's development deal with AstraZeneca for NKTR-118 netted it $125 million up-front and gives it the opportunity to earn an additional $1.5 billion in milestone payments. Another collaboration with Bayer Healthcare is working on development and commercialization of an inhaled antibiotic in clinical trials for the treatment of certain pneumonias.

Nektar can also elect to sell its future royalties to raise cash as it did in 2012 when it sold Royalty Pharma future royalty payments on Cimzia and Mircera from UCB and Roche respectively for about $124 million.

In 2012 the company moved to reduce costs by closing its Alabama research location and consolidating US R&D at its California headquarters.

EXECUTIVES

President CEO and Director, Howard W. Robin, age 67, $892,620 total compensation
SVP and COO, John Nicholson, age 68, $563,100 total compensation
SVP and CFO, Gil M. Labrucherie, age 48, $546,500 total compensation
SVP Pharmaceutical Development and Manufacturing Operations, Maninder Hora, $430,600 total compensation
SVP Drug Development and Chief Medical Officer, Ivan P. Gergel, $621,000 total compensation
Senior Vice President Research and Development and Chief Research and Development Officer, Stephen Doberstein
Vice President of Information Technology, John Cummings
Vice President Legal Commercial and Regulatory, Frank Curtis
VP Quality, Henk Kocken
Vice President Project Management, Camille Deluca-flaherty
VP Clinical Science, Brian Kotzin
Vp Regulatory Affairs And Product Safety, Carlo Difonzo
Senior Vice President Finance And Chief Accounting Officer, Jill Thomsen
Senior Vice President, Mingxiu Hu
Vp Clinical Science, Wei Lin
Chairman, Robert B. Chess, age 63
Secretary, Ashley Acosta
Auditors: Ernst & Young LLP

LOCATIONS

HQ: Nektar Therapeutics
455 Mission Bay Boulevard South, San Francisco, CA 94158
Phone: 415 482-5300
Web: www.nektar.com

PRODUCTS/OPERATIONS

2015 Revenues

	$ mil.	% of total
Product sales	40.2	17
Non-cash royalty revenue related to sale of future royalties	22.1	10
Royalties	2.9	1
License collaboration and other revenue	165.6	72
Total	**230.8**	**100**

COMPETITORS

Agenus	Novo Nordisk
Bristol-Myers Squibb	Pfizer
CTI BioPharma	Progenics
Dr. Reddy's	Pharmaceuticals
Enzon	Roche Holding

GlaxoSmithKline
NOF
Neose Technologies
Novartis
Salix Pharmaceuticals
Sucampo
Takeda Pharmaceutical

HISTORICAL FINANCIALS
Company Type: Public

Income Statement   FYE: December 31

	REVENUE ($ mil.)	NET INCOME ($ mil.)	NET PROFIT MARGIN	EMPLOYEES
12/18	1,193.3	681.3	57.1%	618
12/17	307.7	(96.6)	—	509
12/16	165.4	(153.5)	—	468
12/15	230.7	(81.1)	—	425
12/14	200.7	(53.9)	—	438
Annual Growth	56.2%			9.0%

2018 Year-End Financials

Debt ratio: 11.4%   No. of shares (mil.): 173.5
Return on equity: 75.4%   Dividends
Cash ($ mil.): 194.9   Yield: —
Current ratio: 17.53   Payout: —
Long-term debt ($ mil.): 246.9   Market value ($ mil.): 5,704.0

	STOCK PRICE ($) FY Close	P/E High/Low		PER SHARE ($) Earnings	Dividends	Book Value
12/18	32.87	27	8	3.78	0.00	9.90
12/17	59.72	—	—	(0.62)	0.00	0.55
12/16	12.27	—	—	(1.10)	0.00	0.58
12/15	16.85	—	—	(0.61)	0.00	0.05
12/14	15.50	—	—	(0.42)	0.00	0.28
Annual Growth	20.7%			—	—	144.5%

Nelnet Inc

Got Ivy League tastes on a community college budget? Nelnet may be able to help. The education planning and financing company helps students and parents plan and pay for college educations. Nelnet is mostly known for servicing federal student loans. The firm manages about $76 billion in student loan assets most of which are government loans. However in light of regulatory changes to the student lending market Nelnet is increasingly expanding its fee-based education services. It serves the K-12 and higher education marketplace providing long-term payment plans college enrollment services and software and technology services. It acquired in 2018 Great Lakes Educational Loan Services for $150 million. The firm is part of financial holding company Farmers & Merchants Investment.

Operations

Nelnet provides innovative educational services in loan servicing payment processing education planning and asset management for families and educational institutions. The Company's four operating segments offer a broad range of services designed to simplify education planning and financing for students and families and the administrative and financial processes for schools and financial institutions.

The largest is Asset Generation and Management which acquires and manages Nelnet's student loan holdings. The portfolio includes Nelnet's existing loans originated under the now-defunct Federal Family Education Loan Program (FFELP). However in efforts to diversify its fee-based business and lessen its dependence on student loans the company is focused on developing new products and growing in areas such as tuition payment processing and lead generation products and services such as enrollment management and test prep services.

The three fee-based segments include Student Loan and Guaranty Servicing which services FFELP and other third-party loans writes and services private student loans and provides loan servicing software. (Nelnet is one of four companies providing servicing for the Department of Education.) Tuition Payment Processing and Campus Commerce serves the K-12 market as well as higher education providing financing for families and processing services for schools. Enrollment Services works to connect students with schools by providing marketing for schools and publishing school directories and test preparation study guides for potential students.

Geographic Reach

The company has offices in the US and Canada.

Sales and Marketing

The company's customers include students and families colleges and universities specifically financial aid business and admissions offices K-12 schools lenders state agencies and government entities.

Financial Performance

Nelnet has seen steady growth in revenues in the last few years. In 2013 the company's revenue increased to $1.14 billion (compared to $923.7 million in 2012) primarily due to an increase in Student Loan and Guaranty Servicing (as the result of growth in servicing volume under the company's contract with the Department of Education) and an increase in collection revenues from defaulted FFELP loan assets on behalf of guaranty agencies. Tuition Payment Processing and Campus Commerce revenues grew due to a higher number of managed tuition payment plans as a result of providing more plans at existing schools and obtaining new school customers.

Net income increased to $302.7 million in 2013 (from $117.8 million in 2012) due to higher revenues and lower operating costs (the result of a decrease in depreciation and amortization costs).

In 2013 Nelnet's operating cash flow increased to $387.2 million (compared to $299.3 million in 2012) due to higher net income and proceeds from the termination of one of the company's cross-currency interest rate swaps. The increase in cash provided by operating activities was partially offset by the impacts of changes in non-cash fair value adjustments for derivatives.

Strategy

The company grows organically and through acquisitions.

Mergers and Acquisitions

To strengthen its student loans business Nelnet purchased in 2018 Great Lakes Educational Loan Services for $150 million and in 2014 acquired CIT's student lending business for $1.1 billion.

In 2014 FACTS Management brand a part of Nelnet's Tuition Payment Processing and Campus Commerce segment and the leader in payment plan services for K-12 schools acquired RenWeb School Management Software one of the leading school information systems for private and faith-based schools. RenWeb currently helps over 3000 schools automate administrative processes like admissions scheduling student billing attendance and grade book management. By automating these tasks RenWeb gives teachers more time to shape the lives of students while saving money and resources. FACTS helps over 6500 schools with tuition management billing and financial aid assessment services.

Company Background

Nelnet has been through a turbulent few years as student loan reform and the financial crisis disrupted business and sent revenues down. The company's ability to adapt to the economic pressures and policy changes have helped it land face-up following the recession. Measures taken including laying off staff and tightening lending practices helped boost profits despite lower revenues. Although non-FFELP servicing income and payment processing revenues grew in 2011 FFELP servicing revenues declined as the portfolio further shrunk and school marketing sales decreased as schools cut back on spending. As a result revenues fell that year by 8% to $979 million. Net income increased 8% (to $204 million) in 2011 compared to 2010 when the company had expenses related to restructuring. Also in 2010 Nelnet paid the US government $55 million to settle a lawsuit claiming it had made false statements to receive extra subsidies.

In a blow to the student lending industry President Barack Obama eliminated the FFELP and prohibited private lenders from making federal student loans in 2010. All new federal student loans began going directly through the Department of Education's Direct Loan Program. As a result Nelnet no longer originates new FFELP loans.

But the change didn't put an end to Nelnet. The company was awarded a five-year servicing contract for federally owned student loans including existing FFELP loans. Nelnet also began servicing new loans generated directly under the Federal Direct Loan Program. The contract was a major win for the company. Nelnet expects that its fee-based revenue will increase as the servicing volume for these loans increases (while the FFELP portfolio declines). The company is also focusing on improving its customer service to increase the allotted percentage of new government loans it services.

CEO Michael Dunlap controls the company holding 68% of the voting power for Nelnet. Dunlap and his family also own Farmers & Merchants Investment.

EXECUTIVES

COO, Terry J. Heimes, age 55, $550,000 total compensation
CEO, Jeffrey R. (Jeff) Noordhoek, age 53, $550,000 total compensation
President, Timothy A. (Tim) Tewes, age 60, $375,000 total compensation
CFO, James D. (Jim) Kruger, $375,000 total compensation
Regional Vice President, Jon Potter
Regional Vice President Of Sales K 12 Mi, Mike Spanier
REGIONAL VICE PRESIDENT, Roy Chernikoff
Vice President Campus Solutions, Anne Delplato
Executive Chairman, Michael S. (Mike) Dunlap, age 56
Vice Chairman, Stephen F. (Steve) Butterfield, age 67
Auditors: KPMG LLP

LOCATIONS

HQ: Nelnet Inc
121 South 13th Street, Suite 100, Lincoln, NE 68508
Phone: 402 458-2370
Web: www.nelnetinvestors.com

PRODUCTS/OPERATIONS

2015 Sales

	$ mil.	% of total
Interest		
Loans	726.3	60
Investments	7.8	1
Noninterest		
Loan & guaranty servicing	239.9	20
Enrollment services	70.7	6
Tuition payment processing & campus commerce revenue	120.4	10
Gains on sale of loans & debt repurchases net	5.1	1
Other	32.0	2
Total	**1,202.2**	**100**

COMPETITORS

American Student Assistance
Bank of America
Brazos Higher Education Service Corp.
College Loan Corporation
First Marblehead
Great Lakes Higher Education
JPMorgan Chase
Pennsylvania Higher Education Assistance Agency
Sallie Mae
Texas Guaranteed
Wells Fargo

HISTORICAL FINANCIALS

Company Type: Public

Income Statement
FYE: December 31

	ASSETS ($ mil.)	NET INCOME ($ mil.)	INCOME AS % OF ASSETS	EMPLOYEES
12/18	25,220.9	227.9	0.9%	6,200
12/17	23,964.4	173.1	0.7%	4,300
12/16	27,180.1	256.7	0.9%	3,700
12/15	30,485.9	267.9	0.9%	3,400
12/14	30,098.1	307.6	1.0%	3,100
Annual Growth	(4.3%)	(7.2%)	—	18.9%

2018 Year-End Financials

Return on assets: 0.9%
Return on equity: 10.2%
Long-term debt ($ mil.): —
No. of shares (mil.): 40.2
Sales ($ mil): 1,756.8
Dividends
Yield: 1.2%
Payout: 11.8%
Market value ($ mil.): 2,107.0

	STOCK PRICE ($) FY Close	P/E High/Low		Earnings	PER SHARE ($) Dividends	Book Value
12/18	52.34	11	9	5.57	0.66	57.24
12/17	54.78	14	9	4.14	0.58	52.67
12/16	50.75	9	5	6.02	0.50	48.96
12/15	33.57	8	5	5.89	0.42	42.87
12/14	46.33	7	5	6.62	0.40	37.31
Annual Growth	3.1%	—	—	(4.2%)	13.3%	11.3%

Neogen Corp

Bacteriophobes have a friend in Neogen a maker of products for the food safety and animal health markets. Its food safety testing products are used by the food industry to make sure our edibles are clean unspoiled and free of toxins pathogens and allergens. In core markets in the Americas and Europe Neogen reaches end users (including dairies meat processors and animal feed producers) through a direct sales force; it uses distributors elsewhere. On the animal health front Neogen produces drugs vaccines diagnostics and instruments for the veterinary market; it also makes rat poisons and disinfectants used in animal production plants and diagnostic products for research laboratories.

Operations

Some of Neogen's best-selling food-safety testing products include its Reveal and Alert tests used by meat poultry and seafood processors to detect food-borne bacteria. Others include its Veratox Agre-Screen and Reveal tests which are used by grain producers to detect mycotoxins (toxins produced by fungi).

When it comes to animals lead products include PanaKare a digestive aid; RenaKare a supplement for potassium deficiency in cats and dogs; and the NeogenVet brand including Vita-15 and Liver 7 which are used for the treatment and prevention of nutritional deficiencies in horses. Sales in its Animal Safety unit account for more than half of Neogen's revenue.

Geographic Reach

Neogen's animal products are sold to distributors around the world as well as through farm supply retailers in North America. International sales of all of its products account for about 40% of Neogen's revenue.

The company has manufacturing plants in Michigan Kentucky Wisconsin North Carolina and Iowa as well as in Scotland.

Sales and Marketing

Neogen sells its products through a direct sales force in North America parts of Europe Mexico Brazil and China. Elsewhere it sells through independent distributors. The company has some 20000 customers.

Strategy

Though Neogen has primarily used acquisitions to achieve relatively rapid growth the company is also looking for organic growth over the longer term through new product introductions higher sales of existing products international expansion efforts (it has made strides in India and China as of late) and the formation of strategic alliances. Neogen has ongoing development projects for new diagnostic tests and other complementary products for both the food safety and animal safety markets. The company also sees its over-the-counter animal health products as being particularly ripe for growth so it seeks to increase its line of rodenticides disinfectants instruments and horse care products.

Mergers and Acquisitions

In early 2019 Neogen acquired Canadian animal genomics laboratory Delta Genomics which specializes in beef and cattle testing. After that purchase the group operates five such labs around the world.

In 2018 Neogen acquired Virginia-based Livestock Genetic Services which provides evaluation and data management for cattle breeding groups. The deal boosted Neogen's in-house genetic evaluation abilities.

The prior year Neogen acquired Queensland Animal Genetics Laboratory (AGL) the largest animal genomics lab in Australia. That purchase expanded Neogen's genomics operations in the Asia/Pacific region. AGL provides services for region's large cattle market as well as the sheep goat alpaca and other markets. The lab was renamed GeneSeek Australasia.

EXECUTIVES

VP and CFO, Steven J. (Steve) Quinlan, age 56, $191,000 total compensation
VP Food Safety Operations, Edward L. Bradley, age 59, $167,000 total compensation
VP Animal Safety Operations, Terri A. Morrical, age 54, $165,000 total compensation
President and CEO, John E. Adent, age 51
Vice President International Business, Jason Lilly
Vice President Support Services, Melissa Herbert
Vice President Animal Safety Manufacturing, Dwight Schroedter
Board Member, Jack Parnell
Chairman, James L. Herbert, age 79
Board Of Directors, William Boehm
Board Member, Bruce Papesh
Auditors: BDO USA, LLP

LOCATIONS

HQ: Neogen Corp
   620 Lesher Place, Lansing, MI 48912
Phone: 517 372-9200
Web: www.neogen.com

PRODUCTS/OPERATIONS

2015 Sales

	$ mil.	% of total
Animal safety	151.6	54
Food safety	131.5	46
Total	**283.1**	**100**

2015 Sales

	$ mil.	% of total
Food safety		
Natural toxins allergans drug residues	60.6	21
Dehydrated culture media & other	41.1	15
Bacterial & general sanitation	29.8	11
Animal safety		
Rodenticides insecticides & disinfectants	45.9	16
Animal care & other	35.0	12
Veterinary instruments & disposables	34.3	12
DNA testing	27.7	10
Life sciences & other	8.7	3
Total	**283.1**	**100**

Selected Products

Food safety
   AccuClean (detects proteins and sugars)
   AccuPoint (rapid sanitation test)
   AgriScreen (detects mycotoxins)
   Alert (detects food-borne bacteria food allergens)
   Beta Star (detects antibiotics in milk)
   BioKits (detects allergens in food; also used for species identification)
   GeneQuence (detects food-borne bacteria)
   Reveal (detects food-borne bacteria food allergens ruminant by-products)
   Soleris (detects spoilage organisms)
   Veratox (detects mycotoxins food allergens)
Animal safety
   AgTek (Kane) products (apparel accessories etc.)
   BioSentry (chemicals)
   CyKill (rodent control)
   Di-Kill (rodent control)
   ElectroJac (automated semen collection)
   Havoc (rodenticide)
   Ideal (animal health products and instruments)
   NeogenVet (animal health products)
   Prozap (rodenticide)
   Ramik (rodenticide)
   Rodex (rodenticide)
   Squire (animal health products)

COMPETITORS

American Animal Health
Bayer Animal Health
Celldex Therapeutics
Ecolab
Eurofins Scientific
Hartz Mountain
Heska
IDEXX Labs
Life Technologies Corporation
Merck
Merck Animal Health
Merial
Novartis
Orchid Cellmark
Pfizer
Phibro Animal Health
Sdix
Silliker
Telesta
Virbac Corporation

HISTORICAL FINANCIALS
Company Type: Public

Income Statement   FYE: May 31

	REVENUE ($ mil.)	NET INCOME ($ mil.)	NET PROFIT MARGIN	EMPLOYEES
05/19	414.1	60.1	14.5%	1,682
05/18	402.2	63.1	15.7%	1,546
05/17	361.5	43.7	12.1%	1,413
05/16	321.2	36.5	11.4%	1,235
05/15	283.0	33.5	11.8%	1,062
Annual Growth	**10.0%**	**15.7%**	**—**	**12.2%**

2019 Year-End Financials

Debt ratio: —
Return on equity: 10.0%
Cash ($ mil.): 41.6
Current ratio: 11.75
Long-term debt ($ mil.): —
No. of shares (mil.): 52.3
Dividends
  Yield: —
  Payout: —
Market value ($ mil.): 2,942.0

	STOCK PRICE ($) FY Close	P/E High/Low		PER SHARE ($) Earnings	Dividends	Book Value
05/19	56.35	83	45	1.15	0.00	12.22
05/18	75.71	69	44	1.21	0.00	10.83
05/17	63.29	79	57	0.86	0.00	9.26
05/16	49.37	83	60	0.73	0.00	8.07
05/15	46.74	76	54	0.68	0.00	7.09
Annual Growth	**4.8%**	—	—	**14.2%**	—	**14.6%**

Network-1 Technologies, Inc

EXECUTIVES

Chb-ceo-sec, Corey M Horowitz
Executive Vice President, Jon Greene
Auditors: Friedman LLP

LOCATIONS

HQ: Network-1 Technologies, Inc
   445 Park Avenue, Suite 912, New York, NY 10022
Phone: 212 829-5770   **Fax:** 212 829-5771
Web: www.network-1.com

HISTORICAL FINANCIALS
Company Type: Public

Income Statement   FYE: December 31

	REVENUE ($ mil.)	NET INCOME ($ mil.)	NET PROFIT MARGIN	EMPLOYEES
12/18	22.1	7.7	34.9%	3
12/17	16.4	4.1	25.1%	5
12/16	65.0	23.2	35.7%	3
12/15	16.5	4.1	24.8%	4
12/14	12.3	1.7	14.3%	4
Annual Growth	**15.8%**	**44.5%**	**—**	**(6.9%)**

2018 Year-End Financials

Debt ratio: —
Return on equity: 13.6%
Cash ($ mil.): 18.6
Current ratio: 26.95
Long-term debt ($ mil.): —
No. of shares (mil.): 23.7
Dividends
  Yield: 4.4%
  Payout: 33.3%
Market value ($ mil.): 53.0

	STOCK PRICE ($) FY Close	P/E High/Low		PER SHARE ($) Earnings	Dividends	Book Value
12/18	2.23	10	7	0.30	0.10	2.45
12/17	2.40	29	14	0.16	0.10	2.28
12/16	3.40	3	2	0.93	0.00	2.23
12/15	2.09	16	10	0.17	0.00	1.24
12/14	2.20	34	21	0.07	0.00	1.11
Annual Growth	**0.3%**	—	—	**43.9%**	—	**21.9%**

New Residential Investment Corp

EXECUTIVES

Ceo-pres, Kenneth Riis
Auditors: Ernst & Young LLP

LOCATIONS

HQ: New Residential Investment Corp
   1345 Avenue of the Americas, New York, NY 10105
Phone: 212 798-3150
Web: www.newresi.com

HISTORICAL FINANCIALS
Company Type: Public

Income Statement   FYE: December 31

	REVENUE ($ mil.)	NET INCOME ($ mil.)	NET PROFIT MARGIN	EMPLOYEES
12/18	2,237.5	963.9	43.1%	0
12/17	2,151.8	957.5	44.5%	0
12/16	1,257.2	504.4	40.1%	0
12/15	687.1	268.6	39.1%	0
12/14	721.9	352.8	48.9%	0
Annual Growth	**32.7%**	**28.6%**	**—**	**—**

2018 Year-End Financials

Debt ratio: 22.4%
Return on equity: 18.0%
Cash ($ mil.): 251.0
Current ratio: 0.41
Long-term debt ($ mil.): 7,102.2
No. of shares (mil.): 369.1
Dividends
  Yield: 14.0%
  Payout: 71.1%
Market value ($ mil.): 5,245.0

	STOCK PRICE ($) FY Close	P/E High/Low		PER SHARE ($) Earnings	Dividends	Book Value
12/18	14.21	7	5	2.81	2.00	16.25
12/17	17.88	6	5	3.15	1.98	15.26
12/16	15.72	8	5	2.12	1.84	13.00
12/15	12.16	13	8	1.32	1.75	12.13
12/14	12.77	5	2	2.53	0.38	11.28
Annual Growth	2.7%	—	—	2.7%	51.5%	9.5%

Newmark Group Inc

Auditors: Ernst & Young LLP

LOCATIONS
HQ: Newmark Group Inc
125 Park Avenue, New York, NY 10017
Phone: 212 372-2000
Web: www.ngkf.com

HISTORICAL FINANCIALS
Company Type: Public

Income Statement — FYE: December 31

	REVENUE ($ mil.)	NET INCOME ($ mil.)	NET PROFIT MARGIN	EMPLOYEES
12/18	2,047.5	106.7	5.2%	5,200
12/17	1,596.4	144.4	9.1%	4,800
12/16	1,349.9	168.4	12.5%	4,600
12/15	1,200.2	(2.8)	—	0
Annual Growth	19.5%	—	—	—

2018 Year-End Financials
Debt ratio: 44.1%
Return on equity: 24.3%
Cash ($ mil.): 122.4
Current ratio: 1.06
Long-term debt ($ mil.): 537.9
No. of shares (mil.): 178.2
Dividends
  Yield: 3.3%
  Payout: 42.1%
Market value ($ mil.): 1,429.0

	STOCK PRICE ($) FY Close	P/E High/Low		PER SHARE ($) Earnings	Dividends	Book Value
12/18	8.02	26	12	0.64	0.27	3.33
12/17	15.90	15	13	0.85	0.00	1.82
12/16	0.00	—	—	(0.00)	0.00	(0.00)
Annual Growth	—	—	—	—	—	—

NextEra Energy Partners LP

Auditors: DELOITTE & TOUCHE LLP

LOCATIONS
HQ: NextEra Energy Partners LP
700 Universe Boulevard, Juno Beach, FL 33408
Phone: 561 694-4000
Web: www.nexteraenergypartners.com

HISTORICAL FINANCIALS
Company Type: Public

Income Statement — FYE: December 31

	REVENUE ($ mil.)	NET INCOME ($ mil.)	NET PROFIT MARGIN	EMPLOYEES
12/18	771.0	192.0	24.9%	0
12/17	807.0	(62.0)	—	0
12/16	715.0	82.0	11.5%	0
12/15	471.0	10.0	2.1%	0
12/14	301.0	3.0	1.0%	0
Annual Growth	26.5%	182.8%	—	—

2018 Year-End Financials
Debt ratio: 36.8%
Return on equity: 8.4%
Cash ($ mil.): 147.0
Current ratio: 0.40
Long-term debt ($ mil.): 2,762.0
No. of shares (mil.): 56.1
Dividends
  Yield: 3.9%
  Payout: 58.8%
Market value ($ mil.): 2,415.0

	STOCK PRICE ($) FY Close	P/E High/Low		PER SHARE ($) Earnings	Dividends	Book Value
12/18	43.05	16	12	2.91	1.71	41.82
12/17	43.11	—	—	(1.20)	1.49	40.29
12/16	25.54	17	13	1.88	1.30	32.16
12/15	29.85	104	43	0.46	0.91	30.36
12/14	33.75	236	186	0.16	0.19	29.47
Annual Growth	6.3%	—	—	106.5%	73.8%	9.1%

NexTier Oilfield Solutions Inc

Auditors: KPMG LLP

LOCATIONS
HQ: NexTier Oilfield Solutions Inc
1800 Post Oak Boulevard, Suite 450, Houston, TX 77056
Phone: 713 357-9490
Web: www.keanegrp.com

HISTORICAL FINANCIALS
Company Type: Public

Income Statement — FYE: December 31

	REVENUE ($ mil.)	NET INCOME ($ mil.)	NET PROFIT MARGIN	EMPLOYEES
12/18	2,137.0	59.3	2.8%	2,833
12/17	1,542.0	(28.2)	—	2,748
12/16	420.5	(187.0)	—	1,401
12/15	366.1	(64.6)	—	1,251
12/14	395.8	(45.5)	—	0
Annual Growth	52.4%	—	—	—

2018 Year-End Financials
Debt ratio: 33.3%
Return on equity: 11.8%
Cash ($ mil.): 80.2
Current ratio: 1.51
Long-term debt ($ mil.): 343.5
No. of shares (mil.): 104.1
Dividends
  Yield: —
  Payout: —
Market value ($ mil.): 852.0

	STOCK PRICE ($) FY Close	P/E High/Low		PER SHARE ($) Earnings	Dividends	Book Value
12/18	8.18	36	15	0.54	0.00	4.68
12/17	19.01	—	—	(0.34)	0.00	4.59
Annual Growth	(57.0%)	—	—	—	—	1.9%

NI Holdings Inc

Auditors: Mazars USA LLP

LOCATIONS
HQ: NI Holdings Inc
1101 First Avenue North, Fargo, ND 58102
Phone: 701 298-4200
Web: www.niholdingsinc.com

HISTORICAL FINANCIALS
Company Type: Public

Income Statement — FYE: December 31

	ASSETS ($ mil.)	NET INCOME ($ mil.)	INCOME AS % OF ASSETS	EMPLOYEES
12/18	458.4	31.0	6.8%	178
12/17	376.9	15.9	4.2%	136
12/16	278.7	4.5	1.6%	129
12/15	258.6	17.4	6.7%	126
12/14	247.2	13.7	5.6%	0
Annual Growth	16.7%	22.6%	—	—

2018 Year-End Financials
Return on assets: 7.4%
Return on equity: 11.8%
Long-term debt ($ mil.): —
No. of shares (mil.): 22.1
Sales ($ mil): 212.3
Dividends
  Yield: —
  Payout: —
Market value ($ mil.): 349.0

	STOCK PRICE ($) FY Close	P/E High/Low		PER SHARE ($) Earnings	Dividends	Book Value
12/18	15.73	13	11	1.39	0.00	12.28
12/17	16.98	26	20	0.71	0.00	11.30
Annual Growth	(7.4%)	—	—	95.8%	—	8.7%

Nicolet Bankshares Inc

EXECUTIVES
Pres-ceo, Robert Atwell
Vice President Commercial Banking, Trent Willihnganz
Board Member, Michael Gilson
Auditors: Wipfli LLP

LOCATIONS
HQ: Nicolet Bankshares Inc
111 North Washington Street, Green Bay, WI 54301
Phone: 920 430-1400
Web: www.nicoletbank.com

NMI Holdings Inc

NMI Holdings provides mortgage insurance through two primary subsids - National Mortgage Insurance Corp (NMIC) and National Mortgage Reinsurance Inc. One (Re One). NMIC is its primary insurance subsidiary approved to write coverage in all 50 states and Washington DC. Re One provides reinsurance to NMIC on insured loans with coverage levels in excess of 25%. The company also provides outsourced loan review services to mortgage loan originators through NMI Services. Mortgage insurance protects lenders and investors from default-related losses.

Operations
NMI Holdings offers primary mortgage insurance which provides protection on individual mortgage loans. Mortgages are insured on a case-by-case basis at the time of origination. The company previously offered pool insurance which covers the excess of loss on defaulted mortgages not covered under primary mortgage insurance. It didn't write any pool insurance in 2017 and doesn't expect to do much in that business line in the near future.

Geographic Reach
NMI Holdings gets all of its revenue in the US. Ten states account for more than half of its total risk-in-force (RIF) or the total dollar amount of claims it expects to receive during the year. California, Texas and Virginia account for about 15% 10% and 5% of RIF respectively.

Financial Performance
NIH's revenues have been climbing rapidly over the past five years but net income has been up and down. The company lost money in 2013 2014 and 2015 but was in the black in 2016 and 2017.

Revenue increased 47% to $178.6 million in 2017. Net premiums earned rose thanks to the company's growing insurance in-force. Investment income also rose that year.

Net income dropped 65% to $22.1 million in 2017 as operating expenses primarily insurance claims and claims expenses increased.

The company ended 2017 with $19.2 million in cash and cash equivalents 60% less than it had at the beginning of the year. Although operating cash flow provided $67.8 million cash from investments used $93.1 million.

Strategy
NMI Holdings is one of six private mortgage insurers operating in the US; the others are Arch Capital Essent Group Genworth Financial MGIC Investment Corporation and Radian Group. (Many others went out of business following the financial crisis of 2008.) However the company also competes with federal government agencies who filled the void left by private companies.

The company is working to increase its position in the private mortgage insurance market. It seeks to expand its customer base and strengthen its portfolio of high-quality assets largely through deepening its existing customer relationships.

EXECUTIVES

Chairman and CEO, Bradley M. (Brad) Shuster, age 64
EVP and Chief Risk Officer, Patrick L. Mathis, age 59
EVP and COO, Claudia J. Merkle
CFO, Glenn Farrell
EVP and General Counsel, William J. Leatherberry
Auditors: BDO USA, LLP

LOCATIONS

HQ: NMI Holdings Inc
2100 Powell Street, Emeryville, CA 94608
Phone: 855 530-6642
Web: www.nationalmi.com

PRODUCTS/OPERATIONS

2017 Sales

	% of total
Net premiums earned	91
Net investment income	9
Net realized investment gains	.
Other	.
Total	**100**

COMPETITORS

Arch Capital
Genworth Mortgage Insurance
MGIC Investment
Radian Group

HISTORICAL FINANCIALS

Company Type: Public

Income Statement — FYE: December 31

	ASSETS ($ mil.)	NET INCOME ($ mil.)	INCOME AS % OF ASSETS	EMPLOYEES
12/18	1,092.0	107.9	9.9%	304
12/17	894.8	22.0	2.5%	299
12/16	841.8	65.8	7.8%	276
12/15	662.4	(27.7)	—	243
12/14	463.2	(48.9)	—	189
Annual Growth	23.9%	—	—	12.6%

HISTORICAL FINANCIALS

Company Type: Public

Income Statement — FYE: December 31

	ASSETS ($ mil.)	NET INCOME ($ mil.)	INCOME AS % OF ASSETS	EMPLOYEES
12/18	3,096.5	41.0	1.3%	550
12/17	2,932.4	33.1	1.1%	535
12/16	2,300.8	18.4	0.8%	480
12/15	1,214.4	11.4	0.9%	280
12/14	1,215.2	9.9	0.8%	280
Annual Growth	26.3%	42.5%	—	18.4%

2018 Year-End Financials

Return on assets: 1.3%
Return on equity: 10.9%
Long-term debt ($ mil.): —
No. of shares (mil.): 9.5
Sales ($ mil): 165.0
Dividends
 Yield: —
 Payout: —
Market value ($ mil.): 463.0

	STOCK PRICE ($) FY Close	P/E High/Low		PER SHARE ($) Earnings	Dividends	Book Value
12/18	48.80	14	11	4.12	0.00	40.72
12/17	54.74	17	13	3.33	0.00	37.09
12/16	47.69	19	12	2.37	0.00	32.26
12/15	31.79	12	9	2.57	0.00	26.36
12/14	25.00	11	7	2.25	0.00	27.35
Annual Growth	18.2%	—	—	16.3%	—	10.5%

2018 Year-End Financials

Return on assets: 10.8%
Return on equity: 17.8%
Long-term debt ($ mil.): —
No. of shares (mil.): 66.3
Sales ($ mil): 275.0
Dividends
 Yield: —
 Payout: —
Market value ($ mil.): 1,184.0

	STOCK PRICE ($) FY Close	P/E High/Low		PER SHARE ($) Earnings	Dividends	Book Value
12/18	17.85	14	8	1.60	0.00	10.58
12/17	17.00	48	27	0.35	0.00	8.41
12/16	10.65	10	4	1.08	0.00	8.07
12/15	6.77	—	—	(0.47)	0.00	6.85
12/14	9.13	—	—	(0.84)	0.00	7.31
Annual Growth	18.2%	—	—	—	—	9.7%

Nobility Homes, Inc.

EXECUTIVES

Secretary, Jean Etheredge
Auditors: Daszkal Bolton LLP

LOCATIONS

HQ: Nobility Homes, Inc.
3741 S.W. 7th Street, Ocala, FL 34474
Phone: 352 732-5157
Web: www.nobilityhomes.com

COMPETITORS

American Homestar
Cavalier Homes
Cavco
Champion Home Builders
Clayton Homes
Four Seasons Housing
Giles Industries
Liberty Homes
Skyline
Southern Energy Homes

HISTORICAL FINANCIALS

Company Type: Public

Income Statement — FYE: November 2

	REVENUE ($ mil.)	NET INCOME ($ mil.)	NET PROFIT MARGIN	EMPLOYEES
11/19	46.3	8.8	19.0%	139
11/18	42.8	4.9	11.6%	149
11/17	37.5	3.3	8.8%	147
11/16*	34.0	5.9	17.5%	140
10/15	27.8	2.9	10.5%	129
Annual Growth	13.6%	31.8%	—	1.9%

*Fiscal year change

2019 Year-End Financials

Debt ratio: —
Return on equity: 17.9%
Cash ($ mil.): 22.5
Current ratio: 5.23
Long-term debt ($ mil.): —
No. of shares (mil.): 3.6
Dividends
 Yield: 0.0%
 Payout: 43.1%
Market value ($ mil.): 91.0

	STOCK PRICE ($) FY Close	P/E High/Low		PER SHARE ($) Earnings	Dividends	Book Value
11/19	24.75	11	8	2.32	1.00	13.50
11/18	23.00	19	13	1.27	0.20	12.67
11/17	17.00	22	18	0.83	0.15	11.86
11/16*	15.50	11	8	1.48	0.00	11.16
10/15	12.85	18	13	0.72	0.00	9.70
Annual Growth	17.8%	—	—	34.0%	—	8.6%

*Fiscal year change

Noble Midstream Partners LP

Auditors: KPMG LLP

LOCATIONS

HQ: Noble Midstream Partners LP
1001 Noble Energy Way, Houston, TX 77070
Phone: 281 872-3100
Web: www.NBLMidstream.com

HISTORICAL FINANCIALS
Company Type: Public

Income Statement — FYE: December 31

	REVENUE ($ mil.)	NET INCOME ($ mil.)	NET PROFIT MARGIN	EMPLOYEES
12/18	495.5	162.7	32.8%	160
12/17	239.2	140.5	58.7%	143
12/16	160.7	85.5	53.2%	90
12/15	92.4	38.0	41.1%	80
12/14	5.8	(15.0)	—	0
Annual Growth	202.9%	—	—	—

2018 Year-End Financials
Debt ratio: 27.9%
Return on equity: —
Cash ($ mil.): 11.6
Current ratio: 0.68
Long-term debt ($ mil.): 559.0
No. of shares (mil.): 39.6
Dividends
  Yield: 7.2%
  Payout: 52.8%
Market value ($ mil.): 1,144.0

	STOCK PRICE ($) FY Close	P/E High/Low	Earnings	Dividends	Book Value
12/18	28.84	14 7	3.96	2.09	14.42
12/17	50.00	13 9	4.10	1.76	11.99
12/16	36.00	43 29	0.89	0.00	8.54
Annual Growth	(10.5%)	—	—110.9%	—	30.0%

Northeast Bank (ME)

EXECUTIVES

Clerk Northeast Bank, Suzanne M. Carney, age 54
President CEO and Director Northeast Bancorp and Northeast Bank, James D. Delamater, age 64, $268,434 total compensation
COO Northeast Bank, Marcel C. Blais, age 56, $146,692 total compensation
CFO Northeast Bancorp and Northeast Bank, Robert S. Johnson, age 63, $146,692 total compensation
SVP Chief Risk Officer and Director, Pender J. Lazenby, age 66, $155,590 total compensation
SVP, Leslie L. Couper, $121,849 total compensation
SVP Northeast Bank Insurance Group, Craig Linscott
Director Marketing, Chris Delamater
Sales Manager and Mortgage Loan Officer Portland Branch, Greg Dauphinee
Vp And Enterprise Risk Manager, William DiFulvio
Chief Financial Officer; Chief Operating Officer; Treasurer, Claire Bean
Senior Vice President, Colette Twigg-Rowse
Chief Administrative Officer; Secretary, Heather Campion
Director of Human Resources, Heidi Jacques
Corporate Controller, Jason Stephens
Independent Chairman of the Board, Robert Glauber
President; Chief Executive Officer; Director, Richard Wayne
Auditors: RSM US LLP

LOCATIONS

HQ: Northeast Bank (ME)
500 Canal Street, Lewiston, ME 04240
Phone: 207 786-3245
Web: www.northeastbank.com

COMPETITORS

Bar Harbor Bankshares
Camden National
KeyCorp
Norway Bancorp
TD Bank USA
The First Bancorp

HISTORICAL FINANCIALS
Company Type: Public

Income Statement — FYE: June 30

	ASSETS ($ mil.)	NET INCOME ($ mil.)	INCOME AS % OF ASSETS	EMPLOYEES
06/19	1,153.8	13.8	1.2%	183
06/18	1,157.7	16.1	1.4%	185
06/17	1,076.8	12.3	1.1%	195
06/16	986.1	7.6	0.8%	203
06/15	850.8	7.1	0.8%	191
Annual Growth	7.9%	18.1%	—	(1.1%)

2019 Year-End Financials
Return on assets: 1.2%
Return on equity: 9.5%
Long-term debt ($ mil.): —
No. of shares (mil.): 9.0
Sales ($ mil): 87.9
Dividends
  Yield: 0.0%
  Payout: 2.6%
Market value ($ mil.): 249.0

	STOCK PRICE ($) FY Close	P/E High/Low	Earnings	Dividends	Book Value
06/19	27.58	18 10	1.52	0.04	16.98
06/18	21.80	16 11	1.77	0.04	15.49
06/17	20.35	15 8	1.38	0.04	13.90
06/16	11.25	15 12	0.80	0.04	12.51
06/15	9.95	14 12	0.72	0.04	11.77
Annual Growth	29.0%	—	20.5%	(0.0%)	9.6%

Northeast Community Bancorp Inc

EXECUTIVES

EVP CFO and Director, Salvatore Randazzo, age 48, $173,265 total compensation
Chairman President and CEO, Kenneth A. Martinek, age 63, $273,837 total compensation
Chief Operating Officer; Executive Vice President; Chief Information Officer, Jose Collazo
Auditors: BDO USA, LLP

LOCATIONS

HQ: Northeast Community Bancorp Inc
325 Hamilton Avenue, White Plains, NY 10601
Phone: 914 684-2500
Web: www.necommunitybank.com

COMPETITORS

Bank of America
Citigroup
HSBC USA
JPMorgan Chase
KeyCorp
New York Community Bancorp
TrustCo Bank Corp NY
Wells Fargo

HISTORICAL FINANCIALS
Company Type: Public

Income Statement — FYE: December 31

	ASSETS ($ mil.)	NET INCOME ($ mil.)	INCOME AS % OF ASSETS	EMPLOYEES
12/17	814.8	8.0	1.0%	0
12/16	734.5	5.0	0.7%	0
12/15	593.6	2.3	0.4%	0
12/14	515.4	1.7	0.3%	96
12/13	458.2	1.1	0.2%	104
Annual Growth	15.5%	63.1%	—	—

2017 Year-End Financials
Return on assets: 1.0%
Return on equity: 7.1%
Long-term debt ($ mil.): —
No. of shares (mil.): 12.1
Sales ($ mil): 39.5
Dividends
  Yield: 0.0%
  Payout: 17.9%
Market value ($ mil.): 123.0

	STOCK PRICE ($) FY Close	P/E High/Low	Earnings	Dividends	Book Value
12/17	10.10	15 11	0.67	0.12	9.59
12/16	7.90	19 15	0.42	0.12	8.96
12/15	7.12	40 34	0.20	0.12	8.59
12/14	7.22	53 48	0.14	0.12	8.42
12/13	7.22	87 59	0.09	0.09	8.29
Annual Growth	8.8%	—	65.2%	7.5%	3.7%

Northfield Bancorp Inc (DE)

Auditors: KPMG LLP

LOCATIONS

HQ: Northfield Bancorp Inc (DE)
581 Main Street, Woodbridge, NJ 07095
Phone: 732 499-7200
Web: www.eNorthfield.com

HISTORICAL FINANCIALS
Company Type: Public

Income Statement — FYE: December 31

	ASSETS ($ mil.)	NET INCOME ($ mil.)	INCOME AS % OF ASSETS	EMPLOYEES
12/18	4,408.4	40.0	0.9%	368
12/17	3,991.4	24.7	0.6%	352
12/16	3,850.0	26.1	0.7%	366
12/15	3,202.5	19.5	0.6%	306
12/14	3,020.8	20.2	0.7%	321
Annual Growth	9.9%	18.6%	—	3.5%

2018 Year-End Financials

Return on assets: 0.9%
Return on equity: 6.1%
Long-term debt ($ mil.): —
No. of shares (mil.): 49.6
Sales ($ mil): 155.4
Dividends
Yield: 2.9%
Payout: 66.6%
Market value ($ mil.): 673.0

	STOCK PRICE ($) FY Close	P/E High/Low		PER SHARE ($) Earnings	Dividends	Book Value
12/18	13.55	20	15	0.85	0.40	13.43
12/17	17.08	37	28	0.53	0.34	13.09
12/16	19.97	35	24	0.57	0.31	12.80
12/15	15.92	36	31	0.45	0.28	12.29
12/14	14.80	36	30	0.41	0.26	12.27
Annual Growth	(2.2%)	—	—	20.0%	11.4%	2.3%

Northwest Indiana Bancorp

EXECUTIVES

Assistant Vice President Loan Operations, Antoinette Shettles
Assistant Vice President And Wealth Management Officer, Lisa Morris
ASSISTANT VICE PRESIDENT APPLICATION AND DATABASE ADMINISTRATOR, Kimberlee Klisiak
Assistant Vice President Mortgage Sales Manager, Michael Sowards
Vice President Wealth Management Officer, Thomas Devine
Board Member, Joel Gorelick
Auditors: Plante & Moran, PLLC

LOCATIONS

HQ: Northwest Indiana Bancorp
9204 Columbia Avenue, Munster, IN 46321
Phone: 219 836-4400
Web: www.ibankpeoples.com

COMPETITORS

AMB Financial	First Midwest Bancorp
Bank of America	Harris
Fifth Third	Huntington Bancshares

HISTORICAL FINANCIALS

Company Type: Public

Income Statement FYE: December 31

	ASSETS ($ mil.)	NET INCOME ($ mil.)	INCOME AS % OF ASSETS	EMPLOYEES
12/18	1,096.1	9.3	0.9%	276
12/17	927.2	8.9	1.0%	217
12/16	913.6	9.1	1.0%	216
12/15	864.8	7.8	0.9%	215
12/14	775.0	7.3	1.0%	195
Annual Growth	9.1%	6.0%	—	9.1%

2018 Year-End Financials

Return on assets: 0.9%
Return on equity: 9.6%
Long-term debt ($ mil.): —
No. of shares (mil.): 3.0
Sales ($ mil): 48.5
Dividends
Yield: 2.7%
Payout: 40.0%
Market value ($ mil.): 130.0

	STOCK PRICE ($) FY Close	P/E High/Low		PER SHARE ($) Earnings	Dividends	Book Value
12/18	43.00	15	13	3.17	1.19	33.50
12/17	44.50	14	12	3.13	1.15	32.14
12/16	38.85	12	9	3.20	1.11	29.41
12/15	30.80	12	10	2.75	1.06	28.38
12/14	26.50	11	10	2.60	0.97	26.78
Annual Growth	12.9%	—	—	5.1%	5.2%	5.8%

Norwood Financial Corp.

EXECUTIVES

Executive Vice President, Ken Doolittle
Vice President Deposit Operations, Joann Fuller
Auditors: S.R. Snodgrass, P.C.

LOCATIONS

HQ: Norwood Financial Corp.
717 Main Street, Honesdale, PA 18431
Phone: 570 253-1455
Web: www.waynebank.com

COMPETITORS

Citizens Financial Group	Fidelity D & D
	NBT Bancorp
ESSA Bancorp	PNC Financial

HISTORICAL FINANCIALS

Company Type: Public

Income Statement FYE: December 31

	ASSETS ($ mil.)	NET INCOME ($ mil.)	INCOME AS % OF ASSETS	EMPLOYEES
12/18	1,184.5	13.6	1.2%	210
12/17	1,132.9	8.2	0.7%	214
12/16	1,111.1	6.7	0.6%	215
12/15	750.5	5.9	0.8%	145
12/14	711.6	7.6	1.1%	141
Annual Growth	13.6%	15.6%	—	10.5%

2018 Year-End Financials

Return on assets: 1.1%
Return on equity: 11.4%
Long-term debt ($ mil.): —
No. of shares (mil.): 6.2
Sales ($ mil): 49.5
Dividends
Yield: 2.6%
Payout: 52.6%
Market value ($ mil.): 208.0

	STOCK PRICE ($) FY Close	P/E High/Low		PER SHARE ($) Earnings	Dividends	Book Value
12/18	33.00	18	13	2.17	0.88	19.43
12/17	33.00	34	21	1.31	0.86	18.51
12/16	33.14	30	23	1.15	0.83	17.80
12/15	28.75	29	26	1.07	0.82	18.19
12/14	29.05	23	19	1.40	0.80	17.95
Annual Growth	3.2%	—	—	11.6%	2.4%	2.0%

Novanta Inc

Novanta's business is laser focused. The company uses its expertise in laser and motion control technologies to design and manufacture sets of products that are geared to the medical and healthcare and advanced industrial markets. Sealed CO2 lasers ultrafast lasers and optical light engines are sold primarily to the industrial and scientific markets. Novanta supplies lasers optics encoders and air bearing spindles to the healthcare and medical markets as well as the aerospace market for high-precision cutting drilling marking and measuring. The company changed its name to Novanta from GSI Group in mid-2016. International customers account for about 60% of sales.

Operations

Novanta conducts business through three primary segments: Photonics (45% of net sales) Vision (35%) and Precision Motion (20%).

Photonics designs makes and sells photonics-based tools that include laser scanning and laser beam delivery instruments CO2 lasers continuous wave and ultrafast lasers and optical light engine products.

The Vision segment makes and sells a range of medical technologies including medical insufflators (tools for pumping powder or gas into a body cavity) pumps and related disposables; surgical displays and operating room integration technologies; optical data collection and machine vision technologies; radio frequency identification (RFID) technologies; thermal printers; spectrometry technologies; and embedded touch screens.

The Precision Motion segment's products include optical encoders precision motor and motion control technology air bearing spindles and precision machines components.

Novanta operates through several trade names that include Cambridge Technology Lincoln Laser Synrad Laser Quantum WOM Reach Technology JADAK ThingMagic Photo Research Celera Motion Applimotion and Westwind.

Geographic Reach

Novanta based in Bedford Massachusetts operates from about 20 locations in Europe the Asia/Pacific and the US. Geographically the US generates Novanta's largest amount of sales (more than 40%) followed by Europe (about 30%) and China and other countries in the Asia/Pacific region (about 30%).

Sales and Marketing

Novanta sells its products worldwide through a direct sales force and through resellers or distributors who in turn sell to OEMs that integrate Novanta's products into their own systems. Novanta primarily customers are in the medical and advanced industrial markets.

Financial Performance

After several years of revenue increasing at about a 2% rate Novanta's revenue jumped 35% in 2017 thanks largely to acquisitions made in the past two years. Each segment posted higher sales in 2017 leading to revenue of $521 million. Acquisitions boosted sales for the Photonics and Vision businesses while increased demand in the advanced industrial and medical markets pushed Precision Motion sales higher.

Net income rose to $61 million in 2017 from $22 million in 2016 from higher revenue and as the company kept expenses at or close to previous levels as a percentage of revenue.

Novanta had about $100 million in cash in 2017 up from some $68 million in 2016. The increase came from cash provided by operating activities and money borrowed under its revolving credit facility. The company spent money on the WOM ThingMagic and Laser Quantum acquisitions debt repayments and capital expenditures.

Strategy
Novanta's general strategy includes focusing on scanning products fiber lasers and medical components and building more business in emerging markets through creating more internal sales channels and developing relationships with external channel partners. Part of that strategy involves acquisitions and divesting non-core businesses. Novanta bought three companies in 2016 and 2016 which added more than $100 million in sales in 2017 while shutting down its line of Dome brand radiology products in 2016.

With about 60% of revenue from international customers Novanta runs the risk of getting caught in possible trade wars. China has been a particular target of the US government and that's where Novanta has done increasing business through sales and production outsourcing.

Novanta's push into medical markets has helped increase revenue but the continued uncertainty of the US Patient Protection and Affordable Care Act could interfere with that strategy by changing what health and medical institutions buy and how they do it.

Mergers and Acquisitions
INovanta boosted its products for the medical market through a series of acquisitions.

In 2017 Novanta acquired Germany-based World of Medicine GmbH a provider of medical insufflators (for blowing gas or powder into a body cavity) pumps and related disposables for OEMs for ?118.1 million.

Also in 2017 the company increased it ownership of Laser Quantum to more than 75% with the purchase of additional shares for Â 25.5 million. Laser Quantum provides solid state continuous wave lasers femtosecond lasers and optical light engines to OEMs in the medical market.

The 2017 acquisition of ThingMagic for about $19 million added ultra-high frequency (UHF) radio frequency identification (RFID) modules and finished RFID readers to Novanta's offerings for OEMs.

In 2016 Novanta bought California-based Reach Technology Inc. a provider of embedded touch screen technology products to OEMs for more than $9 million.

EXECUTIVES

CFO, Robert Buckley, age 45, $378,762 total compensation
CEO and Director, Matthijs Glastra, $410,955 total compensation
Vice President Global Information Technology, Scott Rehner
Chairman, Stephen W. Bershad, age 77
Board Member, Thomas Secor
Auditors: PricewaterhouseCoopers LLP

LOCATIONS

HQ: Novanta Inc
  125 Middlesex Turnpike, Bedford, MA 01730
Phone: 781 266-5700   **Fax:** 781 266-5114
Web: www.gsig.com

PRODUCTS/OPERATIONS

2017 sales

	$ mil.	% of total
Photonics	232.4	45
Vision	183.0	35
Precision Motion	105.8	20
Total	**521.2**	**100**

Selected Products and Brands
Laser products
  Lasers and laser-based systems (Synrad)
  Light and color measurement systems (Photo Research Inc.)
  Optics (The Optical Corporation)
  Scanners (Cambridge Technology)
Precision motion
  Encoders (MicroE Systems)
  Lasers (eCO2 Lasers Spectron Lasers)
  Optics (ExoTec Precision)
  Printed circuit board spindles (Westwind Air Bearings)
Medical technologies
Visualizations solutions
Imaging Informatics

COMPETITORS

Analogic	Newport Corp.
Blue Sky Research	OMRON
Coherent Inc.	Omron Electronics
CyberOptics	ProPhotonix
Cymer	Quantel
Electro Scientific Industries	Renishaw
	Spectra-Physics
HEIDENHAIN Corp.	Swatch
Hitachi	TOPCON
II-VI	TRUMPF
IPG Photonics	Virtek Vision
JMAR Technologies	Zygo

HISTORICAL FINANCIALS
Company Type: Public

Income Statement   FYE: December 31

	REVENUE ($ mil.)	NET INCOME ($ mil.)	NET PROFIT MARGIN	EMPLOYEES
12/18	614.3	49.1	8.0%	2,133
12/17	521.2	60.0	11.5%	2,034
12/16	384.7	22.0	5.7%	1,269
12/15	373.6	35.6	9.5%	1,355
12/14	364.7	(24.2)	—	1,418
Annual Growth	13.9%	—	—	10.7%

2018 Year-End Financials
Debt ratio: 28.8%   No. of shares (mil.): 34.8
Return on equity: 14.4%   Dividends
Cash ($ mil.): 82.0   Yield: —
Current ratio: 2.70   Payout: —
Long-term debt ($ mil.): 202.8   Market value ($ mil.): 2,198.0

	STOCK PRICE ($) FY Close	P/E High/Low	PER SHARE ($) Earnings	Dividends	Book Value
12/18	63.00	54 33	1.43	0.00	10.56
12/17	50.00	48 18	1.13	0.00	9.01
12/16	21.00	34 19	0.63	0.00	7.51
12/15	13.62	15 12	1.02	0.00	7.12
12/14	14.72	— —	(0.70)	0.00	6.16
Annual Growth	43.8%		— —	—	14.4%

Novation Companies Inc

EXECUTIVES

Chairman President and CEO, W. Lance Anderson, age 55, $665,784 total compensation
SVP and CFO, Rodney E. Schwatken, age 53, $165,000 total compensation
CEO StreetLinks, Steve Haslam
Chief Information Officer, Matthew Lautz
Director, Barry Igdaloff, age 60
Director, Gregory T. (Greg) Barmore, age 72
Director, Art N. Burtscher, age 64
Director, Edward W. (Ed) Mehrer Jr., age 76
Director, Howard M. Amster, age 67
Auditors: Boulay PLLP

LOCATIONS

HQ: Novation Companies Inc
  9229 Ward Parkway, Suite 340, Kansas City, MO 64114
Phone: 816 237-7000
Web: www.novationcompanies.com

COMPETITORS

DFC Global	FirstCash
EZCORP	Stewart Information Services
First American	

HISTORICAL FINANCIALS
Company Type: Public

Income Statement   FYE: December 31

	REVENUE ($ mil.)	NET INCOME ($ mil.)	NET PROFIT MARGIN	EMPLOYEES
12/18	55.1	6.1	11.1%	2,269
12/17	27.9	(10.8)	—	1,999
12/16	5.0	5.2	103.0%	5
12/15	6.1	(28.7)	—	115
12/14	12.0	30.9	256.4%	169
Annual Growth	46.2%	(33.3%)	—	91.4%

2018 Year-End Financials
Debt ratio: 282.4%   No. of shares (mil.): 99.1
Return on equity: —   Dividends
Cash ($ mil.): 9.2   Yield: —
Current ratio: 2.22   Payout: —
Long-term debt ($ mil.): 85.9   Market value ($ mil.): 2.0

	STOCK PRICE ($) FY Close	P/E High/Low	PER SHARE ($) Earnings	Dividends	Book Value
12/18	0.02	1 0	0.06	0.00	(0.64)
12/17	0.07	— —	(0.12)	0.00	(0.60)
12/16	0.05	2 1	0.06	0.00	(0.53)
12/15	0.13	— —	(0.32)	0.00	(0.67)
12/14	0.28	1 1	0.34	0.00	(0.36)
Annual Growth	(47.1%)		— (35.2%)	—	—

Nuvasive Inc

When a back is seriously out of whack NuVasive has some options. The company makes and markets medical devices for the surgical treatment of spinal disorders. NuVasive's products are primarily used in spinal restoration and fusion surgeries. Its minimally disruptive Maximum Access Surgery (MAS) platform enables surgeons to access the spine from the side of the body instead of from the front or back helping them to avoid hitting nerves. NuVasive also features a line of biologic bone grafting materials — both allograft and synthetic — and has a cervical disc replacement system in development. The company sells its FDA-approved products through a network of exclusive sales agents supported by an in-house sales team.

Operations
NuVasive offers more than 80 products for procedures in the lumbar thoracic and cervical regions including the mesh plates screws and biological implants used with its MAS system. Its Osteocel product is an adult stem-cell bone graft used for bone regeneration in orthopedic procedures and at one point was the only commercially available stem-cell product in the US.

NuVasive's revenues primarily come from the sale of disposable materials and implants. The full system of software and instruments are loaned to hospitals for free as long as they keep ordering disposables and implants though a small portion of the company's revenues are from the sale of instruments and systems. Revenues from its monitoring services come from hospitals and are also billed through various payers.

Geographic Reach
NuVasive maintains a facility in California where it trains doctors in the use of its products. It ships its products directly to doctors overnight from a distribution facility in Tennessee; other US facilities are located in New Jersey Ohio and Maryland. International offices are located in Australia Brazil Germany Japan the Netherlands and the UK.

The US accounts for the majority of NuVasive's sales but the company is working to establish its products in Europe and Asia. The first hurdle is obtaining regulatory approval for all of the components in its platform for each country it seeks to enter.

Sales and Marketing
NuVasive sells its products through its own direct sales force and through exclusive distributors and independent sales agents.

Financial Performance
NuVasive's revenues have steadily increased as it has grown through increased product sales new product additions and acquisitions including a 19% jump to $962.1 million in fiscal 2016. That year's growth was driven by increased spinal hardware product sales which rose 20% and higher surgical support sales which rose 14%.

Net income has fluctuated in recent years. In 2016 it fell 44% to $37.1 million — despite the higher revenue — as operating expenses such as sales and marketing and R&D costs rose.

Strategy
NuVasive's goal is to make its products and services part of the standard procedure for minimally invasive surgery up and down the entire spine. The firm is focused on expanding the reach of its MAS platform through marketing and sales force efforts to increase market penetration. It also conducts research and development efforts to improve existing offerings to make them more adaptable for surgeons and hospitals.

R&D efforts create new products as well. As cervical disc replacement technology — the holy grail for spinal device makers — is advancing rapidly NuVasive has several cervical disc replacement devices in late-stage development.

Mergers and Acquisitions
In mid-2016 NuVasive acquired Biotronic NeuroNetwork which provides intraoperative neurophysiological monitoring services for $98 million. That deal which more than doubled NuVasive's neurophysiology footprint extended the operations of the company's newly established NuVasive Clinical Services division. That unit now provides monitoring services for more than 75000 cases each year.

Also that year the company acquired Ellipse Technologies which developed magnetic growing rod implant systems for $380 million; those products which eliminate the need for repeat surgeries as pediatric patients grow are now sold by NuVasive Specialized Orthopedics. In yet another deal it purchased the LessRay software suite which enhances image quality while helping health care providers manage radiation exposure.

In 2017 NuVasive agreed to buy SafePassage which provides intraoperative neurophysiological monitoring (IONM) services for an undisclosed amount. SafePassage will join its Clinical Services division; it will expand the company's IONM business into new markets especially on the East Coast.

EXECUTIVES

Chairman and CEO, Gregory T. Lucier
EVP Asia Pacific, Takaaki Tanaka
EVP Global Operations, Tyler P. Lipschultz
EVP International, Russell Powers
EVP Strategic Sales and Operations, Scott Durall
EVP Strategy Technology and Corporate Development, Matthew W. (Matt) Link, age 44, $375,000 total compensation
EVP Corporate Affairs and Human Resources, Carol Cox
CIO, Johnson Lai
EVP Global Process Transformation, Stephen Rozow, age 50
EVP and CFO, Rajesh J. (Raj) Asarpota
Executive Vice President International, Skip Kiil
Executive Vice President People and Culture, Pete Leddy
Vice President Chief Intellectual Property Counsel, Michael Doyle
Executive Vice President Global Commercial, Harry Kiil
Vice Chairman, Patrick (Pat) Miles
Auditors: Ernst & Young LLP

LOCATIONS

HQ: Nuvasive Inc
7475 Lusk Boulevard, San Diego, CA 92121
Phone: 858 909-1800   **Fax:** 800 475-9134
Web: www.nuvasive.com

PRODUCTS/OPERATIONS

2016 Sales

	% of total
Spinal Hardware	70
Surgical Support	30
Total	**100**

Selected Acquisitions

COMPETITORS

Alphatec Spine	Natus Medical
CareFusion	Orthofix
DePuy Spine	Stryker
Globus Medical	Synthes
Integra LifeSciences	Zimmer Biomet
Interpore	
Medtronic Sofamor Danek	

HISTORICAL FINANCIALS
Company Type: Public

Income Statement   FYE: December 31

	REVENUE ($ mil.)	NET INCOME ($ mil.)	NET PROFIT MARGIN	EMPLOYEES
12/18	1,101.7	12.4	1.1%	2,600
12/17	1,029.5	83.0	8.1%	2,600
12/16	962.0	37.1	3.9%	2,200
12/15	811.1	66.2	8.2%	1,600
12/14	762.4	(16.7)	—	1,500
Annual Growth	9.6%	—	—	14.7%

2018 Year-End Financials
Debt ratio: 35.2%   No. of shares (mil.): 56.6
Return on equity: 1.5%   Dividends
Cash ($ mil.): 117.8   Yield: —
Current ratio: 3.44   Payout: —
Long-term debt ($ mil.): 602.5   Market value ($ mil.): 2,807.0

	STOCK PRICE ($) FY Close	P/E High/Low	PER SHARE ($) Earnings	Dividends	Book Value
12/18	49.56	298 192	0.24	0.00	14.73
12/17	58.49	50 31	1.50	0.00	14.16
12/16	67.36	92 53	0.69	0.00	12.59
12/15	54.11	41 31	1.26	0.00	13.21
12/14	47.16	— —	(0.36)	0.00	13.42
Annual Growth	1.2%	— —	—	—	2.4%

Nuvera Communications Inc

EXECUTIVES

Director Media Relations, Amy Bauer
Auditors: Olsen Thielen & Co., Ltd.

LOCATIONS

HQ: Nuvera Communications Inc
27 North Minnesota Street, New Ulm, MN 56073
Phone: 507 354-4111
Web: www.nuvera.net

COMPETITORS

AT&T	T-Mobile USA
AT&T Mobility	Verizon
CenturyLink	Verizon Wireless Inc.
Sprint Communications	

HISTORICAL FINANCIALS
Company Type: Public

Income Statement — FYE: December 31

	REVENUE ($ mil.)	NET INCOME ($ mil.)	NET PROFIT MARGIN	EMPLOYEES
12/18	56.6	7.7	13.7%	172
12/17	46.8	9.9	21.2%	134
12/16	42.3	2.8	6.7%	145
12/15	41.6	2.6	6.4%	146
12/14	39.9	2.7	6.9%	148
Annual Growth	9.1%	29.7%	—	3.8%

2018 Year-End Financials
Debt ratio: 38.4%
Return on equity: 10.8%
Cash ($ mil.): 1.5
Current ratio: 0.84
Long-term debt ($ mil.): 57.0
No. of shares (mil.): 5.1
Dividends
  Yield: 2.4%
  Payout: 22.3%
Market value ($ mil.): 95.0

	STOCK PRICE ($) FY Close	P/E High/Low	PER SHARE ($) Earnings	Dividends	Book Value
12/18	18.29	13 11	1.50	0.44	14.41
12/17	17.72	9 5	1.93	0.40	13.27
12/16	9.69	17 12	0.56	0.36	11.72
12/15	7.30	15 13	0.52	0.34	11.54
12/14	7.30	15 12	0.54	0.34	11.38
Annual Growth	25.8%	—	29.1%	6.7%	6.1%

NV5 Global Inc

NV5 Global wants the world to envy its engineering services. It offers infrastructure engineering support and consulting services as well as construction quality assurance and asset management. Customers include government agencies along with quasi-public and private firms in education health care and energy. NV5's enviable projects have included the international terminal at Philadelphia International Airport UC Santa Barbara's Marine Center the New Jersey Devils Arena San Diego's Manchester Grand Hyatt and a wind turbine manufacturing plant in Colorado. The company works from about 20 offices in California Colorado Florida New Jersey and Utah. It was formed in 2011 and filed to go public in 2013.

IPO
The company plans to use its anticipated $6.9 million in IPO proceeds for general corporate purposes including working capital sales and marketing and acquisitions.

Operations
NV5 divides its business into what it calls its five vertical offerings. They are- infrastructure engineering and support services; construction quality assurance; public and private consulting and outsourcing; asset management consulting; and occupational health safety and environmental consulting.

It has traditionally focused on the first two service verticals but is expanding into the others and plans to focus on those going forward.

Financial Performance
NV5's revenues have generally been increasing while its costs have held steady except for acquisitions. The company hasn't reported 2012 numbers yet but in 2011 it nearly doubled revenue and increased net income nearly tenfold. Nolte Associates acquired during 2010 contributed all of the company's revenue for 2011.

Strategy
Going forward NV5 intends to continue to focus on public sector clients which account for about 60% of revenue while working to grow its private sector accounts. It also plans to look for strategic acquisitions and invest in attracting training and retaining personnel.

Mergers and Acquisitions
In 2011 NV5 completed a reorganization to incorporate Nolte Associates acquired the previous year. In 2012 it purchased engineering firm Kaderabek (Kaco) for about $3.5 million.

EXECUTIVES

Director; EVP Strategic Growth NV5, Donald C. (Don) Alford, age 75, $240,000 total compensation
Chairman and CEO, Dickerson Wright, age 73, $400,000 total compensation
VP and CFO, Michael P. Rama, age 53, $178,077 total compensation
Executive Vice President and General Counsel, Richard Tong, age 51, $230,000 total compensation
President and COO, Alexander A. Hockman, age 62, $290,385 total compensation
Executive Vice President and Chief Administrative Officer, Mary Jo OA'Brien, age 57
Vice President of Buildings Energy and Science, Amanda Weir
Vice President Occupational Health Safety And Environmental Services, Steven Lipson
Vice President Of Code Compliance Se Us, Wayne Dean
Auditors: Deloitte & Touche LLP

LOCATIONS
HQ: NV5 Global Inc
200 South Park Road, Suite 350, Hollywood, FL 33021
Phone: 954 495-2112
Web: www.nv5.com

COMPETITORS

AECOM	Terracon
Amec Foster Wheeler	Tetra Tech
Bureau Veritas	The Kleinfelder Group Inc.
Cardno	WS Atkins
Intertek	Willdan Group
Jacobs Engineering	
TRC Companies	

HISTORICAL FINANCIALS
Company Type: Public

Income Statement — FYE: December 29

	REVENUE ($ mil.)	NET INCOME ($ mil.)	NET PROFIT MARGIN	EMPLOYEES
12/18	418.0	26.8	6.4%	2,384
12/17	333.0	24.0	7.2%	2,023
12/16	223.9	11.6	5.2%	1,532
12/15	154.6	8.4	5.5%	975
12/14	108.3	4.8	4.5%	649
Annual Growth	40.1%	53.1%	—	38.4%

2018 Year-End Financials
Debt ratio: 10.6%
Return on equity: 10.8%
Cash ($ mil.): 40.7
Current ratio: 2.54
Long-term debt ($ mil.): 29.8
No. of shares (mil.): 12.5
Dividends
  Yield: —
  Payout: —
Market value ($ mil.): 731.0

	STOCK PRICE ($) FY Close	P/E High/Low	PER SHARE ($) Earnings	Dividends	Book Value
12/18	58.24	37 17	2.33	0.00	25.30
12/17	54.15	25 14	2.23	0.00	16.62
12/16	33.40	29 12	1.22	0.00	14.02
12/15	21.98	22 8	1.18	0.00	9.83
12/14	13.00	15 8	0.87	0.00	6.19
Annual Growth	45.5%	—	27.9%	—	42.2%

Oak Valley Bancorp (Oakdale, CA)

Auditors: RSM US LLP

LOCATIONS
HQ: Oak Valley Bancorp (Oakdale, CA)
125 N. Third Ave., Oakdale, CA 95361
Phone: 209 848-2265
Web: www.ovcb.com

COMPETITORS

Bank of America	U.S. Bancorp
Bank of the West	Wells Fargo
Citibank	Westamerica
MUFG Americas Holdings	

HISTORICAL FINANCIALS
Company Type: Public

Income Statement — FYE: December 31

	ASSETS ($ mil.)	NET INCOME ($ mil.)	INCOME AS % OF ASSETS	EMPLOYEES
12/18	1,094.8	11.5	1.1%	186
12/17	1,034.8	9.0	0.9%	175
12/16	1,002.1	7.6	0.8%	169
12/15	897.0	4.9	0.5%	167
12/14	749.6	7.1	1.0%	157
Annual Growth	9.9%	12.8%	—	4.3%

2018 Year-End Financials
Return on assets: 1.0%
Return on equity: 12.1%
Long-term debt ($ mil.): —
No. of shares (mil.): 8.1
Sales ($ mil): 44.8
Dividends
  Yield: 1.4%
  Payout: 20.6%
Market value ($ mil.): 150.0

	STOCK PRICE ($) FY Close	P/E High/Low	PER SHARE ($) Earnings	Dividends	Book Value
12/18	18.30	17 12	1.42	0.26	12.09
12/17	19.54	18 11	1.13	0.25	11.21
12/16	12.55	13 10	0.95	0.24	10.19
12/15	10.40	18 15	0.61	0.21	9.69
12/14	10.16	12 9	0.89	0.17	9.29
Annual Growth	15.8%	—	12.4%	12.0%	6.8%

Oasis Midstream Partners LP

Auditors: PricewaterhouseCoopers LLP

LOCATIONS
HQ: Oasis Midstream Partners LP
  1001 Fannin Street, Suite 1500, Houston, TX 77002
Phone: 281 404-9500
Web: www.oasismidstream.com

HISTORICAL FINANCIALS
Company Type: Public

Income Statement — FYE: December 31

	REVENUE ($ mil.)	NET INCOME ($ mil.)	NET PROFIT MARGIN	EMPLOYEES
12/18	271.6	50.0	18.4%	0
12/17	182.2	11.6	6.4%	67
12/16	120.8	0.0	—	50
12/15	104.7	0.0	—	0
Annual Growth	37.4%	—	—	—

2018 Year-End Financials
Debt ratio: 32.9%
Return on equity: —
Cash ($ mil.): 6.6
Current ratio: 0.98
Long-term debt ($ mil.): 318.0
No. of shares (mil.): 33.7
Dividends
  Yield: 10.2%
  Payout: 89.6%
Market value ($ mil.): 540.0

	STOCK PRICE ($) FY Close	P/E High/Low		PER SHARE ($) Earnings	Dividends	Book Value
12/18	15.99	13	8	1.82	1.63	7.06
12/17	17.44	22	19	0.85	0.00	8.96
12/16	0.00	—	—	(0.00)	0.00	(0.00)
Annual Growth	—			—	—	—

OceanFirst Financial Corp

Ask the folks at OceanFirst Bank for a home loan and they might say "shore." The subsidiary of holding company OceanFirst Financial operates 25 branches in the coastal New Jersey counties of Middlesex Monmouth and Ocean. The community-oriented bank caters to individuals and small to midsized businesses in the Jersey Shore area offering standard products such as checking and savings accounts CDs and IRAs. It uses funds from deposits mainly to invest in mortgages loans and securities. One- to four-family residential mortgages make up more than half of OceanFirst Financial's loan portfolio which also includes commercial real estate (about 30%) business construction and consumer loans.

Operations
The Bank's principal business is attracting deposits from the general public in the communities surrounding its branch offices and investing those deposits primarily in single-family owner-occupied residential mortgage loans and commercial real estate loans. It active subsidiaries include OceanFirst Services LLC OceanFirst REIT Holdings Inc. and 975 Holdings LLC.

Geographic Reach
OceanFirst has operations in the New Jersey counties of Middlesex Monmouth and Ocean.

Financial Performance
OceanFirst's revenues dropped by 4% in 2012 due to decrease in loans and mortgage-backed securities partially offset by higher revenues from investment securities and other.

Net income declined by 3% in 2012 due to an increase in provision for loan losses and non-interest expenses (higher professional fees).

Strategy
OceanFirst seeks to grow commercial loans receivable by offering commercial lending services to local businesses; grow core deposits through broader product offerings andbranch expansion; and increase non-interest income by expanding its fee-based products and services.

Part of the company's strategy for growth includes expanding its fee-based offerings. The bank for example offers trust and asset management services. Company subsidiary OceanFirst Services sells mutual funds annuities and insurance products from third-party vendors. OceanFirst is also seeking opportunities to grow by opening new branch locations within its existing markets.

In 2013 the Bank opened a full service Financial Solutions Center in Red Bank New Jersey offering deposit lending and asset management services. It also opened an additional branch office in Jackson New Jersey.

Since 1995 OceanFirst has opened sixteen branch offices (twelve in Ocean County and four in Monmouth County).

Mergers and Acquisitions
In January 2016 OceanFirst Financial agreed to buy Cape Bancorp— along with its 22 branches in central and southern New Jersey counties $1.1 billion in loans and $1.3 billion in deposits — for $208.1 million. The deal would grow OceanFirst's total total assets by over 60% and nearly double the size of its branch network.

Company Background
OceanFirst Bank's employee stock option plan owns more than 10% of OceanFirst Financial's shares. The company's charitable foundation OceanFirst Foundation owns 7%.

The Bank was founded as a state-chartered building and loan association in 1902. It converted to a Federal savings and loan association in 1945 and became a Federally-chartered mutual savings bank in 1989.

EXECUTIVES
EVP and CFO, Michael J. Fitzpatrick, age 62, $285,577 total compensation
EVP and Chief Administrative Officer, Joseph R. Iantosca, age 57, $284,808 total compensation
EVP and Chief Lending Officer, Joseph J. Lebel, age 55, $284,808 total compensation
First SVP General Counsel and Corporate Secretary, Steven J. Tsimbinos, $252,798 total compensation
Chairman President and CEO, Christopher D. Maher, age 51, $566,346 total compensation
Avp Information Technology, Elizabeth Alexander
Vice President Bank Counsel, Denise Horner
Assistant Vice President OceanFirst Bank, Karen Rack
Vice President Loan Servicing Operations Manager, Christine Schiess
Senior Vice President and Director Human Resources, Anne Johnson
Senior Vice President, Brad Fouss
Assistant Vice President Project Manager, David Mowder
Vice President, Lauren Dezzi
Assistant Vice President Collections Department, Karen Farrell
Vice President Senior Marketing Officer Strategy, Lisa Natale
Senior Vice President, Nancy Mazza
Board Member, Jack Farris
Auditors: KPMG LLP

LOCATIONS
HQ: OceanFirst Financial Corp
  110 West Front Street, Red Bank, NJ 07701
Phone: 732 240-4500
Web: www.oceanfirst.com

PRODUCTS/OPERATIONS
2016 sales

	% of total
Interest Income	
Loans	80
Mortgage-backed securities	4
Investment securities & other	2
Non-interest	
Bankcard services revenue	3
Wealth management revenue	2
Fees & service charges	7
Loan Servicing income	-
Net gains on sales of loans	1
Net loss from other real estate operations	-
Income from Bank owned Life Insurance	1
Other	-
Total	**100**

COMPETITORS
Bank of America
Cape Bancorp
Citibank
Hudson City Bancorp
Investors Bancorp
JPMorgan Chase
PNC Financial
Sovereign Bank
TD Bank USA
Valley National Bancorp

HISTORICAL FINANCIALS
Company Type: Public

Income Statement — FYE: December 31

	ASSETS ($ mil.)	NET INCOME ($ mil.)	INCOME AS % OF ASSETS	EMPLOYEES
12/18	7,516.1	71.9	1.0%	892
12/17	5,416.0	42.4	0.8%	684
12/16	5,167.0	23.0	0.4%	797
12/15	2,593.0	20.3	0.8%	393
12/14	2,356.7	19.9	0.8%	376
Annual Growth	33.6%	37.9%	—	24.1%

2018 Year-End Financials
Return on assets: 1.1%
Return on equity: 8.7%
Long-term debt ($ mil.): —
No. of shares (mil.): 47.9
Sales ($ mil): 311.4
Dividends
  Yield: 2.7%
  Payout: 41.0%
Market value ($ mil.): 1,079.0

	STOCK PRICE ($) FY Close	P/E High/Low	PER SHARE ($) Earnings	Dividends	Book Value
12/18	22.51	20 14	1.51	0.62	21.68
12/17	26.25	23 18	1.28	0.60	18.47
12/16	30.03	30 16	0.98	0.54	17.80
12/15	20.03	17 13	1.21	0.52	13.79
12/14	17.14	16 13	1.19	0.49	12.91
Annual Growth	7.1%	— —	6.1%	6.1%	13.8%

Old National Bancorp (Evansville, IN)

Old National Bank is old but it's not quite national. Founded in 1834 the main subsidiary of Old National Bancorp operates about 200 bank centers across Indiana Kentucky Michigan and Illinois. The bank serves consumers and business customers offering standard checking and savings accounts credit cards and loans. Its treasury segment manages investments for bank and commercial clients. Business loans commercial and residential mortgages and consumer loans account for most of Old National's lending activity. The company also sells insurance manages wealth for high-net-worth clients and offers investment and retirement services through third-party provider LPL Financial.

Operations
Old National Bancorp operates two main segments: Banking which generates the bulk of Old National's revenue and provides traditional loan and deposit products as well as wealth management services; and Insurance which provides commercial property and casualty surety loss control services employee benefits consulting and administration as well as personal insurance.

The bank generated 51% of its revenue from loan interest (including fees) in 2014 while another 14% came from interest on investment securities. Insurance premiums and commissions contributed 7% to the company's total revenues that year while wealth management fees made up another 5%.

Geographic Reach
The bank's nearly 200 banking centers are located across four Midwestern states and Kentucky. Most are in the central northern and southern parts of Indiana; while others are in central Illinois; Western Kentucky and Louisville; Grand Rapids Southeastern and Southwestern Michigan; and Ohio.

Sales and Marketing
Old National has identified metropolitan areas within its market including Indianapolis; Louisville Kentucky; and Lafayette Indiana for growth within its core community banking segment.

The company spent $9.59 million on marketing in 2014 up from $7.21 million and $7.45 million in 2013 and 2012 respectively.

Financial Performance
Old National Bancorp's revenues and profits have been on the uptrend for the past several years thanks to new loan business from a series of bank acquisitions and declining loan loss provisions as its loan portfolio's credit quality has improved with the strengthened economy.

The company's revenue rose by 5% to $554.86 million in 2014 mostly thanks to new loan business stemming from the bank's acquisitions of Tower Financial United Bancorp and LSB Financial during the year along with organic loan growth. Higher revenue in 2014 coupled with strong cost controls lower interest on deposits and a continued decline in loan loss provisions drove Old National's net income higher by 3% to $103.62 million for the year.

Old National's operating cash fell by 21% to $199.72 million after adjusting its earnings for non-cash items related to its net sales proceeds from the sale of its residential real estate loans held-for-sale.

Strategy
Old National continues to seek out additional branch and whole bank acquisitions to grow its loan business and expand its geographic reach. Its acquisition of United Bancorp in mid-2014 for example added nearly $1 billion in new loan business and $869 million in wealth management assets under management while doubling Old National's presence in Michigan to 36 total branches.

The company is also pursuing growth by increasing its focus on commercial banking and cross-selling its insurance and wealth management offerings. To this end Old National in 2014 bought the insurance accounts (consisting of mostly commercial property/casualty accounts) serviced by the Evansville branch office of Wells Fargo Insurance.

Meanwhile it is also selectively exiting markets that haven't been profitable. In early 2015 as part of its ongoing efficiency improvement efforts the bank announced that it would sell 17 of its banking centers including all twelve of its branches in Southern Illinois and close or consolidate another 19 branches in other states over the following months.

Mergers and Acquisitions
In December 2014 Old National agreed to acquire Founders Financial Corporation along with its Founders Bank & Trust subsidiary in Grand Rapids Michigan for $91.7 million which would add nearly $460 million in total assets and four branches in Kent County.

In November 2014 the company purchased LSB Financial and its Lafayette Savings Bank subsidiary for $51.8 million adding five branches near Lafayette Indiana.

In July 2014 the company acquired Ann Arbor-based United Bancorp along with United Bank & Trust for a total of $122 million adding 18 branches in Michigan nearly $919 million in total assets a $963 million loan servicing portfolio and $688 million in trust assets under management.

In April 2014 Old National purchased Indiana-based Tower Financial along with its Tower Bank & Trust subsidiary adding seven new branches and some $556 million in trust assets under management.

In 2013 the bank bolstered its presence in Michigan after acquiring two dozen Bank of America branches in northern Indiana and southwest Michigan. The previous year the bank purchased Indiana Community Bancorp which added 17 branches in the southeastern part of the state. The transaction was valued at nearly $80 million.

EXECUTIVES

Chairman President and CEO, Robert G. (Bob) Jones, age 62, $668,269 total compensation
SVP and Corporate Secretary, Jeffrey L. (Jeff) Knight, age 59, $321,051 total compensation
EVP and Chief Credit Officer, Daryl D. Moore, age 61, $305,040 total compensation
CEO North Central Region, Mark D. Bradford, age 61
EVP and Chief Client Services Officer, Annette W. Hudgions, age 61, $250,016 total compensation
President and CEO Wealth Management, Caroline J. Ellspermann, age 51
CEO Eastern Region, Dennis P. Heishman
SEVP and CFO, Christopher A. (Chris) Wolking, age 59, $364,730 total compensation
EVP and Chief Community Relations and Social Responsibility Officer, Kathy A. Schoettlin
Region CEO Old National Bank, Randall (Randy) Reichmann
CEO Central and Western Michigan Region, Todd C. Clark, age 49
EVP and Chief Risk Officer, Candice J. Rickard, age 55
Regional CEO Southern, James Sandgren, $357,673 total compensation
CEO Central Region, Dan L. Doan
EVP and Director Corporate Strategy, James C. Ryan, age 47
EVP and CIO, John R. Kamin
EVP Associate Engagement and Integrations, Kendra L. Vanzo
EVP Chief Auditing Executive and Chief Ethics Officer, Richard W. (Dick) Dubé
President ONB Investment Services, Kenneth J. Ellspermann
President Old National Insurance, Scott J. Evernham
CEO Southern Region, Sara L. Miller
President and COO, Jim Sandgren
President North Central Region, Scott Shishman
Vice President Administration, Gloria Reinhart
Vice President Commercial Banking, Brian Henning
Vice President Associate Counsel, Tom Washburne
Assistant Vice President Mortgage Origination, Lynn Greulich
Vice President Commercial Lending, Kathy Cooper
Vice President Estate And Business Planning, Gary Mccall
Vice President And Client Advisor, Steve Hackman
Senior Vice President of Marketing, Scott Adams
Assistant Vice President, Sandy Keen
Assistant Vice President, Gidget Rowe
Vice President, Amanda Castaneda
Vice President Sarbanes Oxley Analyst, Denise Rexing
Vice President, Randy Lilly
Assistant Vice President, Jenny Clark
Assistant Vice President Mortgage Loan Officer, Debra Fulkerson
Vp Lpl Financial Advisor, Gary Shelton
Vice President Commercial Banking, Rob Snyder
Vice President Project Manager, Helen Cook
Assistant Vice President Retail Center Manager, Sabrina Mancuso
Private Banker II Vice President, Tony Patrick
Vice President Assistant Treasurer, Mike Loyd
Vice President Commercial Lender, Tim Helber
Assistant Vice President Branch Manager, Geoff Thompson
Senior Vice President Treasurer, Jennifer Guzman
Vice President, Jason Etter
Vice President Corporate Banking, James Tutt
Vice President Mortgage Lending, Steve Anderson
Vice President of Community Banking and Office V, Tammy Hall

Vice President and Trust Officer, Melanie Newkirk
Assistant Vice President Secondary Marketing, Chris Weiberg
Senior Vice President Commercial Banking, James Barnum
Senior Vice President, Lynell Walton
Human Resources Operations Manager Vice President, Ann Claspell
Svp Mortgage Sales Manager, Joel Van Elderen
Vp Client Advisor Corporate Trust Manager, Shannon Perry
Senior Vice President Assistant General Counsel, Gary Case
Vice President and Financial Center Manager, Cathy Stidham
Vice President Treasury Management, Dana Lackey
Vice President Server Systems, John Knight
Senior Vice President, Tommy Elliott
Vice President, Robert Ogburn
Vice President, Rob Triplett
PRIVATE BANKER L VICE PRESIDENT, Becky Robledo
Vice President Information Technology, Brad Callahan
Senior Vice President and Commercial Relationship Team Leader, Troy Briggs
Vice President Cash Management, Andrea Solis
Volunteer And Work Life Programs Manager Avp, Amy Mpsa
Vp and Commercial Real Estate, Regina Levchets
Senior Vice President, Marty Richardson
VICE PRESIDENT, Jeff Kleinschmidt
VICE PRESIDENT, Jame Tutt
CLIENT ADVISOR LL VICE PRESIDENT, Michael Wiederkehr
CLIENT ADVISOR II VICE PRESIDENT, Tamra Inman
VICE PRESIDENT DIRECTOR AND ASSISTANT CONTROLLER, Treadweay Todd
VICE PRESIDENT DATA ANALYTICS AND LOAN ACQUISITION MARKETING MANAGER, Karen Ellison
Executive Vice President and Chief Legal Counsel, Jefferey Knight
Vice President Compliance Audit Manager, Sonja Kriegsmann
Vice President Director Of Information Technology Risk Management, Luke Zeller
Vice President Commercial Relationship Manager, James Kilsdonk
Senior Vice President Security, Shari Krutulis
Vp Portfolio Manager III Commercial Real Estate, Dan Ryan
Senior Vice President Operational Risk Director, Sherry Schneider
Vice President Senior Special Assets Officer, Doug Mitcheson
Vice President Client Advisor, Rebecca Grasmeyer
Board Member, Alan Braun
Board Member, Randall Shepard
Board Member, Rebecca Skillman
Board Member, Jerome Henry
Board Member, Katherine White
Auditors: Crowe LLP

LOCATIONS

HQ: Old National Bancorp (Evansville, IN)
One Main Street, Evansville, IN 47708
Phone: 800 731-2265
Web: www.oldnational.com

PRODUCTS/OPERATIONS

2014 Sales

	$ mil.	% of total
Interest		
Loans including fees	306.3	51
Investment securities	83.4	14
Noninterest		
Service charges on deposit accounts	47.5	8
Insurance premiums & commissions	41.5	7
Wealth management fees	28.8	5
ATM Fees	25.8	4
Investment product fees	17.1	3
Mortgage banking revenue	6.0	1
Other	41.8	7
Adjustments	(43.3)	-
Total	**554.9**	**100**

COMPETITORS

Fifth Third
First Financial (IN)
German American Bancorp
Huntington Bancshares
JPMorgan Chase
PNC Financial
Peoples Bancorp (IN)
U.S. Bancorp

HISTORICAL FINANCIALS

Company Type: Public

Income Statement
FYE: December 31

	ASSETS ($ mil.)	NET INCOME ($ mil.)	INCOME AS % OF ASSETS	EMPLOYEES
12/18	19,728.4	190.8	1.0%	2,892
12/17	17,518.2	95.7	0.5%	2,801
12/16	14,860.2	134.2	0.9%	2,733
12/15	11,991.5	116.7	1.0%	2,652
12/14	11,647.5	103.6	0.9%	2,938
Annual Growth	14.1%	16.5%	—	(0.4%)

2018 Year-End Financials

Return on assets: 1.0%
Return on equity: 7.8%
Long-term debt ($ mil.): —
No. of shares (mil.): 175.1
Sales ($ mil): 827.3
Dividends
Yield: 3.3%
Payout: 65.8%
Market value ($ mil.): 2,697.0

	STOCK PRICE ($) FY Close	P/E High/Low		PER SHARE ($) Earnings	Dividends	Book Value
12/18	15.40	17	12	1.22	0.52	15.36
12/17	17.45	27	23	0.69	0.52	14.17
12/16	18.15	17	10	1.05	0.52	13.42
12/15	13.56	15	13	1.00	0.48	13.05
12/14	14.88	16	13	0.95	0.44	12.54
Annual Growth	0.9%	—		6.5%	4.3%	5.2%

Old Second Bancorp., Inc. (Aurora, Ill.)

Old Second won't settle for a silver finish when it comes to community banking around Chicago. Old Second Bancorp is the holding company for Old Second National Bank which serves the Chicago metropolitan area through 25 branches in Kane Kendall DeKalb DuPage LaSalle Will and Cook counties. The bank provides standard services such as checking and savings accounts credit and debit cards CDs mortgages loans and trust services to consumers and business clients. Subsidiary River Street Advisors offers investment management and advisory services. Another unit Old Second Affordable Housing Fund provides home-buying assistance to lower-income customers.

Operations

Commercial real estate loans accounted for 53% of Old Second's loan portfolio at the end of 2015 while residential mortgages made up another 31%. The rest was made up of general commercial loans (12% of loan assets) and construction lending (2%).

Roughly 70% of the bank's revenue comes from interest income. About 54% of its revenue came from loan interest (including fees) during 2015 with another 15% coming from interest on investment securities. The remainder of Old Second's revenue came from deposit account service charges (7%) trust income (6%) mortgage loan sale gains (6%) secondary mortgage fees (1%) and other sources.

Geographic Reach

The bank mostly serves customers in Aurora Illinois (which is 40 miles west of Chicago) and surrounding communities. Its 24 branches are located in the Kane Kendall DeKalb DuPage LaSalle Will and Cook counties of Illinois.

Sales and Marketing

Old Second has been ramping up its advertising spend in recent years. It spent $1.34 million on advertising in 2015 up from $1.28 million and $1.23 million in 2014 and 2013 respectively.

Financial Performance

Old Second's annual revenues have fallen 20% since 2011 as it's had to sell of many of its non-performing loan assets to de-risk its loan portfolio. The company's profits however have been on the mend as its de-risking measures have led to declining loan loss provisions.

The bank's revenue rebounded by less than 1% to $97.46 million during 2015 as its average loans including loans held for sale grew by 2% for the year.

Revenue growth in 2015 combined with lower interest and amortization costs on deposits drove Old Second Bancorp's net income up by over 50% to $15.39 million. The bank's operating cash levels jumped sharply to $21.14 million (operations had used $6.3 million in 2014) partially thanks to earnings growth but mostly thanks to positive working capital changes related to sales proceeds from loans held for sale and changes in accrued interest payable and other liabilities.

Strategy

Old Second Bancorp continued in 2016 to focus on shedding riskier loan assets that led it to deep losses in 2011 while focusing on securing high-quality loans with more creditworthiness. Its efforts began to pay off in 2015 as its average loan balances and revenues began to grow again after years of being in decline.

EXECUTIVES

ASSISTANT VICE PRESIDENT OPERATIONS, Brian Bermes
EVP CFO and Director, J. Douglas Cheatham, age 63, $252,000 total compensation
CEO and Director Old Second Bancorp Inc. and Old Second National Bank, James L. Eccher, age 54, $325,000 total compensation
Vice President, Jeff Downs

Assistant Vice President, Janet Mutz
Vice President, Robin Hill
Senior Vice President Personal Trust, Andy Roche
Senior Vice President and Treasurer, Stan Faries
Executive Vice President Human Resources, Robert Dicosola
Senior Vice President, Chris Barry
AVP RESIDENTIAL LENDER, Terri Hanson
Vice President, Peggy Nelson
Executive Vice President, Don Pilmer
Vice President Treasury Management, John Annis
Vice President, Jocelyn Retz
Vice President, Scott Trandel
Vice President Residential Lending, Michelle Domson
Vice President, Troy Langeness
Vice President, Jeri Ott
Assistant Vice President, Ana Torres
Vice President commercial Banking, Kristin Zell
Vice President Commercial Banker, Vanessa Aguirre
Senior Vice President Commercial Lending, Mark Fleming
Vice President Residential Lending, Michelle Almond
Assistant Vice President Branch Manager, Nancy Baker
First Vice President, Chris Hainey
Assistant Vice President Retail Manager, Julie Fuller
First Vice President Commercial Banking Director Of Treasury Management, Juwana Zanayed
Senior Vice President, Peter Harrison
Vice President Operations, Carlos Arroyo
Vp, Denise Rogers
Assistant Vice President, Joseph Gordon
First Vice President, Jacqueline Volkert
Vice President Loan Administration, Jason Evans
Chairman Old Second Bancorp Inc. and Old Second National Bank, William B. Skoglund, age 69
Vice Chairman, Gary S. Collins, age 61
Board Member, John Ladowicz
Auditors: Plante & Moran PLLC

LOCATIONS

HQ: Old Second Bancorp., Inc. (Aurora, Ill.)
37 South River Street, Aurora, IL 60507
Phone: 630 892-0202
Web: www.oldsecond.com

PRODUCTS/OPERATIONS

2015 sales

	% of total
Interest and dividend income	
Loans including fees	54
Taxable	14
Tax exempt	1
Non-interest income	
Service charges on deposits	7
Trust income	6
Net gain on sales of mortgage loans	6
Debit card interchange income	4
Secondary mortgage fees	1
Increase in cash surrender value of bank-owned life insurance	1
Other income	6
Total	**100**

Products/Services
Personal Banking
Card Services
Checking
Loans
Money Services
Online and Mobile Banking
Prime Time Club
Retirement Services
Savings
Loans
Auto and Personal Loans
Home Equity Loans
Home Loans
Mortgage Lenders
Required Documents
SAFE Act
Business Banking
Commercial Banking
Online and Mobile Banking
Small Business Banking
Wealth Management
Business Plan Options
Real Estate Services
Retirement Services

COMPETITORS

Bank of America
BankFinancial
Fifth Third
First Midwest Bancorp
Harris
MB Financial
Northern Trust
West Suburban Bancorp

HISTORICAL FINANCIALS
Company Type: Public

Income Statement — FYE: December 31

	ASSETS ($ mil.)	NET INCOME ($ mil.)	INCOME AS % OF ASSETS	EMPLOYEES
12/18	2,676.0	34.0	1.3%	518
12/17	2,383.4	15.1	0.6%	450
12/16	2,251.1	15.6	0.7%	467
12/15	2,077.8	15.3	0.7%	450
12/14	2,061.7	10.1	0.5%	485
Annual Growth	6.7%	35.3%	—	1.7%

2018 Year-End Financials
Return on assets: 1.3%
Return on equity: 15.8%
Long-term debt ($ mil.): —
No. of shares (mil.): 29.7
Sales ($ mil): 138.9
Dividends
Yield: 0.3%
Payout: 5.3%
Market value ($ mil.): 387.0

	STOCK PRICE ($) FY Close	P/E High/Low	PER SHARE ($) Earnings	Dividends	Book Value
12/18	13.00	14 11	1.12	0.04	7.70
12/17	13.65	28 20	0.50	0.04	6.76
12/16	11.05	22 12	0.53	0.03	5.93
12/15	7.84	18 11	0.46	0.00	5.29
12/14	5.37	12 10	0.46	0.00	6.59
Annual Growth	24.7%	— —	24.9%	—	3.9%

Ollie's Bargain Outlet Holdings Inc

Auditors: KPMG LLP

LOCATIONS

HQ: Ollie's Bargain Outlet Holdings Inc
6295 Allentown Boulevard, Suite 1, Harrisburg, PA 17112
Phone: 717 657-2300
Web: www.ollies.us

HISTORICAL FINANCIALS
Company Type: Public

Income Statement — FYE: February 2

	REVENUE ($ mil.)	NET INCOME ($ mil.)	NET PROFIT MARGIN	EMPLOYEES
02/19	1,241.3	135.0	10.9%	7,700
02/18*	1,077.0	127.5	11.8%	6,700
01/17	890.3	59.7	6.7%	5,500
01/16	762.3	35.8	4.7%	5,000
01/15	637.9	26.9	4.2%	5,000
Annual Growth	18.1%	49.7%	—	11.4%

*Fiscal year change

2019 Year-End Financials
Debt ratio: 0.0%
Return on equity: 15.5%
Cash ($ mil.): 51.9
Current ratio: 2.37
Long-term debt ($ mil.): 0.4
No. of shares (mil.): 63.0
Dividends
Yield: —
Payout: —
Market value ($ mil.): 5,000.0

	STOCK PRICE ($) FY Close	P/E High/Low	PER SHARE ($) Earnings	Dividends	Book Value
02/19	79.35	45 24	2.05	0.00	14.96
02/18*	53.75	28 14	1.96	0.00	12.85
01/17	29.35	33 19	0.96	0.00	10.72
01/16	22.35	33 23	0.64	1.01	9.56
Annual Growth	52.6%	— —	47.4%	—	16.1%

*Fiscal year change

Omega Healthcare Investors, Inc.

Omega Healthcare Investors can put an end to the burdens of real-estate management. The self-administered real estate investment trust (REIT) invests in health care facilities throughout the US. It owns some 900 properties primarily long-term care facilities in more than 40 states. The REIT specializes in sales/leaseback transactions in which it purchases properties owned by health care providers and leases them back to those companies (thereby freeing the health care companies from the responsibilities of real estate management). The REIT's properties are operated by third-party health care operating companies including Genesis HealthCare System and CommuniCare Health Services.

Geographic Reach

The Maryland-based REITs largest markets are Florida Indiana and Ohio. Texas is another important market for the firm. Overall Omega Healthcare Investors has holdings in 41 states.

Sales and Marketing

The REIT's largest tenants include New Ark Investment Genesis Healthcare and CommuniCare Health Services which together represent about a third of its portfolio.

Financial Performance

Omega Healthcare Investors (OHI) reported revenue of $418.7 million in 2013 a 19% increase versus 2012. Driving the double-digit gain was rising rental income generated by investments made in 2013 and 2012. Net income grew 43% to

$172.5 million on higher rental income. Both revenue and cash flow has increased steadily over the past four years and profitability has rebounded.

Strategy

The REIT is investing aggressively in the health care sector as demand for senior living facilities grows in tandem with the aging population and the real estate market makes a comeback. Indeed in 2013 the firm completed transactions totaling about $622 million in new investments. Its core portfolio consists of long-term lease and mortgage agreements. All of its leases are "triple-net" leases which require the tenants to pay all property related expenses. The REIT's mortgage revenue comes from fixed-rate loans. Omega Healthcare's geographically diverse portfolio comprises 476 skilled nursing facilities 18 assisted living locations and 11 specialty facilities such as rehabilitation hospitals. Its properties are operated by third parties.

Mergers and Acquisitions

In mid-2015 Omega acquired Aviv REIT in a deal valued at some $3 billion. The combined company is one of the largest REITs focused on skilled nursing facilities.

EXECUTIVES

CEO and Director, C. Taylor Pickett, age 57, $750,000 total compensation
COO, Daniel J. Booth, age 55, $485,000 total compensation
CFO, Robert O. Stephenson, age 55, $465,000 total compensation
Chief Accounting Officer, Michael D. Ritz, age 50, $320,000 total compensation
Vice President Of Operations, Megan Krull
Svp Of Development, Vikas Gupta
Svp, Matthew Gourmand
Chairman, Craig R. Callen, age 63
Board Member, Edward Lowenthal
Auditors: Ernst & Young LLP

LOCATIONS

HQ: Omega Healthcare Investors, Inc.
303 International Circle, Suite 200, Hunt Valley, MD 21030
Phone: 410 427-1700   **Fax:** 410 427-8800
Web: www.omegahealthcare.com

PRODUCTS/OPERATIONS

2015 Sales

	$ mil.	% of total
Rental income	606.0	81
Mortgage interest	68.9	9
Income from direct financing leases	59.9	8
Others	8.8	2
Total	**743.6**	**100**

COMPETITORS

G&L Realty Properties
HCP
Healthcare Realty Trust
LTC Properties
National Health Investors
Senior Housing Properties
Ventas
Welltower

HISTORICAL FINANCIALS

Company Type: Public

Income Statement — FYE: December 31

	REVENUE ($ mil.)	NET INCOME ($ mil.)	NET PROFIT MARGIN	EMPLOYEES
12/18	881.6	281.5	31.9%	51
12/17	908.3	100.4	11.1%	59
12/16	900.8	366.4	40.7%	60
12/15	743.6	224.5	30.2%	58
12/14	504.7	221.3	43.9%	27
Annual Growth	15.0%	6.2%	—	17.2%

2018 Year-End Financials

Debt ratio: 52.8%
Return on equity: 8.0%
Cash ($ mil.): 10.3
Current ratio: 26.40
Long-term debt ($ mil.): 4,540.6
No. of shares (mil.): 202.3
Dividends
  Yield: 7.5%
  Payout: 188.5%
Market value ($ mil.): 7,112.0

	STOCK PRICE ($) FY Close	P/E High/Low		PER SHARE ($) Earnings	Dividends	Book Value
12/18	35.15	27	18	1.40	2.64	17.02
12/17	27.54	69	53	0.51	2.54	17.93
12/16	31.26	20	14	1.90	2.36	19.67
12/15	34.98	35	25	1.29	2.18	19.95
12/14	39.07	23	17	1.74	2.02	10.98
Annual Growth	(2.6%)	—	—	(5.3%)	6.9%	11.6%

Omnicell Inc

Omnicell wants to be indispensable when it comes to dispensing drugs. The company makes systems that automate delivery of drugs to patients in hospitals homes long-term care centers and other medical healthcare settings. Pharmacies and medical facilities use its mobile cabinets and workstations to automatically dispense doses of medication and surgical supplies to help reduce errors and increase patient safety. More than 4000 hospitals use automation and analytics products such as the Omnicell XT Automated Dispensing Cabinet and Singlepointe software. Omnicell's medications adherence products that include specific-count blister packs help patients take the drugs they're supposed to when they're supposed to.

Operations

Omnicell's Automation and Analytics segment more than 80% of revenue is organized around the design manufacturing sales and servicing of medication and supply dispensing systems pharmacy inventory management systems and related software. The company's products provide predictive analytics from its systems' employment of artificial intelligence and cloud computing. Omnicell deploys robotics systems as well.

Its Medication Adherence segment about 20% of sales includes the manufacturing and selling of consumable medication blister cards packaging equipment and ancillary products and services. These products manage medication administration outside the hospital and include products under the MTS SureMed and Omnicell brands.

Omnicell also makes money from servicing and supporting its products.

The company has parlayed the technology behind its medication-dispensing cabinets into other hospital products that keep track of inventory and supplies. It makes a secure dispensing system for anesthesia supplies used in the operating room as well as a barcode inventory management system for controlled substances.

Geographic Reach

Omnicell based in Mountain View California generates more than 85% of sales in the US with other sales to customers throughout the world. The company has research and development facilities in Mountain View Cranberry Woods Pennsylvania St. Petersburg Florida Raleigh North Carolina and Warrendale Pennsylvania in the US and overseas in Beijing Bochum Germany Lancing UK and Trieste Italy.

Sales and Marketing

Omnicell's sales force is organized by geographic region in the US and Canada. The company deploys a direct sales force for Non-Acute Care products in Australia. For other geographies the company's products are sold through distributors and resellers.

Its Automation and Analytics segment has more than 4000 customers while the Medication Adherence segment's products are used by more than 32000 institutional and retail pharmacies worldwide. Customers include Brigham and Women's Hospital the Cleveland Clinic King Faisal Specialist Hospital & Research Center and Carilion Clinic.

Financial Performance

Omnicell delivered 18% annual revenue growth over the past five years. In 2017 however growth slowed to 3% at $716 million from 2016. Automation and Analytics segment sales fell about $20 million due to the introduction of the new XT series of products in the fourth quarter of 2016. The Medication Adherence segment's sales increased in 2017 from 2016 with the help of the Ateb acquisition (in 2016) and the introduction of the VBM product series in late 2016. The installed customer base pushed service revenue 20% higher in 2017 from 2016.

The company's profit improved to more than $20 million in 2017 from less than $1 million in 2016 due to a $21.5 million tax benefit from the US Tax Cuts and Jobs Act. Before taxes in 2017 the company had a $900000 loss compared to a $1.9 million pre-tax loss in 2016.

Cash on hand stood at about $32 million for 2017 down about $22 million from 2016.

Strategy

Omnicell's growth strategy centers on developing new products and enhancing existing products. The company in 2018 released the XR2 Automated Central Pharmacy System and the IVX Workflow products which have greater automation for compounding and prepared intravenous (IV) treatments.

The company is also building its customer roster with gains among institutions new to automation while current customers have increased the pace at which they add other Omnicell products to their existing portfolios.

Omnicell has been adding to its product lineup through in-house research and development (R&D) averages $55 million over three years) and acquisitions. The 2016 acquisition of Aesynt bolstered Omnicell's robotic and automation offerings.

Mergers and Acquisitions

In 2017 Omnicell acquired InPharmics a developer of medication-use process cost analytics and regulatory compliance systems for acute care hospital pharmacies. The InPharmics technology adds clinical and compliance analytics to Omnicell's Performance Center offering.

In 2016 Omnicell bought Aesynt a provider of central pharmacy robotics and IV compounding automation systems. The Aesynt products and services extended Omnicell's lineup.

Also in 2016 Omnicell acquired Ateb a provider of pharmacy-based patient care products and medication synchronization to independent and chain retail pharmacies a market in which Omnicell had no penetration. The company paired Ateb's Time My Meds product with Omnicell's SureMed medication adherence packaging.

EXECUTIVES

EVP International and Global Quality and Manufacturing, Robin G. (Rob) Seim, age 59, $302,769 total compensation
EVP; Chief Legal and Administrative Officer, Dan S. Johnston, age 55, $270,154 total compensation
Chairman President and CEO, Randall A. Lipps, age 61, $551,538 total compensation
EVP Sales and Marketing, J. Christopher (Chris) Drew, age 53, $322,462 total compensation
EVP Strategy and Business Development, Nhat H. Ngo, age 46, $273,539 total compensation
EVP and CFO, Peter Kuipers, age 47
EVP of Engineering, Jorge R. Taborga, age 59
EVP and Chief Legal and Administrative Officer, Daniel Johnston
Vice President Human Resources, Susan Moriconi
Vice President of Engineering, Chalapathi Rao
Vice President Field Operations, Pat Diresta
Vice President Of Engineering, Nathaniel Moody
Vice President Hardware Engineering, Edith Wilson
Vice President Quality and Regulatory, David Vanella
Executive Vice President Chief Commercial Officer, Scott Seidelmann
VICE PRESIDENT MANUFACTURING, Corinne Augustine
VICE PRESIDENT FINANCE AND ACCOUNTING, Lisa Lamb
Vice President Finance, Mohit Bhatia
Board Member, James Judson
Auditors: Deloitte & Touche LLP

LOCATIONS

HQ: Omnicell Inc
590 East Middlefield Road, Mountain View, CA 94043
Phone: 650 251-6100
Web: www.omnicell.com

PRODUCTS/OPERATIONS

2017 Sales

	$ mil.	% of total
United States	617.3	86
Foreign Countries	98.9	14
Total	**716.2**	**100**

2017 Sales

	$ mil.	% of total
Product revenue	506.2	71
Service and other revenue	210.0	29
Total	**716.2**	**100**

2017 Sales

	$ mil.	% of total
Automation and Analytics	590.4	82
Medication Adherence	125.8	18
Total	**716.2**	**100**

COMPETITORS

Allscripts	Ergotron
AmerisourceBergen	Infor Global
Becton Dickinson	McKesson
CareFusion	SciQuest
Cerner	Siemens Healthcare
Emerson Electric	Swisslog

HISTORICAL FINANCIALS
Company Type: Public

Income Statement   FYE: December 31

	REVENUE ($ mil.)	NET INCOME ($ mil.)	NET PROFIT MARGIN	EMPLOYEES
12/18	787.3	37.7	4.8%	2,480
12/17	716.1	20.6	2.9%	2,350
12/16	692.6	0.6	0.1%	2,444
12/15	484.5	30.7	6.3%	1,451
12/14	440.9	30.5	6.9%	1,236
Annual Growth	15.6%	5.4%		19.0%

2018 Year-End Financials

Debt ratio: 12.5%
Return on equity: 6.3%
Cash ($ mil.): 67.1
Current ratio: 1.94
Long-term debt ($ mil.): 135.4
No. of shares (mil.): 40.3
Dividends
  Yield: —
  Payout: —
Market value ($ mil.): 2,470.0

	STOCK PRICE ($) FY Close	P/E High/Low	PER SHARE ($) Earnings	Dividends	Book Value
12/18	61.24	80 42	0.93	0.00	16.85
12/17	48.50	99 58	0.53	0.00	13.46
12/16	33.90	2020 1272	0.02	0.00	11.78
12/15	31.08	47 31	0.84	0.00	11.30
12/14	33.12	39 29	0.83	0.00	10.89
Annual Growth	16.6%	— —	2.9%	—	11.5%

On Deck Capital Inc

Auditors: Ernst & Young LLP

LOCATIONS

HQ: On Deck Capital Inc
1400 Broadway, 25th Floor, New York, NY 10018
Phone: 888 269-4246
Web: www.ondeck.com

HISTORICAL FINANCIALS
Company Type: Public

Income Statement   FYE: December 31

	ASSETS ($ mil.)	NET INCOME ($ mil.)	INCOME AS % OF ASSETS	EMPLOYEES
12/18	1,161.5	27.6	2.4%	587
12/17	996.0	(11.5)	—	475
12/16	1,064.0	(82.9)	—	708
12/15	749.2	(1.2)	—	638
12/14	729.6	(18.7)	—	444
Annual Growth	12.3%	—		7.2%

2018 Year-End Financials

Return on assets: 2.5%
Return on equity: 9.8%
Long-term debt ($ mil.): —
No. of shares (mil.): 75.3
Sales ($ mil): 398.3
Dividends
  Yield: —
  Payout: —
Market value ($ mil.): 445.0

	STOCK PRICE ($) FY Close	P/E High/Low	PER SHARE ($) Earnings	Dividends	Book Value
12/18	5.90	24 11	0.35	0.00	3.98
12/17	5.74	— —	(0.16)	0.00	3.55
12/16	4.63	— —	(1.17)	0.00	3.62
12/15	10.30	— —	(0.02)	0.00	4.61
12/14	22.43	— —	(0.60)	0.00	4.50
Annual Growth	(28.4%)	— —	—	—	(3.0%)

Onto Innovation Inc

Nanometrics works on a nano scale for electronics manufacturers that need their goods to measure up. The company provides thin-film metrology and inspection systems used by makers of precision electronic gear. These stand-alone integrated and tabletop measurement devices gauge the thickness and consistency of film materials used in making semiconductors LEDs data storage components and power management components. Its systems are used throughout the fabrication process from substrate manufacturing to advanced wafer-scale packaging. Top customers include Samsung Electronics Intel and SK Hynix. Nanometrics generates most of its sales in Asia. Nanometrics and Rudolph Technologies agreed to merge in 2019.

Change in Company Type

Nanometrics and Rudolph Technologies agreed to merge in 2019 to offer a more comprehensive package of services. The merged company would combine complementary offerings to provide end-to-end metrology inspection process control software and lithography equipment. Rudolph stockholders will receive 0.8042 shares of Nanometrics common stock for each Rudolph share. Upon completion current Nanometrics stockholders will own about 50% and current Rudolph stockholders will own about 50% of the combined company. The deal was expected to close in 2019.

Operations

Nanometrics gets about 60% of its revenue from its automated systems such as the Atlas series with integrated systems including the IMPULSE line accounting for about 15% and its materials characterization systems such as the RPMBlue less than 10%. The remaining revenue comes from the company's service operations. The company also offers software applications that include NanoDiffract and SpectraProbe.

The company makes most of its automated and integrated products at its factory and it send some work to third-party contractors.

Geographic Reach

Nanometrics is based in Milpitas California and it has field and support operations in China France Germany Israel Italy Japan South Korea Singapore and Taiwan.

The company's sales are concentrated in Asia with some 35% going to South Korea about 15% to Japan and more than 10% to China. The US accounts for nearly 15% of the company's revenue.

Nanometrics has a manufacturing operation in California and it uses uses contract manufacturers in China Israel Japan and the US for subassembly tasks.

Sales and Marketing
Customers include semiconductor manufacturers and equipment suppliers producers of high brightness-LEDs solar PVs data storage devices silicon wafers and photomasks. Its top three customers — Samsung Electronics Intel and Micron - together account for about 50% of sales.

Nanometrics sells its products through a direct sales force.

Financial Performance
Nanometrics has ridden a robust semiconductor industry to annual average increases of about 14% since 2013. The company beat the average with a 17% increase to more than $258 million in 2017 from 2016 as customers bought instruments for making 3D-NAND and DRAM chips. The Atlas III Nanometrics' newest version of its flagship line accounted for nearly two-thirds of the revenue increase.

Nanometrics reported a lower profit of $30 million in 2017 compared to $44 million in 2016 due to money set aside to comply with the US Tax Cuts and Jobs Act. Before taxes operating income in 2017 was about $43 million compared to $29 million the year before.

The company had $117 million in cash at the end of 2017 compared to $130 million in 2016. Cash from operations fell $25 million in 2017 from 2016 because of higher inventory levels and a higher accounts receivable balance due to record fourth quarter revenue in 2017.

Strategy
Nanometrics has released new versions of key products such as its Atlas metrology systems as the semiconductor industry looks for ways to make smaller and smaller chips. The Atlas III released in 2017 offers improved precision and higher throughput compared to the previous model. Sales of the system boosted Nanometrics' revenue in 2017 and the company expects the Atlas drive revenue in 2018.

The company has added software and analytics capabilities to its portfolio to generate more revenue and provide more services to customers. Its service revenue has increased as its base of installed products has grown.

With a higher percentage of its sales to customers in Asia Nanometrics is susceptible from disruptions if trade issues become a concern and tariffs are implemented.

Mergers and Acquisitions
In 2018 Nanometrics agreed to buy 4D Technology Corp. for about $40 million. The addition of 4D's interferometric measurement and inspection systems should bolster the offerings from Nanometrics while enabling the company to enter new markets. 4D is to become a business unit within Nanometrics when the deal closes probably by the end of 2018.

EXECUTIVES
CFO, Jeffrey (Jeff) Andreson, age 57
President CEO and Director, Timothy J. Stultz, age 71, $465,000 total compensation
SVP Strategic Marketing and Business Development, Kevin Heidrich, age 48
EVP Business Operations, S. Mark Borowicz, age 46
Senior Vice President Commercial Operations, Rollin Kocher
Senior Vice President, Mark Borowicz
Vice President Applications Engineering, Nagesh Avadhany
Vice President Safety, Michael Weber
Vice President Global Human Resources, Dawn Laplante
Vice President Information Technology, Marcy McKee
Vice President Engineering, Rodney Smedt
Vice President Global Operations, Michael Shaughnessy
Vice President Information Technology, Venkat Gopalakrishnan
Vice President Global Human Resources, Philip Ziman
Vice President Service, Randy Tully
Vice President Supply Chain Management, Shane Smith
Svp Of Operations, James Barnhart
Vp Of Engineering, Avi Ray-chaudhuri
Vp Gm Automated Metrology Business Unit, Sudhakar Raman
Chairman, Bruce C. Rhine, age 61
Auditors: Ernst & Young LLP

LOCATIONS
HQ: Onto Innovation Inc
16 Jonspin Road, Wilmington, MA 01887
Phone: 978 253-6200
Web: www.nanometrics.com

PRODUCTS/OPERATIONS
2017 Sales

	$ mil.	% of total
Products		
Automated systems	151.4	59
Integrated System	42.2	16
Material characterization systems	21.3	17
Service	43.7	17
Total	**258.6**	**100**

COMPETITORS

ASM International	Qcept Technologies
Applied Materials	Rudolph Technologies
Bio-Rad Labs	SCREEN Holdings
KLA-Tencor	Tokyo Electron
Nova Measuring	Zygo

HISTORICAL FINANCIALS
Company Type: Public

Income Statement				FYE: December 29
	REVENUE ($ mil.)	NET INCOME ($ mil.)	NET PROFIT MARGIN	EMPLOYEES
12/18	324.5	57.6	17.8%	701
12/17	258.6	30.2	11.7%	592
12/16	221.1	44.0	19.9%	532
12/15	187.3	2.9	1.6%	518
12/14	166.4	(31.1)	—	525
Annual Growth	18.2%	—	—	7.5%

2018 Year-End Financials
Debt ratio: —
Return on equity: 20.1%
Cash ($ mil.): 151.7
Current ratio: 4.53
Long-term debt ($ mil.): —
No. of shares (mil.): 24.3
Dividends
　Yield: —
　Payout: —
Market value ($ mil.): 674.0

	STOCK PRICE ($) FY Close	P/E High/Low		PER SHARE ($) Earnings	Dividends	Book Value
12/18	27.65	19	10	2.34	0.00	12.84
12/17	24.92	27	20	1.17	0.00	10.65
12/16	25.06	14	7	1.75	0.00	9.72
12/15	15.79	155	101	0.12	0.00	7.73
12/14	16.59	—	—	(1.30)	0.00	7.54
Annual Growth	13.6%	—	—	—	—	14.2%

OP Bancorp

Auditors: Crowe LLP

LOCATIONS
HQ: OP Bancorp
1000 Wilshire Blvd., Suite 500, Los Angeles, CA 90017
Phone: 213 892-9999
Web: www.myopenbank.com

HISTORICAL FINANCIALS
Company Type: Public

Income Statement				FYE: December 31
	ASSETS ($ mil.)	NET INCOME ($ mil.)	INCOME AS % OF ASSETS	EMPLOYEES
12/18	1,044.1	14.2	1.4%	154
12/17	901.0	9.2	1.0%	129
12/16	761.2	7.4	1.0%	0
12/15	617.3	5.9	1.0%	0
12/14	528.1	4.4	0.8%	0
Annual Growth	18.6%	33.5%	—	—

2018 Year-End Financials
Return on assets: 1.4%
Return on equity: 12.8%
Long-term debt ($ mil.): —
No. of shares (mil.): 15.8
Sales ($ mil): 59.4
Dividends
　Yield: —
　Payout: —
Market value ($ mil.): 141.0

	STOCK PRICE ($) FY Close	P/E High/Low		PER SHARE ($) Earnings	Dividends	Book Value
12/18	8.87	15	9	0.89	0.00	8.18
12/17	9.80	15	10	0.66	0.00	6.94
12/16	7.70	14	10	0.53	0.00	6.30
12/15	6.55	15	12	0.46	0.00	5.71
12/14	7.10	—	—	(0.00)	0.00	5.27
Annual Growth	5.7%	—	—	—	—	11.6%

Opus Bank (Irvine, CA)

Auditors: RSM US LLP

LOCATIONS
HQ: Opus Bank (Irvine, CA)
19900 MacArthur Blvd., 12th Floor, Irvine, CA 92612
Phone: 949 250-9800
Web: www.opusbank.com

HISTORICAL FINANCIALS
Company Type: Public

Income Statement FYE: December 31

	ASSETS ($ mil.)	NET INCOME ($ mil.)	INCOME AS % OF ASSETS	EMPLOYEES
12/18	7,180.9	30.9	0.4%	845
12/17	7,486.8	47.6	0.6%	797
12/16	7,882.5	11.4	0.1%	835
12/15	6,649.8	59.9	0.9%	661
12/14	5,084.9	43.8	0.9%	585
Annual Growth	9.0%	(8.4%)	—	9.6%

2018 Year-End Financials
Return on assets: 0.4%
Return on equity: 3.0%
Long-term debt ($ mil.): —
No. of shares (mil.): 36.0
Sales ($ mil): 287.8
Dividends
Yield: 2.2%
Payout: 42.1%
Market value ($ mil.): 706.0

	STOCK PRICE ($) FY Close	P/E High/Low	PER SHARE ($) Earnings	Dividends	Book Value
12/18	19.59	37 22	0.81	0.43	28.86
12/17	27.30	23 14	1.26	0.00	28.50
12/16	30.05	112 58	0.33	0.53	27.01
12/15	36.97	21 13	1.79	0.34	26.68
12/14	28.37	22 18	1.38	0.00	28.41
Annual Growth	(8.8%)	—	(12.5%)	—	0.4%

OraSure Technologies Inc.

When it comes to diagnostic tests OraSure is certain it can deliver results. The oral specimen kits and other diagnostic tests developed by OraSure Technologies are designed to detect drug use and certain infectious diseases namely HIV and hepatitis C. Its OraSure products use oral specimens rather than traditional blood or urine based methods to test for HIV. The Intercept line uses oral samples to test for marijuana cocaine opiates PCP and amphetamines. OraSure has also developed a rapid HIV blood diagnostic testing method and it has entered the genetic testing market through its DNAG subsidiary. OraSure sells its products in the US and internationally to health care facilities and medical laboratories.

Operations
Products include tests that detect antibodies to the HIV and HCV viruses and tests for drug abuse detection. OraSure operates in two primary segments: Its OSUR business (70% of revenue) develops manufactures and sells diagnostic products specimen collection devices and genetic testing devices. Meanwhile OraSure Technologies makes and sells enzyme immunoassay test kits and oral fluid collection devices for insurance laboratories; these products are used to assess the health and behavior of insurance applicants.

In addition to diagnostic tests and specimen kits OraSure's Histofreezer cryosurgical removal system treats a range of different types of skin lesions including plantar and genital warts and other common benign skin lesions. OraSure also sells an OTC wart remover under the Freeze n' Clear brand.

Geographic Reach
Only about 25% of OraSure's sales come from abroad but the company is expanding its international sales efforts. Subsidiary DNAG leases a 23500 sq. ft. facility in Ottawa Canada.

OraSure's products are available across North America South America Europe and Australia.

Sales and Marketing
OraSure uses direct agents collaborative partners and independent distributors to market its products in the US and abroad. Marketing techniques include trade shows distributor promotions and print advertisements. Customers include public health clinics hospitals pathology laboratory operators and doctors' offices.

In fiscal 2014 the company spent $6910 on advertising down from $17142 spent in 2013.

Financial Performance
The company's revenues have been steadily climbing for the past five years. Revenue increased 8% to $106 million in 2014 on higher sales especially of its Oragene molecular collection systems HCV detection products and cyrosurgical systems products. Additionally licensing and product development earnings rose due to OraSure's co-promotion agreement with AbbVie for the HCV line.

To date OraSure hasn't been profitable. Net losses declined 59% to $5 million in 2014 though due to the firm's higher revenue and lower marketing expenses. Cash flow from operations which had spiked in 2013 due to settlement payment from Roche declined marginally in 2014 to $7 million. That decline was primarily due to an increase in inventory of its OraQuick HCV product as well as higher expenses.

Strategy
In addition to geographic expansion OraSure is also increasing its product offerings by developing diagnostic tests for other infectious diseases. In 2014 R&D activities were focused primarily on developing its next-generation Intercept i2 collection device testing a new rapid Ebola test using the OraQuick platform and support for its existing products.

OraSure's growth strategy also consists of pursuing additional FDA approvals and European registrations for its best-selling product lines OraQuick and Intercept. In partnership with Thermo Fisher it develops and supplies oral fluid drugs of abuse assays to be used with its Intercept i2 collection device. The company entered an agreement with AbbVie in 2014 to co-promote OraQuick in the US and abroad. Additionally OraSure Technologies and AbbVie joined together with the Healthy Trucking Association of America to educate truckers about the hepatitis C virus.

Additionally the company is starting to offer some existing products over-the-counter. It already sells some of its cryosurgical wart removal kits on an OTC basis in Central America and Europe.

Mergers and Acquisitions
To enter the molecular diagnostics market while keeping its emphasis on oral fluids OraSure acquired private Canadian firm DNA Genotek (DNAG) in 2011. In exchange for some $53 million OraSure obtained DNA Genotek and its oral fluid collection products including the Oragene DNA sample collection kit which is used in a range of settings including academic research labs and personal genetics testing.

EXECUTIVES
COO and CFO, Ronald H. Spair, age 63, $486,243 total compensation
SVP Finance Controller and Assistant Secretary, Mark L. Kuna, age 56, $356,826 total compensation
President and CEO, Douglas A. Michels, age 62, $619,054 total compensation
EVP Sales and Marketing, Anthony (Tony) Zezzo, age 65, $398,403 total compensation
SVP and General Manager Consumer Products, Kathleen Weber
SVP Research and Development and Chief Science Officer, Michael Reed
SVP and General Manager Molecular Collection Systems, Brian Smith
Vice President of Sales, Pat Reis
Vice President, Jill Thompson
Senior Vice President Operations, Nancy McLane
Chairman, Stephen S. Tang, age 58
Auditors: KPMG LLP

LOCATIONS
HQ: OraSure Technologies Inc.
220 East First Street, Bethlehem, PA 18015
Phone: 610 882-1820
Web: www.orasure.com

PRODUCTS/OPERATIONS
2016 Sales

	$ mil.	% of total
OSUR	96.0	75
DNAG	32.2	25
Total	128.2	100

Selected Products
AUTO-LYTE (enzyme immunoassay tests for insurance lab drug testing)
Histofreezer (cryosurgical wart removal system)
Freeze 'n Clear Skin Clinic (wart remover)
Intercept (saliva-based substance abuse testing)
MICRO-PLATE (plasma screening immunoassay tests for drug testing)
Oragene (DNA tests)
OraQuick HCV (rapid antibody test)
OraQuick ADVANCE HIV-1/2 (blood sample HIV test)
OraSure HIV-1 (oral HIV test)
QED Saliva Alcohol Test
QuickFlu Rapid Flu A+B (influenza)
Pointts Wart Remover (Central America OTC cryosurgical wart treatment)
Scholl Freeze Verruca & Wart Remover (Europe OTC cryosurgical wart treatment)

COMPETITORS
ANSYS
Abbott Labs
AcuNetx
Bio-Rad Labs
Calypte Biomedical
Johnson & Johnson
Medtox Scientific
Merck
Olympus Corporation of the Americas
Orgenics
Prestige Brands
Psychemedics
Quest Diagnostics
Quidel
Roche Diagnostics
Siemens Healthcare
Trinity Biotech
eScreen

HISTORICAL FINANCIALS
Company Type: Public

Income Statement   FYE: December 31

	REVENUE ($ mil.)	NET INCOME ($ mil.)	NET PROFIT MARGIN	EMPLOYEES
12/18	181.7	20.4	11.2%	398
12/17	167.0	30.9	18.5%	377
12/16	128.2	19.7	15.4%	325
12/15	119.7	8.1	6.8%	326
12/14	106.4	(4.6)	—	320
Annual Growth	14.3%	—	—	5.6%

2018 Year-End Financials
Debt ratio: —
Return on equity: 7.5%
Cash ($ mil.): 88.4
Current ratio: 7.84
Long-term debt ($ mil.): —
No. of shares (mil.): 61.2
Dividends
  Yield: —
  Payout: —
Market value ($ mil.): 716.0

	STOCK PRICE ($) FY Close	P/E High/Low	PER SHARE ($) Earnings	Dividends	Book Value
12/18	11.68	67 32	0.33	0.00	4.62
12/17	18.86	44 16	0.51	0.00	4.25
12/16	8.78	27 15	0.35	0.00	3.32
12/15	6.44	75 32	0.14	0.00	2.86
12/14	10.14	— —	(0.08)	0.00	2.82
Annual Growth	3.6%		—	—	13.1%

HISTORICAL FINANCIALS
Company Type: Public

Income Statement   FYE: December 31

	ASSETS ($ mil.)	NET INCOME ($ mil.)	INCOME AS % OF ASSETS	EMPLOYEES
12/18	1,934.3	12.8	0.7%	386
12/17	1,558.8	8.0	0.5%	338
12/16	1,414.5	6.6	0.5%	327
12/15	1,292.8	7.8	0.6%	306
12/14	1,190.4	29.1	2.4%	312
Annual Growth	12.9%	(18.6%)	—	5.5%

2018 Year-End Financials
Return on assets: 0.7%
Return on equity: 8.0%
Long-term debt ($ mil.): —
No. of shares (mil.): 9.4
Sales ($ mil): 86.6
Dividends
  Yield: 2.8%
  Payout: 34.0%
Market value ($ mil.): 172.0

	STOCK PRICE ($) FY Close	P/E High/Low	PER SHARE ($) Earnings	Dividends	Book Value
12/18	18.21	18 12	1.50	0.51	18.39
12/17	25.25	27 20	0.98	0.42	17.34
12/16	22.40	29 20	0.81	0.35	16.28
12/15	17.84	19 16	0.97	0.22	16.08
12/14	17.00	5 4	3.59	0.00	15.40
Annual Growth	1.7%		— (19.6%)	—	4.5%

2018 Year-End Financials
Debt ratio: —
Return on equity: 107.5%
Cash ($ mil.): 28.8
Current ratio: 1.61
Long-term debt ($ mil.): —
No. of shares (mil.): 11.5
Dividends
  Yield: 4.2%
  Payout: 96.8%
Market value ($ mil.): 335.0

	STOCK PRICE ($) FY Close	P/E High/Low	PER SHARE ($) Earnings	Dividends	Book Value
12/18	29.04	23 17	1.36	1.23	1.42
12/17	29.05	29 17	1.06	1.16	1.21
12/16	23.00	25 16	0.90	1.16	1.36
12/15	16.30	18 15	0.88	1.08	1.55
12/14	14.36	21 11	0.69	0.37	1.62
Annual Growth	19.3%		— —	18.5% 35.0%	(3.3%)

Pacific Mercantile Bancorp

Pacific Mercantile is banking on southern California businesses. Pacific Mercantile Bancorp is the holding company for Pacific Mercantile Bank which operates more than a dozen branches in southern California's Los Angeles Orange San Bernardino and San Diego counties. Serving area consumers and businesses the bank provides standard services including checking savings and money market accounts CDs and IRAs as well as online banking and bill payment. It uses deposits primarily to fund business loans including commercial mortgages which account for some 65% of the bank's loan portfolio. The bank also offers residential mortgages construction land development and consumer loans.

Financial Performance
Increases in non-interest income drove the Pacific Mercantile's total revenue up 34% in 2012. The bank's non-interest income included revenue earned from mortgage banking fees and proceeds from the sale of mortgage loans tied to its retail mortgage business as well as its wholesale mortgage business which it exited in 2012. Other non-interest income increases that year were attributable to gains from securities the bank sold. Pacific Mercantile's revenue increase was partially offset by a decline in interest income which was caused in part by lower interest rates set by the Fed.

Orrstown Financial Services, Inc.

EXECUTIVES
Vice President Of Regional Senior Loan Officer, Samuel Smith
Senior Vice President Director Of Commer, Andrew Johnson
Vice President Credit Officer, David Chajkowski
Auditors: Crowe LLP

LOCATIONS
HQ: Orrstown Financial Services, Inc.
77 East King Street, P.O. Box 250, Shippensburg, PA 17257
Phone: 717 532-6114
Web: www.orrstown.com

COMPETITORS
Citizens Financial Group
Franklin Financial Services
M&T Bank
PNC Financial
Sovereign Bank

OTC Markets Group Inc

EXECUTIVES
Pres-ceo, R C Coulson
ASSISTANT VICE PRESIDENT, Jason Paltrowitz
Vice President Advisor Relations, Andrew Kyzyk
Vice President, Chris King
Vice President Corporate Services, Bill Karsh
Assistant Vice President Senior Accountant, Jeff Jin
Vice President, Robert Power
Auditors: Deloitte & Touche LLP

LOCATIONS
HQ: OTC Markets Group Inc
300 Vesey Street, 12th Floor, New York, NY 10282
Phone: 212 896-4400   **Fax:** 212 868-3848
Web: www.otcmarkets.com

HISTORICAL FINANCIALS
Company Type: Public

Income Statement   FYE: December 31

	REVENUE ($ mil.)	NET INCOME ($ mil.)	NET PROFIT MARGIN	EMPLOYEES
12/18	59.2	16.2	27.4%	93
12/17	54.6	12.5	23.0%	90
12/16	50.8	10.5	20.7%	88
12/15	49.9	10.2	20.6%	89
12/14	42.2	7.8	18.7%	85
Annual Growth	8.9%	19.8%	—	2.3%

EXECUTIVES
Vice President Operations Manager, Jimmy Hornsby
Assistant Vice President Portfolio Manager, Adam McCann
Vp Fair Lending Compliance Officer, Kimberly Valley
Assistant Vice President Senior Credit Analyst, Yulia Davydova
Senior Vice President Senior Credit Administrator, David Quizon
Vice President Relationship Manager, Jeanette Melton
Vice President Post Closing, Jacqui Irvine
Senior Vice President Regional Manager, Ross Macdonald
Evp And Manager, Tom Wagner

Senior Vice President, Adrian Ward
Senior Vice President Relationship Manager, D'Ann Lungberg
Vice President Senior Relationship Manager, Mark Martinez
Vice President Senior Human Resources Generalist, Kathleen Wiesinger
Vice President Corporate Finance, Chris Lieber
Senior Vice President And Director Financial Reporting, Jen Lyons
Executive Vice President Head Of Cash Management, Cindy Verity
Avp Senior Credit Analyst, Scott Shimozawa
Senior Vice President Loan Operations, George Younes
Vice President Treasury Management Advisor, Shamara Vizcarra
Vice President Credit Card Operations, William Hickox
Senior Vice President Chief Appraiser, Jose Mai
VICE PRESIDENT ASSISTANT CONTROLLER, Christopher Lopez
SENIOR VICE PRESIDENT DIRECTOR OF FINANCIAL REPORTING, Jennifer Lyons
Vice President, Santos Janbeth
VICE PRESIDENT MANAGER OF COLLATERAL SUPPORT, Soledad Huizar
ASSISTANT VICE PRESIDENT CENTRAL OPERATIONS MANAGER, Ck Kothari
Vice President Compliance And Privacy Officer, Maryann Hopp
Svp Director Of Financial Reporting, Jen Mallon
Vice President Relationship Manager, Alice Harris
Treasurer, Tom Stellar
Auditors: RSM US LLP

LOCATIONS

HQ: Pacific Mercantile Bancorp
949 South Coast Drive, Suite 300, Costa Mesa, CA 92626
Phone: 714 438-2500   Fax: 714 438-1059
Web: www.pmbank.com

COMPETITORS

Bank of America	City National
Bank of the West	JPMorgan Chase
California Bank & Trust	MUFG Americas Holdings
Citigroup	U.S. Bancorp

HISTORICAL FINANCIALS
Company Type: Public

Income Statement — FYE: December 31

	ASSETS ($ mil.)	NET INCOME ($ mil.)	INCOME AS % OF ASSETS	EMPLOYEES
12/18	1,349.3	27.3	2.0%	160
12/17	1,322.6	10.4	0.8%	168
12/16	1,140.6	(34.6)	—	169
12/15	1,062.3	12.4	1.2%	160
12/14	1,099.6	0.3	0.0%	168
Annual Growth	5.2%	195.8%	—	(1.2%)

2018 Year-End Financials

Return on assets: 2.0%
Return on equity: 21.5%
Long-term debt ($ mil.): —
No. of shares (mil.): 21.9
Sales ($ mil): 67.1
Dividends
 Yield: —
 Payout: —
Market value ($ mil.): 157.0

	STOCK PRICE ($) FY Close	P/E High/Low	PER SHARE ($) Earnings	Dividends	Book Value
12/18	7.15	9 6	1.16	0.00	6.45
12/17	8.75	22 16	0.45	0.00	4.86
12/16	7.30	— —	(1.51)	0.00	4.33
12/15	7.13	14 12	0.53	0.00	5.87
12/14	7.04	— —	(0.04)	0.00	6.13
Annual Growth	0.4%	— —	—	—	1.3%

Pacific Premier Bancorp Inc

Auditors: Crowe LLP

LOCATIONS

HQ: Pacific Premier Bancorp Inc
17901 Von Karman Avenue, Suite 1200, Irvine, CA 92614
Phone: 949 864-8000
Web: www.ppbi.com

HISTORICAL FINANCIALS
Company Type: Public

Income Statement — FYE: December 31

	ASSETS ($ mil.)	NET INCOME ($ mil.)	INCOME AS % OF ASSETS	EMPLOYEES
12/18	11,487.3	123.3	1.1%	1,030
12/17	8,024.5	60.1	0.7%	846
12/16	4,036.3	40.1	1.0%	448
12/15	2,790.6	25.5	0.9%	335
12/14	2,038.9	16.6	0.8%	285
Annual Growth	54.1%	65.1%	—	37.9%

2018 Year-End Financials

Return on assets: 1.2%
Return on equity: 7.6%
Long-term debt ($ mil.): —
No. of shares (mil.): 62.4
Sales ($ mil): 479.4
Dividends
 Yield: —
 Payout: —
Market value ($ mil.): 1,595.0

	STOCK PRICE ($) FY Close	P/E High/Low	PER SHARE ($) Earnings	Dividends	Book Value
12/18	25.52	20 10	2.26	0.00	31.52
12/17	40.00	26 20	1.56	0.00	26.86
12/16	35.35	24 13	1.46	0.00	16.54
12/15	21.25	20 12	1.19	0.00	13.86
12/14	17.33	18 14	0.96	0.00	11.81
Annual Growth	10.2%	— —	23.9%	—	27.8%

PacWest Bancorp

PacWest Bancorp is the holding company for Pacific Western Bank which operates about 80 branches mostly in southern and central California plus an additional branch in Durham North Carolina. The $21 billion-asset bank caters to small and midsized businesses and their owners and employees offering traditional deposit and loan products and services. Commercial real estate mortgages make up more than 30% of its loan portfolio while cash flow- and asset-based business loans make up another 40%. The bank also originates residential mortgage real estate construction and land loans venture capital equipment finance and consumer loans. PacWest offers investment services and international banking through agreements with correspondent banks.

Operations

Like other retail banks PacWest generates the bulk of its revenue from interest income. About 83% of its total revenue came from interest income on loans and leases during 2015 while another 7% came from interest income on investments. The rest of its revenue came from leased equipment income (3% of revenue) deposit account service charges (1%) other commissions and fees (3%) and other miscellaneous income sources.

The bank's Square 1 Bank Division caters to entrepreneurial businesses and their venture capital and private equity investors while its CapitalSource Division provides cash flow asset-based equipment and real estate loans and leases as well as treasury management services to established middle-market businesses across the country.

Geographic Reach

PWB's branches are located across California in Los Angeles Orange Riverside San Bernardino Santa Barbara San Diego San Francisco San Luis Obispo San Mateo and Ventura Counties. It also has a branch in Durham North Carolina.

Financial Performance

PacWest's acquisitions in 2014 and 2015 boosted its interest-earning loan asset balances more than three-fold which sent its revenues and profits soaring during those years.

The bank's revenue jumped 30% to $968.3 million during 2015 mostly as newly acquired loans from its CapitalSource boosted its interest income during the year.

Strong revenue growth coupled with lower acquisition integration and reorganization costs in 2015 drove PacWest's net income up 77% to $300 million. Its operating cash levels spiked 79% to $594 million with the rise in cash-denominated earnings.

Strategy

PacWest has grown its loan and deposit business as well as its branch network through acquisitions of California community banks and specialized financial services companies. It has made 28 acquisitions since 2000 with some of its most recent being the Square 1 acquisition in 2015 and the CapitalSource Inc. acquisition in 2014.

Mergers and Acquisitions

In October 2015 PacWest purchased $4.6 billion-asset Square 1 and its Square 1 Bank subsidiary for $849 million forming the Square 1 Bank Division of the Bank. The deal boosted its core deposits expanded its national lending platform and bolstered its presence in the technology and life-sciences markets.

In April 2014 the bank bought $10.7 billion-asset CapitalSource Inc. and its CapitalSource Bank (CSB) subsidiary.

In May 2013 PacWest acquired $1.7 billion-asset First California Financial Group operator of First California Bank for $237 million. The purchase added six branches (after consolidation) in Los

Angeles Orange Riverside San Bernardino San Diego San Luis Obispo and Ventura Counties.

Company Background

During the economic downturn PacWest took advantage of a rash of bank failures through FDIC-assisted transactions. The acquired institutions were merged into Pacific Western Bank. Under the loss-sharing deals the FDIC agreed to reimburse PacWest for future losses tied to the acquisitions. In a 2012 non-FDIC-assisted deal PacWest bought American Perspective Bank adding two branches and a loan office in the Central Coast area.

EXECUTIVES

EVP and Director the Company and Pacific Western Bank, Daniel B. Platt, age 72, $52,500 total compensation
EVP and Chief Risk Officer, Suzanne R. Brennan, age 68, $165,000 total compensation
CEO, Matthew P. (Matt) Wagner, age 62, $754,167 total compensation
EVP and CFO Pacific Western Bank, Patrick J. (Pat) Rusnak, age 55
EVP and Chief Accounting Officer, Lynn M. Hopkins, age 51
EVP; Director Human Resources, Christopher D. Blake, age 59, $298,958 total compensation
EVP and Chief Credit Officer, Bryan M. Corsini, age 57, $375,624 total compensation
EVP; President CapitalSource, James J. (Jim) Pieczynski, age 56, $554,539 total compensation
EVP Operations and Systems, Mark Christian
EVP General Counsel and Corporate Secretary, Kori L. Ogrosky
Senior Vice President Information Systems Manager, Norma Lopez
Senior Vice President, Scott Foote
Vice President Operations Manager, Arbi John
Vice President Regional Manager, Shari Schiavone
Vice President, Sue Thomas
Vice President Bsa Officer, Sali Tice
Senior Vice President, John Braunschweiger
Executive Vice President, Jeffrey Lizar
Senior Vice President Financial Planning, Peter Fan
Senior Vice President Group Manager Government Guaranteed Lending Group, Amy Conner
Vice President Business Development Officer, Michelle Coberly
Vice President Operations Executive, Doug Bradley
Senior Vice President Tax, Grace Keegan
Senior Vice President and Controller, Kathy Bailey
VICE PRESIDENT COML INV AND ASSET MANAGER, Kevin Powelson
Chairman, John M. Eggemeyer, age 73
Treasurer, Victor Santoro
Board Member, Paul Burke
Auditors: KPMG LLP

LOCATIONS

HQ: PacWest Bancorp
9701 Wilshire Blvd., Suite 700, Beverly Hills, CA 90212
Phone: 310 887-8500
Web: www.pacwestbancorp.com

PRODUCTS/OPERATIONS

2015 Sales

	% of total
Interest income	
Loans and leases	87
Investment securities & other	7
Noninterest income	
Other commissions and fees	3
Leased equipment income	3
Service charges on deposit accounts	1
Other	3
FDIC loss sharing expense net	-
Total	**100**

Selected Mergers & Acquisitions

COMPETITORS

Bank of America
CVB Financial
California Bank & Trust
City National
JPMorgan Chase
MUFG Americas Holdings
Rabobank America
San Diego County Credit Union
U.S. Bancorp
Wells Fargo
Westamerica

HISTORICAL FINANCIALS
Company Type: Public

Income Statement — FYE: December 31

	ASSETS ($ mil.)	NET INCOME ($ mil.)	INCOME AS % OF ASSETS	EMPLOYEES
12/18	25,731.3	465.3	1.8%	1,833
12/17	24,994.8	357.8	1.4%	1,786
12/16	21,869.7	352.1	1.6%	1,669
12/15	21,288.4	299.6	1.4%	1,670
12/14	16,234.8	168.9	1.0%	1,443
Annual Growth	12.2%	28.8%	—	6.2%

2018 Year-End Financials

Return on assets: 1.8%
Return on equity: 9.4%
Long-term debt ($ mil.): —
No. of shares (mil.): 123.1
Sales ($ mil): 1,310.3
Dividends
Yield: 6.9%
Payout: 66.8%
Market value ($ mil.): 4,100.0

	STOCK PRICE ($) FY Close	P/E High/Low		PER SHARE ($) Earnings	Dividends	Book Value
12/18	33.28	15	8	3.72	2.30	39.17
12/17	50.40	20	15	2.91	2.00	38.65
12/16	54.44	19	10	2.90	2.00	36.93
12/15	43.10	17	14	2.79	2.00	36.22
12/14	45.46	25	20	1.92	1.25	34.04
Annual Growth	(7.5%)	—	—	18.0%	16.5%	3.6%

Palatin Technologies Inc

EXECUTIVES

Vice President Of Research, John Dodd
Auditors: KPMG LLP

LOCATIONS

HQ: Palatin Technologies Inc
4B Cedar Brook Drive, Cranbury, NJ 08512
Phone: 609 495-2200
Web: www.palatin.com

COMPETITORS

Arena Pharmaceuticals
Bayer HealthCare
Cordis
Eli Lilly
GE Healthcare Medical Diagnostics
Pfizer
Repros Therapeutics
Roche Holding
Scios
Takeda Pharmaceutical
VIVUS

HISTORICAL FINANCIALS
Company Type: Public

Income Statement — FYE: June 30

	REVENUE ($ mil.)	NET INCOME ($ mil.)	NET PROFIT MARGIN	EMPLOYEES
06/19	60.3	35.7	59.3%	18
06/18	67.1	24.7	36.8%	19
06/17	44.7	(13.3)	—	22
06/16	0.0	(51.7)	—	22
06/15	12.9	(17.6)	—	18
Annual Growth	46.9%			0.0%

2019 Year-End Financials

Debt ratio: 0.3%
Return on equity: 56.1%
Cash ($ mil.): 43.5
Current ratio: 24.94
Long-term debt ($ mil.): —
No. of shares (mil.): 226.8
Dividends
Yield: —
Payout: —
Market value ($ mil.): 263.0

	STOCK PRICE ($) FY Close	P/E High/Low		PER SHARE ($) Earnings	Dividends	Book Value
06/19	1.16	10	4	0.16	0.00	0.44
06/18	0.97	12	3	0.12	0.00	0.13
06/17	0.43	—	—	(0.07)	0.00	(0.03)
06/16	0.44	—	—	(0.33)	0.00	(0.26)
06/15	0.89	—	—	(0.15)	0.00	0.21
Annual Growth	6.8%	—	—	—	—	20.0%

Parade Technologies Ltd.

Auditors: PricewaterhouseCoopers, Taiwan

LOCATIONS

HQ: Parade Technologies Ltd.
2720 Orchard Parkway, San Jose, CA 95134
Phone: 408 329-5540   **Fax:** 408 329-5541
Web: www.paradetech.com

HISTORICAL FINANCIALS
Company Type: Public

Income Statement — FYE: December 31

	REVENUE ($ mil.)	NET INCOME ($ mil.)	NET PROFIT MARGIN	EMPLOYEES
12/18	338.8	64.3	19.0%	0
12/17	349.1	65.1	18.7%	0
12/16	281.4	41.9	14.9%	0
12/15	218.7	34.8	15.9%	393
12/14	196.6	38.7	19.7%	293
Annual Growth	14.6%	13.6%	—	—

Paramount Group Inc

Auditors: DELOITTE & TOUCHE LLP

LOCATIONS

HQ: Paramount Group Inc
1633 Broadway, Suite 1801, New York, NY 10019
Phone: 212 237-3100
Web: www.paramount-group.com

HISTORICAL FINANCIALS
Company Type: Public

Income Statement — FYE: December 31

	REVENUE ($ mil.)	NET INCOME ($ mil.)	NET PROFIT MARGIN	EMPLOYEES
12/18	758.9	9.1	1.2%	321
12/17	718.9	86.3	12.0%	327
12/16	683.3	(9.9)	—	334
12/15	662.4	(4.4)	—	319
12/14	66.1	57.3	86.7%	219
Annual Growth	84.1%	(36.8%)	—	10.0%

2018 Year-End Financials

Debt ratio: 40.7%
Return on equity: 0.2%
Cash ($ mil.): 388.0
Current ratio: 4.50
Long-term debt ($ mil.): 3,566.9
No. of shares (mil.): 233.1
Dividends
  Yield: 3.1%
  Payout: 1,000.0%
Market value ($ mil.): 2,928.0

	STOCK PRICE ($) FY Close	P/E High/Low	PER SHARE ($) Earnings	Dividends	Book Value
12/18	12.56	399 308	0.04	0.40	17.16
12/17	15.85	47 41	0.37	0.38	17.37
12/16	15.99	— —	(0.05)	0.38	17.35
12/15	18.10	— —	(0.02)	0.42	17.73
12/14	18.59	70 67	0.27	0.00	18.44
Annual Growth	(9.3%)	— —	(38.0%)	—	(1.8%)

Parke Bancorp Inc

EXECUTIVES

Vice President Business Development, Jaime Brooks
Vice President, Kathleen Conover
Auditors: RSM US LLP

LOCATIONS

HQ: Parke Bancorp Inc
601 Delsea Drive, Washington Township, NJ 08080
Phone: 856 256-2500
Web: www.parkebank.com

COMPETITORS

Bank of America
Hudson City Bancorp
Ocean Shore
PNC Financial
TD Bank USA

HISTORICAL FINANCIALS
Company Type: Public

Income Statement — FYE: December 31

	ASSETS ($ mil.)	NET INCOME ($ mil.)	INCOME AS % OF ASSETS	EMPLOYEES
12/18	1,467.4	24.8	1.7%	98
12/17	1,137.4	11.8	1.0%	91
12/16	1,016.1	18.5	1.8%	86
12/15	885.1	10.7	1.2%	84
12/14	821.7	10.4	1.3%	70
Annual Growth	15.6%	24.1%	—	8.8%

2018 Year-End Financials

Return on assets: 1.9%
Return on equity: 17.2%
Long-term debt ($ mil.): —
No. of shares (mil.): 10.6
Sales ($ mil): 65.2
Dividends
  Yield: 2.6%
  Payout: 21.8%
Market value ($ mil.): 200.0

	STOCK PRICE ($) FY Close	P/E High/Low	PER SHARE ($) Earnings	Dividends	Book Value
12/18	18.72	10 7	2.28	0.50	14.39
12/17	20.55	19 14	1.13	0.38	15.28
12/16	20.15	10 5	1.70	0.24	15.31
12/15	12.48	12 10	1.01	0.18	13.53
12/14	11.55	10 8	0.99	0.08	12.89
Annual Growth	12.8%	— —	23.1%	60.5%	2.8%

Parsley Energy Inc

Auditors: KPMG LLP

LOCATIONS

HQ: Parsley Energy Inc
303 Colorado Street, Suite 3000, Austin, TX 78701
Phone: 737 704-2300
Web: www.parsleyenergy.com

HISTORICAL FINANCIALS
Company Type: Public

Income Statement — FYE: December 31

	REVENUE ($ mil.)	NET INCOME ($ mil.)	NET PROFIT MARGIN	EMPLOYEES
12/18	1,826.4	369.1	20.2%	427
12/17	967.0	106.7	11.0%	460
12/16	457.7	(74.1)	—	298
12/15	266.0	(50.4)	—	212
12/14	301.7	23.4	7.8%	174
Annual Growth	56.9%	99.2%	—	25.2%

2018 Year-End Financials

Debt ratio: 23.2%
Return on equity: 7.1%
Cash ($ mil.): 163.2
Current ratio: 0.83
Long-term debt ($ mil.): 2,181.6
No. of shares (mil.): 316.7
Dividends
  Yield: —
  Payout: —
Market value ($ mil.): 5,062.0

	STOCK PRICE ($) FY Close	P/E High/Low	PER SHARE ($) Earnings	Dividends	Book Value
12/18	15.98	24 11	1.35	0.00	17.58
12/17	29.44	84 54	0.42	0.00	14.99
12/16	35.24	— —	(0.46)	0.00	10.07
12/15	18.45	— —	(0.45)	0.00	7.49
12/14	15.96	60 27	0.42	0.00	5.61
Annual Growth	0.0%	— —	33.9%	—	33.0%

Patrick Industries Inc

A recreational vehicle is just an empty motor home until Patrick Industries adds the finishing interior touches. The company makes and distributes a range of building materials and prefinished products primarily for the manufactured home (MH) recreational vehicle (RV) and marine industries. Patrick Industries manufactures decorative paper and vinyl panels moldings countertops doors and cabinet and slotwall components. In addition to these the firm distributes roofing siding flooring drywall ceiling and wall panels household electronics electrical and plumbing supplies and adhesives. Founded in 1959 the company operates more 100 manufacturing plants and more than 40 distribution centers and warehouses in about two dozen US states China Canada and the Netherlands.

Operations

Patrick Industries operates over 100 manufacturing plants where it makes furniture shelving wall counter and cabinet products mouldings interior passage doors and slotwall panels and components among other products. Its manufacturing segment contributes over three-quarters of its annual revenue.

The company also distributes prefinished wall and ceiling panels drywall and drywall finishing products electronics wiring electrical and plumbing products shower doors fireplaces and other miscellaneous products from more than 40 warehouse and distribution facilities. Distribution accounts for the remaining revenue.

Geographic Reach

Patrick Industries is based in Elkhart Indiana where a number of RV makers are clustered. The company operates facilities in nearly two dozen states as well as internationally in Canada China and the Nethlerlands.

Sales and Marketing

Patrick Industries counts most of the major manufactured housing (MH) and recreational vehicle (RV) manufacturers among its clientele but it also serves customers in the kitchen cabinet office and household furniture fixtures and commercial furnishings markets. The company has over 2400 active customers of which two (Forest River and Thor) account for about 50% of its sales.

The RV industry represents nearly 65% of the company's sales while the manufactured housing industrial and marine markets each account for approximately 10%.

Financial Performance

Patrick Industries has been moving along for several years with robust revenue and profit gains.

The company's revenue jumped nearly 40% higher in fiscal year 2018 to $2.2 billion from about $1.6 billion in fiscal year 2017. The increase can be attributed to large increases across all of its segments in particular the marine and industrial markets. It also reflected the revenue contribution of 2018 acquisitions.

Net income was $119.8 million in fiscal year 2018 an increase from $85.7 million in fiscal year 2017. Selling general and administrative expenses grew 41% in fiscal 2018 to $128.2 million.

Cash provided by operating activities was $200 million in fiscal 2018 while investing activities used $371.4 million. Financing activities provided another $175.5 million.

Strategy

With 65% of sales coming from the RV industry Patrick Industries is looking to further diversify its product portfolio for a better balance.

The company has expanded to other industrial commercial marine and institutional markets primarily through acquisitions. Patrick Industries made nine acquisitions in 2018 and has made more than 40 acquisitions since 2010.

While some acquisitions have helped the company grow its content for the RV industry others have focused on newer markets. For example Patrick Industries acquired marine product maker Engineered Metals and Composites in 2018. The South Carolina-based company designs and manufactures custom marine towers frames and other fabricated component products for the marine industry.

Patrick Industries is also tightening its operations by managing its cost structure driving efficiencies across all functions and seeking synergies throughout the company.

Mergers and Acquisitions

Over the last three years the company has invested approximately $734 million to complete 23 acquisitions involving 34 companies.

In late 2018 Patrick Industries completed the acquisition of Arran Isle and its subsidiaries for approximately $34 million. Based in Elkhart Indiana LaSalle Bristol is a supplier of plumbing flooring tile lighting air handling and building products to the manufactured housing recreational vehicle and industrial markets.

Other recent acquisitions include the Metal Moulding Corporation Aluminum Metals Company Indiana Marine Products Holdings Collins & Company Inc. Dehco Dowco Marine Accessories Corporation and Engineered Metals and Composites.

EXECUTIVES

President, Andy L. Nemeth, age 50, $271,730 total compensation
CEO, Todd M. Cleveland, age 51, $555,770 total compensation
VP Human Resources, Courtney A. Blosser, $203,537 total compensation
EVP Sales and Chief Sales Officer, Jeffrey M. Rodino, age 49, $276,517 total compensation
CFO, Joshua A. Boone, age 40
EVP Operations and COO, Kip B. Ellis, age 45
Vice President Sales, Jimmy Ritchey
Chairman, Paul E. Hassler, age 72
Auditors: DELOITTE & TOUCHE LLP

LOCATIONS

HQ: Patrick Industries Inc
107 West Franklin Street, P.O. Box 638, Elkhart, IN 46515
Phone: 574 294-7511
Web: www.patrickind.com

PRODUCTS/OPERATIONS

Selected Products:
Adorn
AIA Countertops
Better Way Products
Carrera Custom Painting
Charleston
Creative Wood Designs
Custom Vinyls
Décor Manufacturing
Foremost Fabricators
Frontline Manufacturing
Gravure Ink Praxis Group
Gustafson Lighting
Infinity GraphicsInte

2015 sales

	$ mil.	% of total
Manufacturing	720.4	78
Distribution	199.9	22
Total	920.3	100

2015 Sales by Customer Type

	% of total
RV industry	75
Manufactured housing	14
Industrial market	11
Total	100

COMPETITORS

Decorator Industries
Flexsteel
HD Supply
LCI Industries
LaSalle Bristol
Lowe's
Quanex Building Products
Saint-Gobain

HISTORICAL FINANCIALS

Company Type: Public

Income Statement
FYE: December 31

	REVENUE ($ mil.)	NET INCOME ($ mil.)	NET PROFIT MARGIN	EMPLOYEES
12/18	2,263.0	119.8	5.3%	8,113
12/17	1,635.6	85.7	5.2%	6,721
12/16	1,221.8	55.5	4.5%	4,497
12/15	920.3	42.2	4.6%	3,542
12/14	735.7	30.6	4.2%	2,799
Annual Growth	32.4%	40.6%	—	30.5%

2018 Year-End Financials

Debt ratio: 51.2%
Return on equity: 30.7%
Cash ($ mil.): 6.9
Current ratio: 2.44
Long-term debt ($ mil.): 621.7
No. of shares (mil.): 23.5
Dividends
 Yield: —
 Payout: —
Market value ($ mil.): 697.0

	STOCK PRICE ($) FY Close	P/E High/Low		PER SHARE ($) Earnings	Dividends	Book Value
12/18	29.61	14	6	4.93	0.00	17.37
12/17	69.45	29	17	3.48	0.00	14.63
12/16	76.30	32	12	2.43	0.00	8.07
12/15	43.50	35	19	1.81	0.00	5.65
12/14	43.98	37	22	1.28	0.00	4.42
Annual Growth	(9.4%)		—	40.2%	—	40.8%

Pattern Energy Group Inc

EXECUTIVES

President and CEO, Michael M. Garland, $420,250 total compensation
EVP Business Development, Hunter H. Armistead, $341,453 total compensation
EVP and General Counsel, Daniel M. Elkort, $304,681 total compensation
CFO, Michael J. Lyon, $242,300 total compensation
SVP Operations, Christopher M. Shugart
Vice President Engineering And, Kevin Deters
Chairman, Alan R. Batkin, age 74
Auditors: PricewaterhouseCoopers LLP

LOCATIONS

HQ: Pattern Energy Group Inc
1088 Sansome Street, San Francisco, CA 94111
Phone: 415 283-4000
Web: www.patternenergy.com

PRODUCTS/OPERATIONS

2016 sales

	% of total
Electricity sales	97
Related party revenue	1
other revenue	1
Total	100

COMPETITORS

AES Wind Generation
Algonquin
Berkshire Hathaway Energy
Brookfield Renewable Energy
EDP Renewables North America LLC
First Wind Holdings
Green Mountain Energy
NRG Yield
Navitas Energy
NextEra Energy
Sea Breeze Power

HISTORICAL FINANCIALS

Company Type: Public

Income Statement
FYE: December 31

	REVENUE ($ mil.)	NET INCOME ($ mil.)	NET PROFIT MARGIN	EMPLOYEES
12/18	483.0	142.0	29.4%	209
12/17	411.3	(17.9)	—	210
12/16	354.0	(17.1)	—	140
12/15	329.8	(32.5)	—	116
12/14	265.4	(31.2)	—	69
Annual Growth	16.1%	—	—	31.9%

2018 Year-End Financials

Debt ratio: 43.1%
Return on equity: 13.2%
Cash ($ mil.): 101.0
Current ratio: 0.44
Long-term debt ($ mil.): 2,029.0
No. of shares (mil.): 98.0
Dividends
 Yield: 9.0%
 Payout: 116.4%
Market value ($ mil.): 1,826.0

	STOCK PRICE ($) FY Close	P/E High/Low	Earnings	Dividends	Book Value
12/18	18.62	19 12	1.45	1.69	10.68
12/17	21.49	— —	(0.20)	1.67	11.18
12/16	18.99	— —	(0.22)	1.58	11.30
12/15	20.91	— —	(0.46)	1.43	11.14
12/14	24.66	— —	(0.56)	1.30	10.22
Annual Growth	(6.8%)	— —		6.8%	1.1%

Paycom Software Inc

Auditors: Grant Thornton LLP

LOCATIONS

HQ: Paycom Software Inc
7501 W. Memorial Road, Oklahoma City, OK 73142
Phone: 405 722-6900
Web: www.paycom.com

HISTORICAL FINANCIALS
Company Type: Public

Income Statement FYE: December 31

	REVENUE ($ mil.)	NET INCOME ($ mil.)	NET PROFIT MARGIN	EMPLOYEES
12/18	566.3	137.0	24.2%	3,050
12/17	433.0	66.8	15.4%	2,548
12/16	329.1	43.8	13.3%	2,075
12/15	224.6	20.9	9.3%	1,461
12/14	150.9	5.6	3.8%	1,021
Annual Growth	39.2%	121.8%	—	31.5%

2018 Year-End Financials

Debt ratio: 2.2%
Return on equity: 58.3%
Cash ($ mil.): 45.7
Current ratio: 1.03
Long-term debt ($ mil.): 32.6

No. of shares (mil.): 57.2
Dividends
  Yield: —
  Payout: —
Market value ($ mil.): 7,014.0

	STOCK PRICE ($) FY Close	P/E High/Low	Earnings	Dividends	Book Value
12/18	122.45	69 34	2.34	0.00	5.84
12/17	80.33	74 38	1.13	0.00	2.34
12/16	45.49	69 30	0.74	0.00	2.03
12/15	37.63	124 63	0.36	0.00	1.72
12/14	26.33	261 113	0.11	0.00	1.38
Annual Growth	46.9%	—	114.8%	—	43.5%

Paylocity Holding Corp

Auditors: KPMG LLP

LOCATIONS

HQ: Paylocity Holding Corp
1400 American Lane, Schaumburg, IL 60173
Phone: 847 463-3200
Web: www.paylocity.com

HISTORICAL FINANCIALS
Company Type: Public

Income Statement FYE: June 30

	REVENUE ($ mil.)	NET INCOME ($ mil.)	NET PROFIT MARGIN	EMPLOYEES
06/19	467.6	53.8	11.5%	3,050
06/18	377.5	38.6	10.2%	2,600
06/17	300.0	6.7	2.2%	2,115
06/16	230.7	(3.8)	—	1,800
06/15	152.7	(13.9)	—	1,320
Annual Growth	32.3%	—	—	23.3%

2019 Year-End Financials

Debt ratio: —
Return on equity: 20.6%
Cash ($ mil.): 132.4
Current ratio: 1.10
Long-term debt ($ mil.): —

No. of shares (mil.): 53.0
Dividends
  Yield: —
  Payout: —
Market value ($ mil.): 4,979.0

	STOCK PRICE ($) FY Close	P/E High/Low	Earnings	Dividends	Book Value
06/19	93.82	101 53	0.97	0.00	5.80
06/18	58.86	86 58	0.70	0.00	4.03
06/17	45.18	378 230	0.12	0.00	2.85
06/16	43.20	— —	(0.08)	0.00	2.34
06/15	35.85	— —	(0.28)	0.00	2.12
Annual Growth	27.2%	— —	—	—	28.6%

PBF Logistics LP

Auditors: DELOITTE & TOUCHE LLP

LOCATIONS

HQ: PBF Logistics LP
One Sylvan Way, Second Floor, Parsippany, NJ 07054
Phone: 973 455-7500
Web: www.pbflogistics.com

HISTORICAL FINANCIALS
Company Type: Public

Income Statement FYE: December 31

	REVENUE ($ mil.)	NET INCOME ($ mil.)	NET PROFIT MARGIN	EMPLOYEES
12/18	283.4	121.1	42.7%	82
12/17	254.8	129.4	50.8%	39
12/16	187.3	87.3	46.6%	0
12/15	142.1	76.4	53.8%	0
12/14	49.8	(3.3)	—	0
Annual Growth	54.4%	—	—	—

2018 Year-End Financials

Debt ratio: 70.4%
Return on equity: 2,718.2%
Cash ($ mil.): 19.9
Current ratio: 1.05
Long-term debt ($ mil.): 673.3

No. of shares (mil.): 45.3
Dividends
  Yield: 9.8%
  Payout: 113.8%
Market value ($ mil.): 912.0

	STOCK PRICE ($) FY Close	P/E High/Low	Earnings	Dividends	Book Value
12/18	20.10	13 11	1.73	1.97	0.52
12/17	20.95	10 9	2.17	1.86	(0.35)
12/16	18.20	12 8	2.01	1.70	(0.80)
12/15	21.36	12 8	2.18	1.44	(5.40)
12/14	21.35	31 20	0.94	0.46	(3.65)
Annual Growth	(1.5%)	— —	16.5%	43.9%	—

PCB Bancorp

Auditors: Crowe LLP

LOCATIONS

HQ: PCB Bancorp
3701 Wilshire Boulevard, Suite 900, Los Angeles, CA 90010
Phone: 213 210-2000
Web: www.paccitybank.com

HISTORICAL FINANCIALS
Company Type: Public

Income Statement FYE: December 31

	ASSETS ($ mil.)	NET INCOME ($ mil.)	INCOME AS % OF ASSETS	EMPLOYEES
12/18	1,697.0	24.3	1.4%	248
12/17	1,442.0	16.4	1.1%	228
12/16	1,226.6	14.0	1.1%	0
12/15	1,042.5	12.1	1.2%	0
12/14	893.9	11.8	1.3%	0
Annual Growth	17.4%	19.7%	—	—

2018 Year-End Financials

Return on assets: 1.5%
Return on equity: 13.7%
Long-term debt ($ mil.): —
No. of shares (mil.): 15.9
Sales ($ mil): 94.1

Dividends
  Yield: 0.7%
  Payout: 7.2%
Market value ($ mil.): 250.0

	STOCK PRICE ($) FY Close	P/E High/Low	Earnings	Dividends	Book Value
12/18	15.65	12 8	1.65	0.12	13.16
12/17	15.50	13 10	1.21	0.12	10.60
12/16	13.00	12 9	1.11	0.11	9.48
12/15	12.85	15 12	1.02	0.07	8.26
12/14	12.38	14 4	1.00	0.00	7.31
Annual Growth	6.0%	— —	13.3%	—	15.8%

PCSB Financial Corp

Auditors: Crowe LLP

LOCATIONS

HQ: PCSB Financial Corp
2651 Strang Blvd., Suite 100, Yorktown Heights, NY 10598
Phone: 914 248-7272
Web: www.pcsb.com

HISTORICAL FINANCIALS
Company Type: Public

Income Statement   FYE: June 30

	ASSETS ($ mil.)	NET INCOME ($ mil.)	INCOME AS % OF ASSETS	EMPLOYEES
06/19	1,637.5	8.3	0.5%	182
06/18	1,480.1	6.6	0.4%	183
06/17	1,426.4	3.2	0.2%	184
06/16	1,262.0	2.9	0.2%	177
06/15	1,200.7	0.5	0.0%	0
Annual Growth	8.1%	101.2%	—	—

2019 Year-End Financials

Return on assets: 0.5%
Return on equity: 2.9%
Long-term debt ($ mil.): —
No. of shares (mil.): 17.8
Sales ($ mil): 56.5

Dividends
Yield: 0.0%
Payout: 26.0%
Market value ($ mil.): 361.0

	STOCK PRICE ($) FY Close	P/E High/Low	PER SHARE ($) Earnings	Dividends	Book Value
06/19	20.25	42 37	0.50	0.13	15.80
06/18	19.87	56 43	0.39	0.03	15.83
06/17	17.06	— —	(0.00)	0.00	15.41
Annual Growth	8.9%	— —	—	—	1.3%

Peapack-Gladstone Financial Corp.

Peapack-Gladstone Financial is the $3.4 billion-asset holding company for the near-century-old Peapack-Gladstone Bank which operates more than 20 branches in New Jersey's Hunterdon Morris Somerset Middlesex and Union counties. Founded in 1921 the bank provides traditional deposit accounts credit cards and loans to individuals and small businesses as well as trust and investment management services through its PGB Trust and Investments unit. Multifamily residential mortgages represent nearly 50% of the company's loan portfolio while commercial mortgages make up around 15%. The bank also originates construction consumer and business loans.

Operations
Peapack-Gladstone Financial operates two main divisions: Banking which offers traditional deposit and loan services merchant card services; and Wealth Management which boasts more than $3.3 billion in assets under administration (as of early 2016) and operates through PGB Trust and Investments which offers asset management services for individuals and institutions as well as personal trust services. More than 80% of the bank's total revenue came from interest income (mostly on its loans) during 2015 while 14% came from its wealth management fee income and 3% came from service charges and fees.

Multifamily residential mortgages represented nearly 50% of the company's loan portfolio at the end of 2015 while commercial mortgages made up another 15%. The rest of its portfolio was made up of construction consumer and business loans.

Geographic Reach
The bank's branches are located across New Jersey in Somerset Morris Hunterdon Middlesex and Union counties Its private banking and wealth management locations are located in Bedminster Morristown Princeton and Teaneck.

Sales and Marketing
The bank's commercial banking business serves business owners professionals retailers contractors and real estate investors. Its wealth management division serves individuals families foundations endowments trusts and estates.

Peapack-Gladstone has been ramping up its advertising spend in recent years. It spent $637000 on advertising during 2015 up from $594000 and $519000 in 2014 and 2013 respectively.

Financial Performance
Peapack-Gladstone's annual revenues and profits have swelled more than 60% since 2011 as its nearly tripled its loan assets to over $2.9 billion.

The bank's revenue jumped 27% to $122.86 million during 2015 mostly thanks to higher interest income as its loan assets grew by 30% with exceptional increases in its multifamily mortgage and commercial loan volumes. Peapack-Gladstone's wealth management division income grew 20% with increases in securities gains service charges and other non-interest income.

Strong revenue growth in 2015 drove Peapack-Gladstone's net income up 34% to $19.97 million. The bank's operating cash levels climbed 11% to $30.31 million thanks to a rise in cash-based earnings.

Strategy
Peapack-Gladstone Financial continued in 2016 to focus on: enhancing its risk management to keep its loan provisions at a minimum and its profits up; expanding its multi-family loans as well as its commercial real estate loans (to a lesser extent); growing its commercial and industrial (C&I) lending business through its private banking divisions; and expanding its wealth management business which now accounts for 15% of its annual revenue.

Mergers and Acquisitions
In May 2015 Peapack-Gladstone bolstered its wealth management division after buying Morristown-based Wealth Management Consultants LLC for $2.8 million. The deal boosted the bank's assets under advisement and administration to $3.5 billion.

EXECUTIVES

SEVP and CFO Peapack-Gladstone Financial and Peapack-Gladstone Bank, Jeffrey J. Carfora, age 61
EVP and COO, Robert A. (Bob) Plante, age 60
President and CEO Peapack-Gladstone Financial and Peapack-Gladstone Bank, Douglas L. Kennedy, age 60
EVP CIO and Head of Banking Services Peapack-Gladstone Bank, Kevin B. Runyon
SEVP Chief Strategy Officer and General Counsel, Finn M.W. Casperson, age 49
EVP and Head of Retail Banking Peapack-Gladstone Bank, Anthony V. Bilotta, age 59
EVP and Head of Commercial Real Estate Peapack-Gladstone Bank, Vincent A. Spero
SEVP and President Private Wealth Management, John P. Babcock
EVP and Chief Credit Officer Peapack-Gladstone Bank, Lisa Chalkan
EVP and Director Human Capital Peapack-Gladstone Bank, Philip Portantino
EVP and President Wealth Management Consultants Peapack-Gladstone Bank, Thomas J. Ross
EVP and Head of Commercial Banking Peapack-Gladstone Bank, Eric H. Waser
SVP and Head of Residential and Consumer Lending Peapack-Gladstone, Glenn R. Straffi
Vice President Director of Corporate Learning, Doreen Macchiarola
Senior Vice President, Charles Adornetto
Vp Sales Distribution Leader, Dominic Sedicino
Vice President, Sean Martin
Vice President And Trust Officer, Kim Czyzewski
Vice President, Glenn Carroll
Private Banker Vice President, Ryan Beltz
Vice President Portfolio Manager, Sarah Krieger
Vice President, Georgette Barnes
Svp Head Of Asset Management At Peapack Capital, David Santom
Assistant Vice President And Senior Loan Administrator, Ana Ribeiro
Assistant Vice President And Senior Custody Officer, Amanda Pullizzi
Svp Senior Underwriter, Christian Gaudioso
Assistant Vice President And Mortgage Consultant, Stephanie Chu
Vice President Financial Analyst, Renee Skuraton
Vice President, David Oddo
Senior Vp Head Of Loan Operations, Lisa Ciampi
Vp Retail Private Banker, Anna Calles
Assistant Vice President And Senior Staff Accountant And Technical Support, Jennifer Greenwood
Chairman, F. Duffield (Duff) Meyercord, age 72
Board Member, Susan Cole
Board Member, Richard Daingerfield
Auditors: Crowe LLP

LOCATIONS
HQ: Peapack-Gladstone Financial Corp.
500 Hills Drive, Suite 300, Bedminster, NJ 07921-0700
Phone: 908 234-0700
Web: www.pgbank.com

PRODUCTS/OPERATIONS

2015 Sales

	$ mil.	% of total
Interest Income		
Loans including fees	94.3	77
Securities available for sale	4.6	4
Other	0.3	-
Other Income		
Wealth management fee income	17.0	14
Service charges and fees	3.3	3
Bank owned life insurance	1.3	1
Other Income	1.0	1
Other	1.1	-
Total	122.9	100

COMPETITORS

Bank of America
Hudson City Bancorp
JPMorgan Chase
MSB Financial

PNC Financial
TD Bank USA
Valley National Bancorp

HISTORICAL FINANCIALS
Company Type: Public

Income Statement   FYE: December 31

	ASSETS ($ mil.)	NET INCOME ($ mil.)	INCOME AS % OF ASSETS	EMPLOYEES
12/18	4,617.8	44.1	1.0%	409
12/17	4,260.5	36.5	0.9%	384
12/16	3,878.6	26.4	0.7%	338
12/15	3,364.6	19.9	0.6%	316
12/14	2,702.4	14.8	0.6%	306
Annual Growth	14.3%	31.2%	—	7.5%

2018 Year-End Financials
Return on assets: 1.0%
Return on equity: 10.1%
Long-term debt ($ mil.): —
No. of shares (mil.): 19.3
Sales ($ mil): 203.8
Dividends
  Yield: 0.7%
  Payout: 8.6%
Market value ($ mil.): 487.0

	STOCK PRICE ($) FY Close	P/E High/Low	PER SHARE ($) Earnings	Dividends	Book Value
12/18	25.18	16 10	2.31	0.20	24.25
12/17	35.02	18 14	2.03	0.20	21.68
12/16	30.88	20 10	1.60	0.20	18.79
12/15	20.62	18 14	1.29	0.20	17.16
12/14	18.56	18 14	1.22	0.20	15.99
Annual Growth	7.9%	— —	17.3%	(0.0%)	11.0%

Pebblebrook Hotel Trust

Pebblebrook Hotel Trust wants the term staycation to take a vacation. The self-managed real estate investment trust (REIT) acquires and manages upscale hotels in the US targeting mostly full-service and select-service luxury properties that don't need major renovation in major US gateway cities. The REIT owns more than 30 hotels (with 7400 rooms) across 11 states and has a 49% interest in six more hotels spanning nearly 1800 rooms through its Manhattan Collection joint venture. Nearly 70% of its revenue comes from room fees while the remainder comes from food and beverage services. Pebblebrook Hotel Trust is the brainchild of CEO Jon Bortz who also founded LaSalle Hotel Properties.

Geographic Reach
Pebblebrook Hotel Trust's properties are in major cities spread across 11 US states. Most are in California (in San Francisco Los Angeles and surrounding areas and San Diego) while most of the others are in Boston Bethesda Minneapolis Miami Nashville New York City Philadelphia Portland and Seattle.

Financial Performance
Pebblebrook's revenues and profits have skyrocketed over the past several years as it has expanded its property portfolio through acquisitions and has charged higher room rates as the economy has strengthened.

The REIT's revenue jumped 22% to $598.8 billion in 2014 mostly thanks to $81 million in new room revenue from its recently acquired properties. Its comparable property revenues added an additional $28.6 million in growth to its top-line thanks to strong performance in its West Coast properties from increases in ADR (average daily rate) and an increase in revenue from its Hotel Zetta (which had been closed in 2012 and part of 2013).

Higher revenue and higher equity earnings on its joint venture properties drove Pebblebrook's net income higher by 70% to $72.9 million. The REIT's operating cash levels rose by 50% to $161.3 million thanks to higher cash earnings.

Strategy
Pebblebrook Hotel Trust has been actively building up its hotel portfolio as the lodging industry has strengthened with the overall economy. The REIT targets hotel property investments in "major gateway urban markets" with high barriers-to-entry and "diverse sources of meeting and room night demand generators." It also sometimes targets investment opportunities in upscale resort destinations in south Florida and southern California. In addition Pebblebrook regularly renovates its properties to add value and be able to charge more revenue per room.

During 2014 the REIT spent $626.8 million to acquire six properties in target markets including: the Prescott Hotel in San Francisco; The Nines a Luxury Collection Hotel in Portland; The Westin Colonnade Coral Gables in Miami; the Revere Hotel Boston Common; and leasehold interests in both the Hotel Palomar Los Angeles-Westwood in Los Angeles and the Union Station Hotel Autograph Collection in Nashville.

Company Background
Pebblebrook had its initial public offering (IPO) in December 2009 raising more than $350 million. The REIT used the proceeds from the offering to buy properties to grow its portfolio which then consisted of around 10 hotels.

EXECUTIVES
Chairman President and CEO, Jon E. Bortz, age 62, $300,000 total compensation
EVP CFO Treasurer and Secretary, Raymond D. Martz, age 48, $250,000 total compensation
EVP and Chief Investment Officer, Thomas C. Fisher, $243,151 total compensation
Vice President Asset Management, Steve Coe
Vice President Asset Management, Wendy Heineke
Vice President Investments, Max Leinweber
Auditors: KPMG LLP

LOCATIONS
HQ: Pebblebrook Hotel Trust
4747 Bethesda Avenue 1100, Bethesda, MD 20814
Phone: 240 507-1300
Web: www.pebblebrookhotels.com

PRODUCTS/OPERATIONS

2014 Sales

	$ mil.	% of total
Rooms	410.6	68
Food & beverage	148.1	25
Other	40.1	7
Total	598.8	100

Selected Properties
Argonaut Hotel (San Francisco)
DoubleTree by Hilton Bethesda- Washington DC
The Grand Hotel (Minneapolis)
InterContinental Buckhead Hotel (Atlanta)
Monaco Washington DC
Sheraton Delfina (Philadelphia)
Sir Francis Drake (San Francisco)
Skamania Lodge and Conference Center (Stevenson WA)

COMPETITORS
Ashford Hospitality Trust
Chesapeake Lodging
Condor Hospitality
DiamondRock Hospitality
FelCor
HMG/Courtland Properties
Hersha Hospitality
Hospitality Properties Trust
Host Hotels & Resorts
Innkeepers USA
MHI Hospitality
Strategic Hotels

HISTORICAL FINANCIALS
Company Type: Public

Income Statement   FYE: December 31

	REVENUE ($ mil.)	NET INCOME ($ mil.)	NET PROFIT MARGIN	EMPLOYEES
12/18	828.6	13.3	1.6%	50
12/17	769.3	99.8	13.0%	28
12/16	816.4	73.7	9.0%	26
12/15	770.8	94.6	12.3%	27
12/14	598.7	72.8	12.2%	27
Annual Growth	8.5%	(34.5%)	—	16.7%

2018 Year-End Financials
Debt ratio: 39.3%
Return on equity: 0.5%
Cash ($ mil.): 83.3
Current ratio: 0.36
Long-term debt ($ mil.): 2,746.9
No. of shares (mil.): 130.3
Dividends
  Yield: 5.3%
  Payout: —
Market value ($ mil.): 3,689.0

	STOCK PRICE ($) FY Close	P/E High/Low	PER SHARE ($) Earnings	Dividends	Book Value
12/18	28.31	— —	(0.06)	1.52	28.85
12/17	37.17	32 23	1.19	1.52	21.78
12/16	29.75	48 34	0.64	1.52	22.33
12/15	28.02	53 29	0.95	1.24	24.51
12/14	45.63	65 41	0.71	0.92	24.89
Annual Growth	(11.2%)	— —	—	13.4%	3.8%

Pegasystems Inc

Pegasystems helps companies fly through business changes without being reined in by their old processes. The company provides a range of enterprise software applications that include customer relationship management business process management business rules management systems and more. The company's Pega Platform serves as the base for its software development and is licensed to customers for their development needs. Pegasystems targets companies in the financial services insurance and health care industries. Established in 1983 Pegasystems also offers cloud-based systems software maintenance consulting and training. International customers account for about 45% of the company's revenue.

Operations
Pegasystems offers a range of software and services with the goal of helping its customers serve their customers better. The foundation is the Pega Platform on which the company builds its applications. It also licenses the platform to customers who want to develop their own applications. The platform uses process models predictive analytics

user experience designs decision logic and other tools to build applications.

Software licenses account for about 35% of revenue. Term licenses (recurring) account for 51% of license revenue while perpetual licenses account for the rest. Other revenue comes from maintenance and consulting and training services which account for about 30% each and cloud sales which supply about 5% of revenue.

Geographic Reach
Pegasystems is headquartered in Cambridge Massachusetts and has about 10 other offices across the US. The company also had locations around the world. The US accounts for more than 55% of sales; Europe including the UK makes up more than 25%; and the Asia/Pacific region brings in more than 10%.

Sales and Marketing
Pegasystems sells through its direct sales force as well as through distributors resellers and trade shows (including the PegaWorld user conference). Its target market is the Global 3000 and the company claims customers among the largest healthcare and insurance companies well as the biggest banks and communications service providers. It also has US government agencies on its client roster. Customers include JP Morgan Chase Aeon Anthem Talk Talk Sanofi Intel and Coca-Cola.

Pegasystems also teams up with major IT services and software providers to extend its reach. Its strategic partners include Accenture Capgemini Cognizant Infosys Mahindra Tata Consultancy Services Virtusa Atos Ernst & Young and Wipro.

Financial Performance
Pegasystems continued its decade of increasing revenue in 2017 when it posted about $840 million in sales a 12% rise from 2016. The company reported higher revenue from term licenses which grew 11% in 2017 from 2016. At the same time perpetual license revenue decreased 4%. Services revenue rose 23% on increases in consulting and training and cloud. Maintenance revenue was up 11%. Strong growth in Europe (up 41%) and the Asia/Pacific region (up 57%) added more money to the top line than did 11% growth in the US. Sales declined in the Americas outside the US and in the UK.

Net income rose 22% to about $33 million in 2017 from 2016. While Pegasystems spent more money on sales and marketing and research and development the percentages were the same year-to-year.

Cash from operations jumped to $158 million in 2017 from about $40 million in 2016 from net income and trade accounts receivable which were boosted by increased cash collections and the timing of billings.

Strategy
Pegasystems' strategy of gaining entree to a customer by selling one product or service and then selling more and more is well founded. The company's array of CRM BPM and other types of software gives it a well-stocked warehouse from which to draw.

Along with just about every other software company Pegasystems is shifting to the business model of selling subscriptions to its products and services as well as running software in the cloud. Each year recurring revenue accounts for a larger portion of the total. It rose to 51% in 2017 from 47% in 2016 and 40% in 2015.

Pegasystems has hired more sales people in recent years to deepen relationships with existing accounts and expand into new industries and geographical areas.

Mergers and Acquisitions
In 2019 Pegasystems acquired In The Chat a digital customer service platform provider that unifies text messaging social media live chat email messengers and chatbots. Pegasystems intends to integrate the capability into its customer engagement tools.

In 2016 Pegasystems acquired OpenSpan a privately held software provider of robotic process automation and workforce analytics software for about $50 million. Following the acquisition the company unified the Pega Robotic Automation with its Pega Platform for Case and Business Process Management and its CRM portfolio.

EXECUTIVES

SVP Human Resources, Jeff Yanagi
Chairman and CEO, Alan Trefler, age 63, $456,000 total compensation
SVP Engineering and Product Development, Michael R. (Mike) Pyle, age 64, $348,000 total compensation
SVP Global Customer Success, Douglas I. (Doug) Kra, age 56, $343,000 total compensation
SVP Corporate Development, Max Mayer, $255,000 total compensation
SVP Products, Kerim Akgonul
CFO and Chief Administrative Officer, Ken Stillwell
SVP and Chief Marketing Officer, Tom Libretto
Vice President Marketing, Dave Donelan
Vp Sales Communications Media And Consumer Services North America, Pat Dwyer
Vp Product Pega Marketing, Shoel Perelman
Area Vice President Sales, Jim Alcina
Vice President Global Sales Operations, Jeff Farley
Chief People Officer, Adriana Bokel Herde
Vice President Australia And New Zealand, Michael Evans
Auditors: DELOITTE & TOUCHE LLP

LOCATIONS

HQ: Pegasystems Inc
One Rogers Street, Cambridge, MA 02142-1209
Phone: 617 374-9600
Web: www.pega.com

PRODUCTS/OPERATIONS

2017 Sales

	$ mil.	% of total
Software licenses	288.3	34
Maintenance	244.3	29
Services	307.9	37
Total	**840.6**	**100**

Selected Software
PegaCloud
PegaCRM
Pega Decision Management
PegaRULES Process Commander
Solutions Frameworks

COMPETITORS

Appian	SAP
EMC	Software AG
Fair Isaac	SunGard
Guidewire Software	TIBCO Software
IBM	TriZetto
Microsoft Dynamics	Trintech
Oracle	salesforce.com
Progress Software	

HISTORICAL FINANCIALS
Company Type: Public

Income Statement
FYE: December 31

	REVENUE ($ mil.)	NET INCOME ($ mil.)	NET PROFIT MARGIN	EMPLOYEES
12/18	891.5	10.6	1.2%	4,650
12/17	840.5	32.9	3.9%	4,237
12/16	750.2	26.9	3.6%	3,908
12/15	682.7	36.3	5.3%	3,333
12/14	590.0	33.2	5.6%	2,970
Annual Growth	10.9%	(24.8%)	—	11.9%

2018 Year-End Financials
Debt ratio: —   No. of shares (mil.): 78.5
Return on equity: 2.1%   Dividends
Cash ($ mil.): 114.4   Yield: 0.2%
Current ratio: 1.84   Payout: 92.3%
Long-term debt ($ mil.): —   Market value ($ mil.): 3,756.0

	STOCK PRICE ($) FY Close	P/E High/Low	PER SHARE ($) Earnings	Dividends	Book Value
12/18	47.83	469 315	0.13	0.12	7.91
12/17	47.15	148 83	0.40	0.12	4.75
12/16	36.00	105 59	0.34	0.12	4.39
12/15	27.50	64 41	0.46	0.12	4.22
12/14	20.77	112 36	0.42	0.11	3.86
Annual Growth	23.2%	—	(25.4%)	3.4%	19.7%

Pendrell Corp

EXECUTIVES

EVP Chief Strategy Officer and Director, R. Gerard (Gerry) Salemme, age 62
Chairman President and CEO, Benjamin G. (Ben) Wolff, age 47
Vice President and Corporate Counsel, Timothy M. Dozois, age 54
Vice President for Investor Relations and Public Relations for Pendrell formerly ICO Global Communications, Christopher Doherty
Vice President General Counsel Corporate Secretary, Robert Jaffe
Vice President Chief Financial Officer, Tom Neary
Vice President Chief Scientist, Robert G. Mechaley
Vice President Chief People Officer, Mark Fanning
Vice President Licensing for Pendrell Technologies, Mario Obeidat
Chief IP Officer, Joseph Siino
Director, Craig O. McCaw, age 66
Director, H. Brian Thompson, age 76
Director, Richard P. (Rick) Fox, age 69
Director, Nicolas Kauser, age 76
Director, Barry L. Rowan, age 58
Director, Stuart M. Sloan, age 72
EVP Chief Strategy Officer and Director, R. Gerard (Gerry) Salemme, age 62
Director, Richard P. Emerson, age 59
Auditors: Grant Thornton LLP

LOCATIONS

HQ: Pendrell Corp
2300 Carillon Point, Kirkland, WA 98033
Phone: 425 278-7100
Web: www.pendrell.com

COMPETITORS

ARM Holdings	MoSys
Acacia Research	Quarterhill
Aware Inc.	RPX
Bain & Company	Rambus
Boston Consulting	Rovi
MOSAID Technologies	

HISTORICAL FINANCIALS
Company Type: Public

Income Statement — FYE: December 31

	REVENUE ($ mil.)	NET INCOME ($ mil.)	NET PROFIT MARGIN	EMPLOYEES
12/17	42.7	19.0	44.6%	12
12/16	59.0	17.7	30.1%	14
12/15	43.5	(109.6)	—	16
12/14	42.5	(51.0)	—	57
12/13	13.1	(55.0)	—	73
Annual Growth	34.4%	—	—	(36.3%)

2017 Year-End Financials

Debt ratio: —
Return on equity: 9.3%
Cash ($ mil.): 184.4
Current ratio: 22.73
Long-term debt ($ mil.): —
No. of shares (mil.): 0.0
Dividends
Yield: 68.1%
Payout: 16.6%
Market value ($ mil.): 1.0

	STOCK PRICE ($) FY Close	P/E High/Low	PER SHARE ($) Earnings	Dividends	Book Value
12/17	575.00	0	018,555.00	3,080.00	211,964.04
12/16	6.75	0	016,000.00	0.00	187,848.83
12/15	0.50	—	(102,500.00)	0.00	168,270.00
12/14	1.38	—	(47,500.00)	0.00	266,679.79
12/13	2.01	—	(52,500.00)	0.00	304,855.32
Annual Growth	311.3%	—	—	—	(8.7%)

Penn Virginia Corp (New)

EXECUTIVES
Vice President, Jill T Zivley
Vice President, Katherine Ryan
Senior Vice President Operations and Engineering, Ben Mathis
Auditors: Grant Thornton LLP

LOCATIONS
HQ: Penn Virginia Corp (New)
16285 Park Ten Place, Suite 500, Houston, TX 77084
Phone: 713 722-6500
Web: www.pennvirginia.com

PRODUCTS/OPERATIONS

2014 Sales

	% of total
crude oil	66
Natural gas liquid	5
Natural gas	9
Gain on sale of property	19
other	1
Total	**100**

COMPETITORS

Belden & Blake	Goodrich Petroleum
Cabot Oil & Gas	Matador Resources
Chesapeake Energy	PDC Energy
EQT Corporation	Petrohawk Energy
Energy & Exploration Partners Inc.	Pioneer Natural Resources
Energy Corporation of America	PrimeEnergy
	Range Resources
Freeport-McMoRan Oil & Gas LLC	SM Energy
	Southwestern Energy
Golden Eagle International	

HISTORICAL FINANCIALS
Company Type: Public

Income Statement — FYE: December 31

	REVENUE ($ mil.)	NET INCOME ($ mil.)	NET PROFIT MARGIN	EMPLOYEES
12/18	440.8	224.7	51.0%	95
12/17	160.0	32.6	20.4%	80
12/16*	39.0	(5.3)	—	59
09/16	94.3	1,054.6	1118.2%	0
12/15	305.3	(1,582.9)	—	112
Annual Growth	9.6%	—	—	(4.0%)

*Fiscal year change

2018 Year-End Financials

Debt ratio: 47.8%
Return on equity: 67.2%
Cash ($ mil.): 17.8
Current ratio: 1.21
Long-term debt ($ mil.): 511.3
No. of shares (mil.): 15.0
Dividends
Yield: —
Payout: —
Market value ($ mil.): 815.0

	STOCK PRICE ($) FY Close	P/E High/Low	PER SHARE ($) Earnings	Dividends	Book Value
12/18	54.06	6 2	14.70	0.00	29.66
12/17	39.11	27 15	2.17	0.00	14.76
12/16*	49.00	— —	(0.35)	0.00	12.38
Annual Growth	5.0%	—	—	—	54.8%

*Fiscal year change

PennyMac Financial Services Inc (New)

If you're thinking residential mortgage this company has more than a penny for your thoughts. The parent of investment management loan services and investment trust companies PennyMac Financial Services (PennyMac) focuses on the US residential mortgage market offering loans and investment management services. Through its Private National Mortgage Acceptance Company the company's PennyMac Loan Services (PLS) originates home loans in 45 states and DC and services loans in 49 states DC and the US Virgin Islands. PLS's counterpart PNMAC Capital Management acts as investment manager and advisor. The companies service and advise PennyMac Mortgage Investment Trust (PMT). PennyMac went public in 2013.

IPO

PennyMac hoped to raise $287.5 million in its IPO but investors responded with $199.9 million. The company plans to use the proceeds to fund growth of its mortgage business through Private National Mortgage Acceptance Company. It will also use the funds for general corporate purposes.

Operations

PennyMac's mortgage banking segment includes correspondent lending retail lending and loan servicing. The correspondent line includes conventional residential mortgages acquired by PMT as well as those guaranteed by FreddieMac FannieMae and other government agencies. The company has more than 140 approved sellers; in 2012 it had $13 billion in conventional loans and $8.4 billion in government-insured loans. Retail lending originates new prime residential conventional and government-backed mortgage loans for purchasing or refinancing homes. PennyMac uses the Internet and a call center rather than traditional branch locations for direct-to-consumer approach. The company's loan servicing business includes the back office work of loan administration collection and default activities. It serves PennyMac subsidiaries and other mortgage companies. The unit handles prime credit and distress loans under the prime servicing and special servicing headings respectively.

PennyMac's investment management segment operates as an investment manager through PNMAC Capital Management (PCM). PCM handles the $1.8 billion in combined assets from PMT and PennyMac's other investment funds. PMT is a publicly traded real estate investment trust (REIT).

Geographic Reach

While PennyMac serves nearly the entire US its portfolio is heavily weighted toward California (38%) Florida (5%) and Colorado (5%).

Financial Performance

The company's revenue has increased on the strength of gains in both the loan servicing and management segments. Other operating metrics include net assets under management total mortgage loans serviced and total mortgage loan production; all have increased in the last three years. PennyMac reported lower net income for 2012 due to amortization and impairment charges and higher spending on compensation. It sold and repurchased loans loans and earned interest on investments to more than double its cash flow for the same period.

Strategy

Since PennyMac was formed during the financial crisis it hasn't had to scramble and adapt like many of its competitors. As many mortgage shoppers turn away from large banks the company believes its poised to take advantage of growth and a lack of stringent regulations imposed on banks. For growth the company intends to focus on expanding its servicing business organically and through acquisitions increasing the number of loan sellers from which it purchases loans and leveraging its servicing portfolio to increase refinance and loan servicing opportunities.

EXECUTIVES

Senior Managing Director and Chief Enterprise Operations Officer, Anne D. McCallion, age 64
President and CEO, David A. Spector, age 56, $503,370 total compensation
President PennyMac Loan Services, Douglas E. (Doug) Jones, age 62, $325,000 total compensation
Senior Managing Director and Chief Risk Officer, David M. (Dave) Walker, age 63
Senior Managing Director and Chief Mortgage Operations Officer, Steve R. Bailey, age 57
Senior Managing Director and CFO, Andrew S. Chang, age 41
Senior Managing Director and Chief Capital Markets Officer, Vandad Fartaj, age 44
Senior Managing Director and Chief Administrative and Legal Officer, Jeffrey P. Grogin, age 58
Senior Managing Director and Deputy CFO, Daniel S. Perotti, age 38
Chairman and CEO PennyMac Financial Services Inc. and Private National Mortgage Acceptance Company LLC, Stanford L. Kurland, age 66
Auditors: DELOITTE & TOUCHE LLP

LOCATIONS

HQ: PennyMac Financial Services Inc (New)
3043 Townsgate Road, Westlake Village, CA 91361
Phone: 818 224-7442
Web: www.pennymacusa.com

COMPETITORS

Bank of America
Citigroup
JPMorgan Chase
Nationstar Mortgage
Ocwen Financial
Quicken Loans
Stonegate Mortgage
U.S. Bancorp
Wells Fargo

HISTORICAL FINANCIALS

Company Type: Public

Income Statement — FYE: December 31

	ASSETS ($ mil.)	NET INCOME ($ mil.)	INCOME AS % OF ASSETS	EMPLOYEES
12/18	7,478.5	87.6	1.2%	3,460
12/17	7,368.0	100.7	1.4%	3,189
12/16	5,133.9	66.0	1.3%	3,038
12/15	3,505.2	47.2	1.3%	2,509
12/14	2,507.1	36.8	1.5%	1,816
Annual Growth	31.4%	24.2%	—	17.5%

2018 Year-End Financials
Return on assets: 1.1%
Return on equity: 8.2%
Long-term debt ($ mil.): —
No. of shares (mil.): 77.4
Sales ($ mil): 1,129.2
Dividends
  Yield: 0.0%
  Payout: 15.4%
Market value ($ mil.): 1,648.0

	STOCK PRICE ($) FY Close	P/E High/Low		PER SHARE ($) Earnings	Dividends	Book Value
12/18	21.26	9	7	2.59	0.40	21.34
12/17	22.35	5	4	4.03	0.00	19.95
12/16	16.65	6	4	2.94	0.00	15.49
12/15	15.36	9	7	2.17	0.00	12.32
12/14	17.30	11	8	1.73	0.00	9.92
Annual Growth	5.3%	—	—	10.6%	—	21.1%

Penumbra Inc

Auditors: Deloitte & Touche LLP

LOCATIONS

HQ: Penumbra Inc
One Penumbra Place, Alameda, CA 94502
Phone: 510 748-3200
Web: www.penumbrainc.com

HISTORICAL FINANCIALS

Company Type: Public

Income Statement — FYE: December 31

	REVENUE ($ mil.)	NET INCOME ($ mil.)	NET PROFIT MARGIN	EMPLOYEES
12/18	444.9	6.6	1.5%	2,200
12/17	333.7	4.6	1.4%	1,700
12/16	263.3	14.8	5.6%	1,500
12/15	186.1	2.3	1.3%	1,100
12/14	125.5	2.2	1.8%	1,000
Annual Growth	37.2%	30.9%	—	21.8%

2018 Year-End Financials
Debt ratio: —
Return on equity: 1.6%
Cash ($ mil.): 67.8
Current ratio: 6.22
Long-term debt ($ mil.): —
No. of shares (mil.): 34.4
Dividends
  Yield: —
  Payout: —
Market value ($ mil.): 4,208.0

	STOCK PRICE ($) FY Close	P/E High/Low	PER SHARE ($) Earnings	Dividends	Book Value
12/18	122.20	87 3445	0.18	0.00	12.26
12/17	94.10	82 8458	0.13	0.00	11.89
12/16	63.80	162 86	0.44	0.00	8.57
12/15	53.81	61 8406	0.08	0.00	7.78
Annual Growth	31.4%	— —	31.0%	—	16.4%

People's United Financial Inc

People's United Financial is the holding company for People's United Bank (formerly People's Bank) which boasts more than 400 traditional branches supermarket branches commercial banking offices investment and brokerage offices and equipment leasing offices across New England and eastern New York. In addition to retail and commercial banking services the bank offers trust wealth management brokerage and insurance services. Its lending activities consist mainly of commercial mortgages (more than a third of its loan portfolio) commercial and industrial loans (more than a quarter) residential mortgages equipment financing and home equity loans. Founded in 1842 the bank has $36 billion in assets.

Operations
People's United operates two core business segments Retail Banking and Commercial Banking which both share duties of the bank's now-defunct Wealth Management division. The bank also has a non-core Treasury division that manages the company's securities portfolio and other investments.

Commercial Banking which makes up more than half of the company's total revenue provides business loans equipment financing (through People's Capital and Leasing Corp. or PCLC and People's United Equipment Finance Corp or PUEFC) and municipal banking as well as trust services for corporations and institutions and private banking services for wealthy individuals.

Retail Banking which makes up around 20% of total revenues provides deposit services residential mortgages and home equity loans financial advisory and investment management services as well as life insurance through People's United Insurance Agency.

Overall the bank generated 68% of its total revenue from loan interest in 2014 and 7% from interest on securities. About 10% of total revenues came from bank service charges while investment management fees commercial banking lending fees insurance revenue and brokerage commissions each made up less than 3% of overall revenue for the year.

Geographic Reach
People's United has more than 400 branches across Connecticut southeastern New York Massachusetts Vermont New Hampshire and Maine. Connecticut is its largest lending market with 27% of the bank's loan portfolio being extended to consumers and businesses in the region in 2014. New York and Massachusetts are the bank's next largest markets with a 19% and 18% share of its loan portfolio.

Sales and Marketing
The bank sells its products and services through investment and brokerage offices commercial branches online banking and investment trading and through its 24-hour telephone banking service. The company's PCLC and PUEFC affiliates have a sales presence in 16 states to support equipment financing operations throughout the US.

People's United spent $13 million on advertising in 2014 compared to $15.4 million and $17.7 million in 2013 and 2012 respectively.

Strategy
People's United emphasizes cross-selling financial products by developing client relationships and has increasingly tied employee compensation to this ability. The company is particularly focused on building its small business lending wealth management and insurance business. It also continues to open new branches and seeks acquisition targets for further growth.

One other key element of its strategy involves boosting its deposit assets through its expanded convenient store reach. In early 2015 the company boasted nearly 150 full-service branches in Stop & Shop supermarkets across Connecticut and southeastern New York which comprised 36% of the bank's total branch network and held 14% of its total deposits. Much of this is attributed to a key acquisition in 2012 when the company purchased nearly 60 branches (many within Stop & Shop supermarkets) in the New York metro area from RBS Citizens. People's United already had more than 80 Stop & Shop branches in Connecticut so the deal strengthened its relationship with the retailer and expanded its presence in the New York market.

Mergers and Acquisitions
In 2019 People's United Financial acquired BSB Bancorp the holding company for Belmont Savings

Bank for about $330 million. Belmont Massachusetts-headquartered Bemont Savings Bank holds about $3 billion in assets and has six branches in the Greater Boston area. The acquisition deepens People's United's presence in the area. That year the company also agreed to buy United Financial Bancorp in a transaction valued at around $760 million. United Financial is the holding company for United Bank a Hartford-based community bank with $7.3 billion in assets and roughly 60 branches in central Connecticut and western Massachusetts.

People's United acquired independent leasing and finance company VAR Technology Finance in early 2019. VAR uses its software platform to finance commercial and public sector customers of large technology manufacturers. The company will maintain its brand but become a division of People's United's LEAF Commercial Capital subsidiary. VAR originated $180 million in loans in 2018.

In 2018 People's United agreed to acquire First Connecticut Bancorp in an all-stock transaction valued at $544 million. The acquisition will further enhance People's United's established presence in the northeastern US. First Connecticut Bancorp is the holding company of Farmington Bank which operates nearly 30 community bank locations across Connecticut and in western Massachusetts.

Company Background

One of the main goals of People's United has been to build its presence in the two largest metropolitan areas in its market New York City and Boston. One of the largest in the Boston area Danvers Bancorp added some 30 branches and carried a price tag of approximately $493 million. People's United also acquired LSB Corporation and Butler Bank the latter in an FDIC-assisted transaction that included a loss-sharing agreement with the regulator covering all acquired loans and foreclosed real estate of the failed bank bringing in another 10 branches in the Boston area. In 2010 People's United bought Bank of Smithtown which had about 30 branches primarily on Long Island in New York.

People's United Financial acquired commercial lender Financial Federal Corporation in 2010 (now People's United Equipment Finance) which provides financing and leasing to small and midsized business nationwide.

People's United Financial underwent significant transformation in past years. The company demutualized and converted to a stock holding company in 2007 and early the following year acquired multibank holding company Chittenden Corporation. The deal added some 140 branches doubling People's United Bank's branch network and expanding its reach beyond Connecticut and New York and into the rest of New England.

EXECUTIVES

Vp Marketing, Cindy Belak
President and CEO, John P. (Jack) Barnes, age 63, $890,384 total compensation
SEVP Corporate Development and Strategic Planning, Kirk W. Walters, age 64, $468,461 total compensation
SVP and President Merrill Bank, William P. (Bill) Lucy, age 60
Chief Financial Officer, R. David Rosato, age 57
EVP Marketing and Regional Banking People's United Bank, Robert R. (Bob) D'Amore, age 66, $429,323 total compensation
President Vermont, Michael L. Seaver
SEVP Wealth Management, Louise T. Sandberg, age 67
President Massachusetts, Timothy P. Crimmins
Market Leader New York, Sara M. Longobardi
President Northern Connecticut, Michael J. Casparino
SEVP Human Resources, David K. Norton, age 64, $411,231 total compensation
SEVP Commercial Banking, Jeffrey J. (Jeff) Tengel, age 56, $408,654 total compensation
SVP and Division President People's United Bank Southern Connecticut, Armando F. Goncalves
SEVP and General Counsel, Robert E. Trautmann, age 65
SEVP and Chief Administrative Officer, Lee C. Powlus
SVP; President Ocean Bank Division, Dianne M. Mercier
President Southern Maine, Daniel P. (Dan) Thornton
Vice President Information Technology, Carol Anderson
Vice President Information Technology, Roy Allison
Vice President, Kon Khongkham
Vice President Information Technology, Albert Sanna
Vice President Financial Services Manager, Cheryl Nickerson
Vice President Sales Aviation Finance, Jim Pulie
Vice President Of Sales, Jeffrey Morrison
Vice President Market Research, Craig Noble
First Vice President Wealth Management, John Lescure
Senior Vice President Human Resources, Michelle McNeil
Senior Vice President and Market Development Officer, Brian Shea
Vice President, Peter Martinez
Vp Call Center, David Weber
Divisional Vice President, Peter Brestovan
Assistant Vice President, Patrick Talcott
Vice President Capital Markets, Russ Hardy
Svp, Doug Smith
Vice President Customer Experience Manager, Thomas Griesing
Vice President Commercial Relationship Manager, Kasi White
Vice President Director of Tax, Kathleen Jones
Vp Operations Manager Commercial Services, Keara Piscitelli
Market Manager Assistant Vice President, Alice Baird
Vice President Commercial Lending, Edgar Auchincloss
Senior Vice President And Director Marketing, Kathleen Schirling
Vice President Customer Service Manager, Joan Foster
Senior Vice President, Robert Maquat
Vice President, Daniel Reilly
Vice President Market Manager, David Conner
Vice President, Elaine Khu
Vice President, Patrick Lorent
Vice President Business Banking Portfolio Management, Louis Paffumi
Assistant Vice President Customer Service, Ana Saraiva
Assistant Vice President, Kasey Franzoni
Senior Vice President, Kathleen Lepak
Vice President Financial Analyst, Rita Rivers
Vice President Finance, Brian Connery
Vice President Purchasing, Theresa Knies
Assistant Vice President, David Schalk
Financial Services Mananger Assistant Vice President, Amy Pasquarelli
Assistant Vice President, Francine Grandmaison
Executive Vice President And Market Mana, John Bundschuh
Vice President, Kurtis Denison
Vice President, Bethany Dubuque
Vice President, Lisa Rollins
Senior Vice President, Jody Cole
Vice President Market Manager, David Cavanaugh
Senior Vice President Commercial Lending, Tom Wolcott
Vice President, Michael Ciborowski
Relationship Manager Vice President, Steven Wurtz
Vice President, Rose Morgan
Senior Vice President And Enterprise Security Officer, Jane Stowell
Senior Vice President Senior Commercial Real Estate Lender, Suzanne Wakeen
Vice President Commercial Lending, Debbie Boyle
Vice President Financial Services Manager, Jennifer Lynch
Vice President, Joanne Murgalo
Senior Vice President, Marilyn Hardacre
Vice President, Sheila Moran
Region Manager Senior Vice President Commercial Real Estate Finance, Kathleen Hayes
Senior Lender Vice President, Peter Lange
Svp And Regional Manager Wealth Management, Sylvia Mackinnon
Vice President, Darrin Fodor
Vice President, James Bucko
Assistant Vice President Financial Services Manager, Angela Gallagher
Vice President, Timothy B Hodges
Vice President, Michael Rispoli
Senior Vice President, Mark Leonardi
Vice President Commercial Banking, Deborah Quirk
Senior Vice President Relationship Manager, Vincent Bergin
Executive Vice President Mid Corporate, Dexter Freeman
Financial Services Manager Assistant Vice President, Cheryl Hagmann
Financial Services Manager Assistant Vice President, Alex Slootskiy
Assistant Vice President Financial Services Manager, Robert Duffus
Commercial Portfolio Manager Assistant Vice President, James Davenport
Vice President Customer Service Manager, Scott Zimmerman
Fixed Income Strategist Senior Vice President, Karissa McDonough
Assistant Vice President Branch Manager, Kristen Lavallee
Vice President Financial Services Manager, Kristen Keil
Market Manager Vice President, Renee Goupille
Financial Services Manager Assistant Vice President, Cathy Ferreira-Golino
Assistant Vice President Customer Service Manager, Sylvana Chiluisa
Senior Vice President Senior Portfolio Manager, James Witterschein
Vice President Model Validation And Risk Management, Julien Lee
Vice President Financial Services Manager, Joseph Perun
Vice President Senior Market Manager, Christina Veziris
ASSISTANT VICE PRESIDENT MORTGAGE ACCOUNT OFFICER, Richard Klein
Executive Vice President Chief Credit Officer, David Barey
Team Leader Vice President Senior Commercial Review Appraiser, Michelle Gamache
Vice President Comm Lending, Frank Cory

V P Sales, Roger Allcorn
Senior Vice President And Senior Relationship Manager, Ellery Perkinson
Senior Vice President, Patrick Lee
Vice President, Brian Boyaji
Assistant Vice President Customer Service Manager, Krupali Doshi
Vice President Sales and Leasing, Rick Curtiss
Vice President, Tom Emery
Assistant Vice President, Ana Espinal
Vice President, Michael Mancuso
Assistant Vice President, Miriam James
Regional Vice President, Gary Fisher
Vice President and Sr.Market Manager Bridgeport Market, Virgilio Lopez
Senior Vice President Senior Relationship Manager New York CRE, Ted Dalton
VICE PRESIDENT, Justin Jennings
Vice President Corporate Communications, Steven Bodakowski
Senior Vice President Head of Wealth Strategy Product and Marketing, Daniel Darst
Vice President Wealth Management Marketing, Sara Sparks
First Vice President Digital Marketing, James Roy
Vice President Wealth Management Marketing Bank Brand and Advertising, Christine Stafstrom
Senior Market Manager Vice President, Raymond DiPresso
Avp Bank Manager, Flawer Bardales
Assistant Vice President Customer Service Manager, Danielle Lutz
Vice President, Elizabeth Dougherty
Vice President, Justin Mills
VICE PRESIDENT, Kenneth Vaccaro
VICE PRESIDENT CUSTOMER SERVICE MANAGER, Lacey Bicknell
First Vice President, Maria Kastanis
Vice President Information Technology, Michael Kirven
Senior Vice President, Mark Danie
Vice President Treasury Management Sales Officer, Elaine Canton
Senior Vice President Commercial Banking, David Estes
Vice President Market Manager, Benish Shah
Senior Vice President, Phil Cohen
Vice President Customer Service Manager, Silveras Sboui
Business Banker Vice President, Colin Branon
Assistant Vice President Bank Manager, Andrew Matarese
Senior Vice President, Mary McLemore
Senior Portfolio Manager Senior Vice President, Richard Casselman
Senior Vice President Healthcare Financial Services, Walter Unangst
Vice President, Douglas Olsen
Senior Vice President Senior Private Banker, Al Falco
Vice President Senior Private Banker, Sarah Haley
Vice President, Theodore Horan
Assistant Vice President, Rosalind Rubin
N.a. Vice President, Kimberly Alty
Vice President Senior Market Manager, Dean Debiase
Associate Vice President Documentation, Raquel Harduby
Vice President T Community Development and Clinical Research Associate Officer New York, Elizabeth Custodio
Senior Vice President Regional Manager Massachusetts, Veronica Ctfa
Vice President, Kevin Dougherty
Vice President Business Banking, Michael Tardella
Vice President Financial Services Manager, Jeanie Szostek
Vice President, Timothy Mcmachen
Senior Vice President, Patricia Camelio
Senior Vice President Commercial Relationship Manager, Michael Lavoie
Vice President Private Banking Administration, Katharine Bosley
Vice President Commercial Lending, Matthew Harrison
First Vice President Senior Credit Officer, David Sherrill
Senior Vice President, Jeff Warminsky
Assistant Vice President Mortgage Account Officer, Darren Ginas
Vice President, John Bernhardt
Senior Vice President Region Manager, Joseph Paoletta
Senior Vice President Relationship Manager, Kevin Kelly
Assitant Vice President Branch Manager, Sue Racicot
Vice President Employee Benefits Division, Adam Zebian
Vice President, Robert C Bursey
Senior Vice President, Katherine Jenkins
Senior Vice President, Robert Smedley
Svp, Adam Seiden
Senior Vice President, Jared Morris
Senior Vice President Treasury Management Services, Jacqueline Brown
Financial Services Manager Vice President, Sandra Allyn-gauthier
Senior Vice President, Greenfield Laura
SENIOR VICE PRESIDENT, Jim Riley
SENIOR VICE PRESIDENT, Michael Cox
Vice President, Betsey Mustaka
Vice President, Gabrielle Corsetti
Senior Vice President Chief Appraiser, Phil Foundos
Vice President Loan Resolution, Craig Lougee
Assistant Vice President Financial Services Manager, Richard Fry
Senior Vice President Commercial Real Estate Finance, Kim Phelps
Vice President, Cynthia D'andrea-neely
Assistant Vice President Mortgage Account Officer, Helen Lambropoulos
Vice President Market Manager, Angela Reese
Chairman, George P. Carter, age 82
Secretary, Patricia Chonko
Auditors: KPMG LLP

LOCATIONS

HQ: People's United Financial Inc
850 Main Street, Bridgeport, CT 06604
Phone: 203 338-7171   **Fax:** 203 338-2545
Web: www.peoples.com

PRODUCTS/OPERATIONS

2014 Sales

	$ mil.	% of total
Interest & dividends		
Loans		
Commercial real estate	354.2	26
Commercial	351.0	26
Residential mortgage	153.5	12
Consumer	73.9	5
Securities	96.8	7
Other	1.2	—
Noninterest		
Bank service charges	128.6	10
Investment management fees	41.6	3
Operating lease income	41.6	3
Commercial banking lending fees	33.4	2
Insurance revenue	29.9	2
Other	76.6	4
Adjustment	(0.9)	—
Total	**1,381.4**	**100**

COMPETITORS

Bank of America
Citibank
Citizens Financial Group
Fairfield County Bank
KeyCorp
Liberty Bank
Sovereign Bank
TD Bank USA
Webster Financial

HISTORICAL FINANCIALS

Company Type: Public

Income Statement
FYE: December 31

	ASSETS ($ mil.)	NET INCOME ($ mil.)	INCOME AS % OF ASSETS	EMPLOYEES
12/18	47,877.3	468.1	1.0%	5,920
12/17	44,453.4	337.2	0.8%	5,584
12/16	40,609.8	281.0	0.7%	5,173
12/15	38,877.4	260.1	0.7%	5,139
12/14	35,997.1	251.7	0.7%	5,397
Annual Growth	7.4%	16.8%	—	2.3%

2018 Year-End Financials
Return on assets: 1.0%
Return on equity: 7.5%
Long-term debt ($ mil.): —
No. of shares (mil.): 377.3
Sales ($ mil): 1,885.4
Dividends
 Yield: 4.8%
 Payout: 54.0%
Market value ($ mil.): 5,444.0

	STOCK PRICE ($) FY Close	P/E High/Low		PER SHARE ($) Earnings	Dividends	Book Value
12/18	14.43	16	11	1.29	0.70	17.32
12/17	18.70	20	16	0.97	0.69	16.79
12/16	19.36	22	15	0.92	0.68	16.28
12/15	16.15	20	16	0.86	0.67	15.26
12/14	15.18	19	16	0.84	0.66	15.05
Annual Growth	(1.3%)	—	—	11.3%	1.5%	3.6%

People's Utah Bancorp

Auditors: Moss Adams LLP

LOCATIONS

HQ: People's Utah Bancorp
1 East Main Street, American Fork, UT 84003
Phone: 801 642-3998
Web: www.peoplesutah.com

HISTORICAL FINANCIALS

Company Type: Public

Income Statement
FYE: December 31

	ASSETS ($ mil.)	NET INCOME ($ mil.)	INCOME AS % OF ASSETS	EMPLOYEES
12/18	2,184.2	40.6	1.9%	459
12/17	2,123.5	19.8	0.9%	483
12/16	1,665.9	23.6	1.4%	430
12/15	1,555.9	19.6	1.3%	414
12/14	1,367.1	14.9	1.1%	367
Annual Growth	12.4%	28.5%	—	5.8%

2018 Year-End Financials
Return on assets: 1.8%
Return on equity: 14.8%
Long-term debt ($ mil.): —
No. of shares (mil.): 18.7
Sales ($ mil): 130.4
Dividends
 Yield: 1.3%
 Payout: 25.4%
Market value ($ mil.): 565.0

	STOCK PRICE ($) FY Close	P/E High/Low	PER SHARE ($) Earnings	Dividends	Book Value
12/18	30.15	18 13	2.14	0.41	15.49
12/17	30.30	30 22	1.08	0.34	13.91
12/16	26.85	21 11	1.30	0.22	12.82
12/15	17.21	15 13	1.17	0.18	11.92
Annual Growth	20.6%	— —	22.3%	31.6%	9.1%

Peoples Bancorp Inc (Marietta, OH)

Peoples Bancorp offers banking for the people by the people and of the people. The holding company owns Peoples Bank which has about 50 branches in rural and small urban markets in Ohio Kentucky and West Virginia. The bank offers traditional services such as checking and savings accounts CDs loans and trust services. Commercial and agricultural loans including those secured by commercial real estate account for the majority of the bank's lending activities. Its Peoples Financial Advisors division offers investment management services while Peoples Insurance sells life health and property/casualty coverage.

Operations
Credit cards and brokerage services are offered through third-party providers.

Financial Performance
The company's revenue increased from $103.7 million in fiscal 2012 up to $104.6 million for fiscal 2013. However despite the slight spike in annual revenue Peoples Bancorp's net income decreased from $29.9 million in fiscal 2012 down to $29 million for fiscal 2013.

The company's cash on hand decreased by about $1 million in fiscal 2013 compared to fiscal 2012 levels.

Strategy
Peoples Bancorp is looking to increase its revenue from service changes and other fees and commissions particularly from insurance and wealth management which are not reliant on fluctuating interest rate margins.

The company is also looking to strengthen its brand and build deeper relationships with its clients.

EXECUTIVES

EVP and Chief Administrative Officer Peoples Bancorp and EVP Chief Administrative Officer and CashierPeoples Bank N.A., Carol A. Schneeberger, age 62, $233,000 total compensation
EVP and Chief Commercial Lending Officer Peoples Bancorp and Peoples Bank N.A., Daniel K. (Dan) McGill, age 64, $250,000 total compensation
EVP and Chief Credit Officer Peoples Bancorp and Peoples Bank N.A., Timothy H. Kirtley, age 49, $221,500 total compensation
President CEO and Director Peoples Bancorp and Peoples Bank N.A., Charles W. Sulerzyski, age 61, $500,000 total compensation
EVP CFO and Treasurer Peoples Bancorp and Peoples Bank N.A., John C. Rogers, age 59, $26,136 total compensation
Vice President, Steven Nulter
Assistant Vice President Branch Market Manager, Candace Frump
Branch Market Manager Assistant Vice President, Peggy Scott-Morgan
Vice President and Controller, Jeffrey Baran
VICE PRESIDENT, Randy Barengo
Chairman Peoples Bancorp and Peoples Bank N.A., David L. Mead, age 64
Auditors: Ernst & Young LLP

LOCATIONS
HQ: Peoples Bancorp Inc (Marietta, OH)
138 Putnam Street, P.O. Box 738, Marietta, OH 45750
Phone: 740 373-3155
Web: www.peoplesbancorp.com

PRODUCTS/OPERATIONS

2016 Sales

	$ mil.	% of total
Interest Income:		
Interest and fees on loans	93.9	56
Interest and dividends on taxable investment securities	18.5	11
Interest on tax-exempt investment securities	3.2	2
Other Income:		
Insurance income	13.9	8
Deposit account service charges	10.7	6
Trust and investment income	10.5	6
Electronic banking income	10.3	6
Bank owned life insurance income	1.4	1
Mortgage banking income	1.3	1
Commercial loan swap fee income	1.0	1
Net gain on investment securities	0.9	1
Net loss on asset disposals and other transactions	(1.1)	—
Other	1.8	1
Total	**166.3**	**100**

COMPETITORS

1st West Virginia Bancorp	Huntington Bancshares
BB&T	Ohio Valley Banc
Fifth Third	U.S. Bancorp
	United Bankshares

HISTORICAL FINANCIALS
Company Type: Public

Income Statement   FYE: December 31

	ASSETS ($ mil.)	NET INCOME ($ mil.)	INCOME AS % OF ASSETS	EMPLOYEES
12/18	3,991.4	46.2	1.2%	871
12/17	3,581.6	38.4	1.1%	774
12/16	3,432.3	31.1	0.9%	782
12/15	3,258.9	10.9	0.3%	817
12/14	2,567.7	16.6	0.6%	699
Annual Growth	11.7%	29.0%	—	5.7%

2018 Year-End Financials
Return on assets: 1.2%
Return on equity: 9.4%
Long-term debt ($ mil.): —
No. of shares (mil.): 19.5
Sales ($ mil): 208.0
Dividends
Yield: 3.7%
Payout: 51.1%
Market value ($ mil.): 588.0

	STOCK PRICE ($) FY Close	P/E High/Low	PER SHARE ($) Earnings	Dividends	Book Value
12/18	30.10	16 12	2.41	1.12	26.64
12/17	32.62	16 14	2.10	0.84	25.13
12/16	32.46	19 10	1.71	0.64	23.99
12/15	18.84	42 30	0.61	0.60	22.88
12/14	25.93	20 15	1.36	0.60	22.92
Annual Growth	3.8%	— —	15.4%	16.9%	3.8%

PGT Innovations Inc

PGT helps Floridians weather their storms. The company makes and sells WinGuard and PremierVue impact-resistant doors and windows for the residential market. The energy-efficient customizable doors and windows are made of aluminum or vinyl with laminated glass and are designed to withstand hurricane-strength winds. PGT also makes Eze-Breeze porch enclosure panels and garage door screens SpectraGuard vinyl replacement windows and PGT Architectural Systems windows for high-rises. The company has two manufacturing facilities in Florida and North Carolina. PGT sells its products through some 1200 window distributors dealers and contractors in the Southeastern US Canada Central America and the Caribbean.

Operations
The company's manufacturing facility is located in North Venice Florida where it makes customized impact-resistant windows and doors.

Geographic Reach
Florida-based PGT rings up more than 95% of its sales in storm-prone areas of the US. Indeed Florida is the company's largest market representing the majority of its sales. Other markets include the southeastern Gulf Coast and coastal Mid-Atlantic regions of the US as well as the Caribbean Central America and Canada.

Sales and Marketing
The company distributes its products through multiple channels including about 1200 window distributors building supply distributors window replacement dealers and enclosure contractors. The residential new construction and home repair and remodeling end markets represented about 41% and 59% of its sales respectively during 2015.

PGT markets its products through print and web-based advertising consumer dealer and builder promotions and selling and collateral materials. It markets its products based on quality building code compliance outstanding service shorter lead times and on-time delivery utilizing its fleet of trucks and trailers.

Financial Performance
PGT has achieved unprecedented growth over the years with revenues peaking at a record-setting $390 million in 2015. The historic growth was due to a spike in the sale of impact-resistant window and door products in addition to non-impact window and door products. These product lines were helped by additional sales of WinGuard and Storefront products coupled with additional sales from a previous acquisition.

Net income surged by 44% to reach $24 million in 2015 mainly due to the steep rise in sales and profits to improvement in the housing market (both new home construction and remodels) and aggressive marketing of its WinGuard product line. Cash flow from operations has risen along with sales and profits jumping 46% during 2015.

Strategy

PGT is focused on its core market — Florida — where it's looking to gain market share through promotional activities. The company also has programs and partnerships with national accounts to increase sales. The firm is focused on growing in both the new construction and remodeling markets.

In 2015 it launched Vinyl WinGuard and EnergyVue its new line of vinyl impact-resistant and non-impact energy saving windows. The company intends for the product line to replace various existing lines of vinyl impact-resistant and energy saving windows.

PGT's prospects for growth rely in part on demand during adverse weather conditions and also on the enforcement of building codes that mandate the use of impact-resistant windows and doors. The company began to pioneer such products in the aftermath of Hurricane Andrew in 1992.

Mergers and Acquisitions

In 2016 PGT purchased WinDoor a provider of high-performance impact-resistant windows and doors for five-star resorts luxury high-rise condominiums hotels and custom residential homes. The deal increased its penetration into the commercial and high-end fenestration markets and added a line of thermally-broken products and new sliding and swing door product lines.

In September 2014 PGT acquired CGI Windows & Doors Holdings of Miami a local rival for $111 million. With $45 million in annual sales CGI will continue manufacturing and selling its own brand of storm-resistant products and operate as a subsidiary of PGT. The purchase of CGI which was the company's first major acquisition strengthens PGT's product line and should help it compete against national suppliers. CGI is expected to add to earnings in 2015.

EXECUTIVES

Chairman and CEO, Rodney (Rod) Hershberger, age 62, $476,100 total compensation
President and COO, Jeffrey T. (Jeff) Jackson, age 53, $427,268 total compensation
VP and General Counsel, Mario Ferrucci, age 55, $233,155 total compensation
SVP and CFO, Bradley (Brad) West, age 49, $219,270 total compensation
VP; General Manager Glass Operations, Martin Bracamonte
VP and General Manager PGT Custom Windows+Doors, Bob Keller
Vp Customer Care, Benji Hershberger
Vp Supply Chain And Logistics, John Bonacci
Vp Product And Management, Dean Ruark
Vp Operations Cgi, Kevin Huber
Svp Shared Services And Commercial, Ted Rock
Vp And Corporate Controller, Raoul Quijada
Senior Vice President Human Resources, Debbie L Lapinska
Vice President Of Human Resources, Rachel Evans
Auditors: KPMG LLP

LOCATIONS

HQ: PGT Innovations Inc
1070 Technology Drive, North Venice, FL 34275
Phone: 941 480-1600
Web: www.pgtinnovations.com

PRODUCTS/OPERATIONS

2013 Sales

	$ mil.	% of total
Impact window and door products	183.4	77
Other window & door products	56.9	23
Total	239.3	100

COMPETITORS

Andersen Corporation
Atrium
JELD-WEN
Keller Manufacturing
MI Windows and Doors
Nor-Dec
Pella
Quanex Building Products
Silver Line Building Products
Simonton Windows Inc.
TRACO

HISTORICAL FINANCIALS

Company Type: Public

Income Statement — FYE: December 29

	REVENUE ($ mil.)	NET INCOME ($ mil.)	NET PROFIT MARGIN	EMPLOYEES
12/18	698.4	53.9	7.7%	3,000
12/17	511.0	39.8	7.8%	2,700
12/16*	458.5	23.7	5.2%	2,600
01/16	389.8	23.5	6.0%	2,300
01/15	306.3	16.4	5.4%	1,900
Annual Growth	22.9%	34.7%	—	12.1%

*Fiscal year change

2018 Year-End Financials
Debt ratio: 42.5%
Return on equity: 19.2%
Cash ($ mil.): 52.6
Current ratio: 2.85
Long-term debt ($ mil.): 366.6
No. of shares (mil.): 58.0
Dividends
 Yield: —
 Payout: —
Market value ($ mil.): 913.0

	STOCK PRICE ($) FY Close	P/E High/Low		PER SHARE ($) Earnings	Dividends	Book Value
12/18	15.72	25	14	1.00	0.00	6.64
12/17	16.85	21	13	0.77	0.00	3.52
12/16*	11.45	25	18	0.47	0.00	2.69
01/16	11.39	33	17	0.47	0.00	2.19
01/15	9.76	35	21	0.33	0.00	1.55
Annual Growth	12.7%	—	—	31.9%	—	43.8%

*Fiscal year change

Phillips 66 Partners LP

EXECUTIVES

Board Member, Gary Adams
Board Member, David Bairrington
Auditors: Ernst & Young LLP

LOCATIONS

HQ: Phillips 66 Partners LP
2331 CityWest Blvd., Houston, TX 77042
Phone: 855 283-9237
Web: www.phillips66partners.com

COMPETITORS

Buckeye Partners
EnLink Midstream Partners
Energy Transfer
Enterprise Products
K-Sea Transportation
Kinder Morgan Energy Partners
Plains All American Pipeline
Sunoco Logistics
TransMontaigne
Williams Companies

HISTORICAL FINANCIALS

Company Type: Public

Income Statement — FYE: December 31

	REVENUE ($ mil.)	NET INCOME ($ mil.)	NET PROFIT MARGIN	EMPLOYEES
12/18	1,486.0	796.0	53.6%	0
12/17	1,169.0	524.0	44.8%	0
12/16	873.0	408.0	46.7%	0
12/15	348.1	194.2	55.8%	0
12/14	229.1	124.4	54.3%	0
Annual Growth	59.6%	59.0%	—	—

2018 Year-End Financials
Debt ratio: 52.3%
Return on equity: —
Cash ($ mil.): 1.0
Current ratio: 0.48
Long-term debt ($ mil.): 2,998.0
No. of shares (mil.): 126.5
Dividends
 Yield: 6.9%
 Payout: 73.4%
Market value ($ mil.): 5,330.0

	STOCK PRICE ($) FY Close	P/E High/Low		PER SHARE ($) Earnings	Dividends	Book Value
12/18	42.11	13	10	4.00	2.94	19.82
12/17	52.35	22	17	2.59	2.41	17.42
12/16	48.64	29	20	2.20	1.98	14.32
12/15	61.40	24	14	3.26	1.54	4.63
12/14	68.93	27	12	2.93	1.12	0.94
Annual Growth	(11.6%)	—	—	8.1%	27.3%	114.1%

Phillips Edison & Co Inc

Auditors: Deloitte & Touche LLP

LOCATIONS

HQ: Phillips Edison & Co Inc
11501 Northlake Drive, Cincinnati, OH 45249
Phone: 513 554-1110
Web: www.phillipsedison.com

HISTORICAL FINANCIALS

Company Type: Public

Income Statement — FYE: December 31

	REVENUE ($ mil.)	NET INCOME ($ mil.)	NET PROFIT MARGIN	EMPLOYEES
12/18	430.3	39.1	9.1%	300
12/17	311.5	(38.3)	—	304
12/16	257.7	8.9	3.5%	0
12/15	242.1	13.3	5.5%	0
12/14	188.2	(22.6)	—	0
Annual Growth	23.0%	—	—	—

2018 Year-End Financials
Debt ratio: 47.2%
Return on equity: 2.5%
Cash ($ mil.): 16.7
Current ratio: 0.56
Long-term debt ($ mil.): 2,438.8
No. of shares (mil.): 279.8
Dividends
 Yield: —
 Payout: 335.0%
Market value ($ mil.): —

Physicians Realty Trust

EXECUTIVES

EVP and Chief Investment Officer, John W. Sweet, $255,385 total compensation
President and CEO, John T. Thomas, $630,769 total compensation
SVP and Principal Accounting and Reporting Officer, John W. Lucey, $240,000 total compensation
SVP Asset and Investment Management, Mark D. Theine, $249,231 total compensation
EVP and CFO, Jeff Theiler, $375,000 total compensation
EVP Investments, D. Deeni Taylor
Chairman, Tommy G. Thompson
Auditors: Ernst & Young LLP

LOCATIONS

HQ: Physicians Realty Trust
309 N. Water Street, Suite 500, Milwaukee, WI 53202
Phone: 414 367-5600
Web: www.docreit.com

COMPETITORS

HCP
Healthcare Realty Trust
Legacy Healthcare
Medical Properties Trust
National Health Investors
Sabra Health Care
Tiptree
Universal Health Realty
Ventas
Welltower

HISTORICAL FINANCIALS

Company Type: Public

Income Statement
FYE: December 31

	REVENUE ($ mil.)	NET INCOME ($ mil.)	NET PROFIT MARGIN	EMPLOYEES
12/18	422.5	56.2	13.3%	70
12/17	343.5	38.1	11.1%	63
12/16	241.0	29.9	12.4%	41
12/15	129.4	11.7	9.1%	25
12/14	53.3	(4.0)	—	14
Annual Growth	67.8%	—		49.5%

2018 Year-End Financials

Debt ratio: 37.0%
Return on equity: 2.3%
Cash ($ mil.): 19.1
Current ratio: 0.59
Long-term debt ($ mil.): 1,532.8
No. of shares (mil.): 182.4
Dividends
Yield: 5.7%
Payout: 306.6%
Market value ($ mil.): 2,924.0

	STOCK PRICE ($) FY Close	P/E High/Low	PER SHARE ($) Earnings	Dividends	Book Value
12/18	16.03	60 48	0.30	0.92	13.04
12/17	17.99	95 75	0.23	0.91	13.63
12/16	18.96	100 72	0.22	0.90	12.79
12/15	16.86	119 94	0.15	0.90	11.76
12/14	16.60	— —	(0.12)	0.90	10.56
Annual Growth	(0.9%)	— —	—	0.6%	5.4%

Pinnacle Financial Partners Inc

Pinnacle Financial Partners works to be at the top of the community banking mountain in central Tennessee. It's the holding company for Tennessee-based Pinnacle Bank which has grown to some 40 branches in the Nashville and Knoxville areas since its founding in 2000. Serving consumers and small- to mid-sized business the $9 billion financial institution provides standard services such as checking and savings accounts CDs credit cards and loans and mortgages. The company also offers investment and trust services through Pinnacle Asset Management while its insurance brokerage subsidiary Miller Loughry Beach specializes in property/casualty policies. Pinnacle agreed to merge with North Carolina-based BNC Bancorp in 2017.

Operations

Pinnacle Financial Partners' commercial and industrial loans and commercial real estate loans account for nearly 40% and 20% respectively of its total portfolio of loans.

As part of its primary services to both individual and commercial clients Tennessee-based subsidiary Pinnacle Bank provides core deposits including savings checking interest-bearing checking money market and certificate of deposit accounts.

The bank's lending products include commercial real estate and consumer loans to individuals and small- to medium-sized businesses and professional entities. Pinnacle Bank Partners also offers auto dealer finance services to certain automobile dealers and their customers. Additionally it offers Pinnacle-branded consumer credit cards to select clients.

Its convenience-centered products and services include 24-hour telephone and Internet banking debit and credit cards direct deposit and cash management services.

Geographic Reach

Based in Tennessee Pinnacle Financial Partners has become the second-largest bank holding company in the state with nearly 35 offices in eight Middle Tennessee counties and four Knoxville offices. It boasts locations in Nashville Knoxville Murfreesboro Dickson Ashland City Mt. Juliet Lebanon Franklin Brentwood Hendersonville Goodlettsville Smyrna and Shelbyville.

Sales and Marketing

Pinnacle Bank traditionally has obtained its deposits through personal solicitation by its officers and directors although it has used media advertising more in recent years due to its advertising and banking sponsorship with the Tennessee Titans NFL Football team. While it would prefer its customers to bank in person the institution allows customers to bank remotely.

Its marketing and other business development costs have risen in recent years: $4.13 million $3.639 million and $3.636 million in 2014 2013 and 2012 respectively.

Financial Performance

Pinnacle Financial Partners has enjoyed steady revenue and profit growth for the past several years thanks to positive loan growth. Revenue in 2014 rose by 9% to a record $258.77 million mostly to thanks to 9% growth in interest income from loans as the bank's loan assets grew by double digits. Pinnacle also saw double-digit growth in its fee income from service charges on deposit accounts as deposit balances grew and double-digit growth in its investment services income and trust fees as brokerage and trust account balances grew.

Higher revenue drove net income up by 22% to a record $70.47 million. Operations provided $95.06 million or 25% less cash than in 2013 primarily because the bank collected roughly $30 million less in proceeds from its mortgage loans held for sale than it did the year before.

Strategy

Pinnacle's goal is to become the dominant bank in its home market of the Southeast. In 2016 it acquired Avenue Financial Holdings for $200 million and followed up the acquisition by agreeing to merge with regional rival BNC Bancorp of North Carolina in 2017. Once the merger completes the combined company will be the biggest in the region.

Pinnacle Financial Partners been looking to diversify its revenue streams through strategic investments in recent years. In early 2015 for example Tennessee-based subsidiary Pinnacle Bank purchased a 30% membership interest in Bankers Healthcare Group LLC which makes term loans to healthcare professionals and practices for $75 million.

Primarily serving small- to medium-sized businesses in the Nashville and Knoxville areas the company in 2013 began extending its reach in its primary markets by opening its fourth full-service banking location in the Knoxville market in the Cedar Bluff area.

Mergers and Acquisitions

In 2017 Pinnacle agreed to merge with BNC Bancorp. The combined company will have assets of some $20 billion and a presence in four states and in 12 of the largest metropolitan markets in the Southeast.

In 2016 Pinnacle acquired Avenue Financial Holdings (holding company of Avenue Bank with five banking locations in Nashville); the transaction was valued at some $201.4 million. Avenue Bank will operate as a division of Pinnacle Bank for a few months after which the companies will combine operations.

EXECUTIVES

President and CEO, M. Terry Turner, age 63, $784,700 total compensation
EVP and Chief Administrative Officer, Hugh M. Queener, age 63, $376,700 total compensation
EVP and Senior Lending Officer; Manager Client Advisory Group Nashville, J. Edward (Ed) White, age 69, $145,000 total compensation
EVP and Director Assocaite and Client Experience, Joanne B. Jackson, age 62, $117,000 total compensation
CFO, Harold R. Carpenter, age 60, $376,700 total compensation
SVP and Manager Trust and Investment Advisory, Robert Newman
President Pinnacle Knoxville, Mike DiStefano
Chief Credit Officer; President Pinnacle Knoxville, J. Harvey White, $283,800 total compensation
EVP and Manager Pinnacle Asset Management, Gary Collier
SVP and Senior Credit Officer Real Estate, Mike Hendren
SVP and Senior Credit Officer, Tim Huestis

SVP and CIO, Randy Withrow
President and CEO PNFP Capital Markets, Roger Osborne
SVP and Manager Residential Mortgage Services, Ross Kinney
EVP and Area Executive Rutherford County, Bill Jones
Chief Investment Officer, Mac Johnston
SVP Small Business Banking, Chip Higgins
EVP and Financial Advisor, Jerry Hampton
President Pinnacle Memphis, Damon Bell
Senior Vice President and financial advisor in Nashville, Lynn Kendrick
Senior Vice President, Scott Mccabe
Senior Vice President, Kay Mcalister
Financial Advisor Senior Vice President, Brad Byrd
Vice President, Tyane Powell
Senior Vice President, Kevin Marchetti
Senior Vice President Financial Advisor, Cynthia Oliva
Senior Vice President Mortgage Advisor, Jeff Anderson
Senior Vice President Financial Advisor, Lynn Lassiter
Senior Vice President, Michael G Lindseth
Senior Vice President, David Edwards
Senior Vice President, Steve Horn
Senior Vice President, Brande Thomas
Senior Vice President And Mortgage Advisor, Jamie Lacy
Senior Vice President, Eric Kruse
Senior Vice President, Gail Outland
Senior Vice President, Larry Trabue
Senior Vice President, Steve Uebelhor
Senior Vice President, Sarah Teague
Senior Vice President, Kirk Garrett
Senior Vice President Financial Advisor, David Ligon
Senior Vice President, Natalie Readett
Svp and Mortgage Advisor, Laurel Mckenzie
Senior Vice President, Rob Masengill
Credit Advisor Vice President Sba, Pamela Holmes
Sr Vice President, Tina Hoke
Senior Vice President, William Diehl
Senior Vice President Financial Advisor, Kim Ciukowski
Vice President Automotive Finance, Jeff Rhodes
Svp Mortgage Advisor, Luciano Scala
Chief People Officer, Rachel West
Vice President, Shelly Donohoo
Senior Vice President, Todd Carter
SRVP; Mortgage Advisor, Scott Ractliffe
Svp Mortgage Advisor, Deon Ducey
Svp and Office Leader, Sherrie Hicks
Senior Vice President Financial Advisor, Cindy Oliva
Executive Vice President And Chief Financial Officerand#8230; Alan Haefele
Senior Vice President, Sherry McHaffie
Senior Vice President, Clark Cox
Senior Vice President And Financial Adviser In Commercial Real Estate, Thomas Vester
Senior Vice President, Lucy Foutch
Executive Vice President and Senior credit Officer, Edward White
Senior Vice President, Robert Denovo
Vice President Administration, Beth Hobbs
Senior Vice President, Donna Taylor
Senior Vice President Financial Advisor, Keely Ritchie
Senior Vice President, Allison Jones
Vice President Of Training And Development, Eddie Alford
Senior Vice President Trust And Investment Advisor, Keith B Davis

Senior Vice President Financial Advisor, Stacey Richards
Senior Vice President, Amy Charles
Senior Vice President, Bryan Bean
Vice President, Gary Green
SENIOR VICE PRESIDENT AND FINANCIAL ADVISOR, Samuel King
Senior Vice President, Chris Rippy
Senior Vice President, Nathan Matheson
Senior Vice President And Portfolio Manager, Christopher Bricker
Senior Vice President And Financial Advisor, Ashley Preskenis
Senior Vice President And Financial Advisor, Nancy Benskin
Senior Vice President Credit Advisor, Stacey Fantom
Senior Vice President Credit Advisor, Kendria Northcutt
Senior Vice President, Sam King
SENIOR VICE PRESIDENT, Tom Dozier
Senior Vice President, Gina Scott
Senior Vice President Private Client Services Community Banker, Janine Stinnett
Senior Vice President and Trust Officer, Scott Lindsey
Senior Vice President, Ron Stinson
Senior Vice President Financial Advisor, Tim Bewley
Senior Vice President, Jason Reierson
Senior Vp, Chris Howe
Executive Vice President, Kent Cleaver
Senior Vice President, Lisa Baskette
Svp Mortgage Advisor, Bridget Mounger
Vice President, Bob Stimson
Senior Vice President, John Douglas
Executive Vice President, Phil Stevenson
Senior Vice President, Cooper Samuels
Senior Vice President Financial Advisor, Amy Campbell
Assistant Vice President, Alan Gauger
Senior Vice President, Diane Jones
Vice President: Treasury Management Advisor, Joy Bowen
CMB Senior Vice President, Jeff Tucker
Senior Vice President Mortgage Advisor, Clint Porter
Senior Vice President Credit Advisor, Katherine Graham
Senior Vice President, Ryan Murphy
CTFA Senior Vice President Financial Advisor, Steve Scott
Senior Vice President Financial Advisor, Bryant Lecroy
Svp And Mortgage Advisor, Donathan Cassidy
Senior Vice President, Bob Lawhon
Senior Vice President Mortgage Advisor, Becky Fiedler
Senior Vice President, Debbie Morgan
SENIOR VICE PRESIDENT MANAGING DIRECTOR, Nathan Kurita
Senior Vice President, Jeff East
Senior Vice President, Rick Nelson
Senior Vice President, Jimmy Moncrief
Evp and Music and Entertainment Director, Andy Moats
Senior Vice President, Dan Neumann
Senior Vice President Mortgage Advisor, Todd Flynn
Vice President, Cheryl Plummer
Senior Vice President, Donna Edwards
Senior Vice President, Glenn Layne
Svp Group Banking Manager, Lucy Daugherty
Svp Financial Advisory, Richard Harris
Senior Vice President Financial Advisor, Debbie Indermuehle

Vp Sba Business Development Officer, Janet Matthew
Vice President, Rick Lalance
Mortgage Adv Sor Vice President, Debbie Del Corro
Executive Vice President Director Of Client Services, Andy Boyer
Senior Vice President Financial Advisor, Danny Hester
Svp Fice Leader, Michael Colyer
Senior Vice President Financial Advisor, Bob Johnson
Senior Vice President Credit Advisor, Warren Jackson
Senior Vice President, Regina Jennings
Svp And Area Manager, Eddie Blount
Senior Vice President Financial Advisor, Peggy Hollandsworth
Senior Vice President, Peter Gentry
Senior Vice President, Brad Medcalf
Vice President Mortgage Advisor, Brandon Caldwell
Senior Vice President Financial Consultant, Doug Jones
Senior Vice President Financial Advisor, Edwin Pugh
Senior Vice President, Eric Barrett
Svp Client Service Center Director, Gerry Barber
Senior Vice President Financial Advisor, Jennifer Finnell
Senior Vice President Financial Advisor, John Moore
Svp Area Executive, Mary Garcia
Vp Appraisal Process Manager, Peter Kapetanakis
Credit Advisor Senior Vice President, Rachel Mitchell
Executive Vice President Regional President, Reid Marks
Vp Credit Advisor, Richard Pierce
Senior Credit Officer Vice President, Richmond Moore
Senior Vice President, Ryan Earwaker
Senior Vice President Of Commercial Banking, Shannon Miller
Senior Vice President Financial Advisor, Stephen Ratterman
Senior Vice President Financial Advisor, Stewart Holmes
Senior Vice President, Todd Quinton
Senior Vice President Managing Director, Nate Fowler
Senior Vice President Sc Upstate Regional President, Ed Stein
Senior Vice President Credit Advisor, Aaron Eaquinto
Vice President Mortgage Manager, Kyle Russell
Portfolio Manager Trust Services Advisor Svp, Danny Gork
Vp Sba Portfolio Manager, Nisha Desai
Svp and Office Leader, Karen Coward
Senior Vice President, Jim Going
Senior Vice President Financial Advisor, Brandon Deering
Svp Trust Operations and Systems Manager, Lisa Foster
Vice Chairman, Ed C. Loughry, age 76
Chairman, Robert A. (Rob) McCabe, age 68
Auditors: Crowe LLP

LOCATIONS

HQ: Pinnacle Financial Partners Inc
150 Third Avenue South, Suite 900, Nashville, TN 37201
Phone: 615 744-3700
Web: www.pnfp.com

PRODUCTS/OPERATIONS

2014 Revenue

	% of total
Interest Income	80
Non-interest Income	20
Total	100

Selected Subsidiaries
Pinnacle Advisory Services Inc.
Pinnacle Credit Enhancement Holdings Inc.
Pinnacle National Bank
    Miller & Loughry Inc. (dba Miller Loughry Beach)
    PFP Title Company
    Pinnacle Community Development Corporation
    Pinnacle Nashville Real Estate Inc.
    Pinnacle Rutherford Real Estate Inc.
    Pinnacle Rutherford Towers Inc.
    Pinnacle Service Company Inc.
PNFP Insurance Inc.

COMPETITORS

BB&T	Regions Financial
Bank of America	SunTrust
Fifth Third	U.S. Bancorp
First Horizon	

HISTORICAL FINANCIALS
Company Type: Public

Income Statement   FYE: December 31

	ASSETS ($ mil.)	NET INCOME ($ mil.)	INCOME AS % OF ASSETS	EMPLOYEES
12/18	25,031.0	359.4	1.4%	2,297
12/17	22,205.7	173.9	0.8%	2,132
12/16	11,194.6	127.2	1.1%	1,180
12/15	8,715.4	95.5	1.1%	1,065
12/14	6,018.2	70.4	1.2%	767
Annual Growth	42.8%	50.3%	—	31.6%

2018 Year-End Financials
Return on assets: 1.5%
Return on equity: 9.3%
Long-term debt ($ mil.): —
No. of shares (mil.): 77.4
Sales ($ mil): 1,147.5
Dividends
  Yield: 1.2%
  Payout: 15.8%
Market value ($ mil.): 3,572.0

	STOCK PRICE ($) FY Close	P/E High/Low		PER SHARE ($) Earnings	Dividends	Book Value
12/18	46.10	15	9	4.64	0.58	51.18
12/17	66.30	26	21	2.70	0.56	47.70
12/16	69.30	24	15	2.91	0.56	32.28
12/15	51.36	22	14	2.52	0.48	28.25
12/14	39.54	20	15	2.01	0.32	22.46
Annual Growth	3.9%	—	—	23.3%	16.0%	22.9%

PJT Partners Inc

Auditors: DELOITTE & TOUCHE LLP

LOCATIONS
HQ: PJT Partners Inc
  280 Park Avenue, New York, NY 10017
Phone: 212 364-7800
Web: www.pjtpartners.com

HISTORICAL FINANCIALS
Company Type: Public

Income Statement   FYE: December 31

	REVENUE ($ mil.)	NET INCOME ($ mil.)	NET PROFIT MARGIN	EMPLOYEES
12/18	580.2	27.1	4.7%	590
12/17	499.2	(32.5)	—	473
12/16	499.4	(3.0)	—	419
12/15	405.9	7.5	1.9%	353
12/14	401.0	4.4	1.1%	291
Annual Growth	9.7%	56.8%	—	19.3%

2018 Year-End Financials
Debt ratio: 4.4%
Return on equity: —
Cash ($ mil.): 106.1
Current ratio: 2.51
Long-term debt ($ mil.): 30.0
No. of shares (mil.): 22.5
Dividends
  Yield: 0.5%
  Payout: 17.2%
Market value ($ mil.): 875.0

	STOCK PRICE ($) FY Close	P/E High/Low		PER SHARE ($) Earnings	Dividends	Book Value
12/18	38.76	49	29	1.16	0.20	(3.83)
12/17	45.60	—	—	(1.73)	0.20	(8.48)
12/16	30.88	—	—	(0.17)	0.20	(0.48)
12/15	28.29	—	—	(0.61)	0.00	1.79
Annual Growth	11.1%			—	—	—

Planet Fitness Inc

Auditors: KPMG LLP

LOCATIONS
HQ: Planet Fitness Inc
  4 Liberty Lane West, Hampton, NH 03842
Phone: 603 750-0001
Web: www.planetfitness.com

HISTORICAL FINANCIALS
Company Type: Public

Income Statement   FYE: December 31

	REVENUE ($ mil.)	NET INCOME ($ mil.)	NET PROFIT MARGIN	EMPLOYEES
12/18	572.9	88.0	15.4%	1,052
12/17	429.9	33.1	7.7%	1,046
12/16	378.2	21.5	5.7%	963
12/15	330.5	18.5	5.6%	936
12/14	279.7	36.8	13.2%	842
Annual Growth	19.6%	24.4%	—	5.7%

2018 Year-End Financials
Debt ratio: 86.6%
Return on equity: —
Cash ($ mil.): 289.4
Current ratio: 2.96
Long-term debt ($ mil.): 1,160.1
No. of shares (mil.): 93.0
Dividends
  Yield: —
  Payout: —
Market value ($ mil.): 4,988.0

	STOCK PRICE ($) FY Close	P/E High/Low		PER SHARE ($) Earnings	Dividends	Book Value
12/18	53.62	56	29	1.00	0.00	(4.03)
12/17	34.63	83	44	0.42	0.00	(1.21)
12/16	20.10	49	27	0.50	2.78	(1.33)
12/15	15.63	174	136	0.11	0.00	(0.16)
Annual Growth	50.8%	—	—	108.7%	—	—

Plumas Bancorp Inc

EXECUTIVES
ASSISTANT VICE PRESIDENT ADMIN SERVICES MANAGER, Kathy Beatty
Vice President SBA Underwriter, John Rash
Auditors: Eide Bailly LLP

LOCATIONS
HQ: Plumas Bancorp Inc
  35 South Lindan Avenue, Quincy, CA 95971
Phone: 530 283-7305
Web: www.plumasbank.com

COMPETITORS

Bank of America	Scott Valley Bank
Bank of Commerce	TriCo Bancshares
Bank of the West	U.S. Bancorp
North Valley Bancorp	Wells Fargo

HISTORICAL FINANCIALS
Company Type: Public

Income Statement   FYE: December 31

	ASSETS ($ mil.)	NET INCOME ($ mil.)	INCOME AS % OF ASSETS	EMPLOYEES
12/18	824.4	13.9	1.7%	174
12/17	745.4	8.1	1.1%	161
12/16	657.9	7.4	1.1%	155
12/15	599.2	5.8	1.0%	151
12/14	538.8	4.7	0.9%	155
Annual Growth	11.2%	31.1%	—	2.9%

2018 Year-End Financials
Return on assets: 1.7%
Return on equity: 22.8%
Long-term debt ($ mil.): —
No. of shares (mil.): 5.1
Sales ($ mil): 43.2
Dividends
  Yield: 1.5%
  Payout: 16.2%
Market value ($ mil.): 117.0

	STOCK PRICE ($) FY Close	P/E High/Low		PER SHARE ($) Earnings	Dividends	Book Value
12/18	22.71	11	8	2.68	0.36	13.03
12/17	23.20	14	10	1.58	0.28	11.00
12/16	19.00	12	5	1.47	0.10	9.80
12/15	8.68	8	6	1.15	0.00	8.79
12/14	7.99	8	6	0.95	0.00	7.60
Annual Growth	29.9%	—	—	29.6%	—	14.4%

Polaris Infrastructure Inc

Auditors: PricewaterhouseCoopers LLP

LOCATIONS
HQ: Polaris Infrastructure Inc
  401 Ryland Street, Reno, NV 89502
Phone: 775 398-3711   Fax: 775 398-3741
Web: www.polarisinfrastructure.com

HISTORICAL FINANCIALS
Company Type: Public

Income Statement
FYE: December 31

	REVENUE ($ mil.)	NET INCOME ($ mil.)	NET PROFIT MARGIN	EMPLOYEES
12/18	68.8	12.1	17.6%	134
12/17	60.1	1.6	2.8%	162
12/16	54.6	(4.2)	—	128
12/15	50.1	(37.4)	—	118
12/14	48.1	(23.8)	—	118
Annual Growth	9.3%	—	—	3.2%

2018 Year-End Financials
Debt ratio: 40.0%
Return on equity: 6.2%
Cash ($ mil.): 37.8
Current ratio: 1.34
Long-term debt ($ mil.): 172.7
No. of shares (mil.): 15.6
Dividends
 Yield: 0.0%
 Payout: 81.0%
Market value ($ mil.): 107.0

	STOCK PRICE ($) FY Close	P/E High/Low		PER SHARE ($) Earnings	Dividends	Book Value
12/18	6.80	22	8	0.74	0.60	12.68
12/17	13.59	131	91	0.11	0.53	11.97
12/16	11.34	—	—	(0.27)	0.31	12.44
12/15	5.88	—	—	(3.78)	0.00	13.09
12/14	0.00	—	—	(120.00)	0.00	746.35
Annual Growth	509.2% (63.9%)	—	—	—	—	—

PotlatchDeltic Corp

"Potlatch" is Chinook for giving but you'll have to pay for Potlatch's wood products. The real estate investment trust (REIT) harvests timber from some 1.6 million acres of hardwood and softwood forestland in Alabama Arkansas Idaho Mississippi and Minnesota; it claims to be the largest private landowner in Idaho. Potlatch operates sawmills in five states that produce logs and fiber and lumber and panels. Beyond wood product sales the company generates revenue by leasing its land for hunting recreation mineral rights biomass production and carbon sequestration. It also sells real estate through Potlatch TRS. In 2018 it completed its acquisition of Arkansas-based Deltic Timber Corporation.

Operations
Potlatch operates three main business segments. Its Wood Products segment which made up 53% of its sales during 2015 makes and sells lumber plywood and residual products. Its Resources segment (42% of sales) manages timberland leases it for hunting recreation mineral rights biomass production and carbon sequestration. The real estate segment (5% of sales) sells non-strategic or low-revenue generating land holdings through Potlatch TRS.

Geographic Reach
Washington-based Potlatch harvested 99% of its revenue from sales in the US during 2015. Combined Canada and Mexico accounted for only about half of 1% of sales. The REIT has sawmills in Alabama Arkansas Idaho Michigan and Minnesota.

Sales and Marketing
The company sells its products directly through its sales offices to end users retailers or national wholesalers. Its products are mostly used in home building industrial products or other construction.

Financial Performance
Potlatch has been enjoying strong demand for its Resource and Wood Products segments with the uptick in housing starts over the last several years which has led to rising revenues and profits.

The REIT's sales changed course in 2015 however falling 5% to $575 million for the year as its Wood Product sales slumped 11% as lumber prices tumbled and as lumber shipments declined on down time to balance supply with demand and down time for large capital projects installations at each of its four lumber mills. Its Real Estate sales shrank 28% for the year as the segment sold less acreage in Minnesota and Idaho despite higher acreage sales in the South.

Revenue declines in 2015 combined with higher logging hauling depreciation depletion and amotization costs that stemmed from recent (2014) timberland acquisitions in Alabama and Mississippi caused Potlatch's net income to fall 66% to $31.71 million for the year. The company's operating cash levels dove 44% to $74 million in 2015 due to the fall in cash earnings.

Strategy
Potlatch continues to focus on acquiring new timberland to support its future growth. In 2018 it completed its acquisition of Deltic Timber a company with more than 900000 timberland acres sawmill capacity of 630 million board feet and excellent growth opportunities in the fast-growing Texas housing market.

The REIT also has been optimizing its revenue from every acre of its land to keep revenue growing. It planned to harvest some 4.4 million tons of timberland for 2016 up from 3.8 million tons in 2014.

The company touts its environmental sustainability initiatives but its motives are not entirely altruistic: Logs that come from timberlands that are certified by the Forest Stewardship Council or International Standardization Organization sell at higher-than-average prices. The same goes for lumber and plywood.

HISTORY
Lumber magnate Frederick Weyerhaeuser led a swarm of midwestern lumber companies into virgin northern Idaho forests at the turn of the 20th century. Two primary rivals — William Deary of Northland Pine Company (a firm helped by Weyerhaeuser) and Henry Turrish of Wisconsin Log & Lumber — bought thousands of acres of white pine around the state's Palouse Potlatch and Elk river basins. They kept land prices down by purchasing it together. In 1903 they merged more than 100000 acres and created Potlatch Lumber. Weyerhaeuser's son Charles served as president.

Potlatch struggled for three decades in the high-risk lumber business. Maintaining a mill and a company town (Potlatch Idaho) was expensive and the company's policy of harvesting all tree varieties instead of those in demand didn't help. With the opening of the Panama Canal in 1914 Pacific Coast companies were able to undercut Potlatch in eastern markets by using the cheap transportation alternative. Before his death in 1914 Weyerhaeuser reportedly referred to Potlatch as an appropriate name for a company that spent piles of money with miniscule returns. To survive the Depression the company merged with two major competitors Clearwater and Edward Rutledge in 1931. The new company Potlatch Forests was headed by Weyerhaeuser's descendants.

The WWII boom helped Potlatch raise badly needed profits from lumber orders. Afterwards the company introduced new products including paperboard used in milk cartons plywood and laminated decking. It expanded its timber reserves through acquisitions in Arkansas and Minnesota. In the 1960s Potlatch bought Clearwater Tissue Mills. The company moved its headquarters to San Francisco in 1965 and changed its name in 1973 to Potlatch Corporation.

Richard Madden became chairman and CEO in 1971 and reduced operations from 20 product lines to four — wood printed papers pulp and paperboard and tissue. The company emphasized capital expenditures such as its 1981 construction of the first US plant to make plywood-alternative oriented strand board.

In 1994 Madden retired and COO Pendleton Siegel succeeded him. In 1997 the company moved its headquarters to Spokane Washington; the following year it announced plans to spend more than $200 million to modernize and expand its Cloquet Minnesota pulp mill.

Potlatch and Anderson-Tully Company hatched a plan in 1998 to combine their Arkansas timber holdings into the Timberland Growth Corporation the first public real estate investment trust (REIT) to focus on timber ownership. The plan fell apart in 1999 however because of a weak timber market in Asia and weakened confidence in US markets after declines in the autumn of 1998.

The company's upgrade of its Cloquet pulp mill (including a new pulp machine) was completed in late 1999. Poor performance by the company's Minnesota pulp and paper division in 2000 led the company to trim about 300 jobs. It eliminated an additional 124 positions early in 2001.

In 2002 Potlatch sold its Cloquet Minnesota coated fine pulp and printing papers facilities to a subsidiary of Sappi Limited for $480 million in cash. Early the next year the company sold its Brainerd Minnesota paper mill and related assets to Missota Paper Company for $4.44 million in cash.

The company reorganized itself as a REIT in 2006. Under this arrangement Potlatch was able to derive tax benefits from its timberland holdings without having to divest its non-real estate operations. It handled those operations through taxable subsidiary Potlatch Forest Products. As a result much of the company's activities became geared toward shifting around its forestland holdings.

Pendleton Siegel stepped down as chairman and CEO in 2006. He was succeeded by Michael Covey a 23-year veteran of competitor Plum Creek Timber.

In 2007 Potlatch acquired more than 75000 acres of Wisconsin forestland in a deal worth about $65 million. It picked up more forestland the following year when it acquired about 180000 acres in central Idaho from Western Pacific Timber.

Soon after the 2008 financial crisis softened demand in the US brought on by the weak housing market compelled the company to curtail some of its plywood and lumber production operations. It cut or halted production at many of its facilities in 2009 (but did not do so in 2010). It closed down an Arkansas lumber mill in 2008 and sold the property two years later. The company also sold its particleboard plant and a railroad in Idaho in 2010.

In 2012 the REIT completed two timberland purchases — totaling 9285 acres — in and around land it owns in Arkansas for a total consideration of $11.8 million.

EXECUTIVES

Chairman and CEO, Michael J. Covey, age 61, $715,020 total compensation
President and COO, Eric J. Cremers, age 56, $442,558 total compensation
Vice President - Wood Products and Arkansas Resource, Thomas J. Temple, age 63, $274,537 total compensation
Vice President - Real Estate and Lake States Resource, William R. DeReu, age 53, $193,629 total compensation
VP and CFO, Jerald W. (Jerry) Richards
Vice President Resource, Darin Ball
Vice President, Tom Temple
Vice President Public Affairs, Anna Torma
Auditors: KPMG LLP

LOCATIONS

HQ: PotlatchDeltic Corp
601 West First Avenue, Suite 1600, Spokane, WA 99201
Phone: 509 835-1500
Web: www.potlatch.com

PRODUCTS/OPERATIONS

2015 Sales

	$ mil.	% of total
Wood Products	336.3	53
Resource	263.9	42
Real estate	29.0	5
Intersegment eliminations	(53.7)	-
Total	575.3	100

COMPETITORS

CatchMark	Svenska Cellulosa
Deltic Timber	UPM-Kymmene
International Paper	West Fraser Timber
Louisiana-Pacific	Weyerhaeuser
Rayonier	
Roseburg Forest Products	

HISTORICAL FINANCIALS
Company Type: Public

Income Statement
FYE: December 31

	REVENUE ($ mil.)	NET INCOME ($ mil.)	NET PROFIT MARGIN	EMPLOYEES
12/18	974.5	122.8	12.6%	1,471
12/17	678.6	86.4	12.7%	963
12/16	599.1	10.9	1.8%	953
12/15	575.3	31.7	5.5%	927
12/14	606.9	89.9	14.8%	887
Annual Growth	12.6%	8.1%	—	13.5%

2018 Year-End Financials

Debt ratio: 32.4%
Return on equity: 16.2%
Cash ($ mil.): 76.6
Current ratio: 1.92
Long-term debt ($ mil.): 715.3
No. of shares (mil.): 67.5
Dividends
 Yield: 16.2%
 Payout: 258.2%
Market value ($ mil.): 2,138.0

	STOCK PRICE ($) FY Close	P/E High/Low	PER SHARE ($) Earnings	Dividends	Book Value
12/18	31.64	27 14	1.99	5.14	19.46
12/17	49.90	25 19	2.10	1.53	4.94
12/16	41.65	161 91	0.27	1.50	3.86
12/15	30.24	55 36	0.77	1.50	5.01
12/14	41.87	20 17	2.20	1.43	5.54
Annual Growth	(6.8%)	— —	—	(2.5%)	37.8% 36.9%

PQ Group Holdings Inc

Auditors: PricewaterhouseCoopers LLP

LOCATIONS

HQ: PQ Group Holdings Inc
300 Lindenwood Drive, Malvern, PA 19355
Phone: 610 651-4400
Web: www.pqcorp.com

HISTORICAL FINANCIALS
Company Type: Public

Income Statement
FYE: December 31

	REVENUE ($ mil.)	NET INCOME ($ mil.)	NET PROFIT MARGIN	EMPLOYEES
12/18	1,608.1	58.3	3.6%	3,188
12/17	1,472.1	57.6	3.9%	3,149
12/16	1,064.1	(79.7)	—	2,949
12/15	388.8	11.4	2.9%	0
12/14	35.5	(22.0)	—	0
Annual Growth	159.4%	—	—	—

2018 Year-End Financials

Debt ratio: 48.8%
Return on equity: 3.5%
Cash ($ mil.): 57.8
Current ratio: 2.19
Long-term debt ($ mil.): 2,106.7
No. of shares (mil.): 135.5
Dividends
 Yield: —
 Payout: —
Market value ($ mil.): 2,008.0

	STOCK PRICE ($) FY Close	P/E High/Low	PER SHARE ($) Earnings	Dividends	Book Value
12/18	14.81	42 30	0.43	0.00	12.24
12/17	16.45	34 29	0.52	0.00	12.04
Annual Growth	(10.0%)	—	(17.3%)	—	1.7%

Preferred Apartment Communities Inc.

Preferred Apartment Communities prefers to own retail properties with multifamily ones. The real estate investment trust (REIT) owns nearly 20 multifamily communities with 6100-plus units as well as some 20 grocery-anchored retail shopping centers with some 2 million sq. ft. of leasable space in major metro areas including Atlanta Austin Dallas Houston Nashville Orlando and Philadelphia. Its largest retail tenants include Publix Kroger and Tom Thumb. The REIT also buys senior mortgage loans or mezzanine debt and membership or partnership interests in multifamily properties. Preferred Apartment Communities was formed in 2009 and went public in 2011.

Operations
The REIT operates three business segments: Multifamily which made up 60% of its total revenue during 2015 and generates rental income from its 19 owned multifamily apartment communities; Financing (28% of revenue) which generates interest income from its investment portfolio of real estate loans bridge loans and other development financing-related instruments; and Retail (12% of revenue) which collects rental income from its portfolio of 14 grocery-anchored shopping centers.

Some of Preferred Apartment Communities' subsidiaries include: Preferred Residential Management Preferred Campus Management Main Street Apartment Homes New Market Properties LLC and Preferred Capital Securities.

Geographic Reach
Atlanta-based Preferred had properties in 24 cities across 11 states at the end of 2015 mostly in large metropolitan cities including major metro areas including Atlanta Austin Dallas Houston Nashville Orlando and Philadelphia.

Sales and Marketing
More than 50% of the REIT's retail portfolio (by gross leasable area or GLA) was occupied by grocery anchor tenants at the end of 2015 which included Publix (27% of GLA) Kroger (15%) Bi-Lo (5%) Tom Thumb of Safeway (3%) and The Fresh Market (2%).

Financial Performance
Preferred Apartment Communities' revenues have risen ten-fold since 2011 mostly as new property acquisitions have spurred higher rental income. The REIT's bottom line has been fluctuating between losses and profitable years despite consistently reporting operating income growth mainly as it's had to pay for growth-supporting financing costs.

The REIT's revenue nearly doubled to $109.3 million during 2015 mainly as to new multifamily property acquisitions continued to boost rental revenues. Retail revenue also quadrupled for the year on new property acquisitions while financing revenue grew by 41% as the REIT purchased 10 real estate loans and bridge loans.

Despite exceptional revenue growth in 2015 Preferred reported a loss of $2.43 million as it paid more in interest expenses on finances used to support its acquisitions. The REIT's operating cash levels more than doubled to $35.2 million as cash-denominated rental income rose during the year.

Strategy
Preferred Apartment Communities has been acquiring more retail properties in recent years to diversify beyond its core apartment holdings. The REIT prefers to buy properties in fast-growing metropolitan markets around the US which attract plenty of new renters and command higher rental prices over time as demand increases.

In late 2017 and early 2018 the company went on a buying spree. Between November and February it purchased in Atlanta a 310-unit multifamily community a class A office building and a grocery-anchored shopping center. It also bought a 265-unit multifamily facility in Jacksonville FL a 255-unit community in Richmond VA a student housing complex in Waco TX (near Baylor University) and a grocery-anchored shopping center in Naples FL.

In mid-2016 the REIT acquired another seven shopping centers (with some 650400 sq. ft. of rentable space) for $158 million

During 2015 Preferred bought nine multifamily communities — nearly doubling its existing multifamily portfolio — with 2810 units in Orlando Nashville San Antonio Charlotte Sarasota and Houston. Adding to its retail property portfolio that year it spent $88 million toward buying four grocery-anchored shopping centers with 585000 sq. ft. of GLA in the Atlanta Dallas and Chattanooga markets.

Company Background

Preferred Apartment Communities went public in 2011 raising some $45 million in its initial public offering somewhat less than the $75 million it was aiming for. Preferred used net proceeds from the offering to acquire new properties and place certain proceeds in interest-bearing short-term investments intended to help it qualify as a real estate investment trust (REIT).

CEO John A. Williams controls both Preferred Apartment Communities and its manager Preferred Apartment Advisors. Williams is also founder of US REIT Post Properties.

EXECUTIVES

Executive Vice President Chief Distribution Officer, Albert Haworth
Senior Vice President Asset Management, Carl Dickson
Vice President renovations Capital Projects, Jeff Boy
Auditors: PricewaterhouseCoopers LLP

LOCATIONS

HQ: Preferred Apartment Communities Inc.
3284 Northside Parkway N.W., Suite 150, Atlanta, GA 30327
Phone: 770 818-4100
Web: www.pacapts.com

COMPETITORS

Apartment Investment and Management	Home Properties
Equity Residential	MAA
Essex Property Trust	Steadfast Companies
	UDR

HISTORICAL FINANCIALS

Company Type: Public

Income Statement FYE: December 31

	REVENUE ($ mil.)	NET INCOME ($ mil.)	NET PROFIT MARGIN	EMPLOYEES
12/18	397.2	43.4	10.9%	0
12/17	294.0	27.6	9.4%	0
12/16	200.1	(9.5)	—	0
12/15	109.3	(2.4)	—	0
12/14	56.5	2.0	3.7%	0
Annual Growth	62.8%	113.5%	—	—

2018 Year-End Financials

Debt ratio: 53.4%
Return on equity: 3.0%
Cash ($ mil.): 38.9
Current ratio: 0.85
Long-term debt ($ mil.): 2,299.6
No. of shares (mil.): 41.7
Dividends
 Yield: 7.2%
 Payout: —
Market value ($ mil.): 587.0

	STOCK PRICE ($) FY Close	P/E High/Low	PER SHARE ($) Earnings	Dividends	Book Value
12/18	14.06	— —	(1.08)	1.02	38.49
12/17	20.25	— —	(1.13)	0.94	33.08
12/16	14.91	— —	(2.11)	0.82	33.35
12/15	13.08	— —	(0.95)	0.73	22.98
12/14	9.10	— —	(0.31)	0.66	13.53
Annual Growth	11.5%	— —	—	11.7%	29.9%

Preferred Bank (Los Angeles, CA)

Preferred Bank wants to be the bank of choice of Chinese-Americans in Southern California. Employing a multilingual staff the bank provides international banking services to companies doing business in the Asia/Pacific region. It targets middle-market businesses typically manufacturing service distribution and real estate firms as well as entrepreneurs professionals and high-net-worth individuals through about a dozen branches in Los Angeles Orange and San Francisco Counties. Preferred Bank offers standard deposit products such as checking accounts savings money market and NOW accounts. Specialized services include private banking and international trade finance.

Geographic Reach

Preferred Bank markets its services in half a dozen Southern Californian counties: Los Angeles Orange Riverside San Bernardino San Francisco and Ventura.

Financial Performance

In 2013 Preferred Bank reported about $72 million in revenue up just more than 10% from the prior year. The increase was solely from interest income as non-interest income (a very small part of overall revenue anyway) fell more than 40%. The company saw growth in its loan portfolio that year as well as overall deposit growth. Net income fell 20% to $19 million; the decline was primarily related to a boost in net income for 2012 because of a $20 million income tax benefit (compared to income tax expense of $12 million in 2013).

Strategy

Historically the company was focused on the Chinese-American market and although it continues to cater to that clientele most of its current customer base is from the diversified mainstream market.

EXECUTIVES

EVP and CFO, Edward J. Czajka
President and COO, Wellington Chen, age 59
Chairman and CEO, Li Yu, age 78
Vice President Commercial Real ESATE LOAN Officer, Sally Chang
Vice President, William Ko
Senior Vice President, Jim Belanic
Assistant Vice President Credit Administration, Margaret King
Senior Vice President, John C Stipanov
Vice President, Debbie White
First Vice President, Madelyn Hayashi
Vice President, Barbara Gordon
Vice President Real Estate Industries Group, Greg Hahn
Senior Vice President And Corporate Banking Manager, Christina Ching
Vice President, Craig Miller
Avp Senior Bsa Analyst, Joshua Barron
Vp Assistant Bsa Officer, Kristie Yang
Executive Vice President Head Of Northern California, Alice Huang
Senior Vice President, Pamela Lau
Vice President, Sofia Huang
Vice President Financial Reporting, Brandon George
First Vice President, Johnny Hsu
Vice President Lending, Luey Couto
Senior Vice President, Ann Cheung
Vice President, Wayne Chow
Vice President Human Resources Manager, Karen Cangey
Senior Vice President Internal Audit, Jenny Own
Senior Vice President And Controller, Debbie Kong
Vp Internal Audit Manager, Carlo Garcia
Vice President Commercial Banking, Ricken Li
Vice President Assistant Compliance Officer, Florence Hsu
Vice President, Silvia Espinoza
First Vice President, Philip Wong
Vice President Product Manager, John Wong
Vice President And Portfolio Manager, Welmer Jurado
Senior Vice President, Bill Oberholzer
Executive Vice President Chief Credit Officer, Jonathan Sigal
Assistant Vice President Operations Officer, Patty Artavia
Avp, Xiao Wells
First Vice President, Jean Ou
Vice President Relationship Manager, Eddie Ong
Vice President Financial Intelligence Unit Manager, Krishan Sirimane
Vice President Portfolio Manager, Judy Chang
Senior Vice President Head Of International Banking And Commercial Industrial Lending, Samuel Leung
VICE PRESIDENT, Clara Moore
Vice President, Winny Lo
Senior Vice President, Ann J Cheung
Board Member, Clark Hsu
Fvp Treasurer, Eric Chen
Auditors: Crowe LLP

LOCATIONS

HQ: Preferred Bank (Los Angeles, CA)
601 S. Figueroa Street, 48th Floor, Los Angeles, CA 90017
Phone: 213 891-1188
Web: www.preferredbank.com

PRODUCTS/OPERATIONS

2015 Sales

	% of total
Interest income	
Loans and leases	90
Investment securities available for sale	6
Federal funds sold	-
Non-interest income	
Fees and service charges on deposit accounts	1
Trade finance income	2
BOLI income	
Other income	1
Total	**100**

COMPETITORS

Bank of America	City National
Bank of the West	East West Bancorp
Broadway Financial	Far East National Bank
Cathay General Bancorp	Hanmi Financial
Citigroup	MUFG Americas Holdings

HISTORICAL FINANCIALS
Company Type: Public

Income Statement — FYE: December 31

	ASSETS ($ mil.)	NET INCOME ($ mil.)	INCOME AS % OF ASSETS	EMPLOYEES
12/18	4,216.4	70.9	1.7%	263
12/17	3,769.8	43.3	1.2%	238
12/16	3,221.6	36.3	1.1%	218
12/15	2,598.8	29.7	1.1%	205
12/14	2,054.1	24.5	1.2%	163
Annual Growth	19.7%	30.3%	—	12.7%

2018 Year-End Financials

Return on assets: 1.7%
Return on equity: 18.4%
Long-term debt ($ mil.): —
No. of shares (mil.): 15.3
Sales ($ mil): 204.5
Dividends
 Yield: 2.1%
 Payout: 23.8%
Market value ($ mil.): 664.0

	STOCK PRICE ($) FY Close	P/E High/Low		PER SHARE ($) Earnings	Dividends	Book Value
12/18	43.35	15	9	4.64	0.94	27.22
12/17	58.78	22	16	2.96	0.76	23.48
12/16	52.42	20	10	2.56	0.60	20.94
12/15	33.02	17	12	2.14	0.46	19.02
12/14	27.89	15	11	1.78	0.10	17.40
Annual Growth	11.7%	—	—	27.1%	75.1%	11.8%

Primerica Inc

Auditors: KPMG LLP

LOCATIONS
HQ: Primerica Inc
 1 Primerica Parkway, Duluth, GA 30099
Phone: 770 381-1000
Web: www.primerica.com

HISTORICAL FINANCIALS
Company Type: Public

Income Statement — FYE: December 31

	ASSETS ($ mil.)	NET INCOME ($ mil.)	INCOME AS % OF ASSETS	EMPLOYEES
12/18	12,595.0	324.0	2.6%	2,699
12/17	12,460.7	350.2	2.8%	2,718
12/16	11,438.9	219.4	1.9%	2,662
12/15	10,612.1	189.8	1.8%	2,626
12/14	10,738.1	181.4	1.7%	2,579
Annual Growth	4.1%	15.6%	—	1.1%

2018 Year-End Financials

Return on assets: 2.5%
Return on equity: 22.5%
Long-term debt ($ mil.): —
No. of shares (mil.): 42.6
Sales ($ mil): 1,899.8
Dividends
 Yield: 1.0%
 Payout: 13.6%
Market value ($ mil.): 4,172.0

	STOCK PRICE ($) FY Close	P/E High/Low		PER SHARE ($) Earnings	Dividends	Book Value
12/18	97.71	17	12	7.33	1.00	34.23
12/17	101.55	14	9	7.61	0.78	32.07
12/16	69.15	16	9	4.59	0.70	26.71
12/15	47.23	15	11	3.70	0.64	23.72
12/14	54.26	17	12	3.29	0.48	23.87
Annual Growth	15.8%	—	—	22.2%	20.1%	9.4%

ProPetro Holding Corp

Auditors: DELOITTE & TOUCHE LLP

LOCATIONS
HQ: ProPetro Holding Corp
 1706 South Midkiff, Bldg. B, Midland, TX 79701
Phone: 432 688-0012
Web: www.propetroservices.com

HISTORICAL FINANCIALS
Company Type: Public

Income Statement — FYE: December 31

	REVENUE ($ mil.)	NET INCOME ($ mil.)	NET PROFIT MARGIN	EMPLOYEES
12/18	1,704.5	173.8	10.2%	1,579
12/17	981.8	12.6	1.3%	986
12/16	436.9	(53.1)	—	642
12/15	569.6	(45.8)	—	0
Annual Growth	44.1%	—	—	—

2018 Year-End Financials

Debt ratio: 5.4%
Return on equity: 28.7%
Cash ($ mil.): 132.7
Current ratio: 0.99
Long-term debt ($ mil.): 70.0
No. of shares (mil.): 100.1
Dividends
 Yield: —
 Payout: —
Market value ($ mil.): 1,234.0

	STOCK PRICE ($) FY Close	P/E High/Low		PER SHARE ($) Earnings	Dividends	Book Value
12/18	12.32	11	6	2.00	0.00	7.96
12/17	20.16	121	65	0.16	0.00	4.98
12/16	0.00	—	—	(1.19)	0.00	4.20
Annual Growth	—	—	—	—	—	37.7%

Proto Labs Inc

Proto Labs creates custom parts in quick turnaround for prototypes and short-run production. The company's web-based interface allows customers to upload a 3D CAD file and Proto Labs' software can quickly quote a price. The Injection Molded division (47% of sales) produces aluminum molds for production of plastic and rubber injection-molded parts. Proto Labs' CNC Machining segment (35% of sales) uses milling machinery to produce custom products. The 3D Printing division (12% of sales) makes plastic and metal parts. The company's Sheet Metal segment (6% of sales) can produce between one and 500 precision metal products. The US accounts for about 80% of Proto Labs' sales.

Financial Performance

Proto Labs' revenue has more than doubled over the last five years. Growth has been boosted by acquisitions which have helped the company expand into new geographic markets and offer a wider variety of manufacturing technologies and materials.

Sales in 2018 increased 29% to $445.6 million compared to $344.5 million in 2017. Growth in 2018 was fueled by the rising volume of product developers and engineers Proto Labs served. All the company's operating segments saw strong growth especially the sheet metal unit which benefited from the 2017 purchase of RAPID which bolstered the company's sheet metal and CNC machining offerings.

Net income increased 17.2% to $76.6 million in 2018 compared to 2017 primarily due to a stronger customer base and a broader array of product capabilities.

Cash at the end of 2018 was $85 million an increase of $48.3 million from the prior year. Cash from operations contributed $122.9 million to the coffers while investing activities used $63.3 million mainly for capital expenditures and marketable securities purchases. Financing activities used $10.4 million primarily for stock repurchases and payments on debt.

Strategy

Proto Labs has rapidly added new customers. Between 2016 and 2018 the number of unique product developers and engineers the company serves has risen 46%. The company targets companies where developers and engineers have already used Proto Labs' products and builds on those relationships to add new users largely through word-of-mouth. Proto Labs' sales and marketing teams also target new customers in geographic regions where product developers and engineers are most highly concentrated — the US Europe and Japan.

The company plans to enhance the functionality of its web-based platform while increasing the level of automation to meet customers' evolving needs. To that end Proto Labs is also extending its product lines to grow the range size design geometries materials and complexity of the parts it can produce.

Company Background

Proto Labs began as The Protomold Company (molded plastic parts) but added CNC metal part machining its Firstcut business in 2007. In 2009 both branches began operating under the Proto Labs banner. It all started when founder and computer geek Lawrence Lukis started a desktop printer design business and was astounded at the long turnaround (weeks) and cost (thousands) for prototype parts. He turned his computer skills to solving the problem and found a way to completely automate the entire process and produce a part in a day for prices starting at $1500.

EXECUTIVES

Vice President Marketing, William M Dietrick
EVP and CTO, Donald G. Krantz, age 64, $286,083 total compensation
President and CEO, Victoria M. (Vicki) Holt, age 61, $514,539 total compensation
CFO, John A. Way, $290,000 total compensation

VP and General Manager and Managing Director - Europe Middle East and Africa, John B. Tumelty, age 48, $189,268 total compensation
CTO, Rich Baker
VP and General Manager Americas, Robert Bodor, age 46, $249,323 total compensation
National Account Manager, Todd Martin
Vice President Marketing, Bill Dietrick
Vice President Managing Director, Bjoern Klaas
Chairman, Lawrence J. Lukis, age 71
Board Member, Rainer Gawlick
Board Member, Douglas Kohrs
Auditors: Ernst & Young LLP

LOCATIONS

HQ: Proto Labs Inc
  5540 Pioneer Creek Drive, Maple Plain, MN 55359
Phone: 763 479-3680
Web: www.protolabs.com

PRODUCTS/OPERATIONS

2013 Sales

	$ mil.	% of total
Protomold	115.1	71
Firstcut	48.0	29
Total	**163.1**	**100**

COMPETITORS

Ajax United Patterns and Molds
Anchor Mfg. Group
Deswell
Materialise
Richco
Total Plastics

HISTORICAL FINANCIALS
Company Type: Public

Income Statement
FYE: December 31

	REVENUE ($ mil.)	NET INCOME ($ mil.)	NET PROFIT MARGIN	EMPLOYEES
12/18	445.6	76.5	17.2%	2,487
12/17	344.4	51.7	15.0%	2,266
12/16	298.0	42.7	14.3%	1,700
12/15	264.1	46.5	17.6%	1,549
12/14	209.5	41.6	19.9%	1,077
Annual Growth	**20.8%**	**16.5%**	**—**	**23.3%**

2018 Year-End Financials

Debt ratio: —
Return on equity: 15.2%
Cash ($ mil.): 85.0
Current ratio: 4.08
Long-term debt ($ mil.): —
No. of shares (mil.): 26.9
Dividends
  Yield: —
  Payout: —
Market value ($ mil.): 3,044.0

	STOCK PRICE ($) FY Close	P/E High/Low		PER SHARE ($) Earnings	Dividends	Book Value
12/18	112.79	58	36	2.81	0.00	20.07
12/17	103.00	55	25	1.93	0.00	17.19
12/16	51.35	50	27	1.61	0.00	14.33
12/15	63.69	44	32	1.77	0.00	12.51
12/14	67.16	53	36	1.60	0.00	10.28
Annual Growth	**13.8%**	—	—	**15.1%**	—	**18.2%**

Provident Bancorp Inc (MD)

Auditors: Whittlesey PC

LOCATIONS

HQ: Provident Bancorp Inc (MD)
  5 Market Street, Amesbury, MA 01913
Phone: 978 834-8555
Web: www.theprovidentbank.com

HISTORICAL FINANCIALS
Company Type: Public

Income Statement
FYE: December 31

	ASSETS ($ mil.)	NET INCOME ($ mil.)	INCOME AS % OF ASSETS	EMPLOYEES
12/18	974.0	9.3	1.0%	132
12/17	902.2	7.9	0.9%	135
12/16	795.5	6.3	0.8%	128
12/15	743.4	3.8	0.5%	115
12/14	658.6	4.5	0.7%	116
Annual Growth	**10.3%**	**19.6%**	—	**3.3%**

2018 Year-End Financials

Return on assets: 0.9%
Return on equity: 7.7%
Long-term debt ($ mil.): —
No. of shares (mil.): 9.6
Sales ($ mil): 46.5
Dividends
  Yield: —
  Payout: —
Market value ($ mil.): 209.0

	STOCK PRICE ($) FY Close	P/E High/Low		PER SHARE ($) Earnings	Dividends	Book Value
12/18	21.68	30	20	1.00	0.00	13.05
12/17	26.45	31	20	0.86	0.00	12.02
12/16	17.90	28	19	0.69	0.00	11.31
12/15	12.99	—	—	(0.00)	0.00	10.68
Annual Growth	**18.6%**	—	—	—	—	**6.9%**

Prudential Bancorp Inc (New)

Auditors: S.R. Snodgrass, P.C.

LOCATIONS

HQ: Prudential Bancorp Inc (New)
  1834 West Oregon Avenue, Philadelphia, PA 19145
Phone: 215 755-1500
Web: www.prudentialsavingsbank.com

HISTORICAL FINANCIALS
Company Type: Public

Income Statement
FYE: September 30

	ASSETS ($ mil.)	NET INCOME ($ mil.)	INCOME AS % OF ASSETS	EMPLOYEES
09/19	1,289.4	9.5	0.7%	88
09/18	1,081.1	7.0	0.7%	83
09/17	899.5	2.7	0.3%	87
09/16	559.4	2.7	0.5%	63
09/15	487.1	2.2	0.5%	71
Annual Growth	**27.5%**	**43.7%**	—	**5.5%**

2019 Year-End Financials

Return on assets: 0.8%
Return on equity: 7.1%
Long-term debt ($ mil.): —
No. of shares (mil.): 8.8
Sales ($ mil): 47.1
Dividends
  Yield: 3.8%
  Payout: 61.9%
Market value ($ mil.): 151.0

	STOCK PRICE ($) FY Close	P/E High/Low		PER SHARE ($) Earnings	Dividends	Book Value
09/19	17.01	17	14	1.07	0.65	15.71
09/18	17.31	25	21	0.78	0.70	14.29
09/17	18.53	57	44	0.32	0.12	15.12
09/16	14.48	43	38	0.36	0.12	14.17
09/15	14.41	56	44	0.26	0.27	13.85
Annual Growth	**4.2%**	—	—	**42.4%**	**24.6%**	**3.2%**

Pzena Investment Management Inc

EXECUTIVES

Chairman CEO and Co-Chief Investment Officer, Richard S. Pzena, age 60, $377,500 total compensation
President and Co-Chief Investment Officer, John P. Goetz, age 61, $377,500 total compensation
President and Head of Business Development and Client Service, William L. Lipsey, age 60, $377,500 total compensation
COO, Gary J. Bachman, age 51, $350,000 total compensation
EVP and Portfolio Manager Global Focused Value International (ex-US) Focused Value International (ex-US) Expanded Value Global Expanded Value and European Focused Value, Michael D. Peterson, age 54, $377,500 total compensation
Manager Financial Reporting, Jessica R. Doran
Auditors: PricewaterhouseCoopers LLP

LOCATIONS

HQ: Pzena Investment Management Inc
  320 Park Avenue, New York, NY 10022
Phone: 212 355-1600
Web: www.pzena.com

COMPETITORS

AllianceBernstein
BlackRock
FMR
Morgan Stanley Investment Management
Principal Global
State Street

HISTORICAL FINANCIALS
Company Type: Public

Income Statement
FYE: December 31

	REVENUE ($ mil.)	NET INCOME ($ mil.)	NET PROFIT MARGIN	EMPLOYEES
12/18	153.5	13.7	9.0%	106
12/17	141.3	6.9	4.9%	105
12/16	108.3	16.1	14.9%	100
12/15	116.6	7.6	6.6%	88
12/14	112.5	8.1	7.2%	81
Annual Growth	**8.1%**	**14.2%**	—	**7.0%**

QCR Holdings Inc

Quad City is muscling in on the community banking scene in the Midwest. QCR Holdings is the holding company for Quad City Bank & Trust Cedar Rapids Bank & Trust Rockford Bank & Trust and Community State Bank. Together the banks have about 20 offices serving the Quad City area of Illinois and Iowa as well as the communities of Cedar Rapids Iowa; Rockford Illinois; and Milwaukee. The banks offer traditional deposit products and services and concentrate their lending activities on local businesses: Commercial real estate loans make up about half of the loan portfolio; commercial loans and leases make up another third.

Operations
QCR Holdings' Bancard subsidiary provides credit card processing services; its majority-owned M2 Lease Funds leases machinery and equipment to commercial and industrial businesses.

Strategy
QCR Holdings has grown by launching operations in new geographic markets and then building upon them. It also expands through acquisitions. In mid-2016 the company acquired Iowa-based Community State Bank which operates some 10 branches in the Des Moines area.

EXECUTIVES
Senior Vice President And Director Dep, Kathleen M Francque
President and CEO, Douglas M. (Doug) Hultquist, age 64, $290,000 total compensation
Director; President and CEO Cedar Rapids Bank and Trust, Larry J. Helling, age 63, $251,899 total compensation
EVP and Chief Credit Officer, Dana L. Nichols
EVP COO and CFO, Todd A. Gipple, age 56, $251,899 total compensation
EVP Corporate Strategy Human Resources and Branding, Cathie Whiteside, $162,000 total compensation
President and CEO Rockford Bank and Trust, Thomas D. Budd, $172,000 total compensation
President and CEO Quad City Bank and Trust, John H. Anderson, $200,000 total compensation
EVP Deposit Operations and Information Services, John A. Rodriguez
SVP and CIO, Michael J. Wyffels

EVP and Chief Operations Officer, John R. McEvoy
President and CEO Community Bank and Trust, Stacey Bentley
President m2 Lease Funds, Richard W. Couch
Chairman and CEO m2 Lease Funds, John R. Engelbrecht
EVP and Chief Investment Officer, M. Randolph (Rand) Westlund
Vice President Operations Manager, Sherrie L Larson
Senior Vice President Director Of Hum, Jill Dekeyser
Senior Vice President Marketing and Co, Cathy Whiteside
Vice President Controller, Jeri Vandervinne
Vice President And Controller, Nick Anderson
Assistant Vice President Compliance, Thomas King
Vice President, William Grimes
Vice President Product, Gregory Braid
Senior Vice President Treasury Management, Lori Diaz
ASSISTANT VICE PRESIDENT MARKETING AND PUBLIC RELATIONS OFFICER, Stacey L Keller
ASSISTANT VICE PRESIDENT MARKETING AND PUBLIC RELATIONS OFFICER, Stacey Keller
Executive Vice President Corporate Strategy and Branding, S Whiteside
Chairman, Patrick S. (Pat) Baird, age 66
Vice Chairman of the Board, Marie Ziegler
Board Member, Donna Sorensen
Auditors: RSM US LLP

LOCATIONS
HQ: QCR Holdings Inc
3551 7th Street, Moline, IL 61265
Phone: 309 736-3580
Web: www.qcrh.com

PRODUCTS/OPERATIONS

2015 Sales

	$ mil.	% of total
Quad City Bank & Trust	52.8	46
Cedar Rapids Bank & Trust	37.5	32
Rockford Bank & Trust	14.8	13
Wealth Management	9.1	8
All other	0.7	1
Inter-company Eliminations	(0.4)	-
Total	**114.5**	**100**

COMPETITORS
Bank of America
Blackhawk Bancorp
First Business Financial
First Midwest Bancorp
First National of Nebraska
MidWestOne
U.S. Bancorp

HISTORICAL FINANCIALS
Company Type: Public

Income Statement FYE: December 31

	ASSETS ($ mil.)	NET INCOME ($ mil.)	INCOME AS % OF ASSETS	EMPLOYEES
12/18	4,949.7	43.1	0.9%	755
12/17	3,982.6	35.7	0.9%	641
12/16	3,301.9	27.6	0.8%	572
12/15	2,593.2	16.9	0.7%	406
12/14	2,524.9	14.9	0.6%	409
Annual Growth	18.3%	30.3%	—	16.6%

2018 Year-End Financials
Debt ratio: —
Return on equity: 42.2%
Cash ($ mil.): 38.1
Current ratio: 3.37
Long-term debt ($ mil.): —
No. of shares (mil.): 69.6
Dividends
Yield: 5.9%
Payout: 66.2%
Market value ($ mil.): 602.0

	STOCK PRICE ($) FY Close	P/E High/Low		PER SHARE ($) Earnings	Dividends	Book Value
12/18	8.65	17	11	0.77	0.51	0.47
12/17	10.67	30	21	0.40	0.37	0.47
12/16	11.11	11	6	0.58	0.41	0.42
12/15	8.60	21	14	0.50	0.41	0.27
12/14	9.46	19	13	0.53	0.35	0.28
Annual Growth	(2.2%)	—	—	9.8%	9.9%	14.1%

Qualys, Inc.

Qualys tries to calm customers' qualms about cybersecurity. The Qualys Cloud Platform is a cloud security and compliance management software suite of about 20 applications that automates security weakness detection and network security asset auditing. Its biggest product Vulnerability Management includes continuous monitoring threat protection and IT asset tracking through a cloud agent. Its products keep watch over networks with hardware and software sensors. The company counts more than 12200 customers in some 130 countries. Qualys reaches many customers through partnerships with managed service providers consultants and resellers including IBM Fujitsu Optiv and Verizon Communications.

Financial Performance
Qualys has delivered robust revenue increases with sales more than doubling from 2014-2018. The company's net income also jumped boasting profit margins of 17% in 2017 and 20% in 2018.

In 2018 revenue rose to $278.9 million up $48.1 million from 2017 driven by additional revenue from existing customers as well as revenue from new customers. Existing customers provided about $36 million of the increase while new customers contributed about $12 million. Geographically international customers accounted for just more than half of the increase.

Higher sales led to net income of $57.3 million in 2018 compared to $40.4 million in 2017.

Qualys' treasury held $42.2 million in cash in 2018 compared to $87.8 million in 2017. Its operations generated $125.5 million in 2018 while investing activities used $93.5 million and financing activities used $77.5 million.

Strategy
Qualys intends to grow by growing. That is the company is building out its portfolio of applications to attract additional dollars from current customers. In 2018 Qualys offered new applications for container security cloud inventory cloud security assessment certificate inventory and certificate assessment. It also released an AI cloud app that provides customers single source of identification of IT assets within hybrid cloud environments.

The company develops some new capabilities in-house but obtains others through acquisitions. The deal for 1Mobility provides information about mobile devices owned by Qualys customers and

2018 Year-End Financials
Return on assets: 0.9%
Return on equity: 10.4%
Long-term debt ($ mil.): —
No. of shares (mil.): 15.7
Sales ($ mil): 224.4
Dividends
Yield: 0.7%
Payout: 8.8%
Market value ($ mil.): 504.0

	STOCK PRICE ($) FY Close	P/E High/Low		PER SHARE ($) Earnings	Dividends	Book Value
12/18	32.09	17	10	2.86	0.24	30.10
12/17	42.85	18	15	2.61	0.20	25.38
12/16	43.30	20	10	2.17	0.16	21.82
12/15	24.29	15	11	1.61	0.08	19.21
12/14	17.86	10	10	1.72	0.08	18.12
Annual Growth	15.8%	—	—	13.6%	31.6%	13.5%

their employees. The Layered Insight acquisition brought container security capabilities to Qualys. Through the acquisition of Adya Qualys can provide security and compliance audits of SaaS applications.

Qualys has expanded relationships with partners including Amazon Web Services IBM and Microsoft. In its partnership with Carahsoft Qualys could increase its penetration of the federal government market with the FedRAMP-authorized Qualys Gov Platform.

Qualys relies on US customers for two-thirds of its sales. Efforts to cultivate international markets could be paying off with as international customers accounted for more than half of growth from new customers in 2018.

EXECUTIVES

VP General Counsel and Corporate Secretary, Bruce K. Posey, age 68, $250,000 total compensation
Chairman and CEO, Philippe F. Courtot, age 74, $350,000 total compensation
VP Marketing, Amer S. Deeba, age 52, $250,000 total compensation
CTO, Wolfgang Kandek
EVP Worldwide Field Operations, Dan Barahona
Chief Product Officer, Sumedh S. Thakar, age 43, $260,417 total compensation
CFO, Melissa Fisher
Vice President and General Manager Global SME and SMB Sales, Fuad Najjar
Vice President Field Operations, Michael Yee
Vp Engineering, Dilip Bachwani
Vice President Global Business Process and Applications, Grayson Williams
VP Product Management Cloud Agent Platform, Chris Carlson
Vice President Channel And Business Development, Michael Guglielmi
Vice President FP and A and Investor Relations, joo Kim
Vp And General Manager Federal Division, Bill Solms
Board Member, Sandra Bergeron
Board Member, Jeffrey Hank
Member Board Of Directors, Kristi Rogers
Board Member, Todd Headley
Board Member, Patricia Hatter
Auditors: Grant Thornton LLP

LOCATIONS

HQ: Qualys, Inc.
919 E. Hillsdale Boulevard, 4th Floor, Foster City, CA 94404
Phone: 650 801-6100
Web: www.qualys.com

PRODUCTS/OPERATIONS

2018 Sales

	% of total
Direct	59
Partner	41
Total	100

COMPETITORS

Barracuda Networks	McAfee
BeyondTrust	Micro Focus
CA Inc.	Rapid7
Check Point Software	Symantec
FireEye	Tenable Holdings
IBM	Trustwave Holdings
Imperva	

HISTORICAL FINANCIALS

Company Type: Public

Income Statement — FYE: December 31

	REVENUE ($ mil.)	NET INCOME ($ mil.)	NET PROFIT MARGIN	EMPLOYEES
12/18	278.8	57.3	20.5%	1,194
12/17	230.8	40.4	17.5%	869
12/16	197.9	19.2	9.7%	684
12/15	164.2	15.8	9.7%	510
12/14	133.5	30.2	22.6%	431
Annual Growth	20.2%	17.3%	—	29.0%

2018 Year-End Financials
Debt ratio: 0.2%
Return on equity: 16.3%
Cash ($ mil.): 41.0
Current ratio: 1.92
Long-term debt ($ mil.): —
No. of shares (mil.): 39.0
Dividends
 Yield: —
 Payout: —
Market value ($ mil.): 2,916.0

	STOCK PRICE ($) FY Close	P/E High/Low		PER SHARE ($) Earnings	Dividends	Book Value
12/18	74.74	66	40	1.37	0.00	9.18
12/17	59.35	57	30	1.01	0.00	8.90
12/16	31.65	71	32	0.50	0.00	7.21
12/15	33.09	117	59	0.42	0.00	5.68
12/14	37.75	44	20	0.81	0.00	4.52
Annual Growth	18.6%	—	—	14.0%	—	19.4%

Quidel Corp.

Is it the flu or are you pregnant? Quidel can tell you quickly enough. The company makes rapid diagnostic in vitro test products used at the point-of-care (POC) usually at a doctor's office or other outpatient setting. Unlike tests sent off to a lab POC tests can be read on the spot. Quidel's leading products are diagnostics for infectious diseases (such as influenza and strep throat) and reproductive health sold under the QuickVue D3 Direct Detection and Thyretain brands. The company also makes diagnostics for streptococci chlamydia and the ulcer-causing H. pylori bacterium as well as Sofia a next generation rapid immunofluorescence-based point-of-care diagnostic test system.

Operations

The company's new AmpliVue is the first hand-held molecular device approved by the FDA. It tests for infectious diarrhea group B streptococcus and herpes simplex one and two; Quidel is always exploring additional uses. Another new product is Lyra a real-time test for flu (A and B) strep and other viruses. AmpliVue and Lyra are both part of the company's molecular diagnostics line.

Quidel's Specialty Products Group (SPG) makes research and clinical assays (the latter in the areas of bone health and inflammatory disease) used in research (but not patient diagnosis) and sells them to labs under the MicroVue and TECOmedical brand names. The SPG division focuses its research on biomarkers that hold potential for developing rapid POC assays in the future.

Tests for infectious diseases make up about 70% of sales.

Geographic Reach

The company markets its products in the US through a network of national and regional distributors and a direct sales force. Internationally it sells and markets in Asia-Pacific primarily Japan and Europe through distributor arrangements.

Quidel manufactures its products at facilities in California and Ohio and in Germany. It has R&D facilities in Ohio and Massachusetts as well as in Germany.

International sales account for about 13% of revenue.

Sales and Marketing

Quidel sells its products in the US through national and regional distributors including Cardinal Health and McKesson Corp. It also sells products directly to end users and distributors for professional use in physician offices hospitals clinical laboratories reference laboratories leading universities retail clinics and wellness screening centers.

Internationally Quidel focuses on markets in Japan (where its QuickVue flu tests are popular) and Europe. To help penetrate foreign markets which have been less receptive to POC diagnostics than the US Quidel enters into agreements with international distributors.

Financial Performance

The company's revenues were up in 2013 due to an increase in demand for its flu tests. Products to test for infectious disease like the flu account for about 70% of the company's revenues.

Quidel reported a 48% spike in net income in 2013 after the company received a favorable ruling from the IRS and released about $3.5 million it was holding in reserved pending the outcome. Operating cash flow followed revenue and showed a modest $6 million gain as it paid to relocate some facilities.

Strategy

The company is looking to become a broader-based diagnostic company with products in market segments in which it has significant expertise and know-how. It is leveraging its infrastructure to develop and launch lateral flow and Direct Fluorescent Antibody (DFA) products such as the Sofia Analyzer. It is also developing its Lyra and AmpliVue molecular diagnostics franchise and is strengthening its position with distribution partners and customers in order to sell more products.

In addition the company leverages acquisitions to expand its product line. In 2013 it acquired BioHelix a former partner with which it co-developed an isothermal test for C. difficile viral infections for about $10 million. It also purchased AndiaTec a Germany maker of molecular assays for about $3 million. The deal gave the company its Germany R&D facility.

Mergers and Acquisitions

In mid-2017 Quidel agreed to buy certain assets of Alere for $440 million. The assets to be acquired include Alere's Triage MeterPro cardiovascular and toxicology business and its B-type Naturietic Peptide assay line.

EXECUTIVES

SVP Clinical and Regulatory Affairs, John D. Tamerius, age 73, $297,544 total compensation
President and CEO, Douglas C. (Doug) Bryant, age 61, $524,378 total compensation
SVP Business Development General Counsel and Corporate Secretary, Robert J. Bujarski, age 51, $334,299 total compensation

SVP Operations, Scot M. McLeod, age 54, $258,440 total compensation
CFO, Randall J. (Randy) Steward, age 64, $331,923 total compensation
SVP Research and Development, Werner Kroll, age 62, $195,462 total compensation
Vice President Us Sales, Peter Troija
Vice President, Adonis Stassinopoulos
Vice President Of Global Distribution, Chuck Mckinley
Chairman, Kenneth F. (Ken) Buechler, age 66
Auditors: Ernst & Young LLP

LOCATIONS

HQ: Quidel Corp.
 12544 High Bluff Drive, Suite 200, San Diego, CA 92130
Phone: 858 552-1100
Web: www.quidel.com

PRODUCTS/OPERATIONS

2015 Sales

	$ mil.	% of total
Infectious disease products	141.8	72
Women's health products	37.2	19
Gastrointestinal disease products	7.2	4
Royalty license fees and grants	6.2	3
Other products	3.7	2
Total	**196.1**	**100**

Selected Subsidiaries
BioHelix Corporation
Diagnostic Hybrids Inc.
Litmus Concepts Inc.
Metra Biosystems Inc.
Osteo Sciences Corporation
Pacific Biotech Inc.
Quidel China Ltd.
Quidel Germany GmbH
Quidel International LLC

Selected Brands
AmpliVue
Copan
D3 Direct Detection
ELVIS
Lyra brands
QuickVue
Sofia
Thyretain

COMPETITORS

ACON Laboratories	Meridian Bioscience
Axis-Shield	Roche Diagnostics
Beckman Coulter	Sekisui Diagnostics
Becton Dickinson	Thermo Fisher Scientific
Church & Dwight	Trinity Biotech
McNeil Consumer Healthcare	bioMérieux

HISTORICAL FINANCIALS

Company Type: Public

Income Statement
FYE: December 31

	REVENUE ($ mil.)	NET INCOME ($ mil.)	NET PROFIT MARGIN	EMPLOYEES
12/18	522.2	74.1	14.2%	1,224
12/17	277.7	(8.1)	—	1,193
12/16	191.6	(13.8)	—	627
12/15	196.1	(6.0)	—	624
12/14	182.6	(7.0)	—	610
Annual Growth	**30.0%**	—	—	**19.0%**

2018 Year-End Financials
Debt ratio: 13.3%
Return on equity: 22.7%
Cash ($ mil.): 43.7
Current ratio: 1.21
Long-term debt ($ mil.): 53.1
No. of shares (mil.): 39.3
Dividends
 Yield: —
 Payout: —
Market value ($ mil.): 1,923.0

	STOCK PRICE ($) FY Close	P/E High/Low		PER SHARE ($) Earnings	Dividends	Book Value
12/18	48.82	39	21	1.86	0.00	10.81
12/17	43.35	—	—	(0.24)	0.00	6.58
12/16	21.42	—	—	(0.42)	0.00	6.10
12/15	21.20	—	—	(0.18)	0.00	6.56
12/14	28.92	—	—	(0.21)	0.00	7.12
Annual Growth	**14.0%**	—	—	—	—	**11.0%**

QuinStreet, Inc.

QuinStreet connects companies with potential customers through the information superhighway. The online direct marketing company uses proprietary technologies to provide leads to companies. Clients use the leads as the targets of their direct marketing campaigns. As a sign of its confidence in its quality QuinStreet has adopted a pay-for-performance model of pricing in which customers are charged based on lead performance. Catering mainly to the education and financial services sectors its customers have included big organizations such as DeVry and ADT. QuinStreet has offices in the US Brazil and India. The company was founded in 1999.

Operations
QuinStreet's two largest client verticals are financial services and education. Its financial services segment represented 62% of revenue in fiscal 2017. QuinStreet's education client vertical represented 24% of revenue in fiscal 2017 while the company's other client verticals consisting of home services business-to-business technology and medical represented the remainder of revenue.

Geographic Reach
QuinStreet's corporate headquarters are located in Foster City California with additional offices in the US Brazil and India. Nearly all of the company's revenues (98%) come from the US.

Sales and Marketing
QuinStreet generates revenue from fees earned through the delivery of qualified leads clicks inquiries calls customers and display advertisements.

Financial Performance
QuinStreet has enjoyed steady revenue growth year-over-year. The company reported $299 million in revenue for fiscal 2017 up from $297 million the previous fiscal year (an increase of $2.1 million or 1%).

QuinStreet's financial services segment revenue increased $29.6 million or 19% primarily due to an enhanced product set. The company's education client segment's revenue decreased by $18 million or 20% primarily due to a reduction in clients . Revenue from QuinStreet's other client verticals decreased $9.5 million or 18% primarily due to decreased client demand.

Despite the top line revenue growth in fiscal 2017 QuinStreet suffered a net loss of $12.2 million. The company has suffered net losses in the past several fiscal years as its expenses overshadow its revenue.

QuinStreet reported $18.5 billion in cash from operations at the end of fiscal 2017 up from $1 billion at the close of fiscal 2016. Cash provided by operating activities in fiscal 2017 included the net loss of $12.2 million which included a restructuring charge of $2.4 million offset by non-cash adjustments of $23 million. There was also a net increase in cash from changes in working capital of $7.8 million during fiscal 2017 compared to the prior fiscal period.

Strategy
Education and financial services remain QuinStreet's largest vertical markets bringing in the majority of its revenue. The company's growth strategy is to increase the number of verticals it serves while also entering new verticals. It does so primarily acquisitions and has spent the last few years snapping up marketing and media firms. Other industries served include of business-to-business technology home services and medical sectors.

QuinStreet believes marketing approaches are changing as budgets continue to shift from offline analog advertising media to digital advertising media and internet marketing.

EXECUTIVES

Chairman and CEO, Douglas (Doug) Valenti, age 60, $525,000 total compensation
CTO, Nina Bhanap, age 46, $362,000 total compensation
CFO, Gregory Wong, $262,771 total compensation
General Counsel and Head of Compliance and Corporate Development, Martin J. (Marty) Collins, $75,000 total compensation
Senior Vice President and Category Head of Financial Services, Andreja Stevanovic
Vice President PPC and SEO Education Vertical, Jeremy Crisp
Senior Vice President Category Head Of Financial Services, Brett Moses
Auditors: PricewaterhouseCoopers LLP

LOCATIONS

HQ: QuinStreet, Inc.
 950 Tower Lane, 6th Floor, Foster City, CA 94404
Phone: 650 587-7700
Web: www.quinstreet.com

PRODUCTS/OPERATIONS

Selected Industries Served
Financial services
Education
Business-to-business technology
Home services
Medical

COMPETITORS

About.com	Leaf Group Ltd.
Agency.com	Marchex
Aptimus	Monster Worldwide
Conversant	Proven Direct
DigitasLBi	Yahoo!
Google	

HISTORICAL FINANCIALS
Company Type: Public

Income Statement — FYE: June 30

	REVENUE ($ mil.)	NET INCOME ($ mil.)	NET PROFIT MARGIN	EMPLOYEES
06/19	455.1	62.4	13.7%	637
06/18	404.3	15.9	3.9%	506
06/17	299.7	(12.2)	—	469
06/16	297.7	(19.4)	—	601
06/15	282.1	(20.0)	—	638
Annual Growth	12.7%	—	—	(0.0%)

2019 Year-End Financials
Debt ratio: —
Return on equity: 33.6%
Cash ($ mil.): 62.5
Current ratio: 1.71
Long-term debt ($ mil.): —
No. of shares (mil.): 50.5
Dividends
Yield: —
Payout: —
Market value ($ mil.): 801.0

	STOCK PRICE ($) FY Close	P/E High	P/E Low	Earnings	Dividends	Book Value
06/19	15.85	16	10	1.18	0.00	4.41
06/18	12.70	43	10	0.32	0.00	3.08
06/17	4.17	—	—	(0.27)	0.00	2.60
06/16	3.55	—	—	(0.43)	0.00	2.74
06/15	6.45	—	—	(0.45)	0.00	3.04
Annual Growth	25.2%		—	—	—	9.8%

Radiant Logistics, Inc.

EXECUTIVES
Chairman and CEO, Bohn H. Crain, age 54, $325,000 total compensation
COO Freight Forwarding Operations, E. Joseph (Joe) Bento
SVP and CFO, Todd E. Macomber, age 54, $200,000 total compensation
Chief Commercial Officer and COO Service By Air Inc. (SBA), Arnie Goldstein
Vice President Business Development, Philippe Gabay
VICE PRESIDENT STATION OPERATIONS SUPPORT, Tim Kolkmeyer
NATIONAL ACCOUNT MANAGER, Connie Banks
Vice President Risk Management, Paul Kwiatkowski
Auditors: BDO USA, LLP

LOCATIONS
HQ: Radiant Logistics, Inc.
405 114th Ave S.E., Third Floor, Bellevue, WA 98404
Phone: 425 943-4599 **Fax:** 425 462-0768
Web: www.radiantdelivers.com

COMPETITORS
AIT Worldwide Logistics
APL Logistics
CEVA Logistics
DHL
Landstar System
UPS Supply Chain Solutions

HISTORICAL FINANCIALS
Company Type: Public

Income Statement — FYE: June 30

	REVENUE ($ mil.)	NET INCOME ($ mil.)	NET PROFIT MARGIN	EMPLOYEES
06/19	890.5	16.3	1.8%	708
06/18	842.4	10.1	1.2%	728
06/17	777.6	4.8	0.6%	758
06/16	782.5	(3.5)	—	640
06/15	502.6	5.8	1.2%	760
Annual Growth	15.4%	29.2%	—	(1.8%)

2019 Year-End Financials
Debt ratio: 13.6%
Return on equity: 12.5%
Cash ($ mil.): 5.4
Current ratio: 1.27
Long-term debt ($ mil.): 32.5
No. of shares (mil.): 49.5
Dividends
Yield: —
Payout: —
Market value ($ mil.): 304.0

	STOCK PRICE ($) FY Close	P/E High	P/E Low	Earnings	Dividends	Book Value
06/19	6.14	26	14	0.27	0.00	2.56
06/18	3.91	33	21	0.16	0.00	2.70
06/17	5.38	107	41	0.06	0.00	2.51
06/16	3.00	—	—	(0.11)	0.00	2.44
06/15	7.31	72	27	0.10	0.00	1.98
Annual Growth	(4.3%)		—	28.2%	—	6.6%

Rand Worldwide Inc.

Auditors: Dixon Hughes Goodman LLP

LOCATIONS
HQ: Rand Worldwide Inc.
11201 Dolfield Boulevard, Suite 112, Owings Mills, MD 21117
Phone: 410 581-8080
Web: www.rand.com

HISTORICAL FINANCIALS
Company Type: Public

Income Statement — FYE: June 30

	REVENUE ($ mil.)	NET INCOME ($ mil.)	NET PROFIT MARGIN	EMPLOYEES
06/19	222.4	12.0	5.4%	0
06/18	116.4	2.6	2.2%	0
06/17	81.0	3.6	4.5%	0
06/16	85.2	5.5	6.5%	0
06/15	86.7	2.0	2.4%	345
Annual Growth	26.6%	55.8%	—	—

2019 Year-End Financials
Debt ratio: 23.6%
Return on equity: 39.2%
Cash ($ mil.): 0.6
Current ratio: 0.91
Long-term debt ($ mil.): 15.2
No. of shares (mil.): 31.4
Dividends
Yield: —
Payout: —
Market value ($ mil.): 211.0

	STOCK PRICE ($) FY Close	P/E High	P/E Low	Earnings	Dividends	Book Value
06/19	6.70	—	—	(0.00)	0.00	1.17
06/18	3.14	—	—	(0.00)	0.00	0.79
06/17	2.70	—	—	(0.00)	0.00	0.71
06/16	2.02	—	—	(0.00)	0.00	0.59
06/15	2.13	45	22	0.05	0.00	0.43
Annual Growth	33.2%		—	—	—	28.0%

Rayonier Advanced Materials Inc

Auditors: Grant Thornton LLP

LOCATIONS
HQ: Rayonier Advanced Materials Inc
1301 Riverplace Boulevard, Suite 2300, Jacksonville, FL 32207
Phone: 904 357-4600
Web: www.rayonieram.com

HISTORICAL FINANCIALS
Company Type: Public

Income Statement — FYE: December 31

	REVENUE ($ mil.)	NET INCOME ($ mil.)	NET PROFIT MARGIN	EMPLOYEES
12/18	2,134.4	128.4	6.0%	4,200
12/17	961.3	324.9	33.8%	4,200
12/16	868.7	73.2	8.4%	1,200
12/15	941.3	55.2	5.9%	1,200
12/14	957.6	31.6	3.3%	1,300
Annual Growth	22.2%	41.9%	—	34.1%

2018 Year-End Financials
Debt ratio: 44.3%
Return on equity: 18.3%
Cash ($ mil.): 108.9
Current ratio: 1.93
Long-term debt ($ mil.): 1,173.1
No. of shares (mil.): 49.2
Dividends
Yield: 2.6%
Payout: 14.2%
Market value ($ mil.): 525.0

	STOCK PRICE ($) FY Close	P/E High	P/E Low	Earnings	Dividends	Book Value
12/18	10.65	10	4	1.96	0.28	14.34
12/17	20.45	3	2	5.81	0.28	13.41
12/16	15.46	10	4	1.55	0.28	4.89
12/15	9.79	18	5	1.30	0.28	(0.40)
12/14	22.30	58	29	0.75	0.14	(1.46)
Annual Growth	(16.9%)		—	—	27.1%	18.9%	—

RBB Bancorp

Auditors: Eide Bailly LLP

LOCATIONS

HQ: RBB Bancorp
1055 Wilshire Blvd., Suite 1200, Los Angeles, CA 90017
Phone: 213 627-9888
Web: www.royalbusinessbankusa.com

HISTORICAL FINANCIALS

Company Type: Public

Income Statement
FYE: December 31

	ASSETS ($ mil.)	NET INCOME ($ mil.)	INCOME AS % OF ASSETS	EMPLOYEES
12/18	2,974.0	36.1	1.2%	365
12/17	1,691.0	25.5	1.5%	203
12/16	1,395.5	19.0	1.4%	177
12/15	1,023.0	12.9	1.3%	0
12/14	0.0	10.4**************%		0
Annual Growth	—	36.4%	—	—

2018 Year-End Financials

Return on assets: 1.5%
Return on equity: 11.2%
Long-term debt ($ mil.): —
No. of shares (mil.): 20.0
Sales ($ mil): 114.9

Dividends
Yield: 2.4%
Payout: 21.3%
Market value ($ mil.): 351.0

	STOCK PRICE ($) FY Close	P/E High/Low	PER SHARE ($) Earnings	Dividends	Book Value
12/18	17.57	16 8	2.01	0.43	18.73
12/17	27.37	15 12	1.68	0.08	16.67
Annual Growth	(35.8%)	— —	19.6%	437.5%	12.4%

RBC Bearings Inc

RBC Bearings keeps businesses on a roll. The company makes an array of plain roller and ball bearing products. It specializes in regulated bearings used by OEMs and their aftermarkets of commercial/military aircraft automobiles and commercial trucks industrial/agricultural machinery as well as air turbines. Targeting high-end markets its precision lineup satisfies thousands of applications from engine controls to radar systems mining tools and gear pumps. RBC's top customers include Boeing GE Lockheed Martin and the US Department of Defense. RBC Bearings has grown since 1919 to some 30 manufacturing facilities in Europe and North America.

Operations

RBC operates through four reportable business segments: Plain Bearings Engineered Products Roller Bearings and Ball Bearings. Plain Bearings represents 45% of total revenue and is used in aircraft controls helicopter rotors or in heavy mining and construction equipment.

Engineered Products consists of highly engineered hydraulics fasteners collets and precision components used in aerospace marine and industrial applications. Roller Bearings are anti-friction bearings that use rollers in place of balls. The company manufactures four basic types of roller bearings: heavy duty needle roller bearings with inner rings tapered roller bearings track rollers and aircraft roller bearings.

Ball Bearings makes four basic types of ball bearings: high precision aerospace airframe control thin section and commercial ball bearings which are used in high-speed rotational applications.

Geographic Reach

The company operates about 30 facilities in the US and has international operations in Canada Switzerland Mexico and Poland. RBC's warehouses reside in the Midwest Southwest and on the East and West coasts of the US as well as in France and Switzerland. The US is its largest market accounting for more than 85% of total sales.

Sales and Marketing

The company sells its products through a direct sales force located in North America Europe Asia and Latin America. It also utilizes marketing managers product managers customer service representatives product application engineers and a global network of industrial and aerospace distributors. The aerospace and defense markets account for more than 65% of total sales. Sales to its top 10 customers generate 33% of total sales.

Financial Performance

RBC has experienced unprecedented growth over the last few years. Its revenues climbed 34% $445 million in 2015 to $597 million in 2016. Profits also jumped 10% from $58 million in 2015 to $64 million in 2016. Both these totals represented historic milestones for the company.

The historic growth for 2016 was driven by an explosive 439% surge in sales from Engineered Products largely due to additional revenue from its Sargent acquisition. Through the purchase RBC enjoyed impressive growth within the aerospace and industrial markets. Related to these factors sales from the US sales also climbed by 29% in 2016.

From 2015 to 2016 the company's cash flow spiked from $72 million to $84 million mainly due to favorable changes in inventory.

Strategy

RBC has managed to increase its sales to the aftermarket. Bearings which are indispensable for a machine's operating efficiency periodically wear out which creates a second stream of replacement parts sales. During 2016 aftermarket sales of replacement parts for installed equipment accounted for nearly 45% of RBC's revenues. Aerospace and defense customers also promise a particularly reliable opportunity for replacement business.

Mergers and Acquisitions

The company makes acquisitions in order to further develop its offerings end-markets and geographic footprint. In early 2016 the company acquired Arizona-based Sargent an expert in precision-engineered products services and repairs for aircraft airframes and engines rotorcraft submarines and land vehicles for $500 million in cash. The deal enhanced RBC's product portfolio and engineering technologies and added exponentially to its Plain Bearings and Engineering Products segments.

Company Background

RBC Bearings is an amalgamation of companies merged and acquired. The company got its start in 1919 making ball bearings; by the 1940s it became the sole supplier for landing gear bearings on military aircraft made by Ford Motor Company. In 2005 the company jetted onto the public investor market.

EXECUTIVES

Chairman President and CEO, Michael J. Hartnett, age 72, $922,643 total compensation
VP; General Manager RBC Division, Richard J. Edwards, age 62, $306,000 total compensation
VP COO and CFO, Daniel A. (Dan) Bergeron, age 58, $370,000 total compensation
VP; General Manager Heim Bearings and Schaublin, Thomas C. Crainer, age 60, $314,000 total compensation
Vice President Sales, Karen De Mestrio
Vice President General Manager, Patrick Bannon
Auditors: Ernst & Young LLP

LOCATIONS

HQ: RBC Bearings Inc
One Tribology Center, Oxford, CT 06478
Phone: 203 267-7001
Web: www.rbcbearings.com

PRODUCTS/OPERATIONS

2016 Sales

	$ mil.	% of total
Plain	270.5	45
Engineered Products	161.3	27
Roller	112.0	19
Ball	53.7	9
Total	597.5	100

2016 Sales

	% of total
Aerospace market	66
Industrial market	34
Total	100

PRODUCTS
AEROSPACE
Airframe Control Ball Bearings
Airframe Control Needle Track Rollers
Ball Bearing Rod Ends
Gear Box and Engine and Roller Ball Bearings
Journal Bearings
Links and Assemblies
Machined Components
Radial Ball Bearings
Rod End Plain Bearings
Spherical Plain Bearings
Stud Type Track Roller Bearings
Swage Tubes and Control Rods
Thin Section Ball Bearings
INDUSTRIAL
Ball Bearings
Cam Followers
Collets/Toolholders
Heavy Duty Fleet Customers
Heavy Duty Needle Roller Bearings
Pins Rollers Shafts
Rod Ends
Self-Lubricating Bearings
Spherical Plain Bearings
Tapered/Tapered Thrust Roller Bearings
Thin Section Ball Bearings

COMPETITORS

Emerson Electric	Rexnord
General Bearing	SKF USA
Kaydon	Timken
MinebeaMitsumi	
NTN Bearing Corp. of America	

HISTORICAL FINANCIALS

Company Type: Public

Income Statement — FYE: March 30

	REVENUE ($ mil.)	NET INCOME ($ mil.)	NET PROFIT MARGIN	EMPLOYEES
03/19	702.5	105.1	15.0%	3,764
03/18*	674.9	87.1	12.9%	3,466
04/17	615.3	70.6	11.5%	3,401
04/16	597.4	63.8	10.7%	3,277
03/15	445.2	58.2	13.1%	2,490
Annual Growth	12.1%	15.9%	—	10.9%

*Fiscal year change

2019 Year-End Financials

Debt ratio: 3.8%
Return on equity: 11.7%
Cash ($ mil.): 29.8
Current ratio: 5.58
Long-term debt ($ mil.): 43.1
No. of shares (mil.): 24.8
Dividends
Yield: —
Payout: —
Market value ($ mil.): 3,161.0

	STOCK PRICE ($) FY Close	P/E High/Low	PER SHARE ($) Earnings	Dividends	Book Value
03/19	127.17	39 26	4.26	0.00	38.97
03/18*	124.20	37 25	3.58	0.00	34.62
04/17	97.09	32 23	2.97	0.00	29.77
04/16	73.65	28 20	2.72	0.00	26.37
03/15	75.58	30 21	2.49	2.00	23.49
Annual Growth	13.9%	— —	14.4%	—	13.5%

*Fiscal year change

Ready Capital Corp

Auditors: DELOITTE & TOUCHE LLP

LOCATIONS

HQ: Ready Capital Corp
1251 Avenue of the Americas, 50th Floor, New York, NY 10020
Phone: 212 257-4600
Web: www.readycapital.com

COMPETITORS

American Capital Agency Corp.
Anworth Mortgage Asset
Capital Trust
Capstead Mortgage
Drive Shack
Five Oaks
Hatteras Financial
Invesco Mortgage Capital
MFA Financial
Starwood Property

HISTORICAL FINANCIALS

Company Type: Public

Income Statement — FYE: December 31

	REVENUE ($ mil.)	NET INCOME ($ mil.)	NET PROFIT MARGIN	EMPLOYEES
12/18	295.1	59.2	20.1%	4
12/17	211.4	43.2	20.5%	0
12/16	171.4	49.1	28.7%	0
12/15	72.7	(1.2)	—	246
12/14	65.2	26.7	41.0%	216
Annual Growth	45.8%	22.0%	—	(63.1%)

2018 Year-End Financials

Debt ratio: 75.9%
Return on equity: 10.9%
Cash ($ mil.): 54.4
Current ratio: 1.91
Long-term debt ($ mil.): 2,306.9
No. of shares (mil.): 32.1
Dividends
Yield: 11.3%
Payout: 85.3%
Market value ($ mil.): 444.0

	STOCK PRICE ($) FY Close	P/E High/Low	PER SHARE ($) Earnings	Dividends	Book Value
12/18	13.83	9 7	1.84	1.57	16.97
12/17	15.15	12 9	1.38	1.48	16.75
12/16	13.45	8 7	1.85	1.55	16.80
12/15	15.08	— —	(0.16)	1.60	19.98
12/14	17.25	6 5	3.08	1.60	21.73
Annual Growth	(5.4%)	— —	(12.1%)	(0.5%)	(6.0%)

RealPage Inc

RealPage's keeps real estate operations on the same page for property managers. The company's on-demand software platform is designed to make the property management process more efficient enabling owners and managers of single- and multifamily rental properties to oversee their accounting leasing marketing pricing and screening operations from a single shared database. The centralized system helps with managing incoming and outgoing residents and overseeing property functions from hiring plumbers to training staff. Its customers include all of the top 10 largest multifamily property management companies in the US.

Operations

RealPage's on-demand software (96% of sales) is its primary revenue segment and consists of an integrated software platform that provides a single point of access containing data on residents prospects and properties. The software is generally licensed under one-year customer subscription agreements. A smaller portion of the company's revenue is generated from professional services which include consulting training and implementation services.

Sales and Marketing

RealPage sells its software and services through an in-house direct sales organization. The firm promotes its products via online marketing activities including email campaigns online advertising Web campaigns webinars and social media (blogging Facebook and Twitter). Advertising cost totaled $15.1 million in 2014 vs. $11.4 million in 2013.

In 2014 more than 10700 customers used one of more of the company's on-demand software products to help manage the operations of some 9.6 million rental housing units.

Financial Performance

RealPage's revenue has climbed steadily each year and it reached $404 million in 2014 a 7% gain from $337 million in 2013. Sales of its cloud-based on-demand products continued to grow (up 8% in 2014) while sales of the on-premise version which the company no longer actively sells have diminished. Despite a reliable revenue rise profits have been less dependable as the company has spent more money generating and supporting sales. RealPage posted a loss of $10 million in 2014 after posting $20.7 million in net income in 2013. Headcount increased 16% in 2014 from new hires and acquisitions. Cash flow from operations inched higher to $70 million in 2014 from $69 million the previous year.

Strategy

Most of RealPage's strategy to push growth can be summed up in four words: acquire buy purchase and integrate. The company has bought some 30 firms since 2002 which has enabled it to expand its platform and offerings expand the number and types of property markets it serves and expand its customer base. As it looks ahead RealPage focuses on offering (as well as acquiring) cloud-based software. It no longer markets its on-premise software to new customers.

Mergers and Acquisitions

RealPage bought American Utility Management (AUM) a provider of utility and energy management services for the multifamily housing industry for about $70 million in June 2017. RealPage expands its Resident Utility Management (RUM) platform that provides billing invoice processing and bill payment services. RealPage intends to combine the data it collects with those of AUM to create the industry's largest database of utility consumption and cost data.

In 2014 RealPage bought two vacation rental management companies for a total of about $45 million and in 2015 combined them into one platform. The first acquisition was Bookt LLC and its InstaManager product for $9.2 million. InstaManager a Software-as-a-Service (SaaS) vacation rental booking system that offers marketing websites online pricing and availability online booking automated reservations payment processing and insurance sales. Then RealPage spent about $36 million on Kigo Inc. also a SaaS vacation rental booking system. The company combined the acquisitions under the name Kigo and offers the package of services for licensing.

Other recent acquisitions included Virtual Maintenance Manager a SaaS application that facilitates the management of the end-to-end maintenance life cycle for single-family and multifamily rental properties; Notivus Multi-Family which offers vendor risk management and compliance software; and ICIM Corp. (trade named Indatus) a suite of cloud-based automation and routing solutions for handling maintenance calls.

Company Background

RealPage was formed in 1998 to acquire Rent Roll Inc. which marketed and sold on-premise property management systems for certain multifamily housing markets. Three years later it released OneSite its first on-demand property management system.

EXECUTIVES

Chairman and CEO, Stephen T. (Steve) Winn, age 72, $500,000 total compensation
EVP Enterprise Solutions, William P. Chaney, age 48, $366,667 total compensation
EVP and CFO, W. Bryan Hill, age 52, $365,000 total compensation
EVP and Chief Revenue Officer, Ashley Glover
EVP Chief Legal Officer and Secretary, David G. Monk, age 52, $314,639 total compensation
Senior Vice President, Andrea Massey
Chief People Officer, Kurt Twining
Senior Vice President Sales, Jason Russell
Vice President Investor Relations, Rhett Butler
Vice President I, Tracy Turner

Vice President Enterprise Sales, Ryan Bratcher
Vice President Of Engineering, Sudip Shekhawat
Senior Vice President Product Engineering, Steve Deford
Vp Gm Screening, James Hilliard
Vice President, Kevin Cleveland
Auditors: Ernst & Young LLP

LOCATIONS

HQ: RealPage Inc
 2201 Lakeside Blvd., Richardson, TX 75082-4305
Phone: 972 820-3000
Web: www.realpage.com

PRODUCTS/OPERATIONS

2014 Sales

	$ mil.	% of total
On-demand	390.6	96
Professional & other	10.9	3
On-premise	3.1	1
Total	**404.6**	**100**

Products
Apartment Marketing
Contact Center
Electronic Payments
Market Research
Property Management
Renter's Insurance
Resident Portal
Resident Screening
Revenue Management
Spend Management
Utility Management
Vendor Credentialing Services
Business Intelligence
Client Portal
Housing Compliance
Professional Services
RealPage Exchange
RealPage Training
Support Services
Technology as a service
Technology Services
Vendor Services
Solutions
Affordable
Conventional
Commercial
Single Family
Senior Living
Student Housing
Military Housing
Vacation Rentals

COMPETITORS

Archibus
Assurant
Chase Paymentech Solutions
Communities Group
First Advantage
First Data
Fiserv
Infor Global
MoneyGram International
PROS Holdings
SiteStuff
TransUnion
Who's Calling
Yardi Systems

HISTORICAL FINANCIALS
Company Type: Public

Income Statement
FYE: December 31

	REVENUE ($ mil.)	NET INCOME ($ mil.)	NET PROFIT MARGIN	EMPLOYEES
12/18	869.4	34.7	4.0%	6,200
12/17	670.9	0.3	0.1%	5,400
12/16	568.1	16.6	2.9%	4,400
12/15	468.5	(9.2)	—	4,122
12/14	404.5	(10.2)	—	3,875
Annual Growth	**21.1%**	—	—	**12.5%**

2018 Year-End Financials
Debt ratio: 31.2%
Return on equity: 4.4%
Cash ($ mil.): 228.1
Current ratio: 1.31
Long-term debt ($ mil.): 591.3
No. of shares (mil.): 93.6
Dividends
 Yield: —
 Payout: —
Market value ($ mil.): 4,513.0

	STOCK PRICE ($) FY Close	P/E High/Low	PER SHARE ($) Earnings	Dividends	Book Value
12/18	48.19	165 112	0.38	0.00	11.35
12/17	44.30	— —	(0.00)	0.00	6.03
12/16	30.00	140 74	0.21	0.00	4.75
12/15	22.45	— —	(0.12)	0.00	4.14
12/14	21.96	— —	(0.13)	0.00	4.16
Annual Growth	**21.7%**	—	—	—	**28.5%**

Realty Income Corp

Retail real estate is a reality for Realty Income Corporation. The self-administered real estate investment trust (REIT) acquires owns and manages primarily free-standing highly-occupied single-tenant properties which it leases to regional and national consumer retail and service chains. Realty Income owns more than 4320 (mostly retail) properties spanning some 71 million sq. ft. of leasable space across every US state except Hawaii though nearly half of the REIT's rental revenue comes from its properties in Texas California Florida Minnesota Georgia Illinois and Virginia. Realty Income's top five tenants include Walgreens FedEx Dollar General LA Fitness and Family Dollar.

Operations
Realty Income owned more than 4320 properties during 2014 nearly 79% of which were Retail and the rest being Industrial and distribution (10%) Office (nearly 7%) Manufacturing (2%) and Agricultural related properties. Subsidiary Crest Net owns properties which are held for sale rather than for long-term investment.

Geographic Reach
California-based Realty Income's largest markets include Texas California Florida Minnesota Georgia Illinois and Virginia. More than 10% of its rental revenue came from properties in California in 2014 while properties in Texas contributed another nearly 10%.

Sales and Marketing
Realty Income's occupancy rate has been above 96% every year since its 1969 founding; its properties were 98.4% occupied in 2014 with an average remaining lease term of 10.2 years.

Its tenants have included owners of restaurants convenience stores theaters child care providers automotive care centers health and fitness facilities grocery stores and drug stores. Realty Income's top five tenants — Walgreens FedEx Dollar General LA Fitness and Family Dollar — combined generated nearly 25% of its total revenue in 2014. About 10% of its client types were owners of convenience stores.

Strategy
Realty Income's investment strategy involves acting as a source of capital to regional and national tenants. As such it focuses on long-term sale-leaseback transactions in which the tenant is responsible for taxes and maintenance. And when considering its investment targets the REIT looks to acquire what its tenants consider important toward the successful operation of their businesses.

Realty Income has traditionally grown its revenue through high-quality property acquisitions (with above 96% occupancy rates and existing long-term lease arrangements). It often sells properties with the intent to reinvest the proceeds in new real estate with the potential for higher returns.

Mergers and Acquisitions
In 2019 Realty Income purchased 454 single tenant properties from an affiliate of CIM Group in a deal worth $1.2 billion.

EXECUTIVES

EVP General Counsel and Secretary, Michael R. Pfeiffer, age 58, $375,000 total compensation
SVP Research, Robert J. Israel, age 59
Vice President Asset Management, Jenette O'brien
EVP CFO and Treasurer, Paul M. Meurer, age 53, $400,000 total compensation
President CEO and Director, John P. Case, age 55, $800,000 total compensation
President and COO, Sumit Roy, age 49, $406,250 total compensation
VP Information Technology, Clint Schmucker
SVP Investments, Neil Abraham
Associate Vice President Director Of Research, Scott Kohnen
Vp Assistant Controller Systems, Jill Cossaboom
Associate Vice President Acquisitions Director, Greg Smith
Vp And Head Capital Markets And Investor Relations, Jonathan Pong
Vp Acquisitions, April Little
Vice President Of Real Estate Acquisit, Cary J Wenthur
Chairman, Michael D. McKee
Auditors: KPMG LLP

LOCATIONS

HQ: Realty Income Corp
 11995 El Camino Real, San Diego, CA 92130
Phone: 858 284-5000
Web: www.realtyincome.com

PRODUCTS/OPERATIONS

2014 Properties

	No.	% of rental revenue
Retail	4.1	79
Industrial and distribution	82.0	10
Office	44.0	7
Manufacturing	14.0	2
Agriculture	15.0	2
Total	**4,327.0**	**100**

2014 Sales	
	% of total
Rental	96
Tenant reimbursement	4
Others	-
Total	100

COMPETITORS

Acadia Realty Trust
Capital Automotive
DDR
EPR Properties
Federal Realty Investment
Kimco Realty
National Retail Properties
One Liberty Properties
Regency Centers
Simon Property Group
The Blackstone Group
Weingarten Realty

HISTORICAL FINANCIALS
Company Type: Public

Income Statement   FYE: December 31

	REVENUE ($ mil.)	NET INCOME ($ mil.)	NET PROFIT MARGIN	EMPLOYEES
12/18	1,327.8	363.6	27.4%	165
12/17	1,215.7	318.8	26.2%	152
12/16	1,103.1	315.5	28.6%	146
12/15	1,023.2	283.7	27.7%	132
12/14	933.5	270.6	29.0%	125
Annual Growth	9.2%	7.7%	—	7.2%

2018 Year-End Financials

Debt ratio: 42.6%
Return on equity: 4.7%
Cash ($ mil.): 10.3
Current ratio: 0.47
Long-term debt ($ mil.): 6,499.9
No. of shares (mil.): 303.7
Dividends
 Yield: 4.1%
 Payout: 209.4%
Market value ($ mil.): 19,148.0

	STOCK PRICE ($) FY Close	P/E High/Low		PER SHARE ($) Earnings	Dividends	Book Value
12/18	63.04	53	38	1.26	2.64	26.63
12/17	57.02	57	48	1.10	2.54	25.94
12/16	57.48	64	45	1.13	2.40	26.01
12/15	51.63	51	40	1.09	2.28	26.08
12/14	47.71	48	36	1.04	2.19	24.96
Annual Growth	7.2%	—	—	4.9%	4.7%	1.6%

Redwood Trust Inc

Redwood Trust is cultivating a forest of real estate mortgage assets. The real estate investment trust (REIT) finances manages and invests in residential real estate mortgages and securities backed by such loans. It also invests in commercial real estate loans and securities. Redwood acquires assets throughout the US but has a concentration of credit risk in California Texas Massachusetts Florida and New York which hold some of the US' most active real estate markets. Redwood Trust slowed loan origination acquisition and securitization during the most recent recession but has picked up those activities as the economy has recovered.

Operations

Redwood Trust invests in real estate related assets that have the potential to provide attractive cash flows over a long time period and distribute attractive levels of dividends to stockholders. The mortgage-backed securities the company typically invests in include senior securities. Redwood Trust also invests in other assets securities and instruments that are related to residential and commercial real estate.

About 43% of Redwood's total revenue came from interest income on its real estate securities in 2014 while interest income on its residential loans and commercial loans made up 24% and 16% of total revenue that year respectively. The rest of its revenue (about 12%) came from its mortgage banking activities which involves buying and selling mortgage loans. The bank had a staff of 221 people at the end of 2014.

Geographic Reach

Redwood primarily concentrates on supplying loans to the markets of California Texas Massachusetts Virginia Florida and New York — which held 70% of its credit held for sale and 53% of its credit held-for-investment in 2014. The REIT has offices in California Colorado and New York.

Financial Performance

Redwood Trust has struggled to grow its revenues and profits over the past few years mostly as its mortgage banking business and other non-interest income sources have declined (an industry-wide problem for mortgage banking businesses). Its interest income however has been on the rise as it's acquired more interest-earning assets over time.

The company's revenue fell 25% to $278.1 million in 2014 mostly as its residential mortgage banking income declined by $67 million with fewer originations as potential interest rate hikes scared borrowers away during the year and put "pressure on margins and profitability" according to the company.

Revenue declines in 2014 caused Redwood's net income to plummet 42% to $100.6 million. Its cash levels fell further than in the prior year with operations using $1.79 billion mostly because the the REIT used more of its cash toward purchasing loans and generated less from proceeds from loan sales.

Strategy

Redwood Trust continues to acquire prime jumbo residential loans on a flow basis for the subsequent securitization of those loans and to a lesser extent for sale to third parties. The company is focusing on building a franchise business model that would get it ready to capitalize on the expected eventual reform of government agencies Fannie Mae and Freddie Mac.

The company has shifted its strategy in recent years to transition toward originating senior commercial loans and increasing gain-on-sale or fee income. Its long-term strategy is to to add additional loan sellers loan products and capital sources. To this end in mid-2014 Redwood Trust established a new subsidiary that could access "attractive long-term financing from the Federal Home Loan Bank of Chicago (FHLBC) for residential mortgage loans" with the intention to acquire residential mortgage loans to hold as long-term investments.

EXECUTIVES

CEO, Martin S. (Marty) Hughes, age 61, $750,000 total compensation
President, Christopher J. Abate, age 39, $425,000 total compensation
EVP General Counsel and Secretary, Andrew P. Stone, age 48, $375,000 total compensation
CFO, Collin Cochrane, age 43
EVP Commercial Investments and Finance, Fred J. Matera, age 55, $500,000 total compensation
EVP, Dashiell Robinson
Vice President, Fred Ty
Vice President Credit Policy Manager, Jennifer Adams
Assistant Vice President, Jason Moutray
Associate Vice President, Jennifer Wolff
Vice Chairman, Douglas B. Hansen, age 61
Chairman, Richard D. Baum, age 72
Auditors: Grant Thornton LLP

LOCATIONS

HQ: Redwood Trust Inc
 One Belvedere Place, Suite 300, Mill Valley, CA 94941
Phone: 415 389-7373
Web: www.redwoodtrust.com

PRODUCTS/OPERATIONS

2014 Sales

	$ mil.	% of total
Interest income		
Real estate securities	125.5	43
Residential loans	68.9	24
Commercial loans	47.6	16
Others	0.1	-
Non-interest income		
Mortgage banking activities	34.9	12
Realized Gains	15.5	5
Adjustments	(14.4)	-
Total	278.1	100

COMPETITORS

Annaly Capital Management
Bank of America
Capstead Mortgage
Duff & Phelps
Dynex Capital
Hercules Technology
MFA Financial
Main Street Capital
NewStar Financial
Starwood Property
Triangle Capital
iStar Financial Inc

HISTORICAL FINANCIALS
Company Type: Public

Income Statement   FYE: December 31

	ASSETS ($ mil.)	NET INCOME ($ mil.)	INCOME AS % OF ASSETS	EMPLOYEES
12/18	11,937.4	119.6	1.0%	149
12/17	7,039.8	140.4	2.0%	120
12/16	5,483.4	131.2	2.4%	125
12/15	6,231.0	102.0	1.6%	211
12/14	5,918.9	100.5	1.7%	221
Annual Growth	19.2%	4.4%	—	(9.4%)

2018 Year-End Financials

Return on assets: 1.2%
Return on equity: 9.3%
Long-term debt ($ mil.): —
No. of shares (mil.): 84.8
Sales ($ mil): 452.5
Dividends
 Yield: 7.8%
 Payout: 88.0%
Market value ($ mil.): 1,279.0

	STOCK PRICE ($) FY Close	P/E High/Low		PER SHARE ($) Earnings	Dividends	Book Value
12/18	15.07	12	10	1.34	1.18	15.89
12/17	14.82	10	8	1.60	1.12	15.83
12/16	15.21	10	6	1.54	1.12	14.96
12/15	13.20	17	10	1.18	1.12	14.67
12/14	19.70	18	14	1.15	1.12	15.05
Annual Growth	(6.5%)	—	—	3.9%	1.3%	1.4%

Regency Centers Corp

Regency Centers' bread and butter comes from grocery stores. A real estate investment trust (REIT) the firm owns manages and develops neighborhood shopping centers in about two dozen states and Washington DC many of them anchored by a Kroger Publix or Safeway supermarket. Other tenants include retailers restaurants and professional services firms. The REIT wholly owns or has interests in about 330 properties measuring more than 44 million sq. ft. of leaseable space. The REIT focuses on high-growth areas in states including California Florida Texas Georgia and Colorado home to the majority of its wholly-owned holdings.

Geographic Reach
Florida-based Regency Centers has grocery-anchored shopping centers in 23 states and the District of Columbia. California Florida and Texas account for more than 10% of the firm's operating income.

Sales and Marketing
Grocery giants Kroger Florida-based Publix and Safeway are the REIT's largest clients contributing 5% 4% and 3% of its annualized base rent respectively.

Financial Performance
Regency's revenue declined by nearly 2% in 2013 versus 2012 to $489 million. Net income soared 479% over the same period to $149.8 million. The decline in revenue reflects the sale of a 15-property portfolio in July 2012 that resulted in a decrease in recoveries from tenants and other income in 2013. The huge bump in net income was due to the gain on the sale of the properties.

Strategy
The REIT grows its shopping center portfolio through acquisitions of existing shopping centers and new development. New development is customer driven in that the REIT generally has an executed lease from the anchor tenant before it breaks ground. Since 2000 the company has developed some 215 properties and acquired more than 100 more though such activity slowed during the recession. With the US economy on the mend Regency is actively acquiring developing and re-developing properties in high-growth and affluent areas. Indeed in April 2014 Regency opened a new shopping center in South Los Angeles called the Juanita Tate Marketplace. The new development is anchored by Hispanic grocery chain Gonzalez Market.

While the REIT wholly owns about two-thirds of its properties about 125 others are partially owned by Regency Centers through joint ventures with other institutional investors such as CalSTRS and USAA.

Mergers and Acquisitions
In March 2017 Equity One merged with and into Regency with Regency continuing as the surviving public company. The merger formed a combined company with a total market capitalization of approximately $16 billion.

EXECUTIVES

Managing Director Texas Southern California Cincinnati and Columbus, John S. Delatour, $350,000 total compensation
Managing Director Operations East, James D. (Jim) Thompson, age 63, $395,000 total compensation
Chairman and CEO, Martin E. (Hap) Stein, age 66, $790,000 total compensation
Managing Director Pacific Northwest and Northern California, H. Craig Ramey
Managing Director East, Alan T. Roth
President and CFO, Lisa Palmer, age 51, $455,000 total compensation
SVP and CIO, Dale Johnston
EVP Development, Dan M. (Mac) Chandler, age 51, $375,000 total compensation
Managing Director Chicago Minneapolis and Colorado, Nick Wibbenmeyer
Senior Vice President Transactions, Barry E Argalas
Vice President Construction, John Hayes
Executive Vice President of Investments, Mac Chandler
Vice President Investments, James Reuter
Vice President Of Capital Markets, Patrick Johnson
Vice President, Scott Porter
Vice President Market Officer, Patrick Mckinley
Vice President Regional Officer, Andre Koleszar
Vice President Financial Services Central Region, Dave Mcnulty
Senior Vice President Senior Market Officer, Patrick Krejs
Vice President of Construction, Scott Wilson
Vice President Investments, Paul Maxwell
Senior Vice President Financial Services And Tax, Kathy Miller
Vp Investments, John Mehigan
Vice President, James Chiang
Vice President, Andy Hofheimer
Vice President, Christopher Widmayer
Senior Vice President Senior Market Officer, Doug Shaffer
Senior Vice President Senior Market Officer, Krista Di Iaconi
Vice President acquisitions dispositions, Stuart Brackenridge
Vice President Finance, Chris Leavitt
Director of Nursing, Tracy Vick
Senior Vice President, Rafael Muniz
Vice Chairman COO, Mary Fiala
Auditors: KPMG LLP

LOCATIONS

HQ: Regency Centers Corp
One Independent Drive, Suite 114, Jacksonville, FL 32602
Phone: 904 598-7000
Web: www.regencycenters.com

PRODUCTS/OPERATIONS

2016 Sales

	$ mil.	% of total
Minimum rent	444.3	72
Recoveries from tenants & other income	140.6	23
Management acquisition & other fees	25.4	4
Percentage rent	4.1	1
Total	**614.4**	**100**

COMPETITORS

CBL & Associates Properties	Kimco Realty
Cousins Properties	Macerich
DDR	Vornado Realty
Federal Realty Investment	Weingarten Realty

HISTORICAL FINANCIALS
Company Type: Public

Income Statement
FYE: December 31

	REVENUE ($ mil.)	NET INCOME ($ mil.)	NET PROFIT MARGIN	EMPLOYEES
12/18	1,120.9	249.1	22.2%	446
12/17	984.3	176.0	17.9%	446
12/16	614.3	164.9	26.8%	371
12/15	569.7	150.0	26.3%	371
12/14	537.9	187.3	34.8%	370
Annual Growth	20.2%	7.4%	—	4.8%

2018 Year-End Financials
Debt ratio: 33.9%
Return on equity: 3.8%
Cash ($ mil.): 42.5
Current ratio: 0.13
Long-term debt ($ mil.): 3,715.2
No. of shares (mil.): 167.5
Dividends
 Yield: 3.7%
 Payout: 152.0%
Market value ($ mil.): 9,830.0

	STOCK PRICE ($) FY Close	P/E High/Low	PER SHARE ($) Earnings	Dividends	Book Value
12/18	58.68	47 38	1.46	2.22	38.19
12/17	69.18	72 59	1.00	2.10	39.14
12/16	68.95	60 46	1.42	2.00	24.88
12/15	68.12	51 42	1.36	1.94	21.22
12/14	63.78	36 26	1.80	1.88	20.35
Annual Growth	(2.1%)	— —	(5.1%)	4.2%	17.0%

REGENXBIO Inc

Auditors: PricewaterhouseCoopers LLP

LOCATIONS

HQ: REGENXBIO Inc
9600 Blackwell Road, Suite 210, Rockville, MD 20850
Phone: 240 552-8181
Web: www.regenxbio.com

HISTORICAL FINANCIALS
Company Type: Public

Income Statement
FYE: December 31

	REVENUE ($ mil.)	NET INCOME ($ mil.)	NET PROFIT MARGIN	EMPLOYEES
12/18	218.5	99.9	45.7%	192
12/17	10.3	(73.1)	—	139
12/16	4.5	(62.9)	—	107
12/15	7.5	(22.8)	—	56
12/14	6.1	(4.0)	—	19
Annual Growth	144.4%	—	—	78.3%

2018 Year-End Financials
Debt ratio: 1.0%
Return on equity: 28.8%
Cash ($ mil.): 75.5
Current ratio: 15.24
Long-term debt ($ mil.): 5.8
No. of shares (mil.): 36.1
Dividends
 Yield: —
 Payout: —
Market value ($ mil.): 1,515.0

Regional Management Corp

Regional Management is looking to give credit where credit is due. Consumer finance company Regional Management provides secured personal loans (up to $27500) auto loans and furniture and appliance loans to consumers who may otherwise have limited access to credit through banks and other traditional lenders. The company which operates under the Regional Finance RMC Financial Services Anchor Finance and Sun Finance banners among others has some 265 branch locations in eight states in the south and southwest. It also provides loans through pre-screened live check mailings auto dealerships and its e-commerce site. Founded in 1987 Regional Management went public via an IPO in 2012.

IPO
The company intends to use a portion of the proceeds from its March 2012 IPO ($63 million down from what the $80 million it expected) to repay debt and for general corporate purposes. It also plans to use some of the proceeds to make a one-time payment to pre-IPO owners to terminate a consulting agreement. Prior to the IPO private equity firm Palladium Equity Partners held a 48% stake in the company and Parallel 2005 Equity Fund held a 28% stake.

Operations
The consumer finance company makes small installment loans (ranging from $300 to $2500) large installment loans (between $2500 and $20000) and automobile purchase loans (up to $27500). It also makes loans to finance retail purchases of up to $7500 that are secured by the purchased item. Regional Management also sells insurance on its loans. Most of its loan activity consists of small installment and auto purchase loans.

Geographic Reach
South Carolina-based Regional Management makes loans in the Carolinas Texas Georgia Tennessee Alabama Oklahoma and New Mexico.

Financial Performance
In its first full year as a public company Regional Management reported sales of $170.6 million in 2013 an increase of 25% versus the prior year on rising interest and fee income. Net income grew 14% to $28.8 million over the same period. Indeed the finance company's sales and profits have been rising in lockstep since 2008 as the company opened new branches. In 2013 about 75% of the firm's loans were classified as current with 17% between 1 to 29 days delinquent.

Strategy
Regional Management targets non-prime and underbanked consumers who have limited access to credit from traditional channels such as banks and credit card companies. While the population of such customers has grown in recent years the supply of consumer credit to them has contracted presenting Regional Management with a growth market for its installment auto and retail purchase loans.

As a key component of its growth strategy Regional Management has been busy opening new branches in new and existing markets. Indeed the company's branch network has more than doubled in size from 117 branches in 2009 to about 265 in 2013. In 2013 the firm opened or acquired 43 new branches including its first branches in Georgia. Regional Management is eyeing several states outside its present footprint with favorable interest rate and regulatory climates such as Kentucky Louisiana Mississippi Missouri and Virginia. The company also plans to bolster its other lending channels including driving traffic to its e-commerce website through marketing and advertising initiatives and by leveraging search engine optimization technologies.

EXECUTIVES
EVP and CFO, Donald E. (Don) Thomas, age 60, $332,000 total compensation
CEO, Peter R. Knitzer, age 60, $221,557 total compensation
SVP and Chief Risk Officer, Daniel J. Taggart, age 46, $308,000 total compensation
VP General Counsel and Secretary, Brian J. Fisher, age 35, $230,000 total compensation
COO, John D. Schachtel
Vice President Auto Products, Brian Switalski
Vice President Of Operations South Carolina, Scott Juvelier
Chairman, Alvaro G. (Al) de Molina, age 61
Auditors: RSM US LLP

LOCATIONS
HQ: Regional Management Corp
979 Batesville Road, Suite B, Greer, SC 29651
Phone: 864 448-7000
Web: www.regionalmanagement.com

PRODUCTS/OPERATIONS

2015 Sales

	% of total
Interest and fee income	90
Insurance income net	5
Other	5
Total	**100**

COMPETITORS

1st Franklin Financial	DFC Global
Advance America	Nicholas Financial
Capital One Auto Finance	OneMain
Check 'n Go	QC Holdings
Check Into Cash	World Acceptance
Community Choice Financial	Xponential

HISTORICAL FINANCIALS
Company Type: Public

Income Statement — FYE: December 31

	ASSETS ($ mil.)	NET INCOME ($ mil.)	INCOME AS % OF ASSETS	EMPLOYEES
12/18	956.4	35.3	3.7%	1,535
12/17	829.4	29.9	3.6%	1,448
12/16	712.2	24.0	3.4%	1,363
12/15	629.0	23.3	3.7%	1,421
12/14	530.2	14.8	2.8%	1,443
Annual Growth	15.9%	24.3%	—	1.6%

2018 Year-End Financials
Return on assets: 3.9%
Return on equity: 13.6%
Long-term debt ($ mil.): —
No. of shares (mil.): 11.7
Sales ($ mil): 306.7
Dividends
Yield: —
Payout: —
Market value ($ mil.): 283.0

	STOCK PRICE ($) FY Close	P/E High	P/E Low	PER SHARE ($) Earnings	Dividends	Book Value
12/18	24.05	12	8	2.93	0.00	23.70
12/17	26.31	10	7	2.54	0.00	20.53
12/16	26.28	13	6	1.99	0.00	18.12
12/15	15.47	11	8	1.79	0.00	15.89
12/14	15.81	31	10	1.14	0.00	13.99
Annual Growth	11.1%	—	—	26.6%	—	14.1%

(Regional Management table at top of page:)

	STOCK PRICE ($) FY Close	P/E High	P/E Low	PER SHARE ($) Earnings	Dividends	Book Value
12/18	41.95	27	8	2.73	0.00	14.09
12/17	33.25	—	—	(2.45)	0.00	5.85
12/16	18.55	—	—	(2.38)	0.00	6.11
12/15	16.60	—	—	(2.59)	0.00	8.24
Annual Growth	36.2%	—	—	—	—	19.6%

Reliant Bancorp Inc

Auditors: Maggart & Associates, P.C.

LOCATIONS
HQ: Reliant Bancorp Inc
1736 Carothers Parkway, Suite 100, Brentwood, TN 37027
Phone: 615 221-2020

HISTORICAL FINANCIALS
Company Type: Public

Income Statement — FYE: December 31

	ASSETS ($ mil.)	NET INCOME ($ mil.)	INCOME AS % OF ASSETS	EMPLOYEES
12/18	1,724.3	14.0	0.8%	263
12/17	1,125.0	7.2	0.6%	168
12/16	911.9	8.9	1.0%	143
12/15	876.4	5.5	0.6%	226
12/14	295.7	2.1	0.7%	47
Annual Growth	55.4%	59.7%	—	53.8%

2018 Year-End Financials
Return on assets: 0.9%
Return on equity: 8.0%
Long-term debt ($ mil.): —
No. of shares (mil.): 11.5
Sales ($ mil): 78.8
Dividends
Yield: 1.3%
Payout: 24.3%
Market value ($ mil.): 266.0

Renasant Corp

Those who are cognizant of their finances may want to do business with Renasant Corporation. The holding company owns Renasant Bank which serves consumers and local business through about 80 locations in Alabama Georgia Mississippi and Tennessee. The bank offers standard products such as checking and savings accounts CDs credit cards and loans and mortgages as well as trust retail brokerage and retirement plan services. Its loan portfolio is dominated by residential and commercial real estate loans. The bank also offers agricultural business construction and consumer loans and lease financing. Subsidiary Renasant Insurance sells personal and business coverage. Shareholders approved a merger with Metropolitan Bank in mid-2017.

Financial Performance
The company's revenue increased in fiscal 2013 compared to the prior year. It reported revenue of $252.6 million for fiscal 2013 up from $228 million in revenue for fiscal 2012.

Renasant's net income also went up in fiscal 2013 compared to the previous fiscal period. It reported net income of about $33.5 million for fiscal 2013 up from net income of $26.6 million in fiscal 2012.

The company's cash on hand decreased by about $24 million in fiscal 2013 compared to fiscal 2012 levels.

Strategy
Renasant has looked to diversify its loan portfolio. The bank has reduced its amount of loans for construction and land development — a sector that has been hit particularly hard — by tightening its underwriting standards.

It's also been growing through acquistions. In late 2014 for example Renasant purchased Heritage Financial Group in an all stock merger deal that amounted to $258 million. The move added $1.9 billion in assets $1.2 billion in loan assets and $1.3 billion in deposit assets to Renasant's collection. In addition the move significantly expanded the bank's geographic reach adding 48 banking mortgage and investment offices in Alabama Florida and Georgia. All told the deal made Renasant one of the largest community banks in the Southeast region of the United States.

Mergers and Acquisitions
In 2017 Renasant agreed to a $190 million merger with Metropolitan Bank.

EXECUTIVES

EVP, Stuart R. Johnson, age 66, $250,000 total compensation
Chairman President and CEO, E. Robinson (Robin) McGraw, age 72, $750,000 total compensation
EVP, James W. Gray, age 63, $230,000 total compensation
President and COO, C. Mitchell (Mitch) Waycaster, age 61, $450,000 total compensation
EVP, Mary J. Witt, age 60
EVP, W. Mark Williams, age 56
EVP, R. Rick Hart, age 71, $496,000 total compensation
EVP and General Counsel, Stephen M. Corban, age 64, $75,000 total compensation
EVP; President Eastern Region Renasant Bank, O. Leonard (Len) Dorminey, age 66, $213,285 total compensation
EVP and CFO, Kevin D. Chapman, age 44, $375,000 total compensation
EVP; President Western Region Renasant Bank, J. Scott Cochran, age 56
First Vice President Director Of Corporate Communication And Ir Contact, John Oxford
Executive Vice President, Danny Gladney
Assistant Vice President, Kent Dees
Vice President And Trust Officer, Allison Youngblood
Executive Vice President, Craig Gardella
Senior Vice President Corporate Banking, Will Smithhart
Assistant Vice President Account Executive, Brian Gagel
Vice President, Josh Sullivan
Senior Vice President, Donna Wade
Senior Vice President, Robert Hankins
Senior Vice President And Business Development Officer, Bobby Harper
Vice President Commercial Banker, Larry Finkel
Executive Vice President Credit Administration, Stuart Weise
Senior Vice President, Scott Rossman
Vice President, Jack Stuart
Vice President Relationship Officer, Danny Crabtree
Senior Vice President Commercial Banking, David Harwell
Senior Vice President, Jason McClimans
Division President Executive Vice President, Raymond Vannorman
Vice President Client Portfolio Manager Asset Manage Ement Renasant Asset Management, Matt Legg
Vice President Appraisal Officer Card, Lisa Wells
Central Monitoring Department Manager Vice President, Tracey Aldridge
Senior Vice President Director of Senior Business Analyst Lending, John Daly
Vice President, Raakhi Phillips
First Vice President Associate Counsel, Jared Carrubba
Vice President, Brian Porter
Vice President, Michael Wiegert
Small Business Lending Division Manager Senior Vice President, Butch Lyle
Assistant Vice President Senior Business Analyst Portfolio Manager, Kathy Davis
Senior Vice President, Phil Smith
Executive Vice President, Mark Jeanfreau
Assistant Vice President And To, Crystal Tucker
Senior Vice President, Melanie Kurn
Division President Senior Vice President, Ed Hutchinson
Senior Vice President Mortgage Controller, Bryan Morelli
Vice President, Jon Appel
Senior Vice President, John Temple
Assistant Vice President Mortgage Lender, Brenda Pearce
Assistant Vice President Treasury Management Specialist, Chrissy Aubin
Vice President Special Assets Officer, Scott Williams
Board Member, Richard Heyer
Auditors: Horne LLP

LOCATIONS
HQ: Renasant Corp
209 Troy Street, Tupelo, MS 38804-4827
Phone: 662 680-1001
Web: www.renasant.com

PRODUCTS/OPERATIONS

2015 Sales

	$ mil.	% of total
Interest income		
Loans	236.3	64
Securities	26.5	7
Other	0.2	-
Non-interest income		
Mortgage banking income	35.8	10
Service charges on deposit accounts	29.3	8
Fees and commissions	16.1	4
Wealth management	9.8	3
Other	17.3	4
Total	**371.3**	**100**

COMPETITORS

BBVA Compass Bancshares	First Horizon
BancorpSouth	Hancock Holding
Citizens Holding	Regions Financial
Citizens National Bank of Meridian	Trustmark

HISTORICAL FINANCIALS
Company Type: Public

Income Statement
FYE: December 31

	ASSETS ($ mil.)	NET INCOME ($ mil.)	INCOME AS % OF ASSETS	EMPLOYEES
12/18	12,934.8	146.9	1.1%	2,359
12/17	9,829.9	92.1	0.9%	2,102
12/16	8,699.8	90.9	1.0%	1,965
12/15	7,926.5	68.0	0.9%	1,996
12/14	5,805.1	59.5	1.0%	1,471
Annual Growth	22.2%	25.3%	—	12.5%

2018 Year-End Financials
Return on assets: 1.2%
Return on equity: 8.2%
Long-term debt ($ mil.): —
No. of shares (mil.): 58.5
Sales ($ mil): 605.8
Dividends
 Yield: 2.6%
 Payout: 34.0%
Market value ($ mil.): 1,767.0

	STOCK PRICE ($) FY Close	P/E High/Low	PER SHARE ($) Earnings	Dividends	Book Value
12/18	30.18	18 10	2.79	0.80	34.91
12/17	40.89	23 19	1.96	0.73	30.72
12/16	42.22	20 14	2.17	0.71	27.81
12/15	34.41	20 14	1.88	0.68	25.73
12/14	28.93	17 14	1.88	0.68	22.56
Annual Growth	1.1%	— —	10.4%	4.1%	11.5%

	STOCK PRICE ($) FY Close	P/E High/Low	PER SHARE ($) Earnings	Dividends	Book Value
12/18	23.04	24 17	1.23	0.30	18.07
12/17	25.64	29 24	0.88	0.40	15.51
12/16	21.51	19 11	1.16	0.20	13.75
12/15	13.71	17 15	0.86	0.20	13.29
12/14	13.00	18 14	0.69	0.40	11.74
Annual Growth	15.4%	— —	15.5%	(6.9%)	11.4%

Renewable Energy Group, Inc.

Renewable Energy Group (REG) is North America's largest advanced biofuels producers converting natural fats oils and greases into lower carbon intensive products such as heating oil ultra-low sulfur diesel and blended fuel. The company sells some 650 million gallons of biofuels yearly through some 15 refineries in the US and Germany. REG is also working to develop renewable chemicals from fatty acids and other raw materials. Vertically integrated REG sells to municipalities transportation fleets fuel wholesalers and convenience stores and industries like mining and agriculture. The company generates nearly all its revenue in the US.

Operations
The production of biomass-based diesel (traditional and renewable) accounts for 95% of Renewable Energy Group's (REG) sales. It produces cleaner biodiesel by converting feedstock like inedible corn oil used cooking oil or rendered animal fat from vendors across North America.

REG's service segment manages third-party biodiesel facility construction and operations bringing in some 5% of revenue.

Geographic Reach
Headquartered in Ames Iowa REG sells its products in across the US as well as in six Canadian provinces and around 20 other companies around the world.

It has 14 biorefineries?12 in North America and two in Germany. Additionally REG has testing and research facilities at its HQ in Iowa as well as in Tulsa Oklahoma. It produces renewable diesel at its Geismar Louisiana plant.

More than 90% of REG revenues come from the United States while Germany accounts for most of the rest.

Sales and Marketing
Advertising its fuel up to 50% cleaner than diesel REG sells almost 650 million gallons of biofuel per year through a national distribution system in the US. Terminals are equipped variously with on-site rail loading system truck loading system direct barge access or deep-water ship loading capabilities. For the smooth running of its distribution operation it leases more than 1100 railcars and diesel storage tanks at some 45 terminals.

REG sells branded BioHeat blended fuel petroleum-based heating oil and ultra-low sulfur diesel (ULSD) biofuel blends in the Northeast and Midwest. These blended products allow REG to reach a wider customer base such as those operating in cold climates.

It has a diverse customer base. Its finished products are sold in convenience stores to major petroleum industry players and other distributors.

Financial Performance
REG has seen exponential growth doubling its revenue in the last six years. In contrast REG's profit has fluctuated wildly year-over-year. In the last decade it has had five profitable years and five years of losses. In 2018 REG posted its higher ever revenue and its highest ever profits.

Sales grew 11% to $2.4 billion largely due to the "federal biodiesel mixture excise tax credit" (BTC) being restated in 2017 but recognized in Q1 2018. The BTC provides a $1 refundable tax credit per gallon. REG also saw an 11% increase in gallons sold partially offset by a lower average selling price.

Net income of $295.8 billion represented a swing back to profit after a $66.3 million loss in 2017. Cost of goods sold dropped from 96% of sales to 82% largely due to the reinstatement of the BTC (worth $205 million) lower feedstock costs and gains from risk management.

REG's cash balance is relatively weak and in the last few years the company has had to issue debt and take on borrowings to support liquidity. REG's cash balance improved during 2018 ending the year $49.1 million higher at $126.6 million. The company's operating activities generated cash of $365.5 million while investing activities used $97.2 million and financing activities $219.2 million. REG's primary cash uses were capital expenditures cash paid on debt and borrowing repayments.

Strategy
With the sharp rise of renewable fuels in the energy market and the consequent decrease in production costs (biofuels would grow from a $8 billion market in 2016 to $100 billion in 2023) REG's constantly improving revenue positions it well for the future. The International Energy Agency predicts that by 2040 40% of global power generation will comprise renewable energy.

REG's strategy of recycling carbon-intense products to supply cleaner fuel has enabled it to grow into one of the top performers in the US. The company has actively integrated production technologies to lower operating costs while expanding usage of lower cost feedstocks.

Of the 14 biorefineries REG owns around ten are "multi-feedstock capable" allowing for the processing of a broad range of lower cost feedstocks unlike its competitors who use costlier alternatives. REG added 10 terminal expansions in 2017 and 8 fleet customers. The company has further plans to expand terminals in the US for blended fuel petroleum and biodiesel.

REG also has ambitious plans to scale-up production of renewable diesel a more expensive product that offers higher margins. The company is investigating the viability of partnerships with other major oil industry players such as Phillips 66 to set up a large-scale renewable diesel plant. An alternative option would be expanding the existing plant in Geismar.

Company Background
The company was formed in 2003 by West Central Cooperative.

EXECUTIVES

President and CEO, Daniel J. Oh, age 54, $570,000 total compensation
VP Manufacturing, Brad Albin, age 56, $295,962 total compensation
VP Supply Chain Management, David Elsenbast, age 58, $243,654 total compensation
VP Sales and Marketing, Gary Haer, age 65, $283,654 total compensation
CFO, Chad Stone, age 49, $295,962 total compensation
Chairman, Jeffrey (Jeff) Stroburg, age 69
Vice Chairman Of The Board, Chris Sorrells
Assistant Treasurer, Vincent Perez
Board Member, Peter Harding
Auditors: DELOITTE & TOUCHE LLP

LOCATIONS
HQ: Renewable Energy Group, Inc.
416 South Bell Avenue, Ames, IA 50010
Phone: 515 239-8000
Web: www.regi.com

PRODUCTS/OPERATIONS

2018 Sales

	$ mil.	% of total
Biomass-based diesel	2,157.9	93
Services	93.3	4
Corporate and other	249.2	10
Inter-segment	(117.4)	-
Total	**2,383.0**	**100**

Selected Products
Biodiesel
Bioheat
Co-Product Purchase Inquiries
Feedstock Supplier Inquiries
Glycerin
Other Products

Selected Services
Construction/Upgrades
Conversion to Fuel
Feedstock Development
Fuel Distribution
Fuel Marketing
Operations Management

COMPETITORS
ADM
Abengoa Bioenergy
BP
Cargill
Extreme Biodiesel
GeoBio Energy
Green Brick Partners
Hawkeye Energy Holdings
Owensboro Grain
Valero Energy

HISTORICAL FINANCIALS
Company Type: Public

Income Statement — FYE: December 31

	REVENUE ($ mil.)	NET INCOME ($ mil.)	NET PROFIT MARGIN	EMPLOYEES
12/18	2,382.9	292.3	12.3%	850
12/17	2,158.2	(79.0)	—	727
12/16	2,041.2	44.3	2.2%	703
12/15	1,387.3	(151.3)	—	597
12/14	1,273.8	82.6	6.5%	502
Annual Growth	17.0%	37.2%	—	14.1%

2018 Year-End Financials
Debt ratio: 17.9%
Return on equity: 43.8%
Cash ($ mil.): 174.5
Current ratio: 1.58
Long-term debt ($ mil.): 35.6
No. of shares (mil.): 37.3
Dividends
  Yield: —
  Payout: —
Market value ($ mil.): 959.0

	STOCK PRICE ($) FY Close	P/E High	P/E Low	PER SHARE ($) Earnings	PER SHARE ($) Dividends	PER SHARE ($) Book Value
12/18	25.70	4	1	6.48	0.00	20.51
12/17	11.80	—	—	(2.04)	0.00	14.61
12/16	9.70	10	6	1.06	0.00	15.75
12/15	9.29	—	—	(3.44)	0.00	13.94
12/14	9.71	6	4	1.99	0.00	17.33
Annual Growth	27.5%	—	—	34.3%	—	4.3%

Repligen Corp.

Repligen supplies bio-engineered drug ingredients to the pharmaceutical industry. The company's bioprocessing business develops and commercializes proteins and other agents used in the production of biopharmaceuticals. Repligen is a major supplier of Protein A a recombinant protein used in the production of monoclonal antibodies and other biopharmaceutical manufacturing applications. Its product portfolio also includes filtration products and chromatography devices. Repligen's largest customer is GE Healthcare with which it has a multi-year supply agreement. The US accounts for about half of the company's total revenue.

Geographic Reach
Repligen is headquartered in Massachusetts. The company has manufacturing facilities in the US (Massachusetts California Nevada and Texas) Sweden Germany the Netherlands China India Korea and Japan. It has sales and distribution facilities in India China Korea the Netherlands and Japan.

The company's two largest single markets are the US which accounts for about 45% of revenue and Sweden which brings in another 20%.

Sales and Marketing
Repligen uses its own direct sales force and partners including GE Healthcare MilliporeSigma and Purolite to sell its products to life sciences and biopharma companies.

Financial Performance
Repligen's revenue have been generally rising for the past five years. Net income fell in 2014 but has been recovering since.

In 2017 revenue increased 35% to $141.2 million. Two factors drove that gain — higher sales of filtration and chromatography products and the added income from recently acquired firms Spectrum Laboratories Atoll and TangenX Technology.

Net income rose 143% to $28.4 million in 2017 thanks partly to the higher revenue that year but also thanks to a $21.1 income tax benefit.

The company ended 2017 with $173.8 million in net cash about $50 million more than it had at the end of 2016. Financing activities — largely the issuance of common stock — provided $129.3 million while operating activities provided another $17.5 million. Investing activities used $98.2 million.

Strategy
Historically Repligen did most of its business selling products to antibody purification companies who would then sell their products to the pharmaceutical sector. Now the company is increasingly selling products directly to pharmaceuticals and contract research organizations. In fact direct sales make up more than 60% of the firm's product revenue. This shift in strategy has been beneficial as R&D spending by pharmaceuticals continues to rise.

However Repligen is a relatively small contender in the bioprocessing field and several of its competitors enjoy brand name recognition greater access to large amounts of capital and even more experience developing innovative products. This makes the company somewhat vulnerable to such threats as lower prices for competing products. Additionally Repligen has certain key customers which are also competitors. The loss of one of those customers due to new competing products (or any number of reasons) could significantly impact the company's finances.

To counteract these challenges the company aims to deliver products that can address unmet needs in bioprocessing. It utilizes its internal development expertise with an eye toward getting its products to key customers early. By doing so Repligen products have the potential to serve as foundational elements in customers' processes. The firm is investing in its core proteins franchise as well as developing products to support its filtration and chromatography lines. In addition to developing products internally Repligen keeps an eye out for potential acquisition targets such as Spectrum Laboratories (2017) the purchase of which strengthened the company's filtration business.

The company is also working to expand its operations geographically especially in the US Europe and Asia.

Mergers and Acquisitions
In 2017 Repligen bought California-based Spectrum Laboratories for $359 million. Spectrum makes products that filter isolate purify and concentrate protein-based drugs as well as vaccines and cell therapies. That deal strengthened Repligen's filtration business and its position in the single-use and continuous manufacturing technologies sector.

In 2016 Repligen bought German manufacturer Atoll which makes MediaScout pre-packed chromatography columns used in the clinical manufacturing of biologic drugs. The deal was valued at $22.5 million. With that purchase the company expanded its pre-packed column chromatography portfolio into high throughput process development screening.

Later in 2016 the company acquired TangenX Technology Corporation from Novasep for $39 million. TangenX develops and markets tangential flow filtration (TFF) technologies including the single-use Sius which are used in the manufacturing of biopharmaceuticals.

EXECUTIVES

SVP Research and Development, James R. Rusche, age 66, $311,000 total compensation
VP Sales and Marketing, Stephen Tingley
VP Business Development, Howard Benjamin, $279,000 total compensation
President and CEO, Tony J. Hunt, $403,846 total compensation
CFO, Jon K. Snodgres, $330,000 total compensation
VP and Managing Director Repligen GmbH, Martin Reuter
VP Human Resources, Kelly Capra
Vice President, Vikas Gupta
Vice President, John Bonham-Carter
Vice President Global Operations, Steve Curran
Vice President Business Development, Marc Centrella
Vice President, Gautam Choudhary
Senior Vice President, Anthony Macdonald
Chairman, Karen A. Dawes
Auditors: Ernst & Young LLP

LOCATIONS

HQ: Repligen Corp.
41 Seyon Street, Bldg. 1, Suite 100, Waltham, MA 02453
Phone: 781 250-0111   **Fax:** 781 250-0115
Web: www.repligen.com

PRODUCTS/OPERATIONS

2017 Sales

	$ mil.	% of total
Product revenue		
Protein products	54.0	38
Filtration products	49.0	35
Chromatography products	36.3	26
Other	1.8	1
Royalties & other	0.1	-
Total	**141.2**	**100**

COMPETITORS

Abbott Labs   Incyte
Asahi Kasei   NeuroNova
Bio-Rad Labs   PDL BioPharma
Danaher

HISTORICAL FINANCIALS
Company Type: Public

Income Statement   FYE: December 31

	REVENUE ($ mil.)	NET INCOME ($ mil.)	NET PROFIT MARGIN	EMPLOYEES
12/18	194.0	16.6	8.6%	548
12/17	141.2	28.3	20.1%	476
12/16	104.5	11.6	11.2%	236
12/15	83.5	9.3	11.2%	168
12/14	63.5	8.1	12.9%	136
Annual Growth	32.2%	19.4%	—	41.7%

2018 Year-End Financials

Debt ratio: 13.3%   No. of shares (mil.): 43.9
Return on equity: 2.7%   Dividends
Cash ($ mil.): 193.8   Yield: —
Current ratio: 2.12   Payout: —
Long-term debt ($ mil.): —   Market value ($ mil.): 2,316.0

	STOCK PRICE ($) FY Close	P/E High/Low		PER SHARE ($) Earnings	Dividends	Book Value
12/18	52.74	181	81	0.37	0.00	14.02
12/17	36.28	62	39	0.72	0.00	13.57
12/16	30.82	97	60	0.34	0.00	4.99
12/15	28.29	151	71	0.28	0.00	3.73
12/14	19.80	102	49	0.25	0.00	3.41
Annual Growth	27.8%	—	—	10.3%	—	42.4%

Republic Bancorp, Inc. (KY)

As one of the top five bank holding companies based in Kentucky $4 billion-asset Republic Bancorp is the parent of Republic Bank & Trust (formerly First Commercial Bank) which offers deposit accounts loans and mortgages credit cards private banking and trust services through more than 30 branches in across Kentucky and around 10 more in southern Indiana Nashville Tampa and Cincinnati Ohio. About one-third of the bank's $3 billion-loan portfolio is tied to residential real estate while another 25% is made up of commercial real estate loans. Warehouse lines of credit home equity loans and commercial and industrial loans make up most of the rest. The company also offers short-term consumer loans and tax refund loans.

Operations

Republic Bancorp operates three "core banking" segments: Traditional Banking which generated more than 80% of the company's total profit during 2015; Warehouse (almost 20% of profit) and Mortgage Banking (less than 1%). Its Warehouse lending business offers short-term credit facilities secured by single-family residences to mortgage bankers nationwide. Its Republic Processing Group segment offers short-term consumer loans prepaid debit cards and tax refund loans.

The bank made 75% of its total revenue from interest income almost entirely from loans during 2015 though a small percentage came from taxed investments and Federal Home Loan Bank stock. The rest of its revenue came from net refund transfer fees from its Republic Processing Group segment (9% of revenue) deposit account service charges (7%) interchange fee income (4%) mortgage banking income (2%) and other miscellaneous income sources.

Subsidiary Republic Insurance Services (also known as the Captive) provides property and casualty insurance coverage to the company and eight other third-party insurance captives for which insurance may not be available or cost effective.

Geographic Reach

The company had 40 RB&T branches at the end of 2015 including 32 in Kentucky mostly in the Louisville Metro area and others in the Central Western and Northern parts of the state. It had 3 branches in southern Indiana (in Floyds Knobs Jeffersonville and New Albany); two branches in the Tampa Florida metro area; two branches in the Nashville Tennessee metro area; and one more in the Cincinnati Ohio metro area.

Sales and Marketing

Republic spent $3.16 million on marketing and development expenses during 2015 compared to $3.26 million and $3.11 million in 2014 and 2013 respectively.

Financial Performance

Republic Bancorp's revenues and profits have been trending higher since 2013 as its loan assets have risen more than 30% over the period.

The company's revenue climbed 9% to $190 million during 2015 mostly thanks to higher interest income as its loan assets grew by 9% to $3.33 billion with commercial loans (real estate and business loans) and residential mortgage loans and lines of credit driving most of the growth.

Strong revenue growth in 2015 drove Republic's net income up 22% to $35 million for the year. The company's operating cash levels nearly doubled to $50 million after adjusting its earnings for non-cash items related to mortgage loan sales and thanks to favorable working capital changes related to changes in other liabilities.

Strategy

Republic Bancorp is moving toward building its commercial loans business launching a Corporate Banking division in 2015 to originate commercial loans with amounts ranging from $2.5 million to $25 million to borrowers with the highest credit ratings in its existing geographic markets. It also acquires smaller community banks to expand into new geographic markets while building its loan and deposit business.

Additionally Republic Bancorp has been moving into other revolving credit lines while also looking to take advantage of the rapidly growing prepaid card market. During 2015 for example it partnered with netSpend to become a pilot issuer of netSpend-branded prepaid cards; and partnered with ClearBalance to originate revolving lines of credit nationally for hospital receivables.

Mergers and Acquisitions

In October 2015 Republic Bancorp expanded its presence in Florida and grew its loan business after agreeing to buy $250 million-asset Cornerstone Bancorp along its four Cornerstone Community Bank branches in the Tampa Florida metro area $190 million in loans and $200 million in deposits. The deal was expected to be completed in the first half of 2016.

Company Background

In 2012 Republic Bancorp entered the Nashville and Minneapolis market through the FDIC-assisted acquisitions of the failed Tennessee Commerce Bank and First Commercial Bank respectively.

EXECUTIVES

Vice Chairman; President Republic Bank & Trust, A. Scott Trager, age 66, $350,000 total compensation
President and CEO; CEO Republic Bank & Trust, Steven E. (Steve) Trager, age 58, $353,000 total compensation
EVP CFO and Chief Accounting Officer Republic Bancorp and Republic Bank & Trust, Kevin Sipes, age 47, $281,500 total compensation
Vice President and Risk Manager, Bryan Hendrick
Assistant Vice President, Mike Long
Vice President, Susan Smith
Assistant Vice President Accounting Supervisor, Denise Witten
Senior Vice President, Lisa Butcher
Assistant Vice President Technology Services Managerand#8230, Scott Estes
Vice President Project Services Manager, Michelle Cunningham
Vice President Retail Collections, Lori Forbes
Executive Vice President and Chief Risk Officer of Republic Bank and Trust Company, John Rippy
Avp Banking Center Supervisor, Robin Verenna
Vice President Retail Collections Supervisor, Jaree Glass
Senior Vice President, David Buchanon
Vice President Director of Business Intelligence, Deb Reese
Assistant Vice President, Philip Thomas
Vice President, Karen McGee
Vice President Senior Manager of Technology Services, Sean O'Mahoney
Assistant Vice President, Amy Quinn
Vice President Mortgage Warehouse Lending, Tim Poole
Vice President Senior Private Banking Officer, Steven Sharp
Vice President Contact Center Director Of Client Experience, Robinson Damion
Vice President Treasury Management, Tamara McCain
Vice President, Scott Lee
Vice President Mortgage Warehouse Lending, Scott Davis
Assistant Vice President Business Development Manager, Wende Cosby
Vice President Of Dealer Floor Plan Services, Gina Robinson
Vice President Relationship Manager, Steven Shields
Vice President Loan Operations, Donna Blincoe
Chairman, Bernard M. Trager, age 90
Secretary, Madhurie Nagir
Auditors: Crowe LLP

LOCATIONS

HQ: Republic Bancorp, Inc. (KY)
 601 West Market Street, Louisville, KY 40202
Phone: 502 584-3600
Web: www.republicbank.com

PRODUCTS/OPERATIONS

2015 Sales

	$ mil.	% of total
Interest		
Loans including fees	134.0	70
Taxable investment securities	7.0	4
Other	1.4	1
Noninterest		
Net refund transfer fees	17.4	9
Service charges on deposit accounts	13.0	7
Interchange fee income	8.4	4
Mortgage banking	4.4	2
Other	5.1	3
Adjustments	(0.3)	-
Total	**190.4**	**100**

Selected Services
Checking
Credit & Debit Cards
Internet & Mobile Banking
Lending
Private Banking & Wealth Management
Savings & Investing

COMPETITORS

BB&T	KeyCorp
Bank of America	PNC Financial
Community Trust	Stock Yards Bancorp
Fifth Third	U.S. Bancorp
Home Federal	

HISTORICAL FINANCIALS

Company Type: Public

Income Statement FYE: December 31

	ASSETS ($ mil.)	NET INCOME ($ mil.)	INCOME AS % OF ASSETS	EMPLOYEES
12/18	5,240.4	77.8	1.5%	1,064
12/17	5,085.3	45.6	0.9%	1,009
12/16	4,816.3	45.9	1.0%	954
12/15	4,230.2	35.1	0.8%	799
12/14	3,747.0	28.7	0.8%	735
Annual Growth	8.7%	28.2%	—	9.7%

2018 Year-End Financials

Return on assets: 1.5%
Return on equity: 11.7%
Long-term debt ($ mil.): —
No. of shares (mil.): 20.8
Sales ($ mil): 319.6
Dividends
 Yield: 2.5%
 Payout: 25.8%
Market value ($ mil.): 809.0

	STOCK PRICE ($) FY Close	P/E High/Low		PER SHARE ($) Earnings	Dividends	Book Value
12/18	38.72	7	5	3.74	0.97	33.03
12/17	38.02	19	15	2.20	0.87	30.33
12/16	39.54	18	11	2.22	0.83	28.97
12/15	26.41	16	13	1.70	0.78	27.59
12/14	24.72	18	16	1.38	0.74	26.80
Annual Growth	11.9%	—	—	28.3%	7.1%	5.4%

Republic First Bancorp, Inc.

Republic First Bancorp is the holding company for Republic Bank which serves the Greater Philadelphia area and southern New Jersey from more than 15 branches. Boasting over $1 billion in assets the bank targets individuals and small to midsized businesses offering standard deposit products including checking and savings accounts money market accounts IRAs and CDs. Commercial mortgages account for more than 70% of the company's loan portfolio which also includes consumer loans business loans and residential mortgages. Republic has been transitioning from a commercial bank into a major regional retail and commercial bank.

Operations
The bank's loan portfolio is made up of mostly commercial loans including commercial real estate loans construction and land development loans commercial and industrial loans as well as owner occupied real estate loans consumer-related loans and residential mortgages. As of 2015 each its commercial loans typically ranged from $250000 to $5 million though it sometimes lent up to its legal limit of $19.9 million.

About 72% of Republic First Bancorp's total revenue came from loan interest (including fees) in 2014 while another 11% came from interest and dividends on its taxable and tax-exempt investment securities. The rest of its revenue came from gains on sales of SBA loans (10%) loan advisory and servicing fees (3%) service fees on deposit accounts (3%) and other miscellaneous income sources. The bank had a staff of 235 full-time employees at the end of 2014.

Geographic Reach
Republic First boasts more than 15 branch offices in Pennsylvania (in Abington Ardmore Bala Cynwyd Plymouth Meeting Media and Philadelphia) and New Jersey (in Berlin Cherry Hill Glassboro Haddonfield Marlton and Voorhees).

Sales and Marketing
The bank's commercial loans are mostly made to small and medium-sized businesses as well as professionals who need working capital financing for asset acquisitions or other financial services.

Republic First has been ramping up its advertising spend in recent years. It spent $597 thousand on advertising in 2014 compared to $447 thousand and $307 thousand in 2013 and 2012 respectively.

Financial Performance
The company has struggled to consistently grow its revenues in recent years due to shrinking interest margins on loans amidst the low-interest environment. Republic First has been steadily climbing out from prior years of losses (2013 2011 2010) however thanks to declining interest expenses and lower loan loss provisions as its loan portfolio's credit quality has improved with higher property valuations in the strengthened economy.

Republic First's revenue rose by 4% to $48.4 million in 2014 mostly thanks to an 8% jump in interest income as loan balances increased during the year. The bank's non-interest income fell on lower sales of SBA loans with fewer SBA loan originations which offset some of its top-line growth.

The company shot back into the black with a $2.4 million profit in 2014 (compared to a net loss of $3.5 million in 2013) mostly because in 2013 it had suffered a non-recurring $3.6 million loan loss on a bad loan as well as a non-recurring $1.9 million charge related to a legal settlement. Republic First's operating cash levels also skyrocketed to $9.7 million mostly on higher cash earnings.

Strategy
Republic Bank which had historically been known for its business and commercial lending has been focused on retail banking in the past few years and is working to become a major regional retail and commercial bank. As part of this strategy the bank has restructured its loan portfolio to reduce its emphasis on commercial real estate loans and has pursued a "retail-focused" strategy by offering customers "extended store hours absolutely free checking and coin counting more than 55000 surcharge ATMs and free VISA gift cards" according to the company's CEO letter included in the 2014 annual report.

The company has been expanding organically through new branch openings in recent years. In 2015 for example Republic Bank opened three new branches in South New Jersey in Berlin Marlton and Glassboro. In April of that year the company also sold $45 million in common stock through a private placement offering to cover its "aggressive expansion plans in 2015 and beyond."

EXECUTIVES

Assistant Vice President Network Engineer, John Rudolph
Svp Human Resources Director, Janine Zangrilli
Senior Vice President Chief Risk Officer, Tracie Young
Vice President And Marketing Manager, Katie Michaleski
Vice President Loan Administration, Lisa Iannello
Vice President Of Consumer Lending, Dan Charyna
Senior Vice President and Retail Market Manager, Leslie DiLuigi
Vice President Senior Business Development Officer, Judy Rosner
Vice President, Krista Collings
Vice President, Amy Osborn
Senior Vice President, Brennan Charlene
Assistant Vice President Loan Closer Sba Division, Camille Oldenburg
Board Member, Brian Tierney
Board Member, Theodore Flocco
Auditors: BDO USA, LLP

LOCATIONS

HQ: Republic First Bancorp, Inc.
50 South 16th Street, Philadelphia, PA 19102
Phone: 215 735-4422
Web: www.myrepublicbank.com

PRODUCTS/OPERATIONS

2014 Sales

	$ mil.	% of total
Interest income		
Interest and fees on taxable loans	34.5	71
Interest and dividends on taxable investment securities	5.1	10
Interest and fees on tax-exempt loans	0.3	1
Interest and dividends on tax-exempt investment securities	0.3	1
Interest on federal funds sold and other interest-earning assets	0.1	0
Non interest		
Gain on sales of SBA loans	4.7	10
Loan advisory and servicing fees	1.4	3
Service fees on deposit accounts	1.2	3
Gain on sale of investment securities	0.4	1
Legal settlements	0.0	0
Other-than-temporary impairment	0.0	0
Portion recognized in other comprehensive income (before taxes)	(0.03)	0
Net impairment loss on investment securities	0.0	0
Bank owned life insurance income	0.0	0
Other non-interest income	0.1	0
Total	**48.5**	**100**

COMPETITORS

Bank of America	Sovereign Bank
Citizens Financial Group	Sun Bancorp (NJ)
	TD Bank USA
PNC Financial	TF Financial
Prudential Bancorp	Wells Fargo
Royal Bancshares	

HISTORICAL FINANCIALS

Company Type: Public

Income Statement — FYE: December 31

	ASSETS ($ mil.)	NET INCOME ($ mil.)	INCOME AS % OF ASSETS	EMPLOYEES
12/18	2,753.3	8.6	0.3%	531
12/17	2,322.3	8.9	0.4%	448
12/16	1,923.9	4.9	0.3%	306
12/15	1,439.4	2.4	0.2%	277
12/14	1,214.6	2.4	0.2%	235
Annual Growth	22.7%	37.1%	—	22.6%

2018 Year-End Financials

Return on assets: 0.3%
Return on equity: 3.6%
Long-term debt ($ mil.): —
No. of shares (mil.): 58.7
Sales ($ mil): 112.4
Dividends Yield: —
Payout: —
Market value ($ mil.): 351.0

	STOCK PRICE ($) FY Close	P/E High/Low		PER SHARE ($) Earnings	Dividends	Book Value
12/18	5.97	62	39	0.15	0.00	4.17
12/17	8.45	62	47	0.15	0.00	3.97
12/16	8.35	69	29	0.12	0.00	3.79
12/15	4.33	77	55	0.06	0.00	3.00
12/14	3.75	76	43	0.07	0.00	2.98
Annual Growth	12.3%	—	—	21.0%	—	8.8%

Retail Opportunity Investments Corp

For this company opportunity knocking sounds a lot like a neighborhood shopping center. Retail Opportunity Investments (ROIC) true to its name invests in owns leases and manages shopping centers. It targets densely populated middle and upper class markets and looks for centers anchored by large grocery or drug stores. The self-managed real estate investment trust (REIT) owns more than 50 shopping centers comprising 5.5 million sq. ft. in Oregon Washington and California. It makes money from rent management expenses and mortgage interest. ROIC was formed in 2007 as an acquisition company. It purchased NRDC Capital Management in 2009 and took its current name in 2010.

Financial Performance
Increases in base rents drove ROIC's revenue up 45% in 2012 over 2011. The company saw its net income drop 18% during the same period due in part to high operating and depreciation and amortization expenses as well as to expenditures related to the company's headquarters relocation from New York to California.

Strategy
ROIC's strategy includes renovating its properties and making lease agreement adjustments to keep its occupancy rates high. The company occasionally bolsters its portfolio with acquisitions of properties in its target markets. Between fiscal 2011 and 2013 the company added nearly three dozen properties to its portfolio. While it has focused its investments along the West Coast (California Washington and Oregon) ROIC is also eying properties in the Northeast.

Company Background
The company began operating in late 2009 and immediately commenced building out its portfolio purchasing a 95000-square-foot shopping center in Los Angeles County anchored by Rite Aid. In its second year it boosted its holdings after acquiring another dozen properties.

EXECUTIVES

CFO, Michael B. (Mike) Haines, age 57, $290,000 total compensation
President CEO and Director, Stuart A. Tanz, age 60, $775,000 total compensation
COO, Richard K. Schoebel, age 52, $340,000 total compensation
Chairman, Richard A. Baker, age 52
Board Member, Edward Meyer
Board Member, Eric Zorn
Board Member, Lee Neibart
Board Member, Laura Pomerantz
Auditors: Ernst & Young LLP

LOCATIONS

HQ: Retail Opportunity Investments Corp
11250 El Camino Real, Suite 200, San Diego, CA 92130
Phone: 858 677-0900
Web: www.roireit.net

PRODUCTS/OPERATIONS

2015 Sales

	$ mil.	% of total
Base Rents	148.6	77
Recoveries from tenants other	44.1	23
Total	192.7	100

Selected Properties

California
  Claremont Center
  Deser Springs Marketplace
  Gateway Village
  Marketplace Del Rio
  Nimbus Winery Village
  Norwood Shopping Center
  Paramount Plaza
  Phillips Village
  Pinole Vista
  Pleasant Hill Marketplace
  Santa Ana Downtown Plaza
  Sycamore Creek
Oregon
  Cascade Summit
  Division Crossing
  Halsey Crossing
  Happy Valley Town Center
  Oregon City Point
  Wilsonville Old Town Square
Washington
  Crossroads
  Heritage Market Center
  Meridian Valley Plaza
  The Market at Lake Stevens
  Vancouver Market Center

COMPETITORS

Kimco Realty
Macerich
Regency Centers
Simon Property Group
Vornado Realty
Weingarten Realty

HISTORICAL FINANCIALS
Company Type: Public

Income Statement — FYE: December 31

	REVENUE ($ mil.)	NET INCOME ($ mil.)	NET PROFIT MARGIN	EMPLOYEES
12/18	295.8	42.7	14.4%	71
12/17	273.2	38.4	14.1%	73
12/16	237.1	32.7	13.8%	71
12/15	192.7	23.8	12.4%	69
12/14	155.8	20.3	13.0%	65
Annual Growth	17.4%	20.5%	—	2.2%

2018 Year-End Financials

Debt ratio: 49.3%
Return on equity: 3.5%
Cash ($ mil.): 6.0
Current ratio: 0.06
Long-term debt ($ mil.): 1,482.7
No. of shares (mil.): 113.9
Dividends
  Yield: 4.9%
  Payout: 210.8%
Market value ($ mil.): 1,810.0

	STOCK PRICE ($) FY Close	P/E High/Low		PER SHARE ($) Earnings	Dividends	Book Value
12/18	15.88	53	41	0.38	0.78	10.42
12/17	19.95	64	51	0.35	0.75	10.72
12/16	21.13	74	56	0.31	0.72	10.87
12/15	17.90	74	62	0.25	0.68	10.42
12/14	16.79	71	59	0.24	0.64	9.93
Annual Growth	(1.4%)	—	—	12.2%	5.1%	1.2%

Revere Bank (Laurel, MD)

Auditors: Dixon Hughes Goodman LLP

LOCATIONS

HQ: Revere Bank (Laurel, MD)
2101 Gaither Road, Suite 600, Rockville, MD 20850
Phone: 301 841-9600   **Fax:** 301 841-9601
Web: www.reverebank.com

HISTORICAL FINANCIALS
Company Type: Public

Income Statement — FYE: December 31

	REVENUE ($ mil.)	NET INCOME ($ mil.)	NET PROFIT MARGIN	EMPLOYEES
12/18	109.2	27.6	25.3%	0
12/17	90.5	16.2	18.0%	0
12/16	58.4	8.7	15.0%	0
12/15	34.6	6.2	17.9%	0
Annual Growth	46.6%	64.5%	—	—

2018 Year-End Financials

Debt ratio: 3.8%
Return on equity: 12.1%
Cash ($ mil.): 136.4
Current ratio: 0.07
Long-term debt ($ mil.): 94.1
No. of shares (mil.): 11.8
Dividends
  Yield: —
  Payout: —
Market value ($ mil.): 337.0

	STOCK PRICE ($) FY Close	P/E High/Low		PER SHARE ($) Earnings	Dividends	Book Value
12/18	28.50	12	10	2.52	0.00	22.42
12/17	28.05	19	11	1.59	0.00	19.11
12/16	17.55	15	12	1.17	0.00	17.51
12/15	10.65	—	—	1.16	0.00	13.75
/0.00	—	—(0.00)		0.00	(0.00)	
Annual Growth	—	—	—	—	—	—

Rexford Industrial Realty Inc

Rexford Industrial Realty knows that there's more to business in Southern California than moviemaking and fashion. A real estate investment trust or REIT Rexford Industrial owns and manages a portfolio of nearly 70 industrial properties in Los Angeles County and surrounding areas. Its portfolio comprises about 7.6 million sq. ft. of warehouse distribution and light manufacturing space that's leased to small and midsized businesses. It manages 20 more properties — altogether comprising 1.2 million sq. ft. of rentable space. A self-administered and self-managed REIT Rexford Industrial was formed in 2013 from the assets of its predecessor. In mid-2013 the company went public.

IPO

Rexford Industrial intends to use a portion of the $224 million in proceeds to repay debt much of which is secured by various properties.

Operations
Rexford Industrial's portfolio spans several California counties including Los Angeles Orange Ventura San Bernadino Riverside and San Diego.

Financial Performance
Revenue rose for Rexford Industrial by 27% in fiscal 2012 to $34 million from 2011's $28 million thanks to increases in rental revenue and tenant reimbursements from rising occupancy rates and a boost in revenues from properties it acquired during both 2012 and 2011. Rexford Industrial logged 64% increases in revenue from management leasing and development services due to the additional third-party management fees.

Strategy
Rexford Industrial is seeking to acquire equity stakes and debt in stable and distressed industrial properties in infill markets (i.e. highly developed urban centers) in Los Angeles Orange San Diego and Ventura counties and the West Inland Empire to the east. The REIT is also looking to manage properties located in these same areas that are owned by third parties.

The REIT has been buying properties throughout Southern California particularly in the cities of Van Nuys and Tarzana as well as in Glenview Illinois. It looks to purchase both newer and older vintage properties as well as single (40% of its portfolio) and multi-tenant (60%) projects. The REIT invests in every category of industrial property. Tenants are typically small and medium-sized businesses that are tied to the Southern California economy. Rexford Industrial boasts an average tenant size of about 9000 sq. ft. Nearly 70% of its tenants occupy fewer than 50000 sq. ft. apiece.

EXECUTIVES
Co-CEO and Director, Howard Schwimmer, $495,000 total compensation
Co-CEO and Director, Michael S. Frankel, age 56, $495,000 total compensation
CFO, Adeel Khan, $315,000 total compensation
Vice President And Assistant General Counsel, Laura Mask
Chairman, Richard S. Ziman, age 76
Auditors: Ernst & Young LLP

LOCATIONS
HQ: Rexford Industrial Realty Inc
11620 Wilshire Boulevard, Suite 1000, Los Angeles, CA 90025
Phone: 310 966-1680
Web: www.rexfordindustrial.com

PRODUCTS/OPERATIONS
2015 Revenue

	$ mil.	% of total
Rental		
Rental Revenues	81.1	86
Tenant Reimbursements	10.5	11
Management Leasing & Development Services	0.6	1
Other Income	1.0	1
Interest Income	0.7	1
Total	**93.9**	**100**

Selected Property Categories
Core
Core Plus
First Mortgages Tied to Target Industrial Property
Value Add

COMPETITORS
Brandywine Realty
PS Business Parks
Prologis
Terreno Realty

HISTORICAL FINANCIALS
Company Type: Public

Income Statement — FYE: December 31

	REVENUE ($ mil.)	NET INCOME ($ mil.)	NET PROFIT MARGIN	EMPLOYEES
12/18	212.4	46.2	21.7%	108
12/17	161.3	40.7	25.2%	98
12/16	126.1	25.1	19.9%	90
12/15	93.9	1.8	2.0%	70
12/14	66.5	0.9	1.3%	48
Annual Growth	33.7%	168.0%	—	22.5%

2018 Year-End Financials
Debt ratio: 27.1%
Return on equity: 2.8%
Cash ($ mil.): 180.6
Current ratio: 1.52
Long-term debt ($ mil.): 757.3
No. of shares (mil.): 96.8
Dividends
Yield: 2.1%
Payout: 156.1%
Market value ($ mil.): 2,853.0

	STOCK PRICE ($) FY Close	P/E High/Low	PER SHARE ($) Earnings	Dividends	Book Value
12/18	29.47	79 63	0.41	0.64	19.38
12/17	29.16	66 45	0.48	0.58	17.07
12/16	23.19	65 43	0.36	0.54	14.13
12/15	16.36	556423	0.03	0.51	12.09
12/14	15.71	800642	0.02	0.48	11.89
Annual Growth	17.0%	—	—112.8%	7.5%	13.0%

Ring Energy Inc

Auditors: Eide Bailly LLP

LOCATIONS
HQ: Ring Energy Inc
901 West Wall St., 3rd Floor, Midland, TX 79701
Phone: 432 682-7464
Web: www.ringenergy.com

HISTORICAL FINANCIALS
Company Type: Public

Income Statement — FYE: December 31

	REVENUE ($ mil.)	NET INCOME ($ mil.)	NET PROFIT MARGIN	EMPLOYEES
12/18	120.0	9.0	7.5%	42
12/17	66.7	1.7	2.6%	37
12/16	30.8	(37.6)	—	30
12/15	31.0	(9.0)	—	31
12/14	38.0	8.4	22.1%	22
Annual Growth	33.2%	1.7%	—	17.5%

2018 Year-End Financials
Debt ratio: 6.9%
Return on equity: 2.2%
Cash ($ mil.): 3.3
Current ratio: 0.32
Long-term debt ($ mil.): 39.5
No. of shares (mil.): 63.2
Dividends
Yield: —
Payout: —
Market value ($ mil.): 321.0

	STOCK PRICE ($) FY Close	P/E High/Low	PER SHARE ($) Earnings	Dividends	Book Value
12/18	5.08	114 28	0.15	0.00	7.32
12/17	13.90	493315	0.03	0.00	6.58
12/16	12.99	— —	(0.97)	0.00	5.92
12/15	7.05	— —	(0.32)	0.00	6.13
12/14	10.50	60 23	0.33	0.00	5.54
Annual Growth	(16.6%)	—	—(17.9%)	—	7.2%

River Financial Corp

Auditors: Mauldin & Jenkins, LLC

LOCATIONS
HQ: River Financial Corp
2611 Legends Drive, Prattville, AL 36066
Phone: 334 290-1012
Web: www.riverbankandtrust.com

HISTORICAL FINANCIALS
Company Type: Public

Income Statement — FYE: December 31

	REVENUE ($ mil.)	NET INCOME ($ mil.)	NET PROFIT MARGIN	EMPLOYEES
12/18	43.5	8.5	19.5%	195
12/17	38.4	8.3	21.6%	151
12/16	35.2	7.9	22.5%	134
12/15	19.2	2.3	12.3%	129
12/14	17.9	3.4	19.4%	0
Annual Growth	24.8%	25.0%	—	—

2018 Year-End Financials
Debt ratio: 4.3%
Return on equity: 8.4%
Cash ($ mil.): 47.5
Current ratio: 0.32
Long-term debt ($ mil.): 46.9
No. of shares (mil.): 5.6
Dividends
Yield: 0.0%
Payout: 16.8%
Market value ($ mil.): 171.0

	STOCK PRICE ($) FY Close	P/E High/Low	PER SHARE ($) Earnings	Dividends	Book Value
12/18	30.00	18 13	1.60	0.27	19.60
Annual Growth	—	—	—	—	—

Riverview Bancorp, Inc.

EXECUTIVES
Vice President And Cash Management Officer Vice President Cash Management Officer, Diana Fitzpatrick
Vice President Special Assets, Greg Brown
Vice President Operations, Tony Hays
Senior Vice President, Cheri Smith
Vice President And Corporate Secretary, Teri Baker

Vice President And Audit Manager, Ronald Sines
Vice President Business Development Officer, Farhad Dadkho
SENIOR VICE PRESIDENT AND COMMERCIAL TEAM LEADER, Steve Plambeck
VICE PRESIDENT TRUST OFFICER, Margaret Dent
Senior Vice President Operations And Systems, Jule Webster
Auditors: Delap LLP

LOCATIONS

HQ: Riverview Bancorp, Inc.
900 Washington St., Ste. 900, Vancouver, WA 98660
Phone: 360 693-6650
Web: www.riverviewbank.com

COMPETITORS

Bank of America	Merchants Bancorp
Banner Corp	The Commerce Bank of Oregon
FS Bancorp	U.S. Bancorp
Heritage Financial	Umpqua Holdings
JPMorgan Chase	
KeyCorp	

HISTORICAL FINANCIALS
Company Type: Public

Income Statement   FYE: March 31

	ASSETS ($ mil.)	NET INCOME ($ mil.)	INCOME AS % OF ASSETS	EMPLOYEES
03/19	1,156.9	17.2	1.5%	250
03/18	1,151.5	10.2	0.9%	258
03/17	1,133.9	7.4	0.7%	260
03/16	921.2	6.3	0.7%	229
03/15	858.7	4.4	0.5%	231
Annual Growth	7.7%	40.0%	—	2.0%

2019 Year-End Financials
Return on assets: 1.5%   Dividends
Return on equity: 13.8%   Yield: 0.0%
Long-term debt ($ mil.): —   Payout: 18.4%
No. of shares (mil.): 22.6   Market value ($ mil.): 165.0
Sales ($ mil): 60.9

	STOCK PRICE ($) FY Close	P/E High/Low	PER SHARE ($) Earnings	Dividends	Book Value
03/19	7.31	13 9	0.76	0.14	5.89
03/18	9.34	22 14	0.45	0.10	5.18
03/17	7.15	24 13	0.33	0.08	4.94
03/16	4.20	18 15	0.28	0.06	4.81
03/15	4.50	24 17	0.20	0.01	4.62
Annual Growth	12.9%	— —	39.6%	87.8%	6.3%

Riverview Financial Corp (New)

Auditors: Dixon Hughes Goodman LLP

LOCATIONS

HQ: Riverview Financial Corp (New)
3901 North Front Street, Harrisburg, PA 17110
Phone: 717 957-2196

HISTORICAL FINANCIALS
Company Type: Public

Income Statement   FYE: December 31

	ASSETS ($ mil.)	NET INCOME ($ mil.)	INCOME AS % OF ASSETS	EMPLOYEES
12/18	1,137.6	10.8	1.0%	310
12/17	1,163.6	(4.9)	—	297
12/16	543.0	3.0	0.6%	137
12/15	549.4	(0.7)	—	115
12/14	436.1	2.7	0.6%	116
Annual Growth	27.1%	41.3%	—	27.9%

2018 Year-End Financials
Return on assets: 0.9%   Dividends
Return on equity: 9.8%   Yield: 2.7%
Long-term debt ($ mil.): —   Payout: 25.2%
No. of shares (mil.): 9.1   Market value ($ mil.): 99.0
Sales ($ mil): 52.7

	STOCK PRICE ($) FY Close	P/E High/Low	PER SHARE ($) Earnings	Dividends	Book Value
12/18	10.90	12 8	1.19	0.30	12.49
12/17	13.15	— —	(0.91)	0.55	11.72
12/16	11.60	14 12	0.95	0.55	12.95
12/15	13.20	— —	(0.28)	0.55	13.20
12/14	15.25	15 9	1.00	0.55	14.10
Annual Growth	(8.1%)	— —	4.4%	(14.1%)	(3.0%)

RLJ Lodging Trust

Auditors: PricewaterhouseCoopers LLP

LOCATIONS

HQ: RLJ Lodging Trust
3 Bethesda Metro Center, Suite 1000, Bethesda, MD 20814
Phone: 301 280-7777
Web: www.rljlodgingtrust.com

HISTORICAL FINANCIALS
Company Type: Public

Income Statement   FYE: December 31

	REVENUE ($ mil.)	NET INCOME ($ mil.)	NET PROFIT MARGIN	EMPLOYEES
12/18	1,761.2	190.1	10.8%	84
12/17	1,356.2	75.3	5.6%	99
12/16	1,160.0	200.3	17.3%	58
12/15	1,136.3	218.2	19.2%	56
12/14	1,109.2	135.4	12.2%	56
Annual Growth	12.3%	8.8%	—	10.7%

2018 Year-End Financials
Debt ratio: 36.6%   No. of shares (mil.): 174.0
Return on equity: 5.4%   Dividends
Cash ($ mil.): 384.8   Yield: 8.0%
Current ratio: 1.58   Payout: 141.9%
Long-term debt ($ mil.): 2,202.6   Market value ($ mil.): 2,854.0

	STOCK PRICE ($) FY Close	P/E High/Low	PER SHARE ($) Earnings	Dividends	Book Value
12/18	16.40	26 17	0.93	1.32	19.96
12/17	21.97	53 41	0.47	1.32	20.29
12/16	24.49	15 11	1.61	1.32	17.87
12/15	21.63	21 13	1.68	1.32	17.51
12/14	33.53	32 23	1.06	1.04	17.89
Annual Growth	(16.4%)	— —	(3.2%)	6.1%	2.8%

RMR Group Inc (The)

Auditors: Ernst & Young LLP

LOCATIONS

HQ: RMR Group Inc (The)
Two Newton Place, 255 Washington Street, Suite 300, Newton, MA 02458-1634
Phone: 617 796-8230
Web: www.rmrgroup.com

HISTORICAL FINANCIALS
Company Type: Public

Income Statement   FYE: September 30

	REVENUE ($ mil.)	NET INCOME ($ mil.)	NET PROFIT MARGIN	EMPLOYEES
09/19	713.3	74.5	10.5%	50,600
09/18	404.9	96.0	23.7%	52,600
09/17	271.7	42.2	15.6%	53,475
09/16	266.9	37.2	14.0%	52,450
09/15	192.9	7.3	3.8%	50,400
Annual Growth	38.7%	78.8%	—	0.1%

2019 Year-End Financials
Debt ratio: —   No. of shares (mil.): 31.3
Return on equity: 28.6%   Dividends
Cash ($ mil.): 358.4   Yield: 3.0%
Current ratio: 4.74   Payout: 30.5%
Long-term debt ($ mil.): —   Market value ($ mil.): 1,424.0

	STOCK PRICE ($) FY Close	P/E High/Low	PER SHARE ($) Earnings	Dividends	Book Value
09/19	45.48	20 9	4.59	1.40	9.22
09/18	92.80	16 9	5.92	1.00	7.45
09/17	51.35	21 13	2.63	1.00	4.80
09/16	37.94	17 5	2.33	0.55	3.92
Annual Growth	6.2%	— —	25.4%	36.6%	33.0%

Rogers Corp.

Rogers Corp. makes and sell specialty materials used for connecting and cushioning as well as managing power in electronic industrial and consumer products. The company's connectivity products are circuit materials used in telecommunications infrastructure automotive applications and consumer electronics. Its polyurethane and silicone products provide cushioning sealing and vibration management in smart phones automotive and aerospace applications and shoes. Its ceramic substrate materials are used in power-related applications like variable frequency drives vehicle electrification and renewable energy. International customers generate about 70% of the Chandler Arizona-based company's revenue.

Financial Performance

Roger's revenue grew an average of 9% a year from 2014-2018 punctuated by a 25% jump in 2016-2017 when each segment generated record sales with contributions from the DeWal and Diversified Silicone Products acquisitions.

Rogers' sales rose 7% to $879 million in 2018 up $58 million from 2017. The company's Elastomeric Material Solutions segment's sales rose about 9% due to stronger sales of electric and hybrid electric vehicles and the Power Electronics Solutions segment's revenue grew about 21% on higher sales of portable electronics and automotive applications. Meanwhile the Advanced Connectivity Solutions segment's sales dipped 2% from lower sales of wireless 4G LTE and portable electronics applications. The acquisition of Griswold added about $14 million to the year-over-year increase.

Rising costs ate up the higher 2018 sales leaving the company with a pre-tax profit of $110.6 million compared to about $133 million in 2017. Rogers paid less in taxes in 2018 however leaving it with net income of $87.7 million compared to $80.5 million in 2017.

Rogers had $167.7 million in cash in 2018 compared to $181.2 million in 2017. The company's operating activities generated $66.8 million in 2018 while investing activities used $167.4 million and financing activities provided $88.7 million.

Strategy

Rogers in 2018 stepped on the gas to expand production capacity to meet the rising market demand in the mobility (electric vehicles) and connectivity (5G networks) markets that it expects. Rogers reckons that 5G infrastructure would use five times more Rogers material than 4G/LTE designs while in the automotive area Rogers expects more business as automated driver assist systems expand into mass-market vehicles and automakers boost production of electric vehicles. As part of its production expansion the company bought a plant in Chandler Arizona and outfitted it to make 5G-related materials.

Since 2016 Rogers has made three acquisitions designed to boost its growth. Griswold (2018) brought engineered cellular elastomer and microcellular polyurethane products; Diversified Silicone Products (2017) provided the company with custom silicone product development and manufacturing; and DeWAL Industries (2016) added a round of films pressure-sensitive tapes and specialty products for the industrial aerospace automotive and electronics markets.

With about a third of its sales going to customers in China Rogers has felt the impact of the US-China trade war. A related element is the company's relationship with Huawei the Chinese telecom company that the US has tried to freeze out from 5G work. While Huawei accounts for less than 10% of its business its loss as a customer could hurt Rogers.

Company Background

In Asia it formed a strategic alliance with Hitachi Chemical in 2011 to provide high-speed digital printed circuit materials. The materials produced help meet the growing demand for increased speed in Internet data and video transmission.

In 2011 Rogers acquired Curamik Electronics a manufacturer of power electronic substrate products in Eschenbach Germany for $153 million. Curamik Electronics is a global leader for the development of direct copper bonded ceramic substrate products which are used in industrial motor drives wind and solar energy converters and hybrid electric vehicle drive systems. The acquisition enhanced Rogers' existing power electronic products portfolio.

In late 2011 Rogers ceased operations at its underperforming Thermal Management Solutions segment after failing to gain traction in the market and having problems with the manufacturing process. With the acquisition of Curamik Electronics in 2011 Rogers restructured its business segments to add Power Electronics Solutions as one of its three core strategic units along with High Performance Foams and Printed Circuit Materials. Curamik Electronic Solutions and Power Distribution Systems comprise the Power Electronics Solutions business segment.

Rogers was founded in 1832 as a materials manufacturer for the textile industry by Peter Rogers.

EXECUTIVES

Vice President Sales And Marketing, Mario Kerr
SVP and CTO, Robert C. (Bob) Daigle, age 56, $320,016 total compensation
CFO, Janice E. Stipp, age 59
President and CEO, Bruce D. Hoechner, age 58, $490,773 total compensation
President Enterprise Business Unit, Nitin Kawale
VP Advanced Circuit Materials Division, Jeffrey M. Grudzien, age 57, $276,543 total compensation
VP High Performance Foams Division, John C. Quinn
VP Power Electronics Solutions; President Rogers Asia, Helen Zhang
Chief Human Resource Officer Senior Vice President, Gary Glandon
Board Member, Michael Barry
Board Member, Carol Jensen
Board Member, Peter Wallace
Board Member, Helene Simonet
Board Member, Ganesh Moorthy
Board Member, Keith Barnes
Auditors: PricewaterhouseCoopers LLP

LOCATIONS

HQ: Rogers Corp.
2225 W. Chandler Blvd., Chandler, AZ 85224-6155
Phone: 480 917-6000
Web: www.rogerscorp.com

PRODUCTS/OPERATIONS

2018 Sales

	$ mil.	% of total
Elastomeric Material Solutions	341.0	39
Advanced Connectivity Solutions	294.1	34
Power Electronics Solutions	223.4	25
Other	20.2	2
Total	879.1	100

Selected Products and Brands

High Performance Foams
  Plate backing and mounts for printing plates (R/bak)
  Silicon foams and sponges (BISCO)
  Urethane and silicon foams for high-impact cushioning gaskets and seals portable communications devices computers (PORON)

Printed Circuit Materials
  Flexible circuit materials (R/flex)
  Printed circuit board materials (DUROID ULTRALAM)
Power Electronics Solutions
  Curamik Electronics Solutions
  Direct copper bonded (DCB) ceramic substrate products
  Power distribution systems
  Busbar products used in mass transit and clean technology (RO-LINX)
Other Polymer Products
  Elastomer rollers and belts (ENDUR)
  Floats for fuel-level sensors (NITROPHYL)

COMPETITORS

Hexcel	Kingboard
Honeywell Electronic Materials	Park Electrochemical
	Plexus
Insulectro	Vesuvius

HISTORICAL FINANCIALS

Company Type: Public

Income Statement FYE: December 31

	REVENUE ($ mil.)	NET INCOME ($ mil.)	NET PROFIT MARGIN	EMPLOYEES
12/18	879.0	87.6	10.0%	3,700
12/17	821.0	80.4	9.8%	3,400
12/16	656.3	48.2	7.4%	3,100
12/15	641.4	46.3	7.2%	2,800
12/14	610.9	52.8	8.7%	2,800
Annual Growth	9.5%	13.5%	—	7.2%

2018 Year-End Financials

Debt ratio: 18.2%   No. of shares (mil.): 18.4
Return on equity: 10.8%   Dividends
Cash ($ mil.): 167.7   Yield: —
Current ratio: 4.53   Payout: —
Long-term debt ($ mil.): 233.1   Market value ($ mil.): 1,822.0

	STOCK PRICE ($) FY Close	P/E High/Low	PER SHARE ($) Earnings	Dividends	Book Value
12/18	99.06	37 19	4.70	0.00	46.12
12/17	161.92	38 17	4.34	0.00	41.99
12/16	76.81	29 16	2.65	0.00	35.28
12/15	51.57	33 18	2.48	0.00	32.55
12/14	81.44	28 18	2.83	0.00	31.62
Annual Growth	5.0%	— —	13.5%	—	9.9%

Royal Gold Inc

Royal Gold loves royalties. Rather than operating gold mines the company buys the right to collect royalties and stream finance (a purchase arrangement that provides in exchange for an upfront deposit the right to purchase metal production from a mine at a price determined for the term of the agreement) from mine operators. This approach allows Royal Gold to minimize its exposure to the costs of mineral exploration and development. It owns interests in more than 190 properties (including producing exploration and development-stage projects) on six continents. Its operations in Chile accounts for about 15% of the company's revenues; operations in Canada 35%.

Operations
Royal Gold is a precious metals royalty and stream company engaged in the acquisition and management of precious metal royalties streams and similar production based interests. Its principal producing properties includes - Andacollo (Chile) Canadian Malartic (Canada) Cortez (US) Holt (Canada) and Mulatos and Peñasquito (Mexico).

Development-stage properties include Mt. Milligan (British Columbia) and Pascua-Lama Project (Chile).

The stream segment accounts for more than 65% of sales.

Geographic Reach
The company owns interests in more than 190 properties on six continents including interests in about 34 producing mines and 21 development-stage projects.

Financial Performance
Royal Gold's revenue increased by 29% in fiscal 2016 (June year end) to $359.8 million primarily as a result of higher stream revenue due to growth in production at Mount Milligan and new production from recently acquired streams Wassa and Prestea Pueblo Viejo and Andacollo.

Royalty revenue decreased due to lower average metal prices the sale of an Andacollo royalty and production decreases at Peñasquito and Cortez.

Despite the higher overall revenue the company reported a net loss of $82.2 million in fiscal 2016 (compared to net income of $52.7 million a year earlier) due to an increase in expenses including costs of sales and exploration costs; depreciation depletion and amortization; and impairments of stream and royalty interests and royalty receivables.

In fiscal 2016 Royal Gold's net cash provided by operations decreased to $191.1 million from $169.9 million due to an increase in income taxes of $55.8 million related to the sale of an Andacollo royalty; an increase in exploration costs of $6.4 million; and a $7.3 million increase in interest paid. These declines were partially offset by higher proceeds from stream and royalty interest interests net of production taxes and cost of sales of $47.5 million.

Strategy
Royal Gold grows by acquiring and managing stakes in precious metal royalties and production streams. This approach offers lower risk investment opportunities while retaining upside value. The advantages of this business model include portfolio diversification no-cost exploration upside geopolitical stability fixed-cost investments and inherent growth.

The company's growth strategy includes providing capital for the exploration development and construction of precious metals mines in exchange for royalties; monetizing precious metals by-product streams from base metals operations in development or operation; and offering acquisition finance in partnership with operating companies in return for a royalty or metal stream on acquired properties.

In 2016 Royal Gold owned stream interests in four producing properties and three development stage properties. That fiscal year it invested $1.3 billion in stream interests including stream interests relating to Pueblo Viejo Carmen de Andacollo Wassa and Prestea and Rainy River.

Mergers and Acquisitions
In 2016 the company acquired a 3.75% royalty covering a significant area of Barrick Gold's Cortez gold mine in the US from a private party seller for $70 million. Other 2016 acquisitions included a gold and silver stream on the Pueblo Viejo mine in the Dominican Republic; a gold stream on the Andacollo copper-gold mine located in Chile; a gold stream on the Wassa and Prestea mines in Ghana; and a gold and silver stream on the Rainy River Project in Canada.

EXECUTIVES
President and CEO, Tony Jensen, age 57, $700,000 total compensation
CFO and Treasurer, Stefan L. Wenger, age 46, $425,000 total compensation
VP General Counsel and Secretary, Bruce C. Kirchhoff, age 60, $375,000 total compensation
VP Investor Relations, Karli Anderson, $310,000 total compensation
VP Corporate Development, William Heissenbuttel, age 54, $450,000 total compensation
VP Operations, Mark E. Isto
Chairman, William M. (Bill) Hayes, age 74
Auditors: Ernst & Young LLP

LOCATIONS
HQ: Royal Gold Inc
1144 15th Street, Suite 2500, Denver, CO 80202
Phone: 303 573-1660
Web: www.royalgold.com

PRODUCTS/OPERATIONS

2013 Sales by Property

	% of total
Andacollo	28
Voisey's Bay	11
Pe?asquito	10
Holt	7
Mulatos	6
Robinson	5
Cortez	3
Canadian Malartic	3
Las Cruces	2
Other	25
Total	**100**

COMPETITORS
Anglo American
AngloGold Ashanti
BHP Billiton
Franco-Nevada
Rio Tinto Limited

HISTORICAL FINANCIALS
Company Type: Public

Income Statement FYE: June 30

	REVENUE ($ mil.)	NET INCOME ($ mil.)	NET PROFIT MARGIN	EMPLOYEES
06/19	423.0	93.8	22.2%	23
06/18	459.0	(113.1)	—	23
06/17	440.8	101.5	23.0%	23
06/16	359.7	(77.1)	—	21
06/15	278.0	51.9	18.7%	20
Annual Growth	11.1%	15.9%	—	3.6%

	STOCK PRICE ($) FY Close	P/E High/Low	PER SHARE ($) Earnings	Dividends	Book Value
06/19	102.49	72 50	1.43	1.03	32.65
06/18	92.84	— —	(1.73)	0.98	32.16
06/17	78.17	55 40	1.55	0.94	34.91
06/16	72.02	— —	(1.18)	0.91	34.24
06/15	61.59	103 71	0.80	0.87	36.18
Annual Growth	13.6%	— —	15.6%	4.3%	(2.5%)

2019 Year-End Financials
Debt ratio: 8.4%
Return on equity: 4.4%
Cash ($ mil.): 119.4
Current ratio: 4.60
Long-term debt ($ mil.): 214.5
No. of shares (mil.): 65.4
Dividends
Yield: 0.0%
Payout: 72.0%
Market value ($ mil.): 6,707.0

S & T Bancorp Inc (Indiana, PA)

S&T Bancorp is the bank holding company for S&T Bank which boasts nearly $5 billion in assets and serves customers from some 60 branch offices in western Pennsylvania. Targeting individuals and local businesses the bank offers such standard retail products as checking savings and money market accounts CDs and credit cards. Business loans including commercial mortgages make up more than 80% of the company's loan portfolio. The bank also originates residential mortgages construction loans and consumer loans. Through subsidiaries S&T Bank sells life disability and commercial property/casualty insurance provides investment management services and advises the Stewart Capital Mid Cap Fund.

Operations
S&T Bancorp operates through three main business segments: Community Banking which offers traditional banking services and commercial and consumer loans; Wealth Management which boasts $2 billion in assets under management and administration and provides brokerage services trust and custodial services and investment advisory for affluent individuals and institutions; and Insurance which offers commercial property and casualty insurance group life and health coverage employee benefit services and personal insurance products through S&T Insurance Group LLC.

Its S&T Bancholding subsidiary provides investment services in the Wealth Management segment while its Stewart Capital Advisors subsidiary provides investment advisory services in the segment.

Overall S&T Bancorp generated 72% of its total revenue from loan interest (including fees) in 2014 plus another 6% from interest on its investment securities. About 10% of its total revenue came from debit and credit card fees and deposit account service charges while wealth management fees and insurance fees made up 6% and 3% of total revenue that year respectively.

Geographic Reach
Headquartered in Indiana Pennsylvania S&T Bancorp boasts branches in a dozen counties in the state including: Allegheny Armstrong Blair Butler Cambria Centre Clarion Clearfield Indiana Jefferson Washington and Westmoreland counties. It also has loan production offices in northeast and central Ohio and in western New York.

Sales and Marketing
Targeting both individuals and local businesses S&T Bancorp spent $3.32 million on marketing in

2014 up from the $2.93 million and $3.21 million it spent in 2013 and 2012 respectively.

Financial Performance

S&T Bancorp's revenue has slowly declined in recent years due to shrinking interest margins on loans amidst the low-interest environment. The firm's profits however have been rising thanks to declining loan loss provisions as its loan portfolio's credit quality has improved with the strengthened economy.

Following several years of top-line declines the bank's revenue inched up by nearly 1% to $206.86 million in 2014. The rise was mostly thanks to higher interest income as overall earning-asset balances grew by nearly 7% during the year reflecting the bank's growing loan business and increased investment securities assets. Wealth Management fees also continued to grow rising by 6% during the year.

Higher revenue coupled with lower interest expenses on deposits and a $6.6 million reduction in loan loss provisions in 2014 drove S&T Bancorp's net income higher by 15% to $57.91 million. S&T's operating cash levels fell by 9% to $78.1 million for the year after adjusting its earnings for non-cash items mostly related to its net proceeds from sales of its mortgage loans originated-for-sale.

Strategy

S&T Bancorp reiterated in 2015 that its growth strategy is centered around organic growth in existing and new markets and growth through strategic acquisitions that introduce new lines of business. Its 2015 acquisition of Integrity Bancshares for example expanded S&T's footprint eastward across four counties in Pennsylvania and added millions of dollars worth of new loan business. Also that year the bank entered the western part of New York for the first time with the opening of a new loan production office in the region.

In late 2012 the bank extended its operations into its neighbor Ohio when it opened a handful of branches in Akron. That same year the bank acquired Mainline Bancorp and Gateway Bank of Pennsylvania bolstering its presence in its core western Pennsylvania market.

Mergers and Acquisitions

In March 2015 S&T Bancorp purchased Camp Hill-based Integrity Bancshares for $155 million adding $860 million in assets and eight branches expanding S&T's geographic footprint eastward into Cumberland Dauphin Lancaster and York counties in Pennsylvania. S&T added that the acquisition positioned the bank in high-growth markets within the state and added experienced members to the bank's loan team.

In 2012 the bank acquired Mainline Bancorp and Gateway Bank of Pennsylvania. Both transactions served to expand S&T's presence in western Pennsylvania.

EXECUTIVES

SEVP and COO, David P. Ruddock, age 57, $265,000 total compensation
President and CEO S&T and S&T Bank, Todd D. Brice, age 56, $525,000 total compensation
EVP and Retail Banking Division Manager, Richard A. (Rich) Fiscus
SEVP and CFO, Mark Kochvar, age 58, $278,000 total compensation
SEVP and Chief Lending Officer, David G. Antolik, age 52, $302,000 total compensation
EVP and Chief Investment Officer Wealth Management, Malcolm E. Polley, age 56
SEVP Chief Risk Officer and Secretary, Ernest J. Draganza
EVP and Deputy Chief Credit Officer, William (Bill) Kametz
SEVP and Chief Credit Officer, Patrick Haberfield
SEVP and Chief Banking Officer, Rebecca Stapleton
EVP and Commercial Loan Officer, Steve Drahnak
EVP and Chief Audit Executive, LaDawn D. Yesho
EVP, David Richards
EVP Marketing Division Manager, Rob Jorgenson
EVP and CIO, Jim Mill
EVP and Manager, Robert Jogrenson
SEVP and Market Executive, Thomas J. Sposito
Market President Central Pennsylvania, Jordan Space
Market President Northeast Ohio, Steve Hendricks
Vice President Mortgage Underwriting Manager, Christine Rumbaugh
Vice President Marketing, Kelly Thomas
Vice President Credit Analysis Operation Manager, Dennis Scott
Senior Vice President Banking Operations, Robert Coleman
Vice President Marketing, Kelly Corrinne
Evp And Chief Risk Officer, Ernie Draganza
Vice President Of Information Technology, Ron Rodman
Vice President Regional Manager, Megan White
Assistant Vice President SBA Commercial Loan, Becky Oldenski
Evp And Chief Security Officer, Kevin Dodds
Svp Regional Busines Banking SandT Bank, Sean Dockery
Svp Commercial Banker SandT Bank, Jeffrey Bierlein
Svp Commercial Banker SandT Bank, David D'angelo
Vice President Special Assets Officer, Peter Talarovich
Vice President Business Banker, Cathleen Campriani-square
VICE PRESIDENT AND RELATIONSHIP MANAGER, Ronald Barner
ASSISTANT VICE PRESIDENT DATA MANAGEMENT MANAGER, Matthew Mann
SENIOR VICE PRESIDENT COMMERCIAL BANKER, Paul Kelly
ASSISTANT VICE PRESIDENT SENIOR OPERATIONS ACCOUNTANT, Travis Mazon
VICE PRESIDENT, Kevin Hurley
VICE PRESIDENT PLATFORMS SUPPORT MANAGER, Debbie Silveri
Chairman S&T and S&T Bank, Charles G. Urtin
Vice Chairman S&T and S&T Bank, Christine J. Toretti, age 62
Board Member, Jeffrey D Grube
Auditors: Ernst & Young LLP

LOCATIONS

HQ: S & T Bancorp Inc (Indiana, PA)
800 Philadelphia Street, Indiana, PA 15701
Phone: 800 325-2265
Web: www.stbancorp.com

PRODUCTS/OPERATIONS

2014 Sales

	% of total
Interest	
Loans including fees	72
Investment securities & other	6
Noninterest	
Wealth management fees	6
Debit and credit card fees	5
Service charges on deposit accounts	5
Insurance fees	3
Others	3
Total	**100**

Selected Subsidiaries

9th Street Holdings Inc.
Commonwealth Trust Credit Life Insurance Company (50%)
S&T Bank
  S&T Insurance Group LLC
  S&T-Evergreen Insurance LLC
  S&T Bancholdings Inc.
  S&T Professional Resources Group LLC
  S&T Settlement Services LLC
  Stewart Capital Advisors LLC

COMPETITORS

AmeriServ Financial
Citizens Financial Group
F.N.B. (PA)
Fidelity Bancorp (PA)
First Commonwealth Financial
Northwest Bancshares
PNC Financial

HISTORICAL FINANCIALS

Company Type: Public

Income Statement
FYE: December 31

	ASSETS ($ mil.)	NET INCOME ($ mil.)	INCOME AS % OF ASSETS	EMPLOYEES
12/18	7,252.2	105.3	1.5%	1,040
12/17	7,060.2	72.9	1.0%	1,080
12/16	6,943.0	71.3	1.0%	1,080
12/14	4,964.6	57.9	1.2%	945
12/13	4,533.1	50.5	1.1%	948
Annual Growth	12.5%	20.2%	—	2.3%

2018 Year-End Financials

Return on assets: 1.4%
Return on equity: 11.5%
Long-term debt ($ mil.): —
No. of shares (mil.): 34.6
Sales ($ mil): 339.0
Dividends
  Yield: 2.6%
  Payout: 32.8%
Market value ($ mil.): 1,312.0

	STOCK PRICE ($) FY Close	P/E High/Low	PER SHARE ($) Earnings	Dividends	Book Value
12/18	37.84	16 12	3.01	0.99	26.98
12/17	39.81	21 16	2.09	0.82	25.28
12/16	39.04	19 11	2.05	0.77	24.12
12/14	29.81	16 11	1.95	0.68	20.42
12/13	25.31	15 10	1.70	0.61	19.21
Annual Growth	10.6%	— —	15.4%	12.9%	8.9%

Sabra Health Care REIT Inc

Sabra Health Care REIT doesn't mind a little healthy competition in the real estate sector. The company invests in income-producing health care facilities in the US. The REIT's investment portfolio includes about 180 properties most of which are skilled nursing/post-acute centers. It also invests in assisted living and independent living facilities and hospitals. Sabra's facilities house more than 18300 beds and are located in 35-plus states. Substantially all of the properties are leased to and operated by subsidiaries of Sun Healthcare Group which spun off its real estate assets to form Sabra Health Care REIT in 2010. In mid-2017 Sabra acquired Care Capital Properties for approximately $2.1 billion more than doubling the REIT's size.

Operations
Sabra owned 180 real estate properties that were leased to operates and tenants under triple-net lease agreements during 2015 with nearly 60% of them being skilled nursing/transitional care facilities and most of the rest being senior housing facilities.

Geographic Reach
The REIT has licensed beds in 37 US states with its three largest markets being New Hampshire Texas and Connecticut.

Financial Performance
Sabra's annual revenues have almost tripled since 2011 as it has expanded its property portfolio through acquisitions and has charged higher rental rates as the real estate market has strengthened. Meanwhile it annual profits have risen more than five-fold as it's been able to keep a lid on its overhead costs.

The REIT's revenue jumped 30% to $238.86 million during 2015 mostly thanks to added rental income from newly acquired properties (acquired after January 1 2014).

Strong revenue growth in 2015 drove Sabra's net income up 69% to $79.41 million for the year. The REIT's operating cash levels climbed 42% to $121.1 million mostly as its cash earnings rose during the year.

Strategy
Sabra aims to profit from the aging of the US population and increasing life expectancy both of which are driving demand for long-term care services. The REIT is focused on growing its geographically diverse portfolio primarily through the purchase of senior housing and memory care facilities with a secondary emphasis on acquiring skilled nursing homes. In mid-2015 for example Sabra Health Care REIT agreed to buy four Maryland-based skilled nursing facilities — which specialized in transitional care and medically complex post-surgical ventilator and dialysis patients — consisting of 678 beds for $234 million.

EXECUTIVES
Chairman and CEO, Richard K. Matros, age 65, $725,000 total compensation
Chief Investment Officer, Talya Nevo-Hacohen, $350,000 total compensation
EVP and CFO, Harold W. Andrews, age 55, $350,000 total compensation
Chief Technology Officer, Galen Warren

Chief Operating Officer, Nick Cafferillo
Executive Vice President Portfolio Manager, Chappell Brent
Auditors: PricewaterhouseCoopers LLP

LOCATIONS
HQ: Sabra Health Care REIT Inc
18500 Von Karman Avenue, Suite 550, Irvine, CA 92612
Phone: 888 393-8248
Web: www.sabrahealth.com

PRODUCTS/OPERATIONS

2015 Sales
	$ mil.	% of total
Rental income	209.9	88
Interest and other income	25.5	11
Resident fees and services	3.5	1
Total	**238.9**	**100**

COMPETITORS
Extendicare
HCP
Healthcare Realty Trust
LTC Properties
National Health Investors
Omega Healthcare Investors
Senior Housing Properties
Ventas
Welltower

HISTORICAL FINANCIALS
Company Type: Public

Income Statement — FYE: December 31

	REVENUE ($ mil.)	NET INCOME ($ mil.)	NET PROFIT MARGIN	EMPLOYEES
12/18	623.4	279.0	44.8%	31
12/17	405.6	158.3	39.0%	61
12/16	260.5	70.2	27.0%	14
12/15	238.8	79.4	33.2%	13
12/14	183.5	46.9	25.6%	11
Annual Growth	35.8%	56.1%	—	29.6%

2018 Year-End Financials
Debt ratio: 48.4%
Return on equity: 8.3%
Cash ($ mil.): 50.2
Current ratio: 2.39
Long-term debt ($ mil.): 3,232.0
No. of shares (mil.): 178.3
Dividends
 Yield: 10.9%
 Payout: 73.4%
Market value ($ mil.): 2,938.0

	STOCK PRICE ($) FY Close	P/E High/Low		PER SHARE ($) Earnings	Dividends	Book Value
12/18	16.48	16	11	1.51	1.80	18.23
12/17	18.77	21	13	1.40	1.73	19.26
12/16	24.42	29	16	0.92	1.67	15.56
12/15	20.23	31	17	1.11	1.60	16.17
12/14	30.37	39	31	0.78	1.51	15.95
Annual Growth	(14.2%)		—	18.0%	4.5%	3.4%

Sachem Capital Corp

Auditors: Hoberman & Lesser, CPA's, LLP

LOCATIONS
HQ: Sachem Capital Corp
698 Main Street, Branford, CT 06405
Phone: 203 433-4736
Web: www.sachemcapitalcorp.com

HISTORICAL FINANCIALS
Company Type: Public

Income Statement — FYE: December 31

	REVENUE ($ mil.)	NET INCOME ($ mil.)	NET PROFIT MARGIN	EMPLOYEES
12/18	11.7	7.7	66.3%	11
12/17	7.0	4.8	69.5%	7
12/16	4.1	3.0	73.8%	0
12/15	2.7	2.3	82.8%	2
12/14	1.5	0.0	—	0
Annual Growth	65.6%	—	—	—

2018 Year-End Financials
Debt ratio: 31.9%
Return on equity: 14.4%
Cash ($ mil.): 0.1
Current ratio: 14.26
Long-term debt ($ mil.): 27.5
No. of shares (mil.): 15.4
Dividends
 Yield: 15.6%
 Payout: 117.3%
Market value ($ mil.): 60.0

	STOCK PRICE ($) FY Close	P/E High/Low		PER SHARE ($) Earnings	Dividends	Book Value
12/18	3.91	9	7	0.50	0.61	3.42
12/17	3.94	14	10	0.38	0.26	3.54
Annual Growth	(0.8%)		—	31.6%	134.6%	(3.4%)

Safehold Inc

Auditors: DELOITTE & TOUCHE LLP

LOCATIONS
HQ: Safehold Inc
1114 Avenue of the Americas, 39th Floor, New York, NY 10036
Phone: 212 930-9400
Web: www.safetyincomegrowth.com

HISTORICAL FINANCIALS
Company Type: Public

Income Statement — FYE: December 31

	REVENUE ($ mil.)	NET INCOME ($ mil.)	NET PROFIT MARGIN	EMPLOYEES
12/18	49.7	11.7	23.6%	0
12/17*	17.2	(3.6)	—	0
04/17	6.0	1.8	30.6%	0
12/16	21.7	6.6	30.4%	0
12/15	18.5	5.3	28.8%	0
Annual Growth	27.9%	21.7%		

*Fiscal year change

2018 Year-End Financials
Debt ratio: 55.5%
Return on equity: 3.3%
Cash ($ mil.): 16.4
Current ratio: 5.33
Long-term debt ($ mil.): 543.9
No. of shares (mil.): 18.2
Dividends
 Yield: 3.1%
 Payout: 93.7%
Market value ($ mil.): 344.0

	STOCK PRICE ($) FY Close	P/E High/Low		PER SHARE ($) Earnings	Dividends	Book Value
12/18	18.81	31	24	0.64	0.60	19.44
12/17*	17.60	—	—	(0.25)	0.31	19.57
Annual Growth	6.9%		—	—	95.7%	(0.6%)

*Fiscal year change

Salisbury Bancorp, Inc.

EXECUTIVES
Senior Vice President, Amy Raymond
Auditors: Baker Newman & Noyes LLC

LOCATIONS
HQ: Salisbury Bancorp, Inc.
5 Bissell Street, Lakeville, CT 6039
Phone: 860 435-9801
Web: www.salisburybank.com

COMPETITORS
Berkshire Hills Bancorp
KeyCorp
M&T Bank
TD Bank USA
Webster Financial

HISTORICAL FINANCIALS
Company Type: Public

Income Statement — FYE: December 31

	ASSETS ($ mil.)	NET INCOME ($ mil.)	INCOME AS % OF ASSETS	EMPLOYEES
12/18	1,121.5	8.8	0.8%	198
12/17	986.9	6.2	0.6%	194
12/16	935.3	6.6	0.7%	187
12/15	891.1	8.4	0.9%	188
12/14	855.4	2.5	0.3%	182
Annual Growth	7.0%	36.8%	—	2.1%

2018 Year-End Financials
Return on assets: 0.8%
Return on equity: 8.7%
Long-term debt ($ mil.): —
No. of shares (mil.): 2.8
Sales ($ mil.): 49.3
Dividends
Yield: 3.1%
Payout: 42.7%
Market value ($ mil.): 102.0

	STOCK PRICE ($) FY Close	P/E High/Low	PER SHARE ($) Earnings	Dividends	Book Value
12/18	36.18	16 11	3.13	1.12	36.86
12/17	44.65	21 16	2.24	1.12	35.01
12/16	37.50	16 12	2.41	1.12	34.08
12/15	33.48	11 9	3.02	1.12	33.13
12/14	27.34	23 20	1.32	1.12	37.42
Annual Growth	7.3%	— —	24.1%	(0.0%)	(0.4%)

Sanchez Energy Corp.

The Sanchez family has been around South Texas almost as long as the oil found in the Eagle Ford Shale. Sanchez Energy is a spin off from Sanchez Oil & Gas Corporation (SOG) a private firm owned by the Sanchez family who trace their family history back to the founding of Laredo in 1755. Sanchez Energy was formed in 2011 to take over almost 39000 acres (about 60 sq. mi.) of land in the oil-rich Eagle Ford Shale in South Texas. In 2013 it had 140000 net acres in the Eagle Ford play and 40000 net acres in the Tuscaloosa Marine Shale in Louisiana. It also has undeveloped acreage in Montana. The company filed Chapter 11 in 2019.

Bankruptcy
Amid low commodity prices and mounting debt Sanchez Energy voluntarily entered Chapter 11 bankruptcy protection in 2019.

Sales and Marketing
Three customers accounted for 97% of the company's revenues in 2012 (one for 66%).

Financial Performance
Sanchez Energy's revenue increased by 197% in 2012 primarily due to the higher oil and natural gas production and higher oil prices partially offset by lower natural gas prices.

The company reported a net Loss of $16.2 million (compared to net income of $2 million in 2011) due to increased operating costs.

Strategy
Supported by strong oil prices the company is focused on developing oil shale plays in Texas and Louisiana.

The company improved its liquidity with a $345 million midstream asset sale in 2015.

Mergers and Acquisitions
In 2017 Anadarko Petroleum agreed to sell its South Texas oil-and-gas assets to Sanchez Energy and Blackstone Group for $2.3 billion. The deal includes 155000 net acres located next to Sanchez Energy's existing assets with 130 gross drilled but uncompleted wells.

In 2013 the company acquired 43000 net acres in the Eagle Ford Shale in South Texas from Hess for $265 million. The assets Dimmit Frio LaSalle and Zavala Counties included 50 gross wells producing 4500 barrels of oil equivalent per day. It completed another Eagle Ford purchase the Wycross acquisition for $230.1 million. That deal added production of 2000 barrels of barrels of oil equivalent per day.

Moving into a new area in 2013 the company bought 40000 net undeveloped acres in the Tuscaloosa Marine Shale.

Company Background
Sanchez Energy went public in 2011 with a $203 million IPO.

Following the offering SOG subsidiary Sanchez Energy Partners I (SEPI) transferred the acreage assets to Sanchez Energy. SEP I began acquiring leases in the Eagle Ford Shale area in 2008 the same year Petrohawk Energy announced its discovery of the oil deposit. (Fortunately the Sanchez businesses have a storied history with South Texas and wasted no time buying land leases).

EXECUTIVES
President and CEO, Antonio R. (Tony) Sanchez, age 45, $650,000 total compensation
EVP and CFO, Howard J. Thill, age 61
SVP and COO, Christopher D. Heinson, age 36, $250,000 total compensation
President, Eduardo A. Sanchez, age 39, $72,958 total compensation
Vice President of Geoscience, William Satterfield
Chairman, A. R. (Tony) Sanchez, age 76
Auditors: KPMG LLP

LOCATIONS
HQ: Sanchez Energy Corp.
1000 Main Street, Suite 3000, Houston, TX 77002
Phone: 713 783-8000
Web: www.sanchezenergycorp.com

PRODUCTS/OPERATIONS

2015 sales
	% of total
Oil sales	65
Natural gas liquid sales	14
Natural gas sales	21
Total	**100**

COMPETITORS
Abraxas Petroleum
Alta Mesa Holdings
Anadarko Petroleum
Apache
BP
Cabot Oil & Gas
Carrizo Oil & Gas
Chesapeake Energy
Clayton Williams Energy
Comstock Resources
Freeport-McMoRan Oil & Gas LLC
Magnum Hunter Resources
Petrohawk Energy
Repsol Oil & Gas
Rosetta Resources Inc.
SM Energy
Swift Energy

HISTORICAL FINANCIALS
Company Type: Public

Income Statement — FYE: December 31

	REVENUE ($ mil.)	NET INCOME ($ mil.)	NET PROFIT MARGIN	EMPLOYEES
12/18	1,056.9	85.2	8.1%	0
12/17	740.3	43.1	5.8%	0
12/16	431.3	(256.9)	—	0
12/15	475.7	(1,454.6)	—	0
12/14	666.0	(21.7)	—	0
Annual Growth	12.2%	—	—	—

2018 Year-End Financials
Debt ratio: 84.9%
Return on equity: —
Cash ($ mil.): 197.6
Current ratio: 1.07
Long-term debt ($ mil.): 2,395.4
No. of shares (mil.): 87.3
Dividends
Yield: 0.2%
Payout: —
Market value ($ mil.): 153.0

	STOCK PRICE ($) FY Close	P/E High/Low	PER SHARE ($) Earnings	Dividends	Book Value
12/18	1.75	— —	(0.04)	2.44	0.10
12/17	17.63	— —	(0.46)	0.00	(0.50)
12/16	33.38	— —	(4.63)	0.81	(10.52)
12/15	11.19	— —	(25.70)	3.25	(7.37)
12/14	34.69	— —	(1.06)	2.44	17.06
Annual Growth	(52.6%) (72.7%)	— —	—	(0.0%)	

Sandy Spring Bancorp Inc

Sandy Spring Bancorp is the holding company for Sandy Spring Bank which operates around 50 branches in the Baltimore and Washington DC metropolitan areas. Founded in 1868 the bank is one of the largest and oldest headquartered in Maryland. It provides standard deposit services including checking and savings accounts money market accounts and CDs. Commercial and residential real estate loans account for nearly three-quarters of the company's loan portfolio; the remainder is a mix of consumer loans business loans and equipment leases. The company also offers personal investing services wealth management trust services insurance and retirement planning.

Operations

Sandy Spring Bancorp's nonbank subsidiaries include money manager West Financial Services and Sandy Spring Insurance which sells annuities and operates insurance agencies Chesapeake Insurance Group and Neff & Associates.

Financial Performance

The company's revenue increased in fiscal 2013 compared to the previous year. It reported $196.9 million in revenue for fiscal 2013 after bringing in revenue of $190.8 million in fiscal 2012.

The company's net income also went up in fiscal 2013 compared to the prior period. It claimed a profit of about $44 million in fiscal 2013 after netting a little more than $36 million in fiscal 2012.

Sandy Spring Bancorp's cash on hand increased by about $43 million in fiscal 2013 compared to fiscal 2012 levels.

Mergers and Acquisitions

In 2012 Sandy Spring Bancorp acquired CommerceFirst Bancorp a small Maryland bank with a strong Small Business Administration lending practice. The $25.4 million transaction added five branches to Sandy Spring Bank's network.

EXECUTIVES

EVP General Counsel and Secretary, Ronald E. Kuykendall, age 66, $279,039 total compensation
EVP Wealth Management Insurance Mortgage, R. Louis (Lou) Caceres, age 56, $333,865 total compensation
President and CEO Bancorp and Bank, Daniel J. (Dan) Schrider, age 54, $600,692 total compensation
EVP and CFO Bancorp and Bank, Philip J. Mantua, age 60, $333,192 total compensation
EVP and CIO, John D. Sadowski, age 55
EVP Commercial and Retail Banking, Joseph O'Brien, $355,038 total compensation
EVP and Chief Credit Officer, Ronda M. McDowell
Vice President, Brian Schott
Vice President Private Banking Relationship Manager, Victor Emeogo
Vice President, Christopher Huang
Senior Business Analyst Assistant Vice President, Stephen Marsico
Vice President Marketing Communications Manager, Jennifer Schell
Assistant Vice President Team Leader, Tamika Daniels
Vice President, Denise Kratz
Vice President HRIS Project Administrator, Patti Boyle
Vice President, Isaac Sterbenz
Vice President Commercial Lending, Heather Burke
Assistant Vice President Public Relations Specialist, Amanda Walsh
Senior Vice President, Scott Sims
Vice President, William Grahe
Senior Vice President Commercial Relatio, Wendy Lance
Senior Vice President, Glen Buco
Vice President eCommerce, Lisa Johnson
Assistant Vice President Branch Manager, Phil Hicks
Vice President and Underwriter, Jacqueline Gerhart
Vice President, James Holochuk
Vice President Facilities, Thomas Gemmell
Senior Vice President Alternative Delivery, Don Haasen

Vice President Debit and Credit Card Product Manager, Ron Waters
Vice President, Michael Mckeon
Vice President Commercial Relationship Manager, James Bear
Executive Vice President, Lou Caceres
Senior Vice President, Laurie Kramer
Vice President, Christine Wilson
Vice President Corporate Paralegal, Lori Shipley
Vice President, Cave Katie
VICE PRESIDENT AND INSURANCE AND SURETY BONDING, Fred Hildebrand
SENIOR VICE PRESIDENT DIRECTOR OF REGULATORY MANAGEMENT, Diane Slack
SENIOR VICE PRESIDENT MARKETING, Amalia G Kastberg
Assistant Vice President, Alexis Vining
Vice President, Todd Levine
Vice President Mortgage Banker, Jeff Starcher
SENIOR VICE PRESIDENT MARKETING, Amalia Kastberg
Card Systems And Operations Manager Vice President, Rebecca Kruse
Senior Vice President, Michael Acton
Senior Vice President Financial Reporting, Joseph Dennis
Vice President, Philip Fish
Vice President, Jackie Yankanich
Vice President, Asma Iqbal
Vice President, Dushanti Peiris
Vice President, Michael Groft
Vice President Commercial Banking Treasury Management Division, Monica Tressler
Vice President Senior Mortgage Banker, Doug Benner
Senior Vice President, Michelle Levenson
Chairman, Robert L. Orndorff, age 63
Auditors: Ernst & Young LLP

LOCATIONS

HQ: Sandy Spring Bancorp Inc
17801 Georgia Avenue, Olney, MD 20832
Phone: 301 774-6400
Web: www.sandyspringbank.com

PRODUCTS/OPERATIONS

2015 Sales

	$ mil.	% of total
Interest Income:		
Interest and fees on loans and leases	135.2	65
Interest and dividends on investment securities	22.5	11
Other	0.6	-
Non-interest Income:		
Wealth management income	19.9	10
Service charges on deposit accounts	7.6	4
Insurance agency commissions	5.2	2
Bank card fees	4.7	2
Mortgage banking activities	3.1	2
Other Income	9.4	4
Total	208.2	100

COMPETITORS

BB&T
Bank of America
Bay Bancorp
Capital One
Fulton Financial
OBA Financial Services
PNC Financial
SunTrust

HISTORICAL FINANCIALS
Company Type: Public

Income Statement — FYE: December 31

	ASSETS ($ mil.)	NET INCOME ($ mil.)	INCOME AS % OF ASSETS	EMPLOYEES
12/18	8,243.2	100.8	1.2%	932
12/17	5,446.6	53.2	1.0%	754
12/16	5,091.3	48.2	0.9%	752
12/15	4,655.3	45.3	1.0%	737
12/14	4,397.1	38.2	0.9%	727
Annual Growth	17.0%	27.5%	—	6.4%

2018 Year-End Financials

Return on assets: 1.4%
Return on equity: 12.3%
Long-term debt ($ mil.): —
No. of shares (mil.): 35.5
Sales ($ mil): 385.1
Dividends
Yield: 3.5%
Payout: 44.9%
Market value ($ mil.): 1,114.0

	STOCK PRICE ($) FY Close	P/E High/Low		PER SHARE ($) Earnings	Dividends	Book Value
12/18	31.34	15	11	2.82	1.10	30.06
12/17	39.02	21	17	2.20	1.04	23.50
12/16	39.99	20	12	2.00	0.98	22.32
12/15	26.96	16	13	1.84	0.90	21.58
12/14	26.08	18	15	1.52	0.76	20.83
Annual Growth	4.7%	—	—	16.7%	9.7%	9.6%

Santa Cruz County Bank (CA)

Auditors: Crowe Horwath LLP

LOCATIONS

HQ: Santa Cruz County Bank (CA)
740 Front Street Ste 220, Santa Cruz, CA 95060
Phone: 831 457-5000
Web: www.sccountybank.com

HISTORICAL FINANCIALS
Company Type: Public

Income Statement — FYE: December 31

	ASSETS ($ mil.)	NET INCOME ($ mil.)	INCOME AS % OF ASSETS	EMPLOYEES
12/17	629.9	6.7	1.1%	0
12/16	588.2	6.4	1.1%	0
12/15	513.3	5.4	1.1%	0
12/14	459.7	4.3	1.0%	0
12/13	398.5	3.3	0.8%	0
Annual Growth	12.1%	19.5%	—	—

2017 Year-End Financials

Return on assets: 1.1%
Return on equity: 12.5%
Long-term debt ($ mil.): —
No. of shares (mil.): 2.4
Sales ($ mil): 29.6
Dividends
Yield: 0.0%
Payout: 6.7%
Market value ($ mil.): 119.0

	STOCK PRICE ($) FY Close	P/E High/Low		PER SHARE ($) Earnings	Dividends	Book Value
12/17	48.95	18	14	2.76	0.19	23.64
12/16	39.50	15	10	2.67	0.18	21.05
12/15	28.60	13	9	2.26	0.18	18.52
12/14	21.42	12	9	1.84	0.18	16.40
12/13	17.75	13	9	1.47	0.14	14.91
Annual Growth	28.9%	—	—	17.0%	8.1%	12.2%

SB Financial Group Inc

EXECUTIVES

EVP and CFO Rurban Financial and The State Bank and Trust, Anthony V. (Tony) Cosentino, age 54
EVP and Senior Lender The State Bank and Trust, Jonathan R. Gathman
Chairman, Richard L. Hardgrove, age 77
President CEO and Director Rurban Financial and The State Bank and Trust, Mark A. Klein, age 61, $212,320 total compensation
EVP and Chief Retail Officer The State Bank and Trust, Steven R. Grube
Director, Thomas A. Buis, age 78
Director, Robert A. Fawcett Jr., age 74
Director, Gaylyn J. Finn, age 66
Chairman, Richard L. Hardgrove, age 77
Director, Rita A. Kissner, age 70
Director, Thomas L. Sauer, age 68
President CEO and Director Rurban Financial and The State Bank and Trust, Mark A. Klein, age 61
Director, Timothy J. Stolly
Independent Director, Lynn Isaac
Auditors: BKD, LLP

LOCATIONS

HQ: SB Financial Group Inc
401 Clinton Street, Defiance, OH 43512
Phone: 419 783-8950
Web: www.yourSBFinancial.com

PRODUCTS/OPERATIONS

Selected Subsidiaries and Divisions
The State Bank and Trust Company
Reliance Financial Services
RDSI Banking Systems

COMPETITORS

Fifth Third
First Defiance Financial
First Financial Bancorp
Huntington Bancshares
KeyCorp
United Bancshares

HISTORICAL FINANCIALS

Company Type: Public

Income Statement
FYE: December 31

	ASSETS ($ mil.)	NET INCOME ($ mil.)	INCOME AS % OF ASSETS	EMPLOYEES
12/18	986.8	11.6	1.2%	250
12/17	876.6	11.0	1.3%	234
12/16	816.0	8.7	1.1%	227
12/15	733.0	7.6	1.0%	214
12/14	684.2	5.2	0.8%	190
Annual Growth	9.6%	21.9%	—	7.1%

2018 Year-End Financials
Return on assets: 1.2%
Return on equity: 10.3%
Long-term debt ($ mil.): —
No. of shares (mil.): 6.5
Sales ($ mil): 56.1
Dividends
Yield: 1.9%
Payout: 21.1%
Market value ($ mil.): 107.0

	STOCK PRICE ($) FY Close	P/E High/Low		PER SHARE ($) Earnings	Dividends	Book Value
12/18	16.45	12	9	1.51	0.32	20.06
12/17	18.49	9	7	1.74	0.28	19.61
12/16	16.05	11	6	1.38	0.24	17.87
12/15	11.14	8	7	1.19	0.20	16.61
12/14	9.40	9	7	1.08	0.16	15.52
Annual Growth	15.0%	—	—	8.7%	18.9%	6.6%

SB One Bancorp

EXECUTIVES

Vice President Business Development Officer, Ariana Anguiano
Vice President, James Imbro
Auditors: BDO USA, LLP

LOCATIONS

HQ: SB One Bancorp
95 State Route 17, Paramus, NJ 07652
Phone: 844 256-7328
Web: www.sussexbank.com

COMPETITORS

Bank of America
Bank of New York Mellon
Hudson City Bancorp
Lakeland Bancorp
PNC Financial
Sovereign Bank
TD Bank USA
Valley National Bancorp

HISTORICAL FINANCIALS

Company Type: Public

Income Statement
FYE: December 31

	ASSETS ($ mil.)	NET INCOME ($ mil.)	INCOME AS % OF ASSETS	EMPLOYEES
12/18	1,795.7	9.9	0.6%	237
12/17	979.3	5.6	0.6%	156
12/16	848.7	5.5	0.7%	148
12/15	684.5	3.7	0.5%	139
12/14	595.9	2.6	0.4%	136
Annual Growth	31.8%	39.8%	—	14.9%

2018 Year-End Financials
Return on assets: 0.7%
Return on equity: 7.1%
Long-term debt ($ mil.): —
No. of shares (mil.): 9.5
Sales ($ mil): 67.4
Dividends
Yield: 1.3%
Payout: 28.2%
Market value ($ mil.): 195.0

	STOCK PRICE ($) FY Close	P/E High/Low		PER SHARE ($) Earnings	Dividends	Book Value
12/18	20.44	25	16	1.25	0.29	19.45
12/17	26.85	26	19	1.05	0.22	15.59
12/16	20.90	18	10	1.19	0.16	12.67
12/15	13.09	17	12	0.81	0.16	11.61
12/14	10.20	19	13	0.57	0.09	10.99
Annual Growth	19.0%	—	—	21.7%	33.4%	15.4%

Scripps (EW) Company (The)

You might say this media company tries to be appealing to both newspaper readers and television viewers. The E. W. Scripps Company is a venerable newspaper publisher with a portfolio of more than 15 dailies including The Commercial Appeal (Memphis Tennessee) the Knoxville News Sentinel (Tennessee) and the Ventura County Star (California). Scripps also owns some 60 local TV stations in 42 markets most of which are affiliated with ABC and NBC. Subsidiaries Scripps Howard News Service and United Media distribute syndicated content including news columns editorial cartoons and such comic strips Peanuts. The Scripps family controls the company through various trusts.

Operations

Scripps' portfolio of content holdings includes Newsy a next-generation national news network; podcast distributor Stitcher; national broadcast networks Bounce Grit Escape Laff and Court TV; and Triton s provider of digital audio technology and measurement services.

The compay also runs an investigative reporting newsroom in Washington D.C. and is the steward of the Scripps National Spelling Bee.

Geographic Reach

The Cincinatti Ohio-based E. W. Scripps has 60 stations in 42 markets. It also has an investigative reporting newsroom in Washington D.C.

Strategy

Like other ad-supported media businesses E. W. Scripps struggled during the recession as advertisers reined in their spending. Its newspapers meanwhile are losing readers in parallel with that industry's long slow decline. In response the company has had to take actions to cut expenses including wage and staff reductions at its papers. Its growth strategy involves acquisitions in other areas of content including broadcasting and digital holdings.

Mergers and Acquisitions

In 2019 E W Scripps Company acquired eight television stations in seven markets from the Nexstar Media Group. The acquisition grew the Scripps local television station footprint to 60 stations in 42 markets making it the nation's fourth-largest independent broadcaster with a reach of 31% of US TV households.

HISTORY

Edward Willis "E. W." Scripps launched a newspaper empire in 1878 with his creation of The Penny Press in Cleveland. While adding to his string of inexpensive newspapers Scripps demonstrated his fondness for economy by shunning "extras" such as toilet paper and pencils for his employees.

In 1907 Scripps gave the Associated Press a new rival combining three wire services to form United Press. E. W. Scripps' health began deteriorating in the 1920s and Roy Howard was named chairman. Howard's contribution to the burgeoning media enterprise soon was acknowledged when the company's name was changed to the Scripps Howard League. E. W. Scripps died in 1926 leaving a newspaper chain second in size only to Hearst.

In the 1930s Scripps made a foray into radio buying WCPO (Cincinnati) and KNOX (Knoxville Tennessee). Roy Howard placed his son Jack in charge of Scripps' radio holdings; under Jack's leadership Scripps branched into TV. Its first TV station Cleveland's WEWS began broadcasting in 1947. Scripps also made Charlie Brown a household name when it launched the Peanuts comic strip in 1950. By the time Charles Scripps (E. W.'s grandson) became chairman and Jack Howard was appointed president in 1953 the company had amassed 19 newspapers and a handful of radio and TV stations.

United Press merged with Hearst's International News Service in 1958 to become United Press International (UPI). In 1963 Scripps took its broadcasting holdings public as Scripps Howard Broadcasting Company (Scripps retained controlling interest). Scripps Howard Broadcasting expanded its TV station portfolio in the 1970s and 1980s buying KJRH (Tulsa Oklahoma; 1971) KSHB (Kansas City; 1977) KNXV (Phoenix; 1985) WFTS (Tampa; 1986) and WXYZ (Detroit; 1986).

With UPI facing mounting losses Scripps sold the news service in 1982. Under leadership of chief executive Lawrence Leser Scripps began streamlining jettisoning extraneous investments and refocusing on its core business lines. In 1988 after decades of family ownership the company went public as The E. W. Scripps Company (the Scripps family retained a controlling interest).

In 1994 Scripps Howard Broadcasting merged back into E. W. Scripps Company. That year Scripps branched into cable TV when its Home & Garden Television network went on the air. Former newspaper editor William Burleigh became CEO in 1996. Scripps' 1997 purchase of the newspaper and broadcast operations of Harte-Hanks marked the largest acquisition in its history. Scripps promptly traded Harte-Hanks' broadcasting operations for a controlling interest in the Food Network.

Scripps sold television production unit Scripps Howard Productions in 1998. The company sold its Dallas Community Newspaper Group in 1999 and launched the Do It Yourself cable network and affiliated Web site later that year. In 2000 Scripps' financially struggling Rocky Mountain News entered into a joint operating agreement with rival The Denver Post (owned by MediaNews). The Justice Department approved the agreement in 2001. Scripps launched cable channel Fine Living in 2002 aimed at affluent households. (Fine Living was rebranded as the Cooking Channel in 2010.) That year the company shuttered its Scripps Ventures fund which invested in Internet and online commerce businesses.

In late 2002 the company bought a 70% stake in home shopping network company Summit America Television (owner of the Shop At Home cable network) for $49 million. It bought the remaining 30% of the company in 2004.

The Shop At Home network came to an end in 2006 when Scripps shut down the network after several years of nothing but losses at the channel. Scripps later sold its five Shop At Home affiliate television stations to Multicultural Television Broadcasting for $170 million.

Former chairman Charles Scripps died in 2007. At the end of that year the company shuttered the Cincinnati Post and the following year it ceased publication of The Albuquerque Tribune . E. W. Scripps spun off its cable TV operations as Scripps Networks Interactive later in 2008. It shuttered the Rocky Mountain News early in 2009 after attempts to sell the money-losing paper failed.

EXECUTIVES

VP Radio, Steve Wexler
SVP CFO and Treasurer, Timothy M. (Tim) Wesolowski, age 61, $410,000 total compensation
SVP and General Counsel, William (Bill) Appleton, age 70, $410,000 total compensation
VP and General Manager WPTV (West Palm Beach FL), Brian G. Lawlor, age 52, $500,000 total compensation
SVP and Chief Administrative Officer, Lisa A. Knutson, age 54, $410,000 total compensation
President and CEO, Adam P. Symson, age 45
Vice President Senior Human Resources Business Partner, Candace Anderson
Vice President and GM WMAR (Baltimore MD), Bill Hooper
Chief Financial Officer Senior Vice President, Timothy Williams
Vice President Marketing, Jessica Rappaport
Vice President Communications International, Cecelia Bender
Vice President of Marketing Newsy, Eric Svenson
Vice President of News, Sean McLaughlin
Vice President Deputy General Counsel, Dave Giles
National Sales Manager, Sarah Linden
Vp And General Manager Wgba And Wacy Green Bay Wi, Joe Antonelli
Vice President Sales Radio Vice President General Manager Knoxville Operations, Chris Protzman
Vice President General Manager, Leon Clark
Vice President Planning, Jason Combs
Senior Vice President Legal Scripps Ne, Cynthia Gibson
Vice President General Manager, David Abel
Vice President Chief Diversity Officer, Danyelle St Wright
VICE PRESIDENT OPERATIONS, Vincent Gullotto
Vice President Of Corporate Communications And Investor Relations, Carolyn Pione
Vp Engineering, Ray Thurber
Vice President Product, Tony Brown
Vice President Global Business Systems and Information Technology Planning, Patrick Browning
Chairman, Richard A. (Rich) Boehne, age 63
Board Member, Roger Ogden
Board Member, Kelly Conlin
Auditors: DELOITTE & TOUCHE LLP

LOCATIONS

HQ: Scripps (EW) Company (The)
312 Walnut Street, Cincinnati, OH 45202
Phone: 513 977-3000
Web: www.scripps.com

PRODUCTS/OPERATIONS

Selected Operations
Newspapers
   Abilene Reporter-News (Texas)
   Anderson Independent-Mail (South Carolina)
   Corpus Christi Caller-Times (Texas)
   Evansville Courier & Press (Indiana)
   Ft. Pierce Tribune (Florida)
   Henderson Gleaner (Kentucky)
   Kitsap Sun (Washington)
   Knoxville News Sentinel (Tennessee)
   Memphis Commercial Appeal (Tennessee)
   Naples Daily News (Florida)
   Redding Record-Searchlight (California)
   San Angelo Standard-Times (Texas)
   Stuart News (Florida)
   Ventura County Star (California)
   Wichita Falls Times Record News (Texas)
Television stations
   KJRH (NBC; Tulsa OK)
   KMCI (Ind; Lawrence KS)
   KNXV (ABC Phoenix)
   KSHB (NBC Kansas City)
   WCPO (ABC Cincinnati)
   WEWS (ABC Cleveland)
   WFTS (ABC Tampa)
   WMAR (ABC Baltimore)
   WPTV (NBC; West Palm Beach FL)
   WXYZ (ABC Detroit)

COMPETITORS

A. H. Belo	Meredith Corporation
Andrews McMeel Universal	New York Times Newport Television
CBS	Raycom Media
Graham Holdings	Sinclair Broadcast Group
Hearst Corporation	
Local TV	TEGNA
McClatchy Company	Times Publishing Co.
Media General	Tribune Media

HISTORICAL FINANCIALS

Company Type: Public

Income Statement　　　　　　　　　　FYE: December 31

	REVENUE ($ mil.)	NET INCOME ($ mil.)	NET PROFIT MARGIN	EMPLOYEES
12/18	1,208.4	20.3	1.7%	3,950
12/17	864.8	(13.1)	—	4,100
12/16	943.0	67.2	7.1%	4,100
12/15	715.6	(82.4)	—	3,800
12/14	869.0	10.5	1.2%	4,800
Annual Growth	8.6%	18.0%	—	(4.8%)

2018 Year-End Financials

Debt ratio: 32.3%　　　　　　No. of shares (mil.): 80.6
Return on equity: 2.1%　　　Dividends
Cash ($ mil.): 107.1　　　　　　Yield: 1.2%
Current ratio: 2.38　　　　　　Payout: 500.0%
Long-term debt ($ mil.): 685.7　Market value ($ mil.): 1,269.0

	STOCK PRICE ($) FY Close	P/E High/Low		PER SHARE ($) Earnings	Dividends	Book Value
12/18	15.73	71	43	0.24	0.20	11.48
12/17	15.63	—	—	(0.16)	0.00	11.48
12/16	19.33	24	16	0.79	0.00	11.54
12/15	19.00	—	—	(1.06)	1.03	10.75
12/14	22.35	129	85	0.18	0.00	9.09
Annual Growth	(8.4%)	—	—	7.5%	—	6.0%

Seacoast Banking Corp. of Florida

Seacoast Banking Corporation is the holding company for Seacoast National Bank. It operates some 50 branches in Florida with a concentration in four large city markets. Serving individuals and businesses the bank offers a range of financial products and services including deposit accounts credit cards trust services and private banking. Commercial and residential real estate loans make up most of the bank's lending activities; to a lesser extent it also originates business and consumer loans.

Operations
Seacoast Bank offers traditional banking products such as deposit accounts checking & savings accounts CDs business loans home mortgages and the like. It also makes available to its customers brokerage and annuity services along with insurance products. A division of the bank Seacoast Marine Finance specializes in boat loans which it typically originates itself and then sells into the secondary market.

Geographic Reach
Seacoast National Bank has some 50 branches in 14 counties across Florida stretching from Broward County north through the Treasure Coast and into Orlando and west to Okeechobee and surrounding counties. Its primary markets are Tampa Orlando Port St. Lucie and West Palm Beach/Ft. Lauderdale.

Financial Performance
Seacoast Banking Corporation has done well in recent years steadily growing interest income to nearly $200 million in 2017 up from a low of $70 million just four years prior. The bank registered positive earnings from 2013 forward albeit the results fluctuated wildly.

In 2017 interest income grew 30% to $192 million and non-interest income improved by 25% to $170 million. Its loan portfolio grew ? through organic means as well as via acquisitions ? by almost 30% against which it earned additional interest income. The bank's average net interest margin rose 10 basis points to 3.73%.

Net income also lodged an excellent year increasing 48% from the prior year to $43 million. Although the company incurred an $8.6 million impairment of its deferred tax assets due to the change in US Federal tax law the increase in revenue along with a $15 million gain on the sale an investment it made in Visa company stock pushed up yearly earnings.

Cash at the end of the year was $109 million unchanged from 2016. Financing activities contributed $196 million mostly from an increase in deposits from acquisitions. Investing activities used $246 million in the process of buying and selling securities and originating new loans. Operating activities added $49 million.

Strategy
Seacoast Bank has grown mostly through acquisitions in recent years. Since 2014 it opened one new office and acquired 49 branches (19 of which were subsequently shuttered). Orlando has been a hot destination for it as it transformed its presence there just a few branches to the largest Florida-based bank in the market by 2017. The bank anticipates continued geographic growth in Florida through organic means but also through acquisition if the right opportunity arises as with the 2017 purchases of NorthStar Banking and Palm Beach Community Bank.

Although it caters to personal customers as well as business clients the focus on businesses has sparked significant growth in the associated loan portfolio. The company tends to commercial clients with revenues exceeding $5 million in specific industry verticals. It takes a comprehensive relationship approach by providing business treasury lending and wealth management services. The commercial loan portfolio grew nearly 300% between year-end 2013 and year-end 2017 from $632 million to $2.5 billion.

The bank significantly expanded its banking technology platform by introducing digital deposit capture on smartphones updating its mobile platforms for consumer and business customers and enhancing its ATM capabilities. Customers have taken to the online functionality and in 2017 the bank processed more digital transactions than it did through its physical branch network.

Mergers and Acquisitions
In 2017 Seacoast purchased NorthStar Banking Corporation adding more than $200 million in assets $170 million in deposits and nearly $140 million in loans to Seacoast's balance sheet. In the same year it acquired Palm Beach Community Bank for some $70 million adding $270 million in loans and four bank branches to Seacoast's operations.

EXECUTIVES

Chairman and CEO, Dennis S. (Denny) Hudson, age 63, $537,852 total compensation
EVP and Residential Lending Executive, Michael J. (Mike) Sonego
EVP and Commercial Banking Executive, Charles K. Cross, age 61, $273,333 total compensation
EVP and Chief Risk and Credit Officer, David D. Houdeshell, age 58, $262,500 total compensation
EVP Enterprise Services and Initiatives, Kathleen (Kathy) Cavicchioli
EVP and Chief Marketing Officer, Jeffery (Jeff) Lee
EVP Service and Operations, Jeffery (Jeff) Bray
EVP and Chief Human Resources Officer, Daniel G. (Dan) Chappell
CFO and Head of Strategy, Charles M. (Chuck) Shaffer, age 45, $248,333 total compensation
EVP Community Banking, Julie Kleffel
Senior Vice President Marketing Director, Susan Bergstrom
Senior Vice President Human Resources Director, Charles Olsson
Vp Sba Portfolio Manager, Maureen Swierkowski
Executive Vice President Chief Human Resources Officer, Dan Chappell
Executive Vice President, William Hahl
Assistant Vice President and Call Center Manager, Joni Wyszkowski
Vice President Financial Advisor, Carl Newton
EXECUTIVE VICE PRESIDENT, Tom Hall
Senior Vice President Community Banking Director, Eileen Hatt
Vice President Business Banking Manager, Theresa Vazquez
Svp Senior Fiduciary and Risk Officer Cfp Clu, Peter Lowery
AVP Banking Center Manager, Amber Shirk
Senior Vice President Commercial Banking, Thomas Dargan
Assistant Vice President Corporate Finance, Zev Zaretsky
Vice President Commercial Banking, David Beckey
Vice President Cra Officer, Iris Jones
Vice President And Treasury Management, Jacci Watson
Vice President Leadership Development Manager, Angel Birch
Vice President Senior Market Leader, Tom Popieski
Vice President Market Manager, Hart Donovan
Vice President, Travis Engebretsen
Vice President Business Banker, Stephen Markham
Senior Market Manager Vice President, Monika Krumbock
Vice President Senior Small Business Banker, Jack Gould
Vice President Collection and Recovery Manager, Gary Albert
Vice President Residential Lending, Steve Bilbo
Vp Of Seacoast Bank Commercial Banking, Greg Peters
Vice President Commercial Banking, Daniel Lightfritz
VICE PRESIDENT AND MARKET MANAGER, Lee Jeff
Vice President Mortgage Banking Officer, Grace Monforte
Vice President Mortgage Lending Area Manager, Megan Martinez
Vice President Commercial Banking, Brian Wickman
Assistant Vice President Commercial Loan Officer, Ronnie Houck
Vice President Business Banker, Joe Ritchie
Vp Small Business Banking and Commercial Banking, Gilbert Russell
Vp Regional Business Banking Manager, Phil Fitzpatrick
Senior Vice President Commercial Banker, Jennifer Potter
Vice President Commercial Banker, Shane McCutchen
Board Director, Dennis Arczynski
Board Member, Maryann Goebel
Board Member, Herbert Lurie
Board Member, Jacqueline Bradley
Board Member, Tim Huval
Auditors: Crowe LLP

LOCATIONS

HQ: Seacoast Banking Corp. of Florida
815 Colorado Avenue, Stuart, FL 34994
Phone: 772 287-4000
Web: www.seacoastbanking.com

PRODUCTS/OPERATIONS

Selected Services
Commercial and retail banking
Mortgage services
Wealth management

COMPETITORS

BB&T	PNC Financial
BBX Capital	Regions Financial
Bank of America	SunTrust
BankUnited	Suncoast Schools FCU
CenterState Banks	Wells Fargo
EverBank Financial	

HISTORICAL FINANCIALS
Company Type: Public

Income Statement FYE: December 31

	ASSETS ($ mil.)	NET INCOME ($ mil.)	INCOME AS % OF ASSETS	EMPLOYEES
12/18	6,747.6	67.2	1.0%	902
12/17	5,810.1	42.8	0.7%	805
12/16	4,680.9	29.2	0.6%	725
12/15	3,534.7	22.1	0.6%	665
12/14	3,093.3	5.7	0.2%	579
Annual Growth	21.5%	85.4%	—	11.7%

2018 Year-End Financials
Return on assets: 1.0%
Return on equity: 8.6%
Long-term debt ($ mil.): —
No. of shares (mil.): 51.3
Sales ($ mil): 291.4
Dividends
  Yield: —
  Payout: —
Market value ($ mil.): 1,336.0

	STOCK PRICE ($) FY Close	P/E High/Low		PER SHARE ($) Earnings	Dividends	Book Value
12/18	26.02	24	17	1.38	0.00	16.83
12/17	25.21	26	21	0.99	0.00	14.70
12/16	22.06	29	17	0.78	0.00	11.45
12/15	14.98	25	18	0.66	0.00	10.29
12/14	13.75	68	48	0.21	0.00	9.44
Annual Growth	17.3%		—	60.1%	—	15.6%

Select Bancorp Inc (New)

EXECUTIVES

President CEO and Director New Century Bancorp; President New Century Bank South and New Century Bank, William L. (Bill) Hedgepeth II, age 54, $231,000 total compensation
EVP COO and CFO; EVP and CFO New Century Bank and New Century Bank South, Lisa F. Campbell, age 48, $169,400 total compensation
EVP; Chief Banking Officer New Century Bank and New Century Bank South, Kevin S. Bunn, age 54, $145,517 total compensation
EVP and Chief Deposit Operations Officer New Century Bank and New Century Bank South, Joan I. Patterson, age 69, $121,275 total compensation
Vice Chairman, C. Lee (Bozie) Tart Jr., age 81
Chairman, J. Gary Ciccone, age 69
EVP and Chief Credit Officer New Century Bancorp New Century Bank and New Century Bank South, J. Daniel (Danny) Fisher, age 67
SVP Human Resources New Century Bank, Lynn Johnson
Executive Vice President Chief Credit Officer, David Richard
Executive Vice President and Chief Credit Officer of the Company and New Century Bank, David Tobin
President CEO and Director New Century Bancorp; President New Century Bank South and New Century Bank, William L. (Bill) Hedgepeth II, age 54

Vice Chairman, C. Lee (Bozie) Tart Jr., age 81
Independent Director, Oscar N. Harris, age 77
Independent Director, John W. McCauley, age 48
Independent Director, Carlie C. McLamb, age 79
Independent Director, Dan McNeill
Independent Director, Larry Keen
Independent Director, Ralph Huff
Independent Director, Ronald Jackson
Auditors: Dixon Hughes Goodman LLP

LOCATIONS
HQ: Select Bancorp Inc (New)
  700 W. Cumberland Street, Dunn, NC 28334
Phone: 910 892-7080
Web: www.selectbank.com

COMPETITORS
BB&T
Bank of America
Capital Bank
First Citizens BancShares
First South Bancorp (NC)
Four Oaks Fincorp
KS Bancorp
North State Bancorp
Southern BancShares
Wake Forest Bancshares

HISTORICAL FINANCIALS
Company Type: Public

Income Statement FYE: December 31

	ASSETS ($ mil.)	NET INCOME ($ mil.)	INCOME AS % OF ASSETS	EMPLOYEES
12/18	1,258.5	13.7	1.1%	2,050
12/17	1,194.1	3.1	0.3%	202
12/16	846.6	6.7	0.8%	150
12/15	817.0	6.5	0.8%	153
12/14	766.1	2.3	0.3%	154
Annual Growth	13.2%	55.5%	—	91.0%

2018 Year-End Financials
Return on assets: 1.1%
Return on equity: 7.9%
Long-term debt ($ mil.): —
No. of shares (mil.): 19.3
Sales ($ mil): 61.5
Dividends
  Yield: —
  Payout: —
Market value ($ mil.): 239.0

	STOCK PRICE ($) FY Close	P/E High/Low		PER SHARE ($) Earnings	Dividends	Book Value
12/18	12.38	16	13	0.87	0.00	10.85
12/17	12.64	47	36	0.27	0.00	9.72
12/16	9.85	18	13	0.58	0.00	8.95
12/15	8.09	15	12	0.56	0.00	9.04
12/14	7.37	41	24	0.26	0.00	8.59
Annual Growth	13.8%		—	35.2%	—	6.0%

Select Energy Services Inc

Auditors: Grant Thornton LLP

LOCATIONS
HQ: Select Energy Services Inc
  1233 W. Loop South, Suite 1400, Houston, TX 77027
Phone: 713 235-9600
Web: www.selectenergyservices.com

HISTORICAL FINANCIALS
Company Type: Public

Income Statement FYE: December 31

	REVENUE ($ mil.)	NET INCOME ($ mil.)	NET PROFIT MARGIN	EMPLOYEES
12/18	1,528.9	36.5	2.4%	5,300
12/17	692.4	(16.8)	—	5,100
12/16	302.4	(307.5)	—	1,700
12/15	535.5	(80.8)	—	0
Annual Growth	41.9%	—	—	—

2018 Year-End Financials
Debt ratio: 3.3%
Return on equity: 4.9%
Cash ($ mil.): 17.2
Current ratio: 2.40
Long-term debt ($ mil.): 45.0
No. of shares (mil.): 104.9
Dividends
  Yield: —
  Payout: —
Market value ($ mil.): 663.0

	STOCK PRICE ($) FY Close	P/E High/Low		PER SHARE ($) Earnings	Dividends	Book Value
12/18	6.32	44	13	0.49	0.00	7.93
12/17	18.24	—	—	(0.51)	0.00	6.18
12/16	0.00	—	—	(0.05)	0.00	1.93
Annual Growth	102.7%		—	—	—	—

ServisFirst Bancshares Inc

ServisFirst Bancshares is a bank holding company for ServisFirst Bank a regional commercial bank with about a dozen branches located in Alabama and the Florida panhandle. The bank also has a loan office in Nashville. ServisFirst Bank targets privately-held businesses with $2 million to $250 million in annual sales as well as professionals and affluent customers. The bank focuses on traditional commercial banking services including loan origination deposits and electronic banking services such as online and mobile banking. Founded in 2005 by its chairman and CEO Thomas Broughton III the bank went public in 2014 with an offering valued at nearly $57 million.
IPO
ServisFirst Bancshares sold 625000 shares priced at $91 per share. Proceeds from the May 2014 IPO will be used to support the bank's growth plans both in Alabama and in other states.
Geographic Reach
Birmingham-based ServisFirst Bank has branches in Birmingham Huntsville Montgomery Mobile Dothan Pensacola and Nashville.
Financial Performance
The bank reported net income of $41.2 million in 2013 compared with $34 million in 2012. The increase was primarily due to an increase in net interest income which rose nearly 20% to $112.5 million. Noninterest income increased 4% to $10 million in 2013.
As of March 2014 the bank had total assets of approximately $3.6 billion total loans of $2.9 billion and total deposits of about $3.0 billion.

EXECUTIVES

President and CEO ServisFirst Bancshares and ServisFirst Bank, Thomas A. (Tom) Broughton, age 63, $350,000 total compensation
EVP and COO ServisFirst Bancshares and ServisFirst Bank, Clarence C. Pouncey, age 62, $263,000 total compensation
EVP CFO Treasurer and Secretary ServisFirst Bancshares and ServisFirst Bank, William M. Foshee, age 64, $230,000 total compensation
EVP ServisFirst Bancshares and President and CEO ServisFirst Bank of Huntsville, Andrew N. (Andy) Kattos, age 49
President and CEO ServisFirst Bank of Mobile, William (Bibb) Lamar, age 75
EVP ServisFirst Bancshares and President and CEO ServisFirst Bank of Montgomery, G. Carlton (Carl) Barker, age 64
EVP ServisFirst Bancshares and President and CEO ServisFirst Bank of Pensacola, Rex D. McKinney, age 56
EVP Correspondent Banking ServisFirst Bancshares and ServisFirst Bank, Rodney E. Rushing, age 61, $245,000 total compensation
SVP and Chief Credit Officer ServisFirst Bancshares and ServisFirst Bank, Don G. Owens, age 67, $187,200 total compensation
President and CEO ServisFirst Bank of Atlanta, Ken Barber
EVP and Chief Lending Officer, Doug Rehm
CEO ServisFirst Bank Dothan, B. Harrison Morris, age 42
First Vice President, Lee McKinnon
Senior Vice President Commercial Lending, Chad Thomason
Senior Vice President Of Commerical Banking, David Hearne
SENIOR VICE PRESIDENT COMMERCIAL BANKING, Jeff Johnson
Vice President, John Peacock
Senior Vice President Commercial Banking Team Lead, Lawson Kirkland
VICE PRESIDENT RETAIL BANKING CENTER MANAGER, Crystal Lee
Senior Vice President Commercial Relationship Manager, Jim Gardner
Senior Vice President, Justin Fontenot
Vice President, Kiley Elmore
Senior Vice President of Commercial Banking, Walter Brand
Senior Vice President Private Banking, Patricia Griner
Assistant Vice President, Debbie Crook
Vice President Portfolio Manager, Gary Allen
FVP Commercial Banking, Cheryl Dunn
Executive Vice President, Brad Armagost
Vice President, Barry Devane
Vice President, Bart Mcbride
Vice President Correspondent Banking, Andrew Barrett
Vice President and Commercial Lender, Max Coblentz
Vice President Commercial Banking, Marshall Darneille
SENIOR VICE PRESIDENT, Samantha S Curd
VICE PRESIDENT CREDIT OFFICER, Stacy B Suddeth
Vice President, Sam Scott
Senior Vice President, Hill Womble
Senior Vice President Commercial Banking, Will Clay
Senior Vice President, Michael Stephens
Assistant Vice President Cash Management Services, Loretta Shapiro
Vice President Credit Officer, Stacy Suddeth
Senior Vice President, Bryan Neth
Vice President Portfolio Manager, Jill Alvarez
Vice President Of Cash Management, Delbert Madison
Chairman ServisFirst Bancshares and ServisFirst Bank, Stanley M. (Skip) Brock, age 68
Auditors: Dixon Hughes Goodman LLP

LOCATIONS

HQ: ServisFirst Bancshares Inc
2500 Woodcrest Place, Birmingham, AL 35209
Phone: 205 949-0302
Web: www.servisfirstbank.com

COMPETITORS

Bank of America Wells Fargo
Bank of the Ozarks

HISTORICAL FINANCIALS
Company Type: Public

Income Statement FYE: December 31

	ASSETS ($ mil.)	NET INCOME ($ mil.)	INCOME AS % OF ASSETS	EMPLOYEES
12/18	8,007.3	136.9	1.7%	473
12/17	7,082.3	93.0	1.3%	434
12/16	6,370.4	81.4	1.3%	420
12/15	5,095.5	63.5	1.2%	371
12/14	4,098.6	52.3	1.3%	298
Annual Growth	18.2%	27.2%	—	12.2%

2018 Year-End Financials
Return on assets: 1.8%
Return on equity: 20.7%
Long-term debt ($ mil.): —
No. of shares (mil.): 53.3
Sales ($ mil): 346.0
Dividends
Yield: 1.5%
Payout: 21.3%
Market value ($ mil.): 1,701.0

	STOCK PRICE ($) FY Close	P/E High/Low		PER SHARE ($) Earnings	Dividends	Book Value
12/18	31.87	17	12	2.53	0.48	13.39
12/17	41.50	25	19	1.72	0.20	11.46
12/16	37.44	48	23	1.52	0.19	9.93
12/15	47.53	40	24	1.20	0.12	8.64
12/14	32.95	83	26	1.05	0.16	8.20
Annual Growth	(0.8%)	—	—	24.7%	32.0%	13.0%

Shake Shack Inc

Auditors: Ernst & Young LLP

LOCATIONS

HQ: Shake Shack Inc
225 Varick Street, Suite 301, New York, NY 10014
Phone: 646 747-7200
Web: www.shakeshack.com

HISTORICAL FINANCIALS
Company Type: Public

Income Statement FYE: December 26

	REVENUE ($ mil.)	NET INCOME ($ mil.)	NET PROFIT MARGIN	EMPLOYEES
12/18	459.3	15.1	3.3%	6,101
12/17	358.8	(0.3)	—	4,440
12/16	268.4	12.4	4.6%	3,521
12/15	190.5	(8.7)	—	2,215
12/14	118.5	2.1	1.8%	1,680
Annual Growth	40.3%	63.6%	—	38.0%

2018 Year-End Financials
Debt ratio: —
Return on equity: 7.7%
Cash ($ mil.): 24.7
Current ratio: 1.69
Long-term debt ($ mil.): —
No. of shares (mil.): 37.0
Dividends
Yield: —
Payout: —
Market value ($ mil.): 1,602.0

	STOCK PRICE ($) FY Close	P/E High/Low		PER SHARE ($) Earnings	Dividends	Book Value
12/18	43.21	128	69	0.52	0.00	6.10
12/17	44.34	—	—	(0.01)	0.00	4.61
12/16	36.83	78	58	0.53	0.00	4.18
12/15	39.96	—	—	(0.65)	0.00	2.78
Annual Growth	2.6%	—	—	—	—	30.0%

Shell Midstream Partners LP

Auditors: Ernst & Young LLP

LOCATIONS

HQ: Shell Midstream Partners LP
150 N. Dairy Ashford, Houston, TX 77079
Phone: 832 337-2034
Web: www.shellmidstreampartners.com

HISTORICAL FINANCIALS
Company Type: Public

Income Statement FYE: December 31

	REVENUE ($ mil.)	NET INCOME ($ mil.)	NET PROFIT MARGIN	EMPLOYEES
12/18	524.7	464.1	88.5%	0
12/17	470.1	295.3	62.8%	0
12/16	291.3	244.9	84.1%	0
12/15	326.5	167.1	51.2%	0
12/14	182.4	13.4	7.3%	0
Annual Growth	30.2%	142.6%		

2018 Year-End Financials
Debt ratio: 110.5%
Return on equity: —
Cash ($ mil.): 208.0
Current ratio: 5.43
Long-term debt ($ mil.): 2,115.8
No. of shares (mil.): 228.3
Dividends
Yield: 8.7%
Payout: 95.2%
Market value ($ mil.): 3,748.0

	STOCK PRICE ($)	P/E	PER SHARE ($)		
	FY Close	High/Low	Earnings	Dividends	Book Value
12/18	16.41	20 11	1.50	1.43	(1.24)
12/17	29.82	27 20	1.28	1.19	(3.07)
12/16	29.09	32 20	1.32	0.97	0.54
12/15	41.52	42 22	1.16	0.67	0.64
12/14	40.98	395320	0.10	0.00	3.03
Annual Growth	(20.5%)	— —	96.8%	—	—

Shenandoah Telecommunications Co

If Virginia is for lovers Shenandoah Telecommunications must carry some interesting conversations. Through subsidiaries the company (which does business as Shentel) provides telecom services in the Shenandoah Valley and beyond. Shenandoah Telephone has more than 20500 access lines in service. As a Sprint affiliate subsidiary Shenandoah Personal Communications offers wireless services to more than 262000 customers. The company's cable TV unit serves about 115000 customers while about 13000 households subscribe to its dial-up and broadband Internet access.

Operations
Recognizing that the market for wireline service is shrinking from the rise of mobile phones as a primary phone and VoIP technology Shentel is now primarily a wireless provider. Some 56% of sales come from its being a Sprint affiliate. (It also offers prepaid wireless service from Sprint subsidiaries Virgin Mobile and Boost.) Cable services account for about 26% of sales and its wireline service (which includes Internet service) makes up the remaining 18%.

Geographic Reach
Shentel's wireless segment provides digital wireless service to a portion of a four-state area covering the region from Harrisburg York and Altoona Pennsylvania to Harrisonburg Virginia. Its wireline cable and Internet services are offered throughout Shenandoah County and portions of northwestern Augusta County Virginia.

Financial Performance
Overall sales grew 5% in 2015 to $342.5 million from 2014 due to increases prepaid subscribers and a higher average revenue per subscriber from a richer product mix. all segments grew in 2015 with the cable operation increasing 15%.

The rise in revenue fueled a 21% increase in profit to $40.8 million in 2015. Cash from operations was $120 million in 2015 compared to $115 million in 2014.

Strategy
In order to focus on its core communications offerings in 2013 the company sold off its Shentel Converged Services business that provided local and long distance voice video and Internet services to off-campus college student housing throughout the southeastern United States.

Mergers and Acquisitions
Shenandoah is buying NTELOS Holdings Corp. for some $208 million. The deal was agreed to in 2015 and was to be finalized in 2016. Shenandoah acquired the NTELOS' wireless network assets retail stores and nearly 300000 retail subscribers in the nTELOS western markets. Shentel will complete plans to close down nTELOS' Eastern markets. The acquisition doubles Shentel's wireless customer base expands its footprint in the Mid-Atlantic region and strengthens its partnership with Sprint.

In 2016 Shentel acquired Colane Cable a video Internet and home phone-service provider in West Virginia for $2.4 million. Colane's operations are adjacent to areas served by Shentel.

EXECUTIVES
SVP Wireless, William L. (Willy) Pirtle, age 60, $262,787 total compensation
Chairman President and CEO, Christopher E. (Chris) French, age 61, $559,602 total compensation
EVP and COO, Earle A. MacKenzie, age 67, $370,565 total compensation
VP Finance CFO and Treasurer, Adele M. Skolits, age 60, $292,977 total compensation
VP Information Technology, Richard A. Baughman, age 51
VP Wireline and Engineering, Edward H. McKay, age 46
SVP Cable, Thomas A. (Tom) Whitaker, age 58, $217,308 total compensation
Vp Wireless Network Development, Dan Meenan
Board Member, Leigh Schultz
Auditors: KPMG LLP

LOCATIONS
HQ: Shenandoah Telecommunications Co
500 Shentel Way, Edinburg, VA 22824
Phone: 540 984-4141
Web: www.shentel.com

PRODUCTS/OPERATIONS
2015 Sales

	$ mil.	% of total
Wireless	208.8	56
Cable	97.6	26
Wireline	67.4	18
Adjustments	(31.4)	-
Total	342.5	100

Selected Services
Business telephone products
Cable TV
Cellular products and services
Centrex
Fiber-optic capacity
Internet access
ISDN
Local telephone access
Long-distance
Paging
Security systems

COMPETITORS
AT&T	Suddenlink Communications
Aquis Communications Group	T-Mobile USA
Comcast	Time Warner Cable
DISH Network	U.S. Cellular
EarthLink	Verizon
Lumos	Verizon Wireless Inc.

HISTORICAL FINANCIALS
Company Type: Public

Income Statement   FYE: December 31

	REVENUE ($ mil.)	NET INCOME ($ mil.)	NET PROFIT MARGIN	EMPLOYEES
12/18	630.8	46.6	7.4%	1,029
12/17	611.9	66.3	10.8%	1,066
12/16	535.2	(0.9)	—	1,236
12/15	342.4	40.8	11.9%	730
12/14	326.9	33.8	10.4%	708
Annual Growth	17.9%	8.3%		9.8%

2018 Year-End Financials
Debt ratio: 51.8%   No. of shares (mil.): 49.6
Return on equity: 11.7%   Dividends
Cash ($ mil.): 85.0   Yield: 0.6%
Current ratio: 2.37   Payout: 15.1%
Long-term debt ($ mil.): 749.6   Market value ($ mil.): 2,196.0

	STOCK PRICE ($)	P/E	PER SHARE ($)		
	FY Close	High/Low	Earnings	Dividends	Book Value
12/18	44.25	54 32	0.93	0.27	8.91
12/17	33.80	30 19	1.33	0.26	7.10
12/16	27.30	— —	(0.02)	0.25	6.05
12/15	43.05	60 33	0.83	0.24	5.98
12/14	31.25	47 33	0.70	0.24	5.35
Annual Growth	9.1%	— —	7.6%	3.5%	13.6%

Shutterstock Inc

Shutterstock brings the online marketplace mentality to the world of digital images illustrations and videos. Its 35000+ contributors have uploaded more than 19 millions bits of content perused by 550000 subscribers. The company's primary customers include marketing agencies media organizations and communications departments of businesses that subscribe to single downloads a set number of images or unlimited downloads for a month or a year; average cost per image is $3. Shutterstock's marketplace is available in 10 languages and 150 countries where its images are used for corporate communications websites ads and books and other published materials. Formed in 2007 the company went public in 2012.

IPO
The company plans to use its $76 million in IPO proceeds for general corporate purposes including possible acquisitions though nothing specific is in the works. Shutterstock had initially valued its IPO at $115 million.

Financial Performance
Shutterstock has seen its revenue grow steadily doubling between 2009 and 2011. Not only has the company's library and number of downloads grown during that time its revenue per download has also increased from $1.80 to $2.05.

Strategy
Going forward Shutterstock's growth strategies include increased localization of content to meet specific ethnic and culture media requirements and pursuing new content types as they become available. It also intends to move from mostly word-of-mouth to focused marketing in order to improve its penetration of both the small-to-medium-size

business segment (a majority of sales) and large agencies and enterprises.

EXECUTIVES

CFO, Steven Berns, age 54, $144,231 total compensation
Chairman and CEO, Jonathan (Jon) Oringer, age 45, $1 total compensation
Chief Product Officer, Catherine Ulrich, $324,423 total compensation
CEO WebDAM, Jody Vandergriff
Vice President And General Counsel, Michael Lesser
Senior Vice President Technology, Dan McCormick
Vice President Sales Operations and Development, Kate Pignata
Vice President Infrastructure and Data, Chris Coluzzi
Vp Head Of Delivery, Anne Islan
Vice President, Laura Gorham
Board Member, Nina Fry
Auditors: PricewaterhouseCoopers LLP

LOCATIONS

HQ: Shutterstock Inc
350 Fifth Avenue, 21st Floor, New York, NY 10118
Phone: 646 710-3417
Web: www.shutterstock.com

COMPETITORS

AG Interactive	New York Times
Agence France-Presse	PR Newswire
Associated Press	Piksel
Cartoon Bank	Reuters
Corbis	Rex Features
Facebook	Sipa Press
Getty Images	The NewsMarket
Masterfile	Wazee Digital
National Geographic	Zuma Press

HISTORICAL FINANCIALS
Company Type: Public

Income Statement   FYE: December 31

	REVENUE ($ mil.)	NET INCOME ($ mil.)	NET PROFIT MARGIN	EMPLOYEES
12/18	623.2	54.6	8.8%	1,029
12/17	557.1	16.7	3.0%	1,130
12/16	494.3	32.6	6.6%	858
12/15	425.1	19.5	4.6%	621
12/14	327.9	22.0	6.7%	512
Annual Growth	17.4%	25.4%	—	19.1%

2018 Year-End Financials

Debt ratio: —
Return on equity: 18.1%
Cash ($ mil.): 230.8
Current ratio: 1.37
Long-term debt ($ mil.): —
No. of shares (mil.): 35.0
Dividends
  Yield: 8.3%
  Payout: 256.4%
Market value ($ mil.): 1,263.0

	STOCK PRICE ($) FY Close	P/E High/Low	PER SHARE ($) Earnings	Dividends	Book Value
12/18	36.01	35 21	1.54	3.00	8.18
12/17	43.03	114 66	0.47	0.00	9.06
12/16	47.52	70 28	0.91	0.00	8.23
12/15	32.34	137 52	0.54	0.00	8.09
12/14	69.10	163 99	0.61	0.00	7.06
Annual Growth	(15.0%)	— —	26.1%	—	3.7%

Siebert Financial Corp

EXECUTIVES

Vice President Institutional Sales and Trading, Bryce Young
Senior Vice President, Christopher Myer
Vice President, Angelo Guerriero
Svp Investments, John Mcguinness
Auditors: Baker Tilly Virchow Krause, LLP

LOCATIONS

HQ: Siebert Financial Corp
120 Wall Street, New York, NY 10005
Phone: 212 644-2400
Web: www.siebertnet.com

COMPETITORS

Charles Schwab	Scottrade
E*TRADE Financial	ShareBuilder
Edward Jones	TD Ameritrade
FMR	The Vanguard Group

HISTORICAL FINANCIALS
Company Type: Public

Income Statement   FYE: December 31

	REVENUE ($ mil.)	NET INCOME ($ mil.)	NET PROFIT MARGIN	EMPLOYEES
12/18	30.0	11.9	39.8%	76
12/17	13.1	2.1	16.5%	80
12/16	9.8	(5.5)	—	31
12/15	10.1	(2.8)	—	43
12/14	15.8	(6.5)	—	48
Annual Growth	17.4%	—	—	12.2%

2018 Year-End Financials

Debt ratio: —
Return on equity: 106.8%
Cash ($ mil.): 7.2
Current ratio: 9.23
Long-term debt ($ mil.): —
No. of shares (mil.): 27.1
Dividends
  Yield: —
  Payout: —
Market value ($ mil.): 393.0

	STOCK PRICE ($) FY Close	P/E High/Low	PER SHARE ($) Earnings	Dividends	Book Value
12/18	14.46	47 17	0.44	0.00	0.63
12/17	13.50	200 26	0.10	0.00	0.19
12/16	2.98	— —	(0.25)	0.20	0.10
12/15	1.29	— —	(0.13)	0.00	0.71
12/14	2.20	— —	(0.30)	0.00	0.84
Annual Growth	60.1%	— —	—	—	(6.9%)

Sierra Bancorp

Sierra Bancorp is the holding company for the nearly $2 billion-asset Bank of the Sierra which operates approximately 30 branches in Central California's San Joaquin Valley between (and including) Bakersfield and Fresno. The bank offers traditional deposit products and loans to individuals and small and mid-size businesses. About 70% of its loan portfolio is made up of real estate loans while another 15% is made up of mortgage warehouse loans and a further 10% is tied to commercial and industrial loans (including SBA loans and direct finance leases). The bank also issues agricultural loans and consumer loans.

Operations
Bank of the Sierra makes almost 80% of its revenue from interest income. About 64% of its total revenue came from interest income on loans and leases (including fees) during 2015 while another 14% came from interest income on taxed and tax-exempt securities. The rest of its revenue came from deposit account service charges (12% of revenue) checkcard fees (5%) and other non-interest income sources.

Geographic Reach
The Porterville California-based bank operates branches and offices mostly in the San Joaquin Valley in Porterville Arroyo Grande Atascadero Bakersfield California City Clovis Delano Dinuba Exeter Farmersville Fillmore Fresno Hanford Lindsay Oxnard Paso Robles Reedley San Luis Obispo Santa Clarita Santa Paula Selma Tehachapi Three Rivers Visalia and Tulare.

Sales and Marketing
Bank of the Sierra has been gradually increasing its advertising spend in recent years. It spent $2.3 million on advertising and promotion in 2015 up from $2.2 million and $1.9 million in 2014 and 2013 respectively.

Financial Performance
The bank's revenue has been steadily rising over the past few years mostly as bank acquisitions and organic loan business growth has spurred higher interest income. Meanwhile its profits have more than doubled since 2011 thanks to declining loan loss provisions as its loan portfolio's credit quality has improved with higher property valuations in the strengthened economy.

Sierra Bancorp's revenue jumped 13% to $80.4 million during 2015 thanks to higher interest income from continued double-digit loan asset growth led by a jump in mortgage warehouse lines from increased line utilization a first-quarter purchase of residential mortgage loans and strong organic growth in non-farm real estate and agricultural production loans. Deposit account service fees also grew thanks to organic deposit client growth.

Strong revenue growth and lower acquisition costs in 2015 drove the bank's net income up 19% to $18 million. Sierra's operating cash levels rose 4% to $29.78 million during the year as its cash-based earnings increased.

Strategy
While the Bank of Sierra has traditionally grown organically by opening around one new branch per year in the Central Valley it has more recently acquired small area banks and individual branches to bolster its deposit and loan business while expanding into untapped markets such as further south into the Santa Clara Valley.

Mergers and Acquisitions
In July 2016 the bank bought $145 million-asset Coast Bancorp and its Coast National Bank branches in San Luis Obispo Paso Robles Arroyo Grande and Atascadero California.

In November 2014 Sierra Bancorp bought $129 million-asset Santa Clara Valley Bank N.A. and its branches in Santa Paula Santa Clarita and Fillmore in California for $15 million. the deal expanded Sierra's reach outside of its traditional market for the first time more south into the Santa Clara Valley of California.

EXECUTIVES

EVP and CFO, Kenneth R. (Ken) Taylor, age 59, $242,500 total compensation
EVP and Chief Credit Officer, James F. (Jim) Gardunio, age 68, $197,600 total compensation
VP and Manager Hanford Bank of the Sierra, Kevin J. McPhaill, age 46, $185,000 total compensation
Senior Vice President Specialized Lending, Michael McLennan
Senior Vp, Matthew Hessler
Senior Vice President of Tulare County and Manager of Tulare County, David Soares
Vice President Assistant Risk Manager, Cyndi Carmichael
Chairman, Morris A. Tharp, age 79
Auditors: Eide Bailly LLP

LOCATIONS

HQ: Sierra Bancorp
86 North Main Street, Porterville, CA 93257
Phone: 559 782-4900
Web: www.bankofthesierra.com

COMPETITORS

Bank of America
Bank of the West
Central Valley Community Bancorp
Citibank
Comerica
JPMorgan Chase
MUFG Americas Holdings
United Security Bancshares
Wells Fargo
Westamerica
Zions Bancorporation

HISTORICAL FINANCIALS
Company Type: Public

Income Statement — FYE: December 31

	ASSETS ($ mil.)	NET INCOME ($ mil.)	INCOME AS % OF ASSETS	EMPLOYEES
12/18	2,522.5	29.6	1.2%	556
12/17	2,340.3	19.5	0.8%	576
12/16	2,032.8	17.5	0.9%	497
12/15	1,796.5	18.0	1.0%	431
12/14	1,637.3	15.2	0.9%	437
Annual Growth	11.4%	18.1%	—	6.2%

2018 Year-End Financials
Return on assets: 1.2%
Return on equity: 11.2%
Long-term debt ($ mil.): —
No. of shares (mil.): 15.3
Sales ($ mil): 123.2
Dividends
  Yield: 2.6%
  Payout: 38.3%
Market value ($ mil.): 368.0

	STOCK PRICE ($) FY Close	P/E High/Low		PER SHARE ($) Earnings	Dividends	Book Value
12/18	24.03	16	12	1.92	0.64	17.84
12/17	26.56	21	17	1.36	0.56	16.81
12/16	26.59	20	12	1.29	0.48	14.94
12/15	17.65	14	11	1.33	0.42	14.36
12/14	17.56	16	14	1.08	0.34	13.67
Annual Growth	8.2%	—	—	15.5%	17.1%	6.9%

SIGA Technologies Inc

EXECUTIVES

Chief Scientific Officer, Dennis E. Hruby, $250,000 total compensation
Chairman and CEO, Eric A. Rose, $400,000 total compensation
EVP and General Counsel, William J. Haynes II
EVP and CFO, Daniel J. Luckshire
Director, Bruce Slovin, age 80
Director, James J. Antal, age 65
Director, Thomas E. Constance, age 79
Director, Michael A. Weiner, age 69
Director, Michael J. Bayer, age 68
Director, Joseph W. (Chip) Marshall III, age 63
Director, Paul G. Savas, age 53
Director, Judy S. Slotkin, age 61
Director, Steven L. Fasman, age 52
Director, Scott M. Hammer, age 68
Independent Director, Andrew Stern
Independent Director, Frances Townsend
Independent Director, William Bevins
Auditors: PricewaterhouseCoopers LLP

LOCATIONS

HQ: SIGA Technologies Inc
31 East 62nd Street, New York, NY 10065
Phone: 212 672-9100
Web: www.siga.com

COMPETITORS

Achillion
Bavarian Nordic A/S
Celldex Therapeutics
Chimerix
Emergent BioSolutions
GlaxoSmithKline
Novartis
Sanofi

HISTORICAL FINANCIALS
Company Type: Public

Income Statement — FYE: December 31

	REVENUE ($ mil.)	NET INCOME ($ mil.)	NET PROFIT MARGIN	EMPLOYEES
12/18	477.0	421.8	88.4%	41
12/17	12.2	(36.2)	—	37
12/16	14.9	(39.7)	—	36
12/15	8.1	(39.4)	—	29
12/14	3.1	(265.4)	—	34
Annual Growth	251.1%	—	—	4.8%

2018 Year-End Financials
Debt ratio: 37.1%
Return on equity: —
Cash ($ mil.): 100.6
Current ratio: 10.70
Long-term debt ($ mil.): 75.5
No. of shares (mil.): 80.7
Dividends
  Yield: —
  Payout: —
Market value ($ mil.): 638.0

	STOCK PRICE ($) FY Close	P/E High/Low		PER SHARE ($) Earnings	Dividends	Book Value
12/18	7.90	2	1	5.18	0.00	1.27
12/17	4.85	—	—	(0.46)	0.00	(4.09)
12/16	2.88	—	—	(0.69)	0.00	(3.65)
12/15	0.42	—	—	(0.73)	0.00	(5.26)
12/14	1.44	—	—	(4.97)	0.00	(4.61)
Annual Growth	53.0%	—	—	—	—	—

Signature Bank (New York, NY)

Signature Bank marks the spot where some professional New Yorkers bank. The institution provides customized banking and financial services to smaller private businesses their owners and their top executives through 30 branches across the New York metropolitan area including all five boroughs Long Island and affluent Westchester County. The bank's lending activities mainly entail real estate and business loans. Subsidiary Signature Securities offers wealth management financial planning brokerage services asset management and insurance while its Signature Financial subsidiary offers equipment financing and leasing. Founded in 2001 the bank now boasts assets of roughly $29 billion.

Operations
Mortgage loans including commercial real estate loans multifamily residential mortgages home loans and lines of credit and construction and land loans comprise the bulk of Signature Bank's loan portfolio (and much of its asset base as well).

The bank which staffed some 1010 employees at the end of 2014 generated 68% of its revenue from interest on loans and leases that year while 20% came from interest on its securities available-for-sale and 7% came from securities held-to-maturity. The remainder of its revenue came from fees and service charges (2%) and various other miscellaneous sources.

Geographic Reach
The bank's nearly 30 branch offices are mostly in the New York metropolitan area which includes Manhattan Brooklyn Westchester Long Island Queens the Bronx Staten Island and Connecticut.

Sales and Marketing
Signature Bank mostly serves privately-owned businesses their owners and senior managers (typically with a net worth between $500000 and $20 million).

Financial Performance
The company's revenues and profits have risen in recent years thanks to strong organic loan business growth and declining loan loss provisions as its loan portfolio's credit quality has improved with higher property valuations in the strengthened economy.

Signature's revenue jumped by 22% to a record $959.3 million in 2014 mostly as loan interest (on commercial loans mortgages and leases) and security interest income continued to grow as the bank built up its interest-earning assets during the year.

Higher revenue and a continued decline and loan loss provisions in 2014 boosted the bank's net income by 30% to a record $296.7 million. Signature's operating cash levels more than doubled to $421 million on higher cash earnings.

Strategy
Signature Bank has long targeted privately-held businesses that have fewer than 1000 employees and revenues of less than $200 million. Some of its target clients include real estate owners/companies law firms accounting firms entertainment business managers medical professionals retail establishments money management firms and nonprofit foundations.

The bank continues to expand its service lines particularly focusing on specialty financing to grow its business organically. In 2015 it planned to offer direct commercial vehicle financing through a network of approved commercial vehicle dealerships in New York's Tri-State area with loans targeting small and mid-size business borrowers looking to acquire commercial vehicles and fleets. Also that year it formed its Maryland-based Signature Public Funding Corp subsidiary to provide municipal finance and tax-exempt lending and leasing products to local state and federal government agencies nationwide.

Company Background

The bank's emphasis on personal service helped it to grow its deposit base and loan portfolio in 2011. During a time when many other banks struggled under the weight of bad loans in a bad economy Signature Bank achieved record earnings for the fourth consecutive year.

Founded in 2001 as an alternative to megabanks Signature Bank was spun off from Bank Hapoalim in 2004.

EXECUTIVES

President CEO and Director, Joseph J. DePaolo, $577,500 total compensation
SVP and CFO, Vito Susca
President CEO and Director, Michael G. O'Rourke
EVP, Kevin P. Bastuga
EVP, Bryan D. Duncan
VP Retail Operations Manager, Ella Riordan-Pacheco
Vice President, John C Spagnuolo
Vice President, Joseph Fingerman
Group Director Senior Vice President, Kevin Hardiman
Vice President Commercial Banking, Ross Thomson
Senior Vice President Group Director, Salvatore Costa
SVP, Maria Hegi
Chairman and Director, Leonard S. Caronia
Auditors: KPMG LLP

LOCATIONS

HQ: Signature Bank (New York, NY)
565 Fifth Avenue, New York, NY 10017
Phone: 646 822-1500
Web: www.signatureny.com

PRODUCTS/OPERATIONS

2014 Sales

	$ mil.	% of total
Interest		
Loans net	655.6	68
Securities available for sale	193.6	20
Securities held to maturity	69.8	7
Other	5.3	1
Noninterest		
Fees & service charges	19.3	2
Commissions	10.6	1
Net gains on sales of loans	5.4	1
Net gains on sales of securities	5.3	-
Other	2.2	-
Adjustments	(7.8)	-
Total	**959.3**	**100**

COMPETITORS

Apple Bank for Savings	Herald National Bank
Astoria Financial	JPMorgan Chase
Bank Leumi USA	New York Community Bancorp
Capital One	
Citigroup	Safra Bank
HSBC USA	TD Bank USA

HISTORICAL FINANCIALS
Company Type: Public

Income Statement — FYE: December 31

	ASSETS ($ mil.)	NET INCOME ($ mil.)	INCOME AS % OF ASSETS	EMPLOYEES
12/18	47,364.8	505.3	1.1%	1,393
12/17	43,117.7	387.2	0.9%	1,305
12/16	39,047.6	396.3	1.0%	1,218
12/15	33,450.5	373.0	1.1%	1,122
12/14	27,318.6	296.7	1.1%	1,010
Annual Growth	14.7%	14.2%	—	8.4%

2018 Year-End Financials

Return on assets: 1.1%
Return on equity: 11.9%
Long-term debt ($ mil.): —
No. of shares (mil.): 55.0
Sales ($ mil): 1,732.2
Dividends
  Yield: 1.0%
  Payout: 13.3%
Market value ($ mil.): 5,659.0

	STOCK PRICE ($) FY Close	P/E High/Low	PER SHARE ($) Earnings	Dividends	Book Value
12/18	102.81	17 11	9.23	1.12	80.07
12/17	137.26	23 17	7.12	0.00	73.33
12/16	150.20	21 15	7.37	0.00	66.15
12/15	153.37	22 16	7.27	0.00	56.81
12/14	125.96	22 17	5.95	0.00	49.61
Annual Growth	(5.0%)	—	11.6%	—	12.7%

Silvercrest Asset Management Group Inc

Auditors: DELOITTE & TOUCHE LLP

LOCATIONS

HQ: Silvercrest Asset Management Group Inc
1330 Avenue of the Americas, 38th Floor, New York, NY 10019
Phone: 212 649-0600

HISTORICAL FINANCIALS
Company Type: Public

Income Statement — FYE: December 31

	REVENUE ($ mil.)	NET INCOME ($ mil.)	NET PROFIT MARGIN	EMPLOYEES
12/18	98.6	9.6	9.8%	125
12/17	91.3	5.3	5.8%	122
12/16	80.2	5.0	6.2%	119
12/15	75.1	5.3	7.1%	113
12/14	69.4	4.7	6.9%	97
Annual Growth	9.2%	19.2%	—	6.5%

2018 Year-End Financials

Debt ratio: —
Return on equity: 18.3%
Cash ($ mil.): 69.2
Current ratio: 2.25
Long-term debt ($ mil.): —
No. of shares (mil.): 13.4
Dividends
  Yield: 4.2%
  Payout: 70.0%
Market value ($ mil.): 178.0

	STOCK PRICE ($) FY Close	P/E High/Low	PER SHARE ($) Earnings	Dividends	Book Value
12/18	13.23	15 10	1.16	0.56	4.17
12/17	16.05	25 18	0.66	0.48	3.72
12/16	13.15	22 16	0.62	0.48	3.66
12/15	11.89	23 16	0.68	0.48	3.61
12/14	15.65	29 21	0.63	0.48	3.46
Annual Growth	(4.1%)	—	16.5%	3.9%	4.8%

Simmons First National Corp

Simmons First National thinks it's only natural it should be one of the largest financial institutions in The Natural State. The $8.1 billion-asset holding company owns Simmons First National Bank and seven other community banks that bear the Simmons First Bank name and maintain local identities; together they operate around 150 branches throughout Arkansas and in Kansas Tennessee and Missouri. Serving consumers and area businesses the banks offer standard deposit products like checking and savings accounts IRAs and CDs. Lending activities mainly consist of commercial real estate loans single-family mortgages and consumer loans such as credit card and student loans.

Operations

In addition to Simmons First National Bank the company owns Simmons First Bank of Jonesboro Simmons First Bank of South Arkansas Simmons First Bank of Northwest Arkansas Simmons First Bank of Russellville Simmons First Bank of Searcy Simmons First Bank of El Dorado and Simmons First Bank of Hot Springs. Simmons First Trust Company a subsidiary of Simmons First National Bank provides trust and fiduciary services; Simmons First Investment Group offers broker-dealer services.

Like other retail banks Simmons makes the bulk of its money from interest income. About 65% of its total revenue came from loan interest during 2015 while another 8% came from interest on investment securities. The rest of its revenue came from service charges on deposit accounts (8% of revenue) debit and credit card fees (6%) mortgage lending income (3%) trust income (2%) investment banking income (1%) and other non-interest income sources.

Geographic Reach

The bank has around 150 branches mostly in Arkansas but also in Kansas Missouri and Tennessee.

Financial Performance

Simmons First National Bank's annual revenues and profits have been rising mostly thanks to new loan business from rapid bank expansion (mostly stemming from acquisitions).

The bank's revenue jumped 60% to $396.8 million during 2015 mostly thanks to 58% growth in legacy loans and growth in acquired loan business from the acquisitions of Liberty and Community First. Non-interest income grew 54% thanks to rising trust service charges deposit fees mortgage lending income all also tied to its recent acquisitions.

Revenue growth in 2015 more than doubled Simmons' net income to $74.36 million. The bank's operating cash levels spiked eight-fold to $88.7 million for the year thanks to a rise in cash-based earnings and favorable changes in working capital.

Strategy

Simmons tries to differentiate itself from smaller competitors by offering a wider array of products while striving to provide more personalized service than larger regional banks. The company also likes to acquire banks to grow its loan and deposit business while expanding into new geographic markets. Between 1990 and 2015 Simmons made 11 whole bank acquisitions and a handful of branch deals with other banks adding some 125 branches to its total branch network.

Mergers and Acquisitions

In 2019 Simmons First National acquired Reliance Bancshares a bank holding company with more than 20 branches in the St. Louis Missouri metropolitan area. The acquisition brings Simmons total assets to $17.6 billion and its total number of branches to more than 200 across Arkansas Colorado Illinois Kansas Missouri Oklahoma Tennessee and Texas. That year the company also purchased The Landrum Company the parent of Landmark Bank. Landrum brings with it approximately $3.3 billion in assets $2.1 billion in loans $3 billion in deposits and 40 branches in Missouri Oklahoma and Texas.

EXECUTIVES

EVP Organizational Development, Stephen C. Massanelli, age 63
Chairman and CEO, George A. Makris, age 62, $502,500 total compensation
SEVP CFO and Treasurer, Robert A. Fehlman, age 54, $306,614 total compensation
EVP and Central and Northeast Arkansas Regional Chairman Simmons First National Bank, Barry K. Ledbetter
President and Chief Credit Officer Simmons First National Bank, N. Craig Hunt
EVP and South Arkansas Regional Chairman Simmons First National Bank, Freddie G. Black
EVP Corporate Strategy and Performance and Secretary, Susan F. Smith, age 57
President Chief Banking Officer and Director, David L. Bartlett, age 67, $376,142 total compensation
EVP, Marty D. Casteel, age 67, $304,180 total compensation
EVP Controller Chief Accounting Officer and Investment Relations Officer, David W. Garner, age 49
EVP of Marketing, Robert C. Dill, age 76, $179,393 total compensation
EVP and Chief Risk Officer, Tina M. Groves, age 49
EVP Technology and Operations Simmons First National Bank, Lisa W. Hunter
SVP and Marketing Director Simmons First National Bank, Amy W. Johnson
President El Dorado Community Bank, Robert L. Robinson
Chairman Russellville Community Chairman, Ronald B. (Ron) Jackson
President Hot Springs Community Bank, Steven W. (Steve) Trusty
President Conway Community Bank, Jason Culpepper
EVP and General Counsel, Patrick A. Burrow, age 65
EVP Specialty Lending Simmons First National Bank, Larry L. Bates
EVP and Tennessee Regional Chairman Simmons First National Bank, John C. Clark
EVP and Kansas and Missouri Regional Chairman Simmons First National Bank, Gary E. Metsger
Vice President, Clint Parton
Vice President and Personnel Manager, Leigh Cockrum
Vice President, Pam Lawshe
Vp Of Mortgage, Deana Powell
Assistant Vice President Branch Manager, Emily Ferguson
Assistant Vice President Loans, Esther Chapman
Senior Vice President Director Of Marketing And Communications, Elizabeth Machen
Vice President, Chad Pittillo
Executive Vice President Operations, Glenda Tolson
Vice President Regional Manager, Zilpha Wilson
Vice President, Rick Pierce
Senior Vice President, Adam Mitchell
Vice President Financial Analysis Manager, Donna Renfro
Senior Vice President Regulatory and Consumer Affairs, Kevin Archer
Vice President Market Manager, Dorvan Wiley
Vice President and Trust Officer, Robin Thornton
Vice President Administration, David Rushing
Vice President Equipment Finance, Michael Childers
Assistant Vice President And Trust Officer, Karen Cash
Vice President Customer Service, Barbara Jacks
Vice President Mortgage Lending Manager, Justin Moore
Vice President Regional Manager, Michael Ramsey
Vice President, Roland Getchell
Vice President Commercial Lending, Wayne Wilson
Assistant Vice President and Investment Officer, Kelton Harrison
Vice President Administration, Brent Martin
Senior Vice President, Steve Landry
Assistant Vice President, Chris Rittelmeyer
Vice President Commercial Lending, Vernon Scott
Assistant Vice President Atm Operations, Karla Dial
VICE PRESIDENT FACILITIES MANAGEMENT, Anita Murrell
EXECUTIVE VICE PRESIDENT FINANCIAL SERVICES, Phillip Tappan
Vice President Manager Personal Trust, Cathy Roper
Svp Dtr Of Community Dev, Martie North
VICE PRESIDENT FINANCIAL ADVISOR, James Watkins
SENIOR VICE PRESIDENT AND SENIOR CREDIT OFFICER, Stephen Landry
Executive Vice President Chief People Marketing Officer Assistant General Counsel, Jennifer Compton
Executive Vp, Tina Graves
Senior Vice President, David Seal
SENIOR VICE PRESIDENT COMMERCIAL LENDING, Shane Strahl
Board Member, Edward Drilling
Board Member, Eugene Hunt
Board Member, Brandy West
Board Member, Christopher Kirkland
Board Member, Mark Doramus
Board Member, Scott Mcgeorge
Auditors: BKD, LLP

LOCATIONS

HQ: Simmons First National Corp
501 Main Street, Pine Bluff, AR 71601
Phone: 870 541-1000
Web: www.simmonsbank.com

PRODUCTS/OPERATIONS

2015 Sales

	$ mil.	% of total
Interest Income		
Loans	268.4	65
Investment securities	30.6	8
Others	2.0	-
Non-interest income		
Service charges on deposit accounts	31.0	8
Debit and credit card fees	26.7	6
Mortgage lending income	11.4	3
Trust income	9.2	2
Other service charges and fees	9.9	2
others	22.4	6
Net (loss) gain on assets covered by FDIC loss share agreements	(14.8)	
Total	**396.8**	**100**

COMPETITORS

Arvest Bank	Bear State Financial
BOK Financial	Home BancShares
BancorpSouth	IBERIABANK
Bank of America	Regions Financial
Bank of the Ozarks	U.S. Bancorp

HISTORICAL FINANCIALS

Company Type: Public

Income Statement
FYE: December 31

	ASSETS ($ mil.)	NET INCOME ($ mil.)	INCOME AS % OF ASSETS	EMPLOYEES
12/18	16,543.3	215.7	1.3%	2,654
12/17	15,055.8	92.9	0.6%	2,640
12/16	8,400.0	96.8	1.2%	1,875
12/15	7,559.6	74.3	1.0%	1,946
12/14	4,643.3	35.6	0.8%	1,331
Annual Growth	37.4%	56.8%	—	18.8%

2018 Year-End Financials

Return on assets: 1.3%
Return on equity: 9.9%
Long-term debt ($ mil.): —
No. of shares (mil.): 92.3
Sales ($ mil): 824.5
Dividends
Yield: 2.4%
Payout: 25.8%
Market value ($ mil.): 2,228.0

	STOCK PRICE ($) FY Close	P/E High/Low		PER SHARE ($)		
			Earnings	Dividends	Book Value
12/18	24.13	26 10	2.32	0.60	24.33
12/17	57.10	47 37	1.33	0.50	22.65
12/16	62.15	42 25	1.57	0.48	18.40
12/15	51.36	44 27	1.32	0.46	17.78
12/14	40.65	41 31	1.06	0.44	13.69
Annual Growth	(12.2%)	— —	21.8%	8.1%	15.5%

Simpson Manufacturing Co., Inc. (DE)

Through its subsidiaries Simpson Manufacturing makes connectors and venting systems for the building remodeling and do-it-yourself industries. Subsidiary Simpson Strong-Tie (SST) makes more than 15000 types of standard and custom products that are used to connect and reinforce joints between wood concrete and masonry building components which the company markets globally and distributes through home centers and a network of contractor and dealer distributors. The company's products are sold primarily in Canada Europe Asia the US and the South Pacific.

Operations
Simpson divides its product lines across two main categories: wood construction (85% of net sales) and concrete construction (15%).

Geographic Reach
The company has around 20 manufacturing locations in Canada France Denmark Germany Switzerland Poland Portugal China the UK and the US. North America accounted for 85% of its revenue in 2015.

Sales and Marketing
Simpson sells its products through an extensive distribution system comprising dealer distributors supplying thousands of retail locations nationwide contractor distributors home centers lumber dealers manufacturers of engineered wood products and specialized contractors such as roof framers. SST markets its products to the residential construction light industrial and commercial construction remodeling and do-it-yourself (DIY) markets.

Financial Performance
The company's revenues climbed 6% from $752 million in 2014 to $794 million in 2015 its highest total in about seven years. The growth for 2015 was driven by a 10% spike in North America that were mostly due to an increase in sales volume and from acquisitions primarily within the US.

Profits also jumped 7% from $64 million in 2014 to $68 million in 2015. Simpson's operating cash flow has fluctuated the last two years; after declining sharply in 2014 cash flow skyrocketed by 70% during 2015.

Strategy
Simpson's long-term strategy has relied on capturing additional market share in both the wood construction and concrete construction product groups by continuing to invest in mobile and web applications for customers. It is also utilizing social media blog posts and videos to connect and engage with its customers and to help them do their jobs more efficiently.

In March 2015 the company closed sales offices in China Dubai and Thailand due to continued losses in these operations.

Mergers and Acquisitions
The company also makes relatively small acquisitions to grow its product lines. In late 2015 it purchased the two businesses of Blue Heron Enterprises and Fox Chase Enterprises for $3.4 million. Both companies manufactured and sold hidden deck clips and associated products and systems.

EXECUTIVES
VP, Jeffrey E. Mackenzie, age 58, $181,830 total compensation
President and CEO, Karen W. Colonias, age 62, $350,000 total compensation
CFO Treasurer and Secretary, Brian J. Magstadt, age 51, $243,337 total compensation
President North American Sales Simpson Strong-Tie Company, Roger Dankel, age 55, $166,455 total compensation
COO Simpson Strong-Tie Company Inc, Ricardo M. Arevalo, age 62, $191,276 total compensation
Vice President Human Resources, Jennifer Lutz
Chairman, Peter N. Louras, age 70
Vice Chairman, Thomas J. (Tom) Fitzmyers, age 79
Board Member, Celeste Ford
Board Member, Michael Bless
Auditors: Grant Thornton LLP

LOCATIONS
HQ: Simpson Manufacturing Co., Inc. (DE)
5956 W. Las Positas Blvd., Pleasanton, CA 94588
Phone: 925 560-9000   **Fax:** 925 833-1496
Web: www.simpsonmfg.com

PRODUCTS/OPERATIONS

2015 Sales

	% of total
Wood construction	85
Concrete construction	15
Other	-
Total	**100**

Selected Products
Simpson Strong-Tie
  Adhesives
  Mechanical anchors
  Powder-actuated tools
  Screw fastening systems
  Shearwalls
  Wood-to-concrete connectors
  Wood-to-masonry connectors
  Wood-to-wood connectors

Selected Subsidiaries
Simpson Strong-Tie Australia Inc.
Simpson Strong-Tie Canada Limited
Simpson Strong-Tie Company Inc.
Simpson Strong-Tie Europe EURL
Simpson Strong-Tie International Inc.
Simpson Strong-Tie Japan Inc.

COMPETITORS

Action Industries	MSC Industrial Direct
Anaheim Manufacturing	MacLean-Fogg
Boral	Masco
Dayton Superior	W rth Group
Kemco Systems	

HISTORICAL FINANCIALS
Company Type: Public

Income Statement   FYE: December 31

	REVENUE ($ mil.)	NET INCOME ($ mil.)	NET PROFIT MARGIN	EMPLOYEES
12/18	1,078.8	126.6	11.7%	3,135
12/17	977.0	92.6	9.5%	2,902
12/16	860.6	89.7	10.4%	2,647
12/15	794.0	67.8	8.5%	2,498
12/14	752.1	63.5	8.4%	2,434
Annual Growth	9.4%	18.8%	—	6.5%

2018 Year-End Financials
Debt ratio: —   No. of shares (mil.): 45.0
Return on equity: 14.5%   Dividends
Cash ($ mil.): 160.1   Yield: 1.5%
Current ratio: 3.96   Payout: 31.6%
Long-term debt ($ mil.): —   Market value ($ mil.): 2,436.0

	STOCK PRICE ($) FY Close	P/E High/Low		PER SHARE ($) Earnings	Dividends	Book Value
12/18	54.13	28	18	2.72	0.86	19.01
12/17	57.41	31	21	1.94	0.78	18.93
12/16	43.75	26	16	1.86	0.68	18.25
12/15	34.15	28	23	1.38	0.60	17.64
12/14	34.60	28	22	1.29	0.53	17.63
Annual Growth 11.8%		—	—	20.5%	12.9%	1.9%

Simulations Plus Inc.

EXECUTIVES
CFO and Director Human Resources Facilities and Equipment; CFO Words+, Momoko A. Beran, age 64, $135,000 total compensation
Chairman President and CEO, Walter S. (Walt) Woltosz, age 71, $250,000 total compensation
President Words+, Jeffrey A. (Jeff) Dahlen, age 55, $100,000 total compensation
Investor Relations Director, Renee Bouche
Director Life Sciences, Robert D. Clark
Team Leader Discovery Informatics, David Miller
Manager Marketing and Sales, John DiBella
Secretary Treasurer and Director, Virginia E. Woltosz, age 63
Director, David Z. D'Argenio, age 65
Director, Richard R. Weiss, age 81
Director, H. Wayne Rosenberger, age 76
Independent Director, David DArgenio
Auditors: Rose, Snyder & Jacobs LLP

LOCATIONS
HQ: Simulations Plus Inc.
42505 Tenth Street West, Lancaster, CA 93534-7059
Phone: 661 723-7723   **Fax:** 661 723-5524
Web: www.simulations-plus.com

PRODUCTS/OPERATIONS

Selected Products
Augmentative Communication Products
  Cyberlink
  E Z Keys for Windows
  Freedom 2000
  HeadMouse
  MessageMate
  SoftSwitch
  Talking Screen for Windows
  Tracker One
  TuffTalker
Educational Software
  Circuits for Physical Science
  Gravity for Physical Science
  Ideal Gas for Chemistry
  Optics for Physical Science
  Universal Gravitation for Physical Science
Pharmaceutical Applications
  GastroPlus
  QMPRchitect
  QMPRPlus

COMPETITORS

Cyprotex
DynaVox
Entelos
Fonix
Nuance Communications

HISTORICAL FINANCIALS
Company Type: Public

Income Statement FYE: August 31

	REVENUE ($ mil.)	NET INCOME ($ mil.)	NET PROFIT MARGIN	EMPLOYEES
08/19	33.9	8.5	25.3%	111
08/18	29.6	8.9	30.1%	95
08/17	24.1	5.7	24.0%	86
08/16	19.9	4.9	24.8%	63
08/15	18.3	3.8	21.0%	60
Annual Growth	16.7%	22.2%	—	16.6%

2019 Year-End Financials
Debt ratio: —
Return on equity: 24.6%
Cash ($ mil.): 11.4
Current ratio: 4.42
Long-term debt ($ mil.): —
No. of shares (mil.): 17.5
Dividends
  Yield: 0.0%
  Payout: 50.0%
Market value ($ mil.): 635.0

	STOCK PRICE ($) FY Close	P/E High/Low	PER SHARE ($) Earnings	Dividends	Book Value
08/19	36.11	85 36	0.48	0.24	2.14
08/18	20.85	46 28	0.50	0.24	1.83
08/17	14.50	47 25	0.33	0.20	1.49
08/16	8.62	39 23	0.29	0.20	1.32
08/15	6.75	30 25	0.23	0.20	1.15
Annual Growth	52.1%	—	20.2%	4.7%	16.8%

SiteOne Landscape Supply Inc

Auditors: Deloitte & Touche LLP

LOCATIONS
HQ: SiteOne Landscape Supply Inc
300 Colonial Center Parkway, Suite 600, Roswell, GA 30076
Phone: 470 277-7000
Web: www.siteone.com

HISTORICAL FINANCIALS
Company Type: Public

Income Statement FYE: December 30

	REVENUE ($ mil.)	NET INCOME ($ mil.)	NET PROFIT MARGIN	EMPLOYEES
12/18	2,112.3	73.9	3.5%	4,300
12/17*	1,861.7	54.6	2.9%	3,800
01/17	1,648.2	30.6	1.9%	3,300
01/16	1,451.6	28.9	2.0%	2,850
12/14	1,176.6	21.7	1.8%	0
Annual Growth	15.8%	35.8%	—	—

*Fiscal year change

2018 Year-End Financials
Debt ratio: 49.0%
Return on equity: 28.8%
Cash ($ mil.): 17.3
Current ratio: 2.71
Long-term debt ($ mil.): 563.2
No. of shares (mil.): 40.8
Dividends
  Yield: —
  Payout: —
Market value ($ mil.): 2,273.0

	STOCK PRICE ($) FY Close	P/E High/Low	PER SHARE ($) Earnings	Dividends	Book Value
12/18	55.59	52 28	1.73	0.00	7.38
12/17*	76.70	56 26	1.29	0.00	5.33
01/17	34.73	— —	(3.01)	0.00	3.76
Annual Growth	26.5%	—	—	—	40.1%

*Fiscal year change

SLM Corp.

If SLM doesn't seem familiar perhaps you know it by its more common moniker Sallie Mae. Holding more than $8 billion in student loans SLM's main subsidiary Sallie Mae Bank is one of the nation's largest education loan providers and specializes in originating acquiring financing and servicing private student loans which are not guaranteed by the government. The company also earns fees for its processing and administrative offerings through various subsidiaries.

HISTORY

The Student Loan Marketing Association was chartered in 1972 as a response to problems in the Guaranteed Student Loan Program of 1965. For years the GSL program had tinkered with rates to induce banks to make loans but servicing the small loans was expensive and troublesome. Sallie Mae began operations in 1973 buying loans from their originators; its size provided economies of scale in loan servicing.

Originally only institutions making educational or student loans were allowed to own stock in Sallie Mae. This was later changed so that anyone could buy nonvoting stock. In 1993 voting stock was listed on the NYSE.

Sallie Mae was always a political football altered again and again to reflect the education policies of the party in power. When it was founded during the Nixon administration its loans were restricted by a needs test which was repealed during the Carter years. The Reagan administration reimposed the needs test and at the same time sped up the schedule under which the company was to become self-supporting which it did by late 1981.

Forced to rely on its own resources Sallie Mae turned to creative financing. One of its traditional advantages was that its loan interest rates were linked to Treasury bills traditionally about 3% above the T-bill rate. The company became a master at riding the spread between its cost of funds and the interest rates it charged.

Between 1983 and 1992 Sallie Mae's assets swelled by more than 400% and its income rose by almost 500%. As the firm grew management became more visible with high pay and extravagant perks. Although salaries were not inconsistent with those of executives at comparable private corporations the remuneration level and perks irked Congress. But Sallie Mae kept growing — in 1992 it expanded its facilities and added 900 new staff members.

The 1993 Omnibus Budget Reconciliation Act with its transfer of the student loan program directly to the government and its surcharge on Sallie Mae began to adversely affect earnings in 1994. While awaiting permission to alter its charter the company stepped up its marketing efforts especially to school loan officers who advised students on loan options.

In 1995 then-COO Albert Lord led a group of stockholders in a push to cut operating expenses and repackage student loans as securities la Freddie Mac and Fannie Mae. Lord and some of his supporters won seats on the board (as well as the enmity of Lawrence Hough who resigned as CEO in the midst of the melee). That year Sallie Mae bought HICA Holding one of two private insurers of education loans. In 1996 Congress passed legislation forcing Sallie Mae's privatization.

Despite SLM's rising stock shareholders were unhappy with chairman William Arceneaux's status quo business plan. Lord gained control in 1997.

In 1998 the organization became SLM Holding. Assets and earnings were muted that year when unfavorable market conditions prevented Sallie Mae from securitizing its loans.

The firm the next year expanded its lending operations by buying Nellie Mae. Also in 1999 Sallie Mae teamed with Answer Financial to sell insurance. Growth continued in 2000 when the company bought loan servicer Student Loan Funding Resources as well as the marketing student loan servicing and administrative operations of USA Group; the company changed its name to USA Education following the acquisition. The company also cut some 1700 jobs approximately 25% of its workforce.

The following year Sallie Mae teamed with Intuit allowing the financial software company access to Sallie Mae's 7 million customers. It also launched online recruiting service TrueCareers that year.

In 2002 it bought Pioneer Credit Recovery and General Revenue Corporation two of the nation's largest student loan collection agencies. It also reverted to the SLM moniker to reconnect with the name by which it has so long been known.

The privatization plan put into place in the mid-'90s (orchestrated in large part by then-CEO Lord) came to fruition nearly four years ahead of schedule when SLM transitioned to a private organization in December 2004.

In 2007 SLM saw its stock values plummet to their lowest levels in about a decade. A number of industry-wide factors figured into the losses not the least of which was the downturn in the credit market. Also affecting the company was the signing into law of the College Cost Reduction and Access Act (CCRAA). Intended to reform student lending and cut costs for borrowers the act slashed subsidies for lenders participating in the Federal Family Education Loan Program (FFELP). The reform cut into the company's interest-earning operations. As a result SLM increased its focus on higher-yielding private education loans which carry a lower risk.

Additionally SLM that year became ensnared in a student-lending industry probe led by New York attorney general Andrew Cuomo. The company agreed to a $2 million settlement and to abide by a code of conduct regarding its dealings with college employees.

One of the most dramatic results of the troubles was the collapse of a planned acquisition by a consortium of investment firms. The planned $8.8 billion deal included buyers J.C. Flowers (which was to own about a half of SLM) Bank of America and JPMorgan Chase. In the midst of the industry probe J.C. Flowers sought a change in SLM's leadership in an effort to secure regulatory approval for the acquisition; Thomas J. (Tim) Fitzpatrick was ousted as CEO. Ultimately the buyers canceled the deal citing the reduced potential value of SLM. The student lender filed a lawsuit to challenge the termination but eventually dropped the suit. It later cut more than 10% of its workforce.

EXECUTIVES

Vp Federal Government Relations, Tim Morrison
Senior Vice President Loan Operations, Michael Maier
Chairman and CEO, Raymond J. Quinlan, $600,000 total compensation
EVP and General Counsel, Laurent C. Lutz, $525,000 total compensation
EVP and CFO, Steven J. McGarry, $375,000 total compensation
SVP and Chief Risk Officer, Jeffery F. Dale, age 57, $400,000 total compensation
EVP and Chief Marketing Officer, Charles P. Rocha, $375,000 total compensation
Svp And Chief Compliance Officer, Jim Truitt
Vice President West Region Head, Robin Famiglietti
Svp Corporate Development, Paul Mayer
Svp And Chief Risk Officer, Jeffrey Dale
Assistant Vice President Network Services, Peter Tropf
Vice President, Jonathan Boyles
Senior Vice President General Counsel, Nicolas Jafarieh
Vice President Finance Other Credit, Doug Maurer
Vice President Finance and Treasurer, Christopher Lynch
Vice President And Associate General Counsel, Anne Milem
Executive Vice President Administration, Joni Reich
Vice President, Lynn M Langdon
Vice President Information Technology Credit Origination, Michael Migliore
Senior Executive Administrative Assistant for Senior Vice President Corporate Finance, Kathleen Mullaney
Svp Banking And Campus Solutions, Kelly Christiano
Vice President Information Technology Risk and Compliance, Karen Delozier
Svp And Chief Security Officer, Jerry Archer
Vice President Product Development, John Lazzati
Senior VP, Tamara Belkin
Senior Vice President Chief Regulatory Counsel and Assistant Corporate Secretary, Rick Nelson
Auditors: KPMG LLP

LOCATIONS

HQ: SLM Corp.
 300 Continental Drive, Newark, DE 19713
Phone: 302 451-0200
Web: www.salliemae.com

PRODUCTS/OPERATIONS

2016 Sales

	$ mil.	% of total
Interest		
Lons	1,060.5	79
Investments	9.2	1
Cash & cash equivalents	7.6	1
Non-Interest income		
Gain on sale of loans	0.2	14
(Losses) gains on derivatives and hedging activities net	(0.9)	5
Other income	69.5	—
Total	**1,146.1**	**100**

Selected Subsidiaries
HICA Holding
Sallie Mae Bank
Sallie Mae Inc.
SLM Education Credit Finance Corporation
 Bull Run I LLC
 SLM Education Credit Funding LLC
SLM Investment Corporation
Southwest Student Services Corporation

COMPETITORS
Bank of America
Brazos Higher Education Service Corp.
Citizens Financial Group
Discover
Educational Funding of The South
First Marblehead
FirstCity Financial
Great Lakes Higher Education
KeyCorp
Mohela
Nelnet
PNC Financial
Pennsylvania Higher Education Assistance Agency
SunTrust
Texas Guaranteed

HISTORICAL FINANCIALS
Company Type: Public

Income Statement FYE: December 31

	ASSETS ($ mil.)	NET INCOME ($ mil.)	INCOME AS % OF ASSETS	EMPLOYEES
12/18	26,638.1	487.4	1.8%	1,700
12/17	21,779.5	288.9	1.3%	1,500
12/16	18,533.0	250.3	1.4%	1,300
12/15	15,214.1	274.2	1.8%	1,200
12/14	12,972.2	194.2	1.5%	1,000
Annual Growth	19.7%	25.9%	—	14.2%

2018 Year-End Financials
Return on assets: 2.0%
Return on equity: 17.9%
Long-term debt ($ mil.): —
No. of shares (mil.): 435.6
Sales ($ mil): 1,883.4
Dividends
 Yield: —
 Payout: —
Market value ($ mil.): 3,621.0

	STOCK PRICE ($) FY Close	P/E High/Low		PER SHARE ($) Earnings	Dividends	Book Value
12/18	8.31	11	8	1.07	0.00	6.82
12/17	11.30	20	16	0.62	0.00	5.72
12/16	11.02	21	10	0.53	0.00	5.47
12/15	6.52	18	11	0.59	0.00	4.92
12/14	10.19	63	19	0.42	0.60	4.32
Annual Growth	(5.0%)	—	—	26.3%	—	12.1%

Smart Sand Inc

Auditors: Grant Thornton LLP

LOCATIONS

HQ: Smart Sand Inc
 1725 Hughes Landing Blvd, Suite 800, The Woodlands, TX 77380
Phone: 281 231-2660

HISTORICAL FINANCIALS
Company Type: Public

Income Statement FYE: December 31

	REVENUE ($ mil.)	NET INCOME ($ mil.)	NET PROFIT MARGIN	EMPLOYEES
12/18	212.4	18.6	8.8%	323
12/17	137.2	21.5	15.7%	198
12/16	59.2	10.3	17.5%	103
12/15	47.7	4.9	10.5%	97
12/14	68.1	7.5	11.1%	0
Annual Growth	32.9%	25.4%	—	—

2018 Year-End Financials
Debt ratio: 15.2%
Return on equity: 9.3%
Cash ($ mil.): 1.4
Current ratio: 2.03
Long-term debt ($ mil.): 47.8
No. of shares (mil.): 39.9
Dividends
 Yield: —
 Payout: —
Market value ($ mil.): 89.0

	STOCK PRICE ($) FY Close	P/E High/Low		PER SHARE ($) Earnings	Dividends	Book Value
12/18	2.22	24	4	0.46	0.00	5.24
12/17	8.66	39	9	0.53	0.00	4.70
12/16	16.55	38	25	0.42	0.00	3.67
Annual Growth	(63.4%)	—	—	4.7%	—	19.5%

SmartFinancial Inc

EXECUTIVES

Senior Vice President Knoxville Area Market Executive, Mike Honeycutt
Regional President Alabama And Florida, Robert Kuhn
Auditors: Dixon Hughes Goodman LLP

LOCATIONS

HQ: SmartFinancial Inc
 5401 Kingston Pike, Suite 600, Knoxville, TN 37919
Phone: 865 437-5700
Web: www.smartfinancialinc.com

COMPETITORS

Bank of America
First Horizon
First Security Group
Home Federal Bank (TN)
Regions Financial
SunTrust
Tennessee Valley Financial Holdings

HISTORICAL FINANCIALS
Company Type: Public

Income Statement — FYE: December 31

	ASSETS ($ mil.)	NET INCOME ($ mil.)	INCOME AS % OF ASSETS	EMPLOYEES
12/18	2,274.4	18.1	0.8%	387
12/17	1,720.7	5.0	0.3%	343
12/16	1,062.4	5.8	0.5%	222
12/15	1,023.9	1.5	0.1%	225
12/14	415.7	1.6	0.4%	104
Annual Growth	52.9%	82.3%	—	38.9%

2018 Year-End Financials
Return on assets: 0.9%
Return on equity: 7.4%
Long-term debt ($ mil.): —
No. of shares (mil.): 13.9
Sales ($ mil): 98.7
Dividends
 Yield: —
 Payout: —
Market value ($ mil.): 255.0

	STOCK PRICE ($) FY Close	P/E High/Low		PER SHARE ($) Earnings	Dividends	Book Value
12/18	18.27	19	12	1.45	0.00	20.31
12/17	21.70	47	33	0.55	0.00	18.46
12/16	18.56	24	18	0.78	0.00	17.85
12/15	16.09	46	9	0.32	0.00	17.25
12/14	3.31	93	58	0.04	0.00	24.54
Annual Growth	53.3%	—		145.4%	—	(4.6%)

Solaris Oilfield Infrastructure Inc

Auditors: BDO USA, LLP

LOCATIONS
HQ: Solaris Oilfield Infrastructure Inc
9811 Katy Freeway, Suite 700, Houston, TX 77024
Phone: 281 501-3070
Web: www.solarisoilfield.com

HISTORICAL FINANCIALS
Company Type: Public

Income Statement — FYE: December 31

	REVENUE ($ mil.)	NET INCOME ($ mil.)	NET PROFIT MARGIN	EMPLOYEES
12/18	197.2	42.4	21.5%	382
12/17	67.4	3.6	5.4%	266
12/16	18.1	2.8	15.4%	101
12/15	14.2	(1.3)	—	0
Annual Growth	140.3%			

2018 Year-End Financials
Debt ratio: 3.1%
Return on equity: 28.8%
Cash ($ mil.): 25.0
Current ratio: 2.29
Long-term debt ($ mil.): 13.1
No. of shares (mil.): 46.6
Dividends
 Yield: 0.8%
 Payout: 6.2%
Market value ($ mil.): 564.0

	STOCK PRICE ($) FY Close	P/E High/Low		PER SHARE ($) Earnings	Dividends	Book Value
12/18	12.09	15	7	1.59	0.10	3.61
12/17	21.41	77	36	0.27	0.00	2.73
12/16	0.00	—	—	(0.23)	0.00	(0.00)
Annual Growth	—			—	—	—

Somero Enterprises Inc

EXECUTIVES
Pres, Jack Cooney
Auditors: Whitley Penn LLP

LOCATIONS
HQ: Somero Enterprises Inc
14530 Global Parkway, Fort Myers, FL 33913
Phone: 239 210-6500 Fax: 239 210-6600
Web: www.somero.com

HISTORICAL FINANCIALS
Company Type: Public

Income Statement — FYE: December 31

	REVENUE ($ mil.)	NET INCOME ($ mil.)	NET PROFIT MARGIN	EMPLOYEES
12/18	94.0	21.5	22.9%	190
12/17	85.6	18.4	21.5%	177
12/16	79.3	14.2	18.0%	178
12/15	70.2	11.5	16.4%	165
12/14	59.4	14.5	24.5%	165
Annual Growth	12.2%	10.3%	—	3.6%

2018 Year-End Financials
Debt ratio: —
Return on equity: 41.8%
Cash ($ mil.): 28.2
Current ratio: 4.40
Long-term debt ($ mil.): —
No. of shares (mil.): 56.2
Dividends
 Yield: —
 Payout: 50.0%
Market value ($ mil.): —

Sound Financial Bancorp Inc

Auditors: Moss Adams, LLP

LOCATIONS
HQ: Sound Financial Bancorp Inc
2400 3rd Avenue, Suite 150, Seattle, WA 98121
Phone: 206 448-0884
Web: www.soundcb.com

HISTORICAL FINANCIALS
Company Type: Public

Income Statement — FYE: December 31

	ASSETS ($ mil.)	NET INCOME ($ mil.)	INCOME AS % OF ASSETS	EMPLOYEES
12/18	716.7	7.0	1.0%	119
12/17	645.2	5.1	0.8%	121
12/16	588.3	5.3	0.9%	106
12/15	540.7	4.7	0.9%	111
12/14	495.1	4.2	0.9%	97
Annual Growth	9.7%	13.5%	—	5.2%

2018 Year-End Financials
Return on assets: 1.0%
Return on equity: 10.2%
Long-term debt ($ mil.): —
No. of shares (mil.): 2.5
Sales ($ mil): 37.4
Dividends
 Yield: 1.6%
 Payout: 21.0%
Market value ($ mil.): 83.0

	STOCK PRICE ($) FY Close	P/E High/Low		PER SHARE ($) Earnings	Dividends	Book Value
12/18	32.55	14	12	2.74	0.54	28.15
12/17	34.02	17	13	2.00	0.60	25.95
12/16	28.00	14	10	2.09	0.30	24.12
12/15	22.64	12	9	1.86	0.23	22.08
12/14	18.85	11	10	1.63	0.20	20.06
Annual Growth	14.6%	—	—	13.9%	28.2%	8.8%

South Jersey Industries Inc

South Jersey Industries (SJI) is Atlantic City's answer to cold casino nights. In 2014 its main subsidiary South Jersey Gas (SJG) provided natural gas to 342155 residents 24253 commercial customers and 446 industrial customers in southern New Jersey including Atlantic City. The utility has more than 6000 miles of transmission and distribution mains; it also sells and transports wholesale gas. SJI's deregulated retail supplier South Jersey Energy (SJE) provides retail gas electricity and energy management services. Its South Jersey Resources (SJR) unit is a wholesale gas marketer and services provider in the Southeast US. Subsidiary Marina Energy develops and operates on-site energy projects. In 2017 subsidiary South Jersey Gas agreed to purchase for $1.7 billion Elizabethtown Gas and Elkton Gas from a subsidiary of The Southern Company adding nearly 300000 new gas customers.

Operations
SJI operates in several different operating segments. Its SJG gas utility operations consist primarily of natural gas distribution to residential commercial and industrial customers; Wholesale energy operations include the activities of SJR and South Jersey Exploration (SJEX); SJE is involved in both retail gas and retail electric activities include natural gas acquisition and transportation service business lines electricity acquisition and transportation to commercial and industrial customers; On-Site energy production consists of Marina Energy's thermal energy facility and other energy-re-

lated projects; Appliance service operations includes South Jersey Energy Service Plus (SJESP)'s servicing of appliances under warranty via a subcontractor arrangement as well as on a time and materials basis. SJG accounted for 68.5% of SJI's revenues in 2014.

SJE provides services for the acquisition and transportation of natural gas and electricity for retail end users and markets total energy management services. SJR markets natural gas storage commodity and transportation assets on a wholesale basis mainly in mid-Atlantic Appalachian and southern regions of the country. SJEX owns oil gas and mineral rights in the Marcellus Shale region of Pennsylvania Marina Energy develops and operates energy-related projects. Marina's largest wholly owned operating project provides cooling heating and emergency power to the Borgata Hotel Casino & Spa in Atlantic City. SJESP services residential and small commercial HVAC systems installs small commercial HVAC systems provides plumbing services and services appliances under warranty via a subcontractor arrangement as well as on a time and materials basis.

SJI also has a joint venture with Connective to offer meter-reading services through Millennium Account Services.

Sales and Marketing

SJG makes wholesale gas sales to gas marketers for resale and ultimate delivery to end users. Customers for SJG grew 1.3% for 2014 as SJG increased its focus on customer conversions. Consumers converting to fuels such as electric propane or oil represented more than 69% of the total new customer acquisitions for the year.

The total number of customers in SJG's service territory purchasing natural gas from a marketer averaged 41837 46872 and 39398 during 2014 2013 and 2012 respectively.

Geographic Reach

SJI's South Jersey Gas service territory covers 2500 square miles in southern New Jersey including 117 towns and cities in Atlantic Cape May Cumberland and Salem counties and portions of Burlington Camden and Gloucester counties. SJI also markets natural gas storage commodity and transportation assets on a wholesale basis in the mid-Atlantic Appalachia and the southern US.

Financial Performance

In 2014 SJI's net revenues increased by 21%. Gas Utility revenues grew due to higher firm sales and Off-System Sales colder weather additional customers and certain capital investments into base rates.

Retail gas sales increased due to a higher monthly New York Mercantile Exchange settle price along with a increase in sales volumes. Sales from retail electric operations decreased due to price volatility. Revenues from wholesale energy operations rose mainly due to higher margins on daily energy trading activities along with a 44% increase in storage volumes sold.

Revenues from on-site energy grew as the result of several new renewable energy projects along with higher hot water production and electricity sales at the wholly-owned thermal facility due to colder temperatures. Sales from appliance service operations decreased primarily due to lower installation jobs compared to the prior year.

SJI's net income increased by 19% due to a decrease in Energy and Other Taxes (as the result of the elimination of gas utility operations) and changes in income taxes.

In 2014 cash from operating activities increased by 1%.

Strategy

The company looks for steady growth by maintaining its core regulated-utility businesses and pursuing acquisitions and partnerships that complement its focus on energy and energy services.

The company expects strong performance in its regulatory businesses where customer growth and infrastructure investment in the utility and returns from their investment in the much needed Penneast pipeline will contribute the bulk of SJI's earnings. SJI Midstream LLC was formed in 2014 to invest in this project to build a 100-mile natural gas pipeline in Pennsylvania and New Jersey.

In 2012 SJE expanded its portfolio of customers by acquiring marketing assets from CenterPoint Energy in Pennsylvania. In a move to grow its energy assets in 2011 SJI teamed up with Clean Energy Fuels agreeing to build a compressed natural gas fueling station on a South Jersey Gas property in Glassboro. SJG opened its third CNG station in 2014.

EXECUTIVES

Director Business and Product Development, Michael J. Renna, age 52, $528,846 total compensation
EVP and CFO, Stephen H. Clark, $347,692 total compensation
EVP and COO, Jeffrey E. (Jeff) DuBois, age 57, $388,769 total compensation
President South Jersey Gas, David Robbins
SVP and Chief Administrative Officer, Kathleen A. McEndy, $299,231 total compensation
SVP and Chief Risk Officer, Kenneth Lynch
SVP General Counsel and Corporate Secretary, Gina Merritt-Epps, $334,539 total compensation
SVP South Jersey Energy Solutions, Gregory Nuzzo
Vice President, Ken Depriest
Vice president, Judi Hall
Vice President, William Shiminske
Vice President of Marketing, Carlos Navarro
Vice President Marketing, David Irussi
Chairman, Walter M. (Walt) Higgins, age 75
Secretary B, Gina Kell
Auditors: DELOITTE & TOUCHE LLP

LOCATIONS

HQ: South Jersey Industries Inc
1 South Jersey Plaza, Folsom, NJ 08037
Phone: 609 561-9000
Web: www.sjiindustries.com

PRODUCTS/OPERATIONS

2014 Sales

	$ mil.	% of total
Gas utility	501.9	57
Energy Group:		
Retail Gas and other operations	127.0	14
Retail electricity operation	123.8	14
Wholesale energy operation	77.0	9
Energy Services:		
On-Site energy production	56.1	6
Corporate & services	30.2	3
Appliance service operations	10.5	1
Adjustment (intersegment sales) (39.5) (4)		
Total	887.0	100

Selected Subsidiaries

Marina Energy LLC (energy project development)
South Jersey Energy Company (retail energy marketer energy management services)
South Jersey Energy Service Plus LLC (HVAC systems installation and appliance servicing)
South Jersey Exploration LLC (oil and gas assets)
South Jersey Gas Company (natural gas utility)
South Jersey Resources Group LLC (wholesale natural gas marketing trading transportation and management services)

COMPETITORS

Con Edison
Delmarva Power
Integrys Energy Services
National Grid USA
New Jersey Resources
PPL Corporation
Public Service Enterprise Group
UGI

HISTORICAL FINANCIALS

Company Type: Public

Income Statement — FYE: December 31

	REVENUE ($ mil.)	NET INCOME ($ mil.)	NET PROFIT MARGIN	EMPLOYEES
12/18	1,641.3	17.6	1.1%	1,100
12/17	1,243.0	(3.4)	—	760
12/16	1,036.5	118.8	11.5%	750
12/15	959.5	105.1	11.0%	720
12/14	887.0	97.0	10.9%	700
Annual Growth	16.6%	(34.7%)	—	12.0%

2018 Year-End Financials

Debt ratio: 47.6%
Return on equity: 1.4%
Cash ($ mil.): 30.0
Current ratio: 0.42
Long-term debt ($ mil.): 2,106.8
No. of shares (mil.): 85.5
Dividends
Yield: 4.0%
Payout: 536.9%
Market value ($ mil.): 2,377.0

	STOCK PRICE ($) FY Close	P/E High/Low		PER SHARE ($) Earnings	Dividends	Book Value
12/18	27.80	172	124	0.21	1.13	14.82
12/17	31.23	—	—	(0.04)	1.10	14.99
12/16	33.69	22	15	1.56	1.06	16.22
12/15	23.52	40	14	1.53	1.02	14.62
12/14	58.93	42	36	1.46	0.96	13.65
Annual Growth	(17.1%)	—	—	(38.4%)	4.1%	2.1%

South State Corp

South State Corporation (formerly First Financial Holdings) is the holding company for South State Bank (formerly South Carolina Bank and Trust and South Carolina Bank and Trust of the Piedmont both known as SCBT). The bank operates branches throughout the Palmetto state as well as in select counties in Georgia and North Carolina. Serving retail and business customers the banks provide deposit accounts loans and mortgages as well as trust and investment planning services. More than half of the firm's loan portfolio is devoted to commercial mortgages while consumer real estate loans make up more than a quarter. South State plans to merge with Southeastern Bank Financial parent of Georgia Bank & Trust.

Operations

Beyond its retail and commercial banking mortgage lending consumer finance and trust and investment businesses the bank operates registered investment advisors Minis & Co. and First Southeast 401K Fiduciaries as well as limited-purpose broker-dealer First Southeast Investor Services.

South State Corporation generated 70% of its total revenue from loan interest (including fees) in 2014 while another 4% came from interest income on investment securities. Service charges and Bankcard services income made up another 14% of total revenue while trust and investment services income and mortgage banking income each contributed roughly 4% during the year.

Geographic Reach
South State Corporation boasts nearly 130 branches across nearly 20 counties in South Carolina a handful of counties in North Carolina and about a dozen counties in the northeast and coastal regions of Georgia.

Financial Performance
South State Corporation's revenues and profits have been on the rise over the past few years mostly thanks to continued growth of its loan business and declining loan loss provisions as its loan portfolio's credit quality has improved with the strengthened economy.

The company's revenue jumped by 28% to $436.72 million in 2014 which was mostly driven by 20% growth in its loan interest income as its average loan asset balances swelled by a similar percentage. South State's non-interest income also swelled by 76% thanks to higher deposit account service charge bankcard service trust and investment service and mortgage banking fees from overall growth in the business through acquisitions and organic initiatives.

Higher revenue and controlled operating costs in 2014 drove the bank's net income higher by 53% to $75.44 million. South State's operating cash levels declined by 51% to $118.65 million for the year after adjusting its earnings for non-cash net sales proceeds from its mortgage loans held-for-sale and as the bank spent more cash toward its accrued income taxes.

Strategy
Though it does sometimes expand or relocate its existing branches to better position its locations for more growth South State Corporation has been mostly growing its loan business and branch network through strategic bank and branch acquisitions. Its 2015 acquisition of 13 branch locations from Bank of America for example extended South State's reach into six new markets and three existing markets while adding millions of dollars worth of new loan business. Then in mid-2016 South State Corporation agreed to buy Southeastern Bank Financial the holding company of Georgia Bank & Trust (which also operates in South Carolina as Southern Bank & Trust). The combined company will operate more than 130 branches in Georgia and the Carolinas.

Mergers and Acquisitions
In 2015 South State Corporation agreed to purchase 12 South Carolina branches and one Georgia branch from Bank of America expanding its reach into six new markets. The acquired branches were located in Hartwell Georgia; as well as Florence Greenwood Orangeburg Sumter Newberry Batesburg-Leesville Abbeville and Hartsville in South Carolina.

Company Background
South State Corporation and South State Bank changed their names from First Financial Holdings and South Carolina Bank and Trust respectively in 2014. The change was designed to better promote the South State brand with customers.

EXECUTIVES
CEO, Robert R. Hill, age 52, $645,000 total compensation
Vice President of Public Relations, Donna Pullen
CFO and COO, John C. Pollok, age 53, $442,000 total compensation
Regional President Upstate, John F. Windley, age 67, $315,000 total compensation
Chief Credit Officer and Chief Risk Officer, Joseph Burns, $295,000 total compensation
President, R. Wayne Hall, $203,405 total compensation
EVP and Corporate Secretary, William C. Bochette
Vice President, Reid Davis
Senior Vice President Technology, Ross Bagley
Senior Executive Vice President, Dane H Murray
Vice President, Stacy Cannon
Senior Vice President Corporate Counsel, Nici Comer
Senior Vice President Chief Compliance Officer, Lora Jex
Chairman, Robert R. Horger, age 68
Vice Chairman, Paula Harper Bethea
Board Member, Kevin Walker
Board Member, Cynthia Hartley
Board Member, Robert Demere
Auditors: Dixon Hughes Goodman LLP

LOCATIONS
HQ: South State Corp
520 Gervais Street, Columbia, SC 29201
Phone: 800 277-2175
Web: www.southstatebank.com

PRODUCTS/OPERATIONS

2011 Sales

	$ mil.	% of total
Interest		
Loans including fees	319.9	70
Investment securities	20.3	4
Other	1.8	-
Noninterest		
Service charges on deposit accounts	36.2	10
Bankcard services income	29.6	6
Trust and investment services income	18.3	4
Mortgage banking	16.2	4
Securities gains net	-	0
Amortization of FDIC indemnification asset	(21.9)	0
Other	16.2	4
Total	**436.7**	**100**

COMPETITORS

BB&T	Regions Financial
Bank of America	Security Federal
Bank of South Carolina	
First Citizens Bancorporation	

HISTORICAL FINANCIALS
Company Type: Public

Income Statement — FYE: December 31

	ASSETS ($ mil.)	NET INCOME ($ mil.)	INCOME AS % OF ASSETS	EMPLOYEES
12/18	14,676.3	178.8	1.2%	2,602
12/17	14,466.5	87.5	0.6%	2,719
12/16	8,900.5	101.2	1.1%	2,055
12/15	8,557.3	99.4	1.2%	2,058
12/14	7,826.2	75.4	1.0%	2,081
Annual Growth	17.0%	24.1%	—	5.7%

2018 Year-End Financials
Return on assets: 1.2%
Return on equity: 7.6%
Long-term debt ($ mil.): —
No. of shares (mil.): 35.8
Sales ($ mil): 712.9
Dividends
Yield: 2.3%
Payout: 38.8%
Market value ($ mil.): 2,148.0

	STOCK PRICE ($) FY Close	P/E High/Low	PER SHARE ($) Earnings	Dividends	Book Value
12/18	59.95	19 12	4.86	1.38	66.04
12/17	87.15	32 27	2.93	1.32	62.81
12/16	87.40	22 14	4.18	1.21	46.83
12/15	71.95	19 14	4.11	0.98	43.84
12/14	67.08	22 18	3.08	0.82	40.78
Annual Growth	(2.8%)	— —	12.1%	13.9%	12.8%

Southeastern Banking Corp. (Darien, GA)

Auditors: Mauldin & Jenkins, LLC

LOCATIONS
HQ: Southeastern Banking Corp. (Darien, GA)
1010 North Way, Darien, GA 31305
Phone: 912 437-4141
Web: www.southeasternbank.com

HISTORICAL FINANCIALS
Company Type: Public

Income Statement — FYE: December 31

	ASSETS ($ mil.)	NET INCOME ($ mil.)	INCOME AS % OF ASSETS	EMPLOYEES
12/18	419.5	6.8	1.6%	0
12/17	431.0	2.9	0.7%	0
12/16	414.1	3.8	0.9%	0
12/15	403.3	2.6	0.7%	0
12/14	389.7	7.9	2.0%	0
Annual Growth	1.9%	(3.6%)	—	—

2018 Year-End Financials
Return on assets: 1.6%
Return on equity: 12.9%
Long-term debt ($ mil.): —
No. of shares (mil.): 3.1
Sales ($ mil): 21.7
Dividends
Yield: 0.0%
Payout: 20.1%
Market value ($ mil.): 55.0

	STOCK PRICE ($)	P/E	PER SHARE ($)		
	FY Close	High/Low	Earnings	Dividends	Book Value
12/18	17.50	10 8	2.18	0.44	17.64
12/17	19.75	21 14	0.93	0.40	16.15
12/16	13.25	11 8	1.24	0.34	15.60
12/15	10.35	12 10	0.85	0.16	14.76
12/14	9.00	4 3	2.53	0.00	14.20
Annual Growth	18.1%	— —	(3.7%)	—	5.6%

Southern First Bancshares, Inc.

EXECUTIVES

Senior Vice President, Shannon Smoak
Board Member, Rudolph Johnstone
Board Member, Fred Gilmer
Auditors: Elliott Davis, LLC

LOCATIONS

HQ: Southern First Bancshares, Inc.
100 Verdae Boulevard, Suite 100, Greenville, SC 29607
Phone: 864 679-9000
Web: www.southernfirst.com

COMPETITORS

BB&T
Bank of America
First Citizens Bancorporation
Regions Financial

HISTORICAL FINANCIALS

Company Type: Public

Income Statement — FYE: December 31

	ASSETS ($ mil.)	NET INCOME ($ mil.)	INCOME AS % OF ASSETS	EMPLOYEES
12/18	1,900.6	22.2	1.2%	229
12/17	1,624.6	13.0	0.8%	198
12/16	1,340.9	13.0	1.0%	179
12/15	1,217.2	10.1	0.8%	167
12/14	1,029.8	6.6	0.6%	155
Annual Growth	16.6%	35.4%	—	10.2%

2018 Year-End Financials

Return on assets: 1.2%
Return on equity: 13.7%
Long-term debt ($ mil.): —
No. of shares (mil.): 7.4
Sales ($ mil): 86.8
Dividends
Yield: —
Payout: —
Market value ($ mil.): 239.0

	STOCK PRICE ($)	P/E	PER SHARE ($)		
	FY Close	High/Low	Earnings	Dividends	Book Value
12/18	32.07	16 10	2.88	0.00	23.29
12/17	41.25	23 17	1.76	0.00	20.37
12/16	36.00	18 11	1.94	0.00	17.00
12/15	22.70	14 10	1.55	0.00	14.98
12/14	17.02	15 11	1.10	0.00	13.34
Annual Growth	17.2%	— —	27.2%	—	14.9%

Southern Missouri Bancorp, Inc.

EXECUTIVES

Vice President, Mel Jackson
Vice President Loan Officer, Jon Holman
Vp, Tiffany Jenkins
Vice President of Deposit Operations, Tiffany Beaton
Auditors: BKD, LLP

LOCATIONS

HQ: Southern Missouri Bancorp, Inc.
2991 Oak Grove Road, Poplar Bluff, MO 63901
Phone: 573 778-1800
Web: www.bankwithsouthern.com

COMPETITORS

Bank of America
Commerce Bancshares
IBERIABANK
Regions Financial
U.S. Bancorp
UMB Financial

HISTORICAL FINANCIALS

Company Type: Public

Income Statement — FYE: June 30

	ASSETS ($ mil.)	NET INCOME ($ mil.)	INCOME AS % OF ASSETS	EMPLOYEES
06/19	2,214.4	28.9	1.3%	470
06/18	1,886.1	20.9	1.1%	415
06/17	1,707.7	15.5	0.9%	390
06/16	1,403.9	14.8	1.1%	342
06/15	1,300.0	13.6	1.1%	327
Annual Growth	14.2%	20.6%	—	9.5%

2019 Year-End Financials

Return on assets: 1.4%
Return on equity: 13.1%
Long-term debt ($ mil.): —
No. of shares (mil.): 9.2
Sales ($ mil): 112.6
Dividends
Yield: 0.0%
Payout: 16.5%
Market value ($ mil.): 324.0

	STOCK PRICE ($)	P/E	PER SHARE ($)		
	FY Close	High/Low	Earnings	Dividends	Book Value
06/19	34.83	13 10	3.14	0.52	25.66
06/18	39.02	17 13	2.39	0.44	22.31
06/17	32.26	18 11	2.07	0.40	20.15
06/16	23.53	12 9	1.98	0.36	16.94
06/15	18.85	22 10	1.79	0.34	17.88
Annual Growth	16.6%	— —	15.1%	11.2%	9.5%

Southern National Bancorp Of Virginia Inc

EXECUTIVES

Senior Vice President, Linda Sandridge
Vice President Senior Lending Officer, Marie Leibson
Senior Vice President and Chief Credit Officer of the Company and the Bank, Tom Baker
Assistant Vice President, Sharon Tyson
Auditors: Dixon Hughes Goodman LLP

LOCATIONS

HQ: Southern National Bancorp Of Virginia Inc
6830 Old Dominion Drive, McLean, VA 22101
Phone: 703 893-7400
Web: www.sonabank.com

COMPETITORS

BB&T
Bank of America
Burke & Herbert Bank
Capital One
PNC Financial
SunTrust
Virginia Commerce Bancorp
Wells Fargo

HISTORICAL FINANCIALS

Company Type: Public

Income Statement — FYE: December 31

	ASSETS ($ mil.)	NET INCOME ($ mil.)	INCOME AS % OF ASSETS	EMPLOYEES
12/18	2,701.3	33.6	1.2%	348
12/17	2,614.2	2.4	0.1%	393
12/16	1,142.4	10.3	0.9%	162
12/15	1,036.1	9.2	0.9%	181
12/14	916.6	7.4	0.8%	173
Annual Growth	31.0%	45.7%	—	19.1%

2018 Year-End Financials

Return on assets: 1.2%
Return on equity: 10.0%
Long-term debt ($ mil.): —
No. of shares (mil.): 24.0
Sales ($ mil): 129.1
Dividends
Yield: 2.4%
Payout: 32.3%
Market value ($ mil.): 318.0

	STOCK PRICE ($)	P/E	PER SHARE ($)		
	FY Close	High/Low	Earnings	Dividends	Book Value
12/18	13.22	13 9	1.39	0.32	14.48
12/17	16.03	142 118	0.13	0.32	13.48
12/16	16.34	20 14	0.83	0.32	10.30
12/15	13.06	17 15	0.75	0.52	9.78
12/14	11.34	19 16	0.63	0.60	9.33
Annual Growth	3.9%	— —	21.9%	(14.5%)	11.6%

Southern Power Co

Southern Power provides power for the burgeoning population in the South. The company owns builds acquires and markets energy in the competitive wholesale supply business. It develops and operates independent power plants in the southeastern US. The company which is part of Southern Company's generation and energy marketing operations has more than 10500 MW of primarily fossil-fueled facilities generating capacity operating or under construction in Alabama California Florida Georgia Nevada North Carolina Texas and New Mexico. Southern Power's electricity output is marketed to wholesale customers in the region. It is growing by acquiring and developing solar power facilities.

Operations

The company is a wholesale energy provider serving electricity needs of municipalities electric cooperatives and investor-owned utilities. Southern Power and its subsidiaries owns and/or operates

35 facilities in nine states. Its renewable assets include biomass and solar.

Thanks to solar facilities under construction and the acquisitions of Calipatria Solar and Grant Wind as well as other capacity and energy contracts the Southern Power has an average of 75% of its available demonstrated capacity covered through 2020 and an average of 70% of its available demonstrated capacity covered through 2025.

Geographic Reach
Southern Power has operations Alabama California Florida Georgia Nevada New Mexico North Carolina Oklahoma and Texas.

Financial Performance
In fiscal 2015 Southern Power's net sales decreased by $111 million compared to 2014. Power purchase agreements (PPA) energy revenues declined due to lower energy prices driven by a drop in natural gas prices which was passed through in fuel revenues.

Wholesale revenues and non-affiliates revenues declined due to lower energy and capacity revenues.

In 2015 net income increased by 25% due to lower fuel expenses and purchased power partially offset by decreased sales.

Fuel expense decreased due to lower natural gas generation costs.

Purchased power expenses decreased primarily due to a drop in volume of KWhs purchased as well as a decrease associated with the average cost of purchased power.

Net cash provided by the operating activities increased by 66% due to higher income tax benefits received and higher revenues from new PPAs including solar PPAs.

Strategy
The company is expanding its regional generation portfolio (primarily with solar power plants) in order to boost its overall generating capacity to almost 10000 MW.

Mergers and Acquisitions
Growing its solar power assets in 2016 Southern Power acquired the 120-MW East Pecos solar facility (Southern Power's second solar project in Texas).

That year Southern Power and Turner Renewable Energy jointly bought the 20-MW Calipatria solar facility from Solar Frontier Americas. (Southern Power's 10th solar facility in California).

In 2015 Southern Power acquired a controlling interest in the 200-MW Garland solar facility under construction in California from Recurrent Energy a subsidiary of Canadian Solar Inc.

In 2014 Southern Power and Turner Renewable Energy acquired the largest solar facility in New Mexico the 50-MW Macho Springs Solar Facility. The Southern Power-Turner Renewable Energy partnership's seventh solar project and its second-largest overall the plant is expected to generate enough electricity to power more than 18000 homes.

EXECUTIVES
SVP and COO, John G. Trawick
Vice President of Construction, Keith Russell
Senior Vice President Compliance Officer, Thomas Bishop
Board Member, Larry Thompson
Auditors: DELOITTE & TOUCHE LLP

LOCATIONS
HQ: Southern Power Co
30 Ivan Allen Jr. Boulevard, N.W., Atlanta, GA 30308
Phone: 404 506-5000

PRODUCTS/OPERATIONS
2015 Sales

	$ mil.	% of total
Wholesale revenues non-affiliates	964.0	69
Wholesale revenues affiliates	417.0	30
Other revenues	9.0	1
Total	1,390.0	100

COMPETITORS
AEP	Duke Energy
AES	Entergy
Calpine	NextEra Energy

HISTORICAL FINANCIALS
Company Type: Public

Income Statement — FYE: December 31

	REVENUE ($ mil.)	NET INCOME ($ mil.)	NET PROFIT MARGIN	EMPLOYEES
12/18	2,205.0	187.0	8.5%	491
12/17	2,075.0	1,071.0	51.6%	541
12/16	1,577.0	338.0	21.4%	0
12/15	1,390.0	215.0	15.5%	0
12/14	1,501.2	172.3	11.5%	0
Annual Growth	10.1%	2.1%	—	—

2018 Year-End Financials
Debt ratio: 33.7%
Return on equity: 4.6%
Cash ($ mil.): 181.0
Current ratio: 0.72
Long-term debt ($ mil.): 4,418.0
No. of shares (mil.): 0.0
Dividends
Yield: —
Payout: 166.8%
Market value ($ mil.): —

Southside Bancshares, Inc.

Southside Bancshares is the holding company for Southside Bank which boasts nearly 65 branches across East North and Central Texas with many around the cities of Tyler and Longview. About one-third of its branches are located in supermarkets (including Albertsons and Brookshire stores) and 40% are motor bank facilities. The bank provides traditional services such as savings money market and checking accounts CDs and other deposit products as well as trust and wealth management services. Real estate loans primarily residential mortgages make up about half of the company's loan portfolio which also includes business consumer and municipal loans. The bank has total assets exceeding $4.8 billion.

Operations
Southside generated 48% of its total revenue from loan interest in 2014 while interest income on taxable investment securities and mortgage-backed securities made up 16% and 19% respectively. About 9% of its revenue came from deposit service fees and another 2% came from trust income.

Geographic Reach
The bank's branches are located in East North and Central Texas. Its main markets are in East Texas the greater Fort Worth area and the greater Austin area. It is also an affiliate with more than 55000 foreign ATMs worldwide.

Sales and Marketing
Southside which staffed 813 employees at 2014's end serves individuals businesses municipal entities and non-profit organizations in local communities.

Financial Performance
Southside Bancshares' revenues and profits have been falling over the past several years despite consistent growth in loan and investment interest income mostly because the bank's gains on securities held-for-sale have declined.

The company's revenue dipped by 4% to $148.3 million in 2014 mostly due to a $5.6 million decline in gains on the sale of its AFS securities and a $2.8 million impairment of equity related to its investment in SFG Finance stemming from the sale of loans purchased by SFG and the repossessed assets.

Lower revenue and an uptick in loan loss provisions in 2014 caused Southside's net income to tumble 49% to $20.8 million for the year while its operating cash levels dipped by 6% to $56 million on lower cash earnings.

Strategy
Southside looks to acquire financial institutions to grow its loan business and expand its geographic reach outside of its existing markets. Its 2014 acquisition of OmniAmerican Bank alone helped boost its loan assets by more than 60% to $2.17 billion while adding 14 branches in a new market (Dallas/Fort Worth).

To grow its deposits and deepen its presence in the markets it serves the company has also been expanding its network of banking locations — both in-store and full-service branches.

Mergers and Acquisitions
In December 2014 the company acquired OmniAmerican Bank to boost its loan business and expand its footprint to the Dallas area. The deal added 14 full-service branches in the 12-county Dallas/Fort Worth metroplex and more than $763 million in new loan business.

EXECUTIVES
Senior Executive Vice President, Jeryl Story
President and CEO Southside Bancshares and Southside Bank, Lee R. Gibson, age 62, $493,325 total compensation
Regional President North Texas Southside Bank, Tim Carter, age 64
Regional President Central Texas Southside Bank, Peter M. Boyd, age 63, $435,510 total compensation
EVP and Chief Credit Officer Southside Bank, Earl W. (Bill) Clawater, age 65, $265,000 total compensation
EVP and Chief Analytics Officer Southside Bank and Company Secretary, Brian K. McCabe, age 58, $228,385 total compensation
Regional President East Texas Southside Bank, Tim Alexander, age 62
EVP and CFO, Julie N. Shamburger, age 56
Assistant Vice President Marketing, Jill Payne
Assistant Vice President, Julie A Brown
Vice President, Jeff Quesenberry

Vice President, Cindy Davis
Senior Vice President, Michael Custer
Senior Vice President, Kim Partin
Vice President Branch Manager, Tara Suttle
Executive Vice President, Debra Rutledge
Vp Of Information Technology, Gina Heppel
Senior Vice President, Zelton Harvey
Senior Vice President, Doug Cassidy
Vice President, Julie Hunter
Assistant Vice President, Tanya Merritt
Senior Vice President, Mary Mclarry
VP Internal Audit, Misty de Wet
Vice President Business Services, Grant Williams
Senior Vice President, Landon Brim
Senior Vice President Loan Operations, Krystyna Alexander
Vp Sr. Credit Analyst, Ken Hetherington
Vp Commercial Lending, Ryan Reeve
Executive Vice President, Brad Browder
Vice President Special Assets, Ginger Hines
Vp Mortgage Loan Officer, Gary Gardner
Assistant Vice President Project Management, Niki Hughes
Vice President, Bradan Myrick
Vice Chairman, John R. (Bob) Garrett, age 66
Chairman, W.D. (Joe) Norton, age 82
Board Member, Elaine Anderson
Auditors: Ernst & Young LLP

LOCATIONS

HQ: Southside Bancshares, Inc.
1201 S. Beckham Avenue, Tyler, TX 75701
Phone: 903 531-7111
Web: www.southside.com

PRODUCTS/OPERATIONS

2014 Sales

	$ mil.	% of total
Interest		
Loans	70.6	48
Mortgage-backed & related securities	28.2	19
Investment securities	24.7	16
Other	0.3	—
Non-interest		
Deposit services	15.3	9
Gain on sale of securities	2.9	2
Trust income	3.1	2
Back owned life insurance income	1.4	1
Gain on sale of loans	0.3	—
Other	4.3	3
Adjustments	(2.8)	—
Total	**148.3**	**100**

COMPETITORS

Bank of America	Jacksonville Bancorp of Illinois
Capital One	
East Texas Financial	Regions Financial

HISTORICAL FINANCIALS

Company Type: Public

Income Statement — FYE: December 31

	ASSETS ($ mil.)	NET INCOME ($ mil.)	INCOME AS % OF ASSETS	EMPLOYEES
12/18	6,123.4	74.1	1.2%	820
12/17	6,498.1	54.3	0.8%	855
12/16	5,563.7	49.3	0.9%	679
12/15	5,162.0	44.0	0.9%	683
12/14	4,807.2	20.8	0.4%	813
Annual Growth	6.2%	37.3%	—	0.2%

2018 Year-End Financials

Return on assets: 1.1%
Return on equity: 9.9%
Long-term debt ($ mil.): —
No. of shares (mil.): 33.7
Sales ($ mil): 269.9
Dividends Yield: 3.7%
Payout: 62.1%
Market value ($ mil.): 1,071.0

	STOCK PRICE ($) FY Close	P/E High/Low	PER SHARE ($) Earnings	Dividends	Book Value
12/18	31.75	17 14	2.11	1.20	21.68
12/17	33.68	21 17	1.81	1.10	21.55
12/16	37.67	21 11	1.81	0.96	17.71
12/15	24.02	19 15	1.61	0.92	16.25
12/14	28.91	36 26	0.96	0.84	15.61
Annual Growth	2.4%	— —	21.6%	9.3%	8.6%

Spartan Motors, Inc.

Spartan Motors has built itself on the foundation of its chassis. Founded in 1975 Spartan Motors (through its core Spartan Chassis unit) makes custom chassis for fire trucks motor homes and other specialty vehicles including mine resistant and light armored vehicles for the US military. The company also manufactures emergency vehicles through Spartan USA which was formed with the 2016 merger of three subsidiaries: Crimson Fire Aerials Crimson Fire and Utilimaster. Other operations manufacture chassis and other products to customer specifications for use in the package delivery one-way truck rental bakery and snack delivery utility and linen and uniform rental sectors.

Operations
Spartan operates through three reportable segments: Emergency Response Vehicles (34% of sales) Delivery and Service Vehicles (41%) and Specialty Chassis and Vehicles (25%).

Geographic Reach
The company has facilities in Michigan Pennsylvania South Dakota and Indiana. Spartan markets its products throughout the US and Canada as well as select markets in South America and Asia.

Sales and Marketing
Spartan markets its products primarily through the direct contact of our sales department with OEMs dealers and end users to the recreational vehicle (RV) emergency response government services defense and delivery and service markets.

Strategy
To mitigate its losses Spartan has been streamlining its organizational structure. In 2015 its former Spartan Motors Chassis subsidiary (which operated its Charlotte Michigan location) and its former Crimson Fire Aerials subsidiary (which operated its Ephrata Pennsylvania location) were merged into Spartan USA. In early 2016 its former Utilimaster Corporation subsidiary (which operated its Bristol and Wakarusa Indiana locations) was also merged into Spartan USA.

Mergers and Acquisitions
Spartan bought Royal Truck Body a maker of service truck bodies and accessories in 2019. The deal expanded Spartan's product line within its Specialty Chassis and Vehicles segment while extending the company's footprint in California Arizona and Texas.

In 2018 Spartan acquired Florida-based Strobes-R-Us a provider of upfit services for government and non-government vehicles. The acquisition expands Spartan's product offerings in the fleet and emergency response market and broadens its reach in the southeastern US. The Strobes-R-Us business will operate under Spartan's Fleet Vehicles and Services (FVS) business unit.

Company Background
Spartan Motors was founded in 1975 by George Sztykiel a former lead engineer at Chrysler's heavy truck division along with William Foster Jerry Geary and John Knox. Funded with second mortgages Spartan started by building chassis for customized fire trucks.

EXECUTIVES

Vice President Manufacturing, Art Dickes
President and CEO, Daryl M. Adams, age 58, $620,385 total compensation
President Specialty Vehicles, Steve Guillaume, age 51
CFO, Frederick (Rick) Sohm, age 49, $269,231 total compensation
President Spartan Emergency Response, John W. Slawson, age 53, $250,000 total compensation
President Fleet Vehicles and Services (FVS), Tom Ninneman
Vice President Of Ft Sales, Bill Foster
Chairman, James A. (Jim) Sharman, age 60
Auditors: BDO USA, LLP

LOCATIONS

HQ: Spartan Motors, Inc.
1541 Reynolds Road, Charlotte, MI 48813
Phone: 517 543-6400
Web: www.SpartanMotors.com

PRODUCTS/OPERATIONS

2015 Sales

	$ mil.	% of total
Delivery and services vehicles	227.7	41
Emergency response vehicles	187.1	34
Specialty chassis and vehicles	135.6	25
Total	**550.4**	**100**

2015 Sales by market

	% of total
Emergency response vehicles	34
Aftermarket parts and assemblies	3
Defense vehicles	1
Total	**0**
Delivery and service vehicles	41
Motor home chassis	19
Other vehicles	2
Total	**100**

Selected Products

Spartan Chassis
Assembly and component integration for military vehicles including Mine Resistant Ambush
Custom cabs and chassis for fire apparatusCustom chassis for Class A motorhomesProtected or MRAP program and Iraqi Light Armored Vehic
Classic Fire LLC
Crimson Fire Aerials Inc.
Crimson Fire Inc.
Spartan Motors Chassis Inc.
Utilimaster Corporation

COMPETITORS

Alamo Group	Mack Trucks
Collins Industries	Navistar International
Daimler	Oshkosh Truck
E-ONE	Pierce Manufacturing

Federal Signal
Ford Motor
Freightliner Custom Chassis
LCI Industries
Supreme Industries
Terex
Thor Industries
Volvo
Winnebago

HISTORICAL FINANCIALS
Company Type: Public

Income Statement — FYE: December 31

	REVENUE ($ mil.)	NET INCOME ($ mil.)	NET PROFIT MARGIN	EMPLOYEES
12/18	816.1	15.0	1.8%	2,338
12/17	707.1	15.9	2.3%	2,327
12/16	590.7	8.6	1.5%	2,340
12/15	550.4	(16.9)	—	1,900
12/14	506.7	1.1	0.2%	1,600
Annual Growth	12.7%	89.1%	—	9.9%

2018 Year-End Financials
Debt ratio: 7.2%
Return on equity: 8.4%
Cash ($ mil.): 27.4
Current ratio: 1.78
Long-term debt ($ mil.): 25.5
No. of shares (mil.): 35.3
Dividends
  Yield: 1.3%
  Payout: 22.2%
Market value ($ mil.): 255.0

	STOCK PRICE ($) FY Close	P/E High/Low	PER SHARE ($) Earnings	Dividends	Book Value
12/18	7.23	43 16	0.43	0.10	5.29
12/17	15.75	38 14	0.46	0.10	4.81
12/16	9.25	39 11	0.25	0.10	4.47
12/15	3.11	— —	(0.50)	0.10	4.35
12/14	5.26	226 143	0.03	0.10	4.95
Annual Growth	8.3%	—	94.6%	(0.0%)	1.7%

SPS Commerce, Inc.

SPS Commerce answers the supply chain SOS. Founded in 1987 as St. Paul Software the company offers an Internet-based suite of supply chain management software to consumer goods suppliers retailers distributors and logistics companies in North America. Its software which is maintained and delivered as a service via the cloud is used by customers to manage place and fill orders and track the shipments of goods. Customers can electronically send invoices shipping notices and purchase orders automate shipment functions and evaluate the performance of their vendors or suppliers. Best Buy Costco and Callaway Golf are among SPS's thousands of customers.

Geographic Reach
The company operates in New Jersey and internationally in China India Australia and the UK. It has sales offices in North America as well as in China Hong Kong and Australia.

Sales and Marketing
SPS boasts 60000 customers many of which are small-to mid-sized suppliers in the consumer packaging industry. Its sales force is organized into teams that target customers in different industries including retail and supply companies.

Financial Performance
SPS maintained its chain of years with strong revenue increases in 2014. Revenue rose 23% to $128 million with more recurring revenue customers and higher revenue per customers. The average recurring revenue per recurring revenue customer (the company condenses it to "wallet") was $5525 in 2014 compared to $4920 in 2013. The number of such customers was about 21000 in 2014 up from 19700 in 2013.

Profit was up 157% to $2.7 million in 2014 on the higher revenue and other income from operations. Cash flow from operations slipped to $16.8 million in 2014 from $18.24 million the previous year.

Mergers and Acquisitions
SPS's acquisition strategy looks for businesses that will bring in new customers offer compelling potential for expanding into new regions or sectors or boost product functionality.

The company's 2018 acquisition of CovalentWorks a provider of cloud-based EDI software brought about 2000 small and medium-sized businesses to SPS. The deal was valued at about $23 million.

EXECUTIVES

President and CEO, Archie C. Black, age 57, $370,000 total compensation
EVP and COO, James J. (Jim) Frome, age 54, $271,025 total compensation
EVP and CFO, Kimberly K. (Kim) Nelson, age 52, $270,000 total compensation
SVP and Chief Marketing Offcier, Peter Zaballos
SVP and Chief Technology Officer, Jamie Thingelstad
Vice President Information Systems, Richard Perrin
Divisional Vice President Of Finance And Operations, Nick Ilacqua
Auditors: KPMG LLP

LOCATIONS

HQ: SPS Commerce, Inc.
333 South Seventh Street, Suite 1000, Minneapolis, MN 55402
Phone: 612 435-9400
Web: www.spscommerce.com

COMPETITORS

GXS
IBM
Open EC
Seeburger
TIBCO Software

HISTORICAL FINANCIALS
Company Type: Public

Income Statement — FYE: December 31

	REVENUE ($ mil.)	NET INCOME ($ mil.)	NET PROFIT MARGIN	EMPLOYEES
12/18	248.2	23.8	9.6%	1,231
12/17	220.5	(2.4)	—	1,336
12/16	193.3	5.7	3.0%	1,217
12/15	158.5	4.6	2.9%	1,046
12/14	127.9	2.7	2.1%	943
Annual Growth	18.0%	72.4%	—	6.9%

2018 Year-End Financials
Debt ratio: —
Return on equity: 8.0%
Cash ($ mil.): 133.8
Current ratio: 4.42
Long-term debt ($ mil.): —
No. of shares (mil.): 34.6
Dividends
  Yield: —
  Payout: —
Market value ($ mil.): 2,858.0

	STOCK PRICE ($) FY Close	P/E High/Low	PER SHARE ($) Earnings	Dividends	Book Value
12/18	82.38	144 70	0.68	0.00	9.19
12/17	48.59	— —	(0.07)	0.00	8.08
12/16	69.89	436 231	0.17	0.00	7.30
12/15	70.21	552 385	0.14	0.00	6.64
12/14	56.63	837 569	0.08	0.00	6.27
Annual Growth	9.8%	—	70.7%	—	10.0%

STAG Industrial Inc

If STAG Industrial were to show up alone at a party it would likely be on the hunt for single tenants looking to lease industrial space. The self-managed and self-administered real estate investment trust (REIT) has built a business acquiring and managing single-tenant industrial properties located across more than 35 states. The company's portfolio consists primarily of 50 million sq. ft. of leasable warehouse distribution manufacturing and office space located in secondary markets. STAG conducts most of its business through its operating partner STAG Industrial Operating Partnership. The Massachusetts-based REIT went public in 2011.

Operations
STAG's property portfolio consists of 265 buildings spanning some 54 million sq. ft. across 37 states. More than 83% of its rental income comes from its warehouse/distribution building properties while some 10% comes from its light manufacturing building properties. The rest of its rental revenue comes from its flex-office buildings. Its properties are about 95% leased to a collective 227 tenants.

Key subsidiaries include STAG Industrial Operating Partnership STAG Industrial GP STAG Industrial Management STAG Industrial TRS and STAG Investments Holdings III among others.

Geographic Reach
Based in Massachusetts STAG owns and manages single-tenant industrial properties across 30-plus states. Nearly 40% of its rental income came from its properties in the states of North Carolina Ohio Illinois Pennsylvania and Texas.

Sales and Marketing
STAG made over 50% of its rental income from tenants out of five industries including: Automotive; Industrial Equipment Components & Metals; Containers & Packaging; Air Freight and Logistics; and Food and Beverages. While none of its tenants accounted for more than 3% of its total rental income its top five customers in 2014 included Deckers Outdoor Corporation Solo Cup Company International Paper Company Bank of America and Exel Logistics.

Financial Performance
STAG Industrial's revenues have nearly quadrupled since 2011 as it has expanded its property portfolio through acquisitions and has charged higher rental rates as the economy has strengthened. The REIT has also suffered losses in recent years mostly as its interest expenses on its long-term debt have been higher than its operating profits.

The REIT's revenue jumped 30% to a record $173.82 million in 2014 thanks to continued growth in rental income from newly acquired properties. STAG's same store rental revenue declined by less than 1% mostly due to vacancies and tenants downsizing their spaces. Same store occupancy rates declined by two percentage points to 92.7%.

Despite generating higher revenue in 2014 STAG suffered a $4 million loss during the year mostly due to a $20.5 million increase in depreciation and amortization expenses stemming from its acquired properties. Its interest expenses increased by $4.8 million as its debt levels grew also hurting the company's bottom line. STAG's operating cash levels grew by 17% to $96.7 million in 2014 mostly thanks to higher cash revenue stemming from its property acquisitions.

Strategy

STAG Industrial acquires direct and indirect ownership of industrial space in secondary markets across the US — including small cities and towns and suburban areas — to grow its rental revenue. STAG typically purchases individual Class B single-tenant industrial properties located in secondary markets nationwide with its purchase prices ranging from $5 million to $25 million.

During 2014 the REIT acquired 43 industrial buildings spanning 9.3 million sq. ft. for $425 million while its pipeline of potential acquisitions included some 85 industrial buildings exceeding $1.1 billion in value. In mid-2013 STAG acquired eight warehouse and distribution facilities located in Belvidere Illinois and two light manufacturing facilities located near Grand Rapids Michigan. Altogether the 10 properties comprise more than 1.1 million sq. ft.

Some of its other recent purchases include its late 2012 buy of a Massachusetts warehouse and distribution facility containing a total of 217000 sq. ft. and a Michigan light manufacturing and warehouse facility that comprises a total of 108000 sq. ft. (both deals for $13.4 million); a portfolio of 31 primarily single tenant industrial buildings (for about $129 million); and three industrial buildings containing a total of 518838 sq. ft. ($19.8 million).

Company Background

The company's CEO and founder Benjamin S. Butcher founded STAG Industrial's predecessor companies in 2003. Butcher and other investors formed STAG Industrial to consolidate the companies' assets under a REIT umbrella for tax purposes and to raise public funds.

EXECUTIVES

EVP and COO, Stephen C. Mecke, age 56, $309,000 total compensation
Chairman President and CEO, Benjamin S. Butcher, age 66, $515,000 total compensation
EVP and Director Real Estate Operations, David G. King, age 51, $272,950 total compensation
CFO, William R. Crooker
EVP General Counsel and Secretary, Jeffrey M. Sullivan
SVP Data Analytics and Technology, Peter S. Fearey
SVP and Regional Director East, David A. Barker
Auditors: PricewaterhouseCoopers LLP

LOCATIONS

HQ: STAG Industrial Inc
One Federal Street, 23rd Floor, Boston, MA 02110
Phone: 617 574-4777   **Fax:** 617 574-0052
Web: www.stagindustrial.com

PRODUCTS/OPERATIONS

2014 Sales

	$ mil.	% of total
Rental income	149.5	86
Tenant recoveries	23.6	14
Others	0.7	—
Total	**173.8**	**100**

COMPETITORS

First Industrial Realty
Liberty Property Trust
Monmouth Real Estate
Prologis
Welsh Property Trust

HISTORICAL FINANCIALS

Company Type: Public

Income Statement FYE: December 31

	REVENUE ($ mil.)	NET INCOME ($ mil.)	NET PROFIT MARGIN	EMPLOYEES
12/18	350.9	92.9	26.5%	73
12/17	301.0	31.2	10.4%	72
12/16	250.2	34.5	13.8%	68
12/15	218.6	(29.4)	—	68
12/14	173.8	(4.0)	—	54
Annual Growth	19.2%	—	—	7.8%

2018 Year-End Financials

Debt ratio: 42.7%
Return on equity: 6.2%
Cash ($ mil.): 7.9
Current ratio: 0.76
Long-term debt ($ mil.): 1,325.9
No. of shares (mil.): 112.1
Dividends
  Yield: 5.7%
  Payout: 179.7%
Market value ($ mil.): 2,791.0

	STOCK PRICE ($) FY Close	P/E High/Low	PER SHARE ($) Earnings	Dividends	Book Value
12/18	24.88	36 28	0.79	1.42	14.39
12/17	27.33	120 95	0.23	1.41	14.01
12/16	23.87	88 52	0.29	1.39	12.78
12/15	18.45	— —	(0.61)	1.37	12.05
12/14	24.50	— —	(0.28)	1.29	13.41
Annual Growth	0.4%	—	—	2.4%	1.8%

Stamps.com Inc.

Stamps.com hopes its customers keep putting letters in the mail. Its PC Postage Service lets registered users who have downloaded Stamps.com software buy stamps online and print the postage directly onto envelopes and labels. Customers can order US Postal Service options such as registered mail certified mail and delivery confirmation as well as print custom stamps using virtually any image through its PhotoStamps.com website. Stamps.com charges a monthly fee for its service which is aimed at consumers home offices and small businesses. In addition customers can buy mailing labels scales and dedicated postage printers from Stamps.com. Postage fees are sent directly to the US Postal Service.

Operations

The company operates through the single segment of Internet Mailing and Shipping Services offering customized postage under the PhotoStamps and PictureItPostage brand names. Revenue from services accounted for 83% in 2015.

Sales and Marketing

Stamps.com taps several channels to market its business. It relies on affiliated channels direct mail direct sales offline marketing programs partnerships traditional media and online advertising. Its target niche customer continues to be small businesses individuals home offices mid-sized businesses and large enterprises. It services to more than 600000 customers.

Financial Performance

Stamps.com has experienced significant revenue growth over the years with revenues peaking at a record-setting $214 million in 2015. However it suffered its first net loss ($2.4 million) in at least 10 years in 2015. After rising for several straight years the company's operating cash flow declined by 11% during 2015.

The historic revenue growth for 2015 was fueled by substantial increases in services (53%) insurance (27%) customized postage (33%) and other (78%) revenue. Services increased due to a surge in annual average paid customers and an increase in annual average service revenue per paid customer. Product revenue increased due to additional sales of mailing and shipping labels and label printers as those businesses continued to grow their customer base. Other product lines grew through acquisitions.

Its net loss for 2015 was fueled by a surge in general and administrative expenses related to its ShipStation ShipWorks and Endicia acquisitions increases in headcount and expenses related to infrastructure investments.

Mergers and Acquisitions

Stamps.com also seeks add-on acquisitions to grow its business organically. In 2015 it obtained PSI Systems a California corporation doing business as Endicia. Endicia is a provider of high volume shipping technologies and services for shipping with the USPS and was purchased for $215 million in cash. The deal accelerated its high volume and e-commerce shipping capabilities.

Adding both new customers and a couple of brand names to its portfolio Stamps.com in 2014 acquired Austin Texas-based ShipStation for about $50 million in cash. The business offers monthly subscription-based e-commerce shipping software primarily under the ShipStation and Auctane brands.

Company Background

Stamps.com was founded as StampMaster in 1996. The company changed its name to Stamps.com in 1998 and went public the following year.

EXECUTIVES

Vice President Marketing, Mark Krojansky
Chairman and CEO, Kenneth (Ken) McBride, age 52, $595,833 total compensation
President, Kyle Huebner, age 49, $364,583 total compensation
VP Postal Technology and Affairs, J.P. Leon, $185,691 total compensation
Chief Product and Strategy Officer, John Clem, age 48, $287,083 total compensation

CTO, Michael Biswas, age 42, $279,167 total compensation
VP Information Technology, Michael Patchen
CFO, Jeff Carberry, age 45
Vice President, Leslie Loomans
Senior Vice President And General Manager, Doug Walner
Board Member, Bradford Jones
SECRETARY, John W Owen
SECRETARY, John Owen
Auditors: Ernst & Young LLP

LOCATIONS
HQ: Stamps.com Inc.
1990 E. Grand Avenue, El Segundo, CA 90245
Phone: 310 482-5800
Web: www.stamps.com

PRODUCTS/OPERATIONS

SELECTED PRODUCTS & SERVICES:
USPS Mailing and Shipping Services
Multi-Carrier Shipping Services
Mailing and Shipping Integrations
Mailing & Shipping Supplies Stores
Branded Insurance
International

2015 Sales

	$ mil.	% of total
Service	176.6	83
Product	18.2	9
Insurance	11.7	5
Customized postage revenue	7.1	3
Other	0.4	-
Total	214.0	100

BRANDS
Stamps.com
Endicia
ShipStation
ShipWorks
PRODUCT CATEGORIES
Products
Small Office Mailers
Online Sellers
Warehouse Shippers
Corporate Postage Solutions
PhotoStamps
Supplies

COMPETITORS
Endicia	Pitney Bowes
FedEx	UPS
Neopost USA	US Postal Service
Newell Brands	eBay

HISTORICAL FINANCIALS
Company Type: Public

Income Statement — FYE: December 31

	REVENUE ($ mil.)	NET INCOME ($ mil.)	NET PROFIT MARGIN	EMPLOYEES
12/18	586.9	168.6	28.7%	1,179
12/17	468.7	150.6	32.1%	825
12/16	364.3	75.2	20.7%	700
12/15	213.9	(4.2)	—	600
12/14	147.2	36.8	25.0%	343
Annual Growth	41.3%	46.2%	—	36.2%

2018 Year-End Financials
Debt ratio: 7.1%
Return on equity: 30.3%
Cash ($ mil.): 113.7
Current ratio: 1.52
Long-term debt ($ mil.): 50.1
No. of shares (mil.): 17.6
Dividends
  Yield: —
  Payout: —
Market value ($ mil.): 2,749.0

	STOCK PRICE ($) FY Close	P/E High/Low	PER SHARE ($) Earnings	Dividends	Book Value
12/18	155.64	30 15	8.99	0.00	34.74
12/17	188.00	26 12	8.19	0.00	28.33
12/16	114.65	28 16	4.12	0.00	22.06
12/15	109.61	— —	(0.26)	0.00	14.31
12/14	47.99	22 13	2.25	0.00	12.82
Annual Growth	34.2%	— —	41.4%	—	28.3%

Standard AVB Financial Corp

EXECUTIVES
Vice Chairman, Dale A. Walker, age 66
President CEO and Director Standard Financial Corp. and Standard Bank, Timothy K. Zimmerman, age 65, $217,885 total compensation
SVP and CFO Standard Financial Corp. and Standard Bank, Colleen M. Brown, age 57, $96,687 total compensation
SVP and Chief Commercial Loan Officer Standard Financial Corp. and Standard Bank, Paul A. Knapp, age 62, $89,008 total compensation
Chairman, Terence L. Graft, age 66
Director and Business Development Coordinator Standard Bank, David C. Mathews, age 61
Marketing Manager, Vanessa Saxton
VP Director of Technology, Sheila D. Crystaloski
VP Controller, Susan A. Parente
Vice Chairman, Dale A. Walker, age 66
President CEO and Director Standard Financial Corp. and Standard Bank, Timothy K. Zimmerman, age 65
Director, Horace G. Cofer, age 78
Director, William T. Ferri, age 71
Director and Business Development Coordinator Standard Bank, David C. Mathews, age 61
Director, Thomas J. Rennie, age 66
Auditors: S.R. Snodgrass, P.C.

LOCATIONS
HQ: Standard AVB Financial Corp
2640 Monroeville Boulevard, Monroeville, PA 15146
Phone: 412 856-0363
Web: www.standardbankpa.com

COMPETITORS
Ally Bank	M&T Bank
Citizens Financial Corp.	PNC Financial
Dollar Bank	S&T Bancorp
First Commonwealth Financial	SunTrust
	Wells Fargo

HISTORICAL FINANCIALS
Company Type: Public

Income Statement — FYE: December 31

	ASSETS ($ mil.)	NET INCOME ($ mil.)	INCOME AS % OF ASSETS	EMPLOYEES
12/18	971.8	8.8	0.9%	158
12/17	972.6	4.3	0.4%	144
12/16*	488.0	0.5	0.1%	0
09/16	495.2	3.0	0.6%	0
09/15	468.2	3.5	0.8%	0
Annual Growth	20.0%	25.6%	—	—

*Fiscal year change

2018 Year-End Financials
Return on assets: 0.9%
Return on equity: 6.4%
Long-term debt ($ mil.): —
No. of shares (mil.): 4.8
Sales ($ mil): 41.1
Dividends
  Yield: 2.9%
  Payout: 48.8%
Market value ($ mil.): 144.0

	STOCK PRICE ($) FY Close	P/E High/Low	PER SHARE ($) Earnings	Dividends	Book Value
12/18	29.88	18 15	1.88	0.88	28.65
12/17	30.08	28 23	1.05	0.77	27.97
12/16*	25.20	111 99	0.23	0.11	28.00
09/16	22.80	21 18	1.22	0.42	28.24
09/15	23.50	17 15	1.37	0.24	27.24
Annual Growth	6.2%	— —	8.2%	38.5%	1.3%

*Fiscal year change

Starwood Property Trust Inc.

Starwood Property Trust hopes to shine brightly in the world of mortgages. A real estate investment trust (REIT) the company originates finances and manages US commercial and residential mortgage loans commercial mortgage-backed securities and other commercial real estate debt investments. It acquires discounted loans from failed banks and financial institutions some through the FDIC which typically auctions off large pools of loan portfolios. Starwood Property Trust is externally managed by SPT Management LLC an affiliate of Starwood Capital Group. As a REIT the trust is exempt from paying federal income tax so long as it distributes quarterly dividends to shareholders.

Financial Performance
Overall revenues grew 63% in 2012 to $327 million up from $201 million in 2011. The trust primarily earns money on interest income from mortgage-backed securities and loans.

Mergers and Acquisitions
In 2013 Starwood Property Trust bought LNR Property LLC a real estate investment finance management and development firm. The trust paid $862 million for LNR's US special servicer the US investment securities portfolio Archetype Mortgage Capital (now Starwood Mortgage Capital) Archetype Financial Institution Services LNR Europe and 50% of LNR's interest in Auction.com.

Later that year it moved to spin off its single-family residential business as a new REIT named

Starwood Waypoint Residential Trust. The trust which will be affiliated with Waypoint Homes will invest own and operate single-family rental homes and non-performing residential mortgage loans in the US.

EXECUTIVES

Chairman and CEO, Barry S. Sternlicht, age 56
EVP and Interim Principal Financial Officer, Jerome C. (Jerry) Silvey, age 58
COO and General Counsel, Andrew J. Sossen, age 39
President and Managing Director, Boyd W. Fellows
CFO, Stew Ward
Chief Credit Officer and Managing Director, Chris Tokarski
Lead Independent Director, Richard Bronson
Chief Originations Officer and Managing Director, Warren de Haan
Independent Director, Camille J. Douglas
Independent Director, Jeffrey DiModica
Independent Director, Strauss Zelnick
Auditors: Deloitte & Touche LLP

LOCATIONS

HQ: Starwood Property Trust Inc.
591 West Putnam Avenue, Greenwich, CT 06830
Phone: 203 422-7700
Web: www.starwoodpropertytrust.com

COMPETITORS

American Capital Agency Corp.	JER Investors Trust
Annaly Capital Management	MFA Financial
	PennyMac Mortgage
Arbor Realty Trust	Petra Real Estate
Colony Northstar	RAIT Financial Trust
Drive Shack	Realty Finance Corporation
Hatteras Financial	Redwood Trust
Invesco Mortgage Capital	Two Harbors
	iStar Financial Inc

HISTORICAL FINANCIALS
Company Type: Public

| Income Statement | | | FYE: December 31 |
	ASSETS ($ mil.)	NET INCOME ($ mil.)	INCOME AS % OF ASSETS	EMPLOYEES
12/18	68,262.4	385.8	0.6%	290
12/17	62,941.2	400.7	0.6%	312
12/16	77,256.2	365.1	0.5%	340
12/15	85,738.1	450.7	0.5%	450
12/14	116,099.3	495.0	0.4%	468
Annual Growth	(12.4%)	(6.0%)	—	(11.3%)

2018 Year-End Financials
Return on assets: 0.5%
Return on equity: 8.5%
Long-term debt ($ mil.): —
No. of shares (mil.): 275.6
Sales ($ mil): 1,109.2
Dividends
  Yield: 9.7%
  Payout: 135.2%
Market value ($ mil.): 5,433.0

	STOCK PRICE ($) FY Close	P/E High/Low	PER SHARE ($) Earnings	Dividends	Book Value
12/18	19.71	16 13	1.42	1.92	16.70
12/17	21.35	15 14	1.52	1.92	17.13
12/16	21.95	15 11	1.50	1.92	17.44
12/15	20.56	13 10	1.91	1.92	17.43
12/14	23.24	13 10	2.24	1.92	17.27
Annual Growth	(4.0%)	—	(10.8%)	(0.0%)	(0.8%)

Sterling Bancorp (DE)

EXECUTIVES

Chief Administrative Officer Senior Executive Vice President, Rodney Whitwell
Executive Vice President General Counsel Chief Legal Officer, James Blose
Executive Vice President Marketing, Anthony Burke
Senior Managing Director And Svp, Tammy Leisen
Vice President Managing Director, Michael Gogitidze
Assistant Vice President Client Service Manager, Jason Solow
Vice President Managing Director, Lisa Congemi-doutney
Vp and Director Compliance Assurance, Dawn Arenella
Vp Director Facilities Procurement And Vendor Management, Michele Miuta
Svp Director Consumer Banking Network, James Griffin
Svp Director Consumer Banking Administration, Michael Lechleider
Vice President And Managing Director, Craig Levy
Vice President Senior Credit Officer Leg, James Schanter
Assistant Vice President Secondary Marketing Analyst, Michelle Bobrow
Operations Workflow Integration Leader Vp, Krista Gulalo
Auditors: Crowe LLP

LOCATIONS

HQ: Sterling Bancorp (DE)
400 Rella Boulevard, Montebello, NY 10901
Phone: 845 369-8040
Web: www.sterlingbancorp.com

COMPETITORS

Capital One	JPMorgan Chase
Citibank	KeyCorp
HSBC USA	M&T Bank

HISTORICAL FINANCIALS
Company Type: Public

| Income Statement | | | FYE: December 31 |
	ASSETS ($ mil.)	NET INCOME ($ mil.)	INCOME AS % OF ASSETS	EMPLOYEES
12/18	31,383.3	447.2	1.4%	1,907
12/17	30,359.5	93.0	0.3%	2,076
12/16	14,178.4	139.9	1.0%	970
12/15	11,955.9	66.1	0.6%	1,089
12/14	7,424.8	17.0	0.2%	829
Annual Growth	43.4%	126.5%	—	23.2%

2018 Year-End Financials
Return on assets: 1.4%
Return on equity: 10.3%
Long-term debt ($ mil.): —
No. of shares (mil.): 216.2
Sales ($ mil): 1,299.8
Dividends
  Yield: 1.7%
  Payout: 14.3%
Market value ($ mil.): 3,570.0

	STOCK PRICE ($) FY Close	P/E High/Low	PER SHARE ($) Earnings	Dividends	Book Value
12/18	16.51	13 8	1.95	0.28	20.48
12/17	24.60	45 36	0.58	0.28	18.86
12/16	23.40	23 13	1.07	0.28	13.72
12/15	16.22	29 22	0.60	0.28	12.81
12/14	14.38	72 63	0.20	0.28	11.62
Annual Growth	3.5%	—	76.7%	(0.0%)	15.2%

Sterling Bancorp Inc (MI)

Auditors: Crowe LLP

LOCATIONS

HQ: Sterling Bancorp Inc (MI)
One Towne Square, Suite 1900, Southfield, MI 48076
Phone: 248 355-2400
Web: www.sterlingbank.com

HISTORICAL FINANCIALS
Company Type: Public

| Income Statement | | | FYE: December 31 |
	ASSETS ($ mil.)	NET INCOME ($ mil.)	INCOME AS % OF ASSETS	EMPLOYEES
12/18	3,196.7	63.4	2.0%	352
12/17	2,961.9	37.9	1.3%	308
12/16	2,163.6	33.2	1.5%	294
12/15	1,712.0	22.5	1.3%	0
Annual Growth	23.1%	41.3%	—	—

2018 Year-End Financials
Return on assets: 2.0%
Return on equity: 20.8%
Long-term debt ($ mil.): —
No. of shares (mil.): 53.0
Sales ($ mil): 183.8
Dividends
  Yield: 0.5%
  Payout: 3.8%
Market value ($ mil.): 368.0

	STOCK PRICE ($) FY Close	P/E High/Low	PER SHARE ($) Earnings	Dividends	Book Value
12/18	6.95	12 6	1.20	0.04	6.32
12/17	12.70	16 15	0.82	0.21	5.16
12/16	0.00	— —	0.73	0.19	3.58
Annual Growth	—	—	—	28.2% (54.1%)	32.8%

Sterling Construction Co Inc

Sterling Construction company specializes in the building reconstruction and repair of transportation and water infrastructure. It also works on specialty projects such as excavation shoring and drilling. The heavy civil construction company and its subsidiaries (Texas Sterling Construction Ralph L. Wadsworth Contractors RDI Foundation Drilling Myers and Sons Banicki Construction and Road and Highway Builders) primarily serve public sector clients throughout the Southwest and West. Transportation projects include excavation and asphalt paving as well as construction of bridges and rail systems. Water projects include work on sewers and storm drainage systems.

Geographic Reach

Houston-based Sterling Construction and its subsidiaries operate from offices in Texas California Arizona Utah and Nevada. The firm's major markets include Texas Utah and Nevada.

Financial Performance

The economic recession and prolonged recovery has taken its toll on Sterling Construction. The company reported a net loss of $297 million in 2012 following a loss of $36 million in 2011. The company attributed the losses which continued in 2013 primarily to additional write-downs on three large projects booked prior to 2012 in Texas that continue to have a negative impact on profitability. Sterling says it expects the projects to be substantially complete by mid-2014.

Revenue is improving however. In 2012 sales increased 26% compared with 2011 to $630.5 million driven by projects in in Arizona and California. Indeed 2012 marked the third consecutive year of rising sales for the firm. While the revenue picture is brighter profits are still expected to suffer as Sterling faces increased competitive pressure to bid low for construction projects.

Strategy

Sterling Construction and other companies that rely heavily on government highway work have been hurt buy Congress' inability to pass the Federal Highway Bill. Without new legislation new projects and funding for the work is uncertain. In response to the uncertain outlook Sterling refocused on project execution and conservative bidding. The company also sold some equipment in order to raise cash to upgrade its fleet.

Sterling Construction's long-term strategy is to expand its geographic footprint to attractive markets. The company also seeks to add to its construction capabilities. It has mostly used acquisitions to achieve those goals.

Increased competition has sent Sterling looking for work in new markets. As a result it has landed contracts in places such as Hawaii Montana Idaho and Louisiana. Sterling also expanded its operations in Texas to include El Paso and Corpus Christi. The company continues to seek opportunities in new markets in western southwestern and southeastern states. Sterling also is seeking to work on larger higher-margin design/build projects by entering joint ventures. One example is Ralph L. Wadsworth Contractors' joint venture with Fluor and two other companies to build a $1.2 billion project on I-15 in Utah.

Mergers and Acquisitions

In January 2013 the firm acquired the remaining 20% interest in Ralph L. Wadsworth Construction Co. from its management for $23.1 million. In 2011 Sterling expanded into Arizona and California with the acquisition of J. Banicki Construction. Also that year Sterling bought a 50% stake in California-based Myer & Sons Construction.

EXECUTIVES

Senior Vice President Chief Compliance And Administration Officer, Craig Allen
Vice President Special Projects, Joseph Malucci
SENIOR VICE PRESIDENT ENVIRONMENTAL HEALTH AND SAFETY AND OQ, Todd Johnson
Executive Vice President General Counsel Secretary, Richard Chandler
Vice President And Chief Talent Officer, Kate Sberna
Board Member, Richard Schaum
Board Member, Raymond Messer
Auditors: Grant Thornton LLP

LOCATIONS

HQ: Sterling Construction Co Inc
1800 Hughes Landing Blvd., The Woodlands, TX 77380
Phone: 281 214-0800
Web: www.strlco.com

PRODUCTS/OPERATIONS

Selected Subsidiaries
J. Banicki Construction Inc. (Banicki)
Myers and Sons Construction
Ralph L. Wadsworth Contractors LLC (RLW)
RDI Foundation Drilling (RDI)
Road and Highway Builders LLC (RHB)
Road and Highway Builders of California (RHBCa)
Texas Sterling Construction Co. (TSC)

COMPETITORS

Austin Industries
Bechtel
Boh Bros Construction
Clyde Companies
Fluor
Furmanite
Holloman
Insituform Technologies
J.D. Abrams
McCarthy Building
Meadow Valley
Michael Baker
Peter Kiewit Sons'
Williams Brothers Construction
Zachry Inc.

HISTORICAL FINANCIALS
Company Type: Public

Income Statement   FYE: December 31

	REVENUE ($ mil.)	NET INCOME ($ mil.)	NET PROFIT MARGIN	EMPLOYEES
12/18	1,037.6	25.1	2.4%	1,935
12/17	957.9	11.6	1.2%	1,740
12/16	690.1	(9.2)	—	1,684
12/15	623.6	(20.4)	—	1,565
12/14	672.2	(9.7)	—	1,799
Annual Growth	11.5%	—	—	1.8%

2018 Year-End Financials
Debt ratio: 17.0%
Return on equity: 16.4%
Cash ($ mil.): 94.1
Current ratio: 1.69
Long-term debt ($ mil.): 79.1
No. of shares (mil.): 26.6
Dividends
 Yield: —
 Payout: —
Market value ($ mil.): 290.0

	STOCK PRICE ($) FY Close	P/E High/Low	PER SHARE ($) Earnings	Dividends	Book Value
12/18	10.89	17 11	0.93	0.00	6.18
12/17	16.28	41 18	0.43	0.00	5.22
12/16	8.46	— —	(0.40)	0.00	4.30
12/15	6.08	— —	(2.02)	0.00	4.85
12/14	6.39	— —	(0.54)	0.00	7.11
Annual Growth	14.3%	— —	—	—	(3.4%)

Stitch Fix Inc

Auditors: DELOITTE & TOUCHE LLP

LOCATIONS

HQ: Stitch Fix Inc
1 Montgomery Street, Suite 1500, San Francisco, CA 94104
Phone: 415 882-7765
Web: www.stitchfix.com

HISTORICAL FINANCIALS
Company Type: Public

Income Statement   FYE: August 3

	REVENUE ($ mil.)	NET INCOME ($ mil.)	NET PROFIT MARGIN	EMPLOYEES
08/19*	1,577.5	36.8	2.3%	8,000
07/18	1,226.5	44.9	3.7%	6,600
07/17	977.1	(0.5)	—	5,800
07/16	730.3	33.1	4.5%	0
Annual Growth	29.3%	3.6%	—	—

*Fiscal year change

2019 Year-End Financials
Debt ratio: —
Return on equity: 10.2%
Cash ($ mil.): 170.9
Current ratio: 2.64
Long-term debt ($ mil.): —
No. of shares (mil.): 101.4
Dividends
 Yield: —
 Payout: —
Market value ($ mil.): 2,518.0

	STOCK PRICE ($) FY Close	P/E High/Low	PER SHARE ($) Earnings	Dividends	Book Value
08/19*	24.83	138 45	0.36	0.00	3.91
07/18	29.51	73 32	0.34	0.00	3.19
07/17	0.00	— —	(0.02)	0.00	3.88
Annual Growth	—	— —	—	—	0.3%

*Fiscal year change

Stock Yards Bancorp Inc

Stock Yards Bancorp is the holding company of Stock Yards Bank & Trust which operates about 35 branches mostly in Louisville Kentucky but also in Indianapolis and Cincinnati. Founded in 1904 the $3 billion-asset bank targets individuals and regional business customers offering standard retail services such as checking and savings accounts credit cards certificates of deposit and IRAs. It also provides trust services while brokerage and credit card services are offered through agreements with other banks. Commercial real estate mortgages make up 40% of the bank's loan portfolio which also includes commercial and industrial loans (30%) residential mortgages (15%) construction loans and consumer loans.

Operations

Stock Yards Bank & Trust operates two main business lines: Commercial Banking which provides loans and deposits to individual consumers and businesses as well as mortgage origination and company brokerage activity; and Investment Management and Trust which provides wealth management services such as investment management trust estate administration and retirement plan services.

About 63% of the company's total revenue came from loan interest during 2015 while another 7% came from interest income on its securities. The rest came from its investment management and trust services (13% of revenue) deposit account service charges (7%) bankcard transaction revenue (4%) mortgage banking revenue (3%) brokerage commissions and fees (1%) and other non-interest sources.

Geographic Reach
Kentucky-based Stock Yards Bancorp had 37 branches at the end of 2015 including 28 branches in the Louisville Kentucky metro area and the rest in the Indianapolis Indiana and Cincinnati Ohio metro areas.

Financial Performance
Stock Yards' annual revenues have risen 11% since 2011 thanks to a combination of mostly organic loan growth and investment management and trust services fee growth. Meanwhile its annual profits have grown more than 55% on declining loan loss provisions as its loan portfolio's credit quality has improved with higher property valuations in the strengthened economy.

The bank's revenue climbed 4% to a record $133.12 million during 2015 on higher interest income mostly as its loan assets grew 9% to $2 billion with record loan production.

Revenue growth and a decline in interest expense on deposits in 2015 drove Stock Yard's net income up 7% to a record $34.82 million. The bank's operating cash levels jumped 8% to $43.17 million mostly thanks to the increase in cash-based earnings.

Strategy
Stock Yards outlined its plans for 2016 and beyond to maintain stable net interest margins achieve near-double digit loan growth manage credit quality to keep loan loss provisions down and increasing its regulatory readiness.

Mergers and Acquisitions
In 2013 the bank extended the reach of its operations into Oldham County through its purchase of $146 million-asset The BANcorp Inc. and its five THE BANK branches in the region for $19.9 million.

EXECUTIVES

SEVP, Kathy C. Thompson, age 57, $345,000 total compensation
Chairman and CEO, David P. Heintzman, age 59, $535,000 total compensation
EVP Secretary Treasurer and CFO, Nancy B. Davis, age 63, $232,000 total compensation
EVP and Chief Lending Officer, Philip S. Poindexter, age 53, $270,000 total compensation
President, James A. (Ja) Hillebrand, age 50, $375,000 total compensation
EVP and Chief Risk Officer, William M. Dishman, age 57
EVP and Chief Strategic Officer, Clay Stinnett
EVP Retail Banking Brokerage and Business Banking, Michael J. Croce
Assistant Vice President Deposit Operations, Marcia Sweat
Vice President Private Banking, Dan Thacker
Vice President Commercial Lending, Kevin Mccullough
Assistant Vice President, June Schenk
Vice President Commerical Lending, Jason Morgan
Board Member, Richard Northern
Auditors: BKD LLP

LOCATIONS
HQ: Stock Yards Bancorp Inc
1040 East Main Street, Louisville, KY 40206
Phone: 502 582-2571
Web: www.syb.com

PRODUCTS/OPERATIONS

2015 Revenues by Category
	$ mil.	% of total
Interest income	93.1	70
Non-interest income	40.0	30
Total	133.1	100

Selected Products & Services
Personal Banking
  Banking
  Personal Lending
  Personal Investing & Wealth Management Services
Business Banking
  Credit Loans & Leasing
  Deposit Services
  Treasury Management
  Business Retirement Plans
Wealth Management Services
  Investment Management
  Financial Planning
  Trust & Estate Services
  Brokerage Service

COMPETITORS
Fifth Third
First Capital
Home Federal
PNC Financial
Porter Bancorp
Republic Bancorp
U.S. Bancorp

HISTORICAL FINANCIALS
Company Type: Public

Income Statement — FYE: December 31

	ASSETS ($ mil.)	NET INCOME ($ mil.)	INCOME AS % OF ASSETS	EMPLOYEES
12/18	3,302.9	55.5	1.7%	591
12/17	3,239.6	38.0	1.2%	580
12/16	3,039.4	41.0	1.3%	578
12/15	2,816.8	37.1	1.3%	555
12/14	2,563.8	34.8	1.4%	524
Annual Growth	6.5%	12.4%	—	3.1%

2018 Year-End Financials
Return on assets: 1.7%
Return on equity: 15.8%
Long-term debt ($ mil.): —
No. of shares (mil.): 22.7
Sales ($ mil): 175.1
Dividends
  Yield: 2.9%
  Payout: 48.2%
Market value ($ mil.): 746.0

	STOCK PRICE ($) FY Close	P/E High	P/E Low	Earnings	Dividends	Book Value
12/18	32.80	17	12	2.42	0.96	16.11
12/17	37.70	28	19	1.66	0.80	14.71
12/16	46.95	26	15	1.80	0.72	13.88
12/15	37.79	24	18	1.65	0.64	12.80
12/14	33.34	21	17	1.57	0.59	11.75
Annual Growth	(0.4%)	—	—	11.4%	13.1%	8.2%

STORE Capital Corp

Auditors: Ernst & Young LLP

LOCATIONS
HQ: STORE Capital Corp
8377 East Hartford Drive, Suite 100, Scottsdale, AZ 85255
Phone: 480 256-1100
Web: www.storecapital.com

HISTORICAL FINANCIALS
Company Type: Public

Income Statement — FYE: December 31

	REVENUE ($ mil.)	NET INCOME ($ mil.)	NET PROFIT MARGIN	EMPLOYEES
12/18	540.7	216.9	40.1%	90
12/17	452.8	162.0	35.8%	80
12/16	376.3	123.3	32.8%	68
12/15	284.7	83.7	29.4%	60
12/14	190.4	48.1	25.3%	50
Annual Growth	29.8%	45.7%	—	15.8%

2018 Year-End Financials
Debt ratio: 43.0%
Return on equity: 6.1%
Cash ($ mil.): 27.5
Current ratio: 0.13
Long-term debt ($ mil.): 2,925.3
No. of shares (mil.): 221.0
Dividends
  Yield: 4.5%
  Payout: 120.7%
Market value ($ mil.): 6,259.0

	STOCK PRICE ($) FY Close	P/E High	P/E Low	Earnings	Dividends	Book Value
12/18	28.31	29	21	1.06	1.28	17.48
12/17	26.04	29	22	0.90	1.20	16.36
12/16	24.71	38	27	0.82	1.12	15.58
12/15	23.20	35	29	0.68	1.04	14.62
12/14	21.61	36	32	0.61	0.11	13.74
Annual Growth	7.0%	—	—	14.8%	83.1%	6.2%

Summit Financial Group Inc

EXECUTIVES

Senior Vice President and Chief of Credit Administration, Patrick Frye
Senior Vice President Commercial Lending, Jason Hicks
Senior Vice President Commercial Lending, Lisa Dennison
Executive Vice President of Business Development, Jack Rossi
SENIOR VICE PRESIDENT AND TRUST OFFICER, Julie H Johnson
VICE PRESIDENT COMMERICAL LOANS, Anna B Abbey
VICE PRESIDENT OF MORTGAGE ORIGINATIONS, Oguz Sengul
VICE PRESIDENT COMMERICAL LOANS, Anna Abbey
Senior Vice President And Trust Officer, Julie Johnson

Senior Vice President Commercial Lending, Jim Rodgers
Secretary Independent Director, Phoebe Heishman
Board Member, Scott Bridgeforth
Auditors: Yount, Hyde & Barbour, P.C.

LOCATIONS

HQ: Summit Financial Group Inc
300 North Main Street, Moorefield, WV 26836
Phone: 304 530-1000
Web: www.summitfgi.com

COMPETITORS

Allegheny Bancshares
BB&T
F & M Bank
Fauquier Bankshares
Highlands Bankshares Inc.
SunTrust

HISTORICAL FINANCIALS
Company Type: Public

Income Statement FYE: December 31

	ASSETS ($ mil.)	NET INCOME ($ mil.)	INCOME AS % OF ASSETS	EMPLOYEES
12/18	2,200.5	28.0	1.3%	371
12/17	2,134.2	11.9	0.6%	349
12/16	1,758.6	17.3	1.0%	251
12/15	1,492.4	16.1	1.1%	231
12/14	1,443.5	11.3	0.8%	222
Annual Growth	11.1%	25.4%	—	13.7%

2018 Year-End Financials
Return on assets: 1.3%
Return on equity: 13.3%
Long-term debt ($ mil.): —
No. of shares (mil.): 12.3
Sales ($ mil): 112.8
Dividends
  Yield: 2.7%
  Payout: 28.6%
Market value ($ mil.): 238.0

	STOCK PRICE ($) FY Close	P/E High/Low		PER SHARE ($) Earnings	Dividends	Book Value
12/18	19.31	12	8	2.26	0.53	17.85
12/17	26.32	28	19	1.00	0.44	16.30
12/16	27.53	18	7	1.61	0.40	14.47
12/15	11.88	8	7	1.50	0.32	13.47
12/14	11.90	9	7	1.17	0.00	15.86
Annual Growth	12.9%	—		17.9%	—	3.0%

Summit Hotel Properties Inc

From the southern states to the Mountain States Summit Hotel Properties has plenty of room for US travelers. Operating through its subsidiaries Summit Hotel is a self-advised real estate investment trust (REIT) that holds a portfolio of almost 90 midscale and upscale hotels with 11400-plus rooms across 24 states including major markets in western and southern states like Arizona California Colorado Idaho and Texas. More than 60% of its hotels operated under the Marriott International and Hilton brands during 2015 while the rest mostly operated under the Hyatt and Intercontinental Hotel brands. Summit Hotel was formed in 2010 and went public in 2011.

Operations
Summit's property portfolio consisted of 87 hotel properties with 11420 rooms in 24 states at the end of 2015. About 64% of the rooms were tied to the company's Marriott and Hilton branded properties while the rest of the rooms were tied to the Hyatt (22% of rooms) Intercontinental Hotel (11%) Carlson (less than 1%) and Starwood (less than 1%) brands.

Geographic Reach
Austin Texas-based Summit Hotel Properties has its hotel properties in 24 states including major markets in western and southern states like Arizona California Colorado Idaho and Texas.

Strategy
Summit Hotel continues to focus on acquiring premium-branded select-service hotels to grow its portfolio and boost its total room revenue. It also looks to bolster its portfolio's value through property renovation repositioning and asset management efforts. Summit believes that because its properties operate under multiple leading hotel brands in markets suited to the hospitality industry (near tourist attractions corporate headquarters conventions centers etc.) it is well-positioned to reap strong returns in the hotel industry for the foreseeable future.

The REIT has been acquiring properties in hot real estate markets in recent years. In 2019 the company acquired four hotels on the West Coast in high-growth markets such as Portland San Francisco and San Jose. Other recent acquisitions include hotel properties in growing cities such as Minneapolis Boston Baltimore Miami and Atlanta.

Company Background
The company and its operating company Summit Hotel OP were formed in 2010 to acquire and operate the hotel portfolio of predecessor company Summit Hotel Properties LLC. It used the more than $250 million that it raised in its IPO to repay debt fund capital improvements at its properties and for general corporate purposes.

EXECUTIVES

EVP CFO and Treasurer, Greg A. Dowell, age 56, $360,000 total compensation
Chairman President and CEO, Daniel P. Hansen, age 50, $575,000 total compensation
EVP and COO, Craig J. Aniszewski, age 56, $375,000 total compensation
EVP General Counsel and Chief Risk Officer, Christopher R. Eng, age 48, $260,000 total compensation
Auditors: Ernst & Young LLP

LOCATIONS

HQ: Summit Hotel Properties Inc
13215 Bee Cave Parkway, Suite B-300, Austin, TX 78738
Phone: 512 538-2300
Web: www.shpreit.com

PRODUCTS/OPERATIONS

2015

	% of total
Room	94
Other hotel operations revenue	6
Total	**100**

COMPETITORS

Ashford Hospitality Trust
FelCor
Hospitality Properties Trust
Host Hotels & Resorts
LaSalle Hotel Properties

HISTORICAL FINANCIALS
Company Type: Public

Income Statement FYE: December 31

	REVENUE ($ mil.)	NET INCOME ($ mil.)	NET PROFIT MARGIN	EMPLOYEES
12/18	567.2	90.9	16.0%	57
12/17	515.3	99.2	19.3%	49
12/16	473.9	107.8	22.7%	44
12/15	463.4	124.4	26.8%	40
12/14	403.4	20.8	5.2%	39
Annual Growth	8.9%	44.5%	—	10.0%

2018 Year-End Financials
Debt ratio: 43.1%
Return on equity: 7.3%
Cash ($ mil.): 44.0
Current ratio: 1.35
Long-term debt ($ mil.): 958.7
No. of shares (mil.): 104.7
Dividends
  Yield: 7.4%
  Payout: 105.8%
Market value ($ mil.): 1,020.0

	STOCK PRICE ($) FY Close	P/E High/Low		PER SHARE ($) Earnings	Dividends	Book Value
12/18	9.73	24	14	0.68	0.72	11.36
12/17	15.23	24	18	0.79	0.67	12.22
12/16	16.03	16	9	1.00	0.55	10.80
12/15	11.95	12	9	1.24	0.47	9.82
12/14	12.44	254	174	0.05	0.46	9.05
Annual Growth	(6.0%)	—		92.0%	11.9%	5.8%

Summit Materials Inc

Auditors: KPMG LLP

LOCATIONS

HQ: Summit Materials Inc
1550 Wynkoop Street, 3rd Floor, Denver, CO 80202
Phone: 303 893-0012
Web: www.summit-materials.com

HISTORICAL FINANCIALS
Company Type: Public

Income Statement FYE: December 28

	REVENUE ($ mil.)	NET INCOME ($ mil.)	NET PROFIT MARGIN	EMPLOYEES
12/19	2,222.1	61.1	2.8%	6,000
12/18	2,101.0	36.3	1.7%	6,000
12/17	1,932.5	125.8	6.5%	6,000
12/16*	1,626.0	46.1	2.8%	5,000
01/16	1,432.3	3.3	0.2%	4,300
Annual Growth	11.6%	107.3%	—	8.7%

*Fiscal year change

2019 Year-End Financials
Debt ratio: 45.7%
Return on equity: 4.4%
Cash ($ mil.): 311.3
Current ratio: 2.66
Long-term debt ($ mil.): 1,851.0
No. of shares (mil.): 113.3
Dividends
  Yield: —
  Payout: —
Market value ($ mil.): 2,701.0

	STOCK PRICE ($)	P/E	PER SHARE ($)		
	FY Close	High/Low	Earnings	Dividends	Book Value
12/19	23.84	47 23	0.52	0.00	12.60
12/18	12.30	112 38	0.30	0.00	11.89
12/17	31.44	29 21	1.11	0.00	11.40
12/16*	23.79	47 26	0.52	0.00	8.65
01/16	20.04	40 25	0.50	0.00	5.16
Annual Growth	4.4%	— —	0.8%	—	25.0%

*Fiscal year change

Summit Midstream Partners LP

Auditors: DELOITTE & TOUCHE LLP

LOCATIONS

HQ: Summit Midstream Partners LP
1790 Hughes Landing Blvd., Suite 500, The Woodlands, TX 77380
Phone: 832 413-4770
Web: www.summitmidstream.com

HISTORICAL FINANCIALS
Company Type: Public

Income Statement   FYE: December 31

	REVENUE ($ mil.)	NET INCOME ($ mil.)	NET PROFIT MARGIN	EMPLOYEES
12/18	506.6	42.1	8.3%	0
12/17	488.7	85.6	17.5%	0
12/16	402.3	(38.1)	—	0
12/15	371.3	(186.8)	—	0
12/14	330.6	(21.1)	—	0
Annual Growth	11.3%	—	—	—

2018 Year-End Financials
Debt ratio: 41.6%
Return on equity: —
Cash ($ mil.): 4.3
Current ratio: 0.97
Long-term debt ($ mil.): 1,257.7
No. of shares (mil.): 74.8
Dividends
  Yield: 22.8%
  Payout: 3,833.3%
Market value ($ mil.): 753.0

	STOCK PRICE ($)	P/E	PER SHARE ($)		
	FY Close	High/Low	Earnings	Dividends	Book Value
12/18	10.05	377 178	0.06	2.30	16.31
12/17	20.50	27 19	0.98	2.30	18.63
12/16	25.15	— —	(0.71)	2.30	15.90
12/15	18.73	— —	(6.08)	2.27	14.51
12/14	38.00	— —	(0.93)	2.04	16.10
Annual Growth	(28.3%)	— —	—	3.0%	0.3%

Summit State Bank (Santa Rosa, CA)

EXECUTIVES

VP Branch Manager, Candy Yandell
Avp Sr. Operations And Utility Manager, Marjorie Peterson
Vice President And Marketing Director, Roni Brown
Vice President Director Of Branch And Deposit Operations, Genie Del Secco
Evp Chief Credit Officer, Brandy Seppi
Vp Of Information Security And Risk Management Officer, Aaron Lucey
Assistant Vice President Of Senior Branch Operations Officer, Liliana Lopez
Executive Vice President, Camille Kazarian
Auditors: Moss Adams LLP

LOCATIONS

HQ: Summit State Bank (Santa Rosa, CA)
500 Bicentennial Way, Santa Rosa, CA 95403
Phone: 707 568-6000
Web: www.summitstatebank.com

COMPETITORS

Bank of America
Bank of Marin
Bank of the West
Exchange Bank
Wells Fargo
Westamerica

HISTORICAL FINANCIALS
Company Type: Public

Income Statement   FYE: December 31

	ASSETS ($ mil.)	NET INCOME ($ mil.)	INCOME AS % OF ASSETS	EMPLOYEES
12/18	622.1	5.8	0.9%	89
12/17	610.8	3.2	0.5%	78
12/16	513.7	4.9	1.0%	74
12/15	513.3	6.0	1.2%	67
12/14	459.6	5.4	1.2%	61
Annual Growth	7.9%	1.5%	—	9.9%

2018 Year-End Financials
Return on assets: 0.9%
Return on equity: 9.6%
Long-term debt ($ mil.): —
No. of shares (mil.): 6.0
Sales ($ mil): 27.8
Dividends
  Yield: 4.0%
  Payout: 55.8%
Market value ($ mil.): 71.0

	STOCK PRICE ($)	P/E	PER SHARE ($)		
	FY Close	High/Low	Earnings	Dividends	Book Value
12/18	11.77	17 12	0.96	0.48	10.14
12/17	12.60	33 22	0.54	0.46	9.88
12/16	15.00	18 16	0.82	0.38	9.74
12/15	13.76	14 13	0.98	0.38	9.59
12/14	13.88	16 11	0.89	0.35	11.31
Annual Growth	(4.0%)	— —	2.0%	8.1%	(2.7%)

Sun Communities Inc

Sun Communities helps residents in the Sunshine State and around the US. The self-managed real estate investment trust (REIT) owns develops and operates manufactured housing communities (trailer and recreation vehicle parks) in nearly 30 states. Its portfolio includes more than 200 properties with nearly 80000 developed manufactured home and RV sites. Its Sun Home Services unit sells new and used homes for placement on its properties the majority of which are in Michigan Florida Indiana Texas and Ohio. Sun Communities also acquires at a discount and resells mobile homes that have been repossessed by lenders in its communities.

Operations
Sun Communities operates two lines of business: Real property and homes sales and rentals.

The Real Property business which generates roughly 75% of the company's total revenue owns operates and develops manufactured home (MH) and RV communities and is in the business of acquiring and expanding those communities to grow revenue.

The Home Sales and Rentals segment which operates under the company's Sun Home Services subsidiary sells manufactured homes and provides leasing services to consumers looking to live in their communities.

The company's properties have trained on-site property managers and maintenance personnel as well as such amenities as clubhouses laundry facilities and swimming pools. At the end of 2014 the company owned and operated 217 properties in 29 states including 183 manufactured housing communities 25 RV communities and 9 properties containing both manufactured housing and RV sites. That year Sun Homes Services had 10973 occupied leased homes in its portfolio and boasted an average renewal rate for residents in Sun Communities' rental program of 59%.

Geographic Reach
Sun Communities has nearly 220 properties across 29 states. Around 30% of these properties were in Michigan in 2014 while 17% were in Florida. Texas Indiana and Ohio each held 5% or more of the company's properties. About 20% of properties were in other states in the Northeast and the Southwest.

Sales and Marketing
Sun Communities spent $3.2 million on advertising in 2014 compared to $2.9 million and $2.5 million in 2013 and 2012 respectively.

Financial Performance
Sun Communities has enjoyed years of healthy revenue and profit growth thanks to aggressively property acquisitions and expansions with revenue nearly doubling over the past five years.

The company's revenue grew by 14% to $471.68 million in 2014 mostly thanks to a 14% increase in income from its Real Property segment as the REIT raised its rental rates by 3% during the year and continued to grow its occupied home sites. Rental home revenue also swelled by 20% as more residents took to the company's Rental Program and thanks to higher monthly rental rates. Home sales fell slightly for the company despite higher new home sales mostly as the company sold its pre-owned homes at lower prices during the year.

Higher revenue coupled with a $17.7 million gain on the sale of 10 MH properties in 2014 drove the REIT's net income up by 71% to a record $28.51 million while its operating cash rose by 16% to $133.32 million thanks to higher cash earnings.

Strategy

Sun Communities' main strategy toward growth has been to acquire highly-occupied and high-quality MH and RV communities with attractive amenities that support more potential occupancy and rent growth. Typically these are family or retirement communities with at least 200 home sites located near cities with populations exceeding 100000. In 2015 for example the REIT made two acquisitions totaling more than $1.5 billion (one was its largest acquisition ever) which spread its property portfolio business further into the fast-growing markets of Florida and Arizona.

Sun Communities' solid performance is in part due to increased demand from retiring adults a growing demographic. The company also points to its rental program as key to its success during the recession. Home rentals have become a popular and affordable alternative to customers.

Mergers and Acquisitions

In April 2015 the REIT completed its largest acquisition to date with the $1.3 billion-plus purchase of the Green Courte properties which spanned 59 MH communities across 19000 sites in the fast-growing markets of Florida and Arizona.

Additionally in early 2015 Sun Communities purchased seven large manufactured housing communities in the Orlando Florida area for $257 million which spanned 3150 manufactured housing sites (approximately 60% of these were in age-restricted communities) and were 96% occupied. Management believed that the purchase further strengthened its portfolio of high-quality communities particularly in age-restricted communities which it said were essential toward the REIT's sustained growth.

In early 2013 the company acquired ten RV communities (Gwynns Island RV Resort LLC Indian Creek RV Resort LLC Lake Laurie RV Resort LLC Newpoint RV Resort LLC Peters Pond RV Resort Inc. Seaport LLC Virginia Tent LLC Wagon Wheel Maine LLC Westward Ho RV Resort LLC and Wild Acres LLC) with 3700 sites in Connecticut Maine Massachusetts New Jersey Ohio Virginia and Wisconsin for $112.8 million.

In 2012 Sun Communities made seven acquisitions (which included 14 properties in total seven manufactured housing communities five RV communities and two communities containing both manufactured housing and RV communities. The acquisitions included Three Lakes RV Resort Blueberry Hill RV Resort and Grand Lake Estates located in Florida; Blazing Star RV Resort (260 sites located in San Antonio Texas); Northville Crossing Manufactured Home Community (756 sites in Northville Michigan); Rainbow RV Resort (500 sites in Frostproof Florida); four manufactured home communities (the Rudgate Acquisition Properties) in southeast Michigan and Palm Creek Golf & RV Resort (283 manufactured home sites 1580 RV sites and the expansion potential of 550 manufactured housing or 990 RV sites) in Casa Grande Arizona.

EXECUTIVES

Executive Vice President, Jonathan Colman
Vice President, Chelsey Bannister
Regional Vice President, Michael Machikas
RVP, Ken Kuiper
Vice President, Monica Slider
Regional Vice President of Operations and Sales, Melinda Graulau
Senior Vice President Human Resources, Laura Messa
Board Member, Clunet Lewis
Board Member, Ronald Klein
Board Member, Brian Hermelin
Board Member, Meghan Baivier
Auditors: Grant Thornton LLP

LOCATIONS

HQ: Sun Communities Inc
27777 Franklin Rd., Suite 200, Southfield, MI 48034
Phone: 248 208-2500
Web: www.suncommunities.com

PRODUCTS/OPERATIONS

2014 Sales

	$ mil.	% of total
Real property income	357.7	77
Home sales	54.0	11
Home rentals	39.2	8
Interest and other	19.8	4
Brokerage commission and other income	1.0	—
Total	**471.7**	**100**

Selected Mergers and Acquisitions

COMPETITORS

American Land Lease
Equity Lifestyle Properties
Hometown America
Nobility Homes
Outdoor Resorts
UMH Properties

HISTORICAL FINANCIALS

Company Type: Public

Income Statement — FYE: December 31

	REVENUE ($ mil.)	NET INCOME ($ mil.)	NET PROFIT MARGIN	EMPLOYEES
12/18	1,126.8	111.7	9.9%	2,784
12/17	982.5	76.7	7.8%	2,727
12/16	833.7	31.3	3.8%	2,679
12/15	674.7	160.4	23.8%	1,790
12/14	471.6	31.4	6.7%	1,525
Annual Growth	24.3%	37.3%	—	16.2%

2018 Year-End Financials

Debt ratio: 46.0%
Return on equity: 3.8%
Cash ($ mil.): 50.3
Current ratio: 0.39
Long-term debt ($ mil.): 2,961.0
No. of shares (mil.): 86.3
Dividends
  Yield: 2.7%
  Payout: 220.1%
Market value ($ mil.): 8,783.0

	STOCK PRICE ($) FY Close	P/E High/Low		PER SHARE ($) Earnings	Dividends	Book Value
12/18	101.71	84	65	1.29	2.84	36.71
12/17	92.78	112	90	0.85	2.68	33.15
12/16	76.61	302	236	0.26	2.60	32.27
12/15	68.53	28	24	2.52	2.60	26.35
12/14	60.46	118	78	0.54	2.60	18.36
Annual Growth	13.9%	—	—	24.3%	2.2%	18.9%

Suncrest Bank (Visalia, CA)

Auditors: Varinek, Trine, Day & Co., LLP

LOCATIONS

HQ: Suncrest Bank (Visalia, CA)
501 West Main Street, Visalia, CA 93291
Phone: 559 802-1000
Web: www.suncrestbank.com

HISTORICAL FINANCIALS

Company Type: Public

Income Statement — FYE: December 31

	ASSETS ($ mil.)	NET INCOME ($ mil.)	INCOME AS % OF ASSETS	EMPLOYEES
12/18	928.6	9.8	1.1%	0
12/17	528.9	3.3	0.6%	0
12/16	447.6	1.7	0.4%	0
12/15	296.8	0.9	0.3%	0
12/14	188.6	0.4	0.2%	0
Annual Growth	49.0%	123.4%	—	—

2018 Year-End Financials

Return on assets: 1.3%
Return on equity: 10.1%
Long-term debt ($ mil.): —
No. of shares (mil.): 12.4
Sales ($ mil): 36.0
Dividends
  Yield: —
  Payout: —
Market value ($ mil.): 134.0

	STOCK PRICE ($) FY Close	P/E High/Low		PER SHARE ($) Earnings	Dividends	Book Value
12/18	10.75	14	11	0.94	0.00	10.71
12/17	11.07	24	19	0.48	0.00	8.68
12/16	10.50	34	21	0.34	0.00	8.21
12/15	7.32	34	26	0.25	0.00	7.87
12/14	6.75	50	33	0.18	0.00	8.26
Annual Growth	12.3%	—	—	51.2%	—	6.7%

Sunrun Inc

Auditors: Ernst & Young LLP

LOCATIONS

HQ: Sunrun Inc
225 Bush Street, Suite 1400, San Francisco, CA 94104
Phone: 415 580-6900
Web: www.sunrun.com

HISTORICAL FINANCIALS

Company Type: Public

Income Statement — FYE: December 31

	REVENUE ($ mil.)	NET INCOME ($ mil.)	NET PROFIT MARGIN	EMPLOYEES
12/18	759.9	26.6	3.5%	4,400
12/17	529.7	124.5	23.5%	3,260
12/16	453.9	91.6	20.2%	3,020
12/15	304.6	(28.2)	—	3,380
12/14	198.5	(70.8)	—	1,700
Annual Growth	39.9%	—	—	26.8%

Superior Group of Companies Inc

Superior Uniform Group works to keep its business all sewn up. The company makes work clothing and accessories for US employees in several industries. The apparel firm designs makes and markets uniforms for employees in the medical and health fields as well as those who work in hotels fast food joints and other restaurants and public safety industrial and commercial markets. About half of its products are sold under the Fashion Seal brand. The company also makes and distributes specialty labels such as Martin's Worklon Blade and UniVogue. Chairman Gerald Benstock and his son CEO Michael run company which began as Superior Surgical Mfg. Co. in 1920.

Operations
The company operates its business through two reportable segments: Uniforms and Related Products (97% of sales) and Remote Staffing Solutions which includes The Office Gurus and TOG an affiliate firm that offers cost effective bilingual telemarketing and office support services.

Geographic Reach
From its headquarters in Florida Superior Uniform serves to outfit companies and customers nationwide boasting manufacturing operations overseas. Suppliers in Central American typically produce more than 50% of the company's products. It operates in El Salvador Costa Rica and the US through its The Office Gurus businesses and an affiliate entity in Belize added to its operations at the end of 2012.

Financial Performance
Due to a boost in market penetration Superior Uniform logged a 6% net sales increase in fiscal 2012 as compared to 2011 across its Uniforms and Related Products unit and 9% from its Remote Staffing Solutions. Net income for the same reporting period declined 27% due to the rising cost of goods sold — primarily related to cotton shortages in the Uniforms and Related Products business — and increasing payroll-related costs across the Remote Staffing Solutions segment.

Strategy
Demand for Superior's uniforms and service apparel largely depends on the health of the economy. The economic downturn in the US negatively impacted the uniform supplier's customers who closed locations reduced headcounts or eliminated uniforms to save money.

In addition to the challenging economic climate the dramatic rise in cotton prices has the potential to pinch Superior Uniform's profit margin. While the company has been able to compensate for its higher materials costs by raising prices it warns at times that gross margins could be negatively impacted.

Mergers and Acquisitions
In March 2016 Superior Uniform acquired BAMKO Inc. a Los Angeles-based merchandise sourcing and promotional products company. It acquired BAMKO and its China Brazil and England subsidiaries as well as an India affiliate for $15.8 million in cash. BAMKO's products complement Superior Uniform's; however the acquisition expands the company's presence in China and India particularly its branded merchandise and promotional product offerings. Superior Uniform operates BAMKO as a subsidiary.

EXECUTIVES

Vice President Business Develo, Ron Klepner
EVP; President Fashion Seal Healthcare, Peter Benstock, age 57, $251,248 total compensation
CEO, Michael Benstock, age 63, $513,133 total compensation
COO CFO and Treasurer, Andrew D. Demott, age 55, $324,454 total compensation
VP Marketing and President Superior I.D., David Schechter
Chairperson, Sidney Kirschner, age 84
Assistant Treasurer, Jerry Chiovaro
Board Member, Robin Hensley
Board Member, Todd Siegel
Auditors: Mayer Hoffman McCann P.C.

LOCATIONS
HQ: Superior Group of Companies Inc
10055 Seminole Boulevard, Seminole, FL 33772-2539
Phone: 727 397-9611
Web: www.superiorgroupofcompanies.com

PRODUCTS/OPERATIONS

2016 sales

	% of total
Uniforms and related products	82
Promotional Products	11
Remote staffing solutions	7
Inter-segment elimination	-
Total	**100**

Selected Brands
Blade
Fashion Seal
Fashion Seal Healthcare
Martin's
Worklon
UniVogue

COMPETITORS

ARAMARK	Convergys
Accenture	Fujitsu America
Alsco	G&K Services
Angelica Corporation	Sitel Worldwide
Broder Bros.	StarTek
Capgemini North America	Sykes Enterprises
	TeleTech
Cintas	UniFirst

2018 Year-End Financials
Debt ratio: 44.8%
Return on equity: 3.0%
Cash ($ mil.): 226.6
Current ratio: 1.24
Long-term debt ($ mil.): 2,060.7
No. of shares (mil.): 113.1
Dividends
 Yield: —
 Payout: —
Market value ($ mil.): 1,232.0

	STOCK PRICE ($) FY Close	P/E High/Low		PER SHARE ($) Earnings	Dividends	Book Value
12/18	10.89	67	22	0.23	0.00	8.38
12/17	5.90	6	4	1.15	0.00	7.56
12/16	5.31	13	5	0.87	0.00	6.45
12/15	11.77	—	—	(0.96)	0.00	5.47
Annual Growth	(2.6%)	—	—	—	—	15.3%

Superior Industries International, Inc.

Superior Industries International is one of the world's largest makers of cast aluminum wheels for passenger cars and light trucks holding the #1 position in North America. The company has the capacity to make approximately 21 million wheels annually at its nine manufacturing facilities located in Arkansas Mexico Poland and Germany. It sells to the ten largest original equipment manufacturers (OEMs) in the world however sales to Ford General Motors Volkswagen and Toyota represent more than 55% of net sales. Wheels are primarily sold for factory installation but in Europe Superior sells aftermarket brands under the ATS RIAL ALUTEC and ANZIO brands. North America represents about 55% of net sales while Europe accounts for about 45%. In North America Mexico generates almost 85% of sales with the remaining 15% coming from the US. In Europe Poland and Germany are its major markets.

Financial Performance
Superior Industries' sales have been growing by leaps and bounds with the addition of the European operations of Uniwheels acquired in 2017. Overall revenue has increased by more than 100% since 2014.

Sales in 2018 reached $1.5 billion up 36% compared with $1.1 billion in 2017. In addition to five more months of sales from its new European operations the increase in 2018 reflected a higher average selling price per wheel and improved product mix from larger diameter wheels and premium finishes. The company also cited increased alu-

---

HISTORICAL FINANCIALS
Company Type: Public

Income Statement
FYE: December 31

	REVENUE ($ mil.)	NET INCOME ($ mil.)	NET PROFIT MARGIN	EMPLOYEES
12/18	346.3	16.9	4.9%	2,906
12/17	266.8	15.0	5.6%	2,280
12/16	252.6	14.6	5.8%	1,632
12/15	210.3	13.0	6.2%	1,278
12/14	196.2	11.3	5.8%	1,055
Annual Growth	15.3%	10.6%	—	28.8%

2018 Year-End Financials
Debt ratio: 35.0%
Return on equity: 12.3%
Cash ($ mil.): 5.3
Current ratio: 4.25
Long-term debt ($ mil.): 111.5
No. of shares (mil.): 15.2
Dividends
 Yield: 2.2%
 Payout: 42.3%
Market value ($ mil.): 268.0

	STOCK PRICE ($) FY Close	P/E High/Low		PER SHARE ($) Earnings	Dividends	Book Value
12/18	17.65	25	14	1.10	0.39	9.93
12/17	26.71	27	16	0.99	0.37	8.29
12/16	19.62	20	14	0.98	0.34	7.62
12/15	16.98	40	17	0.90	0.32	6.66
12/14	29.37	35	17	0.82	0.29	5.95
Annual Growth	(12.0%)	—	—	7.6%	8.2%	13.7%

minum prices which were passed on to its customers.

The company posted net income of $26.0 million in 2018 after a profit loss of $6.0 million the previous year. The increase was mostly due to higher sales in 2018.

Cash at the end of fiscal 2018 was $47.5 million an increase of $1.1 million from the prior year. Cash from operations contributed $156.1 million to the coffers while investing activities used $77.1 million mainly for additions to property plant and equipment. Financing activities used another $76.3 million for loan payments and the company's stock repurchase program.

Strategy

Superior Industries' strategy for growth includes expanding its market share in Europe and focusing on larger diameter wheels and premium finishes. The acquisition in 2017 of Uniwheels the largest wheel manufacturer in Europe launched Superior into the European market and added significant customer share with OEMs such as BMW-Mini Daimler AG Jaguar-Land Rover VW and Volvo.

The company aims to follow the trend for increased demand for more stylish larger diameter wheels (19 inches or more) with more complex finishes especially for the electric vehicle and hybrid vehicle markets. In 2019 it introduced its lightweight AluLite wheels designed to make up for any added weight associated with the bigger wheels. The AluLite wheels reduce weight by three pounds per wheel resulting in higher fuel efficiency.

EXECUTIVES

President and CEO, Donald J. (Don) Stebbins, age 60, $900,000 total compensation
SVP Sales Marketing and Product Development, Parveen Kakar, age 53, $385,962 total compensation
SVP Operations, Robert M. Tykal, age 57
EVP and CFO, Nadeem Moiz, age 48
Svp Of Business Operations, James Sistek
Senior Vice President, Wolfgang Hiller
Chairman, Timothy C. McQuay, age 68
Auditors: DELOITTE & TOUCHE LLP

LOCATIONS

HQ: Superior Industries International, Inc.
26600 Telegraph Road, Suite 400, Southfield, MI 48033
Phone: 248 352-7300 **Fax:** 818 780-3500
Web: www.supind.com

COMPETITORS

Accuride
American Eagle Wheel
Arconic
CITIC Ltd.
CRAGAR
Carlisle Tire & Wheel
Iochpe-Maxion
Meritor
NGK INSULATORS
Topy
YHI
wheel pros

HISTORICAL FINANCIALS
Company Type: Public

Income Statement FYE: December 31

	REVENUE ($ mil.)	NET INCOME ($ mil.)	NET PROFIT MARGIN	EMPLOYEES
12/18	1,501.8	25.9	1.7%	8,260
12/17	1,108.0	(6.2)	—	8,150
12/16	732.6	41.3	5.6%	4,189
12/15	727.9	23.9	3.3%	3,050
12/14	745.4	8.8	1.2%	3,000
Annual Growth	19.1%	31.0%	—	28.8%

2018 Year-End Financials
Debt ratio: 45.7%
Return on equity: 4.8%
Cash ($ mil.): 47.4
Current ratio: 2.08
Long-term debt ($ mil.): 661.4
No. of shares (mil.): 25.0
Dividends
  Yield: 7.4%
  Payout: 124.1%
Market value ($ mil.): 120.0

	STOCK PRICE ($) FY Close	P/E High/Low		PER SHARE ($) Earnings	Dividends	Book Value
12/18	4.81	78	16	0.29	0.36	21.25
12/17	14.85	—	—	(1.01)	0.54	21.61
12/16	26.85	19	10	1.62	0.72	15.84
12/15	18.87	23	19	0.90	0.72	15.86
12/14	19.79	66	52	0.33	0.72	16.42
Annual Growth	(29.8%)	—	—	(3.2%)	(15.9%)	6.6%

Supernus Pharmaceuticals Inc

Supernus Pharmaceuticals wouldn't mind being a drug-maker superhero of sorts to epileptics. As a specialty pharmaceutical company Supernus develops treatments for epilepsy and other central nervous system disorders. It has two marketed products for treating epilepsy: Oxtellar XR and Trokendi XR. In addition it is developing a number of candidates to treat such ailments as attention deficit hyperactivity disorder (ADHD) impulsive aggression in patients with ADHD autism bipolar disorder schizophrenia depression and dementia. The company utilizes third-party commercial manufacturing organizations (CMOs) for all of its manufacturing.

Geographic Reach
Supernus Pharmaceuticals has its corporate office and laboratory space in Maryland.

Sales and Marketing
Supernus markets its products through more than 150 sales representatives and distributes them through wholesalers and pharmaceutical distributors. Supernus primarily targets neurologists to grow sales of its epilepsy franchise.

In 2015 advertising costs totaled $19.3 million up from $14.8 million in 2014 and $14.6 million in 2013.

Financial Performance
Supernus began earning product revenue in 2013 when it launched Oxtellar XR. The 2014 launch of Trokendi led to further gains in revenues. In 2015 revenue increased 18% to $144 million as more prescriptions of its two medications were issued.

Net income spiked in 2014 but declined 29% to $14 million the following year. This drop was related to increased sales and marketing spend for its two products as well as higher R&D costs for additional pre-clinical and clinical trials. Additionally Supernus was hit with tax expenses for the first time in 2015 which further cut into the bottom line. As of the end of 2015 the company had an accumulated deficit of some $144.6 million.

Cash flow from operations has risen sharply over the past couple of years. In 2015 it increased 315% to $32 million due to several factors including changes in accounts payable and an increase in cash provided by accrued sales deductions.

Strategy
Supernus is focused on growing its epilepsy franchise in the US and in getting its pipeline products on the market. It also has a licensing and royalty agreements with other firms which helps boost its overall earnings.

Mergers and Acquisitions
In 2018 Supernus agreed to buy privately held Biscayne Neurotherapeutics which is developing a treatment for epilepsy for an upfront payment of $15 million plus some $170 million in development and sales milestone payments. SPN-817 has been given the Orphan Drug designation in the US for the treatment of Dravet Syndrome a rare form of epilepsy in children.

EXECUTIVES

President CEO and Director, Jack A. Khattar, age 58, $523,403 total compensation
SVP Sales and Marketing, Victor Vaughn, age 61, $291,635 total compensation
SVP Intellectual Property and Chief Scientific Officer, Padmanabh P. Bhatt, age 62, $337,443 total compensation
VP Finance and CFO, Gregory S. Patrick, age 67, $330,470 total compensation
EVP Research and Development and Chief Medical Officer, Stefan K. F. Schwabe, age 67, $356,411 total compensation
Vice President Marketing, Todd Horich
Vice President Marketing, Stefan Antonsson
Vice President Corporate Development, Bryan Roecklein
Chairman, Charles W. (Chuck) Newhall, age 74
Auditors: KPMG LLP

LOCATIONS

HQ: Supernus Pharmaceuticals Inc
1550 East Gude Drive, Rockville, MD 20850
Phone: 301 838-2500
Web: www.supernus.com

PRODUCTS/OPERATIONS

2015 Sales

	$ mil.	% of total
Net product sales	143.5	99
Revenue from royalty agreement	-	-
Licensing revenue	0.9	1
Total	144.4	100

Selected Products
Oxtellar XR (marketed)
SPN-809 (under trail)
SPN-810 (under trail)
SPN-812 (under trail)
Trokendi XR (marketed)

COMPETITORS

Abbott Labs
AstraZeneca
Eisai Inc.
GlaxoSmithKline
Johnson & Johnson
Mylan Pharmaceuticals
Noven Pharmaceuticals
Shire
UCB
Upsher-Smith

HISTORICAL FINANCIALS
Company Type: Public

Income Statement — FYE: December 31

	REVENUE ($ mil.)	NET INCOME ($ mil.)	NET PROFIT MARGIN	EMPLOYEES
12/18	408.9	110.9	27.1%	448
12/17	302.2	57.2	19.0%	422
12/16	215.0	91.2	42.4%	363
12/15	144.4	14.0	9.7%	344
12/14	122.0	19.8	16.3%	309
Annual Growth	35.3%	53.7%	—	9.7%

2018 Year-End Financials

Debt ratio: 33.6%
Return on equity: 30.8%
Cash ($ mil.): 192.2
Current ratio: 3.06
Long-term debt ($ mil.): 329.4
No. of shares (mil.): 52.3
Dividends
  Yield: —
  Payout: —
Market value ($ mil.): 1,738.0

	STOCK PRICE ($) FY Close	P/E High/Low	PER SHARE ($) Earnings	Dividends	Book Value
12/18	33.22	28 14	2.05	0.00	8.66
12/17	39.85	44 21	1.08	0.00	5.21
12/16	25.25	15 6	1.76	0.00	3.84
12/15	13.44	71 27	0.28	0.00	2.43
12/14	8.30	24 16	0.32	0.00	1.66
Annual Growth	41.4%	— —	59.1%	—	51.1%

Surmodics Inc

SurModics doesn't want to scratch the surface of the medical device market — it just wants to coat it with its own special agent. The company's medical device unit makes special coatings that make the devices easier to use less traumatic to the body and even useful in delivering drugs to patients. For example it is developing drug-coated balloons designed to treat peripheral artery disease which causes narrowing of the arteries. SurModics' in vitro diagnostics (IVD) unit handles diagnostic test and research kits and products. Three scientists formed the company in 1979.

Operations
SurModics makes about half of its money from licensing and royalty deals under which medical device makers and drug companies use its technologies in their products. Within licensing and royalties the company divides its business between medical devices and IVD with medical devices taking the lion's share — about three-fourths of total revenue.

Product sales accounts for about 40% of the company's revenue while R&D and other activities bring in the rest.

Geographic Reach
SurModics has operations in Minnesota (2) and in Ireland.

The US is the company's largest market accounting for some 80% of total revenue.

Sales and Marketing
SurModics uses a global direct sales force and online sales to ply its wares. Medtronic is the company's largest customer; it accounts for about one quarter of sales.

Financial Performance
Revenue for SurModics has been rising for the past five years. In fiscal 2016 (ended September) revenue rose 15% to $71.4 million largely on higher product sales. Royalties license fees and R&D revenue also rose that year. Both the medical device and IVD segments saw double-digit growth due to increasing demand for the company's products and services as well as limited product price increases.

Net income has been more volatile peaking at $15.2 million in fiscal 2013 but dropping 16% to $10 million in fiscal 2016. That decline was due to higher operating costs including product costs R&D expenses and selling general and administrative expenses.

Strategy
SurModics looks to grow by enlisting more licensing customers (it makes about half of its revenue from royalties and fees) and by expanding its product line. It is also working to move beyond being a provider of coating technologies to offering whole-product systems to its medical device customers particularly in the vascular market. During fiscal 2016 (ended September) the company began a first in-human early study of its SurVeil drug-coated balloon. Early the following fiscal year SurModics completed the expansion of an R&D and manufacturing facility to further support its growth.

Mergers and Acquisitions
In 2015 SurModics acquired Irish firm Creagh Medical which makes balloon catheters for angioplasties for $32 million. That purchase fit in with its focus on expanding beyond its traditional medical device coating technologies. The following year SurModics bought development firm Normedix which focuses on minimally invasive catheter technologies for $14 million.

EXECUTIVES

SVP and General Manager Medical Device, Charles W. (Charlie) Olson, $280,000 total compensation
VP and General Manager In Vitro Diagnostics, Joseph J. (Joe) Stich, $236,900 total compensation
President and CEO, Gary R. Maharaj, $435,000 total compensation
VP Finance and CFO, Andrew D. C. (Andy) LaFrence, $162,599 total compensation
Vice President, Joe Stich
Chairman, Scott R. Ward, age 82
Auditors: DELOITTE & TOUCHE LLP

LOCATIONS

HQ: Surmodics Inc
9924 West, 74th Street, Eden Prairie, MN 55344
Phone: 952 500-7000
Web: www.surmodics.com

PRODUCTS/OPERATIONS

2013 Revenues

	$ mil.	% of total
Royalties & licensing fees	29.8	53
Product sales	22.5	40
Research & development	3.8	7
Total	**56.1**	**100**

2013 Revenues

	$ mil.	% of total
Medical device	41.1	73
In Vitro Diagnostics	15.0	27
Total	**56.1**	**100**

COMPETITORS

Alimera
Biocompatibles
DURECT
Hydromer
Novelion Therapeutics
Spire Corp.
W.L. Gore
alchimer
pSivida

HISTORICAL FINANCIALS
Company Type: Public

Income Statement — FYE: September 30

	REVENUE ($ mil.)	NET INCOME ($ mil.)	NET PROFIT MARGIN	EMPLOYEES
09/19	100.0	7.5	7.6%	369
09/18	81.3	(4.4)	—	338
09/17	73.1	3.9	5.4%	257
09/16	71.3	9.9	14.0%	219
09/15	61.9	11.9	19.3%	168
Annual Growth	12.8%	(10.7%)	—	21.7%

2019 Year-End Financials

Debt ratio: —
Return on equity: 6.5%
Cash ($ mil.): 30.3
Current ratio: 4.03
Long-term debt ($ mil.): —
No. of shares (mil.): 13.5
Dividends
  Yield: —
  Payout: —
Market value ($ mil.): 618.0

	STOCK PRICE ($) FY Close	P/E High/Low	PER SHARE ($) Earnings	Dividends	Book Value
09/19	45.74	129 67	0.55	0.00	9.07
09/18	74.65	— —	(0.34)	0.00	8.11
09/17	31.00	104 75	0.29	0.00	8.52
09/16	30.09	39 23	0.76	0.00	8.09
09/15	21.84	30 20	0.90	0.00	7.10
Annual Growth	20.3%	— —	(11.6%)	—	6.3%

SWK Holdings Corp

Auditors: BPM LLP

LOCATIONS

HQ: SWK Holdings Corp
14755 Preston Road, Suite 105, Dallas, TX 75254
Phone: 972 687-7250
Web: www.swkhold.com

HISTORICAL FINANCIALS
Company Type: Public

Income Statement — FYE: December 31

	REVENUE ($ mil.)	NET INCOME ($ mil.)	NET PROFIT MARGIN	EMPLOYEES
12/18	25.9	6.2	23.8%	5
12/17	37.4	3.0	8.1%	4
12/16	22.3	28.8	129.1%	4
12/15	23.4	(7.3)	—	4
12/14	17.4	20.7	119.3%	4
Annual Growth	10.6%	(26.1%)	—	5.7%

Synalloy Corp.

2018 Year-End Financials
Debt ratio: —
Return on equity: 2.9%
Cash ($ mil.): 20.2
Current ratio: 8.65
Long-term debt ($ mil.): —
No. of shares (mil.): 12.9
Dividends
Yield: —
Payout: —
Market value ($ mil.): 123.0

	STOCK PRICE ($) FY Close	P/E High/Low		PER SHARE ($) Earnings	Dividends	Book Value
12/18	9.50	24	20	0.47	0.00	16.47
12/17	10.90	50	43	0.23	0.00	15.93
12/16	10.40	5	4	2.22	0.00	15.54
12/15	11.10	—	—	(0.57)	0.00	13.35
12/14	1.32	0	0	3.20	0.00	13.89
Annual Growth	63.8%	—	—	(38.1%)	—	4.4%

EXECUTIVES
Chairman, James G. Lane Jr., age 81, $15,000 total compensation
Corporate Secretary, Cheryl C. Carter, age 64, $88,833 total compensation
VP Finance and CFO, Richard D. (Rick) Sieradzki, age 60
President Piping Systems Division, Michael D. Boling, age 59, $150,000 total compensation
CEO President and Director, Craig C. Bram, age 56
EVP and General Manager Organic Pigments, R. Gary Wulf
COO, Daniel (Dan) Shauger
Technical Director Organic Pigments, Andy Farley
Purchasing and Customer Service Manager Organic Pigments, Daisy Lugardo
President Bristol Metals, J. Kyle Pennington, age 56
President; Chief Executive Officer; Director, Ronald Frankel
Chief Operating Officer, Scott Bailey
Chief Financial Officer, William Stuart
Executive Vice President - Sales and Marketing, George Chamoun
Independent Chairman of the Board, Jordan Levy
Director, Ronald H. Braam, age 71
Director, Carroll D. Vinson, age 74
Director, Sibyl N. Fishburn, age 79
Director, Murray H. Wright, age 69
CEO President and Director, Craig C. Bram, age 56
Independent Director, Marwan Fawaz
Independent Director, Michael Montgomery
Independent Director, Gary Ginsberg
Independent Director, Henry Guy
Independent Director, James Terry
Auditors: KPMG LLP

LOCATIONS
HQ: Synalloy Corp.
4510 Cox Road, Suite 201, Richmond, VA 23060
Phone: 804 822-3260
Web: www.synalloy.com

PRODUCTS/OPERATIONS

Selected Subsidiaries
Manufacturers Soap and Chemicals Company
Manufacturers Chemical LLC
Ram-Fab LLC
Synalloy Metals Inc.
Bristol Metals LLC

COMPETITORS
AK Steel Holding Corporation
Berg Steel Pipe
Dalmine
Earle M. Jorgensen
Matrix Service
Robbins & Myers
Tubacex
Webco Industries

HISTORICAL FINANCIALS
Company Type: Public

Income Statement   FYE: December 31

	REVENUE ($ mil.)	NET INCOME ($ mil.)	NET PROFIT MARGIN	EMPLOYEES
12/18	280.8	13.1	4.7%	607
12/17	201.1	1.3	0.7%	533
12/16	138.5	(7.0)	—	412
12/15*	175.4	(11.5)	—	411
01/15	199.5	5.4	2.7%	464
Annual Growth	8.9%	24.4%	—	6.9%

*Fiscal year change

2018 Year-End Financials
Debt ratio: 33.5%
Return on equity: 13.6%
Cash ($ mil.): 2.2
Current ratio: 4.50
Long-term debt ($ mil.): 76.4
No. of shares (mil.): 8.8
Dividends
Yield: 1.5%
Payout: 16.4%
Market value ($ mil.): 147.0

	STOCK PRICE ($) FY Close	P/E High/Low		PER SHARE ($) Earnings	Dividends	Book Value
12/18	16.59	16	8	1.48	0.25	11.55
12/17	13.40	101	67	0.15	0.13	10.27
12/16	10.95	—	—	(0.82)	0.00	10.22
12/15*	6.88	—	—	(1.32)	0.30	11.02
01/15	17.67	29	21	0.63	0.30	12.57
Annual Growth	(1.6%)	—	—	23.8%	(4.5%)	(2.1%)

*Fiscal year change

Synovus Financial Corp

Synovus Financial has a nose for community banking. The holding company owns flagship subsidiary Synovus Bank and more than 25 locally branded banking divisions that offer deposit accounts and consumer and business loans in Alabama Florida Georgia South Carolina and Tennessee. Through more than 280 branches the bank provides checking and savings accounts loans and mortgages and credit cards. Other divisions offer insurance private banking wealth and asset management and other financial services. Nonbank subsidiaries include Synovus Mortgage Synovus Trust investment bank and brokerage Synovus Securities and GLOBALT which provides asset management and financial planning services.

Geographic Reach
Georgia-based Synovus Financial has about 130 bank branches in Georgia. Florida is the bank's second largest market with nearly 50 branches while Alabama and South Carolina are home to more than 40 each.

Financial Performance
While the bank reported a 10% decline in revenue in 2013 versus 2012 to $1.18 billion and an 81% plunge in net income (to $159.4 million) it did make some progress on the long road to recovery. Significantly the bank redeemed its obligations under TARP (troubled asset relief program) in July 2013 funding more than two-thirds of the TARP redemption with internally available funds. The firm redeemed the remainder with proceeds from offerings of its common and preferred stock. Its loan portfolio grew by about $516 million up nearly 3% versus 2012. Credit quality also continued to improve while the bank lowered expenses.

Synovus blamed its continuing revenue slide on lower interest and non-interest income in 2013 versus 2012. Interest income fell on lower income on loans and investment securities. Non-interest income suffered relative to 2012 when the bank experienced higher levels of investment securities gains and gains on private equity investments as well as a decline in income from mortgage banking.

Strategy
Synovus has been cutting costs raising capital and improving efficiency in the aftermath of the residential and commercial real estate bust that hit the southeastern US particularly hard. During the dark days of the banking crisis (2008 to 2009) the company slashed about 10% of its workforce and it cut approximately 10% more in 2010 and 2011. It also closed nearly 40 branches and consolidated others.

Also Synovus which has traditionally maintained separate charters and local boards of directors for its subsidiary banks consolidated all of its charters into one in 2010 in order to reduce complexity and improve efficiency. Synovus also consolidated by merging some of its banks in Georgia and Florida; two of its Florida banking subsidiaries (one de novo and the other formed in the merger of three subsidiaries' banking charters) have taken the Synovus Bank brand a new strategy for the company.

The company returned to profitability in 2012 and remained profitable (although considerably less so) in 2013. To right itself Synovus has deemphasized commercial real estate lending and increased its focus on commercial and industrial banking including specialized services such as asset-based lending international banking and treasury management in an effort to increase revenue. The company is courting large corporate clients in the health care manufacturing distribution financial services natural resources and transportation sectors. Among smaller enterprises it targets professional practices such as physicians attorneys and accountants particularly for its private banking business.

Mergers and Acquisitions
In May 2013 Synovus assumed $56.8 million in deposits that belonged to failed Sunrise Bank from its receiver the FDIC. As part of the deal the bank acquired $492000 in loans.

The company bought specialty finance firm Entaire Global in October 2016. Entaire a private life insurance premium finance lender primarily serves small businesses. Synovus which is aiming to diversify its loan portfolio with the purchase paid an initial $30 million; it will pay extra earnings-based payments over a period of up to five years.

EXECUTIVES

EVP and COO, Allen J. Gula, age 64, $434,192 total compensation
EVP and Chief Risk Officer, Mark G. Holladay, age 63, $428,454 total compensation
EVP and Chief Retail Banking Officer, D. Wayne Akins, age 56
Chairman and CEO, Kessel D. Stelling, age 63, $962,269 total compensation
EVP Financial Management Services, J. Barton Singleton, age 55, $390,606 total compensation
EVP and Chief Credit Officer, Kevin J. Howard, age 54
EVP and Chief Community Banking Officer, R. Dallis (Roy) Copeland, age 50, $412,336 total compensation
EVP and Chief Corporate Banking Officer, Curtis J. Perry, age 56
EVP and CFO, Kevin S. Blair
CIO, Renee S. Roth
CTO, Santosh Kokate
EVP General Counsel and Secretary, Allan E. Kamensky, age 58, $417,229 total compensation
Chief Information Security Officer, Kevin P. Gowen
Vice President Of Regional Sales, Ron Ward
Executive Vice President Corporate Affairs, Calvin Smyre
Senior Vice President Deputy General Counsel, Michael Smith
Senior Vice President Diversity and Career Resources, Audrey Hollingsworth
Senior Vice President Private Wealth Advisor, Michelle Mcclellan
Senior Vice President, Edward Deitz
Executive Vice President Risk and Compliance, John Latimer
Vice President, Susan Pitts
Vice President Product Management, Lynn White
Executive Vice President Retail Branches Columbus Band And Trust, Carolynn Obleton
Senior Vice President And Chief Audit Executive, Stephen Sawyer
Vice President Accounting Manager, Liz Gobbel
Vice President Tax Compliance Manager, Jim Buchs
Senior Vice President, Robbie Jones
Vice President and Director Compliance, Deborah Kent-Cochran
Senior Vice President, Brick F Luke
Executive Vice President, Jon Dodds
Senior Vice President, Jason Ninas
Executive Vice President, David Kimrey
Senior Vice President Facility Management Division, Mike Webb
Vice President Of Human Resources, Ronald Carr
Senior Vice President, Eric Tikkanen
Vice President Commercial Banking, Michael Harley
Vice President Retail Market Manager, Stephan Hollis
Vice President Finance Account Manager, Richard Pettit
Vice President Senior Business Analyst Lender, Alvena Pareja
Senior Vice President, Dan Summers
Vice President Commercial Real Estate, Mark Mathews
Senior Vice President Director of Correspondent Banking, Richard Lane
Senior Vice President and Director LCBG East, Michael Sawicki
Vice President, Phyllis Lyons
Vice President, Sandy Gowan
Evp Commercial Real Estate Division, Paige Collier
Vice President Commercial Banking, Patrick Ahern
Senior Vice President, David O'rear
Senior Vice President, Jeff Bauer
Evp And President Florida, Kent Ellert
Assistant Vice President Retail Market Manager, Leteria Waters
Senior Vice President, Wayne Gray
Vp and Commercial Banker, Gregory Alt
Senior Vice President Corporate Banking, Brad Beard
Assistant Vice President Branch Manager, Eileen Burton
Senior Vice President Market President, Patrick Murphy
Assistant Vice President, Janice Vagner
Treasurer, Joseph Lowery
Board Member, Jennifer Brooke
Auditors: KPMG LLP

LOCATIONS

HQ: Synovus Financial Corp
1111 Bay Avenue, Suite 500, Columbus, GA 31901
Phone: 706 649-2311
Web: www.synovus.com

PRODUCTS/OPERATIONS

2016 Sales

	$ mil.	% of total
Interest income:		
Loans including fees	944.2	73
Investment securities available for sale	67.5	5
Trading account assets	0.1	-
Mortgage loans held for sale	2.6	-
Federal Reserve Bank balances	4.4	-
Other earning assets	4.0	-
Non-interest income:		
Service charges on deposit accounts	81.4	6
Fiduciary and asset management fees	46.6	4
Bankcard fees	33.3	3
Other non-interest income	34.3	3
Brokerage revenue	27.0	2
Mortgage banking income	24.3	2
Other fee income	20.2	2
Investment securities gains net	6.0	-
Total	**1,296.0**	**100**

COMPETITORS

BB&T	First Citizens BancShares
BBVA Compass Bancshares	First Horizon
BBX Capital	Regions Financial
BancorpSouth	SunTrust
Bank of America	Trustmark
Citigroup	Wells Fargo

HISTORICAL FINANCIALS

Company Type: Public

Income Statement
FYE: December 31

	ASSETS ($ mil.)	NET INCOME ($ mil.)	INCOME AS % OF ASSETS	EMPLOYEES
12/18	32,669.1	428.4	1.3%	4,651
12/17	31,221.8	275.4	0.9%	4,541
12/16	30,104.0	246.7	0.8%	4,436
12/15	28,792.6	226.0	0.8%	4,452
12/14	27,051.2	195.2	0.7%	4,511
Annual Growth	4.8%	21.7%	—	0.8%

2018 Year-End Financials

Return on assets: 1.3%
Return on equity: 14.0%
Long-term debt ($ mil.): —
No. of shares (mil.): 115.8
Sales ($ mil): 1,624.4
Dividends
 Yield: 3.1%
 Payout: 28.8%
Market value ($ mil.): 3,707.0

	STOCK PRICE ($) FY Close	P/E High/Low		PER SHARE ($) Earnings	Dividends	Book Value
12/18	31.99	16	9	3.47	1.00	27.05
12/17	47.94	23	18	2.17	0.60	24.91
12/16	41.08	22	14	1.89	0.48	23.95
12/15	32.38	21	15	1.62	0.42	23.16
12/14	27.09	21	2	1.33	0.24	22.34
Annual Growth	4.2%	—	—	27.1%	42.9%	4.9%

Tactile Systems Technology Inc

Auditors: Grant Thornton LLP

LOCATIONS

HQ: Tactile Systems Technology Inc
3701 Wayzata Blvd, Suite 300, Minneapolis, MN 55416
Phone: 612 355-5100
Web: www.tactilemedical.com

HISTORICAL FINANCIALS

Company Type: Public

Income Statement
FYE: December 31

	REVENUE ($ mil.)	NET INCOME ($ mil.)	NET PROFIT MARGIN	EMPLOYEES
12/18	143.7	6.6	4.6%	499
12/17	109.2	5.8	5.4%	406
12/16	84.5	2.8	3.4%	335
12/15	62.8	1.3	2.2%	275
12/14	47.7	2.0	4.3%	0
Annual Growth	31.7%	33.7%	—	—

2018 Year-End Financials

Debt ratio: —
Return on equity: 8.1%
Cash ($ mil.): 20.1
Current ratio: 5.28
Long-term debt ($ mil.): —
No. of shares (mil.): 18.6
Dividends
 Yield: —
 Payout: —
Market value ($ mil.): 849.0

	STOCK PRICE ($) FY Close	P/E High/Low		PER SHARE ($) Earnings	Dividends	Book Value
12/18	45.55	197	78	0.34	0.00	4.79
12/17	28.98	108	44	0.31	0.00	4.08
12/16	16.41	112	62	0.15	0.00	3.54
Annual Growth	66.6%	—	—	50.6%	—	16.3%

Tallgrass Energy LP

Auditors: DELOITTE & TOUCHE LLP

LOCATIONS

HQ: Tallgrass Energy LP
4200 W. 115th Street, Suite 350, Leawood, KS 66211
Phone: 913 928-6060
Web: www.tallgrassenergy.com

HISTORICAL FINANCIALS
Company Type: Public

Income Statement
FYE: December 31

	REVENUE ($ mil.)	NET INCOME ($ mil.)	NET PROFIT MARGIN	EMPLOYEES
12/18	793.2	137.1	17.3%	750
12/17	655.9	(128.7)	—	0
12/16	605.1	26.7	4.4%	0
12/15	536.2	31.9	6.0%	0
12/14	371.5	70.6	19.0%	0
Annual Growth	20.9%	18.0%	—	—

2018 Year-End Financials
Debt ratio: 54.4%
Return on equity: —
Cash ($ mil.): 9.6
Current ratio: 0.67
Long-term debt ($ mil.): 3,205.9
No. of shares (mil.): 280.2
Dividends
Yield: 7.6%
Payout: 146.6%
Market value ($ mil.): 6,820.0

	STOCK PRICE ($) FY Close	P/E High/Low		PER SHARE ($) Earnings	Dividends	Book Value
12/18	24.34	21	14	1.27	1.86	6.16
12/17	25.74	—	—	(2.22)	1.26	0.31
12/16	26.80	49	19	0.55	0.89	1.60
12/15	15.97	65	27	0.51	0.22	2.69
Annual Growth	15.1%	—	—	35.5%	104.7%	31.9%

Talos Energy Inc

Auditors: Ernst & Young LLP

LOCATIONS
HQ: Talos Energy Inc
333 Clay Street, Suite 3300, Houston, TX 77002
Phone: 713 328-3000
Web: www.stoneenergy.com

HISTORICAL FINANCIALS
Company Type: Public

Income Statement
FYE: December 31

	REVENUE ($ mil.)	NET INCOME ($ mil.)	NET PROFIT MARGIN	EMPLOYEES
12/18	891.2	221.5	24.9%	374
12/17	412.8	(62.8)	—	238
12/16	258.7	(208.0)	—	0
12/15	315.6	(646.6)	—	0
12/14	561.5	309.4	55.1%	0
Annual Growth	12.2%	(8.0%)	—	—

2018 Year-End Financials
Debt ratio: 29.2%
Return on equity: 46.4%
Cash ($ mil.): 139.9
Current ratio: 1.10
Long-term debt ($ mil.): 654.8
No. of shares (mil.): 54.1
Dividends
Yield: —
Payout: —
Market value ($ mil.): 884.0

	STOCK PRICE ($) FY Close	P/E High/Low		PER SHARE ($) Earnings	Dividends	Book Value
12/18	16.32	8	3	4.81	0.00	18.60
Annual Growth	—	—	—	—	—	—

TCF Financial Corp (New)

Chemical Financial has banking down to a science. It's the holding company for Chemical Bank which provides standard services such as checking and savings accounts CDs and IRAs credit and debit cards and loans and mortgages to individuals and businesses through nearly 190 branches in the lower peninsula of Michigan. The majority of the bank's loan portfolio is made up of commercial loans while consumer loans make up the remainder. Boasting assets of $9 billion Chemical is the second largest bank in Michigan. The company also offers trust investment management brokerage and title insurance services through subsidiaries.

Operations

Its Wealth Management division which has some $4 billion in assets under custody offers trust services estate planning investment management and employee benefit programs. Chemical Financial Advisors offers mutual funds and marketable securities while CFC Title Services issues title insurance for mortgage properties. CFC Capital manages the company's municipal investment securities portfolio.

About 72% of Chemical Financial's total revenue came from loan interest (including fees) in 2014 while another 6% came from interest on its investment securities. The rest of its revenue came from deposit account service charges and fees (8%) wealth management revenue (6%) mortgage banking income (2%) and other miscellaneous sources of income.

Sales and Marketing

Chemical Financial spent $3.45 million on advertising in 2014 up from $2.97 million and $3.11 million in 2013 and 2012 respectively.

Financial Performance

Chemical Financial's revenues and profits have been rising over the past few years thanks growing loan and deposit business from acquisitions lower interest expenses on deposits and declining loan loss provisions as its loan portfolio's credit quality has improved with higher property valuations in the strengthened economy.

The bank's revenue rose by 6% to $290.4 million in 2014 as the bank as its acquisition of Northwestern Bancorp boosted its loan business during the year. Higher revenue lower interest expenses and a continued decline in loan loss provisions drove the bank's net income up by 9% to a record $62.1 million. The bank's operating cash levels inched higher to $89.9 million on higher cash earnings.

Strategy

The bank follows an aggressive acquisition strategy to boost its loan and deposit business while expanding its branch network into key parts of Michigan. Indeed its acquisitions in 2015 and 2014 boosted the bank's presence in northwestern Michigan and along the Michigan-Indiana border. By the end of 2014 the bank had acquired some 21 community banks and 36 branch bank offices.

Mergers and Acquisitions

Chemical Financial agreed in January 2019 to merge with Minnesota-based TCF Financial to form a Midwest bank with about $45 billion in assets $34 billion in total deposits and more than 500 branches in nine states. TCF's large deposit base and national wholesale lending business will complement Chemical's commercial lending and wealth management activities. The combined company which is to retain the TCF brand will have a more diversified deposit mix between retail and commercial lines and a more balanced loan portfolio across geographies asset classes and industries. Following the merger TCF shareholders will have a controlling interest in the combined company.

Company Background

In late 2012 the company acquired 21 branches in northeastern Michigan and Battle Creek from Independent Bank. That more than $8-million transaction further expands Chemical Bank's presence geographically. Additional acquisitions including FDIC-assisted takeovers of failed banks are possible.

EXECUTIVES

SVP CFO and Treasurer, Lori A. Gwizdala, age 61, $344,720 total compensation
Vice Chairman and President Chemical Bank, Thomas C. (Tom) Shafer, age 60
EVP and Senior Credit Officer Chemical Bank, James E. Tomczyk, age 67, $225,504 total compensation
Vice Chairman Chemical Bank and CEO InSite Capital LLC, Thomas W. Kohn, age 65, $329,174 total compensation
EVP Commercial Lending Chemical Bank, Daniel W. Terpsma, age 65
EVP and CFO Chemical Financial and Chemical Bank, Dennis L. Klaeser, age 61, $183,483 total compensation
President and CEO, David T. Provost
Director Chemical Financial and Chairman Chemical Bank, Franklin C. Wheatlake, age 71
EVP and COO Business Operations Chemical Bank, Leonardo Amat, age 50, $309,477 total compensation
EVP and Chief Risk Officer Chemical Bank, Lynn M. Kerber, age 50
EVP General Counsel and Secretary, William C. Collins, age 66
EVP and COO Customer Experience Chemical Bank, Robert S. Rathbun, age 55, $309,477 total compensation
SVP and CIO, Greg Meidt
Vice President of Customer Service, Sue Lynde
Vice President, Robert O Burgess
Assistant Vice President Product Development, Jim Hubinger
Vice President Commercial Loan Officer, Jeff Hyde
Executive Vice President Chief Operating Officer, James Milroy
Senior Vice President of Investments, Pavel Konecny
Vice President Information Systems, Laurie Soren
Senior Vice President and Trust Officer, Jude Patnaude
Vice President Information Technology, Gary Richard
Vice President Senior Financial Advisor East Region Sales Manager, Brenda Rajewski
Vice President Data Services, Brian Beall
First Vice President, David Vermilye
Vice President, Robin Grove
Vice President and Trust Investment Officer, Glen Matz
Mortgage Officer Assistant Vice President, Sue Moody

Vice President Information Technology, Annette Rus
Executive Vice President, Diane M Schweigert
Vice President and Community Reinvestment Act Officer, Robert BurgessJr
Vice President Commerical Loans, Scott Harris
Vice President, John Laman
Vice President Commercial Loans, EARL VANOPSTALL
Vice President Trust Investment Officer, Duane Carpenter
Vice President Treasury Management And Business Development, Marc Cesere
Vice President Treasury Management, Tammy Kerr
Vice President Commercial Lending, David Kiekintveld
Vice President Mortgage Originator, Krista Martiny
Assistant Vice President Electronic Banking Services, Mary Green
Vice President Commercial Banking Relationship Manager Commerce Park Interim Vice, Ron Cordaro
Vice President First, Michael Debo
Assistant Vice President Treasury Management Sales Advisor, Julie Kuchnicki
Executive Vice President Chief Delivery Officer, Gregory Bixby
Assistant Vice President And Branch Operations Specialist, Barb Hartman
Vice President And Trust Officer, Pamela Dolezan
Assistant Vice President Branch Manager, Sharon Langenberg
Senior Vice President Business Banking Credit Director, Nita Cohen
Vice President And Personal Trust Officer, Joanna Keenan
Chairman, Gary H. Torgow, age 61
Treasurer, Cheryl Whitman
Board Member, James Fitterling
Auditors: KPMG LLP

LOCATIONS

HQ: TCF Financial Corp (New)
  333 W. Fort Street, Suite 1800, Detroit, MI 48226
Phone: 800 867-9757
Web: www.chemicalbank.com

PRODUCTS/OPERATIONS

2014 Sales

	$ mil.	% of total
Interest		
Loans including fees	209.4	72
Investment securities	17.4	6
Other	0.4	-
Non-interest		
Service charges on deposit accounts	22.3	8
Wealth management revenue	16.0	6
Other customer service charges & fees	18.6	6
Other	6.1	2
Total	**290.4**	**100**

COMPETITORS

1st Source Corporation
Bank of America
Comerica
Fifth Third
Firstbank
Flagstar Bancorp
Huntington Bancshares
Independent Bank (MI)
Mercantile Bank

HISTORICAL FINANCIALS
Company Type: Public

Income Statement
FYE: December 31

	ASSETS ($ mil.)	NET INCOME ($ mil.)	INCOME AS % OF ASSETS	EMPLOYEES
12/18	21,498.3	284.0	1.3%	3,100
12/17	19,280.8	149.5	0.8%	3,000
12/16	17,355.1	108.0	0.6%	3,300
12/15	9,188.8	86.8	0.9%	2,100
12/14	7,322.1	62.1	0.8%	2,000
Annual Growth	30.9%	46.2%	—	11.6%

2018 Year-End Financials
Return on assets: 1.3%
Return on equity: 10.3%
Long-term debt ($ mil.): —
No. of shares (mil.): 71.4
Sales ($ mil): 924.5
Dividends
  Yield: 3.3%
  Payout: 31.4%
Market value ($ mil.): 2,616.0

	STOCK PRICE ($) FY Close	P/E High/Low		PER SHARE ($) Earnings	Dividends	Book Value
12/18	36.61	15	9	3.94	1.24	39.69
12/17	53.47	27	21	2.08	1.10	37.48
12/16	54.17	25	13	2.17	1.06	36.57
12/15	34.27	15	12	2.39	1.00	26.62
12/14	30.64	17	13	1.97	0.94	24.32
Annual Growth	4.6%	—	—	18.9%	7.2%	13.0%

Tennant Co.

Tennant is one of the world's leading manufacturers of industrial floor maintenance equipment. It makes specialty surface coatings and cleaning machines including extractors scrubbers sweepers and vacuums. Parts and supplies are also offered along with maintenance and repair services. Its products are used to clean up surfaces at airports factories offices parking garages stadiums supermarkets warehouses and other high-traffic areas. Brand names include Alfa Tennant Nobles and Orbio. The Americas account for about 60% of sales.

Financial Performance

Tennant's sales have been a bit choppy over the last five years but have risen since 2016. Revenue increased more than 36% between 2014 and 2018. Higher sales over the last two years have been driven chiefly by higher sales volumes and a 2017 acquisition that expanded its footprint in Europe.

Sales in 2018 increased 12% to $1.1 billion compared to $1 billion in 2017. Growth in 2018 was fueled by higher volumes and pricing across all the geographic regions the company serves particularly the Americas. Sales were also strong in Germany France China and Australia.

Net income increased to $33.4 million in 2018 compared to a loss of $6.2 million in 2017 primarily due to higher sales lower taxes resulting from the Tax Cuts and Jobs Act and acquisition costs that contributed to the net income loss in 2017.

Cash at the end of 2018 was $86.1 million an increase of $27 million from the prior year. Cash from operations contributed $80 million to the coffers while investing activities used $16 million mainly for capital expenditures. Financing activities used $32.8 million primarily for payment of long-term debt.

Strategy

After making a couple of acquisitions aimed at extending its global reach Tennant is focused on innovating new products and growing its roster of large-contract customers. In early 2019 the company bought China-based Gaomei Cleaning Equipment Company. The deal expanded Tennant's manufacturing footprint and brand offerings. The company's $353 million acquisition of Italy's IPC Group a manufacturer of professional cleaning equipment in mid-2017 also addressed Tennant's goals of geographically diversifying its revenue.

Tennant is betting on the future of automated floor cleaning equipment. In mid-2019 the company struck a deal with Walmart to provide the retailer with Tennant's T7AMR autonomous floor cleaners. Tennant hopes to strike similar deals as big box retailers shopping centers and airports increasingly make significant investments in automated cleaning equipment to free workers to perform more customer-facing tasks increase cleaning speed and better track equipment performance.

HISTORY

Irish immigrant George Tennant founded Tennant Company in 1870 to make wooden architectural products such as hardwood flooring. The company was formally incorporated in 1909. In 1932 a high school janitor demonstrated a homemade floor scourer powered by a washing machine motor. The company was sold on the idea and by 1940 Tennant was focusing its manufacturing efforts on floor care machines and floor sealers. Seven years later a Tennant engineer invented the first vacuumized power industrial sweeper a product that revolutionized industrial floor maintenance.

Tennant went public in 1969. Over the course of its history Tennant's cleaning products have scoured such famous places as the White House Grand Central Station Yankee Stadium and the holy cities of Mecca and Medina Saudi Arabia.

EXECUTIVES

SVP and CFO, Thomas (Tom) Paulson, age 63, $376,027 total compensation
President and CEO, H. Chris Killingstad, age 63, $664,577 total compensation
President CEO and Director, Chris Killingstad, age 63, $622,694 total compensation
VP Global Operations, Don B. Westman, age 65, $348,925 total compensation
SVP and CTO Global Research and Development, Michael W. (Mike) Schaefer, age 58
Vice President North America Sales, Brian Leland
Senior Vice President EMEA APAC Global Marketing and Operations, Dave Huml
Auditors: KPMG LLP

LOCATIONS

HQ: Tennant Co.
  701 North Lilac Drive, P.O. Box 1452, Minneapolis, MN 55440
Phone: 763 540-1200
Web: www.tennantco.com

PRODUCTS/OPERATIONS

2015 sales

	$ mil.	% of total
Equipment	499.6	62
Parts & consumables	175.6	22
Service & other	112.6	14
Specialty surface coatings	23.8	2
Total	811.7	100

Selected Industries
Automotive
Aviation / Transportation
Cleaning Professionals
Education
Electronics
Food and Beverage
Government Institutions
Health Care
Hospitality
Manufacturing
Mining
Municipalities
Pharmaceutical
Retail
Warehousing and Logistics

Selected Products
Commercial floor maintenance equipment
  Buffers
  Burnishers
  Carpet extractors
  Polishers
  Vacuums
  Walk-behind sweepers and scrubbers
Floor coatings
  Products that treat repair and upgrade concrete and wood floors
Industrial floor maintenance equipment
  Scrubbers (rider and walk-behind)
  Sweepers
Outdoor floor maintenance equipment
  Rider brooms
  Vacuum sweepers

COMPETITORS

Alfred Karcher
Federal Signal
Minuteman International
NSS Enterprises
Nilfisk-Advance
RPM International
Royal Appliance
TYMCO

HISTORICAL FINANCIALS
Company Type: Public

Income Statement
FYE: December 31

	REVENUE ($ mil.)	NET INCOME ($ mil.)	NET PROFIT MARGIN	EMPLOYEES
12/18	1,123.5	33.4	3.0%	4,300
12/17	1,003.0	(6.2)	—	4,300
12/16	808.5	46.6	5.8%	3,236
12/15	811.8	32.0	4.0%	3,164
12/14	821.9	50.6	6.2%	3,087
Annual Growth	8.1%	(9.9%)	—	8.6%

2018 Year-End Financials
Debt ratio: 35.7%
Return on equity: 10.9%
Cash ($ mil.): 85.6
Current ratio: 1.88
Long-term debt ($ mil.): 328.0
No. of shares (mil.): 18.1
Dividends
  Yield: 1.6%
  Payout: 46.7%
Market value ($ mil.): 945.0

	STOCK PRICE ($) FY Close	P/E High/Low		Earnings	Dividends	Book Value
12/18	52.11	45	27	1.82	0.85	17.35
12/17	72.65	—	—	(0.35)	0.84	16.58
12/16	71.20	29	17	2.59	0.81	15.75
12/15	56.26	41	31	1.74	0.80	14.21
12/14	72.17	28	21	2.70	0.78	15.24
Annual Growth	(7.8%)	—	—	(9.4%)	2.2%	3.3%

TerraForm Power Inc

Auditors: Ernst & Young LLP

LOCATIONS
HQ: TerraForm Power Inc
200 Liberty Street, 14th Floor, New York, NY 10281
Phone: 646 992-2400
Web: www.terraformpower.com

HISTORICAL FINANCIALS
Company Type: Public

Income Statement
FYE: December 31

	REVENUE ($ mil.)	NET INCOME ($ mil.)	NET PROFIT MARGIN	EMPLOYEES
12/18	766.5	12.3	1.6%	177
12/17	610.4	(164.1)	—	119
12/16	654.5	(129.8)	—	0
12/15	469.5	(79.8)	—	0
12/14	125.8	(25.6)	—	0
Annual Growth	57.1%	—	—	—

2018 Year-End Financials
Debt ratio: 61.7%
Return on equity: 0.6%
Cash ($ mil.): 248.5
Current ratio: 0.73
Long-term debt ($ mil.): 5,297.5
No. of shares (mil.): 209.1
Dividends
  Yield: 6.7%
  Payout: 1,085.7%
Market value ($ mil.): 2,347.0

	STOCK PRICE ($) FY Close	P/E High/Low		Earnings	Dividends	Book Value
12/18	11.22	172	142	0.07	0.76	9.89
12/17	11.96	—	—	(1.65)	0.00	10.20
12/16	12.81	—	—	(1.47)	0.00	8.92
12/15	12.58	—	—	(1.25)	0.00	8.46
12/14	30.88	—	—	(0.87)	0.00	4.19
Annual Growth	(22.4%)	—	—	—	—	24.0%

Terreno Realty Corp

Terreno Realty has its eyes set on acquiring industrial real estate. The real estate investment trust (REIT) invests in and operates industrial properties in major US coastal markets including Los Angeles San Francisco Bay Area Seattle Miami Northern New Jersey/New York City and Washington DC/Baltimore. The REIT typically invests in warehouse and distribution facilities flex buildings for light manufacturing and research and development and transportation and shipping centers. The company owns more than 125 buildings spanning 9.3 million square feet and two improved land parcels totaling 3.5 acres.

Operations
About 89% of Terreno Realty's property portfolio consisted of warehouse/distribution properties while flex buildings (including light industrial and R&D facilities) made up another 9%. Trans-shipment properties made up the rest.

Sales and Marketing
Some of Terreno Realty's tenants include FedEx Cepheid Northrop Grumman HD Smith Wholesale Drug Company Home Depot and the US government.

Financial Performance
Terreno Realty's revenues and profits have rising at a healthy clip in recent years as its rental income has increased with new property acquisitions.

The REIT's revenue rose by 51% to a record $68.9 million in 2014 thanks to new rental income from property acquisitions made in 2014 and 2013. Same-store revenue grew as well as it increased rental rates by 8% and as occupancy rates increased to 97.1% from 96.3% the year before.

Higher revenue in 2014 drove the REIT's net income higher by 61% to $10.7 million while its operating cash levels more than doubled to $29.3 million thanks to higher cash earnings.

Strategy
Terreno Realty seeks long-term earnings growth by increasing rents and operating income at its existing properties and by acquiring new properties in its six target geographic markets. In 2015 it spent on $115.5 million on properties in Washington DC while it also purchased properties in Annapolis Junction Maryland; Medley Florida; Union City California; Tukwila Washington; and Kent Washington. During 2014 it spent $235.7 million on 29 industrial buildings spanning 2.27 million sq. ft. and one improved land parcel (1.2 acres) growing its property portfolio's square footage by 33%.

In 2012 the company acquired 22 industrial buildings (containing almost 1.8 million square feet) for $180.9 million. Properties included Global Plaza in Sterling Virginia; Garfield in Commerce California; Caribbean in Sunnyvale California; and South Main in Carson California.

Company Background
The company took itself public in February 2010 in an effort to capitalize on a distressed market ripe with foreclosures and troubled loans. Portions of the net proceeds from its public offering were used to invest in interest-bearing short-term securities to help it gain REIT status.

EXECUTIVES

President, Michael A. (Mike) Coke, age 51, $541,667 total compensation
Chairman and CEO, W. Blake Baird, age 58, $541,667 total compensation
Executive Vice President Jaime J. Cannon, Andrew T. Burke
SVP and CFO, Jaime J. Cannon, $245,000 total compensation
Vice President, Gregory N Spencer
Auditors: Ernst & Young LLP

LOCATIONS

HQ: Terreno Realty Corp
101 Montgomery Street, Suite 200, San Francisco, CA 94104
Phone: 415 655-4580
Web: www.terreno.com

PRODUCTS/OPERATIONS

2012 Sales

	$ mil.	% of total
Rental	24.5	78
Tenant expense reimbursements	6.7	22
Total	31.2	100

COMPETITORS

DCT Industrial Trust
Duke Realty
EastGroup Properties
First Industrial Realty
First Potomac Realty
Liberty Property Trust
Mack-Cali
Monmouth Real Estate
PS Business Parks
Prologis

HISTORICAL FINANCIALS

Company Type: Public

Income Statement — FYE: December 31

	REVENUE ($ mil.)	NET INCOME ($ mil.)	NET PROFIT MARGIN	EMPLOYEES
12/19	171.0	55.5	32.5%	24
12/18	151.6	63.2	41.7%	23
12/17	132.4	53.1	40.1%	22
12/16	108.4	15.1	13.9%	19
12/15	95.9	14.6	15.2%	18
Annual Growth	15.6%	39.6%	—	7.5%

2019 Year-End Financials

Debt ratio: 23.3%
Return on equity: 4.0%
Cash ($ mil.): 110.0
Current ratio: 1.57
Long-term debt ($ mil.): 491.5
No. of shares (mil.): 67.2
Dividends
 Yield: 1.8%
 Payout: 100.9%
Market value ($ mil.): 3,641.0

	STOCK PRICE ($) FY Close	P/E High/Low	PER SHARE ($) Earnings	Dividends	Book Value
12/19	54.14	67 40	0.85	1.02	22.56
12/18	35.17	36 29	1.09	0.92	20.45
12/17	35.06	40 28	0.95	0.84	18.56
12/16	28.49	111 80	0.26	0.76	17.12
12/15	22.62	92 75	0.26	0.66	16.93
Annual Growth	24.4%	—	34.5%	11.5%	7.4%

Tetra Tech Inc

Tetra Tech is a global leader in providing consulting design and engineering services in the fields of water environment infrastructure energy and development. Its solutions span the entire life cycle of consulting and engineering projects and include applied science data analytics research engineering design construction management and operations and maintenance. The US government is one of Tetra's biggest clients along with development agencies and commercial clients in oil and gas energy utilities and mining industries. Based in the US Tetra engages in projects worldwide. The company likes to do business under time-and-materials fixed-price and cost-plus contracts.

Operations

Tetra reports through two business segments. The company's Government Services Group (more than 55% of sales) provides consulting and engineering services for a broad range of water environment and infrastructure-related needs.

Its Commercial/International Services Group (nearly 45% of revenue) provides consulting and engineering services worldwide for a broad range of water environment and infrastructure-related needs. This segment also supports commercial clients by providing design services to renovate upgrade and modernize industrial water supplies and address industrial water treatment and water reuse needs. Tetra conducts industrial water treatment projects throughout the world.

Geographic Reach

Headquartered in Pasadena California Tetra delivers projects across the US and in some 100 countries worldwide including Canada Brazil Chile Australia and New Zealand. The company owns three US facilities and leases about 400 more in the US and foreign locations.

Some 75% of revenue comes from the US; Canada and Australia are the company's primary international markets.

Sales and Marketing

Tetra provides consulting services to all levels of the US government (half of company revenue) its biggest client. Within the government USAID (roughly 15%) and Department of Defense (about 10%) are its biggest clients. The company also works with development agencies and commercial clients across many industries. Services are performed under three types of contracts: time-and-materials (accounts for 45% of revenue) fixed-price (35%) and cost-plus (20%).

Tetra maintains centralized business development resources to develop corporate branding and marketing materials support proposal preparation and planning conduct market research and manage promotional and professional activities.

Financial Performance

Tetra's revenue has maintained an upward trajectory in the last five years growing from $2.4 billion in 2014 to $2.9 billion in 2018. Sales climbed 8% in 2018 (ended September) from $2.7 billion in 2017. The growth came mostly from the acquisitions of Glumac and Norman Disney & Young plus from proceeds from the divestment of utility field services operations. Organic revenue grew 3.8% thanks to municipal water infrastructure work in the metropolitan areas of California Texas and Florida.

Net income grew marginally from $117 million in 2017 to $136 million in 2018 the difference mostly stemming from a YOY $14 million fall in income tax expenses.

Cash holdings declined from $189 million at the end of 2017 to $146 million a year later. Operations provided $176 million offset by $42 million going towards investments and a further $173 million used in financial activities (mostly in payments of long-term debt).

Strategy

Tetra Tech's main strategy has been investing in innovation or as the company calls it "leading with Science". Tetra boasts expertise in innovative water treatment technologies with significant projects in California (groundwater reliability improvement) Texas (desalination plant) and Florida (direct potable reuse program). These projects registered the highest revenue growth in 2018 some 14%. Furthermore with demand of high-end infrastructure business on the rise especially in water solutions and environmental response the company is expected considerable visibility going into the future.

To accommodate growing demand the company has acquired two companies in 2018 (Glumac and Norman Disney & Young) to add to its infrastructure engineering expertise and increase access to local government contracts (which brings in most of its revenue). A bold move was to expand into the aviation services space with the acquisition of BridgeNet. Its acquisition in Australia (ELA) points towards boosting quality service consultation in the Asia Pacific region.

Tetra also reorganized its business in 2018 to into two renamed reportable segments to provide quicker and targeted consulting and technical solutions. Government Services Group will focus on serving the US government clients (federal state and local) and activities with development agencies worldwide. Meanwhile the Commercial/International Services Group is geared towards private clients.

Mergers and Acquisitions

Tetra tech has been busy acquiring promising companies to better position itself in the markets it operates in.

In early 2018 Tetra Tech purchased BridgeNet a California-based aviation technology systems provider. The combination will help the company expand its ability to deliver platforms for ground and airspace support aviation demand forecasting and modeling and other lifecycle aviation services.

Later that year Tetra Tech also acquired two other companies to boost its infrastructure engineering offerings. Both Glumac and Norman Disney & Young will help Tetra to incorporate incorporates innovative technologies and solutions into its products that use less energy.

In 2017 the company also acquired the Australian consulting firm ELA that provides innovative high-end environmental and ecological services.

Company Background

Tetra Tech Inc. was founded in 1966 to provide engineering services related to waterways harbors and coastal areas. Tetra Tech went public in 1991. For more than 50 years the company has substantially increased the size and scope of its business and expanded its service offerings through a series of strategic acquisitions and internal growth.

HISTORY

Tetra Tech was founded in 1966 by Nicholas Boratynski as a coastal and marine engineering firm. One of its first jobs was measuring water waves to determine the damage an offshore nuclear bomb could do to the coastline. The company developed expertise in water management in the 1970s. Honeywell bought the company in 1982 and Tetra Tech management in turn bought out Honeywell in 1988. Tetra Tech went public in 1991.

Since 1993 Tetra Tech has grown largely through acquisitions. In 1997 the company expanded into infrastructure and telecommunications. Tetra Tech acquired two site development firms — CommSite Development Corp. and Whalen & Company — to capitalize on the growing telecom market. It also enlarged its environmental business with the purchase of Halliburton's Brown & Root and Halliburton NUS environmental service units.

Continuing to build up its telecom business in 1998 it bought Sentrex Cen-Comm Communications Systems an engineering firm serving the cable TV telephone and data networking industries.

A year later the company won a $105 million contract from the US Department of Energy to help monitor the nation's nuclear weapons stockpile. In 2000 Tetra Tech won a $375 million contract from WideOpenWest a leading broadband wired access provider in the Denver area. It also snapped up nine companies that fiscal year.

In 2001 Tetra Tech expanded its energy services to include power plant relicensing projects in the US. The company also expanded its consulting services to the energy and mining industries through acquisitions. In 2002 the company acquired The Thomas Group a leading designer of educational and health care facilities. It also picked up Florida-based consulting engineering firm Ardaman & Associates adding to its water resources management operations.

The next year the group expanded even more by acquiring nearly all the assets of environmental services management firm Foster Wheeler Environmental Corp. a unit of Foster Wheeler. Tetra Tech renamed the group which provides hazardous and nuclear waste management primarily to the federal government Tetra Tech FW. In 2003 it strengthened its position in the federal market even more by acquiring California-based engineering firm Engineering Management Concepts (EMC) which provides weapons test range services and systems logistics support to the Department of Defense.

The group was buying again in 2004 with its purchase of Advanced Management Technology Inc. which enhanced its position in the security and defense market. In 2005 however Tetra Tech exited the wireless communications arena and began consolidating its infrastructure operations.

Tetra Tech builds out its skill set and product offerings through acquisitions — such as the 2008 purchase of Vermont-based international engineering consulting firm ARD and of Tennessee-based nuclear services provider Haselwood Enterprises the next year. In 2009 the company also acquired construction management firm Tesoro Corporation environmental consulting firm Mussetter Engineering of Fort Collins Canadian power engineering specialists ACI Engineering and the Californian consulting and engineering firm Bryan A. Stirrat.

Tetra Tech expanded its international energy and infrastructure consulting services by purchasing the US-based international development consulting business practice from London-based PA Consulting Group in 2010. The deal doubled Tetra Tech's energy management consulting business. That year the company also acquired Alberta-based EBA Engineering Consultants and BPR a Quebec-based scientific and engineering firm expanding its Canadian holdings.

Growing its US assets in 2013 Tetra Tech acquired solid waste management specialist American Environmental Group Ltd. of Richfield Ohio and Rooney Engineering Inc. an oil and gas pipeline planning and engineering firm based in Colorado.

That year the company agreed to buy Parkland Pipeline an Alberta-based company that serves the oil and gas industry in Western Canada.

EXECUTIVES

Senior Vice President Corporate Human Resources and Leadership Development, Kevin McDonald
Chairman President and CEO, Dan L. Batrack, $900,000 total compensation
SVP and CIO, Craig L. Christensen
EVP CFO and Treasurer, Steven M. Burdick, $446,154 total compensation
SVP Enterprise Risk Management Officer, William R. Brownlie
EVP Resource Management and Energy, Ronald J. Chu, $454,231 total compensation
EVP Water Environment and Infrastructure, Leslie L. Shoemaker, $368,414 total compensation
Vice President Engineering and Architectural Services, Dave George
Vice President Oil Gas and Chemicals, Mark Moderski
Vice President Resource Management, Eric Dohner
Vice President, Nick Benedico
Senior Vice President, Jane Carpenito
Vice President, Melissa Koob
Vice President, Gary Revoir
Vice President, Sean Reardon
Vice President Infrastructure Western Region, Mark Bush
Vice President, Thomas Villeneuve
Senior Vice President Enterprise Risk Management, Brendan O'rourke
Auditors: PricewaterhouseCoopers LLP

LOCATIONS

HQ: Tetra Tech Inc
3475 East Foothill Boulevard, Pasadena, CA 91107
Phone: 626 351-4664
Web: www.tetratech.com

PRODUCTS/OPERATIONS

2018 Sales

	% of total
U.S commercial	26
U.S. federal government	33
International	25
U.S. state and local government	16
Total	**100**

SELECTED SUBSIDIARIES

Advanced Management Technology Inc.
AEG West Inc.
America's Schoolhouse Consulting Services Inc.
American Environmental Group Ltd.
ARD Inc.
Ardaman & Associates Inc.
BFP Consultants Pty Ltd
BIOCNG LLC
Bovell Freeman Holley (Pty) Ltd
BPR-Énergie Inc.
SERVICES
Consulting and Technical Services
Design and Engineering
Program and Construction Management

COMPETITORS

AECOM	EA Engineering
ARCADIS	Jacobs Engineering
Amec Foster Wheeler	MWH Global
Black & Veatch	Stantec
Brown and Caldwell	TRC Companies
Camp Dresser McKee	Weston Solutions

HISTORICAL FINANCIALS
Company Type: Public

Income Statement FYE: September 29

	REVENUE ($ mil.)	NET INCOME ($ mil.)	NET PROFIT MARGIN	EMPLOYEES
09/19	2,389.6	158.6	6.6%	20,000
09/18*	2,200.7	136.8	6.2%	17,000
10/17	2,034.0	117.8	5.8%	16,000
10/16	1,929.2	83.7	4.3%	16,000
09/15	1,718.7	39.0	2.3%	13,000
Annual Growth	8.6%	42.0%	—	11.4%

*Fiscal year change

2019 Year-End Financials

Debt ratio: 12.8%   No. of shares (mil.): 54.5
Return on equity: 16.2%   Dividends
Cash ($ mil.): 120.7   Yield: 0.0%
Current ratio: 1.40   Payout: 19.0%
Long-term debt ($ mil.): 263.9   Market value ($ mil.): 4,635.0

	STOCK PRICE ($) FY Close	P/E High/Low		PER SHARE ($) Earnings	Dividends	Book Value
09/19	84.94	30	17	2.84	0.54	17.62
09/18*	68.30	29	18	2.42	0.44	17.47
10/17	46.55	23	17	2.04	0.38	16.62
10/16	35.47	25	16	1.42	0.34	15.24
09/15	24.92	43	36	0.64	0.30	14.42
Annual Growth	35.9%	—	—	45.1%	15.8%	5.1%

*Fiscal year change

Texas Capital Bancshares Inc

Texas Capital Bancshares is the parent company of Texas Capital Bank with more than 10 branches in Austin Dallas Fort Worth Houston and San Antonio. The bank targets high-net-worth individuals and Texas-based businesses with more than $5 million in annual revenue with a focus on the real estate financial services transportation communications petrochemicals and mining sectors. Striving for personalized services for its clients the bank offers deposit accounts Visa credit cards commercial loans and mortgages equipment leasing wealth management and trust services. Its BankDirect division provides online banking services. Founded in 1998 Texas Capital Bancshares has about $11.7 billion in assets.

Financial Performance

The bank reported $488.6 million in revenue in 2013 an nearly 11% increase versus 2012. Net income was flat at about $121 million after posting three consecutive years of gains. Cash flow from operations continued its steep three year decline. The bank's total assets increased 11% from about $10.5 billion in 2012 to $11.7 billion in 2013. Total deposits increased 24% year over year to about $9.3 billion.

Strategy

Headquartered in Dallas Texas Capital Bank (TCB) believes that its Texas roots give it a competitive advantage over larger competitors that are headquartered out of state. Indeed TCB is gaining market share and is expanding by hiring experienced bankers and support staff. The bank is looking to grow within its main metropolitan markets but has also branched out beyond the borders of its home state. The bank has an Cayman Islands branch to offer offshore cash management and deposit products to it core clientele.

EXECUTIVES

President and CEO Texas Capital Bancshares Inc. President and CEO Texas Capital Bank, C. Keith Cargill, age 66, $825,000 total compensation
EVP and Chief Lending Officer Dallas Region, Vince A. Ackerson, age 62, $454,166 total compensation
Managing Director Regional and Specialty Banking Texas Capital Bank Austin Fort Worth and San Antonio and Commercial Real Estate and Builder Finance, Mark M. Johnson
EVP Austin Region Texas Capital Bank, Kerry L. Hall
Regional President Texas Capital Bank Dallas, Russell Hartsfield
Chief Risk Officer Texas Capital Bancshares Inc. and Texas Capital Bank, John D. Hudgens, age 63, $455,833 total compensation
Managing Director Specialty and Regional Banking Texas Capital Bank Dallas and Syndicated Finance Lender Finance Leasing and Financial Institutions, James D. (Jim) Recer
Regional Chairman Texas Capital Bank Houston, Bill Wilson
Regional President Texas Capital Bank San Antonio, David Pope
Managing Director Regional and Specialty Banking Texas Capital Bank Houston, John C. Sarvadi
Controller and Chief Accounting Officer Texas Capital Bancshares and CFO Texas Capital Bank, Julie L. Anderson, age 50, $355,000 total compensation
Regional Chairman Texas Capital Bank San Antonio, Shaun Kennedy
Regional Chairman Texas Capital Bank Fort Worth, Robin Hamilton
Regional President Texas Capital Bank Fort Worth, David Williams
EVP Builder Finance, Melissa Abel
EVP Asset Based Lending, Chris Capriotti
EVP Commercial Real Estate, Rob Delph
EVP Lender Finance, David Fricke
EVP Energy/Oil and Gas Syndicated Finance and Financial Institutions, Lester Keliher
EVP Financial Institutions, Peter Stringer
President Mortgage Finance, Gary Ort
EVP Technology Operations Enterprise Planning and Information Security Texas Capital Bank, Kirk Coleman
EVP SBA Lending, John Gannon
EVP Public Finance, Paul Howell
EVP Strategic Sales and Marketing, Greg Lewis
President Private Wealth Advisors, Alan L. Miller
Vice President Manager Credit Underwriting, Anthony Violi
Senior Vice President Compensation Director, Chris Gullo
Vice President, Lela Naggar
Vice President, Raul Cantu
Vice President Deposit Operations, Leslie Marsh
Vice President of Information Technology Infrastructure, Randy Tiegs
Senior Vice President and Deposit Operation, Connie Couch
Vice President, Jenny Downey
Vice President Corp Security and Investigations, Cary Wicker
Vice President Fraud Investigator, Jamie Burud
Vice President Security, Neal Baker
Executive Vice President, Brent Johnston
Executive Vice President, Ronald Baker
Vice President Planning, Prasad Varma
Executive Vice President Human Resources and LD, Cara McDaniel
Executive Vice President Director of Operations, James White
Senior Vice President and CRA Manager, Phil Aslin
Chairman, Larry L. Helm, age 71
Board Member, Elysia Ragusa
Board Member, James Browning
Board Member, Robert Stallings
Board Member, Steven Rosenberg
Auditors: Ernst & Young LLP

LOCATIONS

HQ: Texas Capital Bancshares Inc
2000 McKinney Avenue, Suite 700, Dallas, TX 75201
Phone: 214 932-6600
Web: www.texascapitalbank.com

PRODUCTS/OPERATIONS

2015 Sales

	% of total
Interest income	
Interest and fees on loans	92
Other	1
Non-interest income	
Brokered loan fees	3
Service charges on deposit accounts	1
Trust fee income	1
Swap fees	1
Other	1
Total	**100**

Selected Services
Association capital bank
Bankdirect
Business services
Mortgage business finance
Online services
Personal banking
Private wealth advisors
Treasury and liquidity

COMPETITORS

Amegy	Comerica
BBVA Compass Bancshares	Cullen/Frost Bankers
	JPMorgan Chase
BOK Financial	Prosperity Bancshares
Bank of America	Wells Fargo

HISTORICAL FINANCIALS
Company Type: Public

Income Statement — FYE: December 31

	ASSETS ($ mil.)	NET INCOME ($ mil.)	INCOME AS % OF ASSETS	EMPLOYEES
12/18	28,257.7	300.8	1.1%	1,641
12/17	25,075.6	197.0	0.8%	1,564
12/16	21,697.1	155.1	0.7%	1,442
12/15	18,909.1	144.8	0.8%	1,329
12/14	15,899.9	136.3	0.9%	1,142
Annual Growth	15.5%	21.9%	—	9.5%

2018 Year-End Financials
Return on assets: 1.1%
Return on equity: 12.7%
Long-term debt ($ mil.): —
No. of shares (mil.): 50.2
Sales ($ mil): 1,242.2
Dividends
Yield: —
Payout: —
Market value ($ mil.): 2,565.0

	STOCK PRICE ($) FY Close	P/E High/Low	PER SHARE ($) Earnings	Dividends	Book Value
12/18	51.09	18 8	5.79	0.00	49.81
12/17	88.90	25 19	3.73	0.00	44.37
12/16	78.40	26 10	3.11	0.00	40.59
12/15	49.42	21 14	2.91	0.00	35.39
12/14	54.33	23 17	2.88	0.00	32.45
Annual Growth	(1.5%)	— —	19.1%	—	11.3%

Texas Pacific Land Trust

EXECUTIVES

Co-General Agent CEO and Secretary, Tyler Glover, age 34
Co-General Agent and CFO, Robert J. Packer, age 50, $127,083 total compensation
Chairman, Maurice Meyer, age 84
Auditors: Lane Gorman Trubitt, LLC

LOCATIONS

HQ: Texas Pacific Land Trust
1700 Pacific Avenue, Suite 2900, Dallas, TX 75201
Phone: 214 969-5530 **Fax:** 214 871-7139
Web: www.TPLTrust.com

PRODUCTS/OPERATIONS

2015 sales

		% of total
Easements and sundry income		40
Oil and gas royalties		31
Land sales	22.6	28
Grazing lease rentals	0.5	1
Interest income from notes receivable	0.0	—
Total	**79.4**	**100**

COMPETITORS

American Realty Investors	Koch Industries Inc.
	Permian Basin

HISTORICAL FINANCIALS
Company Type: Public

Income Statement — FYE: December 31

	REVENUE ($ mil.)	NET INCOME ($ mil.)	NET PROFIT MARGIN	EMPLOYEES
12/18	300.2	209.7	69.9%	71
12/17	132.3	76.3	57.7%	32
12/16	59.9	37.2	62.2%	10
12/15	79.4	50.0	63.0%	8
12/14	55.2	34.7	63.0%	8
Annual Growth	52.7%	56.7%	—	72.6%

2018 Year-End Financials
Debt ratio: —
Return on equity: 129.5%
Cash ($ mil.): 119.6
Current ratio: 6.98
Long-term debt ($ mil.): —
No. of shares (mil.): 7.7
Dividends
Yield: 0.1%
Payout: 15.0%
Market value ($ mil.): 4,204.0

	STOCK PRICE ($)	P/E	PER SHARE ($)		
	FY Close	High/Low	Earnings	Dividends	Book Value
12/18	541.63	32 16	26.93	4.05	31.52
12/17	446.63	46 27	9.72	1.35	10.12
12/16	296.77	65 24	4.66	0.31	6.01
12/15	130.92	27 18	6.10	0.29	5.63
12/14	118.00	56 23	4.14	0.27	3.21
Annual Growth	46.4%	— —	59.7%	96.8%	77.0%

Texas Roadhouse Inc

Texas Roadhouse operates a leading full-service casual dining restaurant chain with about 590 company-owned and franchised locations in nearly 50 US states and 10 countries. The Southwest-themed eatery serves a variety of steaks ribs chicken pork chops and seafood entrees along with sandwiches chili starters and a selection of side dishes. The company also operates a few restaurants under the name Bubba's 33 that specializes in burgers pizza and wings. Despite its name Texas Roadhouse was founded in Clarksville Indiana in 1993.

Operations
About 495 of Texas Roadhouse's restaurants are company-owned; around 90 are franchised. The company garners nearly all its revenue from company-owned and operated units. It operates some 465 locations under the Texas Roadhouse brand?a Southwest-themed steakhouse that also sells a range of other beef pork seafood and chicken dishes. Roughly 25 of Texas Roadhouse's locations are branded as family-friendly sports restaurant Bubba's 33. That chain serves wings pizza burgers beer and other pub fare.

Geographic Reach
Louisville Kentucky-headquartered Texas Roadhouse has about 580 company-owned and franchised restaurants in just under 50 US states and 10 countries. Its locations are concentrated in the Midwest and Southeast. Roughly 70 of the company's restaurants are in Texas. It also has about 25 franchise restaurants in about 10 countries outside the US including in the Middle East Taiwan the Philippines Mexico China and South Korea.

Sales and Marketing
Targeting the casual dining sector Texas Roadhouse's namesake chain focuses on offering mid-priced menu items in a family-friendly dining atmosphere. The chain is primarily interested in serving the dinner segment offering its lunch menu only on weekends. Its over-the-top Texas décor including down-home touches such as jukeboxes and complimentary in-the-shell peanuts helps the chain distinguish itself in a crowded field of competitors that includes Logan's Roadhouse and Lone Star Steakhouse & Saloon. Texas Roadhouse also faces stiff competition from industry heavyweights Chili's and Outback Steakhouse.

Financial Performance
Over the last five years Texas Roadhouse has posted impressive improvements across several key performance metrics as it accelerates restaurant openings and sales. The company's revenue increased more than 50% while net income gained greater than 80%. Meanwhile it expanded its cash by nearly 150% and almost completely eradicated its long-term debt.

Texas Roadhouse's revenue grew by 11% to $2.5 billion in 2018 on rising sales volume at its growing restaurant base.

Net income increased by 20% to end the year at $158.2 million. Greater average unit volume sales growth restaurant openings and margins drove the improvements.

The company added $59.2 million to its cash for total stores of $210.1 million at the end of 2018. Operations brought in $352.9 million. Investments?almost all property and equipment?used $158.1 million and financing activities ate up $135.5 million. Financing spend was mostly for dividend payments and principal payments on long-term debt and capital lease obligations.

Strategy
Texas Roadhouse's growth strategy mainly involves expanding its owned restaurants as opposed to franchising which gives the corporation tighter control over its operations and a larger share of its returns. It plans to open about 30 Texas Roadhouse locations annually.

The company owns around 500 restaurants and franchises about 90. It franchises to a select group: about 75% of its franchise restaurants are operated by only nine franchisees each of which runs 15 restaurants or fewer. Its franchisees plan to open no more than eight restaurants in 2019. Furthermore they are expected to be international locations where franchisees may have better insight into local markets.

Texas Roadhouse relies on specially priced value menu items and targets its marketing message toward cost-conscious families looking for affordable dining options. It aims to garner new customers and bring in new ones through local marketing initiatives. The company also increases the throughput of its guests by emphasizing service speed and expanding seats and parking.

Company Background
Founder and chairman Kent Taylor opened the first Texas Roadhouse in 1993. A veteran of the restaurant business he previously served with chains including Bennigan's Hooters and KFC.

EXECUTIVES

President and CFO, Scott M. Colosi, age 54, $400,000 total compensation
Chairman and CEO, W. Kent Taylor, age 63, $525,000 total compensation
General Counsel and Corporate Secretary, Celia P. Catlett, $200,000 total compensation
Vice President Manager Director, Brian Wathen
Vice President Manager Director, Anne Gossman
Vice President Training And People Development, James Scholz
Auditors: KPMG LLP

LOCATIONS

HQ: Texas Roadhouse Inc
6040 Dutchmans Lane, Suite 200, Louisville, KY 40205
Phone: 502 426-9984

PRODUCTS/OPERATIONS

2018 Sales

	$ mil.	% of total
Restaurant sales and other	2,437.1	99
Franchise royalties and fees	20.3	1
Total	2,457.4	100

COMPETITORS

Applebee's International	LRI Holdings
Brinker	Landry's
Buffets Inc	Lone Star Steakhouse
Carlson Restaurants	O'Charley's
Cracker Barrel	OSI Restaurant Partners
Darden	P.F. Chang's
Golden Corral	Ruby Tuesday
Hooters	
Ignite Restaurant Group	

HISTORICAL FINANCIALS
Company Type: Public

Income Statement — FYE: December 25

	REVENUE ($ mil.)	NET INCOME ($ mil.)	NET PROFIT MARGIN	EMPLOYEES
12/18	2,457.4	158.2	6.4%	64,900
12/17	2,219.5	131.5	5.9%	56,300
12/16	1,990.7	115.6	5.8%	52,500
12/15	1,807.3	96.8	5.4%	47,900
12/14	1,582.1	87.0	5.5%	43,300
Annual Growth	11.6%	16.1%	—	10.6%

2018 Year-End Financials
Debt ratio: 0.1% No. of shares (mil.): 71.6
Return on equity: 17.7% Dividends
Cash ($ mil.): 210.1 Yield: 0.0%
Current ratio: 0.90 Payout: 45.4%
Long-term debt ($ mil.): 2.0 Market value ($ mil.): 4,069.0

	STOCK PRICE ($)	P/E	PER SHARE ($)		
	FY Close	High/Low	Earnings	Dividends	Book Value
12/18	56.81	34 24	2.20	1.00	13.20
12/17	54.08	30 22	1.84	0.84	11.79
12/16	49.56	31 21	1.63	0.76	10.62
12/15	36.06	30 24	1.37	0.68	9.55
12/14	33.78	27 19	1.23	0.60	8.73
Annual Growth	13.9%	— —	15.6%	13.6%	10.9%

TGR Financial, Inc

Auditors: RSM US LLP

LOCATIONS
HQ: TGR Financial, Inc
P.O Box 10910, Naples, FL 34101
Phone: 239 348-8000 **Fax:** 239 213-3342
Web: www.ffibank.com

HISTORICAL FINANCIALS
Company Type: Public

Income Statement — FYE: December 31

	REVENUE ($ mil.)	NET INCOME ($ mil.)	NET PROFIT MARGIN	EMPLOYEES
12/18	57.6	15.0	26.1%	0
12/17	49.3	8.1	16.5%	0
12/16	42.1	5.7	13.5%	0
12/15	36.6	4.6	12.8%	0
12/14	30.8	1.6	5.2%	0
Annual Growth	17.0%	75.1%	—	—

2018 Year-End Financials

Debt ratio: —
Return on equity: 12.2%
Cash ($ mil.): 92.7
Current ratio: 0.07
Long-term debt ($ mil.): —
No. of shares (mil.): 17.3
Dividends
Yield: —
Payout: —
Market value ($ mil.): 179.0

	STOCK PRICE ($) FY Close	P/E High/Low		PER SHARE ($) Earnings	Dividends	Book Value
12/18	10.37	15	12	0.78	0.00	7.48
12/17	11.35	24	17	0.43	0.00	6.72
12/16	7.80	39	17	0.30	0.00	6.18
Annual Growth	15.3%	—	—	61.2%	—	10.0%

The Bancorp Inc

The Bancorp is — what else? — the holding company for The Bancorp Bank which provides financial services in the virtual world. Targeting nonbank financial service companies across the US and Europe from start-ups to small and midsized businesses underserved by larger banks in the market The Bancorp Bank provides private-label online banking to 200 affinity groups; offers specialty lending; issues prepaid debit cards; and processes ACH and merchant credit card transactions. Its specialty lending products include securities backed lines of credit (SBLOC) auto fleet and equipment leasing SBA loans and commercial mortgage loans for sale in capital markets.

Operations

The Bancorp and The Bancorp Bank operate three business segments: Payments which made up 45% of the bank's total revenue in 2015 and provides prepaid cards card payments and ACH processing services; Specialty Finance (31% of revenue) which consists of commercial mortgage loan sales small business administration (SBA) loans leasing and security backed lines of credit and related deposit business; and Corporate (24% of revenue) which includes the company's investment portfolio.

Unlike other banks which rely on interest income The Bancorp makes more than 60% of its revenue from fee-based income. About 38% of its total revenue came from loan interest (including fees) during 2015 while another 14% came from interest income on investment securities. The rest of its revenue came from prepaid card fees (22% of revenue) service fees on deposit accounts (3%) card payment and ACH processing fees (3%) leasing income (1%) debit card income (1%) affinity fees (2%) and non-recurring gains from the sale of its loans investment securities and health savings portfolio (27%).

Geographic Reach

Wilmington Delaware-based The Bancorp serves customers in the US and Europe from 16 offices in the two regions and Southeast Asia.

Sales and Marketing

The company targets non-bank financial services companies including start-ups small and medium businesses underserved by large banks and Fortune 500 companies. It spent $387000 on advertising during 2015 down from $621000 and $706000 in 2014 and 2013 respectively.

Financial Performance

The Bancorp's annual revenues and profits have nearly doubled since 2011 mostly as its Payments business income has nearly quadrupled over the period. Its loan assets have also nearly tripled spurring additional interest income growth.

The company's revenue jumped 39% to $216.5 million during 2015 thanks largely to a $33.5 million gain on the sale of the majority of its health savings business and a $14.4 million gain on the sale of its tax-exempt municipal bonds portfolio. The Bancorp's loan interest revenue was also up 37% as its specialty lending balances continued to grow with new SBLOC SBA leasing and loans-for-sale business.

Despite strong revenue growth in 2015 The Bancorp's net income plunged more than 75% to $13.43 million mostly as its discontinued operations (its discontinued Philadelphia commercial loan business) generated $27 million less in revenue than the year before and because in 2014 it had collected a $14.5 million income tax benefit from a reversal of valuation allowances. The company's operations used $234.8 million or more than four times more cash than in 2014 mainly on a steep decline cash-based earnings especially after accounting for net proceeds from sales of its loans-originated-for-resale.

Strategy

The Bancorp and The Bancorp Bank has been winding down its non-core operations in recent years to concentrate more in its national specialty lending business. In October 2015 the bank sold its $400 million-HSA portfolio to HealthEquity for $34..4 million after selling its regional Commercial Lending business in 2014. As a result the bank noted that its discontinued operations were reduced by 50% at the end of 2015 and expected its discontinued loan portfolio to shrink from there through loan repayments and opportunistic loan sales.

On the growth side The Bancorp continues to buy specialty financing assets from other financial companies to bolster its loan assets and extend its geographic reach. In December 2015 it expanded its commercial fleet leasing presence in the West Coast with a new California office after buying the commercial leasing assets of Ellis Brooks Leasing Inc.

EXECUTIVES

EVP Strategy CFO and Secretary, Paul Frenkiel, age 67, $312,200 total compensation
President and CEO, Damian Kozlowski, age 52
EVP and Chief Credit Officer The Bancorp Inc. and The Bancorp Bank, Donald F. (Don) McGraw, age 62, $317,500 total compensation
EVP Commercial Fleet Leasing and Chief Lending Officer, Scott R. Megargee, age 67, $202,541 total compensation
EVP and CIO, Peter (Pete) Chiccino
SVP; Managing Director Payment Solutions, Jeremy L. Kuiper, $458,060 total compensation
SVP and General Counsel, Thomas G. Pareigat, $347,500 total compensation
EVP and COO, Gail S. Ball
EVP and Chief Risk Officer, Steven Turowski
EVP Commercial Mortgage Securitization, Ron Wechsler
First Vp Loan Committee, Genevieve Johnson
Senior Vice President Chief Information Security Officer, Anthony Meholic
Vice President Information Security Officer, Darin Wipf
First Vice President And Bro, Michael Terroni
VICE PRESIDENT CREDIT RISK, Dennis Day
FIRST VICE PRESIDENT, Elizabeth Roy
VICE PRESIDENT, Carole Turansky
VICE PRESIDENT SBA PORTFOLIO MANAGER, John Morgenthaler
Vp And Sba Business Development Officer, Jeffrey Fulcher
Vp Vendor Manager II, Michael Meiskey
Assistant Vice President Senior Risk Analyst, Craig Tabun
Vice President Threat And Vulnerability Management Officer, Peter Iancic
Chairman The Bancorp Inc. and The Bancorp Bank, Daniel G. Cohen, age 49
Board Member, John Chrystal
Auditors: Grant Thornton LLP

LOCATIONS

HQ: The Bancorp Inc
409 Silverside Road, Wilmington, DE 19809
Phone: 302 385-5000
Web: www.thebancorp.com

PRODUCTS/OPERATIONS

2015 sales

	$ mil.	% of total
Payments	98.0	45
Specialty finance	67.6	31
Corporate	51.0	24
Total	216.6	100

2015 Sales

	$ mil.	% of total
Interest income		
Loans including fees	49.9	23
Interest on investment securities:	30.7	14
Federal funds sold/securities purchased under agreements to resell	0.6	-
Interest earning deposits	2.3	1
Non-interest income		
Prepaid card fees	47.5	22
Gain on sale of health savings portfolio	33.6	15
Gain on sale of investment securities	14.4	7
Gain on sale of loans	10.1	5
Service fees on deposit accounts	7.5	3
Card payment and ACH processing fees	5.7	3
Affinity fees	3.4	2
Other	5.3	2
Change in value of investment in unconsolidated entity	1.7	1
Leasing income	2.3	1
Debit card income	1.6	1
Total	216.6	100

COMPETITORS

Citizens Financial Group
E*TRADE Bank
M&T Bank
PNC Financial
Republic First Bank
Royal Bancshares
Sovereign Bank
Sun Bancorp (NJ)
TD Bank USA
WSFS Financial

HISTORICAL FINANCIALS

Company Type: Public

Income Statement
FYE: December 31

	ASSETS ($ mil.)	NET INCOME ($ mil.)	INCOME AS % OF ASSETS	EMPLOYEES
12/18	4,437.9	88.6	2.0%	589
12/17	4,708.1	21.6	0.5%	538
12/16	4,858.1	(96.4)	—	589
12/15	4,765.8	13.4	0.3%	762
12/14	4,986.3	57.1	1.1%	684
Annual Growth	(2.9%)	11.6%	—	(3.7%)

2018 Year-End Financials

Return on assets: 1.9% Dividends
Return on equity: 24.2% Yield: —
Long-term debt ($ mil.): — Payout: —
No. of shares (mil.): 56.3 Market value ($ mil.): 449.0
Sales ($ mil): 301.7

	STOCK PRICE ($) FY Close	P/E High/Low		PER SHARE ($) Earnings	Dividends	Book Value
12/18	7.96	7	5	1.55	0.00	7.22
12/17	9.88	26	12	0.39	0.00	5.81
12/16	7.86	—	—	(2.17)	0.00	5.40
12/15	6.37	31	18	0.35	0.00	8.47
12/14	10.89	13	5	1.49	0.00	8.46
Annual Growth	(7.5%)			1.0%	—	(3.9%)

The Trade Desk Inc

Auditors: PricewaterhouseCoopers LLP

LOCATIONS
HQ: The Trade Desk Inc
42 N. Chestnut Street, Ventura, CA 93001
Phone: 805 585-3434
Web: www.thetradedesk.com

HISTORICAL FINANCIALS
Company Type: Public

Income Statement   FYE: December 31

	REVENUE ($ mil.)	NET INCOME ($ mil.)	NET PROFIT MARGIN	EMPLOYEES
12/18	477.2	176.2	36.9%	944
12/17	308.2	101.6	33.0%	713
12/16	202.9	(6.2)	—	467
12/15	113.8	24.6	21.7%	387
12/14	44.5	0.0	0.0%	0
Annual Growth	80.9%	1270.3%	—	—

2018 Year-End Financials

Debt ratio: — No. of shares (mil.): 43.8
Return on equity: 55.0% Dividends
Cash ($ mil.): 207.2 Yield: —
Current ratio: 1.48 Payout: —
Long-term debt ($ mil.): — Market value ($ mil.): 5,091.0

	STOCK PRICE ($) FY Close	P/E High/Low		PER SHARE ($) Earnings	Dividends	Book Value
12/18	116.06	75	21	1.92	0.00	9.00
12/17	45.73	53	21	1.15	0.00	5.90
12/16	27.67	—	—	(1.46)	0.00	4.20
Annual Growth	104.8%			—	—	46.3%

Thomasville Bancshares, Inc.

Auditors: Mauldin & Jenkins, LLC

LOCATIONS
HQ: Thomasville Bancshares, Inc.
301 North Broad Street, Thomasville, GA 31792
Phone: 229 226-3300
Web: www.tnbank.com

COMPETITORS
Ameris   SunTrust
Bank of America   Synovus
Capital City Bank

HISTORICAL FINANCIALS
Company Type: Public

Income Statement   FYE: December 31

	ASSETS ($ mil.)	NET INCOME ($ mil.)	INCOME AS % OF ASSETS	EMPLOYEES
12/18	880.5	16.8	1.9%	0
12/17	806.4	12.0	1.5%	0
12/16	780.2	11.8	1.5%	0
12/15	753.5	9.6	1.3%	0
12/14	650.2	8.4	1.3%	0
Annual Growth	7.9%	19.0%	—	—

2018 Year-End Financials

Return on assets: 2.0% Dividends
Return on equity: 22.1% Yield: 0.0%
Long-term debt ($ mil.): — Payout: 50.7%
No. of shares (mil.): 5.9 Market value ($ mil.): 244.0
Sales ($ mil): 51.9

	STOCK PRICE ($) FY Close	P/E High/Low		PER SHARE ($) Earnings	Dividends	Book Value
12/18	40.99	15	14	2.56	1.30	13.60
12/17	40.00	20	17	1.83	1.00	12.05
12/16	35.00	18	14	1.81	0.85	11.10
12/15	28.75	18	16	1.48	0.75	9.96
12/14	29.50	29	15	1.30	0.65	9.14
Annual Growth	8.6%			18.5%	18.9%	10.5%

Tile Shop Holdings Inc

EXECUTIVES
Senior Vice President Of Operations, Joe Kinder
Auditors: Ernst & Young LLP

LOCATIONS
HQ: Tile Shop Holdings Inc
14000 Carlson Parkway, Plymouth, MN 55441
Phone: 763 852-2950
Web: www.tileshop.com

HISTORICAL FINANCIALS
Company Type: Public

Income Statement   FYE: December 31

	REVENUE ($ mil.)	NET INCOME ($ mil.)	NET PROFIT MARGIN	EMPLOYEES
12/18	357.2	10.4	2.9%	1,738
12/17	344.6	10.8	3.1%	1,634
12/16	324.1	18.4	5.7%	1,448
12/15	292.9	15.7	5.4%	1,410
12/14	257.1	10.5	4.1%	1,190
Annual Growth	8.6%	(0.2%)	—	9.9%

2018 Year-End Financials

Debt ratio: 17.9% No. of shares (mil.): 52.7
Return on equity: 7.2% Dividends
Cash ($ mil.): 5.5 Yield: 3.6%
Current ratio: 2.58 Payout: 100.0%
Long-term debt ($ mil.): 53.4 Market value ($ mil.): 289.0

	STOCK PRICE ($) FY Close	P/E High/Low		PER SHARE ($) Earnings	Dividends	Book Value
12/18	5.48	52	26	0.20	0.20	2.78
12/17	9.60	104	39	0.21	0.20	2.76
12/16	19.55	59	35	0.36	0.00	2.69
12/15	16.40	56	23	0.31	0.00	2.24
12/14	8.88	88	38	0.21	0.00	1.83
Annual Growth	(11.4%)			(1.2%)	—	11.0%

Timberland Bancorp, Inc.

EXECUTIVES
Vice President Executive Admin. Secretary Appraisal Officer, Rexann Napoleon
ASSISTANT VICE PRESIDENT COMMERCIAL UNDERWRITER, Samantha Neuzil
Auditors: Delap LLP

LOCATIONS
HQ: Timberland Bancorp, Inc.
624 Simpson Avenue, Hoquiam, WA 98550
Phone: 360 533-4747
Web: www.timberlandbank.com

COMPETITORS
Bank of America   KeyCorp
Columbia Banking   Washington Federal
JPMorgan Chase   Wells Fargo

HISTORICAL FINANCIALS
Company Type: Public

Income Statement   FYE: September 30

	ASSETS ($ mil.)	NET INCOME ($ mil.)	INCOME AS % OF ASSETS	EMPLOYEES
09/19	1,247.1	24.0	1.9%	298
09/18	1,018.2	16.7	1.6%	268
09/17	952.0	14.1	1.5%	274
09/16	891.3	10.1	1.1%	269
09/15	815.8	8.2	1.0%	253
Annual Growth	11.2%	30.5%	—	4.2%

2019 Year-End Financials

Return on assets: 2.1% Dividends
Return on equity: 16.2% Yield: 2.8%
Long-term debt ($ mil.): — Payout: 29.3%
No. of shares (mil.): 8.3 Market value ($ mil.): 229.0
Sales ($ mil): 70.0

	STOCK PRICE ($) FY Close	P/E High/Low		PER SHARE ($) Earnings	Dividends	Book Value
09/19	27.50	11	8	2.84	0.78	20.54
09/18	31.24	17	12	2.22	0.60	16.84
09/17	31.34	16	8	1.92	0.50	15.08
09/16	15.75	11	7	1.43	0.37	13.95
09/15	10.89	10	8	1.17	0.24	12.76
Annual Growth	26.1%			24.8%	34.3%	12.6%

Tiptree Inc

Tiptree Financial is a holding company for primarily financial service firms. It holds majority interests in operating companies Fortegra (insurance and insurance services) Telos (asset management and specialty finance) and Luxury Mortgage and Reliance First Capital (residential mortgage origination). The company sold in early 2018 its Care Investment Trust REIT to Invesque for US$425 million.

EXECUTIVES

CEO and Director, Jonathan Ilany, age 65, $350,000 total compensation
CFO, Sandra E. Bell, age 62, $200,000 total compensation
CFO and Secretary, Julia Wyatt, age 61, $350,000 total compensation
VP General Counsel and Secretary Tiptree Financial Inc. and Tiptree Operating Company LLC, Neil C. Rifkind, $375,000 total compensation
Vice President, Robert A Masucci
Vice President Of Fleet Planning And Technical Ser, Scott Waltman
Senior Vice President, Joseph Lux
Vp Finance, Aashitha Ashokkumar
Chairman, Michael G. Barnes, age 53
Auditors: KPMG LLP

LOCATIONS

HQ: Tiptree Inc
299 Park Avenue, 13th Floor, New York, NY 10171
Phone: 212 446-1400
Web: www.tiptreefinancial.com

PRODUCTS/OPERATIONS

2012 Sales

	% of total
Rental income	86
Reimbursable income	9
Income from loans & investments	5
Total	**100**

Selected Subsidiaries

Asset Management:
 Muni Capital Management LLC
 TAMCO
 Telos
 Tiptree Capital Management LLC
 TREIT
Insurance:
 Philadelphia Financial Administration Services Company
 Philadelphia Financial Agency Inc.
 Philadelphia Financial Distribution Company
 Philadelphia Financial Life Assurance Company
 Philadelphia Financial Life Assurance Company of New York
Real Estate:
 Care Investment Trust LLC
Specialty Finance:
 Muni Funding Company of America
 Siena Capital Finance

COMPETITORS

AXA Financial
Extendicare
HCP
Healthcare Realty Trust
MetLife
National Health Investors
Omega Healthcare Investors
Prudential
Senior Housing Properties
Ventas
Welltower

HISTORICAL FINANCIALS
Company Type: Public

Income Statement
FYE: December 31

	REVENUE ($ mil.)	NET INCOME ($ mil.)	NET PROFIT MARGIN	EMPLOYEES
12/18	625.8	23.9	3.8%	393
12/17	581.8	3.6	0.6%	1,011
12/16	567.1	25.3	4.5%	1,042
12/15	440.1	5.7	1.3%	929
12/14	80.3	(1.7)	—	761
Annual Growth	67.1%	—	—	(15.2%)

2018 Year-End Financials

Debt ratio: 18.9%
Return on equity: 6.9%
Cash ($ mil.): 86.0
Current ratio: —
Long-term debt ($ mil.): 354.0
No. of shares (mil.): 35.8
Dividends
 Yield: 2.4%
 Payout: 12.0%
Market value ($ mil.): 201.0

	STOCK PRICE ($) FY Close	P/E High/Low		PER SHARE ($) Earnings	Dividends	Book Value
12/18	5.59	10	7	0.69	0.14	10.79
12/17	5.95	62	48	0.11	0.12	6.97
12/16	6.15	9	6	0.78	0.10	6.82
12/15	6.14	48	31	0.17	0.10	7.28
12/14	8.10	—	—	(0.10)	0.18	6.84
Annual Growth	(8.9%)	—	—	—	(6.3%)	12.1%

TopBuild Corp

Auditors: PricewaterhouseCoopers LLP

LOCATIONS

HQ: TopBuild Corp
475 North Williamson Boulevard, Daytona Beach, FL 32114
Phone: 386 304-2200
Web: www.topbuild.com

HISTORICAL FINANCIALS
Company Type: Public

Income Statement
FYE: December 31

	REVENUE ($ mil.)	NET INCOME ($ mil.)	NET PROFIT MARGIN	EMPLOYEES
12/18	2,384.2	134.7	5.7%	10,300
12/17	1,906.2	158.1	8.3%	8,400
12/16	1,742.8	72.6	4.2%	7,900
12/15	1,616.5	78.9	4.9%	8,000
12/14	1,512.0	9.4	0.6%	7,800
Annual Growth	12.1%	94.6%	—	7.2%

2018 Year-End Financials

Debt ratio: 30.2%
Return on equity: 13.0%
Cash ($ mil.): 100.9
Current ratio: 1.59
Long-term debt ($ mil.): 716.6
No. of shares (mil.): 34.5
Dividends
 Yield: —
 Payout: —
Market value ($ mil.): 1,556.0

	STOCK PRICE ($) FY Close	P/E High/Low		PER SHARE ($) Earnings	Dividends	Book Value
12/18	45.00	23	11	3.78	0.00	31.01
12/17	75.74	17	8	4.32	0.00	28.00
12/16	35.60	20	12	1.92	0.00	25.72
12/15	30.77	17	11	2.09	0.00	24.30
Annual Growth	13.5%	—	—	21.8%	—	8.5%

TowneBank

Auditors: Dixon Hughes Goodman LLP

LOCATIONS

HQ: TowneBank
5716 High Street, Portsmouth, VA 23703
Phone: 757 638-7500
Web: www.townebank.com

HISTORICAL FINANCIALS
Company Type: Public

Income Statement
FYE: December 31

	ASSETS ($ mil.)	NET INCOME ($ mil.)	INCOME AS % OF ASSETS	EMPLOYEES
12/18	11,163.0	133.7	1.2%	2,897
12/17	8,522.1	87.6	1.0%	2,727
12/16	7,973.9	67.2	0.8%	2,529
12/15	6,296.5	62.3	1.0%	1,903
12/14	4,982.4	42.1	0.8%	1,737
Annual Growth	22.3%	33.5%	—	13.6%

2018 Year-End Financials

Return on assets: 1.3%
Return on equity: 10.0%
Long-term debt ($ mil.): —
No. of shares (mil.): 72.4
Sales ($ mil): 613.4
Dividends
 Yield: 2.5%
 Payout: 39.4%
Market value ($ mil.): 1,736.0

	STOCK PRICE ($) FY Close	P/E High/Low		PER SHARE ($) Earnings	Dividends	Book Value
12/18	23.95	18	12	1.88	0.62	21.05
12/17	30.75	25	21	1.41	0.55	18.06
12/16	33.25	29	14	1.18	0.51	17.20
12/15	20.87	18	12	1.22	0.47	15.71
12/14	15.12	14	11	1.18	0.43	17.02
Annual Growth	12.2%	—	—	12.3%	9.6%	5.5%

TPG RE Finance Trust Inc

Auditors: DELOITTE & TOUCHE LLP

LOCATIONS

HQ: TPG RE Finance Trust Inc
888 Seventh Avenue, 35th Floor, New York, NY 10106
Phone: 212 601-4700
Web: www.tpgrefinance.com

HISTORICAL FINANCIALS
Company Type: Public

Income Statement
FYE: December 31

	REVENUE ($ mil.)	NET INCOME ($ mil.)	NET PROFIT MARGIN	EMPLOYEES
12/18	266.9	106.9	40.1%	0
12/17	200.6	94.3	47.0%	0
12/16	154.0	69.9	45.4%	0
12/15	128.7	59.3	46.1%	0
12/14	1.8	(8.2)	—	0
Annual Growth	246.7%	—	—	—

HOOVER'S HANDBOOK OF EMERGING COMPANIES 2020

TPG Specialty Lending Inc

Auditors: KPMG LLP

LOCATIONS

HQ: TPG Specialty Lending Inc
301 Commerce Street, Suite 3300, Fort Worth, TX 76102
Phone: 817 871-4000   **Fax:** 817 871-4001
Web: www.tpgspecialtylending.com

HISTORICAL FINANCIALS

Company Type: Public

Income Statement   FYE: December 31

	ASSETS ($ mil.)	NET INCOME ($ mil.)	INCOME AS % OF ASSETS	EMPLOYEES
12/18	1,730.3	143.8	8.3%	0
12/17	1,720.2	120.2	7.0%	0
12/16	1,675.5	107.3	6.4%	0
12/15	1,516.9	95.3	6.3%	0
12/14	1,303.7	104.4	8.0%	0
Annual Growth	7.3%	8.3%	—	

2018 Year-End Financials

Return on assets: 8.3%   Dividends
Return on equity: 14.1%   Yield: 9.8%
Long-term debt ($ mil.): —   Payout: 79.1%
No. of shares (mil.): 65.4   Market value ($ mil.): 1,183.0
Sales ($ mil): 261.9

	STOCK PRICE ($) FY Close	P/E High/Low	PER SHARE ($) Earnings	Dividends	Book Value
12/18	18.09	9 8	2.25	1.78	16.25
12/17	19.80	11 9	2.00	1.75	16.09
12/16	18.68	10 8	1.83	1.56	15.95
12/15	16.22	16 14	1.18	1.56	15.15
12/14	16.82	14 9	1.68	1.53	15.53
Annual Growth	1.8%	— —	7.6%	3.9%	1.1%

2018 Year-End Financials (Transamerica)

Debt ratio: 69.5%   No. of shares (mil.): 67.1
Return on equity: 8.4%   Dividends
Cash ($ mil.): 39.7   Yield: 9.3%
Current ratio: 3.18   Payout: 100.5%
Long-term debt ($ mil.): 3,149.8 Market value ($ mil.): 1,228.0

	STOCK PRICE ($) FY Close	P/E High/Low	PER SHARE ($) Earnings	Dividends	Book Value
12/18	18.28	12 11	1.70	1.71	19.76
12/17	19.05	12 11	1.74	0.71	19.82
Annual Growth	(4.0%)	— —	(2.3%)	140.8%	(0.3%)

Transamerica Advisors Life Insurance Co

EXECUTIVES

Pres, Marilyn Carp
Auditors: PricewaterhouseCoopers LLP

LOCATIONS

HQ: Transamerica Advisors Life Insurance Co
4333 Edgewood Road, NE, Cedar Rapids, IA 52499-0001
Phone: 800 346-3677
Web: www.transamerica.com

HISTORICAL FINANCIALS

Company Type: Public

Income Statement   FYE: December 31

	ASSETS ($ mil.)	NET INCOME ($ mil.)	INCOME AS % OF ASSETS	EMPLOYEES
12/17	8,621.8	99.4	1.2%	0
12/16	8,670.2	(20.5)	—	0
12/15	9,165.9	13.6	0.1%	0
12/14	10,108.4	33.5	0.3%	0
12/13	10,555.8	(254.4)	—	0
Annual Growth	(4.9%)			

2017 Year-End Financials

Return on assets: 1.1%   Dividends
Return on equity: 9.2%   Yield: —
Long-term debt ($ mil.): —   Payout: 140.8%
No. of shares (mil.): 0.2   Market value ($ mil.): —
Sales ($ mil): 216.8

Transcontinental Realty Investors, Inc.

EXECUTIVES

EVP CFO and Chief Accounting Officer; Chairman President CEO and CFO New Concept Energy, Gene S. Bertcher, age 64
EVP General and Tax Counsel and Secretary, Louis J. Corna, age 65
Chairman, Henry A. Butler, age 63
EVP Residential Construction, Alfred Crozier, age 60
President and COO, Daniel J. (Danny) Moos, age 62
Treasurer; Treasurer American Realty Investors and Income Opportunity Realty Investors, Daeho Kim, age 36
Director, Ted R. Munselle, age 56
Independent Director, Sharon Hunt, age 73
Director, Robert A. Jakuszewski, age 51
Director, Martha C. Stephens, age 67
Director; VP Project Development Prime, RL S. Lemke, age 57
Auditors: Farmer, Fuqua & Huff, P.C.

LOCATIONS

HQ: Transcontinental Realty Investors, Inc.
1603 Lyndon B. Johnson Freeway, Suite 800, Dallas, TX 75234
Phone: 469 522-4200
Web: www.transconrealty-invest.com

COMPETITORS

AIMCO Properties   Equity Residential
Camden Property   Highwoods Properties
CapLease   TVO Groupe
DVL   Tarragon
Equity Office

HISTORICAL FINANCIALS

Company Type: Public

Income Statement   FYE: December 31

	REVENUE ($ mil.)	NET INCOME ($ mil.)	NET PROFIT MARGIN	EMPLOYEES
12/18	120.9	181.4	150.0%	0
12/17	125.2	(15.8)	—	0
12/16	118.4	0.0	0.0%	0
12/15	102.2	(7.6)	—	0
12/14	75.8	41.5	54.8%	0
Annual Growth	12.4%	44.5%	—	—

2018 Year-End Financials

Debt ratio: 50.5%   No. of shares (mil.): 8.7
Return on equity: 66.1%   Dividends
Cash ($ mil.): 36.3   Yield: —
Current ratio: 4.30   Payout: —
Long-term debt ($ mil.): 435.8   Market value ($ mil.): 247.0

	STOCK PRICE ($) FY Close	P/E High/Low	PER SHARE ($) Earnings	Dividends	Book Value
12/18	28.32	2 1	20.71	0.00	41.26
12/17	31.32	— —	(1.92)	0.00	21.70
12/16	12.02	— —	(0.10)	0.00	23.62
12/15	10.30	— —	(0.98)	0.00	23.72
12/14	10.30	4 2	4.74	0.00	24.69
Annual Growth	28.8%	— —	44.6%	—	13.7%

TransUnion

Auditors: Ernst & Young LLP

LOCATIONS

HQ: TransUnion
555 West Adams, Chicago, IL 60661
Phone: 312 985-2000
Web: www.transunion.com

HISTORICAL FINANCIALS

Company Type: Public

Income Statement   FYE: December 31

	REVENUE ($ mil.)	NET INCOME ($ mil.)	NET PROFIT MARGIN	EMPLOYEES
12/18	2,317.2	276.6	11.9%	7,100
12/17	1,933.8	441.2	22.8%	5,100
12/16	1,704.9	120.6	7.1%	4,700
12/15	1,506.8	5.9	0.4%	4,200
12/14	1,304.7	(12.5)	—	4,200
Annual Growth	15.4%	—	—	14.0%

2018 Year-End Financials

Debt ratio: 57.5%
Return on equity: 15.2%
Cash ($ mil.): 187.4
Current ratio: 1.53
Long-term debt ($ mil.): 3,976.4
No. of shares (mil.): 185.7
Dividends
  Yield: 0.4%
  Payout: 15.5%
Market value ($ mil.): 10,548.0

	STOCK PRICE ($) FY Close	P/E High/Low	PER SHARE ($) Earnings	Dividends	Book Value
12/18	56.80	51 35	1.45	0.23	10.18
12/17	54.96	23 13	2.32	0.00	9.44
12/16	30.93	54 32	0.65	0.00	7.44
12/15	27.57	700 580	0.04	0.00	6.75
Annual Growth	27.2%	—	231.0%	—	14.6%

Trex Co Inc

Trex Company is all decked out with plenty of places to go. It's the world's largest maker of wood-alternative decking and railing products which are used in the construction of residential and commercial decks rails and trims. Marketed under the Trex name products resemble wood and have the workability of wood but require less long-term maintenance. The Trex Wood-Polymer composite is made of waste wood fibers and reclaimed plastic. Trex serves professional installation contractors and do-it-yourselfers through about 90 wholesale distribution centers which in turn sell to retailers including Home Depot and Lowe's. Trex products are available in more than 5500 locations primarily in the US and Canada.

Operations

Trex produces five principal decking products: Trex Transcend Trex Enhance Trex Select Trex Accents and Trex Escapes. Its two railing products include Trex Designer Series Railing and Trex Transcend Railing. The company's collection also includes Trex Transcend Porch Flooring and Railing System (a porch product) Trex Elevations (a steel deck framing system) Trex Seclusions (a fencing product) Trex DeckLighting (a deck lighting system) TrexTrim (a cellular PVC outdoor trim product) and Trex Hideaway (a hidden fastening system for specially grooved boards). Its newest product is polyethylene pellets made from recycled plastic that it sells to plastic bag sheet and film makers.

The company converts millions of pounds of recycled and reclaimed plastic and waste wood each year into Trex products. Its raw materials come from recovered plastic grocery bags plastic film and waste wood fiber. As part of its operations the company each year purchases about 300 million pounds of both used polyethylene and hardwood sawdust. It recycles more than 1.3 billion grocery retail bags annually.

Geographic Reach

Based in Virginia Trex has manufacturing facilities in Winchester Virginia and Fernley Nevada. It operates globally through international retailers.

Sales and Marketing

Trex serves both professional installers and those who prefer to do it themselves. Through some 90 wholesale distribution centers the company sells its products to big-box home improvement retailers including Lowe's and Home Depot.

It markets its products as having "unmatched good looks and longevity" — products that "will never rot crack or splinter." Its wood is also the only composite lumber to be code-listed by the nation's three major building code agencies.

A majority of Trex's net sales come from its vast network of wholesale distributors. In 2014 Boise Cascade accounted for more than 10% of sales. The company has extended its reach by providing some of its lines to international retailers.

Financial Performance

Revenue has been climbing at Trex since 2010. In 2014 it grew 14% to $392 million from $342 the previous year. Stronger demand from existing customers and new distributors lead to higher sales volume though a revamped pricing strategy caused lower average prices per unit.

Profits have been growing since 2012 and the bump in revenue helped net income top $41.5 million in 2014 a 20% increase over 2013's $34.6 million. Cash from operations also grew by $45.21 million to hit $58.64 million.

Strategy

Trex generates most of its sales by selling Trex products to wholesale distributors who market to retail lumber outlets. While Trex sells to both homeowners and contractors it focuses on sales to contractors remodelers and homebuilders because their installations are generally larger and feature professional craftsmanship.

The company chooses to sell through a wholesale distribution network for its higher value products and contractor-oriented lumber yards and other retail outlets. Typically Trex appoints a distributor on a non-exclusive basis to distribute its products within a specific area. The distributor in general purchases its products at the sales price the day it ships to the distributor.

Home improvement stores purchase Trex products directly from the company and through wholesale distributors for special orders placed by consumers. In 2014 the company moved online when it began offering its outdoor lighting products through Amazon.com. Trex licensees were already selling the company's outdoor furniture pergolas and deck drainage systems on the retail site.

Trex works to bring new products to the marketplace. Through research and development Trex is interested in creating products that are durable low maintenance and easy to install such as its cellular PVC fire-resistant deck board and outdoor trim products (including mouldings and millwork). The company has built on its high-performance Trex Transcend collection with a range of railing options for all its customer segments. Research and development expenses in 2014 came in at $2.3 million down from $2.9 million the previous two years.

Company Background

Trex was formed in 1996 through a buyout of a division of Mobil Corporation. It went public in 1999.

EXECUTIVES

SVP and CFO, James E. Cline, age 68, $289,100 total compensation
VP Marketing, Adam D. Zambanini
VP and CFO, Bryan H. Fairbanks
VP Operations, Jay Scripter
Vp Marketing, Leslie Adkins
Vice President Sales, Chris Gerhard
Chairman, Ronald W. (Ron) Kaplan, age 68

Board Member, Patricia Robinson
Auditors: Ernst & Young LLP

LOCATIONS

HQ: Trex Co Inc
160 Exeter Drive, Winchester, VA 22603-8605
Phone: 540 542-6300
Web: www.trex.com

PRODUCTS/OPERATIONS

Selected Brands

Decking
  Trex Accents
  Trex Enhance
  Trex Escapes
  Trex Select
  Trex Transcend
  Deck Lighting System
  Trex DeckLighting
Fencing
  Trex Seclusions
  Hidden Fastening System
  Trex Hideaway
Porch
  Trex Transcend Porch Flooring & Railing System
  PVC Outdoor Trim
  TrexTrim
Railing
  Trex Designer Series
  Trex Transcend
  Steel Deck Framing System
  Trex Elevations

Selected Products

Decking
Fencing
Railing
Trim

COMPETITORS

Advanced Environmental Recycling
CPG International
CertainTeed
Huttig Building Products
Louisiana-Pacific
NEW Plastics
TAMKO
Tumac Lumber
Universal Forest Products
Weyerhaeuser

HISTORICAL FINANCIALS

Company Type: Public

Income Statement   FYE: December 31

	REVENUE ($ mil.)	NET INCOME ($ mil.)	NET PROFIT MARGIN	EMPLOYEES
12/18	684.2	134.5	19.7%	1,214
12/17	565.1	95.1	16.8%	815
12/16	479.6	67.8	14.1%	830
12/15	440.8	48.1	10.9%	700
12/14	391.6	41.5	10.6%	630
Annual Growth	15.0%	34.2%	—	17.8%

2018 Year-End Financials

Debt ratio: —
Return on equity: 46.8%
Cash ($ mil.): 105.7
Current ratio: 2.91
Long-term debt ($ mil.): —
No. of shares (mil.): 58.5
Dividends
  Yield: —
  Payout: —
Market value ($ mil.): 3,476.0

	STOCK PRICE ($) FY Close	P/E High/Low		PER SHARE ($) Earnings	Dividends	Book Value
12/18	59.36	56	23	2.28	0.00	5.86
12/17	108.39	73	39	1.61	0.00	3.93
12/16	64.40	61	28	1.15	0.00	2.28
12/15	38.04	74	42	0.76	0.00	1.88
12/14	42.58	129	41	0.64	0.00	1.77
Annual Growth	8.7%	—	—	37.7%	—	34.9%

TriCo Bancshares (Chico, CA)

People looking for a community bank in California's Sacramento Valley can try TriCo. TriCo Bancshares is the holding company for Tri Counties Bank which serves customers through some 65 traditional and in-store branches in 23 counties in Northern and Central California. Founded in 1974 Tri Counties Bank provides a variety of deposit services including checking and savings accounts money market accounts and CDs. Most patrons are retail customers and small to midsized businesses. The bank primarily originates real estate mortgages which account for about 65% of its loan portfolio; consumer loans contribute about 25%. TriCo has agreed to acquire rival North Valley Bancorp.

Operations

In addition to its retail banking products and services the company provides wholesale banking and investment services; TriCo offers brokerage services through an arrangement with Raymond James Financial. The company does not provide trust or international banking services.

Geographic Reach

Based in Chico California Tri Counties Bank operates 66 branches (41 traditional branches and 25 in-store branches) in 23 counties in Northern and central California including Fresno Kern Mendocino Napa Sacramento and Yuba counties.

Financial Performance

In 2013 net interest income the company's primary source of revenue rose 0.6% compared with 2012 to $102.2 million. The slight increase in net interest income was mainly due to a decrease in average balance of other borrowings a shift in deposit balances from relatively high interest rate earning time deposits to noninterest-earning demand and savings deposits an increase in the average balance of investments securities and an increase in the average balance of loans; all of which were substantially offset by a decrease in the average yield on loans.

Strategy

The bank's growth has been fueled by acquisitions and the opening of new branches; it frequently opens branches within grocery stores or other retailers including Wal-Mart. TriCo in 2010 acquired the three branches of Granite Community Bank which had been seized by regulators. The transaction which also included most of the failed bank's assets and deposits was facilitated by the FDIC and includes a loss-sharing agreement with the agency. The following year TriCo acquired Citizens Bank of Northern California. The FDIC-assisted deal included seven branches. The acquisitions are part of TriCo's strategy of adding new customers.

Mergers and Acquisitions

TriCo in January 2014 announced plans to buy its rival in Northern California North Valley Bancorp (NVB) for about $178.4 million. NVB is the parent company of North Valley Bank which had about $918 million in assets and 22 commercial banking offices across eight Northern California counties at the end of 2013. At closing which is expected in the second or third quarter of 2014 NVB will be merged into Tri Counties Bank. The combined bank would have about $3.6 billion in assets.

EXECUTIVES

EVP and CFO TriCo Bancshares and Tri Counties Bank, Thomas J. (Tom) Reddish, age 59, $309,601 total compensation
EVP and Chief Credit Officer, Craig B. Carney, age 60, $274,932 total compensation
EVP Wholesale Banking, Richard B. O'Sullivan, age 62, $260,890 total compensation
President and CEO, Richard P. Smith, age 61, $549,846 total compensation
EVP and COO, John S. Fleshood, age 57
EVP and Chief Retail Banking Officer, Daniel K. (Dan) Bailey, age 50, $268,335 total compensation
SVP and CIO, Bruce Barnett
Vice President Facilities Expansion MA, Chimene Sonsteng
Vice President Marketing, Dan Herbert
Senior Vice President Special Assets Manager, Steve Macrae
Senior Vice President, Mark Davis
Senior Vice President, Brent Mcclure
Chairman, William J. Casey, age 74
Vice Chairman, Michael W. Koehnen, age 58
Auditors: Moss Adams LLP

LOCATIONS

HQ: TriCo Bancshares (Chico, CA)
63 Constitution Drive, Chico, CA 95973
Phone: 530 898-0300
Web: www.tcbk.com

PRODUCTS/OPERATIONS

2015 Sales

	$ mil.	% of total
Interest		
Loans including fees	131.8	64
Debt securities	26.8	13
Dividends	2.1	1
Other	0.7	-
Noninterest		
Service charges & fees	31.8	16
Commissions	3.4	2
Gain on sale of loans	3.1	1
Other	7.1	3
Total	**206.8**	**100**

Selected Services

Business debit cards
Business online banking
Business workshops
Cash management
Education savings and CDs
Loans and credits
Merchant services
Order checks
Overdraft services
Pension and retirement
Personal certificates of deposit
Personal checking
Personal savings and money market
Retirement savings and CDs

COMPETITORS

Bank of America
Bank of the West
Central Valley Community Bancorp
MUFG Americas Holdings
PremierWest
Wells Fargo
Westamerica

HISTORICAL FINANCIALS

Company Type: Public

Income Statement — FYE: December 31

	ASSETS ($ mil.)	NET INCOME ($ mil.)	INCOME AS % OF ASSETS	EMPLOYEES
12/18	6,352.4	68.3	1.1%	1,174
12/17	4,761.3	40.5	0.9%	1,023
12/16	4,517.9	44.8	1.0%	1,063
12/15	4,220.7	43.8	1.0%	1,011
12/14	3,916.4	26.1	0.7%	1,009
Annual Growth	12.9%	27.2%	—	3.9%

2018 Year-End Financials

Return on assets: 1.2%
Return on equity: 10.2%
Long-term debt ($ mil.): —
No. of shares (mil.): 30.4
Sales ($ mil): 277.5
Dividends
Yield: 2.0%
Payout: 36.8%
Market value ($ mil.): 1,028.0

	STOCK PRICE ($) FY Close	P/E High/Low		PER SHARE ($) Earnings	Dividends	Book Value
12/18	33.79	16	12	2.54	0.70	27.20
12/17	37.86	25	19	1.74	0.66	22.03
12/16	34.18	18	12	1.94	0.60	20.87
12/15	27.44	15	12	1.91	0.52	19.85
12/14	24.70	19	15	1.46	0.44	18.41
Annual Growth	8.1%	—	—	14.8%	12.3%	10.3%

TriState Capital Holdings Inc

TriState Capital Holdings has found its niche right in the middle of the banking industry. The holding company owns TriState Capital Bank a regional business bank that caters to midsized businesses or those annually earning between $5 million and $300 million. TriState Capital also offers private banking services nationally to high-net-worth individuals. Its loan portfolio consists of about 50% commercial loans 30% commercial real estate loans and 20% private banking-personal loans. The bank serves clients from branches in Cleveland; New Jersey; New York City Philadelphia and Pittsburgh. Altogether it has some $2 billion in assets. TriState Capital went public in mid-2013.

IPO

The company does not have any specific plans outlined for its proceeds but will likely use it for general corporate purposes which might include maintaining liquidity at the holding company providing equity capital to the bank to fund balance sheet growth and possibly investing in or acquiring wealth management businesses.

Strategy

The company's founders saw an opportunity in serving what they perceived was an underserved market – midsized businesses. Consolidation had left major national banks catering to individuals and large businesses while community banks served individuals and small businesses.

Company Background

TriState Capital was founded in 2007 by two banking industry executives — chairman and CEO James Getz who spent 20 years at Federated Investors and vice chairman William Schenck the former secretary of banking for Pennsylvania.

EXECUTIVES

Chairman President and CEO, James F. (Jim) Getz, $1,500,000 total compensation
President Commercial Banking, David A. Molnar
Vice Chairman and CFO, Mark L. Sullivan, $425,000 total compensation
Regional President New Jersey, Kenneth R. Orchard
Regional President New York, Thomas N. Gilmartin
Regional President Ohio, John D. Barrett
Regional President Eastern Pennsylvania, Joseph M. Finley
Regional President Western Pennsylvania, Vince Locher
President Private Bank Team, Charles C. Fawcett
President and CEO TriState Capital Bank, Brian S. Fetterolf
Senior Vice President Relationship Manager, Michael Blasko
Senior Vice President, Sheila Roberts
SENIOR VICE PRESIDENT, John Buglione
Senior Vice President Commercial Real Estate Finance, David Segal
Senior Vice President, Tim Moriarity
Senior Vice President, Paul Steiger
Vice Chairman, A. William (Bill) Schenck
Auditors: KPMG LLP

LOCATIONS

HQ: TriState Capital Holdings Inc
One Oxford Centre, 301 Grant Street, Suite 2700, Pittsburgh, PA 15219
Phone: 412 304-0304 **Fax:** 412 304-0391
Web: www.tristatecapitalbank.com

PRODUCTS/OPERATIONS

2015 Sales	% of total
Interest income	
Loans	67
Investments	3
Interest-earning deposits	.
Noninterest income	
Investment management fees	25
Commitment and other fees	2
Other income	3
Total	**100**

COMPETITORS

Bank of America	HSBC Private Bank
Bank of New York Mellon	Herald National Bank
	JPMorgan Private Bank
Boston Private	Julius Baer
Brown Brothers Harriman	Lakeland Bancorp
	M&T Bank
Citigroup	Safra Bank
Citigroup Private Bank	U.S. Trust
First Republic (CA)	

HISTORICAL FINANCIALS
Company Type: Public

Income Statement   FYE: December 31

	ASSETS ($ mil.)	NET INCOME ($ mil.)	INCOME AS % OF ASSETS	EMPLOYEES
12/18	6,035.6	54.4	0.9%	257
12/17	4,777.9	37.9	0.8%	230
12/16	3,930.4	28.6	0.7%	224
12/15	3,302.8	22.4	0.7%	192
12/14	2,846.8	15.9	0.6%	182
Annual Growth	20.7%	36.0%	—	9.0%

2018 Year-End Financials

Return on assets: 1.0%
Return on equity: 12.5%
Long-term debt ($ mil.): —
No. of shares (mil.): 28.8
Sales ($ mil): 247.7
Dividends
  Yield: —
  Payout: —
Market value ($ mil.): 562.0

	STOCK PRICE ($) FY Close	P/E High/Low	PER SHARE ($) Earnings	Dividends	Book Value
12/18	19.46	16 10	1.81	0.00	16.60
12/17	23.00	18 15	1.32	0.00	13.61
12/16	22.10	22 11	1.01	0.00	12.38
12/15	13.99	18 12	0.80	0.00	11.62
12/14	10.24	26 16	0.55	0.00	10.88
Annual Growth	17.4%	— —	34.7%	—	11.1%

Triumph Bancorp Inc

Auditors: Crowe LLP

LOCATIONS

HQ: Triumph Bancorp Inc
12700 Park Central Drive, Suite 1700, Dallas, TX 75251
Phone: 214 365-6900
Web: www.triumphbancorp.com

HISTORICAL FINANCIALS
Company Type: Public

Income Statement   FYE: December 31

	ASSETS ($ mil.)	NET INCOME ($ mil.)	INCOME AS % OF ASSETS	EMPLOYEES
12/18	4,559.7	51.7	1.1%	1,121
12/17	3,499.0	36.2	1.0%	820
12/16	2,641.0	20.7	0.8%	705
12/15	1,691.3	29.1	1.7%	500
12/14	1,447.9	17.7	1.2%	466
Annual Growth	33.2%	30.7%	—	24.6%

2018 Year-End Financials

Return on assets: 1.2%
Return on equity: 10.0%
Long-term debt ($ mil.): —
No. of shares (mil.): 26.9
Sales ($ mil): 285.9
Dividends
  Yield: —
  Payout: —
Market value ($ mil.): 800.0

	STOCK PRICE ($) FY Close	P/E High/Low	PER SHARE ($) Earnings	Dividends	Book Value
12/18	29.70	22 13	2.03	0.00	23.62
12/17	31.50	19 11	1.81	0.00	18.81
12/16	26.15	24 12	1.10	0.00	16.01
12/15	16.50	11 8	1.57	0.00	14.88
12/14	13.55	10 8	1.52	0.00	13.22
Annual Growth	21.7%	— —	7.5%	—	15.6%

Turning Point Brands Inc

Auditors: RSM US LLP

LOCATIONS

HQ: Turning Point Brands Inc
5201 Interchange Way, Louisville, KY 40229
Phone: 502 778-4421
Web: www.turningpointbrands.com

HISTORICAL FINANCIALS
Company Type: Public

Income Statement   FYE: December 31

	REVENUE ($ mil.)	NET INCOME ($ mil.)	NET PROFIT MARGIN	EMPLOYEES
12/18	332.6	25.2	7.6%	520
12/17	285.7	20.2	7.1%	289
12/16	206.2	26.9	13.1%	286
12/15	197.2	9.1	4.6%	231
12/14	200.3	(29.4)	—	0
Annual Growth	13.5%	—	—	—

2018 Year-End Financials

Debt ratio: 65.0%
Return on equity: 37.2%
Cash ($ mil.): 3.3
Current ratio: 1.75
Long-term debt ($ mil.): 186.7
No. of shares (mil.): 19.5
Dividends
  Yield: 0.6%
  Payout: 12.8%
Market value ($ mil.): 532.0

	STOCK PRICE ($) FY Close	P/E High/Low	PER SHARE ($) Earnings	Dividends	Book Value
12/18	27.22	34 15	1.28	0.17	4.23
12/17	21.13	20 12	1.04	0.04	2.78
12/16	12.25	10 4	1.49	0.00	1.85
Annual Growth 49.1%		— —	(7.3%)	—	51.1%

Turtle Beach Corp

EXECUTIVES

Vice President Of Operations, Scott Rankin
Vice President International Marketing, David Roberton
Vice President Global Operations, Jose Rosado
Auditors: BDO USA, LLP

LOCATIONS

HQ: Turtle Beach Corp
  11011 Via Frontera, Suite A/B, San Diego, CA 92127
Phone: 888 496-8001
Web: www.parametricsound.com

COMPETITORS

Bose
Boston Acoustics
Harman International
Klipsch
Mitsubishi Corp.
Pioneer Corporation
Polk Audio
Sony USA

HISTORICAL FINANCIALS
Company Type: Public

Income Statement
FYE: December 31

	REVENUE ($ mil.)	NET INCOME ($ mil.)	NET PROFIT MARGIN	EMPLOYEES
12/18	287.4	39.1	13.6%	154
12/17	149.1	(3.2)	—	135
12/16	173.9	(87.1)	—	172
12/15	162.7	(82.9)	—	221
12/14	186.1	(15.4)	—	161
Annual Growth	11.5%	—	—	(1.1%)

2018 Year-End Financials

Debt ratio: 30.6%
Return on equity: 510.9%
Cash ($ mil.): 7.0
Current ratio: 1.55
Long-term debt ($ mil.): —
No. of shares (mil.): 14.2
Dividends
  Yield: —
  Payout: —
Market value ($ mil.): 204.0

	STOCK PRICE ($) FY Close	P/E High/Low		PER SHARE ($) Earnings	Dividends	Book Value
12/18	14.27	11	0	2.74	0.00	2.63
12/17	0.45	—	—	(0.28)	0.00	(1.79)
12/16	1.31	—	—	(7.16)	0.00	(1.68)
12/15	2.01	—	—	(7.84)	0.00	5.33
12/14	3.19	—	—	(1.56)	0.00	12.49
Annual Growth	45.4% (32.3%)	—	—	—		

Tyler Technologies, Inc.

Tyler Technologies doesn't want local governments tied up in red tape. The company provides software and services intended to help state and local government offices operate more efficiently. Specializing in applications for local governments and public schools Tyler's products include software for accounting and financial management filing court documents electronically tracking and managing court cases and automating appraisals and assessments. Other products include applications that allow citizens to access utility accounts or pay traffic fines online. Tyler complements its software with hosting support and maintenance services. The company counts more than 13000 government and school customers in all 50 states Canada the Caribbean and the UK.

Operations
The company divides its operations into two segments — enterprise software and appraisal and tax software. Enterprise software which accounts for 88% of sales provides local governments and schools with software and services for back-office functions such as financial management and courts and justice processes. Appraisal and tax software which makes up the other 11% of sales is used by local governments and taxing authorities to automate property appraisal and assessment including physical inspection data collection property valuation preparing tax rolls and arbitration.

The company's technology partners include Microsoft and ESRI.

Geographic Reach
Tyler Technologies operates from about 20 offices in the US and one in Canada.

Sales and Marketing
The company uses a direct sales force. It participates in government associations and attends annual meetings trade shows and educational events to attract new customers. Its customers are primarily county and municipal agencies school districts and other local government offices.

Financial Performance
Tyler Technologies has been on a tear in revenue growth and it continued in 2014. Revenue jumped 18% to $493 million because of growth throughout its offerings. It posted 40% growth in subscriptions 22% in software services and 20% growth in software licenses and royalties from current customers and new ones. A particular driver of subscription-based services revenue came from a contract with the Texas Office of Court Administration for the company's Odyssey File and Serve e-filing system. Overall local government spending loosened as economic conditions improved.

Tyler Technologies converted the revenue growth into a 59% increase in profit. It rose to $59 million in 2014 from $39 million in 2013.

Cash flow from operations also jumped rising to $123 million in 2014 from $66 million in 2013.

Strategy
In addition to acquisitions the company expands its software product line with new offerings and product upgrades including the Odyssey judicial case management system and public-use Internet portals that enable users to pay property taxes utility bills and complete other transactions electronically. The company is also looking to grow by selling new products and services to its existing customer base expanding its market focus to include larger customers and entering new geographic regions.

Mergers and Acquisitions
Tyler acquired MicroPact a provider of specialized case management and business process management software for government from Arlington Capital Partners for about $185 million in 2019. The deal helps move Tyler into the health and human services market and gain customers in the federal government. MicroPact's clients include the US Department of Justice Department of the Treasury Social Security Administration and the NASA.

In early 2015 Tyler Technologies acquired 20% of Record Holdings an Australian company specializing in digitizing the spoken word in courts. Also in 2015 Tyler Technologies bought Brazos Technology Corp. a provider of mobile hand-held products used by law enforcement agencies for field accident reporting and electronically issuing citations. Toward the end of 2015 Tyler Technologies bought New World Systems Corp. a provider of public safety and financial products. Tyler Technologies paid $360 million in cash and about 2.1 million shares of Tyler's stock.

Company Background
Formerly an auto parts and supplies company established in 1966 Tyler sold its chain of auto parts stores in 1999 and used acquisitions to transform itself into a provider of software for the local government and education markets.

EXECUTIVES

EVP CFO and Treasurer, Brian K. Miller, age 60, $323,000 total compensation
Chairman and CEO, John S. Marr, age 60, $512,000 total compensation
President, H. Lynn Moore, age 51, $323,000 total compensation
EVP and President Local Government Division, Dustin R. Womble, age 60, $430,000 total compensation
VP and CIO, Matthew (Matt) Bieri
President Courts and Justice Division, Jeff Puckett
VP and Chief Marketing Officer, Samantha Crosby
President Appraisal and Tax Division, Andrew D. Teed
President ERP and School Division, Christopher P. (Chris) Hepburn
President Justice Group, Bret Dixon
President Public Safety Division, Greg Sebastian
Vice President Of Implementation For The Local Gov, Elven Corder
Chief Sales Officer, Brett Cate
Vice President For Information Systems, Paul Ilami
Vice President, Stefan Werdegar
Sr. Vice President, Ted Thien
Vice President Software Strategy and Development, Brian Leary
Vice President of EnerGov Operations, Mark Beverly
National Sales Manager, Brian Baker
Senior Vice President Operations Public Safety Division, Bryan Proctor
Vice President Of East Division, Todd Cloutier
VICE PRESIDENT, Steve Magoun
BOARD MEMBER PROJECT IMPLEMENTATION MANAGER, Malcolm Logan
Board Member, Christopher King
Auditors: Ernst & Young LLP

LOCATIONS

HQ: Tyler Technologies, Inc.
  5101 Tennyson Parkway, Plano, TX 75024
Phone: 972 713-3700
Web: www.tylertech.com

PRODUCTS/OPERATIONS

2014 Sales

	% of total
Enterprise software	89
Appraisal & tax software	11
Corporate	-
Total	**100**

2014 Sales

% of total	$ mil
Maintenance	43
Software services	23
Subscriptions	18
Software licenses and royalties	10
Appraisal services	4
Hardware & other	2
Total	**100**

Selected Products
Appraisal and assessment software (property appraisal and assessment)
Criminal justice software (court case tracking and management)
Document management and recording software (image storage and retrieval)
Education software
Finance and accounting software
Law enforcement and corrections software (police dispatch records and jail management)
Municipal court software (case management)
Odyssey (case and court management)
Public Records and content management
Tax collections software (tax collections office operations)
Utility billing software (billing and collections)

Selected Services
Information technology and professional services
Maintenance
Outsourced property appraisals for tax jurisdictions

COMPETITORS

CACI International	Official Payments Holdings
Constellation Software	Oracle
DynTek	SAP
HP Enterprise Services	SunGard
IBM	USTI
MAXIMUS	Xerox
Manatron	

HISTORICAL FINANCIALS
Company Type: Public

Income Statement
FYE: December 31

	REVENUE ($ mil.)	NET INCOME ($ mil.)	NET PROFIT MARGIN	EMPLOYEES
12/18	935.2	147.4	15.8%	4,525
12/17	840.6	163.9	19.5%	4,069
12/16	756.0	109.8	14.5%	3,831
12/15	591.0	64.8	11.0%	3,586
12/14	493.1	58.9	12.0%	2,856
Annual Growth	17.4%	25.8%	—	12.2%

2018 Year-End Financials
Debt ratio: —
Return on equity: 11.8%
Cash ($ mil.): 134.2
Current ratio: 1.22
Long-term debt ($ mil.): —
No. of shares (mil.): 38.2
Dividends
  Yield: —
  Payout: —
Market value ($ mil.): 7,112.0

	STOCK PRICE ($) FY Close	P/E High/Low		PER SHARE ($) Earnings	Dividends	Book Value
12/18	185.82	65	45	3.68	0.00	34.61
12/17	177.05	42	33	4.18	0.00	30.81
12/16	142.77	58	40	2.82	0.00	24.90
12/15	174.32	95	55	1.77	0.00	23.35
12/14	109.44	64	42	1.66	0.00	10.07
Annual Growth	14.2%			22.0%	—	36.2%

U.S. Physical Therapy, Inc.

U.S. Physical Therapy (USPh) through its subsidiaries lends a hand to injured workers athletes and others in need of some TLC. With some 560 outpatient clinics in more than 40 states USPh provides physical therapy services for work-related and sports injuries trauma orthopedic conditions osteoarthritis treatment and post-surgical rehabilitation. The clinics operate under a number of local or regional brands including Red River Valley Physical Therapy and Pioneer Physical Therapy. USPh also operates 22 physical therapy facilities for third parties including physician groups and hospitals.

Operations
Most of USPh's clinics are joint ventures in which the company owns a majority stake and the licensed therapists/clinic managers own a minority stake. Other facilities are wholly owned by the company but are operated through profit-sharing agreements with physical therapists. The company also manages a handful of physician-owned and hospital-owned clinics on a contract basis.

USPh relies on its therapist-managers to maintain relationships with local physicians who refer patients to the clinics. Services are paid for by commercial health insurance managed care programs Medicare workers' compensation insurance or proceeds from personal injury cases.

Geographic Reach
USPh has clinics in 42 states. The company has a significant presence in Georgia Maryland Michigan Pennsylvania Tennessee Texas Virginia Washington and Wisconsin.

Sales and Marketing
The company markets its activities to orthopedic surgeons neurosurgeons podiatrists occupational medicine physicians and other physicians.

In 2015 commercial health insurance accounted for 28% of USPh's net patient revenue. This was followed by Medicare and Medicaid (25% of net patient revenue) managed care programs (23%) workers' compensation (18%) and other (6%).

Financial Performance
Revenues for USPh have continued to increase over the years as the company has expanded its network of clinics. In 2015 revenues increased 9% to $331 million due to an increase in patient visits (3 million up from 2.8 million in 2014) at both new and mature clinics. The acquisition of additional clinics also boosted revenues.

Net income which had declined in 2012 and 2013 has risen over the past couple of years. In 2015 it increased 7% to $22 million thanks to the higher revenue but this was partially offset by an increase in clinic operating expenses. Cash flow from operations had been trending upward until 2015 when it fell 9% to $41 million. This decline was primarily due to a decrease in accounts payable and accrued expenses as well as an increase in cash used in accounts receivable.

Strategy
USPh grows by developing and acquiring new clinics throughout the US. In 2015 the company acquired a total of 21 clinics for some $21 million. It plans to continue buying and developing additional facilities as well as opening satellite clinics in suitable locations.

Along with developing new partnerships and opening new clinics USPh seeks to increase its market share by upping its patient volume through marketing campaigns and by adding new services. It also works to recruit and retain physical therapists that have strong relationships with referring physicians by offering competitive salaries and opportunities to own a stake in or share profits in the clinics where they work.

Mergers and Acquisitions
In 2017 USPh paid about $6.6 million for a 55% stake in a company that provides industrial clients with onsite injury prevention and rehabilitation performance optimization and ergonomic assessments. It purchased a 65% stake in a similar firm for $9 million in 2018.

The company has also grown through the purchase of clinical practices throughout the nation. In 2016 it acquired a 55% stake in an eight-clinic physical therapy practice for $14 million and a 60% stake in a 12-clinic group for $11.5 million. Early the following year the company bought a 70% stake in a 17-clinic physical therapy practice for $11.4 million and a 60% stake in a nine-clinic practice for $16.3 million.

EXECUTIVES
CFO, Lawrance W. (Larry) McAfee, age 64, $409,577 total compensation
CEO, Christopher J. (Chris) Reading, age 55, $558,730 total compensation
COO, Glenn McDowell, age 63, $363,942 total compensation
Vice President of Operations, Darryl Gotwalt
Vice President Of Operations, Mary Dimick
Vice President, Kelly Drake
Chairman, Jerald L. Pullins, age 77
Board Member, Mark Brookner
Auditors: Grant Thornton LLP

LOCATIONS
HQ: U.S. Physical Therapy, Inc.
  1300 West Sam Houston Parkway South, Suite 300, Houston, TX 77042
Phone: 713 297-7000
Web: www.usph.com

PRODUCTS/OPERATIONS

2015 Sales

	$ mil.	% of total
Patient revenue		
Commercial insurance	91.8	28
Medicare/Medicaid	79.3	24
Managed care	73.5	22
Workers' compensation	60.1	18
Other patient revenue	19.5	6
Other	7.0	2
Total	331.3	100

COMPETITORS
Concentra
Five Star Senior Living
Physiotherapy Associates
RehabCare
Select Medical
Spaulding Rehabilitation Hospital
U.S. HealthWorks

HISTORICAL FINANCIALS
Company Type: Public

Income Statement
FYE: December 31

	REVENUE ($ mil.)	NET INCOME ($ mil.)	NET PROFIT MARGIN	EMPLOYEES
12/18	453.9	34.8	7.7%	4,600
12/17	414.0	22.2	5.4%	4,300
12/16	356.5	20.5	5.8%	3,800
12/15	331.3	22.2	6.7%	3,400
12/14	305.0	20.8	6.8%	3,151
Annual Growth	10.4%	13.7%	—	9.9%

2018 Year-End Financials

Debt ratio: 8.9%
Return on equity: 16.5%
Cash ($ mil.): 23.3
Current ratio: 1.89
Long-term debt ($ mil.): 38.4
No. of shares (mil.): 12.6
Dividends
  Yield: 0.9%
  Payout: 70.2%
Market value ($ mil.): 1,298.0

	STOCK PRICE ($) FY Close	P/E High/Low	PER SHARE ($) Earnings	Dividends	Book Value
12/18	102.35	98 55	1.31	0.92	17.02
12/17	72.20	44 32	1.76	0.80	16.27
12/16	70.20	44 28	1.64	0.68	14.98
12/15	53.68	32 22	1.77	0.60	13.11
12/14	41.96	27 19	1.62	0.48	11.92
Annual Growth	25.0%	— —	(5.2%)	17.7%	9.3%

Ubiquiti Inc

Auditors: KPMG LLP

LOCATIONS

HQ: Ubiquiti Inc
685 Third Avenue, 27th Floor, New York, NY 10017
Phone: 646 780-7958
Web: www.ubnt.com

HISTORICAL FINANCIALS

Company Type: Public

Income Statement — FYE: June 30

	REVENUE ($ mil.)	NET INCOME ($ mil.)	NET PROFIT MARGIN	EMPLOYEES
06/19	1,161.7	322.6	27.8%	955
06/18	1,016.8	196.2	19.3%	843
06/17	865.2	257.5	29.8%	725
06/16	666.4	213.6	32.1%	537
06/15	595.9	129.6	21.8%	435
Annual Growth	18.2%	25.6%	—	21.7%

2019 Year-End Financials

Debt ratio: 56.5%
Return on equity: 155.5%
Cash ($ mil.): 238.1
Current ratio: 4.21
Long-term debt ($ mil.): 464.7
No. of shares (mil.): 69.4
Dividends
  Yield: 0.0%
  Payout: 22.1%
Market value ($ mil.): 9,136.0

	STOCK PRICE ($) FY Close	P/E High/Low	PER SHARE ($) Earnings	Dividends	Book Value
06/19	131.50	38 18	4.51	1.00	1.43
06/18	84.72	35 20	2.51	0.00	4.26
06/17	51.97	20 12	3.09	0.00	7.50
06/16	38.66	16 11	2.49	0.00	5.39
06/15	31.92	34 18	1.45	0.17	4.83
Annual Growth	42.5% (26.2%)	— —	32.8%	—	55.7%

UFP Technologies Inc.

As a maker of polyethylene polyurethane and polystyrene foam products UFP Technologies peddles the primary P's of plastics. Its engineered foam operations makes car interior parts gaskets and filters carrying cases soundproofing toys beauty products and components for medical diagnostic equipment. It also makes cushion packaging and molded fiber packaging products for automotive computer electronics industrial medical and pharmaceutical manufacturers. UFP uses cross-linked polyethylene foams to laminate fabrics for footwear backpacks and gun holsters. The company also makes recycled paper packaging for computer components medical devices and electronics.

Geographic Reach

The company is headquartered in Newburyport Massachusetts and has a presence in Georgia Alabama Michigan California Colorado New Jersey Florida Texas and Iowa.

Sales and Marketing

UFP caters to the main markets of medical (41% of net sales) automotive (19%) consumer (12%) electronics (10%) aerospace and defense (9%) and industrial (8%). Its top 10 customers represented nearly 26% of its total sales in 2015.

Financial Performance

UFP's revenues remained flat from 2013 to 2015. The flat revenue for 2015 was fueled by sales decreases to customers in the electronics (17%) industrial (17%) and aerospace and defense (13%) markets. This was offset by a sales spike to customers in the medical market (15%).

Like its revenues UFP's net income remained consistent form 2014 to 2015 hovering around the the $7.5 million mark for both years. In addition UFP's operating cash flow has fluctuated over the years; after declining in 2015 cash flow surged by 18% during 2015.

Strategy

UFP aims to jump-start its static balance sheet by adding capacity in order to enhance operate inefficiencies in its manufacturing plants. In 2015 it announced plans to cease operations at its Raritan New Jersey plant and consolidate operations into its Newburyport Massachusetts facility and other UFP facilities. The move was in response to a continued decline in business at its Raritan facility and the recent purchase of a 137000-sq.-ft. facility in Newburyport.

EXECUTIVES

SVP CFO and Treasurer, Ronald J. Lataille, age 57, $230,000 total compensation
SVP Sales and Marketing, Mitchell C. Rock, age 52, $230,000 total compensation
Chairman President and CEO, R. Jeffrey Bailly, $450,000 total compensation
SVP Operations, W. David Smith, $88,442 total compensation
Senior Vice President Operations, David Smith
Vice President Operations, William Smith
Auditors: Grant Thornton LLP

LOCATIONS

HQ: UFP Technologies Inc.
100 Hale Street, Newburyport, MA 01950
Phone: 978 352-2200
Web: www.ufpt.com

PRODUCTS/OPERATIONS

2015 Sales by Market

	% of total
Medical	41
Automotive	19
Consumer	12
Electronics	10
Aerospace & Defense	10
Industrial	8
Total	**100**

Selected Component Products

Abrasive nail files
Athletic and industrial safety belts
Automotive interior trim
Medical diagnostic equipment components
Shock absorbing inserts used in athletic and leisure footwear

Selected Packaging Products

Antistatic foam packs for printed circuit boards
Corner blocks for telecommunications consoles
Die-cut or routed inserts for attaché cases
End-cap packs for computers
Plastic trays for medical devices and components

Selected Services

Assembling
Cutting
Engineering
Laminating
Molding
Prototyping
Vacuum forming

Selected Subsidiaries

Moulded Fibre Technology Inc.
Patterson Properties Corporation
Simco Automotive Trim Inc.
Simco Industries Inc.
Stephenson & Lawyer Inc.
United Development Company Limited (26%)

COMPETITORS

Dow Corning
FXI Holdings
MSA Foams
Pactiv
Sealed Air Corp.
Toray Plastics

HISTORICAL FINANCIALS

Company Type: Public

Income Statement — FYE: December 31

	REVENUE ($ mil.)	NET INCOME ($ mil.)	NET PROFIT MARGIN	EMPLOYEES
12/18	190.4	14.3	7.5%	1,051
12/17	147.8	9.2	6.2%	796
12/16	146.1	7.9	5.5%	805
12/15	138.8	7.5	5.5%	722
12/14	139.3	7.5	5.4%	658
Annual Growth	8.1%	17.3%	—	12.4%

2018 Year-End Financials

Debt ratio: 13.2%
Return on equity: 10.8%
Cash ($ mil.): 3.2
Current ratio: 2.69
Long-term debt ($ mil.): 22.2
No. of shares (mil.): 7.3
Dividends
  Yield: —
  Payout: —
Market value ($ mil.): 222.0

	STOCK PRICE ($) FY Close	P/E High/Low	PER SHARE ($) Earnings	Dividends	Book Value
12/18	30.04	20 14	1.93	0.00	19.02
12/17	27.80	25 18	1.26	0.00	16.99
12/16	25.45	24 18	1.10	0.00	15.67
12/15	23.82	24 18	1.05	0.00	14.44
12/14	24.59	25 19	1.05	0.00	13.44
Annual Growth	5.1%	— —	16.4%	—	9.1%

Ultra Clean Holdings Inc

Ultra Clean Holdings is a pure play in helping computer chip makers keep their manufacturing conditions pristine. The company which does business as Ultra Clean Technology (UCT) designs engineers manufactures and tests customized gas liquid and catalytic steam generation delivery systems used primarily in the production of semiconductors. The company also provides third-party manufacturing services. UCT has extended its know-how in the semiconductor industry to move into flat-panel display medical research and energy markets. The company's three biggest customers account for about 85% of revenue.

Operations
Ultra Clean Technology functions through wholly owned subsidiaries: Ultra Clean Technology Systems and Service Inc. AIT LLC Ultra Clean Micro-Electronics Equipment (Shanghai) Co. Ltd. Ultra Clean Asia Pacific Pte Ltd. Marchi and Miconex. The company places its factories near its customers' plants in the US and Asia because of the tight integration of UCT tools into its customers' processes.

The company's products perform functions throughout a semiconductor fabrication plant. Products include gas delivery systems liquid delivery systems precision robotics and process modules.

Geographic Reach
Ultra Clean Technology has international operations in China Singapore the Philippines Austria the Czech Republic and in California Arizona and Texas in the US. Manufacturing is done at all locations while engineering functions are also conducted at its California headquarters in Hayward and Austin Texas. A bit more than half of the company's sales are made to customers headquartered in the US while the rest are to international customers.

Sales and Marketing
Ultra Clean Technology relies on a direct sales force of sales directors account managers and sales support staff to work closely with customers. The sales staff includes technical sales support and engineers stationed at customers' factories. After several round of consolidation in the semiconductor industry just three customers account for about 85% of UCT's revenue. They are LAM Research (50%) Applied Materials (25%) and ASM (about 10%).

Financial Performance
The record of Ultra Clean Tech's revenue and profit for the past decade reflects the ups-and-downs on the semiconductor industry. The company had an up year in 2016 posting stronger revenue and a profit after a loss in 2015.

The company's sales increased 20% to about $563 million in 2016 from about $470 million in 2015. The company shipped more products in 2016 to meet higher customer demand. Its semiconductor-related business accounted for about 80% of the sales increase while the rest came from the flat panel medical and energy work it does. Sales to US customers dropped by half in 2016 while sales to foreign customers jumped 48%. The foreign sales increase was due to the Miconex acquisition of 2015 and the continuing shift of business to UCT's Singapore operations by a US customer. Sales generated by UCT's Singapore site have increased 220% from 2014 to 2016.

UCT flipped a $10 million loss in 2015 to a $10 million profit in 2016. The turnaround came from higher revenue in 2016 along with lower expenses as the company maintained a tight rein on costs and had a lower tax bill in 2015.

Cash flow from operations jumped to about $18 million in 2016 from about $926000 in 2015. Sources of cash were non-cash activities such as depreciation of equipment and leasehold improvements amortization of intangible assets as well as decreases in prepaid expenses and other and deferred tax assets net and increases in accounts payable and accrued compensation.

Strategy
Ultra Clean Tech's rode more investment more capacity and stronger demand in the semiconductor industry to higher revenue and profit in 2016 and the company looks for the trend to continue in 2017. Semiconductor makers are racing to keep up with consumer demand for more electronics and that means more business for UCT.

Customers look to UCT for manufacturing capacity as they max out their production facilities as well as make equipment for new facilities. And the company's expansion beyond clean technologies has enlarged its addressable market. The company expects demand for its flat-panel capabilities to grow as they did in 2016 when flat panel revenue doubled from 2015.

Mergers and Acquisitions
In 2019 Ultra Clean acquired Dynamic Manufacturing Solutions a provider of welding servces for the semiconductor industry for about $30 million. DMS offers contract welding manufacturing UHP weld assemblies gas and chemical delivery process and facility modules engineering services and electrical and mechanical design and assembly. DMS complements Ultra Clean's products and services.

Ultra Clean Tech made two acquisitions in 2015 that expanded its product lineup and geographic foot print.

In August 2015 UCT acquired Miconex a Czech Republic-based provider of advanced precision fabrication of plastics for about $15 million. The acquisition expands company's capabilities in specialty manufacturing processes the semiconductor equipment market and adjacent markets.

Also in 2015 UCT acquired Marchi a designer and manufacturer of specialty thermocouples heaters and temperature controllers for $30 million in cash. The acquisition expanded UCT's offerings.

EXECUTIVES

CEO, James P. (Jim) Scholhamer, age 53, $370,577 total compensation
SVP Asia, Lavi A. Lev, age 63, $247,199 total compensation
SVP Supply Chain Management and Machining Operations, Mark G. Bingaman, age 64, $271,314 total compensation
SVP Finance CFO Secretary Principal Financial Officer and Chief Accounting Officer, Sheri Brumm, age 49
SVP Engineering, Michael Henderson
Vice President Global Information Technology, Victor Gonzalez
Chairman, Clarence L. Granger, age 71
Board Member, Emily Liggett
Board Member, Barbara Scherer
Board Member, Thomas Edman
Auditors: Moss Adams LLP

LOCATIONS

HQ: Ultra Clean Holdings Inc
26462 Corporate Avenue, Hayward, CA 94545
Phone: 510 576-4400
Web: www.uct.com

COMPETITORS

ATMI	L'Air Liquide
Air Products	Matheson Tri-Gas
Allegro MicroSystems	Praxair
Ebara	Sanmina
Flextronics	Wolfe Engineering

HISTORICAL FINANCIALS
Company Type: Public

Income Statement FYE: December 28

	REVENUE ($ mil.)	NET INCOME ($ mil.)	NET PROFIT MARGIN	EMPLOYEES
12/18	1,096.5	36.6	3.3%	4,280
12/17	924.3	75.0	8.1%	2,747
12/16	562.7	10.0	1.8%	2,183
12/15	469.1	(10.7)	—	1,817
12/14	513.9	11.3	2.2%	1,546
Annual Growth	20.9%	34.0%	—	29.0%

2018 Year-End Financials

Debt ratio: 35.3%
Return on equity: 9.9%
Cash ($ mil.): 144.1
Current ratio: 3.32
Long-term debt ($ mil.): 331.5
No. of shares (mil.): 39.0
Dividends
 Yield: —
 Payout: —
Market value ($ mil.): 321.0

	STOCK PRICE ($) FY Close	P/E High/Low		PER SHARE ($) Earnings	Dividends	Book Value
12/18	8.21	28	8	0.94	0.00	11.17
12/17	23.09	15	4	2.19	0.00	8.92
12/16	9.70	34	15	0.30	0.00	6.56
12/15	5.38	—	—	(0.34)	0.00	6.23
12/14	9.38	38	19	0.38	0.00	6.38
Annual Growth	(3.3%)	—	—	25.4%	—	15.0%

Union Bank (Greenville, NC)

Auditors: Dixon Hughes Goodman LLP

LOCATIONS

HQ: Union Bank (Greenville, NC)
804 Carey Road, P.O. Box 279, Kinston, NC 28501-0279
Phone: 252 939-3900
Web: www.thelittlebank.com

HISTORICAL FINANCIALS
Company Type: Public

Income Statement　　　　　　　　　　FYE: December 31

	ASSETS ($ mil.)	NET INCOME ($ mil.)	INCOME AS % OF ASSETS	EMPLOYEES
12/18	745.1	6.7	0.9%	0
12/17	702.5	2.6	0.4%	0
12/16	362.0	3.0	0.9%	0
12/15	362.1	3.1	0.9%	0
12/14	339.0	2.9	0.9%	0
Annual Growth	21.8%	23.2%	—	—

2018 Year-End Financials
Return on assets: 0.9%
Return on equity: 8.9%
Long-term debt ($ mil.): —
No. of shares (mil.): 6.0
Sales ($ mil): 33.9
Dividends
  Yield: 1.3%
  Payout: 18.4%
Market value ($ mil.): 86.0

	STOCK PRICE ($) FY Close	P/E High/Low		PER SHARE ($) Earnings	Dividends	Book Value
12/18	14.40	17	13	1.12	0.19	13.04
12/17	16.60	36	23	0.55	0.17	12.22
12/16	13.10	16	14	0.86	0.16	10.28
12/15	12.25	14	12	0.87	0.14	9.70
12/14	12.68	15	12	0.84	0.13	9.50
Annual Growth	3.2%	—	—	7.3%	10.6%	8.2%

United Bancshares Inc. (OH)

EXECUTIVES
Senior Vice President, Norman Schnipke
Executive Vice President Marketing, Amy Reese
Vice President Loan Operations, Donna Brown
Vice President, Paul Walker
Assistant Vice President Commercial Lender, Chase Doll
Vice President Of Call Centre, Erin Hardesty
Senior Vice President Chief Credit Officer, Teresa Deitering
Vice President Commercial Lending Sba And Government Programs, Rose Roman
Vp Mortgage Banking, Ben Stewart
Board Member, Robert Benroth
Board Member, David Roach
Auditors: CliftonLarsonAllen LLP

LOCATIONS
HQ: United Bancshares Inc. (OH)
105 Progressive Drive, Columbus Grove, OH 45830
Phone: 419 659-2141
Web: www.theubank.com

COMPETITORS
Commercial Bancshares
Fifth Third
First Defiance Financial
Huntington Bancshares
JPMorgan Chase
Peoples-Sidney
SB Financial Group
U.S. Bancorp

HISTORICAL FINANCIALS
Company Type: Public

Income Statement　　　　　　　　　　FYE: December 31

	ASSETS ($ mil.)	NET INCOME ($ mil.)	INCOME AS % OF ASSETS	EMPLOYEES
12/18	830.3	8.2	1.0%	179
12/17	780.4	3.8	0.5%	177
12/16	633.1	5.5	0.9%	155
12/15	608.6	5.9	1.0%	151
12/14	650.2	4.3	0.7%	142
Annual Growth	6.3%	17.5%	—	6.0%

2018 Year-End Financials
Return on assets: 1.0%
Return on equity: 10.4%
Long-term debt ($ mil.): —
No. of shares (mil.): 3.2
Sales ($ mil): 43.7
Dividends
  Yield: 2.4%
  Payout: 23.5%
Market value ($ mil.): 65.0

	STOCK PRICE ($) FY Close	P/E High/Low		PER SHARE ($) Earnings	Dividends	Book Value
12/18	20.02	9	7	2.51	0.48	24.76
12/17	22.20	20	17	1.18	0.48	23.17
12/16	21.42	13	10	1.68	0.44	22.21
12/15	18.24	10	8	1.77	0.36	21.62
12/14	14.45	13	10	1.27	0.35	20.12
Annual Growth	8.5%	—	—	18.6%	8.2%	5.3%

United Bankshares Inc

United Bankshares (no relation to Ohio's United Bancshares) keeps it together as the holding company for two subsidiaries doing business as United Bank (WV) and United Bank (VA). Combined the banks boast some $12 billion in assets and operate roughly 130 branches that serve West Virginia Virginia and Washington DC as well as nearby portions of Maryland Pennsylvania and Ohio. The branches offer traditional deposit trust and lending services with a focus on residential mortgages and commercial loans. United Bankshares also owns United Brokerage Services which provides investments asset management and financial planning in addition to brokerage services.

Operations
The company's loan portfolio is made up of commercial and construction commercial and residential real estate and consumer loans (including credit card and home equity loans).

United Bankshares generated 75% of its total revenue from interest and fees on loans in 2014 plus an additional 7% from interest and dividends on its investment securities. The company generated about 9% of its total revenue from deposit services fees and another 4% from trust and brokerage services fees.

Geographic Reach
United Bankshares boasts some 130 full-service branches including more than 55 across the state of West Virginia nearly 70 in the Shenendoah Valley region of Virginia and the Northern Virginia Maryland and Washington DC metro area and a handful of branches split between southwestern Pennsylvania and southeastern Ohio.

Sales and Marketing
The company spent $4.76 million on advertising in 2014 up from $3.78 million and $4.27 million spent in 2013 and 2012 respectively.

Financial Performance
United Bankshares' revenues and profits have trended higher over the past few years thanks to growth in its loan business from acquisitions increased trust and brokerage services fee income and declining interest expense on deposits amidst the low-interest environment.

The company's revenue jumped by nearly 34% to a record $499.50 million in 2014 mostly as its interest income spiked by 37% after its Virginia Commerce acquisition added new interest-earning assets and increased the average yields on its loans investments and security assets. United Bankshare's non-interest income also swelled by 22% thanks to higher income from fees from trust and brokerage services bankcard fees and merchant discounts and net gains on investment securities.

Higher revenue in 2014 boosted the company's profits by 52% to a record $129.89 million while the company's operating cash grew by 2% thanks to higher cash earnings.

Strategy
United Bankshares has historically expanded through small bank and branch acquisitions closing nearly 30 bank purchases in the past quarter-century. Its growth strategy has mainly been focused in on the Washington DC/suburban Maryland/northern Virginia market though its also expanded into Pennsylvania in recent years as well. In 2014 for example the company extended its reach into Washington DC while boosting its loan business by $2 billion after completing its largest-ever acquisition of Virginia Commerce Bancorp.

In 2016 the company agreed to buy Cardinal Financial which has some $4.2 billion in assets and operates 30 branches in Virginia Maryland and Washington DC.

Mergers and Acquisitions
In January 2014 United Bankshares acquired Arlington-based Virginia Commerce Bancorp for a total cost of $585.53 million. The deal expanded United's reach into the Washington DC metropolitan area and added $2.07 billion in new loan business and $2.02 billion in deposits.

Company Background
The 2011 acquisition of West Virginia-based Centra Financial Holdings gave United Bankshares its first branches in Pennsylvania and entry into the Pittsburgh market.

EXECUTIVES
EVP the Company and United Bank and WV, James B. Hayhurst, age 73, $225,000 total compensation
President, Richard M. Adams, age 51, $328,846 total compensation
COO, James J. Consagra, age 59, $334,462 total compensation
EVP and COO United Bank (VA), Craige L. Smith, age 67, $243,750 total compensation
EVP and CFO, W. Mark Tatterson, age 44
EVP, Darren K. Williams
Vice President Risk Management, Connie Stone
Assistant Vice President Information Technology Audit Manager, Jason Moore
Senior Vice President, Dale Homan
Vice President Internal Audit Manager, Steve Hizak

Assistant Vice President Corporate Security Officer, Rachel Wilson
Assistant Vice President and C, Erica Fowler
Vp Financial Advisor, Cameron Stewart
Board Member, Peter Converse
Auditors: Ernst & Young LLP

LOCATIONS

HQ: United Bankshares Inc
300 United Center, 500 Virginia Street, East,
Charleston, WV 25301
Phone: 304 424-8716
Web: www.ubsi-inc.com

PRODUCTS/OPERATIONS

2014 Sales

	$ mil.	% of total
Interest		
Loans including fees	383.7	75
Interest and dividends on securities	33.9	7
Other	0.9	-
Noninterest		
Fees from deposit services	42.4	9
Fees from trust & brokerage services	18.1	4
Other	28.9	5
Adjustment (losses)	(8.4)	-
Total	**499.5**	**100**

COMPETITORS

BB&T	JPMorgan Chase
Bank of America	M&T Bank
Burke & Herbert Bank	PNC Financial
Cardinal Financial	SunTrust
City Holding	United Bancorp
Fifth Third	Virginia Commerce
Fulton Financial	Bancorp
Huntington Bancshares	WesBanco

HISTORICAL FINANCIALS

Company Type: Public

Income Statement FYE: December 31

	ASSETS ($ mil.)	NET INCOME ($ mil.)	INCOME AS % OF ASSETS	EMPLOYEES
12/18	19,250.5	256.3	1.3%	2,230
12/17	19,058.9	150.5	0.8%	2,381
12/16	14,508.8	147.0	1.0%	1,701
12/15	12,577.9	137.9	1.1%	1,701
12/14	12,328.8	129.8	1.1%	1,703
Annual Growth	11.8%	18.5%	—	7.0%

2018 Year-End Financials

Return on assets: 1.3%
Return on equity: 7.9%
Long-term debt ($ mil.): —
No. of shares (mil.): 102.3
Sales ($ mil): 846.4
Dividends
 Yield: 4.3%
 Payout: 68.3%
Market value ($ mil.): 3,183.0

	STOCK PRICE ($) FY Close	P/E High/Low		PER SHARE ($)		
				Earnings	Dividends	Book Value
12/18	31.11	16	12	2.45	1.36	31.78
12/17	34.75	30	21	1.54	1.33	30.85
12/16	46.25	25	16	1.99	1.32	27.59
12/15	36.99	22	17	1.98	1.29	24.61
12/14	37.45	20	15	1.92	1.28	23.90
Annual Growth	(4.5%)	—	—	6.3%	1.5%	7.4%

United Community Banks Inc (Blairsville, GA)

United Community Banks is the holding company for United Community Bank (UCB). UCB provides consumer and business banking products and services through nearly 150 branches across Georgia North Carolina Tennessee and South Carolina. Commercial loans including construction loans and mortgages account for the largest portion of UCB's loan portfolio (more than 50%); residential mortgages make up 30%. The company which boasts roughly $10 billion in assets also has a mortgage lending division and provides insurance through its United Community Insurance Services subsidiary (aka United Community Advisory Services).

Operations
The bank's retail mortgage lending division United Community Mortgage Services (UCMS) sells and services mortgages for Fannie Mae and Freddie Mac and provides fixed and adjustable-rate home mortgages. It also offers retail brokerage services through an affiliation with a third-party broker/dealer.

About 65% of UCB's total revenue came from loan interest (including fees) in 2014 while another 16% came from taxable investments. The rest of its revenue came from service charges and fees (10%) mortgage loan fees (2%) and brokerage fees (2%) among other sources.

Geographic Reach
UCB's nearly 105 branches are located in Georgia (in the north the Atlanta-Sandy Springs-Roswell metro area Gainsville metro area and coastal areas); western North Carolina; eastern and central Tennessee; and South Carolina (in the Greenville-Anderson-Mauldin metro area).

Sales and Marketing
The bank provides community banking services for individuals small businesses and corporations.

Financial Performance
UCB has struggled to consistently grow its revenues in recent years due to shrinking interest margins on loans amidst the low-interest environment. Its profits however have been rising thanks to declining loan loss provisions as its loan portfolio's credit quality has improved with higher property valuations in the strengthened economy.

The bank's revenue inched higher by 1% to $304 million in 2014 thanks to an increase in interest income stemming from strategic business growth initiatives designed to add new business lines and expand into new markets as well as balance sheet management and restructuring actions taken in the second quarter of the year.

Despite higher revenue in 2014 UCB's net income dove 75% to $67.6 million mostly because in 2013 it had received a non-recurring income tax benefit of $238 million stemming from reversal of a deferred tax valuation allowance. Not counting this item however the bank's profit before taxes nearly tripled during the year. UCB's operating cash levels dropped by 47% to $101.9 million in 2014 due to lower cash earnings.

Strategy
UCB has been concentrating on growing its small business lending business in recent years. In 2014 it made "significant investments" in its SBA business after acquiring Business Carolina which specialized in SBA and USDA lending.

It also continues to pursue bank acquisitions to expand its reach in its existing core markets and boost its loan and deposit business. Its acquisitions in 2015 and 2014 alone have added over $1 billion in new loan business and $1.3 billion in new deposits.

Mergers and Acquisitions
In 2016 United Community Banks expanded into key markets in coastal South Carolina after buying Mt. Pleasant-based Tidelands and its seven Tidelands Bank branches in the Charleston Myrtle Beach and Hilton Head areas.

In 2015 UCB bought Tennessee-based MoneyTree Corporation and its 10 First National Bank branches in east Tennessee. The deal added $425 million in assets $354 million in deposits and $253 million in new loan business to UCB's books.

In 2014 the company purchased Palmetto Bancshares and its Palmetto Bank branches expanding its footprint into "major" southeastern metro markets in Greenville and the Upstate South Carolina area. The deal also added $1.2 billion in assets $832 million in loans and $967 million in deposits.

Also in 2014 UCB purchased Columbia-based Business Carolina a commercial lender that specialized in SBA and USDA loans for $31.3 million in cash. The deal included $25 million in loans $6 million in other assets and substantially all of the company's employees.

EXECUTIVES

President of Specialized Lending, Richard W. Bradshaw, age 57
Chairman and CEO, Jimmy C. Tallent, age 66, $750,000 total compensation
President Community Banking, William M. (Bill) Gilbert, age 66, $308,334 total compensation
President and Director United Community Banks Inc. and President CEO and Director United Community Bank, H. Lynn Harton, age 57, $575,000 total compensation
EVP General Counsel and Chief Risk Officer, Bradley J. (Brad) Miller, age 48
EVP and Chief Credit Officer, Robert A. (Rob) Edwards, age 54, $305,000 total compensation
EVP and CFO United Community Banks Inc. and United Community Bank, Jefferson L. Harralson
Senior Vice President, Robert Head
Vice President Mortgage Origination, Lisa Mericle
Vice President, Casey Brogdon
Vice President, Ronney Dixon
Avp Mortgage Loan Officer, Tabitha Helms
Senior Vice President, David Shelnutt
Assistant Vice President Incentive Marketing Manager, Diana White
Senior Vice President, Ron Altman
Assistant Vice President, Wendy Cawthon
Vice President Mortgage Banker, Angie Abston
Vice President Of Business Development And Marketing, Elaine Bell
Senior Vice President Commercial Lending, Sam Churchill
Vice President Commercial Lending, Brian Hill
Senior Vice President, Donald Harris
Senior Vice President Corporate Services Support, Jeanette Garrett
VP Marketing, Greg Stephens

Senior Vice President Senior Risk Officer, Shep Calhoun
Vice President, Jane Callihan
Assistant Vice President Business Banking Underwriting, Eric Rivenbark
Vice President, Nick Harty
Senior Vice President Commercial Banking, Ben Walker
Senior Vice President, Phil Beaudette
Assistant Vice President, Rob Andrews
Executive Vice President Commercial lender, Bud Turner
Executive Vice President, Wayne Lowrey
Vice President Commercial Banking, Michael Emigh
Senior Vice President, Alan Kumler
Senior Vice President Builder Finance, Scott Ernest
Vice President, Darryl Meadows
Vice President, Tyler White
Vice President, Anne Wade
VICE PRESIDENT AND PRIVATE BANKER, Terra Winter
Senior Vice President Commercial Lending, Fred Faulkner
Senior Vice President, Jessie Marolis
VICE PRESIDENT BRANCH MANAGER, Wendy Martin
Vice President Commercial Lender, Donna Clark
VICE PRESIDENT, David Brindley
VICE PRESIDENT CRAFT BEVERAGE LENDING, Ken Jernigan
Vice President, Shad Hill
Vice President Franchise Lending, Mike Stone
Senior Vice President United Community Bank, Dennis McBride
SENIOR VICE PRESIDENT, Sheila Stolorena
Vice President, Jeff Wilson
Vice President, David Ball
Senior Vice President And Corporate Controller, Alan H Kumler
Vice President Branch Manager, Liz Bowen
SENIOR VICE PRESIDENT, Will Ferguson
VICE PRESIDENT COMMERCIAL RELATIONSHIP MANAGER, William Marcus
Vice President, Sandra Brown
VICE PRESIDENT COMMERCIAL RELATIONSHIP MANAGER, Laura Hodge
VICE PRESIDENT UNDERWRITING, Linda Durden
ASSISTANT VICE PRESIDENT BRANCH MANAGER, Michelle Galarza
ASSISTANT VICE PRESIDENT AND MORTGAGE PROCESSING MANAGER, Nalann Moss
VICE PRESIDENT, Frank Scott
Vice President Corporate Banking, James Boccardo
VICE PRESIDENT CUSTOMER CONTACT CENTER TEAM MANAGER SC, Jeanie Roberts
VICE PRESIDENT, Kirby Butler
VICE PRESIDENT AND MORTGAGE ORIGINATION SUPPORT MANAGER, Darin Scheidly
Vice President Relationship Management, Nate Rohler
Vice President Sba Business Development Officer, Lisa Morgan
Assistant Treasurer, Mitchell Bleske
Board Member, Kenneth Daniels
Board Member, David Wilkins
Board Member, David Shaver
Auditors: PricewaterhouseCoopers LLP

LOCATIONS

HQ: United Community Banks Inc (Blairsville, GA)
125 Highway 515 East, Blairsville, GA 30512
Phone: 706 781-2265
Web: www.ucbi.com

PRODUCTS/OPERATIONS

2011 Sales

	$ mil.	% of total
Interest		
Loans including fees	239.1	69
Taxable investment securities	55.2	16
Other	3.3	1
Noninterest		
Service charges & fees	29.1	8
Mortgage loans & related fees	5.4	2
Brokerage fees	3.0	1
Net securities gains	0.8	—
Other	12.3	3
Adjustment	(0.7)	—
Total	**347.5**	**100**

COMPETITORS

Atlantic Coast Financial
BB&T
Bank of America
Bank of Oak Ridge
First Citizens BancShares
Georgia Bancshares
Georgia-Carolina Bancshares
Peoples Bancorp (NC)
Regions Financial
Southeastern Bank Financial
Southeastern Banking
SunTrust
Synovus
WGNB

HISTORICAL FINANCIALS

Company Type: Public

Income Statement

FYE: December 31

	ASSETS ($ mil.)	NET INCOME ($ mil.)	INCOME AS % OF ASSETS	EMPLOYEES
12/18	12,573.1	166.1	1.3%	2,312
12/17	11,915.4	67.8	0.6%	2,137
12/16	10,708.6	100.6	0.9%	1,916
12/15	9,626.1	71.5	0.7%	1,883
12/14	7,566.9	67.6	0.9%	1,506
Annual Growth	13.5%	25.2%	—	11.3%

2018 Year-End Financials

Return on assets: 1.3%
Return on equity: 12.0%
Long-term debt ($ mil.): —
No. of shares (mil.): 79.2
Sales ($ mil): 593.0
Dividends
Yield: 2.7%
Payout: 28.0%
Market value ($ mil.): 1,700.0

	STOCK PRICE ($) FY Close	P/E High/Low	PER SHARE ($) Earnings	Dividends	Book Value
12/18	21.46	16 10	2.07	0.58	18.40
12/17	28.14	33 27	0.92	0.38	16.80
12/16	29.62	21 11	1.40	0.30	15.17
12/15	19.49	20 15	1.09	0.22	14.24
12/14	18.94	18 14	1.11	0.11	12.27
Annual Growth	3.2%	— —	16.9%	51.5%	10.6%

United Security Bancshares (CA)

EXECUTIVES

Chairman President and CEO United Security Bancshares and United Security Bank, Dennis R. Woods, age 68, $368,036 total compensation
EVP and Chief Administrative Officer United Security Bancshares and United Security Bank, Kenneth L. (Ken) Donahue, age 67, $145,414 total compensation
SVP and COO United Security Bancshares and United Security Bank, David L. (Dave) Eytcheson, age 75, $142,815 total compensation
Secretary and Director, Robert G. Bitter, age 77
Vice Chairman, Ronnie D. Miller, age 74
SVP and CFO United Security Bancshares and United Security Bank, Richard Shupe
Secretary and Director, Robert G. Bitter, age 77
Vice Chairman, Ronnie D. Miller, age 74
Independent Director, Stanley J. Cavalla, age 65
Independent Director, Tom Ellithorpe, age 73
Independent Director, Walter Reinhard, age 86
Independent Director, John Terzian, age 83
Independent Director, Michael T. (Mike) Woolf, age 60
Independent Director, Robert M. Mochizuki, age 67
Independent Director, Todd Henry
Auditors: Moss Adams LLP

LOCATIONS

HQ: United Security Bancshares (CA)
2126 Inyo Street, Fresno, CA 93721
Phone: 559 248-4943   **Fax:** 559 248-5088
Web: www.unitedsecuritybank.com

COMPETITORS

Bank of America
First Hawaiian
MUFG Americas Holdings
Sierra Bancorp
Westamerica
Zions Bancorporation

HISTORICAL FINANCIALS

Company Type: Public

Income Statement

FYE: December 31

	ASSETS ($ mil.)	NET INCOME ($ mil.)	INCOME AS % OF ASSETS	EMPLOYEES
12/18	933.0	14.0	1.5%	125
12/17	805.8	8.6	1.1%	128
12/16	787.9	7.3	0.9%	132
12/15	725.6	6.8	0.9%	129
12/14	663.1	6.2	0.9%	132
Annual Growth	8.9%	22.5%	—	(1.4%)

2018 Year-End Financials

Return on assets: 1.6%
Return on equity: 13.3%
Long-term debt ($ mil.): —
No. of shares (mil.): 16.9
Sales ($ mil): 41.2
Dividends
Yield: 3.6%
Payout: 50.0%
Market value ($ mil.): 162.0

	STOCK PRICE ($)	P/E	PER SHARE ($)		
	FY Close	High/Low	Earnings	Dividends	Book Value
12/18	9.58	14 11	0.83	0.35	6.45
12/17	11.00	22 14	0.51	0.17	6.00
12/16	7.75	19 11	0.44	0.00	5.73
12/15	5.35	14 12	0.40	0.00	5.31
12/14	5.46	16 13	0.37	0.00	4.91
Annual Growth	15.1%	— —	22.7%	—	7.0%

Uniti Group Inc

Auditors: PricewaterhouseCoopers LLP

LOCATIONS

HQ: Uniti Group Inc
10802 Executive Center Drive, Benton Building Suite 300, Little Rock, AR 72211
Phone: 501 850-0820
Web: www.uniti.com

HISTORICAL FINANCIALS

Company Type: Public

Income Statement				FYE: December 31
	REVENUE ($ mil.)	NET INCOME ($ mil.)	NET PROFIT MARGIN	EMPLOYEES
12/18	1,017.6	16.1	1.6%	798
12/17	916.0	(9.4)	—	654
12/16	770.4	(0.2)	—	316
12/15	476.3	24.8	5.2%	37
Annual Growth	28.8%	(13.3%)	—	178.4%

2018 Year-End Financials

Debt ratio: 105.5%
Return on equity: —
Cash ($ mil.): 38.0
Current ratio: 0.15
Long-term debt ($ mil.): 4,846.2
No. of shares (mil.): 180.5
Dividends
  Yield: 15.4%
  Payout: 2,400.0%
Market value ($ mil.): 2,811.0

	STOCK PRICE ($)	P/E	PER SHARE ($)		
	FY Close	High/Low	Earnings	Dividends	Book Value
12/18	15.57	465 283	0.04	2.40	(8.30)
12/17	17.79	— —	(0.13)	2.40	(7.01)
12/16	25.41	— —	(0.04)	2.40	(8.52)
12/15	18.69	190 109	0.16	1.64	(7.79)
/0.00	—	— (0.00)	0.00	(0.00)	
Annual Growth					

Unity Bancorp, Inc.

EXECUTIVES

Assistant Vice President Senior Network Administrator, Jonathan Sheehy
Vice President Branch Sales Manager, Sarika Sikand
Board Member, Raj Patel
Board Member, Aaron Tucker
Auditors: RSM US LLP

LOCATIONS

HQ: Unity Bancorp, Inc.
64 Old Highway 22, Clinton, NJ 08809
Phone: 908 730-7630
Web: www.unitybank.com

PRODUCTS/OPERATIONS

Selected Subsidiaries
Unity Bank
  Unity Financial Services Inc.
  Unity Investment Company Inc.

COMPETITORS

1st Constitution Bancorp
Amboy Bancorp
Bank of America
Bank of New York Mellon
Brunswick Bancorp
Fox Chase Bancorp
Investors Bancorp
Magyar Bancorp
Peapack-Gladstone Financial
Roma Financial
TD Bank USA
TF Financial
Valley National Bancorp

HISTORICAL FINANCIALS

Company Type: Public

Income Statement				FYE: December 31
	ASSETS ($ mil.)	NET INCOME ($ mil.)	INCOME AS % OF ASSETS	EMPLOYEES
12/18	1,579.1	21.9	1.4%	207
12/17	1,455.5	12.8	0.9%	208
12/16	1,189.9	13.2	1.1%	194
12/15	1,084.8	9.5	0.9%	173
12/14	1,008.7	6.4	0.6%	183
Annual Growth	11.9%	36.0%	—	3.1%

2018 Year-End Financials

Return on assets: 1.4%
Return on equity: 17.0%
Long-term debt ($ mil.): —
No. of shares (mil.): 10.7
Sales ($ mil): 76.2
Dividends
  Yield: 1.3%
  Payout: 15.8%
Market value ($ mil.): 224.0

	STOCK PRICE ($)	P/E	PER SHARE ($)		
	FY Close	High/Low	Earnings	Dividends	Book Value
12/18	20.76	12 9	2.01	0.27	12.85
12/17	19.75	17 13	1.20	0.23	11.13
12/16	15.70	12 7	1.38	0.17	10.15
12/15	12.47	12 9	1.02	0.13	8.46
12/14	9.43	14 10	0.74	0.09	7.60
Annual Growth	21.8%	— —	28.5%	31.3%	14.0%

Universal Insurance Holdings Inc

While some companies shy away from insuring homes in hurricane-prone Florida Universal Insurance Holdings is right at home there. Operating through its Universal Property & Casualty Insurance Company (UPCIC) and American Platinum Property and Casualty Insurance Company (APPCIC) subsidiaries the company underwrites distributes and administers homeowners property and personal liability insurance. The company's additional subsidiaries process claims perform claims adjustments and property inspections provide administrative duties and negotiate reinsurance. All together the group services some 765000 insurance policies.

Operations

Universal Insurance is Florida's largest private residential homeowners' insurance provider by direct written premiums in-force with some 10% of the market share.

In addition to UPCIC and APPCIC the company owns Universal Risk Advisors (managing general agent) Universal Inspection Corporation (underwriting inspections) Universal Adjusting Corporation (claims processing) and Blue Atlantic Reinsurance (reinsurance intermediary).

Through Universal Insurance's Universal Direct platform consumers in all states the group operates in are able to directly purchase homeowners policies online without meeting an intermediary face-to-face.

Geographic Reach

Universal Insurance's UPCIC unit has taken its expertise in flood and wind coverage to other markets. While Florida remains its largest market it also operates in 15 other states: Alabama Delaware Florida Georgia Hawaii Indiana Maryland Massachusetts Michigan Minnesota New Hampshire New Jersey New York North Carolina Pennsylvania South Carolina and Virginia. Although not yet active in Illinois Iowa New Hampshire or West Virginia the company is licensed in those states.

APPCIC writes homeowners multi-peril insurance for homes worth more than $1 million in Florida.

Sales and Marketing

Universal Insurance distributes its products through a network of some 8800 independent agents. It also sells its policies through its online platform Universal Direct.

Financial Performance

Universal Insurance's revenues have been rising for the past five years. In 2017 revenue increased 10% to $751.9 million as net premiums earned rose 9% commissions rose 20% and net investment income rose 41%. Policy fees and other revenue also grew in 2017. Direct premiums written increased 11% within Florida and 40% in other states.

With the higher revenue net income rose 8% to $106.9 million. Operating cash flow followed suit more than doubling to $245 million. Factors driving that growth included positive changes to unpaid losses and loss adjustment expenses net reinsurance payable and liabilities and accrued expenses.

Strategy

Universal Insurance has been rapidly and organically expanding its operations beyond Florida especially in states with underserved homeowners markets. It has also introduced new types of coverage such as fire commercial multi-peril and other liability. With this diversification the company is less vulnerable to the catastrophes that have been the bane of Florida insurers. However because it does the majority of its business in Florida Universal Insurance has been hit hard with property/casualty claims in certain years — including in 2017 with the appearance of Hurricane Irma.

Additionally the company has seen an increase in lawsuits against it including suits originating in South Florida. As other insurers shy away from

Florida business Universal Insurance remains committed to the state and to offset rising claims has sought approval to raise its rates some 10% across most of South Florida.

Personal residential homeowners insurance is the company's bread and butter but Universal Insurance is increasingly diving into commercial policies particularly commercial residential coverage in Florida.

EXECUTIVES

Chairman and CEO, Sean P. Downes, age 49, $2,278,015 total compensation
COO, Stephen J. Donaghy, $802,514 total compensation
President and Chief Risk Officer, Jon W. Springer, age 49, $1,337,416 total compensation
CFO and Principal Accounting Officer, Frank C Wilcox, $350,000 total compensation
CIO, Kimberly Cooper, $196,923 total compensation
Senior Vice President of Taxation, Tom Redmond
Auditors: Plante & Moran, PLLC

LOCATIONS

HQ: Universal Insurance Holdings Inc
1110 West Commercial Blvd., Fort Lauderdale, FL 33309
Phone: 954 958-1200
Web: www.universalinsuranceholdings.com

PRODUCTS/OPERATIONS

2017 Sales

	$ mil.	% of total
Net premiums earned	688.8	92
Commissions	21.2	3
Policy fees	18.8	2
Net investment income	13.5	2
Net realized gains on investments	2.6	-
Other	7.0	1
Total	751.9	100

Selected Products and Services
Condominium policy
Dwelling coverage
Dwelling fire policy
Homeowners policy
Other structures coverage
Personal liability coverage
Personal property coverage
Renter's policy

COMPETITORS

Allstate
Citizens Property Insurance
Federated National Holding
HCI Group
Heritage Insurance Holdings
Liberty Mutual
Progressive Corporation
State Farm
Travelers Companies
USAA
United Insurance Holdings

HISTORICAL FINANCIALS
Company Type: Public

Income Statement — FYE: December 31

	ASSETS ($ mil.)	NET INCOME ($ mil.)	INCOME AS % OF ASSETS	EMPLOYEES
12/18	1,858.3	117.0	6.3%	734
12/17	1,455.0	106.9	7.3%	558
12/16	1,060.0	99.4	9.4%	483
12/15	993.5	106.4	10.7%	392
12/14	911.7	72.9	8.0%	335
Annual Growth	19.5%	12.5%	—	21.7%

2018 Year-End Financials
Return on assets: 7.0%
Return on equity: 24.8%
Long-term debt ($ mil.): —
No. of shares (mil.): 34.7
Sales ($ mil): 823.8
Dividends
Yield: 1.5%
Payout: 22.3%
Market value ($ mil.): 1,319.0

	STOCK PRICE ($) FY Close	P/E High/Low		Earnings	PER SHARE ($) Dividends	Book Value
12/18	37.92	15	8	3.27	0.73	14.42
12/17	27.35	9	5	2.99	0.69	12.67
12/16	28.40	10	6	2.79	0.69	10.59
12/15	23.18	12	6	2.97	0.63	8.35
12/14	20.45	10	5	2.08	0.55	6.24
Annual Growth	16.7%	—	—	12.0%	7.3%	23.3%

Univest Financial Corp

Univest Corporation of Pennsylvania will keep your money close to its vest. The holding company owns $3 billion-asset Univest Bank and Trust which serves the southeastern part of the Keystone State and the broader Mid-Atlantic region online and though 30 branches and provides standard retail and commercial banking services such as checking and savings accounts CDs IRAs and credit cards. Subsidiary Univest Capital provides small-ticket commercial financing while Univest Insurance offers personal and commercial coverage. Univest Investments which boasts some $3 billion in assets under management offers brokerage and investment advisory services.

Operations
Univest operates three main business segments: Banking which accounted for 79% of the company's total revenue during 2015 and provides traditional banking services to consumers businesses and government entities through Univest Bank and Trust; Wealth Management (12% of revenue) which offers investment advisory retirement plan trust municipal pension and broker/dealer services through Univest Investments; and Insurance (9% of revenue) which offers commercial and personal insurance lines as well as benefits and human resources consulting through Univest Insurance.

Broadly speaking Univest Corporation gets more than 60% of its revenue from interest income. About 61% of its total revenue came from loan interest (including fees on loans and leases) during 2015 while another 5% came from interest on its investment securities. The rest of its revenue came from insurance commissions and fees (8% of revenue) investment advisory commission and fee income (7%) trust fee income (5%) deposit account service charges (3%) mortgage banking sales (3%) and other miscellaneous income sources.

More than 40% of the company's loan portfolio was made up of commercial real estate loans at the end of 2015 while another 23% of loan assets were made up of commercial loans that were financial or agricultural-related. The remainder of the portfolio was made up of loans tied to residential properties secured for business purposes (10% of loan assets) residential properties for personal purposes (8%) lease financings (7%) construction real estate loans (4%) and loans to individuals (less than 2%).

Geographic Reach
Souderton Pennsylvania-based Univest Corporation and its subsidiaries serve clients across the Mid-Atlantic region. The company has around 30 bank branches and nearly 20 offices in the Montgomery Bucks Philadelphia Chester Berks Lehigh and Delaware counties of Pennsylvania as well as in Calvert County in Maryland Camden County in New Jersey and Lee County in Florida.

Sales and Marketing
Univest Corporation serves individuals businesses municipalities and non-profit organizations. It spent $2.25 million on marketing and advertising during 2015 to reach these clients up from $1.88 million and $1.95 million in 2014 and 2013 respectively.

Financial Performance
The bank's revenues and profits have been trending higher over the past several years thanks to 50% loan asset growth and 50% non-interest revenue growth since 2011 along with a continued reduction in loan loss provisions as its loan portfolio's credit quality has improved with higher property valuations in the strengthened economy.

Univest Corporation's revenue jumped 24% to a record $154.41 million during 2015 mostly as 35% loan asset growth (loan balances swelled to $2.16 billion) stemming from its Valley Green Bank acquisition helped boost interest income. The company's non-interest income also rose 9% as its mortgage banking gains doubled during the year on higher volumes and as its insurance commissions and fee income rose 20% after acquiring Sterner Insurance in mid-2014.

Strong revenue growth in 2015 drove the company's net income up 23% to $27.27 million for the year. Univest Corporation's operating cash levels climbed 12% to $35.63 thanks to the rise in earnings.

Strategy
Univest Corporation has been expanding its service lines and building its loan and deposit businesses by strategically acquiring other banks and investment or insurance-related financial firms.

Mergers and Acquisitions
In December 2015 Univest Corporation agreed to buy Fox Chase Bancorp along with its $1.1 billion in assets $768 million in loans $765 million in deposits and several Fox Chase Bank branches in Pennsylvania and New Jersey for a price exceeding $240 million. The deal would also expand Univest's presence in Bucks Chester Philadelphia and Montgomery counties in Pennsylvania as well as into Atlantic and Cape May counties in New Jersey.

In January 2015 the company purchased Valley Green Bank as well as its three branches and two loan production offices in the greater Philadelphia market for $77 million.

In July 2014 Univest bolstered its Univest Insurance subsidiary after acquiring Sterner Insurance Associates a full-service insurance and consultative risk management firm that served individuals and businesses across the Lehigh Valley Berks Bucks and Montgomery counties.

In January 2014 flagship subsidiary Univest Bank and Trust Co. bought registered investment advisory firm Girard Partners Ltd. as well as its $500 million in assets under management. The deal boosted Univest's assets under management by 20% to a total of $3 billion after the acquisition.

EXECUTIVES

President Corporate Banking, Philip C. (Phil) Jackson, $250,000 total compensation
SEVP and Chief Risk Officer, Duane J. Brobst, $200,000 total compensation
President and CEO, Jeffrey M Schweitzer, $450,000 total compensation
SEVP and CFO, Michael S Keim, $270,000 total compensation
Executive Vice President, John Duerksen
Vice President, Barry Keck
Senior Vice President In Credit Administration, Tami Garber
Senior Vice President, Karen Tejkl
Vice President Account Executive, Chip Schofield
Executive Vice President Chief Experience Officer and Director Corporate Planning, Annette Szygiel
Senior Vice President, Leanne Hayes
Senior Vice President, Richard Pearce
Vice President Relationship Manager Corporate Banking, Randall Beaman
VICE PRESIDENT, Brett Chesmar
VICE PRESIDENT AREA MANAGER, Gregory Taber
SENIOR VICE PRESIDENT EMPLOYEE BENEFITS PRACTICE LEADER, Dennis Boyle
Vice President, Barton Skurbe
VICE PRESIDENT AND OPERATIONS MANAGER, Roxanne Tornetta
Senior Vice President Director Of Commercial Lending, Bryan Moyer
Vice President Business Banking, Patrick Mullen
National Accounts Manager, Kyle Hirsch
SVP Director Bank Systems, Jeffrey Groff
Vice President and Senior Benefits Consultant, Rick Mack
Vice President, Joe Panepresso
Vice President Relationship Manager, Nicholas Yelicanin
Vice President Commercial Lending, Andrew Leaman
VICE PRESIDENT BUSINESS BANKING, Nan Kelly
Executive Vice President General Counsel and Chief Risk Officer of the Corporation and the Bank, Megan Santana
Assistant Vice President Finance Business Unit Analytics, Mary Beth Osbeck
SENIOR VICE PRESIDENT RELATIONSHIP MANAGER, John Thomas
VICE PRESIDENT, David Henrich
SENIOR VICE PRESIDENT FINANCE, Denise Joyce
VICE PRESIDENT RELATIONSHIP MANAGER, Samantha Arland
VICE PRESIDENT ASSET RECOVERY, Kevin Boyer
Vice President Commercial Lending, Ramzi Dagher
Vice President Commercial Lending, John P Hogan
Senior Vice President Commerical Lending, Joseph Gennett
Executive Vice President Chief Information Officer Of The Corporation And Of The Bank, Eric Deacon
Chairman, William S. Aichele, age 68
Board Member, Mark Schlosser
Treasurer, Bill Shelley
Board Member, Glenn Moyer
Auditors: KPMG LLP

LOCATIONS

HQ: Univest Financial Corp
14 North Main Street, Souderton, PA 18964
Phone: 215 721-2400
Web: www.univest.net

PRODUCTS/OPERATIONS

2015 sales

	$ mil.	% of total
Banking	120.9	79
Wealth Management	18.9	12
Insurance	14.4	9
Other	0.3	-
Total	**154.5**	**100**

COMPETITORS

Citizens Financial Group
Fulton Financial
Harleysville Savings
M&T Bank
PNC Financial
QNB Corp.
Royal Bancshares
Sovereign Bank

HISTORICAL FINANCIALS

Company Type: Public

Income Statement
FYE: December 31

	ASSETS ($ mil.)	NET INCOME ($ mil.)	INCOME AS % OF ASSETS	EMPLOYEES
12/18	4,984.3	50.5	1.0%	841
12/17	4,554.8	44.0	1.0%	855
12/16	4,230.5	19.5	0.5%	840
12/15	2,879.4	27.2	0.9%	717
12/14	2,235.3	22.2	1.0%	638
Annual Growth	22.2%	22.8%	—	7.2%

2018 Year-End Financials

Return on assets: 1.0%
Return on equity: 8.2%
Long-term debt ($ mil.): —
No. of shares (mil.): 29.2
Sales ($ mil): 250.6
Dividends
Yield: 0.0%
Payout: 46.5%
Market value ($ mil.): 631.0

	STOCK PRICE ($) FY Close	P/E High/Low		PER SHARE ($) Earnings	Dividends	Book Value
12/18	21.57	17	12	1.72	0.80	21.32
12/17	28.05	20	16	1.64	0.80	20.57
12/16	30.90	37	22	0.84	0.80	19.00
12/15	20.86	15	13	1.39	0.80	18.51
12/14	20.24	16	13	1.36	0.80	17.54
Annual Growth	1.6%	—	—	6.0%	(0.0%)	5.0%

US Concrete Inc

When things get hard U.S. Concrete's products get even harder. The company produces ready-mixed concrete precast concrete and related materials and services for commercial residential and infrastructure construction projects. U.S. Concrete has a fleet of about 1360 mixer trucks and about 145 ready-mixed concrete concrete block and 10 aggregate plants. During 2015 the company produced some 7 million cu. yd. of concrete and more than 4.9 million tons of aggregates; concrete accounts for about 90% of the company's sales. U.S. Concrete concentrates on major markets such as California New Jersey/New York and Texas. In 2017 the company agreed to purchase Polaris Materials for CAD$309 million.

Operations

U.S. Concrete operates primarily through the two segments of ready-mixed concrete and aggregate products. It has a fleet of over 1360 owned and leased mixer trucks and over 1325 other rolling stock and vehicles. Ready-mixed concrete accounted for about 90% of the revenue in 2015.

Geographic Reach

The company operates principally in Texas California and New Jersey/New York with those markets representing approximately 40% 29% and 26% respectively in 2015. It provides its ready-mixed concrete and concrete-related products from its operations in north and west Texas; northern California; New Jersey; New York; Washington DC; and Oklahoma. In addition U.S. Concrete produces precast concrete products at one plant in Pennsylvania.

Sales and Marketing

The company's customers include contractors for commercial and industrial residential street and highway and other public works construction. Concrete product revenue by type of construction activity for 2015 was commercial and industrial (57%); residential (15%); and street highway and other public works (15%).

Financial Performance

U.S. Concrete saw its revenues jump 39% from $704 million in 2014 to a record-setting $975 million in 2015. Its profits also climbed 24% from $21 million in 2014 to $26 million in 2015 mainly due to an income tax benefit it earned. The historic revenues for 2015 were driven by growth in sales of ready-mixed concrete and additional revenue from acquisitions.

Mergers and Acquisitions

U.S. Concrete has achieved milestone revenues over the years in part by acquiring smaller operators — part of its continuous growth strategy.

In 2017 the company expanded its aggregates business with the acquisition of Leon River Aggregate Material LLC a Texas-based sand and gravel producer along with its state-of-the-art processing plant.

In 2016 U.S. Concrete acquired the assets of NYCON Supply Corp. a ready-mixed concrete producer headquartered in the Long Island City neighborhood of Queens New York. NYCON's premier location widened its footprint to serve the New York City market and expanded its regional customer base. Also in 2016 U.S. Concrete obtained the assets of Greco Brothers Concrete a ready-mixed concrete producer located in Brooklyn New York. The deal is expected to offer new opportunities to service its expanded customer base optimize service efficiencies and enhance raw material purchasing savings.

EXECUTIVES

President CEO and Director, William J. (Bill) Sandbrook, age 61, $816,788 total compensation
VP Marketing and Sales, Wallace H. Johnson, age 71
VP and General Manager West Region, Jeff L. Davis, age 68, $245,400 total compensation
VP and General Manager Ingram Concrete, Jeffrey W. Roberts, age 52, $246,248 total compensation
Principal Accounting Officer, Kevin R. Kohutek, age 46, $260,250 total compensation
EVP South East Division, Niel L. Poulsen, age 65, $282,500 total compensation
SVP General Counsel and Corporate Secretary, Paul M. Jolas, age 54, $300,850 total compensation
SVP and COO, Ronnie Pruitt, age 48
Vice President Human Resources, Mark Peabody
Vice President And General Manager, Matt Emmert
Chairman, Eugene I. (Gene) Davis, age 64
Board Member, Kurt Cellar
Board Member, Robert M Rayner
Board Member, Theodore Rossi
Auditors: Ernst & Young LLP

LOCATIONS

HQ: US Concrete Inc
331 N. Main Street, Euless, TX 76039
Phone: 817 835-4105
Web: www.us-concrete.com

PRODUCTS/OPERATIONS

2015 Sales

	% of total
Ready-mixed concrete	90
Aggregates	6
Other products	4
Total	**100**

2015 Sales by Product

	% of total
Ready-mixed concrete	90
Aggregates	3
Aggregate distribution	3
Lime	2
Hauling	1
Building materials	1
Other	-
Total	**100**

2015 Sales by Market

	% of total
Residential construction	22
Street & highway construction & paving	20
Commercial & industrial construction	18
Other public works & infrastructure construction	40
Total	**100**

Selected Products

Aggregate
  Granite
  Sand
Concrete Masonry
  Cinder blocks
  Concrete blocks
Building Materials
  Color Products
  Fasteners
  Concrete Forms
  Hand Tools
  Liquid Products
  Lumber
  Power Tools
  Safety Gear and Products
  Sand & Rock
  Tools & Accessories
  Fiber
  Waterproofing Material

Ready-Mixed Concrete
  Site Set
  Site Fill
  Site Fresh
  Construct-Lite

COMPETITORS

Ash Grove Cement	Lattimore Materials
Buzzi Unicem USA	Lehigh Hanson
CEMEX	Oldcastle
Eagle Materials	Superior Ready Mix
Holcim (US)	TXI
Lafarge North America	

HISTORICAL FINANCIALS

Company Type: Public

Income Statement   FYE: December 31

	REVENUE ($ mil.)	NET INCOME ($ mil.)	NET PROFIT MARGIN	EMPLOYEES
12/18	1,506.4	30.0	2.0%	3,301
12/17	1,336.0	25.5	1.9%	3,070
12/16	1,168.1	8.8	0.8%	643
12/15	974.7	25.5	2.6%	2,700
12/14	703.7	20.5	2.9%	2,144
Annual Growth	21.0%	9.9%	—	11.4%

2018 Year-End Financials

Debt ratio: 52.0%
Return on equity: 10.1%
Cash ($ mil.): 20.0
Current ratio: 1.28
Long-term debt ($ mil.): 683.3
No. of shares (mil.): 16.6
Dividends
  Yield: —
  Payout: —
Market value ($ mil.): 587.0

	STOCK PRICE ($) FY Close	P/E High/Low	PER SHARE ($) Earnings	Dividends	Book Value
12/18	35.28	46 16	1.82	0.00	18.78
12/17	83.65	53 37	1.53	0.00	16.84
12/16	65.50	116 71	0.55	0.00	12.03
12/15	52.66	33 14	1.64	0.00	11.09
12/14	28.45	19 14	1.48	0.00	7.26
Annual Growth	5.5%	— —	5.3%	—	26.8%

USANA Health Sciences Inc

Health is a matter of science at USANA Health Sciences. The company makes nutritional personal care and weight management products selling them through a direct-sales network marketing system of some 290000 independent distributors or associates. USANA Health Sciences also sells directly to "preferred" customers who buy its products for personal use; it has some 275000 active preferred customers. USANA's associates operate throughout North America as well as the Asia/Pacific region. The company's product portfolio includes nutritional supplements and foods sold under the USANA brand and skin and hair care products marketed under the Celavive and Sensé labels. Chairman and founder Myron Wentz controls nearly half of USANA.

Operations
USANA manufactures all of its tablet products and its beauty products in-house. It also develops capsules drink mixes nutrition bars and personal care items.

Sales to associates or independent distributors represent about 60% of the company's total revenue. Preferred customers — those who buy products for their own personal use — account for the remainder of sales.

Geographic Reach
USANA divides its operations into two regions: North America/Europe and Asia/Pacific. Together those regions cover about 25 markets. The company has a European headquarters in Paris where the company manages growth in newer markets including Germany Italy Spain and Romania markets it entered in 2018. Greater China is the group's largest single market bringing in about half of total sales.

The company makes most of its products at its facilities in Utah.

Sales and Marketing
USANA intends to fight sagging sales by increasing brand awareness — for instance it introduced a new social sharing platform in 2018 — and acquiring more associates and preferred customers. Advertising expenses totaled $11503 in 2017 compared to $12266 in 2016 and $13766 in 2015.

Along with direct selling USANA sells its products in natural health food retail stores via mail order and the internet and in drug stores and supermarkets.

Financial Performance
USANA's revenue has been steadily climbing for the past five years thanks largely to growth in the Asia/Pacific region. Net income has been more turbulent though rising and falling as the company's spending varies.

Revenue increased a modest 4% to $1.05 billion in 2017; that increase was primarily due to growth in the Asia/Pacific region especially through its associate customers. Sales in South Korea rose 27% while sales in China rose 9%. This was partially offset by slight decline in North American sales.

Net income fell 38% to $62.5 million in 2017. A one-time charge of $30 million related to US tax reform hurt the company's bottom line that year.

USANA ended 2017 with $247.1 million in net cash an increase of more than 70% from the prior year. Operating activities provided $123.8 million while investing activities used $12.9 million and financing activities used $50.3 million.

Strategy
USANA is focused on growing its active customer base especially targeting preferred customers who buy its products for their own personal use. It is increasingly personalizing customer experiences to build loyalty and increase sales. However as with all direct selling companies USANA is heavily reliant on attracting and retaining customers. The company does face a high level of customer turnover each year which hampers earnings.

China is among its most important markets for future growth and the company is working to expand into new regions in that country. With China being its largest market though the company is vulnerable to possible regulatory changes in that country which could negatively impact its business there. Other target markets for growth include Australia New Zealand and the Philippines.

Sales in North America and Europe have been lagging so USANA is increasing its marketing efforts in those markets. It is sponsoring athletes and athletic teams to make its brand more familiar to the public. It also has a partnership with television personality Dr. Mehmet Oz of the Dr. Oz show.

The company boasts that it gleans the latest scientific findings to help in its product development activities. For example in early 2018 it launched the Celavive skincare product line based on its new Incelligence platform that delivers key phytonutrients to the body's cells. Once the Celavive roll-out is successful USANA plans to phase out its Sensé product line.

USANA is open to making acquisitions to expand its product portfolio and customer base.

EXECUTIVES

CFO and Chief Leadership Development Officer, Paul A. Jones, age 55, $348,042 total compensation
CEO and Director, Kevin G. Guest, age 56, $608,516 total compensation
President Asia, Deborah Woo, age 65, $592,305 total compensation
Chief Legal Officer and Corporate Secretary, James H. (Jim) Bramble, age 49, $388,032 total compensation
President and COO, Jim Brown, age 50
Chief Scientific Officer, Robert (Rob) Sinnott
EVP Field Development Americas and Chief Communications Officer, Daniel A. (Dan) Macuga, age 49
CIO, Walter Noot
Chairman, Myron W. Wentz, age 78
Auditors: KPMG LLP

LOCATIONS

HQ: USANA Health Sciences Inc
3838 West Parkway Blvd., Salt Lake City, UT 84120
Phone: 801 954-7100
Web: www.usanahealthsciences.com

COMPETITORS

AIM International	Melaleuca
AMS Health Sciences	Nature's Sunshine
Amazon Herb	Nu Skin
Amway	Reliv' International
GNC	Shaklee
Herbalife Ltd.	Sunrider
Mannatech	

HISTORICAL FINANCIALS
Company Type: Public

Income Statement				FYE: December 29
	REVENUE ($ mil.)	NET INCOME ($ mil.)	NET PROFIT MARGIN	EMPLOYEES
12/18	1,189.2	126.2	10.6%	1,911
12/17	1,047.2	62.5	6.0%	1,810
12/16*	1,006.0	100.0	9.9%	1,788
01/16	918.5	94.6	10.3%	1,664
01/15	790.4	76.6	9.7%	1,527
Annual Growth	10.8%	13.3%	—	5.8%

*Fiscal year change

2018 Year-End Financials
Debt ratio: —
Return on equity: 33.5%
Cash ($ mil.): 214.3
Current ratio: 2.64
Long-term debt ($ mil.): —
No. of shares (mil.): 23.5
Dividends
  Yield: —
  Payout: —
Market value ($ mil.): 2,709.0

	STOCK PRICE ($) FY Close	P/E High/Low	PER SHARE ($) Earnings	Dividends	Book Value
12/18	114.96	26 14	5.12	0.00	16.60
12/17	74.05	29 21	2.53	0.00	15.12
12/16*	61.20	36 14	3.99	0.00	13.29
01/16	127.75	47 26	3.59	0.00	11.24
01/15	102.28	41 20	2.80	0.00	9.11
Annual Growth	3.0%		16.3%	—	16.2%

*Fiscal year change

USD Partners LP

Auditors: BDO USA, LLP

LOCATIONS

HQ: USD Partners LP
811 Main Street, Suite 2800, Houston, TX 77002
Phone: 281 291-0510
Web: www.usdpartners.com

HISTORICAL FINANCIALS
Company Type: Public

Income Statement				FYE: December 31
	REVENUE ($ mil.)	NET INCOME ($ mil.)	NET PROFIT MARGIN	EMPLOYEES
12/18	119.2	21.1	17.7%	0
12/17	111.3	22.2	19.9%	0
12/16	111.1	24.1	21.8%	0
12/15	81.7	17.6	21.6%	0
12/14	36.1	(7.6)	—	0
Annual Growth	34.8%	—	—	—

2018 Year-End Financials
Debt ratio: 71.5%
Return on equity: —
Cash ($ mil.): 6.4
Current ratio: 1.82
Long-term debt ($ mil.): 205.5
No. of shares (mil.): 26.6
Dividends
  Yield: 13.5%
  Payout: 183.7%
Market value ($ mil.): 278.0

	STOCK PRICE ($) FY Close	P/E High/Low	PER SHARE ($) Earnings	Dividends	Book Value
12/18	10.45	15 12	0.77	1.42	2.61
12/17	11.25	19 11	0.88	1.35	2.78
12/16	15.80	15 5	1.06	1.25	2.02
12/15	7.24	18 7	0.83	1.11	2.16
12/14	14.17	— —	(0.29)	0.00	1.91
Annual Growth	(7.3%)		—	—	8.2%

Vail Resorts Inc

One of North America's leading ski resort operators Vail Resorts owns or manages 15 mountain resorts primarily in the US. Half of its properties are in Colorado and Utah popular destinations for skiers and winter vacationers. Key resorts include Breckenridge Mountain Resort Crested Butte Mountain and Vail Mountain. Other properties are located in Lake Tahoe on the California/Nevada border Vermont New Hampshire and a handful of other northern states. It also owns or manages lodges condominiums and hotels as well as 15 golf courses in and around the company's resorts. In addition to its US properties Vail operates the Whistler Blackcomb Resort in British Columbia Canada and the Perisher Ski Resort in Australia.

Financial Performance
Vail Resorts' revenue has been on the rise in recent years. Over the past five years revenue has increased an average of 12% annually. Acquisitions made during the period contributed significantly to the results.

The company's 2018 results fell below the 12% annual five-year trend. Vail's revenue increased 5% to top $2 billion in 2018 compared to the previous year. Skier visitation increased overall which drove higher ski lift dining lodging and other lines-of-business revenue. The company's acquisition of Stowe Mountain Resort in Vermont also pushed revenue higher. These results were partially offset by lower snowfall rates at Vail's western resorts which limited skiing activity and ultimately impacted revenue across all lines of business at the resorts.

Higher revenue along with a favorable income tax provision in 2018 pushed net income to $379.8 million a $169.3 million increase (80% jump) from 2017.

Total cash at the end of the period increased $60.7 million to $178.1 million. Cash flow from operations added $551.6 to the coffers while investing activities used $134.5 million and financing activities used $350.7 million.

Strategy
Peak operating season for Vail Resorts is of course ski season which lasts from mid-November through mid-April. The company's largest source of revenue is its Mountain segment which makes most of its money from the sale of lift tickets (including season passes). Lift tickets represent about 50% of the Mountain segment's net revenue.

Like many of its rival ski operators the company markets its ski properties as year-round operations in an effort to offset steep declines in business during the offseason. Vail Resorts promotes the use of its resorts for summer activities such as mountain biking zip lines ropes courses golf tennis and fishing to woo warm-weather visitors.

To maintain resort operations and enhance the ski and ride experience for its guests the company allocates about $150 million each year for capital expenditures. Vail Resorts also leverages acquisitions of ski resorts to expand into new markets and diversify its resorts portfolio both which help the company bolster its top line and mitigate risks caused by unfavorable regional weather conditions.

Mergers and Acquisitions
In 2019 Vail Resorts expanded its portfolio when it agreed to acquire Peak Resorts which

owns 17 ski resorts in the Northeast and Midwest for $264 million.

Vail Resorts completed its acquisition of Whistler Blackcomb Holdings Inc. (Whistler Blackcomb) in late 2016 for about $1.1 billion. Whistler Blackcomb operates the Whistler Blackcomb resort a year round mountain resort.

HISTORY

Vail Mountain resort was first developed by New Hampshire native Pete Seibert and opened in 1962. In 1966 Seibert's Vail Associates went public and later bought Beaver Creek Mountain in 1971. But in 1976 a gondola accident killed four skiers (the worst US skiing accident at the time) and lawsuits forced Vail Associates to sell a controlling interest to Texas oil magnate Harry Bass for $13 million. A row with his children ousted Bass in 1984 and the next year Vail was bought for $130 million by businessman George Gillett.

Gillett Holdings declared bankruptcy in 1991 however and the next year it was acquired by Wall Street deal maker Leon Black's Apollo Advisors. Gillett was allowed to stay on as chairman of Vail but left in 1996. Norwegian Cruise Lines president Adam Aron was named chairman and CEO that year (he departed in 2006). The company's acquisition of the Breckenridge Keystone and Arapahoe Basin resorts from Ralcorp in 1997 made it the nation's top ski resort company. (It later divested Arapahoe Basin at the request of the FTC.) Vail Resorts went public that year and later it acquired the Breckenridge Hilton the area's largest hotel and the 61-room Lodge at Vail.

In 1998 days after the company cleared trees to begin work on an ecologically disputed expansion at Vail Mountain multiple fires caused $12 million in damage and completely destroyed a restaurant ski patrol headquarters and a picnic area. Environmental group Earth Liberation Front claimed responsibility for the fires. Poor weather that winter added to the company's woes and it lost its top ranking to Canada's Intrawest.

The following year Vail bought three resorts in Grand Teton National Park at Jackson Hole Wyoming for $50 million from CSX Corp. As Internet marketing became increasingly important the company also bought Colorado ISP VailNet and Web services firm InterNetWorks. Early in 2000 Vail opened its contested Blue Sky Basin expansion. Later that year the company bought 51% of the Renaissance Resort and Spa (renamed Snake River Lodge and Spa) in Jackson Hole Wyoming.

As part of Vail's efforts to become less dependent on seasonality the firm in 2001 bought Rock-Resorts International which operated 11 resort hotels across the US. Also that year it bought the 349-room Vail Marriott Mountain Resort from Host Marriott for $49.5 million. In 2002 the company acquired Heavenly Ski Resort located on the Nevada/California border for about $102 million.

The company sold its Vail Marriott Mountain Resort in 2005 to DiamondRock Hospitality for $62 million while retaining a management agreement to run the property through 2020. The following year chairman and CEO Aron decided that his ten year anniversary was a good time to call it quits and he did. Robert Katz was appointed CEO in 2006.

In 2008 Vail Resorts acquired CME a shuttle business that offers year-round ground transportation from Denver International Airport and Eagle County Airport to resorts in Vail Aspen and Summit County Colorado.

In 2010 the company added a sixth ski resort to its portfolio: Northstar-at-Tahoe. Vail Resorts acquired a long-term lease on the property — owned by CNL Lifestyle Properties (part of CNL Financial Group) — from Vail-based Booth Creek Ski Holdings for some $63 million. The purchase allowed Vail Resorts to move into the North Shore of Lake Tahoe. (Its other property in the area Heavenly Mountain is on the South Shore.)

Also in 2010 the company acquired Mountain News Corporation which operates the online snow sports portal OnTheSnow.com and resort guide information provider MountainGetaway.com. Vail Resorts made the purchase worth nearly $16 million to reach the nearly 400000 skiers snowboarders and resort travelers who subscribe to Mountain News' websites.

In 2012 the company expanded its resort holdings when it acquired Kirkwood Mountain Resort in Lake Tahoe California for about $18 million. Also that year OnTheSnow.com expanded through the purchase of Skiinfo.com.

In 2016 the company paid about $1.1 billion to acquire Whistler Blackcomb Holdings Inc.

EXECUTIVES

Senior Vice President General Counsel, Fiona Arnold
Chairman and CEO, Robert A. (Rob) Katz, age 52, $869,341 total compensation
EVP and CIO, Robert N. Urwiler
SVP and COO Vail Mountain Division, Christopher E. (Chris) Jarnot
EVP and CFO, Michael Z. Barkin, age 41, $399,900 total compensation
President Mountain Division, Patricia A. (Pat) Campbell, age 56, $390,000 total compensation
EVP and Chief People Officer, Mark R. Gasta
EVP General Counsel and Secretary, David T. Shapiro, age 49, $375,794 total compensation
EVP and Chief Marketing Officer Vail Resorts Management Company, Kirsten A. Lynch, age 51, $399,900 total compensation
SVP and COO Hospitality, James C. O'Donnell
COO Retail, Greg Sullivan
Vice President Information Technology, Tim April
Vice President Assistant Controller, Wayne Wasechek
Vice President Internal Audit, Shawn Tebben
Vice President Company Operations, Rick Sramek
Vice President Of Mountain Operations, James Grant
Vice President of Mountain Finance, Angela Korch
Vice President, David Reed
Vp Hospiitality, John Dawsey
Svp Chief Operating Officer Mountain, Bill Rock
Vice President Of Retail Operations, Glenn Stahlman
National Sales Manager, Cheryl Braucht
Vice President Finance, Flora Ferraro
VICE PRESIDENT HEALTH AND SAFETY, Ken Colonna
Vice President Of Mountain Planning, Tim Beck
Board Member, John Redmond
Board Member, Roland Hernandez
Auditors: PricewaterhouseCoopers LLP

LOCATIONS

HQ: Vail Resorts Inc
  390 Interlocken Crescent, Broomfield, CO 80021
Phone: 303 404-1800 **Fax:** 303 404-6415
Web: www.vailresorts.com

PRODUCTS/OPERATIONS

2018 Charts

	$ mil.	% of total
Mountain		
Lift tickets	880.3	44
Retail/rental	296.5	15
Ski school	189.9	9
Dining	161.4	8
Other	194.9	10
Lodging	284.6	14
Real Estate	4.0	—
Total	**2,011.6**	**100**

Selected Operations

Skiing
  Beaver Creek Resort (Colorado)
  Breckenridge Ski Resort (Colorado)
  Heavenly Mountain Resort (Lake Tahoe NV)
  Keystone Resort (Colorado)
  Vail Mountain (Colorado)
Resorts
  The Arrabelle at Vail Square (Colorado)
  Austria Haus Hotel (Vail CO)
  Breckenridge Mountain Lodge (Colorado)
  The Great Divide Lodge (Breckenridge CO)
  Hotel Jerome (Aspen CO)
  The Keystone Lodge (Colorado)
  The Landings St. Lucia (West Indies)
  The Lodge at Vail (Colorado)
  Mountain Thunder Lodge (Breckenridge CO)
  The Osprey at Beaver Creek (Colorado)
  The Pines Lodge (Beaver Creek CO)
  Ski Tip Lodge (Keystone CO)
  Snake River Lodge & Spa (Teton Village WY)
  Vail Marriott Mountain Resort & Spa (Colorado)
  Village Hotel (Breckenridge CO)
  Whistler Blackcomb (Whisler BC Canada)

COMPETITORS

Aspen Skiing	Mammoth Mountain
Booth Creek Ski	Sinclair Oil
Holdings	Snowdance
Boyne USA	The Resort Company
Club Med	Winter Sports
International Leisure	

HISTORICAL FINANCIALS

Company Type: Public

Income Statement   FYE: July 31

	REVENUE ($ mil.)	NET INCOME ($ mil.)	NET PROFIT MARGIN	EMPLOYEES
07/19	2,271.5	301.1	13.3%	38,500
07/18	2,011.5	379.9	18.9%	33,300
07/17	1,907.2	210.5	11.0%	33,500
07/16	1,601.2	149.7	9.4%	27,000
07/15	1,399.9	114.7	8.2%	21,613
Annual Growth	12.9%	27.3%	—	15.5%

2019 Year-End Financials

Debt ratio: 35.6%	No. of shares (mil.): 40.3
Return on equity: 19.4%	Dividends
Cash ($ mil.): 108.8	Yield: 2.6%
Current ratio: 0.73	Payout: 86.3%
Long-term debt ($ mil.): 1,527.7	Market value ($ mil.): 9,945.0

	STOCK PRICE ($) FY Close	P/E High/Low		PER SHARE ($) Earnings	Dividends	Book Value
07/19	246.52	40	24	7.32	6.46	37.20
07/18	276.87	31	22	9.13	5.05	39.22
07/17	210.76	40	27	5.22	3.73	39.20
07/16	143.07	35	25	4.01	2.87	24.17
07/15	109.69	35	23	3.07	2.08	23.73
Annual Growth	22.4%	—	—	24.3%	32.8%	11.9%

Valley National Bancorp (NJ)

Valley National Bancorp is high on New Jersey and New York. The holding company owns Valley National Bank which serves commercial and retail clients through more than 200 branches in northern and central New Jersey and in the New York City boroughs of Manhattan Brooklyn and Queens as well as on Long Island. The bank provides standard services like checking and savings accounts loans and mortgages credit cards and trust services. Subsidiaries offer asset management mortgage and auto loan servicing title insurance asset-based lending and property/casualty life and health insurance. Founded as The Passaic Park Trust Company in 1927 Valley National is looking to expand in Florida.

Operations
In addition to its commercial and retail banking operations Valley National Bancorp through its subsidiaries operates: an all-line insurance agency that offers property and casualty life and health insurance; a wealth management advisory business; title insurance agencies in New York and New Jersey. It also specializes in general aviation financing commercial equipment leasing and custom financing for health care professionals and law firms.

Financial Performance
Valley National reported revenue of $744.7 million in 2013 a decline of 6% versus 2012 on lower interest income caused by lower yields on average interest earning assets as a result of low long-term market interest rates. Net income fell 8% over the same period to about $132 million on lower revenue and an increase in non-interest expenses.

Strategy
One of the leading commercial banks in the New York and New Jersey metro areas Valley National has set its sights on Florida with its proposed acquisition of Boca Raton-based 1st United Bankcorp the largest commercial bank in Palm Beach County. The deal which is valued at $312 million would add a 21 branch network covering urban banking markets in Florida and approximately $1.7 billion in assets. Combined the two companies will have about $18.1 billion in assets nearly $13 billion in loans and $12.7 billion in deposits. The deal is expected to close in late 2014.

Commercial real estate and construction loans account for the largest portion of Valley's loan portfolio (47%). However the bank has ramped up its residential lending and has been actively marketing its home loan refinancing products amid continued low interest rates.

Mergers and Acquisitions
Valley National completed its approximately $222 million acquisition of New York-based bank holding company State Bancorp at the beginning of 2012. The deal which brought in 17 branches is part of Valley's overall strategy to expand its presence throughout New York City metropolitan area. It marked the company's first foray in Long Island and added locations in Manhattan and Queens as well. It also provides an opportunity to build retail relationships in new markets as State Bancorp focused more on commercial clients. Valley typically targets consumers disillusioned with larger banks.

In 2010 the company acquired the branches and most of the assets and deposits of failed Manhattan-based financial institutions LibertyPointe Bank and Park Avenue Bank in FDIC-assisted transactions. It also opened a loan production office in Bethlehem Pennsylvania to offer residential mortgages and title insurance. Valley continues to look for additional expansion opportunities.

EXECUTIVES

President and Chief Banking Officer Valley National Bank, Rudy E. Schupp, age 68, $425,000 total compensation
SEVP and CFO, Alan D. Eskow, age 71, $545,750 total compensation
Chairman President and CEO, Gerald H. Lipkin, age 79, $1,123,500 total compensation
EVP and Chief Retail Lending Officer, Albert L. Engel, age 71, $440,000 total compensation
SVP Shareholder and Public Relations, Dianne M. Grenz
EVP and Senior Community Reinvestment Act Officer, Bernadette M. Mueller, age 60
SEVP and Treasurer, Ira Robbins, age 44, $425,000 total compensation
EVP and Chief Administrative Officer, Andrea Onorato
EVP and CIO, Robert J. Bardusch
EVP and Chief Risk Officer, Melissa Scofield
Senior Vice President Human Resources Benefits, Terry Gehrke
Assistant Vice President Commercial Loans, John Kenny
Vice President, Peter Alvarez
Assistant Vice President, Tony Dibenedetto
Vice President, Dave Denoya
Vice President, Timothy Tierney
Assistant Vice President Branch Sales Manager, Marie Castro
Vice President, Claudia Orourke
Assistant Vice President Business Development Commercial Loans, Kristen Upadek
Vice President Sales Manager, Veronica Valentine
Vice President Community Lending, Angela Brauer
Vice President Territory Sales Manager, Melvin Madera
Senior Vice President Commercial Lending, John Murphy
Vice President Retail Training, Mary Black
Senior Vice President, Chip Woodbury
Vice President, Mark Stanek
Vice President, Karen Conway
Assistant Vice President, Paul Cronen
Vice President, Barbara Santos
First Vice President and Chief Compliance Officer, Manfred Brockmann
Vice President, Janet Knipfing
Vice President and Senior Counsel, Gary Michael
Vice President, Jennifer Yager
Vice President, Ruth A Finn
Senior Corporate Management Vice President GM, Ralph Passafiume
Vice President, John Cina
Vice President and Branch Sales Manager, Tina Brand
First Senior Vice President, Wayne Fritsch
Senior Vice President, Eileen Sackman
Vice President, Tony Zeleszko
Senior Vice President; Regional Manager, Steven Vitale
Vice President, Geriann Smith
Vice President, Luba Gelman
VICE PRESIDENT SENIOR MARKETING MANAGER, Jeffery Doberman
Vice President of Sales, John Siberio
Vice President Commercial Lender, Janice Brunson
Vice President, Mark Sabow
Assistant Vice President Operations, Frank Reyes
Vice President Commercial Lending, Catherine Keller
Executive Vice President Chief Financial Officer and Chief Operating Officer, Stan Pinkham
Avp Branch Sales Manager, Robert Grasso
Vice President and Credit Officer, Peter Tomasi
Vice President Commercial Lender, Maggie Gonzalez
Vice President Commercial Middle Market Banking, Dan Smith
Vice President Territory Sales Manager, Mary Beltz
Senior Executive Vice President; Chief Lending Officer of Valley National Bank, Thomas Iadanza
Regional Vice President, Drita Kukic
Senior Vice President Director of Association Banking and Treasury Management, Marc Nuzzolo
First Vice President District Sales Manager, Nestor Roldan
Executive Vice President and Chief Credit Officer, Mark Saeger
Vice President, Joe Gargiulo
Senior Vice President Market Executive, Ivete Pinheiro
Vice President Commercial Relationship Manager, Cindy Dunlop
Vice President, Thomas Russo
Vice President, Mikel Sharpe
Vice President Commercial Lending, Art Shelley
Vice President, Oscar Hernandez
Senior Vice President, Valerie Pickert
Assistant Vice President Assistant Banking Office Manager One North Federal Highway Boca Raton, Ann Longworth
Vice President Branch Manager Residential Mortgage, Robert Nardone
Vice President Commercial Lending Valley National Bank Florida Division, Gus Treichel
Vice President Territory Sales Manager, Eddie Beylin
First Vice President, Martha Soper
Vice President Territory Sales Manager, Matthew Coppola
Vice President, Linda Diaz
Vp Aml Bsa Compliance, Rahsan Mumcuoglu
Vice President, Alan Gilman
Vice President, Daniel Maes
Vice President Director Of Sales, Amanda Miller
Vice President New Business Underwriting, Joseph Klapkowski
Vice President, David Beil
Vp and Residential Mortgage Project Manager, Scott Honey
Assistant Vice President Training, Jim Hatcher
Vice President Network Operations, Kenneth Aul
Vp Territory Sales Manager, Ijaz Mughal
Cfsa And Senior Auditor And Assistant Vice President, Colleen Moriarty
Vp and Territory Manager, Lee Stevenson
First Vice President Commercial Loan Team Leader, Dan Sorrell
First Vice President, Ron Fraser
First Senior Vice President, Dorothy Kahlau
First Senior Vice President, Russ Murawski
Board Member, Marc Lenner
Board Member, Peter Baum
Auditors: KPMG LLP

LOCATIONS

HQ: Valley National Bancorp (NJ)
One Penn Plaza, New York, NY 10119
Phone: 973 305-8800
Web: www.valleynationalbank.com

PRODUCTS/OPERATIONS

2016 Sales

	$ mil.	% of total
Interest Income		
Interest and fees on loans	685.9	79
Interest and dividends on investment securities	79.9	9
Interest on federal funds sold and other short-term investments	1.1	0
Non-Interest Income		
Gains on sales of loans net	22.0	3
Service charges on deposit accounts	20.9	2
Insurance commissions	19.1	2
Trust and investment services	10.3	1
Bank owned life insurance	6.7	1
Fees from loan servicing	6.4	1
Gains on sales of assets net	1.4	0
Gains on securities transactions net	0.8	0
Change in FDIC loss-share receivable	(1.3)	0
Other	16.9	2
Total	**870.1**	**100**

COMPETITORS

Bank of America	JPMorgan Chase
Capital One	New York Community Bancorp
Citigroup	
Dime Community Bancshares	PNC Financial
	TD Bank USA
Hudson City Bancorp	Wells Fargo

HISTORICAL FINANCIALS

Company Type: Public

Income Statement — FYE: December 31

	ASSETS ($ mil.)	NET INCOME ($ mil.)	INCOME AS % OF ASSETS	EMPLOYEES
12/18	31,863.0	261.4	0.8%	3,192
12/17	24,002.3	161.9	0.7%	2,842
12/16	22,864.4	168.1	0.7%	2,828
12/15	21,612.6	102.9	0.5%	2,929
12/14	18,793.8	116.1	0.6%	2,907
Annual Growth	14.1%	22.5%	—	2.4%

2018 Year-End Financials

Return on assets: 0.9%
Return on equity: 8.8%
Long-term debt ($ mil.): —
No. of shares (mil.): 331.4
Sales ($ mil): 1,293.3
Dividends
  Yield: 4.9%
  Payout: 58.6%
Market value ($ mil.): 2,943.0

	STOCK PRICE ($) FY Close	P/E High/Low	PER SHARE ($) Earnings	Dividends	Book Value
12/18	8.88	18 11	0.75	0.44	10.11
12/17	11.22	22 18	0.58	0.44	9.58
12/16	11.64	19 13	0.63	0.44	9.02
12/15	9.85	27 22	0.42	0.44	8.70
12/14	9.71	19 16	0.56	0.44	8.03
Annual Growth	(2.2%)	— —	7.6%	(0.0%)	5.9%

Valley Republic Bancorp

Auditors: Vavrinek, Trine, Day & Co., L.L.P.

LOCATIONS

HQ: Valley Republic Bancorp
5000 California Avenue, Suite 110, Bakersfield, CA 93309
Phone: 661 371-2000 **Fax:** 661 371-2010
Web: www.valleyrepublicbank.com

HISTORICAL FINANCIALS

Company Type: Public

Income Statement — FYE: December 31

	REVENUE ($ mil.)	NET INCOME ($ mil.)	NET PROFIT MARGIN	EMPLOYEES
12/18	28.7	8.9	31.1%	0
12/17	23.2	5.2	22.6%	0
12/16	18.7	4.4	23.8%	0
12/15	15.9	3.5	22.1%	0
12/14	13.3	2.7	20.3%	0
Annual Growth	21.1%	34.7%	—	—

2018 Year-End Financials

Debt ratio: —
Return on equity: 14.4%
Cash ($ mil.): 74.8
Current ratio: 0.11
Long-term debt ($ mil.): —
No. of shares (mil.): 3.9
Dividends
  Yield: —
  Payout: —
Market value ($ mil.): 125.0

	STOCK PRICE ($) FY Close	P/E High/Low	PER SHARE ($) Earnings	Dividends	Book Value
12/18	31.50	15 12	2.14	0.00	16.87
12/17	29.00	21 12	1.29	0.00	14.94
12/16	16.80	14 11	1.16	0.00	13.60
12/15	14.80	17 15	0.92	0.00	12.36
12/14	15.55	26 20	0.70	0.00	11.39
Annual Growth	19.3%	— —	32.0%	—	10.3%

Vanda Pharmaceuticals Inc

Vanda Pharmaceuticals is a pharmaceutical company that is developing several drugs for disorders of the central nervous system. The company's first commercial drug was schizophrenia treatment Fanapt (iloperidone). Another drug Hetlioz (tasimelteon) was launched in the US in 2014 for the treatment of non-24-hour sleep-wake disorder; it received European Commission approval in 2015. Other drug candidates are treatments for sleep disorders including insomnia and sleep apnea as well as anxiety and depression. Vanda typically licenses development and commercialization rights for its compounds from (and to) companies including Bristol-Myers Squibb Eli Lilly and Novartis.

Operations

Vanda's product pipeline includes Tradipitant which is in development for the treatment of chronic itching in atopic dermatitis; Trichostatin A for the treatment of cancer; and AQW051 for the treatment of schizophrenia.

Fanapt accounts for 60% of the company's revenue while Hetlioz brings in the remaining 40%.

Geographic Reach

Vanda commercializes its two products in the US and Canada. Its distribution partners launched Fanapt in Israel and Mexico in 2014. Vanda began rolling out Hetlioz in Europe in 2016.

Sales and Marketing

Fanapt and Hetlioz are marketed in the US and Canada. Vanda's top six customers all based in the US accounted for 94% of its revenue in fiscal 2015.

The company spent $3.4 million on branded advertising in 2015 down from $5 million in 2014.

Financial Performance

While Fanapt sales provided steady growth for the firm since its 2009 FDA approval revenue really grew when the company launched Hetlioz in 2014. In fiscal 2015 revenue more than doubled to $110 million. Also contributing to that growth was the firm's acquisition of the commercial rights of Fanapt in the US and Canada from Novartis.

However the company returned to the red in 2015 when it lost a net $40 million due to higher research and development activities. At the end of 2015 Vanda had an accumulated deficit of $327.8 million.

Cash flow from operations has been fluctuating for the past five years. After reporting a cash outflow in 2014 Vanda had a cash inflow of $12 million in 2015 due to cash generated from government and other rebates and accounts payable.

Strategy

Vanda intends to pursue additional partnership agreements to extend its product marketing efforts internationally as well as to commercialize other product candidates once they are approved. The company intends to develop or license additional product candidates as well.

With its two drugs bringing in a modest $100 million in sales in 2015 (in particular Fanapt sales have never been that strong) the company is also seeking options such as a possible sale in the lively M&A market.

Company Background

The company was established in 2003 by Dr. Mihael Polymeropoulos Vanda's CEO and a former researcher for Novartis.

EXECUTIVES

President CEO and Director, Mihael H. Polymeropoulos, age 60, $461,147 total compensation
SVP CFO Treasurer and Secretary, James P. Kelly, $15,163 total compensation
Senior Vice President Chief Commercial Officer, Gian Piero Reverberi
Senior Vice President Business Development, Gunther Birznieks
Chairman, Howard H. Pien, age 60
Board Member, Richard Dugan
Auditors: PricewaterhouseCoopers LLP

LOCATIONS

HQ: Vanda Pharmaceuticals Inc
2200 Pennsylvania Avenue, N.W., Suite 300 E,
Washington, DC 20037
Phone: 202 734-3400
Web: www.vandapharma.com

PRODUCTS/OPERATIONS

2015 Sales

	% of total
Fanapt	60
Hetlioz	40
Total	100

COMPETITORS

ACADIA Pharmaceuticals	Merck
Abbott Labs	Neurocrine Biosciences
AstraZeneca	Novartis
Bristol-Myers Squibb	Otsuka Pharmaceutical
Cephalon	Pfizer
Eli Lilly	Sanofi
GlaxoSmithKline	Solvay
H. Lundbeck	Somaxon
Jazz Pharmaceuticals	Sunovion
Johnson & Johnson	Takeda Pharmaceutical

HISTORICAL FINANCIALS

Company Type: Public

Income Statement
FYE: December 31

	REVENUE ($ mil.)	NET INCOME ($ mil.)	NET PROFIT MARGIN	EMPLOYEES
12/18	193.1	25.2	13.1%	270
12/17	165.0	(15.5)	—	273
12/16	146.0	(18.0)	—	142
12/15	109.9	(39.8)	—	118
12/14	50.1	20.1	40.2%	64
Annual Growth	40.1%	5.7%	—	43.3%

2018 Year-End Financials

Debt ratio: 0.0%
Return on equity: 12.3%
Cash ($ mil.): 61.0
Current ratio: 5.64
Long-term debt ($ mil.): —
No. of shares (mil.): 52.4
Dividends
 Yield: —
 Payout: —
Market value ($ mil.): 1,371.0

	STOCK PRICE ($) FY Close	P/E High/Low		PER SHARE ($) Earnings	Dividends	Book Value
12/18	26.13	63	28	0.48	0.00	5.25
12/17	15.20	—	—	(0.35)	0.00	2.92
12/16	15.95	—	—	(0.41)	0.00	2.98
12/15	9.31	—	—	(0.94)	0.00	3.11
12/14	14.32	32	15	0.55	0.00	3.88
Annual Growth	16.2%	—	—	(3.3%)	—	7.9%

Veeva Systems Inc

Veeva Systems is breathing new life into software for the health care industry. Its cloud-based software and mobile apps are used by pharmaceutical and biotechnology companies to manage critical business functions. Veeva Systems' customer relationship management software uses Salesforce's platform to manage sales and marketing functions. Its Veeva Vault provides content management and collaboration software for quality management in clinical trials and regulatory compliance for new drug submissions. Its software is used in 75 countries and available in more than 25 languages but North America is its largest market. Founded in 2007 Veeva Systems went public in 2013.

Operations

Veeva sells its products through subscriptions and they account for about three-quarters of its business. The rest comes from professional services it provides for installing and training on its software.

Geographic Reach

Veeva Systems operates from three offices in the US and one in Canada. It also has locations in China Japan and Spain. North America is its largest market accounting for 55% of sales. Europe makes up another 26% while customers in Asia account for about 20% of sales. Sales outside North American increased about 64% in 2015 (ended January).

The company runs its software on data centers in California Illinois and Virginia and Germany Japan and the UK.

Sales and Marketing

The company uses a direct sales force with representatives in more than a dozen countries. Veeva Systems counts about 275 customers including global pharmaceutical companies such as Bayer Boehringer Ingelheim Eli Lilly Gilead Sciences Merck and Novartis.

Financial Performance

Veeva Systems has posted big gains in revenue since 2011. Sales zoomed from $30 million in fiscal 2011 (year-end January) to $313 million in 2015. In addition it has been consistently profitable which is uncommon for a relatively new and growing company. Profit increased almost 50% in 2015. While the company has increased spending on research and development and sales and marketing revenue growth covered the higher spending and then some.

Strategy

The company makes 95% of sales from its Veeva CRM customer relationship management software but new products are also being developed. Its latest software offering is Veeva Network a customer master solution that creates and maintains healthcare provider and organization master data. Veeva Network also contains a proprietary database of people and companies in China and the US using data gathered from state federal and industry sources.

While Veeva Systems currently focuses on the life sciences industry specifically pharmaceutical and biotechnology companies it would like to expand to other specialized companies such as contract research organizations (CROs) and contract manufacturing organizations (CMOs).

Mergers and Acquisitions

In 2015 Veeva acquired Qforma CrowdLink a developer of key opinion leader (KOL) data and services for life sciences' brand medical and market access teams. Veeva introduced a product based on Qforma technology to help its customers get more sophisticated information for introducing products.

EXECUTIVES

Vice President Of Product Marketing, Paul Shawah
Vice President Professional Services Europe, Will Larter
VICE PRESIDENT, Rebecca Silver
VICE PRESIDENT SOLUTION CONSULTING AND SALES ENGINEERING, Michael Longo
Vice President, Jennifer Goldsmith
VICE PRESIDENT CUSTOMER SUCCESS MANAGEMENT, Nate Gazaway
Vice President, John Lawrie
Vice President Commercial Strategy, Jan Van Den Burg
Vice President Of Finance And Corporate Controller, Michele Oconnor
Vice President Engineering, Dan Soble
Vice President Global Sales Operations, Mike King
Vp, Alan Mateo
Vice President Commercial Strategy, Jamie Morris
Vice President Corporate Communications, Roger Villareal
Vice President Product Marketing, Ligia Zamora
Senior Vice President Global Customer Services, Frederic Lequient
Vice President Marketing Europe, Kelly Brown
Vice President Global Customer Support, Hind Roubos
Vice President Global Medical Strategy, Robert Groebel
Vice President Vault Quality, Jovanis Mike
Vice President Rd Sales, Mike Davies
Vice President Sales And Marketing, Erta Muca
Vice President Products And Technology Veeva Network, Wong Stan
Auditors: KPMG LLP

LOCATIONS

HQ: Veeva Systems Inc
4280 Hacienda Drive, Pleasanton, CA 94588
Phone: 925 452-6500   Fax: 925 452-6504
Web: www.veeva.com

PRODUCTS/OPERATIONS

2015 Sales

	% of total
Subscription fees	74
Professional services	26
Total	100

Selected Products

Veeva CRM (customer relationship management)
 Veeva CLM (closed-loop marketing)
 Veeva iRep (mobile app for Apple products)
 Veeva CRM Approved Email (tracks regulatory compliant emails between sales reps and physicians)
Veeva Vault (content management and collaboration software)
 Veeva Vault eTMF (document management for clinical trials)
 Veeva Vault Investigator Portal (secure file exchange for clinical trials)
 Veeva Vault MedComms (medical content management)
 Veeva Vault PromoMats (promotional materials management)
 Veeva Vault QualityDocs (quality management)
 Veeva Vault Submissions (document management for regulatory submissions)
Veeva Network (master software and data stewardship)
 Veeva Network Provider Database (proprietary database of people and companies in China and the US)
 Veeva Network Customer Master (cleanse and match people and company data)
 Veeva Network Data Stewardship Services (data management)

COMPETITORS

Advanced Health Media	Microsoft
Allscripts	Open Text

Computer Sciences Corp.
EMC
IMS Health
Oracle
SDI Health
StayinFront

HISTORICAL FINANCIALS
Company Type: Public

Income Statement   FYE: January 31

	REVENUE ($ mil.)	NET INCOME ($ mil.)	NET PROFIT MARGIN	EMPLOYEES
01/19	862.2	229.8	26.7%	2,553
01/18	685.5	141.9	20.7%	2,171
01/17	544.0	68.8	12.6%	1,794
01/16	409.2	54.4	13.3%	1,474
01/15	313.2	40.3	12.9%	951
Annual Growth	28.8%	54.5%	—	28.0%

2019 Year-End Financials

Debt ratio: —
Return on equity: 21.7%
Cash ($ mil.): 550.9
Current ratio: 3.57
Long-term debt ($ mil.): —
No. of shares (mil.): 146.1
Dividends
  Yield: —
  Payout: —
Market value ($ mil.): 15,943.0

	STOCK PRICE ($) FY Close	P/E High/Low		PER SHARE ($) Earnings	Dividends	Book Value
01/19	109.06	69	34	1.47	0.00	8.47
01/18	62.86	66	42	0.92	0.00	6.13
01/17	42.33	93	40	0.47	0.00	4.74
01/16	24.10	80	56	0.38	0.00	3.78
01/15	28.76	122	58	0.28	0.00	3.10
Annual Growth	39.5%	—	—	51.4%	—	28.5%

Verisk Analytics Inc

Insurance is a risky business and Verisk Analytics is in the business of helping to manage that risk. The company compiles and analyzes data to detect fraud economic headwinds and catastrophe weather risk. It uses what it finds to predict losses for clients in the insurance energy and specialized markets and financial services industries. Verisk's customers include the top property/casualty insurers in the US; leading credit card issuers in North America the UK and Australia; and the world's largest energy companies. Verisk was created by subsidiary Insurance Services Office (ISO) in 2008 as a means of going public.

Operations
Verisk is experiencing steady revenue growth in both of its main business segments — Decision Analytics and Risk Assessment — as businesses pay ever-increasing attention to risk management and loss control.

The Decision Analytics segment (which accounts for more than 60% of revenues) has three divisions: Insurance Energy and Specialized Markets and Financial Services. The Insurance business which brings in nearly 40% of total revenue offers analytics in fraud detection catastrophe modeling underwriting and loss estimation. Energy and Specialized Markets provides analytics for customers in the global energy chemicals and mining and metals industries; it represents another 20% of Verisk's sales. Financial Services provides financial institutions regulators payment processors lenders and merchants with competitive benchmarking business intelligence and customized analytics.

The Risk Assessment segment which includes flagship subsidiary ISO and several other units provide data software and information services. Its customers include property/casualty insurers and reinsurers in the US and abroad. The segment accounts for nearly 40% of Verisk's revenues.

Verisk has approximately 10 petabytes (10 million gigabytes) of risk information including 19 billion commercial and personal records detailed information on 3.7 million commercial buildings an insurance fraud database with more than 1 billion claims natural hazard models covering more than 100 countries 4.75 million material safety data sheets on hazardous chemicals and depersonalized data on 1.6 billion debit and credit card accounts.

The company's brands include ISO Xactware Argus AIR Worldwide and Wood Mackenzie.

Geographic Reach
Verisk has offices in more than 20 US states as well as international locations in more than 25 countries across the Americas Asia Europe and the Middle East.

Sales and Marketing
A majority of Verisk's revenue is generated through annual subscriptions and long-term agreements within the US property/casualty insurance industry. Major customers in this category include AIG Allstate Hartford and Liberty Mutual. The company sells its products and services through a direct sales force and technical consultants. Verisk also serves select clients in the supply chain human resources and risk management industries.

Advertising costs from branding and promotional activities totaled $6.9 million in fiscal 2017 versus $6.5 million in 2016 and $5.9 million in 2015.

Financial Performance
Verisk has seen strong revenue and net income growth over the past five years. In 2017 revenue rose 8% to $2.1 billion as both primary segments saw had higher sales. Decision Analytics rose 8% (thanks primarily to growth in the insurance market) while Risk Assessment rose 6%. This growth was largely driven by added income from the company's recently acquired subsidiaries including Wood Mackenzie Greentech Media and MarketStance.

Despite the higher revenue net income fell 23% to $555.1 million in 2017. Operating expenses related to the company's spate of acquisitions rose that year largely due to increases in salaries and benefits for added personnel. An absence of income from discontinued operations also cut into the bottom line.

Cash flow from operations increased 29% to $743.5 million in 2017 partially due to positive changes in accounts payable and deferred revenues.

Strategy
Verisk's strategy for further growth includes increasing sales to insurance energy and financial services customers; developing proprietary data sets and predictive analytics; continuing to acquire complementary businesses; and leveraging its intellectual property into new markets. Towards those ends the company has acquired a number of companies recently including Wood Mackenzie Arium and Greentech Media. It has increasingly focused on key insurance coverages as drones and Ebola-style viruses in addition to weather and climate risks.

On the organic growth side Verisk conducts internal programs to create new and enhanced products. In fact the company strives to be the first to bring new types of products to the market. Its product development process incorporates market research internal software development and alliances with other information providers and technology companies.

In addition to launching new offerings the company also works to deepen its engagement with customers embedding its products into customer workflows. This helps clients better manage their risk as well as cementing its relationships with clients.

As a data-driven company Verisk has to manage its own risk levels. It relies on third parties for its data and if a vendor decides to deny access to its resources its customer offerings could be negatively impacted. Furthermore Verisk has to stay steadfast in securing its data as cyber attacks can cause customers to run the other way.

Switching its focus to the energy market Verisk sold its Verisk Health division in 2016 for $714.6 million.

Mergers and Acquisitions
Verisk has been making a number of acquisitions to enter new markets (such as global energy) expand its international operations and broaden its offerings. With the help of several years' worth of rising revenues the company has acquired more than 20 businesses since 2013. Building its renewable energy and electricity data offerings the company purchased Greentech Media in 2016. Also that year the company acquired UK-based geographic data specialist GeoInformation Group and insurance data and analytics firm MarketStance.

The firm had a very active year in 2017. Early that year it acquired Arium (Architects for Risk Identification Understanding and Management) which specializes in liability risk modeling and decision support. That purchase boosted the firm's casualty analytics offerings. Later the company bought G2 Web Services a specialist in merchant risk intelligence for payment system providers for $112 million. It also acquired London-based insurance software specialist Sequel for $323 million and California-based bankruptcy risk prediction firm LCI for $151 million.

Verisk's other deals in 2017 included the acquisitions of UK-based Emergent Network Intelligence and Healix Risk Rating India-based Fintellix and Denmark-based MAKE.

Company Background
Verisk traces its roots back to 1971 when ISO was created by an association of insurance companies. Verisk went public in 2009 in one of the largest offerings of the year raising almost $2 billion.

EXECUTIVES

Chairman President and CEO, Scott G. Stephenson, age 62, $1,000,000 total compensation
EVP General Counsel and Corporate Secretary, Kenneth E. Thompson, age 59, $451,800 total compensation
EVP and COO, Mark V. Anquillare, age 53, $530,200 total compensation

VP and Chief Marketing Officer, Christopher H. Perini
President Underwriting Solutions, Neil Spector
President Verisk Health, Nadine Hays
SVP Corporate Development and Strategy, Vincent de P. McCarthy, age 55, $430,400 total compensation
President ISO Claims Analytics, Richard Della Rocca
President ISO Solutions, Beth Fitzgerald
Chief Analytics Officer; President Argus Information and Advisory Services, Nana Banerjee, age 50, $515,000 total compensation
Group President Wood Mackenzie 3E Co. and Verisk Maplecroft, Steve Halliday
SVP and CIO, Nicholas Daffan
President Xactware Solutions, Mike Fulton
President AIR Worldwide, Bill Churney
Chief Internal Auditor, Joanna Gassoso
EVP and CFO, Lee M. Shavel
Vice President Verisk Underwriting, John Cantwell
Vice President, Anthony Canale
Assistant Vice President Sales: Verisk Insurance, Spencer Prahl
Vice President Learn Information Technology Solutions, Rich Dibenedetto
Senior Vice President Compliance, Mark Magath
Vice President, Eric Schneider
Vp Commercial Underwriting Products, Rick Stoll
Vice President Corporate Development, Yang Chen
Assistant Vice President, Joe Louwagie
Sales Vice President, Jeffrey Meissner
Regional Vice President, Michael Simonian
Vice President Enterprise Technology Operations, Chuck Moon
Vice President Engineering, Jim Despelteau
Vice President, Scott Cooper
Vice President, Steve Lekas
Assistant Vice President Property Claim Services, Gary Kerney
Assistant Vice President Iot Telematics, Joe Wodark
Vice President of Strategic Data Operations, Tracy Spadola
Vice President and Senior Analyst, Erik Hanley
Vice President Marketing and Customer Service, Brenda Kelly
Vice President, Patrick Pollard
SVP Marketing, Matt Weir
Vp Engineering, Jeff Lewis
Vice President of Analytics, Shane De Zilwa
Assistant Vice President Development Commercial Property Division, Timothy Coyle
Vice President Global Talent Acquisition, Danelle DiLibero
Assistant Vice President Support Services Xactware Solutions Inc., Brian Gibb
Vice President of Business Development and Logistics Services, Sal Marino
Vice President Corporate Development And Strategy, John Mcilwaine
VICE PRESIDENT, Pieprzyca Mark
Assistant Vice President Human Resources, Karlyn Norton
Vice President Coverage Products And Operations, Jeff De Turris
Vice President Analytics Solutions, Vikas Vats
Assistant Vice President Customer Strategy and Solutions, Scott West
Senior Vice President Claims Analytics, Karthik Balakrishnan
Vice President Of Tax, Jeff Louis
Board Director, Bruce Hansen
Auditors: DELOITTE & TOUCHE LLP

LOCATIONS
HQ: Verisk Analytics Inc
545 Washington Boulevard, Jersey City, NJ 07310-1686
Phone: 201 469-3000
Web: www.verisk.com

PRODUCTS/OPERATIONS

2017 Sales by Segment

	$ mil.	% of total
Decision Analytics		
Insurance	784.7	36
Energy & specialized markets	444.7	21
Financial services	145.5	7
Risk Assessment		
Industry-standard insurance programs	593.6	28
Property-specific rating & underwriting	176.7	8
Total	**2,145.2**	**100**

Selected Markets:
P/C Insurance
Energy Metals and Mining
Financial Services
Supply Chain
HR Departments
Retail
Commercial Real Estate
Community Hazard Mitigation

COMPETITORS

CoreLogic
DMG Information
Deloitte Consulting
Fair Isaac
IHS Markit
LexisNexis
Solera Holdings
Willis Towers Watson

HISTORICAL FINANCIALS
Company Type: Public

Income Statement — FYE: December 31

	REVENUE ($ mil.)	NET INCOME ($ mil.)	NET PROFIT MARGIN	EMPLOYEES
12/18	2,395.1	598.7	25.0%	8,184
12/17	2,145.2	555.1	25.9%	7,304
12/16	1,995.2	591.2	29.6%	6,314
12/15	2,068.0	507.5	24.5%	7,918
12/14	1,746.7	400.0	22.9%	6,550
Annual Growth	8.2%	10.6%	—	5.7%

2018 Year-End Financials

Debt ratio: 46.1%
Return on equity: 29.9%
Cash ($ mil.): 139.5
Current ratio: 0.49
Long-term debt ($ mil.): 2,050.5
No. of shares (mil.): 163.9
Dividends
  Yield: —
  Payout: —
Market value ($ mil.): 17,879.0

	STOCK PRICE ($) FY Close	P/E High/Low		PER SHARE ($) Earnings	Dividends	Book Value
12/18	109.04	34	25	3.56	0.00	12.63
12/17	96.00	29	23	3.29	0.00	11.68
12/16	81.17	24	19	3.45	0.00	7.98
12/15	76.88	27	20	3.01	0.00	8.10
12/14	64.05	27	23	2.37	0.00	1.34
Annual Growth	14.2%	—	—	10.7%	—	75.3%

Veritex Holdings Inc

Auditors: Grant Thornton LLP

LOCATIONS
HQ: Veritex Holdings Inc
8214 Westchester Drive, Suite 800, Dallas, TX 75225
Phone: 972 349-6200
Web: www.veritexbank.com

HISTORICAL FINANCIALS
Company Type: Public

Income Statement — FYE: December 31

	ASSETS ($ mil.)	NET INCOME ($ mil.)	INCOME AS % OF ASSETS	EMPLOYEES
12/18	3,208.5	39.3	1.2%	330
12/17	2,945.5	15.1	0.5%	324
12/16	1,408.5	12.5	0.9%	171
12/15	1,039.6	8.7	0.8%	149
12/14	802.2	5.2	0.6%	125
Annual Growth	41.4%	65.8%	—	27.5%

2018 Year-End Financials

Return on assets: 1.2%
Return on equity: 7.7%
Long-term debt ($ mil.): —
No. of shares (mil.): 24.2
Sales ($ mil): 156.1
Dividends
  Yield: —
  Payout: —
Market value ($ mil.): 519.0

	STOCK PRICE ($) FY Close	P/E High/Low		PER SHARE ($) Earnings	Dividends	Book Value
12/18	21.38	20	13	1.60	0.00	21.88
12/17	27.59	36	30	0.80	0.00	20.28
12/16	26.71	23	11	1.13	0.00	15.73
12/15	16.21	20	15	0.84	0.00	12.33
12/14	14.17	23	18	0.72	0.00	11.96
Annual Growth	10.8%	—	—	22.1%	—	16.3%

VICI Properties Inc

Auditors: DELOITTE & TOUCHE LLP

LOCATIONS
HQ: VICI Properties Inc
430 Park Avenue, 8th Floor, New York, NY 10022
Phone: 646 949-4631
Web: www.viciproperties.com

HISTORICAL FINANCIALS
Company Type: Public

Income Statement — FYE: December 31

	REVENUE ($ mil.)	NET INCOME ($ mil.)	NET PROFIT MARGIN	EMPLOYEES
12/18	897.9	523.6	58.3%	140
12/17	187.6	42.6	22.7%	140
12/16	18.7	0.0	—	140
12/15	18.0	0.0	0.0%	0
12/14	18.9	0.0	0.0%	0
Annual Growth	162.5%	1802.1%	—	—

Victory Capital Holdings Inc (DE)

Auditors: Ernst & Young LLP

LOCATIONS

HQ: Victory Capital Holdings Inc (DE)
 4900 Tiedeman Road 4th Floor, Brooklyn, OH 44144
Phone: 216 898-2400
Web: www.vcm.com

HISTORICAL FINANCIALS
Company Type: Public

Income Statement — FYE: December 31

	REVENUE ($ mil.)	NET INCOME ($ mil.)	NET PROFIT MARGIN	EMPLOYEES
12/18	413.4	63.7	15.4%	263
12/17	409.6	25.8	6.3%	267
12/16	297.8	(6.0)	—	276
12/15	240.7	3.8	1.6%	0
Annual Growth	19.7%	155.9%	—	—

2018 Year-End Financials
Debt ratio: 33.5%
Return on equity: 18.5%
Cash ($ mil.): 51.4
Current ratio: 1.74
Long-term debt ($ mil.): 268.8
No. of shares (mil.): 67.5
Dividends
 Yield: —
 Payout: 1.3%
Market value ($ mil.): 690.0

	STOCK PRICE ($) FY Close	P/E High/Low	PER SHARE ($) Earnings	Dividends	Book Value
12/18	10.22	14 8	0.90	0.00	6.74
12/17	0.00	— —	0.43	2.42	4.19
Annual Growth	—	—	109.3%	—	60.8%

Viper Energy Partners LP

Auditors: Grant Thornton LLP

LOCATIONS

HQ: Viper Energy Partners LP
 500 West Texas, Suite 1200, Midland, TX 79701
Phone: 432 221-7400
Web: www.viperenergy.com

2018 Year-End Financials
Debt ratio: 36.3%
Return on equity: 9.1%
Cash ($ mil.): 598.4
Current ratio: 5.91
Long-term debt ($ mil.): 4,122.2
No. of shares (mil.): 404.7
Dividends
 Yield: 5.3%
 Payout: 69.7%
Market value ($ mil.): 7,601.0

	STOCK PRICE ($) FY Close	P/E High/Low	PER SHARE ($) Earnings	Dividends	Book Value
12/18	18.78	16 12	1.43	1.00	16.84
12/17	20.50	111 95	0.19	0.00	15.62
Annual Growth	(8.4%)	—	652.6%	—	7.8%

Virginia National Bankshares Corp

EXECUTIVES

Chb, Hunter Craig
Director Of Retail Banking and Executive Vice President, Jennifer Matheny
Executive Vice President Retail Banking Director, Alan Williams
Auditors: Yount, Hyde & Barbour, P.C.

LOCATIONS

HQ: Virginia National Bankshares Corp
 404 People Place, Charlottesville, VA 22911
Phone: 434 817-8621
Web: www.vnb.com

HISTORICAL FINANCIALS
Company Type: Public

Income Statement — FYE: December 31

	ASSETS ($ mil.)	NET INCOME ($ mil.)	INCOME AS % OF ASSETS	EMPLOYEES
12/18	644.8	8.4	1.3%	86
12/17	643.8	6.5	1.0%	81
12/16	605.0	5.7	1.0%	85
12/15	567.4	3.1	0.6%	94
12/14	537.0	1.9	0.4%	101
Annual Growth	4.7%	45.3%	—	(3.9%)

HISTORICAL FINANCIALS
Company Type: Public

Income Statement — FYE: December 31

	REVENUE ($ mil.)	NET INCOME ($ mil.)	NET PROFIT MARGIN	EMPLOYEES
12/18	288.8	143.9	49.8%	0
12/17	172.0	111.4	64.8%	0
12/16	79.1	(10.9)	—	0
12/15	74.8	24.4	32.6%	0
12/14	77.7	29.6	38.1%	0
Annual Growth	38.8%	48.5%	—	—

2018 Year-End Financials
Debt ratio: 24.8%
Return on equity: —
Cash ($ mil.): 22.6
Current ratio: 10.83
Long-term debt ($ mil.): 411.0
No. of shares (mil.): 124.0
Dividends
 Yield: 8.1%
 Payout: 98.1%
Market value ($ mil.): 3,231.0

	STOCK PRICE ($) FY Close	P/E High/Low	PER SHARE ($) Earnings	Dividends	Book Value
12/18	26.04	22 11	2.01	2.12	4.37
12/17	23.33	22 14	1.07	1.23	8.03
12/16	16.00	— —	(0.13)	0.77	6.24
12/15	13.96	69 44	0.31	0.86	6.21
12/14	18.13	118 50	0.29	0.25	6.72
Annual Growth (10.2%)	9.5%	—	62.3%	70.6%	

2018 Year-End Financials
Return on assets: 1.3%
Return on equity: 12.4%
Long-term debt ($ mil.): —
No. of shares (mil.): 2.6
Sales ($ mil): 31.2
Dividends
 Yield: 3.3%
 Payout: 34.5%
Market value ($ mil.): 92.0

	STOCK PRICE ($) FY Close	P/E High/Low	PER SHARE ($) Earnings	Dividends	Book Value
12/18	34.51	17 11	3.15	1.09	26.49
12/17	39.00	16 11	2.46	0.61	24.50
12/16	28.50	13 10	2.19	0.47	22.61
12/15	24.05	23 19	1.12	0.36	21.17
12/14	22.70	37 28	0.64	0.26	20.46
Annual Growth	11.0%	—	49.3%	42.8%	6.7%

Virtusa Corp

Virtusa believes that virtually any business can improve its technology. The company provides a variety of offshore-based software development and information technology services including digitization cloud computing software engineering application development application outsourcing maintenance systems integration and legacy asset management. Virtusa's customers come from industries such as banking financial services insurance telecommunications entertainment media and healthcare. Customers in North America generate about 70% of Virtusa's revenue.

Financial Performance

Virtusa's revenue rose steadily from 2015-2019 increasing an average of better than 30% a year. The company has made money for the past five years but the amount of profit has been lower in the past three years.

In 2019 (ended March) revenue advanced 20% to more than $1 billion up about $227 from 2018 driven by the eTouch acquisition and growth in the banking insurance and healthcare industry groups. North American revenue was about 33% higher and Europeans sales rose 8%.

Virtusa turned a profit of $16.1 million in 2019 compared to $1.3 million profit in 2018 on higher revenue and lower taxes.

The company's treasury held $195 million in cash at the end of 2019 a $50 million increase from 2018. Operations generated $68.6 million in 2019 while investing activities used $74.7 million and financing activities provided $14.7 million.

Strategy

Virtusa is putting its strategic attention and investment toward its business of helping clients digitize their businesses. The company has focused its recent investments on deepening its industry knowledge and expanding its digital engineering capabilities. The digitization focus can bring other benefits. Virtusa's work in helping a major bank improve the functionality of its online and mobile operations led to other business with the client that turned into a multi-year relationship.

The acquisition eTouch in 2018 expanded Virtusa's engineering and service offerings digital marketing cloud analytics and data security. The acquisition also beefed up Virtusa's customer list bringing along a Silicon Valley-based multinational internet company which became one of Virtusa's top-10 clients.

The company has strong reliance on a limited number of customers. It biggest Citi accounts for nearly 20% of revenue while the 10 biggest customers account for 50% of revenue. The loss of revenue from any one of its major clients could weaken Virtusa's financial condition.

EXECUTIVES

Chairman and CEO, Kris A. Canekeratne, age 53, $462,500 total compensation
EVP and Chief Strategy Officer, Thomas R. (Tom) Holler, age 56, $332,500 total compensation
EVP and COO, Roger K. (Keith) Modder, age 55, $256,858 total compensation
EVP Client Services and Business Development, John Gillis
President Enterprise Technology and Solutions, Raj Rajgopal, age 59, $372,500 total compensation
EVP Insurance Healthcare Media & Entertainment and Diversified Business Units North America, Jim Francis
EVP and CFO, Ranjan Kalia, age 59, $352,500 total compensation
VP General Counsel and Assistant Secretary, Paul D. Tutun
President, Samir Dhir, age 49
EVP Global Digital Solutions, Frank Palermo
EVP and Global Head of Telecoms and Managing Director Middle East and Asia, Srinivasan Jayaraman
SVP and Global Head of Transformational Outsourcing Solutions, Sreekanth Lapala
SVP and Global Head of SAP Practice, Zlatan Lipovaca
EVP and Global Head of Engineering, Chandika Mendis
SVP and Global Head of Human Resources, Sundararajan (Sundar) Narayanan
EVP CIO and Head of Business Process Excellence, Madu Ratnayake
EVP and Global Head of Business Consulting and Business Process Transformation, Tim Wright
Executive Vice President Head Global New Business Development, Vasan Srinivasan
Vice President of Sales, Dan Kielar
Vice President, Sumita Ohri
Senior Vice President Head Of Isv And Technology Business Unit, Harsha Liyanage
Vice President Business Consulting, David Cirnigliaro
Senior Vice President Delivery, Pragash Krishnamoorthy
Vp User Experience Practice, David Katz
Vice President, Sunny Bathla
Vice President Of Sales, Joseph Walsh
Vice President Delivery, Kartik Iyengar
Vice President, Kishore Dubagunta
Vice President Business Development, Rob Oyler
Vice President Engineering, Ravi Govil
Vice President Shared Services, Robert Sutton
Auditors: KPMG LLP

LOCATIONS

HQ: Virtusa Corp
132 Turnpike Rd, Southborough, MA 01772
Phone: 508 389-7300
Web: www.virtusa.com

PRODUCTS/OPERATIONS

2019 Sales

	% of total
Banking Financial Services Insurance	62
Communications and Technology	29
Media Information and Other	9
Total	**100**

COMPETITORS

Accenture	IBM Global Services
Capgemini	Infosys
Cognizant Tech Solutions	Sapient
	Sirius Computer Solutions
Computer Sciences Corp.	Tata Consultancy
Deloitte Consulting	Tech Mahindra
HCL Technologies	Wipro
HP Enterprise Services	

HISTORICAL FINANCIALS

Company Type: Public

Income Statement   FYE: March 31

	REVENUE ($ mil.)	NET INCOME ($ mil.)	NET PROFIT MARGIN	EMPLOYEES
03/19	1,247.8	16.1	1.3%	21,745
03/18	1,020.6	1.2	0.1%	20,491
03/17	858.7	11.8	1.4%	17,750
03/16	600.3	44.8	7.5%	18,226
03/15	478.9	42.4	8.9%	9,247
Annual Growth	27.0%	(21.5%)	—	23.8%

2019 Year-End Financials

Debt ratio: 32.0%   No. of shares (mil.): 30.1
Return on equity: 3.1%   Dividends
Cash ($ mil.): 189.6   Yield: —
Current ratio: 2.71   Payout: —
Long-term debt ($ mil.): 351.3   Market value ($ mil.): 1,611.0

	STOCK PRICE ($) FY Close	P/E High/Low		PER SHARE ($) Earnings	Dividends	Book Value
03/19	53.45	146	95	0.38	0.00	16.52
03/18	48.46	—	—	(0.09)	0.00	17.76
03/17	30.22	95	46	0.39	0.00	16.62
03/16	37.46	38	21	1.49	0.00	16.14
03/15	41.38	29	21	1.44	0.00	14.61
Annual Growth	6.6%	—	—	(28.3%)	—	3.1%

VSE Corp.

VSE brings military hand-me-downs back into fashion. The company provides engineering testing and logistics services for the US Army the US Navy and other government agencies on a contract basis. VSE operates through various subsidiaries and divisions that comprise its core federal group segment (engineering logistics communications and management services) and its international group (fleet maintenance and foreign military sales). Other segments include IT energy and management consulting (technical and consulting services for civilian government) and infrastructure (engineering and construction services). VSE generates about half of its revenues from the Department of Defense (DOD).

Operations
The company's Supply Chain Management Group provides sourcing acquisition scheduling transportation shipping logistics data management and other services to assist our clients with supply chain management efforts. This group consists of its Wheeler Bros. Inc. (WBI) subsidiary.

The company's federal group segment operates through divisions that are dedicated to serving major military customers. Its communications & engineering engineering & logistics field support services and systems engineering divisions manage various aspects of its logistics and engineering contracts with the US Army Army Reserves and Marine Corps. VSE Services International on the other hand provides engineering industrial logistics and foreign military sales services primarily to the US military through its GLOBAL and fleet maintenance divisions. The GLOBAL division reactivates old Navy ships for transfer to other countries.

Conversely VSE divides its work in its non-federal group and international segments between a handful of subsidiaries that serve mostly civilian government agencies. Its Energetics subsidiary part of the IT energy and management consulting segment serves agencies concerned with energy and environmental issues. Another IT consulting subsidiary Virginia-based G&B provides information technology services to various civilian-based government agencies. Subsidiary Akimeka LLC also offers services in these fields. The infrastructure group's ICRC unit offers diversified technical and management services to the US Department of Transportation and similar government agencies.

In 2013 Supply Chain accounted for 33% of VSE's revenues; International 31%; Federal 20%; and IT Energy and Management Consulting 16%.

Geographic Reach
VSE has operations in Arkansas California Colorado Florida Georgia Guam Hawaii Maryland Michigan Mississippi New Jersey North Carolina Oklahoma Oregon Pennsylvania South Carolina Texas Utah Virginia Wisconsin and Washington DC.

Sales and Marketing
The company's services are performed for the US government various federal civilian agencies and other clients. Its largest customers are the DOD and the USPS.

Supply Chain Management Group supplies vehicle parts for the USPS truck fleet and direct sales to other clients. International Group provides its services to the US Navy Department of Treasury Air Force Department of Justice and Bureau of Alcohol Tobacco Firearms and Explosives (ATF).

The Managed Inventory Program (supplying truck replacement parts for the USPS fleet) the Foreign Military Sales Program for the US Navy and its vehicle and equipment refurbishment work for the US Army Reserve are VSE's three largest revenue generators accounting for 30% 20% and 13% respectively of its 2013 revenues.

Financial Performance
The company has seen a continuous decline in revenues since 2009. Revenues dipped by 14% in 2013 due to a 33% decline in revenues from the Federal Group segment primarily due to the expiration of a contract to provide mechanical maintenance services for Mine Resistance Ambush Protected vehicles and systems in Kuwait and to a reduction in revenues from its vehicle and equipment refurbishment work for the US Army Reserve

due to the interruption of contract coverage. International Group segment sales declined by 12% as the result a decline of $18 million in pass-through work provided on engineering and technical services task orders and to due to a lesser decline in revenues from CFT Program services. Also IT Energy and Management Consulting Group decreased by 21% due to a decrease in services performed due to contract expirations and a decline in services ordered by clients on continuing contracts. The drop was partially offset by increase in revenues from the Supply Chain Management thanks to a stronger year for Wheeler Brothers' Managed Inventory Program with USPS.

Net income increased by 7% in 2013 as the result of the absence of impairment of intangible assets and a decline in interest expense due to reductions in the level of borrowing (the company paid down its bank loan during 2013) and a less severe loss from discontinued operations.

Operating cash flow decreased by $3 million to $57 million in 2013 due to changes in the levels of operating assets and liabilities; a decrease of a $3.6 million in depreciation and amortization and other non-cash operating activities; and an increase of $1.6 million in cash provided by net income.

Strategy

For the company which offers very few of its services to commercial clients relying on government contracts can be a bit like walking a mine field. VSE often faces funding delays terminations and political moratoriums and is subject to fluctuations in demand from its core customers. In an effort to curtail vulnerabilities inherent to such fluctuations the company makes acquisitions of complementary businesses that help bring in new customers and expand its services.

During 2013 the company abandoned the construction management operations of its wholly owned subsidiary Integrated Concepts and Research Corporation (ICRC). ICRC participated in an arrangement to provide performance and payment bonding services for certain small business prime contractors associated with ICRC's construction management business. Under the arrangement ICRC received subcontractor work from the small business prime contractors in exchange for indemnifying the surety company in respect of the performance and payment bonds it provided for the small business prime contractors.

Company Background

In 2011 VSE acquired Wheeler Bros. Inc. (WBI) a supply chain management company for roughly $180 million. WBI provides vehicle parts primarily to the USPS and the DOD. The takeover added fleet management for the USPS and expanded VSE's supply chain service offerings to existing customers. WBI also helps the company compensate for lost business from the DOD as it undergoes budget adjustments. The previous year the company bolstered its G&B unit with the acquisition of Hawaii-based Akimeka for $38 million. Akimeka is a health services information technology consulting group that came with a strong US government client base.

Besides acquisitions the company has been pursuing growth by developing new contracts to succeed fading deals. Included among these new agreements is a 2011 award that will make up for lost work from the discontinued R2 contract.

VSE was established in Virginia in 1959 with three employees; its first contract provided the US Navy with a competitive bidding package for missile rocket motors.

EXECUTIVES

EVP and CFO, Thomas R. (Tom) Loftus, age 63, $311,610 total compensation
VP General Counsel and Secretary, Thomas M. Kiernan, $249,174 total compensation
President CEO COO and Director, Maurice A. Gauthier, age 71, $700,000 total compensation
President Energetics Inc. and Akimeka LLC, Nancy Margolis, age 63, $214,240 total compensation
President and COO Wheeler Bros. Inc., Chad Wheeler, age 44, $250,000 total compensation
President and COO VSE Aviation Inc., Paul W. Goffredi, age 61
President Federal Services Group, Joseph R. (JR) Brown, age 62
CIO, Matthew (Matt) Mullenix
Chairman, Clifford M. Kendall, age 88
Board Member, John Potter
Board Member, Admiral Mark Ferguson
Auditors: Ernst & Young LLP

LOCATIONS

HQ: VSE Corp.
6348 Walker Lane, Alexandria, VA 22310
Phone: 703 960-4600   Fax: 703 960-2688
Web: www.vsecorp.com

PRODUCTS/OPERATIONS

2016 sales

	$ mil.	% of total
Supply Chain Management Group	205.4	30
Aviation Group	133.4	19
Federal Services Group	306.1	44
ITEnergy and Management consulting Group	46.7	7
Total	691.7	100

2016 sales

	$ mil.	% of total
U.S.Postal Service	181.2	26
DOD		
U.S.Navy	190.1	27
U.S.Army	139.7	20
U.S Air Force	3.4	1
Commercial		
Commercial Aviation	131.0	19
Other Commercial	10.7	2
Other Civilian Agencies		
Department of Energy	11.7	2
Social Security Administration	9.7	1
Other Government	13.9	2
Total	691.7	100

Selected Subsidiaries
Air Parts & Supply Co.
Akimeka LLC
CT Aerospace LLC
Energetics Incorporated
G&B Solutions Inc.
Integrated Concepts and Research Corporation
Kansas Aviation of Independence L.L.C.
Prime Turbines LLC
VSE Aviation Inc.
Wheeler Bros. Inc

Selected Projects
Energy conservation projects
Engineering support for military vehicles and combat trailers
Large-scale port engineering development and construction management
Life cycle support for ships
Logistics management support
Machinery condition analysis
Military equipment refurbishment and modification
Ship communication systems
Ship force crew training
Ship maintenance overhaul and follow-on technical support
Specification preparation for ship alterations

Selected Operating Units
Supply Chain Group
Acquisition Management
   Configuration Management
   Obsolescence Management
   Prototyping & Fabrication
   Logistics
   Reserve Engineering
Federal Group
   Communications and Engineering Division
   Engineering and Logistics Division
   Field Support Services Division
   Systems Engineering Division
International Group
   GLOBAL Division
   Fleet Maintenance Division (global field engineering and logistics)
IT Energy and Management Consulting Group
   Akimeka
   Energetics Incorporated
   G&B Solutions

COMPETITORS

Boeing   Lockheed Martin
Force Protection   Northrop Grumman
General Dynamics   Todd Shipyards

HISTORICAL FINANCIALS

Company Type: Public

Income Statement   FYE: December 31

	REVENUE ($ mil.)	NET INCOME ($ mil.)	NET PROFIT MARGIN	EMPLOYEES
12/18	697.2	35.0	5.0%	2,228
12/17	760.1	39.1	5.1%	2,306
12/16	691.7	26.7	3.9%	2,523
12/15	533.9	24.9	4.7%	2,057
12/14	424.0	19.3	4.6%	1,589
Annual Growth	13.2%	16.0%	—	8.8%

2018 Year-End Financials

Debt ratio: 28.1%   No. of shares (mil.): 10.8
Return on equity: 11.2%   Dividends
Cash ($ mil.): 0.1   Yield: 1.0%
Current ratio: 2.68   Payout: 7.5%
Long-term debt ($ mil.): 170.0 Market value ($ mil.): 326.0

	STOCK PRICE ($) FY Close	P/E High/Low		PER SHARE ($) Earnings	Dividends	Book Value
12/18	29.91	17	8	3.21	0.30	30.17
12/17	48.43	16	10	3.60	0.26	27.04
12/16	38.84	30	12	2.47	0.23	23.63
12/15	62.18	36	15	2.31	0.42	21.33
12/14	65.90	41	23	1.81	0.38	19.17
Annual Growth	(17.9%)	—	—	15.5%	(5.7%)	12.0%

Walker & Dunlop Inc

When it comes to its commercial real estate loans Walker & Dunlop has the government on its side. The company provides commercial real estate financial services — mainly multifamily loans for apartments health care properties and student housing — to real estate owners and developers across the US. It originates and sells its products (e.g. mortgages supplemental financing construction loans and mezzanine loans) primarily through government-sponsored enterprises (GSEs) like Fannie Mae and Freddie Mac as well as through HUD. To a lesser extent the company originates loans for insurance companies banks and institutional investors.

Operations
The company generates its revenue from five main revenue streams: mortgage banking (62% of total revenue) servicing fees (about 30%) warehouse interest (5%) escrow earnings (1%) and other (5%).

Geographic Reach
Walker & Dunlop operates through 26 offices across the country with locations residing in Atlanta; Chicago; Dallas; Ft. Lauderdale Florida; Irvine California; Nashville Tennessee; New Orleans; New York; Seattle; San Francisco; Needham Massachusetts; and Walnut Creek California.

Sales and Marketing
Walker & Dunlop originates and sells loans through the programs of the Federal National Mortgage Association the Federal Home Loan Mortgage Corporation the Government National Mortgage Association and the Federal Housing Administration a division of the US Department of Housing and Urban Development.

Financial Performance
Walker & Dunlop has enjoyed record-setting revenue growth over the last few years. In 2014 revenue grew 13% to $360.8 million as all primary business categories saw growth. The largest category mortgage banking rose 9% that year on greater loan origination volume. Servicing fees revenue also rose 9% due to a larger average servicing portfolio.

Net income has also been on the rise as of late with the exception of 2012 when it took a slight dip. In 2014 profits rose 24% to $51.4 million largely due to the increased revenue. However Walker & Dunlop posted a cash outflow of $729.5 million that year (an improvement over the $836.9 million outflow posted in 2013) primarily due to changes in working capital.

Strategy
Walker & Dunlop has shaped its growth strategy around certain opportunities in the commercial real estate market on which it believes it can capitalize. It intends to invest in origination activities and products to meet the expected increase in demand for real estate financing. In addition Walker & Dunlop's focus on growing its services to health care facilities is centered on an expected rise in the demand for health care real estate loans. It hopes to serve an expected increased demand for such facilities as baby boomers reach retirement age. The company is also motivated by the fact that many commercial health care loans are sought after through GSE and HUD programs.

To further grow its loan origination and servicing operations Walker & Dunlop acquired certain assets of Johnson Capital Group for some $23.5 million in late 2014. That deal added 30 new loan originators to its capital markets team which the company intends to keep expanding in order to meet expected demand in the coming years. It also plans to open additional capital markets offices throughout the nation to increasingly tap into the commercial real estate market.

Company Background
Walker & Dunlop's relationship with government-related housing finance companies began in the late 1980s after it started originating underwriting and selling loans through Fannie Mae. In 2008 it began working with Freddie Mac and HUD after acquiring a loan servicing portfolio worth $5 billion from Column Guaranteed LLC. The acquisition served to widen Walker & Dunlop's revenue base and increase its sales volume.

EXECUTIVES

Chairman and CEO, William M. (Willy) Walker, age 53, $750,000 total compensation
Vice Chairman Capital Markets, Guy K. Johnson
EVP General Counsel and Secretary, Richard M. (Rich) Lucas, age 54, $400,000 total compensation
President, Howard W. Smith, age 60, $500,000 total compensation
EVP and Chief Credit Officer, Richard C. Warner, age 64, $400,000 total compensation
EVP and CFO, Stephen P. Theobald, $400,000 total compensation
EVP and Chief Production Officer Multifamily Finance, Donald P. King
EVP Proprietary Capital, Jeffrey M. (Jeff) Goodman
CTO, Bill Granger
EVP and Group Head FHA Finance, Michelle Warner
SVP Walker & Dunlop Investment Sales (WDIS), Rob Coleman
EVP and Managing Director Capital Markets, James Cope
CEO and Managing Director Walker & Dunlop Investment Sales, Greg Engler
Senior Vice President, David Redmond
Vice President, Mark Plenge
Vice President, Alex Iman
Assistant Vice President, Michael Liefer
Senior Vice President, David Gahagan
Avp And Underwriter Hud Underwriting, Jennifer Eisenbrandt
Vice President, Matthew Wallach
Assistant Vice President, Doug Hart
Vice President, Debbie Casale
Senior Vice President, Brendan Coleman
Vice President, Benjamin Krosin
Assistant Vice President, Kevin Bohm
Vice President Accounting Operations Proprietary Capital, Lacey Bowman
Vice President Asset Management, Suzanne Collins
Vice President Multifamily Finance, Dustin Swartz
Vice President, Kimberly Riordan
Vice President, Kevin Walsh
Senior Vice President Real Estate Finance, Chris Charboneau
Vice President, Tom Meunier
Assistant Vice President, Kristin Layden
Senior Vice President, Dan Martin
Vice President Capital Markets, Demetrius Ware
Assistant Vice President, Pete Rowan
Vice President Loan Servicing, Bob Watson
Assistant Vice President, Josh West
Vice President, Margret Caufield
Senior Vice President, Patrick Dempsey
ASSISTANT VICE PRESIDENT, Mary Hui
Vice President Closing, Veronica Veraldi
Vice President, Matthew Baldwin
Senior Vice President, Roberto Pesant
SENIOR VICE PRESIDENT, Brad Burns
Senior Vice President, Thomas Sigrist
SENIOR VICE PRESIDENT, Levi Brooker
Vice President, Veronica Langhofer
Vice President and Deputy Chief Underwriter HUD Underwriting, Charles Conkling
Assistant Vice President Manager, Judy DiRienzo
Vice President, Jacob Cohen
Vice President, Jeff Berger
Vice President, Jeff Baik
VP and DEPUTY CHIEF UNDERWRITER, Breck Nolley
Assistant Vice President Real Estate Finance, Laura Woltanski
Senior Vice President, Jim Cope
Vice President, Curtis Kaufman
Senior Vice President, Steven Hinds
Assistant Vice President Capital Markets, Mark Vinitsky
Senior Vice President, Craig Mueller
VICE PRESIDENT, James Chapman
SENIOR VICE PRESIDENT AND DEPUTY CHIEF UNDERWRITER, Joe Tarantino
ASSISTANT VICE PRESIDENT, Riley Manke
ASSISTANT VICE PRESIDENT, Rob Buelow
VICE PRESIDENT CM, Ryan Chapman
ASSISTANT VICE PRESIDENT, Scott Oeser
Senior Vice President, By Cartmell
VICE PRESIDENT, Brian Kaufman
ASSISTANT VICE PRESIDENT, Jason Taylor
SENIOR VICE PRESIDENT, James Pierson
SENIOR VICE PRESIDENT, Keaton Merrell
SENIOR VICE PRESIDENT, Michael Presser
ASSISTANT VICE PRESIDENT, Robert Quarton
ASSISTANT VICE PRESIDENT CAPITAL MARKETS, Luke Erlandson
Senior Vice President, Aaron Rosenfeld
ASSISTANT VICE PRESIDENT, Toni Copeland
ASSISTANT VICE PRESIDENT AND SENIOR CLOSING OFFICER, Donna Potember
Vice President And Team Leader, Guevara Michelle
Vice President Marketing, Chris Zegal
Vice President Capital Markets, Shannon Hersker
Svp Capital Markets, Shannon Rex
Svp And Managing Director Mutifamily Finance Group, John Gilmore
Svp, Bobby Gatling
Vp Capital Markets, Stephanie Sawyer Fletcher
Vp Fha Finance, Charlie Krisfalusi
Senior Vice President Asset Management, Marsha Palmer
Svp, Javier Rivera
Vice President Capital Markets, Ralph Wurzburger
Vice President Software Engineering, Michael Glick
Avp Talent Acquisition Manager, Becky Natiello
Vice President Information Technology, Schuyler Manson
Assistant Vice President Capital Markets, Bonnie Goldberg
Vice President, Nicole Brickhouse
Vice President Originations, Kimberly Schmitz
Senior Vice President And Deputy Chief Underwriter, Charley Conkling
Auditors: KPMG LLP

LOCATIONS

HQ: Walker & Dunlop Inc
7501 Wisconsin Avenue, Suite 1200E, Bethesda, MD 20814
Phone: 301 215-5500
Web: www.walkerdunlop.com

PRODUCTS/OPERATIONS

2014 Sales

	% of total
Gains from mortgage banking activities	62
Servicing fees	27
Net warehouse interest income	5
Escrow earnings & other interest income	1
Other	5
Total	**100**

Selected Products and Services
- Capital Markets and Investment Services
- Construction loans
- Equity investments
- FHA Finance
- First mortgage loans
- Healthcare Finance
- Mezzanine loans
- Multifamily Finance
- Second trust loans
- Supplemental financings
- Underwriting

COMPETITORS

American Capital	MetLife
Arbor Commercial	NewStar Financial
CapitalSource	Ocwen Financial
Centerline Holding Co.	Pzena Investment Management
Deutsche Bank	Redwood Trust
Deutsche Bank Berkshire Mortgage	Walter Investment Management
Encore Capital Group	
Kennedy-Wilson	Wells Fargo

HISTORICAL FINANCIALS
Company Type: Public

Income Statement — FYE: December 31

	REVENUE ($ mil.)	NET INCOME ($ mil.)	NET PROFIT MARGIN	EMPLOYEES
12/18	725.2	161.4	22.3%	723
12/17	711.8	211.1	29.7%	623
12/16	575.2	113.9	19.8%	550
12/15	468.2	82.1	17.5%	504
12/14	360.7	51.4	14.3%	465
Annual Growth	19.1%	33.1%	—	11.7%

2018 Year-End Financials
Debt ratio: 52.3%
Return on equity: 18.8%
Cash ($ mil.): 90.0
Current ratio: 0.53
Long-term debt ($ mil.): 1,457.3
No. of shares (mil.): 29.5
Dividends
Yield: 2.3%
Payout: 20.1%
Market value ($ mil.): 1,276.0

	STOCK PRICE ($) FY Close	P/E High	P/E Low	PER SHARE ($) Earnings	Dividends	Book Value
12/18	43.25	12	7	4.96	1.00	30.58
12/17	47.50	8	4	6.56	0.00	26.97
12/16	31.20	8	5	3.65	0.00	20.65
12/15	28.81	12	6	2.65	0.00	16.56
12/14	17.54	11	8	1.58	0.00	13.62
Annual Growth	25.3%	—	—	33.1%	—	22.4%

Warrior Met Coal Inc

Auditors: Ernst & Young LLP

LOCATIONS
HQ: Warrior Met Coal Inc
16243 Highway 216, Brookwood, AL 35444
Phone: 205 554-6150
Web: www.warriormetcoal.com

HISTORICAL FINANCIALS
Company Type: Public

Income Statement — FYE: December 31

	REVENUE ($ mil.)	NET INCOME ($ mil.)	NET PROFIT MARGIN	EMPLOYEES
12/18	1,378.0	696.7	50.6%	1,395
12/17	1,169.0	455.0	38.9%	1,354
12/16*	297.6	(49.6)	—	1,130
03/16	71.3	(61.8)	—	0
12/15	544.7	(310.5)	—	0
Annual Growth	26.1%			

*Fiscal year change

2018 Year-End Financials
Debt ratio: 33.8%
Return on equity: 123.8%
Cash ($ mil.): 205.5
Current ratio: 3.77
Long-term debt ($ mil.): 468.2
No. of shares (mil.): 51.6
Dividends
Yield: 74.4%
Payout: 136.2%
Market value ($ mil.): 1,245.0

	STOCK PRICE ($) FY Close	P/E High	P/E Low	PER SHARE ($) Earnings	Dividends	Book Value
12/18	24.11	3	2	13.17	17.94	13.80
12/17	25.15	3	2	8.62	11.36	7.75
Annual Growth	(4.1%)	—	—	52.8%	57.9%	78.1%

Webster Financial Corp (Waterbury, Conn)

Webster Financial is the holding company for Webster Bank which operates about 170 branches in southern New England primarily in Connecticut but also in Massachusetts New York and Rhode Island. The bank provides commercial and retail services such as deposit accounts loans and mortgages and consumer finance as well as government and institutional banking services. It performs asset-based lending through its Webster Business Credit subsidiary and equipment financing through Webster Capital Finance. The company's HSA Bank division offers health savings accounts nationwide. Webster Bank provides brokerage and investment services through an agreement with UVEST a division of LPL Financial.

Operations
Webster Financial operates in three segments: Commercial Banking HSA Bank and Community Banking.

Commercial Banking provides lending deposit and treasury and payment services.

Community Banking services consist of personal and business banking. It operates about 170 banking centers more than 330 ATMs a customer care center and web and mobile banking services.

HSA Bank is focused on health savings accounts as well as providing health reimbursement arrangements flexible spending and commuter benefit account administration services to employers and individuals in all 50 states.

Geographic Reach
Webster's largest market is Connecticut with about 115 branches. Massachusetts has about 35 branches; Rhode Island about 10; and New York fewer than 10. Customers can conduct transactions at some 330 ATMs across throughout New England.

Financial Performance
Webster Financial's revenue and net income have appreciated in recent years. In 2017 the bank's revenue rose to $1.05 billion from $983 million in 2016 while net income rose to $255 million from $207 million.

Webster credited strong loan growth funded with growth in low-cost long-duration HSA deposits for achieving higher net interest margin in 2017. Net interest income increased about $78 million while provision for loan and lease losses dropped about $15 million. The bank reported that non-interest expense rose about $38 million and that it had one-time gain of about $7 million on the sale of an asset in 2016.

Strategy
Webster focuses on building its community banking and health savings account businesses. The community banking unit is expansion in several metro areas led by Boston where the bank is on pace to meet its goal of $1 billion in new deposits and $500 million in loans over five years. While it faces fierce pricing competition in the Boston market it sees steady deposit growth in the core franchise there.

In the HSA Bank business Webster has invested in sales staff which helped drive compensation costs about $27 million higher in 2017 from 2016 and relationship management to gather new clients. The investment seems to be paying off with growth in clients and deposits and some $6 billion under administration. Webster uses deposits made in the HSA Bank to fund lending in its other businesses.

EXECUTIVES

Vice President Association Financial Services, Jordan Arovas

Chairman and CEO Webster Financial Corporation and Webster Bank N.A., James C. (Jim) Smith, age 69, $882,435 total compensation

EVP General Counsel and Corporate Secretary Webster Financial Corporation and Webster Bank N.A., Harriet M. Wolfe, age 65

President and COO Webster Business Credit Corporation (WBCC), Warren K. Mino

Regional President Boston Webster Bank N.A., Paul F. Mollica

EVP and Chief Human Resources Officer Webster Financial Corporation and Webster Bank N.A., Bernard M. Garrigues, age 60

EVP and Chief Marketing Officer Webster Financial Corporation and Webster Bank N.A., Dawn C. Morris, age 51

Regional President New Haven Conn. Webster Bank N.A., Jeffrey A. (Jeff) Klaus

EVP Commercial Banking; Chairman of Regional Presidents' Council, John R. Ciulla, age 53, $363,479 total compensation

EVP and Head of Community Banking, Nitin J. Mhatre, age 48, $358,521 total compensation

EVP and CFO Webster Financial Corporation and Webster Bank N.A., Glenn I. MacInnes, age 57, $453,310 total compensation

EVP and CIO Webster Financial Corporation and Webster Bank N.A., Colin D. Eccles, age 60

EVP Consumer Deposits Investments and Network Management Webster Bank N.A., David D. Miree

EVP and Chief Risk Officer Webster Financial Corporation and Webster Bank N.A., Daniel H. Bley, age 50
EVP and Head of Private Banking Webster Financial Corporation and Webster Bank N.A., Daniel M. (Dan) FitzPatrick, age 60, $300,000 total compensation
EVP Commercial Real Estate, William E. Wrang
EVP Webster Financial Corporation and Webster Bank N.A. and Head of HSA Bank, Charles L. (Chad) Wilkins, age 57
Regional President Metro New York, Abby Parsonnet
Regional President Southern Massachusetts and Rhode Island Webster Bank N.A., Douglas E. (Doug) Scala
Regional President Waterbury Conn. Webster Bank N.A., Michael L. (Mike) O'Connor
Regional President for Pennsylvania Webster Bank N.A., Scott C. Meves
Regional President Hartford Conn. Webster Bank N.A., Timothy D. Bergstrom
EVP Middle Market Banking Webster Bank N.A., Christopher J. (Chris) Motl
Vice President Information Technology, Tom Clark
Vice President Human Resources Technology, Chris Muller
Vice President Information Technology Applications, Jay Clark
Vice President Corporate Facilities Operations, Mark Nisbett
Senior Vice President Director of Corporate Security, Michael Wolf
Vice President Loan Operations, Terri O'sullivan
Vice President Marketing, Joanne Renna
Vice President eBanking, Chris Barlow
Vice President External Communications, Sarah Barr
Vice President Database, Jennifer Zbell
Vice President Finance, Shelly Abdella
Senior Vice President Middle Market Commercial Banking Webster Bank, Stephen Corcoran
Vice President Commercial Banking, Joe Pelliccia
Vice President Human Resources, Laura Chandler
Senior Vice President, Kevin Collins
Senior Vice President and Director Business and Professional Banking, John Guy
Senior Vice President Compensation Benefits and Hris, Carole Hynes
Senior Vice President, Torres Gilbert
Vice Chairman Webster Financial Corporation and Webster Bank N.A., Joseph J. (Joe) Savage, age 66
Board Member, Mark Pettie
Board Member, Lauren States
Board Member, Elizabeth Flynn
Board Member, William Atwell
Auditors: KPMG LLP

LOCATIONS

HQ: Webster Financial Corp (Waterbury, Conn)
  145 Bank Street, Waterbury, CT 06702
Phone: 203 578-2202
Web: www.websterbank.com

PRODUCTS/OPERATIONS

2017 Sales

	$ mil.	% of total
Interest		
Interest and fees on loans and leases	708.6	57
Taxable interest and dividends on securities	181.1	17
Non-taxable interest on securities	22.9	2
Loans held for sale	1.0	-
Non-interest		
Deposit service fees	151.2	13
Loan and lease related fees	26.4	3
Wealth and investment services	31.0	3
Mortgage banking activities	9.9	1
Increase in cash surrender value of life insurance policies	14.6	1
Gain on sale of investment securities net	—	-
Impairment loss on securities recognized in earnings	(0.13)	-
Other income	26.4	3
Total	**1,055.8**	**100**

COMPETITORS

Bank of America
Citibank
Citizens Financial Group
Fairfield County Bank
First Connecticut Bancorp
JPMorgan Chase
KeyCorp
Liberty Bank
New England Bancshares
Patriot National Bancorp
People's United Financial
SBT Bancorp Inc.
SI Financial
TD Bank USA
Washington Trust Bancorp

HISTORICAL FINANCIALS
Company Type: Public

Income Statement
FYE: December 31

	ASSETS ($ mil.)	NET INCOME ($ mil.)	INCOME AS % OF ASSETS	EMPLOYEES
12/18	27,610.3	360.4	1.3%	3,265
12/17	26,487.6	255.4	1.0%	3,302
12/16	26,072.5	207.1	0.8%	3,168
12/15	24,677.8	206.3	0.8%	2,946
12/14	22,533.0	199.7	0.9%	2,764
Annual Growth	5.2%	15.9%	—	4.3%

2018 Year-End Financials

Return on assets: 1.3%
Return on equity: 12.9%
Long-term debt ($ mil.): —
No. of shares (mil.): 92.1
Sales ($ mil): 1,337.7
Dividends
  Yield: 2.5%
  Payout: 32.8%
Market value ($ mil.): 4,543.0

	STOCK PRICE ($) FY Close	P/E High/Low	PER SHARE ($) Earnings	Dividends	Book Value
12/18	49.29	18 12	3.81	1.25	31.31
12/17	56.16	22 17	2.67	1.03	29.36
12/16	54.28	25 14	2.16	0.98	27.54
12/15	37.19	19 13	2.15	0.89	26.38
12/14	32.53	16 13	2.08	0.75	25.70
Annual Growth	10.9%	— —	16.3%	13.6%	5.1%

Wellesley Bancorp Inc.

Auditors: Wolf & Company, P.C.

LOCATIONS

HQ: Wellesley Bancorp Inc.
  100 Worcester Street, Suite 300, Wellesley, MA 02481
Phone: 781 235-2550
Web: www.wellesleybank.com

HISTORICAL FINANCIALS
Company Type: Public

Income Statement
FYE: December 31

	ASSETS ($ mil.)	NET INCOME ($ mil.)	INCOME AS % OF ASSETS	EMPLOYEES
12/18	871.4	5.9	0.7%	79
12/17	805.4	3.1	0.4%	72
12/16	695.2	2.9	0.4%	73
12/15	621.1	2.6	0.4%	70
12/14	535.1	1.7	0.3%	72
Annual Growth	13.0%	35.5%	—	2.3%

2018 Year-End Financials

Return on assets: 0.7%
Return on equity: 9.6%
Long-term debt ($ mil.): —
No. of shares (mil.): 2.5
Sales ($ mil): 36.2
Dividends
  Yield: 0.7%
  Payout: 11.6%
Market value ($ mil.): 70.0

	STOCK PRICE ($) FY Close	P/E High/Low	PER SHARE ($) Earnings	Dividends	Book Value
12/18	27.74	14 11	2.40	0.22	25.79
12/17	29.70	22 19	1.30	0.19	23.64
12/16	27.75	22 14	1.24	0.15	22.22
12/15	19.00	18 16	1.14	0.12	21.22
12/14	19.19	26 23	0.77	0.08	20.07
Annual Growth	9.6%	— —	32.9%	30.1%	6.5%

Wells Fargo Real Estate Investment Corp

Auditors: KPMG LLP

LOCATIONS

HQ: Wells Fargo Real Estate Investment Corp
  90 South 7th Street, Minneapolis, MN 55402
Phone: 855 825-1437
Web: www.wellsfargo.com/invest_relations/filings

WesBanco Inc

WesBanco wants to be the "BesBanco" for its customers. The holding company owns WesBanco Bank which has about 210 branches in Indiana Kentucky Ohio Pennsylvania and West Virginia. In addition to providing traditional services such as deposits and loans the bank operates a wealth management department with offices in West Virginia and Ohio and some $4.7 billion of assets under management and custody including the company's proprietary WesMark mutual funds. Other units include brokerage firm WesBanco Securities and multi-line insurance provider WesBanco Insurance Services.

Operations
Commercial loans including real estate and operating loans account for more than half of WesBanco's loan portfolio. Its retail portfolio mainly consists of home equity loans and deposit overdraft limits. The bank usually sells new residential mortgages that it originates into the secondary market. It plans to continue to grow its portfolio of commercial and industrial loans.

Strategy
WesBanco likes to purchase smaller banks to expand its reach into new geographic markets while bolstering its loan and deposit business. It's acquired more than 50 banks and financial services firms in the past 25 years.

Mergers and Acquisitions
The company agreed in 2019 to acquire Old Line Bancshares for $500 million. The combined company will have about $15.6 billion in total assets and about 235 branches in more than five states. The deal give WesBanco more than 35 new offices primarily in Baltimore and Washington DC.

In 2018 WesBanco acquired Kentucky-based Farmers Capital Bank Corporation for $429.8 million and West Virginia-based First Sentry Bancshares for $107.5 million.

EXECUTIVES

EVP Treasury and Strategic Planning, Brent E. Richmond, age 56
EVP and Chief Credit Officer, Peter W. Jaworski, age 64, $212,101 total compensation
EVP and CFO, Robert H. Young, age 63, $269,363 total compensation
President and CEO, Todd F. Clossin, age 57, $466,923 total compensation
EVP and Chief Risk & Administrative Officer, Michael L. Perkins
EVP Retail Delivery, Lynn D. Asensio
EVP and Senior Operations Officer, Gregory A. Dugan
EVP Wealth Management, Jonathan D. Dargusch, age 61, $230,270 total compensation
EVP Human Resources Management, Anthony F. Pietranton
EVP and Chief Lending Officer, Jayson M. Zatta
Market President Kanawha Region, David L. Sayre
Vice President District Sales Manager, Nick Taylor
Senior Vice President Human Resources, Lee Blundon
Vice President Finance, Luanne Bush
Vice President And Manager Human Resources, Sheri Clarke
Vice President Risk Management Security Officer, James Thompson
Senior Vice President, Howard Bertram
Vice President Commercial Real Estate, Traci Boeing
Assistant Vice President, Bruce Bandi
Vice President, Allen Retton
Vice President, Tom Medovic
Senior Vice President Credit Risk Management, Edward Polli
Vice President Electronic Banking Manager, Jason Plotner
Assistant Vice President Business Development Manager, Lycia Maurits
Assistant Vice President Information Technology Services, W Terrance Naughton
Vice President Of Information Technology, Mike Robbins
Vice President Investments, Steve Kellas
Senior Vice President, Robert Booth
Executive Vice President Commercial Banking, Jay Zatta
Vice President Retail Operations, Lisa Copley
Senior Vice President Senior Lender, Bob Friend
Vice President and Loan Review Officer, Diane Todd
Vice President Business Development Officer, Neal Jackson
Senior Vice President Investments, Michael Klick
Assistant Vice President Commercial Banking Officer, Randall Trickett
Senior Vice President and Senior Credit Officer, David Knuth
Assistant Vice President Private Banker, Kerrie Smith
Vice President of Commercial Banking, Michael Mistovich
VICE PRESIDENT AND BUSINESS BANKING OFFICER, Nathan Mcvicker
Assistant Vice President Branch Manager, Tom Wiggershaus
Banking Center Manager Assistant Vice President, Nicholas Beresh
Vice President Residential Lending, David Bendis
Vice President Secondary Marketing Manager, Ryan Freimark
Senior Vice President Corporate Banking, Charles Wharton
Vice President, Sabra Thomas Kershaw
Senior Vice President Enterprise Services, Jan Pattishall
Vice President Business Banking, John Mcdonough
Assistant Vice President Financial Advisor, Josh Schmalz
VICE PRESIDENT COMMERCIAL LENDING, Kurt Bevan
Vice President Credit Risk Management, Ryan Potts
Vice President, James Bish
Assistant Vice President, Anthony Habbit
Senior Vice President, Jeff Ferry
Assistant Vice President Information Technology, John Busack
Assistant Vice President BCM Business Development, Jason Lucarelli
Vice President Corporate Banking, Harry J Silvis
Vice President and Manger, Mary Bryson
Senior Vice President, Thomas Ziacik
Assistant Vice President Senior Underwriter, Tim Robinson
Assistant Vice President, Dan Baxter
Vice President, Brent Dapper
Assistant Vice President Banking Center Manager, Linda Yon
Vice President, Michael Puzausky
Vice President, Nathan Schoetz
Vice President Business Banking, Maherdickerson Stephanie
Vice President Quality Assurance Manager, Pamela Jones
Vice President Corporate Banking, Jack Green
VICE PRESIDENT PRIVATE BANKER, Leslie D Witzel
Vice President And Commercial Banker, Michael Epperley
SENIOR VICE PRESIDENT AND SENIOR COMMERCIAL BANKER, Michael T Misich
VICE PRESIDENT COMMERCIAL LENDER, Robert E Krzeminski
VICE PRESIDENT TREASURY MANAGEMENT SALES, Stacy Graf
VICE PRESIDENT SENIOR TRUST OFFICER, Thomas D Barsody
VICE PRESIDENT COMMERCIAL LENDING, Kurt C Bevan
VICE PRESIDENT COMMERCIAL BANKER, Camde Skidmore
SENIOR VICE PRESIDENT, Ed Hensley
VICE PRESIDENT AND TECHNOLOGY SERVICES COORDINATOR, Stephanie Skivington
VICE PRESIDENT COMMERCIAL BANKING, Daniel Hindman
Vice President Senior Trust Officer, Thomas Barsody
VICE PRESIDENT PRIVATE BANKER, Leslie Witzel
SENIOR VICE PRESIDENT AND SENIOR COMMERCIAL BANKER, Michael Misich
ASSISTANT VICE PRESIDENT AND APPRAISAL REVIEW OFFICER, Ann Scranton
Svp Financial Advisor Crc, Sherri Libersat
Vice President, Jeff Davis
Evp, David Ellwood Cfa
Evp Senior Operations Officer, Greg Dugan
Senior Vice President Private Client Services, Andy Mayer
Chairman, James C. (Jim) Gardill, age 73
Secretary, Cindy Dailer

HISTORICAL FINANCIALS
Company Type: Public

Income Statement
FYE: December 31

	REVENUE ($ mil.)	NET INCOME ($ mil.)	NET PROFIT MARGIN	EMPLOYEES
12/18	1,379.4	1,237.6	89.7%	2
12/17	1,353.0	1,218.6	90.1%	2
12/16	899.9	783.8	87.1%	2
12/15	680.8	645.9	94.9%	2
12/14	697.0	637.9	91.5%	2
Annual Growth	18.6%	18.0%	—	0.0%

2018 Year-End Financials
Debt ratio: 8.6%
Return on equity: 3.8%
Cash ($ mil.): —
Current ratio: —
Long-term debt ($ mil.): 3,054.7
No. of shares (mil.): 34.0
Dividends
  Yield: 6.3%
  Payout: 4.4%
Market value ($ mil.): 853.0

	STOCK PRICE ($) FY Close	P/E High	P/E Low	PER SHARE ($) Earnings	PER SHARE ($) Dividends	PER SHARE ($) Book Value
12/18	25.05	1	1	35.82	1.59	951.77
12/17	26.49	1	1	35.27	1.59	951.03
12/16	25.17	1	1	37.75	1.59	951.15
12/15	26.16	1	1	48.71	1.69	962.24
12/14	25.35	1	1	49.37	46.74	957.87
Annual Growth	(0.3%)	—	—	(7.7%)	(57.0%)	(0.2%)

Board Member, Ronald Owen
Board Member, Denise Knouse-snyder
Auditors: Ernst & Young LLP

LOCATIONS

HQ: WesBanco Inc
1 Bank Plaza, Wheeling, WV 26003
Phone: 304 234-9000
Web: www.wesbanco.com

PRODUCTS/OPERATIONS

2016 Sales

	$ mil.	% of total
Interest and Dividend Income		
Loans including fees	227.0	61
Interest and dividends on securities	56.9	15
Other interest income	2.2	1
Non-Interest Income		
Trust fees	21.6	6
Service charges on deposits	18.3	5
Electronic banking fees	15.6	4
Net securities brokerage	6.4	2
Bank-owned life insurance	4.1	1
Net gains on sales of mortgage loans	2.5	1
Net securities gains	2.4	1
Net gain / (loss) on other real estate owned and other assets	0.8	-
others	9.8	3
Total	**367.6**	**100**

Selected Products and Services
Personal Banking
Internet Banking
Checking
Savings
Time Deposits
Debit Cards
Credit Cards
Loans
Mortgage Lending
Other Services
Business
Internet Banking
Checking
Savings
Time Deposits
Credit Cards
Loans
Treasury Management
Insurance Services
Wealth Management

COMPETITORS

1st West Virginia Bancorp	Huntington Bancshares
BB&T	Ohio Valley Banc
Bank of America	PNC Financial
Cheviot Financial	United Bancorp
City Holding	United Bankshares
First Community Bancshares	

HISTORICAL FINANCIALS

Company Type: Public

Income Statement
FYE: December 31

	ASSETS ($ mil.)	NET INCOME ($ mil.)	INCOME AS % OF ASSETS	EMPLOYEES
12/18	12,458.6	143.1	1.1%	2,383
12/17	9,816.1	94.4	1.0%	1,940
12/16	9,790.8	86.6	0.9%	1,928
12/15	8,470.3	80.7	1.0%	1,633
12/14	6,296.5	69.9	1.1%	1,448
Annual Growth	18.6%	19.6%	—	13.3%

2018 Year-End Financials

Return on assets: 1.2%
Return on equity: 8.4%
Long-term debt ($ mil.): —
No. of shares (mil.): 54.6
Sales ($ mil): 515.2
Dividends
Yield: 3.1%
Payout: 46.9%
Market value ($ mil.): 2,003.0

	STOCK PRICE ($) FY Close	P/E High/Low	PER SHARE ($) Earnings	Dividends	Book Value
12/18	36.69	17 12	2.92	1.16	36.24
12/17	40.65	20 16	2.14	1.04	31.68
12/16	43.06	20 13	2.16	0.96	30.53
12/15	30.02	17 14	2.15	0.92	29.18
12/14	34.80	15 11	2.39	0.88	26.90
Annual Growth	1.3%	— —	5.1%	7.2%	7.7%

West Bancorporation, Inc.

West Bancorporation is the holding company for West Bank which serves individuals and small to midsized businesses through about a dozen branches mainly in the Des Moines and Iowa City Iowa areas. Founded in 1893 the bank offers checking savings and money market accounts CDs Visa credit cards and trust services. The bank's lending activities primarily consist of commercial mortgages; construction land and land development loans; and business loans such as revolving lines of credit inventory and accounts receivable financing equipment financing and capital expenditure loans to borrowers in Iowa.

Sales and Marketing
West Bank focuses on small to medium-sized businesses in its local markets. The thinking is that smaller local firms want to develop an exclusive relationship with a single bank.

Financial Performance
The company's revenue has been remarkably consistent year-over-year. It reported $61.2 million in annual revenue for fiscal 2013 after claiming $61.7 million in fiscal 2012 and $64.1 million in fiscal 2011.

Net income has also remained very consistent in recent years. The bank reported net income of $16.8 million for fiscal 2013 after clearing $16 million in fiscal 2012 and $15.27 million in fiscal 2011.

The company's net cash on hand has decreased dramatically in recent fiscal years however mostly as a result of property investments.

Strategy
West Bank has slowly but surely been expanding its territory. The company is working on building a new headquarters building and expanding into Minnesota.

EXECUTIVES

EVP; President West Bank, Brad L. Winterbottom, age 63, $275,000 total compensation
EVP CFO and Treasurer, Douglas R. (Doug) Gulling, age 66, $275,000 total compensation
President and CEO, David D. (Dave) Nelson, age 59, $400,000 total compensation
EVP and Chief Risk Officer, Harlee N. Olafson, age 62, $275,000 total compensation
Vice President, Donavon Paulson
Vice President, Nancy Behmer
Senior Vice President, Keith Kurth
Chairman, David R. Milligan
Board Member, Steven Gaer
Board Member, Kaye Lozier
Board Member, Lou Ann Sandburg
Member Board of Directors, Sean McMurray
Auditors: RSM US LLP

LOCATIONS

HQ: West Bancorporation, Inc.
1601 22nd Street, West Des Moines, IA 50266
Phone: 515 222-2300
Web: www.westbankstrong.com

PRODUCTS/OPERATIONS

2015 Sales

	$ mil.	% of total
Interest		
Loans including fees	52.5	77
Taxable investment Securities	4.4	6
Tax-exempt investment Securities	3.2	5
Federal funds sold	0.0	-
Noninterest		
Service charges on deposit accounts	2.6	4
Debit card usage fees	1.8	3
Trust services	1.3	2
Revenue from residential mortgage banking	0.1	-
Increase in cash value of bank-owned life insurance	0.7	1
Realized investment securities gains net	0.0	-
Other income	1.6	2
Total	**68.4**	**100**

COMPETITORS

BTC Financial	Regions Financial
Bank of America	U.S. Bancorp
Bank of the West	Wells Fargo
MidWestOne	

HISTORICAL FINANCIALS

Company Type: Public

Income Statement
FYE: December 31

	ASSETS ($ mil.)	NET INCOME ($ mil.)	INCOME AS % OF ASSETS	EMPLOYEES
12/18	2,296.5	28.5	1.2%	163
12/17	2,114.3	23.0	1.1%	162
12/16	1,854.2	23.0	1.2%	165
12/15	1,748.6	21.7	1.2%	174
12/14	1,615.8	20.0	1.2%	178
Annual Growth	9.2%	9.2%	—	(2.2%)

2018 Year-End Financials

Return on assets: 1.2%
Return on equity: 15.4%
Long-term debt ($ mil.): —
No. of shares (mil.): 16.3
Sales ($ mil.): 92.5
Dividends
Yield: 4.0%
Payout: 50.6%
Market value ($ mil.): 311.0

	STOCK PRICE ($) FY Close	P/E High/Low	PER SHARE ($) Earnings	Dividends	Book Value
12/18	19.09	15 10	1.74	0.78	11.72
12/17	25.15	20 15	1.41	0.71	10.98
12/16	24.70	17 11	1.42	0.67	10.25
12/15	19.75	15 12	1.35	0.62	9.49
12/14	17.02	14 11	1.25	0.49	8.75
Annual Growth	2.9%	— —	8.6%	12.3%	7.6%

Westbury Bancorp Inc

EXECUTIVES

Chm-ceo; Pres Ceo, Raymond Lipman
Vice President Controller, Steve Sinner
Assistant Vice President Marketing, Noe Pacheco
Senior Vice President, Joe Schaefer
Assistant Vice President Accounting Manager, Tammy Pyka
Senior Vice President Commercial Lending, Joe Pieper
Vice President Employee Benefits Trust Officer, Rob Reynolds
Auditors: CliftonLarsonAllen LLP

LOCATIONS

HQ: Westbury Bancorp Inc
200 South Main Street, West Bend, WI 53095
Phone: 262 334-5563
Web: www.westburybankwi.com

HISTORICAL FINANCIALS

Company Type: Public

Income Statement — FYE: September 30

	ASSETS ($ mil.)	NET INCOME ($ mil.)	INCOME AS % OF ASSETS	EMPLOYEES
09/19	855.6	6.8	0.8%	0
09/18	816.3	4.2	0.5%	0
09/17	790.2	2.8	0.4%	125
09/16	702.6	3.4	0.5%	133
09/15	638.9	3.5	0.6%	128
Annual Growth	7.6%	18.2%	—	—

2019 Year-End Financials

Return on assets: 0.8%
Return on equity: 8.6%
Long-term debt ($ mil.): —
No. of shares (mil.): 3.3
Sales ($ mil): 38.6
Dividends
Yield: —
Payout: —
Market value ($ mil.): 86.0

	STOCK PRICE ($) FY Close	P/E High/Low	PER SHARE ($) Earnings	Dividends	Book Value
09/19	25.60	12 9	2.09	0.00	24.46
09/18	22.00	21 16	1.18	0.00	21.03
09/17	19.95	29 25	0.76	0.00	20.23
09/16	19.53	22 18	0.93	0.00	19.43
09/15	17.82	22 17	0.85	0.00	18.21
Annual Growth	9.5%	— —	25.2%	—	7.7%

Western Alliance Bancorporation

Western Alliance Bancorporation and its flagship Western Alliance Bank (WAB) have an alliance with several bank brands in the West operating as the Alliance Bank of Arizona; Bank of Nevada; First Independent Bank (Nevada); as well as Bridge Bank and Torrey Pines Bank which are both located across California. Combined the banks operate nearly 50 branches that provide standard consumer and business deposit and loan products. About half of the Western Alliance's loan portfolio is made up of commercial and industrial loans while another 40% is made up of commercial real estate loans. It also makes land development loans and consumer residential mortgages and other lines of credit.

Operations
Western Alliance focuses on commercial lending. About 46% of the bank's loan portfolio consisted of commercial and industrial loans at the end of 2015 while another 39% was made up of commercial real estate loans. The bank also had construction and land development loans (10% of loan assets) residential mortgages (3%) commercial leases (1%) and consumer loans (less than 1%).

More than 90% of the bank's revenue comes from interest income. About 86% of its total revenue came from loan interest during 2015 while another 9% came from interest or dividends on investment securities. The remainder of its revenue came from service charges and fees (2% of revenue) card income (1%) and other miscellaneous sources.

Geographic Reach
Western Alliance's 40 branches and seven loan offices are spread across Arizona Nevada and California as well as Boston Dallas and Reston Virginia. At the end of 2015 its loan business was concentrated in the Los Angeles San Francisco San Jose Phoenix Tuscon Reno and Las Vegas metropolitan areas.

Sales and Marketing
The bank serves local businesses real estate developers and investors not-for-profit organizations and consumers. It specializes in lending to such customers operating in the healthcare professional services manufacturing and distribution resorts and timeshares technology and startups municipalities and local governments non-profit and renewable energy markets. Some of its clients (as of early 2016) include Cutter Aviation FNF Construction Hollenbeck Palms New American Funding and Signature Healthcare Services.

Western Alliance spent $2.89 million on marketing in 2015 up from $2.30 million and $2.58 million in 2014 and 2013 respectively.

Financial Performance
Western Alliance's annual revenues have risen nearly 70% since 2011 as its loan business has swelled. Meanwhile the bank's annual profits have ballooned more than five-fold as its credit portfolio's credit quality has improved with higher property valuations in the strengthened economy.

The group's revenue jumped 26% to $555 million during 2015 mostly thanks to new loan business more than half of which was obtained from the Bridge Bank acquisition which spurred more interest income for the year. Non-interest income especially service charges and lending-related fees grew by double digits during the year also thanks to the acquisition as well as from more organic deposit business growth.

Strong revenue growth and a continued decline in credit loss provisions in 2015 drove Western Alliance's net income up by 31% to $194 million for the year. The company's operating cash levels climbed 30% to $213 million mostly thanks to the rise in cash earnings.

Strategy
Western Alliance Bancorporation looks to expand its branch network and selectively acquire other banks to boost its loan and deposit business and extend its geographic reach. The bank may also buy other financial services businesses to bolster its line of service offerings.

Mergers and Acquisitions
In June 2015 Western Alliance bought $13 billion-asset Bridge Capital Holdings along with its 48 Bridge Bank branches in California Arizona and Nevada in a deal worth about $425 million. The purchase brought expertise in technology and international banking among other areas and expands Western Alliance's market into Northern California.

EXECUTIVES

EVP and Chief Credit Officer, Robert R. (Bob) McAuslan, age 66
Chairman and CEO, Robert G. Sarver, age 58, $830,000 total compensation
EVP and CFO, Dale M. Gibbons, age 58, $400,000 total compensation
EVP Northern California Administration and President and CEO Bridge Bank division, Daniel P. (Dan) Myers, age 58, $212,885 total compensation
EVP Southern Nevada Administration and CEO Bank of Nevada Division, John Guedry
EVP and CIO, John P. Peckham
EVP California Administration and President Torrey Pines Bank, Gerald A. (Gary) Cady, age 64, $360,000 total compensation
EVP and Chief Risk Officer, Patricia A. Taylor
EVP and General Counsel, Randall S. Theisen
EVP and COO, Jim Haught
EVP Arizona Administration and CEO Alliance Bank of Arizona, Don Garner
Senior Vice President, Seth Davis
Vice President, Jennifer Holyoak
Senior Credit Analyst Vice President Warehouse Lending, Bryan Brooks
Chief Human Resource Officer Executive Vice President, Barbara Kennedy
Vp Of Relationship Manager Of Bank Of Nevada, Melanie Maviglia
Evp Bank Of Nevada, Bill Oakley
Board Member, Cary Mack
Board Member, Marianne Johnson
Board Member, William Boyd
Auditors: RSM US LLP

LOCATIONS

HQ: Western Alliance Bancorporation
One E. Washington Street, Suite 1400, Phoenix, AZ 85004
Phone: 602 389-3500
Web: www.westernalliancebancorporation.com

PRODUCTS/OPERATIONS

2015 Sales

	% of total
Interest income	
Loans including fees	86
Investment securities	7
Dividends	2
Other	-
Non-interest income	
Service charges and fees	2
Income from bank owned life insurance	1
Card income	1
Other	1
Total	100

Selected Services
Business Checking & Savings
Business Loans & Credit
Card Services
International Banking
Personal Banking
Treasury Management

COMPETITORS

Bank of America
Bank of the West
Desert Schools FCU
First Banks
MUFG Americas Holdings
PacWest Bancorp
U.S. Bancorp
Wells Fargo
Westamerica
Zions Bancorporation

HISTORICAL FINANCIALS
Company Type: Public

Income Statement — FYE: December 31

	ASSETS ($ mil.)	NET INCOME ($ mil.)	INCOME AS % OF ASSETS	EMPLOYEES
12/18	23,109.4	435.7	1.9%	1,787
12/17	20,329.0	325.4	1.6%	1,725
12/16	17,200.8	259.8	1.5%	1,557
12/15	14,275.0	194.2	1.4%	1,446
12/14	10,600.5	147.9	1.4%	1,131
Annual Growth	21.5%	31.0%	—	12.1%

2018 Year-End Financials
Return on assets: 2.0%
Return on equity: 18.0%
Long-term debt ($ mil.): —
No. of shares (mil.): 104.9
Sales ($ mil.): 1,076.6
Dividends
  Yield: —
  Payout: —
Market value ($ mil.): 4,144.0

	STOCK PRICE ($) FY Close	P/E High/Low		PER SHARE ($) Earnings	Dividends	Book Value
12/18	39.49	15	9	4.14	0.00	24.90
12/17	56.62	19	14	3.10	0.00	21.14
12/16	48.71	20	11	2.50	0.00	18.00
12/15	35.86	19	12	2.03	0.00	15.44
12/14	27.80	17	12	1.67	0.00	11.29
Annual Growth	9.2%	—	—	25.5%	—	21.9%

Western Asset Mortgage Capital Corp

Auditors: PricewaterhouseCoopers LLP

LOCATIONS

HQ: Western Asset Mortgage Capital Corp
  385 East Colorado Boulevard, Pasadena, CA 91101
Phone: 626 844-9400
Web: www.westernassetmcc.com

HISTORICAL FINANCIALS
Company Type: Public

Income Statement — FYE: December 31

	ASSETS ($ mil.)	NET INCOME ($ mil.)	INCOME AS % OF ASSETS	EMPLOYEES
12/18	4,497.4	26.4	0.6%	0
12/17	3,886.9	85.1	2.2%	0
12/16	3,156.0	(25.0)	—	0
12/15	3,414.5	(9.4)	—	0
12/14	4,909.2	100.7	2.1%	1
Annual Growth	(2.2%)	(28.4%)	—	—

2018 Year-End Financials
Return on assets: 0.6%
Return on equity: 5.4%
Long-term debt ($ mil.): —
No. of shares (mil.): 48.1
Sales ($ mil): 199.2
Dividends
  Yield: 14.8%
  Payout: 203.2%
Market value ($ mil.): 401.0

	STOCK PRICE ($) FY Close	P/E High/Low		PER SHARE ($) Earnings	Dividends	Book Value
12/18	8.34	19	14	0.61	1.24	10.45
12/17	9.95	5	5	2.03	1.24	11.15
12/16	10.07	—	—	(0.61)	1.38	10.27
12/15	10.22	—	—	(0.25)	2.49	12.21
12/14	14.70	6	5	2.67	2.74	14.94
Annual Growth	(13.2%) (8.5%)	—	—	(30.9%)	(18.0%)	—

Western Midstream Partners LP

Auditors: KPMG LLP

LOCATIONS

HQ: Western Midstream Partners LP
  1201 Lake Robbins Drive, The Woodlands, TX 77380
Phone: 832 636-6000
Web: www.westerngas.com

PRODUCTS/OPERATIONS

2011 Sales

	$ mil.	% of total
Natural gas NGLs and condensate sales	502.4	61
Gathering processing & transporation of natural gas & NGLs	301.3	36
Equity income & other	19.6	3
Total	**823.3**	**100**

COMPETITORS

DCP Midstream Partners
Dominion Questar
Enbridge Energy
Kinder Morgan Energy Partners
ONEOK Partners
XTO Energy

HISTORICAL FINANCIALS
Company Type: Public

Income Statement — FYE: December 31

	REVENUE ($ mil.)	NET INCOME ($ mil.)	NET PROFIT MARGIN	EMPLOYEES
12/18	1,990.2	369.4	18.6%	0
12/17	2,248.3	376.6	16.8%	0
12/16	1,804.2	345.7	19.2%	0
12/15	1,561.3	87.8	5.6%	0
12/14	1,273.7	221.9	17.4%	0
Annual Growth	11.8%	13.6%	—	—

2018 Year-End Financials
Debt ratio: 52.1%
Return on equity: —
Cash ($ mil.): 92.1
Current ratio: 0.63
Long-term debt ($ mil.): 4,787.3
No. of shares (mil.): 218.9
Dividends
  Yield: 8.2%
  Payout: 135.8%
Market value ($ mil.): 6,071.0

	STOCK PRICE ($) FY Close	P/E High/Low		PER SHARE ($) Earnings	Dividends	Book Value
12/18	27.73	25	16	1.69	2.30	4.35
12/17	37.16	28	20	1.72	2.02	4.85
12/16	42.35	30	13	1.53	1.71	4.79
12/15	36.29	167	77	0.39	1.40	4.85
12/14	60.23	64	37	1.02	1.04	5.76
Annual Growth	(17.6%)	—	—	13.5%	21.8%	(6.8%)

Western New England Bancorp Inc

EXECUTIVES

Vice President Retail Banking, Kevin O'Connor
AVP Residential Lending, Michael Laga
ASSISTANT VICE PRESIDENT FINANCIAL SERVICES, Libiszewski Darlene
Senior Vice President Of Retail Banking, Cidalia Inacio
Vice President Commercial Lender, Richard Hanchett
Vice President, Matthew Manganelli
Auditors: Wolf & Company, P.C.

LOCATIONS

HQ: Western New England Bancorp Inc
  141 Elm Street, Westfield, MA 01086
Phone: 413 568-1911
Web: www.westfieldbank.com

COMPETITORS

Bank of America
Citizens Financial Group
Sovereign Bank
TD Bank USA

HISTORICAL FINANCIALS
Company Type: Public

Income Statement   FYE: December 31

	ASSETS ($ mil.)	NET INCOME ($ mil.)	INCOME AS % OF ASSETS	EMPLOYEES
12/18	2,118.8	16.4	0.8%	320
12/17	2,083.0	12.3	0.6%	317
12/16	2,076.0	4.8	0.2%	310
12/15	1,339.9	5.7	0.4%	195
12/14	1,320.1	6.1	0.5%	200
Annual Growth	12.6%	27.7%	—	12.5%

2018 Year-End Financials
Return on assets: 0.7%
Return on equity: 6.7%
Long-term debt ($ mil.): —
No. of shares (mil.): 28.3
Sales ($ mil): 88.2
Dividends
  Yield: 1.5%
  Payout: 37.2%
Market value ($ mil.): 285.0

	STOCK PRICE ($) FY Close	P/E High/Low	PER SHARE ($) Earnings	Dividends	Book Value
12/18	10.04	20 16	0.57	0.16	8.35
12/17	10.90	27 22	0.41	0.12	8.11
12/16	9.35	38 30	0.24	0.03	7.85
12/15	8.40	25 22	0.33	0.12	7.63
12/14	7.34	23 20	0.34	0.21	7.61
Annual Growth	8.1%	—	13.8%	(6.6%)	2.3%

Wex Inc

WEX (formerly Wright Express) provides payment processing and information management services to commercial and government vehicle fleets through a network that tracks purchases made on fleet charge cards throughout the US Canada Australia New Zealand and Europe. The company provides clients with transaction data analysis tools and purchase control capabilities for every vehicle in their fleets. Data collected at the point of sale include expenditures lists of items purchased odometer readings and driver vehicle and vendor identification. Around 12.5 million vehicles use WEX for fleet management. The company also offers health and employee benefits payment platforms in Brazil and corporate purchasing and payment products.

Financial Performance
WEX's sales have climbed steadily in recent years rising more than 80% since 2014 driven by a growing customer base resulting from acquisitions and organic growth; higher gas prices in 2017 and 2018 also pushed up revenue. The company's net income has declined nearly 20% in the last five years: a near seven-fold jump in 2017 wasn't enough to bring the company back from major declines the previous two years when expense growth (particularly financing interest salary and other personnel and service fees) outpaced sales growth.

WEX's revenue increased 20% to $1.5 billion in 2018. Contributing factors included an 8% increase in average number of serviced vehicles an organic 7% addition in processed fuel transactions and an 18% rise in US gas prices.

The company's net income gained 5% to $168 million that year on the strength of its revenue.

WEX added $32.6 million to its cash on hand in 2018 to end the year with $555 million. Operations provided $400.2 million; investments (primarily acquisitions and property equipment and software purchases) used $254.2 million and financing activities (mainly repayments on its revolving credit facility) used $102.7 million. Exchange rates reduced stores a further $10.7 million.

Strategy
Aided by income from substantial organic growth WEX is expanding its business in recent years through frequent strategic acquisitions.

In 2019 WEX purchased Go Fuel Card the fuel card business of European fuel and convenience store company EG Group. The deal deepened WEX's reach in the Netherlands France Belgium and Luxembourg?where some 200000 Go Fuel cards are in circulation. The company also expanded its healthcare benefits account technology through its acquisition employee benefits administrator Discovery Benefits for $425 million. Furthermore WEX widened its corporate payments business when it bought the Noventis commercial electronic bill and invoice payment network which was already one of WEX's virtual payment card suppliers.

The year prior WEX began integrating Chevron's Chevron and Texaco Business Card customer portfolio into its own operations in a $223.4 million deal. The collaboration was originally announced in 2016 and extended in 2017 to cover Singapore Hong Kong Malaysia Thailand and the Philippines.

In 2017 WEX acquired AOC a commercial payments technology company. The transaction grew its customer base and enhanced its payment processing technology platforms.

EXECUTIVES
CTO, David Cooper
President CEO and Director, Melissa D. Smith, age 50, $578,317 total compensation
SVP General Counsel and Corporate Secretary, Hilary A. Rapkin, age 52, $362,884 total compensation
SVP International, George W. Hogan, age 58, $318,308 total compensation
SVP and General Manager North American Fleet, Kenneth W. (Ken) Janosick, age 57, $320,000 total compensation
CFO, Roberto R. Simon, age 44
SVP and General Manager Virtual Payments, Jim Pratt
SVP and General Manager WEX Health, Jeff Young
SVP and General Manager EFS, Scott Phillips
Vice President Global Sales Operations, Jason Hanley
Vice President Strategic Relations, Brian Fournier
Vice President Product Management (Acting), Wayne Arthur
Senior Vice President Sales Marketing, David Maxsiimc
Vice President Corporate Controller, Robin Sawyer
Global Vp Of Technology Wex Corporate Payments, Ryan Taylor
Vp Operations Strategy And Technology, Amy Dunckelmann
Vp and Business Manager, Kevin Thomson
Vice Chairman, Rowland T. (Row) Moriarty, age 72
Chairman, Michael E. Dubyak, age 68
Auditors: DELOITTE & TOUCHE LLP

LOCATIONS
HQ: Wex Inc
  1 Hancock Street, Portland, ME 04101
Phone: 207 773-8171
Web: www.wexinc.com

PRODUCTS/OPERATIONS
2018 Revenue

	$ mil.	% of total
Payment processing revenue	724.0	48
Account servicing revenue	308.1	21
Finance fee revenue	208.6	14
Other revenue	251.9	17
Total	1,492.6	100

COMPETITORS
Comdata   Retail Decisions
FleetCor   U.S. Bancorp
Multi Service

HISTORICAL FINANCIALS
Company Type: Public

Income Statement   FYE: December 31

	REVENUE ($ mil.)	NET INCOME ($ mil.)	NET PROFIT MARGIN	EMPLOYEES
12/18	1,492.6	168.3	11.3%	3,700
12/17	1,250.5	160.2	12.8%	3,300
12/16	1,018.4	60.6	6.0%	2,600
12/15	854.6	111.3	13.0%	2,265
12/14	817.6	202.2	24.7%	2,004
Annual Growth	16.2%	(4.5%)	—	16.6%

2018 Year-End Financials
Debt ratio: 34.7%
Return on equity: 9.6%
Cash ($ mil.): 541.5
Current ratio: 1.47
Long-term debt ($ mil.): 2,133.9
No. of shares (mil.): 43.1
Dividends
  Yield: —
  Payout: —
Market value ($ mil.): 6,041.0

	STOCK PRICE ($) FY Close	P/E High/Low	PER SHARE ($) Earnings	Dividends	Book Value
12/18	140.06	51 34	3.86	0.00	41.40
12/17	141.23	38 26	3.72	0.00	39.78
12/16	111.60	78 39	1.48	0.00	34.95
12/15	88.40	45 32	2.62	0.00	27.96
12/14	98.92	23 15	5.18	0.00	27.26
Annual Growth	9.1%	— —	(7.1%)	—	11.0%

Whitestone REIT

Whitestone REIT is out to make a name for itself in real estate. The self-managed real estate investment trust owns leases and operates around 70 retail office and warehouse properties in Texas (Houston is the company's largest market) Illinois and Arizona totaling 6 million sq. ft. Whitestone focuses on what it calls community-centered properties or high-visibility properties in established or developing culturally diverse neighborhoods. It recruits retail grocery financial services and other tenants to its Whitestone branded commercial centers. Some of its top tenants include Safeway Dollar Tree Wells Fargo Walgreens University of Phoenix and Alamo Drafthouse.

Geographic Reach
Whitestone REIT had 70 commercial properties in three states at the end of 2015 including 30 properties in Houston Texas and 25 properties in the Phoenix metro area of Arizona. The rest of its properties were located in Dallas-Fort Worth (7 properties) Austin Texas (4) San Antonio (3) and Buffalo grove near Chicago Illinois (1).

Sales and Marketing
The REIT's tenant base is made up of a diverse mix of mostly retail clients with some banks and university clients sprinkled in. While none of Whitestone's tenants contributed more than 2.6% to its total revenue during 2015 its five largest tenants by revenue for the year included: Safeway Stores Bashas' Inc. Haggens Food & Pharmacy Wells Fargo & Company and Alamo Drafthouse Cinema.

Financial Performance
Whitestone REIT has tripled its revenues and boosted its profits sixfold since 2011 mostly as it has expanded its property portfolio through acquisitions and has raised its average rent per square foot by more than 40%.

The REIT's revenue jumped 29% to $93.4 million during 2015 mostly thanks to 12 new property acquisitions made from January 2014 through the end of 2015. Its "Same Store" comparable sales for existing properties grew during the year as its revenue rate per average leased square foot rose 4% to $17.28 per foot. Occupancy rates dipped slightly but remained mostly around 87%.

Despite strong revenue growth in 2015 Whitestone REIT's net income shrank 11% to $6.75 million for the year mostly because in 2014 it generated a non-recurring $1.9 million gain from property sales. The REIT's operating cash levels climbed 44% to $36.1 million during 2015 as its cash-based earnings increased.

Strategy
Whitestone REIT's strategically acquires commercial properties in high growth markets with densely populated and culturally diverse neighborhoods in and around Austin Chicago Dallas-Fort-Worth Houston Phoenix and San Antonio.

During 2015 it targeted acquisitions of "neighborhood- or community- retail properties" near master planned communities such as Quinlan Crossing (for $37.5 million) and Parkside Village South ($32.5 million) in Austin Texas; a single-tenant 14600 sq. ft. property in Gilbert Tuscany Village ($1.7 million); and the 93500 sq. ft. Keller Place property in the Keller suburb of Ft. Worth Texas. In mid-2014 it added Heritage Trace Plaza in Fort Worth Texas to its portfolio. It acquired half a dozen or so properties in 2013 including Market Street at DC Ranch in Scottsdale Arizona and Headquarters Village Shopping Center in Plano Texas.

EXECUTIVES
Chairman and CEO, James C. Mastandrea, age 76, $400,000 total compensation
COO, John J. Dee, age 68, $205,289 total compensation
CFO, David K. Holeman, age 56, $250,000 total compensation
VP Acquisitions and Asset Management, Bradford D. Johnson, $184,616 total compensation

VP Product Strategy and Market Research, Christine J. Mastandrea, $154,231 total compensation
Auditors: Pannell Kerr Forster of Texas, P.C.

LOCATIONS
HQ: Whitestone REIT
2600 South Gessner, Suite 500, Houston, TX 77063
Phone: 713 827-9595   **Fax:** 713 465-8847
Web: www.whitestonereit.com

PRODUCTS/OPERATIONS

2015 Sales

	$ mil.	% of total
Rental	71.8	77
Other	21.6	23
Total	**93.4**	**100**

COMPETITORS
GGP   Simon Property Group
IRC Retail Centers   Weingarten Realty

HISTORICAL FINANCIALS
Company Type: Public

Income Statement   FYE: December 31

	REVENUE ($ mil.)	NET INCOME ($ mil.)	NET PROFIT MARGIN	EMPLOYEES
12/18	119.8	21.4	17.9%	98
12/17	125.9	8.3	6.6%	103
12/16	104.4	7.9	7.6%	106
12/15	93.4	6.7	7.2%	95
12/14	72.3	7.5	10.5%	81
Annual Growth	13.4%	29.6%	—	4.9%

2018 Year-End Financials
Debt ratio: 60.0%   No. of shares (mil.): 39.7
Return on equity: 6.1%   Dividends
Cash ($ mil.): 13.6   Yield: 9.3%
Current ratio: 0.96   Payout: 219.2%
Long-term debt ($ mil.): 618.2   Market value ($ mil.): 488.0

	STOCK PRICE ($) FY Close	P/E High/Low		PER SHARE ($) Earnings	Dividends	Book Value
12/18	12.26	27	19	0.52	1.14	8.81
12/17	14.41	68	51	0.22	1.14	9.14
12/16	14.38	62	38	0.26	1.24	9.08
12/15	12.01	65	44	0.24	1.14	9.00
12/14	15.11	47	40	0.32	1.14	9.20
Annual Growth	(5.1%)	—	—	12.9%	(0.0%)	(1.1%)

Willdan Group Inc

Willdan Group can and will do what it takes to meet its customers' numerous engineering needs. The company has four operating service segments: engineering (Willdan Engineering) energy efficiency (Willdan Energy Solutions) public finance (Willdan Financial Services) and homeland security (Willdan Homeland Solutions). Clients include federal and local governments school districts public utilities and some private industries. Willdan focuses on small- to mid-sized clients that may fall below the radar of larger competitors. The company was founded in 1964.

Operations
Willdan Group's engineering services which account for about a third of revenues are provided by subsidiaries Willdan Engineering and Public Agency Resources. Its public finance subsidiary Willdan Financial Services offers consulting services to municipalities and other public entities; its offerings include economic impact analyses facility financing plans and special district formation.

Willdan Energy Solutions provides energy efficiency and sustainability services to companies and agencies seeking to implement environmental strategies for conservation. (The high-growth business was split off from the engineering operations to its own segment in 2011.) Another subsidiary Willdan Homeland Solutions helps cities counties and communities protect infrastructure and personnel against terrorist attacks and natural disasters. The unit offers public safety consulting and management consulting services.

Geographic Reach
Willdan serves clients located predominantly in New York and California. Other locations reside in Arizona; Florida; Texas; Washington; and Washington DC.

Sales and Marketing
Willdan serves about 750 clients. Two clients — the Consolidated Edison Company of New York and the City of Elk Grove — accounted for 21% and 10% of its total revenue in 2012 respectively.

Financial Performance
After two straight years of revenue growth and positive net income Willdan saw its revenues decline by 13% from $107 million in 2011 to $93 million in 2012. It also posted a net loss of $17 million for 2012.

The revenue decline was driven by a 21% dip in its energy efficiency segment resulting from a decrease in the direct installation of energy efficiency measures in New York and California and contract renewal delays from those populous states. Willdan was also hurt by revenue decreases from its Willdan Homeland Solutions operations during 2012.

Its net loss for 2012 was due to higher general and administrative expenses associated with a $15 million goodwill impairment charge it paid related to its energy efficiency segment.

Strategy
Willdan Group looks for opportunities in areas that have increased demand for services as well as population growth which will place strain on existing infrastructure and prompt the need for new structures or the rehabilitation of aging systems. Additionally the company stands to benefit from the heightened need for homeland security as several of the markets it serves have received federal funding for preparedness initiatives.

Mergers and Acquisitions
Willdan Group agreed to acquire Onsite Energy Corporation in June 2019. The acquisition of Onsite an energy services company focused on industrial customers allows Willdan to expand its market.

EXECUTIVES
Vice President of Training and Exercises, Jim Bailey
Senior Vice President, Eric Woychik
Vice President, Adel Freij
Executive Vice President, Kim Early

Vice President Energy Project Development, Arthur Vertner
Vice President Of Operations, David Daniel
VICE PRESIDENT OF ENERGY PROJECT DEVELOPMENT, Chuck Spiker
Board Member, Arne Lovnaseth
Board Member, Tom D Brisbin
Auditors: Crowe LLP

LOCATIONS

HQ: Willdan Group Inc
2401 East Katella Avenue, Suite 300, Anaheim, CA 92806
Phone: 800 424-9144
Web: www.willdan.com

COMPETITORS

AECOM	Langdon Wilson
Bureau Veritas	Lime Energy
Ernst & Young LLP	Michael Baker
HDR	Parsons Brinckerhoff
Harley Ellis Devereaux	Psomas
ICF International	RBF Consulting
Jacobs Engineering	Stantec
Kimley-Horn and Associates	TRC Companies
	Tetra Tech

HISTORICAL FINANCIALS
Company Type: Public

Income Statement — FYE: December 28

	REVENUE ($ mil.)	NET INCOME ($ mil.)	NET PROFIT MARGIN	EMPLOYEES
12/18	272.2	10.0	3.7%	1,202
12/17	273.3	12.1	4.4%	882
12/16*	208.9	8.3	4.0%	831
01/16	135.1	4.2	3.2%	688
01/15	108.0	9.4	8.7%	637
Annual Growth	26.0%	1.6%	—	17.2%

*Fiscal year change

2018 Year-End Financials
Debt ratio: 23.9%   No. of shares (mil.): 10.9
Return on equity: 9.3%   Dividends
Cash ($ mil.): 15.2   Yield: —
Current ratio: 1.49   Payout: —
Long-term debt ($ mil.): 63.3   Market value ($ mil.): 373.0

	STOCK PRICE ($) FY Close	P/E High/Low		PER SHARE ($) Earnings	Dividends	Book Value
12/18	34.00	35	18	1.03	0.00	13.16
12/17	23.94	26	15	1.32	0.00	8.03
12/16*	22.59	26	7	0.97	0.00	5.98
01/16	8.38	30	15	0.52	0.00	4.76
01/15	14.50	15	4	1.22	0.00	3.98
Annual Growth	23.7%	—	—	(4.1%)	—	34.8%

*Fiscal year change

Willis Lease Finance Corp.

Hey buddy got any spare Pratt & Whitneys? Willis Lease Finance buys and sells aircraft engines that it leases to commercial airlines air cargo carriers and maintenance/repair/overhaul organizations in some 30 countries. Its portfolio includes about 180 aircraft engines and related equipment made by Pratt & Whitney Rolls-Royce CFMI GE Aviation and International Aero. The engine models in the company's portfolio are used on popular Airbus and Boeing aircraft. The Willis Lease portfolio also includes four de Havilland DHC-8 commuter aircraft. Customers include Island Air Alaska Airlines American Airlines and Southwest Airlines. Almost 80% of the company's engines are leased and operated outside the US.

Operations
The company divides its revenue streams across three segments. Lease rent accounted for 64% of its total sales in 2012 while maintenance reserve generated 28%. The gain of sale on leased equipment and other operations contribute the remainder of revenue.

Geographic Reach
Willis Lease has operations in Africa Asia Canada Europe Mexico the Middle East and the US. The majority of lease revenue comes from Europe (37% of total lease revenue in 2012) Asia (20%) the US (12%) and South America (10%).

Financial Performance
After experiencing revenue and profit increases in 2011 Willis Lease suffered a 6% drop in net revenue and a massive 90% nosedive in profits during 2012. From 2011 to 2012 its revenues dipped from $157 million to $148 million while its profits slipped from $14.5 million to $1.5 million.

The decrease in revenues was attributed a 10% decline in lease rent revenues. This slump reflected lower portfolio utilization in 2012 and a decrease in the average size of the lease portfolio (which translated into a lower amount of equipment on lease). In addition the lower revenue translated to a decrease on the sale of leased equipment which was $5 million in 2012 compared with $11 million in 2011.

The plunge in profits was mainly due to a $15 million loss stemming from the extinguish of debt and derivative instruments.

Strategy
Growth in the spare engine leasing industry is contingent on the number of commercial aircraft in the market and the proportion of leased versus owned engines. Willis Lease is on the flip-side of most companies during economic downturns because it offers cash-strapped businesses a more affordable route — to lease engines rather than buying or repairing them. The company explains that engine repairs can cost as much as $3 million while leasing an engine may cost only $80000.

With fluctuating fuel costs an airline can spend the difference between maintenance and leasing on the cost of fuel. Additionally industry experts estimate that approximately 36000 aircraft will be in flight in less than 20 years. Growth is expected in both established markets as well as emerging markets especially Asia which is showing extraordinary growth in both passenger and cargo traffic.

EXECUTIVES

Vice President Information Technology, Jennifer Torlone
Senior Vice President General Counsel Secretary, Dean Poulakidas
Auditors: KPMG LLP

LOCATIONS

HQ: Willis Lease Finance Corp.
4700 Lyons Technology Parkway, Coconut Creek, FL 33073
Phone: 561 349-9989
Web: www.willislease.com

COMPETITORS

AAR Corp.	ILFC
AerCap	Jetscape
AeroCentury	Kellstrom Industries
Boeing Capital	
GE Capital Aviation Services	

HISTORICAL FINANCIALS
Company Type: Public

Income Statement — FYE: December 31

	REVENUE ($ mil.)	NET INCOME ($ mil.)	NET PROFIT MARGIN	EMPLOYEES
12/18	348.3	43.2	12.4%	175
12/17	274.8	62.1	22.6%	155
12/16	207.2	14.0	6.8%	147
12/15	199.6	7.3	3.7%	104
12/14	174.2	7.2	4.2%	99
Annual Growth	18.9%	56.3%	—	15.3%

2018 Year-End Financials
Debt ratio: 69.1%   No. of shares (mil.): 6.1
Return on equity: 13.4%   Dividends
Cash ($ mil.): 11.6   Yield: —
Current ratio: 0.96   Payout: —
Long-term debt ($ mil.): 1,337.3   Market value ($ mil.): 214.0

	STOCK PRICE ($) FY Close	P/E High/Low		PER SHARE ($) Earnings	Dividends	Book Value
12/18	34.60	6	4	6.60	0.00	54.46
12/17	24.97	3	2	9.69	0.00	48.04
12/16	25.58	13	8	2.05	0.00	33.74
12/15	20.10	23	16	0.92	0.00	27.86
12/14	21.90	27	18	0.89	0.00	25.98
Annual Growth	12.1%	—	—	65.0%	—	20.3%

Wilson Bank Holding Co.

EXECUTIVES

Chairman; Chairman Of The Board, John Freeman
Vice President and Loan Officer Carthage, Lisa Gregory
Vice President and Marketing Director Main Office, Rebecca Jennings
Vice President and Loan Officer Smithville, Chad Colwell
Auditors: Maggart & Associates, P.C.

LOCATIONS

HQ: Wilson Bank Holding Co.
623 West Main Street, Lebanon, TN 37087
Phone: 615 444-2265
Web: www.wilsonbank.com

HISTORICAL FINANCIALS
Company Type: Public

Income Statement
FYE: December 31

	ASSETS ($ mil.)	NET INCOME ($ mil.)	INCOME AS % OF ASSETS	EMPLOYEES
12/18	2,543.6	32.5	1.3%	487
12/17	2,317.0	23.5	1.0%	471
12/16	2,198.0	25.6	1.2%	444
12/15	2,021.6	23.8	1.2%	446
12/14	1,873.2	20.7	1.1%	406
Annual Growth	7.9%	11.9%	—	4.7%

2018 Year-End Financials
Return on assets: 1.3%
Return on equity: 11.5%
Long-term debt ($ mil.): —
No. of shares (mil.): 10.6
Sales ($ mil): 128.7
Dividends
Yield: —
Payout: 29.2%
Market value ($ mil.): —

Wingstop Inc

Auditors: KPMG LLP

LOCATIONS
HQ: Wingstop Inc
5501 LBJ Freeway, 5th Floor, Dallas, TX 75240
Phone: 972 686-6500
Web: www.wingstop.com

HISTORICAL FINANCIALS
Company Type: Public

Income Statement
FYE: December 29

	REVENUE ($ mil.)	NET INCOME ($ mil.)	NET PROFIT MARGIN	EMPLOYEES
12/18	153.1	21.7	14.2%	661
12/17	105.5	27.3	25.9%	530
12/16	91.3	15.4	16.9%	479
12/15	77.9	10.1	13.0%	428
12/14	67.4	8.9	13.3%	366
Annual Growth	22.8%	24.7%	—	15.9%

2018 Year-End Financials
Debt ratio: 223.1%
Return on equity: —
Cash ($ mil.): 12.4
Current ratio: 1.13
Long-term debt ($ mil.): 309.3
No. of shares (mil.): 29.3
Dividends
Yield: 0.1%
Payout: 895.8%
Market value ($ mil.): 1,894.0

	STOCK PRICE ($) FY Close	P/E High/Low		PER SHARE ($) Earnings	Dividends	Book Value
12/18	64.64	100	53	0.73	6.54	(7.67)
12/17	38.98	45	27	0.93	0.14	(1.66)
12/16	29.59	61	39	0.53	2.90	(2.60)
12/15	22.56	95	55	0.36	1.83	(0.34)
Annual Growth	42.0%	—	—	26.6%	52.9%	—

Winnebago Industries, Inc.

A pioneer in the world of recreational vehicles Winnebago Industries makes products intended to encourage exploration. Almost all the company's sales come from its motor homes and towables which are sold via independent dealers throughout the US and Canada under brands including Winnebago Adventurer Sightseer Grand Design and Minnie Winnie. Winnebago Industries also sells RV parts and provides related services. The company also builds custom specialty vehicles for uses including mobile law enforcement command centers and mobile medical units. In 2018 Winnebago purchased Chris-Craft a manufacturer of recreational power boats. More than 90% of the company's sales are in the US. Winnebago traces its roots back to the 1950s.

Operations
Winnebago's towable offerings (56% of sales) are comprised of travel trailers (which hook up to a hitch on the vehicle's frame) and fifth wheels (which attach to the vehicle with a special fifth wheel hitch). The company's motor homes portfolio (43% of sales) includes three main product lines: Class A (conventional motor homes) Class B (panel-type vans) and Class C (motor homes built on van-type chassis). Specialty vehicles and Chris-Craft boats account for about 1% of sales.

Geographic Reach
Winnebago is based in Forest City Iowa. It owns facilities in Middlebury Forest City Lake Mills Charles City and Waverly Iowa; Junction City Oregon; Middlebury Indiana; and Sarasota Florida.

Sales and Marketing
The company markets its RVs on a wholesale basis to a diversified independent dealer network located throughout the US and to a limited extent in Canada Africa Asia Europe Australia and South America. The RV dealer network in the US and Canada includes about 550 motorized and towable physical dealer locations with some 75 of these locations carrying both Winnebago motorized and towable products. La Mesa RV Center with 11 dealer locations accounted for 10% of Winnebago's total revenue in fiscal 2018.

Financial Performance
Excepting fiscal 2016 when Winnebago's revenue growth was flat the company has seen steady growth over the last five years. Between 2014 and 2018 revenue more than doubled. Growth has been driven by increased demand for towable products and the acquisition of Grand Design.

Sales increased more than 30% to $2.0 billion in fiscal 2018 compared to $1.5 billion the prior year. Revenues for the towable segment saw the strongest growth with a rise of nearly 65% in fiscal 2018. Towable growth was spurred by organic demand as well as the addition of the Grand Design brand. Motorhome sales growth was subdued growing just under 1% in fiscal 2018.

Winnebago's net income rose 44% to 102.4 million in fiscal 2018 mainly due to higher sales in the towable segment and reduced tax liability.

The company's cash and equivalents stood at $2.3 million at the end of fiscal 2018 compared to $35.9 million the year before. Cash from operations contributed $83.3 million to the coffers while investing activities used $111.8 million mainly for the Chris-Craft acquisition and for capital expenditures to expand manufacturing capacity in the towable segment. Financing activities used $5.2 million primarily for payments on the credit agreement used to finance the Grand Design acquisition stock repurchases and shareholder dividends.

Strategy
Winnebago is focused on expanding the company's product offerings particularly in the fast-growing towable product segment. To that end late in 2016 the company bought Grand Design a manufacturer of towable RVs for about $500 million in cash and Winnebago shares. In 2018 the company acquired Chris-Craft which expanded Winnebago's offerings to include recreational power boats.

The company is also working to build more technology into its products. In 2019 Winnebago formed a new Advanced Technology Group which will work with each of the company's business segments to identify develop and commercialize emerging technologies. Initial efforts of the Advanced Technology Group will be to increase electrification and connectivity of Winnebago's products and use data gathered from products to enhance customer experience.

Mergers and Acquisitions
In 2019 Winnebago agreed to acquire fellow RV manufacturer Newmar Corporation for about $344 million. The addition of Newmar will increase Winnebago's offerings in the Class A and Super C motorized RV categories and supports Winnebago's efforts to grow its line-up of motorized RV products.

Company Background
During a mid-1950s economic downturn furniture store owner John Hanson convinced Forest City officials to welcome a local subsidiary of California trailer maker Modernistic Industries. The company's first trailer rolled off the line in 1958. Hanson later bought the plant and in 1960 named the business Winnebago Industries after Forest City's home county. Winnebago Industries went public in 1966. Sales took off when the company offered less-expensive RVs than its competitors.

EXECUTIVES
President and CEO, Michael J. Happe, age 48, $338,461 total compensation
VP; President Grand Design RV, Donald J. Clark
VP; General Manager Towables Business, S. Scott Degnan, age 54, $309,614 total compensation
VP Information Technology and CIO, Jeff Kubacki, age 62
VP; General Manager Motorhome Business, Brian Hazelton, age 54
VP and CFO, Bryan Hughes, age 51
VP Operations, Chris West, age 47
V Pres Mfg, Daryl W Krieger
Vice President Strategic Planning and Development, Ashis Bhattacharya
VICE PRESIDENT ADMINISTRATION, Bret A Woodson
Vice President General Manager Towables Business, S Scott Degnan
Vice President and General Manager Towables Business, Steven Degnan
Chairman, Robert M. (Bob) Chiusano, age 68
Board Member, William Fisher
Auditors: DELOITTE & TOUCHE LLP

LOCATIONS

HQ: Winnebago Industries, Inc.
P.O. Box 152, Forest City, IA 50436
Phone: 641 585-3535   Fax: 641 585-6966
Web: www.winnebagoind.com

PRODUCTS/OPERATIONS

2016 Sales

	$ mil.	% of total
Motorhomes parts and service	875.0	90
Towables and parts	89.4	9
Other manufactured products	10.8	1
Total	975.2	100

Selected Products

ERA
  ERA
Itasca
  Cambria
  Ellipse
  Impulse
  Impulse Silver
  Meridian
  Meridian V Class
  Navion
  Navion IQ
  Reyo
  Suncruiser
  Sunova
  Sunstar
Winnebago
  Access
  Access Premier
  Adventurer
  Aspect
  Journey
  Journey Express
  Sightseer
  Tour
  Via
  View
  View Profile
  Vista

COMPETITORS

Airstream
Elixir Industries
Featherlite
Forest River
Gulf Stream Coach
Jayco Inc.
Keystone RV
Motor Coach Industries
Newmar Corporation
Patrick Industries
Prevost Car
Rexhall Industries
Skyline
Supreme Industries
TRIGANO
Thor Industries
Tiffin Motorhomes

HISTORICAL FINANCIALS

Company Type: Public

Income Statement
FYE: August 31

	REVENUE ($ mil.)	NET INCOME ($ mil.)	NET PROFIT MARGIN	EMPLOYEES
08/19	1,985.6	111.8	5.6%	4,500
08/18	2,016.8	102.3	5.1%	4,700
08/17	1,547.1	71.3	4.6%	4,060
08/16	975.2	45.5	4.7%	3,050
08/15	976.5	41.2	4.2%	2,900
Annual Growth	19.4%	28.3%	—	11.6%

2019 Year-End Financials

Debt ratio: 23.0%
Return on equity: 18.8%
Cash ($ mil.): 37.4
Current ratio: 2.08
Long-term debt ($ mil.): 245.4
No. of shares (mil.): 31.5
Dividends
  Yield: 0.0%
  Payout: 12.2%
Market value ($ mil.): 1,009.0

Stock Price / Per Share

	STOCK PRICE ($) FY Close	P/E High/Low		PER SHARE ($) Earnings	Dividends	Book Value
08/19	32.02	11	6	3.52	0.43	20.06
08/18	37.30	18	11	3.22	0.40	16.95
08/17	34.55	16	9	2.32	0.40	13.98
08/16	23.91	14	10	1.68	0.40	9.98
08/15	20.42	17	12	1.52	0.36	8.20
Annual Growth	11.9%	—	—	23.4%	4.5%	25.1%

Wintrust Financial Corp (IL)

Wintrust Financial is a holding company for 15 subsidiary banks (mostly named after the individual communities they serve) with more than 150 branches primarily in the metropolitan Chicago and southern Wisconsin (including Milwaukee) markets. Boasting assets of more than $23 billion the banks offer personal and commercial banking wealth management and specialty lending services with business and commercial real estate loans making up 60% of the company's loan portfolio. Wintrust's banks target small business customers though some of Wintrust's banks also provide niche lending for homeowners associations medical practices franchisees and municipalities.

Operations

Wintrust operates three business segments: Community Banking which accounted for 77% of total revenue in 2015 and serves individuals and small businesses; Specialty Finance (13% of revenue) operating through First Insurance Funding and First Insurance Funding of Canada which provide financing for commercial insurance and life insurance premiums in the US and Canada respectively; and Wealth Management (10% of revenue) which offers financial planning and brokerage services through The Chicago Trust Company N.A. Wayne Hummer Investments LLC and Great Lakes Advisors LLC.

Wintrust makes more than 70% of its revenue from interest income. About 66% of its total revenue came from loan interest (including fees) during 2015 while another 6% came from interest on investment securities. The rest of its revenue came from mortgage banking (12%) wealth management services (7%) deposit account service charges (3%) and other miscellaneous income sources.

Geographic Reach

Wintrust's banks operate more than 150 branches and 220-plus automatic teller machines mostly located in communities throughout the Chicago metropolitan area and southern Wisconsin. Its wealth management offices are in Chicago; Appleton Wisconsin; and Safety Harbor Florida. Its Wintrust Mortgage subsidiary has 55 locations in a dozen states while its insurance subsidiaries have locations in Northbrook Illinois; Jersey City; Long Island New York; Toronto; Mississauga Ontario; and Vancouver.

Sales and Marketing

The bank's customers include individuals small to mid-sized businesses local governmental units and institutional clients residing primarily in the banks' local service areas.

Wintrust has been ramping up its advertising spend in recent years. It spent $21.9 million on advertising during 2015 up from $13.6 million and $11.1 million in 2014 and 2013 respectively.

Financial Performance

Wintrust Financial's annual revenues have risen more than 40% since 2011 as its loan assets have swelled by nearly 70% with rapid branch expansion. Its annual profits have doubled over the same period.

The banking group's revenue jumped 12% to $990.1 million during 2015 mostly as its average loan balances grew by 15% for the year. Mortgage banking revenue increased 26% for the year thanks to higher origination volumes and purchases on a more favorable mortgage banking environment also helping buoy the company's top-line growth.

Strong revenue growth in 2015 drove Wintrust's net income up 4% to $156.75 million despite a rise in acquisition-related professional and legal fees. The group's operating cash levels fell 82% to $37.95 million due to unfavorable working capital changes mainly tied to an increase in accrued interest receivable and other assets.

Strategy

Wintrust has developed its community-based banking franchise through rapid branch expansion stemming from either through new openings or small bank acquisitions. Indeed the bank's branch count has flourished by more than 50% since 2011 from 99 back then to 152 branches at the end of 2015.

Beyond branch expansion the company remains focused on making new loans especially of the commercial and commercial real estate type where opportunities that meet its underwriting standards exist.

Mergers and Acquisitions

In January 2016 Wintrust Financial expanded into Pewaukee Wisconsin after agreeing to buy Generations Bancorp and its Foundations Bank subsidiary. Later that year the company finalized the $33.5 million purchase of First Community Financial Corporation the holding company of First Community Bank (which operates two branches in Elgin Illinois).

In July 2015 the company purchased Community Financial Shares Inc. and its four Community Bank of Wheaton/Glen Ellyn bank branches in the respective communities they serve in Illinois for a total of $42.4 million.

Also in July 2015 the company bought $118 million-asset North Bank and its two branches in Chicago.

In April 2015 Wintrust acquired Suburban Illinois Bancorp and its 10 Suburban Bank & Trust Company (SBT) branches in Chicago and surrounding suburbs for $12.5 million. The SBT locations would operate under Wintrust's Hinsdale Bank & Trust Company subsidiary.

In January 2015 the bank group purchased $224 million-asset Delavan Bancshares Inc. and its Community Bank CBD subsidiary.

Company Background

In 2012 Wintrust expanded its premium funding business into Canada with the acquisition of Macquarie Premium Funding Inc which was a subsidiary of Macquarie Group. The deal marked Wintrust's first international venture.

EXECUTIVES

EVP Technology; President Wintrust Information Technology Services, Lloyd M. Bowden, age 66, $167,333 total compensation
EVP CFO Secretary and Treasurer, David A. Dykstra, age 59, $759,167 total compensation
President CEO and Director, Edward J. Wehmer, age 64, $1,100,000 total compensation
EVP and Regional Market Head, Frank J. Burke
EVP and Chief Credit Officer, Richard B. Murphy, age 60, $509,167 total compensation
EVP and Chief Administration Officer, Leona A. Gleason
SVP Finance, David L. Stoehr, age 60, $419,167 total compensation
EVP and Regional Market Head, Timothy S. (Tim) Crane, age 57
EVP Wealth Management, Thomas P. (Tom) Zidar
EVP General Counsel and Secretary, Lisa J. Pattis, $446,167 total compensation
EVP and Regional Market Head, David L. Larson
EVP and COO Wintrust Commercial Finance (WCF), Joseph F. Thompson
Vice President Compliance, Kellie Oostendorp
Group Vp; Treasury Management Sales, Sarah Grooms
Executive Vice President, Ursula Moncau
Vice President Bsa Officer, Kathleen Franklin
Senior Vice President Middle Market, Dave Killpack
Vice President Managed Assets Division, Sandy Durek
Vice President Loan Operations, Sharon Hiller
Vice President Managed Assets Division, Irene Calzadilla
Vice President, Philip Sheridan
Senior Vice President Finance Credit Reporting, Mario Nudo
Senior Vice President Commercial Lender, Gregory Pinter
Avp Treasury Management, Judy Majon
Assistant Vice President Financial System Management, Marty Lavin
Avp Middle Market Treasury Management Sales, Lauren Hess
Vice President, Mary Koehler
Senior Vice President, Rhonda Pokoj
Vice President Marketing, Todd Younger
Vice President Wealth Services, Anna Fedus
Vice President Commercial Banking, Roy Gibson
Vice President Compliance, Christine Wujek
Assistant Vice President, Robert Murphy
Vice President, Sarah Withrow
Vice President Real Estate Services, Trey Meers
Vice President Commercial Banking, Jason Girardin
Senior Vice President, Darragh Griffin
Senior Vice President Planning, Scott Ernsteen
Senior Vice President Commercial Real Estate, Nick Cannon
Senior Vice President, George Reimnitz
Vice President Operations, Colleen Toft
Vice President, Joseph Ach
Senior Vice President Commercial Banking, Sean Dunn
Vice President, Sara Staniszewski
Vice President Commercial Banking, Michael Roman
Senior Vice President, Ryan Witte
Senior Vice President, William Robin
Vice President, Jon Swanson
Assistant Vice President Investments, Scott Weichle
Vice President Regulatory Reporting, Anita Chakravarthy
Assistant Vice President Commercial Real Estate, Kim Curschman
Senior Vice President Investments, David Galvan
Vice President Fair Lending Officer, Teresa Handley
Assistant Vice President Branch Management, Rick Butterly
Vice President, Caroline Gonos
Vice President Commercial Real Estate, Zornitsa Titova
Assistant Vice President, Todd Shifrin
Vice President Managed Assets Division, Hany Morsy
Vice President Human Resources, Janet Huffman
Vice President Marketing, Wendy Schenker
Assistant Vice President, Jeffrey Eversden
Vice President Assistant Counsel Litigation, Cindy Stuyvesant
Vice President Finance Regulatory Reporting, James Oranga
Executive Vice President and Chief Credit Officer, Paul Hallauer
Vice President Operations Manager Private Banker, Nicole Cox
Executive Vice President, Matthew Doucet
Vice President, Paul Varga
Executive Vice President, Christine Smith
Assistant Vice President, Darren Jamriska
Senior Vice President, Anish Saran
Senior Vice President Commercial Loan Review Manager, Cindy Bauer
Vice President, Nick Koricanac
Vice President Operations, Susan Puraleski
Vice President Loan Operations, Racquel Clemente
Vice President Assistant Controller, Dana French
Senior Vice President Sales, Steve Cusick
Vice President Executive, Sharon Moeller
Assistant Vice President Commercial Product Manager, Karon Gater
Assistant Vice President Retail Digital Product Manager, Natalie Fedus
Vice President, Jeffery Wolinski
Vice President Operations, Lisa Johnson
Vice President Credit, Juan Cabrera
Senior Vice President Information Services, Mike Nathan
Vice President Finance, Derek Ramsden
Assistant Vice President, Katie Cagney
Assistant Vice President Branch Manager, Anthony Scott
Senior Vice President, Joe Gensor
Senior Vice President Sales, Tom Forbes
Vice President, Kim Endsley
Vice President, Sharon Sagert
Vice President Risk, Tim Doran
Senior Vice President Treasury Management, Chris Lantman
Senior Vice President, Brian de la Houssaye
Assistant Vice President, Edward Semik
Vice President of Operations Wintrust Commercial Finance, Lisa McNeme
Vice President Business Banking, Chris Dana
Senior Vice President Commercial Real Estate, Daniel Lawlor
Assistant Vice President, Richard Eber
Vice President Construction And Engineering Division, Chris Vantassel
Senior Vice President Commercial Real Estate, Joe Nitti
Senior Vice President Risk, Evan Bossard
Vice President Government Nonprofit Healthcare Lender, Erinn Siegel
Vp Eft Services, Crystal Tabar
Vice President Commercial Banking, Christopher Sobey
Assistant Vice President, Dhaval Gandhi
Vice President, Tara Fedorko
Vice President, Rafiq Harris
Senior Vice President, Dawn Mase
Vice President Business Lending, Katie Moore
Assistant Vice President Commercial Real Estate, Lauren Barnard
Senior Vice President, Tom Carlson
Vice President Senior Commercial Underwriter, Sean Little
Vice President of Marketing, Jennifer Bohnen
Senior Vice President Of Operations, Anna Jimenez
Senior Vice President Operations, Stephen Milota
Assistant Vice President Bsa Compliance, Amber Schoenauer
Senior Vice President Of Commercial Banking, Lena Dawson
Vice President, Timmer John
Vice President Capital Markets, Clark Brian
Avp Eeo Compliance, Mary Rivers
Svp, Joseph Gregoire
Vp Senior Manager, Joseph White
Vice President, Rob Lewis
Vp New Business Development Wintrust Commercial Finance Irvine, Robert Harris
Assistant Vice President Learning And Development, Douglas Campbell
Assistant Vice President Marketing Commercial Banking, Kim Nagy
Vp Reconciliation Manager, Catherine Costanza
Vice President, Laura Sepulveda
Vice President Risk, Thomas Benkoske
Senior Vice President Commercial Banking, Vishal Patel
Vice President, Patrice Louis
Vice President Risk Management, Shipra Sethi
Vice President And Audit Manager, Paul Beierwaltes
Assistant Vice President Consumer Loan Documentation Manager, Christy Niemietz
Vice President And Assistant General Counsel, Erik Hsu
Assistant Vice President Default Servicing, Paul Hennessy
Senior Vice President, Ronald Calandra
Senior Vice President Of Finance, Daniel Tuerk
Senior Vice President Wealth Services, Kendra L Castelloni
Vice President Human Resources, Norah Larke Mba
Avp Fair Lending, Matt Sabatino
Senior Vice President, Brad Schotanus
Group Senior Vice President, Glenn Margraff
Vice President Vice Retail Branch Manager, Agnes Lyko
Vice President Cashier controller, Lynn Dohnalik
Senior Vice President, Nicholas Begley
Vice President Business Banking, Sean Daly
Vice President, Tom Groth
Assistant Vice President Commercial Banking, Benjamin Johnson
Vice President Commercial Real Estate, John Koranda
Senior Vice President Managing Director, Richard Howard
Vp and Director Enterprise Risk Management, Jennifer Lamalfa
Vice President Consolidated Deposit Operations, Debbie Szmurlo
Svp Sr Mortgage Risk Officer, Kevin Stanley
Vice President, Eric Gross
Senior Vice President, Joel Gordon
Chairman, Peter D. Crist, age 68
Board Member, Michele Murphy
Auditors: Ernst & Young LLP

LOCATIONS

HQ: Wintrust Financial Corp (IL)
9700 W. Higgins Road, Suite 800, Rosemont, IL 60018
Phone: 847 939-9000   Fax: 847 615-4091
Web: www.wintrust.com

PRODUCTS/OPERATIONS

2015 Sales

	$ mil.	% of total
Interest		
Loans including fees	651.8	66
Securities	61.0	6
Other	5.6	-
Non-interest		
Mortgage banking	115.0	12
Wealth management	73.5	7
Service charges on deposit accounts	27.4	3
Fees from covered call options	15.4	2
Other	40.6	4
Trading (losses) gains net	(0.2)	-
Total	**990.1**	**100**

Selected Subsidiaries and Affiliates

Banking
 Barrington Bank & Trust Company N.A.
 Beverly Bank & Trust Company N.A.
 Crystal Lake Bank & Trust Company N.A.
 Hinsdale Bank & Trust Company
 Lake Forest Bank & Trust Company
 Libertyville Bank & Trust Company
 North Shore Community Bank & Trust Company
 Northbrook Bank & Trust Company
 Old Plank Trail Community Bank N.A.
 Schaumburg Bank & Trust Company N.A.
 St. Charles Bank & Trust
 State Bank of The Lakes
 Town Bank
 Village Bank & Trust
 Wheaton Bank and Trust Company
Non-banking
 Chicago Trust Company N.A.
 First Insurance Funding Corporation
 Great Lakes Advisors LLC
 Tricom Inc. of Milwaukee
 Wayne Hummer Asset Management Company
 Wayne Hummer Investments LLC
 Wayne Hummer Trust Company N.A.
 Wintrust Information Technology Services Company
 Wintrust Mortgage Corporation (formerly WestAmerica Mortgage Company)

COMPETITORS

Associated Banc-Corp
Bank of America
Citigroup
Citizens Financial Group
Fifth Third
First Midwest Bancorp
Harris
JPMorgan Chase
MB Financial
Northern Trust
PrivateBank
U.S. Bancorp

HISTORICAL FINANCIALS

Company Type: Public

Income Statement   FYE: December 31

	ASSETS ($ mil.)	NET INCOME ($ mil.)	INCOME AS % OF ASSETS	EMPLOYEES
12/18	31,244.8	343.1	1.1%	4,727
12/17	27,915.9	257.6	0.9%	4,075
12/16	25,668.5	206.8	0.8%	3,878
12/15	22,917.1	156.7	0.7%	3,770
12/14	20,010.7	151.4	0.8%	3,491
Annual Growth	11.8%	22.7%	—	7.9%

2018 Year-End Financials

Return on assets: 1.1%
Return on equity: 10.9%
Long-term debt ($ mil.): —
No. of shares (mil.): 56.4
Sales ($ mil.): 1,526.9
Dividends
Yield: 1.1%
Payout: 13.4%
Market value ($ mil.): 3,751.0

	STOCK PRICE ($) FY Close	P/E High/Low		PER SHARE ($) Earnings	Dividends	Book Value
12/18	66.49	16	11	5.86	0.76	57.93
12/17	82.37	19	14	4.40	0.56	53.19
12/16	72.57	19	10	3.66	0.48	51.96
12/15	48.52	18	14	2.93	0.44	48.62
12/14	46.76	16	14	2.98	0.40	44.22
Annual Growth	9.2%	—	—	18.4%	17.4%	7.0%

WisdomTree Investments, Inc.

Asset management firm WisdomTree Investments specializes in exchange-traded funds (ETFs). (ETFs are funds that track indexes such as the S&P 500 or DJIA.) Through subsidiaries WisdomTree Trust and WisdomTree Asset Management the company manages more than 90 ETFs that invest in domestic and international equities currencies fixed-income and alternatives. It provides an alternative to funds weighted by market capitalization by focusing on fundamentals such as earnings dividends and industry. Serving both individual and institutional investors fast-growing WisdomTree Investments has about $46 billion in ETF assets under management about 65% of which are tied to international hedged equities (as of early 2016).

Operations

The asset manager makes almost all of its income from ETF advisory fees which are tied to managed assets. About 60% of the company's assets under management (AUM) and 60% of revenues in 2015 were tied to two of its US listed ETFs: WisdomTree Europe Hedged Equity Fund (HEDJ) and WisdomTree Japan Hedged Equity Fund (DXJ).

Sales and Marketing

The firm distributes its ETFs through all major channels within the asset management industry including registered investment advisers wirehouses institutional investors private wealth managers and discount brokers. The firm features its research through its professional sales force online through its websitevia targeted emails to financial advisers and financial media outlets such as Barron's Pensions & Investments Investor's Business Daily CNBC and Bloomberg.

WisdomTree increased its advertising and marketing spend by 16% to $13.37 million in 2015 versus 2014 as it boosted television print and online advertising support.

Financial Performance

Thanks to rising financial markets and a growing investor base driven by the popularity of ETFs WisdomTree has more than tripled its assets under management (AUM) since 2011 — from $12.2 billion to $51.6 billion at the end of 2015 — which has led strong fee and advisory income growth over the past several years. Its revenues have more than quadrupled over that period while its profits have grown more than 26-fold.

WisdomTree's revenue spiked 63% to $298.94 million during 2015 as its AUM balances rose more than 30% mostly on higher inflows from new customer business.

Strong revenue growth in 2015 drove the asset manager's net income up 31% to $80 million. The company's operating cash levels climbed 88% to $155 million as its cash-based operating revenue rose during the year.

Strategy

WisdomTree is banking on the continued growing popularity of ETFs around the world to grow its asset-based business. While ETFs have been around since the early 1980s their low fees have made them increasingly popular to investors over the past decade.

This factor combined with appreciating financial markets have boosted WisdomTree's assets under management from just shy of $10 billion at the end of 2010 to $51.6 billion in at the end of 2015. Its ETF annual net inflows from investors have also skyrocketed from $3.1 billion to $16.9 billion over the same period. Overall as of early 2016 fast-growing WisdomTree ranked as the fifth-largest US ETF sponsor with an 8% inflow market share (up from the 11th largest in 2009).

The asset manager regularly adds to its ETF offerings and expands its global distribution network (on its own through partnerships or by acquiring smaller asset managers) to attract new investors and their capital. The company also relies on strong investment performance from its teams to ensure its customers keep coming back.

Mergers and Acquisitions

In January 2016 WisdomTree expanded its commodity-based fund offerings after acquiring GreenHaven Commodity Services LLC — along with its GreenHaven Continuous Commodity Index Fund and GreenHaven Coal Services LLC and GreenHaven Coal Fund (to be rebranded as The WisdomTree Continuous Commodity Index Fund (GCC) and the WisdomTree Coal Fund (TONS) respectively) — for $12 million.

In April 2014 the firm expanded its distribution network in Europe after acquiring a 75% majority investment in UK-based exchange-traded product (ETP) provider Boost ETP LLP. The provider was renamed WisdomTree Europe and lists 12 branded UCITS ETFs on the London Stock Exchange and other prominent exchanges across Europe. WisdomTree will acquire the remaining 25% stake in Boost by March 31 2018.

HISTORY

The son of onetime corporate raider Saul Steinberg Jonathan Steinberg won The Wall Street Journal 's investing contest multiple times while still in his 20s. He founded Financial Data Systems in 1985 and bought The Penny Stock Journal in 1988.

The company launched the Special Situations Report newsletter in 1989; the following year The Penny Stock Journal became Individual Investor. Financial Data Systems went public in 1991 and adopted the Individual Investor Group moniker in 1993. It branched into hedge funds in 1994 by creating Wisdom Tree fund.

In 1996 Individual Investor introduced Ticker magazine. It launched the Individual Investor Web site the next year. In 1998 Individual Investor dissolved the ailing Wisdom Tree hedge fund and bought InsiderTrader.com. It took a stake in VentureHighway.com in 1999.

With its financial picture looking bleak the company took minority stakes in ReverseAuction.com and Tradeworx.com in exchange for advertising in 2000. Later that year the company engaged investment banking firm The Jordan Edmiston Group to find alternatives for buttressing its drooping financial position. It also sold the Insider-Trader.com Web site to Edgar Online. In 2001 Individual Investor cut its staff by 20% and was delisted from the Nasdaq exchange. Later that year the company closed Individual Investor. The company then merged its Web site with the WallStreetCity.com site owned by INVESTools (now thinkorswim). In 2002 the company changed its name to Index Development Partners and sold its print division including its newsletter Special Situations Report .

In 2005 the company changed its name to WisdomTree Investments and reinvented itself.

EXECUTIVES

CIO, A. David Yates
CEO and President, Jonathan L. (Jono) Steinberg, $230,000 total compensation
EVP Business and Legal Affairs and Chief Legal Officer, Peter M. Ziemba
EVP Finance and CFO, Amit Muni
EVP Operations and COO, Gregory Barton
EVP Head Sales and Chief Investment Strategist, Luciano Siracusano
CEO WisdomTree Japan K.K., Jesper Koll
Chairman, Michael H. Steinhardt
Vice Chairman, Bruce Lavine
Auditors: Ernst & Young LLP

LOCATIONS

HQ: WisdomTree Investments, Inc.
245 Park Avenue, 35th Floor, New York, NY 10167
Phone: 212 801-2080
Web: www.wisdomtree.com

PRODUCTS/OPERATIONS

Selected Products
U.S. Listed Products
Alternative Strategy ETFs
Commodity ETFs
Currency ETFs
Equity ETFs
Fixed Income ETFs
International Hedged Equity ETFs
Non-U.S. Listed Products
Boost Short and Leveraged ETPs
WisdomTree UCITS ETFs

COMPETITORS

American Century	Legg Mason
BlackRock	MassMutual
E*TRADE Financial	Putnam
FMR	T. Rowe Price
Franklin Templeton	TD Ameritrade
Invesco	The Vanguard Group

HISTORICAL FINANCIALS
Company Type: Public

Income Statement — FYE: December 31

	REVENUE ($ mil.)	NET INCOME ($ mil.)	NET PROFIT MARGIN	EMPLOYEES
12/18	274.1	36.6	13.4%	228
12/17	237.4	27.2	11.5%	204
12/16	219.4	26.1	11.9%	209
12/15	298.9	80.0	26.8%	177
12/14	183.7	61.0	33.2%	124
Annual Growth	10.5%	(12.0%)	—	16.4%

2018 Year-End Financials

Debt ratio: 20.7%
Return on equity: 10.7%
Cash ($ mil.): 77.7
Current ratio: 1.88
Long-term debt ($ mil.): 194.5
No. of shares (mil.): 153.2
Dividends
 Yield: 1.8%
 Payout: 40.0%
Market value ($ mil.): 1,019.0

	STOCK PRICE ($) FY Close	P/E High/Low		PER SHARE ($) Earnings	Dividends	Book Value
12/18	6.65	58	27	0.23	0.12	3.20
12/17	12.55	63	41	0.20	0.32	1.41
12/16	11.14	83	44	0.19	0.32	1.48
12/15	15.68	45	25	0.58	0.57	1.71
12/14	15.68	40	21	0.44	0.08	1.38
Annual Growth	(19.3%)	—	—	(15.0%)	10.7%	23.4%

World Wrestling Entertainment Inc

The action might be fake but the business of World Wrestling Entertainment (WWE) is very real. The company is a leading producer and promoter of wrestling matches for TV and live audiences exhibiting more than 350 matches each year across the globe. Its WWE Network available on a variety of digital streaming and mobile devices has more than 1.5 million paying subscribers. Its most famous live pay-per-view event is its flagship program WrestleMania. Other core content includes RAW and SmackDown Live. WWE also licenses characters for merchandise and sells videos and DVDs. Two-time WWE world champion Vince McMahon has about 80% voting control of the company.

Financial Performance

Throughout the five-year period ending in 2018 WWE reported year-over-year revenue growth. During that same period profits also rose except for a slight dip in 2017. While WWE has recently reported strong growth in media the firm has admitted that its live events aren't drawing people as they once did.

The company reported $930.2 million in revenue for 2018 a 16% increase from $801.0 million in 2017. Growth was attributed to a 28% increase in Media revenue offset by a 5% revenue decline from Live Events and a 10% drop from Consumer Products. Within Media content rights fees tied to distribution agreements of core programs Raw and SmackDown Live grew 10%. Advertising and sponsorships revenues also grew as did network revenue which include revenue from WWE Network subscriptions and pay-per-view. In 2018 the company reported growth in number of average paid subscribers all of which pay $9.99 per month to access the WWE Network.

Net income was $99.6 million in 2018 up from $32.6 million the prior year. During 2018 WWE recognized an income tax benefit of $22.5 million as compared to $1.6 million during 2017.

Cash at the end of 2018 was $167.5 million. Cash from operations was $186.7 million while investing activities used $66.1 million. Financing activities used $90.9 million.

Strategy

WWE does business through three segments: Media (including the WWE Network pay television digital and social media and filmed entertainment) Live Events (wrestling matches) and Consumer Products (merchandising of WWE-branded products such as video games toys and apparel).

Media revenue which principally consists of content rights fees subscriptions to the WWE Network and advertising and sponsorships accounts for 73% of sales. Live Event revenue (16% of sales) primarily comes from ticket sales including primary and secondary distribution revenue from events for which WWE receives a fixed fee and the sale of event travel packages. Royalties and licensee fees related to WWE branded products and sales of merchandise distributed at live events and through e-commerce platforms account for most of Consumer Product revenue (11% of sales).

While WWE is a diversified media company its livelihood stems from the live wrestling matches it produces around the country. Live Event operations account for a relatively small portion of sales but the segment drives the company's other revenue streams including TV shows pay-per-view events video games DVDs and other ancillary products. The company faces competition from Monday Night Football and other sporting events that target similar audiences.

The company also focuses on developing and promoting its wrestling talent which it calls "Superstars." WWE has about 215 Superstars under contract. The strengthening of WWE's content distribution agreements is another of WWE's primary long-term growth drivers.

HISTORY

Jesse McMahon made a name for himself as a boxing promoter in the 1940s before switching to wrestling. His son Vincent joined him in the business and they founded the World Wide Wrestling Federation in 1963. The company operated in Northeastern cities such as New York Philadelphia and Washington DC remaining a regional operation until the early 1980s (it dropped Wide from its name in 1979).

Vince McMahon Jr. inherited control of the WWF from his sick father in 1982 changed its name to Titan Sports and focused on gaining national exposure. McMahon made wrestling hugely popular but angered promoters as well as some fans with his nontraditional ideas. He embraced the idea of wrestling as show business instead of sport involving celebrities such as Cyndi Lauper and Mr. T and pursued a presence on cable TV. McMahon also purchased or put out of business many regional promoters as he spread the business across the US.

In the mid-1980s McMahon hit the jackpot with a former bodybuilder named Terry Gene Bollea.

Christened Hulk Hogan he quickly became lord of the ring making the cover of Sports Illustrated and performing for sellout crowds across the US. His likeness spawned toys clothing and a Saturday morning cartoon. Titan set a record for attracting the largest indoor crowd (more than 93000 fans packed Detroit's Pontiac Silverdome for Wrestlemania III) in 1987 and by the following year was selling $80 million in tickets annually.

Titan was body slammed in 1993 when competitor World Championship Wrestling (WCW formed in 1988 by Ted Turner to broadcast on his TBS network) lured away several major stars including Hogan. Also that year the US government charged Titan with illegal distribution of steroids. The company was acquitted in 1994 but the bad press along with the star defections allowed WCW to take the ratings lead by 1996.

Titan's refashioning of the WWF with more violence and sexual innuendo unleashed a hailstorm of criticism but returned it to the top spot by mid-1998; meanwhile former WWF star Jesse "The Body" Ventura was elected governor of Minnesota. Titan was named a defendant in a wrongful death suit in 1999 filed by the family of wrestler Owen Hart who fell to his death during a pay-per-view event (the case was settled in 2000). The company also changed its name to World Wrestling Federation Entertainment (WWFE) and went public that year. The company later licensed the WWF name for a theme restaurant in New York City.

WWFE continued its bone-crunching ways in 2000 by launching XFL a professional football league that played in the winter following the NFL season. Still smarting from the loss of the NFL broadcast rights to CBS NBC bought half of the new league and broadcast the games on its network. The deal also gave NBC a 3% stake in WWF. The league was a disaster during its first season and it quickly folded. (The company repurchased NBC's shares in 2002.)

Later that year the firm bought the WWF New York Times Square Entertainment Complex from its licensee for $24.5 million. (It closed the location in 2003.) It also abandoned its broadcasting contract with USA Networks (now IAC/InterActiveCorp) in favor of a more lucrative deal with Viacom which also took a 3% stake in the company. (Viacom sold the stake back to the company in 2003.) In 2001 WWFE put a headlock on the wrestling world when it bought the WCW from Turner Broadcasting.

In 2002 WWE received the smackdown in a court battle with the World Wildlife Fund which claimed the company (formerly WWF) lifted the animal preservation group's initials. The company had to change its name from World Wrestling Federation Entertainment to World Wrestling Entertainment as part of a settlement.

After ending its partnership with Viacom's Spike TV in 2005 the WWE cut a deal with NBCUniversal to air Monday Night Raw on the USA Network and on Spanish-language network Telemundo. The following year after The WB and the UPN merged to form The CW Network WWE inked a deal with the upstart broadcaster to air Friday Night SmackDown . (The show moved to MyNetworkTV owned by News Corporation in 2008.) It also created a new show ECW: Extreme Championship Wrestling for NBCUniversal's SCI FI Channel (now Syfy).

The company inked a lucrative toy licensing partnership with Mattel in 2010.

EXECUTIVES

Vp Public Relations, Jim Brown
Vp Home Entertainment And Retail Marketing, Joel Satin
Chairman, Vincent K. (Vince) McMahon, age 74, $1,239,923 total compensation
EVP Global Sales and Partnerships, John S. Brody
EVP Television Production, Kevin Dunn, age 58, $859,904 total compensation
Chief Strategy and Financial Officer, George A. Barrios, age 53, $723,692 total compensation
Chief Brand Officer, Stephanie McMahon, age 42
EVP Talent Live Events and Creative, Paul Levesque, age 49, $573,269 total compensation
President WWE Studios, Michael Luisi, age 53
Svp Consumer Products, James Connelly
Vice President, Peggy Waldo
Vice President Research and Technology, Kevin Quinn
Evp-content, Lisa F Lee
VP, Larry Smith
Vice President of Creative WWE Network, Julie Sbuttoni
Vice President Talent Brand Management, Christopher Handy
Vice President Tv Programming, Jennifer Good
Executive Vice President, Brett Hart
Vice President Of Event Booking Global Touring, Denis Sullivan
Senior Vice President And General Manager Digital Media, Brian Kalinowski
Vice President Legal And Business Affairs, Scott Amann
Vice President Post Production, Nancy Hirami
Vice President E Commerce And Retail Marketing, John Bancroft
Executive Vice President Consumer Products, Casey Collins
VICE PRESIDENT FINANCIAL REPORTING AND ACCOUNTING, Lisa Rundle
Vice President and General Manager WWE India, Sheetesh Srivastava
SVP TV and Network Operations, Tracey Arrowood
Vice President Of Digital Media Content, Joseph Bonsignore
VICE PRESIDENT TRAVEL AND EVENT PLANNING, Emma Rubinov
Senior Vp Enterprise Technology, Colette Rubio
Vp Operations And Global Consumer Products, Sylvia Lee
Svp Consumer Products, Sarah Cummins
Board Member, Frank Riddick
Auditors: DELOITTE & TOUCHE LLP

LOCATIONS

HQ: World Wrestling Entertainment Inc
1241 East Main Street, Stamford, CT 06902
Phone: 203 352-8600
Web: www.wwe.com

PRODUCTS/OPERATIONS

Selected Operations
Live and televised entertainment
  Live wrestling events
  Pay-per-view programming
  Television programming
  A.M. RAW (USA Network)
  Friday Night SmackDown (Syfy)
  Monday Night Raw (USA Network)
  WWE NXT (WWE.com)
  WWE Superstars (WGN America)
  WWE Classics On Demand (video on demand service)
Consumer products
  Home video
  Magazines
  Product licensing
Digital media
  WWE.com
  WWEShop
WWE Studios (film production)

COMPETITORS

Harlem Globetrotters	NASCAR
Live Nation Entertainment	NBA
	NFL
Major League Baseball	NHL

HISTORICAL FINANCIALS

Company Type: Public

Income Statement   FYE: December 31

	REVENUE ($ mil.)	NET INCOME ($ mil.)	NET PROFIT MARGIN	EMPLOYEES
12/18	930.1	99.5	10.7%	915
12/17	800.9	32.6	4.1%	850
12/16	729.2	33.8	4.6%	870
12/15	658.7	24.1	3.7%	840
12/14	542.6	(30.0)	—	761
Annual Growth	14.4%	—	—	4.7%

2018 Year-End Financials

Debt ratio: 30.5%   No. of shares (mil.): 78.0
Return on equity: 34.9%   Dividends
Cash ($ mil.): 167.4   Yield: 0.6%
Current ratio: 1.33   Payout: 42.8%
Long-term debt ($ mil.): 25.7   Market value ($ mil.): 5,830.0

	STOCK PRICE ($) FY Close	P/E High/Low		PER SHARE ($) Earnings	Dividends	Book Value
12/18	74.72	76	24	1.12	0.48	4.05
12/17	30.58	77	42	0.42	0.48	3.28
12/16	18.40	48	33	0.44	0.48	3.14
12/15	17.84	72	31	0.32	0.48	2.76
12/14	12.34	—	—	(0.40)	0.48	2.73
Annual Growth	56.9%		—	—	(0.0%)	10.4%

WSFS Financial Corp

WSFS isn't a radio station but it is tuned to the banking needs of Delaware. WSFS Financial is the holding company for Wilmington Savings Fund Society (WSFS Bank) a thrift with nearly $5 billion in assets and more than 75 branches mostly in Delaware and Pennsylvania. Founded in 1832 WSFS Bank attracts deposits from individuals and local businesses by offering standard products like checking and savings accounts CDs and IRAs. The bank uses funds primarily to lend to businesses: Commercial loans and mortgages account for about 85% of its loan portfolio. Bank subsidiaries Christiana Trust Cypress Capital Management and WSFS Wealth Investment provide trust and investment advisory services to wealthy clients and institutional investors.

Operations

Its Christiana Trust division boasts nearly $9 billion in assets under administration and provides investment fiduciary agency bankruptcy and commercial domicile services from offices in Delaware and Nevada.

The company's Cash Connect division operates more than 450 ATMs for WSFS Bank which boasts the largest branded ATM network in Delaware. The division also manages some $490 million of vault cash in approximately 15000 ATMs nationwide and provides online reporting and ATM cash management predictive cash ordering armored carrier management and ATM processing and equipment sales.

Overall the bank generated roughly 57% of its total revenue from interest and fees on loans in 2014 plus an additional 10% from interest on its mortgage-back and other investment securities. About 7% of its total revenue came from wealth management income while mortgage banking income contributed another 2%. The majority of the remaining revenue came from credit/debit card and ATM income and deposit service charges.

Geographic Reach

WSFS Bank has 45 branches throughout Delaware nearly 10 branches in Pennsylvania one branch in Nevada and one in Virginia.

Financial Performance

WSFS Financial's revenues and profits have been trending higher in recent years thanks to sustained growth in its lending business organically and through acquisitions and thanks to declining loan loss provisions as its loan portfolio's credit quality has improved with the strengthened economy.

The company's revenue rose by 5% to $238.62 million in 2014 thanks to interest income growth mostly driven by increased loan business and higher securities interest; which stemmed from a combination of the bank's First Wyoming Financial Corporation acquisition improvements in its balance sheet mix and additional income from its reverse mortgage-related assets.

Higher revenue and a continued decline in loan loss provisions in 2014 pushed WSFS Financial's net income up by 15% to $53.73 million during the year while the company's operating cash levels jumped by 17% to $67.06 million thanks to higher cash earnings.

Strategy

WSFS Financial reiterated its long-term growth strategy in 2015 which included growing the bank's lending business boosting its Trust and Wealth Management group's assets under administration and expanding Cash Connect's ATM customer base and customer cross-sell.

Beyond utilizing its community-oriented and local commercial lending teams the company has been growing its loan business and its branch reach through strategic acquisitions of banks and bank branches in target markets with preference toward markets in southeastern Pennsylvania. Its 2014 acquisition of First Wyoming Financial Corp for example bolstered WSFS' presence in Kent county while strengthening its position as the one of Delaware's top independent community banks.

Mergers and Acquisitions

In mid-2018 WSFS Financial agreed to purchase Philadelphia-based Beneficial Bancorp in a deal worth $1.5 billion. The transaction will create the largest locally headquartered community bank in the Greater Delaware Valley region with about $13 billion in assets.

EXECUTIVES

Chairman President and CEO, Mark A. Turner, age 56, $639,336 total compensation
EVP and Chief Risk Officer, Thomas W. Kearney
EVP and Chief Retail Banking Officer, Richard M. (Rick) Wright, age 66, $337,173 total compensation
EVP and COO, Rodger Levenson, age 57, $348,721 total compensation
EVP and Chief Human Capital Officer, Peggy H. Eddens, age 63
EVP and Chief Wealth Officer, Paul D. Geraghty, $310,671 total compensation
EVP and CTO, S. James (Jim) Mazarakis, $337,173 total compensation
President Cash Connect, Tom Stevenson
CFO, Dominic Canuso
Vice President Retail Banking, Adrienne Hawes
Senior Vice President And General Counsel, John Olsen
Senior Vice President Middle Market Team Leader, James Gise
Senior Vice President, Dennis Matarangas
Executive Vice President Human Resources, Robert Silwa
Vp Division Controller, Ruth Mcdevitt
Assistant Vice President Network Services Director, Jason Berkowitz
Vice President Audit Manager, Rene Lopez
Vice President Retail Office Manager, Patricia Frechette
Executive Vice President, Cynthia Cole
Executive Vice President Chief Commercial Banking Officer, Steve Clark
Assistant Vice President Small business Lender Retail Office Manager, Carol Brindle
Senior Vice President Commercial R E Lending, Joseph C Walker
Executive Vice President and Chief Commercial Banking Officer, Stephen Null Clark
Vice President Financial Advisor, Nick Frake
Assistant Vice President, Paul Roughton
AVP Facilities Manager, Bill Hornung
Senior Vice President and Director, Steven G Kochie
Assistant Vice President Digital Banking And Payments Solutions Manager, Chris Zupko
Assistant Vice President T, Nicole Monroe-cole
Assistant Vice President Senior Training Specialist, Marcedes Carter
Avp Asset Recovery Relationship Manager, William Madgey
Vice President Credit Card Product Management, Paul Brutsche
Vp Directorgovernment Guaranteed Lending, Candice Caruso
Vice President Small Business Relationship Manager, Amy Flynn
Vice President Sba Lending, Tom Dowling
Avp Retail Office Manager, Chris Graham
Vice President Regional Manager, Jeremy Shackleford
Board Member, Marvin Schoenhals
Vice Chairman, Charles G. Cheleden, age 75
Board Member, David Turner
Board Member, Jennifer Davis
Board Member, Eleuthere Du Pont
Board Member, Christopher Ghysens
Auditors: KPMG LLP

LOCATIONS

HQ: WSFS Financial Corp
500 Delaware Avenue, Wilmington, DE 19801
Phone: 302 792-6000
Web: www.wsfsbank.com

PRODUCTS/OPERATIONS

2014 Sales

	$ mil.	% of total
Interest		
Loans including fees	137.0	57
Mortgage-backed securities	13.5	6
Investment securities	9.8	4
Noninterest		
Credit/debit card & ATM income	24.1	11
Deposit service charges	17.1	7
Wealth management income	17.4	7
Mortgage baning activities	4.0	2
Other	15.7	6
Total	238.6	100

COMPETITORS

Bank of America	M&T Bank
Citizens Financial Group	PNC Financial Sovereign Bank
Fulton Financial	TD Bank USA
JPMorgan Chase	The Bancorp

HISTORICAL FINANCIALS

Company Type: Public

Income Statement
FYE: December 31

	ASSETS ($ mil.)	NET INCOME ($ mil.)	INCOME AS % OF ASSETS	EMPLOYEES
12/18	7,248.8	134.7	1.9%	1,177
12/17	6,999.5	50.2	0.7%	1,159
12/16	6,765.2	64.0	0.9%	1,116
12/15	5,585.9	53.5	1.0%	947
12/14	4,853.3	53.7	1.1%	841
Annual Growth	10.5%	25.8%	—	8.8%

2018 Year-End Financials

Return on assets: 1.8%
Return on equity: 17.4%
Long-term debt ($ mil.): —
No. of shares (mil.): 31.3
Sales ($ mil): 455.5
Dividends
Yield: 1.1%
Payout: 10.0%
Market value ($ mil.): 1,189.0

	STOCK PRICE ($) FY Close	P/E High/Low		PER SHARE ($)		
				Earnings	Dividends	Book Value
12/18	37.91	13	9	4.19	0.42	26.17
12/17	47.85	33	27	1.56	0.30	23.05
12/16	46.35	22	13	2.06	0.25	21.90
12/15	32.36	42	13	1.85	0.31	19.50
12/14	76.89	40	33	1.93	0.17	17.34
Annual Growth	(16.2%)	—	—	21.4%	25.4%	10.8%

Wyndham Hotels & Resorts Inc

Auditors: DELOITTE & TOUCHE LLP

LOCATIONS

HQ: Wyndham Hotels & Resorts Inc
22 Sylvan Way, Parsippany, NJ 07054
Phone: 973 753-6000
Web: www.wyndham.com

HISTORICAL FINANCIALS

Company Type: Public

Income Statement
FYE: December 31

	REVENUE ($ mil.)	NET INCOME ($ mil.)	NET PROFIT MARGIN	EMPLOYEES
12/18	1,868.0	162.0	8.7%	16,200
12/17	1,347.0	243.0	18.0%	8,700
12/16	1,312.0	172.0	13.1%	0
12/15	1,301.0	149.0	11.5%	0
Annual Growth	12.8%	2.8%	—	—

2018 Year-End Financials

Debt ratio: 43.0%
Return on equity: 11.9%
Cash ($ mil.): 366.0
Current ratio: 1.23
Long-term debt ($ mil.): 2,120.0
No. of shares (mil.): 98.0
Dividends
  Yield: 1.6%
  Payout: 46.3%
Market value ($ mil.): 4,450.0

	STOCK PRICE ($) FY Close	P/E High/Low	PER SHARE ($) Earnings	Dividends	Book Value
12/18	45.37	41 27	1.62	0.75	14.46
12/17	0.00	— —	(0.00)	0.00	(0.00)
Annual Growth	—		—	—	—

XPEL Inc

Auditors: Baker Tilly Virchow Krause, LLP

LOCATIONS

HQ: XPEL Inc
618 W. Sunset Road, San Antonio, TX 78216
Phone: 210 678-3700 Fax: 210 678-3701

HISTORICAL FINANCIALS

Company Type: Public

Income Statement
FYE: December 31

	REVENUE ($ mil.)	NET INCOME ($ mil.)	NET PROFIT MARGIN	EMPLOYEES
12/18	109.9	8.7	7.9%	0
12/17	67.7	1.1	1.8%	0
12/16	51.7	2.2	4.3%	0
12/15	41.4	1.5	3.7%	0
12/14	29.6	3.1	10.5%	0
Annual Growth	38.8%	29.5%	—	—

2018 Year-End Financials

Debt ratio: 5.9%
Return on equity: 50.1%
Cash ($ mil.): 3.9
Current ratio: 2.48
Long-term debt ($ mil.): 0.9
No. of shares (mil.): 27.6
Dividends
  Yield: —
  Payout: —
Market value ($ mil.): 168.0

	STOCK PRICE ($) FY Close	P/E High/Low	PER SHARE ($) Earnings	Dividends	Book Value
12/18	6.10	22 4	0.32	0.00	0.75
12/17	1.40	57 32	0.04	0.00	0.51
12/16	1.40	17 8	0.08	0.00	0.40
12/15	1.01	64 20	0.06	0.00	0.32
12/14	3.05	32 10	0.12	0.00	0.29
Annual Growth	18.9%	— —	27.8%	—	27.3%

Yelp Inc

Yelp offers user-generated reviews and information on local businesses and service providers through its website and mobile app. Its content covers restaurants and bars spas and salons doctors and retail establishments as well as a host of other business and consumer service providers. It includes more than 177 million consumer reviews and is primarily ad-supported. The site has a social media-friendly interface — users can create and maintain profiles (complete with friend networks and photos) where they can blog on experiences with businesses. Yelp has a presence in cities across the US Canada and Europe. The firm was founded in 2004 by former PayPal engineers Jeremy Stoppelman and Russel Simmons.

Financial Performance

Yelp has seen sizable growth in its revenue since 2014 though its net income has fluctuated and profits took a hit in 2015 and 2016 when the company reported losses. Yelp hit some snags with competition for talented workers and credibility issues following reports about fake reviews but the firm has since recovered.

During 2018 the company generated net revenue of $942.8 million representing 11% growth over 2017. The spike was due to a significant increase in the number of paying advertising accounts. Yelp attributes this increase to its switch from longer fixed-term contracts to shorter non-term agreements that let advertisers cancel their ad campaigns at any time.

Net income was $55.4 million in 2018 down from $152.9 million in 2017. Higher general and administrative costs as well as an increase in product development expenses contributed to the decline. Also in 2017 the company benefited from a pre-tax gain on proceeds from the sale of Eat24.

In 2018 cash and cash equivalents were $332.8 million while net cash provided by operating activities was $160.2 million. Net cash used in investing activities was $164.4 million and net cash used in financing activities was $207.7 million.

Strategy

Yelp considers its competitive advantages to be its brand its large audience of intent-driven consumers its content and the network dynamics on its platform. The company is highly dependent on advertising sales which account for nearly all revenues.

The firm has added capabilities that allow consumers to transact with local businesses primarily through integrations with partners in key verticals. Its largest category in this area by revenue and volume is online food ordering available through a partnership with Grubhub. Similarly consumers can book auto repairs (RepairPal) make spa and salon appointments (Vagaro) schedule legal consultations (LegalZoom) and order flowers (BloomNation) through Yelp. Consumers can also message businesses to directly request quotes for products and services.

Yelp is working to refine its advertising products. In 2018 it launched the Yelp Ads Certified Partners Program. Through the program Yelp partners with independent marketing agencies that have a direct line to Yelp and have been trained on all aspects of managing ad campaigns on the service. Yelp claims it is more efficient for partner agencies to manage ad campaigns on behalf of their small and medium-sized business clients.

The company which has historically relied on local ads plans to expand its national accounts. It is also enhancing its self-serve channel which lets businesses purchase ads directly through Yelp's website. Yelp states that the channel generates high-margin revenue with less involvement from its sales force.

EXECUTIVES

CFO, Charles C. (Lanny) Baker, age 52
CEO, Jeremy Stoppelman, age 42, $1 total compensation
SVP Marketing, Andrea Rubin
COO, Joseph R. (Jed) Nachman, age 47, $325,000 total compensation
SVP Legal and User Operations General Counsel and Secretary, Laurence Wilson, age 47, $325,000 total compensation
CEO Yelp Eat24, Mike Ghaffary
VP Corporate Infrastructure, Todd Miner
Vice President New Markets, Miriam Warren
Vice President Corporate Communications, Vince Sollitto
Vice President Consumer and Mobile Products, Eric Singley
National Account Manager, Kathryn Usie
National Account Manager, Jeffrey Lonski
Vice President Community Marketing, Colleen Curtis
Director Of Government Relations, Luther Lowe
National Account Manager, Shila Birkmann
Vice President, Cindy Mesaros
National Account Manager, Michelle Chin
Senior Vice President Business and Corporate Development, Chad Richard
Vice President Consumer Marketing, Brian Osborn
National Account Manager, Candice Chambers
Vice President of Corporate Communications, Shannon Eis
National Sales Manager, Michael Shu
Vice President Customer Success, Jami Zakem
Vice President National Sales, Tom Foran
Senior Vice President Marketing, Dan Kimball
Board Member, Geoff Donaker
Auditors: DELOITTE & TOUCHE LLP

LOCATIONS

HQ: Yelp Inc
140 New Montgomery Street, 9th Floor, San Francisco, CA 94105
Phone: 415 908-3801
Web: www.yelp.com

PRODUCTS/OPERATIONS

2014 Sales

	$ mil.	% of total
Local advertisig	319.1	83
Brand advertising	34.5	12
Other	23.9	5
Total	377.5	100

2014 Reviewed Businesses

	% of total
Shopping	26
Restaurants	21
Home & local services	12
Beauty & fitness	10
Health	6
Auto	5
Nightlife	4
Travel & hotel	4
Other	12
Total	100

2014 Reviews

	% of total
Restaurants	40
Shopping	22
Nightlife	9
Beauty & fitness	8
Home & local services	6
Auto	3
Health	3
Travel & hotel	3
Other	6
Total	**100**

Selected Business Categories
Arts entertainment & events
Automotive
Beauty & fitness
Health
Hotel & travel
Nightlife
Restaurants
Shopping

COMPETITORS

AOL	MSN
Better Business Bureaus	OpenTable
	Restaurant.com
CityGrid Media	Time Out Group
Consumers Union	TripAdvisor
Facebook	Yahoo!
Google	Yellowbook
Groupon	Zagat
LivingSocial	craigslist

HISTORICAL FINANCIALS
Company Type: Public

Income Statement — FYE: December 31

	REVENUE ($ mil.)	NET INCOME ($ mil.)	NET PROFIT MARGIN	EMPLOYEES
12/18	942.7	55.3	5.9%	6,030
12/17	846.8	152.8	18.1%	5,323
12/16	713.0	(4.6)	—	4,256
12/15	549.7	(32.9)	—	2,220
12/14	377.5	36.4	9.7%	2,711
Annual Growth	25.7%	11.0%	—	22.1%

2018 Year-End Financials
Debt ratio: —
Return on equity: 5.0%
Cash ($ mil.): 332.7
Current ratio: 13.25
Long-term debt ($ mil.): —
No. of shares (mil.): 82.0
Dividends
 Yield: —
 Payout: —
Market value ($ mil.): 2,869.0

	STOCK PRICE ($) FY Close	P/E High/Low	PER SHARE ($) Earnings	Dividends	Book Value
12/18	34.99	79 46	0.62	0.00	13.12
12/17	41.96	25 15	1.75	0.00	13.13
12/16	38.13	— —	(0.06)	0.00	10.16
12/15	28.80	— —	(0.44)	0.00	9.13
12/14	54.73	192 98	0.48	0.00	8.07
Annual Growth	(10.6%)	— —	6.6%	—	12.9%

Yeti Holdings Inc

Auditors: Grant Thornton LLP

LOCATIONS
HQ: Yeti Holdings Inc
7601 Southwest Parkway, Austin, TX 78735
Phone: 512 394-9384
Web: www.yeti.com

HISTORICAL FINANCIALS
Company Type: Public

Income Statement — FYE: December 29

	REVENUE ($ mil.)	NET INCOME ($ mil.)	NET PROFIT MARGIN	EMPLOYEES
12/18	778.8	57.7	7.4%	647
12/17	639.2	15.4	2.4%	565
12/16	818.9	47.9	5.9%	0
12/15	468.9	74.2	15.8%	0
Annual Growth	18.4%	(8.0%)	—	—

2018 Year-End Financials
Debt ratio: 63.7%
Return on equity: —
Cash ($ mil.): 80.0
Current ratio: 1.59
Long-term debt ($ mil.): 284.3
No. of shares (mil.): 84.2
Dividends
 Yield: —
 Payout: 2.9%
Market value ($ mil.): 1,248.0

	STOCK PRICE ($) FY Close	P/E High/Low	PER SHARE ($) Earnings	Dividends	Book Value
12/18	14.82	27 18	0.69	0.00	0.34
12/17	0.00	— —	0.19	0.00	(0.93)
Annual Growth	—	—	263.2%	—	—

ZAGG Inc

ZAGG makes items to protect power and improve mobile products. It generates more than half its revenue from smart phone and tablet screen protectors and cases marketed primarily under the InvisibleShield name. The company's other products include power stations and wireless chargers; earbuds headphones and speakers; and keyboards and other accessories. ZAGG sells its products primarily through big-box retailers electronics stores and other indirect channels; it also operates e-commerce websites and works with third-party franchisees. The US is the company's largest market.

Operations
Zagg's operations are divided into four product segments. The largest accounting for about 55% of total sales is Protection which includes smart phone and tablet screen protectors and cases under the InvisibleShield brand name. The company is one of the leading providers of mobile protection products in the US. The segment also includes the Gear4 brand of smartphone cases that are #1 in the UK.

Its Power Management segment accounts for about a third of sales and includes power stations power cases and wireless chargers; mophie and HALO are the leading brands in this segment.

The Audio (earbuds headphones speakers) and Productivity (keyboards accessories) segments each contribute about 5% of Zagg's sales. Top brands include IFROGS and BRAVEN for headphones and speakers and ZAGG for keyboards and other mobile accessories.

Geographic Reach
Utah-based ZAGG generates about 85% of sales in the US; Europe accounts for about 10%.

It has office space in the US (California Florida Michigan and Utah) as well as in England Ireland and China.

Sales and Marketing
Zagg's markets its products to consumers of electronic and hand-held devices through retail partners and distributors (nearly 90% of sales) as well as directly through websites (nearly 10%) and via franchisees (less than 5%). Items for Apple iPhones and iPads and Samsung Galaxy smartphones and tablets are its biggest sellers but it is diversifying to suit other manufacturers as their market shares increases.

The company relies heavily on a handful of customers with the top three accounting for nearly 40% of total revenue — wireless products supplier Superior Communications (nearly 25%) retailer Best Buy (about 10%) and distributor GENCO (about 5%).

Financial Performance
Amid the proliferation of mobile devices Zagg has seen strong revenue over the past five years. Sales have more than doubled since 2014. Net income has been a little more sporadic falling into the red in 2016 before bouncing back the past two years.

In 2018 the company reported revenue of $538.2 million up 4% from the prior year. Growth in screen protection spurred on by the launch of a new iPhone and wireless charging boosted the results.

Net income was $39.2 million that year more than double the 2017 figure as a result of revenue growth and a lower income tax provision.

Cash at the end of 2018 was $15.8 million a decrease of $9.2 million from the prior year. Cash from operations contributed $25.9 million to the coffers while investing activities used $40 million mainly for the purchase of Gear4. Financing activities added another $5.6 million from proceeds from revolving credit.

Strategy
Zagg has been aided in its growth by the increasing number of mobile devices in the world. There seems to be a smart phone or tablet in every hand and all those devices need protection and power. To keep its momentum going the company is focused on expanding its product offerings and entering new domestic and global markets.

It has introduced a plethora of new products in 2018 and 2019 including screen protectors with EyeSafe technology that filters out harmful light clear cases that allow for the quick swapping of designs battery cases providing advanced impact protection and backlit laptop-style keyboards for iPad models. The company has also added new product lines via acquisition.

Zagg made a big move in the UK market with the late 2018 purchase of that country's leading smartphone case brand Gear4.

Mergers and Acquisitions
In early 2019 Zagg paid $43 million in cash and stock for HALO which makes mobile accessories such as wireless chargers and portable power

products. The deal expands Zagg's IP portfolio and establishes a relationship with home shopping and e-commerce leader QVC.

The prior year the company purchased UK's top smartphone case brand Gear4 (for about $40 million) and Bluetooth audio products maker BRAVEN.

EXECUTIVES

CEO, Randall L. Hales, $696,400 total compensation
CFO, Bradley J. Holiday, $128,461 total compensation
President, Brian Stech
President mophie and International, Chris Ahern
VP Operations, Marshall Clark
Vice President of Marketing, Brad Bell
National Sales Manager, Jordan Sagona
Vice President, Chris Paterson
Senior Vice President Americas, Jonathan Downer
Chairman, Cheryl A. Larabee
Auditors: KPMG LLP

LOCATIONS

HQ: ZAGG Inc
910 West Legacy Center Way, Suite 500, Midvale, UT 84047
Phone: 801 263-0699
Web: www.zagg.com

PRODUCTS/OPERATIONS

2018 Sales

	% of total
Screen protection	57
Power management	26
Power cases	6
Audio	5
Keyboards	5
Other	1
Total	**100**

COMPETITORS

Apple Inc.	Kyocera Communications
Bose	Motorola Mobility
Dooney & Bourke	Otterbox
Forward Industries	Plantronics

HISTORICAL FINANCIALS

Company Type: Public

Income Statement
FYE: December 31

	REVENUE ($ mil.)	NET INCOME ($ mil.)	NET PROFIT MARGIN	EMPLOYEES
12/18	538.2	39.1	7.3%	618
12/17	519.5	15.1	2.9%	543
12/16	401.8	(15.5)	—	431
12/15	269.3	15.5	5.8%	234
12/14	261.5	10.4	4.0%	220
Annual Growth	19.8%	39.1%	—	29.5%

2018 Year-End Financials

Debt ratio: 15.4%
Return on equity: 26.6%
Cash ($ mil.): 15.7
Current ratio: 1.68
Long-term debt ($ mil.): 58.3
No. of shares (mil.): 27.4
Dividends
  Yield: —
  Payout: —
Market value ($ mil.): 269.0

Stock Price / P/E / Per Share

	STOCK PRICE ($) FY Close	P/E High/Low		PER SHARE ($) Earnings	Dividends	Book Value
12/18	9.78	14	6	1.38	0.00	5.77
12/17	18.45	43	11	0.53	0.00	4.85
12/16	7.10	—	—	(0.56)	0.00	4.19
12/15	10.94	23	11	0.54	0.00	4.74
12/14	6.79	20	11	0.34	0.00	4.36
Annual Growth	9.6%	—	—	41.9%	—	7.2%

Zix Corp

Zix wants to nix unauthorized clicks or any other untoward use of your e-mail. The company offers a full-range of email security products and services that include email encryption advanced threat protection archiving Bring-Your-Own-Device security and data loss prevention. Customers can buy them as standalone products or in bundles. Zix targets customers in the health care financial services insurance and government sectors (including financial regulatory agencies). Zix delivers more than 1.5 million encrypted messages on a usual business day. The company built out its email security portfolio through acquisitions made in 2017.

Operations

Zix maintains security and ease-of-use through its ZixDirectory an email encryption community of some 60 million members. The company's Best Method of Delivery is designed to deliver email securely to the recipient and ZixEncrypt automatically encrypts and decrypts messages with sensitive content.

With the acquisition of Greenview in 2017 Zix offered the ZixProtect and ZixArchive products. ZixProtect defends against the likes of zero-day malware ransomware phishing CEO fraud W-2 phishing attacks spam and viruses. ZixArchive is a cloud-based email retention service that enables user retrieval compliance and eDiscovery.

ZixOne is a mobile security application that addresses Bring-Your-Own-Device issues.

Geographic Reach

Zix is headquartered in Dallas and it has offices in Burlington Massachusetts and Ottawa Canada. Zix has virtually no penetration of international markets with almost all of its sales made to US customers.

Sales and Marketing

Zix sells its Email Encryption SaaS through a direct sales staff that zeroes in on larger businesses while a telesales force caters to small and midsized accounts. Also Zix generates sales through a diverse network of value-added resellers original equipment manufacturers and third-party distribution channels. Together they account for more than 55% of sales. Google Inc. is the largest third-party reseller representing about 5% of sales.

About half of Zix's sales are concentrated in one industry healthcare while financial services serve up about 30% of revenue. Government customers and those clustered under "Other" contribute 7% and about 15% respectively.

Financial Performance

Zix adds about $5 million in revenue year after year with sales increasing an average of 7% a year since 2013. In 2017 revenue increased 9% to about $66 million from 2016 driven by the Greenview Data acquisition new subscribers and subscription renewals by current customers.

Zix managed costs in 2017 with the growth in sales and marketing expenses about matching the revenue growth rate and a decrease in administrative expenses. Research and development costs rose about 15% with the addition of Greenview employees. While Zix will have a lower tax rate in 2018 from the US Tax Cuts and Jobs Act it got hit with a $12 million tax bill in 2017 sending the company to a loss of $8 million after posting a $5.8 million profit in 2016.

The company generated cash flow from operations of about $18 million in 2017 a 9% increase from 2016. Its cash and cash equivalents hit $33 million at the end of 2017 up from $26.5 million at the end of 2016.

Strategy

In 2018 Zix acquired AppRiver a provider of cloud-based cybersecurity tools for about $275 million. Zix made the deal to bolster its security offerings and cloud platform. The company plans to sell technologies from Zix and App River to each other's customers. To pay for the transaction Zix took on debt and an investment from True Wind Capital.

In two acquisitions in 2017 Zix moved beyond niche email encryption to offer a more comprehensive line of email security products. The move brings a greater market opportunity as well as exposure to more competition.

The $6.5 million acquisition of Greenview Data brought Greenview's advanced threat protection antivirus anti-spam and archiving capabilities to Zix's platform allowing it to offer a comprehensive portfolio of email security products. Following the acquisition Zix introduced ZixProtect and ZixArchive broadening its range of products.

Zix then bought the Entelligence Messaging Server (EMS) technology from Entrust Datacard to bolster its email encryption technologies and delivery methods. Zix followed in 2018 with the acquisition of Erado to add to its archiving and compliance capabilities.

While opening Zix to a total addressable market nearly 12 times bigger than its previous market the product expansion opens the company to greater competition. The company is thrust into battle with heavyweights like Microsoft and IBM while continuing to battle smaller companies such as Virtru and MobileIron.

Mergers and Acquisitions

In 2019 Zix acquired the assets of Cirius Messaging Inc. and its wholly owned subsidiary DeliverySlip Inc. related to the DeliverySlip product for $14 million. DeliverySlip provides email encryption e-signatures and secure file sharing. The deal adds those capabilities to Zix's offerings and eliminates the third party royalty paid by AppRiver to DeliverySlip.

Zix agreed to buy AppRiver a provider of cloud-based email security tools for $275 million in 2019. The deal combines Zix's product delivery capabilities with AppRiver's customer support while expanding the customer base of the combined company. The companies said growth should accelerate with the combination.

The 2018 acquisition of Erado enabled Zix to offer cloud-based archiving for a wider range of digital communications including social media instant messaging audio and video.

In 2017 Zix bought Greenview Data for $6.5 million for Greenview's wide range of email security products.

The 2017 acquisition of Entelligence Messaging Service (EMS) technologies from Entrust Datacard. EMS offered advanced message tracking PDF statement delivery high availability on-premises architecture and standards-based end-to-end encryption.

EXECUTIVES

VP Engineering, David J. Robertson, age 60, $250,000 total compensation
VP Client Services, Russell J. Morgan, age 59, $208,311 total compensation
President CEO and Director, David Wagner
CFO, David Rockvam
VP Marketing, Geoffrey R. (Geoff) Bibby
Chairman, Robert C. (Bob) Hausmann, age 56
Auditors: Whitley Penn LLP

LOCATIONS

HQ: Zix Corp
2711 North Haskell Avenue, Suite 2200, LB 36, Dallas, TX 75204-2960
Phone: 214 370-2000   **Fax:** 214 370-2070
Web: www.zixcorp.com

PRODUCTS/OPERATIONS

2017 Sales by Market

	% of total
Healthcare	49
Financial Services	28
Government	7
Other	16
Total	100

COMPETITORS

Barracuda Networks	MobileIron
Cisco Systems	Proofpoint
Citrix Systems	Sophos
EMC	Symantec
IBM	Trend Micro
McAfee	VMware
Microsoft	Voltage Security

HISTORICAL FINANCIALS
Company Type: Public

Income Statement
FYE: December 31

	REVENUE ($ mil.)	NET INCOME ($ mil.)	NET PROFIT MARGIN	EMPLOYEES
12/18	70.4	15.4	21.9%	265
12/17	65.6	(8.0)	—	233
12/16	60.1	5.8	9.7%	201
12/15	54.7	5.0	9.2%	192
12/14	50.3	4.1	8.1%	198
Annual Growth	8.8%	39.3%	—	7.6%

2018 Year-End Financials

Debt ratio: —
Return on equity: 29.5%
Cash ($ mil.): 27.1
Current ratio: 0.81
Long-term debt ($ mil.): —
No. of shares (mil.): 54.1
Dividends
  Yield: —
  Payout: —
Market value ($ mil.): 310.0

	STOCK PRICE ($) FY Close	P/E High/Low	PER SHARE ($) Earnings	Dividends	Book Value
12/18	5.73	24 13	0.29	0.00	1.12
12/17	4.38	— —	(0.15)	0.00	0.80
12/16	4.94	46 31	0.11	0.00	0.91
12/15	5.08	64 38	0.09	0.00	1.00
12/14	3.60	70 42	0.07	0.00	0.99
Annual Growth	12.3%	— —	42.7%	—	3.3%

Zynex Inc

EXECUTIVES

Vp Technical Operations, Robert Cozart
Vice President Operations, David Mogill
Vp Of Sales and Marketing, Christopher Brown
Board Member, Joshua Disbrow
Auditors: Plante & Moran, PLLC

LOCATIONS

HQ: Zynex Inc
9555 Maroon Circle, Englewood, CO 80112
Phone: 303 703-4906
Web: www.zynex.com

HISTORICAL FINANCIALS
Company Type: Public

Income Statement
FYE: December 31

	REVENUE ($ mil.)	NET INCOME ($ mil.)	NET PROFIT MARGIN	EMPLOYEES
12/18	31.9	9.5	29.9%	182
12/17	23.4	7.3	31.4%	109
12/16	13.3	0.0	0.5%	106
12/15	11.6	(2.9)	—	121
12/14	11.1	(6.2)	—	92
Annual Growth	30.2%	—	—	18.6%

2018 Year-End Financials

Debt ratio: —
Return on equity: 132.8%
Cash ($ mil.): 10.1
Current ratio: 2.25
Long-term debt ($ mil.): —
No. of shares (mil.): 32.2
Dividends
  Yield: 2.3%
  Payout: 21.8%
Market value ($ mil.): 95.0

	STOCK PRICE ($) FY Close	P/E High/Low	PER SHARE ($) Earnings	Dividends	Book Value
12/18	2.94	19 8	0.28	0.07	0.29
12/17	3.18	14 1	0.23	0.00	0.15
12/16	0.30	— —	(0.00)	0.00	(0.12)
12/15	0.45	— —	(0.09)	0.00	(0.13)
12/14	0.17	— —	(0.20)	0.00	(0.04)
Annual Growth	105.5%	— —	—	—	—

Hoover's Handbook of Emerging Companies

2020 Indexes

Hoovers™
A D&B COMPANY

Austin, Texas

Index by Headquarters

ARE

Abu Dhabi
Emirates Telecommunications Group Company PJSC W148
Etisalat W157
First Abu Dhabi Bank PJSC W162
Abu Dhabi Commercial Bank W3
Abu Dhabi Islamic Bank W4

Dubai
Dubai Islamic Bank Ltd W142
Mashreqbank W249

AUS

Brisbane
Suncorp Group Ltd. W373

Docklands
Australia & New Zealand Banking Group Ltd W39

Hawthorn East
Coles Group Ltd (New) W112

Melbourne
BHP Group Ltd W67
Rio Tinto Ltd W324
National Australia Bank Ltd. W269
Telstra Corp., Ltd. W387

Newstead
Bank of Queensland Ltd W54

Perth
Wesfarmers Ltd. W422

Sydney
Woolworths Group Ltd W425
Commonwealth Bank of Australia W113
Westpac Banking Corp W423
Caltex Australia Ltd. W83
Macquarie Group Ltd W242
QBE Insurance Group Ltd. W316
AMP Ltd. W27

AUT

Linz
voestalpine AG W417

Vienna
OMV AG (Austria) W294
Strabag SE-BR W365
Erste Group Bank AG W156
UNIQA Versicherungen AG (Austria) W411
Oesterreichische Nationalbank W292
BAWAG Group AG W60

BEL

Brussels
Umicore SA W405
Ageas NV W12
KBC Group NV W217
Dexia SA W139
Dexia Bank Belgium S.A. (Belgium) W139
Banque Nationale de Belgique (National Bank of Belgium) W55

Leuven
Anheuser-Busch InBev SA/NV W29

BHR

Manama
Ahli United Bank W13

BMU

Hamilton
Brookfield Business Partners LP W81
Jardine Strategic Holdings Ltd (Bermuda) W209

Pembroke
Athene Holding Ltd W38
Arch Capital Group Ltd W33

BRA

Rio de Janeiro
Petroleo Brasiliero SA W302
Vale SA W412

Sao Paulo
Itau Unibanco Holding S.A. W205
JBS SA W210
Banco Bradesco SA W44
Ultrapar Participacoes SA W404
Banco Santander Brasil SA W45

CAN

Aurora
Magna International Inc W243

Brampton
Loblaw Companies Ltd W239

Calgary
Enbridge Inc W149
Suncor Energy Inc W372
Imperial Oil Ltd W196
Husky Energy Inc W190
Canadian Natural Resources Ltd W85
Cenovus Energy Inc. W92

Halifax
Bank of Nova Scotia Halifax W52

Laval
Alimentation Couche-Tard Inc W21

Levis
Desjardins Group W132

Montreal
Power Corp. of Canada W312
Power Financial Corp W313
Bank of Montreal (Quebec) W52
Bombardier Inc. W73
National Bank of Canada W270
Laurentian Bank of Canada W232

Ottawa
Bank of Canada (Ottawa) W50

Quebec City
IA Financial Corp Inc W193

Stellarton
Empire Co Ltd W148

Toronto
Brookfield Asset Management Inc W79
Royal Bank of Canada (Montreal, Quebec) W330
Manufacturers Life Insurance Co. (Toronto, Canada) W246
Toronto Dominion Bank W395
Weston (George) Ltd W422
Manulife Financial Corp W246
ONEX Corp (Canada) W295
Canadian Imperial Bank Of Commerce (Toronto, Ontario) W84
Sun Life Financial Inc W370
Sun Life Assurance Co Canada - Insurance Products W370
Fairfax Financial Holdings Ltd W158
Sun Life Assurance Company of Canada W370

Vancouver
HSBC Bank Canada W187

Verdun
BCE Inc W65

Winnipeg
Great-West Lifeco Inc W174
Great-West Life Assurance Co W173

CHE

Baar
Glencore PLC W172

Basel
Roche Holding Ltd W327
Novartis AG Basel W289
Baloise Holding AG W42
Bank Sarasin & Co W54

Geneva
Compagnie Financiere Richemont AG W114

Jona
LafargeHolcim Ltd W229

Lausanne
Banque Cantonale Vaudoise W55

Schindellegi
Kuehne & Nagel International AG W227

Vevey
Nestle SA W276

Zurich
Zurich Insurance Group AG W435
UBS Group AG W404
Swiss Re Ltd W378
Chubb Ltd W105
ABB Ltd W2
Adecco Group AG W6
Credit Suisse Group AG W119
Swiss Life Holding AG W378
Swiss Life (UK) plc (United Kingdom) W378

CHL

Santiago
Cementos Bio-Bio S.A. (Chile) W91
Empresas COPEC SA W149
AntarChile S.A. (Chile) W29
Corporacion Nacional del Cobre de Chile W117
Banco Santander Chile W46
Banco de Chile W44
Itau CorpBanca W204

CHN

FIH Mobile Ltd W162

Anshan City
Angang Steel Co Ltd W28

Baoding
Great Wall Motor Co Ltd W173

Beijing
China Petroleum & Chemical Corp W100
PetroChina Co Ltd W301
Industrial and Commercial Bank of China Ltd W198
China Construction Bank Corp W97
Agricultural Bank of China Ltd W12
China Railway Group Ltd W101
China Railway Construction Corp Ltd W101

INDEX BY HEADQUARTERS LOCATION

```
A = AMERICAN BUSINESS
E = EMERGING COMPANIES
P = PRIVATE COMPANIES
W = WORLD BUSINESS
```

China Communications Constructions Group Ltd W97
JD.com, Inc. W210
Metallurgical Corp China Ltd W255
China Shenhua Energy Co., Ltd. W102
CRRC Corp Ltd W122
Aluminum Corp of China Ltd. W25
Xiaomi Corp W429
Huaneng Power International Inc W190
New China Life Insurance Co Ltd W277
China National Building Material Co Ltd W99
Longfor Group Holdings Ltd W239
China Life Insurance Co Ltd W98
China Coal Energy Co Ltd W96
Baidu Inc W42
BOE Technology Group Co Ltd W72

Dalian
China Grand Automotive Services Co Ltd W98
Zhongsheng Group Holdings Ltd. W434

Guangzhou
Poly Real Estate Group Co., Ltd. W310
China Southern Airlines Co Ltd W103

Hangzhou
Zhejiang Material Industrial Zhongda Yuantong Group Co., Ltd. W434

Huizhou
TCL Corp W384

Longyan
Zijin Mining Group Co Ltd W434

Nanchang
Jiangxi Copper Co., Ltd. W211

Nanjing
Suning.com Co Ltd W373

Qingdao
Qingdao Haier Co Ltd W317

Shanghai
SAIC Motor Corp Ltd W336
China Pacific Insurance (Group) Co., Ltd. W100
Shanghai Jinfeng Investment Co Ltd W347
Baoshan Iron & Steel Co Ltd W56
China United Network Communications Ltd W104
Shanghai Construction Group Co., Ltd. W347
Shanghai Pharmaceuticals Holding Co Ltd W347
Huayu Automotive Systems Company Ltd W190
China Eastern Airlines Corp., Ltd. W97
Sinopec Shanghai Petrochemical Co., Ltd. W354

Shenzhen
Ping An Insurance (Group) Co of China Ltd. W306
China Evergrande Group W98
Tencent Holdings Ltd. W388
China Vanke Co Ltd W104

Shijiazhuang
Hebei Iron & Steel Co Ltd W179

Tianjin
Tianjin Tianhai Investment Co Ltd W392
Sunac China Holdings Ltd W372
COSCO Shipping Holdings Co Ltd W118

Weifang
Weichai Power Co Ltd W421

Wuhan
China Gezhouba Group Co., Ltd. W98

Wuhu City
Anhui Conch Cement Co Ltd W29

Xiamen
Xiamen C & D Inc W428
Xiamen Xiangyu Co Ltd W429
Xiamen International Trade Group Corp Ltd W429

Zhuhai
Gree Electric Appliances Inc Of Zhuhai W174

Zoucheng
Yanzhou Coal Mining Co Ltd W431

COL

Bogota
Ecopetrol SA W144

Envigado
Almacenes Exito S.A. W24

Medellin
BanColombia SA W48

CSK

Prague 1
Komercni Banka AS (Czech Republic) W222

DEU

Bad Homburg
Fresenius SE & Co KGaA W166
Fresenius Medical Care AG & Co KGaA W165

Berlin
Deutscher Sparkassen-und Giroverband e.V. (Germany, Fed. Rep.) W138
Deutsche Bahn AG W132

Bonn
Deutsche Telekom AG W137
Deutsche Post AG W136
Deutsche Postbank AG W137

Cologne
Rewe-Zentral AG (Germany, Fed. Rep.) W322
Gothaer Versicherungsbank VVaG (Germany, Fed. Rep.) W173

Darmstadt
Merck KGaA (Germany) W254

Duesseldorf
Ceconomy AG W90
Henkel AG & Co KGAA W181

Dusseldorf
Uniper SE W410
Metro AG (New) W255

Erlangen
Siemens Healthineers AG W353

Essen
ThyssenKrupp AG W391
innogy SE W201
E.ON SE W142
Hochtief AG W183
Evonik Industries AG W158
RWE AG W334
Brenntag AG, Muehleim/Ruhr W77

Frankfurt
Deutsche Lufthansa AG (Germany, Fed. Rep.) W135
Dekabank Deutsche Girozentrale W131

Frankfurt am Main
Deutsche Bank AG W133
Commerzbank AG W112
Kreditanstalt Fuer Wiederaufbau (Germany, Fed. Rep.) W225
Landesbank Hessen-Thueringen Girozentrale (Helaba) (Germany, Fed. Rep.) W231
Landwirtschaftliche Rentenbank (Germany, Fed. Rep.) W231

Friedrichshafen
ZF Friedrichshafen AG (Germany) W432

Gerlingen-Schillerhoehe
Bosch (Robert) GmbH (Germany Fed. Rep.) W74

Guetersloh
Bertelsmann AG (Germany, Fed. Rep.) W66

Hamburg
Otto Versand (GmbH & Co.) (Germany, Fed. Rep.) W299
Marquard & Bahls AG (Germany) W248
Hamburger Sparkasse (Germany, Fed. Rep.) W177

Hannover
Talanx AG W382
Hannover Rueckversicherung SE W178

Hanover
Continental AG (Germany, Fed. Rep.) W116
TUI AG W401

Heidelberg
HeidelbergCement AG W179

Herzogenaurach
Adidas AG W7

Ingolstadt
AUDI AG W39

Karlsruhe
ENBW Energie Baden-Wuerttemberg AG W150

Leverkusen
Bayer AG W60
Covestro AG W119

Ludwigshafen
BASF SE W58

Munich
Allianz SE W23
Bayerische Motoren Werke AG W62
Siemens AG (Germany) W352
Muenchener Rueckversicherungs-Gesellschaft AG (Germany) W267
BAYWA Bayerische Warenvermittlung Landwirtschaftlicher Genossenschaften AG W64
Bayerische Landesbank (Germany) W61
Muenchener Hypothekenbank EG (Germany, Fed. Rep.) W267

Stuttgart
Daimler AG W125
McKesson Europe AG W250
Landesbank Baden-Wurttemberg W230
Mahle GmbH (Germany) W245

Walldorf
SAP SE W339

Wiesbaden
Aareal Bank AG W2

Wolfsburg
Volkswagen AG W418

DNK

Bagsvaerd
Novo-Nordisk AS W290

Copenhagen K
A.P. Moller - Maersk A/S W1
Danske Bank A/S W128

Silkeborg
Jyske Bank A/S W214

ESP

Alicante
Banco De Sabadell SA W44

Bilbao
Banco Bilbao Vizcaya Argentaria SA (BBVA) W43
Iberdrola SA W194

La Coruna
Industria De Diseno Textil (Inditex) SA W197

Madrid
Aedas Homes SAU W9
Banco Santander SA (Spain) W46
Repsol S.A. W320
Telefonica SA W387
ACS Actividades de Construccion y Servicios, S.A. W5
International Consolidated Airlines Group SA W201
Naturgy Energy Group SA W274
Mapfre SA W248
Endesa S.A. W151
Bankia S A W55
Bankinter, S.A. W55

FIN

Copenhagen
Danske Bank Plc W129

Espoo
Nokia Corp W284
Neste Oyj W275

Helsinki
Varma Mutual Pension Insurance Co W413

FRA

Bezons
Atos Origin W38

Boulogne-Billancourt
Carrefour S.A. W87
Renault S.A. (France) W320
Colas SA Boulogne W111

INDEX BY HEADQUARTERS LOCATION

Clermont-Ferrand
Compagnie Generale des Etablissements Michelin SCA W115

Courbevoie
Total SA W397
Engie SA W153
Compagnie de Saint-Gobain W114
Thales W389
Esso SA W157

Ergue-Gaberic
Financiere De L Odet SA (France) W162

Issy-les-Moulineaux
Sodexo W357

Marseille
Holding CMA-CGM (France) W184

Montrouge
Credit Agricole SA W119

Nanterre
Faurecia SA (France) W160

Paris
AXA SA W41
EDF Trading Ltd W145
Electricite de France W147
BNP Paribas (France) W70
Societe Generale W357
CNP Assurances S.A. W110
LVMH Moet Hennessy Louis Vuitton W240
Christian Dior SE W104
Orange W296
Rallye S.A. Neuilly-Sur-Seine W318
Sanofi W339
Bouygues S.A. W75
Schlumberger Ltd W343
L'Oreal S.A. (France) W229
Air France-KLM W14
Veolia Environnement W414
Danone W127
Safran SA W336
L'Air Liquide S.A. (France) W229
Valeo SA W413
SCOR S.E. (France) W345
NATIXIS SA W274
Vivendi W415
Kering SA W217
Rexel S.A. W323
Capgemini SE W86

Paris La Defense
SUEZ SA W366

Puteaux
Bollore SA W73

Rueil-Malmaison
Peugeot SA W304
Vinci SA W414
Schneider Electric SE W343

Saint-Etienne
Casino Guichard Perrachon S.A. W89

Velizy-Villacoublay
Eiffage SA W146

GBR

Phoenix Group Holdings PLC W305

Bradford
Morrison (Wm.) Supermarkets Plc W264
Yorkshire Building Society W432

Brentford
GlaxoSmithKline Plc W170

Bristol
Imperial Brands PLC W196

Cambridge
AstraZeneca Plc W37

Chertsey
Compass Group PLC (United Kingdom) W116

Edinburgh
Royal Bank of Scotland Group Plc W331

Glasgow
Clydesdale Bank PLC (United Kingdom) W109

Guildford
Linde plc W237

London
BP PLC W77
Fiat Chrysler Automobiles NV W162
HSBC Holdings Plc W188
Unilever Plc (United Kingdom) W408
BHP Group Plc W69
Rio Tinto Plc W326
LyondellBasell Industries NV W242
J Sainsbury PLC W206
Barclays PLC W56
Lloyds Banking Group Plc W239
British American Tobacco Plc (United Kingdom) W78
BT Group Plc W81
CNH Industrial NV W110
Lloyds Bank plc W238
Anglo American Plc (United Kingdom) W28
HSBC Bank Plc (United Kingdom) W188
Barclays Bank Plc W56
Aviva Plc (United Kingdom) W39
BAE Systems Plc W41
Rolls-Royce Holdings Plc W329
WPP Plc (New) W426
Associated British Foods Plc W35
National Grid plc W272
Diageo Plc W139
Kingfisher PLC W219
Bupa Finance plc W82
National Westminster Bank Plc W273
Johnson Matthey Plc (United Kingdom) W211
TSB Banking Group PLC W401
Legal & General Group PLC (United Kingdom) W233

Newbury
Vodafone Group Plc W416

Slough
Reckitt Benckiser Group Plc W319

Southhampton
Carnival Plc W86

Welwyn Garden City
Tesco PLC (United Kingdom) W388

Windsor
Centrica Plc W93

Wokingham
Ferguson PLC (New) W161

GRC

Athens
National Bank Of Greece S A W271
Alpha Bank SA W25
Eurobank Ergasias SA W157
Piraeus Bank SA W307

HKG

China Mobile Limited W99
CITIC Ltd W108
Alibaba Group Holding Ltd W20
Country Garden Holdings Co Ltd W118
Lenovo Group Ltd W234
Jardine Matheson Holdings Ltd. W209
China Unicom (Hong Kong) Ltd W103
Hongkong & Shanghai Banking Corp Ltd W187
AIA Group Ltd. W13
CK Hutchison Holdings Ltd W109
Cnooc Ltd. W110
Prudential Plc W314
China Taiping Insurance Holding Co., Ltd. W103
China Resources Pharmaceutical Group Ltd W102
Standard Chartered Plc W363
WH Group Ltd W424
China Overseas Land & Investment Ltd W100
BYD Co Ltd W82
China Resources Land Ltd W102
Fosun International Ltd W165
Geely Automobile Holdings Ltd W170
Kunlun Energy Co., Ltd. W227
Sun Art Retail Group Ltd. W370
Cathay Pacific Airways Ltd. W90
Boc Hong Kong Holdings Ltd W72
Hang Seng Bank Ltd. W177
Bank of East Asia Ltd. W50
Far East Horizon Ltd. W159
DBS Bank (Hong Kong) Limited W130
Dah Sing Financial Holdings Ltd. W123

HUN

Budapest
MOL Magyar Olaj es Gazipari Reszvenytar W263

IDN

Jakarta
P.T. Astra International TBK W299
PT Bank Negara (Indonesia) W315

IND

Gurugram
Vedanta Ltd W413

Mumbai
Reliance Industries Ltd W320
Indian Oil Corp., Ltd. (India) W197
State Bank of India W365
Tata Motors Ltd W383
Tata Steel Ltd W384
Larsen & Toubro Ltd W231
Tata Consultancy Services Ltd W383
ICICI Bank Ltd (India) W194
HDFC Bank Ltd W179
Mahindra & Mahindra Ltd W245

IRL

Cork
Johnson Controls International plc W211

Dublin
Accenture plc W4
CRH Plc W121
Medtronic PLC W253
DCC Plc W130
Allergan PLC W21
Aptiv PLC W30
Bank of Ireland Group plc W51
AIB Group PLC W14
Central Bank of Ireland (Ireland) W93

Dublin 1
Adient Plc W9

Dublin 4
Eaton Corp plc W144

Swords
Ingersoll-Rand Plc W201

ISR

Petach Tikva
Teva Pharmaceutical Industries Ltd W388

Ramat Gan
Mizrahi Tefahot Bank Ltd W263

Tel-Aviv
Bank Hapoalim B.M. (Israel) W49
Bank Leumi Le-Israel B.M. W49
Israel Discount Bank Ltd. W203
FIBI Holdings Ltd. W162
First International Bank of Israel W163

ITA

Bergamo
Unione Di Banche Italiane SpA W409

Bologna
Unipol Gruppo SpA W410
UnipolSai Assicurazioni SpA W411

Milan
Telecom Italia SpA W385
Mediobanca Banca Di Credito Finanziario SpA W251

Milano
Unicredito SpA W406

Modena
BPER Banca SpA W77

Reggio Emilia
Credito Emiliano Spa Credem Reggio Emilia W121

Rome
ENI S.p.A. W154
Enel Societa Per Azioni W151
Poste Italiane SpA W312
Leonardo SpA W235

Sondrio
Banca Popolare di Sondrio Societa Cooperativa a.r.l. (Italy) W43
Credito Valtellinese Scarl Sondri W121

Torino
Intesa Sanpaolo S.P.A. W201

Trieste
Assicurazioni Generali S.p.A. W34

JPN

Aki-gun
Mazda Motor Corp. (Japan) W249

INDEX BY HEADQUARTERS LOCATION

```
A = AMERICAN BUSINESS
E = EMERGING COMPANIES
P = PRIVATE COMPANIES
W = WORLD BUSINESS
```

Chiba
Aeon Co. Ltd. (Japan) W11
Chiba Bank, Ltd W96
Keiyo Bank, Ltd. (The) (Japan) W217

Fukuoka
Kyushu Electric Power Co Inc W228

Fukushima
Toho Bank, Ltd. (The) W392

Gifu
Juroku Bank, Ltd. W213

Hamamatsu
Suzuki Motor Corp. (Japan) W375

Hino
Hino Motors, Ltd. W182

Hiroshima
Hiroshima Bank Ltd (The) (Japan) W183

Iwata
Yamaha Motor Co Ltd W429

Kadoma
Panasonic Corp W300

Kanazawa
Hokkoku Bank, Ltd. (The) (Japan) W184

Kariya
Denso Corp. (Japan) W131
Aisin Seiki Co Ltd W17
Toyota Industries Corporation (Japan) W398

Kobe
Kobe Steel Ltd (Japan) W220
Kawasaki Heavy Industries Ltd (Japan) W216

Kofu
Yamanashi Chuo Bank, Ltd. (Japan) W430

Kyoto
Kyocera Corp W228
Bank of Kyoto Ltd (Japan) W52

Maebashi
Gunma Bank Ltd (The) W176

Matsue
San-In Godo Bank, Ltd. (The) (Japan) W339

Matsuyama
Iyo Bank, Ltd. (Japan) W205

Morioka
Bank of Iwate, Ltd. (The) (Japan) W51

Nagano
Hachijuni Bank, Ltd. (Japan) W177

Nagaokakyo
Murata Manufacturing Co Ltd W268

Nagoya
Toyota Tsusho Corp W401
Chubu Electric Power Co Inc W106
Suzuken Co Ltd W375
Central Japan Railway Co. W93
Bank of Nagoya, Ltd. W52

Nara
Nanto Bank, Ltd. W269

Numazu
Suruga Bank, Ltd. W375

Ogaki
Ogaki Kyoritsu Bank, Ltd. W292

Oita
Oita Bank Ltd (Japan) W293

Okayama
Chugoku Bank, Ltd. (The) W107

Osaka
ITOCHU Corp (Japan) W205
Nippon Life Insurance Co. (Japan) W278
Daiwa House Industry Co Ltd W126
Sumitomo Life Insurance Co. (Japan) W368
Kansai Electric Power Co., Inc. (Kansai Denryoku K. K.) (Japan) W215
Sumitomo Electric Industries, Ltd. (Japan) W367
Daikin Industries Ltd W123
Suntory Holdings Ltd W373
Sekisui House, Ltd. (Japan) W345
Kubota Corp. (Japan) W226

Otsu
Shiga Bank, Ltd. W348

Saitama
Musashino Bank, Ltd. W268

Sakai
Sharp Corp (Japan) W347

Sapporo
North Pacific Bank Ltd W289

Sendai
Tohoku Electric Power Co., Inc. (Japan) W392
77 Bank, Ltd. (The) (Japan) W1

Shizuoka
Shizuoka Bank Ltd (Japan) W351

Takamatsu
Hyakujushi Bank, Ltd. W191

Takasaki
Yamada Denki Co Ltd W429

Tokushima
Awa Bank, Ltd. W40

Tokyo
Mitsubishi Corp W256
Honda Motor Co., Ltd.(Honda Giken Kogyo Kabushiki Kaisha) (Japan) W185
Japan Post Holdings Co Ltd W207
Nippon Telegraph & Telephone Corp (Japan) W281
JXTG Holdings Inc W213
SoftBank Group Corp W358
Hitachi, Ltd. W183
Sony Corp W361
Japan Post Insurance Co Ltd W207
Marubeni Corp. W248
Mitsui & Co., Ltd. W262
Seven & i Holdings Co. Ltd. W346
Dai-ichi Life Holdings Inc W123
Tokyo Electric Power Company Holdings Inc W394
Nippon Steel Corp (New) W279
MS&AD Insurance Group Holdings W266
Tokio Marine Holdings Inc W392
Mitsubishi UFJ Financial Group Inc W261
Sumitomo Corp. (Japan) W367
KDDI Corp W217
Sumitomo Mitsui Financial Group Inc Tokyo W369
Mitsubishi Electric Corp W257
Idemitsu Kosan Co Ltd W195
Mitsubishi Heavy Industries Ltd W258
Canon Inc W86
Meiji Yasuda Life Insurance Co. W253
Fujitsu Ltd W168
Mitsubishi Chemical Holdings Corp W255
JFE Holdings Inc W210
Toshiba Corp W397
SoftBank Corp (New) W358
Bridgestone Corp (Japan) W78
Sompo Holdings Inc W360
Medipal Holdings Corp W252
Subaru Corporation W365
East Japan Railway Co. W143
NEC Corp W
Cosmo Energy Holdings Co Ltd W118
Komatsu Ltd W222
Alfresa Holdings Corp Tokyo W20
Mitsubishi Shokuhin Co., Ltd. W260
Nippon Steel Trading Corp W281
Mitsubishi Motors Corp. (Japan) W259
Orix Corp W298
FUJIFILM Holdings Corp W168
Bank of Japan W51
Toray Industries, Inc. W395
Fast Retailing Co., Ltd. W159
Sumitomo Chemical Co., Ltd. W367
Recruit Holdings Co Ltd W319
Japan Tobacco Inc. W207
Asahi Kasei Corp W34
NTT Data Corp W291
Isuzu Motors, Ltd. (Japan) W204
Nippon Express Co Ltd W277
Asahi Group Holdings Ltd. W34
Takeda Pharmaceutical Co Ltd W380
Hanwa Co Ltd (Japan) W178
ANA Holdings Inc W27
Obayashi Corp W291
T&D Holdings Inc W378
Ricoh Co Ltd W324
Kajima Corp. (Japan) W214
Tokyo Gas Co Ltd W395
Kirin Holdings Co Ltd W220
Mitsui Fudosan Co Ltd W262
Sojitz Corp W359
Japan Post Bank Co Ltd W207
Lixil Group Corp W237
Nippon Yusen Kabushiki Kaisha W282
Shimizu Corp. W348
Mitsubishi Materials Corp. W259
Taisei Corp W379
Yamato Holdings Co., Ltd. W430
Sony Financial Holdings, Inc. W362
Shin-Etsu Chemical Co., Ltd. W349
Daito Trust Construction Co., Ltd. W126
Oji Holdings Corp W293
Sumitomo Mitsui Trust Holdings Inc W370
Sony Life Insurance Co., Ltd. (Japan) W362
Sumitomo Mitsui Trust Bank Ltd W369
Nomura Holdings Inc W285
Resona Holdings Inc Osaka W321
Fukoku Mutual Life Insurance Co (Japan) W169
Asahi Mutual Life Insurance Co. (Japan) W34
Shinsei Bank Ltd W350
Shoko Chukin Bank (The) (Japan) W351
Aozora Bank Ltd W30

Toyama
Hokuhoku Financial Group Inc W184

Toyota
Toyota Motor Corp W399

Tsu
Hyakugo Bank Ltd. (Japan) W191

Yokohama
Nissan Motor Co., Ltd. W282

KOR

Busan
BNK Financial Group Inc W70

Daegu
Korea Gas Corp. (South Korea) W224
DGB Financial Group Co Ltd W139

Icheon-si
SK Hynix Inc W354

Incheon
Hyundai Steel Co W193

Naju-si
Korea Electric Power Corp W224

Pohang-si
POSCO (South Korea) W311

Seongnam
SK C&C Co Ltd W354

Seongnam-si
KT Corp (Korea) W226

Seoul
Hyundai Motor Co., Ltd. W192
LG Electronics Inc W236
Kia Motors Corp. (South Korea) W218
SK Innovation Co Ltd W355
Hanwha Corp W178
Hyundai Mobis Co Ltd (South Korea) W192
Samsung Life Insurance Co Ltd W338
Samsung C&T Corp (New) W337
KB Financial Group, Inc. W216
CJ Corp (Korea) W108
S-Oil Corp W335
Posco Daewoo Corp W312
LG Display Co Ltd W236
Hanwha Life Insurance Co., Ltd. W178
Samsung Fire & Marine Insurance (South Korea) W337
CJ CheilJedang Corporation W108
Doosan Corp. (Korea) W141
Lotte Shopping Co Ltd W240
GS Holdings Co., Ltd W176
E-MART Co Ltd W142
SK Telecom Co Ltd (South Korea) W355
Hyundai Glovis Co., Ltd. W191
Hyundai Engineering & Construction Co., Ltd. (South Korea) W191
Lotte Chemical Corp W239
Woori Financial Group Inc W426

Suwon-si
Samsung Electronics Co Ltd W337

LBN

Beirut
Bank Audi SAL W49
Blom Bank SAL W70

LUX

Luxembourg
ArcelorMittal SA W31
European Investment Bank W157

INDEX BY HEADQUARTERS LOCATION

MAR

Casablanca
Banque Centrale Populaire W55

MEX

Mexico City
Petroleos Mexicanos (Pemex) (Mexico) W303
America Movil SAB de CV W25
Wal-Mart de Mexico S.A.B. de C.V. W420
Grupo Bimbo SAB de CV (Mexico) W175
Grupo Financiero Banorte S.A. BDE C V W176
Banco Santander Mexico SA, Institucion de Banca Multiple, Grupo Financiero Santander Mexico W46

Monterrey
Fomento Economico Mexicano, S.A.B. de C.V. W164

San Pedro Garza Garcia
ALFA SAB de CV W19
Cemex S.A.B. de C.V. W91

MYS

Kuala Lumpur
Malayan Banking Berhad W245
CIMB Group Holdings Bhd W107
Public Bank Berhad (Malaysia) W316
RHB Bank Berhad W323
Hong Leong Bank Berhad W186
AMMB Holdings BHD W27

NLD

Amsterdam
ING Groep NV W199
Heineken Holding NV (Netherlands) W180
Heineken NV (Netherlands) W181
NN Group NV (Netherlands) W283
X5 Retail Group NV W428
Koninklijke Philips NV W224
Altice Europe NV W25

Diemen
Randstad NV W318

Leiden
Airbus SE W15

Rotterdam
Unilever N.V. W407

The Hague
Royal Dutch Shell Plc W333
AEGON NV W9

Zaandam
Koninklijke Ahold Delhaize NV W223

NOR

Lysaker
Storebrand ASA W365

Oslo
Norsk Hydro ASA W288
DNB ASA W140
Kommunalbanken A/S (Norway) W222

Stavanger
Equinor ASA W155

OMN

Seeb
Bank Muscat S.A.O.G W49

PER

Lima
CrediCorp Ltd. W119

PHL

Makati City
BDO Unibank Inc. W66
Metropolitan Bank & Trust Co. (Philippines) W255
Bank of the Philippine Islands W54

Mandaluyong City
San Miguel Corp W338

POL

Katowice
ING Bank Slaski SA (Poland) W199

Plock
Polski Koncern Naftowy Orlen S.A. W310

Warsaw
Powszechny Zaklad Ubezpieczen SA W314
Bank Polska Kasa Opieki SA W54
mBank SA W250

PRT

Lisbon
Galp Energia, SGPS, SA W169
EDP Energias de Portugal S.A. W145

Porto
Banco Comercial Portugues SA W44

QAT

Doha
Qatar National Bank W316
Commercial Bank of Qatar W112
Qatar Islamic Bank W316

RUS

Krasnodar
Magnit PJSC W245

Moscow
PJSC Gazprom W307
Rosneft Oil Co OJSC (Moscow) W329
PJSC Lukoil W309
Sberbank Of Russia W342
PJSC Rosseti W310
Transneft W401

St. Petersburg
Gazprom Neft PJSC W169
JSC VTB Bank W213

Tyumenskaya Oblast
Surgutneftegas PJSC W374

SAU

Riyadh
Saudi Basic Industries Corp - SABIC (Saudi Arabia) W342
Saudi Electricity Co W342
Riyad Bank (Saudi Arabia) W327
Samba Financial Group W336
Arab National Bank W31
Saudi British Bank (The) W342

SGP

Wilmar International Ltd W424
Flex Ltd W163
Olam International Ltd. W293
China Aviation Oil Singapore Corp Ltd W96
Oversea-Chinese Banking Corp. Ltd. (Singapore) W299
Jardine Cycle & Carriage Ltd W208
DBS Group Holdings Ltd. W130
United Overseas Bank Ltd. (Singapore) W411
Great Eastern Holdings Ltd (Singapore) W173

SWE

Goeteborg
Volvo AB W419

Gothenburg
Volvo Car Corp. (Sweden) W420

Stockholm
Telefonaktiebolaget LM Ericsson (Sweden) W386
Ericsson W156
Hennes & Mauritz AB W182
Skanska AB W357
Vattenfall AB W413
Nordea Bank ABp W286
Alecta pensionsforsakring, omsesidigt (Sweden) W19
Skandinaviska Enskilda Banken W356
Svenska Handelsbanken W376
Sveriges Riksbank (Sweden) W377

Sundbyberg
Swedbank AB W377

THA

Bangkok
PTT Public Co Ltd W315
Charoen Pokphand Foods Public Co., Ltd. (Thailand) W95
C.P. All Public Co Ltd W83
PTT Global Chemical Public Co Ltd W315
Siam Cement Public Co. Ltd. W351
Kasikornbank Public Co Ltd W216
Siam Commercial Bank Public Co Ltd (The) W351
Bangkok Bank Public Co., Ltd. (Thailand) W48
Krung Thai Bank Public Co. Ltd. W226
Bank of Ayudhya Public Co Ltd W50
Thanachart Capital Public Co Ltd W390

Nonthaburi
Electricity Generating Authority of Thailand W148

TUR

Istanbul
Koc Holdings AS W221
Turkiye Is Bankasi AS W403
Haci Omer Sabanci Holding AS W177
Turkiye Garanti Bankasi AS W402
Yapi Ve Kredi Bankasi AS W431
AKBANK W18

TWN

Hsinchu
Taiwan Semiconductor Manufacturing Co., Ltd. W379
Wistron Corp W425

New Taipei
Hon Hai Precision Industry Co Ltd W184

Tainan
Uni-President Enterprises Corp. W406

Taipei
Pegatron Corp W301
Compal Electronics Inc W115
Cathay Financial Holding Co W89
Inventec Corp W203
CTBC Financial Holdings Co Ltd W123
E Sun Financial Holdings Co Ltd W142
Taiwan Cooperative Bank W379

Taoyuan
Quanta Computer Inc W317

Yunlin County
Formosa Petrochemical Corp W165

ZAF

Johannesburg
Standard Bank Group Ltd W362
Absa Group Ltd (New) W3
Nedbank Group Ltd W275

Pretoria
South African Reserve Bank W362

Sandton
ESKOM (South Africa) W156
Sasol Ltd. W340
Investec Ltd W203

USA

ALABAMA

ALEXANDER CITY
Medco, L.l.c. P320

ANDALUSIA
Powersouth Energy Cooperative P426

AUBURN
Auburn University P54

BESSEMER
Piggly Wiggly Alabama Distributing Co., Inc. P418

BIRMINGHAM
Regions Financial Corp (new) A711
Alabama Power Co A27
Protective Life Insurance Co A683
Proassurance Corp A678
Servisfirst Bancshares Inc A754 E368
Southern Nuclear Operating Company, Inc. P506

INDEX BY HEADQUARTERS LOCATION

```
A = AMERICAN BUSINESS
E = EMERGING COMPANIES
P = PRIVATE COMPANIES
W = WORLD BUSINESS
```

Mayer Electric Supply Company, Inc. P316
B.l. Harbert Holdings, L.l.c. P58
B.l. Harbert International, L.l.c. P58
The Children's Hospital Of Alabama P559
University Of Alabama Health Services Foundation, P.c. P624
The Southeastern Conference P590
Navigate Affordable Housing Partners, Inc P360
Baptist Health System, Inc. P63
Consolidated Pipe & Supply Company, Inc. P156
Spire Alabama Inc. P510
Medical Properties Trust Inc E273
Servisfirst Bancshares Inc A754 E368
Diversified Gas & Oil Plc E113

BROOKWOOD
Warrior Met Coal Inc E434

DOTHAN
Aaa Cooper Transportation P1
Construction Partners Inc E95

HUNTSVILLE
The Health Care Authority Of The City Of Huntsville P571
Huntsville Hospital Health System P247
Huntsville Utilities P247

MOBILE
Infirmary Health System, Inc. P252
University Of South Alabama P637
Computer Programs & Systems Inc E92

NORTHPORT
Southfresh Aquaculture, Llc P506

PRATTVILLE
River Financial Corp E357

SCOTTSBORO
American Associated Pharmacies P31

TUSCALOOSA
University Of Alabama P623
The Dch Health Care Authority P564
Century Health Alliance Joint Venture P122

ALASKA

ANCHORAGE
First National Bank Alaska A347
Arctic Slope Regional Corporation P43
Nana Development Corporation P356
Petro Star Inc. P414
Chugach Alaska Corporation P134
Anchorage School District P38
Chenega Corporation P125
Gci, Llc P213
Alaska Native Tribal Health Consortium P16
Crowley Petroleum Dist Inc P166

JUNEAU
Alaska Permanent Fund Corporation A29 P16

KOTZEBUE
Nana Regional Corporation, Inc., P356

ARIZONA

CHANDLER
Microchip Technology Inc A563
Rogers Corp. E358

GLENDALE
Don Ford Sanderson Inc P184

MESA
Banner Health A116 P60
Empire Southwest, Llc P195
Mesa Unified School District 4 P333
City Of Mesa P138
Banner Health A116 P60

PEORIA
R. Directional Drilling & Underground Technology, Inc. A700 P436

PHOENIX
Avnet Inc A99
Freeport-mcmoran Inc A365
Republic Services Inc A720
Southern Copper Corp A771
On Semiconductor Corp A627
Knight-swift Transportation Holdings Inc A495
Sprouts Farmers Market Inc A775
Western Alliance Bancorporation A912 E438
Banner Health A116 P60
Shamrock Foods Company P487
Mercy Care P327
Blue Cross And Blue Shield Of Arizona, Inc. P89
Phoenix Children's Hospital, Inc. P417
Shell Medical Plan P492
John C. Lincoln Health Network P266
Western Alliance Bancorporation A912 E438
Cavco Industries Inc (de) E69
Cole Credit Property Trust Iv Inc E86

SCOTTSDALE
Magellan Health Inc. A531
Scottsdale Healthcare Corp. P478
Scottsdale Healthcare Hospitals P479
Vitalant P654
Healthcare Trust Of America Inc E203
Store Capital Corp E389
Axon Enterprise Inc E30

SUN CITY
Banner Health A116 P60

TEMPE
Insight Enterprises Inc. A457
Drivetime Automotive Group, Inc. P185
Salt River Project Agricultural Improvement And Power District P468
Arizona State University P44
Sundt Construction, Inc. P532
United Dairymen Of Arizona P619

TOLLESON
Russell Sigler, Inc. P459

TUCSON
The Sundt Companies Inc P590
Pima County P420
Tucson Medical Center P611
Banner-university Medical Center Tucson Campus Llc P61

YUMA
Yuma Regional Medical Center Inc P677

ARKANSAS

BENTONVILLE
Walmart Inc A900
Walton Family Foundation Inc P657

CONWAY
Home Bancshares Inc A426 E213

EL DORADO
Murphy Usa Inc A579

JONESBORO
St. Bernards Healthcare P514

LITTLE ROCK
Dillard's Inc. A267
Windstream Holdings Inc A923
Bank Ozk A113 E35
University Of Arkansas System P624
Baptist Health P62
Arkansas Electric Cooperatives, Inc. P45
Arkansas Children's Hospital P45
Bank Ozk A113 E35
Uniti Group Inc E419

LOWELL
Hunt (j.b.) Transport Services, Inc. A441

NORTH LITTLE ROCK
Comfort Systems Usa (arkansas), Inc. P149
Bruce Oakley, Inc. P102

PINE BLUFF
Simmons First National Corp A759 E373

SPRINGDALE
Tyson Foods Inc A854

STUTTGART
Riceland Foods, Inc. P448

CALIFORNIA

AGOURA HILLS
American Homes 4 Rent E16

ALAMEDA
Exelixis Inc E139
Penumbra Inc E328

ALHAMBRA
Apollo Medical Holdings Inc E24

ANAHEIM
Willdan Group Inc E441
Eaco Corp E116
Bridgford Foods Corp. E50

APPLE VALLEY
St. Mary Medical Center P522

BAKERSFIELD
Jaco Oil Company P263
Kern High School Dst P276
Valley Republic Bancorp E426

BEVERLY HILLS
Live Nation Entertainment Inc A521
Pacwest Bancorp A638 E319
Mgm Holdings Inc. P337
Pacwest Bancorp A638 E319
Kennedy-wilson Holdings Inc E244

BREA
Sun Mar Management Services P532

BURBANK
Disney (walt) Co. (the) A271

BURLINGAME
Mills-peninsula Health Services P341
Innoviva Inc E230

CALABASAS
Marcus & Millichap Inc E267

CARLSBAD
Bergelectric Corp. P77
Callaway Golf Co (de) E59
Ionis Pharmaceuticals Inc E237
Natural Alternatives International, Inc. E297

CARMICHAEL
San Juan Unified School District P471

CERRITOS
First Choice Bancorp E156

CHICO
Trico Bancshares (chico, Ca) A846 E410

CHINO HILLS
Victory International Group, Llc P650

CHULA VISTA
Chg Foundation P126
Sweetwater Union High School District P537

CITY OF INDUSTRY
America Chung Nam (group) Holdings Llc P30

COLTON
Arrowhead Regional Medical Center P46

CONCORD
Ufcw & Employers Trust Llc P615

CORONA
Monster Beverage 1990 Corporation P347

COSTA MESA
Pacific Mercantile Bancorp E318

COVINA
Citrus Valley Health Partners, Inc. P136

CUPERTINO
Apple Inc A72

DAVIS
University Of California, Davis P624

DIXON
First Northern Community Bancorp E168

DOWNEY
Los Angeles County Office Of Education P299

DUBLIN
Ross Stores Inc A730

EAST PALO ALTO
Finjan Holdings Inc E152

EL SEGUNDO
The Aerospace Corporation P553
Mega Brands America, Inc. P322
Icrest International Llc P248
Stamps.com Inc. E385
Landmark Infrastructure Partners Lp E252

ELK GROVE
Grove Elk Unified School District P223

EMERYVILLE
Nmi Holdings Inc E304

ENCINO
National Cement Company, Inc. P357

INDEX BY HEADQUARTERS LOCATION

FAIRFIELD
Northbay Healthcare Group P383
FONTANA
California Steel Industries, Inc. P107
Fontana Unified School District P205
FOSTER CITY
Gilead Sciences Inc A385
Quinstreet, Inc. E343
Qualys, Inc. E341
FOUNTAIN VALLEY
Memorial Health Services P323
FREMONT
Synnex Corp A794
Lam Research Corp A505
Asi Computer Technologies Inc P48
Washington Township Healthcare District P659
Ichor Holdings Ltd E221
Acm Research Inc E3
FRESNO
Community Hospitals Of Central California P152
Fresno Community Hospital And Medical Center P210
Community Hospitals Of Central California P152
Dairyamerica, Inc. P170
California's Valued Trust P107
Fresno Unified School District P211
Saint Agnes Medical Center P462
Central Valley Community Bancorp E73
United Security Bancshares (ca) E418
Communities First Financial Corp E89
FULLERTON
St. Jude Hospital P519
GARDEN GROVE
Garden Grove Unified School District P212
GLENDALE
Avery Dennison Corp A96
GOLETA
Inogen, Inc E230
Community West Bancshares E91
GUADALUPE
Curation Foods, Inc. P168
HAYWARD
Ultra Clean Holdings Inc E415
HUNTINGTON BEACH
Boardriders, Inc. P93
IMPERIAL
Imperial Irrigation District P250
IRVINE
Pacific Premier Bancorp Inc A636 E319
Opus Bank (irvine, Ca) A631 E316
First Foundation Inc A342 E162
Pacific Premier Bank A636 P403
St. Joseph Health System P517
Vizio, Inc. P654
Newport Corporation P373
Irvine Unified School Distict P259
Pacific Premier Bank A636 P403
Masimo Corp. E271
Boot Barn Holdings Inc E49
Sabra Health Care Reit Inc E362
Pacific Premier Bancorp Inc A636 E319
Calamp Corp E57
Opus Bank (irvine, Ca) A631 E316
Alteryx Inc E11

First Foundation Inc A342 E162
IRWINDALE
Superior Communications, Inc. P534
KENTFIELD
Marin General Hospital P307
LA CANADA FLINTRIDGE
Allen Lund Company, Llc P24
LA JOLLA
Silvergate Capital Corp A759
LA MESA
Grossmont Hospital Foundation P222
LAKE FOREST
Del Taco Restaurants Inc (new) E111
LANCASTER
Simulations Plus Inc. E375
LIVERMORE
Formfactor Inc E177
LODI
Farmers & Merchants Bancorp (lodi, Ca) A313 E144
Pacific Coast Producers P403
Farmers & Merchants Bancorp (lodi, Ca) A313 E144
LONG BEACH
Molina Healthcare Inc A570
Farmers & Merchants Bank Of Long Beach (ca) A313
Ta Chen International, Inc. P540
City Of Long Beach P138
Long Beach Memorial Medical Center P297
Apro, Llc P43
St. Mary Medical Center P522
LOS ALTOS
The David And Lucile Packard Foundation P564
LOS ANGELES
Cbre Group Inc A174
Aecom A15
Reliance Steel & Aluminum Co. A716
Mercury General Corp. A555
Cathay General Bancorp A174 E68
Hope Bancorp Inc A431 E216
Hanmi Financial Corp. A403 E198
Preferred Bank (los Angeles, Ca) A675 E338
Rbb Bancorp A707 E344
American Business Bank (los Angeles, Ca) A50 E15
Capital Income Builder, Inc. A166 P111
American High Income Trust A56 P33
Amcap Fund Inc A45 P30
Capital Income Builder, Inc. A166 P111
The Childrens Hospital Los Angeles P559
Aids Healthcare Foundation P12
Los Angeles Department Of Water And Power P299
American High Income Trust A56 P33
Amcap Fund Inc A45 P30
Los Angeles Lomod Corporation P300
Korn Ferry E247
Air Lease Corp E6
J2 Global Inc (new) E240
Houlihan Lokey Inc E217
Ares Management Corp E24
Kilroy Realty L.p. E246
Kilroy Realty Corp E245
Hudson Pacific Properties Inc E218
Cathay General Bancorp A174 E68
Hope Bancorp Inc A431 E216
Hanmi Financial Corp. A403 E198

Rexford Industrial Realty Inc E356
Preferred Bank (los Angeles, Ca) A675 E338
Rbb Bancorp A707 E344
Pcb Bancorp E323
American Business Bank (los Angeles, Ca) A50 E15
Cbb Bancorp Inc E69
Op Bancorp E316
LOS GATOS
Netflix Inc A586
LYNWOOD
St. Francis Medical Center P515
MADERA
Valley Children's Healthcare P646
Valley Children's Hospital P647
MENLO PARK
Facebook Inc A310
Robert Half International Inc. A725
Novo Construction, Inc. P391
Corcept Therapeutics Inc E96
MILL VALLEY
Redwood Trust Inc A709 E348
Four Corners Property Trust Inc E180
MILPITAS
Devcon Construction Incorporated P179
Silicon Graphics International Corp. P494
Renesas Electronics America Inc. P446
MISSION VIEJO
Mission Hospital Regional Medical Center Inc P343
MODESTO
Stan Boyett & Son, Inc. P524
Doctors Medical Center Of Modesto, Inc. P184
MONTEREY
Community Hospital Of The Monterey Peninsula P152
MOUNTAIN VIEW
Alphabet Inc A38
Intuit Inc A470
Omnicell Inc E314
NEWPORT BEACH
Chipotle Mexican Grill Inc A192
Hoag Memorial Hospital Presbyterian P241
NORCO
Corona-norco Unified School District P160
NOVATO
Bank Of Marin Bancorp A110
OAKDALE
Oak Valley Bancorp (oakdale, Ca) E309
OAKLAND
Clorox Co (the) A207
Kaiser Foundation Hospitals Inc A484 P271
Chevron Federal Credit Union A191
Kaiser Foundation Hospitals Inc A484 P271
Kaiser Fdn Health Plan Of Colorado P271
Kfhp Of The Mid-atlantic States Inc. P278
Oakland Unified School District P392
San Francisco Bay Area Rapid Transit District P470

E.l.f. Beauty Inc E116
California Bancorp E59
ONTARIO
Cvb Financial Corp A249 E108
ORANGE
Orange County Health Authority, A Public Agency P397
St. Joseph Hospital Of Orange P517
Orange County Transportation Authority P398
Children's Hospital Of Orange County P129
Chapman University P123
PALO ALTO
Hp Inc A437
Tesla Inc A817
Vmware Inc A896
Lucile Salter Packard Children's Hospital At Stanford P302
PASADENA
East West Bancorp, Inc A284 E119
Western Asset Mortgage Capital Corp A913 E439
California Institute Of Technology P106
Schaumbond Group, Inc. P475
Huntington Hospital P246
Pasadena Hospital Association, Ltd. P408
Tetra Tech Inc E401
East West Bancorp, Inc A284 E119
Alexandria Real Estate Equities Inc E8
Green Dot Corp E193
Western Asset Mortgage Capital Corp A913 E439
Arrowhead Pharmaceuticals Inc E25
PERRIS
Val Verde Unified Sch Dis P646
PETALUMA
Frontrow Calypso Llc P211
PITTSBURG
Uss-posco Industries, A California Joint Venture P645
PLEASANTON
Simpson Manufacturing Co., Inc. (de) E375
Veeva Systems Inc E427
PORTERVILLE
Sierra Bancorp A757 E371
R. M. Parks, Inc. P436
Sierra Bancorp A757 E371
QUINCY
Plumas Bancorp Inc E335
RANCHO CORDOVA
Dignity Health Medical Foundation P182
REDWOOD CITY
Oracle Corp A632
Dpr Construction, Inc. P184
RICHMOND
West Contra Costa Unified School District P662
RIVERSIDE
County Of Riverside P161
Riverside Unified School District P451
ROCKLIN
Farm Credit West A313 P200
ROSEMEAD
Edison International A289
Southern California Edison Co. A769

INDEX BY HEADQUARTERS LOCATION

```
A = AMERICAN BUSINESS
E = EMERGING COMPANIES
P = PRIVATE COMPANIES
W = WORLD BUSINESS
```

ROSEVILLE
Adventist Health System/west P6
Sutter Roseville Medical Center P536

SACRAMENTO
State Of California A782 P525
Sutter Health A791 P535
State Of California A782 P525
Sutter Health A791 P535
Sutter Health Sacramento Sierra Region P536
Sacramento Municipal Utility District P461
Alston Construction Company, Inc. P28
Sacramento City Unified School District P461
River City Petroleum, Inc. P450
Sutter Valley Medical Foundation P536
Bank Of Commerce Holdings (ca) E35

SALINAS
Salinas Valley Memorial Healthcare Systems P468

SAN BERNARDINO
San Bernardino City Unified School District P470
Inland Counties Regional Center, Inc. P253

SAN CARLOS
Rudolph And Sletten, Inc. P458

SAN CLEMENTE
Icu Medical Inc E221
Caretrust Reit Inc E65

SAN DIEGO
Qualcomm Inc A694
Sempra Energy A752
Axos Bank A100 P58
American Assets Trust, Inc. A48
Sharp Healthcare P489
Scripps Health P479
Rady Children's Hospital And Health Center P437
Sharp Memorial Hospital P490
Mercy Scripps Hospital P332
Southern Cal Schools Vol Emp Benefits Assoc P503
Rady Children's Hospital-san Diego P437
Axos Bank A100 P58
Amn Healthcare Services Inc E20
Realty Income Corp E347
Nuvasive Inc E308
Quidel Corp. E342
Retail Opportunity Investments Corp E356
Turtle Beach Corp E411
Ligand Pharmaceuticals Inc E257
Cv Sciences Inc E108

SAN FRANCISCO
Wells Fargo & Co (new) A908
Visa Inc A895
Pg&e Corp (holding Co) A659
The Gap Inc A825
Federal Reserve Bank Of San Francisco, Dist. No. 12 A321
Salesforce.com Inc A738
Uber Technologies Inc A856
Schwab (charles) Corp (the) A745
Levi Strauss & Co. A513 P292
Williams Sonoma Inc A921

First Republic Bank (san Francisco, Ca) A349
Federal Home Loan Bank Of San Francisco A318
Lendingclub Corp A511
Dignity Health A265 P181
Levi Strauss & Co. A513 P292
American Balanced Fund, Inc. A50 P31
The Irvine James Foundation A827
Levi Strauss & Co. A513 P292
Dignity Health A265 P181
Levi Strauss & Co. A513 P292
The Income Fund Of America Inc P572
Swinerton Incorporated P538
Swinerton Builders P538
Schwab Charitable Fund P477
Wilbur-ellis Holdings Ii, Inc. P669
American Balanced Fund, Inc. A50 P31
Sutter Bay Hospitals P534
Ilwu-pma Welfare Trust P249
Stitch Fix Inc E388
Nektar Therapeutics E299
Yelp Inc E450
Sunrun Inc E392
Pattern Energy Group Inc E322
Cai International Inc E56
Terreno Realty Corp E400
Ishares S&p Gsci Commodity-indexed Trust E240

SAN JOSE
Cisco Systems Inc A197
Hewlett Packard Enterprise Co A419
Paypal Holdings Inc A643
Western Digital Corp A913
Adobe Inc A11
Ebay Inc. A286
Sanmina Corp A741
Heritage Commerce Corp A414 E208
Atmel Corporation P52
Good Samaritan Hospital, L.p. P218
Santa Clara Valley Medical Center P472
Cypress Semiconductor Corp. E109
Align Technology Inc E9
Fair Isaac Corp E144
Parade Technologies Ltd. E320
Heritage Commerce Corp A414 E208
Immersion Corp E225

SAN JUAN CAPISTRANO
Capistrano Unified School District P110
Ensign Group Inc E127

SAN LEANDRO
Energy Recovery Inc E126

SAN MATEO
Franklin Resources Inc A362
Tesla Energy Operations, Inc. P546
Essex Property Trust Inc E136
Guidewire Software Inc E196

SAN PEDRO
Port Of Los Angeles P424

SAN RAFAEL
Westamerica Bancorporation A911

SAN RAMON
Chevron Corporation A189
Hill Physicians Medical Group, Inc. P240

SANTA ANA
First American Financial Corp A331
Banc Of California Inc A103

SANTA BARBARA
Santa Barbara Cottage Hospital P472
Appfolio Inc E24

SANTA CLARA
Intel Corp A459
Applied Materials, Inc. A73
Nvidia Corp A612
Advanced Micro Devices Inc A13
Agilent Technologies, Inc. A22
Svb Financial Group A792
Avaya Holdings Corp. P56
Asiainfo-linkage, Inc. P49
Arista Networks Inc E25
Coherent Inc E85

SANTA CRUZ
Santa Cruz County Bank (ca) E364

SANTA MONICA
Activision Blizzard, Inc. A9
Anworth Mortgage Asset Corp. A70
Ucla Medical Center P615
City Of Santa Monica P138
Douglas Emmett Inc E114

SANTA PAULA
Calavo Growers, Inc. E58

SANTA ROSA
Luther Burbank Corp A529 E262
Exchange Bank (santa Rosa, Ca) A303 E139
Redwood Credit Union A709 P442
Santa Rosa Memorial Hospital Inc P472
Redwood Credit Union A709 P442
Luther Burbank Corp A529 E262
Exchange Bank (santa Rosa, Ca) A303 E139
Summit State Bank (santa Rosa, Ca) E391

STANFORD
Leland Stanford Junior University A510 P289
Stanford Health Care P524
Stanford Health Services P525

STOCKTON
Coastal Pacific Food Distributors, Inc. P142
Stockton Unified School District P530
St. Josephs Medical Center Inc P519

STUDIO CITY
Motion Picture Industry Health Plan P350

SUNNYVALE
Netapp, Inc. A586
Hcl America Inc. P230
Fortinet Inc E178

THOUSAND OAKS
Amgen Inc A64
Los Robles Hospital & Medical Center P300

TORRANCE
American Honda Finance Corporation A56 P33
Harbor-ucla Medical Center P228

TURLOCK
Yosemite Farm Credit, Aca A936

TUSTIN
Humax Usa, Inc P246

VALENCIA
Sunkist Growers, Inc. P533

VAN NUYS
North La County Regional Center Inc P379

VENTURA
The Trade Desk Inc E406

VERNON
Lawrence Wholesale, Llc P286

VISALIA
Kaweah Delta Health Care District P274
Suncrest Bank (visalia, Ca) E392

WALNUT
Shea Homes Limited Partnership, A California Limited Partnership P492

WALNUT CREEK
John Muir Health P267
Central Garden & Pet Co E70
Baycom Corp E41

WEST COVINA
Citrus Valley Medical Center, Inc. P137

WEST HOLLYWOOD
Cedars-sinai Medical Center P118

WEST SACRAMENTO
Raley's P438

WESTLAKE VILLAGE
Pennymac Financial Services Inc (new) A648 E327
Ltc Properties, Inc. E260

WHITTIER
County Sanitation District No. 2 Of Los Angeles County P162
Pih Health Hospital - Whittier P419

WOODLAND HILLS
B Riley Financial Inc E32

COLORADO

AURORA
University Of Colorado Health P626
Children's Hospital Colorado P127
Aurora Public Schools P55

BOULDER
The Regents Of The University Of Colorado P586

BROOMFIELD
Ball Corp A102
Whitewave Foods Company P668
Mwh Global, Inc. P355
Flatiron Constructors, Inc. P202
Vail Resorts Inc E423
Dmc Global Inc E113

CASTLE ROCK
Douglas County School District P184

CENTENNIAL
Arrow Electronics, Inc. A81

COLORADO SPRINGS
Colorado Springs Utilities P147
Compassion International Inc P153
Memorial Hospital Corporation P324

DENVER
Davita Inc A256
Dcp Midstream Lp A257
Western Union Co A915
Colorado Housing And Finance Authority A219
University Of Colorado P626
Pcl Construction Enterprises, Inc. P409
Denver Health And Hospitals Authority Inc P178
Colorado State University System P148
University Of Colorado Hospital Authority P626
St. Joseph Hospital, Inc. P518

INDEX BY HEADQUARTERS LOCATION

Mercy Housing, Inc. P331
Colorado Seminary P146
Saint Joseph Hospital, Inc P464
Summit Materials Inc E390
Liberty Oilfield Services Inc E256
Extraction Oil & Gas Inc E142
Coresite Realty Corp E97
Royal Gold Inc E359
Antero Midstream Corp E23
Farmland Partners Inc E145
Carbon Energy Corp (de) E65

DURANGO
Saddle Butte Pipeline Llc P462

ENGELWOOD
Liberty Media Corp (de) A516

ENGLEWOOD
Qurate Retail Inc A698
Dish Network Corp A270
Qurate Retail Inc A698
Liberty Media Corp (de) A516
Catholic Health Initiatives Colorado P117
American Furniture Warehouse Co Inc P32
Kiewit Building Group Inc. P279
Innospec Inc E229
Zynex Inc E453

FORT COLLINS
Colorado State University P147
Poudre Valley Health Care, Inc. P425

GLENWOOD SPRINGS
Alpine Banks Of Colorado E11

GOLDEN
Jefferson County School District No. R-1 P265

GRAND JUNCTION
St. Mary's Hospital & Medical Center, Inc. P523

GREELEY
Pilgrims Pride Corp. A663
Hensel Phelps Construction Co. P237

GREENWOOD VILLAGE
Vf Corp. A890
Newmont Corp A594
Great West Life & Annuity Insurance Co - Insurance Products A397
National Bank Holdings Corp A580 E293
Cobank, Acb A213 P143
Air Methods Corporation P12
Cherry Creek School District 5 P126
Century Communities Inc E74
National Storage Affiliates Trust E297
National Bank Holdings Corp A580 E293

HIGHLANDS RANCH
Advanced Emissions Solutions Inc E4

LAKEWOOD
Rockies Express Pipeline Llc P456
Natural Grocers By Vitamin Cottage Inc E298
Mesa Laboratories, Inc. P279

LITTLETON
Thompson Creek Metals Company Usa P604
Stillwater Mining Company P529

LOVELAND
Heska Corp. E209

WHEAT RIDGE
Scl Health - Front Range, Inc. P477

CONNECTICUT

BLOOMFIELD
Cigna Corp (new) A194

BRANFORD
Sachem Capital Corp E362

BRIDGEPORT
People's United Financial Inc A650 E328
Bridgeport Hospital P97
People's United Financial Inc A650 E328

CHESHIRE
Bozzuto's, Inc. P96
Lane Industries Incorporated P285
The Lane Construction Corporation P573

DANBURY
Western Connecticut Health Network, Inc. P664
Western Connecticut Health Network Foundation, Inc. P664

FAIRFIELD
Save The Children Federation, Inc. P474

FARMINGTON
United Technologies Corp A874

GREENWICH
Xpo Logistics, Inc. A934
Berkley (wr) Corp A125
Starwood Property Trust Inc. A780 E386
Interactive Brokers Group Inc E234
Starwood Property Trust Inc. A780 E386

HARTFORD
Hartford Financial Services Group Inc. A407
Hartford Healthcare Corporation P229
Hartford Hospital P229
Eversource Energy Service Company P198
Saint Francis Hospital And Medical Center Foundation, Inc. P464

LAKEVILLE
Salisbury Bancorp, Inc. E363

MANCHESTER
Lydall, Inc. E263

MILFORD
Doctor's Associates Inc. P183

NAUGATUCK
Eastern Co. E120

NEW BRITAIN
Stanley Black & Decker Inc A777

NEW CANAAN
Csc Sugar, Llc P167
Bankwell Financial Group Inc E38

NEW HAVEN
Knights Of Columbus A495 P281
Yale University P675
Yale-new Haven Hospital, Inc. P676
Knights Of Columbus A495 P281
The United Illuminating Company P593

NORWALK
Booking Holdings Inc A142
Xerox Holdings Corp A932
Frontier Communications Corp A366
Emcor Group, Inc. A291
Factset Research Systems Inc. E142

OLD GREENWICH
Ellington Financial Inc E124

ORANGE
Avangrid Inc A96

OXFORD
Rbc Bearings Inc E345

RIDGEFIELD
Chefs' Warehouse Inc (the) E76

SHELTON
Prudential Annuities Life Assurance Corp A684

SOUTH WINDSOR
Gerber Scientific Products Inc P216

STAMFORD
Charter Communications Inc (new) A186
Synchrony Financial A794
United Rentals Inc A871
Equinor Marketing & Trading (us) Inc. A301 P196
Lexa International Corporation P293
Equinor Natural Gas Llc P197
Tudor Investment Corporation P611
Americares Foundation, Inc. P37
City Of Stamford P138
World Wrestling Entertainment Inc E447
Eagle Bulk Shipping Inc E117

WALLINGFORD
Amphenol Corp. A65

WATERBURY
Webster Financial Corp (waterbury, Conn) A906 E434

WESTPORT
Terex Corp. A815

WILTON
Blue Buffalo Pet Products, Inc. P87

WINDSOR
Talcott Resolution Life Insurance Co A800

DELAWARE

DOVER
Bayhealth Medical Center, Inc. P70
Chesapeake Utilities Corp. E78

NEWARK
Slm Corp. A763 E376
Christiana Care Health Services, Inc. P132
University Of Delaware P626
Slm Corp. A763 E376

WILMINGTON
Chemours Co (the) A186
Navient Corp A582
Wsfs Financial Corp A928 E448
The Bancorp Inc A822 E405
Barclays Bank Delaware A118 P66
Comenity Bank A220 P149
Wilmington Trust Company A922 P671
Balfour Beatty, Llc P60
Barclays Bank Delaware A118 P66
Comenity Bank A220 P149
Alfred I.dupont Hospital For Children P22
Gannett Fleming Affiliates, Inc. P212
Wilmington Trust Company A922 P671
Incyte Corporation E226
Wsfs Financial Corp A928 E448
The Bancorp Inc A822 E405

DISTRICT OF COLUMBIA

WASHINGTON
Fannie Mae A311
Federal Reserve System A321
Danaher Corp A253
Federal Agricultural Mortgage Corp A316 E145
Securities Investor Protection Corporation A750 P481
Wgl Holdings, Inc. P666
Aarp P2
Smithsonian Institution P497
National Association Of Letter Carriers P357
Pan American Health Organization Inc P404
The Georgetown University P570
The George Washington University P569
Washington Hospital Center Corporation P658
Children's Hospital P127
Childrens Hospital P131
Financial Industry Regulatory Authority, Inc. P201
Medstar-georgetown Medical Center, Inc. P322
Dc Water And Sewer Authority P174
Population Services International P424
American Chemical Society P32
Patient Access Network Foundation P409
Children's National Medical Center P130
Corporation For Public Broadcasting P160
The George Washington University Hospital P570
American Institutes For Research In The Behavioral Sciences P33
Securities Investor Protection Corporation A750 P481
Costar Group, Inc. E98
Federal Agricultural Mortgage Corp A316 E145
Cogent Communications Holdings, Inc. E84
Vanda Pharmaceuticals Inc E426
Easterly Government Properties Inc E120

FLORIDA

ALTAMONTE SPRINGS
Adventist Health System Sunbelt Healthcare Corporation A14 P6

BARTOW
Polk County School District P423

BOCA RATON
Office Depot, Inc. A619
Johnson Controls Fire Protection Lp P269
Dcr Workforce, Inc. P174
Geo Group Inc (the) (new) E184

BOYNTON BEACH
Bethesda Hospital, Inc. P81

BRADENTON
Beall's, Inc. P73

CLEARWATER
Tech Data Corp. A808
Morton Plant Hospital Association, Inc. P349
Baycare Health System, Inc. P70
Marinemax Inc E269

INDEX BY HEADQUARTERS LOCATION

```
A = AMERICAN BUSINESS
E = EMERGING COMPANIES
P = PRIVATE COMPANIES
W = WORLD BUSINESS
```

Heritage Insurance Holdings Inc E209

COCOA
Southeast Petro Distributors, Inc. P503

COCONUT CREEK
Food For The Poor, Inc. P205
Willis Lease Finance Corp. E442

CORAL GABLES
Mastec Inc. (fl) A542
Amerant Bancorp Inc A45 E15

DADE CITY
Withlacoochee River Electric Cooperative Inc P673

DAVIE
Nova Southeastern University, Inc. P389

DAYTONA BEACH
Topbuild Corp E407
Consolidated-tomoka Land Co. E94

DELRAY BEACH
Morse Operations, Inc. P349

ESTERO
Hertz Global Holdings Inc (new) A417
The Hertz Corporation A827 P571

FORT LAUDERDALE
Autonation, Inc. A93
School Board Of Broward County, The (inc) P476
Broward County Public Schools P101
North Broward Hospital District P377
Brandsmart Usa Of Henry County, Llc P96
Holy Cross Hospital, Inc. P243
Broward General Medical Center P101
Kemet Corp. E243
National Beverage Corp. E294
Bbx Capital Corp (new) E41
Universal Insurance Holdings Inc E419

FORT MYERS
Lee Memorial Health System Foundation, Inc. P286
21st Century Oncology Holdings, Inc. P1
Lee Memorial Hospital, Inc. P287
Somero Enterprises Inc E378
Finemark Holdings Inc E152

GAINESVILLE
University Of Florida P627
Shands Teaching Hospital And Clinics, Inc. P488
Florida Clinical Practice Association, Inc. P203
Infinite Energy, Inc. P252

HOLLYWOOD
South Broward Hospital District P500
Interbond Corporation Of America P255
Heico Corp E206
Nv5 Global Inc E309

JACKSONVILLE
Csx Corp A245
Fidelity National Information Services Inc A326
Fidelity National Financial Inc A324

Equity One, Inc. A302
Crowley Maritime Corporation P166
Jea P264
Baptist Health System, Inc. P63
Southern Baptist Hospital Of Florida Inc. P503
Duval County Public Schools P188
Shands Jacksonville Healthcare, Inc. P488
Shands Jacksonville Medical Center, Inc. P488
Mayo Clinic Jacksonville (a Nonprofit Corporation) P317
The Stellar Companies Inc P590
St. Vincent's Medical Center, Inc P523
Beaver Street Fisheries, Inc. P75
Rayonier Advanced Materials Inc E344
Regency Centers Corp E349

JUNO BEACH
Nextera Energy Inc A597
Florida Power & Light Co. A353
Nextera Energy Partners Lp E303

KISSIMMEE
The School District Of Osceola County Fl P588

LAKELAND
Publix Super Markets, Inc. A688 P434
Midflorida Federal Credit Union A566
Publix Super Markets, Inc. A688 P434
Lakeland Regional Medical Center, Inc. P285
Lakeland Regional Health Systems, Inc. P284

MELBOURNE
L3harris Technologies Inc A500

MIAMI
World Fuel Services Corp. A926
Lennar Corp A511
Ryder System, Inc. A734
The School Board Of Miami-dade County P588
Public Health Trust Of Miami Dade County P433
Baptist Hospital Of Miami, Inc. P65
Variety Children's Hospital P648
Regent Seven Seas Cruises, Inc. P443
Perez Trading Company, Inc. P412
Ladenburg Thalmann Financial Services Inc E249

MIAMI BEACH
Mount Sinai Medical Center Of Florida, Inc. P351

MIAMI LAKES
Bankunited Inc. A114 E37

MULBERRY
W.s. Badcock Corporation P655

NAPLES
The School District Of Collier County Fl P588
Naples Community Hospital Inc P357
Beasley Broadcast Group Inc E42
Tgr Financial, Inc E404

NORTH VENICE
Pgt Innovations Inc E331

OCALA
Nobility Homes, Inc. E304

ORLANDO
Darden Restaurants, Inc. A255
The Orange County Public School District P582
School Board Of Orange County Florida P476
Orlando Health, Inc. P399

Campus Crusade For Christ Inc P108
Central Florida Expressway Authority P120
Hilton Grand Vacations Inc E210
National Retail Properties Inc E296
Gencor Industries Inc E183

PONTE VEDRA BEACH
Pga Tour, Inc. P415

ROCKLEDGE
Health First, Inc. P232

SAINT PETERSBURG
Raymond James & Associates Inc A703 P439
Pscu Incorporated P431

SANFORD
The School Board Of Seminole County Florida P588

SARASOTA
Roper Technologies Inc A729
Sarasota County Public Hospital District P473
Helios Technologies Inc E207

SEMINOLE
Superior Group Of Companies Inc E393

SOUTH MIAMI
Baptist Health South Florida, Inc. P62
South Miami Hospital, Inc. P501

ST. PETERSBURG
Jabil Inc A475
Raymond James Financial, Inc. A703
United Insurance Holdings Corp A868

STUART
Seacoast Banking Corp. Of Florida A749 E367
Martin Memorial Health Systems, Inc. P310
Martin Memorial Medical Center, Inc P311
Seacoast Banking Corp. Of Florida A749 E367

SUNRISE
Fednat Holding Co E149

TALLAHASSEE
Capital City Bank Group, Inc. A165
Florida Housing Finance Corp A353 P204
Florida State University P204
Tallahassee Memorial Healthcare, Inc. P540
Mainline Information Systems, Inc. P306
Florida Housing Finance Corp A353 P204

TAMPA
Mosaic Co (the) A575
Hillsborough County School District P240
County Of Hillsborough P161
Florida Health Sciences Center Inc P203
H. Lee Moffitt Cancer Center And Research Institute, Inc. P227
Seminole Electric Cooperative, Inc. P483
St. Joseph's Hospital, Inc. P519
University Of South Florida P637
University Community Hospital, Inc. P621
Helm Fertilizer Corporation (florida) P235
Avi-spl Holdings, Inc. P57

Health Insurance Innovations Inc E202

VERO BEACH
Armour Residential Reit Inc. A79
Orchid Island Capital, Inc. A632

VIERA
School Board Of Brevard County P476

WELLINGTON
Klx Energy Services Holdings Inc E247

WEST PALM BEACH
The School District Of West Palm Beach County P589
School Board Of Palm Beach County P476
South Florida Water Management District Leasing Corp. P501
Kast Construction Company Llc P274
Chatham Lodging Trust E76

WINTER HAVEN
Centerstate Bank Corp A181 E69

WINTER PARK
Mission Health System, Inc. P343

WINTER SPRINGS
Iradimed Corp E239

GEORGIA

ACWORTH
Cobb County Public Schools P144

ALBANY
Phoebe Putney Memorial Hospital, Inc. P416

ALPHARETTA
National Christian Charitable P358
Colonial Pipeline Company P145
Jackson Healthcare, Llc P262

ATHENS
University Of Georgia P628

ATLANTA
Home Depot Inc A427
United Parcel Service Inc A870
Delta Air Lines Inc (de) A261
Coca-cola Co (the) A214
Southern Company (the) A770
Genuine Parts Co. A379
Westrock Co A917
Pultegroup Inc A690
Veritiv Corp A889
Newell Brands Inc A593
Georgia Power Co A382
Federal Reserve Bank Of Atlanta, Dist. No. 6 A319
Intercontinental Exchange Inc A462
Ncr Corp A585
Hd Supply Holdings Inc A412
Graphic Packaging Holding Co A394
Ameris Bancorp A61 E19
Invesco Mortgage Capital Inc A472
Atlantic Capital Bancshares Inc A90 E28
Board Of Regents Of The University System Of Georgia A139 P93
Lettie Pate Evans Foundation A513
Board Of Regents Of The University System Of Georgia A139 P93
Heartland Payment Systems, Llc P234
Northside Hospital, Inc. P386
Action Capital Corporation P5
Grady Memorial Hospital Corporation P219
Logisticare Solutions, Llc P297

INDEX BY HEADQUARTERS LOCATION

Fulton County Board Of
  Education P212
Unipro Foodservice, Inc P618
Windstream Eagle Holdings, Llc P672
Piedmont Hospital, Inc. P418
Altisource Solutions, Inc. P29
Emory University Hospital
  Midtown P194
Municipal Electric Authority Of
  Georgia P353
Cooperative For Assistance And Relief
  Everywhere, Inc. (care) P158
Wells Real Estate Investment Trust
  Ii P662
Balfour Beatty Infrastructure,
  Inc. P59
Purchasing Power, Llc P435
Ntg Investment Partners, Inc P392
Southern Power Co E381
Floor & Decor Holdings Inc E175
Gray Television Inc E192
Cousins Properties Inc E99
Ameris Bancorp A61 E19
Greensky Inc E195
Preferred Apartment Communities
  Inc. E337
Marine Products Corp E268
Atlantic Capital Bancshares Inc A90
  E28

BLAIRSVILLE
United Community Banks Inc
  (blairsville, Ga) A866 E417

BRASELTON
Fox Factory Holding Corp E180

BROOKHAVEN
The Salvation Army P587

BRUNSWICK
Map International (inc.) P307

CALHOUN
Mohawk Industries, Inc. A568

COLUMBUS
Aflac Inc A18
Synovus Financial Corp A795 E396

CONYERS
Pratt Corrugated Holdings, Inc. P427

CUMMING
Forsyth County Board Of
  Education P206

DARIEN
Southeastern Banking Corp. (darien,
  Ga) E380

DECATUR
Global Health Solutions Inc P217
County Of Dekalb P161
Dekalb County Public Library P176
Dekalb Regional Health System,
  Inc. P177

DORAVILLE
Metrocity Bankshares Inc E281

DULUTH
Agco Corp. A20
Asbury Automotive Group Inc A82
Primerica Inc A676 E339
National Vision Holdings Inc E297

GAINESVILLE
Northeast Georgia Medical Center,
  Inc. P383

JEFFERSON
Jackson Electric Membership
  Corporation P262

JOHNS CREEK
Ebix Inc E121

LAWRENCEVILLE
Gwinnett Hospital System, Inc. P226

MACON
The Medical Center Of Central
  Georgia Inc P575

MARIETTA
Cobb County Board Of
  Education P144
The Conlan Company P563
Kennestone Hospital Inc P275
Cobb Electric Membership
  Corporation P144
Kennestone Hospital At Windy Hill,
  Inc. P275

MCDONOUGH
Henry County Board Of
  Education P235

NORCROSS
Intelligent Systems Corp. E234

PEACHTREE CORNERS
Fleetcor Technologies Inc E173

PENDERGRASS
Royal Ten Cate (usa), Inc. P458

RICHMOND HILL
The Sommers Company P590

ROSWELL
Siteone Landscape Supply Inc E376

SAVANNAH
Memorial Health, Inc. P323
Savannah-chatham County Board Of
  Education P474
Savannah Health Services, Llc P473

STONE MOUNTAIN
Dekalb County Board Of
  Education P176

SUWANEE
Gwinnett County Board Of
  Education P226

THOMASVILLE
Thomasville Bancshares, Inc. E406

WEST POINT
Hyundai Transys Georgia Powertrain,
  Inc. P248

HAWAII

HONOLULU
First Hawaiian Inc A342
Bank Of Hawaii Corp A109
Central Pacific Financial Corp A182
Territorial Bancorp Inc A816
Servco Pacific Inc. P485
Hawai I Pacific Health P230
The Queen's Health Systems P585
Suasin Cancer Care Inc. P530
University Of Hawaii Systems P628
University Of Hawai'i Of Manoa P628
Trustees Of The Estate Of Bernice
  Pauahi Bishop P610

IDAHO

BOISE
Albertsons Companies Inc A30
Micron Technology Inc. A564
Albertsons Companies, Inc. A30 P19
Winco Holdings, Inc. P672
St. Luke's Health System, Ltd. P520
St. Luke's Regional Medical Center,
  Ltd. P522
The Amalgamated Sugar Company
  Llc P553
Saint Alphonsus Regional Medical
  Center Inc. P463
Snake River Sugar Company P498
Dbsi Inc P174
Saint Alphonsus Regional Medical
  Center, Inc. P463
Employers Resource Management
  Company P195

COEUR D ALENE
Kootenai Hospital District P282

HAILEY
Power Engineers, Incorporated P425

ILLINOIS

ABBOTT PARK
Abbott Laboratories A4

AURORA
Old Second Bancorp., Inc. (aurora,
  Ill.) A622 E312
Indian Prairie Community Unit
  School District P251
Cabot Microelectronics Corp E55
Old Second Bancorp., Inc. (aurora,
  Ill.) A622 E312

BLOOMINGTON
Hbt Financial Inc A409
Growmark, Inc. A399 P223

BOLINGBROOK
Ulta Beauty Inc A858

BROADVIEW
Robert Bosch Llc A724 P451

CARBONDALE
Southern Illinois Healthcare
  Enterprises, Inc. P504
Southern Illinois University Inc P504
Southern Illinois Healthcare E P504

CARMI
Martin & Bayley, Inc. P310

CHAMPAIGN
First Busey Corp A335 E154

CHICAGO
Boeing Co. (the) A139
Archer Daniels Midland Co. A76
United Airlines Holdings Inc A864
Exelon Corp A304
Mcdonald's Corp A548
Jones Lang Lasalle Inc A481
Lkq Corp A523
Cna Financial Corp A209
Conagra Brands Inc A231
Motorola Solutions Inc A576
Donnelley (rr) & Sons Company A276
Northern Trust Corp A604
Old Republic International
  Corp. A622
Telephone & Data Systems Inc A809
Kemper Corp (de) A488
First Midwest Bancorp, Inc.
  (naperville, Il) A346 E167
Byline Bancorp Inc A159 E55
Commonspirit Health A225 P149
Board Of Education Of City Of
  Chicago A139 P92
Ggp, Inc. A384 P216
Hometown America Management
  Corp. A429
Christian Brothers Investment
  Services, Inc. A193
Commonspirit Health A225 P149
Board Of Education Of City Of
  Chicago A139 P92
The Walsh Group Ltd P600
University Of Chicago P625
Ggp, Inc. A384 P216
Rush University Medical Center P459
The University Of Chicago Medical
  Center P593
Walsh Construction Company P657
Northwestern Memorial
  Hospital P388
The Pepper Companies Inc P584
Pepper Construction Group, Llc P412
Metropolitan Water Reclamation
  District Of Greater Chicago P336
Pepper Construction Company P412
Crowe Llp P165
Central Steel And Wire
  Company P121
Ann & Robert H. Lurie Children's
  Hospital Of Chicago P38
Regional Transportation
  Authority P445
Chicago Transit Authority P126
Loyola University Of Chicago
  Inc P301
Blue Cross & Blue Shield
  Association P88
De Paul University P174
Family Health Network, Inc. P199
Newark Corporation P372
Newark Electronics Corporation P372
North Advocate Side Health
  Network P376
Seyfarth Shaw Llp P486
Echo Global Logistics Inc E123
Federal Home Loan Bank
  Chicago E147
Transunion E408
John Bean Technologies Corp E241
Littelfuse Inc E257
Enova International Inc E127
Grubhub Inc E195
Envestnet Inc E130
Heidrick & Struggles International,
  Inc. E207
First Midwest Bancorp, Inc.
  (naperville, Il) A346 E167
Cars.com Inc E67
Byline Bancorp Inc A159 E55

DEERFIELD
Walgreens Boots Alliance Inc A899
Caterpillar Inc. A173
Mondelez International Inc A572
Baxter International Inc A119
Fortune Brands Home & Security,
  Inc. A361
Scai Holdings, Llc P475

DES PLAINES
Brg Sports, Inc. P97

DOWNERS GROVE
Univar Solutions Inc A878
Dover Corp A277
Invesco Db Commodity Index
  Tracking Fund A472 E235
Advocate Health Care Network A15
  P8
Advocate Health And Hospitals
  Corporation A15 P7
Advocate Health Care Network A15
  P8
Advocate Health And Hospitals
  Corporation A15 P7
Midwestern University P340
Invesco Db Commodity Index
  Tracking Fund A472 E235

EDWARDSVILLE
Prairie Farms Dairy, Inc. P426

INDEX BY HEADQUARTERS LOCATION

```
A = AMERICAN BUSINESS
E = EMERGING COMPANIES
P = PRIVATE COMPANIES
W = WORLD BUSINESS
```

EFFINGHAM
Midland States Bancorp Inc A566 E282

ELK GROVE VILLAGE
Alexian Brothers Medical Center Inc P22

EVANSTON
Northwestern University P388
Northshore University Healthsystem P385
North Shore University Health System P381
Rotary International P457

FRANKLIN PARK
Hill/ahern Fire Protection, Llc A420 P240

GLENVIEW
Illinois Tool Works, Inc. A453
Anixter International Inc A68

HOFFMAN ESTATES
Sears Holdings Corp A750

JOLIET
Central Grocers, Inc. P121

LAKE FOREST
Tenneco Inc A812
Grainger (w.w.) Inc. A393
Packaging Corp Of America A637

LIBERTYVILLE
Brightstar Us, Inc. P97

LINCOLNSHIRE
Cdw Corp A176

LISLE
Navistar International Corp. A583

MATTOON
First Mid Bancshares Inc A345 E166

MAYWOOD
Loyola University Medical Center P301

METTAWA
Brunswick Corp. A153

MILAN
Group O, Inc. P222

MOLINE
Deere & Co. A260
Qcr Holdings Inc A693 E341

NAPERVILLE
Edward-elmhurst Healthcare P192
Edward Hospital P191

NORTH CHICAGO
Abbvie Inc A5

NORTHBROOK
Allstate Corp A34

OAK BROOK
Treehouse Foods Inc A845
Ace Hardware Corporation A8 P4
Federal Signal Corp. E148

PARIS
North American Lighting, Inc. P376

PARK RIDGE
Advocate Health And Hospitals Corporation A15 P7

PEORIA
Rli Corp A723
Osf Healthcare System P401
Core Construction Group, Ltd. P159

RIVERWOODS
Discover Financial Services A269

ROCK ISLAND
Modern Woodmen Of America A568 P345

ROCKFORD
Swedishamerican Hospital P537
Rockford, Board Of Education P456

ROLLING MEADOWS
Gallagher (arthur J.) & Co. A368
Kimball Hill Inc P280
Myr Group Inc E292

ROSEMONT
Us Foods Holding Corp A886
Wintrust Financial Corp (il) A924 E444
The Big Ten Conference Inc P555
Wintrust Financial Corp (il) A924 E444

SCHAUMBURG
Paylocity Holding Corp E323

SPRINGFIELD
Horace Mann Educators Corp. A432
Tom Lange Company, Inc. P605

TINLEY PARK
Panduit Corp. P404

URBANA
Carle Foundation Hospital P113

VERNON HILLS
Graham Enterprise, Inc. P219

WESTCHESTER
Ingredion Inc A456

INDIANA

BLOOMINGTON
Trustees Of Indiana University P609
Indiana University P251
Hoosier Energy Rural Electric Cooperative Inc. P243

CARMEL
Cno Financial Group Inc A211
Merchants Bancorp (indiana) A553 E276
Indiana Municipal Power Agency P251
Merchants Bancorp (indiana) A553 E276

CLARKSVILLE
First Savings Financial Group Inc E170

COLUMBUS
Cummins, Inc. A247

CORYDON
First Capital Inc. E156

DANVILLE
Hendricks County Hospital P235

ELKHART
Thor Industries, Inc. A833
Lci Industries E252
Patrick Industries Inc E321

EVANSVILLE
Berry Global Group Inc A128
Onemain Holdings Inc A628

Old National Bancorp (evansville, In) A620 E311
Deaconess Health System, Inc. P175
Atlas World Group, Inc. P52
Deaconess Hospital Inc P176
Van Atlas Lines Inc P647
Southern Indiana Gas & Electric Company P505
St. Mary's Health, Inc. P522
Old National Bancorp (evansville, In) A620 E311

FISHERS
First Internet Bancorp A343 E164

FORT WAYNE
Steel Dynamics Inc. A785
Do It Best Corp. P182
Petroleum Traders Corporation P415

HIGHLAND
Strack And Van Til Super Market Inc. P530

INDIANAPOLIS
Anthem Inc A69
Lilly (eli) & Co A517
Simon Property Group, Inc. A760
Oneamerica Financial Partners, Inc. A628 P396
Community Health Network, Inc. P151
Indiana University Health, Inc. P251
The Finish Line Inc P567
Countrymark Cooperative Holding Corporation P160
Oneamerica Financial Partners, Inc. A628 P396
National Collegiate Athletic Association P358
Citizens Energy Group P136
Wabash Valley Power Association Inc P656
Renaissance Charitable Foundation Inc. P446
Bmw Constructors, Inc. P91
Federal Home Loan Bank Indianapolis E147

JASPER
German American Bancorp Inc A383 E186
Kimball Electronics Inc E246
German American Bancorp Inc A383 E186

LA GRANGE
Fs Bancorp (indiana) E181

MERRILLVILLE
Nisource Inc. (holding Co.) A600
Northern Indiana Public Service Company P384

MICHIGAN CITY
Horizon Bancorp Inc A433 E216

MISHAWAKA
Franciscan Alliance, Inc. P207

MUNCIE
First Merchants Corp A344 E165
Mutualfirst Financial Inc A580 E292
First Merchants Corp A344 E165
Mutualfirst Financial Inc A580 E292

MUNSTER
Community Foundation Of Northwest Indiana, Inc. P150
Munster Medical Research Foundation, Inc P354
Northwest Indiana Bancorp E306

SOUTH BEND
1st Source Corp A1 E1

TERRE HAUTE
First Financial Corp. (in) A341
Union Hospital, Inc. P617

WARSAW
Zimmer Biomet Holdings Inc A938
Lakeland Financial Corp A504 E251

IOWA

AMES
Danfoss Power Solutions Inc. P173
Iowa State University Of Science And Technology P259
Renewable Energy Group, Inc. E352

ANKENY
Casey's General Stores, Inc. A172
Perishable Distributors Of Iowa, Ltd. P412

CEDAR RAPIDS
United Fire Group, Inc. A867
Transamerica Advisors Life Insurance Co A841 E408
Crst International, Inc. P167
Transamerica Advisors Life Insurance Co A841 E408

CRAIG
Farmers Cooperative Company P200

DAVENPORT
Genesis Health System P215

DES MOINES
Principal Financial Group Inc A676
Federal Home Loan Bank Of Des Moines A318
Central Iowa Hospital Corp P121
Catholic Health Initiatives - Iowa, Corp. P117
Iowa Physicians Clinic Medical Foundation P258

DUBUQUE
Heartland Financial Usa, Inc. (dubuque, Ia) A412 E204

FARNHAMVILLE
Farmers Cooperative Company P200

FOREST CITY
Winnebago Industries, Inc. E443

HILLS
Hills Bancorporation A420

IOWA CITY
Midwestone Financial Group, Inc. A567 E283
The University Of Iowa P594
University Of Iowa Hospitals And Clinics P629
Midwestone Financial Group, Inc. A567 E283

JOHNSTON
Iowa Physicians Clinic Medical Foundation P258

MASON CITY
Mercy Health Services-iowa, Corp. P329

MONTICELLO
Innovative Ag Services Co. P253

ROLAND
Key Cooperative P277

WATERLOO
Covenant Medical Center, Inc. P163

WEST BURLINGTON
Big River Resources, Llc. P82

INDEX BY HEADQUARTERS LOCATION

WEST DES MOINES
American Equity Investment Life Holding Co A52
Fbl Financial Group Inc A316
West Bancorporation, Inc. A911 E437
Hy-vee, Inc. A447 P247
Iowa Health System P258
Heartland Co-op P233
West Bancorporation, Inc. A911 E437

KANSAS

KANSAS CITY
Dairy Farmers Of America, Inc. A252 P169
Associated Wholesale Grocers, Inc. A86 P50
Dairy Farmers Of America, Inc. A252 P169
Associated Wholesale Grocers, Inc. A86 P50
The University Of Kansas Hospital P595

LEAWOOD
Amc Entertainment Holdings Inc. A44
Crossfirst Bankshares Inc A243
Amc Entertainment Inc. P30
Tallgrass Energy Lp E397

MANHATTAN
Kansas State University P273

MCPHERSON
Chs Mcpherson Refinery Inc. P133

MERRIAM
Seaboard Corp. A747

MOUNDRIDGE
Mid-kansas Cooperative Association P340

OVERLAND PARK
Sprint Corp (new) A775
Black & Veatch Holding Company P86
Bvh, Inc. P104
Npc Restaurant Holdings, Llc P391
Black & Veatch Corporation P85
Black & Veatch International Company P86

SHAWNEE MISSION
Shawnee Mission Medical Center, Inc. P491

TOPEKA
Capitol Federal Financial Inc A168
Stormont-vail Healthcare, Inc. P530
Federal Home Loan Bank Topeka E148

WICHITA
Spirit Aerosystems Holdings Inc A774
Equity Bancshares Inc A302 E134
Unified School District 259 P617
Wesley Medical Center, Llc P662
Ascension Via Christi Hospitals Wichita, Inc. P48
Equity Bancshares Inc A302 E134

KENTUCKY

ASHLAND
King's Daughters Health System, Inc. P280

BOWLING GREEN
Houchens Industries, Inc. P244

EDGEWOOD
Saint Elizabeth Medical Center, Inc. P463

FRANKLIN
Keystops, Llc P278

HENDERSON
Big Rivers Electric Corporation P83

LEXINGTON
Appalachian Regional Healthcare, Inc. P41

LOUISVILLE
Humana Inc. A440
Yum! Brands Inc A937
Republic Bancorp, Inc. (ky) A718 E353
Stock Yards Bancorp Inc A788 E388
Baptist Healthcare System, Inc. P64
Norton Hospitals, Inc P389
Jefferson County Board Of Education P264
University Health Care Inc P621
Almost Family, Inc. P27
University Of Louisville P629
University Medical Center Inc P623
Texas Roadhouse Inc E404
Turning Point Brands Inc E411
Republic Bancorp, Inc. (ky) A718 E353
Stock Yards Bancorp Inc A788 E388

PARIS
Kentucky Bancshares Inc E245

PIKEVILLE
Community Trust Bancorp, Inc. A229
Pikeville Medical Center, Inc. P419

LOUISIANA

ABBEVILLE
Coastal Chemical Co., L.l.c. P142

BATON ROUGE
Business First Bancshares Inc A159 E55
Franciscan Missionaries Of Our Lady Health System, Inc. P209
Our Lady Of The Lake Hospital, Inc. P401
Universities Of Louisiana System P621
Mmr Group, Inc. P345
Mmr Constructors, Inc. P344
Cajun Industries, Llc P105
The Newtron Group L L C P581
Cajun Industries, Llc P105
Amedisys, Inc. E13
Business First Bancshares Inc A159 E55
Investar Holding Corp E235

CHALMETTE
Chalmette Refining, L.l.c. A186 P123

COVINGTON
Zen-noh Grain Corporation A938 P678
Consolidated Grain & Barge Company A235 P156
Zen-noh Grain Corporation A938 P678
Consolidated Grain & Barge Company A235 P156
Saint Tammany Parish School Board P467

HAMMOND
First Guaranty Bancshares, Inc. E162

HARVEY
Jefferson Parish School Board Inc P265

LAFAYETTE
Iberiabank Corp A448 E219
Home Bancorp Inc A425 E212
Lafayette General Health System, Inc. P284
Lafayette General Medical Center, Inc. P284
Lhc Group Inc E255
Iberiabank Corp A448 E219
Home Bancorp Inc A425 E212

LAKE CHARLES
Central Crude, Inc. P120

MONROE
Centurylink Inc A183
Qwest Corp A699
Allied Building Stores, Inc. P25

NEW ORLEANS
Entergy Corp A295
Ochsner Clinic Foundation A619 P393
Ochsner Health System P394
Louisiana Childrens Medical Center, Inc P300
Entergy Services, Inc. P196
The Administrators Of The Tulane Educational Fund P552
Walton Construction - A Core Company, Llc P657
Children's Hospital P127

RUSTON
Origin Bancorp Inc A632

SHREVEPORT
Willis-knighton Medical Center P670
Biomedical Research Foundation Of Northwest Louisiana P85
Caddo Parish School Board P105

THIBODAUX
Rouse's Enterprises, L.l.c. P458

MAINE

AUGUSTA
Mainegeneral Medical Center P305

BANGOR
Eastern Maine Medical Center P190

BAR HARBOR
Bar Harbor Bankshares A117 E39

BREWER
Eastern Maine Healthcare Systems P190

CAMDEN
Camden National Corp. (me) A162 E61

DAMARISCOTTA
Miles Health Care, Inc P341

LEWISTON
Northeast Bank (me) E305

ORONO
University Of Maine System P630

PORTLAND
Mainehealth P305
Martin's Point Health Care, Inc. P312
Wex Inc A440

WESTBROOK
Idexx Laboratories, Inc. E222

YORK
York Hospital P677

MARYLAND

ADELPHI
University System Of Maryland P641

ANNAPOLIS
Anne Arundel County Board Of Education P39
Anne Arundel Medical Center, Inc. P39
Hannon Armstrong Sustainable Infrastructure Capital Inc E199

BALTIMORE
T Rowe Price Group Inc A798
Under Armour Inc A861
Howard Bancorp Inc A437
Johns Hopkins University A478 P268
The Whiting-turner Contracting Company A830 P601
Johns Hopkins University A478 P268
The Whiting-turner Contracting Company A830 P601
Johns Hopkins Hospital P268
Lifebridge Health, Inc. P295
Baltimore City Public Schools P60
University Of Maryland Medical System Corporation P630
Maryland Transportation Authority P313
Sinai Hospital Of Baltimore, Inc. P494
Mercy Health Services, Inc. P329
Johns Hopkins Bayview Medical Center, Inc. P268
Gbmc Healthcare, Inc. P213
Franklin Square Hospital Center, Inc. P209
Mercy Medical Center, Inc. P332
Medifast Inc E274

BEL AIR
County Of Harford P161
Harford County Board Of Education (inc) P228

BETHESDA
Lockheed Martin Corp A524
Marriott International, Inc. A536
Host Hotels & Resorts Inc A436
Agnc Investment Corp A23 E5
Eagle Bancorp Inc (md) A283 E116
Rlj Lodging Trust E358
Agnc Investment Corp A23 E5
Pebblebrook Hotel Trust E325
Walker & Dunlop Inc E432
Enviva Partners Lp E132
Eagle Bancorp Inc (md) A283 E116
Global Medical Reit Inc E189

CHEVY CHASE
Jbg Smith Properties E241

COLLEGE PARK
University Of Maryland, College Park P631

COLUMBIA
Medstar Health, Inc. A551 P321
Maxim Healthcare Services, Inc. P315

GAITHERSBURG
Adventist Healthcare, Inc. P7
Emergent Biosolutions Inc E125

GLEN BURNIE
R. E. Michel Company, Llc P436

GREENBELT
Sgt, Llc P487

INDEX BY HEADQUARTERS LOCATION

```
A = AMERICAN BUSINESS
E = EMERGING COMPANIES
P = PRIVATE COMPANIES
W = WORLD BUSINESS
```

HANOVER
Allegis Group, Inc. A32 P23
Aerotek, Inc. A17 P8
Allegis Group, Inc. A32 P23
Aerotek, Inc. A17 P8
Maryland Department Of Transportation P313
Teksystems, Inc. P544

HUGHESVILLE
Maryland Southern Electric Cooperative Inc P313

HUNT VALLEY
Mccormick & Co Inc A546
Omega Healthcare Investors, Inc. E313

LA PLATA
The Wills Group Inc P602
Smo, Incorporated P498

LAUREL
Washington Suburban Sanitary Commission (inc) P658

MARRIOTTSVILLE
Bon Secours Mercy Health, Inc. P94

OLNEY
Sandy Spring Bancorp Inc A740 E363

OWINGS MILLS
Rand Worldwide Inc. E344

ROCKVILLE
County Of Montgomery P161
Westat, Inc. P663
Choice Hotels International, Inc. E79
Supernus Pharmaceuticals Inc E394
Regenxbio Inc E349
Revere Bank (laurel, Md) E356
Capital Bancorp Inc (md) E63

SILVER SPRING
Discovery Inc A269
Holy Cross Health, Inc. P242

UPPER MARLBORO
Prince George's County Public Schools P429

WALDORF
Community Financial Corp (the) E91

MASSACHUSETTS

AMESBURY
Provident Bancorp Inc (md) E340

ANDOVER
Mks Instruments Inc E285
Mercury Systems Inc E276
Casa Systems Inc E67

AUBURNDALE
Atrius Health, Inc. P53

BEDFORD
Interactive Data Corporation A461 P255
The Mitre Corporation P577
Interactive Data Corporation A461 P255
Irobot Corp E239
Novanta Inc E306

BEVERLY
Axcelis Technologies Inc E29

BILLERICA
Entegris Inc E128

BOSTON
General Electric Co A373
State Street Corp. A783
Santander Holdings Usa Inc. A743
American Tower Corp (new) A58
Wayfair Inc A905
Lpl Financial Holdings Inc. A527
Berkshire Hills Bancorp Inc A128 E42
Boston Private Financial Holdings, Inc. A147
Brookline Bancorp Inc (de) A152 E51
Partners Healthcare System, Inc. A641 P406
The President And Fellows Of Harvard College P585
City Of Boston P138
Suffolk Construction Company, Inc. P531
University Of Massachusetts P631
The Massachusetts General Hospital P574
The Brigham And Women's Hospital Inc P556
Boston University P96
Fidelity Inv Charitable Gift Fund P201
The Children's Hospital Corporation P558
Boston Medical Center Corporation P95
Beth Israel Deaconess Medical Center, Inc. P79
Northeastern University P383
Tufts Medical Center, Inc. P612
Shawmut Woodworking & Supply, Inc. P490
Massachusetts School Building Authority P315
Dana-farber Cancer Institute, Inc. P172
Massachusetts Port Authority P314
Harvard Management Private Equity Corporation P229
Federal Home Loan Bank Boston E146
Logmein Inc E259
Berkshire Hills Bancorp Inc A128 E42
Cra International Inc E101
Stag Industrial Inc E384
Brookline Bancorp Inc (de) A152 E51

BRAINTREE
Altra Industrial Motion Corp E11

BROCKTON
Harborone Bancorp Inc (new) A406 E200

BURLINGTON
Keurig Dr Pepper Inc A489
Lahey Clinic Hospital, Inc. P284
Cerence Inc E74
Lemaitre Vascular Inc E253

CAMBRIDGE
Biogen Inc A132
Cambridge Bancorp A161 E61
Massachusetts Institute Of Technology P313
The Charles Stark Draper Laboratory Inc P556
The Broad Institute Inc P556
Pegasystems Inc E325
Cargurus Inc E66
Cambridge Bancorp A161 E61

CANTON
Dunkin' Brands Group Inc E115

CHELMSFORD
Brooks Automation Inc E52

CHESTNUT HILL
Trustees Of Boston College P608

CHICOPEE
Consumer Product Distributors, Inc. P156

CONCORD
Welch Foods Inc., A Cooperative P661

DANVERS
Abiomed, Inc. E2

FALL RIVER
Southcoast Hospitals Group, Inc. P502

FRAMINGHAM
Tjx Companies, Inc. A834

HANOVER
Independent Bank Corp (ma) A454 E227

HINGHAM
Hingham Institution For Savings A423 E211

HYANNIS
Cape Cod Healthcare, Inc. P109
Cape Cod Hospital P109

LOWELL
Enterprise Bancorp, Inc. (ma) A297 E129
Circle Health, Inc. P135
Lowell General Hospital P300
Enterprise Bancorp, Inc. (ma) A297 E129

LYNNFIELD
New England Petroleum Limited Partnership P363
Babcock Power Inc. P58

MARLBOROUGH
Boston Scientific Corp. A148

MEDFORD
Century Bancorp, Inc. A183 E73

MIDDLEBORO
Ocean Spray Cranberries, Inc. P393

MILFORD
Consigli Construction Co Inc. P155

NATICK
Cognex Corp E84

NEWBURYPORT
Ufp Technologies Inc. E414

NEWTON
Rmr Group Inc (the) E358

NORWOOD
Analog Devices Inc A66

OXFORD
Ipg Photonics Corp E237

PEABODY
Meridian Bancorp Inc A556 E277

QUINCY
Granite Telecommunications Llc P220
J.jill Inc E240

SOMERVILLE
Allways Health Partners, Inc. P27
Trustees Of Tufts College P610

SOUTH WEYMOUTH
South Shore Hospital, Inc. P502

SOUTHBOROUGH
Virtusa Corp E430

SPRINGFIELD
Eversource Energy A302
Baystate Health System Health Services, Inc. P72
Baystate Health Inc. P72

TAUNTON
Dennis K. Burke Inc. P178

TEWKSBURY
Covenant Health, Inc. P163

WALTHAM
Raytheon Co. A705
Thermo Fisher Scientific Inc A831
Global Partners Lp A387
Parexel International Corporation P404
Repligen Corp. E353
Care.com Inc E65

WATERTOWN
Bright Horizons Family Solutions, Inc E51

WELLESLEY
Wellesley Bancorp Inc. E435

WESTBOROUGH
Bj's Wholesale Club Holdings Inc A134

WESTFIELD
Western New England Bancorp Inc A914 E439

WESTFORD
Kadant Inc E242

WILMINGTON
Charles River Laboratories International Inc. E74
Onto Innovation Inc E315

WORCESTER
Hanover Insurance Group Inc A404
Umass Memorial Health Care Inc And Affiliates Group Return P616
Umass Memorial Health Care, Inc. P616
Umass Memorial Medical Center, Inc. P616
Umass Memorial Community Medical Group, Inc. P616

MICHIGAN

ADA
Alticor Inc. A39 P28
Solstice Holdings Inc. A766 P500
Alticor Inc. A39 P28
Solstice Holdings Inc. A766 P500
Access Business Group Llc P3

ANN ARBOR
Regents Of The University Of Michigan A710 P444
Tecumseh Products Company Llc P543
Truven Holding Corp. P611

AUBURN HILLS
Borgwarner Inc A146
Commercial Contracting Group, Inc. P149

BATTLE CREEK
Kellogg Co A486

BEAR LAKE
Blarney Castle Oil Co. P87

BENTON HARBOR
Whirlpool Corp A919

INDEX BY HEADQUARTERS LOCATION

BLOOMFIELD HILLS
Penske Automotive Group Inc A649
Agree Realty Corp. E5

CADILLAC
Wolverine Power Supply Cooperative, Inc. P673

CENTER LINE
Father Murray Nursing Center P201

CHARLOTTE
Spartan Motors, Inc. E383

DEARBORN
Ford Motor Co. (de) A359

DETROIT
General Motors Co A377
Dte Energy Co A279
Ally Financial Inc A37
American Axle & Manufacturing Holdings Inc A49
Dte Electric Company A278
Tcf Financial Corp (new) A805 E398
Henry Ford Health System A413 P236
Uaw Retiree Medical Benefits Trust A856 P614
Henry Ford Health System A413 P236
Uaw Retiree Medical Benefits Trust A856 P614
Detroit Wayne Mental Health Authority P179
Wayne State University P659
The Detroit Institute Of Arts P565
Pressure Vessel Service, Inc. P429
Tcf Financial Corp (new) A805 E398

EAST LANSING
Greenstone Farm Credit Services Aca A398 P222
Michigan State University P339
Greenstone Farm Credit Services Aca A398 P222

FARMINGTON HILLS
Orleans International, Inc. P400
Level One Bancorp Inc E254

FENTON
Fentura Financial Inc E150

FLINT
Mott, Charles Stewart Foundation Inc A578

GRAND RAPIDS
Spartannash Co. A773
Independent Bank Corporation (ionia, Mi) A455 E228
Mercantile Bank Corp. A552 E275
Spectrum Health System A774 P510
Spectrum Health Hospitals P509
Meritage Hospitality Group Inc E279
Independent Bank Corporation (ionia, Mi) A455 E228
Mercantile Bank Corp. A552 E275

HILLSDALE
Cnb Community Bancorp Inc E82

HOLLAND
Macatawa Bank Corp. E265

JACKSON
Cms Energy Corp A208
Consumers Energy Co. A237
Henry Ford Allegiance Health System P235

KALAMAZOO
Stryker Corp A788
Bronson Health Care Group, Inc. P99
Bronson Methodist Hospital Inc P99

LANSING
Sparrow Health System P507

Neogen Corp E301

LIVONIA
Masco Corp. A541
Trinity Health Corporation A847 P606
Trinity Health-michigan P607
Mercy Health Services-iowa, Corp. P329

MADISON HEIGHTS
Mcnaughton-mckay Electric Co. P320

MANISTIQUE
Mackinac Financial Corp E265

MIDDLEVILLE
Hps Llc P246

MIDLAND
Dow Inc A278

MOUNT CLEMENS
Henry Ford Macomb Hospitals P237

MOUNT PLEASANT
American Mitsuba Corporation P34

MUSKEGON
Mercy Health Partners P329

NOVI
Nhk International Corporation P375
Michigan Milk Producers Association P339

PORT HURON
Semco Energy, Inc. P482

ROYAL OAK
Beaumont Health P74
William Beaumont Hospital P670
Barrick Enterprises, Inc. P67

SAGINAW
Covenant Medical Center, Inc. P163

SOUTHFIELD
Lear Corp. A507
Sterling Bancorp Inc (mi) A786 E387
Federal-mogul Holdings Llc A322 P201
Metaldyne Performance Group Inc. P334
Barton Malow Enterprises, Inc. P68
Barton Malow Company P68
Ascension Providence Hospital P47
Superior Industries International, Inc. E393
Credit Acceptance Corp (mi) E103
Sun Communities Inc E391
Sterling Bancorp Inc (mi) A786 E387

TAYLOR
Atlas Oil Company P52

TRAVERSE CITY
Munson Healthcare P353
Munson Medical Center P354

TROY
Kelly Services, Inc. A488
Flagstar Bancorp, Inc. A352 E172
Altair Engineering Inc E11

WARREN
St. John Hospital And Medical Center P516

MINNESOTA

AUSTIN
Hormel Foods Corp. A433

BAUDETTE
Ani Pharmaceuticals Inc E21

BLOOMINGTON
Healthpartners, Inc. A412 P233

Lamex Foods Inc. P285

BREWSTER
Minnesota Soybean Processors P343

BURNSVILLE
Ames Construction, Inc. P37

DULUTH
Smdc Medical Center P496
St. Luke's Hospital Of Duluth P521

EDEN PRAIRIE
Robinson (c.h.) Worldwide, Inc. A727
Mts Systems Corp E291
Surmodics Inc E395

EDINA
Production Technologies, Inc. P430

HERMANTOWN
Miners Incorporated P342

INVER GROVE HEIGHTS
Chs Inc A193

LITCHFIELD
The First District Association P568

MAPLE GROVE
Great River Energy P220

MAPLE PLAIN
Proto Labs Inc E339

MEDINA
Polaris Inc A669

MINNEAPOLIS
Target Corp A803
Us Bancorp (de) A883
General Mills Inc A375
Ameriprise Financial Inc A59
Xcel Energy Inc A931
Riversource Life Insurance Co A723
Fairview Health Services A311 P199
Allina Health System P26
Regions Hospital P445
Cliftonlarsonallen Llp P141
Minneapolis Public School District P343
North Memorial Health Care P379
University Of Minnesota Physicians P632
Apogee Enterprises Inc E23
Wells Fargo Real Estate Investment Corp E435
Tennant Co. E399
Bio-techne Corp E44
Sps Commerce, Inc. E384
Tactile Systems Technology Inc E397

MINNETONKA
Unitedhealth Group Inc A876

NEW ULM
Nuvera Communications Inc E308

PLYMOUTH
Tile Shop Holdings Inc E406

RICHFIELD
Best Buy Inc A129

ROCHESTER
Mayo Clinic Hospital-rochester A545 P317
Saint Marys Hospital P467
Mayo Foundation For Medical Education And Research P318
Hmn Financial Inc. E211

ROSEVILLE
Hawkins Inc E201

SAINT CLOUD
Coborn's, Incorporated P144
The Saint Cloud Hospital P587

SAINT LOUIS PARK
Park Nicollet Methodist Hospital P406

SAINT PAUL
Api Group Inc. P41
Hmo Minnesota P241
Augustana Health Care Center Of Apple Valley P55
Independent School Dist 625 P250
Regions Hospital Foundation P445
Merrill Corporation P332

ST. PAUL
3m Co A1
Ecolab Inc A288
Patterson Companies Inc A642

WINONA
Fastenal Co. A314

MISSISSIPPI

GREENVILLE
Farmers Grain Terminal, Inc. P201

GREENWOOD
Staple Cotton Cooperative Association P525

GULFPORT
Hancock Whitney Corp A401 E198

HATTIESBURG
First Bancshares Inc (ms) A334 E153
Cooperative Energy, A Mississippi Electric Cooperative P158
The Merchants Company P575
First Bancshares Inc (ms) A334 E153

JACKSON
Trustmark Corp A852
Board Of Trustees Of State Institutions Of Higher Learning P93
University Of Mississippi Medical Center P632
St. Dominic-jackson Memorial Hospital P514
Entergy Operations, Inc. P196

MERIDIAN
Southern Pipe & Supply Company, Inc. P506

MISSISSIPPI STATE
Mississippi State University P344

RIDGELAND
Eastgroup Properties Inc E121

TUPELO
Bancorpsouth Bank (tupelo, Ms) A105
Renasant Corp A717 E351
North Mississippi Health Services, Inc. P380
North Mississippi Medical Center, Inc. P381
Renasant Corp A717 E351

UNIVERSITY
University Of Mississippi P632

MISSOURI

CHESTERFIELD
Reinsurance Group Of America, Inc. A714
Mercy Health A555 P328
St. Luke's Episcopal-presbyterian Hospitals P520

CLAYTON
Olin Corp. A623

HOOVER'S HANDBOOK OF EMERGING COMPANIES 2020

INDEX BY HEADQUARTERS LOCATION

```
A = AMERICAN BUSINESS
E = EMERGING COMPANIES
P = PRIVATE COMPANIES
W = WORLD BUSINESS
```

Enterprise Financial Services Corp A298 E130

COLUMBIA
University Of Missouri System P633
Mfa Incorporated P337
M. F. A. Oil Company P302
University Of Missouri Health Care P633

DES PERES
Jones Financial Companies Lllp A480

FENTON
Maritz Holdings Inc. P308

GRANDVIEW
Nasb Financial Inc A580 E293

JOPLIN
Freeman Health System P209
The Empire District Electric Company P565

KANSAS CITY
Commerce Bancshares Inc A223
Umb Financial Corp A858
Kansas City Life Insurance Co (kansas City, Mo) A485
J.e. Dunn Construction Group, Inc. P261
J.e. Dunn Construction Company P260
Dst Systems, Inc. P186
Saint Luke's Health System, Inc. P466
Mercy Children's Hospital P327
Kcp&l Greater Missouri Operations Company P274
Saint Luke's Hospital Of Kansas City P467
St Luke's Hospital Of Kansas City P514
Truman Medical Center, Incorporated P607
Epr Properties E133
Corenergy Infrastructure Trust Inc E97
Novation Companies Inc E307

NORTH KANSAS CITY
Cerner Corp. A185
North Kansas City Hospital P379
Maxus Realty Trust Inc E273

POPLAR BLUFF
Southern Missouri Bancorp, Inc. A771 E381

SAINT JOSEPH
Heartland Health P234
Mosaic Life Care P349

SAINT LOUIS
Ascension Health Alliance A84 P47
World Wide Technology Holding Co., Llc A928 P673
Ssm Health Care Corporation A776 P512
World Wide Technology, Llc A928 P674
Ascension Health Alliance A84 P47
World Wide Technology Holding Co., Llc A928 P673
Ssm Health Care Corporation A776 P512
World Wide Technology, Llc A928 P674
Mccarthy Holdings, Inc. P319
Mccarthy Building Companies, Inc. P318
The Washington University P600
Barnes-jewish Hospital P67
Alberici Corporation P18
Spire Missouri Inc. P510
Barry-wehmiller Group, Inc. P67
Mercy Hospitals East Communities P331
Cic Group, Inc. P134
Alberici Group, Inc. P19
Alberici Constructors, Inc. P18
Saint Louis University P465
St Louis Children's Hospital P513
Missouri Baptist Medical Center P344
Special School District Of St. Louis County P508
Mercy Hospital South P330

SIKESTON
Food Giant Supermarkets, Inc. P205

SPRINGFIELD
O'reilly Automotive, Inc. A615
Great Southern Bancorp, Inc. A396
New Prime, Inc. P363
Mercy Hospital Springfield P331
Hiland Dairy Foods Company., Llc P239
Lester E. Cox Medical Centers P291
City Utilities Of Springfield Mo P139
Src Holdings Corporation P511
Guaranty Federal Bancshares Inc (springfield, Mo) E195

ST. LOUIS
Centene Corp A178
Emerson Electric Co. A292
Graybar Electric Co., Inc. A395
Ameren Corp A46
Post Holdings Inc A671
Peabody Energy Corp (new) A644
Stifel Financial Corp A787
Energizer Holdings Inc (new) E126
Bellring Brands Inc E42
Esco Technologies, Inc. E135

MONTANA

BILLINGS
First Interstate Bancsystem Inc A344 E164
Billings Clinic P84
St. Vincent Healthcare P523
First Interstate Bancsystem Inc A344 E164

GREAT FALLS
Benefis Hospitals, Inc P77

KALISPELL
Glacier Bancorp, Inc. A386 E188
Cityservicevalcon, Llc P139
Kalispell Regional Healthcare System P273
Glacier Bancorp, Inc. A386 E188

LEWISTOWN
Sports, Inc. P511

SIDNEY
Upper Missouri G & T Electric Co-operative Inc P644

NEBRASKA

COLUMBUS
Nebraska Public Power District P362

DORCHESTER
Farmers Cooperative P200

LINCOLN
Nelnet Inc A585 E300
Union Bank And Trust Company A862 P617
Board Of Regents Of The University Of Nebraska P92
Crete Carrier Corporation P165
Bryan Health P103
Bryan Medical Center P103
Union Bank And Trust Company A862 P617
Nelnet Inc A585 E300

NORFOLK
Affiliated Foods Midwest Cooperative, Inc. P9

OMAHA
Berkshire Hathaway Inc A127
Union Pacific Corp A863
Td Ameritrade Holding Corp A806
Kiewit Corporation A492 P279
Peter Kiewit Sons', Inc. A655 P413
Tenaska Marketing Ventures A810 P546
Farm Credit Services Of America A313 P200
Kiewit Corporation A492 P279
Peter Kiewit Sons', Inc. A655 P413
Tenaska Marketing Ventures A810 P546
The Scoular Company P589
Kiewit Industrial Group Inc P279
Ag Processing Inc A Cooperative P10
Hdr, Inc. P231
Kiewit Infrastructure West Co. P280
Hdr Engineering, Inc. P230
The Nebraska Medical Center P579
Sapp Bros., Inc. P473
Omaha Public Power District P396
Farm Credit Services Of America A313 P200
Kiewit Infrastructure Co. P279
Omaha Public Schools P396
Alegent Health- Bergan Mercy Health System P21
Northern Natural Gas Company P384
Tenaska Energy, Inc. P546
Kiewit Infrastructure South Co. P279
Nebraska Methodist Hospital Inc P362
Creighton Alegent Health P164
Warren Distribution, Inc. P658
Green Plains Partners Lp E194
America First Multifamily Investors Lp E15

WAVERLY
Farmers Cooperative Company P200

NEVADA

LAS VEGAS
Las Vegas Sands Corp A506
Mgm Resorts International A561
Caesars Entertainment Corp A159
Wynn Resorts Ltd A929
Axos Financial Inc A100 E31
Clark County School District P140
County Of Clark P160
City Center Holdings, Llc P137
University Medical Center Of Southern Nevada P623
Cannery Casino Resorts, Llc P108
Allegiant Travel Company E10
Axos Financial Inc A100 E31
Live Ventures Inc E259

RENO
Employers Holdings Inc A293
Nevada System Of Higher Education P362
Washoe County School District P659
Eldorado Resorts Inc E124
Polaris Infrastructure Inc E335

SPARKS
Sierra Nevada Corporation P493

NEW HAMPSHIRE

CONCORD
University System Of New Hampshire P642
Concord Hospital, Inc. P154

HAMPTON
Planet Fitness Inc E335

HANOVER
Trustees Of Dartmouth College P609
Dartmouth College P173

LEBANON
Dartmouth-hitchcock Health P173
Maxifacial Dental Surgery P315

MANCHESTER
Allegro Microsystems, Llc A24
Elliot Health System P193
Cmc Healthcare System P142

NEW JERSEY

ATLANTIC CITY
Marina District Development Company, Llc P308

BAYONNE
Bcb Bancorp Inc A120 E41

BEDMINSTER
Peapack-gladstone Financial Corp. A646 E324

BRANCHVILLE
Selective Insurance Group Inc A751

BRIDGETON
Inspira Medical Centers, Inc. P254

BRIDGEWATER
Brother International Corporation P100

BURLINGTON
Burlington Stores Inc A157

CAMDEN
Campbell Soup Co A163
The Cooper Health System P563
Virtua-west Jersey Health System, Inc. P653

CLINTON
Unity Bancorp, Inc. E419

CRANBURY
Palatin Technologies Inc E320
1st Constitution Bancorp E1

CRANFORD
Weeks Marine, Inc. P660

EAST BRUNSWICK
Wipro, Llc P672

EAST HANOVER
Novartis Pharmaceuticals Corporation A609 P391

EDISON
Hmh Hospitals Corporation P241
Jfk Health System, Inc. P266
The Community Hospital Group Inc P562
Larsen & Toubro Infotech Limited P286

INDEX BY HEADQUARTERS LOCATION

ENGLEWOOD CLIFFS
Connectone Bancorp Inc (new) A233 E94
Avio Inc. P57
Connectone Bancorp Inc (new) A233 E94

EWING
New Jersey Transportation Trust Fund Authority P363

FAIR LAWN
Columbia Financial Inc A220 E87

FAIRFIELD
Kearny Financial Corp (md) A486 E243

FARMINGDALE
Cherry Hill Mortgage Investment Corp E77

FLORHAM PARK
Conduent Inc A233

FOLSOM
South Jersey Industries Inc E378

FORT LEE
Empire Resources, Inc. P194

FRANKLIN LAKES
Becton, Dickinson & Co A122

HAMILTON
First Bank (williamstown, Nj) E154

HOBOKEN
Jarden Llc A477 P263

HOLMDEL
Monmouth Real Estate Investment Corp E287

ISELIN
Macdonald Mott Group Inc P303

JERSEY CITY
Provident Financial Services Inc A684
Verisk Analytics Inc E428

KEASBEY
Wakefern Food Corp. A898 P656

KENILWORTH
Merck & Co Inc A553

LINDEN
Turtle & Hughes, Inc P613

LITTLE FALLS
Cantel Medical Corp E62

LIVINGSTON
St Barnabas Medical Center (inc) P513

LONG BRANCH
Monmouth Medical Center Inc. P346

MADISON
Realogy Holdings Corp A707
Realogy Group Llc A707

MAHWAH
Ascena Retail Group Inc A83

MATAWAN
Creative Management Inc P164

MONTVALE
Berry Global Films, Llc P78

MORRIS PLAINS
Honeywell International Inc A430

MORRISTOWN
Prosight Global Inc A682
Ahs Hospital Corp. P12
Majesco E266

MOUNT LAUREL
Marlin Business Services Corp E270

NEPTUNE
Meridian Hospitals Corporation P332

NEW BRUNSWICK
Johnson & Johnson A479
Robert Wood Johnson University Hospital, Inc. P454
Johnson & Johnson Patient Assistance Foundation Inc P269

NEWARK
Prudential Financial Inc A685
Public Service Enterprise Group Inc A687
The New Jersey Transit Corporation P579
Newark Beth Israel Medical Center Inc. P371

OAK RIDGE
Lakeland Bancorp, Inc. A503 E250

PARAMUS
Sb One Bancorp E365

PARSIPPANY
Pbf Energy Inc A643
Avis Budget Group Inc A97
Zoetis Inc A941
Wyndham Hotels & Resorts Inc E449
B&g Foods Inc E32
Pbf Logistics Lp E323

PATERSON
St. Joseph's University Medical Center Inc P519
Paterson Public School District P409

PENNINGTON
Zydus Pharmaceuticals Usa Inc P678

PLAINSBORO
Integra Lifesciences Holdings Corp E233

POMONA
Atlanticare Regional Medical Center P51

PRINCETON
Nrg Energy Inc A610
The Trustees Of Princeton University P591
Educational Testing Service Inc P191
Clearway Energy Inc E81

RED BANK
Oceanfirst Financial Corp A618 E310

RIDGEWOOD
The Valley Hospital Inc P598

ROSELAND
Automatic Data Processing Inc. A93

SECAUCUS
Quest Diagnostics, Inc. A697
Njmhmc Llc P376

SHORT HILLS
Investors Bancorp Inc (new) A472 E236

SOMERSET
Shi International Corp. A757 P492

TEANECK
Cognizant Technology Solutions Corp. A216

UNION
Bed, Bath & Beyond, Inc. A124

VOORHEES
Kennedy Memorial Hospital University Medical Center Inc P275

WASHINGTON TOWNSHIP
Parke Bancorp Inc E321

WEST ORANGE
A-1 Specialized Services & Supplies, Inc. P1
Barnabas Health, Inc. P66

WHIPPANY
Stephen Gould Corporation P527

WOODBRIDGE
Northfield Bancorp Inc (de) A607 E305
Dhpc Technologies, Inc. A264 P180
New Jersey Turnpike Authority Inc P363
Northfield Bancorp Inc (de) A607 E305

WOODBURY
Inspira Medical Centers, Inc. P254

WOODCLIFF LAKE
Eagle Pharmaceuticals, Inc. E118

NEW MEXICO

ALBUQUERQUE
University Of New Mexico P633
Albuquerque Municipal School District Number 12 P20

ESPANOLA
Akal Security, Inc. P15

NEW YORK

ALBANY
State University Of New York A784 P526
Sefcu Services, Llc A751 P482
State University Of New York A784 P526
Dormitory Authority - State Of New York P184
St. Peter's Health Care Services P523
Capital District Physicians' Health Plan, Inc. P110
The Research Foundation For The State University Of New York P586
Albany Medical Center Hospital P18
Thruway Authority Of New York State P604
Albany Medical Center P17
New York State Environmental Facilities Corp P369
Sefcu Services, Llc A751 P482

ARMONK
International Business Machines Corp A464

BALLSTON SPA
Stewart's Shops Corp. P529

BINGHAMTON
United Health Services Hospital, Inc. P619

BRIDGEHAMPTON
Bridge Bancorp, Inc. (bridgehampton, Ny) A149 E50

BRONX
Montefiore Medical Center P348
Bronxcare Health System P99
Fordham University P205
Lincoln Medical And Mental Health Center P296

BROOKLYN
Dime Community Bancshares, Inc A268
Newyork-presbyterian/brooklyn Methodist P374
Maimonides Medical Center P304
The Brookdale Hospital Medical Center P556
Etsy Inc E137

BUFFALO
M & T Bank Corp A529
Rich Products Corporation P449
Kaleida Health P272
Buffalo City School District P103
Erie County Medical Center Corp. P197

CAMDEN
International Wire Group, Inc. P257

CATSKILL
Greene County Bancorp Inc E194

COOPERSTOWN
The Mary Imogene Bassett Hospital P574

CORNING
Corning Inc A239

DEWITT
Community Bank System Inc A226 E90

EAST ELMHURST
Skanska Usa Civil Inc. P495
Skanska Usa Civil Northeast Inc. P496

EAST SYRACUSE
D/l Cooperative Inc. P168

FLUSHING
Newyork-presbyterian/queens P374

GETZVILLE
Columbus Mckinnon Corp. (ny) E87

GLEN HEAD
First Of Long Island Corp A348 E169

GLENS FALLS
Arrow Financial Corp. A82

GLENVILLE
Trustco Bank Corp. (n.y.) A851

GREAT NECK
Brt Apartments Corp E53

HAMBURG
Evans Bancorp, Inc. E137

HAUPPAUGE
County Of Suffolk P162

HICKSVILLE
National Grid Generation Llc P359

ITHACA
Tompkins Financial Corp A838
Tompkins Trust Company A839
Cornell University P159

JAMAICA
St. John's University P517

JERICHO
Getty Realty Corp. E187
Esquire Financial Holdings Inc E135

LAGRANGEVILLE
Health Quest Systems, Inc. P233

LIVERPOOL
Raymours Furniture Company, Inc. P440

LONG ISLAND CITY
Altice Usa Inc A39

INDEX BY HEADQUARTERS LOCATION

```
A = AMERICAN BUSINESS
E = EMERGING COMPANIES
P = PRIVATE COMPANIES
W = WORLD BUSINESS
```

Jetblue Airways Corp A477
New York City School Construction Authority P366

LYNBROOK
Biospecifics Technologies Corp. E45

MANHASSET
North Shore University Hospital P382

MELVILLE
Schein (henry) Inc A743
Comtech Telecommunications Corp. E93

MENANDS
Health Research, Inc. P233

MINEOLA
Nassua County Interim Finance Authority P357

MONTEBELLO
Sterling Bancorp (de) A786 E387

NEW HYDE PARK
Long Island Jewish Medical Center P298

NEW YORK
Jpmorgan Chase & Co A482
Verizon Communications Inc A889
Citigroup Inc A202
Metlife Inc A558
Federal Reserve Bank Of New York, Dist. No. 2 A319
Pfizer Inc A657
Goldman Sachs Group Inc A389
Morgan Stanley A573
American International Group Inc A57
American Express Co. A53
Intl Fcstone Inc. A469
Travelers Companies Inc (the) A843
Philip Morris International Inc A660
Bristol-myers Squibb Co. A151
Bank Of New York Mellon Corp A111
Colgate-palmolive Co. A217
Omnicom Group, Inc. A625
Marsh & Mclennan Companies Inc. A539
Lauder (estee) Cos., Inc. (the) A507
Viacomcbs Inc A892
Blackrock Inc A134
Loews Corp. A524
Consolidated Edison Inc A234
Equitable Holdings Inc A301
Icahn Enterprises Lp A450
Fox Corp A362
Consolidated Edison Co. Of New York, Inc. A234
News Corp (new) A595
Interpublic Group Of Companies Inc. A468
Pvh Corp A691
Coty, Inc. A242
Voya Financial Inc A898
Assurant Inc A87
Foot Locker, Inc. A358
Sirius Xm Holdings Inc A762
Alleghany Corp. A31
Blackstone Group Inc (the) A136
S&p Global Inc A737
Hsbc Usa, Inc. A439
Nielsen Holdings Plc A599 P376
Abm Industries, Inc. A7
Hess Corp A418
Ralph Lauren Corp A701
Tapestry Inc A801

National General Holdings Corp A581
Federal Home Loan Bank New York A317
Cit Group Inc (new) A199
E*trade Financial Corp A282
Annaly Capital Management Inc A68
Signature Bank (new York, Ny) A758 E372
Valley National Bancorp (nj) A887 E425
Chimera Investment Corp A191 E79
Two Harbors Investment Corp A853
Ladder Capital Corp A503 E249
Ambac Financial Group, Inc. A43 E12
Metropolitan Bank Holding Corp A560 E281
Ag Mortgage Investment Trust Inc A20
The Turner Corporation A829 P592
Turner Construction Company Inc A853 P612
New York City Health And Hospitals Corporation A588 P365
Metropolitan Transportation Authority A560 P336
New York University A591 P369
The New York And Presbyterian Hospital A827 P580
Tata America International Corporation A805 P542
Nielsen Holdings Plc A599 P376
New York University A591 P369
Signature Financial Llc A759 P493
Reckson Operating Partnership, L.p. A708 P441
Virtu Financial Llc A895 P653
The Simons Foundation Inc A829 P589
The Ford Foundation A825 P568
Brixmor Llc A152 P98
New York Community Trust And Community Funds Inc A590
State Of New York Mortgage Agency A782 P525
Nielsen Holdings Plc A599 P376
The Turner Corporation A829 P592
Turner Construction Company Inc A853 P612
New York City Health And Hospitals Corporation A588 P365
Metropolitan Transportation Authority A560 P336
New York University A591 P369
The New York And Presbyterian Hospital A827 P580
Tata America International Corporation A805 P542
Nielsen Holdings Plc A599 P376
New York City Transit Authority P366
Lukoil Pan Americas, Llc P302
Memorial Sloan-kettering Cancer Center P325
New York University A591 P369
Trammo, Inc. P605
Axel Johnson Inc. P57
Icahn School Of Medicine At Mount Sinai P248
Memorial Hospital For Cancer And Allied Diseases P325
Mount Sinai Hospitals Group, Inc. P351
Triborough Bridge & Tunnel Authority P606
Genpact Limited P216
Signature Financial Llc A759 P493
Vns Choice P655
Beth Israel Medical Center P80
The Bloomberg Family Foundation Inc P555
Newmark & Company Real Estate, Inc. P372
Nfp Corp. P375

Lenox Hill Hospital P291
Lhh Corporation P294
Guildnet, Inc. P225
St Luke's-roosevelt Hospital Center P514
Reckson Operating Partnership, L.p. A708 P441
Blue Tee Corp. P90
Hunter Roberts Construction Group Llc P246
New York City Economic Development Corporation P364
International Rescue Committee, Inc. P257
Catholic Medical Mission Board Inc P117
Virtu Financial Llc A895 P653
Management-ila Managed Health Care Trust Fund P307
The Simons Foundation Inc A829 P589
Henry Modell & Company, Inc. P237
United States Fund For Unicef P620
New York State Housing Finance Agency P369
Metro-north Commuter Railroad Co Inc P335
The Associated Press P554
New York-presbyterian Fund Inc P371
The Ford Foundation A825 P568
New York Blood Center, Inc. P364
Visiting Nurse Service Of New York Home Care Ii P654
Jewish Communal Fund P265
Logicalis Us Holdings, Inc. P297
Brixmor Llc A152 P98
State Of New York Mortgage Agency A782 P525
Kkr & Co Inc E246
New Residential Investment Corp E302
Evercore Inc E137
Newmark Group Inc E303
Hc2 Holdings Inc E201
Signature Bank (new York, Ny) A758 E372
Madison Square Garden Co (the) (new) E266
Gannett Co Inc (new) E182
American Express Credit Corp. E15
Msci Inc E290
Valley National Bancorp (nj) A887 E425
Chimera Investment Corp A191 E79
Ubiquiti Inc E414
Cowen Inc E100
Vici Properties Inc E429
Moelis & Co E287
Exlservice Holdings Inc E140
Terraform Power Inc E400
Paramount Group Inc E321
Blackstone Mortgage Trust Inc E48
Tiptree Inc E407
Shutterstock Inc E370
Carey Watermark Investors Inc E66
Ladder Capital Corp A503 E249
Pjt Partners Inc E335
Ambac Financial Group, Inc. A43 E12
Siga Technologies Inc E372
Shake Shack Inc E369
Marketaxess Holdings Inc. E270
On Deck Capital Inc E315
Fortress Transportation & Infrastructure Investors Llc E179
Ready Capital Corp E346
Global Net Lease Inc E189
Wisdomtree Investments, Inc. E446
Tpg Re Finance Trust Inc E407
Corporate Property Associates 18 Global Inc E98
Kkr Real Estate Finance Trust Inc E247

Pzena Investment Management Inc E340
Goldman Sachs Bdc Inc E191
Silvercrest Asset Management Group Inc E373
Metropolitan Bank Holding Corp A560 E281
Otc Markets Group Inc E318
Safehold Inc E362
Mesabi Trust E280
Siebert Financial Corp E371
Network-1 Technologies, Inc E302

NORWICH
Nbt Bancorp. Inc. A583

OCEANSIDE
South Nassau Communities Hospital Inc P502

PEARL RIVER
Orange And Rockland Utilities Inc P397

POUGHKEEPSIE
Central Hudson Gas & Electric Corporation P121
Vassar Brothers Hospital P649

PURCHASE
Pepsico Inc A653
Mastercard Inc A543
Mbia Inc. A546

REGO PARK
New York State Catholic Health Plan, Inc. A590 P368

ROCHESTER
Home Properties, Limited Partnership A428 P243
Rochester General Hospital Inc P455
Rochester Gas And Electric Corporation P455
Rochester City School District P454
Rochester Institute Of Technology (inc) P455
Home Properties, Limited Partnership A428 P243
The Unity Hospital Of Rochester P593

ROSLYN
St. Francis Hospital, Roslyn, New York P515

RYE BROOK
Xylem Inc A935
Rusal America Corp. P458

SCHENECTADY
The Golub Corporation P570
Mvp Health Plan, Inc. P355

STATEN ISLAND
Key Food Stores Co-operative, Inc. P277
Staten Island University Hospital P527

SYRACUSE
Srctec, Llc P512
St. Joseph's Hospital Health Center P518
Syracuse City School District P539
Carrols Restaurant Group Inc E66

TARRYTOWN
Regeneron Pharmaceuticals, Inc. A709
Db Us Holding Corporation P174

UNIONDALE
Flushing Financial Corp. A356
Long Island Power Authority P298
Arbor Realty Trust Inc E24

INDEX BY HEADQUARTERS LOCATION

VALHALLA
Westchester County Health Care Corporation P664

VICTOR
Constellation Brands Inc A236

WARSAW
Financial Institutions Inc. A330 E151

WEST ISLIP
Good Samaritan Hospital Medical Center P217

WEST NYACK
The Salvation Army P587

WESTBURY
New York Community Bancorp Inc. A589
North Shore-long Island Jewish Health Care P382

WESTFIELD
National Grape Co-operative Association, Inc. P358

WHITE PLAINS
New York Power Authority P367
White Plains Hospital Medical Center P667
Northeast Community Bancorp Inc E305

WILLIAMSVILLE
Life Storage Inc E256

YORKTOWN HEIGHTS
Pcsb Financial Corp E323

NORTH CAROLINA

ASHEVILLE
Hometrust Bancshares Inc. A430 E215
Mission Hospital, Inc. P343
Hometrust Bancshares Inc. A430 E215

BOONE
Samaritan's Purse P469

BURLINGTON
Laboratory Corporation Of America Holdings A502

CARY
Ply Gem Holdings, Inc. P423
Coc Properties, Inc. P145
Cary Oil Co., Inc. P115
Wake County Public School System P656

CHAPEL HILL
University Of North Carolina Hospitals P635
The University Of North Carolina P595
University Of North Carolina At Chapel Hill P634

CHARLOTTE
Bank Of America Corp A106
Nucor Corp. A611
Duke Energy Corp A280
Sonic Automotive, Inc. A766
Brighthouse Financial Inc A150
Brighthouse Life Insurance Co - Insurance Products A150
Duke Energy Carolinas Llc A280
The Charlotte-mecklenburg Hospital Authority A823 P557
Snyder's-lance, Inc. P498
Presbyterian Hospital P428

Parsons Environment & Infrastructure Group Inc. P406
Premier Healthcare Alliance, L.p. P428
Lendingtree Inc (new) E254

CONCORD
Carolinas Medical Center Northeast P114
Cmc-northeast, Inc. P142

DUNN
Select Bancorp Inc (new) E368

DURHAM
Iqvia Holdings Inc A473
Duke University P186
Duke University Health System, Inc. P187
The North Carolina Mutual Wholesale Drug Company P581
Research Triangle Institute Inc P447

FAYETTEVILLE
Carolina Healthcare Center Of Cumberland Lp P114
Cape Fear Valley Medical Center P110
Cumberland County Hospital System, Inc. P167

GASTONIA
Mann+hummel Filtration Technology Intermediate Holdings Inc. P307
Caromont Health, Inc. P115

GREENSBORO
The Moses H Cone Memorial Hospital P578
The Fresh Market Inc P568
Guilford County School System P225

GREENVILLE
Pitt County Memorial Hospital, Incorporated P420

HICKORY
Alex Lee, Inc. P21

HUNTERSVILLE
American Tire Distributors Holdings, Inc. P35

KINSTON
Hillco, Ltd. P240
Union Bank (greenville, Nc) E415

LEXINGTON
Lexington Medical Center P294

MOORESVILLE
Lowe's Companies Inc A526

PINEHURST
Moore Regional Hospital, Inc. P349

RALEIGH
Advance Auto Parts Inc A12
First Citizens Bancshares Inc (nc) A335 E156
Coastal Federal Credit Union A213
County Of Wake P162
North Carolina Electric Membership Corporation P378
Rex Hospital, Inc. P448
Suntory International Corp. P534
Rex Healthcare, Inc. P447
North Carolina Eastern Municipal Power Agency P378
First Citizens Bancshares Inc (nc) A335 E156
Bandwidth Inc E35

SOUTHERN PINES
First Bancorp (nc) A334 E153

WILMINGTON
Live Oak Bancshares Inc A523 E259
Live Oak Banking Company A523

Live Oak Bancshares Inc A523 E259

WINSTON SALEM
Novant Health, Inc. P390
North Carolina Baptist Hospital P377
Quality Oil Company, Llc P435
Winston-salem/forsyth County Schools P672

WINSTON-SALEM
Truist Financial Corp A848
Hanesbrands Inc A402

NORTH DAKOTA

BISMARCK
Basin Electric Power Cooperative P68

FARGO
Sanford P471
North Dakota University System P378
Sanford North P472
Ni Holdings Inc E303

GRAND FORKS
Alerus Financial Corp A31 E8
Altru Health System P29
Alerus Financial Corp A31 E8

MINOT
Trinity Health P606

WEST FARGO
Clark Equipment Company P140

OHIO

AKRON
Goodyear Tire & Rubber Co. A391
Firstenergy Corp A350
Jersey Central Power & Light Company P265
Ohio Edison Company P394
West Penn Power Company P662
The Cleveland Electric Illuminating Company P562
Pennsylvania Electric Company P411
Metropolitan Edison Company P336
Childrens Hospital Medical Center Of Akron P131
American Transmission Systems, Incorporated P37
Akron General Medical Center Inc P15

BROOKLYN
Victory Capital Holdings Inc (de) E430

BROOKLYN HEIGHTS
Graftech International Ltd E191

CANFIELD
Farmers National Banc Corp. (canfield,oh) A314 E144

CANTON
Mercy Medical Center, Inc. P332

CHILLICOTHE
Adena Health System P5

CINCINNATI
Kroger Co (the) A497
Procter & Gamble Company (the) A679
Macy's Inc A531
Fifth Third Bancorp (cincinnati, Oh) A327
American Financial Group Inc A55
Cintas Corporation A196
Federal Home Loan Bank Of Cincinnati A318 E147

First Financial Bancorp (oh) A339 E160
General Electric International, Inc. A375 P215
Mercy Health A555 P328
Phillips Edison - Arc Shopping Center Reit Inc. A663
General Electric International, Inc. A375 P215
Mercy Health A555 P328
Uc Health, Llc. P614
Children's Hospital Medical Center P128
Kgbo Holdings, Inc P278
University Of Cincinnati P625
Messer Construction Co. P334
General Electric International Operations Company, Inc. P215
The Christ Hospital P559
University Of Cincinnati Medical Center, Llc P625
Cincinnati Public Schools P135
Bethesda, Inc. P81
Bethesda Hospital, Inc. P81
Good Samaritan Hospital Of Cincinnati P218
Federal Home Loan Bank Of Cincinnati A318 E147
Scripps (ew) Company (the) E365
Medpace Holdings Inc E275
First Financial Bancorp (oh) A339 E160
Phillips Edison & Co Inc E332

CLEVELAND
Sherwin-williams Co (the) A755
Parker Hannifin Corp A639
Keycorp A490
Transdigm Group Inc A841
Tfs Financial Corp A822
The Cleveland Clinic Foundation A824 P561
Eaton Corporation A286 P190
The Cleveland Clinic Foundation A824 P561
Eaton Corporation A286 P190
Case Western Reserve University P116
Cleveland Municipal School District P141
The Metrohealth System P576
Metrohealth Medical Center P335
Bearing Distributors, Inc. P74

COLUMBUS
American Electric Power Co Inc A50
L Brands, Inc A499
Alliance Data Systems Corp. A33
Huntington Bancshares Inc A443
Big Lots, Inc. A131
State Auto Financial Corp. A781
Battelle Memorial Institute P70
Ohiohealth Corporation P394
The Ohio State University Wexner Medical Center P581
Nationwide Children's Hospital P359
Mount Carmel Health System P350
American Electric Power Service Corporation P32
Franklin County Board Of Commissioners P209
Ohiohealth Riverside Methodist Hospital P395
American Municipal Power, Inc. P34
Columbus City School District P148
Columbia Gas Of Ohio, Inc. P148
Mount Carmel Health System P350
Mount Carmel Health Plan Medig P350
M/i Homes Inc E263
Installed Building Products Inc E231
Diamond Hill Investment Group Inc. E111

INDEX BY HEADQUARTERS LOCATION

```
A = AMERICAN BUSINESS
E = EMERGING COMPANIES
P = PRIVATE COMPANIES
W = WORLD BUSINESS
```

COLUMBUS GROVE
United Bancshares Inc. (oh) E416

DAYTON
Kettering Adventist Healthcare P276
Med America Health Systems Corporation P320
Miami Valley Hospital P338

DEFIANCE
First Defiance Financial Corp A339 E159
Sb Financial Group Inc E365

DELPHOS
K & M Tire, Inc. P270

DUBLIN
Cardinal Health, Inc. A169

FAIRFIELD
Cincinnati Financial Corp. A194

FINDLAY
Marathon Petroleum Corp. A534
Mplx Lp A578

GAHANNA
Heartland Banccorp E204

HUDSON
The American Endowment Foundation P554

HURON
Huron Health Care Center, Inc P247

INDEPENDENCE
Apple American Group Llc P42

KENT
Carter-jones Companies, Inc. P115
Kent State University P275

KETTERING
Kettering Medical Center P277

MARIETTA
Peoples Bancorp Inc (marietta, Oh) A652 E331
Marietta Area Health Care Inc P307
Peoples Bancorp Inc (marietta, Oh) A652 E331

MASSILLON
Fresh Mark, Inc. P210

MAUMEE
Dana Inc A253

MAYFIELD HEIGHTS
Ferro Corp E150

MAYFIELD VILLAGE
Progressive Corp. (oh) A680

MEDINA
Rpm International Inc (de) A732

MIDDLEFIELD
Middlefield Banc Corp. E282

NEWARK
Park National Corp (newark, Oh) A639

NORTH RIDGEVILLE
Invacare Corporation (tw) P257

ORRVILLE
Smucker (j.m.) Co. A764

OXFORD
Miami University P337

PERRYSBURG
O-i Glass Inc A616

RICHFIELD
Element14 Us Holdings Inc P193

SANDUSKY
Civista Bancshares Inc A206 E81

SHAKER HEIGHTS
University Hospitals Health System, Inc. P622

TOLEDO
Owens Corning A634
Pilkington North America, Inc. P419
The Toledo Hospital P591
The University Of Toledo P596
Mercy Health St Vincent Med Llc P330
Toledo Public Schools P605

WALBRIDGE
The Rudolph/libbe Companies Inc P587

WARREN
Anderson And Dubose, Inc. P38

WEST CHESTER
Ak Steel Holding Corp. A26

WESTLAKE
Travelcenters Of America Inc A842

WILMINGTON
Air Transport Services Group, Inc. E7

YOUNGSTOWN
Forge Industries, Inc. P206

OKLAHOMA

ANADARKO
Western Farmers Electric Cooperative P665

CATOOSA
Cherokee Nation Businesses Llc P126

OKLAHOMA CITY
Devon Energy Corp. A263
Chesapeake Energy Corp. A188
Bancfirst Corp. (oklahoma City, Okla) A104 E33
Candid Color Systems, Inc. A165 P108
State Of Oklahoma A782 P526
Candid Color Systems, Inc. A165 P108
State Of Oklahoma A782 P526
Hobby Lobby Stores, Inc. P242
Express Services Inc P198
Integris Health, Inc. P254
Seventy Seven Energy Llc P485
Integris Baptist Medical Center, Inc. P254
Kirby - Smith Machinery, Inc. P281
Ssm Health Care Of Oklahoma, Inc. P513
Mammoth Energy Services Inc E266
Gulfport Energy Corp. E196
Paycom Software Inc E323
Bancfirst Corp. (oklahoma City, Okla) A104 E33

STILLWATER
Oklahoma State University P395

TAHLEQUAH
The Cherokee Nation P558

TULSA
Ngl Energy Partners Lp A598
Oneok Inc A629
Williams Cos Inc (the) A921
Bok Financial Corp A141 E48
Oneok Partners, L.p. A631 P396
Continuum Energy Services, L.l.c. P157
Continuum Midstream, L.l.c. P157
St. John Health System, Inc. P515
Saint Francis Hospital, Inc. P464
Magellan Pipeline Company, L.p. P303
T. D. Williamson, Inc. P539
Ahs Hillcrest Medical Center, Llc P12
Bok Financial Corp A141 E48
Laredo Petroleum, Inc E252
Educational Development Corp. E124

OREGON

BEAVERTON
Nike Inc A599
Beaverton School District P76

BEND
St. Charles Health System, Inc. P514

CORVALLIS
Samaritan Health Services, Inc. P469

ESTACADA
Portland General Electric Comp P424

EUGENE
Oregon University System P399
University Of Oregon P635
Bi-mart Acquisition Corp. P82

MEDFORD
Lithia Motors Inc A520
C & K Market, Inc. P104

MONMOUTH
Western Oregon University P665

PORTLAND
Umpqua Holdings Corp A860
Precision Castparts Corp. A674 P427
Uti, (u.s.) Holdings, Inc. P646
Oregon Health & Science University P398
Legacy Health P288
Fctg Holdings, Inc. P201
Careoregon, Inc. P112
Portland Public Schools P425
Blount International, Inc. P87
Fortis Construction, Inc. P207
Legacy Emanuel Hospital & Health Center P287
Familycare, Inc. P199

ROSEBURG
Mercy Medical Center, Inc. P332

SALEM
Oregon State Lottery P399
Salem-keizer School District 24j P467

WILSONVILLE
Mentor Graphics Corporation P326

PENNSYLVANIA

ABINGTON
Abington Memorial Hospital Inc P3

ALLENTOWN
Air Products & Chemicals Inc A23
Ppl Corp A673
Lehigh Valley Health Network, Inc. P289
Talen Energy Supply, Llc P540
Lehigh Gas Corporation P288

AUDUBON
Globus Medical Inc E190

BALA CYNWYD
Philadelphia Consolidated Holding Corp. A660 P416
Hamilton Lane Inc E197

BEAVER
Heritage Valley Health System, Inc. P238

BENSALEM
Healthcare Services Group, Inc. E202

BETHLEHEM
St. Luke's Health Network, Inc. P520
Saint Luke's Hospital Of Bethlehem, Pennsylvania P466
St Luke's Hospital & Health Network Inc P513
Orasure Technologies Inc. E317
Embassy Bancorp Inc E125

BRYN MAWR
Bryn Mawr Bank Corp A154 E54
Main Line Hospitals, Inc. P305
Bryn Mawr Bank Corp A154 E54

CAMP HILL
Rite Aid Corp A721

CANONSBURG
Centimark Corporation P119
Ansys Inc. E22
Cnx Midstream Partners Lp E83

CARMICHAELS
Cb Financial Services Inc E69

CHAMBERSBURG
Summit Health P531

CHESTERBROOK
Amerisourcebergen Corp. A63

CLEARFIELD
Cnb Financial Corp. (clearfield, Pa) A210 E82

CLIFTON HEIGHTS
Harlee Manor, Inc. P228

CONSHOHOCKEN
Allied Security Holdings Llc P26
Mercy Health System Of Southeastern Pennsylvania P330

CORAOPOLIS
Dick's Sporting Goods, Inc A264

DANVILLE
Geisinger Health A371 P213
Geisinger Health Plan P214
Grandview Health Homes, Inc. P219
Geisinger Medical Center P214
The Geisinger Clinic P569
Geisinger System Services P214

DENVER
Ugi Utilities, Inc. P615

DUNCANSVILLE
Value Drug Company P647

DUNMORE
Fidelity D&d Bancorp Inc E151

GETTYSBURG
Acnb Corp E3

GREENSBURG
Westmoreland Regional Hospital P666

HARRISBURG
Pennsylvania Housing Finance Agency A648 P411
Pinnacle Health Hospital P420
United Concordia Life And Health Insurance Company P618
Upmc Pinnacle Hospitals P644

INDEX BY HEADQUARTERS LOCATION

Pennsylvania Housing Finance Agency A648 P411
Ollie's Bargain Outlet Holdings Inc E313
Riverview Financial Corp (new) E358

HERSHEY
Hershey Company (the) A416
Pennsylvania - American Water Company P411
Milton Hershey School & School Trust P342

HONESDALE
Norwood Financial Corp. E306

HORSHAM
Toll Brothers Inc. A836

INDIANA
First Commonwealth Financial Corp (indiana, Pa) A337 E158
S & T Bancorp Inc (indiana, Pa) A736 E360
First Commonwealth Financial Corp (indiana, Pa) A337 E158
S & T Bancorp Inc (indiana, Pa) A736 E360

KENNETT SQUARE
Exelon Generation Co Llc A305

KING OF PRUSSIA
Universal Health Services, Inc. A878
Ugi Corp. A856

LANCASTER
Fulton Financial Corp. (pa) A367
The Lancaster General Hospital P572

LANGHORNE
St. Mary Medical Center P522

LANSDALE
Skf Usa Inc. P496

MALVERN
Vanguard Charitable Endowment Program P648
Pq Group Holdings Inc E337
Cubesmart E103
Biotelemetry Inc E46

MANHEIM
Worley & Obetz, Inc. P674

MANSFIELD
Citizens Financial Services Inc E80

MILLERSBURG
Mid Penn Bancorp Inc A566 E281

MILTON
Kramm Healthcare Center, Inc P282

MONROEVILLE
Standard Avb Financial Corp E386

MOON TOWNSHIP
Calgon Carbon Corporation P106
Mastech Digital Inc E272

NEWTOWN
Epam Systems, Inc. E132

PAOLI
Malvern Bancorp Inc E266

PHILADELPHIA
Comcast Corp A220
Aramark A74
Radian Group, Inc. A700
Republic First Bancorp, Inc. A719 E355
University Of Pennsylvania A879 P636
The William Penn Foundation A831
University Of Pennsylvania A879 P636
Thomas Jefferson University P603

The School District Of Philadelphia P588
Temple University-of The Commonwealth System Of Higher Education P545
Hospital Of The University Of Pennsylvania P244
Thomas Jefferson University Hospitals, Inc. P603
Temple University Health System, Inc. P545
Community Behavioral Health P150
Health Partners Plans, Inc. P232
Albert Einstein Medical Center P19
The Pew Charitable Trusts P585
Albert Einstein Medical Associates, Inc. P19
Southeastern Pennsylvania Transportation Authority P503
Five Below Inc E171
Independence Realty Trust Inc E227
Republic First Bancorp, Inc. A719 E355
Prudential Bancorp Inc (new) E340

PITTSBURGH
Kraft Heinz Co (the) A496
Pnc Financial Services Group (the) A668
Ppg Industries Inc A672
United States Steel Corp. A873
Arconic Inc A78
Alcoa Corporation A31
Wesco International, Inc. A909
Fnb Corp A357 E175
Tristate Capital Holdings Inc A848 E410
Upmc Presbyterian Shadyside A883 P644
University Of Pittsburgh P636
Smmh Practice Plan, Inc. P498
Carnegie Mellon University P113
Duquesne Light Company P188
Magee-womens Hospital Of Upmc P303
Allegheny General Hospital Inc P23
Pittsburgh School District P421
Board Of Public Education School District Of Pittsburgh (inc) P92
Upmc P643
Federal Home Loan Bank Of Pittsburgh E147
Equitrans Midstream Corp E134
Eqm Midstream Partners Lp E134
Fnb Corp A357 E175
Tristate Capital Holdings Inc A848 E410

PITTSTON
Benco Dental Supply Co. P76

RADNOR
Lincoln National Corp. A519
Avantor Inc A96
Airgas, Inc. A24 P13
Main Line Health System P304

READING
Boscov's, Inc. P95
Redner's Markets, Inc. P442
Reading Hospital P440

SAXONBURG
Ii-vi Inc E224

SCRANTON
Peoples Financial Services Corp A653

SHIPPENSBURG
Orrstown Financial Services, Inc. E318

SOUDERTON
Univest Financial Corp A880 E420

TREVOSE
Broder Bros., Co. P98

UNIVERSITY PARK
The Pennsylvania State University A828 P584

UPPER CHICHESTER
Sunoco Pipeline L.p. P533

WARREN
Northwest Bancshares, Inc. (md) A609

WILKES BARRE
Geisinger Wyoming Valley Medical Center P215

WORCESTER
Allan Myers, Inc. P22

WYOMISSING
Customers Bancorp Inc A247 E106
Gaming & Leisure Properties, Inc E182
Customers Bancorp Inc A247 E106

YARDLEY
Crown Holdings Inc A244

YORK
York Hospital P677
Codorus Valley Bancorp, Inc. E83

PUERTO RICO

RIO GRANDE
Desarolladora Del Norte S E P179

SAN JUAN
Popular Inc. A670

TOA BAJA
Best Petroleum Corporation P79

RHODE ISLAND

LINCOLN
Narragansett Electric Comp P357

PAWTUCKET
Teknor Apex Company P544

PROVIDENCE
United Natural Foods Inc. A868
Textron Inc A820
Citizens Financial Group Inc (new) A204
State Of Rhode Island And Providence Plantations A782 P526
Gilbane Building Company A384 P216
State Of Rhode Island And Providence Plantations A782 P526
Gilbane Building Company A384 P216
Care New England Health System Inc P111
Rhode Island Hospital P448
Women & Infants Hospital Of Rhode Island P673

WARWICK
Plan International, Inc. P422

WEST WARWICK
Astronova Inc E27

WESTERLY
Washington Trust Bancorp, Inc. A903

WOONSOCKET
Cvs Health Corporation A250

SOUTH CAROLINA

ANDERSON
Anmed Health P38

CHARLESTON
Carolina Financial Corp (new) A172 E66
The Medical University Of South Carolina P575
Carealliance Health Services P111
Medical University Hospital Authority P321
Blackbaud, Inc. E47
Carolina Financial Corp (new) A172 E66

COLUMBIA
South State Corp A769 E379
Agfirst Farm Credit Bank A22 P10
Central Electric Power Cooperative, Inc. P120
Agfirst Farm Credit Bank A22 P10
South State Corp A769 E379

CONWAY
Horry County School District P244

DILLON
Saint Eugene Medical Center P464

FORT MILL
Domtar Corp A275

GREENVILLE
Athene Annuity & Life Assurance Company A90 P51
Prisma Health-upstate P429
Athene Annuity & Life Assurance Company A90 P51
Southern First Bancshares, Inc. E381

GREER
Regional Management Corp E350

HARTSVILLE
Sonoco Products Co. A767

LEXINGTON
First Community Corp (sc) E159

MONCKS CORNER
South Carolina Public Service Authority (inc) P500

SPARTANBURG
J M Smith Corporation P259
Security Group, Inc. P481
Security Finance Corporation Of Spartanburg P481

SUMMERVILLE
Advanced Technology International P5

WEST COLUMBIA
Lexington Medical Center P294
Lexington County Health Services District, Inc. P293

SOUTH DAKOTA

ABERDEEN
Dacotah Banks Inc. A252
Agtegra Cooperative P11

RAPID CITY
Regional Health, Inc. P445
Rapid City Regional Hospital, Inc. P439

SIOUX FALLS
Great Western Bancorp Inc A397 E192
Meta Financial Group Inc A557 E280
Sanford Health P471

INDEX BY HEADQUARTERS LOCATION

```
A = AMERICAN BUSINESS
E = EMERGING COMPANIES
P = PRIVATE COMPANIES
W = WORLD BUSINESS
```

The Evangelical Lutheran Good
  Samaritan Society P566
Great Western Bancorp Inc A397
  E192
Meta Financial Group Inc A557 E280

TENNESSEE

BRENTWOOD
Delek Us Holdings Inc (new) A260
Tractor Supply Co. A840
Premise Health Holding Corp. P428
Reliant Bancorp Inc E350

BRISTOL
Contura Energy Inc E95

CHATTANOOGA
Unum Group A881
Hamilton Chattanooga County
  Hospital Authority P227
Emj Corporation P194
Electric Power Board Of
  Chattanooga P193
Memorial Health Care System,
  Inc. P323

CLARKSVILLE
First Advantage Bancorp E153

COOKEVILLE
Averitt Express Incorporated P56
Averitt Express, Inc. P56

FRANKLIN
Community Health Systems,
  Inc. A227
Franklin Financial Network Inc A362
  E181
Clarcor Inc. P139
Franklin Financial Network Inc A362
  E181

GERMANTOWN
Mid-america Apartment Communities
  Inc E282

GOODLETTSVILLE
Dollar General Corp A272

GREENEVILLE
Forward Air Corp E179

JACKSON
Jackson-madison County General
  Hospital District P263

KINGSPORT
Eastman Chemical Co A285
Wellmont Health System P661

KNOXVILLE
Tennessee Valley Authority A814
Smartfinancial Inc A764 E377
Cfj Properties Llc A186 P123
Educational Funding Of The South,
  Inc. A290
Cfj Properties Llc A186 P123
Scripps Networks Interactive,
  Inc. P480
Regal Entertainment Group P443
Covenant Health P162
University Of Tennessee P638
Smartfinancial Inc A764 E377
Mountain Commerce Bancorp
  Inc E289

LEBANON
Wilson Bank Holding Co. A923 E442

LOUDON
Malibu Boats Inc E266

MEMPHIS
Fedex Corp A322
International Paper Co A466
Autozone, Inc. A94
First Horizon National Corp A342
  E163
Methodist Healthcare Memphis
  Hospitals P335
American Lebanese Syrian Associated
  Charities, Inc. P34
Board Of Education-memphis City
  Schools P92
Baptist Memorial Hospital P65
Monogram Food Solutions, Llc P347
First Horizon National Corp A342
  E163
Frontdoor Inc E181

MURFREESBORO
The Middle Tennessee Electric
  Membership Corporation P577
National Health Investors, Inc. E295

NASHVILLE
Hca Healthcare Inc A410
Pinnacle Financial Partners Inc A664
  E333
Fb Financial Corp A315 E145
Ryman Hospitality Properties,
  Inc. A735 P459
Vanderbilt University Medical
  Center P648
The Vanderbilt University P599
Ryman Hospitality Properties,
  Inc. A735 P459
Dialysis Clinic, Inc. P180
Tri Star Energy, Llc P606
Saint Thomas Hospital P467
Lifeway Christian Resources Of The
  Southern Baptist Convention P295
Delta Dental Of Tennessee P177
Pinnacle Financial Partners Inc A664
  E333
Fb Financial Corp A315 E145
Capstar Financial Holdings Inc E64
Harrow Health Inc E200

OOLTEWAH
Miller Industries Inc. (tn) E284

VONORE
Mastercraft Boat Holdings Inc E272

TEXAS

ABILENE
First Financial Bankshares, Inc. A340
  E161
Hendrick Medical Center P235
First Financial Bankshares, Inc. A340
  E161

ADDISON
Guaranty Bancshares Inc A400 E195

AMARILLO
Affiliated Foods, Inc. P9
Bruckner Truck Sales, Inc. P102
Baptist St. Anthony's Hospital
  Corporation P66

ARLINGTON
Horton (dr) Inc A435
Texas Health Resources P550
Arlington Independent School District
  (inc) P46
Forestar Group Inc (new) E176

AUSTIN
National Western Life Group
  Inc A582
State Of Texas A782 P526
Whole Foods Market, Inc. A920 P668
Texas Permanent School Fund
  Management Company, Inc. A820
  P551
Texas County And District Retirement
  System A819 P549
Farm Credit Bank Of Texas A312 P199
State Of Texas A782 P526
Whole Foods Market, Inc. A920 P668
Texas Permanent School Fund
  Management Company, Inc. A820
  P551
Texas County And District Retirement
  System A819 P549
Permanent University Fund P413
Austin Independent School District
  (inc) P56
Lower Colorado River Authority P301
Texas State University System P552
Attorney General, Texas P54
Farm Credit Bank Of Texas A312 P199
Parsley Energy Inc P321
Yeti Holdings Inc E451
Summit Hotel Properties Inc E390
Luminex Corp E261

BEAUMONT
Communitybank Of Texas National
  Association A229

BROWNSVILLE
Brownsville Independent School
  District P102

CARROLLTON
Hilite International, Inc. P239
The Brandt Companies Llc P556

CONROE
Conroe Independent School
  District P155

COPPELL
Mr Cooper Group Inc A578 E289

DALLAS
At&t Inc A88
Energy Transfer Operating Lp A295
Energy Transfer Lp A293
Southwest Airlines Co A773
Kimberly-clark Corp. A493
Tenet Healthcare Corp. A811
Hollyfrontier Corp A424
Sunoco Lp A790
Texas Instruments Inc. A819
Jacobs Engineering Group, Inc. A476
Dean Foods Co. A258
Builders Firstsource Inc. A155
Enlink Midstream Llc A295
Santander Consumer Usa Holdings
  Inc A742
Comerica, Inc. A221
Hilltop Holdings, Inc. A421
Texas Capital Bancshares Inc A818
  E402
Triumph Bancorp Inc A848 E411
Capstead Mortgage Corp. A168
Veritex Holdings Inc A888 E429
Baylor Scott & White Holdings A120
  P71
Army & Air Force Exchange
  Service A80 P46
Spirit Realty Capital, Inc. A775 P511
Baylor Scott & White Holdings A120
  P71
Army & Air Force Exchange
  Service A80 P46
Placid Refining Company Llc P421
Placid Holding Company P421

Balfour Beatty Construction Group,
  Inc. P58
Balfour Beatty Construction, Llc P59
Bearingpoint, Inc. P74
Dallas County Hospital District P170
Baylor University Medical Center P71
Steward Health Care System Llc P528
Children's Medical Center Of
  Dallas P129
Mv Transportation, Inc. P354
Spirit Realty Capital, Inc. A775 P511
Stevens Transport, Inc. P527
Southern Methodist University
  Inc P505
Copart Inc E95
Match Group Inc E273
Dave & Busters Entertainment
  Inc E110
Texas Capital Bancshares Inc A818
  E402
Howard Hughes Corp E217
Matador Resources Co E273
Berry Petroleum Corp E43
Holly Energy Partners Lp E212
Texas Pacific Land Trust E403
Triumph Bancorp Inc A848 E411
Ashford Inc (holding Co) E26
Veritex Holdings Inc A888 E429
Wingstop Inc E443
Transcontinental Realty Investors,
  Inc. E408
Zix Corp E452
Capital Southwest Corp. E64
Swk Holdings Corp E395

DEER PARK
Deer Park Refining Limited
  Partnership P176

DENTON
University Of North Texas
  System P635

DFW AIRPORT
Dallas/fort Worth International
  Airport P171

EDINBURG
Doctors Hospital At Renaissance,
  Ltd. P183

EL PASO
El Paso Independent School District
  Education Foundation P192
El Paso County Hospital District P192
Ysleta Independent School
  District P677
Socorro Independent School
  District P499

EULESS
Us Concrete Inc E421

FORT WORTH
American Airlines Group Inc A47
Burlington Northern & Santa Fe
  Railway Co. (the) A156
Bnsf Railway Group A138 P91
Fort Worth Independent School
  District P206
Texas Health Harris Methodist
  Hospital Fort Worth P550
Cook Children's Medical Center P157
Tarrant County Hospital District P541
County Of Tarrant P162
Texas Christian University Inc P548
Cook Children's Health Plan P157
Firstcash Inc E170
Elevate Credit Inc E124
Tpg Specialty Lending Inc E408
Lonestar Resources Us Inc E260

FRISCO
Addus Homecare Corp E3

INDEX BY HEADQUARTERS LOCATION

GAINESVILLE
Ses Holdings, Llc P485
Select Energy Services, Llc P482

GALVESTON
American National Insurance Co. (galveston, Tx) A57

GARLAND
Garland Independent School District P212

GRAPEVINE
Gamestop Corp A370

HOUSTON
Phillips 66 A662
Sysco Corp A796
Conocophillips A233
Enterprise Products Partners L.p. A298
Plains All American Pipeline Lp A667
Plains Gp Holdings Lp A668
Halliburton Company A400
Baker Hughes Company A101
Occidental Petroleum Corp A617
Eog Resources, Inc. A300
Waste Management, Inc. (de) A904
Kinder Morgan Inc. A494
Group 1 Automotive, Inc. A398
Quanta Services, Inc. A696
Centerpoint Energy, Inc A180
Targa Resources Corp A802
Westlake Chemical Corp A916
National Oilwell Varco Inc A581
Cheniere Energy Inc. A187
Apache Corp A70
Centerpoint Energy Resources Corp. A180
Marathon Oil Corp. A533
Cheniere Energy Partners L P A188
Crown Castle International Corp (new) A244
Prosperity Bancshares Inc. A682
Cadence Bancorporation A159 E56
Allegiance Bancshares Inc A32 E10
Cbtx Inc A176
Citgo Petroleum Corporation A201 P135
Cameron International Corporation A163 P108
Memorial Hermann Health System A552 P324
Citgo Petroleum Corporation A201 P135
Cameron International Corporation A163 P108
Memorial Hermann Health System A552 P324
Spectra Energy Corp P509
Tauber Oil Company P542
Biourja Trading, Llc P85
Houston Methodist Hospital P245
Memorial Hermann Healthcare System P324
Houston Independent School District P245
Chemium International Corp. P125
Midcoast Energy Partners, L.p. P340
United Space Alliance, Llc P620
Texas Children's Hospital P548
Methodist Health Care System P334
Texas Eastern Transmission, Lp P549
Technip Usa, Inc. P543
Texla Energy Management, Inc. P552
Cypress-fairbanks Independent School District P168
Kraton Polymers U.s. Llc P282
Cima Energy, Lp P135
Sun Coast Resources, Inc. P531
Financial Trader Corporation P202
Plains Pipeline, L.p. P422
Community Health Choice, Inc. P151

Florida Gas Transmission Company, Llc P203
Geokinetics Inc. P216
Anr Pipeline Company P40
Aldine Independent School District P21
Centerpoint Energy Services Retail Llc P119
Natural Gas Pipeline Company Of America Llc P360
S & B Engineers And Constructors, Ltd. P460
Enterprise Te Products Pipeline Company Llc P196
El Paso Natural Gas Company, L.l.c. P193
Southern Natural Gas Company, L.l.c. P506
University Of Houston System P629
Enterprise Crude Pipeline Llc P196
Mid-america Pipeline Company, Llc P340
Alief Independent School District P22
Tmh Physician Organization P604
The University Of Texas Health Science Center At Houston P595
Spring Branch Independent School District (inc) P511
Algonquin Gas Transmission, Llc P22
U.s. Pipeline, Inc. P613
Enable Gas Transmission, Llc P195
Lone Star Ngl Pipeline Lp P297
Texas Aromatics, Lp P547
Houston Methodist Hospital P245
Comfort Systems Usa Inc E88
Nextier Oilfield Solutions Inc E303
Kraton Corp E248
Select Energy Services Inc E368
Phillips 66 Partners Lp E332
Ies Holdings Inc E223
Sanchez Energy Corp. E363
Talos Energy Inc E398
Hi-crush Inc E210
Cadence Bancorporation A159 E56
Callon Petroleum Co. (de) E60
Cactus Inc E56
Shell Midstream Partners Lp E369
Noble Midstream Partners Lp E305
U.s. Physical Therapy, Inc. E413
Penn Virginia Corp (new) E327
Oasis Midstream Partners Lp E310
Solaris Oilfield Infrastructure Inc E378
Allegiance Bancshares Inc A32 E10
Whitestone Reit E440
Usd Partners Lp E423
Evolution Petroleum Corp E138

HUMBLE
Humble Independent School District P246

IRVING
Exxon Mobil Corp A308
Mckesson Corp A549
Fluor Corp. A354
Pioneer Natural Resources Co A665
Vistra Energy Corp A896
Celanese Corp (de) A177
Commercial Metals Co. A225
Michaels Companies Inc A563
Federal Home Loan Bank Of Dallas A318 E147
Christus Health International P132
Gruma Corporation P224
Nch Corporation P361
Jp Energy Partners Lp P270
Federal Home Loan Bank Of Dallas A318 E147
Montage Resource Corp E289

JOHNSON CITY
Pedernales Electric Cooperative, Inc. P410

KATY
Katy Independent School District P274

KILGORE
Martin Resource Management Corporation P311
Martin Product Sales Llc P311

KILLEEN
Killeen Independent School District P280

LAREDO
International Bancshares Corp. A463
United Independent School District P620

LEAGUE CITY
The Clear Creek Independent School District P561

LEANDER
Leander Independent School District P286

LEWISVILLE
Kmm Telecommunications P281

LUBBOCK
South Plains Financial Inc A768
Plains Cotton Cooperative Association P422
Pro Petroleum, Inc. P430
Covenant Health System P163
Texas Tech University Health Sciences Center P552
Lubbock County Hospital District P302

MCKINNEY
Globe Life Inc A388
Independent Bank Group Inc. A455 E228

MESQUITE
Mesquite Independent School District P333

MIDLAND
Wtg Gas Processing, L.p. P674
Diamondback Energy, Inc. E112
Propetro Holding Corp E339
Viper Energy Partners Lp E430
Ring Energy Inc E357

NEW BRAUNFELS
Rush Enterprises Inc. A733

PASADENA
Floworks International Llc P204
Pasadena Independent School District P408
Sunbelt Supply L.p. P532

PLANO
Toyota Motor Credit Corp. A839
Penney (j.c.) Co.,inc. (holding Co.) A647
Yum China Holdings Inc A936
Plano Independent School District P422
Integer Holdings Corp E232
Diodes, Inc. E112
At Home Group Inc E28
Tyler Technologies, Inc. E412
Green Brick Partners Inc E193
Bg Staffing Inc E43

RICHARDSON
Realpage Inc E346

ROUND ROCK
Dell Technologies Inc A261
Round Rock Independent School District (inc) P457

SAN ANTONIO
Valero Energy Corp A886
Iheartmedia Inc A451
Cullen/frost Bankers, Inc. A246 E104
Cps Energy P164
Bexar County Hospital District P81
Northside Independent School District P387
The University Of Texas Health Science Center At San Antonio P596
North East Independent School District P378
San Antonio Water System P469
San Antonio Independent School District Fac P469
Christus Santa Rosa Health Care Corporation P133
Southwest Research Institute Inc P507
Joeris General Contractors, Ltd. P266
Cullen/frost Bankers, Inc. A246 E104
Biglari Holdings Inc (new) E43
Xpel Inc E450

SAN MARCOS
Texas State University P551

SELMA
Spaw Glass Holding, L.p. P508

SPRING
Klein Independent School District P281
American Bureau Of Shipping P31

SUGAR LAND
Cvr Energy Inc A250
Noble Holding (u.s.) Corporation P376
Meglobal Americas Inc. P322

TEMPLE
Mclane Company, Inc. A550 P319
Scott & White Memorial Hospital P478
Scott & White Health Plan P477

TEXARKANA
Truman Arnold Companies P607
Yates Group, Inc. P676

THE WOODLANDS
Huntsman Corp A446
Chevron Phillips Chemical Company Lp A191 P126
Oxbow Sulphur Inc. P403
Western Midstream Partners Lp E439
Lgi Homes, Inc. E255
Sterling Construction Co Inc E387
Summit Midstream Partners Lp E391
Smart Sand Inc E377
Earthstone Energy Inc E119

TYLER
Southside Bancshares, Inc. A772 E382
East Texas Medical Center Regional Healthcare Syst P189
Christus Trinity Mother Frances Health System P133
Southside Bancshares, Inc. A772 E382

VICTORIA
South Texas Electric Cooperative, Inc. P502

WACO
Brazos Electric Power Cooperative, Inc. P96

INDEX BY HEADQUARTERS LOCATION

```
A = AMERICAN BUSINESS
E = EMERGING COMPANIES
P = PRIVATE COMPANIES
W = WORLD BUSINESS
```

Baylor University P71

WEBSTER
Clear Lake Regional Medical Center, Inc. P141

WEST LAKE HILLS
The Drees Company P565

WESTLAKE
Core Mark Holding Co Inc A238

WICHITA FALLS
The Priddy Foundation A829 P585

WYLIE
North Texas Municipal Water District P382

UTAH

AMERICAN FORK
People's Utah Bancorp A652 E330
Alpine School District P28
People's Utah Bancorp A652 E330

CENTERVILLE
Management & Training Corporation P306

DRAPER
Healthequity Inc E204

FARMINGTON
Davis School District P173

HURRICANE
Dats Trucking, Inc. P173

LOGAN
Utah State University P646

MIDVALE
Ally Bank A36 P27
Zagg Inc E451

NORTH SALT LAKE
Big West Oil, Llc P83

OGDEN
Big West Of California, Llc P83
Afj, Llc P10

SALT LAKE CITY
Zions Bancorporation, N.a. A939
Intermountain Health Care Inc A462 P256
The University Of Utah P597
Associated Food Stores, Inc. P50
C.r. England, Inc. P104
University Of Utah Health Hospitals And Clinics P639
Alsco Inc. P28
R.c. Willey Home Furnishings P437
Granite School District P220
Garff Enterprises, Inc. P212
Big-d Construction Corp. P83
Extra Space Storage Inc E141
Usana Health Sciences Inc E422

SOUTH JORDAN
Merit Medical Systems, Inc. E277

ST GEORGE
Ihc Health Services, Inc. A451 P249

WEST JORDAN
Jordan School District P270

VERMONT

BURLINGTON
The University Of Vermont Health Network Inc P597
The University Of Vermont Medical Center Inc P598
University Of Vermont & State Agricultural College P639

COLCHESTER
Green Mountain Power Corporation P221

RUTLAND
Casella Waste Systems, Inc. E67

VIRGIN ISLANDS

CHRISTIANSTED
Limetree Bay Terminals Llc A518 P296

VIRGINIA

ALEXANDRIA
City Of Alexandria P137
Vse Corp. E431

ARLINGTON
Aes Corp. A17
The Nature Conservancy P578
Ceb Inc. P117
Virginia Hospital Center Arlington Health System P650
Partnership For Supply Chain Management, Inc. P408
Virginia Hospital Center Arlington Health System P650
Public Broadcasting Service P432

BLACKSBURG
Virginia Polytechnic Institute & State University P652

BLUEFIELD
First Community Bankshares Inc (va) A338

BROADLANDS
Loudoun County Public School District P300

CENTREVILLE
The Parsons Corporation P582

CHARLOTTESVILLE
Rector & Visitors Of The University Of Virginia P441
Virginia National Bankshares Corp E430

CHESAPEAKE
Dollar Tree Inc A273
Fincantieri Marine Systems North America, Inc. A331 P202

CHRISTIANSBURG
Carilion New River Valley Medical Center P112

DANVILLE
American National Bankshares, Inc. (danville, Va) E16

EDINBURG
Shenandoah Telecommunications Co E370

FAIRFAX
Fairfax County Virginia P199
Guest Services, Inc. P224
Fvcbankcorp Inc E182

FALLS CHURCH
Northrop Grumman Corp A607
Inova Health Care Services P253
Inova Health System Foundation P253

GLEN ALLEN
Markel Corp (holding Co) A535

GLOUCESTER
Riverside Middle Peninsula Hospital, Inc. P451

HERNDON
Beacon Roofing Supply Inc A121

LYNCHBURG
Liberty University, Inc. P295
Centra Health, Inc. P119

MANASSAS
Prince William County Public Schools P429
Northern Virginia Electric Cooperative P385

MARTINSVILLE
Carter Bank & Trust (martinsville, Va) A172
Hooker Furniture Corp E215

MC LEAN
Dyncorp International Llc P189
Delta Tucker Holdings, Inc. P177
Immixtechnology, Inc. P250
Immixgroup, Inc. P249

MCLEAN
Freddie Mac A363
Capital One Financial Corp A166
Hilton Worldwide Holdings Inc A422
Booz Allen Hamilton Holding Corp. A143
Southern National Bancorp Of Virginia Inc A772 E381
Gladstone Commercial Corp E188

MECHANICSVILLE
Owens & Minor, Inc. A633

NEWPORT NEWS
Huntington Ingalls Industries, Inc. A445
Riverside Healthcare Association, Inc. P450
Riverside Hospital, Inc. P450
Riverside Regional Medial Center P451

NORFOLK
Norfolk Southern Corp A603
Sentara Healthcare A753 P483
Sentara Hospitals - Norfolk P484
Virginia International Terminals, Llc P652

PORTSMOUTH
Townebank A839 E407

RESTON
General Dynamics Corp A372
Leidos Holdings Inc A509
Nvr Inc. A614
Idemia Identity & Security Usa Llc P248
John Marshall Bancorp Inc E242

RICHMOND
Altria Group Inc A40
Performance Food Group Co A655
Carmax Inc. A170
Dominion Energy Inc (new) A274
Genworth Financial, Inc. (holding Co) A380
Virginia Electric & Power Co. A894

Federal Reserve Bank Of Richmond, Dist. No. 5 A320
Atlantic Union Bankshares Corp A91 E29
Apple Hospitality Reit, Inc. A71 P43
Virginia Housing Development Authority A894 P651
Virginia College Building Authority A894 P650
Vcu Health System Authority P649
Virginia Department Of Transportation P650
Estes Express Lines, Inc. P197
Virginia Premier Health Plan, Inc. P653
Gpm Investments, Llc P219
Apple Hospitality Reit, Inc. A71 P43
Virginia Commonwealth University P650
Virginia Housing Development Authority A894 P651
Virginia College Building Authority A894 P650
Apple Hospitality Reit Inc E24
Atlantic Union Bankshares Corp A91 E29
Synalloy Corp. E396
Kinsale Capital Group Inc E246

ROANOKE
Carilion Medical Center P112
Carilion Services, Inc. P112
Luna Innovations Inc E262

STRASBURG
First National Corp. (strasburg, Va) E168

TIMBERVILLE
F & M Bank Corp. E142

TYSONS
Dxc Technology Co A281
Computer Sciences Corporation A230 P153
Alarm.com Holdings Inc E8

VIRGINIA BEACH
Navy Exchange Service Command P360
Atlantic Diving Supply, Inc. P51

WINCHESTER
Valley Health System Group Return P647
Winchester Medical Center P671
Winchester Medical Center Auxiliary, Inc. P672
American Woodmark Corp. E18
Trex Co Inc E409

WASHINGTON

BELLEVUE
T-mobile Us Inc A800
Paccar Inc. A635
Expedia Group Inc A306
Overlake Hospital Association P402
Overlake Hospital Medical Center P402
Radiant Logistics, Inc. E344

BELLINGHAM
Haggen, Inc. P227

EVERETT
Fortive Corp A360
Public Utility District 1 Of Snohomish County P434
Funko Inc E182

HOQUIAM
Timberland Bancorp, Inc. E406

INDEX BY HEADQUARTERS LOCATION

ISSAQUAH
Costco Wholesale Corp A240
Naes Corporation P356

KENT
Petrocard, Inc. P415

KIRKLAND
King County Public Hospital District 2 P280
Monolithic Power Systems Inc E288
Pendrell Corp E326

LONGVIEW
North Pacific Paper Company, Llc P381

MOUNTLAKE TERRACE
Fs Bancorp Inc (washington) E181

OLYMPIA
Heritage Financial Corp (wa) A415 E208
Providence Health And Services P431
Heritage Financial Corp (wa) A415 E208

PORT ANGELES
First Northwest Bancorp E169

REDMOND
Microsoft Corporation A565

RENTON
Providence Health & Services A683 P431
Providence Health & Services - Oregon P431
Providence Health & Services-washington P431
Public Hospital District 1 Of King County P433
First Financial Northwest Inc E162

RICHLAND
Kadlec Regional Medical Center P270

SEATTLE
Amazon.com Inc A41
Starbucks Corp. A778
Nordstrom, Inc. A601
Alaska Air Group, Inc. A28
Expeditors International Of Washington, Inc. A307
Weyerhaeuser Co A917
Washington Federal Inc A903
Homestreet Inc A428 E214
University Of Washington Inc A880 P640
Swedish Health Services P537
Northwest Dairy Association P387
Group Health Community Foundation P222
Virginia Mason Medical Center P652
Seattle Public Schools P481
The City Of Seattle-city Light Department P560
Port Of Seattle P424
Ocean Beauty Seafoods Llc P392
Homestreet Inc A428 E214
Sound Financial Bancorp Inc E378

SPOKANE
Northwest Farm Credit Services A609 P387
Urm Stores, Inc. P645
Northwest Farm Credit Services A609 P387
Spokane Public Schools P511
Potlatchdeltic Corp E336

TACOMA
Columbia Banking System Inc A219 E86
Multicare Health System P352
Franciscan Health System P208
Tacoma Public Schools P540
Franciscan Medical Group P208
Columbia Banking System Inc A219 E86

VANCOUVER
Peacehealth P409
Southwest Washington Health System P507
Public Utility District 1 Of Clark County P433
Barrett Business Services, Inc. E40
Nautilus Inc E299
Riverview Bancorp, Inc. E357

WALLA WALLA
Banner Corp. A115 E38

YAKIMA
Yakima Valley Memorial Hospital Association Inc P674

WEST VIRGINIA

CHARLES TOWN
Jefferson County Board Of Education P264

CHARLESTON
United Bankshares Inc A865 E416
City Holding Co. A206
Charleston Area Medical Center, Inc. P124
United Bankshares Inc A865 E416

FAIRMONT
Monongahela Power Company P347
Mvb Financial Corp E292

FOLLANSBEE
Wheeling-nisshin, Inc. P667

HUNTINGTON
Cabell Huntington Hospital Inc P105

MOOREFIELD
Summit Financial Group Inc A790 E389

MORGANTOWN
West Virginia United Health System, Inc. P663
Virginia West University Hospitals Inc P653
West Virginia University P663

WHEELING
Wesbanco Inc A908 E436

WISCONSIN

APPLETON
U.s. Venture, Inc. A855 P614
Thedacare, Inc. P602
The Boldt Group Inc P555

BEAVER DAM
United Cooperative P618

BELOIT
Blackhawk Bancorp Inc E48

BROOKFIELD
Fiserv Inc A351

CLINTON
The Delong Co Inc P564

FITCHBURG
Certco, Inc. P122

FOND DU LAC
Agnesian Healthcare, Inc. P11

GLENDALE
Wheaton Franciscan Services, Inc. P667

GREEN BAY
Associated Banc-corp A85 E26
Nicolet Bankshares Inc A599 E303
Krueger International, Inc. P283
Bellin Health Systems, Inc. P76
Bellin Memorial Hospital, Inc. P76
Associated Banc-corp A85 E26
Nicolet Bankshares Inc A599 E303

JANESVILLE
Mercy Health System Corporation P330

LA CROSSE
Kwik Trip, Inc. P283
Gundersen Lutheran Medical Center, Inc. P225
Dairyland Power Cooperative P170
Mayo Clinic Health System-franciscan Medical Center, Inc. P316

LA FARGE
Cooperative Regions Of Organic Producer Pools P158

MADISON
Wisconsin Housing And Economic Development Authority A926
University Of Wisconsin System P641
Meriter Hospital, Inc. P332
First Business Financial Services, Inc. E155

MANITOWOC
Bank First Corp E35
County Bancorp, Inc. E99

MARSHFIELD
Marshfield Clinic Health System, Inc. P309
Security Health Plan Of Wisconsin, Inc. P482
Marshfield Clinic, Inc. P310

MENASHA
Network Health System Inc P362

MENOMONEE FALLS
Kohl's Corp. A496

MEQUON
Charter Manufacturing Company, Inc. P124

MIDDLETON
University Of Wisconsin Medical Foundation, Inc. P640

MILWAUKEE
Manpowergroup Inc A532
Wec Energy Group Inc A907
Rockwell Automation, Inc. A729
Harley-davidson Inc A406
Mgic Investment Corp. (wi) A560
Johnson Controls, Inc. A480 P270
Aurora Health Care, Inc. A91 P55
Robert W. Baird & Co. Incorporated A726 P452
Johnson Controls, Inc. A480 P270
Aurora Health Care, Inc. A91 P55
Aurora Health Care Metro, Inc P55
Milwaukee Public Schools (inc) P342
Froedtert Memorial Lutheran Hospital, Inc. P211
Robert W. Baird & Co. Incorporated A726 P452
Children's Hospital Of Wisconsin, Inc P129
Marquette University P309
Marcus Corp. (the) E267
Douglas Dynamics, Inc. E114
Physicians Realty Trust E333

MOUNT HOREB
Duluth Holdings Inc E115

OSHKOSH
Oshkosh Corp (new) A632

RACINE
Modine Manufacturing Co E286

RIPON
Alliance Laundry Holdings Llc P25

SUN PRAIRIE
Independent Pharmacy Cooperative P250

WAUKESHA
American Transmission Company, Llc P36
Waukesha Memorial Hospital, Inc. P659
Generac Holdings Inc E184

WAUSAU
Aspirus, Inc. P49
Aspirus Wausau Hospital, Inc. P49

WEST BEND
Westbury Bancorp Inc E438

WYOMING

GILLETTE
Cloud Peak Energy Resources Llc P142

Index of Executives

A

A, Wright Nathan P610
A, Sun W306
Aaefedt, Matthew A877
Aaholm, Sherry A A247
Aakre, Scott A434
Aaldering, Mark P572
Aaron, Thomas J. (Tom) A228
Aaron, Susan A433
Aaron, Carol P410
Aaron, Todd P528
Aaron, Susan E217
Aaronson, Diane P300
Aarup-Andersen, Jacob W129
Aase, Rune A301
Aase, Rune P196
Aasheim, Hilde M. W289
Aass, Luke A25
Aass, Luke P14
Abad, Rafael Lopez A771
Abadie, Laurent W301
Abadir, Jeffrey A242
Abadir, Jeff A242
Abarca, Jose A654
Abate, Victor (Vic) A374
Abate, Christopher J. A709
Abate, Christopher J. E348
Abba, Diego A10
Abbal, Frédéric W344
Abbamondi, Desa A921
Abbamondi, Desa P669
Abbasi, Azher A319
Abbate, Mark L. A556
Abbate, Sam A608
Abbate, Mark L. E277
Abbeele, Annick D. Van den P172
Abbene, David A540
Abberton, James P382
Abbey, Jared A126
Abbey, Anna B A790
Abbey, Anna A790
Abbey, Anna B E389
Abbey, Anna E389
Abbondante, Joseph A726
Abbott, Lynn A60
Abbott, Todd A533
Abbott, Sarah A562
Abbott, Beth A686
Abbott, Mark A704
Abbott, Dean A715
Abbott, Greg A782
Abbott, Mary J P265
Abbott, Greg P526
Abbott, Dave P559
Abbott, John W334
Abbott, Darren E132
Abbott, Erik E143
Abboud, Andy A506
Abboud, Ali El A783
Abdallah, Chaouki T. P634
Abdel-Kerim, Ahmed P41
Abdelhafiz, Gada M P229
Abdelhak, Mervat P636
Abdella, Shelly A906

Abdella, Shelly E435
Abdo, Marcus P316
Abdo, John E41
Abdoo, Elizabeth A. A436
Abdraboh, Seif P164
Abduljalil, Hala P517
Abdullah, Rao A401
Abdullah, Sakinah P494
Abdun-Nabi, Daniel J. E125
Abe, Karrie A791
Abe, Karrie P535
Abe, Toshinori W345
Abedin, AJ E7
Abel, Greg A127
Abel, Donna A248
Abel, Brandi A437
Abel, Bryon A528
Abel, Melissa A818
Abel, Scott P300
Abel, Nir W203
Abel, Donna E107
Abel, Ryan E272
Abel, Robert E281
Abel, David E366
Abel, Melissa E403
Abel-Hodges, Cheryl A692
Abela, John A559
Abell, Elaine A450
Abellera, Philip A723
Abelli, Donna L. A455
Abelli, Donna L. E227
Abello, Marc P A222
Abelman, David A722
Abelsen, James N P496
Abelson, David J. P406
Abercrombie, John A771
Abercrombie, Les P210
Abercrombie, Barbara P635
Abergel, Danny E267
Aberle, Jim P675
Abernathy, Gill P253
Abernathy, Cammy P627
Abernathy, Andrew Mark P632
Abhyankar, Vivek P325
Abiteboul, Jean A187
Abji, Minaz B. A436
Abkin, Kimberly A325
Abler, Bill A296
Ables, Grady L. A71
Ables, Dorothy M. P509
Abney, David P. A870
Aboaf, Eric A783
Abood, Steven A715
Aboody, Linda P325
Aboulafia, Joseph A111
Aboumrad, Daniel Hajj W26
Abraham, Jai A242
Abraham, JJ A512
Abraham, Frank A569
Abraham, Biju A895
Abraham, Karen P90
Abraham, Laurence J P206
Abraham, John P276
Abraham, Christine P280
Abraham, Neil E347
Abrahamson, Laura A16

Abrahamson, Tom P283
Abramowicz, Daniel A. A245
Abramowitz, Bernard H P369
Abrams, Sarah A147
Abrams, Murray A166
Abrams, Ed A465
Abrams, Dave P86
Abrams, Robin P230
Abrams, Paul P254
Abrams, Mark E79
Abrams, John E285
Abrams, Jack E285
Abreu, Yolanda P368
Abreu, Christopher A408
Abreu, Ant- - nio Manuel Barreto Pita de W146
Abreu, Rodrigo Modesto W385
Abston, Chris L A599
Abston, Angie A866
Abston, Angie E417
Abts, Brad A85
Abts, Joy A885
Abts, Brad E27
Abu-Hadba, Walid E22
Abulaban, Majdi B. W31
Abutaleb, Sam A831
Abutaleb, Sam P601
Accogli, Giuseppe A119
Accordino, Daniel T. E66
Accum, Claude A. W371
Aceituno, Walter P286
Acereda, Alberto P191
Aceto, Jay P651
Acevedo, Alejandro A538
Acevedo, Ellen P2
Acevedo, Debby P457
Ach, J. Wickliffe A340
Ach, J A340
Ach, Joseph A925
ach, W6
Ach, J. Wickliffe E160
Ach, J E160
Ach, Joseph E445
Achary, Michael M. A401
Achary, Michael M. E198
Acharya, Guru A927
Achat, Catherine P161
Achenbach, Mark A509
Achkire, Debra A349
Achleitner, Paul W135
Achten, Dominik von W180
Acikalin, Faik W222
Acito, Paiul A3
Acito, Joe A329
Ackerly, Nelson E246
Ackerman, Michelle A36
Ackerman, Joel A257
Ackerman, Brian A482
Ackerman, Dean M A508
Ackerman, John P171
Ackerman, Jeffrey (Jeff) P568
Ackerman, Thomas F. E75
Ackermann, Peter A107
Ackermann, Bryan E248
Ackerson, Vince A. A818
Ackerson, Vince A. E403

Acklin, Mark P404
Ackroyd, Jim A9
Ackroyd, Jim P4
Acoca, Bernard A779
Acosta, Jennifer A483
Acosta, Navia A590
Acosta, Philip A P499
Acosta, Ashley E300
Acosta-Trant, Ivette P65
Acott, Sarah A137
Acquafredda, Rita A744
Acres, Harold R P163
Acton, Michael A741
Acton, Bryan P91
Acton, Michael E364
Acutt, Nicola A897
Adachi, Mitsuo W127
Adair, Charles A389
Adair, Bryan A465
Adair, Charles A809
Adair, A. Jayson E96
Adali, Erhan W403
Adam, Rolf A458
Adam, David A606
Adam, Bradley J P506
Adam, Joseph E143
Adamczyk, Darius A431
Adame, Pedro A921
Adame, Theresa P22
Adame, Pedro A669
Adames, Ivan P175
Adamich, John A843
Adamo, Terri A325
Adamo, John A686
Adamos, Tara A452
Adamoski, Rob E96
Adams, Dennis A36
Adams, John A85
Adams, Brian A91
Adams, Douglas A100
Adams, Michael A154
Adams, Robert A171
Adams, Kraig A215
Adams, Kevin D A235
Adams, Melissa A246
Adams, Bruce A249
Adams, Craig L. A304
Adams, Isaac A409
Adams, Lisan A413
Adams, Michael A444
Adams, Joseph A460
Adams, David A462
Adams, Gregory A. A485
Adams, Amy A525
Adams, Calvin A527
Adams, Romaneo A540
Adams, Jennifer A540
Adams, Fay A571
Adams, John A590
Adams, Erin A592
Adams, Ann A604
Adams, Annie A604
Adams, Matt A606
Adams, Scott A621
Adams, Cathryn A658
Adams, D. Scott A683

HOOVER'S HANDBOOK OF EMERGING COMPANIES 2020

COMBINED HOOVER'S HANDBOOK INDEX OF EXECUTIVES

```
A = AMERICAN BUSINESS
E = EMERGING COMPANIES
P = PRIVATE COMPANIES
W = WORLD BUSINESS
```

Adams, Jennifer A709
Adams, Wayne A714
Adams, Patricia (Trish) A804
Adams, Trish A804
Adams, Tim A811
Adams, Dian A811
Adams, Jess A859
Adams, Richard M. A865
Adams, Gayle A876
Adams, Sherry A902
Adams, Nicholas A922
Adams, J Phillip P10
Adams, John V P22
Adams, James R. P82
Adams, Cathy P144
Adams, Kevin D P156
Adams, Marsha P179
Adams, Scott P212
Adams, David P256
Adams, William P264
Adams, Gregory A. P271
Adams, Joe M P274
Adams, H E P279
Adams, H E P280
Adams, Martin L. P299
Adams, Andy P329
Adams, Joseph (Joe) P355
Adams, Walter P361
Adams, Erin P371
Adams, Todd P389
Adams, Kendra P425
Adams, Melody P448
Adams, Mary P454
Adams, Michele P511
Adams, Valerie P573
Adams, Justin P579
Adams, Garold B. (Gary) P582
Adams, Ashley P597
Adams, Cecelia P605
Adams, Mary Jane P623
Adams, Bart P639
Adams, Cody P670
Adams, Nicholas P671
Adams, Trevor W275
Adams, John E27
Adams, Brian E29
Adams, Lisa E80
Adams, Melissa E105
Adams, Bruce E108
Adams, Kurt P. E174
Adams, Lisan E205
Adams, W. Andrew (Andy) E296
Adams, Scott E311
Adams, Gary E332
Adams, Jennifer E348
Adams, Daryl M. E383
Adams, Richard M. E416
Adamson, Nancy A117
Adamson, Adam A133
Adamson, Nancy P61
Adamson, Mark E114
Adan, Paul A538
Adcock, Robert H. A426
Adcock, Richard P515
Adcock, Robert H. E213
Addiego, Gino A74
Addison, Linda A389
Addison, Ann M. A509
Addison, James A538
Addison, John A676
Addison, Paul P394
Addoh, Carla P508
Adduci, Rich W273
Addy, R Mark A663
Adebo, Olo P174
Adelgren, Paul E189
Adelman, Marty A16
Adelman, Fredie P497
Adelman, Jeffrey D. (Jeff) E240

Adelman, Jeff E240
Adelson, Sarah A319
Adelson, Sheldon G. A506
Aden, Chandler P274
Adent, John E. E302
Adepeder, Suzanne P175
Ades, Susan P497
Adesnik, Ryan A510
Adesnik, Ryan P290
Adger, Ellis A354
Adham, Allen A10
Adiletta, Mark A530
Adkerson, Richard C. A365
Adkins, Dan A228
Adkins, Chuck A461
Adkins, Rodney A674
Adkins, Rodney A871
Adkins, Chuck P255
Adkins, Greg P618
Adkins, Leslie E409
Adkison, Jeffrey A481
Adler, Dean S A125
Adler, Paul F. A197
Adler, Don P300
Adler, Robert P304
Adler, Michael M. P351
Adome, Amy P489
Adorjan, J. Joe P465
Adornato, Theodore C. (Ted) A774
Adornetto, Charles A646
Adornetto, Charles E324
Adreani, Lou A784
Adriance, Glenn E. E279
Adsuar, Natalie P285
Advani, Navin A798
Adzema, Gregg D. E100
Aertker, Gayle A158
Afable, Richard P517
Affrique, Antoine de Saint W408
Agaj, Indrid E282
Agarwal, Anil A54
Agarwal, Pankaj A203
Agarwal, Sahil A484
Agarwal, Achal A493
Agarwal, Manu A574
Agarwal, Parag A628
Agarwal, Jitin E133
Agata, Shintaro W298
Agate, Chris A731
Agathoklis, Mariana A890
Agee, Nancy Howell P112
Agee, Andy E16
Agen, Brian E286
Aggarwal, Rohit A447
Aggarwal, Lokesh A784
Aggarwal, Prateek P230
Aggus, Gary L. P239
Aghai-Yazdy, Dana A794
Aghili, Aziz S A253
Agiasotis, Kerry A915
Agnello, Alexis A530
Agnes, Pierre P93
Agnew, John A921
Agnew, John P669
Agnos, Alexandra A751
Agnos, Alexandra P482
Agocs, Michele P596
Agostini, Joseph A877
Agostino, Rich A804
Agostino, Jason E123
Agrawal, Nancy A554
Agrawal, Rajesh K. (Raj) A915
Agrawal, Gail B. P594
Agree, Joey E6
Agree, Richard E6
Agresta, Richard A751
Agricola, Michael A329
Agroskin, Daniel A156
Agudio, Sharon A704
Agugliaro, Aubrey P103
Aguiar, Michael W. E230
Aguila, Alex A902
Aguilar, Alfredo A219
Aguilar, Douglas A318
Aguilar, Edgard Corrales A771

Aguilar, Corinna A780
Aguilar, Ashley P107
Aguilar, Jesse P276
Aguilar, Shannon P356
Aguilar, Gayla P378
Aguilar, Leslie P477
Aguilar, Juan Antonio W26
Aguilar, Alfredo E87
Aguinaga, Liz A525
Aguirre, Pascal A216
Aguirre, Edward A489
Aguirre, Jean A540
Aguirre, Vanessa A623
Aguirre, Adrian A921
Aguirre, Adriana P499
Aguirre, Rodney E77
Aguirre, Vanessa E313
Agulnek, Barbara A409
Agusti, Sandra A107
Agust-n, Juan P. San W91
Agyen, George A405
Aharony, Nadav P314
Ahearn, Tracey A527
Ahee, Joseph A444
Ahern, R A320
Ahern, Michael A390
Ahern, Patrick A796
Ahern, Paula P197
Ahern, Michael P198
Ahern, F. Gregory P202
Ahern, Gregory P202
Ahern, Patrick E397
Ahern, Chris E452
Ahlgrimm, Marijo P34
Ahlmann, Kaj A723
Ahmad, Usman A613
Ahmad-Taylor, Ty A310
Ahmar, Wasim A14
Ahmar, Wasim P6
Ahmed, Anwar A111
Ahmed, Riffat K A414
Ahmed, Sohail U. A460
Ahmed, Michael A855
Ahmed, Waseem P171
Ahmed, Riffat K P236
Ahmed, Riaz E. W396
Ahn, Sang A432
Ahn, Janice A793
Ahn, Jean P72
Ahn, Henry P480
Ahn, Timothy P628
Ahn, Francis P655
Ahn, Sang E216
Aho, Todd R A414
Aho, Dustin P6
Aho, Todd R P236
Ahrendts, Angela A72
Ahrens, Shelly A538
Ahrens, Steve A686
Ahrens, Blake A723
Ahrens, Chris P140
Ahrens, Jere M P196
Ahrens, Charles E. P470
Ahsan, Jawad E31
Ahuja, Deepak A818
Ahuja, Kishore P376
Ahuja, Rohit P448
Ahuja, Naresh P504
Ai, Lin P627
Aiba, Yasunori W374
Aichele, William S. A881
Aichele, William S. E421
Aicher, Allison A713
Aidi, Ali A544
Aiguo, Lin W301
Aiken, Jim A19
Aiken, Jason W. A373
Aiken, Scott A933
Aiken, Jefferson K. (Jeff) P289
Aiken, Paul P593
Aikens, Jason P248
Aikens-allen, Karla P432
Aili, Liu W99
Aimee, Heeter P610
Aing, Melissa A552

Aing, Melissa P324
Ainslie, Carolyn N. P591
Ainsworth, Julie A750
Aiosa, Lisa A701
Air, Dorothy P625
Air, David A. E183
Aird, Dan P512
Aires, Dave A460
Aishman, Lisa P255
Aitken, Murray L. A474
Aizawa, Zengo W394
Ajdaharian, Paul A761
Ajmani, Deep P389
Akalaeva, Nailya P459
Akalski, Frank J. A356
Akamatsu, Yayoi P375
Akashi, Masaru W127
Akatsuka, Yo W286
Akbar, Mehrdad A902
Akbarzadeh, Hosai A167
Akers, David (Dave) P104
Akers, Harlan P469
Akers, Sally P611
Akers, Brian E57
Akey, Douglas P333
Akgonul, Kerim E326
Akhtar, Muhammad A530
Akiba, Junichi W127
Akikawa, Tadashi W169
Akin, Virginia A367
Akin, Stacie A682
Akin, Rich P461
Akin, Terry P578
Akins, Nicholas K. (Nick) A51
Akins, D. Wayne A796
Akins, Nicholas K P32
Akins, D. Wayne E397
Akinwande, Wale A738
Akita, Seiichiro W50
Akiya, Fumio W349
Akiyama, Tomofumi W169
Akiyoshi, Mitsuru W249
Akman, Jeffrey S. P569
Akolawala, Joher A573
Akotia, Dennis A571
Akpik, Debbie P43
Akpoguma, Andrea P76
Akroush, Ghada P276
Akrout, Chekib A14
Aksdal, Roy A166
Aksyutin, Oleg E. W308
Al-Amoudi, Omar A. W342
Al-Benyan, Yousef A. W342
Al-Ghamdi, Othman W335
Al-Ghanoudi, Ashirf P218
Al-Haffar, Maher W91
Al-Humaid, Abdulaziz S. W342
Al-Issa, Abdullah Mohammed Ibrahim W327
Al-joulani, Omar A522
Al-Khudhair, Mariam A251
Al-Mady, Mohamed H. W342
Al-Maker, Awadh W342
Al-Mana, Khaled W342
Al-Naim, Najib Abdulaziz W344
Al-Ohali, Mosaed W342
Al-Rabeeah, Abdullah S. W342
Al-Saud, Saud bin Abdullah bin Thenayan W342
Al-Sheaibi, Fahad W342
Al-Zamel, Yousef W342
Alabran, Jeffrey A211
Alabran, Jeffrey E83
Alack, Marisa M P284
Alaimo, Chris P309
Alaix, Juan R. A941
Alam, Mahmood A658
Alam, Danesh A877
Alama, Bernie A109
Alameddine, Rima A613
Alaniz, Carol P486
alarcon, Alessandro De P128
Alarcon, Mari P183
Alas, Alejandra P646
Alba, Alex P536

COMBINED HOOVER'S HANDBOOK INDEX OF EXECUTIVES

Alban, Carlos A6
Alban, Susan A922
Alban, Susan P671
Albanel, Christine W297
Albanese, William A449
Albanese, Gerard A536
Albanese, William E220
Albanesi, David A885
Albarado, Rose A296
Alber, Laura A921
Alberici, John S P18
Alberici, John S P19
Alberico, Robert A742
Albers, Lisa A142
Albers, Lisa E49
Albert, Don A287
Albert, Scott A391
Albert, Justin A727
Albert, Gary A749
Albert, James A845
Albert, Justin P453
Albert, Elizabeth P517
Albert, Gary E367
Albertine, John E243
Alberto, Carl P520
Alberts, Jim P274
Albertson, Paul A588
Albertson, Paul P365
Albi, Chris A498
Albin, Brad E352
Albinson, Brock A93
Albo, Giuseppina W267
Albonetti, Susan P625
Albor, John A352
Albouy, Laurent A692
Albrecht, Vicki A63
Albrecht, Geoffrey A698
Albrecht, Julie A768
Albrecht, Raymond P P340
Albrecht, W. Steve E110
Albrechtsen, John P. E127
Albright, Steven A782
Albright, Dave P379
Albright, Linda P451
Albright, Steven P526
Albright, John P. E94
Alchin, John R A702
Alcina, Jim E326
Alcock, Charles R. P497
Alcorn, Lee A528
Aldag, Edward K. E274
Alday, Truitt A481
Alday, Joseph P459
Aldeborgh, John E. E30
Alden, John A871
Alderman, Keith A123
Alderman, Mark A540
Alderman, Marian A852
Alderoty, Stuart A200
Aldersley, Stephen P456
Alderson, Christopher D. A799
Alderson, Tony P119
Alderson, Philip O. P465
Aldous, David E113
Aldous, Hugh E229
Aldred, Linda P548
Aldrete, Eddie A463
Aldrich, Sister Barbara P523
Aldrich, Bernard P. (Bernie) E23
Aldridge, Tracey A717
Aldridge, Bryan P56
Aldridge, Don P282
Aldridge, Tracey E351
Aleardi, Keith P A368
Alec, Pittman A905
Alekperov, Vagit Y. W309
Alekseeva, Marina B A461
Aleksic, Aleksandar A15
Aleksic, Aleksandar P7
Aleman-Bermudez, Aurelio A333
Alemany, Ellen R. A200
Alena, Luz A164
Alers, Scott A747
Ales, Donna P284
Alesci, Megan A449

Alesci, Megan E221
Alesina, Susan P558
Aletrakis, Timothy A356
Aletta, Joseph A264
Aletta, Joseph P180
Alex, Bodney P415
Alexaitis, Irene P489
Alexander, Susan H. A133
Alexander, Mark R. A164
Alexander, Robert M. A166
Alexander, Leslie A180
Alexander, Karin A192
Alexander, Natasha A248
Alexander, Bob A250
Alexander, Gaylord A414
Alexander, Forbes I. J. A475
Alexander, Paul A493
Alexander, Juliet A530
Alexander, Nathan A574
Alexander, Elizabeth A618
Alexander, Barbara A695
Alexander, Bob A702
Alexander, Robert A761
Alexander, Tim A772
Alexander, Krystyna A772
Alexander, Alan A799
Alexander, John A838
Alexander, Cory B. A876
Alexander, Bill A936
Alexander, Bruce K. A940
Alexander, Nick P5
Alexander, Jackie P27
Alexander, Craig P170
Alexander, Allen P174
Alexander, Gaylord P236
Alexander, Lisa P291
Alexander, Sherrie P334
Alexander, James P346
Alexander, Jim P411
Alexander, Kelly P508
Alexander, Randy P606
Alexander, Pamala P617
Alexander, Gordon P647
Alexander, Koler Dan W49
Alexander, Deborah M. W53
Alexander, Denny E106
Alexander, Natasha E107
Alexander, Angie E264
Alexander, Elizabeth E310
Alexander, Tim E382
Alexander, Krystyna E383
Alexandre, Patrick W15
Alexiou, Joy P472
Alfano, Nicholas (Nick) A289
Alfano, Nick A289
Alff, Christopher E174
ALFIERI, CLAUDIA W121
Alfonso, Diana A203
Alford, Bradley A97
Alford, Eddie A665
Alford, William C. P87
Alford, Katherine P480
Alford, Barbara P541
Alford, Bobby P548
Alford, Richard E72
Alford, Donald C. (Don) E309
Alford, Eddie E334
Alfred, Richard L. P486
Alger, Eugene K. A308
Alger, Robert P285
Algiere, Dennis L A904
Algoe, Eric P551
Alhadeff, Kathie P418
Ali, Syed Arbab A414
Ali, Alam A577
Ali, Syed A P64
Ali, Syed Arbab P236
Ali, Mohamad E239
Ali-Ahmad, Walid A695
Aliabadi, Paymon A304
Alicandri, John P246
Alice, Quiros A571
Alicea, Maria P97
Alicea, Marisa P175
Alicea, Jaime P539

Aligheri, Tim P262
Aliperti-urbielewicz, Michelle A210
Alissandratos, Dimitrios A839
Alkemade, Maurice A846
Alkemade, Moe A900
Alkire, Joseph A891
Alkire, Michael P428
Allain, Dwayne P578
Allaire, Bella Loykhter A704
Allaire, Melanie A731
Allam, Anthony P68
Allan, Donald (Don) A778
Allani, Pramod A900
Allard, Scott M. E10
Allard, Kristin E131
Allbright, Justin A114
Allbright, Justin E37
Allcorn, Roger A651
Allcorn, Roger E330
Alldian, David P P90
Allemand, Anita A251
Allen, Hubert L. A5
Allen, Gary A19
Allen, Jeremy A85
Allen, Diana A91
Allen, Blane A105
Allen, Andrew A133
Allen, Bertrand-Marc (Marc) A140
Allen, Lee A142
Allen, Thad W. A144
Allen, Tom A165
Allen, Lawren A167
Allen, Susan A191
Allen, Julianne A200
Allen, Warren A200
Allen, Tom A210
Allen, Dana A212
Allen, Jeremy A224
Allen, James A246
Allen, Douglas A257
Allen, Samuel R A260
Allen, Mark A323
Allen, Cynthia D A323
Allen, Valena A329
Allen, Gregory R. A339
Allen, Christopher A345
Allen, Jim A392
Allen, Lorl A409
Allen, Jodi A417
Allen, Ashley A421
Allen, Sherri A428
Allen, Madalyn A449
Allen, George A452
Allen, Robert A462
Allen, Yorke A482
Allen, Matson A540
Allen, Jeffrey A544
Allen, Jon A556
Allen, Douglas A571
Allen, Scott R A586
Allen, Walter A630
Allen, Don A692
Allen, Daniel A704
Allen, Michael E. A716
Allen, Barbara A723
Allen, Gary A735
Allen, Patrick A744
Allen, Vanessa A750
Allen, Gary A755
Allen, Aaron A804
Allen, Jodi J A827
Allen, Christine A902
Allen, Matt A902
Allen, Etta A912
Allen, Michael D. P13
Allen, Amy P45
Allen, Les P82
Allen, Jeff P151
Allen, Jennifer P162
Allen, James P202
Allen, Herbert P204
Allen, Robert P256
Allen, Daniel P P258
Allen, Stephen P P279

Allen, Clay M P284
Allen, Jon P328
Allen, Steve P359
Allen, David J. P374
Allen, Erin P387
Allen, Mark P422
Allen, Traci P423
Allen, Trina P445
Allen, Kim P490
Allen, Gloria P530
Allen, Cindy P541
Allen, Jodi J P571
Allen, Elizabeth Heller P576
Allen, Richard D P587
Allen, Greg P627
Allen, Dee P631
Allen, Gary K. P633
Allen, Ricci P638
Allen, Ken W137
Allen, Stephen W243
Allen, Jeremy E27
Allen, Diana E29
Allen, Blane E34
Allen, Lee E49
Allen, Fritz E53
Allen, Ryan E81
Allen, James E105
Allen, Stephanie E106
Allen, David R. (Dave) E152
Allen, Gregory R. E159
Allen, Christopher E165
Allen, Laura E168
Allen, Madalyn E221
Allen, Gary E369
Allen, Craig E388
Allensworth, Tami A442
Alleva, Frank A137
Alley, Alex A327
Alley, Sherri A383
Alley, Sherri E186
Allinger, Wesley E180
Allinson, Brooke A701
Allison, Jeffrey A198
Allison, John W. A426
Allison, Michael A620
Allison, Roy A651
Allison, Paul D. A704
Allison, Glenn A840
Allison, Jeff A895
Allison, Les P225
Allison, David P302
Allison, Stephen P308
Allison, William P360
Allison, Julie P361
Allison, John P617
Allison, Brian R. W173
Allison, Brad W190
Allison, R. Dirk E4
Allison, John W. E213
Allison, Roy E329
Allman, Keith J. A541
Allman, Dora P56
Allocca, Lori P502
Allocco, Steve A171
Allouche, Danny A97
Allred, Justin P58
Allshouse, Scott A921
Allshouse, Scott P669
Allums, LaShaunda A799
Ally, Desiree A574
Allyn-gauthier, Sandra E330
Almanzor, Aj A452
Almaraz, Frank P164
Almazan, Cynthia A695
Almazan, Robert A934
Almedhychy, Ali A170
Almeida, Ayesha A53
Almeida, José E. (Joe) A119
Almeida, Nelson A487
Almeida, Ashok A613
Almeida, Derek A793
Almeida, Jose A900
Almeida, Odilon A915
Almirantearena, Evangelina A461
Almog, Yael W49

COMBINED HOOVER'S HANDBOOK INDEX OF EXECUTIVES

A = AMERICAN BUSINESS
E = EMERGING COMPANIES
P = PRIVATE COMPANIES
W = WORLD BUSINESS

Almon, Lorie E. P486
Almond, William A347
Almond, Michelle A623
Almond, Karen P588
Almond, William E168
Almond, Michelle E313
Almoro, Lynn A54
Aloia, Sal A137
Alomar, Melissa A203
Alonso, Jose A114
Alonso, German A243
Alonso, Victor Ventimilla W343
Alonso, Jose E37
Alonzo, Leonicio P59
Alpay, John M P110
Alpen, Joachim W357
Alper, Cenk W177
Alperstein, Janet A592
Alperstein, Janet P370
Alpert, Marc A525
Alpert-Romm, Adria A270
Alptekin, Alper A554
als, W364
Alsip, Bryan P82
Alsman, Floyd A383
Alsman, Floyd E186
Alspaw, Mark P308
Alstead, Troy A407
Alstrom, Eric P173
Alt, Steven A686
Alt, Gregory A796
Alt, Aaron A804
Alt, Gregory E397
Altaras, June P537
Altarriba, Ariel A573
Altenborf, Mike P182
Altendorf, Michael J. (Mike) P182
Alter, Stewart A469
Alter, Ed A784
Alter, Tom P415
Alteri, Joseph P586
Alters, Alan E240
Altes, Wallace W. E43
Althauser, Chris A396
Althoff, Kirsten A155
Althoff, Sven W178
Althoff, Kirsten E54
Altier, Eric A390
Altieri, Len P420
Altig, David E. A319
Altman, Richard I. (Rick) A700
Altman, Stanley J. (Stan) A716
Altman, Dara F. A762
Altman, Ron A866
Altman, Roger C. E138
Altman, Amy L. E261
Altman, Ron E417
Alton, Gregg H. A385
Altoro, Joaquin A926
Altozano, Angel Manuel Garcia W6
Altre-Kerber, Alison A491
Altrogge, Jeannine A63
Altschul, Larry A562
Altschuler, Glenn C. P159
Altstadt, Dale A383
Altstadt, Dale E186
Altvater, Kurt A175
Alty, Kimberly A651
Alty, Kimberly E330
Altz, Jean A544
Aluisio, Frank V P578
Alvarado, Rosa A18
Alvarado, Jose A115
Alvarado, Roger A191
Alvarado, Elizabeth A222
Alvarado, Jennifer A463
Alvarado, Paulina P161
Alvarado, Angelita P250

Alvarado, Douglas P404
Alvarado, Rodrigo Huidobro W149
Alvarado, Jose E37
Alvarez, Aida A438
Alvarez, Raul A527
Alvarez, Miguel I. A616
Alvarez, Jill A755
Alvarez, Peter A888
Alvarez, Carolina P299
Alvarez, Sorita P325
Alvarez, Terry P518
Alvarez, Victor P677
Alvarez, Jose Antonio W48
Alvarez, Ernesto E185
Alvarez, Jill E369
Alvarez, Peter E425
alver, P159
Alverson, Michael A600
Alves, Nuno M. Pestana de Almeida W145
Alvey, Jack P251
Alvey, Jennifer P252
Alviani, Joseph D A641
Alviani, Joseph D P407
Alvior, Rudy A109
Aviti, Paulette R. A359
Alwan, Basil W284
Alwood, Amy P581
Alyea, Ryan P119
Alzamora, Esteban P404
Amaba, Jane A323
Amador, Richard A166
Amadou, Teddy P242
Amadu, Sule P193
Amamiya, Masayoshi W51
Amanda, Nesmith A604
Amann, Scott E448
Amano, Luciana A544
Amanullah, Aman P19
Amaro, Luis A680
Amaro, Denise P244
Amass, Leslie A658
Amat, Leonardo A806
Amat, Leonardo E398
Amato, Lisa A113
Amato, Dina A405
Amato, Gavin A727
Amato, Elizabeth B. A875
Amato, David P140
Amato, Gavin P453
Amato, Lisa E36
Amaya, Rosa A147
Ambach, Robert F. (Bob) P625
Ambe, Kazushi W361
Amble, Mike A327
Amble, Marcy A548
Ambrecht, Kenneth A56
Ambrose, Sherie A266
Ambrose, Steve A279
Ambrose, Steven A279
Ambrose, Steven A330
Ambrose, Curtis L A390
Ambrose, Nick A530
Ambrose, Julia A893
Ambrose, Sherie P182
Ambrose, Kelly P298
Ambrose, Steven E152
Ambroseo, John R. E86
Ambrosino, Richard P643
Ambrosio, Anthony G. A892
Ambrosio, Michael A899
Ambrosio, Michael P657
Ambrosio, Ken E143
Ambrosius, Jorg A783
Ambrowiak, Alice A727
Ambrowiak, Alice P453
Ameden, Paul E183
Ameismeier, Donna P459
Amejorado, Josie A682
Amel, Benjamin A149
Ameli, Mehrnaz M. E274
Amelio, William J. (Bill) A99
Amen, Darrell S. van A429
Amen, Darrell S. van E214
Amend, Chris A312

Amend, Michael A647
Amend, Kurt A706
Amend, Matt P25
Amend, Chris P199
Amenson, Valencia A180
America, James P146
Americas, Levi Strauss A514
Americas, Levi Strauss A516
Americas, Levi Strauss P293
Amerine, Teri P462
Amerongen, Marcel V A177
Amerson, Leon T. (Timmy) A22
Amerson, Leon T. (Timmy) P11
Amerson-Allman, Aneidre A713
Ames, Marissa A115
Ames, Richard P196
Ames, Marissa E37
Amezquita, Juan A616
Amicarella, Ana E180
Amici, Joseph E123
Amick, W. Michael A467
Amin, Nick W40
Amine, James L. W120
Amirat, Cherif P572
Amirpoor, Laurie A179
Ammann, Daniel (Dan) A378
Ammann, Vincent L. P666
Amon, Cristiano R. A694
Amon, Jim E172
Amornkiatkajorn, Boobpha W316
Amorim, Paula W169
Amoroso, Michael A137
Amoroso, Josephine A356
Amoruso, Robert C P519
Amos, Daniel P. (Dan) A19
Amos, Paul S. A19
Amos, Sister Helen P332
Amos, Gregg P491
Amosson, Brett A835
Amoussou, Ben P422
Amparan, Oscar L. P550
Amranand, Piyasvasti W316
Amrik, Nicole P19
Ams, Matt E100
Amsell, David P459
Amstel, Hans P. van W7
Amster, Howard M. E307
Amstutz, Karen A532
Amuthan, Bala E290
An, Peter A176
An, Weizhe P336
An, Wang W96
An, Tong-Il W311
Ana, Coleen Santa A754
Ana, Coleen Santa P484
Anaiscourt, Dawn A770
Analdo, Stephen F P411
Anand, Manish P230
Anand, Lawrence P230
Ananthanarayanan, Arul A695
Ananyev, Sergei A. W375
Anastas, Jonathan A10
Anastasi, Michelle A641
Anastasi, Shane A739
Anastasi, Michelle P407
Anastasio, Richard A376
Anatrella, Louis J E78
Anaya, Pedro A871
Anaya, Jose Antonio Gonzalez W304
Ancell, Murray T. P386
Ancher-Jensen, Henrik A22
Andeer, Kyle A72
Andel, Steve Van A40
Andel, Stephen Van A766
Andel, Steve Van P29
Andel, Stephen Van P500
Anderman, Craig A13
Anders, Kim A85
Anders, Mark A360
Anders, Bob A480
Anders, Dave A602
Anders, Bob P270
Anders, Marjorie P335
Anders, Kim E26
Andersen, Bryan A155

Andersen, Ric A491
Andersen, Christina A662
Andersen, Keith A845
Andersen, Carl A896
Andersen, Paul P246
Andersen, Tonny Thierry W129
Andersen, Ole G. W129
Andersen, Bryan E54
Anderskouv, Niels A820
Anderskow, Jerry A25
Anderskow, Jerry P14
Anderson, James R. (Jim) A14
Anderson, Bruce A34
Anderson, Bryan A35
Anderson, Valerie A43
Anderson, Janelle A47
Anderson, Christine A53
Anderson, Tracy A60
Anderson, Nancy A60
Anderson, Kristen A65
Anderson, Anthony A97
Anderson, Gaylin D. A104
Anderson, John A105
Anderson, Terri A116
Anderson, Beth A140
Anderson, John A142
Anderson, Kristine Martin A145
Anderson, William A222
Anderson, Bob A235
Anderson, Peter W A247
Anderson, Christopher A259
Anderson, Jeff A271
Anderson, Gerard M. A279
Anderson, Melissa H. A281
Anderson, Fred A287
Anderson, Lars C. A329
Anderson, Megan A329
Anderson, Michael A351
Anderson, Paul Alan A405
Anderson, Charlotte A421
Anderson, Joe A444
Anderson, Cevin A448
Anderson, Laura A460
Anderson, A. Scott A462
Anderson, Miles A481
Anderson, Zach A481
Anderson, Christine A492
Anderson, Ian D. A494
Anderson, Carl A. A495
Anderson, Alyssa A507
Anderson, Carol S A538
Anderson, James A545
Anderson, Traci K. A551
Anderson, Don Anderson Don A559
Anderson, Lori A583
Anderson, Brad R A586
Anderson, Shawn A600
Anderson, Steve A621
Anderson, John C. A629
Anderson, Scott A640
Anderson, Shelly A642
Anderson, Carol A651
Anderson, Jeff A664
Anderson, Yvonne A692
Anderson, John H. A693
Anderson, Nick A693
Anderson, Roger W A706
Anderson, Shane A707
Anderson, Scott A728
Anderson, Greg A730
Anderson, David A742
Anderson, Steven H. (Steve) A746
Anderson, Steve A747
Anderson, Allen A751
Anderson, Jill A770
Anderson, Elaine A773
Anderson, Christy A809
Anderson, Julie L. A818
Anderson, Stephen A. (Steve) A820
Anderson, Jeremy A835
Anderson, Kenneth A877
Anderson, Jane A879
Anderson, Llewellyn C. A894
Anderson, Bradbury H. (Brad) A905
Anderson, Jennifer A922

Anderson, A. Scott (Scott) A940
Anderson, Howard A940
Anderson, Warren P38
Anderson, Erik P49
Anderson, Eric P49
Anderson, Colleen P59
Anderson, Michael P64
Anderson, Thomas R P78
Anderson, Doug P85
Anderson, Lois P97
Anderson, Lois P110
Anderson, Markham J J P121
Anderson, David P128
Anderson, Sharon P132
Anderson, Staci P153
Anderson, Tricia P184
Anderson, C. Colt P206
Anderson, Barbara P207
Anderson, Rebecca P212
Anderson, Janet P215
Anderson, Anjanette P220
Anderson, Lcpl P244
Anderson, Cevin P247
Anderson, Don P250
Anderson, Larry P255
Anderson, A. Scott P256
Anderson, Kenneth W P258
Anderson, Ronnie K P281
Anderson, Carl A. P282
Anderson, Steven P285
Anderson, Allyson P288
Anderson, Gregory A P310
Anderson, Traci K. P321
Anderson, Angela P362
Anderson, Jill P367
Anderson, Terry Sam P382
Anderson, Shelly P407
Anderson, Jim P415
Anderson, Richard P415
Anderson, Joe Dean P419
Anderson, Carole P433
Anderson, Cheryl P451
Anderson, Richard A P466
Anderson, Terry D P467
Anderson, Misty P471
Anderson, Richard A P513
Anderson, Julie P515
Anderson, Charles K P522
Anderson, Geri P525
Anderson, Gregory P546
Anderson, Sophie P549
Anderson, Stephanie J P552
Anderson, Amanda P561
Anderson, Audrey J. P599
Anderson, Gerri P604
Anderson, Eric P610
Anderson, Jane P636
Anderson, Llewellyn C. P651
Anderson, Suzanne P652
Anderson, Leha P653
Anderson, Jennifer P671
Anderson, William D. (Bill) W371
Anderson, Darby E4
Anderson, Gregory C. E10
Anderson, Valerie E13
Anderson, John E34
Anderson, Terri E39
Anderson, John E49
Anderson, Christopher E114
Anderson, Robert J. E119
Anderson, Andina E132
Anderson, Joel D. E172
Anderson, N. Leigh E262
Anderson, David J. (Dave) E291
Anderson, W. Lance E307
Anderson, Steve E311
Anderson, Carol E329
Anderson, Jeff E334
Anderson, John H. E341
Anderson, Nick E341
Anderson, Karli E360
Anderson, Candace E366
Anderson, Elaine E383
Anderson, Julie L. E403
Anderson-loague, Michelle A235

Andersson, Roland P405
Andersson, Johan W357
Anderton, Amanda A228
Anderton, Judd A713
Andes, John P511
Anding, Julie A407
Andino, Peter A465
Ando, Kenji W258
Ando, Goran W290
Andolina, Mark P625
Andrabi, Imran A P330
Andrada, Marissa A779
Andrade, Mauro A301
Andrade, Mauro P196
Andrade, Juan C. W106
Andrade, Miguel Stilwell de W146
Andre, Michel W91
Andre-Brunet, Marc A495
Andre-Brunet, Marc P282
Andrekus, Brad A489
Andrekus, Bradley A489
Andresen, Andy P215
Andresen, Elena P399
Andreski, Lynne P513
Andresky, Christa A853
Andresky, Christa P612
Andreson, Jeffrey (Jeff) E316
Andrew, Cooley A340
Andrew, Jim A654
Andrew, Briggs P112
Andrew, Cooley E160
Andrews, Nathan J. A301
Andrews, Suzanne A559
Andrews, Kirkland B. A610
Andrews, Shaun A699
Andrews, Wayne (Keith) A724
Andrews, Rob A866
Andrews, Briggs P112
Andrews, Nancy C. P187
Andrews, Stephanie P252
Andrews, Haven P315
Andrews, Bill P369
Andrews, Susan Mc P451
Andrews, Wayne (Keith) P452
Andrews, Josh P552
Andrews, Felicia P561
Andrews, Sue P574
Andrews, Teresa P610
Andrews, Arthur P638
Andrews, Cindy P650
Andrews, Thomas J. E8
Andrews, Michael E47
Andrews, Kirkland B. E81
Andrews, Chip E100
Andrews, Harold W. E362
Andrews, Rob E418
Andreyka, Timothy A29
Andreyka, Timothy P16
Andrichik, Kenneth P202
Andrietti, Bernadette A460
Andro, Ronald P23
Andronikakis, Spiros A. W25
Aneaknithi, Pipit W216
Anello, Neil P255
Anfinnsen, Tor Martin P197
Ang, Ramon S. W338
Angehrn, Urban W435
Angel, Joseph A347
Angel, Joseph E167
Angela, Wallave A145
Angelastro, Philip J. A626
Angelico, Michael D P97
Angelina, Michael A723
Angelini, Michael P. A405
Angelis, Yamynn De A249
Angelis, Yamynn De E108
Angell, Janice A3
Angell, Jan A3
Angelle, Bryant P142
Angelo, Paula A409
Angelo, Jesse A596
Angelo, Tami A933
Angerer, Erin A793
Angilan, Jason A844
Angle, Greg P300

Angle, Colin M. E239
Angley, James P369
Anglin, Kyle A167
Angotta, Paul A112
Angotti, Liz A859
Anguiano, Ricardo Padilla W175
Anguiano, Ariana E365
Angulo, Carlos P265
Angulo, Christine Stiltner P501
Angus, Jeff P189
Anicetti, Richard A. (Rick) P568
Anis, Joseph A374
Aniszewski, Craig J. E390
Anita, Kroll A810
Ankrum, Bob P333
Ann, Peggy A72
Anna, Gregory J. E80
Annabathula, Santhi A605
Annamalai, Deva A940
Annan, Roland A167
Annecharico, Mary Alice A414
Annecharico, Mary Alice P236
Anello, Gretchen A884
Annese, Gretchen A152
Annese, Gretchen E52
Annis, John A623
Annis, John E313
Annunziato, Frank P546
Anquillare, Mark V. E428
Ansari, Ansar A896
Anschell, Jonathan H. A892
Anschutz, J Barron P117
Ansell, Jeffery D. (Jeff) A778
Anselmino, Silvia A123
Anson, Betty P515
Anspach, Angela P117
Anstice, Martin B. A505
Ansuini, Jason A562
Ansusinha, Panop W216
Antal, James J. A181
Antal, James J. E70
Antal, James J. E372
Antell, James A584
Antes, John P344
Anthony, Dapp A877
Anthony, Jon E A891
Anthony, Satrick A918
Anthony, Donna P254
Anthony, Tim P360
Anthony, Jim P405
Anthony, David P456
Anthos, James A849
Antis, Connie P518
Antishin, Dennis A933
Antkowiak, Patrick M. A608
Antolik, David G. A737
Antolik, David G. E361
Anton, Daniela P43
Anton, John J P124
Anton, Michael E P124
Antonace, William A177
Antonelli, Pierluigi A554
Antonelli, Cecille A782
Antonelli, Cecille P526
Antonelli, Giovanni W411
Antonelli, Joe E366
Antongeorgi, Monica A115
Antongeorgi, Monica E37
Antoniello, Angela P383
Antonini, Alberto P611
Antonino, John A264
Antonino, John P180
Antonsson, Stefan E394
Antonucci, Toni A711
Antonucci, Toni P444
Antony, Bejoy A198
Antoun, Georges A199
Antrobus, Mike A519
Antunes, Lionel A349
Anunda, Sydney P627
Anvar, Saba A135
Anvar, Saba A574
Anzaldua, Erika A309
Anzaldua, Ricardo A. A559
Anzaldua, Adolfo A742

Anzalone, John M. A472
Anzalone, Christopher (Chris) E25
Aoki, Takeo W286
Aoun, Joseph E. P383
Aoyama, Andrew A559
Aoyama, Shinji W186
Aoyama, Hidehiko W293
Ao'brien, Kathryn P175
Aparin, Vladimir A695
Apatoff, Robert A36
Apfalter, Guenther W244
Apfel, Ken A32
Apicerno, Ken A833
Apitz, Marcus P655
Apker, Mike E131
Aplington, David P513
Apodaca, Rod A175
Apodaca, Aaron A550
Apoliona, Haunani A110
Apollonio, Carlos A778
Apostolou, Carrie A446
Appel, Jon A717
Appel, Jeff P43
Appel, Ron P43
Appel, Frank W137
Appel, Dennis P E286
Appel, Dennis E286
Appel, Jon E351
Appelbaum, Kristin A200
Appelt, Thomas A240
Apperson, Kevin P315
Appia, Janey P354
Applbaum, Hilda L A50
Applbaum, Hilda L P31
Apple, Robert E. (Bob) A543
Applebee, Tim A428
Appleberg, Brett A798
Appleby, Leslie P677
Applefeld, Jack P478
Applegate, Beth A312
Applegate, John S. P609
Appleton, William (Bill) E366
Appleyard, Joseph P608
Appold, Stacy R P161
Appolonia, John A25
Appolonia, Jack A25
Appolonia, John P14
Appolonia, Jack P14
April, Tim E424
Apte, Chaitanya A50
Aquilla, Dave A933
Aquino, Rosemarie A109
Aquino, Marlene A145
Aquino, Osvaldo A591
Aquino, Michelle P37
Aquino, Osvaldo P369
Arabie, Cheryl P467
Aragon, Manuela P537
Aragon, Patrick P546
Araiza, Ron E58
Araki, Holly A109
Araki, Gavin P399
Aramaki, Tomoyuki W228
Aran, Pete P464
Arand, Donna P276
Aranda, Jose A606
Aranda, Marc P212
Aranguren-trellez, Luis A457
Aranha, Brian W33
Arapoff, Susan A835
Araujo, George A466
Aravena, Jose A756
Aravindakshan, Santhosh A559
Arbaugh, Brad A140
Arbide, Donna P569
Arboleda, Zara P646
Arbuckle, Barry P298
Arcalgud, Anil A289
Arcand, Tom A259
Arcand, Alfred P111
Arcaro, Katri P202
Arcaro, John P610
Archambeau, Shellye A602
Archer, Pmp A10
Archer, Keith A10

COMBINED HOOVER'S HANDBOOK INDEX OF EXECUTIVES

A = AMERICAN BUSINESS
E = EMERGING COMPANIES
P = PRIVATE COMPANIES
W = WORLD BUSINESS

Archer, Brandi A15
Archer, Timothy M. (Tim) A505
Archer, Ed A742
Archer, Kevin A760
Archer, Jerry A763
Archer, Dominick A858
Archer, Brandi P8
Archer, Donna P274
Archer, Kuan E194
Archer, Kevin E374
Archer, Jerry E377
Archibald, Nolan D. A447
Archibald, Sandra A880
Archibald, Sandra P640
Archie, Thomas A25
Archie, Thomas P14
Arcidiacono, Salvator A584
Arczynski, Dennis A749
Arczynski, Dennis E367
Ard, Jay J A215
Ardalkar, Prashant P286
Ardezzone, Anthony A590
Ardill, John A309
Ardisonne, Ron A94
Ardizzone, Ann A29
Ardoin, Elizabeth A. (Beth) A449
Ardoin, Beth A449
Ardoin, Elizabeth A. (Beth) E220
Ardoin, Beth E220
Arduini, Peter J. E233
Arebalos, Ish A215
Areeratchakul, Tanawong W351
Arellano, Luis R A746
Arellano, Richard P410
Arellano, Augusto E138
Arenas, Charles A492
Arendt, Peter A444
Arendt, Brian A545
Arendt, Brian P317
Arenella, Dawn A786
Arenella, Dawn E387
Arenivas, Jesse A494
Arevalo, Ruth M A683
Arevalo, Ruth M P431
Arevalo, Ricardo M. E375
Arey, Paris A198
Arey, George P608
Argalas, James A101
Argalas, James E32
Argalas, Barry E E349
Argao, Selene A746
Argent, Heather A402
Argent, Heather E198
Argento, Frances A204
Argo, Kristi A826
Argodale, George A840
Argue, David P231
Arguello, Felipe A135
Arias, Michael A870
Aried, Nada A500
Arief, Armand B. W411
Arif, Abu A61
Arihara, Masahiko W258
Arii, Carrie P437
Arikat, Yazeed P519
ARIKUNI, MICHIO W375
Arima, Koji W132
Arimanithaya, Sreehanth Krishnan A230
Arimanithaya, Sreehanth Krishnan P154
Arinelli, Wilmar A245
Arison, Micky W87
Aristone, Angel A452
Arivukkarasu, Purushothaman A212
Arizmendi, Pablo A779
Ark, Jon Vander A721
Arkilahti, Nina W377
Arko, John A520

Arkof, Anna P259
Arland, Samantha A881
Arland, Samantha E421
Arledge, David A. W150
Arm, Amy Steele P125
Armacost, Samuel H. E59
Armagost, Brad A755
Armagost, Brad E369
Armater, Ann P233
Armato, Carl S. P390
Armato, Carl P428
Armbruster, Leslie P677
Arment, Daniel J. (Dan) P97
Armentano, Vincent J A845
Armentrout, Sharon A797
Armentrout, Tracy A P391
Armer, Douglas E48
Armes, Tonia A704
Armfield, Jeff P501
Armini, Michael P383
Armistead, Hunter H. E322
Armitage, Courtney A165
Armlin, Patricia E168
Armogan, Nathan A161
Armour, Norm A914
Armour, Meri P335
Arms, William C P515
Armstrong, Jason A117
Armstrong, Tim A143
Armstrong, Dean A193
Armstrong, Paula A319
Armstrong, Christopher A319
Armstrong, Steven A359
Armstrong, Kim A442
Armstrong, Ann K A460
Armstrong, Keith D. A556
Armstrong, Scott A590
Armstrong, Ronald E. (Ron) A636
Armstrong, Greg L. A668
Armstrong, Greg L A668
Armstrong, Susie A695
Armstrong, Jason P61
Armstrong, Scott A. P172
Armstrong, Wayne P186
Armstrong, Kevin R P252
Armstrong, Greg L P422
Armstrong, Mary P487
Armstrong, Katrina A. P574
Armstrong, William P630
Armstrong, Philip W173
Armstrong, Keith D. E277
Armstrong, Nate E285
ARNABOLDI, LETIZIA MARIA BRICHETTO W410
Arnault, Bernard W105
Arnault, Bernard W241
Arndt, Kenneth A. A366
Arndt, Gerald P225
Arner, Steve P112
Arneson, Georgene P429
Arneson, Craig P431
Arnett, Gevan A212
Arnett, Harry E59
Arnn, Roger P199
Arnold, Sarah A60
Arnold, Steve A87
Arnold, Scott A94
Arnold, Ken A100
Arnold, Colleen A170
Arnold, Vance A246
Arnold, Craig A286
Arnold, Michael J. A365
Arnold, Christy A458
Arnold, Jeffrey A487
Arnold, Michael A519
Arnold, Dan H. A528
Arnold, Charles A559
Arnold, Keith A663
Arnold, Doug A724
Arnold, Charlotte A835
Arnold, Timothy G. (Tim) A882
Arnold, Steve P50
Arnold, Jeff P83
Arnold, Bradley P126
Arnold, Jason P134

Arnold, Craig P190
Arnold, Kay K P196
Arnold, Sandra P206
Arnold, David P258
Arnold, Doug P452
Arnold, Gregory A. (Greg) P607
Arnold, Truman P607
Arnold, Vance E105
Arnold, Fiona E424
Arnoldussen, Ludger W267
Arnoult, Mike A900
Arnow, Bruce A510
Arnow, Bruce P290
Arntzen, Corry P511
Aroesty, Jason E210
Aromando, Nicholas A112
Aron, Adam M. A45
Aronis, George C. W25
Aronne, Brian P246
Aronov, Tina P108
Aronowitz, Scott A325
Aronson, Sandy A702
Aronson, Michele E114
Aronzon, Nicole A468
Aronzon, Daniel P649
Aroonratskul, Weera E290
Arora, Deepak A54
Arora, Ankush W283
Arora, Anil E132
Arous, Gérard Ben A592
Arous, Gérard Ben P370
Arovas, Jordan A906
Arovas, Jordan E434
Aroy, Jeffrey E102
Arquette, Andy E123
Arrata, Philippe A130
Arredondo, Fabiola A164
Arrell, Sarah A804
Arriaga, Rene A463
Arrighi, Theresa A850
Arrington, Leslie A312
Arrington, Pat P261
Arrington, Courtney P606
Arriola, Dennis V. A753
Arronte, Melissa A205
Arrowood, Tracey E448
Arrowsmith, Andrea A125
Arroyo, F. Thaddeus A89
Arroyo, Carlos A623
Arroyo, Jesus A746
Arroyo, Ana A827
Arroyo, Ana P580
Arroyo, Alan E96
Arroyo, Carlos E313
Arsenault, Julie P454
Arseneault, Michael A892
Arseneault, Tom W42
Arstark, Reid A744
Art, Perez A740
Artalejo, Henry A457
Artavia, Patty A676
Artavia, Patty E338
Arters, Doug A467
Arthachinda, Nick A859
Arthur, Sarbah A43
Arthur, Vicki B. A768
Arthur, Gary A887
Arthur, Randal P36
Arthur, Kory P293
Arthur, Mark W193
Arthur, John W424
Arthur, Sarbah E13
Arthur, Wayne E440
Arthurs, Mike P556
Artino, Sarah A590
Artman, John A544
Artman, Michael P327
Arts, Sander P53
Artusi, Daniel A461
Artz, Peyton A752
Artz, Eric A869
Arunratana, Siripong W95
Arvin, Ann Margaret A510
Arvin, Ann Margaret P290
Arwari, Andy P113

Arway, Pamela A416
as, W321
Asada, Teruo W249
Asai, Eriko A374
Asakowicz, Steven M. E210
Asano, Kikuo W253
Asare, Charles E237
Asarpota, Rajesh J. (Raj) E308
Asbury, John C. A91
Asbury, Stephanie A107
Asbury, Tad A538
Asbury, John C. E29
Ascher, Michael C P606
Asenkerschbaumer, Stefan W75
Asensio, Lynn D. A908
Asensio, Lynn D. E436
Ash, Bruce A272
Ash, David A756
Ashabolu, Ahmet W222
Ashby, Michael A754
Ashby, Valerie S. P187
Ashby, Michael P484
Ashenbrenner, Fred A236
Ashenfelter, Lacey P359
Asher, Linda A145
Ashida, Jun W348
Ashley, Richard W A5
Ashley, Dennis A57
Ashley, David A199
Ashley, Cathleen A199
Ashley, Andrew A492
Ashley, Anthony A494
Ashley, David A536
Ashley, Pamela A713
Ashley, Dennis P33
Ashley, Marion P161
Ashley, Stanley W P556
Ashley, Steven W286
Ashlock, Richard A797
Ashlyn, Sowell A478
Ashlyn, Sowell P269
Ashmeade-Brown, Jamila P21
Ashokkumar, Aashitha E407
Ashtary, Mishel P34
Ashtiani, Kaihan A505
Ashton, Joseph A378
Ashton, Martin A460
Ashton, Melinda P230
Ashton, Bill E172
Ashue, Meghan A922
Ashue, Meghan P671
Ashworth, Richard M. A899
Askey, Daniel A380
Asleson, Brett A434
Aslett, Mark E277
Aslin, Phil A818
Aslin, Phil E403
Asmar, Joseph A540
Asmus, Sharon A736
Asmus, Sharon P460
Asnani, Anil A502
Asnani, Manish A896
Asp, Jim P579
Aspinwall, Glenn A482
Asplund, Dale A. A872
Asrat, Mack P494
Assaf, Michal P229
Assaf, Ronald G. P390
Assaf, Samir W189
Assalone, Kim A626
Assef, Eduardo A202
Assef, Eduardo P136
Asselberg, Mark A628
Asthana, Sandeep W371
Astle, Stephen E144
Astor, Frank P357
Astroth, Joseph A910
Ata, Sana P284
ATAKA, TATEKI W184
Atalay, Hakan A692
Atarashi, Akira W348
Atcherman, S Jeffrey P334
Atcheson, Michael E93
Atchison, Pierre A742
Atchley, Kecia P431

Atchue, Nancy A835
Atcovitz, Michael A722
Aten, Derek A222
Athanasia, Dean C. A107
Athanasopoulos, Athanasios I. W25
Athanassopoulos, Theodoros I. W25
Athavale, Atul P230
Atherton, Andrea P425
Athreya, Kartik A320
Atieno, Juliana A871
Atiya, Sami W3
Atkins, Margaret A255
Atkins, Bruce A387
Atkins, Damien A416
Atkins, Patricia J P489
Atkins, E Morrey A151
Atkinson, Jonathan A319
Atkinson, Ralph A413
Atkinson, Luanne A482
Atkinson, Cliff A562
Atkinson, Heather A740
Atkinson, Tracy A783
Atkinson, Mike P6
Atkinson, Corrinne P231
Atkinson, Ralph E205
Atmore, Gillian P362
Atsumi, Naoki W215
Attal, Jeremy A232
Attanasio, John B. P505
Attar, Rias A161
Attarian, Howard W A865
Attaway, David A90
Attaway, John A. A688
Attaway, John A. A689
Attaway, David P51
Attaway, John A. P435
Attea, Robert J. E256
Attebery, Tim P662
Attia, Naguib A465
Attick, Carlene A271
Attig, Kelley A530
Attili, Srinivas A465
Attiyah, Abdullah Bin Khalifa Al W112
Attrill, Ed P180
Attrovio, Matteo W235
Attwood, Dorothy A271
Atwell, Robert A599
Atwell, William A906
Atwell, Robert E303
Atwell, William E435
Atwood, Paul P220
Atwood, Anita P245
Atwood, Denver P506
Au, Joseph A284
Au, Reynette K A461
Au, Reynette A565
Au, Lawrence A605
Au, Mei P375
Au, Joseph E120
Aubin, Chrissy A718
Aubin, Michael D. P63
Aubin, Chrissy E351
Aubrey, William E. A653
Aubry, Olivier A245
Aubuchon, Michael A246
Aubuchon, Michael E105
Auchincloss, Edgar A651
Auchincloss, Edgar E329
Auckland, Nick A526
Auclair, Robert E131
Auclair, Bob E132
Aucoin, Gary P197
Audette, Matthew J. (Matt) A528
Audiffred, Doug P318
Audiffred, J Douglas P319
Augdahl, Mark E23
Auger, Stephen A353
Auger, Stephen P204
Augostini, Christopher P570
Augsburger, Tod P293
August-deWilde, Katherine A349
Augustine, Lesley A726
Augustine, Lesley P453
Augustine, Corinne E315
Augustino, Philip P194

Augustsson, Tommy A373
Augustyn-Fierg, Laurie A846
Aul, Kenneth A888
Aul, Christopher P168
Aul, Kenneth E425
Auld, David V. A435
Auld, Maureen A922
Auld, Maureen P671
Aulph, Karen A335
Aulph, Karen E155
Aultmon, Gisela P409
Aument, Tonya A367
Aunan, Erik A3
Auque, Fran-§ois W17
Aurand, Martin P114
Aurilio, Lisa P131
Auris, Jan-Dirk W181
Aurora, Dana A135
Ausdall, Sean Van E64
Ausenhus, Dennis A447
Ausenhus, Dennis P247
Ausere, Michael J P198
Ausman, Sara A31
Ausman, Gary A807
Ausman, Sara E8
Ausmus, Guy A600
Aust, Dee P402
Austen, Karla P355
Austin, Roxanne A5
Austin, Danielle A100
Austin, Karen A. A659
Austin, Earl C. (Duke) A696
Austin, Danielle P58
Austin, Scott P343
Austin, Joe P417
Austin, Jennifer P476
Austin, Pam P511
Austin, Scott P563
Austin, John D. E77
Autenried, Paul von A151
Auth, Christopher P A461
Autio, Ann P619
Autrey, Marty A902
Auvil, Adam A212
Auyeung, Rex A677
AuYeung, Benjamin E88
Avadhany, Nagesh E316
Avdic, Kenan E132
Avena, Allan E132
Averbach, Rob A922
Averbach, Rob P671
Averett, Addison A804
Averett, J W P506
Averette, Joseph W P458
Averill, Chris P412
Averill, Christopher R P584
Avery, Linda A390
Avery, Mary A922
Avery, Emily P122
Avery, Jeffrey P195
Avery, Jonathan P288
Avery, Sonja P302
Avery, Thomas P517
Avery, Lois P660
Avery, Mary P671
Avery, Chris E106
Avetikov, Albert P459
Avila, Erin De A107
Avila, Veronica A345
Avila, Rene A463
Avila, Luisa P107
Avila, José A. W117
Avila, Veronica E165
Aviles, Alan D. A588
Aviles, Alan D. P365
Aviotti, Michael E222
Avis, Nancy P377
Awad, Greg A312
Awad, Anwar A460
Awada, Hassan A242
Awada, Kaled A813
Awadallah, Ehab A166
Awan, Zoya P570
Awells, Rebecca P175
Axelrod, Susan F. P202

Axenson, Tanya A33
Axenson, Tanya P24
Axford, Eric W373
Axtell, Tom P432
Axtman, Renee P29
Ayala, Jaime Augusto Zobel De W54
Ayala-Gonzalez, Oscar P638
Ayar, Alper P496
AYATA, YUJIRO W191
Aycock, Angela W A222
Aydinli, --brahim W403
Aye, Chris A702
Ayele, Wouleta A780
Ayer, William S. (Bill) A880
Ayer, William S. (Bill) P640
Ayers, Stephen A739
Ayers, Joshua P280
Ayers, Lori P349
Ayers, Mark P361
Ayers, Jonathan W. (Jon) E223
Ayla, Ahmet Fuat W18
Ayllon, Christina E658
Aylor, James H. P442
Ayoub, Johnny A145
Ayoub, Ellen A793
Ayres, Maria A13
Ayscue, Charles F P344
Ayuthaya, Chirayu Isarangkun Na W351
Ayyar, Shekar A897
Azadian, Rosa A722
Azam, Asif P287
Azar, Sam A613
Azar, Mark A835
Azar, Mario P86
Azar, Gordon P386
Azar, Robert B P389
Azare, Monica E256
Azarela, Michael (Mike) P531
Azerang, Ramin A602
Azinovic, Drago A661
Aznaurova, Lolitta P491
Aznavorian, Rosemarie P551
Azoulay, Salomon A658
Azoulay, Jack W305
Azuara, Katherine A120
Azzi, Shane A493
Azzinaro, James A100

B

Baak, Lauren P638
Baatar, Bold W325
Baatar, Bold W327
Baba, Shinsuke W30
Babaeva, Inna P225
Babaria, Dharmesh P482
Babb, Ralph W. A221
Babb, Ovid A327
Babb, Ivy P93
Babcock, John P. A646
Babcock, Calvin P65
Babcock, Thomas E. P503
Babcock, John P. E324
Babiak, Janice A900
Babik, Amber A444
Babikian, Jeffrey C A175
Babin, Brian A842
Babineau, Thomas A146
Babinski, Steve A347
Babinski, Steve E167
Babka, Kim A701
Babos, Constance P138
Babou, Stephanie A784
Babst, Gordon P123
Babu, Santhosh A204
Babu, Benson P523
Babu, Biju E131
Bach, Tommy A325
Bach, Jeremy A506
Bachaalani, Issam A218
Bachand, Kelly P199
Bachand, Deborah P306
Bache-Wiig, Ben P26

Bachelder, Stuart A257
Bachman, Theresa A367
Bachman, Robert J P194
Bachman, Mike P253
Bachman, Page P417
Bachman, Gary J. E340
Bachmann, Lisa M. A132
Bachmann, Steve A140
Bachmeyer, Christy E105
Bachrach, William E E291
Bachus, Kevin E111
Bachwani, Dilip E342
Baciarelli, Renato P133
Bacigalupo, Richard J P445
Back, Tekla A654
Back, Jan Erik W356
Back, Steve E261
Backman, Mats A92
Backman, Eli P642
Backus, Marcia E. A618
Backus, Harroll (Hop) P2
Bacon, Gwen A29
Bacon, Graham W. A299
Bacon, Ashley A483
Bacon, Jennie A492
Bacon, James P303
Bacon, Alan P361
Bacon, Ernest P486
Bacus, Lisa A194
Badalament, Michael A508
Badame, Anne P302
Badar, Ruben A574
Badders, Matt A246
Badders, Matt E105
Badeer, Nancy A559
Bader, Jeffrey A565
Bader, Feras P597
Baderman, Catherine E207
Badger, Austin A793
Badgley, Lisa A900
Badgley, Jeffrey I. (Jeff) E284
Badi, Mohammed A53
Badowska, Eva P206
Badrinath, Vivek W417
Badu, Kofi P281
Baehren, James W. (Jim) A616
Baer, Nick A481
Baer, Richard N. (Rich) A699
Baer, TimothyR A804
Baer, Tim A804
Baer, Tammy P160
Baer, Donald A. (Don) P432
Baer, Daniel E3
Baer, Marc E7
Baerlocher, Shawn A501
Baeslack, William A. (Bud) P116
Baetz, Sheri P507
Baeva, Alla P517
Baez-Toro, Eduardo A480
Bagai, Pavan E140
Bagattini, Roy A514
Bagattini, Roy A516
Bagattini, Roy P293
Bagby, Allan A782
Bagby, Carolyn L P105
Bagby, Allan P526
Bagel-Trah, Simone W181
Bagemihl, Katherine P211
Bagg, Halsey P619
Baginski, Mark E123
Bagley, Chris A. A106
Bagley, Shannon A179
Bagley, Daniel A218
Bagley, Don A309
Bagley, Ross A769
Bagley, William A882
Bagley, David A922
Bagley, David P456
Bagley, David P671
Bagley, Ross E380
Baglivo, Mary L. P388
Bagnall, Roger A592
Bagnall, Roger P370
Bagnell, Neil P429
Bagno, Craig A469

COMBINED HOOVER'S HANDBOOK INDEX OF EXECUTIVES

A = AMERICAN BUSINESS
E = EMERGING COMPANIES
P = PRIVATE COMPANIES
W = WORLD BUSINESS

Bagnoli, Mark P. A114
Bagnoli, Mark P. E37
Bagozzi, David A672
Bagshaw, Seth H. E285
Bague, Hugo W325
Bague, Hugo W327
Bagus, Laura P39
Bagwell, Norman P. A141
Bagwell, Norman P. E49
Bahadourian, Haro E290
Baham, Desiree P21
Bahl, Himani A108
Bahl, William A196
Bahl, Tracy L. A251
Bahlool, Hossam E225
Bahner, Craig A487
Bahnlein, Carl B P651
Bahorich, Michaels A71
Bahr, Antony M. A213
Bahr, Stephanie A312
Bahr, Antony M. P143
Bahra, Paul A329
Baier, Robin P312
Baik, Jeff E433
Bail, Jennifer P228
Bailer, Scott A629
Bailey, Jennifer A72
Bailey, Michael A179
Bailey, Clay A184
Bailey, James A200
Bailey, Sandra A296
Bailey, Kristin A325
Bailey, Holly A346
Bailey, Richard A438
Bailey, Brett A444
Bailey, Todd A444
Bailey, Erin A447
Bailey, Todd A483
Bailey, Caleb A565
Bailey, Daniel A567
Bailey, Rosie A574
Bailey, Todd A578
Bailey, Joseph A626
Bailey, Kathy A638
Bailey, Steve R. A648
Bailey, Freida A702
Bailey, Travis A707
Bailey, Daniel K. (Dan) A847
Bailey, Lee A887
Bailey, Kevin D. A891
Bailey, Brooke A900
Bailey, Joanna P108
Bailey, David E. P141
Bailey, Georgette P160
Bailey, Brad P184
Bailey, David P229
Bailey, Erin P247
Bailey, Matt P252
Bailey, Larry P252
Bailey, Rickey P281
Bailey, Brandi P340
Bailey, Jeff P422
Bailey, Don P447
Bailey, Colonel B P587
Bailey, Jean Ann P652
Bailey, A. Robert D. W23
Bailey, David W196
Bailey, Holly E166
Bailey, Daniel E284
Bailey, Todd E289
Bailey, Kathy E320
Bailey, Steve R. E328
Bailey, Scott E396
Bailey, Daniel K. (Dan) E410
Bailey, Jim E441
Baileys, Kristen A883
Baileys, Kristen P644
Bailie, David A447
Bailie, David P247

Bailie, Mark W333
Bailin, Mitchell P570
Baillie, Thomas A880
Baillie, Thomas P640
Bailly, Jean-Philippe W218
Bailly, R. Jeffrey E414
Baima, Anthony A335
Baima, Anthony E155
Bain, Earle A6
Bain, Adrienne A205
Baine, Edward Ed A275
Baines, Heather U. A70
Baines, Chelsea P436
Bains, Michael E116
Bainum, Stewart E80
Baio, Richard M. A126
Baiocco, John A839
Bair, Sheila A436
Baird, Howard A56
Baird, H Kim A56
Baird, Allison A147
Baird, Andrea A326
Baird, Lisa A466
Baird, Brent A531
Baird, Alice A651
Baird, Patrick S. (Pat) A693
Baird, Jim P296
Baird, Bob I. W190
Baird, Alice E329
Baird, Patrick S. (Pat) E341
Baird, W. Blake E400
Bairrington, David E332
Baisiwala, Udai P290
Baisley, David P114
Baitcher, Howard P8
Baiunco, Joseph A833
Baivier, Meghan E392
Baja, Mahoney P147
Bajaj, Lalit P127
Bajpay, Pari A89
Bajraktari, Leta A203
Bajus, Paul P547
Baker, Bill A25
Baker, Charles E. A103
Baker, Charles A112
Baker, Lloyd W. A116
Baker, Scott A117
Baker, Aj A161
Baker, Rodney A171
Baker, Roger A194
Baker, Sibylle A203
Baker, Mary Ellen A205
Baker, Trishia A224
Baker, Aaron A225
Baker, Jill A240
Baker, Wayne A246
Baker, Scott A251
Baker, Douglas M. (Doug) A289
Baker, Peter A292
Baker, Paula A323
Baker, Sherry A327
Baker, Tricia A337
Baker, Sally W A364
Baker, Jeffrey R. A434
Baker, Peter A460
Baker, Paula A465
Baker, Deborah A478
Baker, Dan A479
Baker, Delores A571
Baker, Charles A589
Baker, Judson A606
Baker, Nancy A623
Baker, Tom A772
Baker, Neal A818
Baker, Ronald A818
Baker, Jessica A828
Baker, Todd A833
Baker, Doug A882
Baker, Joseph A922
Baker, Jared A935
Baker, James A P10
Baker, Bill P14
Baker, J Craig P32
Baker, Scott P61
Baker, Mike P86

Baker, Bill John P126
Baker, Emily A P137
Baker, Hannelore P162
Baker, Paula P210
Baker, Mewesette P212
Baker, Ron P264
Baker, Deborah P269
Baker, Veronica P272
Baker, Dan P273
Baker, Alun P333
Baker, John P339
Baker, Karen P349
Baker, Greg P446
Baker, Tori Budgeon P456
Baker, Kay P467
Baker, Denis P473
Baker, Gary E. P478
Baker, Gary P479
Baker, Stephen W. (Steve) P509
Baker, Jessica P584
Baker, Frederic P616
Baker, Brandon P646
Baker, Joseph P671
Baker, Jeff W323
Baker, Lloyd W. E39
Baker, Wayne E105
Baker, Gordon E149
Baker, Tricia E158
Baker, Nancy E313
Baker, Rich E340
Baker, Richard A. E356
Baker, Teri E357
Baker, Tom E381
Baker, Neal E403
Baker, Ronald E403
Baker, Brian E412
Baker, Charles C. (Lanny) E450
Baker-Greene, Edward E143
Baker-Nel, Deena A97
Bakken, A. Christopher (Chris) A296
Bakken, Chris A296
Bakken, Kyle A885
Bakr, Nahiyan A711
Bakr, Nahiyan P444
Bakshi, Hemant W408
Bala, Aru A778
Balaban, David A65
Balachandran, Madhavan A64
Balakrishnan, Govind A11
Balakrishnan, Karthik E429
Balal, Sarah P383
Balandran, Adriana P499
Balara, Curt A846
Balas, Egon P114
Balasubramaniam, Priya A72
Balasubramanian, Ruma A199
Balasubramanian, Gopal A784
Balasubramanian, Mallathur P672
Balawajder, Charles G. A873
Balazik, Matthew P650
Balbirnie, Michael A713
Balbosa, Suzanne P65
Balcer, Holly P112
Balcezak, Thomas J. P676
Baldasare, Joseph A356
Baldassaro, Sarah P569
Balde, Mamadou P459
Balderson, Diane A608
Baldorossi, Dana E172
Baldridge, Don A258
Balduzzi, Michael A P196
Baldwin, Jay A91
Baldwin, James L A489
Baldwin, Valerie A509
Baldwin, Robert H. A562
Baldwin, Paul A606
Baldwin, Dianne A678
Baldwin, Penny A694
Baldwin, Robert A770
Baldwin, Jo A801
Baldwin, Sean P74
Baldwin, Todd P225
Baldwin, Lawanda P342
Baldwin, Molly P564

Baldwin, Patricia P596
Baldwin, Jay E29
Baldwin, Steve R. E197
Baldwin, Matthew E433
Balena, Alfredo A309
Bales, Jim A465
Bales, Brian A. A721
Bales, Jayson C A726
Bales, Jayson C P453
Balfour, Scott A40
Balfour, Scott P29
Balhoff, William E P401
Bali, Adnan W404
Baline, Lorraine A301
Balius, Shary A711
Balius, Shary P444
Ball, John A1
Ball, Martin A114
Ball, Emanuel A155
Ball, Vicki A246
Ball, Susan M. A250
Ball, Mindy A444
Ball, Zane A460
Ball, Tracey A483
Ball, Gail S. A823
Ball, David A867
Ball, Jon W. P238
Ball, Parke D P279
Ball, Andrew J. (Andy) P531
Ball, George L. P582
Ball, John E1
Ball, Martin E36
Ball, Emanuel E54
Ball, Vicki E105
Ball, Darin E337
Ball, Gail S. E405
Ball, David E418
Ballan, Wassim P417
Ballance, Tom P308
Ballance, Robert E41
Ballantine, Alex A727
Ballantine, Alex P453
Ballard, Eugene G. A126
Ballard, Shari L. A130
Ballard, Joe A368
Ballard, Mark A710
Ballard, Amanda A891
Ballard, Gary P201
Ballard, Tim P506
Ballard, Jeff E219
Ballarin, John A744
Ballas, Kelly A484
Ballenger, Jeremy A176
Ballesteros, Walter P161
Ballinas, Carlos P329
Ballinger, Kevin J. A149
Ballock, Steven P77
Ballou, Amanda P5
Ballou, Doug P391
Balloun, James S. A472
Ballow, Tracey A538
Ballsrud, Robert A335
Ballsrud, Robert E155
Ballweg, Sallyanne K. A348
Ballweg, Sallyanne K. E169
Balmuth, Michael A. A731
Balogun, Stephen A121
Balogun, Kelvin A215
Balot, Cheryl A619
Balot, Cheryl P393
Balousek, Jon A207
Balow, Michael E110
Balsasty, Gerald A880
Balsasty, Gerald P640
Balseiro, Liana A200
Balser, Kathy A580
Balser, Jeffrey R. P599
Balser, Jeffrey R. P648
Balser, Kathy E292
Balsera, Manuel A61
Balte, Tom A654
Balter, Bruce P558
Balthrop, Patrick J. E261
Baltimore, David P556
Baltodano-Dubey, Monica P265

Baltzley, Michael P665
Bamert, Ryan E132
Bamford, Roger A386
Bamford, William A P587
Bamford, Roger E188
Bamfordiii, William A P587
Ban, Hubert A739
Banati, Amit A487
Banbury, Colby P627
Bancarz, Gloria P6
Banchoff, Tom P570
Bancroft, Charles A. A151
Bancroft, Philip V. W106
Bancroft, John E448
Band, Alexandra A704
Banda, Jose P461
Banda, Kassandra P552
Bandaru, Ravi A784
Bandaru, Murali P36
Bandas, Mark P599
Bandel, Jason A799
Bandi, Bruce A908
Bandi, Bruce E436
Bandini, Marzia A801
Bandla, Madhuri A222
Bando, Colin A799
Banducci, Bradford (Brad) W426
Bane, Julie A482
Banens, Tania A544
Banerjea, Atish A310
Banerjee, Aunoy A784
Banerjee, Prith W344
Banerjee, Nana E429
Banes, Michele A580
Banes, Michele E292
Bang, Derek P165
Bang, Carl S. W371
Banga, Ajaypal S. (Ajay) A544
Bangs, Richard A702
Bania, Beth P429
Banic, Susanna A686
Banigo, Awoala P82
Banis, R. Daniel A249
Banis, Daniel A249
Banis, William P388
Banis, R. Daniel E108
Banis, Daniel E108
Banister, Brian A695
Banister, Gaurdie E A855
Baniszewski, Daniel P525
Bank, David A893
Banker, Jennifer A108
Bankhead, Tammie P566
Banks, Tony A315
Banks, Tony A452
Banks, Mia A507
Banks, Lee C. A640
Banks, Maureen A641
Banks, Joseph A756
Banks, Samuel A855
Banks, Gary P117
Banks, Melinda P122
Banks, Maureen P407
Banks, Jeffrey P534
Banks, Kenneth B P575
Banks, David P579
Banks, Jennifer J. E8
Banks, Heather E19
Banks, Connie E344
Banner, Jon A654
Bannister, Clive C R W306
Bannister, Chelsey E392
Bannon, Patrick E345
Banos, Ed P82
Bansal, Shiv A850
Bansal, Abhishek P610
Bansal, Arun W386
Bansky, Alyssa A164
Banta, Walter J A368
Banta, Walter A368
Banta, David E194
Bantegnie, Eric E22
Bantz, Charles R. P609
Bao, David A391
Bao-Lang, Chen W165

Bapna, Deepak A896
Baptist, Kevin A109
Baptista, Antonio P399
Baptiste, Ernest J. A588
Baptiste, Ernest J. P365
Baptiste, Sandra P500
Baque-stanton, Vanessa A731
Bar-Adon, Eshel A100
Bar-Adon, Eshel A101
Bar-Adon, Eshel P58
Bar-Adon, Eshel E32
Barabino, Joseph P586
Baraddon, Cynthia A738
Barahona, Dan E342
Barak, Angela P554
Baraldi, Raymond L. P563
Baran, Tonya A22
Baran, Jeffrey A652
Baran, Lance A702
Baran, Jeffrey E331
Baranov, Vitaliy W169
Baranovsky, Leon A199
Barash, Yona P536
Baratta, Joseph P. A137
Baratta, Julie A642
Baratta, Julie P407
Baratz, Meredith A877
Barazandeh, Farzin A632
Barba, James J. P17
Barba, James J P18
Barba, J. Brendan P78
Barbagallo, John A. A681
Barbagallo, Michel P325
Barbar-tzadik, Smadar W163
Barbara, Walters A337
Barbara, Walters E158
Barbarick, Steve K. A840
Barbeau-Leonard, Geraldine P228
Barbeauld, Rob P146
Barbella, Al A470
Barber, Anthony A75
Barber, Timothy C. A308
Barber, Tim A444
Barber, Walter A476
Barber, Gerry A665
Barber, Ken A755
Barber, James J. (Jim) A870
Barber, Ken A882
Barber, Mike P106
Barber, Dennis P159
Barber, David P260
Barber, Gary P337
Barber, Chris P514
Barber, Roger L P589
Barber, Gerry E334
Barber, Ken E369
Barber-Tzadik, Smadar W162
Barbera, Vanesa A381
Barbera, John A674
Barbera, Mike E8
Barbercheck, Richard S. A340
Barbercheck, Richard S. E160
Barberesi, Vincent A137
Barberi, Carlos A271
Barberot, David A854
Barbier, Robert P P623
Barbier, Fran-§ois W164
Barbieri, Roberta A654
Barbieri, Eric P332
Barbieri, Mark P335
Barbizet, Patricia W218
Barbo, William D. E75
Barbone, Ray A115
Barbone, Ray E38
Barcalow, Sharon A91
Barcalow, Sharon E29
Barcelos, Elcio A312
Barch, Frank A754
Barch, Frank P484
Barchan, Olexander P383
Barchus, Carl A592
Barchus, Carl P370
Barclay, Lynn A492
Barclay, Bruce A562
Barclay, Alyson S. E135

Bardales, Flawer A651
Bardales, Flawer E330
Bardazzi, Marco W155
Barditch, Larry A452
Bardos, Kevin E260
Bardot, Rob A60
Bardsley, Mark A879
Bardsley, Mark P636
Bardusch, Robert J. A888
Bardusch, Robert J. E425
Bared, Amparo A734
Barefoot, Becky A850
Bareford, Steven A320
Bareilles, Mary P405
Bareis, Janet A371
Barengo, Randy A652
Barengo, Randy E331
Barenkamp, John P513
Barer, Sol J. W389
Baresich, Michael A37
Barey, David A651
Barey, David E329
Barfield, David P21
Barfield, Kelle J P196
Barfield, Regina P291
Barfield, Lowry E5
Barganski, John A421
Barger, Andrew A173
Barger, Dawn A544
Barger, Dennis L A751
Bargull, Raymond C P590
Barhaug, Michael A724
Barhaug, Michael P452
Barhorst, Matthew A528
Baribeau, Nathan B P24
Baricaua, Geoffrey A817
Baril, Thierry W17
Bariquit, Teri A602
Barkdull, Kris P83
Barker, Alberta A1
Barker, Greg A28
Barker, Phyllis A410
Barker, Bill A452
Barker, Debra A584
Barker, G. Carlton (Carl) A755
Barker, Ellen L. A820
Barker, Nick A853
Barker, Kurtis A872
Barker, James P P161
Barker, Annalesa P409
Barker, Nick P612
Barker, Alberta E1
Barker, Nicholas E272
Barker, G. Carlton (Carl) E369
Barker, David A. E385
Barkey, Carl A53
Barkin, Michael Z. E424
Barkinge, Michele A481
Barkley, Chris A103
Barkley, Michael A636
Barks, Brad A715
Barksdale, Myrla P546
Barlak, Paul M P193
Barlak, Paul M P372
Barleaza, Jean-Phillipe A897
Barley, Hattie A320
Barley, Debbi A511
Barley, J Patrick P270
Barley, Debbi P290
Barley, Amy P626
Barlow, Jeff D. A570
Barlow, Debra A844
Barlow, Chris A906
Barlow, Chris E435
Barlowe, Jamie P596
Barmore, Gregory T. (Greg) E307
Barna, Thomas A371
Barna, Thomas P213
Barnaba, Michael A842
Barnard, Ray F. A355
Barnard, Christine A532
Barnard, Natashe A545
Barnard, Tony A903
Barnard, Lauren A925
Barnard, Rikki P74

Barnard, Keith P204
Barnard, John P359
Barnard, Lauren E445
Barnash, Chris A352
Barnefield, John A727
Barnefield, John P453
Barner, Sharon R A247
Barner, Ronald A737
Barner, Ronald E361
Barnes, Joseph A112
Barnes, Dave A265
Barnes, John A305
Barnes, Dave A417
Barnes, Robert B. (Bob) A463
Barnes, Emily A470
Barnes, Melissa Stapleton A517
Barnes, Georgette A646
Barnes, John P. (Jack) A650
Barnes, Donald A837
Barnes, Lamar A850
Barnes, Lucinda P258
Barnes, David G. P355
Barnes, Nicole P447
Barnes, Maureen P. P563
Barnes, Virginia A. (Ginger) P620
Barnes, James R P648
Barnes, Susan L. P654
Barnes, Erin P665
Barnes, Tom E172
Barnes, Georgette E324
Barnes, John P. (Jack) E329
Barnes, Keith E359
Barnes, Michael G. E407
Barnett, Lamar A19
Barnett, Mark A112
Barnett, Sheila A225
Barnett, Thomas A528
Barnett, June A688
Barnett, Hoyt R. (Barney) A688
Barnett, Hoyt R. (Barney) A689
Barnett, Bruce A847
Barnett, Marty A885
Barnett, Jay A893
Barnett, Rob A922
Barnett, Robert A922
Barnett, Alan P371
Barnett, Hoyt R. (Barney) P435
Barnett, Phillip P440
Barnett, Adam P476
Barnett, Elaine P523
Barnett, Rob P671
Barnett, Robert P671
Barnett, Bill E270
Barnett, Bruce E410
Barnett-Sarpalius, Jenny P300
Barnette, Mary K A227
Barnette, Kimberly P126
Barnette, Wesley P278
Barnette, Mary K E90
Barney, Karina A537
Barnhart, Eric A809
Barnhart, Cynthia P314
Barnhart, Glenn P537
Barnhart, Dale G. E263
Barnhart, James E316
Barnhill, Jerry A258
Barns, Mitch A599
Barns, Mitch P376
Barnum, James A621
Barnum, James E312
Baroldi, Joseph E237
Baron, Wayne A543
Baron, Harold P392
Baron, Nir W389
Barone, Frank A264
Barone, Vincent A756
Barone, Christine A779
Barone, Steve A922
Barone, Laura A922
Barone, Ed A922
Barone, Frank P180
Barone, Joel P308
Barone, Steve P671
Barone, Laura P671
Barone, Ed P671

COMBINED HOOVER'S HANDBOOK INDEX OF EXECUTIVES

```
A = AMERICAN BUSINESS
E = EMERGING COMPANIES
P = PRIVATE COMPANIES
W = WORLD BUSINESS
```

Baroni, Jason E143
Baronian, Nicholas A320
Barquist, Richard A559
Barr, David A75
Barr, Simon A135
Barr, Scott A145
Barr, William A275
Barr, Sarah A906
Barr, Mike P261
Barr, Sarah E435
Barra, Hugo A310
Barra, Mary T. A378
Barra, Ornella A899
Barranco, David A43
Barranco, David E13
Barrentine, Curt A484
Barrera, John A315
Barrera, Triccia A935
Barrera, Benjelyn P437
Barret, Jay A483
Barreto, Sue A346
Barreto, Sue E167
Barrett, Noel A119
Barrett, Kayla A139
Barrett, Jeanne A147
Barrett, George S. A170
Barrett, Clay A383
Barrett, Eric A665
Barrett, Lausanne A682
Barrett, Geoffrey (Geoff) A692
Barrett, Andrew A755
Barrett, Genevieve A835
Barrett, John D. A848
Barrett, Kevin A850
Barrett, Jennifer A928
Barrett, Kayla P93
Barrett, Michael P142
Barrett, Karin A P180
Barrett, Bill P237
Barrett, Kevin P246
Barrett, Robert P260
Barrett, David P284
Barrett, Mark P285
Barrett, Barbara M. P553
Barrett, John A. P596
Barrett, William P615
Barrett, Jennifer P673
Barrett, Rick E143
Barrett, Clay E186
Barrett, Eric E334
Barrett, Andrew E369
Barrett, John D. E411
Barrick, Bob A785
Barrick, Robert L P67
Barrick, Karen P637
Barriere, Steve E230
Barrila, Craig A657
Barringer, Chris A823
Barringer, Chris P557
Barringhaus, Tim A298
Barringhaus, Tim E130
Barrington, Martin J. (Marty) A41
Barrinson, Tom P461
Barrios, Alfredo (Alf) W325
Barrios, Alfredo W327
Barrios, George A. E448
Barriss, Jay A882
Barroca, Nadine A191
Barron, John A16
Barron, Joshua A676
Barron, Eric J. A828
Barron, James A. (Andy) A901
Barron, Wayne P430
Barron, Eric J. P584
Barron, Todd P677
Barron, Shelton E282
Barron, Joshua E338
Barros, Marion De A859
Barros, Carlos P422

Barros, D. Benjamin P596
Barros, Daniel Feldmann W26
Barroso, Carlos J. A164
Barrow, Shannon A329
Barrows, John A98
Barrows, Karen P456
Barrs, Craig A382
Barry, Corie S. A130
Barry, Edie Feilce A511
Barry, Chris A623
Barry, Kyle A922
Barry, Edie Feilce P290
Barry, Ellen P336
Barry, Jim P409
Barry, Thomas E P505
Barry, Kyle P671
Barry, Erin E278
Barry, Chris E313
Barry, Michael E359
Barsanti, Ronald G P420
Barsby, Anna W266
Barsody, Thomas D A909
Barsody, Thomas A909
Barsody, Thomas D E436
Barsody, Thomas E436
Barstad, Melanie A197
Barstow, Debbie A298
Barstow, Debbie E130
Bart, Kelly P315
Bartczak, Amy P604
Bartee, Chris A171
Bartek, David A526
Bartek, Adam P549
Bartel, Tony D. A371
Bartel, Trish P242
Bartel, Ricardo W45
Bartels, Heidi A686
Barter, Jim P128
Barth, Jill A25
Barth, Dawn A161
Barth, Kevin G. A224
Barth, Kate A413
Barth, Werner A661
Barth, Kevin A893
Barth, Jill P14
Barth, Jan E48
Barth, Kate E205
Barthel, Brett A891
Bartholomew, Stephen A752
Bartkowski, Paul A922
Bartkowski, Paul P671
Bartle, Simon A381
Bartleson, Linda E51
Bartlett, Thomas A. (Tom) A59
Bartlett, Thomas A325
Bartlett, Tom A326
Bartlett, Matthew A743
Bartlett, David L. A760
Bartlett, Charles A809
Bartlett, Russ A821
Bartlett, Michael A833
Bartlett, Daniel J. (Dan) A901
Bartlett, Joe E282
Bartlett, David L. E374
Bartolini, Huey A337
Bartolini, Huey E158
Bartolomei, Tom P356
Bartolomeo, Melissa A337
Bartolomeo, Melissa E158
Bartolozzi, Arthur P583
Bartolucci, Tony A17
Bartolucci, Anthony A17
Bartolucci, Tony P9
Bartolucci, Anthony P9
Barton, Robert F. A48
Barton, Lisa M. A51
Barton, Michael A97
Barton, Richard B. A116
Barton, Ellen A226
Barton, Louis A246
Barton, Sally A492
Barton, Nina A497
Barton, Rich A587
Barton, John A712

Barton, Linda A713
Barton, Kurt A840
Barton, Jacqueline K. P107
Barton, Ellen P150
Barton, Stancil E. (Stan) P375
Barton, Richard B. E39
Barton, Louis E105
Barton, Christopher J. E219
Barton, Gregory E447
Bartone, Michael A778
Bartos, Scott A933
Bartosh, Robert J. P69
Bartosz, Carol A530
Bartsch, Matthew P537
Bartschat, Michael A480
Bartschat, Michael P270
Bartz, Lisa A680
Baruffi, Kumi Yamamoto A219
Baruffi, Kumi Yamamoto E87
Barwood, Marlene A P265
Baryshnikov, Vladislav W169
Barzilay, Jonathan P432
Bas, Didem W403
Basch, Kenneth P116
Basche, Todd E30
Basden, Carl A543
Basden, Daniel P126
Baseden, Candice A692
Baseler, Theodor P. (Ted) A41
Baselga, José P325
Baser, Didem Din-Şer W403
Basey, Jim A413
Basey, Jim E205
Basford, Nick A871
Basford, Matt P443
Bashaw, Michael A921
Bashaw, Michael P669
Basher, Linda A203
Basil, Jack P463
Basilio, Karin A74
Basilio, Paulo A496
Basilio, Esther P519
Basilotto, Steve P211
Basinger, Tracy A321
Basir, Khadija A167
Baske, Jim W33
Basker, Vr A654
Baskerville, Bob P480
Baskette, Lisa A665
Baskette, Lisa E334
Baskin, Jeremy A605
Baskin, Scott E18
Basler, Uwe A842
Basney, Barbara A933
Basom, Jean P463
Basom, Joanne P644
Bason, John G. W36
Bass, Bill A272
Bass, Brenda A479
Bass, Maureen A844
Bass, Everett A905
Bass, William L. P120
Bass, Mike P162
Bass, Justin P165
Bass, Theodore P488
Bass, Patrick W391
Bassano, Lori A540
Basse, Gloria A941
Bassett, Gretta A58
Bassett, Lawton E. A62
Bassett, Julie A236
Bassett, Chance A469
Bassett, Donal J P356
Bassett, Claire M P548
Bassett, Mary Beth P654
Bassett, Kira P673
Bassett, Lawton E. E20
Bassett, William E100
Bassham, Terry D P274
Bassin, Darin A893
Bassler, Dennis A30
Bassler, Bonnie A710
Bassler, Dennis P20
Basso, Maurizio W35
Bassoni, Mario P605

Basta, Amaya P522
Bastian, Ben A175
Bastian, Edward H. (Ed) A262
Bastings, Arthur A270
Basto, Edgar W68
Bastug, Recep W403
Bastuga, Kevin P. A759
Bastuga, Kevin P. E373
Basu, Devjit A135
Basu, Gourab A895
Basulto, Jose P500
Batanian, Michael A137
Batato, Magdi W276
Batchelder, Eugene L. (Gene) A618
Batchelder, Peter E264
Batcheler, Colleen A232
Batchelor, Phil A119
Batchelor, Steve A905
Batchelor, E Dale P467
Batelaan, Richard A90
Bateman, Jerry A323
Bateman, Melody A629
Bateman, Mark T. P462
Bateman, Christopher M P529
Bates, Tony A198
Bates, Robert A561
Bates, Alex A595
Bates, Larry L. A760
Bates, Jonathan R. (Jon) P45
Bates, Crandall P59
Bates, Paul P126
Bates, Martin W P220
Bates, Ondrea P235
Bates, Peter W. P305
Bates, Ruth P332
Bates, Chris P544
Bates, Laurence W. W238
Bates, Larry L. E374
Batey, Alan S. A378
Bath, Margaret A487
Bath, Chuck E112
Bathgate, Brian E75
Bathla, Sunny E431
Batista, Wesley Mendon-§a A663
Batkin, Alan R. E322
Batman, Colleen A409
Bator, Susan P573
Batra, Radhika A673
Batra, Udit W254
Batrack, Dan L. E402
Batres, Grace A887
Batres, Francisco P153
Batri, Nadim A145
Batshaw, Mark P130
Batson, Andrew A919
Batson, Charles H. (Chuck) E156
Batt, Douglas A. P405
Battaglia, Alex A478
Battaglia, Giancarlo E101
Battaglini, Stephen A930
Battas, Sandy A859
Batten, Brian A137
Battenfield, Keith P119
Battey, Margaret P639
Battifarano, Leonard A540
Battle, Seymour A887
Battle, Cheryll P253
Battle, A. George (Skip) E144
Baty, Darren A447
Baty, Darren P247
Batzri, Ilab W163
Bauche, Douglas N. A298
Bauche, Douglas N. E130
Baucum, Carlton E P245
Bauda, John A839
Baudach, Detlev A450
Baude, Bruce K. A212
Bauder, Charles J A704
Bauder, Douglas R. A770
Baudoin, Mark A526
Baudouin, Richard E7
Bauer, Ryan A58
Bauer, Pete A101
Bauer, Brett C. A129
Bauer, Judy A179

COMBINED HOOVER'S HANDBOOK INDEX OF EXECUTIVES

Bauer, Michael P. (Mike) A361
Bauer, W S A463
Bauer, Jeff A796
Bauer, Tom A799
Bauer, Daniel (Dan) A831
Bauer, John A835
Bauer, David A837
Bauer, Kris B. A864
Bauer, Cindy A925
Bauer, Mark P176
Bauer, Brad P514
Bauer, Daniel (Dan) P601
Bauer, Sabine W9
Bauer, Pete E32
Bauer, Amy E308
Bauer, Jeff E397
Bauer, Cindy E445
Bauerlein, Alison E231
Baughan, Michael B. P390
Baughman, Michael A119
Baughman, Karen A123
Baughman, Michael J A292
Baughman, Richard A. E370
Bauhofer, Scott A13
Baum, James A36
Baum, Don A702
Baum, Richard D. A709
Baum, Peter A888
Baum, Jeff A897
Baum, Shannon P503
Baum, Mark L E200
Baum, Richard D. E348
Baum, Peter E425
Bauman, James L. (Jim) A3
Bauman, Steve A538
Bauman, Brian A905
Baumann, Caroline P497
Baumann, Joseph P673
Baumann, Werner W61
Baumgardner, Jeffrey P96
Baumgarten, Jennifer A391
Baumgarten, Alan S P344
Baumgartl, Wolf-Dieter W382
Baumgartner, Michael A. P64
Baumgartner, Robert V. E45
Baumli, Heather A452
Baures, Robert P456
Bausch, Rebecca A877
Bauters, Fred J P165
Bautista, Estela P137
Bautista, Javier Velez P224
Bautista, Jeremy P450
Bauwel, Chantal Van P95
Bavazls, Marcelo P46
Baverman, Charlie P128
Baverso, Louis P644
Bavouset, Jim A512
Bavrica, Karime A90
Bawale, Ajay A695
Bawol, Jeff A99
Baxley, Thomas P111
Baxley, Doug E250
Baxter, Warner L. A46
Baxter, Dave A281
Baxter, Joel D. A756
Baxter, Peter A761
Baxter, Jeffrey A831
Baxter, Scott H. A891
Baxter, Dan A909
Baxter, John P190
Baxter, Rob P487
Baxter, Jeffrey P601
Baxter, Matt E290
Baxter, Dan E436
Bay, Annell A71
Bayardo, Jose A A581
Baybars, Ilker P114
Baye, Cheryl A112
Bayer, Terry P. A570
Bayer, Dan A787
Bayer, Buddy A924
Bayer, James P2
Bayer, Paul E. E296
Bayer, Michael J. E372
Bayha, Deborah A325

Bayle, Jan A727
Bayle, Jan P453
Bayles, Autumn A75
Bayless, Django A522
Bayless, Victoria W P40
Bayless, George P213
Baylor, Denise A371
Baylor, Denise P213
Bayne, Edward A140
Bayne, Teresa A804
Bays, Claudia A452
Baysinger, Jared A885
Baytos, David P335
Bazan, Fernando E45
Bazante, Jennifer A440
Bazarko, Dawn A877
Bazemore, Teresa A. Bryce A700
Bazile, Yamilee P371
Bazinet, Martin A547
Bazire, Nicolas W241
Bazluke, Francine P639
Bazoli, Giovanni W202
Bazzoli, Jana P128
Bea, Javon R P330
Beabout, Brent A602
Beach, Joan A266
Beach, Mark A654
Beach, Brian C. A797
Beach, Joan P181
Beacham, Renee A107
Beacham, Michael A255
Beachey, Brenda A859
Beadie, William M P41
Beahm, Paul A902
Beair, Duane A525
Beal, Bob A453
Beal, Jamie A752
Beal, Neda P11
Beal, Steven P323
Beal, Graham W J P565
Beal, Rebecca E134
Beale, G. William (Billy) A91
Beale, G. William (Billy) E29
Bealer, Christopher A920
Beall, Brian A806
Beall, Brian E398
Beam, Chris T. A51
Beam, Eric A186
Beam, Diane A339
Beam, Garrett A528
Beam, Eric P123
Beam, Dawn P636
Beam, Diane E159
Beaman, Randall A881
Beaman, Jamie P675
Beaman, Randall E421
Beams, Mike P315
Beams, Jutta P564
Bean, Blu A142
Bean, Robert A559
Bean, Bryan A665
Bean, Lincoln A. P16
Bean, Darlene P190
Bean, James C. P383
Bean, Paul W358
Bean, Blu E49
Bean, Claire E305
Bean, Bryan E334
Bear, James A741
Bear, James E364
Beard, Patty A264
Beard, Deanne A345
Beard, Brad A796
Beard, Robert F. (Bob) A857
Beard, Robert P32
Beard, Dave P184
Beard, Gregory P643
Beard, Simon E10
Beard, Ronald S. E59
Beard, Deanne E165
Beard, Stephen W. E207
Beard, JW E222
Beard, Brad E397
Beardall, Brent J. A903

Bearden, Matt P508
Beardi, James A530
Beardsley, Bruce A369
Beardsley, Kirk M. A602
Bearese, Andrew A739
Bearison, Daniel A626
Beasley, Marsha P406
Beasley, Barnie P506
Beasley, Scott P552
Beasley, Ralph D P609
Beason, Amy P306
Beato, Jacqueline A160
Beaton, Tiffany A771
Beaton, Tiffany E381
Beattie, Kathryn P522
Beattie, Greg E75
Beatty, Mark A133
Beatty, Donald A218
Beatty, Patrick A606
Beatty, Jana A709
Beatty, Jonathan A746
Beatty, Vincent L. A903
Beatty, Lee P237
Beatty, Jana P442
Beatty, Ellen M. P553
Beatty, Kathy E335
Beaty, Brian A175
Beaty, Julie A452
Beauchamp, Alexander A559
Beauchamp, Janice A658
Beaudette, Phil A866
Beaudette, Phil E418
Beaudoin, Marc Phillipe A380
Beaudoin, Edward P24
Beaudoin, Pierre W73
Beaudreault, Jim P96
Beaumont, Simon A465
Beaumont, Carol A835
Beaumont, Glenn W150
Beaune, Geoff P658
Beauregard, Colleen A835
Beausoleil, Barbara T P616
Beauvoir, Lynnie P161
Beaven, Peter W68
Beaven, Peter W69
Beaver, Steven A19
Beaver, Rick A859
Beazley, Eric P96
Beazley, Frank P462
Beazley, Dorothy P612
Bebawi, Michael A574
Bebber, David L. Van A855
Beberness, Benjamin P434
Bebout, John A872
Beccarelli, Lou E115
Becerra, Enrique A798
Becerra, Enrique X A798
Bech, Douglas A425
Bech, Douglas Y. E240
Bechar, Yossi W203
Bechard, Armond A36
Bechler, Kent P160
Becht, Lambertus J. H. (Bart) A243
Becht, Gerd W133
Bechtel, Pamela A828
Bechtel, Kathleen P211
Bechtel, Pamela P584
Bechtle, Mavis P576
Bechtol, Nancy P497
Bechu, Sophie A465
Becil, Carlos A801
Beck, Andrew H. (Andy) A21
Beck, Gary L. A29
Beck, Lance A34
Beck, Douglas A72
Beck, Ken A184
Beck, Gregory A235
Beck, Christophe A289
Beck, David E. (Dave) A320
Beck, Connie A368
Beck, Joe A416
Beck, Amy A444
Beck, Elisabeth A474
Beck, Christian A746
Beck, Drake A746

Beck, Jeff A752
Beck, Daniel A793
Beck, Angela P75
Beck, David P95
Beck, Gretchen P114
Beck, Gregory P156
Beck, Jason P175
Beck, Monica P205
Beck, Art P277
Beck, Thomas P521
Beck, Teresa P579
Beck, Mary P635
Beck, Rebecca P662
Beck, Emily E168
Beck, Ralf E286
Beck, Tim E424
Beck-Codner, Iris W389
Beckel, Jaime E143
Becker, Robert A36
Becker, Cathleen A137
Becker, Jen A327
Becker, Christopher A348
Becker, Susan A525
Becker, Lisa A595
Becker, Dave A604
Becker, Steven A677
Becker, David A748
Becker, Yin C. A789
Becker, Gregory W. (Greg) A793
Becker, Russell P41
Becker, Pete P429
Becker, Bernard P530
Becker, Taffee P541
Becker, Pamela P615
Becker, Kendall P662
Becker, W. Marston (Marty) W317
Becker, Christopher E169
Becker, William C. E291
Beckerle, Katy P18
Becketti, Sean A364
Beckey, David A749
Beckey, David E367
Beckham, William A22
Beckham, William P11
Beckley, Debra A19
Beckley, Michael A537
Beckley, Jason A702
Beckman, Kim A195
Beckman, Lawrence P21
Beckman, Jason P133
Beckman, Joni P666
Beckman, Per W377
Beckmann, Barbara A356
Beckmann, Laura A882
Beckmann, Kai W254
Beckmeyer, Laura P174
Beckom, Daria A902
Beckum, Renee P174
Beckwith, Patricia A309
Beckwith, Tina A559
Beckwith, Robert P127
Beckwith, Richard P353
Beckwitt, Richard (Rick) A512
Beckworth, Brandon P506
Becky, Solmirin A368
Bedard, Natalie A658
Bedard, Amy A774
Bedard, Tim A895
Beddes, Hallie A540
Bedeau, Theresa A167
Bedel, Vicki A883
Bedel, Vicki P644
Beder-yee, Janice A561
Bedessem, Mike P158
Bedford, Charles E. P579
Bedingfield, Kenneth L. A608
Bednar, Alexander A412
Bednarek, Amy A84
Bednarovsky, Jessica A807
Bednarski, Teresa A A107
Bedore, James M A585
Bedros, Suzanne A885
Beebe, Robert A199
Beebe, Brian A294
Beebe, Mike A426

COMBINED HOOVER'S HANDBOOK INDEX OF EXECUTIVES

A = AMERICAN BUSINESS
E = EMERGING COMPANIES
P = PRIVATE COMPANIES
W = WORLD BUSINESS

Beebe, Calvin P318
Beebe, Mike E213
Beecher, Barbara P108
Beecher, Bradley P. P566
Beecher, Shirley P598
Beede, Katherine A835
Beehler, Brice E72
Beeken, Scott A56
Beekman, Sheri P352
Beeler, John A739
Beeler, Don P133
Beeman, Tom P467
Beeman, Thomas E. (Tom) P573
Beene, Delwin P151
Beer, Lori A. A483
Beer, James A. A549
Beer, Sander De A658
Beer, Ron A924
Beer, Megan W27
Beer-christensen, Debbie A692
Beerle, Gail P184
Beers, Marlene A674
Beers, David P245
Beery, Joseph C. (Joe) A832
Beery, Cindy P581
Beery, Joe E223
Beeson, John N A922
Beeson, John N P671
Beetson, Deborah P185
Beeuwsaert, Dirk W154
Begam, Thomas A329
Begg, Brian A910
Begg, Patrick E264
Begle, Curt L. A129
Begley, Jody L. A41
Begley, Nicholas A926
Begley, Nicholas E445
Beguiristain, Frank A938
Beguiristain, Frank P678
Behal, Raj P524
Behan, Mark A82
Behl, Navneet A71
Behling, Kristen P173
Behm, Michael J. A711
Behm, Michael J. P444
Behmer, Nancy A911
Behmer, Nancy E437
Behnk, Karin A859
Behr, Dr. Giorgio W433
Behrens, David A. A58
Behrens, Michael A325
Behrens, Matt P258
Behring, Alexandre (Alex) A497
Behringer, Brad A195
Behrle, Jim A376
Beidelman, Jason A649
Beierwaltes, Paul A925
Beierwaltes, Paul E445
Beil, David A888
Beil, David E425
Beine, William A161
Beine, Beverly P386
Beirne, Nazli A484
Beiter, Stephanie P455
Beithon, Patricia A. E23
Beitler, Ken A590
Belak, Cindy A650
Belak, Cindy E329
Belalcazar, Angel Dario A218
Belanger, Dave A446
Belanic, Jim A676
Belanic, Jim E338
Belanoff, Joseph K. E96
Belardi, James R A90
Belardi, James R P51
Belardo, Joseph P60
Belasco, Kent S. A346
Belasco, Kent S. E167
Belavic, Jennifer P643

Belcher, Patricia A135
Belcher, Samuel L. A351
Belcher, Kelly A793
Belcher, Megan P589
Belcourt, Tracey A361
Belden, Scott A844
Belden, Doug P146
Belden, Richard P390
Belekewicz, William D. A353
Belekewicz, William D. E173
Belen, Andy A879
Beletti, Chris A236
Belfort, Michael A. P548
Belger, Brenda A. E4
Belgya, Mark R. A765
Belhadj, Hafed A661
Belhouse, Brad A160
Belisle, Jocelyn A778
Belitsky, Lee J. A264
Belitz, Robert P246
Beliveau-dunn, Jeanne A199
Belk, William A767
Belkin, Tamara A764
Belkin, Tamara E377
Bell, Patricia A A19
Bell, Bernice E A23
Bell, Thomas A140
Bell, Gretchen A150
Bell, Brad A222
Bell, Mike A240
Bell, Katherine Button A292
Bell, Doug A383
Bell, Christie A449
Bell, Teri A481
Bell, David A484
Bell, Steve A489
Bell, Mark A520
Bell, George A559
Bell, Del A571
Bell, Thomas A604
Bell, Ken A605
Bell, Des A659
Bell, David A663
Bell, Damon A664
Bell, Gina A791
Bell, Ted A793
Bell, Elaine A866
Bell, Barbara A880
Bell, Sheila P76
Bell, Douglas P84
Bell, Alastair P95
Bell, Kristine P259
Bell, Scott P265
Bell, Deborah P342
Bell, Malcolm P442
Bell, Brent P513
Bell, Jack P523
Bell, Gina P535
Bell, Bonnie P550
Bell, Donald P587
Bell, Kathy P594
Bell, Charlton P606
Bell, Jill P622
Bell, Barbara P640
Bell, Juliette B. P642
Bell, Susie P672
Bell, Jeff W95
Bell, Gregory E102
Bell, Shane E168
Bell, Doug E186
Bell, Christie E221
Bell, Michael E239
Bell, Damon E334
Bell, Sandra E. E407
Bell, Elaine E417
Bell, Brad E452
Bellack, Janis P. A641
Bellack, Janis P. P407
Bellamy, Adrian A921
Bellamy, Billie P454
Bellanti, Tim A87
Bellanti, Tim P50
Belle, Marty A393
Belle, Leah P430
Bellemare, Alain M. W73

Bellettini, Francesca W218
Bellinger, Delaney M. A447
Bellino, Nick A358
Bellino, Nick E176
Belliot, Laura A327
Bellitti, Jeff A482
Bello, Gaetano P248
Bello, Stephen P502
Bello, Kathy P593
Belloma, Kevin A224
Bellon, Sophie W358
Bellone, Steven P162
Belloni, Antonio (Toni) W241
Bellos, Alex A921
Belmonte, Lawrence A54
Belochi, Franck A692
Beloff, Hardie A P228
Beloff, Leland P228
Beloff, Jean P228
Belotto, Kathleen P174
Belous, Scott A54
Below, Ellen A409
Belshe, Mike A442
Belsher, Geoffrey (Geoff) W85
Belton, Paul P489
Beltowsk, Hann Candi A337
Beltowsk, Hann Candi E158
Beltrametti, Monica A933
Beltran, Christina A104
Beltran, Clemente (Clay) E113
Beltre, Milca A137
BeltrAn, Eduardo Navarro W149
Beltz, Ryan A646
Beltz, Mary A888
Beltz, Ryan E324
Beltz, Mary E425
Belvaux, Eric P421
Belzowski, Anne P615
Bem, David S. A673
Bemiller, Todd A922
Bemiller, Todd P671
Bemis, Mark A. A77
Ben, Mark P608
Benali, Karim E2
Benattia, Isma A65
Benavides, David A314
Benavides, David E145
Benavidez, Janet P492
Benbow, Camilla P599
Bencher, Susan D A409
Benchoff, Nancy A390
Bencosme, Thomas A574
Benda, Birgitta A658
Bendalin, Ken E218
Bender, Jim A94
Bender, Jason C. A349
Bender, Jeremy A385
Bender, Paul A695
Bender, Michael J A736
Bender, Andria A782
Bender, M. Steven (Steve) A917
Bender, Fred A430
Bender, Judy P456
Bender, Michael J P460
Bender, Andria P526
Bender, Cecelia E366
Benderman, Mimi A8
Bendis, David A909
Bendis, David E436
Bendler, Matt P10
Bendotti, Charles A661
Beneby, Doyle N A306
Beneby, Doyle N. P164
Benedettini, Natalie E123
Benedetto, Ben Di A538
Benedetto, Florence Di A791
Benedetto, Florence Di P535
Benedico, Nick E402
Benedict, John A184
Benedict, Karen P611
Benedict, Rod P646
Benefield, John A21
Benefield, Donna A610
Benegal, Jay A205
Beneke, Jim A100

Beneke, Jenny A695
Beneke, Andrea P633
Benenati, Susan V P649
Benet, Jay S. A844
Benett, Halle J A104
Beneventano, David A391
Benfer, Michelle E260
Beng, Na Wu W299
Bengs, Mike A602
Bengston, Robert A. A636
Bengston, Kelly A779
Bengston, Rusty P196
Benham, Ayisha P662
Benioff, Marc A739
Benito, Michael E. A414
Benito, David Pastrana A750
Benito, Michael E. E208
Benjamin, Rachel A200
Benjamin, Charles A203
Benjamin, Andre A391
Benjamin, Gerald A. A744
Benjamin, Peter A835
Benjamin, Howard E353
Benko, Brittany A189
Benkoske, Thomas A925
Benkoske, Thomas E445
Benn, Markham A463
Benn, Keith A618
Benn, David P. A791
Benn, David P. P535
Bennack, Frank A. A827
Bennack, Frank A. P580
Benner, David A475
Benner, Doug A741
Benner, Doug E364
Bennett, Rick A3
Bennett, Chap A62
Bennett, Bruce A63
Bennett, Shayne A74
Bennett, Karen A89
Bennett, Douglas M. A116
Bennett, Jeffrey A129
Bennett, Darlene A181
Bennett, Brian A236
Bennett, Lance J. A268
Bennett, Charles A337
Bennett, Vicki A367
Bennett, Jonathan R. A408
Bennett, Steven A752
Bennett, Dan A797
Bennett, Kris A824
Bennett, Rick A859
Bennett, Terry A902
Bennett, Susan P112
Bennett, J. Bradley P202
Bennett, W. Bradley (Brad) P315
Bennett, Chris P349
Bennett, Graham F P436
Bennett, Leon S P505
Bennett, Christopher P543
Bennett, Kris P562
Bennett, Julie P662
Bennett, Glenn W9
Bennett, Brad W106
Bennett, Adam W114
Bennett, Chap E20
Bennett, Douglas M. E39
Bennett, Darlene E102
Bennett, Matthew E102
Bennett, Charles E158
Bennett, C. Frank E237
Bennie, Michael E414
Bennington, Todd A146
Bennion, Richard W. H. (Rich) A429
Bennion, Richard W. H. (Rich) E214
Bennis, Raul E272
Benns, Norris A179
Benoist, Gilles W111
Benoit, Cole A850
Benoit, Robert P344
Benoit, John P405
Benoit, James P604
Benowitz, Leigh A745
Benroth, Robert E416
Bensalah, Nocair E126

Bense, Allan A382
Bensema, David J. P64
Bensignor, Laurence E. A283
Bensignor, Laurence E. E117
Bension, Ronald (Ron) A522
Benskin, Nancy A665
Benskin, Nancy E334
Benso, Mike E106
Benson, Don A133
Benson, Nigel A135
Benson, Mark A262
Benson, David C. A312
Benson, Ed A312
Benson, Jodi A376
Benson, Mike A376
Benson, DEA A707
Benson, Aaron A727
Benson, Marta A921
Benson, Ed P199
Benson, Leon P386
Benson, Rebecca P415
Benson, Teresa P431
Benson, Aaron P453
Benson, Chris P550
Benson, Lora J P591
Benson, Nick P594
Benson, Richard P652
Bensoussan, Arnaud A686
Bensoussan, Albert W218
Benstock, Peter E393
Benstock, Michael E393
Benter, Bob B682
Bentestuen, Trond W140
Bentkover, Adam E206
Bentley, Elizabeth M. A91
Bentley, Lee A444
Bentley, Stacey A693
Bentley, Philip A902
Bentley, Joshua P657
Bentley, Elizabeth M. E29
Bentley, Stacey E341
Bento, E. Joseph (Joe) E344
Benton, Antonio A337
Benton, David A853
Benton, Cory P198
Benton, Brent P205
Benton, Shelisa P212
Benton, David P285
Benton, Rae P386
Benton, David P612
Benton, Antonio E158
Bents, Fran P664
Bentz, Barbara P471
Benveniste, Madison P549
Benvenuto, Joe A747
Benvenuto, Joe P68
Benz, John A692
Benza, Holly P333
Benzaia, Alice P561
Benzin, Sandy A286
Benzin, Sandy P190
Benzon, Jennie A538
Bené, Thomas L. (Tom) A797
Bepler, Stephen E P572
Beppler, Bev P358
Bequette, Marcia A714
Beracha, Barry A827
Beracha, Barry P571
Beran, Momoko A. E375
Berard, Sarah A409
Berard, Patrick W323
Berberian, Lance V. A502
Berce, Daniel E. (Dan) A378
Berchtold, Joe A522
Berchtold, Tim A654
Bercovici, Nancy A320
Berdan, Barclay E. P550
Berdine, Winona A715
Bereche, Alfred C P359
Berend, Anne A465
Berendsen, Michael A919
Berendsen, Nancy A919
Berendsen, Jay Michael A919
Berenis, Joseph P120
Berensen, Nannette A462

Berensen, Nannette P256
Berenson, Harris A405
Berenzweig, Harold P551
Beresford, Michael P337
Beresh, Nicholas A909
Beresh, Nicholas E436
BERETTA, PIETRO GUSSALLI W410
Berg, John A61
Berg, Charles G. (Chuck) A257
Berg, Tracey L. A293
Berg, Bryce A571
Berg, Mark S. A666
Berg, John P. von A668
Berg, John A668
Berg, Justin A726
Berg, Tim A544
Berg, Joel H. A880
Berg, Jessica P116
Berg, Deborah P253
Berg, Sarah P463
Berg, Joel H. P640
Berg, James P675
Berg, Achim W66
Berg, William E140
Bergamini, Nancy A538
Bergan, Chad A252
Bergantzel, Matthew P185
Berger, David A60
Berger, Larry L. A289
Berger, Joe A423
Berger, Tim A544
Berger, Debra A592
Berger, Manuela A658
Berger, Hilary A702
Berger, Jeff P163
Berger, Debra P370
Berger, David P574
Berger, Tom E1
Berger, Jeff E433
Bergerand, Christophe W305
Bergeron, Kate A72
Bergeron, Ornella P202
Bergeron, Sandra E342
Bergeron, Daniel A. (Dan) E345
Bergers, David P. A528
Berges, James G A412
Berges-Gonzalez, Orlando A333
Bergeson, Jan A37
Bergeson, Steven P26
Bergeson, Jan P27
Bergevin, Paul A460
Bergh, Charles V. (Chip) A438
Bergh, Charles V. (Chip) A514
Bergh, Charles V. (Chip) A516
Bergh, Charles V. (Chip) P293
Berghs, Jim A884
Bergin, Cynthia A163
Bergin, James P. A319
Bergin, Vincent A651
Bergin, Cynthia E62
Bergin, Vincent E329
Berglund, Steven A86
Berglund, Bryn A893
Berglund, Steven E27
Berglund, Robert C E280
Bergman, Barbara A248
Bergman, Stanley M. A744
Bergman, Laurie A A857
Bergman, David E. A862
Bergman, Brandon P312
Bergman, William T P545
Bergman, William P546
Bergman, Chris P560
Bergman, Jessica P596
Bergman, Barbara E107
Bergman, Judson (Jud) E131
Bergmann, Steven R. P80
Bergquist, Derek A819
Bergquist, Lauren P438
Bergquist, Derek P549
Bergqvist, Yonnie W377
Bergstrom, Susan A749
Bergstrom, Timothy D. A906
Bergstrom, Susan E367
Bergstrom, Timothy D. E435
Bergstrom, Henrik A673

Bergthold, Michelle A606
Bergthold, Steven P153
Beri, Rajive A89
Berina, Leslie P408
Berisford, John L. A738
Berk, Donald A605
Berk, Eric V P343
Berkay, H Sinan P515
Berke, Ethan M P173
Berkebile, Dean A936
Berkeu, Jason E A781
Berkley, W. Robert (Rob) A126
Berkley, William R. (Bill) A126
Berkley, William R. (Bill) A592
Berkley, Teresa P335
Berkley, William R. (Bill) P370
Berkman, Charles S. E257
Berkompas, Duane P509
Berkowitz, Gideon A506
Berkowitz, Jason A929
Berkowitz, Martin A P588
Berkowitz, Jason A449
Berlamino, Betty E A892
Berle, Dolf E111
Berlin, Brian A237
Berlin, Warren A329
Berlin, Grant W80
Berloe-Buch, Wendy A702
Berman, Ross A6
Berman, Walter S. A60
Berman, Adam A266
Berman, Ira A373
Berman, Adam A374
Berman, Richard A456
Berman, Ann A526
Berman, Geoffrey A574
Berman, Bridget A593
Berman, Adam P181
Berman, Glenn S P206
Berman, Natalie P363
Berman, Joel P390
Berman, Mandy E51
Berman, Bobby E106
Berman, Richard E228
Berman, Brian E312
Bermel, Seth A349
Bermes, Brian A623
Bermes, Brian E312
Bermudez, Lorena P102
Bernacki, Jeanette M P522
Bernadett, Martha Molina A570
Bernadett, Mary A571
Bernal, Linda A109
Bernal, Alejandro A941
Bernard, Andrea A218
Bernard, Peter C A574
Bernard, Nicole A606
Bernard, Scott A722
Bernard, Edward C. A799
Bernard, Charles W A900
Bernard, Hans P636
Bernard, Daniel W219
Bernardo, Napoleon P536
Bernardo, Thomas E80
Bernardy, Nancy P479
Bernd, Suzanna A82
Bernd, David L P484
Berndsen, Don A25
Berndsen, Don P14
Berndt, Wolfgang C. W295
Berne, Robert (Bob) A592
Berne, Robert (Bob) P370
Bernet, Martin A608
Bernet, Charlie A775
Bernet, Charlie P511
Bernhardt, Chris P178
Bernhardt, Hans W231
Bernhardt, John E330
Bernica, Andrea C P86
Bernier, Keith A179
Bernier, Danielle A692
Bernier, Jody P582
Bernier, Jean W21
Bernier, Gregg E140
Berning, Allen E211
Bernis, Valérie W154

Bernon, Alan J. A253
Bernon, Alan J. P169
Bernotat, Wulf H. W24
Berns, Jason A702
Berns, Harvey A845
Berns, Steven E371
Bernstein, Dean A152
Bernstein, Daniel A200
Bernstein, Scot A569
Bernstein, Mark J. A711
Bernstein, David A746
Bernstein, Brian P32
Bernstein, Dean P98
Bernstein, Michael P433
Bernstein, Mark J. P444
Bernstein, Mathew P638
Bernstein, David W87
Bernstein, Kenneth F. E53
Bernstein, H. Carol E56
Bernsten, James R. A213
Bernsten, James R. P143
Beronio, David A415
Beronio, David E208
Berotti, John A831
Berotti, John P601
Berquist, Carl A537
Berra, John A735
Berradia, Jamal A680
Berridge, Jeff A405
Berrios, Marcelino P440
Berroeta, aki W417
Berry, Katy A69
Berry, Dana A101
Berry, Teri A107
Berry, Daphne A222
Berry, Hussein A262
Berry, Dottie A323
Berry, John A325
Berry, Kay A340
Berry, Alicia A383
Berry, Liz A405
Berry, Samantha Thomas A487
Berry, Mary A540
Berry, Jennifer A545
Berry, Gene P A628
Berry, Bob A882
Berry, Debra A922
Berry, David T. P45
Berry, Robert P83
Berry, Bob P126
Berry, Richard E P168
Berry, Greg P184
Berry, Richard W. P202
Berry, Janet P359
Berry, Gene P P396
Berry, Peter P476
Berry, Ray P568
Berry, Pat P605
Berry, Jessica P626
Berry, Lisa P663
Berry, Debra P671
Berry, Dana E32
Berry, Kay E161
Berry, Alicia E186
Berryman, Kevin C. A476
Bershad, Stephen W. A292
Bershad, Stephen W. E307
Bert, Dave A189
Bert, John Di W73
Bertcher, Gene S. E408
Bertelli, Luca W155
Bertero, Gerardo A914
Berthaut, Chris A449
Berthaut, Chris E220
Berthiaume, Mark L. A405
Bertholf, Leigh P21
Bertholf, Leigh P323
Bertiere, Francois W76
Bertke, Monika P143
Bertolami, Charles N. A592
Bertolami, Charles N. P370
Bertolet-Duff, Dianne A409
Bertoli, Jose A457
Bertolissi, Mario W202
Bertolla, Fernando A740

COMBINED HOOVER'S HANDBOOK INDEX OF EXECUTIVES

A = AMERICAN BUSINESS
E = EMERGING COMPANIES
P = PRIVATE COMPANIES
W = WORLD BUSINESS

Bertoluzzo, Paolo W417
Bertoni, Diana A369
Bertoni, Anthony E207
Bertorelli, Carlo A833
Bertot, Susan A63
Bertot, Barbara P500
Bertram, Luc A457
Bertram, Howard A908
Bertram, Howard E436
Bertrand, Mark A140
Bertrand, Greg D. A797
Bertrand, Diane P464
Bertrand, Marc L P609
Bertsch, Jan A146
Bertsch, Jan A. A616
Bertscha, Noreen A686
Bertucci, Nancy A800
Bertucci, John R. E285
Berube, Stephen A514
Berube, Stephen A516
Berube, Stephen P293
Berube, Rachel P639
Berus, Floyd A327
Berus, Lisa P475
Berwager, Emily P499
Berwick, Tracy A489
Besack, Jim A315
Besanko, Bruce A496
Beseda, Leslie A456
Beseda, Leslie E228
Beshah, Guenet A166
Beshar, Peter J. A539
Beshaw, Beth A530
Besley, Ben P300
Beslity, James A151
Besman, Eric A408
Bespalov, Alexander D. W308
Bessant, Catherine P. (Cathy) A107
Bessant, Jennifer P244
Besse, Eric A64
Bessel, Polly A89
Bessette, Andy F. A844
Bessette, Stephen A904
Bessey, John A663
Bessey, Kerry P325
Bessey, Linda A E205
Best, C. Munroe A121
Best, Amy A305
Best, John A470
Best, James A716
Best, Stephen P261
Bestic, Gregory A314
Bestic, Gregory E145
Bestland, Jennifer P330
Betancourt, Sofia A900
Betancourt, Tommie P349
Betanzos, Fernando P646
Beth, Marconi A428
Bethay, Ronnie A852
Bethea, Elizabeth A452
Bethea, Paula Harper A769
Bethea, Lorenzo P386
Bethea, Paula Harper E380
Bethke, Tom A643
Betlesky, Scott A405
Betsworth, Sonia E148
Bettenbrock, James P340
Bettencourt, Bernadette P530
Betteridge, Neil E196
Betterly, Luke A922
Betterly, Luke P671
Bettinger, Douglas R. (Doug) A505
Bettinger, Walter W. (Walt) A746
Bettinger-buckingham, Lisa A520
Bettis, Shannon A449
Bettis, Shannon E221
Bettridge, Ellen A54
Betts, Wendy A605
Betts, Randy P242

Betz, Peter P120
Betz, Robert P318
Beuke, Richard A673
Beumee, Gary A752
Beurden, Ben van W334
Beutin, Brian A117
Beutin, Brian P61
Bevan, Kurt A909
Bevan, Kurt C A909
Bevan, Paul E57
Bevan, Kurt E436
Bevan, Kurt C E436
Bevente, Guy A89
Beveridge, Roy A. A440
Beverly, Mark E412
Beville, Lisa A325
Bevins, William E372
Bewley, Tim A665
Bewley, Peter A840
Bewley, Ed P57
Bewley, Tim E334
Beyene, Merykokeb A900
Beyer, Gary J A222
Beyer, Kevin A320
Beyer, Ruth A. A675
Beyer, Ruth A. P428
Beyer, Nicole P569
Beyersdorfer, Jeffrey S. E5
Beylin, Eddie A888
Beylin, Eddie E425
Bezar, Farrukh A A245
Bezich, Louis S. P563
Bezjak, Rob A396
Bezos, Jeffrey P. (Jeff) A42
Bezrucik, Peter P150
Bhagat, Dave A793
Bhagat, Sarah P284
Bhakey, Rajeshwar A203
Bhakhri, Sandeep A301
Bhalla, Anant A150
Bhalla, Ajay A544
Bhalla, Vikas E140
Bhanap, Nina E343
Bhandari, Amit P85
Bhandari, Arpita P85
Bhanot, Sanjay E237
Bharadia, Vijay Vithal A137
Bharara, Ashish A902
Bharatwaj, Shekar A218
Bhardwaj, Yogesh A75
Bhargava, Vic A84
Bhargava, Manish A108
Bhargava, Amit A541
Bhasin, Puneet A905
Bhat, Sanjay A571
Bhatia, Sujata A54
Bhatia, Qamar S A431
Bhatia, Arv A498
Bhatia, Manish A565
Bhatia, Prashant A807
Bhatia, Manish A914
Bhatia, Mohit E315
Bhatt, Padmanabh P. E394
Bhattacharjee, Manash A544
Bhattacharya, Parthasarathi A107
Bhattacharya, Churni A349
Bhattacharya, Ashis E443
Bhatti, Hammad P488
Bhavanishankar, Chinmayi P114
Bhir, Ravi A744
Bhogal, Madhu A266
Bhogal, Madhu P181
Bhojwani, Gary C. A212
Bholai, Ian P642
Bhullar, Parampal P430
Bhumbla, Ravinder A191
Bhushan, Varun E143
Bhutani, Aman A307
Biala, Gerry P475
Bialick, Jim E272
Bialosky, David L. (Dave) A392
Bianchi, Dean P116
Bianchi, August P252
Bianchi, Robert J P360
Bianchi, Luis P501

Bianchi, Christophe M. W381
Bianco, Lawrence A829
Bianco, Lawrence P589
Bias, Alicia A414
Bias, Alicia P236
Bibbo, Paul A835
Bibby, Geoffrey R. (Geoff) E453
Bibic, Mirko W65
Bible, Daryl N. A849
Bibliowicz, Jessica M. P375
Biblo, Lee P211
Bibus, Parker P259
Bichelmeier, Hans-Peter W115
Bick, Karen A790
Bickel, Michael A142
Bickel, Michael E49
Bickerstaff, Robert A200
Bickerstaff, Bob E64
Bickerton, Michael A609
Bickett, Brent B. A325
Bickham, Brandon P564
Bickham, W. Bradley E4
Bickley, Ian A801
Bickley, Craig P148
Bicknase, Lynn A15
Bicknase, Lynn P8
Bicknell, Lacey A651
Bicknell, Lacey E330
Bieber, Stephen A343
Bieber, Martin A P515
Bieber, Corey B. W85
Bieber, Stephen E164
Biedermann, Wynn P330
Biediger, Michael P293
Biegger, Dave A232
Biegler, Jack A169
Biehler, Jefry M P649
Bieker, Lois P102
Bielan, Judith Q. E41
Bielar, James A89
Bielawski, Nicole A41
Bielen, Richard J. A683
Bien, James P252
Bienaime, Jean-jacques E226
Bier, Nicole A492
Bierer, Barbara P172
Bieri, Matthew (Matt) E412
Bierlein, Jeffrey A737
Bierlein, Jeffrey E361
Bierman, James A812
Biermann, Frederick P19
Biermann, Dave E98
Biernbaum, Robert P352
Biesterfeld, Robert C. A728
Bietsch, Julie A266
Bietsch, Julie P181
Bifone, Patrick P496
Bigaouette, Terry A728
Bigelow, Lawrence A205
Bigelow, Steven T. P97
Bigelow, Teresa P537
Biggers, Candi A682
Biggins, Lillie P550
Biggs, Morgan A125
Biggs, M. Brett A901
Biggs, Ray P481
Biggs, Randy E88
Biglari, Sardar E44
Bigley, Jamie A682
BIGLIOLI, PAOLO W43
Bignotti, Donald A847
Bignotti, Donald P606
Bigos, Christopher A367
Bihlmier, Joseph A54
Bijun, Wu W118
Bike, Brent A246
Bike, Brent E105
Bilanin, Jared A135
Bilbo, Steve A749
Bilbo, Steve E367
Bilbrey, John A218
Bilbrey, John P. (J.P.) A416
Bilbrey, Ryan E102
Bilderack, Brandy A855
Bildstein, Cole P505

Biles, Steve P606
Bilicki, Judy P94
Bilko, David G. (Dave) A91
Bilko, David G. (Dave) E29
Bill, Buckner A364
Bill, Shreve A933
Bill, Puckett P357
Billak, Ann A483
Billera, Patrick P646
Billig, Edward P P78
Billig, David P664
Billing, Michael A481
Billings, Craig S. A930
Billings, Mary P371
Billings, Brian P451
Billingsley, Rob A432
Billington, William A362
Billiot, Susan A797
Billman, Diane A248
Billman, Diane E107
Billotte, Mike P619
Bills, Matthew A367
Bills, Elizabeth A711
Bills, Elizabeth P444
Billups, Ramsey A3
Billups, Lamarr P570
Bilney, Jody L. A440
Bilney, Jod A441
Bilotta, Anthony V. A646
Bilotta, Anthony V. E324
Bilotti-Peterson, Christine A405
Bily, Shirley A890
Bimson, Stephen A160
Bin, Mo W118
Bin, Ong Eng W299
Binbasgil, Hakan W18
Bincoletto, Cintia A920
Binda, Marc E8
Bindelglass, David P97
Binder, Steven G. A434
Binder, Kurt P655
Binderman, Judi P153
Bindra, Akhil A824
Bindra, Paveljit P137
Bindra, Akhil P562
Bindschatel, Nikki P340
Binette, Nathalie A562
Biney, Yvonne P348
Bing, Shang W99
Bingaman, Peter A465
Bingaman, Christopher (Chris) E112
Bingaman, Mark G. E415
Bingham, Kim R. A174
Bingham, Patty A263
Bingham, Rob A383
Bingham, Paul A442
Bingham, Paula A835
Bingham, Kim R. E68
Bingham, Rob E186
Bingold, Michael A356
Binick, Emily Goodman A54
Binkleysenior, David A919
Binkowski, Chuck P68
Binnendijk, Maurits A813
Binnie, Lisa A405
Binnie, Bob P107
Binns, Justin T. A756
Bino, Gil W162
Bintz, John P233
Bintz, William (Bill) E30
Binvel, Yannick E248
Binzer, Ann A196
Binzer, Greg P664
Bion, Joel A198
Biondi, Paul A151
Biossat, William A449
Biossat, William E220
Birch, Robert F. A426
Birch, Angel A749
Birch, Mark P59
Birch, Sue P99
Birch, Robert F. E213
Birch, Angel E367
Birchmeier, Cindy A398
Birchmeier, Cindy P222

COMBINED HOOVER'S HANDBOOK INDEX OF EXECUTIVES

Bird, Roger M. A5
Bird, Kim A145
Bird, Stephen A203
Bird, Kristin A855
Bird, Lauren A887
Bird, Michael P131
Bird, Jeff P252
Bird, J. Richard W150
Bird, Graham R. W173
Birdwell, Cameron A390
Birge, Greg P435
Birkelo, Jeff A903
Birkenholtz, Brad A108
Birkenstock, Timothy L P129
Birkenstock, Tim M P649
Birkenstock, Timothy P649
Birkett, Kathryn P251
Birkett, Bernard E278
Birkholz, Shelly A408
Birkholz, Jeff A715
Birkmann, Shila E450
Birkmeyer, David A871
Birla, Nita A391
Birling, Melissa A86
Birling, Melissa E27
Birmingham, Martin K. A330
Birmingham, Martin K. E152
Birmingham-Byrd, Melody A281
Birnbaum, David A575
Birnbaum, Jason A865
Birnbaum, Ing. Leonhard W143
Birnbrich, Pamela A444
Birner, Ulrike A423
Birnie, Jennifer A740
Birns, Ira M. A927
Biron, Ziv W203
Birznieks, Gunther E426
Bisaccia, Lisa A251
Bisaccio, Brian A838
Bisaro, Paul M. W23
Biscardi, Joseph P1
Bischmann, Joanne M. A407
Bischof, Tim A212
Bischofberger, Norbert W. A385
Bischoff, Lou P47
Bischoff, David P618
Bischoff, Werner W117
Bischoff, Manfred W125
Biscotti, John A680
Bisegna, Anthony C. A783
Bish, James A909
Bish, James E436
Bishop, Daniel A86
Bishop, John A512
Bishop, Marissa A596
Bishop, Steven D. (Steve) A679
Bishop, James A740
Bishop, Thomas A771
Bishop, Amy A819
Bishop, Rachel R. A846
Bishop, Kendall A877
Bishop, Bridgette A879
Bishop, Barry A924
Bishop, Deena P38
Bishop, William (Billy) P88
Bishop, Ken P125
Bishop, Lisa P338
Bishop, Amy P549
Bishop, Carmena P673
Bishop, Tim W243
Bishop, Daniel E27
Bishop, Thomas E382
Bisselberg, Stephanie A27
Biswas, Yogini A150
Biswas, Michael E386
Bittarelli, Jason A784
Bittel, Philip A713
Bitter, Robert G. E418
Bittinger, Jana A25
Bittinger, Jana P14
Bittner, Edward P618
Bittner, Elaine B. E78
Bitzer, Marc R. A919
Bivens-rose, Gail A727
Bivens-rose, Gail P453

Bixby, R. Philip A485
Bixby, Walter E. (Web) A485
Bixby, Gregory A806
Bixby, Gregory E399
Bixenman, Bob P458
Bixler, Tony P677
Bizzard, Kenneth A713
Bizzarri, Marco W218
Bjerke, Mark A729
Bjerknes, Dan A226
Bjerknes, Dan P150
Bjorkman, Karen S. P596
Bjornholt, J. Eric A564
Bjornstad, Geir P197
Black, Krystl A88
Black, David F A159
Black, Willa A198
Black, Dennis A222
Black, Alan A336
Black, Chris A362
Black, Bonnie A666
Black, Peter A695
Black, Ken A722
Black, Freddie G. A760
Black, Katy A811
Black, Katherine A815
Black, Mary A888
Black, Chastity A891
Black, Nadine A922
Black, Christopher A928
Black, Anthony P104
Black, Kim P162
Black, Douglas P344
Black, Ronald P506
Black, Michael E P596
Black, Madison P597
Black, Nadine P671
Black, Christopher P674
Black, Randall E. (Randy) E80
Black, Randall E. (Randy) E81
Black, Buzz E138
Black, Alan E157
Black, Freddie G. E374
Black, Archie C. E384
Black, Mary E425
Blackburn, Fred K. A144
Blackburn, Andy A199
Blackburn, Patrick A334
Blackburn, Stella A474
Blackburn, Lezlee A744
Blackburn, Robert A778
Blackburn, Rosie A850
Blackburn, Patrick E153
Blackford, David E. A940
Blackhurst, Janis L. (Jan) Jones A160
Blackhurst, Jan Jones A161
Blackhurst, Eric A433
Blackhurst, Jason A896
Blackhurst, Eric E217
Blackley, R. Scott A166
Blackman, Scott A222
Blackmon, Keith A799
Blackmore, Brad P128
Blackmore, Milton C. (Bud) E229
Blackson, Jordan P213
Blackstead, Alexis A915
Blackston, Stevie C A922
Blackston, Stevie C P671
Blackstone, Robin P478
Blackwelder, John A167
Blackwelder, Megan P389
Blackwell, James A642
Blackwell, Patrick P183
Blackwell, James P407
Blackwood, Brian A25
Blackwood, Hank A240
Blackwood, Elizabeth A479
Blackwood, Eric A647
Blackwood, Brian P14
Blaesing, Jeff P260
Blagg, Richard A16
Blain, Robert (Rob) A175
Blain, September A467
Blain, Nicole P99
Blain, Keith P376

Blair, Ingrid A3
Blair, Rainer M. A254
Blair, Gavin A405
Blair, David G A425
Blair, Scott A507
Blair, Matthew A540
Blair, Timothy A606
Blair, Bradley A713
Blair, Kevin S. A796
Blair, Colin A809
Blair, Karen A856
Blair, Paul A915
Blair, Chuck P119
Blair, Linda P162
Blair, Jane E P259
Blair, Bill P274
Blair, Karen P614
Blair, Carrie W371
Blair, Kevin S. E397
Blais, Greg A598
Blais, Marc A936
Blais, Marcel C. E305
Blaise, Timothy A255
Blaise, Michelle A305
Blaising, Rachel A179
Blake, Victoria A36
Blake, Tony A117
Blake, Amy A137
Blake, Nancy A222
Blake, Francis S. (Frank) A262
Blake, Frank A428
Blake, Winston A440
Blake, Patrick J. (Pat) A549
Blake, Tim A630
Blake, Christopher D. A638
Blake, David M. A677
Blake, Lynn S. A783
Blake, Ellen A891
Blake, Vanessa P38
Blake, Tony P61
Blake, Joe P148
Blake, Woods P228
Blake, Randy P253
Blake, Stephen E141
Blake, Christopher D. E320
Blakely, Cameron E99
Blakemore, Jim A232
Blakemore, Anthony A770
Blakemore, Dominic W116
Blakeney, John A224
Blakewood, Benjamin F. A22
Blakewood, Benjamin F. P11
Blakey, Rachel P382
Blakey, Choling P606
Blakley, Linda P175
Blaku, Sherif P257
Blalock, Pam A559
Blanc, Farron A715
Blanc, Christian A936
Blanc, Jean-Louis W154
Blanc, Robert M. (Bobby) Le W296
Blancas, Monica P192
Blanchard, Dan A262
Blanchard, Brent A518
Blanchard, Dantre A458
Blanchard, Lydia P552
Blanchard, David W409
Blanchet, Paul J. E212
Blanchette, Alan P68
Blanchette, Bob P193
Blanco, Alex A289
Blanco, Juan SebastiAn Moreno W46
Bland, Maryanne A153
Bland, Christine A343
Bland, Mickey A458
Bland, Tim P31
Bland, Jeffry P312
Bland, Maryanne E52
Bland, Christine E164
Blank, Dr Josef P174
Blank, Gary P463
Blank, Rebecca M. P641
Blankenburg, Evie P240
Blankenship, Charles P. (Chip) A79
Blankenship, Dave A538

Blankenship, Stu P212
Blankenship, Jeffrey P263
Blankfein, Lloyd C. A390
Blankmeyer, Erik A807
Blanks, Richard P462
Blanton, Hamilton A166
Blanton, Mack P175
Blase, William A. (Bill) A89
Blaser, Brian J. A5
Blaser, Richard P252
Blasingame, David T. P600
Blasini, David P A167
Blaske, Stephen A60
Blasko, Michael A848
Blasko, Michael E411
Blatcher, Kevin A164
Blattman, Barry W80
Blaufuss, Mark P334
Blaug, Suzanne A64
Blaya, Richard A891
Blaylock, Isaac A756
Blazejewski, Steve A169
Blazer, Robert A536
Blazquez, Nicholas B. (Nick) W140
Blazye, Andrew R. E174
Bleck, Regina P570
Bledsoe, Vallerie M A324
Bledsoe, Steve A400
Bledsoe, Matthew A713
Bledsoe, Linda P625
Bledsoe, Steve E195
Bleeker, Gary L. P231
Blegen, Bernie E288
Blehm, Julie P471
Bleisch, N. David A620
Bleming, Jim E203
Blerman, Mike A811
Bleske, Mitchell A867
Bleske, Mitchell E418
Bless, Michael A210
Bless, Michael E375
Blestowe, James A59
Blevins, Tony A72
Blevins, P. Rodney A275
Blevins, Meriem A329
Blew, Clinton J. (C.J.) A194
Bley, Daniel H. A906
Bley, Daniel H. E435
Bleyl, Steven A462
Bleyl, Steven P256
Blickenstaff, Scott P554
Blidner, Jeffrey M. (Jeff) W80
Blihovde, Valerie A804
Blincoe, Donna A719
Blincoe, Donna E354
Blinder, Warren A800
Blinn, Tom P536
Blissett, Julian A378
Blitz, Gil P371
Blitzer, David S. A137
Blivice, Marni A137
Bloch, Jeremy A180
Bloch, Nick A831
Bloch, Nick P601
Block, Robert A36
Block, Seth A296
Block, Keith G. A739
Block, Dan P170
Block, Joanna P193
Block, Steven P377
Block, Anita P630
Blocker, Jeff A527
Blocker, Jeffrey A527
Blocker, Adrian M. A918
Bloj, Ricardo W234
Blom, David P. P395
Blome, James W61
Blondia, Jeanne A789
Blood, Richard A544
Bloodgood, Debra A609
Bloodgood, Debra P391
Bloodworth, Shannon P223
Bloom, Leah A7
Bloom, Brent A74
Bloom, Richard S A213

HOOVER'S HANDBOOK OF EMERGING COMPANIES 2020

COMBINED HOOVER'S HANDBOOK INDEX OF EXECUTIVES

A = AMERICAN BUSINESS
E = EMERGING COMPANIES
P = PRIVATE COMPANIES
W = WORLD BUSINESS

Bloom, William A. (Bill) A408
Bloom, Alfred H. A592
Bloom, Ronnie A831
Bloom, Alfred H. P370
Bloom, Mark W10
Bloomquist, Cathy P250
Blose, James A786
Blose, James E387
Blosser, Courtney A. E322
Blotz, Gerald R. E40
Blough, Lynn E A460
Blount, Sally A5
Blount, Eddie A665
Blount, Sally E. P388
Blount, Eddie E334
Bloxam, Richard A481
Bludau, Laurence A228
Bludworth, Jed A72
Blue, Robert M. (Bob) A275
Blue, Tamara A746
Blue, Robert M. A894
Blue, Dan P471
Blue, Tracy P541
Blue, Karen E99
Blum, Jeffrey A271
Blum, Donald W. A684
Blum, Jason A746
Blum, Audrey P135
Blum, Olivier W344
Blum, Keith E264
Blume, Brent A885
Blumenfeld, Stephen A391
Blumenfeld, Barry P305
Blumenfeld, Amy P508
Blumensaadt, Karen A713
Blumer, David J. A135
Blumeyer, Greg A215
Blumhardt, James A910
Blunck, Thomas W267
Blundell, Alan A527
Blundon, Lee A908
Blundon, Lee E436
Blunt, Chris A137
Blunt, Mary L. A754
Blunt, Mary J. P484
Blute, Michael L. P574
Bluth, Tom A173
Blutman, Gary A505
Blye, Jeffrey C A320
Blyth, Lord A68
Blyth, Lesley A779
Blyth, Myrna P2
Blythe, Douglas P161
Blyze, Scott A264
Bo, Yao W306
Bo, Yang W373
Boada, Robert C A770
Boals, Richard L. (Rich) P90
Boardman, David P546
Boas, Nancy A702
Boasberg, Tom P476
Boatright, Michael A686
Boatwright, Peter P114
Bob, Archuleta P94
Bobb, Stevan B. A138
Bobb, Stevan B. A157
Bobb, Stevan B. P91
Bobbie, Frances D A727
Bobbie, Frances D P453
Bober, Sharon A641
Bober, Sharon P407
Boberg, Peter E102
Bobitz, Ward E. A381
Bobko, Gary P78
Bobo, Jennifer P629
Bobrow, Michelle A786
Bobrow, Michelle E387
Bobrowsky, Bill A711
Bobrowsky, Bill P444

Boccalandro, Cristina P596
Boccaletti, Giulio P579
BOCCARDELLI, PAOLO W410
Boccardo, James A867
Boccardo, James E418
Boccolini, Giovanni W202
Bochette, William C. A769
Bochette, William C. E380
Bochynski, Edward P382
Bocian, Pete P361
Bock, Kurt W. W59
Bockhorst, Daniel E. A181
Bockhorst, Cheri A203
Bockhorst, Daniel E. E70
Bockus, Keith E102
Bodakowski, Steven A651
Bodakowski, Steven E330
Bodansky, Robert L. P486
Bodapati, Ramesh A199
Boden, Alison L. P591
Bodenhafer, Scott A520
Bodenheimer, George A762
Bodenheimer, Henry C. P80
Bodgs, Lynn P428
Bodhuin, Francois P254
Bodi, Attila A254
Bodin, Susan P301
Bodine, Bruce A576
Bodisch, Laurie A368
Bodman, Ryan A544
Bodmer, Chris P315
Bodnar, Vincent A381
Bodnar, Michael P300
Bodor, Robert E340
Body, Frederick A885
Boe, Ryan A571
Boe, Douglas A885
Boeck, Karel Gerard De W307
Boeckenstedt, Jon P175
Boedeker, Kenneth W. A301
Boegner, Scott A837
Boehler, Bill P165
Boehm, William E302
Boehme, Linda P507
Boehn, Michael A224
Boehne, Richard A. (Rich) E366
Boehnlein, Glenn A789
Boeing, Traci A908
Boeing, Traci E436
Boeka, Amy A452
Boelstler, Doreen A222
Boelte, Katherine P386
Boelter, Ben E123
Boening, Bj A533
Boer, A. Dick W223
Boeren, Leni W15
Boersma, Brad A329
Boersma, Wendy P235
Boesch, Marc A835
Boesch, Donald F. (Don) P642
Boeshaar, Brad A859
Boeshore, Samantha P269
Boesiger, Brian P463
Boettcher, Eileen M. P578
Boezeman, Alex M. E59
Boff, Linda E115
Bogan, Gary A444
Bogan, Joyce P351
Bogan, Heather P390
Bogdan, Rick E290
Bogdanoff, Debra P162
Bogdanov, Vladimir L. W375
Bogdanovich, Peter P610
Boggess, Michael A108
Boggetto, Brian A305
Boggs, Gregory A170
Boggs, Rod A559
Boggs, Darrell A613
Bogle, Jill P76
Bogler, John A. A104
Bogler, Carl P464
Bognar, Paul A920
Bogner, Kevin P86
Bogosta, Charles E. (Chuck) P643
Bogoyevac, Steve E267

Bogue, Greg P308
Bogusch, Brandon P528
Boguski, Michael L. A678
Bohaboy, Scott A119
Bohannon, Jason A442
Bohannon, Donald P508
Bohanon, Chris A317
Bohanon, Debbie P473
Bohanon, Chris E146
Bohaty, Brian R. A35
Bohbrink, Marshall A399
Bohbrink, Marshall P223
Boheman, Fredrik W356
Bohen, Mark P74
Bohen, Sean W38
Bohl, Chris A219
Bohl, Nicki A226
Bohl, Nicki P150
Bohl, Howard P618
Bohl, Chris E87
Bohleber, Amanda P175
Bohlen, Patricia P51
Bohling, Brian A418
Bohlinger, Thomas A175
Bohlke, Sherri A725
Bohm, David A321
Bohm, Kevin E433
Bohmler, April A540
Bohn, William M. A85
Bohn, Don A479
Bohn, William M. E26
Bohnen, Jennifer A925
Bohnen, Jennifer A445
Bohnenkamp, Martin P429
Bohnsack, Gary A494
Bohrer, Scott A428
Boid, Jonathan P135
Boigegrain, Barbara A347
Boigegrain, Barbara E168
Boike, Brian D.J. A353
Boike, Brian D.J. E173
Boillat, Pascal W135
Boim, Dave A571
Bois, Michel W111
Boisier, Pierre A123
Boisseau, Philippe W398
Boisten, Bernd A724
Boisten, Bernd P452
Boisvert, Laura A281
Boisvert, Gerald P229
Boisvert, Gerry P229
Boitano, Robert A327
Boitumelo, Patrick W327
Bojanowski, Mark A686
Bojdak, Robert J. A530
Bok, Cathleen A204
Bokan, Mike A565
Bokar, Cathy A858
Bokerman, Grant A137
Bokina, Erin A686
Bokorney, Mark B. E208
Bolander, Larry Bolander Larry A355
Bolanos, Steve A640
Bold, William A694
Boldea, Lucian A285
Bolden, Tod A126
Boldt, Oscar C P555
Boldt, Thomas J P555
Bolduc, Ellyn A751
Bolduc, Ellyn P482
Bolen, Michael D. (Mike) P318
Bolen, Michael D P319
Boles, Tim A713
Boles, Andrea P506
Bolg, Julee P558
Bolgar, Paulo A120
Bolger, Andrea A36
Bolger, Rod W331
Bolick, Patrick A481
Bolin, Amy A812
Boline, Chad A224
Boling, Keith A713
Boling, Michael D. E396
Bolis, Ken P500
Bolisay, Eric A799

Boller, Judy P477
Bollin, Bonnie A413
Bollin, Bonnie E205
Bollinger, Kathy A117
Bollinger, Lee C. A320
Bollinger, Paul A509
Bollinger, Kathy P61
Bollinger, Jennifer P394
Bollini, Marco W155
Bolloré, Vincent W162
Bolloré, Vincent W416
Bologna, Matt A933
Bols, Ivo A24
Bolster, Jennifer Reschke P518
Bolt, Cynthia A739
Bolt, Gregg A813
Bolt, Carmen P508
Bolt, Jennifer E232
Bolton, C. Anderson (Andy) A245
Bolton, Jon A727
Bolton, Karen A885
Bolton, Jon P453
Bolton, Scott P507
Bolton, Dave E232
Bolton, H. Eric E282
Bolton, James E295
Bolts, George A550
Bolts, George P319
Boltz, William P A527
Bolwerk, Dave A86
Bolwerk, Dave E27
Boly, Sarah P76
Bolze, Steve A374
Boman, P-or W377
Bomar, Alice A920
Bombara, Beth A. A408
Bombard, Tate P448
Bombardier, J. R. André W73
Bomboy, David A334
Bomboy, David E153
Bomhard, jur. Nikolaus von W267
Bommarito, Bruce A160
Bommentre, Frank A248
Bommentre, Frank E67
Bompard, Alexandre W88
Bona, Robin A893
Bonacci, John E332
Bonadio, Bill A140
Bonalle, David A53
Bonamoe, John F P371
Bonanno, Kelly A369
Bonano, Charles A329
Bonanotte, Gino A. A577
Bonarti, Michael A A93
Bonck, Michael P208
Bond, Simon A468
Bond, Richard E A583
Bond, Richard A690
Bond, Robert W. (Bob) A640
Bond, Martine A783
Bond, Carol A850
Bond, Ray P59
Bond, Matt P86
Bond, Bradley P116
Bond, James P117
Bond, Harrison P155
Bond, Jeffrey C. (Jeff) P291
Bond, Jack P662
Bondada, Vijay A281
Bonde, Brian P471
Bondel, Mary Lou A538
Bonderoff, Scott P574
Bondeson, Rusty A258
Bondi, Paolo W151
Bondi, Stephen E207
Bonds, Michael P. (Mike) A865
Bonds, John E80
Bondur, Thomas A505
Bondurant, Robert D P311
Bone, Ronald A550
Bone, Doug A795
Boneberg, Sandra P272
Bonfanti, Brian A298
Bonfanti, Brian E130
Bonfield, Andrew R J A173

Bonfield, Andrew R. J. W273
Bonfiglio, Joanne P60
Bongiorno, Anthony A893
Bongiovanni, Bobbi P508
Bongiovi, Joseph A540
Bonham, Jeff A180
Bonham, Randy P57
Bonham, David W159
Bonham-Carter, John E353
Bonhomme, Thierry W297
Bonick, Martin J. A228
Boniface, William P161
Bonilla, Eduardo A704
Bonilla, Myfanwy A922
Bonilla, Myfanwy P671
Bonin, Deb P27
Bonn, Nicholas T. (Nick) A783
Bonn, Karen A922
Bonn, Karen P671
Bonnafé, Jean-Laurent W71
Bonneau, Jacques Q. W106
Bonnefont, Yves W305
Bonnell, William W270
Bonner, Bill P160
Bonner, Dr Jim P624
Bonner, Darryl E100
Bonner, James E172
Bonnett, John W A414
Bonnett, John W P236
Bonney, Joseph A198
Bonnick, Peter A722
Bonniwell, Kent E132
Bonomo, Stuart A284
Bonomo, Stuart E120
Bonsall, Mark B. P418
Bonsall, Mark B. P468
Bonsignore, Joseph E448
Bontcheva, Milena A271
Bonza, Craig A417
Bonzani, Andrew A468
Boocock, Richard A24
Boogaards, Arjan A289
Boogerd, Ginger P509
Booher, David A778
Booher, Kathy A867
Booker, Martin W. A66
Booker, Robert A876
Booles, Angela A36
Boom, Marc L P245
Boom, Marc L P604
Boomer, Stephen L. A339
Boomer, Stephen L. E159
Boon, Philip J. (Phil) E229
Boondoungprasert, Prasit W95
Boone, Michael A179
Boone, Kevin A245
Boone, Elsie A246
Boone, Elwood B. (Bernie) A754
Boone, Jerry E P219
Boone, Michele P219
Boone, Elwood B. (Bernie) P484
Boone, Torrence P567
Boone, Elsie E105
Boone, Joshua A. E322
Boonnoon, Anek W95
Boor, Kathryn J. P159
Boor, Anthony W. (Tony) E47
Boor, William C. (Bill) E69
Boor, Gina E81
Boortz, Kevin A442
Boosin, Greg A544
Boote, John A175
Booth, William A167
Booth, Steven G. (Steve) A726
Booth, Mike A739
Booth, Robert A908
Booth, Chris P311
Booth, Steven G. (Steve) P453
Booth, Sheryl P578
Booth, Steve P630
Booth, Kenneth S. E103
Booth, Daniel J. E314
Booth, Robert E436
Boothby, Justin E174
Boothe, Dorrett A114

Boothe, Steven A799
Boothe, Dorrett E37
Bootsma, Pieter W15
Boozer, Leslie P205
Bor, Chris A485
Borade, Vidhya A928
Borade, Vidhya P673
Boragine, Ellie A54
Boran, Anne P288
Boras, Stephen A329
Borba, George A. A249
Borba, George A. E109
Borchardt, Randall A885
Borcherding, Tricia A212
Borchers, Bradford D. A629
Borchers, Susan C. A716
Borchers, Amy P20
Borcke, Wulff-Erik von A6
Borda, Oscar W26
Bordelon, John W A426
Bordelon, Jennifer A449
Bordelon, John W. E212
Bordelon, Jennifer E220
Borden, Alexia A28
Borden, Rob A140
Borden, Ian A548
Borden, Rebecca A893
Borden, Jane P191
Borden, Vic P610
Bordenave, Philippe W71
Bordenave, Thierry E233
Borders, Carolynne A744
Borders, Charlie P280
Bordes, Michael P. (Mike) A292
Bordo, Julie A371
Bordo, Julie P213
Borduas, Ted P588
Boren, Kevin P332
Borer, Mark A258
Borg, April M P464
Borgen, Thomas F. W129
Borger, Janet P330
Borges, Steven D. (Steve) A475
Borgklint, Per G. W386
Borglund, Patricia P24
Borgman, Charles L A219
Borgmann, Kevin S. A166
Borgne, Gilles Le W305
Borgonah, Darryl P552
Borgonovi, Barbara A706
Borgstrom, Marna P. P676
Boring, Daniel A176
Borino, Melissa Borino Melissa A884
Borisenko, David P240
Borisenko, Natalia W309
Boriskey, Karen A448
Boriskey, Karen P247
Borja, Paul D. A353
Borja, Paul D. E173
Borkowski, Tim A315
Borkowski, Jane P393
Borling, Jeff P521
Borman, J Richard A380
Bormann, Scott A554
Bornhorst, Donald A262
Bornhost, Michael P558
Bornhurst, Don A262
Bornibus, Francois W234
Bornmann, David E. A688
Bornmann, David E. A689
Bornmann, David E. P435
Borns, Lisa A449
Borns, Chad E27
Borotto, Fausto E138
Boroughs, Timothy A. W106
Borowicz, S. Mark E316
Borowicz, Mark E316
Borowiecki, Jeff A179
Borowy, Don A220
Borowy, Don P149
Borque, Suzonne E255
Borrego, Susan E. A711
Borrego, Susan E. P444
Borrelli, Jerry A32
Borschuk, Richard P213

Borsello, Fabrice A915
Borst, Walter G A583
Borton, Chad M. A329
Bortz, Jon E. E325
Borucki, Bethany A804
Boruff, Brian E. E47
Borum, Andrea A704
Borup, Steve A481
Borwankar, Satish B. W383
Boryla, Stephanie A859
Borzi, James A123
Borzileri, Darcey A219
Boschelli, John M. A489
Boschini, Victor J. P549
Bosco, Paul A198
Bosco, Teresa A222
Bosco, Sara Y A292
Bosco, Michael A481
Boscov, Albert P95
Bose, Robert A44
Bose, Supratim A149
Bose, Debarati P192
Bose, Robert E13
Boshoff, Chris A658
Bosi, Benoit A686
Bosler, Chris A502
Bosley, Marvenia P148
Bosley, Katharine E330
Bosma, Laura A484
Bosmat, Hana Ben Zvi W49
Boss, Daniel A299
Boss, R Daniel A299
Boss, Jane P110
Bossard, Evan A925
Bossard, Evan E445
Bosscher, James A847
Bosscher, James P606
Bosse, J A385
Bosserman, David P395
Bosshart, Andrea A228
Bossidy, Lawrence A. (Larry) E42
Bossmann, Lori A9
Bossmann, Lori P4
Bosso, Leonard A590
Bossone, Carla A835
Bossong, Bob P618
Bost, Philippe A10
Bostic, Raphael W. A319
Bostock, Nathan M. W333
Boston, Steve A27
Boston, Michelle A108
Boston, Tracy P396
Bostrom, Robert A364
Bostrom, Brent A399
Bostrom, Brent P223
Bostwick, Tony P198
Bosway, William T. A277
Boswood, Mike P611
Bosworth, Jim P115
Bosworth, Jim P145
Botbol, Michel A701
Botfield, Helen A800
Bothe, Albert A371
Bothe, Albert P213
Bothmann, Larry P532
Bothner, Carl R A933
Bothner, Joan P127
Botifoll, Jordi A198
Botker, Maria P471
Botnick, Alex A893
Botsford, Tom A60
Bott, Lisa A449
Bott, Lisa E221
Bott, Louise E278
Botta, G. Andrea A187
Botte, Jeff A835
Botteon, Greg A831
Botteon, Greg P601
Botti, Jean J. W17
Botticelli, Louis A536
Botticelli, Anne P103
Bottineau, Deborah A726
Bottoms, Derek W A428
Bottoms, Bill P249
Bottoms, Bill P250

Bot- n, Ana P. W48
Bouboulis, Panagiota A112
Bouc, Herve Le W76
Bouc, Hervé Le W112
Bouch, Gary A323
Bouchard, Alain W21
Bouche, Renee E375
Boucher, Harold A219
Boucher, Francine A686
Boucher, Michelle A882
Boucher, Kelley E2
Boucher, Harold E87
Bouchereau, Sabine A114
Bouchereau, Valerie A374
Bouchereau, Sabine E37
Bouchiat, Pascal W390
Bouck, Chad P28
Boudani, Nabil N A60
Boudewyns, Tom A877
Boudreau, Thomas A408
Boudreau, Helen A609
Boudreau, Jeffrey A735
Boudreau, Helen P391
Boudreaux, Trish A58
Boudreaux, Gail K. A69
Boudreaux, Greg A349
Boudreaux, Bryan A902
Boughman, Joann P642
Boughner, Bob P308
Boukalik, Brian A813
Boulais, Nicole P456
Boulanger, Normand A P186
Boulanger, Bernard P576
Boulanger, Steve E65
Bouldin, Brent E80
Boulding, William F. P186
Bouley, Nathan A461
Bouley, Nathan P255
Bouley, Sally E285
Boulos, Jeff A347
Boulos, Tala A799
Boulos, Paul F. P355
Boulos, Jeff E167
Boulton, Gina A519
Boulware, Omar M. P658
Boumann, Cynthia A277
Bounds, Hank M. P92
Bounds, Hank P93
Bounsy, Ryan A658
Bouongiono, Michael P305
Bourgeois, Richard J A426
Bourgeois, Eugene J. (Gene) P551
Bourgeois, Richard J. E212
Bourget, Chris A835
Bourgon, Jocelyne W193
Bourla, Albert A657
Bourne, Robert W A71
Bourne, Jeremy P160
Bourne, Meredith E138
Bourque, Robert H. A245
Bourque, Simon A380
Bourque, Michael P608
Bourquin, Daniel E184
Boursier, Jean-Marc W366
Bourzutschky, Marc A746
Bousbib, Ari A474
Boushek, Aaron A52
Bousquet, Gilles P641
Boutros, Akram P576
Boutross, Joseph A524
Boutte, Tracie A296
Bouvin, Anders W377
Bouygues, Olivier W76
Bouygues, Martin W76
Bouée, Pierre-Olivier W120
Bove, Joyce A590
Bove, Victor E24
Bovender, Jack O. P187
Bover, J P647
Boward, Kylea A54
Bowden, James A364
Bowden, Daniel A754
Bowden, Bryson A859
Bowden, Lloyd M. A925
Bowden, Daniel P484

COMBINED HOOVER'S HANDBOOK INDEX OF EXECUTIVES

A = AMERICAN BUSINESS
E = EMERGING COMPANIES
P = PRIVATE COMPANIES
W = WORLD BUSINESS

Bowden, Lloyd M. E445
Bowe, Dan A692
Bowe, Eydie P255
Bowe, Richard P417
Bowen, William A62
Bowen, Robert A100
Bowen, Doug A117
Bowen, John A126
Bowen, Richard A309
Bowen, Michelle A327
Bowen, Andrew A491
Bowen, Cara A536
Bowen, Matt A550
Bowen, Joy A665
Bowen, Liz A867
Bowen, Arthur N. (Art) A894
Bowen, John J A904
Bowen, Doug P61
Bowen, Jack P194
Bowen, Tim P255
Bowen, Elizabeth P304
Bowen, Jennifer P308
Bowen, Matt P319
Bowen, José A. P505
Bowen, Arthur N. (Art) P651
Bowen, Zhang W227
Bowen, William E20
Bowen, Brent E278
Bowen, Joy E334
Bowen, Liz E418
Boweolsen, Maria A305
Bower, Huw S. A154
Bower, Joseph B. A211
Bower, Joseph A526
Bower, Robert C. A872
Bower, Curtis P582
Bower, Joseph B. E82
Bowerman, James A571
Bowers, David A19
Bowers, William A28
Bowers, Ann A72
Bowers, Douglas H. (Doug) A104
Bowers, Matthew A161
Bowers, Christopher D. A179
Bowers, Chris A179
Bowers, Paul A382
Bowers, David A524
Bowers, Elizabeth A612
Bowers, Brad A700
Bowers, Mike A776
Bowers, Jeff A859
Bowers, Scott A891
Bowers, Catherine P151
Bowers, Alisa P419
Bowers, Mike P512
Bowers, Shawn E190
Bowersock, Tim A242
Bowersox, Dennis A388
Bowersox, Jim A512
Bowes, Timothy E. (Tim) A49
Bowes, Ken P198
Bowie, Paul J. A33
Bowie, Paul J. P24
Bowie, Cathy P651
Bowlby, Jeffrey L. A678
Bowler, Joseph A912
Bowler, Rodney M P235
Bowles, Janae P6
Bowles, W Bryan P173
Bowles, Julie P507
Bowles, Sharon P662
Bowles, Jack W79
Bowlin, John E184
Bowling, Brian A319
Bowling, Douglas P111
Bowling, Charlene E215
Bowman, Cynthia A108
Bowman, Arthur A170
Bowman, Andrew A248

Bowman, Gina A250
Bowman, Richard A409
Bowman, Giles A428
Bowman, Steve A431
Bowman, Jeff A549
Bowman, Stephen B. (Biff) A605
Bowman, William A640
Bowman, Gayle A879
Bowman, Jeff P158
Bowman, Darryl P233
Bowman, Cheri P329
Bowman, Elaine P585
Bowman, Andrew E107
Bowman, Paula E222
Bowman, Theresa E290
Bowman, Mike E290
Bowman, Lacey E433
Bowry, Oran A670
Bowser, Scott L. E286
Bowyer, Joan A890
Box, Laurie A859
Box, Aa Jewel P518
Boxer, Mark A194
Boy, Jeff E338
Boyaji, Brian A651
Boyaji, Brian E330
Boyce, Paula A109
Boyce, Gregory A533
Boyce, Jill A765
Boyce, David S. A838
Boyce, Jane E23
Boyd, Jeffery H. (Jeff) A143
Boyd, Tom A218
Boyd, Skiles A279
Boyd, John J. A301
Boyd, Michael A385
Boyd, Jeff A390
Boyd, Pete A507
Boyd, Jeff A527
Boyd, Ben A543
Boyd, Joseph A672
Boyd, Peter M. A772
Boyd, William A913
Boyd, Robert A924
Boyd, Terry P148
Boyd, David P153
Boyd, Barbara P429
Boyd, Kelsey P546
Boyd, Alison E105
Boyd, Peter M. E382
Boyd, William E438
Boyden, Tracey A658
Boyer, Gregg A119
Boyer, Jason A224
Boyer, Blake A227
Boyer, Mikey A337
Boyer, Jonathan A491
Boyer, Andy A665
Boyer, Jeffrey A715
Boyer, Kevin A881
Boyer, Craig P273
Boyer, Tamara P449
Boyer, Jean-Michel W71
Boyer, Bradley S. (Brad) E19
Boyer, Blake E90
Boyer, Mikey E158
Boyer, Steven E281
Boyer, Andy E334
Boyer, Kevin E421
Boyes, John C A313
Boyes, John C P200
Boyett, Dale P524
Boyette, Gaye A530
Boyette, Richard P78
Boyette, Scott P361
Boykas, Paul A654
Boyken, James W A465
Boykin, Frank H. A569
Boykin, Susan P548
Boykins, Lamont A60
Boylan, Laura A660
Boylan, Laura P416
Boylan, Peter C P464
Boylan, Deirdre F P630
Boyland, Gloria A324

Boyle, Amy A61
Boyle, Hugh F. A104
Boyle, Chris A364
Boyle, Karen A530
Boyle, Kevin A550
Boyle, Terence A602
Boyle, Debbie A651
Boyle, Patti A741
Boyle, Stephen J. (Steve) A807
Boyle, Mark A. A853
Boyle, Dennis A881
Boyle, Tom A933
Boyle, Kathy P179
Boyle, Brian P423
Boyle, Jodell J P469
Boyle, Jodell P469
Boyle, Nadine P547
Boyle, Mark A. P612
Boyle, Debbie E329
Boyle, Mark A. E364
Boyle, Patti E364
Boyle, Dennis E421
Boyles, Andrew A109
Boyles, Kathryn A391
Boyles, Kevin A757
Boyles, Jonathan A763
Boyles, Kevin P214
Boyles, Kevin P492
Boyles, Peter W. W189
Boyles, Jonathan E377
Boylston, Brianna P418
Boynton, Timothy J P284
Boynton, Andrew C. P608
Boynton, Susan E25
Boysen, Harry A251
Boysen, Doug P469
Boza, Xavier A164
Bozard, John P400
Bozek, Kathy A86
Bozek, Kathy E27
Bozeman, Keith P545
Bozgo, Paul A137
Bozzi, Bryan A897
Bozzoli, Carlo W153
Bozzolo, Albert A356
Bozzuto, Michael A. P96
Braam, Ronald H. E396
Braathen, Kjerstin W140
Braatz, Jay P175
Brabant, Steven A175
Brabec, Chris A915
Brabec-Lagrange, Claire W154
Brabham, Dave P273
Brabson, Charles A299
Braca, Greg W396
Bracamonte, Martin E332
Brace, George A429
Brace, Terri A838
Brace, George E214
Bracey, Brent A654
Bracher, Paul H. A246
Bracher, Pierre-Alain W54
Bracher, Candido Botelho W205
Bracher, Paul H. E105
Brachet, Anne W15
Bracht, Berend A724
Bracht, Berend P452
Bracken, Richard A251
Bracken, Chris A543
Bracken, Sam P212
Bracken, George R. E295
Brackenbury, Katie A137
Brackenridge, Stuart E349
Brackett, Rebecca P305
Brackett, Melanie M P587
Brackin, D. Wayne P63
Bracy, Kevin A442
Bracy, Raymond A902
Brad, Macdougall A583
Bradac, Joe A902
Braddy, Cheryl A800
Bradehoft, Nancy P343
Braden, Monica A366
Braden, Scott A550
Braden, Scott P319
Brader, Andy P82

Bradford, Douglas A103
Bradford, Don A465
Bradford, Hope A488
Bradford, Mark D. A621
Bradford, Hannah A702
Bradford, Tim A704
Bradford, Mark D. E311
Bradham, Sue A753
Bradish, Bob A51
Bradley, Mike A100
Bradley, Myles A165
Bradley, William E. (Bill) A184
Bradley, Jen A224
Bradley, Nancy A343
Bradley, John A483
Bradley, Elizabeth A587
Bradley, Doug A638
Bradley, John A686
Bradley, Jeff A713
Bradley, Pat A715
Bradley, Jacqueline A749
Bradley, David A791
Bradley, Scott A804
Bradley, W. Bennett A849
Bradley, Kristi A852
Bradley, Kevin P. A873
Bradley, Patrick A921
Bradley, Philip C P199
Bradley, Peg P212
Bradley, Constance (Connie) P232
Bradley, Tonya P268
Bradley, Megan P280
Bradley, David A P282
Bradley, Maureen P287
Bradley, Carol P288
Bradley, Mark J. P309
Bradley, Joseph P330
Bradley, Russell P334
Bradley, Greg P335
Bradley, Dana P389
Bradley, Walter P433
Bradley, David P535
Bradley, Glen P571
Bradley, Martha P597
Bradley, Patrick P669
Bradley, Bill E35
Bradley, Nancy E164
Bradley, Allen E183
Bradley, Russell W. E261
Bradley, Edward L. E302
Bradley, Doug E320
Bradley, Jacqueline E367
Bradshaw, Steven G. (Steve) A141
Bradshaw, Jim A498
Bradshaw, Richard W. A866
Bradshaw, Susan P477
Bradshaw, Steven G. (Steve) E49
Bradshaw, Richard W. E417
Bradvica, Michael A16
Bradway, Robert A. (Bob) A64
Bradwell, Hollis (Terry) P2
Brady, Sean A1
Brady, Kevin A51
Brady, Molly A54
Brady, Paul A363
Brady, Holly Gibson A363
Brady, Christopher J A373
Brady, Deanna T. A434
Brady, Amy G. A491
Brady, Christopher A492
Brady, Robert T. (Bob) A531
Brady, John A606
Brady, Linda A674
Brady, Elizabeth S. (Beth) A677
Brady, Emanuel A706
Brady, Christian M. M. A828
Brady, Melissa P423
Brady, Lisa P519
Brady, Patrick P536
Brady, Christian M. M. P584
Brady, Sean E1
Brady, Chris E290
Braemer, Richard A837
Brager, David A. A249
Brager, David A. E108

Bragg, Chris A113
Bragg, Dorry A325
Bragg, Michael B. A880
Bragg, Alisha P140
Bragg, Amy P635
Bragg, Michael B. P640
Bragg, Chris E36
Brahm, Bernard P80
Braid, Gregory A693
Braid, Gregory E341
Brailer, David A900
Braine, Bruce H A51
Braine, Bill A544
Braine, Michael A801
Brainerd, Mary A412
Brainerd, Mary A790
Brainerd, Mary P233
Braithwaite, Robert P242
Braitsch, Pete A161
Brake, Gene P103
Brakeville, Barry A859
Bram, Greg A887
Bram, Craig C. E396
Bramble, James H. (Jim) E423
Brames, Anne A924
Bramlage, Stephen P. (Steve) A75
Bramlett, E Chandler P252
Bramman, Anne L. A602
Bramow, Karen P259
Branca, Frank A872
Branch, Gregory C. A868
Branch, Matthew P343
Brand, Meir A39
Brand, Dennis L. A105
Brand, Walter A755
Brand, Tina A888
Brand, Rick P200
Brand, Christian W231
Brand, Dennis L. E34
Brand, David E51
Brand, Daniel E102
Brand, Walter E369
Brand, Tina E425
Brandano, Anthony P58
Brandel, Daniel A175
Brandenberg, Frank G. E244
Brandenburg, Pat A713
Brandenburg, Joel A861
Brandenburg, Julie P549
Brandenstein, Kendra P160
Brandenstein, Daniel C. (Dan) P620
Brandgaard, Jesper W290
Brandl, Linda A863
Brandolph, Larry P546
Brandom, Jessica A85
Brandom, Jessica E27
Brandon, Joseph P. A32
Brandon, Rush A364
Brandon, David P258
Brandow, Peter B. P443
Brands, Andrew D. W173
Brands, Andrew D. W174
Brandt, Ric A175
Brandt, Kristi A412
Brandt, James A. A527
Brandt, Tim A540
Brandt, Bryan K A632
Brandt, Genise A727
Brandt, Tom A876
Brandt, Kristi P233
Brandt, Douglas P234
Brandt, Michael P405
Brandt, Genise P453
Brandt, Paul P547
Brandt, Kristen E153
Brandtzaeg, Svein R. W289
Branham, Charlie E159
Branigin, John A319
Branion, Andrew W53
Brank, Roger P226
Brannan, Joseph A520
Brannemo, Tomas A936
Brannen, James P. (Jim) A316
Brannon, Jeff A170
Brannon, Kenna A176

Brannon, B C A619
Brannon, Bobby A619
Brannon, James A767
Brannon, B C P393
Brannon, Bobby P393
Branon, Bethany A882
Branon, Colin E330
Branscome, Andrea A849
Branscum, John E93
Branson, Marianne P490
Branson, Jeff P529
Brant, Kevin A481
Brantley, Todd A349
Brantley, John P120
Brantley, Chris P572
Branz, Sandra A409
Branzburg, Paul A784
Brasfield, Shirley P45
Brash, David L. P661
Braskamp, Steve A167
Braskamp, Larry P301
Bratcher, Ryan E347
Brathole, Kristin I P592
Brathwaite, Chris A813
Bratman, Fred A872
Bratspies, Steve A901
Bratt, Mikael A92
Bratt, Mikael W420
Bratton, Justin P78
Braucht, Drew E138
Braucht, Cheryl E424
Braud, Ken A401
Braude, Katie P299
Brauer, Mark A447
Brauer, Angela A888
Brauer, Mark P247
Brauer, Stephen F. P601
Brauer, Angela E425
Brault, Tom P76
Braun, Dennis A170
Braun, Eric A329
Braun, Randall L. A383
Braun, Lee A421
Braun, Alan A621
Braun, Peggy A754
Braun, Ray P116
Braun, Robert P162
Braun, Matthew P261
Braun, Annabelle P343
Braun, Peggy P484
Braun, Robert P513
Braun, Donald E149
Braun, Michael H. E149
Braun, Randall L. E186
Braun, Alan E312
Braun-Kolbe, Karl A530
Braunagel, Pat P281
Braunig, Gunther W225
Braunscheidel, Stephen A530
Braunschweiger, John A638
Braunschweiger, John E320
Brause, Kenneth A200
Brautigan, Bernard (Bernie) A731
Brautlacht, Gerald A530
Braveman, Peter P118
Braverman, Alan N A271
Bravo, Eduardo A407
Bravo, Giovanna P582
Brawley, Mark A46
Bray, Jeffrey A203
Bray, Jeffery (Jeff) A749
Bray, Karen A754
Bray, David A855
Bray, Karen P484
Bray, Dee L P529
Bray, Jeffery (Jeff) E367
Brayboy, Regina P P652
Brayer, Frank A522
Braylovskiy, Olga A471
Brayshaw, Bettina A798
Brazell, Chris A25
Brazell, Joe A602
Brazell, Chris P14
Brazil, Ben W243
Brda, Bruce W. A577

Bready, Bruce A504
Bready, Linda E131
Bready, Bruce E251
Breakefield, Xandra A642
Breakefield, Xandra P407
Breakey, Mark D. A211
Breakey, Mark D. E82
Breakie, Shane E E78
Bream, Stephanie E132
Breanna, Cypers P597
Breard, Jack A176
Breault, Debra P180
Breaux, Randall A379
Breaux, Holly A494
Breaux, Charles P523
Breber, Pierre R. A190
Brecheisen, Bruce A748
Brecher, Mark A502
Brecker, Nicholas L. A69
Breckon, Curt A559
Bredar, Randall A260
Bredow, Eugene J. A614
Bree, Margaret Van P448
Breeden, Gregory A442
Breeding, Todd E106
Breeman, Steven A504
Breeman, Steven E251
Breen, Timothy P. (Tim) A379
Breen, Chuck A381
Breen, Margaret P153
Breen, Bryan A475
Breen, Jennifer P678
Breezee, Jack P536
Brega, Jo--o Carlos A919
Bregier, Fabrice W17
Brehm, Susan P337
Breier, Barbara P551
Breig, John P135
Breight, Matthew A222
Breihan, Beth A870
Breitenbach, Kerry A681
Breitenbach, T G P320
Breitenbach, Ellen P647
Breitling, John A444
Breivogel, Donald A629
Brekelmans, Harry W334
Brekke, Liz P30
Brell, Mark A246
Brell, Mark E105
Bremar, Nancy P663
Bremm, Dirk W59
Bremner, John P509
Bremser, Brett A447
Bremser, Brett P247
Brenan, Kathryn P553
Brenda, Montgomery A456
Brenda, Huff P94
Brenda, Montgomery E228
Brendis, Janet A369
Brendle, Jim A125
Brendzal, Michael A877
Breneman, Jill P411
Breneman, Darcus E168
Brennan, Daniel J. (Dan) A149
Brennan, Troyen A. A251
Brennan, Thomas A347
Brennan, Matthew A347
Brennan, Kevin F. A371
Brennan, Mark A592
Brennan, Suzanne R. A638
Brennan, James A797
Brennan, Brian A799
Brennan, Jennifer A22
Brennan, Kevin F. P213
Brennan, Murray F. P325
Brennan, Maire P325
Brennan, Jim P356
Brennan, Thomas P362
Brennan, Mark P370
Brennan, James P468
Brennan, Tara E77
Brennan, Thomas E167
Brennan, Matthew E167
Brennan, Suzanne R. E320
Brenner, Timothy L. A584

Brenner, Dean A695
Brenner, Alena A734
Brenner, Glen A835
Brenner, Faith P369
Brenner, Catherine W27
Brenner, Hans-Dieter W231
Brensinger, Donald A722
Brent, Jacques A360
Brent, Arthur P159
Brent, Chappell E362
Brenton, Flint A199
Breon, Richard C A774
Breon, Richard C P510
Bres, Thomas A. (Tom) P508
Bres, Tom P508
Brescione, Richard P153
Breshears, Eric A349
Breshears, Betty P291
Bresky, Steven J. A748
Breslau, Carol P331
Breslauer, Jacque A200
Breslawski, James P. A744
Breslin, David A349
Breslow, Jeff P160
Bresnahan, John A725
Bresnahan, Rodney A843
Bresnan, Debra A374
Bress, Tracy A526
Bressette, Sharon P596
Bressler, Richard J. A452
Bressler, Allan A893
Brestovan, Peter A651
Brestovan, Peter E329
Breter, Greg A882
Brethauer, Craig P519
Brett, Anne Liners P291
Brett, John L. W33
Brettler, Dan A880
Brettler, Dan P640
Breuel, Chuck A544
Breuillac, Arnaud W398
Breunig, Charlene E156
Breux, Ken Le A605
Breves, Christine S. A873
Brewer, Allen M. A356
Brewer, Russell A511
Brewer, Dominic A592
Brewer, Janet J. A815
Brewer, Linda P157
Brewer, Kelley P254
Brewer, Russell P290
Brewer, Tracy P360
Brewer, Dominic P370
Brewer, Melanie P624
Brewer, Kevin J. E50
Brewer, Oliver G. (Chip) E59
Brewers, Doug A61
Brewster, James P6
Brewster, Deana P458
Breyer, Michael K P279
Brezden, Alexander A137
Brian, Clark A925
Brian, Clark E445
Briand, Remy E290
Briathwaite, Robert P242
Brice, Todd D. A737
Brice, Todd D. E361
Bricker, Christopher A665
Bricker, Jodi A826
Bricker, Terri P658
Bricker, Christopher E334
Brickhaus, David A89
Brickhouse, Nicole E433
Brickles, Stephen P446
Brickley, Liam A155
Brickley, David A831
Brickley, David P601
Brickley, Liam E54
Brickman, David M. A364
Brickman, Jay P166
Brickman, James R. E193
Bridarolli, Shelley A146
Bridelli, Guido A575
Bridenbaugh, Carl A351
Bridge, Tracy B. A180

COMBINED HOOVER'S HANDBOOK INDEX OF EXECUTIVES

A = AMERICAN BUSINESS
E = EMERGING COMPANIES
P = PRIVATE COMPANIES
W = WORLD BUSINESS

Bridge, Byard A470
Bridge-Cook, Jeremy E261
Bridgeforth, Scott A790
Bridgeforth, Scott E390
Bridgens, Katie A828
Bridgens, Katie P584
Bridges, David A22
Bridges, Kimberly A224
Bridges, Terri A449
Bridges, Jennifer A579
Bridges, Linda A599
Bridges, John A688
Bridges, Kristopher A712
Bridges, Kris A713
Bridges, David P11
Bridges, Kay P265
Bridges, Danielle P325
Bridges, Paul P405
Bridges, Carolyn P423
Bridges, Richele P471
Bridges, Susan A P481
Bridges, Darin P511
Bridges, Terri E221
Bridgette, Welch P162
Bridgford, Bruce H. E51
Bridgford, R.H. E51
Bridgford, Blaine K. E51
Bridgford, Allan L. E51
Bridgford, Hugh William E51
Bridgford, William L. (Bill) E51
Bridgham, Jerry A. P64
Brien, Jack O' P522
Brien, Lowell P613
Brienza, David A151
Brier, Jeff A16
Briesemeister, Eric P258
Briest, Neal P318
Brigantic, Patricia E A575
Brigden, John A198
Brigety, Reuben E. P569
Briggs, Tammy A19
Briggs, Ashlea A105
Briggs, Michael A380
Briggs, Jon A544
Briggs, Troy A621
Briggs, Larry A706
Briggs, Brent A940
Briggs, Craig A P279
Briggs, Stacy P412
Briggs, Susan P611
Briggs, Andy W40
Briggs, Ashlea E34
Briggs, Troy E312
Brigham, F Gorham A205
Brigham, Matthew P A379
Bright, Christopher A56
Bright, Tobias A140
Bright, Vonette Z P108
Brightman, Allison A893
Briglia, Jennifer A884
Brigman, Vince A505
Brignoni, Gregory P299
Brill, Matthew A213
Brill, Scott A804
Brill, David P86
Brill, Matthew P143
Brill, Cheryl P643
Brilli, Richard J. P359
Brim, Landon A772
Brim, Landon E383
Brimberry, Jared A29
Brimberry, Jared P16
Brimhall, Matt A628
Brimmer, Jana A177
Brinberg, Simeon E53
Brinch, Brian A317
Brinch, Brian E146
Brinckerhoff, Ron A809
Brindle, Carol A929

Brindle, Carol E449
Brindley, David A867
Brindley, Roger P638
Brindley, David E418
Bringe, Chad E73
Bringhurst, Richard A642
Bringhurst, Richard P407
Brink, Evert Van Den A784
Brink, Darin P199
Brink, James P574
Brinker, Mark A654
Brinkley, Cynthia J. (Cindy) A179
Brinkley, Ruth W. A226
Brinkley, Stephen A804
Brinkley, Ruth W. P150
Brinkley, Kevin P422
Brinkley, David L. E230
Brinkman, Rob L P655
Brinkmann, Mike P470
Brinkworth, Heather P476
Brinner, Scott A704
Brinton, Geraldine R. A791
Brinton, Geraldine R. P535
Brisbin, Tom D E442
Briscoe, Debi A142
Briscoe, Deb E49
Brisebois, Martin A380
Bristow, Peter M. A336
Bristow, Peter M. E157
Britell, Jenne K. A872
Brito, Michael A251
Brito, Josefa A654
Britsch, Sheryl A319
Britsch, Kristy A922
Britsch, Kristy P671
Britt, Pat A266
Britt, Annasivia A522
Britt, Vickie A682
Britt, Angela A850
Britt, Pat P181
Britt, Stuart P378
Britt, Douglas (Doug) W164
Brittain, Kevin A168
Brittain, Jim A355
Brittingham, Ch A837
Britto, Hugo A93
Britto, Maria P128
Britton, Paula A255
Britton, Carl A341
Britton, Lynn A556
Britton, William P22
Britton, Lynn P328
Britton, Adriene P593
Brizan, Audrey P138
Brizard, Jean C P454
Brnilovich, Bob P85
Broad, David A203
Broaddus, Alfred A536
Broadfield, Shawn A35
Broadnax, Robert E102
Broadway, Andy E46
Broas, Matthew A761
Brobst, Duane J. A881
Brobst, Duane J. E421
Brocato, Melissa A184
Brocato, Mike A230
Brocato, Mike P154
Brochick, George A649
Brock, Charisse A232
Brock, Anthony A574
Brock, Stanley M. (Skip) A755
Brock, Nancy A876
Brock, Wendy A885
Brock, Lisa P402
Brock, Jeffrey E103
Brock, Stanley M. (Skip) E369
Brockelbank, Russ P185
Brockett, Trina E256
Brockman, Dawn E61
Brockman, Henry A362
Brockmann, Manfred A888
Brockmann, Manfred E425
Brod, Beth P425
Broderick, Todd A30
Broderick, Craig W. A390

Broderick, Deborah A592
Broderick, Todd P20
Broderick, Deborah P370
Broderson, Tiffany A779
Brodeur, Tyler P259
Brodhead, Richard H. (Dick) P186
Brodie, Dianne A115
Brodie, Dianne E38
Brodigan, Darla J P316
Brodowski, Carolyn P257
Brodrick, Anita A189
Brodsky, Victor P118
Brodsky, Harry P384
Brodsky, William J P388
Brody, Sharon S A687
Brody, Robert C. (Bob) A844
Brody, Paul J. E235
Brody, John S. E448
Brodzeller, Jeff P667
Broeder, Karen P523
Broek, Jacques van den W319
Broen, Martin A654
Broendell, Jane E P357
Broening, Mercedes A349
Broerman, Robert A. (Rob) A754
Broerman, Robert A. (Rob) P484
Broermann, Robert A P484
Brogan, Joseph J A120
Brogan, John J A120
Brogan, Mike A835
Brogan, Lowell P288
Brogan, Joseph E41
Brogdon, Casey A866
Brogdon, Casey E417
Brok, Martin A779
Broll, Frank A58
Broman, Craig P587
Bromley, Craig R. W247
Bronczek, David J. A323
Bronder, Debra A585
Bronet, Frances P636
Brongiel, Daniel E225
Bronkella, Adam A128
Bronner, James P. A126
Brons-Poulsen, Peter A218
Bronsdon, Phillip A184
Bronson, David L. A824
Bronson, Ellen A882
Bronson, David L. P561
Bronson, Richard E387
Bronstein, Howard A702
Bronstein, David P402
Brook, Melissa P338
Brook, Meredith P390
Brooke, Jennifer A796
Brooke, Paul A E226
Brooke, Jennifer E397
Brooker, Wes A612
Brooker, Aaron P396
Brooker, Levi E433
Brookes, Andy A5
Brookfield, David A86
Brookfield, David E27
Brookman, Robert P544
Brookner, Mark E413
Brooks, Mark J. A179
Brooks, Jessa A266
Brooks, Brian P. A312
Brooks, Landie A325
Brooks, Keith A432
Brooks, Jessica A442
Brooks, Roland A444
Brooks, Josh A452
Brooks, David R. A455
Brooks, Daniel W. A456
Brooks, Wendell M. A460
Brooks, Bill A466
Brooks, Charles T. A489
Brooks, Kerry A520
Brooks, Ashley T. A524
Brooks, Raymond L. A534
Brooks, Annie A538
Brooks, Michele A559
Brooks, Rebekah A596
Brooks, Byron A654

Brooks, Steve A658
Brooks, Brian A713
Brooks, Andy A799
Brooks, Espen S. A831
Brooks, Jason A840
Brooks, Dan A855
Brooks, Elaine A893
Brooks, Bryan A913
Brooks, Tony A934
Brooks, Michael P64
Brooks, Steve P64
Brooks, Eve P146
Brooks, Roy P162
Brooks, Jessa P182
Brooks, Dawn P205
Brooks, Dick P401
Brooks, Espen S. P601
Brooks, Margaret P635
Brooks, David R. E228
Brooks, Daniel W. E228
Brooks, Jaime E321
Brooks, Bryan E438
Brooks-Williams, Denise A414
Brooks-Williams, Denise P236
Brookshire, William A. P461
Broome, Sharon A36
Broome, Richard D. A160
Broome, Tol A850
Broome, Marion E. P187
Broome, Belinda P306
Broome, Michael C P581
Broome, Mike P581
Broomfield, Robert A876
Brophy, Joseph A405
Broque, Eric A827
Broquet, Bruce L P213
Bros, Warner E240
Broseker, Bob A559
Brosnahan, Maria A167
Brosnan, David J. (Dave) A210
Brosnan, Michael W166
Brossart, Tim A932
Brosseau, Phil A175
Brosseau, Guy A795
Brost, Mike P264
Brost, Arin E223
Brothers, Sara A56
Brothers, Grace A212
Brothers, Lisa A345
Brothers, Norm A870
Brothers, Norman A871
Brothers, Lisa E165
Brothman, Dan E272
Brotman, Marc A658
Brotman, Adam A779
Brouaux, Marie-No-«lle W88
Brough, Rob A940
Broughman, Wade D P450
Broughton, Jack A489
Broughton, Thomas A. (Tom) A755
Broughton, Bruce P205
Broughton, Tracy E105
Broughton, Thomas A. (Tom) E369
Brouillette, Elizabeth P337
Broumidis, Haris W118
Broun, Elizabeth (Betsy) P497
Broussard, Bruce D. A440
Broussard, Bonnie P142
Brow, Betty A109
Browder, Brad A772
Browder, Brad E383
Brower, David A380
Brown, Harlan A3
Brown, Thomas A5
Brown, Chad A29
Brown, Jeffrey J A37
Brown, Jeffrey J. (JB) A37
Brown, Bradley A37
Brown, Scott A43
Brown, Jason A54
Brown, Judy Gawlik A65
Brown, Eric A75
Brown, Jim A82
Brown, Caitlin A89
Brown, M. Dean A91

COMBINED HOOVER'S HANDBOOK INDEX OF EXECUTIVES

Brown, Jeff A135
Brown, Cj A137
Brown, Ian A143
Brown, James C. A147
Brown, Danielle A154
Brown, William A177
Brown, Debra A200
Brown, Michael A205
Brown, Adriane A240
Brown, Karen A251
Brown, William E. A268
Brown, Darrell A289
Brown, Marcus V. A296
Brown, Michael A309
Brown, Anita A319
Brown, Shannon A323
Brown, Jill A323
Brown, Marianne C. A327
Brown, Rod A329
Brown, Trish A332
Brown, David D. A338
Brown, Todd A338
Brown, Douglas A358
Brown, Treg A379
Brown, James S. (Jim) A401
Brown, Angie A410
Brown, Hamish A418
Brown, Doug A435
Brown, Keith A442
Brown, Maureen A445
Brown, Michael J. (Mike) A449
Brown, Michelle A452
Brown, Robin A457
Brown, Dora A463
Brown, Jack A465
Brown, Michael A478
Brown, Dan A484
Brown, David A491
Brown, William M. (Bill) A501
Brown, Sheila A530
Brown, James A546
Brown, David A550
Brown, Tim A559
Brown, Ashley A569
Brown, Gregory Q. (Greg) A577
Brown, Robert A589
Brown, Donald E. A600
Brown, Meg A600
Brown, Jennifer Jackson A602
Brown, Holly A606
Brown, Stephen A606
Brown, Keegan A613
Brown, Kathryn A626
Brown, Bartholomew A628
Brown, Brien H. A630
Brown, Ron A647
Brown, Paul A647
Brown, Lori A672
Brown, David A678
Brown, Joyce A702
Brown, Dan A711
Brown, Diane A722
Brown, Thomas L. A723
Brown, Gerald A735
Brown, Jeff A747
Brown, Kevin A750
Brown, Nancy A751
Brown, Susan L A752
Brown, Maryam A753
Brown, Julie A A772
Brown, Seth A776
Brown, Joel E. A781
Brown, Marc P. A783
Brown, Adam A799
Brown, Melinda A801
Brown, Robert A816
Brown, Kimberly A833
Brown, Gasford A849
Brown, Matthew A850
Brown, Janice A852
Brown, Calvin A852
Brown, Derek A853
Brown, Sandra A867
Brown, Janice A879
Brown, Trevor A884

Brown, Mike A903
BROWN, MIKE A915
Brown, Erin A919
Brown, Mike A928
Brown, Marty A930
Brown, Jimmy A933
Brown, Scott A942
Brown, Chad P16
Brown, Pamela P17
Brown, Donna P19
Brown, Doug P22
Brown, Jeffrey J P27
Brown, Leah P34
Brown, William A. P64
Brown, Jennifer P68
Brown, David P84
Brown, Charles H. P94
Brown, Robert P96
Brown, Tracy P104
Brown, Jeremy P112
Brown, Carolyn P112
Brown, Emily P120
Brown, Hannah P123
Brown, Michael P161
Brown, Kevin P162
Brown, Casey P173
Brown, Alexander P175
Brown, Doris P175
Brown, Dhannetta P179
Brown, Garry P196
Brown, Marcus V P196
Brown, Deirdre A P203
Brown, Marilyn P209
Brown, Tom P212
Brown, Eric P225
Brown, Jim P228
Brown, Janet P237
Brown, Amy P255
Brown, Jeff P255
Brown, Michael P268
Brown, James D P280
Brown, George J. P288
Brown, Cathy A P296
Brown, Kevin P299
Brown, Diona P323
Brown, Kim P327
Brown, Dan P358
Brown, Luke P359
Brown, Leonard P361
Brown, Michael P373
Brown, Jane P383
Brown, Kathleen P396
Brown, Bartholomew P396
Brown, Kevin P418
Brown, Geoff P418
Brown, Janine P418
Brown, Dr Kenneth P429
Brown, Brian P440
Brown, Dan P444
Brown, Carole P445
Brown, Drew P478
Brown, Robin B. P479
Brown, Cassie P480
Brown, Nancy P482
Brown, Venessa P486
Brown, W P501
Brown, Daniel A. P551
Brown, Eric P559
Brown, Michael W P571
Brown, Vance M P574
Brown, David FM P574
Brown, David A P582
Brown, Edith P589
Brown, Charlie P594
Brown, Chani P597
Brown, Derek P612
Brown, Jay P615
Brown, Janice P636
Brown, Virginia L P643
Brown, Mike P673
Brown, Richard P677
Brown, Charles W65
Brown, Gary W. W85
Brown, Michael W. T. (Mike) W275
Brown, Jason W317

Brown, Jim W333
Brown, Andrew W334
Brown, Randolph B. (Randy) W371
Brown, Scott E13
Brown, M. Dean E29
Brown, Roger H E51
Brown, Kevin E51
Brown, Marc E58
Brown, William E. (Bill) E72
Brown, Lorraine E81
Brown, Steve E123
Brown, Christen E131
Brown, Douglas E176
Brown, Kelly E180
Brown, Craig E181
Brown, Molly Z E204
Brown, Michael J. (Mike) E220
Brown, Toya E255
Brown, Jacqueline E330
Brown, Greg E357
Brown, Tony E366
Brown, Julie A E382
Brown, Colleen M. E386
Brown, Roni E391
Brown, Donna E416
Brown, Sandra E418
Brown, Jim E423
Brown, Kelly E427
Brown, Joseph R. (JR) E432
Brown, Jim E448
Brown, Christopher E453
Brown-philpot, Stacy A438
Browne, Stacey E128
Browne, Paul A414
Browne, Robert P. (Bob) A605
Browne, Dalya A626
Browne, Paul T. A811
Browne, Colin A862
Browne, Mark P162
Browne, Paul P236
Browne, Janelle P551
Browne, Michael A. (Mike) E58
Brownell, Kelly D. P187
Brownell, Mark P395
Brownie, Susan P488
Browning, Nicholas A444
Browning, Bill P485
Browning, James A819
Browning, Michael A831
Browning, Jay D. A887
Browning, Deborah P128
Browning, Chris P128
Browning, Chris P351
Browning, Allan P371
Browning, Debbie P424
Browning, Michael P601
Browning, Patrick E366
Browning, James P403
Brownlee, James P638
Brownlee, Ben E47
Brownlie, William R. E402
Brownsberger, Tina P633
Broxton, Sonnie A798
Broyles, Rhonda A804
Broyles, Rob P204
Broyles, Andy P480
Broz, Steven A. (Steve) A681
Brozyna, Roman A200
Brubacher, Kevin E102
Brubaker, Katie A428
Brubaker, Terry Lee E189
Bruce, Timothy A152
Bruce, Howard A373
Bruce, Carrie A709
Bruce, David A734
Bruce, Wendy A855
Bruce, Jim A871
Bruce, Harry A880
Bruce, Timothy P98
Bruce, Carrie P442
Bruce, Anne P493
Bruce, Harry P640
Bruce, Sally W27
Bruchman, Robert P30
Bruck, Lori A A810

Bruck, Lori A P546
Bruckner, Brian M P102
Bruckner, Chris B P102
Bruder, Michael A19
Bruder, David A501
Bruder, Eric P610
Bruder, Karen P638
Brudermuller, Martin W59
Brudnicki, Gary P664
Brudzynski, Daniel A279
Brueck, Margaret P486
Brueckman, Brian A877
Bruen, Phil A559
Bruggeman, Kevin A922
Bruggeman, Kevin P671
Bruggen, Danielle Ver A135
Bruhin, Joseph D. (Joe) A236
Bruhmuller, Arthur A559
Bruhn, Carl A315
Bruhn, Michelle P471
Bruil, Wouter A135
Brukardt, David P641
Brum, Cristina A167
Brumagim, Jeannie P429
Brumbaugh, Mary A798
Brumberg, Leonard A152
Brumberg, Leonard P98
Brumfield, Chris N A313
Brumfield, Chris N P200
Brumitt, David E14
Brumley, Susan P175
Brumley, Blake P549
Brumm, Jennifer L P316
Brumm, Sheri E415
Brummer, Derek V. A700
Brummit, John A448
Brummit, John P247
Brummitt, Charles A91
Brummitt, Charles P55
Brumsted, John P597
Brumsted, John R. P598
Brun, Scott A6
Brun, Philip A876
Brundage, Barry A222
Brundige, Cynthia P513
Brune, Donna A682
Brunel, Patrick A661
Brunelle, Eric A681
Bruner, Robert F. P442
Bruni, Daniel J. A776
Bruni, Frank A804
Brunk, John A219
Brunk, Debbie P186
Brunk, John E87
Brunken, Muriel A318
Brunl, Frank A804
Brunn, Carsten W61
Brunner, Steve A452
Brunner, Mary P625
Brunner, Brian E83
Brunner, Rob E102
Bruno, Marc A75
Bruno, Christopher J A460
Bruno, Stephen A587
Bruno, James E. A873
Bruno, John P P519
Bruno, Rosemary P607
BRUNO, RICCARDO W121
Bruns, Marilee A228
Bruns, Timothy D. A489
Brunschwig, Serge W105
Brunson, Janice A888
Brunson, Janice E425
Brunt, Jeff Van A856
Brunt, Jeff Van P614
Brunton, Patty E240
Brus, David A885
Brusadelli, Maurizio A573
Bruskotter, Kurt A512
Brust, Andrew L A567
Brust, Andrew L E284
Bruton, Steve A742
Brutsche, Paul A929
Brutsche, Paul E449
Bruun, Ed P508

A = AMERICAN BUSINESS
E = EMERGING COMPANIES
P = PRIVATE COMPANIES
W = WORLD BUSINESS

Bruxvoort, Keith P530
Bruyn, Leon De A191
Bruza, John M P583
Bruzzano, Marco A279
Bryan, Kathleen A109
Bryan, Cary A199
Bryan, Devon A319
Bryan, J. Randolph A449
Bryan, Glynis A. A458
Bryan, Vere A752
Bryan, Vincent A845
Bryan, Joe P162
Bryan, Lawana P383
Bryan, Deborah P597
Bryan, John P604
Bryan, Elizabeth W84
Bryan, Jason E19
Bryan, J. Randolph E220
Bryant, Sterling A165
Bryant, Warren A272
Bryant, Diane M. A460
Bryant, John A. A487
Bryant, James A790
Bryant, Thaire A797
Bryant, Mike A871
Bryant, Bruce A900
Bryant, Greg A933
Bryant, Phil P263
Bryant, Mary P263
Bryant, Kevin E P274
Bryant, Bret P281
Bryant, Jay P312
Bryant, Dawn P379
Bryant, Douglas C. (Doug) E342
Bryar, Alex P300
Bryce, Kristin Jones P631
Brycz, Kim A378
Brycz, Kimberly kim A378
Bryke, Christine P79
Brynelsen, Chuck A5
Brysch, Paul P502
Bryson, Philip A537
Bryson, Mary A909
Bryson, Mary E436
Brzezicki, Paul A A790
Brzoskowski, Ryszard P544
Brungger, Renata Jungo W125
Bsirske, Frank W335
Buafo, Charles P575
Bubb, David A747
Bubnov, Sergey P458
Bucci, Don A482
Buchanan, Jim A3
Buchanan, Travis A168
Buchanan, John D. A221
Buchanan, Stephen G. (Steve) A736
Buchanan, Ashley A901
Buchanan, Brooke A921
Buchanan, Jason P98
Buchanan, Kenneth (Ken) P171
Buchanan, Maxine P174
Buchanan, Jennifer P204
Buchanan, Kathryn P334
Buchanan, Stephen G. (Steve) P460
Buchanan, Jamie P640
Buchanan, Brooke P669
Buchanan, Malcolm W333
Buchanon, Kent A501
Buchanon, David A718
Buchanon, David E354
Buchband, Richard D A532
Buchbinder, David K P129
Buchenau, Blaine P207
Bucher, Ryan A394
Bucher, Jennifer A466
Bucher, Charles P159
Bucher, Al P197
Bucher, Mary Kaye P636
Buchert, Mark E156

Buchholtz, Chris P447
Buchholz, Thomas P479
Buchmeier, Peter A199
Buchner, Renee A922
Buchner, Renee P671
Buchness, Brett A135
Buchs, Jim A796
Buchs, Jim E397
Buchwald, Hyman A936
Buchwald, Darren E126
Buck, Robert R. A121
Buck, Michele G. A416
Buck, Danny A581
Buck, John D. A643
Buck, Haydee P183
Buck, Catherine (Cathy) P211
Buck, Sean P261
Buck, Tiffany P547
Buckalew, Steve A399
Buckalew, Steve P223
Buckelew, Alan B. W87
Bucker, Robert P505
Buckheit, Scott A162
Buckheit, Scott E62
Buckingham, Andrew A215
Buckingham, Lisa M. A519
Buckingham, Rob P381
Buckingham, Phil P611
Buckiso, David A337
Buckiso, Scott D. A873
Buckiso, David E158
Bucklee, Andrew A519
Buckley, David P A71
Buckley, Brad A183
Buckley, Bradford J A183
Buckley, John A251
Buckley, John A379
Buckley, Michael A405
Buckley, Michael A536
Buckley, Raegan A540
Buckley, John A608
Buckley, Richard E A686
Buckley, Michael C. A725
Buckley, Erin A751
Buckley, George W. A778
Buckley, David P P43
Buckley, Morgan P155
Buckley, John L. P423
Buckley, Gerard J. P456
Buckley, Erin P482
Buckley, Guy G. P509
Buckley, Kerry P578
Buckley, Adam P. P598
Buckley, Linda P632
Buckley, Brad E74
Buckley, Bradford J E74
Buckley, Robert E307
Bucklin, Patricia P586
Buckman, Tim E59
Buckman, Michael E174
Buckminster, Douglas E. A53
Buckner, Alma A15
Buckner, Alma P8
Buckner, Emma P624
Bucko, James A651
Bucko, James E329
Buco, Glen A741
Buco, Glen E364
Buczko, Brian A449
Buczko, Brian E220
Buday, Ernie A327
Budd, Stephen A647
Budd, Thomas D. A693
Budd, Thomas D. E341
Budesilich, Casey A827
Budraitis, Alyssa A. A24
Budroe, James A672
Budzinski, Jeff A292
Buechel, Jason A921
Buechel, Jason P669
Buechler, Mark A85
Buechler, Mark E27
Buechler, Kenneth F. (Ken) E343
Buechse, Oliver A85
Buechse, Oliver E26

Buehler, James A692
Buehler, Charlie A922
Buehler, Ralf P193
Buehler, Charlie P671
Buelow, Dawn A540
Buelow, Rob E433
Buenaseda, Jude A592
Buenaseda, Jude P370
Buendia, Robin A489
Buenker, Kenneth A871
Buer, Gene P. E88
Buergel, Erich P326
Bueschen, Anton P624
Buescher, John P318
Buese, Nancy K. A595
Buesinger, Robert F. A917
Bueter, Brian A51
Buffa, Damiano A137
Buffa, Sandra M. E298
Buffalo, Bill A161
Bufferd, Allan S P79
Bufferd, Allan P314
Buffett, Warren E. A127
Buffi, Cindy A835
Buffie, Craig A. A491
Buffington, Heidi P465
Buffmire, Andrew P639
Buffon, Mike A871
Buffoni, Chris A509
Buffy, Birrittella A702
Bufkin, Lucy A824
Buford, Mark A228
Bugaj, Rick A329
Bugatto, David J. A32
Bugh, Stan A598
Bugh, Frank A704
Bugher, Mark D. P309
Bugher, Daniel P505
Buglione, John A848
Buglione, John E411
Buhay, Rene A374
Buhl, Reinhard W433
Buhler, Marlene A62
Buhler, Marlene E20
Buhr, Jeffrey L. A1
Buhr, Steve P78
Buhr, Jeffrey L. E1
Bui, Vanesa A562
Bui-Thompson, Nancy P462
Buijs, Peter P158
Buis, Thomas A. E365
Buisson, Steve A850
Buit, Tim A588
Buit, Tim P365
Buit, Ron E265
Buitrago, Gus A356
Bujarski, Robert J. E342
Bujold-Lee, Sue A15
Bujold-Lee, Sue P8
Bukiewicz, Ralph P587
Bukiewicz, Susan P587
Bula, Patrice W276
Bulaich, Nick A421
Bulakul, Surong W315
Bulanda, Mark J A292
Bulander, Rolf W75
Bulandr, Peter A85
Bulandr, Peter E26
Bulanov, Alexander N. W375
Bulawa, Bryan F. A299
Bulawa, Bryan F P340
Bulcke, Paul W276
Bull, Steven A850
Bull, Harry P126
Bull, Mick P457
Bull, Kenneth R. E172
Bullard, James B. A322
Bullard, Trey A728
Bullard, Coby P104
Bullen, Derrik A559
Buller, Katja A133
Bullinger, Phil A914
Bullington, Amy P105
Bullion, Diana A683
Bullion, Diana P431

Bullock, Brian H. A297
Bullock, James A393
Bullock, Diana P193
Bullock, Timothy P302
Bullock, Gregory P631
Bullock, Erik E32
Bullock, Brian H. E129
Bullock, John E203
Bulmash, Mark E218
Bulmer, William H A686
Bulpin, Andrew A554
Bulpitt, Amy P516
Bultman, Gary A505
Bulusu, Bhaskar A489
Bumgardner, Beth A P573
Bumgarner, David L. A206
Bumpus, Ray A640
Bunch, Tara A72
Bunch, Charles A534
Bunch, Lonnie G. P497
Bunch, Jaclyn P637
Bunder, Lawrence A592
Bunder, Lawrence P370
Bundschuh, John A651
Bundschuh, Russell G. W106
Bundschuh, John E329
Bundy, Orrin A828
Bundy, Michael P109
Bundy, Orrin P584
Bung-ju, Kwon W176
Bunger, Steven G. E69
Bunk, Craig A463
Bunker, Matthew B A564
Bunker, Mike P112
Bunn, Mike A155
Bunn, Mike E54
Bunn, Kevin S. E368
Bunnell, Ronald R. (Ron) A117
Bunnell, Ronald R. (Ron) P61
Bunnell, Craig A. P172
Bunsness, Joe P98
Bunte, Brent A470
Bunting, Glenn A71
Bunting, Theodore H. (Theo) A296
Bunting, Chris A559
Bunting, Glenn P43
Bunton, Robert A175
Bunton, Kris P549
Bunyard, Heather A374
Bunyard, Steve P395
Bunzel, Theodore A135
Buonaiuto, Joe A51
Buonanno, Bernie P2
Buonaura, Vincenzo Calandra W407
Buonforte, Jeffrey J. A504
Buonforte, Jeffrey J. E251
Buongiorno, Michael P305
Buono, Tim P475
Buonpastore, Andy A592
Buonpastore, Andy P370
Buquicchio, Gerard A704
Burak, Mark A110
Buran, John R. A356
Buranakanonda, Charcrie W316
Burba, Deron P497
Burbach, Nicole P250
Burback, Katie P15
Burbage, Lois P201
Burby, Chris P529
Burch, William A713
Burch, Eric P251
Burch, Stephen A. P631
Burch, Brian E244
Burchart, Nathalie De Vos P85
Burchett, Katheryn A647
Burchett, Ronald P419
Burchette, Mary A885
Burchfield, Carol A180
Burckhart, Camille A670
Burd, Travis A145
Burda, Brian E58
Burdakin, David C. E241
Burdalski, Dan A161
Burdett, Judith A824
Burdett, Judith P562

Burdett, H W P565
Burdick, Don A242
Burdick, Kevin L. A630
Burdick, Steven A877
Burdick, Christian P619
Burdick, Steven M. E402
Burdiek, Michael J. E58
Burdiss, Paul E. A940
Burdjalov, Vladimir A824
Burdjalov, Vladimir P561
Burdolski, Jane P491
Burelli, Laura P395
Burer, Dan A382
Buresti, Francesco W153
Burfitt, Gregory H P117
Burg, Jan Van Den E427
Burgard, Louis-Roch W415
Burgdoerfer, Stuart B. A500
Burge, Debbie A680
Burge, Patty P45
Burgess, David A68
Burgess, John A379
Burgess, Shari L A508
Burgess, Brian A583
Burgess, Robert O A806
Burgess, Jo Lynn A850
Burgess, Conal P405
Burgess, Patrice P463
Burgess, Robert O E398
BurgessJr, Robert A806
BurgessJr, Robert E399
Burget, Mark P579
Burghart, Julia E148
Burgher, Cedric W. A618
Burgis, David A36
Burgoon, David A715
Burgos, Sonia P203
Burik, Jeff A224
Burington, Judy A90
Burington, Judy P51
Burkard, Joe P283
Burkart, John F. E136
Burke, Michael S. (Mike) A16
Burke, Ed A25
Burke, Glenn A98
Burke, James T. A110
Burke, Sean A147
Burke, Zane M. A185
Burke, Stephen B A220
Burke, George J A227
Burke, Kevin A234
Burke, Brian A347
Burke, Ken A364
Burke, Susan A364
Burke, Patrick J. (Pat) A439
Burke, Sean A473
Burke, Edward J. (E.J.) A491
Burke, Geoffrey A574
Burke, William A. (Bill) A593
Burke, James J. (Jim) A598
Burke, John A606
Burke, Paul A638
Burke, Lucas A700
Burke, Donna A708
Burke, Heather A741
Burke, Jason A746
Burke, Anthony A786
Burke, Paul A902
Burke, Frank J. A925
Burke, Ed P14
Burke, Michael W P19
Burke, Ryan P137
Burke, Edmund F P178
Burke, Timothy J. (Tim) P396
Burke, John P440
Burke, Gerald P442
Burke, Thomas M. P464
Burke, James F. P478
Burke, James F P479
Burke, Alan P514
Burke, Janice P603
Burke, John D. P608
Burke, Patrick J. (Pat) W189
Burke, Michael W241
Burke, George J E90

Burke, Gary E113
Burke, Sean E123
Burke, Joan A. E156
Burke, Brian E167
Burke, Sean E236
Burke, Thomas A. (Tom) E286
Burke, Paul E320
Burke, Heather E364
Burke, Anthony E387
Burke, Andrew T. E400
Burke, Frank J. E445
Burkel, Terri P417
Burkett, Steven P228
Burkett, Lynn P441
Burkhalter, Brandy A179
Burkhardt, Steve P5
Burkhardt, Andrew P597
Burkhart, Megan D. A222
Burkhart, Kimberly A877
Burkhart, James R. P203
Burkhart, Craig P524
Burkholder, Michael P412
Burks, Trinidad E123
Burlage, David P. A213
Burlage, David P. P143
Burlando, Fabrizio A544
Burleigh, Clarence A112
Burleson, Tom E177
Burlingame, Nathan A167
Burlog, Chris A872
Burlowski, John A329
Burls, Chris P354
Burman, Darryl M. A398
Burmaster, Brad P297
Burmester, Mark A P362
Burnell, Lawrence A433
Burnell, James A933
Burnell, Jody P402
Burnell, Lawrence E217
Burnett, Brian A254
Burnett, Connie A263
Burnett, Kent A267
Burnett, Jason A774
Burnett, Bonnie P21
Burnett, Janice P94
Burnett, Archie P96
Burnett, Don P160
Burnett, Walter P174
Burnett, Mark P337
Burnett, Kevin M P532
Burnett, Kevin M P590
Burnett, Brian D. P633
Burnette, Don P160
Burnette, Peg P179
Burney, Bryan A522
Burney, Pete P261
Burnfield, Richard G. P503
Burnham, Suzy A686
Burnham-snyder, Eben A188
Burnich, Jeffrey A791
Burnich, Jeffrey P535
Burnim, Mickey L. P642
Burnip, Douglas A882
Burnison, Gary D. E248
Burnosky, James A591
Burnosky, James P369
Burns, Nisha A6
Burns, Frederick A51
Burns, Ward A115
Burns, Kevin A137
Burns, Ned A175
Burns, Austin A246
Burns, John A257
Burns, Jennifer J. A320
Burns, Shira A325
Burns, Matthew A346
Burns, Jean A349
Burns, Larry A355
Burns, Mark L. A373
Burns, Mary A413
Burns, Nellson D. A425
Burns, Stephanie A487
Burns, Chris A561
Burns, David A573
Burns, Gay A714

Burns, Joseph A769
Burns, Michelle A780
Burns, Sheri T. A861
Burns, Anna A871
Burns, Glenn P59
Burns, Steve P245
Burns, Mandy P333
Burns, Patricia P344
Burns, Joseph E P462
Burns, Sister Miriam P514
Burns, Ryan P543
Burns, James P608
Burns, Jacqueline P627
Burns, Jon P. P630
Burns, Ward E38
Burns, Austin E105
Burns, Matthew E167
Burns, Mary E205
Burns, Joseph E380
Burns, Brad E433
Burnside, Sara A340
Burnside, Bob A449
Burnside, Sara E161
Burnside, Bob E221
Burnson, Bob A672
Burnstein, Mark I A414
Burnstein, Mark I P236
Buro, Geoff A877
Burpee, Steve P457
Burrell, Cheryl A782
Burrell, Carol P383
Burrell, Cheryl P526
Burrescia, Dominic A727
Burrescia, Dominic P453
Burrin, Stephen E P553
Burris, Alex A512
Burris, Ellen A859
Burris, Brian P281
Burris, Lee E16
Burriss, Steve P448
Burritt, David B. (Dave) A873
Burroughs, Margaret A6
Burroughs, Michael A382
Burroughs, Phil A501
Burroughs, Philip A890
Burroughs, Clint P106
Burroughs, Lisa P481
Burrow, Lynne M. A162
Burrow, Patrick A. A760
Burrow, Mark P646
Burrow, Carl E58
Burrow, Lynne M. E61
Burrow, Patrick A. E374
Burrowes, Todd A255
Burrows, Matthew R A196
Burrows, Adam A740
Burrows, Clifford (Cliff) A779
Burrows, Richard W79
Burrows, Robert E126
Burrus, Victoria P648
Burry, Todd P176
Bursey, Robert C E330
Burson, Arthur A554
Burson, Michael L P135
Burt, David A637
Burt, Brady T. A639
Burt, Jessica A654
Burt, Jeff A804
Burt, Linda K P362
Burt, Suzie P646
Burt, Richard L. E93
Burtis, Andy A550
Burtis, Michelle E102
Burton, Brian A112
Burton, Lynn A197
Burton, James A216
Burton, Craig A331
Burton, Mary A711
Burton, Eileen A785
Burton, Becky A885
Burton, Laura A893
Burton, Steven L P105
Burton, Marianne P129
Burton, Christa P276
Burton, Mary P331

Burton, Mary P444
Burton, Carol P476
Burton, Pam P639
Burton, Teresa P677
Burton, Spencer E127
Burton, David E138
Burton, Craig E152
Burton, Andrew E260
Burton, Eileen E397
Burtscher, Art N. E307
Burtt, Susan A527
Burud, Jamie A818
Burud, Jamie E403
Burvall, Pether W377
Burvill, Martin A890
Burwell, Brian E102
Bury, Randy P566
Busacca, Brian P263
Busack, John A909
Busack, John E436
Busam, James A384
Busam, James P217
Busannagari, Chandra A784
Busateri, Annette A532
Busby, Todd A51
Buscaglia, Nick A530
Busch, Eric A374
Busch, Tina A493
Busch, Kathryn A528
Busch, Jonathan A709
Busch, Pat A756
Busch, Todd P166
Busch, Jonathan P442
Busch, Roland W353
Busch, Henry William E212
Busch, Christopher E226
Buschkowiak, Boris P674
Buseman, Michael D. (Mike) A99
Buser, Darin A119
Busey, Ricky A161
Bush, Julie A54
Bush, Richard A60
Bush, James A367
Bush, Stephanie A408
Bush, Mary A538
Bush, Antoinette (Toni) A596
Bush, Wesley G. (Wes) A608
Bush, Luanne A908
Bush, Frederick S Steve P22
Bush, Emily P56
Bush, Vicki P289
Bush, Stephen P478
Bush, William L P509
Bush, Mark E402
Bush, Luanne E436
Bushmaker, Jessie A85
Bushmaker, Jessie E26
Bushman, Julie L. A3
Buskey, Michael T. (Mike) A371
Buskey, Mike A371
Buss, Jessica E. A781
Busse, Keith E. A785
Busse, Thomas A877
Bussel, Marina P405
Bussell, Rosemary A301
Bussells, Walter P264
Bussey, Tonya A678
Busson, Donald A145
Bussy, Jean-Franois P153
Bustamante, Jose L. M. A355
Bustamante, Jose Luis A355
Bustamante, Jolito A508
Bustamante, Tracey A704
Buster, Bob P161
Bustle, Nick A115
Bustle, Nick E38
Butala, Reema A204
Butcher, Art A149
Butcher, Lisa A718
Butcher, Lisa E354
Butcher, Benjamin S. E385
Butchko, Jason A821
Buteaux, Paul A199
Butier, Mitchell R. A97
Butina, Barry A922

COMBINED HOOVER'S HANDBOOK INDEX OF EXECUTIVES

```
A = AMERICAN BUSINESS
E = EMERGING COMPANIES
P = PRIVATE COMPANIES
W = WORLD BUSINESS
```

Butina, Barry P671
Butkovich, Joe A893
Butkus, Sean A390
Butler, Kent A21
Butler, Charl L. A22
Butler, Pat A147
Butler, John A209
Butler, Brittany A222
Butler, John M. A238
Butler, Keith G. A281
Butler, Gregory B. A303
Butler, Calvin G. A304
Butler, Ronald D. (Ron) A340
Butler, Maurice A449
Butler, Mark A475
Butler, David A492
Butler, Traci A502
Butler, Eric L A600
Butler, Brad A715
Butler, Timothy A727
Butler, Amy A833
Butler, Eric L. A863
Butler, Kirby A867
Butler, Charl L. P11
Butler, Paul Edd P83
Butler, Rich P132
Butler, Steve P183
Butler, Annmarie P259
Butler, Alice P332
Butler, Mike P431
Butler, Michael P431
Butler, Linda P448
Butler, Timothy P453
Butler, June P558
Butler, P. Barry P594
Butler, Connie P596
Butler, Michael C P616
Butler, Richard P617
Butler, Gary P618
Butler, Karis P657
Butler, David P672
Butler, Gerard W106
Butler, Jason E99
Butler, Ronald D. (Ron) E161
Butler, Maurice E220
Butler, Richard D. E259
Butler, Rhett E346
Butler, Henry A. E408
Butler, Kirby E418
Butsch, Tom A850
Butschek, Gunter W17
Butschek, Guenter W383
Butte, Grease P265
Butterfield, Bridget A360
Butterfield, Stephen F. (Steve) A586
Butterfield, Stephen F. (Steve) E301
Butterly, Rick A925
Butterly, Rick E445
Butters, Sheri P235
Butterworth, Warren A329
Butterworth, Liam W31
Butto, Joseph A838
Butolph, Dan A327
Buttrick, Tony A353
Buttrick, Tony E173
Buttrill, Stephanie A626
Buuren, Johannes Van P652
Buxton, Sandra P616
Buytenhuys, Sheldon A739
Buzachero, Vic P479
Buzby, Timothy L. (Tim) A317
Buzby, Timothy L. (Tim) E146
Buzzell, Mark A360
Buzzo, Ann A759
Buzzo, Ann P493
Byard, Sarah P632
Bybee, Gary A103
Byck, David P474
Byers, Bryan A1

Byers, Jay A191
Byers, Allison A247
Byers, Douglas A609
Byers, Kelli A915
Byers, Eric P83
Byers, Bryan E1
Byers, Allison E105
Byerwalter, Mariann A363
Bygott, Stephen A882
Byington, Tony A447
Byington, Tony P247
Byington, Beth E290
Bykoned, Margo P537
Bykoriz, Vlad A658
Byl, John A552
Byl, John E275
Bylen, Hans Van W181
Bynoe, Linda A68
Bynum, Laura A713
Bynum, Rufus A850
Bynum, Shaun P119
Bynum, Cherlyn P244
Byrd, Stacy A181
Byrd, Joanie A267
Byrd, Laurie A334
Byrd, Daryl G. A449
Byrd, Jerry A649
Byrd, Brad A664
Byrd, Heath R. A766
Byrd, Danny A797
Byrd, Lu P84
Byrd, William D P265
Byrd, Jacqueline P423
Byrd, Jane P448
Byrd, Michael P489
Byrd, Mark P660
Byrd, Stacy E137
Byrd, Laurie E153
Byrd, Daryl G. E220
Byrd, Brad E334
Byrne, Alice A35
Byrne, Garvan A65
Byrne, Sara A267
Byrne, Mike A606
Byrne, Mike A658
Byrne, Timothy (Tim) A726
Byrne, Julie P55
Byrne, Jolene P92
Byrne, Barbara P192
Byrne, Bobbie P192
Byrne, Timothy (Tim) P453
Byrne, Jolene P474
Byrne, Richard J. P578
Byrne, Donal W93
Byrne, Peter E58
Byrne, Noel E106
Byrne, Penny E156
Byrnes, Timothy A115
Byrnes, Terry A160
Byrnes, Larry A254
Byrnes, James J. A838
Byrnes, James A839
Byrnes, Timothy E37
Byrns, Laurette P76
Byrns, James E132
Byrum, Stan A63
Byrwa, Joy A329
Bytner, Mark A465
Byunn, Jay A140
B-ote, Oliver W24
Buchele, Wolfgang W254
Bucker, Michael W62
Bédier, Jér-'me W88
Béharel, Fran-§ois W319
Bénacin, Philippe W416
Bézard, Yannick W305

C

C, Victoria P209
Caamano, John A177
Cab, Sandy A191
Cabalitasan, Carina A775
Cabalitasan, Carina P511

Caballero, Diana A160
Caban, John A835
Cabanas, Juan A575
Cabbil, Nathan A721
Cabezuela, Zaide P499
Cable, Carol A142
Cable, Carol E49
Cabrales, Steven X P152
Cabrera, Juan A925
Cabrera, Kayla P134
Cabrera, Juan P192
Cabrera, Maria P501
Cabrera, Alicia P530
Cabrera, Juan E445
Cabuso, Nita A606
Caccamo, Frank A680
Caccivio, James C. A783
Caceres, R. Louis (Lou) A741
Caceres, Lou A741
Caceres, Celia P668
Caceres, R. Louis (Lou) E364
Caceres, Lou E364
Cadavona, Karen A770
Caddell, Kari P396
Cadden, Mike A402
Cadden, Mike E198
Cade, Curtis A466
Cadena, Adrian E105
Cadieux, Marc C. A793
Cadieux, Melissa P190
Cadiz, Bruce J A140
Cadley, Carola P558
Cadlo, Mitch A774
Cadman, Justin A704
Cadoret, Francois A380
Cadwallader, Brian J A480
Cadwallader, Brian J P270
Cady, Gerald A. (Gary) A913
Cady, Gerald A. (Gary) E438
Cafferillo, Nick E362
Caffery, David A688
Caffrey, Robert A89
Cafiero, Luca A198
Cafiso, Giovanni A801
Caforio, Giovanni A151
Cage, Jeff A452
Cagle, Lorita A108
Cagle, Chris C A329
Cagle, Kevin A449
Cagle, Farris A569
Cagle, Dawn E73
Cagle, Kevin E221
Cagney, Katie A925
Cagney, Katie E445
Cahill, William A405
Cahill, Ann A485
Cahill, John T. A497
Cahill, Laura A877
Cahill, Thomas P128
Cahill, Sr Helen P209
Cahill, Eileen P242
Cahill, Ann P271
Cahill, Joseph P502
Cahill, Gerald R. (Gerry) W87
Cahill, Antony W270
Cahill, Brian E118
Cahillane, Steven A. (Steve) A487
Cahir, B.P. (Bart) W196
Cahlin, Jim A481
Cahlstadt, Timothy A530
Cahoj, Nicholas P48
Cahuzac, Antoine W148
Cai-Lee, Wendy A284
Cai-Lee, Wendy E120
Cain, Scott A218
Cain, Michael S A246
Cain, Debbie A323
Cain, James A727
Cain, Angela P104
Cain, Kelli P117
Cain, Jessica P198
Cain, James P453
Cain, Kristen P511
Cain, Matthew P628
Cain, Michael S E105

Caine, Patrice W390
Caines, Brett A523
Caiola, Vincent P285
Caires, Olivia A800
Cairns, Ann A544
Cairns, Gillian A205
Cairns, Chuck A727
Cairns, Chuck P453
Cairns, Gordon M. W426
Cairns, Kim E115
Cairo, Chris A194
Cajigas, Veronica A270
Cal, Bryant E132
Calabio, Travis A784
Calabrese, Kevin J A105
Calabrese, Vincent J. A357
Calabrese, Kevin J E34
Calabrese, Vincent J. E175
Calabretta, Chris A164
Calaman, Diane P170
Calandra, Ronald A925
Calandra, Ronald E445
Calantzopoulos, André A661
Calarco, Daniel P610
Calbert, Michael M. A272
Calbert, Robert (Bo) P318
Calbone, Kathie P254
Calcagni, Mark A442
Calcagno, Keith P35
Calcaterra, Ronald J P120
Calcote, Colby A852
Caldarelli, Brian P432
Caldart, Gilberto A544
Calder, Tracy A528
Calder, Jennifer P138
Calderon, Fabricio A203
Calderon, Larry P389
Calderon, Aurora T. W338
Calderon, Leonard E105
Calderone, Matthew A145
Calderone, Tina P588
Calderwood, Tom A84
Caldwell, John E. A14
Caldwell, William J. A432
Caldwell, Bill A432
Caldwell, Cathleen A449
Caldwell, Melody A452
Caldwell, Christopher A580
Caldwell, Angie L A602
Caldwell, Brandon A665
Caldwell, Christopher (Chris) A794
Caldwell, Michael R A798
Caldwell, Troy A831
Caldwell, Barry A905
Caldwell, Pete P244
Caldwell, Rose P422
Caldwell, Brian P451
Caldwell, Troy P601
Caldwell, Cathleen E220
Caldwell, Christopher E292
Caldwell, Brandon E334
Caldwell, David L. (Dave) A137
Calhoun, Matt A530
Calhoun, Chris A799
Calhoun, Shep A866
Calhoun, Erin A893
Calhoun, Mike P7
Calhoun, Jay P114
Calhoun, Bill P232
Calhoun, Jaci E264
Calhoun, Shep E418
Cali, Jim A487
Calisto, Jodi A761
Caliva, Jeffrey E250
Calkins, Steve A620
Call, Sherry A69
Call, Barbara A227
Call, Kevin P155
Call, Douglas P424
Call, Barbara E90
Callaghan, James P207
Callaghan, Lisa P637
Callagy, Catherine P368
Callahan, Timothy A19
Callahan, Michael A125

Callahan, Barbara A200
Callahan, Don A203
Callahan, Rebecca A222
Callahan, Daniel D. A224
Callahan, Michael A281
Callahan, Donald A391
Callahan, Tom A417
Callahan, Brian A452
Callahan, Brendan A481
Callahan, Brad A621
Callahan, Patrick K. (Pat) A681
Callahan, Matt A690
Callahan, David A747
Callahan, James A784
Callahan, Andrew P. (Andy) A855
Callahan, Eve A860
Callahan, Chris A902
Callahan, Emily P34
Callahan, Sean P117
Callahan, Mark P207
Callahan, Clara A. P603
Callahan, Brad E312
Callan, Edward A304
Callanan, Kim A405
Callanan, Kevin P647
Callander, David P118
Callari, Denise A877
Callaway, Antone A513
Callaway, Brenda P89
Callecod, David P284
Callen, Craig R. E314
Callender, Scott A332
Calles, Anna A646
Calles, Anna E324
Callicott, Bevan A170
Callier, Theodore A267
Callihan, Jane A866
Callihan, Jane E418
Callinicos, Sean A170
Callis, Gaynor P450
Callison, Steven A170
Callison, Tim P436
Callison, Marilyn P436
Callum, Sean A349
Callum, Moray A360
Callum, Michael G. P528
Calmes, Mark E A77
Calombo, Antonio A191
Caltabiano, Justin P479
Caltagirone, Francesco G. W35
Calvio, Sal P481
Calvo, Cesar P125
Calvo-sanchez, Tammi A713
Calzada, Pablo P433
Calzadilla, Irene A925
Calzadilla, Irene E445
Cama, Domenick A. A473
Cama, Domenick A. E236
Camarata, Pete A508
Camber, Susan A880
Camber, Susan P640
Cambridge, Derek P86
Camelio, Patricia E330
Camero, John A248
Camero, John E107
Cameron, Art A140
Cameron, Lee A352
Cameron, Stewart A355
Cameron, Richard A613
Cameron, Terry K A810
Cameron, James A910
Cameron, Jennifer P127
Cameron, Mark P220
Cameron, Donna P284
Cameron, Carol P486
Cameron, Terry K P546
Cameron, Michael A. W373
Camilleri, Peter A205
Camilleri, Louis C. A661
Cammaker, Shelly A292
Cammarano, Terri Wagner P118
Cammarata, Marie A782
Cammarata, Marie P526
Cammaroto, Gerilyn A54
Cammer, Matt A213

Cammer, Matt P143
Cammisecra, Antonio W153
Cammorata, Andrew A784
Camoscio, Catalina A686
Camp, James A22
Camp, Elizabeth A380
Camp, James P11
Camp, Anne Van P497
Camp, David P525
Campagna, Peter A575
Campana, Mark A522
Campanella, Edward J. A82
Campanella, Jeanne P553
Campanello, Russell J. (Russ) E239
Campany, Daniel A409
Campbell, Jeffrey C. (Jeff) A53
Campbell, Scott A58
Campbell, Michael P. A88
Campbell, Mary A142
Campbell, Scott A160
Campbell, Joanne T. A162
Campbell, Linda A196
Campbell, Craig A205
Campbell, Roger A. A241
Campbell, Mario A248
Campbell, Ryan D A260
Campbell, Michael A262
Campbell, Bruce L. A270
Campbell, Nell A319
Campbell, Kevin A325
Campbell, Tabitha A325
Campbell, Jimmy A402
Campbell, Kristin A. A423
Campbell, Ann-Marie A428
Campbell, Patrick D A477
Campbell, Claude A520
Campbell, Carla A532
Campbell, Patricia A538
Campbell, Kerrie A576
Campbell, Robert A592
Campbell, Kristin A620
Campbell, Alan A628
Campbell, Amy A665
Campbell, Marion A686
Campbell, John P A727
Campbell, Todd A765
Campbell, Andrew A816
Campbell, Melanie A835
Campbell, Bonnie A839
Campbell, Mitchell A852
Campbell, Sean A880
Campbell, Karen A890
Campbell, Travis A891
Campbell, Steven A914
Campbell, Douglas A925
Campbell, Kevin P13
Campbell, Sabrina V P32
Campbell, Anna P32
Campbell, Lori P48
Campbell, Cynthia P54
Campbell, Rocky P104
Campbell, Danny P108
Campbell, Ryan P115
Campbell, Cynthia P162
Campbell, Patrick D P263
Campbell, Andrina P296
Campbell, Krista P306
Campbell, Barbara P312
Campbell, Shane P315
Campbell, Bobby P319
Campbell, Jane P347
Campbell, Graham P356
Campbell, Robert P370
Campbell, Geoff P387
Campbell, Bob P417
Campbell, Joe P432
Campbell, Kimberly P436
Campbell, John P P453
Campbell, Margaret H P513
Campbell, Carol P549
Campbell, Juan P588
Campbell, Ballard C P610
Campbell, Sean P640
Campbell, Marianne P659
Campbell, Norie C. W396

Campbell, R. Perry E18
Campbell, Mary E49
Campbell, Joanne T. E62
Campbell, Kathleen M. E80
Campbell, Mario E107
Campbell, Bruce A. E180
Campbell, Jimmy E198
Campbell, Laura E219
Campbell, Albert M. (Al) E282
Campbell, Amy E334
Campbell, Lisa F. E368
Campbell, Patricia A. (Pat) E424
Campbell, Douglas E445
Campese, Mike P197
Campion, Andrew A599
Campion, Heather E305
Campione, Bob A807
Campisi, David J. (Dave) A132
Campisi, Anthony A356
Campisi, Vince A875
Camplwell, Jeff P261
Campo, Carlos A922
Campobasso, Deb P250
Campos, Melisza P454
Campos, Sergio L. W80
Campot, Peter P531
Campriani-square, Cathleen A737
Campriani-square, Cathleen E361
Camps, Josep Pique i W17
Camunez, Michael A290
Camus, Julie A894
Camus, Julie P651
Can, Alp A781
Can, Hakan A828
Can, Charles Mc P263
Can, Hakan P584
Canaday, Charles T. E16
Canafax, Daniel M. E230
Canal, Judy P135
Canale, Anthony E429
Canales, Art E105
Canavan, John A191
Canavan, Pat A851
Canavan, Dana E53
Canavera, Glen P356
Canavesio, Mark A704
Canazaro, Chris A793
Cancelloni, Frank A692
Cancelmi, Daniel J. (Dan) A811
Cancila, Peter A161
Cancino, Diane P138
Candelario, Larry A115
Candelario, Larry E38
Canden, Hugh P197
Cane, Michael A158
Caneer, Mary E100
Canekeratne, Kris A. E431
Canel, Brad A230
Canel, Brad P154
Canestrari, Ken A835
Cangemi, Thomas R. (Tom) A589
Cangey, Karen A676
Cangey, Karen E338
Canipe, Rick A850
Canizares, Isabel P617
Cankat, Burc A218
Cann, Ryan P94
Cannaday, Billy K. P442
Cannady, Ed P46
Cannan, Rich A326
Cannariato, Lawrence A167
Cannata, Sebastian A115
Cannata, Sebastian E38
Cannatelli, Len A831
Cannatelli, Brian A933
Cannatelli, Len P601
Cannavo, Ann A52
Cannell, Robert P677
Cannella, Carol P502
Cannestra, Paul E184
Canney, Jacqueline P. (Jacqui) A901
Cannici, Joe P336
Canning, David A871
Canning, Daniel A915
Canning, John J P5

Canning, John P5
Canning, Lori P476
Cannizzo, Lauren A740
Cannizzo, Mike P529
Cannon, Marc A94
Cannon, Ed A135
Cannon, Jessie A170
Cannon, Maria A199
Cannon, Darren A312
Cannon, John A364
Cannon, Eric A409
Cannon, Don A451
Cannon, Eric A462
Cannon, Alexander (Alex) A692
Cannon, Stacy A769
Cannon, Tim A799
Cannon, Nick A925
Cannon, Marivette P117
Cannon, Peter P173
Cannon, Darren P199
Cannon, Don P249
Cannon, Eric P256
Cannon, Maryann L P330
Cannon, Courtney P558
Cannon, Michael R. P600
Cannon, Chris P637
Cannon, Janis E80
Cannon, Stacy E380
Cannon, Jaime J. E400
Cannon, Nick E445
Cano, Lorraine P246
Canose, Jeffrey L. P551
Cantalejo, Pedro José Moreno W46
Cantarell, Luis W276
Cantera, Jose Garcia W48
Cantillon, Tom A746
Cantillon, Maria A783
Canton, Elaine A651
Canton, Elaine E330
Cantone, Fabienne Freymond W55
Cantor, Nancy A462
Cantor, Nancy P256
Cantor, Ilene P508
Cantor, David P664
Cantow, Don P326
Cantrell, Stephen A75
Cantrell, Gary L. A475
Cantrell, James M. A567
Cantrell, Jane P235
Cantrell, Bruce P430
Cantrell, David P559
Cantrell, James M. E283
Cantres, Wanda A354
Cantu, Dave A171
Cantu, Ernesto Torres A203
Cantu, Mary A414
Cantu, Raul A818
Cantu, Becky P151
Cantu, Mary P236
Cantu, Martha P511
Cantu, Alejandro Ramirez W91
Cantu, Raul E403
Cantuniar, Niculae W324
Cantus, Charles P74
Cantwell, Richard A199
Cantwell, Robert C. (Bob) E33
Cantwell, John E429
Canty, Kristi P327
Canup, Steven C. (Steve) A104
Canup, Ed A165
Canup, Steven A431
Canup, Steven E216
Canuso, Dominic A929
Canuso, Dominic E449
Canzoneri, Mike A119
Cao, Tuqiang A198
Cao, Thinh P227
Cao, Peixi W190
Caoagas, Rachelle A711
Caoagas, Rachelle P444
Caparros, Alain W322
Capatides, Michael G. W85
Capek, John M. A5
Capek, Thomas A240
Capek, Glen P200

COMBINED HOOVER'S HANDBOOK INDEX OF EXECUTIVES

```
A = AMERICAN BUSINESS
E = EMERGING COMPANIES
P = PRIVATE COMPANIES
W = WORLD BUSINESS
```

Capel, Burt A285
Capell, Peter J A376
Capellas, Michael D. W164
Capello, Jeffrey D. (Jeff) A133
Capener, John P538
Capers, Jacquelyn A108
Capetillo, Carlos A222
Capitulo, Andrew A137
Capizzi, Steve A112
Caplan, Craig A358
Caplan, Deborah H. A597
Caplan, Michael S. P386
Caplan, Craig E176
Caplin, Barry A311
Caplin, Barry P199
Caplovitz, Michael E218
Capobianco, Marie-Claire W71
Capodici, Lisa A170
Capolarello, Debra A559
Capone, Jeff A428
Caporella, Joseph G. (Joe) E295
Caporella, Nick A. E295
Capossela, Christopher C A565
Capote, David A184
Capots, Larry A524
Capozzola, Peter A82
Capozzoli, Robert A684
Capparelli, Robert A137
Cappello, Joseph A64
Cappello, Allison A701
Capper, Joseph H. (Joe) E46
Capps, Allen C P22
Capps, Brant P66
Capps, Richard P430
Capra, Kelly E353
Capriotti, Chris A818
Capriotti, Chris E403
Capron, Christopher P55
Capuano, Linda A A533
Capuano, Anthony G. (Tony) A537
Capuano, Terry P289
Caputo, Marco A146
Caputo, Melissa A224
Caputo, Lisa M. A844
Caputo, Anthony M P40
Caputo, Mark P243
Caputo, Michael J. P575
Caputo, Michael P. (Mike) P600
Capuzzo, Maria Paula A218
Cara, Jose A658
Caraballo, Barbara A452
Caraccio, Vito A331
Caraccio, Don P353
Caraccio, Vito E152
Carafello, Gregory A349
Caragher, Nick A934
Caram, Meredith A89
Caranfa, John A844
Carano, Carl A409
Carapella, Victor A346
Carapella, Victor E167
Carapezzi, William A658
Caras, Chris A175
Caravati, Martin P639
Caraway, Troy P258
Carbajal, José Antonio Fernandez W164
Carbajal, Gabino Miguel G--mez W175
Carballo, Tyson A115
Carballo, Tyson E37
Carberry, Ellen P570
Carberry, Jeff E386
Carbo, Angelique A751
Carbone, A A375
Carbone, Michael P A478
Carbone, A P215
Carbone, Raymond (Ray) P315
Carbone, Philip E6
Carbone, Egidio E59

Carbonell, Nelson A. P569
Carcache, Sonia A812
Carchedi, Francis (Frank) E99
Cardamone, Susan P368
Cardeli-Arroyo, Barbara A592
Cardeli-Arroyo, Barbara P370
Cardello, Margherita A722
Cardenas, Ricardo (Rick) A255
Cardenas, Javier A266
Cardenas, Alberto de A543
Cardenas, Christopher A674
Cardenas, Javier P182
Cardenas, Diana P433
Cardenas, Mitzi P607
Carder, Bryce A117
Carder, Bryce P61
Carder, Jennifer P356
Cardillo, James A636
Cardinal, Tim A682
Cardinal, Tony P511
Cardinali, Sergio P389
Cardona, Jairo A115
Cardona, Jairo E38
Cardoso, Joe A544
Cardoso, Carlos A778
Cardoza, Fernando P673
Caret, Leanne G. A140
Caret, Robert L. P631
Carew, Thomas J. A592
Carew, Patrick J. P267
Carew, Thomas J. P370
Carey, Karen E A232
Carey, K Kristann A237
Carey, Bridget A262
Carey, Susan A324
Carey, Brian A408
Carey, Matthew A. (Matt) A428
Carey, Matt A428
Carey, Albert A428
Carey, Sean A587
Carey, Thomas A626
Carey, Albert P. (Al) A654
Carey, Liz A702
Carey, Anthony A783
Carey, David R A800
Carey, Pat A894
Carey, Russell C. P101
Carey, Ann P523
Carey, Mark P615
Carey, Pat P651
Carey, James H. E7
Carfora, Jeffrey J. A646
Carfora, Jeffrey J. E324
Cargan, Sonia A54
Cargile, Richard A258
Cargile, Charles F. (Chuck) P374
Cargill, Robyn A531
Cargill, C. Keith A818
Cargill, Sharon P15
Cargill, Jon P242
Cargill, C. Keith E403
Carhill, Norm A498
Cariello, Lou A880
Cariello, Lou P640
CARINCI, WILLIAM A391
Carl, David A87
Carl, Holowaty A715
Carl, David P50
Carlander, Magnus W420
Carle, Judy A266
Carle, Judy P182
Carle, Liz P399
Carleton, Mark D. A699
Carleton, Rob E80
Carley, John P158
Carli, Maurizio A897
Carlin, Arthur A414
Carlin, Arthur P236
Carling, Shelly A15
Carling, Timothy A409
Carling, Shelly P7
Carlino, Anthony P66
Carlisi, Rob P582
Carlisle, Heidi A19
Carlisle, Gordon A228

Carlisle, Lee A272
Carlisle, Peggy A323
Carlisle, Jennifer P45
Carlisle, Natalie P205
Carll, Thomas W. E28
Carlo, Anibal A151
Carlo, Francesca Di W153
Carlock, Craig E180
Carlos, Cisneros A36
Carlson, Dawn A7
Carlson, Jan A92
Carlson, Carl M. A152
Carlson, Chante A181
Carlson, W. Erik A271
Carlson, Brenda A335
Carlson, Ann A376
Carlson, Toni A437
Carlson, Chris A606
Carlson, J.D. A649
Carlson, LeRoy T. (Ted) A810
Carlson, Walter C. D. A810
Carlson, Chris A831
Carlson, Kevin A877
Carlson, Stephen A879
Carlson, Jennie P. A884
Carlson, Tom A925
Carlson, Lisa P5
Carlson, Kerry P29
Carlson, Edward P354
Carlson, Spencer P389
Carlson, Pamela J. P417
Carlson, Lori P457
Carlson, Lisa P472
Carlson, Carolyn P573
Carlson, Chris P601
Carlson, Kathleen P639
Carlson, Debra E16
Carlson, Carl M. E52
Carlson, Chante E70
Carlson, Bill E80
Carlson, Brenda E155
Carlson, Chris E342
Carlson, Tom E445
Carlsson, Magnus W356
Carlton, Brent A704
Carlton, Steve P625
Carlucci, Carl P. P629
Carmack, Timothy W P302
Carmack, Kelli P638
Carman, Amy A797
Carman, Stephen E154
Carmean, Lisa P148
Carmichael, Brendan A224
Carmichael, Greg D. A329
Carmichael, Cyndi A758
Carmichael, Amanda A933
Carmichael, Cyndi E372
Carmicheal, Samuel P52
Carmin, Cheryl P581
Carminati, Catherine A63
Carmines, Sheila A167
Carmody, Glenn A170
Carmody, Christine M. (Chris) A303
Carmody, Kevin A390
Carmody, Cora L. A476
Carmouche, Sue P264
Carnaghi, Jill P465
Carnathan, Kevin A713
Carnegie-Brown, Bruce N. W48
Carneiro, Marcia A108
Carnes, Kenneth P367
Carney, James A203
Carney, Craig B. A847
Carney, Mary Ellen A884
Carney, Rita D A902
Carney, Patricia P406
Carney, Suzanne M. E305
Carney, Craig B. E410
Carnifax, Rod A641
Carnifax, Rod P407
Carnwath, Alison A636
Caro, Jennifer A654
Caro, Jodi J A858
Caro, Jaime P478
Carol, Vanslyke A69

Carol, Canington A165
Carol, Annalise A626
Carol, Amanda P672
Carolan, Edward L. (Ed) A164
Carolan, Milou A608
Carolan, Susan P175
Carole, Hackett P604
Carollo, Gail A409
Carollo, Chris P235
Caron, Taylor A747
Caron, James A793
Caron, William L. P306
Caronia, Leonard S. A759
Caronia, Leonard S. E373
Carosi, Nicholas P253
Carotenuto, Michael A162
Carotenuto, Michael E61
Carp, Jeffrey N. A783
Carp, Marilyn A841
Carp, Marilyn E408
Carpenito, Jane E402
Carpenter, Wesley A89
Carpenter, William A109
Carpenter, Kaye A247
Carpenter, Angie A497
Carpenter, Curtis A550
Carpenter, James J. A589
Carpenter, Bruce A613
Carpenter, Harold R. A664
Carpenter, Jonathan A750
Carpenter, Christopher A752
Carpenter, Lonny J. A789
Carpenter, Duane A806
Carpenter, Nancy A835
Carpenter, Scott A850
Carpenter, Benjamin A885
Carpenter, Andrew A895
Carpenter, Angie M P162
Carpenter, Guy P198
Carpenter, Curtis P319
Carpenter, Stan P551
Carpenter, Vinay E22
Carpenter, Kaye E105
Carpenter, Melanie E282
Carpenter, Harold R. E333
Carpenter, Duane E399
Carper, Patricia A831
Carper, Howell P. (Hal) A855
Carper, Patricia P601
Carpino, Patti P272
Carpinone, Jean A357
Carpinone, Jean E176
Carr, John A32
Carr, Muneera S. A222
Carr, Ian A309
Carr, Dennis A355
Carr, Bryan A440
Carr, Chris A779
Carr, Ronald A796
Carr, Judy A839
Carr, Dan A844
Carr, Carolyn P131
Carr, Nora K P225
Carr, Robert O P234
Carr, Jim P235
Carr, Aileen P489
Carr, Concetta M P638
Carr, Frances P639
Carr, Roger W42
Carr, Jeff W223
Carr, Jeff E80
Carr, Ronald E397
Carrasco, Jorge P560
Carrasquillo, Jose A742
Carraway, Gary A871
Carre, Eric A401
Carrel, Edson A556
Carrel, Edson P328
Carrelli, Donna A56
Carrero, Franklin A167
Carretta, Robert P346
Carrico, Lucy A363
Carrico, Stephen J. (Steve) P238
Carrier, Brian A871
Carrier, Patrick B P133

Carrig, John A A233
Carrigan, Lee P394
Carrigg, Terri P75
Carrillo, Julian A189
Carrillo, Sue A715
Carrillo, Alicia P620
Carrillo, David E72
Carrillo, Louis E185
Carrington, Ron P425
Carri--n, Richard L. A670
Carroll, Frank A9
Carroll, David A54
Carroll, Leo A127
Carroll, George A147
Carroll, Michael A152
Carroll, Milton A180
Carroll, Barry A222
Carroll, William A262
Carroll, Thomas M. A276
Carroll, Elizabeth A356
Carroll, Kirta A359
Carroll, Kevin A399
Carroll, Christopher F. A468
Carroll, Pamela A479
Carroll, Jay A543
Carroll, John A. A556
Carroll, Glenn A646
Carroll, Rhonda L. A682
Carroll, Matthew A700
Carroll, Johnnie A884
Carroll, Scott A902
Carroll, Frank P4
Carroll, Mary Beth P15
Carroll, Mark P23
Carroll, Karana P93
Carroll, Michael P98
Carroll, Allen P111
Carroll, Kevin P146
Carroll, Kevin P223
Carroll, Andrew W P227
Carroll, Lorraine P304
Carroll, Mary P336
Carroll, Amy P481
Carroll, Christopher P503
Carroll, Clayton P508
Carroll, Kathleen P555
Carroll, Jeff P558
Carroll, Shannon P677
Carroll, Robert E218
Carroll, John A. E277
Carroll, Glenn E324
Carrubba, Carmelo A635
Carrubba, Jared A717
Carrubba, Jared E351
Carruth, Mary A519
Carruth, Linsley A800
Carruth, Janet P546
Carruthers, Susan A246
Carruthers, Scott P12
Carruthers, Susan E105
Carson, Candace F A375
Carson, Shaun A415
Carson, Brian M. A569
Carson, John C. A704
Carson, Candace F P215
Carson, Lorenzo P417
Carson, Dawn P429
Carson, Steven P546
Carson, Shaun E209
Carswell, Demario A530
Carter, Scott A1
Carter, David A6
Carter, Cyndi A170
Carter, Van C A246
Carter, Peter W. A262
Carter, Allan A262
Carter, John A320
Carter, Robert B. (Rob) A323
Carter, Racheal A341
Carter, Susan A381
Carter, Ian R. A423
Carter, Cindy A552
Carter, Anita A571
Carter, Charles J. (Jack) A637
Carter, Todd A664

Carter, Chrystah A668
Carter, Jimmy A692
Carter, Joann A695
Carter, Mary Randolph A702
Carter, Andrea A702
Carter, Ron A746
Carter, Mark A770
Carter, Tim A772
Carter, J Braxton A800
Carter, Lugeion Y A827
Carter, Benjamin A847
Carter, Steven A871
Carter, Dave A875
Carter, Marcedes A929
Carter, Mitzi P122
Carter, Angela P161
Carter, Jan P186
Carter, Paul P193
Carter, Anthony P P206
Carter, Jonathan P244
Carter, Donald E P276
Carter, Don P276
Carter, Gregory P473
Carter, Lonnie N. P501
Carter, Elizabeth P541
Carter, Richard P560
Carter, Lennie P570
Carter, Lugeion Y P580
Carter, Benjamin P606
Carter, Julien P611
Carter, Lauren P626
Carter, Glenn P627
Carter, Lisa P641
Carter, Bob W400
Carter, Scott E1
Carter, Van C E105
Carter, Cindy E276
Carter, Melanie E282
Carter, Kelly C E282
Carter, George P. E330
Carter, Todd E334
Carter, Tim E382
Carter, Cheryl C. E396
Carter, Marcedes E449
Carter-miller, Jocelyn A469
Carter-Robertson, Kira P508
Carthew, Geoffrey P356
Cartier, Guillaume W260
Cartmell, By E433
Carton, Maeve W122
Cartwright, Charlie A456
Cartwright, Charlie E228
Carty, Brian P528
Carucci, Richard A891
Caruselle, Nicholas P527
Caruso, Robert A125
Caruso, Dominic J. A479
Caruso, Christopher R. A673
Caruso, Kelly A804
Caruso, Candice A929
Caruso, Michael P497
Caruso, Michael E265
Caruso, Candice E449
Caruthers, Judy A482
Carvajal, Taylor A137
Carvajal, Maria Elisa A218
Carvajal, Oscar Von Chrismar W46
Carvalho, Fabiana Pires A942
Carvalho, Luiz Nelson Guedes de W303
Carvallo, Jorge P114
Carvelli, Joe P549
Carver, William A442
Carver, Bill A442
Carver, Carla E A672
Carver, Carla A672
Carver, Deb P677
Carver, Cathryn W270
Carveth, Reggie A837
Carveth, Barbara P626
Carwein, Vicky L. P610
Carwell, Mark P155
Cary, Glen A125
Cary, Clay A246
Cary, Bill A364
Cary, Curtis P228

Cary, Mark P232
Cary, John P508
Cary, Clay E105
Caryn, Wilson A642
Caryn, Wilson P407
Casa, Federico A740
Casaccio, Tenee A82
Casale, Mike A715
Casale, Thomas P638
Casale, Debbie E433
Casalegno, Gina P114
Casalino, Denise A16
Casanova, Pascal W230
Casati, Gianfranco W5
Casazza, Louise A540
Casazza, Rich P304
Casbon, Scott A345
Casbon, Scott E166
Cascino, Laura A262
Cascio, Michael A451
Cascio, Michael P249
Case, Kendra A179
Case, Melissa A219
Case, David A330
Case, Rob A479
Case, Gary A621
Case, Ken A885
Case, Melissa E87
Case, David E152
Case, Gary E311
Case, John P. E347
Casella, John W. E68
Caselli, Mike A313
Caselli, Mike E144
Cases, Juan Santamaria W6
Cases-villablanca, Jesse P639
Casey, Donald M. (Don) A169
Casey, David A251
Casey, John P. A373
Casey, Ryan A608
Casey, Donald J. (Don) A708
Casey, Katie A747
Casey, William J. A847
Casey, Margaret P74
Casey, Lois P107
Casey, Joseph M. (Joe) P503
Casey, Donna P505
Casey, Margaret P670
Casey, William J. E410
Cash, Ryan A167
Cash, W. Larry A228
Cash, Larry A228
Cash, Linda A360
Cash, Karen A760
Cash, Kriner P103
Cash, Jordan P254
Cash, Karen E374
Cashaw, Brad A259
Cashen, Dennis A695
Cashen, Karen A746
Cashill, Robert M. A473
Cashill, Robert M. E236
Cashin, Amanda E8
Cashion, Tana A263
Cashman, George D. A200
Cashman, Ed A704
Cashman, James E. (Jim) E22
Cashman, Charles A. (Chuck) E269
Casimiro, Michael A559
Casini, Victor A524
Casino, Alfred A444
Caslin, Cindy A369
Casner, Matt A325
Cason, Randall A935
Caspar, Christoph A199
Casparino, Michael J. A651
Casparino, Michael J. E329
Casper, Ben A481
Casper, Marc N. A832
Casper, Steve E174
Caspero, Mark A850
Casperson, Finn M.W. A646
Casperson, Finn E324
Cassandra, Frank A559
Cassano, Richard A25

Cassano, Richard P14
Casseb, George A229
Cassel, Paul A323
Cassel, Kari P489
Cassel, Mat-as Domeyko W149
Cassella, Renee A481
Casselman, Richard A651
Casselman, Richard E330
Cassels, Scott L A492
Cassels, Scott L P279
Cassels, Scott L P280
Cassels, Bill P594
Casser, Ann A390
Cassidy, Shawn A325
Cassidy, Donathan A665
Cassidy, Doug A772
Cassidy, Philip A795
Cassidy, Rick W380
Cassidy, Donathan E334
Cassidy, Doug E383
Cassin, Joe A905
Casson, Justin P555
Cast, Mike A168
Cast, Carter A487
Cast, William R. P610
Castagna, Eugene A. (Gene) A125
Castaneda, Amanda A621
Castaneda, Hugo P133
Castaneda, Carla A P550
Castaneda, Amanda E311
Castanon, Adrian A713
Castanon, Paul A811
Casteel, Beth A323
Casteel, Marty D. A760
Casteel, Aaron A761
Casteel, Marty D. E374
Castellano, Christen A117
Castellano, Gail A590
Castellano, Christen P61
Castellano, Jerry P400
Castellano, Donna E131
Castellanos, Lydia P450
Castelloni, Kendra L A925
Castelloni, Kendra L E445
Castell--, Juan L. Pier A527
Casten, Peter G P564
Castiello, John A700
Castille, Philip P629
Castillo, Eloise A418
Castillo, Claudia A484
Castillo, Narges A835
Castillo, Christine P66
Castillo, Juan E185
Castle, Michael A115
Castle, Don P415
Castle, Scott P524
Castle, Michael E38
Castleberry, Chris A882
Castman, Rich A112
Castoral, Roger A135
Castrejana, Josie P297
Castrejon, Eugene A449
Castrejon, Eugene E220
Castro, Sylvia A205
Castro, Anselmo A463
Castro, Michael A746
Castro, Lorraine A879
Castro, Marie A888
Castro, Chris A893
Castro, Craig S. P153
Castro, Ricardo P257
Castro, Mercedes P570
Castro, Christopher E84
Castro, Marie E425
Castrucci, Pamela A882
Casula, Roberto W155
Caswell, Angie A479
Caswell, Lee A897
Caswell, Jim P276
Catalano, Jamie A204
Catalano, Anna A425
Catalano, Mark J. A928
Catalano, Anna P282
Catalano, Robert P514
Catalano, Mark J. P674

COMBINED HOOVER'S HANDBOOK INDEX OF EXECUTIVES

```
A = AMERICAN BUSINESS
E = EMERGING COMPANIES
P = PRIVATE COMPANIES
W = WORLD BUSINESS
```

Cataldo, Bob A867
Catalfo, R O A452
Catalona, William P388
Catanzariti, Joe A512
Catapano, Richard A158
Catapano, Michael A850
Cataudella, Mary P304
Cate, Brett E412
Catedral, Manuel A544
Cater, Kevin A696
Cates, Rebecca A161
Cates, Mark A484
Cates, Ron A564
Cates, Brandon A750
Cathcart, David A804
Catherine, Annis A16
Cathey, James A695
Cathey, Marcus E64
Catino, David A410
Catlender, Katie P27
Catlett, Jack A91
Catlett, Sheri A859
Catlett, Jack E29
Catlett, Celia P. E404
Catlin, Ray P194
Cato, Dawn A203
Catoir, Christophe W7
Caton, Jay A742
Catran, Ricardo Isaac W405
Catsicas, Stefan W276
Catt, Michael A494
Cattaneo, Flavio W385
Cattin, James P190
Catton, Mark W333
Catts, Michael E138
Catz, Safra A A632
Cauce, Ana Mari A880
Cauce, Ana Mari P640
Caudell, Scott A461
Caudell, Scott P255
Caudill, Jay A132
Caudill, Larry A398
Caudullo, Al A704
Caufield, Margret E433
Caughey, Andrew P235
Caughman, S Wright P194
Cauley, Robert E. A632
Causey, Robert A381
Cauthon, Denise E148
Cava, Anthony V. P454
Cavagnaro, Charles E. P73
Cavaleri, Greg E190
Cavaliere, Joseph W. A593
Cavaliere, Carl A845
Cavalini, Renato W80
Cavalla, Stanley J. E418
Cavallaro, Joe A254
Cavallaro, Anthony P202
Cavallaro, Richard P496
CAVALLETTI, BELLINI LETIZIA W410
Cavallo, Lucy A893
Cavallo-Miller, Linda P515
Cavallucci, Eugene A501
Cavanagh, Lisa A125
Cavanagh, Michael J A220
Cavanah, Michael P534
Cavanaugh, Kathleen A167
Cavanaugh, David A651
Cavanaugh, Steven M. P596
Cavanaugh, Kevin P648
Cavanaugh, Steve E293
Cavanaugh, David E329
Cavaness, Joel D. A369
Cavazos, Raul A442
Cavazos, Jacob E106
Cave, Michael A103
Cave, Michael J. (Mike) A407
Cave, George H. (Sonny) A627
Cave, Steven A723

Cavender, Jack A206
Caveney, John E. (Jack) P404
Cavicchioli, Kathleen (Kathy) A749
Cavicchioli, Kathleen (Kathy) E367
Cawley, Timothy P. A235
Cawley, Christopher A526
Cawley, Patrick J. P575
Cawthon, Wendy A866
Cawthon, Wendy E417
Caylor, Mark A. A608
Cayson, Patrick A713
Cazar, Jorge L. W106
Cazares, Sara L P530
Cazenave, Bruce M. E299
Cazer, David A140
Cbet, John P394
Cbet, Fred A P459
Ccim, Jennifer A62
Ccim, Jennifer E20
Cctc, Jennifer P302
Cecalek, Karen E106
Cecava, Eric P5
Cecchi, Joseph L. P634
Ceccio, Cathy P15
Cecere, Andrew A884
Cecil, Coleen A482
Cecilia, Ernest E A155
Cecilia, Manuel Manrique W321
Cecilia, Ernest E E54
Cecoltan, Sergiu A544
Cederholm, Wayne P104
Cefalo, Richard A609
Cefalu, Anthony A379
Cefalu, Kathy A810
Ceiley, Glen F. E116
Celestin, Angela A629
Celi, Ivo E88
Cella, Peter L A191
Cella, Peter L P126
Cellar, Kurt E422
Cellard, Vincent A100
Cellini, Chris A767
Cellucci, Annemarie P304
Ceman, Jamie P123
Cemper, Ctibor E101
Centeno, Betsy P229
Centore, Susan P539
Centrella, Marc E353
Centrone, Anthony P66
Cepeda, Claudia A142
Cepeda, Claudia E49
Ceragioli, Teresa P606
Ceraolo, Brian P228
Cerbone, Dominick E77
Cercone, Cindy A835
Cercone, Gemma P56
Cerda, Christian E239
Cerepak, Brad M. A277
Cerifko, Susan E83
Cerio, Shelly A613
Cerio, Sigrid P110
Cerise, Frederick P. (Fred) P171
Cerna, Hector J. A463
Cerniglia, Gregg A327
Cerniglia, Linda P300
Cernugel, Carol A538
Cerny, Amy A15
Cerny, Amy P7
Cerone, Luciano A374
Cerqueira, Rosemary P616
Ceruti, Anne A97
Cervini, August P558
Cervini, Gus P558
Cervone, Antonio A378
Cesario, Jeff E207
Cesarz, Mike A549
Ceschia, Piero A262
Cesere, Marc A806
Cesere, Marc E399
Cesheshyan, Emelina P257
Cevis, Eric A890
Cezar, Gamez P537
Cfa, David Ellwood A909
Cfa, David Ellwood E436
Cha, Sam Ho P248

Cha, Elaine P591
Chabal, Grace P594
Chabino, Doug P303
Chabot, René W193
Chack, Dennis M. A350
Chacon, Ernest A846
Chaconas, Ed A108
Chac--n, Chanda Cashen P548
Chac--n, a W26
Chadbourne, Christopher A877
Chadbourne, Elizabeth P312
Chadderton, Megan A137
Chadderton, Cheryl P409
Chaderton, Sean A115
Chaderton, Sean E38
Chadha, Sanjeev A654
Chadwich, Jerry P225
Chadwick, Edward G. (Ed) A414
Chadwick, David T A676
Chadwick, Norman A688
Chadwick, Edward G. (Ed) P236
Chae, Michael S. A137
Chaffin, Paul B. A289
Chaffin, Patrick A736
Chaffin, Patrick P460
Chaffinch, Randy A678
Chaffins, Randall A245
Chaganti, Nitika A915
Chagnon, Michael L. A509
Chahin, Jaime P551
Chai, David A198
Chai, Dan E102
Chaiken, Rochelle A658
Chaiko, Warren P230
Chaimengyew, David A418
Chaisson, Mary P162
Chajkowski, David E318
Chakraborty, Prabal A149
Chakravarthy, Anita A925
Chakravarthy, Anita E445
Chalamalasetti, Rajesh A677
Chalanick, Brett A137
Chalkan, Lisa A646
Chalkan, Lisa E324
Chalke, Dennis W. P73
Challon-Kemoun, Adeline W15
Chalons-Browne, Roland W. W353
Chaloux, Debra A882
Chaltraw, William P646
Chalut, Sylvain W50
Chambas, Corey A. E155
Chamberlain, John W. A48
Chamberlain, Charles A844
Chambers, Margaret W. (Megan) A147
Chambers, Boyd J A312
Chambers, Connor A444
Chambers, Adrienne A544
Chambers, Bradley S. A551
Chambers, Brian D. A635
Chambers, Susan A902
Chambers, Elizabeth G. (Libby) A915
Chambers, H D P22
Chambers, Boyd J P199
Chambers, Bradley S. P321
Chambers, Richard P397
Chambers, Larry P456
Chambers, Yohna P549
Chambers, Norman P597
Chambers, Vanessa P646
Chambers, Stuart W29
Chambers, Candice E450
Chamblin, James A736
Chamblin, James P460
Chamoun, George E396
Champ, Matt A170
Champion, Stephen A750
Champion, Traylor A918
Champion, Bret A P281
Champion, Bret A P286
Champion, Natalie P623
Champlin, James P417
Chan, Arvan A179
Chan, Alex A193
Chan, Owen A198
Chan, Donna A203

Chan, Quay A258
Chan, May A349
Chan, Stephen A390
Chan, Simon A460
Chan, Alice A480
Chan, Jenny A484
Chan, Garrett A512
Chan, Katherine A609
Chan, Ava A725
Chan, Kenyon S. A880
Chan, Kurt A914
Chan, Katherine P391
Chan, Margaret P486
Chan, Jake P517
Chan, Aubrey C P629
Chan, Kenyon S. P640
Chan, Eric W208
Chanana, Mohit A191
Chanana, Mohit P126
Chance, Diane A498
Chance, Kenneth B. P116
Chance, Linda P212
Chancellor, James P264
Chand, Sujeet A729
Chandel, Nitin A896
Chandler, David A121
Chandler, John A206
Chandler, Jimmy A340
Chandler, Roger A460
Chandler, Amber A520
Chandler, Willy A569
Chandler, Don A793
Chandler, Laura A906
Chandler, Catherine A922
Chandler, Mark P35
Chandler, Austin P55
Chandler, Carla P343
Chandler, Willis P616
Chandler, Timothy J.L. P642
Chandler, Catherine P671
Chandler, Jimmy E160
Chandler, Dan M. (Mac) E349
Chandler, Mac E349
Chandler, Richard E388
Chandler, Laura E435
Chandoha, Marie A. A746
Chandok, Vijay W194
Chandra, Sumeer A438
Chandra, Gautam P666
Chandrani, Mic A54
Chandrasekaran, Ramakrishnan A216
Chandrasekaran, Rajiv A779
Chandrasekaran, Suja A902
Chandrasekaran, Natarajan (Chandra) W383
Chandrasekaran, Natarajan (Chandra) W384
Chandrasekhar, Arun A460
Chandratre, Mandar P286
Chandrayana, Kartik A740
Chandwani, Manesh A200
Chanen, Daniel P342
Chaney, Glynn A502
Chaney, Laura P209
Chaney, William P. E346
Chang, Annabel A29
Chang, Shen A53
Chang, Mike A126
Chang, Daniel A137
Chang, Jennifer A137
Chang, Herman A182
Chang, Chris A255
Chang, Sam A575
Chang, Andrew S. A648
Chang, Sally A676
Chang, Judy A676
Chang, Eddie A694
Chang, Emily A780
Chang, Helen P225
Chang, Florence P352
Chang, Derek P480
Chang, James P540
Chang, Andrew P540
Chang, Jason C P585
Chang, Lay Nam P652

Chang, Fa-Te W89
Chang, In-Hwa W311
Chang, Morris W380
Chang, Pierce E7
Chang, Norman E22
Chang, Andrew S. E328
Chang, Sally E338
Chang, Judy E338
Changshun, Wang W103
Channawi, Omar A680
Channick, Colleen P615
Chant, Rick P546
Chanter, Keith A292
Chanthaphasouk, Thomas A692
Chao, Bo A518
Chao, Albert A917
Chao, James Y. A917
Chao, Jon P199
Chao, Gong W12
Chapa, Ram--n A. Leal W19
Chapa, Jaime G. Elizondo W91
Chapados, Gregory F P213
Chapanar, Marilyn A392
Chapin, Libby A329
Chapin, David A482
Chapin, Kurt A797
Chapin, Susan P511
Chapman, Ryan A137
Chapman, Robert A151
Chapman, Keith A232
Chapman, Steven M A247
Chapman, Rhonda A336
Chapman, Martin A449
Chapman, Kevin D. A717
Chapman, Chuck A752
Chapman, Esther A760
Chapman, Paul A826
Chapman, Ken A844
Chapman, Garrett A891
Chapman, Timothy M. A894
Chapman, Michele A935
Chapman, Janet P65
Chapman, Robert H. (Bob) P67
Chapman, Asa P174
Chapman, Archie J P320
Chapman, Carl L P505
Chapman, Catherine A P595
Chapman, Timothy M. P651
Chapman, Adrian P. P666
Chapman, Barbara W113
Chapman, David W193
Chapman, Rhonda E157
Chapman, Martin E221
Chapman, Kevin D. E351
Chapman, Esther E374
Chapman, James E433
Chapman, Ryan E433
Chapp, Cori A839
Chappel, Myguail P176
Chappell, Daniel G. (Dan) A749
Chappell, Dan A749
Chappell, Robert W. E81
Chappell, Brent P. E261
Chappell, Daniel G. (Dan) E367
Chappell, Dan E367
Chappini, Tom P512
Char, Rashmi A695
Charalambous, Ioannis A. A618
Charalampidis, Damianos I. W25
Charalampidis, Damianos W272
Charboneau, Diane P315
Charboneau, Chris E433
Charbonneau, Tracy A409
Charbonneau, Ed A695
Charbonneau, Edward A695
Charbonneau, Brett P257
Chard, David P505
Chard, Daniel R. (Dan) E274
Charest, Laurie A205
Charest, Teri A884
Charest, Yvon W193
Charette, Scott P30
Charette, Gary C P40
Charette, Bill P300
Chargois, Trevor A533

Charity, Alicia A60
Charlat, Martin P479
Charlene, Brennan A719
Charlene, Brennan E355
Charles, Victor A19
Charles, Ronald A179
Charles, Anthony St A229
Charles, Robert A340
Charles, Audrey A505
Charles, Doug A509
Charles, R Lynn A525
Charles, Amy A665
Charles, Stephen P249
Charles, Steve P250
Charles, John P314
Charles, Robert E161
Charles, Doug E248
Charles, Amy E334
Charlet, Barbara A782
Charlet, Barbara P526
Charlotte, Hooks A36
Charlton, Mark A692
Charlton, R. Scott A797
Charlton, Scott A798
Charmatz, Jeff A112
Charnas, Robert A710
Charneski, Brian S. A415
Charneski, Brian S. E209
Charney, Eugene A540
Charney, Dennis P248
Charoenanusorn, Apiphan W352
Charon, Ben E138
Charos, Rae P519
Charreton, Didier W29
Charri, Ali A255
Charrier, Richard P672
Charsha, Dianne P563
Charton, Daryl A3
Charuchinda, Nuttachat W315
Charvat, Peter P519
Charvat, Peter P587
Charyna, Dan A719
Charyna, Dan E355
Chase, William A5
Chase, William J. A6
Chase, Amy A16
Chase, Jonathan A331
Chase, Wendy A520
Chase, P. Kevin A753
Chase, Linda P252
Chase, Libby E131
Chase, Brian E147
Chase, Jonathan E152
Chasney, Laura A799
Chasse, Floyd P228
Chastain, Megan A390
Chastain, Stephen A482
Chastain, Douglas A933
Chateauneuf, Rob E131
Chatfield, Jeff E222
Chatillon, Jean-Baptiste de W305
Chatman, Mary P474
Chatoian, Cathy E73
Chatry, Stephen P660
Chatterjee, Koushik W384
Chatterton, David A740
Chattopadhyay, Sanat A554
Chau, Celia A135
Chaubal, Prasad A484
Chaudhry, Jawad A473
Chaudhry, Jawad E236
Chauhan, Abhishek A262
Chauhan, Ranveer S. W294
Chaussade, Jean-Louis W154
Chaussade, Jean-Louis W366
Chausse, Jean W370
Chauvin, Robert F. (Bob) P269
Chauvin, Mark R. W396
Chavanne, Patrick B A507
Chavez, Joann A279
Chavez, R. Martin A390
Chavez, Mauricio A550
Chavez, Don A608
Chavez, Earl A709
Chavez, Eileen A828

Chavez, Cara P20
Chavez, Frank P410
Chavez, Earl P442
Chavez, Eileen P580
Chavez, Victor W390
Chavez, Pablo E7
Chavis, Eva A325
Chawla, Sona A496
Chawla, Vikas A574
Chawla, Subodh A654
Chawla, Ashish P672
Chazen, Stephen A289
Chazin, Steve A199
Chea, Jun A492
Chean, Kevin A559
Cheap, Richard A. A444
Chearavanont, Dhanin W83
Chearavanont, Dhanin W95
Cheatham, J. Douglas A623
Cheatham, Tim A902
Cheatham, Ollie P364
Cheatham, J. Douglas E312
Cheatman, Lora C P274
Cheatwood, Chris J. A666
Checketts, John A478
Checketts, Lannie P463
Checketts, Lannie P606
Checki, Terrence J. A319
Cheek, Bruce D. A52
Cheek, Bryan A713
Cheek, Sally P230
Cheema, Amy A702
Cheers, Lisa P175
Cheeseman, Michael A401
Cheesewright, David A901
Chegini, Ali P409
Chehrazi, Claire P405
Cheleden, Charles G. A929
Cheleden, Charles G. E449
Chelewski, Tom A449
Chelewski, Tom E220
Chelminiak, Lee A641
Chelminiak, Lee P407
Chelminski, Piotr W310
Chen, Lei A54
Chen, Donald A77
Chen, Alexander A120
Chen, Sophie A137
Chen, Kuohsin A137
Chen, Heng W. A174
Chen, Jennifer A203
Chen, Nia A285
Chen, Simone A559
Chen, David A641
Chen, Wellington A676
Chen, Eric A676
Chen, Roawen A695
Chen, Patgun A702
Chen, John A728
Chen, George A742
Chen, David A744
Chen, Ming A746
Chen, James A818
Chen, George A922
Chen, Linda A930
Chen, Heidi C. A941
Chen, Dan P82
Chen, Kenneth P111
Chen, Shiming P270
Chen, Chunguang P371
Chen, Jarvis P383
Chen, David P407
Chen, Solomon P534
Chen, Robert P534
Chen, Branndon P627
Chen, George P671
Chen, Grace W89
Chen, Tsu-Pei W89
Chen, Yusheng W97
Chen, James W123
Chen, Yong Jin W123
Chen, James Y.G. W123
Chen, Ching Chuan W123
Chen, Jida W434
Chen, Jie E7

Chen, Heng W. E68
Chen, C. H. E113
Chen, Nia E120
Chen, Wellington E338
Chen, Eric E338
Chen, Yang E429
Chenevert, Don P511
Cheney, Andrew B. (Andy) A62
Cheney, John A512
Cheney, Andrew B. (Andy) E19
Cheng, Laurence A65
Cheng, Johnny A284
Cheng, Al A285
Cheng, Andrew A385
Cheng, Henry A519
Cheng, Marn K. A579
Cheng, Marco P331
Cheng, Pam W38
Cheng, Jack T.K. W123
Cheng, Johnny E120
Cheng, Al E120
Cheng, Michael E143
Chenore, Elizabeth A345
Chenore, Elizabeth E166
Cheong, Hoe Wai P85
Cheong, Tony W173
Cheong, Wee Ee W411
Chepurnoy, Oleg W401
Cherecwich, Peter B. A605
Cherepanov, Vsevolod W308
Cherewko, Greg A922
Cherewko, Greg P671
Cherian, Kuruvilla A89
Chermak, Jerome P389
Cherner, Anatoly W169
Chernett, Kevin A522
Chernikoff, Roy A586
Chernikoff, Roy E301
Cheroux, Roch W366
Cherry, Kimberley C. (Kim) A343
Cherry, Pedro A382
Cherry, Don J. A386
Cherry, Craig A837
Cherry, Melody P507
Cherry, Kimberley C. (Kim) E163
Cherry, Don J. E188
Cherry, Karen E218
Chersky, Susan P92
Cherukuri, Ravikrishna A199
Chery, Sulexan A44
Chery, Sulexan E13
Chesbro, Derek P157
Cheshire, Brent A419
Cheshire, Ian W58
Chesler, Randall M. (Randy) A386
Chesler, Robert A470
Chesler, Randall M. (Randy) E188
Chesley, Bruce A140
Chesley, Yonnie A410
Chesley, Philip P446
Chesmar, Brett A881
Chesmar, Brett E421
Chesna, Peter A855
Chesney, Susan A726
Chesnut, Jeff A34
Chesnutt, Jim P399
Chess, Robert B. E300
Chessare, John B P213
Chester, Doris P541
Chester, Timothy M P628
Chestnutt, Roy H. A889
Cheung, Nina A112
Cheung, Annie A465
Cheung, Ann A676
Cheung, Ann J A676
Cheung, Sue A747
Cheung, Teresa P30
Cheung, Yan P30
Cheung, Keith P233
Cheung, Ava P534
Cheung, Ann E338
Cheung, Ann J E338
Chevalier, John T A680
Chevardi-`re, Patrick de La W398
Chevrette, John P85

COMBINED HOOVER'S HANDBOOK INDEX OF EXECUTIVES

```
A = AMERICAN BUSINESS
E = EMERGING COMPANIES
P = PRIVATE COMPANIES
W = WORLD BUSINESS
```

Chew, Lee Fang A74
Chew, Simon A135
Chew, Roy P277
Chew, Allen E64
Chewens, Michael J. A584
ChFC, Brooke A58
Chhean, Forster P615
Chheda, Nimesh A799
Chhibbar, Vishal E140
Chhikara, Vishal A800
Chhina, Harbir S. W92
Chi, David A71
Chi, Cindy A431
Chi, Kung Yeung (Ann) Yun W72
Chi, Cindy E216
Chia, Donny A574
Chia, Yip-fong E96
Chiang, Lidia A262
Chiang, Ellen A284
Chiang, Hwai Hai (HH) A475
Chiang, Ron A738
Chiang, Calvin P455
Chiang, Ellen E120
Chiang, James E349
Chiappetta, Mark E239
Chiappone, Charles A484
Chiarella, Sharon A42
Chiarelli, Linda A592
Chiarelli, Linda P370
Chiarini, Alberto W155
Chibesa, Felix P117
Chicas, Carlos P110
Chiccino, Peter (Pete) A823
Chiccino, Peter (Pete) E405
Chichester, David A779
Chickering, Mark P49
Chico, Michael Chico Michael A605
Chicoine, Gerry A89
Chicoine, Jerry L. A316
Chicoine, James P604
Chidley, Shelley A746
Chien, David A65
Chier, Jim A393
Chiesa, John A391
Chikahisa, Cindy A776
Chikaraishi, Koichi W282
Chikhale, Caroline L. (Cece) E261
Child, Jeffrey S. (Jeff) P437
Child, Curtis P437
Child, William H. (Bill) P437
Childers, Cecil A682
Childers, Michael A760
Childers, David A809
Childers, Michael E374
Childress, Josh P102
Childs, Torrance A147
Childs, Jeffrey J A858
Childs, Craig P337
Childs, Shanna P430
Chiles, Thomas P608
Chilewitz, Mark A484
Chill, Martha O. P662
Chillemi, John A610
Chillo, Laura A882
Chilton, Mike A18
Chilton, Jim A140
Chiluisa, Sylvana A651
Chiluisa, Sylvana E329
Chilwan, Adnan Abdusshakoor W142
Chima, Ron A722
Chiminski, Matthew E233
Chin, Marc A135
Chin, Mary A204
Chin, Francis A546
Chin, Patrick A793
Chin, Caroline P534
Chin, Brian W121
Chin, Kee Min W208
Chin, Frederick V. F. W411

Chin, Michelle E450
China, John D. A793
Chindemi, Craig P311
Chinea, Manuel A670
Ching, K.C. (Glenn) A182
Ching, Christina A676
Ching, Christina E338
Chini, Marc A496
Chinigo, Chin A441
Chinn, Linda A695
Chinn, Michael A. (Mike) A738
Chinn, Barbara P12
Chinn, Terri P523
Chinn, Gregg E105
Chinniah, Nim P388
Chintamaneni, Ramakrishna Prasad A216
Chinyamutangira, Kelvin E290
Chiolan, Robert A135
Chion, Verona A249
Chion, Verona E109
Chiovaro, Jerry E393
Chip, Kingsley P313
Chiprany, David P144
Chirachanakul, Prasert A391
Chirakitcharern, Paisan W95
Chirekos, Nicholas A645
Chirico, Emanuel (Manny) A692
Chirolas, William A559
Chisholm, Jessica A336
Chisholm, Craig A369
Chisholm, Hugh A390
Chisholm, Moody L. A462
Chisholm, Ron A680
Chisholm, Effie P177
Chisholm, Moody L. P256
Chisholm, Simon E102
Chisholm, Jessica E157
Chisholm-krosnicki, Christine A905
Chism, James P200
Chisolm, Moody P523
Chithambaram, Kalimuthu A530
Chiu, Andrew A695
Chiu, Lisa P116
Chiu, Elisa P199
Chiu, Amanda P314
Chiu, Melissa P497
Chiusano, Robert M. (Bob) E443
Chivavibul, Somsak A583
Chivinski, Beth Ann L. A367
Chlebicki, Marilee A360
Cho, Brandie A325
Cho, Alex A432
Cho, Alex A438
Cho, SungHwan A450
Cho, Jane A801
Cho, Chung-Myong W311
Cho, Yong E112
Cho, Alex E216
Choakpichitchai, Prapoj W95
Choate, Mike A715
Choate, David P102
Choate, Mark P412
Chodak, Paul A51
Chodroff, Charles P677
Choe, Liz A404
Choe, Hyelim A431
Choe, Yong A722
Choe, Liz E199
Choe, Hyelim E216
Choeff, Sonya A704
Choi, Justin C A68
Choi, Mike A104
Choi, Sonia A385
Choi, Gina A432
Choi, Carolynn A592
Choi, Alison A893
Choi, Augustine M.K. P159
Choi, Carolynn P370
Choi, Hyung-Seok W236
Choi, Young Moo W337
Choi, Jin Mook E138
Choi, Gina E216
Chojnowski, Tammy A784
Chojnowski, Daniel P312

Chokron, Jeni A114
Chokron, Jeni E36
Cholger, Melissa P353
Cholley, Jeff A444
Chomienne, Kathleen A374
Chon, Hyoung A175
Chong, Francis A740
Chonko, Marcie A824
Chonko, Marcie P562
Chonko, Patricia E330
Choo, Kangsoo W224
Choo, Vincent W299
Choong, Wong Kim W411
Choowatanapakorn, Somkuan W95
Chopey, Stephen A782
Chopey, Stephen P525
Chopra, Rahul A596
Chopra, Saurabh A895
Chorley, Michael A727
Chorley, Michael P453
Chornohos, Chris A482
Chosy, James L. A884
Choto, Miguel A484
Chotsuparach, Praderm W95
Chou, John G. A63
Chou, Mike A850
Chou, Anita P419
Choudhary, Ken R. A355
Choudhary, Gautam E353
Choudhury, Awanish A784
Choudry, Tauseef P356
Choufuku, Yasuhiro W252
Choutka, Michael J. P238
Chovanec, Tony A299
Chovanec, Anthony C A299
Chovit, Bradley A609
Chow, Donald S. A174
Chow, Yu Teong A461
Chow, Jonathan A522
Chow, David A627
Chow, Jean A657
Chow, Wayne A676
Chow, Lisa A686
Chow, Marjorie P627
Chow, Nancy P655
Chow, Donald S. E68
Chow, Wayne E338
Chowdhury, Ashfaque A934
Choy, Alex A793
Chrest, Travis P502
Chris, Redmond A16
Chris, Lockerman A75
Chris, Lobdell A740
Chris, Carmello P248
Chris, Fjellstad P572
Chrislaw, Cathy P564
Chrisman, George P505
Chrismar, Oscar E. Von W45
Christakes, Jennifer A481
Christakos, Bretta A181
Christakos, Bretta E70
Christal, Nancya R A251
Christanday, Geoffrey E2
Christanto, Jevri A778
Christen, Amy A198
Christensen, Natalie A5
Christensen, Michelle A132
Christensen, Wesley J. A630
Christensen, Dirk A934
Christensen, John P92
Christensen, Mylia P112
Christensen, Cindy P129
Christensen, Jesper V P173
Christensen, Dianne P270
Christensen, Marc P. P505
Christensen, Alana P511
Christensen, Angela P665
Christensen, Christopher R. E127
Christensen, Roy E. E127
Christensen, Craig L. E402
Christenson, Daniel A25
Christenson, Peter A61
Christenson, Wesley A630
Christenson, Daniel P14
Christenson, Greg S. P668

Christenson, Carl R. E12
Christey, Bob A575
Christian, David A. A275
Christian, Edward A329
Christian, Lester A379
Christian, Laurie A481
Christian, Mark A638
Christian, Douglas A692
Christian, Ronald A727
Christian, Dan P1
Christian, Kellee P429
Christian, Ronald P453
Christian, Ronald E P505
Christian, Ralf W353
Christian, Voigtlander E222
Christian, Mark E320
Christiano, Kelly A763
Christiano, Kelly E377
Christiansen, Cynthia P129
Christiansen, Dave P340
Christiansen, Amira P537
Christiansen, Douglas L. P599
Christiansen, Jeppe W290
Christianson, Larry A408
Christie, William T. A319
Christie, Brad A798
Christin, Mcmanu P415
Christman, Kelli A859
Christmann, John J. A71
Christmas, Charles E. (Chuck) A552
Christmas, Charles E. (Chuck) E275
Christodoulou, Petros W272
Christodoulou, Nikos W272
Christoferson, Will A340
Christoferson, Will E161
Christoff, Paul W345
Christofferson, Carla J. A16
Christoforo, John P79
Christoph, Schell A438
Christophe, Pierrot A375
Christophe, Pierrot P215
Christopher, Melissa A170
Christopher, John Y A418
Christopher, Sue P64
Christopher, Norman C. P131
Christopher, Rugg P135
Christopher, Megan P610
Christopoulou, Constantina A218
Christou, Lorri E80
Christy, Lisa R A339
Christy, James A684
Christy, Lisa R E159
Chriszt, Michael A319
Chronowic, Peter A366
Chrystal, Curtis A413
Chrystal, John A823
Chrystal, Curtis E205
Chrystal, John E405
Chrystie, Dale A323
Chrzan, Michael A711
Chrzan, Michael P444
Chu, William A99
Chu, Gary A376
Chu, Joshua A431
Chu, Melvin A481
Chu, Sophia A484
Chu, Benjamin K. A485
Chu, Christine A522
Chu, Julie A540
Chu, Stephanie A646
Chu, Tom A692
Chu, Kenny P248
Chu, Benjamin K. P271
Chu, William W123
Chu, Joshua E216
Chu, Stephanie E324
Chu, Ronald J. E402
Chuang, Dorothy A175
Chuang, Hans P H A461
Chubb, Jack P153
Chubb, Stephen E75
Chucri, Theresa P333
Chuderewicz, Leonard A873
Chugg, Juliana A376
Chugh, Davinder W33

Chui, Bennett A284
Chui, Bennett E120
Chuisano, Joe A890
Chulick, Michele P130
Chulos, Nicholas J. A346
Chulos, Nicholas J. E167
Chumakov, George A487
Chumbley, Bud P49
Chumley, Robert J. (Rob) A579
Chumley, Rob A579
Chun, Jean A74
Chun, Millie A544
Chun, Dan A593
Chun, Semin P248
Chun, Gregory H. (Greg) P320
Chun-Soo, Han W219
Chung, Lianne A63
Chung, John A248
Chung, Michael H. K. A285
Chung, Bora A287
Chung, Annie A404
Chung, Anna A404
Chung, Brian A431
Chung, Felix A540
Chung, Yoon (Michael) A640
Chung, Karen L A700
Chung, Paul W. A803
Chung, Alexander N P77
Chung, David P229
Chung, John E107
Chung, Brian E138
Chung, Annie E199
Chung, Anna E199
Chung, Brian E216
Chung, My E262
Chunyan, Wang W96
Chupa, Tammy A935
Chupina, Yulia G. W343
Chuprevich, Tammy E51
Church, Brian A335
Church, John R. A376
Church, Kathryn A485
Church, Tonya A844
Church, Craig P514
Church, Beverly P610
Church, Brian E155
Churchill, Clinton A110
Churchill, Susanne A642
Churchill, Sam A866
Churchill, Arthur L P233
Churchill, Susanne P407
Churchill, Gary P412
Churchill, Laurie A. E253
Churchill, Sam E417
Churchouse, Robin W432
Churchwell, Kevin P558
Churchwell, Keith P676
Churney, Bill E429
Chuslo, Steven L. (Steve) E200
Chutima, Sarunthorn W351
Chutkan, Wayne P351
Chvez, Dr Jess H P457
Chwee, Kenny B. H. W424
Chynoweth, Kathleen P147
Chythlook, Joseph P415
Ch-'vre, Claude W178
Chéreau, Xavier W305
Ciafardini, Mary A101
Ciafardini, Mary E32
Ciambrone, Anthony A36
Ciamillo, Rich A544
Ciampa, Dominick A590
Ciampi, Lisa A646
Ciampi, Lisa E324
Cianchini, Michelle A670
Ciancimino, Paul A530
Cianciolo, Joseph M. E117
Ciano, Lori E53
Ciardi, Julie A465
Ciarlariello, Mark P270
Ciavaglia, Fabian E184
Cibelli, Steve A405
Ciborowski, Michael A651
Ciborowski, Michael E329
Ciccini, Roger A735

Ciccone, J. Gary E368
Cicconi, Fiona W38
Cichocki, Andrew R. (Andy) A25
Cichocki, Andrew R. (Andy) P14
Cichon, Monica A491
Cichowski, Lorraine P555
Ciello, Ronald Del P330
Cieri, Martin P208
Cieslak, Kim E253
Cilento, Robert A506
Ciliberti, Angelo P630
Cillo, Sherry A91
Cillo, Sherry E29
Cimalore, Steven A922
Cimalore, Steven P671
Cimbri, Carlo W411
Cimen, Cenk W222
Ciminello, William A323
Cimino, Rob P304
Cimmino, Dom A90
Cimock, Kristen A327
Cina, John A888
Cina, John E425
Cincera, Matthew Matt A262
Cinco-abela, Tracy A698
Cincotta, Tiffany A5
Cincotta, Tiffany A6
Cintra, George E232
Cioffoletti, Dominic A801
Ciolli, Vince A842
Ciongoli, Adam G. A164
Ciotoli, Carlo A592
Ciotoli, Carlo P370
Cipollini, Auggie P308
Cipolloni, Steven A137
Cipriano, Fred A145
Cipriano, Gino E131
Ciprich, Tresa A828
Ciprich, Tresa P584
Ciraulo, Richard A893
Cirelli, Jean-Fran-§ois W154
Cirillo, Janice A922
Cirillo, Janice P671
Cirin-, Luciano W35
Cirksena, Mark P185
Cirnigliaro, David E431
Ciroli, James K. A353
Ciroli, James K. E173
Cirri, Dawn A811
Cisarik, James A A299
Ciserani, Giovanni A679
Cisi, Laura A207
Ciskowski, Michael S. (Mike) A887
Cisneros, Tamara A900
Citrino, Mary A438
City, Jeanne M. E274
Ciucci, Jillian A859
Ciukowski, Kim A664
Ciukowski, Kim A334
Ciulla, John R. A906
Ciulla, John R. E434
Civello, Stephen A236
Civello, Linda P552
Civgin, Don A35
Civil, Timothy F A654
Claar, Terri E16
Claassens, Christo E132
Clabaugh, Samuel F. P564
Clabby, Joseph S. (Joe) W106
Clack, Alan A892
Claes, Hilde A479
Clagett, Carol A334
Clagett, Carol E153
Clair, Joyce St. A605
Clair, Joyce A605
Clair, Mark A816
Clair, Joseph E143
Claire, Wayne P146
Claisse, Elizabeth A114
Claisse, Elizabeth E37
Clancey, Elizabeth A203
Clancy, Rick A222
Clancy, John P. (Jack) A297
Clancy, Sean A690
Clancy, Kevin P199

Clancy, Makkie P338
Clancy, Peter P424
Clancy, Brian P469
Clancy, Edward (Ed) W106
Clancy, John P. (Jack) E129
Clancy, Paul E226
Clapp, Dale A345
Clapp, Bud A604
Clapp, Dale E165
Clappin, James P. A240
Claps, Francis X P167
Clardy, Donna P202
Clardy, David P245
Clare, Jack E115
Clariana, Roy A828
Clariana, Roy P584
Clark, Matt A16
Clark, Dennis A30
Clark, James B A51
Clark, James A51
Clark, Greg A51
Clark, Gina K. A63
Clark, Bessie A69
Clark, Doug A89
Clark, Jim A123
Clark, Frank A139
Clark, Ginny A236
Clark, James A251
Clark, Scott A284
Clark, Etta A285
Clark, Benjamin A308
Clark, Mark A351
Clark, David A376
Clark, Jack A438
Clark, Neil S A444
Clark, Wade A481
Clark, Michael A524
Clark, Morris A533
Clark, Ron A550
Clark, Richard A613
Clark, Bryan A619
Clark, Todd C. A621
Clark, Jenny A621
Clark, Shelagh A680
Clark, Brian A688
Clark, Christopher A715
Clark, Bernard J. A746
Clark, John C. A760
Clark, John B A785
Clark, Terri L A798
Clark, Cathy A809
Clark, Kerry A821
Clark, Tanya A827
Clark, Judy A846
Clark, Donna A867
Clark, Denise A869
Clark, Rhonda A870
Clark, Terry M. A876
Clark, Cassie A902
Clark, Tom A906
Clark, Jay A906
Clark, Adam A921
Clark, Steve A929
Clark, Stephen Null A929
Clark, Christopher B. (Chris) A932
Clark, Dennis P20
Clark, Frank P92
Clark, Rick P96
Clark, Kelly J P110
Clark, Buster P115
Clark, Vonelle P155
Clark, Talisa R P161
Clark, Donald P163
Clark, Dedra P205
Clark, R. Mel P254
Clark, Karri P281
Clark, Kimberly P308
Clark, Ron P319
Clark, Mark T P336
Clark, Susan P337
Clark, Carrie P338
Clark, Greg P356
Clark, Kathy P377
Clark, Mitchell P390
Clark, Bryan P393

Clark, Gary C P395
Clark, Mark T P411
Clark, Edward Stuart P428
Clark, Joseph T. (Joe) P475
Clark, Joe P475
Clark, Alma P481
Clark, Virginia B. (Ginny) P497
Clark, John B P526
Clark, Joan S. P550
Clark, Mark T P562
Clark, Tanya P580
Clark, Holly Symonds P630
Clark, Carol P633
Clark, Don P638
Clark, Eric P639
Clark, Dale P662
Clark, Lori P677
Clark, Kevin P. W31
Clark, Richard B. (Ric) W80
Clark, Allen E16
Clark, Larry E18
Clark, Donald E47
Clark, Chris E73
Clark, Scott E117
Clark, Bill E172
Clark, Kathy E194
Clark, Karin E262
Clark, Doug E282
Clark, Todd C. E311
Clark, Jenny E311
Clark, Leon E366
Clark, John C. E374
Clark, Robert D. E375
Clark, Stephen H. E379
Clark, Donna E418
Clark, Tom E435
Clark, Jay E435
Clark, Donald J. E443
Clark, Steve E449
Clark, Stephen Null E449
Clark, Marshall E452
Clarke, Dean A56
Clarke, Michael A63
Clarke, Michael B A82
Clarke, Peter A309
Clarke, Patrick A465
Clarke, Troy A A583
Clarke, Jeanne A692
Clarke, Andrew C. A728
Clarke, Terry A810
Clarke, Sheri A908
Clarke, Stephen L P40
Clarke, David P458
Clarke, Tamara Jampo P487
Clarke, Terry P546
Clarke, Cyril P652
Clarke, Peter W159
Clarke, Tracy W364
Clarke, Ronald F. (Ron) E174
Clarke, Thomas J. (Tom) E259
Clarke, Sheri E436
Clarkson, Thomas F. A35
Clarkson, Caroline A323
Clarkson, Daniel P51
Clarkson, Dan P51
Clarkson, Frances E P632
Clasen, Sebastian Gil W149
Claspell, Ann A621
Claspell, Ann E312
Class, Kristin A222
Clatch, Linda E265
Clatterbaugh, Carol P650
Clatterbuck, Janice E. A320
Clatterbuck, Michelle A471
Claudio, Natalie A670
Clauer, Janice A596
Clausen, Jorgen M P173
Claussen, Jennifer P251
Clawater, Earl W. (Bill) A772
Clawater, Earl W. (Bill) E382
Claxon, Christi P242
Clay, Brian A115
Clay, Richard A519
Clay, Will A755
Clay, Reed A782

COMBINED HOOVER'S HANDBOOK INDEX OF EXECUTIVES

A = AMERICAN BUSINESS
E = EMERGING COMPANIES
P = PRIVATE COMPANIES
W = WORLD BUSINESS

Clay, Sharon Ten P141
Clay, Judy P417
Clay, Robert P474
Clay, Amy P478
Clay, Reed P526
Clay, Brian E38
Clay, Will E369
Claybrook, Robert A125
Claypool, Pamela J. (Pam) A25
Claypool, Pamela J. (Pam) P14
Claypool, Forrest P126
Claypool, Blain P523
Clayton, Chris A213
Clayton, Christian A213
Clayton, Douglas A489
Clayton, Michelle A728
Clayton, Chris P143
Clayton, Christian P143
Clayton, Donald E. P252
Clayton, James B. (Jim) P480
Clayton, Annette K. W344
Clear, Nicola A658
Cleare, Christy A320
Cleary, James F. (Jim) A63
Cleary, Michael L A246
Cleary, Don A537
Cleary, Patrick A850
Cleary, James J P193
Cleary, Timothy J P279
Cleary, Stephanie P309
Cleary, Valentina P546
Cleary, Michael L E105
Cleaver, Kent A665
Cleaver, Chuck P311
Cleaver, Bruce W28
Cleaver, Kent E334
Clebsch, Bill A510
Clebsch, Bill P290
Cleek, Don A285
Cleeve, Karen A688
Clegg, Catherine A378
Cleland, Richard C P197
Clem, Mike A21
Clem, John E385
Clemens, Chris A332
Clemens, Paul F. A346
Clemens, Peter P475
Clemens, Reinhard W138
Clemens, Paul F. E167
Clement, Michael A155
Clement, Mark P455
Clement, Mike P632
Clement, Richard W. P634
Clement, Michael E55
Clement-Holmes, Linda W. A679
Clemente, Racquel A925
Clemente, Racquel E445
Clementi, Erich A465
Clements, Jeff A177
Clements, Todd A844
Clements, Janet A859
Clements, Malissa P7
Clements, David P91
Clements, David P424
Clemeson, Marry A45
Clemeson, Marry P30
Cleminson, Ian P. E229
Clemmensen, Christopher N. E123
Clemmenson, Larry A56
Clemmenson, Larry P33
Clemmons, Scott A181
Clemmons, Scott E70
Clemons, Garrett A599
Clemons, Rick A605
Clemons, Jaquetta P255
Clemons, George W55
Clendenin, Don A538
Clerico, John A. E124
Clesceri, Shannon P112

Cleveland, Linda A347
Cleveland, Brian K. A716
Cleveland, Linda E168
Cleveland, Todd M. E322
Cleveland, Kevin E347
Clevenger, Michael A850
Clevenger, Josh P96
Clevenger, Megan P282
Cleves, Thomas A467
CLICK, ELIZABETH P116
Clickner, Kris A754
Clickner, Kris P484
Clifford, Scott S. A396
Clifford, Joseph A674
Clifford, Paul R. A756
Clifford, John P. A844
Clifford, Daniel A919
Clifford, Laurae A930
Clifford, Tim P505
Clifford, Robert P604
Clifford, Peter G. E63
Clifford, John E132
Clift, Ruth P401
Clifton, Dena A345
Clifton, Thu-Quyen A380
Clifton, Nicole A871
Clifton, Karmar P116
Clifton, Dena E166
Clinaz, Rick A872
Cline, Colleen A62
Cline, Richard A429
Cline, Kimberly R A785
Cline, Jon P343
Cline, Kimberly R P526
Cline, Colleen E20
Cline, James E. E409
Clingen, Steve A347
Clingen, Steve E167
Clingenpeel, Chris A799
Clinger, Phillip W. P597
Clinton, Tim A56
Clinton, Angeline A281
Clinton, Adam A492
Clinton, Brenden P337
Clinton, Shaun P551
Clippinger, Michael P260
Clodfelter, Bill A891
Cloer, Michael G. A872
Cloninger, Kriss A19
Clontz, Jerry L. A498
Cloonan, Brian A686
Clopton, George A702
Close, Jay A191
Close, Karla A257
Close, Brett P523
Closs, Diane A804
Clossin, Todd F. A908
Clossin, Todd F. E436
Closter, Harold A. P497
Clott, Jeffrey H A687
Cloud, Andrew A922
Cloud, Mike P260
Cloud, Carol P302
Cloud, Andrew P671
Cloues, Edward P653
Clouse, Steve P470
Clouse, Steven (Steve) P470
Clouthier, Marie A309
Cloutier, Jean W159
Cloutier, Todd E412
Clouzard, Pascal W88
Clowdus, Susan A713
Clowes, Simon A65
Cluff, Tad A845
Clukey, Kristi P463
Clulow, Christopher C A247
Clune, Anna A205
Clute, Daniel A877
Clutterbuck, James P31
Clyde, R. Andrew A579
Cmil, Jennifer A595
Coad, Scott A915
Coady, Shawn W. A598
Coakley, John P151
Coard, Shawn A713

Coates, Steve A112
Coates, Etta P7
Coates, Robert P198
Coates, Spencer P205
Coates, Spencer A. P245
Coats, Sylvia A108
Coats, Brian A483
Coats, Sam P171
Coats, William E194
Cobb, Tamara A142
Cobb, Kathy A727
Cobb, Brian A885
Cobb, Amanda P225
Cobb, Kathy P453
Cobb, Russ E47
Cobb, Tamara E49
Coben, Lawrence S. A610
Coberly, Michelle A638
Coberly, Michelle E320
Cobine, Stew P610
Coble, Fred A704
Coble, Paul P162
Coblentz, Max A755
Coblentz, Max E369
Coborn, Chris P145
Cobos, Patricio A877
Coburn, Chris A642
Coburn, Tom A726
Coburn, Chris P407
Coburn, Tom P453
Coburn, Quinn J. E191
Cocca, Michael P529
Coccagno, James A. P106
Coccagno, Jim P106
Cocero, Nanette A657
Cochran, Sandra A272
Cochran, George A489
Cochran, Larry A492
Cochran, Sandra A527
Cochran, Scott D. A714
Cochran, J. Scott A717
Cochran, Larry P279
Cochran, Sharlet P285
Cochran, Karen P464
Cochran, Barry S. P564
Cochran, Eric P670
Cochran, J. Scott E351
Cochrane, Lisa A36
Cochrane, Lisad A36
Cochrane, Terah A532
Cochrane, James A654
Cochrane, Collin A709
Cochrane, John Gregory P359
Cochrane, Andy P379
Cochrane, Collin E348
Cockayne, Matt E132
Cockcroft, Adrian A42
Cockerham, Greg E91
Cockrell, Housto Earl A112
Cockrell, Harry A768
Cockrell, Matt A902
Cockrell, Kevin P25
Cockrell, Phillip P596
Cockrum, Dirk A494
Cockrum, Leigh A760
Cockrum, Leigh E374
Coco, Debbie P56
Coco, Denae P135
Cocorullo, L Mark P311
Coder, Forrest David A158
Coder, Derrick P201
Codispoti, Pam A54
Codsi, Jean-marc A287
Cody, William M. (Bill) A681
Cody, Bill Cody Bill A781
Cody, Thomas G. P128
Cody, April E290
Coe, Nicholas P.M. (Nick) A500
Coe, Steve E325
Coelho, Paulo E138
Coen, Bill P337
Cofer, Tim A573
Cofer, Horace G. E386
Coffey, Patricia A35
Coffey, Timothy P. A68

Coffey, Hal A329
Coffey, Linda A527
Coffey, Pamela P508
Coffey, Philip (Phil) W424
Coffin, Joanne P80
Coffin, Mark W. P486
Coffman, George C A437
Coffman, Dionisia A484
Coffman, Thomas P187
Cofield, James A882
Cofré, Daniel Rodr- guez W164
Cogdill, Matthew P294
Cogdill, Richard A. (Rick) P589
Coggins, Jeff P86
Coghlan, Suzie A421
Cogliano, Michael A784
Cohan, Martin E267
Cohart, Kevin P91
Cohen, Sharon A3
Cohen, Daniel A6
Cohen, Barry A83
Cohen, Gary M. A123
Cohen, Jalie A179
Cohen, Lisa A188
Cohen, David L A220
Cohen, Stephanie A323
Cohen, Rob A326
Cohen, Chad A349
Cohen, Doreen A509
Cohen, Harvey A522
Cohen, Jodi A540
Cohen, David A574
Cohen, Tiffany A589
Cohen, Elisa A592
Cohen, Phil A651
Cohen, Jon R. A697
Cohen, Angela A702
Cohen, Mike A702
Cohen, Robin A726
Cohen, Don A744
Cohen, Steve A762
Cohen, Andre A801
Cohen, Ira A801
Cohen, Nita A806
Cohen, Eric I. A815
COHEN, MARTIN A822
Cohen, Daniel G. A823
Cohen, Patti A893
Cohen, Howard P132
Cohen, Sheldon P153
Cohen, Dennis P162
Cohen, Caitlin P226
Cohen, Bob P245
Cohen, David I. P304
Cohen, Evan P357
Cohen, Elisa P370
Cohen, Andrew P448
Cohen, Daniela P472
Cohen, Brian P612
Cohen, Cliff P643
Cohen, David W113
Cohen, Peter A. E101
Cohen, Iosef E179
Cohen, Phil E330
Cohen, Nita E399
Cohen, Daniel G. E405
Cohen, Jacob E433
Cohen-Hillel, Avi A74
Cohill, Mike A791
Cohill, Mike P535
Cohlmia, Peter P86
Cohn, Marc A559
Cohn, Arthur A658
Cohn, Leslie P60
Cohodes, Jeffery D. A605
Cojbasic, Ivana A327
Cojuangco, Eduardo M. (Danding) W338
Coke, Michael A. (Mike) E400
Coker, Jimmy A170
Coker, R. Howard A768
Coker, David A934
Cokyuksel, Aysun A167
Col, Richard Dal P110
Colaiacovo, Judith A692

Colaizzi, Barbara A837
Colaizzi, Meredith P303
Colandrea, Joe P206
Colanero, Stephen A. A45
Colangelo, Carmon P600
Colao, Vittorio A. W417
Colarusso, David A752
Colarusso, Roz P666
Colasurdo, Giuseppe N P595
Colberg, Alan B. A88
Colbert, Theodore (Ted) A140
Colbert, Charles E A938
Colbert, Charles E P678
Colburn, Susan A90
Colburn, Martin P. P202
Colburn, James D P310
Colburn, Russell E131
Colby, Robert (Rob) P93
Colby, Bryon P435
Coldiron, Jenny P213
Coldiron, Den Ellen P623
Coldren, Jade E41
Coldrey, Andrew A728
Coldwell, Michael A319
Coldwell, Adam E147
Cole, Russell G. A152
Cole, Michel A168
Cole, David D. A184
Cole, Grey A222
Cole, Tracey A540
Cole, Kenneth G. A541
Cole, Susan A646
Cole, Jody A651
Cole, David D A699
Cole, Brad A704
Cole, Lauren A793
Cole, Frank A871
Cole, David A871
Cole, Cori A879
Cole, Cynthia A929
Cole, Charles T. P111
Cole, Paris P174
Cole, Chris P260
Cole, George P278
Cole, Bennie L P387
Cole, Johnnetta B. P497
Cole, David P575
Cole, Emma P594
Cole, James P651
Cole, Michael W65
Cole, Hart E8
Cole, Russell G. E52
Cole, Lecil E. (Lee) E58
Cole, Jason E174
Cole, Matthew J. E258
Cole, Susan E324
Cole, Jody E329
Cole, Cynthia E449
Coleal, David M. W73
Colella, Carmine P349
Colella, Gerald G. E285
Coleman, Ed A46
Coleman, Casey A90
Coleman, Justin A104
Coleman, Russell F. A259
Coleman, Caretha A266
Coleman, Jim A301
Coleman, Kenny A382
Coleman, Gary L. A389
Coleman, Gary A408
Coleman, Leonard A419
Coleman, Scott A442
Coleman, Jay A491
Coleman, Laura A589
Coleman, Donna A604
Coleman, Allison A605
Coleman, Robert A737
Coleman, Kirk A818
Coleman, Chris A876
Coleman, Laura A882
Coleman, Timothy A883
Coleman, Erin P39
Coleman, Caretha P182
Coleman, Jack P199
Coleman, Kia P360

Coleman, Beverly P546
Coleman, Brandon P588
Coleman, Willi P639
Coleman, Timothy P644
Coleman, Adria P676
Coleman, Michael J. W106
Coleman, John F. E121
Coleman, Victor J. E219
Coleman, Glenn E233
Coleman, Jon E272
Coleman, Robert E361
Coleman, Kirk E403
Coleman, Rob E433
Coleman, Brendan E433
Coles, Lauren A550
Coles, Gus P188
Colestock, Richard E A672
Coletta, Jackie P273
Coletta, Edmond R. (Ned) E68
Coletti, Robert A197
Coletti, Janet M. A530
Colf, Richard W A492
Colf, Richard W P279
Colgan, Meegan A702
Colgan, Sheila E144
Colgate, Brenda A242
Colin, Mark A3
Colin, Rath A61
Colino, John A870
Colisto, Nicholas R. A936
Colistra, David A465
Collar, Gary L. A21
Collar, Steven M. (Steve) P166
Collar, Steve P166
Collard, Steve P74
Collazo, Jose E305
Colleen, Keilty A642
Colleen, Keilty P407
College, Eugene A313
College, Eugene P200
Colleran, Don A323
Colleran, Donald F A323
Collett, Lee A919
Collette, David P195
Colli, Alison A409
Collier, Alita A36
Collier, Erin A452
Collier, Dirk A480
Collier, Gary A664
Collier, Stephanie A683
Collier, Paige A796
Collier, Daniel A887
Collier, Bradley W P264
Collier, Christopher E. (Chris) W164
Collier, Dwayne E224
Collier, Gary E333
Collier, Paige E397
Colligan, Robert A191
Collignon, Dan A383
Collignon, Dan E186
Collin, Aimee A469
Collings, Krista A719
Collings, Krista E355
Collingsworth, J M P340
Collins, Tomago A94
Collins, Heidi A116
Collins, Bill A140
Collins, Whitley A175
Collins, Al A180
Collins, Daniel A240
Collins, Jim A248
Collins, Jonathan M A253
Collins, Chris A262
Collins, Ellis A310
Collins, Robert A327
Collins, Randy A373
Collins, Christopher A392
Collins, Barclay A418
Collins, Mark A455
Collins, Kevin A472
Collins, Chris A484
Collins, Rodger L A489
Collins, David A574
Collins, Olga A590
Collins, Gary S. A623

Collins, Christian A649
Collins, Daniel A715
Collins, William C. A806
Collins, Terry A852
Collins, Steve A859
Collins, Kevin A906
Collins, Robert A922
Collins, Joshua L. (Josh) P87
Collins, Lance R. P159
Collins, Michael P261
Collins, Michael P265
Collins, Barbara P398
Collins, Diane P445
Collins, Tommy H. P461
Collins, Bill P588
Collins, Michael F. P631
Collins, Robert P671
Collins, Heidi E39
Collins, James E. E41
Collins, Jim E107
Collins, Steven C. E119
Collins, Mark E228
Collins, Gary S. E313
Collins, Martin J. (Marty) E343
Collins, William C. E398
Collins, Suzanne E433
Collins, Kevin E435
Collins, Casey E448
Collinson, Michael A692
Collinson, Tammy P396
Collinsworth, Paul A444
Collis, Steven H. A63
Collischan, Michael A902
Collopy, Fred P116
Collura, Corren P531
Colman, Robin A287
Colman, Jonathan E392
Colmers, John A478
Colmers, John P269
Cologero, Mary A128
Colom, Rebeca P536
Colombo, Russell A. (Russ) A110
Colombo, William J. (Bill) A265
Colombo, Beatrice A658
Colombo, Benjermin A793
Colombo, Costantino (Chris) P314
Colombo, Paolo E22
Colon, Tara A89
Colon, Rebecc A440
Colon, Trinity A762
Colon, Ruth P367
Colon-Kolacko, Rosa M P132
Colondres, Jose A798
Colonges, Guillaume de W88
Colonias, Karen W. E375
Colonna, Jerome P76
Colonna, Joe P418
Colonna, Nicholas E245
Colonna, Ken E424
Colorito, Donna A762
Colosi, Scott M. E404
Colpack, Michael J P279
Colpaert, Gary P211
Colpo, Charles C. A634
Colquhoun, Debby A540
Colter, David A118
Colter, David E40
Colton, Sabine P445
Colton, Jeffrey M. (Jeff) E59
Coltrane, Scott P636
Colucci, Anthony J P197
Colucciello, Michael P429
Coluzzi, Chris E371
Colvin, Jeff A17
Colvin, Marlow A305
Colvin, Ben A545
Colvin, Donald A628
Colvin, John A704
Colvin, Jeff P9
Colvin, Garren P463
Colwell, Chad A923
Colwell, Gale R P670
Colwell, Michael E243
Colwell, Chad E442
Colyandro, Anthony A559

Colyar, Michelle A420
Colyar, Michelle P240
Colyer, Michael A665
Colyer, Michael E334
Comarsh-Hein, Michele A528
Comas, Daniel L. A254
Comay, Josh A893
Combe, Daniela A465
Combs, Al A606
Combs, Brian A723
Combs, Nicole P586
Combs, Joseph D. P599
Combs, Stephen P662
Combs, Jason E366
Comeau, Carol P38
Comeaux, Preston P421
Comegys, Glenn P140
Comella, Thomas A384
Comella, Thomas P217
Comer, Hugh A309
Comer, Nici A769
Comer, Nici E380
Comerford, Dick P147
Comia, Rowell A109
Cominiello, Kristeen A220
Comiskey, Patrick P532
Comitale, Jim A722
Comizzoli, Pierre P498
Commesser, Jay A728
Commins-Tzoumakas, Kimberly P1
Comnenus, Maurizia Angelo W252
Comnick, Terry P470
Compher, Matt A696
Compton, Brian A135
Compton, Kip A198
Compton, Bob A252
Compton, Tania A327
Compton, Richard A613
Compton, Jennifer A760
Compton, Kevin A761
Compton, Lisa A779
Compton, Teresa A902
Compton, Kris P30
Compton, James M P158
Compton, Mary P523
Compton, Rocky P523
Compton, Paul W56
Compton, Paul W58
Compton, Jennifer E374
Comstock, Karolyn P532
Comyn, Matt W113
Conant, Douglas A64
Conaty, Kelly P166
Conaway, Samuel A149
Conaway, Mary Ann A211
Conaway, Mary Ann E82
Conboy, Diane A684
Concannon, William F. (Bill) A175
Concannon, Michael (Mike) A408
Conceicao, Cassio P494
Concordia, Elizabeth B. P643
Condegni, Anthony A93
Condia, Anthony P615
Condina, Jim A200
Condo, Connie A444
Condoleo, Edward A16
Condon, Joy A512
Condon, Jeff A522
Condon, Bill A893
Condon, Michael A. P505
Condon, Liam W61
Condran, Georgina A367
Condren, Dave A844
Condren, Barbara P302
Condron, Gary D P563
Cone, Steve P2
Cone, Barbara P392
Coneset, Marianne A346
Coneset, Marianne E167
Conetta, Tony A425
Coneway, Mary P56
Coney, Jason E265
Coney, Jason ME E265
Confalone, Pat N. P32
Conforti, James E. A791

COMBINED HOOVER'S HANDBOOK INDEX OF EXECUTIVES

```
A = AMERICAN BUSINESS
E = EMERGING COMPANIES
P = PRIVATE COMPANIES
W = WORLD BUSINESS
```

Conforti, James E. P535
Congemi-doutney, Lisa A786
Congemi-doutney, Lisa E387
Conger, Harry M. (Red) A365
Conger, Ann P394
Congleton, Brian A89
Congleton, Gregg A540
Congoran, Thomas M. P54
Coniaris, Jeffrey A654
Coniaris, Jeff A654
Conine, Shelley A36
Conklin, Jeff A151
Conklin, Kevin A219
Conklin, Joseph A243
Conklin, Patrick A680
Conklin, Carla P64
Conklin, George S. P132
Conklin, Kevin E87
Conkling, Charles E433
Conkling, Charley E433
Conlen, Chuck A279
Conley, Ann P76
Conley, John P260
Conley, Amber P333
Conley, Melinda S. E249
Conlin, Kelly E366
Conlon, Paul F A847
Conlon, Paul F P606
Conn, Iain C. W95
Conn, Mitzi P. E60
Connatser, Gayle A509
Connell, Hope Holding A336
Connell, Bruce A536
Connell, Ben P104
Connell, Amy P488
Connell, Hope Holding E157
Connelly, James M. A414
Connelly, Margery A502
Connelly, Deirdre A520
Connelly, Rebecca A575
Connelly, Natalie A626
Connelly, Thomas M. (Tom) P32
Connelly, James M. P236
Connelly, Joshua P543
Connelly, Ryan H. E253
Connelly, James E448
Connely, Patrick P242
Conner, R David A88
Conner, Peter J. A116
Conner, Raymond L. (Ray) A140
Conner, Brad L. A205
Conner, Jack W. A415
Conner, Amy A638
Conner, David A651
Conner, Anne A839
Conner, David E. A867
Conner, Thomas O P336
Conner, Mark P608
Conner, Peter J. E39
Conner, Bill E106
Conner, Jack W. E208
Conner, Amy E320
Conner, David E329
Conners-Copeland, Ryan A575
Connery, Raymond A112
Connery, Brian A651
Connery, Brian E329
Connolly, Thomas A63
Connolly, Sean M. A232
Connolly, Joy A592
Connolly, Paul A784
Connolly, Landon P119
Connolly, Lois P211
Connolly, Dennis P252
Connolly, Joy P370
Connolly, Adrian L P513
Connolly, Brian P670
Connolly, Edward T. W190
Connolly, Patrick E. (Pat) W358

Connolly, M. Colin E100
Connor, Mark A147
Connor, Robert A267
Connor, Kevin A484
Connor, Frank T. A821
Connor, Martin P. (Marty) A837
Connor, Scott P418
Connor, David P524
Connor, Daniel P654
Connor, Sue P664
Connor, Roger W171
Connor, Dean W370
Connor, Dean A. W371
Connor, Mark E264
Connors, Denise A484
Connors, Susan A544
Connors, Timothy A616
Connors, John A640
Connors, Michael L. P109
Connors, Alfred F. P576
Conoley, Brittani A683
Conophy, Thomas M. (Tom) A94
Conover, David A494
Conover, Jeffrey W A605
Conover, Bob A686
Conover, Kathleen E321
Conrad, Susan A381
Conrad, Mary Jo P103
Conrad, David P594
Conrad, Jeffrey A P656
Conrado, Eduardo F. A577
Conran, Brent A461
Conroy, Donal A72
Conroy, Alexandre A123
Conroy, Courtney A893
Consagra, James J. A865
Consagra, James J. E416
Considine, William A61
Considine, Marty A645
Considine, William H. (Bill) P131
Consigli, Anthony M P155
Consigli, Matthew D P155
Consing, Cezar W54
Consolino, Joseph E. (Jeff) A55
Constable, David E. W341
Constance, Thomas E. E372
Constant, Mark A363
Constant, Jean P57
Constant, Jean-Paul W219
Constant, Christopher J. E187
Constantine, Tom A100
Constantine, Thomas A101
Constantine, Sandra A801
Constantine, Tom P58
Constantine, Thomas E32
Constantino, Chris A588
Constantino, Chris P365
Constantino, Christopher P539
Constantino, Ferdinand K. W338
Contat, Kevin A444
Conte, John A910
Conteras, Jaime A5
Conterno, Enrique A. A517
Conti, Stephanie A246
Conti, Stephanie E105
Continenza, James V. (Jim) P333
Contis, David J. A761
Contractor, Raj A436
Contreras, Jaime A5
Contreras, Luis A561
Contreras, Mary P153
Contreras, Juan P196
Contreras, Sharon L P225
Contreras, Sharon P225
Contreras-Soto, Alex P433
Contrerasn, Sharon P539
Converse, Peter A865
Converse, Peter E417
Convit, Rafael P658
Conway, Trish A126
Conway, John W. A245
Conway, William A. A414
Conway, Dennis A444
Conway, Christian A740
Conway, Michael A779

Conway, Jeffrey D. A783
Conway, Karen A888
Conway, Christopher L. P140
Conway, Victoria P162
Conway, Linda P176
Conway, William A. P236
Conway, Craig A. E196
Conway, Karen E425
Conyers, Sally A345
Conyers, Lois P137
Conyers, Larry P160
Conyers, Al P378
Conyers, Sally E166
Cook, James A25
Cook, Randy A89
Cook, David A112
Cook, Ian M. A217
Cook, Thomas A224
Cook, Jill E A247
Cook, Dave A313
Cook, Christopher A320
Cook, Robert A346
Cook, Tracey A355
Cook, Frank A369
Cook, Jennifer A397
Cook, Jerry A403
Cook, Jay A465
Cook, Bill A484
Cook, Stuart A559
Cook, Mitchell W. A567
Cook, Derek A575
Cook, Helen A621
Cook, Sandy A678
Cook, Houston A713
Cook, David A727
Cook, Michael A747
Cook, Stephen R. (Steve) A762
Cook, Ben A804
Cook, Mike A901
Cook, James P14
Cook, Keith P114
Cook, Christopher P117
Cook, Dave P200
Cook, Robert W. P202
Cook, Bill P205
Cook, Matthew P252
Cook, Darin P252
Cook, Jason P252
Cook, Paul P253
Cook, Katherine P303
Cook, Troy D P391
Cook, David P453
Cook, Jill P561
Cook, Cindy P567
Cook, James E. (Jim) P578
Cook, Angela P595
Cook, Will P626
Cook, Larry P629
Cook, Christine P629
Cook, Derek E19
Cook, Kathryn E42
Cook, Robert E166
Cook, Mitchell W. E283
Cook, Helen E311
Cooke, Dennis C. A734
Cooke, Daniel A765
Cooke, Gary A924
Cooke, David J. P406
Cool, Jonathan M. E262
Cooledge, Deborah A876
Cooley, Sheila A449
Cooley, Kem P376
Cooley, Philip L (Phil) E44
Cooley, Sheila E221
Cooman, Lynn A69
Coombe, Gary A679
Coombe, Robert D. (Bob) P146
Cooney, Vicki A863
Cooney, Jack E378
Coonrod, Julie P634
Coons, Kenneth A484
Coons, Sandra A919
Coons, Rick P656
Cooper, Mark A17
Cooper, Ross D. A121

Cooper, Matt A140
Cooper, Mark A156
Cooper, Debra A179
Cooper, Pamela A196
Cooper, John A205
Cooper, Denise A227
Cooper, Allen A232
Cooper, Mark A255
Cooper, Rich A277
Cooper, Michael A371
Cooper, James A376
Cooper, Edith W. A390
Cooper, Ansley Oliver A449
Cooper, Angus A450
Cooper, Marianne A465
Cooper, John A513
Cooper, Ellen A519
Cooper, Geoffrey A561
Cooper, Kathy A621
Cooper, Michael A663
Cooper, Don A677
Cooper, Sandra A702
Cooper, Frederick A837
Cooper, Allen A846
Cooper, Douglas W A853
Cooper, Troy A. A934
Cooper, Mark P9
Cooper, Mark A. P119
Cooper, Gary P126
Cooper, Dorothy P163
Cooper, Robyn P286
Cooper, Kerri Jo P298
Cooper, Troye P312
Cooper, Malcolm Charles P359
Cooper, Warren P469
Cooper, Darryl P487
Cooper, Shelby S P574
Cooper, Christopher J. P596
Cooper, Jack P606
Cooper, Douglas W P612
Cooper, Simon W364
Cooper, Brad W424
Cooper, Beth W. E78
Cooper, Denise E90
Cooper, Roman E105
Cooper, Emilio E154
Cooper, Buzz E189
Cooper, Ansley Oliver E221
Cooper, Angus E221
Cooper, Skyler E267
Cooper, Tod E293
Cooper, Kathy E311
Cooper, Kimberly E420
Cooper, Scott E429
Cooper, David E440
Cooper-Boone, Deborah P207
Cooperstein, Marci A893
Coopshaw, Elaine P596
Coore, Becky P652
Coorigan, Micheal P184
Cope, George A. W65
Cope, James E433
Cope, Jim E433
Copeland, Scott A105
Copeland, John G. A106
Copeland, Reed A250
Copeland, Rex A. A397
Copeland, R. Dallis (Roy) A796
Copeland, Jon P31
Copeland, Bonnie S P60
Copeland, Alan P440
Copeland, Scott E34
Copeland, R. Dallis (Roy) E397
Copeland, Toni E433
Copelin, Bill A442
Copello, Corinne A602
Copello, Corinne E A602
Copfer, Ronald P116
Copher, Ron J. A386
Copher, Ron J. E188
Copier, Judy A452
Copley, Lisa A908
Copley, Lisa E436
Coponen, Bonnie A398
Coponen, Bonnie P222

COMBINED HOOVER'S HANDBOOK INDEX OF EXECUTIVES

Coppedge, Kathleen P130
Coppey, Pierre W415
Coppola, Matthew A888
Coppola, Matthew E425
Copsey, Andrew W377
Cora-Bramble, Denice P130
Corace, Robert E133
Coradine, Sedare A828
Coradine, Sedare P580
Coranet, Mike P247
Corasanti, Joseph J. (Joe) E224
Corban, Stephen M. A717
Corban, Stephen M. E351
Corbat, Michael L. A203
Corbett, Maribeth A22
Corbett, Kevin A36
Corbett, Michael A86
Corbett, John A181
Corbett, ED A236
Corbett, Dennis A793
Corbett, Maribeth P11
Corbett, William P616
Corbett, S. Mark W174
Corbett, Michael E27
Corbett, John E70
Corbin, John A444
Corbin, Randell P35
Corbin, Lee Anne P227
Corbo, Michael A. (Mike) A217
Corbridge, Nancy P402
Corbusier, Drue A267
Corcoran, Mary A405
Corcoran, Doug A835
Corcoran, Stephen A906
Corcoran, Stephen E435
Cordani, David A194
Cordani, David A376
Cordano, Michael D. A914
Cordaro, Ron A806
Cordaro, Joe E226
Cordaro, Ron E399
Cordeiro, Sharen P610
Corder, Paul P552
Corder, Elven E412
Cordero, Saul P171
Cordero, Jose P630
Cordero, Ivette E296
Cordes, Laura P450
Cordier, Emile De P95
Cordova, Deanna P549
Corely, Catherine A902
Corey, Gloria A89
Corey, Lee A574
Corey, Toby P547
Corey, Kevin E292
Corielli, Emanuela P371
Corirossi, David A716
Corkill, Krista E106
Corkran, Shawn A296
Corl, Curtis A272
Corleto, Jose A695
Corlett, David A257
Corlew, Joe E153
Corley, Donna A364
Corley, John A933
Corley, William E. (Bill) P151
Corley, Robin P626
Corley, John Jason E193
Corman, Bob A828
Corman, Bob P584
Cormier, Kipp E131
Corn, Ron A191
Corn, Ron P126
Corna, Louis J. E408
Cornelious, Derrick A112
Cornelius, Marcus A176
Cornelius, Craig A610
Cornelius, Jim A726
Cornelius, Lynn A733
Cornelius, Jessica A840
Cornelius, Jim P453
Cornell, Daniel C. A41
Cornell, Brad A528
Cornell, Brian C. A804
Cornell, Steve A915

Cornell, Theodore P376
Cornell, Stephen W341
Cornett, Maggie P253
Cornew, Kenneth W. (Ken) A304
Corney, Glenn E290
Cornish, Thomas M. A114
Cornish, Thomas M. E37
Cornuelle, Valerie P107
Cornwall, Kevin A248
Cornwall, Kevin E107
Corona, George S A488
Corporatio, United States Steel P645
Corr, Edwin G P307
Corr, David E183
Corradetti, Sandra A471
CORRADI, ENRICO W121
Corrado, Richard F. (Rich) E7
Corrales, Nils P638
Corran, Robert P639
Corrato, Joe A686
Correa, Jaime A715
Correa, Craig A762
Correa, Bonnie P325
Corredera, Crystal P513
Corredor, Nathalie A423
Correll, Craig P336
Corrigan, Dennis A478
Corrigan, Frank A574
Corrigan, Thomas L P132
Corrigan, Joanna P223
Corrigan, George M P501
Corrinne, Kelly A737
Corrinne, Kelly E361
Corritore, Janet A810
Corritore, Janet P546
Corritori, Mark A544
Corro, Debbie Del A665
Corro, Debbie Del E334
Corry, David M P295
Corry, Sandra P637
Corsetti, Gabrielle E330
Corsini, Bryan M. A638
Corsini, Bryan M. E320
Corson, B. W. A309
Corson, Brad A309
Cortelyou, Bob A262
Cortes, Fernando A489
Cortese, Buddy A312
Cortese, Buddy P200
Cortez, Juan A346
Cortez, Juan E167
Cortina, Ignacio A A632
Cortés-Vazquez, Lorraine P2
Corum, Bethany H. (Beth) A165
Corvi, Carolyn P652
Corvino, Mike A900
Corwin, Kraig A169
Corwin, Steven J. (Steve) A827
Corwin, Steven J. (Steve) P580
Cory, Nick A366
Cory, Frank A651
Cory, Thompson P508
Cory, Barry P511
Cory, Frank E329
Cosby, Wende A719
Cosby, Wende E354
Coselli, Joseph P548
Cosentino, Luca W155
Cosentino, Anthony V. (Tony) E365
Cosenza, Mark Cosenza Mark A388
Cosenzo, Donna P227
Cosey, Cathy A713
Cosgrove, Delos M. (Toby) A824
Cosgrove, Cole P166
Cosgrove, Delos M. (Toby) P561
Cosman, James M. A152
Cosman, James M. E52
Coss, David P353
Cossaboom, Jill E347
Cosset, Yael A498
Cossetti, Tony E172
Cosslett, Andy W219
Cost, Mike P534
Costa, Mark J. A285
Costa, Roland A320

Costa, Alan Null A751
Costa, Salvatore A759
Costa, Robert A816
Costa, Patricio Tapia W29
Costa, Ant- - nio Fernando Melo Martins da W146
Costa, José Carlos da Silva W169
Costa, Salvatore E373
Costantino, Danielle A135
Costanza, Catherine A925
Costanza, Catherine E445
Costanzo, Dan A778
Costanzo, Sherry A922
Costanzo, Sherry P671
Costella, Margaret F P573
Costello, Kat A91
Costello, Jason A115
Costello, Michael A207
Costello, Christopher A228
Costello, Suzanna A319
Costello, Kristen A325
Costello, Thomas A374
Costello, Fred A394
Costello, Richard A409
Costello, Kevin A465
Costello, Daniel A596
Costello, Meg A641
Costello, Jordana A877
Costello, Meg P407
Costello, Joseph G P445
Costello, Kat E29
Costello, Jason E37
Costello, Richard J. A. E193
Costesso, Dennis P498
Costigan, Conor W131
Costopoulos, Spyro A160
Cote, Donna A16
Cote, David M. (Dave) A431
Cote, Kathleen A914
Cote, Joe P178
Cote, Mike P285
Cote, Bryce E260
Coterillo, Fernando Julio Arias W194
Cothran, April A329
Coticchia, Mark P116
Cotich, Kristin P337
Cotner, Kimberly P548
Coto, Patricia Raquel Hevia W26
Cotoni, Paul A449
Cotoni, Paul E220
Cotran, Paul R P284
Cotrone, Kris A376
Cotta, Rick E223
Cotten, Eugene P83
Cotter, Ruth A14
Cotter, Martin A67
Cotter, Dick A739
Cotti, Shanna E75
Cottington, Eric M. P325
Cotto, Carlos P454
Cotton, Charles A452
Cotton, Benjamin A856
Cotton, Benjamin P614
Cotton, Gwendolyn P660
Cottrell, Christopher E. E119
Cottrell, Elizabeth H E168
Cotts, Nick A595
Couch, Joey A421
Couch, Richard W. A693
Couch, Brett D. A712
Couch, David deS. (Dave) A774
Couch, Connie A818
Couch, Laverne P524
Couch, Robert E5
Couch, Richard W. E341
Couch, Connie E403
Coudrelle, Laurent A613
Couger, Scott A405
Coughlan, Ian M. A930
Coughlin, Thomas M A120
Coughlin, Ron A438
Coughlin, Margaret P558
Coughlin, Thomas M. E41
Coughlin, John S. E174
Couglin, John E174

Cougoule, Jeff A349
Couitt, Michael A842
Coulson, R C E318
Coultas, Tonya P570
Coulter, Ryan A135
Coulter, Roxanne A179
Coulter, Cuan A783
Coulter, John P610
Counihan, Kevin J. A179
Counts, John A797
Coupe, Nick A378
Coupe, Mike W206
Couper, Leslie L. E305
Courant, Paul N. A711
Courant, Paul N. P444
Coureil, Hervé W344
Court, James A101
Court, James E32
Courtay, Rena P475
Courter, Traci A552
Courter, Traci E276
Courtney, Rob A761
Courtney, Matthew A780
Courtois, Jean-Philippe A565
Courtois, Frédéric de W35
Courtot, Philippe F. E342
Courville, Isabelle W232
Couse, Anthony A481
Cousino, Mark A279
Cousins, Patricia A538
Cousins, Katherine A891
Cousins, Erica P329
Cousins, Richard J. W116
Coutchie, Peggy A552
Coutchie, Peggy E276
Couto, Luey A676
Couto, Luey E338
Coutu, Pat A205
Couture, Elaine S A321
Couture, Ken P221
Covella, Robert P78
Covello, John P250
Covert, Michael H. A226
Covert, Brian A647
Covert, Charlie A870
Covert, Michael H. P150
Covert, Brent E177
Covey, Michael J. E337
Covietz, Kristopher A711
Covietz, Kristopher P444
Covington, J. Curtis A317
Covington, Mark A833
Covington, J. Curtis E146
Covino, Greg A133
Covre, André W405
Cowan, Chad A524
Cowan, Joshua P6
Cowan, James P58
Cowans, Sabrina P548
Coward, Robert A933
Coward, Karen E334
Cowden, Christy P195
Cowden, John P327
Cowell, Andrew M. P446
Cowen, Karen E101
Cowgill, Dan A326
Cowhig, Michael T. A593
Cowie, Frederick A379
Cowing, Chris A704
Cowles, James C. A203
Cowles, Darby P270
Cowley, David P646
Cowman, Craig A169
Cowper, Matthew E42
Cowperthwait, David P449
Cox, Frank A62
Cox, Ed A168
Cox, Kevin A171
Cox, Donna A198
Cox, Thomas A209
Cox, Shirley A246
Cox, Chris A251
Cox, Brian A271
Cox, Shawn A284
Cox, Mark K. A285

COMBINED HOOVER'S HANDBOOK INDEX OF EXECUTIVES

A = AMERICAN BUSINESS
E = EMERGING COMPANIES
P = PRIVATE COMPANIES
W = WORLD BUSINESS

Cox, Christopher K. (Chris) A310
Cox, Mark A324
Cox, B. Guille A341
Cox, James W. A352
Cox, Laura J A353
Cox, Rhydian H. A439
Cox, Clay A442
Cox, John A608
Cox, Clark A665
Cox, Yolanda A683
Cox, Ryan A727
Cox, John A744
Cox, Stuart A762
Cox, Matthew A774
Cox, Philip C. A793
Cox, Keith A794
Cox, Carrie A820
Cox, John A835
Cox, Nicole A925
Cox, Christopher P62
Cox, Bob P166
Cox, Laura J P204
Cox, Terence C P230
Cox, Terry P230
Cox, Terence C. (Terry) P231
Cox, Larry P244
Cox, Karen P327
Cox, Judy P349
Cox, George P358
Cox, Russell F P389
Cox, Douglas P446
Cox, Ryan P453
Cox, Ted P465
Cox, Gregory P493
Cox, Matthew P510
Cox, Dudley P605
Cox, Michael E P609
Cox, Diana P659
Cox, John J. E8
Cox, Frank E20
Cox, Shirley E105
Cox, Shawn E117
Cox, Carol E308
Cox, Michael E330
Cox, Clark E334
Cox, Nicole E445
Coxall, Dan P127
Coy, Thomas P210
Coyle, Jamie A36
Coyle, John A40
Coyle, Kevin A405
Coyle, Michael J. A413
Coyle, Lori A752
Coyle, John P29
Coyle, Jennifer P420
Coyle, Michael J. E205
Coyle, Timothy E429
Coyle-ikemoto, Gayle A877
Coyne, John A10
Coyne, E A25
Coyne, Patrick A320
Coyne, Brian A532
Coyne, John A845
Coyne, E P14
Coyne, Gwen P177
Coyne, Michelle P233
Coyne, Lynn P610
Coyner, Sheri A69
Cozad, Stacy A774
Cozart, Meri P157
Cozart, Robert E453
Cozza, Keith A450
Cozzolino, Christina A628
Cozzolino, Christina P396
Cozzone, Robert D. A455
Cozzone, Robert D. E227
Crabb, Taryn A528
Crabb, Joel A804
Crabbe, Amy A347

Crabbe, Amy E168
Crable, Kathleen P135
Crabtree, Thomas A145
Crabtree, Jennifer A246
Crabtree, Danny A717
Crabtree, Monte A P140
Crabtree, Dave P529
Crabtree, Gordon P639
Crabtree, Jennifer E105
Crabtree, Danny E351
Cracchiolo, James M. (Jim) A60
Crace, David A891
Cracolici, Frank P514
Craft, Frank A680
Craft, Robert A799
Craft, John P280
Crafter, Lochiel A784
Crager, Kyle E47
Crager, William (Bill) E131
Cragg, Christopher A299
Cragg, John A649
Craig, Pommels A255
Craig, Hamish A327
Craig, Kim A398
Craig, Marian A527
Craig, Christopher A738
Craig, Jonathan M. A746
Craig, Brett A804
Craig, Gloria A852
Craig, David P161
Craig, C C P201
Craig, Alex P246
Craig, Valerie P252
Craig, Allen P307
Craig, Kerry P552
Craig, Andr--nico Luksic W44
Craig, Jim E187
Craig, Thomas E223
Craig, Hunter E430
Crain, Robert B. A21
Crain, Becky A713
Crain, Steven P291
Crain, John P621
Crain, Bohn H. E344
Craine, Barry A60
Craine, Randy A156
Craine, Eric A859
Craine, Ann P481
Crainer, Thomas C. E345
Craker, Robin P618
Cralle, Chris A203
Cramer, Errol A35
Cramer, Denise A530
Cramer, James R. (Jim) P478
Cramer, David P618
Cramer, Ralf W117
Cramer, Stuart E245
Crandall, Brett A137
Crandall, Douglas A727
Crandall, Tracy A732
Crandall, Janice A890
Crandall, Debbie P262
Crandall, Douglas P453
Crandall, Cynthia E131
Crandell, Sarah A75
Crandon, Mark P389
Crane, Christopher M. (Chris) A304
Crane, Christopher M A306
Crane, Jill A711
Crane, Eric A859
Crane, Timothy S. (Tim) A925
Crane, Jill P444
Crane, Timothy S. (Tim) E445
Cranmer, Mark A246
Cranmer, Mark E105
Cranner, Chris A893
Cranny, Joe A526
Cranor, Ben P469
Crater, Ann A200
Craven, Katherine P315
Craven, Dennis M. E76
Craver, Theodore A281
Craw, Theresa A544
Crawford, Frederick J. (Fred) A19
Crawford, Gordon A45

Crawford, Victor L. A75
Crawford, Matthew A114
Crawford, Stephen S. (Steve) A166
Crawford, Rhonda A262
Crawford, Stephen G. (Steve) A285
Crawford, Cree A310
Crawford, Anne A314
Crawford, James C. A334
Crawford, Earl A349
Crawford, Bruce A626
Crawford, Kermit R. A722
Crawford, Charles A744
Crawford, Peter A746
Crawford, David A783
Crawford, Joe A785
Crawford, Stan A850
Crawford, Gordon P30
Crawford, Brian P32
Crawford, Lynn P64
Crawford, Sophie P94
Crawford, Tony P119
Crawford, Gary P147
Crawford, Nolan P506
Crawford, Gregory K (Greg) P578
Crawford, Beverly P653
Crawford, James D. P670
Crawford, Matthew E37
Crawford, Anne E145
Crawford, James C. E153
Crawley, Joyce A418
Crawley, Thomas E73
Cray, Charlesetta Mc P625
Craychee, Patrick P222
Crcm, Jean Prazecky A338
Crea, Patricia P206
Creach, Andrea A782
Creach, Rod P68
Creach, Andrea P526
Creagh, Gerard (Gerry) E79
Creamer, Michele A554
Creamer, Eunice P51
Creamons, Joe A347
Creamons, Joe E167
Creary, Mike Mc A556
Creary, Mike Mc P328
Creatura, Nick A210
Creaturo, Craig A. E224
Credle, Eric P. A334
Credle, Eric P. E153
Creech, Matt A520
Creech, Denise P32
Creech, Dale P320
Creed, Greg A920
Creed, Greg A937
Creedon, Michael A13
Creek, Phillip G. E264
Creely, Mark A688
Creery, Thomas G. A425
Creery, Tom A425
Creevy, William P95
Creger, Angie P329
Cregg, Daniel J. (Dan) A687
Cremers, Eric J. E337
Cremin, Mary C A56
Cremin, Mary C P33
Crenshaw, William E. (Ed) A688
Crenshaw, William E. (Ed) A689
Crenshaw, William E. (Ed) P435
Creque, Patricia P95
Cresap, Jennifer P471
Cresci, Robert J. E240
Cress, Yevette P617
Cressman, Jonathan A686
Cresswell, Alex W390
Creus, Jose Oliu W45
Crevak, Maureen P666
Crew, Matt A105
Crew, Morgan A466
Crew, Debra A A477
Crew, Debra A573
Crew, Debra A593
Crew, Debra A P263
Crew, Matt E34
Crews, Mark A28
Crews, Terrell A77

Crews, Terrell A434
Crews, Kirk A597
Crewse, Britt P187
Cribb, Gary A731
Cribbs, Kyle A65
Cribbs, Kevin A337
Cribbs, Steven A838
Cribbs, Kevin E158
Crichton, Peter A845
Crider, Perry A271
Criger, Sara P26
Crigler, Forest A367
Crim, Dave A1
Crim, Dave E1
Crimmins, Timothy P. A651
Crimmins, Mike A924
Crimmins, Thomas P. E33
Crimmins, Timothy P. E329
Crines, James T A939
Cripe, Kimberly P129
Cripps, Tony W189
Crisci, Robert A730
Crisci, Rob A730
Criscione, David A42
Criscuolo, Adolfo P573
Crisman, Michael A630
Crismer, Cindy A104
Crisp, Stanley A321
Crisp, Jeremy E343
Criss, Mike A355
Crist, Peter D. E445
Cristall, Joel P449
Cristman, Jim A202
Cristman, Jim P136
Cristoforo, Albert J. (Jerry) A783
Crites, James M. (Jim) P171
Critikos, John A837
Crnkovich, Sean A540
Crocco, M. Scott A24
Croce, Dan A30
Croce, Michael J. A788
Croce, Dan P20
Croce, Denise P232
Croce, Michael J. E389
Crocker, Janet A448
Crocker, Janet P247
Crockett, Joan A36
Crockett, Shawn P117
Crockett, Gary P397
Croessmann, Philip P356
Croft, Bryan P118
Crofts, Sharon M. A109
Croger, Scott A645
Croley, Matthew P332
Croley, Alan E105
Croll, David D. P159
Crombleholme, Timothy M. P127
Cromer, Fred S. W73
Cromme, Gerhard W353
Cromwell, Dennis P610
Cron, Robert P78
Crone, Anna A327
Crone, Michael A469
Cronen, Paul A888
Cronen, Paul E425
Croney, Michael P270
Croney, Barbara P469
Cronin, John A60
Cronin, Douglas A149
Cronin, Thomas A545
Cronin, James A706
Cronin, Raphael A706
Cronin, Julie P86
Cronin, Brian P391
Cronister, Becky J P5
Cronk, Trent A105
Cronk, Trent E34
Crook, Debbie A755
Crook, Debbie E369
Crooke, Robert B. A460
Crooke, Stanley T. E237
Crooker, William R. E385
Crookshanks, Denise A680
Crookston, Jesse A92
Croom, Marshall A. A527

Cros, Christophe W366
Crosbie, Debbie W109
Crosby, William A468
Crosby, Michael J. A927
Crosby, Michael P501
Crosby, Jim E105
Crosby, Samantha E412
Croson, Rachel P632
Cross, Jeffrey A51
Cross, Karen A62
Cross, Don A86
Cross, Charles K. A749
Cross, Jeffrey D P32
Cross, Coleen P212
Cross, Maya P548
Cross, Kevin P581
Cross, Karen E20
Cross, Don E27
Cross, Richard E66
Cross, Charles K. E367
Crosson, Mike A713
Crosswhite, Mark A28
Croston, J. Kevin P379
Croteau, Daniel A414
Croteau, Daniel P236
Croteau, Ray P341
Crotteau, Patrick A149
Crotts, Matthew P542
Crotty, Marty A18
Crotty, Theresa A642
Crotty, David A799
Crotty, Theresa P407
Crouch, M. Andrew (Drew) A103
Crouch, Tami A335
Crouch, Genie A902
Crouch, Kaye A922
Crouch, J Brady P482
Crouch, Kaye P671
Crouch, Robert P. (Bob) W7
Crouch, Tami E155
Crouse, Michael A497
Crouse, Jerry K P546
Crouser, Mark P60
Croushore, Susan P560
Crout, Steve A695
Crout, Megan P409
Crout, Randy P409
Crouter, Ann C. (Nan) A828
Crouter, Ann C. (Nan) P584
Crow, M. Chad A156
Crow, John A195
Crow, Jeff A320
Crow, Timothy M. (Tim) A428
Crow, Stan A608
Crow, Michael M. P44
Crowder, Andy P479
Crowe, Richard A145
Crowe, Mike A218
Crowe, Maria A517
Crowe, Ronald P429
Crowell, Wyatt E A439
Crowell, Eric P121
Crowell, Ed P144
Crowell, Eric P258
Crowell, Keri E197
Crowley, Larry A115
Crowley, F. Michael A536
Crowley, Margaret A561
Crowley, JD A893
Crowley, Thomas B. (Tom) P166
Crowley, Richard D. (Rick) P446
Crowley, Rick P446
Crowley, Larry E37
Crown, Timothy A. (Tim) A458
Crown, Donna A641
Crown, Donna P407
Crown, Brian P439
Crownover, Shannon P579
Crowther, David A98
Crowther, Chip P81
Croxall, Clifford A321
Croxton, Kristen A167
Croxton, Cheryl A312
Croy, Bobbi A502
Croyle, Mike P351

Crozier, Barry P60
Crozier, Susan P307
Crozier, Alfred E408
Cruce, Andrea A179
Cruikshank, J. David A111
Cruise, Karen A849
Crum, Bill A444
Crumby, Brian A161
Crummy, Kevin A. E114
Crump, Darin A224
Crump, Julie A456
Crump, Scott A752
Crump, Carol P475
Crump, Julie E228
Crusinberry, Dawn E73
Crutcher, Brian T. A820
Crutchfield, Lisa A368
Crutchfield, Steven A524
Crutchfield, David P651
Cruz, Edia A203
Cruz, Julie A242
Cruz, Sergio A493
Cruz, Kenneth A701
Cruz, Jesus A704
Cruz, Ray A872
Cruz, Paul P56
Cruz, Michael P66
Cruz, Tawna P83
Cruz, Carl P147
Cruz, Roberto de la P171
Cruz, Mike De La P223
Cruz, Milagros P257
Cruz, Bob P304
Cruz, Jose P454
Cruz, Paulo P659
Cruz, Jo- - o Manuel Ver- ssimo Marques da W146
Cruz, A.B. E126
Cruzan, Jeff P254
Cryan, John W135
Cryer, Edward P356
Crystal, Richard P567
Crystal, Jon P639
Crystaloski, Sheila D. E386
Crépin, Frédéric R. W416
Csabon, Robin P307
Csapo, Peter P. P13
Cseh, Bela W264
Csoma, Stephan W405
Csonger, Rob A613
Csont, Dan P432
Ctfa, Veronica E330
CU, Jennipher P162
Cuaboucher, Genevive P377
Cubbage, Gary C. A144
Cubbon, Henry W131
Cubias, Carlos A871
Cuccia, Tony A323
Cuccias, Brian A446
Cucco, Wayne A58
Cuccurullo, Sara P563
Cudd, Steven A882
Cuddihy, Robert A65
Cuddy, Christopher M. (Chris) A77
Cuddy, Rhonda P633
Cudkowicz, Merit Ester P574
Cudmore, Tony W68
Cudmore, Tony W69
Cue, Eduardo H. (Eddy) A72
Cuellar, William A463
Cuervo, Larry A401
Cuervo, Carlos A927
Cuervo, Larry E198
Cuevas, Jason A382
Cuevas, Diego Gaxiola W175
Cuff, Rich A540
Cuffe, Michael S. A410
Cugini, Dominic A491
Cuilla, Michelle A574
Culak, Bob A797
Culang, Howard A700
Culbert, John P175
Culbertson, Darian A34
Culbertson, Leslie S. A460
Culbreath, John P417

Culbreth, John A272
Culbreth, M. Scott E19
Culhaci, Hayri W19
Culham, Harry W85
Cull, Shawn P199
Cullen, Thomas A. (Tom) A271
Cullen, Susan A356
Cullen, William A501
Cullen, Michael P502
Culling, Robert (Doug) A754
Culling, Robert (Doug) P484
Culloch, Cathy Mc P474
Culman, Shirley A158
Culnan, Mary Beth P523
Culos, Joe A337
Culos, Joe E158
Culp, John A478
Culp, Patricia A504
Culp, Patricia E251
Culpepper, Lenore A108
Culpepper, Paul A739
Culpepper, Jason A760
Culpepper, Lee A902
Culpepper, Jason E374
Culver, Curt S. A561
Culver, John A779
Culver, Kevin A855
Culwell, Curtis P212
Cumbaa, Charlie E47
Cumbaa, Charles T E47
Cumming, Christine M. A319
Cummings, Matthew A16
Cummings, Tammy A319
Cummings, Sean J. A407
Cummings, Kevin A473
Cummings, Sean A483
Cummings, Bob A804
Cummings, Brian A591
Cummings, Harold A768
Cummings, Scott A842
Cummings, Dan A877
Cummings, Jerilin A879
Cummings, Michelle P30
Cummings, Emily P229
Cummings, Ricardo P279
Cummings, Heather P281
Cummings, Brian P369
Cummings, Steven P535
Cummings, Sue W396
Cummings, Kevin E236
Cummings, John E300
Cummins, Michael A756
Cummins, Diane M P566
Cummins, Sarah E448
Cummiskey, Chris A382
Cummisky, Olivia A921
Cunanan, Jennifer P663
Cune, Bill A240
Cunfer, Todd A416
Cunha, Paulo Guliherme Aguiar W405
Cuningham, David P530
Cunneen, Carmela P325
Cunney, Michael A536
Cunningham, Benjamin A135
Cunningham, Shirley A194
Cunningham, Thomas A321
Cunningham, David L. A323
Cunningham, Tom A468
Cunningham, Joe A477
Cunningham, William H. A520
Cunningham, Carmen A580
Cunningham, Everett V. A698
Cunningham, Michelle A718
Cunningham, Vickie A828
Cunningham, Melissa A880
Cunningham, Belinda A922
Cunningham, Mike P25
Cunningham, Bridgett P105
Cunningham, Shirley P133
Cunningham, Joe P263
Cunningham, Jerry P332
Cunningham, Sandra P354
Cunningham, Kim P397
Cunningham, Vickie P584
Cunningham, Alicia P631

Cunningham, John P631
Cunningham, Melissa P640
Cunningham, Phil P660
Cunningham, Belinda P671
Cunningham, John H. E8
Cunningham, Daniel N E73
Cunningham, Kelly E264
Cunningham, Carmen E293
Cunningham, Michelle E354
Cupelli, Kim A855
Cupp, Dondi A711
Cupp, Dondi P444
Cupp, Scott P552
Cupp, Ronnie P563
Cuppernull, Patty A863
Cupps, Pete A158
Cupps, Donald L. P633
Curaca, Eduardo P404
Curatolo, Tom A429
Curcio, Michael J. A283
Curd, Samantha S A755
Curd, Samantha S E369
Cure, James P120
Cure, Carlos W144
Curet, Carrie A449
Curet, Carrie E220
Cureton, Jesse P390
Curley, Charles A327
Curley, Michael A349
Curley, Shannon A481
Curley, Jeffrey A520
Curley, Abby A702
Curley, Kevin A851
Curley, Tim P646
Curley, Robert M. E43
Curnow, Randy P329
Curoe, Tim A804
Curphy, Rona A117
Curphy, Rona P61
Currall, Steven P505
Curran, Richard A1
Curran, Mary A A104
Curran, Kaori A137
Curran, Michael A175
Curran, Martin J. (Marty) A240
Curran, Teresa M. A321
Curran, Ryan A368
Curran, Bob A466
Curran, Michael J. A551
Curran, Shawn A826
Curran, Michael J. P321
Curran, Greg P613
Curran, Maria P649
Curran, David W424
Curran, Richard E1
Curran, John J. E85
Curran, Steve E353
Currarino, Giancarlo A616
Curren, John A746
Currens, Bill A281
Currie, Calvin A795
Currie, Dean W. P107
Currie, John P361
Currie, Theresa L. (Teri) W396
Currie, Gordon A.M. W422
Currier, Rand P220
Curry, John A483
Curry, Ruthanna A518
Curry, Angie A520
Curry, Mike Mc A556
Curry, Robert P137
Curry, Denise P153
Curry, Wanda C P196
Curry, Randal P212
Curry, Maridee P320
Curry, Mike Mc P328
Curry, Kevin P439
Curry, John P443
Curry, Susan J. P594
Curry, Jeffrey T P666
Curry-Briggs, Doreen P40
Curschman, Rick A833
Curschman, Kim A925
Curschman, Kim E445
Curti, Darlene A115

COMBINED HOOVER'S HANDBOOK INDEX OF EXECUTIVES

A = AMERICAN BUSINESS
E = EMERGING COMPANIES
P = PRIVATE COMPANIES
W = WORLD BUSINESS

Curti, Joseph Tate P193
Curti, Darlene E38
Curtin, Jim A103
Curtin, David A135
Curtin, Mike A855
Curtis, Williams A171
Curtis, Roger A238
Curtis, Mark D. A348
Curtis, Lynda D. A588
Curtis, Scott A. A704
Curtis, Jack A859
Curtis, Michael P312
Curtis, Lynda D. P365
Curtis, Lucy P418
Curtis, Yvonne P425
Curtis, Mark D. E169
Curtis, Frank E300
Curtis, Colleen E450
Curtiss, Jennifer A54
Curtiss, Rick A651
Curtiss, Lisa A702
Curtiss, Rick E330
Curto, Chris P239
Curtwright, Lois P128
Cury, Devon A341
Cury, Jason P307
Cush, Tom A702
Cush, Thomas A702
Cusher, Andrew P615
Cushing, Robert B. (Bob) A13
Cushing, Robert P17
Cushing, Don E148
Cushing, Donald E148
Cushman, Bob A296
Cushman, Deann A550
Cushman, Audrey P315
Cushman, John C. E59
Cusick, Steve A925
Cusick, Steve E445
Cusimano, Kristine A179
Cuskaden, Trisha P662
Cussen, Laura A484
Custer, Timothy R. A71
Custer, Scott A523
Custer, Michael A772
Custer, John A845
Custer, Jami P558
Custer, Michael E383
Custodio, Elizabeth E330
Cutchins, Alexis G P194
Cutifani, Mark W29
Cutillo, Gian Piero W235
Cutino, Camille G. E57
Cutler, Scott A287
Cutler, Paul A597
Cutler, Juanita P116
Cutler, Brian P555
Cutliff, Scott A703
Cutliff, Scott P439
Cutlip, Robert G. E189
Cutt, Timothy J. (Tim) W69
Cutter, Brian P157
Cutter, David P475
Cutter, David W140
Cutting, Tim A761
Cuviello, David A530
Cuyk, Ryun Van A85
Cuyk, Ryun Van E27
Cuzzi, Gregory A678
Cyganiak, Dave A606
Cymrot, Andrew A538
Cypher, Morgan A337
Cypher, Morgan E158
Cyphert, Mark J. A683
Cyr, Michael A544
Cyrus, Alicia A179
Czaja, Mark A640
Czaja, Stacey E106
Czajka, Edward J. A676

Czajka, Edward J. E338
Czajkowski, Andrew P241
Czak, Kim A366
Czarnecki, Kevin A374
Czarnecki, Walter P A649
Czarnetzki, Theresa P216
Czebotar, Jerry A P358
Czech, Eric A538
Czosnowski, Marc A437
Czumak, Michael P325
Czyz, Danielle A605
Czyzewski, Kim A646
Czyzewski, Kim E324

D

D, Pedro Cazabon M P394
D, Eric Dickson M P616
Dabagia, Robert C. A433
Dabagia, Robert C. E217
Dabbs, Lorrie P246
Dabi, Chris A538
Daboval, Wendy A191
Dachenbach, Angie A448
Dachenbach, Angie P247
Dachman, Richard A797
Daco, Katherine A137
Dacosta, John E110
Dacunha, Kathleen A259
Dacus, Scott A765
Dadey, Bryan P596
Dadkho, Farhad E358
Daehnke, Arno W363
Daeihagh, Pirouz P377
Daffan, Nicholas E429
Daffey, Michael D. A390
Dagher, Ramzi A658
Dagher, Ramzi A881
Dagher, Ramzi E421
Dague, Brandi E206
Dahan, René W223
Dahl, Roslyn P18
Dahlberg, Edwin P522
Dahlen, Jeffrey A. (Jeff) E375
Dahlgren, Peter W357
Dahlmann, David S. (Dave) A337
Dahlmann, David S. (Dave) E158
Dahlstrom, Richard (Rick) P320
Dahua, Shi W101
Dahut, Karen M. A144
Dai, Michael A3
Dai, Changhong A460
Dai, Hai-Lung P546
Daigle, Gregory A880
Daigle, Gregory P640
Daigle, Robert C. (Bob) E359
Daignault, Jesse A65
Daik, Sam P543
Dailer, Cindy A909
Dailer, Cindy E436
Dailey, Mike P385
Dailey, John P480
Dailey, John R. (Jack) P497
Dailey, Jeffrey J. (Jeff) W435
Daingerfield, Richard A646
Daingerfield, Richard E324
Daiss, Ann A382
Dajany, Adam P28
Dake, Gary C P529
Dake, William P P529
Dakey, Alan W. A653
Dalal, Amit A606
Dalal, Kosha P202
Dale, Jeffery F. A763
Dale, Jeffrey A763
Dale, Amanda A804
Dale, Nancy P300
Dale, Ken P555
Dale, Christopher P646
Dale, Jeffery F. E377
Dale, Jeffrey E377
Dalecki, Cristin A390
Daleo, Robert D. (Bob) P206
Dales, Kira A11

Dalessandro, Nick A654
Daley, Larry A164
Daley, Elvia A247
Daley, Dorian E A632
Daley, Elvia E105
Daley, Troy E290
Dalgleish, Glen A143
Dalgleish, Glen A243
Dalhouse, Warner E262
Dalia, Randall A465
Dall, Trisha A452
Dalla, Anna A702
Dallago, Lou A657
Dallago-Iohan, Deneen A752
Dallaire, Seth A42
Dallala, Daniel P114
Dallas, Mike P599
Dallman, Carla P671
Dalrymple, Christopher K. A32
Dalrymple, Jeff A933
Dalrymple, Jeffrey A933
Dalrymple, Cara P160
Dalsky, David P116
Dalton, Hector A3
Dalton, Gregory W. A118
Dalton, Alexandra A260
Dalton, Bary A320
Dalton, Lashawn A491
Dalton, Ted A651
Dalton, James T. A711
Dalton, Justin A798
Dalton, Genus A845
Dalton, Willam S P226
Dalton, William P227
Dalton, Chuck P386
Dalton, James T. P444
Dalton, Jay P539
Dalton, Mark F. P599
Dalton, Karen P607
Dalton, Gregory W. E40
Dalton, Mark L. E81
Dalton, Ted E330
Daly, Brendan P. A121
Daly, James A303
Daly, Andrew A409
Daly, Colleen A491
Daly, David M. A688
Daly, John A717
Daly, Shawn A830
Daly, Jim A849
Daly, Marty A893
Daly, Sean A926
Daly, Ronald E. P2
Daly, Marilyn P27
Daly, Kevin P96
Daly, Eric P246
Daly, Ashley P327
Daly, Patricia P330
Daly, Shawn P593
Daly, Michael P. E42
Daly, Michael P. E43
Daly, Brian G E143
Daly, James M. (Jim) E226
Daly, John E351
Daly, Sean E445
Damanaki, Maria P579
Damashek, Yumiko E56
Dambach, Michael A133
Dambrosio, Nancy A135
Damen, Shannon A500
Dameron, Keith A449
Dameron, Jeffrey C P124
Dameron, Keith E220
Dames, Peter P485
Damian, John A700
Damiano, William P642
Damico, Jennifer A658
Damico, Anthony P489
Damion, Robinson A718
Damion, Robinson E354
Damiris, George J. A425
Damm, Jon A508
Damme, Niek Jan Van W138
Dammon, Robert M. P114
Damon, Carrie A915

Damon, Lisa J. P486
Damore, Joseph P344
Damrongchietanon, Prasopsuk W216
Damschroder, Patricia P596
Dan, Yang A374
Dan, Chad A452
Dan, Jackson P383
Dana, Terry A259
Dana, Chris A925
Dana, Ashley P165
Dana, Michal Carmi W49
Dana, Michael W296
Dana, Chris E445
Danahy, John A740
Dandorph, Michael J P459
Daneau, Guy W193
Danes, Mike A87
Danes, Mike P50
Daney, Jennifer M P48
Dang, Nelson A109
Dang, Van A198
Dang, Doan A248
Dang, Kimberly A. (Kim) A494
Dang, Doan E107
Dangel, Wolfgang H. E208
Dangelo, Kathryn P546
Danheiser, Geoff E98
Dani, Shaila A592
Dani, Shaila P370
Danica, Hostettler A518
Danie, Mark A651
Danie, Mark E330
Daniel, James R. A105
Daniel, Marvin A200
Daniel, Karen L A224
Daniel, William K. (Dan) A254
Daniel, Yolanda A319
Daniel, John M. A343
Daniel, Annette A605
Daniel, Karen L. P85
Daniel, Becky P551
Daniel, Chris Mc P596
Daniel, Terrie P638
Daniel, Patrick D. W92
Daniel, James R. E34
Daniel, Roark E53
Daniel, Sabbas A. E110
Daniel, John M. E163
Daniel, David E442
Daniels, J. Todd A19
Daniels, Cheryl A54
Daniels, Jon G. A171
Daniels, Bill A181
Daniels, Nancy A270
Daniels, Ronald J. (Ron) A478
Daniels, Matthew A520
Daniels, Brady A604
Daniels, Scott A686
Daniels, Tamika A741
Daniels, Christina A784
Daniels, Peter A835
Daniels, Kenneth A867
Daniels, Erik A884
Daniels, Stephen P127
Daniels, Andria P161
Daniels, Ronald J. (Ron) P268
Daniels, Jacqueline R. P390
Daniels, Vince P487
Daniels, Mark P511
Daniels, Bobbi P632
Daniels, Bill E70
Daniels, Stefan E132
Daniels, Jeffery J E267
Daniels, Tamika E364
Daniels, Kenneth E418
Danielson, Sandra P357
Danilewitz, Dale A63
Danilson, Dean A855
Danis, Mark A207
Dankel, Roger E375
Dankner, Wayne P405
Danley, Derek A571
Danmeter, Debbie A246
Danmeter, Debbie E105
Dann, Diane A544

Danna, Scott A137
Dannenfeldt, Thomas W138
Danner, Nicole A315
Danner, Mary A731
Danner, Rosalin A738
Dannewitz, Charles V. (Chuck) A809
Dannov, David M. A748
Danon, Saar P298
Dansermsuk, Sukhawat W95
Dantani, Shigeki W360
Dantas, Bruno P51
Dantilio, Derek E285
Dantzler, Rhonda D A222
Daochai, Predee W216
Dapaah, Janine A325
Dapeer, Jonathan E8
Dapp, Anthony A877
Dapper, Brent A909
Dapper, Brent E436
Daprile, Joseph R P193
Daprile, Jospeh R P372
Dara, Thomas A135
Darby, Gerard A84
Darby, Maria A144
Darby, Paul P208
Darcy, Mike A230
Darcy, Mike P154
Dardari, Davide P572
Darden, Calvin A170
Darden, J. Matthew A389
Darden, James A389
Darendinger, Steve A199
Daretta, Bob A480
Dargan, Thomas A749
Dargan, Susan A783
Dargan, Thomas E367
DArgenio, David E375
Darger, Ford STANFORD P375
Dargie, John A351
Darguesse, Frederic A695
Dargusch, Jonathan D. A908
Dargusch, Jonathan D. E436
Darin, Bob A251
Darji, Rajesh A724
Darji, Rajesh P452
Dark, Zachary A713
Dark, Dana P578
Darlene, Libiszewski A914
Darlene, Libiszewski E439
Darling, Michael A391
Darlington, Stefanie A374
Darlington, Angela W40
Darmon, Marc W390
Darne, Michael A538
Darneille, Marshall A755
Darneille, Marshall E369
Darnill, Jill E131
Darnold, Jenny A383
Darnold, Jenny E186
Darnow, Tamara A491
Darr, Alex A711
Darr, Alex P444
Darr, Ryan E131
Darrell, Dyson A894
Darrell, Dyson P651
Darren, Weston A480
Darrenkamp, Kevin A524
Darricarrére, Yves-Louis W398
Darrow, Mark A654
Darrow, Bruce P351
Darrow, Rebecca P511
Darsey, James R. A612
Darst, Daniel A651
Darst, Daniel E330
Dart, Richard C. P179
Daruwala, Zarin W194
Daruwala, Zarin W364
Darwin, Pam A309
Darwin, Steven A813
Das, Kaustubh A198
Das, Sushanto A438
Das, Sugata P678
Dasari, Praveen A135
Dasgupta, Satarupa P371
Dashwood, John A309

Dasic, Gorana A658
DaSilva, Jack A830
DaSilva, Jack P601
Daskalos, Paul P469
Dasossa, Mag P176
Dastugue, Michael P. A901
Datar, Srikant A790
Datema, Scott P87
Dato, Sandra A167
Dattilo, Thomas A501
Daubner, Thomas P604
Dauch, David C. A49
Dauer, Jennifer P128
Dauger, Jean-Marie W154
Daugherty, Michael A327
Daugherty, Wayne A421
Daugherty, Doug A508
Daugherty, Gary A618
Daugherty, Christine A654
Daugherty, Lucy A665
Daugherty, Michael P553
Daugherty, Paul W5
Daugherty, Lucy E334
Daugiala, Alfredas P496
Daum, Martin W125
Dauphine, Jon P2
Dauphinee, Greg E305
Daurio, Nancy P304
Dauterive, F Ralph P394
Dave, Naimesh P140
Dave, Rajesh P619
Davenport, Rodney A34
Davenport, Michael A63
Davenport, Nancy A559
Davenport, Brian A686
Davenport, Leslie A692
Davenport, Bobby A850
Davenport, DeWitt P109
Davenport, John P303
Davenport, Charles P408
Davenport, Beverly P625
Davenport, Jacquie P645
Davenport, Mely P675
Davenport, James E329
Davert, Marshall P356
Daveu, Marie Claire W218
Davey, Deirdre A60
Davey, James E. (Jim) A408
Davi, Susanna A686
Davich, Joe P176
David, Gregory A75
David, Doerr A120
David, Paula A218
David, Cathy A327
David, Rose Marie A429
David, Harmon A501
David, Svitek A571
David, Evan A642
David, Scott B. A799
David, Glenn C. A941
David, Mark P126
David, Prabu P340
David, Steven P371
David, Evan P407
David, Laurent W71
David, Caio Ibrahim W205
David, Rose Marie E214
David, Cliff E267
David-Borha, Sola W363
Davidar, David D. E190
Davidek, Donna A449
Davidek, Donna E220
Davidman, Jeff A262
Davidoff, Ravin P95
Davidoni, Giorgio A518
Davidovicz, Paul A722
Davids, Jody R. A654
Davidson, Bruce A181
Davidson, Cindy A358
Davidson, Wendy A487
Davidson, Michael A600
Davidson, Linda A692
Davidson, Julie P184
Davidson, Robert G P332
Davidson, Candi P477

Davidson, Jay P506
Davidson, Martin D P506
Davidson, Brian P523
Davidson, Gary P573
Davidson, Bruce E70
Davidson, Cindy E176
Davidson, Michelle E290
Davidsson, Peter A920
Davies, Erik Null A29
Davies, Colin A418
Davies, Richard A593
Davies, Neal P333
Davies, Howard J. W333
Davies, John E43
Davies, Mike E427
Davila, Marco A636
Davila, Diana P245
Davila, Rosa P344
Davila, Melinda P620
Davilla, Nancy P486
Davis, Lori A10
Davis, Julia K. A19
Davis, James C. (Jim) A33
Davis, Robert A74
Davis, Chris A85
Davis, Helene B A109
Davis, Cindy A125
Davis, Michael A137
Davis, Darryl W. A140
Davis, Kathy A142
Davis, J. Kimbrough (Kim) A165
Davis, Angela A170
Davis, John A171
Davis, Jessica A180
Davis, Tony A184
Davis, John A195
Davis, Patrick A204
Davis, Pat A206
Davis, Mike A246
Davis, Georgetta A278
Davis, Robert A281
Davis, Damon A309
Davis, Debby A323
Davis, Chad A327
Davis, Lou J. A336
Davis, C William A338
Davis, Sharon L. A339
Davis, Claude E. A340
Davis, Alicia Boler A378
Davis, Timothy A380
Davis, Jana J. A410
Davis, Joe A413
Davis, Anyee A416
Davis, Jeffery Chad A430
Davis, John R. A449
Davis, Tom A452
Davis, Douglas L. (Doug) A460
Davis, Doug A460
Davis, Martina Del Raso A497
Davis, Ryan A500
Davis, Robert M. A554
Davis, Jeff A569
Davis, Doug A569
Davis, James A575
Davis, Latia A592
Davis, Ian A618
Davis, Erika T. A634
Davis, Timothy Paul A644
Davis, Jeffrey (Jeff) A647
Davis, Keith B A665
Davis, George S. A694
Davis, James E. A698
Davis, Glenn A700
Davis, Pam A713
Davis, Kathy A717
Davis, Scott A719
Davis, Bart A723
Davis, Cory A726
Davis, Dan A739
Davis, Steven D. A753
Davis, Jonathan S. A754
Davis, Charles A761
Davis, Reid A769
Davis, Cindy A772
Davis, Nancy B. A788

Davis, Jodi A791
Davis, Chris A798
Davis, Gillian A818
Davis, Terrell A835
Davis, Robert D. (Bob) A838
Davis, Mark A847
Davis, John A850
Davis, Robert A850
Davis, Raymond P. (Ray) A861
Davis, Kern A868
Davis, Raymond A879
Davis, Stephanie A A887
Davis, Gigi A893
Davis, Kurt A893
Davis, Jeff A909
Davis, Seth A913
Davis, Jennifer A929
Davis, Derek A939
Davis, Yolanda P9
Davis, James C. (Jim) P24
Davis, Chris P64
Davis, Mary P77
Davis, Joan P89
Davis, Jason P105
Davis, Benjamin P113
Davis, Pamela Bowles P116
Davis, Carolyn P131
Davis, Scott P134
Davis, Ellen F. P187
Davis, Adora P188
Davis, Pamela P191
Davis, Brian P192
Davis, Matt P205
Davis, Gary P206
Davis, Becky P209
Davis, Chris P235
Davis, Ken P248
Davis, Shirley P250
Davis, Auston P302
Davis, Leslie C P303
Davis, Kenneth L P351
Davis, Jed P361
Davis, Latia P370
Davis, Richard E. P389
Davis, Mark P395
Davis, Tim P417
Davis, Belinda P420
Davis, Debbie P451
Davis, Cory P453
Davis, Paul P475
Davis, Crystal P482
Davis, Jonathan S. P484
Davis, Jodi P535
Davis, Myra P548
Davis, Shawn P548
Davis, Muzzet P551
Davis, Dawn P554
Davis, Joan S. P563
Davis, Greg P567
Davis, Anne P571
Davis, Patricia P574
Davis, Jeff P574
Davis, Thomas P P581
Davis, Debra A. P596
Davis, John P602
Davis, Michael P607
Davis, Elizabeth P625
Davis, Tyler P639
Davis, Leslie C. P643
Davis, Deborah P649
Davis, A. Jack P652
Davis, Traci P659
Davis, James L P674
Davis, Darrell W21
Davis, Gareth W161
Davis, Lisa W353
Davis, Sarah R. W422
Davis, Morris A. E5
Davis, Chris E27
Davis, John B. E43
Davis, Kathy E49
Davis, Todd E80
Davis, Mike E105
Davis, Meloni E106
Davis, Lou J. E157

COMBINED HOOVER'S HANDBOOK INDEX OF EXECUTIVES

A = AMERICAN BUSINESS
E = EMERGING COMPANIES
P = PRIVATE COMPANIES
W = WORLD BUSINESS

Davis, Sharon L. E159
Davis, Claude E. E160
Davis, Kirk A. E183
Davis, Blake E185
Davis, Joe E205
Davis, Andrew E218
Davis, John R. E220
Davis, Robert T. E233
Davis, Desiree E264
Davis, Larry E282
Davis, Keith B E334
Davis, Kathy E351
Davis, Scott E354
Davis, Reid E380
Davis, Cindy E383
Davis, Nancy B. E389
Davis, Mark E410
Davis, Jeff L. E422
Davis, Eugene I. (Gene) E422
Davis, Jeff E436
Davis, Seth E438
Davis, Jennifer E449
Davis-Kubofcik, Deborah P575
Davis-Smith, Amy A797
Davison, Brian A232
Davison, Steve A373
Davison, J Scott A628
Davison, Paul J A688
Davison, Corey A811
Davison, J Scott P396
Davisson, Robert J. A756
Davoren, Peter J A830
Davoren, Peter J. A853
Davoren, Peter J P593
Davoren, Peter J. P612
Davoren, Peter J. W6
Davy, Alan P443
Davy, Alan W79
Davydova, Yulia E318
Daw, Peter A361
Dawes, James A196
Dawes, Leah A306
Dawes, Christopher A510
Dawes, Christopher P290
Dawes, Christopher P302
Dawes, Karen A. E353
Dawkins, Linda A284
Dawkins, Linda E117
Dawley, Mary P54
Dawoodbhai, Moiz A91
Dawoodbhai, Moiz P55
Dawsey, John E424
Dawson, Robert A111
Dawson, Mike A364
Dawson, Pat D. A624
Dawson, Lena A925
Dawson, Lena E445
Day, Mike A213
Day, Alan A219
Day, Ray A360
Day, Thomas R. A434
Day, Zane A498
Day, Kate A559
Day, Edward A590
Day, Geoff A750
Day, Diana A753
Day, J. Randal A765
Day, J Randal A765
Day, William B. (Bill) A797
Day, Dennis A823
Day, Sarah A924
Day, Timothy P80
Day, Terri P277
Day, Debbie P352
Day, Lynn Carmen P451
Day, James H P607
Day, Sarah P672
Day, Anthony W373
Day, Alan E87

Day, Ken E268
Day, Paulee C. E269
Day, Dennis E405
Day-Salo, Ann A222
Dayal, Gaurov A776
Dayal, Gaurov P512
Dayhoff, Diane A428
Dayon, Alexandre (Alex) A739
Days, Karen P359
DC, Sister Bernice Coreil A84
DC, Sister Maureen McGuire A84
DC, Sister Bernice Coreil P47
DC, Sister Maureen McGuire P47
DDS, Will Daniels P77
DDS, L Kenneth Heuler P129
DDS, Edwin Zechman P131
DDS, Phillip Wenk P177
De, Rossi Gabriel A571
De, Monica P102
Deacon, Mary Ann A504
Deacon, Eric A881
Deacon, Mary Ann E251
Deacon, Eric E421
Deakin, Scott M. E263
Deal, Stanley A. (Stan) A140
Deal, Helena A418
Deal, Richard S. E144
deAlcuaz, Joseph E51
deAlcuaz, Joe E51
Dealmeida, Isabel A205
Dealy, Richard P. (Rich) A666
Deambrogio, Roberto W153
Dean, Aaron A100
Dean, Kim A167
Dean, Robert A176
Dean, John C. A182
Dean, Lloyd H. A266
Dean, Roger A274
Dean, Clay A345
Dean, Lynda A456
Dean, Robert A581
Dean, Andrea A723
Dean, Steve A735
Dean, DOT P28
Dean, Edward P58
Dean, James D P85
Dean, Jerry P168
Dean, Lloyd H. P181
Dean, Doug P193
Dean, Gregory P202
Dean, Pam P377
Dean, Lesley P396
Dean, Antoinette P465
Dean, Susanne P532
Dean, Christina P610
Dean, Robert E98
Dean, Lisa E123
Dean, James E131
Dean, Clay E166
Dean, Lynda E228
Dean, Alison E239
Dean, Robert E294
Dean, Wayne E309
Dean-Hammel, Bridget A135
Deane, Stephen A408
Deangelo, Lucia A248
Deangelo, Joseph J A412
Deangelo, Lucia A107
DeAngelo, Lawrence J. (Larry) E271
Deanhardt, Jill A850
Dearborn, Grant P232
Deardorff, Kevin L. A504
Deardorff, Kevin L. E251
Dearman, Paul A135
Dearth, Randall S. (Randy) P106
Deases, Rene E106
Deason, Richard A509
Deaton, Craig A933
Deaton, John P160
Deaton, Eric P662
Deaver, W. Scott A98
Deaver, Scott A98
Deb, Stone P111
DeBarger, Candace A544
DeBarros, Garfield A137

Debenedetti, Pablo G. P591
Debertin, Jay D. A194
Debertin, Jay P133
Debiase, Dean E330
Deblaere, Johan G. (Jo) W5
Debnam, Henry A501
Debo, Michael A806
Debo, Michael E399
DeBoer, Bryan B. A521
DeBoer, Sidney B. (Sid) A521
Deboer, Greg A797
Debon, Marie-Ange W366
Debono, Paul A222
Debord, Wes A329
Debra, Scammon P597
Debrecht, Ken P18
Debrier, Jurgen A744
Debruin, Christopher P531
Debruyne, Luc W171
Decardenas, Eva P561
Decaria, Amanda A155
Decaria, Amanda E54
Decastro, Ramon A800
Decastro, Victoria P128
December, Katrina P642
Dechaene, Tom W55
Dechant, Suzanne A779
Dechant, Maria P636
Decher, Peter A863
Dechiara, Michael A89
Dechiro, Carlo V P509
Decicco, Carl A151
Decicco, Dawn A727
Decicco, Dawn P453
Deck, Richard A692
Deck, Brian A. E241
Deckard, Bill A756
Decker, Susan A242
Decker, Casey A316
Decker, T Blair A373
Decker, Edward P. (Ted) A428
Decker, Julie A715
Decker, Patrick K. A936
Decker, Andrea P330
Decker, Jeff E21
DeClaris, Wade N. A927
Declas, Jean-Luc A934
Decoeur, Dan P673
Decolli, Chris A3
DeConinck, Louis H. W193
Decourcey, Lynn A530
Decraene, Dave A345
Decraene, Stefaan W71
Decraene, Dave E165
Dedicoat, Chris A198
Dedinsky, John G. A640
Dedominicis, Kim A799
Dee, Jane A620
Dee, Tim P404
Dee, Fabian W255
Dee, John J. A441
Deeba, Amer S. E342
Deegan, Glenn E. E12
Deely, Brendan E252
Deering, Michael P299
Deering, Brandon E334
Dees, Kent A717
Dees, Chuck A905
Dees, Kent E351
Deese, Willie A688
Deevy, Will A793
Defalco, Joseph A137
Defazio, Gary M A123
Defeciani, Patrick A203
Defeis, Nicholas A686
Defenbaugh, Raymond E P82
Defilippis, Victor A635
Defilippo, Ken A484
Definis, Karen A575
DeFonce, Dave E143
Defontnouvelle, Patrick A322
DeFord, Drexel P528
Deford, Steve E347
DeFranco, James (Jim) A271
Defranco, Jim A271

DeFreese, Susan A449
DeFreese, Susan E221
DeFreitas, Shannie A115
DeFreitas, Shannie E38
Degeer, Randy E102
Degenhart, Elmar W117
DeGiorgio, Kenneth D. A332
Degliantoni, Lori A895
Deglopper, Julie A530
Degnan, S. Scott A443
Degnan, S Scott E443
Degnan, Steven E443
Degodt, Nathan E14
Degoede, Arthur P168
Degraff, Cheryl A222
DeGrand, Robert P211
DeGregorio, Ronald J. (Ron) A304
Degroot, Scott A493
Deguia, Edgar A260
Dehahn, Erin P659
Dehaven, Judy A893
Dehaven, Michael P513
Dehaze, Alain W7
Dehli, Sharon A352
Dehring, Tim A600
Deibert, Karen P399
Deigl, Jeffrey A36
Deignan, Joanne A135
Deignan, Kathleen P591
Dein, Brian A722
Deis, Tiffany A A233
Deis, Ron A457
Deis, Colin P496
Deisinger, Jennifer A108
Deitch, Sally A811
Deitering, Teresa E416
Deitz, Robert A75
Deitz, Edward A796
Deitz, Edward E397
Deiure, Giovannella E253
Dejarme, Lindy P70
DeJong, Nick A69
Dejong, Paul A768
Dejurnett, Mikki A507
Dekay, Sam A112
Dekay, Donald F P257
Dekay, Barry P362
Dekeyser, Jill A693
Dekeyser, Paul P356
Dekeyser, Jill E341
Dekker, Karen A60
Dekker, Hans A355
Dekker, Wout W319
Dekkers, Marijn W409
Dekoch, Bob P555
Dekorte, Jeff A161
DeKosky, Steven T. (Steve) P442
Delabriere, Yann W161
Delac, Frank A63
Delacour, Alia P481
Delacruz, Cedric A409
Delafuente, Laura A482
Delagardelle, Pam P258
Delagi, R. Gregory (Greg) A820
Delahunt, Susan A183
Delahunt, Peter A704
Delahunt, Susan E73
Delamater, James D. E305
Delamater, Chris E305
Delancey, Virginia P389
Delaney, John A147
Delaney, Steve A175
Delaney, BradleyBrad A195
Delaney, Bradley A195
Delaney, Chris A392
Delaney, Kristen A452
Delaney, Thomas A. (Tom) A592
Delaney, William A742
DeLaney, William J. (Bill) A797
Delaney, Thomas A. (Tom) P370
Delaney, Michelle Anne P497
Delaney, Ed P618
Delaney, Mary P664
Delano, Joe A584
Delano, Laurie A. P566

Delanois, Gary P1
Delany, Jim P555
Delarge, Steven P. W238
DeLaTorre, Katy A804
Delatorre, Xavier P677
Delatour, John S. E349
Delattre, James A828
Delattre, James P584
Delauder, Brad P161
DeLawder, C. Daniel (Dan) A639
Delawder, Bruce A831
Delawder, Bruce P601
Delay, Mary G P596
Delay, Emmanuel W305
Delcastro, Dennis A493
Delcorse, Jeff E131
Delellis, Michael A692
Delellis, Ronald A P448
Delena, Daniel A465
deLeon, Rudy A373
Deleon, Marcos A478
Deleon, Leo A754
Deleon, Marcos P269
Deleon, Leo P484
Deleonardis, Doreen P664
Delessio, Linda P215
Delfassy, Gilles A628
Delgadillo, Joe P387
Delgado, Joaquin A3
Delgado, Gilberto P582
Delgatti, Michael W. E215
Delgiudice, Tim A706
Delie, Vincent J. (Vince) A357
Delie, Vincent J. (Vince) E175
deLima, Pia A915
Delimitros, Maria A155
Delimitros, Maria E54
DeLine, Robert A460
Delio, Anthony P. (Tony) A457
DeLise, Antonio L. (Tony) E270
Delity, Dan E122
Delker, Jed A352
Dell, Joseph E. A211
Dell, Michael S. A897
Dell, Joseph E. E83
Dell, Linda E118
Dellaglio, Vincent A135
Dellantonia, Dean A702
Dellapina, Megan A337
Dellapina, Megan E158
Dellaquila, Frank J A292
Dellaselva, Chris P138
Dellazoppa, Steve A835
Dellinger, Lisa P312
Dellosa, Vince A702
Dell'Osso, Domenic J. (Nick) A189
Delmenhorst, Fred E268
DeLoach, Thomas C. A83
DeLoach, Harris E. A768
DeLoach, Scott A927
Deloach, Darlene P508
Deloatch, Sidney A329
Delombarde, Joey P235
Delone, Carrie L A371
Delone, Carrie L P213
Delong, David P564
Delong, William C P564
Delong, Charles R P564
Delong, Bo P564
Delong, Mary Lou P608
Delong, Bob E51
DeLongchamps, Peter C. A398
Delorenz, Don A933
DeLorenzo, Michael A61
Delorenzo, Marc A169
Delorenzo, Marianne A218
Delorenzo, Rhonda A356
Delorimier, John A440
Delorme, Philippe W344
Delotta, Debbie P500
Delozier, Karen A763
Delozier, Sharon P449
Delozier, Karen E377
Delp, Robert D. (Rob) A939
Delph, Chuck A99

Delph, Rob A818
Delph, Rob E403
Delplato, Anne A586
Delplato, Anne E301
Delpropoto, Zachary A414
Delpropoto, Zachary P236
Delrosso, Irene P409
Deltenre, Ingrid W55
DeLuca, Richard R. A554
Deluca, Vince P297
Deluca-flaherty, Camille E300
DeLucia, Cathy A132
Deluke, Linda A751
Deluke, Linda P482
Deluz, Donna P628
Delvecchio, Michael A468
Delvecchio, Steve P2
Demahy, Anita P481
Demange, Vincent W323
DeMarco, David S. (Dave) A82
Demarco, David A690
Demarcus, Mark A430
Demarcus, W Mark A430
DeMaria, Jacqueline M. A914
Demarie, John P70
Demartino, John A63
Dematas, Teri P252
DeMatteo, Daniel A. A371
DeMay, Brian A899
Demay, David P274
Demay, Renee E22
Dembitz, Terry A914
Demchak, William S A668
Demchak, Robert A761
Deme, Zoltan E290
DeMeester, Chris E172
Demel, Herbert W244
Demello, Daphne P417
Dement, Jason A329
Demere, Robert A769
Demere, Robert E380
Demetriou, Steven J. A476
Demetsky, Nate A482
DeMichiei, Robert A. P643
Demild, Brian A368
Deming, Peggy P82
Demirovski, Fluturi P445
Demise, Mesfin E202
Demita, Tab A329
Demko, Chris A367
Demme, Kendra P101
Demmerle, Stefan A146
Demmers, Dan E73
Demmings, Keith W. A88
Demoleas, John P P527
Demont, Melanie A60
Demont, Adam A86
Demont, Adam E27
Demos, Mark C A105
Demos, Mike A132
Demos, Mark C E34
Demott, Andrew D. E393
Demourkas, Cat P472
Dempsey, Maureen A69
Dempsey, Joan A. A145
Dempsey, Paul A830
Dempsey, Paul P593
Dempsey, Patrick E433
Dempster, Graham Wayne W275
Demski, Renee A478
Demski, Renee P269
Demski, David M. (Dave) E190
Demuro, Gerard A373
Demuro, Mike A613
Demuro, Jerry W42
Demuth, Phil A352
Den, Sara P465
Denadel, Matt E185
Denahan, A. Alexandra E79
Denault, Leo P. A296
Denault, Leo P P196
Denbaum, Larry A111
denBoer, Marten P175
Denby, Farrell A135
Denby, Kristy A222

Dendinger, Bradley M A461
Denecke, Sue A540
Denenberg, Dave A125
DeNezza, Matthew R. E289
Deng, Tania A445
Dengbang, Gao W29
Dengel, Kaye A538
Denges, Jim P530
Dengg, Robb A462
Dengg, Robb P256
Denham, Heather A260
Denham, Amber P623
Denholm, David J. A487
Deni, Rob A146
DeNichilo, Nicholas P303
Deninger, Matthew P315
Denise, Mccauley P574
Denison, Kurtis A651
Denison, Jessica P564
Denison, Kurtis E329
Denizard, Patrice E85
Denizli, Alexandra P459
Denk, Peter A724
Denk, Peter P452
Denka, Andrew A726
Denker, Claude H. (Bud) A649
Denman, Kenneth A577
Dennemann, Kelly A335
Dennemann, Kelly E155
Denner, Volkmar W75
Denning, Ryan A409
Denningham, Wayne A. A30
Denningham, Wayne A. P20
Dennis, Young A52
Dennis, Bob A61
Dennis, Debbie A62
Dennis, Bruce A140
Dennis, Crystal A222
Dennis, Ott A320
Dennis, Stephen A415
Dennis, Joseph A741
Dennis, Dan A859
Dennis, Patricia A874
Dennis, Lakisha P137
Dennis, Patrick P261
Dennis, Everette E. P388
Dennis, Tyler P415
Dennis, Monica P420
Dennis, Debbie E20
Dennis, Jason E143
Dennis, Thomas (Tom) St. E177
Dennis, Stephen E209
Dennis, Joseph E364
Dennison, Lisa A790
Dennison, Kay P40
Dennison, Mike W164
Dennison, Lisa E389
Denny, Lindell A63
Denny, Coleen P662
Denoble, Ubavka P405
Denovo, Robert A665
Denovo, Robert E334
Denoya, Dave A888
Denoya, Dave E425
Denoyel, Eric A374
Densham, Edward P469
Dent, Pamela A364
Dent, Mary J. E194
Dent, Margaret E358
Dente, Lisa A530
Denti, Aldo A479
Denton, David M. (Dave) A251
Denton, Bill A452
Denton, Kelly P264
Denty, Kimberly P187
Denzer, Carol A723
Denzer, Bill E31
Deo, Rajat P244
Deoliveira, Jessica A592
Deoliveira, Mark A835
Deoliveira, Jessica P370
Deon, Pasquale T. (Pat) P503
Depagnier, Thom A36
Depail, Jean-Claude W154
DePaolo, Joseph J. A759

Depaolo, Joseph J A759
Depaolo, Joseph J P493
Depaolo, Mary-beth P496
DePaolo, Joseph J. E373
Deparle, Nancy-ann A251
dePasquale, Caterina A356
DePauw, Karen P. P652
DePell, Fred (Fred) A609
DePell, Fred (Fred) P387
DePiano, Frank P389
DePina, Stuart E131
DePinto, Joseph I. A169
DePinto, Joseph M. (Joe) W346
Depot, Dennis A428
Depowski, Robert A484
Deppe, Erik A325
DEPPERU, DONATELLA W43
Deprey, Matthew A270
Depriest, Jennifer A746
Depriest, Ken E379
Deprospero, Joe E111
Deputy, Christine F. A602
Der, Channing P595
Derba, Laura A921
Derba, Laura P669
Derby, Cindy P513
DeReu, William R. E337
Deris, John A734
Derita, Nancy P516
DeRito, John A. A206
Dermanuelian, Nareg A203
Dermody, Michael A112
Dermody, John A161
Dernoncourt, Jean-Baptiste W88
Deroche, Lynne A538
DeRosa, Mike A357
Derosa, Peter P138
DeRosa, Mike E176
Derpinghaus, Patrick J. A85
Derpinghaus, Patrick J. E26
Derr, Michael A784
Derr, David P411
Derrick, Brian P19
Derrick, Brian P326
Derstine, Mike A381
DeRue, Scott A711
DeRue, Scott P444
Deruiter, Kathie A A433
Deruiter, Kathie A E217
Derwinski, Janet P404
Dery, William E150
Deryckere, Bernard P. J. P668
Derzypolski, Stephanie P541
Desai, Darpan A69
Desai, Ankit A188
Desai, Bobby A369
Desai, Gary A450
Desai, Ashit A540
Desai, Paritosh A804
Desai, Jinali A902
Desai, Anup P349
Desai, Nisha E334
Desal, Parltosh A804
Desalvo, Tom A750
DeSantis, Caitlin A391
Desantis, Mark A658
DeSantis, Chris A905
Desanto, John A207
Desanto, John E81
Desarno, Fred P294
Descalzi, Claudio W155
Deschamps, Frederic (Fred) A417
Deschamps, Ignacio (Nacho) W53
Descheneaux, Michael R. (Mike) A793
Deschon, Beverly P618
Desfosses, Kristina E287
Deshaies, Roger P598
Deshazo, Nina P130
Deshon, Michelle A491
Deshong, Leanne P117
Deshpande, Anant A198
Deshpande, Jayant K. P45
Desiderio, Kathleen A204
Desilva, Philip A75
Desilva, Shelley A167

COMBINED HOOVER'S HANDBOOK INDEX OF EXECUTIVES

```
A = AMERICAN BUSINESS
E = EMERGING COMPANIES
P = PRIVATE COMPANIES
W = WORLD BUSINESS
```

deSilva, Peter A807
Desimas, Danny P274
Desimone, John A706
Desimone, Marianne E154
Desire, Jean-Luc A813
Desisto, Donna P473
Deskins, Juanita P419
Desmarais, Brian A782
Desmarais, Brian P525
Desmarais, André R. W313
Desmarais, Paul W313
Desmarais, André R. W313
Desmarais, Paul W313
Desmartis, Charles W88
Desmond, James A716
Desmond, Neil P390
Desmond, Margaret P596
Desmond-hellmann, Susan A310
Desoer, Barbara J. A203
Desorbo, Louis A179
Desormeaux, Joseph A375
Desormeaux, Joseph P215
DeSousa, Dennis E. A396
DeSouza, Jacqui A512
Despain, Daniel E123
Despeaux, Kimberly H P196
Despelteau, Jim E429
DeSpirt, Christa A530
Desrosiers, Mark A740
Dessen, Flo A701
Deste, Dario A331
Deste, Dario P202
DeStefano, Joseph (Joe) A387
DeStefano, Lisa A428
DeStefano, Joanne M. P159
Destler, William W. (Bill) P456
Destro, Steven A530
Detavernier, Andrew A915
Dete, Brendan P5
Deters, Deborah A413
Deters, Deborah E205
Deters, Kevin E322
Detlaff, Lee A327
Detmer, Don P442
Detommaso, Michael A248
Detommaso, Michael E107
Detwiler, James A140
Detwiler, Stefanie A596
Deuel, Jeffrey J. (Jeff) A415
Deuel, Jeffrey J. (Jeff) E209
Deuprey, Charleen A109
Deuschle, James R. (Jim) P449
Deutsch, Clayton G. (Clay) A147
Deutsch, Emilie A893
Deutsch, Esther W203
Deutsch, Andy E290
Dev, Raj P547
Devader, Julie M E148
Devane, Barry A755
Devane, Barry E369
Devaney, Edward A251
Devaney, Jack P74
Devaraju, Ramasamy W208
Devarajulu, Krishna A884
DeVard, Jerri L. A620
Devard, Jerri A862
Devault, David V. A904
Deveaux, Kenneth A205
Devendran, Anand A835
Deveno, Paul A428
Devens, Michael P185
Devera-duncan, Leslie A690
Deverell, Tom A369
Devereux, Patricia A544
Devers, Shannon E237
Deveson, Gregory S. (Greg) A49
Devienne, Frederic A21
Devilbiss, Lisamarie A484

Deville, Marc A107
Devine, Jeff A199
Devine, Michael P. A268
Devine, Dan A418
Devine, Daniel A418
Devine, Danielle A479
Devine, Catherine A479
Devine, Dennis A. A491
Devine, Amy A530
Devine, David P360
Devine, Thomas E306
Devine-Pride, Anne A809
Devitt, John A702
Devivo, Zita P366
Devlin, Kelly A484
Devlin, Jason A575
Devlin, Dennis P569
Devlin, Dave P618
Devoe, Clint A168
Devoe, Michael P52
Devoe, Ellen P96
Devoney, William P191
DeVoney, Michael P613
Devooght, Shawn P233
Devore, Susan P428
DeVos, Doug A40
DeVos, Mr Doug L A766
DeVos, Doug P29
Devos, Mr Doug L P500
Devries, Bailey A799
Dew, Lyndol A526
Dewaard, Roelant A360
Dewald, Julius P388
Dewalt, Karen A428
Dewan, Rohit A629
Dewane, Sherry A147
Dewar, Patrick M A524
Dewbre, Jim A189
Dewerff, Mike P258
Dewey, Barbara I. A828
Dewey, Duane A. A852
Dewey, Susan F. A894
Dewey, Barbara I. P584
Dewey, Susan F. P651
Dewhurst, Moray P. A354
DeWilder, Dean E123
Dewitt, Kimberly A531
Dewolf, John E218
DeWolfe, Richard B. W247
Dews, Maria A100
Dews, Maria P58
Dews, Teri E120
Dexian, Chen W306
Dexter, Brad A442
Dey, Eric R. E174
Dezenzo, Rosemarie A738
Dezern, Craig A423
Dezzi, Lauren A618
Dezzi, Lauren E310
Dhagat, Aditi A471
Dhalla, Cyrus A608
Dhamodharan, Raj A544
Dhanapal, Kishore P286
Dhanda, Anuj A30
Dhanda, Anuj P20
Dhandapani, Chandra A175
Dhanjee, Bhaveer A722
Dhawan, Mahasweta A54
Dhawan, Neha A135
Dhawan, Ravinder A554
Dhillon, Janet L. A158
Dhingra, Amit A444
Dhingra, Ajay A933
Dhir, Samir E431
Dholakia, Paras A378
Dhooge, Dirk A842
Di, Kim A702
Diab, Rob A868
Diacont, Chad A893
Diakov, Peter P630
Dial, Karla A760
Dial, Karla E374
Dials, Kelly P359
Dialto, Margaret P527

Diamond, Lee A175
Diamond, Mark C A414
Diamond, Rachael A828
Diamond, Gene P207
Diamond, Mark C P236
Diamond, Margae P477
Diamond, Lester P514
Diamond, Rachael P584
Diamond, Vicky P677
Diamond, Larry J. E8
Diamond, Jeremy E79
Diamond-wells, Tammy R P45
Dian, Ali P493
Diana, Charles E101
Diao, Charles A230
Diao, Charles P154
Dias, André Pires de Oliveira W405
Diasio, Anthony P325
Diaz, Fernando A103
Diaz, Andy A173
Diaz, Guillermo A198
Diaz, Paul A257
Diaz, Carlos A378
Diaz, Pedro A449
Diaz, Michael A481
Diaz, Raymond A560
Diaz, Lori A693
Diaz, Jose Antonio A782
Diaz, Octavio J. (Tavi) A811
Diaz, Miguel A867
Diaz, Linda A888
Diaz, Raymond P336
Diaz, Jesse P417
Diaz, Jose Antonio P525
Diaz, Mark P569
Diaz, Jorge E P587
Diaz, Robert P671
Diaz, Frederic E131
Diaz, Fred E131
Diaz, Pedro E220
Diaz, Lori E341
Diaz, Linda E425
Diaz-infante, Alfred P468
Diaz-Matos, Andrew A409
Dibattista, Cj A756
Dibattista, Vincent P229
DiBella, John E375
Dibenedetto, Tony A888
Dibenedetto, Tony E425
Dibenedetto, Rich E429
DiBernardi, John A532
DiBianca, Suzanne A739
DiBiase, Ronald A337
DiBiase, Ronald E158
Dibkey, Brett A919
Dibky, Brett A920
Dibonaventura, Lynn A922
Dibonaventura, Lynn P671
Dibrell, Henry P274
Dicesare, Thor P119
DiChiaro, Steven J. (Steve) A389
DiCicco, Sean A161
Dicicco, Aimee A323
Dicicco, Aimee L A323
DiCicco, Wendy F. E225
Diciurcio, John P202
DiCiurcio, John A. W6
Dickel, Susan P573
Dickens, Dave P108
Dickens-hunter, Deborah A752
Dickenson, Bill A369
Dickenson, James P264
Dicker, Derek A565
Dicker, Joshua E187
Dickerson, Gary E. A74
Dickerson, Rita A359
Dickerson, John C. P301
Dickerson, Staci P489
Dickes, Art E383
Dickey, Bill A281
Dickey, Elbert P92
Dickherber, Alice P465
Dickie, Robert W435
Dickinson, Barbara A91
Dickinson, Andrew A385

Dickinson, Clay A481
Dickinson, Laurie A491
Dickinson, Paul A509
Dickinson, Marty J. A861
Dickinson, Barbara E29
Dickman, Randy A540
Dickman, Susan F P265
Dickman, Paul P417
Dicks, Cindy A677
Dickseski, Jerri Fuller A446
Dickson, Tom A117
Dickson, Steve A262
Dickson, Jenny A540
Dickson, David A924
Dickson, Tom P61
Dickson, Kevin P199
Dickson, Jim E149
Dickson, Bruce F. E177
Dickson, Carl E338
Dicosola, Robert A623
Dicosola, Robert E313
Dicus, John B. A168
Didawick, Kathy P89
Diddee, Anu P284
Didden, Andrew P202
Diderich, Jeroen A97
Didomenico, Vincent A120
Didonato, Ray A54
Didonato, Thomas A508
Diebolt, Dennis A711
Diebolt, Dennis P444
Dieckmann, Anita P235
Diederich, Tom P417
Diedrich, David A573
Diefenderfer, Joe A266
Diefenderfer, William M. A583
Diefenderfer, Joe P181
Diefenderfer, William M. E104
Diefenthaler, Aaron P. A723
Diegan, Brian A357
Diegan, Brian E175
Diehl, William A664
Diehl, Valerie P117
Diehl, William E334
Diehl-boyle, Constance A89
Diehm, Russell C P95
Diekmann, Michael W59
Diemer, John W A726
Diemer, John W P453
Diennen, Rob P491
Diercks, Dwight A613
Dieringer, Brian A442
Diesch, Siegfried A661
Diesel, R Wayne A785
Diesel, R Wayne P526
Diess, Herbert W418
Dieter, Claus W151
Dietert, Jeff A662
Dietrich, Lavonne A253
Dietrich, Todd A368
Dietrich, Martin A. A584
Dietrich, Paul A723
Dietrich, Peter T. A770
Dietrich, William S A883
Dietrich, Lavonne P169
Dietrich, Bob P384
Dietrich, Katherine P523
Dietrich, William S P644
Dietrich, Greg E271
Dietrick, William M E339
Dietrick, Bill E340
Dietsch, Johannes W61
Dietsche, Jim P76
Dietz, Robert J P212
Dietz, Edward R. E271
Dietze, Steven J. P670
Dietzen, Joseph A912
Dietzler, David A219
Dietzler, David E87
Diez, John J. A734
Diez, Janice E127
DiFerdinando, John E179
Difinizio, Antoinette A590
Difonzo, Carlo E300
Difrancesco, Ray A574

DiFrancesco, Paul A868
DiFulvio, William E305
DiGaetani, Mark A200
Diganci, Todd T. P202
Diggelmann, Roland W328
Diggins, Patty P231
Dighe, Prafad P519
Digiovanni, Mark E172
Dignam, Chris A715
DiGrande, Sebastian A826
Digregorio, Michael A922
Digregorio, Michael P671
Diguilio, Ralph A447
Dijk, Carol Van P341
Dikeman, Marcy P604
Diker, Charles A526
Diker, Charles M. E63
Dilan, Jose P369
Dile, Brenda E14
Dilger, Jason A452
DiLibero, Danelle E429
Diliberto, Matthew J A708
Diliberto, Matthew J P441
Dilisi, Jeffrey P651
Dilka, Krystal P525
Dill, Richard A213
Dill, Robert C. A760
Dill, Matt A895
Dill, Richard P143
Dill, Julie P549
Dill, Robert C. E374
Dillard, James E. (Jim) A41
Dillard, Maria A89
Dillard, Mike A267
Dillard, Alex A267
Dillard, William (Bill) A267
Dillard, Monica P551
Dille, Eric A301
Diller, Barry A307
Diller, Lisa R. P172
Dillingham, Frederick E150
Dillion, Kevin P595
Dillon, Michael A. (Mike) A11
Dillon, Julie A218
Dillon, Donna A229
Dillon, Mary N A858
Dillon, Daniel P44
Dillon, Tim P246
Dillon, Danel P319
Dillon, Deborah P556
Dillon, Kevin P596
Dillon, Roderick H. (Ric) E112
DiLorenzo, Dennis A592
DiLorenzo, Dennis P370
Dilts, Sandra P500
DiLuigi, Leslie A719
DiLuigi, Leslie E355
Dilworth, Robert A780
DiMaio, Joseph J A155
DiMaio, Rick A620
Dimaio, Joseph J E54
DiPrima, Natasha P389
Dimarco, Tony P116
Dimarco, Dana P409
DiMarco, Bret M. E86
Dimaria, Dina A707
Dimas, Constantine A525
Dimas, Michelle P138
Dimauro, Bernice P673
Dimech, Johnpaul W358
Dimicco, Daniel A281
Dimick, Mary E413
Dimino, Sal A125
Dimino, John A531
Dimitian, Diana A514
Dimitian, Diana A516
Dimitian, Diana P293
Dimitrova, Roza A44
Dimitrova, Roza E13
Dimitry, Irene A279
Dimmick, Ruth P21
Dimmick, Scott W P284
Dimmitt, Elizabeth P677
Dimock, Rodney C. E42
Dimodica, Jeffrey F A780
DiModica, Jeffrey E387

Dimon, James (Jamie) A483
Dimond, Bob A30
Dimond, Bob P20
Dimopoulos, Dimitrios G. W272
Dimuccio, Robert A904
DiNapoli, Mark L. P531
DiNapoli, Michael (Mike) P531
DiNapoli, Michael P531
Dinardo, Mary A668
Dinda, Kelly A108
Dindigal, Anil A739
Dindoffer, Joan A222
DiNello, Alessandro P. A353
DiNello, Alessandro P. E173
Dinesman, Jonathan A179
Ding, Yanzhang W98
Ding, Guangmu W431
Dingemans, Simon W171
Dinger, Stephanie A862
Dinger, Stephanie P617
Dinges, Victoria A35
Dinges, Dan A874
Dingess, Cheryl A885
Dingle, David K. W87
Dinh, Trang A54
Dinis, Filipe W50
Diniz, Cem P395
Dinjian, Randy A405
Dinn, Colin R. W351
Dinnage, Susanna A270
Dinner, Larry A176
Dinnie, Holly P72
Dinshaw, Behram M. A844
Dinsmore, Walter A137
Dinsmore, Richard A331
Dinsmore, Richard P202
Din-Şer, Suzan Sabanci W19
Din-Şer, Haluk W177
Diodati, Joe A199
Diokno, Ananias P670
Diomedes, David A161
Dion, Stephane A875
Dion, Richard E131
Dionisio, Mike A263
Dionne, Michael P590
Dionne, Mike P590
DiPalma, Greg A934
Dipalma, Theresa Alberghini P598
Dipaolo, Joseph A P12
Dipaolo, Michael P495
DiPento, Melissa A108
Diperna, Kathy A437
Dipetrio, Kenneth A133
DiPiazza, Robert A902
DiPietro, Kenneth A. (Ken) A133
Dipp, Margaret E8
Dippolito, Tom A268
Dipre, Sharon E143
DiPresso, Raymond A651
DiPresso, Raymond E330
DiPrima, Natasha P389
DiPrisco, Dan P548
Director, Goodin A117
Director, Goodin P61
Direnzo, Patrick A248
Direnzo, Patrick E107
Diresta, Pat E315
DiRienzo, Judy E433
Dirik, Akin E196
Dirks, Douglas D. A293
Dirks, Ryan A329
Dirkschneider, Kathryn A A706
Dirmyer, Richard P456
Dirscherl, Dan P246
DiRusso, Lonny R. A732
Disanti, Joseph A114
Disanti, Joseph E37
DiSanto, Edmund (Ed) A59
Disanto, Salvatore A702
Disarlo, Lorraine P646
Disbrow, Joshua E453
Discola, Christine A574
Dishaw, Michael P68
Dishaw, Michael F P68
Dishman, William M. A788

Dishman, Pam P177
Dishman, Roy P445
Dishman, William M. E389
DiSilvestro, Anthony P. A164
Disilvestro, Carlo A A853
Disilvestro, Carlo A P612
Disimone, Vincent A752
Disney, Ed A142
Disney, David L P261
Disney, Ed E49
Dison, Rick A444
Dispensa, James V A139
Dispensa, James V P92
Disser, Peter A600
Dissinger, Debra E. A653
Distad, Pete A72
Distasio, Lynne A559
Distaso, John C. A666
DiStefano, Jim A530
DiStefano, Mike A664
Distefano, Michael E248
DiStefano, Mike E333
Distelrath, James W. E150
Ditmars, John A345
Ditmars, John E165
Ditmore, Jim W179
Dittemore, Karen P234
Dittmar, Brian P297
Dittmer, Joseph A831
Dittmer, Joseph P601
Dittrich, Deven A205
Dittrich, Tom A596
DiTullio, Steve P557
Diven, Cathy P70
Divine, Jon P625
Diwa, Portia A791
Diwa, Portia P535
Dix, Dennis A293
Dixon, Gordon A58
Dixon, Robert L A69
Dixon, Susan A169
Dixon, Cheryl A243
Dixon, David A604
Dixon, Donna A866
Dixon, Ronney A866
Dixon, Kenneth (Ken) A889
Dixon, Heather A900
Dixon, Emily E P81
Dixon, Cora P168
Dixon, Anastasia P188
Dixon, Jonathan P203
Dixon, April P225
Dixon, Yolanda P401
Dixon, Wendy E226
Dixon, Bret E412
Dixon, Ronney E417
Dixon-Williams, Sherrie P576
Diya, Kevin A46
Djalali, Chaden P594
DMD, Steven Kramm P282
Do, Orlando Chapa P157
Doak, Mark A22
Doan, Dan L. A621
Doan, Peter P55
Doan, Dan L. E311
Dobbe, Steven A58
Dobbelaere, Jeff P306
Dobbelaere, Arthur G P341
Dobber, Ruud W38
Dobbins, Donnie A449
Dobbins, John A924
Dobbins, John P672
Dobbins, R. Helm E16
Dobbins, Donnie E220
Dobbs, Dennis A209
Dobbs, Lori A520
Dobbs, Randy E. E5
Dobelbower, Peter P242
Doberman, Jeffery A888
Doberman, Jeffery E425
Doberstein, Stephen E300
Dobkin, Arkadiy E133
Dobranski, Edward J. A349
Dobrauc, Christian A599
Dobre, Mircea A727

Dobre, Mircea P453
Dobrinov, Mihail A677
Dobrinski, Everett M. A213
Dobrinski, Everett M. P143
Dobronski, Dave A232
Dobson, Robert A468
Docken, Lori P641
Dockery, Mike A195
Dockery, Sean A737
Dockery, Sean E361
Dockins, Cynthia P550
Docobo, Angel P349
Docter, Judith M. A85
Docter, Judy A85
Docter, Judith M. E26
Docter, Judy E27
Dodd, Jay A145
Dodd, Alida A179
Dodd, David A381
Dodd, Jerry A608
Dodd, Susan P467
Dodd, John E320
Dodds, Carla A544
Dodds, Kevin A737
Dodds, Jon A796
Dodds, Vince P331
Dodds, Alexander W264
Dodds, Jeff E59
Dodds, Kevin E361
Dodds, Jon E397
Dodenhoff, Steven W. A458
Dodge, R. Stanton A271
Dodge, Paul A512
Dodge, Richard E. P389
Dodi, Joe P232
Dodig, Victor W85
Dods, Sarah A740
Dodson, Marti A385
DOE, Cindy P240
Doebele, Luke A36
Doebler, Carl P230
Doecke, Beverly P613
Doehner, Mauricio W91
Doelling, Bruce A103
Doerfler, Max A166
Doering, Richard P242
Doering, Lina P259
Doering, Kimberly B. (Kim) P620
Doerr, David M. P13
Doerr, David P13
Doerr, Andrea P422
Doerrer, Ann P378
Doherty, William J. A66
Doherty, Chris A313
Doherty, Maureen A381
Doherty, Catherine T. A698
Doherty, Chris P200
Doherty, Thomas P304
Doherty, Paul P491
Doherty, John E285
Doherty, Christopher E326
Dohle, Markus W66
Dohman, Pammie P472
Dohnalek, David A140
Dohnalik, Lynn A926
Dohnalik, Lynn E445
Dohner, Eric E402
Dohzen, Shirley P553
Doi, Michael A213
DOI, NOBUHIRO W52
Doig, Russ P213
Doig, John W53
Doignet, Cedric A81
Dojcak, Dena A112
Dokich, Sretenka P438
Dokmecioglu, Ozan A489
Dolan, Paula D. A330
Dolan, Terrance R. (Terry) A884
Dolan, John A897
Dolan, Kelly P22
Dolan, Cole B P316
Dolan, Jill S. P591
Dolan, Paula D. E152
Dolan-wilson, Allison P314
Dolbec, Brad A166

COMBINED HOOVER'S HANDBOOK INDEX OF EXECUTIVES

```
A = AMERICAN BUSINESS
E = EMERGING COMPANIES
P = PRIVATE COMPANIES
W = WORLD BUSINESS
```

Dolce, Diane A167
Dolce, Jeff A420
Dolen, Jim P185
Dolezan, Pamela A806
Dolezan, Pamela E399
Doligale, Anne A759
Doligale, Anne P493
Doliner, Susan P306
Doliner, Peggy P306
Dolinski, Maria A112
Doll, Cynthia P635
Doll, Chase E416
Dollaghan, Jim P184
Dolling, David S. P569
Dolly, Lisa A111
Dolson, Jed E193
Dolsten, Mikael A657
Domanico, Ronald J A412
Domaschuk, Lindsay A654
Dombchewsky, Orest P51
DomBourian, Melkon P127
Domenech, Manuel A119
Domenick, Joseph A835
Domersant, Rachmani P205
Domill-maltese, Alana A356
Dominach, Sandy A236
Dominguez, Letty A246
Dominguez, Joseph A304
Dominguez, Hector A423
Dominguez, Alexus A452
Dominguez, Michael A562
Dominguez, Oscar P499
Dominguez, Leanna P611
Dominguez, Maria P620
Dominguez, Letty E105
Dominic, Gwen A246
Dominic, Gwen E105
Dominick, Jay P591
Dominski, Chris A290
Domit, Carlos Slim W26
Domit, Patrick Slim W26
Domke, Tracey A61
Domson, Michelle A623
Domson, Michelle E313
Dom-nguez, Jaime Muguiro W91
Don, Boelling E162
Donado, Yvette P191
Donaghue, Jason M P516
Donaghy, Gerald A137
Donaghy, Sean T. E122
Donaghy, Stephen J. E420
Donahoe, Tim A550
Donahoe, Tim P319
Donahoe, Keith E105
Donahoo, Mark P185
Donahue, Brian D. A227
Donahue, Timothy J. A245
Donahue, Joseph A281
Donahue, David A315
Donahue, Mike A327
Donahue, Hugh O A365
Donahue, Paul D. A379
Donahue, Joseph A538
Donahue, Amie A559
Donahue, Terry A850
Donahue, Jeanine A876
Donahue, Michael P190
Donahue, Brian D. E90
Donahue, Michael E259
Donahue, Kenneth L. (Ken) E418
Donaker, Geoff E450
Donald, Arnold A245
Donald, Kirkland A296
Donald, Bruce Mc P97
Donald, Arnold W. W87
Donald, Ian W276
Donaldson, Melinda A140
Donaldson, Michael P. A301
Donaldson, Jason A668

Donaldson, Rob A803
Donaldson, David P163
Donaldson, Amy P247
Donarski, Dave A884
Donath, Dan E102
Donato, Valorie A731
Donatone, Lorna C. W358
Donatsch, Reto W55
Donavan, James P341
Dondanville, Ted J. A249
Dondanville, Ted J. E108
Donder, Daniel J P342
Dondero, Cort J. E183
Donegan, Mark A675
Donegan, Mark P428
Donegan, Lynda P608
Donelan, Cindy P131
Donelan, Dave E326
Donelson, Rob A784
Donenberg, Phillip B. E21
Dong, Hanh A319
Dong, Vicky P57
Dong, Ren Ji W103
Dong, Hyunsoo W141
Dong, Mingzhu W174
Dongjin, Wang W301
Dongsheng, Wang W72
Dongsheng, Li W385
Donina, Pete A626
Donley, Jeffrey P115
Donley, Michael B. P553
Donley, Patrick M P657
Donlin, Paul A191
Donlin, Paul E79
Donlon, Patrick A324
Donnell, Steve A312
Donnell, Cathy Mc P129
Donnell, Steve P199
Donnellan, James A559
Donnellan, Kevin P2
Donnelly, Mark A72
Donnelly, Michael J. (Mike) A498
Donnelly, Brent A540
Donnelly, Mary Beth A595
Donnelly, Patrick L. A762
Donnelly, Scott C. A821
Donnelly, Lorra A885
Donnelly, Sean A936
Donnelly, Mel P270
Donnelly, Thomas P333
Donnelly, April P579
Donnelly, Deb E81
Donnelly, Bob E282
Donner, Fred R. A844
Donner, Lee P296
Donnet, Philippe W35
Dono, Robert A724
Dono, Robert P452
Donofrio, Paul M. A107
Donoghue, Tom A569
Donohoo, Shelly A664
Donohoo, Shelly E334
Donohue, Sarah A89
Donohue, Martin A191
Donohue, Jessica A783
Donohue, John A824
Donohue, Sean P. P171
Donohue, John P562
Donovan, John M. A89
Donovan, Jim A155
Donovan, Timothy R. (Tim) A160
Donovan, Margaret A248
Donovan, Peggy A284
Donovan, Jim A452
Donovan, Gerald A481
Donovan, Hart A749
Donovan, Paul P79
Donovan, Thomas C. (Tom) P404
Donovan, Mike P480
Donovan, R. Nowell P549
Donovan, Susan P579
Donovan, Patrick E51
Donovan, Jim E54
Donovan, Margaret E107
Donovan, Peggy E120

Donovan, Hart E367
Doo, Lim Ah W294
Doody, Kevin A135
Dooher, Peter P485
Doolan, Pat A309
Dooley, Wendy A135
Dooley, Brian A175
Dooley, Meta A226
Dooley, Meta P150
Dooley, Bill P155
Dooley, John E. P652
Doolittle, Kirsen E265
Doolittle, Ken E306
Doonan, Tom A456
Doonan, Tom E228
Doordan, Martin L P40
Doors, Stanley A778
Dopson, Nicole P634
Dor, Sigal A179
Dorado, Louis A132
Doram, Keith R P6
Doramus, Mark E374
Doran, James A13
Doran, Debbie A460
Doran, John A540
Doran, Tim A925
Doran, Pat E148
Doran, Jessica R. E340
Doran, Tim E445
Dorch, A. Verona A645
Dorchester, Wendy P298
Dorcheus, Shane A30
Dorcheus, Shane P20
Doren, Craig P51
Dorer, Benno A207
Dores, Daniel P628
Dorfler, Robert P604
Dorfman, Debra A526
Dorgan, David M A729
Dori, Holnagel P242
Doria, Guillermo A115
Doria, Guillermo E38
Dorig, Rolf W7
Dority, Matt A224
Dorkofikis, Constantinos R. W25
Dorman, David W. (Dave) A251
Dorman, Kim A488
Dorminey, O. Leonard (Len) A717
Dorminey, O. Leonard (Len) E351
Dormo, Cindy P131
Dorne, Eric A. A869
Dorner, Steve A695
Dorofeev, Dmitry W428
Doros, Jonathan A476
Dorph, Martin S. A592
Dorph, Martin S. P370
Dorrance, Robert E. (Bob) W396
Dorris, Keith A726
Dorris, Jim A872
Dorris, Keith P453
Dorroh, Tina P623
Dortch, Thomas W P219
Dorto, Joseph P652
Dorward-King, Elaine A595
Dosal, Paul J P638
Dosch, Theodore A A68
Dosch, Theodore A857
Doshi, Gunjan A109
Doshi, Pranav S A414
Doshi, Tejas A590
Doshi, Krupali A651
Doshi, Pranav S P236
Doshi, Krupali E330
Dosi, Abhishek A791
Dosi, Abhishek P535
Doss, Sanjeev A150
Doss, Michael P. A395
Doss, David P432
Dossani, Imran P613
Dostal, Drew A117
Dostal, Drew P61
Doto, Michael A835
Dotson, Judith H. (Judi) A144
Dotson, Tony P228
Dotson, Sonya P429

Dotto, John A54
Dottori-Attanasio, Laura W85
Doty, David D P104
Doty, David P104
Doty, Rob P251
Doty, Larry P421
Doty, William S P505
Doty, Travis P625
Dotzenrath, Anja W143
Doucet, Matthew A925
Doucet, Réal J.H. W85
Doucet, Matthew E445
Doucette, Elmer P190
Doucette, Jami P428
Doucette, Mike J P450
Doud, Art A371
Doud, Terri A799
Douds, Haley A167
Dougherty, Robert A. A25
Dougherty, Edward A112
Dougherty, Siiri A158
Dougherty, Michael A434
Dougherty, Elizabeth A651
Dougherty, Michael D. A669
Dougherty, Thomas A902
Dougherty, Robert A. P14
Dougherty, James P58
Dougherty, Kirsten P291
Dougherty, Kevin P. W371
Dougherty, Elizabeth E330
Dougherty, Kevin E330
Doughman, Ted W A195
Doughty, Thomas A686
Doughty, Ron A686
Douglas, Kevin A6
Douglas, Welter A86
Douglas, Toby A179
Douglas, J. Alexander M. (Sandy) A215
Douglas, Sean A447
Douglas, John A665
Douglas, Laurie Z. A688
Douglas, Laurie Z. A689
Douglas, Keith A831
Douglas, Iain A891
Douglas, Matthew P375
Douglas, Dan P384
Douglas, Laurie Z. P435
Douglas, Brian P597
Douglas, Keith P601
Douglas, Paul C. W396
Douglas, Welter E27
Douglas, J. Boyd E92
Douglas, John E334
Douglas, Camille J. E387
Douglass, Dorothy A580
Douglass, Stephen B P108
Douglass, Travis L P232
Douglass, Dorothy E292
Douillet, Alban A613
Doukas, Peter P546
Doull, Jim P85
Doumas, Michael A934
Doupe, Tom A481
Dour, Joanne P518
Dourlias, George A933
Doustdar, Maziar Mike W290
Douthard, Ross P408
Dove, Timothy L. (Tim) A666
Dove, Kimberly A838
Dove, Reid P1
Dover, Steve P193
Dovey, Stephen A520
Dow, Sandy A325
Dow, Melinda A791
Dow, Trish A924
Dow, Melinda P535
Dowd, Jennifer A540
Dowd, Lacey P539
Dowdell, Robert (Bob) A682
Dowden, Patrick A704
Dowdle, Jeffrey A. (Jeff) A704
Dowell, Greg A. E390
Dowidar, Hatem W417
Dowler, Lynette A279

COMBINED HOOVER'S HANDBOOK INDEX OF EXECUTIVES

Dowling, Ruth A59
Dowling, Steve A72
Dowling, Carol A519
Dowling, Courtney A885
Dowling, Tom A929
Dowling, Joseph L. P102
Dowling, Dennis P382
Dowling, Caroline W164
Dowling, Joseph E224
Dowling, Tom E449
Down, James A123
Downe, Andrew J. W243
Downer, Michael J A56
Downer, Michael J P33
Downer, Jonathan E452
Downes, Sean P. E420
Downey, Todd A185
Downey, Frank A727
Downey, Jenny A818
Downey, Ken A835
Downey, William B P450
Downey, William P451
Downey, Frank P453
Downey, Charles P P658
Downey, Roger W412
Downey, Jenny E403
Downie, Sara P467
Downing, Forrest A56
Downing, Denise A835
Downing, Denise P122
Downing, Mark A. P446
Downing, Helen Dean P474
Downs, Ryan A287
Downs, Allen A466
Downs, Jeff A623
Downs, Mary P602
Downs, Yvette P658
Downs, Keith E8
Downs, Jordan E72
Downs, Jeff E312
Dox, James A222
Doxey, Tom A865
Doyal, Brian S. A726
Doyal, Brian S. P453
Doyle, Larry A22
Doyle, Colleen A54
Doyle, John D A84
Doyle, Fred A103
Doyle, Fredrick A103
Doyle, Scott E. A180
Doyle, James A232
Doyle, Kevin A369
Doyle, Aimee A532
Doyle, John Q. A539
Doyle, John A539
Doyle, John A660
Doyle, Liam A740
Doyle, Michael A790
Doyle, Larry P11
Doyle, John D P47
Doyle, Jim P142
Doyle, Johnna P148
Doyle, James P175
Doyle, John P190
Doyle, Brian P334
Doyle, John P416
Doyle, Terry A P461
Doyle, Mary E P479
Doyle, Noreen W121
Doyle, Michael E308
Dozier, C. Michael A636
Dozier, Tom A665
Dozier, Michael P284
Dozier, Luann P552
Dozier, Tom E334
Dozois, Timothy M. E326
Dozono, Elisa P399
Do--mo, Daniel W344
Draa, Mark A765
Draeger, Jeffrey S A460
Dragalin, Vladimir A480
Draganza, Ernest J. A737
Draganza, Ernie A737
Draganza, Ernest J. E361
Draganza, Ernie E361

Dragas, Helen E. P442
Dragisich, Dominic E. E80
Drago, William P220
Drago, Allyson P626
Dragone, Domingos A778
Drahnak, Steve A737
Drahnak, Steve E361
Drakaki, Alexandra P615
Drake, Jim A108
Drake, Darrell A203
Drake, Michael A219
Drake, Richard A405
Drake, Shelley A530
Drake, Kelrick A592
Drake, George A630
Drake, Debra A645
Drake, Raymond A871
Drake, Kelrick P371
Drake, Daniel P421
Drake, Michael V P581
Drake, Michael E87
Drake, Tonya E239
Drake, Kelly E413
Dransfield, Gary W373
Draper, Jackie A320
Draper, Derrick P86
Drapkin, Shelly A761
Drass, M. Joy A551
Drass, M. Joy P321
Draughn, James B. (Jim) A229
Draut, Eric A489
Dravenstott, Rob A271
Draves, Brad A742
Draxler, David A885
Draxler, Deb P49
Drazkowski, William J. A315
Drazkowski, Bill A315
Dreal, John Van P467
Drebin, Jeffrey A. P325
Drees, Christopher A154
Drees, Dennis A723
Drees, Ralph P565
Drees, David P565
Drefs, Cheryl A782
Drefs, Cheryl P525
Dreier, Gregory A246
Dreier, Gregory E105
Dreiling, Richard A487
Dreiling, Richard A691
Drell, Persis S. A510
Drell, Persis S. P290
Dremel, Ralf A701
Drengler, Kathy P49
Drennan, Molly A605
Drennen, Bill A419
Drennen, Chris A704
Dressel, David A135
Dressel, Bruce P51
Drew, Brian A75
Drew, Ryan A862
Drew, Theresa A922
Drew, Swazenne P7
Drew, Joel P110
Drew, Alton P199
Drew, Theresa P671
Drew, J. Christopher (Chris) E315
Drewes, Kevin P359
Dreyer, Doug A466
Dreyer, Matthew A686
Dreyer, Michael L. A793
Dreyer, Anna A799
Dreyfus, Andrew P89
Dreyfus, Lee E267
Drezek, Maria P555
Driban, John A922
Driban, John P671
Dries, William A842
Driggers, Timothy K. A301
Driggers, Jason P428
Driggs, Terry A723
Driggs, Taylor E194
Drilling, Edward E374
Drillings, Robert M P369
Drinan, Beth A36
Driscoll, Jennifer A167

Driscoll, Cameron A481
Driscoll, Michael A536
Driscoll, Jennifer A606
Driscoll, Stephen P2
Driscoll, Paul P202
Driscoll, Jeff P375
Driscoll, Brian J. P499
Driscoll, Edward P611
Driver, Bill A562
Driver, Darienne P342
Driver, Jeff P524
Drolet, Patricia P382
Drone, Nicole P227
Drop, Jeffrey S. A226
Drop, Jeffrey S. P150
Drossaert, Wim P356
Drotman, Jim A360
Drouin, Joseph L. A690
Drouse, Lisa P155
Drozdetski, Eugene A135
Drozdowski, Colin A69
Druckenmiller, Al A329
Drufner, Jean A844
Druitt, John A145
Drum, Jason A137
Drum, Melissa A323
Drum, James A590
Drum, Craig E180
Drumm, Ann P314
Drummond, Brad C. A75
Drummond, Danielle P284
Drummond, Donna P382
Drury, Frank A391
Drury, Scott D. A753
Drusin, Lewis P368
Druten, Robert J. E134
Druzbik, James R. A398
Dryden, Kristi A89
Dsa, Roy A444
Dsena, Bruce P572
Dsouza, Sandesh E290
Dsylva, Brenda P137
Dua, Naveen P174
Duane, Mandy A189
Duane, Francis K. (Ken) A692
Duane, Graupman A936
Duarte, Alexandre A43
Duarte, Gianni A267
Duarte, Alexandre E13
Duato, Joaquin A479
Dubagunta, Kishore E431
Duban, Heike A226
Duban, Heike P150
DuBard, Dennis A373
Dubauskas, Keith A704
Dubczak, Roman W85
Dube, Sandeep A262
Dube, Lori A845
Dube, Joyce P467
Duberstein, Kenneth A312
Dubes, Christopher P93
Dubik, Nikolay N. W308
Dubin, James M P225
Dubinksi, Dawn E268
Dubler, Josh E203
Dublin, Ardenia P19
Dubois, Eric A72
Dubois, Erin A398
Dubois, Erin P222
DuBois, Raymond N. P575
Dubois, Guy E22
DuBois, Jeffrey E. (Jeff) E379
Dubose, Cory P55
Dubose, Jack P163
Dubourdieu, Derric E219
Dubovoy, Hugo A394
Dubreuil, Stéphane W173
Dubuc, Manuel Pérez A18
Dubuche, Karl Von P609
Dubuisson, Betty A559
Dubuque, Bethany A651
Dubuque, Bethany E329
Dubyak, Michael E. A440
Dubé, Richard W. (Dick) A621
Dubé, Richard W. (Dick) E311

Duc, Bernard le W65
Duca, Michael A. A162
Duca, Michael A. E61
Ducasse, Romain P660
Ducato, Patty A313
Ducato, Patty E144
Duce, Ronald C P279
Ducey, Deon A664
Ducey, Bj A696
Ducey, Scott A723
Ducey, Leslie P474
Ducey, Deon E334
DuCharme, L. D. A309
Duchatellier, Christophe W7
Ducher, Daniel P358
Duchossois, Craig J. P594
Duchow, Tim A726
Duchow, Tim P453
Duck, Kevin A171
Duck, Barbara F. A849
Ducker, Michael L. A323
Duckett, W. David (Dave) A668
Duckett, Carl A742
Duckworth, David A520
Duckworth, Jana P491
Ducourty, Kelly A438
Ducros, Gary A654
Ducré, Henri W154
Duda, Laura A392
Dudek, Tony A95
Dudick, David E A376
Dudik, Dale A323
Dudish, Sherry P226
Dudkin, Gregory N. A674
Dudley, Stuart A108
Dudley, William C. A319
Dudley, William C. A322
Dudley, Michael M. A754
Dudley, Warren P327
Dudley, Michael M. P484
Dudley, Jenny P548
Dudley-Eshbach, Janet P631
Dudley-Eshbach, Janet P642
Dudonis, Chris A43
Dudonis, Chris E13
Dudsdeemaytha, Surasak W216
Duenas, Jose A255
Duenig, Mark A856
Duenig, Mark P614
Duerk, Jeffrey P116
Duerksen, Craig A224
Duerksen, John A881
Duerksen, John E421
Dueser, F. Scott A340
Dueser, F. Scott E161
Dufala, George D. (Chip) A489
Duff, Sammy A166
Duff, Michael A510
Duff, Scott K A581
Duff, Martin A891
Duff, Michael P290
Duff, John P291
Duffany, Dennis A374
Duffelen, Mark A933
Duffell, Christopher A934
Duffenbach, Chris A315
Duffey, Jason A260
Duffey, Barbara P597
Duffin, N. W. A309
Duffin, Neil A309
Duffle, Denise A105
Duffle, Denise E34
Dufford, Shawn P465
Duffus, Robert A651
Duffus, Robert E329
Duffy, Jack A89
Duffy, James J. (Jim) A200
Duffy, Mark A232
Duffy, Terrence A347
Duffy, Robert L. A501
Duffy, Shelley A700
Duffy, Richard A833
Duffy, Stephen W P282
Duffy, Brian J. P496
Duffy, Matthew P662

COMBINED HOOVER'S HANDBOOK INDEX OF EXECUTIVES

A = AMERICAN BUSINESS
E = EMERGING COMPANIES
P = PRIVATE COMPANIES
W = WORLD BUSINESS

Duffy, David W109
Duffy, Brian W340
Duffy, Terrence E168
Duffy, W. Leslie E263
Dufour, Pierre A25
Dufour, Pierre A77
Dufour, Gregory A. (Greg) A162
Dufour, Pierre P14
Dufour, Victoria P516
Dufour, Jannette P552
Dufour, Gregory A. (Greg) E62
Dufresne, Richard W422
Dufur, Todd E184
Dufétel, Céline A799
Dugan, Peter A175
Dugan, Gregory A. A908
Dugan, Greg A909
Dugan, Edna P159
Dugan, Richard E426
Dugan, Gregory A. E436
Dugan, Greg E436
Dugar, Pankaj A438
Dugdale, Jason A746
Dugenske, John A35
Dugent, Paul P197
Duggan, Conor A713
Duggan, Scott P568
Duggan, Frank W3
Dugo, Corrado A3
Duhamel, Mary A751
Duhamel, Mary P482
Duhamel, Philippe W390
Duke, Roger A349
Duke, Timothy R. (Tim) A785
Duke, Stacey A803
Duke, Steven P92
Duke, Tom P555
Duke, Lee M. P573
Dukeman, Van A. A335
Dukeman, Van A. E154
Dukes, Jw A62
Dukes, Jw E20
Dulac, Fabienne W297
Dulak, Catherine P103
Dulmaine, Jean P279
Dumais, Lynn A A150
Dumais, Michael R. (Mike) A875
Dumas, Ellie A606
Dumas, José Tomas Guzman W29
Dumbauld, Tim A842
Dumelle, Peter A114
Dumelle, Peter E37
Dumesnil, Diana P586
Dumler, James A180
Dumond, Susan A16
Dumont, Patrick A506
Dumont, Serge A626
Dumont, Stephanie P202
Dumonte, Brian E131
Dumora, Renaud W71
Dunagin, Martin A418
Dunaway, William J. (Bill) A470
Dunaway, Barry C. A765
Dunaway, Mike P316
Dunbar, Pete A491
Dunbar, Timothy M. (Tim) A677
Dunbar, Roger F. A793
Dunbar, Kent P157
Duncan, Greg A84
Duncan, George L. A297
Duncan, Philip J A679
Duncan, Bryan D. A759
Duncan, Michele A877
Duncan, Jim P84
Duncan, Gary P205
Duncan, Ronald P213
Duncan, Andy P356
Duncan, Jonathan P358
Duncan, Traci P383

Duncan, Janelle P431
Duncan, Amy P477
Duncan, Todd P625
Duncan, Kim E105
Duncan, George L. E129
Duncan, Fred E148
Duncan, Bryan D. E373
Dunckelmann, Amy E440
Dunevant, Karen A86
Dunevant, Karen E27
Dungee, Khalefia P653
Dunham, Kara P121
Dunigan-wernke, Jennifer A329
Dunkelman, David P26
Dunkle, Jason P184
Dunlaevy, Williar A128
Dunlaevy, Williar E43
Dunlap, Kevin A19
Dunlap, James E. (Jim) A444
Dunlap, Michael S. (Mike) A586
Dunlap, Stan A740
Dunlap, David L. P111
Dunlap, Edward B. P119
Dunlap, Timothy M. P119
Dunlap, Patrick P119
Dunlap, Ray P443
Dunlap, Joe W. W193
Dunlap, Michael S. (Mike) E301
Dunleavy, J.K. W212
Dunlop, Cindy A888
Dunlop, Cindy E425
Dunn, Ann A62
Dunn, Gary S. A104
Dunn, Colleen A130
Dunn, Stacey A A181
Dunn, Kenneth A184
Dunn, Tony A195
Dunn, Allison A213
Dunn, Dan A222
Dunn, Kenneth E. A301
Dunn, Jordan A332
Dunn, Marc A369
Dunn, Patrick A A418
Dunn, Cind M A441
Dunn, Cind A441
Dunn, Tammy A452
Dunn, Patrick A455
Dunn, Shawna A726
Dunn, Cheryl A755
Dunn, James A762
Dunn, Bradford A835
Dunn, Sheila A871
Dunn, Sam A902
Dunn, Sean A925
Dunn, Allison P143
Dunn, Jim P171
Dunn, Cindy P220
Dunn, Amy P225
Dunn, Terry P261
Dunn, William H P261
Dunn, Steve P261
Dunn, William H. (Bill) P261
Dunn, Bob P261
Dunn, Stephen D. (Steve) P261
Dunn, Greg P308
Dunn, James P314
Dunn, Steve P351
Dunn, Gregory W. (Greg) P443
Dunn, Donna P478
Dunn, Randy J P504
Dunn, Edward P662
Dunn, Ann E20
Dunn, Stacey A E70
Dunn, Colin E75
Dunn, Patrick E228
Dunn, Steve E240
Dunn, Cheryl E369
Dunn, Sean E445
Dunn, Kevin E448
Dunn-Krause, Debbie P301
Dunne, Viola A135
Dunne, Melanie A540
Dunne, Deidre A701
Dunne, Ronan A889
Dunne, Thomas P206

Dunne, Liz P410
Dunne, Laura E132
Dunnie, Tookie P15
Dunning, Simon A74
Dunoyer, Marc W37
Dunson, Tom A345
Dunson, Susan A824
Dunson, Susan P562
Dunson, Tom E165
Dunster, William A673
Dunston, S. Cary E19
Dunton, Shirby P652
Dunworth, James A657
Dunyon, Aaron E127
Duong, Julie A104
Duong, Tran Ba W208
Dupaquier, Marc A466
Duperow, Megan A604
Duperron, Christian A654
Duplaix, Jean Marc W218
Dupler, Scott A444
Duplessis, Chad P106
Dupont, Michael R P363
Dupont, Christine P536
Dupont, Philippe W54
Duprat, Pierre-Christophe A77
Dupre, Mike E123
duPreez, Jan A565
Duprey, Lauren A133
Duprez, Debra A835
Dupuis, Marie Claire A380
Dupuis, Mike A692
Dupuy, Sheila P287
Durako, Steve P664
Durall, Scott E308
Duran, Joe A508
Duran, George A522
Duran, Susan P449
Duran, Alejandro P530
Durand, Bob A87
Durand, Michael A872
Durand, Bob P50
Durand, Pierre P300
Durant, Luke A613
Durant, Romules P605
Durant, Alison E260
Durante, Nicandro W79
Durbin, Bill A497
Durbin, Patrick M. A833
Durburg, Jack A175
Durcan, Deborah A. (Debbie) P641
Durden, Linda A867
Durden, Linda E418
Durek, Sandy A925
Durek, Sandy E445
Durfee, Thomas A224
Durfey, Jim A48
Durgin, Linda P311
Durham, Freeman A56
Durham, Bill A811
Durham, Ronald A934
Durham, Pamala P160
Durham, Karin E172
Durkee, Matthew K. A584
Durkin, Dennis A10
Durkin, James W. (Jim) A369
Durkin, Sam A482
Durkin, Sean E102
Durkovic, Svelana P409
Durn, Daniel (Dan) A74
Durnell, Shawn P108
Durnell, Keith P618
Durocher, Philip A218
Durocher, Stephen A686
Durr, Paul P489
Durr, Kristi P514
Durrans, Jan A101
Durrans, Jan E32
Durre, Edmond A401
Durrence, Neiciee A36
Dusang, Nina P122
Duseux, Francis W157
Dussert, Bertrand A934
Dustzadeh, Justin A896
Dutcher, Phillip C P357

Dutcher, Phillip P357
Dutchyshyn, Tom A853
Dutchyshyn, Tom P612
Dutertre, Jey A526
Dutkowsky, Robert M. A809
Dutra, Kasey P662
Dutt, Shilpa A319
Dutt, Asha P129
Dutta, Kara A462
Dutta, Soumitra P159
Dutta, Rahul E138
Dutton, Rob A263
Dutton, Jim P82
Dutton, John P536
Duty, Earnie P280
Duva, Judith P401
Duval, Scott A740
Duval, Melany P172
Duval, John P649
Duvvur, Amarendra A6
Duvvuri, Kumar A135
Dvm, Prem Paul P103
Dvorchak, Steve A620
Dvorkin, Victor E133
Dweck, Carrie A544
Dwight, Craig M. A433
Dwight, Craig M. E217
Dworkin, James A433
Dworkin, Aaron A711
Dworkin, Darren P118
Dworkin, Aaron P444
Dworkin, James E217
Dwyer, Anita A347
Dwyer, Robert A543
Dwyer, James E. (Jim) A672
Dwyer, Maria F. A783
Dwyer, Jay P76
Dwyer, Michael P410
Dwyer, Shannon P431
Dwyer, Shannon P517
Dwyer, Anita E167
Dwyer, Pat E326
Dych, Jennifer P25
Dyck, Earl A25
Dyck, Earl P14
Dycus, Chris A179
Dye, Justin A30
Dye, Alan A72
Dye, John R. A915
Dye, Kathleen P5
Dye, Justin P20
Dye, David A. E92
Dyer, Jay A170
Dyer, Chris A799
Dyer, Jonathon A915
Dyer, Emily P363
Dyer, Adam P422
Dyer, William B. E79
Dygert, Brian E80
Dygert, Cassy E81
Dyke, Concetta Van A125
Dyke, Frank J. (Jeff) A766
Dyke, Colin A778
Dyke, William R. (Bill) Van P85
Dyke, David P103
Dyke, Frances P636
Dykes, Menia P93
Dykes, Bradford W. P252
Dykes, Melissa P264
Dykes, Mary H. P417
Dykes, Jimmy E99
Dykstra, Karen A897
Dykstra, David A. A925
Dykstra, David A. E445
Dym, Kevin E264
Dymally, Alice A204
Dyme, Jeremy A54
Dymtrow, Brice A210
Dynes, David A313
Dynes, David P200
Dyslin, Bradley E. A19
Dyson, Sam A203
Dyukov, Alexander V. W169
Dziadzio, Richard S. A88
Dzialo, Joseph A891

Dziedzic, Chad A135
Dziegielewski, Greg A146
Dziekciowski, Dan A60
Dzielak, Robert A307
Dzierzbinski, Danusia P257
Dziuba, Michael A700
Dziuk, David A A412
Dziuk, David A P233
Dziwis, Carolyn P576
D'Agnese, Luca W153
D'Agostino, John A704
D'aiutolo, Michael A91
D'aiutolo, Michael E29
D'Alessandro, Carl A501
D'ambrose, Michael A77
D'Amelio, Frank A. A657
D'amelio, Frank A942
D'Amore, Robert R. (Bob) A651
D'Amore, Diana A686
D'Amore, Robert R. (Bob) E329
D'andrea, Elena A544
D'andrea-neely, Cynthia E330
D'Angelo, Franco A161
D'Angelo, John A530
D'angelo, David A737
D'Angelo, John P254
D'Angelo, Larry E260
D'Angelo, Lawrence E260
D'angelo, David E361
D'Aniello, Gianluca P555
d'Apice, Leon E122
D'Aquila, Richard P676
d'Archirafi, Francesco Vanni A203
D'Arezzo, Gloria A933
D'Argenio, David Z. E375
D'Arienzo, Annette Marino P90
D'Arrigo, Daniel J. A562
D'Arrigo, Peter (Pete) E131
D'Ascoli, Fred P364
D'auria, Jay A200
D'Aveni, Richard P173
D'Cruz, Candice A538
D'errico, Michael E260
d'Esparbes, Eric E230
d'Estaing, Antoine Giscard W89
d'Estais, Jacques W71
D'Lugos, Steve A89
D'ornellas, Inigo A245
D'Ouville, Paul A605
D'Souza, Francisco A216
D- az, Eduardo P497
Duren, Aydin W403

E

E, Thomas Kevin P356
Eade-Viele, Carol P22
Eadie, Cynthia M P183
Eager, Pamela P114
Ealet, Isabelle A390
Ealy, Carleton A467
Eames, Tristyn A746
Eames, Frederick P18
Eames, Andy P511
Eaquinto, Aaron E334
Earhart, Cynthia C. (Cindy) A603
Earl, David A569
Earl, Nancy P489
Earl, Ashlee M P556
Earl, Dustin P672
Earle, Cletis P272
Earley, Jean McNicholas A112
Earley, Caroline A452
Earley, Sid A809
Earley, Steve A940
Earley, Franklin P P652
Early, Betsy A754
Early, Charles P360
Early, Betsy P484
Early, Johnnie L. P596
Early, Kim E441
Earnest, Josh A865
Earnest, Morgan G. (Jerry) E134
Earnhart, Michele P153

Earnshaw, Bill A695
Earwaker, Ryan A665
Earwaker, Ryan E334
Easley, Matthew A90
Easley, Ed A512
Easley, Matthew A715
Easley, Matthew P51
Easley, Stephen T P274
Eason, J. Cliff A715
Eason, David P469
East, Jeff A665
East, Jeff E334
Easterbrook, Stephen J. (Steve) A548
Easterlin, Edward P147
Easterlin, Edward E. P396
Easterling, Lynn A198
Easterling, William E. A828
Easterling, William E. P584
Easterwood, Scott A801
Eastham, Mark A550
Eastin, David A598
Eastling, Darel A686
Eastman, Stephen L. A669
Eastman, Meggin E290
Easton, Diane A227
Easton, Mark A465
Easton, Diane E90
Eaton, Belinda A108
Eaton, Mary Jo A175
Eaton, Robert A276
Eaton, Bob A360
Eaton, Danny A522
Eaton, Dave A880
Eaton, Roger G. A937
Eaton, Carrie P259
Eaton, Dave P640
Eaton, Rachel E255
Eaves, Christina E132
Ebb, David P574
Ebbesberg, Kjetil M. W289
Ebbs, Brian A613
Ebel, Gregory L. (Greg) P509
Eber, Bob A859
Eber, Richard A925
Eber, Richard E445
Eberhardt, Jack A598
Eberhart, Dan P442
Eberle, Jon J. E211
Eberlein, Michael P594
Eberly, Carolyn A84
Ebermann, Wolfgang A458
Ebers, Kevin H A126
Ebers, Kevin A126
Ebert, Horst A392
Ebert, Todd A700
Ebert, Paul A799
Ebert, Kevin A922
Ebert, Deborah P298
Ebert, Kevin P671
Eberts, F. Samuel A502
Eberwein, Elise R. A47
Ebken, Stephanie P128
Ebner, R. M. A309
Ebrahim, Linda A44
Ebrahim, Linda E13
Eby, Amy A519
Eby, Tom A565
Eby, Edith A657
Ebye, Amanya P257
Eccard, Bryan R A500
Eccell, Julius A246
Eccell, Julius E105
Eccher, James L. A623
Eccher, James L. E312
Eccles, Daniel A762
Eccles, Colin D. A906
Eccles, Colin D. E434
Eccleshare, C. William A452
Echavarria, Vivian P16
Echevarria, Ricardo J A460
Echiverri, Henry C P192
Echols, Matthew T A215
Echols, Jimmie A628
Echols, Lee P386
Echols, Edwin P547

Eck, Brian A465
Eck, Robert A735
Eck, Stefan P239
Eck, Chris P567
Eckel, Ryan A264
Eckel, Elizabeth B A904
Eckel, Robert A. (Bob) P248
Eckel, James A E106
Eckel, Jeffrey W. E200
Ecker, Dana A746
Ecker, Kraig A928
Ecker, Jeffrey Lawrence (Jeff) P574
Ecker, Kraig P674
Eckert, Matthew P55
Eckert, Bob P251
Eckert, Liz P409
Eckhardt, Laura A246
Eckhardt, Laura E105
Eckhart, Bradley A701
Eckhart, Brad P567
Eckhart, Gloria P605
Eckle, Ryan A265
Eddens, Peggy H. A929
Eddens, Peggy H. E449
Eddinger, Ronnie P95
Eddins, Allison A768
Eddins, Brad A819
Eddins, Brad P549
Eddowes, Geoffrey W. P573
Edds, Michael P572
Eddy, Jodi A149
Eddy, Ashley A562
Eddy, Bruce A933
Eddy, Lee A P45
Eddy, Janet P94
Edeker, Randy A447
Edeker, Randy P247
Edel, John A200
Edelberg, Erik A505
Edelman, Deane A145
Edelson, David B. A525
Edelstein, Martin P P382
Edelstein, Stewart P642
Edema, Douglas P508
Edens, Wesley R. (Wes) A629
Edens, Wesley R. (Wes) E183
Eder, George A658
Eder, Wolfgang W417
Edfors, Patricia A762
Edgar, Robert V A590
Edgar, Robin P329
Edgar, James E174
Edge, Judy A323
Edge, Jillian P302
Edgehill, Beverly A835
Edgell, Eleonore A711
Edgell, Garland P361
Edgell, Eleonore P444
Edgeller, Kristin E106
Edgerton, Ivis P358
Edgett, Paul W. A226
Edgett, Paul W. P150
Edgington, Michael A922
Edgington, Michael P671
Edgmond, Wanda A224
Edicola, Mike A119
Edin, Ebru Dildar W403
Edison, Jeffrey S A663
Edith, Martinez-kidde P638
Edler, Marie P475
Edlund, Monte G. A447
Edlund, Todd E128
Edman, Thomas E415
Edminster, Susan P11
Edmonds, Jennifer P573
Edmonds, Bonnie P596
Edmondson, Rhonda A324
Edmunds, Coleman A94
Edmunds, Cynthia P631
Edmunds, Karen P666
Edmundson, Chad P567
Edney, Jerry A87
Edney, Jerry P50
Edris, Warren A492
Edson, Kent A252

Edson, David A575
Edson, Pam P359
Edwards, Jon S. A62
Edwards, Nate A89
Edwards, Bill A95
Edwards, Rob A107
Edwards, Peter G. A177
Edwards, Lisa M A218
Edwards, Jon A272
Edwards, Patricia L. A301
Edwards, Jennifer A325
Edwards, Wade A329
Edwards, Martin A418
Edwards, Thomas H. A433
Edwards, Bill A449
Edwards, Ben A465
Edwards, Tom A466
Edwards, Nick A492
Edwards, Dean A516
Edwards, William A527
Edwards, Zalise A550
Edwards, Mark A550
Edwards, Lori A569
Edwards, Julie A630
Edwards, Darren A649
Edwards, David A664
Edwards, Donna A665
Edwards, Chris A690
Edwards, Teresa L. (Terrie) A754
Edwards, Bonnie A850
Edwards, Ben A852
Edwards, Robert A. (Rob) A866
Edwards, Steven L. P85
Edwards, Steven L P86
Edwards, Steve P86
Edwards, Steve L P104
Edwards, Mary P112
Edwards, Michael P116
Edwards, Thomas K P135
Edwards, Bill P260
Edwards, Katherine P269
Edwards, Gordon P288
Edwards, Steven D. (Steve) P291
Edwards, Dean P293
Edwards, Marcie L. P299
Edwards, Brady P301
Edwards, Gordon T. P309
Edwards, Janet P405
Edwards, Pearse P424
Edwards, Gerry P446
Edwards, Jennifer P451
Edwards, Rebecca P456
Edwards, Clarence P481
Edwards, Teresa L. (Terrie) P484
Edwards, Sherman P664
Edwards, N. Murray W85
Edwards, Jon S. E19
Edwards, Harold E59
Edwards, Kip E72
Edwards, Geoff E102
Edwards, Crawford E106
Edwards, Thomas H. E217
Edwards, Bill E220
Edwards, Jeffrey w. E232
Edwards, David E334
Edwards, Donna E334
Edwards, Richard J. E345
Edwards, Robert A. (Rob) E417
Effenheim, John A859
Effinger, Jason E192
Effron, Seth P229
Eftink, Mike A680
Egan, Brian A319
Egan, Anne A574
Egan, William A606
Egan, Scott A833
Egan, Tom A919
Egan, Karen P190
Egan, Luisa P642
Egan, Joe P646
Egashira, Toshiaki W266
Egashira, Tetsuya W431
Egbert, Charles A853
Egbert, Charles P612
Egbujor, Michael A415

COMBINED HOOVER'S HANDBOOK INDEX OF EXECUTIVES

A = AMERICAN BUSINESS
E = EMERGING COMPANIES
P = PRIVATE COMPANIES
W = WORLD BUSINESS

Egbujor, Michael E208
Ege, Fred P364
Ege, Patrick P633
Egerdal, J E E291
Eggemeyer, John M. A638
Eggemeyer, John M. E320
Eggers, Daniel A305
Eggers, Drew A609
Eggers, Drew P387
Eggli, Doug A416
Egidi, Kenneth P412
Eglen, Richard A240
Eglinton, Mia A481
Egloff, Tim A329
Egloff, German W43
Egyhazy, Sonia E80
Ehlers, Michael D. (Mike) A133
Ehlers, Marc A528
Ehlers, James A798
Ehlers, Mary P55
Ehlert, Ryan A129
Ehlert, Kimberly P463
Ehlert, Angela P511
Ehling, Allen A799
Ehlinger, Jon D P185
Ehren, Jean A85
Ehren, Jean E26
Ehrenberg, James A. E280
Ehrenpreis, Ira A818
Ehrhart, Ryan A240
Ehrle, Markus A740
Ehrler, Richard P403
Ehrlich, Derinda A100
Ehrlich, Whitney A135
Ehrlich, Donald A254
Ehrlich, Robert P313
Ehrlich, Beth P400
Ehrling, Marie W287
Ehrman, Thomas A259
Ehrman, Larry P302
Ehrmann, Jacques W88
Ehst, Richard A. A248
Ehst, Richard A. E107
Eibensteiner, Herbert W417
Eibling, David A571
Eichelberger, Mitch A191
Eichelberger, Mitch P126
Eichenberger, Matt A695
Eichenlaub, John P573
Eichenseer, Tim E177
Eichenstein, Izzy A175
Eichert, Alison A155
Eichert, Alison E54
Eichfeld, R Andrew A269
Eichfeld, William P504
Eichler, Kelly P624
Eichner, Andrew A137
Eichorn, Mark A574
Eickenhorst, Thorsten A133
Eickhoff, Patti E51
Eickholt, Jochen W353
Eide, Tina A54
Eide, Kjell A301
Eide, Kjell P196
Eidson, Dennis A774
Eifler, Robert W P376
Eijsink, Jeroen A728
Eiland, Mattie P505
Eilander, Derek A326
Eiler, Justin P447
Einseln, Matt A16
Eippert, Debbie A246
Eippert, Debbie E105
Eis, Shannon E450
Eisbart, Benjamin A785
Eisen, Robert A348
Eisen, Robert E169
Eisenbarth, Jeff A98
Eisenbeis, Tara A60

Eisenberg, Paul R. A64
Eisenberg, Warren A125
Eisenberg, Alissa A135
Eisenberg, Steven D. A290
Eisenberg, Stacey A452
Eisenberg, Glenn A. A502
Eisenberg, Ron A831
Eisenberg, Burton P242
Eisenberg, Debra P382
Eisenberg, Ron P601
Eisenbrandt, Peter P303
Eisenbrandt, Jennifer E433
Eisenhart, Jeff A562
Eisenkraft, James P351
Eisenschmid, Christin A460
Eisentrout, Craig P81
Eisgruber, Christopher L. P591
Eisleben, Elisabeth A13
Eismann, Charles E634
Eisman, Robert B. A43
Eisman, Robert B. E13
Eisner, Paul A501
Eissenstat, Everett A378
Ekabut, Chaovalit W351
Ekarius, Michele A108
Ekbom, Carol P652
Ekholm, Borje E. W386
Ekici, Tuncay A658
Ekman, Eric W287
Ekvall, Susan A179
El-Hibri, Fuad E126
El-Khoury, Hassane E110
Elachi, Charles P107
Elam, Lisa A165
Elam, Mike A746
Elam, Laura P588
Elamine, A K P502
Elbaum, Richard P118
Elberfeld, Adrienne P563
Elbers, Pieter W15
Elbert, Robert A859
Elborne, Cy A744
Elcar, Per W377
Eldayrie, Elias G. P627
Elder, Mark A236
Elder, Daniel A320
Elder, Larry P83
Elder, Krystle P116
Elderen, Joel Van A621
Elderen, Joel Van E312
Elderkin, Greg A774
Elderkin, Greg P510
Eldern, Leonard Van A936
Eldridge, Benjamin E177
Elebash, Joe P306
Elefther, George A125
Eleser, Karen A167
Eleswarpu, Lakshmi A140
Elezovski, Manfred A391
Elgart, Natalie A243
Elghanayan, Shahram A167
Elgin, Jeff A166
Elgin, Steve A373
Elgohary, Nivin A213
Elgohary, Nivin P143
Elia, Maryellen P240
Elias, Jack A. P101
Eliasen, Mark A29
Eliason, William A630
Elices, Simone P549
Elich, Michael L. (Mike) E40
Elicker, John A151
Eline, William G. (Bill) A640
Eling, Greg A197
Elio, Suzanne A320
Eliopoulos, Deirdre A626
Elisabeth, Ricci A642
Elisabeth, Ricci P407
Elizabeth, Caroline A879
Elizabeth, Caroline P636
Elizondo, Carlos José Garc-a Moreno W26
Eljaiek, Lester A754
Eljaiek, Lester P484
Elkeles, Tamar A695

Elkin, Ilyas A613
Elkin, Neil A711
Elkin, Neil P444
Elkin, Jim P606
Elkins, Carla P471
Elkinson, Ken P357
Elkort, Daniel M. E322
Elkott, Matt E101
Ellard, Craig A165
Ellard, Beth P2
Ellefsen, Eric P660
Ellehuus, Christoffer P117
Ellen, Maclauglin A642
Ellen, Hanson P230
Ellen, Maclauglin P407
Ellenbecker, Brian A727
Ellenbecker, Brian P453
Ellenbogen, Marc A39
Eller, Jeff P6
Eller, Zeke E278
Ellerbrook, Niel C P505
Ellerin, Jack A885
Ellert, Kent A796
Ellert, Kent E397
Ellinger, Deborah E239
Ellinghausen, James R. (Jim) A690
Ellingsen, Catharine D. A721
Ellingson, Rachel A939
Ellingson, Kari P597
Ellington, Kim A A345
Ellington, Debbie A467
Ellington, Bryon A708
Ellington, Chris P635
Ellington, Kim A E165
Elliot, Erin A36
Elliot, John A206
Elliot, Douglas G. (Doug) A408
Elliot, Cynthia P454
Elliot, Charles P536
Elliott, Lane A101
Elliott, Ryann A210
Elliott, Jeff A242
Elliott, Anita A272
Elliott, Vanessa A325
Elliott, Robin N. A335
Elliott, Laura A444
Elliott, Mike A478
Elliott, Joseph C. A618
Elliott, Tommy A621
Elliott, Steven G A674
Elliott, Douglas G A676
Elliott, Danielle A687
Elliott, Wayne P83
Elliott, Tj P191
Elliott, Carla P253
Elliott, Brett P347
Elliott, Steven P542
Elliott, Bruce P575
Elliott, Lane E32
Elliott, Robin N. E154
Elliott, Marc G. E183
Elliott, E. J. (Mike) E183
Elliott, Marc G. E183
Elliott, Jay P. E232
Elliott, Eric E255
Elliott, Tommy E312
Ellis, Mike A65
Ellis, Justin A117
Ellis, Hannah A137
Ellis, Chris A145
Ellis, Beverly A165
Ellis, Rob A180
Ellis, Lance A512
Ellis, Kathleen A526
Ellis, Brian A569
Ellis, Sabrina A592
Ellis, Kate A596
Ellis, Gary A658
Ellis, Mark A675
Ellis, CynthiaLynn A711
Ellis, Charles A740
Ellis, Raquel A784
Ellis, George A816
Ellis, Damon A831
Ellis, Matthew D. (Matt) A890

Ellis, Justin P61
Ellis, Beverly P108
Ellis, Richard P132
Ellis, David P162
Ellis, John W P213
Ellis, Colleen P251
Ellis, Karen P330
Ellis, David P337
Ellis, Sabrina P370
Ellis, Bret P382
Ellis, Mark P428
Ellis, CynthiaLynn P444
Ellis, Kevin S P571
Ellis, Clyde P582
Ellis, Stephen P587
Ellis, Damon P601
Ellis, George P638
Ellis, J. Thad E100
Ellis, Kip B. E322
Ellison, Dave A108
Ellison, Brian A471
Ellison, Edward A485
Ellison, Seth M. A514
Ellison, Seth M. A516
Ellison, Karen A621
Ellison, Lawrence J A632
Ellison, Marvin R. A647
Ellison, Edward P271
Ellison, Seth M. P293
Ellison, Karen E312
Ellithorpe, Tom E418
Ells, M. Steven (Steve) A192
Ellspermann, Caroline J. A621
Ellspermann, Kenneth J. A621
Ellspermann, Caroline J. E311
Ellspermann, Kenneth J. E311
Ellwood, Michelle A171
Ellwood, Paul A587
Elman, Ryan A137
Elmasri, Fakhir F P285
Elming, Gregory B. (Greg) A677
Elmo, Kim E3
Elmore, Doug A181
Elmore, Julie A272
Elmore, Greg A329
Elmore, Samuel A338
Elmore, Jennifer A726
Elmore, Kiley A755
Elmore, John R. A884
Elmore, Doug E70
Elmore, Kiley E369
Elmquist, David A483
Elnashai, Amr S. A828
Elnashai, Amr S. P584
Eloranta, Jorma W275
Elrich, Marc P161
Elrod, David P185
Elrod, James K P670
Elrod, Michael E14
Elsaesser, Ford A219
Elsaesser, Ford E87
Elsbrock, Natalie P128
Else, Ryan P26
Elsenbast, David E352
Elser, Chrisanna A413
Elser, Mark A855
Elser, Chrisanna E205
Elsner, Deanie A487
Elson, Clifford P355
Elsroth, Thomas A16
Elstad, Rob A61
Elster, Nanette P301
Elstott, John B. A921
Elstrott, John B. P669
Elswick, Darin A834
Elswick, Shannon P400
Elvekrog, John P564
Elwell, William A409
Elwood, Stephen A526
Elwyn, Tashtego S. (Tash) A704
Ely, Lisa P469
Elzie, Matt A565
Emami, Azita A880
Emami, Azita P640
Emans, Jedd P35

Embree, Wayne A781
Embry, Kevin P161
Emel, Aaron A859
Emelonye, Ken A900
Emeogo, Victor A741
Emeogo, Victor E364
Emerson, Matt A109
Emerson, Mark A191
Emerson, Michael A491
Emerson, Ralph W A530
Emerson, Rob P508
Emerson, Richard P. E326
Emery, Glenn A294
Emery, Tom A651
Emery, Tama A725
Emery, Bruce A774
Emery, Andrea P512
Emery, Mary P648
Emery, Tom E330
Emigh, Michael A867
Emigh, Michael E418
Eminovic, Sead P257
Emiris, Ioannis M. W25
Emison, Kevin A398
Emison, Kevin P222
Emler, Jessica P180
Emley, Charles A104
Emmans, John P108
Emmendorfer, Melissa A126
Emmerich, I. Robert (Bob) A337
Emmerich, Matthew J. A669
Emmerich, I. Robert (Bob) E158
Emmert, Matt E422
Emmett, Nicholas A492
Emmett, Dan A. E114
Emmons, Brian A345
Emmons, George A491
Emmons, Elizabeth A700
Emmons, Christopher W. P306
Emmons, Michael P508
Emmons, Brian E166
Emory, Beverly P672
Empey, Dennis P606
Empson, Douglas A859
Emrich, Richard P389
Emrich, Clark E229
Emswiler, Shane E22
Enberg, Steve A728
Enbody, Justin E245
Ence, Russell A569
Endebrock, Eric A565
Enders, Thomas (Tom) W17
Endersby, Jeff A16
Enderson, Taryl P343
Endres, Bill A16
Endres, Helmut A21
Endres, Jeff A444
Endresen, Heather A104
Endresen, William D. A429
Endresen, William D. E214
Endries, Kari A191
Endsley, Kim A925
Endsley, Kim E445
Eng, Chester A56
Eng, Sharon A203
Eng, Phil A560
Eng, Stephanie A722
Eng, Steve A850
Eng, Phil P336
Eng, Christopher R. E390
Engebretsen, Travis A749
Engebretsen, Travis E367
Engel, Lior A74
Engel, Robert B. A213
Engel, Randy A595
Engel, John A874
Engel, Albert L. A888
Engel, John J. A910
Engel, Robert B. P143
Engel, Robin P625
Engel, Hans-Ulrich W59
Engel, Marc W409
Engel, Kelsey E272
Engel, Albert L. E425
Engelbrecht, John R. A693

Engelbrecht, John R. E341
Engelen, Peter W402
Engelhard, Bob A879
Engelhardt, Fredrik A179
Engelhardt, Mark A434
Engelhardt, Brent P457
Engelhardt, Jeff E237
Engelhart, James A859
Engelking, Brian A61
Engelman, Craig A528
Engelman, Dan P72
Engels, Trevor A844
Engelstoft, Morten H. W1
Engen-pazdera, Judy A856
Engen-pazdera, Judy P614
Enger, Mark P399
Engerer, Jill A345
Engerer, Jill E165
England, Donna M A278
England, Jan A850
England, Todd D. P104
England, Corey D. P104
England, Chad P104
England, Josh P104
England, Zach P104
England, Dustin P104
England, Daniel E. (Dan) P104
England, Dean D. P104
Engle, Bridget E. A111
Engle, Barry A378
Englebright, Jane D. A410
Englehardt, Scott A704
Engleman, Laurie A879
Engleman, Laurie P636
Engler, Greg E433
Englert, Mitch A165
Englert, Brian A340
Englert, Richard M P545
Englert, Brian E160
Engles, Gregg L. P668
English, James A386
English, Shaileen A657
English, Steven E. A781
English, Rebecca A799
English, Francine P242
English, James E188
Engrav, Mary A571
Engskov, Kris A779
Engstrom, Kathryn A811
Engstrom, Mark A893
Engstrom, Rick P644
Enigl, Debra A571
Enk, Theresa A596
Enna, James A811
Ennerfelt, P Goeran P293
Ennerfelt, Goeran P P293
Ennico, Dolores A624
Ennis, Daniel G. A478
Ennis, Cheryl A492
Ennis, Robert A596
Ennis, Catherine A778
Ennis, Elizabeth P64
Ennis, Daniel G. P268
Ennis, Niall W131
Enomoto, Hideto P375
Enos, Deborah C. A641
Enos, Deborah C. P407
Enqvist, Toby J A865
Enright, Daniel A305
Enriquez, Oscar A616
Ensinger, Colleen A357
Ensinger, Colleen E176
Ensley, Matt A200
Enslin, Robert (Rob) W340
Enslow, Beth A540
Enterline, Larry L. E180
Entner, Peter A799
Entwisle, Beverly J P609
Entwistle, David P524
Entwistle, David P639
Epidendio, Steve A921
Epidendio, Steve P669
Epley, Diane A540
Epp, Melanie A850
Epperlein, Susann A702

Epperley, Michael A909
Epperley, Michael E436
Eppert, Mark A215
Eppes, Lionel A200
Eppich, Timothy P116
Eppinger, David A355
Epple, Carl A502
Eppler, Klaus A125
Epps, Mike A682
Epps, Barry L. A716
Epps, Jeremy A872
Epps, JoAnne A. P546
Epstein, Lauren A163
Epstein, Janet A746
Epstein, Norman P P531
Epstein, Lauren E62
Eraly, Satish A133
Eran, Oded W49
Erb, Tricia A316
Erb, David B. A449
Erb, Jane A641
Erb, Jane P389
Erb, Jane P407
Erb, David B. E220
Erber, Ralph P175
Erbil, Ali Fuat W403
Erdman, Leonard P101
Erdoes, Mary Callahan A483
Erekson, O. Homer P549
Erel, Husnu W403
Eremenko, Paul A875
Erfourth, Michael A552
Erfourth, Michael E276
Ergastolo, Patrick P594
Ergen, Charles W. (Charlie) A271
Ericksen, John A668
Erickson, Randall J. A85
Erickson, Lynn A91
Erickson, Jon A194
Erickson, Cindy A205
Erickson, Wendy A246
Erickson, Peter C. A376
Erickson, Jesse A449
Erickson, Joseph A507
Erickson, Lynne A530
Erickson, Karen A549
Erickson, Pam A706
Erickson, Andrew A783
Erickson, Scott P26
Erickson, Lynn P55
Erickson, Zachary P107
Erickson, Elizabeth P138
Erickson, Sue P332
Erickson, Tina P576
Erickson, John R. E5
Erickson, Randall J. E26
Erickson, Wendy E105
Erickson, Matt E131
Erickson, Jesse E221
Ericson, Brady D. A146
Ericson, Brent A399
Ericson, Brent P223
Ericson, Magnus W377
Erik, Shank A642
Erik, Shank P407
Erika, Hofmann A641
Erika, Hofmann P407
Eriksen, Jim A530
Erikson, Lynn A684
Erkan, Hafize Gaye (Gaye) A349
Erlandson, Dean A846
Erlandson, Luke E433
Erlich, Morton E8
Erlinger, James H. (Jim) A474
Erlinger, Joe A548
Ermatinger, William R. (Bill) A446
Ermine-Baer, Kristin A883
Ermine-Baer, Kristin P644
ERMOLD, SHAWNA A872
Ernest, Scott A599
Ernest, Scott A. A821
Ernest, Scott A867
Ernest, William P404
Ernest, Scott E418
Ernie, Barry P505

Ernst, Joe A135
Ernst, Mark A. A352
Ernst, Steven A575
Ernst, Barbara A686
Ernst, Barrie W. A867
Ernsteen, Scott A925
Ernsteen, Scott E445
Erny, Michelle A484
Ernzen, Kim A706
Erokhin, Vladimir P. W375
Erokhin, Yuri E238
Erpenbach, Michelle P566
Erpenbeck, Donald A P356
Errera, Mike A67
Ersek, Hikmet A915
Erskine, Carolyn E14
Ertel, Elizabeth A195
Ertzeid, Ottar W140
Ervin, Juanita D A139
Ervin, Chuck A401
Ervin, Amy A552
Ervin, Juanita D P93
Ervin, Amy E275
Erwin, Tami A890
Erwin, Duane P49
Erwin, Duane L. P49
Erwin, Steven P103
Erwin, Michael A P176
Erwin, Terry P308
Erzen, Rob A369
Erun, Gokhan W403
Esamann, Douglas F. (Doug) A281
Esarte, Marty A902
Escalera, Elizabeth A41
Escallon, Alvaro Jaramillo W44
Escamilla, Edward P164
Escarrer, Gabriel P179
Escasa-Haigh, Jo Ann P431
Escasa-Halgh, Jo Ann P517
Escatel, Martin A798
Esch, Cort P212
Esch, Alyson P422
Eschenauer, Robert P517
Escobar, Mike A36
Escobar, Amanda A358
Escobar, Amanda E176
Escossi, Julio A21
Escover, Norman P356
Escudero, Jaime P412
Escuyer, Vincent P233
Esernio, Anthony W396
Esfahani, Sam P432
Esfarjani, Keyvan A460
Esham, David A574
Eshelbrenner, Adam A831
Eshelbrenner, Adam P601
Eshghi, Fleur P206
Eskandarian, Ali P569
Eskew, Michael A36
Esko, Courtney A846
Eskow, Alan D. A888
Eskow, Alan D. E425
Eskue, Kyle A502
Esler, Jennifer A449
Esler, Jennifer E221
Eslick, Rob A447
Eslick, Rob P247
Esparza, Lisa A177
Esparza, Mary Lou L P102
Esparza, Ryan P262
Espeland, Curtis E. (Curt) A285
Esper, Eric A417
Esper, Richard E A827
Esper, Richard E P571
Espeskog, Geir A135
Espey-English, Patricia P664
Espinal, Ana A651
Espinal, Ana E330
Espindola, Mauricio Lara A135
Espinosa, Wanda A168
Espinosa, M Angelica A753
Espinosa, Carlos P60
Espinosa, Rafael W144
Espinoza, Silvia A676
Espinoza, Aurora P408

COMBINED HOOVER'S HANDBOOK INDEX OF EXECUTIVES

```
A = AMERICAN BUSINESS
E = EMERGING COMPANIES
P = PRIVATE COMPANIES
W = WORLD BUSINESS
```

Espinoza, Jose P499
Espinoza, Edna P537
Espinoza, Silvia E338
Esplin, J. Kimo A447
Esplin, J Kimo A447
Esposito, Maria A205
Esposito, Joe A262
Esposito, Chris A347
Esposito, Mike A390
Esposito, Michael A782
Esposito, Frank P266
Esposito, Michael P525
Esposito, Chris E167
Espy, Kevan P144
Esquibel, Emilio P476
Esquith, Stephen L. (Steve) P339
Esquivel, Grisselda A58
Esquivel, Amada P596
Esrael, Craig P432
Esrig, Cynthia P248
Esselman, Tom A60
Essenberg, Janice P76
Essenmacher, Brian E184
Esser, Manfred W322
Essex, Kim A626
Essex, Susan E105
Essig, Marshall A213
Essig, Marshall P143
Essig, Stuart M. E234
Esslinger, Steve A804
Esson, Margo A60
Esta, Linda P589
Estabrook, David A349
Estabrook, James B. A402
Estabrook, Madeleine P383
Estabrook, James B. E198
Estampes, Jerome A243
Estby, Becky P145
Esteban, Carmen A429
Esteban, A. Gabriel P175
Esteban, Carmen E214
Estep, Julie A340
Estep, Missie A828
Estep, Seth A840
Estep, Missie P584
Estep, Greg W294
Estep, Julie E160
Esterman, Michelle P29
Estes, Charlie A253
Estes, William B A319
Estes, David A651
Estes, Scott A718
Estes, Rob W. P197
Estes, David P308
Estes, Melinda L. P466
Estes, David E330
Estes, Scott E354
Esteves, Robert A593
Estevez, Carlos A658
Esther, Chet A399
Esther, Chet P224
Estrella, Guilherme W303
Estridge, Sherry A894
Estridge, Sherry P651
Estus, Ian E202
Etchemendy, John W. A510
Etchemendy, John W. P290
Etchemendy, Kathi P467
Etchison, Ron A262
Etes, Tim A452
Etheredge, Charles T. (Tom) E177
Etheredge, Jean E304
Etheridge, Don P358
Ethiraj, Devi A137
Ethridge, Mary A713
Etienne, Carissa P404
Etoh, Kimihiro W51
Etten, Peter Van P187
Ettenger, Kreg P630

Etter, Jason A621
Etter, Carl J. P479
Etter, Jason E311
Etti-williams, Jimmy P549
Ettl, Robert A P229
Etzel, Steven W A729
Etzel, Tom A940
Etzell, Joan A791
Etzell, Joan P535
Eubanks, Russell A319
Eubanks, Brent A522
Eubanks, Clifford P196
Eudy, John D. E136
Eugley, Alan A352
Eugster, Cris P164
Eui-Sun, Chung W192
Eulacio, Ramon A18
Eulate, Borja Prado W151
Eulau, Robert K. (Bob) A742
Euler, Jeff A323
Eulich, John S. A298
Eulich, John S. E130
Eun-Yeon, Hwang W311
Eung-sik, Kim W176
Eureste, Ralph A36
Eusden, Alan A240
Eustace, Joan P611
Euston, Carmen A429
Evan, Griffith A305
Evangel, Lori M. A381
Evangelista, Guy A142
Evangelista, Paul A. A183
Evangelista, W. Scott A474
Evangelista, Guy E49
Evangelista, Paul A. E73
Evanko, Brian C A194
Evans, Michael A1
Evans, Bruce A67
Evans, Joseph W A159
Evans, Steve A189
Evans, Laurence A204
Evans, Michael A219
Evans, Dan A222
Evans, Mark A232
Evans, Charisse A262
Evans, Charles L. (Charlie) A322
Evans, Morris A325
Evans, Jill A325
Evans, Michelle A329
Evans, Janel A402
Evans, Gerald W. A403
Evans, Godfrey B. A429
Evans, Aicha S. A460
Evans, Katrina M. (Trina) A491
Evans, Glenn A507
Evans, Carnot A538
Evans, Stephen R. T. A551
Evans, Ed A559
Evans, John A567
Evans, Robert A602
Evans, Terry A604
Evans, Jason A623
Evans, Richard D. A654
Evans, Beckey A668
Evans, John A690
Evans, Joseph A704
Evans, James A704
Evans, Marlin A713
Evans, Norman A742
Evans, Deanna A744
Evans, Russ A766
Evans, J. Eric A811
Evans, V. Lynn A815
Evans, Karen A831
Evans, Jack B. A868
Evans, Sean P32
Evans, Doug P126
Evans, Jeremy P174
Evans, Crystal P194
Evans, Dave P214
Evans, Robert P242
Evans, Jeremy S P282
Evans, Stephen R. T. P321
Evans, Donnie W P409

Evans, Steve P415
Evans, Malik P454
Evans, Peggy P484
Evans, Scott P489
Evans, Russ P500
Evans, Kimberly P532
Evans, Scott P571
Evans, Karen P601
Evans, Palmer P611
Evans, Arthur T P625
Evans, Gene P636
Evans, Sharon P637
Evans, Brandy P645
Evans, Mariah P659
Evans, Michael E1
Evans, Michael E87
Evans, Drew E123
Evans, William E147
Evans, Bruce R E174
Evans, Brian R. E185
Evans, Janel E198
Evans, Godfrey B. E214
Evans, John E284
Evans, Jason E313
Evans, Michael E326
Evans, Rachel E332
Evanson, Brynn L. A647
Evanson, Jeff A818
Evanson, Jeff K A818
Evanson, Paul J A347
Evanson, Douglas (Doug) P470
Evelhoch, Jeffrey A554
Evenzwig, Michael A559
Everett, Nora M. A677
Everett, Bryan A722
Everett, Greg P333
Everette, James P70
Everhart, Matt A941
Everhart, Martin P454
Everitt, Derek A816
Everling, Jeffrey A498
Evernham, Scott J. A621
Evernham, Scott J. E311
Evers, Peter P155
Eversden, Jeffrey A925
Eversden, Jeffrey E445
Eversman, Paul A85
Eversman, Paul E27
Everson, Carolyn A310
Evert, Nancy P445
Eves, David L. A931
Evey, Lee P548
Evitts, Aaron A191
Evitts, Aaron P126
Evola, Peter J A75
Evon, Scott A762
Ewald, Linda A63
Ewaldsson, Ulf W386
Ewens, Peter A A800
Ewert, Beth A859
Ewert, Brian H P310
Ewert, Phil P469
Ewig, Randall G. A404
Ewig, Randall G. E199
Ewing, Justin A30
Ewing, William A112
Ewing, Gregory A170
Ewing, Wylie A283
Ewing, Clay W. A383
Ewing, Jane A902
Ewing, Justin P20
Ewing, Marilyn E P253
Ewing, Clay W. E186
Ewing, Robert E255
Exnicios, Joseph S. A401
Exnicios, Joseph S. E198
Exshaw, Christian W85
Exton, Martha A179
Ey, Nick A357
Ey, Nick E176
Eyeington, Thomas P499
Eyken-sluyters, Eric A740
Eyl, Steven M. (Steve) E210
Eyl, Steve E210
Eyler, David A608

Eynon, Eric P449
Eyre, Brik V. A119
Eyre, Brandon P55
Eytcheson, David L. (Dave) E418
Eyzaguirre, Tatiana A115
Eyzaguirre, Tatiana E37
ez, A921
ez, P669
Ezell, Todd A449
Ezell, James A481
Ezell, Todd E221
Ezer, Dorit Ben P129
Ezzard, Milt A10

F

F, Yvonne P102
Fabara, Paul D. A53
Faber, Heather A604
Faber, Emmanuel W128
Fabian, Bruce A200
Fabilli, Dominic A491
Fabis, Joe A420
Fabis, Joe P240
Fabregas, Edgardo A479
Facchin, Claudio W3
Fache, Jameson Smith P117
Fache, Adrienne Palmer P318
Facheris, Maurizio A7
Facktor, Debra D A103
Factor, Saul P260
Factora, Faith A824
Factora, Faith P562
Fadahunsi, Ajibola A530
Fadden, Thomas Mc A500
Fadem, Steve P555
Fadool, Joseph F. A146
Fafoglia, Nick A224
Fagan, Elizabeth A900
Fagan, Cathlyn P382
Fagan, Charles P432
Fagan, Mary P438
Fagan, Tiffani P464
Fagan, Shiraz M. P479
Fagen, Richard E. (Rich) P107
Fagenstrom, Billie A586
Fagerstrom, Brad A877
Fagg, Jenny W85
Faggard, Steve A191
Fagin, Michelle P122
Fagnani, Jennifer A266
Fagnani, Jennifer P182
Fagnoule, Dominique W270
Faherty, Sean A408
Fahey, Mike A176
Fahey, Joe A922
Fahey, Lisbeth P127
Fahey, Walter J. P304
Fahey, Joe P671
Fahim, Shafei P55
Fahner, Dawn P337
Fahrig, Siegmund A539
Fahrney, Nicholas E131
Fai, Lee Wai W411
Faile, Ann E255
Fails, Ashley P313
Fain, Eric S. A5
Fain, William A790
Fain, Jonathan D. P544
Faintuch, Amir A460
Faiola, Francesco E290
Fair, Sonia P22
Fairbairn, Robert W. (Rob) A135
Fairbank, Richard D. (Rich) A166
Fairbanks, Donald P344
Fairbanks, Bryan H. E409
Fairbrother, Priscilla A882
Fairburn, Judy W92
Fairchild, Larry A312
Fairchild, Mark A329
Fairchild, Larry P200
Fairchild, Nancy E261
Faircloth, Michael E. A403
Faircloth, David A465

Fairey, Chris A734
Fairhurst, David A548
Fairweather, George R. A899
Faison, Lauren P541
Faisst, Georg A692
Fait, Laura P597
Faith, John A91
Faith, David M. P589
Faith, John E29
Fajardo, Hector A191
Fakhry, Robert A135
Fakude, Nolitha W341
Fakult, James V. A351
Falag-ey, Michael E290
Falaguerra, Robert J. (Bob) P464
Falb, Mark C. A413
Falb, Derek J P134
Falb, Mark C. E205
Falbo, Michael P641
Falci, Mark A727
Falci, Mark P453
FALCK, FEDERICO W43
Falco, Al A651
Falco, John A684
Falco, Al E330
Falcone, Brian A243
Falcone, Joseph C P358
Falcone, Joseph C. P661
Falcone, Maria P678
Falcone, Philip E202
Falcone, Ron E226
Fale, Mr Robert P11
Falgoust, Stephen A668
Falgout, David A938
Falgout, David P678
Falk, Thomas J. (Tom) A493
Falk, Chip A849
Falk, Linda P76
Falk, Samantha P524
Falk, Megan P662
Falk, Karin W420
Falkengren, Annika W356
Falkin, Bruce A112
Falkner, Keon P64
Falkowitz, Mary A827
Falkowitz, Mary P580
Fall, Clinton P568
Fallan, James A630
Fallen, Kelly A850
Fallen, Wendy P555
Faller, Marcia R. E21
Fallert, Bill E122
Fallo, Monica E174
Fallon, Sean A212
Fallon, Katie A423
Fallon, William C. (Bill) A546
Fallon, Jeanne M. P109
Fallon, David J. P140
Fallon, Lynnette C. E30
Falotico, Joy A360
Falstad, Daniel T P196
Falvey, Katie E268
Falzon, Robert M. A686
Falzon, Michael A686
Famiglietti, Michael A649
Famiglietti, Robin A763
Famiglietti, Robin E377
Famuyiwa, Oluyemisi O P242
Fan, Peter A638
Fan, Jiansheng P650
Fan, Peter E320
Fanale, James P111
Fanale, James P673
Fanchar, Brent P471
Fancher, Geoff A198
Fanelli, Arcangelo A198
Fanelli, John A613
Fanelli, Denise P253
Faneuf, Allan A797
Faneuil, Jesse A126
Faneuil, Edward J. A387
Fang, Greg A436
Fang, AJ A793
Fang, Bin P227
Fang, Zhang Zi W103

Fang, Ting E290
Fang-ming, Lu W185
Fannin, Charity P615
Fanning, Thomas A. (Tom) A319
Fanning, Brock A837
Fanning, Thomas A P506
Fanning, Mark E326
Fanqiu, Meng W96
Fansler, Janet P284
Fant, Christopher A329
Fantauzzi, Kathy A870
Fantle, Jean P628
Fantom, Stacey A665
Fantom, Stacey E334
Fantorno, Carla P540
Fanucchi, Margaret A P472
Farabet, Clment A613
Farah, Pedro A902
Farah, Jean Claude A915
Farah, Pedro W421
Farber, Jeffrey M. (Jeff) A405
Farber, Nancy P659
Farbes, Hubert A. P179
Fardella, Amy A835
Farden, John P474
Fare, Julia A740
Fare, Brenda P177
Fares, Nancy A695
Fargo, Thomas B. A446
Farhat, Jerry A16
Farias, Gil A109
Fariello, Teri A865
Fariello, Terri A865
Faries, Stan A623
Faries, Stan E313
Farineau, Don A312
Farkas, Chris P240
Farkouh, Stephen A924
Farland, Bill P147
Farland, Kenn Mc P343
Farley, Ryan A149
Farley, Jack A281
Farley, Brian A351
Farley, James D. (Jim) A359
Farley, Jim A360
Farley, Dan A783
Farley, Nate A859
Farley, Lucille P31
Farley, Joseph M P110
Farley, Leigh P333
Farley, Jeff E326
Farley, Andy E396
Farmer, Scott A129
Farmer, Scott D. A197
Farmer, Curtis C. A221
Farmer, Marc A222
Farmer, Dennis A399
Farmer, Dom A694
Farmer, Paul J P167
Farmer, Dennis P223
Farnan, Patrick A329
Farnay, Matt A381
Farner, Kim A877
Farner, David M. P643
Farney, Cheryl P333
Farnin, Paul A170
Farnsworth, Bryan D. A434
Farnsworth, Ronald L. (Ron) A860
Farnum, Marissa P191
Farnum, Allan P252
Faroughi, Cheryl A571
Farquhar, Laurie A54
Farr, David N A292
Farr, Rich P104
Farr, David P529
Farr, Paul A P540
Farrall, Ann A606
Farrand, Stephen A554
Farrant, M. A. A309
Farrant, Malcolm A309
Farrar, Jeffrey W. A91
Farrar, Rick A701
Farrar, Jeffrey W. E29
Farrel, Miles A54
Farrell, Lynn A75

Farrell, Peter A112
Farrell, Debra A251
Farrell, Thomas F. A275
Farrell, Pamela A374
Farrell, Mary A A384
Farrell, Todd A512
Farrell, William J. (Bill) A530
Farrell, Kristina A531
Farrell, Karen A618
Farrell, Alison A722
Farrell, William A827
Farrell, Mike A835
Farrell, Breege A. A882
Farrell, Scott A884
Farrell, Bill A922
Farrell, Mary A P217
Farrell, Edward P306
Farrell, William P580
Farrell, Bill P671
Farrell, Mary C. P676
Farrell, Garry W243
Farrell, Joanne W325
Farrell, Joanne W327
Farrell, Glenn E304
Farrell, Karen E310
Farren, John P554
Farrier, Joe P361
Farrimond, Katherine P378
Farrington, Duane A637
Farrington, Joanne A784
Farrington, Shannon P428
Farris, J. Matt A435
Farris, Jack A619
Farris, Kristofer M. A716
Farris, Bain P465
Farris, Bain J P465
Farris, Bain J P518
Farris, Jack E310
Fartaj, Vandad A648
Fartaj, Vandad E328
Farthing, Gary A61
Farthing, Dana A444
Fasano, Rebecca A140
Fasano, Gerard A. (Gerry) A509
Fash, Boni P664
Fasino, Jeffrey A220
Fasino, Jeffrey P649
Fasman, Steven L. E372
Fasolo, Peter M. A479
Fass, Peter A534
Fassberg, Maxine A460
Fassig, Gerry E98
Fateh, Kiran P215
Fathers, Bill A897
Fatovic, Robert D. A734
Fattore, Charles A276
Fattore, Doreen A390
Fattori, Ruth A654
Fauber, Skip A797
Faucher, John A218
Fauchet, Philippe P599
Faujour, Olivier A376
Faul, Mark A831
Faul, Mark P601
Faulconer, Kyle A654
Faulds, Jason P476
Faulk, Brian A523
Faulker, Kim A218
Faulkingham, Dell A133
Faulkner, Jonathan A452
Faulkner, Nigel A799
Faulkner, Fred A867
Faulkner, Archimedes P333
Faulkner, Aaron E35
Faulkner, Fred E418
Faulkner-macdonagh, Chris A800
Faury, Guillaume W17
Faust, Daniel A16
Faust, James A195
Faust, Phil A702
Faustino, Aimee A921
Favale, Vincent A893
Favarelli, Andrea P75
Favors, Jim A647
Favre, Michel W160

Favuzza, Steven P P593
Fawaz, Hussein A74
Fawaz, Mike A508
Fawaz, Ramzi A595
Fawaz, Marwan E396
Fawcett, John J. A200
Fawcett, Matthew K A586
Fawcett, Charles C. A848
Fawcett, Karen W364
Fawcett, Robert A. E365
Fawcett, Charles C. E411
Fay, Gerald W. (Gerry) A99
Fay, Laura A613
Fayad, Walid A145
Fayard, Gary A380
Faz, Patricia A702
Fazio, Giulio W153
Fazzari, Francesca A191
Fazzino, Tabitha P588
Fazzone, Paul A897
Feagin, Amy A456
Feagin, Amy E228
Fealk, Sharry A222
Fearey, Peter S. E385
Fearing, Dru A364
Fearon, Richard A286
Fearon, Matthew (Matt) A816
Fearon, Richard P190
Feathers, Eric A341
Feazell, Glenn A527
Febo, Lawrence A191
Febus, Francelia A469
Fechushak, John A262
Fecker, Alicia P425
Feczko, Peter J A414
Feczko, Peter J P236
Fedacsek, Joseph S A606
Fedele, Christopher E233
Feder, Eric A512
Federenko, Garvin P16
Federici, John A530
Federico, Peter J A23
Federico, Jim A407
Federico, David A835
Federico, Peter E5
Federighi, Craig A72
Fedgechin, Michele A520
Fedor, Marc A795
Fedorchak, Bill A442
Fedorenko, Pasha A254
Fedorko, Tara A925
Fedorko, Tara E445
Fedus, Anna A925
Fedus, Natalie A925
Fedus, Anna E445
Fedus, Natalie E445
Fedyszyn, Karen A9
Fedyszyn, Karen P4
Fedzhora, Liliya P650
Fee, Troy A857
Feely, Terri P253
Feeney, Brian J. A183
Feeney, Eileen A469
Feeney, Paul M. P78
Feeney, Brian J. E74
Feenstra, Gregory A89
Fees, Nick P475
Feese, Kelly A325
Feher, William A292
Fehlman, Robert A. A760
Fehlman, Robert A. E374
Fehnel, Stephen H P441
Feidner, Susan P129
Feigh, Gregg A343
Feigh, Gregg E164
Feight, R. Preston A636
Feil, Alex A842
Feiler, Leonard A323
Fein, David A304
Fein, Alan P556
Feinberg, David M. A51
Feinberg, Melody A317
Feinberg, David T. A371
Feinberg, Hill A. A421
Feinberg, David A. P172

COMBINED HOOVER'S HANDBOOK INDEX OF EXECUTIVES

A = AMERICAN BUSINESS
E = EMERGING COMPANIES
P = PRIVATE COMPANIES
W = WORLD BUSINESS

Feinberg, David T. P213
Feinberg, David P615
Feiner, Barbara A. P600
Feinstein, Leonard (Lenny) A125
Feistauer, Marcelo A25
Feistauer, Marcelo P14
Fejer, Paul A418
Fejes, Balazs E133
Felberg, Bret A481
Felcht, Utz-Hellmuth W133
Feld, John P480
Feldhaus, Peter W391
Feldman, Darrah A201
Feldman, Dan A812
Feldman, Michael (Mike) A933
Feldman, Dorothy P382
Feldmann, Robert P616
Feldmer, Joachim A744
Feldmeyer, Kristopher A345
Feldmeyer, Kristopher E166
Feleccia, Annie A335
Feleccia, Annie E155
Felenstein, Craig A270
Felice, Gregorio de W202
Felicelli, Robert A120
Feliciano, Stephanie P552
Felis, Sandra L. P598
Felix, Natalie A337
Felix, Deborah A835
Felix, Ruth P437
Felix, Jorge P459
Felix, Jose P582
Felix, Natalie E158
Felkey, Tana P596
Felkins, Jay A177
Felkner, Joseph (Joe) P232
Fellahi, Khalid A915
Feller, Gordon A198
Fellinger, Robert E. (Bob) P198
Fellows, Steven P472
Fellows, Boyd W. E387
Fellure, Diana A89
Felsinger, Donald A77
Feltman, Rusk A713
Felton, Jerry A871
Felton, Glenn A882
Felton, Alison P46
Felton, Tom P318
Felts, Revis A527
Felts, Marcia P505
Fender, Brooke P329
Feng, Larry A702
Fenley, Michelle P333
Fenn, Scott P64
Fennell, Laura A. A471
Fenneman, Catherine A608
Fenner, Simon P302
Fennessy, Michael A418
Fennimore, Judy A538
Fenster, Jeanne A409
Fenstermacher, John E203
Fenstermaker, William H. A449
Fenstermaker, William H. E221
Fenton, Andrew A941
Fenton, George E30
Fenton, Rick E76
Fenwick, Sandra L. P558
Fenzel, Paul P261
Feola, Francis A112
Feragne, Mark A P24
Ferando, Jim A117
Ferando, Jim P61
Ferber, Scott A465
Ferbert, Dal E258
Ferbet, Charlie P308
Ferch, Wayne P6
Ferdschneider, Marcy A592
Ferdschneider, Marcy P370
Ferencz, Steven M. P119

Feret, Peter P480
Ferger, Mike A530
Ferguson, Roy C. A105
Ferguson, T. Ritson A175
Ferguson, Elizabeth A251
Ferguson, Jim A324
Ferguson, Tim A327
Ferguson, Brad A338
Ferguson, Bob A449
Ferguson, Mike A549
Ferguson, Carley A569
Ferguson, Sharon A580
Ferguson, James A606
Ferguson, Emily A760
Ferguson, Kelly A850
Ferguson, Rhonda S. A863
Ferguson, Will A867
Ferguson, Denise A882
Ferguson, Stewart P16
Ferguson, Gary P132
Ferguson, Brent P260
Ferguson, Joel I. P340
Ferguson, Amy P481
Ferguson, Jeff P508
Ferguson, John R. P551
Ferguson, Deedra P630
Ferguson, Roy C. E34
Ferguson, Bob E221
Ferguson, Mark E278
Ferguson, Sharon E292
Ferguson, Emily E374
Ferguson, Will E418
Ferguson, Admiral Mark E432
Ferguson-McHugh, Mary L. A679
Ferlita, Christine P476
Fermo, Anthony A166
Fernald, John A321
Fernandes, Savio A203
Fernandes, Paulo A545
Fernandes, Al P613
Fernandes, Sidney P638
Fernandez, Miguel A99
Fernandez, Carlos A203
Fernandez, George A245
Fernandez, Jeff A441
Fernandez, Jennifer A458
Fernandez, Luis A465
Fernandez, Yadilsa A540
Fernandez, Andre J A585
Fernandez, Samantha A704
Fernandez, Jan A829
Fernandez, Manny A895
Fernandez, Mary P298
Fernandez, Aurelio M. P500
Fernandez, Jan P589
Fernandez, Daniel W88
Fernandez, Ramon W297
Fernandez, Freddy E57
Fernandez, Gene E143
Fernandez, Madeline E194
Fernandez, Henry A. E290
Ferndinand, Norma P573
Ferniany, Will P624
Fernandez, José Luis A474
Fernandez, Ignacio Madridejos W91
Fernandez, V-ctor Turpaud W149
Feroz, Noorani A456
Feroz, Noorani E228
Ferracone, Robin A. P187
Ferrando, Jonathan A94
Ferrang, Jennifer A169
Ferranti, Andrea A528
Ferranti, Richard M. P449
Ferrar, Stephen P240
Ferrara, Albert A873
Ferrara, Enzo P638
Ferrara, John P652
Ferrara, Cid E260
Ferrari, Richard A227
Ferrari, Lisa A441
Ferrari, Daniele A447
Ferrari, Dominic A668
Ferrari, Mauro P334
Ferrari, Richard E90
Ferraro, Joseph A. (Joe) A98

Ferraro, Ralph A520
Ferraro, Paul A706
Ferraro, James A859
Ferraro, Flora E424
Ferree, Gregory A290
Ferree, Gregory M. A770
Ferree, Greg A770
Ferree, John N. P478
Ferreira, Chris A482
Ferreira, Luisa P642
Ferreira-Golino, Cathy E329
Ferrell, Lee A58
Ferrell, Malcolm A167
Ferrell, James A668
Ferrell, Patrick A723
Ferrell, Ashley P56
Ferrell, Tyler P102
Ferrell, Ronnie P201
Ferrell, Woody P281
Ferrer, Javier D. A670
Ferrer, Stephanie P558
Ferrer, Antonio Garc-a W6
Ferreri, Anthony C P527
Ferrero, Adam P546
Ferreter, Randy A257
Ferretti, Gerald P116
Ferretti, Nicole P442
Ferri, Nicolas A262
Ferri, Vince A856
Ferri, Vince P614
Ferri, William T. E386
Ferrie, John A708
Ferriman, Robert A726
Ferriman, Robert P453
Ferriola, John J. A612
Ferris, Frederick A195
Ferris, Rick A195
Ferris, Kelly A797
Ferris, Cindi P554
Ferrise, Sam P140
Ferro, Anthony A85
Ferro, Anthony E27
Ferrucci, Mario E332
Ferrufino, Jimena P125
Ferry, Jeff A909
Ferry, Thomas P22
Ferry, Michael J. E42
Ferry, Jeff E436
Ferran, Javier W140
Feruson, Frank E268
Fesen, Michael A604
Fesko, Frankie P150
Fesko, Frankie L P354
Fesmire, David A398
Festa, Stephen V. A293
Fetsko, Francis M. A838
Fetter, Victor P. A528
Fetter, Elizabeth E180
Fetterolf, Brian S. A848
Fetterolf, Brian S. E411
Fettig, Jeff M. A920
Fetzer, Ryan A327
Feucht, Terry A329
Feuer, Michael J. P569
Feuerstein, Jeff A545
Feuring, Joerge P239
Feus, Andrea P341
Fey, Alan A936
Feygin, David A149
Ffolkes, Marie A24
Fiala, Mary E349
Fiatte, Traci L. W319
Ficalora, Rob A438
Ficalora, Joseph R. A589
Fichadia, Ashok A863
Fichtel, Howard P359
Fichter, Darren M. W85
Ficke, Cliff A695
Fickler, Susan A168
Ficklin, Steve A198
FIDANZA, SILVIA W410
Fiddelke, Michael A804
Fiddler, Kawika A109
Fiddler, Lori P441
Fidler, John A492

Fiedler, William A289
Fiedler, Becky A665
Fiedler, Steven A927
Fiedler, Uwe P405
Fiedler, Becky E334
Fiedorek, R. Mark P509
Field, Doug A72
Field, Catherine A440
Field, Sam P447
Fielding, Ron A434
Fielding, Danion E187
Fields, Anna A137
Fields, Steven A444
Fields, Bruce A470
Fields, Aurora A695
Fields, Nicole A801
Fields, Karin P199
Fields, Sherry P264
Fields, Diana P276
Fields, Dana P428
Fields, Randolph H. E183
Fields, Brian E263
Fiene, Bryan A727
Fiene, Bryan P453
Fier, Jim A247
Fierens, Louis J A847
Fierens, Louis J P606
Fierke, Carol A. A711
Fierke, Carol A. P444
Fifarek, Kelly E174
Fife, Brady A54
Fifer, Tad A520
Fifer, Joseph J P509
Fifick, Anne A686
Fifield, Trent A747
Figer, Rich A897
Figge, Cherie A859
Fighs, Charles P499
Figliola, Steve A779
Figliuolo, Steve A353
Figliuolo, Steve E173
Figueredo, Jorge L. A549
Figueroa, George A571
Figueroa, John A717
Figueroa, Juan P552
Figulski, Michael A845
Fihla, Kenny W363
Fikaris, George A200
Fikry, Christopher A698
Fiksdahl, Liv W140
Fikse, David A228
Filaretos, Spyros N. W25
Filas, Melanie A170
Filbin, Michael E A746
Filetti, Robert A727
Filetti, Robert P453
Filho, Benjamin M. Baptista W33
Filho, Alfredo Egydio Arruda Villela W205
Filho, Pedro Jorge W405
Filho, Leocadio Antunes de Almeida W405
Filho, Lucio de Castro Andrade W405
Filipov, Stoyan (Steve) A815
Filipov, Douglas P113
Filippo, Pasquale A. (Pat) Di A853
Filippo, Pasquale A. (Pat) Di P612
Filipski, Kevin A658
Filkins, Heather A482
Fillis, James A16
Fillman, Jennifer A169
Fillmore, Randall A571
Filosa, Kirsten A135
Filthaut, Rich A409
Filton, Steve G. A878
Filtz, Joe P119
Fimiani, Jaime A114
Fimiani, Jaime E37
Finacchio, Daniel A835
Finale, Lucio A801
Finan, Irial A215
Finberg, Robert P616
Finch, Mary E. A16
Finch, Elizabeth A323
Finch, Felesha A449

COMBINED HOOVER'S HANDBOOK INDEX OF EXECUTIVES

Finch, Veleka A713
Finch, Bob P277
Finch, Kathleen P480
Finch, Bill P604
Finch, Duncan W233
Finch, Steven A. (Steve) W247
Finch, Felesha E221
Finchem, Timothy W. (Tim) P415
Fincher, C. Anderson A277
Fincher, Murray A852
Findlay, D. Cameron A77
Findlay, Debbie A441
Findlay, David M. A504
Findlay, Russell P597
Findlay, David W286
Findlay, David M. E251
Findley, Mary A340
Findley, Mary P171
Findley, Mary E160
Findling, Mark A747
Findlow, David A746
Fine, Peter S. A117
Fine, Keith A528
Fine, Eric A540
Fine, Rick A746
Fine, Kim P17
Fine, Peter S. P61
Fine, Michael H P451
Finer, Jeffrey T. E230
Finestone, Mark A. A95
Finger, Jennifer A912
Fingerman, Joseph A759
Fingerman, Joseph E373
Finholt, Thomas A. A711
Finholt, Thomas A. P444
Fini, Salvatore De A57
Finis, Mario P356
Finissi, Mike A600
Finizio, John A484
Fink, Laurence D. (Larry) A135
Fink, Charles A296
Fink, Nicholas I. A361
Fink, Anne A654
Fink, Martin A914
Fink, Michael P472
Fink, Robert P552
Finkel, Seth A16
Finkel, Larry A717
Finkel, Peter A922
Finkel, Peter P671
Finkel, Larry E351
Finkelstein, David L. A68
Finkelstein, Mark A219
Finkelstein, Andy P232
Finkelstein, David P513
Finkelstein, Mark E87
Finks, Jay A250
Finley, Tammy M. A13
Finley, John G. A137
Finley, Brett A361
Finley, Marcy A727
Finley, Joseph M. A848
Finley, Teresa M. A870
Finley, Wayne P161
Finley, Lowell P233
Finley, Marcy P453
Finley, Rebecca S. P603
Finley, Joseph M. E411
Finn, Tim A449
Finn, Thomas M. A679
Finn, Michael A877
Finn, Ruth A A888
Finn, William A. P501
Finn, Tim E221
Finn, Gaylyn J. E365
Finn, Ruth A E425
Finnegan, John A89
Finnegan, Daniel J. A143
Finnegan, Brian A318
Finnegan, Mike A522
Finnegan, Deb A606
Finnegan, Sean E172
Finnell, Jennifer A665
Finnell, Jennifer E334
Finneran, John G. A166

Finnerty, Ted A147
Finnerty, Shaun A470
Finnerty, Jennifer A686
Finnerty, Ken A870
Finney, Dwayne A205
Finney, Michele A811
Finnie, Cherie P667
Finnin, Jeffrey S. (Jeff) E97
Finz, David A540
Fioravanti, Mark A736
Fioravanti, Perry A781
Fioravanti, Mark P460
Fiore, Thomas A161
Fiore, Michael A544
Fiore, Maria A899
Fiore, Maria P657
Fiorelli, Bill P125
Fiorentino, Paolo W407
Fiori, Debra P406
Fiorilli, Matthew A125
Fiorini, Monica P653
Fiorvento, Bruno A482
Fipps, Paul A862
Firdaus, Dave P90
Fireman, Cassie P308
Firestone, James A392
Firestone, Marc S. A661
Firestone, Robert A754
Firestone, Robert P484
Firmender, Seth T P573
Firmery, Steve P78
Firmin, Lynne P552
Firouzdehghan, Sima A571
Firpo, Jan P456
Fisackerly, Haley R. A296
Fischer, Jean-Luc A218
Fischer, Thomas A245
Fischer, Robert A248
Fischer, Maylin A262
Fischer, Stanley A322
Fischer, Thomas J. (Tom) A512
Fischer, John E. A624
Fischer, Mark D. A692
Fischer, Avery A702
Fischer, Dave A715
Fischer, Carolyn A835
Fischer, Anthony J. (Tony) A859
Fischer, George J. A889
Fischer, Michael R. (Mike) P59
Fischer, Steven P79
Fischer, Alex P359
Fischer, Susan P372
Fischer, Jennifer P402
Fischer, Sam W140
Fischer, Robert E107
Fischer-Kinney, Julie P596
Fisco, Bob A491
Fiscus, Richard A. (Rich) A737
Fiscus, Bruce A740
Fiscus, Richard A. (Rich) E361
Fish, Mike A408
Fish, Patrick A491
Fish, Kathleen B. (Kathy) A679
Fish, Philip A741
Fish, James C. (Jim) A905
Fish, Mark P355
Fish, Kathleen P355
Fish, John F. P531
Fish, John F. P608
Fish, Philip E364
Fishbein, Daniel R. W371
Fishburn, Sibyl N. E396
Fishel, Rick E272
Fisher, Michael A19
Fisher, Brad A56
Fisher, Daniel W. A103
Fisher, Benjamin A115
Fisher, Tiffanie A152
Fisher, Joe A222
Fisher, Stephen (Steve) A287
Fisher, M Ross A409
Fisher, Ruth A414
Fisher, Douglas W. (Doug) A460
Fisher, John A467
Fisher, Nick A479

Fisher, James A538
Fisher, Heidi A584
Fisher, Susan A590
Fisher, Jeff A613
Fisher, Gary A651
Fisher, Amy A702
Fisher, Steve A754
Fisher, Derek A799
Fisher, Richard A812
Fisher, Robert J. (Bob) A826
Fisher, Scott A850
Fisher, John (Scott) A872
Fisher, Eric A887
Fisher, Marlise G. A903
Fisher, Mary A905
Fisher, Mary A922
Fisher, Phoebe P22
Fisher, Tiffanie P98
Fisher, Robby P102
Fisher, Michael P128
Fisher, Scott P197
Fisher, Alexandra P206
Fisher, Seth P215
Fisher, Ruth P236
Fisher, Sherri R P242
Fisher, Donald P302
Fisher, Morris P306
Fisher, Kyle P390
Fisher, Michelle P418
Fisher, James P456
Fisher, Steve P484
Fisher, Scott W. P541
Fisher, Rand P553
Fisher, David E. P574
Fisher, Ben P610
Fisher, Mary P671
Fisher, Benjamin E38
Fisher, Jeffrey H. E76
Fisher, Geoff E102
Fisher, Thomas C. E325
Fisher, Gary E330
Fisher, Melissa E342
Fisher, Brian J. E350
Fisher, J. Daniel (Danny) E368
Fisher, William E443
Fishman, Eric A419
Fishman, Alan H. A503
Fishman, Robert A711
Fishman, Matthew E. P27
Fishman, Robert E P356
Fishman, Robert P444
Fishman, Robert S. E96
Fishman, Alan H. E249
Fishstein, Donald E224
Fisk, Tim E132
Fissore, Sergio A628
Fitch, Deborah A227
Fitch, Karl A642
Fitch, Karl P407
Fitch, Carl P662
Fitch, Deborah E90
Fitchett, Hank P672
Fithian, Jeff E113
Fitschen, Jurgen W135
Fitterling, James A806
Fitterling, James E399
Fittro, John A329
Fitts, Lee A95
Fitts, Tina A309
Fitz, Chris A713
Fitz, Grant A933
Fitz, Stefan W208
Fitzgerald, Murdoch A81
Fitzgerald, Rich A100
Fitzgerald, Timothy A112
Fitzgerald, James A137
Fitzgerald, Shannon A145
Fitzgerald, Joseph M. (Joe) A149
Fitzgerald, Brian A222
Fitzgerald, Patrick A324
Fitzgerald, Bill A410
Fitzgerald, Anne A641
Fitzgerald, Jay A692
Fitzgerald, Patrick A762
FitzGerald, Scott R. A783

Fitzgerald, Timothy P214
Fitzgerald, Timothy P215
Fitzgerald, Anne P407
Fitzgerald, Kevin P472
Fitzgerald, Rob E80
Fitzgerald, Joe E104
Fitzgerald, Beth E429
Fitzgerald-mays, Linda P75
Fitzgibbons, Michael A A630
Fitzgibbons, Michael A A631
Fitzgibbons, Carol A P253
Fitzgibbons, Carol P253
Fitzgibbons, Michael A P397
Fitzgibbons, Timothy P P616
Fitzharris, Greg A171
Fitzmyers, Thomas J. (Tom) E375
Fitzpatrick, Pete A222
Fitzpatrick, Michael A232
Fitzpatrick, Maggie A305
Fitzpatrick, Michael J. A618
Fitzpatrick, Meg A626
Fitzpatrick, Phil A749
FitzPatrick, Daniel M. (Dan) A906
Fitzpatrick, David P12
Fitzpatrick, Sean P523
FitzPatrick, Mark T. W315
Fitzpatrick, Alex E123
Fitzpatrick, John E131
Fitzpatrick, Michael J. E310
Fitzpatrick, Diana E357
Fitzpatrick, Phil E367
FitzPatrick, Daniel M. (Dan) E435
Fitzsimmons, Ellen A46
Fitzsimmons, Brooks A89
Fitzsimmons, Bill P156
Fitzsimmons, William P156
Fitzsimmons, Rhiannon P268
Fitzsimons, Patricia Sue P676
Fixer, Mike A409
Fiz, Alex A538
Fizer, Kevin A604
Fjelsted, Craig A160
Flach, Christian W248
Flack, Kerry A36
Flack, Cheryl A606
Flacke, Jennifer A161
Flaharty, Paul A725
Flaherty, Janice A418
Flaherty, Eileen A642
Flaherty, Chuck A924
Flaherty, Joe P220
Flaherty, Maureen P325
Flaherty, Eileen P407
Flaherty, Robert E47
Flaherty, Michael E223
Flaherty-Oxler, Karen P573
Flake, Rick A347
Flakes-Cuffee, Alicia P74
Flaks, Jeffrey A P229
Flanagan, Michael A89
Flanagan, Robert A421
Flanagan, Jennifer A519
Flanagan, Bill A604
Flanagan, Patrick A761
Flanagan, Kevin A921
Flanagan, Dennis P653
Flanagan, Joseph F. (Joe) E232
Flanders, Sam P74
Flanders, Paul R. E66
Flanigan, John A17
Flanigan, John A272
Flanigan, Dan A329
Flanigan, Brent A723
Flanigan, John P9
Flannelly, Barry P. E226
Flannery, John L. A374
Flannery, Matthew J. A872
Flannery, Rhonda P291
Flannery, Robert P640
Flannery, Mark P655
Flannery, David A. E153
Flannigan, Michael A645
Flappan, Bob A89
Flareau, Bruce P70
Flatley, Jay E86

HOOVER'S HANDBOOK OF EMERGING COMPANIES 2020

COMBINED HOOVER'S HANDBOOK INDEX OF EXECUTIVES

```
A = AMERICAN BUSINESS
E = EMERGING COMPANIES
P = PRIVATE COMPANIES
W = WORLD BUSINESS
```

Flatt, Chrisann A930
Flatt, J. Bruce W80
Flattery, Bill P112
Flattery, William J P112
Flaugh, Jenny P311
Flaugher, Brett A624
Flavin, Laura A217
Flavin, Patrick A835
Flavin, Karen P22
Flaws, Brandan P235
Flax, Samuel A. E5
Flaxman, Jon E. A438
Fleagle, Steve R. P594
Fleary, Samantha A137
Fleck, Marcie A562
Fleckenstein, Michele A126
Fleeger, Russell A939
Fleet, Clifford B. (Cliff) A41
Fleet, Peter A360
Fleisch, Chris A829
Fleisch, Chris P589
Fleischer, Michael R P604
Fleischman, Natalie P569
Fleites, Fernando P94
Flemate, Willa A794
Fleming, Hans A54
Fleming, Paul A105
Fleming, Kat A112
Fleming, Michael A140
Fleming, Denise Russell A140
Fleming, Kenzel A203
Fleming, Thomas A465
Fleming, Daniel A602
Fleming, Robert A608
Fleming, Mark A623
Fleming, Paul A783
Fleming, Gerald P120
Fleming, Nancy P173
Fleming, Stan P356
Fleming, Lee Ann P400
Fleming, Dave P532
Fleming, Scott P544
Fleming, John P551
Fleming, Rhonda P552
Fleming, Rita P624
Fleming, Paul E34
Fleming, Mark E313
Flescher, Mark A782
Flescher, Mark P525
Fleshood, John S. A847
Fleshood, John S. E410
Fletcher, Tom A79
Fletcher, Verna A246
Fletcher, Barry A446
Fletcher, Jeremy A615
Fletcher, Whitney A747
Fletcher, Donna A884
Fletcher, J. Kevin A907
Fletcher, John P. A924
Fletcher, Neil P284
Fletcher, Andrea P306
Fletcher, Gary P522
Fletcher, John P672
Fletcher, Chad E80
Fletcher, Pamela E86
Fletcher, Verna E105
Fletcher, Stephanie Sawyer E433
Fletterich, Michael W254
Fleurant, Jacques W187
Fleuriet, Cathy P552
Fleury, Gustave A592
Fleury, Lynda A882
Fleury, Gustave P370
Fleury, Alison J P490
Flewelling, Brian A492
Flewelling, Matt A893
Flewelling, Linda P155
Flickinger, Bill A22
Flickinger, Brent A77

Fling, Mary A903
Flinn, James A176
Flinois, Xavier P405
Flint, Gavin T A578
Flint, Christopher A798
Flint, John W189
Flinton, David A936
Flippin, Mark A58
Fliss, Jon A140
Flissler, Allen A626
Flitman, David E P347
Flitt, Vito A530
Flive, Michael P590
Floberg, Charlie A482
Flocco, Theodore A719
Flocco, Theodore E355
Flood, Amy A385
Flood, Michael G A413
Flood, Michael A413
Flood, Gary J. A544
Flood, Peter A605
Flood, Michael A660
Flood, Nina A891
Flood, Donna L. P97
Flood, Michael P416
Flood, Rory P428
Flood, Michael G E205
Flood, Michael E205
Flood-Shaffer, Kellie P541
Florance, Andrew C. E98
Florea, Stephen A105
Florea, Stephen E34
Florell, Ann A804
Florence, John A768
Florence, Jared P175
Florence, Shelley P571
Florence, Cristian W45
Florentine, Mary P384
Flores, Bryan A104
Flores, Debbie A117
Flores, Stacy L A246
Flores, Jose A325
Flores, Doug A514
Flores, Doug A516
Flores, Debra A. A754
Flores, Toribio A824
Flores, Jose A845
Flores, Sara A859
Flores, Joshuah P. A872
Flores, Debbie P61
Flores, Mary P102
Flores, Jeanne P118
Flores, Noel P183
Flores, Doug P293
Flores, Hector P456
Flores, Dr Steven P457
Flores, Debra A. P484
Flores, Eloisa P486
Flores, Toribio P562
Flores, Alberto P587
Flores, William V. (Bill) P629
Flores, Nidia E24
Flores, Stacy L E105
Floress, Rick A327
Florey, Reinhard W295
Flori, Lou A677
Florida, John P577
Florin, Daniel P. (Dan) A939
Florio, Joseph A200
Florio, Carlo V. di P202
Floris, Karla P265
Florness, Daniel L. (Dan) A315
Flory, Brett A465
Flory, Kevin A613
Flounders, John A392
Flowe, Aaron A428
Flower, Karl A723
Flowers, Randy A202
Flowers, Garry W. A355
Flowers, Dennis A606
Flowers, Toni P112
Flowers, Randy P136
Flowers, Edtra P175
Flowers, Carolyn P354
Flowers, Laurie P596

Flowers, Steve P670
Floyd, Dennis A140
Floyd, Benjamin A161
Floyd, Patrick A735
Floyd, David K. A789
Floyd, P P112
Floyd, Jay P501
Floyd, Gary P541
Floyd, Denise P645
Flugstad, Daniel A501
Fluhler, Stephan H. A345
Fluhler, Stephan H. E165
Flum, Joshua (Josh) A251
Flury, Elizabeth P130
Flury, L. Richard E60
Fly, Daniel P354
Flygar, Brent A109
Flynn, Barbara A14
Flynn, Philip B. (Phil) A85
Flynn, Dwayne A175
Flynn, James A183
Flynn, Paul A205
Flynn, Paul G. A299
Flynn, Shannon A349
Flynn, Rick A371
Flynn, Dennis A379
Flynn, Thomas L. A413
Flynn, Michael J A414
Flynn, Joseph A458
Flynn, Brian M A504
Flynn, Julie M A578
Flynn, Todd A665
Flynn, Michael A692
Flynn, Pamela A702
Flynn, Eric A746
Flynn, Sue A836
Flynn, Amy A929
Flynn, Barbara P6
Flynn, Lynn P74
Flynn, Lauren P123
Flynn, Rick P213
Flynn, Jennifer P215
Flynn, Michael J P236
Flynn, Colleen P329
Flynn, Philip B. (Phil) E26
Flynn, Mike E72
Flynn, James E74
Flynn, Thomas L. E205
Flynn, Brian M E251
Flynn, Todd E334
Flynn, Elizabeth E435
Flynn, Amy E449
Foad, Jon P458
Fobbs, Shari P45
Fodor, Darrin A651
Fodor, Darrin E329
Foehr, Matthew W. E257
Foering, Jeff A723
Foff, John E148
Fogarty, Steve A218
Fogarty, John P79
Fogarty, Kevin M P282
Fogarty, James P604
Fogarty, Michael J. E211
Fogarty, Kevin M. E248
Fogel, Richard A84
Fogel, Glenn D. A143
Fogel, Arthur A522
Fogel, Richard P47
Fogg, Bryan A702
Foggio, Richard A702
Fogle, Natalie A109
Fogt, Andrew A224
Fohringer, Ken A828
Fohringer, Ken P584
Fojo, Carlos P750
Fojtasek, Georgia P235
Fok, Canning K. N. W190
Foley, Sean A103
Foley, John A156
Foley, Michael E. A283
Foley, Beth A303
Foley, Shannon A442
Foley, Sheena Null A500
Foley, Brendan M. A547

Foley, Patrick M A628
Foley, Joseph R. (Joe) A882
Foley, Patrick M P396
Foley, Anne P486
Foley, D Sue P587
Foley, Henry C. (Hank) P633
Foley, Brad P636
Foley, John W315
Foley, Mike W435
Folgado, Nicolas P125
Folger, Karen A724
Folger, Karen P452
Folger, Sherrie P511
Foli, Elsie P302
Folkins, Brad P450
Folks, Jacqueline P115
Folks, John P387
Follansbee, Russell A793
Follett, Ray A257
Folliard, Thomas J. (Tom) A171
Folliard, Thomas A691
Follis, Bob P233
Follis, Mike E99
Follmer, Brian A509
Follmer, Cathy P329
Follon, Stacey A358
Folse, William P467
Folsom, John A219
Folsom, Suzanne R. A873
Folsom, John E87
Foltz, Aleesa P644
Folz, Gregory P176
Fomby, Rod A812
Fonacier, Femy A198
Fong, Ivan A3
Fong, Terence A891
Fonseca, Lidia A698
Font, Juan E98
Fontaine, Julie A587
Fontaine, Michael A783
Fontaine, Keith P229
Fontaine, Dorrie K. P442
Fontaine, Jean-Louis W73
Fontanez, Carmen A179
Fontanilla, Tiara E290
Fontano, Anthony A686
Fontem, Franklin P383
Fontenot, Justin A755
Fontenot, Justin E369
Foo, Seehack A74
Foo, Chok-Pin P307
Foo, Peter M. T. W411
Foody, Paul A905
Fook, Hou Wey W130
Foote, James M A245
Foote, Trevor A530
Foote, Scott A638
Foote, Warren A642
Foote, Warren P407
Foote, Scott E320
Fopma, Rick P277
Foraker, Randy P. A105
Foraker, John M. A376
Foraker, Randy P. E34
Foran, Bob A16
Foran, Robert E. (Bob) A560
Foran, Gregory S. (Greg) A901
Foran, Robert E. (Bob) P336
Foran, Tom E450
Forant, Jim A798
Forbes, Chris A104
Forbes, Jeffrey A147
Forbes, Jeff A147
Forbes, Lori A718
Forbes, Tom A925
Forbes, Kelli P7
Forbes, Jeff S P196
Forbes, Stephen J. W85
Forbes, Lori E354
Forbes, Tom E445
Forbes-roberts, Victoria A262
Forche, Kurt A487
Ford, Robert B. A5
Ford, Mary A56
Ford, Thomas V A112

COMBINED HOOVER'S HANDBOOK INDEX OF EXECUTIVES

Ford, Susan A240
Ford, Kevin A338
Ford, William C. (Bill) A360
Ford, Gerald J. A365
Ford, Brett A397
Ford, Jeremy B. A421
Ford, Gerald J. A421
Ford, Kevin A483
Ford, Marianne A629
Ford, Karen A702
Ford, Rodney A713
Ford, Heather A922
Ford, Darrell L. A933
Ford, Tom A934
Ford, Kale P120
Ford, Mike P185
Ford, Gary P334
Ford, Tim P379
Ford, Dorvetta P448
Ford, Tracey P595
Ford, Deborah (Debbie) P641
Ford, Heather P671
Ford, Michael W317
Ford, W. Sean E259
Ford, W E260
Ford, Celeste E375
Forde, Terry P7
Forde, Wayne P116
Fordham, Mark A779
Fordham, Yolanda P371
Fordham, Pam P588
Fore, Delbert A299
Fore, Henrietta A309
Foreman, Nicholas A859
Foreman, Kelly A940
Foreman, Jeff P260
Foreman, Jennifer P351
Foreman, Ken P443
Foreman, Anne E185
Forero, Juan A657
Forese, James A. (Jim) A203
Forese, Laura L. A827
Forese, Laura L. P580
Foresman, Stephen E203
Forestier, Jean-Pierre W390
Foret, Nathan A61
Forger, James (Jim) P339
Forgette, Steve A835
Foris, Nico P225
Forkish, Jennifer A161
Forlenza, Vincent A. (Vince) A123
Forman, James A613
Forman, Eric C. E99
Formella, Nancy P79
Fornas, Bernard W115
Fornberg, Anders P104
Forney, John L. A868
Forney, Stephen P163
Forrest, Frank R. A329
Forrest, Michael A460
Forrest, John A481
Forrest, Stephen A711
Forrest, Dawn P138
Forrest, Beth P147
Forrest, Stephen P444
Forrest, Ella P555
Forrey, Kevin A752
Fors, Rudy A885
Forsgren, Kent A371
Forst, Israel A739
Forster, Eric James A711
Forster, Eric James P444
Forster, Ann P483
Forsyth, John A120
Forsythe, Claire A313
Forsythe, Cameron P596
Forsythe, Claire E144
Forsythe, Patrick E184
Fort, Bob A754
Fort, Stephen W. A853
Fort, Bob P484
Fort, Stephen W. P612
Forte, Jacquelynn A284
Forte, Jacquelynn E120
Forthman, Michael A P213

Fortin, Mary Jane B. A35
Fortin, Jennifer A179
Fortin, David A522
Fortino, Joseph A512
Fortna, Bob E179
Fortner, Jack L. P634
Fortuna, Robert A109
Fortuna, David A885
Fortunas, Paula P541
Fortunato, Kim Fremont A164
Fortunato, Joseph A776
Fortunato, Steve E33
Fortune, Erica A132
Fortwangler, Robert P106
Forward, Bill A668
Forzano, Mauricette A739
Forziati, Gina A135
Foschi, Pier Luigi W87
Foshee, William M. A755
Foshee, Kevin P31
Foshee, William M. E369
Foss, Eric J. A75
Foss, Kimberly A408
Foss, Bob A643
Foss, Donald A. E103
Fossati, Massimiliano W407
Fossett, Sheryl P312
Foster, Sarah A112
Foster, Jesse G. A116
Foster, Nancy A200
Foster, James A207
Foster, David A218
Foster, Sara E. A224
Foster, Sean A243
Foster, Richard A246
Foster, David A286
Foster, A Mickey A323
Foster, Colleen A329
Foster, Holly M. A340
Foster, Rodney A340
Foster, Daphne H. A387
Foster, Jon M. A410
Foster, Mark A465
Foster, Bryan A528
Foster, Joan A651
Foster, Mike A715
Foster, Louise A831
Foster, Larry A835
Foster, Delecia P12
Foster, Chris P105
Foster, Chris P117
Foster, Andrew P139
Foster, Scott P160
Foster, David P190
Foster, Michael P237
Foster, Paul D. P262
Foster, Janet P293
Foster, Andy P306
Foster, Richard P347
Foster, Pamela P478
Foster, Robert F P499
Foster, Randall P589
Foster, Jesse G. E39
Foster, James C. E75
Foster, Richard E105
Foster, Kelly E156
Foster, Holly M. E160
Foster, Rodney E161
Foster, Andrea E268
Foster, Joan E329
Foster, Lisa E334
Foster, Bill E383
Fosz, Lea A381
Foti, Joe P309
Foti, Alessandro W407
Fotiades, George L. E63
Fotiou, John A155
Fotiou, John E54
Fouberg, Robert A252
Fouche, Andy A243
Foulds, Tom A776
Foulke, Elvia P137
Foulkes, David M. A154
Foulkes, Helena B. A251
Foulkes, Anne A673

Foulston, Matthew J. A846
Foundos, Phil E330
Fountain, David B. A281
Fountain, Jason A442
Fountain, JoAnn A462
Fountain, JoAnn P256
Fouque, Jorge Andueza W29
Fournier, Martha A133
Fournier, Dave P391
Fournier, Michele P405
Fournier, Ron P590
Fournier, Dominique E249
Fournier, Brian E440
Fouse, Jacqualyn E226
Fouss, Brad A618
Fouss, Brad E310
Foust, Eric A491
Foutch, Lucy A665
Foutch, Lucy E334
Fouty, Dennis P629
Fowinkle, Ron A89
Fowke, Benjamin G. S. (Ben) A931
Fowle, John A405
Fowler, Ross A198
Fowler, Bryan A278
Fowler, W. Randall (Randy) A299
Fowler, John M A470
Fowler, Kevin A533
Fowler, Terry A571
Fowler, Doug A654
Fowler, Edward A681
Fowler, Maggie A776
Fowler, Erica A865
Fowler, Charles D. (Chuck) P116
Fowler, W Randall P196
Fowler, Bob P197
Fowler, W Randall P340
Fowler, James C P391
Fowler, Jim P391
Fowler, Maggie P512
Fowler, John C P552
Fowler, Mike P610
Fowler, Alice P649
Fowler, J. B. W212
Fowler, Christopher L. E92
Fowler, Nate E334
Fowler, Erica E417
Fowles, Mike A447
Fowlkes, Harold A409
Fox, Jeffrey A98
Fox, Karen A107
Fox, Gregory C. A138
Fox, Gregory C. A157
Fox, Joseph A177
Fox, John N A216
Fox, Matt A233
Fox, Vicki A337
Fox, John A343
Fox, Barbara A364
Fox, Christopher A403
Fox, Brian J. A413
Fox, Tom A481
Fox, Sheldon J. A501
Fox, Marc A. A503
Fox, Andrea A520
Fox, John A731
Fox, Steve A833
Fox, Hannah P56
Fox, Gregory C. P91
Fox, Leana P94
Fox, John T P194
Fox, Rebecca P274
Fox, Robin P300
Fox, Tricia P518
Fox, Jamie P580
Fox, Andrew P596
Fox, Susan P667
Fox, Brett M. W80
Fox, Vicki E158
Fox, John E164
Fox, Brian J. E205
Fox, Marc A. E249
Fox, Duane E291
Fox, Richard P. (Rick) E326
Fox-andrews, Dana P215

Fox-Martin, Adaire W340
Foy, Pete A327
Foy, Bryan E203
Foye, Brian A255
Foye, Rona A324
Foyles, Kirsten A334
Foyles, Kirsten E153
Frable, Anna A609
Frable, Anna P391
Fracchia, Joe E282
Fraczkiewicz, Robert J A388
Fraczkowski, Kurt A220
Fraczkowski, Kurt P149
Fradkin, Steven L. (Steve) A605
Fraenkel, Martin A738
Fraenkel, Fred S. E101
Fraga, Francisco A164
Fraga, Amanda A522
Fragale, Michael P160
Fragkiadakis, Leonidas W272
Fragnoli, Dellanie A242
Fragnoli, Stephen P149
Frahm, Monty A608
Frahm, Eric P339
Frain, Michelle A347
Frain, Michael A589
Frain, Diane P244
Frake, Nick A929
Frake, Nick E449
Fraley, Dave A355
Fraley, Alton P274
Fralick, Julie P536
Frame, Randall A. A351
Framke, Gregory A. (Greg) W247
Frampton, Marcus A29
Frampton, Cathy A482
Frampton, Robin A695
Frampton, Marcus P16
Frampton, John P547
France, Robert A240
Franceschi, Janice P588
Franceschini, Luca W155
Francesconi, Louise A790
Francesconi, Michael A870
Francia, Chris P148
Francic, Nick A482
Francioli, Richard W415
Francione, Brian A835
Francis, Laith A222
Francis, Charles P. A266
Francis, Charlie A266
Francis, John A327
Francis, Shaun J. A354
Francis, James A403
Francis, Scott A540
Francis, Julian A635
Francis, Robert E. (Bob) A785
Francis, Timothy A845
Francis, Beth P64
Francis, Maxine James P101
Francis, Charles P. P181
Francis, Charlie P181
Francis, Robert P286
Francis, Evette P348
Francis, Michael P511
Francis, Jim E431
Francisco, Michelle A877
Franco, Joe A176
Franco, Joseph A476
Franco, Patty A713
Franco, Javier Augusto Gonzalez W175
Franco, Ashley E122
Francois, Holly P308
Francque, Kathleen M A693
Francque, Kathleen M E341
Franczek, Carol P386
Franey, Bill A108
Franey, Henry J. P630
Franey, Hank P630
Frangetis, Dimitris W272
Frangione, Thomas A77
Frank, Janet D. (Jan) A32
Frank, Brian A35
Frank, Elizabeth A45
Frank, Edward A67

COMBINED HOOVER'S HANDBOOK INDEX OF EXECUTIVES

A = AMERICAN BUSINESS
E = EMERGING COMPANIES
P = PRIVATE COMPANIES
W = WORLD BUSINESS

Frank, Barbara A137
Frank, Malcolm A216
Frank, Dave A222
Frank, Andy A224
Frank, Terry A246
Frank, Billy A343
Frank, Aaron A349
Frank, Norm A399
Frank, Matthew A507
Frank, Larry A686
Frank, Malcangio A695
Frank, Ben A824
Frank, Maxine A827
Frank, Aaron P70
Frank, Edward H. (Ed) P114
Frank, Isabelle P206
Frank, Norm P223
Frank, Ben P561
Frank, Maxine P580
Frank, James S. (Jim) P594
Frank, Robert G. P634
Frank, Debra P643
Frank, Howard S. W87
Frank, Terry E105
Frank, Malcolm E143
Frank, Billy E163
Frank, Thomas A. J. E235
Frank-lightfoot, Lorraine P353
Franke, Charlene A711
Franke, James A890
Franke, Jerold P. A907
Franke, Mark A928
Franke, Paul P16
Franke, Charlene P444
Franke, Mark P674
Frankel, Bonnie P174
Frankel, Adam B. E138
Frankel, Michael S. E357
Frankel, Ronald E396
Frankiline, John A360
Franklin, Ed A107
Franklin, Jack A346
Franklin, Matthew A732
Franklin, Kathleen A925
Franklin, Carol P245
Franklin, William H. P262
Franklin, Tamara P480
Franklin, William E. E96
Franklin, Jack E166
Franklin, Kathleen E445
Frankovich, Chris A219
Frankovich, Chris E87
Franks, Brent J. A75
Franks, Michael A179
Franks, Kim E105
Frantz, Thom A341
Frantz, Byron A380
Frantz, T K P110
Frantz, Rita A. P594
Franz, Christoph W328
Franzi, Cristiano A120
Franzino, Michael E248
Franzoni, Kasey A651
Franzoni, Greg A799
Franzoni, Kasey E329
Fraser, Jim A104
Fraser, Jane A203
Fraser, Carrie A444
Fraser, Stephen A708
Fraser, John A797
Fraser, Chuck A797
Fraser, John J A798
Fraser, Ron A888
Fraser, Carol P298
Fraser, John M P362
Fraser, Gertrude P442
Fraser, Mike W68
Fraser, Nancy E. E144
Fraser, Ron E425

Frasier, Edie A165
Frasier, Timothy (Tim) A724
Frasier, Timothy (Tim) P452
Fratamico, John J. A509
Fratanduono, Sal A167
Fratantoni, Karen P130
Frates, Caton A242
Fratini, Adrienne M P308
Fratus, Mark A784
Fraumann, Timothy A905
Frawley, Patrick J A179
Frawley, Caroline A319
Frawley, Owen P282
Frayer, Becky A680
Frayha, Najla A882
Frazer, Beverly P225
Frazier, Seth A414
Frazier, Spencer A442
Frazier, Kenneth C. (Ken) A554
Frazier, Seth P236
Frazier, Bryan P532
Frazis, George W424
Frear, David J. A762
Frech, Christopher W E126
Frechette, Patricia A929
Frechette, Patricia E449
Frecker, Richard A417
Freddino, Robert A746
Fredell, Thomas P333
Frederick, Bob A164
Frederick, Brian A258
Frederick, Chad A315
Frederick, Lori P333
Frederick, Jeff P447
Fredericks, David A103
Fredericks, Jay A161
Fredericks, Raymond P266
Frederickson, Trevor A893
Fredin, Steven (Steve) A92
Fredrick, Robert P591
FREEBORN, TIM A521
Freed, Brian W. A71
Freed, Todd P261
Freed, Dean P326
Freedman, Jill A479
Freedman, Barry P19
Freedman, Stephen P206
Freedman, Mark P664
Freedman, Jamie W37
Freedman, Joseph S. (Joe) W80
Freel, John A605
Freeland, Steve E73
Freeley, Katherine A218
Freeman, Cathy S. A106
Freeman, Mark A129
Freeman, William A201
Freeman, Mark A246
Freeman, Bruce A307
Freeman, Mark A491
Freeman, Charles A550
Freeman, Jim A562
Freeman, Dexter A651
Freeman, Lori A695
Freeman, John A923
Freeman, Joshua P117
Freeman, Richard P190
Freeman, Dennis M. P314
Freeman, Charles P319
Freeman, Amy P332
Freeman, Marcus P378
Freeman, Todd P391
Freeman, Richard P489
Freeman, Jim P617
Freeman, Nikki P662
Freeman, Thomas E. E81
Freeman, Mark E105
Freeman, Richard E177
Freeman, Terry E224
Freeman, Dexter E329
Freeman, John E442
Freemon, Mildred P552
Freer, Rudell S P299
Freesmeyer, Sam A21
Frei, Reto A391
Frei, Theresa A791

Frei, Theresa P535
Freiberg, Gregory W. (Greg) E183
Freiburg, Debbie P130
Freidenfelds, Lauris P459
Freihoefer, Cori A413
Freihoefer, Cori E205
Freij, Adel E441
Freilich, Helen A801
Freimark, Barry — A466
Freimark, Ryan A909
Freimark, Ryan E436
Freireich, Neil P644
Freisleben, Ron A727
Freisleben, Ron P453
Freitag, Randal J. A519
Freitag, Kristine P524
Freitas, Mike A765
Freitas, Humberto W412
Freixe, Laurent W276
Frelka, Greg A746
Fremar, Leanne A779
Fremont, Philippe A100
French, Tracy M. A426
French, Lesa A482
French, Richard A574
French, Amber A711
French, Dana A925
French, Susan P97
French, Robert W P202
French, Constance P399
French, Amber P444
French, Hadley Mack P670
French, Seamus W29
French, Tracy M. E213
French, Christopher E. (Chris) E370
French, Dana E445
Freni, Sam E123
Frenkel, Jacob A526
Frenkiel, Paul A823
Frenkiel, Paul E405
Frent, Marty A158
Frenzel, Robert C. (Bob) A932
Frenzel, Michael W402
Frere, Edward A884
Frescura, Andi A444
Frescura, Louis P285
Frese, Calvin W. (Cal) A175
Frese, Brian A867
Frese, Mark W91
Freshour, Kimberly P486
Fretheim, Scott A233
Fretwell, Roger P210
Fretz, Deborah M E172
Freudmann, Axel A845
Freund, Lothar P P282
Freund, Charles R. E174
Freund, Lothar P. E248
Freundlich, Todd A452
Frey, Charles A294
Frey, James A839
Frey, Daniel P157
Frey, Michelle P336
Frey, James P336
Frey, R P463
Frey, Pamela P519
Freyling, Sylvia A325
Freyne, Colm J. W371
Freyou, Jason P A426
Freytas, Denise A112
Frias, Cristina A114
Frias, James D. (Jim) A612
Frias, Yanela C A684
Frias, Cristina E37
Frick, Mark A233
Frick, Wendy P596
Fricke, David A818
Fricke, Lisa A922
Fricke, Lisa P671
Fricke, David E403
Fricker, Michael P220
Frickle, T A386
Frickle, T J A386
Frickle, T E188
Frickle, T J E188
Friday, Gary P305

Friebis, Dawn P359
Fried, David A505
Fried, Arthur P527
Fried, David W317
Fried, Richard E219
Friedel, Bobby P508
Friedell, Andrew P315
Friedland, Jd A744
Friedlander, Steven A893
Friedman, Richard A. A390
Friedman, Farley A391
Friedman, Mark A460
Friedman, Dan A466
Friedman, Leonard A484
Friedman, Howard A496
Friedman, Howard H. A678
Friedman, Diana A744
Friedman, Paula J. A776
Friedman, Michael A782
Friedman, Mark A877
Friedman, Paul A893
Friedman, Seth A895
Friedman, Wayne P487
Friedman, Paula J. P512
Friedman, Michael P525
Friedman, Hanan W49
Friedman, Jeremy A. E232
Friedmann, Paul P72
Friedmann, Glenon P630
Friedrich, Amy C. A677
Friel, Emily A526
Friemel, Jake A222
Friend, Mark A364
Friend, Grant A444
Friend, Michelle A444
Friend, Sean A449
Friend, Zoe A587
Friend, Matthew A896
Friend, Bob A908
Friend, Gwyn P175
Friend, Sean E220
Friend, Bob E436
Frierson, Henry T. P627
Fries, Rick P23
Fries, James P173
Fries, Robert P477
Friesen, Ernie A397
Friesen, Debbie A912
Friesen, Carol P401
Friesen, Scott E123
Frieson, Don A902
Friess, Robert A74
Frigeria, Vincent A688
Friman, Maija-Liisa W275
Frimpong, Stephen A493
Frint, Yhonis P481
Frioux, George E278
Frisbee, Kimberly P45
Frisch, Ann A588
Frisch, Scott P2
Frisch, Steven M. P17
Frisch, Stephen P17
Frisch, Hans P75
Frisch, Benjamin P75
Frisch, Mark P75
Frisch, Ann P365
Frisch, Melissa P630
Frishman, Arik W203
Frisk, Patrik A862
Frissora, Mark P. A160
Frist, Thomas A410
Fritsch, Wayne A888
Fritsch, Wayne E425
Fritts, William A212
Fritz, Peter A3
Fritz, Lance M. A863
Fritz, James S. P64
Fritz, Susan M. P92
Frizzell, Benjamin P524
Froc, Jay E. W85
Frock, Charles T P349
Froehlich, Patti P209
Froehlich, Mark P648
Froggatt, Mark E262
Frome, James J. (Jim) E384

Fromille, Carla P228
Fromm, Daniel A137
Fron, David A713
Fronduti, John A56
Fronheiser, Jason A329
Fronk, Chris A605
Fronmuller, Mark A46
Frons, Marc A596
Frontczak, Deborah P116
Frontz, Marilyn A6
Frontz, Eric P677
Fronzaglio, Joseph A425
Frooman, Thomas E. A197
Frossmo, Kristin A602
Frost, Robert A54
Frost, Christopher A109
Frost, Robert A227
Frost, Patrick B. (Pat) A246
Frost, Jack A387
Frost, Donna A449
Frost, Chase A713
Frost, David P305
Frost, Robert E90
Frost, Patrick B. (Pat) E104
Frost, Donna E221
Frost, Phillip E250
Frost, Ronald A. E278
Fruehauf, Richard A873
Fruhling, Julian L P479
Frumkin, Theodore E. (Ted) A776
Frumkin, Howard A880
Frumkin, Howard P640
Frump, Candace A652
Frump, Candace E331
Frustaci, Dominick E232
Fry, Earl A182
Fry, Patrick E P536
Fry, Shane E290
Fry, Richard E330
Fry, Nina E371
Frydrych, Tim A849
Frye, Andrew A120
Frye, John A226
Frye, Dawn A327
Frye, Arthur A482
Frye, Patrick A790
Frye, John P150
Frye, Deborah P596
Frye, Patrick E389
Fryett, Terry W53
Fryfogle, Jim A668
Frykhammar, Jan W386
Fryson, David P663
Fryz, Mike P74
Fr-ondberg, Sofia W420
Fu, Frederick A99
Fu, Cary E258
Fucci, John T. E245
Fuchigami, Kazuo W293
Fuchs, Rainer A133
Fuchs, Rob A271
Fuchs, Jim A319
Fuchs, Rick A465
Fuchs, Barbara A686
Fuchs, Michael A833
Fuchs, Mary Ann P187
Fuchs, W. Kent P627
Fudge, Duncan A574
Fuente, Maria Eugenia de la W45
Fuentes, Antonia A72
Fuentes, Christopher A891
Fuerst, Aaron A219
Fuerst, Edward A577
Fuerstenberg, Jeffrey P302
Fuetsch, Andre E64
Fugger, Edward F. P668
Fugina, Annette A559
Fugui, Xu W301
Fuguitt, Gayle A376
Fuhrman, Stephen E P122
Fujibayashi, Kiyotaka W262
Fujie, Naofumi W18
Fujii, Hideaki P34
Fujikura, Masato W360
Fujimoto, Masayoshi W360

Fujino, Michimasa W186
Fujita, Minoru W127
Fujita, Katsuyuki W127
Fujita, Yoshitaka W268
FUJIWARA, ICHIRO W52
Fujiwara, Hiroaki W221
Fujiwara, Kiyoshi W250
Fujiwara, Shoji W293
FUKAI, AKIHIKO W176
Fukasawa, Yuji W143
Fukuda, Makoto W30
Fukuhara, Kazuyuki W250
Fukui, Soichi W259
Fukuichi, Tokuo W400
Fukushima, Meigan A544
Fukuzawa, Toshihiko A19
Fulcher, Jeffrey A823
Fulcher, Jeffrey E405
Fulghum, Lisa A713
Fulk, Sue A455
Fulk, Gary A629
Fulkerson, Mike A538
Fulkerson, Debra A621
Fulkerson, Ed A746
Fulkerson, William J. P187
Fulkerson, Perry P204
Fulkerson, Rick P212
Fulkerson, Debra E311
Fuller, Sherrika A135
Fuller, Jeff A246
Fuller, Scott A266
Fuller, Gregory A319
Fuller, David A329
Fuller, Lynn B. A413
Fuller, Gary A425
Fuller, Wilford H. (Will) A519
Fuller, Amy A544
Fuller, Bryan A544
Fuller, Debra A552
Fuller, Julie A623
Fuller, Jake A654
Fuller, Rodger D. A768
Fuller, Gail A850
Fuller, Robert A936
Fuller, Scott P181
Fuller, Jim P353
Fuller, Jeff E105
Fuller, Tony E149
Fuller, Lynn B. E205
Fuller, Debra E276
Fuller, Joann E306
Fuller, Julie E313
Fuller-Andrews, Lynne A403
Fullerton, Rob P670
Fulmer, James W. (Jim) A838
Fulmer, Jeff E97
Fulton, Howard A53
Fulton, Marshall A115
Fulton, Cedrick A560
Fulton, Mark P306
Fulton, Cedrick P336
Fulton, Matthew P371
Fulton, Marshall E38
Fulton, Tricia L. E208
Fulton, Mike E429
Fultz, Kelli P5
Fumelle, Michael A85
Fumelle, Michael E26
Funai, Edmund P638
Funaoka, Akihiko W262
Funato, Takashi W258
Funayama, Norio W350
Fund, Steven L. A460
Funderburk, William W. P299
Fung, Linda A686
Fung, Vincent P536
Funk, Dan A87
Funk, Charles N. A567
Funk, Dan P50
Funk, Robert A. P198
Funk, Justin P506
Funk, Michael E168
Funk, Charles N. E283
Funkhouser, Cameron K. P202
Funston, Linda P475

Funston, Karen P525
Fuqua, Barbara A483
Fura, Embry A222
Furbee, Shari A358
Furbee, Shari E176
Furby, David W106
Furey, Shawn A179
Furey, Jan A219
Furey, Michael A606
Furey, Adrian A939
Furey, Jan E87
Furgal, Scott A575
Furlong, Mark A147
Furlong, Fred A321
Furlong, Frederick T A321
Furlong, Bryan A713
Furman, Maria D. P631
Furner, John A901
Furnish, Kyle P215
Furniss, Kristin E296
Furnstahl, Lawrence J. P399
Furr, William B. A421
Furr, David A616
Furtado, Larissa P597
Furtek, Kathryn A605
Furuichi, Takeshi W279
Furukawa, Shinya W398
Furuto, Gordon P628
Furuya, Katsumasa W169
Furuya, Kazuki W346
Fusco, Jeff A115
Fusco, Jack A. A187
Fusco, Joseph A540
Fusco, Art P120
Fusco, Jeff E38
Fushen, Li W103
Fushitani, Kiyoshi W298
Fusillo, Robert A902
Fuson, Micah P168
Fussell, Stephen R. (Steve) A5
Futamiya, Masaya W360
Futhey, Tracy P186
Fybel, Gary G. P479
Fynan, Tamara J. A765
Fyodorov, Igor Y. W308
Fyodorov, Pavel W330
Félix, José Ant-´nio Guaraldi W26

G

Gaal, Sheri A835
Gabanna, Louis W112
Gabay, Philippe E344
Gabbard, Brian A75
Gabbard, Brian A103
Gabel, Barry A522
Gabel, Steve A616
Gabel, Karen A756
Gabel, Timothy J. (Tim) P447
Gaber, Sharon L. P596
Gabilondo, Natalia F P329
Gable, Deborah A61
Gable, Steve A366
Gabriel, Gerry A309
Gabriel, Christina A900
Gabriel, Kaigham (Ken) P557
Gabriel, Emigda P576
Gabriel, Yves W76
Gabrielle, With A604
Gabrielson, Rick A527
Gabrys, Gerard T. P224
Gachot, Robert A616
Gack, Bruce A498
Gacke, Brad P462
Gacsy, Timothy A528
Gadberry, Kirk P376
Gadd, Philip L A461
Gaddes, Kathy H. A63
Gaddis, Byron J. A675
Gaddis, Byron J. P428
Gaden, Nancy P95
Gadgil, Beena A126
Gadis, David L P174
Gadol, Boris A589

Gadow, Julie P537
Gadzinski, Norman P356
Gaeckle, Joseph A520
Gaemperle, Chantal W241
Gaeng, Chris A799
Gaer, Steven A911
Gaer, Steven E437
Gaeta, Mary P97
Gaffney, Dan A112
Gaffney, Paul J. A264
Gaffney, Michael A379
Gaffney, Paul A496
Gaffney, Michael A761
Gaffney, Kathy A837
Gaffney, Marie P418
Gage, Marlyss J. A844
Gage, Timothy M. E69
Gagel, Brian A717
Gagel, Brian E351
Gagey, Frédéric W15
Gagliano, Joe A54
Gagliano, Mario A657
Gagliardi, Frank A189
Gagliardotto, David A574
Gagne, John A530
GAGNON, BRENDA A196
Gagnon, Carl A882
Gagnon, Martin W270
Gagua, Irina P218
Gahagan, David E433
Gaherty, John B. A242
Gai, Michael P85
Gaiennie, Liz A296
Gain, Tom A928
Gain, Tom P674
Gaines, Bennett L. A350
Gaines, Zach P412
Gaines, Kristin S. E296
Gainor, Sue A140
Gainsburg, Daniel P248
Gairing, Peter A704
Gaither, Kevin A767
Gaither, J. Michael (Mike) P35
Gaither, Chris P450
Gaizutis, Jennifer A824
Gaizutis, Jennifer P562
Gal, Shimon W49
Galainena, M David A827
Galainena, M David P571
Galante, Edward A177
Galanti, Richard A. A242
Galarza, Charles A726
Galarza, Michelle A867
Galarza, Adrian P114
Galarza, Maria P383
Galarza, Charles P453
Galarza, Michelle E418
Galasso, Mario E180
Galatali, Saltik W18
Galbraith, John F P117
Galbraith, Katie P187
Galbreath, Kristen P646
GALBUSERA, CRISTINA W43
Gale, Janelle A310
Gale, Samuel A376
Gale, Fournier J. (Boots) A712
Gale, Barry E147
Galen, Dean Van P641
Gales, Amy H. A213
Gales, Amy H. P143
Galhotra, A. Kumar A360
Galifi, Vincent J. W244
Galik, Milan E235
Galin, Tomi A228
Galinat, Walter W254
Galindo, Sergio A616
Galindo, Thomas A636
Galindo, Thomas A637
Galindo, Esther A919
Galindo, Esther Berrozpe A919
Galindo, Susan P378
Galindo, Thomas P403
Galipeau, Linda W319
Galit, Scott A557
Galit, Scott E281

COMBINED HOOVER'S HANDBOOK INDEX OF EXECUTIVES

```
A = AMERICAN BUSINESS
E = EMERGING COMPANIES
P = PRIVATE COMPANIES
W = WORLD BUSINESS
```

Galiuk, Andrey A277
Gall, David W270
Gallagher, Patricia A112
Gallagher, John A123
Gallagher, Lorraine A167
Gallagher, Kathryn A205
Gallagher, Kevin A325
Gallagher, J. Patrick (Pat) A369
Gallagher, Thomas J. (Tom) A369
Gallagher, Thomas C. (Tom) A380
Gallagher, Michael A549
Gallagher, Angela A590
Gallagher, Sean A616
Gallagher, Angela A651
Gallagher, Marie A654
Gallagher, Norman A740
Gallagher, Linda A859
Gallagher, Duncan P. P26
Gallagher, Kevin P114
Gallagher, Meghan P116
Gallagher, Sally P129
Gallagher, Emily P261
Gallagher, Rick P364
Gallagher, Gerald (J.P.) P386
Gallagher, Elaine P476
Gallagher, James D. (Jim) W247
Gallagher, Maurice J. (Maury) E10
Gallagher, Angela E329
Gallant, John P608
Gallas, Carla A A561
Gallas, Melissa P359
Gallatin, David P666
Galle, Jean-Lo--c W390
Gallego, Alex P472
Gallegos, Heather A695
Gallegos, James P505
Gallen, Michelle P441
Gallett, Scott D. A146
Galletta, Joanna P254
Galletti, Michael E93
Galley, John P643
Galligan, Matthew E. (Matt) A200
Galligan, Peter A205
Galligan, Brendan A715
Gallik, Diana P124
Gallimore, Alec D. A711
Gallimore, Alec D. P444
Gallina, John E. A69
Gallino, Matthew A483
Gallo, Tom A8
Gallo, Laurene (Laurie) A144
Gallo, Horst A465
Gallo, Dominick A574
Gallo, Silvina A658
Gallo, A. C. A921
Gallo, A. C. P669
Gallo, Livio W153
Gallois, Louis W305
Gallop, Melanie A692
Gallops, Wayne P215
Galloway, Ian A57
Galloway, Shannon A464
Galloway, Brandi P137
Galloway, Heather C. P551
Galpin, Susan A628
Galsnte, Alena A797
Galst, Sandra A89
Galuppi, Barb A369
Galuppo, Gail A. A19
Galusha, Rachel A492
Galvan, David A925
Galvan, Roxann P445
Galvan, Angel P558
Galvan, David E445
Galvez, Jean-Marc A129
Galvez, Jose D. Bogas W151
Galvin, Walter A46
Galvin, William A A68
Galvin, Dana A248

Galvin, Daniel A686
Galvin, Anthony A801
Galvin, Suzanne A885
Galvin, William J P300
Galvin, Dana E107
Galway, Dan A352
Gamache, Michelle A651
Gamache, Michelle E329
Gamage, Jennifer A779
Gamarra, Cesar A890
Gambatese, Marlene P116
Gambhir, Snehil A647
Gambhir, Vandana P330
Gambill, Ron A290
Gamble, Rob Gamble Rob A36
Gamble, Daniel A536
Gamble, Leighann P176
Gamboa, Ivan A926
Gamboa, Arturo Natho W149
Gambrell, Yolanda P366
Gambuzza, Nat A176
Games, Stephanie A835
Gamez, Yenisel A167
Gamgort, Robert A489
Gamiel, Robert A89
Gamis, Mark A145
Gammelin, Johann-Caspar W158
Gammiere, Tom P479
Gammieri, Jerry A48
Gammons, Lynda A540
Ganassin, Bob E201
Ganatra, Manish A60
Ganatra, Gigi A602
Gandarilla, Daniel P551
Gandarillas, David A264
Gandarillas, David P180
Gandhi, Shyama A571
Gandhi, Dhaval A925
Gandhi, Sanjeev W59
Gandhi, Dhaval E445
Gandolfo, Joanne A686
Gandre, Tom P432
Gandy, Jason A312
Gandy, Jason P200
Gandy, Patrick W P284
Ganeev, Oleg W343
Ganem, Adriana A511
Ganem, Adriana P290
Ganger, Sonja P353
Gangestad, Nicholas C. A3
Gangone, Lynn P146
Gangwer, Patricia A171
Gann, John W A425
Gannaway, Shelly A222
Gannfors, John W. A620
Gannon, Stephen T. (Steve) A205
Gannon, John A818
Gannon, John E403
Gannotta, Richard J P388
Gans, Alan A103
Gans, Stephan A654
Gant, Beth A590
Ganti, Surya A695
Ganti, Andrew A879
Gantman, Alex A695
Gantner, Diane A85
Gantner, John P454
Gantner, Diane E27
Gantsho, Mandla Sizwe Vulindlela W341
Gantt, Jim P144
Ganz, Dale A9
Ganz, Dale P4
Ganzlin, Karen A807
Gao, Ning P636
Gao, Dennis E259
Gaor, Matt A649
Gapontsev, Valentin P. E238
Garafola, Lana A554
Garafola, Rachael P476
Garantiva, Fabian A113
Garantiva, Fabian E36
Garanzini, Michael J. P301
Garber, David A329
Garber, Tami A881

Garber, Ken P34
Garber, Tami E421
Garceau, Eric De A571
Garcia, Arturo A8
Garcia, Carlos A16
Garcia, Eduardo Gomez A54
Garcia, James P A109
Garcia, Pedro A114
Garcia, Luis A115
Garcia, Cesar A125
Garcia, Lindsay A161
Garcia, Gavin A188
Garcia, Mary A325
Garcia, Dennis A363
Garcia, Arlene A465
Garcia, Jeanne A483
Garcia, Jaime A484
Garcia, Mary Alice A571
Garcia, Gabriel A610
Garcia, Mary A665
Garcia, Fabio A670
Garcia, Carlo A676
Garcia, Art A. A734
Garcia, Jose A774
Garcia, Kelly P A798
Garcia, Kelly A798
Garcia, Christina A827
Garcia, Donna A850
Garcia, G Gary A857
Garcia, Teri P56
Garcia, Roland P63
Garcia, Jose P74
Garcia, Paul P96
Garcia, Julian P101
Garcia, Sergio P102
Garcia, Maria P164
Garcia, Joseph P184
Garcia, Ernest C P185
Garcia, Ace P302
Garcia, Diana P335
Garcia, Robert P461
Garcia, Al P483
Garcia, Henry P489
Garcia, Ramona P499
Garcia, Martha P524
Garcia, David P659
Garcia, Felix W128
Garcia, Pedro E37
Garcia, Luis E38
Garcia, Victor M. E57
Garcia, Richard G. E78
Garcia, Carol E168
Garcia, Mike E206
Garcia, Cristina E290
Garcia, Mary E334
Garcia, Carlo E338
Garcia-Barbon, Jennifer A115
Garcia-Barbon, Jennifer E37
Garcia-Velez, Calixto A333
Garc-a, Federico Reyes W164
Garde, Sameer A198
Gardea, Theresa P205
Gardella, Craig A717
Gardella, Craig E351
Gardial, Sarah A868
Gardial, Sarah Fisher P594
Gardill, James C. (Jim) A909
Gardill, James C. (Jim) E436
Gardiner, Brendan A77
Gardner, Karen A36
Gardner, Kent C. A121
Gardner, Brian A329
Gardner, Danny A364
Gardner, Shannon A444
Gardner, Freda A571
Gardner, Steven R A636
Gardner, Tom A739
Gardner, Jim A755
Gardner, Gary P773
Gardner, Jonathan A779
Gardner, Victoria A798
Gardner, Tammy A809
Gardner, Jon A840
Gardner, Charles A893
Gardner, Jean P333

Gardner, Thomas R P347
Gardner, Steven R P403
Gardner, James P659
Gardner, Paul W373
Gardner, Brandon A123
Gardner, Jim E369
Gardner, Gary E383
Gardunio, James F. (Jim) A758
Gardunio, James F. (Jim) E372
Garell, Tyler P392
Garff, Robert P212
Garff, John P212
Garff, Matthew P212
Garfield, Mark A11
Garfield, David R. A746
Garfield, Alicia A835
Garfinkle, Andrew A147
Garfinkle, Marni A686
Garg, Vivek A59
Garg, Rahul A149
Garg, Subhek A390
Garg, Abhishek P383
Garger, Stavros A702
Gargiulo, Joe A888
Gargiulo, Joe P505
Gargiulo, Joe E425
Gargrave, Maria E264
Garijo, Belén W254
Garimella, Suresh E286
Garison, Cathy A246
Garison, Cathy E105
Garito, Bonnie A211
Garito, Bonnie E83
Garland, Sheryl A602
Garland, Greg C. A662
Garland, Lorie A850
Garland, Jeffrey P627
Garland, Michael M. E322
Garlington, Cody P25
Garma-Fernandez, Emilio A704
Garman, Patrick P493
Garnadt, Karl U. W136
Garner, Sharon A58
Garner, Mason A91
Garner, Curtis (Curt) A192
Garner, Denise A207
Garner, Ed A346
Garner, Nancy A360
Garner, James A713
Garner, David W. A760
Garner, Steven A839
Garner, Sarah A853
Garner, Don A913
Garner, Stephen A933
Garner, Cicero P5
Garner, Brenda P464
Garner, Quintin P594
Garner, Sarah P612
Garner, Katherine W371
Garner, Mason E29
Garner, Ed E167
Garner, David W. E374
Garner, Don E438
Garnett, Timothy A518
Garnett, Chris A550
Garnett, Becky P112
Garnett, Valerie P337
Garnett, Sherman W. P339
Garnier, Thierry W88
Garniewski, Joe A922
Garniewski, Joe P671
Garofalo, Jill A559
Garofalo, Martin (Marty) A596
Garofalo, Marty A596
Garofalo, Michele A702
Garoff, Stephen P114
Garozzo, Scott A835
Garrabants, Greg A100
Garrabants, Greg P58
Garrabrant, Nancy A337
Garrabrant, Nancy E158
Garrabrants, Gregory A101
Garrabrants, Gregory E32
Garratt, John W. A272
Garrelts, James P48

COMBINED HOOVER'S HANDBOOK INDEX OF EXECUTIVES

Garrett, Mark S. A11
Garrett, Laurie A75
Garrett, Cristie A165
Garrett, Valerie A335
Garrett, Rob A345
Garrett, Dave A346
Garrett, Kirk A664
Garrett, John R. (Bob) A773
Garrett, Jeanette A866
Garrett, Richard A887
Garrett, Patrick P7
Garrett, Aaron P96
Garrett, James H. P114
Garrett, Melinda P245
Garrett, Amy P358
Garrett, John R P651
Garrett, Michelle E131
Garrett, Valerie E155
Garrett, Rob E166
Garrett, Dave E166
Garrett, Darren E229
Garrett, Kirk E334
Garrett, John R. (Bob) E383
Garrett, Jeanette E417
Garrigan, Allison A374
Garrigues, Bernard M. A906
Garrigues, Gretchen H. W247
Garrigues, Bernard M. E434
Garringer, Jesse A744
Garrison, Jerry A225
Garrison, Brad A345
Garrison, Thomas A460
Garrison, John L. A815
Garrison, Nickole A922
Garrison, Lori P379
Garrison, William P616
Garrison, Nickole P671
Garrison, Brad E165
Garrote-torra, Ivonne A571
Garry, Kyle A835
Garside, Geoffrey A537
Garsin, Danielle P596
Garske, Rick A103
Garst, Kevin A731
Garsys, Lucia P161
Gartland, Chuck A121
Gartner, James J. (Jim) A229
Garver, Jenny P252
Garver, David P582
Garvey, Paul A54
Garvey, Elaine A324
Garvey, Matthew A835
Garvin, Robert M. (Bert) A907
Garvin, Jean P497
Garvin, Michele P558
Garvin, Laura E265
Gary, Lehman A345
Gary, Sandra A727
Gary, Steven P197
Gary, Lee P426
Gary, Sandra P453
Gary, Lehman E166
Garza, Monica A25
Garza, Jana A344
Garza, Bernardo De La A463
Garza, Mario A571
Garza, Monica P14
Garza, Tiffany P64
Garza, Molly P205
Garza, Ed P469
Garza, --lvaro Fernandez W19
Garza, Alfonso Garza W164
Garza, Jana E165
Gasaway, Bill A442
Gascho, Dwith P246
Gaskins, Sherman L. P119
Gaspar, Pamela A249
Gaspar, Pamela E109
Gasparovic, John J. A146
Gasparro, Michael A16
Gasper, Jim P119
Gasper, David P150
Gass, Michelle A496
Gass, Rhonda O. A778
Gassen, Michael W31

Gassoso, Joanna E429
Gasta, Mark R. E424
Gaster, Scott P25
Gaster, Beth P147
Gastevich, Donna P625
Gastfriend, Jody E65
Gaston, Patrick R A125
Gatchalian, Ryan A512
Gatens, Paul A380
Gater, Karon A925
Gater, Karon E445
Gates, David A87
Gates, Scott A248
Gates, David A355
Gates, Dennis A559
Gates, Beth A804
Gates, Tim A921
Gates, David P50
Gates, John P225
Gates, Gail P395
Gates, W. Gary P396
Gates, Gabriel P442
Gates, Michelle P646
Gates, Tim P669
Gates, Ken E106
Gates, Scott E107
Gathing, Ayo A571
Gathman, Jonathan R. E365
Gathof, Larry A937
Gathright, Kristian M A71
Gathright, Kristian A71
Gathright, Kristian M P43
Gathright, Kristian P43
Gatliff, Peggy P386
Gatling, Bobby E433
Gatmaitan, Al W. P252
Gatons, Rhonda A346
Gatons, Rhonda E166
Gatta, Lawrence A272
Gattinella, Lori A409
Gattle, William H. (Bill) A501
Gatto, Pamela A. P232
Gatto, Joseph C. E60
Gatz, Ronald F. P566
Gaub, Chris P363
Gauba, Gary A184
Gaudet, Jason A160
Gaudet, Gordon J. A751
Gaudette, Kevin P210
Gaudiosi, Monica M. A857
Gaudioso, Christian A646
Gaudioso, Christian E324
Gaudreau, Charles E131
Gauger, Kelly A180
Gauger, George A332
Gauger, Alan A665
Gauger, Alan E334
Gaughan, John A347
Gaughan, John E167
Gaughen, Robert H. A424
Gaughen, Robert H. E211
Gault, James S. (Jim) A369
Gaura, Frank A735
Gaus, Otto A25
Gaus, Otto P14
Gaus, Gregory J P340
Gause, Garry A811
Gause, James E298
Gausman, Loren A797
Gaut, Steven A871
Gautam, Rajeev A431
Gautam, Alka A715
Gauthier, Eugene A390
Gauthier, Joyce V P433
Gauthier, Daniel W180
Gauthier, -%oric W323
Gauthier, Maurice A. E432
Gauvin, Tim A108
Gavazzi, Alberto W140
Gavegnano, Richard J. A556
Gavegnano, Richard J. E277
Gavel, Anne A876
Gavell, Stefan M. A783
Gavelle, Jean-Luc A66
Gavenchak, Genie A592

Gavenchak, Genie A596
Gavenchak, Genie P370
Gavens, Mark R. P118
Gavica, Marcos Alejandro Mart--nez W46
Gavigan, John A340
Gavigan, John E160
Gavin, James R A120
Gavin, Gary A467
Gavin, Michael E. A504
Gavin, Lawrence E88
Gavin, Michael E. E251
Gavitt, Dan P358
Gavrilenya, Alexey E174
Gawinski, Michelle M P555
Gawlick, Rainer E340
Gawne, Berc P560
Gawron, Mark A501
Gawron, Kinga A686
Gay, Pamela A165
Gay, Mary Chris A562
Gay, Gregory A885
Gay, Susan P204
Gay, Caroline P284
Gay, Andrew P356
Gaye, Omar A921
Gaye, Omar P669
Gayle, Troy A432
Gayne, William P658
Gayner, Thomas S. A536
Gaysunas, Clifford A248
Gaysunas, Clifford E107
Gazarian, Ed P314
Gazarik, Michael A103
Gazaway, Brad A. P478
Gazaway, Nate E427
Gazitua, John A323
Gazivoda, Lola A530
Gazula, Srinivas A877
Gcabashe, Thulani W363
Geagea, Joseph C. (Joe) A190
Geannacopulos, Nick C. P486
Gearhart, Jeffrey J. (Jeff) A901
Gearheart, Lisa A907
Gearheart, Lisa E107
Gearing, John A891
Geary, William C A68
Geary, Michael J A375
Geary, Michael J P215
Geary, Richard S. E237
Geatens, Fran A554
Gebauer, Peter R. E253
Gebb, Luke A54
Gebers, Bart A492
Gebo, Kate A865
Geckle, Geraldine Johnson A879
Geczik, Tom A301
Geczik, Tom P196
Geddes, F Michael P479
Geddes, Deanna P546
Geddes, Paul W333
Gedrich, Chris P531
Geduldig, Courtney A738
Gee, Kevin A137
Gee, Patrick A845
Gee, Mike E16
Geekie, Matthew W. A396
Geelen, Eddy A245
Geer, Lauren A797
Geer, Stacey K A676
Geer, Matt E81
Geffken, Barbara P674
Gegerson, Kelly A449
Gegerson, Kelly E221
Geha, Sam E110
Gehlen, Greg E8
Gehman, William A A172
Gehring, John F. A232
Gehrke, Terry A888
Gehrke, Terry E425
Geibel, John P675
Geier, Ross A452
Geier, Kristina A487
Geiersbach, Rik A140
Geiger, Linda A180

Geiger, Jeffrey S. A373
Geiger, Brooks A882
Geiger, Philippa P110
Geiger, Denise P286
Geiger, Eric P296
Geisert, Dawn P75
Geisinger, Kathleen P94
Geisler, Dana A121
Geisler, Jennifer A928
Geisler, James E. P178
Geisler, Karen P350
Geisler, Jennifer P673
Geiss, Cindy P49
Geissinger, John W A193
Geist, Stephen (Steve) W85
Gelbard, Wendy P456
Gelbcke, Alex A813
Geldzahler, Seth A125
Gelfand, Dan E138
Gelinas, Raymond P604
Gellart, Kathleen P197
Gelle, James A492
Gellens, Maggie A120
Geller, David A6
Geller, Jeff A554
Geller, Michal A654
Geller, Jorg M. E75
Geller, Stacey E143
Geller, David E290
Gellerstedt, Lawrence L. E100
Gelman, Jack A479
Gelman, Mesh A780
Gelman, Luba A888
Gelman, Lawrence P183
Gelman, Luba E425
Gelok, Brian A203
Gelsinger, Patrick P. (Pat) A897
Gelsomin, Lynn A88
Gelston, Kevin A271
Gelwix, Steve A267
Gembicki, Mark P74
Gembler, Dawn P379
Gemignani, Gino J. A831
Gemignani, Gino J. P601
Gemmell, Patrick A167
Gemmell, Thomas A741
Gemmell, Thomas E364
Gemmill, Glenn A215
Gemrich, John A885
Gendell, David B E224
Gendelman, Berry P152
Genden, Eric P351
Gendler, Gordon A859
Gendreau, Donna A409
Gendron, Daniel A704
General, Dean A846
Generale, Paul P132
Generous, Robin A409
Genestar, Thierry W112
Geng, Tan Wan W103
Genis, Arnaud P. A635
Genius, Just A6
Gennaro, Susan P608
Gennaro, Giovanni De W235
Gennett, Joseph A881
Gennett, Joseph E421
Genola, Gabriele Galateri di W35
Genovesi, Diane A483
Genshaft, Judy L. P638
Gensler, Melanie A452
Genso, Gueitiro Matsuo W412
Gensor, Joe A925
Gensor, Joe E445
Gentile, Mario A158
Gentile, Bob A694
Gentile, Thomas C A774
Gentle, Meg A. A188
Gentry, Art A227
Gentry, Peter A665
Gentry, Michael A754
Gentry, Daniel A797
Gentry, Craig P312
Gentry, Michael P484
Gentry, Tony P653
Gentry, Art E90

COMBINED HOOVER'S HANDBOOK INDEX OF EXECUTIVES

```
A = AMERICAN BUSINESS
E = EMERGING COMPANIES
P = PRIVATE COMPANIES
W = WORLD BUSINESS
```

Gentry, Peter E334
Gentsch, Benjamin W345
Gentzkow, Paul F. A725
Gentzler, Rollie A434
Genzink, Larry A774
Genzink, Larry P510
Gen-§, Onur W403
Geofroy, Diana A218
Geoghegan, Kevin A347
Geoghegan, Kevin E168
George, David C. (Dave) A255
George, Ester L. A322
George, Marlon A452
George, Martin (Marty) St. A478
George, Cherian A479
George, Brandon A676
George, Andrew A713
George, Sumesh A804
George, Boyd L. P21
George, Brian P21
George, Richard P67
George, Dennis St P174
George, Carl St P213
George, William S. P232
George, Denise P233
George, Jason P276
George, Susan P356
George, Pascal P364
George, Jessica P394
George, Zachary P430
George, Thomas F. (Tom) P633
George, Roger E. E9
George, William E89
George, Mark St E137
George, Michael E264
George, Brandon E338
George, Dave E402
Georges, Laura P192
Gephart, Craig A444
Gephart, Beth P235
Geppert, Michael P231
Ger, Kevin A29
Gera, Chris A543
Gerace, Christopher P. A724
Gerace, Christopher P. P452
Geraci, Greg A175
Geraci, Gaspere A571
Geraghty, Joanna A478
Geraghty, Timothy A605
Geraghty, Paul D. A929
Geraghty, Paul D. E449
Gerard, Jeff A791
Gerard, Jeff P535
Gerard, Christopher E14
Gerarde, Roberta P299
Gerardi, Marlene A374
Gerardi, Dave A522
Gerarve, Robin A938
Gerarve, Robin P678
Gerba, Emin A739
Gerber, Chuck P555
Gerber-Vecsey, Karen P417
Gerberding, Julie L. A554
Gerdeman, Aaron A327
Gerdes, Jurgen W137
Gerety, Peggy E51
Gergel, Andrew A575
Gergel, Ivan P. E300
Gerguis, Steven P141
Gerhard, Chris E409
Gerhart, Scott A69
Gerhart, John A248
Gerhart, Jacqueline A741
Gerhart, Bobbie P338
Gerhart, John E107
Gerhart, Jacqueline E364
Gericke, Johan A167
Gering, William A922
Gering, William P671

Gerken, Tim P600
Gerlach, Alysa P384
Gerlock, Cynthia P504
German, Scott A336
German, Scott E157
German, Robert D. E224
Germann, Jim A13
Germano, Don A264
Germano, Donald A264
Gernandt, Karl W227
Gernath, Eric W366
Gernhart, Diana P399
Gero, James F. E252
Geronimno, Mark Di P266
Gerow, Cheryl P113
Gerr, Marina A722
Gerrard, Ron A447
Gerrard, Dave P652
Gerrell, Matthew P232
Gers, Alison E. A155
Gers, Alison E. E54
Gersema, George H P195
Gersema, Douglas W P195
Gersema, Mary D P195
Gershenhorn, Alan A870
Gershkowitz, Todd A783
Gershman, Jennifer A109
Gershon, Richard P389
Gershon, Peter W273
Gershowitz, Diane E268
Gerspach, John C. A203
Gersten, Gary A482
Gerstenkorn, Petra W402
Gerster, Brennan A452
Gerstle, Douglas A680
Gerula, Christine A115
Gerula, Christine E37
Gervasi, Martha (Marty) A408
Gervasio, Mike A654
Gerwert, Bernhard W17
Gesing, Stefan W391
Gessel, James P597
Gestin, Denis A5
Getchell, Shawn A935
Getchell, Christa P406
Getchell, Roland E374
Getman, George J. A227
Getman, George J. E90
Getz, James F. (Jim) A848
Getz, Heather C. E46
Getz, James F. (Jim) E411
Getzfrid, Lisa P232
Gevondyan, Hilary A349
Gewirtz, Henry A544
Geyer, Debi A778
Geyer, Deb A778
Geyer, Krista E265
Geyzel, David Van A32
Ghaffarian, Kam P487
Ghaffary, Mike E450
Ghai, Rahul A501
Ghan, P Mark P363
Ghanayem, Steve A74
Ghanem, Salma P175
Ghartey-Tagoe, Kodwo A281
Ghasemi, Seifi A24
Ghayalod, Raj P206
Ghazi, Leili A213
Ghazi, Julie L. P143
Ghia, Filippo A114
Ghia, Filippo E37
Ghio, Esther P46
Ghion, Christopher P7
Ghislier, Andres Carlos Ferrero A771
Ghodsi, Ramin A565
Ghose, Mohit A571
Ghosh, Anirvan A133
Ghosh, Sourav A436
Ghosh, Bhaskar W5
Ghosh, Asim W190
Ghosn, Carlos W283
Ghost, Lisa E168
Ghysens, Christopher A929
Ghysens, Christopher E449
Giacobbe, Scott A8

Giacobbe, Ken A79
Giacobbe, George A264
Giacomelli, Barbara A550
Giacomin, Jon A169
Giacomini, Thomas W. E241
Giamalis, John A408
Giametta, Lauren A135
Giammatteo, Robb A84
Giamouridis, Kostas A658
Giampietro, Lawrence A784
Gianarkis, Dean A658
Giancola, Tom A34
Gianetti, Dave A684
Gianfortune, Tammy A846
Giangola, Louis A522
Giangrande, Michele A799
Giangrasso, Tina P13
Giannantoni, Leslie A115
Giannantoni, Leslie E38
Gianneschi, Stephanie P55
Giannone, Domenico A320
Giannone, Gregory A884
Gianoni, Michael P. (Mike) E47
Gianoulis, Julee A405
Giard, Diane W270
Giardina, Kelly A571
Gibala, Susan P315
Gibaldi, Paul A540
Gibb, Randall P84
Gibb, Brian E429
Gibbons, Thomas P. (Todd) A111
Gibbons, James A145
Gibbons, Tom A251
Gibbons, Sean A652
Gibbons, Terry A776
Gibbons, Dale M. A913
Gibbons, Thomas F. E388
Gibbons, Michael P600
Gibbons, Dale M. E438
Gibbs, Brian A267
Gibbs, Jon A309
Gibbs, Dennis A380
Gibbs, Robert A548
Gibbs, Steve A855
Gibbs, Jackie A894
Gibbs, Dawn A926
Gibbs, David W. A937
Gibbs, Kenneth P304
Gibbs, Jackie P651
Gibellini, Yasmine E126
Giberson, Sandra A726
Gibin, Leslie A349
Gibler, Bryan P625
Giblin, Mike P604
Gibney, Ronald A200
Gibralter, Jonathan C. P642
Gibson, W Daniel A103
Gibson, Art A120
Gibson, Cicely A257
Gibson, Don A323
Gibson, Gregory L A341
Gibson, Justin A349
Gibson, Andrew A349
Gibson, Kim A401
Gibson, Sandra A566
Gibson, John W. A630
Gibson, Amy A715
Gibson, Blaine A727
Gibson, Lee R. A772
Gibson, Andy A900
Gibson, Roy A925
Gibson, Belinda P66
Gibson, Sandra Lee P90
Gibson, Lawrence P116
Gibson, Cathy P155
Gibson, Elizabeth C. P364
Gibson, James J. (Jim) P447
Gibson, Blaine P453
Gibson, Cynthia L. P480
Gibson, John P590
Gibson, Shirley P650
Gibson, Laura P651
Gibson, Kim E198
Gibson, Cynthia E366
Gibson, Lee R. E382

Gibson, Roy E445
Gick, Daniel J A345
Gick, Daniel J E165
Giddens, Ron A340
Giddiens, Ron E161
Giddings, Andy A326
Gideon, Richard A. (Rick) A263
Gidner, Bjorn A374
Giedlin, Tom A571
Giedlin, Thomas A571
Gier, Vanessa De P517
Giesbert, Jurgen A538
Gieseman, Greg P82
Giesige, Steve A339
Giesige, Steve E159
Giffard, Susan A163
Giffard, Susan E62
Gifford, William F. (Billy) A41
Gifford, Jenny A105
Gifford, Gerard H (Jerry) A245
Gifford, Richard A264
Gifford, Bill A387
Gifford, Linda A414
Gifford, Adam A524
Gifford, Richard P180
Gifford, Linda P236
Giglia, Garret A349
Giglia, Joseph T P197
Giglio, Gaby A53
Giglio, Gabriella A54
Giglio, Theresa A162
Giglio, William A227
Giglio, Theresa E61
Giglio, William E90
Gigliotti, Patti A883
Gigliotti, Steven J. (Steve) P480
Gigliotti, Mike P487
Gigliotti, Ron P522
Gigliotti, Patti P644
Gil, Bikram P164
Gilardino, Ned P126
Gilbane, William J. (Bill) A384
Gilbane, Thomas F. (Tom) A384
Gilbane, William J. (Bill) P217
Gilbane, Thomas F. (Tom) P217
Gilbert, Christopher A36
Gilbert, James A126
Gilbert, Matthew A163
Gilbert, George A203
Gilbert, Don A405
Gilbert, Lesli A456
Gilbert, E. Scott A539
Gilbert, Scott E A540
Gilbert, Bob A551
Gilbert, Huw A654
Gilbert, Andrew A695
Gilbert, Mikel A804
Gilbert, William M. (Bill) A866
Gilbert, Steve A887
Gilbert, Paul A893
Gilbert, Torres A906
Gilbert, Cammy P5
Gilbert, Ozzie P219
Gilbert, Denis P P231
Gilbert, David P234
Gilbert, Deanne P280
Gilbert, Bob P321
Gilbert, Christopher B P466
Gilbert, Taco P493
Gilbert, Christopher P513
Gilbert, Peter N. P615
Gilbert, Michael P626
Gilbert, Tom P642
Gilbert, John W137
Gilbert, Matthew E62
Gilbert, Lesli E228
Gilbert, William M. (Bill) E417
Gilbert, Torres E435
Gilbertson, Bruce P191
Gilbertson, Roger L P472
Gilbertson, Gene W233
Gilbreath, Lorry A219
Gilbreath, Lorry E87
Gilbride, Bob A890
Gilchrist, David A179

Gilchrist, Grant A418
Gilchrist, Richard I A775
Gilchrist, Richard I P511
Gilchrist, Gregory P596
Gildard, Matthew A484
Gildea, Patrick P155
Gildea, Edward J. (Ed) E152
Gilder, Sandy A369
Gileadi, Ido A327
Giles, William T. (Bill) A95
Giles, Daniel A112
Giles, Chantal A135
Giles, Dee A444
Giles, Bobbi P523
Giles, Dave E366
Gilinski, Saul E250
Gilio, Teresa E73
Gilkerson, Dennis A222
Gilkey, Steven P198
Gill, Mark A67
Gill, Sukhbir A135
Gill, Brian A602
Gill, Manjit A695
Gill, Vijay A740
Gill, G. Andrew (Andy) A746
Gill, Charles D. A875
Gill, Joanna A895
Gill, Varinder P85
Gill, Kashmir P164
Gill, Maureen P243
Gill, Margaret P474
Gill, Michelle P524
Gill, Valerie E14
Gill, Darla R. E278
Gillan-Myer, Maureen A. A439
Gillaspie, Michael A630
Gillean, John A. P132
Gillern, Jeffry H. (Jeff) von A884
Gillespie, Rob A224
Gillespie, Scot A393
Gillespie, Peter K. A444
Gillespie, Shertina A544
Gillespie, Phillip S. A783
Gillespie, Charla P429
Gillespie, Michael P558
Gillespie, Julie P638
Gillet, Vincent A417
Gillett, Mike A512
Gillett, Nancy A. E75
Gillette, Allen D E184
Gilley, Mike A624
Gillham, Simon W416
Gilliam, Kyle A106
Gilliam, Scott A195
Gilliam, Theron I A512
Gilliam, Derek P150
Gilliam, Marilyn P390
Gilliam, Dabney T. P. (Dexter) E16
Gillian, Cheri A347
Gillies, Iris A58
Gilligan, Peggy A498
Gilligan, Matt A706
Gilligan, Thomas A756
Gilliland, M. Amy A373
Gilliland, Terry A754
Gilliland, Terry P484
Gilliland, Ryan E148
Gillin, Greg A522
Gillingham, Aaron P75
Gillis, Kathy A13
Gillis, Michelle A. (Shelly) A55
Gillis, Kemp A512
Gillis, Jim A778
Gillis, Laurel P2
Gillis, Robert P37
Gillis, Anne D P242
Gillis, Don P600
Gillis, John E431
Gillman, Heike A798
Gillman, David D A810
Gillmon, Brett A540
Gillmore, Ron A559
Gillock, Timothy A224
Gillrie, Dave P. P87
Gillund, Chris P140

Gilman, Alan A888
Gilman, Fred P114
Gilman, Alan E425
Gilmartin, Thomas N. A848
Gilmartin, Thomas N. E411
Gilmer, Fred E381
Gilmore, Jamie A179
Gilmore, Dennis J. A332
Gilmore, John A559
Gilmore, Sam A656
Gilmore, Sally A678
Gilmore, Rob A695
Gilmore, Elizabeth A893
Gilmore, Grover C. (Cleve) P116
Gilmore, Sam P414
Gilmore, John E22
Gilmore, John E433
Gilson, Michael A599
Gilson, Michael E303
Gilster, Megan P594
Gilstrap, Jamie K P48
Gilstrap, Mike P575
Giltner, F. Phillips (Phil) E487
Gilvarry, Siobhan P486
Gilyard, Scott P583
Gim, Mark K. W. A904
Gimbel, Amy A536
Ginaldi, Joel A165
Ginas, Darren E330
Gincavage, Ray A388
Gindy, David A709
Gindy, David P442
Gineris, Peter A175
Gines, Joan P597
Ginger, Elliott A190
Gingerich, Bradley A175
Gingras, France M. A738
Gingras, David P329
Gingras, Mercy P597
Ginieczki, Chris A613
Ginley, Karen A824
Ginley, Karen P562
Ginn, Cheryl A940
Ginn, Donnie P86
Ginn, William (Bill) P579
Ginsberg, Michelle P325
Ginsberg, Alan S. E117
Ginsberg, Gary E396
Ginsburg, Greg A207
Ginsburg, Josh A761
Ginsburg, Alan H. E53
Ginter, Matt A3
Ginter, Melissa A369
Gintoli, George E185
Gintzburger, Emmanuel W218
Gioia, Ellen A115
Gioia, Ellen E37
Gionfriddo, Robert P. (Bob) A414
Gionfriddo, Robert P. (Bob) E208
Giordano, Susie A460
Giordano, Alison A544
Giordano, Doug A658
Giordano, Michele A797
Giordano, Michael E143
Giorelli, Michela A270
Giorgianni, Kathryn A42
Giornelli, Lillian C. E100
Giovanelli, Gabriele E222
Giovani, John Di' P519
Giovanni, Christopher A520
Giovanniello, Joseph E250
Giovi, Martin P108
Giovinazzi, Brian A684
Gipe, David E264
Gipple, Todd A. A693
Gipple, Todd A. E341
Gipson, Matthew P223
Gipson, James (Jimmie) P245
Gira, Thomas R. P202
GIRALDO, CARLOS MARIO W24
Girard, Steven A205
Girard, Sebastien P171
Girard, Jon D P338
Girard, Mark P528
Girardin, Jason A925

Girardin, Jason E445
Girgis, Pete E58
Giri, Vineet A460
Girod, Curtis A216
Giroir, Pat P157
Girolamo, Michael A704
Giromonte, Ron A112
Girouard, Denis W270
Giroux, Marc A240
Girre, Xavier W148
Girsch, Jerry A524
Girten, Damian P618
Girton, Tani A110
Girton, Drew A877
Gise, James A929
Gise, James E449
Gisel, William G. (Bill) P449
Gisler, Mona E114
Gist, Stan A713
Gitlin, David L. A875
Gitlitz, Edward A98
Gitter, Gina A327
Gitter, Daniel A398
Gitter, Daniel P222
Gittleman, Kelly A452
Giudice, William (Bill) P541
Giuffra, Robert P31
Giuffre, Matthew A409
Giuffre, Mark A871
Giust, Flavio A491
Givans, Natalie A145
Given, Barbara P508
Givertz, Michael P556
Givler, Gary A195
Givler, Sean A196
Giza, Chris A544
Gjervik, Staale A309
Glacken, Gary A559
Glad, Lauren A107
Gladden, Brian T. A573
Glade, Doug A253
Glade, Doug P169
Gladieux, Keely A877
Gladney, Karen A222
Gladney, Danny A717
Gladney, Danny E351
Gladstein, Lina A319
Gladstone, Gini A538
Gladstone, David J. E189
Gladu, Robert A859
Gladys, Taylor P116
Glaetzer, Sam A237
Glandon, Gary E359
Glanvill, Derek W. P318
Glaros, Dean A478
Glaros, Dean P268
Glas, Jason A62
Glas, Jason E20
Glasco, Cal A397
Glasel, Dan A264
Glasel, Dan P180
Glasenberg, Ivan W172
Glaser, Daniel S. (Dan) A539
Glaser, Tom A891
Glaser, Thomas A. A891
Glaser, Garry P152
Glaser, William D P279
Glasgow, Dane A287
Glasgow, Mark A565
Glasgow, Diane P163
Glasman, Zvi E180
Glass, Linda A340
Glass, Steven A356
Glass, Shannon A500
Glass, Dennis R. A519
Glass, Jaree A718
Glass, Robert W. A725
Glass, Gene A819
Glass, Steven C. A824
Glass, William A850
Glass, Cynthia P463
Glass, Gene P549
Glass, Steven C. P561
Glass, Kevin W85
Glass, Lynda E3

Glass, Linda E160
Glass, Jaree E354
Glassberg, Dean A346
Glassberg, Dean E167
Glasscock, James S. A634
Glasscock, Larry C. A939
Glasscock, Melbern G P547
Glasser, Ted P64
Glassman, Jerry P332
Glastra, Matthijs E307
Glauber, Robert E305
Glaunert, Curtis P659
Glavaz, Bridget A347
Glavaz, Bridget E167
Glavey, Patrick P355
Glazier, Tony A152
Glazier, Paula P19
Glazier, Steve P400
Glazier, Tony E52
Gleason, George G. A113
GLEASON, SUSAN A414
Gleason, Patrick A584
Gleason, John J. A734
Gleason, Leona A. A925
Gleason, Hugh P197
GLEASON, SUSAN P236
Gleason, George G. E36
Gleason, Matt E98
Gleason, Leona A. E445
Gledhill, David W130
Gleeson, Sam A137
Gleeson, Richard E86
Gleiser, Betsy A246
Gleiser, Betsy E105
Gleissle, Karin A933
Gleit, Naomi A310
Glendinning, Stewart F. A855
Glenn, R Alexander A281
Glenn, T. Michael A323
Glenn, Michael A323
Glenn, Andrew C A329
Glenn, Staci A444
Glenn, Tim A482
Glenn, Greg A778
Glenn, Richard K. P43
Glenn, Nicholls P116
Glenn, Ellie P513
Glenn, David E263
Glenney, Chris P133
Glennie, Nigel A423
Glenzinski, Derek A846
Glew, James P. E69
Glick, Jason A266
Glick, Reuven A321
Glick, Andrew A606
Glick, Jason P181
Glick, Madeleine P572
Glick, Michael E433
Glicker, Joanna A880
Glicker, Joanna P640
Glicksman, Marci A692
Glidden, Craig B. A378
Glied, Sherry A. A592
Glied, Sherry A. P370
Glimcher, Paul A592
Glimcher, Laurie H. P172
Glimcher, Paul P370
Glinton, Robin A740
Glisan, Bre A160
Glisson, Britton L. (Britt) A536
Globa, Kseniia A137
Global, Akal P15
Glockner, Jacqueline A60
Glod, Dan P415
Glod, David P597
Glooch, Karen A799
Gloor, Wendy P410
Gloria, Doriane P364
Glorioso, Jeanne A246
Glorioso, Jeanne E105
Glover, William A367
Glover, Ric A540
Glover, Kate A552
Glover, Marcus A562
Glover, Amanda A722

COMBINED HOOVER'S HANDBOOK INDEX OF EXECUTIVES

> A = AMERICAN BUSINESS
> E = EMERGING COMPANIES
> P = PRIVATE COMPANIES
> W = WORLD BUSINESS

Glover, Lisa A884
Glover, Connie P56
Glover, Joseph (Joe) P627
Glover, Kofi P638
Glover, Kate E276
Glover, Ashley E346
Glover, Tyler E403
Gluck, Jason P229
Gluckman, Jon A86
Gluckman, Thomas A108
Gluckman, Michael Mike A590
Gluckman, Jon E27
Gluski, Andrés R. A18
Gmelich, Justin G. A390
Gmuer, Stefan A783
Gnetz, Patricia A884
Gnodde, Richard J. A390
Goar, Michael P343
Goarcke, Nathan A394
Goare, Douglas M. (Doug) A548
Gobbel, Liz A796
Gobbel, Liz E397
Goben, Randy A189
Goble, Joy A528
Goble, Jonathan P252
Goceljak, John A658
Gockel, Douglas A389
Gockley, Loretta P368
Goddard, Marcia J A469
Goddard, Steven P672
Gode, Pierre W241
Godecke, Rebecca A602
Godenzi, Alberto P608
Godfrey, Brian A746
Godfrey, Todd P203
Godin, Barb A713
Godina, Susie P499
Godinez, Alberto A15
Godinez, Alberto P7
Godinho, Sergio A922
Godinho, Sergio P671
Godinho, Ester E290
Godla, Brian E123
Godlewski, Daniel A491
Godoy, Marcelo A595
Godridge, Leslie V. A884
Godsell, Peter A360
Godshaw, Gary A390
Godusky, Brenda P618
Godwin, Hank A327
Godwin, Cristina A526
Godwin, Jim D. A849
Godwin, John T. P119
Goebel, Maryann A749
Goebel, Sheila P631
Goebel, Maryann E367
Goedderz, Ralph A654
Goedecke, Nancy Collat P316
Goedecke, Glenn P316
Goedhart, Saskia W27
Goeke, George A89
Goel, Dipti A885
Goel, Vishal P505
Goelkel, Chris A602
Goelzer, Angela P202
Goenn, Elizabeth P550
Goeppinger, Kathleen H P340
Goers, Brent A713
Goeschel, Burkhard W244
Goeta-Kreisler, Kevin P611
Goetz, Victor A518
Goetz, James A612
Goetz, William W. (Bill) A797
Goetz, Bill A797
Goetz, John E64
Goetz, John P. E340
Goetz-Krummel, Melissa A480
Goetz-Krummel, Melissa P270
Goff, Corinne Le A64

Goff, Stacey W. A184
Goff, Elizabeth A201
Goff, Mike P86
Goffaux, Denis W405
Goffnett, Carol P49
Goffney, Dr Latonya P21
Goffredi, Paul W. E432
Goforth, Patricia A144
Gogan, Don A407
Goggin, Patrick (Pat) A140
Goggins, Brock A383
Goggins, Brock E186
Gogitidze, Michael A786
Gogitidze, Michael E387
Goh, Martin A540
Goh, Eng Lim P494
Goh, Linus T. L. W299
Gohman, Katie A801
Gohsman, Jim A774
Goicouria, Luis P415
Going, Jim E334
Goins, Randy A374
Goist, Brad A487
Gokhale, Pradeep A61
Golan, Ela W163
Golanowski, Marie P55
Golato, Andrea P551
Golba, Curtis P260
Golbasarians, Albert E122
Golbus, Joseph P386
Gold, Victor A54
Gold, Andre A84
Gold, Stephen J. A251
Gold, Baba A465
Gold, Richard S. A530
Gold, Jeffrey P. P92
Gold, Gary P164
Gold, Barbara P632
Goldberg, Scott L. A212
Goldberg, Linda A234
Goldberg, Rebecca A320
Goldberg, Wendy A452
Goldberg, Micah A452
Goldberg, Bruce A484
Goldberg, Richard A551
Goldberg, Gary J. A595
Goldberg, Howard A885
Goldberg, Jonathan P27
Goldberg, Carla P38
Goldberg, Michael P204
Goldberg, Richard P321
Goldberg, Mark A. P405
Goldberg, Neil P440
Goldberg, Michael P440
Goldberg, Steven P440
Goldberg, Bonnie E433
Goldberger, Mayer A409
Goldblatt, Ronald P586
Golden, Theonie A115
Golden, Adam A449
Golden, Deborah A567
Golden, Elizabeth A657
Golden, Greg A922
Golden, Becky S P279
Golden, John P527
Golden, Andrew K. P591
Golden, Robert P640
Golden, Greg P671
Golden, Theonie E38
Golden, Adam E221
Golden, Deborah E283
Goldenberg, Scott A835
Goldenstein, Ihno W250
Golder, George E7
Goldey, Donna E91
Goldfarb, Timothy M. P489
Goldgeier, Eileen P102
Goldgut, Harry A. W80
Goldhaber, Dale P639
Goldhaber, Jeanne P639
Goldhahn, Laura P77
Goldin, Adam A484
Goldin, Derek P390
Goldman, Nathan D A245
Goldman, David A391

Goldman, Jeffrey A457
Goldman, Lonnie A484
Goldman, Kissel A527
Goldman, Howard A827
Goldman, Marc P208
Goldman, Joshua E31
Goldman, Michael N. P375
Goldman, Lynn R. P569
Goldman, Howard P580
Goldring, Steven P368
Goldsberry, John A742
Goldsberry, Brian P220
Goldschmidt, Guy A452
Goldschmidt, Lawrence E P225
Goldschmidt, Nancy P399
Goldsman, Helene A877
Goldsmith, Leo L A592
Goldsmith, Spencer A884
Goldsmith, Ilyse A885
Goldsmith, David L. P267
Goldsmith, Leo L P370
Goldsmith, Stephen P567
Goldsmith, Marisha P581
Goldsmith, Gray E16
Goldsmith, Jennifer E427
Goldstein, Lawrence A. (Larry) A129
Goldstein, Rob L. A135
Goldstein, Robert G. (Rob) A506
Goldstein, Mary A511
Goldstein, Bruce A692
Goldstein, Adam P126
Goldstein, Lewis P158
Goldstein, Mary P290
Goldstein, Lisa A P368
Goldstein, Allan Moises P574
Goldstein, Brian P P635
Goldstein, Jeff E64
Goldstein, Arnie E344
Goldstine, Abner A50
Goldstine, Abner P31
Goldstone, Steven F. (Steve) A232
Goldszer, Robert C. P351
Goldwater, John K. A126
Goldwin, Richard P623
Golestani, Clark A554
Golia, Jet A458
Golisano, Courtney A575
Goliyad, Yuriy E133
Golkiewicz, Tamara P596
Gollert, Barb A514
Gollert, Barb A516
Gollert, Barb P293
Gollisz, Gustav A203
Goloubef, Mike A833
Golston, Allan A407
Golston, Jeremiah A695
Golub, Bennett W. A135
Golub, Scott A135
Golub, Neal A175
Golub, Todd P556
Golub, Jerel T. (Jerry) P571
Golub, Mona J. P571
Golub, David P571
Golub, Jerry P571
Golub, Neil M. P571
Golz, Judy Briscoe P153
Gomer, Jay A444
Gomes, Sheila Haunani A109
Gomes, Maria P299
Gomes, Carlos W305
Gomes, Fernando Jorge Buso W412
Gomez, Jorge M. A169
Gomez, Jaime A219
Gomez, Maribeth A222
Gomez, Mark A271
Gomez, Debbie A294
Gomez, Henry A420
Gomez, Rick H. A804
Gomez, Carlos A920
Gomez, Rick P183
Gomez, Jim Gaton P351
Gomez, Julie P445
Gomez, Maria P581
Gomez, Garrett E106

Gomez-sanchez, Juan A512
Gomi, Hideki A565
Gominiak, Matt A559
Gomulka, Robert P619
Goncalves, Armando F. A651
Goncalves, Armando F. E329
Gonchar, Tony A262
Gongora, Ben A746
Gongxun, Lv W301
Gonick, Lev S. P44
Gonick, Lev P116
Gonick, Denise V. P355
Gonnella, Thomas A200
Gonos, Caroline A925
Gonos, Caroline E445
Gonsalves, Rodney A22
Gonsior, Tim A369
Gonyea, Paula P598
Gonyea, Dave P655
Gonzales, Chad A54
Gonzales, Yolanda A246
Gonzales, Bob A260
Gonzales, Domingo A682
Gonzales, Joe A725
Gonzales, Phil A893
Gonzales, Darolyn P286
Gonzales, Erika P537
Gonzales, Gil P634
Gonzales, Yolanda E105
Gonzales, Randall B E263
Gonzalez, Richard A. (Rick) A6
Gonzalez, Carlos A107
Gonzalez, Ricardo A126
Gonzalez, Luis A181
Gonzalez, Alex A222
Gonzalez, Adan A222
Gonzalez, Jaime A242
Gonzalez, Melissa A271
Gonzalez, Richard A401
Gonzalez, Shari A452
Gonzalez, Eliza A463
Gonzalez, Carlos A512
Gonzalez, Edward A. (Eddie) A748
Gonzalez, Charles A859
Gonzalez, Alfonso A885
Gonzalez, Maggie A888
Gonzalez, Arthur A. P179
Gonzalez, Angel P205
Gonzalez, Andres P211
Gonzalez, Jorge P312
Gonzalez, Zocima P351
Gonzalez, Catalina P390
Gonzalez, Eva P507
Gonzalez, Tina P558
Gonzalez, Shawn P571
Gonzalez, Christina P611
Gonzalez, Fernando P613
Gonzalez, Patty P620
Gonzalez, Jacqueline L P649
Gonzalez, Marina P677
Gonzalez, Luis E70
Gonzalez, Tony E232
Gonzalez, Victor E415
Gonzalez, Maggie E425
Gonzalez-Flores, Elizabeth P409
Gonzalez-scarano, Francisco P583
Gonzalez, Mario H. Paez W19
Gonzalez, José A. W91
Goo, Lisa A109
Gooch, Mark A. A229
Goocher, Robert P505
Good, Jim A103
Good, David A140
Good, George A175
Good, Jeff A272
Good, Lynn J. A281
Good, Tina A785
Good, Sue P131
Good, Michael P P360
Good, Tina P526
Good, Michael P627
Good, Glenn E. P627
Good, Jennifer E448
Goodall, Laura A126
Goodarzi, Sasan K. A471

Goode, Travis A368
Goode, Jeff P124
Goode, Wilson S P652
Goodell, Josh A89
Goodell, Jeffrey A478
Gooden, Narcissis P563
Gooderham, JP P552
Goodes, David A8
Goodfellow, Kathy P220
Goodger, Simon A658
Goodhall, Gary A448
Goodhall, Gary P247
Goodhart, Scott A18
Goodhew, Ian A880
Goodhew, Ian P640
Goodhew, J. William (Bill) E234
Goodhue, Todd A222
Goodine, Paul A269
Gooding, Marie C. A319
Goodman, Sean D. A83
Goodman, Bennett J. A137
Goodman, Scott R. A298
Goodman, Stacey A364
Goodman, Saul A381
Goodman, Laurie A484
Goodman, Nessa A536
Goodman, Gregg M. A761
Goodman, Lindsay P206
Goodman, Gary J P479
Goodman, Wayne H. P553
Goodman, Andrew E114
Goodman, Scott R. E130
Goodman, Jeffrey M. (Jeff) E433
Goodnow, John P77
Goodpaster, Keith A329
Goodreau, Randy A480
Goodrich, Donna C. A849
Goodridge, Brenda P630
Goodrow, Carolyn A243
Goodrum, Ryan P552
Goodsir, Michelle A200
Goodson, Joey A21
Goodspeed, Sharon A160
Goodspeed, Randy A260
Goodwin, Annie A386
Goodwin, Dustin A451
Goodwin, Kellie A896
Goodwin, Jean P333
Goodwin, Linda P395
Goodwin, Deanna P543
Goodwin, Karen P625
Goodwin, Annie E188
Goodwyn, Bill A270
Goody, James A347
Goody, James E168
Goold, Alex P28
Gooley, Thomas (Tom) A528
Goolsby, Steven P115
Goon, Julie A69
Goone, David S A462
Goorevich, Charlie P487
Gopal, Ajei S. E22
Gopalakrishnan, Raja A327
Gopalakrishnan, Venkat E316
Gopalswamy, Sudhir E110
Gopaul, Natasha A137
Gopffarth, Lance P194
Gopie, Lon A115
Gopie, Lon E38
Gopinath, Brijesh P286
Gorab, Dave A762
Goran, Steve E184
Goranson, Mark A627
Gorbunov, Igor N. W375
Gorden, Ed A259
Gorden, Bill A438
Gorder, Joseph W. (Joe) A887
Gorder, Christopher D. Van P479
Gordin, Peggy P513
Gordon, Robert A. (Bob) A30
Gordon, Marc D. A53
Gordon, Murdo A151
Gordon, Derek A. A218
Gordon, Ilene S. A457
Gordon, Bruce A481

Gordon, Bancroft S A538
Gordon, Erin A571
Gordon, Ben A571
Gordon, Andrew A592
Gordon, Joseph A623
Gordon, Barbara A676
Gordon, Russell L. A732
Gordon, Tom A793
Gordon, Cima A799
Gordon, Howard A922
Gordon, Crystal L P13
Gordon, Jeffrey P17
Gordon, Robert A. (Bob) P20
Gordon, Scott R. P45
Gordon, Dan P85
Gordon, Ora P118
Gordon, Thomas D P118
Gordon, Pam P135
Gordon, Eric P141
Gordon, Vivian P237
Gordon, Bernard P284
Gordon, Andrew P370
Gordon, Sean P648
Gordon, Howard P671
Gordon, Susan E96
Gordon, Michael (Mike) E144
Gordon, Drew B. E219
Gordon, Barry E267
Gordon, Joseph E313
Gordon, Barbara E338
Gordon, Joel E445
Gore, Clark A176
Gore, Steve P423
Gorecki, Teresa A479
Gorelick, Joel E306
Gorenc, Jim E172
Goret, Michelle A197
Gorham, Roger B. A32
Gorham, Bo A53
Gorham, Tracey A305
Gorham, Doug P572
Gorham, Laura E371
Gori, Roy W247
Gorillo, Rodrigo Echenique W48
Gorin, Ariane A307
Gorin, Joanna P191
Goris, Patrick A729
Gork, Danny E334
Gorman, Norma A35
Gorman, Robert M. (Rob) A91
Gorman, Mark A198
Gorman, Charlie A232
Gorman, Jeffrey A367
Gorman, Christopher M. (Chris) A491
Gorman, Paul A A545
Gorman, James P. A574
Gorman, Stephen A645
Gorman, Mark J. A668
Gorman, Mark J A668
Gorman, Patty A809
Gorman, Frank A859
Gorman, Cheryl A875
Gorman, Eric P119
Gorman, Kathleen E. Chavanu P130
Gorman, Kathleen Chavanu P130
Gorman, Donna P298
Gorman, Paul A P317
Gorman, Luke P551
Gorman, Robert M. (Rob) E29
Gormley, William A161
Gormley, Thomas A877
Gormley, Alice P309
Gorney, David J. P553
Gorostiza, Georg A780
Gorrall, Garth A222
Gorrie, Thomas M. P187
Gorriz, Michael W364
Gorska, Anna A183
Gorska, Anna E74
Gorski, Jim A327
Gorski, Bill P537
Gorsky, Alex A479
Gorsky, Alex A609
Gorsky, Alex P391

Gorti, Bhaskar M. W284
Gorton, Elizabeth A545
Gosch, Kenneth L A252
Gosebruch, Henry O. A6
Gosian, Jonathan P220
Gosney, Laura L P559
Goss, David A678
Goss, Jeanne P254
Goss, Andreas J. W391
Gossard, Cheryl P270
Gosse, Lynn P602
Gosselin, Gene A692
Gosselink, Robert A126
Gossen, Michael A346
Gossen, Michael E167
Gossett, Paul A30
Gossett, Paul P20
Gossett, Barry P. P642
Gossett, Bret E8
Gossman, Anne E404
Gostin, Jill P572
Goswami, Chitra A257
Gothard, Ann A745
Gothard, Joe P250
Gothard, Butch E229
Goto, Noriaki W50
Goto, Katsuhiro A346
Goto, Masao W360
Gottardy, Brian G P378
Gottesfeld, Stephen P. A595
Gottlieb, Robert A642
Gottlieb, Jonathan E. P252
Gottlieb, Robert P407
Gottschalk, Marla A132
Gottschalk, Adrian A133
Gottschling, Andreas W156
Gottscho, Richard A. (Rick) A505
Gottsegen, Jonathan M A872
Gottstein, Thomas P. W121
Gottwals, Bill A344
Gottwals, Bill E165
Gotwals, Janet W A105
Gotwals, Janet W E34
Gotwalt, Darryl E413
Gou, Terry T.M. W185
Goudreau, Christopher A465
Gough, A Gaius A380
Gough, Jim P59
Gough, Fredric P383
Gough, Michael W P389
Gouin, Kevin A327
Goulart, Steven J. A559
Gould, R Marcia A50
Gould, Jason A207
Gould, Mark A. A321
Gould, John A334
Gould, Rob A354
Gould, Melissa A392
Gould, Dan A596
Gould, Vicky A678
Gould, Jack A749
Gould, Karen A830
Gould, Karen O. A853
Gould, Cristie P12
Gould, R Marcia P31
Gould, Rod P138
Gould, Karen P593
Gould, Karen O. P612
Gould, Matthew J. E53
Gould, Jeffrey A. E53
Gould, Fredric H. E53
Gould, Mitchell K. E53
Gould, Jeffrey A. E53
Gould, Jason E108
Gould, Gerard H. (Gerry) E153
Gould, John E153
Gould, Sharon E260
Gould, Jack E367
Goulding, Philip L P347
Goulet, Beverly K. A47
Goulet, Ken A69
Goulet, Kenneth A69
Goulet, Shelly A833
Goumans, Marcus W181
Goupille, Renee A651

Goupille, Renee E329
Gourdine, Jerome P392
Gourio, Francois P96
Gourlay, Denise A14
Gourlay, Alexander W. (Alex) A899
Gourley, Fletcher P426
Gourmand, Matthew E314
Gouveia, Jeffrey P531
Govan, Christopher A. (Chris) W296
Gove, Matt P418
Govender, Munsamy A484
Govil, Charu A390
Govil, Anita P19
Govil, Ravi E431
Govin, Dan A696
Gow, Joe P641
Gowan, Dennis A281
Gowan, Sandy A796
Gowan, Sandy E397
Gowen, Nick A442
Gowen, Kevin P. A796
Gowen, Kevin P. E397
Gower, Greg E58
Goyal, Harsh A203
Goyal, Rahul A460
Goyanes, Everardo P422
Goyette, Karen P229
Gozon, Richard C. P603
Gozzarino, Katie P517
GP, Energy T A295
GP, Ealmoor P674
Graaf, Bill Van de A218
Grab, Edward L P230
Grabenstein, Alan E290
Graber, Tim P343
Grabusic, Cynthia P546
Graca, Amy A160
Grace, Helen A54
Grace, Sean A112
Grace, Garrett A182
Grace, William A222
Grace, Amy A402
Grace, Bob A853
Grace, Raymond A862
Grace, Ted A872
Grace, Bob P612
Grace, Raymond P617
Grace, William M P652
Grace, Adrian W10
Grace, Liz E134
Grace, Amy E198
Grachek, Joseph A242
Gracias, Antonio P547
Graczewski, Cheryl P34
Gradassi, Christina A801
Graddick-weir, Mirian A143
Graddick-Weir, Mirian M. A554
Graddick-weir, Mirian A937
Graddy, Gwendolyn A414
Graddy, Steven P210
Graddy, Gwendolyn P236
Grade, Joel T. A797
Gradert, Scott A756
Gradnik, Amy A895
Grady, Christopher A90
Grady, Gerry A325
Grady, Melissa A559
Grady, Seamus A742
Grady, Christopher P51
Grady, Max P276
Grady, Jason P383
Grady, James P514
Grady, Philips P671
Graebner, Clark P333
Graeff, Scott A. E262
Graf, Alan B. A323
Graf, Erik A692
Graf, Stacy A909
Graf, Jane P331
Graf, Stacy E436
Graff, Michael J. (Mike) A25
Graff, K E A313
Graff, Jeffrey P6
Graff, Michael J. (Mike) P14
Graff, Ed P38

COMBINED HOOVER'S HANDBOOK INDEX OF EXECUTIVES

A = AMERICAN BUSINESS
E = EMERGING COMPANIES
P = PRIVATE COMPANIES
W = WORLD BUSINESS

Graff, K E P200
Graff, Richard E113
Grafman, Laura R. P478
Graft, Terence L. E386
Gragg, Jodi P352
Graham, Jonathan P. A64
Graham, Jon A71
Graham, Colleen A147
Graham, John A222
Graham, Kristin A307
Graham, Paul A319
Graham, Brad A466
Graham, Timothy A528
Graham, Derek A598
Graham, Katherine A665
Graham, John A692
Graham, Melissa A757
Graham, Stephen P A780
Graham, Christopher A. (Chris) A785
Graham, Ned A872
Graham, Ginger A900
Graham, Mark A A922
Graham, Chris A929
Graham, Anthony A935
Graham, Jeffrey J. P5
Graham, Louis P66
Graham, John C P219
Graham, Eugene W P219
Graham, Matthew X P219
Graham, Patrick T P219
Graham, Dionne P230
Graham, Ed P338
Graham, Randolph P358
Graham, Paul P373
Graham, Franklin P469
Graham, Melissa P492
Graham, Peter P508
Graham, Kim P607
Graham, Dale P662
Graham, Mark A P671
Graham, Roger C. E81
Graham, Katherine E334
Graham, Chris E449
Grahe, William A741
Grahe, William E364
Grainger, Guy A481
Grainger, Jo P570
Grajeda, Jessica A642
Grajeda, Jessica P407
Graley, David P105
Gram, Dwight P449
Grambart, Sean P113
Grambo, Francis P228
Gramlich, Tom A470
Granado, Alejandro A202
Granado, Alejandro P136
Granata, Thomas A58
Granath, Herbert A P206
Granato, Jerome A226
Granato, Jerome P150
Granberry, Debbie A230
Granberry, Debbie P154
Granchi, Annie A392
Grande, Christine A686
Grandia, Larry D P428
Grandisson, Marc W33
Grandmaison, Francine A651
Grandmaison, Francine E329
Grandmont, Scott A715
Granese, Jamie A559
Graney, Kevin M. A373
Granger, Darren A187
Granger, Chris A750
Granger, Jason P189
Granger, Harvey P503
Granger, Carolyn P616
Granger, Dennis A E100
Granger, Clarence L. E415
Granger, Bill E433

Graninger, Clark D. W30
Grannis, Dick A695
Gransbery, Wayne P529
Grant, Belinda A14
Grant, Lee A16
Grant, Jennifer A24
Grant, Timothy A75
Grant, Marilee A149
Grant, Andy A170
Grant, Shane A215
Grant, Joan A283
Grant, Melanie A351
Grant, Dan A421
Grant, Colleen A452
Grant, Jeffrey A608
Grant, Tiffany A893
Grant, Belinda P6
Grant, Thomas P7
Grant, Susan P75
Grant, Diana P161
Grant, Jack P265
Grant, Duane P498
Grant, Alan P652
Grant, Shari E101
Grant, Joan E117
Grant, James E424
Grant-anderson, Belinda A89
Grant-anderson, Belinda P599
Grantham, Connee A768
Granville, Caroline A544
Granzyk, Steve A179
Graphos, Ted A449
Graphos, Ted E220
Grasela, Wayne T P588
Grasmeyer, Rebecca A621
Grasmeyer, Rebecca E312
Grass, Stephanie A715
Grasshoff, Michaela A540
Grassi, Alexa A882
Grassi, Louis C. (Lou) E53
Grassie, Neil A205
Grassinger, Maxine P491
Grassmick, Clint A543
Grasso, Maria A. A356
Grasso, Janine A465
Grasso, Robert A888
Grasso, Robert E425
Gratton, September A161
Grau, Dominique P A22
Grauer, Scott B. A142
Grauer, Scott B. E49
Graugnard, Milton P105
Graugnard, Milton P106
Graulau, Melinda E392
Graumlich, Lisa A880
Graumlich, Lisa P640
Grauze, Sarah A3
Gravanis, Georges A97
Gravel, Karine A658
Gravel, Monique W85
Gravelle, Michael L. (Mike) A325
Graver, Barbie A587
Graves, William W. A95
Graves, Quentin A481
Graves, Christopher A555
Graves, Mayra A683
Graves, Tina A760
Graves, Karolyn A930
Graves, Gerry P6
Graves, Marti P244
Graves, Mayra P431
Graves, Jeanne E111
Graves, Michael (Mike) E118
Graves, Gregory B. (Greg) E128
Graves, Jeffrey A. (Jeff) E291
Graves, Tina E374
Gravilla, Katie P456
Gravino, Ronald P363
Graviss, Jonathan A452
Grawe, George A36
Grawey, Vickie A502
Gray, Sean A A128
Gray, Jonathan D. A137
Gray, Harry W A140

Gray, Maria A363
Gray, Jonathan D. A423
Gray, Patrick A425
Gray, Robert D A430
Gray, Brandon A447
Gray, James D. (Jim) A457
Gray, Rick A543
Gray, Dan A550
Gray, Diedre A672
Gray, James W. A717
Gray, Wayne A796
Gray, David J. A828
Gray, Myron A. A870
Gray, M Joel A917
Gray, Linsey P38
Gray, David L. P64
Gray, Larry W. P64
Gray, Darcey P188
Gray, Thomas L P274
Gray, Jake P316
Gray, Nancy P333
Gray, Brent P419
Gray, John P497
Gray, Tracey P530
Gray, Monica P570
Gray, Jarrod P576
Gray, David J. P584
Gray, Gary W267
Gray, Larry E7
Gray, Sean A. E42
Gray, David C. E53
Gray, William D. (Bill) E121
Gray, James W. E351
Gray, Wayne E397
Graybeal, R Steven P312
Grayer, Loren E185
Grayfer, Valery I. W310
Graylin, Peter A218
Graysmark, Phil A816
Grazer, Mike A643
Graziano, Nicholas F. (Nick) E144
Greasheimer, Sharon A170
Greathouse, Steven R. E94
Grebb, Joye A824
Grebb, Joye P562
Grebe, Douglas A56
Grebe, Charles P228
Grebenc, Jane A337
Grebenc, Jane E158
Grebow, Peter E. E118
Grebstein, Marci A647
Grecco, Robert A702
Grech, Jim A352
Grech, Joe A613
Greck, Sonya B P343
Greco, Thomas R. (Tom) A13
Greco, Denise A243
Greco, Joe A482
Greco, Ignazio A559
Greco, John R. A640
Greco, Joe A752
Greco, Suzanne P183
Greco, Donna P219
Greco, Mario W435
Gredys, Joan E24
Greek, Matt P69
Greelish, James P115
Green, Mark A18
Green, Anthony C. A68
Green, Joseph A89
Green, Christopher A147
Green, Gerry A160
Green, Saryia A200
Green, Keturah A224
Green, Phillip D. A246
Green, Frederec A260
Green, Logan A287
Green, Joe A405
Green, Markham A421
Green, Andy A446
Green, O'Neil A461
Green, Michael A483
Green, Matthew A484
Green, Mark A. A489
Green, Brady A528

Green, Rosanne A528
Green, Elizabeth A538
Green, Phil A575
Green, Bryan A584
Green, Allyson A592
Green, Peter A658
Green, Gary A665
Green, Mark A692
Green, Crickett A709
Green, Jeff A712
Green, Clara A713
Green, William A738
Green, Jim A740
Green, Tammy A780
Green, Barbara A797
Green, Niki A799
Green, Mary A806
Green, Nancy A826
Green, Miguale A859
Green, Paul S. A869
Green, Tara A902
Green, Jack A909
Green, Dee P6
Green, Jon P30
Green, Ronnie P92
Green, Teresa P117
Green, Greg P135
Green, Thomas B P140
Green, Ann P147
Green, Mike P161
Green, Judy P161
Green, David P242
Green, Steve P242
Green, Mart P242
Green, Lance P284
Green, Marie P356
Green, Allyson P370
Green, James P375
Green, Wendy P392
Green, Crickett P442
Green, Jane P448
Green, Gene E P502
Green, Teressia P508
Green, Beth P563
Green, Mary P659
Green, Kevin P678
Green, Gary R. W116
Green, John M. W317
Green, Kevin E81
Green, Ben E98
Green, Phillip D. E104
Green, Karen E106
Green, Yasemin E132
Green, Patrick E147
Green, Janet E290
Green, William H. E293
Green, Gary E334
Green, Mary E399
Green, Jack E436
Greenan, Joe A16
Greenbaum, Veronica A784
Greenberg, Lon R A64
Greenberg, Joe A69
Greenberg, Dan A702
Greenberg, Ari A738
Greenberg, Richard P19
Greenberg, Lawrence P553
Greenberg, Lon R P615
Greenberg, Evan G. W106
Greenberg, Jordan E33
Greenberg, Sarah E290
Greenblatt, David A. E69
Greene, Alexander A44
Greene, Mike A60
Greene, Brian A108
Greene, Jason K. A129
Greene, Thomas (Tom) A218
Greene, John T A269
Greene, Matt A286
Greene, Brian A647
Greene, Gregory A734
Greene, Greg A734
Greene, A. Hugh P63
Greene, Tim P109
Greene, John P157

COMBINED HOOVER'S HANDBOOK INDEX OF EXECUTIVES

Greene, Michael P175
Greene, Sonja P182
Greene, Matt P190
Greene, Graham F P284
Greene, Charles J P356
Greene, Toni P476
Greene, Queen P477
Greene, Hugh P503
Greene, Alexander E13
Greene, Steve E174
Greene, Richard W. E207
Greene, Jon E302
Greene-Campbell, Allyson P589
Greener, Todd A13
Greener, Geoffrey S. A107
Greener, Charles A900
Greener, Fred P83
Greener, Fred L P83
Greenfield, Eric A175
Greenfield, Jeremy A571
Greenfield, Karen P429
Greenfield, Andrew J. E2
Greenglass, Alan S P132
Greengold, Alexander A552
Greengold, Alexander P324
Greenhaw, Mark A113
Greenhaw, Mark E36
Greenier, Ryan A432
Greening, Oliver A449
Greening, Oliver E221
Greenleaf, Lari A491
Greenleaf, Chris A538
Greenlees, Sharon A6
Greenlees, Jim P664
Greenspon, Tom A144
Greenstein, Scott A. A762
Greenstein, Sara A. A873
Greenstein, Bruce E256
Greenstreet, Michelle M A775
Greenstreet, Michelle M P511
Greensweig, Gary P472
Greenup, Marion A829
Greenup, Marion P589
Greenwald, Vicki P112
Greenwald, Judy P541
Greenwalt, Rodgers K. A129
Greenway, Mark A442
Greenwell, Melissa P567
Greenwood, John A246
Greenwood, Jennifer A646
Greenwood, Alison A699
Greenwood, John E105
Greenwood, Jennifer E324
Greer, K. Gordon A105
Greer, Jeff A170
Greer, Emily A371
Greer, Steven K. A389
Greer, Pam A779
Greer, Louis E. A852
Greer, Emily S P34
Greer, Jon P343
Greer, Jeanne P563
Greer, K. Gordon E34
Gref, Herman W343
Grefe, Roger A704
Greff, Brian A475
Grefstad, Odd Arild W365
Greg, Dosedel A877
Greg, Perticone P268
Grega, Jocelyn A882
Greger, Gene P604
Gregg, Mark A340
Gregg, Mark E160
Gregoire, Kevin P. A352
Gregoire, Christopher J A524
Gregoire, Daniel N. (Dan) A532
Gregoire, Joseph A925
Gregoire, Andrew J. E256
Gregoire, Joseph E445
Gregoris, Daniel E190
Gregory, William A195
Gregory, Johnson A320
Gregory, Lentz A345
Gregory, Catherine A409
Gregory, Sherman A695

Gregory, Paul C. A696
Gregory, Audrey A811
Gregory, Dave A897
Gregory, Lisa A923
Gregory, Sean J. P410
Gregory, Christy P478
Gregory, Robert P505
Gregory, Linsey P595
Gregory, Matt P597
Gregory, Lentz E165
Gregory, Lisa E442
Greiff, David E122
Greig, Jeffrey P186
Greindl, Jean-Marie A673
Greiner, Paul A509
Greiner, James (Jim) P13
Grella, Christopher A61
Grelling, Susan A643
Grenfell, Bob A296
Grenfell, Alistair A474
Grenon, Yves P405
Grensteiner, Ronald J. (Ron) A52
Grenz, Dianne M. A888
Grenz, Dianne M. E425
Grescovich, Mark J. A116
Grescovich, Mark J. E39
Grese, Frank A398
Greslick, Richard L A211
Greslick, Rich A211
Greslick, Richard L E82
Greslick, Rich E83
Gress, William J. A154
Grether, James A940
Greubel, Scott P185
Greuel, Norm A512
Greuel, Norman A512
Greulich, Lynn A621
Greulich, Lynn E311
Greve, Norman de A251
Grewal, Paul A310
Grewal, Gulsher S A460
Grewal, Harjinder P70
Grewcock, Bruce E A492
Grewcock, Bruce E. A656
Grewcock, Bruce E P279
Grewcock, Bruce P279
Grewcock, Bruce E. P414
Grewe, Patrick A885
Grewe, Jerry P443
GREWE, MELISSA P471
Greyber, Rob A307
Gribbin, Mary A592
Gribbin, Mary P370
Grice, Bill A481
Grider, Daniel A428
Gridley, Maryanne P184
Grieco, Patrizia W153
Grieder, Daniel A692
Griego, Kathleen A798
Grier, Rosa P546
Grierson, Matthew A880
Grierson, Matthew P640
Grieshaber, Joe A498
Griesing, Thomas A651
Griesing, Thomas E329
Griessenauer, Christoph P215
Griff, Christine A654
Griffeth, Jack T P383
Griffin, Jayson A62
Griffin, Brian T. A69
Griffin, Ronald B. (Ron) A95
Griffin, Jeremy A140
Griffin, Corey A. A147
Griffin, Stacey A442
Griffin, Robyn A444
Griffin, Alyson A460
Griffin, Kevin A481
Griffin, Minnie A637
Griffin, Monty J. A756
Griffin, John A783
Griffin, James A786
Griffin, Sean F. A869
Griffin, Darragh A925
Griffin, Michael P6
Griffin, Donnie P86

Griffin, James D. P172
Griffin, Caroline P184
Griffin, Anthony H P199
Griffin, Mike P235
Griffin, April P240
Griffin, Justin P260
Griffin, Charles P274
Griffin, Marcus P430
Griffin, B R P430
Griffin, Doug P456
Griffin, Noelle P468
Griffin, Alison P505
Griffin, Walt P588
Griffin, Jayson E20
Griffin, Gretchen E156
Griffin, Leland E212
Griffin, James E387
Griffin, Darragh E445
Griffis, Mark P1
Griffis, Mark E80
Griffith, John B. A1
Griffith, Bob A324
Griffith, Brian A408
Griffith, Beth A519
Griffith, Timothy T. A534
Griffith, Jill A654
Griffith, S. Patricia (Tricia) A681
Griffith, Derek A722
Griffith, Donna H P311
Griffith, J. Brian P337
Griffith, John P383
Griffith, Bob P615
Griffith, Chris W29
Griffith, John B. E1
Griffith, Doreen E250
Griffith, Scott E264
Griffiths, Stephen A877
Griffiths, Guy W42
Griffiths, Peter L. W206
Griffo, Michael A357
Griffo, Michael A176
Grigaux, Paul J. A770
Griger, David T P574
Grigg, Robert A484
Grigg, Richard R P37
Grigg, William P210
Griggs, Malcolm D. A205
Griggs, Rebecca A257
Griggs, Karessa P551
Griggs, Kathleen M. (Kathy) E240
Grignon, Perianne A750
Grigsby, Todd P105
Grigsby, Lane P105
Grigsby, Todd P106
Grigsby, L Lane P106
Grill, Neil A112
Grill, Donald L. E150
Grilli, Francesco A695
Grillo, Kathleen A890
Grillo, Loraine P366
Grillo, Anthony P514
Grillo, Anthony E258
Grillot, Larry A666
Grima, Crocefissa A590
Grima, Edward P74
Griman, Emilio A465
Grime, Ben A934
Grimes, Jennifer A246
Grimes, William A693
Grimes, Joseph P. (Joe) A815
Grimes, Joe A815
Grimes, Sally A855
Grimes, Matt A877
Grimes, Robert R. P206
Grimes, Cynda P551
Grimes, Patricia E100
Grimes, Jennifer E105
Grimes, Thomas L. (Tom) E282
Grimes, William E341
Grimet, Howard P274
Grimm, Susan P116
Grimm, Carol P301
Grimm, Douglas P334
Grimm, Paul E105
Grimm, David M. E177

Grimmer, Steven A308
Grimmer, Lee E290
Grimmett, Gail A262
Grimminger, Kurt A928
Grimminger, Kurt P674
Grimshaw, Matt A226
Grimshaw, Matt P150
Grimsley, Diane P618
Grimsman, Randall A175
Grimstone, Gerry W56
Grimstone, Gerry W58
Grinberg, Paul J. A101
Grinberg, Paul J. E32
Grindal, Corey A188
Grindberg, Guy A877
Griner, Patricia A755
Griner, Patricia E369
Grinis, Scott E131
Grinnell, Bruce A320
Grinthal, Karen P480
Grintsvayg, Greg E131
Grisez, Todd P131
Grisham, Dorothy P150
Grisko, David A494
Grissen, David J. A537
Griswold, Ryan P A484
Griswold, Venus A859
Grizzard, Bryon A571
Grizzard, Maynard A831
Grizzard, Maynard P601
Groat, Jeff A934
Grob, Trena A463
Grob, Matthew S. (Matt) A694
Grobler, Fleetwood W341
Groch, James R. (Jim) A175
Grodin, Joshua A735
Grodowski, Jenie P527
Groebel, Robert E427
Groendyke, John E77
Groenewold, John A484
Groeschel, Craig E197
Groetelaars, John A123
Groetken, Doug A915
Groff, Stacey A448
Groff, Rick A746
Groff, Michael R. (Mike) A839
Groff, Mike A859
Groff, Jeffrey A881
Groff, Stacey P247
Groff, Jeffrey E421
Groft, Michael A741
Groft, Michael E364
Grogan, Edwin A506
Grogin, Jeffrey P. A648
Grogin, SScott A893
Grogin, Jeffrey P. E328
Groh, Kelly L. A381
Groh, Paul P351
Grohe, Mark A232
Groll, Jeanine P103
Grolman, David A658
Gronbach, Tyler A833
Groneman, Joseph L P174
Gronke, Mark A325
Gronow, Tom P626
Groom, Steve A362
Groom, Scott P574
Grooms, Terry A329
Grooms, Sarah A925
Grooms, Sarah E445
Groot, René de W15
Groppi, Shannon A784
Gros-Pietro, Gian Maria W202
Grosby, Karen P389
Grosfield, Howard A53
Gross, Jeff A436
Gross, Bob A481
Gross, Bruce E. A512
Gross, Linda A522
Gross, Gary A527
Gross, Roger A885
Gross, Kevin P12
Gross, Arthur P17
Gross, Anne P172
Gross, Roy P333

HOOVER'S HANDBOOK OF EMERGING COMPANIES 2020

COMBINED HOOVER'S HANDBOOK INDEX OF EXECUTIVES

```
A = AMERICAN BUSINESS
E = EMERGING COMPANIES
P = PRIVATE COMPANIES
W = WORLD BUSINESS
```

Gross, Daniel L. (Dan) P489
Gross, Nsharra E100
Gross, Eric E445
Grossenbacher, John A536
Grosser, Joy M. P258
Grossi, Stephen D. A142
Grossi, Therese A170
Grossi, Adriana A784
Grossi, Stephen D. E49
Grossman, Rick A266
Grossman, Robert I. A592
Grossman, Jeff A600
Grossman, Rick P181
Grossman, Robert I. P370
Grossman, Divina P631
Grossman, Jean E115
Grosso, Steve A893
Grosvenor, John C. A104
Grosvenor, Mark P375
Grote, Joe A842
Grote, Kathleen E148
Groth, Tom A926
Groth, Tom E445
Grottenthaler, Bob P68
Grottkau, Jennifer A441
Grotzinger, John P. P107
Grove, Hannah A783
Grove, Robin A806
Grove, Gerri P89
Grove, Scott P96
Grove, Robin E398
Grover, Michael A179
Grover, Rajeev A199
Grover, Amar A358
Grover, Owen A452
Grover, Purva A824
Grover, Rishi A875
Grover, Purva P562
Grover, Amar E176
Groves, Mary A453
Groves, Tina M. A760
Groves, S Van P279
Groves, Ned P325
Groves, Allen P442
Groves, Jennifer P556
Groves, Jason L. E274
Groves, Tina M. E374
Grow, Erin H A107
Grow, Bradford A933
Grozier, Paul A119
Grube, Pat A714
Grube, Rudiger W133
Grube, Jeffrey D E361
Grube, Steven R. E365
Gruber, Mark A80
Gruber, William A657
Gruber, Julie A826
Gruber, Scott L. A838
Grubic, Robert C A566
Grubic, Robert C. E281
Grudzien, Wayne A405
Grudzien, Jeffrey M. E359
Gruener, Gregory P39
Gruenfeld, Chris A219
Gruenfeld, Chris E87
Gruenke, Scott A885
Gruenthal, Michael P17
Grugan, Anne P19
Grunder, Mark A850
Grundt, Bruce A512
Grune, Thomas J A564
Grune, Robert B. (Rob) P166
Gruner, Greg A91
Gruner, Dean P602
Gruner, Greg E29
Grunfeld, Joseph A575
Grunig, Jared A922
Grunig, Jared P671
Grunow, Tamie P625

Gruntz, Cory P196
Grunwald, Stefan A169
Grunwald, Gerald B. P603
Grussendorf, Christi A29
Grussendorf, Christi P16
Grynberg, Marc W405
Grynspan, Devora P389
Gryska, David W. (Dave) E226
Gryzbek, Thomas P207
Grzechowiak, Robin A530
Gr-ober, Jurgen W178
Gu, Yaobin (Richard) A66
Gu, Yueru A606
Gu, Hanson A692
Guadagnoli, Donald A. P109
Guagliardo, Paul (Guyardo) A270
Guajardo, Dante Contreras W118
Gualdoni, Donald P35
Guan, Pua Seck W424
Guangyu, Yuan W110
Guardia, Juan P625
Guardino, Lenny A538
Guardino, Christopher A922
Guardino, Christopher P671
Guardiola, Charlie A158
Guarin, Fernando P572
Guarino, Mary P193
Guarino, Alan E77
Guarisco, Pete P209
Guarneschelli, Philip P420
Guastella, Lily P627
Guatam, Anjali P114
Guatero, Montha A326
Guay, Martin A778
Guay, Marty A778
Gubitosi, David A203
Gubler, Jocelyn A761
Gubler, Blaise P529
Gude, David A435
Gudgel, Jane A746
Gudgell, Kay E127
Gudibande, Aroon A742
Gudipalli, Subbarao A804
Guedry, John A913
Guedry, John E438
Guell, Miguel Montes W45
Guenault, Karl A474
Guenther, Cindy A36
Guenther, Stephen A442
Guenther, Christopher A596
Guenther, Greg A893
Guenthner, Kevin J. A344
Guenthner, Steven P27
Guenthner, Kevin J. E165
Guerci, Alan P515
Guericke, Keith R. E136
Guerin, Olivier A746
Guerlain, Eric W105
Guerra, Michael A305
Guerra, R. David A463
Guerra, Robert A761
Guerra, Andrea A801
Guerra, Homero P31
Guerra, Joe P242
Guerra, Dylan P505
Guerrazzi, Mark A198
Guerreri, John E127
Guerrero, Juan O. A670
Guerrero, Ismael P678
Guerrero, --ngel Alija W26
Guerrero, Pedro Guerrero W55
Guerrieri, Gary A357
Guerrieri, Gina P594
Guerrieri, Gary E175
Guerriero, Angelo E371
Guerrini, Martino Scabbia A891
Guerry, Bernie A373
Guertler, Walter A92
Guest, Kevin G. E423
Guevara, Alfredo P649
Guge, Brett P107
Guggemos, Michael A458
Guggemos, Julie A804
Guggenheim, Paul A. A643
Guggenheimer, Ron A204

Guggina, William H. W31
Gugino, Matthew A254
Gugino, Ann B. A643
Gugino, Michael E138
Guglielmi, Joseph M A577
Guglielmi, Michael E342
Guglielmo, Michael P546
Guha, Krishna A319
Guhe, Joachim A640
Guichard, Kent B. E19
Guidi, Richard A184
Guidotti, Michael A453
Guidry, Darren E. E212
Guilbaud, Jean-Jacques W398
Guiley, Thomas E P184
Guilfoile, Peter W. A222
Guilfoile, Mary A469
Guillaume, Steve E383
Guillemette, Gilles A744
Guillen, Ernesto A85
Guillen, Ernesto E27
Guillory, Lloyd A309
Guillory, Cory A713
Guillot, Stephen A543
Guillotte, Gwen E256
Guillouard, Catherine W323
Guillén, Federico W284
Guinan, Tom A109
Guinan, Mark J. A698
Guindo, Chirfi A133
Guinee, Arnaud P140
Guiony, Jean-Jacques W241
Guiot, Oliver A. E201
Guire, Peter Mc P465
Gul, Zartash P625
Gula, Allen J. A795
Gula, Allen J. E397
Gulalo, Krista A786
Gulalo, Krista E387
Gulbin, Michael A893
Gulden, Bjorn W218
Gulinello, Jim A405
Gullbrants, Brian A930
Gulley, Janet A824
Gulley, Janet P562
Gulling, Douglas R. (Doug) A911
Gulling, Douglas R. (Doug) E437
Gulliver, Stuart T. W189
Gullo, Kristine A112
Gullo, Samuel M A331
Gullo, Chris A818
Gullo, Samuel M E152
Gullo, Chris E403
Gullotto, Vincent E366
Gulmon, Gary A794
Gulrajani, Linda E267
Gulson, Scott A68
Gumaer, Andy E32
Gumbar, Gitika A390
Gumbert, Jack A509
Gumbs, Jason A220
Gumbs, Milton A P100
Gumeringer, Bert P548
Gumm, Gary P658
Gummey, Charles A922
Gummey, Charles P671
Gums, Cary A809
Gundacker, Mark A740
Gunderman, Robert E. (Bob) A924
Gunderman, Bob P672
Gundersen, Curtis P184
Gundotra, Vic A39
Gunkel, Damon A452
Gunn, Deborah P164
Gunn, William B P609
Gunnison, Kyle A704
Gunter, Thomas A492
Gunter, Jim P82
Gunter, Marcus P331
Gunter, C. Scott W106
Gunther, Guy A184
Gunther, Conrad J. A268
Gunther, Jeffery A425
Gunthner, Richard A544
Guntupalli, Ajay A432

Guntupalli, Ajay E216
Gunupure, Suresh A559
Guo, Peng (Patrick) A813
Guo, Lin P642
Guo, George W385
Guo, Lucy E101
Guohua, Zhang W110
Guoxiong, Wei W198
Gupta, Sanjay A35
Gupta, Suren A35
Gupta, Anchal A54
Gupta, Vineet A135
Gupta, Vishad A327
Gupta, Sanjiv A378
Gupta, Rocky A378
Gupta, Rohit A381
Gupta, Rajneesh A471
Gupta, Pranjal A478
Gupta, Ayan Das A530
Gupta, Anu A804
Gupta, Amit P70
Gupta, Pranjal P269
Gupta, Sunny P446
Gupta, Vinayak P547
Gupta, Mahendra R. P600
Gupta, Rajiv L. (Raj) W31
Gupta, Piyush W130
Gupta, Sanjeev W350
Gupta, Vikram E110
Gupta, Anuj E132
Gupta, Pranav E138
Gupta, Vikas E314
Gupta, Vikas E353
Gupton, Donna P2
Gur, Sharon W49
Gurander, Jan W420
Gurgens, Cydney A859
Gurgovits, Stephen J. (Steve) A358
Gurgovits, Stephen J. (Steve) E176
Gurian, Daniela A722
Gurin, Steve A118
Gurin, Patricia B P34
Gurin, Steve E40
Gurk, Kevin Mc P76
Gurkan, Tarkan A654
Gurley, Tony P162
Gurley, William E263
Gurnani, Roger A889
Gurri, Mia P253
Gurtman, Jeff P159
Gurumurthy, Vivek A890
Gurvitz, Howard A36
Guse, Brad A926
Gushie, Steve A13
Gusho, Mike P607
Gusomano, Laura P595
Guss, Fred P392
Gust, Don P283
Gustafson, Paul A222
Gustafson, Todd A438
Gustafson, Dan A593
Gustafson, Joel A598
Gustafson, John P32
Gustafson, Lynn P96
Gustas, Lisa P120
Gustavson, Timothy B A707
Gustavsson, Niklas W420
Gutch, Matthew P529
Gutgesell, Emily P250
Gutgutia, Virag A707
Guth, Amy P188
Guthery, Christopher A271
Guthneck, Griffin A482
Guthrie, Steve A442
Guthrie, Linda P389
Guthrie, Kevin P389
Guthrie, Chris P599
Guthrie, Wayne P627
Gutierrez, Harvey A246
Gutierrez, Guillermo A467
Gutierrez, Frank A522
Gutierrez, Mauricio A610
Gutierrez, John A746
Gutierrez, Brian G. P549
Gutierrez, Mauricio E81

COMBINED HOOVER'S HANDBOOK INDEX OF EXECUTIVES

Gutierrez, Harvey E105
Gutierrez, Carlos E105
Gutman, Luisa P243
Gutmann, Bernard A627
Gutmann, Kathleen A871
Gutmann, Amy A879
Gutmann, Amy P636
Gutnick, Michael P. P325
Gutsch, James L. (Jim) A748
Gutt, Jack A320
Gutteridge, Thomas G. (Tom) P596
Guttery, John A289
Guttman, Tim G. A63
Gutz, Phyllis P661
Guy, Jennifer A179
Guy, Jerry A369
Guy, John A906
Guy, Barbara P502
Guy, Kimberly P519
Guy, Henry E396
Guy, John E435
Guyaux, Joseph A147
Guyett, Gregory L. A284
Guyett, Gregory L. E120
Guynn, Kevin P583
Guyon, Robert E. (Bob) P528
Guyot, Hervé W160
Guyse, Clyde A106
Guyton, Jeffrey H. W250
Guziak, James A850
Guzick, David S. P489
Guzick, David S. P627
Guzik, Bill A9
Guzik, Bill P4
Guzman, Marta A213
Guzman, Jennifer A621
Guzman, Francisco A728
Guzman, Manuel P32
Guzman, Melissa P253
Guzman, Rafael W144
Guzman, Jorge Andres Saieh W204
Guzman, Douglas A. W331
Guzman, Jennifer E311
Guzman-Petter, Teresa P472
Guzzi, Anthony J. (Tony) A292
Guzzie-peck, Peggy A479
Gwalani, Sanjay A54
Gwebster, Richard A305
Gwillim, Ryan M A154
Gwilt, Edward A222
Gwin, Andrew A84
Gwin, Marie A126
Gwin, Andrew P47
Gwinn, Nancy E. P497
Gwizdala, Lori A. A805
Gwizdala, Lori A. E398
Gwydir, Tom E290
Gyarmaty, Mike A434
Gysbers, Niki A567
Gysbers, Niki E284
Gyurci, John P333
Gyurisin, Margie P531
Galvez, José Damian Bogas W153
G--mez, Eugenio Llorente W6
G--mez, Carlos G--mez y W46
Gonensin, Turgay W403
Gorg, Werner W173
Go-şmen, Mehmet W177
Guney, Turgut W18
Gur, Kaan W18
Gélard, Yves Le W154
Généreux, Claude W313
Gérardin, Yann W71

H

Ha, Bao P456
Haacker, Kristin P586
Haag, Natalie A168
Haagenson, Deb A226
Haagenson, Deb P150
Haahr, J. Tyler A557
Haahr, J. Tyler E281
Haake, Anne P456

Haaland, Corey L A804
Haan, Taco de A355
Haan, Patti A530
Haan, Warren de E387
Haas, Tracie A6
Haas, William A502
Haas, G. Hunter A632
Haas, David A831
Haas, Mark P. P339
Haas, Nancy P360
Haas, Gerard P502
Haas, Herbert K. W178
Haas, Herbert K. W382
Haas, Christopher E224
Haas, Tara E260
Haas-Kogan, Daphne P172
Haase, Joseph A410
Haasen, Don A741
Haasen, Don E364
Haave, Christopher A706
Habak, Charles A145
Habbit, Anthony A909
Habbit, Anthony E436
Habeck, Bryan A219
Habeck, Heather P602
Habeck, Bryan E87
Haber, Daniel A. P574
Haberfield, Patrick A737
Haberfield, Patrick E361
Haberkamp, Dean A329
Haberkorn, David A797
Haberman, Michael A877
Haberman, Shelley P11
Haberman, Bruce P506
Habermann, Eric A436
Habib, Hadi P210
Habib, Reza P504
Habicht, Kevin B. E296
Habingreither, Robert P551
Hablitzel, Thomas C. A756
Haby, Jeff P470
Hachenburg, Douglas A670
Hachey, Barbara P261
Hachey, Barb P261
Hachigo, Takahiro W186
Hacikamiloglu, Mehmet W177
Hackenberg, Amy L. A339
Hackenberg, Kim P214
Hackenberg, Amy L. E159
Hackenson, Elizabeth A18
Hacker, Harold A420
Hacker, Mark S. A577
Hacker, Howard A811
Hacker, Harold P240
Hackerman, Nancy P494
Hackett, William F. (Bill) A236
Hackett, Jim A360
Hackett, Ann A631
Hackett, Margaux A536
Hackett, Steven G. (Steve) A675
Hackett, John A756
Hackett, Steven G. (Steve) P428
Hackett, Sylvia P448
Hackett, Gail P650
Hackman, Steve A621
Hackman, Mark P351
Hackman, Jeff E126
Hackman, Steve E311
Hackney, Carol P446
Hackstadt, Kent A787
Hadad, Henry A151
Hadar, Janet P595
Hadavi, Judith A658
Haddad, Michael A63
Haddad, Nathalie A97
Haddad, AL A574
Haddad, Gabriel G. P438
Haddad, Ghassan P501
Haddox, Matthew P266
Hadjiliadis, Dennis P244
Hadjisotiriou, Paula N. W272
Hadley, Stephen A706
Hadley, David P254
Hadley, Lester P356
Hadley, Philip A. E143

Hadsell, Charlie A292
Haeberlein, Samantha A133
Haefele, Alan A665
Haefele, Alan E334
Haefner, Larry A. A210
Haefner, Jeremy A. P456
Haela, Randi E162
Haelsig, Claus-Peter A355
Haensel, Douglas P. E118
Haer, Gary E352
Haessler, Laura A271
Haeussler, Mark A98
Hafer, Michael A915
Hafer, Greg P461
Hafertepen, Eric A492
Haffenreffer, Joan A204
Haffner, Paul A701
Hafford, Daniel A801
Hafner, Steve A143
Hafner, Jennifer A747
Haft, Ian A44
Haft, Steven A893
Haft, Ian E13
Hafter, Jeffrey M. (Jeff) A126
Hagan, Robert A329
Hagan, Michael A428
Hagan, Kevin A449
Hagan, Roland A465
Hagan, Benjamin A616
Hagan, Willard A842
Hagan, Christine A893
Hagan, Nicole P51
Hagan, Diane P258
Hagan, Kevin E221
Hagans, Robert R. P2
Hageboeck, Charles R. (Skip) A206
Hagedoorn, Amy A255
Hagedorn, C Kristopher A578
Hagedorn, Michael D. (Mike) A858
Hagekyriakou, Luke A72
Hagel, Shawn R. A675
Hagel, Shawn R. P428
Hagelin, Carl A112
Hagelin, Keith E114
Hagemann, Robert A735
HAGEMANN, DAVID E105
Hagemeister, Eric A680
Hagen, Terence D. A476
Hagen, Mary A556
Hagen, Russell S. A918
Hagen, Kelly P30
Hagen, Bruce P395
Hagen, Mary E277
Hagens, William P505
Hager, Dan A100
Hager, David A. (Dave) A263
Hager, Tim A452
Hager, Dan P58
Hagerman, Yvonne P137
Hagerty, Jim A181
Hagerty, James A904
Hagerty, Jim E70
Hagerty, Thomas E174
Hagey, Michelle P419
Haggen, Brad P227
Hagger, Andrew W270
Haggerty, Kathleen A54
Haggerty, Patrick A793
Haggy, Bret A444
Hagio, Keiji W278
Hagiwara, Takeshi W257
Hagler, Mendel A588
Hagler, Mendel P365
Haglund, Matt A61
Hagmann, Cheryl A651
Hagmann, Cheryl E329
Hagner, Nancy A922
Hagner, Nancy P671
Hagy, Michelle P419
Hahl, William A749
Hahl, Barbara P351
Hahl, William E367
Hahn, Gregory A329
Hahn, Terrence S. A431
Hahn, Craig A452

Hahn, Greg A676
Hahn, William C. P172
Hahn, Brian F P546
Hahn, Michelle E272
Hahn, Greg E338
Hai, Zhu W344
Haibi, Jason E290
Haidamus, Ramzi W284
Haidar, Wael P94
Haidu, James A36
Haight, Mark A A716
Haijun, Wu W354
Haile, Kempton C. A831
Haile, Elizabeth P592
Haile, Kempton C. P601
Hailey, Bill A682
Hailey, Fernanda A713
Hailey, Clint A811
Hailey, Robert P157
Hain, Craig A816
Haines, Ann A527
Haines, Michelle A850
Haines, Gary A903
Haines, Paul P318
Haines, Mike P347
Haines, Cynthia P558
Haines, Gerald M. (Gerry) E277
Haines, Michael B. (Mike) E356
Hainey, Chris A623
Hainey, Chris E313
Hair, Ken P246
Haire, Gary P204
Haire, Stephen I P349
Haire, Gary E232
Hairston, John M. A401
Hairston, Michelle A690
Hairston, John M. E198
Hajdik, Brock A418
Hajny, Mark P536
Hak, Seo Kang W193
Hakanson, David P465
Hake, Sharon A368
Hake, James P379
Hakim, Shazmah A538
Hakim, Veronique A560
Hakim, Dorith A640
Hakim, Veronique P336
Hakim, Veronique (Ronnie) P580
Hakman, Joseph E8
Hakso, Chelsea A793
Hakulin, Ruth P642
Halamka, John D. P79
Halberg, Richard A227
Halberg, Phil A450
Halberg, Richard E91
Halberstadt, Geoffrey L. A155
Halberstadt, Geoffrey L. E54
Haldeman, Frances A368
Haldeman, Charles E. (Ed) A738
Haldeman, Greg P185
Halderen, Tracy Van P511
Halderman, Robert R A345
Halderman, Robert R E166
Hale, Karen A6
Hale, Jean R. A229
Hale, Betty A323
Hale, Stephen A455
Hale, Jordan A782
Hale, Stacy A804
Hale, Kenneston P196
Hale, Robert T. (Rob) P220
Hale, Philip P301
Hale, Kathleen P306
Hale, Daniel G P329
Hale, David F. P438
Hale, Mark S. P480
Hale, Jordan P526
Hale, Blake P542
Hale, Randy E106
Hale, Stephen E228
Halepete, Sameer A613
Hales, Kim A610
Hales, Randall L. E452
Haley, Christopher A248
Haley, Chris A319

HOOVER'S HANDBOOK OF EMERGING COMPANIES 2020

COMBINED HOOVER'S HANDBOOK INDEX OF EXECUTIVES

```
A = AMERICAN BUSINESS
E = EMERGING COMPANIES
P = PRIVATE COMPANIES
W = WORLD BUSINESS
```

Haley, Colleen A325
Haley, Tim M A412
Haley, Colleen A640
Haley, Sarah A651
Haley, Tim M P233
Haley, Michael P252
Haley, Jeffrey V. E16
Haley, Michael E16
Haley, Christopher E107
Haley, Sarah E330
Halford, Andy W364
Haliburton, Valerie A218
Halinski, Bob A879
Halkos, Elizabeth P435
Hall, Tom A36
Hall, William (Bill) A37
Hall, Mary C A45
Hall, Prentiss A75
Hall, Jill A142
Hall, Adam A150
Hall, Stephanie A179
Hall, Mark A201
Hall, Ryan A203
Hall, Michael A205
Hall, Tammy A345
Hall, Duncan A381
Hall, Charles J. (Chuck) A410
Hall, Veronica M. A414
Hall, Neil A526
Hall, Ladd R. A612
Hall, Tammy A621
Hall, William M. (Bill) A627
Hall, Bill A628
Hall, Kathryn A642
Hall, Bill A645
Hall, Chris A654
Hall, J. D. A666
Hall, J D A666
Hall, Leslie (Les) A692
Hall, J. Franklin (Frank) A700
Hall, Julie A739
Hall, Tom A749
Hall, John A765
Hall, R. Wayne A769
Hall, Paul A775
Hall, Bill A804
Hall, John G A810
Hall, Jack A813
Hall, Kerry L. A818
Hall, Bradley C. A857
Hall, Keith A871
Hall, Reggie A872
Hall, Brian A896
Hall, Jonathan A902
Hall, Richard P16
Hall, Steve P21
Hall, Mary C P30
Hall, R Alan P58
Hall, Marc P80
Hall, Jim P82
Hall, Tracy P124
Hall, Tony P161
Hall, Ryan P162
Hall, Russell P187
Hall, Christopher P194
Hall, Brian P196
Hall, Trudy P209
Hall, Veronica M. P236
Hall, Stacy P250
Hall, Barbara P259
Hall, Bryan P349
Hall, Gairy P383
Hall, Jesse Peterson P386
Hall, Jim P404
Hall, Kathryn P407
Hall, Roger P415
Hall, Vera P463
Hall, John G P546
Hall, Mark P552

Hall, John P581
Hall, Kathryn A. P592
Hall, Daniel P629
Hall, Derwin E16
Hall, Jill E49
Hall, Adam E50
Hall, Tammy E165
Hall, Amy E172
Hall, Jason E184
Hall, Brian M. E252
Hall, Tammy E311
Hall, Tom E367
Hall, Judi E379
Hall, R. Wayne E380
Hall, Kerry L. E403
Hallada, Tony P141
Hallagan, Pamela A559
Hallahan, Molly P610
Hallak-Serwatka, Mary Ann A584
Hallauer, Paul A925
Hallauer, Paul E445
Halle, Ray P469
Hallee, Christopher A205
Hallenbeck, Joshua A595
Haller, Tom A8
Haller, Monique A751
Haller, Monique P482
Hallett, Mark P410
Halley, Mary P617
Hallford, Brad P417
Halliburton, Shirley A296
Halliday, Sarah A. A584
Halliday, Steve E429
Halligan, Donald A P313
Hallinan, Patrick D. A361
Hallis, Marwan A583
Halliwell, Stephen W233
Halliwill, Donald P112
Hallman, Dwayne D. A432
Hallmark, Michael A449
Hallmark, Michael E220
Hallock, Kevin F. P159
Halloran, Michael A727
Halloran, Michael P453
Halloran, Angela P616
Hallquist, Raymond D P279
Hallum, Kathy A782
Hallum, Kathy A526
Halmy, Christopher A. A37
Halnon, Bill A721
Halper, John A468
Halper, Lisa A654
Halperin, Kenneth P498
Halpern, Kellye P387
Halpern, Howard P594
Halpern, Lonnie E53
Halpern, Janice E102
Halpin, Edward D. (Ed) A659
Halpin, Kevin A924
Halpin, Jean P395
Halprin, Joe A545
Halsey, Drew P194
Halsey, Casey S. P260
Halsey, Casey S. P261
Halsey, Mark P642
Halstrom, Danielle A151
Halter, Bob A36
Halter, Patrick G. (Pat) A677
Halter, Michael P. (Mike) A811
Halverson, Thomas A213
Halverson, John P55
Halverson, Thomas P143
Halvorson, Elise A218
Halvorson, Christine A315
Haly, Gregg A175
Ham, Ning A483
Hamalainen, Jim A60
Hamann, Edward A325
Hamano, Wayne Y. A109
Hamaoui, Elie P304
Hamblin, Vicky A850
Hambrecht, Jurgen W59
Hambrick, Thomas A408
Hamburg, Marc D. A127
Hamby, Donna P38

Hamby, Leigh S. P418
Hamdy, Walid A694
Hamel, Brian A465
Hamel, Cathy P213
Hamers, Ralph A. J. G. W200
Hames, Danette R A222
Hamid, Hind P564
Hamill, Laura A64
Hamill, Michael A119
Hamill, Laura A385
Hamill, Tim A481
Hamill, Geoffrey S P344
Hamilton, Adam A1
Hamilton, Jerome A3
Hamilton, Holly A54
Hamilton, Alfred A108
Hamilton, Forey A140
Hamilton, Charles S A145
Hamilton, Booz A A145
Hamilton, John A175
Hamilton, Julie A215
Hamilton, David A246
Hamilton, Jon A327
Hamilton, Lisa A380
Hamilton, Joanne G. A436
Hamilton, Scott A452
Hamilton, George Null A462
Hamilton, Andrew A592
Hamilton, Nancy A605
Hamilton, Robin A818
Hamilton, Colin A835
Hamilton, Sam A896
Hamilton, Patrick A902
Hamilton, Mark P43
Hamilton, Andrea P117
Hamilton, Kathy P223
Hamilton, Marta P232
Hamilton, Larry P244
Hamilton, George Null P256
Hamilton, Todd P275
Hamilton, Andrew P370
Hamilton, Shaya P382
Hamilton, Scott P412
Hamilton, John R P419
Hamilton, Katie P549
Hamilton, Lanandra P551
Hamilton, Jennifer P604
Hamilton, Rick P606
Hamilton, Samantha P637
Hamilton, Adam E1
Hamilton, David E105
Hamilton, Scott E223
Hamilton, Robin E403
Hamlin, Phil A455
Hamlin, Scott J. P128
Hamlin, Stephen E. P542
Hamlin, Phil E228
Hamline, Steve P260
Hamline, Steve P261
Hamm, Bradley P388
Hammad, Rania A526
Hammer, Beth A277
Hammer, Ziv A461
Hammer, Doug A462
Hammer, Karl P239
Hammer, Doug P256
Hammgren, Scott M. E372
Hammergren, John H. A549
Hammergren, John H. W250
Hammerstone, Jim P116
Hammes, Eric A3
Hammes, Chris P254
Hammon, Amy A327
Hammond, Carol A114
Hammond, P A A441
Hammond, John A442
Hammond, Harlan A462
Hammond, Peter A726
Hammond, Lee W P2
Hammond, Scott P120
Hammond, Jane P159
Hammond, Harlan P256
Hammond, Peter P453
Hammond, Ruby P546
Hammond, Star P653

Hammond, Carol E37
Hammond, Jake E229
Hammonds, Kristen A137
Hammonds, Kim W135
Hammons, John P1
Hammons, Matt P92
Hamner, Stephanie P386
Hamner, R. Steven E274
Hamory, Bruce H. A371
Hamory, Bruce H. P213
Hampson, Chad P265
Hampton, Mike A200
Hampton, Karen A360
Hampton, Eve A397
Hampton, Jerry A664
Hampton, Vanessa A850
Hampton, Monica P179
Hampton, Jason P308
Hampton, Shondra P306
Hampton, Kelly P412
Hampton, Philip W171
Hampton, Jerry E334
Hamre, Lasse A452
Hamre, John J. P578
Hamri, Abdel A692
Hamrick, Janet P115
Hamrock, Joseph (Joe) A600
Han, Vivian — A100
Han, Bernard L. (Bernie) A271
Han, Sang A356
Han, Joseph A505
Han, James A527
Han, Jeff A747
Han, Ying P49
Han, Joseph P484
Han, Kevin P530
Han, Yoon Gap W192
Han, Sang-Beom W236
Hanafin, Mark W95
Hanagarth, Heike W133
Hanak, Christopher P222
Hanavec, Jeree A928
Hanavec, Jeree P674
Hanback, Patricia A145
Hanbury, George L. P389
Hance, Dave Null P98
Hance, Michael L. E180
Hanchett, Richard A914
Hanchett, Richard E439
Hanchey, William A184
Hancock, Paul A126
Hancock, C. Wayne A229
Hancock, K. Kelly A824
Hancock, Sue A852
Hancock, Tiffany A852
Hancock, William P28
Hancock, Todd P132
Hancock, K. Kelly P561
Hancox, Steven E208
Hand, Fred A158
Hand, Jason A484
Hand, Steven P642
Handanyan, Lynne A658
Handler, Jonathan A120
Handlesman, Ralph P673
Handley, Terry W. A173
Handley, Thomas W. (Tom) A289
Handley, Bill W A484
Handley, Teresa A925
Handley, Gail P96
Handley, Jack P280
Handley, Teresa E445
Handlon, Carolyn B. A537
Handren, Scott A133
Handscombe, Jason E290
Handshuh, Harold P515
Handt, Scott A512
Handy, Edward O. (Ned) A904
Handy, Elsie P653
Handy, Christopher E448
Handzo, Michael A61
Hane, Laurie A897
Hanemann, Kim A688
Hanes, Vladimir A65
Hanes, Marilyn A403

Hanes, Madlyn A828
Hanes, Lesley P462
Hanes, Madlyn P584
Haney, Joe A739
Haney, Annette P150
Hang, Edward A813
Hanggi, Brad A740
Hanichak, Mark P454
Haniel, Franz M. W91
Hanif, Farina A167
Hanighen, John A13
Haning, Tony A481
Hank, Jeffrey E342
Hanke-baier, Petra A680
Hankerd, John A85
Hankerd, John E27
Hankins, Anthony P. A447
Hankins, Robert A717
Hankins, Steven A855
Hankins, Tad P149
Hankins, Robert E351
Hankinso, Beverly E106
Hanko, Edward A75
Hanks, W. Bruce A184
Hanks, Randy A248
Hanks, Craig P554
Hanks, Randy E107
Hanley, Doug A125
Hanley, Brian A449
Hanley, Walter P. A524
Hanley, Colleen A684
Hanley, Joseph R. A810
Hanley, Richard J P163
Hanley, Karen P667
Hanley, Brian E221
Hanley, Erik E429
Hanley, Jason E440
Hanlon, Paul A205
Hanlon, Crystal A428
Hanlon, Philip J P609
Hanlon, David P628
Hanlon, Deborah E135
Hanly, Donna P395
Hanman, Emma A54
Hanna, Melad A16
Hanna, Brad A85
Hanna, Pat A137
Hanna, Bill A419
Hanna, Kathy A498
Hanna, Mark A722
Hanna, Chris P340
Hanna, Gia P356
Hanna, Brad E27
Hanna, Jack E69
Hanna, Ally E101
Hanna, Wade E156
Hannaford, Thomas A444
Hannah, D. Jay A105
Hannah, Mark A859
Hannah, D. Jay E34
Hannah, Robert E58
Hannan, Renee A412
Hannan, Renee P233
Hannasch, Brian P. W21
Hannegan, David A934
Hanner, John A75
Hannigan, Andrew A484
Hannigan, Anne A510
Hannigan, Anne P290
Hannon, Mary A112
Hannon, Timothy A199
Hannon, Chris A347
Hannon, Tom P311
Hannon, Rita P315
Hannon, Chris E167
Hannum, Nancy P581
Hanny, Mark A466
Hanrahan, Ann M A3
Hanrahan, Jack A332
Hanrahan, Brian A727
Hanrahan, Brian P453
Hansberry, Kristin P330
Hanscom, Heather Null A60
Hansel, Gary E219
Hansen, Mike A17

Hansen, John A77
Hansen, Albert A108
Hansen, J. Michael (Mike) A197
Hansen, Russell A200
Hansen, Denise A232
Hansen, Kathy A248
Hansen, Kara A272
Hansen, Marshall A313
Hansen, Jodi A326
Hansen, John A366
Hansen, Donna A403
Hansen, Mike A415
Hansen, Faith A444
Hansen, Heather A462
Hansen, Terry A483
Hansen, Steven A492
Hansen, Becky A568
Hansen, Linda A606
Hansen, Peter A627
Hansen, Tim A704
Hansen, Douglas B. A709
Hansen, Geert A816
Hansen, Corey A885
Hansen, Dennis R. A912
Hansen, Mike P9
Hansen, Marshall P200
Hansen, Heather P256
Hansen, Steven P279
Hansen, Becky P345
Hansen, William P425
Hansen, Dr David P451
Hansen, Jan P607
Hansen, Inge K. W289
Hansen, Jorgen B. E63
Hansen, Kathy E107
Hansen, Mike E208
Hansen, Douglas B. E348
Hansen, Daniel P. E390
Hansen, Bruce E429
Hanson, Ash A75
Hanson, Breck F. A85
Hanson, Noreen A203
Hanson, Jay A287
Hanson, Bryan C. A304
Hanson, Bryan A306
Hanson, Bryan C A306
Hanson, Greg A388
Hanson, Laura A408
Hanson, Bradley C. (Brad) A557
Hanson, Terri A623
Hanson, Eric A654
Hanson, Ronald A761
Hanson, Milagros A804
Hanson, Shawna P50
Hanson, Stephen C. P64
Hanson, Deb P140
Hanson, Dena P157
Hanson, Michael P211
Hanson, Vicki P456
Hanson, Breck F. E26
Hanson, Bradley C. (Brad) E281
Hanson, Terri E313
Hantke, William A610
Hantman, Perla Tabares P588
Hantzinikolaou, George Petros W307
Hanzel, Kevin A301
Hanzelik, Daniel P228
Happe, Michael J. E443
Happel, Charles T. A316
Haqqani, Farrukh P651
Haque, Nadia A414
Haque, Nadia P236
Haque, Nawal P563
Hara, Debra O P428
Hara, Susumu W214
Hara, Toshiki W321
Hara, Takashi W360
Harada, Masaaki W30
Harada, Ken W127
Harada, Yuji W250
Harada, Shozo W292
Harada, Hiroya W392
Haran, Jim A605
Haran, Edward A738
Harari, Olivier A710

Haray, Richard A468
Harayama, Yasuhito W376
Harbach, F Edwin P74
Harbager, Claude P514
Harbarger, Claude W P514
Harbaugh, Todd W421
Harbert, Billy P58
Harbour, Shawn A859
Harchuck, Amanda E143
Harczak, Harry J A809
Hardacre, Marilyn A651
Hardacre, Marilyn E329
Hardee, Sandra P430
Hardeman, Kasonya P22
Harden, Billy P158
Harden, James P325
Harden, M C P503
Harden, Robert P551
Harden, Thomas P641
Harder, Chris A276
Hardesty, Erin E416
Hardgrove, Richard L. E365
Hardie, James R. A838
Hardig, John J. A934
Hardiman, Kevin A759
Hardiman, Kevin E373
Hardin, P Russell A380
Hardin, Matt A405
Hardin, Brad A452
Hardin, Alice A609
Hardin, Geoffrey A799
Hardin, Marie A828
Hardin, Scott P55
Hardin, Ed P211
Hardin, Alice P387
Hardin, Kathrine P472
Hardin, Marie P584
Hardin, Bill E102
Harding, John D A368
Harding, John A368
Harding, P Russell A513
Harding, James A. (Jim) A744
Harding, Debra A871
Harding, Joe A924
Harding, Douglas J P58
Harding, Scott P113
Harding, Harry P442
Harding, Joe P672
Harding, Peter E352
Hardison, Ann A849
Hardister, Hal P532
Hardman, Susan J. P446
Hardof, Tamir E179
Hardtke, Mark A606
Harduby, Raquel E330
Hardwick, Mark K. A345
Hardwick, M Susan P505
Hardwick, Mark K. E165
Hardy, Jody A91
Hardy, Stephen G. A227
Hardy, Karen A449
Hardy, Brent A451
Hardy, Thomas A518
Hardy, Russ A651
Hardy, James A783
Hardy, Cody P126
Hardy, Brent P249
Hardy, Benjamin P515
Hardy, Jody E29
Hardy, Stephen G. E90
Hardy, Karen E221
Hardy, Russ E329
Hardy-decuir, Beverly P171
Hare, Joshua A200
Hare, Diane A715
Hare, Brad A837
Hare, Douglas A859
Harel, Jonathan A746
Haren, Deborah P112
Harford, Simon N. R. P405
Hargadon, Donald A922
Hargadon, Donald P671
Hargenes, Donna P264
Hargens, Donna P264
Hargett, Carla A704

Hargett, Fred M. P390
Hargis, Michael A540
Hargrove, Robin S. (Rob) A573
Hariharan, Subramanian A658
Harik, Mario A. A934
Harika, Michelle A137
Haring, Dawn P103
Haring, Don P537
Harion, Jean Marc W297
Hariri, Abdi A505
Haris, Clint E128
Harker, Patrick T. A322
Harker, Victoria A446
Harker, Timothy A746
Harkey, Jean A413
Harkey, Jean E205
Harkins, David A56
Harkins, Bonnie P153
Harkness, Gordon A462
Harkness, David C. A931
Harkness, Gordon P256
Harkness, Teresa P567
Harlacher, Donna A530
Harlan, Jim A798
Harlan, Kristy A918
Harland, James P314
Harlem, Peter P501
Harless, Lisa A713
Harley, Michael A796
Harley, Richard P677
Harley, Michael E397
Harlovic, Michael P23
Harlow, David R. A105
Harlow, Leslie A327
Harlow, Bryce A892
Harlow, David R. E34
Harlowe, Michael P252
Harman, Gregory A394
Harmening, Jeffrey L. A376
Harmon, Damien A130
Harmon, David A179
Harmon, Gordon A286
Harmon, Gordon P190
Harmon, Robert P475
Harmon, Cindy P633
Harms, Timothy W A262
Harms, Brian K A695
Harms, Ole W419
Harness, Carl P161
Harnett, James A491
Harnett, Suzanne A635
Harney, Thomas A503
Harney, John P. P626
Harney, Thomas E249
Haron, C Daniel A251
Haroutunian, Karen P606
Harp, Matt A105
Harp, Vicky A855
Harp, Laurie P564
Harp, Matt E34
Harper, Toya A58
Harper, Sean E. A64
Harper, Chad A320
Harper, Jennifer A340
Harper, Derrick A414
Harper, Craig A442
Harper, Lori A446
Harper, Ginger A449
Harper, Peter A522
Harper, Stacey A522
Harper, Ron A647
Harper, Bobby A717
Harper, Gregory P195
Harper, Derrick P236
Harper, David P356
Harper, Raymond P461
Harper, C. Gregory (Greg) W150
Harper, Jane E147
Harper, Jennifer E161
Harper, Ginger E220
Harper, Bobby E351
Harra, Robert A922
Harra, Robert P671
Harrall, Chris A544
Harralson, Jefferson L. A866

COMBINED HOOVER'S HANDBOOK INDEX OF EXECUTIVES

```
A = AMERICAN BUSINESS
E = EMERGING COMPANIES
P = PRIVATE COMPANIES
W = WORLD BUSINESS
```

Harralson, Jefferson L. E417
Harreld, J. Bruce P594
Harrell, Erick A160
Harrell, James A. A768
Harrell, Robert A915
Harrell, Kim P201
Harrell, Leslie P262
Harrell, Colleen P330
Harrelson, Rhonda A298
Harrelson, Rhonda E130
Harrigan, PJ A700
Harriger, Tim A936
Harriger, Matt P54
Harring, Jeff A704
Harrington, Ben A105
Harrington, Michael W. (Mike) A155
Harrington, Dennis A303
Harrington, Barbara J. A335
Harrington, Michael J. A349
Harrington, Michael J. A517
Harrington, Neal A530
Harrington, Michael A713
Harrington, Liam A934
Harrington, Paul E. P97
Harrington, Jeff P127
Harrington, Jeffrey P127
Harrington, John P206
Harrington, Carol P232
Harrington, Charles L. (Chuck) P582
Harrington, Ben E34
Harrington, Michael W. (Mike) E54
Harrington, Barbara J. E154
Harris, David A44
Harris, Matt A53
Harris, Stephen A59
Harris, Angelee J. A104
Harris, Mitchell E. A111
Harris, Mary A114
Harris, Michael A126
Harris, Timothy A133
Harris, Wendy Guthrie A135
Harris, Michael A140
Harris, Henriette Henriette A167
Harris, Terrie A167
Harris, Diane A200
Harris, William A205
Harris, Crystal A218
Harris, Edmond L A245
Harris, Wes A250
Harris, David G. A263
Harris, Mattison W A320
Harris, Bobbye A325
Harris, Timothy K. (Tim) A339
Harris, Julie A339
Harris, Steven A345
Harris, Nigel A360
Harris, Ronald A380
Harris, Paul N. A491
Harris, Brian R. A503
Harris, Jeff A512
Harris, Steve A520
Harris, Walter A526
Harris, Christina A540
Harris, Jennifer A552
Harris, Yvette A562
Harris, Joe A592
Harris, Glenn A632
Harris, Jeff A637
Harris, Valerie A647
Harris, Val A647
Harris, James A649
Harris, Richard A665
Harris, Michael A682
Harris, Mike A682
Harris, Timothy P. A686
Harris, Paul A691
Harris, Jan A695
Harris, John D. A706
Harris, Tenesha A706

Harris, Todd A713
Harris, Paul V A723
Harris, Henry (Sandy) A754
Harris, Rick A804
Harris, Scott A806
Harris, C. Martin A824
Harris, Susan A839
Harris, Jenna A859
Harris, Donald A866
Harris, Sandra A891
Harris, Jeff M. A905
Harris, Erica-Nicole A908
Harris, Rafiq A925
Harris, Robert A925
Harris, Walter P2
Harris, Bill P25
Harris, Jeff P32
Harris, Holly P42
Harris, Hollie P42
Harris, Glenda P66
Harris, Patty P77
Harris, Shanetta P141
Harris, Gene T P148
Harris, Peter P175
Harris, Sally P240
Harris, Mark A. P305
Harris, Joe P370
Harris, Stacy P375
Harris, David P415
Harris, Spencer P420
Harris, Mark P426
Harris, Henry (Sandy) P484
Harris, John P485
Harris, William P514
Harris, Christian P533
Harris, C. Martin P561
Harris, Bruce P589
Harris, Ila P632
Harris, Brendan P644
Harris, David E13
Harris, Mary E37
Harris, Matthew E77
Harris, David E148
Harris, Timothy K. (Tim) E159
Harris, Julie E159
Harris, Steven E166
Harris, Kevin E226
Harris, John E232
Harris, Michael W. E240
Harris, Brian R. E249
Harris, Jennifer E275
Harris, Alice E319
Harris, Richard E334
Harris, Oscar N. E368
Harris, Scott E399
Harris, Donald E417
Harris, Rafiq E445
Harris, Robert E445
Harris-johnson, Ann A922
Harris-johnson, Ann P671
Harrison, Andrew R. A29
Harrison, Christopher A121
Harrison, Miranda A135
Harrison, Gregory A144
Harrison, David A199
Harrison, Suzan F. A217
Harrison, Olga A246
Harrison, Leslie A357
Harrison, Keith A423
Harrison, Gator A452
Harrison, A. Marc A462
Harrison, Scott A482
Harrison, Winifred A525
Harrison, Peter A623
Harrison, Dan L A630
Harrison, Justin A677
Harrison, Kelton A760
Harrison, Robert A804
Harrison, A. Marc A824
Harrison, Kent A855
Harrison, Jason A859
Harrison, Bo A861
Harrison, Linda A933
Harrison, Brandon P104
Harrison, Robert S. P159

Harrison, Kimberly P229
Harrison, A. Marc P256
Harrison, Matthew P262
Harrison, Patrick P337
Harrison, Dean P388
Harrison, A. Marc P561
Harrison, Hal P581
Harrison, Wayne P618
Harrison, Don P625
Harrison, Keith P637
Harrison, Marianne W247
Harrison, M. Ponder E10
Harrison, Barry E72
Harrison, Olga E105
Harrison, Leslie E175
Harrison, Thomas E234
Harrison, Steven B. E291
Harrison, Peter E313
Harrison, Matthew E330
Harrison, Kelton E374
Harrod, Tricia A470
Harrod, Lawrence A879
Harrod, Laurence A879
Harrod, James P461
Harrop, Thomas P616
Harry, Roger P369
Harshaw, Andy W33
Harshbarger, Catherine A117
Harshbarger, Catherine P61
Harston, Renee A462
Harston, Renee P256
Hart, Shannon A108
Hart, Christopher A112
Hart, Steven A114
Hart, Craig A132
Hart, Amy A219
Hart, Angela A347
Hart, Kevin A374
Hart, Christina A512
Hart, Mark J. A640
Hart, Laura A695
Hart, R. Rick A717
Hart, Sharon E. Donovan A783
Hart, Tom A791
Hart, David A846
Hart, Allen A852
Hart, Craig A855
Hart, Brett J. A864
Hart, Gregory L. (Greg) A864
Hart, Will A902
Hart, Michael P45
Hart, Joy P378
Hart, Charles P439
Hart, Charles E P445
Hart, Sharon Y. P456
Hart, Tom P535
Hart, Brent P605
Hart, Joy P629
Hart, Stephen P. W53
Hart, Eric H. E33
Hart, Steven E37
Hart, Amy E87
Hart, Angela E167
Hart, Richard E196
Hart, R. Rick E351
Hart, Doug E433
Hart, Brett E448
Hartert, Daniel W61
Hartery, Nicky W122
Hartfield, Jerry A855
Hartford, James M P659
Hartigan, Eric P541
Hartings, Benjamin J A345
Hartings, Benjamin J E166
Hartke, Raymond P49
Hartke, Gerhardt P318
Hartl, Thomas A574
Hartley, Karen A61
Hartley, Jerry A329
Hartley, Andrew A380
Hartley, Cynthia A769
Hartley, Regina A871
Hartley, Cynthia E380
Hartman, John S A83
Hartman, Bret A198

Hartman, Cathy A538
Hartman, Ursula A640
Hartman, Carl A754
Hartman, Art A789
Hartman, Barb A806
Hartman, Richard T. (Rick) A837
Hartman, Michael A933
Hartman, Scott V P284
Hartman, Donna P298
Hartman, Carl P484
Hartman, Philip S. (Phil) P549
Hartman, Barb E399
Hartmann, Michael A224
Hartmann, Ronald A356
Hartmann, Greg A423
Hartmann, William L. (Bill) A491
Hartmann, Margot A641
Hartmann, Kelly P212
Hartmann, Margot P407
Hartmann, Peter P677
Hartmann, Judith W154
Hartmann, Nancy E212
Hartnett, Patricia A162
Hartnett, John R. A453
Hartnett, Chad M P231
Hartnett, Mary Pat P512
Hartnett, W.J. (Bill) W196
Hartnett, Patricia E61
Hartnett, Michael J. E345
Hartog, Byran Den P439
Harton, H. Lynn A866
Harton, H. Lynn E417
Hartpence, Melissa P613
Hartsell, Ruth P465
Hartsfield, Russell A818
Hartsfield, Lois P38
Hartsfield, Russell E403
Hartshorn, Michael J. A731
Hartung, John R. (Jack) A192
Hartung, Stefan W75
Harty, Harriet K. A35
Harty, Mike A161
Harty, Nick A866
Harty, Nick E418
Hartz, Gregory J. A838
Hartz, Scott S. W247
Hartz, Jan E171
Hartzel, Cynthia E51
Hartzell, Robert A31
Hartzell, Robert E8
Hartzer, Brian C. W424
Harvey, J Dale A50
Harvey, Staci A167
Harvey, David C. A249
Harvey, Anna L. A592
Harvey, Gene A605
Harvey, Zelton A772
Harvey, Dave A773
Harvey, J Dale P31
Harvey, Jonathan P180
Harvey, Stephen P248
Harvey, Sara P309
Harvey, Anna L. P370
Harvey, Ken P380
Harvey, Gerald P493
Harvey, Len P541
Harvey, Brent F. P582
Harvey, Gayla P615
Harvey, Larry K. E5
Harvey, Seth E91
Harvey, David C. E108
Harvey, Zelton E383
Harvill, Howard P209
Harvill, Kim P375
Harward, Randy A862
Harward, Kay P597
Harwell, Ed A442
Harwell, David A717
Harwell, Scott P546
Harwell, David E351
Harwood, Randall R. A396
Harwood, Dave P308
Hasan, Muhammad A484
Hasbrouck, Margaret P26
Hasegawa, Lise A559

COMBINED HOOVER'S HANDBOOK INDEX OF EXECUTIVES

Hasegawa, Takuro W252
Hasegawa, Koji W258
Hasegawa, Yoshisuke W348
Hasegawa, Yasuchika W381
Hasenmiller, Stephen A432
Haser, H. William A813
Hash, John A467
Hashimoto, Takashi W269
Hashimoto, Masahiro W368
Hashmoto, Eiji W280
Hasimoglu, Tamer W222
Haskell, Simon A514
Haskell, Simon A516
Haskell, Simon P293
Haskell, Jeanne P450
Haskett, David A379
Haslam, Steve E307
Hasner, Adam E185
Hasold-Schilter, Marianne W53
Hasper, Greg A672
Hass, Brenda P212
Hass, Josh E102
Hassani, Ali P383
Hassanin, Ahmed P626
Hassard, Charles P174
Hasse, Patricia A483
Hasse, William A P354
Hassebrock, David P277
Hasselbarth, William C. P17
Hassell, Gerald L. A111
Hassett, Joseph (John) A67
Hassett, Tom A265
Hassett, Gerry W173
Hassfurther, Thomas A. (Tom) A637
Hassing, Ben A902
Hassler, Gregg A905
Hassler, Paul E. E322
Hassman, Vicki P174
Hassmann, Jill P406
Hast, Marty A748
Hasten, Laurie P P360
Hastie, Brent A215
Hasting, Reed A587
Hasting, Willeen P335
Hastings, Scott A113
Hastings, Warren A170
Hastings, Lee A267
Hastings, Douglas P574
Hastings, Scott E36
Haswell, Mike A723
Hatate, Mark A903
Hatch, Jessica A540
Hatch, Michael A567
Hatch, Ed P83
Hatch, Michael E284
Hatcher, Kristi A86
Hatcher, Desiree A319
Hatcher, Jim A888
Hatcher, Melanie P101
Hatcher, Doreen P273
Hatcher, Melanie P377
Hatcher, Kristi E27
Hatcher, Jim E425
Hatchett, Judy A311
Hatchett, Judy P199
Hatfield, Josh E219
Hathaisattayapong, Rewat W95
Hathaway, Scot C. A275
Hathaway, Tammy A512
Hathaway, Stephanie P116
Hathaway, Stephen J P237
Hathaway, William R P343
Hathi, Neesha A746
Hathy, Tim A723
Hatmaker, Brian A229
Hatt, Eileen A749
Hatt, Eileen E367
Hattem, Marita P49
Hatter, Patricia E342
Hattey, Steve A222
Hatton, Teresa A84
Hatton, Amy A626
Hatton, Teresa P47
Hattori, Atsushi W215
Hatzenbuehler, Anthony E98

Hau, Robert W. (Bob) A352
Hauck, Ryan A512
Haudrich, John A616
Hauenstein, Glen W. A262
Hauer, Norma A216
Hauer, Patsy A902
Hauersperger, Joe A383
Hauersperger, Joe E186
Haug, Laural P163
Haugen, Robert W. A250
Haugen, Darren A330
Haugen, John A376
Haugen, Robert A451
Haugen, Barbara Hayden P521
Haugen, Darren E152
Haugen, David E180
Haugh, Samantha A104
Haught, Deanna A567
Haught, Jim A913
Haught, Deanna E283
Haught, Jim E438
Haugli, Brian A405
Hauk, Jeff E126
Haulman, Jean A880
Haulman, Jean P640
Haun, Michael A139
Haun, Michael P93
Haun, Dennis M P140
Hauner, Axel A842
Haupert, Sue A867
Haupert, John M P219
Haupt, Helen P563
Hauser, David A474
Hauser, Mark J P65
Hausfeld, Jackie P128
Haushalter, Todd A562
Hausman, William A711
Hausman, Rick A924
Hausman, Rick P211
Hausman, William P444
Hausman, Alice P546
Hausmann, Jena P127
Hausmann, Robert C. (Bob) E453
Havalotti, Jessica A57
Havalotti, Jessica P33
Havard, Robert A479
Havel, John A550
Havel, John P319
Havelock, Kevin W408
Havelock, Kevin W409
Haven, Kelly P252
Havener, Wendy A112
Havenga, Barb P486
Haverkamp, Michael F P81
Haverlock, Scott A75
Haverlock, Scott E133
Havern, Lindsay A658
Haverstick, Donald A922
Haverstick, Donald P671
Haverty, Hunter A198
Haverty-Stacke, Dylan A54
Havey, Adam R. E126
Haviland, Christophe A934
Havlisch, Rebecca A847
Havlisch, Rebecca P606
Haw, Kate P497
Hawes, Adrienne A929
Hawes, Adrienne E449
Hawk, Ken A910
Hawk, Dan P157
Hawken, Jeffrey C. E245
Hawkes, Troy A36
Hawkes, Geoffrey A675
Hawkes, Geoffrey P428
Hawkins, Amy A138
Hawkins, Amy A157
Hawkins, James jay A189
Hawkins, Ken A228
Hawkins, Steve J. A343
Hawkins, Richard J A374
Hawkins, John A413
Hawkins, Jay A565
Hawkins, Scott A685
Hawkins, Randall A704
Hawkins, Mark J. A739

Hawkins, Amy A856
Hawkins, Alphonso A884
Hawkins, J. Michael A894
Hawkins, Rodney A924
Hawkins, Krista P76
Hawkins, Amy P91
Hawkins, Jennifer P133
Hawkins, Robert P153
Hawkins, Linda P160
Hawkins, Linda P184
Hawkins, Jeff P291
Hawkins, Ronald E P295
Hawkins, Amy P614
Hawkins, J. Michael P651
Hawkins, Barbara P659
Hawkins, Andy E110
Hawkins, Steve J. E163
Hawkins, Patrick H. E201
Hawkins, John E205
Hawkins, John E284
Hawks, Howard L A810
Hawks, Lisa A877
Hawks, Howard L. P92
Hawks, Howard L P546
Hawksley, Lee A740
Hawley, Amanda A528
Hawley, Rick P210
Hawley, Sue P536
Hawley, Chad P555
Hawley, Austin E112
Haworth, Kirk A173
Haworth, Albert E338
Hawthorne, Bruce A446
Hawthorne, Will P120
Hawthorne, Rick P204
Hay, Lewis (Lew) A354
Hay, Niall A649
Hayakawa, Etsuo W268
Hayakawa, Shigeru W400
Hayashi, Madelyn A576
Hayashi, Toshihiro W169
Hayashi, Haruki W257
Hayashi, Takeshi W279
Hayashi, Takuji W346
Hayashi, Madelyn E338
Hayashida, Eiji W210
Hayden, John A715
Hayden, Thomas A727
Hayden, Don P430
Hayden, Thomas P453
Hayden, Donna P616
Hayden, Michael W389
Hayden-Cook, Melissa P489
Haydon, John B. A698
Haydon, Trey A704
Haydon, Emily P389
Hayduk, Ken A373
Hayek, Andrew P. P475
Hayes, John A. A103
Hayes, Brian A167
Hayes, Rejji P. A209
Hayes, Matt A228
Hayes, James M A228
Hayes, John A265
Hayes, James A320
Hayes, Maria Reeves A465
Hayes, Robin A478
Hayes, Joy A484
Hayes, Jeff A550
Hayes, Jennifer A596
Hayes, Kathleen A651
Hayes, Holly A704
Hayes, Kristin A747
Hayes, Nicole A752
Hayes, Francine A784
Hayes, Christina A804
Hayes, Tom A835
Hayes, Thomas P. (Tom) A855
Hayes, Todd M. A872
Hayes, Gregory J. A875
Hayes, Leanne A881
Hayes, Janet A921
Hayes, Michele P60
Hayes, Caroline P259
Hayes, Jeff P319

Hayes, William (Billy) P386
Hayes, Paul P433
Hayes, Jacqui P456
Hayes, Deborah (Debbie) P560
Hayes, Brett P633
Hayes, John E102
Hayes, Kathleen E329
Hayes, John E349
Hayes, William M. (Bill) E360
Hayes, Leanne E421
Hayes-badon, Connie A937
Hayford, Michael D A585
Haygood, Vanessa P578
Hayhurst, Michael A303
Hayhurst, James B. A865
Hayhurst, James B. E416
Hayim, Ilan W54
Haymond, Sherri A544
Hayne, Bill P563
Haynes, Jana A434
Haynes, Joan E. A609
Haynes, Brian A715
Haynes, Lawrence P57
Haynes, Joan E. P387
Haynes, Jim P425
Haynes, Jenna P489
Haynes, William J. E372
Haynie, Tammy A200
Haynie, Mary P677
Hayon, Jack P191
Hays, Dan A165
Hays, Ed A215
Hays, Von A222
Hays, Paul A236
Hays, Matthew A405
Hays, Robert C A460
Hays, Andrew A663
Hays, Lindstrom P98
Hays, Dan P108
Hays, Chuck P305
Hays, Charles P305
Hays, Ryan M P625
Hays, Sara L. E23
Hays, Tony E357
Hays, Nadine E429
Hayslip, Paul P15
Haytaian, Peter D. A69
Haythornthwaite, Richard (Rick) W95
Hayutin, David L P534
Hayward, Jeffery R. A312
Hayward, Michelle A784
Hayward, Lani A860
Hayward, Thomas P584
Hayward, Anthony B. (Tony) W172
Haywood, Cathy A713
Haywood, Trent P89
Haywood, Ken P242
Hazard, Stephen A709
Hazard, Sharon A835
Hazard, Stephen P442
Hazboun, Alex A522
Hazel, Mark A147
Hazelip, Rex P278
Hazelton, Brian E443
Hazelwood, Lauris N P476
Hazen, Samuel N. (Sam) A410
Hazen, Andrea P437
Hazinski, Rich A63
Hazlin, John A218
He, Dennis A793
He, Yong W190
Heacock, David A. A275
Head, Robert A866
Head, Betty P511
Head, Julie P610
Head, Robert E417
Headley, Todd E342
Headrick, Chris A492
Heady, Christopher (Chris) A137
Heald, Christopher B E68
Healey, Melanie A423
Healey, Don A686
Healey, Megan A804
Healton, Cheryl G. A592
Healton, Cheryl G. P370

COMBINED HOOVER'S HANDBOOK INDEX OF EXECUTIVES

A = AMERICAN BUSINESS
E = EMERGING COMPANIES
P = PRIVATE COMPANIES
W = WORLD BUSINESS

Healy, Cornelius A69
Healy, Luke A246
Healy, Denis A356
Healy, Tom A390
Healy, Mark A428
Healy, Russell A447
Healy, James A451
Healy, Colm A695
Healy, Peter P79
Healy, Greg P93
Healy, Dan P198
Healy, Anthony J. W270
Healy, Luke E105
Heaney, Bradley G A461
Heaney, Joe A559
Heaney, Kevin P592
Heaphy, Leslie P276
Heaps, John W432
Heard, Mike A212
Heard, Peter A845
Hearn, David A353
Hearn, Sabrina L P164
Hearn, David P204
Hearn, Shandlyn P551
Hearne, Darrell A236
Hearne, David A755
Hearne, David E369
Hearrell, Jeff P379
Heart, Cherri A171
Heasley, Teena A492
Heater, Nicole A716
Heath, Chad A85
Heath, Ross A880
Heath, Christine P130
Heath, George P194
Heath, Ross P640
Heath, Chad E27
Heath, Larry E53
Heather, Roach A761
Heatherington, Jeff P199
Heaton, Richard A199
Heaton, Gregory L. (Greg) A357
Heaton, Gregg A645
Heaton, Tracey A895
Heaton, Andrew P364
Heaton, Gregory L. (Greg) E175
Heavner, Laurie P35
Hebard, Barbara P608
Heber, Amy A177
Hebert, Jason A852
Hebert, Teresa P157
Hebert-myrick, Debra E256
Hecht, William F. P289
Hechtner, Mike A213
Hechtner, Mike P143
Heck, Christopher B. (Chris) A281
Heck, Matthew A746
Heck, Scott A871
Heck, Lee A880
Heck, John P589
Heck, Lee P640
Hecker, Rob A882
Heckler, Lynn P432
Heckler, Chris P581
Heckman, Pam A481
Heckman, Michael P624
Hecox, Penny A180
Hector, Joshua P552
Heda, Bhushan A471
Hedderich, Michael A450
Hedgebeth, Reggie A533
Hedgebeth, Reginald A533
Hedgebeth, Reginald D A533
Hedgebeth, Reginald D. (Reggie) P509
Hedgepeth, Samuel P196
Hedgepeth, Blair P653
Hedgepeth, William L. (Bill) E368
Hedges, Kari P89
Hedges, Kathleen P513

Hedgpeth, Amanda P291
Hedien, Jason P356
Hediger, Gary A559
Hedin, Maria W377
Hedley, Christopher G P408
Hedley, Mark E143
Hedman, Britt A510
Hedman, Britt P290
Hedrick, Stephen A872
Hee, Lee Won W192
Heeman, Jaime P240
Heenan, Palmer T. A353
Heenan, Palmer T. E173
Heersink, Ewout R. (Eve) W296
Hees, Bernardo V. A496
Hefel, Victoria A867
Hefel, Rachael P309
Hefferle, Brian A319
Heffernan, Edward J. (Ed) A34
Heffernan, Terri-beth A850
Heffernan, John H P58
Heffington, John A175
Heffler, Mava K. A292
Hefflinger, Jeffrey A90
Heffron, Tom A902
Hefter, Marcia Z. A150
Hefter, Marcia Z. E50
Hegarty, Kevin P. A711
Hegarty, Kieran A816
Hegarty, Kevin P. P444
Hegde, Ashok W294
Hegde, Sharath S. E230
Hegeler, Fran A16
Heger, Mary P. A46
Heger, Tom P260
Heggen, Elmar W66
Hegi, Maria A759
Hegi, Maria E373
Hegstrom, Scott A821
Hegwood, Neil A569
Hehn, Gunther P411
Heib, Adam P492
Heiba, Ibrahim A285
Heidari, Farnaz A722
Heidari, Faye P398
Heidel, Cindy A326
Heidi, Salyer P615
Heidingsfelder, Rachel A575
Heidrich, Kevin E316
Heidrick, Richard A227
Heidrick, Richard E90
Heidt, Alex A501
Heidtbrink, Scott P274
Heier, Timothy C. A746
Heijden, R. L. P. J. van der W212
Heikkila, Seth A482
Heil, Tim A259
Heil, Susan P34
Heil, Kevan P303
Heilbron, Jim A28
Heilman, Chandra P. P497
Heim, Michael A. A803
Heiman, Scott A504
Heiman, Scott E251
Heimbach, Liz P657
Heimback, John A530
Heimberger, Brandon P588
Heimburger, David P465
Heimes, Terry J. A586
Heimes, Terry J. E301
Heimeshoff, Volker A902
Hein, Jon A85
Hein, Leland J. (Lee) A315
Hein, Chris P81
Hein, Dan P410
Hein, Jon E26
Hein, David E132
Heine, Uwe A502
Heine, Robert A518
Heine, Chris E278
Heineke, Wendy E325
Heinicke, John A16
Heiniluoma, Roger P135
Heinrich, Daniel A103
Heinrich, Josh A859

Heinrich, Gregor E185
Heinson, Christopher D. E363
Heintz, Ginger A325
Heintz, Karen A726
Heintz, Karen P453
Heintz, Elizabeth B P467
Heintz, Elizabeth P467
Heintze, Michael P552
Heintzman, David P. A788
Heintzman, David P. E389
Heinz, Karl A347
Heinz, Michael W59
Heinzelmann, Nick A520
Heinzmann, David W. E258
Heise, Arthur G. (Art) A85
Heise, Richard A224
Heise, Angela L. A509
Heise, Rus P179
Heise, Arthur G. (Art) E26
Heisel, James P147
Heiser, Julia A522
Heiser, Karen P359
Heiser, Robert P630
Heisey, John L. P119
Heisey, Shirley P573
Heisey, Jennifer P625
Heisey, Kristen E83
Heishman, Dennis P. A621
Heishman, Phoebe A790
Heishman, Dennis P. E311
Heishman, Phoebe E390
Heisler, Tom A252
Heissenbuttel, William E360
Heist, John A702
Heist, Matt P39
Heitin, Mark A835
Heizer, Jan P465
Heizmann, Jochem W418
Hejl, Jeremy A329
Hejmadi, Daaman A461
Hekmaty, Cyrus A452
Hekster, Odette P424
Helal, Ivette A833
Helber, Tim A621
Helber, Andreas W64
Helber, Tim E311
Helding, Erik M. A212
Heldman, Chris A571
Heldman, Susan P477
Hele, John C. R. A559
Heleen, Mark L. A583
Heleen, Mark L A583
Helfer, Peter E218
Helfgott, Alan A530
Helgerson, Bryce P288
Helgesen, Roald P16
Helle, Joel A251
Hellebust, Solveig W140
Hellebust, Kent E93
Hellem, Bob A232
Heller, Stacie A63
Heller, Adam A125
Heller, Stephanie A319
Heller, Richard A403
Heller, Paul G. A444
Heller, Marc A596
Heller, Jeffrey A604
Heller, Gene A744
Heller, Paul P12
Heller, Donald E. P339
Heller, Elizabeth P382
Heller, Andra P611
Heller, Matt P642
Hellighausen, John P540
Helliker, Carol A180
Helling, Larry J. A693
Helling, Larry J. E341
Hellman, Peter S A120
Hellman, Thomas A533
Hellmann, Chris A215
Hellmich, Thomas P467
Helm, Ron A204
Helm, Bob A373
Helm, Ariel A437
Helm, James A540

Helm, Lucy Lee A779
Helm, Larry L. A818
Helm, Cathy P497
Helm, Roshonda P550
Helm, Larry L. E403
Helmandollar, Carole P127
Helmer, Richard P397
Helmerick, Shelley A746
Helmers, Maik D. E253
Helminiak, Deanna A85
Helminiak, Deanna E26
Helmreich, Anne P549
Helmrich, Klaus W353
Helms, Lloyd W. (Bill) A301
Helms, Cory A301
Helms, Heather A713
Helms, Tabitha A866
Helms, Janet E172
Helms, Tabitha E417
Helmuth, Heather P150
Helon, Ryan A781
Helow, Ronald A432
Helsel, Christopher A392
Helt, Peter A112
Hem, Pannah A115
Hem, Pannah E38
Hemade, Sagar A813
Hemberger, Lawson P340
Hembry, Daryl A491
Hemelryck, Tom Van A903
Hemenway, Wanda A219
Hemenway, Wanda E87
Heminger, Gary R. A534
Heminger, Gary A673
Hemingway-Marion, Sonya A403
Hemink, David C. E63
Hemker, David J. (Dave) A505
Hemler, Alan J A658
Hemmer, Tara A905
Hemmingsen, Claus V. W1
Hempen, Rande A170
Hemphill, Teresa A160
Hemphill, Stuart R. A770
Hemphill, Norine P127
Hemphill, Todd E174
Hempton, Sue A348
Hempton, Sue E169
Hemstead, Louise P158
Henbest, Bob P195
Hench, Amy P420
Henck, Dan P464
Henckel, Joel A544
Henderschedt, Robert A14
Henderschedt, Robert P6
Henderson, Greg A67
Henderson, Chris A133
Henderson, Mark A155
Henderson, Brantley A165
Henderson, Terrance A222
Henderson, Theodore A271
Henderson, Douglas A329
Henderson, Richie A442
Henderson, Paula A530
Henderson, Mike A533
Henderson, Leah A683
Henderson, Susan A722
Henderson, Bob A842
Henderson, Robert S. A842
Henderson, Adam A885
Henderson, Roger P21
Henderson, Bill P100
Henderson, Bruce A P176
Henderson, Cecilia P205
Henderson, Jeff P251
Henderson, Jane P377
Henderson, Harry P489
Henderson, James P641
Henderson, Jason W187
Henderson, Ralph S. E21
Henderson, Mark E54
Henderson, Michael E415
Hendery, Suzanne P72
Hendon, Terry A228
Hendren, Bradley A115
Hendren, Mike A664

COMBINED HOOVER'S HANDBOOK INDEX OF EXECUTIVES

Hendren, Bradley E37
Hendren, Mike E333
Hendrian, Catherine A209
Hendrick, Marcia A414
Hendrick, John A520
Hendrick, Bryan A718
Hendrick, Stephen E144
Hendrick, Bryan E354
Hendricks, John A175
Hendricks, Mike A358
Hendricks, Thomas A467
Hendricks, Steve A737
Hendricks, Martin A813
Hendricks, Irene P159
Hendricks, William A. (Andy) P486
Hendricks, Thomas E P546
Hendricks, Mike E176
Hendricks, Steve E361
Hendricksen, Matthew A293
Hendrickson, Nancy A836
Hendrikse, Pieter A481
Hendrikse, Danny A658
Hendrix, Heidi A608
Hendry, Andrew A218
Hendry, Carol A228
Hendry, John A. E212
Heneberry, Richard A36
Heneghan, Daniel A501
Heneghan, James A605
Heneghan, Steven P574
Heng, Jiunn P547
Heng, Ming W173
Hengst, Dean A304
Hengst, Carla E255
Hengster, Ingrid W225
Henigin, Susan A337
Henigin, Susan E158
Henin, Jonathan A767
Henk, Michael A660
Henk, Michael P416
Henke, Daniel F A196
Henke, Mary-Margaret A915
Henkel, Robert J A84
Henkel, Robert J P47
Henkel, Thomas P56
Henkel, Lisa P285
Henley, Robert W. A614
Henley, Jeffrey O E632
Henley, Chandra A863
Henley, Diane P246
Henley, Dale P439
Henley, David P622
Henley, Kyle P636
Henly, Julie A836
Henn, Anthony A195
Henn, Tony A195
Hennelly, Ben J P57
Hennelly, Patricia P298
Hennenfent, Paul A5
Hennenfent, Joel P608
Hennessey, Karen P296
Hennessey, Ruth P515
Hennessy, Patricia A200
Hennessy, John L. A510
Hennessy, John A525
Hennessy, Lisa A680
Hennessy, Ray A692
Hennessy, Paul A925
Hennessy, James J. P206
Hennessy, John L. P290
Hennessy, Michael J. P551
Hennessy, John E143
Hennessy, Paul E445
Hennigan, Nathan A104
Hennigan, Mike A534
Henning, James P. (Jim) A281
Henning, Brian A621
Henning, Glenn P404
Henning, Brian E311
Henninger, Tadd J A674
Henningfield, Nancy A347
Henningfield, Nancy E168
Henningsen, Dan A494
Henoch, Malcolm P74
Henrich, David A881

Henrich, William L P596
Henrich, David E421
Henrichsen, Kim A462
Henrichsen, Kim P256
Henrickson, Pamela Q. P633
Henriksson, Mats W167
Henrot, Fran-§ois W323
Henry, Maurice A87
Henry, Kelly A294
Henry, Nicholas A332
Henry, Douglass A436
Henry, Brian A463
Henry, Maria G. A493
Henry, Daniel A548
Henry, Christopher A562
Henry, Peter B. A592
Henry, Jerome A621
Henry, Christopher A791
Henry, Mildred A850
Henry, Jeff A893
Henry, Celia P32
Henry, Maurice P50
Henry, Michael P93
Henry, Mark P168
Henry, Richard A. (Rich) P318
Henry, Lori P356
Henry, Peter B. P370
Henry, Donna Price P442
Henry, Jake P464
Henry, Christopher P535
Henry, Geneva P569
Henry, Dana P588
Henry, Brent L. P592
Henry, Gretchen P630
Henry, Mary Anne P646
Henry, Mike W53
Henry, Mike W68
Henry, Mike W69
Henry, Kenneth R. (Ken) W270
Henry, Pierre W358
Henry, Kimberley E49
Henry, Charles W E120
Henry, Jerome E312
Henry, Todd E418
Hensel, Robert A200
Henseler, Glenn D A706
Hensey, Bernard A140
Henshaw, Carrie A313
Henshaw, Vern P28
Henshaw, Carrie E144
Hensing, John A117
Hensing, John P61
Henslee, Gregory L. (Greg) A615
Hensley, Pat A448
Hensley, Dan A467
Hensley, Scott A606
Hensley, Ed A909
Hensley, Charles P153
Hensley, Pat P247
Hensley, Richard A. P334
Hensley, Harvey P461
Hensley, Robin E393
Hensley, Ed E436
Henson, Curtis A25
Henson, Robert A224
Henson, Cindi A323
Henson, Doug A756
Henson, Christopher L. (Chris) A849
Henson, Erica A902
Henson, Meghan A. A934
Henson, Curtis P14
Henson, Vaughn P511
Henson, Thomas O P587
Hentzen, Peter P623
Henwood, Patricia A642
Henwood, Patricia P407
Henze, Daryl A470
Henzi, Scott A654
Hepburn, Cc A498
Hepburn, Aaron A924
Hepburn, Matthew A924
Hepburn, Christopher P. (Chris) E412
Hepner, Adrian E118
Heppel, Gina A772
Heppel, Gina E383

Heppenstall, C. Talbot P643
Heppenstall, C Talbot P643
Hepworth, Simon W84
Herbel, Vern D. A389
Herbert, Chris A25
Herbert, Toni A270
Herbert, James H. A349
Herbert, Courtney A530
Herbert, Dan A847
Herbert, Chris P14
Herbert, Greg P54
Herbert, Michael P74
Herbert, Clayton W373
Herbert, Melissa E302
Herbert, James L. E302
Herbert, Dan E410
Herbes, William F. (Bill) E33
Herbes, Bill E33
Herbst, Gary P274
Herbst, Lawrence P565
Herd, Callie P2
Herd, Carl G. P64
Herde, Adriana Bokel E326
Herdener, Anthony M P383
Herdiech, Edward K. (Ed) E259
Heredia, Tony A804
Hereford, James P524
Herena, Monique R. A111
Herencia, Roberto R. A333
Hereng, Patrick W398
Hergenroether, Craig P67
Herget, Stephen A152
Herget, Stephen P98
Herington, Dave A3
Herlehy, Ann Harie P22
Herlin, Robert S. E139
Herling, Alfred W135
Herlocker, Jon A897
Herman, Martin A200
Herman, Mark I. A210
Herman, Robert A. (Bob) A662
Herman, Matthew A663
Herman, Scott A893
Herman, Ron P30
Herman, Linda P161
Herman, Greg P254
Herman, Amy P494
Herman, Jay P604
Hermance, Frank A857
Hermandev-Lichto, Javier P501
Hermann, Christopher A327
Hermann, Valérie A701
Hermann, Bill P2
Hermann, Chris P18
Hermann, Colleen P308
Hermann, Steve P647
Hermann, Alex W348
Hermanson, Karen P351
Hermel, Oren A877
Hermelin, Brian E392
Hermes, Joe A774
Hermida, Adam A137
Hermiz, Laith M. E6
Hermon, Christopher J. A834
Hermonat, Karl A877
Hernandez, Calvin A109
Hernandez, John A114
Hernandez, Laurie A119
Hernandez, Cynthia A200
Hernandez, Abdon A236
Hernandez, Mariela A246
Hernandez, Martin A248
Hernandez, Carlos M. A355
Hernandez, Patrice A415
Hernandez, Yogi A441
Hernandez, Dolores A449
Hernandez, Wendie A528
Hernandez, Enrique (Rick) A548
Hernandez, Dodie A621
Hernandez, Emmanuel A628
Hernandez, Anthony A713
Hernandez, Michelle A727
Hernandez, Dennis A797
Hernandez, Oscar A888

Hernandez, Victor A902
Hernandez, Debbie P75
Hernandez, George B. P82
Hernandez, Zoyla P125
Hernandez, Marco P239
Hernandez, Mary P253
Hernandez, Amber P253
Hernandez, Carol P354
Hernandez, Enrique P357
Hernandez, Michelle P453
Hernandez, Linda P456
Hernandez, Olga M P469
Hernandez, Awilda P567
Hernandez, Beatrice P588
Hernandez, Tomas W144
Hernandez, John E37
Hernandez, Mariela E105
Hernandez, Martin E107
Hernandez, Patrice E209
Hernandez, Dolores E220
Hernandez, Roland E424
Hernandez, Oscar E425
Hernandez-blades, Catherine A19
Hernas, Carl A801
Hernberg, Philip A. P78
Herndon, Wendy L A19
Herndon, Lori P51
Hernquist, Thomas A416
Hernandez, Juan G. A355
Hernandez, Luis W91
Herold, Rich A595
Heron, Doug P187
Heron, W. David P389
Heron, Dwight P644
Heroux, Ben E47
Herr, Frederick M A319
Herr, Adam A329
Herr, Tracy P176
Herr, Scott E264
Herr-Wilczek, Teri P310
Herrema, Gregory J. (Greg) A832
Herrema, Greg A833
Herrema, Donald J. E245
Herrenbruck, David W A329
Herrera, Milciades A115
Herrera, Fernando A686
Herrera, Ana P588
Herrera, Gina P665
Herrera, Jes--s V. Gonzalez W91
Herrera, Milciades E37
Herrera, Tammy E105
Herrero, Jose A355
Herrick, Patricia A215
Herrick, Brian A492
Herrick, Glen W. A557
Herrick, Doug P603
Herrick, James E42
Herrick, Glen W. E281
Herridge, David A692
Herrin, Debbie P672
Herring, Julie A1
Herring, Jim A79
Herring, Kip A536
Herring, Jamie A575
Herring, Thomas A922
Herring, Jennifer P235
Herring, Marsha P486
Herring, David J. P634
Herring, Thomas P671
Herring, Julie E1
Herrington, Doug C A215
Herrington, Matthew E141
Herrman, Ernie A835
Herrman, Eddie P254
Herrmann, Tracey A272
Herrmann, Gunnar A360
Herrmann, Bernie J. A716
Herrmann, Tom A897
Herron, Kevin A379
Herron, Dallas I. A386
Herron, Olivia A711
Herron, C. Keith A712
Herron, Paul A891
Herron, Cherry P144
Herron, Olivia P444

COMBINED HOOVER'S HANDBOOK INDEX OF EXECUTIVES

A = AMERICAN BUSINESS
E = EMERGING COMPANIES
P = PRIVATE COMPANIES
W = WORLD BUSINESS

Herron, Brent P595
Herron, Dallas I. E188
Herron, J. Brendan E200
Herron, Bonnie L. E234
Herschel, Tom A893
Herschman, Ray A185
Hersey, Jonathan P356
Hershberger, Rodney (Rod) E332
Hershberger, Benji E332
Hershey, Dale R. A22
Hershey, Dale R. P11
Hershey, Milton P342
Hersker, Shannon E433
Herskovitz, Rachel A452
Herteg, Diane A782
Herteg, Diane P525
Hertogh, Mark De P422
Hertz, Sally A481
Hertz, Sandy P313
Hertzog, Rory A530
Hervey, Michael D P299
Herweck, Peter W344
Herwig, Chris A859
Herzberg, Caspar W344
Herziger-Snider, Kathy A352
Herzmark, Paula P179
Herzog, Katie A135
Herzog, Laura A930
Herzog, Don E256
Heseltine, Cathy A779
Heskin, John A200
Heslin, Kevin A196
Heslop, Steve A794
Hess, William H. (Hal) A59
Hess, Jeffrey A60
Hess, Rick D. A67
Hess, Karen A259
Hess, John B. A418
Hess, Carol A438
Hess, Lauren A925
Hess, Jim P334
Hess, Marybeth P478
Hess, Jan P520
Hess, Steve P597
Hess, Steve P626
Hess, Marc W137
Hess, Beat W. W230
Hess, Derek E72
Hess, Lauren E445
Hesse, Thomas W66
Hessekiel, Jeffrey J. E140
Hesser, Gregory T P18
Hession, Eric A160
Hession, Michael A409
Hessler, Matthew A758
Hessler, Matthew E372
Hessner, Cathy E229
Hester, Kevin D. A426
Hester, David A447
Hester, Danny A665
Hester, Randy D. A682
Hester, Darin A770
Hester, Jim P415
Hester, Kevin D. E213
Hester, Danny E334
Hesterberg, Earl J. A398
Hesterbrink, Christoph A893
Hestnes, Erik P480
Heston, Mary A739
Hete, Joseph C. (Joe) E7
Hetherington, Ken A772
Hetherington, Ken E383
Hett, Matthew A50
Hetterich, F. Paul A236
Hetterich, Paul A237
Hettler, Gary A747
Hetzke, Gregor W158
Hetzler, Dustin A715
Heuberger, Celeste A325

Heuer, Steve A592
Heuer, Steve P370
Heuring, Shirley P541
Heutink, Chris W319
Heuvel, William A196
Hevrony, Nathan P58
Hewatt, Russell A113
Hewatt, Michael P220
Hewatt, Russell E36
Hewes, Donna A882
Hewes, Kim P156
Hewett, Mark A. P385
Hewitt, Robert C. A126
Hewitt, Ariel A437
Hewitt, Dennis E. A626
Hewitt, Rod A891
Hewitt, Kathryn P161
Hewitt, William P371
Hexter, Ralph J. P624
Hey-Hadavi, Judith A658
HEYA, TOSHIO W183
Heyde, Charles Von Der A663
Heydlauff, Dale E. A51
Heydlauff, Dale E P32
Heydon, Amy A53
Heyer, Richard A718
Heyer, Richard E351
Heyman, William H. (Bill) A845
Heyman, Neal A877
Heyrich, George P522
Heyrman, Tracie P31
Hezlep, John A272
Hiatt, Clare A61
Hiatt, Ruth A686
Hibbard, Keith A179
Hibbard, Richard A686
Hibbert, Brad A398
Hibbert, Brad P222
Hice, Alan A115
Hice, Alan E38
Hickerson, Marcus A425
Hickey, Scott S. A85
Hickey, Dennis J. A217
Hickey, Adam R A225
Hickey, Michael A. (Mike) A289
Hickey, Brian E. A530
Hickey, JP A713
Hickey, Renee A784
Hickey, Kevin P120
Hickey, Tim P159
Hickey, Wayne P531
Hickey, Paul R. P558
Hickey, Patricia P558
Hickey, Scott S. E26
Hickman, Phillip A85
Hickman, Angie A626
Hickman, George T. P17
Hickman, Tanya P566
Hickman, Phillip E26
Hickman, Thomas E232
Hickok, Christopher A922
Hickok, Lori A. P480
Hickok, Christopher P671
Hickox, Michelle S. A456
Hickox, Michelle S. E228
Hickox, William E319
Hicks, Weston M. A32
Hicks, Malcolm A113
Hicks, JO A224
Hicks, Andrew A446
Hicks, Lucas A446
Hicks, Kirkland L. A519
Hicks, Jeff A552
Hicks, Douglas A574
Hicks, Sherrie A664
Hicks, Phil A741
Hicks, Sarah A782
Hicks, Adam A784
Hicks, Jason A790
Hicks, Roland A890
Hicks, Charles A922
Hicks, Gilbert P56
Hicks, Tom P56
Hicks, John D P66
Hicks, Allyson P155

Hicks, Karen P187
Hicks, Dana P226
Hicks, Jeff P261
Hicks, Holly P450
Hicks, Ashley P499
Hicks, Sarah P526
Hicks, Charles P671
Hicks, Malcolm E36
Hicks, David Y. E121
Hicks, Randy E150
Hicks, Jeff E275
Hicks, Sherrie E334
Hicks, Phil E364
Hicks, Jason E389
Hidayat, Amir A191
Hideshima, Nobuya W430
Hieb, Alan P566
Hiel, Rudolph J. van der E81
Hiel, Rudolph E81
Hier, Lars A301
Hier, Lars P196
Hierholzer, John A544
Hiers, Bobby A566
Hiesinger, Heinrich W391
Hiffa, Michael P262
Higa, Jill A109
Higa, Janelle A109
Higa, Marie A199
Higashi, Mitchell A151
Higashi, Kazuhiro W321
Higbie, Allison A215
Higdon, Dan A263
Higginbotham, Herbert A16
Higginbotham, John A142
Higginbotham, Lesley B A222
Higginbotham, Cole A224
Higginbotham, Ronald A401
Higginbotham, Candace A713
Higginbotham, Robert A799
Higginbotham, John E49
Higgins, Martha T. A147
Higgins, Tom A167
Higgins, Brian A306
Higgins, Christopher A390
Higgins, Jeanne A484
Higgins, Alan A484
Higgins, Kathy A527
Higgins, Sam A530
Higgins, David A620
Higgins, Chip A664
Higgins, Amy A750
Higgins, Scott F. A844
Higgins, Thomas P72
Higgins, Zach P183
Higgins, John P204
Higgins, Jeanette P327
Higgins, Julie P330
Higgins, Trina P543
Higgins, John L. E257
Higgins, Chip E334
Higgins, Walter M. (Walt) E379
Higginson, Rick A871
Higginson, David P417
Higginson, Andrew T. W266
Higgs, Currie P263
High, Joseph C. A393
High, Michael P82
Highbear, Danielle P439
Highet, David A123
Highland, Mary Anne P515
Highley, Duane P45
Highley, Ian E258
Hight, Greg P83
Hightman, Carrie J. A600
Higuchi, Takeo W127
Hilado, Maria Teresa (Tessa) W23
Hilal, Paul C A245
Hilbelink, Garrett P204
Hilburn, Charles P623
Hildebrand, J. Bruce A340
Hildebrand, Fred A741
Hildebrand, J. Bruce E161
Hildebrand, Fred E364
Hildebrandt, Stephanie A299
Hildebrandt, Michael P478

Hilderbrand, John P188
Hildreth, Christopher A727
Hildreth, Christopher P453
Hildum, Ty A604
Hile, Chris A482
Hileman, Donald P. A339
Hileman, Donald P. E159
Hiley, Patricia A554
Hiley, Erin A571
Hiley, David B. E117
Hilferty, Daniel J. P89
Hilgart, Bret A536
Hilger, Andy A33
Hilger, Andrew A33
Hilger, James K. (Jim) A257
Hilger, Andy P24
Hilger, Andrew P24
Hilgers, Berna P184
Hilken, Lou P431
Hilkner, Cristiane A465
Hill, W. Guy A35
Hill, Guy W A36
Hill, Lloyd A45
Hill, Anne A97
Hill, Sandy A101
Hill, Bonnie G A104
Hill, Justin A125
Hill, J. Tomilson A137
Hill, Daniel A140
Hill, Jean Marie A158
Hill, Edwin J. (Ed) A171
Hill, Ed A171
Hill, Kathryn A177
Hill, Tim A191
Hill, Vicki A195
Hill, Pam A224
Hill, Todd A228
Hill, Kimberly A262
Hill, George A264
Hill, Rodney A315
Hill, Craig D. A316
Hill, Gwen A318
Hill, Julie A323
Hill, Cathy A382
Hill, Mark A385
Hill, Maureen A390
Hill, Monica A392
Hill, Gregory P. (Greg) A418
Hill, Greg A418
Hill, Tom A435
Hill, Herbert A452
Hill, Scott A A461
Hill, Scott A A462
Hill, Peter A478
Hill, Keith A478
Hill, Fran A509
Hill, Dan A569
Hill, Brian A583
Hill, Robert A584
Hill, David R. A610
Hill, Robin A623
Hill, Charles H. (Chuck) A657
Hill, Kimberly A690
Hill, Stephanie A738
Hill, Robert R. A769
Hill, Scot A833
Hill, Brian A866
Hill, Shad A867
Hill, Allen A871
Hill, Deryl A871
Hill, Stephanie A879
Hill, Becky A885
Hill, John A887
Hill, Cindy P45
Hill, Lisa P72
Hill, Tim P126
Hill, Ashley D P131
Hill, Brianne P140
Hill, Christopher R. P146
Hill, Dan P178
Hill, Steven P240
Hill, Greg P240
Hill, Lucy P240
Hill, Scott A P255
Hill, Peter P268

Hill, Keith P268
Hill, Tim P296
Hill, Melissa P316
Hill, Frederick W P364
Hill, Dan P372
Hill, Malcolm P383
Hill, Sam P422
Hill, Pat P429
Hill, Richard P467
Hill, Ryan P571
Hill, Lisa P613
Hill, Sandy E32
Hill, Susan M. E43
Hill, Tim E47
Hill, Thomas E78
Hill, David R. E81
Hill, George E172
Hill, Randy E238
Hill, Brad E282
Hill, Robin E313
Hill, W. Bryan E346
Hill, Robert R. E380
Hill, Brian E417
Hill, Shad E418
Hillard, Zach A335
Hillard, Zach E155
Hillary, Caitlin P402
Hille, James R. P549
Hillebrand, Lana L. A51
Hillebrand, James A. (Ja) A788
Hillebrand, James A. (Ja) E389
Hillebrandt, Mark A744
Hillebrecht, Chris A657
Hillemeier, A. Craig A828
Hillemeier, A. Craig P584
Hillen, Sally A649
Hillenmeyer, Taylor A175
Hiller, Todd A799
Hiller, Sharon A925
Hiller, Wolfgang E394
Hiller, Sharon E445
Hillery, Martin A81
Hilliard, Belinda P606
Hilliard, Sheffie E106
Hilliard, James E347
Hillier, Scott A. A521
Hillier, Luke P51
Hillis, Lin A444
Hillman, Michael A332
Hillman, Cindy A835
Hillman, David A893
Hillman, John P549
Hillman, Randy E256
Hillmann, Jeffrey P311
Hills, Malina M P553
Hillsman, Ann A91
Hillsman, Ann E29
Hillyer, Christopher D. P364
Hiltbrand, Ray A283
Hilton, Calvin A34
Hilton, Susan A158
Hilton, Christopher A348
Hilton, Michael A735
Hilton, Thomas P399
Hilton, James L. P442
Hilton, Christopher E169
Hiltz, Kenneth A P74
Hiltzer, James P658
Hilzenrath, Robert P375
Hilzinger, Kurt J. A441
Hilzinger, Jeffrey A. E271
Himelfarb, Richard J. A787
Himes, Andrew P251
Himes, Vicki P415
Himes, Geoff P576
Himesvicki, L P415
Himle, Karen L. E211
Himler, Bob A722
Himpe, Robrecht W33
Himpler, Donna A219
Himpler, Donna E87
Hinago, Takashi W215
Hincker, Lawrence G P112
Hinckle, Veronica A171
Hinckle, Robert D. E92

Hinckley, Robert P110
Hinckley, Gregory K. (Greg) P326
Hind, John A246
Hind, John E105
Hinde, Jason A303
Hinde, Jason E139
Hindel, Joanne A329
Hinderhofer, Kathryn A205
Hinderstein, Chase A727
Hinderstein, Chase P453
Hindley-smith, Sheron A726
Hindman, Daniel A909
Hindman, Daniel E436
Hinds, Tom A933
Hinds, Tanya P130
Hinds, Rick P615
Hinds, Steven E433
Hindsbo, Mark E22
Hinduja, Anil A364
Hine, Louise A880
Hine, Mark P295
Hine, Louise P640
Hines, Michael A175
Hines, Eric A487
Hines, Ginger A773
Hines, William H P394
Hines, Anson (Tuck) P497
Hines, Frances P511
Hines, Linda P653
Hines, Ginger E383
Hinger, Chris A701
Hingl, John P128
Hingsbergen, Michael A195
Hingston, Alex A606
Hingtgen, Tim L. A228
Hinkel, Robert W190
Hinkle, James A426
Hinkle, Eric A713
Hinkle, Allen J. P355
Hinkle, James E213
Hinkleman, Jon P358
Hinkley, Richard A199
Hinkley, Leo E41
Hinnant, Charlie A850
Hinnenkamp, Paul D. A296
Hinojosa, Heather A112
Hinojosa, Conrado E244
Hinrichs, Peter A272
Hinrichs, Joseph R. (Joe) A359
Hinrichs, Jon P103
Hinsch, Ronda P471
Hinshaw, Janice A512
Hinshaw, Ken A893
Hinson, Ed A259
Hinson, W. Ron A382
Hinson, Donald J. A415
Hinson, Jeffrey T. A924
Hinson, Donald J. E209
Hintermeister, Kim P587
Hinton, Michelle A245
Hinton, Patricia A369
Hinton, Wade A882
Hinton, Shirley P25
Hinton, Phillip P210
Hintze, Paul P331
Hintzen, Daniel A606
Hinz, Erica A519
Hiott, Niurka A115
Hiott, Craig A228
Hiott, Niurka E37
Hippe, Patricia A219
Hippe, Alan W328
Hipskind, Jennifer A647
Hipwell, Todd A264
Hirai, Kenji W169
Hirai, Kazuo (Kaz) W361
Hirakawa, Masaatsu W360
Hiraki, Justin A797
Hirako, Yuji W27
Hirakuri, Simone A497
Hirami, Nancy E448
Hirani, Imran A204
Hirano, Peter P485
Hirano, Hajime W257
Hirano, Nobuyuki W262

Hirashima, Takayuki W374
Hirata, Vernon A816
Hirbe, Richard P515
Hire, W. Jeffrey E232
Hirji, Rahim W247
Hirko, Andrew A271
Hiroe, Mutsuo W258
Hirono, Yutaka W348
Hirons, Michael L E134
Hirose, Naomi W394
Hiroshige, Cliff P47
Hirota, Yasuhito W257
Hirsch, Larry A123
Hirsch, Tracey A449
Hirsch, Barbara A469
Hirsch, Kyle A881
Hirsch, Karen P96
Hirsch, Constance P161
Hirsch, Bonnie P175
Hirsch, Jim P422
Hirsch, Tracey E220
Hirsch, Kyle E421
Hirschman, Bill A833
Hirsh, Peter A135
Hirsh, Michael P616
Hirshberg, Eric A10
Hirshberg, Gary W128
Hirst, Daniel A63
Hirst, Terri A91
Hirst, William A248
Hirst, Alistair D. A487
Hirst, Terri E29
Hirst, William E107
Hirtle, Beverly A320
Hirtz, Deborah P130
Hiscoe, Les P491
Hisel, Jerremy A528
Hishta, John P2
Hitch, Brad A188
Hitchcock, Rob A179
Hitchings, Stephen A734
Hitchner, Kenneth W. A390
Hite, Amanda A107
Hite, Bill A267
Hitt, Gregory A A275
Hitt, David A670
Hitt, Greg A902
Hitt, Charles A934
Hitt, Kathy P46
Hitter, E. Paul P334
Hiwatari, Kenji W281
Hixson, Richard A483
Hizak, Steve A865
Hizak, Steve E416
Hizkiaho, Rony W163
Hizuka, Shinichiro W374
Hjelm, Christopher T. (Chris) A498
Hladek, Keith E202
Hladki, Matt A935
Hlivka, John A325
Hnat, Jim A478
Hnat, James G. (Jim) A478
Hnatek, Gene A695
HO, Duong A8
Ho, Ivan A100
Ho, Peter S. A109
Ho, Emily A137
Ho, Raymond A218
Ho, Karen A390
Ho, Frank A722
Ho, Cynthia A804
Ho, Stephanie P337
Ho, Kevin P391
Ho, Clifton P446
Ho, Lora W380
Hoag, Erik A327
Hoag, Jay A587
Hoag, Darci A711
Hoag, Darci P444
Hoak, Tabatha P530
Hoak, David C. E226
Hoang, Lananh A54
Hobart, Lauren R. A264
Hobart, Brian E. A456
Hobart, Brian E. E228

Hobbs, Franklin W. (Fritz) A37
Hobbs, Nicholas (Nick) A442
Hobbs, Beth A665
Hobbs, Rodney A778
Hobbs, Lee P40
Hobbs, Lee G P40
Hobbs, Richard P151
Hobbs, Timothy L. P151
Hobbs, Richard F P609
Hobbs, Beth E334
Hobby, Jean E232
Hobgood, Tiffanie A325
Hobin, Peggy L. A903
Hobson, Christopher K. (Chris) A239
Hobson, Debra P147
Hobson, James M P323
Hobson, James P323
Hobson, Spencer P364
Hobson, John P610
Hocevar, Christopher J A194
Hoch, Erich A475
Hoch, Russell A935
Hochberg, Steven P80
Hochberg, Stanley P95
Hochgesang, Mark A112
Hochgesang, Luke P610
Hochheiser, Felicia A466
Hochman, Alan A84
Hochman, Rod A683
Hochman, Rod P431
Hochman, Rodney P431
Hochschild, Roger C A269
Hochstein, Craig P70
Hockenberry, Melissa P272
Hockenbroch, Karen P214
Hockenson, Tod A448
Hockenson, Tod P247
Hockers, Joseph A86
Hockers, Joseph E27
Hockey, Timothy D. (Tim) A807
Hockfield, Susan P314
Hockman, Alexander A. E309
Hoddy, Ian A800
Hodes, Jack A374
Hodes, Adam A559
Hodge, Bernice A224
Hodge, Terry A837
Hodge, Laura A867
Hodge, Chris P539
Hodge, Debra P543
Hodge, Joe P551
Hodge, Laura E418
Hodges, James R. A106
Hodges, Simon A275
Hodges, Ernest M A313
Hodges, Timothy B A651
Hodges, Ernest M P200
Hodges, James P314
Hodges, Thomas H. P386
Hodges, Sheila P389
Hodges, Joe P513
Hodges, Bruce M. W35
Hodges, Patrick E47
Hodges, Timothy B E329
Hodgins, Steve A352
Hodgkinson, Kimberly P410
Hodgkinson, Andrew E253
Hodgson, Robert A704
Hodgson, Deborah P486
Hodne, Nate A855
Hodnett, David W. P. W3
Hodous, Brian A10
Hodsden, Jennifer A200
Hodson, John W377
Hodulich, David P578
Hoechner, Bruce D. E359
Hoedl, Dean P364
Hoefer, Maury P133
Hoefler, Brenda P253
Hoehler, Rainer E110
Hoehne, Brent A715
Hoellein, Ken P19
Hoellen, Jay P546
Hoelzle, Richard A837
Hoen, Corey A885

COMBINED HOOVER'S HANDBOOK INDEX OF EXECUTIVES

A = AMERICAN BUSINESS
E = EMERGING COMPANIES
P = PRIVATE COMPANIES
W = WORLD BUSINESS

Hoencamp, Jeroen W417
Hoene, Scott A86
Hoene, William A. (Bill) Von A304
Hoene, Scott E27
Hoenger, Andreas P626
Hoepf, Jeff A205
Hoereth, Anthony A934
Hoerl, Jonathan P126
Hoerth, Scott A85
Hoerth, Scott E27
Hoesch, Josh E156
Hoesen, Peter Van P24
Hoesten, Mark P361
Hoey, Ellen A115
Hoey, Bob A465
Hoey, Amy P300
Hoey, Ellen E37
Hof, Thomas A859
Hofe, Chris P68
Hofelich, Kurt A754
Hofelich, Kurt P484
Hofemeier, Ulf A460
Hofer, Nicholas A.R. A147
Hofer, Patti A323
Hoff, Linda P288
Hoff, Jeremy E215
Hoffer, Theresa A195
Hoffler, Valerie A165
Hoffman, Roger A77
Hoffman, Steve A98
Hoffman, Julie A135
Hoffman, Peter A140
Hoffman, Mark A145
Hoffman, Nate A167
Hoffman, Christopher A222
Hoffman, Francis A325
Hoffman, David A327
Hoffman, John A479
Hoffman, Marc A538
Hoffman, Basha A559
Hoffman, Rachel A640
Hoffman, Mike A657
Hoffman, Kathleen A686
Hoffman, James D. A716
Hoffman, Alex A785
Hoffman, Susan A882
Hoffman, Dave A920
Hoffman, Angela P85
Hoffman, Bruce P220
Hoffman, Chris P305
Hoffman, Mary J P318
Hoffman, Rany P349
Hoffman, Andrew P429
Hoffman, Brad P491
Hoffman, Annette P523
Hoffman, André W328
Hoffman, Joseph E66
Hoffmann, Daryl A246
Hoffmann, Wayne A540
Hoffmann, Marc W143
Hoffmann, Daryl E105
Hoffmann, David L. (Dave) E115
Hoffmeister, Bruce A537
Hoffmeister, Jan A684
Hoffmeyer, Stig W1
Hofgard, Jefferson A140
Hofheimer, Andy E349
Hofheins, Todd A412
Hofheins, Todd A683
Hofheins, Todd P233
Hofheins, Todd P431
Hofmann, Scott A105
Hofmann, Robert A218
Hofmann, Kevin A428
Hofmann, Herb E. A525
Hofmann, Richard A554
Hofmann, Scott E34
Hofstadler, Paul P326
Hogan, Shane A34

Hogan, William Josep A58
Hogan, Mark D A120
Hogan, James D. A248
Hogan, Patrick A327
Hogan, Ed A360
Hogan, Michael P. (Mike) A371
Hogan, Rob A446
Hogan, Sean A466
Hogan, Kathleen T A565
Hogan, David P. A629
Hogan, John P A881
Hogan, Tom A893
Hogan, Noel P17
Hogan, Laurie P127
Hogan, Laurie P130
Hogan, Larry P313
Hogan, Patrick D. P442
Hogan, Gillian P549
Hogan, Erin P627
Hogan, Joseph M. (Joe) E9
Hogan, Mark D. E41
Hogan, James D. E107
Hogan, John P E421
Hogan, George W. E440
Hogarth, Hillary A209
Hogarty, Lisa P558
Hogenmiller, Mike A428
Hogg, Charlotte M. A895
Hogg, Chris W273
Hogle, Scott A452
Hoglund, Robert N. A234
Hoglund, Robert N. A235
Hogue, John A444
Hogue, Steven A657
Hogue, Herbert L P299
Hoheisel, Dirk W75
Hohmann, Paul P487
Hohmeister, Harry W136
Hohn, Diedrich P138
Hohndel, Dirk A897
Hohndorf, Mike E57
Hohnstein, John P233
Hoke, Margaret A345
Hoke, Tina A664
Hoke, Margaret E165
Hoke, Tina E334
Hokenson, Erik A877
Holani, Kimberly A109
Holappa, Bruce A794
Holbrook, Austin A203
Holbrook, Amy A337
Holbrook, Mark A381
Holbrook, Jenni A426
Holbrook, Jimmy A726
Holbrook, Judy P518
Holbrook, Amy E158
Holbrook, Jenni E213
Holcomb, Michele A169
Holcomb, Debbie A206
Holcomb, John A804
Holcomb, George W. P327
Holcomb, David P548
Holcomb, Alexandra W424
Holda, Margaret P502
Holden, Robert A22
Holden, Chauncey A205
Holden, Zachery A748
Holden, James A762
Holden, Christopher P1
Holden, Robert P11
Holden, Peter J. P79
Holden, Kenneth R P80
Holden, Teresa P140
Holden, Ross J P366
Holden, E. Wayne P447
Holden-williams, Rebecca A324
Holder, Luke A135
Holder, Julie A285
Holder, John A380
Holder, Sonia A590
Holder, Christine A704
Holder, Sophia G P558
Holder, Diane P. P643
Holder, Cindy E224
Holderman, Wanda P153

Holding, Frank B. A336
Holding, Frank B. E157
Holdings, Midcoast P340
Holdorf, Diane A487
Holdorff, Sharon P141
Holdridge, Carl A569
Hole, James A195
Hole, David E190
Holeksa, Jurgen W433
Holeman, David K. E441
Holgerson, William A641
Holgerson, William P407
Holiday, Edith A742
Holiday, Bradley J. (Brad) E59
Holiday, Bradley J. E452
Holien, Patrick P606
Holifield, Mark Q. A428
Holinsky, Ronald A520
Holker, Matthew P41
Holladay, Mark G. A796
Holladay, Mark G. E397
Hollan, Michael A252
Holland, Peter A112
Holland, David A198
Holland, Bob A218
Holland, Tom A323
Holland, Ricky T. A336
Holland, Leslie A345
Holland, Jim A360
Holland, Christine A444
Holland, Clifford A479
Holland, James A494
Holland, Leslie A522
Holland, Arlene A527
Holland, Ralph A569
Holland, Cindy A587
Holland, George A935
Holland, Cindy P45
Holland, Robert P208
Holland, Lynn P500
Holland, Julie E113
Holland, Ricky T. E157
Holland, Leslie E165
Hollander, Pam A35
Hollander, Rich A658
Hollander, Martin A752
Hollander, Gail E183
Hollandsworth, Peggy A665
Hollandsworth, Peggy E334
Hollandt, Andrea P174
Hollaway, David A682
Hollenbeck, Martin F. A195
Hollenbeck, Rupal Shah A461
Hollenbeck, Jennifer A861
Hollenbush, Kevin A934
Holler, Drew A902
Holler, Glenn J P257
Holler, Cindy P331
Holler, Thomas R. (Tom) E431
Holleran, Kevin P. A821
Holley, Rick A145
Holley, Jeffrey D A628
Holley, Peter A850
Holley, Rick R. A918
Holley, Jeffrey D P396
Holliday, Bob A89
Holliday, Susan A331
Holliday, Brian A431
Holliday, Carl A630
Holliday, Marc A708
Holliday, Marc P441
Holliday, Charles O. (Chad) W334
Holliday, Susan E152
Hollifield, Matthew A527
Hollihan, Walter P72
Hollingbery, Aaron A837
Hollinger, Dennis E3
Hollingsworth, Rebecca A42
Hollingsworth, Pamela A467
Hollingsworth, Laura A736
Hollingsworth, Audrey A796
Hollingsworth, Laura P460
Hollingsworth, Jarvis V. P629
Hollingsworth, Todd E18
Hollingsworth, Audrey E397

Hollinsworth, John A879
Hollis, Curtis A491
Hollis, Stephan A796
Hollis, Stephan E397
Holloman, J. Phillip A197
Holloway, Duane D. A84
Holloway, Bavan A140
Holloway, Duane D A873
Holloway, John B. P111
Holloway, April P140
Holloway, Brandi P455
Hollub, Vicki A. A618
Holm, Andrea P12
Holm, Peter P36
Holman, Gene A113
Holman, Brian A179
Holman, Rick A727
Holman, Jon A771
Holman, Jeff P303
Holman, Rick P453
Holman, Gene E36
Holman, Jon E381
Holme, Sarah A826
Holmen, Hans A233
Holmen, James P610
Holmes, John A16
Holmes, Donald N A260
Holmes, Bradley A294
Holmes, William A538
Holmes, John A547
Holmes, Debra A610
Holmes, Pamela A664
Holmes, Robert A691
Holmes, James A692
Holmes, Jim A692
Holmes, Gloria A695
Holmes, Terraca A811
Holmes, James A850
Holmes, John P183
Holmes, Brad P203
Holmes, Gerald T P231
Holmes, Angela P263
Holmes, Ann P354
Holmes, Kim P375
Holmes, Nicholas P437
Holmes, Nicholas P438
Holmes, Rochelle P445
Holmes, Norman G P506
Holmes, Robin P564
Holmes, Chip P598
Holmes, Dan P613
Holmes, John P677
Holmes, Thomas E3
Holmes, Janet E81
Holmes, John E101
Holmes, Chad E102
Holmes, Juanita E168
Holmes, Scott M E267
Holmes, Pamela E334
Holmes, Stewart E334
Holmgren, Thor A60
Holmstrom, Torbjorn W420
Holochuk, James A741
Holochuk, James E364
Holodak, Stephen A251
Holschbach, Leon J. A567
Holschbach, Leon J. E283
Holscher, Russ A120
Holscher, Michael P424
Holsclaw, Janet A727
Holsclaw, Janet P453
Holshouser, Susan A452
Holsinger, Brent E264
Holstebro, Jens P211
Holstein, Kate P412
Holsten, Joseph M. A524
Holston, Michael J. A554
Holstrom, June P383
Holt, Alan A61
Holt, John A142
Holt, Gregs A533
Holt, Katie A647
Holt, Brian A774
Holt, Melinda A905
Holt, Kasha P1

558

HOOVER'S HANDBOOK OF EMERGING COMPANIES 2020

COMBINED HOOVER'S HANDBOOK INDEX OF EXECUTIVES

Holt, Jason P115
Holt, Patrick P654
Holt, Tim O. W353
Holt, John E49
Holt, Victoria M. (Vicki) E339
Holte, James A316
Holthaus, Scott E35
Holthausen, Robert E102
Holthouser, James E. (Jim) A423
Holton, Adam A194
Holton, Ginger A449
Holton, Alex A481
Holton, Terry J. A748
Holton, Ginger E221
Holton, Micah E282
Holtrup, Kevin E123
Holtschneider, Patty A577
Holtz, Dave A262
Holtz, Bryan A824
Holtz, Curt A891
Holtz, Bryan P562
Holy, Jeff A917
Holyoak, Jennifer A913
Holyoak, Steven P140
Holyoak, Jennifer E438
Holz, John A466
Holz, Alissa A715
Holzem, John D A797
Holzer, Damon A89
Holzer, Phil A151
Holzer, Sunita A707
Holzer, Sunita A708
Holzhauer, Daniel A86
Holzhauer, Daniel E27
Holzmann, Thomas P125
Holzshu, Christopher (Chris) A521
Hom, Erwin A349
Hom, John A686
Homan, Paige A115
Homan, Richard P. A853
Homan, Dale A865
Homan, Ken P477
Homan, Richard P. P612
Homan, Jan W156
Homan, Paige E37
Homan, Dale E416
Homayouni, Bryan P120
Homem, Manuel A125
Homenuik, Terry A397
Homer, David P. (Dave) A376
Homma, Koji W431
Homsey, Harvey P198
Hon-shing, Tong W50
Honculada, Amy P299
Honda, Amy A109
Honda, Osamu W376
Honda, Shinji W381
Hondlik, Carol A60
Hone, Dennis A63
Honer, Pete E111
Honey, Scott A888
Honey, Debra P162
Honey, Scott E425
Honeycutt, John A270
Honeycutt, Mike A764
Honeycutt, Mike E377
Honeyman, Joel P140
Hong, Peter A79
Hong, Sung-Dae A833
Hong, Z P206
Hong, Chong P246
Hong, Mark P329
Hong, Ching Wei W299
Hong, Chen W336
Hong, Kuok Khoon W424
Hongli, Zhang W198
Hongola, Michael A811
Honig, Peter A658
Honig, Lyle P12
Honjo, Masaya W368
Honma, Clesio A724
Honma, Clesio P452
Honnette, Chelsea A21
Honnold, Wes A746
Honold, Doris W364

Honor, Steve A46
Honore, Babette A571
Hood, Chris A487
Hood, Amy E A565
Hood, Byron A574
Hoogenboom, Paul G. P. A732
Hoogenkamp, Eric E7
Hoogeveen, Kevin A335
Hoogeveen, Kevin E155
Hooi, Ng Keng W14
Hook, Rich A649
Hook, Thomas J. E232
Hooker, Thomas A199
Hooks, Brenda A213
Hooley, Joseph L. (Jay) A783
Hooper, Anthony C. (Tony) A64
Hooper, Tony A65
Hooper, Ana A255
Hooper, Mike A799
Hooper, Brandy P31
Hooper, Lucelia P300
Hooper, Mike P384
Hooper, Bill E366
Hoopes, John R. P468
Hoopes, Sue P524
Hoops, Fred A222
Hooser, Steve Van A258
Hooser, David Van P467
Hoover, Sheila A337
Hoover, Travis A448
Hoover, Craig A522
Hoover, Stephen (Steve) A933
Hoover, Jewell P2
Hoover, Travis P247
Hoover, Wayne P276
Hoover, Michael P390
Hoover, Johanna Hammond P480
Hoover, G Michael P532
Hoover, Mike P590
Hoover, Linda M P609
Hoover, Sheila E158
Hoovers, Brian A722
Hope, Walter A63
Hope, Jim A797
Hope, Mark A852
Hope, Henry P458
Hopf, Clarence J. (Joe) P540
Hopfer, Rick A570
Hopfinger, Mark M A715
Hopke, Debra P640
Hopkin, Vincent A628
Hopkins, Tim A142
Hopkins, Linda A246
Hopkins, Herbert A489
Hopkins, Lynn M. A638
Hopkins, Kevin A824
Hopkins, Will P83
Hopkins, Gloria P277
Hopkins, Kevin P561
Hopkins, Mary Ann P582
Hopkins, Tim E49
Hopkins, Geoff E57
Hopkins, Linda E105
Hopkins, Jack E267
Hopkins, Roger R. E296
Hopkins, Lynn M. E320
Hopmans, John A522
Hopp, Daniel A433
Hopp, Jason P442
Hopp, Daniel E217
Hopp, Maryann E319
Hoppe, Jonn D P284
Hoppe, Beth P432
Hoppe, Christoph W390
Hoppenot, Herve E226
Hopper, Sidney A30
Hopper, Doyle A612
Hopper, Sidney P20
Hopper, Tim P134
Hopper, Karen P335
Hopper, Steven P641
Hopson, Jeffrey A715
Hora, Maninder E300
Horan, Michael A91
Horan, Cindy Horan A224

Horan, Theodore A651
Horan, Terry A732
Horan, Craig A873
Horan, Michael E29
Horan, Theodore E330
Horber, Patrick A6
Hore, David T. E291
Horgan, Kathryn M. (Kathy) A783
Horger, Robert R. A769
Horger, Robert R. E380
Hori, Fran A637
Horich, Todd E394
Horikami, Brian P485
Horiszny, Laurene A146
Horiuchi, Kirk A482
Horky, Robert P493
Horn, Charles L. A34
Horn, Lindsay A227
Horn, Justin A552
Horn, Steve A664
Horn, Joe Van A887
Horn, Lindsay E90
Horn, Justin E276
Horn, Stephen A. E296
Horn, Steve E334
Hornbuckle, William J. A562
Hornby, William P. A183
Hornby, William P. E74
Horne, Lewis A175
Horne, Mike A176
Horne, Jeff P543
Horne, Marilyn P610
Horner, Leigh E A416
Horner, Mike A481
Horner, Denise A618
Horner, Shawn A640
Horner, Matt A928
Horner, Henry P356
Horner, Greg P594
Horner, Matt P674
Horner, Denise E310
Horng, Susanna A686
Horning, Sharon A584
Horning, Brian P115
Horning, Susan P517
Hornsby, Jimmy E318
Hornstein, Andreas L A320
Hornung, Bill A929
Hornung, Andrew P505
Hornung, Bill E449
Horowitz, Paul A135
Horowitz, Alex A137
Horowitz, Paul A575
Horowitz, Zane P399
Horowitz, Corey M E302
Horsch, Betsy P587
Horseman, Neil A895
Horst, Mark A922
Horst, Mark P671
Horst, Darren E72
Horstman, Gregory A167
Horstmann, Douglas J. A413
Horstmann, David L. A413
Horstmann, Douglas J. E205
Horstmann, David L. E205
Hortman, Edwin W. (Ed) A62
Hortman, Edwin W. (Ed) E19
Horton, Chelsea A86
Horton, Rick A435
Horton, Donald R. A435
Horton, David A506
Horton, Tonia A562
Horton, Michael A673
Horton, Kelly A680
Horton, William E. (Bill) A712
Horton, Katherine P378
Horton, Lilla P596
Horton, Chelsea E27
Horvath, Elizabeth A409
Horvath, Lori A482
Horvath, Michael A761
Horvath, Jeff P514
Horvathpeterson, Sandra P570
Horwedel, Gregory P161
Hosch, Pete A448

Hosch, Pete P247
Hosea, Kristina A590
Hosey, Dr Ashley P144
Hosfield, Rick A376
Hosford, Karlene P296
Hoshii, Susumu W349
Hoshino, Yoshihiko W431
Hoskins, Walter A165
Hoskins, Roni P596
Hoskins, Brad E110
Hoskinson, James W A140
Hosoi, Susumu W204
Hosono, Katsuya W30
Hosoya, Kazuo W366
Hossack, Michael A329
Hossack, Brad A789
Hossle, Dwight A252
Host, Gerard R. (Jerry) A852
Hoste, Renee A711
Hoste, Renee P444
Hosten, Shani P2
Hoster, David H. E121
Hostetler, Matt A385
Hostetter, David A367
Hostetter, Margaret P128
Hosticka, Carl A636
Hosty, Neil J. A530
Hosty, Tom P358
Hotaling, Michael A309
Hotaling, Michael A469
Hotarek, George A793
Hotchkiss, James P. A346
Hotchkiss, Dan P260
Hotchkiss, James P. E167
Hotsuki, Keishi A574
Hottges, Timotheus A800
Hottges, Timotheus W138
Hotwani, Vishal P174
Hou, Jung-Lung W406
Houchens, Paul P476
Houck, Sherry A206
Houck, Ronnie A749
Houck, Ronnie E367
Houdayer, Pascal W181
Houde, Jean W270
Houdeshell, David D. A749
Houdeshell, David D. E367
Hougen, Elizabeth L. E237
Houghton, Nicole A462
Houghton, Robert A728
Houghton, Bob A728
Houghton, Nicole P256
Houghton, Mike P297
Houghton, Andrew E8
Houk, Beverly P163
Houlditch, Geoffrey A449
Houlditch, Geoffrey E220
Houliang, Dai W101
Houlihan, Robert A555
Houlihan, Cathy A702
Hourigan, John A81
Hourigan, Tim A427
Hourigan, Michael P202
Hourihan, John P. P166
Hours, Bernard W128
House, James L. (Jim) A71
House, Rebecca W A729
House, Gerry P191
House, Deb P471
House, Morgan P552
House, Paula P623
House, Andrew M361
House, Todd W. E174
Householder, Thomas A51
Householder, Joseph A. (Joe) A753
Householder, Adam A862
Householder, Jeffry M. E78
Houseman, Jeff P215
Houser, Denise A882
Houser, Susan P70
Houserman, Lynne E93
Housianitis, Lisa A658
Houska, Mark A199
Houssaye, Brian de la A925
Houssaye, Brian de la E445

HOOVER'S HANDBOOK OF EMERGING COMPANIES 2020

COMBINED HOOVER'S HANDBOOK INDEX OF EXECUTIVES

A = AMERICAN BUSINESS
E = EMERGING COMPANIES
P = PRIVATE COMPANIES
W = WORLD BUSINESS

Houston, Monica A340
Houston, Helga S. A444
Houston, Daniel J. (Dan) A677
Houston, Stacy W A704
Houston, Melanie A883
Houston, Sally H. P203
Houston, Bronwyn P288
Houston, Don P337
Houston, John P643
Houston, Melanie P644
Houston, Monica E161
Houston, David L. E197
Housworth, Elizabeth P610
Houten, Matthew Van A89
Houten, Diana Van P244
Houweling, Tara Van A168
Hovanec, Sandy P678
Hovanessian, Angel P137
Hove, Bart P661
Hovious, Jeff A859
Howard, Linda A10
Howard, Cheryl A155
Howard, Paul A205
Howard, Gary A374
Howard, John L. A393
Howard, Jeff A452
Howard, Dennie A708
Howard, Mary A727
Howard, Connie A738
Howard, Dennis A746
Howard, Chris A776
Howard, Kevin J. A796
Howard, Terence A799
Howard, Donald A827
Howard, Kim A827
Howard, Claude A844
Howard, Laura A856
Howard, John A882
Howard, J. Kyle A894
Howard, Richard A926
Howard, Martin P96
Howard, Nancy A P184
Howard, Greggory P280
Howard, John P430
Howard, Mary P453
Howard, Dan P505
Howard, Chris P512
Howard, Laura P614
Howard, Michael P629
Howard, J. Kyle P651
Howard, Stephen R P670
Howard, Cheryl E54
Howard, Josephus E105
Howard, Kevin J. E397
Howard, Richard E445
Howarth, Anne A654
Howarth, Joan W. P339
Howat, Dan A483
Howdeshell, Mike P361
Howdyshell, Cathy A320
Howe, Dave A205
Howe, Reed A266
Howe, Douglas A496
Howe, Chris A665
Howe, Roman A740
Howe, Reed P181
Howe, Becky P228
Howe, William P304
Howe, William P508
Howe, Jeff P672
Howe, Stephen W65
Howe, Kenneth R. E6
Howe, Chris E334
Howell, Peyton R. A63
Howell, Lloyd W. A144
Howell, John A179
Howell, Susie A246
Howell, Terry A362
Howell, Douglas K. (Doug) A369

Howell, Melissa A487
Howell, James A. A602
Howell, Sandra K A713
Howell, Eric A759
Howell, Robert A797
Howell, Paul A818
Howell, Sysun P266
Howell, Joel P376
Howell, Sylvia P377
Howell, Katherine A. (Kathy) P466
Howell, Eric P493
Howell, Stephen (Steve) P579
Howell, Kevin P595
Howell, Susie E105
Howell, Hilton H. E192
Howell, Sarah E194
Howell, Paul E403
Howenstine, Debra P633
Howes, Joshua A167
Howes, David P312
Howie, Neil E59
Howland, Edward P382
Howlett, C. C. W212
Howley, W. Nicholas (Nick) A842
Howley, Michael G. E2
Howson, David A200
Howze, Marc A A260
Hoxsie, Katherine A904
Hoy, Thomas L. A82
Hoy, Joann P101
Hoyle, Kevin P117
Hoyle, Simon P375
Hoyme, Sharon P617
Hoysan, Mandy A722
Hozouri, Cecile P479
Hpenterprise, Synnex A795
Hrabowski, Freeman A. P642
Hrina, Sharon P131
Hrina, Sharin P131
Hrinak, David P288
Hrountas, Stacey P489
Hruby, Dennis E. E372
Hrusovszky, James P619
Hrusovszky, Jimco P619
Hrybenko, Michael E93
Hschneider, Joseph P252
Hsiao, Chiu Bin P197
Hsieh, John A465
Hsieh, Jackson A775
Hsieh, Jackson P511
Hsieh, Johnny P540
Hsing, Michael R. E288
Hsiung, Ken A590
Hsiung, Ming-Ho W89
Hsu, Joyce A391
Hsu, Christopher P. (Chris) A420
Hsu, Michael D. A493
Hsu, Johnny A676
Hsu, Florence A676
Hsu, Clark A676
Hsu, Erik A925
Hsu, Kevin P475
Hsu, Penny P610
Hsu, J. H. W89
Hsu, Larry W123
Hsu, Boshan W123
Hsu, David W209
Hsu, Judy W364
Hsu, Johnny E338
Hsu, Florence E338
Hsu, Clark E338
Hsu, Erik E445
Hu, Kathryn A166
Hu, Anna A182
Hu, Bradford A203
Hu, Hao A204
Hu, Soomin A390
Hu, Mandy A592
Hu, S. Jack A711
Hu, Kaijie P114
Hu, Mandy P370
Hu, S. Jack P444
Hu, Arthur W234
Hu, Mingxiu E300
Hua, Zhong W110

Hua, Yang W110
Hua, Hsieh Fu W411
Huang, Yu A167
Huang, Victor A376
Huang, Gene A484
Huang, Jen-Hsun A613
Huang, Alice A676
Huang, Sofia A676
Huang, Lily A686
Huang, Christopher A741
Huang, Janice P591
Huang, Tao W98
Huang, Yung Jen W142
Huang, Peter M.T. W370
Huang, Chao-Kai W406
Huang, Wen Zhou W428
Huang, Alice E338
Huang, Sofia E338
Huang, Christopher E364
Huat, Peter Seah Lim W130
Huaxiang, Cai W12
Hubbard, Richard A142
Hubbard, Joel A224
Hubbard, Latonya A922
Hubbard, Skip P94
Hubbard, Maryann P343
Hubbard, Bart P471
Hubbard, Latonya P671
Hubbard, Richard E49
Hubbard, Brandon E123
Hubbell, Michael A267
Hubbell, Richard A. E268
Hubbs, Arthur C. E75
Hubbuch, Chris A919
Huber, Gary E A132
Huber, Ed A207
Huber, Edgar O. A243
Huber, Marie Oh A287
Huber, John A329
Huber, Michael A390
Huber, J. Kendall A405
Huber, Thomas A723
Huber, Tom A723
Huber, Kathyrn P612
Huber, Reid M. E226
Huber, Kevin E332
Hubert, Angela St P101
Huberty, John A3
Hubinger, Jim A806
Hubinger, Jim E398
Hubka, Tim E203
Hubr, Gary Null A132
Huch, Jamie A224
Huch, David P618
Huck, Jack P103
Huckabay, Evan A222
Huckabay, David A522
Huckabay, Kent P168
Huckaby, Hank A139
Huckaby, Hank P93
Huckelberry, Chuck P420
Huckfeldt, Paul A. E215
Huckle, Amanda A135
Hudak, James L. (Jim) A200
Hudak, John A346
Hudak, Tom E134
Hudak, John E167
Huddart, Andrew E248
Huddleston, Rose A930
Hudgens, John D. A818
Hudgens, Liz A922
Hudgens, Liz P671
Hudgens, John D. E403
Hudgins, Jessie P647
Hudgions, Annette W. A621
Hudgions, Annette W. E311
Hudnall, Matt A405
Hudon, Isabelle W371
Hudson, Thomas A6
Hudson, David W. A182
Hudson, Jennifer A232
Hudson, Thomas A287
Hudson, Jody A332
Hudson, Patty A345
Hudson, Scott R. A369

Hudson, Brenda A458
Hudson, Dennis S. (Denny) A749
Hudson, Rob A750
Hudson, Jeremiah A853
Hudson, Jamie A861
Hudson, Roz A879
Hudson, Ray A921
Hudson, David T. A932
Hudson, William P267
Hudson, Wayne P313
Hudson, Keeba P335
Hudson, Amanda P478
Hudson, R. Guy P537
Hudson, Elisabeth P599
Hudson, Jeremiah P612
Hudson, Ray P669
Hudson, Ian A. E149
Hudson, Patty E166
Hudson, Mark E286
Hudson, Dennis S. (Denny) E367
Hueber, Stu A259
Huebner, Kyle E385
Hueners, Jeff P125
Huerta, Liliana A85
Huerta, Miguel A831
Huerta, Miguel P601
Huerta, Liliana E27
Huesser, Larry P502
Huestis, Tim A664
Huestis, Tim E333
Huet, Jean-michel E290
Huether, Jim A744
Huey, Cindy A119
Huey, Byron P392
Huey, Kevin E110
Huff, Shelly A140
Huff, Steve A168
Huff, Jerry A900
Huff, Scott A901
Huff, Signe P308
Huff, Lisa P429
Huff, Justin P514
Huff, Joe P554
Huff, Ralph E368
Huffer, Linda R. A754
Huffer, Linda R. P484
Huffer, Russell E23
Huffines, James R. A421
Huffman, Nina A218
Huffman, Mona A550
Huffman, Janet A925
Huffman, Ryan P123
Huffman, Hoyt P170
Huffman, Mona P319
Huffman, Janet E445
Hufford, Bob A87
Hufford, Bob P50
Hufford, Dustin P563
Hufman, Chris A799
Hugger, Erin E226
Huggins, M J A172
Huggins, John A250
Huggins, Angela A527
Hugh, Bryan Iv A101
Hugh, Bryan Iv E32
Hugh-Pugh, Beverly P647
Hughes, Janet A1
Hughes, Ted A52
Hughes, Sharon A60
Hughes, Tom A89
Hughes, Shannon A112
Hughes, Peter A115
Hughes, Giselle A151
Hughes, Kellie A156
Hughes, Tony A158
Hughes, Sharon A206
Hughes, Brian D A269
Hughes, Gareth A271
Hughes, Bryan A289
Hughes, Frederick P A355
Hughes, Edmond E A446
Hughes, Philandria A467
Hughes, Erik A543
Hughes, Jay A561
Hughes, Robert K. A588

COMBINED HOOVER'S HANDBOOK INDEX OF EXECUTIVES

Hughes, Martin S. (Marty) A709
Hughes, Jeffrey A. (Jeff) A721
Hughes, Niki A773
Hughes, Michael A775
Hughes, Christine A824
Hughes, Kate A835
Hughes, Johnny A855
Hughes, Bill P40
Hughes, Wilson P213
Hughes, Scott P221
Hughes, Stephen P253
Hughes, James P253
Hughes, Michael P P272
Hughes, Robert K. P365
Hughes, Mark P415
Hughes, Roddy P422
Hughes, Julie P478
Hughes, Ron P502
Hughes, Michael P511
Hughes, Jessica M P511
Hughes, Tanya P536
Hughes, Mark P551
Hughes, Christine P562
Hughes, John P639
Hughes, Mark W331
Hughes, Janet E1
Hughes, Peter E38
Hughes, Robert E41
Hughes, Sharon E132
Hughes, Ryan E156
Hughes, Martin S. (Marty) E348
Hughes, Niki E383
Hughes, Bryan E443
Hughey, Sandy P378
Hughte, Carol A654
Huguenard, Charles W P483
Hui, Stella A747
Hui, Edward P615
Hui, Ka Yan W98
Hui, Chng Sok W130
Hui, Mary E433
Huibers, Paul A518
Huidekoper, Elizabeth C. P101
Huie, Robert P670
Huillard, Xavier W415
Huiman, Yi W198
Huiskens, Terry A165
Huiyan, Yang W118
Huizar, Soledad E319
Hukkelhoven, Mathias A151
Hulbert, Thomas A219
Hulbert, Thomas E87
Hulburd, Jon P418
Hulburt, Jeff P79
Hulburt, Benjamin W. E289
Hulburt, Christopher K. E289
Hulen, Randy A600
Huling, Becky A323
Huling, Rebecca A323
Hull, Stacey A179
Hull, Ted Hull Ted A199
Hull, Chad A257
Hull, Charles F A323
Hull, George A476
Hull, Steve A509
Hull, Anthony E A707
Hull, Anthony E. (Tony) A708
Hullinger, Jaime A53
Hullings, Ken A528
Hulse, Walter S. A630
Hulse, Walter S A631
Hulse, Lew P233
Hulse, Walter S P397
Hulsey, Jason P210
Hult, David W. A83
Hultman, Jeff A413
Hultman, Jeff E205
Hultquist, Douglas M. (Doug) A693
Hultquist, Douglas M. (Doug) E341
Hum, Robert P326
Humbert, Robert A16
Hume, Christopher A562
Hume, Sophie A779
Hume, Richard T. (Rich) A809
Humes, Chelsi P245

Humes, Thomas H. (Tom) P625
Huml, Dave E399
Humm, David A212
Humm, Philipp W417
Hummel, Robert A114
Hummel, William A329
Hummel, Tracy A809
Hummel, John M. A869
Hummel, Chris A872
Hummel, Christopher K A872
Hummel, Dennis P308
Hummel, Mike P468
Hummel, Robert E37
Hummell, Liz A156
Hummingbird, Ruth P558
Humpal, Jen A54
Humphrey, Christopher A227
Humphrey, Melissa A398
Humphrey, Malcolm A565
Humphrey, Jamie A850
Humphrey, John J. A872
Humphrey, Chad P167
Humphrey, Richard P171
Humphrey, Mike P185
Humphrey, Eric P211
Humphrey, Melissa P222
Humphrey, Kate P230
Humphrey, David P296
Humphrey, Christopher E90
Humphrey, Scott E210
Humphreys, James A698
Humphries, Kent A798
Humphries, Paul J. W164
Hunckler, Stephen P. A781
Hund, Kenneth A167
Hund, Lawrence G. A407
Hund-Mejean, Martina A544
Hundzinski, Ronald T. (Ron) A146
Hung, Ho-fung P610
Hung, Benjamin P. C. (Ben) W364
Hung, Priscilla E196
Hungria, Cristina P90
Hunkeler, Robert A467
Hunn, L. Neil A730
Hunn, Jean P137
Hunnicutt, Tyna P610
Hunniford, Michael A605
Hunsaker, Michelle A902
Hunsaker, Rebecca P631
Hunsberger, Scott A678
Hunt, David A46
Hunt, James A161
Hunt, Jim A303
Hunt, Thomas A379
Hunt, Neil A587
Hunt, Lisa Kidd A746
Hunt, N. Craig A760
Hunt, Amy A857
Hunt, Sandy A861
Hunt, Doris P157
Hunt, Robert P174
Hunt, David P191
Hunt, Markelle P203
Hunt, Deborah P294
Hunt, Nicole P322
Hunt, Cheri P327
Hunt, Stephen J P369
Hunt, Adeanya P395
Hunt, Dustin P545
Hunt, Linda P610
Hunt, Melissa P610
Hunt, Gary P625
Hunt, Terry P636
Hunt, Joseph P664
Hunt, John E58
Hunt, Dennis B. E183
Hunt, Tony J. E353
Hunt, N. Craig E374
Hunt, Eugene E374
Hunt, Sharon E408
Hunter, Jennifer A41
Hunter, Kelli A. A60
Hunter, Renee A69
Hunter, Jesse N. A179
Hunter, Barbara A326

Hunter, Alisa A329
Hunter, George A329
Hunter, Jocelyn A428
Hunter, Christopher H. (Chris) A440
Hunter, Martin A461
Hunter, Kelli A723
Hunter, Lisa W. A760
Hunter, Julie A772
Hunter, Rhonda C. A918
Hunter, Scott A942
Hunter, David P74
Hunter, Martin P255
Hunter, Jen P308
Hunter, Dan E86
Hunter, John E206
Hunter, Gordon B. E258
Hunter, Lisa W. E374
Hunter, Julie E383
Hunter-perkins, Paula A435
Huntington, Bradford A688
Huntley, David S. A89
Huntley, Monique P428
Huntsberry, Cody P276
Huntsman, Peter R. A447
Huntsman, Jon M. A447
Hunzeker, Fred R A810
Hunzeker, Fred R P546
Hupka, Yanina A751
Hupp, Billy P197
Huppertz, Julie P250
Hur, Lucy A779
Hurand, Gary E53
Hurd, Pat A177
Hurd, Terri A224
Hurd, Mark V A632
Hurd, Heather E106
Huret, Robert A110
Hurlbert, Terry P114
Hurlbut, Rich P546
Hurley, Mike A340
Hurley, Kyle A398
Hurley, ToniRae A449
Hurley, Kevin A737
Hurley, Thomas A776
Hurley, John J A922
Hurley, Kyle P222
Hurley, Jimmy P556
Hurley, John J P671
Hurley, Mike E160
Hurley, John M. E185
Hurley, ToniRae E221
Hurley, Kevin E361
Hurn, Patricia D. A711
Hurn, Patricia D. P444
Hurst, Trent A243
Hurst, David A259
Hurst, Kevin A287
Hurst, Peter A381
Hurst, David A462
Hurst, George A501
Hurst, Tony A647
Hurst, Jessica A893
Hurst, David P256
Hurst, Gregory A. (Greg) P418
Hurst, Ron P421
Hurst, Chuck P480
Hurst, A. C. W212
Hurt, George A. P120
Hurtado, Cesar A191
Hurtado, Anna P537
Hurtak, Erica E106
Hurte, Vernon P259
Hurttbateman, Patricia P287
Hurvitz, Elizabeth A895
Hurwitz, John P P472
Hurzeler, Robert A. A629
Husain, Bazmi W3
Huse, Mark A494
Huseman, Kim P281
Hushbeck, Scott P670
Husk, Lacy A713
Huskins, Keith A403
Huskins, Lee P267
Huson, Chris P314
Huspeni, Jeffrey A595

Huss, Eric P232
Hussain, Aamir A184
Hussey, Kevin A240
Huston, Martha A170
Huston, John J A218
Huston, Michael A344
Huston, Michael E165
Hutchcraft, Mitch P501
Hutcheson, Jennifer A736
Hutcheson, David A837
Hutcheson, Jennifer P460
Hutchins, Jay A19
Hutchins, Michael A364
Hutchins, Brian P155
Hutchins, Ronald P442
Hutchins, Mark P673
Hutchinson, Tom A39
Hutchinson, William R. A86
Hutchinson, Debra A248
Hutchinson, Randy A296
Hutchinson, Mark A374
Hutchinson, Ed A717
Hutchinson, Anna P246
Hutchinson, Ishion P597
Hutchinson, Jeff W73
Hutchinson, William R. E27
Hutchinson, Debra E107
Hutchinson, Ed E351
Hutchison, Larry M. A389
Hutchison, John A658
Hutchison, Corey A897
Hutchison, Randall P214
Hutchison, Harry P514
Hutmacher, Dustin A900
Hutson, Andy A728
Hutson, Marc P260
Huttenlocher, Daniel P. P159
Hutter, Dustin A726
Hutter, Dustin P453
Hutto, Richard A28
Hutton, Rob A240
Hutton, Peter A270
Hutton, Rob A512
Hutton, Jennifer A686
Hutton, William L. A714
Hutton, Chuck P412
Hutton, Scot E8
Huval, Timothy S. (Tim) A440
Huval, Tim A749
Huval, Tim E367
Huxtable, Russell W E148
Huynh, Chinh P41
Huza, Callie P332
Hu- «t, Jean Marc W408
Hwang, Cindy A137
Hwang, Jina A378
Hwang, Angela A657
Hwang, Christine P570
Hwang, Yong-Kee W236
Hwang, Robert P. T. W425
Hwang, Donald W425
Hwang, Jason E147
Hwee, Susan W. C. W411
Hybl, Greg A54
Hyde, Len A325
Hyde, Steve A487
Hyde, Jeff A806
Hyde, Andrew A885
Hyde, Jeff E398
Hyden, Georgine A209
Hyder, Brent A826
Hyder, Syed P643
Hyder, Rima E143
Hyland, Donna A380
Hyland, Jason P. A562
Hyland, Michael A690
Hylen, Theresa P182
Hylton, Emsley A115
Hylton, Tracy A206
Hylton, Emsley E38
Hyman, Shana A323
Hyman, Deborah A871
Hyman, Edward S. (Ed) E138
Hyman, Linda E248
Hymel, Gwen A296

COMBINED HOOVER'S HANDBOOK INDEX OF EXECUTIVES

```
A = AMERICAN BUSINESS
E = EMERGING COMPANIES
P = PRIVATE COMPANIES
W = WORLD BUSINESS
```

Hymer, Maggie P280
Hymes, Camille A779
Hynes, William A114
Hynes, Timothy (Tim) A583
Hynes, Carole A906
Hynes, John P111
Hynes, William E37
Hynes, Carole E435
Hyslip, Mark A67
Hyslop, Gregory L. (Greg) A140
Hytinen, Barry A. A403
Hyun, Sung Chul W338
Hyun-Ko, You A692
Hyung-soon, Kim W176
H-orter, Daniel W433
H-ousler, Gerd W62
Holz, Martin W391
Hopke, Doris W267
Hovell-Patrizi, Allegra van W10
H-idahl, Hans-Olav W21
H-ltermand, Peter W357
Hébert, Brigitte W270

I

Iaconi, Krista Di E349
Iacovazzi, Vito A922
Iacovazzi, Vito P671
Iadanza, Thomas A888
Iadanza, Thomas E425
Iampietro, Steve A63
Iancic, Peter A823
Iancic, Peter E405
Iannaccone, Robert P513
Iannarone, Thomas A137
Iannelli, Josephine A118
Iannelli, Josephine E40
Iannello, Lisa A719
Iannello, Lisa E355
Ianni, Julie P262
Ianniciello, Raffaela A592
Ianniciello, Raffaela P370
Ianniello, Joseph R. A892
Iannone, Jamie A901
Iannone, Michael E296
Iannotti, Thomas J. (Tom) A74
Iantosca, Joseph R. A618
Iantosca, Joseph R. E310
Iasonides, John A903
Iasparro, Kelly P532
Ibach, Jason D A368
Ibach, Jason A368
Ibarra, Erick A746
Ibarra, Francisco A921
Ibarra, Francisco P669
Ibata, Naoki P248
Ibbotson, Mark A901
Ibeh, Dozie P546
Ibrahim, Marko A620
Ibrahim, Tommy P255
Ibrahimpasic, Elvir A192
Icahn, Carl C. A250
Icahn, Carl C. A451
Ice, Carl R. A138
Ice, Carl R. A157
Ice, Carl R. P91
Ichihashi, Yasuhiko W182
Ichikawa, Alan P307
Ichikawa, Evan P320
Ichikawa, Masakazu W182
Ichimiya, Tadao W429
Ichinaga, Stephen A794
Ichinaga, Steve A795
Ichino, Atsushi W431
Ichinokawa, Takashi P34
Ichiura, Yoichi W260
Ickes, Jane P276

Idalski, Derek A63
Idemoto, Derek A198
Idiodi, Christian P333
Idrissi, Mehdi A592
Idrissi, Mehdi P370
Ierna, Diane A36
Ierulli, Laura A348
Ierulli, Laura E169
Ifuku, Masahiro W253
Igarashi, Tetsuo W176
Igdaloff, Barry E307
Igel, Bill P261
Iger, Robert A A271
Iglesias, Axel A467
Iglesias, Lisa G. A882
Igli, Kevin A855
Igo, Jim P255
Igoe, Christine A828
Igoe, Paul G P186
Igoe, Christine P584
Ihamuotila, Timo W3
Ihara, Yasumori W18
Ihm, Steve A36
IHORI, EISHIN W184
Ii, William Smith A717
Ii, Eric P119
Iida, Osamu W259
Iii, James Dillard A41
Iii, Eric Reinke A608
Iinuma, Yoshiaki W262
Iiyama, Toshiyasu W286
Ijima, Masaru P534
Ikeda, Miki A109
Ikeda, Kyle P639
Ikeda, Hajime W286
Ikegaya, Mikio W262
Ikeya, Koji W260
Ikoma, Masao W215
Iku, Tetsuo W345
Ilacqua, Nick E384
Ilami, Paul E412
Ilan, Haviv A820
Ilany, Jonathan E407
Ilderem, Vida A460
Ilkka, Heikki W287
Ill, Charles L. (Charlie) E144
Illig, Clifford W. (Cliff) A185
Imamura, Masashi W361
Iman, Alex E433
Imanuel, Ofer A391
Imaya, Akihiko W348
Imber, Curt A649
Imbrescia, Wayne P597
Imbrescia, Wayne P639
Imbriale-Holubec, Mary A203
Imbro, James E365
Imfree, Karen E249
Imhof, Doug P205
Imig, John P396
Imitatesdog, Shawn A522
Immaneni, Aravind A329
Immler, Mike A80
Immler, Mike P46
Imparato, Jean Philippe W305
Imperato, Thomas A596
Impicciche, Joseph A84
Impicciche, Joseph R A84
Impicciche, Joseph P47
Impicciche, Joseph R P47
Imundi, Christine A702
Imuro, Keiko A715
Inaba, Nobuo W324
Inacio, Cidalia A914
Inacio, Cidalia E439
Inagaki, Shiro W345
Inaguchi, Toshinori W127
Inamoto, Nobuhide W250
Incandela, Nicholas P51
Incorvaia, A.J. P326
Indaravijaya, Kattiya W216
Indermuehle, Debbie A665
Indermuehle, Debbie E334
Indresano, Michael A42
Infeld, Michael P576
Ingarra, Frank P293

Ingerslev, Christian M. W1
Ingersoll, Don A934
Ingersoll, Christopher D. P596
Ingle, Abhi A89
Ingle, Gary P333
Ingold, Edward A575
Ingoldsby, Jim A610
Ingraham, Jim P193
Ingram, Bill A11
Ingram, Robert A389
Ingram, Carolyn A571
Ingram, Susan R P378
Ingram, Sharon P399
Ingram, George P546
Ingram, Beth F. P594
Ingram, Anita P625
Ingvardsen, Henrik P361
Inkley, Robert P10
Inlander, Todd L. A290
Inlander, Todd L. A770
Inman, David A149
Inman, Tamra A621
Inman, Kent A885
Inman, Tamra E312
Innes, Kim W389
Innocenti, Joe A337
Innocenti, John A883
Innocenti, John P644
Innocenti, Joe E158
Inoue, Yasuhide A740
Inoue, Shin A938
Inoue, Shin P678
Inoue, Noriyuki W124
Inoue, Katsushi W186
Inoue, Tooru W262
Inoue, Toru W268
Inoue, Makoto W298
Inouye, Glenn P485
Insalaco, Sue A751
Insall, Gerard A98
Insch, Gary S. P596
Inscho, Bill A347
Inserra, Andrea A145
Inserra, Lawrence A504
Inserra, Lawrence E251
Inskeep, Lauren A799
Insley, Patricia A520
Insley, Guy P326
Insolia, Matthew T. P499
Intemann, Chris A329
Intili, Louis P664
Inzana, Lugene P306
Inzina, Tommy P70
Inzina, Tommy P519
Iona, Tara A828
Iona, Tara P584
Iordanou, Constantine W33
Ioriatti, Roberto A262
Ip, Norman Ka Cheung W173
Ipp, Alan P357
Ippolito, Peter J. A756
Ippolito, John E285
Iqbal, Farhan A85
Iqbal, Asma A741
Iqbal, Javeria A329
Iqbal, Farhan E27
Iqbal, Asma E364
Ireland, Scott A179
Ireland, Jay W. A374
Ireland, Frieda A810
Irick, Jaime A. A154
Iris, Krug A179
Irish, Stephen J. A297
Irish, William J A723
Irish, Stephen J. E129
Irizarry, Laurens A235
Irizarry, Enid A457
Irsik, Cynthia P633
Irtel, Konrad W267
Irussi, Bruce G. A756
Irussi, David E379
Irvin, Vernon L. A184
Irvin, Nancy A566
Irvin, Richard A855

Irvin, Jenner P456
Irvine, Jeffrey A54
Irvine, James A686
Irvine, Jacqui E318
Irwin, Shannon A211
Irwin, John A444
Irwin, Mike A784
Irwin, Larry (Don) A872
Irwin, Robert A454
Irwin, Brian P598
Irwin, Bradley C. P661
Irwin, Shannon E83
Irwin, Thomas S. E206
Isaac, Alberto P451
Isaac, Jon E259
Isaac, Lynn E365
Isaacson, Irit W162
Isaacson, Irit W163
Isabell, Emily A780
Isabella, Paul M. A121
Isabella, Barb P576
Isais, Geraldine Forbes P634
Isaka, Ryuichi W346
Isakowitz, Steven J. (Steve) P553
Isbell, Ken A224
Ise, Kiyotaka W400
Isely, Kemper E298
Isely, Zephyr E298
Isely, Heather E298
Isely, Elizabeth E298
Iseman, Jay C. A429
Iseman, Andrew J. (Andy) A858
Iseman, Jay C. E214
Iserman, Lance A94
Ishibashi, Takuya W127
Ishibashi, Tamio W127
Ishida, Yoshihisa W348
Ishigami, Hiroyuki W262
Ishiguro, Tadashi P100
Ishiguro, Denroku W20
Ishihara, Toshinobu W349
Ishii, Masashi P415
Ishii, Takuya W126
Ishikawa, Brian A109
ISHIMARU, FUMIO W339
Ishizaki, Yoshiyuki W394
Ishizuka, Hiroaki W256
Ishizuka, Shigeki W361
Ishmael, Cheryl P184
Iskalis, Thomas A605
Isla, Pablo W197
Islam, Munib A120
Islam, Mohammed A711
Islam, Mohammed P444
Islam, Naimul E78
Islan, Anne E371
Ismail, Amid I. P546
Isner, Josh E30
Isom, Robert D. A47
Isom, Bill A225
Isom, Matt A299
Ison, Todd A726
Isono, Denis K. A182
Isono, Tadahisa W400
Israel, Leonard (Len) A353
Israel, Leslie P299
Israel, Michael D P664
Israel, Leonard (Len) E173
Israel, Robert J. E347
Isserman, Jacob P351
Isto, Mark E. E360
Isturiz, Raul A658
Italiano, Deborah P524
Ito, Craig A109
Ito, Val A109
Ito, Shinichiro W27
ITO, TOSHIYASU W191
Ito, Kazuhiko W204
Ito, Takashi W253
Ito, Yujiro W369
Itoyama, Masaaki W205
Iturrey, Albert A543
Itzhaki, Yair W163
Iunghuhn, Cathy A761
IV, R H Holmes A159

COMBINED HOOVER'S HANDBOOK INDEX OF EXECUTIVES

IV, Calvin Thomas P219
Ivanis, Milena A844
Ivannikov, Alexander W308
Ivanova, Detelina A167
Ivashkiv, Lionel B P368
Ive, Jonathan A72
Ive, Jony A72
Iversen, Bernt G. A842
Iverson, Mark A884
Iverson, Kirk P6
Ives, Gray A713
Ives, Stephanie P546
Ives, Tim P595
Ivey, Craig S. A234
Ivey, Brian A382
Ivey, John A452
Ivler, Neil E143
Ivory, Laura P646
Iwane, Shigeki W215
Iwasa, Hiromichi W262
Iwasaki, Toshihiro W286
Iwasaki, Masato W381
Iwatsubo, Hiroshi W268
Iwatsuki, Takashi W376
Iwegbue, Jennifer A900
Iyengar, Sridhar R A461
Iyengar, Sudarshan A564
Iyengar, Jayanthi (Jay) A936
Iyengar, Kartik E431
Iyer, Sethu A108
Iyer, Chandresh A111
Iyer, Shankar Kasi Viswanatha A135
Iyer, Gopal A216
Iyer, Subrmanian A349
Iyer, Seema A420
Iyer, Prasad A544
Iyer, Ranjita A545
Iyer, Bask A897
Iyer, Kris P242
Izaguirre, Luis-Angel Gomez A934
Izaki, Kazuhiro W228
Izurieta, Laura A793
Izutani, Koji W360
Izzo, Mark A444
Izzo, Ralph A687

J

Jabbar, Omar A287
Jabbour, Anthony M. A327
Jaber, Adeeb P40
Jablin, Burton F. P480
Jablonski, Dawn P355
Jablonski, Jeffrey P363
Jablonski, Sue P395
Jabro, Mark P489
Jabs, Jacob P32
Jack, Angela A870
Jackey, Chris A125
Jacklin, Charles A212
Jackman, Lorraine A222
Jackman, Earl A440
Jackman, Aaron P337
Jackman, Lisa P598
Jackowiak, Mary A606
Jackowski, Julia L. (Julie) A173
Jackowski, Jessica P511
Jacks, Barbara A760
Jacks, Jean P315
Jacks, Barbara E374
Jackson, James A69
Jackson, Michael J. (Mike) A94
Jackson, Peter A156
Jackson, Lydia A166
Jackson, Rick C. A168
Jackson, Dan A181
Jackson, Delu A232
Jackson, Brian A251
Jackson, Carolyn A253
Jackson, Clifton A262
Jackson, Jeanne A262
Jackson, Michael J. (Mike) A319
Jackson, Mitchell A323
Jackson, Paul A325

Jackson, Lisa A332
Jackson, Allen A347
Jackson, Kevin A388
Jackson, Jamere A417
Jackson, Brian A426
Jackson, Matt A458
Jackson, Benjamin R A462
Jackson, Monique A463
Jackson, Doris A559
Jackson, Richard A583
Jackson, Keith D. A627
Jackson, Don A663
Jackson, Joanne B. A664
Jackson, Warren A665
Jackson, Alexander A683
Jackson, Jennifer A713
Jackson, Doris A715
Jackson, Bill A722
Jackson, Lori A726
Jackson, Ronald B. (Ron) A760
Jackson, Mel A771
Jackson, Jamere A827
Jackson, Lori A830
Jackson, Denise A840
Jackson, Keri A850
Jackson, Philip C. (Phil) A881
Jackson, Cj A882
Jackson, Neal A909
Jackson, Daniel P32
Jackson, Paul P77
Jackson, Bobby P161
Jackson, James P162
Jackson, Corey P171
Jackson, Shayla P174
Jackson, Rosa P P193
Jackson, Anthony P199
Jackson, Paige P199
Jackson, Scott P204
Jackson, Richard L. P262
Jackson, R. Shane P262
Jackson, Fred P280
Jackson, Gary P281
Jackson, Andrea P300
Jackson, Glen P303
Jackson, Jolinda P315
Jackson, Drew P318
Jackson, Timothy P320
Jackson, Laurisa P327
Jackson, Larry P329
Jackson, Melissa P331
Jackson, Gina P367
Jackson, Maureen P417
Jackson, Karin P418
Jackson, Cynthia P428
Jackson, Alexander P431
Jackson, Lori P453
Jackson, Lisa P456
Jackson, Janet P467
Jackson, Rosa P P506
Jackson, Scott P532
Jackson, Roger P543
Jackson, Tommy P550
Jackson, Angela P550
Jackson, David P551
Jackson, Claire P552
Jackson, Blair P566
Jackson, Alyssa P567
Jackson, Jamere P571
Jackson, Lori P593
Jackson, Linda W305
Jackson, Mary Ann E23
Jackson, Dan E70
Jackson, W. James E125
Jackson, Brian E205
Jackson, Brian E213
Jackson, Jeffrey T. (Jeff) E332
Jackson, Joanne B. E333
Jackson, Warren E334
Jackson, Ronald E368
Jackson, Ronald B. (Ron) E374
Jackson, Mel E381
Jackson, Philip C. (Phil) E421
Jackson, Neal E436
Jackson-Elmoore, Cynthia P339
Jacob, Bobby A246

Jacob, Gregg A263
Jacob, Ovadiah A390
Jacob, Bijesh A540
Jacob, Randy A877
Jacob, Ken P105
Jacob, Mark C P136
Jacob, Brett P344
Jacob, Jeffrey P364
Jacob, Sitt W162
Jacob, Bobby E105
Jacober, Richard P86
Jacobfeuerborn, Bruno W138
Jacobi, Jacqueline A571
Jacobs, Kerry J. A32
Jacobs, Chris A67
Jacobs, Bonnie A69
Jacobs, David A213
Jacobs, Robert A246
Jacobs, Joshua A251
Jacobs, Donna A296
Jacobs, Shirley A298
Jacobs, Stephen D. (Jake) A359
Jacobs, Kevin J. A423
Jacobs, Susan A446
Jacobs, John A460
Jacobs, Lawrence A. (Lon) A506
Jacobs, Caroline A588
JAcobs, Leonore A658
Jacobs, Paul E. A695
Jacobs, Bill A774
Jacobs, Kristine A852
Jacobs, Jennifer A882
Jacobs, Bradley S. A934
Jacobs, Richard F. P45
Jacobs, Michael P116
Jacobs, Richard B. P118
Jacobs, Rick P118
Jacobs, Brian P130
Jacobs, Jill P137
Jacobs, Ronald D P242
Jacobs, John P260
Jacobs, John P261
Jacobs, Stefanie P325
Jacobs, Caroline P365
Jacobs, Louis H P418
Jacobs, Joel P578
Jacobs, Cory P619
Jacobs, Andrew D P652
Jacobs, James K P657
Jacobs, Robert E105
Jacobs, Cindy E105
Jacobs, Shirley E130
Jacobs, William I. E194
Jacobs, Thomas W. E264
Jacobsen, Rene A8
Jacobsen, Donald A630
Jacobsen, Lennart W287
Jacobson, Sandy A226
Jacobson, Paul A. A262
Jacobson, Kristin A267
Jacobson, Steve A272
Jacobson, Jeff A. A481
Jacobson, Scott A722
Jacobson, Jack A903
Jacobson, Jeffrey (Jeff) A933
Jacobson, Carlton P6
Jacobson, Sandy P150
Jacobson, Catherine A. P211
Jacobson, David P586
Jacobson, Roy P643
Jacobson-Aaron E8
Jacobson-Landon, Stephanie P570
Jacoby, Rebecca J. A198
Jacoby, Christy A654
Jacoby, Rebecca A738
Jacques, Dale A727
Jacques, Carolyn P120
Jacques, Dale P453
Jacques, Jean-Sebastien W325
Jacques, Jean-Sébastien W327
Jacques, Heidi E305
Jacquez, Erica P300
Jacquinot, Bob P260
Jacquinot, Robert P261
Jadin, Ronald L. A393

Jadlowski, Mary P168
Jadot, Maxime (Max) W71
Jaeger, Timothy A176
Jaegers, Christine P214
Jafa, Krishna P424
Jafarieh, Nicolas A763
Jafarieh, Nicolas E377
Jafarnia, Korsh P334
Jaffe, David R. A84
Jaffe, Jonathan M. (Jon) A512
Jaffe, Seth R. A514
Jaffe, Seth R. A516
Jaffe, Eric D. A750
Jaffe, Victor A812
Jaffe, Ian P187
Jaffe, Seth R. P293
Jaffe, Harry J P386
Jaffe, Robert E326
Jaffery, Farhan A484
Jaffray, Dawn M. A867
Jafry, Syed A. A832
Jagdfeld, Aaron E184
Jagger, Hal A757
Jagger, Hal P492
Jaggers, Richard P59
Jaglall, Andy A574
Jahanian, Farnam P114
Jahn, Jill P25
Jahn, Timothy P64
Jahn, Barb P465
Jahn, Barb P477
Jahn, Barb P518
Jahnel, Ferdinand A540
Jahnsson, Olli P422
Jaikumar, Srikanth P563
Jaime, Alex A620
Jain, Ajit A127
Jain, Sudarshan A137
Jain, Nitin A179
Jain, Vishal A369
Jain, Vishal A687
Jain, Vikas A695
Jain, Sujit A724
Jain, Renu P22
Jain, Abhi Shek P85
Jain, Sahil P114
Jain, Alok P286
Jain, Manisha P296
Jain, Anshu P344
Jain, Sujit P452
Jain, Ritesh W71
Jain, Vivek E222
Jaiswal, Jyoti P127
Jakeman, Kelly A63
Jakeman, Brad A654
Jakeway, Sarah A544
Jakobsen, Henning A218
Jakobsen, Mads G. W287
Jakosky, Donn A636
Jakosky, Donn P403
Jakstys, Kristina A606
Jakubik, Chris A497
Jakuszewski, Robert A. E408
Jakwani, Asif A628
Jalace-vasold, Melissa A922
Jalace-vasold, Melissa P671
Jalil, Mohammed A278
Jalil, Ovais A877
Jallal, Bahija W37
Jalona, Sanjay P286
Jamal, Arshil W173
Jambor, Joan A89
Jameel, Hasan A637
Jamerson, Joe A36
James, Karen A105
James, Gillian A126
James, Hamilton E. (Tony) A137
James, David A213
James, Fred A286
James, Austin A326
James, Ates A364
James, Schlosser A444
James, Donna A500
James, Galeota A554
James, Phyllis A. A562

HOOVER'S HANDBOOK OF EMERGING COMPANIES 2020

COMBINED HOOVER'S HANDBOOK INDEX OF EXECUTIVES

A = AMERICAN BUSINESS
E = EMERGING COMPANIES
P = PRIVATE COMPANIES
W = WORLD BUSINESS

James, Dick A600
James, Thomas A606
James, Miriam A651
James, Hunt A704
James, Bradley G. A838
James, Al A850
James, Courtney A893
James, Josh A922
James, Dianne R. A940
James, Carl G P74
James, Marianne F. P128
James, David P143
James, Eric P177
James, Fred P190
James, Jeff P204
James, William T P206
James, W Thomas P206
James, Carl G P206
James, Autumn P395
James, Jan P425
James, Rank P455
James, Drew P512
James, Laura P522
James, Anthony P532
James, Josh P671
James, Penny W315
James, Karen E34
James, Susan E86
James, Miriam E330
James-Francis, Ma P377
Jameson, Steven E. (Steve) A229
Jamieson, Robert A1
Jamieson, Dick P116
Jamieson, T J P263
Jamieson, Lee P263
Jamieson, Robert E1
Jamil, Dhiaa M. A281
Jamison, Gary A434
Jamison, Cynthia A620
Jamison, Cynthia T. A840
Jamriska, Darren A925
Jamriska, Darren E445
Jamrozek, Jim P376
Jamsa, Kevin E123
Jan, Couturier A444
Jan, Ng A799
Janacek, Angela P626
Janaillac, Jean-Marc W15
Janas, Grzegorz W54
Janatsch, Adam A272
Janbeth, Santos E319
Janchar, Jim A160
Jandacek, Ed A305
Jandrue, Patricia A325
Jane, Mara A559
Janell, Joseph E P97
Janes, Maria N A904
Janesz, Brandon P449
Jang, Jeanne A283
Janiga, Kathy A255
Janik, James L. E114
Janis, Robert (Bob) P174
Janise, Carlton P105
Janish, Thomas P40
Janisko, Jenny P45
Janitzky, Amanda P456
Janke, Kenneth S. (Ken) A19
Janke, Kenneth S A19
Janke, Grant A863
Janke, AnnMarie A885
Janke, Harry P6
Janki, Daniel A374
Janki, Daniel A375
Janki, Daniel P215
Jankos, Dianna P346
Jankowski, Simona A613
Jankowski, John A673
Jankowski, Michelle A686
Jankowski, Ed A910

Jankowski, Gary P310
Jankowski, Cecelia P572
Jannah, Shekar G. A489
Jannasch, Charlyn P409
Janney, Laura A602
Janney, Michelle P252
Janney, Karen P537
Janosick, Kenneth W. (Ken) E440
Jansen, Jean-paul A243
Jansen, Robert A264
Jansen, James C. (Cory) A315
Jansen, Corey A315
Jansen, Kevin A319
Jansen, Jacqueline A804
Jansen, Robert P180
Jansen, Chad E222
Jansen, Paul R. E272
Janson, Julie S. A281
Janssen, Gwendolyn A5
Janssen, Marilyn A160
Janssen, Ann A301
Janssen, Jerimiah E156
Janssen, Carol E162
Janssens, Tom A917
Jansson, Helena A324
Jansson, Urban W357
Jante, Adam A338
Janthanakul, Voravit W95
Jantzen, Daniel P173
Janus, Tami A833
Japy, Nicholas W358
Jaquay, Joseph A109
Jaques, Attica A862
Jara, Armando P534
Jaramillo, Chris A325
Jaramillo, Richard P313
Jaramillo, Gilbert P385
Jarell, Tim P144
Jarlsjo, Bengt A696
Jarman, Samuel Y P28
Jarnot, Christopher E. (Chris) E424
Jaro, Vic P498
Jarosz, Mike A637
Jarrell, Blake A63
Jarrell, Paul A616
Jarrett, Dr Ehren P456
Jarrett, Craig P646
Jarrold, Tom A702
Jarvis, Glenn A54
Jarvis, Hunter A259
Jarvis, Anita A314
Jarvis, Candice A592
Jarvis, Jim A845
Jarvis, Candice P370
Jarvis, Erin P439
Jarvis, Kevin P501
Jarvis, Guy W150
Jarvis, Anita E145
Jarzabek, Gerald A727
Jarzabek, Gerald P453
Jarznyka, David E53
Jarzynka, David E. E53
Jasa, Matt A519
Jashnani, Yogi A13
Jasin, Clarence A199
Jasinowski, Mike A132
Jasinski, Wojciech W310
Jaskiewicz, Courtney A512
Jaskunas, Jeremy W P332
Jason, Aldrich A36
Jaspers, Allen P253
Jaspon, Kate E115
Jassy, Andrew R. (Andy) A42
Jastrem, Thomas A248
Jastrem, Thomas E107
Jastrow, Michael A60
Jastrow, Bill P251
Jauch, Mike A416
Jaurequi, Pat P471
Javaid, Mohammad E91
Javallana, Maria P548
Javorka, Tony P151
Jawad, Muhammad P400
Jawor, Wojciech A522
Jaworowska, Sabina Bigos W54

Jaworski, Peter W. A908
Jaworski, Peter W. E436
Jay, Dennis A465
Jay, Colleen E. A679
Jay, John C. W160
Jay-Young, Chung W355
Jayaraman, Jay A218
Jayaraman, Srinivasan E431
Jaycox, Ken A797
Jaynes, Jeff A432
Jazayeri, Akbar A290
JD, Howard R Grant P284
Jeamel, Scott A747
Jean-Luc, Bohbot W424
Jeanfreau, Mark A717
Jeanfreau, Mark E351
Jeanniot, Lynn W270
Jeannotte, Allison A706
Jedlicki, Anne P632
Jedrzejczyk, Slawomir R. W310
Jeevan, Siddharth A784
Jeff, Lee A749
Jeff, Lee E367
Jeffcoat, Sally P463
Jeffers, Colleen A839
Jeffers, Linda P153
Jeffers, Lewis P426
Jefferson, Kirby A460
Jefferson, Timothy P219
Jeffrey, David A739
Jeffrey, Hanks P160
Jeffrey, David E P587
Jeffrey, David P587
Jeffries, Allen A11
Jeffries, Kevin A89
Jeffries, Alex P554
Jeffries, Pamela R. P569
Jeffs, Mike P153
Jehl, Charles D. (Chuck) E177
Jehle, Kent L. A567
Jehle, Kent L. E283
Jehn, David A478
Jejdling, Fredrik W386
Jejurikar, Shailesh G. A680
Jelenchick, Erin A727
Jelenchick, Erin P453
Jelinek, W. Craig A241
Jelinek, Maggie P658
Jelks, Dionne P589
Jelle, Lorraine P84
Jellerson, David A576
Jellison, Brian D. A730
Jelly, Maecy P645
Jelmini, David A425
Jen, Grace A824
Jen, Grace P562
Jeng-wu, Tai W348
Jenisch, Jan W230
Jenkin, Thomas M. (Tom) A160
Jenkins, Vonshe A108
Jenkins, Eben A254
JENKINS, WORTH A512
Jenkins, Brian A519
Jenkins, Scott A527
Jenkins, Troy A562
Jenkins, Jesse A626
Jenkins, Flo A636
Jenkins, Flo A637
Jenkins, Kevin A658
Jenkins, Alitha A683
Jenkins, Guy A740
Jenkins, Stephanie A761
Jenkins, Tiffany A771
Jenkins, Scott A784
Jenkins, Jeff A791
Jenkins, Dustee T A804
Jenkins, Doug A933
Jenkins, Jo Ann C. P2
Jenkins, Gina P177
Jenkins, Ladenea P270
Jenkins, Kerri P379
Jenkins, Flo P403
Jenkins, Lori P417
Jenkins, Margaret L. P430
Jenkins, Alitha P431

Jenkins, Buddy P436
Jenkins, Matt P447
Jenkins, A. Dale P448
Jenkins, Barbara M P476
Jenkins, Malinda P506
Jenkins, Jeff P535
Jenkins, Katherine P558
Jenkins, Barbara P582
Jenkins, Brian A. E111
Jenkins, April E134
Jenkins, R. Scott E232
Jenkins, Bill E232
Jenkins, Katherine E330
Jenkins, Tiffany E381
Jenks, Mark A140
Jenks, Cliff A715
Jenks, Maria P274
Jenner, Christopher A160
Jenner, Cindy P573
Jenness, Calvin E. P87
Jennifer, Shade A835
Jennifer, Faase P477
Jennings, Gary A87
Jennings, Jennifer A160
Jennings, Bill A199
Jennings, Michael C. A425
Jennings, Michael A449
Jennings, Stacy A462
Jennings, Kevin A505
Jennings, Justin A651
Jennings, Regina A665
Jennings, Scott A687
Jennings, Dick A734
Jennings, Rebecca A923
Jennings, Dick A933
Jennings, Sarah P2
Jennings, Gary P50
Jennings, William M P97
Jennings, Stacy P256
Jennings, Denyse P323
Jennings, Stephen P438
Jennings, Andrew N. E144
Jennings, Gordan E149
Jennings, Michael E221
Jennings, Justin E330
Jennings, Regina E334
Jennings, Rebecca E442
Jenrette, John P118
Jensen, Scott A126
Jensen, Christopher W. (Chris) A177
Jensen, Jane A184
Jensen, Barry A455
Jensen, Bevan A462
Jensen, Donald A598
Jensen, Don A599
Jensen, Shea A602
Jensen, Shea D A602
Jensen, Derrick A. A696
Jensen, Eric A779
Jensen, Neil D A853
Jensen, Linda A P198
Jensen, Bevan P256
Jensen, Karen P400
Jensen, Jennifer P493
Jensen, Ken P597
Jensen, Espen P610
Jensen, Neil D P612
Jensen, Mira E127
Jensen, Barry E227
Jensen, Carol E359
Jensen, Tony E360
Jenson, James A498
Jenson, Susy P173
Jent, Dave P610
Jentsch, Dieter W. W53
Jentz, Alan P618
Jeong, Kyong-Deuk W236
Jeong, Tak W311
Jeppesen, Jon A A71
Jeppesen, Poul P496
Jeppson, Patricia P597
Jepson, Helene A349
Jepson, Brian D. P395
Jepson, Brian D P395
Jerabek, Judy A545

Jerabek, Judy P317
Jereb, Denise E73
Jergenson, Dana A885
Jermhansa, Noppawan W216
Jernigan, Donald A14
Jernigan, Janet A108
Jernigan, Wyatt A250
Jernigan, Ken A867
Jernigan, Donald P6
Jernigan, Jeff P58
Jernigan, Ken E418
Jernstedt, Tiffin A692
Jerome, Christopher J. (Chris) A882
Jerome, Brian S P282
Jerome, Karen P658
Jerome-Resnick, Cynthia A205
Jerosch-herold, Michael A642
Jerosch-herold, Michael P407
Jerpe, David P411
Jerry, O'hara A569
Jerry, Estimable A642
Jerry, Estimable P407
Jervis, Olivia A782
Jervis, Olivia P525
Jesel, Eugene P469
Jesiolowski, Craig A. P528
Jeske, Ryan E184
Jesko, Danielle P144
Jesse, Lisa A811
Jessee, William P465
Jesselson, Michael A935
Jessup, Sara A834
Jester, Clyde A P149
Jesudason, Rob W113
Jesus, Carmencita De P298
Jesus, Angelo D P532
Jesus, Joe De P546
Jeter, Daniel B. A62
Jeter, Daniel B. E20
Jetnil, Anthony E143
Jett, Stephanie A92
Jett, Robert A715
Jett, Nicole A861
Jett, Betsy P364
Jetter, Martin A465
Jetter, Frederick A727
Jetter, Frederick P453
Jetty, Sathish P5
Jewell, Sarika A189
Jewell, Meg P430
Jewell, John B P606
Jewell, Rob P606
Jewell, Matthew J. E180
Jewett, Joshua R. (Josh) A273
Jewkes, Roger S. A325
Jeworrek, Torsten W267
Jex, Lora A769
Jex, Lora E380
Jez, Karen A312
Jezic, Nina A305
Jha, Bijoy A154
Jha, Ranjeet A203
Jha, Rakesh W194
Jhanji, Shweta A60
Jhaveri, Vishu P90
Jia, Xiaotong A112
Jia, Keith A484
Jiaheng, Wang W72
Jiambalvo, James A880
Jiambalvo, James P640
Jian, Yu W102
Jian, Liu W110
Jian, Qiao W234
Jiandani, Soni A198
Jiang, Richard A391
Jiang, Tina A511
Jiang, Tina P290
Jiang, Shibo P364
Jiang, Joseph P502
Jianguo, Yan W100
Jianguo, Han W102
Jianhua, Zhang W301
Jick, Daniel P79
Jiga, Anthony A592
Jiga, Anthony P370

Jiganti, Jeanine M. A257
Jilg, Robyn P624
Jimenez, Tomas A108
Jimenez, Frank R. A706
Jimenez, Anna A925
Jimenez, Laura P164
Jimenez, Ed P489
Jimenez, Carmen P530
Jimenez, Hector E290
Jimenez, Anna E445
Jimerson, Rori P55
Jimerson, Estee E132
Jin, Jeoung (A. J.) A356
Jin, Na A444
Jin, Julie A522
Jin, Yadong P49
Jin, Jeff E318
Jindal, Meenu P430
Jingdong, Wang W198
Jinghui, Tian W301
Jinglei, Cheng W336
Jingnan, Liu P187
Jingzhen, Lin W72
Jinks, Mark P137
Jinping, Gao W354
Jiong, Wang W108
Jishi, Mohannad A530
Jitjang, Krit W216
Jivanov, Iasmina P287
Jivrajani, Jayish A391
Jiwani, Zahra P266
Joachim, Steven A. (Steve) P202
Jobalia, Amul P472
Jobanputra, Rakesh A596
Jobe, Meredith P6
Jockett, Joan P605
Jocson, Carlito A255
Jodar, Luis A658
Joe, Stephanie A897
Joe, David E139
Joergenrud, Odd A724
Joergenrud, Odd P452
Joeris, Gary P266
Joerres, Jeffrey A. A915
Joffe, Eb P572
Joffrion, Barry P421
Jogaib, Julio A114
Jogaib, Julio E37
Jogrenson, Robert A737
Jogrenson, Robert E361
Johann, Joseph A839
Johanneman, Ben P318
Johansen, Kurt A60
Johansen, Jakob V P194
Johansson, Leif W38
Johansson, Leif W386
Johl, Jugraj A722
John, Feury A16
John, Kevin St A61
John, Michelle A107
John, Ryan A137
John, Binny A550
John, Alan A602
John, Arbi A638
John, Jarratt A692
John, Gregory St A710
John, Todd St A871
John, Timmer A925
John, Beulah P392
John, Kreidler P450
John, Preston St P653
John, Arbi E320
John, Timmer E445
Johndroe, Gordon A140
Johnk, Kellee P471
Johnnie, Mark P59
Johns, John A380
Johns, Leena A559
Johns, John D. A683
Johns, Bobbie P188
Johnsen, Tim P254
Johnsen, Nola P465
Johnsen, David C. P594
Johnsgaard, Dag A301

Johnsgaard, Dag P196
Johnson, Collister (Coddy) A10
Johnson, Jace A11
Johnson, Kristina A18
Johnson, Douglas A19
Johnson, Craig A. A41
Johnson, Stephen L. (Steve) A47
Johnson, Ted M. A52
Johnson, Howard A53
Johnson, Matt A63
Johnson, Laurie A86
Johnson, Michael A91
Johnson, Brad A100
Johnson, Jared A115
Johnson, Kurt A120
Johnson, Jennifer A127
Johnson, Timothy A. (Tim) A132
Johnson, Dannis A138
Johnson, Lynn A140
Johnson, Dick A145
Johnson, Dannis A157
Johnson, Warren A158
Johnson, Thomas A. A162
Johnson, Jeffrey A168
Johnson, Mary A170
Johnson, Cheryl C A173
Johnson, Nancy A175
Johnson, Bennett A176
Johnson, Monte A184
Johnson, James W. (Jay) A190
Johnson, Lynden E. A194
Johnson, Jim A197
Johnson, Jamie A197
Johnson, Cliff A198
Johnson, Beth A205
Johnson, Eric R. A212
Johnson, Avery A219
Johnson, Annie A237
Johnson, J David A240
Johnson, Colleen A242
Johnson, Bill A258
Johnson, William A258
Johnson, Chris B. A267
Johnson, Don A270
Johnson, Richard A285
Johnson, Kimberly H. A312
Johnson, Daniel A315
Johnson, Michael A319
Johnson, Christine A319
Johnson, Margie A329
Johnson, Darin A343
Johnson, Darlene A345
Johnson, Richard A. (Dick) A359
Johnson, Gregory E. A363
Johnson, Jennifer M. A363
Johnson, Rupert H. A363
Johnson, James J A364
Johnson, Daniel A369
Johnson, S. Daniel (Dan) A373
Johnson, S Daniel A373
Johnson, Jill A374
Johnson, Phillip A380
Johnson, Steven A389
Johnson, Brandon A390
Johnson, James A405
Johnson, Coleman A405
Johnson, Brion A408
Johnson, R. Milton A410
Johnson, Kelly J. A413
Johnson, Gary A421
Johnson, Wes A440
Johnson, Scott A444
Johnson, Kathryn A452
Johnson, Jay A467
Johnson, A A467
Johnson, Erin A480
Johnson, Guy A487
Johnson, Lacy A489
Johnson, Gina A500
Johnson, Edwin A502
Johnson, Erik S A513
Johnson, Philip A518
Johnson, Eric A520
Johnson, Robert A527
Johnson, Emily A546

Johnson, Oliver M. A551
Johnson, Melonie A562
Johnson, Margaret L A565
Johnson, Gregory D. (Greg) A615
Johnson, Anne A618
Johnson, Steve A630
Johnson, James W A632
Johnson, Phil A635
Johnson, Jodie A647
Johnson, Dennis A647
Johnson, Jam A654
Johnson, Rady A. A657
Johnson, Paula A. A662
Johnson, Bob A665
Johnson, Christine A677
Johnson, Paul A691
Johnson, Peggy L A695
Johnson, Stuart R. A717
Johnson, Don A723
Johnson, Tim A726
Johnson, Samuel H A735
Johnson, Lisa A741
Johnson, Steve A747
Johnson, Jeff A755
Johnson, Amy W. A760
Johnson, David A761
Johnson, Robert A774
Johnson, Kevin R. A779
Johnson, Aimee A779
Johnson, Julie H A790
Johnson, Julie A790
Johnson, Patrick A793
Johnson, Tom A797
Johnson, Brion S A800
Johnson, Bob A809
Johnson, William D. (Bill) A815
Johnson, Chris A816
Johnson, Mark M. A818
Johnson, Cheryl H. A821
Johnson, Genevieve A823
Johnson, Bret A833
Johnson, Laura A835
Johnson, Robert J. A849
Johnson, Steve A853
Johnson, Shannon A. A859
Johnson, Debbie A859
Johnson, Sarah A859
Johnson, Kelly A860
Johnson, Joseph A867
Johnson, Willie A871
Johnson, Todd A877
Johnson, Stephen A885
Johnson, Alan A895
Johnson, Clay A901
Johnson, Jason A922
Johnson, Lisa A925
Johnson, Benjamin A926
Johnson, Tracy A933
Johnson, Darrin A933
Johnson, Adam R. A939
Johnson, Marta P31
Johnson, Charlotte P45
Johnson, Nicole Conley P56
Johnson, George P56
Johnson, Antonia Axson P57
Johnson, Dennis P64
Johnson, John H P86
Johnson, Gerald D. (Jerry) P87
Johnson, Dannis P91
Johnson, Bobby P96
Johnson, Peter S P101
Johnson, Paul P102
Johnson, Pete P108
Johnson, Bret P111
Johnson, Tod S. P114
Johnson, Kelly M. P127
Johnson, John P134
Johnson, Charles P137
Johnson, Larue P148
Johnson, Kathryn P150
Johnson, J D P162
Johnson, Bruce E. P172
Johnson, Stacey P174
Johnson, H Keith P180
Johnson, Deborah C P190

COMBINED HOOVER'S HANDBOOK INDEX OF EXECUTIVES

```
A = AMERICAN BUSINESS
E = EMERGING COMPANIES
P = PRIVATE COMPANIES
W = WORLD BUSINESS
```

Johnson, David P193
Johnson, Jt P197
Johnson, Steven P. P232
Johnson, Don P237
Johnson, Patsy P244
Johnson, Kimberly P244
Johnson, Michelle R P250
Johnson, Mark P258
Johnson, Donna P260
Johnson, Patrice P270
Johnson, Neil P280
Johnson, Antonia Axson P293
Johnson, Carrie P302
Johnson, Colleen P313
Johnson, Kimiko P320
Johnson, Oliver M. P321
Johnson, Mark P329
Johnson, Rodney D. P333
Johnson, Cato P335
Johnson, Barbara P338
Johnson, Karen D P340
Johnson, Bernadeia P343
Johnson, Karen P355
Johnson, David D P358
Johnson, Ryan P379
Johnson, Tracy P383
Johnson, Hattie P388
Johnson, Tony P395
Johnson, Pamela P402
Johnson, Andrew P425
Johnson, Joey P428
Johnson, J Keith P429
Johnson, Sandra P456
Johnson, Dale P462
Johnson, Jani L. P466
Johnson, Lisa P466
Johnson, Jani L P467
Johnson, Ken P478
Johnson, Robert C P479
Johnson, Carol P481
Johnson, Kirk P497
Johnson, Bryan P523
Johnson, Sara P531
Johnson, Frank P532
Johnson, Raymond P546
Johnson, Mark L. P549
Johnson, Willie P551
Johnson, Maurice P552
Johnson, Brian P552
Johnson, Ray F P553
Johnson, Rosalyn P594
Johnson, M. Eric P599
Johnson, Allen (Al) P607
Johnson, Steve P612
Johnson, Kirk P616
Johnson, Julia P616
Johnson, Julie A. P627
Johnson, Sylvia Smith P630
Johnson, Mary P632
Johnson, John P653
Johnson, Jerry N. P658
Johnson, Josephine J P659
Johnson, April P670
Johnson, Jason P671
JOHNSON, ERIN P675
Johnson, Sidney W31
Johnson, Chris W276
Johnson, David T. E18
Johnson, Gary R. E23
Johnson, Laurie E27
Johnson, Michael E29
Johnson, Jared E38
Johnson, William S. (Bill) E56
Johnson, Thomas A. E61
Johnson, Ray E64
Johnson, Edwin D. (Ed) E68
Johnson, Shari E81
Johnson, Avery E87
Johnson, Martin E99

Johnson, Rhett E102
Johnson, Vanessa E106
Johnson, Cheryl E123
Johnson, Phinesia E132
Johnson, Leonard F E143
Johnson, Lynn E144
Johnson, Darin E164
Johnson, Darlene E166
Johnson, Paul E172
Johnson, Charles E197
Johnson, Kelly J. E205
Johnson, Carl J. E224
Johnson, Nicholas E275
Johnson, Alex E290
Johnson, David E291
Johnson, Betty R. E293
Johnson, Gary E293
Johnson, M. Carl E299
Johnson, Robert S. E305
Johnson, Anne E310
Johnson, Andrew E318
Johnson, Bob E334
Johnson, Patrick E349
Johnson, Stuart R. E351
Johnson, Lisa E364
Johnson, Lynn E368
Johnson, Jeff E369
Johnson, Amy W. E374
Johnson, Todd E388
Johnson, Julie H E389
Johnson, Julie E389
Johnson, Mark M. E403
Johnson, Genevieve E405
Johnson, Wallace H. E422
Johnson, Guy K. E433
Johnson, Marianne E438
Johnson, Bradford D. E441
Johnson, Lisa E445
Johnson, Benjamin E445
Johnston, Mark A25
Johnston, Rob A71
Johnston, Mary A105
Johnston, Steve A108
Johnston, Lori A. A177
Johnston, Steven J. A195
Johnston, Bryan L A222
Johnston, Andy A232
Johnston, Michael F. (Mike) A277
Johnston, Gregory A319
Johnston, Kelly A349
Johnston, William A530
Johnston, Hugh F. A654
Johnston, Mac A664
Johnston, David A686
Johnston, Maryann A738
Johnston, Brent A818
Johnston, Richard A887
Johnston, Greg A902
Johnston, Mark P14
Johnston, Adriane P32
Johnston, Greg P64
Johnston, Kenneth P66
Johnston, Craig P201
Johnston, Christine P285
Johnston, Jeffrey P331
Johnston, Diann P346
Johnston, Andy P487
Johnston, James W. P499
Johnston, Lisa P596
Johnston, J. Dave W174
Johnston, Dave W174
Johnston, Russell (Russ) W317
Johnston, Steve W373
Johnston, Colleen M. W396
Johnston, Mary E34
Johnston, Linda A. E42
Johnston, Rene E131
Johnston, Dan S. E315
Johnston, Daniel E315
Johnston, Mac E334
Johnston, Dale E349
Johnston, Brent E403
Johnstone, William O. A105
Johnstone, Robert A140
Johnstone, William O. E34

Johnstone, Rudolph E381
Johnstun, Paul A413
Johnstun, Paul E205
Johri, Akhil A875
Johst, David P. E75
Joiner, Brad A319
Joiner, Mary A877
Joins, Spille P582
Jojo, Linda P. A864
Jokerst, Russell P520
Jolas, Paul M. E422
Jolin, Joanne A248
Jolin, Joanne E107
Joling, Scott A859
Jolkovsky, Richard P587
Jolley, Jennifer A940
Jolley, Burke P270
Jolly, Ed A352
Joly, Hubert A130
Joly, Hubert A702
Jonas, Richard P130
Jones, Greg A17
Jones, Douglas L. (Doug) A25
Jones, Ross A25
Jones, Katie R A36
Jones, Gregg A56
Jones, Brian A63
Jones, Wesley A63
Jones, Bob A72
Jones, Jennifer A89
Jones, John P A93
Jones, Alicia A108
Jones, Cary A112
Jones, Jeremy A135
Jones, Lacey A140
Jones, Ken A143
Jones, Mike A149
Jones, Jonathan A160
Jones, Nicole A194
Jones, Rosalyn A200
Jones, Thomas A222
Jones, Anthony A226
Jones, Larry W. A229
Jones, D. Andrew A229
Jones, David A229
Jones, Bill A242
Jones, Clay A246
Jones, Summara A255
Jones, Tim A259
Jones, Mary K W A260
Jones, Shane A262
Jones, Laurie A262
Jones, Paul R A262
Jones, Paul A262
Jones, Keri A264
Jones, Wendy A287
Jones, Karla A296
Jones, Jeanne A305
Jones, Katrina A312
Jones, Jeffrey A A329
Jones, Alex A345
Jones, Charles E. (Chuck) A350
Jones, J Myers A362
Jones, Randy A364
Jones, Paul J. A407
Jones, Bruce A420
Jones, Katrina A423
Jones, Adrienne F A441
Jones, Kevin A444
Jones, Carolyn A444
Jones, Earl A452
Jones, Franklin B A460
Jones, Sheri A462
Jones, Buff A466
Jones, Mamie A471
Jones, Dave A487
Jones, Suzan A492
Jones, Steve A498
Jones, Paul A500
Jones, David A510
Jones, René F. A530
Jones, Deanna L. A533
Jones, Beth A538
Jones, Cynthia A562
Jones, Kevin A566

Jones, Amanda A566
Jones, Kim A573
Jones, Jessica A578
Jones, Mae A606
Jones, Christopher T. A608
Jones, Robert G. (Bob) A621
Jones, Wilson R A632
Jones, Jeff C A636
Jones, Douglas E. (Doug) A648
Jones, Kathleen A651
Jones, Laura A654
Jones, Bill A664
Jones, Allison A665
Jones, Diane A665
Jones, Doug A665
Jones, Randall T. (Todd) A688
Jones, Larry A688
Jones, Randall T. (Todd) A689
Jones, Larry A689
Jones, Bob A704
Jones, Ellen S. A712
Jones, Karen M. A734
Jones, Tom A735
Jones, Iris A749
Jones, William A753
Jones, Jeffrey A761
Jones, Barbara A782
Jones, Andrea A793
Jones, Robbie A796
Jones, Tracy A798
Jones, Alicia A800
Jones, Elizabeth A820
Jones, Nicholas P. A828
Jones, Chris A835
Jones, Roger V. A842
Jones, Lisa A843
Jones, Bruce R. A844
Jones, Stuart A849
Jones, Mike A871
Jones, Linda A873
Jones, Brian A880
Jones, Anthony A887
Jones, Jeffrey L A887
Jones, Tony A887
Jones, Richard M. A892
Jones, Rosetta A896
Jones, Pamela A909
Jones, Mindy A922
Jones, Eddie A935
Jones, Don P6
Jones, Greg P9
Jones, Douglas L. (Doug) P14
Jones, Ross P14
Jones, Sandra S P19
Jones, Lynwood A P22
Jones, Gala P46
Jones, Doug P59
Jones, Theresa P60
Jones, C. Todd P64
Jones, Stephen P66
Jones, Lakeisha P105
Jones, Michael P109
Jones, Christopher P116
Jones, Melody L P117
Jones, Michael P129
Jones, Bruce P142
Jones, Anthony P150
Jones, Timothy P P155
Jones, Ross P157
Jones, Vernon P161
Jones, Amy P168
Jones, Scott P186
Jones, Dan P206
Jones, Chris P209
Jones, Jim P221
Jones, Theresa P223
Jones, Kearline P232
Jones, Jeff P233
Jones, Stephanie P235
Jones, Sheri P256
Jones, Brian P258
Jones, Mark A P265
Jones, Evan C P284
Jones, David P290
Jones, Charles E P336

Jones, Barbara P337
Jones, Gordon L P344
Jones, Suzanne P375
Jones, Mark A. P400
Jones, Jeff C P403
Jones, Jacqueline P409
Jones, Charles E P411
Jones, Janel P412
Jones, Misty P417
Jones, Randall T. (Todd) P435
Jones, Larry P435
Jones, Marna P448
Jones, Dylan P. P480
Jones, Harold P517
Jones, Mike P522
Jones, Sterling P525
Jones, Barbara P526
Jones, Lisa P546
Jones, Elizabeth P551
Jones, Bryson P555
Jones, Marc P568
Jones, Jeff P578
Jones, Robert P582
Jones, Nicholas P. P584
Jones, Tammie P593
Jones, Barbara P608
Jones, Linda P617
Jones, Christopher P623
Jones, Reed F P624
Jones, Daniel W P632
Jones, Lindsey P638
Jones, Brian P640
Jones, Alison P650
Jones, Mindy P671
Jones, Garth W14
Jones, Den W212
Jones, Tiffany E14
Jones, Keith E80
Jones, Marsha E81
Jones, Steven M. E103
Jones, Clay E105
Jones, Becky E123
Jones, Ryan E127
Jones, Gregory E143
Jones, Alex E165
Jones, Rob E197
Jones, Barbara E256
Jones, Greg E264
Jones, Robert G. (Bob) E311
Jones, Douglas E. (Doug) E328
Jones, Kathleen E329
Jones, Bill E334
Jones, Allison E334
Jones, Diane E334
Jones, Doug E334
Jones, Iris E367
Jones, Bradford E386
Jones, Robbie E397
Jones, Paul A. E423
Jones, Pamela E436
Jong, Annemieke De P556
Jonker, Coenraad (Coen) W114
Jonske, James A36
Jooma, Imran P567
Joon, Lee Won W240
Jope, Alan W408
Jope, Alan W409
Joplin, Joe P382
Jorandby, Kendra P309
Jord, Scar A321
Jordahl, Mark S. P26
Jordan, Michael A60
Jordan, James A80
Jordan, Simon A133
Jordan, Deborah A. A162
Jordan, Michelle A167
Jordan, Rusty A171
Jordan, D. Bryan A343
Jordan, Chris A381
Jordan, Nancy A520
Jordan, Tom A592
Jordan, Randy A630
Jordan, Gregory B A668
Jordan, Barry A702
Jordan, Joe A713

Jordan, Steve A850
Jordan, Bill A921
Jordan, Darren A922
Jordan, James P46
Jordan, Steve P120
Jordan, George P120
Jordan, Patrick P173
Jordan, Denisha P188
Jordan, Arthur P189
Jordan, Javoris P280
Jordan, Marie K. (Kim) P289
Jordan, Tom P370
Jordan, Will P577
Jordan, David P610
Jordan, Bill P669
Jordan, Darren P671
Jordan, Deborah A. E62
Jordan, Sheila E143
Jordan, Ronald E149
Jordan, D. Bryan E163
Jordan-smith, Gavin A933
Jordon, Stacy P481
Jorgensen, Ben A13
Jorgensen, Helen A436
Jorgensen, Jeff A448
Jorgensen, Jay T. A901
Jorgensen, Helge P173
Jorgensen, Jeff P247
Jorgensen, Mary P298
Jorgensen, Dwain C. E211
Jorgenson, Rob A737
Jorgenson, Kenneth A747
Jorgenson, Robert E181
Jorgenson, Rob E361
Josan, Jose Luis A289
Jose, Fran A158
Jose, Alberto A507
Joseph, Gregory A56
Joseph, Loretta A65
Joseph, Ritesh A135
Joseph, Oliver A264
Joseph, Tommy S. A467
Joseph, George A555
Joseph, Philip A895
Joseph, Cathy P212
Joseph, Simone P325
Joseph, Dennis P405
Joseph, Jason E53
Joshi, Abhay A460
Joshi, Amit P433
Joshi, Pravin E290
Joshua, Eto A381
Josias, Mike A179
Joslin, Tim A. P153
Joslin, Tim P153
Joslin, Tim A P210
Joslyn, Scott P298
Josowitz, Barry A481
Jost, Paul A915
Jotwani, Juhi A465
Joulwan, George E126
Jovanovic, Veka P75
Joyal, David A243
Joyce, Deborah A181
Joyce, Thomas P. A254
Joyce, Teresa A349
Joyce, David L. A374
Joyce, Robert J. (Bob) A489
Joyce, Denise A881
Joyce, Katherine A P656
Joyce, Deborah E70
Joyce, Denise E421
Joyner, Dee A224
Joyner, J. David A251
Joyner, John A251
Joyner, Andre A500
Joyner, Ken A604
Joyner, Matt P540
Joysizemore, Dian A105
Joysizemore, Dian E34
Jozwik, Mary P642
Jr, Paul G Haaga A45
Jr, Paul G Haaga A50
Jr, George Pierce A56
Jr, Paul B Murphy A159

Jr, Jack E Counts A165
Jr, Domenic Dell'osso A189
Jr, James Spellings A309
Jr, W Michael Amick A467
Jr, C Thomas Evans A489
Jr, Robert E Swaney A578
Jr, Ray Napolitan A612
Jr, George West A636
Jr, Ronald J Nicolas A636
Jr, Phillip D Joseph A775
Jr, Lawrence C Franklin A782
Jr, John B King A785
Jr, William Berry A790
Jr, Richard L Smith A830
Jr, Thomas B Gerlach A830
Jr, John Pelusi A883
Jr, Brooks Von Arx A922
Jr, Hugh Inman P5
Jr, Leroy J Stromberg P19
Jr, Richard Kruse P22
Jr, Walter Sullivan P24
Jr, Paul G Haaga P30
Jr, Paul G Haaga P31
Jr, Donald M Clements P32
Jr, Rick Shadyac P34
Jr, Richard K Trowbridge P37
Jr, John A Miller P38
Jr, James F McEncaney P40
Jr, William J Ferguson P58
Jr, J James Pearce P81
Jr, John F George P85
Jr, Joseph Sarpy P85
Jr, Andrew Hove P103
Jr, Floyd Eharlow P105
Jr, Jack E Counts P108
Jr, George Robert Vaughan P112
Jr, Arthur C Evans P150
Jr, Robert Rosene P157
Jr, Robert B Rosene P157
Jr, John Kennedy P162
Jr, Joseph P Santucci P165
Jr, John C Fryer P188
Jr, Theo Bunting P196
Jr, Herbert H Huddleston P201
Jr, Glenn D Steele P214
Jr, Albert Bothe P214
Jr, Glenn D Steele P214
Jr, Glenn D Steele P215
Jr, Robert Hill P240
Jr, Ewing Werlein P245
Jr, Ernest J Novak P265
Jr, Howard L Barton P279
Jr, Stephen Paul Carter P279
Jr, Carlos Cole P280
Jr, Jerry Lamon Falwell P295
Jr, Martin Salinas P297
Jr, Robert L Lord P310
Jr, Charles A Collat P316
Jr, John M Starcher P329
Jr, Thomas M Dono P334
Jr, Norris L Hodgins P349
Jr, David D Desper P349
Jr, Robert Blount P387
Jr, Theodore T Myre P389
Jr, Charles E Jones P394
Jr, Ronald J Nicolas P403
Jr, Richard C Owens P408
Jr, Michael Perrone P423
Jr, Glenn Steel P428
Jr, Donald Anderson P431
Jr, Robert Allen P439
Jr, Thomas J McCraken P445
Jr, Walter W Austin P450
Jr, William Delong P466
Jr, J Harry Haslam P474
Jr, Jerome A Benkert P505
Jr, Phillip D Joseph P511
Jr, Lawrence C Franklin P526
Jr, John B King P526
Jr, Elmo M Cavin P552
Jr, William Michael Warren P559
Jr, Eugene A Gargaro P565
Jr, Glenn D Steele P569
Jr, Virgil E Cooper P575
Jr, Kenneth O Johnson P587

Jr, William Hite P588
Jr, Richard L Smith P593
Jr, Thomas B Gerlach P593
Jr, Donald Campbell P595
Jr, James W Dean P642
Jr, John Pelusi P644
Jr, Anthony Rizzo P664
Jr, Brooks Von Arx P671
Ju, Jennifer P534
Juarez, Alfonso P250
Juby, Alyce A491
Jucha, Piotr A548
Jucker, Bernhard W3
Juday, Mark A37
Juday, Ryan A834
Juday, Mark P27
Judd, Jim A608
Jude, Justin L. A524
Judge, Christopher A34
Judge, James J. (Jim) A303
Judge, Kenan A447
Judge, Kenan P247
Judge, Daniel P P268
Judge, Kathy E147
Judice, Marc W. E212
Judson, James E315
Judy, Ryan A69
Jue, Don A465
Jueckstock, Rainer A813
Juergensen, Colleen A498
Juett, Phillip P333
Jugo, Rita A109
Jugoon, Peter A744
Juinio, Gilbert A586
Jula, Peg A329
Julian, Paul C. A549
Julian, Sylvie A695
Julian, Steve A754
Julian, Kenneth D. A834
Julian, Steve P484
Julian, James R. P631
Julian, Heather San P647
Juliano, Mark A506
Julie, Campbell P137
Julie, Norton P383
Julien, Jeffrey P. (Jeff) A704
Julien, Robert P274
Julien, Marc--%otienne W319
Jump, Belinda A385
Jump, Jamie E99
Jun, Albert P268
Jun-Ho, Kim W354
Junck, Mary E. P555
Junco, Kirk P285
Juneau, Jeff A780
Jung, Yoosung P248
Jung, Holger R P282
Jung, Soo-Hyun W191
Jung, Dong-chang W311
Jung, Holger R. E248
Jung, Pete E279
Jung-ho, Park W355
Junglas, Steve A398
Junglas, Steve P222
Jungwirth, Rebecca A260
Juniper, Brooke A575
Junius, Daniel E223
Junk, Luke A727
Junk, Luke P453
Junker, Heinz K. W245
Junkins, Lowell L. A317
Junkins, Lowell L. E146
Junming, Guo W190
Junod, Vincent A744
Junqueira, Patricia E159
Juntti, Debbie P308
Jupe, Joel — P164
Jurado, Welmer A676
Jurado, Welmer E338
Jurco, Tim A598
Jurczyk, Andrew D. P486
Jurgens, Michael A448
Jurgens, Michael P247
Jurrens, Erika A170
Jurrjens, George A390

COMBINED HOOVER'S HANDBOOK INDEX OF EXECUTIVES

A = AMERICAN BUSINESS
E = EMERGING COMPANIES
P = PRIVATE COMPANIES
W = WORLD BUSINESS

Jurs, Peter A329
Jusino, Arnaldo P86
Jusko, James P553
Jussame, Raymond P340
Juster, Andrew A. (Andy) A761
Justesen, Jon E40
Justice, Peggy Rasnick P419
Justice, Lorraine P456
Justice, Ronald L. E150
Justus, Luiza P608
Juszczyszyn, Kyle A175
Jutras, Mary E147
Jutze, Roy A327
Juve, Kathy A795
Juvelier, Scott E350
Jyothinagaram, Sathya A117
Jyothinagaram, Sathya P61
J-okel, Julia W66
J-rgensen, Torsten Hagen W287
J-rgensen, Lars Fruergaard W290
Jégo-Laveissi-"re, Mari-No-«lle W297

K

K, Sandvik Helvi P356
K, Ajit E131
Kaaihue, Herb P112
Kaalund, Sekou H A484
Kaare, Rae P49
Kaatman, Nancy J A140
Kaban, Leonard P574
Kabani, Farhan E267
Kabat, Amanda A15
Kabat, Kevin T. A882
Kabat, Amanda P7
Kabay, Laura P110
Kablawi, Hani A111
Kabrick, Elizabeth P516
Kacavas, John P173
Kacewicz, Marek A190
Kachel, Vic A360
Kachurka, Matt A248
Kachurka, Matt E107
Kacich, Gary A645
Kacmarek, Robert P574
Kaczkowski, Brian A496
Kaczmarek, Larry A405
Kaczmarek, Walter T. (Walt) A414
Kaczmarek, Jessica A827
Kaczmarek, Walter T. (Walt) E208
Kaczoruk, Stanislaw Ryszard W54
Kaczynski, Thomas A534
Kaddoura, Maher A329
Kaden, Ellen O A164
Kadien, Thomas G. (Tom) A467
Kadlec, Tom A804
Kadnar, Julie A55
Kadokami, Ei W258
Kadouchi, Hitoshi W126
Kadre, Manuel A721
Kaeding, Nate A567
Kaeding, Nate E284
Kaelin, Michael H. (Mike) A447
Kaepernik, Daniel E64
Kaese, Torben A79
Kaeser, Richard A480
Kaeser, Joe W353
Kaestner, Angie P465
Kaewrungruang, Wallaya W351
Kafer, Ann A399
Kafer, Ann P223
Kafer, Tim P306
Kafka, Donald L. A333
Kagan, Amber A374
Kaganis, Perry A590
Kagawa, Jiro W215
Kagitcibasi, Elif A97

Kahan, Rich A746
Kahanek, Jacob P196
Kahanek, Sheila P532
Kahanek, Debra P548
Kahl, Cathy P313
Kahla, Vuyo W341
Kahlau, Dorothy A888
Kahlau, Dorothy E425
Kahlich, Randy P432
Kahn, Brad A25
Kahn, Cheryl A170
Kahn, Dale A797
Kahn, Wendy A801
Kahn, Todd A801
Kahn, Benjamin A882
Kahn, Brad P14
Kahne, Michael A345
Kahne, Michael E165
Kai, Keishi W279
Kaighn, Chris A84
Kail, Marilyn P114
Kain, Gary D A23
Kain, Peter A584
Kain, Gary D. E5
Kainersdorfer, Franz W417
Kairis, Phil A610
Kaiser, George B. A142
Kaiser, Laura S. A462
Kaiser, Jim A530
Kaiser, Frances A590
Kaiser, Nicole P174
Kaiser, Michael P193
Kaiser, Laura S. P256
Kaiser, Cindy P266
Kaiser, Daphne P282
Kaiser, Larry R. P546
Kaiser, Ken P546
Kaiser, Larrty R P595
Kaiser, George B. E49
Kaiser, Daniel E264
Kaiserman, David J. A512
Kaiwa, Makoto W392
Kaji, Lucy P198
Kajioka, Jenny A109
Kajueter, Henrik A97
Kakar, Parveen E394
Kakiuchi, Takehiko W257
Kakiya, Tatsuo W349
Kakkis, Jane P323
Kakogiannis, Efstathios A. W25
Kaku, Masatoshi W293
Kakuda, Kevin A226
Kakuda, Kevin P150
Kalafatis, Lara P116
Kalafut, Thomas A922
Kalafut, Thomas P671
Kalakkad, Dinesh A505
Kalamaras, Paul A473
Kalamaras, Paul E236
Kalambur, Ganesh P604
Kalanihuia, Janice P585
Kalanovic, Daniel A658
Kalaria, Brij A137
Kalaria, Brijesh A137
Kalathur, Rajesh A260
Kalavakuri, Hari A93
Kalayjian, Nick A818
Kalbaugh, J. Andrew (Andy) A528
Kalchik, Mona A114
Kalchik, Mona E36
Kalchuri, Shantanu A613
Kale, Kimberly P180
Kale, Rahul W424
Kalen, Michael A686
Kali, Thomas A137
Kalia, Ranjan E431
Kaliappan, Eswaramoorthy P445
Kalin, Robert A571
Kalinoski, Joe P97
Kalinowski, Tracy P500
Kalinowski, Brian E448
Kalisek, Brian A565
Kalish, Carol P473
Kalish, David W. E53
Kalkwarf, Lane P200

Kallas, Anjie A799
Kallenbach, Charles P234
Kallevik, Eivind W289
Kallsen, Terri R. A746
Kalmin, Steven W172
Kalnin, Andrew J P581
Kalonder, Liz A893
Kaloussis, Evangelos J. W25
Kaloustian, Maral A155
Kaloustian, Maral E54
Kalp, Dirk P666
Kalsbeck, Brad Van P281
Kalsbeek, David P175
Kalscheur, Gregory P608
Kalstein, Michele A320
Kaltner, Savilla E290
Kaluarachchi, Pubudu P638
Kalvaitis, Jennifer A484
Kam, Keith P534
Kamada, Kazuhiko W293
Kamal, Mostafa M. A532
Kamalbatcha, Shajahan A209
Kamano, Michel P422
Kamara, Abdul A170
Kamara, Ernest T P383
Kamath, Harish A135
Kamath, Vijita A711
Kamath, Vijita P444
Kambe, Shiro W361
Kamber, Martin A137
Kamdar, Devyani A137
Kamei, Katsunobu W298
Kamei, Atsushi W346
Kamel, Hany P654
Kamell, Ralph P300
Kamenash, Tracey A409
Kamensky, Allan E. A796
Kamensky, Allan E. E397
Kamerling, Allison P258
Kametz, William (Bill) A737
Kametz, William (Bill) E361
Kamford, Peter A126
Kamijo, Masahito W321
Kamiliotis, Daniela A702
Kamin, Cynthia A175
Kamin, John R. A621
Kamin, John R. E311
Kaminski, Jennifer A85
Kaminski, Tom A502
Kaminski, Irene A540
Kaminski, Robert B. A552
Kaminski, Mark V. A717
Kaminski, Douglas A746
Kaminski, Karen A843
Kaminski, Jennifer E27
Kaminski, Robert B. E275
Kamitaki, Wayne A182
Kamke, Trent G. E253
Kamlani, Kunal S P443
Kamm, Terry A140
Kammerer, Richard F. P560
Kammerman, Susan P405
Kamminga, Duane A345
Kamminga, Duane E166
Kammonen, Osmo W275
Kamp, W. Taylor E271
Kampf, Mark A706
Kamphaus, Randy P636
Kamps, Jordan E143
Kamra, Kush A559
Kamran, Nadia A469
Kamsickas, James K A253
Kan, Tetsuya W321
Kanaan, Matthew P187
Kanagawa, Chihiro W349
Kanaglekar, Indraneel A939
Kanai, Randy A602
Kanai, Seita W250
Kanai, Makoto W292
Kanakubo, Atsushi W127
Kanamori, Hitoshi W431
Kanas, John A. A115
Kanas, John A. E38
Kanazawa, Yugo W238
Kanbur, Charu A43

Kanbur, Charu E13
Kanda, Haruo W430
Kandarian, Steven A. (Steve) A559
Kandek, Wolfgang E342
Kandt, Debbie P617
Kane, Courtney A112
Kane, Thomas M. (Tom) A236
Kane, Thomas A326
Kane, Brian A405
Kane, Brian A. A440
Kane, Edward A444
Kane, Terri A462
Kane, John A583
Kane, Jim A608
Kane, Julie A609
Kane, Martha A641
Kane, Eric A797
Kane, Patrick P A867
Kane, Peter A893
Kane, Patrick P109
Kane, Jenny P193
Kane, Maggie P255
Kane, Terri P256
Kane, Kenneth P299
Kane, Julie P391
Kane, Martha P407
Kane, Allen R. P497
Kaneb, Gary P363
Kanefsky, Andrea A126
Kaneko, Shin W93
Kaneko, Hiroshi W215
Kaneshige, Jason P628
Kang, Byung A228
Kang, Katelyn A432
Kang, Hyun C P472
Kang, In-Byeong W236
Kang, Yu Sig W236
Kang, Katelyn E216
Kanis, Jordan A793
Kanis, Karla P405
Kannan, N. S. W194
Kanome, Hiroyuki W20
Kansara, Dushyant P85
Kansky, Bill P178
Kant, Surya A805
Kant, Surya P542
Kantamneni, Raje A606
Kantenberger, Curtis A263
Kanter, Maurissa A347
Kanter, Maurissa E168
Kantola, Kevin A877
Kantor, Jonathan D. (Jon) A210
Kantor, Hans P237
Kanwal, Ayesha P637
Kanwal, Ajay W364
Kao, Roger W123
Kaohi, Cheryl A109
Kaperi, Ari W287
Kapetanakis, Peter A665
Kapetanakis, Peter E334
Kapito, Robert S. (Rob) A135
Kapki, Nick Kapki Nick A884
Kapla, Bob A85
Kapla, Bob E27
Kaplan, Marlena A137
Kaplan, Ronald A158
Kaplan, Joel A310
Kaplan, Robert S. (Rob) A322
Kaplan, Valentin D A461
Kaplan, Andrew A589
Kaplan, Mike A740
Kaplan, Ryan A747
Kaplan, Robert A783
Kaplan, Dean A893
Kaplan, Bob A893
Kaplan, Paul P185
Kaplan, Matthew P343
Kaplan, Ross P399
Kaplan, Mark P627
Kaplan, Alan P640
Kaplan, Gary S P652
Kaplan, Marc E99
Kaplan, Jordan L. E114
Kaplan, Ronald W. (Ron) E409
Kaplanis, Donna P665

COMBINED HOOVER'S HANDBOOK INDEX OF EXECUTIVES

Kaplin, Leo A107
Kaplon, Sari P346
Kapoor, Rishi A562
Kapoor, Samir A695
Kapoor, Pragati P357
Kapoor, Rohit E140
Kappel, Angie A86
Kappel, Angie E27
Kappele, Brian P590
Kapre, Ravi E110
Kapsner, Richard A728
Kapur, Anuj A199
Kapur, Patricia P615
Kapur, Sangita P625
Kapusinski, Victor A884
Kar, Scott Van Der E59
Karachalios, Konstantinos P572
Karachi, Tracy P608
Karadere, Nafiz W403
Karafin, Thomas A686
Karageorges, Carolyn P128
Karalis, Cathy A590
Karamanoukian, Henry A680
Karami, Ladan A167
Karamouzis, Nikolaos Basil W157
Karanam, Raj A254
Karandikar, Nitin P594
Karanjkar, Ashish A654
Karas, Donald A421
Karasawa, Yasuyoshi W266
Karasick, Michael A466
Karatha, Padmanabhan A222
Karatsu, Masanori W256
Karavias, Fokion Christos W157
Karavolos, Nick P381
Karcz, Adam P252
Karczewski, Alicia P477
Kardis, Phillip J A191
Kareiva, Peter P579
Karen, Friedman A933
Kargar, Peyman W283
Karl, James A16
Karl, Patricia P163
Karlovich, Robert W. (Trey) A598
Karls, Lori A856
Karls, Lori P614
Karlsson, HAkan W420
Karlsten, Peter W420
Karn, Alice A491
Karn, Heather A824
Karn, Randy A920
Karn, Heather P562
Karner, Sabine P136
Karnes, Merle A682
Karnik, Nihar A606
Karnuta, Daniel A812
Karo, Rachel P428
Karolis, George C. A83
Karp, Caroline A120
Karp, Peter A147
Karp, Harold M P543
Karp, Stephen R. P558
Karpiak, Peter A708
Karpiak, Stephen P371
Karpik, Mike A783
Karpinski, John A452
Karr, Kathi A432
Karr, Michael A636
Karr, Michael P403
Karras, Athanasios A431
Karrazzi, Alia E290
Karrer, Joy P389
Karrip, Brian A337
Karrip, Brian E158
Karros, Kirt A420
Karsanbhai, Lal A292
Karsh, Bill E318
Karsner, Alexander A74
Karst, Darren W. A722
Karstens, Kevin A115
Karstens, Kevin E38
Karstensen, Steen S. W1
Kartson, Marianne A444
Karu, Zoher A287
Karytinos, Aristotelis W272

Kasai, Yoshiyuki W93
Kasai, Masahiro W366
Kasanoff, Howard A246
Kasanoff, Howard E105
Kasargod, Sameer A551
Kasargod, Sameer P321
Kasbar, Michael J. A927
Kase, Yutaka W360
Kaseman, Sheila P127
Kasen, Stewart A536
Kasendorf, Leonard A559
Kasey, Jay P351
Kashian, Alan E218
Kashiwagi, Yasuo W286
Kashkari, Neel T. A322
Kashner, John E3
Kaska, Tony A447
Kaska, Tony P247
Kasman, Glenn P352
Kasmiersky, Donna A449
Kasmiersky, Donna E221
Kasner, Ken A409
Kasper, Michael A36
Kasper, Andrea A686
Kasper, Kimberly A726
Kasprowicz, Michael A158
Kass, Jordan T. A728
Kassab, Leanne D. A211
Kassab, Leanne D. E83
Kassem, Rona P332
Kasser, James P558
Kassir, Abdul P153
Kassirer, Lacey E132
Kastanis, Maria A651
Kastanis, Maria E330
Kastberg, Amalia G A741
Kastberg, Amalia A741
Kastberg, Amalia G E364
Kastberg, Amalia E364
Kastendick, Kurt A859
Kastner, Evelyn A258
Kastner, Kevin A382
Kastner, Christopher D. A446
Kastner, Christopher K. A541
Kastner, Janeen B. A732
Kasturia, Sanjay A695
Kasuya, Tsuyoshi W221
Kaszowski, Richard P394
Kaszuba, Tracy A726
Kaszynski, Michal Rafal W54
Katahira, Satoru W298
Kataoka, Kazunori W298
Katayama, James P248
Katayama, Masanori W204
Katcher, Keith A613
Katehi, Linda P.B. P624
Kates, Kenneth P P629
Kath, Sean A686
Katherman, William H. (Bill) E180
Kathryn, Conde A480
Katie, Cave A741
Katie, Cave E364
Katims, Susan A158
Katkade, Vaibhav A658
Kato, Junichiro A135
Kato, Takeshi W51
KATO, SADANORI W107
Kato, Minoru W186
Kato, Kazuyasu W220
Kato, Hideaki W360
Kato, Toshizumi W430
Katoh, Nobuaki W132
Katrib, Tony A526
Katseli, Louka T. W272
Katsoudas, Francine A198
Katsouleas, Thomas C. P442
Katsoyannis, George P459
Katsuno, Satoru W107
Katsura, Yasuo W300
Katt, Faye A120
Kattan, Omar P615
Katterheinrich, Lean P148
Kattos, Andrew N. (Andy) A755
Kattos, Andrew N. (Andy) E369
Katyal, Navin A658

Katz, Richard A58
Katz, Heidi A65
Katz, Marc D. A158
Katz, Jerome A199
Katz, Mark A421
Katz, Robert L. (Bobby) A475
Katz, Todd A559
Katz, Maxine A588
Katz, Erin A711
Katz, Kelly A799
Katz, Jason P34
Katz, Ellen P81
Katz, Martin J. (Marty) P146
Katz, Maxine P365
Katz, Kevin P386
Katz, Erin P444
Katz, Kristine P524
Katz, Louis H. P569
Katz, Robert A. (Rob) E424
Katz, David E431
Katzav, Adir E117
Kauder, Frank P578
Kauffman, Holly C A351
Kauffman, Keith A452
Kauffman, Andy A538
Kauffman, Catherine A850
Kaufman, Jules P. A243
Kaufman, Victor A. A307
Kaufman, Neil A390
Kaufman, Jordan A390
Kaufman, Nick A498
Kaufman, Al A512
Kaufman, Richard A641
Kaufman, Michael J A686
Kaufman, Valerie A715
Kaufman, Adam A835
Kaufman, Dan P260
Kaufman, Dan P261
Kaufman, Charles P340
Kaufman, Richard P407
Kaufman, Irvin A P437
Kaufman, Irvin A. P438
Kaufman, Brett H. E250
Kaufman, Curtis E433
Kaufman, Brian E433
Kaufmann, Michael C. (Mike) A169
Kaufmann, Kevin A590
Kaukali, Chris T P628
Kaul, John A394
Kaul, Will P221
Kaup, Chad A339
Kaup, Nicholas P595
Kaup, Chad E159
Kaupa, Michael B. P406
Kaur, Primal A65
Kausch, Thomas P456
Kauser, Nicolas E326
Kaushal, Sunil W364
Kavanagh, Anthony A51
Kavanagh, Tony A51
Kavanagh, Ben A246
Kavanagh, Ben E105
Kavanaugh, John A230
Kavanaugh, James J. A465
Kavanaugh, James P A928
Kavanaugh, James P. (Jim) A928
Kavanaugh, John P154
Kavanaugh, James P P673
Kavanaugh, James P. (Jim) P674
Kavassalis, Tom A933
Kavin, Emily A362
Kavthekar, Suhas P502
Kawahara, Makoto W204
Kawai, Shuji W126
Kawai, Katsutomo W127
Kawai, Masanori W278
Kawai, Hideaki W301
Kawai, Fumiyoshi W368
Kawai, Mitsuru W400
Kawakami, Hiroshi W227
Kawale, Nitin E359
Kawamoto, Ryuichi W238
Kawamoto, Shoichiro W262
Kawamura, Dean A182
Kawamura, Yumiko W182

Kawamura, Takashi W394
Kawasaki, Hiroyuki A938
Kawasaki, Hiroyuki P678
Kawasaki, Hiroya W221
Kawasaki, Yasuyuki W369
Kawasaki, Masuo W374
Kawata, Hiro P218
Kawiecki, Michele A345
Kawiecki, Michele E166
Kay, Susan A114
Kay, Linda Sloane A183
Kay, Julie A185
Kay, Sue A484
Kay, Mary P627
Kay, Susan E37
Kay, Linda Sloane E74
Kayatta, Dominic P304
Kaye, David J. A147
Kaye, Stephen E248
Kays, Karmy A399
Kays, Karmy P224
Kayser, C. Dallas A206
Kayser, Catherine A797
Kayser, Karen P630
Kaza, Srini E10
Kazakevich, Vadim A112
Kazarian, Kristina A A578
Kazarian, Camille E391
Kazazian, Haig A478
Kazazian, Haig P268
Kazerounian, Reza P53
Kazi, Iftekhar P643
Kazmerick, Richard A227
Kazmerick, Richard E90
Kboudi, Caryn A230
Kboudi, Caryn P154
Keables, Michael P146
Keach, Michael A492
Keach, Camillia P546
Keady, Thomas P608
Kealey, Katie P304
Kealy, Mary V P300
Kean, Steven J. (Steve) A494
Kean, Stve A494
Kean, Ryan A498
Kean, Steve P360
Keane, Denise F. A41
Keane, John A51
Keane, Stella A132
Keane, Valerie A754
Keane, Conor A784
Keane, John B P32
Keane, Merry P410
Keane, Valerie P484
Keane, Sean E170
Keaney, Ellen P280
Kearline, Jones P232
Kearney, Daniel A. P352
Kearney, Daniel A405
Kearney, Christopher A612
Kearney, Tim A835
Kearney, Thomas W. A929
Kearney, Rick P306
Kearney, Thomas W. E449
Kearns, Richard A87
Kearns, Jim P28
Kearns, Richard P50
Kearns, Donald B P437
Kearns, Donald P438
Kearns, Brian E190
Kearny, Ric A167
Kearson, Margaretta P500
Keat, Cheong Jin W14
Keating, Leslie A13
Keating, Kim A89
Keating, Thomas P A120
Keating, Mark R. A783
Keating, Valerie A933
Keating, Mary J P198
Keating, Michael P333
Keating, Patrick J. P608
Keating, Todd P616
Keaveny, Mark P496
Keck, Barry A881
Keck, Barry E421

HOOVER'S HANDBOOK OF EMERGING COMPANIES 2020

COMBINED HOOVER'S HANDBOOK INDEX OF EXECUTIVES

```
A = AMERICAN BUSINESS
E = EMERGING COMPANIES
P = PRIVATE COMPANIES
W = WORLD BUSINESS
```

Keckeis, Thomas M. (Tom) P334
Keddy, Asha A460
Kedia, Gunjan A784
Kedia, Gunjan A884
Kee, Rob A457
Kee, Marlow A829
Kee, Timothy A919
Kee, Marlow P589
Kee, Kristine E282
Keecheril, Mathew A540
Keefauver, David A442
Keefe, Tom A388
Keefe, Peter A452
Keefe, Ray A715
Keefe, Dennis D P673
Keefer, Joseph G. (Joe) A155
Keefer, Elizabeth P116
Keefer, Ben P425
Keefer, Joseph G. (Joe) E54
Keefer-Hugill, J A155
Keefer-Hugill, J E54
Keegan, Margaret A474
Keegan, Grace A638
Keegan, Robert J. (Bob) A933
Keegan, Michael P439
Keegan, Grace E320
Keehn, Jeremiah A289
Keel, Errol A935
Keele, Philip A. W85
Keeler, Pamela A347
Keeler, Brian P161
Keeler, Tracy P246
Keeley, Greg A54
Keeley, Karen A940
Keeley, Brian E. P63
Keeley, John P96
Keeley, Jim E203
Keeling, Rob A167
Keeling, E F P399
Keeling, Kelli P665
Keen, Sandy A621
Keen, Joseph A877
Keen, Eric L P230
Keen, Eric L. P231
Keen, Sandy E311
Keen, Larry E368
Keenan, Steven J. A71
Keenan, Vince A100
Keenan, David A352
Keenan, Rob A544
Keenan, John A686
Keenan, David R. (Dave) A712
Keenan, Karen D. A783
Keenan, Joanna A806
Keenan, Joseph (Joe) P579
Keenan, Joe P579
Keenan, Paul A. E79
Keenan, Joanna E399
Keene, Mark P13
Keene, Kristi P387
Keener, Ken A600
Keener, Pat A649
Keener, Larry E69
Keenley, Michael P678
Keesee, Don A113
Keesee, Don E36
Keesling, Becky A142
Keesling, Becky E49
Keesling, Dennis E110
Keetch, Chad A. E127
Keeton, Winn A181
Keeton, Winn E70
Keeton, Brogiin E138
Kefeli, Hulya W18
Kefer, Volker W133
Keffer, Michelle P456
Kegley, Clark P479
Kehl, Eric A383
Kehl, Eric E186

Kehler, Grant A161
Kehlet, Jim A494
Kehoe, Anne Marie A902
Kehoe, Kendra P233
Kehoe, James W381
Kehui, Zhang W102
Keiffer, Mark A89
Keil, Michael A588
Keil, Kristen A651
Keil, Andrew A704
Keil, Michael P365
Keil, Richard P532
Keil, Virginia P596
Keil, Kristen E329
Keilen, Joyce A452
Keilin, Eugene J. P304
Keim, Mark L. A405
Keim, Mark L A571
Keim, Michael S A881
Keim, Marco W10
Keim, Michael S E421
Keiper, Joel A414
Keiper, Joel P236
Keippela, Jeremy A526
Keipper, Phil A423
Keiser, Kenneth A. A248
Keiser, Harold P196
Keiser, Rosemary P625
Keiser, Kenneth A. E107
Keith, Glenda A196
Keith, Elizabeth A266
Keith, Christopher A376
Keith, R. Alexandra A680
Keith, Elizabeth P181
Keithgiordano, Mary P489
Keivani, Beth P386
Keivens, Patrick E237
Keizer, Henry R. A417
Keizer, Henry R A827
Keizer, Henry R P571
Kekoolani, Kaleo A109
Kelej, Rasha A554
Kelems, Theresa A700
Keliher, Lester A818
Keliher, Lester E403
Kell, Gina E379
Kellagher, Dennis A778
Kellam, Richard A392
Kellar, Brian A117
Kellar, Michael A520
Kellar, Brian P61
Kellas, Steve A908
Kellas, Steve E436
Kelleher, Ann B. A460
Kelleher, Dan A538
Kelleher, Colm A574
Kelleher, Kevin J. A708
Kelleher, Margaret Ann P349
Kelleher, Kathleen P639
Kelleman, Joe E275
Kellen, Vincent P175
Keller, Ken A65
Keller, Stephen A97
Keller, Brett A143
Keller, Shawn A236
Keller, Kevin A409
Keller, Robert A584
Keller, Kurt A. A640
Keller, Stacey L A693
Keller, Stacey A693
Keller, Erika A702
Keller, Steven L. (Steve) A733
Keller, Scott A779
Keller, Greg A797
Keller, Kimberly A862
Keller, Catherine A888
Keller, Jonell P22
Keller, San P34
Keller, Kevin P231
Keller, John C. P594
Keller, Kimberly P617
Keller, Hans E122
Keller, Thomas J. E201
Keller, Doreen E293
Keller, Bob E332

Keller, Stacey L E341
Keller, Stacey E341
Keller, Catherine E425
Keller-Comte, Jean-Philippe A450
Kellerhals, Patricia R A224
Kellerhouse, James P17
Kellermann, Doug P249
Kellermann, James P581
Kellett, James D A253
Kellett, James A715
Kelley, Mark A16
Kelley, Lisa A100
Kelley, Patrick M A125
Kelley, Daniel T. (Dan) A213
Kelley, Tim A298
Kelley, Thomas A533
Kelley, Thomas M. (Tom) A534
Kelley, Tom A534
Kelley, Daniel A540
Kelley, Laurie A683
Kelley, Levern A920
Kelley, Bridgett P5
Kelley, Jennifer P12
Kelley, Laura P120
Kelley, Daniel T. (Dan) P143
Kelley, H. Lynn P291
Kelley, Brian P315
Kelley, Susan P423
Kelley, Laurie P431
Kelley, Mike P432
Kelley, Trenton L P547
Kelley, Tim E130
Kelligrew, James B. A884
Kellison, Keith A871
Kellman, Christianna A933
Kellmer, Matthias E141
Kellner, Bob A885
Kello, Jason A509
Kellogg, James A622
Kellow, Glenn L. A645
Kelly, Brian G. A10
Kelly, Shawn A16
Kelly, Thomas B. (Tom) A17
Kelly, Kendra A58
Kelly, Michael A. A64
Kelly, Pat A115
Kelly, William A160
Kelly, Keith A205
Kelly, John A206
Kelly, Thomas A. A245
Kelly, Edward J A245
Kelly, Barbara A247
Kelly, Cargile A289
Kelly, John A290
Kelly, Theresa A356
Kelly, Catherine T. (Kate) A413
Kelly, Anastasia A446
Kelly, Nicolette A452
Kelly, Joel A452
Kelly, Andy A452
Kelly, John E. A465
Kelly, Patrick E. A495
Kelly, Melissa A536
Kelly, Marcella A559
Kelly, Tom A559
Kelly, Amber A566
Kelly, Scott A600
Kelly, Brian A654
Kelly, Michael A660
Kelly, Michael (Mike) A692
Kelly, Paul A737
Kelly, Gary C A773
Kelly, Carol A782
Kelly, Alicia A835
Kelly, Ann P A857
Kelly, John A877
Kelly, Nan A881
Kelly, Alfred F. (Al) A895
Kelly, John J. P3
Kelly, Thomas B. (Tom) P9
Kelly, Gail P12
Kelly, William M P90
Kelly, Jhon P96
Kelly, Mike P120

Kelly, Karen P149
Kelly, Patty P250
Kelly, Patrick E. P282
Kelly, Thomas P301
Kelly, Julie P316
Kelly, Joseph J P331
Kelly, Paul P384
Kelly, Michael P416
Kelly, Jane P418
Kelly, Angela P426
Kelly, Michael J. (Mike) P432
Kelly, Carstens P477
Kelly, Alan P478
Kelly, Alan B P479
Kelly, Dennis P497
Kelly, Robin P519
Kelly, Carol P525
Kelly, Frank J P665
Kelly, Pat E37
Kelly, Barbara E105
Kelly, Edmund E131
Kelly, Jim E132
Kelly, Catherine T. (Kate) E205
Kelly, Kevin E330
Kelly, Paul E361
Kelly, Nan E421
Kelly, James P. E426
Kelly, Brenda E429
Kelseth, Carrie P362
Kelsey, Paul A482
Kelso, J. Pete A19
Kelso, April A386
Kelso, Bill A436
Kelso, Brian A727
Kelso, Brian P453
Kelso, April E188
Kelty, Matt A793
Kelvinton, William C P411
Kely, Jim A465
Kemer, Dan A522
Kemery, Maegan A879
Kemick, Allura A754
Kemick, Allura P484
Kemp, Terri M A49
Kemp, Rory A444
Kemp, Stephen J. A669
Kemp, Nicole P332
Kemp, Matthew P336
Kemp, Chuck P425
Kemp, Anne P513
Kemp, Kelly P561
Kempczinski, Chris (Chris K) A548
Kempen, Wouter T. van A258
Kemper, David W. A224
Kemper, John W. A224
Kemper, Jonathan M. A224
Kemper, J. Mariner A858
Kemper, David W. P600
Kemper, Talfourd H. E262
Kempic, Mark A600
Kemppel, Denali P43
Kemps, Steven J. (Steve) A738
Kenagy, John P288
Kenas, Jamie A54
Kendall, Dale A910
Kendall, Randolph L. (Randy) P553
Kendall, Clifford M. E432
Kendra, Chris P239
Kendrew, Jeff W80
Kendrick, Robin A146
Kendrick, Lynn A664
Kendrick, David P122
Kendrick, Kenny P246
Kendrick, Andrew W106
Kendrick, Lynn E334
Kendricks, Samuel B. A401
Kendricks, Samuel B. E198
Keneally, Sean A69
Kenefick, Jeffrey P. A330
Kenefick, Jeffrey P. E152
Kennamore, Jackie P105
Kennard, William A281
Kennard, Corey P516
Kenneally, Anthony P220
Kennedy, Brad A17

Kennedy, Bryan J. A34
Kennedy, Castlen A71
Kennedy, Steve A75
Kennedy, Teri A204
Kennedy, Peter A222
Kennedy, Lisa A248
Kennedy, John A251
Kennedy, Paul A258
Kennedy, Jonathan A262
Kennedy, Greg A262
Kennedy, Marie A266
Kennedy, Cathy A325
Kennedy, Michael A332
Kennedy, Parker S. A332
Kennedy, Tanya A469
Kennedy, Chris A500
Kennedy, James E. (Jim) A596
Kennedy, Joanne A602
Kennedy, Douglas L. A646
Kennedy, Stacey A661
Kennedy, Thomas A. (Tom) A706
Kennedy, Aniel O A723
Kennedy, Scott A804
Kennedy, Kevin A809
Kennedy, Shaun A818
Kennedy, Beverly A835
Kennedy, Al A892
Kennedy, Barbara A913
Kennedy, Blake P5
Kennedy, Brad P9
Kennedy, Charles A. P114
Kennedy, Marie P182
Kennedy, Dannie P240
Kennedy, Bruce P334
Kennedy, Peter P386
Kennedy, Danny P449
Kennedy, Deborah P477
Kennedy, Steven L. P486
Kennedy, James P610
Kennedy, John W140
Kennedy, Brian W275
Kennedy, Melissa J. W371
Kennedy, Lisa E107
Kennedy, Laura K E126
Kennedy, Mark E234
Kennedy, Douglas L. E324
Kennedy, Shaun E403
Kennedy, Barbara E438
Kennemer, Derek A442
Kenner, Steve A72
Kenner, Shane A398
Kenner, Andrew A917
Kenner, Shane P222
Kenneth, Andrews P237
Kenney, Jeanne A296
Kenney, Anthony R. (Tony) A534
Kenney, David A852
Kenney, Tom A903
Kenney, George P546
Kennon, S. Gary A277
Kenny, Aaron A19
Kenny, Katharine A171
Kenny, David W. A465
Kenny, Natalie A540
Kenny, Mark A804
Kenny, John A888
Kenny, Maureen E. P608
Kenny, Joe W294
Kenny, John E425
Kenoyer, Jason A101
Kenoyer, Jason E32
Kensey, Gary A54
Kent, Alicia A75
Kent, Cindy A130
Kent, John A135
Kent, Muhtar A215
Kent, Torion A319
Kent, James L. (Jim) A550
Kent, Rodney D P257
Kent, Geoff P257
Kent, James L. (Jim) P319
Kent, Peter P415
Kent-Cochran, Deborah A796
Kent-Cochran, Deborah E397
Kent-Sheehan, Kate A349

Kentfield, Ian A842
Kenvin, Kenny A421
Kenyon, John A115
Kenyon, Christopher N A461
Kenyon, Bill A872
Kenyon, Robert P52
Kenyon, John E37
Kenzie, Lesa Mc P465
Keogh, Tracy S. A438
Keogh, John W. W106
Keough, Susan — A756
Keough, Adam P117
Keown, James A89
Keown, Karen A877
Kepley, Gail A606
Kepp, Scott P587
Keppel, Mary Ann P233
Kepple, Yann P233
Kepron, David A538
Keqiang, Xu W110
Kerber, Lynn M. A806
Kerber, Lynn M. E398
Kerbeshian, Marie P594
Kerby, Michael P83
Kereere, Suzan A54
Kerger, Paula A. P432
Kerins, Sean J. A81
Kerk, Julie P211
Kerkhoff, Guido W391
Kerkow, Audra A877
Kerley, Jay A74
Kern, Jason A449
Kern, Geri A518
Kern, Jeffrey A575
Kern, Howard P. A754
Kern, Howard P. P484
Kern, Howard P484
Kern, Georges W115
Kern, Andreas W180
Kern, Jason E220
Kernaghan, Paul W24
Kernan, Michael A105
Kernan, Michael E34
Kerndl, John P75
Kerney, Gary E429
Kerns, Jim A294
Keroack, Mark A. P72
Keroack, Mark A. P73
Kerouani, Farida P404
Kerr, Derek J. A47
Kerr, William A112
Kerr, William A469
Kerr, Tammy A806
Kerr, Mary E. P116
Kerr, Robert P156
Kerr, Donald M. P578
Kerr, Mario E359
Kerr, Tammy E399
Kerrigan, Robert M A294
Kerris, Robert F. (Bob) E122
Kerschner, Barry A540
Kershaw, Gary A461
Kershaw, David A838
Kershaw, Sabra Thomas A909
Kershaw, Hayley E144
Kershaw, Sabra Thomas E436
Kersten, Dale A742
Kersten, Rebecca P45
Kerstetter, Mitzie P214
Kerth, Rob P462
Kerwin, George P76
Kesavan, Sudhakar A8
Keshava, Jagannath A460
Keshava, Sudarshan A695
Keshvari, Keivan A14
Keskar, Dinesh A. A140
Kesler, Andrew A160
Kesler-Arnold, Kimberly P356
Kess, Avrohom J. A845
Kess, Thomas P597
Kessel, Steve A42
Kessel, Cindy A309
Kessel, Kathryn A559
Kessel, Donna Van P496
Kesseler, Brian A813

Kesselman, Marc L. A937
Kessler, Ben A104
Kessler, Bethmara A164
Kessler, Marla A474
Kessler, Cesiah A532
Kessler, Joe P151
Kessler, Andrea P252
Kessler, Bruce L. W106
Kessler, Michael W106
Kessler, Denis W345
Kessler-Sanders, Michelle A692
Kestel, Idania A181
Kestel, Idania E70
Kester, Jenny P184
Keswick, Ben W209
Keswick, Adam W209
Keswick, Henry W209
Keswick, Ben W209
Keswick, Henry W209
Keswick, Paul D. E110
Ketchum, John A522
Ketchum, John A597
Ketell, Greg A415
Ketell, Greg E208
Ketler, Jeff A89
Ketola, Todd P68
Ketter, Andrew A727
Ketter, Andrew P453
Ketterling, Terry L P498
Kettler, Tamara P379
Keucher, Stephen P610
Keucher, Steve P610
Keuer, Steve P133
Keung, Yeung Kwok W118
Keup, Gregory P41
Keuten, John P670
Kevern, Dave A324
Keville, Doreen A835
Kevin, Liney A660
Kevin, Liney P416
Kevin, Dunnigan E19
Key, Daniel A213
Key, George A399
Key, Jason A519
Key, Daniel P143
Key, George P223
Key, Lester P278
Key, Charles P278
Keyes, Kevin G. A68
Keyes, Greg A798
Keyes, Gregory S A798
Keyes, J. Patrick A907
Keyes, Jim A915
Keyler, Joseph A345
Keyler, Joseph E165
Keys, Thomas C A800
Keys, Randall D. E139
Keyser, Richard A837
Khaira, Jay A438
Khairallah, Joseph S. E267
Khait-Palant, Olga V P433
Khalaf, Michel A559
Khaleghi, Trisha P489
Khalil, Omar A119
Khalil, Ik A177
Khalil, Basil A323
Khalsa, Mehtab P15
Khamseh, Ladan P397
Khan, Nadeem G. A19
Khan, Sohail A200
Khan, Suleman A204
Khan, Rona A222
Khan, Sabrina A391
Khan, Raheel A460
Khan, Fareed A. A487
Khan, Mehmood A654
Khan, Kanwar Nasir A658
Khan, Atif A702
Khan, Nasir P89
Khan, Karen P114
Khan, Nazeer P189
Khan, Adil P215
Khan, S S P500
Khan, M Aness P519
Khan, Iqbal W121

Khan, Adeel E357
Khandpur, Ashish K. A3
Khang, Chris A374
Khanna, Tarun A18
Khanna, Sanjay A54
Khanna, Nikhil A391
Khare, Anupam A632
Khasis, Lev W343
Khater, Sam A364
Khatib, Bassil A271
Khatib, Riad P516
Khatibi, Alex E7
Khator, Renu P629
Khatri, Aashish A318
Khattar, Jack A. E394
Khavarani, Anthony A747
Khawaja, Wajhiuddin P664
Khazanchi, Shal P456
Kheirolomoom, Ali E196
Khelghatian, Raffi A222
Khemka, Vivek A271
Khera, Neha A149
Khesin, Eugene A318
Khichi, Samrat A123
Khillan, Gaurav A544
Khilnani, Vinod E135
Kho, Dicky A680
Khokar, Ghazala P663
Khom, Alexander P206
Khongkham, Kon A651
Khongkham, Kon E329
Khoo, Mei A680
Khorasani, Mohammad P182
Khordodi, Mehran E8
Khosla, Suresh P1
Khosla, Ashok K P1
Khosla, Leena P1
Khosrowshahi, Kaveh A94
Khosrowshahi, Amir A460
Khouri, Lara M P559
Khourie, Matt A175
Khoury, Raymond A145
Khoury, Nabil A414
Khoury, Johnny A740
Khoury, John A746
Khoury, Nabil P236
Khoury, Aldo P519
Khrimian, Tigran P202
Khu, Elaine A651
Khu, Elaine E329
Khudainatov, Eduard W330
Khurana, Rajiv A575
Khurana, Sanjay P2
Kiam, Raphael A137
Kiamos, James P199
Kiani, Joe E. E272
Kibbey, Anthony E295
Kibler, Tom A919
Kicia, Kenneth A509
Kick, Richard A348
Kick, Richard E169
Kickbusch, Laura P119
Kiczuk, William A706
Kidd, Michael A3
Kidd, Herbert A329
Kidd, Brandon A683
Kido, Tomoyuki W127
Kidwell, Stephen A46
Kidwell, Heather A939
Kiebzak, Michael A575
Kieffer, Steve P74
Kieffer, Amy P225
Kiekintveld, David A806
Kiekintveld, David E399
Kielar, Dan E431
Kieli, Kasia A270
Kielty, Iain A218
Kiely, Peter A784
Kiener, Mary P449
Kiener, Pascal W55
Kiernan, Steve A784
Kiernan, Jeff A893
Kiernan, Thomas M. E432
Kieselstein, Shahaf A460
Kieser, Cliff E48

COMBINED HOOVER'S HANDBOOK INDEX OF EXECUTIVES

A = AMERICAN BUSINESS
E = EMERGING COMPANIES
P = PRIVATE COMPANIES
W = WORLD BUSINESS

Kiesewetter, Scott P35
Kigawa, Makoto W431
Kiger, Kris A469
Kight, Rob A262
Kight, Seth E47
Kight, Peter E47
Kiida, Mike A500
Kiil, Skip E308
Kiil, Harry E308
Kijewski, Peter P325
Kiker, William A. (Bill) A872
Kiker, Bill A872
Kiksman, Allen P471
Kikuchi, Kent P230
Kikumoto, C. David P13
Kikut, Janusz P598
Kilbane, Kevin A704
Kilberg, James A. (Jim) A918
Kilborn, Jim P31
Kilbourne, Edwin A509
Kilbride, Marc A180
Kilbride, Marc P195
Kilburn, Garth A224
Kilby, Jay E110
Kilcoyne, Adrian A895
Kildare, Gary A465
Kilduff, Cydney A487
Kilduff, Jennifer P111
Kile, Pam K P140
Kiley, Ernie P10
Kiley, Tom P314
Kilgallon, Lisa A692
Kilgour, John A170
Kiliper, Cathy A731
Kilkenny, Rosemary P570
Killabrew, Mike A453
Killeen, Greg A390
Killeen, Steve P200
Killeen, Tom P333
Killeen, Edward F. E256
Killen, Kevin A574
Killian, Don A179
Killian, Ann E. E151
Killinger, Elizabeth A610
Killingstad, H. Chris E399
Killingstad, Chris E399
Killingsworth, Mark A267
Killman, Scott A852
Killmer, Jonathon P241
Killmer, John E18
Killmeyer, Susan P643
Killpack, Dave A925
Killpack, Dave E445
Kilmer, Raymond J. (Ray) A79
Kilpatrick, David B A16
Kilpatrick, David A187
Kilpatrick, Carole A247
Kilpatrick, Elena A366
Kilpatrick, Dona P34
Kilpatrick, C P650
Kilpatrick, Charles A P650
Kilpatrick, Carole E105
Kilpin, Timothy J. (Tim) A10
Kilroy, Jill A432
Kilroy, Thomas M A460
Kilroy, John B. E245
Kilsby, Susan A361
Kilsdonk, James A621
Kilsdonk, James E312
Kim, Kyo Yung (K Y) A24
Kim, Ta Won A74
Kim, Rob A103
Kim, Edward A109
Kim, Anna A135
Kim, Jaysen A182
Kim, Cynthia A200
Kim, Song A210
Kim, Charles G. (Chuck) A224
Kim, John A307

Kim, Claudia A317
Kim, Jamie A332
Kim, Jin A356
Kim, Jane A390
Kim, Greg D. A404
Kim, Anthony A404
Kim, Sue A404
Kim, Kathy A404
Kim, Kyu A431
Kim, Kay A431
Kim, Chris A432
Kim, Sylvester A432
Kim, Linda A432
Kim, Alex A432
Kim, Patti A522
Kim, Sarah A559
Kim, Olivia A602
Kim, Annie A637
Kim, Chino A645
Kim, Knox A686
Kim, Mary A726
Kim, Ann A793
Kim, Jeff A896
Kim, Charlie A930
Kim, Joe P118
Kim, Ginny P118
Kim, Taeeuk P248
Kim, Changyoung P248
Kim, Chung P296
Kim, Phillip P305
Kim, Dong Eun P361
Kim, Bill P419
Kim, Robert P488
Kim, Helen P546
Kim, Y S P645
Kim, Cheol Ha W108
Kim, Hong Ki W108
Kim, Yeon Bae W178
Kim, Kyung Bae W191
Kim, Sang-Don W236
Kim, Won-Hoi W239
Kim, Jin-Il W311
Kim, Hag-Dong W311
Kim, Jhi-Yong W311
Kim, Hong-Soo W311
Kim, Min Chul W354
Kim, Jun W355
Kim, Jennie E32
Kim, Michael E102
Kim, Greg D. E199
Kim, Anthony E199
Kim, Sue E199
Kim, Kathy E199
Kim, Kyu E216
Kim, Kay E216
Kim, Chris E216
Kim, Sylvester E216
Kim, Linda E216
Kim, Alex E216
Kim, joo E342
Kim, Daeho E408
Kimata, Masatoshi W227
Kimball, Brent A347
Kimball, Kenny A498
Kimball, John A567
Kimball, Scott P642
Kimball, John E284
Kimball, Dan E450
Kimbell, David C A858
Kimbell, Jimmy P38
Kimble, Lewis P. A359
Kimble, Sally P A362
Kimble, Chandra A444
Kimble, Donald R. A491
Kimble, Sarah P308
Kimbrel, Kelly A156
Kime, Jeffery L. (Jeff) A834
Kimelman, Andrew E123
Kimm, David A807
Kimm, Christopher A890
Kimmel, Bradford P149
Kimmerle, David P184
Kimmerle, Sandra Sue P184
Kimmet, Pamela O. (Pam) A169
Kimmich, Jeff A797

Kimmitt, Joseph H A632
Kimmons, Herb P438
Kimpton, Jay A701
Kimrey, David A796
Kimrey, David E397
KIMURA, HIROKI W34
Kimura, Yasushi W214
Kimura, Shigeru W227
Kimura, Tomohiko W252
Kimura, Kazuaki W258
Kimura, Yoshihiko W259
Kimura, Hikaru W259
Kimura, Kenji W286
Kimura, Takaaki W430
Kimzey, Megan A859
Kin, Lam Kun W299
Kinaitis, Eric P554
Kinak, Mett A799
Kinasewich, Rob A147
Kinate, Pat A3
Kincaid, John A850
Kindelan, Brian E42
Kinder, Kurt A29
Kinder, Richard D. (Rich) A494
Kinder, Lauren A692
Kinder, Richard D P360
Kinder, Joe E406
Kindig, Susan A518
Kindle, Fred W435
Kindler, Mark A727
Kindler, Thomas A885
Kindler, Mark P453
Kindlick, David P653
Kindred, Betty A682
Kindred, Bryan N. P564
Kindy, Mike A272
King, Steve A35
King, Timothy A51
King, Kathleen A53
King, Michael A60
King, Andrew D. (Andy) A81
King, Steve A119
King, Carter A167
King, Thomas A205
King, Timothy A220
King, Stephen A248
King, Benjamin A251
King, Brandon A257
King, Timothy B. A268
King, Justin A292
King, Sam A293
King, Jason A340
King, W Russell A365
King, Jerry A375
King, Adam A461
King, Lisa M A489
King, David P. (Dave) A502
King, Caroline A526
King, Darren J. A530
King, Marie A530
King, Jeffrey A571
King, Patricia A589
King, Toni A658
King, Martin G. A661
King, Samuel A665
King, Sam A665
King, Margaret A676
King, Thomas A693
King, Suzanne A727
King, Robert A727
King, Jake A746
King, Glenn A801
King, Kelly S. A849
King, Stacy A859
King, John A882
King, Jeremy A901
King, David A921
King, Daniel A924
King, Jeff P96
King, Gena P133
King, Randy P142
King, Timothy P149
King, Letitia P160
King, Yolanda P160
King, Vanessa P168

King, Jerry P215
King, Victoria P220
King, Michele P303
King, Victoria P410
King, Andrea P415
King, Suzanne P453
King, Robert P453
King, Jared P466
King, Bernard F P467
King, Jeffrey P484
King, Kathleen P506
King, Kirk P551
King, Charles P563
King, David P575
King, Mark W9
King, Aaron W123
King, Peter W424
King, Stephen E107
King, Stephen M. E111
King, Mark A. E113
King, Jason E160
King, Alan E174
King, Michael E192
King, Gina E201
King, Kevin E267
King, Jon E282
King, Terry E290
King, Chris E318
King, Samuel E334
King, Sam E334
King, Margaret E338
King, Thomas E341
King, David G. E385
King, Christopher E412
King, Mike E427
King, Donald P. E433
King-Shaw, Ruben J. P631
Kingbury, Mike P210
Kingham, Jennifer A598
Kingman, John W233
Kingsbury, Thomas A. (Tom) A158
Kingsbury, Charles A405
Kingsley, Scott A. A227
Kingsley, Georgia A686
Kingsley, Stephen A761
Kingsley, Scott P505
Kingsley, Scott A. E90
Kingsley, Lawrence E223
Kingsmill, Stephani E. W247
Kingsmore, Stephen P438
Kingston, Robert E. P574
Kingston, Brian W80
Kingswell-smith, Charles A668
Kini, Narendra M P649
Kininsberg, Jorge Alberto W54
Kinlin, Clark S. A240
Kinman, Thomas P128
Kinman, Mary P551
Kinnaird, Jeff A428
Kinneer, Mike P148
Kinner, Michael A271
Kinner, Scott P86
Kinney, John A408
Kinney, Virginia A610
Kinney, Ross A664
Kinney, Patrick J. A844
Kinney, Stephanie P128
Kinney, Anthony P425
Kinney, Julie E143
Kinney, Ross E334
Kinnison, Chris A677
Kinoshita, Yoshio W127
Kinsella, Paul E240
Kinser, Christine A465
Kinsey, Joseph A195
Kinsey, Sherri A449
Kinsey, Jon P193
Kinsey, Sherri E221
Kinsley, Bryce A735
Kinslow, Anthony D P116
Kintigh, Denise P467
Kinton, Diane A530
Kinville, Richard A686
Kinyo, Doug P336
Kinzel, Beth A224

COMBINED HOOVER'S HANDBOOK INDEX OF EXECUTIVES

Kip, Pinar A784
Kipcak, Husnu A687
Kipp, Melana C A882
Kippenberger, Michael A722
Kippenhan, Matthew P389
Kipperman, Bruce A184
Kiraly, Robert G. (Bob) A356
Kiranandana, Khunying Suchada W216
Kirane, Ryan P478
Kirby, Jefferson W. A32
Kirby, Cheryl A91
Kirby, Mary A272
Kirby, Brent G. A527
Kirby, J. Scott A864
Kirby, Jamie P23
Kirby, Phil P68
Kirby, Ed P281
Kirby, Jeffrey P306
Kirby, Tracy P379
Kirby, Rex B. P531
Kirby, Adrienne P563
Kirby, Cheryl E29
Kirch, Bob A774
Kirchgaessner, Rainer W106
Kirchhardt, Erin A532
Kirchhoefer, Kari A863
Kirchhoff, Steve A309
Kirchhoff, Micha A724
Kirchhoff, Mary P32
Kirchhoff, Micha P452
Kirchhoff, Bruce C. E360
Kirchner, Mike A60
Kirchner, Timothy A125
Kirchner, Jeffrey P573
Kirgan, Danielle A255
Kirihara, Wayne H. A182
Kirikova, Vera W327
Kirk, Debbie A107
Kirk, Richard A248
Kirk, Mathew A409
Kirk, Jennifer A618
Kirk, Tiffany A713
Kirk, Melvin (Mel) A734
Kirk, Warren J. A811
Kirk, Denise P146
Kirk, Joyce P162
Kirk, Warren J P184
Kirk, Joseph P210
Kirk, Bruce M P295
Kirk, Patrick T P329
Kirk, Christopher P356
Kirk, Richard E107
Kirk, Spencer E141
Kirkeeng, Erin A381
Kirkegaard, Ulrika Stolt W377
Kirkemo, Erik A301
Kirkemo, Erik P196
Kirkendall, Eric A794
Kirkendall, Bill P567
Kirker, Barry P103
Kirkevold, Dee P540
Kirkland, Tracy A327
Kirkland, Richard G A524
Kirkland, Lawson A755
Kirkland, Rhea P167
Kirkland, Lawson E369
Kirkland, Christopher E374
Kirkpatrick, Paul K A225
Kirkpatrick, Kevin A484
Kirkpatrick, Maureen A853
Kirkpatrick, R. James P339
Kirkpatrick, Timothy J P395
Kirkpatrick, Maureen P612
Kirkwood, Tom A219
Kirkwood, John A465
Kirkwood, Karen A832
Kirkwood, Tom E87
Kirousis, Marni A833
Kirsch, Eric M. A19
Kirsch, Peter P195
Kirsch, Steven E285
Kirschling, Ryan A793
Kirschner, Sid P418
Kirschner, Timo P435
Kirschner, Ron P579

Kirschner, Sidney E393
Kirshner, Alan I. A536
Kirsis, Karlis P A935
Kirsner, James D. (Jim) E144
Kirstetter, Axel P333
Kirtley, Timothy H. A652
Kirtley, Timothy H. E331
Kirven, Michael A651
Kirven, Michael E330
Kirwan, Jeff A826
Kirwan, William E. P642
Kisaka, Ryuichi W293
Kisber, Michael E. A343
Kisber, Michael E. E163
Kiscaden, Bradley J. A536
Kiser, Jason A271
Kiser, Carly A793
Kish, Donald A364
Kish, Jeff P567
Kishan, Neel P114
Kishi, Jamal Al W135
Kishida, Makoto W292
Kishimoto, Sumiyuki W210
Kishor, Seetharaman A530
Kishore, Ashok P605
Kishpaugh-stotz, Jennifer A161
Kislow, Anthony P116
Kissell, Mason E102
Kissinger, Jeff P480
Kissinger, Tom E268
Kissire, Debbie A626
Kissler, Courtney A779
Kissling, Lou A247
Kissling, Lou E105
Kissner, Rita A. E365
Kist, Jonathan A470
Kistler, Matthew A902
Kistner, Tim P196
Kitagawa, Allan S. A816
Kitahara, Yoshikazu W262
Kitamura, Sam A325
Kitamura, Takumi W286
KITAMURA, SEISHI W392
Kitazawa, Toshifumi W393
Kitchell, Ryan C. P252
Kitcher, Ron A315
Kitchin, Mark A859
Kitlen, John A595
Kitrilakis, Periklis M. W25
Kitson, Damian A816
Kitt, Jennifer A511
Kitt, Jennifer P290
Kitterman, Aaron A774
Kittilstved, Sherri A861
Kittner, Lisa A574
Kittredge, Teri A657
Kitzman, Felicia P565
Kitzmann, Jessica A167
Kitzmiller, Kenneth G. A555
Kiyono, Jolene A182
Kizer, Kim A819
Kizer, Kim P549
Kizer, Jay E248
Kjellberg, Henrik V. A307
Kjenes, Atle A301
Kjenes, Atle P196
Klaas, Bjoern E340
Klabe, Jim A922
Klabe, Jim P671
Klaczak, Robert A520
Kladakis, Stephanie P23
Klados, Charalabos A218
Klaeser, Dennis L. A806
Klaeser, Dennis L. E398
Klahre, Robert A559
Klaich, Daniel P363
Klammer, Thoma P A441
Klapkowski, Joseph A888
Klapkowski, Joseph E425
Klappa, Gale E. A907
Klasko, Stephen K. P603
Klatte, Erika E123
Klauber, Arnold A8
Klauck, James P211

Klaus, Jeffrey A. (Jeff) A906
Klaus, Jeffrey A. (Jeff) E434
Klausner, Herbert W353
Klava, William P471
Klavsons, David A418
Klawitter, Jerry E233
Klebba, AJ A656
Klebba, Philip A739
Klebba, Michael A746
Klebba, AJ P414
Klecker, Donna A544
Klee, Evan A346
Klee, Brian A658
Klee, Evan E167
Kleefisch, Brett A501
Kleeman, Steven P81
Kleespies, Kurt A891
Kleffel, Julie A749
Kleffel, Julie E367
Kleiman, Dr Michael P266
Kleiman, Angela E136
Klein, Kearney A24
Klein, Gene A25
Klein, Bruce A198
Klein, John E. A216
Klein, David A236
Klein, Steven A A246
Klein, John A326
Klein, Christopher J. (Chris) A361
Klein, Aaron A491
Klein, Richard A651
Klein, Pete A729
Klein, Susan A799
Klein, Mike A837
Klein, Gerald J. A838
Klein, Michael F. A844
Klein, David A919
Klein, Gene P14
Klein, Jason P325
Klein, Cathy P342
Klein, Steve P434
Klein, Paul P449
Klein, Michael L. P546
Klein, Robert P572
Klein, Bobbie P586
Klein, Bonita P640
Klein, Joseph P648
Klein, John A. E23
Klein, Michael R. E99
Klein, Steven A E105
Klein, Richard E329
Klein, Mark A. E365
Klein, Ronald E392
Klein-Magar, Margret W340
Kleinemeier, Michael W340
Kleinhample, Ken A920
Kleinhaut, Mark A491
Kleinhemple, Ken A920
Kleinhenz, Matt A765
Kleinman, Kent P159
Kleinman, Ronald Ellis P574
Kleinschmidt, Jeff A621
Kleinschmidt, Jeff E312
Kleisterlee, Gerard J. W417
Kleitz, Shawn P546
Klemashevich, Fred A323
Klemencic, Joy A218
Klene, Brian A565
Klenk, Jeffrey P. (Jeff) A844
Klepner, Ron E393
Klerk, Wim de W33
Kleski, Vickie P94
Klesyk, Andrzej Piotr W314
Kletter, David A144
Klevorn, Marcy A360
Kleweno, Elizabeth P522
Kley, Karl-Ludwig W63
Kley, Karl-Ludwig W143
Kleyle, Tom A212
Klick, Michael A909
Klick, Michael E436
Kliethermes, Craig W. A723
Klimchak, Joseph A715
Klimczak, Bob A552
Klimczak, Bob E276

Klimonek, Barbara P15
Kline, Betsy A75
Kline, Sharon A175
Kline, Gary J A195
Kline, Clayton A481
Kline, Mark A775
Kline, Sam P220
Kline, Douglas B. P262
Kline, Carla P282
Kline, Daniel P518
Kline, Mark W. P548
Kling, David A310
Kling, Jonathan P357
Klingenberg, Bernard E. W341
Klinger, David A371
Klinger, Glenn A922
Klinger, David P213
Klinger, James M P448
Klinger, Glenn P671
Klinger, Randall L. E281
Klingler, David P493
Klinitchek, Darryl P502
Klink, Phil A327
Klinkner, Kim A85
Klinkner, Kim E26
Klinovskaya, Taisiya W375
Klipp, Todd P96
Klisiak, Kimberlee E306
Klisures, George A559
Kloak, Cindy A712
Kloberdanz, Mark P412
Klobnak, Jennifer L. A723
Klockenga, Kevin P517
Klockhaus, Werner W91
Klode, Peter A726
Klode, Peter P453
Klodnicki, Jessica P97
Kloecker, Edward A205
Kloehn, Steve P114
Klontz, Richard P619
Kloostra, Jim A552
Kloostra, Jim E276
Kloppenburg, Norbert W225
Klosson, Michael P474
Klosterboer, Robert A. (Bob) A627
Klotz, Jim A752
Klotzbach, Kevin B. A330
Klotzbach, Kevin B. E152
Klotzbier, Edward P383
Klowden, Larry P388
Kluber, Bill A692
Klubert, Laura P22
Klucevek, Doug B A460
Klueg, Steven P P307
Kluemper, Steve A398
Kluemper, Steve P222
Kluesener, Adam P625
Klug, Loren C. A439
Klug, Sue A721
Kluga, Mary P286
Klugherz, Greg P445
Klugherz, Greg P587
Klusik, Hartmut W61
Kluth, Doreen P523
Klutsch, Gwen E14
Kluyver, Cornelis A. (Kees) de P636
Klyce, Harvey A484
Klyn, Pamela A920
Klo--, Susanne W137
Kmiecik, Thomas T P334
Kmietek, Kathy A409
Knackstedt, Beth P356
Knapke, Murph A340
Knapke, Murph E160
Knapp, Tracy W. A485
Knapp, Gary A492
Knapp, Michael A565
Knapp, Ken Knapp Ken A713
Knapp, Debra P49
Knapp, Brian P76
Knapp, Steven P569
Knapp, Jean E81
Knapp, Paul A. E386
Knapper, Anastacia P610
Knatz, Courtney A799

HOOVER'S HANDBOOK OF EMERGING COMPANIES 2020

COMBINED HOOVER'S HANDBOOK INDEX OF EXECUTIVES

```
A = AMERICAN BUSINESS
E = EMERGING COMPANIES
P = PRIVATE COMPANIES
W = WORLD BUSINESS
```

Knauss, Donald A487
Knauss, Bob A857
Knavish, Timothy M. A673
Knazur, John A323
Knecht, Michael E P371
Kneeland, Michael J. A872
Kneessy, Amy P476
Kneidinger, Michael (Mike) A255
Kneipp, Carla A180
Kneiser, Patti P211
Knel, Wendy A135
Knelly, Shirley J P40
Knepp, Lynn E P212
Knepper, Chris P153
Knesek, Michael J P340
Knickerbocker, Rick A571
Knickrehm, Mark A. W5
Knies, Theresa A651
Knies, Theresa E329
Kniffin, Ogden A704
Kniffley, Steven P630
Knight, Bobbie A28
Knight, Justin G A71
Knight, Glade M A71
Knight, Nelson G A71
Knight, Angela A222
Knight, Andrea A246
Knight, Mike A296
Knight, William A379
Knight, M Keith A379
Knight, Jeffrey W. A397
Knight, Michael A484
Knight, Jeffrey L. (Jeff) A621
Knight, John A621
Knight, Jefferey A621
Knight, Kimberly A682
Knight, Christine A686
Knight, Robert M. A863
Knight, Justin G P43
Knight, Glade M P43
Knight, Nelson G P43
Knight, Napoleon P113
Knight, Kristi P144
Knight, Yvonne P214
Knight, Keith P261
Knight, Calvin (Cal) P267
Knight, Alton P615
Knight, Kevin E47
Knight, Andrea E105
Knight, Jeffrey L. (Jeff) E311
Knight, John E312
Knight, Jefferey E312
Knightly, Kevin C. A474
Knipfer, Shannon P595
Knipfing, Janet A888
Knipfing, Janet E425
Knirsch, Charles A657
Knisely, Amy P206
Knisely, Alaina E81
Knitzer, Peter R. E350
Knobel, Jeffrey A A103
Knobel, Carsten W181
Knobloch, George P278
Knoblock, Bruce A E136
Knoll, Lisa E143
Knoll-finn, Mj A592
Knoll-finn, Mj P370
Knopf, Matthew A262
Knopf, David A497
Knopf, Keith P439
Knott, Timothy A485
Knott, Greg A734
Knott, Irene A831
Knott, Irene P601
Knotts, Daniel L. (Dan) A276
Knouse, Sabrina A797
Knouse-snyder, Denise A909
Knouse-snyder, Denise E437
Knowles, Debie A58

Knowles, Leo A232
Knowles, Brock P78
Knowles, Laura P259
Knowling, Doug A715
Knox, Bradley A19
Knox, Shontell A108
Knox, Fred A879
Knuckles, Beth A500
Knudsen, Mary A380
Knudsen, Jeannette A765
Knudsen, Jackie P104
Knudstorp, Jorgen A780
Knue, Gregory A109
Knueven, Matthew A713
Knupp, Catherine A. (Cathy) A941
Knuth, David A909
Knuth, Barbara A. P159
Knuth, David E436
Knutson, Brian A329
Knutson, Lisa A. E366
Knupling, Frieder W345
Ko, Al A471
Ko, William A676
Ko, Steven R P446
Ko, Suk-Bum W311
Ko, William E338
Koban, Mark A483
Kobashi, Kozo W349
Kobashigawa, Scot A746
Kobayakawa, Tomoaki W394
Kobayashi, Edison A109
KOBAYASHI, HIDEFUMI W1
Kobayashi, Katsuma W126
Kobayashi, Koji W132
Kobayashi, Hirotake W220
Kobayashi, Yoshimitsu W256
Kobayashi, Ken W257
Kobayashi, Kazuo W279
Kobayashi, Toshiaki W300
Kobayashi, Yotaro E59
Koble, Keith A111
Kobori, Michael A514
Kobori, Michael A516
Kobori, Michael P293
Kobylak, Gene P340
Koc, Mehmet O. W222
Koc, Yildirim A. W222
Koc, Yildirim Ali W432
Koch, Daniel A87
Koch, Matt A371
Koch, Stephen P. (Steve) A716
Koch, Jonathan A745
Koch, Daniel P50
Koch, Cheryl P268
Koch, Amanda P511
Koch, Angela P513
Koch, Olaf W91
Koch, Monte E80
Kochalski, Miroslaw W310
Kochanov, Oleg A115
Kochanov, Oleg E37
Kochem, Gary J. P17
Kochem, Gary J P18
Kocher, Isabelle W154
Kocher, Rollin E316
Kocherlakota, Swamy A738
Kochhar, Chanda D. W194
Kochie, Steven A922
Kochie, Steven G A929
Kochie, Steven P671
Kochie, Steven G E449
Kochvar, Mark A737
Kochvar, Mark E361
Kociancic, Mark W345
Kocken, Henk E300
Koczko, Mike A893
Kodama, Hugh P352
Kodama, Yukio W258
Koder, Tim P330
Kodish, Joel A100
Kodish, Joel P58
Kody, Michael A63
Koebler, Ellen A283
Koehler, Mike A304
Koehler, Mary A925

Koehler, Hailee P626
Koehler, Christine P659
Koehler, Mary E445
Koehly, Hank A224
Koehnen, Michael W. A847
Koehnen, Michael W. E410
Koel, Mike A856
Koel, Mike P614
Koellner, Meliss A A440
Koelmel, John R. P367
Koen, Kenneth A893
Koenig, Ronald A69
Koenig, Paul A88
Koenig, Jim A175
Koenig, Ron A224
Koenig, Karl A379
Koenig, Bill A394
Koenig, Douglas J A862
Koenig, Joseph G. (Joe) A928
Koenig, Douglas J P617
Koenig, Joseph G. (Joe) P674
Koening, John A501
Koepcke, Oliver E235
Koepke, Ashley A86
Koepke, Diane P76
Koepke, Ashley E27
Koeppe, Adam A890
Koering, Adam A876
Koeppel, Holly P32
Koerner, Spencer P118
Koerschner, Carl P334
Koertner, William A. (Bill) E293
Koerwer, Joseph A554
Koestler, Robert J. P497
Koetting, Paul A928
Koetting, Paul P673
Koffer, Danielle A218
Kofsky, David E72
Koga, Akira W250
Kogai, Masamichi W250
Kogan, Allan A441
Kogan, David P252
Kogen, Barbara A98
Koger, Brett A225
Koguchi, Masanori W258
Koh, Peter A431
Koh, Peter E216
Kohava, Avraham W49
Kohl, Karen A859
Kohler, Kayleen A116
Kohler, Lori A859
Kohler, David A940
Kohler, Kayleen E39
Kohler, Reto E102
Kohler, Matt E194
Kohli, Vimal A265
Kohli, Anna A540
Kohlscheen, Kevin P546
Kohn, Thomas W. A806
Kohn, Emily P66
Kohn, Kate P486
Kohn, Thomas W. E398
Kohnen, Scott E347
Kohner, Jody A739
Kohr, Jeff A85
Kohr, Jeff E27
Kohrs, Douglas E340
Kohutek, Kevin R. E422
Koizumi, Atsushi (Windy) W374
Kojima, Yuichi W268
Kojima, Kazuo W298
Kojima, Koji W374
Kojima, Takashi W374
Kojima, Yoichiro W430
Kokaji, Hiroshi W182
Kokate, Bhupesh A203
Kokate, Santosh A796
Kokate, Santosh E397
Kokemiller, Paula P259
Kokke, Jorgen A457
Kokubu, Fumiya W249
Koladis, Randall A175
Kolakowska, Malgorzata W199
Kolatkar, Neil A175
Kolavo, Joe P530

Kolb, John A319
Kolb, Dianne C. P109
Kolb, Kenneth P133
Kolbe, Martin W227
Kolberg, Rita A797
Kolbus, Timothy A81
Kolcum, Jeff A798
Kolcz, Crystal A329
Koleilat, Majed P175
Kolesha, Kurt A248
Kolesha, Kurt E107
Koleszar, Andre E349
Kolker, Dov P351
Kolkmeyer, Tim E344
Koll, Jesper E447
Kollat, David A500
Kollatz, Christoph A79
Koller, Bridgit A512
Koller, Patrick W160
Kolli, Sreelakshmi E10
Kolling, Susan K. E211
Kolluri, Rama A19
Kolodgie, Keith P305
Kolodgy, Robert J. (Bob) P89
Kolodzieski, Ed A902
Kolosky, Jack P226
Kolpasky, Paul A414
Kolpasky, Paul P236
Kolpin, Linda E127
Koltookian, Aram A834
Kolytiris, Valerie A332
Komar, June P479
Komata, Lillian A206
Komer, Rick A485
Kometani, Hanbei W184
Komidar, John A844
Komine, Francine A182
Komiske, Bruce P228
Kommala, Dheerendra A120
Komoda, Masanobu W262
Komori, Shigetaka W168
Komos, Tom A843
Kompkoff, Lloyd P125
Komula, Thomas A91
Komula, Thomas P55
Komuniecki, Patricia R. P596
Komura, Yoshifumi W204
Konczaty, Michel W71
Kondap, Kedar A694
Kondo, Shiro W324
Kondo, Jun W366
Kondrotis, Krisstie A774
Konecny, Pavel A806
Konecny, Pavel E325
Koneru, Sridhar A502
Kong, Debbie A676
Kong, Boon W173
Kong, Ho Kiam W424
Kong, Debbie E338
Kongsubto, Gaesenee P19
Kongyingyong, Phanporn W352
Konidari, Penelope E. W25
Koning, Todd E272
Konings, Frank A479
Konkel, Kevin P438
Konkle, Jeff E6
Konkolics, Charles A831
Konkolics, Charles P601
Konner, Karon A641
Konner, Karon P407
Konort, Phil A54
Konrad, Jocelyn A722
Konst, Dave P449
Konstantinovsky, Irina A119
Kontul, Dean A491
Konyn, Mark W14
Konzelman, Sharon P278
Konzen, Jerry A104
Koob, Melissa E402
Koocher, Gerald P. P175
Kooda-chizek, Kristin A60
Kooistra, Toni A324
Koonce, Scott A25
Koonce, Paul D. A275
Koonce, Scott P14

Koons, Michael A199
Koontz, Robert A364
Koontz, Dan A512
Koop, Alvin A766
Koop, Alvin P500
Koopman, Ray A936
Kopchinski, Richard A668
Kopcho, Darcy P572
Kopelman, Donna A484
Kopfensteiner, Thomas R. A226
Kopfensteiner, Thomas R. P150
Kopil, Edward A125
Kopin, Jeffrey P389
Kopitsky, Christopher A837
Koplovitz, Jonathan A525
Koplow, Ellen L. S. A807
Kopp, Betsy P420
Koppen, Lynda P150
Kopper, Carolyn L A408
Kopriva, John A327
Kopstain, Eric P599
Koptak, Haley P501
Kopycinski, Gloria A247
Kopycinski, Gloria E105
Korajkic, Jasko A222
Koranda, Erica A797
Koranda, John A926
Koranda, John E445
Korbelak, Stacy P39
Korch, Angela E424
Korchak, William M A482
Korczynski, Sherry E118
Kordahi, Rony C. A634
Korde, Kishore E7
Kordes, Shelli P252
Koremans, Robert W389
Koren, Vladimir P109
Korenberg, Matthew A390
Korenek, Joe A301
Koretzky, Gary P159
Korey, Lowder P306
Koricanac, Nick A925
Koricanac, Nick E445
Korins, Danielle A692
Kornberg, Fred V. E93
Kornbluth, Sally P187
Korneffel, Laurie A184
Korner, Barbara O. A828
Korner, Barbara O. P584
Kornobis, Theodore A575
Kornowski-Bonnet, Sophie W328
Koro, Mark A694
Korolog, George A742
Korologos, Ann A436
Korona, Jim A161
Korsapati, Venka A43
Korsapati, Venka E13
Korsch, Marija G. W2
Korsh, Les B. A643
Korshun, Sergei P458
Korsmeyer, Mark A253
Korsmeyer, Mark P169
Korsok, Ed A492
Kort, Keesje A654
Korte, Daniel A673
Kortegast, Candice P652
Kortfelt, Doug A210
Korth, Beth E156
Kortum, Joe P507
Korzec-Brown, Joan A835
Korzekwa, Christi A840
Korzekwinski, Francis W. (Frank) A356
Kos, Heather A457
Kosakai, Kenkichi W256
Kosasa, Paul J A182
Koseki, Yoshiki W293
Koseoglu, Ata W177
Koser, Michael P667
Koshansky, Deborah E51
Kosharek, Jamie A704
Koshkin, Joe E224
Kosiek, Patrick A204
Kosinski, Anthony A277
Kosinski, Ken A540
Kosiyangkakul, Tai P462

Kosko, Michael A120
Koskull, Casper von W287
Koslow, John A54
Kosowski, Brent P82
Koss, James A410
Koss, Kristen K P529
Kost, Beth P275
Kostantos, Roland W208
Koster, Corneel A262
Koster, Teresa A369
Koster, Barbara G. A686
Koster, James A779
Koster, John P431
Kostosky, Robert A A722
Kostroske, Randy E218
Kosydor, Vicki A319
Kotagiri, Seetarama W244
Kotara, Vivian E105
Kotch, Noah E103
Koth, Dan A727
Koth, Dan P453
Kothakota, Aishwarya A409
Kothari, Neelam A69
Kothari, Ck E319
Kothe, Kelly P330
Kotick, Robert A. (Bobby) A10
Kotler, Dov W49
Kotlikoff, Michael I. P159
Kotsenas, Peter A351
Kotsopoulos, Peter W371
Kottler, Robert M. (Bob) A449
Kottler, Robert M. (Bob) E220
Kottman, Bill P191
Kotwal, Gautam A31
Kotwal, Shailesh M. A884
Kotwal, Gautam P20
Kotzbach, Kevin A331
Kotzbach, Kevin E152
Kotzin, Brian A64
Kotzin, Brian E300
Koudouris, Maria P164
Kouduki, Kazuo W393
Koulisis, Christo P208
Koulouris, Richard R. A672
Koumouris, Rick A355
Kounalakis, Eleni A782
Kounalakis, Eleni P525
Kouri, Stephen A765
Koury, Emile A401
Koury, Jeffrey (Jeff) A811
Koury, Emile E198
Koushik, Srinivas (Srini) A532
Kouyate, Bengaly P58
Kouzmenko, Roman E290
Kovac, Carrie A283
Kovach, Andrew L P12
Kovacs, Kris A213
Koval, Kathy A751
Kovalcik, Derek A919
Koviak, Jeff A813
Kovoch, Dan P68
Kowal, Dave A160
Kowaleski, Tim A209
Kowalski, Kevin P. A551
Kowalski, Kevin P. P321
Kowalski, Patrick P625
Kowbel, Kevin B. W85
Kowkabany, Rob A62
Kowkabany, Rob E20
Kowler, Kathy A590
Kowlzan, Mark W. A637
Koyama, Tomoyuki W282
Koza, Edward A877
Kozai, Gerald P515
Kozak, Dave A447
Kozak, Dennis A658
Kozak, Colleen A750
Kozak, Patricia A879
Kozak, Charlie P43
Kozak, Dave P247
Kozak, Patricia P636
Kozakov, Alex A175
Kozanian, Hagop A820
Kozano, Yoshiaki W350
Kozar, Paul Kozar Paul A884

Kozarich, John W. E257
Kozel, David F. (Dave) A692
Kozich, Gregory H A668
Kozicz, Gregory J P18
Kozicz, Gregory J P19
Kozik, Thom A538
Koziol, Patrick A112
Koziol, Patty A844
Koziol, Michael P305
Kozlow, Steve A61
Kozlowski, Damian A823
Kozlowski, Annmarie A824
Kozlowski, Mike A924
Kozlowski, Eric P73
Kozlowski, Annmarie P562
Kozlowski, Damian E405
Kozoman, Robert L. (Bob) P174
Kozulla, Allison A360
Kra, Douglas I. (Doug) E326
Kraats, Robert-Jan van de W319
Krabbe, Mark A258
Krabbenhoft, Kelby K P471
Krackeler, Chris E47
Krackenberger, Melissa A449
Krackenberger, Melissa E220
Kracov, Eric A590
Kraemer, Theodore A145
Kraetsch, Jeff P168
Krafft, Chris P86
Kraft, Robert O. (Rocky) A251
Kraft, Ted A413
Kraft, Christopher A750
Kraft, Jennifer A865
Kraft, John P627
Kraft, Ted E205
Krage, David A449
Krage, David E220
Krajicek, Cathy A533
Krakowsky, Christina A161
Krakowsky, Philippe A468
Kralingen, Bridget A. van A465
Krall, Donna M. A353
Krall, Donna M. E173
Kralovic, Damon A824
Kralovic, Damon P562
Kramer, Derek A51
Kramer, Kelly A. A198
Kramer, Richard J. (Rich) A392
Kramer, Kevin A567
Kramer, Curt A A583
Kramer, Phillip D. (Phil) A668
Kramer, Phil A668
Kramer, Phil D A668
Kramer, Mark A722
Kramer, Laurie A741
Kramer, Steve A884
Kramer, David A. P104
Kramer, Karen P291
Kramer, Don P451
Kramer, Bill P512
Kramer, Ken P551
Kramer, Markus W59
Kramer, Marcus W62
Kramer, Christina W85
Kramer, Gary E40
Kramer, Robert G. (Bob) E126
Kramer, Marty E149
Kramer, Francis J. E224
Kramer, Francis J. E225
Kramer, Kevin E283
Kramer, Laurie E364
Kramm, Jeffrey P282
Kramm, Randall L P282
Krane, Hilary K A599
Krane, Jeffrey P556
Krantz, Donald G. E339
Kranzo, Alan A774
Kranzo, Alan P510
Krapels, Marco P547
Krapf, Howard J P288
Krasner, Stephen A510
Krasner, Stephen P290
Krasno, Richard E250
Krasnoff, Jeffrey P. (Jeff) A512
Krasowski, Janet D. A684

Krass, Lauren P273
Krasula, Jason A686
Kraszewski, Andrew P368
Kratky, Kay W136
Kratz, Denise A741
Kratz, Denise E364
Kratzer, Doug A405
Kratzert, Niki A495
Kratzert, Niki P282
Kraus, Eric A327
Kraus, Frederick A506
Kraus, Kim A680
Kraus, Carl A768
Kraus, Ronald P405
Kraus, Jason P552
Kraus, Cedar P588
Krause, John A176
Krause, Douglas P. A284
Krause, Matt A530
Krause, Jessica A626
Krause, Teresa P76
Krause, Melissa P133
Krause, Alan J. A355
Krause, Catherine P634
Krause, L William E86
Krause, Douglas P. E119
Krauss, Soheir A200
Krauss, Jim A754
Krauss, Jim P484
Kraut, Jeffrey A. P382
Kravchenko, Kirill W169
Krawchuk, Sandy A465
Krawczyk, Tammy A922
Krawczyk, Tammy P671
Krawiec, Ronald P197
Kreatsoulas, John A460
Krebber, Markus W335
Krebs, Donald E. (Don) A485
Krebs, Don A485
Krebsbach, Karen P606
Krech, Joyce A126
Kreeke, Jeffrey Van De P211
Kreft, Wesley P408
Kreger, John M. P578
Krehbiel, Bruce A470
Krehbiel, Bradley C. E211
Kreider, Torsten A245
Kreider, Carole A267
Kreigh, Dave E180
Krein, Jeffrey A574
Kreiner, Lynne A530
Kreips, Christopher A730
Kreis, Melanie W137
Krejs, Patrick E349
Kremberg, Jeffrey A201
Kremer, Lisa A540
Kremer, Wesley D. A706
Kremer, Melissa A804
Kremer, Thomas W138
Kremin, Donald H. (Don) A434
Kremke, Kevin L A260
Krempl, Stephen A779
Krenk, Chris P112
Krenke, Gary A86
Krenke, Brian P283
Krenke, Gary E27
Krenz, William C. (Willie) P553
Kreppel, Rick A536
Kreppel, Rick E190
Kresge, Kevin A137
Kresl, Michael A58
Kress, Jean A385
Kress, Colette M. A613
Kretzinger, Cut P234
Kretzmer, William B. (Brian) E240
Kreuzbauer, Georg A64
Krevans, Sarah A791
Krevans, Sarah P535
Krew, David A681
Krey, Doug A423
Krhovsky, David M P509
Kriakov, Ivan A391
Krick, Robert A332
Krick, Gerd W166
Krick, Gerd W167

COMBINED HOOVER'S HANDBOOK INDEX OF EXECUTIVES

```
A = AMERICAN BUSINESS
E = EMERGING COMPANIES
P = PRIVATE COMPANIES
W = WORLD BUSINESS
```

Krider, Jack P395
Krieble, William A341
Krieg, Susan A452
Krieger, Sandra C. (Sandy) A319
Krieger, Sarah A646
Krieger, Noah E131
Krieger, Sarah E324
Krieger, Daryl W E443
Kriegesmann, Holly A928
Kriegesmann, Holly P673
Kriegner, Martin W230
Kriegsmann, Sonja A621
Kriegsmann, Sonja E312
Kriesberg, Barry P229
Krikorian, Lazarus A63
Krikorian, Mark A64
Krill, Steven L. E118
Krimbill, H. Michael A598
Kring, Steven C. A433
Kring, Kent P347
Kring, Steven C. E217
Krinsky, Lewis A727
Krinsky, Lewis P453
Kripalu, Anand W140
Krippner, Brian A859
Krisel, Bob P404
Krisfalusi, Charlie E433
Krish, Bharani A571
Krishen, Ashok W294
Krishna, Srinivasan P100
Krishna, R. Murali P254
Krishna, Siva P594
Krishnamoorthy, Vinodh A137
Krishnamoorthy, Dheepa A203
Krishnamoorthy, Pragash E431
Krishnamurthi, Gopal A323
Krishnamurthy, Aparna A240
Krishnamurthy, Nikki A307
Krishnamurthy, Ram A527
Krishnan, Chidu A695
Krishnan, Ramayya P114
Krishnan, Sridhar W294
Kriss, Scott A620
Kristen, Kirby P588
Kristensen, Douglas A. (Doug) P92
Kristiansen, Thore A301
Kristiansen, Thore P196
Kristiansen, Thore E. W169
Kristic, Nik A63
Kristich, John A744
Kristjanson, Stefan W173
Kristoff, David A595
Kristollari, Viljan A722
Kristovich, Joe P375
Kritskij, Juriy L. W401
Krivacek, Laura P570
Krivo, George P189
Krizelman, Jill A692
Krmpotic, Deb A117
Krmpotic, Deb P61
Krna, Catherine P524
Kroehler, Jon A583
Kroeker, Harrald F. A75
Kroeker, Curtis M. E99
Kroeper, Jon P202
Krojansky, Mark E385
Krol, Wojciech A218
Krolewicz, Randall A530
Krolick, Mark A865
Kroll, Elaine A347
Kroll, Austin E105
Kroll, Werner E343
Krone, Roger A. A509
Kronenberger, Carolyn P71
Kroos, Karsten W391
Kropf, Jonathan A349
Kropf, Susan A801
Kropiunik, Frank C P18
Kropp, Susan A700

Krosby, Lars E269
Krosin, Benjamin E433
Krouse, Michael P395
Krow, Elizabeth A135
Kruczlnicki, David A82
Kruegel, William A179
Krueger, John A85
Krueger, Pam A89
Krueger, Alan A175
Krueger, Steve A449
Krueger, Robert A688
Krueger, Paul A722
Krueger, Jason P556
Krueger, John E27
Krueger, Steve E220
Krug, Paul A799
Krug, Erik P642
Krugel, Mike A381
Kruger, James D. (Jim) A586
Kruger, Bob A809
Kruger, Bill A871
Kruger, Cory P475
Kruger, R. M. (Rich) W196
Kruger, Ben W363
Kruger, James D. (Jim) E301
Kruglov, Lisa A452
Kruk, Janice A893
Krulewitch, Jerry A548
Krull, Megan E314
Krum, David A91
Krum, David P55
Krumbock, Monika A749
Krumbock, Monika E367
Krumholz, Stephen A272
Krummenacher, Cornel W276
Krump, Paul J. W106
Krunic, Nancy E261
Krupinski, Michal Tomasz W54
Krupinski, Dave E65
Kruse, Kevin A156
Kruse, Karen A343
Kruse, Cory A361
Kruse, Shelly A399
Kruse, Karl A448
Kruse, Tony A449
Kruse, Trent A647
Kruse, Brent A660
Kruse, Eric A664
Kruse, Christi A877
Kruse, Shelly P223
Kruse, Lowell P234
Kruse, Karl P247
Kruse, Brent P416
Kruse, Richard P549
Kruse, Stein W87
Kruse, Richard E96
Kruse, Karen E164
Kruse, Tony E221
Kruse, Eric E334
Kruse, Rebecca E364
Krusi, Alan P E89
Kruszewski, Ronald J. (Ron) A787
Kruthaupt, Bob A680
Krutka, April A462
Krutka, April P256
Krutulis, Shari A621
Krutulis, Shari E312
Kruythoff, Kees W409
Kruzner, Melinda P P293
Krych, Ron P599
Krygoski, Haide A752
Krylo, Angie A747
Krynauw, Pieter A431
Krysiak, Lauren A444
Kryska, Mark P52
Krysler, Kevan A897
Krystopolski, Ruth P471
Krzeminski, Robert E A909
Krzeminski, Robert E E436
Krzmarzick, Brent P632
Krzysiak, Honorata A233
Krzyzanowski, Bobby P650
Kruger, Harald W63
Kruger, Roland W283
Ksenak, Stephen M. A43

Ksenak, Stephen M. E13
Ksoll, Chris A347
Ksoll, Chris E167
Ku, Pao P177
Kuang, Ooi Sang W299
Kubacki, Michael L. A504
Kubacki, Michael L. E251
Kubacki, Jeff E443
Kubba, Omar A332
Kubiak, Connie P542
Kubick, David E260
Kubiesa, Susan A606
Kubik, Michele A530
Kubista, Jennifer P540
Kubo, Taizo W20
Kubo, Toshihiro W227
Kubo, Ken W369
Kubota, Hironobu W227
Kucera, Randall A400
Kucera, Randall E195
Kuchar, Trey A180
Kucharski, Joseph A658
Kuchnicki, Julie A806
Kuchnicki, Julie E399
Kuczmanski, John D. P320
Kudithipudi, Vinay E96
Kudla, Keith P199
Kudler, Douglas A559
Kudler, Neil P72
Kudo, Sumio W93
Kudo, Yasumi W282
Kudrna, Casey A859
Kudzman, Susan W232
Kuebel, Todd P567
Kuebel, Christoph W75
Kueber, Ken A212
Kuehl, Christopher J A23
Kuehl, Thomas W283
Kuehl, Christopher E5
Kuehn, Gina A3
Kuehn, Vern A16
Kueker, Derek A715
Kuelbs, Brian P. A104
Kuenzle, Sheila P94
Kueper, Martin A724
Kueper, Martin P452
Kugel, Irene A112
Kugler, Alexander A64
Kuhl, Barbara A P310
Kuhl, Shelly E48
Kuhlow, John A442
Kuhn, Rebecca (Becky) A117
Kuhn, Christian A423
Kuhn, Michael A465
Kuhn, Robert A764
Kuhn, Rebecca (Becky) P61
Kuhn, William P67
Kuhn, Don P78
Kuhn, Tom P415
Kuhn, Robert E377
Kuhnert, Marcus W254
Kuick, Ken A161
Kuick, Kenneth A161
Kuiper, Jeremy L. A823
Kuiper, Ken E392
Kuiper, Jeremy L. E405
Kuipers, Peter E315
Kujirai, Yoichi W258
Kukic, Drita A888
Kukic, Drita E425
Kukkal, Pankaj A695
Kukura, Sergei P. W309
Kukurin, James A746
Kula, Tom P382
Kularski, Patty A405
Kulas, Chad A171
Kulas, Michael G A862
Kulas, Michael G P617
Kulatham, Sarakorn W316
Kulchitskaya, Yanina A203
Kuligowski, Michal E226
Kulkarni, Santosh A200
Kulkarni, Shridhar A654
Kulkarni, Sanjeev R. P591
Kulkarni, Vic E22

Kulkin, Harvey A756
Kull, Steven A347
Kull, Mike A561
Kull, Steven E167
Kulle, David A408
Kullmann, Christian W158
Kulma, Maria P189
Kum, Chong Guk (C. G.) A404
Kum, Chong Guk (C. G.) E199
KUMAGAI, TOSHIYUKI W217
Kumakiri, Naomi W126
Kumar, Devinder A14
Kumar, Atul A135
Kumar, Ram A203
Kumar, Gopa A321
Kumar, Sunil A478
Kumar, Seema A479
Kumar, Vanitha A695
Kumar, Rajesh A722
Kumar, Rick A742
Kumar, Krish A833
Kumar, Ashok P1
Kumar, Arvind P215
Kumar, Anish P239
Kumar, Sunil P268
Kumar, Pratik S P673
Kumar, Santhosh E115
Kumar, Sujit E290
Kumar, Santosh E290
Kumaraswamy, Subra A896
Kumasaki, Sally A855
Kumbier, Michelle A. A407
Kumer, Kathleen A622
Kumler, Alan A867
Kumler, Alan H A867
Kumler, Alan E418
Kumler, Alan H E418
Kumm, Wendy A85
Kumm, Wendy E26
Kummeth, Janet P211
Kummeth, Charles R. (Chuck) E45
Kumpas, James A356
Kumpula, Jim P537
Kumro, Mark A530
Kuna, Mark L. A317
Kunash, Amanda P22
Kunath, Jan W322
Kunda, Dolores P567
Kunde, Gerald A798
Kunde, Chip A798
Kunde, Grace E141
Kundurthy, Praveen A460
Kunduru, Sree A854
Kunibe, Takeshi W369
Kunii, Yoshihiro W160
Kunik, Raymond A417
Kunimoto, Yoshihiko P534
Kunisaki, Tom P488
Kunk, James E. A444
Kunkel, Ted A115
Kunkel, Heidi A423
Kunkel, Jay K. A508
Kunkel, Thomas M. (Tom) A844
Kunkel, Ted E37
Kunst, Jeff A240
Kuntz, William A176
Kuntz, John F. A684
Kuntz, Michael J. (Mike) A853
Kuntz, Louann P17
Kuntz, Kevin P318
Kuntz, Michael J. (Mike) P612
Kunz, Thomas W128
Kunze, Shane A688
Kunze, Shane A689
Kunze, Shane P435
Kupbens, Bob A287
Kupchak, Kyle A452
Kuper, Debra A21
Kuperman, Maxim E290
Kupetz, Dan A893
Kupka, Alyssa P175
Kupper, Randy A60
Kuppuswamy, Murali A417
Kuppuswamy, Murali A827
Kuppuswamy, Murali P571

Kurahara, Fumiaki W369
Kuraishi, Hideaki W30
Kuraishi, Seiji W186
Kurali, Andreas A661
Kurani, Maheboob A404
Kurani, Maheboob E199
Kurapati, Raja A135
Kurapka, David A135
Kurdas, Meral E. W177
Kurdle, Florence B P40
Kurek, Robert A491
Kurian, George A586
Kurin, Richard P497
Kurisu, Toshizo W430
Kurita, Nathan A665
Kurita, Nathan E334
Kuritani, Kevin E114
Kuritsky, Lloyd P489
Kuritzkes, Andrew A783
Kurizaki, Sheryl A182
Kurland, Stanford L. A648
Kurland, Stanford L. E328
Kurlapski, Matthew A915
Kurn, Melanie A717
Kurn, Melanie E351
Kurnick, Robert H. A649
Kurnik, David A743
Kuroda, Haruhiko W51
Kuroda, Tadashi W262
Kuropas, Stephen A605
Kurosawa, Seikichi W349
Kurow, Dave A347
Kurow, Dave E167
Kurth, Keith A911
Kurth, Keith E437
Kurtis, Wilkerson A224
Kurtov, Ines A590
Kurtz, Aaron A227
Kurtz, Ronald D A571
Kurtz, Martin A746
Kurtz, Kevin A835
Kurtz, Erin A934
Kurtz, Jeffrey P86
Kurtz, William P429
Kurtz, Aaron E90
Kurzius, Lawrence E. A547
Kuselias, Jason A409
Kush, Andrew E203
Kushel, J. Richard (Rich) A135
Kushida, Seiji W127
Kuslits, Thomas R. A353
Kuslits, Thomas R. E173
Kusserow, Paul B. E14
Kustenbauter, Jim A828
Kustenbauter, Jim P584
Kuster, Robson J. (Rob) A472
Kuster, Kristin A731
Kusterer, Thomas W151
Kustor, Chris A577
Kutac, Mary-Katherine A179
Kutam, Sreeni A93
Kutateladze, Andrei P146
Kutch, John M P606
Kutchera, Kris A29
Kutina, Kenneth P116
Kutz, Tim E123
Kuwabara, Shigehiro W51
Kuwahara, Takao W160
Kuwahara, Masahiro W262
Kuwano, Mitsumasa W429
Kuye, Olabisi A877
Kuykendall, Debbie A105
Kuykendall, Ronald E. A741
Kuykendall, Debbie E34
Kuykendall, Ronald E. E364
Kuypers, Tom A125
Kuzas, Betsy P417
Kuzbel, Jeffrey A167
Kuzee, Willem A654
Kuzmak, Beth A549
Kuznetsov, Sergey A191
Kuznetsov, Stanislav K. W343
Kvadus, Glen A877
Kvasnikoff, Wayne P392
Kvistad, Gregg P146

Kvochak, Gregg E248
Kwak, Jin P248
Kwan, Irene E B A109
Kwas, Richard A813
Kwasnica, Christina A266
Kwasnica, Christina P181
Kwasnowski, Lisa A574
Kwawu, Sena M A780
Kwawu, Sena A780
Kwiatkowski, Paul E344
Kwitchoff, Jim E256
Kwok, John A107
Kwok, Daphne P2
Kwon, Mea A349
Kwon, Oh Hyung A695
Kwon, Kenneth P343
Kwon, Bong-Suk W237
Kwon, Oh-Joon W311
Kwong, Melsen P118
Kyff, Emilia A559
Kylberg, Richard A81
Kyle, Rex A113
Kyle, Rick A691
Kyle, Rex E36
Kyle, Mithchin E180
Kymes, Stacy C. A141
Kymes, Stacy C. E49
Kyoya, Yutaka W257
Kyprianou, Annette P576
Kyriacos, Zoe P642
Kyriakidis, Alex A537
Kyzyk, Andrew E318
K-ollenius, Ola W125
Kohler, Roland W230

L

L, Green Jacob P569
La, Mai A137
La, Paul De P404
Laan, Ron Van Der A112
Laan, Sander van der W223
Labar, Frank A237
Labarba, Frank A905
LaBarge, Jeffrey A237
Labban, Ziad A902
LaBelle, James P479
Laben, Nancy J. A145
Labeyrie, Christian W415
Labi, Abdul A850
Labian, Paula C A430
Labib, Joseph A684
Labonte, Chip P356
Laborde, Thierry W71
LaBorde, Ronald A. E14
Labosky, Laura P138
Labovich, Gary D. A144
Labrador, Leslie A682
Labrecque, Andre G P24
Labrecque, Christine P300
Labrique, Steve A69
Labrosse, Derek A114
Labrosse, Derek E36
Labrot, Andy E122
Labrucherie, Gil M. E300
Labus, Gregory E A141
Lacaille, Rick A783
Lacassagne, Gtraudmarie A243
Lacerda, Michael A137
Lacey, Diane E. A588
Lacey, Diane E. P365
Lacey, Cheryl E14
Lachance, Margaret P. (Meg) A692
Lachenmeyer, William E263
Lacher, Joseph P. (Joe) A489
Lachica, Carlos De E106
Lachman, Barry P171
Lachman, Sandy P445
Lacina, Diane A421
Lacker, Jeffrey M. (Jeff) A322
Lackey, Michael A355
Lackey, Dana A621
Lackey, Dana E312
Lackhouse, Gary A89

Lacombe, Elizabeth A882
Lacombe, Philip P72
Lacour, Raymond A704
Lacroix, Richard A216
Lacroix, Chris A248
Lacroix, Didier E85
Lacroix, Chris E107
Lacroix, David E126
Lacroix, Rob E225
Lacy, James A89
Lacy, Jamie A664
Lacy, Alan J. E111
Lacy, Jamie E334
Laczi, Chris E256
Lad, Nitin E290
Ladd, Tim A552
Ladd, Edward H. (Ted) P79
Ladd, Kevin P205
Ladd, Steven P223
Ladd, Tim E276
Lade, Herb E85
Lader, Philip W427
Laderman, Gerald (Gerry) A864
Ladiwala, Shiraz A833
Ladouceur, Jacinthe A54
Ladowicz, John A623
Ladowicz, John E313
Laduke, David A481
Laeng, Leslie A362
Laenger, William A713
Laferle, Michael A428
Lafferty, Kevin A263
Lafferty, Jack A933
Lafferty, William P677
Laffin, Nathan A647
Laffoon, Chris A522
Lafiandra, Craig A877
Lafitte, Michael J. (Mike) A175
Laflamme, Renée W193
Lafloure, Thomas P134
LaFollette, Christopher A69
Lafon, Emily P665
Lafond, Dan A89
Lafond, Michelle A882
Lafont, Bruno W230
Lafontaine, Micheline P598
Lafontaine, Henri W148
Lafontant, Edouard A670
LaForgia, Felicia A884
Lafrance, Dan A497
LaFrence, Andrew D. C. (Andy) E395
LaFreniere, Kevin A409
Laga, Michael A914
Laga, Michael E439
Lagano, Roxanne A941
Lagarde, Michel A833
Lagarrigue, Emmanuel W344
LaGatta, Loreen A. A91
LaGatta, Loreen A. E29
Lage, Jose L. P505
Lager, Jeffrey T A50
Lager, Jeffrey T P31
Lagerlef, Brenda P422
Lagestee, Mark A937
Laginess, Meredith A265
Laginestra, Charles A175
Lagioia, Andrea A218
Lagnado, Silvia A548
Lago, Jim A286
Lago, Virginia Del A540
Lago, Jim P190
Lagomarcino, Mark A677
Lagoy, Ned P166
Lagreca, Gregory A837
Lagrone, Craig A599
Lagrone, Bart A608
Laguarta, Ramon A654
Lague, Richard C P329
LaHaise, James A. A62
LaHaise, James A. E20
Lahanas, Nicholas (Niko) E72
Lahrs, Claus-Dietrich W218
Lai, Nathan A200
Lai, King-chung A695
Lai, Julius P30

Lai, Chong Ta W379
Lai, Johnson E308
Laigneau, Marianne W148
Laine, Jim A343
Laine, Jim E164
Laing, Sheila A447
Laing, Sheila P247
Laing, Melanie W114
Laipple, Chad A885
Laird, Bruce A198
Laird, Fiona A593
Laird, William P301
Laird, Brian E121
Laixuthai, Adit W216
Lajos, Jaroslav E290
Lake, Charles D. A19
Lake, Robert A264
Lake, Stuart A419
Lake, Marianne A483
Lake, Jeffrey A584
Lake, Robert P180
Lake, Marcelino P249
Lake, Frederick E265
Lakely, Brock A219
Lakely, Brock E87
Lakhani, Shereen A574
Lakhtman, Lilia P604
Lakin, Kenneth S P95
Lakin, Peter D P95
Lakin, Edwin A P95
Lakshmaihgari, Raj A647
Lakshman, Girish A750
Lakshminarayan, Ramesh A216
Lal, Pradeep W417
Lalance, Rick A665
Lalance, Rick E334
Lalanne, Jean-Christophe W15
Lalas, Jose W P160
Laliberty, Tom A706
Lalime, Yvonne A155
Lalime, Yvonne E54
Lalithakumar, Ananth A179
Lally, James B. A298
Lally, Thomas P475
Lally, Devin P625
Lally, James B. E130
Lalonde, Mary P574
Lalonde, Kenn W. W396
Lalor, Angela S. A254
Lalor, William P58
Lalwani, Ellen A504
Lalwani, Ellen E251
Lam, Margaret A79
Lam, Michael A112
Lam, Samsonz A284
Lam, Ricky A284
Lam, Sophia A285
Lam, Josiah A484
Lam, Alethea A538
Lam, Winnie A784
Lam, Karen A817
Lam, Barry W317
Lam, Samsonz E120
Lam, Ricky E120
Lam, Sophia E120
Lamacchio, Tom A704
Lamalfa, Jennifer E445
Laman, John A806
Laman, John E399
Lamanno, Lori A859
Lamar, William (Bibb) A755
Lamar, Jim P218
Lamar, William (Bibb) E369
Lamarche, Robert A715
Lamarre, Anne P204
Lamas, Terry P102
Lamb, Todd A170
Lamb, Brian A329
Lamb, Gerry A373
Lamb, Scott A692
Lamb, Robert A744
Lamb, Todd A782
Lamb, Jim P120
Lamb, Eric P185
Lamb, John P309

COMBINED HOOVER'S HANDBOOK INDEX OF EXECUTIVES

```
A = AMERICAN BUSINESS
E = EMERGING COMPANIES
P = PRIVATE COMPANIES
W = WORLD BUSINESS
```

Lamb, Michael P376
Lamb, Mark P506
Lamb, Todd P526
Lamb, Jureen P541
Lamb, Brian D. P638
Lamb, Peter E140
Lamb, Trisha M E194
Lamb, Scott E. E222
Lamb, Lisa E315
Lambert, Danielle A72
Lambert, Jeff A135
Lambert, Michael A347
Lambert, Jeff A581
Lambert, Brett A608
Lambert, Richard F. A686
Lambert, Cameron A702
Lambert, Matthew A706
Lambert, Jay A934
Lambert, Phil P488
Lambert, Jér- 'me W115
Lambert, Nick W417
Lambert, Michael E167
Lambert, Sandra L. E243
Lamberti, Hermann-Josef M. W200
Lambertson, Stephen A831
Lambertson, Stephen P601
Lambeth, Tracy A569
Lambiase, Matthew A191
Lambiase, Matthew E79
Lamble, Mark P246
Lambropoulos, Helen E330
Lambros, Cindy P122
LAMEY, KRISTEN A602
Laming, Michael S. A381
Lamkin, Bryan A11
Lamm, Kim A850
Lamm, Kimberly P450
Lammas, Mark T. E219
Lammers, John A95
Lammers, Dave A264
Lammers, James A320
Lammers, Kent A397
Lamneck, Kenneth T. (Ken) A458
Lamoreaux, Brent A451
Lamoreaux, Roy I A668
Lamoreaux, Brent P249
Lamotte, Joseph A396
Lamparski, Jerry A36
Lampe, Adam P319
Lampen, Richard J. (Dick) E250
Lampereur, Andrew E184
Lampert, Edward S. (Eddie) A750
Lampert, Steven P54
Lampier, Carol A246
Lampier, Carol E105
Lampley, Marcus A56
Lampman, Rusty A312
Lampman, Rusty P199
Lampmann, Rich A692
Lampo, Craig A. A66
Lampone, Salvatore W235
Lamppa, Lindsey A804
Lamprecht, Charlotte A695
Lampropoulos, Fred P. E278
Lampropoulos, Justin E278
Lamsam, Banthoon W216
Lamsam, Krisada W216
LaMue, Julian A85
LaMue, Julian E26
Lamy, David W366
Lanahan, Judith A325
Lancaster, Tim A340
Lancaster, Christopher A409
Lancaster, Robert A548
Lancaster, Kim A715
Lancaster, Rick P221
Lancaster, Tim E161
Lance, Ryan M A233
Lance, Wendy A741

Lance, Phil P254
Lance, Donald W P587
Lance, Fletcher P648
Lance, Wendy E364
Lanci, Gianfranco W234
Lancia, Pete A694
Lanctot, Chris A170
Lancy, Raymond F. E51
Land, Jeff A266
Land, Jeff P181
Landa, Jon A522
Landa, Dara A575
Landa, Howard A791
Landa, Howard P535
Landaker, Larry P410
Landau, Glenn R. A467
Landau, Igor W9
Landau, Steve E1
Lande, Ruth P325
Lander, John A620
Lander, Jamie A682
Lander, Ryan P422
Lander, Eric P556
Landers, Richard A164
Landers, Linda K A222
Landers, Joseph A793
Landers, Lisa P27
Landers, Peter P613
Landes, Barbara L. P432
Landever, Alan P198
Landewee, Cassy P337
Landis, Todd A835
Landis, Chris E80
Landless, David E229
Landmark, Greg A844
Landow, Ali E275
Landre, Jay E613
Landreth, Laura P554
Landroche, Jeff A115
Landroche, Jeff E37
Landrum, Tom A604
Landrum, Marilyn P141
Landry, Mark A355
Landry, Ed A547
Landry, Robert E. A710
Landry, Steve A760
Landry, Stephen A760
Landry, Chris A859
Landry, Doug P384
Landry, Steve E374
Landry, Stephen E374
Landschulz, Mark A353
Landschulz, Mark E173
Landsgard, Carson A804
Landsman, Liza K. A901
Landstrom, G A847
Landstrom, G P606
Landy, Nancy A414
Landy, Nancy E208
Landy, Michael P. E287
Landy, Eugene W. E287
Lane, Andrew H. A5
Lane, Danny A87
Lane, Janet A247
Lane, Eric S. A390
Lane, Jeffrey H. A561
Lane, Mike A628
Lane, Michael A715
Lane, J. Bret A753
Lane, Colin A775
Lane, Richard A796
Lane, Danny P50
Lane, Conan P234
Lane, Becca P259
Lane, Linda P421
Lane, Colin P511
Lane, Charles E. P627
Lane, Timothy W50
Lane, Brian E. E89
Lane, Janet E105
Lane, Mike E223
Lane, Christine E223
Lane, James A. E268
Lane, John D E282
Lane, James G. E396

Lane, Richard E397
Lanese, Katherine P116
Lanesey, Rob A471
Laney, G. Timothy (Tim) A581
Laney, Mark P234
Laney, Mark P349
Laney, D. Randy P566
Laney, G. Timothy (Tim) E294
Lang, Rick A63
Lang, Nicholas A126
Lang, Steve A199
Lang, Robert A257
Lang, Michael (Mike) A270
Lang, Rick A347
Lang, Richard A364
Lang, Patrick A507
Lang, Edward A A721
Lang, Rebecca A A859
Lang, Rebecca A859
Lang, Marcina P637
Lang, Joe E89
Lang, Rick E167
Langan, Tom A678
Langberg, Michael L. P118
Langberg, Joanna P199
Langdale, Paul A456
Langdale, Paul E228
Langdon, Lynn M A763
Langdon, Lynn M E377
Lange, Wade A48
Lange, Jeffrey A409
Lange, Peter A651
Lange, Julie P46
Lange, Donald H P134
Lange, Gerald P404
Lange, Kelley E293
Lange, Peter E329
Langel, Craig A A386
Langel, Craig A E188
Langella, Steve A170
Langen, D Bryce Bryce A690
Langenberg, Sharon A806
Langenberg, Sharon E399
Langenderfer, Randy P548
Langendonk, Dave A920
Langeness, Troy A623
Langeness, Troy E313
Langenfeld, Jon A. A726
Langenfeld, Jon A. P453
Langenfeld, Josh E184
Langenhan, Anna A158
Langenus, John A69
Langer, C E286
Langer, Steve E286
Langevin, Eric T. E243
Langford, Barbara P28
Langford, Stephen P76
Langford, Mark D P279
Langford, Ron E102
Langhals, Ken P270
Langham, Catherine P567
Langham, Jacquelyn P639
Langhofer, Veronica E433
Langlais, Tracy P110
Langley, David A224
Langley, W. John P315
Langley, John P315
Langlois, Jennifer P86
Langone, Elizabeth A559
Langone, Joey A726
Langston, Scott A724
Langston, Lewis A904
Langston, Scott P452
Langston, Mark P475
Lanham, Don A687
Lanier, Lawrence A323
Lanier, Gina P55
Laniewski, Jeffrey E179
Lankler, Douglas M. (Doug) A657
Lankton, Madelyn A844
Lannie, P. Anthony A71
Lannie, Panthony A71
Lannie, P Anthony A71
Lanning, Justin A933
Lannon, David A921

Lannon, David P669
Lanoha, Richard A P279
Lansbury, Stephen A364
Lansesey, Rob A471
Lansford, Gordon E. P260
Lansford, Gordon E. P261
Lansing, Linda P475
Lansing, William J. (Will) E144
Lant, Stephen P121
Lant, Todd E47
Lanter, Greg A345
Lanter, Greg E165
Lantman, Chris A925
Lantman, Chris E445
Lantos, Phyllis R. A827
Lantos, Phyllis P371
Lantos, Phyllis R. P580
Lantrip, Reese T. A301
Lantta, Kimberly E48
Lantz, Tina A170
Lantz, Brian A361
Lantz, Penelope P569
Lantzsch, Thomas P. (Tom) A460
Lantzsch, Tom A460
Lantzy, Mark P252
Lanusse, Adrien A587
Lanza, Steve A505
Lanza, Lorie A686
Lanza, Michael H. A751
Lanzer, Kris A332
Lanzetta, Keri A784
Lanzillo, Dante A722
Lanzoni, Nancy A115
Lanzoni, Nancy E38
Lao, Peter A391
Laokwansatit, Anucha W351
Lapala, Sreekanth E431
Lapcevic, Misha A538
Lapczynski, Susan A135
Lapenta, Robert A158
Laperriere, Nick P175
Lapeyre, Elizabeth A619
Lapeyre, Elizabeth P393
Lapiana, John K. P497
Lapidas, Gary P616
Lapierre, Steve A149
Lapierre, Jamie P639
Lapinska, Debbie L E332
LaPlante, Frank A910
LaPlante, William P578
Laplante, Dawn E316
Lapoint, Shelly A85
Lapoint, Aaron A271
Lapoint, Shelly E26
Lapointe, Johanne A118
LaPointe, Mike A160
Lapointe, Margot A414
Lapointe, Kimberly A686
LAPOINTE, BEN A704
Lapointe, Margot P236
Lapointe, Johanne E40
Lapolice, Matt A728
LaPorta, Cosimo A779
LaPorte, Todd P478
Laporte, Todd P479
Lappala, Kris A656
Lappala, Kris P414
LaPrade, Frank G. A166
Laprade, Ken A501
Laprade, Patricia P59
Lapuente, Chris de W241
Larabee, Cheryl A. E452
Laramie, Jay A654
Laratonda, Susan A922
Laratonda, Susan P671
Laraway, Dennis L. A117
Laraway, Dennis P552
Laraway, Dennis L. P61
Laraway, Dennis P324
Larch, Amy A108
Larchrid, Jim A86
Larchrid, Jim E27
Lardy, Dave A643
Lareau, Doug P491
Lareau, Richard G. E280
Largent, Jessica A595

HOOVER'S HANDBOOK OF EMERGING COMPANIES 2020

Larger, Cary P127
Larkey, Sheila A859
Larkin, Paul A428
Larkin, Deanna A439
Larkin, Gary A452
Larkin, Terrence B. (Terry) A508
Larkin, Frank P166
Larkin, C. Raymond E10
Larkins, Thomas F. A74
Larkln, Joyce A179
Larnaudie-Eiffel, Xavier W111
Larocca, Prue B A23
LaRocca, Andrew A590
LaRocca, John E118
LaRocco, Michael E. (Mike) A781
Larochelle, Steven R. A297
Larochelle, Steven R. E129
Larocque, Jim A271
Larocque, Brett A325
Larocque, Peter A794
Larocque, Lynda P633
LaRose, Jason A862
LaRossa, Ralph A. A687
Laroyia, Varun A524
Larrimore, Randall A624
Larsen, Kenneth A. (Ken) A116
Larsen, James A161
Larsen, Jill A199
Larsen, Shild A301
Larsen, Michael M. A453
Larsen, Marshall A527
Larsen, Sallie R. A528
Larsen, Mark A902
Larsen, Burke P173
Larsen, Shild P196
Larsen, Brian P316
Larsen, Daniel P478
Larsen, Matthew P497
Larsen, Keri P607
Larsen, Hans J- rgen W214
Larsen, Kenneth A. (Ken) E39
Larsen, Don E226
Larsh, Roger A765
Larsh, Herbert P471
Larsh, Kurtis A60
Larson, Jan A72
Larson, Erik A113
Larson, Gloria A147
Larson, Paul A210
Larson, Maxwell A257
Larson, Greg A391
Larson, Gregory J. (Greg) A436
Larson, Greg A436
Larson, Michael A626
Larson, Randall A630
Larson, Pamela A637
Larson, Timothy M. A669
Larson, Don A672
Larson, Sherrie L A693
Larson, Todd C. A714
Larson, Michael A761
Larson, Steve A799
Larson, David L. A925
Larson, Kent T. A931
Larson, Steve P28
Larson, Les P41
Larson, Lawrence P102
Larson, John P213
Larson, Elwin P231
Larson, Earl P393
Larson, Warren P471
Larson, Todd P478
Larson, Tom P573
Larson, Mike P633
Larson, Lynette P659
Larson, Luke E30
Larson, Erik E36
Larson, Todd L E48
Larson, Sherrie L E341
Larson, David L. E445
Larsson, Naya A544
Larsson, John P361
Larter, Will E427
Lartigue, Donna A711
Lartigue, Donna P444

LaRussa, Baldo A702
Lasaga, Manuel P65
Lasane, Karlos A161
Lasarre, Al A369
Lascari, Scott A325
Laschinger, Mary A487
Lasecki, Marilyn A537
Lash, James H. (Jim) A351
Lash, Joan P276
Lashier, Mark E A191
Lashier, Mark E P126
Lashin, Joanne A751
Lashin, Joanne P482
Lashley, Joseph A380
Lashmet, Craig A739
LaShoto, Kathleen A835
Laskawy, Philip A526
Laskey, Sara P576
Lasko, Jonathan P156
Laskowski, Alicia A371
Laskowski, Robert P132
Laskowski, Alicia P213
Lasky, Charles A351
Lasky, Lawrence P357
Lasky, Jeffrey E219
Laslavic, Anthony A816
Lasota, Stephen A. E101
Laspisa, Jerry A530
Laspisa, Esther A933
Lass, John J. A366
Lassa, Bradley J P316
Lassar, Alex A481
Lassere, Vicki E106
Lassise, Noel A115
Lassise, Noel E38
Lassiter, Margaret A135
Lassiter, Wright L. A414
Lassiter, Lynn A664
Lassiter, Wright L. P236
Lassiter, Lynn E334
Laster, Annette P448
Laszlo, Matt A207
Latacki, Nancy A455
Lataille, Ronald J. E414
Latchford, Robert A871
Lateef, Omar P459
Latek, Kevin P. E192
Latella, Robert N. A331
Latella, Robert N. E152
Latham, Lara A789
Lathan, Grenita P245
Lathrop, Ann P165
Latimer, John A796
Latimer, John E397
Latsko, Felicia P127
Lattal, Frank W106
Lattanzio, Nicole P522
Lattari, Steve A67
Lattmann, Susan E. A125
Latuga, Tina A870
Laturell, Johnny E72
Latushie, Dick P439
Latza, Torben A135
Lau, Timothy J. A85
Lau, Malcom A109
Lau, Cindy A167
Lau, Stephen A218
Lau, Betty A319
Lau, Jacky A475
Lau, James A511
Lau, Elizabeth A571
Lau, Pamela A676
Lau, Paul P462
Lau, Timothy J. E26
Lau, Pamela E338
Laub, Jeff A158
Laubach, Lorene A804
Laubach, Harold E. P389
Laubacher, Pat P554
Lauber, Scott J. A907
Laubert, Joyce A544
Laudenslager, Kevin W. E281
Lauder, Est E A507
Lauderdale, Mark E194

Lauer, Trevor F. A279
Lauer, Kelley A859
Lauf, Michael K. (Mike) P109
Laufenberg, Wade P73
Laughlin, Terence P. (Terry) A107
Laughlin, Bill A598
Laughlin, John P. A714
Laughridge, Alan P418
Laughton, Kim P477
Launer, Justin A349
Laur, James P118
Laura, Hess A332
Laura, Kasch P638
Laura, Greenfield E330
Laureano, Karen A65
Lauren, Ralph A702
Lauren, David A702
Laurence, Scott A478
Laurenti, Rich P666
Laures, Karen P318
Lauria, Kristen A465
Lauria, Lynnette A761
Lauria, Joe P356
Laurie, Bob A100
Laurie, David A654
Lauriello, Johnathan P633
Laurin, Sean A358
Laurin, Michael W193
Laurin, Fran- §ois W232
Laurin, Sean A176
Lauring, Josh P268
Laurito, James P217
Lauritzen, Greg A833
Lauro, Carolyn A112
Lauro, Jeff A615
Laursen, Thomas E. A940
Laury, Véronique W219
Laut, Steve W. W85
Lautmann, Max A793
Lautsch, Robert A722
Lautz, Matthew E307
Lauzon, Shannon A731
Lavallee, Kristen A631
Lavallee, Paul A882
Lavallee, Kristen E329
Lavan, Maryanne R P206
Lavas, Helen P374
Lavaty, Brad E77
Laveck, Bill P512
Lavelli, Lucinda P627
Lavenberg, Stephanie A367
Lavender, Shelley K. A140
Lavender, Greg — A198
Lavender, Sunee P623
Laver, Michael A592
Laver, Michael P370
Laverdi, Barb A236
Lavergne, Angelica A670
Laverne, Heather A423
Laverty, David A. E59
Lavery, Michelle P471
Lavey, Bob A16
Lavey, Richard W. (Dick) A405
Lavigne, Joe A147
Lavin, Marty A925
Lavin, Pablo Granifo W44
Lavin, Marty E445
Lavinay, Gérard W88
Lavine, Bruce E447
Lavizzo-mourey, Risa A419
Lavoie, Karen A642
Lavoie, Blair P356
Lavoie, Karen P407
Lavoie, Michael E330
Law, Beth A108
Law, Christina A376
Law, Simon E99
Law, Richard E274
Lawal, Lekan A571
Lawenda, David A893
Lawerence, John A933
Lawhead, Casey A449
Lawhead, Brian A492
Lawhead, Casey E221

Lawhon, Bob A665
Lawhon, Pres A724
Lawhon, Pres P452
Lawhon, Bob E334
Lawhorn, Alex A727
Lawhorn, Andy A837
Lawhorn, Wesley L P102
Lawhorn, Alex P453
Lawicki, Pat A583
Lawing, Douglas A494
Lawit, Jason A A606
Lawler, Robert D. (Doug) A189
Lawler, Keith A409
Lawler, Nelda P197
Lawler, Michael A P234
Lawless, Cari A738
Lawless, Stephen T P22
Lawlor, Daniel A925
Lawlor, Dave P309
Lawlor, Edward F. P600
Lawlor, Dave P624
Lawlor, Sean E132
Lawlor, Brian G. E366
Lawlor, Daniel E445
Lawonn, Ken P489
Lawonn, Ken P490
Lawrence, Doug A61
Lawrence, Kevin A105
Lawrence, Ralph A145
Lawrence, Tim A145
Lawrence, Stephen A163
Lawrence, Steve A170
Lawrence, Paul J A225
Lawrence, Ryan A482
Lawrence, Guy A559
Lawrence, Edward P. A642
Lawrence, Taylor W. A706
Lawrence, Allison A778
Lawrence, Sherry A852
Lawrence, Ronald A891
Lawrence, Terri P11
Lawrence, Ida P191
Lawrence, Bruce P254
Lawrence, Heather P298
Lawrence, Mike P312
Lawrence, Sandra A. J. P327
Lawrence, Elin P333
Lawrence, Edward P. P407
Lawrence, Joseph P428
Lawrence, Beth P480
Lawrence, William B. P505
Lawrence, Kenneth P546
Lawrence, Silvana P548
Lawrence, Kevin E34
Lawrence, Stephen E62
Lawrence, Levy F E111
Lawrence, Rob E260
Lawrence-tarr, Cheryl A6
Lawrie, John E427
Laws, Matt A195
Laws, John A374
Laws, Dale A919
Lawshe, Pam A760
Lawshe, Pam E374
Lawson, Linda A87
Lawson, David C. (Dave) A219
Lawson, Rodger A. A283
Lawson, Mark A298
Lawson, Scott P. A595
Lawson, Linda P50
Lawson, Ralph E. P63
Lawson, Ralph P65
Lawson, James W. (Jim) P67
Lawson, Ken P245
Lawson, Carmen P286
Lawson, Matt P318
Lawson, Matthew P319
Lawson, Michael P395
Lawson, Sherri P511
Lawson, John W P650
Lawson, Marian W53
Lawson, Brian D. W80
Lawson, Stuart W333
Lawson, Douglas A. (Doug) E30
Lawson, David C. (Dave) E87

COMBINED HOOVER'S HANDBOOK INDEX OF EXECUTIVES

```
A = AMERICAN BUSINESS
E = EMERGING COMPANIES
P = PRIVATE COMPANIES
W = WORLD BUSINESS
```

Lawson, Mark E130
Lawton, Harry A. (Hal) A287
Lawton, Patrick S. (Pat) A726
Lawton, Patrick S. (Pat) P453
Lawton, Michael P488
Laxer, Richard A. (Rich) A374
Laxton, Gregory A140
Lay, Garry A16
Lay, Linda A296
Lay, Jeri A462
Lay, Jeri P256
Laychak, Heather P553
Layden, Kristin E433
Layman, Mark P59
Laymon, Joe A645
Layne, Glenn A665
Layne, Beverly A682
Layne, Christopher P354
Layne, Glenn E334
Layne-farrar, Anne E102
Laytart, David P329
Layton, Donald H. (Don) A364
Layton, Robert P189
Layton, Mary Jo P266
Lazar, Paula A349
Lazarczyk, Scott E72
Lazaridis, Nick A438
Lazarus, Larry S. A117
Lazarus, Franz E. A241
Lazarus, Larry S. P61
Lazenby, Pender J. E305
Lazo, Marusya P424
Lazrus, Paula P517
Lazzaris, Diane E. A910
Lazzati, John A764
Lazzati, John E377
Lazzi, Gianluca P597
Le, Hung A57
Le, Andy A592
Le, Vickie-hanh A722
Le, Sara A885
Le, Hung P33
Le, Christian P152
Le, Andy P371
Le, Brian P441
Lea, Andy A526
Lea, Jenny P282
Leach, Cliff A409
Leach, Mary Anne P127
Leach, Joy P305
Leach, Todd P642
Leach, Charles N. E42
Leackfeldt, Stephen M. A118
Leackfeldt, Stephen M. E40
Leadbeater, Seth M. A224
Leahy, John A60
Leahy, Mary P94
Leahy, Kevin P207
Leahy, William P. P608
Leahy, Marilyn E72
Leal, Danny A246
Leal, Cynthia A747
Leal, Santiago P12
Leal, Alexis P626
Leal, Danny E105
Leaman, Andrew A881
Leaman, Andrew E421
LeaMond, Nancy A. P2
Leamy, Audrey P18
Leandre, Liza A480
Leandro, Andre A722
Leanza, Chris A893
Lear, Mark A844
Leary, Alison A592
Leary, Warren A686
Leary, Mike A762
Leary, John F. A842
Leary, Michael A885
Leary, Alison P370

Leary, Angus P531
Leary, Matt P662
Leary, Brian E412
Leatherberry, William J. E304
Leatherman, Janelle A52
Leatherman, Jacob P52
Leavell, Christopher M. A332
Leavell, Bill E. A389
Leavenworth, Elaine R. A5
Leavitt, Todd A608
Leavitt, Chris E349
Leavy, David C. A270
Leavy, Jack A677
Lebaredian, Rev A613
Lebaron, Dawn P598
Lebby, Paul P647
Lebda, Douglas R. (Doug) E254
Lebeau, Christina A383
Lebeau, Christina E186
Lebel, Joseph J. A618
Lebel, Joseph J. E310
Lebens, Michael C P546
Leber, Charlie P493
LeBlanc, Claude L. A43
Leblanc, Jeff A205
LeBlanc, Jeffrey A205
Leblanc, Robert J. A465
Leblanc, Edmond A595
Leblanc, Richard A715
Leblanc, Deirdre P171
Leblanc, Stephen P173
Leblanc, Fernis P394
LeBlanc, Thomas J. P569
Leblanc, Paul A P623
LeBlanc, Claude L. E13
LeBlanc-Burley, Jelynne P164
Lebleu, Tom E122
Lebold, Suzanne A6
Lebowits, Michelle P265
Lebowitz, John A789
Lechleider, Michael A786
Lechleider, Michael E387
Lechleiter, John C. A518
Lechliter, Katarzyna M P40
Lechner, Kim A259
Lechner, David E. P92
Lechner, David P638
Leckman, Linda C. A462
Leckman, Linda C. P256
Leclair, Michael D P58
LeClaire, Brian P. A440
LeClaire, Greg A. E259
Lecorgne, R Paker P394
Lecoz, Abbie A179
Lecroy, Bryant A665
Lecroy, Jason E203
Lecroy, Bryant E334
Ledbetter, David H. A371
Ledbetter, Barry K. A760
Ledbetter, David H. P213
Ledbetter, Barry K. E374
Leddy, Kim A296
Leddy, Courtney A626
Leddy, Pete E308
Lederer, John A900
Lederer, Bertram M. P544
Lederman, Ira S. A126
Lederman, Mark P333
Lederman, Marvin P355
Ledesma, Monica A670
Ledford, Carolyn P337
Ledford-Crissey, Lisa A69
Ledgister, Mahon P325
Ledien, Randy P653
Ledoux, Marque A604
Leduc, Sylvain A321
Leduc, Robert F. A875
Ledyard, Robin P151
Lee, Jamie A19
Lee, Bonnie A36
Lee, Daniel A51
Lee, Lori M. A89
Lee, Jeremy A135
Lee, Henry A135

Lee, Ned A155
Lee, Gene A160
Lee, Diane A167
Lee, Trina Hoppin A171
Lee, Janet A191
Lee, Emmelene A201
Lee, Don A203
Lee, Ellen A226
Lee, Melinda A240
Lee, Eugene I. (Gene) A255
Lee, Shreve A262
Lee, Adam S A275
Lee, John M. A284
Lee, Jay A287
Lee, Bruce A312
Lee, Virginia A336
Lee, Helen A349
Lee, Thomas A364
Lee, Alice A376
Lee, E Chadwick A380
Lee, William A. A385
Lee, Bonita I. (Bonnie) A404
Lee, Nancy A404
Lee, Yusin A404
Lee, Mike A405
Lee, Bruce K. A413
Lee, Lisa A432
Lee, Eric A432
Lee, Sam A466
Lee, Charlotte A485
Lee, Amy A507
Lee, Hana A510
Lee, Al A512
Lee, Melanie A526
Lee, Lara L. A527
Lee, David A530
Lee, Peter A532
Lee, Nancy A538
Lee, Debra A538
Lee, Natasha A551
Lee, Esther A559
Lee, Rachel A559
Lee, Anne A571
Lee, Jeff A590
Lee, Sam A600
Lee, Thomas H. A641
Lee, Sean A647
Lee, Julien A651
Lee, Patrick A651
Lee, Jeff A687
Lee, Pearl A692
Lee, Chip A704
Lee, Shiuh A711
Lee, Scott A719
Lee, Jonathan A745
Lee, Jeffery (Jeff) A749
Lee, Schavrien A753
Lee, Crystal A755
Lee, Thai A757
Lee, Tom A774
Lee, Yongheon A799
Lee, Debra A812
Lee, William A827
Lee, Michael A862
Lee, Tracy A865
Lee, David A871
Lee, Sang A896
Lee, Julie P2
Lee, James G. P7
Lee, Stephen P64
Lee, Terry G. P97
Lee, David L. P107
Lee, Ted P114
Lee, Judy P115
Lee, Ronald P125
Lee, Ellen P150
Lee, Daniel P162
Lee, Chris P176
Lee, Eric P180
Lee, Yauk P182
Lee, Micheal P207
Lee, Ken P232
Lee, Do Hyun P248
Lee, G Scott P282
Lee, Hana P290

Lee, Mary P340
Lee, Angela Y P389
Lee, Thomas H. P407
Lee, Davis P419
Lee, Shiuh P444
Lee, Sandy P461
Lee, John P485
Lee, Thai P492
Lee, Felecia P549
Lee, William P580
Lee, Terry P586
Lee, David P586
Lee, David S. P591
Lee, Vivian S. P597
Lee, Gentry Patrick P610
Lee, Daniel P615
Lee, Robin P625
Lee, Joyce W61
Lee, Chang-Ken W89
Lee, Alan W89
Lee, Albert W123
Lee, Jae Kyung W141
Lee, Richard W203
Lee, Hyoung-Keun (Hank) W219
Lee, Yeong-Il W239
Lee, Young-Hoon W311
Lee, Woo-Kyu W311
Lee, Tae-Ju W311
Lee, Francis C. Y. W411
Lee, Gwang Goo W426
Lee, Ned E54
Lee, Bob E102
Lee, Jeff E110
Lee, John M. E119
Lee, Virginia E157
Lee, Bonita I. (Bonnie) E199
Lee, Nancy E199
Lee, Yusin E199
Lee, Bruce K. E205
Lee, Lisa E216
Lee, Eric E216
Lee, Yongsam E272
Lee, John T. C. E285
Lee, Yilin E290
Lee, Patrick E290
Lee, Julien E329
Lee, Patrick E330
Lee, Scott E354
Lee, Jeffery (Jeff) E367
Lee, Crystal E369
Lee, Lisa F E448
Lee, Sylvia E448
Lee-Vester, Kris P263
Leech, Kim A449
Leech, Wilson A605
Leech, Tony W358
Leech, Kim E221
Leedom, David W. A557
Leedom, David W. E281
Leedy, Lori P531
Leedy, Brian P644
Leef, Serge P326
Leeming, Rosemary P214
Leenen, Renee P170
Leer, Julie A761
Lees, Susan L. A35
Lees, Richard A P393
Leete, Elizabeth A801
Lefeber, Marilyn Stein A578
Lefebvre, Denise A654
Lefebvre, David P85
Lefebvre, Jocelyn W313
Lefevre, Gordon W27
Leff, Mike A90
Lefferson, C. Douglas (Doug) A340
Lefferson, C. Douglas (Doug) E160
Leffier, Bill A176
Leffler, Stephen P598
Lefko, Kim A9
Lefko, Kim P4
LeFort, Alan A460
Lefrancois, Remi A135
Legallo, Tim E183
Leganza, Nannette A371

Leganza, Nannette P213
Legault, Richard W80
Legault, Richard W193
Leger, Tamela A449
Leger, Tamela E221
Legere, John J A800
Legg, Matt A717
Legg, Russell P55
Legg, Matt E351
Legge, Jeffrey D. (Jeff) A206
Legge, Jeff A206
Leggett, Derrick A45
Leggett, Maria A95
Leggett, Robert A391
Leggett, Pat A467
Leggett, Karen W270
Leggio, John A613
Legin, Joel A100
Legler, Robert C. E296
Lego, Catherine A505
Legorburo, José Ignacio W183
Legoretta, Alfredo P308
Legrand, Thomas A58
Legrand, Joseph A804
Legrand, Jeff P204
Legris, Monique A444
Legro, Jeffrey P442
Legters, Robert A327
Lehman, Daniel A168
Lehman, Jeffrey S. A592
Lehman, Jay A837
Lehman, Jeffrey S. P370
Lehman, Donald P569
Lehman, Jim E18
Lehmann, Mary A65
Lehmann, Jonathan A790
Lehmann, Leslie P558
Lehmann, Michal Piotr W54
Lehmus, Matti W275
Lehmuth, Rich P417
Lehn, Chuck A117
Lehn, Chuck P61
Lehne, Kathy P532
Lehne, Kyle P532
Lehner, Jon A784
Lehner, Ulrich W143
Lehner, Ulrich W391
Lehotsky, Ed A188
Lehoux, Becky P163
Lehrer, Ronald A589
Lehrer, Deborah P351
Leib, Mallory A391
Leibel, Stephen A195
Leiber, Phil P299
Leibman, Maya A47
Leibow, Steve A692
Leibrock, Edeltraud W225
Leibson, Marie A772
Leibson, Marie E381
Leiderman, Roni P390
Leidesdorf, William A451
Leidinger, Michael A423
Leidwinger, Kevin A210
Leifheit, Kurt P113
Leigh, Howard A538
Leigh, Stacey A727
Leigh, Stacey P453
Leighton, Russell A458
Leighty, Scott P329
Leijssenaar, Jacques A865
Leikhim, William P322
Lein, Maureen A276
Leinenbach, Keith A. A383
Leinenbach, Keith A. E186
Leinroth, Peter A468
Leinweber, Max E325
Leipzig, Inna A835
Leisen, Tammy A786
Leisen, John A804
Leisen, Tammy E387
Leish, Becca A626
Leisle, Dan A325
Leissring, Kevin A444
Leist, Drew P59
Leitch, Kari A41

Leitch, Glenn R. A434
Leitch, Andrew M. E47
Leite, Adriana A218
Leith, Andrew P300
Leithauser, Jeffrey A329
Leiting, Jim P82
Leitman, Steven A686
Leitner, Lars P202
Leitner, Manfred W295
Leitzell, Jeff P301
Leiva, Michele P185
Lejeune, Judi A449
Lejeune, Judi E220
Lekas, Steve E429
Lekberg, Roger A934
Leketa, Anthony F. (Tony) P582
Lekhraj, Sharda A135
Lekkala, Maneesh P114
Leland, Todd A390
Leland, Tim A695
Leland, Brian E399
Lelonek, Susan A444
Lemaitre, Philippe J. E208
LeMaitre, George W. E253
Lemann, Jorge A497
Lemay, Lori P503
Lemay, Brian E237
Lemberger, Michael A895
Lembo, Philip J. (Phil) A303
Lembo, Phillip A303
Lemchak, Joseph J. A227
Lemchak, Joseph J. E90
Lemelin, Tracey A520
Lemierre, Jean W71
Leming, Rudy P166
Lemire, Debbie A57
Lemire, Anne A58
Lemire, John A520
Lemire, Debbie P33
Lemkau, Gregg R. A390
Lemke, Jude A240
Lemke, James P. (Jim) A728
Lemke, RL S. E408
Lemly, Chris A156
Lemmer, Jeff A360
Lemmer, Teresa P445
Lemmon, David J. A765
Lemoine, Kevin A167
Lemoine, Frederick P405
Lemois, Xilma P638
Lemon, Paulette A429
Lemon, Robert P652
Lemon, Paulette E214
Lemonius, John A54
Lemons, Cynthia A179
Lemons, Brian A936
Lemperle, John P18
Lempka, Joseph R P279
Lemppenau, Joachim W417
Lemyze, Christine A465
Lenahan, Kevin P12
Lenahan, Anna W114
Lenckos, John A108
Lencquesaing, Aymar de W234
Lencsak, Christian A596
Lenertz, Renae P606
Lengel, John A312
Lenhardt, David A173
Lenhart, Tom A532
Lenhart, Chris A885
Lenhoff, Timothy K. A268
Lennen, Anthony P151
Lenner, Marc E425
Lennie, William G. (Bill) A428
Lennon, Kevin P358
Lennon, Gary W270
Lenok, Amanda A137
Lenson, Celia P308
Lentell, Troy P554
Lenti-Ponsetto, Jean P175
Lentini, Matt P68
Lentz, Mike E. A436
Lentz, Rick A604
Lentz, Bobby A608
Lentz, Darrell P49

Lenz, Rob A65
Lenz, Matt A361
Lenzen, John A805
Lenzen, John P542
Leo, Sheri A368
Leo, Bruno V. Di A465
Leo, Koguan A757
Leo, Christina P272
Leo, Koguan P492
Leon, Sonny A87
Leon, Mercedes M A590
Leon, Rebecca A713
Leon, Lori De A793
Leon, Regan A885
Leon, Sonny P50
Leon, Andres De P378
Leon, Monica Ponce de P591
Leon, Fredy De P646
Leon, Jorge A. W30
Leon, J.P. E385
Leonard, David E. (Dave) A32
Leonard, Jack A115
Leonard, Joesph A320
Leonard, Tim A323
Leonard, James C. A329
Leonard, Dennis A374
Leonard, Margaret A591
Leonard, William A654
Leonard, Robert M. A851
Leonard, Gayle A879
Leonard, Mark P74
Leonard, James C. P113
Leonard, Pat P364
Leonard, Margaret P369
Leonard, Jim P431
Leonard, Jim P462
Leonard, Judith E. P497
Leonard, Roger P662
Leonard, Edward F P667
Leonard, Jack E38
Leonard, Michael E144
Leonard, Thomas E243
Leonardi, Mark A651
Leonardi, Phil P382
Leonardi, Mark E329
Leonardis, Jim A126
Leonardo, Michael A492
Leondakis, Mia A897
Leone, Bob A461
Leone, Roger E. A793
Leone, Joe A930
Leone, Bob P255
Leone, Timothy P420
Leone, Peter E25
Leonetti, Debbie E233
Leonetti, Deborah E234
Leong, Jamie A318
Leong, Chris W344
Leong, Amy E177
Leonhardt, Darrell T. P45
Leonhart, Patrick A34
Leonti, Joseph R. A640
Leopold, Diane G. A275
Leopold, David A364
Leopold, Jay P185
Leopold, Lance E226
Lepage, Vivienne A537
Lepage, Mark A P310
Lepak, Kathleen A651
Lepak, Kathleen E329
LePenske, Amy A530
Lepeu, Richard W115
Lepiane, Gary A912
Lepley, John P329
Lepore, Jonathan A799
Leprince, Igor W284
LeProhon, Scott A380
Lequient, Frederic E427
Lequin, Stan A458
Lerner, Arnold S. A297
Lerner, Richard A390
Lerner, Mark A879
Lerner, J Scott P155
Lerner, Scott E. E33
Lerner, Arnold S. E129

Lerner, Steven E226
Lerose, Frank A324
Leroux, Bertrand A10
Leroux, Monique A738
Leroy, Didier W400
Lertratanakul, Apinya A7
Lesar, David J. (Dave) A401
Lescoeur, Bruno W148
Lescure, John A651
Lescure, John E329
Leshan, Tim P383
Leshe, Lynn A112
Lesiak, Peg A409
Lesieur, David A845
Lesjak, Catherine A. (Cathie) A438
Lesko, Dirk A373
Leskoski, Darren P31
Leskowitz, Mark A51
Leslie, Claudia A112
Leslie, Naomi A391
Leslie, Andy A852
Leslie, Sam A891
Leslie, Paul P171
Leslie, Andy P361
Leslie, James P582
Lesner, Scott A797
Lesneski, Gary J. P563
Lesperance, Thomas F P25
Lesser, Brian A89
Lesser, Todd A740
Lesser, Michael E371
Lessler, Becky P383
Lessner, Philip M. (Phil) E244
Lestang, Martin W154
Lester, William P103
Lester, Mark C. P551
Lestourgeon, Paul A195
LeSueur, Andrew E207
Lesukoski, Paul E42
Lete, Laura A512
Letendre, John A706
Letendre, Donald E. P594
LeTexier, Matthew A380
Letier, Scott P354
Letinsky, Daniel P433
Leto, Francis J. A155
Leto, Lara P240
Leto, Francis J. E54
Letov, Slava A462
Letson, Alicia P237
Lett, Rosalind K P194
Lett, Stan P242
Lettero, Tom P108
Lettieri, Jerry E290
Lettman, Dennis S. P596
Letts, Shannon A902
Leuhmann, John A444
Leukert, Bernd W340
Leung, Sandra A151
Leung, Juo A182
Leung, David A470
Leung, Samuel A676
Leung, Pak (Steven) A936
Leung, C.C. W317
Leung, Samuel E338
Leupold, Mary P230
Lev, Leonid E238
Lev, Lavi A. E415
Levander, Carl W. A600
Levar, Mary E A727
Levar, Mary E P453
Levasseur, Dennis B A155
Levasseur, Rita P243
Levasseur, INA P312
Levasseur, Dennis B E54
Levatich, Matthew S. (Matt) A407
Levchets, Regina A621
Levchets, Regina E312
Leveille, Mark A222
Levenick, Stuart A296
Levenick, Stuart A394
Levenson, Susan A538
Levenson, Michelle A741
Levenson, Rodger A929
Levenson, David W80

COMBINED HOOVER'S HANDBOOK INDEX OF EXECUTIVES

A = AMERICAN BUSINESS
E = EMERGING COMPANIES
P = PRIVATE COMPANIES
W = WORLD BUSINESS

Levenson, Michelle E364
Levenson, Rodger E449
Leventhal, Dana A575
Leverett, Allen L. A907
Levesque, Carla P598
Levesque, Paul E448
Levey, Caryn A85
Levey, Caryn E27
Levi, David F. P187
Levi, Donna P610
Levielle, Eric A380
Levin, David A25
Levin, Bob A559
Levin, Alan G A658
Levin, David P14
Levin, Jesse P117
Levin, Rosalyn P304
Levin, Roy P361
Levin, Barry F P494
Levin, Justine P556
Levin, Kerry P664
Levin, Uri W203
Levin, Donna E65
Levine, Jonathan M. A126
Levine, Eric A204
Levine, Jeff A390
Levine, Britt A452
Levine, Jeremy A522
Levine, Robert A592
Levine, Jay N. A629
Levine, Alec A704
Levine, Todd A741
Levine, Layne L. A924
Levine, Jordan P32
Levine, Mel P299
Levine, Stephen P300
Levine, Robert P370
Levine, Peter H P616
Levine, Helen D P638
Levine, Todd E364
Levings, Stuart A381
Levingston, Charles D. A283
Levingston, Charles D. E117
Levinson, Arthur D. (Art) A72
Levinson, Sara A407
Levinson, Andrew A463
Levinson, Linda A827
Levinson, Linda P571
Levit, Polina P191
Levitt, Evan A412
Levitt, Brian M. W396
Levy, Gwen A6
Levy, Susan Nestor A84
Levy, Paul S. A156
Levy, Jeffrey A227
Levy, Dan A310
Levy, Stephen A319
Levy, Lance A327
Levy, Roger A381
Levy, Anthony A405
Levy, Jay A410
Levy, Rich A522
Levy, Jeffrey M. A584
Levy, Susan C. A605
Levy, Stuart A721
Levy, Craig A786
Levy, Andrew C. A864
Levy, Adam A893
Levy, Geoff A924
Levy, Robert A933
Levy, Susan Nestor P47
Levy, Ofer P125
Levy, Michael P160
Levy, Ann P361
Levy, Lester A P361
Levy, Judd S P369
Levy, Sharon P558
Levy, Ofer W49
Levy, Avi W203

Levy, Avraham W203
Levy, Grant E7
Levy, Jeffrey E91
Levy, Richard S. E226
Levy, Tao E272
Levy, Craig E387
Levy, Jordan E396
Levzow, Erin E268
Lew, George E132
Lewan, Len A850
Lewandowski, Christopher A414
Lewandowski, Rick A561
Lewandowski, Joel P149
Lewandowski, Christopher P236
Lewandowski, Jay P597
Lewbel, Gary A151
Lewey, Robert W. E224
Lewia, David A476
Lewin, Cindy P2
Lewis, Cindi H. A62
Lewis, Jeff A89
Lewis, Scott A105
Lewis, Kimberly A107
Lewis, D A179
Lewis, Liz A224
Lewis, Chris A258
Lewis, Michael A. A281
Lewis, Jay A296
Lewis, Holden A315
Lewis, Margaret G. A320
Lewis, Valerie A326
Lewis, John D. A353
Lewis, Kenneth A. A363
Lewis, Linda A365
Lewis, Nicolle A391
Lewis, Michael A405
Lewis, Daniel A408
Lewis, Scott A409
Lewis, Daniel J A409
Lewis, Barry A417
Lewis, Greg A431
Lewis, Tamara A462
Lewis, Patricia A466
Lewis, Jenae A467
Lewis, Derek A509
Lewis, John A530
Lewis, Lemuel A536
Lewis, Cecilia A538
Lewis, Melanie A550
Lewis, Maria A575
Lewis, William (Will) A596
Lewis, Andrew A606
Lewis, Haston A654
Lewis, Tyler A654
Lewis, Rudy A706
Lewis, Karla R. A716
Lewis, Carlos A752
Lewis, Stacey A761
Lewis, Allan A784
Lewis, Amy A797
Lewis, Greg A818
Lewis, Celine A835
Lewis, Mark A852
Lewis, Joshua A861
Lewis, Kim A877
Lewis, George A893
Lewis, Randall A893
Lewis, Michael A902
Lewis, Lisa A922
Lewis, Rob A925
Lewis, Clinton A. (Clint) A941
Lewis, Michael P2
Lewis, Sherry P25
Lewis, Flint P32
Lewis, Derrick P34
Lewis, James R. (Jim) P85
Lewis, Lisa P164
Lewis, Eric P196
Lewis, David P198
Lewis, Curtis P219
Lewis, Jonathan P233
Lewis, Jake P250
Lewis, Tamara P256
Lewis, Melanie P319
Lewis, Tony P361

Lewis, John P363
Lewis, Dr Kirk P408
Lewis, Ky P489
Lewis, Kelli P518
Lewis, Seth P556
Lewis, Hilton P572
Lewis, Daniel K. P576
Lewis, Erin P594
Lewis, Robert P608
Lewis, Kim P646
Lewis, Joseph P667
Lewis, Lisa P671
Lewis, Stuart W135
Lewis, Michael W143
Lewis, Jonathan W286
Lewis, Stevan W371
Lewis, Cindi H. E19
Lewis, Scott E34
Lewis, Suzi E73
Lewis, Marva E100
Lewis, Cheryl E106
Lewis, James F. E124
Lewis, John D. E173
Lewis, Tom E184
Lewis, Adam A E267
Lewis, Josh E296
Lewis, Clunet E392
Lewis, Greg E403
Lewis, Jeff E429
Lewis, Rob E445
Lewis-Hall, Freda C. A657
Lewnard, John J E78
Lewnes, Ann A11
Lewton, Zachary R P472
Lexis, Pete A930
Ley, A. Lily A636
Leyden, Bob A409
Leyder, Dennis E. E150
Leyendecker, R. Greg A413
Leyendecker, R. Greg E205
Leygraaf, Greg A837
Leyoub, Caprice P621
Leysen, Thomas W405
Leyvi, Michael A540
Leyvi, Michele A540
Lezon, Stanley A686
Lherault, George E156
Lhota, Joseph J. A560
Lhota, Joseph J. P336
Li, Susan A29
Li, Daniel A109
Li, Ying A135
Li, Danshi A151
Li, Xuemei A151
Li, Haiyan A222
Li, Zhenqin A574
Li, Ricken A676
Li, William A701
Li, Ruohao A711
LI, Jie P49
LI, WEI P49
Li, Ruohao P444
Li, Mehra P489
LI, Heng P556
Li, Hengguang P660
Li, David K. P. W50
Li, Samson K. C. W50
Li, Adrian David M. K. W50
Li, Brian David M. B. W50
Li, Arthur K. C. W50
Li, Morris W123
Li, Victor T. K. W190
Li, Baomin W211
Li, Weijian W392
Li, David H. E56
Li, Ricken E338
Li-owens, Chris A859
Lian, Eric V. F. W411
Liang, Liwen A53
Liang, Justin A101
Liang, Kai A200
Liang, George C. A521
Liang, Feng W97
Liang, Weikang W98
Liang, Luo W100

Liang, Justin E32
Lianming, Bo W385
Liano, Martha A479
Liao, Samuel A254
Liao, James A452
Liao, Daniel A505
Liao, Frances A711
Liao, Frances P444
Liao, Edward P502
Liarikos, Angelo P366
Liaw, Betty A284
Liaw, Jeffrey E96
Liaw, Betty E120
Liban, Lisa A352
Libbra, Todd A902
Libby, Russell T. A797
Liberatore, Nick A640
Liberatore, Thomas S. E289
Libersat, Sherri A909
Libersat, Sherri E436
Libertino, John P284
Libler, Gary A746
Libretto, Tom E326
Libstag, Gwen R. A390
Licalzi, Maria P357
Licata, Joseph A742
Licata, Vince E77
Lich, Brad A. A285
Licho, Gary A797
Licht, Valdirene Bastos A457
Lichtendahl, Kenneth A196
Lichtenstein, Jodee A283
Lichtenstein, Jodee E117
Lichtenwalner, Thomas P P466
Lichtenwalner, Rthomas P P513
Lichtman, David B. A349
Lichty, Sheila A854
Liddell, Katrina A935
Liddelow, Kane A526
Liddy, Casey P395
Liding, Lawrence (Larry) A892
Liding, Larry A893
Liebel, Hartmut A475
Lieber, Chris E319
Lieberman, Jonathan A20
Lieberman, Jessica A54
Lieberman, David A61
Liebert, Rebecca A673
Liebhardt, Tom A756
Liebler, Patrick A75
Liebler, William Bill A465
Liebowitz, Jeremy A593
Liebowitz, Richard S. A827
Liebowitz, Jacalyn A879
Liebowitz, Richard S. P580
Liebowitz, Leo E187
Liebross, Adam A104
Liedberg, Douglas H A253
Liede, Kathryn P314
Liedel, Christopher P497
Liedl, Duane A135
Liedtke, Eric W9
Liefer, Michael E433
Liekar, John P119
Lieke, Yang W96
Lienhart, Ross A675
Lienhart, Ross P428
Liepold, Stephen A746
Liesegang, Skip P250
Lieshout, Marc Van A467
Liesman, Jerry E106
Lievonen, Matti W275
Liewen, Mike A654
Lifka, David P159
Lifton, Ilyse A571
Liggett, Nadine A444
Liggett, Emily E415
Light, Darla P206
Light, Amber P469
Lightfoot, Emily D A63
Lightfoot, Will A176
Lightfoot, Jeremy A312
Lightfoot, Bill A879
Lightfoot, Kevin A933
Lightfoot, Jeremy P199

Lightfoot, Lance P548
Lightfoot, David E144
Lightfritz, Daniel A749
Lightfritz, Daniel E367
Lighthart, Mike A575
Lightner, Margaret P75
Lighty, Josh A125
Ligon, David A664
Ligon, David E334
Liguori, Thomas (Tom) A99
Liguori, Kathryn P66
Lihua, Wang W301
Liimatainen, Sherman P221
Lijun, Zhao W99
Likes, Bill A284
Likes, Robert A491
Likes, Bill E120
Likins, Steven A831
Likins, Steve A831
Likins, Steven P601
Likins, Steve P601
Lilek, Ronald P75
Liles, Don P311
Liles, Scott P477
Lilja, Mathias A544
Lilja, Agneta W377
Lill, Thorsten A505
Lillemoe, Keith D. P574
Lilles, Paul P647
Lilley, Brandon A746
Lilli, Maria E290
Lillian, Robles P230
Lilliquist, John A452
Lillis, Terrance A677
Lillis, Charles M. (Chuck) P636
Lilly, Brian A203
Lilly, Rob A319
Lilly, E. Stephen (Steve) A338
Lilly, Brian F. A581
Lilly, Randy A621
Lilly, Tim A933
Lilly, Brian F. E294
Lilly, Jason E302
Lilly, Randy E311
Lim, James A123
Lim, Elsie A170
Lim, John A205
Lim, Douglas A384
Lim, Jean A404
Lim, Rachel A432
Lim, Dennis A626
Lim, Aerin A793
Lim, Douglas P217
Lim, Jolene P402
Lim, Rina P404
Lim, Sim S W130
Lim, Jean E199
Lim, Rachel E216
Lim-Johnson, Hannah S A488
Lima, Alexandre A173
Lima, Renato A203
Lima, Candido A640
Limbaugh, N Joe A379
Limberg, Joachim W391
Limehouse, Capers P112
Limerick, Thomas A62
Limerick, Thomas S. (Stan) A340
Limerick, Thomas E20
Limerick, Thomas S. (Stan) E161
Limjoco, Adrianne A727
Limjoco, Adrianne P453
Lin, Stan A16
Lin, Alexander A19
Lin, Isaac A266
Lin, Li-chung A461
Lin, Benny A701
Lin, Isaac P182
Lin, Wilson W. P374
Lin, Maria P388
Lin, Tian P395
Lin, Senshang P517
Lin, Kathryn P610
Lin, Bruce P659
Lin, Fan W103
Lin, Amy H.C. W123

Lin, J.K. W380
Lin, Henry W425
Lin, Simon H. M. W425
Lin, Wei E300
Linares, Tony A69
Lincoln, Blanche L A296
Lincoln, Charles A833
Lincoln, Butch P43
Lincoln, David R P163
Lincoln, Bonni P264
Lincoln, Dood P356
Lincoln, David E267
Lind, Sharon A117
Lind, Roger A246
Lind, Sharon P61
Lind, Amy P625
Lind, Roger E105
Linda, Doherty A641
Linda, Rasero A882
Linda, Doherty P407
Lindahl, Richard S P117
Lindahl, Lennart P501
Lindauer, Jeff P610
Lindberg, Bonita A838
Lindberg, Chuck P200
Lindblad, Anders W386
Lindblom, Mike P531
Lindbloom, Chad M. A728
Linde, Tamara L. A687
Linde, Ronald K. P107
Lindeen, Denise A877
Lindekugel, Jon T. A3
Lindell, Erik A885
Lindell, James P356
Lindeman, B. John E58
Lindemann, Deven P333
Linden, Andrew A831
Linden, Andrew P601
Linden, Sarah E366
Linder, Kellye A347
Linder, Brian A635
Linder, James P92
Linder, Charlie P282
Linder, Bob E136
Linderman, LeeAnne B. A940
Linders, Ryan A921
Linders, Ryan P669
Lindfors, Lars P. W275
Lindgren, Chris A862
Lindh, Hans G A75
Lindholm, Wayne S. P238
Lindley, Don A494
Lindley, Melissa P138
Lindley, Randy P387
Lindley, Michael E268
Lindner, S. Craig A55
Lindner, Carl H. A55
Lindsay, Steven A505
Lindsay, Karen A544
Lindsay, Kristin A797
Lindsay, Mike P25
Lindsay, Jeff P253
Lindsay, Jeff P390
Lindsay, Candy E14
Lindseth, Michael G A664
Lindseth, Alfred A. (Al) A668
Lindseth, Michael G E334
Lindsey, Scot A169
Lindsey, Scott A665
Lindsey, Mark P35
Lindsey, H. Eugene (Gene) P54
Lindsey, Steven L P510
Lindsey, Don P541
Lindsey, Scott E334
Lindstrom, David A567
Lindstrom, Merl R. A662
Lindstrom, Donnie P261
Lindstrom, David E284
Line, Ann P49
Line, Thomas E. (Tom) E112
Linebarger, N Thomas A247
Lineberger, Terry A727
Lineberger, Terry P453
Linehan, Peter A390
Liner, David A730

Liner, Sallye A. P390
Ling, Christopher A144
Ling, Sam A170
Ling, Mei A198
Ling, Walt A465
Ling, Hai A544
Ling, Karen W23
Lingenfelter, Terry A337
Lingenfelter, Terry E158
Lingerfeldt, Lezli P251
Lingerfelt, Lisa P185
Lingg, Danielle P162
Link, Ron A251
Link, Doug A436
Link, Jeff A491
Link, Molly A654
Link, Scott A701
Link, Charles A723
Link, Janet M A778
Link, Denise W P141
Link, Dave P471
Link, Matthew W. (Matt) E308
Linkenhoker, Gina A320
Links, Mark A201
Linn, Aaron E134
Linnartz, Stephanie C. A537
Linnemann, Andrew A779
Linnen, Edward P. (Ned) A98
Linnenbringer, Jean A212
Linnenbrink, John A203
Linney, Brian P312
Linnington, Max E99
Linscott, Craig E305
Linsky, Wendy A809
Linss, Roxanne P212
Lintag, Ronald A137
Linton, Jason A530
Linton, Brandon A538
Linville, Jud A203
Linzer, Daniel I. P388
Linzey, Bob A559
Lioi, Vittorio Corbo W45
Lioi, Vittorio Corbo W46
Liollio, Dean A668
Lionello, Gemma A602
Lionnet, Stephane A218
Lionnet, Stephane A218
Liotine, Joseph T. A919
Liotta, Gary P. A356
Lipani, Laura P333
Lipar, Eric E255
Lipar, Jack E255
Lipasek, Steven A835
Lipert, John P176
Lipinski, John J. (Jack) A250
Lipira, Lisa A530
Lipka, Lauri A21
Lipke, Kenneth A114
Lipke, Kenneth E37
Lipker, Stephen A36
Lipkin, Gerald H. A888
Lipkin, Gerald H. E425
Lipman, Raymond E438
Lipner, Zachary P66
Lipomi, Jack P109
Lipovaca, Zlatan E431
Lippa, Stacy A804
Lippard, Nicole P91
Lippert, Martin J. (Marty) A559
Lippert, Jason D. E252
Lippi, Chris A478
Lippincott, Constance P653
Lippincott, Rodney A. E210
Lippman, Frederick P389
Lippmann, Patrick A A105
Lippmann, Patrick A E34
Lippoldt, Timothy A835
Lippoldt, Diana P662
Lipps, Randall A. E315
Lipschultz, Tyler P. E308
Lipscomb, Jean P206
Lipsey, William L. E340
Lipsitz, Stuart P556
Lipski, Mike A446
Lipsky, Matt P555

Lipson, Michael A364
Lipson, Steven E309
Lipstein, Steven A46
Liptak, John A845
Lipworth, Celeste A734
Lis, Angela A779
Lisa, Cost P588
Lisboa, Persio V A583
Liscidini, Fabio P496
Liscinsky, Erik E123
Lisek, Jon E123
Lisenby, Jeffrey P. A678
Lish, Ethan P202
Lisi, Louise A111
Lisi, Ben A702
Lisi, Douglas E80
Lisio, Frank Di A167
Liska, Matt A156
Liskay, Alice P576
Lisle, William W14
Lison, Karen P531
Lisowski, Sheryl A. A315
Lisowski, Jason A351
Lissalde, Frédéric B. A146
Lissowski, Antoine W111
List-stoll, Teri A254
List-Stoll, Teri L. A826
Listenbee, Rashaan P539
Listengart, Joseph P360
Lister, Noel P446
Lister, Anna E282
Liszt, Mark P286
Liszt, Max P286
Litavec, Viliam P206
Litchfield, David A281
Litchfield, R A354
Litchford, Susan P70
Litchy, William P318
Litteken, Luke A932
Littell, Morgan A859
Littell, John A930
Litterer, Bob A133
Little, Frank R. A3
Little, Mark A67
Little, Richard A147
Little, Keith A188
Little, Marinda A222
Little, Patricia A. A416
Little, R Parrish A430
Little, Charles A473
Little, T. Mitchell (Mitch) A533
Little, Mitch A533
Little, Daniel F. (Dan) A602
Little, Daniel A711
Little, Glenn A713
Little, Sean A925
Little, Steve P11
Little, George A P230
Little, George P230
Little, George A. P231
Little, Daniel P444
Little, Tom W65
Little, Mark W373
Little, Charles E236
Little, Rob E256
Little, April E347
Little, Sean E445
Little-tranter, Lisa A518
Littlefair, Andrew A421
Littlefield, Mark D A313
Littlefield, Jerod A323
Littlefield, Mark D P200
Littlefield, Nate E138
Littleford, Frankie A478
Littlejohn, Bill P489
Littman, Owen E101
Litton, Wayne P106
Littrell, Wesley A228
Littrell, J. Scott E92
Litwin, Barry A884
Litwin, Jim P250
Litzelman, Michele E81
Litzinger, Ronald L. A290
Liu, Chang A104
Liu, Stanley A167

COMBINED HOOVER'S HANDBOOK INDEX OF EXECUTIVES

A = AMERICAN BUSINESS
E = EMERGING COMPANIES
P = PRIVATE COMPANIES
W = WORLD BUSINESS

Liu, Manni A284
Liu, Kelly A323
Liu, Herng A460
Liu, Chang A571
Liu, Jeffrey A657
Liu, Don H. A804
Liu, Anthony P129
Liu, Catherine P368
Liu, Guangliang P501
Liu, Manuel M P649
Liu, Yuzhi W98
Liu, I. Cheng W123
Liu, Fei W164
Liu, Guoyue W190
Liu, Mark W380
Liu, Chun W431
Liu, Joseph E113
Liu, Manni E120
Liutkus, Tom A843
Liuwen, Tian W97
Lively, Kelly A540
Lively, Scott A887
Lively, David P389
Liverani, Giovanni W35
Livermore, Karen A337
Livermore, Karen E158
Livesay, Bruce A. A343
Livesay, Jackie J P160
Livesay, Bruce A. E163
Livingood, Jack P83
Livingston, John T. A16
Livingston, Wendy A140
Livingston, Robert A. (Bob) A277
Livingston, Tanner A449
Livingston, Randall S. (Randy) A510
Livingston, Wyvetter A690
Livingston, Kathleen A692
Livingston, Sandra A882
Livingston, Larry P35
Livingston, Randall S. (Randy) P290
Livingston, Lee P371
Livingston, Kim P558
Livingston, Keith P602
Livingston, Tanner E221
Livingston, Robert E226
Livingstone, Jennifer A210
Livingstone, Catherine B. W114
Livne, Omer A460
Liyanage, Harsha E431
Lizar, Jeffrey A638
Lizar, Jeffrey E320
Lizardi, Rafael R. A820
Lizardi, Lizette A890
Lize, Franck W164
Lizhong, Yu A592
Lizhong, Yu P370
Ljungqvist, Katarina W377
LLandreth, David A250
Llanes, Raul A115
Llanes, Raul E38
LLC, Wyoming Acquisition GP A708
LLC, Wyoming Acquisition GP P441
LLC, SES Holdings P482
Lleras, Mateo A544
Llinas, Javier A218
Llope, Richard A450
Lloyd, Gary A14
Lloyd, Scott A257
Lloyd, Robert A. (Rob) A371
Lloyd, Steve A386
Lloyd, Jack A413
Lloyd, Tim P102
Lloyd, Kathy P160
Lloyd, John R P251
Lloyd, Lisa Kay P551
Lloyd, James P627
Lloyd, Daniel E133
Lloyd, Steve E188
Lloyd, Jack E205

Lo, Alice A484
Lo, Winny A676
Lo, Hermand A924
Lo, Elaine A930
Lo, Chih-Hsien W406
Lo, James E194
Lo, Winny E338
Loach, Jon E143
Lobach, David M E125
Lobaugh, Mike P227
Lobel, Elie W297
Lobo, Carolina A64
Lobo, Kevin A. A789
Lochan, Donie A528
Lochen, Richard S. A653
Locher, Duane A224
Locher, Jim A610
Locher, Vince A848
Locher, Vince E411
Lochner, David A444
Lochner, Karl Manfred W231
Lochocki, Sharon A492
Locke, Pat A54
Locke, Betsy A531
Locke, Justin P164
Locke, Jay E P277
Locker, David A458
Locker, Brad A522
Lockery, Michael A167
Lockett, Traishon E127
Lockhart, Gerald A62
Lockhart, Dennis P. A322
Lockhart, Laura S A488
Lockhart, Ann A619
Lockhart, Marvin P189
Lockhart, Ann P393
Lockhart, Clayton P442
Lockhart, John P506
Lockhart, Amy P588
Lockhart, Gerald E20
Lockington, Eric A846
Locklear, Samuel A355
Lockley, Jason P409
Lockridge, Greg P559
Lockwood, Charles J. P203
Lockwood, Amanda P306
Loconsolo, Mike A200
Loder, Greg A686
Lodes, Terry A915
Lodesani, Eliano Omar W202
Lodge, Terry L. A25
Lodge, Terry L. P14
Lodge, Simon W377
Lodhi, Mujib P658
Lodzinski, Frank A. E119
Loeb, Marshall A. E121
Loeber, Gary A251
Loeber, Jurguen W144
Loebsack, Grita W218
Loeffler, Martin H. A66
Loeffler, William P272
Loeffler, Jay S. P574
Loehr, Steve P284
Loera, Patricia A880
Loera, Patricia P640
Loewald, Thomas W. (Tom) A832
Loewen, Randy A457
Loewen, Bernd W225
Loewenbaum, G. Walter E261
Loffler, Alicia P389
Loffredo, Joseph P456
Loffredo, Joe P456
Lofgren, Diane Gage P489
Lofgren, Richard P. P615
Lofgren, Bruce E73
Lofrumento, Michael A851
Lofties, Paul E250
Loftin, Paul J. A716
Loftis, William A196
Lofton, Kevin E. A226
Lofton, Kevin E P117
Lofton, Kevin E. P150
Lofton, Margaret P381
Loftspring, Peter P85
Loftspring, Peter D P86

Loftus, Mike A371
Loftus, Gary A533
Loftus, Phillip A776
Loftus, Phillip P512
Loftus, Thomas R. (Tom) E432
Lofurno, Alan P87
Logan, Jonathan B. A213
Logan, Jason A222
Logan, Erik A270
Logan, Patrick A315
Logan, Stephanie A336
Logan, Donna A357
Logan, Stephen A409
Logan, Stephen A460
Logan, John A840
Logan, Jonathan B. P143
Logan, Dwayne P336
Logan, Cheryl P396
Logan, Roger P417
Logan, Candace C P523
Logan, Stephanie E157
Logan, Donna E176
Logan, Don E229
Logan, Malcolm E412
Logatto, Vincent P527
Logeman, Scott A452
Logeman, David P120
Loges, Michael P148
Logiudice, Salvatore A827
Logiudice, Salvatore P580
Logothetis, Peter A36
Logoyda, Steve A540
Logsdon, John A312
Logsdon, David A905
Logsdon, John P199
Logue, Joseph (Joe) A144
Logue, Amanda P284
Logue, David P415
Loh, Evan A658
Loh, Gordon A658
Loh, Wallace P631
Loh, Wallace D. P642
Lohan, Jim A816
Lohawatanakul, Chingchai W95
Lohkamp, Irene P84
Lohman, Andrew A452
Lohmar, Rachel A140
Lohmeier, Michelle J A774
Lohmeyer, Mark A897
Lohrer, Joe A137
Lohrer, Bernadette P476
Loiacono, Jim A744
Loiacono, Joseph P218
Lokay, Jon P739
Lokke, Scott A160
Lokken, Holly P202
Loliger, Hans A245
Lollar, Chris A713
Lollar, Donald P399
Lollini, Claudio E244
Lomas, Terry A108
Lomas, Todd A569
Lomax, Manning A380
Lombard, Eric W35
Lombardi, Todd A264
Lombardi, Len A337
Lombardi, Bill A409
Lombardi, Michael J. A843
Lombardi, Len E158
Lombardo, Kevin A501
Lombardo, Chad A797
Lombardo, Anthony P186
Lombardo, Patrick P528
Lomboy, Sheila A347
Lomeli, Bernardo A830
Lomeli, Bernardo P593
Lomel-n, Carlos Salazar W164
Lomeo, Jody L P197
Loncar, Patrick A321
London, Qiana A711
London, Adam A893
London, Qiana P444
London, Kim P563
London, Daniel T. (Dan) W5
Lonergan, Robert A. A88

Lones, Darling P536
Loney, Andrew A29
Loney, Andrew P16
Long, Ann A5
Long, Michael J. (Mike) A81
Long, Suzanne A135
Long, Suzette M A173
Long, Tony A175
Long, Rodney A179
Long, Jon A222
Long, Jeffrey R. A242
Long, Brett V A248
Long, Thomas E. (Tom) A294
Long, William A530
Long, Ray A610
Long, James A682
Long, Deborah J. A683
Long, Michael A685
Long, Ted A704
Long, Ellie A713
Long, Mike A718
Long, Ross A724
Long, Andy A833
Long, Paul A877
Long, Mike A887
Long, Susan A902
Long, Mark P. A914
Long, Tao P49
Long, William P94
Long, Helene P146
Long, Laura P235
Long, Theresa P429
Long, Ross P452
Long, Terry P477
Long, Denise P489
Long, Ronald R. (Ron) P550
Long, Nathan P560
Long, Greg P602
Long, John W. P638
Long, Courtney P648
Long, Annabelle Yu W66
Long, Peter W402
Long, Brad E99
Long, Brett V E107
Long, Robert E143
Long, Mike E354
Longe, Thomas A426
Longe, Thomas E213
Longenderfer, Roger P420
Longfield, Charles L. (Chuck) E47
Longhi, William G P397
Longhofer, T. Luke A340
Longhofer, T. Luke E161
Longhurst, Sherri A462
Longhurst, Sherri P256
Longmier, Mark A259
Longmore, Mike A482
Longo, Chris A686
Longo, Jeffrey A844
Longo, Christie A922
Longo, Kevin P6
Longo, Christie P671
Longo, Michael E427
Longobardi, Sara M. A651
Longobardi, Sara M. E329
Longood, Ross A171
Longstaff, William P470
Longstreet, Christopher P309
Longsworth, Nora P596
Longwell, Char P325
Longwith, Jana P379
Longworth, Ann A888
Longworth, Ann E425
Lonski, Jeffrey E450
Loof, Per-Olof E244
Look, Chuck A198
Looker, Travis P608
Looknanan, Lydia E168
Loomans, Leslie E386
Loomis, Timothy A695
Loomis, Nate A933
Loomis, Anna P352
Loos, Nicholas P424
Looser, Mary P597
Lootens, Ken A222

Loparco, Michael J. A475
Loparrino, Rosemarie A115
Loparrino, Rosemarie E38
Loper, D. Shane A401
Loper, D. Shane E198
Lopes, Luiz Ildefonso Sim-µes W80
Lopez, Christian A36
Lopez, Emilia A167
Lopez, Albert A167
Lopez, Gabby A200
Lopez, Samuel A247
Lopez, Tom A496
Lopez, Andres A. A616
Lopez, Norma A638
Lopez, Virgilio A651
Lopez, Frank A879
Lopez, Rene A929
Lopez, Jesus P12
Lopez, Amy P133
Lopez, David S. P171
Lopez, Edith P199
Lopez, Tom P235
Lopez, Barbara P244
Lopez, Ann P315
Lopez, Jorge P325
Lopez, Marcela P456
Lopez, Julio P505
Lopez, Jorge P511
Lopez, Nestor A Ramirez P516
Lopez, Mary P620
Lopez, Andreu Plaza W48
Lopez, Samuel E105
Lopez, George A. E222
Lopez, Christopher E319
Lopez, Norma E320
Lopez, Virgilio E330
Lopez, Liliana E391
Lopez, Rene E449
Lopez-Hodoyan, Mauricio E694
Lopez-Lay, Ginoris A333
Lopman, Abe P676
Loppatto, Gregory A870
Lorbeck, Jeff A695
Lorber, Howard M. E250
Lorberbaum, Jeffrey S. A569
Lord, Pat A505
Lord, Jack A683
Lord, Ellen A821
Lord, Paul P387
Lord, W. Leighton P501
Lore, Marc A901
Loredan, Luca A900
Loree, James M. (Jim) A778
Loree, James A920
Lorei, Greg P260
Lorei, Greg P261
Lorensen, Erik A8
Lorenson, Donna A480
Lorenson, Katie A. A567
Lorenson, Katie A. E283
Lorent, Patrick A651
Lorent, Patrick E329
Lorentson, Jeff A345
Lorentson, Jeffery B. A345
Lorentson, Jeffrey A345
Lorentson, Jeff E165
Lorentson, Jeffery B. E165
Lorentson, Jeffrey E165
Lorenz, Donald A112
Lorenz, Lori P36
Lorenz, Paul E P472
Lorenzen, Jeffrey D. (Jeff) A52
Lorenzen, Angela A921
Lorenzen, Angela P669
Lorenzo, Alejandro R. A573
Lorenzo, Antonio Alvarez A915
Lorenzo, Lisa P565
Lores, Enrique A438
Loreto, Michael J Di P47
Loreto, Sheila P573
Lorge, Timothy J. (Tim) A245
Lori, William E. A495
Lori, Michael A884
Lori, William E. P282
Loriggio, Louann A545

Lorino, Joseph A827
Lorino, Joseph P580
Lorraine, Metzka A518
Lorsson, Devin A502
Lorton, Andrea P104
Lorton, Donald E P112
Lorts, Angela P128
Lortz, Andre A186
Lortz, Andre P10
Lortz, Andre P123
Losacco, Vinicius A587
Losch, William C. (BJ) A343
Losch, William C. (BJ) E163
Loschelder, Todd A842
Losee, Mark D. E291
Losekamp, Karen P625
Losenegger, Michael J. E155
Losh, J. Michael (Mike) A541
Loshin, David S. P390
Loshitzer, Zohar E240
Losik, Dennis A100
Losntos, Juan De P379
Lotfi, Azin A188
Loth, Melissa A804
Lott, Tanya P112
Lott, Charles E69
Lotte, Evelina A112
Lottner, Jens W351
Lotvin, Alan M. A251
Lotze, Timothy P548
Lotzer, John A86
Lotzer, John E27
Loucks, Andrew A487
Loucks, Brian A489
Loudermilk, Robert A380
Loudermilk, Tony A383
Loudermilk, Kerry P417
Loudermilk, Tony E186
Louette, Pierre W297
Loufman, Donna A704
Louge, Michael W. (Mike) P395
Lougee, Craig E330
Loughman, Tim A928
Loughman, Tim P674
Loughran, Joseph P435
Loughrey, Kevin P604
Loughridge, Jerome A782
Loughridge, Jerome P526
Loughry, Ed C. E334
Louie, Joe A108
Louie, David A135
Louie, Bryan A807
Louis, David A337
Louis, Kathy St A518
Louis, Patrice A925
Louis, David N. P574
Louis, Tom P586
Louis, David E158
Louis, Jeff E429
Louis, Patrice E445
Loukotka, Jonathan A713
Louks, Jeff E267
Lounsbury, Chuck A735
Loup, Stephen P467
Louras, Peter N. E375
Loureiro, Guilherme W421
Louton, Beth A879
Louton, Alysa P20
Louttit, Gordon P553
Louvet, Patrice J. L. A701
Louwagie, Joe E429
Lovaglio, Luigi W407
Love, Talvis A170
Love, Kelli A170
Love, Marcella A191
Love, Judith S. A221
Love, Joe A340
Love, David A514
Love, David A516
Love, Peggy A702
Love, Zachary A879
Love, George A933
Love, Debra P27
Love, Ron P133
Love, Karen P151

Love, Bruce P166
Love, David P293
Love, Claudia P551
Love, Joe E161
Lovejoy, Madeline A325
Lovelace, James B A166
Lovelace, Lia A567
Lovelace, James B P111
Lovelace, Lia E284
Loveless, Steve P523
Lovell, Michael P641
Lovely, Dave A871
Lovering, Sheree A528
Lovern, Edward P418
Lovett, Robert P605
Lovins, Gregory S. (Greg) A97
Lovnaseth, Arne E442
Lovrien, Phyllis A727
Lovrien, Phyllis P453
Lovvorn, Lindsay A525
Low, Julianne A167
Low, Jim A457
Low, Sylvia A618
Low, Lewis P288
Low, Robert E. P364
Lowber, John M P213
Lowden, Cynthia A88
Lowden, Simon A654
Lowder, James P395
Lowder, Dr Steve P530
Lowe, Heather A6
Lowe, John E. A71
Lowe, Meg A270
Lowe, Rich A410
Lowe, John A410
Lowe, Chad A444
Lowe, Bill A522
Lowe, Wendy A574
Lowe, Edward A. (Sandy) A618
Lowe, Michael A704
Lowe, Corey H. A733
Lowe, Gregory A761
Lowe, Terrill P152
Lowe, Terrill P152
Lowe, Tamara P173
Lowe, Amy P209
Lowe, Patricia P229
Lowe, Kenneth W. (Ken) P480
Lowe, William J. P610
Lowe, Nick W377
Lowe, William M. E244
Lowe, Luther E450
Lowenberg, John P311
Lowenfeld, Ed A508
Lowenstein, Arnie E102
Lowenthal, Edward E314
Lower, Joseph T. (Joe) A620
Lower, Dennis P85
Lowery, Richard M. A126
Lowery, Jason A171
Lowery, Norman D. A341
Lowery, Peter A749
Lowery, Joseph A796
Lowery, Frederick M. (Fred) A832
Lowery, Kelli A877
Lowery, Blanche P559
Lowery, Jeremy E131
Lowery, Peter E367
Lowery, Joseph E397
Lowery-Yilmaz, Barbara A418
Lowman, David B. (Dave) A364
Lowman, Eric A850
Lowman, Tim P436
Lowman, Amy E16
Lown, Christian A583
Lowney, Peter E156
Lowrance, Randy A384
Lowrance, Randy P217
Lowrey, Carmen A583
Lowrey, Charles F. (Charlie) A686
Lowrey, Wayne A867
Lowrey, Wayne E418
Lowrie, Dan A444
Lowrimore, Bonnie A167
Lowth, Simon W82

Lowther, Aaron P126
Lowther, Patrick P652
Lowthers, Bruce A327
Lowy, Laura A114
Lowy, Susanna A893
Lowy, Laura E37
Loxton, Michelle A409
Loy, Teresa A141
Loy, Bertrand E128
Loyd, Mike A621
Loyd, Mike E311
Loyola, Connie P300
Lozada, Cristal P433
Lozada, Leonardo J. P466
Lozano, Erika A58
Lozano, Natividad A463
Lozano, Debra A464
Lozano, Miguel A779
Lozano, Rogelio Zambrano W91
Lozano-corona, Marina P175
Lozier, Kaye A911
Lozier, Kaye E437
LP, John F Shea P492
Lu, Eugene Y. C. A24
LU, Laura A140
Lu, Chris A174
Lu, Gary W115
Lu, Chris E68
Lu, Keh-Shew E113
Lubbers, Paul A36
Lubeley, Aaron R. P486
Lubelli, Luigi W35
Lubenow, Darrell E123
Luber, Jean E293
Lubert, Ira M. A828
Lubert, Ira M. P584
Lubeski, Damien P304
Lubi, Garry A181
Lubi, Garry E70
Lubian, Patricia A114
Lubian, Patricia E37
Lubitz, Allan A555
Lubkemann, Jamee A53
Luboff, Sharon A123
Lubow, Stuart H. A268
Luburic, Dan A361
Luburic, Danny A361
Luc, Phuong A900
Lucado, Joseph E264
Lucareli, Michael B. E286
Lucarelli, Jason A909
Lucarelli, Jason E436
Lucas, James A320
Lucas, John T. A392
Lucas, Julie A444
Lucas, Don A449
Lucas, Claudia A500
Lucas, Daniel A518
Lucas, Wonya A647
Lucas, Rebecca A692
Lucas, Mike A752
Lucas, Thomas J. (Tom) A756
Lucas, John P136
Lucas, Robert P285
Lucas, Bruce P351
Lucas, Dawn P456
Lucas, Bryan P549
Lucas, Laura P581
Lucas, Alfredo Escobar San W26
Lucas, Patrice W305
Lucas, Roger C. E45
Lucas, Lonnie E99
Lucas, Don E221
Lucas, Richard M. (Rich) E433
Lucas-Bull, Wendy E. W3
Luce, Amy A115
Luce, Amy E38
Lucero, Ben P147
Lucey, Matthew C. A644
Lucey, John W. E333
Lucey, Aaron E391
Luchini, Joseph P198
Luchtel, Pat A196
Lucia, Carol De P465
Lucia, Amy E47

COMBINED HOOVER'S HANDBOOK INDEX OF EXECUTIVES

```
A = AMERICAN BUSINESS
E = EMERGING COMPANIES
P = PRIVATE COMPANIES
W = WORLD BUSINESS
```

Luciano, Juan R. A77
Luciano, Louis A835
Luciano, Melba P588
Lucido, Michael P465
Lucido, Mary P513
Lucien, Kent T. A109
Lucien, Arthur A204
Lucier, Christopher P639
Lucier, Gregory T. E308
Luck, David A209
Luck, John P119
Luckas, Nancy P150
Luckenbach, Myron A8
Luckenbill, Patti P441
Luckett, Artra P56
Luckoff, Jeff A452
Lucks, Cheryl W. P359
Luckshire, Daniel J. E372
Lucore, Charles P516
Lucy, William P. (Bill) A650
Lucy, William P. (Bill) E329
Ludden, Paul W. P505
Ludeman, Christopher R. A175
Ludeman, Ross P112
Ludford, Brad P465
Ludington, Bob P589
Ludka, Andrea P354
Ludwig, Jeff A65
Ludwig, Richard A112
Ludwig, Brett A170
Ludwig, Debbie A222
Ludwig, Logan A495
Ludwig, Jeffrey G. A567
Ludwig, Dan A672
Ludwig, Logan P282
Ludwig, Michael M. E177
Ludwig, Jeffrey G. E283
Ludwig-Beymer, Patti P192
Lueck, Kim M. E267
Luecke, Edward A575
Lueckenhoff, Joe A90
Luecking, William A800
Luedeman, Lars P68
Luersman, Abby A920
Luettke, Maura P596
Luff, Paula P175
Lugardo, Daisy E396
Lugo, Luz P514
Lui, Lucian A147
Lui, Simon A575
Luippold, Wayne P432
Luis, Victor A801
Luisa, Jennifer F A405
Luisi, Michael E448
Lujan, Alfonso P164
Luka-Lognoné, Ida W24
Lukacs, Colleen A A368
Lukacs, Colleen A368
Lukas, Ron A266
Lukas, Ron P182
Lukasheva, Oksana A405
Lukatch, Heath E231
Lukcso, Andrew A444
Luke, Brick F A796
Luke, Dolores P42
Luke, Julie P206
Luke, Jacquelyn R P356
Luke, Richard P357
Luke, Brick F E397
Luken, Lauren A498
Luken, Ellen P187
Luker, Michael A885
Lukes, Donald P610
Lukis, Lawrence J. E340
Lukow, Bradley S. (Brad) A776
Lulla, Pankaj A198
Lulu, Karl Michael A747
Lumb, Richard A. W5
Lumbard, Lisa P120

Lumberg, James W. E131
Lumpkin, Mark E119
Lumpkins, Robert L. A576
Lumsden, Chris A. A754
Lumsden, Chris A. P484
Lunak, Leslie N. A114
Lunak, Leslie N. E37
Lund, Elizabeth A140
Lund, Henrik A418
Lund, Ed P25
Lund, Mary P170
Lund, Per P211
Lund, Dennis P. P417
Lund, Cathy N P657
Lund-Jurgensen, Kirsten A657
Lundberg, Fredrik W377
Lundeberg, Greta A140
Lundequam, Michael P430
Lundergan, Dan K. P639
Lundgren, David J. A401
Lundgren, Tamara A735
LUNDGREN, DAVID P208
Lundgren, John F. E59
Lundgren, David J. E198
Lundquist, Steve A170
Lundquist, Nicholas J. (Nick) A315
Lundquist, Jane L. A455
Lundquist, Stephanie A. A804
Lundquist, Curt A887
Lundquist, Joel P85
Lundquist, Jane L. E227
Lundy, Sal P375
Lundy, Mark H. E53
Lungberg, D'Ann E319
Lunn, Eric P29
Lunsford, Betsy P150
Luo, Jason A359
Luo, Susan A784
Luong, Bruce E77
Lupacchino, Gerard P229
Lupica, John J. W106
Lupkas, Scott A706
Lupo, Terri A382
Lupo, Hope P244
Lupo-Adams, Linda P111
Lupone, E. Robert A821
Luppino, Justin A346
Luppino, Justin E167
Luquette, Gary P A191
Luquette, Nancy A738
Luridas, Angela A15
Luridas, Angela P8
Lurie, Lindsey A466
Lurie, Herbert A749
Lurie, Robert F. P367
Lurie, Herbert E367
Lurker, Nancy A609
Lurker, Nancy P391
Lusardi, Greg A630
Lusch, Lynn A86
Lusch, Lynn E27
Lusco, C. Matthew A712
Luscombe, Caroline W230
Lush, Steve E215
Lusher, Jill P112
Lusignan, Cindy L A540
Lusk, John M. A363
Lusk, Sherri A482
Lusk, Keith A797
Lussier, Mark A835
Lustgarten, Joyce P183
Lusztyn, Marek Grzegorz W54
Lutek, Ben W. A389
Lutero, Lu P650
Lutgen, Garrett A935
Luthanen, Donn A751
Luthanen, Donn P482
Luthar, Vikram A77
Luther, Thomas A62
Luther, Scott A232
Luther, Lisa C. A602
Luther, John A879
Luther, Thomas E20
Luthi, Francesca A88
Luthringer, Lifford P676

Luton, Shan A259
Lutostanski, Lou A100
Luttig, J. Michael (Mike) A140
Luttig, J M A140
Lutton, Lorraine P519
Luty, Thomas A540
Lutz, John A1
Lutz, Ron A527
Lutz, Danielle A651
Lutz, Laurent C. A763
Lutz, Tom P563
Lutz, John M. P599
Lutz, Klaus J. W64
Lutz, Richard W133
Lutz, Rolf W433
Lutz, John E1
Lutz, Danielle E330
Lutz, Jennifer E375
Lutz, Laurent C. E377
Luu, Bao Q P479
Lux, Stephen A46
Lux, Mary P216
Lux, Joseph E407
Luxton, Matthew S A373
Luxton, Sam A890
Luz, Eduardo A496
Luzar, Jay A491
Luzzi, Joan A243
Lv, Xiangyang W82
Lyall, Kathy A571
Lyden, Shawn P131
Lydon, Katy A905
Lyerly, Ron P390
Lyga, Joseph E41
Lykins, Gregory B. (Greg) A335
Lykins, Gregory B. (Greg) E155
Lyko, Agnes A926
Lyko, Agnes E445
Lyle, Mike A121
Lyle, David A472
Lyle, Butch A717
Lyle, Rebekah A780
Lyle, Tommy A852
Lyle, John P604
Lyle, Butch E351
Lyles, Lester A373
Lyman, Samantha P266
Lymon, Hari A629
Lynam, Ben A571
Lynas, Peter W42
Lynch, Kevin A72
Lynch, Brian E. A84
Lynch, Ann A112
Lynch, Kim A145
Lynch, Thomas J. A151
Lynch, Thomas A240
Lynch, Charles A308
Lynch, R. Dale A317
Lynch, Kevin A343
Lynch, Christopher S. A364
Lynch, Thomas A391
Lynch, Renee A393
Lynch, Jeffrey A399
Lynch, Richard A418
Lynch, Barry A434
Lynch, Daniel A475
Lynch, Kenneth A492
Lynch, John A509
Lynch, Robert A559
Lynch, Jennifer A651
Lynch, Thomas A674
Lynch, Tom A702
Lynch, Brian A704
Lynch, Timothy G. A711
Lynch, Tom A721
Lynch, Christopher A763
Lynch, Jack A850
Lynch, Bill A891
Lynch, Sharon A902
Lynch, Patrick A912
Lynch, John A928
Lynch, James P74
Lynch, Kaye P105
Lynch, Brian P P174

Lynch, Timothy W P208
Lynch, Jeffrey P224
Lynch, Donald M P265
Lynch, Jack P304
Lynch, Timothy G. P444
Lynch, Dennis P546
Lynch, Ray P639
Lynch, John P674
Lynch, Christopher W325
Lynch, Christopher J. (Chris) W327
Lynch, Yvonne E51
Lynch, William E72
Lynch, Bill E72
Lynch, R. Dale E146
Lynch, Kevin E164
Lynch, Jennifer E329
Lynch, Christopher E377
Lynch, Kenneth E379
Lynch, Kirsten A. E424
Lynd, Michael A228
Lyndaker, Matthew A922
Lyndaker, Matthew P671
Lynde, Sue A806
Lynde, Sue E398
Lyne, Catharine A709
Lyne, Catharine P442
Lynn, Jeffrey A60
Lynn, Jeff A61
Lynn, Mary A293
Lynn, Steven A379
Lynn, Scott J. A736
Lynn, Mary P220
Lynn, Scott J. P460
Lynn, Terry P578
Lyon, Nancy A606
Lyon, Karie P74
Lyon, Mark P227
Lyon, Jim P489
Lyon, Glenn S. P567
Lyon, Michael J. E322
Lyons, Martin J. A46
Lyons, Joseph S A141
Lyons, Kara A167
Lyons, Jeffrey A242
Lyons, Daniel A309
Lyons, Blake A319
Lyons, Terrence A329
Lyons, Chad A347
Lyons, Sarah A369
Lyons, Robert C. A396
Lyons, John A405
Lyons, Garry A544
Lyons, Robert A637
Lyons, Thomas M. A684
Lyons, Daniel A715
Lyons, Brenda A783
Lyons, Bruce A784
Lyons, Steve A793
Lyons, Phyllis A796
Lyons, Shonyel A799
Lyons, Cathy A850
Lyons, Scott P185
Lyons, Mitch P340
Lyons, Biff P582
Lyons, Irving E136
Lyons, Chad E167
Lyons, Jeanne M. E183
Lyons, Jen E319
Lyons, Jennifer E319
Lyons, Phyllis E397
Lyski, James (Jim) A171
Lytle, Jeffrey A200
Lyttle, Lance A424
Lyublanovits, Robert A704
Lyubomirsky, Robert A933
Lyvers, Jason A440
L'Heureux, Scott P262
L- - pez, Humberto Chavez W26
Lofvenholm, Johan A97
Léopold-Metzger, Philippe W115
Lévy, Jean-Marc W79
Lévy, Jean-Bernard W148

M

Ma, Kader A167
Ma, Ziya A461
Ma, Hezhong A715
Maakestad, Paul P385
Maas, Linda A413
Maas, Linda E205
Maas-Brunner, Melanie W59
Maass, Paul T. P589
Maaty, Yehia A933
Mabe, Katherine (Kathy) A35
Mabee, Roger E229
Maberry, Matt A222
Mabry, Steven A279
Macadaeg, Reyne A112
Macak, Jeffrey A125
Macak, Jeff A125
Macali, Ralph A314
Macali, Ralph E145
Macaluso, Diane P24
Macaluso, David P372
Macarthur, Don P220
Macau, Carlos L. E206
Maccarone, Diane P429
Macchiarola, Doreen A646
Macchiarola, Doreen E324
Macchio, Ralph A243
Macchio, Frank A590
Macciocchi, Vince F. A77
Maccluer, Chuck P572
MacConduibh, Sarah P578
Macdermott, Alice A414
Macdermott, Alice P236
Macdonald, Brian A143
MacDonald, W. Timothy A147
Macdonald, Thomas R A460
Macdonald, Beth A527
Macdonald, Eileen B P40
Macdonald, Ngan P89
MacDonald, Walt P191
MacDonald, Mott P303
Macdonald, Carrie P626
Macdonald, Sally W426
MacDonald, Michael C. E275
Macdonald, Ross E318
Macdonald, Anthony E353
Macdougall, Betty P34
Macdougall, Mark P313
MacDougall, Harriett P389
Mace, Steve A482
Mace, Dave A871
Mace, Alexander P505
Macechko, Nicholas A922
Macechko, Nicholas P671
Macedo, Omar E245
Macek, Paul A799
Macellaro, Pat A36
Macewen, Kayla A421
Macgillivray, Diane P383
MacGowan, William N. (Bill) A595
Macgregor, Alastair A16
Macha, Erick A421
Machamer, Virginia A922
Machamer, Virginia P671
Machen, Elizabeth A760
Machen, Robert P34
Machen, Elizabeth E374
Machetti, Claudio W153
Machida, Marissa A109
Machikas, Michael E392
Machozzi, Thomas A879
Machuel, Denis W358
Machuzak, Michael A824
Machuzak, Michael P562
Macias, Annette P137
Macias, Efrain P250
Maciejewski, Gary A647
Maciel, Andre A497
Macina, Tom A704
Macina, Robert P. P573
MacInnes, Glenn I. A906
Macinnes, Dennis M P349
MacInnes, Glenn I. E434

Macintosh, Nancy A72
Macintyre, David A330
Macintyre, David E152
Macioce, Domenic A910
Macip, Marcus D. E255
Mack, Monica A484
Mack, Stephen A485
Mack, Richard L. (Rich) A576
Mack, Robert P. (Bob) A669
Mack, Diane A695
Mack, Jackie A797
Mack, Rick A881
Mack, Cary A913
Mack, Jill P193
Mack, Dave P404
Mack, Clifford P429
Mack, Michael P667
Mack, Rick E421
Mack, Cary E438
Mack-Brooks, Pamela P244
Mackay, Bill A29
Mackay, Ad A361
MacKay, Koley X A482
Mackay, Kevin A559
Mackay, John M P552
Mackay, Iain J. W189
Mackay, Martin E75
Macke, Kevin M. A859
Mackendree, Tammy P226
Mackenzie, Bill A152
MacKenzie, Alexander R. (Rod) A657
Mackenzie, Paula P509
Mackenzie, Bob P542
Mackenzie, Andrew W68
Mackenzie, Andrew W69
MacKenzie, Jason W296
Mackenzie, Bill E52
MacKenzie, Earle A. E370
Mackenzie, Jeffrey E. E375
Mackert, Sandra A545
Mackey, Edward F. A149
Mackey, Melinda A160
Mackey, Helen A255
Mackey, James G. A364
Mackey, John P. A921
Mackey, Sandra P549
Mackey, John P. P669
Mackie, H. Spurgeon A449
Mackie, Adam P38
Mackie, H. Spurgeon E220
MacKimm, James I. A121
MacKinnon, Allan A352
Mackinnon, Sylvia A651
Mackinnon, Maria A695
Mackinnon, Matt P355
Mackinnon, Sylvia E329
Mackler, Mitchell P672
Macko, Emily A879
Macko, David P214
Macko, David P569
Mackovic, Gayle E282
Mackown, Jennifer P454
Macky, Edward A149
Maclagger, Robert P335
Maclaren, Catherine P190
Maclasco, Robert A751
Maclasco, Robert P482
Maclaughlin, Eric P552
MacLean, Brian W. A844
Maclean, Dinah W50
Maclean, Malcolm W190
Maclennon, John P430
Macleod, Rod A789
MacLeod, Robert W212
MacMahon, John P A240
Macmahon, Mike E57
Macmanus, Steve A818
Macmaster, Gregory P394
MacMillan, John A222
MacMillan, Michael A835
Macmillan, Catherine A912
Macmullen, Jennifer E172
Macnee, Walt W. A544
Macnee, Lauren P597
Macneil, Dennis A632

MacNicholas, Garry W173
MacNicholas, Garry W174
Maco, Marylou A198
Macomber, Marina P383
Macomber, Todd E. E344
Macon, Mary A323
Macoun, Jeff W173
Macphail, Winborne P475
Macpherson, Donald G. (D.G.) A393
Macpherson, Andrew E102
MacQuarrie, Dennis A251
MacQuillan, Sandra J. A493
MacRae, Kristine A571
Macrae, Steve A847
Macrae, Steve E410
Macrie, Sari A35
Macrillo, Sam A200
MacRitchie, John A639
MacSween, Mike W373
Macuga, Daniel A. (Dan) E423
Macvey, Matt P130
Macwilliams, Robert A16
Macy, David A293
Madabhushi, Venkata A674
Madalena, Ralph J P369
Madalin, Diane A246
Madalin, Diane E105
Madaya, Jeanette A922
Madaya, Jeanette P671
Maddalone, Dom P501
Maddaloni, Sharon A545
Madden, John F. A104
Madden, Joe A452
Madden, Teresa A645
Madden, James A713
Madden, Mark P533
Madden, Donald P605
Madden, Daryl W24
Madderla, Jayanth K P383
Maddipati, Srikanth A209
Maddock, Dennis A475
Maddock, Ernest E. (Ernie) A565
Maddox, John A160
Maddox, Willie A A368
Maddox, Willie A368
Maddox, Matt A930
Maddox, Mark P115
Maddox, Mark P145
Maddux, Susan A877
Maddy, Brian A782
Maddy, Brian P526
Madeira, Harry R. A155
Madeira, Harry R. E54
Madeley, Paul E A120
Madeley, Paul E P71
Madera, Melvin A888
Madera, Melvin E425
Madge, Larry R. W371
Madgey, William A929
Madgey, William E449
Madi, Dani A492
Madigan, Kevin A756
Madill, Justin P77
Madineedi, Gautam A835
Madison, Thomas A706
Madison, Delbert A755
Madison, Joel P493
Madison, Thomas P604
Madison, Delbert E369
Madon, Cyrus W80
Madonia, Mark A547
Madonia, Frank E284
Madonna, John A255
Madormo, Richard X A461
Madra, Sundeep A360
Madrid, Bethany A438
Madrigal, Miguel A645
Madrigal, Calvin P595
Madrinkian, Alex A734
Madsen, C. Fred A126
Madsen, C A126
Madsen, Tammy A462
Madsen, Mark A905
Madsen, Tammy P256
Madsen, J-,rn W1

Madsen, J-,rn W21
Madson, Tomas R A373
Maduck, Sean E96
Maduri, John A366
Madyun, Adimu P392
Maeda, Eiji W51
Maeder, Jeff A831
Maeder, Jeff P601
Maes, Betty A224
Maes, Daniel A888
Maes, Ann P20
Maes, Daniel E425
Maestas, Karen A16
Maestas, Samantha A326
Maestri, Luca A72
Maestri, Jackie A480
Maestri, Bruno A603
Maez, Patrick P398
Maffei, Gregory B. (Greg) A522
Maffei, Frank A590
Maffei, Gregory B. (Greg) A699
Maffei, Gregory B. (Greg) A762
Maffeo, Vincent A. (Vince) A509
Maffeo, Tracey A626
Maffett, Stephen A219
Maffett, Stephen E87
Maffettone, Biagio A205
Mafi, Gabriela P212
Mafune, Yukio W346
Magann, Rita A54
Maganov, Ravil U. W309
Magaro, Phill P250
Magaru, Riva A309
Magath, Mark E429
Magdziarz, Wayne P39
Magdziarz, Wayne F P301
Magee, James E57
Magee, Ryan E203
Mageli, John P26
Magenheimer, Richard C P253
Magenheimer, Richard P253
Maggelakis, Sophia P456
Magglet, Crystal Call A186
Magglet, Crystal Call P123
Maggio, Michael A479
Maggio, Joseph A706
Maggs, Michelle A468
Maggs, Thomas O. A851
Magid, Larry A727
Magid, Larry P453
Magill, M. Elizabeth A510
Magill, M. Elizabeth P290
Maginnis, Vytas A575
Maglaque, Neal A60
Magleby, Curt A360
Magner, Johnette P85
Magno, Benjamin D P242
Magnus, Keith E138
Magnuson, Michele A433
Magnuson, Richard P26
Magnuson, Michele E217
Mago, Vikram A203
Mago, Angela G. A491
Magoun, Steve E412
Magri, Joseph E246
Magruder, Joan A344
Magruder, Joan P513
Magstadt, Brian J. E375
Maguin, Stephen P162
Maguire, William A296
Maguire, Tim A349
Maguire, Elizabeth A692
Maguire, Justin A740
Maguire, Adam P309
Maguire, Andy W189
Mah, Chester P325
Mahabadi, Hadi A933
Mahaffee, Joseph W. (Joe) A144
Mahaffey, Jenny P228
Mahaffy, Denise A267
Mahajan, Umesh A897
Mahalingam, S. A805
Mahalingam, S. P542
Mahan, Chip A523
Mahan, James S A523

COMBINED HOOVER'S HANDBOOK INDEX OF EXECUTIVES

A = AMERICAN BUSINESS
E = EMERGING COMPANIES
P = PRIVATE COMPANIES
W = WORLD BUSINESS

Mahaney, Sheryl P280
Mahaney, Robert E265
Maharaj, Gary R. E395
Mahendra-Rajah, Prashanth A67
Maher, Dina A319
Maher, Lee A. A379
Maher, Christopher D. A618
Maher, Jeff A645
Maher, Sean A713
Maher, Joshua A722
Maher, Nancy A835
Maher, Steve A855
Maher, Mark A893
Maher, Joseph P528
Maher, Carly E250
Maher, Christopher D. E310
Mahlan, Deirdre A. W140
Mahlen, Jennifer A347
Mahler, William W. (Bill) A726
Mahler, William W. (Bill) P453
Mahler, Carl P541
Mahler, Anthony P664
Mahlich, Ben A398
Mahlich, Ben P222
Mahlman, Jason P445
Mahmood, Fuad A575
Mahmood, Kash P31
Mahmud, Shahzad A914
Mahon, Kenneth J. A268
Mahon, Paul A. W173
Mahon, Paul A. W174
Mahone, Barbara P670
Mahoney, Ryan A16
Mahoney, Michael A120
Mahoney, Michael F. (Mike) A149
Mahoney, Mike A197
Mahoney, Timothy O. (Tim) A431
Mahoney, Adeline A469
Mahoney, Bob A628
Mahoney, Eileen A692
Mahoney, Tom A704
Mahoney, Kathie A762
Mahoney, Kevin A768
Mahoney, Kathleen M. (Kathy) A774
Mahoney, Edward J. P325
Mahoney, Joanne M. P367
Mahoney, Paul G. P442
Mahoney, Carole P578
Mahoney, Cornelius D. E42
Mahoney, Dennis E79
Mahoney, Theresa E147
Mahony, Susan (Sue) A517
Mahtaney, Andrew A167
Mai, Shayne P361
Mai, Jose E319
Maia, Paulo W189
Maibach, Doug P68
Maibach, Ben C. P68
Maibach, Ryan P68
Maibach, Sheryl P68
Maibach, Benjamin C P68
Maibach, Douglas L P68
Maibach, Sheryl B P68
Maier, Henry J. A323
Maier, Richard A512
Maier, Michael A763
Maier, Andrew W P429
Maier, Stuart A. E197
Maier, Charles E295
Maier, Michael E377
Maiers, Mary C A397
Maikisch, Michelle P120
Mail, Ingrid M P307
Mailand, William P295
Mailes-Dineff, Suzanne P204
Mailes-Dineff, Suzanne P532
Mailloux, Marc A409
Main, Richard W. (Dick) A297
Main, Timothy L. (Tim) A475

Main, Joel P70
Main, Richard W. (Dick) E129
Mainer, Matthew A672
Maines, Robert E172
Maingot, Lawrence C. E183
Maio, Mike A112
Maio, Keith D. A940
Maiorana, James A218
Maiorana, Michael A890
Maipoom, Pichit W351
Mair, Nancy A158
Maisano, Anthony E42
Maisonville, Dan P74
Maisonville, Dan P206
Maiuri, Lou A783
Majcher, Marian W54
Majeski, Carl A36
Majewski, Sylwia P57
Majher, Matt E19
Majka, Don A905
Majon, Judy A925
Majon, Judy E445
Major, Paul A60
Major, Cathy P242
Major, John E258
Majors, Teresa A14
Majors, Michael C. A389
Majors, Gregory A704
Majors, Teresa P6
Majors, Charles H. (Charlie) E16
Majumdar, Anurita A518
Majuri, Danielle P563
Mak, Derek A198
Makas, Rebecca A686
Makhlin, Leo A928
Makhlin, Leo P674
Makhulo, Linus A559
Maki, Mark A P340
Maki, Jennifer W412
Makiya, Khalid A188
Maklan, David P664
Makowski, John A176
Makowski, Lisa P129
Makris, George A. A760
Makris, George A. E374
Maksoud, Jane P248
Makulec, Jude P456
Malaeb, Rabih A175
Malakof, Stacey L P368
Malamed, Adam E250
Malan, Jill P513
Malanga, J. D. W212
Malapkowski, Bob P157
Malasto, Thomas A. P151
Malat, Jeff A547
Malat, Scott B. A934
Malatesta, Keith A320
Malave, Tracy A605
Malavé, Andrés P390
Malchin, Kobi W163
Malchoff, Kevin R. P449
Malchuk, Daniel W68
Malchuk, Daniel W69
Malcolm, Gregory A218
Malcolm, Mark A373
Malcolm, Steven J A921
Maldonado, R. Danny A821
Maldonado, Ricardo P183
Maldonado, Matias P508
Maldonado, Norma P540
Maleh, Paul A. E102
Malekkhosravi, Benny A695
Malempati, Ihari P419
Maleno, Christopher A. (Chris) W106
Maley, Michael A25
Maley, Ernie A351
Maley, Michael P14
Maley, Christopher P573
Malhotra, Raghu A544
Malhotra, Kapil A654
Malik, Ben A181
Malik, Asad A414
Malik, Amjad A487
Malik, Saad A778
Malik, Abinta A826

Malik, Asad P236
Malik, Kemal W61
Malik, Ben E70
Malik, Alicia E132
Malin, Clint B. E261
Malina, Joel P159
Malina, Robert E106
Malinaric, Dan A564
Malinowski, Barbara A605
Malinowski, Jim P433
Malizia, Vince A374
Mallah, Isaac P519
Mallak, Brian A224
Mallaney, James A9
Mallaney, James P4
Mallard, Ty A64
Mallard, Ben A442
Mallen, Ben P248
Mallet, Thierry M. W366
Mallett, Belinda P276
Mallett, Chris P383
Malley, Chris A784
Mallick, Imtiaz P233
Mallik, David A831
Mallik, David P601
Mallon, Ed A135
Mallon, Rose A605
Mallon, Mark W38
Mallon, Jen E319
Mallonee, Jim A522
Mallory, Don A142
Mallory, Don E49
Mallott, Philip E. A132
Malloy, Luke A61
Malloy, Betty A554
Malloy, John P. (Jack) A577
Mally, Andrew P104
Malmer, Christoffer W357
Malmgren, Bob A893
Malone, Daniel J. (Dan) A209
Malone, Daniel J. (Dan) A238
Malone, Kevin A270
Malone, Steve A320
Malone, Robert W. A640
Malone, Rob A640
Malone, Robert A. (Bob) A645
Malone, John C. A699
Malone, Mike A727
Malone, David A799
Malone, Ollie P171
Malone, Steve P205
Malone, Richard P266
Malone, Lisa P315
Malone, Mike P334
Malone, Dean P340
Malone, Dean P P340
Malone, Blake P392
Malone, Mike P453
Malone, Kent P461
Malone, Marguerite G. P473
Malone, Michael P651
Malone, Mark E197
Maloney, Dan A36
Maloney, Robert A108
Maloney, Drew A418
Maloney, Deiken A606
Maloney, Matt A793
Maloney, James A922
Maloney, Patrick P207
Maloney, James P671
Maloney, John E138
Malpeli, Laurent A174
Malphurs, Stacy A773
Malte, Bob P280
Maltempo, Robb A230
Maltempo, Robb P154
Maltsbarger, Richard D. A527
Maltz, Richard B. A118
Maltz, David A281
Maltz, Richard B. E40
Maltzman, Forrest P569
Malucci, Joseph E388
Malugen, William C A844
Malverdi, Fabrizio W218
Maly, Rachel P282

Malzahn, Daniel D. A614
Mamerow, Steve A666
Mamet, Michele P331
Mammadov, Emin A496
Mammen, Mathai A230
Mammen, Timothy P. V. E238
Mamo, Martha P92
Managiaracina, Brian A63
Manahan, Thomas J. (Tom) A853
Manahan, Thomas J. (Tom) P612
Manahan-smith, Suzanne A309
Manasia, Anthony P351
Manatt, J R E106
Manazir, Mike A140
Manbeck, Keith A921
Manbeck, Keith P669
Manchanda, Mona E132
Manchandra, Anita A686
Manchester, Paula A255
Manchester, Eric A498
Manchester, Morgan E132
Manchur, Fred P277
Mancini, Michael A22
Mancini, Robert A109
Mancini, Joseph A933
Mancini, Michael P11
Mancini, Shawn P604
Mancini, Wayne E103
Mancl, Dave A465
Manculich, Joshua P552
Mancuso, Alfred A329
Mancuso, Sabrina A621
Mancuso, Michael A651
Mancuso, Anthony P203
Mancuso, Anthony P304
Mancuso, Sabrina E311
Mancuso, Michael A330
Mandable, Terence A145
Mandala, Rocco A175
Mandas, Pat E80
Mandato, Robert A544
Mandava, Sabala R A414
Mandava, Sabala R P236
Mandavilli, Apoorva A829
Mandavilli, Apoorva P589
Mandel, Joseph G. A476
Mandel, Carol A. A592
Mandel, Lisa P314
Mandel, Carol A. P370
Mandel, Adrienne A. P658
Mandell, Michael A203
Mandell, James P558
Mandelli, Maela A692
Manderscheid, David A538
Mandersson, Magnus W386
Mandeville, Kathy P315
Mandine, Béatrice W297
Mandir, Amber A104
Mandon, Daniel A596
Mandraccia, Crocifissa A77
Mandrell, Matthew A368
Mandry, Kyle A895
Mandt, Ingo M. W231
Manduca, Paul W315
Mandy, Bowers A36
Maneker, Amy P131
Maner, Patti A713
Maness, Barry A850
Maness, Robert E102
Manfredonia, Donald L. A348
Manfredonia, Donald L. E169
Mangan, Martina P467
Manganaro, Mike A784
Manganelli, Matthew A914
Manganelli, Matthew E439
Mangel, Allen W. P447
Mangels, Tonya A45
Mangiaracina, Brian A63
Mangieri, Theresa A346
Mangieri, Theresa E166
Manginelli, John A492
Mangino, Lou P77
Mangino, Louis P77
Mango, John A337
Mango, John E158

COMBINED HOOVER'S HANDBOOK INDEX OF EXECUTIVES

Mangrum, Rick A902
Mangu, Anand A722
Mangum, Jesse A482
Manhas, Raj P481
Manheimer, Mark L A775
Manheimer, Mark L P511
Mani, Nat A742
Mania, Kasey P42
Manias, William G P196
Maniates, Zenaida A884
Manifold, Albert W122
Manigan, Elizabeth P206
Manigault, Pierre P112
Manion, Gary P131
Manis, Jonathan (Jon) A791
Manis, Charles P422
Manis, Jonathan (Jon) P535
Maniscalco, Nick A540
Manka, Michael P388
Manke, David A875
Manke, Riley E433
Mankiller, Kristen T P558
Manley, Melissa P435
Manley, Gerard A. (Gerry) W294
Mann, James A17
Mann, Jeff A25
Mann, Natalie A713
Mann, Matthew A737
Mann, James P9
Mann, Jeff P14
Mann, Lindsay K P274
Mann, Edward P277
Mann, Eric P306
Mann, Lisa P436
Mann, Scott P638
Mann, Dorothy P652
Mann, Erica L. W61
Mann, Trevor W260
Mann, Jeff E63
Mann, Matthew E361
Manna, Heidi A164
Mannai, David A688
Mannarino, Frank A. A778
Mannebach, Robert P582
Mannello, Louis J. A397
Mannhardt, Thilo W405
Manning, Joseph (Joe) A5
Manning, Karen A112
Manning, Jennifer A117
Manning, Joyce A158
Manning, Anna A714
Manning, Ben A850
Manning, Tom P49
Manning, Jennifer P61
Manning, Michael P574
Manning, Robert J. (Rob) W371
Manning, John T. (Terry) E23
Mannion, Melissa A325
Mannix, Margaret P2
Manno, Federico A367
Mano, Carl E101
Manocha, Pooja P230
Manocha, Charu E239
Manoharan, Arun P184
Manolovic, Michelle A251
Manotti, Kenneth P325
Manseau, James J. A150
Manseau, James J. E50
Manser, Marlene A500
Mansfield, Bob A72
Mansfield, William P. A396
Manson, Dave P472
Manson, Schuyler E433
Mansuetti, Mike A724
Mansuetti, Mike P452
Mantaring, Rizalina G. W371
Mantella, Philomena V. P383
Manternach, Jill P253
Mantia, Linda P. W247
Mantilla, Julio A835
Manto, Jennifer P645
Manton-jones, Chris E260
Mantovani, Massimo W155
Mantri, Rahul P230
Mantua, Philip J. A741

Mantua, Mitch A746
Mantua, Philip J. E364
Mantz, Gary A170
Mantz, Jay A512
Mantz, Constantine A P1
Mantzounis, Demetrios P. W25
Manuel, Chris A616
Manuel, Ethan P326
Manuel, Shasta P513
Manusos, Nicholas A120
Manville, Ryan K E154
Manwani, Harish A695
Manwani, Harish A920
Manzano, Mike A779
Manzano, Wilhelmina A827
Manzano, Pam P550
Manzano, Wilhelmina P580
Manzella, Jaci A345
Manzella, Jaci E166
Manzi, Rosina A356
Manzo, Gael A809
Manzo, Arnie P66
Manzo, Arnie P513
Mao, Li A479
Mapes, Michelle A313
Mapes, Chris A936
Mapes, Michelle P200
Maples, John T. P499
Mapp, Frederick A14
Maquat, Robert A651
Maquat, Robert E329
Mara, Mike A857
Marable, Natasha P133
Marafioti, Michael A702
Maragos, George A175
Maraist, Michael P A426
Maraist, Michael P. E212
MARAMOTTI, LUIGI W121
Marandola, Crystine A782
Marandola, Crystine P526
Marano, Tom A8
Marantis, Demetrios A895
Marasigan, Glenn A793
Maraziti, Lara A592
Maraziti, Lara P370
Marbach, Kenneth D. A301
Marburg, Mitch A112
Marcantano, Mark P673
MarcAurele, Joseph J. (Joe) A904
Marced, Maria W380
Marcegaglia, Emma W155
Marcela, Sanchez A361
Marcelino, Luis A528
Marcell, Marvin A398
Marcellino, Mark E132
Marcelo, Sheila Lirio E65
Marcey, Tom A171
March, Shayn P E185
March, Shayn E185
Marchael, Tom A862
Marchael, Tom P617
Marchand, Gil A495
Marchand, Gil P282
Marchese, Jason A204
Marchetti, Kevin A664
Marchetti, Kevin E334
Marchick, Jill A75
Marchik, Katie P258
Marchini, Larry A115
Marchini, Larry E38
Marchio, Samuel A69
Marchio, Timothy A752
Marchioni, John J. A751
Marchozzi, Tom P229
Marchuk, Neil A79
Marck, Marianne A779
Marconi, Luis G. A434
Marcos, Vanessa A704
Marcot, Thomas A575
Marcotte, James A. (Jim) A297
Marcotte, James A. (Jim) E129
Marcum, R. Alan A263
Marcum, R Alan A263
Marcum, Lanette A386
Marcum, Dennis P333
Marcum, Lanette E188

Marcus, Judy A137
Marcus, Avi A A622
Marcus, William A867
Marcus, Philip P464
Marcus, Ruth P500
Marcus, W. Andrew P636
Marcus, Joel S. E8
Marcus, George M. E136
Marcus, George A E267
Marcus, Gregory S. E267
Marcus, Stephen H. E268
Marcus, William E418
Marcuz, Lisa A281
Mardany, Herbert A842
Mare, Amanda P625
Marecki, Pam P550
Maredia, Amin N. A776
Marek, Dave A65
Marenghi, Matt A587
Marengo, James A405
Maresca, Kristin A115
Maresca, Kristin E37
Maresch, Wayne P288
Margetts, Marty P132
Marglous, Lauren A596
Margol, Kanoe P585
Margolies, Laurie P248
Margolin, Eric M. A171
Margolis, Joseph D. (Joe) E141
Margolis, Nancy E432
Margraff, Glenn A926
Margraff, Glenn E445
Mari, Marisol P164
Mariani, John A125
Marianna, Boyd A385
Marians, Ken P325
Mariconti, Janet E131
Marien, Philippe W76
Marietta, Richard P141
Marillac, Louise De P47
Marin, Daniele A701
Marinakis, Eric A240
Marine, Ray A325
Marinello, Kathryn V. (Kathy) A417
Marinello, Kathryn V A827
Marinello, Kathryn V P571
Maring, Trent P412
Marinho, Fatima W P404
Marini, Greg A62
Marini, Greg E20
Marinkoski, Robert P119
Marino, Madelyn A54
Marino, Michael A161
Marino, Pamela A791
Marino, Rick A850
Marino, Mary P131
Marino, Georgie P486
Marino, Pamela P535
Marino, Ricardo Villela W204
Marino, Sal E429
Marinow, Nikolai E272
Marins, Rubia A329
Marinus, Sven W358
Marinzel, Ron P487
Marion, Diane A163
Marion, Melissa A922
Marion, Melissa P671
Marion, Diane E62
Mariotti, Marco A661
Maris, George A605
Maritato, Christopher (Chris) A767
Maritz, W. Stephen (Steve) P308
Mark, David A5
Mark, Reisinger A36
Mark, Richard J. A46
Mark, Larry A215
Mark, Hamilton A320
Mark, Corey A421
Mark, Sprague A532
Mark, Kelly A577
Mark, Richard A812
Mark, Pieprzyca E429
Markantonis, George M. A506
Markarian, Michael A869
Markatos, Robert A457

Markel, Tony A536
Markel, Anthony F. A536
Markel, Steven A. A536
Markell, Peter K. A641
Markell, Peter K. P407
Markell, Peter K P574
Markell, Peter K. P608
Marken, James E21
Markewicz, Jeremy P315
Markham, Stephen A749
Markham, Nick P157
Markham, Pat E206
Markham, Stephen E367
Markich, Rich A855
Markinson, Bryan P351
Markis, Randall A442
Markle, Jami P246
Markley, Stephen A491
Markley, Dave A722
Markley, Steve P182
Markofski, Dean A727
Markofski, Dean P453
Markos, Aaron A347
Markos, Aaron E167
Markovich, Nick A444
Markovich, Matt A837
Markovitch, Steve P395
Markowski, Steven A115
Markowski, Steven E38
Marks, Karen A119
Marks, Thomas A530
Marks, Reid A665
Marks, Judy F. A875
Marks, Lisa P301
Marks, Scott W P376
Marks, Stanley W. P500
Marks, Chris W274
Marks, Chris W333
Marks, Francis A. (Frank) E234
Marks, Reid E334
Markus, Richard A65
Markwalter, Jack W85
Marlatt, Geoff T. A634
Marleen, Odonnell P72
Marlette, Tim G. A228
Marley, Charles P677
Marlin, Chris A512
Marlin, Jason A842
Marlin-mha, Cynthia P109
Marlow, Patty P652
Marnick, Cliff A481
Marnick, Samantha J A774
Maroc, Genny P291
Marockie, Felicia A525
Marohn, Steve A210
Marold, Paul E263
Marolis, Jessie A867
Marolis, Jessie E418
Marone, Sal E367
Maroney, Timothy A686
Maroney, Patrick A868
Maroni, Bradley P133
Maroni, Kathy P332
Marotta, Janet A114
Marotta, Richard M A128
Marotta, Michael A410
Marotta, Janet E37
Marotta, Richard M. E42
Marotto, Stephen A349
Maroun, Nabih A144
Maroun, George E147
Marpe, Joel A902
Marquardt, Patti P76
Marquardt, R. Scott P306
Marquardt, Robert P306
Marquardt, Jeanne P608
Marquardt, Rolf W377
Marques, Luis A408
Marques, Roberto A573
Marques, Miguel Athayde W169
Marquess, Dan E230
Marquez, Antonio F. A283
Marquez, Tina P315
Marquez, Melanie P638
Marquez, Antonio F. E117

COMBINED HOOVER'S HANDBOOK INDEX OF EXECUTIVES

A = AMERICAN BUSINESS
E = EMERGING COMPANIES
P = PRIVATE COMPANIES
W = WORLD BUSINESS

Marquis, Mike A835
Marquis, Jeffrey A. P224
Marr, Kelly A215
Marr, Richard R A262
Marr, Kara A715
Marr, David W426
Marr, Christopher P. (Chris) E104
Marr, John S. E412
Marra, Diana A654
Marria, Mohit A191
Marriott, Richard E. A436
Marriott, John A491
Marriott, John W. (Bill) A538
Marriott, Christie A912
Marriott, Brianne P153
Marro, Margareta P12
Marron, Doug A704
Marrone, Alicia A54
Marrone, Joe A479
Marrs, Anna A53
Marrs, Douglas W. (Doug) A397
Marry, Thomas F. (Tom) E286
Marschall, Patrick A120
Marschke, Keith E257
Marsden, Dale P470
Marsh, Kevin A170
Marsh, Nancy M A183
Marsh, Laurie M. A289
Marsh, Andrew S. (Drew) A296
Marsh, Allison A390
Marsh, John T. A403
Marsh, Quentin A715
Marsh, Mike A746
Marsh, Leslie A818
Marsh, Richard A922
Marsh, Amanda P122
Marsh, Andrew P196
Marsh, Randy P361
Marsh, Allen P473
Marsh, Richard P671
Marsh, Nancy M E74
Marsh, Leslie E403
Marshall, Linda A54
Marshall, Steven C. A59
Marshall, James A69
Marshall, Kimberly L A113
Marshall, Jay A447
Marshall, Jason A472
Marshall, Russell A682
Marshall, Ryan R. A690
Marshall, Greg A875
Marshall, David R P118
Marshall, Colin P142
Marshall, Jay P247
Marshall, Steve P402
Marshall, Pamela P418
Marshall, Timon P480
Marshall, Era L. P497
Marshall, Chuck P529
Marshall, Ken P623
Marshall, John L. W7
Marshall, Rick A. E23
Marshall, Kimberly L E36
Marshall, Joseph W. (Chip) E372
Marsico, Stephen A741
Marsico, Stephen E364
Marsiglio, Cindi A902
Marsilio, Jason A108
Marsolais, Christian A744
Marsteller, Brent A P105
Marsters, Karen P190
Marston, Monica A3
Marston, Jed P193
Martchek, Jeffrey D. A614
Martel, Roland M. A453
Martell, Rita A826
Martello, Wan Ling W276
Marten, Lori A602
Martens, Philip R. (Phil) A395

Marthinsen, Jim A436
Martin, Tom A8
Martin, Cheryl A103
Martin, Paul E. A119
Martin, Sean A120
Martin, Paul E A120
Martin, Fenton A162
Martin, Fabian A167
Martin, Rodney A168
Martin, R. Brad A189
Martin, Julia A191
Martin, John A255
Martin, James A276
Martin, Kevin A310
Martin, David A313
Martin, Matthew A. A320
Martin, Chris A325
Martin, John J. A345
Martin, David A374
Martin, G Henry A379
Martin, John C. A385
Martin, Jon A405
Martin, Bradley A432
Martin, Kristin A441
Martin, Sabrena A452
Martin, Robin A460
Martin, Lynn C A462
Martin, Jeff A478
Martin, Phil A484
Martin, Thomas A. (Tom) A494
Martin, James A511
Martin, Roger A520
Martin, Ron A543
Martin, Larry A559
Martin, Antonio A588
Martin, Jules A592
Martin, Kenny A615
Martin, Sean A646
Martin, Steve A647
Martin, Joseph A677
Martin, Christopher P. A684
Martin, Katy A695
Martin, Sandy A704
Martin, Andrew D. A711
Martin, Aubrey A712
Martin, Jeffrey W. A753
Martin, Brent A760
Martin, Ian A783
Martin, Mitchell P. A794
Martin, Robert A828
Martin, Robert W. A834
Martin, Marsha A837
Martin, Erika A861
Martin, Wendy A867
Martin, Michelle A893
Martin, James A902
Martin, Susan H. A907
Martin, Carey A920
Martin, Julia P5
Martin, Jason P7
Martin, Janelle P13
Martin, Michael P46
Martin, Curtis J P86
Martin, John P96
Martin, Keith P102
Martin, Dan P114
Martin, Michelle P114
Martin, Gerard R. P130
Martin, David P138
Martin, Cary W P142
Martin, Michael P148
Martin, Stephen J P156
Martin, Sandy P157
Martin, Kay P177
Martin, David P200
Martin, Michael M. P206
Martin, Brady P220
Martin, James P290
Martin, Ruben S P311
Martin, Kathryn P325
Martin, Augusta P355
Martin, Antonio P365
Martin, Jules P370
Martin, Larry P393
Martin, Tina P394

Martin, Josh P411
Martin, Gisel P412
Martin, Melanie P428
Martin, Mary P430
Martin, Julie P430
Martin, George K. P442
Martin, Andrew D. P444
Martin, Elizabeth P451
Martin, Shereen P468
Martin, James P475
Martin, Lawanda P490
Martin, Diane P516
Martin, James P524
Martin, Kayla P546
Martin, Robert P584
Martin, Michelle P589
Martin, Paula P605
Martin, Hannah P610
Martin, Roy P611
Martin, David P645
Martin, Ashley P649
Martin, Donald L P672
Martin, R. Bradley (Brad) W66
Martin, Eric W71
Martin, Denis W305
Martin, Paolo De W345
Martin, Edward E16
Martin, Joseph R. E53
Martin, Fenton E61
Martin, Jay E103
Martin, Timothy M. (Tim) E104
Martin, David G. E149
Martin, Dennis J. E149
Martin, John J. E165
Martin, Todd E177
Martin, Amber E185
Martin, Bradley E216
Martin, Ronald H. E264
Martin, Bob E265
Martin, Sean E324
Martin, Todd E340
Martin, Brent E374
Martin, Wendy E418
Martin, Dan E433
Martin-Flickinger, Gerri A779
Martinbianco, Dino A704
Martindale, Steven L. (Steve) A453
Martindale, Bob A680
Martinek, Kenneth A. E305
Martinelli, James E224
Martines, Arnold D. A182
Martinez, Juan Gonzalez A7
Martinez, Irma A15
Martinez, Ken A16
Martinez, Dennis A82
Martinez, Charles A108
Martinez, Joel A167
Martinez, Victor A203
Martinez, Vince A219
Martinez, Lori A258
Martinez, Elizandro A360
Martinez, Ozzie A456
Martinez, Alvaro A463
Martinez, Carlos A463
Martinez, Darcy A506
Martinez, Michael A538
Martinez, Steve A562
Martinez, Robert A604
Martinez, Robert E A604
Martinez, Peter A651
Martinez, Brett A709
Martinez, Maria A739
Martinez, Manny A739
Martinez, Megan A749
Martinez, John A852
Martinez, Irma P8
Martinez, Jason P20
Martinez, Abby P21
Martinez, Oscar P149
Martinez, Fernando P160
Martinez, Christy P211
Martinez, Julie P250
Martinez, Jane P423
Martinez, Brett P442
Martinez, Michael P462

Martinez, Kenneth P470
Martinez, Dorothea P507
Martinez, Danielle P594
Martinez, Edward P649
Martinez, Michelle P678
Martinez, Vince E87
Martinez, Ozzie E228
Martinez, Marco E293
Martinez, Mark E319
Martinez, Peter E329
Martinez, Megan E367
Martini, James (Jim) A831
Martini, James (Jim) P601
Martino, Tony A347
Martino, Stephen A562
Martino, Liberino A833
Martino, Tony E167
Martino-Valdes, Emilio A333
Martinovich, Robert F. (Rob) A630
Martinovich, Robert F A631
Martinovich, Robert F P397
Martins, Izzy A98
Martins, Newton A450
Martinson, Chris A831
Martinson, Eric K P585
Martinson, Chris P601
Martiny, Krista A806
Martiny, Krista E399
Martire, Frank R. A327
Martire, Frank R A585
Martire, Diane A658
Marto, Michelle A877
Martocci, Gino A. A530
Martore-Baker, Susan A162
Martore-Baker, Susan E61
Martrenchar, Yves W71
Martucci, Patty A539
Martus, Chris A576
Martuza, Robert L. P574
Marty, Margaret A205
Marty, Angela P341
Marty, Fletcher P628
Marty, Michael E65
Martyn, Derek P556
Martz, Stephen A358
Martz, B. Bradford A868
Martz, Sheila P126
Martz, Stephen E176
Martz, Wes E243
Martz, Raymond D. E325
Mart-n, Miguel Mart-nez San W321
Mart-nez, Enrique R. (Henry) A270
Mart-nez, Armando Tamez W19
Mart-nez, José Formoso W26
Marumoto, Akira W250
Maruna, Mike A395
Maruna, Karen A444
Maruyama, Yoshinori W27
Maruyama, Haruya W132
Maruyama, Hideki W268
Maruyama, Hidetoshi W282
Marvel, G Michael A173
Marventano, David Dave A281
Marventano, David A355
Marvin, Melodye A325
Marvin, Joanne E81
Marvin, James L. E241
Marx, Neal A465
Marx, Michael A498
Marx, Felix A545
Marx, Joseph A677
Marx, Benjamin A859
Marx, Sherri A885
Marx, Douglas P211
Marx, Kara P489
Mary, Howard A449
Mary, Michele St A501
Mary, Mark P425
Mary, Howard E220
Marzan-goble, Alicia A791
Marzan-goble, Alicia P535
Marzec, Robert J. E23
Marzen, Russ A935
Marzilli, Christopher (Chris) A373
Mas, Alberto A123

Mas, José R. A543
Mas, Jorge A543
Masashi, Shigetoh A92
Mascarenhas, Ryan A82
Mascari, Dorine P548
Mascaro, Dan A681
Mascher, Christof W24
Mascia, Angelo A588
Mascia, Jonathan P229
Mascia, Angelo P365
Masciantonio, Vince A831
Masciantonio, Vince P601
Mascolo, Pablo A218
Mase, Steve A574
Mase, Dawn A925
Mase, Dawn E445
Maselko, Stephen A538
Masengill, Rob A664
Masengill, Rob E334
Mash, Lisa A63
Mashani, Sheikh Khalid bin Mustahail Al W49
Mashburn, Alan P78
Mashioff, Michael A512
Masi, Vince A465
Masi, James E123
Masiak, Kamila A661
Masiel, Pete P502
Mask, Laura E357
Maskal, Vanessa E. E33
Maslavets, Nick P202
Masley, Deborah A850
Maslow, Andrew P448
Maslyaev, Ivan W310
Mason, Heather L. A5
Mason, Ben A91
Mason, Jeanne K. A119
Mason, Jeannie K A120
Mason, Steve A169
Mason, Jennifer A248
Mason, Thomas P. A294
Mason, Paul A327
Mason, Robert A340
Mason, Michael A347
Mason, Richard J A368
Mason, Richard A368
Mason, Rich A391
Mason, Mark K. A429
Mason, Craig A A436
Mason, Andrew A466
Mason, Craig A485
Mason, Margaret A491
Mason, Tiffany A527
Mason, Jenifer L A538
Mason, Jim A569
Mason, Simon A608
Mason, Charlie A742
Mason, Tyler A877
Mason, Linda A893
Mason, Tashara P325
Mason, Cheryl P375
Mason, Mariah Null P399
Mason, Michael Atwood P497
Mason, Jonathan P539
Mason, Edward P548
Mason, Robin P616
Mason, Sally P629
Mason, Ben E29
Mason, Jennifer E107
Mason, Robert E160
Mason, Michael E168
Mason, Mark K. E214
Mason, J. Thomas (Tom) E264
Mason, Thomas E264
Mason, J T E264
Masone, Cassie A752
Masrani, Bharat B. W396
Mass, Davey A853
Mass, Davey P612
Massa, Mark P608
Massanelli, Stephen C. A760
Massanelli, Stephen C. E374
Massarelli, John A121
Massarelli, John P206
Massaro, Mark A784

Massaro, Michelle P304
Massaro, Joseph R. W31
Massaro, George E75
Massaron, Paul E. P660
Massato, Louis E80
Masschelin, Paul J. W196
Masse, Paul A452
Massei-rosato, Maria A319
Massengill, Scott R A151
Massengill, Scott A417
Massengill, Matthew E. (Matt) A914
Masser, Keith E. A828
Masser, Keith E. P584
Massery, Joe A713
Massey, Edward A104
Massey, Ken P118
Massey, Andrea E346
Massheder, Alfred A333
MASSIAH, VICTOR W410
Massie, John P504
Massod, Rafeh A265
Masson, Mark A61
Masson, Lisa P118
Massos, William A147
Mast, Jorg A481
Mastandrea, James C. E441
Mastandrea, Christine J. E441
Masterman, Andrew V. A675
Masterman, Andrew V. P428
Masters, Wes A340
Masters, Laurie A491
Masters, Jeff P455
Masters, Wes E161
Masterson, David J. (Dave) A754
Masterson, David J. (Dave) P484
Mastiaux, Frank W151
Mastioni, Marcello P29
Mastrarrigo, Julie A701
Mastro, Thomas J A112
Mastrolia, Angelo A752
Mastromatteo, Marissa P242
Mastromihalis, Eleni A900
Masu, Kazuyuki W257
Masucci, Robert A E407
Masuko, Osamu W260
Masumoto, Kimie A562
Masumoto, Yasuo W227
Matacunas, Michael (Mike) A273
Matarangas, Dennis A929
Matarangas, Dennis E449
Matarese, Andrew A651
Matarese, Andrew E330
Matecko, Lee A921
Matecko, Lee P669
Mateo, Carmen P366
Mateo, Alan E427
Mater, Robert A1
Mater, Derek De La A232
Mater, Robert E1
Mater, Tonya E134
Matera, Fred J. A709
Matera, Fred J. E348
Mathai, John A484
Matheis, Lisa A383
Matheis, Lisa E186
Matheny, Allen A195
Matheny, Drue A267
Matheny, Jennifer E430
Mather, Lisa A218
Mather, Courtney A451
Mathern, Mary A686
Mathers, David W120
Mathes, Sorrell P80
Matheson, Monique S A599
Matheson, Kathryn A654
Matheson, Nathan A665
Matheson, Mark A704
Matheson, Les W333
Matheson, Nathan E334
Mathew, Soni P100
Mathew, Reji P341
Mathew, Santhosh E106
Mathews, Betsy A135
Mathews, Emily A137
Mathews, Rich A195

Mathews, Casey A520
Mathews, Mark A796
Mathews, Rick A935
Mathews, Melanie P312
Mathews, James E72
Mathews, David C. E386
Mathews, Mark E397
Mathias, Ann P114
Mathiesen, Danna A552
Mathiesen, Danna E276
Mathieson, Mark P153
Mathieu, Laura A167
Mathieu, Ronald P153
Mathieu, Cheryl P233
Mathieu, Catherine P671
Mathios, Alan D. P159
Mathis, Archard A329
Mathis, Larry L P334
Mathis, Patrick L. E304
Mathis, Ben E327
Mathison, Doug A891
Mathison, Lora P387
Mathur, Nikhil A135
Mathur, Ashwin A385
Mathur, Rohit A686
Matisak, Phil A756
Matkin, Richard P422
Matley, Robert P. A227
Matley, Robert P. E90
Matlock, Stephanie P245
Matos, Patricia A200
Matousek, James A444
Matovina, John M. A52
Matraki, Farid A562
Matre, Frances P615
Matros, Richard K. E362
Matschi, Helmut W117
Matschullat, Robert W. A896
Matson, Bruce A71
Matson, Shane A184
Matson, Kenneth J. (Ken) A389
Matson, Pamela A510
Matson, Andrea A677
Matson, Timothy (Tim) A714
Matson, Bruce P43
Matson, Angie P133
Matson, Pamela P290
Matsubara, Kazuhiro W107
Matsuda, Naoya E8
Matsui, Shunichi W257
Matsumoto, Toshiya A109
Matsumoto, Randy A109
Matsumoto, Pat A182
Matsumoto, Keith P230
Matsumoto, Yoshiyuki W186
Matsumoto, Yoshihisa W195
Matsumoto, Sachio W238
Matsumoto, Ryu W346
Matsumoto, Masayoshi W368
Matsumoto, Tamiji W379
Matsumura, Harumi W238
Matsumura, Hiroshi W360
Matsushima, Hidekazu W127
Matsushita, Isao W214
Matsushita, Masayuki W301
Matsuura, Masanori W107
Matsuura, Yohzoh W324
Matsuura, Hiroaki W376
Matsuzaki, Takashi W124
Matte, Vana A442
Mattea, Andrea A458
Mattelaer, Alex E122
Matteo, Steve A162
Matteo, Peter P544
Matteo, Steve E62
Matter, Donald (Chad) A872
Mattera, Vincent D. (Chuck) E224
Mattern, Paul A559
Matteson, Larry A444
Matteson, Timothy J. A504
Matteson, Timothy J. E251
Matthei, Brittany A862
Mattheus, Deven P383
Matthew, Byrd A58
Matthew, Janet A665

Matthew, Cooper P17
Matthew, Mussallem P332
Matthew, Janet E334
Matthews, Robert A224
Matthews, Dwayne E A253
Matthews, John A262
Matthews, Kade A340
Matthews, Terrence D. (Terry) A442
Matthews, Ryan A481
Matthews, Thomas A599
Matthews, Jeff A669
Matthews, Jason A850
Matthews, Marcia A859
Matthews, Douglas R. A873
Matthews, Charles R. A907
Matthews, Phil P162
Matthews, Jean P166
Matthews, Caz P179
Matthews, Clint P441
Matthews, David Clint P441
Matthews, Coke P559
Matthews, Ward P587
Matthews, Charles E106
Matthews, Kade E161
Matthews, Steven D. E201
Matthys, Carol A844
Matthys, Joan P22
Matti, Louis A356
Mattia, Tony P359
Mattiacci, John A. P546
Mattiace, Michelle P232
Mattice, Alicia A329
Mattics, Steven C. A602
Mattimore, Mary A596
Mattingly, Timothy P242
Mattingly, Paul P. P486
Mattke, Timothy A561
Mattke, Roger P284
Mattmiller, Michael P560
Matto, Andrew (Drew) Del E178
Mattox, Michael A60
Mattox, David A746
Mattox, Cheryl P233
Mattrisch, Dawn A727
Mattrisch, Dawn P453
Mattson, Courtney A576
Mattson, Steve A804
Mattson, Gayle P379
Mattson, Eric P485
Mattson, Glenn G E250
Mattsson, Michele P597
Matturri, Alexander J. (Alex) A738
Matty, Len P19
Matuga, Ed A784
Matulis, Marc P401
Matuschka, Nikolaus Graf von W6
Matuschka, Nikolaus Graf von W183
Matusic, Diane A784
Matviak, Ivan P783
Matytsyn, Alexander K. W309
Matz, R. Kevin A292
Matz, Glen A806
Matz, Jennifer A922
Matz, Jennifer P671
Matz, Glen E398
Mau, Jeanne A892
Mauch, Robert P. A63
Mauck, Jan P473
Maude, Brian P151
Mauer, Jennifer A554
Mauer, Craig A880
Mauer, Craig P640
Mauler, Michael K. (Mike) A371
Maulsby, Don P326
Maulucci, Jason P639
Maun, Marc C. A141
Maun, Marc C. E49
Maune, Sarah A715
Maune, Jennifer P255
Maurath, Keith P48
Maurel, Laurent W398
Maurer, John A359
Maurer, Mark A470
Maurer, Doug A763
Maurer, Marsha P79

COMBINED HOOVER'S HANDBOOK INDEX OF EXECUTIVES

A = AMERICAN BUSINESS
E = EMERGING COMPANIES
P = PRIVATE COMPANIES
W = WORLD BUSINESS

Maurer, Robert P519
Maurer, Monika W284
Maurer, Doug E377
Maurice, Jean R P296
Maurici, Vito A550
Maurici, Vito P319
Mauriello, Elaine A320
Maurin, Daniel A449
Maurin, Daniel E220
Maurits, Lycia A908
Maurits, Lycia E436
Maurno, Frank A704
Mauro, Cristina Di A114
Mauro, Cristina Di E37
Maury, Kent A538
Mauser, Jason P308
Mavengere, Shingai A877
Maviglia, Melanie A913
Maviglia, Melanie E438
Mavilla, Michael A482
Mavra, Joanne A135
Maw, Scott H. A779
Maxey, Dr Rick P244
Maxfield, Casey A246
Maxfield, Casey E105
Maxsiimc, David E440
Maxsimic, David D. E174
Maxson, Patricia (Trish) A481
Maxsted, Lindsay P. W424
Maxwell, Gary A. A273
Maxwell, David G. A396
Maxwell, Ken A478
Maxwell, Jai A559
Maxwell, Barbara A571
Maxwell, M. Craig A640
Maxwell, Terrance P. (Terry) A726
Maxwell, Jeff A859
Maxwell, Edwin P215
Maxwell, Bob P261
Maxwell, Crissette P364
Maxwell, Kevin P429
Maxwell, Terrance P. (Terry) P453
Maxwell, Beverly P486
Maxwell, Paul E349
May, Christopher J. (Chris) A49
May, Daniel A205
May, John C A260
May, Greg A262
May, Gregory A262
May, Ron A279
May, Phillip R. A296
May, Thomas J. (Tom) A303
May, Marty A412
May, Alan A420
May, Carmalynn A449
May, Karen J. A573
May, J. Phillip (Phill) A630
May, Philip A630
May, Jerry A. A711
May, Richard A756
May, Holly A780
May, Scott A884
May, Lee P161
May, Eric P168
May, Carol P330
May, Brandon P349
May, Nancy P383
May, Walter E P419
May, Jerry A. P444
May, Laurie P664
May, Sean E102
May, Carmalynn E221
May, Monroe E278
May-Stahl, Jeff P420
Mayberry, Michael C. (Mike) A460
Maybury, Mark T A778
Maycott, Cathy S P188
Mayer, Gregory A43
Mayer, Michael A118

Mayer, Jessica L. A169
Mayer, Kevin A A271
Mayer, Michael G. A334
Mayer, Dean A462
Mayer, Paul A583
Mayer, Sandra A688
Mayer, Paul A763
Mayer, Andy A909
Mayer, Michael P66
Mayer, Dean P256
Mayer, Jennifer P473
Mayer, Chris P531
Mayer, Laurel P579
Mayer, Josh E131
Mayer, Michael G. E153
Mayer, Max E326
Mayer, Paul E377
Mayer, Andy E436
Mayeron, John P174
Mayers, Philip A381
Mayes, Greg A807
Mayfield, Richard A901
Mayfield, Thomas P372
Mayhan, Jennifer P551
Mayhew, Nicola A119
Mayhew, William A281
Mayhew, Timothy P. (Tim) P97
Mayle, Steve A376
Maynard, Jim P42
Maynard, Monique W173
Mayne, Julia P22
Mayne, Tommy P572
Mayo, Marc A327
Mayo, Michael A. P63
Mayo, Stephen L. P107
Mayo, Michelle P190
Mayo, Nicole P625
Mayopoulos, Timothy J. (Tim) A312
Mayor, Randy E. A426
Mayor, Randy E. E213
Mayor-Mora, Enrique A171
Mays, Darrell A543
Mays, J A920
Mays, Ann P471
Mayse, Tracy P394
Maysent, Miya A647
Mayshura, Maria E154
Mazadoorian, Lynne P456
Mazany, Marcia A222
Mazarakis, S. James (Jim) A929
Mazarakis, S. James (Jim) E449
Mazeau, Jean-pierre A240
Mazelsky, Jay E223
Mazhar, Mir A126
Mazid, Rami A287
Mazile, Yolette A203
Mazman, Mark A704
Mazon, Travis A737
Mazon, Travis E361
Mazor, Lori A592
Mazor, Lori P370
Mazouch, Nick P340
Mazumdar, Arpita A390
Mazur-Hofsaess, Katarzyna A939
Mazurek, Jennifer A163
Mazurek, Julianne A179
Mazurek, Jennifer E62
Mazurova, Alexandra P459
Mazza, Julie A344
Mazza, Nancy A619
Mazza, Daniel A784
Mazza, Julie E165
Mazza, Nancy E310
Mazzali, Claudio A240
Mazzanti, Fernando A470
Mazzara, Phil P158
Mazzarella, Kathleen M. A396
Mazzeffi, Bob P1
Mazzei, Michael A503
Mazzei, Michael A887
Mazzei, Michael E249
Mazzeo, Anthony A163
Mazzeo, Anthony E62
Mazzocco, Gail P595

Mazzolin, Jacopo A935
Mba, Norah Larke A925
MBA, Susan Wack P300
MBA, Gretchen Long P338
Mba, Norah Larke E445
Mbah, Ndubuisi P494
Mbanda, Laurent P153
Mbazima, Norman B. W29
Mcabee, Beth A203
McAbee, Phillip A924
McAdam, Lowell C. A889
McAdams, Joseph E. A70
McAdams, Joseph Lloyd A70
McAdams, Mark P83
McAdams, Robin P246
Mcadoo, Andrew A629
McAfee, Travis A704
McAfee, Erick P189
McAfee, Cole P220
McAfee, Lawrence W. (Larry) E413
McAleenan, Donald F. A156
Mcalister, Kay A664
McAlister, Diane A476
Mcalister, Kay E334
McAllister, Kevin G. A140
McAllister, Gene A695
Mcallister, Margie A797
McAllister, Barbara A850
McAllister, Jeff A902
McAllister, Andrew P415
McAllister, Marilyn P448
Mcaloon, Tom A274
McAloon, Jane F. W69
Mcalorum, Tom A264
Mcalpine, Cheree A100
McAluey, Daniel P502
McAnally, David P262
McAnder, Michael P418
Mcandrew, Bill E151
McAndrews, James J. A319
Mcaneny, Joe A355
Mcardle, Billy A167
McArdle, Richard A232
McArthur, John A281
Mcarthur, Brendan A482
Mcarthur, Bill A506
McArthur, Tessa A654
McArthur, Kathryn P101
McArthur, Melvin E64
McArtor, Allan W17
McAskin, Dan A60
McAtee, David R. A89
McAuley, Malcolm P267
McAuliffe, Elizabeth A A800
McAuslan, Robert R. (Bob) A913
McAuslan, Robert R. (Bob) E438
McAvoy, John T. A234
McAvoy, John T. A235
McAvoy, Linda A816
McAvoy, John P397
McBeath, Mark A195
Mcbee, Jacquelyn P596
McBride, Martin A119
McBride, Mary E. A213
McBride, Margaret A266
Mcbride, William A305
McBride, R. Perley A366
McBride, Douglas A386
Mcbride, Bart A755
McBride, Dennis A867
McBride, Kate A879
Mcbride, Roger L P37
McBride, Mary E. P143
McBride, Margaret P182
McBride, Beverly J P330
McBride, Kathryn P331
McBride, Dwight A. P388
McBride, Renee P635
Mcbride, Jeff E106
Mcbride, Douglas E188
Mcbride, Bart E369
McBride, Kenneth (Ken) E385
McBride, Dennis E418
McBryan, Michael E. E203
Mcburnie, Karen A825

Mcburnie, Karen P568
McCabe, Brian A61
McCabe, Alan A246
McCabe, Pete A374
Mccabe, Scott A664
McCabe, Kari A722
McCabe, Brian K. A772
McCabe, Catherine A779
McCabe, Alan E105
McCabe, Owen E143
Mccabe, Scott E334
McCabe, Robert A. (Rob) E334
McCabe, Brian K. E382
Mccaddon, Joe A224
McCafferty, Donna A203
Mccaffery, John A150
Mccaffery, John E50
McCaffrey, Sean A193
Mccaffrey, Mary A608
McCaffrey, Dennis A934
McCaffrey, Maura C. P73
McCaffrey, Darrell P93
McCain, Tamara A718
Mccain, Bryan A800
McCain, Tamara E354
McCaleb, Robert A608
Mccall, Michael A176
McCall, Michael W. A404
Mccall, Jeff A512
Mccall, Gary A621
Mccall, Michael A704
McCall, Dennis P13
McCall, Anne E. P146
McCall, Brian P552
McCall, Bron E141
McCall, Michael W. E199
McCall, Tom E222
Mccall, Gary E311
McCallin, Nancy P525
McCallion, Anne D. A648
McCallion, Anne D. E328
McCallister, Michael B. A942
McCallister, Terry D. P253
McCallister, Terry D. P666
McCampbell, Dan A702
Mccance, Charles M P442
McCandless, Derek S. E98
McCane, Colleen A628
Mccann, Kimberly A86
Mccann, Megan A137
McCann, Andy A447
Mccann, Michael V A484
Mccann, Elle Donovan A882
McCann, Andy P247
McCann, Christine P330
McCann, Bart P595
McCann, James W223
Mccann, Kimberly E27
McCann, Adam E318
McCanna, Peter P388
McCarl, Mandy P329
McCarrell, Faye P485
Mccarrie, Michael A248
Mccarrie, Michael E107
Mccarroll, Charles A222
McCarroll, Lisa P360
McCarthy, Jim A25
McCarthy, Gloria M. A69
McCarthy, J. Kevin A111
McCarthy, Jeff A111
McCarthy, Marie A135
McCarthy, Christine M A271
McCarthy, Daniel J. A366
Mccarthy, Dan A366
McCarthy, Don A386
Mccarthy, Mike A536
McCarthy, Peter A744
Mccarthy, Chris A784
Mccarthy, Michael A784
Mccarthy, Susan A801
Mccarthy, Annie A863
McCarthy, Richard A885
Mccarthy, Vince A893
McCarthy, Terence A935
McCarthy, Jim P14

McCarthy, Dennis E P87
McCarthy, William J P87
McCarthy, Helen P87
McCarthy, Patsy P114
Mccarthy, Gene P261
McCarthy, John P306
McCarthy, Teresa P344
McCarthy, John P383
McCarthy, Don E188
Mccarthy, Tim E234
McCarthy, Vincent de P. E429
McCartney, David A13
McCartney, Megan A654
Mccartney, Joseph E203
McCartney, Bryan D. E203
McCartney, Daniel P. E203
Mccarty, Michael A222
McCarty, Craig A258
Mccarty, Jeremy A271
Mccarty, Melissa A325
Mccarty, Toni A325
McCarty, Mary A387
McCarty, Mollie A804
McCarty, Geoffrey E262
Mccaslin, Barbara A224
McCaughan, James P. (Jim) A677
McCaughey, Ryan A203
McCaules, Beth P476
McCauley, Cliff A246
Mccauley, Ryan A484
McCauley, Laurie A711
McCauley, Karen P55
McCauley, Laurie P444
McCauley, Cliff E105
McCauley, John W. E368
McCausland, Maureen P. A551
McCausland, Maureen P. P321
McCaw, Craig O. E326
McCellon-Allen, Venita A51
McChesney, Lee B. A778
McChrystal, William L A171
McClain, Ronald G. (Ron) A494
Mcclain, Ron A494
Mcclain, Wayne A520
Mcclain, Daniel A608
Mcclain, Lauren A692
Mcclain, Kenny A704
Mcclain, John A784
McClain, Paula D. P187
Mcclain, Collin E290
McClanahan, David P119
McClanahan, Marsha P139
McClanahan, David P195
McClary, Diane P120
McClaughlin, Don A198
Mccleary, Dennis A250
Mccleery, Sam A862
McClellan, Lisa A179
McClellan, John W. A228
McClellan, Stephen R. (Steve) A392
Mcclellan, Michelle A796
McClellan, Lawson A807
Mcclellan, Dennis P130
McClellan, Makana P585
Mcclellan, Michelle E397
McClelland, David A360
Mcclelland, Hal A678
McClelland, Norman P487
McClelland, Kent P487
McClenahan, Tom E272
Mcclendon, Lewis A855
Mcclendon, Rodney P114
McClendon, Steve P459
Mcclernon, Mike P308
McCleskey, Robert P548
McClimans, Jason A717
McClimans, Jason E351
McClimon, Patty P359
McClincy, Christopher J. A308
Mcclintic, Corinne A605
Mcclintock, William A74
Mcclintock, Dana A892
McClinton, Stephanie P624
Mccloskey, Shaun A799
McCloskey, Sharon P171

McCloskey, Brian E21
Mccloud, Ron A206
McCloud, Kimball W259
McCloy, Fiona P329
McClung, Linda P132
McClung, Barbara P392
McClung, Brett S. P550
McClung, Dylan E290
McClure, Kathy A240
McClure, Marc A809
Mcclure, Brent A847
Mcclure, Teri A871
McClure, Robert P226
McClure, Jackie P443
McClure, Andrea P505
McClure, Dave W5
Mcclure, Brent E410
McClurg, Tim A61
Mccolgan, Jack A320
McColl, John S. E100
McColley, Seth P281
Mccollough, W Alan A891
Mccollum, Thomas A83
Mccollum, Joanne E102
McComas, David P591
McComb, Scott G E204
McCombe, Mark S. A135
Mccombs, Laura A336
McCombs, Debra P330
McCombs, Gillian M. P505
Mccombs, Laura E157
Mccomish, Jeffrey E8
McComiskey, Mike P555
McConaghy, Daniel E144
Mcconie, Jay A348
Mcconie, Jay E169
Mcconkey, Linda A884
McConnell, Scott A3
McConnell, Kelly A222
Mcconnell, Tom A452
McConnell, Rob A458
McConnell, Sarah Hlavinka A933
McConnell, Donald P. P359
McConnell, John D P377
McConnell, John P. P395
McConnell, Aaron P556
Mcconnell, Jerry E123
McConvey, Katherine P281
McConville, Dan P356
McConville, Jim W306
McCool, James D. A746
McCord, Trey A247
Mccord, Ivy P454
McCord, Trey E105
Mccormac, Paul A107
McCormack, Jim A466
McCormack, Pamela A503
Mccormack, Nicole A540
McCormack, Pamela E249
Mccormick, Joseph A36
Mccormick, Phyllis A54
McCormick, Stanley A247
McCormick, Michael C. A289
Mccormick, Deborah A571
McCormick, Allen A626
Mccormick, Courtney A688
McCormick, Robert J. A851
Mccormick, Kelley A862
McCormick, Bob P175
Mccormick, Bob P443
McCormick, C. Clair P573
McCormick, Timothy P593
McCormick, Peter M. (Pete) E88
McCormick, Stanley E105
Mccormick, Tim E105
McCormick, Robert E114
McCormick, Dan E371
Mccorry, Tom A237
McCorvey, Ann P569
McCory, Alicia A713
McCourt, Angie A809
McCourt, MaryFrances P609
Mccowan, Bobbie A852
Mccoy, Merritt A31
Mccoy, John A120

Mccoy, Albert A150
McCoy, Miranda A193
Mccoy, Mike A434
Mccoy, Michael A452
Mccoy, Lyle A536
Mccoy, Gail A797
Mccoy, Merritt P20
McCoy, R. Craig P94
McCoy, Al P162
McCoy, Antoine P366
McCoy, Thomas A. (Tom) W208
Mccoy, Albert E50
McCoy, Dean A. E295
Mccoy-cosentino, Victoria M A592
Mccoy-cosentino, Victoria M P370
McCracken, Grant A188
Mccracken, Kathy A507
McCracken, Steven C. (Steve) E59
McCranie, Jdaniel E110
Mccrary, Rod A16
Mccrary, Wynetta A262
McCrea, Marshall S. (Mackie) A294
McCrea, Marshall S P297
Mccready, David A641
McCready, Phyllis P382
Mccready, David P407
McCreary, Lynn S. A352
McCreary, Ashley A383
McCreary, William P596
McCreary, Ashley E186
McCree, Donald H. (Don) A205
McCree, Jeanie P357
McCreedy, John P498
McCreedy, John P554
Mccreesh, Michael A391
MCCRINK, GERALD A320
McCrory, Martin P610
McCrossen, Ed A199
McCroy, Jeffrey A193
Mccubbins, John A554
Mccue, Betsy A552
McCue, Brian A574
Mccue, Betsy E276
McCuistion, Randy E177
Mccuiston, Chip A428
McCullen, Erin A108
McCuller, Aliesha P133
Mcculloch, Greg A798
McCulloch, Bryan P77
McCullough, Mark C. A51
McCullough, Gary A260
McCullough, Theodore J. (Ted) A382
McCullough, Howell D. (Mac) A444
McCullough, Bruce A. A533
Mccullough, Kevin A788
Mccullough, Gary A842
McCullough, John P11
McCullough, Michael P48
McCullough, Martha P252
Mccullough, Sandra P489
McCullough, Barbara P659
McCullough, A. J. W212
Mccullough, Kevin E389
Mccune, William P573
McCurdy, Michael W. A152
McCurdy, Chris A320
McCurdy, Alicia P353
McCurdy, Michael W. E52
Mccurley, Steve E168
Mccurrie, Brad A74
McCurry, Michael A556
McCurry, Michael P328
Mccusker, Paul A18
Mccusker, Susan A784
McCuskey, Kenneth D P173
McCutchen, Shane A749
McCutchen, Shane E367
McCutcheon, S. Craig A259
McCutcheon, Stewart H. A289
McDade, Bart P373
McDaniel, Thomas L A19
McDaniel, Cara A818
McDaniel, Marvin E. A931
McDaniel, Brad P182
McDaniel, Kris P209

McDaniel, Jenny P464
McDaniel, Michael P571
Mcdaniel, Traci P596
McDaniel, Anna P627
McDaniel, Ronald T. (Ron) E124
McDaniel, Chad A. E263
McDaniel, Cara E403
McDavid, William H. (Bill) A364
McDearis, Kevin E47
Mcdermitt, David A319
McDermott, Mark A175
McDermott, Samantha A449
McDermott, Michael P. A527
Mcdermott, Christopher A574
McDermott, Mike A657
Mcdermott, Mark P86
Mcdermott, John P544
McDermott, William R. (Bill) W340
McDermott, Samantha E220
McDevitt, Charles B. A397
Mcdevitt, Kelly A877
Mcdevitt, Ruth A929
McDevitt, Mike P559
McDevitt, Valerie P638
Mcdevitt, Ruth E449
McDonagh, Brian A726
McDonagh, Brian P453
McDonald, Mark A. A45
McDonald, John D. A45
Mcdonald, Bruce A215
McDonald, Andrew L. (Andy) A219
Mcdonald, Alisa A281
Mcdonald, John A305
Mcdonald, Paul A325
McDonald, Michael A333
Mcdonald, Thomas Michael A333
McDonald, David W. A351
McDonald, Peter A376
McDonald, Bryan D. A415
Mcdonald, Bobbi A441
Mcdonald, Patricia A A460
McDonald, Angus A523
McDonald, Scott A539
McDonald, Kevin A673
McDonald, Bobbie A797
Mcdonald, Jim A922
Mcdonald, Marc P2
Mcdonald, John P31
McDonald, David P280
McDonald, Thomas P360
McDonald, Meg P389
McDonald, Fredda P432
McDonald, Clarke P518
McDonald, Dr Susan P519
McDonald, Terri P541
McDonald, Thomas M. P576
McDonald, Ruth P665
Mcdonald, Jim P671
McDonald, Don W371
McDonald, Patrick R E65
McDonald, Andrew L. (Andy) E87
McDonald, Bryan D. E209
McDonald, Malcolm W. E211
McDonald, Robert E218
McDonald, Kevin E402
Mcdonel, Michele A329
Mcdonell, Jason A654
McDonie, Patrick J. (Pat) A803
Mcdonnel, Lisa A877
McDonnell, Joseph A461
McDonnell, Michael R. (Mike) A474
McDonnell, Nancy A484
Mcdonnell, Jeffrey A567
Mcdonnell, Edward A740
McDonnell, Robert F A894
Mcdonnell, John P337
McDonnell, John F. P600
McDonnell, Robert F P650
Mcdonnell, Jeffrey E283
McDonough, Thomas A90
Mcdonough, Erin A642
McDonough, Karissa A651
McDonough, Robert J. (Bob) A875
Mcdonough, Becky A879
Mcdonough, John A909

COMBINED HOOVER'S HANDBOOK INDEX OF EXECUTIVES

> A = AMERICAN BUSINESS
> E = EMERGING COMPANIES
> P = PRIVATE COMPANIES
> W = WORLD BUSINESS

McDonough, Michael P389
Mcdonough, Erin P407
Mcdonough, Bob P442
McDonough, Robert P442
McDonough, Kevin P531
McDonough, Rachele E147
McDonough, Karissa E329
Mcdonough, John E436
McDowell, Ronda M. A741
Mcdowell, Magnus Mcdowell Magnus A884
Mcdowell, John A902
McDowell, Donnie P105
McDowell, Robert E80
McDowell, Tammy E265
McDowell, Ronda M. E364
McDowell, Glenn E413
McDunn, David A520
McElaney, Mike P77
McElhinney, Paul A. A374
McElligott, Kathleen D. (Kathy) A549
McElmurry, Julie A600
Mcelroy, David A58
Mcelroy, Crystal A559
McElroy, Paul P264
Mcelroy, Janine P287
McElroy, Wayne P564
Mcelveen, Edward A329
McElwain, Brian A512
McElwee, Dave A296
McElya, James S P307
McElyea, Dawn P149
McEndy, Kathleen A. E379
McEniry, James A58
McEuen, Susie P446
McEvoy, Ashley A. A479
Mcevoy, Marian A545
McEvoy, John R. A693
Mcevoy, Marian P317
McEvoy, John R. E341
McEwan, Ross W333
McEwen, Kevin P309
McFadden, Robert A330
McFadden, Dennis A484
McFadden, David P424
Mcfadden, Patricia P546
McFadden, Robert E152
McFadyen, Kieron W92
McFall, Thomas G. (Tom) A615
McFall, Joanne P622
McFarlan, Susan A112
McFarland, Keith A329
McFarland, Joseph M. (Joe) A647
Mcfarland, Timothy P375
Mcfarlane, Allen A592
Mcfarlane, Allen P370
McFarlane, John W56
McFarlane, John W58
McFarlin, Diane H. P627
McFarling, Harry M. P418
McFatter, Dan P344
Mcferran, Virginia E114
McGann, Bill P57
Mcgarey, Jennifer A608
McGarry, Paul A218
McGarry, Michael H. A673
McGarry, Steven J. A763
McGarry, John F. (Jack) A882
Mcgarry, John E131
McGarry, Steven J. E377
Mcgarvey, Lisa A799
Mcgarvie, Blythe A768
McGary, Skip A843
Mcgary, John A843
McGaugh, Ray A855
McGaughey, Tyler P137
Mcgauran, Megan A526
McGaw, Steve A89
McGaw, Michael A522

McGeary, Roderick C P74
McGee, Orlando A68
McGee, Susan A224
McGee, George A451
McGee, Rick A465
McGee, Richard K. A668
McGee, Callery A702
McGee, Karen A718
McGee, Genemarie A754
McGee, Mike P70
McGee, George P249
McGee, Genemarie P484
Mcgee, Tracey P597
McGee, Karen E354
McGeean, TJ P104
McGeehan, Ann A819
McGeehan, Ann P549
Mcgeorge, Scott E374
Mcgeough, Paul A325
McGettrick, Mark F. A275
Mcghee, James E A229
McGhee, Craig P131
Mcgill, Dean A60
Mcgill, Tom A146
Mcgill, Scott A162
Mcgill, Terrance A299
Mcgill, Donald A329
McGill, Bradley A482
McGill, Daniel K. (Dan) A652
Mcgill, Scott E61
McGill, William H. E269
McGill, William Brett E269
McGill, Daniel K. (Dan) E331
Mcgillicuddy, Sherry A247
Mcgillicuddy, Sherry E105
Mcgillivray, Mark A35
Mcginley, Marilyn A226
McGinley, Paula A408
Mcginley, Marilyn P150
McGinn, John P499
McGinn, Meghan P516
McGinnis, Kelly A514
McGinnis, Kelly A516
McGinnis, John T A532
McGinnis, Tim A742
McGinnis, David A831
McGinnis, Jeffrey S. (Jeff) A872
Mcginnis, Sharon A P121
McGinnis, Kelly P293
McGinnis, David P601
Mcginty, Mark A598
McGinty, Daniel P26
McGivney, Mark C. A539
McGlenon, Andrew A884
Mcglinch, Thomas A877
McGlothin, Randy A704
Mcglynn, Pam A313
McGlynn, Patrick P147
Mcglynn, James E131
Mcglynn, Pam E144
McGoldrick, Margaret M. (Meg) P3
Mcgonigle, James E143
McGough, Thomas M. (Tom) A232
Mcgough, Marlon P579
Mcgough, Anna P627
McGough, W. Thomas (Tom) P643
Mcgovern, Shawn A160
McGovern, Lawrence D. A414
McGovern, Shawn A618
McGovern, Kevin P159
McGovern, Nancy P287
McGovern, Lawrence D. E208
Mcgowan, Patt A155
McGowan, David A337
McGowan, Chris A634
McGowan, Marion A. P573
McGowan, Tim P591
Mcgowan, Patt E54
McGowan, David E158
McGowen, Lonnie A756
McGranaghan, Anna P638
McGranahan, Devin B. A352
Mcgrath, Marlene M A3
McGrath, Helen A89
McGrath, Robert L. (Bob) A354

Mcgrath, Kelley A452
Mcgrath, Caroline A544
McGrath, Kathy A550
Mcgrath, Mark A599
Mcgrath, Elizabeth A641
McGrath, Ted A723
Mcgrath, Dennis A779
McGrath, Mike A835
Mcgrath, Elizabeth P407
McGraw, Deirdre D. A60
Mcgraw, Lisa A639
McGraw, E. Robinson (Robin) A717
McGraw, Donald F. (Don) A823
Mcgraw, Kari P308
McGraw, Lawrence E211
McGraw, E. Robinson (Robin) E351
McGraw, Donald F. (Don) E405
Mcgreevy, David A337
Mcgreevy, David E158
McGregor, Marcus A112
Mcgregor, Thomas A115
Mcgregor, Laura A162
McGregor, Gaylyn A224
McGregor, Sharon A620
McGregor, Robert P131
McGregor, George P503
McGregor, Amy P589
McGregor, A. Douglas W331
Mcgregor, Thomas E37
Mcgregor, Laura E61
McGrew, Michael A236
McGrew, Mary P625
Mcgrew, Aaron P642
McGrory, Ryan A861
McGuckin, Sean W53
McGuckin, John W276
McGuff, Greg A512
McGuffin, Colleen A170
McGuffin-Cawley, James P116
McGuigan, Gary A77
McGuigan, Charles C. (Charlie) A500
McGuigan, Peter S A657
McGuiness, Paula P519
Mcguinness, Bernard A215
McGuinness, Richard A740
Mcguinness, John E371
Mcguire, Chris A16
McGuire, Jim A89
McGuire, Michael A251
Mcguire, Shawn A259
McGuire, Mark A286
Mcguire, Toretha A574
Mcguire, David A641
McGuire, Jim A746
McGuire, Tom A799
Mcguire, David A922
McGuire, Mark P190
McGuire, Keith P263
McGuire, Anne L. P396
McGuire, Jeremy R. P540
Mcguire, David P671
McGuirk, Jim P18
McGunnigle, Michael P408
Mcguone, Peter A175
McGurk, Monica A855
McGurk, Kevin J P76
McGurn, David A369
McHaffie, Sherry A665
McHaffie, Sherry E334
McHale, Myles A530
McHale, Thomas A. (Tom) E5
McHann, Jane P198
Mchart, Jessica P242
Mchenry, Yvonne A871
McHenry, Andrea A252
Mchose, Chris P450
Mchugh, Jim A309
McHugh, Philip R. A329
Mchugh, Joe A654
Mchugh, Mark A704
Mchugh, Katrina P215
McHutchison, John G. A385
McIlrath, Chris P277
Mcilwain, Pinckney P124

Mcilwaine, John E429
McInerney, Thomas J. (Tom) A381
McInerney, Matt A728
McInerney, Ryan A895
McInerney, Patrick S. P499
Mcinnes, Andrew P314
Mcinnis, Karen A784
McInnis, Joanne A882
Mcintosh, Ellen A120
McIntosh, John L. A624
McIntosh, Stephen W325
McIntosh, Stephen W327
McIntyre, Bonnie A393
Mcintyre, Andrew A711
McIntyre, Daniel P229
Mcintyre, Andrew P444
McIntyre, Robert P626
Mciver, William A118
McIver, Don P436
Mciver, William E40
Mcjunkin, Stacey P551
McKague, Kirby P6
McKasson, Craig P428
McKay, Erik A222
Mckay, Gerald A224
McKay, John D. A242
Mckay, Jennifer A248
McKay, Scott J. A381
Mckay, David A418
McKay, John A560
McKay, Susan A716
McKay, Tim P87
McKay, John P336
McKay, Tim S. W85
McKay, David I. (Dave) W331
Mckay, Jennifer E107
McKay, Edward H. E370
McKeag, Bryan R. A413
McKeag, Bryan R. E205
McKeand, Kevin A89
Mckedy, Kelly E14
McKee, Lynn B. A75
Mckee, John A222
Mckee, Marie A281
Mckee, Austin A281
McKee, Daniel J A782
McKee, Gerard P19
McKee, Page W. P185
McKee, Tim P247
Mckee, Amy P405
McKee, Daniel J P526
McKee, Michael V. (Mike) P627
Mckee, Shelley E256
McKee, Marcy E316
McKee, Michael D. E347
Mckeeman, Carly E138
Mckeen, Brian A19
Mckeen, P Douglas A865
McKeever, Neal A842
Mckeever, Stephen W P395
McKelvy, Michael C. (Mike) A384
McKelvy, Michael C. (Mike) P217
McKemie, Karen A767
Mckenna, Michael A724
McKenna, Judith A901
McKenna, Margaret A. P79
McKenna, Trent P149
McKenna, James C P246
Mckenna, Michael P452
McKenna, Quinn L. P524
McKenna, Bertine P574
Mckenna, Pamela P576
McKenna, Frank J. W80
McKenna, Frank J. W396
McKenna, Trent T. E89
McKenney, Josh A345
McKenney, Richard P. (Rick) A882
McKenney, Thomas P. E150
McKenney, Josh E165
McKenney, Michael J. E243
Mckenney, Kaylin E260
McKenzie, Paul A133
Mckenzie, Laurel A664
McKenzie, Barbara A. (Barb) A677
McKenzie, A Kirk A782

COMBINED HOOVER'S HANDBOOK INDEX OF EXECUTIVES

McKenzie, A Kirk P525
McKenzie, Michelle P596
McKenzie, Jonathan W190
McKenzie, William G. E274
Mckenzie, Laurel E334
McKeon, Brian M. A145
Mckeon, Timothy A401
Mckeon, Michael A741
Mckeon, Bill A928
Mckeon, Whitney P632
Mckeon, Bill P674
McKeon, John S. (Jack) E201
McKeon, Brian P. E223
Mckeon, Michael E364
McKeough, Kathleen E A904
McKeown, Patrick A269
Mckeown, Bob A381
McKeown, Colleen A627
Mckeown, Brian A885
McKernan, John A146
Mckernan, Chris E156
McKey, N. Keith E121
McKibbin, Karen S. A602
Mckie, Michael P608
McKiernan, Anthony A546
McKillip, Dean A215
McKim, Anoopa A329
McKinley, Gordon A222
McKinley, David C. (Dave) A744
Mckinley, Chris P35
McKinley, Brian P246
McKinley, Amy P246
McKinley, Janet P572
Mckinley, Chuck E343
Mckinley, Patrick E349
Mckinney, Robert A51
McKinney, Greg A113
McKinney, David E A195
McKinney, James J. A489
Mckinney, Michelle A695
McKinney, Rex D. A755
McKinney, Ivy A933
Mckinney, Mark P310
McKinney, Marcus P464
McKinney, Lisa H P623
McKinney, Greg E36
Mckinney, Dina E110
McKinney, Rex D. E369
McKinnon, Paul A205
McKinnon, Lee A755
McKinnon, Lee E369
McKirahan, Rick A393
Mckissic, Edward A902
McKissick, Steven P280
McKittrick, Stacy P77
Mcknight, Gary A246
Mcknight, Erin A526
McKnight, Bob P93
Mcknight, Gary E105
Mckown, David A388
McKoy, Margot A142
McKoy, Margot E49
Mclain, Dean A804
McLamb, Michael H. (Mike) E269
McLamb, Carlie C. E368
McLane, Nancy E317
McLaren, Christopher A526
McLaren, David A595
Mclaren, Gregory E148
Mclaren, Greg E148
Mclarry, Mary A772
Mclarry, Mary E383
Mclauchlin, Chris A293
McLauchlin, Tracy A. E224
McLaughlin, Robert M. (Bob) A25
Mclaughlin, Walter A116
Mclaughlin, Joshua A151
McLaughlin, Robert A155
McLaughlin, Linda A155
Mclaughlin, Chris A167
McLaughlin, James A205
McLaughlin, Lynn A224
Mclaughlin, Carl A246
McLaughlin, R A330
Mclaughlin, Carl A364

Mclaughlin, Linda A393
McLaughlin, Edward (Ed) A544
McLaughlin, David W. A592
McLaughlin, Michael A668
Mclaughlin, Sean A686
McLaughlin, Randall A727
McLaughlin, John J. A732
McLaughlin, Neal A800
McLaughlin, Neal T. A860
McLaughlin, Kathleen A901
McLaughlin, Robert M. (Bob) P14
McLaughlin, Kevin P102
McLaughlin, Edward W. P159
McLaughlin, Ann P219
McLaughlin, Gary P344
McLaughlin, David W. P370
McLaughlin, Randall P453
Mclaughlin, Matt P632
Mclaughlin, Jay P667
McLaughlin, Michael W243
Mclaughlin, Walter E39
McLaughlin, Robert E54
McLaughlin, Linda E55
Mclaughlin, Carl E105
McLaughlin, Karle E131
McLaughlin, R E152
McLaughlin, Blake E290
McLaughlin, Sean E366
Mclean, Scott A180
McLean, James A704
McLean, Graham A. A789
Mclean, John A837
McLean, Scott J. A940
Mclean, William P72
McLean, Melvin P325
McLean, William H. (Will) P388
McLean, David W424
McLean, Tim E240
McLean, Emmett E. E274
Mclean-shinaman, Kieth P72
McLeland, Allan H. A768
McLellan, Heather A471
Mclelland, Alistair A21
McLelland, Dave A349
McLemore, Mary A651
Mclemore, Heidi A727
Mclemore, Heidi P453
McLemore, Mary E330
Mclenaghan, Sheila P415
Mclennan, Kevin A176
McLennan, Michael A758
McLennan, Michael E372
McLeod, David G. A397
Mcleod, David A647
Mcleod, Ian E2
McLeod, Scot M. E343
Mcloughlin, Karen A130
McLoughlin, Karen A216
Mcmachen, Timothy E330
Mcmahan, Jessica P430
McMahon, Robert W A22
McMahon, John A81
McMahon, Michael A654
McMahon, Brian A657
Mcmahon, Terry A704
Mcmahon, David A882
McMahon, Molly A884
McMahon, Don P195
Mcmahon, Heidi Kahly P215
McMahon, Renee E102
Mcmahon, James E102
McMahon, Daniel K. E200
McMahon, John E210
McMahon, William B. E299
McMahon, Vincent K. (Vince) E448
McMahon, Stephanie E448
McManus, John M. A562
McManus, Paul A850
McManus, Gary P25
McManus, Brian M P112
McManus, Fallon Strother P284
Mcmanus, Jim P352
McManus, Corin P440
Mcmartin, Bill A452
Mcmaster, Debbie A418

Mcmaster, Kevin A837
McMasters, Michael P. (Mike) E78
McMichael, Sharon A850
Mcmillan, Putnam A376
McMillan, Darren A452
McMillan, Marilyn A. A592
Mcmillan, Rob A793
McMillan, Lee P1
McMillan, Michael P234
McMillan, Marilyn A. P370
McMillan, James P585
Mcmillan, Brittany P637
Mcmillen, Ruth Ann A922
McMillen, Steve P607
Mcmillen, Ruth Ann P671
McMillin, Nicole P233
McMillon, C. Douglas (Doug) A901
McMinimee, Dan P265
McMinn, Adam P506
McMorrow, William J. E245
Mcmullan, Hank A840
McMullen, Michael R A22
McMullen, W. Rodney A498
Mcmullen, Sandy A891
Mcmullen, Elizabeth P171
McMullen, Michael J P529
Mcmurray, Darin A512
McMurray, Michael C. A635
McMurray, Sean A911
McMurray, Sean E437
Mcmurry, Fred A334
Mcmurry, Fred E153
McMurtrie, M Todd A380
McMurtry, Nancey M A470
McNab, Paul A198
McNab, Sarah P281
McNabb, Forrest P83
McNac, Loretta P558
McNair, Sherri P396
Mcnally, Rael A135
Mcnally, Sean A170
Mcnally, Maureen A349
Mcnally, David A740
Mcnally, Brennan A877
McNally, Brian P. W323
McNamara, Stephen A89
McNamara, Jim A329
McNamara, Daniel R. (Dan) A460
Mcnamara, Michael A545
McNamara, Michael E. (Mike) A804
McNamara, Patrick P155
McNamara, Ed P428
McNamara, Julia M. P676
McNamara, Kyle W53
McNamara, Michael M. (Mike) W164
McNamara, Kevin E261
McNamee, Brian M. A64
McNamee, Sean A323
Mcnamee, Sean S A323
McNamee, Mark G. P652
McNamee, Paul W106
McNary, Kelli A835
McNaughton, Jarrod P277
Mcneal, Scott A816
McNeal, Gwyn E141
Mcnealis, Anne A485
Mcnealis, Anne P271
Mcnearney, Ryan A470
Mcneil, Kurt A378
McNeil, Michelle A651
McNeil, Caroline A782
McNeil, Caroline P525
McNeil, Michelle E329
Mcneill, Jenna A686
Mcneill, Bryan A891
McNeill, Dan E368
McNeme, Lisa A925
McNeme, Lisa E445
Mcnichols, William A779
McNichols, Bill A780
McNichols, Robin P258
McNiff, Greg A30
McNiff, Mike A267
McNiff, Greg P20
Mcnorton, Terri P94

McNulty, Kelly A69
McNulty, Dave A508
McNulty, Tim P114
Mcnulty, Dave E349
Mcnutt, Robert P604
Mcpadden, Laura A596
McParland, Jeffrey J. (Jeff) A803
Mcpartland, Gerry A115
McPartland, James E. (Bo) A389
Mcpartland, Gerry E37
McPeak, Blaine E. P668
McPeek, Brian P579
Mcphail, Kennth A200
McPhaill, Kevin J. A758
McPhaill, Kevin J. E372
McPhedran, James W53
McPhee, Debra M. P206
Mcphee, Joseph R P573
McPhee, Mark S. P607
McPherson, Robert A126
Mcpherson, Julie A145
McPherson, Scott E. A239
Mcpherson, Kevin J A323
Mcpherson, Kevin A324
McPherson, Amy C. A537
McPherson, Heather A799
McPherson, Cora P344
McPherson, Edward P615
McPherson, Amy E268
McPherson, Kevin E270
Mcphillimy, Betty P389
McQuade, Daniel P. A16
Mcquail, Elizabeth P364
McQuay, Timothy C. E394
McQueen, Jason A105
McQueen, Todd P589
McQueen, Jason E34
Mcqueen, Rob E35
Mcqueeney, David A465
McQuillan, Barbara (Barb) P508
McQuillan, Kevin E291
McQuitty, Blanche P129
McRae, Lawrence D. (Larry) A240
McRae, Mark P469
McRaith, William (Bill) A692
McReynolds, John W. A294
Mcreynolds, Michele A859
McRobbie, Michael A. P609
McRobbie, Ian M. E229
McRoberts, Michael J. A733
McRoy, Lynn P405
McRuy, T J P157
McShane, Jamie A445
McShane, Joseph M. P206
McShane, Ryan P415
McSharry, Joe A232
McShea, Sean F. W371
McSheffrey, Aidan P468
Mcsteen, Harry A335
Mcsteen, Harry E155
Mcswain, Kathryn A117
McSwain, Chris A902
Mcswain, Kathryn P61
Mcswiggan, Anne A461
McSzkowski, Marie E268
Mctaggart, Jim E102
McTague, Teresa Q. A19
Mctavish, Julia A609
McTeer, Brandon P655
McTernan, Bernita A266
McTernan, Bernita P181
McTier, Charles H A513
McTiernan, James A112
McTpavish, Julie A609
McVarish, Judith P517
Mcvay, John A216
Mcveety, Tania A465
Mcveigh, Richard A700
McVeigh, Scott A756
Mcvey, Adam A86
McVey, Mary Jo P215
Mcvey, Adam E27
McVey, Richard M. (Rick) E270
Mcvicker, Melissa A511
Mcvicker, Nathan A909

COMBINED HOOVER'S HANDBOOK INDEX OF EXECUTIVES

```
A = AMERICAN BUSINESS
E = EMERGING COMPANIES
P = PRIVATE COMPANIES
W = WORLD BUSINESS
```

Mcvicker, Melissa P290
Mcvicker, Nathan E436
Mcvinnie, David A414
Mcvinnie, David P236
McWane, Paul A726
McWane, Paul P453
McWatters, Denise C. A425
McWay, Jacob P291
McWay, Michael J. P318
McWhan, Casey D. W85
McWherter, Ron A175
McWhinney, Deborah A355
McWhinney, Robert A476
McWhorter, Haden P428
McWilliams, Jelena A329
Md, Chimeremma A554
Md, R Nicholas Nace A642
Md, R Nicholas Nace P407
Meabon, David P596
Meabon, Jared E80
Meacham, Allen A149
Meacham, Jacky P549
Mead, John A60
Mead, James A135
Mead, David L. A652
Mead, Betsy P519
Mead, David L. E331
Meade, Michael A561
Meade, Kevin E16
Meadinger, Chad P97
Meador, David E. (Dave) A279
Meadows, Mark A10
Meadows, Angela A107
Meadows, Karen C A165
Meadows, Ida A240
Meadows, Perry A371
Meadows, Hugh A859
Meadows, Darryl A867
Meadows, William W. (Bill) P171
Meadows, Perry P213
Meadows, Rick W87
Meadows, Darryl E418
Meahl, Pierre A882
Meakins, Ian W161
Meakins, Ian K. W323
Means, Patrick A746
Means, William L. E116
Meany, Kathleen P336
Meany, Gavin P P587
Mears, Jim A577
Measel, Kevin A527
Mebust, Kimberly P352
Mecca, Ray P280
Mechaley, Robert G. E326
Mecham, Nathan A893
Mecke, Stephen C. E385
Meckes, Scott A115
Meckes, Scott E38
Mecklenburg, Sue A779
Mecklenburg, John R P537
Medaglia, Anthony J E85
Medairy, Brad A145
Medcalf, Brad A665
Medcalf, Brad E334
Medeiros, Richard A170
Medeiros, Sheryl A205
Medellin, Angie P548
Meden, Scott A. A602
Medendorp, Marcia A724
Medendorp, Marcia P452
Medenis, Jim A89
Medford, Beth A25
Medford, Jeffrey S. A567
Medford, Beth P14
Medford, Jeffrey S. E283
Medhat, Ola A877
Mediavilla, Mark A176
Medina, Anthony A326
Medina, Mark A940

Medina, Erlinda P332
Medouris, Deanne A251
Medovic, Tom A908
Medovic, Tom E436
Medrano, Randolph A112
Medrano, Evelyn P511
Medvedev, Alexander I. W308
Medvinsky, Anna A540
Medvinsky, Michael E143
Medwedeff, Rick A538
Mee, David G. A442
Mee, Laurie A695
Meegan, John A609
Meehan, Terry A248
Meehan, Joe A672
Meehan, Susan A893
Meehan, Terry E107
Meehan, Terry E272
Meek, Julie P271
Meek-Wohl, Leslie A544
Meeker, Anthony E40
Meeks, Charles C. (Chuck) E244
Meeks, Chuck E244
Meenan, Dan E370
Meermans, Mike P493
Meers, Trey A925
Meers, Trey E445
Mees, Matthew A83
Mees, Greg A315
Meester, Simon A816
Megalou, Christos John W307
Megan, Reichert A320
Megargee, Scott R. A823
Megargee, Scott R. E405
Megdal, Maria P172
Meggs, Scott E10
Megowan, Tammy A734
Meh, Césaire W50
Mehigan, John E349
Mehler, Phillip S. P179
Mehmood, Bilal E243
Mehnert, Dana A. A501
Meholic, Anthony A823
Meholic, Anthony E405
Mehra, Jyoti A385
Mehra, Asit A626
Mehra, Pankaj A914
Mehran, Alexander R. (Alex) A321
Mehrer, Edward W. (Ed) E307
Mehrle, David A444
Mehrotra, Louise A479
Mehrotra, Sanjay A565
Mehrtens, Anne E219
Mehta, Sachin A61
Mehta, Rajeev (Raj) A216
Mehta, Manan A606
Mehta, Sanjay A695
Mehta, Apurva P157
Mehta, Shreeketa M P433
Mehta, Tarak W3
Mehus, Denise A332
Meidt, Greg A806
Meidt, Greg E398
Meier, Jayme K A309
Meier, Richard A. (Randy) A634
Meier, Niklaus P322
Meier, J O P506
Meier, Jessica E156
Meighan, Shelly A677
Meighan, Dori P182
Meignié, Yves W415
Meijers, Neville A694
Meikke, Scott A505
Meikle, Scott A505
Meikle, Garon A856
Meikle, Garon P614
Meiklejohn, Mark J. A152
Meiklejohn, Mark J. E52
Meilinger, Greg A635
Meiller, Kari A804
Meinert, Beth P578
Meinhardt, Erika A325
Meininger, Gary A480
Meintjes, Charles F. A645
Meis, Daren E96

Meisel, David A696
Meisel, Bruce P580
Meisenbach, John A242
Meiskey, Michael A823
Meiskey, Michael E405
Meisner, Laurie P544
Meissner, Jeffrey E429
Meister, George A502
Meister, Doris P. A530
Meister, Richard P175
Meister, Rudi von W433
Meister, Adam E218
Meitus, Christina A740
Meitz, Ann A3
Meixner, Willi W353
Meiyun, Zhou W354
Mejdell, Dag W289
Mejia, Maria F. A487
Mejia, Gerald P538
Mejzak, Richard A575
Mekler, Mark K A704
Melander, Dave A61
Melander, Paul A324
Melandri, Claudio W45
Melanson, Nancy P72
Melaragno, Mark A491
Melazzini, Jorge P605
Melchior, Eric L P213
Melchisedech, Beverley A180
Melendreras, Ed A296
Meletiou, Andreas W364
Melfi, Mitch H. A226
Melfi, Joe A692
Melfi, Mitch H. P150
Melia, Mark P117
Melillo, Nick P6
Melin, Wendy E72
Meline, David W. A64
Mella, Chas A247
Mella, Joe A391
Mella, Chas E105
Mellado, Santiago P153
Mellander, Carl W386
Melleky, Neil A559
Mellen, Eric E. E183
Meller, Craig W27
Mellert, Doug A575
Mellet, Matt A869
Mellette, Fran A891
Melletz, Steven A337
Melletz, Steven E158
Mellevold, Gene A893
Melley, Elizabeth A647
Mellinger, Roy A69
Melloh, Heather A60
Melmed, Shlomo P118
Meloche, Brandon A711
Meloche, Brandon P444
Melotte, Hans A779
Meloy, Mattthew J. (Matt) A803
Meloy, Mark J. E156
Melrose, Bob W270
Melroy-tucson, Brenda A325
Melsen, Gregory J. (Greg) E45
Melson, Benjamin (Ben) P548
Melton, Stephen A. A62
Melton, Farryn A151
Melton, Steve A A189
Melton, Gaylon A761
Melton, Stephen A. E20
Melton, Jeanette E318
Meltzer, Larry A692
Meltzer, Neil P494
Meltzer, Jamie P569
Melville, Greg A713
Melville, Traci A813
Melville, Jim P28
Melvin, Vincent P. (Vin) A81
Melvin, Gary A346
Melvin, Gary E166
Melzer, Heather A727
Melzer, Heather P453
Memio-ºlu, Erol W222
Memis, Adnan W403
Menard, Mark A402

Menard, Satya-Christophe W358
Menard, Peter E113
Menard, Mark E198
Menchaca, Tara A246
Menchaca, Tara E105
Mendelsohn, Karen R. A569
Mendelsohn, D. Eric E296
Mendelson, Richard P486
Mendelson, Victor H. E206
Mendelson, Eric A. E206
Mendelson, Laurans A. E206
Mendelson, Holly E268
Mendenhall, Tom A701
Mendenhall, Amy A859
Mendes, Roberto A833
Mendes, Rhys R. W50
Mendesh, John A376
Mendez, Roberto D. (Bobby) A289
Mendez, Greg A449
Mendez, Carlos A559
Mendez, Martiza A670
Mendez, Jaime P211
Mendez, Alex P351
Mendez, Lincoln S P501
Mendez, Greg E220
Mendicino, Thomas P304
Mendieta, Adrian A329
Mendillo, Jane L P229
Mendiola, Jeff A628
Mendis, Nancy A835
Mendis, Paul P27
Mendis, Chandika E431
Mendoza, Joseph P12
Mendoza, Lucio P102
Mendoza, Leticia P182
Mendoza, Carlos P220
Mendoza, Annie P398
Mendoza, Frank P537
Mendoza, Kimberly E131
Mendoza, Luis E132
Menear, Craig A. A427
Meneilly, Kim A616
Menelly, Denise M. A200
Menendez, Oscar A200
Menezes, Ivan A801
Menezes, Ivan M. W140
Meng, Francis L Boon A927
Meng, Amanda P650
Mengebier, David G. A209
Menges, Kathrin W181
Menichillo, Brenda A126
Menichini, Ralph A245
Menken, Dennis A677
Menna, John A870
Menne, Simone W136
Mennella, Stephen E132
Menneto, Steven D. A669
Menning, Jeremy A444
Menon, Anil A198
Menon, Geeta A592
Menon, Viju A890
Menon, Akash K P116
Menon, Geeta P370
Mensah, Paul A657
Mensch, Denna A795
Mensching, Charlie A89
Mense, D. Craig A210
Mense, D Craig A526
Menshouse, Georgene P465
Mensing, Stan J A381
Mentis, Angela W270
Mento, Andrew A574
Mentzer, W Eric A461
Mentzer, Kevin P587
Menza, Diane A606
Menzel, Susan L. (Sue) A212
Menzel, Jason A452
Menzel, David B. (Dave) E123
Menziuso, Angela Menziuso A731
Meo, Francesco De W167
Merahn, Steven A179
Mercadel, Demetric A296
Mercado, Kenneth M. A180
Mercado, Anna A463
Mercado, Rosie P486

Mercer, Megan A859
Mercer, Karen P2
Mercer, Dale P25
Mercer, John E123
Merchant, Manisha K. A104
Merchant, Fazal A736
Merchant, Linda P199
Merchant, Fazal P460
Merchant, Rahul N. E144
Mercier, Dianne M. A651
Mercier, Lynn P49
Mercier, Andrew B. (Andy) P576
Mercier, Bruno R. W370
Mercier, Dianne M. E329
Mercolini, James P114
Mercuri, Denise A722
Mercuri, Joe P587
Merdian, Charles E255
Meredith, Ian A149
Meredith, Bobbie A855
Meredith, Michael A859
Meredith, Michael P52
Meredith, Christopher P168
Meredith, Myra P660
Mereness, Scott T. E252
Mergelmeyer, Gene E. A88
Mergenthaler, Frank A468
Mergin, Murat W403
Mergy, John P182
Mericle, Lisa A866
Mericle, Lisa E417
Meriweather, Judie A727
Meriweather, Judie P453
Merk, Thomas E86
Merkadeau, Stuart L. E177
Merkel, Greg P309
Merkel, Frederick P618
Merkel, B.G. W196
Merkens, Hermann J. W2
Merkle, Thomas A329
Merkle, Claudia J. E304
Merkley, David P271
Merkley, Brendon P547
Merkt, Jill A449
Merkt, Debbie P129
Merkt, Jill E221
Merle, Denise M. A918
Merli, Jennifer A544
Merlin, Mike A507
Merline, John P211
Merlino, John A512
Merlis, Larry P603
Merlo, Matt A179
Merlo, Larry J. A251
Merlo, Marie P443
Merrell, Keaton E433
Merrifield, Timothy D. E119
Merrill, Walter A419
Merrill, Allen A481
Merrill, Mark A505
Merrill, Jack A887
Merrill, Rick W P157
Merrill, Mike P161
Merrill, Matt P212
Merrill, Mark H P671
Merriman, Tom A569
Merritt, Necole A296
Merritt, Tanya A772
Merritt, Tom A773
Merritt, Tim A934
Merritt, Norman A940
Merritt, Jill P168
Merritt, Edee P578
Merritt, Tanya E383
Merritt-Epps, Gina E379
Merriwether, John P30
Merry, Shaun A450
Mersky, Seth M. W296
Merten, Jess A36
Merten, Joseph (J.) A210
Merten, Joseph A526
Mertens, George A253
Mertens, George P169
Mertens, Blake A. P566
Mertz, Valerie A29

Mertz, Valerie P16
Merwald, Bernard A706
Merwe, Martin Van Der A236
Mesa, Susan P262
Mesaros, Cindy E450
Meserole, Richard C A355
Meshechek, Gene A135
Meshgin-poosh, Mitra A738
Mesker, Michael P270
Meskiewicz, Paul A112
Mesko, David A197
Mesko, Justin A349
Mesquita, Jorge S. A479
Messa, Laura E392
Message, Tippin P192
Messare, Petros A590
Messenberg, Michelle A804
Messer, Angela M. (Angie) A145
Messer, Rick P471
Messer, Raymond E388
Messerich, John P589
Messersmith, Karen P165
Messina, Debbie A589
Messina, John A740
Messina, Laura P54
Messina, Elizabeth A. P90
Messina, Carlo W202
Messinger, Scott A506
Messler, Tom A103
Messmacher, Alejandro A59
Messman, Cathy P659
Messmann, Boyd A775
Messmann, Boyd P511
Messmer, Harold M. A725
Mester, Loretta J. A322
Mestrallet, Gérard W154
Mestrallet, Gérard W366
Mestre, Eduardo A98
Mestrio, Karen De E345
Mesuda, Ken A198
Metayer, Sylvia W358
Metcalf, Sue A289
Metcalf, Rob A518
Metcalf, Kim A893
Metcalf, Michael P410
Metcalfe, Stacey A258
Metcalfe, Tom A907
Metcalfe, Bonnie A922
Metcalfe, Bonnie P671
Meter, Rex Van P254
Metheny, Mike A158
Methvin, Stephen P96
Metoyer, Grady A798
Metre, Chris Van P5
Metrose, Laurie A893
Metselaar, Gerard A744
Metsger, Gary E. A760
Metsger, Gary E. E374
Metsker, Ron P432
Mettel, Kenneth A872
Mettler, Dan A452
Mettling, Bruno W297
Metz, Randy A367
Metz, Karen A565
Metz, Gunnar W64
Metzger, Christina A36
Metzger, John A112
Metzger, William L. A154
Metzger, Len A224
Metzger, Thomas M. (Tom) A581
Metzger, Doug A877
Metzger, Ralph P5
Metzger, Marianne P515
Metzger, Karen P621
Metzger, Carol P625
Metzger, Thomas M. (Tom) E294
Metzler, Thomas A559
Metzler, Mary A668
Metzler, Mike A810
Metzler, Mike P546
Metzner, Brian A107
Meulder, Jan De W43
Meunier, Tom E433
Meurer, Paul M. E347
Meury, William (Bill) W23

Meuth, Jane P504
Meves, Scott C. A906
Meves, Scott C. E435
Mewhertre, Miles A264
Mewkalo, Dave A205
Mexia, Ant- - nio Lu- s Guerra
  Nunes W145
Meyaard, Daniel E223
Meyer, Janis A133
Meyer, Eric A137
Meyer, Ralph A150
Meyer, David A253
Meyer, Tim A347
Meyer, William A355
Meyer, Michele S. A376
Meyer, David A396
Meyer, Bill A405
Meyer, Steve A448
Meyer, Jonathan A577
Meyer, Dan A723
Meyer, James E. (Jim) A762
Meyer, Jeffrey A893
Meyer, Kenneth (Ken) A921
Meyer, Kenny A921
Meyer, Peggy A927
Meyer, Cal P10
Meyer, Pam P73
Meyer, Lynn P81
Meyer, Dave P145
Meyer, Caitlyn P153
Meyer, David P169
Meyer, Mark P219
Meyer, Steve P247
Meyer, Erin P359
Meyer, Robert L. P417
Meyer, Lisa P566
Meyer, Sarah P640
Meyer, Kenneth (Ken) P669
Meyer, Kenny P669
Meyer, Ralph E50
Meyer, George E57
Meyer, Ryan E106
Meyer, Bryan E136
Meyer, Tim E167
Meyer, Edward E356
Meyer, Maurice E403
Meyer-Davis, Pamela P192
Meyercord, F. Duffield (Duff) A646
Meyercord, F. Duffield (Duff) E324
Meyerrose, Sarah L A362
Meyers, Kevin A419
Meyers, Lynn A824
Meyers, Tony W P37
Meyers, Dorothea P332
Meyers, Sydne P420
Meyers, Jay P456
Meyers, Lynn P562
Meyers, Kimberly P626
Meynard, Craig A262
Meyrowitz, Carol M. A836
Meza, Chantel A765
Mezeul, Patricia A356
Mffiorilli, Matt A125
Mhatre, Nitin J. A906
Mhatre, Nitin J. E434
Mialaret, David A167
Miale, Mark A776
Miano, John A170
Miano, Steve A461
Miano, Jonathan P182
Miano, Steve P255
Mical, Isabelle A243
Micali, James A768
Micali, Enzo A835
Micciche, Peter A203
Micciche, Gaetano W202
Micco, Robin P394
Miceli, Charles P598
Miceli, Samuel E. E149
Michaan, Edmond W54
Michael, Margulis A61
Michael, Puddy A250
Michael, Mcgowan A332
Michael, Kate A711

Michael, Jonathan E. A723
Michael, Rocco A824
Michael, Ryan A850
Michael, Gary A888
Michael, Rubell P12
Michael, Amanya P257
Michael, Lorri P276
Michael, Kate P444
Michael, Rocco P562
Michael, Gary E425
Michaelis, Brian L. P486
Michaels, Charles A391
Michaels, Rich A605
Michalak, Michael H. A221
Michalek, Edward A227
Michalek, Jane A388
Michalek, Kevin P32
Michalek, Edward E90
Michales, Kevin A692
Michaleski, Katie A719
Michaleski, Katie E355
Michalopoulos, Georgios V. W25
Michalski, Rick A1
Michalski, Gail A15
Michalski, Gail P8
Michalski, Gene P670
Michalski, Rick E1
Michalsky, Bryan P274
Michas, Alexis P. A146
Michaud, Tracie A381
Michaud, Thomas B. (Tom) A787
Michaud, Jill P49
Michaud, Peter L. P499
Micheal, Jonathan A723
Michel, Euclid P106
Michel, Susan P166
Michel, Nanette P206
Michel, Howard E. P572
Micheletti, Andrew A100
Micheletti, Andrew A101
Micheletti, Andrew P58
Micheletti, Andrew J. E32
Michelin, Lori A218
Michelle, Guevara E433
Michels, David A494
Michels, Greg A844
Michels, Becky P252
Michels, Hartwig W59
Michels, Douglas A. E317
Michelsen, Christina A109
Michelucci, Aaron J P72
Michitsch, Sharon A590
Michler, Matthew A656
Michler, Matthew P414
Michulka, Natalie P543
Mick, Kathy P308
Mickells, Adrienne P85
Mickey, Aileen P280
Micklewright, Scott E281
Mickus, Steven P330
Middendorf, Tom P568
Middlebrook, Sharlee P489
Middlebrooks, Dan C. A803
Middlebrooks, Guy E104
Middleton, Ana A80
Middleton, Charles A167
Middleton, Larry A433
Middleton, Ana P46
Middleton, Keith P606
Middleton, Mike P633
Middleton, Seth E204
Middleton, Larry E277
Midgley, Clare P556
Midkiff, Scott F. P652
Midler, Laurence H. A175
Midseim, Anne-Lene W289
Midteide, Thomas W140
Miebach, Michael A544
Miedema, Susan A325
Miedema, Andrew A552
Miedema, Andrew E276
Mielak, Gary P191
Mielak, Gary P192
Miels, Luke W38
Miels, Luke W171

COMBINED HOOVER'S HANDBOOK INDEX OF EXECUTIVES

A = AMERICAN BUSINESS
E = EMERGING COMPANIES
P = PRIVATE COMPANIES
W = WORLD BUSINESS

Mielsch, Christian W322
Miers, Mike A630
Mierzwinski, Chris P117
Migielicz, Christina A36
Miglani, Nalin E141
Migliazzo, Frank A574
Migliore, Michael A763
Migliore, Mike P35
Migliore, Michael E377
Migliori, Richard A876
Migliozzi, John A556
Migliozzi, John E277
Mignini, Luca A164
Mignone, Anthony A512
Migoya, Carlos A. P433
Miguel, Josu Jon Imaz San W321
Mihal, Denise P390
Mihaljcic, Jennifer A25
Mihaljcic, Jennifer P14
Mihopoulos, Peter A449
Mihopoulos, Peter E221
Mijango, Manuel A P404
Mika, Tom A409
Mika, Thomas A409
Mikalonis, Kevin P517
Mike, Wheeler A355
Mike, Biliouris A740
Mike, Ralph P81
Mike, Harrigan P408
Mike, Roche P597
Mike, Jovanis E427
Mikells, Kathryn A. W140
Miketa, George A846
Mikkelson, Keith E226
Mikkilineni, Krishna A431
Miklich, Charles A724
Miklich, Charles P452
Miko, John A797
Miko, Mark S P188
Mikolajczak, Bonnie A530
Mikoshiba, Toshiaki W186
Miks, Wai A686
Mikulich, Thomas A562
Mikuriya, Derek A833
Miladinovic, Ana A722
Milakovich, Paul P309
Milam, Steve W132
Milando, Anthony A936
Milano, Shelley A500
Milazzo, Joe P120
Milbourn, Linda P486
Milbrandt, Jean C. P578
Milburn, Mike A740
Milcoff, Joseph A323
Milcoff, Matthew P618
Mildner, Martin W299
Milella, James A111
Milem, Anne A763
Milem, Anne E377
Miles, Mark W. A129
Miles, Lisa A155
Miles, Shelley A872
Miles, Steven P24
Miles, Natalie P270
Miles, David J P279
Miles, David J P280
Miles, Amy E. P443
Miles, Andrew P638
Miles, Lisa E54
Miles, Larry K. E183
Miles, Patrick (Pat) E308
Mileto, Danny P202
Miletti, John A845
Miley, Kevin A784
Milford, Gregory A115
Milford, Gregory E37
Miliband, David P257
Milina, Tracy A58
Milks, Chadd P646

Mill, Jim A737
Mill, Jack De P437
Mill, Georgia P457
Mill, Jim E361
Millane, Martin B. A162
Millane, Martin B. E61
Millar, Jason P642
Millard, Chris A236
Millard, Robert B. P314
Millard, Jayne P613
Millard, Suzanne Turtle P613
Millburn, Tom E148
Miller, Michele A1
Miller, Brian A. A18
Miller, Virgil R A19
Miller, Chris A28
Miller, Robert G. (Bob) A30
Miller, Melisa A. A34
Miller, Steve A36
Miller, Matthew A60
Miller, Jason A60
Miller, Barbara A63
Miller, Rick A63
Miller, Steve A64
Miller, Erin A69
Miller, Dave A79
Miller, Elizabeth A82
Miller, Erin A89
Miller, Judy A89
Miller, Mary A91
Miller, Cheryl A94
Miller, MaryAnn G. A99
Miller, Maryann G A100
Miller, Craig A116
Miller, Guy A125
Miller, John A137
Miller, Grace A140
Miller, Bob A145
Miller, John A169
Miller, Sherry A170
Miller, Terrica A179
Miller, Joseph A182
Miller, Lisa A184
Miller, Todd A184
Miller, Diane A193
Miller, Steve A194
Miller, Thomas A209
Miller, Brad A213
Miller, Katie A215
Miller, Brian A222
Miller, Brent A224
Miller, Christopher M. (Chris) A239
Miller, Steve A240
Miller, Russ A242
Miller, Aaron A245
Miller, Kimberly A248
Miller, Ashlie A251
Miller, Jerome A262
Miller, Neal E A272
Miller, Sara A301
Miller, Evelyn A309
Miller, Charles S. A315
Miller, Donald J A323
Miller, Grant A325
Miller, Kevin A334
Miller, Kathy A339
Miller, David W. A343
Miller, Megan A347
Miller, Bob A360
Miller, Lynn A371
Miller, Jamie S. A374
Miller, Heidi A376
Miller, Joe A382
Miller, Jeffrey A. (Jeff) A401
Miller, Cindy A403
Miller, Archie A438
Miller, Suzan A460
Miller, Cliona A500
Millen, Ben A502
Miller, Stuart A. A512
Miller, Zach A527
Miller, Bruce A528
Miller, Detra A530
Miller, Linda A538
Miller, Lois A544

Miller, Patrick A562
Miller, Dwight A567
Miller, Klaus A574
Miller, Michael A596
Miller, David A613
Miller, Sara L. A621
Miller, Bob A649
Miller, Tracy A657
Miller, Kevin A663
Miller, Craig A676
Miller, Dara A702
Miller, Brian A704
Miller, Daniel A722
Miller, Tony A751
Miller, Lorraine A752
Miller, Josh A774
Miller, Dan A778
Miller, Adam A782
Miller, Amber A799
Miller, David A A800
Miller, Greg A812
Miller, Alan L. A818
Miller, Dane A842
Miller, Carl A844
Miller, James A855
Miller, Shane A855
Miller, Chip A855
Miller, Bradley J. (Brad) A866
Miller, Alan B. A878
Miller, Marc D. A879
Miller, Katherine M. (Kate) A882
Miller, Scott A884
Miller, Amanda A888
Miller, Terri A891
Miller, Steve A891
Miller, Julie A895
Miller, Nic A920
Miller, Al A922
Miller, Erin A922
Miller, Robert G. (Bob) P20
Miller, Sue P26
Miller, Mary P55
Miller, Amanda P58
Miller, Dale P58
Miller, Heather P94
Miller, Corie P94
Miller, Toni P95
Miller, James P101
Miller, Alex P128
Miller, Jonathan P153
Miller, David P175
Miller, Timothy (Tim) P182
Miller, Lynn P213
Miller, Lynn P214
Miller, Deborah P214
Miller, Clark P220
Miller, Dale P235
Miller, Edwin (Glen) P238
Miller, Deloris P242
Miller, Scott P245
Miller, Vickie P250
Miller, James P260
Miller, Diane P260
Miller, Victoria P301
Miller, Chris P309
Miller, Cathy P333
Miller, Allison P333
Miller, Rick P359
Miller, Glenn P371
Miller, Jeff P404
Miller, Patrick P429
Miller, Ronald P436
Miller, Tara P443
Miller, James P456
Miller, Alex P473
Miller, Janice P478
Miller, Tim P478
Miller, Jennifer P479
Miller, Peter C. P486
Miller, Scott P497
Miller, Rob P499
Miller, Barbara P502
Miller, Josh P510
Miller, Tim P514
Miller, Don P519

Miller, Jon P521
Miller, Adam P526
Miller, Kurt P540
Miller, Randy P552
Miller, Franklin C. (Frank) P557
Miller, Pamela P573
Miller, Ezra P588
Miller, Paula P588
Miller, Melissa P595
Miller, Mark P595
Miller, Matthew P596
Miller, Patrice P604
Miller, Martin P618
Miller, Kathleen P633
Miller, Richard P653
Miller, Gary P661
Miller, David P662
Miller, Debbie P670
Miller, Al P671
Miller, Erin P671
Miller, Jim P671
Miller, Klaus W178
Miller, Alexei B. W308
Miller, Michele E1
Miller, Scott E3
Miller, Todd E8
Miller, Craig E39
Miller, Catherine B. E43
Miller, Jason E57
Miller, Jeff E85
Miller, Jim E96
Miller, Bradley E102
Miller, Kimberly E107
Miller, Scott G E143
Miller, Kevin E153
Miller, Kathy E159
Miller, David W. E163
Miller, Megan E167
Miller, John E180
Miller, Michael T. E232
Miller, Todd E264
Miller, Tracy E272
Miller, Dwight E283
Miller, William G. E284
Miller, Kevin S. E287
Miller, Colin E290
Miller, Sara L. E311
Miller, Shannon E334
Miller, Craig E338
Miller, Kathy E349
Miller, David E375
Miller, Alan L. E403
Miller, Brian K. E412
Miller, Bradley J. (Brad) E417
Miller, Ronnie D. E418
Miller, Amanda E425
Millet, Richard A16
Millet, Tim A72
Millett, Mark D. A785
Millette, Steven P626
Milligan, Elaine A140
Milligan, John F. A385
Milligan, Cynthia A487
Milligan, Sandra A554
Milligan, David R. A911
Milligan, Stephen D. (Steve) A914
Milligan, Michael D P57
Milligan, David R. E437
Millikan, J. Scott P84
Milliken, Doug A207
Milliken, Joanna A740
Milliken, Bob P74
Milling, Bill E21
Millington, Manuela A835
Millis, Matt A940
Millman, Bert P105
Millner, Thomas A130
Millon, Jean-pierre A251
Millones, Peter J. A143
Mills, Martin A21
Mills, Amy A36
Mills, Jeff A58
Mills, Bruce A107
Mills, Linda A140
Mills, Ken A145

COMBINED HOOVER'S HANDBOOK INDEX OF EXECUTIVES

Mills, William J. (Bill) A203
Mills, Greg A299
Mills, Claire Kramer A320
Mills, Lucy A327
Mills, Gary R. A338
Mills, Steve A452
Mills, Ralph A576
Mills, Justin A651
Mills, Rob A704
Mills, Tracey A797
Mills, Robert D. A840
Mills, Soren A902
Mills, Curtis P112
Mills, Bryan A. P151
Mills, Chris P245
Mills, Sharrie P253
Mills, David C P254
Mills, Don P337
Mills, Angel P488
Mills, Ed P493
Mills, Jim P577
Mills, Mike E19
Mills, Gregory E267
Mills, Justin E330
Millsap, Mark A448
Millsap, Mark P247
Milne, Tim A804
Milne, Robb A P125
Milner, Mary A112
Milner, Trudie P678
Milone, Theresa A408
Milone-Nuzzo, Paula A828
Milone-Nuzzo, Paula P584
Milonovich, Steve A654
Milosevic, Milos A167
Milot, Marie-Claude P387
Milota, Stephen A925
Milota, Stephen E445
Milotich, Michael A896
Milowski, Nicholas P206
Milroy, James A806
Milroy, James E398
Milstead, Rob A380
Milstein, Jed A83
Milstein, Andrew A158
Milstein, Maxine P230
Milstein, Philip E268
Milton, Alex A165
Milton, David A A222
Milton, B. W. A309
Milton, Mark A. A485
Milton, Marisa A538
Milton, Robert A. A865
Mimicopoulos, Louise A702
Mims, Rod A90
Mims, Verett A140
Mims, Cynthia A845
Mims, Rod P51
Mims, Krystal P551
Min, Christina A460
Min, Kyung-Zoon W311
Mina, Jorge E290
Minaka, Masatsugu W124
Minaki, Kenji W430
Minami, Hikaru W249
Minana, Stephen A332
Minard, Timothy A677
Minardi, Christina A921
Minardi, Christina P669
Minarich, Jacob P362
Minato, Norihiko A474
Minaya, Yohan E138
Minda, Sherry A484
Mindak, Maxwell A489
Minehan, Cathy E. P574
Miner, Darryl A452
Miner, Tim A835
Miner, Brian A885
Miner, Jim P342
Miner, Todd E450
Mines, Michael A. (Mick) P396
Ming, Wong Wai W234
Ming, Tan Wing W299
Mingsheng, Yang W99
Mingzhe, Ma W306

Minhas, Faizan A575
Minich, Jeff A512
Minick, Russell S. (Russ) E184
Minicucci, Benito (Ben) A29
Minicucci, Robert A. A34
Mink, Susan W. A319
Minkel, Scott A. A867
Minnich, Brandt N. A555
Minniti, John P2
Mino, Warren K. A906
Mino, Warren K. E434
Minock, Cheri P607
Minogue, Michael R. E2
Minooka, Ann E110
Minor, Shay A340
Minor, Lloyd A510
Minor, Richard P189
Minor, Vicki P268
Minor, Lloyd P290
Minor, Tony P465
Minor, Timothy A P595
Minor, Shay E161
Minowitz, Robert (Bob) A744
Minsk, Helayna A900
Minter, Doris A296
Minter, Clarence P168
Minter, Gordon P245
Mintner, Christina P171
Mintz, Alan P300
Minutoli, Robert A831
Minutoli, Robert P601
Minzberg, Samuel (Sam) W187
Minzler, Dennis P359
Miosi, Sal A561
Mir, Ali T A140
Mirabelli, Jennifer A10
Mirabelli, Mary A420
Miracle, Dan P25
Miralles, Albert J. (Al) A210
Miralles, Diego A479
Miramontes, Darcy A481
Miranda, Manny A354
Miranda, Rich A744
Miranda, Richard A744
Miranda, Mark P94
Miranda, Milburn E123
Miree, David A906
Miree, David D. E434
Mireles, Oscar A352
Miritello, Suzanne P496
Mirock, Chad A409
Miron, Robert J. (Bob) A270
Miron, Mark A379
Mironichenko, Kristina A722
Mirville, Tatiana A137
Mirviss, Jeff A149
Misawa, Victor A593
Misawa, Naoshi P376
Misback, Ann A322
Mischner, Sam E254
Misencik, Peg A492
Mish, Jonathan A735
Mish, J. Vincent E284
Misheikis, Steve E131
Mishina, Craig P485
Mishoe, Scott M A735
Mishra, Paritosh A18
Mishra, Shantanu A520
Mishra, Ashish A780
Mishra, Rakesh A804
Mishra, Soumyadeep P286
Misiak, Dave A643
Misiaszek, Genevieve A128
Misich, Michael T A909
Misich, Michael A909
Misich, Michael T E436
Misich, Michael E436
Misiewicz, Jack A859
Misiewicz, John A859
Misita, Bill A660
Misita, Bill P416
Mislan, Tim P344
Misra, Sanjay P467
Missall, Melissa A219
Missall, Melissa E87

Missil, Kristin A606
Mistler, Thomas E. E225
Mistovich, Michael A909
Mistovich, Michael E436
Mistretta, Fred A201
Mistretta, John J. E47
Mistri, Alex A419
Mistry, Dinyar B. A659
Mistry, Nilesh A928
Mistry, Nilesh P674
Mistysyn, Allen J. A756
Misunas, Kathleen A809
Mita, Toshio W107
Mitacek, Don A262
Mitarotonda, Robert P503
Mitchal, Karen A75
Mitchel, Chris A189
Mitchell, Meredith A58
Mitchell, Steve A89
Mitchell, Anthony (Tony) A145
Mitchell, David A170
Mitchell, Robert W A171
Mitchell, Jeff A184
Mitchell, Lynne A228
Mitchell, Mary A262
Mitchell, Harvey A322
Mitchell, Michael A324
Mitchell, Duncan A327
Mitchell, D Bryant A358
Mitchell, Zabrina A366
Mitchell, R. Brian A389
Mitchell, Carolyn A435
Mitchell, Christopher A441
Mitchell, Matt A462
Mitchell, Edward A540
Mitchell, Nichole A571
Mitchell, David A586
Mitchell, James A605
Mitchell, Kevin A608
Mitchell, Kevin J. A662
Mitchell, Rachel A665
Mitchell, Robbin A702
Mitchell, Brian A747
Mitchell, Robert A751
Mitchell, Adam A760
Mitchell, Rhett A768
Mitchell, Robert (Rob) A831
Mitchell, Jared A855
Mitchell, Jill A877
Mitchell, Betty A933
Mitchell, Tony P32
Mitchell, Ken P83
Mitchell, Charles P86
Mitchell, Laura P135
Mitchell, Susan P192
Mitchell, Jennifer P202
Mitchell, J. Stuart P232
Mitchell, Jim P252
Mitchell, Matt P256
Mitchell, Michael R P295
Mitchell, John P447
Mitchell, Harmon P456
Mitchell, Herry P506
Mitchell, Jenny P515
Mitchell, Sharon P539
Mitchell, Howard P553
Mitchell, Ginny P597
Mitchell, Robert (Rob) P601
Mitchell, Adrienne P660
Mitchell, Stephen C. E23
Mitchell, Drew E53
Mitchell, William M. (Bill) E115
Mitchell, D Bryant E176
Mitchell, Dara E243
Mitchell, Rachel E334
Mitchell, Adam E374
Mitchem, Steven G. A397
Mitcheson, James A205
Mitcheson, Doug A621
Mitcheson, Doug E312
Mitcho, Carmen E120
Mitchum, Troy A930
Mitra, Sumit A564
Mitra, Sajal A658
Mitrick, Joseph M. (Joe) P63

Mitschke, Gina P286
Mitsuya, Makoto W18
Mittal, Sonu A166
Mittal, Gaurav A545
Mittal, Samir A565
Mittal, Pranay A845
Mittal, Vijay P47
Mittal, Aditya W33
Mittal, Lakshmi N. W33
Mittendorfer, Gernot W156
Mittermaier, Pascal P579
Mitz, Vincent W. E96
Mitzel, Barbara A339
Mitzner, Jennifer P242
Miura, Zenji W324
Miuta, Michele A786
Miuta, Michele E387
Miwa, Akihisa W292
Mix, Heidi P455
Mixon, Shawna A332
Miyabe, Yoshiyuki W301
Miyake, Shunichi W20
Miyake, Senji W220
Miyaki, Masahiko W132
Miyamoto, Melba A936
Miyamoto, Tomoaki W33
Miyamoto, Michael P343
Miyamoto, Gene P523
Miyamoto, Tomoaki P678
Miyamoto, Tsuneo W281
Miyamoto, Ikuo W300
Miyamoto, Yoichi W349
Miyanaga, Shunichi W258
Miyanoya, Atsushi W51
Miyares, Javier P642
Miyashiro, Edward A706
Miyata, Koichi W369
Miyazaki, Brent A16
Miyazawa, Katsumi W93
Mize, Regina A902
Mizell, Steven A554
Mizelle, C A449
Mizelle, C E220
Mizrahi, Karmel A884
Mizuhara, Hidemoto W257
Mizui, Satoshi W360
Mizuki, Gizo W205
Mizuno, Masayuki W51
Mizuno, Akihisa W107
Mizushima, Kenji W282
Mizushima, Shigeaki W348
Mizutani, Ryosuke W107
Mizutani, Hisakazu W258
Mizutani, Tetsu W374
Mladenovic, Jeanette P399
Mlcak, Kim A58
Mlotek, Mark E. A744
Mlsna, Brooke A315
Mlynek, Chris A6
Mnning, Carol P673
MO, Weiwei P642
Moalli, Pamela P303
Moats, Andy A665
Moats, Andy E334
Moazzaz, Mona A559
Moberg, Kirk P113
Mobley, Stacey A467
Mobley, Michael A704
Mocanu, Michael A520
Moccio, Cindy P274
Moceri, Joe A388
Mochida, Masanori A390
Mochizuki, Robert M. E418
Mock, Teresa A P329
Mockabee, William P587
Modawell, Debbie P46
Modde, Margaret Mary P163
Modder, Roger K. (Keith) E431
Modell, Mitchell B. (Mitch) P237
Moderski, Mark E402
Modi, Puja E290
Modoff, Brian T. A694
Mody-Baily, Priti P82
Modzelewski, Sophia P175
Moe, Melinda P55

COMBINED HOOVER'S HANDBOOK INDEX OF EXECUTIVES

```
A = AMERICAN BUSINESS
E = EMERGING COMPANIES
P = PRIVATE COMPANIES
W = WORLD BUSINESS
```

Moehlenbrock, Todd A263
Moehn, Michael L. A46
Moeller, Kyle A203
Moeller, Doug A508
Moeller, Jon R. A679
Moeller, Ryan A807
Moeller, Sharon A925
Moeller, Michael P166
Moeller, Sharon E 445
Moen, Russ P198
Moen, Kari Olrud W140
Moerhing, Mike P310
Moesgaard, Lars W377
Moeslein, Rosanne A484
Moffat, Bob A465
Moffat, Bob A742
Moffet, Brian L P494
Moffett, Patricia A702
Moffett, Debbie P153
Moffett, Randy P621
Moffett, Glen P677
Moffitt, Mary A248
Moffitt, Kevin L. A346
Moffitt, Kevin A620
Moffitt, John P337
Moffitt, Jamie P636
Moffitt, Michael P636
Moffitt, Justin Raoul W243
Moffitt, Mary E107
Moffitt, Kevin L. E167
Mogan, Tom P608
Mogan, Thomas P608
Mogck, Timothy A3
Mogelnicki, Nancy A859
Mogen, Emily A491
Mogg, Jim A630
Mogg, Denise P467
Mogi, Yoshio W360
Mogill, David E453
Moglia, Joseph H. (Joe) A807
Moglia, Peter M. E8
Mohammad, Shamim A171
Mohammed, Hafeza A504
Mohammed, Hafeza E251
Mohan, R. Michael (Mike) A130
Mohan, Raj A203
Mohan, Vamsi A215
Mohan, George A492
Mohan, Maya P286
Mohanty, Devi A408
Mohanty, Prasanna P118
Moharir, Prahlad E177
Mohiuddin, Ashfaq A739
Mohler, Justin A175
Mohler, Orv A559
Mohr, Todd M. A17
Mohr, John R A112
Mohr, Rick A735
Mohr, Edward L A744
Mohr, David A754
Mohr, Mr Michael A766
Mohr, Todd M. P9
Mohr, David P484
Mohr, Mr Michael P500
Mohrman, Mike P458
Mohs, Brad A89
Mohta, Namita A641
Mohta, Namita P407
Moisan, Jerome E47
Moison, Franck J. A218
Moison, Franck A871
Moitra, Aninda A74
Moiz, Nadeem E394
Mojares, Dennis A746
Moje, Elizabeth Birr A711
Moje, Elizabeth Birr P444
Mok, Wilbur W. A24
Mokkarala, Viggy E131
Moktali, Amruta A740

Molbert, Paul P284
Moldovan, Regina P505
Molek, Marcie A36
Molesevich, Patrice P214
Molho, Davide E75
Molin, Tommy A176
Molina, Oscar A246
Molina, Hope S A246
Molina, Luis P179
Molina, Sergio P306
Molina, Oscar E105
Molina, Hope S E105
Molina, Alvaro G. (Al) de E350
Molina-Clark, Cecilia P633
Molina-frias, Maria Null P175
Molinaro, Christopher A419
Molinaro, Frank A811
Molinelli, Gayla A416
Molinelli, Rachael A863
Molinini, Louis A481
Molko, Cindy P467
Moll, Julie A538
Molle, Josephine A414
Molle, Josephine P236
Mollenkopf, Steven M. (Steve) A694
Mollet, Chris P192
Mollica, Jim A67
Mollica, Paul F. A906
Mollica, Paul F. E434
Molligo, Jacqueline A596
Mollin, Amy E196
Mollins, Gregg J. A716
Mollins, Sean A716
Mollon, Fernando A897
Molloy, Ross A893
Molmen, David P29
Molnar, David A. A848
Molnar, Jacqueline A915
Molnar, Cindy P119
Molnar, David A. E411
Moloney, Greg A381
Moloney, Jacquie P631
Moloney, John J. W131
Momper, Matthew J. E232
Mona, Michael E108
Monacelli, Fred A89
Monaco, Al W150
Monaghan, Craig T. A83
Monaghan, Meghan P389
Monaghan, Sophia P558
Monahan, Dennis A91
Monahan, Michael A289
Monahan, Dennis P55
Monahan, Thomas L P117
Monahan, Mike Null P389
Monahan, Jay P415
Monan, J. Donald P608
Moncau, Ursula A925
Moncau, Ursula E445
Moncla, Jean A167
Moncrief, Jimmy A665
Moncrief, Kit Tennison P549
Moncrief, Jimmy E334
Moncur, Dave A654
Mondazzi, Massimo W155
Mondelli, Jeffrey A899
Mondelli, Jeffrey P657
Mondello, Mark T. A475
Mondragon, Brian P138
Monery, Dave E179
Mones, Ann P138
Monfeli, Mike A727
Monfeli, Mike P453
Monfort, Norbert A88
Monforte, Grace A749
Monforte, Grace E367
Monfre, Andy A91
Monfre, Andy P55
Mong, Marla P155
Mong-Koo, Chung W192
Mong-Koo, Chung W219
Monge, Cathie P658
Mongeau, Luc W422
Mongelluzzo, Katlin A575
Mongillo, Stephen A250

Monhart, James A605
Monhaut, Michelle A482
Monia, Brett P. E237
Monich, Allan R A49
Moniguchi, Inacio A50
Moninski, Stacey A107
Monk, David H. A828
Monk, David H. P584
Monk, David G. E346
Monley, Dominic A444
Monroe, Michael A167
Monroe, Marvin A259
Monroe, Charles Chuck A446
Monroe, Rosemary A511
Monroe, Tim P276
Monroe, Rosemary P290
Monroe, Sheila P514
Monroe, Ronald E226
Monroe-cole, Nicole A929
Monroe-cole, Nicole E449
Monsen, Brian A571
Monson, Kim A441
Monson, Kevin W. A567
Monson, Dale D. P145
Monson, Kevin W. E284
Montag, Thomas K. (Tom) A107
Montag, Bernd W353
Montag, Richard E187
Montague, Jason A727
Montague, Jason P443
Montague, Jason P453
Montague, Adrian A. W40
Montague, Mark K. E241
Montalbano, Brian A227
Montalbano, Brian E90
Montana, Gregory G. (Greg) A327
Montana, Peter A794
Montanarello, Marie A296
Montano, Jesus L A559
Montano, Satin A559
Montano, Laz A559
Montano, Chris P20
Monte, Dave A600
Monte, John P327
Monteagudo, Ibzan P667
Monteferrante, Chris A89
Monteforte, Jason A540
Monteiro, Mallika A237
Monteiro, Manuel P95
Monteiro, Ivan de Souza W303
Monteith, Stu A447
Montenegro, Sara P548
Montero, Edward A204
Montero, Alejandro P445
Montes, John A562
Montes, Vannessa A670
Montesdeoca, Carmella A793
Montesino, Orlando C A727
Montesino, Orlando C P453
Montezemolo, Luca Cordero di W407
Montgomery, William A71
Montgomery, Jennifer A108
Montgomery, Norman J. A337
Montgomery, Sheila A449
Montgomery, Michael P5
Montgomery, Carol P175
Montgomery, Angel P239
Montgomery, Toni-Marie P388
Montgomery, Lisa P. P575
Montgomery, Norman J. E158
Montgomery, Sheila E220
Montgomery, Michael E396
Monticup, Thomas A831
Monticup, Thomas P601
Montilus, Pascal A218
Montini, Enio A. (Tony) A722
Montjane, Funeka W363
Montler, Robert A211
Montler, Robert E83
Montminy, Matthew A409
Montminy, Pierre A795
Montoya, Nancy A319
Montoya, Isabel A340
Montoya, Valerie A460
Montoya, Luis A654

Montoya, Veronica P456
Montoya, Isabel E161
Montpetit, David A797
Montull, Daniel Javier Servitje W175
Montz, Renee D. A52
Monz--n, Gilberto F. A670
Moo, Jason A390
Mooar, Tara A890
Moochhala, Zenobia E65
Mood, Shawn P117
Moodey, J. Tucker A307
Moodie, Rebecca A859
Moody, Todd A326
Moody, Sue A806
Moody, Doug P149
Moody, Craig P396
Moody, David S P581
Moody, Rob E184
Moody, Nathaniel E315
Moody, Sue E398
Mooers, Blaine A782
Mooers, Blaine P526
Mooijman, Yannick A871
Moon, Eric A203
Moon, Kimberly P185
Moon, Don P295
Moon, Harry P390
Moon, Jenny P546
Moon, Natasha E8
Moon, Chuck E429
Moonesinghe, Dee P151
Mooney, Jim A100
Mooney, James A191
Mooney, Randy A253
Mooney, Jeff A272
Mooney, Howard F. A335
Mooney, Kathleen A343
Mooney, Beth E. A491
Mooney, James F A762
Mooney, Stephen M. (Steve) A811
Mooney, John P161
Mooney, Randy P169
Mooney, Monica P627
Mooney, Kevin W. E47
Mooney, Matt E100
Mooney, Howard F. E154
Mooney, Kathleen E164
Moonves, Leslie (Les) A892
Moor, Bill A165
Moor, David E105
Mooradian, John E233
Moore, Steven A1
Moore, Ken A13
Moore, Pennie A14
Moore, Jocelyn A47
Moore, Scott A51
Moore, Colin A60
Moore, Patrick A77
Moore, Kevin A89
Moore, John A112
Moore, Bob A113
Moore, Beth A135
Moore, Steve A145
Moore, Colleen A160
Moore, Kevin A168
Moore, Becky A168
Moore, Annah A175
Moore, Christine A222
Moore, Stephen L A226
Moore, Michael A227
Moore, Elizabeth D. A235
Moore, Michael A313
Moore, Terry A314
Moore, Johnnie A320
Moore, Paul A329
Moore, Richard H. A334
Moore, Peter A355
Moore, Nicholas G A385
Moore, Christopher A389
Moore, A. Bruce A410
Moore, Robert A417
Moore, Doris A418
Moore, Jessica A421
Moore, Beth A432
Moore, Amy A449

Moore, Mikelle A462
Moore, Patrick A469
Moore, Thomas A470
Moore, Brad A480
Moore, Mary A480
Moore, Jimmy A526
Moore, Andrew A549
Moore, Amanda A556
Moore, Troy A557
Moore, Frederick V. (Fred) A557
Moore, Nicole A566
Moore, Lorena A571
Moore, Joe A609
Moore, Daryl D. A621
Moore, Gary L A636
Moore, Greg A654
Moore, John A665
Moore, Richmond A665
Moore, Clara A676
Moore, Edward W. A732
Moore, Justin A760
Moore, Scott A809
Moore, Christine A818
Moore, Bob A831
Moore, Jason A839
Moore, Doug A850
Moore, Jason A865
Moore, Scott A891
Moore, Michael S. (Mike) A901
Moore, Craig A921
Moore, Katie A925
Moore, Pennie P6
Moore, Bud P76
Moore, Rob P83
Moore, Cory P83
Moore, Andrew P114
Moore, Dana P127
Moore, Maricela S. PJ132
Moore, Stephen L P150
Moore, Dayna P184
Moore, Joseph P187
Moore, Michael P200
Moore, Kimberly P208
Moore, Matthew P243
Moore, Stephanie P248
Moore, James D. P254
Moore, Mikelle P256
Moore, Mary P270
Moore, William L P274
Moore, Morgan P277
Moore, Robert P312
Moore, Debra L P323
Moore, Amanda P328
Moore, David P337
Moore, Joe P387
Moore, Dana P420
Moore, Rachel P425
Moore, Kim P434
Moore, William M. P447
Moore, Edward P449
Moore, John P456
Moore, Lori P489
Moore, Jason P541
Moore, Gary P552
Moore, Barry P556
Moore, Kelly P596
Moore, Jackson W. P599
Moore, Bob P601
Moore, Dorian P606
Moore, Joy P608
Moore, Madeleine G P608
Moore, Michael P624
Moore, Daphne P657
Moore, Craig P669
Moore, Robert J. W233
Moore, Nicholas W. W243
Moore, Steven E1
Moore, Bob E36
Moore, Rick E64
Moore, James E78
Moore, Michael E90
Moore, Terry E145
Moore, Richard H. E153
Moore, Sean D. E171
Moore, Joby E174

Moore, Michael G. (Mike) E197
Moore, Amy E221
Moore, Jon E268
Moore, Clint E269
Moore, Troy E281
Moore, Frederick V. (Fred) E281
Moore, Larry E286
Moore, Daryl D. E311
Moore, John E334
Moore, Richmond E334
Moore, Clara E338
Moore, Justin E374
Moore, H. Lynn E412
Moore, Jason E416
Moore, Katie E445
Moorehead, Cameron A219
Moorehead, Michael A922
Moorehead, Kimberly P2
Moorehead, Kristen P611
Moorehead, Michael P671
Moorehead, Cameron E87
Moorhead, Keith P179
Moorjani, Shail A167
Moorman, Charles A281
Moorman, Kathy P63
Moorthy, Ganesh A564
Moorthy, Ganesh E359
Moos, Daniel J. (Danny) E408
Moose, Savannah P315
Moose, Selina P356
Moots, Stephanie P57
Moquin, Kelli A325
Moquist, Darren C A877
Mora, Diego A135
Mora, Elizabeth P557
Morabito, Leonardo A656
Morabito, Leonardo P414
Moraci, Pj A879
Moraci, Philip J A879
Morack, Sarah J A398
Morack, Sarah J P222
Morais, Diane E A37
Morais, Diane A37
Morais, Diane E P27
Moraitis, Andreas E96
Moral-Niles, Christopher J. Del A85
Moral-Niles, Christopher J. Del E26
Morales, Wendy A108
Morales, Michael PE A132
Morales, Elisa A374
Morales, Ray A462
Morales, Jimmy A550
Morales, Vincent J. A673
Morales, David P2
Morales, Ray P256
Morales, Jimmy P319
Morales, Jose P350
Morales, Ralph P461
Morales, Javier E285
Morales-jaffe, Marcia A927
Moran, Patrick A18
Moran, Rob A19
Moran, Edward A60
Moran, Mickey A85
Moran, Tim A226
Moran, James A277
Moran, Thomas A286
Moran, Robert A403
Moran, Karina A431
Moran, Tim A522
Moran, Sean A574
Moran, Brian A574
Moran, Colleen A596
Moran, Sheila A651
Moran, Jeff A690
Moran, Jennifer A858
Moran, Michael F. P73
Moran, Tim P150
Moran, Thomas P190
Moran, Veronica P368
Moran, John P387
Moran, James P465
Moran, Karina E216
Moran, Edmund J. E230
Moran, Sheila E329

Morant, Blake D. P569
Morar, August A592
Morar, August P370
Morasutti, Joseph A251
Morathi, Raisibe K. W275
Morawetz, Michael M. E28
Morazzani, Christina A680
Morbi, Farzana A391
Morchak, Chris A824
Morchak, Chris P562
Morche, Ed A184
Morckol, Gina A458
Morde, Vishal A118
Morde, Vishal P66
More, Debrah A849
More, Ed P125
Morea, Joseph A843
Moreau, Maxine L. A184
Moreau, Gary P298
Moree, Scott A891
Morehead, Shawn V A590
Moreira, Julio A919
Morel, Hugo W405
Moreland, Mary A5
Moreland, Jeffrey A138
Moreland, Jeffrey A157
Moreland, Ramal A530
Moreland, Kenneth V. A799
Moreland, Jeffrey P91
Morelli, Kris A275
Morelli, Bryan A717
Morelli, Mark D. E88
Morelli, Bryan E351
Moreno, Raul E. A20
Moreno, Elisabeth A438
Moreno, Vanesa P204
Moreno, Imelda P482
Moreno, Noemi P589
Moreno, Oscar Landerretche W118
Moret, Blake D A729
Moreth, Cary A453
Moretti, Marty P234
Moretti, Darlene P500
Moretz, Drew P595
Morey, Raj A793
Morey, Debra A798
Morford, Craig S. A169
Morgan, Randy A3
Morgan, Donna A36
Morgan, Cindy A222
Morgan, Pat A251
Morgan, Lorie Ann A385
Morgan, Lisa A409
Morgan, William A428
Morgan, Jeff A483
Morgan, Molly A484
Morgan, Mary A494
Morgan, Karen A512
Morgan, Bruce A524
Morgan, James A527
Morgan, James A555
Morgan, Rose A651
Morgan, Kenneth A654
Morgan, Rick A660
Morgan, Robert A660
Morgan, Debbie A665
Morgan, Henry A683
Morgan, Jamie A752
Morgan, Jason A788
Morgan, Hugh A798
Morgan, Bob A798
Morgan, Hugh G A798
Morgan, Dana A799
Morgan, Julie A845
Morgan, Keith A861
Morgan, Lisa A867
Morgan, Julie A891
Morgan, Ada P108
Morgan, Marissa P116
Morgan, Kenneth P153
Morgan, Mark P265
Morgan, Amanda P319
Morgan, Bill P325
Morgan, Shana P331
Morgan, Crystal P334

Morgan, Dianna P400
Morgan, Vickie P408
Morgan, Rick P416
Morgan, Robert P416
Morgan, Henry P431
Morgan, Marsha L. P607
Morgan, Amanda P615
Morgan, John P664
Morgan, Becka P665
Morgan, Flemming W128
Morgan, Jennifer W340
Morgan, Bennett E184
Morgan, James E277
Morgan, Rose E329
Morgan, Debbie E334
Morgan, Jason E389
Morgan, Lisa E418
Morgan, Russell J. E453
Morgano, Scott A325
Morganstein, David P664
Morgante, Elizabeth P222
Morgante, Beth P489
Morganthall, Frederick J. (Fred) A498
Morge, Kenneth A262
Morgenlender, Mark A203
Morgenroth, Matthew J. W424
Morgenstern, H Richard P329
Morgenthaler, John A823
Morgenthaler, John E405
Morgioni, Mike A75
Morgo, Joseph A203
Morhaime, Michael (Mike) A10
Mori, Frank A267
Mori, Yoshiki W11
Mori, Kazuyuki W257
Mori, Chitoshi W259
Moriarity, Tim A848
Moriarity, Tim E411
Moriarty, Linda A60
Moriarty, Thomas M. A251
Moriarty, Michael A323
Moriarty, Brad A448
Moriarty, Selina A492
Moriarty, Colleen A888
Moriarty, Daniel P54
Moriarty, Brad P247
Moriarty, Rowland T. (Row) E102
Moriarty, Brian E134
Moriarty, J.D. E254
Moriarty, Colleen E425
Moriarty, Rowland T. (Row) E440
Morici, John F. E10
Moriconi, Susan E315
Moriguchi, Jaime W428
Morikawa, Taku W160
Morikis, John A361
Morikis, John G. A756
Morimoto, David S. A182
Morimoto, Hiromichi W258
Morimura, Tsutomu W93
Morin, Thomas A391
Morin, Jeff A512
Morin, Jamie P553
Morin, Francois W33
Morissette, Daniel J. A266
Morissette, Daniel J. P181
Morita, Shunsaku W127
Morita, Toshio W286
Moritani, Kazuhiro W348
Moritz, John P473
Moriwaki, Lee Y. A182
Moriyama, Toru W260
Mork, Lee P26
Morken, CeCe A471
Morlacci, Laura P512
Morley, Debra A480
Morley, Bruce A574
Morley, Jim P86
Morley, Debra P270
Morlock, David R. P596
Morningstar, Ashley A331
Morningstar, Ashley P202
Moro, Sonya A114
Moro, Gisele A509
Moro, Masahiro W250

COMBINED HOOVER'S HANDBOOK INDEX OF EXECUTIVES

A = AMERICAN BUSINESS
E = EMERGING COMPANIES
P = PRIVATE COMPANIES
W = WORLD BUSINESS

Moro, Sonya E37
Moroski, Steve A739
Morosov, Anatoly A483
Morozov, Alexander W343
Morra, Elizabeth P595
Morray, Jeffrey P. P417
Morrell, Kelley A200
Morrell, Jeff P567
Morrelli, Keri P168
Morrical, Terri A. E302
Morrill, Angela P425
Morris, Donna A11
Morris, Mark A16
Morris, Susan A30
Morris, Leslie A53
Morris, Gregory A. (Greg) A77
Morris, M. Catherine (Cathy) A81
Morris, M Catherine A81
Morris, Jim A140
Morris, James A168
Morris, Tim A196
Morris, James A205
Morris, Joe A224
Morris, James A290
Morris, Rodney A345
Morris, Gerald A376
Morris, Jerry A376
Morris, James A390
Morris, Brian A397
Morris, Tanya A484
Morris, Michael A488
Morris, Chris A545
Morris, Maria R. A559
Morris, Uri A575
Morris, Pamela A592
Morris, Neil A663
Morris, Jesse E. A696
Morris, Tonia G A727
Morris, B. Harrison A755
Morris, Pete A778
Morris, Gene A784
Morris, John A785
Morris, Edna A840
Morris, Fran A890
Morris, Lisa A902
Morris, John J. A905
Morris, Dawn C. A906
Morris, Michael J. A940
Morris, Susan P20
Morris, Thomas P94
Morris, Kenneth P156
Morris, Kenneth C. P187
Morris, David P213
Morris, Patrick P283
Morris, Walker P349
Morris, Pamela P370
Morris, Christine P433
Morris, Sherrill P436
Morris, Tonia G P453
Morris, Patrick P458
Morris, Dave E81
Morris, Rodney E166
Morris, Michael J. E180
Morris, Alan E264
Morris, Lisa E306
Morris, Jared E330
Morris, B. Harrison E369
Morris, Jamie E427
Morris, Dawn C. E434
Morris-gettings, Juanita A520
Morris-Hipkins, Stuart A634
Morrisett, J. Gregory P159
Morrison, Christina A75
Morrison, Scott C. A103
Morrison, Denise M. A164
Morrison, Patricia B. (Patty) A169
Morrison, Richard A303
Morrison, Elizabeth A522
Morrison, Steve A528

Morrison, Deb A544
Morrison, Trevor A592
Morrison, Jeffrey A651
Morrison, Geri A678
Morrison, Tim A763
Morrison, Julia P22
Morrison, Allen P44
Morrison, Dean P119
Morrison, Dr Bob P212
Morrison, Trevor P370
Morrison, Marni P378
Morrison, Karen P395
Morrison, Tom P445
Morrison, Jeffrey P450
Morrison, Jeffrey E329
Morrison, Tim E377
Morriss, Steve A16
Morriss, John A520
Morrissey, Art A103
Morrissey, William P. (Bill) A528
Morrissey, Sean A575
Morrissey, Deborah A641
Morrissey, Deborah P407
Morrissey, Michael M. E140
Morrisson, Mark A828
Morrisson, Mark P584
Morrow, David L A172
Morrow, Richard A230
Morrow, Duncan A246
Morrow, Anthony A255
Morrow, Bradley A540
Morrow, Jerry A550
Morrow, Carol A592
Morrow, Brian R. A731
Morrow, Bailey A793
Morrow, Sherry P18
Morrow, W. Robert P45
Morrow, W. Robert (Bob) P130
Morrow, Richard P154
Morrow, Kent P235
Morrow, Shawn P323
Morrow, Joseph P354
Morrow, Carol P370
Morrow, Kirk P461
Morrow, Jason P596
Morrow, John P628
Morrow, Ron W50
Morrow, Duncan E105
Morse, John A18
Morse, Sherry A89
Morse, Robert J. (Bob) A160
Morse, David L. A240
Morse, Cheryl A296
Morse, John A436
Morse, Colby A797
Morse, Diane A885
Morse, Candace A932
Morse, Lara P66
Morse, Jim P68
Morse, Alan R P225
Morse, Edward J P349
Morse, Colby E77
Morsi, Deborah S. P54
Morstadt, Mary A347
Morstadt, Mary E167
MORSTOFOLINI, ERNESTINA W121
Morsy, Hany A925
Morsy, Hany E445
Mortensen, Scott A147
Mortensen, Pam A647
Mortensen, Brian P471
Morthland, Lee A704
Morton, Susan A540
Morton, George A879
Morton, Steve A891
Morton, Margaret P198
Morton, Michele P242
Morton, Kerry P395
Morton, Leo E. P633
Morton-rowe, Laura A522
Morway, Joe P487
Mory, Scott P114
Morzaria, Tushar W56
Morzaria, Tushar W58
Mosca, Andrew P250

Moscaritolo, Daniel A393
Moscho, Harold P352
Moscho, Harold P585
Moseley, Jacob A793
Mosemann, Richard P312
Moser, Sheldon A334
Moser, Shane A357
Moser, Chris A610
Moser, Phillip G P15
Moser, Joseph D P40
Moser, Len P68
Moser, Kathy P629
Moser, Sheldon E153
Moser, Linda E172
Moser, Shane E176
Moses, James M A128
Moses, Deborah A329
Moses, Sharon A452
Moses, Christopher A489
Moses, George A797
Moses, Roxanne P148
Moses, Joe E184
Moses, Brett E343
Mosher, Allison A227
Mosher, Jason A452
Mosher, Allison E90
Mosich, Nicholas A. A101
Mosich, Nicholas A. E32
Mosier, Preston A804
Mosingo, Jerry L P543
Moskal, Joseph T P112
Moskowitz, David K A271
Moskowitz, Ken A304
Moskowitz, Samuel E. A551
Moskowitz, Paul T. A797
Moskowitz, Amy P161
Moskowitz, Samuel E. P321
Mosler, Preston A804
Mosley, Christopher R P219
Mosley, Anthony P252
Mosner, Lisa A856
Mosner, Lisa P614
Mosocco, Doris P653
Mosquera, Juan-Miguel P459
Moss, Kaylene A100
Moss, Aaron A290
Moss, Barbara A320
Moss, Linda L. A351
Moss, Deanna A528
Moss, Danielle A702
Moss, Nelvin A726
Moss, Kevin A784
Moss, Nalann A867
Moss, Howard P118
Moss, Jackie P177
Moss, R. Lawrence P359
Moss, Chad P426
Moss, Amanda P507
Moss, Leah P549
Moss, Jacqueline C. W85
Moss, Arvid W289
Moss, Robbie E203
Moss, Nalann E418
Mossallam, Usamah A414
Mossallam, Usamah P236
Mosser, Michael A287
Mossey, Sheila A859
Mosshart, Roger E72
Mosso, Robert B. E80
Mostaert, Christine P319
Mosteller, J Scott A380
Mota-Velasco, German Larrea A771
Motakef, Shahin P478
Mote, Gale P530
Motel, Bernhard A451
Motel, George P96
Motes, Joseph A34
Motl, Christopher J. (Chris) A906
Motl, Christopher J. (Chris) E435
Motley, Edward A476
Motley, Lindsay A690
Motley, J. Keith P631
Mott, Randall D. (Randy) A378
Mott, Joe A462

Mott, Carrie A498
Mott, Joe P256
Motta, Stephen A374
Motta, Edgar P179
Motta, Jorge da W208
Motte, Anne-Marie A218
Motteler, James A61
Motz, Steve A887
Mouadeb, Daniel A167
Moulder, Bill P308
Moulton, Paul G. A241
Moulton, Don P361
Moultrie, Anne P642
Mounger, Bridget A665
Mounger, Bridget E334
Mounir, Ihssane A140
Mount, Alyson A296
Mount, Carl A780
Mountain, James R. A80
Mountain, Gary P672
Mountjoy, Ryan P5
Mourad, Waleed P228
Mourad, Bachar P543
Mourino, Art P650
Moustakakis, John P664
Moutenot, Michael A544
Moutray, Jason A709
Moutray, Jason E348
Movassaghi, Eric A449
Movassaghi, Eric E220
Movva, Sunil A108
Mowder, David A618
Mowder, David E310
Mower, David P28
Mowery, Andy A207
Mowery, Geoffrey A444
Mowery, Jamie P476
Mowreader, Jack P415
Moy, Pamela A110
Moy, Daniel A137
Moy, Steve A160
Moy, Ji W P366
Moye, Ginny A727
Moye, Ginny P453
Moye, Vincent E148
Moyer, Matthew A137
Moyer, Priscilla A363
Moyer, Steve A565
Moyer, Bryan A881
Moyer, Glenn A881
Moyer, Arlene A922
Moyer, Nancy P269
Moyer, Dale P475
Moyer, Angel P653
Moyer, Arlene P671
Moyer, A.J. (Bert) E58
Moyer, Bryan E421
Moyer, Glenn E421
Moyette, Zirley A203
Moyle, James A277
Moynihan, Brian T. A107
Moynihan, Barbara A530
Mozrall, Jacqueline P456
MPA, Charity P12
Mpsa, Amy A621
Mpsa, Amy E312
Mrosik, Jan W353
Mrowczynski, Jeff A242
Mubing, Zhou W12
Muca, Erta E427
Mucci, Ron A630
Mucha, John A414
Mucha, Bob P70
Mucha, John P236
Mucic, Luka W340
Mudge, Rex P530
Mudichintala, Kiran A484
Mudler, Gordon A P329
Mudrick, Christopher A304
Muehlen, Constance Von A29
Mueller, Meg R. A367
Mueller, Kurt A434
Mueller, Erinn A434
Mueller, Richard A530
Mueller, Karl W. A622

Mueller, Perry A683
Mueller, Manfred A724
Mueller, Nadean A804
Mueller, Steven A877
Mueller, Bernadette M. A888
Mueller, Roni A893
Mueller, Christopher P86
Mueller, Ken P439
Mueller, Manfred P452
Mueller, John P508
Mueller, Michael W43
Mueller, Denny E286
Mueller, Bernadette M. E425
Mueller, Craig E433
Muenchau, Jeanne A602
Muenster, Gary E. E135
Muenster, G E135
Muenzer, Melanie P636
Muffler, Joseph A583
Mugavero, Jennifer A467
Mugg, Jason P2
Mughal, Ijaz A888
Mughal, Ijaz E425
Mugnier, Denis W157
Muhammad, Shamim A171
Muhart, Matthew J. P500
Muhlfelder, Teddy P197
Muhlhauser, Jurgen A686
Muilenburg, Dennis A. A140
Muilenburg, Brent A876
Muina, Tomas Varela W45
Muir, William D. (Bill) A475
Muir, Katelyn P597
Muir, Tracy P638
Muirhead, David P227
Mukai, Kazushi W348
Muke, Maureen P329
Mukhamedov, Leonid W344
Mukherjee, Preetika P514
Mukherjee, Kishore P596
Mul, James J P227
Mulae, Sherrin E48
Mulcahey, Terri A649
Mulcunry, Ryan E32
Muldoon, Christine P274
Muldowney, David P284
Mulford, Michael D. A339
Mulford, Michael D. E159
Mulhere, Timothy P. A289
Mulherin, Matthew J. (Matt) A446
Mulhern, Ben P343
Mulholland, Ellen A109
Mulholland, Katie S. P594
Mull, Rohit A751
Mullally, Dan A323
Mullane, Marietta A759
Mullane, Dean A941
Mullane, Marietta P493
Mullaney, Kathleen A763
Mullaney, Tom A781
Mullaney, Kathleen E377
Mullarkey, Pat A873
Mulle, Mike P530
Mullen, Matthew A349
Mullen, Michael A497
Mullen, Frank A735
Mullen, Gregory A784
Mullen, Frederick L A835
Mullen, Patrick A881
Mullen, Tom P116
Mullen, David P126
Mullen, Kay P306
Mullen, Thomas P329
Mullen, Thomas R P332
Mullen, Paddy C P364
Mullen, John R P364
Mullen, Kate P573
Mullen, Patrick E421
Mullendore, Scott P432
Mullenix, Matthew (Matt) E432
Mullens, Amy A538
Muller, Josef A245
Muller, John A287
Muller, Frank A412
Muller, Bart A778

Muller, Liz A779
Muller, Chris A906
Muller, Frank P233
Muller, David P351
Muller, Garrick P513
Muller, Brook P636
Muller, Chris E435
Mullery, Stephen P. A317
Mullery, Stephen P. E146
Mullet, Julie A296
Mulligan, Paul A215
Mulligan, Kevin A296
Mulligan, Donal L. (Don) A376
Mulligan, John J. A804
Mulligan, William C A822
Mullin, Tom A63
Mullin, Thomas J. (Tom) A236
Mullin, Daryl A481
Mullin, Lauren A835
Mullin, Shelly P352
Mullin, Mark W. W10
Mullinix, Mark L. A320
Mullins, Robin A19
Mullins, Brenda A19
Mullins, Clara A206
Mullins, Amy A219
Mullins, Debbie A226
Mullins, Kevin A463
Mullins, Jim A744
Mullins, Debbie P150
Mullins, Dennis P252
Mullins, Karyn P262
Mullins, Amy E87
Mullis, Michael P48
Mullis, Harold W. P638
Mullowney, Ron A734
Mulqueen, Tom A25
Mulqueen, Tom P14
Mulrooney, Byrne K. E248
Mulroy, Thomas P. A787
Mulroy, Molly A907
Mulroy, Kevin P109
Mulsow, Brad A887
Multon, Hervé W390
Mulupi, Meshack A421
Mulva, J J A233
Mulvihill, Bill A885
Mumcuoglu, Rahsan A888
Mumcuoglu, Rahsan E425
Mumford, Mark D. P128
Mumford, Lisa E124
Munari, Andrea W71
Munce, Currie A565
Mundell, Robert A747
Mundie, Linda P167
Mundt-Blum, Walter A613
Mundy, Karen A329
Mundy, Robert P. (Bob) A637
Muneoka, Shoji W280
Munger, Charles T. (Charlie) A127
Muni, Lalesh A349
Muni, Amit E447
Munic-Miller, Donna A824
Munic-Miller, Donna P562
Munich, Mario E239
Muniz, Peter A428
Muniz, Sean M. A643
Muniz, Rafael E349
Munjal, Leena A750
Munk, Anthony W296
Munkelt, Larry L P463
Munley, Keith A248
Munley, Keith E107
Munn, Chuck A798
Munn, Rico P55
Munnelly, Joseph M. (Joe) A75
Munoz, Francisco A218
Munoz, Oscar A864
Munoz, Juan P376
Munoz, Rita P470
Munoz, Jose W283
Munro, Euan W40
Munroe, Twuanna P480
Munsell, Terri A859
Munselle, Ted R. E408

Munsey, Ryan A219
Munsey, Ryan E87
Munson, Michael A219
Munson, Laurie A525
Munson, James A933
Munson, Michael E87
Muntoni, Roby A738
Murabito, John A194
Murai, Kevin M. A794
Murai, Shouhei W11
Murakami, David A817
Murakami, Nobuhiko W366
Murakami, Nobuhiko W400
Murali, Narayana S. P309
Murali, Viji P624
Muramatsu, Iwao W1
Muransky, Edward A314
Muransky, Edward E145
Muraro, Robert A803
MURASE, YUKIO W213
Murata, Tsuneo W268
Muratore, Emiliano W45
Muravski, Rick E254
Murawski, Russ A888
Murawski, Russ E425
Murchy, Jodie P82
Murdoch, Britton H. A155
Murdoch, Lachlan K. A596
Murdoch, K. Rupert A596
Murdoch, Tim A739
Murdoch, Brian P143
Murdoch, Britton H. E54
Murdock, Daniel C A220
Murdock, Robert O. (Rob) E299
Murgado, Mario P649
Murgalo, Joanne A651
Murgalo, Joanne P310
Murhammer, Robyn A296
Muri, Scott R P511
Murias, Manny A512
Murillo, Jorge P501
Murillo, Juan P508
Murino, John P19
Murlless, Craig A108
Muro, David A89
Murphey, Mike P222
Murphy, Christopher J. (Chris) A1
Murphy, Patrick A28
Murphy, Steve A54
Murphy, Siobhan A72
Murphy, Thomas J. (Tom) A82
Murphy, Sean A89
Murphy, Thomas A127
Murphy, William A137
Murphy, Albert B A155
Murphy, Michael A191
Murphy, Denis A191
Murphy, Madison A204
Murphy, John A215
Murphy, Connie A220
Murphy, James P. (Jim) A242
Murphy, Drew A290
Murphy, Edward F. A319
Murphy, Gwenn A349
Murphy, James H. (Jim) A376
Murphy, Christopher A386
Murphy, Edmund F. A397
Murphy, Erica A449
Murphy, Mark A453
Murphy, Michael T A467
Murphy, Michael A467
Murphy, Gerry A484
Murphy, Michael A540
Murphy, Christopher A540
Murphy, Timothy H. (Tim) A544
Murphy, Jerry A561
Murphy, Stacey A561
Murphy, R. Madison A579
Murphy, Daniel A616
Murphy, Kathleen F A626
Murphy, Devin I A663
Murphy, Ryan A665
Murphy, John A681
Murphy, Diane A706
Murphy, Cathy A706

Murphy, Amy A709
Murphy, Chris A715
Murphy, Sheehan A740
Murphy, Kathryn A740
Murphy, James A742
Murphy, Gregory E. A751
Murphy, Daniel A782
Murphy, Patrick A796
Murphy, Sean A833
Murphy, Patrick A842
Murphy, Neil A857
Murphy, Jack A869
Murphy, Marylou A882
Murphy, John A888
Murphy, Brian A893
Murphy, Ken A899
Murphy, Dominic A900
Murphy, Julie A901
Murphy, Richard B. A925
Murphy, Robert A925
Murphy, Mary P7
Murphy, John P57
Murphy, Terry P70
Murphy, John E. P85
Murphy, Lisa P96
Murphy, Brian P102
Murphy, Edward P112
Murphy, Del P115
Murphy, Michael P134
Murphy, Connie P149
Murphy, Karen P214
Murphy, Michelle P220
Murphy, Dennis P252
Murphy, Rebecca S P276
Murphy, Erin P302
Murphy, Mike P306
Murphy, Donna P310
Murphy, Mary P332
Murphy, Amy P442
Murphy, John P448
Murphy, Tony P449
Murphy, Michael W. (Mike) P489
Murphy, Richard J P502
Murphy, Teresa P525
Murphy, Daniel P525
Murphy, Michael P538
Murphy, J Pat P595
Murphy, Teresa P598
Murphy, Tammy P644
Murphy, John M P665
Murphy, Donal W131
Murphy, Christopher J. (Chris) E1
Murphy, Albert B E54
Murphy, Scott E115
Murphy, Anthony E172
Murphy, Christopher E188
Murphy, A. Brett E190
Murphy, Erica E221
Murphy, Edward G. E262
Murphy, Carol E282
Murphy, Bryan E290
Murphy, Ryan E334
Murphy, Patrick E397
Murphy, John E425
Murphy, Richard B. E445
Murphy, Robert E445
Murphy, Michele E445
Murray, James A36
Murray, Dan A36
Murray, Jason A42
Murray, Helen A51
Murray, Jay A60
Murray, Todd A198
Murray, Winona A224
Murray, Jennifer A236
Murray, William A275
Murray, Scott A287
Murray, Craig A299
Murray, Carol A313
Murray, Dawn A327
Murray, Angus A355
Murray, Doug A395
Murray, Renee A428
Murray, Michael A435
Murray, Ron A446

COMBINED HOOVER'S HANDBOOK INDEX OF EXECUTIVES

A = AMERICAN BUSINESS
E = EMERGING COMPANIES
P = PRIVATE COMPANIES
W = WORLD BUSINESS

Murray, Pam A456
Murray, Dermot A466
Murray, Pamela A537
Murray, Cathleen A546
Murray, Brian A596
Murray, John A640
Murray, Jerry A647
Murray, Andrea A692
Murray, Michael A747
Murray, Dane H A769
Murray, John A778
Murray, Theodore A797
Murray, Heather A809
Murray, Peter A862
Murray, Donna A879
Murray, Kathryn L A882
Murray, Gary A894
Murray, Donald P164
Murray, Jonathan P199
Murray, Danny P266
Murray, Miriam P275
Murray, Gerry P425
Murray, Bruce H P509
Murray, William J. (Bill) P544
Murray, Bill P544
Murray, Gary P651
Murray, Richard E105
Murray, Carol E144
Murray, Pam E228
Murray, John E E268
Murray, Dane H E380
Murrell, Anita A760
Murrell, Anita E374
Murren, James J. A562
Murrer, B. A. W212
Murry, Dana P70
Murry, Johnnie P312
Murry, Michael P667
Mursuli, Vivian P547
Murtagh, Nigel J. A746
Murter, Jeffrey A509
Murtha, Mark G. A413
Murtha, Gary A654
Murtha, Joseph P373
Murtha, Mark G. E205
Murto, Risto W413
Murtos, Ryan A108
Murtos, Kristen P386
Mury, Francis M. E119
Musa, Ramsey A595
Musacchia, Jacqueline P116
Musca, Robert A871
Muscala, Tiffany A885
Muscarella, Linda P382
Muscat, Michael K. E92
Musen, Robert M. A714
Musgrave, Brant A267
Musgrove, David P552
Musheno, Donise P219
Musi, Diane E65
Musk, Elon A818
Musk, Elon P547
Musselman, Barry A713
Musselman, Kerri P94
Musselman, Bennett E204
Musser, Eric S. A240
Musser, Jeffrey S. A308
Musser, Paul A545
Musso, Chris A669
Musson, Karen E73
Mustaka, Betsey E330
Musteen, Sheila A902
Musti, Subu A544
Mustian, Morton P197
Mustier, Jean-Pierre W407
Mustos, Carl W193
Mutch, Marcy D. A344
Mutch, Cecile A487
Mutch, Marcy D. E165

Mutcherson, James A P130
Mutchler, Len P613
Muth, Ora A206
Muthler, Craig A357
Muthler, Craig E176
Muthukrishnan, Prakash P435
Muto, Gary P. A84
Muto, Daneen A933
Muto, Naoto W366
Mutti, Joe A255
Mutton, Michelle A538
Mutz, Janet A623
Mutz, Janet E313
Muzaffar, Farooq A933
Muzzy, Carol P597
Mwangi, John A544
Mychalowych, Jerome A554
Myer, John W190
Myer, Christopher E371
Myers, Denise A1
Myers, Bill A3
Myers, Kirstie A54
Myers, Tim D. A79
Myers, Jason A103
Myers, Shirley A105
Myers, Timothy D. (Tim) A110
Myers, Timothy A140
Myers, Brian A176
Myers, Tony A179
Myers, Christopher D. (Chris) A249
Myers, Carol A341
Myers, Cynthia M. A353
Myers, Curtis J. A367
Myers, Eric A409
Myers, Ben A478
Myers, Thomas D. A489
Myers, Bradley A530
Myers, Daniel A573
Myers, Fred A592
Myers, Landon A704
Myers, William E. A843
Myers, Lee A863
Myers, Daniel P. (Dan) A913
Myers, Brock P23
Myers, Joseph P30
Myers, David P34
Myers, Isaac J. P64
Myers, Douglas T. P130
Myers, Todd P142
Myers, Ben P173
Myers, Clint P235
Myers, Becky P259
Myers, Ben P268
Myers, Dwayne P312
Myers, Zach P337
Myers, Seth P364
Myers, Fred P370
Myers, Douglas T. P417
Myers, Johnathon P491
Myers, Leah P657
Myers, Russ P675
Myers, Denise E1
Myers, Shirley E34
Myers, Franklin E89
Myers, Christopher D. (Chris) E108
Myers, Cynthia M. E173
Myers, Byron E231
Myers, Keith G. E255
Myers, Sarah E256
Myers, Randy E261
Myers, Daniel P. (Dan) E438
Myler, Jerold E492
Mylett, James E89
Mylonas, Paul W272
Myochin, Toru W350
Myrick, Bradan A773
Myrick, Bradan E383
Myron, Paul A79
Myron, Thomas R A132
Myszka, Kenneth F. E256
Myszka, Jeffrey E256
Myszka, Jeff E256
Myszkowski, Kenneth (Ken) E25
M-oki-Kala, Jyrki W275
M-rch, Lars Stensgaard W129

Muller, Ralph W137
Muller, Werner W158
Muller, Matthias W418

N

Nabel, Elizabeth G. (Betsy) A641
Nabel, Elizabeth G. (Betsy) P407
Nabel, Elizabeth G P556
Naber, Mike P128
Nace, Jeffrey P252
Nacey, Sean A910
Nachman, Joseph R. (Jed) E450
Nachmann, Marc A390
Nachtigal, Amy P467
Nackers, Gary P182
Nackley, Janey A452
Nadar, Shiv P230
Nadarajan, Gunalan A711
Nadarajan, Gunalan P444
Naddeo, Eric A857
Nadeau, Renee A160
Nadeau, Gerard F. A455
Nadeau, Kim P184
Nadeau, Gerard F. E227
Nadel, Hiyam P574
Nadella, Satya A565
Nader, Tony P253
Nadkarni, Pranay A43
Nadkarni, Pranay E13
Naftaly, Robert A856
Naftaly, Rober A856
Naftaly, Ralph A877
Naftaly, Robert P614
Naftaly, Rober P614
Nagae, Shusaku W301
NAGAHORI, KAZUMASA W268
Nagai, Shigeto W51
Nagai, Koji W286
Nagaishi, Robert A56
Nagamatsu, Shoichi W286
Naganathan, Nagi P596
Nagano, Hisashi W286
Nagano, Tsuyoshi W393
Nagao, Tatsunosuke W205
Nagao, Narumi W228
Nagao, Masahiko W376
Nagao, Yutaka W431
NAGAOKA, SUSUMU W40
Nagaoka, Takashi W262
Nagar, Sumeet A135
Nagarajan, Rajesh A177
Nagarajan, Sundaram (Naga) A453
Nagarajan, Sundaram A768
Nagarkar, Niranjan A135
Nagasawa, Hitoshi W282
Nagata, Ron A410
Nagata, Osamu (Simon) W400
Nagayama, Osamu W328
Nageer, Tarique A540
Nagel, David A376
Nagel, Troy A409
Nagel, Brian A507
Nagel, Brian A872
Nagel, Alberto N. W252
Nagelberg, Allison E287
Nagesh, Reddivalen P235
Naggar, Lela A818
Naggar, Lela E403
Nagir, Madhurie E354
Nagji, Bansi A549
Nagle, Margaret A88
Nagler, Harris M. P80
Nagowski, Michael P168
Nagpal, Pooja P211
Nagra, Erica P99
Nagy, Richard A248
Nagy, Kate A329
Nagy, Shayne A580
Nagy, Kim A925
Nagy, Ryan P252
Nagy, Richard E107
Nagy, Shayne E292
Nagy, Kim E445

Nahata, Babu P163
Nahata, Leena P359
Nahdi, Mohamed Abdulla Al W142
Nahe, Eric P627
Nahhas, Kamal A885
Nahrgang, Stephanie A826
Naidoo, Shirley P390
Naidoo, Vassi W275
Naidu, Tulsi R. W435
Naig, Kris P471
Naik, Sangeeta A54
Naik, Piyush A135
Naik, Harshad A447
Naik, Sundip A804
Nail, Steve P201
Naim, Ahmad E226
Naiman, Catherine P515
Nair, Vas A79
Nair, Raj A360
Nair, Mahesh A502
Nair, Roopa A692
Nair, Suresh A713
Nair, Prasanna P630
Nair, Ajai E104
Naish, Rob P32
Naito, Hiroshi P34
Naito, Tadaaki W282
Naito, Shunichi W374
Naja, Khaled P171
Najbicz, Christopher A161
Najima, Hirotaka W127
Najimi, Parnaz A900
Najjar, Fred A266
Najjar, Ted A390
Najjar, Fred P181
Najjar, Fuad E342
Nakagawa, Hiroshi W204
Nakagawa, Kuniharu W204
Nakagawa, Junko W286
Nakagome, Kenji W379
Nakahara, Tina A109
Nakahara, Steven A109
Nakahara, Sean E57
Nakai, Shogo W262
Nakai, Takuji W282
Nakajima, Shuichi W160
Nakajima, Shigehiro W168
Nakajima, Yuji W214
Nakajima, Hajime W220
Nakajima, Norio W268
Nakajima, Yutaka W286
Nakamae, Koji W321
Nakamine, Yuji W250
Nakamura, Galen A109
Nakamura, Takeshi W51
Nakamura, Mitsuyoshi W215
Nakamura, Akira W228
Nakamura, Jiro W278
Nakamura, Kimiyasu W283
Nakamura, Kunio W301
Nakamura, Yukio W350
Nakamura, Tomomi W366
Nakanishi, Katsuya W257
Nakano, Damon A191
Nakano, Tom A609
Nakano, Tom P387
Nakao, Seiya W400
Nakata, Toru W204
Nakata, Yuji W286
Nakatsuka, Ralph Y. A817
Nakayama, Masaaki W127
Nalamasu, Omkaram (Om) A74
Nalbach, Doug A595
Naldi, Robert P304
Naljayan, Mihran A257
Nalluri, Prathima A135
Nally, Thomas A (Tom) A807
Nam, Sik W311
Nam-Hai, Chua W424
Nama, Veeresh A414
Nama, Veeresh P236
Naman, Ananth E56
Nambiar, Vinod A218
Namenye, Andrew E252
Nan, Feng Hua W103

Nanavaty, Maulik A149
Nance, Jim P160
Nancy, Taussig P474
Nancy, Dunlap P588
Nanda, Ann A686
Nandakumar, Anita A391
Nangia, Nikhil A108
Nannen, John A706
Nanterme, Pierre W5
Nanthawithaya, Arthid W351
Nanty, Jer-ˆme W15
Nantz, Mark S. P94
Naouri, Jean-Charles W89
Naouri, Jean-Charles W318
Napier, Adam P425
Napier, James V. E234
Naples, Richard J. A123
Napol, Marcello A3
Napoleon, Rexann E406
Napoli, Frank A63
Napoli, Gus A436
Napoli, Joe A798
Napoli, Cathleen P333
Napoli, John P. P486
Napolitan, Raymond S. A612
Napolitano, Glen A329
Napolitano, Kenneth (Ken) A936
Napolitano, Jason A. E210
Napper, Terry P171
Nappi, David A933
Nappi, Ralph A. P382
Nappi, Mark P620
Naquin, Robbie A167
Naqvi, Syed P118
Naqvi, Naqi E1
Naraki, Kazuhide W221
Narang, Manu A54
Narang, Steve A117
Narang, Steve P61
Narang, Vic P500
Naranjo, Carlos P525
Narasimhan, Laxman A654
Narasimhan, Ramesh P546
Narayan, Sandeep A332
Narayanan, Lakshmi A216
Narayanan, Gowri A544
Narayanan, Ramanathan P10
Narayanan, Sundararajan
  (Sundar) E431
Narayen, Shantanu A11
Narchi, Robert E267
Nardone, Mary Kaye A504
Nardone, Michael A559
Nardone, Robert A888
Nardone, Mary Kaye E251
Nardone, Robert E425
Narenda, Vish M. A395
Narendran, T. V. W384
Narev, Ian W113
Narisetti, Raju A596
Narla, Mohandas P364
Narmi, Charles A727
Narmi, Charles P453
Narmouq, Samir A608
Narr, Bradly J P316
Narro, Oscar A571
Narula, Veru A201
Narvaez, Lorena A89
Narvekar, Abhijit E290
Narwani, Gaurav A776
Nasci, Kathleen P583
Nash, Nata A85
Nash, William D. (Bill) A171
Nash, Alexis A441
Nash, Joseph A556
Nash, Nick A862
Nash, David P603
Nash, Nick P617
Nash, Nata E27
Nash, Wilson E47
Nash, Daniel E105
Nash, John E144
Nash, Joseph E277
Nashar, Raniya Mahmood
  Abdulwahab W336

Nasir, Paul A798
Naspinski, Ed P542
Nassar, Daniel A14
Nassar, Daniel P6
Nasser, Jacques A. (Jac) W68
Nasser, Jac W69
Nassetta, Christopher J. (Chris) A423
Nassos, John A600
Nasta, David A332
Nastanski, Cynthia A654
Nastase, Mary P165
Nastasi, Richard P31
Natale, J A123
Natale, Tom A343
Natale, Lisa A619
Natale, Peter P337
Natale, Marina W407
Natale, Tom E164
Natale, Lisa E310
Natalizia, Michael J. E28
Natalone, John E24
Natarajan, Sanjay A74
Natarajan, Krishna A575
Natarajan, Stephen A588
Natarajan, Venkata A686
Natarajan, Murali A723
Natarajan, Shekar A804
Natarajan, Stephen P365
Natesan, Ganesh A107
Nath, Deepak A5
Nath, Munindra A200
Nath, Pravene P524
Nathan, Scott A114
Nathan, Mike A925
Nathan, Jim P287
Nathan, Cornell P515
Nathan, Sanders P639
Nathan, Scott E37
Nathan, Mike E445
Nathenson, Michael (Mike) P88
Natiello, Becky E433
Natoli, Jerry A471
Natoli, Joe P63
Natoli, Joseph P63
Natsis, Elaine A170
Nauert, Gary P185
Naughton, Marc G. A185
Naughton, Duncan C. Mac A273
Naughton, Mary A540
Naughton, W Terrance A908
Naughton, Des W79
Naughton, W Terrance E436
Naughton-Gerdes, Joan A36
Naugler, Scott P399
Naumann, Michael A19
Naumann, Peter A877
Nausedas, Darius P122
Nava, Carmen P A89
Nava, Mario A222
Navale, Sunil A608
Navarra, Eric A128
Navarra, Linda P110
Navarre, Christophe W241
Navarro, Jen A373
Navarro, Mary W. A444
Navarro, Imelda A463
Navarro, Jorge A871
Navarro, Carlos E379
Navert, Robin P463
Navia, Frank A156
Navran, Susan H. P90
Nay, Emma P249
Nayak, Vinayak A17
Nayak, Harsh A461
Nayak, Ajit A680
Nayak, Vinayak P9
Nayak, Harsh P255
Nayak, Amol E290
Nayama, Michisuke W258
Nayar, Deepak P258
Nayar, Sid E299
Naylor, Katie A54
Naylor, Lisa A228
Nazak, Keith A358
Nazak, Keith E176

Nazarian, Jeanette A478
Nazarian, Marita Q P45
Nazarian, Jeanette P268
Nazarian, Dana C. E110
Nazza, Larry E292
Nazzaro, Stephen F. (Steve) A783
Ndego, John W417
Ndemanga, Sekai A544
Ndiaye, Abdoulaye P422
Neagle, Kelly A627
Neal, Michelle M. A111
Neal, Annmarie A199
Neal, Krista A200
Neal, Stephen C. A514
Neal, Stephen C. A516
Neal, Cheryl A809
Neal, Gary F. A861
Neal, Joel A900
Neal, Lavone P71
Neal, Mikele P190
Neal, Michael P274
Neal, Stephen C. P293
Neal, Shelly P335
Neal, Jake P549
Neal, Greg P661
Neal, John W317
Neal, Kara E124
Neale, Donna A527
Neale, George A. A751
Neale, Gary L. E286
Nealon, Thomas M A773
Neaman, Mark R. P386
Nearhood, William A329
Neary, Tom E326
Nease, Andrea P459
Neate, James W53
Nebreda, Julian A18
Necas, Kevin P633
Necastro, Daniel Butch A36
Nedbalek, Dwayne P543
Nedder, Michael A356
Nedl, Katie A135
Neeb, Greg Null A761
Neeb, Marc J. W244
Need, Thomas A533
Needel, Jerry E47
Needham, Wendy A380
Needham, Sabine P18
Needham, Judy P207
Needham, Clark P352
Needleman, Scott P249
Needles, Adam A25
Needles, Adam P14
Neeley, Paige P300
Neely, Stephanie A36
Neely, Eric A489
Neely, Tonya P93
Neely, Denise P99
Neely, Wayne P498
Neemuchwala, Abidali P672
Neff, Clay A190
Neff, Doug A224
Neff, Lorraine A246
Neff, Scott A444
Neff, Raymond P116
Neff, Cheryl P117
Neff, Lorraine E105
Negishi, Akio W253
Negro, Jack P97
Negr--n, Eduardo J. A670
Neher, Terry A884
Neibart, Lee E356
Neidenbach, Joseph J P523
Neidenbach, Ann E101
Neidorff, Michael F. A179
Neifert, Kevin T. A706
Neike, Cedrik W353
Neikirk, Chris A604
Neil, Jesse A228
Neil, Carl P201
Neill, James R. (Jim) A379
Neill, Gregory A527
Neilsen, Troy A575
Neilson, Duncan P288
Neilson, Eric G. P388

Neilson, Dutch P493
Neis, Eric A575
Neis, Douglas A. E267
Neizman, Kai A219
Neizman, Kai E87
Nekrasov, Vladimir I. W309
Nell, Steven E. A141
Nell, Steven E. E49
Nellis, Jake P261
Nelms, Cary T A798
Nelms, Cary A798
Nelms, Charlie P610
Nelsen, Keith J. A130
Nelsen, Kathy A325
Nelsen, Denise A779
Nelsen, Mark A895
Nelsen, Karen P252
Nelsen, Suzanne P505
Nelso, Nelson A425
Nelson, Amy A71
Nelson, David A80
Nelson, Ronald L. (Ron) A98
Nelson, Roy A103
Nelson, Shelby A117
Nelson, Christopher (Chris) A121
Nelson, Kevin A168
Nelson, Wade A177
Nelson, Joan A213
Nelson, Rosemary A218
Nelson, Faye A. A279
Nelson, Ann W. A293
Nelson, John P. A293
Nelson, Yvonne A325
Nelson, Christian A349
Nelson, Paul A369
Nelson, Kimberly A. (Kim) A376
Nelson, Rick A399
Nelson, William A451
Nelson, Mike A467
Nelson, Brad A522
Nelson, Steven A525
Nelson, Philip B A536
Nelson, Philip A536
Nelson, John A540
Nelson, Susan K. A551
Nelson, Linda A567
Nelson, Linda A A567
Nelson, Jeff A602
Nelson, Peggy A623
Nelson, Jonathan B. A626
Nelson, Rick A665
Nelson, Ryan A740
Nelson, Travis A747
Nelson, Brian A761
Nelson, Rick A764
Nelson, Scott A804
Nelson, Jon A835
Nelson, Robert A844
Nelson, Christopher A859
Nelson, Michael S. A879
Nelson, David D. (Dave) A911
Nelson, Mary A933
Nelson, Zac A940
Nelson, Baltazar-huntersville P35
Nelson, David P46
Nelson, Kimberly P54
Nelson, Shelby P61
Nelson, Dan P86
Nelson, Kristin P110
Nelson, Sheila P110
Nelson, Carrie P114
Nelson, Beth P140
Nelson, Karen P142
Nelson, David P148
Nelson, Mark W. P159
Nelson, Scott P191
Nelson, Glenn P192
Nelson, Deana L. P203
Nelson, Brent P220
Nelson, Rick P223
Nelson, Gregory V P245
Nelson, William P249
Nelson, Doug P273
Nelson, Connia P296
Nelson, Karen P304

COMBINED HOOVER'S HANDBOOK INDEX OF EXECUTIVES

```
A = AMERICAN BUSINESS
E = EMERGING COMPANIES
P = PRIVATE COMPANIES
W = WORLD BUSINESS
```

Nelson, Susan K. P321
Nelson, Keith P323
Nelson, Krista P327
Nelson, Cynthia P330
Nelson, Carl P375
Nelson, Charlie P375
Nelson, Kristina P429
Nelson, Marie P432
Nelson, Brock P445
Nelson, Becky P471
Nelson, Elaine P550
Nelson, Christian P559
Nelson, Heather P594
Nelson, Laura P597
Nelson, Lorraine P621
Nelson, Kristi A P625
Nelson, Scott M. P654
Nelson, Jesse E8
Nelson, Kendra E35
Nelson, Ken E46
Nelson, Joyce E47
Nelson, Kyle E80
Nelson, Linda E284
Nelson, Linda A E284
Nelson, Peggy E313
Nelson, Rick E334
Nelson, Rick E377
Nelson, Kimberly K. (Kim) E384
Nelson, David D. (Dave) E437
Nemat, Claudia W138
Nemecek, Donna A111
Nemeth, Kathy A115
Nemeth, Matt A320
Nemeth, Jeffery A360
Nemeth, Julio A680
Nemeth, Rudolph A684
Nemeth, Joseph P330
Nemeth, Kathy E38
Nemeth, Andy L. E322
Nemphos, Ann A409
Nemser, Earl H. E235
Nemshick, Scott P412
Nenadal, Cody A793
Nentwig, Robert J. A147
Nenzel, Andrea P410
Nepveux, Kevin A657
Nerbonne, Daniel A668
Nerbonne, Dan A668
Nerenhausen, Frank R A632
Neri, Antonio A420
Neri, Marc A793
Neri, Leticia P151
Nerino, Alfred P336
NESBIT, JONATHAN A784
Nesbit, Jeff A835
Nesbit, Dennis P445
Nesbitt, Stephen R. A439
Nesbitt, Douglas A716
Nesbitt, John W373
Nesci, James D. A684
Nescott, Justin E22
Nesemeyer, Ron A224
Nesi, Victor J. A787
Neske, Rainer W231
Ness, Steve A905
Ness, Jon P282
Ness, Roberta B P596
Nesse, Robert P316
Nesselbush, Robert J P272
Nesselbush, Robert P455
Nesset, Sharon P618
Nesta, Cheryl A405
Nester, Brian A. P289
Nesti, Sarah P384
Nestor, Kat P549
Nestor, James E132
Neth, Bryan A755
Neth, Bryan E369
Netherton, Linda A327

Neto, Paulo A512
Neto, Jo--o Manuel Manso W146
Nette, Claus-Georg W248
Nettesheim, Susan A479
Nettle, Austin E171
Nettles, Kwicha A346
Nettles, Richard A479
Nettles, Kwicha E167
Netto, Armando L. E174
Neufeld, Kathy P340
Neufville, Mortimer H. P642
Neugarten, Lisa A452
Neugent, Christopher J. A672
Neuhaus, Joan P21
Neuman, Jennifer A592
Neuman, John P206
Neuman, Jennifer P370
Neumann, Spencer A10
Neumann, Karl-Thomas A378
Neumann, Dan A665
Neumann, Paul G A847
Neumann, Neal P304
Neumann, Paul G P606
Neumann, Paul W208
Neumann, Dan E334
Neumeister, Irene P468
Neumeyer, Daniel J. A444
Neuzil, Samantha E406
Nevala, Wendy A924
Nevels, Baraka E123
Nevens, T Michael A586
Nevers, Rick L. P49
Neville, Brian A51
Neville, Robert M. A105
Neville, Bob A105
Neville, Robert M. E34
Neville, Bob E34
Nevins, Michael A761
Nevins, Janice P132
Nevo-Hacohen, Talya E362
New, Wayne P161
Newallis, David A57
Newallis, David P33
Newberg, William A902
Newbern, Thomas B. A95
Newberry, Stephen G. (Steve) A505
Newberry, Gary A. E60
Newbery, Michelle M. A527
Newbigging, Alexander W208
Newbould, Tom A843
Newbrough, James P. P395
Newcom, Jeff A347
Newcom, Jeff E167
Newcomb, Jorey A236
Newcomb, Mike P288
Newcomer, Mark A304
Newcomer, John A383
Newcomer, Patti A471
Newcomer, Nate A722
Newcomer, John E186
Newell, John D P629
Newell, Lisa E14
Newey, Jay P646
Newfield, Richard U. A581
Newfield, Richard U. E294
Newhall, Charles W. (Chuck) E394
Newhouse, Greg A491
Newkirk, Christopher T. A166
Newkirk, Jesse A347
Newkirk, Melanie A621
Newkirk, Jesse E167
Newkirk, Melanie E312
Newlands, William A. (Bill) A236
Newlin, Karl A281
Newman, Randy A31
Newman, Kenneth Kenneth Newman A111
Newman, Rebecca A112
Newman, Sallie A246
Newman, Jenifer A306
Newman, Tim A351
Newman, John A352
Newman, Margaret A412
Newman, Deon A419
Newman, Michael A452

Newman, Amy A452
Newman, Deon A465
Newman, Rainer A479
Newman, Mark A482
Newman, Margaret A489
Newman, Gerald A548
Newman, Brian A654
Newman, Robert A664
Newman, Peter A828
Newman, Kurt P127
Newman, Kurt D. P130
Newman, Kurt P131
Newman, Mark F. P187
Newman, Bryan P523
Newman, Peter P584
Newman, Allison P610
Newman, Randy E8
Newman, Giles R. E99
Newman, Sallie E105
Newman, Robert E333
Newmyer, Joyce P6
Newns, Steve E203
Newpol, Jon P611
Newport, Roger K. A27
Newsom, Brittany A58
Newsom, Richard W. (Rick) A229
Newsom, Gavin A782
Newsom, Terri T. P430
Newsom, Gavin P525
Newsome, Mark A8
Newsome, Jana P377
Newton, Opal A23
Newton, Wayne A29
Newton, Vera A360
Newton, Carl A749
Newton, Heather A780
Newton, Julianne P636
Newton, Carl E367
Neyland, Stephen J P340
Neylon, Brian V. A271
Neymon, Denys W366
Nezhat, Ceana P386
Ng, Dominic A284
Ng, Frances A284
Ng, Donna A479
Ng, Stella A484
Ng, Regina A544
Ng, Sonia A742
Ng, Carmen A797
Ng, Dominic E119
Ng, Frances E120
Ng, Chong E248
Ngau, Jonathan W. E253
Ngeow, Susan P368
Ngo, A. Catherine A182
Ngo, Michelle E246
Ngo, Nhat H. E315
Ngt, Steve P392
Nguyen, Thong M. A107
Nguyen, Kim A251
Nguyen, Lan A404
Nguyen, Chao A412
Nguyen, Xuong A470
Nguyen, Tony A559
Nguyen, Hanna A722
Nguyen, Tinh A861
Nguyen, Andy H P162
Nguyen, Phubinh P199
Nguyen, Lan Quoc P212
Nguyen, Steven P212
Nguyen, Chao P233
Nguyen, Derek P246
Nguyen, Mong Thi P530
Nguyen, Tricia P551
Nguyen, Phuong P594
Nguyen, Michelle P655
Nguyen, Thi Mai Thanh W208
Nguyen, Thao E154
Nguyen, Lan E199
Nguyen, Van E264
Nguyen, Chuck E290
Nguyen-Duy, Jonathan E179
Niblock, Robert A. A527
Nicandrou, Nic W315
NICASTRO, ROBERTO W410

Niccol, Brian R. A937
Niccolucci, Dani A830
Niccolucci, Dani P601
Niccum, Tom A857
Nicdao, Nicole A738
Nichipor, Thomas A821
Nichitean, Florin P184
Nichol, Andy A596
Nichol, Jason A855
Nicholas, Ken A9
Nicholas, Georgette C. A381
Nicholas, George A482
Nicholas, Jim A483
Nicholas, Brad A690
Nicholas, Ken P4
Nicholas, Jack P125
Nicholas, Marc P235
Nicholas, Richard P593
Nicholas, Robert P634
Nicholls, Timothy S. (Tim) A467
Nicholls, Robbie A62
NICHOLS, ROB A110
Nichols, Todd A133
Nichols, Lee A165
Nichols, Ronald O. A290
Nichols, Jim A341
Nichols, Aaron A349
Nichols, Alan R. A395
Nichols, Nancy A468
Nichols, Russell A518
Nichols, Rodney P. A534
Nichols, Dana L. A693
Nichols, Ronald O. (R.O.) A770
Nichols, Donald A844
Nichols, Art A924
Nichols, Wanda P122
Nichols, Gretchen P288
Nichols, Jimmy P315
Nichols, Amanda P319
Nichols, Lara P375
Nichols, Julie P477
Nichols, Brandie P548
Nichols, Robert P628
Nichols, Robbie E20
Nichols, Jesse E131
Nichols, Maria E147
Nichols, Dana L. E341
Nicholson, Glenn A195
Nicholson, E. Allen A249
Nicholson, Allen A279
Nicholson, Darryl A479
Nicholson, Marla A540
Nicholson, Lyle A855
Nicholson, James B P429
Nicholson, James M P429
Nicholson, David A P429
Nicholson, E. Allen E108
Nicholson, Allen E108
Nicholson, Steve E260
Nicholson, John E300
Niciu, Carrie P529
Nickel, Daryl A71
Nickel, Jackie P3
Nickel, Daryl P43
Nickele, Christopher J. (Chris) A212
Nickels, Jeff A341
Nickerson, Richard A162
Nickerson, Randy A578
Nickerson, Cheryl A651
Nickerson, Nate P314
Nickerson, Daniel P670
Nickerson, Richard E62
Nickerson, Cheryl P329
Nicki, David A380
Nickles, Jenny A444
Nickless, David P166
Nicklin, Emily P594
Nickman, Gene A170
Nickol, Christopher A751
Nickol, Thomas P282
Nicol, Ronald L P187
Nicola, Cindy A818
Nicolaus, Joseph A608
Nicolelli, Maurizio E143
Nicoletti, Laurie A544

Nicoletti, Ralph J. A593
Nicolino, Lynda P299
Nicols, Maureen P300
Nicosia, Santo V P227
Nidiffer, Douglas P104
Nieden, Paul Zur A327
Niederberger, Mary A642
Niederberger, Mary P407
Niederhuber, John A253
Niedzielski, Vincent P. (Vince) E240
Niedzielski, Vince E240
Niehaus, James A56
Niehaus, Brenda W363
Niehaus, Sheila E51
Niekamp, Cynthia A103
Nields, Rosanne P463
Nielsen, Merilee A15
Nielsen, Dan A179
Nielsen, Joel A360
Nielsen, Mark D. A366
Nielsen, Rob A481
Nielsen, Jane H. A701
Nielsen, Mark D A706
Nielsen, James L. (Jim) A776
Nielsen, Michelle A797
Nielsen, Merilee P8
Nielsen, Paul D. P114
Nielsen, Cindy P566
Nielsen, Peter W333
Nielsen, Chris W400
Nielson, Marlin A524
Nielson, Sephen P481
Niem, Eddie A218
Niemann, Tammy A86
Niemann, Tammy E27
Niemann, Scott E226
Niemaseck, Ken P197
Niemczyk, Todd A325
Niemeyer, Bruce L E284
Niemi, Albert W. P505
Niemietz, Christy A925
Niemietz, Christy E445
Niemoeller, John Arthur A343
Niemoeller, John Arthur E164
Nienaber, Margaret W363
Nienen, Marge P129
Nierenberg, Gregg A98
Niermann, Mark A259
Niermann, Nils W62
Nietfeld, Kathi P148
Nieto, Alejandra A658
Nieto, Luis A735
Nieto, Enrique Pena W304
Nieuwenhuys, Gerard A649
Nieves, Antonio De Jesus P79
Nieves, Frankie P593
Nightingale, Timothy P. A162
Nightingale, Timothy P. E62
Nigon, Bernard E211
Nigrin, Daniel P558
Nigro, David A54
Nigro, Joseph (Joe) A304
Nigro, Stephen (Steve) A438
Nigro, James M. A504
Nigro, Rich A727
Nigro, Rich P453
Nigro, James M. E251
Nihei, Ryo W238
Niinami, Takeshi W374
Nikolov, Anita A606
Niland, Mark A800
Niles, Thomas A574
Niles, Brenda P56
Niles, Amy P409
Nill, Michael R. (Mike) A185
Nilsson, Gunilla P496
Nilsson, Stefan W377
Nimbley, Thomas J A186
Nimbley, Thomas J. A644
Nimbley, Thomas J P123
Ninas, Jason A796
Ninas, Jason E397
Ning, Wilson A507
Ninneman, Tom E383
Niranjan, Tejwantie E138

Nisbett, Mark A906
Nisbett, Mark E435
Nisbit, Toni A345
Nisbit, Toni E166
Nisenbom, Hugo A554
Nisenson, Larry A381
Nishi, Masao A797
Nishida, Mitsuo W368
Nishigori, Yuichi W298
Nishihara, Shigeru W360
Nishikata, Masaaki W266
Nishimoto, Jo A69
Nishimoto, John A924
Nishimura, Tatsushi W127
Nishitani, Hideto W298
Nishiura, Kanji W257
Nishizaki, Tsuyoshi P534
Nishizawa, Keiji W360
Nissen, James A P412
Nissenbaum, Ronen A423
Nissenson, Allen R. A257
Nissley, Amy P644
Nister, David A818
Niswonger, Scott A343
Niswonger, Scott E164
Nitithanprapas, Ekniti W226
Nitsch, Denise P667
Nitti, Joe A925
Nitti, Joe E445
Nitzan, Nachman W163
Niubo, Antonio Brufau W321
Niven, Christine P333
Nivens, Lisa A547
Nix, Jeff A95
Nix, Craig L. A336
Nix, D Mark P252
Nix, Craig L. E157
Nixon, Nicole A429
Nixon, Dennis E. A463
Nixon, Bill A744
Nixon, Ken A850
Nixon, John E. P597
Nixon, Bruce P659
Nixon, Kevin E168
Niyogi, Prosun A647
Nizza, Arthur P258
Nizzari-Mcclain, Cynthia P642
Njonjo, Peter A215
Nkongho, Andrew A702
Nkuhlu, Mfundo W275
Noack, Daniel A668
Noakes, Jackie W233
Nober, Roger A138
Nober, Roger A157
Nober, Roger P91
Noble, Quintin A5
Noble, Jeff A338
Noble, Jen A465
Noble, Craig A651
Noble, Steve P141
Noble, David P219
Noble, Kim P502
Noble, Craig E329
Nobles, Anne P252
Nobles, Melissa P314
Noblett, Monique A605
Nocchiero, Tony E60
Noce, Jen P574
Nocella, Andrew P. A864
Nodar, Aaron A530
Nodiff, Eric W. E63
Noe, Alan A713
Noel, Robert A309
Noel, Molaine A538
Noell, Samantha A592
Noell, Samantha P371
Noelle, Boudler A785
Noethiger, Robert A892
Noetzel, Alex P549
Noga, James W. (Jim) A641
Noga, James W. (Jim) P407
Nogalski, John A485
Nogles, Thomas A409
Noglows, William P E258
Noguchi, Tadahiko W292

Nolan, Peter A10
Nolan, Rebecca A16
Nolan, Bob A232
Nolan, Joseph R. (Joe) A303
Nolan, Robert A309
Nolan, Michael J. (Mike) A325
Nolan, James A391
Nolan, Gary A495
Nolan, Paul A547
Nolan, Elizabeth A784
Nolan, David A. A939
Nolan, Matthew P196
Nolan, Gary P282
Nolan, Carrie P308
Nolan, Kevin P392
Nolan, Peter E102
Nolan, Lynn E172
Nolan, Christopher E250
Nolan, Conor E278
Nolan-maccione, Kelley A877
Noland, William M A313
Noland, Matt A852
Noland, William M P200
Nolasco, Teresa A222
Nolden, Casey A3
Nolen, Steve A184
Nolen, Charles E106
Noletto, Tanya A713
Noll, Kelly A35
Noll, Richard A. (Rich) A403
Noll, Chuck P613
Noller, Rick A285
Nolley, Breck E433
Nolte, Jo A647
Nolte, Jeremy P343
Nolting, John A491
Nomura, Stephanie A109
Nomura, Mitsuru W51
Nomura, Katsuaki W348
Nomura, Tetsuya W349
Nonaka, Susan P230
Nonaka, Toshihiko W186
Nonnemaker, Jason P456
Nonnenkamp, Donald H P658
Nonomura, Rikiya W286
Nooijer, Marcel de W15
Nook, Greg P260
Nook, Gregory E. (Greg) P261
Noonan, Mike A200
Noonan, James R. A504
Noonan, James R. E251
Noordende, Alexander M. (Sander) van't W5
Noordhoek, Jeffrey R. (Jeff) A586
Noordhoek, Jeffrey R. (Jeff) E301
Noot, Walter E423
Nooyi, Indra K. A654
Nopka, Jacqueline A197
Noppenberger, Louis A205
Norberg, Kim P41
Norby, Stephanie L. P497
Norcia, Gerardo (Jerry) A279
Norcross, Gary A. A327
Norcross, Anna A491
Norcross, Jeanne A774
Norcross, George E. P563
Nordby, Hans G. E99
Nordell, Scott A325
Nordin, Brandon P32
Nordli, Lars Johannes W155
Nordlie, Elizabeth M. A376
Nordmeyer, Greg A60
Nordmeyer, Jim A616
Nordstrom, Mike A376
Nordstrom, Blake W. A602
Nordstrom, Peter E. (Pete) A602
Nordstrom, Erik B. A602
Nordstrom, James F. (Jamie) A602
Nordstrom, Jeff A715
Norgren, Jim A479
Noriega, Erica A246
Noriega, Erica E105
Noritz, Garey P359
Nork, Edward A227
Nork, Rick P660

Nork, Edward E90
Norkunas, Kathy P153
Norland, Jerry A30
Norland, Jerry P20
Norling, Richard A P428
Norman, Todd A309
Norman, Paul T. A487
Norman, David A902
Norman, Linda P599
Norman, Dave E72
Normington, Debbie A199
Noro, Yukio W368
Norrington, Lorrie A218
Norris, Derek J. A109
Norris, Blake A449
Norris, Josephine A483
Norris, Betty A523
Norris, Julie A550
Norris, Craig A897
Norris, Michael P195
Norris, Julie P319
Norris, Todd P662
Norris, Blake E221
Norrman, Helena W386
Norrod, Forrest E. A14
North, Paul A501
North, John F. A521
North, Martie A760
North, Scott A775
North, Michael E14
North, Marty E47
North, Martie E374
Northam, Thadd A540
Northam, Jaime E203
Northcutt, Kevin A449
Northcutt, Kendria A665
Northcutt, Kevin E221
Northcutt, Kendria E334
Northern, Richard A788
Northern, Richard E389
Northey, Brian A544
Northorp, Dale P6
Northrop, Ann A349
Norton, Rita A64
Norton, Todd A224
Norton, Rick A399
Norton, Michael F A492
Norton, Johna A518
Norton, Ellen A533
Norton, Robert G. (Bob) A641
Norton, David K. A651
Norton, W.D. (Joe) A773
Norton, Brad A813
Norton, Janet P64
Norton, Andrew J P211
Norton, Rick P223
Norton, Michael F P279
Norton, Melissa P306
Norton, Robert G. (Bob) P407
Norton, Margareta E P437
Norton, Margareta E. (Meg) P438
Norton, Glenn E278
Norton, David K. E329
Norton, W.D. (Joe) E383
Norton, Karlyn E429
Norwitt, Richard A. (Adam) A66
Noseworthy, Darren A658
Noseworthy, John H P318
Noskin, Gary P388
Noskov, Mikhail W402
Nosler, John S. A716
Nosowitz, Barry P496
Nota, Pieter W63
Notaristefani, Carlo de W389
Noth, Thomas W382
Nottage, Lavieria P423
Nourot, Mary P536
Novac, Tim A9
Novac, Tim P4
Novaes, Djalma A245
Novak, Ryan A58
Novak, Matt P237
Novak, Kim P359
Novak, Steve P586
Novak, Elizabeth P622

COMBINED HOOVER'S HANDBOOK INDEX OF EXECUTIVES

A = AMERICAN BUSINESS
E = EMERGING COMPANIES
P = PRIVATE COMPANIES
W = WORLD BUSINESS

Novakovic, Phebe A5
Novakovic, Phebe N. A373
Novakovich, Cathy A812
Novich, Neil A67
Novich, Neil A394
Novielli, Jack A684
Novo, Guillermo A24
Novosel, John A345
Novosel, John E166
Nowell, Ana A15
Nowell, Lauren A893
Nowell, Ana P8
Nowicki, Joseph M. A121
Nowicki, Donald A702
Nowicki, Dan A765
Nowiski, Dave P329
Nowlan, Kevin A146
Nowotny, Ewald W292
Noyes, Mark A235
Nozari, Moe A3
Nozawa, Takashi W293
Nqwababa, Bongani W341
Nthunzi, Godfrey A218
Nuccio, Susan A481
Nuchims, Fran A167
Nudelman, Jenna A596
Nudi, Jonathon J. (Jon) A376
Nudo, Mario A925
Nudo, Mario E445
Nuest, Vaughn P610
Nugent, Cchea P505
Nuki, Masayoshi W228
Nulter, Steven A652
Nulter, Steven E331
Nulty, James E110
Numata, Shigeru W127
Numata, Kaoru W286
Nunes, Jack A508
Nunez, Armando A176
Nunez, Rachel A402
Nunez, Ricardo J A412
Nunez, Felix A571
Nunez, Sylvia P160
Nunez, Milton P296
Nunez, Jeanette P433
Nunez, Rachel E198
Nunez-Mejia, Bibi P409
Nunn, Lucy P611
Nunn, Trudy P659
Nunnari, Nicholas A200
Nurmi, Kelsey P116
Nurse, Paul P325
Nusbaum, Nancy P551
Nuss, Wilden A828
Nuss, Wilden P584
Nuti, William A865
Nutt, Wendy A562
Nutt, Pam P235
Nutt, Raymond P443
Nutt, William V P578
Nutter, Michael A246
Nutter, Michael E105
Nutton, Debra A930
Nuzzo, Carla A877
Nuzzo, Gregory E379
Nuzzolo, Marc A888
Nuzzolo, Marc E425
Nwamadi, Tresia A232
Nwele, Kenneth A201
Nwokeji, Linda A165
Nye, Lara A462
Nye, Angela A704
Nye, Lara P256
Nyeholt, Ron A325
Nyen, Jake A85
Nyen, Jake E27
Nyenhuis, Michael P37
Nykiel, Alan A142
Nykiel, Alan E49

Nykoluk, Tim P168
Nylander, Raye Nae P566
Nylen, Tim P152
Nysschen, Carel Johannes de A378
Nystedt, Johan A232
Nysten, Marcus W357
Nyul, Renata P383
N- ͻger, Lorenz W180
N- !ss, Bj- ͵rn Erik W140
Norenberg, Marco W267
Néemeh, Alain P. A714

O

o, W55
Oaconnor, Stephen A384
Oaconnor, Stephen P217
Oake-libow, Eli A520
Oakes, John A64
Oakes, John P201
Oakland, Steven T. A765
Oakley, Christopher A319
Oakley, Glenn A893
Oakley, Bill A913
Oakley, Bill E438
Oakman, Scott P445
Oaks, Patrick P261
Oaks, Kenneth P278
Oal, Tolga A49
Oancia, Doran A598
Oates, Joseph P. A235
Oates, Michael P. A327
Oathout, Brian A456
Oathout, Brian E228
Oba, Masashi W393
Obana, William G P585
Obando, Glenn A112
Obayashi, Takeo W292
Obeidat, Mario A326
Ober, Tammy P573
Oberacker, Beth P306
Oberbruner, Miriam A810
Oberg, Kathleen K. (Leeny) A537
Oberg, Leeny A538
Oberg, Chris P220
Oberhaus, Michael A314
Oberhaus, Michael E145
Oberholzer, Bill A676
Oberholzer, Bill E338
Obering, Henry A. (Trey) A144
Obermeyer, Frank A195
Obermeyer, Paul R. A221
Obermeyer, Jaime P264
Obermiller, John A810
Obermiller, John P546
Oberoi, Raina E290
Oberosler, Bob A722
Oberry, Greg A429
Obert, William A520
Oberton, Willard D. (Will) A315
Obey, Christopher J. W164
Obie, Nestor A670
Obleton, Carolynn A796
Obleton, Carolynn E397
Oblisk, Sonya Gafsi A921
Oblisk, Sonya Gafsi P669
Obolsky, Mitchel A564
Obolsky, Mitch A564
Obray, Bob P50
Obrian, Diana A405
Obrian, Tom A444
Obrien, James J A61
Obrien, James A61
OBrien, Laura A175
Obrien, Sharon A530
Obrien, Kori A740
OBrien, Kevin M. A872
Obrien, Barbara A922
Obrien, Gary P442
Obrien, John P616
Obrien, Barbara P671
OBrien, John E53
Obryan, Megan P141
Obryant, Sid P552

Obuchowski, Andy E102
Obzud, John A325
Ocampo, Christopher A6
Ocasio-Fant, Diana A468
Occhiello, Ernesto W342
Occhipinti, Tony A626
Och, John P569
Ochi, Hitoshi W256
Ochoa, Vanessa A222
Ochoa, Arthur P118
Ochoa, Andrew P302
Ochoa, S. Hector P634
Ochsner, Brian P78
Ochsner, Lisa Cloud P424
Ochsner, Peter W55
OConnell, Dan A409
Oconnell, Mike A852
OConnell, Rick P462
OConnor, Jim A125
OConnor, Kevin A150
Oconnor, Andrew A740
Oconnor, Joseph A767
Oconnor, Caitlin A782
Oconnor, Kimberly A799
Oconnor, Christopher J P502
Oconnor, Caitlin P526
Oconnor, James P594
Oconnor, Michael P677
Oconnor, Kim P677
OConnor, Kevin E50
Oconnor, Michele E427
Oda, Calla A109
Oda, Syuji W127
Oddleifson, Christopher (Chris) A455
Oddleifson, Christopher (Chris) E227
Oddo, David A646
Oddo, David E324
Odegaard, Richard P223
Odegard, Taylor A176
Odell, Deborah A226
Odell, Lawrence A333
Odell, Peck A333
Odell, David A491
Odell, Deborah P150
Odell, Robert P492
Odinet, Bertrand (Bert) A365
Odisho, Walter A140
Oditt, Alex P252
Odle, Roger A36
Odlis, Mark A682
ODoherty, Patrick A678
Odom, Ronald A69
Odom, Kara A609
Odom, Scott E106
Odonnell, Holly A325
Odonnell, Jim A483
Odonnell, Michelle A692
Odonnell, Julia A922
Odonnell, Joseph A922
Odonnell, Morgan P6
Odonnell, Julia P671
Odonnell, Joseph P671
ODowd, Frank E77
Odriozola, Jose Maria (Chema) A870
Odrzywolski, Jason P125
Oechslin, Joachim W120
Oechsner, Susan P250
Oehlert, Christine P157
Oehling, James P P411
Oelke, Dawn A413
Oelke, Les A413
Oelke, Dawn E205
Oelke, Les E205
Oeser, Scott E433
Oestreich, Patrick A935
Oestreich, Rebecca P511
Oetgen, William J. A551
Oetgen, William J. P321
Oexle, Edward A330
Oexle, Edward E152
Offenberger, Eric J. A716
Offer, D. Scott W164
Offers, Nathan P552
Ofman, Joshua A64
Ofner, Jennifer E91

Oftedal, Siv A301
Oftedal, Siv P196
Oganes, Luis A484
Ogata, Isamu W127
Ogata, Masaki W143
Ogawa, Tetsuji W127
Ogawa, Tetsuo W400
Ogburn, Robert A621
Ogburn, Robert E312
Ogden, Stasia L A120
Ogden, Kylie A211
Ogden, Bob A397
Ogden, Jodi P559
Ogden, Kylie E83
Ogden, Roger E366
Ogg, Tom P131
Ogilvie, Marran E151
Oglesby, John A706
Oglesby, Charles M P135
Oglesby, Charles E269
Ogletree, Dan P419
Ognall, Andrew H. A861
Ogoshi, Tatsuo W253
Ogrady, Shawn P A376
Ogren, Dan P161
Ogrosky, Kori L. A638
Ogrosky, Kori L. E320
Ogundiran, Joke P569
Ogunlesi, Adebayo O. (Bayo) E59
Ogunro, Edward E92
Oguz, Orkun W18
Oguz, Bulent W18
Oh, Irene H. A284
Oh, David A482
Oh, James A919
Oh, In-Hwan W311
Oh, Irene H. E120
Oh, Daniel J. E352
Ohabor, Constantine P183
Ohanian, David A222
OHara, Brooks A398
Ohara, Michele A641
Ohara, Yoshinori A938
Ohara, Ruth P290
Ohara, Michele P407
Ohara, Yoshinori P678
Ohara, Kenichiro W107
Ohare, Tammy A877
Ohea, Eve A744
Ohelo, Doree J A109
Ohemeng-Dapaah, Michael P295
Ohira, Noriyoshi W256
Ohk, Joohee P165
Ohl, Chad A842
Ohlgart, Christiane E179
Ohlinger, Brian P650
Ohmpornnuwat, Pisit W95
Ohno, Tomohiko W107
Ohno, Naotake W127
Oho, Yoshihiro W127
Ohri, Sumita E431
Ohta, Jun W369
Ohtake, Takashi P376
Ohtsubo, Fumio W301
Oi, Terence A933
Ojima, Koichi W182
Okabe, David P230
Okabe, Hitoshi W18
Okabe, Nobuhiro E253
Okada, Terri A109
Okada, Motoya W11
Okada, Yutaka W51
Okada, Kenji W205
Okada, Shinichi W210
Okafor, Kenosa P329
Okai, Lilian A108
Okamoto, Gary A P585
Okamoto, Kunie W279
Okamura, Cindy A109
Okano, Michiyuki W350
Okano, Kinosuke W375
Okanobu, Shinichi W392
Okawa, Kazushi W257
Okawara, Masaki W366
Okazaki, Jason A385

COMBINED HOOVER'S HANDBOOK INDEX OF EXECUTIVES

Okazaki, Soichi W11
Okazaki, Takeshi W160
Okazoe, Kiyoshi W258
Okerlund, Janis A325
Okerstrom, Mark D. A307
Okeson, Todd A329
Oketani, Taimi W348
Okimoto, Michelle A835
Okolie, Patricia P242
Okoroafor, Michael A547
Okpalla, Nneka P406
Okray, Thomas B. (Tom) A13
Okray, Thomas B A394
Oku, Masayuki W369
Okubo, Tsuneo W346
Okuda, Kentaro W286
Okun, Robert B P225
ol, W6
Olaes, John P60
Olafson, Harlee N. A911
Olafson, Harlee N. E437
Olafsson, Sigurdur O. (Siggi) W389
Olander, Kristen P126
Olander, Anastasia P420
Olberding, Elizabeth P522
Olczak, Jacek A661
Old, Tim P499
Olden, Christopher A756
Oldenburg, Camille A719
Oldenburg, Kim M P316
Oldenburg, Phyllis E48
Oldenburg, Camille E355
Oldenkamp, Jeffrey P. E201
Oldenski, Becky A737
Oldenski, Becky E361
Oldfield, Cheryl A835
Oldford, Kirk E290
Oldham, Jon A167
Oldham, Paul P545
Olds, Greg A489
Olds, Debbie P670
Oldsberg, Carl E80
Olear, Mark J. E187
Oleary, Donna A922
Oleary, Donna P671
Olejer, Leigh A246
Olejer, Leigh E105
Olejniczak, Dave P516
Oleksak, Michael J. (Mike) E42
Oleksiak, Peter B A278
Oleksiak, Peter B. A279
Oleksiuk, Mary A. A855
Olenick, Evelyn P417
Oleon, John A327
Oles, Karen P335
Olin, John A. A407
Olinsky, Michael A329
Olion, Marion Gillis P168
Oliphant, Gerald P218
Oliu, Edward A837
Oliva, Rhonda A566
Oliva, Cynthia A664
Oliva, Cindy A665
Oliva, Harvey P68
Oliva, Cynthia E334
Oliva, Cindy E334
Olivan, Javier A310
Olivares, David A390
Olivares, Jacob A619
Olivares, Jacob P393
Olivares, Ana P420
Olive, Stephen R. A634
Oliveira, Marcelo A366
Oliveira, Rafael A497
Oliveira, Victor P109
Oliveira, J. Augusto de E110
Oliver, Gary A89
Oliver, Joel A168
Oliver, Kevin A213
Oliver, Joseph A264
Oliver, Sean A327
Oliver, Timothy A354
Oliver, George R A480
Oliver, David A654
Oliver, Mitch A695

Oliver, George A706
Oliver, Cedric A713
Oliver, Wes A727
Oliver, Kirk R. A857
Oliver, Kevin P143
Oliver, George P269
Oliver, George R P270
Oliver, Wes P453
Oliver, Mark P602
Olivera, Armando A355
Olivera, Michelle A452
Oliveras, Noel P390
Oliverio, Dale P54
Oliverio, John D P667
Olivier, Leon J. (Lee) A303
Olivier, Grégoire W305
Olivier, Leon E135
Olivieri, Fernando A. Gonzalez W91
Olivo, Maria A844
Olivo, Rene P458
Olkowski, Ed A922
Olkowski, Ed P671
Ollagnier, Jean-Marc W5
Oller, Robert S. P390
Ollia, Marshall A704
Olmstead, Cpcu A781
Olnick, Bryan A354
Oloughlin, Jane P70
Olsavsky, Brian T. A42
Olscamp, Karen E. P630
Olsen, Neil A313
Olsen, Erica A391
Olsen, Sonja A472
Olsen, Douglas A651
Olsen, Karl A840
Olsen, John A929
Olsen, Morgan R. P44
Olsen, Neil P200
Olsen, Richelle P208
Olsen, Kathy P240
Olsen, Chelsey P639
Olsen, Douglas E330
Olsen, John E449
Olson, Lisa A6
Olson, W. Kregg A71
Olson, Knute A A89
Olson, John A103
Olson, Tiffany P. A169
Olson, Robert A262
Olson, Eric A369
Olson, Arik A571
Olson, Dan A628
Olson, Laurie J. A657
Olson, Thomas A727
Olson, Aaron A747
Olson, Dave A846
Olson, Kevin A856
Olson, Maribeth P26
Olson, Beth P30
Olson, Greg P284
Olson, Gerald P298
Olson, Kristin P318
Olson, David P354
Olson, Toni P434
Olson, Thomas P453
Olson, Matt P469
Olson, Carrie P476
Olson, Ryan P546
Olson, Tim P602
Olson, Kevin P614
Olson, Paul L. H. E128
Olson, Bruce J E268
Olson, Charles W. (Charlie) E395
Olson-Wilk, Jennifer E10
Olsson, Charles A749
Olsson, Jimmy A902
Olsson, Charles E367
Olthuis, Cameron A893
Oltman, Renee P396
Omalley, Sean A319
Omalley, William P384
Omalley, Kimberly P447
Oman, Mark A332
Omanakuttan, Sudheer A107
Omer, Ziv W49

Omidfar, Bahr A526
Omidyar, Pierre M A287
Omiya, Hideaki W258
Omoss, Mario A242
Omoto, Christiane P146
Omtvedt, Craig P A632
Ondecker, Marilyn A520
Onders, Mike A491
Oneal, Adreanne P251
Oneil, Gary E51
Oneil, Stephen E102
ONeill, Beth A108
Oneill, Bernie A686
Oneill, Tim E84
Onell, Lia P330
Onen, Kudret W222
Ong, Eddie A676
Ong, Ivy A742
Ong, Terence S. E. W411
Ong, Eddie E338
Onishi, Ricky P667
Onishi, Tadashi W253
Onishi, Akira W398
Onisick, Bill A108
Onksen, Bill A125
Ono, Santa J. P625
Ono, Naoki M259
Onoda, Satoshi W107
Onodera, Makoto W380
Onofrey, Debbie A879
Onorato, Andrea A888
Onorato, Andrea E425
Onozawa, Yasuo W262
Onumonu, Ngozi A722
Onzuka, Chris A109
Ooi, Boon A734
Oorschot, Rich van W132
Oosten, Mindy A752
Oostendorp, Kellie A925
Oostendorp, Kellie E445
Oosterman, Linnea P597
Oosterman, Wade W65
Opatrny, David A491
Opdyke, Steve A160
Opedal, Anders A301
Opedal, Tor A544
Opedal, Anders P196
Opelka, George A332
Opembe, Patrick P117
Opengo, Jose E106
Ophaug, Courtney A117
Ophaug, Courtney P61
Opilio, Giuseppe R. W385
Oppenheim, David A29
Oppenheimer, Richard A835
Oppenhuis, Liz A36
Opper, Scott E131
Opperman, Carl P78
Oprea, Martha A580
Oprea, Martha E292
Opstedahl, Deeanna A226
Opstedahl, Deeanna P150
Oran, Baris W177
Oranga, James A925
Oranga, James E445
Oranje, Joop P282
Oratis, Michael W272
Oravetz, Cami E14
Oravitz, Jeffrey J. A673
Orban, Stephen A337
Orban, Stephen E158
Orchard, Curtis A608
Orchard, Lisa A779
Orchard, Kenneth R. A848
Orchard, Arlen P462
Orchard, Kenneth R. E411
Ordemann, William (Bill) A299
Ordukaya, Basar A330
Ordukaya, Basar E152
Orduna, Arthur A98
Orecchio, Maria A752
Orellana, Charles P583
Oren, Gadi A460
Oresick, Mark A337
Oresick, Mark E158

Orf, Mike A448
Orf, Harry A642
Orf, David A733
Orf, Mike P247
Orf, Harry P407
Ori, Indira P364
Orie, James G. A357
Orie, James G. E175
Oringer, Jonathan (Jon) E371
Oriol, Albert P438
Orisek, Philip P536
Orisio, Lori P554
Orlandi, Mario A100
Orlando, Mario A437
Orlando, David A799
Orlando, Lorraine A827
Orlando, John A892
Orlando, Lorraine P580
Orlando, Adolph M P587
Orlikoff, James P652
Orloff, Harvey A200
Orlowski, Chris A859
Ormond, Gia A347
Ormond, Tommy P25
Ormond, Gia E167
Ormsby, Lenard T. A293
Ormuz, Tammy P551
Ornas, Melanie A445
Orndahl, Michael E293
Orndorf, Karen P15
Orndorff, Robert L. A741
Orndorff, Robert L. E364
Ornelas, José Gonzalez W164
Ornelas, Jean E73
Ornella, Gregory A756
Orner, Paul A345
Orner, Paul E166
Ornt, Daniel B. P456
Orol, Santiago P605
Oroschakoff, Michelle A528
Orourke, Kevin M A345
Orourke, Kevin A345
Orourke, Melanie A811
Orourke, Claudia A888
Orourke, Terry P117
Orourke, Kevin M E166
Orourke, Kevin E166
Orourke, Claudia E425
Orozco, Tomas A69
Orozco, Jean-Marc A742
Orozco, Ruben P472
Orr, Mark A399
Orr, Bradley A850
Orr, Shenjin A900
Orr, Lydia A902
Orr, Natassia P101
Orr, Mark P223
Orr, James P311
Orr, R. Jeffrey W173
Orr, R. Jeffrey W313
Orr, R. Douglas (Doug) E171
Orr, Patrick E203
Orsburn, Ken A246
Orsburn, Ken E105
Orscheln, Joseph A176
Orsini, Frank C. A508
Orson, Marshall D P176
Ort, Gary A818
Ort, Gary E403
Ortega, Nadine A249
Ortega, Adela P51
Ortega, Rebecca P486
Ortega, Juan Luis W106
Ortega, Nadine E108
Ortegon, Liisa P604
Ortenstone, Susan A180
Orth, Douglas A590
Orth, Stephanie A739
Orthwein, Peter B. A834
Ortiz, Yolanda A43
Ortiz, Anita A602
Ortiz, Veronica P184
Ortiz, Christine P310
Ortiz, Claudia P404
Ortiz, Ana P672

COMBINED HOOVER'S HANDBOOK INDEX OF EXECUTIVES

A = AMERICAN BUSINESS
E = EMERGING COMPANIES
P = PRIVATE COMPANIES
W = WORLD BUSINESS

Ortiz, Yolanda E13
Ortiz, Dionisio E58
Ortkiese, Nancy A850
Ortmanns, Thomas W2
Orton, Todd A60
Orwick, William E156
Orzechowski, Diane A850
Osada, Yutaka W93
Osada, Hiroshi W127
Osakwe, Franklyn A899
Osano, Hidenori W11
Osawa, Hidetoshi W300
Osawa, Toshiyuki W348
Osbeck, Mary Beth A881
Osbeck, Jason E203
Osbeck, Mary Beth E421
Osberg, Carl A343
Osberg, Carl E164
Osborn, William A5
Osborn, David A196
Osborn, Amy A719
Osborn, Jo A846
Osborn, Richard S P270
Osborn, William A. P389
Osborn, Megan P465
Osborn, Kelly P613
Osborn, Donna P657
Osborn, Kevin B. E131
Osborn, Amy E355
Osborn, Brian E450
Osborne, Ron A16
Osborne, Dean A108
Osborne, Roberta A137
Osborne, Roger A664
Osborne, Casey P417
Osborne, Robert D P459
Osborne, Marci P644
Osborne, Terry B. E80
Osborne, Roger E334
Osbourn, William F. (Bill) A933
Oschmann, Jim A103
Oschmann, Stefan W254
Oscos, Jose E106
Ose, Uriel A190
Osekowsky, Curtis E80
Oshea, Steven A22
Oshea, Daniel A409
Oshea, Steven P11
Oshea, Rebecca P604
Oshima, Yuko A715
Oshiro, Don A830
Oshiro, Don P593
Oskouie, Ali P336
Oskvig, O. H. (Dean) P85
Oslakovic, Gerald A629
OSMINKINA-JONES, Olga A654
Osmon, Jim A340
Osmon, Jim E160
Osofsky, Justin A310
Osorio, Maryluz P101
Osorio, Jonathan P392
Ospina, Reynolds A349
Ossip, Alon W244
Ossowski, James A690
Osswald, Oliver W230
Ostalé, Enrique A901
Ostalé, Enrique W421
Ostapovicz, Christopher A436
Osteen, Debra K. A878
Ostendorf, Todd P379
Oster, Christina A835
Oster, Mike P318
Osterday, Rick P11
Ostergard, Winston P165
Osterhaus, Todd A547
Osterman, Vincent J. A598
Osterman, Michael P631
Ostermeier, Timothy P425
Ostis, Heather A262

Ostler, Gordon A492
Ostler, Clyde E141
Ostrander, Daryl A628
Ostrander, Jane A813
Ostrander, Noam P175
Ostroff, Robert P676
Ostrowski, Steve A482
Ostrowski, Scott A904
Ostrowsky, Ally P586
Ostrowsky, Barry P66
Osullivan, Kevin A654
Osullivan, Sean A692
Osullivan, Jim E206
Osvaldik, Peter A800
Oswald, Kathy A414
Oswald, Kathy P236
Oswald, Robert W59
Oswalt, David A748
Ota, Saedene A182
Ota, Yoko P651
Oteiza, Edgar A153
Oteiza, Edgar E52
Otero, Tony P166
Otey, Brianne P141
Otey, Sarah P358
Othites, Michael A236
Otis, Travis A528
Otis, Alan A559
Otjen, Renee A37
Otjen, Tom A494
Otley, Brian P221
Otoya, Luis A167
Otsuji, Nobuyuki W127
OTSUKA, IWAO W205
Ott, Jennifer A85
Ott, Sonia A86
Ott, Susan A540
Ott, Jeri A623
Ott, Brian A831
Ott, Dusty P83
Ott, Richard A P282
Ott, Brian P601
Ott, Jennifer E27
Ott, Sonia E27
Ott, Tim E138
Ott, Jeri E313
Ottel, Robert W417
Otten, Cherie A850
Ottenbruch, Peter W433
Ottera, Magne A301
Ottera, Magne P196
Otterman, G. P. W212
Ottinger, Joe A436
Ottinger, Eric H. A504
Ottinger, Eric H. E251
Ottino, Julio M. P388
Ottman, Dan P305
Otto, Shawn A108
Otto, Christopher A109
Otto, Noreen A448
Otto, Jeff A879
Otto, Noreen P247
Otto, Greg E264
Ottolenghi, Les A160
Ottolini, Mary P130
Ou, Jean A676
Ou, Jean E338
Ouartarone, Jim A799
Ouchida, Michael P249
Oufnac, Patti A449
Oufnac, Patti E220
Ounesavath, John P210
Ourada, Mark A434
Ourada, Jeanette L E284
Ousdahl, Kimberly A597
Ousley, Peter P126
Outar, Gerald P360
Outland, Gail A664
Outland, Gail E334
Outlaw, Annie A871
Outwater, John A249
Outwater, John E108
Ovalle, Juan A658
Ovel, Jack P327
Overbeck, Jim E179

Overby, Corey A150
Overby, Reed A740
Overcash, Julie Ann A780
Overcast, Judy A386
Overcast, Judy E188
Overhage, Craig A254
Overholser, Patrick E101
Overly, Harry A846
Overstreet, Kelly P120
Overton, Pam A36
Overton, Camie P677
Overturf, James E141
Overway, Ben E265
Ovesen, Jesper W357
Oviedo, Tony E119
Ovokaitys, Daniel S. E156
Ovtchinnikov, Alexander (Alex) E238
Owen, Douglas A112
Owen, Jeffrey C. (Jeff) A272
Owen, Paul A301
Owen, Terry M. A315
Owen, Timothy A575
Owen, John B. A712
Owen, Nehemie A823
Owen, Duncan A839
Owen, Ronald A909
Owen, Julie P66
Owen, Paul P196
Owen, Brad P202
Owen, Nehemie P557
Owen, Bobbi P595
Owen, Marc E. W250
Owen, Rhonda E16
Owen, John W E386
Owen, John E386
Owen, Ronald E437
Owenby, Marcus A89
Owens, Ellen A100
Owens, Bob A161
Owens, Victor A284
Owens, Raymond E A320
Owens, Bob A349
Owens, Leonard A382
Owens, Thaddeus A666
Owens, Melissa A683
Owens, Tom A704
Owens, Don G. A755
Owens, Thomas A. P187
Owens, Fritz P392
Owens, Richard P408
Owens, Ben P514
Owens, Patricia E72
Owens, Victor E120
Owens, Rick E222
Owens, Gary M. E279
Owens, Don G. E369
Owings, Nancy P430
Owlia, Azita P670
Own, Jenny A676
Own, Jenny E338
Ownby, David H. P443
Ownjazayeri, Vahid A16
Owsley, Larry P629
Oxford, John A717
Oxford, John E351
Oxley, Scott P190
Oyadomari, David A109
Oyamada, Takashi W262
Oyler, Rick A64
Oyler, Jason P375
Oyler, Clinton P445
Oyler, Rob E431
Oyo, Naima A114
Oyo, Naima E37
Oyola, Vincent A590
Oz, Ran W49
Ozaki, Ernie A695
Ozaki, Masatoshi W262
Ozaki, Norimichi W268
Ozaki, Tetsu W286
Ozan, Kevin M. A548
Ozcelik, Taner A627
Ozeki, Masatatsu W30
Ozer, Lynn A367
Ozguc, Emre A438

Ozimek, Michael M. A851
Ozmen, Fatih P493
Ozmen, Eren P493
Ozuah, Philip O. P348
Ozuna, Noelia A203
Ozuna, Adrian A682
Ozuna-Richards, Elsa P646
O'Brenden, Robyn A776
O'Brien, Shane A36
O'brien, Deirdre A72
O'brien, Chris A91
O'Brien, Dermot J A93
O'brien, Deborah A108
O'Brien, Gregory A115
O'brien, Sean A258
O'brien, Jim A262
O'Brien, Ken A276
O'brien, Cheryl A323
O'Brien, Richard E. A439
O'Brien, Garry A441
O'Brien, Gregory P. (Greg) A481
O'Brien, Beth A519
O'Brien, Gail A566
O'Brien, Lawrence A571
O'Brien, Frank A624
O'Brien, Michael J. A626
O'Brien, Christopher J. (Chris) A728
O'Brien, Joseph A741
O'Brien, Frank A793
O'brien, Kevin M A872
O'brien, Daniel A919
O'Brien, Lindsay P37
O'Brien, Robert P. (Bob) P106
O'Brien, Charles T P197
O'Brien, Kristine P389
O'Brien, Gary P442
O'Brien, Frances D. W106
O'Brien, Eddie W131
O'Brien, Sean W193
O'Brien, Patrick D. W301
O'brien, Chris E29
O'Brien, Gregory E37
O'brien, Jenette E347
O'Brien, Joseph E364
O'Bryan, Brent P26
O'Byrne, Kevin W206
O'Connell, Pat A60
O'connell, Patrick A60
O'connell, Tom A222
O'connell, Alfred A317
O'Connell, Maureen A369
O'Connell, John A688
O'connell, Diarmuid A818
O'Connell, Timothy A E100
O'Connor, Mark A112
O'Connor, Stephen A137
O'Connor, Kevin M. A150
O'Connor, Mary A175
O'Connor, Jim A281
O'Connor, Vicki A352
O'Connor, Nancy A409
O'connor, James A414
O'Connor, Sean M. A470
O'Connor, Michael J. (Mike) A495
O'Connor, Thomas A532
O'connor, Jennifer A608
O'connor, John A624
O'Connor, Thomas L. A644
O'connor, Rory A658
O'Connor, Richard A767
O'Connor, John A785
O'connor, Craig A835
O'Connor, Michael L. (Mike) A906
O'Connor, Kevin A914
O'Connor, Timothy (Tim) A932
O'Connor, Thomas (Tom) P26
O'Connor, Daniel P156
O'connor, James P236
O'Connor, Michael J. (Mike) P282
O'Connor, Gina P300
O'Connor, John P526
O'Connor, Patrick J. (Pat) P546
O'Connor, Kevin M. E50
O'Connor, Michael E60

COMBINED HOOVER'S HANDBOOK INDEX OF EXECUTIVES

O'Connor, Michael L. (Mike) E435
O'Connor, Kevin E439
O'Conor, Raymond F. (Ray) A82
O'Day, Terence L. A416
O'Day, Daniel W328
O'Dea, Edward P289
O'Dell, Janet A340
O'Dell, Janet E161
O'Donald, Lewis W286
O'donnell, Raymond A16
O'donnell, Mary A34
O'Donnell, Robert G A50
O'donnell, George A481
O'Donnell, Robert F A684
O'Donnell, Peter G. A882
O'Donnell, Robert G P31
O'Donnell, Randall L. P327
O'Donnell, Patrick P531
O'donnell, Susan P608
O'Donnell, Dan E85
O'Donnell, Jeffrey E256
O'Donnell, James C. E424
O'Donoghue, Mary Jo P555
O'Donohoe, Karen A112
O'Dowd, Sarah A. A505
O'Dwyer, Philip A574
O'Dwyer, Fergal W131
O'Farrell, Ray A897
O'Flaherty, Lori L. A213
O'Flaherty, Lori L. P143
O'Flynn, Thomas M. (Tom) A18
O'gara, Kevin P261
O'Grady, Shawn P. A376
O'Grady, Michael G. A605
O'grady, Anne A892
O'Hagen, William E53
O'Hanley, Ronald P. (Ron) A783
O'Hanley, Ronald P. (Ron) P79
O'hara, Brooks A398
O'hara, Michael J A640
O'hare, Dennis P26
O'Haver, Cort A860
O'Herlihy, Christopher (Chris) A453
O'Hern, Jim A538
O'hern, Thomas E114
O'Keefe, Laura A784
O'Keefe, Barbara J. P388
O'Keefe, Daniel P501
O'Keefe, Sharon P594
O'Keeffe, John W140
O'Leary, Christopher D. (Chris) A376
O'Leary, Ray P195
O'Leary, Rand P410
O'Leary, Thomas M P584
O'leary, Brian E56
O'loughlin, Leo A482
O'Mahoney, Sean A718
O'Mahoney, Sean E354
O'malley, Brendan A75
O'Malley, Kevin A452
O'malley, Conor A740
O'mara, Shay P395
O'Meara, Robert P. (Bob) A347
O'Meara, Aidan A891
O'Meara, Patrick P610
O'Meara, Robert P. (Bob) E168
O'melia, Elizabeth A738
O'Neal, Clu Jon A58
O'neal, Ryan A753
O'neil, James A351
O'Neil, John A876
O'Neil, Logan P340
O'Neil, Cheri P642
O'neil, Robert E35
O'Neil, Ellen P. E153
O'Neill, Thomas S A306
O'Neill, Timothy J. A390
O'neill, William A414
O'Neill, Lisa M. A504
O'Neill, Liz A514
O'Neill, Liz A516
O'Neill, Myles A517
O'neill, John A575
O'Neill, John P. A675
O'Neill, Sheila A738

O'Neill, Thomas E. A846
O'neill, William P236
O'Neill, Liz P293
O'Neill, John P. P428
O'Neill, Thomas C. (Tom) W7
O'Neill, Lisa M. E251
O'Quinn, Marvin A266
O'Quinn, Marvin P181
O'Reagan, Richard A541
O'rear, David A796
O'rear, David E397
O'reilly, Michael A536
O'Reilly, Lawrence P. (Larry) A615
O'Reilly, Charles H. A615
O'Reilly, David E. A615
O'Reilly, Brian A660
O'reilly, Sarah A702
O'Reilly, Charles P231
O'Reilly, Brian P416
O'riley, Lila P633
O'Rourke, Joan A251
O'Rourke, James (Joc) A576
O'Rourke, Michael G. A759
O'Rourke, Tracy P530
O'Rourke, Timothy C. P546
O'Rourke, Michael G. E373
O'rourke, Brendan E402
O'Shaughnessy, Robert T. (Bob) A690
O'Shea, Daniel A408
O'Shea, John A809
O'Shell, Michael P458
O'Sullivan, Juliann A137
O'Sullivan, John A501
O'Sullivan, Fergus A658
O'Sullivan, Michael B. A731
O'Sullivan, Richard B. A847
O'sullivan, Terri A906
O'Sullivan, Paul P324
O'sullivan, Joe P361
O'Sullivan, James W53
O'sullivan, Kieran E252
O'Sullivan, Richard B. E410
O'sullivan, Terri E435
O'Tero, Ilene A167
OÂ'Brien, Raymond V. A249
OÂ'Brien, Sean P. A258
OÂ'Brien, Denis P. A304
OÂ'Brien, Anthony F. A706
OÂ'Brien, Martin P326
OÂ'Brien, Raymond V. E109
OÂ'Brien, Mary Jo E309
OÂ'Bryant, G. Mark P541
OÂ'Connell, Brian A205
OÂ'Connell, Joseph P. E28
OÂ'Grady, Sean P386
OÂ'Hara, Ryan A596
OÂ'Keefe, Thomas J. A624
OÂ'Leary, David A381
OÂ'Malley, Edward P375
OÂ'Neill, Michael J. A53
OÂ'Sullivan, James P. A778

P

P, Kern Howard P484
Paar, David A151
Pabor, Paul A905
Pabst, Darlene P625
Paccioretti, Steven A409
Paccone, Steve A215
Pace, Philip A162
Pace, Paul A491
Pace, Sonia P21
Pace, Gerald P342
Pace, Cathy P432
Pace, Philip E61
Pace, Jeff E73
Pace-Burke, Susan A589
Pacelli, Anthony E33
Pacey, David P273
Pacey, John E57
Pachano, Jose M A670
Pacheco, Carmita P668
Pacheco, Noe E438

Pachman, Louis J P231
Pacholke, Tim A599
Pacicco, Daniel A88
Paciero, Karen P594
Pacilio, Michael J. A304
Pacino, John A893
Pacious, Patrick S. E80
Pacis, Joe A249
Pacis, Joe E108
Pack, Mike A13
Pack, Barry P399
PACKARD, GUY C A238
Packard, John A P502
Packard, Greg E241
Packee, Jon A482
Packer, Ginny A573
Packer, Roger J. P130
Packer, Steven J P152
Packer, Robert J. E403
Packwood, Erin A798
Pacula, Joseph A438
Paczkowski, Linda A544
Padbury, Guy A554
Padden, Brian A756
Paddy, Rao A271
Padfield, Larry E229
Padgett, Pamela A364
Padgilwar, Amit A86
Padgilwar, Amit E27
Padgitt, Laura A170
Padierna, Pedro A654
Padilla, Maria A249
Padilla, Hector A428
Padilla, Jose P175
Padilla, Maria E108
Padron, Angelica A463
Padula, Rich A346
Padula, Rich E167
Paelinck, Charley A160
Paeth, Mary P507
Paez, Rene A P501
Paffumi, Louis A651
Paffumi, Louis E329
Pagano, Christopher J. A88
Pagano, William A108
Pagano, Dawn A251
Pagano, Shelly P41
Page, Andrew A13
Page, John A98
Page, Marchetti A320
Page, Ed A442
Page, Jack A442
Page, David A654
Page, Charlie A713
Page, Crystal P112
Page, Elaine P382
Page, Bob P595
Page, James H P630
Page, Darryl W106
Page, Timothy E57
Pagel, Reiner A21
Pagels, George A P467
Pagliaro, Renato W252
Pagliazzo, Charlie P220
Pagliero, Jim E272
Pagnani, Marissa A692
Pagni, Marco A899
Pagovich, Stefanie A692
Pagura, Annie P337
Pahnke, Barb A86
Pahnke, Barb E27
Paich, Keith A367
Paich, Brian A692
Paich, Joyce P184
Paidosh, Laurie A877
Paiewonsky, Steve P265
Paige, Lacie P489
Paik, Elaine A218
Paik, Sanghyun P594
Paillassot, Laurent W297
Pain, Mark A. W432
Paine, Ed A335
Paine, Andrew J. (Randy) A491
Paine, Amy A491
Paine, Ed E155

Painter, Corning F. A24
Painter, Robert A216
Painter, Patty P160
Painter, Jonathan W. (Jon) E243
Pairitz, Peter A433
Pairitz, Peter E217
Pais, Paula A248
Pais, Paula E107
Paisley, James A. (Andy) A13
Paja, David W31
Pak, Nancy A218
Pak, Gene A432
Pak, Chris A592
Pak, Chris P370
Pak, Gene E216
Pala, Amy A312
Pala, Amy P200
Palace, Mike A799
Palacios, Jose A243
Paladino, Steven A744
Palafox, Jose A463
Palagiano, Vincent F. A268
Palan, Martha P664
Palardy, Alan A562
Palasthy, Kristen A879
Palatnik, Kevin S. E86
Palazzo, Frank A184
Palazzolo, Joseph A347
Palazzolo, Joseph E167
Palencia, Melissa A761
Palenzona, Fabrizio W407
Palermo, Frank E431
Paletta, Nilton A474
Palframan, Jessica A271
Palfy, Sandor E259
Palinkos, Michael A205
Palis, Jack A540
Palka, Joe A837
Palkhiwala, Akash A695
Palkoski, Linda P454
Pall, Christine A61
Palla, Wayne A253
Palla, Wayne P169
Pallamary, Richard J P371
Pallas, Tony E80
Pallasch, John A540
Pallone, Philip A391
Pallotta, Eric A587
Palm, Gregory K. A390
Palm, Richard A727
Palm, Richard P453
Palma, Bryan A198
Palmberg, Rob P170
Palmberg, Kent P530
Palmer, Annette A107
Palmer, Johnathan A133
Palmer, Paul A163
Palmer, Eric A194
Palmer, Henry A204
Palmer, April A325
Palmer, Gregory A367
Palmer, Kari A409
Palmer, Anthony A416
Palmer, Anthony J. (Tony) A493
Palmer, C. Michael A534
Palmer, C Michael A534
Palmer, Brian A566
Palmer, Thomas (Tom) A595
Palmer, Tom A595
Palmer, Adam A654
Palmer, Brian A672
Palmer, Gary A684
Palmer, Roberta Ruth A711
Palmer, Frank A831
Palmer, Peter A842
Palmer, Marcia A884
Palmer, Steve P57
Palmer, Mike P197
Palmer, Kelly P443
Palmer, Roberta Ruth P444
Palmer, Harvey P456
Palmer, Bart P480
Palmer, Edna P518
Palmer, Frank P601
Palmer, Paul E62

COMBINED HOOVER'S HANDBOOK INDEX OF EXECUTIVES

```
A = AMERICAN BUSINESS
E = EMERGING COMPANIES
P = PRIVATE COMPANIES
W = WORLD BUSINESS
```

Palmer, Mary E137
Palmer, Ben M. E268
Palmer, Lisa E349
Palmer, Marsha E433
Palmer-ellis, Amy P639
Palmerio, Anthony P371
Palmieri, Paul A935
Palmiero, Ross A533
Palmisano, Thomas J. (Tom) A770
Palmore, Roderick A376
Palmore, Kysten P209
Palomarez, Javier A543
Palombo, Grace M. W173
Palombo, Grace W174
Paltridge, Robert D. E233
Paltrowitz, Jason E318
Paltz, Diana A85
Paltz, Diana E26
Paluch, Heather P103
Paluck, Eric A60
Palughi, Joe A502
Palumbo, Dan A522
Palus, Jean Fran- §ois W218
Palzkill, Leslie P216
Pam, Murray A456
Pam, Murray E228
Pamiljans, Janis G. A608
Pamnani, Ravi A654
Pamulo, Pj A349
Pan, Gordon G. A726
Pan, Gordon G. P453
Pan, Darong W98
Pan, Ning W160
Pana, Camelia P450
Panaccio, Frank P405
Panaccione, Genie A71
Panagos, Costa A474
Panas, George A289
Pancham, Cassan A333
Panchanathan, Sethuraman (Panch) P44
Pancino, Matt P373
Panczyk, Michael E263
Pande, Saumitra A205
Pande, Sunil P286
Pandey, Sharad A135
Pandey, Nirmal A461
Pane, Camillo A243
Pane, Stephanie P676
Panepresso, Joe A881
Panepresso, Joe E421
Panettieri, Christopher P233
Pang, Laurinda Y. A184
Pang, Lisa A559
Pang, Y.K. W209
Pang, Y. K. W209
Pangalos, Menelas (Mene) W38
Pangan, Aileen A6
Pangborn, Robert N. A828
Pangborn, Robert N. P584
Pangburn, Charles P615
Panhans, Chet E174
Paniry, Rina A780
Panizza, Sandro W35
Panizza, Florencia E270
Pankowski, Jason A125
Pankratz, Barbara P417
Pann, Stuart C. A438
Pannacciulli, Mike A893
Panno, Enrico A167
Panthawangkun, Wirawat W216
Panuccio, Susan A596
Panyarachun, Anand W352
Panzarella, Michael E194
Panzer, Kenneth M. (Ken) E114
Panzino, Jodi P155
Paoletta, Joseph E330
Paoletti, Rich P573
Paoli, Alberto De W153

Paolini, Nonce W76
Paolini, David E256
Papa, Athony Tony A450
Papa, Gianni Franco W407
Papadopoulos, Stelios A133
Papadopoulos, Stelios E140
Papagaryfallou, Lazaros A. W25
Papay, Mike A608
Papay, Jen A746
Papazis, Petros A190
Pape, Giovanna A484
Pape, Jeff A885
Pape, Kathy P411
Papenberg, Diane A204
Papera, Michael A137
Papermaster, Mark D. A14
Papesh, Kristin A658
Papesh, Bruce E302
Papiasse, Alain W71
Papillo, Carol A16
Papineni, Srinivasa A887
Papkoff, Jackie A480
Papouras, Julia P131
Papp, Harry A. P90
Pappagallo, Michael A152
Pappagallo, Andrea A450
Pappagallo, Michael P98
Pappas, Stephen A242
Pappas, James A801
Pappas, Thomas P202
Pappas, Natalie P547
Pappas, John E77
Pappu, Bhoga E122
Paquette, Michael S. A293
Parada, Ed A85
Parada, Ed E26
Paradowski, Mark E88
Parag, Prakash J A775
Parag, Prakash J P511
Param, Melina A236
Parameswaran, Prabha A218
Paranjpe, Nitin W408
Paranjpe, Nitin W409
Paras, Heather P486
Parasnis, Abhay A11
Parasole, James A251
Paratte, A. Robert E245
Parazynski, Gail M P548
Parcell, Jordan A793
Parcella, Mike A74
Parcher, Dave A164
Parchisanu, Georgeta A680
Parchment, Nadia P287
Pardee, Charles G. (Chip) A815
Parden, Diana P235
Pardes, Herbert A827
Pardes, Herbert P580
Pardini, Joe A934
Pardo, Marcella A491
Pardo, Emilio P2
Pardo, Felipe Bay- - n W144
Pardon, Tony A649
Pardue, Wendel A713
Pare, Roger A405
Pare, Mark A882
Pare, Jean-Philippe W128
Parece, Andrew E102
Paredes, Alfredo A702
Paredes, Jose A922
Paredes, Jose P671
Paredes, Sebastian W130
Pareek, Mayank W383
Pareigat, Thomas G. A823
Pareigat, Thomas G. E405
Pareja, Alvena A796
Pareja, Alvena E397
Parent, June B. A162
Parent, Bob P356
Parent, Ghislain W270
Parent, June B. E62
Parente, Michael Null A360
Parente, Pedro Pullen W303
Parente, Katherine E143
Parente, Susan A. E386
Parento, Stephen A545

Parfet, Donald R A488
Parihar, Jagdish W294
Parik, Allan W357
Parikh, Rima A251
Parikh, Nilay A722
Parikh, Shamin E143
Parikh, Bhavnish E226
Parimbelli, Alessandro A475
Paris, Glen A666
Paris, Nancy P259
Parish, Glenda P141
Parisi, Mike A453
Parisi, Vince P148
Parisi, Rita P229
Parisi, Jennifer P287
Parisi, Janet P368
Park, Ernie A3
Park, Sun A63
Park, David A104
Park, Danny A201
Park, Jay A310
Park, Anthony J. (Tony) A325
Park, Dave A391
Park, Daniel A404
Park, Aekyung A431
Park, Ellie A432
Park, Joon A505
Park, Burt A571
Park, Peter A658
Park, JI A695
Park, Priscilla K A933
Park, Scott P140
Park, Hyun P347
Park, Jihye P363
Park, Gary P635
Park, Geun Hee W108
Park, In Gyu W139
Park, Jeongwon W141
Park, Geewon W141
Park, Han-Woo W219
Park, Sung-Ho W311
Park, Jeong Ho W354
Park, Daniel E199
Park, Aekyung E216
Park, Ellie E216
Parker, W. Douglas (Doug) A47
Parker, Karen A75
Parker, Alex A89
Parker, Donald T. A142
Parker, Erik A175
Parker, Phil A236
Parker, Greg A246
Parker, M Jayne A271
Parker, Ted A334
Parker, Brandon A442
Parker, Jefferson G. (Jeff) A449
Parker, Karen A540
Parker, Calvin A550
Parker, Mark G A599
Parker, Scott T. A629
Parker, Krystal A630
Parker, Greg A640
Parker, Dorothy A641
Parker, Joy A713
Parker, Janet A713
Parker, Stacy A739
Parker, Gwen A807
Parker, Phillip A853
Parker, Bruce A859
Parker, Shelly A859
Parker, Victoria A880
Parker, Michael A882
Parker, P. William (Bill) A884
Parker, Rob A890
Parker, Brenda A922
Parker, Zachary P11
Parker, Chris P62
Parker, Bobby P133
Parker, Chuck P197
Parker, Karen P209
Parker, Calvin P319
Parker, Beck P337
Parker, Terra P358
Parker, Scott P360
Parker, Jeff P374

Parker, Dorothy P407
Parker, Douglas P523
Parker, Lynz P597
Parker, Phillip P612
Parker, Victoria P640
Parker, Barbara P647
Parker, Brenda P671
Parker, John W377
Parker, Donald T. E49
Parker, Greg E105
Parker, Gregory E105
Parker, Ted E153
Parker, Jefferson G. (Jeff) E220
Parker, David E264
Parkhill, Rik W85
Parkinson, Mike A478
Parkinson, Robert L. P301
Parks, Trenton A125
Parks, Lisa A402
Parks, Jasmine A414
Parks, Karen A839
Parks, Scott A850
Parks, Jasmine P236
Parks, Carolanne A449
Parks, Phil P393
Parks, R M P436
Parks, Grayson P582
Parks, Debbie P588
Parks, Lisa E198
Parks, Carolanne E221
Parlapiano, Donna A94
Parlato, Tanya P272
Parlee, Greg E263
Parlier, Matt A575
Parmar, Sheila A896
Parmenter, Stacey A150
Parmenter, Darren E. A421
Parmentier, Jennifer A. A640
Parnell, Winfred P171
Parnell, Jack E302
Parnes, Jane A64
Parnes, Marvin A711
Parnes, Marvin P444
Parolin, Jo- - o Benjamin W405
Parolisi, John P59
Parr, Gregory L A405
Parr, Ixchel P54
Parr, S. John W85
Parraz, Frank E194
Parrent, Michael A905
Parris, Carla M P206
Parrish, Jeff A170
Parrish, Kelly A438
Parrish, Jackson A540
Parrish, Benjamin F. (Ben) A840
Parrish, Kathleen A871
Parrish, Martin A887
Parrish, David K. P87
Parrish, Harvey P201
Parrish, Mike P379
Parrish, Jim P390
Parrish, Chris P514
Parrott, Mike A727
Parrott, William A746
Parrott, Keith A811
Parrott, Keith P64
Parrott, Mike P453
Parry, Michael J. (Mike) A292
Parry, Heather A522
Parry, Andrew A620
Parshall, B. Lynne E237
Parsley, E William A668
Parsley, Shawn D. P551
Parsley, Elizabeth P589
Parson, Susan A692
Parsonnet, Abby A906
Parsonnet, Abby E435
Parsons, Joe A19
Parsons, Julie A36
Parsons, Colleen A69
Parsons, Romelle K A108
Parsons, Jim A309
Parsons, Jane A340
Parsons, Taft A571
Parsons, Kelli A875

Parsons, Kristen P184
Parsons, Blake P513
Parsons, Jane E161
Partanapat, Pakorn W216
Parthemore, Eric A470
Partida, Austin E184
Partin, Kim A772
Partin, Kim E383
Partlow, Stan A51
Parton, Clint A760
Parton, Clint E374
Partridge, Ronald K. (Ron) P404
Parvor, Mike A734
Paré, Jean-Philippe W128
Pasantes, Andres A352
Pascal, Craig A850
Pascal, Maryann A930
Pascale, John P57
Pascale, John P293
Pascaud, Raphael S. E10
Pascavis, Roger F. E184
Pasch, Coni A884
Pasch, Elaine E73
Pasciak, Joseph A203
Pascoe, Ricardo W270
Pascoe, Kevin C. E296
Pascu, Adrian W128
Pascual, Francisco A333
Pascuzzi, Shelley P369
Pasek, Ronald J A586
Pashamova, Bistra A70
Pasicznyk, John G P184
Pasiechnik, Alexander E41
Pasierb, Debbie A449
Pasierb, Debbie E220
Paske, David A850
Paslawsky, William P466
Pasley, Debi P462
Paslick, P. Martin (Marty) A410
Pasqualicchio, Roderick A559
Pasqualone, Frank E230
Pasquarelli, Amy A651
Pasquarelli, Amy E329
Pasquella, Mark A175
Pasquino, Jennifer A156
Pass, Kara A838
Pass, Chris P267
Passafiume, Ralph A888
Passafiume, Ralph E425
Passaro, David A798
Passas, Isidore S. W25
Passerini, Filippo A872
Passerini, Filippo E232
Passey, BO A680
Passo, Melissa A63
Pasternak, Asaf W203
Pastiu, Alina A114
Pastiu, Alina E37
Pastor, Steve W68
Pastore, Michael A405
Pastore, Martin J P197
Pastorek, Greg A545
Pastorius, Kathy A702
Pastour, Gregoire A97
Pastre, Peter A559
Patak, Dawn A203
Pataria, Jesse A313
Pataria, Jesse A144
Patchen, Michael E386
Patchett, Richard B P310
Pate, R. Hewitt (Hew) A190
Pate, R Hewitt A191
Pate, Robert A509
Pate, Tammy P75
Pate, David C. P521
Patek, Lois P596
Patel, Shreya A53
Patel, Sunit S. A184
Patel, Pankaj S. A198
Patel, Ketul J. A226
Patel, Vijay A251
Patel, Komal A251
Patel, Harsh A251
Patel, Mayank A376
Patel, Suresh C A414

Patel, Sidd A478
Patel, Naimish A489
Patel, Ken A680
Patel, Kirt A722
Patel, Manesh A742
Patel, Bimal A784
Patel, Jigar A793
Patel, Ben A813
Patel, Ajay A897
Patel, Vishal A925
Patel, Ketul J. P150
Patel, Amrish P195
Patel, Suresh C P236
Patel, Sidd P269
Patel, Samir P366
Patel, Saavan P565
Patel, Bhavana P595
Patel, Sandeep P596
Patel, Raj P625
Patel, Kiran E226
Patel, Nikul E254
Patel, Raj E419
Patel, Vishal E445
Pater, Krystian W310
Paterno, Andrew J. A444
Paterno, Tony A444
Paterson, Bruce A713
Paterson, Chris E452
Pathak, Sumit P322
Patil, Sandeep A750
Patilis, Joanna A325
Patin, Al P284
Pating, Christopher P610
Patino, Lynn A540
Patino, Dan P195
Patkotak, Crawford P43
Patmore, Kimberly A915
Patnaik, Rekha A859
Patnala, Sai A135
Patnala, Sreedhar A277
Patnaude, Jude A806
Patnaude, Jude E398
Patonai, Nicolas P595
Patria, Slaughter P588
Patric, Sharon P198
Patrick, Todd A181
Patrick, Denit A397
Patrick, Robert A610
Patrick, Tony A621
Patrick, Ericka A855
Patrick, Cory A884
Patrick, Chad P344
Patrick, Barbara P610
Patrick, Chuck P624
Patrick, Todd E70
Patrick, Immel E92
Patrick, James E131
Patrick, Tony E311
Patrick, Gregory S. E394
Patricoff, Tracey C P501
Patridge, Denise A747
Patruno, Joseph P289
Patry, Dean P40
Patry, Fernando P310
Patsiokas, Stell A762
Patt, Mohan A287
Pattara, Theresa A147
Pattee, Russell A675
Pattee, Russell P428
Patten, Charlene A680
Patten, Brad Van P259
Patten, Liz P592
Patten, Scott P655
Patten, Mark E. E94
Patterson, Frank J. A189
Patterson, Debbie A219
Patterson, Ian A222
Patterson, Michael A360
Patterson, Ryan A392
Patterson, Geoff A414
Patterson, Douglas E A492
Patterson, Eric A519
Patterson, James A744
Patterson, Warren A857
Patterson, Clinton A859

Patterson, Pat P45
Patterson, Dean P116
Patterson, Linda P196
Patterson, Geoff P236
Patterson, Douglas E P279
Patterson, Jason P436
Patterson, Jamie P604
Patterson, Bernie P641
Patterson, Lynn K. W50
Patterson, Gavin W82
Patterson, Kevin J. W85
Patterson, Debbie E87
Patterson, Joan I. E368
Patterson-Randles, Sandra R. P609
Patti, Chris A524
Pattijn, Elbert W130
Pattis, Lisa J. A925
Pattis, Lisa E. E445
Pattishall, Jan A909
Pattishall, Jan E436
Pattison, Terry A271
Patton, Charles R. A51
Patton, Mary A337
Patton, Mark A371
Patton, Gary A465
Patton, Rick A882
Patton, Ross P105
Patton, Alex P265
Patton, Kamela P588
Patton, Mary E158
Pattterson, Jerry P344
Patullo, Rita A540
Patyk, Matt A175
Patz, Melanie P64
Paul, Stamy A25
Paul, Ronald D. A283
Paul, Shannon A329
Paul, Jennifer A409
Paul, Barbara A414
Paul, Michael A482
Paul, Andrew A540
Paul, Cynthia A746
Paul, Stamy P14
Paul, Barbara P236
Paul, Janet P293
Paul, Chausse P306
Paul, Terre P368
Paul, Janelle P491
Paul, Valerie J. P497
Paul, Ann P515
Paul, Hernandez P655
Paul, Lenora P660
Paul, Stefan W227
Paul, Michael W433
Paul, Celentano E86
Paul, Ronald D. E117
Paul, Brian E143
Paul, David C. E190
Paula, Jefferson de W33
Pauley, Lisa A. A103
Pauley, Matthew A374
Pauley, Clarence P615
Paulikas, George P553
Paulino, Arleen A65
Paulk, Steve A850
Paulk, Jennifer P117
Paull, David A314
Paull, David E145
Paulo, Donna Null A516
Paulo, Donna Null P293
Paulos, William J P108
Paulsen, Larry A666
Paulsen, Amy P259
Paulson, Brian A327
Paulson, Ronald A394
Paulson, Donavon A911
Paulson, Dana P286
Paulson, Thomas (Tom) E399
Paulson, Donavon E437
Paulus, Ronald A P343
Paulus, Ronald A P344
Paulus, Faydre P633
Pauly, Greg A727
Pauly, Greg P453
Paus, William W357

Pauzer, Stanley A596
Pavageau, Laurent A538
Pavee, Jean-yves A5
Pavelich, Gerald (Jerry) A118
Pavelich, Gerald (Jerry) P66
Pavelka, Bruce A58
Pavia, Rick A843
Pavlic, Gregory A877
Pavlick, Mongkha A321
Pavone, Alicia P409
Pawar, Manoj A226
Pawar, Manoj P150
Pawlak, Renard A170
Pawley, Patrick P321
Pawley, Barbara P623
Pawlowski, Lisa A530
Pawlus, Chris A891
Pawsat, Karen P334
Pax, Gina A819
Pax, Gina P549
Paxson, Christina H. P102
Paxson, Kara P277
Paxton, Drew A935
Paxton, Ken P54
Paxton, Robert P309
Payette, Denise A170
Payla, Michelle A347
Payla, Michelle E167
Payne, Jim A40
Payne, Amanda A61
Payne, Jon A87
Payne, Mandy A155
Payne, Fiona K A215
Payne, Geoff A222
Payne, Ileana A247
Payne, Kevin M. A290
Payne, Jon A442
Payne, Chris A677
Payne, Raymond A722
Payne, Kevin M. A770
Payne, Jill A772
Payne, Leslie A827
Payne, Jennifer M. A859
Payne, David L. A912
Payne, Jim P29
Payne, Jon P50
Payne, Robert P83
Payne, Phyllis P469
Payne, Penelope (Nell) P497
Payne, Mandy E54
Payne, Hunter E84
Payne, Ileana E105
Payne, David E284
Payne, Jill E382
Paynter, Leslie A155
Paynter, Eric A405
Paynter, Tim A608
Paynter, Leslie E54
Paz, Gustavo Calvo A493
Paz, Milton De La P171
Pazerski, Jill A444
Pazienza, Sharon A348
Pazienza, Sharon E169
Paziora, Debra A751
Peabody, Eric A904
Peabody, Robert A704
Peabody, Robert J. W190
Peabody, Mark E422
Peacher, Stephen C. W371
Peachey, Tim A368
Peachey, Bianca A500
Peacock, Bradley R A323
Peacock, Dan A327
Peacock, Jeff A744
Peacock, John A755
Peacock, William (Bill) A824
Peacock, Douglas A842
Peacock, Danielle A877
Peacock, William (Bill) P561
Peacock, John E369
Peak, Linda A442
Peale, Steve A170
Peale, Cheryl A569
Pean, Sabrina M A654
Pear, David A E111

COMBINED HOOVER'S HANDBOOK INDEX OF EXECUTIVES

A = AMERICAN BUSINESS
E = EMERGING COMPANIES
P = PRIVATE COMPANIES
W = WORLD BUSINESS

Pearce, Dana A219
Pearce, Robert A349
Pearce, Brenda A717
Pearce, Christopher A850
Pearce, Richard A881
Pearce, Zach P155
Pearce, Charles T P273
Pearce, David P471
Pearce, Stephen W29
Pearce, Warren W. E232
Pearce, Brenda E351
Pearce, Richard E421
Pearison, Megan P588
Pearl, Cynthia A482
Pearlberg, Jay A414
Pearlberg, Jay P236
Pearlman, Michael P96
Pearlmutter, David A489
Pearson, Marty A19
Pearson, Bryan A. A34
Pearson, Marina A184
Pearson, Todd A287
Pearson, Lynne A329
Pearson, James F. (Jim) A350
Pearson, Gregory R. (Greg) A460
Pearson, Kevin J. A530
Pearson, Wes A599
Pearson, John A885
Pearson, Jeffrey T P34
Pearson, Kermit P69
Pearson, Tamara P94
Pearson, Kathryn P241
Pearson, Kristian P266
Pearson, Ken P310
Pearson, James F P336
Pearson, James F P394
Pearson, James F P411
Pearson, Bruce P478
Pearson, J F P562
Pearson, Shelli P665
Pearson, Lori W80
Pearson, Simon W345
Pearson, Douglas E E170
Peart, Vereena P331
Pearte, Camille A591
Pearte, Camille P369
Pease, Alexander W. P499
Pease, Robert W92
Peaslee, Gregory P643
Peatman, John B. E234
Peay, D. Anthony (Tony) A91
Peay, D. Anthony (Tony) E29
Pecaric, John P. A276
Peccini, Robert A249
Peccini, Robert E108
Pecenka, Michelle P551
Peceny, Mark P634
Peck, Patrick F. A144
Peck, Denise A198
Peck, John A793
Peck, Arthur (Art) A826
Peck, Richard A835
Peck, John A837
Peck, Raphael A862
Peck, Kristin C. A941
Peck, Lori P49
Peck, Cynthia P152
Peck, Kimberly P332
Peck, Jane P467
Peck, Ty E197
Peckham, Fred A530
Peckham, John P. A913
Peckham, Bob P375
Peckham, Michael P. (Mike) P438
Peckham, John P. E438
Peckinpaugh, David P308
Pecor, Raymond A227
Pecor, Raymond E91
Pecora, Anthony A86

Pecora, Anthony E27
Pecyna, Jim A606
Peden, Mark A75
Pedersen, Karsten A21
Pedersen, Brandon S. A29
Pedersen, Chris E. A217
Pedersen, Jeff A727
Pedersen, Joel P92
Pedersen, Jeff P453
Pedersen-Howard, Matt A645
Pederson, Judy P314
Pedireddi, Prasad A107
Pedley, Matthew A137
Pedlow, Bernadette P17
Pedlow, Frank P574
Pedone, Joe A483
Pedonti, Patrick J P186
Pedra, Christi A170
PEDRANZINI, MARIO ALBERTO W43
Pedraza, Hector A218
Pedrick, Christine A704
Pedroza, Noel A896
Peduzzi, Michael D A566
Peebles, Debbie P611
Peek, Audrey P34
Peel, Matthew P185
Peele, Steven P672
Peeples, Trip A179
Peeples, Jon A660
Peeples, Jon P416
Peer, Tonya A620
Peery, Bryan A71
Peery, Bryan P43
Peeters, Clare P57
Peetris, Tina A506
Pefanis, Harry N. A668
Pefanis, Harry N A668
Pefanis, Harry N P422
Peffer, Deb A711
Peffer, Deb P444
Pegg, William E268
Peggy, Sease P122
Peglar, Robert A565
Pehlke, Richard W. (Rich) E207
Pehota, Joe A88
Pehrson, Timothy T. A462
Pehrson, Timothy T. P256
Peigen, Seth P343
Peigh, Terry D. A468
Peignet, Victor W345
Peikon, Andy A522
Peiris, Sumindi A423
Peiris, Dushanti A741
Peiris, Dushanti E364
Peirson, Nancy A135
Peiser, Mark A596
Pekhazis, Fadoul W208
Pekola, Lenny A723
Pelaez, Marc Y. E. A224
Pelan, Dana A125
Pelayo, Arturo P515
Pelch, Steven J A292
Pelech, Margaret A323
Pelfrey, Harvey P394
Pelham, Peter A110
Pelissero, John P301
Pelka, Deb P22
Pelkey, Diane A862
Pell, Martyn A. A338
Pell, Rachel A828
Pell, Rachel P584
Pellakuru, Gurunatham A409
Pellegrini, Frank P361
Pellegrini, Robert P593
Pellegrino, Joan A243
Pellegrino, Alice A409
Pellegrino, Joseph P. E253
Pelleissone, Eduardo A496
Peller, Holger P425
Pelletier, Mike A449
Pelletier, Stephen (Steve) A686
Pelletier, Mike E220
Pelliccia, Joe A906
Pelliccia, Joe E435
Pelligra, Nicole A112

Pellissier, Gervais W297
Pellot, Lisette P627
Pellowski, Amanda A804
Peloquin, Thomas A409
Pelt, Jason Van A19
Pelt, Megan Van A750
Peltier, Wayne P69
Peluso, Piergiorgio W385
Pelyhes, David A487
Pelz, Christiane E172
Pelzel, Brent P340
Pember, Marvin G. A878
Pemberton, Rick P157
Pembleton, S. Gillian A605
Pempek, Kalynn P49
Pena, Efren A463
Pena, Lisa A835
Pena, Yvette P2
Pena, Kelvin P366
Pena, Rodrigo F. Troni P499
Penberthy, Shannon A251
Pence, Beth A246
Pence, Beth E105
Pender, Teri A666
Pender, Erin P608
Pendergast, Stephen A54
Pendergast, Kevin A405
Pendergast, Lisa A561
Pendergast, Jim P2
Pendergast, Jim P115
Pendergrass, Tom A742
Pendergrass, Lynn S. E9
Pendleton, Linda P151
Pendolino, Sophie A922
Pendolino, Sophie P671
Pendse, Raj A695
Penfield, Susan L. A145
Peng, Stony A613
Peng, Shane A776
Peng, Shane P512
Peng, Zhaofeng W179
Pengeroth, Phil A784
Penk, Werner E248
Penland, Cindy P255
Penley, Jack A355
Penn, Jayson A663
Penn, Douglas A867
Penn, Kevin P334
Penn, Laurence E. E124
Pennacchio, Stephen A657
Pennacchio, Steve A658
Penne, David P354
Pennebaker, Lori A512
Pennella, William A. (Bill) P166
Pennes, David P509
Pennett, Barry A471
Penney, Robert T. P119
Pennington, Trey A175
Pennington, Bob A202
Pennington, Kevin P. A352
Pennington, Bob P136
Pennington, Keith P337
Pennington, Chip P492
Pennington, Kelli P659
PENNINGTON, JON E34
Pennington, Dan E72
Pennington, J. Kyle E396
Penny, Bryan A602
Penny, Alfred F. (Fred) W175
Pennycuff, Toby A421
Penrose, Chris A89
Penrose, Jill A765
Penry, Chuck A855
Pensak, Myles P615
Penske, Roger S. A649
Pentz, Larry C. W212
Penvillo, Jim A393
Peoples, Rasheda P429
Peoples, Chanda P476
Pepe, Joseph P142
Pepenelli, Vince A245
Peppe, Joseph A61
Pepper, J David P412
Pepper, Dave P412

Pepper, J Stanley P584
Pepper, Richard S P584
Pepper, David A. E80
Peppiatt-Combes, James P329
Peraino, Vito C. A55
Peralta, Kristina A793
Peralta, Pennie P111
Perate, Rocco E172
Percarpio, Michael F A688
Perceleanu, Elena E138
Perch, Jeanmarie P429
Perche, Patrice E178
Perdomo, Katie A596
Perdue, Rob A224
Perdue, Richard A449
Perdue, Richard E220
Perea, Jennifer Rosato P175
Perego, Robert A111
Pereira, Jose A202
Pereira, Sam A255
Pereira, Jose P136
Pereira, Alvaro P205
Pereira, Ivan de Sa W303
Pereless, Rob A54
Perelman, Robert M. A503
Perelman, Robert M. E249
Perelman, Shoel E326
Peres, Edison A198
Peretz, Richard N. A870
Perez, Vincent A109
Perez, Cliff A246
Perez, Patricio A246
Perez, Roman A309
Perez, Edward A435
Perez, Corine A460
Perez, Javier A544
Perez, Mario A544
Perez, Michelle A559
Perez, Ariel Camacho A573
Perez, Jose M A688
Perez, Marlene A809
Perez, Juan R. A870
Perez, William D A920
Perez, Marta P7
Perez, Marta Brito P7
Perez, Virginia P21
Perez, Jorge P65
Perez, Roberta P412
Perez, Dr Sylvester Syl P469
Perez, Olga P469
Perez, Cliff E105
Perez, Patricio E105
Perez, Javier E290
Perez, Lizandro E138
Perez, Vincent E352
Perez-Sandi, Alex A173
Perez-Vasquez, Nancy A559
Peria, Yolanda A191
Periago, Mirta P404
Peribere, Jerome A936
Perica, Adrian A72
Perikly, Jaime A571
Peril, Dan A107
Perille, Thomas P518
Perillo, Louis P266
Perini, Christopher H. E429
Periquet, Pepper A540
Perisee, Donn A440
Perkash, Om P1
Perkins, Jim A30
Perkins, Raymond A89
Perkins, Thomas B. A239
Perkins, Kevin A305
Perkins, Jan A487
Perkins, Brenda A559
Perkins, Joe Bob A803
Perkins, Kenneth A872
Perkins, Michael L. A908
Perkins, Jim P20
Perkins, Rhonda P131
Perkins, Paul P274
Perkins, Kevin P282
Perkins, Michael L. E436
Perkinson, Ellery A651
Perkinson, Ellery E330

COMBINED HOOVER'S HANDBOOK INDEX OF EXECUTIVES

Perkovich, Brian P336
Perlewitz, Steven A1
Perlewitz, Kathi P211
Perlewitz, Steven E1
Perlin, Jonathan B. (Jon) A410
Perlman, Bob A369
Perlman, Benjamin A381
Perlman, Harvey S. P92
Perlman, Joel A. A348
Perlmutter, Robert J. A74
Perlmutter, Roger M. A554
Perman, Jay A. P642
Permet, Robert P234
Permut, Howard P335
Pernas, Rick P161
Perng, Danny P326
Perno, Joseph A478
Perno, Joseph P269
Pernosky, Lawrence R. (Larry) E14
Peroceschi, Jacob A746
Perold, Jacques A36
Perotti, Daniel S. A648
Perotti, Daniel S. E328
Perra, Tim A778
Perrault, Erika A60
Perrault, Joseph A64
Perrault, Paul A. A152
Perrault, Paul A. E52
Perreault, Michel G A19
Perreault, Roger A857
Perreira, Lawrence A784
Perren, Katharine P390
Perrette, Jean-Briac (JB) A270
Perretti, Leslie A695
Perri, Linda P206
Perri, Michael G. P627
Perri, Joseph E290
Perricone, Jennifer A799
Perriere, Pierre La A384
Perriere, Pierre La P217
Perrilliat, Javara D. A634
Perrin, Mary P300
Perrin, Richard E384
Perrine, John A442
Perrine, Gerry E99
Perrins, Alexander P425
Perris, Chris P223
Perrochon, Louis A287
Perron, Jacques P604
Perrone, Lauren A530
Perrone, Michael P220
Perroots, Stephen A538
Perry, Debra A88
Perry, Harvey P. A184
Perry, Lance A199
Perry, Jennifer A222
Perry, Michelle A236
Perry, Jim A270
Perry, Glynn A276
Perry, Egbert L. J. A312
Perry, Kenneth M A373
Perry, Rick A382
Perry, Opal G. A417
Perry, Matt A479
Perry, Mark A613
Perry, Shannon A621
Perry, Sean A725
Perry, Curtis J. A796
Perry, Opal G A827
Perry, Doni P13
Perry, Karl E P60
Perry, Jason P76
Perry, Sabrina P80
Perry, Janet P153
Perry, J Thomas P177
Perry, James P180
Perry, Barbara P253
Perry, Tia P280
Perry, Glenn P326
Perry, Tom P415
Perry, Thomas P415
Perry, Thirsty P467
Perry, Carol P530
Perry, Dan P552
Perry, Opal G P571

Perry, Rhonda S P575
Perry, Van P618
Perry, Jonathan E104
Perry, Shannon E312
Perry, Curtis J. E397
Perryman, Tad P607
Persampeiri, David E102
Persante, Patricia E185
Persaud, Gloria A115
Persaud, Donna P171
Persaud, Gloria E37
Perselis, Anna P667
Pershing, John A84
Pershing, Dennis A566
Pershing, David W. P597
Persico, Asid P266
Person, Peter P496
Persons, Philip A358
Persons, Rob A378
Persons, Thomas A438
Persons, Philip E176
Persson, Olof W420
Perun, Joseph A651
Perun, Joseph E329
Peryea, Melissa A227
Peryea, Melissa E90
Pesant, Roberto E433
Pesavento, Jim A368
Pesce, Alex A846
Peschek, Grace A903
Peschel, Daron A319
Pesci, Nello-John (NJ) P480
Peshkin, John A691
Pessin, Bill A740
Pessina, Stefano A899
Pestana, Tiago C--mara W169
Pestello, Fred P. P465
Pester, Marc A686
Pestikas, Jennifer A5
Peter, Joe A65
Peter, John St P11
Peter, Nicolas W63
Peter, Joseph G. (Joe) W283
Peterffy, Thomas E235
Peterman, Kathy A219
Peterman, Patrick A761
Peterman, Alison A797
Peterman, Kathy E87
Peternel, Lisa A283
Peters, Alex A10
Peters, Linda A123
Peters, Adam A179
Peters, Chris A296
Peters, Lauren B. A359
Peters, William E. (Bill) A475
Peters, Phillip A578
Peters, Greg A587
Peters, Rebecca A613
Peters, David A670
Peters, Scott M. A712
Peters, Juergen A724
Peters, Greg A749
Peters, Steve A826
Peters, Harld A870
Peters, Robert A903
Peters, James W. (Jim) A919
Peters, Heather P23
Peters, Theresa P75
Peters, Juergen P452
Peters, Dana P514
Peters, Alexandra P549
Peters, Amy P608
Peters, Ian W95
Peters, Scott D E203
Peters, Greg E367
Peterschick, Shannon P511
Petersen, Andy Kramer A117
Petersen, Kenneth A332
Petersen, Carey A657
Petersen, Beth A854
Petersen, Patrick A934
Petersen, Andy Kramer P61
Petersen, Beth P212
Petersen, Katherine P259
Petersen, Jeffrey P P279

Petersen, Jeffrey P P280
Petersen, Richard W. (Rich) P305
Petersen, Gary P422
Peterson, Sean A54
Peterson, James N. A103
Peterson, Tina A117
Peterson, John A145
Peterson, Richard D A186
Peterson, Richard A186
Peterson, Chuck A224
Peterson, Terry D. A276
Peterson, Bruce A279
Peterson, Joseph A345
Peterson, Paul A386
Peterson, Lloyd A393
Peterson, Mary B A410
PETERSON, ERIC A428
Peterson, Kenzie A451
Peterson, Dean A452
Peterson, Joel C. A478
Peterson, Sandra E. A479
Peterson, Christopher H A593
Peterson, Carl A599
Peterson, Mychelle A605
Peterson, David J A605
Peterson, Robert L. A618
Peterson, Doug A686
Peterson, Douglas L. (Doug) A738
Peterson, Brian A745
Peterson, Kevin A807
Peterson, Sigurd A845
Peterson, Karyn A891
Peterson, Martha A900
Peterson, Richard D P10
Peterson, Barbara P40
Peterson, Tina P61
Peterson, Jeannette P82
Peterson, Richard D P123
Peterson, Richard P123
Peterson, Terry P126
Peterson, Mark P220
Peterson, Tim P241
Peterson, Kenzie P249
Peterson, Ronald P268
Peterson, Erin P375
Peterson, Penelope L. P388
Peterson, Teresa P431
Peterson, James H P443
Peterson, Denise M. P464
Peterson, Ken P492
Peterson, Larry P503
Peterson, Randall P530
Peterson, Randy P530
Peterson, Glenn E P553
Peterson, Mandi P597
Peterson, Fross P646
Peterson, Ross P646
Peterson, Matthew W31
Peterson, Bill R. W85
Peterson, Carl E72
Peterson, Scott E72
Peterson, Mary E91
Peterson, Jason E133
Peterson, Mark A. E134
Peterson, Joseph E166
Peterson, Paul E188
Peterson, Alexander E223
Peterson, Joel E259
Peterson, Neil E317
Peterson, Michael D. E340
Peterson, Marjorie E391
Peterzen, Timothy A797
Petillo, Chris P382
Petit, Parker H. (Pete) E234
Petitgas, Franck A574
Petkov, Boris A161
Petkun, William A151
Petkus, Ed A140
Petmecky, William (Tres) A770
Petno, Douglas B. (Doug) A483
Petracchini, Marco W155
Petraia, Garrett A780
Petran, Ruth A289
Petrarca, Stephen M. E28
Petras, Thomas A683

Petrasso, Mark A940
Petree, Shannon A900
Petrie, Michael J. A224
Petrino, Richard A54
Petritsis, Spiro A683
Petro, Jeff A190
Petro, Sharon E183
Petrocelli, Danielle A588
Petrocelli, Danielle P365
Petrone, Andrew A3
Petropoulos, Michael A409
Petrosino, John P151
Petroske, Jeffrey A922
Petroske, Jeffrey P671
Petrossian, John A798
Petroy, Shelley B A103
Petrozza, Chad A506
Petruccelli, Jennifer A519
Petrullo, Michael A540
Petrusky, Chuck P246
Petry, Joann A922
Petry, Joann P671
Petrzelka, Jamie E123
Petsas, William D. E121
Pettagrue, Brandon A713
Petters, C. Michael (Mike) A446
Pettey, Fred E123
Petti, Filippo P382
Pettie, Mark A906
Pettie, Mark E435
Pettiford, Mark A480
Pettigrew, James (Jim) W109
Pettigrew, John W273
Pettinari, Jaclyn A179
Pettinato, Jeffrey A460
Pettinato, Andrea P558
Pettit, Barbara A155
Pettit, Sam A228
Pettit, Tom A735
Pettit, Richard A796
Pettit, Dirk P140
Pettit, Barbara E54
Pettit, C. D. Baer E290
Pettit, Richard E397
Pettus, John P157
Petty, Lora A556
Petty, Tim A885
Petty, Meredith L P175
Petty, Lora P328
Petty, Trent P541
Petty, Brian P. E150
Petznek, Erwin A236
Petzold, Robert A485
Peuch, Olivier Le A163
Peuch, Olivier Le P108
Peugeot-Roncoroni, Marie-Hél- ̈ne W305
Peverly, Francis P397
Pewitt, Lori A877
Pewonka, Della P644
Peyton, Teresa A340
Peyton, Kevin A402
Peyton, John A708
Peyton, Teresa E160
Peyton, Kevin E198
Peyvan, Bianca P515
Pezzulo, Paolo A331
Pezzulo, Paolo P202
Pfabe, John A750
Pfeffer, Gerald A656
Pfeffer, George P185
Pfeffer, Gerald P414
Pfeifer, John C. A154
Pfeifer, John C A632
Pfeifer, Mark P623
Pfeiffer, Vanessa A257
Pfeiffer, Anne A483
Pfeiffer, Michael R. E347
Pfister, Susan P39
Pfitzenreiter, Axel A745
Pflederer, Kent A. A637
Pflieger, Kristian A90
Pflieger, Kristian P51
Phadnis, Amit S A199
Phalan, Brendan P325

COMBINED HOOVER'S HANDBOOK INDEX OF EXECUTIVES

A = AMERICAN BUSINESS
E = EMERGING COMPANIES
P = PRIVATE COMPANIES
W = WORLD BUSINESS

Phalen, Michael P. (Mike) A149
Phalen, James S. P95
Pham, Hongmai A69
Pham, Hoang Q P141
Pham, Dung P551
Phangaraj, Immanuel P307
Phares, Bob P92
Pharmd, Geoffrey Lawton P117
Pharr, Mark A449
Pharr, Mark E220
PHD, Elaine Joyce Simpkins P85
PHD, Donde Plowman P103
PHD, Steven Daeschner P264
PHD, Charles L Beaty P451
Phebus, Linnie A246
Phebus, Linnie E105
Phegley, Richard L. A472
Phelan, Kim A530
Phelan, David C. A783
Phelan, Paula P111
Phelan, Brandi P619
Phelps, Bill A145
Phelps, Boyd A460
Phelps, Ronald A574
Phelps, Marcy P126
Phelps, David E. E43
Phelps, Kim E330
Phifer, Anthony A408
Philbert, Martin A711
Philbert, Martin P444
Philbin, Gary M. A273
Philibert, Jean A67
Philip, Chairez A58
Philip, Kiran A65
Philip, Anil A466
Philippe, Marc W345
Philippe, Hervé W416
Philippin, Charles J A858
Philippopoulos, Evan A19
Philippou, Jim A165
Philipps, Kate W160
Philips, Peggy A171
Philipson, Ulrik A54
Phillipine, Nicole A700
Phillippy, Robert J. P374
Phillippy, Robert E135
Phillips, Kara A58
Phillips, Judy A89
Phillips, Janice A219
Phillips, Eric A270
Phillips, Twila A313
Phillips, Jackie A313
Phillips, Brett A320
Phillips, J Michael A379
Phillips, Joy A401
Phillips, Eric A447
Phillips, Susan A493
Phillips, Travis A506
Phillips, Jeremy A596
Phillips, John A654
Phillips, David A654
Phillips, Michael C A663
Phillips, David P. A688
Phillips, David P. A689
Phillips, Lynn A715
Phillips, Raakhi A717
Phillips, Mary A784
Phillips, John A794
Phillips, Glenn A837
Phillips, Jane A850
Phillips, Gus A850
Phillips, Clay A859
Phillips, Jacque A930
Phillips, Mark D P40
Phillips, Bill P82
Phillips, Pam P94
Phillips, Robyn P110
Phillips, Betty P115
Phillips, Joan P124

Phillips, Betty P145
Phillips, William P162
Phillips, Sharon P171
Phillips, Steven P183
Phillips, Twila P200
Phillips, Kevin D P281
Phillips, Ross P301
Phillips, Dave P341
Phillips, Chris P375
Phillips, David P. P435
Phillips, Mark T P463
Phillips, John P511
Phillips, Kelly P596
Phillips, Carol P639
Phillips, Eva P672
Phillips, Janice E87
Phillips, Jackie E144
Phillips, Joy E198
Phillips, Raakhi E351
Phillips, Scott E440
Philpot, Buddy P657
Philpott, Peter A727
Philpott, Peter P453
Phinney, Allen A850
Phipps, Gil A498
Phipps, P. Cody A634
Phipps, Chad F. A939
Phiri, John P117
Pho, Danny A491
Phoenix, John E131
Phong, Sam P114
Phr, Jeanine A520
Phr, April P105
Phyfer, Cheri M. A756
Piacenza, Bruno W181
Piacquad, David A65
Piani, Carlos A497
Pianka, Stephanie A592
Pianka, Stephanie P370
Pianta, Robert C. P442
Piatkowski, John P112
Piatt, Janice P417
Picarelli, Sergio W7
Picat, Maxime W305
Picazo, Elias P137
Picazo, Daniel P213
Picca, Bruno W202
Picciano, Robert J. (Bob) A465
Piccini, Gabriele W407
Piccioni, Alysia A522
Picco, Gary A292
Piccolomini, Flavio A539
Piccone, Steve P333
Pichai, Sundar A39
Piche, Mick A593
Picher, Helen Davis A831
Pick, Ted A574
Pick, Jeff A884
Pickard, Samuel A16
Pickel, Michael W178
Pickens, Randi A5
Pickerall, Brian A145
Pickering, Sammy G. A301
Pickert, Valerie A888
Pickert, Valerie E425
Pickett, Denise A53
Pickett, Rodney A762
Pickett, Michael P102
Pickett, Larry E83
Pickett, C. Taylor E314
Pickle, Trevor O A262
Pickus, Nancy A158
Picone, Frank A743
Picone, Joe A871
Piechocka, Hanna A491
Piechoski, Michael J. A656
Piechoski, Michael J P279
Piechoski, Michael J. P414
Pieczynski, James J. (Jim) A638
Pieczynski, James J. (Jim) E320
Piekut, Michael P645
Pielsticker, Bob A175
Piemontese, Thomas A183
Piemontese, Thomas E74
Pien, Howard H. E426

Pieniaszek, Nadine P70
Pientka, Cathy E81
Piepenbring, Brent P27
Pieper, Nat A262
Pieper, Rick E293
Pieper, Joe E438
Piepho, Lindsay A855
Pierce, Christopher A145
Pierce, Chris A145
Pierce, David A. (Dave) A149
Pierce, Cathy A152
Pierce, David A196
Pierce, Joseph A245
Pierce, Sandra E. A444
Pierce, Jeff A448
Pierce, Sandra A649
Pierce, Richard A665
Pierce, Charles E. A679
Pierce, Susan A692
Pierce, Robert A706
Pierce, Todd A739
Pierce, Rick A760
Pierce, Larry A774
Pierce, Tom A922
Pierce, Phil P56
Pierce, Jon P126
Pierce, Roger D P211
Pierce, Jeff P247
Pierce, Wade P435
Pierce, Shelly P504
Pierce, Ken P551
Pierce, Kenneth P552
Pierce, Benjamin R P648
Pierce, Tom P671
Pierce, Cathy E52
Pierce, Tom E174
Pierce, Joseph E278
Pierce, Richard E334
Pierce, Rick E374
Pierdon, Steven B P215
Pieri, Melody A386
Pieri, Melody E188
Pierog, Michael A137
Pieron, James R. A675
Pieron, James R. P428
Pierre, Rony A871
Pierre, Ariel P561
Pierre, Monique St P630
Pierret, John E177
Pierron, Chip A60
Pierron, John A460
Piersol, Andrew P390
Pierson, Ken A200
Pierson, Rob A728
Pierson, Christine A859
Pierson, James E433
Pierz, Brian A409
Pierzchalski, Lawrence J. A561
Pieters, Marten W417
Pietragallo, William A883
Pietragallo, William P303
Pietragallo, William P644
Pietranton, Anthony F. A908
Pietranton, Anthony F. E436
Pietrantoni, Carlos Power A333
Pietropola, Joe A264
Pietrunti, Michael A933
Pietrykowski, Robert P390
Piette, Daniel W241
Pifani, Nick A544
Pifer, Nic A60
Pifer, Rick A164
Pifer, Donald A179
Pifko, Melissa K P596
Pigg, Charles P514
Piggott, Julie A. A138
Piggott, Julie A. A157
Piggott, Neil A419
Piggott, Julie A. P91
Pignata, Kate E371
Pignuolo, Chuck A106
Pigott, M. Jason A189
Pigott, Robert A229
Pigott, Mark C. A636
Pigott, Jeremy E272

Pike, Dana A347
Pike, Julie A514
Pike, Julie A516
Pike, Julie P293
Pike, Audrey P417
Pike, Dana E167
Pikuleva, Irina P116
Pildis, John A550
Pileggi, Ken P613
Pilgreen, Brian P22
Pilgrim, Trip A811
Pilgrim, Tony P458
Pilkington, Mary A272
Pilkington, Kevin A618
Pilla, John A774
Pilla, Rocco A915
Pillai, Gopal A900
Pillans, John P610
Piller, Alan A782
Piller, Alan P526
Pillette, Lisa A702
Pilmer, Don A623
Pilmer, Don E313
Pilnick, Gary H. A487
Pilon, Lawrence A394
Pimentel, Armando A597
Pina, Angelica A11
Pina, Carlos Costa W169
Pinault, Fran-Şois-Henri W218
Pinchera, Matt A237
Pinckney, Nancy A329
Pinder, Kymberly P634
Pineda, Maria A147
Pinedo, Mike A756
Ping, David P233
Ping, Andrew C P332
Pingatore, Holly J. E150
Pingle, Brenda P519
Pingolt, Cindy P311
Pingree, David A571
Pinheiro, Ivete A888
Pinheiro, Ivete E425
Pink, Edward A668
Pinkerton, Greg A107
Pinkerton, Jerry A425
Pinkes, Andrew J. A210
Pinkham, Elizabeth A739
Pinkham, Stan A888
Pinkham, Stan E425
Pinnaro, Catherina P629
Pinnavaia, Ian A135
Pinner, Ian A77
Pinner, Ernest S. (Ernie) A181
Pinner, Ernest S. (Ernie) E70
Pinnix-ragland, Hilda A281
Pinnolis, Michael P54
Pino, Dick E81
Pinocci, Leticia A191
Pinson, Brad A329
Pinson, C. Wright P648
Pinson, Andy P649
Pint, Melissa A647
Pintek, Michael A170
Pintek, Michael F. E261
Pinter, John A151
Pinter, Jeff A599
Pinter, Gregory A925
Pinter, Gregory E445
Pinto, Laura A247
Pinto, Daniel E. A483
Pinto, John J. A589
Pinto, Albert A734
Pinto, Claudia P265
Pinto, Arik W49
Pinto, Laura E105
Pintoff, Craig A. A872
Pione, Carolyn E366
Piorko, Jennifer P202
Pioske, Matthew A876
Piou, Olivier W284
Piper, Patrick E. A142
Piper, Greg A599
Piper, John P199
Piper, Mark P604
Piper, Patrick E. E49

Pipito, Frank A380
Pipkin, Katie L A187
Pipkin, Katie A188
Pippert, Bryce A145
Pippin, William C P247
Pippins, Dakota A434
Piquion, Deena A809
Pirard, Eddy W208
Pires, Luciano Siani W412
Pirie, John A800
Pirog, Christine A125
Piroli, Brad A690
Pirone, Renee A545
Pirro, Carleen E106
Pirrotta, Rich P297
Pirtle, William L. (Willy) E370
Pirwitz, Patrick A85
Pirwitz, Patrick E26
Pisani, William P491
Pisano, Adam A761
Pisarczyk, Karen A439
Pischetsrieder, Ing. Bernd W267
Piscitelli, Keara A651
Piscitelli, Keara E329
Piscitello, Sandy A63
Pisieczko, Alex A327
Pistelli, Lapo W155
Pistor, Robert A857
Pita, George L. A543
Pitasky, Scott A779
Pitcher, Terri A129
Pitcher, Daniel D. A316
Pitchford, Gail P124
Pitcock, Laurie P226
Pitesa, John W. (Bill) A281
Pitkethly, Graeme W409
Pitman, Martha A642
Pitman, Martha P407
Pitofsky, David B. A596
Pitorak, Martin A873
Pitre, Kathleen E A103
Pitt, Douglas A397
Pitt, Bonnie P671
Pittard, Pat A520
Pittel, Kimberly A360
Pittillo, Chad A760
Pittillo, Chad E374
Pittinaro, Scott A838
Pittman, Raymond J. (R.J.) A287
Pittman, Roland A402
Pittman, Carolyn A446
Pittman, Robert W. (Bob) A452
Pittman, Kim A893
Pittman, Mark P380
Pittman, Robin P625
Pittman, Roland E198
Pitton, Kathy A222
Pitts, Alice A58
Pitts, Susan A796
Pitts, Susan E397
Pitz, Jeff A417
Pitzer, Cheryl A444
Piva, Gary R P672
Pivarunas, Sara A251
Pivowar, Michael A734
Pivower, Mike A735
Pizarro, Pedro J. A290
Pizza, Andrew A800
Pizzi, Michael A. A283
Pizzini, Ruby A112
Pizzo, Gregory P305
Pizzuti, Eric E. E28
Pizzuto, Frank A879
Pla, Thomas A115
Pla, Thomas E37
Plaat, Mitch A934
Place, John A591
Place, John P369
Place, Nick P627
Plache, Kim A926
Placone, Ginger P114
Plafker, Jed A363
Plaines, Stephanie A481
Plair, Steve A108
Plaisance, Kevin A449

Plaisance, Kevin E220
Plambeck, Steve E358
Plamondon, William N P185
Planitzer, Warren E23
Plank, Kevin A. A862
Plano, Matt E2
Plansky, John A784
Plant, John C. A79
Plante, Francis A56
Plante, David A90
Plante, David A327
Plante, James A409
Plante, Robert A. (Bob) A646
Plante, Robert A. (Bob) E324
Plass, Mary Ellen P17
Plaster, Joe A891
Platanias, Leon P389
Plate, William A125
Plate, Bill A125
Platek, Stan A103
Plater, Alejandro W26
Platford, Giles W381
Plath, Thomas A467
Platt, Louise A267
Platt, Jim A596
Platt, Daniel B. A638
Platt, Daniel B. E320
Platteeuw, Filip W405
Plattner, Hasso W340
Plaza, Angel A432
Plazas, Diana A538
Pleasant, Kevin A567
Pleasant, Kevin E284
Plecki, Robert F. (Bob) A335
Plecki, Robert F. (Bob) E154
Plecnik, John A592
Plecnik, John P370
Pledger, Joseph A872
Pleininger, Johann W295
Plemons, Rocky A355
Plenge, Mark E433
Pless, Karen E131
Plessis, Esme A376
Plessis, Jan P. du W82
Plessis, Jan P. du W325
Plessis, Jan P. du W327
Plessis-Bélair, Michel W313
Pletcher, Brett A385
Pleuhs, Gerhard (Gerd) A573
Plevritis, Peter A203
Plew, Daniel P. Van A710
Plewniak, Linda A15
Plewniak, Linda P7
Plodzeen, Tom A329
Plonski, Joe A135
Ploszek, Judith M P203
Plotke, Eric P274
Plotkin, David A16
Plotkin, Ben A. A787
Plotner, Jason A908
Plotner, Jason E436
Plourde, Jerry A311
Plourde, Robert A877
Plourde, Jerry P199
Plousis, Mark A660
Plousis, Mark P416
Ploutz-Snyder, Lori A711
Ploutz-Snyder, Lori P444
Plowinske, Sandra Besso A922
Plowinske, Sandra Besso P671
Plowman, Gregory A518
Pluard, Tim P466
Pluchino, Fabrizio P72
Plumart, Marc W358
Plummer, Ken A104
Plummer, Jim A481
Plummer, Wade A544
Plummer, Cheryl A665
Plummer, Teresa A839
Plummer, William B. A872
Plummer, Laura P83
Plummer, Alyson P184
Plummer, Beth P378
Plummer, Scott P391
Plummer, Cheryl E334

Plump, Andrew S. W381
Plunk, Ken A902
Plunk, Bob P335
Plunkett, Patrick A215
Plunkett, Debora A647
Plunkett, J. Michael (Mike) E111
Pluta, Chris A756
Poag, Chris A29
Poag, Chris P16
Poblano, Claudia P677
Poblete, Melissa A109
Poblete, Jose A483
Poch, Andi A893
Pocrnich, Christina A206
Pocsi, Charles A684
Podesta, Charles (Chuck) P598
Podges, Christopher P354
Podgorny, Paul A212
Podgurski, Mike A722
Podsadecki, Thomas A5
Poe, Brock A222
Poe, Shawn K. P423
Poenitske, Jason P P391
Poer, James L. P375
Pofahl, Quinn A702
Poff, Brian W. E4
Pofsky, Robert A319
Pohl, Jeffery P184
Pohlman, Kevin A643
Pohlman, Steve A813
Pohlman, John A P502
Pohly, Glenn E272
Poindexter, Karen A578
Poindexter, Philip S. A788
Poindexter, Philip S. E389
Poinsatte, Richard A785
Poinsatte, Christopher A. P171
Poirier, Dan A337
Poirier, Michel W208
Poirier, Dan E158
Poisson, Keith P213
Pokoj, Rhonda A925
Pokoj, Rhonda E445
Pol, Sanjay A199
Pol, Anne A857
Pol, Dave Vander P277
Polakowski, Frank P122
Polanco, Isaac A725
Polanowicz, John P528
Polans, Eric P333
Polanski, John J. A414
Polanski, John J. P236
Polce, Vincent A176
Polechronis, Stephen A16
Polelle, Mike E196
Polen, Thomas E. A123
Polep, Jeff P156
Poletaev, Maxim W343
Poli, Massimo A218
Poli, Kent A335
Poli, Kent E154
Polignac, Fran-§ois Melchior de W88
Polipnick, Gary A. A315
Poliquin, Cathleen P574
Polis, Cindy P92
Polischak, Allan A891
Polishook, Debra A. W5
Polisknowski, John P503
Politopoulou, Marianna W272
Polizzotto, Lawrence A431
Polizzotto, Len P557
Polk, James C. (Jim) A110
Polk, Michael B. (Mike) A593
Polk, Dennis A794
Polk, Alvia P137
Polk, James Robert P463
Polk, Hiram C P623
Polk, Judy L P638
Poll, Max P479
Pollack, Kenneth L A23
Pollack, Dave A197
Pollack, Michael A892
Pollack, Martha E. P159
Pollack, Murray M. P417

Pollard, Victoria A452
Pollard, Jody A733
Pollard, Michael P138
Pollard, Dennis P211
Pollard, Brian P459
Pollard, Gary S. P660
Pollard, Patrick E429
Pollare, Frank A16
Pollei, Mike A61
Polley, Malcolm E. A737
Polley, Malcolm E. E361
Polli, Edward A908
Polli, Edward E436
Pollitt, Erin P332
POLLOCK, WALLY A175
Pollock, Cynthia A774
Pollock, Cynthia P510
Pollock, Samuel J. B. (Sam) W80
Pollok, John C. A769
Pollok, John C. E380
Polluconi, Ron A219
Polluconi, Ron E87
Polly, John A465
Poll-'s, Jeanne A661
Polman, Paul W408
Polman, Paul W409
Polo, Janice P70
Polohakul, Ampol W216
Polomski, Stan A164
Poloni, Lara A16
Polonsky, Kenneth S. P594
Poloz, Stephen S. W50
Poluch, Tony A155
Poluch, Tony E54
Polymeropoulos, Mihael H. E426
Pomaranski, Joseph A. (Joe) A813
Pomerantz, Amanda A332
Pomerantz, Laura E356
Pomerenke, Steve E8
Pomerleau, Michel A380
Pomerleau, Andrew P98
Pomeroy, John A828
Pomeroy, John P584
Pommellet, Pierre-Eric W390
Pompa, Mark A. A292
Pomplon, Carl A166
Ponce, Martha A249
Ponce, Sue P419
Ponce, Martha E108
Poncia, Peter A605
Ponczoch, John A843
Pond, Randy A198
Pond, Randall A199
Pong, Jonathan E347
Ponnekanti, Hari A74
Pons, Matt A520
Pons, Jaume A658
Pons, Karen P125
Pons, Robert M. E202
Ponsler, Tim A624
Ponsonby, Craig A352
Pont, Eleuthere Du A929
Pont, Eleuthere Du E449
Ponte-Goncalves, Claire A575
Pontzer, Deborah A211
Pontzer, Deborah E83
Pooi, Eric W345
Pool, Taylor A421
Pool, Devin A438
Pool, Dr Dennis P396
Poole, Thomas A219
Poole, Tim A718
Poole, James P440
Poole, Nigeria P666
Poole, Thomas E87
Poole, Tim E354
Poole-yaeger, Amy A179
Poonen, Sanjay A897
Poongkumarn, Prasert W95
Poonia, Mohinder P153
Poonpipat, Suphadej W390
Poor, H. Vincent P591
Pootanasap, Vitit W95
Pope, Gene A42
Pope, John C. (Jack) A276

COMBINED HOOVER'S HANDBOOK INDEX OF EXECUTIVES

A = AMERICAN BUSINESS
E = EMERGING COMPANIES
P = PRIVATE COMPANIES
W = WORLD BUSINESS

Pope, Lawrence J. A401
Pope, Robert A609
Pope, Jeffrey A739
Pope, David A818
Pope, Deborah A P94
Pope, Shannon E268
Pope, David E403
Popeck, Charles A799
Popham, Holly A449
Popham, Matthew A509
Popham, Stacey A846
Popham, Holly E220
Popiela, Diane P375
Popielarski, Laurie A530
Popien, Toni P438
Popieski, Tom A749
Popieski, Tom E367
Poplawski, John P299
Popour, Catherine P607
Popov, Igor P543
Popovich, John A414
Popovich, John P236
Popovici, Silviu A654
Popowycz, Alex P232
Popp, Diana A414
Popp, Diana P236
Poppe, Patricia K. (Patti) A209
Poppe, Patricia K. (Patti) A238
Popper, Jozsi A704
Poppinga, Peter W412
Popwell, David T. A343
Popwell, David T. E163
Porat, Ruth M. A39
Porat, M. Moshe P546
Porcari, John P313
Porcelain, Kim P335
Porcelain, Michael D. E93
Pordon, Anthony R. (Tony) A649
Pordon, Tony A649
Poremba, Steve P316
Porgess, Sam A145
Porporino, Dominic A871
Porras, Edward A246
Porras, Julio Carlos W26
Porras, Edward E105
Porru, Martina A658
Porsa, Esmaeil P171
Port, Stephen A759
Port, Joel P305
Port, Stephen P493
Port, Barry R. E127
Portacci, Michael T. A228
Portalatin, Julio A. A539
Portantino, Philip A646
Portantino, Philip E324
Porte, Susan P161
Porter, Darlene A19
Porter, Lisa Porter Lisa A142
Porter, Cynthia V A222
Porter, Pamela G A222
Porter, Tracy L A225
Porter, Biggs C. A355
Porter, David E. A414
Porter, Todd A418
Porter, Jessica A449
Porter, John A466
Porter, Clint A665
Porter, Jonathan A714
Porter, Brian A717
Porter, Kerrick A723
Porter, Stephen D. A754
Porter, Amanda A782
Porter, Brian A799
Porter, Melvin A859
Porter, Ann A859
Porter, Patrick A887
Porter, Doug P89
Porter, Candace P94
Porter, Reca P146

Porter, Jody P213
Porter, Emily P258
Porter, Jennifer P280
Porter, Annabelle P451
Porter, Frenchie P476
Porter, Stephen D. P484
Porter, Amanda P526
Porter, Andy P556
Porter, Brian J. W53
Porter, James S. E23
Porter, Lisa Porter Lisa E49
Porter, David E. E208
Porter, Jessica E220
Porter, Clint E334
Porter, Scott E339
Porter, Brian E351
Portera, Joseph P. (Joe) A241
Porth, Wilfried W125
Portner, Greg A65
Portner, Marc P513
Portnoy, Barry M. A843
Porto, Silvio W289
Porwal, Hemant A910
Posa, Nicola A933
Posada, Juan F. A680
Posch, Danny P340
Posch, Guillaume de W66
Poselenzny, Anthony A871
Posey, Robert A902
Posey, Bruce K. E342
Poshyanonda, Pipatpong W216
Post, Glen F. A184
Post, Roxanne A704
Post, Jennifer P75
Post, Shelley P152
Post, Kim P478
Post, Janet P657
Postell, Ann A452
Postma, Sidney W P433
Postol, Sean A170
Potashner, Kenneth F. P374
Potasky, Jim E292
Potember, Donna E433
Pothemont, Sharlene P325
Pothoven, Bev P277
Potje, Ivan A686
Pototo, Dan P303
Potsic, Robert A605
Potter, Simon M. A319
Potter, Mary A520
Potter, Beth A585
Potter, Jon A586
Potter, Stephen N. A605
Potter, Jennifer A749
Potter, Silas P481
Potter, Sara E143
Potter, Jon E301
Potter, Jennifer E367
Potter, John E432
Pottorff, James P P92
Potts, David L. A716
Potts, Janna A. A804
Potts, Ryan A909
Potts, Henry P326
Potts, David T. W266
Potts, Robert E279
Potts, Ryan E436
Potvin, Toni A259
Potvin, Brian E264
Poudrier, Ray A630
Poulakidas, Dean E442
Poulakos, Greg A69
Poulin, Benoit A175
Poulliott, Joe P432
Poulsen, Greg A462
Poulsen, David P13
Poulsen, Greg P256
Poulsen, Niel L. E422
Pouncey, Clarence C. A755
Pouncey, Clarence C. E369
Pound, Gregory A598
Pound, Greg A598
Pounds, Walt P586
Pourbaix, Alex W92
Poure, Barbara Tartaglia P596

Pourfallah, Stacy A895
Pouyanné, Patrick W398
Povenmire, Rex A271
Povinelli, Brian A538
Povlinski, Bryan P610
Povolny, Denise A492
Povse, Mat A130
Powell, Sarah A13
Powell, Ann A151
Powell, Carol A151
Powell, Jerry W A159
Powell, Jeffrey A211
Powell, Heather A263
Powell, Bradley S. (Brad) A308
Powell, Jon A329
Powell, Kendall J. (Ken) A376
Powell, Ira A391
Powell, Christine A380
Powell, Bill A378
Powell, Teresa A414
Powell, Cleland A449
Powell, James A528
Powell, Heather A537
Powell, Rebecca A584
Powell, Tyane A664
Powell, Deana A760
Powell, Greg A768
Powell, Sharon A779
Powell, Cynthia A. A781
Powell, Terry A831
Powell, Cindy A849
Powell, Ken A850
Powell, Vincent A852
Powell, Wayne A871
Powell, David A877
Powell, Aaron A880
Powell, Charlie P1
Powell, Casey P55
Powell, Brian K P123
Powell, Gerald P135
Powell, Curt P164
Powell, Caleb P188
Powell, Gennifer P204
Powell, Kenneth P291
Powell, David P308
Powell, Chris P315
Powell, Andrew P374
Powell, Ashley P394
Powell, Willa P454
Powell, Tiffany P505
Powell, Larry E P506
Powell, Tanner P543
Powell, John P598
Powell, Terry P601
Powell, Aaron P640
Powell, Scott E. W48
Powell, William W80
Powell, Rice W166
Powell, Rice W167
Powell, Jeffrey E83
Powell, Teresa E208
Powell, Cleland E220
Powell, Jeffrey L. E243
Powell, Paul T. E256
Powell, Tyane E334
Powell, Deana E374
Powelson, Kevin A638
Powelson, Kevin E320
Power, Joseph A46
Power, Doug A376
Power, Nancy A559
Power, Alan J. (Al) A675
Power, Francis A702
Power, Jamila A711
Power, Donna P226
Power, Michael J P383
Power, Alan J. (Al) P428
Power, Jamila P444
Power, Robert E318
Powers, John A51
Powers, Robert P. (Bob) A51
Powers, Christy A61
Powers, John J. A335
Powers, Greg A401
Powers, Marsha A811

Powers, Gary A922
Powers, John J. P78
Powers, Kevin G P122
Powers, James P165
Powers, Donald S P354
Powers, Sandra P489
Powers, Kevin P501
Powers, Eva P660
Powers, Gary P671
Powers, Steve E96
Powers, John J. E154
Powers, Johnny D. E223
Powers, John E244
Powers, Kathleen E286
Powers, Russell E308
Powers, Hammond R P161
Powlus, Lee C. A651
Powlus, Stephen P214
Powlus, Lee C. E329
Pozarycki, Thomas A903
Pozez, Norman A284
Pozez, Norman E117
Poznak, Oksana E250
Pozotrigo, Albert A476
Pozzi, James E. A58
Pozzi, Joseph A391
Pozzi, Steven R. W106
Prabhakar, Lata E143
Prabhu, Arjun A613
Prabhu, Vasant M. A895
Prabhu, John C. E245
Pradelle, Yann E179
Pradyot, Behera A364
Pragada, Robert V. (Bob) A476
Prager, Richard L. (Richie) A135
Prager, Carol P472
Prahl, Spencer E429
Prahlad, Sheela A347
Prahlad, Sheela E167
Pramaggiore, Anne R. A304
Pramanik, Sharmila P472
Prange, Karen A744
Prasad, Veronica A44
Prasad, Amrita A722
Prasad, Manoj A833
Prasad, Veronica E13
Prashaud, Satie A137
Prather, Steve A767
Prather, Sharon P163
Pratico, Joseph A882
Pratka, Amy P502
Prato, Patrick A444
Pratt, Timothy A. (Tim) A149
Pratt, Paul A362
Pratt, Terresa A444
Pratt, Jill A547
Pratt, Valerie A704
Pratt, William C. (Bill) A762
Pratt, John P184
Pratt, Dan P220
Pratt, Ramona P419
Pratt, Ronald E P543
Pratt, Scott P636
Pratt, Gregory P E222
Pratt, Jim E440
Pravlik, Mari A609
Praw, Jonathan E246
Prebola, Don A717
Precourt, Walter F. (Walt) A576
Preece, Linda P504
Prefach, Nanci P325
Prego, Maria A574
Prego, Joe P23
Preiser, Douglas A491
Preiser, Craig A590
Preisler, Donna P192
Preiss, Tammy P164
Prejean, Joshua A167
Prejean, Jerry A449
Prejean, Jerry E220
Prendergast, David A35
Prendergast, Neil A347
Prendergast, Vincent A819
Prendergast, Ed P60
Prendergast, Mark P220

HOOVER'S HANDBOOK OF EMERGING COMPANIES 2020

COMBINED HOOVER'S HANDBOOK INDEX OF EXECUTIVES

Prendergast, Vincent P549
Prendergast, E. James (Jim) P572
Prendergast, Neil E168
Prenger, Ron P291
Prentice, Bill A258
Prentice, F. Sheldon A584
Prentice, Deborah A. P591
Pres, Thomas J La P246
Prescott, Gary A51
Presecan, Anne P481
Presendor, Pascale P325
Present, Randall C. (Randy) A435
Presenti, Jerome A310
Preska, Robert P285
Preskenis, Donald A336
Preskenis, Ashley A665
Preskenis, Donald E157
Preskenis, Ashley E334
Presnell, Richard P463
Presnell, Bill P532
Presser, Michael E433
Pressimone, Glenn P120
Pressley, Mandell A262
Pressley, W. Michael A389
Pressley, Carol P417
Presson, Michael A469
Prest, Joe A205
Presti, Linda A54
Preston, James A222
Preston, Patricia A313
Preston, Bryan A329
Preston, Patricia A544
Preston, Trish A544
Preston, Carolyn A761
Preston, Bill P77
Preston, Terri P255
Preston, Simeon W14
Preston, Patricia E144
Prestopine, Hillarie A460
Pretasky, Barbara P287
Prete, Thomas A875
Pretorius, Alwyn A595
Pretorius, Sy P405
Prettyman, Peter P251
Preuss, J. Christopher (Chris) W31
Prevade, Michael P106
Previn, Fletcher A465
Prevost, Andrew P375
Prewitt, Connie F. P84
Prez, Norberto A670
Prezelj, Irene A351
Price, Zoila A104
Price, Milton A115
Price, Mitch A187
Price, Deb A236
Price, Frank A251
Price, Thomas Michael (Mike) A337
Price, Harold A353
Price, Michael A444
Price, Jeanine A462
Price, Todd M A552
Price, Michael H. A552
Price, Lisa V A602
Price, Lisa A602
Price, Matthew S. A680
Price, Matt A683
Price, Anthony A746
Price, Scott A871
Price, Scott A901
Price, Paula A914
Price, David P68
Price, David P86
Price, David C P86
Price, Cole P120
Price, James P202
Price, Joseph P202
Price, Harold P204
Price, Jeanine P256
Price, Sinai P295
Price, Todd M P324
Price, Debra P357
Price, Connell P378
Price, Pamela P396
Price, Diane P399
Price, Ronald E P415

Price, Clarissa P428
Price, Matt P431
Price, Barbara P479
Price, Audra P531
Price, Nancy P549
Price, Stuart P563
Price, Milton E37
Price, Thomas Michael (Mike) E158
Price, Colin E207
Price, Michael H. E276
Pricket, Glenn P579
Prickett, Charles (Charlie) P1
Prickett, Glenn T. P579
Pridan, Moshe A762
Priddle, Justin A128
Priebe, Nancy P52
Priebe, Jason P493
Prieshoff, Matt A522
Priess, Tammy P164
Priest, Stephen J. (Steve) A478
Priest, Vincent P239
Priest, Geoffrey P332
Prieto, Robert Bob A281
Prill, Gina A246
Prill, Chris A287
Prill, Gina E105
Primmer, Jan A559
Primrose, Tricia A537
Prince, Scott A107
Prince, Sidney A663
Prince, Brandon A924
Prince, Don P537
Prince, Larry E268
Princen, Marc W381
Principato, Giuseppe P437
Prins, Darrell P469
Prinster, Dan P523
Prinz, Corey A114
Prinz, Corey E37
Prior, Graham E122
Prioux, No-«l W88
Priscak, Dave A628
Prisco, Dale A196
Priselac, Thomas M. (Tom) P118
Prising, Jonas A532
Pritchard, Kelly A326
Pritchard, Deborah A747
Pritchard, Shani P38
Pritchard, Sarah M. P388
Pritchard, Abbie E81
Pritchett, Wanda A519
Pritchett, Patricia P624
Priti, Desai A332
Privett, Phillip A809
Privoznik, Chris P89
Prizner, John S A16
Probst, Marc A462
Probst, Marc P256
Prochaska, Amanda A562
Prochazka, Scott M A180
Prochazka, Scott M. A180
Procida, Thomas A137
Procopio, Russell A63
Procter, Kerrigan W233
Proctor, Jason P133
Proctor, Bryan E412
Profeta, Tommaso W235
Proffitt, Julie A447
Proffitt, Julie P247
Proffitt, Joshua L. E255
Profumo, Alessandro W235
Proia, Gina M. A200
Proll, Douglas A. (Doug) W85
Promes, Jennifer P362
Promo, Joe A554
Promo, Joseph A554
Promutico, Alessandro W71
Pronger, Derk P354
Pronti, Scott A839
Prontnicki, Marianna E132
PROPERSI, ADRIANO W43
Prophater, Kristen A882
Propst, Beverly L. A396
Prosera, Sharon P522
Proske, Donna P527

Prosser, Scott A176
Prosser, Joseph P550
Prosser, Ed P589
Prost, Sarah A862
Prothro, Caren P505
Protzman, Chris E366
Prough, Allen A920
Proulx, Kevin A798
Proust, Elisabeth W398
Prout, Mark A352
Prout, John P81
Prout, John S P218
Provance, Aaron P127
Provelcher, Catherine P642
Provera, Marco Tronchetti W252
Providakes, Jason F. P578
Provost, Kristy A648
Provost, David T. A806
Provost, Kristy P411
Provost, David T. E398
Prows, Mark A562
Prozorov, Sergey W309
Pruden, Gary A479
Prudente, Maryann A559
PrudÂ'homme, Sylvain A527
Prue, Kevin A686
Pruessing, Peter P211
Pruitt, Diana A142
Pruitt, Warren A218
Pruitt, Kristin L. A504
Pruitt, Toni P329
Pruitt, Gary B. P555
Pruitt, Lauren P610
Pruitt, Diana E49
Pruitt, Ron E131
Pruitt, Kristin L. E251
Pruitt, Ronnie E422
Prunchunas, Edward M. P118
Prunesti, Jim A232
Pruniaux, Patrick W218
Prupas, Annie A176
Pruss-Jones, Catherine J A140
Prutzman, Lorna P626
Pruzan, Scott A552
Pruzan, Jonathan A574
Pruzan, Scott P324
Prybylski, Jay A384
Prybylski, Jay P217
Pryce, Richard W317
Pryor, David B A84
Pryor, Felecia A146
Pryor, Tom A484
Pryor, D. Scott A803
Pryor, David B P47
Pryor, Vince P192
Pryor, Robert P478
Przybyl, Arthur S. E21
Przybylowicz, James A251
Przybysz, William P25
Przybyszewski, Barbara P349
Psaltis, Vassillios E. W25
Psihas, Julian Jorge Lazalde A771
Psihas, Julian Lazalde A771
Pu, Andrew A686
Pu, Jian W108
Pucci, Jason A704
Pucci, David A859
Puccio, Joseph P638
Pucel, Kenneth J. (Ken) A669
Puckett, Jon A177
Puckett, Karen A296
Puckett, Kate A528
Puckett, Jeffrey M. (Jeff) P132
Puckett, Doug P252
Puckett, Debbie P419
Puckett, Jeff E412
Puco, Christopher C. E9
Puddy, Michael A250
Pudlo, Joe A119
Puechl, Robert L. A768
Puente, Juan A920
Puente, Robert R. P470
Puetz, Verner A307
Puffinburger, Darren P394
Pugh, Edwin A665

Pugh, Vicki A791
Pugh, William P420
Pugh, Vicki P535
Pugh, Beverly H P647
Pugh, Mike E240
Pugh, Edwin E334
Pugliese, Sandy P222
Pugni, Carl P664
Puhy, Dorothy E. P172
Puishys, Joseph E23
Pukylo, Brian A337
Pukylo, Brian E158
Pulakanti, Abhishek A727
Pulakanti, Abhishek P453
Puleio, Frank E154
Puleo, Paul A357
Puleo, Dominic J P649
Puleo, Paul E175
Pulgini, Margaret A922
Pulgini, Margaret P671
Pulie, Jim A651
Pulie, Jim E329
Pulio, Kristen P7
Pullen, Donna A769
Pullen, Jim P532
Pullen, Donna E380
Pulles, Dianne E103
Pulley, Erika P160
Pulley, Megan P556
Pulliam, Ryan A325
Pulliam, Elizabeth P66
Pullin, Ericka A246
Pullin, Cassandra A600
Pullin, Ericka E105
Pullins, Jerald L. E413
Pullizzi, Amanda A646
Pullizzi, Amanda E324
Pullman, Roger A140
Pullman, Adam A452
Pullola, Kristian W284
Pulsifer, Keith A319
Pulsifer, Gregory A376
Pulsifer, Lindsay P424
Pulsipher, Susan P270
Pum, Michael P283
Puma, Grace A654
Puma, Mary G. E30
Pumeroy, Clarence P522
Pumilia, Claude A730
Pummer, Steve A715
Pun, Carla A465
Pung, Michael J. (Mike) E144
Punja, Ranajoy A198
Punnett, Valerie A827
Punnett, Valerie P580
Punta, Stefano Del W202
Punthong, Chavalit W316
Puntney, Jeff A135
Punyamurthula, Sujan A16
Punzina, Carol La A126
Puraleski, Susan A925
Puraleski, Susan E445
Puranik, Gautam A171
Puranik, Shirish A896
Purcell, Cynthia D. (Cindy) A116
Purcell, Stacey A161
Purcell, Kathleen A416
Purcell, Kreg A524
Purcell, Doug A845
Purcell, David A895
Purcell, Alfred L P234
Purcell, Alfred L P349
Purcell, Pamela P642
Purcell, Cynthia D. (Cindy) E39
Purdon, Luke A458
Purdy, Kimberly A36
Purdy, Donald A137
Purdy, Rick A493
Puri, Ajay K. (Jay) A613
Puri, Jay A613
Purington, Joseph A303
Purington, Matthew A882
Purkey, Jeffrey P151
Purnell, Carissa P468
Purrier, Paul P101

HOOVER'S HANDBOOK OF EMERGING COMPANIES 2020

COMBINED HOOVER'S HANDBOOK INDEX OF EXECUTIVES

A = AMERICAN BUSINESS
E = EMERGING COMPANIES
P = PRIVATE COMPANIES
W = WORLD BUSINESS

Pursch, Jonathan A246
Pursch, Jonathan E105
Purugganan, Michael D. A592
Purugganan, Michael D. P370
Purushothaman, Arvind E263
Purvis, Chuck A213
Purvis, Shawn N. A608
Purvis, Alan P195
Purvis, Michael E226
Purwin, Dave A240
Puryear, Chad A704
Puryear, Alvin N. E5
Pushis, Glenn A. A785
Puskar, Joseph P573
Put, Dirk Van de A573
Puthoff, Dolores P128
Puthussery, Joseph A199
Putman, Jim A884
Putnam, Lori A62
Putnam, Chris A442
Putnam, Robert P386
Putnam, Skip P386
Putnam, Lori E20
Putter, Joshua S. P528
Putterbaugh, Lynn A444
Puttick, James A724
Puttick, James P452
Puttock, Mark E128
Putur, Christine (Chris) A801
Puyfontaine, Arnaud Roy de W385
Puyfontaine, Arnaud Roy de W416
Puzausky, Michael A909
Puzausky, Michael E436
Pyatt, Brent A712
Pyatt, Donald C. E23
Pye, Donna A449
Pye, Ken A564
Pye, Donna E221
Pyer, Doug A245
Pyka, Tammy E438
Pyke, Robert A793
Pyle, Robert D A253
Pyle, Kent P278
Pyle, Clint P590
Pyle, Michael R. (Mike) E326
Pyles, Valarie P276
Pyles, Carolyn P333
Pynchon, Bryan N A167
Pyne, David A692
Pyott, David A97
Pzena, Richard S. E340
Potsch, Hans D. W418
Pécresse, Jér-'me A374
Pépin, Normand W193

Q

Qian, Liu W103
Qiang, Guo Zhi W103
Qin, Huofa W98
Qingping, Li W108
Qingsong, Lan W336
Qingying, Zeng P314
Qing'an, Weng W96
Qiu, Alex E226
Quach, Michael A827
Quackenbush, Scott A369
Quaglia, Joseph H. A809
Quagliana, Steve A857
Quagliata, Joseph A54
Quaglino, Kathleen P138
Quale, Matthew A559
Quallen, Christopher A715
Quallis, Tina-shai A722
Qualls, Kathleen P625
Quam, Bethany C. A376
Quam, Eldon A434

Quam, Lois E. P579
Quan, Patrick F A50
Quan, Patrick F P31
Quan, Patrick F P572
Quandt, Fred A902
Quandt, Stefan W63
Quarles, Christa A143
Quarles, Patrick D. (Pat) A177
Quartarone, Lisa A747
Quarton, Robert E433
Quartuccio, James A686
Quast, Gene E298
Quatrano, Ralph S. P600
Quattrochi, Denise A522
Quay, Martha James P670
Quayle, Jon A89
Quddus, Sheikh A167
Queen, Andy A469
Queen, Elizabeth P395
Queenan, Daniel (Danny) A175
Queener, Hugh M. A664
Queener, Hugh M. E333
Quehl, Richard W A723
Quenell, Eileen A540
Quenneville, Cathy L A37
Quenneville, Cathy L P27
Quercize, Stanislas de W115
Querner, Immo W382
Querrey, Dale L. A696
Query, K Rex A612
Quesenberry, Scott A381
Quesenberry, Jeff A772
Quesenberry, Jeff E382
Quesnoy, Dru P274
Questad, Brian A158
Quick, Paul A366
Quick, Janet M. A413
Quick, James E. P505
Quick, Janet M. E205
Quigley, Brian W. A41
Quigley, James H. (Jim) A419
Quigley, Janet A641
Quigley, Dan A692
Quigley, Robert A700
Quigley, Matt A704
Quigley, Lori A789
Quigley, Janet P407
Quigley, Timothy P502
Quigley, David P608
Quijada, Raoul E332
Quijano, Anna A222
Quijano-Lerma, Mariselle P408
Quiles, Cindy P459
Quillen, David A828
Quillen, David P584
Quillin, M. Kirk A116
Quillin, Susan A855
Quillin, M. Kirk E39
Quilter, George A135
Quin, Gardner A61
Quin, Debra A71
Quin, Debra P43
Quincey, James R. A215
Quine, Allen P242
Quiniones, Gil C. P367
Quinlan, Patrick J A619
Quinlan, Ruth A704
Quinlan, Raymond J. A763
Quinlan, Patrick J P393
Quinlan, Steven J. (Steve) E302
Quinlan, Raymond J. E377
Quinley, Michael E177
quinn, Mary Jo A35
Quinn, Robert W. (Bob) A89
Quinn, Brian A A90
Quinn, Rebecca A135
Quinn, Pat A250
Quinn, Stephen D. A398
Quinn, John S. A524
Quinn, R. Patrick A589
Quinn, T. Kyle A636
Quinn, David A686
Quinn, Amy A718
Quinn, Lisa A833
Quinn, Chris A882

Quinn, Katherine B. A884
Quinn, Christopher A887
Quinn, Robert A922
Quinn, Joseph P206
Quinn, Brandi P432
Quinn, Ronald N P546
Quinn, Edward P570
Quinn, Teresa P605
Quinn, Robert P671
Quinn, Jason W3
Quinn, Peter W131
Quinn, Noel W189
Quinn, George W435
Quinn, Marianne E132
Quinn, Amy E354
Quinn, John C. E359
Quinn, Kevin E448
Quinonez, Tanya P199
Quint, Eric A3
Quint, Jason A125
Quintana, Frank A578
Quintanilla, Abel Coello A245
Quintanilla, David A421
Quintanilla, Gloriane P266
Quinter, Mark P558
Quinto, Wanda A191
Quinto, Marcos de A215
Quinton, Jody P185
Quinton, Todd E334
Quirin, Julie L. P466
Quirk, Raymond R. (Randy) A325
Quirk, Kathleen L. A365
Quirk, Deborah A651
Quirk, Maureen A798
Quirk, Maureen M A798
Quirk, Steven (Steve) A807
Quirk, Sherry A. A815
Quirk, William P130
Quirk, Brian C. E285
Quirk, Deborah E329
Quiroga, Victor A246
Quiroga, Victor E105
Quiroz, Mark A438
Quito, Remy A112
Quizon, David E318
Quon, Gene A198
Qureshi, Furhan P287
Quémard, Jean-Christophe W305

R

R, Katzin Lawrence A271
R, Cynthia P161
Raab, Andrew P530
Raad, Mark P. de E272
Rabanal, Mike E47
Rabb, Marie A738
Rabbitt, Dan A103
Rabe, Ron A774
Rabel, Fernando A934
Rabiller, Olivier A431
Rabinowitz, Terry P598
Rabjohn, Richard A465
Rabkin, Mark A310
Rable, George P77
Raburn, Desiree A105
Raburn, Desiree E34
Raby, Julian P497
Racanelli, Joe A870
Rachide, Mary E174
Rachiele, Pierre A380
Rachman, Sherry P162
Rachmeler, Kim A42
Rachunek, Jana A682
Racicot, Sue E330
Racine, Andrew D. P348
Racioppi, Michael A744
Rack, Karen A618
Rack, Karen E330
Ractliffe, Scott A664
Ractliffe, Scott E334
Racut, Kimberly P116
Racz, Francesca A279
Raczkowski, Carl P254

Radano, Amy P423
Radcliffe, Charles A442
Radde, Donald E. (Don) A433
Radde, Donald E. (Don) E217
Radebe, Maurice W341
Radecki, Brian J. E99
Radelet, Aaron A423
Radeloff, Brent A409
Radeloff, Dean P582
Rademaker, Jennifer A545
Rademan, Riaan F. W341
Raden, Ann A187
Rader, Rodney P364
Rader, Kendall P522
Rader, Sandy P643
Radford, Karen L. W150
Radhakrishnan, Rupkumar A135
Radich, Paula P467
Radisic, Damir A15
Radisic, Damir P7
Radley, Steven A452
Radley, Mary P558
Radliff, David A3
Radloff, Sue A346
Radloff, Diane P47
Radloff, Sue E166
Radous, Barbara A51
Radtke, Jodi P353
Rady, Ernest S. A48
Radziwill, John A470
Radzyminski, Julie P77
Rae, John A. W313
Rae, Brendan P. E25
Rae, Gary E264
Raeber, Leslie A718
Raehl, Deborah P640
Raffa, George A704
Raffenot, Jp A381
Raffensperger, Nick A567
Raffensperger, Nick E284
Rafferty, Nicole A89
Rafferty, Emily K. A320
Rafferty, Steven A618
Rafferty, Dan A902
Rafferty, Patrick P153
Raffetto, Michael A176
Raffile, Sheryl P676
Raffoul, John G P6
Rafkin, Scott W420
Raftery, Michael A556
Raftery, Kelli A893
Raftery, Michael E277
Raftevold, Dan P299
Ragel, Larry P516
Ragen, York A. E184
Rager, R. Scott A622
Raghavan, Vis A483
Raghumandala, Harikrishna A752
Raghuram, Rangarajan (Raghu) A897
Ragineni, Ramesh A739
Ragle, Jake A668
Ragni, Margaret V P303
Ragouzeos, Zoe A592
Ragouzeos, Zoe P370
Ragusa, Elysia A819
Ragusa, Elysia E403
Ragwar, Akello P369
Raha, Samraat S A22
Raher, Tim E46
Rahl, Gary A145
Rahlfs, Gary P635
Rahming, Carmen M P342
Rahmlow, Brad E35
Rahn, Pete K P313
Rahnamay-Azar, Amir P114
Rai, Divya A204
Raia, Kathy A247
Raia, Kathy E105
Raiche, Erica P193
Raikes, Jeffrey A242
Raikes, Donald A275
Raimonde, Michael A. A684
Raimondi, Peter J. A147
Raimondo, Gina M A782
Raimondo, Gina M P526

Raina, Sunita A248
Raina, Sunita E107
Raina, Robin E122
Rainbolt, David E. A105
Rainbolt, David E. E34
Rainbow, Harris P392
Rainer, Sallie A296
Rainer, Thom S. P296
Raines, John A263
Raines, J. Paul A371
Raines, Diane S. P63
Rainey, Mark A77
Rainey, Kim A140
Rainey, Joseph D. (Joe) A401
Rainey, Ava A799
Rainey, Brett E132
Rainford, Annmarie P199
Rainone, Anthony P397
Rains, Delynn A105
Rains, Delynn E34
Rainville, William A. (Bill) E243
Rainwater, Meghan P54
Rainwater, Marvin P280
Raish, John P171
Raj, Atul P412
Raja, Prabu G. A74
Raja, Andaleeb H P296
Rajagopalan, Krishnan E207
Rajalingam, Robert A170
Rajan, Resmi P190
Rajappa, Aswin E271
Rajaratnam, Raj A207
Rajasekar, Sunil A287
Rajewski, Brenda A806
Rajewski, Brenda E398
Rajgopal, Raj E431
Rajkowski, E. Mark A936
Rajpal, Arvind A151
Rakas, Daniel A254
Rakauskas, Greg A740
Rake, Michael A738
Rakes, Kellie A36
Rakes, Wade A179
Rakes, Donna E292
Rakotci, George A702
Rakow, Diana Birkett A29
Raleigh, Billy A854
Rales, Steven M. A254
Raley, Zachary W. A66
Raley, Claire A114
Raley, Leonard R. P642
Raley, Claire E37
Rall, Peter A816
Ralli, Georges W88
Rallis, Kim P203
Ralls, Susan M E168
Ralph, Ginevra P636
Ralston, Patrick R A341
Ralston, Michael A442
Ralston, Chris P625
Rama, Michael P. E309
Ramachandra, Sumant A120
Ramachandran, Sampath A414
Ramachandran, Bhaskar A475
Ramachandran, Ranjith P116
Ramachandran, Sampath P236
Ramachandran, Ramesh P322
Ramadoss, Balaji P203
Ramagano, Cheryl A879
Ramalho, Sean A844
Ramamurthy, Sundar A74
Raman, Sridhar A245
Raman, J.V. W408
Raman, Sudhakar E316
Ramapriya, Jeevan A784
Ramaswami, Rajiv A897
Ramaswamy, Ramki A478
Ramawy, Dennis A483
Rambert, Dan A922
Rambert, Dan P671
Rambis, Mark P13
Ramchandani, John P337
Ramelb, Paul A109
Rames, Jared E123
Ramey, Ray A100

Ramey, Eric A236
Ramey, Curtis E264
Ramey, H. Craig E349
Ramgren, Becky P343
Ramirez, Joe A11
Ramirez, Joseph A11
Ramirez, Terrie A246
Ramirez, Rene A246
Ramirez, Renato A463
Ramirez, Ricardo A463
Ramirez, Rosie A463
Ramirez, Ryan A493
Ramirez, German A746
Ramirez, Jaime A. A778
Ramirez, John A799
Ramirez, Gabriela A833
Ramirez, Angel A865
Ramirez, Jennifer A915
Ramirez, Eduardo P141
Ramirez, Lisa P457
Ramirez, Carmen P489
Ramirez, Danielle P530
Ramirez, Juan Roberto P620
Ramirez, Gabriel P620
Ramirez, Raul P662
Ramirez, Raul E80
Ramirez, Terrie E105
Ramirez, Rene E105
Ramiro, Lucila P203
Ramkumar, Krishnaswamy W194
Ramlo, Randy A. A867
Ramon, David E184
Ramonat, R. Whitfield A649
Ramonet, Alfonso J. A373
Ramos, Clarissa C A60
Ramos, Ricardo (Ricky) A217
Ramos, Rene A236
Ramos, Richard A567
Ramos, Bertha A682
Ramos, Victor A686
Ramos, Jess A746
Ramos, Aida A800
Ramos, Harold P194
Ramos, Rick P308
Ramos, Annette P454
Ramos, Hector P462
Ramos, Gavino P470
Ramos, Hermenegildo P482
Ramos, Aurelio P579
Ramos, Maria W3
Ramos, Raul R. E171
Ramos, Richard E283
Ramoutar, Roxanne A257
Rampinelli, Audrey A A526
Ramraj, Sam A290
Ramsay, Omar A444
Ramsay, Paul D. A527
Ramsay, Timothy A927
Ramsay, Royce P385
Ramsay, Nancy P549
Ramsbottom, Scott A68
Ramsden, Derek A925
Ramsden, Derek E445
Ramsey, Craig R. A45
Ramsey, Dean A89
Ramsey, Warren A104
Ramsey, Matthew S A295
Ramsey, Paul A303
Ramsey, Chris A383
Ramsey, Michael A492
Ramsey, Mark A528
Ramsey, Doug A855
Ramsey, Paul G. A880
Ramsey, Michael P279
Ramsey, Daniel J. P309
Ramsey, Paul G. P640
Ramsey, Charles T P662
Ramsey, Chris E186
Ramsey, Michael E374
Ramstedt, Peter S A853
Ramstedt, Peter S P612
Ramundo, Kate A79
Ramza, Timothy W. W247
Ram-rez, Miguel - -ngel Espinoza W175

Ranck, Bruce E. A696
Ranck, Angela P160
Rancour, Joseph A900
Rand, Allison A676
Rand, Edward L. (Ned) A678
Randall, Rick A16
Randall, Anne L. A147
Randall, Sarah A540
Randall, Chris D A723
Randall, Amy P111
Randall, John P579
Randazzo, James A380
Randazzo, Richard P2
Randazzo, Salvatore E305
Randel, Don A210
Randich, David M. A361
Randich, Steven J. (Steve) P202
Randlett, Brad A203
Randolph, Lanny L A142
Randolph, Diane A858
Randolph, Adrian W. B. P388
Randolph, Ron P467
Randolph, Karsten P491
Randolph, Lanny L E49
Randt, Clark A695
Randt, Clark A871
Randy, Moon P637
Raney, Mike A184
Raney, Steven M. (Steve) A704
Rangana, Anand A784
Rangel, Connie P20
Rangel, Enrique Ortiz de Montellano W26
Rangsiyopash, Roongrote W351
Ranjan, Himani A484
Rankin, Lisa L A54
Rankin, Deanna A247
Rankin, Mark A732
Rankin, David A748
Rankin, Cindy A797
Rankin, Devina A. A905
Rankin, Peter E102
Rankin, Deanna E105
Rankin, Scott E411
Ranney, Timothy P344
Ranque, Cyril A307
Ranque, Denis W17
Ranshaw, Lizzie P505
Ransier, Marc P506
Ransom, Rick A325
Ransom, Mark A329
Ransom, Matt A704
Ransom, Rebecca A706
Ransom, Elizabeth P551
Ranta, Curtis A409
Ranzino, Kirk A167
Rao, Sunil A43
Rao, Venkat A209
Rao, Naveen G. A460
Rao, Anil A460
Rao, Jyothi A826
Rao, Mrutyunjaya A919
RAO, Deepak P196
RAO, Raj P251
RAO, Michael P649
Rao, Sunil E13
Rao, Anil E290
Rao, Chalapathi E315
Raoult, Frédéric W366
Rapaccioli, Donna P206
Rapala, Chris A577
Rapanos, Vasileios T. W25
Rapaport, Marc H. P118
Rapelye, Janet L. P591
Raphael, Carol P2
Rapier, Jared A161
Rapier, Charlie A739
Rapino, Brian A390
Rapino, Michael (Mike) A522
Rapkin, Hilary A. E440
Rapp, Murray A373
Rapp, J D A920
Rapp, Peter F. P399
Rappaport, Jessica E366
Rappe, Kristine A908

Rapple, Susan P556
Rapport, Nicole A200
Rasbach, Kyle E101
Rasbid, Ken A170
Rasche, Steven P P510
Raschke, Uwe W75
Rasco, Jane P623
Rasell, Alan A434
Rash, Ron P672
Rash, John E335
Rashell, Ron P361
Rashid, Mamoon A627
Rask, John E264
Raskin, David P334
Raskopf, Karen E115
Rasmussen, Bart A3
Rasmussen, Mike P26
Rasmussen, Steve P395
Rassouli, Novid E101
Rast, Michele A702
Rastetter, Bruce L. P594
Rasti, Abi A259
Rasula, Jay A60
Rasznski, Andre P649
Ratajczak, Kari A408
Ratajczak, Matthew A732
Ratanabanchuen, Virachai W95
Ratay, Andrea A112
Ratcliff, Phil A230
Ratcliff, Phil P154
Rath, John A504
Rath, John E251
Rathbum, Jim A715
Rathbun, Robert S. A806
Rathbun, Robert S. E398
Rathjen, Errol A204
Rathke, Tom W140
Rathke, David E105
Rathnam, Murali A915
Ratigan, Donal A201
Ratinoff, Edward A101
Ratinoff, Edward E32
Ratkovich, Jason A444
Ratliff, John D. A502
Ratliff, Beth A428
Ratnathicam, Chutta A363
Ratnayake, Madu E431
Ratner, Richard A175
Ratner, Hilary P660
Rattanapian, Chongrak W216
Ratterman, Stephen E334
Rattray, Aaron P613
Ratzan, Scott A479
Ratzi, Robert A226
Ratzi, Robert P150
Ratzlaff, Lori A104
Rau, Jason A360
Rau, Celeste A368
Rau, John P. A927
Rauch, Ari A460
Rauch, Pamela A597
Rauch, Scott L. A641
Rauch, Scott L. P407
Raus, Gregg A481
Rausch, Erin K A63
Rausch, Timothy S. P540
Rausch, Chris P613
Rauscher, Robert J. A224
Rauscher, Eric A224
Rauschl, Christopher A376
Rauschmayer, Joseph (Joe) E110
Rause, Michael A597
Rautenstrauch, Jorg A821
Rauw, Brendan P399
Raval, Anuja A204
Ravanzo, Jason A P310
Raven, Gary A156
Ravener, Robert D. (Bob) A272
Ravi, Anilal E131
Ravichandran, Guruswami P107
Ravindra, Shathabi A271
Ravindran, Rajeev A735
Ravit, Sha Sarraf P610
Ravita, John A325
Ravitz, Shawn A899

COMBINED HOOVER'S HANDBOOK INDEX OF EXECUTIVES

```
A = AMERICAN BUSINESS
E = EMERGING COMPANIES
P = PRIVATE COMPANIES
W = WORLD BUSINESS
```

Ravitz, Shawn P657
Rawas, Mark A212
Rawlings, Rhonda A345
Rawlings, Rick A435
Rawlings, Rhonda E166
Rawlins, Rylan A170
Rawlins, Brian P409
Rawnsley, Derek A219
Rawnsley, Derek E87
Rawot, Billie A286
Rawot, Billie P190
Ray, Terrance A35
Ray, Jorge A115
Ray, Sheila E A159
Ray, Erika A167
Ray, Davina A219
Ray, Steven A298
Ray, Scott A323
Ray, Dee A787
Ray, Neville R A800
Ray, Harry A842
Ray, Debapriya A897
Ray, Michael C. A914
Ray, Nancy P82
Ray, Amy G. P120
Ray, David P184
Ray, Monica P234
Ray, Jim P261
Ray, Gabrielle P298
Ray, Denise P418
Ray, Joel P448
Ray, Chris P472
Ray, Jake P646
Ray, Jorge E38
Ray, Steven E130
Ray-chaudhuri, Avi E316
Ray-kuczynski, Stephanie A727
Ray-kuczynski, Stephanie P453
Raya, Lori A30
Raya, Lori P20
Rayavarapu, Sreehari P314
Rayford, Greg W. A187
Raygani, Mehrasa A884
Raykis, Alex A574
Rayl, Jeffrey P259
Raymond, Jeff A97
Raymond, Christopher A140
Raymond, Arthur A281
Raymond, Stephanie A408
Raymond, John T A668
Raymond, Hans A746
Raymond, Michelle A751
Raymond, Ginette P194
Raymond, Michelle P482
Raymond, Jackie P574
Raymond, Amy E363
Raymoure, Sue A170
Raymund, Steven A475
Rayner, Craig A831
Rayner, Craig P601
Rayner, Robert M E422
Raynes, Zoya P265
Razdan, Shashi P433
Razek, Dean A358
Razek, Dean E176
Razi, Afshin P304
Razzoli, Elisa A518
Razzouk, Theo A207
Rea, Will A419
Rea, Jasmin A630
Read, Charles A74
Read, Colin A82
Read, Nicholas J A143
Read, Harold T A592
Read, Ian C. A657
Read, Sarah A859
Read, Harold T P370
Read, Jason P630
Read, Nicholas J. (Nick) W417

Reade, Jeff A744
Readett, Natalie A664
Readett, Natalie E334
Reading, Christopher J. (Chris) E413
Ready, John P556
Ready, Janeth P649
Reagan, John A379
Reagan, James C. (Jim) A509
Real, Peter A67
Reale, Philippe A120
Reali, Joseph A559
Reames, Scott A699
Reardon, Timothy J. A509
Reardon, Sean E402
Reardon-sayer, Nancy A132
Reat, Daniel J P596
Reavis, Mack P285
Rebecchini, Clemente W35
Rebellius, Matthias W353
Rebello, Cheryl A205
Rebello, Max A492
Reber, Cathy D A54
Rebert, Troy A63
Rebholz, Andrew J. A843
Rebsch, Gary P161
Rebuck, Gail W66
Reca, Thomas P527
Recchi, Giuseppe A375
Recchi, Giuseppe P215
Recchi, Giuseppe W385
Recer, James D. (Jim) A818
Recer, James D. (Jim) E403
Rechin, Michael C. (Mike) A345
Rechin, Michael C. (Mike) E165
Rechtin, James A257
Recile, Shane P105
Recile, Shane P106
Recinto, Ed A469
Reck, Peter A450
Reck, Nate P212
Reck, Una Mae P609
Recker, Chris A512
Recon, Chris A879
Records, Ryan A779
Rector, Jennifer A135
Rector, Christopher A218
Rector, Elizabeth A896
Rector, Nancy P62
Rector, Drew P232
Recupero, Michael A319
Recupero, Patricia R P673
Reda, Guy A835
Redahan, Patrick A262
Redburn, Theresa A309
Redd, David A819
Redd, Mike P401
Redd, Ellis S P505
Redd, David P549
Redd, Glen P581
Redden, Robert L A752
Reddick, Sheila D A165
Reddick, Veder A248
Reddick, Veder E107
Reddin, Tom A83
Redding, Ron A410
Reddington, Sara A846
Reddington, Brian J. P432
Reddish, Thomas J. (Tom) A847
Reddish, Thomas J. (Tom) E410
Reddy, Raj A79
Reddy, Sriram A135
Reddy, Nikhil A390
Reddy, Subhakar A917
Reddy, Mamta P327
Reddy, J. Patrick (Pat) P509
Reddy, Sreenath V P596
Reddy, Sangeeta E143
Reder, William P667
Redfearn, Chuck A768
Redfield, Charles A901
Redi, Jason A706
Reding, Douglas P310
Redinger, Shelley P511
Redmon, Angie A343
Redmon, Angie E164

Redmond, Brian A79
Redmond, Richard L. A279
Redmond, Blake A830
Redmond, Velma A P411
Redmond, Blake P593
Redmond, John T. E10
Redmond, Tom E420
Redmond, John E424
Redmond, David E433
Redoutey, Joseph M. A353
Redoutey, Joseph M. E173
Redpath, J. Douglas A778
Redpath, Tammy A804
Redvers, Chris A484
Redwine, Farrell A602
Reed, Maurice A. A27
Reed, Pamela A36
Reed, LaDonna A86
Reed, Tamara A105
Reed, James T. (Jim) A116
Reed, Chris A152
Reed, Yvonne A165
Reed, Keri A203
Reed, Timothy A292
Reed, Colin A343
Reed, Jane A348
Reed, Steven A433
Reed, Lee A463
Reed, Chris A520
Reed, Kimberly A538
Reed, James M A706
Reed, Colin V. A736
Reed, Debra L. (Debbie) A753
Reed, Robert D. (Bob) A791
Reed, Andrea A799
Reed, Andy A840
Reed, Sam K. A846
Reed, Marc C. A889
Reed, Candice A900
Reed, Richard A935
Reed, Margaret P29
Reed, Kate P70
Reed, Johnna S P94
Reed, Chris P98
Reed, Glenn P245
Reed, Charlene P276
Reed, Daniel C P307
Reed, Connie P307
Reed, Katie N P387
Reed, Colin V. P460
Reed, Brian P514
Reed, Robert D. (Bob) P535
Reed, Mary Poyner P558
Reed, Rick P571
Reed, Dan P597
Reed, Laura P602
Reed, David P635
Reed, Fay P644
Reed, John C. W328
Reed, LaDonna E27
Reed, Tamara E34
Reed, James T. (Jim) E39
Reed, Michael A. E72
Reed, Allan E81
Reed, Colin E164
Reed, Jane E169
Reed, John A. E174
Reed, Michael E. (Mike) E183
Reed, Steven E217
Reed, Michael E317
Reed, David E424
Reed-harper, Shana A335
Reed-harper, Shana E155
Reedy, Thomas W. (Tom) A171
Reedy, Tom A171
Reedy, Raquel Martinez P20
Reel, Stephanie L. A478
Reel, Stephanie L. P268
Reemst, Mary W243
Reen, Elizabeth A203
Reents, Scott A6
Rees, Douglas A276
Rees, Dan W53
Reese, Jay A3
Reese, Bruce T. A462

Reese, Craig A484
Reese, Denyse A606
Reese, Deb A718
Reese, Bertram S. (Bert) A754
Reese, Ken A902
Reese, Steven P28
Reese, Bruce T. P256
Reese, Karin P308
Reese, Cathy P354
Reese, Bertram S. (Bert) P484
Reese, Sherri P536
Reese, Marianne P552
Reese, Nancy P589
Reese, Amanda P640
Reese, Kevin E127
Reese, Angela E330
Reese, Deb E354
Reese, Amy E416
Reesing, Jeffrey E99
Reeve, Pamela D. A. A366
Reeve, Derek A700
Reeve, Ryan A772
Reeve, Derek P436
Reeve, Ryan E383
Reeves, Cindy A246
Reeves, Jim A409
Reeves, Sean A746
Reeves, Bethany A877
Reeves, Rosalind P30
Reeves, Terry P525
Reeves, Greg P655
Reeves, Dale E48
Reeves, Cindy E105
Reffler, Rick P613
Reffner, Robert A351
Regan, Marla A727
Regan, Timothy J. A831
Regan, Meg P314
Regan, Marla P453
Regan, Lora P573
Regan, Timothy J. P601
Regan, Jack W27
Regan, Patrick C. (Pat) W317
Regan, Todd E72
Rege, Ashu A613
Regele, Michael B P259
Regelski, Jennifer A492
Reger, Melissa P153
Regier, Philip P44
Regis, Christine (Chris) P505
Register, Mark A465
Regnier, Stacy A224
Regnier, Mike W432
Regrut, Andrew D E132
Rehm, Doug A755
Rehm, Julie P116
Rehm, Wilhelm W433
Rehm, Doug E369
Rehmke, Bruce C. A413
Rehmke, Bruce C. E205
Rehn, Bill E35
Rehner, Scott E307
Reic, Iskra W38
Reich, Kirk W. A27
Reich, David A528
Reich, Joni A763
Reich, Herman P166
Reich, Joni E377
Reichelt, John A835
Reichenbacher, Bill A315
Reichenberg, Auge A469
Reicher, Terri P202
Reichert, Enid A559
Reichert, Nicole A928
Reichert, Donald P576
Reichert, Nicole P673
Reichfield, Mike P395
Reichle, Paula P508
Reichmann, Randall (Randy) A621
Reichmann, Randall (Randy) E311
Reichmuth, Steve A284
Reichmuth, Steve E120
Reichwein, Tim P573
Reid, Stacy A175
Reid, George A176

Reid, Thomas J A220
Reid, Bill A292
Reid, Gail A391
Reid, Landon A408
Reid, Matthew A449
Reid, John A522
Reid, Jack A540
Reid, Kimberly A571
Reid, Alan M. A742
Reid, Gaetan A784
Reid, John P35
Reid, Charles R. P461
Reid, Michael P627
Reid, Philip P665
Reid, Al W92
Reid, Jacqueline E185
Reid, Matthew E221
Reidy, Christopher R. (Chris) A123
Reidy, M. Bridget A304
Reidy, Kevin P127
Reidy, Andrea P141
Reierson, Jason A665
Reierson, Jason E334
Reif, David A530
Reif, David P. A732
Reif, L. Rafael P314
Reifer, Rick E110
Reifsteck, John A399
Reifsteck, John P223
Reighley, Twila P340
Reiley, Peggy J. P478
Reiling, Jason A61
Reilley, James A613
Reilly, Michael A43
Reilly, Mary A54
Reilly, Thomas A320
Reilly, Mary A484
Reilly, John A528
Reilly, James A559
Reilly, John A604
Reilly, Daniel A651
Reilly, Robert Q A668
Reilly, Paul C. A704
Reilly, Tom A853
Reilly, Joe A940
Reilly, Bob P40
Reilly, Annemarie P117
Reilly, Tom P612
Reilly, Kevin P. P641
Reilly, Michael E13
Reilly, John E79
Reilly, Donald E275
Reilly, Daniel E329
Reiman, Eric (Bill) A117
Reiman, Eric (Bill) P61
Reimann, Kevin A731
Reimer, Seth A492
Reimer, Elizabeth P428
Reimnitz, George A925
Reimnitz, George E445
Rein, Joseph A852
Reinard, Shannon E73
Reinartz, Ronald A540
Reinders, Robert A537
Reinders, Rob A538
Reinemund, Steven A538
Reiner, Jason A604
Reiner, Scott P6
Reiner, Carol P246
Reiners, Derek S. A630
Reingardt, John A449
Reingardt, John E221
Reingold, Melinda A364
Reinhard, Susan P2
Reinhard, Walter E418
Reinhardt, Jerry A272
Reinhardt, Tom P463
Reinhart, Gloria A621
Reinhart, Michael A702
Reinhart, Bill P60
Reinhart, Chris P299
Reinhart, Diane P656
Reinhart, Gloria E311
Reinsch, Phillip A. A169
Reinshagen, Dirk A896

Reis, Andy A51
Reis, Mario A243
Reis, Mischa A254
Reis, Jorge A364
Reis, Paulo A518
Reis, Peter P12
Reis, Brad P610
Reis, Pat E317
Reisch, Emily P569
Reisdorf, Michelle A726
Reisenauer, Brian A885
Reisenbach, Amy A893
Reiser, Jason S. A272
Reiser, Jason A591
Reiser, Trista A596
Reiser, Jason P369
Reisinger, Alan A726
Reisinger, Chris P420
Reisner, John R. A339
Reisner, John R. E159
Reiss, Joel A842
Reiss, Mary P447
Reiten, Mark W A564
Reith, Ian P210
Reithofer, Norbert W63
Reitmeyer, David A831
Reitmeyer, David P601
Reitzle, Wolfgang H. W117
Reitzner, Chris P555
Reizman, Elizabeth A110
Rel, Eric A251
Relic, Zelko E10
Relyea, Morgan P549
Rembde, Martin W66
Remes, Sheila A140
Remiker, Richard (Rich) A444
Remington, Mark A559
Remington, Benjamin P184
Remmel, Brian A740
Remolde, Cheryl P304
Remondi, John F. (Jack) A583
Rempe, John P59
Rempel, Steve A722
Remy, Todd A492
Ren, Yi A813
Ren, Robin A818
Renard, Kerstin W420
Renaudie, Jean-Michel W160
Rencher, Bradley (Brad) A11
RENDA, BENEDETTO GIOVANNI MARIA W121
Rendall, Donald P221
Rendeiro, Martha A465
Rendine-cook, Pamela E174
Rendle, Steven E. (Steve) A891
Rendleman, Linda A809
Renduchintala, Venkata M. (Murthy) A460
Renee, Antoniak A785
Renetzky, Lisa A715
Reney, Michael L. P172
Renfer, Mirco A865
Renfrew, Bill A347
Renfrew, Jonathan P202
Renfro, Donna A760
Renfro, Larry C. A876
Renfro, Donna E374
Renfroe, Brian P357
Rengstorff, Jim A782
Rengstorff, Jim P525
Renna, Joanne A906
Renna, Michael J. E379
Renna, Joanne E435
Rennard, Marc W297
Renner, Denise A727
Renner, Troy A A728
Renner, Denise P453
Renner, Joseph D P678
Rennie, Thomas J. E386
Renninger, Rich A255
Renschler, Andreas W418
Rensel, Elizabeth A544
Renshaw, Thomas A63
Rensing, Willy P157
Rensner, Mark A504

Rensner, Mark E251
Renspie, William A236
Rentch, Sean A799
Rentler, Barbara A731
Renwick, Glenn A352
Renwick, Glenn M. A681
Renz, Trish A89
Renz, Brian A105
Renz, Brian E34
Renzi, Randolph P671
Renzini, Mark A357
Renzini, Mark E175
Renzulli, Carmine E110
Repetz, Brian P466
Repetz, Brian P513
Repique, R. John P433
Repo, Susan J A818
Reppa, Robert A524
Reppy, Glen A320
Requejo, Brian P653
Rerkpibook, Auttapol W316
Resac, Maureen E207
Resch, Richard J. (Dick) P283
Resendez, Cindy P409
Resendez, Edward (Ed) E124
Resheske, Frances A235
Resk, Stacey P80
Reske, James R. A337
Reske, James R. E158
Reskey, Scott E202
Resnick, Jon A474
Resnick, Andrea Shaw A801
Resnick, Jaquie P627
Resnick, Peter E102
Respass, David E47
Ress, Kevin A86
Ress, Kevin E27
Ressel, Teresa A628
Ressler, Alison P102
Ressler, Richard S. E240
Restel, Anthony J. A449
Restel, Anthony J. E220
Restiano, Larry A54
Restivo, Filippo A853
Restivo, Filippo P612
Restrepo, Robert A381
Restrepo, Robert P. (Bob) A781
Restrepo, Ana A870
Restrepo, Nicolas C P671
Resweber, Chris A765
Resyapov, Alexander F. W375
Reto, Joyce P21
Retter, Donna P513
Rettig, Jeff A156
Rettig, Chris P251
Rettig, Claus W158
Retton, Allen A908
Retton, Allen E436
Retz, Jocelyn A623
Retz, Jocelyn E313
Retzer, Ingrid P54
Reuschel, Michael P74
Reuse, Sandy P429
Reuss, Mark L. A378
Reuss, John P140
Reuss, Dan E233
Reuss, Herb J P279
Reuter, Deborah K. (Debbie) A414
Reuter, John A704
Reuter, Heitho P665
Reuter, Deborah K. (Debbie) E208
Reuter, James E349
Reuter, Martin E353
Reuvers, Dan E233
Revell, Mark A512
Revelle, Greg A496
Reverberi, Gian Piero E426
Revilla, Lisa A109
Revington, George E215
Revoir, Gary E402
Rewolinski, Andrew P415
Rex, John A876
Rex, Shannon E433
Rexing, Denise A621
Rexing, Denise E311
Rexroad, Jerold L A172

Rey, Helen A722
Rey, Juan P326
Rey, David E144
Reyes, Laura A222
Reyes, Luciano A447
Reyes, Tisha A456
Reyes, Patrick A469
Reyes, Araceli A502
Reyes, Tarik A608
Reyes, Franklin A713
Reyes, Frank A888
Reyes, Marty P125
Reyes, Isabel P182
Reyes, Donna P298
Reyes, Cecilia W435
Reyes, Tina E106
Reyes, Tisha E228
Reyes, Frank E425
Reymondet, Pascal W405
Reynes, Julia E P409
Reynish, Steve W373
Reynolds, Stephen R. (Steve) A75
Reynolds, Chuck A75
Reynolds, Brent A167
Reynolds, James Frank A179
Reynolds, Mark A184
Reynolds, Eric A207
Reynolds, Catherine M. A209
Reynolds, Donald A224
Reynolds, Jeanne A329
Reynolds, Wendy A337
Reynolds, Dennis A351
Reynolds, Catherine A373
Reynolds, Linda A374
Reynolds, Robert L. A397
Reynolds, Dan A481
Reynolds, Fredric A573
Reynolds, Andrew A608
Reynolds, Meredith A626
Reynolds, Sean A692
Reynolds, Cara A724
Reynolds, Robert A922
Reynolds, Peter A933
Reynolds, Nancy P228
Reynolds, Kathryn P270
Reynolds, Julie P280
Reynolds, Ronald P299
Reynolds, Julie P360
Reynolds, Lynn P368
Reynolds, Sean B. P388
Reynolds, Gregory P390
Reynolds, Chad P404
Reynolds, Cara P452
Reynolds, Dudley C. P510
Reynolds, Kimberly P517
Reynolds, Courtney P547
Reynolds, William P570
Reynolds, Sean P573
Reynolds, Lori P646
Reynolds, Robert P671
Reynolds, Robert L. W174
Reynolds, Christopher P. (Chris) W400
Reynolds, Richard V. E23
Reynolds, Mathew E48
Reynolds, Wendy E158
Reynolds, William H. E267
Reynolds, Rob E438
Reza, Ali P475
Reza, Tony P499
Rezendes, Kelsey P109
Rezet, Penny P19
Reznikova, Irina A784
Rhatigan, Arthur A115
Rhatigan, Arthur E37
Rheaume, Lindsey S. A283
Rheaume, Lindsey S. E117
Rhee, Susan A6
Rhee, James A879
Rhen, Angie A910
Rheney, Susan A180
Rhett, Jeffrey P506
Rhine, Bruce C. E316
Rhines, Walden C. (Wally) P326
Rho, Joseph K. A404
Rho, Joseph K. E199

COMBINED HOOVER'S HANDBOOK INDEX OF EXECUTIVES

A = AMERICAN BUSINESS
E = EMERGING COMPANIES
P = PRIVATE COMPANIES
W = WORLD BUSINESS

Rhoads, Marian A226
Rhoads, Rebecca B. A706
Rhoads, Marian P150
Rhoads, Ann D P428
Rhode, Kathy A412
Rhode, Kathy P233
Rhodebeck, Lyle D. A781
Rhodenbaugh, Linda P496
Rhodes, Sage A89
Rhodes, William C. (Bill) A95
Rhodes, Donna A203
Rhodes, Donnie A357
Rhodes, Rory A371
Rhodes, Michelle A569
Rhodes, Mark A A574
Rhodes, Jeff A664
Rhodes, John A752
Rhodes, Michael P5
Rhodes, Dan P6
Rhodes, Anne P395
Rhodes, Robert P672
Rhodes, Donnie E176
Rhodes, Jeff E334
Rhodewalt, Stacey P311
Rhodin, Michael D. (Mike) A465
Rhoman, Cindy P294
Rhone, Oded A290
Rhone, Denise A899
Rhoten, Alison A277
Rhymer, Ernie P436
Rhynalds, Christian A232
Rhyne, Tommy A849
Rhyne, Jerry P296
Riach, Lorna P131
Rial, Sergio A262
Rial, Francis A574
Rial, Sergio W48
Rianda, Lori A107
Riano, Jewell P342
Rias, Chekedia P38
Ribas, Pablo A53
Ribe, Ken P78
Ribeiro, Monica A115
Ribeiro, Ana A646
Ribeiro, Greg A680
Ribeiro, Monica E38
Ribeiro, Ana E324
Ribieras, Jean-Michel A467
Ribiéras, Jean-Michel A467
Riboud, Franck W128
Ricard, Brenda P608
Ricard, Denis W193
Ricardo, Pedro Carmona de Oliveira W169
Ricca, Mike A660
Ricca, Mike P416
Riccardella, Paul E290
Riccardi, John A3
Ricchetti, Ginger A713
Ricchio, Wesley E156
Ricchione, Louis A167
Ricci, Riccardo A218
Ricciardi, Joe A626
Riccio, Daniel (Dan) A72
Riccio, Louis A589
Riccio, Janet A626
Riccioni, Mich P472
Rice, Jeff A16
Rice, Tom A65
Rice, Amy A115
Rice, Jeff A140
Rice, Brian A170
Rice, Andre A210
Rice, Melanie A222
Rice, Kristin K A262
Rice, Kristin A262
Rice, Charles A296
Rice, Jessica A386
Rice, Mary A449

Rice, James A481
Rice, Brian S. A487
Rice, Condoleezza A511
Rice, Karen A520
Rice, Maggie A600
Rice, Mark A605
Rice, Linda Johnson A626
Rice, Ronald A. A732
Rice, Jacqueline Hourigan A804
Rice, Michael B A812
Rice, Patricia M P22
Rice, Condoleezza P290
Rice, Denise P516
Rice, Jane P531
Rice, Tabitha P548
Rice, Ann Madden P624
Rice, Amy E37
Rice, Jessica E188
Rice, Mary E220
Rice, Michael E224
Rich, Brian F. A209
Rich, Brian F. A238
Rich, Michael A318
Rich, Ronald A341
Rich, Robert A432
Rich, Robert E A432
Rich, Melinda A531
Rich, Robert E. (Bob) A824
Rich, Brad A865
Rich, Patty P27
Rich, Melinda R. (Mindy) P449
Rich, Howard P449
Rich, Paul J P449
Rich, Robert E. (Bob) P449
Rich, Mark P528
Rich, Robert E. (Bob) P562
Rich, Judith F P611
Richard, Laino A3
Richard, Koch A36
Richard, Matijasich A63
Richard, Westerkamp A320
Richard, Roger A574
Richard, Henri A586
Richard, Anita A619
Richard, Paul A645
Richard, Gary A806
Richard, Brian A835
Richard, Grant A934
Richard, Anita P393
Richard, Stéphane W297
Richard, David E368
Richard, Gary E398
Richard, Chad E450
Richards, Steve A16
Richards, Christine A36
Richards, Mark A163
Richards, Todd A270
Richards, Christine P. A323
Richards, Alyson A452
Richards, Patricia R. A462
Richards, Laura A596
Richards, Stacey A665
Richards, Lisa A680
Richards, David A737
Richards, Rachel M. A766
Richards, Michael A783
Richards, Pam A835
Richards, Barry A. A843
Richards, Alison A877
Richards, Jesse P123
Richards, James J P150
Richards, Catherine P209
Richards, Patricia R. P256
Richards, Jeanne P312
Richards, James J P354
Richards, Larry P610
Richards, Thomas P633
Richards, Anne W314
Richards, Leighton E59
Richards, Mark E62
Richards, Stacey E334
Richards, Jerald W. (Jerry) E337
Richards, David E361
Richardsen, Ernest A722
Richardson, George A126

Richardson, David A168
Richardson, Michael R. (Mike) A173
Richardson, Nathan A212
Richardson, Jannie A262
Richardson, Daniel A357
Richardson, Cara A369
Richardson, Cameron A379
Richardson, Carmen A381
Richardson, Matt A423
Richardson, Sean P. A444
Richardson, Peter A481
Richardson, Kim A494
Richardson, Elizabeth A571
Richardson, Levi A590
Richardson, Marty A621
Richardson, Fiona A722
Richardson, Michael A744
Richardson, Jennifer A799
Richardson, Rory A875
Richardson, Todd P49
Richardson, Don P145
Richardson, Greg P197
Richardson, Raven P340
Richardson, Mark P399
Richardson, Barbara P454
Richardson, Cliff P525
Richardson, Robert E. P625
Richardson, David E. P627
Richardson, Stephen A. E8
Richardson, James E8
Richardson, Julie E91
Richardson, Tricia E105
Richardson, Chad E174
Richardson, Daniel E176
Richardson, Frank E215
Richardson, Marty E312
Richardville, Bill P168
Richels, John A263
Richenhagen, Martin H. A21
Richenhagen, Martin A673
Richer, Art P249
Richer, Art P250
Richerson, Michelle P504
Riches, Greg A562
Richeson, Samuel A52
Richey, Ellen A895
Richey, Mike P528
Richey, Bernadina P551
Richey, Jonathan E14
Richey, Victor L. (Vic) E135
Richins, Micah E10
Richlak, Thomas A335
Richlak, Thomas E155
Richland, Scott P107
Richman, David A374
Richmann, Dennis A868
Richmond, Michael A440
Richmond, Brent E. A908
Richmond, Estelle P150
Richmond, Craig P576
Richmond, Brent E. E436
Richter, Brandon A36
Richter, Brian A121
Richter, Phil A859
Richter, Brian A884
Richter, Karen P131
Richter, Michael F P537
Richter, Holly P624
Richter, Audrey P638
Richway, Terri A627
Ricia, Catherine A540
Rick, Frederick A540
Rickard, Candice J. A621
Rickard, Charles P531
Rickard, Candice J. E311
Rickel, John C. A398
Rickel, Todd A. P596
Rickenbach, Josef H. von P405
Ricker, Shawn A692
Ricker, Bob P448
Ricketts, Carlton A A168
Ricketts, Todd A807
Rickey, Christopher A715
Rickman, Michael A392
Ricks, David A. A517

Ricks, Ron A773
Ricks, Michael P242
Ricks, Mary L. E245
Rico, Ricardo A779
Ricotta, Dominic J A71
Ricotta, Eduardo W386
Riddell, Carol A233
Riddick, Frank E448
Riddle, Gregory A285
Riddle, Matthew K P625
Riden, Doug A722
Ridenour, Nancy P634
Rider, Susan A304
Rider, Sue A927
Rider, Matthew J. (Matt) W10
Rider, Mike E59
Ridge, Dakota P265
Ridgeway, Charlene A409
Ridgeway, Alan A522
Riebel, William A824
Riebel, William P562
Riebling, Bill A674
Rieck, Lewis A484
Riecker, Robert A. A750
Riedel, Norbert A119
Riedel, Danielle A824
Riedel, Danielle P562
Riedo, Francis X P280
Riefe, James A746
Riegel, Matthew A606
Rieger, JC A161
Rieger, Ralf W382
Rieke, John P352
Rieker, Karen P513
Riel, Pierre A242
Riel, Susan G. A283
Riel, Kevin A609
Riel, Kevin P387
Riel, Susan G. E117
Riele, Thomas A115
Riele, Thomas E38
Rieley, John F. E240
Rielly, John P. A418
Rielly-gauvin, Katie A6
Riemer, Danny A135
Riemer, Hans P161
Riepe, James S. (Jim) A381
Riepenhoff, Patrick A444
Ries, Kelley A877
Riese, Werner De P302
Riester, Tom P646
Riesterer, Jamie A686
Riesterer-Randa, Laura A11
Rietbroek, Robbert A654
Rieves, Jt A428
Riezler, Norbert A506
Rife, Jeremy A816
Rife, John A. A868
Rifkin, Christine A325
Rifkind, Neil C. E407
Rigatti, Maria A290
Rigby, Mark A895
Rigg, Timothy A167
Riggan, Gisela A682
Riggans, Bonnie P174
Riggieri, Rose A835
Riggin, William A200
Riggins, Quentin A28
Riggle, Carrie A337
Riggle, Carrie E158
Riggleman, Dawn E132
Riggs, David A580
Riggs, Lane A887
Riggs, Teresa P1
Riggs, Kirsten P448
Riggs, Jean P588
Riggs, David E. E118
Riggs, Steven C. (Steve) E222
Riggs, David E292
Rigney, Patrick A114
Rigney, Patrick E37
Riis, Jakob W290
Riis, Kenneth E302
Rijswijk, S.J.A. (Steven) van W200
Riley, Adam A135

Riley, Steve A158
Riley, Mary A160
Riley, Chad D A218
Riley, Karla A247
Riley, Bill A259
Riley, Rick A296
Riley, Josh A340
Riley, Kevin P. A344
Riley, Lynn A386
Riley, Eric A390
Riley, Tami A492
Riley, Paul A661
Riley, Anne A715
Riley, Deon A731
Riley, Wesley A752
Riley, Susan A833
Riley, James A922
Riley, Judith P105
Riley, Tammy P250
Riley, Cheryl P280
Riley, Mike P357
Riley, Trent P428
Riley, Anne P596
Riley, James P671
Riley, Gillian W53
Riley, Kevin P. E42
Riley, Karla E105
Riley, Christina E131
Riley, Josh E160
Riley, Kevin P. E165
Riley, Lynn E188
Riley, Sharon L. E210
Riley, Jim E330
Riley-Brown, Michelle P548
Rim, Heather A16
Rimel, Brian A704
Rimer, Barbara A19
Rimer, Matt P643
Rimmer, Nneka A547
Rimmer, Jeffrey P598
Rimmereid, Paul A322
Rimmereid, Tore Olaf W140
Rimnac, Clare P116
Rinaldi, Joe A356
Rinck, Sara A877
Rindlaub, John A179
Rinehardt, Hank A125
Rinehart, Chris A91
Rinehart, Charles R. A546
Rinehart, Lucy P175
Rinehart, Timm P546
Rinehart, Doug P573
Rinehart, Chris E29
Riney, Stephen J. A71
Riney, Robert G. (Bob) A414
Riney, Robert G. (Bob) P236
Ring, David V A862
Ring, David V P617
Ring, Kenneth R. E280
Ringel, Bob A281
Ringer, Jim A347
Ringer, Jim E167
Ringgenberg, Gina A492
Ringler, Thomas A312
Ringler, Thomas P200
Ringold, Kim A933
Ringsted, Sean W106
Ringwald, Brad A340
Ringwald, Brad E160
Rini, Anthony A491
Rink, Matthew A449
Rink, Matthew E221
Rinker, Jackie A452
Rinn, Russell B. (Russ) A785
Rinna, Dabao A104
Rinne, Susan E96
Rinshed, Rick P423
Rintoul, David J. E191
Rio, Frank Del P443
Riopel, Daniel W193
Riordan, Jeremiah A481
Riordan, Michael C. P430
Riordan, Kimberly E433
Riordan-Pacheco, Ella A759
Riordan-Pacheco, Ella E373

Rios, Mabel P476
Ripoll, Joe A160
Rippy, Richard A115
Rippy, Chris A665
Rippy, John A718
Rippy, Richard E38
Rippy, Chris E334
Rippy, John E354
Ris, Lynn M A222
Risan, Michael P69
Risch, Therace M. A647
Rischar, Kent A63
Rishi, Raj P552
Risio, Derek M. Di A688
Risley, Hank B A455
Risley, Hank B E228
Risoleo, James F. A436
Rispoli, Michael A651
Rispoli, Michael E329
Risse, Thomas P431
Rissman, Michael A721
Rita, Mark P276
Ritch, Jill A Alexander P635
Ritchey, Anne A500
Ritchey, Jimmy E322
Ritchey-Baldwin, Lori P463
Ritchie, Chris A108
Ritchie, Michael T. A222
Ritchie, Robert A240
Ritchie, Ian A403
Ritchie, Rob A457
Ritchie, Julia A497
Ritchie, Graeme A509
Ritchie, Keely A665
Ritchie, Mike A713
Ritchie, Joe A749
Ritchie, Justin A789
Ritchie, Kevin J. A820
Ritchie, Chris A877
Ritchie, Jeffrey A922
Ritchie, Jeffrey P671
Ritchie, Garth W135
Ritchie, Lisa W371
Ritchie, Keely E334
Ritchie, Joe E367
Ritchotte, Alan P156
Ritenour, Jeff L. A263
Ritenour, Daniel A629
Ritenour, Brent A785
Rito, Shane A444
Ritrievi, Rory G A566
Ritrievi, Rory G. E281
Rittelmeyer, Chris A760
Rittelmeyer, Chris E374
Rittenmeyer, Ronald A. (Ron) A811
Ritter, Mark A246
Ritter, Mark A368
Ritter, Bob A522
Ritter, Eric A539
Ritter, William D. (Bill) A712
Ritter, Gretchen P159
Ritter, Thad P523
Ritter, Mark E105
Ritterson, Christoph A126
Rittinger, Hannelore A453
Ritts, Betty P26
Ritz, Michael D. E314
Ritzert, Hans-Josef W158
Rivard, Heather A279
Rivas, Hiram A333
Rivas, Isadore P235
Rivas, Manual P382
Rivas-Javier, Andrea P368
Rivaz, Vincent de W148
Rive, Lyndon R. P547
Rive, Peter J. P547
Rivenbark, Eric A866
Rivenbark, Eric E418
Rivenes, Gary P142
Rivera, Jessica A36
Rivera, Alfredo A215
Rivera, Mario A294
Rivera, Sandra A460
Rivera, Alice A468
Rivera, Guadalupe L A494

Rivera, Pj A538
Rivera, Ana A571
Rivera, Néstor O. A670
Rivera, Gina A A827
Rivera, William P2
Rivera, Joseph P52
Rivera, Yesenia P476
Rivera, Gloria P489
Rivera, Gina A P580
Rivera, Evelyn P588
Rivera, Julio P628
Rivera, Mario P634
Rivera, Luisa Fernanda Lafaurie W144
Rivera, Javier E433
Rivera-Batista, Nayda A333
Rivera-gauthier, Nelida A151
Riveras, John P204
Rivers, Lori A170
Rivers, Rita A651
Rivers, Mary A925
Rivers, Emmanuel P120
Rivers, Bill P429
Rivers, Rita E329
Rivers, Mary E445
Rives, John P58
Rivest, Jeffrey A. P630
Rivet, Jeannine M. A876
Rivett, Paul C. W159
Rivieccio, Lou A870
Rivkin, Natalya A213
Rivkin, Natalya P143
Riza, Emma A525
Rizk, Norman W. P524
Rizza, Franco W45
Rizzardi, Russell A912
Rizzo, Jamie A19
Rizzo, Mario A35
Rizzo, James L. A268
Rizzo, Mark A326
Rizzo, Dan A494
Rizzo, Gregory P509
Rmaile, Hassan A97
Rn, Laura Espinosa PHD P334
Rn, Ann Cella P515
Rnian-bivona, Gail A112
Roach, John A281
Roach, Amy A452
Roach, John A887
Roach, Jen P87
Roach, Jill P604
Roach, Colleen P642
Roach, Frank W161
Roach, Rustin E202
Roach, David E416
Roach, Karen E441
Roads, Scott A605
Roaldsen, Liz A784
Roark, Michaelene A243
Roark, Mark P606
Roballo, Marta A680
Robards, Thomas F. E124
Robb, Stephen M. (Steve) A207
Robb, John A246
Robb, Walter E. A921
Robb, Timothy M. P375
Robb, Becky P429
Robb, Chuck P466
Robb, Walter E. P669
Robb, G. Charles E96
Robb, John E105
Robben, John A649
Robbins, Charles H. (Chuck) A198
Robbins, Joanna P259
Robbins, Hadley S. A219
Robbins, Marshall A228
Robbins, Paige K. A393
Robbins, Michael (Mike) A647
Robbins, Cindy A739
Robbins, Ira A888
Robbins, Mike A908
Robbins, David K P203
Robbins, Allison P259
Robbins, Douglas P578
Robbins, Spencer E41
Robbins, Hadley S. E87
Robbins, David E379

Robbins, Ira E425
Robbins, Mike E436
Robel, Susan M. A371
Robel, Susan M. P213
Robel, Lauren P609
Robens, Cornelius P354
Rober, Stephen A508
Roberge, Scott A877
Roberge, Michael W. W371
Roberson, Brian A135
Roberson, Laura A859
Roberson, Bridgette A877
Roberson, Earl P296
Robert, Angela A449
Robert, Edward P111
Robert, Lucas P161
Robert, Debbie P389
Robert, Nenad P417
Robert, Chris P467
Robert, Angela E220
Roberto, Joseph (Joe) A114
Roberto, Ann P448
Roberto, Joseph (Joe) E37
Roberton, David E411
Roberts, Billy A3
Roberts, Bob A3
Roberts, Brad A5
Roberts, Oz R A19
Roberts, David N. A20
Roberts, Bob A36
Roberts, Stan A61
Roberts, Bart A156
Roberts, Brian L A220
Roberts, Jonathan C. A251
Roberts, Michael A394
Roberts, John N. A442
Roberts, Scott A465
Roberts, Bart A478
Roberts, David A481
Roberts, Jason A481
Roberts, William R. A551
Roberts, Brian A602
Roberts, Elizabeth Watters A626
Roberts, Timothy D. (Tim) A662
Roberts, David A680
Roberts, Antoine A726
Roberts, Lori A846
Roberts, Sheila A848
Roberts, Brian A855
Roberts, Chad A859
Roberts, Jeanie A867
Roberts, Jerome A870
Roberts, Warner A877
Roberts, Karen A901
Roberts, Lynn P112
Roberts, Peter W. P130
Roberts, Phyllis P209
Roberts, Kevin V P214
Roberts, Tara P252
Roberts, Scott P269
Roberts, M. Parker P305
Roberts, William R. P321
Roberts, Fred P408
Roberts, Racquel P435
Roberts, Gregory W. P442
Roberts, John G. P498
Roberts, Alisha P571
Roberts, Shauna R. P607
Roberts, Brad P657
Roberts, Becki E73
Roberts, Stacie L E78
Roberts, Justin E80
Roberts, Brett A. E103
Roberts, Joyce E218
Roberts, Katherine E226
Roberts, David B. (Dave) E253
Roberts, Sheila E411
Roberts, Jeanie E418
Roberts, Jeffrey W. E422
Robertshaw, Patricia P501
Robertson, Laura A117
Robertson, Cliff A. A226
Robertson, Jan A246
Robertson, John A319
Robertson, Karen A325

COMBINED HOOVER'S HANDBOOK INDEX OF EXECUTIVES

```
A = AMERICAN BUSINESS
E = EMERGING COMPANIES
P = PRIVATE COMPANIES
W = WORLD BUSINESS
```

Robertson, Bill   A345
Robertson, John   A378
Robertson, Robert   A449
Robertson, Gina   A545
Robertson, Alan   A605
Robertson, Timothy   A692
Robertson, Elizabeth Aulick   A704
Robertson, Bill   A713
Robertson, Bruce   A754
Robertson, Amy   A774
Robertson, Euan   A829
Robertson, Craig   A934
Robertson, Cliff   P21
Robertson, Ardy   P38
Robertson, Laura   P61
Robertson, Cliff A.   P150
Robertson, Jessica   P214
Robertson, Steve   P230
Robertson, Pamela   P273
Robertson, Gina   P317
Robertson, William G. (Bill)   P352
Robertson, Euan   P364
Robertson, Joseph (Joe)   P399
Robertson, Bruce   P484
Robertson, Amy   P510
Robertson, Russell   P525
Robertson, Euan   P589
Robertson, Jeffrey   P611
Robertson, Struan   E45
Robertson, Lindon G.   E53
Robertson, Jan   E105
Robertson, Ann   E159
Robertson, Bill   E166
Robertson, Robert   E221
Robertson, David J.   E453
Robertucci, Kristin   A337
Robertucci, Kristin   E158
Robichaud, Matthew   A528
Robichaud, Michael   A544
Robie, Robert   E143
Robillard, Tc   A403
Robillard, Jean   P629
Robilotto, Frank   A842
Robin, William   A925
Robin, Howard W.   E300
Robin, William   A445
Robinett, Jesse   A606
Robinette, Ken   A170
Robinette, Gary E.   P423
Robins, Rocky   A132
Robins, Alan   E51
Robinson, Paul   A8
Robinson, Breanna   A57
Robinson, Danielle   A69
Robinson, Harvey G.   A105
Robinson, Bill   A112
Robinson, Tom   A149
Robinson, Lester   A161
Robinson, Reginald   A168
Robinson, Jon   A184
Robinson, Charles   A195
Robinson, Darryl L.   A266
Robinson, Tori   A332
Robinson, Richard   A337
Robinson, Vicki   A353
Robinson, Kiersten   A360
Robinson, David   A374
Robinson, David C.   A408
Robinson, Patricia   A540
Robinson, Lori   A547
Robinson, Tim   A584
Robinson, Don   A598
Robinson, Guilford   A692
Robinson, Dashiell   A709
Robinson, Robert L.   A760
Robinson, Sonal   A765
Robinson, William   A793
Robinson, Larry   A799
Robinson, Christian   A849

Robinson, Randy   A882
Robinson, Tim   A909
Robinson, David L.   A912
Robinson, Rebecca K.   A940
Robinson, Breanna   P33
Robinson, Alan   P60
Robinson, Ron   P63
Robinson, Daniel   P114
Robinson, Brenda   P141
Robinson, Chase   P157
Robinson, Casharol   P168
Robinson, Darryl L.   P181
Robinson, Vicki   P204
Robinson, John R   P218
Robinson, Edmondo   P227
Robinson, Aaron   P232
Robinson, Dan   P240
Robinson, Nina B   P242
Robinson, Rebecca   P242
Robinson, Jane   P315
Robinson, Edward   P354
Robinson, Timothy C.   P359
Robinson, Dan   P421
Robinson, Risa   P456
Robinson, Phil   P462
Robinson, Lisa   P463
Robinson, John   P467
Robinson, Lakisha   P476
Robinson, William J. (Bill)   P489
Robinson, Dick   P537
Robinson, Gail   P541
Robinson, David   P551
Robinson, Boyd   P627
Robinson, Samara   P635
Robinson, Douglas   P635
Robinson, Deborah   P638
Robinson, Harvey G.   E34
Robinson, Jeffrey D.   E51
Robinson, David   E131
Robinson, Thomas   E136
Robinson, Richard   E158
Robinson, Timothy G.   E274
Robinson, Dashiell   E348
Robinson, Gina   E354
Robinson, Robert L.   E374
Robinson, Patricia   E409
Robinson, Tim   E436
Robison, Bruce   P291
Robitaille, Mark   P311
Roble, Mark A.   A726
Roble, Mark A.   P453
Robledo, Becky   A621
Robledo, Grace   P164
Robledo, Becky   E312
Robles, Norberto (Bert)   A588
Robles, Monica   P140
Robles, Norberto (Bert)   P365
Robles, Wilma   P390
Robles, Adriane   P470
Robo, James L. (Jim)   A597
Robotis, Dionyssios   P616
Robottom, David T.   W150
Robson, Ted   A799
Robson, Jeremy   W373
Robusto, Dino E.   A210
Roca, Marco A.   A160
Roca, Silvia De La   P8
Rocca, Richard Della   E429
Rocco, David   A112
Rocco, Michael Del   A115
Rocco, James   A167
Rocco, Michael Del   E37
Roch, Liz   A900
Rocha, Charles P.   A763
Rocha, Oscar Gonzalez   A771
Rocha, Carmen   P333
Rocha, Charles P.   E377
Roche, Vincent T.   A67
Roche, John C. (Jack)   A405
Roche, Bill   A449
Roche, Andy   A623
Roche, Erica   A812
Roche, Jules   A933
Roche, Bob   P119
Roche, Alexandra   P129

Roche, Jamie   P229
Roche, Brian   P264
Roche, Lucy   P474
Roche, Max   W146
Roche, Dan   E64
Roche, Bill   E221
Roche, Andy   E313
Roche-Carter, Noreen   P462
Rochefort, Jeffrey   A584
Rocheleau, Duane   A605
Rocheleau, John   P76
Rocher, Leslie   P74
Rochiell, Sievert Jules   P384
Rochon, Sue   E223
Rochow, Garrick   A209
Rock, Jesse   A374
Rock, Sara   A859
Rock, Rex A.   P43
Rock, Jessica J   P188
Rock, Ted   E332
Rock, Mitchell C.   E414
Rock, Bill   E424
Rocker, Tchernavia   A407
Rockett, Stephanie   P45
Rockey, Anne   P191
Rockholt, Tracy   A804
Rockmore, Bette   A762
Rockvam, David   E453
Rockwood, John D.   A551
Rockwood, John D.   P321
Rocourt, Brittney   P422
Roda, Craig A.   A367
Roda, Ann   P7
Roddick, Catherine   A213
Roddick, Catherine   P143
Rodell, Angela   A29
Rodell, Angela   P16
Roden, George   P347
Roden, Frank   E93
Rodeo, Karen   A784
Roder, Anne   A531
Roder, Stephen B. (Steve)   W247
Roderick, Ryan   P446
Rodewald, Chris   A884
Rodgers, Judy   A16
Rodgers, Ben C   A71
Rodgers, Jodi   A203
Rodgers, Steven R. (Steve)   A460
Rodgers, Debbie   A770
Rodgers, Jim   A790
Rodgers, April   A827
Rodgers, Jill   A835
Rodgers, Randall   A859
Rodgers, Randy   A859
Rodgers, Karri   P479
Rodgers, April   P580
Rodgers, Ron   P642
Rodgers, Courtney   P677
Rodgers, Jim   E390
Rodie, Robert   A347
Rodie, Robert   E167
Rodino, Jeffrey M.   E322
Rodis, John   P464
Rodman, Ron   A737
Rodman, Ron   E361
Rodraguez, Melanie   P646
Rodrig, Tzahi   W164
Rodrigue, Perry   A296
Rodrigues, Allen   A61
Rodrigues, Karen   P486
Rodriguez, Rudy   A61
Rodriguez, Rodolfo   A61
Rodriguez, Michael   A89
Rodriguez, Carlos A   A93
Rodriguez, Aida   A104
Rodriguez, Andres   A203
Rodriguez, Maro   A246
Rodriguez, Anabell   A246
Rodriguez, Javier J.   A257
Rodriguez, Alfredo   A271
Rodriguez, Deanna   A296
Rodriguez, Juan   A309
Rodriguez, Vicki   A312
Rodriguez, Linda   A449
Rodriguez, Cristina   A460

Rodriguez, Gerry   A512
Rodriguez, David A.   A537
Rodriguez, Walter   A544
Rodriguez, Rita E.   A626
Rodriguez, Eduardo   A630
Rodriguez, Leticia   A636
Rodriguez, Liesl A   A670
Rodriguez, Debbie   A682
Rodriguez, Susan   A682
Rodriguez, John A.   A693
Rodriguez, Abigail   A700
Rodriguez, Armando G.   A748
Rodriguez, Maria   A751
Rodriguez, Enrique   A762
Rodriguez, Erin   A784
Rodriguez, Havidan   A785
Rodriguez, Damarie   A793
Rodriguez, Sergio   A842
Rodriguez, Barbara   P162
Rodriguez, Vicki   P199
Rodriguez, Camille   P207
Rodriguez, Rick   P212
Rodriguez, Mandy   P242
Rodriguez, Yolanda   P245
Rodriguez, Manuel   P245
Rodriguez, Daniel B.   P388
Rodriguez, Leticia   P403
Rodriguez, Suzanne   P462
Rodriguez, Barbara   P469
Rodriguez, Domingo C   P501
Rodriguez, Sylvia   P507
Rodriguez, Eddie   P508
Rodriguez, Edwin   P523
Rodriguez, Havidan   P526
Rodriguez, Carlos   P548
Rodriguez, Darlene   P551
Rodriguez, Ricardo   P620
Rodriguez, Henry   P638
Rodriguez, Hilda   P657
Rodriguez, Zulma   P678
Rodriguez, Jose Luis Negro   W45
Rodriguez, Maro   E105
Rodriguez, Anabell   E105
Rodriguez, Joe   E105
Rodriguez, Linda   E221
Rodriguez, Rolando B.   E267
Rodriguez, John A.   E341
Rodriguez-Borjas, Carlos   A716
Rodr- guez, Florentino Pérez   W6
Roe, Jeffrey   A112
Roe, Bob   A125
Roe, Jonathan   A329
Roe, John E.   A356
Roe, Jeff   A590
Roe, Jeffrey   A590
Roe, Scott A.   A891
Roe, Deanna   P115
Roe, Stacy   P525
Roe, Lesa   P635
Roebuck, Mark   P506
Roeck, Seppe De   P95
Roecklein, Bryan   E394
Roed, Andy   A727
Roed, Andy   P453
Roedel, Richard W. (Rich)   E262
Roeder, Bob   A530
Roeder, Dieter   E258
Roederer, Nick   A704
Roegner, Eric V.   A79
Roell, Thomas L. (Tom)   P582
Roeloffs, David   A742
Roembke, Steve   A315
Roemer, Jeff   A323
Roemer, Dennis   P519
Roemer, Dennis R.   P573
Roenna, Molly   A469
Roesch, Matt   A691
Roesch, Richard   A727
Roesch, Richard   P453
Roesel, Larry M.   A95
Roeser, William   P508
Roeske, Richard   A489
Roesle, Scott   P85
Roesner, Daniel   A222
Roesser, Matthew   A60

COMBINED HOOVER'S HANDBOOK INDEX OF EXECUTIVES

Roessle, Randy P613
Roessle, Randall P613
Roessner, Karl A. A283
Roeth, George C. E72
Roett, Michelle P570
Roewe, Gordon A224
Roewe, Randy A340
Roewe, Randy E161
Roffler, Michael J. (Mike) A349
Rogalski, Robert J P666
Rogan, Tim A643
Roger, Fran-§ois-Xavier W276
Rogers, Patrick A36
Rogers, Dean A43
Rogers, J. Michael A105
Rogers, Carol A107
Rogers, William D. (Bill) A180
Rogers, Carolyn A191
Rogers, Duncan A240
Rogers, Josh A271
Rogers, Lawrence S. (Larry) A293
Rogers, Rodney A294
Rogers, Derek A345
Rogers, John F.W. A390
Rogers, R. Scott A392
Rogers, Jim A409
Rogers, Nicholas A419
Rogers, Steve A442
Rogers, Jay A463
Rogers, Clark A492
Rogers, Nancy A519
Rogers, Amy A523
Rogers, Derek A575
Rogers, Denise A623
Rogers, Mark A628
Rogers, Greg A632
Rogers, James A634
Rogers, John C. A652
Rogers, Bill A672
Rogers, Alexander H. (Alex) A694
Rogers, Alex A695
Rogers, Brian A746
Rogers, Ann A799
Rogers, Brian C. A800
Rogers, Tony A901
Rogers, Carolyn P126
Rogers, Lana P142
Rogers, Harlan P158
Rogers, Woody P239
Rogers, Marchel P251
Rogers, John P354
Rogers, Cleveland P360
Rogers, Joseph P377
Rogers, Rich P430
Rogers, Richard P430
Rogers, Bobby P436
Rogers, James E. (Jim) P579
Rogers, John W206
Rogers, Dean E13
Rogers, J. Michael E34
Rogers, Linda A E64
Rogers, Doug E138
Rogers, Thomas E149
Rogers, Derek E166
Rogers, John E223
Rogers, Steven E239
Rogers, David L. E256
Rogers, Denise E313
Rogers, John C. E331
Rogers, Kristi E342
Rogerson, Craig A674
Rogerson, Garry W. E86
Roggekamp, Ruud A140
Roggenbuck, Dreta A508
Roggie, Brent P358
Roginsky, Michael A318
Roginsky, Boris A530
Rogula, Ann A606
Rohan, Mary A147
Rohde, William M. A126
Rohde, Bemina A530
Roheim, John P361
Rohit, Mehra A711
Rohit, Mehra P444
Rohkamm, Eckhard W382

Rohler, Nate A867
Rohler, Nate E418
Rohlfing, Ronald P615
Rohman, Cindy P294
Rohmer, Cheryl P482
Rohner, Urs W121
Rohr, Mark C. A177
Rohr, James E. (Jim) P114
Rohrbaugh, Philmer H. (Phil) A367
Rohrbaugh, Scott E149
Rohrer, Bill A16
Rohrer, Daniel A613
Rohrer, Martin P291
Roig, Ismael A77
Roig, Jorge A670
Roiter, Miriam P611
Roitman, Jonathan A865
Rojas, Eliseo A468
Rojas, Manuel F P79
Rojas, Reynaldo P166
Rojas, Saul P367
Rojas, Héctor Manosalva W144
Rojas, Rigoberto Rojo W149
Rojas, Jorge E127
Rojek, Kenneth J P376
Roknich, Ted A347
Roknich, Ted E167
Rokosky, Dave A452
Roland, Barbara A275
Roland, Thierry A439
Rolando, Steve A465
Rolando, Fredric V P357
Roldan, Nestor A888
Roldan, Nestor E425
Roldan-sanchez, Kim A827
Roldan-sanchez, Kim P580
Rolf, Scott A379
Rolfe, Cynthia P89
Rolfes, Francis A165
Rolfes, Francis M A165
Rolfing, Megan E127
Rolh, Martin A176
Rolheiser, Eric J. A239
Roll-Wallace, Kim A120
Rolland, Rodger A41
Rolland, Martial C. W276
Rolland, Marc W358
Roller, Lance A559
Roller, Mark A628
Roller, Bill P251
Roller, Mark P396
Roller, Ted E259
Rollerson, Monica P19
Rolley, Joseph E233
Rollin, Wilber P385
Rollins, James D. (Dan) A106
Rollins, Lisa A651
Rollins, Barrett J. P172
Rollins, Greg P356
Rollins, Paul P571
Rollins, R. Randall E268
Rollins, Pamela E268
Rollins, Timothy E268
Rollins, Lisa E329
Rollison, Marvin L P274
Rolls, Paul E. A627
Rolon, Gil A850
Rolph, Nancy A218
Romain, Peter A592
Romain, Aja A725
Romain, Peter P370
Romaine, Mark A. A387
Romaine, Stephen S. A838
Roman, Michael F. A3
Roman, David H A120
Roman, Andrew A211
Roman, Nori A219
Roman, Oraida A257
Roman, Joy A837
Roman, Michael A925
Roman, Nelson P206
Roman, Sheila P268
Roman, Anthony P332
Roman, David A. W234
Roman, Andrew E83

Roman, Nori E87
Roman, Rose E416
Roman, Michael E445
Roman-Grimaldi, Angela A405
Romaneiro, Marcos A496
Romanelli, Christopher A203
Romanelli, Jim A210
Romanko, Michael F. E172
Romano, Marilyn A29
Romano, Andrea A161
Romano, Frank A556
Romano, Gregory A890
Romano, Peter P97
Romano, Michael B. W398
Romano, Frank E277
Romanoff, Ari A200
Romanoff, Neil P118
Romanova, Anna A562
Romanowski, Mike A213
Romanowski, Paul A435
Romanowski, Mike P143
Romay, Connie A62
Romay, Connie E20
Rome, Melanie A618
Romei, Regan A702
Romeo, Steven A327
Romeo, Steve E73
Romer, Paul A592
Romer, Paul P370
Romero, Pedro A618
Romero, Robert P253
Romero, Javier P299
Romero, Tifinni P488
Romero, Joy P. W85
Romero, Judy E203
Romesser, Scott E260
Rometty, Virginia M. (Ginni) A465
Romick, Steven P118
Romig, Richard A16
Romig, Timothy D. A248
Romig, Timothy D. E107
Romine, Jeremy A115
Romine, Jane A142
Romine, Bill A722
Romine, Donnie P523
Romine, Jeremy E37
Romine, Jane E49
Romito, Joyce A320
Romm, Mike A386
Romm, Preston A386
Romm, Elisa A544
Romm, Mike E188
Romm, Preston E188
Romo, Tammy A773
Romo, Tammy A812
Romo, Rob E264
Romoff, Jeffrey A. P643
Romojaro, Jaime Guardiola W45
Romond, Jennifer L P653
Ron, Stewart A538
Ronald, Alan A61
Rondon, Manuel P202
Roney, Gary A246
Roney, Gary E105
Rongbin, Zhu W118
Ronis, Dave A88
Ronning, Bruce A813
Ronnow, Jesse Ronnow Jesse A940
Ronzitti, Claudio A195
Rood, Carol P148
Roodman, Richard D P433
Rooney, Tim A315
Rooney, Mary A325
Rooney, Brian A452
Rooney, David A559
Rooney, Jack A559
Rooney, Robert A574
Rooney, James A616
Rooney, Jerome A716
Rooney-Mcmillen, Margaret A89
Roop, Kimberly L A69
Roop, Tim A649
Roos, Jeff A512
Roos, Martha A654
Roos, Martin A702

Roos, Tom A877
Root, Barbara A219
Root, Chris A258
Root, Carole P32
Root, George L P397
Root, Barbara E87
Roper, Margie A266
Roper, W A509
Roper, Cathy A760
Roper, Margie P181
Roper, John P443
Roper, Mark P567
Roper, Bret P613
Roper, Cathy E374
Ropp, Stephen E (Steve) A485
Ropp, Holly A485
Ropp, Steve A485
Ros, Francisco A695
Rosa, Dan De La A498
Rosa, Linda A824
Rosa, Jessica P138
Rosa, Enrica De P245
Rosa, Linda P562
Rosado, Robert P782
Rosado, Robert P525
Rosado, Freddy P678
Rosado, Jose E411
Rosamilia, Thomas W. (Tom) A465
Rosano, Sharon A544
Rosanova, Don A498
Rosario, Elvis P25
Rosario, Angela P225
Rosaschi, Suzanne A530
Rosato, R. David A650
Rosato, R. David E329
Rosborg, Kyle A224
Rosbrough, Martha A331
Rosbrough, Martha P202
Roschelle, Perry A409
Roscoe, Lauren P665
Rose, Matthew K. (Matt) A127
Rose, Matthew K. (Matt) A138
Rose, M. Robert A152
Rose, Matthew K. (Matt) A157
Rose, Sheryl A226
Rose, Timothy L. A241
Rose, Marya M A247
Rose, Anthony J. A268
Rose, Dan A310
Rose, Jim A329
Rose, Dennis E. A339
Rose, Doug A347
Rose, Adam A349
Rose, Michael A425
Rose, David G. A433
Rose, Christopher A538
Rose, Roxane A574
Rose, Greg A694
Rose, Matthew K. (Matt) P91
Rose, Douglas P128
Rose, Sheryl P150
Rose, Virginia P551
Rose, Shawn W53
Rose, Deborah W232
Rose, Alison W333
Rose, M. Robert E52
Rose, Richard E58
Rose, Karen E142
Rose, Dennis E. E159
Rose, Doug E168
Rose, Nathaniel J. E200
Rose, David G. E217
Rose, Tyler H. E245
Rose, Eric A. E372
Roseborough, Teresa W. A428
Rosecrans, Marie A739
Roselli, Paris A530
Rosen, Elaine D. A88
Rosen, Stephanie A135
Rosen, Rebecca A263
Rosen, Rae A319
Rosen, Mitch A381
Rosen, Marc A514
Rosen, Marc A516
Rosen, Lora A799

COMBINED HOOVER'S HANDBOOK INDEX OF EXECUTIVES

A = AMERICAN BUSINESS
E = EMERGING COMPANIES
P = PRIVATE COMPANIES
W = WORLD BUSINESS

Rosen, Marc P293
Rosen, Dan P432
Rosen, Andrew P432
Rosen, Jimmy P610
Rosen, Jodi P648
Rosen, David E63
Rosenbach, Lynn A117
Rosenbach, Lynn P61
Rosenbaum, Thomas F. P107
Rosenbaum, Jerrold Frank P574
Rosenberg, Joshua A319
Rosenberg, Donald J. A694
Rosenberg, Andrew A711
Rosenberg, Steven A819
Rosenberg, Michael A899
Rosenberg, Stuart P79
Rosenberg, Stuart A P230
Rosenberg, Michael P241
Rosenberg, Andrew P444
Rosenberg, Michael P657
Rosenberg, Steven P664
Rosenberg, Steven H P665
Rosenberg, Joachim W420
Rosenberg, Steven E403
Rosenberger, Angie A447
Rosenberger, Ron A811
Rosenberger, T P217
Rosenberger, Thomas P217
Rosenberger, Angie P247
Rosenberger, Larry E. E144
Rosenberger, H. Wayne E375
Rosenblum, Jeffrey A606
Rosenblum, Heather A900
Rosenblum, Don P390
Rosenblum, Gail E101
Rosencrans, Dean A86
Rosencrans, Dean E27
Rosenduft, Len A897
Rosenfeld, Irene B. A573
Rosenfeld, Phil E105
Rosenfeld, Aaron E433
Rosenfield, Eliot M. A158
Rosenfield, Richard L. (Rick) E59
Rosengren, Eric S. A322
Rosenbauer, Joan P117
Rosenman, Ned A135
Rosenstein, Robert A143
Rosenthal, Alison A94
Rosenthal, Gary A538
Rosenthal, Gary E A609
Rosenthal, Robert P94
Rosenthal, Jean-Laurent P107
Rosenthal, Gary E P391
Rosenthal, Daniel P574
Rosenthaler, Albert E. A699
Rosenzweig, Israel E53
Rosero, Barbie P476
Rosetta, Gladys A559
Rosier, W. Grady A550
Rosier, W. Grady P319
Rosinski, Kevin A837
Roslin, Anne E156
Rosman, Jessica A160
Rosman, Scott P619
Rosmarin, Kelly Bayer W114
Rosner, Judy A719
Rosner, Robert L P1
Rosner, Judy E355
Rosowsky, David P639
Ross, Cathy A103
Ross, Wayne A112
Ross, Kim A171
Ross, Michele A218
Ross, Joyce M. A226
Ross, Duncan A266
Ross, Rich A270
Ross, Tim A349
Ross, Renee A444
Ross, Heather A449

Ross, Liam A469
Ross, Brendan A538
Ross, Duncan A591
Ross, Andrew D. A640
Ross, Thomas J. A646
Ross, Stephen M. A711
Ross, Rebecca A727
Ross, Bernadette A727
Ross, Bridget A. A744
Ross, Robert A778
Ross, Dennis E. A783
Ross, James E. (Jim) A783
Ross, Sara A804
Ross, Jeannette P21
Ross, David P64
Ross, Samuel L. P94
Ross, Joyce M. P150
Ross, Ryan P252
Ross, James P263
Ross, Trisha P263
Ross, Duncan P369
Ross, Roxana P390
Ross, Jim P423
Ross, Stephen M. P444
Ross, Rebecca P453
Ross, Bernadette P453
Ross, Sylvia P470
Ross, Don P511
Ross, Robert P514
Ross, Goldberg P574
Ross, James E. P630
Ross, Melanie P638
Ross, Robert S. P658
Ross, Bruce W331
Ross, Chad E122
Ross, Lori E172
Ross, Joy E172
Ross, Paul E184
Ross, Latoya E219
Ross, Heather E221
Ross, Stephen E240
Ross, Brian T. E291
Ross, Thomas J. E324
Rossbauer, Pauline A686
Rosser, Carrene G P307
Rosser, Brian P450
Rosser, Troy E92
Rossero, Daniel A351
Rossetsky, Sandra A835
Rossetsky, Sandy A835
Rossetti, Eugenio W202
Rossetto, Paolo A218
Rossetto, Ronald B. A756
Rossi, Mark A. A109
Rossi, Todd A722
Rossi, Hugo A748
Rossi, Jack A790
Rossi, Christopher P130
Rossi, Roberto Angelini W29
Rossi, Simone W145
Rossi, Roberto Angelini W149
Rossi, Luca W234
ROSSI, SIMONA PEZZOLO DE W410
Rossi, Jean W415
Rossi, Jerome E6
Rossi, Jack E389
Rossi, Theodore E422
Rossignoll, Tom A642
Rossignoll, Tom P407
Rossini, Lynn P464
Rossiter, Ryan A690
Rossman, Scott A717
Rossman, Carol A884
Rossman, Eric P56
Rossman, Scott E351
Rossmann, Barbara W. A414
Rossmann, Barbara W. P236
Rossmccalib, Laureen P221
Rossmont, Paul E272
Rosso, Rick A795
Rossolimo, Katherine E138
Rossomanno, Jennifer P134
Rossotti, Charles O. A18
Rossow, Dustin A86

Rossow, Dustin E27
Rost, Julie A363
Rost, Fred P493
Rostan, Richard H. A308
Rosten, James A. (Jim) E245
Rostiac, Sheila A688
Roston, Moore A862
Rostron, Sean A109
Rota, Kerim W18
Rotaeche, Gonzalo Gortazar W321
Rotch, James E P357
Rotenberg, Lesli P432
Roth, Jay A271
Roth, Michael A318
Roth, Julie A444
Roth, Michael I. A468
Roth, Karen A543
Roth, David A630
Roth, Hugh A654
Roth, Renee S. A796
Roth, Corina A835
Roth, Kevin P41
Roth, Steve P43
Roth, Norman P97
Roth, Greg P133
Roth, Doug P182
Roth, Theodore D. (Ted) P438
Roth, Paul B. P634
Roth, Irit W49
Roth, Heidi R. E245
Roth, Alan T. E349
Roth, Renee S. E397
Rothberger, Richard K. P479
Rothchild, Ellen P116
Rothenberg, Ian A325
Rothenberg, Craig A479
Rothkopf, Douglas M P616
Rothman, Craig A170
Rothman, Fred A512
Rothrock, Sandy A828
Rothrock, Sandy P584
Rothstein, Sharon A779
Rotner, Phil P558
Rotolo, Jill A110
Rotondi, Thomas P65
Rotsch, Jeff A376
Rotter, Franz W417
Roty, Christopher M. (Chris) P64
Roualet, Mark C. A373
Rouanne, Marc W284
Roubos, Hind E427
Rougeau, Vincent P608
Roughton, Paul A929
Roughton, Paul E449
Rouleau, Michael A740
Rouly, Chris A325
Roundhill, John A140
Rounds, Bruce P25
Rounds, Mary D P105
Rountree, Gordon P284
Rountree, Elizabeth E102
Rouppas, Susan P596
Rouse, C Jeff A379
Rouse, Scott A855
Rouse, Anthony A887
Rouse, Brad A934
Rouse, Matt P117
Rouse, Donald J P458
Rouse, Thomas B P458
Rouse, Cecilia E. P591
Roush, Phil A199
Roush, Richard A828
Roush, Richard P584
Roush, John E253
Roussat, Olivier W76
Rousse, Jonathan A391
Rousseau, Michael T. (Mike) A5
Rousseau, Paul A297
Rousseau, David P468
Rousseau, Henri-Paul W313
Rousseau, Paul E129
Roussel, Serge A658
Roussel, Christophe A826
Roussel, Pierre-Yves W241
Roussel, Stéphane W416

Roussos, Michael P141
Routly, Kathy P456
Routs, Robert J. W10
Roux, Yvon Le A199
Roux, Bob A522
Roux, Roger G P437
Roverato, Jean-Fran-§ois W146
Rowan, Barry L. E326
Rowan, Pete E433
Rowatt, Kathleen A528
Rowe, Robert C. A200
Rowe, Sharon A206
Rowe, James A250
Rowe, John W A306
Rowe, Gidget A621
Rowe, Chris A842
Rowe, Zane C. A897
Rowe, Steve P387
Rowe, Robert P610
Rowe, William E218
Rowe, Gidget E311
Rowell, Christine A267
Rowell, Jim A640
Rowland, Ian A164
Rowland, James A713
Rowland, G. Joyce A753
Rowland, David J. P486
Rowland, David P. W5
Rowles, Sean A205
Rowles, Michael G. A522
Rowley, Andrea A296
Rowly, Cade P532
Roy, Abir A61
Roy, John A170
Roy, Debashish A218
Roy, Dawn A485
Roy, Robert A587
Roy, James A651
Roy, Elizabeth A823
Roy, Elizabeth A829
Roy, David A845
Roy, Peter A869
Roy, Steve P1
Roy, Lynne P118
Roy, Elizabeth P589
Roy, Craig E296
Roy, James E330
Roy, Sumit E347
Roy, Elizabeth E405
Royall, Elizabeth P597
Royals, Rhonda A56
Roychowdhury, Suranjan E63
Roycroft, Tammy P581
Royer, Adam P228
Roza, Scott E196
Rozanski, Horacio D. A144
Rozanski, Ron A530
Rozario, Datuk Mark A374
Rozek, Charles P116
Rozek, Robert P. E248
Rozelle, Matt P315
Rozenfeld, Jon A776
Rozenfeld, Keren A827
Rozenfeld, Jon P512
Rozenfeld, Keren P580
Rozich, Bill A170
Rozow, Stephen E308
Rozwadowski, Jeanne P179
Rozzi, Ted P160
Rozzi, Carlo P451
Ro- -, Heinz-Peter W382
Ruark, Joseph A226
Ruark, Joseph P150
Ruark, Dean E332
Rubandhas, Samprabhu E290
Rubanenko, Yoram A242
Rubash, Harry E. P574
Rubel, Howard A A373
Rubenstein, Sam A160
Rubenstein, David M. P187
Rubenstein, Ira P432
Ruberg, Tony A444
Rubiano, Rodrigo A842
Rubin, Bob A56
Rubin, Shelley A132

Rubin, Amir Dan A510
Rubin, Jonathan N. (Jon) A532
Rubin, Patricia Lee A592
Rubin, Jon A596
Rubin, Rosalind A651
Rubin, Bryon A893
Rubin, David P162
Rubin, Allan P249
Rubin, Amir Dan P290
Rubin, Patricia Lee P370
Rubin, Ed P597
Rubin, Larry P641
Rubin, Jeffrey G. E53
Rubin, Rosalind E330
Rubin, Andrea E450
Rubinfeld, Arthur A779
Rubinich, Joshua M A837
Rubino, Kristin A877
Rubinov, Emma E448
Rubinstein, Kerstin A329
Rubinstein, David A739
Rubinstein, Pablo P364
Rubio, Javier A670
Rubio, Fernando P597
Rubio, Colette E448
Ruble, Chris C. E180
Rubocki, Cheri A346
Rubocki, Cheri E167
Rubright, James A. (Jim) E177
Rubritz, Timothy G. A357
Rubritz, Timothy G. E175
Ruchti, Laurie A810
Rucker, Merijoy A921
Rucker, Craig P81
Rucker, Craig P218
Rucker, Rob P251
Rucker, Michael P475
Rucker, Merijoy P669
Rucker, James N.B. (Jim) E270
Rudara, Ajay A532
Rudas, Andreas W66
Rudd, W. Troy A16
Rudd, Windy A219
Rudd, Paul A312
Rudd, Neville A450
Rudd, Paul P199
Rudd, Windy E87
Rudden, Russel A16
Ruddock, David P. A737
Ruddock, David P. E361
Ruddy, Thomas A123
Ruddy, Joseph P P652
Rude, Brian P170
Rude, Tom E156
Rudelius, Jeanne A885
Rudinsky, Charles A. (Chuck) A387
Rudisill, Pamela T. A228
Rudman, Robert H. (Bob) A274
Rudoe, Jon W206
Rudolph, John A719
Rudolph, Lynn A727
Rudolph, Sandra P265
Rudolph, Lynn P453
Rudolph, Barry E19
Rudolph, John E355
Rudow, Dale A727
Rudow, Dale P453
Rudoy, Gregory A388
Rudy, John A17
Rudy, Viscomi A642
Rudy, John P9
Rudy, Viscomi P407
Rudy, Wendy P514
Rudzik, Robert J. P119
Rudzik, John P119
Rue, Lisa La P157
Rueb, Lynn A349
Rueber, Joel P49
Ruebesam, Jeffrey A355
Ruegg, Jason A175
Ruehl, Alison A776
Ruehl, Alison P512
Ruehle, Corey J. A867
Ruelas, Robert A897
Ruello, Warren A538

Ruester, Robert P206
Rueter, Jens P190
Ruf, Dave P260
Ruff, Bernd A146
Ruff, Joan P2
Ruff, Patricia P211
Ruff, Heather P390
Ruffer, Kevin A640
Ruffing, Matthew A482
Ruffing, Thomas E48
Ruffolo, Carmel P309
Rufino, Michael G. P202
Rufo, Gloria P608
Rufolo, Rick A870
Rufus, Gregory A842
Rugani, Gina A794
Rugeley, Kent A142
Rugeley, Kent E49
Ruggeri, Nunzio P23
Ruggieri, Bryce E125
Ruggiero, David A199
Ruggiero, Nick P137
Ruh, William (Bill) A374
Ruhbusch, Alayna M P316
Ruhe, Mark A799
Ruhe, Laura E142
Ruhe, Laura C E143
Ruhmann, Donald A140
Ruhnke, Atalie P259
Ruhnke, Brenda P379
Rui, Estrela A642
Rui, Estrela P407
Rui, Yong W234
Ruisanchez, Raul Jacob A771
Ruiz, Jose M A700
Ruiz, Aurelio A700
Ruiz, Gisel A901
Ruiz, Amanda P160
Ruiz, Ashley A P198
Ruiz, Israel P314
Ruiz, Jose M P436
Ruiz, Aurelio P436
Ruiz, Bernardo P481
Ruiz, Rosa P537
Ruland, Lisa A702
Rule, Scott P541
Rulli, John A761
Ruman, Deborah P298
Rumans, Mark C. P84
Rumbaugh, Christine A737
Rumbaugh, Christine E361
Rumbelow, Kevin A857
Rumble, Jonathan A770
Rumbolz, Michael D. (Mike) A293
Rumer, Rich P546
Rumfola, Annlea A170
Rummel, Leah A877
Rumple, Belinda A527
Runcie, Robert W P101
Runck, Cathy P26
Runckel, Christopher E256
Rundall, Thomas P267
Rundell, Phr A799
Rundle, Lisa E448
Runge, Marschall S. A711
Runge, Marschall S. P444
Rungkasiri, Sarun W315
Runion, Scott P530
Runkel, Mark G. A884
Runnels, Chad A704
Runstadler, James A821
Runyan, Ray A218
Runyan, Kirsten P255
Runyon, Mark A462
Runyon, Kevin B. A646
Runyon, Leah P135
Runyon, Mark P256
Runyon, Kevin B. E324
Ruocco, Jennifer P399
Rupczynski, Bob A548
Rupe, Michael D P135
Rupert, Teresa A552
Rupert, Dennis P116
Rupert, Nora P476

Rupert, J P W115
Rupert, Teresa E275
Rupp, Robert R. A408
Rupp, Dave A538
Rupp, Suzanne A654
Rupp, Tom A696
Ruppel, Jonathan A3
Ruppel, William A417
Ruppert, Paul F. A275
Rus, Annette A806
Rus, Annette E399
Rusch, Paul A233
Rusche, James R. E353
Ruscitti, Tony A318
Rusckowski, Stephen H. (Steve) A697
Rush, Deb A183
Rush, Daniel A562
Rush, David G A702
Rush, W. M. (Rusty) A733
Rush, Tim A795
Rush, Greg P405
Rush, William P445
Rush, Jean E4
Rush, Deb E74
Rushing, Matt A21
Rushing, Rodney E. A755
Rushing, David A760
Rushing, Rodney E. E369
Rushing, David E374
Rushmore, John A112
Rushnak, Jeff A200
Rushton, Dale A186
Rushton, Dale P123
Rusk, Mike A315
Ruske, Ralph E105
Rusnak, Patrick J. (Pat) A638
Rusnak, Gregory J. P430
Rusnak, Patrick J. (Pat) E320
Russ, Ioana A658
Russ, Mark A716
Russ, John A767
Russ, Gary P476
Russeau, Chris A509
Russel, Kristin A440
Russel, Kimberly P103
Russell, Ronnie A58
Russell, Darrel A113
Russell, John G. A209
Russell, Nicholas S. (Nick) A227
Russell, John G. A238
Russell, David A243
Russell, Gregg A279
Russell, Dave A323
Russell, Monya A335
Russell, Craig A480
Russell, John A509
Russell, Diane A520
Russell, David A540
Russell, Donald W A540
Russell, Paula A635
Russell, Gilbert A749
Russell, Dan A765
Russell, Keith A771
Russell, Craig A779
Russell, Suzann A793
Russell, David E. A937
Russell, John P26
Russell, Kevin P119
Russell, Gregg P203
Russell, Caroline P232
Russell, Jon P267
Russell, Bob P429
Russell, Toni P620
Russell, Judith C. P627
Russell, Chelsea P638
Russell, David P643
Russell, Sarah A. C. W10
Russell, Darrel E36
Russell, Nicholas S. (Nick) E90
Russell, Monya E155
Russell, Kyle E334
Russell, Jason E346
Russell, Gilbert E367
Russell, Keith E382
Russi, Timothy M. (Tim) A37

Russll, Mark A706
Russo, Michael A356
Russo, Paul M. A390
Russo, Patricia F. (Pat) A420
Russo, Marie A544
Russo, Kristina A711
Russo, Ezio A740
Russo, Mike A835
Russo, Thomas A888
Russo, Alejandra A900
Russo, Kristina P444
Russo, Ralph P496
Russo, Thomas P569
Russo, Jeffrey P642
Russo, Thomas E425
Rust, Brian A15
Rust, Steven W. (Steve) A116
Rust, Bradley M. A383
Rust, Edward A738
Rust, Brian P8
Rust, Tami P286
Rust, Steven P340
Rust, Melissa P624
Rust, Steven W. (Steve) E39
Rust, Bradley M. E186
Rustad, Stephanie A60
Ruste, Ivor M. W92
Rustowicz, Gregory P. E88
Ruth, Michael J. A716
Ruth, John P74
Rutherford, Angela A89
Rutherford, William B. (Bill) A410
Rutherford, John R. A668
Rutkowski, Claire P356
Rutland, James B P344
Rutledge, Elizabeth A53
Rutledge, Debra A772
Rutledge, Terri P629
Rutledge, Debra E383
Rutschman, Cody A452
Ruttanaporn, Sarut W352
Rutten, Lori A36
Rutter, Kenneth S. P69
Rutz, Michael P. E258
Ruud, David A279
Ruud, Yngve W227
Ruvolo, Susan A369
Ruwe, Curtis P165
Ruwe, Steve P432
Ruzicka, Laura P511
Ryan, Martin A79
Ryan, Rebecca A112
Ryan, William J A128
Ryan, Erik A179
Ryan, Jason A180
Ryan, Eileen A211
Ryan, Todd A215
Ryan, Beth A364
Ryan, Marc A367
Ryan, Diana A390
Ryan, Kevin A452
Ryan, Collin A458
Ryan, Courtney J. A475
Ryan, Keith A495
Ryan, Mike A504
Ryan, Lucy C A608
Ryan, D A612
Ryan, James C. A621
Ryan, Dan A627
Ryan, Paula A641
Ryan, Clay A727
Ryan, Richard J A733
Ryan, Carol A752
Ryan, Matthew A779
Ryan, Catherine A827
Ryan, Robert A831
Ryan, Laura A852
Ryan, Cicely P20
Ryan, Kevin P205
Ryan, Barbara P233
Ryan, Philip J. P260
Ryan, Keith P282
Ryan, Michael P325
Ryan, Paula P407
Ryan, Jackie P417

COMBINED HOOVER'S HANDBOOK INDEX OF EXECUTIVES

```
A = AMERICAN BUSINESS
E = EMERGING COMPANIES
P = PRIVATE COMPANIES
W = WORLD BUSINESS
```

Ryan, Clay P453
Ryan, Tim P462
Ryan, Mickey P476
Ryan, Doug O' P519
Ryan, David P574
Ryan, Catherine P580
Ryan, Robert P601
Ryan, Pat P608
Ryan, John P610
Ryan, John M P652
Ryan, Timothy (Tim) W35
Ryan, Michael W73
Ryan, Leonie W135
Ryan, Daniel J. E8
Ryan, Eileen E83
Ryan, Regan E131
Ryan, James C. (Jim) E192
Ryan, Mike E251
Ryan, James C. E311
Ryan, Dan E312
Ryan, Katherine E327
Rybar, Ronald E150
Rybczynski, Andrea A922
Rybczynski, Andrea P671
Rychlik, Wendell P319
Ryckman, Bonnie A393
Rycyna, Kevin P383
Ryde, Bruce A538
Rydell, David R P537
Ryder, Thomas A112
Ryder, John P31
Ryder, Mark P285
Ryder, Paige P313
Ryder, David S P648
Rydin, Craig A143
Rye, Curtis P252
Rye, Ted P557
Ryea, Alan P639
Ryerson, Lisa M. P2
Ryge, Svend A791
Ryge, Svend P535
Rylee, Tanya A69
Ryman, David P123
Ryman, Craig W27
Ryn, Janice Van P168
Rynaski, Theresa A727
Rynaski, Theresa P453
Rynearson, Debra A345
Rynearson, Debra E165
Ryner, Robert P476
Ryneska, Kim A626
Rynhart, Betsey P155
Ryno, Marrianne A447
Ryno, Marrianne P247
Ryors, Alfred P610
Ryrie, Edward A713
Ryu, Hyungon A613
Ryu, Marcus S. E196
Rzonca, Peter A100
R'bibo, Daniel A369
R--DLER, Friedrich W156
Rudiger, Michael W131
Rémont, Luc W344

S

S, Ishak Waguih A240
S.Gragg, Gary A340
S.Gragg, Gary E161
Sa, Francisco A496
Saag, John A270
Saage, Gary W115
Saar, Janet A127
Saari, Carolyn P301
Saarony, Gadi P405
Sabag, Mark W389
Sabanci, Erol W177

Sabanci, Guler W177
Sabatine, Marc P556
Sabatini, Mary P574
Sabatino, Matt A925
Sabatino, Matt E445
Sabatowski, Karen A. A353
Sabatowski, Karen A. E173
Sabbag, Russ A927
Sabbatini, Brian P646
Sabella, Deborah P512
Sabella, Deb E P512
Saberi, Asif P275
Sabers, Candace P615
Sabharwal, Rajiv W194
Sabin, Julia A765
Sabin, Matthew P672
Sabin, Sheree E138
Sablich, Hanai A713
Sabnani, Janisha A349
Sabo, Elias J. E180
Sabol, Colin R. A936
Saborio, Bernal A218
Sabourin, Jim A882
Sabow, Mark A888
Sabow, Mark E425
Sabutis, Mike P333
Saccaro, James K. A119
Saccaro, Jay A120
Sacco, Henry P100
Sacco, Barbara P284
Sacco, Frank V. P500
Saccone, Robert P486
Sacerio, Joan P488
Sach, Derek S. W333
Sachdev, Arvind A218
Sachs, David A. A816
Sachtleben, Michael C. A551
Sachtleben, Michael C. P321
Sack, Brian P. A319
Sackett, John P7
Sackett, Neil P115
Sackett, Walter P277
Sackman, Eileen A888
Sackman, Eileen E425
Sacristan, Carlos Ruiz A753
Sada, Crystal P592
Sada, Armando Garza W19
Sadana, Sumit A565
Sadaqatmal, Ahmad A882
Sadau, Ernie W. P132
Sadek, Hossam A474
Sadler, Wesley A36
Sadler, Jason D A194
Sadler, Rob A258
Sadler, Kimberly A327
Sadler, Michael A565
Sadler, Tony A722
Sadler, Laurie P272
Sadofsky, Lynn P480
Sadosty, Annie A545
Sadosty, Annie P317
Sadove, Stephen A218
Sadovnik, Lev P493
Sadowski, Peter T. A325
Sadowski, John D. A741
Sadowski, John D. E364
Sadro, Cheryl A P323
Sadro, Cheryl P323
Sadvary, Thomas J. (Tom) P478
Sae-hong, Hur W176
Saeger, Mark A888
Saeger, Mark E425
Saegusa, Tomihiro W346
Saeki, Yasumitsu W280
Saenz, Alexanders A115
Saenz, Luis A782
Saenz, Luis P526
Saenz, Alexanders E37
Safady, Edward Z. (Eddie) A682
Safady, Randolph W. P132
Saferian, Candee M P429
Saff, Eric P153
Saffer, Lori Polep P156
Safi, Arshad P531

Safra, Jacob W54
Safranek, Scott A559
Safriet, Dan A58
Safyer, Steven M. P348
Sagar, Bijoy A789
Sage, Anya A571
Sage, James A657
Sagehorn, David M A632
Sagen, James P189
Sager, Ezmeralda Khalil A145
Sagert, Sharon A925
Sagert, Sharon E445
Saggau, David P221
Sagheer, Omer P589
Sagona, Jordan E452
Sagritanti, Mary A573
Saha, Dhriti A647
Saha, Saugata A738
Saha, Tamal A920
Saha, Samar P96
Sahenk, Ferit Faik W403
Sahin, Meltem W417
Sahu, Sambit A461
Saik, Barry A471
Saikawa, Hiroto W283
Sain, Kelly A850
Saini, Rohit E141
Sainsbury, Paul W27
Saint-val, Serge P220
Saito, Takeo W30
Saito, Hitoshi W262
Saitoh, Yasuhiko W349
Saiyawan, Wasin W352
Sajed, Amer A118
Sajed, Amer P66
Sajet, Kim P497
Saji, Nobutada W374
Sakae, Toshiharu W280
Sakaguchi, Masatoshi W107
Sakai, Hitoshi W169
Sakai, Akio W253
SAKAI, TOSHIYUKI W292
Sakamoo, Kevin A109
Sakamoto, Lynette A109
Sakamoto, Jeanne A827
Sakamoto, Greg P628
Sakamoto, Satoru W227
Sakamoto, Ryuji W269
Sakamoto, Fukashi W282
Sakamoto, Mitsuhiro W392
Sakata, Mark P375
Sakil, Kim P546
Sakimura, Noah E138
Sako, Douglas A337
Sako, Gary A606
Sako, Douglas E158
Sakowicz, Adrian A277
Saksti, Hendri W424
Sakuma, Hiroshi W257
Sakuma, Soichiro W280
Sakurada, Kengo W360
Sakys, John V. E279
Sala, Marcello W202
Saladonis, Melissa P128
Saladrigas, Carlos A281
Salah, Jamil A590
Salame, Pablo J. A390
Salamorin, Emelyn P351
Salanger, Atthew J P619
Salava, Deb P643
Salaverry, David A484
Salcedo, Mirta A463
Salchli, Karen P128
Salcito, Tom A654
Saldana, Arturo A544
Saldana, Julia E106
Saldarelli, John A451
Saldivar, Ricardo E. A427
Saldutti, Michael E131
Sale, Adrian A877
Sale, Paul P326
Saleem, Amer E41
Salehpour, Ali A74
Salek, Mohsen A505
Saleki-Gerhardt, Azita A6

Salem, Charbel P280
Salem, Laura P343
Salem, Deeb P612
Salemme, R. Gerard (Gerry) E326
Salerno, Robert A98
Sales, William K. A716
Saletnik, Laurie A478
Saletnik, Laurie E269
Salgueiro, Sandro P314
Saliba, Carol-Lynn A205
Saligram, Ravi A477
Saligram, Ravi P263
Salinas, Jerry A246
Salinas, Ruben A391
Salinas, Theresa P469
Salinas, Erwin Kaufmann W149
Salinas, Jerry E105
Salinas, Micah E106
Salins, Peter D A785
Salins, Peter D P526
SALISBURY, GREGORY M A238
Salisbury, Julian A390
Salisbury, Barbara P129
Salisbury, Chris W325
Salisbury, Chris W327
Salisbury, Susie E148
Salk, Sarah A318
Salka, Susan R. E21
Salkic, Edin A859
Salkowski, Peter E179
Salla, Francis J. (Frank) La A111
Salle, Andrew Bon A312
Saller, Richard P. A510
Saller, Richard P. P290
Salles, Pedro Moreira W205
Sallstrom, Jim A343
Salmans, Todd L. A421
Salmirs, Scott A8
Salmon, Thomas E. (Tom) A129
Salmon, Renaud A243
Salmon, Kimberly A868
Salnas, Todd P472
Salo, Bob P618
Salomon, Robert P546
Saloner, Garth A510
Saloner, Garth P290
Salot, Kalpesh A108
Salsberry, David P541
Salsbury, Jill P402
Salter, Benjamin A887
Salter, Jerry P556
Saltiel, Albert (Al) A95
Saltzman, Robert A42
Saltzman, Nancy E141
SALUS, JAMES A746
Saluzzo, Brian A53
Salvador, Scot R. A851
Salvador, Michael P356
Salvador, Allan P543
Salvadori, Daniel A5
Salvadori, Rossana A877
Salvage, Neil E254
Salvagno, Rob A198
Salvati, Peter A. P185
Salvatico, Michael E290
Salvatore, Bryan J. A405
Salvatore, David A782
Salvatore, David P526
Salvino, Sonia P116
Salway, Roberta A345
Salway, Roberta E165
Salyer, Stephanie A580
Salyer, Kelly P160
Salyer, Stephanie E292
Salyers, Joan A259
Salyers, Sandy A713
Salzburger, Karl Heinz A891
Salzer, Steve P432
Salzman, Mike A160
Samalapa, Patchara W216
Samant, Rahul A262
Samaroo, Savita P678
Samartsev, Igor E238
Sambar, Christopher A89
Sambasivan, Pallavi A592

HOOVER'S HANDBOOK OF EMERGING COMPANIES 2020

Sambasivan, Pallavi P370
Sambel, Andreas A724
Sambel, Andreas P452
Sambrook, David E99
Samenuk, John A483
Samet, Kenneth A. A551
Samet, Kenneth A. P321
Samia, Dori J A784
Samii, Jason P65
Samiljan, Jordan A793
Samir, Mohamed A679
Samitsu, Masahiro W282
Samitt, Craig E. A69
Sammarco, Michael J P197
Sammon, Alison A491
Sammons, Lisa A329
Sampat, Jitesh A135
Sampat, Samir E290
Sampath, Anand E272
Sample, Phillip A175
Sample, Michelle A602
Sample, Mike P610
Sample, Michele E226
Samples, Jeff A463
Samples, Dustin P22
Samples, Joe P470
Samples, Jim P480
Sampson, Shane A30
Sampson, David A479
Sampson, Bryan A727
Sampson, Shane P20
Sampson, Ley P141
Sampson, Luke P356
Sampson, Bryan P453
Sams, Thomas A226
Sams, Bathsheba A467
Sams, Pam King P130
Sams, Thomas P150
Samson, Edward A317
Samson, Denise A704
Samson, Ley P141
Samsonov, Anastasia P402
Samu, Sriram A902
Samudio, Irma P489
Samuel, David A850
Samuel, Noel N P249
Samuel, Noel P250
Samuels, Nicole A53
Samuels, Gloria A466
Samuels, Cooper A665
Samuels, Carol P116
Samuels, Mark P498
Samuels, Gwen P632
Samuels, Cooper E334
Samuelson, Christopher A271
Samuelson, Bobby A559
Samulewicz, Connie P304
Samworth, Martin A175
Samz, Jeff P247
Sanberg, Paul R. P638
Sances, James P22
Sanches, Sidnei A920
Sanchez, Francisco A77
Sanchez, Marcela A107
Sanchez, Danny A222
Sanchez, Anna A246
Sanchez, Lou A287
Sanchez, Ruben A364
Sanchez, Pablo A439
Sanchez, Calline A465
Sanchez, Jessie A571
Sanchez, Maria A642
Sanchez, Beatriz A658
Sanchez, Tammi A713
Sanchez, Robert E. A734
Sanchez, Cynthia A751
Sanchez, Robert A820
Sanchez, Nadia P137
Sanchez, Debra Tica P160
Sanchez, Christina P259
Sanchez, Maria P407
Sanchez, Michael P513
Sanchez, Abby P588
Sanchez, Enrique W7
Sanchez, Jeanette E21

Sanchez, Anna E105
Sanchez, Marie E105
Sanchez, Antonio R. (Tony) E363
Sanchez, Eduardo A. E363
Sanchez, A. R. (Tony) E363
Sand, Laura A694
Sandberg, Christopher A254
Sandberg, Sheryl K. A310
Sandberg, Louise T. A651
Sandberg, Peter A833
Sandberg, Susan P448
Sandberg, Debbie P536
Sandberg, Louise T. E329
Sandbrook, William J. (Bill) E422
Sandburg, Lou Ann A911
Sandburg, Lou Ann E437
Sande, Marc van W405
Sandeen, Mark P10
Sandelands, Barb A526
Sandeno, Greg P145
Sander, Mark G. A346
Sander, Ed P420
Sander, Louise W377
Sander, Mark G. E167
Sanders, Ron A19
Sanders, Jay D. A104
Sanders, Jeff A142
Sanders, Sarah A168
Sanders, Jeff A246
Sanders, Tina A442
Sanders, Ashley A444
Sanders, Marshall A448
Sanders, Dax A494
Sanders, Stacy A512
Sanders, Corey I. A562
Sanders, Matthew A702
Sanders, Scott A744
Sanders, M. Jack A768
Sanders, Dan A776
Sanders, Shane A890
Sanders, Joann P157
Sanders, Marshall P247
Sanders, Jeffrey D. (Jeff) P305
Sanders, Rachelle P348
Sanders, Brenda P361
Sanders, Leo P580
Sanders, Leotis P580
Sanders, Sandra P582
Sanders, Stephanie P596
Sanders, Carolyn P626
Sanders, Jeff E49
Sanders, Jeff E105
Sanders, John E143
Sanders, Steve E235
Sanderson, Kelly A135
Sanderson, Scott A540
Sanderson, Walt A762
Sanderson, Travee P128
Sanderson, La Verne P184
Sanderson, Brad P239
Sandford, W. F. (Bill) W212
Sandfort, Gregory A. (Greg) A840
Sandfort, Greg A840
Sandgren, James A621
Sandgren, Jim A621
Sandgren, James E311
Sandgren, Jim E311
Sandhu, Tony A130
Sandhu, Dalpinder P153
Sandler, Debra A77
Sandler, Pamela P30
Sandler, Anthony P130
Sandlin, Keith P409
Sandman, Dan A578
Sandor, Chris A442
Sandor, Victor E226
Sandore, Jeff A855
Sandorf, Jeff A855
Sandoval, Patricia A140
Sandoval, Martha A346
Sandoval, Andres A478
Sandoval, Stefano P262
Sandoval, Donald P464
Sandoval, Martha E167
Sandra, Wimberl A395

Sandri, Fabio A663
Sandridge, Linda A772
Sandridge, Linda E381
Sandring, Rebecca E97
Sandrock, Alfred W. A133
Sands, Robert S. (Rob) A236
Sands, Richard A237
Sands, John A246
Sands, George A657
Sands, Timothy D. (Tim) P652
Sands, John E105
Sandstedt, Erik A550
Sandvik, Helvi A29
Sandvik, Helvi P356
Sandy, Jody A447
Sandy, Jody P247
Sanfiel, Joaqu-n Cruz W149
Sanford, Marcus A10
Sanford, Kathleen D. A226
Sanford, Tom A479
Sanford, Greg A840
Sanford, Sandra A843
Sanford, Jonathan A882
Sanford, Daniel A896
Sanford, Kathleen D. P150
Sanford, Deborah P190
Sanford, Julie P476
Sanford, Bart E231
Sanford, William R. (Bill) E232
Sanford, Mike L. E245
Sanford, Morris E255
Sang-bong, Lee W237
Sang-Young, Kim W312
Sanger, Robert A538
Sanger, Steve P400
Sanghavee, Naomi A484
Sanghi, Steve A564
Sanghvi, Binit A156
Sangkanarubordee, Sathit W95
Sangster, Denise A139
Sangster, Denise P92
Sanibelli, --zlen W18
Sankaran, Vivek A654
Sankaran, Vijay A807
Sankarlingam, Velchamy A897
Sankey, Greg P590
Sanman, Randall P P279
Sanna, Albert A651
Sanna, Albert E329
Sannella, Mike A528
Sanner, Lisa A135
Sannizzaro, Peter F A800
Sansone, Thomas A. A475
Sanstrom, Bill A401
Sant, Gursharan A540
Santa, Mari P658
Santacroce, Kevin L. A150
Santacroce, Kevin L. E50
Santana, Megan A881
Santana, Angel P135
Santana, Carlos P482
Santana, Megan E421
Santangelo, Vicky A89
Santangelo, Janine A200
Santangelo, Lillian A388
Santangelo, Joseph A A584
Santarone, Mike P590
Santelises, Sonja B P60
Santelli, Jonathan N. A704
Santi, E. Scott A453
Santiago, Geraldine A135
Santiago, Karen A151
Santiago, Michael A404
Santiago, Jackie E185
Santiago, Michael E199
Santillan, Laura A34
Santillan, Alfredo A P227
Santillana, Alex A702
Santilli, Ann Unkcd P299
Santirocco, Laura A409
Santivisat, Srilawat W216
Santo, Masaji W257
Santoki, Tsutomu P534
Santom, David A646
Santom, David E324

Santomassimo, Michael P. A111
Santoni, Thomas E. E224
Santor, Eric W50
Santoro, Antonio A16
Santoro, Rudolph A150
Santoro, Leonard A175
Santoro, Victor A638
Santoro, Jerry A746
Santoro, Sandy P500
Santoro, Rudolph E50
Santoro, Donalee E223
Santoro, Victor E320
Santos, Bernerd Da A18
Santos, Esteban A64
Santos, Corinne A313
Santos, Nicole A356
Santos, Fernando A463
Santos, Barbara A888
Santos, Edwin A904
Santos, Rebecca P223
Santos, Roberto J P620
Santos, Carlos Hernan Zenteno de los W26
Santos, Corinne E144
Santos, Barbara E425
Santry, Edward A600
Santucci, Karen P675
Santurio, Ryanne A713
Sanz, Erick A501
Sanz, Francisco J. Garc-a W418
Sanzone, Virginia E222
Saperstein, Andy A574
Saperstein, Arnold A588
Saperstein, Karen A750
Saperstein, Arnold P365
Saperstein, Karen P481
Sapiente, Andrew A882
Sapko, Gordon A112
Sapnar, Michael C. (Mike) A32
Sapp, Gene A742
Sappenfield, Joel A855
Sappington, Brian A215
Sappington, Jim A548
Sapra, Puja A658
Sapyta, Tim P113
Saraceno, Elizabeth A337
Saraceno, Elizabeth E158
Saracheck, Liz A452
Saradhi, Vijay A588
Saradhi, Vijay P365
Saraei, Armin P363
Saraf, Tal A779
Sarafianos, Alex A713
Sarafpour, Behn E96
Sarah, Lora A262
Saraiva, Ana A530
Saraiva, Ana A651
Saraiva, Ana E329
Saran, Anish A925
Saran, Anish E445
Sarandos, Ted A587
Saravia, Sam A325
Sardinia, Alex A536
Sargent, Angela M. A367
Sargent, Jennifer A642
Sargent, Jennifer P407
Sargent, Annie P408
Sargent, Darryl P557
Sargent, Kimberly P564
Sargent, Jeannine P. W164
Sarhan, Monty P337
Sari, Robert B. A602
Sarid, Tamar P431
Sarieddine, Majed A654
Saripalli, Rangaraju A722
Sarkar, Avik P195
Sarker, Ari A544
Sarkis, Hashim P314
Sarma, Karthik A514
Sarma, Karthik A516
Sarma, Karthik P293
Sarma, Sanjay P314
Sarner, David A114
Sarner, David E36
Sarno, Michael P384

COMBINED HOOVER'S HANDBOOK INDEX OF EXECUTIVES

A = AMERICAN BUSINESS
E = EMERGING COMPANIES
P = PRIVATE COMPANIES
W = WORLD BUSINESS

Sarosdy, Randall P552
Saroyan, Rob P153
Sarratt, Karin A628
Sarratt, Karin P396
Sarrett, David P650
Sarrow, Jonathan A892
Sarsfield, Luke A390
Sarsfield, Sally P57
Sarstedt, Armin A460
Sartain, Mark A275
Sartor-chicowski, Aline P259
Sartorelli, Kenneth P598
Sartorio, James P496
Sarvadi, John C. A818
Sarvadi, John C. E403
Sarver, M Adam A338
Sarver, Robert G. A913
Sarver, Robert G. E438
Sarvis, James A262
Sasagawa, Toshiro W392
Sasaki, Yuuzou W228
Sasaki, Shiro W324
Sasaki, Kazue W398
Sasaoka, Hiroshi W348
Sasashita, Shigeru W127
Sasich, Keith N P279
Sasmor, Evelyn A762
Sass, Forrest P572
Sass, Steven P608
Sassenfeld, Peter W183
Sasser, Bob A274
Sasser, Gary D P56
Sasser, Gary D. P56
Sassoon, Debby A404
Sassoon, Debby E199
Sastri, Karen A584
Satele, Evelyn P298
Sathe, Kedar A200
Satin, Joel E448
Satine, Alberto L. A49
Sato, Keith A109
Sato, Vicki A146
Sato, Tatsuhiko A149
Sato, Michael A602
Sato, Lisa P402
Sato, Beverly P485
Sato, Samuel M. (Sam) P567
Sato, Hiroshi W221
Sato, Hitomi W350
Sato, Yoji W360
Sato, Yoshio W368
Sato, Kazuhiro W400
Satoh, Kunihiko W324
Satou, Naofumi W228
Satou, Masatoshi W262
Satou, Hironobu W350
Satre, Lindsey P182
Satterfield, William E363
Satterthwaite, Jennifer A107
Satterthwaite, Livingston L A247
Satterwhite, Matthew J. A51
Sattler, John A469
Saucier, Grady P345
Sauer, Brad A855
Sauer, Dave P69
Sauer, Konstantin W433
Sauer, Thomas L. E365
Saueressig, Thomas W340
Sauerland, John P. A681
Sauers, Kyle L. E123
Sauerwalt, Craig A799
Saul, Eileen A325
Saul, David A784
Saul, Paula A919
Saul, J. Philip P359
Saulsberry, Scott A921
Saulsberry, Scott P669
Saun, Bruce Van A205
Saun, Bruce W. Van W333

Saunders, Barry L. A768
Saunders, Jim P360
Saunders, Jane P552
Saunders, Ninfa M P575
Saunders, Kathy P578
Saunders, Brenton L. (Brent) W23
Saunders, Rick W135
Saunders, Mark S. W371
Sauquet, Philippe W398
Saurborn, Jim A158
Sausen, Julie A606
Sautter, Allen A319
Sautter, Bruce A444
Sauu, Kakok A419
Savage, Kelly A40
Savage, William A460
Savage, Douglas A483
Savage, Steve A837
Savage, Joseph J. (Joe) A906
Savage, Stanley D. A940
Savage, Kelly P29
Savage, Renee E73
Savage, Sean E143
Savage, Joseph J. (Joe) E435
Savaiano, Helen A405
Savas, Paul G. E372
Savasta, Marc A877
Savell, Jason P349
Saviers, Lori E151
Saville, Paul C. A614
Savina, James A497
Savino, Leo A381
Savio, Kathleen W435
Savoca, Joe A205
Savoff, Mark T P196
Savoie, Debbie A126
Saw, Choon Seong A24
Sawa, Yoshihiro W400
Sawanoi, Makoto P248
Sawasky, Joseph F. P660
Sawczuk, Lisa A86
Sawczuk, Lisa E27
Sawdey, Mike A58
Sawhney, Ash E122
Sawicki, Michael A796
Sawicki, Joseph P162
Sawicki, Joseph D. (Joe) P326
Sawicki, Joe P326
Sawicki, Michael E397
Sawka, Gary E57
Sawn, John A368
Sawyer, Neil A191
Sawyer, Guy A727
Sawyer, Stephen A796
Sawyer, David P160
Sawyer, Billy P219
Sawyer, Guy P453
Sawyer, Stephen E397
Sawyer, Robin E440
Sawyerr, Wraymond P646
Sawyers, Susan P636
Saxena, Sorabh A673
Saxena, Devashish A673
Saxon, Michael A28
Saxton, Karen A112
Saxton, Carol P353
Saxton, Ron P410
Saxton, Pamela L P604
Saxton, Vanessa E386
Sayavedra, Laura P340
Saybe, Victoria P116
Sayiner, Necip W446
Sayler, Kent E46
Sayles, Andy P436
Saylor, Kurt M. A413
Saylor, Jeb P456
Saylor, Kurt M. E205
Saylor, David E291
Sayre, Madison A206
Sayre, David L. A908
Sayre, Donald L. P51
Sayre, David L. E436
Sbarbaro, Cory P222
Sberna, Kate E388
Sboui, Silveras E330

Sbraccia, Denise A922
Sbraccia, Denise P671
Sbuttoni, Julie E448
Scadina, Mark R. E144
Scaer, Robert P212
Scaggiante, Michele P364
Scaggs, Thomas P113
Scaglione, D. Anthony A8
Scala, Luciano A664
Scala, Douglas E. (Doug) A906
Scala, Luciano E334
Scala, Douglas E. (Doug) E435
Scalabrino, Dan A756
Scales, Sam A360
Scales, John P548
Scales, Ted E80
Scalia, Chris A416
Scalise, Anthony A292
Scalzo, Linda A845
Scalzo, Helen P331
Scamihorn, Randy P144
Scaminace, Joseph M. (Joe) A824
Scaminace, Joseph M. (Joe) P562
Scammahorn, Julie A54
Scanio, Kurt P138
Scanlan, John P141
Scanlon, Meghan A149
Scanlon, Regis A337
Scanlon, Andy A519
Scanlon, Suzy A714
Scanlon, Melissa A804
Scanlon, Ryan P93
Scanlon, John P. P119
Scanlon, Regis E158
Scannell, Timothy J. A789
Scannell, James A845
Scaradavou, Andromachi P364
Scarano, Dean A704
Scarboro, Jim A165
Scarborough, Dean A. A97
Scarborough, Randy A323
Scarborough, Fred P45
Scarborough, Rebecca P637
Scarbrough, Brenda P372
Scardigli, Mark E271
Scardina, Mike A36
Scardina, Barrie A692
Scardino, Kimberly A53
Scarinci, Susan P458
Scarlett, Catherine M. A584
Scarlett, Dale P237
Scarlett, Lynn P579
Scarola, Michael A590
Scarpa, Joseph P94
Scarpella, Michelle A608
Scarton, Ron A357
Scarton, Ron E176
Scattareggia, Joe A924
Scaturo, Michael A137
Scavilla, Daniel T. E190
Scavone, April A98
Scelfo, John A418
Scenti, Louis A319
Sceppaguercio, Maria A489
Scerch, Andrea A544
Schaaf, James A604
Schaaf, Christopher A885
Schaal, Barbara A. P600
Schabacker, Marcus A119
Schaben, Christine M A580
Schaben, Christine M E293
Schaber, Carolina P438
Schach, Eric J P505
Schacher, Milo A198
Schacht, David A761
Schacht, Jessica P488
Schacht, Horst Joachim W227
Schachtel, John D. E350
Schachter, Robert A452
Schacter, Adam A200
Schadt, Angela A368
Schaeberle, Steve A405
Schaefer, Rich A5
Schaefer, Jeffrey A86
Schaefer, Kelly A232

Schaefer, Steven A252
Schaefer, Tammy A329
Schaefer, Aaron A421
Schaefer, Michael A449
Schaefer, Werner G A461
Schaefer, Milena A692
Schaefer, Robbie A887
Schaefer, Ronald P164
Schaefer, Chris P423
Schaefer, Jeffrey E27
Schaefer, Charles E194
Schaefer, Michael E220
Schaefer, Michael W. (Mike) E399
Schaefer, Joe E438
Schaeffer, Melissa A24
Schaeffer, Leonard A900
Schaeffer, Joel P175
Schaeffer, Aaron P278
Schaeffer, Tammi P306
Schaeffer, David (Dave) E84
Schaeffer, Andrew E282
Schaell, Tina A272
Schaeublin, JoAnn A491
Schafer, Todd A184
Schafer, Carol A491
Schafer, Lori A552
Schafer, John A613
Schafer, Scott A724
Schafer, Mark A784
Schafer, Dirk P260
Schafer, Dirk P261
Schafer, Scott P452
Schafer, Dana Lee P588
Schafer, Cathy P633
Schafer, Lori E276
Schaffel, Mary P57
Schaffer, Steve A140
Schaffer, Chris P10
Schaffer, Barbara P175
Schaffmeyer, Maryjeanne P602
Schaffner, Jerry L. A421
Schaffner, Fulton P265
Schager, Marty A17
Schager, Marty P9
Schaible, Jeff A120
Schalk, David A651
Schalk, David E329
Schall, Michael J. (Mike) E136
Schaller, Heinrich W417
Schalliol, Charles E. A345
Schalliol, Charles E. E166
Schamer, David A444
Schamus, Neil A98
Schan, Connie A53
Schandler, Jon B P667
Schanel, Judy P578
Schanter, James A786
Schanter, James E387
Schantz, Keith A835
Schanzer, Julie A544
Schaper, Katie P18
Schapiro, Sara P432
Schapiro, Howard P598
Schapper, Brian P334
Schappert, Rich A573
Schar, Dwight C. A614
Scharbauer, Clarence P549
Scharenberg, Janis A329
Scharf, David A218
Scharf, Michael P. P116
Schark, Janelle L P595
Scharlau, Ed A335
Scharlau, Ed E155
Scharmann, Steve P182
Scharmer, Neal R. A867
Scharnowske, Kevin A345
Scharnowske, Kevin E166
Schartz, Weston P617
Schau, Duane P610
Schaub, Christopher A158
Schaubert, Sharon A567
Schaubert, Sharon E283
Schauder, Paul E259
Schauer, Robert A90
Schauer, Darleen A246

Schauer, Alwin A740
Schauer, Darleen E105
Schaufelberger, John A880
Schaufelberger, John P640
Schaum, Richard E388
Schaumburg, Anne A610
Schaus, Philippe W241
Schebler, Jeff A567
Schebler, Jeff E284
Schechter, Jonathan A469
Schechter, Lori A. A549
Schechter, Adam H. A554
Schechter, Chris P140
Schechter, David E393
Scheder, Valerie A89
Scheeler, Scott A198
Scheer, Marc A893
Scheessele, Marc P465
Scheet, Kelley A352
Schefer, Catherine P356
Scheffel, William A179
Schefft, Bob A58
Scheib, Barbera P378
Scheider, Wolf-Henning W75
Scheidly, Darin A867
Scheidly, Darin E418
Scheidmeir, Thomas A6
Scheifele, Bernd W180
Scheiferstein, Scott A392
Scheines, Richard P114
Scheinkman, Daniel A364
Scheirman, Randy A299
Schek, Judy P202
Schell, Christoph A438
Schell, Jennifer A741
Schell, Kenneth P489
Schell, Jennifer E364
Scheller, Robert E282
Schelling, Christina A686
Schembri, Lawrence L. W50
Schemm, Todd A54
Schemmel, Massie A206
Schemmel, Jason A320
Schemmel, Sarah P507
Schempf, Duff P581
Schenck, Boyd A86
Schenck, A. William (Bill) A848
Schenck, Marcus W135
Schenck, Boyd E27
Schenck, A. William (Bill) E411
Schendel, Jennifer P456
Schenk, June A788
Schenk, Norm A871
Schenk, John P266
Schenk, Dieter W166
Schenk, June E389
Schenkel, Scott F. A287
Schenkel, Kendra A405
Schenkel, Cari P254
Schenkel, Carolyn P330
Schenker, Wendy A925
Schenker, Wendy E445
Scheper, Patrick A793
Scheppke, James B P399
Scher, Kevin A469
Scherba, Lena P517
Scherbakov, Eugene E238
Scherdorf, Ron A747
Scherer, Jacob A195
Scherer, Jf A195
Scherer, Laura A487
Scherer, Chad P356
Scherer, Lori M. P578
Scherer, Barb P655
Scherer, Barbara E415
Scherger, Stephen R. A395
Scherler, Lynn A213
Scherler, Lynn P143
Scherman, Carol E. P93
Schermeier, Olaf W166
Schermer, Carol A119
Scherpbier, Harm P305
Scherr, Stephen M. A390
Scherrer, Philip A510
Scherrer, Philip P290

Scheschuk, Peter A738
Schettini, Marcio W205
Schettler, David N A810
Schettler, David N P546
Scheu, Greg W3
Scheuer, Albert W180
Scheuermann, Rob A290
Scheuermann, Daniel A449
Scheuermann, Daniel E221
Scheuren, Jeffrey J. A367
Scheurich, Steven A296
Scheuring, Steve A25
Scheuring, Steve P14
Schewel, Michael A536
Schexnayder, Stephen P45
Schiavone, Drew A336
Schiavone, Shari A638
Schiavone, Drew E157
Schiavone, Shari E320
Schick, Mike A220
Schick, Art A654
Schick, Brian A723
Schick, Mike P149
Schieck-Solomon, Ann P343
Schieffer, Margaret A425
Schiegg, Brian P393
Schiele, Jeffrey A319
Schier, Joseph P359
Schierenbeck, Andreas W391
Schiesl, Troy P76
Schiess, Christine A618
Schiess, Christine E310
Schievelbein, Thomas A446
Schiff, Vikki A103
Schiff, Thomas A196
Schiffer, Meredith E143
Schiffer, Michael E143
Schiffner, Wayne P254
Schijns, Janet A620
Schildz, Christopher A224
Schillaci, Daniele W283
Schiller, Philip W. A72
Schiller, David A72
Schiller, Steven C. A416
Schiller, Marie A518
Schiller, Robert M. P80
Schiller, Mark P285
Schiller, Guy P405
Schiller, Lisa P448
Schiller, Julian W80
Schiltz, Christine P60
Schimkaitis, John R. E78
Schimmelmann, Wulf von W137
Schimmelpfennig, Katie P521
Schimmenti, Kathleen A540
Schimmoller, Kelly P270
Schindel, Joan E168
Schindler, Ron A666
Schindler, Peter A715
Schinski, James E. (Jim) P540
Schiotis, Yvette M A717
Schipper, Heiko W276
Schippers, Harrie C.A.M. A636
Schirack, David A924
Schirling, Kathleen A651
Schirling, Kathleen E329
Schirm, Carla A844
Schirripa, Melissa A702
Schissler, Corey A108
Schissler, Steve P596
Schittina, Mark A325
Schiurba, John P667
Schlachte, Carl P. E225
Schlaegel, Leslie A511
Schlaegel, Leslie P290
Schlaff, Raymond C P359
Schlag, William A492
Schlanger, Eric A98
Schlanger, Marvin O. A857
Schlapia, Jennifer P396
Schlappich, Julie P441
Schlarb, Ann M. E185
Schlater, Benjamin E151
Schlebusch, Peter W363
Schlechty, Rachael P276

Schleifer, Leonard S. A710
Schleiff, Henry S. A270
Schlein, Michael P364
Schlemmer, David P500
Schleper, Denny P141
Schlesinger, Ed A240
Schlesinger, Barry S. E245
Schleyer, J A89
Schleyer, Lorenzo Gazmuri W149
Schlicht, Monica E156
Schlichting, Warren W. A271
Schlichting, Nancy M. A414
Schlichting, Nancy A900
Schlichting, Nancy M. P236
Schlipmann, Adam P251
Schlissel, Mark S. A711
Schlissel, Mark S. P101
Schlissel, Mark S. P444
Schlitz, Lei Zhang A453
Schlndele, Mark A804
Schlonsky, Michael A. (Mike) A132
Schloss, Howard M A629
Schlosser, Jan A199
Schlosser, John W. A494
Schlosser, Mark A881
Schlosser, Mark E421
Schlossman, Martin L E148
Schlosstein, Ralph L. E138
Schlotman, J. Michael A498
Schlott, Robert N P658
Schlott, Abraham N P658
Schluep, Thomas E25
Schlumberger, Allan P429
Schmalz, Josh A909
Schmalz, Josh E436
Schmauderer, Jennifer P251
Schmaus, Becky P101
Schmechel, Daniel J. (Dan) A289
Schmeltekopf, Mark A887
Schmeltz, Andy A658
Schmid, Lauren P113
Schmid, Larry P221
Schmid, Richard J. P603
Schmid, Stefan W63
Schmid, Hans-Peter W137
Schmid, Justin E58
Schmidl, Kurt P450
Schmidt, Franki A54
Schmidt, Judi A63
Schmidt, Darryl A105
Schmidt, Chris A130
Schmidt, John A130
Schmidt, Dany A218
Schmidt, Brent A226
Schmidt, Barry A399
Schmidt, Derek A463
Schmidt, Monica A470
Schmidt, Sue A713
Schmidt, John A856
Schmidt, Ray A856
Schmidt, Brian A859
Schmidt, Craig A872
Schmidt, Diane Grob P32
Schmidt, Pamela P94
Schmidt, Brent P150
Schmidt, Beth P157
Schmidt, Barry P223
Schmidt, Martin A. P314
Schmidt, Todd P390
Schmidt, William P430
Schmidt, Laura A P480
Schmidt, John P614
Schmidt, Ray P614
Schmidt, Darryl E34
Schmidt, Debora E144
Schmied, Jon A314
Schmied, Jon E145
Schmiedel, Rob P182
Schmiegelow, Brent A855
Schmit, David A277
Schmitdgall, Beth P251
Schmitt, Matthew H A727
Schmitt, Paul A831
Schmitt, Peggy P379
Schmitt, Kay P445

Schmitt, Matthew H P453
Schmitt, Paul P601
Schmitt, Christophe W160
Schmitt, David L. E68
Schmittlein, David C. P314
Schmittou, Greg S E177
Schmitz, Bonnie R P11
Schmitz, Tara P11
Schmitz, John P482
Schmitz, John D P485
Schmitz, Rolf Martin W335
Schmitz, Kimberly E433
Schmoke, Kurt A738
Schmoke, Kurt L. P642
Schmoll, William A3
Schmoll, David N. P423
Schmoll, Dave P423
Schmoyer, Ben A734
Schmucker, Clint E347
Schmukler, Louis S. (Lou) A151
Schnaars, Sue A922
Schnaars, Sue P671
Schnabel, Diane A791
Schnabel, Diane P535
Schnalzer, Michael A135
Schnauffer-mansfield, Christine A761
Schnautz, Tom A604
Schneeberger, Carol A. A652
Schneeberger, Carol A. E331
Schneider, Richard E. (Rick) A66
Schneider, Sonia A86
Schneider, Neal C. A212
Schneider, Scott A232
Schneider, Glenn P A269
Schneider, Donald R. (Donny) A350
Schneider, Tom A360
Schneider, Kevin D. A381
Schneider, Albert A465
Schneider, Mark K. A551
Schneider, Allen A567
Schneider, Sherry A621
Schneider, Elise A702
Schneider, Barry T. A785
Schneider, Mike A813
Schneider, Martin A891
Schneider, Pat P252
Schneider, Robert P276
Schneider, Mark K. P321
Schneider, Brett P375
Schneider, Angela P399
Schneider, Amy P462
Schneider, Jennifer S. P464
Schneider, Michael W62
Schneider, Ulf M. (Mark) W276
Schneider, Sonia E27
Schneider, Jerry E85
Schneider, Victor S. E92
Schneider, Mahlon C. E211
Schneider, Allen E284
Schneider, Sherry E312
Schneider, Eric E429
Schnell, David P673
Schnettler, Gary A329
Schneyer, Mark A658
Schnieders, Kurt J. A264
Schnieders, Kurt A500
Schnieders, James P86
Schnipke, Norman E416
Schnirring, Greg P160
Schnitz, Chad A13
Schnitzer, Alan D. A844
Schnitzer, Jay P578
Schnorr, Joseph A112
Schnorr, Lisa A236
Schnuck, Craig D. P601
Schnuckle, Scott A412
Schnuckle, Scott P233
Schnupp, Craig A887
Schnur, Jason A726
Schnurbusch, Shawnda A902
Schnurr, Russ A329
Schober, Steve A376
Schoch, Dave L. (Dave) A359
Schoch, Manfred W63
Schock, Dan A492

COMBINED HOOVER'S HANDBOOK INDEX OF EXECUTIVES

```
A = AMERICAN BUSINESS
E = EMERGING COMPANIES
P = PRIVATE COMPANIES
W = WORLD BUSINESS
```

Schock, Larry P141
Schodde, Joseph P246
Schoebel, Richard K. E356
Schoel, Fran P638
Schoellkopf, Leah A575
Schoeman, Stephan W341
Schoen, Michelle A413
Schoen, Michelle E205
Schoen, Robert E264
Schoenauer, Amber A925
Schoenauer, Amber E445
Schoenblum, Neil A332
Schoenemann, Maureen P456
Schoenfeld, Lynnette A21
Schoenfelder, Kevin P208
Schoenhals, Marvin A929
Schoenhals, Marvin E449
Schoenherr, Melissa P406
Schoening, Lisa P519
Schoenwaelder, Thom P405
Schoepp, Jan Rune P197
Schoettle, Ryan A69
Schoettlin, Kathy A. A621
Schoettlin, Kathy A. E311
Schoetz, Nathan A909
Schoetz, Nathan E436
Schofield, Mary A325
Schofield, Chip A881
Schofield, Harold E28
Schofield, Chip E421
Scholefield, James A778
Scholefield, Michael W131
Scholes, John A493
Scholhamer, James P. (Jim) E415
Scholl, Jonathan W. A509
Scholl, Barbara P110
Scholten, Gary P. A677
Scholten, Michael A859
Scholten, Danielle E P295
Scholtz, Jennifer P94
Scholtz, Marty P594
Scholz, James E404
Schomaker, Justin A170
Schomber, Joe P134
Schonacher, Bill A463
Schonewolf, Lil P522
Schons, Jeri P471
Schooler, Rosemary M A461
Schooler, Richard D P210
Schooler, Rick P400
Schoolmaster, F. Andrew P549
Schoonman, Gerbert A419
Schoonover, Emerson A335
Schoonover, Mark A. A903
Schoonover, Emerson E155
Schopbach, Colin P333
Schoppa, Melinda A191
Schorer, Emily P109
Schorn, Jerry A740
Schorpion, Marc A479
Schorr, Ryan A170
Schorr, Lawrence A265
Schotanus, Brad A926
Schotanus, Brad E445
Schott, Brian A741
Schott, Stevan R. P106
Schott, Brian E364
Schottenstein, Robert H. E264
Schowengerdt, Anna P474
Schrader, Jon A313
Schrader, Dawn A540
Schrader, Michael P397
Schrader, Cheryl B. P633
Schrader, Jon E144
Schraer, Karl A654
Schrag, Matt A262
Schram, Jacob W21
Schramm, Bernie A327
Schramm, Jim A346

Schramm, James A347
Schramm, William A414
Schramm, William P236
Schramm, Jim E167
Schramm, James E167
Schranz, Tom A103
Schreck, John A565
Schreck, Eric W. A851
Schreck, Edward E24
Schreiber, Steve Schreiber Steve A367
Schreiber, Michelle A414
Schreiber, John A423
Schreiber, Steven A536
Schreiber, Melissa A626
Schreiber, Paul A677
Schreiber, Deborah A877
Schreiber, Pam A880
Schreiber, Edward P. (Ed) A940
Schreiber, John R. P73
Schreiber, Bill P170
Schreiber, Michelle P236
Schreiber, Nicolette P433
Schreiber, Pam P640
Schreiner, Steve Deb A3
Schreiner, Linda A536
Schreiner, Mark A704
Schreiner, Joachim A739
Schreiner, Margaret P221
Schreiner, Jeff P589
Schrempp, Samantha A804
Schrenker, Jessica A287
Schrepfer, Robert E21
Schreuder, Jana R. A605
Schrider, Daniel J. (Dan) A741
Schrider, Daniel J. (Dan) E364
Schriewer, Betty A225
Schriml, Rebecca A56
Schrobilgen, Steve A902
Schroder, Ulrich W225
Schroeder, Karl A30
Schroeder, Ian A175
Schroeder, Frank A263
Schroeder, Linda A367
Schroeder, Mark A. A383
Schroeder, Mark A502
Schroeder, David A561
Schroeder, John A561
Schroeder, Bob A606
Schroeder, Jim A682
Schroeder, Michael J. (Mike) A726
Schroeder, Karl P20
Schroeder, Michael J. (Mike) P453
Schroeder, Mark A. E186
Schroedter, Dwight E302
Schroepfer, Michael (Mike) A310
Schroeter, Martin J. A465
Schromm, William A. (Bill) A627
Schropp, Tobin A P279
Schrum, Roger A768
Schrupp, Susan A226
Schrupp, Susan P150
Schubel, Ronald L E258
Schuch, William A481
Schuchter, Douglas A329
Schueler, Kevin P568
Schueller, Gayle A3
Schueren, Clare E72
Schuerman, Janice P337
Schuette, Matt A686
Schuette, Stuart P35
Schuetze, Joergen P404
Schuh, David A215
Schuh, Michele A347
Schuh, Dennis A780
Schuitema, Kurt A376
Schukar, Shawn E. A46
Schuler, Bill A145
Schuler, Barry A538
Schuler, Tatum A746
Schuler, Roland W64
Schulhof, Michael P. E240
Schull, Thomas E A262
Schull, Janette P445
Schuller, George J. A645
Schulman, Melissa A251

Schulman, Mona P403
Schult, Doug A663
Schulte, Ted P14
Schulte, David J. E97
Schulte-Bockum, Jens W417
Schultheis, Wayne M P300
Schultz, Andrew A63
Schultz, Fred A198
Schultz, Steve A259
Schultz, Rob A346
Schultz, Kevin J. A352
Schultz, John F. A420
Schultz, Anthony A431
Schultz, Jeff A434
Schultz, John A466
Schultz, Katie A530
Schultz, John M. A567
Schultz, Robert A567
Schultz, Janet A605
Schultz, Roy A729
Schultz, Howard D. A780
Schultz, Chip A859
Schultz, Andrea P159
Schultz, Tatiana P300
Schultz, Joshua P405
Schultz, Clayton A459
Schultz, Gus P556
Schultz, Danielle P588
Schultz, KAre W389
Schultz, James H E89
Schultz, Rob E167
Schultz, John M. E283
Schultz, Robert E283
Schultz, Leigh E370
Schultze, Lisa A844
Schulz, Dawn A711
Schulz, David S (Dave) A910
Schulz, Duane A933
Schulz, Patricia P141
Schulz, Matthew P358
Schulz, Dawn P444
Schulze, Trevor A565
Schulze, Bill A596
Schum, Ellen E33
Schumacher, Laura J. A6
Schumacher, Michael A87
Schumacher, Patrick A177
Schumacher, Larry A226
Schumacher, Laura A373
Schumacher, Carol A902
Schumacher, Matt P18
Schumacher, Michael P50
Schumacher, Larry P150
Schumacher, John P242
Schumacher, Patrick E131
Schuman, Theresa A114
Schuman, Scott A893
Schuman, Theresa E37
Schumann, William H. (Bill) A100
Schumann, Vicky A608
Schupp, Matt A756
Schupp, Rudy E. A888
Schupp, Rudy E. E425
Schur, Adam A574
Schur, Thomas P A654
Schurko, Allison P667
Schurman, Kim P363
Schurr, Daniel (Dan) A194
Schuster, Jack A893
Schuster, Michael P361
Schuster, Doug P373
Schuster, Francis B. (Frank) P499
Schutt, Douglas W. (Doug) A242
Schutt, Cherie P564
Schutt, Hannah P644
Schutter, Richard U. De E226
Schutts, William A89
Schutze, Heinrich A135
Schutzer, Michael A. A504
Schutzer, Michael A. E251
Schuyler, Matthew W. (Matt) A423
Schvartsman, Fabio W412
Schwab, Karin A287
Schwab, Patrick A434
Schwab, Heidi P476

Schwab, Peter W417
Schwab, Gisela M. E140
Schwab, Holger E286
Schwab-Pomerantz, Carrie P477
Schwabe, Charles E A437
Schwabe, Stefan K. F. E394
Schwabero, Mark D. A154
Schwager, Charles P360
Schwager, Harald W59
Schwager, Harald W158
Schwaibold, Fred P418
Schwallier, Jerry L. A413
Schwallier, Jerry L. E205
Schwalm, Laura P212
Schwan, Cindy A596
Schwan, Severin W328
Schwaneke, Jeffrey A A179
Schwaninger, Jeff A862
Schwarctz, Laurie P182
Schwartz, Steven A52
Schwartz, Bart R. A88
Schwartz, Ken A97
Schwartz, George G. A147
Schwartz, Marlene A167
Schwartz, Eugene A200
Schwartz, Joel A212
Schwartz, Terrance A262
Schwartz, David A366
Schwartz, Harvey M. A390
Schwartz, Mitchell A452
Schwartz, Jay A474
Schwartz, Kathy A713
Schwartz, Peter A740
Schwartz, Lisa A A835
Schwartz, Peter A845
Schwartz, Anne A871
Schwartz, Tim A877
Schwartz, Joel A885
Schwartz, Gil A892
Schwartz, Steven P96
Schwartz, Hollie P202
Schwartz, James K P391
Schwartz, Kendra L P660
Schwartz, Stephen S. E53
Schwartzberg, Jennifer P57
Schwarz, William A204
Schwarz, Paul A340
Schwarz, Ronald F. A495
Schwarz, Ron A495
Schwarz, Ronald E. (Ron) A504
Schwarz, Tony A695
Schwarz, David A727
Schwarz, Diane K. A821
Schwarz, Anne A833
Schwarz, Ronald F. P282
Schwarz, Ron P282
Schwarz, Amy P332
Schwarz, David P453
Schwarz, Jean-Fran-§ois W55
Schwarz, Paul E160
Schwarz, Ronald E. (Ron) E251
Schwarzbach, Fred A592
Schwarzbach, Fred P370
Schwarzman, Stephen A. A137
Schwatken, Rodney E. E307
Schwebel, Gerardo (Gerald) A463
Schwedhelm, Kevin P21
Schwei, Russell P. (Russ) A726
Schwei, Russell P. (Russ) P453
Schweiger, Werner J. A303
Schweigert, Diane M A806
Schweigert, Diane M E399
Schweinhart, Martin G. (Marty) A228
Schweitzer, Pascal A374
Schweitzer, Robert A374
Schweitzer, Jeffrey M A881
Schweitzer, Jeffrey M E421
Schwenker, Adam A695
Schwerdtle, Willi W9
Schwertner, Chris P508
Schwetz, Amy B. A645
Schwilke, Tom A30
Schwilke, Tom P20
Schwimmer, Stephen A201
Schwimmer, Howard E357

Schwind, Bill A746
Schwinn, Debra P594
Schwister, Jay A726
Schwister, Jay P453
SCHWIZER, PAOLA GINA MARIA W121
Schwoerke, Jacqueline P489
Sch-ofer, Wolfgang W117
Sch-oferkordt, Anke W66
Schurmann, Franz-Josef W7
Schutz, Roland W136
Sciame-Giesecke, Susan P610
Sciammacco, Ann A179
Sciammas, Maurice E288
Scianna, Dina A162
Scianna, Dina E61
Sciara, Craig A413
Sciara, Craig E205
Sciarrolta, Christine A837
Sciortino, Cathy L P160
Scirica, Anthony J. P546
Scobell, Daniel A305
Scobie, Alistair A507
Scofield, Melissa A888
Scofield, Melissa E425
Scoggin, Andrew (Andy) A30
Scoggin, Andrew (Andy) P20
Scolaro, Rob A522
Scoleri, Joey A522
Scolieri, Angela P643
Scoma, SophiaS A711
Scoma, SophiaS P444
Sconzo, Guy M P246
Scordelis, Byron E136
Scorsone, Ada P117
Scotland, Michael A461
Scotland, Michael P255
Scott, Samuel A5
Scott, Marlene A8
Scott, Walter A13
Scott, Hagenbach A61
Scott, Sandra A100
Scott, Ann A103
Scott, Dwight A137
Scott, Andrew A137
Scott, Khary A166
Scott, Hunter A170
Scott, Cheryl A176
Scott, Abigal A206
Scott, Christopher A222
Scott, William A305
Scott, Philip A317
Scott, Phil A318
Scott, Stephen L A320
Scott, David A325
Scott, James R. A344
Scott, Clark A345
Scott, Angela A353
Scott, Louise A382
Scott, John A405
Scott, Matthew A409
Scott, Stuart L. A442
Scott, David A452
Scott, Raymond E. (Ray) A508
Scott, Nathan A522
Scott, Richard W. A525
Scott, Bob A527
Scott, Karla A536
Scott, Curtis A554
Scott, William A562
Scott, Wesley A618
Scott, Leonard A624
Scott, Gina A665
Scott, Steve A665
Scott, David A706
Scott, Dennis A737
Scott, Gibson A740
Scott, Sam A755
Scott, Randy A756
Scott, Vernon A760
Scott, Cameron A. A863
Scott, Frank A867
Scott, David C. A872
Scott, Jeffrey A880
Scott, Cheryl A880

Scott, Anthony A925
Scott, Rob P57
Scott, Sam P104
Scott, Pamela P141
Scott, Mychelle P151
Scott, Yvonne P165
Scott, Angela P204
Scott, Selwyn P220
Scott, Eric M P280
Scott, Joseph P371
Scott, Stacey P375
Scott, Cindy P406
Scott, Susan P418
Scott, Peter M. P447
Scott, Charlene P491
Scott, Majeedah P588
Scott, Steven M. P627
Scott, Jeffrey P640
Scott, Cheryl P640
Scott, Stephanie P647
Scott, Brian M. E21
Scott, David E80
Scott, Brandon E123
Scott, James R. E165
Scott, Clark E166
Scott, Gina E334
Scott, Steve E334
Scott, Dennis E361
Scott, Sam E369
Scott, Vernon E374
Scott, Frank E418
Scott, Anthony E445
Scott-Morgan, Peggy A652
Scott-Morgan, Peggy E331
Scoville, Shane A890
Scozzafava, Ralph P. A259
SCRANTON, BRIAN A469
Scranton, Ann A909
Scranton, Alec B. P594
Scranton, Ann E436
Screnar, Ryan T A386
Screnar, Ryan T E188
Scribner, Wendy A682
Scribner, Kent P206
Scribner, Matt E231
Scripter, Jay E409
Scruggs, Marlo A850
Scudder, Michael L. A346
Scudder, Hal A663
Scudder, Daniel P22
Scudder, Walter P572
Scudder, Michael L. E167
Scullans, Greg A781
Scully, Mary Ann A437
Scully, Jodi A774
Scully, Jodi P510
Scungio, Dan P484
Scurfield, Keith P515
Scutro, Vinny A137
Scyphers, Mike A536
Sczepkowski, Kerry E172
Sczudlo, Raymond S. P130
Sczygelski, Sidney P49
Seabaugh, Greg A62
Seabaugh, Greg E20
Seabold, Jeffrey T. A104
Seabright, Jefferson A215
Seabrooks, Nettie P565
Seabury, Bryan A893
Seade, Héctor Slim W26
Seagren, John A29
Seagren, John P16
Seagroatt, Terri A264
Seal, Jill A191
Seal, David A760
Seal, David E374
Seale, Willie A599
Seale, Hamilton A779
Seales, Shaun A559
Sealey, Stephanie A222
Seals, Paul A61
Seaman, Chuck A448
Seaman, Chuck P247
Seamon, Paul A352
Sear, Steve A262

Seargent, Jennifer A105
Seargent, Jennifer E34
Searle, Nigel A309
Searle, Mark P44
Searles, Sean P356
Searls, Eric A850
Sears, Karl A232
Sears, Steven A349
Sears, James A. A350
Sears, Kathy A580
Sears, Rachael A604
Sears, Mark A686
Sears, Melissa P508
Sears, Janice E136
Sears, Kathy E292
Searson, Robert A850
Seasock, Scott A653
Seastone, Bj A60
Seastrom, Dave P185
Seat, David M. A105
Seat, David M. E34
Seaton, Timothy A203
Seaton, Elizabeth A219
Seaton, Mark E. A332
Seaton, Charlee A335
Seaton, David T. A355
Seaton, Grant A747
Seaton, Bree-Annette P160
Seaton, Elizabeth E87
Seaton, Charlee E154
Seaver, Michael L. A651
Seaver, Michael L. E329
Seavers, Dean S. W273
Seavey, Darryl A704
Seawell, Katie A779
Seay, Renee A363
Sebastian, George A654
Sebastian, Greg E412
Sebastiano, Joanne P653
Sebbar, Sa--d W230
Sebourn, Emily A449
Sebourn, Emily E221
Secco, Genie Del E391
Sechrist, Paul W. E86
Seck, Wai Kwong A783
Seck, Jason P86
Seckinger, Mark P395
Secor, Mark E. A433
Secor, Aleyne P375
Secor, Mark E. E217
Secor, Thomas E307
Secord, Greg L. E174
Secrest, Brent A299
Sedam, Lonna P625
Sederholm, Shawn A902
Sedey, Ray P318
Sedey, Raymond J P319
Sedgwick, Dale A933
Sedicino, Dominic A646
Sedicino, Dominic E324
Sedigh, Massoud A927
Sedivy, Michael A85
Sedivy, Michael E27
Sedlacek, Lanie A859
Sedlak, Dan A593
Sedlak, Andrea P664
Sedmak, Pamela S A571
Sedmak, Thomas P74
Seeberger, Mark A246
Seeberger, Mark E105
Seedig, Landry E21
Seedorf, Herman A644
Seeger, Laureen E. A53
Seeger, Rick A158
Seeger, Britta W125
Seekins, Mike A869
Seele, Jon A605
Seele, Rainer W295
Seeley, William A154
Seeley, Scott A222
Seery, Lisa E132
Seethoff, John A237
Seeyave, Shara E290
Sefcik, James A179
Sefcik, Deborah A449

Sefcik, Deborah E221
Sefzik, Peter L. A222
Segal, David A3
Segal, Karin Eibschitz A461
Segal, David A848
Segal, David P27
Segal, Nancy P191
Segal, Julian W84
Segal, Jeremy E260
Segal, David E411
Segall, Peter P351
Segatto, James P199
Segin, Robert P653
Segredo, John A369
Segreto, Antionette A123
Segura, Michael A401
Sehi, John P232
Sehring, Robert P401
Seianna, Apollonia P478
Seibel, Donald J. (Don) A316
Seibel, Douglas E3
Seibert, William P191
Seidcheck, Thomas A726
Seidcheck, Thomas P453
Seidel, Dave A680
Seidel, Laura P239
Seidel, Andrew P466
Seidel, Deborah L P664
Seidell, Violeta A538
Seidelmann, Scott E315
Seiden, Adam E330
Seidenberger, Eric A903
Seidl, David P337
Seidler, Rick P258
Seidner, Erin P408
Seifert, James J. (Jim) A289
Seifriz, Jennifer A60
Seike, Kouichi W379
Seiler, Dawn A680
Seiler, Gregory A890
Seiler, James P587
Seiler, David R. E156
Seim, Robin G. (Rob) E315
Seino, Satoshi W143
Seinsheimer, Matthew P543
Seis, Todd P588
Seitz, James R. A1
Seitz, Jim A1
Seitz, Charles W P293
Seitz, James R. E1
Seitz, Jim E1
Seitze, David A246
Seitze, David E105
Seivold, Stephen A922
Seivold, Stephen P671
Sejas, Cynthia A738
Sejling, Klaus R. W1
Sekely, Larry E264
Sekerka, Robert P114
Sekhar, Chandra A119
Sekhon, Pinder A540
Seki, Masaki W93
Seki, Daisuke W195
Seki, Hiroshi W195
Seki, Jun W283
SEKI, MITSUYOSHI W430
Sekine, Toshitaka W51
Sekizawa, Yukio W30
Sekmakas, Viktoras R. A673
Selanders, Beth A298
Selanders, Beth E130
Selby, Sam E96
Selby, Thomas E185
Selchan, Benjamin A405
Seldon, Eric B. A19
Selembo, David J A196
Seleznev, Kirill Gennadievich W308
Self, Amy P506
Selfa, Joan A453
Selfridge, Michael D. (Mike) A349
Selian, Paul J. A783
Seligman, Heather L P383
Seljan, Jacob A884
Sell, Robert E. (Bob) W5
Sellas, Susie P470

COMBINED HOOVER'S HANDBOOK INDEX OF EXECUTIVES

```
A = AMERICAN BUSINESS
E = EMERGING COMPANIES
P = PRIVATE COMPANIES
W = WORLD BUSINESS
```

Sellers, Mary E. A109
Sellers, Ronnie A312
Sellers, Angie A353
Sellers, Nancy A368
Sellers, Karl A526
Sellers, John A897
Sellers, Ronnie P200
Sellers, Angie P204
Sellers, Thomas P226
Selley, Clive W82
Sellinger, Howard L A430
Sellitto, Gayle A108
Sells, Jennifer A88
Selman, Thomas M. (Tom) P202
Selnes, Rob A540
Selosse, Eric P326
Selsor, Darlene A246
Selsor, Darlene E105
Seltzer, Jeff A559
Selva, Bert P492
Selverian, Arthur A687
Selvidio, Joseph A391
Selwood, Robert C. A562
Selwood, Jim A933
Semanek, Jamie P77
Semba, Sho W374
Sember, Sarah A530
Sementelli, Richard A702
Semeraro, Nicole P475
Semerdjian, Nancy P386
Semet, Gardner A115
Semet, Gardner E37
Semik, Edward A925
Semik, Edward E445
Semmens, Mark A386
Semmens, Mark E188
Semo, Michael A520
Semple, Matt A325
Semple, Heather A492
Semple, Heather P279
Sen, Paula A793
Sen, Michael W353
Sen-Gupta, Prabir A120
Sence, John A369
Sendler, Robert A354
Senel, Aydin W403
Senese, Dominic A210
Senevy, Steven P207
Seng, Hock W173
Senge, James (Jim) E122
Senger, Joe A252
Sengul, Oguz A790
Sengul, Oguz E389
Senia, Vincent A752
Senior, David A63
Senisse, Alessandra P404
Senke, Gernot A702
Senken, Matt A112
Senker, T. J. A551
Senker, T. J. P321
Senn, Andrew E232
Senner, Christopher J. (Chris) E140
Sennott, John L. (Jack) A32
Senroy, Sid A133
Sensing, J. Steven (Steve) A734
Senske, Thomas A104
Senty, Josh P657
Seok-Hui, Lee W354
Seong, Chan W411
Sepe, Billye P166
Seppi, Brandy E391
Sepulveda, Laura A925
Sepulveda, Juan P432
Sepulveda, Liliana P677
Sepulveda, Laura E445
Sep--Iveda, Eli S. A670
Sequeira, Ramona W381
Sequin, Donny P478
Serafino, Joseph A418

Serago, Michael A100
Serbun, Joseph A227
Serbun, Joseph E90
Serck-hanssen, Sverre A301
Serck-hanssen, Sverre P196
Serck-Hanssen, Harald W140
Sereda, Peter L. A810
Sereda, Dexter P500
Sereni, Judy A160
Serge, Adrian A540
Serhal, Ed P553
Serianni, Charles F. (Chuck) A721
Serkes, Jeffrey David P347
Seroka, Gene P424
Serota, Scott P. P89
Serpa, Fernando A902
Serpico, Donna P489
Serrano, Evelyn A16
SERRANO, SHERRY A110
Serrano, Jose Fernando A218
Serrano, Jose Fernando Fernando A218
Serrano, Michael A332
Serrano, Thea A341
Serrano, Cookie A809
Serrato, Michael A320
Serrato, Pedro P192
Serre, Nicholas P41
Serven, Neal A501
Servodidio, Mark J. A98
Sesana, Marco W35
Seshadri, Raj A544
Seshadri, Sridhar P524
Sessions, Roy B. P80
Sesto, Eric Del A366
Seth, Ajay A425
Sethi, Rajeev A60
Sethi, Parvesh A199
Sethi, Shipra A925
Sethi, Naresh W79
Sethi, Shipra E445
Sethna, Meenal A. E258
Sethov, Inger W289
Setiawan, Rico W208
Setlock, Brandon A746
Seto, Kinya W238
Seto, Shinichirou W350
Setta, Salli A255
Settembri, Marco W276
Settersten, Scott M A858
Settino, Tom A317
Settle, Tom A448
Settle, Peggy A641
Settle, Tom P247
Settle, Judy P389
Settle, Peggy P407
Settle, Diane P473
Setubal, Alfredo Egydio W205
Setzer, Nikolai W117
Seuferer, Kevin A52
Seung-won, Kang W283
Seurynck, Michael A813
Sevenich, John R. E201
Sever, Susan A325
Severance, Matthew P111
Severance, Keith P611
Severance, Dawn E92
Severiano, Gilda P206
Severino, Michael E. A6
Severino, Vittorio M. A439
Severson, Gerald P253
Sevesind, Elizabeth A104
Sevier, John P56
Sevilla, Gene A735
Sevilla, Javier P202
Sevilla-Sacasa, Eugenio A735
Sevilla-Sacasa, Eugene A735
Sevimsavur, Tolgay A658
Sewalls, Travis P465
Seward, Michelle P266
Seward, Robert P333
Sewell, D. Bruce A72
Sewell, Michael J. (Mike) A195
Sewell, David A343
Sewell, David B. A756
Sewell, Leigh P94

Sewell, Denise P656
Sewell, David E164
Sexauer, Nicholas A747
Sexton, Ellen A876
Sexton, Kevin P242
Sexton, John P371
Sey, Jennifer (Jen) A514
Sey, Jennifer (Jen) A516
Sey, Jennifer (Jen) P293
Seybold, Henry P379
Seyer, Laurent E290
Seymour, Kim A54
Seymour, Jeff A89
Seymour, Russell A850
Seymour, Linda W187
Seze, Amaury de W313
Sfamenos, Steve P85
Sferrazza, Bob A167
Sferruzza, Maria A374
Sfiroudis, Steven A574
Sgaglione, Lucille T. A126
Sgammato, Tom A835
Sgro, Gianfranco W227
Shaari, Bahren W299
Shabalala, Sandile W275
Shabot, M. Michael P324
Shabshab, Nabil A123
Shaby, Dave E51
Shackelford, Richard A332
Shackleford, Jeremy A929
Shackleford, Jeremy E449
Shacochis, David A184
Shade, Jennifer A835
Shade, Elizabeth F P40
Shadid, Sean A105
Shadid, Sean E34
Shadix, Michelle A704
Shadle, Roger P531
Shadwick, Susan P325
Shae, Kate A309
Shaeff, Julie S. E89
Shaeffer, Carrie P68
Shaeffer, Rick E73
Shaevsky, Mark P670
Shafer, Ronald A228
Shafer, Craig A376
Shafer, Walter F. A663
Shafer, Walt A663
Shafer, Craig A672
Shafer, Thomas C. (Tom) A805
Shafer, Joan M. A907
Shafer, Thomas C. (Tom) E398
Shaff, Karen E. A677
Shaffer, Ben A63
Shaffer, Richard A343
Shaffer, Elizabeth A378
Shaffer, Michael A. (Mike) A692
Shaffer, Charles M. (Chuck) A749
Shaffer, Stephen A22
Shaffer, Stephen P171
Shaffer, Shelly P247
Shaffer, Rachel P383
Shaffer, Richard E164
Shaffer, Doug E349
Shaffer, Charles M. (Chuck) E367
Shagimuratova, Elvira P408
Shagoury, Antoine A783
Shah, Manan A69
Shah, Ken A167
Shah, Mayank A203
Shah, Manish A228
Shah, Niyant A378
Shah, Yogendra A203
Shah, Abhay A418
Shah, Sanjiv A460
Shah, Raheel A A460
Shah, Aarti A518
Shah, Benish A651
Shah, Neal H A666
Shah, Rushabh A686
Shah, Bhavin A739
Shah, Rajen A783
Shah, Manojkumar A804
Shah, Sanjay A818
Shah, Pratik A899

Shah, Mahesh P503
Shah, Rashmi P503
Shah, Summit P503
Shah, Benish E330
Shaheen, Gabriel L. A432
Shaheen, George T. E248
Shahid, Mohammad P488
Shahin, Gus W164
Shahrestani, Navid A793
Shahri, Masoud A850
Shaibani, H E Mohammad Ibrahim Abdulrahm Al W142
Shaibel, Ruvi W164
Shaik, Shalina P629
Shaikh, Jalil P53
Shakdwipee, Manish E290
Shakeel, Ella A713
Shaker, Mark P338
Shalala, Mark E80
Shalkham, Anna P294
Shallcross, Joanne A155
Shallcross, Joanne E54
Shallow, Andrew A86
Shamber, Mark E. A774
Shamberger, Rick A885
Shamburger, Julie N. A772
Shamburger, Mike A799
Shamburger, Julie N. E382
Shamir, Nachum E261
Shamloo, Brenda A850
Shammo, Brian A25
Shammo, Brian P14
Shamseddine, Adel A900
Shamshoian, John A251
Shamsuarov, Azat W310
Shan, Jia A391
Shan, Tan Su W130
Shanahan, Patrick M. (Pat) A140
Shanahan, Julie A413
Shanahan, Julie E205
Shane, Tarah P273
Shane, Leslie P536
Shang, Mark A147
Shank, Chad A531
Shank, Melissa A799
Shank, Diana P340
Shank, Theresa P362
Shankar, Shashi A530
Shankar, Latha R A571
Shankar, Ram A859
Shanker, Nick P281
Shanks, Robert L. (Bob) A359
Shanks, Ron A797
Shanks, Laura P113
Shanks, Scott P534
Shanley, Edward A540
Shanmugam, Nataraj P182
Shannon, Robert A123
Shannon, John A164
Shannon, John A197
Shannon, Albert A247
Shannon, Sean C A307
Shannon, Jason P35
Shannon, Kelly P301
Shannon, Nicole P457
Shannon, Jetawn P476
Shannon, Jennifer P631
Shannon, Albert E105
Shanteau, Kelly A246
Shanteau, Kelly E105
Shao, Lei A460
Shaoyong, Liu W97
Shaper, Darryl A81
Shapiro, Chuck A10
Shapiro, Glenn T. A35
Shapiro, Marc A525
Shapiro, Jodi A577
Shapiro, Steve A704
Shapiro, Loretta A755
Shapiro, Paul A837
Shapiro, Steven P111
Shapiro, Karin P187
Shapiro, Donna P287
Shapiro, Louis P368
Shapiro, Robert S. (Bob) P382

Shapiro, Morton O. P388
Shapiro, Larry J. P600
Shapiro, Sheri P606
Shapiro, Steven D. P643
Shapiro, Eric E261
Shapiro, Loretta E369
Shapiro, David T. E424
Shapleigh, Greg P97
Shappee, Dave A264
Shappell, James R. (Jim) P582
Shara, Thomas J. A504
Shara, Thomas J. E251
Share, Christopher J. P130
Share, Douglas G. P130
Sharff, Rich P475
Shari, Lord P637
Sharifian, Bahman E179
Sharifzadeh, Shahin P53
Sharkey, Jeff A63
Sharkey, John A240
Sharkey, Andrew A717
Sharkey, Allan P445
Sharma, Amit A59
Sharma, Vishal A289
Sharma, Mayank A391
Sharma, Praveen A865
Sharma, Roger P137
Sharma, Amit P467
Sharma, Mahendra Kumar W194
Sharma, Ritesh E10
Sharma, Pramod E200
Sharma, Praveen E207
Sharman, Sandy W85
Sharman, James A. (Jim) E383
Sharon, Richard A571
Sharon, Bodi S P605
Sharon, Lanier P637
Sharoni, Elan P375
Sharp, Robert T A292
Sharp, John A329
Sharp, Reid A340
Sharp, Erin S. A498
Sharp, Ken A509
Sharp, Steven A718
Sharp, Jeff A891
Sharp, John F P85
Sharp, Joseph P144
Sharp, Mike P215
Sharp, Carissa P233
Sharp, Eddie P410
Sharp, Linda P412
Sharp, Lindsey P448
Sharp, Christopher (Topher) P524
Sharp, Bob P657
Sharp, Reid E161
Sharp, James P. E183
Sharp, Steven E354
Sharpe, Stacy A35
Sharpe, Matthew P. A432
Sharpe, Mikel A888
Sharpe, Ben W9
Sharpe, Mikel E425
Sharpless, Walt A798
Sharr, Michael A405
Shasha, Brian A571
Shashoua, Stanley A761
Shashua, Amnon A460
Shastry, Mira A559
Shattock, Matthew J. (Matt) W374
Shattuck, Mayo A. A305
Shattuck, Mayo A A306
Shatzer, Warren A13
Shauger, Daniel (Dan) E396
Shaughnessy, Michael A706
Shaughnessy, Gary W435
Shaughnessy, Michael E316
Shaukat, Tariq M. A39
Shaukat, Tariq A160
Shaulis, Matthew A658
Shaulis, Charlie P32
Shavel, Lee M. E429
Shaver, David A867
Shaver, Bill P493
Shaver, David E418
Shaw, Diana A29

Shaw, Sean A80
Shaw, John A86
Shaw, G W A89
Shaw, Paula A113
Shaw, Jennifer A139
Shaw, Kenneth A140
Shaw, Keri-Lynne A243
Shaw, Robert K. A397
Shaw, Carl A401
Shaw, Michael A483
Shaw, David A484
Shaw, William A491
Shaw, Christi A517
Shaw, Jeff A530
Shaw, Alan H. A604
Shaw, Jeff M. A615
Shaw, Lynn T A704
Shaw, Mark R A773
Shaw, Terry A879
Shaw, Sean P46
Shaw, Tom P83
Shaw, Jennifer P93
Shaw, Chris P190
Shaw, Angela P199
Shaw, Chuck P476
Shaw, Keeasha P552
Shaw, Diane P606
Shaw, Jen Day P627
Shaw, Gene P677
Shaw, Nicola W273
Shaw, John E27
Shaw, Paula E36
Shaw, Joanne E150
Shaw, Bruce E212
Shawah, Paul E427
Shawdee, Karen A449
Shawdee, Karen E221
Shay, Troy A361
Shaye, Gary P474
Shayegi, Cameron A862
Shea, Kevin A126
Shea, Ann A170
Shea, Katherine A170
Shea, Colleen A298
Shea, Phil A325
Shea, Jim A390
Shea, E. Stewart A450
Shea, Brian A651
Shea, Daniel A660
Shea, Jody A696
Shea, Dennis A784
Shea, David A837
Shea, Dan A870
Shea, Molly A915
Shea, Dennis P175
Shea, Agnes A P337
Shea, Daniel P416
Shea, James L. P642
Shea, Colleen E130
Shea, Jonathan E143
Shea, John E203
Shea, E. Stewart E221
Shea, Brian E329
Sheafe, Scott A654
Sheahan, Denis K. A162
Sheahan, Denis K. E61
Shear, Neal A. A187
Shear, Neal A188
Shearan, Kevin W106
Sheard, Paul A738
Shearer, Maureen A135
Shearer, Bruce A444
Shearer-adams, Jackie A179
Shearrow, Brian E84
Shebik, Steven E. (Steve) A35
Sheckleford-lister, Peter P85
Sheckley, Chris A686
Shedlin, Gary S. A135
Sheedy, William M. (Bill) A895
Sheedy, Linda L P391
Sheehan, John F. A25
Sheehan, John A88
Sheehan, Bill A137
Sheehan, Dennis A359
Sheehan, Daniel J. (Dan) A381

Sheehan, James N. A434
Sheehan, Greg A481
Sheehan, Dan A658
Sheehan, John D. A815
Sheehan, John F. P14
Sheehan, Casey P199
Sheehan, Arlene P302
Sheehan, Timothy P555
Sheehan, Kevin E183
Sheehy, Bill A175
Sheehy, Jonathan E419
Sheeley, Michael J. A867
Sheer, Julie A251
Sheets, Anna P128
Sheets, Brian P235
Sheets, Roger P494
Shefcik, James A893
Sheffield, Tamara A462
Sheffield, Kenneth H. A666
Sheffield, Scott D. A666
Sheffield, Tamara P256
Sheftel, Edward A452
Sheftic, Jeff A520
Shehadi, Ramez A145
Shehee, Virginia K P85
Sheinbaum, Gary A692
Sheinheit, Alvin A559
Shekar, A. W294
Shekhawat, Sudip E347
Shelby, Bryan A137
Shelby, Thomas S. A656
Shelby, Laurie A818
Shelby, Thomas S. P414
Shelby, Laura Wilson P486
Sheldon, Tim A537
Sheldon, Todd N. A690
Sheldon, D. Scott E10
Sheldon, David E143
Shelford, James A668
Sheline, Douglas A530
Shell, Jeffrey A175
Shell, Yvonne A440
Shell, Ellen P96
Shelley, Bill A881
Shelley, Art A888
Shelley, Christine P590
Shelley, Val E206
Shelley, Bill E421
Shelley, Art E425
Shelley-Kessler, Pamela J. (Pam) E261
Shellman, Carolyn E. P164
Shelly, Lisa P135
Shelnutt, David A866
Shelnutt, David E417
Shelowitz, Rachel A243
Shelter, Rolando Zubiran W19
Shelton, Gary A621
Shelton, Afton A668
Shelton, Nakeya A871
Shelton, Jean P121
Shelton, Anna P207
Shelton, Natalie P549
Shelton, M. Dwight P652
Shelton, Gary E311
Shen, Jessica A479
Shen, Sam A511
Shen, Sam P290
Shen, Heting W255
Shen, David W425
Shendell-Falik, Nancy P72
Shendell-Falik, Nancy P73
Shengdong, Zhang W431
Shenkin, Kerri A112
Shenkman, Dov A900
Shenoy, Navin A460
Shepard, Andy A16
Shepard, Ernest A119
Shepard, Gerald A166
Shepard, Andrew A218
Shepard, Chip A330
Shepard, Randall A621
Shepard, Ken P297
Shepard, Alan G P388
Shepard, Chip E152
Shepard, Randall E312

Sheperd, David A926
Shepheard, Hillary P549
Shepherd, Richard P278
Shepherd, Mary P386
Shepherd, Glenn P481
Shepherd, Mary P599
Shepherd, Joel E16
Shepherd, Stacie E96
Shepler, Mary P465
Sheppard, Charles A301
Sheppard, Charlie A301
Sheppard, Valarie A680
Sheppard, Ben A746
Sheppard, Linda P440
Sheppard, Dennis P511
Sheppard, William D P511
Sheppard, William P511
Sheppard, Karen E106
Shepperly, David A151
Shepro, William B P29
Sher, Susan S. P594
Sherbin, Bob A613
Sherbin, Robert A613
Sherer, Jay A195
Sherer, Matt P541
Sheridan, William A200
Sheridan, Jean E A605
Sheridan, Arthur A782
Sheridan, Jerry E. A857
Sheridan, Philip A925
Sheridan, Michael A933
Sheridan, Chris P116
Sheridan, James P335
Sheridan, Arthur P526
Sheridan, John P. P563
Sheridan, Philip E445
Sheriff, Abrar A853
Sheriff, Abrar P612
Sherlock, Kevin A448
Sherlock, Kevin P247
Sherlock, Peter P578
Sherman, Ronald A89
Sherman, Jeffrey S. A123
Sherman, Floyd F A156
Sherman, Catherine A165
Sherman, Patrick A345
Sherman, Matthew A352
Sherman, Arthur A421
Sherman, Peter A626
Sherman, Kim P360
Sherman, Harry P368
Sherman, Mark P479
Sherman, Malcolm L P612
Sherman, Jennifer P642
Sherman, Joseph P642
Sherman, Jennifer L. E149
Sherman, Patrick E166
Sherman, Larry E185
Shermer, Teresa P126
Sherpa, Chheki P190
Sherr, Richard A835
Sherrard, Roger S. A640
Sherrer, Kendell A170
Sherrill, Gregg M. A813
Sherrill, Stephen C. E33
Sherrill, David E330
Sherrod, Melissa A304
Shervington, Allyson P351
Sherwin, R Lawrence P510
Shetti, Victor A108
Shettles, Antoinette E306
Shetty, Prajwal Shetty Prajwal A108
Shetty, Suraj A198
Shetty, Rajesh A198
Shetty, Yeshwant A199
Shetty, Vishwanath E272
Shetye, Rajesh (Raj) E255
Shevchek, James A401
Shevins, Nicole A692
Shevsky, David A37
Sheynblat, Len A695
Shi, Patricia P364
Shi, Diana P475
Shi, Steven W385
Shi, Chengzhong W431

COMBINED HOOVER'S HANDBOOK INDEX OF EXECUTIVES

A = AMERICAN BUSINESS
E = EMERGING COMPANIES
P = PRIVATE COMPANIES
W = WORLD BUSINESS

Shibano, Nobuo W259
Shibasaki, Kenichi W430
Shibata, Kenichi W292
Shibayama, Yoshinari W127
Shickolovich, Bill P612
Shieh, Brian A74
Shiel, James G. A126
Shields, Stephanie A19
Shields, John A137
Shields, Mike A267
Shields, Joe A452
Shields, Jenny A496
Shields, Steven A719
Shields, Kevin A831
Shields, Richard P93
Shields, Christine P135
Shields, Robert P524
Shields, Ed P595
Shields, Kevin P601
Shields, Charles W. (Charlie) P608
Shields, Dennis P641
Shields, Maria T. E22
Shields, Steven E354
Shiels, Julie P358
Shifflett, Porter A538
Shiffman, David A452
Shiffman, Steven B. (Steve) A692
Shifke, Mark E194
Shiflett, Susan A226
Shiflett, Susan P150
Shifrin, Todd A925
Shifrin, Todd E445
Shiga, Toshiyuki W283
Shigemura, Dean Y. A109
Shigenaga, Dean A. E8
Shih, Richard A137
Shih, Elizabeth A266
Shih, Chin A613
Shih, Elizabeth P181
Shih, Frank W123
Shih, Ming-Hsiung W165
Shihara, Yoshito P534
Shikany, Charlie A236
Shillings, Joe A804
Shillman, Robert J. (Bob) E85
Shiltz, LauraA A711
Shiltz, LauraA P444
Shima, Masato W127
Shimabuku, Corey A109
Shimamura, Gemmei W293
Shimanski, Janette A3
Shimberg, David A P428
Shimick, Debby A255
Shiminske, William E379
Shimizu, Seiichi W51
Shimizu, Hiroshi W279
Shimoda, Dale E219
Shimoe, Kazuo W127
Shimonishi, Yasuhara A813
Shimotori, Etsuo W281
Shimozawa, Scott E319
Shin, Hak Cheol (H.C.) A3
Shin, Angie A326
Shin, Nam A637
Shin, Jung-tak A658
Shin, Hak A688
Shin, Sungwon P645
Shin, Sang-Mun W236
Shindo, Kosei W280
Shindo, Kiyotaka W293
Shine, Daniel P. (Dan) A833
Shine, Dan A833
Shiner, Bill E238
Shinichi, Iguchi P670
Shinkle, Kevin A495
Shinkle, Kevin P282
Shinn, Stephanie A120
Shinn, Tom A167
Shinn, David A463

Shinn, Shannon A761
Shinobe, Osamu W27
Shinohara, Minoru W286
Shinohara, Masashi W360
Shinohara, Hidenori W368
Shinozaki, Kozo W430
Shiokawa, Yorihisa W301
Shiomi, Takao W204
Shipek, Melanie P390
Shipley, Susan Baker A205
Shipley, Susan (Susie) Baker A444
Shipley, Kirk A540
Shipley, Lori A741
Shipley, Marcus B A847
Shipley, Stephen A877
Shipley, Marcus B P606
Shipley, Lori E364
Shipman, Melissa A726
Shipp, Vicki P465
Shipp, Bob P637
Shippey, Mike A924
Shippey, Mike P672
Shirai, Haruo W238
Shiraishi, Toru W292
Shiraji, Kozo W260
Shirakuni, Noriyuki W93
Shirato, Masayoshi P34
Shiratsuka, Shigenori W51
Shireman, Mark D E156
Shirey, Lonnie A89
Shirey, Richard T P229
Shirk, Amber A749
Shirk, Brett A897
Shirk, Amber E367
Shirley, Ray A637
Shirley, Kandy A713
Shirley, Linda A850
Shirley, Bard A852
Shirley, Dennis P316
Shirley, Jasmin P377
Shirley, Lee P546
Shirley, David W P552
Shirley, Douglas E. P563
Shirtcliff, Chris P72
Shisheng, Gu W431
Shishman, Scott A621
Shishman, Scott E311
Shishodia, Nagendra E141
Shisler, Jessica P175
Shivamber, Leon A501
Shivanandan, Monique W40
Shively, Kari P356
Shively, Julianne H E105
Shiver, Kim A522
Shivers, William C. A444
Shlomo, Michael Goldfarb W49
Shmerling, James E. P127
Shmulik, Arbel W49
Shnayder, Boris E133
Shoback, Jacqueline S. A147
Shobuda, Kiyotaka W250
Shockley, Harold A463
Shockley, Jennifer E172
Shoeling, Lanny A494
Shoemaker, Carey A591
Shoemaker, Christopher A872
Shoemaker, Jonathan P26
Shoemaker, Carey P369
Shoemaker, Laura E156
Shoemaker, Leslie L. E402
Shoeman, Rosalie A98
Shoener, Scott A891
Shofe, Allen E126
Shogren, Steve A3
Shohet, Lenny E131
Shokes, Brad A481
Sholy, George A16
Shome, Surojit W130
Shomento, Stacy P84
Shomette, Tom A191
Shomette, Tom P126
Shon, Larry D. De A98
Shon, Harim A203
Shono, Hiroshi W281
Shontere, Daniel A61

Shontere, Jim P492
Shook, John A64
Shook, Rhonda P617
Shoop, James A100
Shoop, James P58
Shoopman, Chuck P638
Shope, Juanita A713
Shoquist, Debora C. A613
Shor, David P389
Shore, Barbara A704
Shore, Melissa P172
Shorett, Carl A175
Shori, Yaakov W163
Shorris, James A528
Short, Andrea G. A1
Short, Joe A63
Short, Sandra A146
Short, Edward T A672
Short, Michael J. (Mike) A728
Short, Marianne D. A876
Short, Brian P119
Short, Steve P203
Short, Jason P539
Short, Jeffrey B P568
Short, Andrea G. E1
Shorten, Dermot A698
Shortridge, Wayne A742
Shortt, Thomas A428
Shortt, Vittoria W114
Shotwell, David F. (Dave) A860
Shoulders, Patrick A. P610
Shoup, Jennifer A575
Shouping, Chai W301
Shovel, Robert A722
Shovlin, Kristen A262
Showers, Mark E. A714
Showman, Brian P306
Shows, Susan A513
Shows, W T P158
Showvaker, James E3
Shrader, Ralph W. A145
Shrader, Kelly A484
Shrair, David A P156
Shreiber, Kathleen P134
Shrewsbury, Amber P227
Shriber, Ryan A135
Shrimpton, Sean A5
Shrivastava, Siddharth A390
Shrivastava, Manish M. A690
Shrivastava, Sanjeev A692
Shroff, Hiten A125
Shrout, Steve A559
Shroyer, Christopher M. (Chris) A335
Shroyer, Christopher M. (Chris) E154
Shrum, Kayse P782
Shrum, Kayse P526
Shryack, Christopher A316
Shryne, Michael A530
Shu, Gu W198
Shu, Michael E450
Shuck, Sarah A150
Shuck, Theresa P523
Shucoski, Patricia P563
Shue, Russell E A140
Shufflebarger, Thomas G P559
Shugart, Christopher M. E322
Shugrue, Vincent A373
Shuh, Monson P168
Shui, Conway A893
Shukla, Anand A179
Shukla, Jayant E226
Shuler, Marsha A320
Shuler, Ken A835
Shulick, Brett A115
Shulick, Brett E38
Shull, Thomas C. (Tom) A80
Shull, Greg A171
Shull, Thomas C. (Tom) P46
Shulman, Doug A111
Shulman, Brett P455
Shultheis, Sherri P445
Shultz, Katherine A314
Shultz, Patti A483
Shultz, Jeff A893
Shultz, Katherine E145

Shuma, Douglas D. A810
Shumaker, Dan A16
Shumann, C R P234
Shumard, Candy A345
Shumard, Candy E165
Shumate, Michael A58
Shumate, Carla E254
Shumel, Brad A710
Shumway, April E264
Shunck, Marybeth A339
Shunck, Marybeth E159
Shupe, Rachel P548
Shupe, Richard E418
Shurniak, William W190
Shurts, Wayne A797
Shurtz, Larry A739
Shustak, Michael A175
Shuster, Bradley M. (Brad) E304
Shute, Malcolm A21
Shute, Ryan A862
Shute, Stephen E. W340
Shuttleworth, Edward L. A351
Shuyama, Andres A327
Shytle, Debbie A36
Si, Stephanie L P161
Siak, Stacey A220
Siak, Stacey P149
Siao, Susan A218
Siarkowski, Tracey A329
Sibadan, Sherilene A137
Sibbald, Andrew E138
Siberio, John A888
Siberio, John E425
Sibley, James M A513
Sibley, Karen P102
Sibley, Miriam P171
Sica, Frank V. A478
Sica, Frank V A496
Sichak, Stephen (Steve) A123
Sichel, Hobart (Bart) A158
Siciliano, Betsy A893
Siciliano, Edward J. (Ed) E271
Sickinger, Lauren A467
Sicola, Tom A550
Sicola, Tom P319
Siddhu, Vivek A530
Siddiqi, Sajid A222
Siddique, Omar P631
Siddiqui, Omer P174
Sideras, John F. P116
Sideris, Harry K. A281
Sidhu, Jay S. A248
Sidhu, Libby P223
Sidhu, Jay S. E107
Sidrys, Paul P126
Siebenborn, Bill A253
Siebenborn, Bill P169
Sieber, Thomas W43
Siebers, Eric P555
Siebert, April P179
Siebert, Eric E126
Siedel, Jay A97
Siedlecki, Sandy E265
Sieg, Andy A107
Siegel, Charles J. A70
Siegel, Steven F A152
Siegel, Steven A152
Siegel, Richard A266
Siegel, Kenneth I. A525
Siegel, Michael A571
Siegel, Andrew A893
Siegel, Erinn A925
Siegel, James P94
Siegel, Steven F P98
Siegel, Steven P98
Siegel, Richard P181
Siegel, Deana P540
Siegel, Laurie E143
Siegel, Eric H. E226
Siegel, Todd E393
Siegel, Erinn E445
Sieger, Michael D. (Mike) A681
Siegert, Thomas P572
Siegfried, Scott P466
Siegl, C P572

Siegmund, Jan A93
Siegrist, Robert N. A162
Siegrist, Robert N. E61
Sielak, George P43
Siemer, Julie P463
Siemon, George P158
Sienkiewicz, Mark A479
Sieracki, Julie A538
Sieradzki, Richard D. (Rick) E396
Siereveld, Ryan P A680
Sierra, Joseph A112
Sierras, Jennifer A791
Sierras, Jennifer P535
Siersdorfer, Dietmar W353
Siess, Thorsten E2
Sievers, Hans Christian P235
Sievers, Glen P412
Sievers, Leanne E113
Sievert, G Michael A800
Sievert, Deana P591
Sieving, Charles E. A354
Sieving, Charles E. A597
Siewert, Patrick A97
Sifer, Joseph F. (Joe) A145
Sifer, Joe A145
Sigal, Jonathan A676
Sigal, Jonathan E338
Siggeman, Carlee P456
Sigler, Jon A739
Sigler, John J P459
Sigler, Russell P459
Sigler, Lee Lanning P459
Sigman, Brian C. A20
Sigmon, William L A51
Sigmon, Vaughn A171
Sigmon, William P58
Sigmund, William A123
Signorille, Mary P2
Signorino, Charles A179
Signorio, Mark A506
Sigrist, Thomas E433
Sih, Gil A695
Siilasmaa, Risto W284
Siino, Joseph A98
Siino, Joseph E326
Sikand, Yash P393
Sikand, Sarika E419
Sikela, Jozef W156
Sikora, Justin A255
Sikora, Kaz A606
Sikorski, Fred J. E264
Silagy, Eric E. A354
Silagy, Eric E. A597
Silbaugh, Jason A483
Silberberg, Allison P137
Silberhorn, Tara A635
Silberman, David A893
Silberschlag, Kirstin A887
Silberstein, Edward P625
Silbert, Mark A61
Silcock, Chris A423
Silcock, Christopher A423
Silfa, Betty A203
Silfee, Keith A368
Silfen, Lori P337
Silgen, Karen A877
Silitch, Nicholas C. (Nick) A686
Silitch, Nick A686
Silk, Robert P383
Sill, Scott A668
Sillars, Laura A449
Sillars, Laura E221
Silliman, Craig L. A890
Sills, Stephen J. A32
Sills, James P83
Silos, Richard A16
Silta, Bill P649
Silungan, Chris E123
Silva, Nicole A140
Silva, Amanda A198
Silva, Stephen A198
Silva, Francisco A. Aristeguieta A203
Silva, Marc A204
Silva, Mona A242
Silva, Rodrigo A352

Silva, Joseph M A414
Silva, Rebecca A519
Silva, Eduardo A571
Silva, Anthony A899
Silva, Joseph M P236
Silva, Jan P611
Silva, Eduardo Padilla W164
Silva, Carlos Nuno Gomes da W169
Silva, Filipe Cris--stomo W169
Silva, Randy E106
Silva, Nishan E257
Silvagni, Anthony J. P390
Silveira, Roberto A658
Silver, Mark A829
Silver, Richard P478
Silver, Mark P589
Silver, Christopher P627
Silver, Rebecca E427
Silveri, Debbie A737
Silveri, Debbie E361
Silveria, Richard P95
Silverman, Rob A145
Silverman, Steve A320
Silverman, Jan P23
Silverman, Barry J. P390
Silverman, Daniel C P494
Silvermintz, Sharon A849
Silvernail, Andrew A790
Silvers, David A1
Silvers, J. B. P576
Silvers, David E1
Silvers, Gregory K. (Greg) E134
Silvers, Daniel E177
Silverstein, Martin B. A385
Silverstein, Pamela A692
Silverstein, Ray A780
Silverstein, Joon A801
Silverstein, Marni P173
Silverstein, Douglas M. P386
Silvester, Mike A740
Silvester, Peter A833
Silvestri, Jennifer P546
Silvey, Jerome C. (Jerry) E387
Silvi, Marcus P392
Silvia, Jason A465
Silvia, Phil A793
Silvino, Ant-́nio Rubens Silva W303
Silvis, Harry J A909
Silvis, Harry J E436
Silwa, Robert A929
Silwa, Robert E449
Sim, Edward P63
Simancas, Jose de Jes--s Valdez W19
Simard, Curtis C. A118
Simard, Curtis C. E40
Simberg, Bruce F. E149
Simcoe, Suma A571
Simensen, Hanne W289
Simeone, Giovanni A108
Simeone, Robert A522
Simerly, Rick P260
Simermeyer, Elizabeth A. (Beth) A289
Simhon, Gail P304
Siminoff, Laura A. P546
Siminski, Mike A552
Siminski, Mike E275
Simio, Frank P206
Simitian, Vahe E8
Simitz, Robert A457
Simkhayeva, Liliya A484
Simkins, Amber P625
Simko, David A314
Simko, Chris A893
Simko, David E145
Simkowitz, Daniel A. (Dan) A574
Simmelink, Scott P10
Simmons, Paul A104
Simmons, Angela A255
Simmons, Patrick A376
Simmons, Jodi A462
Simmons, Jeffrey N. (Jeff) A517
Simmons, Tammy A713
Simmons, Brad A787
Simmons, Eileen A883
Simmons, Gary A887

Simmons, Harris H. A940
Simmons, Sharon P101
Simmons, Paul P116
Simmons, Jodi P256
Simmons, Leslie P295
Simmons, Tj P303
Simmons, Elizabeth H. P339
Simmons, Eileen P644
Simmons, John V. E51
Simmons-Oliver, Cheryl P296
Simms, Constance A347
Simms, David A465
Simms, James A654
Simms, Susan P411
Simms, Constance E168
Simoes, Antonio W189
Simon, Jon A218
Simon, Lynn T. A228
Simon, Mindy A232
Simon, Laura A248
Simon, Grigore A595
Simon, John R. A659
Simon, Steve A716
Simon, David A761
Simon, Deborah A761
Simon, Larry A762
Simon, Marianne A824
Simon, Andrea A893
Simon, Sam P52
Simon, Mary P203
Simon, Brian P245
Simon, Debbie P258
Simon, Lou Anna K. P339
Simon, Don P382
Simon, Jolynn P486
Simon, Linda P518
Simon, Marianne P562
Simon, Keri P633
Simon, Angel W366
Simon, Marc E33
Simon, Jonathan H. (Jon) E53
Simon, Laura E107
Simon, William E114
Simon, Ronald I. E124
Simon, David E245
Simon, Herb E250
Simon, Michael K. E260
Simon, Roberto R. E440
Simonds, Michael Q. A882
Simonds, John E265
Simone, Alan Del P662
Simoneau, Ron P491
Simonelli, Lorenzo A374
Simonet, Helene E359
Simonetti, Beth E. A809
Simonian, Michael E429
Simonich, Brent A283
Simonitsch, Allen A921
Simons, Doyle A352
Simons, Marilyn A829
Simons, James H A829
Simons, Sharon A835
Simons, Doyle R. A918
Simons, Marilyn P589
Simons, James H P589
Simonte, Michael K. A49
Simonton, Mark A738
Simpson, Dean A16
Simpson, Austin A113
Simpson, Vincent A145
Simpson, Barry N. A215
Simpson, Richard A330
Simpson, Shelley A442
Simpson, Kristina A491
Simpson, Jay A562
Simpson, Kathryn A608
Simpson, David L. A716
Simpson, Gwynn A776
Simpson, Stewart A789
Simpson, Julie A850
Simpson, Steve A933
Simpson, Joshua P35
Simpson, Jennie P187
Simpson, Jennifer P382
Simpson, Austin E36

Simpson, Jason E80
Simpson, Richard E152
Simpson, Wendy L. E261
Sims, Colleen A107
Sims, C. Randall (Randy) A426
Sims, Heidi A444
Sims, John V. A467
Sims, Robert H A632
Sims, Nicole A726
Sims, Dave A734
Sims, Scott A741
Sims, Damon A828
SIMS, SUZANNE P171
Sims, Dominique P505
Sims, Damon P584
Sims, Mike E179
Sims, C. Randall (Randy) E213
Sims, Scott E364
Simson, Marck A86
Simson, Thomas H. A150
Simson, Marck E27
Simson, Thomas H. E50
Simuro, Frank E98
Sin, Cp A914
Sinagra, Jack P613
Sinatra, Kim A930
Sinchak, David P610
Sinclair, Stephen A198
Sinclair, Julia A641
Sinclair, Donald A713
Sinclair, Rebecca P35
Sinclair, Shannon P253
Sinclair, Julia P407
Sindel, Mehmet W18
Sinden, Jessie A390
Sinden, Shaun A809
Sindoni, James A325
Sines, Ronald E358
Sinesi, Polly A500
Sinewgz, Larry P96
Sing, Goh Ing W424
Singaraju, Prasanna A804
Singelais, B. C. W212
Singer, David A123
Singer, Lori A243
Singer, David A403
Singer, Gadi A460
Singer, Lori A544
Singer, Jolie P368
Singer, Samantha P556
Singer, Janet E P673
Singer, Michael E101
Singh, Rajinder P. (Raj) A114
Singh, Jennifer A137
Singh, Munjeet A145
Singh, Zorawar Biri A198
Singh, Inder A199
Singh, Charan A203
Singh, Manjit A207
Singh, Dk A232
Singh, Sukhvinder A436
Singh, Harmeet A505
Singh, Harmit J. A514
Singh, Harmit J. A516
Singh, Vikram A527
Singh, Jasraj A538
Singh, Bobby A575
Singh, Shaminder A654
Singh, Sanjay A735
Singh, Ajay A897
Singh, Sukhwinder P15
Singh, Gurbir P47
Singh, Rajinder P276
Singh, Ankush P286
Singh, Harmit J. P293
Singh, Harry P364
Singh, Vijayeta P383
Singh, Sabi P629
Singh, Rajinder P. (Raj) E37
Singh, Pally E80
Singh, Anant E143
Singh, Chandrashekhar E290
Singla, Anjali P17
Singler, Craig A465
Singleton, J. Barton A796

COMBINED HOOVER'S HANDBOOK INDEX OF EXECUTIVES

```
A = AMERICAN BUSINESS
E = EMERGING COMPANIES
P = PRIVATE COMPANIES
W = WORLD BUSINESS
```

Singleton, John Knox P253
Singleton, Kali P282
Singleton, Palmer C P354
Singleton, H. Wells P390
Singleton, Arnold R. P501
Singleton, Ray E119
Singleton, J. Barton E397
Singley, Eric E450
Sinha, Santosh A205
Sinha, Dharmendra Kumar A216
Sinha, Sharat A897
Sinha, Manish E22
Sinko, Christopher A151
Sinko, Jim A756
Sinks, Patrick A561
Sinnard, Pat A56
Sinner, Anna P205
Sinner, Steve E438
Sinnott, Eamonn A460
Sinnott, Justin A747
Sinnott, Carrie E179
Sinnott, Robert (Rob) E423
Sinopoli, Angelo P430
Sinowitz, Paul A562
Sinz, Eric A232
Sipe, Adrienne A343
Sipe, Barb A674
Sipe, Adrienne E164
Sipes, Kevin A718
Sipes, Kevin E354
Sipser, Michael P314
Siqing, Chen W72
Siracusa, Giorgio A680
Siracusano, Luciano E447
Siragusa, Paul A660
Siragusa, Paul P416
Sirakos, William A246
Sirakos, William E105
Sirbu, Pete A60
Sirianni, Frank P206
Sirimane, Krishan A676
Sirimane, Krishan E338
Sirkin, Clive A487
Sirkin, David A692
Sirko, Nancy P588
Sirleaf, James P307
Sirmon, Gary L. A116
Sirmon, Gary L. E39
Sirois, Bonnie P96
Sirois, Charles W85
Sironen, Jason P529
Sirota, Gennady A198
Sirota, Bruce A482
Sirridge, Susan A168
Sirstins, Max P184
Sisisky, Richard L P503
Sisitsky, Todd B. P475
Sisneros, Tim A184
Sisney, Dan P532
Sisson, William G. P64
Sistek, James E394
Sistine, Teriann Van A86
Sistine, Teriann Van E27
Sistovaris, Violet G. A600
Sites, Larry P280
Sitherwood, Suzanne P510
Sitohang, Helman W120
Sitorus, Martua W424
Sitzmann, Edith W231
Siu, Wing A120
Siu, Albert P248
Siu, Albert P351
Siu, Shawn W98
Siva, Chokkalingam P633
Sivadasan, Babu E131
Sivagnanam, Kalyana W283
Sivamurthy, Krupa A658
Sivaram, Siva A914
Sivignon, Pierre-Jean W88

Siwek, Janusz A425
Six, Rob A97
Sizemore, Mark A683
Sizemore, Vicki P60
Sizemore, Stephen P162
Sizemore, Jay P228
Sizemore, Mark P431
Sjodin, Cara A877
Sjonell, Peter A702
Sjulin, Susie A258
Sjulin, Renee P103
Skabelund, Hoyt A117
Skabelund, Hoyt P61
Skaggs, Amy L A781
Skaggs, Michael D. (Mike) A815
Skaggs, Sean A884
Skaggs, Stephen A. (Steve) P53
Skaggs, Stephen E86
Skains, Tom A281
Skala, P. Justin A218
Skala, P Justin A218
Skala, Peter A218
Skalnik, Alicia A250
Skandalis, Chris A219
Skandalis, Chris E87
Skarbek, Tabetha A6
Skarda, Ed A934
Skarulis, Patricia C. P325
Skaugen, Kirk B. W234
Skeans, Tracy A937
Skeath, Carter A893
Skeats, Lawrence N. A629
Skeete, Hannah A936
Skelley, Sean A750
Skelly, Mame A155
Skelly, Mame E54
Skelsey, Maral P322
Skelton, Bryndon A222
Skelton, William A421
Skiba, Dennis A538
Skidmore, Timothy A194
Skidmore, Douglas A196
Skidmore, Camde A909
Skidmore, Timothy P133
Skidmore, Constance E89
Skidmore, Camde E436
Skiendzielewski, John P214
Skiendzielewski, John P569
Skiles, Todd A735
Skillern, Raejeanne A460
Skillin, Chris A452
Skillman, Rebecca A621
Skillman, Rebecca E312
Skinner, Elizabeth A325
Skinner, Greg A600
Skinner, Paul A734
Skinner, James A. (Jim) A900
Skinner, Jessica P227
Skinner, Claudia P519
Skinner, Stephen P531
Skinner, Brooks P595
Skinner, A. Chester E94
Skirde, Kevin A896
Skivington, Stephanie A909
Skivington, Stephanie E436
Sklarski, Kate A161
Sklenar, John P230
Skluth, Nancy P333
Skobel, Mark A887
Skoglund, William B. A623
Skoglund, William B. E313
Skogsbergh, James H A15
Skogsbergh, James H P7
Skogsbergh, James H P8
Skokan, Mike A447
Skokan, Mike P247
Skoko, Goran E143
Skolfield, Melissa P585
Skolits, Adele M. E370
Skoog, Keith A204
Skopick, Richard A181
Skopick, Richard E70
Skorkowsky, Patrick P140
Skoro, A T P280
Skorton, David J. P497

Skory, John E. A351
Skory, John E P562
Skou, Soren W1
Skoufalos, Yannis A679
Skov, Thomas A379
Skovran, Patrick A147
Skovronsky, Daniel (Dan) A518
Skrabak, Rachel A922
Skrabak, Rachel P671
Skrivanos, Stephen F P85
Skrocki, Denise P616
Skrzypek, Leslaw P638
Skubis, Ryan A726
Skudutis, Tom W244
Skulina, James A842
Skuraton, Renee A646
Skuraton, Renee E324
Skurbe, Barton A881
Skurbe, Barton E421
Skyler, Edward A203
Slabach, Christopher A346
Slabach, Christopher E166
Slabosz, Lawrence A686
Slack, Diane A741
Slack, Karoliina P471
Slack, Diane E364
Slader, Ami A224
Slaff, Morgan A711
Slaff, Morgan P444
Slager, Donald W. (Don) A721
Slagle, Dennis R. (Denny) W420
Slak, Tom A857
Slanina, John A180
Slate, Larry A140
Slater, Sara A137
Slater, Blake D A195
Slater, David A279
Slater, Catherine I. A467
Slater, Catherine I A467
Slater, Bill A559
Slater, Todd A. A624
Slatkin, Diane A167
Slaton, Shawn P126
Slattery, Steve A198
Slattery, Megan A421
Slaugh, Linden A596
Slaughter, Stephanie A179
Slaughter, Nicole A228
Slaughter, Roy A855
Slaughter, James G. P461
Slaughter, Veronica P620
Slavik, James A394
Slavin, Peter L. A641
Slavin, Peter L. P407
Slavin, Kevin P519
Slavin, Peter L. P574
Slawson, John W. E383
Slaybaugh, Chris A922
Slaybaugh, Chris P671
Sledjeski, Stephanie E131
Sleece, Kelly A115
Sleece, Kelly E38
Sleep, Darryl A65
Sleight, Barbara A658
Sleiman, Adham A145
Slenker, Kirk P493
Slentz, Jayden A340
Slentz, Andrew A418
Slentz, Jayden E161
Slessor, Michael (Mikie) E177
Slevin, Linda E138
Sleyster, Scott G. A686
Slezak, Lee A855
Slider, Monica E392
Slifer, Celeste A33
Slifer, Celeste P24
Slifka, Eric A387
Slifka, Andrew A387
Slifka, Richard A388
Sliger, Jeff A604
Slipy, Scott D A475
Slivinsky, Barry A11
Sliwowski, Michael A753
Sloan, Brian A56
Sloan, David A195

Sloan, Rob A289
Sloan, Rodney L. A413
Sloan, Scott A419
Sloan, Joshua A482
Sloan, Garrett A747
Sloan, Kevin A798
Sloan, Gayle P467
Sloan, Michelle E170
Sloan, Jeffrey E174
Sloan, Rodney L. E205
Sloan, Stuart M. E326
Sloane, Steele A179
Sloane, Barry R. A183
Sloane, Marshall M. A183
Sloane, Scott P155
Sloane, Barry R. E74
Sloane, Marshall M. E74
Sloane, Edward G. (Ed) E156
Sloat, Julie A51
Slobasky, Renee P664
Slocum, Michael C. A166
Slocumb, Travis A706
Slominski, Donald D. (Don) P320
Slomsky, David P531
Slone, Reuben E A13
Slone, Reuben A900
Slootskiy, Alex E329
Slotkin, Judy S. E372
Slotnick, Dianne E282
Slotnik, Joseph J. A153
Slotnik, Joseph J. E52
Sloup, Michael A140
Slovin, Bruce E372
Slubowski, Michael A847
Slubowski, Michael P606
Sluka, Joseph P445
Sluka, Joe P514
Slusher, John F A599
Slutsky, Lorie A A590
Sly, Patrick J. P465
Slyconish, John A784
Smaglick, Dorothy A885
Smagula, William A303
Smail, James A314
Smail, James E145
Small, William J. (Bill) A339
Small, Carolyn A409
Small, Chip A418
Small, Sheila A522
Small, Brown A684
Small, Rob A842
Small, David A889
Small, Jeff A924
Small, David R. P433
Small, J. Radford P547
Small, Susan P583
Small, Deborah A P591
Small, Jeff P672
Small, William J. (Bill) E159
Smallets, Beatrice A530
Smalley, John P315
Smallhouse, Cathy E35
Smalls, Kandi P168
Smallwood, Ricky A799
Smart, George M. A351
Smart, Robert A512
Smart, Denise T. P551
Smart, Justin W. E245
Smeaton, Paul W373
Smedley, Dave A1
Smedley, Dave E1
Smedley, Robert E330
Smedt, Mark De W7
Smedt, Rodney E316
Smet, John H A50
Smet, John H P31
Smet, John P572
Smid, Tony A36
Smiddy, Craig R. A622
Smiley, Tom A431
Smiley, Anwar A491
Smiley, Josh A518
Smiley, Alice P131
Smilie, Karen A606
Smilo, Bettina P74
```

HOOVER'S HANDBOOK OF EMERGING COMPANIES 2020
```

COMBINED HOOVER'S HANDBOOK INDEX OF EXECUTIVES

Smit, Rod P343
Smith, Jen A6
Smith, Jeffrey C. A13
Smith, Rob A21
Smith, Lucinda A21
Smith, Ronald A28
Smith, Mary Pat A33
Smith, Karen A34
Smith, Elizabeth A36
Smith, Larry A36
Smith, A Wade A51
Smith, Stephan A57
Smith, Wayne A58
Smith, Olivia A58
Smith, Ernie A60
Smith, Rodney A A68
Smith, Donna N. A85
Smith, Heidi A86
Smith, David A87
Smith, Michele A89
Smith, Chip A90
Smith, Guy H A90
Smith, L. Duane A91
Smith, Martyn R. A98
Smith, Jennifer A98
Smith, Tyler A105
Smith, Julie A108
Smith, Jason A109
Smith, Joann A114
Smith, Mike A115
Smith, Ryan A117
Smith, A A117
Smith, John C. (Jack) A121
Smith, Larry A123
Smith, Jeffrey A. A135
Smith, Rob A135
Smith, Taylor A139
Smith, Gregory D. (Greg) A140
Smith, Kim A140
Smith, Robert A145
Smith, Drew A155
Smith, William G. (Bill) A165
Smith, Darla A167
Smith, Phillip A180
Smith, Jim A183
Smith, Chris A187
Smith, Kevin A196
Smith, Claire A205
Smith, Peter F. A211
Smith, William F A213
Smith, Brian J. A215
Smith, Douglas A222
Smith, Allan A224
Smith, James G A224
Smith, Barbara R A225
Smith, Wayne T. A228
Smith, P. Paul A228
Smith, Ken A232
Smith, Brenda A246
Smith, Sam A248
Smith, Samuel H A248
Smith, Richard P. (Rick) A253
Smith, Michael A259
Smith, Patrick A260
Smith, Joanne A262
Smith, Anne A262
Smith, Molly A287
Smith, Bob A296
Smith, Raiford A296
Smith, Robert C. A301
Smith, Bobby A301
Smith, Ron A303
Smith, Lane A319
Smith, Edward C. A319
Smith, Frederick W. (Fred) A323
Smith, Carol A324
Smith, Sam A326
Smith, Serena A327
Smith, Lindsey A334
Smith, Linda A335
Smith, Christy A343
Smith, Rita K A345
Smith, Dale A. A349
Smith, Lee M. A353
Smith, Diane A368

Smith, Robert E. (Rob) A373
Smith, Donna A378
Smith, Vickie A379
Smith, Jason A379
Smith, Roger C. A389
Smith, Kimberley A389
Smith, Gregory A389
Smith, Sarah E. A390
Smith, Bryan R A409
Smith, Elizabeth A423
Smith, Mark A432
Smith, Gordon A436
Smith, Mary A444
Smith, Joyce A444
Smith, Michael S. A446
Smith, Amanda A449
Smith, Dan A452
Smith, Lee A452
Smith, Mallory A456
Smith, Stacy J. A460
Smith, David A465
Smith, Dennis A467
Smith, Julieta A469
Smith, Philip A. A470
Smith, Brad D. A471
Smith, Joseph A479
Smith, Evamarie A482
Smith, Gordon A. A483
Smith, Kyle A484
Smith, Sara A491
Smith, Mark A494
Smith, Steve A500
Smith, Jeff A501
Smith, Ryan A512
Smith, Geoffrey A512
Smith, Elizabeth A A513
Smith, Mark A521
Smith, Jared A522
Smith, Bert A523
Smith, Dudley A524
Smith, Jay A526
Smith, Barry M. A532
Smith, Craig S. A537
Smith, Allan A540
Smith, Michael R. A547
Smith, Deborah A550
Smith, Allen A552
Smith, Martin A552
Smith, Sarah A552
Smith, Bradford L A565
Smith, James A575
Smith, Donnie A579
Smith, Susan A580
Smith, Lyle A584
Smith, Teresa A600
Smith, Tricia D. A602
Smith, Carl A608
Smith, David A612
Smith, Gerry P. A620
Smith, Daniel T. (Dan) A635
Smith, Kent A636
Smith, Linda A640
Smith, Allen L. A641
Smith, Doug A651
Smith, Robert A657
Smith, David A658
Smith, Jason A658
Smith, Allan A659
Smith, Richard J A663
Smith, Harmon D. A690
Smith, Beth A704
Smith, Linda Larkin A704
Smith, Kristin A704
Smith, Eugene A706
Smith, Richard A A707
Smith, Richard A. A708
Smith, Monty A708
Smith, Ronald G. (Ronnie) A712
Smith, Scott A. A716
Smith, Matthew L. (Matt) A716
Smith, Phil A717
Smith, Susan A718
Smith, Shawn B A727
Smith, Abbie A735
Smith, Emily A735

Smith, Follin E A735
Smith, Shawn A736
Smith, Darryl A742
Smith, Susan F. A760
Smith, Christopher A761
Smith, Terry A762
Smith, B. Scott A766
Smith, O. Bruton A767
Smith, David B. A767
Smith, Zeta A779
Smith, Maria A780
Smith, Park A787
Smith, Todd A791
Smith, Michael A796
Smith, Brian A797
Smith, Stephen A797
Smith, Rodger A797
Smith, Kristin A798
Smith, Craig A799
Smith, Catherine R. (Cathy) A804
Smith, Ray A819
Smith, Dennis A820
Smith, Mike A827
Smith, Anthony H A833
Smith, Tony A833
Smith, Kim A835
Smith, Kevin C. A844
Smith, Richard P. A847
Smith, Bethany L A852
Smith, Bethany A852
Smith, Dustin A859
Smith, Lisa A859
Smith, Craige L. A865
Smith, Orin C. A880
Smith, Jeff A882
Smith, Geriann A888
Smith, Dan A888
Smith, Karen A891
Smith, S. Dawn A897
Smith, Gregory L. (Greg) A901
Smith, Eileen A902
Smith, Catherine A902
Smith, Linda S A904
Smith, James C. (Jim) A906
Smith, Kerrie A909
Smith, Anna A922
Smith, Drew A924
Smith, Christine A925
Smith, Jeff S. A927
Smith, Paul V. A934
Smith, Jennifer A. A940
Smith, David P7
Smith, Mary Pat P24
Smith, Caitlyn P25
Smith, Lisa P26
Smith, Stephan P33
Smith, Rosi P45
Smith, Judy P49
Smith, David P50
Smith, Chip P51
Smith, Guy H P51
Smith, Ginny P51
Smith, Lamont P54
Smith, Jodi P56
Smith, Ryan P61
Smith, A P61
Smith, Andrew P74
Smith, Stuart P83
Smith, Taylor P93
Smith, Nate P93
Smith, Catherine P97
Smith, Jared M P101
Smith, Shane P102
Smith, Patricia P108
Smith, Charles P160
Smith, Rockwell E. (Rocky) P166
Smith, Rockwell P166
Smith, Richard P. (Rick) P169
Smith, Annette P170
Smith, Sean P173
Smith, Barbara A P173
Smith, Larry P173
Smith, Stephanie P175
Smith, Howard P194
Smith, Jim P195

Smith, Robert P201
Smith, Stephanie P203
Smith, Jane P205
Smith, Christina P212
Smith, Dolois P242
Smith, Lachlan P244
Smith, Brian P246
Smith, Doug P255
Smith, Eugene P261
Smith, Robert P276
Smith, Steven E P281
Smith, Randy Smith Randy P295
Smith, Quiara P302
Smith, Wes P316
Smith, Jeralyn Waller P318
Smith, Amy M P330
Smith, Allen P337
Smith, Alex P344
Smith, Diane R P349
Smith, Brian P351
Smith, David A. P356
Smith, Donald P356
Smith, P P356
Smith, Harold P358
Smith, Doug P363
Smith, Lawrence G. P382
Smith, Steve P383
Smith, Debra P384
Smith, Steven P386
Smith, Ryan P391
Smith, Jim P395
Smith, Kent P403
Smith, Hank P404
Smith, Rob P406
Smith, Allen L. P407
Smith, Van P421
Smith, Eddie P422
Smith, Carole P425
Smith, Suzanne P428
Smith, Michelle Taylor P430
Smith, Martha P430
Smith, Andrew O P433
Smith, Randy P443
Smith, David P450
Smith, Shawn B P453
Smith, Shawn P460
Smith, Linda P463
Smith, Jonathan P465
Smith, Sheryl P465
Smith, Meg P466
Smith, Cydni P467
Smith, Brenda P484
Smith, Tim P489
Smith, Andrea P505
Smith, Astria P505
Smith, Stephen P505
Smith, Kenneth A. (Ken) P510
Smith, Todd P535
Smith, Devonna P546
Smith, Dillon P549
Smith, Ray P549
Smith, Joanne P551
Smith, Elyse P554
Smith, Chad P558
Smith, Larry T P558
Smith, Jill P559
Smith, Greg P561
Smith, Amy P566
Smith, Julia P588
Smith, Mo P596
Smith, Jennifer R. P600
Smith, Richard J. P600
Smith, Elizabeth P604
Smith, Rebekah P607
Smith, Chris P615
Smith, John P637
Smith, Andrew M P638
Smith, Sarah P639
Smith, Orin C. P640
Smith, Brent P641
Smith, Clinton P646
Smith, Bob P657
Smith, James E. P664
Smith, Sharon P P666
Smith, Anna P671

COMBINED HOOVER'S HANDBOOK INDEX OF EXECUTIVES

A = AMERICAN BUSINESS
E = EMERGING COMPANIES
P = PRIVATE COMPANIES
W = WORLD BUSINESS

Smith, Wayne T. W59
Smith, Matt W80
Smith, Gary W84
Smith, Ian W109
Smith, Keith J. W342
Smith, Mark W364
Smith, Kris W373
Smith, Martin W426
Smith, Mark E21
Smith, Donna N. E26
Smith, Heidi E27
Smith, David E28
Smith, L. Duane E29
Smith, Patrick W. (Rick) E30
Smith, Tyler E34
Smith, Joann E36
Smith, Mike E37
Smith, Drew E54
Smith, Karen E73
Smith, Mark E73
Smith, Jim E74
Smith, David R. E75
Smith, Peter F. E83
Smith, Daniel E. E94
Smith, Daniel E96
Smith, Steven J. E98
Smith, Brenda E105
Smith, Sam E107
Smith, Samuel H E107
Smith, Roland E115
Smith, Barry E127
Smith, Lindsey E153
Smith, Linda E155
Smith, Jerome R. (Jerry) E156
Smith, Christy E164
Smith, Rita K E166
Smith, Gerald E168
Smith, Lee M. E173
Smith, Bob E192
Smith, Hugh C. E211
Smith, Mark E216
Smith, Amanda E221
Smith, Mallory E228
Smith, Steven R. (Steve) E241
Smith, Jim E249
Smith, Dan F. E249
Smith, Marsha E255
Smith, Brian C E267
Smith, Allen E276
Smith, Martin E276
Smith, Sarah E276
Smith, Matt E282
Smith, Marcus E290
Smith, Susan E292
Smith, Shane E316
Smith, Brian E317
Smith, Samuel E318
Smith, Doug E329
Smith, Greg E347
Smith, Phil E351
Smith, Susan E354
Smith, Cheri E357
Smith, Susan F. E374
Smith, Michael E397
Smith, Richard P. E410
Smith, W. David E414
Smith, David E414
Smith, William E414
Smith, Craige L. E416
Smith, Geriann E425
Smith, Dan E425
Smith, Howard W. E433
Smith, James C. (Jim) E434
Smith, Kerrie E436
Smith, Melissa D. E440
Smith, Larry E448
Smith-Acuna, Shelly P146
Smith-anoa'i, Tiffany A893

Smith-Calascibetta, Patricia A15
Smith-Calascibetta, Patricia P7
Smith-Hill, Janet P390
Smither, Chris A21
Smithers, Barbara A8
Smithey, Regina P649
Smithhart, Will A717
Smithhart, Will E351
Smithson, Heidi A346
Smithson, Heidi E167
Smithwick, Michael P477
Smithy, M Deron A713
Smits, Lynn A86
Smits, Robert P215
Smits, Lynn E27
Smoak, Shannon E381
Smoke, Tony A28
Smolinski, Brian E293
Smookler, Eric A922
Smookler, Eric P671
Smoot, Raymond D. (Ray) A91
Smoot, Steve A462
Smoot, Rob A897
Smoot, Steve P256
Smoot, Raymond D. (Ray) E29
Smothers, Kevin P7
Smotrys, Ken E245
Smrtic, Mark A67
Smucker, Darrell A314
Smucker, Mark T. A765
Smucker, Richard K. A765
Smucker, Darrell E145
Smuda, Mike A394
Smuland, Brad P333
Smullen, F W P117
Smulski, Gregory A778
Smyklo, Mike A893
Smylie, John P496
Smyre, Calvin A796
Smyre, Calvin E397
Smyrnios, Nicholas P616
Smyth, Cameron A571
Smyth, Maureen A578
Smyth, Declan E232
Snabe, Jim Hagemann W1
Snail, Timothy E102
Snapper, Suzanne D. E127
Snarr, Jack P389
Snead, Ron A281
Snead, Mark A393
Snedaker, Dianne A349
Snee, James P. A434
Snel, Michael A37
Snel, Michael P27
Snell, Lindsay A835
Snelling, Dawn A530
Sng, Yih A813
Snider, Maureen A5
Snider, Dawn A323
Snider, Kim A327
Snider, Diane P7
Snider, Eric P492
Snider, Michael E255
Sniffen, John A51
Sniffin, Ted A145
Snively, Melissa P240
Snoddy, Aimee A782
Snoddy, Brelinda A893
Snoddy, Aimee P526
Snodgrass, Mark A549
Snodgrass, Robert A608
Snodgrass, Greg P552
Snodgres, Jon K. E353
Snow, Michael A91
Snow, Tracey A114
Snow, Ola A170
Snow, Kristine A. (Kris) A198
Snow, Lary A248
Snow, Scott A850
Snow, Stuart P168
Snow, Kimberly P420
Snow, Wayne W306
Snow, Michael E29
Snow, Tracey E37
Snow, Lary E107

Snow, F. Philip E143
Snow, Brad E272
Snowden, Ed A75
Snowden, Joseph I. A675
Snowden, Joseph I. P428
Snowden, Lori E77
Snustad, John P30
Snyder, Scott A63
Snyder, Mary A111
Snyder, Ike A364
Snyder, Tammy A367
Snyder, Amy A368
Snyder, Scott A368
Snyder, Kyle A371
Snyder, Matt A388
Snyder, Matt A397
Snyder, Bill A434
Snyder, Deanna A438
Snyder, Tim A440
Snyder, Judy A488
Snyder, Rob A621
Snyder, Jay A809
Snyder, Mitch A821
Snyder, Jane A922
Snyder, Chandra P38
Snyder, Barbara R. P116
Snyder, Kyle P213
Snyder, Kenneth P272
Snyder, Tammy P430
Snyder, Meredith P626
Snyder, Jane P671
Snyder, Rob E311
So, Stacy A284
So, Stacy E120
Soab, Alan P281
Soares, Denise C. A588
Soares, David A758
Soares, Habiba A933
Soares, Denise C. P365
Soares, David P372
Soave, John S. E103
Sobanet, Henry P148
Sobas, Laurie A170
Sobecki, Lisa P605
Sobel, Brian M. A110
Sobel, Aaron A525
Soben, Gary A574
Sobey, Christopher A925
Sobey, Mark E86
Sobey, Christopher E445
Sobic, Dan A636
Soble, Dan E427
Sobson, Carol L A609
Sobson, Carol L P387
Sobti, Sanjiv A115
Sobti, Sanjiv E38
Socarras, Aleida E78
Socha, Bernie P571
Sochacki, Thomas L P666
Socia, Robert E A378
Sock, Shannon A556
Sock, Shannon P328
Sodano, Kerrie A25
Sodano, Kerrie P14
Soderberg, John L. A315
Soderblom, Len A606
Soderburg, John L. A315
Soderholm, Glenn W129
Soderstrom, Gerry A528
Soderstrom, Gerry P479
Sodo, Michael E189
Sodomick, Karen A827
Sodomick, Karen P580
Soete, Elizabeth P175
Soetenga, Deanne A727
Soetenga, Deanne P453
Soffer, Patricia G P518
Sofia, Ivie Blussette P597
Sofish, Greg A756
Sofko, Gary A544
Sogan, Lance A51
Sogegian, Bob A145
Soghier, Lamia P130
Sognefest, Peter W. E225
Sohm, Frederick (Rick) E383

Sohn, Mike K. A463
Sohn, Regina P405
Sohn, Young P645
Sohn, Stephanie P656
Soifer, B. Thomas P107
Soiffer, Robert J. P172
Soike, Dave P424
Soirat, Arnaud W325
Soirat, Arnaud W327
Sokn, Erick A824
Sokn, Erick P562
Sokobin, Jonathan S. P202
Sokola, Thomas A371
Sokola, Thomas P213
Sokolov, Lisa A592
Sokolov, Richard S. (Rick) A761
Sokolov, Lisa P370
Sola, Jure A742
Solanski, David P234
Solari, Ida A147
Solazzo, Mark J. P382
Solberg, Jeff A399
Solberg, Jeffrey M A399
Solberg, Jeff P223
Solberg, Jeffrey M P223
Soldi, Marinella A270
Soldo, Stephen P462
Soler, Leslie A409
Soler, Leslie A800
Soles, Darren P214
Solfest, Glenn A36
Solheim, Leif A77
Soliman, Fady A722
Solis, Andrea A621
Solis, Raul P168
Solis, Jose P604
Solis, Robert P631
Solis, Andrea E312
Solk, Steven (Steve) A200
Sollars, Pat A645
Sollitto, Vince E450
Solms, Bill E342
Solomita, Mike A198
Solomon, J. Stuart A51
Solomon, John A72
Solomon, David M. A390
Solomon, Rob A417
Solomon, Natan A505
Solomon, Victor A550
Solomon, Lesley P172
Solomon, Sarah P172
Solomon, Lisa P299
Solomon, Jeffrey M. E101
Solomon, Scott E102
Solomon, Sharon E126
Solomon, Kim E226
Solon, Kenneth S. A519
Solotar, Joan A137
Solow, Jason A786
Solow, Barbara E126
Solow, Jason E387
Sol-s, Oscar Von Hauske W26
Somanchi, Subba P326
Somashekar, Vinay A484
Somasundaram, Sivasankaran (Soma) A277
Somavilla-castro, Ivan A90
Somayajula, Srinivas A289
Somerfeld, Jessica A126
Somerhalder, John A180
Somerhalder, John W. P146
Somers, Bob A262
Somers, Jason A325
Somers, Jim E260
Somerville, Linda A565
Somerville, Susan P382
Somma, Joe A161
Sommella, Christine A507
Sommer, Alan A9
Sommer, Clint A444
Sommer, Alan P4
Sommer, Harry P443
Sommer, Stefan W433
Sommer, Tom E73
Sommers, John A9

642

HOOVER'S HANDBOOK OF EMERGING COMPANIES 2020

Sommers, David A571
Sommers, John P4
Sommers, Jimmy F P590
Sommers, Sarah W P590
Sommers, Wynelle P590
Sommers, Randy P590
Sommerville, Gwen P308
Somphanh, Boun E218
Somrak, Sarah E46
Son, David A432
Son, Jamie A933
Son, Gyeong Sik W108
Son, Chang Hwan W311
Son, David E216
Soncini, Bill E32
Sondhi, Samrat E141
Sonecha, Sonia A329
Sonego, Michael J. (Mike) A749
Sonego, Michael J. (Mike) E367
Sonenreich, Steven D. P351
Song, Jeromy A19
Song, J. Jonathan A308
Song, Jonathan A308
Song, David A726
Song, Li A793
Song, Annie A804
Song, Norman P86
Song, Zhiping W99
Song, Lin W104
Song, Guangju W310
Song, Se-Bin W311
Song, Jiehua E207
Songer, Terri P45
Soni, Paul J. A730
Soni, Pipasu A873
Sonneborn, Chris A294
Sonnemaker, Scott A. A797
Sonnenschein, Kai A402
Sonnenschein, Kai E198
Sonnier, Buford P105
Sonntag, Matt A512
Sono, Kiyoshi W262
Sonoda, Satoshi W268
Sonora, Lynn P561
Sonora, Brandi P561
Sonsteby, Charles M. (Chuck) A255
Sonsteng, Chimene A847
Sonsteng, Chimene E410
Sonthalia, Ashok P286
Sontheimer, Dan P291
Sonty, S Sita P493
Soo, Huh Chang W176
Sood, Anjla A6
Sood, Vipan A7
Sood, Arvind A65
Sood, Vijay K A376
Sood, Shailesh A393
Sood, Rohit P405
Sookram, Atma A16
Soon-ky, Hong W176
Soong, Sarah A932
Soong, Raymond E113
Soper, Abigail A222
Soper, Martha A888
Soper, Aaron A922
Soper, Aaron P671
Soper, Martha E425
Sorbara, Nicole W243
Sorber, William P78
Sorbera, Candice A137
Sordillo, Emilia P514
Sorel, Alison A205
Soren, Laurie A806
Soren, Laurie E398
Sorensen, Rob A171
Sorensen, Jeralyn A540
Sorensen, Mark A597
Sorensen, Donna A693
Sorensen, Donn P331
Sorensen, Jim P439
Sorensen, Charles W. P641
Sorensen, Donna E341
Sorenson, Steven P. A35
Sorenson, John B. (Brad) A149
Sorenson, Rob A171

Sorenson, Charles A451
Sorenson, Arne M. A537
Sorenson, Kim A804
Sorenson, Meredith P116
Sorenson, Charles P249
Sorenson, Roger P644
Soreq, Avigal A260
Sorgi, Vincent (Vince) A674
Sori, Henry A905
Sori, Alfredo E P280
Soriano, Lidio V. A670
Sorice, Maria P94
Soriot, Pascal W37
Sorkey, Alan J P670
Soroka, Dina A591
Soroka, Dina P369
Sorrell, Dan A888
Sorrell, Kellie P56
Sorrell, Martin W427
Sorrell, Tracy E12
Sorrell, Dan E425
Sorrells, Chris E352
Sorrentino, Vincent A200
Sorrentino, Renee A642
Sorrentino, Renee P407
Sorrentino, Rob W66
Sorter, Michael P128
Sorto, Rafael P26
Sorvillo, Domenico A331
Sorvillo, Domenico P202
Sosa, Enrique A200
Sosebee, Jane A89
Sosebee, Lori P115
Sosebee, Tim P144
Sosebee, Tina P551
Sosland, Matthew A88
Sosnovy, Richard A84
Soso, Gary P667
Sossen, Andrew J A780
Sossen, Andrew J. E387
Sossi, Frank A230
Sossi, Frank P154
Sotelo, Dan P303
Soterakis, Jack P515
Soteropoulos, Paula E237
Soto, Zoemy A91
Soto, Myrna A209
Soto, Donna A546
Soto, Zoemy P55
Soto, Dannette P286
Sotorp, Kai R. W247
Sotos, Michelle P218
Sotos, Christopher S. (Chris) E81
Sottong, Suzy A343
Sottong, Suzy E164
Soucy, Alicia A800
Souder, Matthew P677
Souders, Michael P297
Soufi, Nerissa A845
Souki, Charif A188
Soukup, Beth P260
Soukup, Beth P261
Soules, Steve A145
Soung, Nisha A899
Sounillac, Jean-Pierre W160
Soupene, John C. (Jay) A173
Souque, Lionel W322
Sourisse, Pascale W390
Sourisseau, Didier A245
Sourry, Amanda W409
Sousa, John A180
Sousa, Jose A483
Soutar, Jeff E103
South, Ronald A744
South, John R P234
Southam, Arthur M. P132
Southard, Bill P347
Southard, Wendy E81
Southern, Jenny P297
Southey, Kristin A10
Southwick, Michael J P587
Soutomaior, Luiz A746
Soutter, Jim E219
Souza, Joseph A86
Souza, Shanae A109

Souza, Fabian A305
Souza, Gustavo De A497
Souza, Nicole A784
Souza, Clinton De P408
Sova, Gregory A329
Sova, Colleen R. A867
Sow, Christine P424
Sowa, Ashley A404
Sowa, Mark P270
Sowa, Ashley E199
Sowards, Michael E306
Sowder, Dianna P75
Sowell, May-Ling E181
Sowers, Jerry A505
Sowinski, Mark A884
Sowmarpet, Mandasmitha P330
Soy, Randall P443
Space, Jordan A737
Space, Jordan E361
Spada, Gerald A784
Spada, Mary A879
Spada, Mary P636
Spadafino, Lisa A166
Spadaro, Christy P586
Spadea, Vincent A850
Spadola, Tracy E429
Spagnuolo, Andrea A552
Spagnuolo, John C A759
Spagnuolo, Andrea E275
Spagnuolo, John C E373
Spahr, Tom A428
Spahr, Dalena P536
Spaid, John L. E296
Spain, Wade A340
Spain, Michael A838
Spain, Wayne P56
Spain, Wade E160
Spain, Wade E161
Spain-Remy, Claire P352
Spair, Ronald H. E317
Spalding, Jennifer A170
Spalding, Jeffrey A401
Spalding, William R P1
Spalding, Susan P171
Span, Barbara A915
Spangler, Mark A340
Spangler, Dan A565
Spangler, Tammy P340
Spangler, Weldon E115
Spangler, Mark E160
Spanier, Mike A586
Spanier, Leslie E51
Spanier, Mike E301
Spann, Scott E218
Spano, Charlie A795
Spanos, Mike A654
Spanswick, Paul W286
Sparacino, Giuseppe A348
Sparacino, Michael A742
Sparacino, Giuseppe E169
Sparer, Cynthia N. P676
Sparger, Mike A729
Spargo, Glenn P163
Sparke, Andrea P333
Sparkman, Ricky D. A229
Sparkman, Julie A711
Sparkman, Julie P444
Sparks, Misty A160
Sparks, Timothy A209
Sparks, David A213
Sparks, Sara A651
Sparks, Kevin P. A876
Sparks, Kenneth A887
Sparks, Tracy A936
Sparks, David P143
Sparks, Lisa P252
Sparks, Danny P392
Sparks, Dennis P464
Sparks, Gary E72
Sparks, Sara E330
Sparolini, Sonia A801
Sparrow, Victor A828
Sparrow, Victor P584
Spartz, Mike A695
Spas, Paula P323

Spaugh, Gary A266
Spaugh, Gary P181
Spaulding, Rick A446
Spaulding, Luke A449
Spaulding, Stephen J A853
Spaulding, Todd A877
Spaulding, Scott A924
Spaulding, Stephen J P612
Spaulding, Luke E221
Spaziano, Greg P111
Spear, Lorna P511
Spearman, Terri P94
Spears, Wendy A115
Spears, Robert R. A169
Spears, Gary A313
Spears, Winsford A630
Spears, L Steven P331
Spears, David P340
Spears, Wendy E37
Spears, Steve E106
Spears, Gary E144
Speas, Dawn A114
Speas, Theodore W A798
Speas, Theodore A798
Speas, Dawn E36
Specht, William A A566
Specht, William A. E281
Specter, Eric M. E172
Spector, David A. A648
Spector, Ruth P218
Spector, David A. E328
Spector, Neil E429
Speer, Stephen A115
Speer, Samantha P114
Speer, Kevin P P235
Speer, Bill P581
Speer, Stephen E38
Speers, Jodie A346
Speers, Jodie E167
Speetzen, Michael T. (Mike) A669
Speicher, Charles A. E277
Speidell, Paul A754
Speidell, Paul P484
Speizer, Howard P447
Spellecy, Mike P308
Speller, Tony E249
Spellicy, Stephen A420
Spence, Susan A323
Spence, Timothy N. A329
Spence, Karis A444
Spence, William H. A674
Spence, Allen A704
Spence, Kenneth F. (Ken) A844
Spence, Jenny P412
Spenceley, James P86
Spencer, Jim A8
Spencer, Steve A28
Spencer, James F. A162
Spencer, Bill A219
Spencer, Robert A345
Spencer, Octavia A461
Spencer, Harry A478
Spencer, Carey A492
Spencer, Katy A512
Spencer, Lance A609
Spencer, Terry K. A630
Spencer, Terry K A631
Spencer, Carlton A681
Spencer, Ipyana A877
Spencer, Ruth A899
Spencer, Lorraine A902
Spencer, Larry A920
Spencer, Dennis A940
Spencer, Ian A940
Spencer, John P28
Spencer, Jill P38
Spencer, Rhonda P67
Spencer, Lorraine P194
Spencer, Kate P206
Spencer, Octavia P255
Spencer, Linda P264
Spencer, Ronald P375
Spencer, Terry K P397
Spencer, James F. E61
Spencer, Robert E165

COMBINED HOOVER'S HANDBOOK INDEX OF EXECUTIVES

A = AMERICAN BUSINESS
E = EMERGING COMPANIES
P = PRIVATE COMPANIES
W = WORLD BUSINESS

Spencer, Gregory N E400
Spengler, Richard S. A473
Spengler, Richard S. E236
Spenner, Richard A520
Spera, Richard P571
Speranza, James A589
Sperber, Julie A561
Sperling, Ed A200
Sperling, Lorraine A390
Spero, Vincent A. A646
Spero, Vincent A. E324
Sperry, Diane P402
Speth, Ralf W383
Spevakov, Eugene E110
Speyer, Sharon S. A444
Speyer, Sharon S. P596
Spicer, Renee A29
Spicer, Bruce A367
Spicer, Randy A877
Spicer, Donald Z. P642
Spicer, Michael G. E63
Spiegel, Isabella A84
Spiegel, Joan A540
Spiegelman, Kathy P383
Spiegler, Eric E72
Spiehler, Mark P647
Spieker, Marc W143
Spieler, Robert A90
Spielman, Amanda A552
Spielman, Amanda P324
Spier, Scott P329
Spier, Dr Scott P332
Spierkel, Gregory M A636
Spiers, Robert H. A22
Spiers, Robert H. P11
Spies, Mike A654
Spiesshofer, Ulrich W3
Spiewak, Brian A3
Spight, Don P399
Spiker, Chuck E442
Spilker, Alan A704
Spillane, Doug A575
Spiller, Elizabeth P652
Spiller, Jeff E203
Spillers, David P247
Spillers, David P571
Spilman, Thomas A491
Spilman, Jeff A538
Spina, Suzana P422
Spinelli, Luis E86
Spinieo, Bob A418
Spinner, Steven L. (Steve) A869
Spiroff, Paul A561
Spitser, Christy A226
Spitser, Christy P150
Spitz, Robert A596
Spitzer, John A613
Spitzer, Anna P P325
Spivey, William A706
Spivey, Ami A902
Spivey, Beth P196
Splain, Steve A152
Splain, Steve P98
Splaine, Thomas F. A504
Splaine, Kevin R P509
Splaine, Thomas F. E251
Splettstaszer, Maureen A884
Spoelder, Eelco W160
Spohn, Benjamin A349
Spohr, Carsten W136
Spolidoro, Laurence A272
Spolver, Michelle E179
Sponenberg, Chris A922
Sponenberg, Chris P671
Spong, Rick A380
Spong, Bernadette P400
Spong, Bernadette P448
Spoon, Alan A254
Spooner, Patty A108

Spore, Brandon P396
Sporing, Eileen P558
Sposito, Thomas J. A737
Sposito, Thomas J. E361
Spott, Erika A857
Spott, Erika A A857
Spotts, Lang P294
Spracher, John A338
Spradley, Scott A855
Spradlin, Diane A605
Spradlin, Shane M. A649
Spragale, Scott A833
Sprague, Joseph A. (Joe) A29
Sprague, Mark A175
Sprague, Raymond J. (Ray) A408
Sprague, Ray A409
Sprague, Brittney P209
Sprague, Neil E. E134
Sprague, Norman F. E280
Sprankle, Diane P131
Spraus, Joyan P212
Spray, Steve A195
Sprecher, Jeffrey C A462
Sprecher, Dennis L P429
Spreen, Paul A474
Spriggs, Elise A781
Spring, Terry P519
Spring, Annabel F. W113
Springer, Barbara A272
Springer, Jon W. E420
Springfield, Susan L. A343
Springfield, Susan L. E163
Springmeyer, Douglas A571
Springuel, Myriam P498
Sprinkle, Beverly P107
Sprouls, Joe A559
Sprouse, Linda P664
Spruce, Robert P179
Sprunk, Eric D A599
Sprunk, Robert P353
Spurbeck, Mark A645
Spurgeon, William W. (Bill) A277
Spurlin, Sharon A668
Spurling, David A. A415
Spurling, David A. E209
Spyridakos, Vangelis A218
Squadere, Bonnie A491
Squaire, Brenda A479
Squeo, Anne Marie A933
Squeri, Stephen J. (Steve) A53
Squeri, Steve A54
Squier, Jenny A218
Squier, Margaret E226
Squier, Peg E226
Squilla, Candy P457
Squire, David A331
Squire, David E152
Squires, Luke A1
Squires, James A. (Jim) A604
Squires, Paula P72
Squires, Jeffrey F. P582
Squires, Luke E1
Sr, Dan Bachovin A879
Sr, Margaret Hadley P242
Sr, Linda Reedy P250
Sr, Jesse T Williams P265
Sr, Anthony J Rouse P458
Sr, Robert Curran P588
Sr, Dan Bachovin P636
Sr., Jerome L. Davis E23
Sramek, Rick E424
Sreca, Ray A379
Sreenivasan, Katepalli R. (Sreeni) A592
Sreenivasan, Katepalli R. (Sreeni) P370
Srichukrin, Narong W351
Srihong, Teeranun W216
Srikrishna, Ajay E110
Srimahunt, Pikun W352
Srinivasan, Mukund A74
Srinivasan, Veena A203
Srinivasan, Kumud A460
Srinivasan, Vasan E431
Sripratak, Adirek W95
Sriram, Divya P409
Srirongmuang, Songphol W95

Srivanich, Payong W226
Srivastava, Sam K. A532
Srivastava, Sulabh P252
Srivastava, Sheetesh E448
Srivathsan, Venkataramani W294
Srivatsan, Nagaraja E141
Sroka, Kenneth P. A126
Sroufe, Dan P403
Srouji, Johny A72
Staalenburg, Leanne A165
Staaterman, Stacey A53
Stabingas, Mark P643
Stabler, Lee P294
Stacey, Brett A336
Stacey, Paul A460
Stacey, Robert A880
Stacey, Brett A880
Stacey, Showerman P631
Stacey, Robert P640
Stacey, Brett P640
Stacey, Brett E157
Stachowiak, Tom A853
Stachowiak, Tom P612
Stack, John A54
Stack, Karen A80
Stack, Kimberly A248
Stack, Edward W. (Ed) A264
Stack, Karen P46
Stack, John P P511
Stack, Kimberly E107
Stackalis, Jack A831
Stackalis, Jack P601
Stacks, Ben A115
Stacks, Ben E38
Stacy, Jill A246
Stacy, Neel A449
Stacy, Jill E105
Stacy, Neel E220
Stacy, Michelle E239
Stade, Nelda E106
Stadler, Rupert W418
Stadtmueller, John A528
Staebler, Ned P660
Staecker, Kim P277
Staehle, Robert A154
Staelens, Kurt C. A750
Staes, Charles A797
Staffieri, Victor A. A674
Stafford, Gloria A167
Stafford, Connell A215
Stafford, William P. A338
Stafford, Vernon H. A343
Stafford, Ron A580
Stafford, Nicole P179
Stafford, Deborah P215
Stafford, Ingrid S. P388
Stafford, Vernon H. E164
Stafford, Ryan K. E258
Stafford, Ron E293
Stafstrom, Christine A651
Stafstrom, Christine E330
Stagg, Kendall W. (Ken) W85
Staggs, Lynn A170
Stagliano, Joseph R. A584
Staglin, Garen K. E141
Stagman, Guy P93
Stahl, Stephanie A274
Stahl, Neil A710
Stahl, Stephanie A801
Stahl, Kent P229
Stahl, Jim P356
Stahler, David A933
Stahler, Sheri P546
Stahlman, Glenn E424
Stain, Michael D A249
Stain, Michael D E108
Staines, Fowler P632
Stajduhar, Tony P262
Stake, James A728
Staker, Janet A462
Staker, Janet P256
Stakolich, Tim P165
Staley, Nina A606
Staley, Sally J. P116
Staley, Jeanette P431

Staley, David P563
Staley, James E. (Jes) W58
Stalick, Theodore R. A555
Stalker, Rebecca A111
Stalker, Robin J. W9
Stall, Hank P502
Stallings, John G. A91
Stallings, Norfleet A91
Stallings, Jay A117
Stallings, Robert A819
Stallings, James B A857
Stallings, Jay P61
Stallings, John G. E29
Stallings, Norfleet E29
Stallings, Robert E403
Stalls, Justin A936
Stalnaker, Jeffrey C. P232
Stalter, Robert A500
Stalzer, Jennifer A544
Stamas, Sharon P276
Stamm, Jessica A727
Stamm, Jeffrey P85
Stamm, Rich P393
Stamm, Jessica P453
Stan, Wong E427
Stanard, Patricia P299
Stanback, Shauna P435
Stanbrough, John A722
Stancel, George M P596
Stancl, Craig Robert P318
Stanczak, Felicia A369
Standeffer, Luke P564
Standing, Shannon P103
Standish, Dr Liz P396
Standlee, Carrie A449
Standlee, Carrie E221
Standley, John T. A722
Standley, Betty P265
Standley, Christopher E14
Standridge, Brant J. A849
Stanek, Mary Ellen A726
Stanek, Mark A888
Stanek, Mary A908
Stanek, Mary Ellen P453
Stanek, Janet P530
Stanek, Mark E425
Stanfield, Par A902
Stanford, Beth P92
Stanford, Kevin P205
Stanford, Gregory G P671
Stanger, Gregg E278
Stangis, Dave A164
Stango, John A745
Stanichev, Frederick A740
Stanislav, Chuck A635
Staniszewski, Sara A925
Staniszewski, Sara P445
Stank, Michael A205
Stankey, John T. A89
Stankey, John A871
Stanley, Karen W. A163
Stanley, Jenny A224
Stanley, Chris A226
Stanley, Allen A319
Stanley, Gina A325
Stanley, Donald A392
Stanley, Shirley A744
Stanley, Chris P150
Stanley, Roger P186
Stanley, John D. P289
Stanley, Kelly P485
Stanley, James E. (Jes) W56
Stanley, Karen W. E62
Stanley, Kevin E445
Stanners, Russell W417
Stansbury, Christopher D. (Chris) A81
Stansbury, Tracy A86
Stansbury, H. Tayloe A471
Stansbury, Tracy E27
Stansel, Armand P245
Stanski, Bruce A. A355
Stanski, Matthew E P588
Stanson, Sarah A747
Stanton, Matt A237
Stanton, Jill A. A340

Stanton, Lisl A483
Stanton, Kevin J. A544
Stanton, Neil A708
Stanton, Matthew A862
Stanton, Tim A884
Stanton, Tammie P448
Stanton, Oliver K. P605
Stanton, Jill A. E160
Stanush, Dan A887
Stanutz, Nicholas G. (Nick) A444
Stanwood, Michael P204
Stanworth, Paul W233
Stanz, Joseph A204
Stanzione, Dominick P304
Staple, Andy E64
Staples, Christopher A329
Staples, Cindy A528
Staples, Miles A536
Staples, Shawna A599
Staples, David M. (Dave) A774
Staples, William A. P629
Stapleton, Jack A224
Stapleton, Michael A552
Stapleton, Rebecca A737
Stapleton, Jason P26
Stapleton, Mary P228
Stapleton, Michael E276
Stapleton, Rebecca E361
Stapley, Holly A325
Starace, Francesco W153
Starcher, Jeff A741
Starcher, Jeff E364
Starck, Jonathan A56
Stark, Ronald J. (Ron) A25
Stark, Ruth A56
Stark, Arthur (Art) A125
Stark, Doug A313
Stark, Deborah A545
Stark, Ronald J. (Ron) P14
Stark, Doug P200
Stark, Deborah P317
Stark, Larry P462
Stark, Tony P566
Stark, Kevin E264
Starke, James A647
Starkey, Destry P196
Starkey, Linda P203
Starkle, Philip A595
Starkovich, John E7
Starling, Curtis P126
Starmer, Samantha A702
Starnes, Lee A240
Starnes, Will A327
Starnes, W. Stancil (Stan) A678
Starnes, Clarke R. A849
Starnes, Karen A850
Starns, Renee P552
Starr, Vennesa A246
Starr, James A380
Starr, G. Gabrielle A592
Starr, Kirk A778
Starr, Patrick P55
Starr, Daniel B. (Dan) P182
Starr, Maureen P358
Starr, G. Gabrielle P370
Starr, Vennesa E105
starr-Howard, Marianne P359
Starsiak, Michael P349
Startin, Michael A481
Stashower, Susan A53
Stasior, Bill A72
Stasior, William A565
Stassi, Phillip J. A476
Stassinopoulos, Adonis E343
Stata, Ray A67
Staten, Jennifer A220
Staten, Jennifer P149
Staten, Karen P308
States, Lauren E435
Stathakopoulos, George A72
Stathes, Garey A305
Staton, Daniel C. A80
Staton, Melissa A440
Statton, Timothy P58
Statuto, Richard J. (Rich) P94

Staub, Steve A351
Staub, Mary A462
Staub, W. Richard A474
Staub, Elizabeth A789
Staub, Lon A935
Staub, Mary P256
Staublin, Valerie A520
Staudt, Donald A688
Staudt, Tom P337
Stauffer, Charlotte A139
Stauffer, Charlotte P93
Stauffer, Russell P220
Stauffer, Mike E245
Staunton, Henry E. W306
Stausberg, Bertram W66
Stausholm, Jakob W1
Stauth, Scott G. W85
Stavig, Amanda P20
Stavinoha, Curtis P266
Stavriotis, Eric A175
Stavropoulos, Nickolas (Nick) A659
Stavros, Chris P587
Stclair, Anne A922
Stclair, Anne P671
Steadham, Clay A798
Stearley, Cheryl P617
Stearn, Joyce A500
Stearn, David A512
Stearns, Pam A1
Stearns, Leah C. A59
Stearns, Caitlin A332
Stearns, Leo P211
Stearns, Stephen P493
Stearns, Pam E1
Stebbins, Donald J. (Don) E394
Stec, Randy A398
Stec, Randy P222
Stec, Jeffery E102
Stech, Brian E452
Stecher, Kenneth W. (Ken) A196
Stecher, Esta E. A390
Steck, Kevin P530
Stedfast, Sarah B. A894
Stedfast, Sarah B. P651
Stedronsky, Gregg A376
Steeber, Mark A850
Steeg, Monica A606
Steele, John A196
Steele, Sally A. A227
Steele, Kelly A364
Steele, Delaney A731
Steele, Drew A761
Steele, Douangchan A798
Steele, Anthony G A850
Steele, Robert P45
Steele, Bob P45
Steele, Paul Edward P128
Steele, Kevin B. P232
Steele, Kate P386
Steele, Athornia P389
Steele, Catherine J. P553
Steele, Mark T. P607
Steele, Darren E30
Steele, Sally A. E91
Steelman, Kecia A858
Steen, John A761
Steen, Ida E106
Steenbergen, Ewout L. A738
Steensen, Erik A530
Steer, Robert L. A748
Steere, William A942
Steere, F William P15
Stefanini, Pierluigi W411
Stefano, Christine P611
Stefanou, Katerina A722
Stefanowicz, Melanie P588
Stefansic, Robert J. (Bob) A457
Stefanski, Mike A890
Steffe, Greg A686
Steffen, Julie A481
Steffen, Mark A606
Steffen, Mark A P159
Steffens, Mikenzie P389
Steffens, Stacy L P595
Steffensen, Mark A439

Steffensen, Dwight A795
Stefonek, Mark P333
Stegeman, John A412
Stegeman, Jeff A491
Stegen, Andrew A526
Steger, Darcy A347
Steger, Troy A413
Steger, Troy E205
Stegman, Melissa A329
Stegmayer, Joseph H. (Joe) E69
Stegner, Robert L. (Bob) A794
Stegner, Bob A795
Stehney, Jane A488
Steichen, Mark P86
Steidel, Michael P114
Steiger, Paul A848
Steiger, Peter P405
Steiger, John P527
Steiger, Paul E411
Steigerwalt, Eric T A150
Steigman, Liz A409
Steil, Jim P93
Steimer, Richard A329
Stein, Gary A43
Stein, Jeffrey S. A44
Stein, David L. A85
Stein, Derek K. A135
Stein, Laura A207
Stein, Clint E. A219
Stein, William G. A239
Stein, Andrew A284
Stein, Rona A319
Stein, Richard A329
Stein, Laura A363
Stein, Stephanie A452
Stein, Eileen A470
Stein, Trudy A474
Stein, Dirk A695
Stein, Kevin M. A842
Stein, Anna A882
Stein, Keith L. P63
Stein, Barry P229
Stein, Rob P237
Stein, Paul P305
Stein, Dennis P361
Stein, Jeff P429
Stein, Gary E13
Stein, Jeffrey S. E13
Stein, David L. E26
Stein, Clint E. E87
Stein, Andrew E120
Stein, Steven H. E226
Stein, Sylvia E286
Stein, Ed E334
Stein, Martin E. (Hap) E349
Steinbach, Justin A247
Steinbach, Justin E105
Steinbacher, Michele P617
Steinbeck, Daryl A831
Steinbeck, Daryl P601
Steinberg, Lewis R A592
Steinberg, Jesse A854
Steinberg, Lewis R P370
Steinberg, Michael P623
Steinberg, Jonathan L. (Jono) E447
Steinborn, Birgit W353
Steinbrech, Patricia C. P578
Steiner, Judy A116
Steiner, Tim A152
Steiner, Troy A158
Steiner, Rachel A413
Steiner, Kristin M A575
Steiner, Melanie A692
Steiner, Curt A885
Steiner, Judy E39
Steiner, Tim E52
Steiner, Rachel E205
Steines, Brian P478
Steinhafel, Arthur W. (Art) P423
Steinhardt, Michael H. E447
Steinhauer, Peter P586
Steinhaus, Tom A413
Steinhaus, Tom E205
Steinhauser, Barbara P298
Steinhoffer, Sara P489

Steinke, Connie A346
Steinke, Connie E167
Steinlauf, Jon P480
Steinmetz, Jay A656
Steinmetz, Bill A838
Steinmetz, Bill A839
Steinmetz, Carol A850
Steinmetz, Robert A896
Steinmetz, Jay P414
Steinmetz, Joseph D E78
Steinour, Stephen D. (Steve) A444
Steinwert, Kent A A313
Steinwert, Kent A E144
Steinwolf, Chad A203
Stella, John A61
Stellar, James A785
Stellar, James P526
Stellar, Tom E319
Stelling, James A58
Stelling, Kessel D. A796
Stelling, Kessel D. E397
Stelly, Donald D. (Don) E255
Stelman, Randee A5
Stelnik, Jeff P90
Stemmer, Ralf W137
Stempki, Jennifer E265
Stencel, Douglas A727
Stencel, Douglas P453
Stendardi, Deborah P456
Stenehjem, David P597
Stengel, Ray A715
Stenger, Michael J. P207
Stenhouse, John A723
Stenman, Eric P59
Stenson, Brian A785
Stensrud, David A828
Stensrud, David P584
Stenz, John A249
Stenz, John E108
Stenzel, Christopher (Chris) A236
Stepanski, Robert A484
Stephan, William P610
Stephanie, Maher-dickerson A909
Stephanie, Ste P344
Stephanie, Maher-dickerson E436
Stephatos, George A835
Stephen, Lomsdalen A61
Stephen, Robert P2
Stephen, Boos P72
Stephen, Antonia P574
Stephens, John J. A89
Stephens, Devin A315
Stephens, Angela A489
Stephens, Michael A755
Stephens, Greg A866
Stephens, Steven D. A940
Stephens, Donna P480
Stephens, Anthony P522
Stephens, Shane P525
Stephens, Sana E290
Stephens, Jason E305
Stephens, Michael E369
Stephens, Martha C. E408
Stephens, Greg E417
Stephenson, Randall L. A89
Stephenson, Britt A598
Stephenson, Todd A756
Stephenson, David P28
Stephenson, Craig P115
Stephenson, Don P115
Stephenson, Rick P115
Stephenson, Adam P115
Stephenson, Harry D P145
Stephenson, Don P145
Stephenson, Craig P145
STEPHENSON, JEAN P242
Stephenson, Steve P258
Stephenson, Roger P356
Stephenson, Mark P405
Stephenson, Anne P489
Stephenson, Robert O. E314
Stephenson, Scott G. E428
Sterbenz, James A164
Sterbenz, Jim A164
Sterbenz, Isaac A741

COMBINED HOOVER'S HANDBOOK INDEX OF EXECUTIVES

```
A = AMERICAN BUSINESS
E = EMERGING COMPANIES
P = PRIVATE COMPANIES
W = WORLD BUSINESS
```

Sterbenz, Isaac E364
Sterchi, Ashley A823
Sterchi, Ashley P557
Sterghos, Nick A569
Sterin, Steven A177
Sterling, Christine A327
Sterling, Michelle A694
Sterling, Kira A837
Sterling, Joseph E138
Sterman, David P369
Stern, Walter A45
Stern, Peter A72
Stern, Brian A112
Stern, Robert A117
Stern, Sonny A262
Stern, Jonathan A356
Stern, Michele A465
Stern, Chris A559
Stern, Walter P30
Stern, Robert P61
Stern, Philip P187
Stern, Zachary E101
Stern, Rachel R. E143
Stern, Paul E264
Stern, Andrew E372
Sternberg, Janae A161
Sterner, Beth A850
Sternlicht, Barry S A780
Sternlicht, Barry S. E387
Stetson, John P639
Stettner, Jennifer A662
Stetz, Gary E41
Stetzer, Ed P296
Steubing, Will E105
Stevanovic, Andreja E343
Steve, Davidsen A7
Steve, Harman A184
Steve, Enos A933
Steve, Kelly P172
Steven, Charles A305
Steven, Johnson A320
Steven, Becker P588
Stevens, Jim A3
Stevens, Timothy (Chip) A19
Stevens, Kelly A54
Stevens, Philip A80
Stevens, Michael A86
Stevens, Andrew A103
Stevens, Mark A114
Stevens, Brian A120
Stevens, Mark A181
Stevens, Craig A227
Stevens, Dominique A327
Stevens, Craig A374
Stevens, Charles K. (Chuck) A378
Stevens, Keith A442
Stevens, Ed A480
Stevens, Cheryl A500
Stevens, Maureen A530
Stevens, Rick A663
Stevens, Denise A762
Stevens, Tara A784
Stevens, W. Arthur A852
Stevens, Simon A876
Stevens, Kristen A902
Stevens, David P34
Stevens, Philip P46
Stevens, Chris P84
Stevens, Craig B P96
Stevens, Ed P270
Stevens, Velinda P273
Stevens, George P379
Stevens, Daniel P421
Stevens, Lynette P435
Stevens, Carla P514
Stevens, Kevin P623
Stevens, Ben W79
Stevens, Lyle G. W85
Stevens, Matthew E7

Stevens, Andrea E14
Stevens, Michael E27
Stevens, Mark E37
Stevens, Mark E70
Stevens, Craig E90
Stevenson, Kimberly A147
Stevenson, Casey A222
Stevenson, Michael A335
Stevenson, Mark A345
Stevenson, Phil A665
Stevenson, Mark P. A832
Stevenson, Jim A844
Stevenson, Karen A879
Stevenson, Lee A888
Stevenson, Tom A929
Stevenson, Cindy P265
Stevenson, Roger P415
Stevenson, Kyle P463
Stevenson, Heather P492
Stevenson, Hollie P626
Stevenson, Karen P636
Stevenson, Tim E. P. W212
Stevenson, Michael E155
Stevenson, Mark E165
Stevenson, Phil E334
Stevenson, Lee E425
Stevenson, Tom E449
Steves, Sonja P288
Steves, Janet P473
Steward, David A928
Steward, David L. A928
Steward, David P673
Steward, David L. P674
Steward, Randall J. (Randy) E343
Stewart, Jeffrey R A6
Stewart, Lisa A71
Stewart, Julia A97
Stewart, William (Bill) A145
Stewart, Janie A165
Stewart, Greg A171
Stewart, Steele A179
Stewart, Alice A179
Stewart, Wayne A181
Stewart, Ricky A185
Stewart, Rob A219
Stewart, Suzanne A267
Stewart, Dave A272
Stewart, Jan A279
Stewart, Eric A290
Stewart, Jamie B A320
Stewart, Kevin A340
Stewart, Michael J. (Mike) A345
Stewart, John F. A356
Stewart, Sheila A358
Stewart, Inez A478
Stewart, Kristy A478
Stewart, Jennifer A484
Stewart, Carol A487
Stewart, Marlene A498
Stewart, Bob A548
Stewart, Heather A592
Stewart, Prue A642
Stewart, Don A658
Stewart, Stephanie D. A666
Stewart, Cheryl A684
Stewart, Terri A704
Stewart, Will A850
Stewart, Cameron A865
Stewart, Leanne M P1
Stewart, James P58
Stewart, Susan P132
Stewart, David P249
Stewart, Traci P259
Stewart, Inez P269
Stewart, Kristy P269
Stewart, Anna P300
Stewart, C Todd P310
Stewart, J P325
Stewart, Heather P370
Stewart, Prue P407
Stewart, Dennis T P418
Stewart, Cindy P472
Stewart, Matt P475
Stewart, Eric P488
Stewart, Lee P639

Stewart, Megan P652
Stewart, Robert A. (Bob) W23
Stewart, R. Bruce E25
Stewart, Wayne E70
Stewart, Jim E72
Stewart, Rob E87
Stewart, Alison J E143
Stewart, Richard A. (Dick) E144
Stewart, Kevin E160
Stewart, Cecelia E164
Stewart, Michael J. (Mike) E165
Stewart, Sheila E176
Stewart, Kevin D E264
Stewart, Ben E416
Stewart, Cameron E417
Stibal, John A882
Stibler, Ellen A545
Stich, Mark P64
Stich, Joseph J. (Joe) E395
Stich, Joe E395
Stichnoth, Roseann A319
Stichter, Don P17
Stickels, Eric E91
Stickland, Davina A135
Stickler, Valerie E81
Stickney, Tim A520
Stickney, Michael L. W193
Sticksel, Amy A599
Stidham, Cathy A621
Stidham, Mark W160
Stidham, Cathy E312
Stidsen, Andrea P574
Stief, Brian A480
Stief, Brian P270
Stiefel, Lester A109
Stiefel, Holly A922
Stiefel, Holly P671
Stiegmann, Gregory V. (Greg) P626
Stienemeier, Marion A692
Stiers, Mark W. A279
Stiff, Cory A658
Stika, Martina P113
Still, Kevin A. A213
Still, Kevin A. P143
Still, Cash P281
Stilla, John A325
Stille, Charles A380
Stille, Goran A377
Stiller, David A444
Stillman, Jamie P650
Stills, David A901
Stillwagon, Troy P477
Stillwell, Scott A855
Stillwell, Kathy P226
Stillwell, Mary-lee E81
Stillwell, Ken E326
Stilwell, Craig G. A206
Stimson, Bob A665
Stimson, Bob E334
Stinde, Mark A647
Stinehart, Korey P343
Stinger, Harold P487
Stingily, Karl A323
Stingl, Jennifer A145
Stinnett, Janine A665
Stinnett, Clay A788
Stinnett, Joseph A873
Stinnett, Hester P546
Stinnett, Janine E334
Stinnett, Clay E389
Stinnette, Mike A569
Stinson, Deirdre A640
Stinson, Ron A665
Stinson, Ceasar P342
Stinson, Ron E334
Stipanov, John C A676
Stipanov, John C E338
Stipanovich, Sasha A704
Stipek, Deborah A510
Stipek, Deborah P290
Stipp, Janice E P543
Stipp, Keith D. W31
Stipp, Janice E. E359
Stippig, Julian A204
Stiritz, William P. (Bill) A672

Stirling, Grant P39
Stirling, Steve P307
Stites, Mark A184
Stites, Jill D P129
Stith, Melvin A19
Stitt, Kimberly A340
Stitt, Kevin A782
Stitt, David P355
Stitt, Kevin P526
Stitt, Kimberly E160
Stiver, Ron P252
Stivers, Betsy A882
Stivers, Richard P176
Stjernholm, Helena W386
Stobak, Michael (Mike) P68
Stober, Renee L A140
Stockdale, Barry A61
Stockdale, Sandra P588
Stocker, Michael A. A588
Stocker, Michael A. P365
Stockman, Jim A487
Stockmann, Bill P445
Stockmeister, Aaron A329
Stocksdale, Thomas A314
Stocksdale, Thomas E145
Stockton, Dmitri L. A374
Stockton, Dmitri A735
Stockton, Don P155
Stockton, Jennifer P274
Stockton, Kathryn P597
Stockton, Charles E105
Stoddard, Daniel G A275
Stoddard, Lorilee A940
Stoddard, Denny P202
Stoddard, Joan P574
Stoddard, Thomas D. (Tom) W40
Stoecker, Chris A793
Stoeckert, Michael A678
Stoeger, Florian A726
Stoeger, Florian P453
Stoehr, Rebecca A137
Stoehr, David L. A925
Stoehr, David L. E445
Stoering, Mark E. A931
Stoffel, Ann A532
Stoffels, Paulus (Paul) A479
Stoffels, Paul A480
Stoffers, Brian F. A175
Stoffregen, Lynn A413
Stoffregen, Tom P536
Stoffregen, Lynn E205
Stokes, Tony A3
Stokes, Russell A374
Stokes, Bobby A410
Stokes, Charles A552
Stokes, Patrick A809
Stokes, Melvina P135
Stokes, Charles P324
Stokes, Charles D. (Chuck) P324
Stokes, Michelle P588
Stolarick, Kenneth A530
Stolfi, Carl A388
Stoll, Debra A677
Stoll, Carol P163
Stoll, Rick E429
Stoller, Tim A647
Stoller, William H. (Bill) P198
Stollings, Anthony M. (Tony) A340
Stollings, Anthony M. (Tony) E160
Stolly, Timothy J. E365
Stolorena, Sheila A867
Stolorena, Sheila E418
Stolper, Edward M. P107
Stoltz, Michael A285
Stolz, Dustin P160
Stolz, Robert H. P390
Stolzenberg, Eric L P543
Stone, Tony A22
Stone, Brett A85
Stone, Brenda A112
Stone, Carol A123
Stone, Robert D. A126
Stone, Richard A262
Stone, Jeffrey A281
Stone, Neil A390

Stone, Paul A417
Stone, David A420
Stone, Denise A444
Stone, Steven M. A500
Stone, Mollie A536
Stone, Samuel G. A552
Stone, Claire A654
Stone, Andrew P. A709
Stone, Scott A715
Stone, Randy A740
Stone, Woodrow A761
Stone, Paul E A827
Stone, Eugene A831
Stone, Connie A865
Stone, Mike A867
Stone, Barry A877
Stone, Kent V. A884
Stone, Nancy A887
Stone, Tony P11
Stone, Jeff P161
Stone, William C P186
Stone, Mike P258
Stone, Susan P489
Stone, Joel P508
Stone, Kevin P551
Stone, Paul E P571
Stone, Christina P574
Stone, Brett E26
Stone, Samuel G. E275
Stone, Andrew P. E348
Stone, Chad E352
Stone, Connie E416
Stone, Mike E418
Stoneham, Gloria A147
Stonehill, Robyn Price A88
Stonell, Keith E196
Stoner, Colin P391
Stoner, Sherry P644
Stonesifer, Timothy C. (Tim) A420
Stonesifer, Kurt P621
Stoness, Scott A494
Stonestreet, Dana L A430
Stonestreet, Jana P168
Stonhaus, Dallas A739
Stonhill, Richard P174
Stonier, Joann A544
Stoothoff, Anthony A37
Stoothoff, Anthony P27
Stopczynski, Pawel W54
STOPPANI, LINO ENRICO W43
Stoppelman, Jeremy E450
Storbeck, Robert A444
Storch, Christian E12
Storer, Carrie A270
Storey, Jeffrey K. (Jeff) A184
Storey, Marie A327
Storey, Dale A376
Storie, Rockey A299
Stork, Ryan D. A135
Stork, Hans A627
Stormer, Ben A170
Stormont, Douglas P525
Storr, Hanns-Peter W137
Storrs, Todd A746
Storset, Snorre W287
Storto, David E. A641
Storto, David E. P407
Storvick, Jim A861
Story, Leo A62
Story, Jeryl A772
Story, Pete A809
Story, Leo E20
Story, Jeryl E382
Stotland, Eve A A590
Stotler, Tracy A420
Stouffer, Ron A36
Stough, Mike A320
Stout, Dawn A355
Stout, Christopher A687
Stout, William P212
Stout, Chris P561
Stout, Rich E7
Stovall, Charles A299
Stovall, Shanobia A552
Stovall, Shanobia P324

Stover, Jim A369
Stover, Patrick A378
Stover, Jeremy A498
Stover, Bill A565
Stover, Gary E7
Stoverock, Linda P359
Stowe, Jay C. A815
Stowe, Barry L. W315
Stowe, Christina E105
Stowell, John A281
Stowell, Jane A651
Stowell, Jane E329
Stoyer, Dean A862
Strabala, Gwen P226
Strable, Deanna A677
Strable-Soethout, Deanna D. A677
Strachan, Ron P151
Strachan-smith, Genie A885
Strachota, Jenny A86
Strachota, Jenny E27
Strack, Jeff P530
Strader, Trisha P359
Strader, H. Gregg E16
Strader, Christopher E194
Straffi, Glenn R. A646
Straffi, Glenn R. E324
Strah, Steven E. (Steve) A350
Strahl, Shane A760
Strahl, Shane E374
Strahlman, Ellen R. A123
Straight, Sharra A598
Strain, Robert D. (Rob) A103
Strain, Charles P175
Strain, Trevor W266
Strain, Kevin D. W371
Strait, Ari A746
Straka, Mary A908
Straker, Gary A627
Straley, Ben A779
Stram, Randy A559
Strampel, William D. P339
Strand, Ivan P610
Strang, Ward A323
Strange, Mallor A441
Strange, Nicholas (Nick) A692
Strange, J. Leland E234
Stranges, Paula A34
Strangeway, Christine P519
Strangfeld, John R. A686
Stranghoener, V. Raymond (Ray) A224
Strassburger, Daniel A701
Stratman, R. Joseph A612
Stratton, Ed A129
Stratton, Mike A160
Stratton, Sarah A222
Stratton, John G. A889
Straub, Maximiliane A724
Straub, Karl P262
Straub, Maximiliane P452
Straubel, Jeffrey B. (JB) A818
Straus, David H. A429
Straus, David H. E214
Strauss, Sarah A167
Strauss, John L A481
Strauss, Cindy P431
Strauss, Frank W137
Strauss, Thomas W. E101
Stravitz, Mitchell A175
Straw, Mona A337
Straw, Chuck A481
Straw, Mona E158
Strayer, Brandon A85
Strayer, Joe P260
Strayer, Brandon E26
Straz, David A. P203
Stream, Kevin A512
Stream, Christopher E35
Streb, Gene A672
Streck, Richard J P15
Stredit-Thomas, Sukari P246
Streed, Ben A704
Street, Brad A30
Street, Jim A686
Street, Doug P9
Street, Brad P20

Streeter, Hope A924
Streeter, Bill P337
Streeter, Monica P459
Streeter, Debra P507
Streett, Sarah A511
Streett, Sarah P290
Streif, Mary P465
Streit, David A301
Streit, Michael A481
Streit, Steven W. E194
Strength, Brent P261
Streton, Michele A405
Strey, Jean P161
Strickland, Hoyt J. A58
Strickland, Sam A145
Strickland, Robert A226
Strickland, Tamara A325
Strickland, Robert P150
Strickler, Gayla A444
Strickler, Natalie E142
Stricklin, Leslie G A713
Stringer, Peter A818
Stringer, Ruth M P161
Stringer, Peter E403
Stringfellow, West A804
Stringham, Daniel A686
Stritikus, Tom A880
Stritikus, Tom P640
Strobel, Marsha P205
Strobel, Victoria L P310
Stroburg, Jeffrey (Jeff) E352
Strock, James A250
Stroeh, Brad A340
Stroeh, Brad E160
Stroh, Rosa A416
Stroh, Elizabeth P253
Strohaver, Deborah P235
Strohecker, Jennifer A571
Strohfus, Joseph P476
Strohl, Kingman P116
Strohmaier, Walter W62
Stroin, Jeff P613
Stroker, Robert T. P546
Strom, Arlene W373
Stromann, Nicholas P160
Stromberg, Stephanie A462
Stromberg, William J. (Bil) A799
Stromberg, Leroy P18
Stromberg, Stephanie P256
Stromski, Christopher P520
Strong, Gary B P157
Strong, David W. P400
Strong, Carol E80
Strongin, Steven H. A390
Strottman, Lori K A316
Stroud, Martin A711
Stroud, Martin P444
Strouse, David A892
Stroz, Barbara A559
Stroz, Edward M. P206
Strozzi, Mary A386
Strozzi, Ken E188
Strubell, Taylor A232
Struble, Lisa A862
Struck, Richard A885
Struecker, Dennis A16
Struik, Eric E59
Strull, Scott P618
Strumwasser, Todd A266
Strumwasser, Todd P181
Strunk, Tom A928
Strunk, Thomas W. (Tom) A928
Strunk, Tom P673
Strunk, Thomas W. (Tom) P674
Struth, Werner A724
Struth, Werner P452
Struth, Werner W75
Struthers, Darren P200
Strycker, Samara A A583
Stryker, David M. A447
Stryker, Ronda A790
Strykowski, Chris A240
Strykowski, Jill P26
Stu, Aaron A198
Stuart, Al A57

Stuart, Christian A160
Stuart, Greg A170
Stuart, Robert J. (Bob) A417
Stuart, Bob A417
Stuart, Susan A604
Stuart, Charles A682
Stuart, Jack A717
Stuart, Tim A721
Stuart, Kirk A896
Stuart, Kelly P94
Stuart, Cindy P240
Stuart, Paul P304
Stuart, Tim P400
Stuart, Rob P432
Stuart, Sandra W187
Stuart, Isabel E290
Stuart, Jack E351
Stuart, William E396
Stubbers, Edward A69
Stubblefield, Joel A108
Stubbs, Willie P196
Stubbs, Henry P430
Stubbs, P. Scott E141
Stubbs, Ed E185
Stuber, Rich P645
Stucky, Duane P504
Studer, Dianne P379
Studt, Amanda P206
Stueve, Jo P327
Stuff, Ronald P532
Stuff, Ronald P590
Stuhr, Kim A409
Stuiver, Jake E138
Stukalin, Felix E238
Stukenborg, John A834
Stulken, Judy P11
Stull, Hilary A246
Stull, Ed A421
Stull, Terrence L P417
Stull, Hilary E105
Stulpin, Anne A155
Stulpin, Anne E54
Stultz, Timothy J. E316
Stumbo, Kevin J. A229
Stump, James M. A425
Stump, Josh A922
Stump, Kate Lucas P278
Stump, Josh P671
Stumpf, Elizabeth P160
Stumpf, Patricia P486
Stumpf, Jeff P610
Stuntz, Linda A290
Stuopis, Cecilia P314
Sturany, Klaus W178
Sturdivant, Lisa A135
Sturgeon, Sara P610
Sturges, Rick A18
Sturges, Anthony P55
Sturgess, David E P307
Sturgill, Keith A285
Sturm, Jacklyn A A460
Sturm, Stephan W167
Sturtevant, John P326
Sturycz, Robert A794
Sturza, Scott G A414
Sturza, Scott G P236
Stutts, Garry A338
Stutts, William A882
Stutz, Byron P228
Stutzman, Paul P220
Stuyvesant, Cindy A925
Stuyvesant, Cindy E445
Styles, Maurice A89
Styles, Michael A933
Styles, Tracy A933
Styons, Connie P541
Stys, Richard P229
Su, Lisa A14
Su, Lisa A67
Su, Cynthia A794
Su, John P309
Su, Meihsun W123
Su, Tsung-Ming W406
Su, John E237
Suanne, Thurman P671

COMBINED HOOVER'S HANDBOOK INDEX OF EXECUTIVES

```
A = AMERICAN BUSINESS
E = EMERGING COMPANIES
P = PRIVATE COMPANIES
W = WORLD BUSINESS
```

Suarez, Jaime A661
Suarez, Jennifer A893
Suarez, Sarah A895
Suarez, JP A901
Suarez, Mar-a Fernanda W144
Suazo, Art E219
Subbaswamy, Kumble R. (Swamy) P631
Subilia, Sam A793
Sublette, Bill P476
Subramaniam, Rajesh A343
Subramaniam, Rajesh E164
Subramanian, Guhan A524
Subzposh, Faiz P215
Succes, Rodney E131
Suchan, Donna A530
Suche, Steve C. W85
Sucher, Theresa P441
Suchy, Gregory A205
Suchy, Frederick J. P127
Suckale, Margret W59
Sud, James (Jim) A921
Sud, James (Jim) P669
Sudbury, Cathy P263
Suddeth, Stacy B A755
Suddeth, Stacy A755
Suddeth, Stacy B E369
Suddeth, Stacy E369
Sudduth, Pam A859
Suderman, Julie P555
Sudmyer, Nancy P539
Sue, Minny A415
Sue, Minny E208
Suemnicht, Brandon E35
Suer, Murat A654
Suess, Robbin A419
Suetens, David A783
Suever, Catherine A. (Cathy) A640
Sufang, Cui A677
Suffern, Janette A845
Suffridge, Guy P461
Sugar, Robert J. A716
Sugarman, Sarah A54
Sugarman, Gary A810
Suggs, Carolyn P341
Sughrue, Timothy P445
Sugiarto, Prijono W208
Sugiura, Junichi W127
Sugiyama, Takashi A395
Sugiyama, Yoshihiro A938
Sugiyama, Deborah P383
Sugiyama, Yoshihiro P678
Sugiyama, Nao W292
Sugra, Chris A367
Suh, Brian E248
Suhl, Randy P547
Suhm, Tom A484
Suhoza, Chris A323
Suhr, Adam E106
Suit, John M P40
Suite, Denzil A880
Suite, Denzil P640
Suiter, Paul A A414
Suiter, Paul A P236
Suits, Bill A482
Sukeno, Kenji W168
Sukhdeo, Rohan A216
Sukut, Paul P69
Sukys, Dan A491
Sula, Lavern A378
Sulentic, Robert E. (Bob) A175
Sulerzyski, Charles W. A652
Sulerzyski, Charles W. E331
Suliman, Virginia A423
Sullivan, Wynn A14
Sullivan, Robert A16
Sullivan, James A16
Sullivan, Christine A36
Sullivan, Steven R A46

Sullivan, Chris A48
Sullivan, Christopher A68
Sullivan, Timothy J. A71
Sullivan, Andrew A90
Sullivan, Martha A97
Sullivan, Darin A101
Sullivan, Kevin M. A118
Sullivan, Travis A140
Sullivan, Lee A149
Sullivan, John A170
Sullivan, Sean A175
Sullivan, Peter A203
Sullivan, Dave A222
Sullivan, Kevin A264
Sullivan, Kathleen A266
Sullivan, William P. (Bill) A290
Sullivan, Jason A458
Sullivan, David A471
Sullivan, John A551
Sullivan, Heidi A555
Sullivan, James A584
Sullivan, Owen J A585
Sullivan, Anne Marie A588
Sullivan, Adam A590
Sullivan, Brian A626
Sullivan, John A649
Sullivan, Trudy A706
Sullivan, Becky A713
Sullivan, Josh A717
Sullivan, Frank C. A732
Sullivan, William A767
Sullivan, George E. A783
Sullivan, Martin A784
Sullivan, Steve A799
Sullivan, Mark L. A848
Sullivan, Brendan A891
Sullivan, Wynn P6
Sullivan, John P32
Sullivan, Sean P64
Sullivan, Kevin M. P66
Sullivan, Tim P67
Sullivan, Joan P72
Sullivan, John P111
Sullivan, Devon P160
Sullivan, Caroline P162
Sullivan, Janelle P165
Sullivan, Jacqueline P171
Sullivan, Kevin P180
Sullivan, Kathleen P181
Sullivan, Paul P220
Sullivan, Chris P303
Sullivan, John P321
Sullivan, Robert A P330
Sullivan, Anne Marie P365
Sullivan, Brian P383
Sullivan, Margaret P389
Sullivan, Timothy F P412
Sullivan, Teresa A. P442
Sullivan, Sharon P569
Sullivan, George P588
Sullivan, Leo P608
Sullivan, Suzanne P626
Sullivan, Blaise P639
Sullivan, John P658
Sullivan, Chris W333
Sullivan, Louis W. E21
Sullivan, Darin E32
Sullivan, Patrick E42
Sullivan, Kathleen E131
Sullivan, Joanne E147
Sullivan, John J. E279
Sullivan, Josh E351
Sullivan, Jeffrey M. E385
Sullivan, Mark L. E411
Sullivan, Greg E424
Sullivan, Denis E448
Sullivan-Marx, Eileen A592
Sullivan-Marx, Eileen P370
Sullivan-yelko, Teri A686
Sulston, Patrick A544
Sult, John R P193
Sult, John R P506
Sultan, Nader A355
Sultemeier, Chris A902
Sumi, Shuzo W393

Sumichrast, Robert T. P652
Summer, Randee A624
Summerford, R. Michael A852
Summerlin, Scott A519
Summers, Kevin V. A99
Summers, Diane M. A104
Summers, Markus A320
Summers, Dan A796
Summers, Curtis P45
Summers, Barbara (Barb) P151
Summers, Dan E397
Summers-brown, Shelly P62
SUMMERSON, NEIL W54
Summit, Shah P503
Sumner, Christopher A522
Sumner, Tom P157
Sumner, Mike P635
Sumoski, David A. A612
Sumpter, Tammy A654
Sumpter, Thomas P92
Sumpter, Nikki P541
Sumrall, Paul P93
Sun, Albert A284
Sun, Gene A323
Sun, Benjamin A391
Sun, Hannah A686
Sun, John A727
Sun, Winnie A795
Sun, Tony A877
Sun, Julie P402
Sun, John A453
Sun, David P. W89
Sun, Jack W380
Sun, Albert E120
Suncine, Kevin A597
Sund, Charlotta W386
Sundal, Deborah A877
Sundara, Ano P498
Sundaram, Eash A478
Sunderland, Judith A902
Sunderland, Matthew E296
Sunderwala, Meeta A287
Sunderwirth, David A112
Sundharam, Mallik P384
Suneson, Ada P692
Sung, Nancy A191
Sung, Keehyuk P246
Sung, C James P673
Sung, Se Hwan W70
Sung-joong, Huh W283
Sung-Wook, Park W354
Sunod, Babu E132
Sunterapak, Todd P647
Suntichok, Pimolpa W352
Suntrapak, Todd P646
Sunu, Virginia A727
Sunu, Virginia P453
Sunywcc, Instructor A479
Supakarapongkul, Viboon W95
Supancik, Kent A518
Supornpaibul, Jirawat W216
Suraci, Armond A89
Suranjan, Magesvaran A680
Suranye, Monique A329
Surdykowski, Andrew J A462
Sureda, Rob A200
Suresh, Subra A438
Suresh, Subra P114
Suresh, Sailaja P392
Suresh, K.C. W294
Surette, Jahn A409
Surface, Michael E148
Suri, Rajeev W284
Surjaudaja, Parwati W299
Surkosky, Shawn A726
Suro, Manuel A480
Surplus, Scott A425
Surratt, Jeanette P656
Surridge, Sally B P327
Suryanarayana, Lalitha E110
Susalla, Mike A360
Susan, Schmidt P431
Susca, Vito A759
Susca, Vito E373
Susel, Allison P38

Susie, White P665
Susik, Daniel A734
Suske, Lori A540
Suskind, Dennis A. A150
Suskind, Dennis A. E50
Susman, Sally A657
Susman, Lynn P558
Susor, Mark A871
Sussan, Georgina A436
Sussman, Andrew J. (Andy) A251
Sustakoski, Marion A179
Sustana, Mark A512
Sutandar, Laurie A647
Sutaris, Joseph E. A227
Sutaris, Joseph E. E90
Sutcliff, Michael R. (Mike) W5
Sutcliffe, Jim A522
Sutera, Albert P567
Sutera, AJ P567
Sutherland, Alden A63
Sutherland, Kenneth A811
Sutherland, David S. (Dave) A873
Sutherland, Jeff A884
Sutherland, Mark A885
Sutherland, Janet P274
Sutisna, Paulus W130
Sutivong, Arak W352
Sutley, Nancy P299
Sutter, David A323
Sutter, Victor A522
Sutter, David A666
Sutter, Betsy A897
Suttle, Tara A772
Suttle, Tara E383
Sutton, Richard A56
Sutton, Dave A87
Sutton, Scott M. A177
Sutton, Mark S. A467
Sutton, Deborah A660
Sutton, Dave P50
Sutton, Denise P315
Sutton, Ellen P387
Sutton, Deborah P416
Sutton, Robin P523
Sutton, Jaqueline P563
Sutton, Scott T. E212
Sutton, Robert E431
Suvalic, Adnan P257
Suyash, Ashu P738
Suzana, Dellisanti A740
Suzui, Stacey A182
Suzuki, Kazi A940
Suzuki, Yoshihiro P24
Suzuki, Kenji W182
Suzuki, Masahito W220
Suzuki, Toru W220
Suzuki, Nobuya W253
Suzuki, Yasunobu W259
Suzuki, Daiichiro W260
Suzuki, Hisahito W266
Suzuki, Tomoyuki W361
Suzuki, Toshihiro W376
Suzuki, Osamu W376
Suzuki, Masaharu W398
Suarez, Joaqu-n M. Estrada W91
Svanberg, Carl-Henric W420
Svanstrom, Johan A307
Sved, Gergely A289
Svendsen, Heidi A877
Svenkerud, Doug A56
Svenson, Eric E366
Svihel, Alice P55
Svillar, Carmen A554
Svoboda, Rachel A222
Svoboda, Frank M. A389
Svoboda, Dan B. A928
Svoboda, Dan B. P674
Svymbersky, Andy P74
Swaan, Tom de W223
Swaan, Tom de W435
Swaby, Jonathan P140
Swader, Matthew A827
Swader, Matthew P580
Swain, Steven E. (Steve) A271
Swain, John P173

Swain, Stacy P343
Swain, Jayme P432
Swain, Debra P476
Swain, Kevin P600
Swain, Paula J. E226
Swais, Ala A347
Swais, Ala E167
Swallow, Michael F A220
Swallow, Michael F P149
Swallow, Edward M. (Ed) P553
Swallow, Ed P553
Swan, Bob A287
Swan, David A325
Swan, Robert H. (Bob) A460
Swan, Mara E A532
Swan, Kyle A793
Swan, Dennis P508
Swan, Beth A. P603
Swanbeck, Ian A355
Swanberg, Dale P202
Swander, Robert P12
Swanepoel, Fred W275
Swango, Gary A399
Swango, Gary P223
Swanholm, John A311
Swanholm, John P199
Swank, C. Eric A121
Swank, Colleen P30
Swann, Lynn A355
Swann, Krista A530
Swann, Patricia A590
Swann, Joan P46
Swanner, Angela A647
Swanson, Paulyn A29
Swanson, Brian A100
Swanson, Brian A101
Swanson, Scott A104
Swanson, Steven A137
Swanson, Duane A195
Swanson, Roxann A199
Swanson, Marc A330
Swanson, Jordan A440
Swanson, Erika A471
Swanson, Al A668
Swanson, Celia A902
Swanson, Jon A925
Swanson, Paulyn P16
Swanson, Brian P58
Swanson, Scott J. P172
Swanson, Al P422
Swanson, Brian E32
Swanson, Kristofer E102
Swanson, Marc E152
Swanson, Jon E445
Swantek, Kevin A520
Swapp, Russell B. P486
Swart, Mackenzie A711
Swart, Mackenzie P444
Swartz, Heidi A352
Swartz, Carol A583
Swartz, Brian P417
Swartz, Marc E99
Swartz, Robert E246
Swartz, Richard S. (Rick) E293
Swartz, Dustin E433
Swarup, Vijay A309
Swaya, Matthew A779
Swayne, Tashaan P140
Swearengin, Mike A615
Swearingen, John S. A534
Swearingen, Stanley A. (Stan) P53
Swearingen, Fritz Null P215
Sweat, Susan A323
Sweat, Marcia A788
Sweat, Marcia E389
Swecker, Carol A69
Swecker, Craig A403
Swecker, Ben P429
Swedberg, Joe A434
Swedberg, Greg A452
Swedish, Joseph R. A69
Sweeney, Jean A3
Sweeney, Joseph E. (Joe) A60
Sweeney, Richard S. A351
Sweeney, Eileen A388

Sweeney, Sue A408
Sweeney, Tim A461
Sweeney, Joseph A465
Sweeney, John A509
Sweeney, Anne A587
Sweeney, Karen A727
Sweeney, Brandon A897
Sweeney, Alex P166
Sweeney, William P204
Sweeney, Tim P255
Sweeney, Chris P310
Sweeney, Karen P453
Sweeney, Nathan P537
SWEENEY, MICHAEL W51
Sweers, Kim A571
Sweet, Joy Ann A36
Sweet, Lindsay S A345
Sweet, Shane A449
Sweet, Rob A880
Sweet, Stephen J. P73
Sweet, Brett P599
Sweet, Rob P640
Sweet, Julie W5
Sweet, Lindsay S E166
Sweet, Shane E221
Sweet, John W. E333
Sweitzer, Caesar A245
Swenarton, Geri P454
Sweney, Elizabeth A647
Swensen, Mark A887
Swenson, Lynn A147
Swenson, Alyssa A219
Swenson, Mark A734
Swenson, Andrew D. (Andy) A868
Swenson, Rod A885
Swenson, Douglas P174
Swenson, Jessica P299
Swenson, Beau J P567
Swenson, Shaun P607
Swenson, Dana P616
Swensson, Eric E265
Swentkowsky, Stacey A112
Swerdlow, Steven A. (Steve) A175
Swestka, Jason A567
Swestka, Jason E284
Swett, Christian R. (Chris) A859
Swevish, Joseph P329
Swieringa, John W. A271
Swierkowski, Maureen A749
Swierkowski, Maureen E367
Swift, Jim A314
Swift, Christopher J. A408
Swift, Malcolm A547
Swift, Jim E145
Swiger, Andrew P. (Andy) A309
Swilley, Lori P226
Swim, Rob A729
Swim, Karmen P639
Swindle, J. Dean A226
Swindle, J. Dean P150
Swinehart, Alice P333
Swinford, Sandy A723
Swinney, Brad A312
Swinney, Brad P199
Swinton, Matt L P280
Swist, Kyle P220
Switalski, Pamela A5
Switalski, Brian E350
Switkowski, Zygmunt W373
Switz, Robert E. (Bob) A565
Switzer, Julie P664
Sword, Billie P615
Swords, Sheridan C. A630
Swygert, Jenny P6
Swyres, Christine P329
Sy, Teresita W66
Syal, Rajeev (Raj) A444
Syamaprasad, Sindhu P66
Sydnor, Walker P. P120
Syed, Khalid A145
Syed, Mamoon P559
Syiek, Mary A571
Sykes, Brian A167
Sykes, John A452
Syko, Donna A126

Sykora, Joe E179
Syler-Jones, Tracy P549
Sylstra, Michael A374
Sylvester, Maryrose T. A374
Sylvester, Andrea A481
Sylvester, Cara A804
Sylvester, Audrey A852
Sylvia-Reardon, Mary A641
Sylvia-Reardon, Mary P407
Symans, Catherine P639
Symeonides, Kara A347
Symeonides, Kara E167
Symmonds, Joslyn P443
Symonds, Taft P422
Symonds, Jonathan W188
Symonds, Rob W. P. W190
Symons, Nigel A583
Symons, Robert A. A674
Symson, Adam P. E366
Synek, Christopher R. A934
Syngal, Sonia A826
Synnamon, Bill A903
Sytsma, Dan P297
Syverud, Kent D. P600
Szabad, David A591
Szabad, David P369
Szablak, Chester J. (Chet) A297
Szablak, Chester J. (Chet) E129
Szablowski, Paul P551
Szabo, Zoltan A151
Szalka, Gergely E290
Szalla, Todd A10
Szaraburak, Deb A409
Szarek, Malgorzata A467
Szarkowski, Amy P230
Szczecina, Camille A692
Szczupak, David T. (Dave) A919
Szczupak, Dave A919
Szebenyi, Steven E. P232
Szekely, Levente A742
Szerlong, Timothy J. (Tim) A210
Szeto, Mon A381
Szilagyi, Paul A414
Szilagyi, Paul P236
Szlamas, Barbara A824
Szlatenyi, Janos E290
Szlosek, Thomas A. (Tom) A431
Szmurlo, Debbie E45
Sznewajs, Robert D. A104
Sznewajs, John G. A541
Szostek, Jeanie E330
Szurek, Paul E. E97
Szurkus, Dennis A754
Szurkus, Dennis P484
Szygiel, Annette A580
Szygiel, Annette E421
Szyjka, Ray A135
Szymanski, Tom A50
Szymanski, David A620
Szymanski, Paul P255
Szymanski, Ken P287
Szymczak, Luke A366
Szymczak, Stephen J P281
Szynal, Michele E59
Sozen, Suleyman W403
S-_rensen, Mikael W377

T

Taaffe, Dan A246
Taaffe, Dan E105
Taal, Renzo A740
Taaveniku, Arja W219
Tabak, Max A368
Tabaka, William A439
Tabar, Crystal A925
Tabar, Crystal E445
Tabb, Kimberly A686
Tabb, Kevin P79
Tabback, John A484
Taben, Charles A381
Taber, Gregory A881
Taber, Rodman P509
Taber, Abram P588

Taber, Gregory E421
Taborda, Marcelo A470
Taborga, Jorge R. E315
Tabun, Craig A823
Tabun, Craig E405
Tacchetti, Greg A781
Tacchetti, Gregory A781
Tachasirinugune, Sommai W95
Tachimori, Takeshi W366
Tachouet, Matthew P646
Tacke, Markus W353
Tackett, Willie A444
Tackett, Candace P663
Tackitt, Susan A147
Tad-Y, Darlene B P626
Tadeo, James A58
Tadeo, Jeff A809
Tadiello, Larissa A491
Tadros, Abdullah A347
Tadros, Abdullah E167
Taets, Joseph D. (Joe) A77
Taffe, Pat P379
Taft, Peter A810
Taft, Matthias W64
Tagaras, Neil A704
Tagg, Sherri P34
Taggart, Richard G. A783
Taggart, Daniel J. E350
Tagliapietra, Ron A696
TAGUCHI, YUKIO W51
Taheri, Paul P598
Tahir, Sumbul P386
Tahvonen, Greg A262
Tai, Pin A174
Tai, Pin E68
Taiclet, James D. (Jim) A59
Taik-Keun, Jung W176
Tailey, Richard A859
Tait, Steven (Steve) A352
Tait, Richard A780
Tait, Joseph M. (Joe) E263
Taiwo, Oyebode A3
Takac, Kevin A491
Takagi, Yoshiyuki W127
Takagi, Ichiro W361
Takahama, Satoru W360
Takahashi, Koichi W124
Takahashi, Tetsu W221
Takahashi, Kenji W280
Takahashi, Toyonori W298
Takahashi, Kunio W346
TAKAHASHI, SHOJIRO W348
Takahashi, Mitsuru W366
Takami, Kazunori W301
Takara, Kurt P326
Takasaka, Masahiko W205
Takashima, Denise A816
Takayama, Yasushi W286
Takeda, Becky P148
Takeda, Tomohisa W51
Takei, Masato W360
Takemoto, Sue P514
Takemura, Shigeyuki W27
Takemura, Hideaki W252
Takemura, Yoshito W268
Takemura, Tsutomu W286
Taketa, Richard P242
Takeuchi, Kyle A462
Takeuchi, Kohei W186
Takeuchi, Akira W259
Takizawa, Soichiro W186
Takizawa, Masahiro W430
Takla, Magdy P563
Talaga, Dana A345
Talaga, Dana E165
Talamas, Stephanie A255
Talan, Melba P296
Talarovich, Peter A737
Talarovich, Peter E361
Talati, Rakesh P72
Talavera, Judith A51
Talavera, Maria A861
Talavera, Alvaro P244
Talbot, Patricia A424
Talbot, Brian A552

COMBINED HOOVER'S HANDBOOK INDEX OF EXECUTIVES

```
A = AMERICAN BUSINESS
E = EMERGING COMPANIES
P = PRIVATE COMPANIES
W = WORLD BUSINESS
```

Talbot, Chris A695
Talbot, Angela P261
Talbot, Patricia E211
Talbot, Brian E275
Talbott, Jeff A799
Talbott, Gregory P228
Talcott, Patrick A651
Talcott, Patrick E329
Talen, Bruce A224
Taletovic, Semir E127
Talhouet, Patrice de A243
Talka, Michele P72
Tallaksen, Jim A778
Tallamraju, Raman A799
Tallent, Jimmy C. A866
Tallent, William P528
Tallent, Jimmy C. E417
Tallet, Eric A695
Talley, Cyndi A410
Talley, Doug A799
Talley, Linda P130
Talley, Erik P325
Talley, Verlinda P633
Tallis, Heather P579
Talonpoika, Nikolas W218
Talreja, Manjula A739
Talty, Blair A922
Talty, Blair P671
Talwar, Vikram A352
Tam, Cherry A203
Tam, Jamie A390
Tama, Christopher A833
Tamagawa, Akio W281
Tamai, Takaaki W393
Tamaka, Hideo A57
Tamaka, Hideo P33
Tamasi, Tony A613
Tambakeras, Markos I. A936
Tamburi, Carlo W153
Tamerius, John D. E342
Tamez, Cesar P620
Tammaro, Vincent P676
Tammy, Miller A381
Tammy, Goslant A882
Tamweber, Eric A789
Tan, Alex A24
Tan, Raymond A269
Tan, Amanda A315
Tan, Phillip A346
Tan, Jenny A680
Tan, Zhaohui W98
Tan, Darren S. P. W299
Tan, Phillip E167
Tanabe, Barbara A110
Tanabe, Jose A543
Tanabe, Masaki W30
Tanabe, Eiichi W257
Tanaka, Bryan P628
Tanaka, Masayasu W205
Tanaka, Jun W221
Tanaka, Seiichi W360
Tanaka, Junichi W360
Tanaka, Yumi E143
Tanaka, Takaaki E308
Tanasijevich, George A506
Tanchoco, Silvino P325
Tancrati, Juliana A114
Tancrati, Juliana E37
Tancredi, Lucy E143
Tande, Brett P472
Tandler, Jaclyn P524
Tandon, Ashish A166
Tandon, Manu P79
Tandy, Sonya A224
Taneja, Rajat A895
Tanenbaum, Donna E99
Tang, Michael A22
Tang, Karen A140

Tang, Kin P366
Tang, Youhua P594
Tang, Vance E89
Tang, Edmund E113
Tang, Francis E113
Tang, Stephen S. E317
Tangney, Eugene A734
Tango, Yasutake W208
Taniguchi, Michihiro W260
Taniguchi, Shinichi W360
Tanikawa, Kei W30
Tanimoto, Dale A109
Tanis, Justin A452
Tankesley, Mark A224
Tankut, Papatya A251
Tannehill, Tom A323
Tannenbaum, Carl A320
Tanner, Ryan A114
Tanner, Julie A193
Tanner, Teresa J. A329
Tanner, Steve A340
Tanner, Kirk A654
Tanner, Geoff A765
Tanner, Edward P268
Tanner, Ryan E36
Tanner, Steve E160
Tannert, Silvio P114
Tannian, Michael A870
Tanory, Todd A598
Tanoue, Donna A. A109
Tans, Gillian A143
Tantikulanan, Thiti W216
Tantivess, Vittavat W95
Tanum, Anne Carine W140
Tanwar, Ankit A108
Tanz, Stuart A. E356
Tanzawa, Hideo W431
Tanzer, David A137
Tanzer, Kim P442
Tanzer, Tobi P445
Tao, Andy E261
Taohai, Xue W99
Taormina, Jo A A133
Tap, Genevieve A744
Taparausky, Kevin A835
Tapia, Eric A394
Tapia, Mark A872
Tapia, Dave P659
Tapler, Howard A745
Taplin, Mary-Ellen P172
Taplin, Bill P356
Taplits, Steven A125
Tapp, Tim P83
Tappan, Phillip A760
Tappan, Hugh P662
Tappan, Phillip E374
Tapper, Lynne A218
Tappert, Tod N. P430
Tarafa, Denise A181
Tarafa, Jose A543
Tarafa, Denise E70
Tarakji, Ahmad P595
Taranenko, Pavlo E290
Tarantino, Joe E433
Taranto, Tony A893
Taraporevala, Cyrus A783
Taras, Jennifer A692
Tarasenko, Kseniya A581
Taraskavage, Joe P87
Tarasov, Aleksey P459
Tarbet, Linda A747
Tarby, Todd A373
Tarchetti, Mark S. A593
Tardella, Michael E330
Taris, Tom A54
Tarling, Michael A140
Tarling, Neil P197
Tarlton, Dudley A599
Tarpey, Michael A784
Tarpey, John P59
Tarrach, Chris E131
Tarriff, Scott L. E118
Tart, C. Lee (Bozie) E368

Tartaglia, Michael A588
Tartaglia, Michael P365
Tartanella, Michael A115
Tartanella, Michael E37
Tarver, Mary A215
Tarvin, Julie A463
Tashiro, Tamiharu W215
Taske, Jim A69
Tasker, Benjamin P193
Tasooji, Michael B. P93
Tassell, Van P650
Tastad, Carolyn A487
Tastad, Carolyn A679
Tata, Lee P574
Tatachar, Gopinath A112
Tate, Marian A91
Tate, Edwin A483
Tate, Greg A739
Tate, Howard M A803
Tate, Marian P55
Tate, Allyson P157
Tate, Mike P386
Tate, Creston P677
Tate, Mike E102
Tatelbaum, Ronald J P649
Tatelbaumm, Ron P233
Tateosian, David A349
Tatera, Robert A218
Tatevosian, Michael A269
Tateyama, Len A104
Tatom, Kim A340
Tatom, Kim E161
Taton, Jacqueline P542
Tatterson, W. Mark A865
Tatterson, W. Mark E416
Taube, Carl A713
Taubeneck, Paul A492
Taubeneck, Brian A880
Taubeneck, Brian P640
Tauber, David W. P542
Tauber, Richard E. P542
Taubert, Jennifer A479
Taubman, Ross E. A678
Taulien, Valarie A119
Taunton, Michael A81
Tauscher, Randall L P311
Tavaglinoe, John P161
Tavakkolizadeh, Ali P556
Tavakoli, Nader A43
Tavakoli, Nader E13
Tavares, Chris A140
Tavares, Luis P229
Tavares, Carlos W305
Tavernier, Jacques W415
Taves, Joel A706
Tavill, Gail A232
Tavolato, Stefanie E143
Tawes, Greg A850
Tawney, Jeff A835
Tay, Talal A246
Tay, Julie E10
Tay, Talal E105
Tayano, Ken W124
Taylor, Mark A1
Taylor, Robert A30
Taylor, J A58
Taylor, Stuart A103
Taylor, Joyce A108
Taylor, Michael A109
Taylor, Steven A126
Taylor, Julie A151
Taylor, Craig A182
Taylor, Todd A195
Taylor, Ellen A205
Taylor, Warren A248
Taylor, Cherylope A262
Taylor, Lyndon C. A263
Taylor, Rhonda M. A272
Taylor, Emily A272
Taylor, Stephen M. (Steve) A289
Taylor, Namisa A309
Taylor, Cheri A325
Taylor, Robert C. A355
Taylor, Robert A386
Taylor, Emma A390

Taylor, Todd A395
Taylor, Pamela J. (Pam) A429
Taylor, Peggy A441
Taylor, Erin A442
Taylor, Jim A446
Taylor, Anna A449
Taylor, Todd J A467
Taylor, Anna A523
Taylor, Jason A544
Taylor, Daniel A562
Taylor, Howard A610
Taylor, Bertha A642
Taylor, Donna A647
Taylor, Tim G. A662
Taylor, Donna A665
Taylor, David S. A679
Taylor, Sharon C. A686
Taylor, Sue A686
Taylor, Moira A702
Taylor, Zachary A704
Taylor, Bob A704
Taylor, Pamela A713
Taylor, Redmond A713
Taylor, Angela Pittman A727
Taylor, Steven A733
Taylor, Bret A739
Taylor, Bill A740
Taylor, Shirley A744
Taylor, Carter A747
Taylor, Michael A754
Taylor, Kenneth R. (Ken) A758
Taylor, Bronwen A789
Taylor, Nathan A799
Taylor, Randy A852
Taylor, Steve A855
Taylor, Renee A859
Taylor, Fritz A862
Taylor, Scott A877
Taylor, Ed A880
Taylor, Stacey A895
Taylor, Nick A908
Taylor, Patricia A. A913
Taylor, Mike P. A928
Taylor, Rebecca A933
Taylor, Robert P20
Taylor, Kari P77
Taylor, Mike P111
Taylor, Cyrus P116
Taylor, Seth P185
Taylor, Monica P210
Taylor, Jennifer P250
Taylor, Mark P300
Taylor, Dana P303
Taylor, Scott P333
Taylor, Denise P357
Taylor, Nikki P378
Taylor, Karen P382
Taylor, Michael P404
Taylor, Bertha P407
Taylor, Spence M. P430
Taylor, Heather P448
Taylor, Angela Pittman P453
Taylor, Starla P457
Taylor, David P461
Taylor, Kim P467
Taylor, R. Stephen P473
Taylor, Julie P480
Taylor, Michael P484
Taylor, Mark P516
Taylor, Shaun P540
Taylor, Michael P546
Taylor, Tangula P548
Taylor, Dana P564
Taylor, Liane P606
Taylor, Kyle P615
Taylor, James P623
Taylor, Phil P625
Taylor, Ed P640
Taylor, Derrick P655
Taylor, Curtis E P656
Taylor, Mike P. P674
Taylor, Kevin W42
Taylor, Joseph M. (Joe) W300
Taylor, Kathleen P. W331
Taylor, Mark E1

Taylor, Greg E47
Taylor, Warren E107
Taylor, Parker E143
Taylor, Robert E188
Taylor, Pamela J. (Pam) E214
Taylor, Anna E221
Taylor, Tammy E222
Taylor, Brenton E231
Taylor, Kelly E290
Taylor, D. Deeni E333
Taylor, Donna E334
Taylor, Kenneth R. (Ken) E372
Taylor, W. Kent E404
Taylor, Jason E433
Taylor, Nick E436
Taylor, Patricia A. E438
Taylor, Ryan E440
Taylor-Gerken, Polly P605
Tazawa, Naoya W282
Teagle, Walter C. A348
Teagle, Walter C. E169
Teague, Eric A114
Teague, Roger A140
Teague, R. Keith A187
Teague, Keith A188
Teague, A. James (Jim) A299
Teague, Sarah A664
Teague, Bart P263
Teague, Justin P412
Teague, Lynn P430
Teague, Eric E36
Teague, Sarah E334
Teahen, Joshua P482
Teare, David W357
Teasdale, Chris W377
Tebben, Thomas E123
Tebben, Shawn E424
Tebeaux, Jeff A435
Tebelman, Tracey A329
Tech, Georgia P114
Tecotzky, Mark E124
Tedder, Tiffani A336
Tedder, Jeff A768
Tedder, Tiffani E157
Tedeschi, Anthony A811
Tedesco, Maria P A91
Tedesco, Janice A444
Tedesco, Amy A686
Tedesco, Arthur N P665
Tedesco, Maria P E29
Tedjarati, Shane W431
Tedrick, Ann P76
Teears, Colleen A700
Teed, Fred A670
Teed, Andrew D. E412
Teel, Lawrence E. (Skip) A917
Teel, Skip A917
Teel, Kerry P262
Teel, Michael J. (Mike) P438
Teepsuwan, Veraphan W208
Teerasoontornwong, Thawee W216
Teets, Richard T A785
Teetz, Robert P359
Teeven, Jeff E97
Tefft-Keller, Kathryn P2
Tegan, Jason A369
Teh, Pearly A14
Teh, Raymond A613
Tehrani, Sean P448
Teirlynck, Yves A609
Teirlynck, Yves P391
Teixeira, Kay P307
Tejada, Albert A266
Tejada, Albert P181
Tejkl, Karen A881
Tejkl, Karen E421
Tekavec, John A91
Tekavec, John E29
Teklemichael, Chernet P467
Telesz, Todd E. A213
Telesz, Todd E. P143
Telfair, Jackie A902
Telfer, Geoff A355
Telfer, Chris P399
Telfer, Richard J. P641

Telford, Ric A465
Tellechea, Julio W248
Telles, Mark A329
Telles, Lisa P538
Tellez, George A325
Tellkamp, Scott A246
Tellkamp, Scott E105
Temares, Steven H. (Steve) A125
Temkin, David A587
Temmen, Diane P633
Tempel, Trent A595
Temperley, Donald A434
Tempesta, Edward A544
Temple, Brett A271
Temple, Mike A369
Temple, Christopher A668
Temple, Michael G. (Mike) A683
Temple, John A717
Temple, Mary P55
Temple, Thomas J. E337
Temple, Tom E337
Temple, John E351
Templeton, Deborah A371
Templeton, Richard K. (Rich) A820
Templeton, Deborah P213
Templeton, Brady E7
Templeton, D. Jeffrey E43
Templeton, Gary E185
Templin, Donald C. (Don) A534
Templin, Roy A919
Tena, Andrea P469
Tendler, Craig A479
Tenebruso, Marc A701
Tenenbaum, Brian M. A716
Teng, Adrian W208
Teng, Ooi Say W371
Tengel, Jeffrey J. (Jeff) A651
Tengel, Jeffrey J. (Jeff) E329
Tengelin, Michael A374
Tengler, Nancy A413
Tengler, Nancy E205
Tenkhoff, Anne P633
Tenn, Steven E102
Tennant, Nancy A919
Tenney, Emily P251
Tenney, Maurice H. (Dusty) E53
Tennis, Karen P26
Tennison, Lynden L. A863
Tennison, Tom P199
Tennity, Jennifer Villa A200
Tennyson, Jeff A700
Tenorio, Orlando A218
Tenpas, Kevin S. A413
Tenpas, Jan P312
Tenpas, Kevin S. E205
Tenuta, Emilio A289
Teo, Jean W96
Teodoro, Antonio A813
Teodosio, Tammy P431
Tepartimargorn, Pitipan W316
Teper, Steven P149
Teplin, Stephen A327
Tepper, Robyn A511
Tepper, Robyn P290
Terabatake, Masamichi W208
Teraguchi, Tomoyuki W286
Terajima, Yoshinori W279
Teran, Tim A204
Terashi, Shigeki W400
Tercek, Mark R. P579
Terebessy, Chris A747
Teresi, Todd A72
Teresi, Rob P223
Terifay, Robert J. A710
Terisse, Pierre-Andre W128
Terlisner, John A723
Terner, Franck W15
Terpsma, Daniel W. A806
Terpsma, Daniel W. E398
TERRACHINI, FRANCO W121
Terranova, Carleen A922
Terranova, Carleen P671
Terrell, Karenann A120
Terrell, Mike A195
Terrell, Felencia A606

Terrell, Ransom P140
Terribile, Jennifer A200
Terris, Maria A695
Terroni, Michael A823
Terroni, Michael E405
Terrott, Pam A536
Terry, Susan A165
Terry, Rick O. A413
Terry, Cheryl A449
Terry, James A584
Terry, Jim A584
Terry, Thomas S. (Tom) A859
Terry, Tom A859
Terry, Lisa P85
Terry, Joshua P108
Terry, Ryan P116
Terry, Rick O. E205
Terry, Cheryl E221
Terry, Tilea E282
Terry, James E396
Terryn, Kristof W435
Terwiesch, Peter W3
Terzian, John E418
Terzioglu, Kaan A199
Tesarova, Katarina A506
Teska, Rich A606
Tessier, Pamela P229
Tessier, Claude W21
Tessitore, Ron A695
Tessitore, Christopher P. (Chris) E296
Tessler, Hervé A933
Testa, Mark A36
Testa, Thomas A379
Testa, Sarah A846
Testa, Christopher P. A869
Testor, Joseph A35
Testy, Kellye A880
Testy, Kellye P640
Tetenman, Scott P367
Tetere, Ieva W357
Teti, Nathaniel A301
Teti, Nathaniel P196
Tetreault, Kristin A409
Tettamanti, Candice P311
Teuber, Andy P16
Teufel, Sharon P148
Tevlin, Marjorie P523
Tew, John P625
Tewes, Timothy A. (Tim) A586
Tewes, Timothy A. (Tim) E301
Teyssen, Johannes W143
Thacher, John P. P670
Thacker, Dan A788
Thacker, Dan E389
Thaden, Terry A654
Thaer, Lewis F. Von P178
Thai, Beth P596
Thakar, Sumedh S. E342
Thalacker, Gail P619
Tham, Russell A74
Tham, Elaine A544
Thaman, Michael H. (Mike) A635
Thaman, Beatrice A711
Thaman, Beatrice P444
Thames, Davis A188
Thames, Thomas B. A754
Thames, Thomas B. P484
Thamm, Michael W87
Thammasart, DVM Sujint W95
Thampatty, Gayathri P190
Thanawiwat, Phillip A747
Thandri, Ananthan P326
Thanh, Mai Trang A431
Thani, Jassim bin Hamad Jassim bin Jabor Al- W316
Thanopoulos, George P334
Thao, MAI P107
Thapar, Manu A902
Tharby, Linda M. A123
Tharmaratnam, Anand A474
Tharp, Debbie A311
Tharp, Morris A. A758
Tharp, Randall A859
Tharp, Beth P151
Tharp, Debbie P199

Tharp, William W P203
Tharp, Morris A. E372
Thatchanamoorth, Aravinth P672
Thaus, Kurt B. A810
Thaw, James P101
Thayer, Jonathan W. (Jack) A304
Thayer, Bud P74
Thayer, Pamela P596
Thaysen, Jacob A22
Theess, Karsten A505
Theiler, Jeff E333
Theine, Mark D. E333
Theis, Axel W24
Theisen, Jen A728
Theisen, Randall S. A913
Theisen, Randall S. E438
Theiss, Paul A606
Theiss, Dave A891
Theleman, David A584
Themelis, Nicholas E270
Thengvall, Kelly A89
Theobald, Neil D. P546
Theobald, Donald E154
Theobald, Tyler E267
Theobald, Stephen P. E433
Theobalds, Kenneth A296
Theodore, Julie A69
Theodoredis, Roger E. P668
Theodoridis, Artemios Ch. W25
Theodorou, Tasos A767
Theodosis, Christian P639
Theofilaktidis, Maria W53
Thepaut, Eric A149
Theriault, Matthew A540
Theriault, Ryan A940
Therrien, Stephane W232
Thezan, Alexander A167
Thiam, Tidjane C. W120
Thiara, Raju P659
Thibaud, Didier M.C. E277
Thibeault, Robert A123
Thibeault, Robert A610
Thibeault, Anne A686
Thibeault, Rick P630
Thibodaux, Penny P458
Thibodeau, Johnathan A654
Thibodeau, David P131
Thibodeaux, Faron J. A71
Thibodeaux, William A871
Thibodeaux, Wayne P549
Thiel, John A107
Thiele, Patricia P519
Thielen, Kent R P318
Thieme, Dennis P363
Thien, Ted E412
Thien-Ngern, Orapong W352
Thienachariya, Thana W352
Thierrin, Brian A837
Thiers, Bernard P. A569
Thies, Jeremy A740
Thiesing, James A476
Thiessen, Jay A637
Thiessen, Eric A751
Thiessen, Allen P644
Thietten, Gary E256
Thigpen, Carl S. A683
Thill, Howard A263
Thill, Howard J. E342
Thillart, Leo van den W80
Thilmany, Andrea P400
Thim, Gene P456
Thingelstad, Jamie E384
Thipavong, Lynda A160
Thirot, Olivier G A488
Thiry, Kent J. A257
Thissen, Karen Wilson A60
Thistlethwaite, Bryan A575
Thiyagarajan, Sakthivel A135
Tho, Lye A575
Thoem, Tyler A449
Thoem, Tyler E221
Thoke, Steve A735
Thole, Nick A40
Thole, Karen A828
Thole, Nick P29

COMBINED HOOVER'S HANDBOOK INDEX OF EXECUTIVES

```
A = AMERICAN BUSINESS
E = EMERGING COMPANIES
P = PRIVATE COMPANIES
W = WORLD BUSINESS
```

Thole, Karen P584
Thom, Patrick P5
Thom, Jonathan P198
Thoma, Ronald A245
Thoma, Joy A544
Thoma, Mark A891
Thoman, Thomas S. A25
Thoman, Thomas S. P14
Thomas, Shantelle A36
Thomas, Toby L. A51
Thomas, David A101
Thomas, Dan A113
Thomas, Michael M. (Mike) A144
Thomas, Mary H. A160
Thomas, Ashley A162
Thomas, Verghese A177
Thomas, Carolyn A179
Thomas, Bill A195
Thomas, Anthony A203
Thomas, Kevin A206
Thomas, Brandi A262
Thomas, David A279
Thomas, William R. A301
Thomas, Gary L. A301
Thomas, Lee A319
Thomas, Pamela A331
Thomas, David M. A361
Thomas, Jamie A368
Thomas, Jim A383
Thomas, Suzanne C. A401
Thomas, Darrell A407
Thomas, Robin A456
Thomas, Michael A491
Thomas, Stephen S A492
Thomas, Rob A509
Thomas, Joseph A527
Thomas, Roni A530
Thomas, Nixon A540
Thomas, Kurt A561
Thomas, Betty A571
Thomas, Tonya A590
Thomas, David A591
Thomas, Sharon A595
Thomas, Geevy S.K. A602
Thomas, Paige L. A602
Thomas, Sue A638
Thomas, Gibu A654
Thomas, Stephen A656
Thomas, Brande A664
Thomas, David A704
Thomas, Laurita A711
Thomas, Philip A718
Thomas, Paul A724
Thomas, Kelly A737
Thomas, Tim A746
Thomas, John M. A815
Thomas, Drue A859
Thomas, Christy A859
Thomas, John A881
Thomas, Karen A885
Thomas, Cheryl A887
Thomas, Gibu A902
Thomas, Andrea A902
Thomas, Anne A902
Thomas, Anthony W. (Tony) A924
Thomas, Joseph P116
Thomas, Ailsa P117
Thomas, Jacob P140
Thomas, Robin P140
Thomas, Michael J P159
Thomas, Will P176
Thomas, Stephanie P179
Thomas, Pamela P202
Thomas, Dean P211
Thomas, Dana P252
Thomas, Lydia P253
Thomas, Michael S. P267
Thomas, Stephen S P279
Thomas, Karen P291

Thomas, Beverly P337
Thomas, Kevin P356
Thomas, David P369
Thomas, Stephen P414
Thomas, Dan P424
Thomas, Laurita P444
Thomas, Paul P452
Thomas, Maggie P540
Thomas, Tony P672
Thomas, Anthony (Tony) W283
Thomas, Ralf P. W353
Thomas, David E32
Thomas, Dan E36
Thomas, Ashley E61
Thomas, Dorothy E73
Thomas, John E86
Thomas, M. Andrew E99
Thomas, Brandon E131
Thomas, Martin E141
Thomas, Jeswin E143
Thomas, Peter T. E151
Thomas, Ed E174
Thomas, Jim E186
Thomas, Suzanne C. E198
Thomas, Jeffrey E223
Thomas, Robin E228
Thomas, Tarca E234
Thomas, Kurt E268
Thomas, Anil E290
Thomas, Sue E320
Thomas, John T. E333
Thomas, Brande E334
Thomas, Donald E. (Don) E350
Thomas, Philip E354
Thomas, Kelly E361
Thomas, John E421
Thomasjr, William A859
Thomason, Mary A142
Thomason, Linton J. (Lin) A397
Thomason, David S. A659
Thomason, Chad A755
Thomason, Jaime P274
Thomason, Mary E49
Thomason, Chad E369
Thome, James A871
Thomford, Mark E143
Thompson, Matthew A. (Matt) A11
Thompson, Matt A11
Thompson, Bridget A29
Thompson, Jeff A36
Thompson, Jeffrey A36
Thompson, Sherene A39
Thompson, John A57
Thompson, Tommy A121
Thompson, Jeffrey D. (Jeff) A129
Thompson, Betty A144
Thompson, Elizabeth M. (Betty) A145
Thompson, Dale A. A165
Thompson, Sherry A165
Thompson, Morris A167
Thompson, Lisa A222
Thompson, Rodney A222
Thompson, Becki A226
Thompson, Christopher A290
Thompson, Mike A315
Thompson, Christine A336
Thompson, Kent T. A339
Thompson, Michael A367
Thompson, Laura K. A392
Thompson, Steve A409
Thompson, Kirk A442
Thompson, Mark E. A444
Thompson, Angel A465
Thompson, Matt A498
Thompson, Rebecca A498
Thompson, Steve A501
Thompson, Stafford A520
Thompson, Craig A554
Thompson, John W A565
Thompson, Kevin L. A567
Thompson, James A567
Thompson, Richard L. (Rich) A600
Thompson, Geoff A621
Thompson, Paul W. A674
Thompson, Bryan A680

Thompson, James H. (Jim) A694
Thompson, Marcy J. A768
Thompson, Larry A771
Thompson, William P. A776
Thompson, Chris A787
Thompson, Kathy C. A788
Thompson, Robert A804
Thompson, Lloyd A859
Thompson, Beryl A890
Thompson, James A908
Thompson, John D. (David) A915
Thompson, Kimberly A919
Thompson, Kenny D A920
Thompson, Ryan A922
Thompson, Joseph F. A925
Thompson, Eric A935
Thompson, Brian P20
Thompson, Doug P27
Thompson, Dwight P29
Thompson, John P33
Thompson, Troy P83
Thompson, Arthur P85
Thompson, Robert P116
Thompson, Bryan P122
Thompson, Becki P150
Thompson, Linda Valdez P171
Thompson, Lisa P173
Thompson, Jerry E P196
Thompson, Matt P200
Thompson, Georgiana P220
Thompson, Katherine P233
Thompson, Bryan P234
Thompson, Angela D P242
Thompson, Matt P246
Thompson, Gloria P250
Thompson, Susan K. P258
Thompson, Elaine P284
Thompson, Craig B P325
Thompson, Craig B. P325
Thompson, Lisa P340
Thompson, Kelly P389
Thompson, Lisa P396
Thompson, David P410
Thompson, Glynn P471
Thompson, Donna P489
Thompson, William P. P512
Thompson, Rebecca P536
Thompson, David P591
Thompson, Ryker P549
Thompson, Chase P627
Thompson, Ann P636
Thompson, Erin P655
Thompson, M Keith P656
Thompson, Ryan P671
Thompson, Johnny W116
Thompson, Regarner E14
Thompson, Stephen C. (Steve) E78
Thompson, Cathy E91
Thompson, Newton E147
Thompson, Christine E157
Thompson, Kent T. E159
Thompson, Andrew E260
Thompson, Kevin L. E283
Thompson, James E283
Thompson, Dennis L. E295
Thompson, Geoff E311
Thompson, Jill E317
Thompson, H. Brian E326
Thompson, Tommy G. E333
Thompson, James D. (Jim) E349
Thompson, Larry E382
Thompson, Kathy C. E389
Thompson, Kenneth E. E428
Thompson, James E436
Thompson, Joseph F. E445
Thomsen, Joseph A564
Thomsen, Mads Krogsgaard W290
Thomsen, Jill E300
Thomson, James A. A27
Thomson, Robert A596
Thomson, Ross A759
Thomson, Andrew J. (Andy) A832
Thomson, Dawn P52
Thomson, Greg P618
Thomson, Phil W171

Thomson, Warren A. W247
Thomson, Ross E373
Thomson, Kevin E440
Thon, Andrew J P309
Thopay, Sudarsan A713
Thorburn, Andrew W270
Thorley, Trevor E72
Thornberry, Richard G. (Rick) A700
Thornburgh, Richard A738
Thornburgh, Richard E. W121
Thorne, Sherri A320
Thorne, Richard A493
Thorne, James A498
Thornhill, Joelle A257
Thornhill, Hugh P395
Thornley, Anthony S. (Tony) E59
Thornton, Mary A86
Thornton, Randolph I. A239
Thornton, Bob A349
Thornton, Christopher A360
Thornton, Janis A540
Thornton, Daniel P. (Dan) A651
Thornton, Curt A695
Thornton, Robin A760
Thornton, Orson P83
Thornton, Brian P114
Thornton, Steve P442
Thornton, Glenda P541
Thornton, Leslie P666
Thornton, Mary E27
Thornton, Daniel P. (Dan) E329
Thornton, Robin E374
Thorogood, Richard A218
Thorp, H. Holden P600
Thorpe, Linda A117
Thorpe, Linda P61
Thorpe, Wendy W27
Thorslund, Katarina W19
Thorson, Robert A. A912
Thorson, Michael P221
Thorup, Schuyler P117
Thottikamath, Sethu A327
Thouin, Stéphane W88
Thouret, Claude G. E117
Thrasher, Vickie A28
Thrasher, Rebecca A115
Thrasher, Kelsey P302
Thrasher, Rebecca E37
Threlkeld, Ashley E106
Throsby, Tim W58
Thu, Wendy A16
Thuillier, Larry A599
Thulin, Inge G. A3
Thull, Todd A242
Thumaty, Kalyan A461
Thuning, Elizabeth A885
Thurber, Robert A797
Thurber, Robert C A798
Thurber, Ray E366
Thurlow, Brenda P472
Thurm, Patrick A744
Thurman, Chris A526
Thurow, Rick A442
Thurston, Brian A859
Thurston, Corydon L. E43
Thurston, John E185
Thuss, Charles A16
Thway, Myint P488
Thygesen, Mikael A761
Thygesen, Henriette H. W1
Thépaut, Eric A149
Tian, Angel A816
Tian, Guoli W72
Tiano, Dick P6
Tiano, Vincent E284
Tibbitts, Betsy P215
Tibbs, E. W. P120
Tiberi, John A688
Tibke, Kathy A519
Tice, Sali A638
Tice, Casandra P116
Tice, Betty P277
Tice, Sali E320
Tichelman, Maurits A460
Tichenor, Jim A645

Tickles, Chuck P274
Ticku, Jonathan P316
Tidd, Diana H. E290
Tiddettes, Shawn P652
Tidwell, Isaiah A520
Tidwell, Janet P122
Tidwell, Kay L. E219
Tieanworn, Min W95
Tiede, Robert C. (Rob) A768
Tiedemann, Edward A694
Tiegs, Randy A818
Tiegs, Randy E403
Tielke, Lori P32
Tiemeier, Greg A723
Tiencken, John P120
Tienor, Dennis E35
Tierney, Brian X. A51
Tierney, Kathleen M. A126
Tierney, John A137
Tierney, William A233
Tierney, Thomas J. (Tom) A287
Tierney, Tim A329
Tierney, Brian A719
Tierney, Bill A773
Tierney, Timothy A888
Tierney, Thomas J. P579
Tierney, Nancy P630
Tierney, William E94
Tierney, Brian E355
Tierney, Timothy E425
Tiesi, Jeffrey P667
Tietjen, Deb P212
Tiews, Matthew A511
Tiews, Matthew P290
Tiggelaar, Thomas P316
Tigges, Kevin A686
Tight, Steven M. A160
Tignor, Chris A320
Tihami, Michele A180
Tiitinen, Pekka W3
Tiitola, Antti W275
Tikkanen, Eric A796
Tikkanen, Eric E397
Tilas, Tom A16
Tilden, Bradley D. (Brad) A29
Tilds, Eric P297
Tilford, Tim P310
Tilghman, Lee A224
Till, Scott A801
Tillemans, Todd W. A416
Tillett, Doug A319
Tilley, Daryl A527
Tillman, Audrey Boone A19
Tillman, Tonia A397
Tillman, Lee M. A533
Tillman, Joseph A871
Tilton, Glenn F A191
Tilton, David P51
Tilton, Jesse C P378
Timanus, H. E. (Tim) A682
Timberlake, Rebecca P523
Timen, Sanford A824
Timen, Sanford P561
Timko, Thomas A374
Timm, Bryan L. A861
Timm, Craig E250
Timmer, Kristin E265
Timmerman, Douglas A37
Timmerman, Gail A484
Timmerman, Timothy T. P301
Timmermans, Koos W200
Timmers, Martha P430
Timmins, Lawrence A112
Timmons, James T. (Jimmy) A512
Timmons, Darla P476
Timms, Diane P51
Timothy, Brad A465
Timothy, Civil A654
Timothy, Melhorn P675
Timpe, Mark P566
Tin, Kng Hwee W299
Tina, Saldana P5
Tindale, Breanne A376
Tindall, Michael A123
Tindall, Adam W27

Ting, Richard A469
Ting, Henry A827
Ting, Henry P580
Tingler, Matthew A727
Tingler, Matthew P453
Tingley, Sandy P431
Tingley, Stephen E353
Tinglum, Kristen A518
Tingstrom, Ulf A684
Tingue, David A63
Tinney, Stephen A583
Tinsley, Will A115
Tinsley, Will E38
Tintori, John A592
Tintori, John P370
Tipayamongkol, Supat A284
Tipayamongkol, Supat E120
Tippett, Leslie P47
Tippie, Henry B E268
Tippit, Mike A312
Tippit, Mike P200
Tippl, Thomas A10
Tippner, Kristie A692
Tipton, Perry A421
Tipton, John (Stephen) A426
Tipton, Mark A449
Tipton, Jennifer A600
Tipton, Paul P675
Tipton, John (Stephen) E213
Tipton, Mark E220
Tirado, Selene P470
Tirador, Gabriel A555
Tirpak, Ronald K A502
Tisack, Gael A711
Tisack, Gael P444
Tisch, Jonathan M. A525
Tisch, James S. A525
Tisch, Andrew H. A526
Tisch, Merryl H A785
Tisch, Thomas J. P102
Tisch, Merryl H P526
Tischler, Mary A893
Tisci, Dante E222
Tishman, Daniel R. (Dan) A16
Tison, Jack P404
Tisone, Bob A933
Titinger, Jorge L. P494
Titova, Zornitsa A925
Titova, Zornitsa E445
Titus, Laurin A108
Titus, Martin E A810
Titus, Martin E P546
Tiwari, Anoop P230
Tjernsmo, Dag W377
Tkalcevic, Joshua A112
Toale, Kevin A918
Toalson, Valerie C A159
Tobar, Cesar A203
Tobe, Dean A739
Tobey, Josh A626
Tobey, Paul P305
Tobi, Kathleen A692
Tobias, Hugh A900
Tobias, Karen P101
Tobin, Bill P189
Tobin, Gail P554
Tobin, James J. (Jim) W244
Tobin, Dominic M. E98
Tobin, David E368
Tobison, Gary A361
Tocher, Catherine S. A397
Toczydlowski, Greg C A844
Toczydlowski, Gregory A845
Todaro, Michael J. A530
Todd, Stephen A277
Todd, Paul A287
Todd, Terry A400
Todd, Amy A513
Todd, Treadway A621
Todd, Brian R A797
Todd, Jeff A877
Todd, Diane A909
Todd, Aaron D. P13
Todd, Timothy J P341
Todd, Ertel P615

Todd, James E48
Todd, Terry E195
Todd, Treadway E312
Todd, Diane E436
Todhanakasem, Kittiya W351
Todhunter, Jeff A429
Todhunter, Jeff E214
Todman, Michael A593
Toellner, Ann P633
Toerpe, William A735
Toerpe, Bill A735
Toevs, Bob A271
Toffey, Bryan A17
Toffey, Bryan P9
Toft, Colleen A925
Toft, Colleen E445
Togami, Kai A902
Togashi, Norio W127
Togawa, Masanori W124
Toh, Ryugo A686
Tohara, Connie P639
Tohrnan, Kathy P519
Toivola, Sakari W275
Tokarev, Nikolai P. W401
Tokarski, Chris E387
Tokash, Tom A264
Tokash, Tom P180
Tokish, Tim A600
Tokito, Mark A109
Tokunaga, Christine P248
Tokunari, Muneaki W262
Toledano, Udi A32
Toledano, Gaby A818
Toledano, Sidney W105
Tolentino, Joel A109
Toler, Chandara A571
Tolivar, Dennis A380
Toll, Nancy A824
Toll, Robert I. A837
Toll, Nancy P562
Tolle, Bev P5
Tollefson, Phillip H P147
Tollett, Preston A580
Tollett, Preston E292
Tolliver, Paula C. A460
Tolomeo, Chris A530
Tolot, Jér- ′me W154
Tolson, Glenda A760
Tolson, Glenda E374
Tom, Teresa A761
Tom, Richard P364
Tom, Crystal P558
Toma, Thor P485
Toma, Shigeki W350
Toma, Mike E141
Tomar, Praveen A327
Tomases, Arthur A440
Tomasi, Peter A888
Tomasi, Peter E425
Tomasik, Andy P340
Tomasky, Susan P32
Tomasson, Jon E118
Tomasuolo, Henry P558
Tomaszewski, Dan P123
Tomazinis, Larry P245
Tomb, Matthew C. (Matt) A337
Tomb, Matthew C. (Matt) E158
Tomc, Stuart E108
Tomczik, Pam A804
Tomczyk, James E. A806
Tomczyk, Martin A856
Tomczyk, Martin P614
Tomczyk, James E. E398
Tome, Carol A871
Tomic, Brano A340
Tomic, Brano E160
Tomita, Jiro W124
Tomita, Tetsuro W143
Tomita, Tetsuji (Mike) W227
Tomiyama, Hideaki W127
Tomkins, David A583
Tomko, Joe A227
Tomko, Joe E90
Tomlin, Fiona A493
Tomlin, Dervla M. W173

Tomlinson, Marc A520
Tomlinson, Eric P377
Tomlinson, R Jason P629
Tomlinson, Kevin W208
Tomlinson, D. J. W212
Tommasi, Eric A531
Tommasini, Martina W60
Tompkins, Randy A179
Tompkins, Cathlyn L. (Cathy) A189
Tompkins, Cathy A189
Tompkins, Michael A326
Tompkins, Kevin E72
Toms, Paul B. E215
Tomsicek, Michael E2
Tomsik, Scott A835
Tomsovic, Robert A482
Tomé, Carol B. A427
Tondreau, Pamela E110
Tonelli, Alfred A479
Toner, Richard A686
Toner, John A686
Toner, Renee P179
Toney, Pam A114
Toney, Frederiek A360
Toney, Charles A555
Toney, Shannon A859
Toney, Deloris P532
Toney, Pam E36
Tong, Ming A212
Tong, Lim Khiang W299
Tong, Richard E309
Tongue, Steve P353
Tonies, Jerry A198
Tonjum, Kurt P139
Tonkin, Susan A877
Tonn, Brian A728
Tonnison, John A809
Tonno, Jim A686
Tonomoto, Kiyoshi W27
Tonon, Viviane A191
Toogood, Rosie W233
Toohey, Sean A289
Tooker, A. Morris (Mo) A408
Tooker, A Morris A409
Tookes, Hansel A735
Tooley, Russell A855
Toomey, Brendan A203
Toomey, John A538
Toomey, Kimberly A708
Toomey, John A810
Toong, Yee Chek W424
Topalian, Noha A654
Toporek, Jill A390
Topp, Jonathan A167
Topper, Joan A371
Topper, Joan P213
Topper, John E P332
Topps, Ed P493
Torbakhov, Alexander W343
Torbert, Ronald J P68
Torch, Kevin A175
Torchiana, David F. A641
Torchiana, David A641
Torchiana, David F. P407
Torchiana, David P407
Torello, William A. (Bill) E153
Toretti, Christine J. A737
Toretti, Christine J. E361
Torgeby, Johan W357
Torgerson, James P P593
Torgow, Gary H. A806
Torgow, Gary H. E399
Torii, Nobuhiro W374
Torii, Shingo W374
Toriumi, Chie W286
Torlone, Jennifer E442
Torma, Anna E337
Tornetta, Roxanne A881
Tornetta, Roxanne E421
Tornga, Mark A137
Torno, Vitaliano A616
Tornquist, Alice A695
Toro, Alex A588
Toro, Alex P365
Toro, Suzan P368

COMBINED HOOVER'S HANDBOOK INDEX OF EXECUTIVES

```
A = AMERICAN BUSINESS
E = EMERGING COMPANIES
P = PRIVATE COMPANIES
W = WORLD BUSINESS
```

Toro, Alphie P373
Torok, Ken A871
Toronto, Ellen A711
Toronto, Ellen P444
Torossian, Lynn M. A414
Torossian, Lynn M. P236
Torrance, Jeffery A695
Torre, Ralph de la P528
Torre, De La P677
Torre, Henry E203
Torreano, Gail A89
Torrence, Chas P194
Torres, Jeff A179
Torres, Lizmary A440
Torres, Mark A512
Torres, Russ A593
Torres, Ana A623
Torres, Debra A654
Torres, Hector A891
Torres, Edgardo A915
Torres, Orlando P72
Torres, Marilyn P336
Torres, Danny P412
Torres, Roberto Mendez W45
Torres, Roberto Mendez W46
Torres, Juan Romero W91
Torres, Max W144
Torres, Elizabeth E106
Torres, Ana E313
Torres-Springer, Maria P364
Torrey, Michael A209
Torrion, Philippe W148
Torrisi-Cartwright, Sharyn A690
Torstendahl, Mats W357
Tortora, Samantha A575
Tortorici, Samuel M A159
Torvick, Stan P164
Torvik, Dan P164
Tory, Jennifer W331
Tosh, Jason A329
Tosheff, Alex A897
Toshikuni, Nobuyuki W227
Tosi, Jeff P313
Tosi, Stephen P616
Tosi-Renna, Barbara Ann A589
Toske, Cheryl P86
Toso, Greg A903
Tosolini, Alessandro A498
Toste, Francisco A554
Toste, Guen A799
Totah, Robyn A682
Toth, Scott A259
Totman, Brad A839
Totoki, Hiroki W361
Totten, Mark A392
Totten, Elizabeth P592
Touchstone, Karen A922
Touchstone, Karen P671
Tougas, Roger C. P491
Toups, Charles A140
Toure, Jennifer A686
Tournadre, David W390
Tournier, Philippe W112
Toussaint, Donald R. A249
Toussaint, Claudia S. A936
Toussaint, Donald R. E108
Tovar, John A9
Tovar, Alexandra A115
Tovar, John P4
Tovar, Alexandra E37
Tow, Heath A458
Towell, Mark A466
Tower, Hess A419
Tower, Erika A835
Towers, Daniel P366
Towers, Kelly P571
Towers, Adele P643
Towler, Fred A467
Town, Erin A880

Town, Erin P640
Towner, Dan A236
Townes, Chad A89
Townes, Noel P94
Townes, Emilie M. P599
Townley, Jerry P486
Townsel, Beadie H P481
Townsend, Kent G. A168
Townsend, Tally A170
Townsend, Dana A181
Townsend, Jeffrey A. (Jeff) A185
Townsend, Carol A205
Townsend, Drew A413
Townsend, Gayle A498
Townsend, Gary A843
Townsend, Adam A892
Townsend, Alan P187
Townsend, Tammy P211
Townsend, Ted P258
Townsend, Dana E70
Townsend, Drew E205
Townsend, Frances E372
Towson, Jeff A199
Toy, Coleen A367
Toy, David A496
Toyoda, Kanshiro W18
Toyoda, Tetsuro W398
Toyoda, Akio W400
Toyomatsu, Hideki W215
Toyoshima, Masaaki W11
Toyoshima, Masanori W205
Toyota, Jun P376
Tozzi, Andre A287
Trabandt, Charles E102
Trabbia, Michael W297
Traboulsi, Nadine E58
Trabue, Larry A664
Trabue, Larry E334
Tracey, Scott A129
Tracey, Patricia A874
Trach, Natalie P377
Trachet, Richard P252
Tracy, Ann A218
Tracy, Mike A232
Tracy, Thomas (Tom) A609
Tracy, Diane A711
Tracy, Eric A882
Tracy, Thomas (Tom) P387
Tracy, Diane P444
Tracy, James A. (Jim) P462
Tracy, Kevin E123
Traczyk, Daniel A804
Traeger, Joseph P252
Traeger, Phil P445
Traff, Rod A524
Traficanti, Joseph J. (Joe) A869
Trafton, Gail A905
Trager, A. Scott A718
Trager, Steven E. (Steve) A718
Trager, Bernard M. A719
Trager, Greg A893
Trager, A. Scott E354
Trager, Steven E. (Steve) E354
Trager, Bernard M. E354
Tragl, Karl A79
Tragni, Lauren M P561
Tragos, Bill A232
Trahan, Claude A235
Trahan, Lindsey A620
Trahtenhertz, Michael A199
Traicoff, Andy A392
Train, Michael H A292
Trainer, Michael P131
Trakimas, Ann A213
Trakimas, Ann P143
Trakulhoon, Kan W351
Tramack, Michael A793
Tramel, Beth P188
Trammell, Kenneth R. (Ken) A813
Trammell, Jeffrey A850
Trammell, Shelly P665
Tramontana, Nick A820
Tramontana, Nick P551

Tramonte, Michael P595
Tramontin, Shannon A552
Tramontin, Shannon E275
Tran, Long A135
Tran, Thi A140
Tran, Henry A222
Tran, JoAnne A251
Tran, Peter P114
Tran, Tram P118
Tran, Dai P174
Tran, Phat P212
Tran, Dana P280
Tran, Vicki P615
Tranchita, Daniel A727
Tranchita, Daniel P453
Trandel, Scott A623
Trandel, Scott E313
Trang, Nguyen A518
Transue, Brannon A75
Transue, Bill A779
Trantallis, Karin A538
Trapani, Joe P281
Trapp, Megan A222
Trapp, Steve A482
Traquina, Perry A36
Trasatt, Andrew A347
Trasatt, Andrew E167
Trask, Tallman P186
Traub, Michael A724
Traub, Michael P452
Traut, Mark A60
Trautchild, John A309
Trauth, Denise M. P551
Trautman, David L. A639
Trautmann, Robert E. A651
Trautmann, Robert E. E329
Travaille, Tim A366
Traver, Christina A512
Travers, Martin G. P85
Travers, Andy E179
Traviolia, Brad P555
Travis, Len A188
Travis, Nigel A620
Travis, Shelley A850
Travis, Troy P337
Travis, Nigel E115
Travisano, Jacqueline A. P390
Trawick, John G. A771
Trawick, John G. E382
Trawicki, Roman A941
Traynham, William W. E16
Traynor, Stephen P A318
Treacy, Chad A859
Treadway, Bryan A262
Treadway, Brandy A647
Treadwell, Robert A115
Treadwell, Melinda P642
Treadwell, Robert E38
Treanor, John A66
Treasure, Jeff P280
Trebilcock, James R A489
Trebuchet, Delphine A581
Trecker, Kristin E. E232
Treenuchagron, Chansin W316
Trefethen, Angela A628
Trefethen, Angela P396
Trefler, Alan E326
Treft, Jason E278
Trefzger, Detlef W227
Treganza, Mat P357
Treibatch, Natalie A491
Treibic, Adam A345
Treibic, Adam E165
Treichel, Gus A888
Treichel, Gus E425
Treichl, Andreas W156
Trella, Ronald A216
Trella, Chris A373
Trella, Kelly A408
Tremann, Nikki E47
Tremblay, Caroline A380
Tremblay, Matthew P31
Tremblay, Stephen E P282
Tremblay, Michel W193
Tremblay, Stephen E. E248

Trembulak, Frank A371
Trembulak, Frank P213
Trembulak, Frank J P214
Trembulak, Frank J P215
Trembulak, Frank J P569
Tremmel, Lothar E226
Tremonti, Yvette P227
Tremoulis, John A444
Trenbeath, Lynn V P173
Trend, Jonathan A559
Trent, Rachel A329
Trent, Layne P207
Trent, Judith P625
Trent, Thad E110
Trent, Evan E207
Trento, Mark A71
Trepa, Kevin M. P87
Trepczyk, Aretina A861
Tresch, Richard P608
Treschow, Michael W408
Trescott, Erin A335
Trescott, Erin E155
Tressler, Charles A657
Tressler, Monica A741
Tressler, Scott A837
Tressler, Monica E364
Tretiak, Gregory D. W313
Trevallion, Emily A405
Trevathan, James E. A905
Trevathan, Jim A905
Trevisan, Suzann A635
Trevisan, Jadran W155
Trevisani, Valter W35
Treworgy, Samantha A139
Treworgy, Samantha P92
Trexler, Shawn A245
Trezise, Scott A. A184
Trezza, Steve P359
TRIACCA, DOMENICO W43
Triano, Charles A658
Tribble, J Lee A513
Tribble, Agnes A852
Trice, David W. A301
Trice, Barry G. P225
Trichur, Vish A184
Trick, David A43
Trick, David E13
Trickett, Randall A909
Trickett, Randall E436
Tricoire, Jean-Pascal W344
Triesenberg, Ryan P563
Trifone, John A809
Trigg, Donald D. A185
Trimble, Craig A569
Trimboli, Debbie P400
Trimbur, Nancy P529
Trimmer, Curtis P233
Trimuel, Joyce A526
Trinh, Roger A5
Trinh, Julie E8
Trinita, Sister Mary P514
Trinske, Mark A834
Tripathi, Vivek A54
Tripeny, R. Tony A240
Triplett, Michael W A194
Triplett, Ethan A409
Triplett, Robin A444
Triplett, Rob A621
Triplett, Timothy W P86
Triplett, Timothy W P104
Triplett, Neal P187
Triplett, Rob E312
Triplitt, Jennifer P472
Tripp, Ann K. A405
Tripp, Mark A. P97
Tripp, Kurt H P582
Tritt, Gary A259
Tritton, Mark J. A804
Tritz, Andrew P496
Trivett, Shari P287
Trivunovich, Nick P638
Troberman, Gayle A452
Troccoli, Alejandro A613
Trocin, Jeffrey E. (Jeff) A704
Trogdon, Sara A222

Trogele, Ulrich (Bob) E18
Troger, Laurent W73
Troija, Peter E343
Trolli, Michele D. A530
Trollope, Rowan M. A198
Trontell, Kathy E30
Tropf, Peter A763
Tropf, Peter E377
Tropp, Tom A369
Trosclair, Andree P45
Troska, Hubertus W125
Trosvig, Kelli A711
Trosvig, Kelli A880
Trosvig, Kelli P444
Trosvig, Kelli P640
Trotter, Christy P344
Troughton, Katrina A465
Troulis, Maria J. P574
Trout, Christopher A442
Trout, Cynthia P430
Trout, John D P609
Trouvain, Joerg A10
Trovato, Salvatore A480
Trovato, Joseph A559
Trovillion, Raleigh A859
Trower, Paul E226
Troxler, Margie P377
Troy, Thomas M. A35
Troy, Tom A36
Troy, Patricia P40
Troy, Kimberly E132
Trubiano, Steve A452
Truby, Beth A219
Truckermiller, Debbie A368
Trudeau, Julie P578
Trudeau, Michel C. W232
TRUDEL, SYLVIE A391
Trudell, Julie A571
Trudell, Cynthia M. A654
Trudell, Andre A859
True, Douglas K. P594
True, Simon W306
Truelove, Brian D. A418
Trueman, Doug A64
Truesdale, Ken E240
Truesdell, Robert A294
Truett, Richard P82
Truitt, Jim A763
Truitt, Jim E377
Trujillo, Javier P126
Trujillo, Becky P330
Trujillo, Daniel P337
Trump, Christine A592
Trump, Christine P370
Trunck, Mike A346
Trunck, Mike E167
Trunfio, Joseph A P12
Trunkett, Camille P199
Truscott, William F. (Ted) A60
Truscott, Tricia P113
Truskey, George P187
Trusley, Jason A602
Trusty, Steven W. (Steve) A760
Trusty, Mike A902
Trusty, Steven W. (Steve) E374
Tryhuss, Gregg P185
Tryniski, Mark E. A227
Tryniski, Mark E. E90
Tryon-smith, Tiffany A756
Trythall, John A508
Trytten, Jennifer P153
Trzcinski, Todd A327
Tsacalis, William A P81
Tsafaridis, George A60
Tsai, Sheng-ta A284
Tsai, Helen A505
Tsai, Jeffrey A893
Tsai, John A905
Tsai, Caroline A915
Tsai, Hong-Tu W89
Tsai, Cheng-Ta W89
Tsai, Cheng-Chiu W89
Tsai, Sheng-ta E120
Tsalikis, Niki A540
Tsang, Michael A484

Tsang, Daniel E8
Tsao, Andy A793
Tscherne, Tiffany P47
Tschetter, Chad E264
Tschudin, Marie-France A609
Tschudin, Marie-France P391
Tse, Cindy A701
Tse, Edmund S.W. W14
Tse-Gonzalez, Mildred A317
Tseng, Vivian S Y P358
Tseng, F. C. W380
Tseng, Charles E248
Tseng, Saria E288
Tshabalala, Simpiwe (Sim) W363
Tshudy, Doug A367
Tsien, Matthew (Matt) A378
Tsien, Samuel N. (Sam) W299
Tsimbinos, Steven J. A618
Tsimbinos, Steven J. E310
Tso, Daphne A592
Tso, Daphne P370
Tso, Stephen T. (Steve) W380
Tsoi, Tracy A562
Tsokova, Olga A349
Tsoshima, Naoti P248
Tsourapas, Panagiotis A217
Tsourapas, George A679
Tsuchida, Yukio P326
Tsuchikane, Takuji W176
Tsuchitani, Yuri A460
Tsuga, Kazuhiro W300
Tsuge, Koei W93
Tsuji, Emi A325
Tsuji, Shinji W360
Tsujimura, Hideo W374
Tsukamoto, Shigeru W350
Tsukioka, Takashi W195
Tsurumaki, Fumio W259
Tsurumi, Seiichi W51
Tsutsui, William M. P505
Tsutsui, Yoshinobu W279
Tsvayberg, Leonid A391
Tsymbalyuk, Michael P502
Tu, Hanh A198
Tu, Amy A855
Tu, Lawrence P. (Larry) A892
Tu, L.C. W380
Tubiolo, Justin P202
Tubridy, Kevin A835
Tuchman, Mendel P130
Tuchscherer, Blaine P555
Tucker, Michael K. A98
Tucker, John A155
Tucker, Mark A181
Tucker, Jason A345
Tucker, Chris A501
Tucker, Douglas A567
Tucker, Jeff A665
Tucker, Crystal A717
Tucker, Joann A828
Tucker, Scott A912
Tucker, Timothy H P55
Tucker, Thomas P184
Tucker, Richard G. P238
Tucker, Joanne P242
Tucker, Joann P584
Tucker, Mark E. W189
Tucker, John E54
Tucker, Mark E70
Tucker, Jason E166
Tucker, Matt E189
Tucker, Douglas E283
Tucker, Jeff E334
Tucker, Crystal E351
Tucker, Aaron E419
Tudor, Sorin A135
Tueckes, Amy A325
Tuerk, Daniel A925
Tuerk, Daniel E445
Tuffaha, Sam A89
Tuffin, Mark A498
Tufo, Lou Del A355
Tuftee, Debbie A222
Tuftee, Carrie P209
Tuggle, Charles T. A343

Tuggle, Deloris Simpson P213
Tuggle, Charles T. E163
Tugwell, Robert P378
Tull, Andrea A179
Tullett, Lindsey A742
Tulliam, Elizabeth P133
Tullier, Kelly M. A895
Tullier, Kelly Mahon A896
Tullis, David P496
Tulloch, Maurice W40
Tully, Herbert B. P670
Tully, William E243
Tully, Randy E316
Tulsi, Japjit A287
Tulsky, James P172
Tulsyan, Ravi A934
Tumelty, John B. E340
Tumma, Madhu A483
Tummillo, Michael A527
Tumminello, Antonette A248
Tumminello, Antonette E107
Tumulty, Timothy A540
Tun, David E181
Tunez, Roland E64
Tung, Caroline A702
Tung, Chao Chin W123
Tung, Tzu Hsien W301
Tunis, Trisha A P209
Tunks, Tom P505
Tuori, Jeffery C A40
Tuori, Jeffery C P29
Turan, Kc P643
Turansky, Carole A823
Turansky, Carole E405
Turbeville, Frank P177
Turchet, Tom A465
Turcke, Mary Ann W65
Turcotte, Katie P569
Turcotte, Denis A. E191
Turetsky, Larisa A112
Turfe, A. Alan P260
Turi, Carol A112
Turi, Karen A828
Turi, Karen P580
Turiano, Vincent C A211
Turiano, Gary A P197
Turiano, Vincent C E83
Turicchi, R. Scott E240
Turits, Michael A704
Turits, Mark A893
Turkienicz, Jose A164
Turley, Susan P183
Turnage, Greg A156
Turnage, Sue A246
Turnage, Casey P93
Turnage, Sue E105
Turnas, Jeff A921
Turnas, Jeff P669
Turnbull, Robert A246
Turnbull, Jim P639
Turnbull, Robert E105
Turner, John A3
Turner, George A25
Turner, Henry A41
Turner, Dustin J A126
Turner, Dustin A126
Turner, Jill A184
Turner, Aprile A191
Turner, Gregory A212
Turner, Greg A212
Turner, Jeffrey A224
Turner, Jim A245
Turner, Jim L. A259
Turner, Keene S. A298
Turner, Greg A315
Turner, Mark A323
Turner, Mark A360
Turner, Matthew A381
Turner, Joseph W. (Joe) A397
Turner, William V. A397
Turner, Michael R. (Mike) A418
Turner, Ladd A432
Turner, Simon A447
Turner, Ethan A452
Turner, Cynthia A496

Turner, John C. A569
Turner, Vince A580
Turner, Debra A584
Turner, Chris A654
Turner, M. Terry A664
Turner, John M. A712
Turner, David J. A712
Turner, Michele A723
Turner, Nicole A735
Turner, Christina A833
Turner, Bud A866
Turner, Steve A899
Turner, Jody A919
Turner, Ryan A924
Turner, Mark A. A929
Turner, George P14
Turner, Aprile P126
Turner, Pete P151
Turner, Mary P177
Turner, Stacey P254
Turner, Aaron P273
Turner, Tabitha P274
Turner, William I P293
Turner, Jennifer P300
Turner, Hugh P308
Turner, Jennifer P315
Turner, Wanda P335
Turner, Rick P463
Turner, R. Gerald P505
Turner, Vickie P551
Turner, Wesley R. P551
Turner, Dorothy P559
Turner, Elaine P627
Turner, Quint O. E7
Turner, Keene S. E130
Turner, Kathy E223
Turner, Vince E292
Turner, M. Terry E333
Turner, Tracy E346
Turner, Bud E418
Turner, Mark A. E449
Turner, David E449
Turnes, Terje W140
Turney, John A606
Turney, Susan L. P309
Turngren, Robert P332
Turowski, Arthur A482
Turowski, Steven A823
Turowski, Steven E405
Turpan, Natalie A692
Turpin, Kevin P563
Turrens, Julio P637
Turrentine, Don A713
Turrentine, Rebecca J P299
Turris, Jeff De E429
Turton, Daniel A296
Turturro, Michael P171
Turvey, Paul E134
Tushaus, Gregg P309
Tushman, Earl P400
Tushman, Lawrence P400
Tushman, Larry P400
Tushman, Reed P400
Tushman, Marc P400
Tuten, Chris A583
Tuthill, Allen A88
Tutin, Ken A245
Tutkovics, Julie C. A444
Tutor, Jonathan A713
Tutson, Tracy A69
Tutt, James A621
Tutt, Jame A621
Tutt, James E311
Tutt, Jame E312
Tuttle, Mark A565
Tuttle, Russ A761
Tutun, Paul D. E431
Tutunjian, Brad A180
Tuzun, Tayfun A329
Tverskoy, Kirill A658
Tveter, Brian A746
Tvinnereim, Mike P565
Twardy, David A877
Tweedie, Eric P306
Tweel, Benjamin A108

COMBINED HOOVER'S HANDBOOK INDEX OF EXECUTIVES

> A = AMERICAN BUSINESS
> E = EMERGING COMPANIES
> P = PRIVATE COMPANIES
> W = WORLD BUSINESS

Twembeke, Willem van W154
Twigg-Rowse, Colette E305
Twining, Kurt E346
Twist, Greg P10
Twist, Krista P276
Twitty, Tim A. E208
Twohig, Paul A779
Twomey, Mike A296
Twornay, Michael A296
Twumasi, Akua P21
Twyman, Rob A921
Twyman, Rob P669
Ty, Fred A709
Ty, Arthur W255
Ty, Fred E348
Tyau, Laurie P242
Tye, Chris A355
Tye, Marc R. P501
Tye, David E219
Tyer, Ethan A893
Tykal, Robert M. E394
Tykocinski, Richard J. P603
Tyle, Craig S. A363
Tyler, Michele A487
Tyler, Robyn A620
Tyler, Gail A704
Tyler, Chris A812
Tyler, Breck W. A852
Tyler, Ollie P105
Tyler, David A. W206
Tylski, Scott A232
Tymchenko, Viktor A460
Tymms, Jason A544
Tynan, Katie P586
Tyner, Benjamin A107
Tynes, Donnie A852
Tyra, Heidi A449
Tyra, Heidi E221
Tyree, Sarah A213
Tyree, Sarah P143
Tyree, Joanne P404
Tyrell, Doug E104
Tyren, Almeda A14
Tyren, Almeda P6
Tyrholm, Laura A135
Tyroller, Peter W75
Tyrrell, Joseph A161
Tyrrell, Linda A326
Tyrrell, Nathan S. A436
Tyrrell, Edward L P604
Tyser, Matthew C A379
Tyson, Vern A403
Tyson, Dylan A686
Tyson, Sharon A772
Tyson, John H. A855
Tyson, Sharon E381
Tywater, TY A748
Tzakou-Lambropoulou, Nelly W272
Tzitzouris, Jim A799
Tozge, A. Galip W18

U

Uanarumit, Wirat W315
Ubagai, Takumi W256
Ubell, Elizabeth A394
Uchida, Kathryn A63
Uchida, Satoru W214
Uchin, Robert A. P390
Uchioke, Fumikiyo W368
Uchiyamada, Takeshi W400
Udnoon, Prajit W95
Udovic, Rev Edward P175
Udpa, Satish P339
Udy, Brad A444
Uebber, Bodo W125
Uebelhor, Steve A664

Uebelhor, Steve E334
Ueda, Takuji W127
Ueda, Takashi W262
Ueda, Masahiro W379
Uehara, Edwina (Eddie) A880
Uehara, Edwina (Eddie) P640
Uei, Takashi W227
Ugalde, Philip A713
Ugarte, Alfonso J A222
Uhl, Michael C A461
Uhl, Michael A465
Uhl, Jessica W334
Uhlir, Beth A346
Uhlir, Beth E167
Ui, Seon Jung W193
Ulander, Peder A198
Ulatowski, Dan E103
Ulbrich, Christian A481
Ulbricht, Will A575
Ulissi, Roberto W155
Ulizzi, Holly A324
Ullan, Chuck P2
Ullmann, Michael H. A479
Ullrich, Michael A54
Ulm, Scott J. A80
Ulp, Greg P212
Ulrey, Sharissa A345
Ulrey, Sharissa E166
Ulrich, Travis A497
Ulrich, Catherine E371
Umaki, Tamio W298
Umanoff, Adam S. A290
Umaoka, Seishu W127
Umberto, Anna M A251
Umfleet, Jason A774
Umfleet, Jason P510
Umlah, Jason A137
Ummersen, Gordon Van A790
Umpleby, D James A173
Unangst, Walter A651
Unangst, Walter E330
Unberger, Dave A227
Unberger, Dave E90
Underberg, Scott A713
Underberg, Sharon E223
Underhill, Kim A493
Underhill, Mike A500
Underwald, Sue P480
Underwood, Michelle A278
Underwood, Jacqueline A414
Underwood, Neil L A523
Underwood, Dawn P123
Underwood, Jacqueline P236
Underwood, Dawn P395
Ung, Brenda A654
Unger, Keith A206
Unkel, John P94
Unkovich, Teresa E123
Unroe, Larry P307
Unrue, William P610
Unthank, Ryan A727
Unthank, Ryan P453
Upadek, Kristen A888
Upadek, Kristen E425
Upchurch, Wes A232
Upchurch, John A281
Upchurch, W. Howard A403
Upfold, Patrick W243
Uppal, Jinny A125
Uppala, Sathyadev A695
Uppugonduri, Krishna E222
Uptain, Brian E103
Upton, Ray A820
Upton, Tom A871
Urabe, Toshimitsu W257
Urban, Lauren A246
Urban, Larry A398
Urban, Thomas A398
Urban, Kevin J. A692
Urban, Sarah P125
Urban, Larry P222
Urban, Thomas P222
Urban, Lauren E105
Urdapilleta, Eduardo A101
Urdapilleta, Eduardo E32

Ure, Christopher P377
Urech, Greg A512
Urena, Tiffany P486
Urena-Raso, Domingo W17
Uribe, Elias A200
URIBE, JUAN CARLOS MORA W48
Uriu, Michiaki W228
Urland, Taisha A538
Urness, Daniel L. E69
Urovsky, Teri A538
Urrabazo, Ignacio A463
Ursat, Xavier W148
Urschel, Ned A778
Urso, Kristen P215
Urso, Joanne E51
Urso-Rio, Kristen A375
Urso-Rio, Kristen P215
Urtheil, Robert H. E270
Urtin, Charles G. A737
Urtin, Charles G. E361
Urtz, Deborah A530
Urunanon, Teerasak W95
Urwiler, Robert N. E424
Ushana, Ramina E73
Ushijima, Arthur A P585
Ushijima, Takeo W292
Ushio, Osamu W400
Ushioda, Yoichiro W238
Usiak, Ryan P283
Usie, Kathryn E450
Usmani, Farukh A462
Usmani, Farukh P256
Usry, Chris P106
Utecht, Darren P59
Utermark, D. Chad A612
Utermark, D A612
Utermark, Chad A612
Utermark, Douglas A612
Utley, Nancy P83
Utley, Mark P430
Utne, Jeff A654
Utrup, Brian A491
Utsude, Tomoya A19
Utsugi, Susan A182
Utt, Bobbi P214
Uttermark, Anne P26
Utz, John A. A85
Utz, John A. E26
Uy, Maria E80
Uyeda, Dean A109
Uzan, Eric W88

V

Vaanchig, Amar P477
Vacanti, Stephen E132
Vaccari, Kim P364
Vaccaro, Frank A54
Vaccaro, Daniel A115
Vaccaro, Kenneth A651
Vaccaro, Daniel E37
Vaccaro, Marco E290
Vaccaro, Kenneth E330
Vachna, Maureen P348
Vachon, Jennifer P89
Vachon, Alain W250
Vachon, Louis W270
Vaddadi, Venkat E122
Vaddi, Kris E226
Vadell, Tomeu A202
Vadell, Tomeu P136
Vadell, Pablo Vallbona W6
Vadlamannati, Ramaparasad (Ram) A673
Vaez-iravani, Mehdi A74
Vagelos, P. Roy A710
Vagner, Janice A796
Vagner, Janice E397
Vagt, Robert A494
Vaidya, Vinay P417
Vaidyanathan, Krishnamurthy A390
Vail, Bob A374
Vail, Angela A641

Vail, Robert P274
Vail, Angela P407
Vailes, Kathy A161
Vaillancourt, Alex P560
Vaillant, Frederic A146
Vaina, Alan A294
Vainisi, William A35
Vaio, Robert A418
Vaishnav, Mike A794
Vajda, Neil A329
Valashinas, Brion E131
Valavanis, Spero A433
Valavanis, Spero E217
Valdes, Susan L P240
Valdes, Roland P630
Valdez, James A18
Valdez, James A246
Valdez, Ruth A642
Valdez, Hernan A657
Valdez, Arthur A804
Valdez, Ruth P407
Valdez, Arthur V P469
Valdez, James E105
Valdivia, Raul P399
Valdovinos, Clariza P299
Valdés, Luis A677
Vale, Michael G. A3
Vale, Mike A255
Vale, MaryAnn A692
Vale, Brenda J. P333
Valenca, Alan A799
Valencia, Rick A695
Valencia, Veronica A731
Valencia, Jacqueline E14
Valente, Dan A528
Valente, Donna A743
Valenti, Natalia A115
Valenti, Franco A243
Valenti, Alessandro A701
Valenti, Susan M. A838
Valenti, Joe A933
Valenti, Natalia E37
Valenti, Javier E138
Valenti, Douglas (Doug) E343
Valentin, Raul A243
Valentin, Ruth P120
Valentin, Josue P244
Valentine, Melinda A112
Valentine, Ken A329
Valentine, Jerry A441
Valentine, Leanne A677
Valentine, Raymond A767
Valentine, Veronica A888
Valentine, Debra P51
Valentine, Beau P122
Valentine, Mike P432
Valentine, Annette P633
Valentine, James E224
Valentine, Veronica E425
Valentino, James A559
Valentzas, Anne A544
Valenzano, Don A573
Valenzuela, Dan A30
Valenzuela, Elvira A285
Valenzuela, Dan P20
Valenzuela, Elvira E120
Valera, Fernando A202
Valera, Fernando P136
Valerius, Barbara P128
Valern, Theresa P243
Valeva, Sanya A492
VALGIURATA, LUCIO IGINO ZANON DI W121
Valianatos, Pete A831
Valianatos, Pete P601
Valine, Yousef A. A343
Valine, Yousef A. E163
Valiton, Robert (Rob) P53
Valitutto, Richard A935
Valiveti, Srihari A784
Valkenburg, Tina Van A552
Valkenburg, Tina Van E275
Valladares, Jorge A842
Vallance, Russell P102
Vallance, Patrick W171

Valle, Dean Della W68
Valle, Dean Della W69
Valle, William (Bill) W166
Vallee, Roy A. A321
Vallejos, Vincent A793
Vallely, Art A649
Valletta, Robert A321
Valley, Richard A258
Valley, Kimberly E318
Vallillo, Anthony J P593
Vallin, Jean-Michel W160
Vallone, James A153
Vallone, Paul A640
Vallone, James E52
Valls, Juan A453
Valovcin, David A465
Valsechini, Monica A891
Vamvalis, Laura A82
Van, David A473
Van, Lynda P255
Van, Bonnie E156
Van, David E236
Van-praag, Mary A243
Vanackere, Steven W55
Vanags, Art A577
Vanamburgh, Suzanne A219
Vanamburgh, Suzanne E87
Vanaselja, Siim A. W65
Vanator, Jonathan P252
Vanburen, Audrey E106
Vance, Tyler A113
Vance, Linda A222
Vance, Daniel A264
Vance, Brian L. A415
Vance, Quonta A428
Vance, David A857
Vance, Anna A910
Vance, Edward Bubba P102
Vance, Daniel P180
Vance, June P623
Vance, Erika P635
Vance, Tyler E36
Vance, Brian L. E209
Vancheeswaran, Pradeep A897
Vancleave, Roger A882
VanCleef, Alan A383
VanCleef, Alan E186
Vancourt, Donna A84
Vancura, Ales P517
Vandebroek, Sophie E223
Vandecasteele, Jeff A260
Vandehei, Kathy P76
Vandekreke, Michael P445
Vandeman, Robert T. P7
Vandenbergh, Robert A. A504
Vandenbergh, Robert A. E251
Vanderford, Roxanne P137
Vanderford, Bob P469
Vandergriff, Jody E371
Vanderhaar, Brett A774
Vanderhaar, Brett P510
Vanderhoff, Margaret P250
Vanderhoff, Bruce P395
Vanderhoof, Ashley A707
Vanderkooi, Joel A487
Vanderlaan, Meg P356
Vanderleest, Elizabeth P329
Vanderlind, Gary A392
Vanderlinden, Dick P672
Vandermeulen, Johan W79
Vanderslice, Doug P558
Vandervinne, Jeri A693
Vandervinne, Jeri E341
Vanderzee, Steven A15
Vanderzee, Steven P7
VanDeVelde, Doug A487
Vandewater, Christopher A309
Vanella, David E315
Vaness, Craig A329
VanEssendelft, Ed P3
Vanfossen, Cymbre E156
Vang, Todd A900
Vangilder, Grant A599
Vangrevenhof, Heather A36
Vanhoff, Kathleen A469

Vanhorsen, Debra P168
Vanichvoranun, Vasin W216
Vankirk, Trudy A90
VanKirk, James A690
Vanlander, Jean-Pierre W157
VanLeuven, Megan A196
VanNess, William C. (Bill) P151
Vanness, Joan P347
Vannest, Nancy P99
Vanneste, Jeffrey H. A508
Vanni, Rob A240
Vannorman, Steven A451
Vannorman, Raymond A717
Vannorman, Steven P249
Vannorman, Raymond E351
VanNoy-Pineda, Kathleen A528
Vanommen, Mike E265
VANOPSTALL, EARL A806
VANOPSTALL, EARL E399
Vanslyke, Lisa P529
Vanstraten, Randy P76
Vantassel, Chris A925
Vantassel, Chris E445
Vantrieste, Martin A65
Vanvleck, Douglas P184
Vanvleet, Mike A789
Vanwallaghen, John A871
Vanwelzen, Jim A613
Vanwormer, Lauri P596
Vanzo, Kendra L. A621
Vanzo, Kendra L. E311
Vara, Raymond A110
Varadarajan, Sesha A505
Varadhan, Ashok A390
Varbero, Blake P613
Varco, Susan P632
Vardas, Michael A605
Vardeleon, Christian A137
Vardeman, Tracy P383
Varela, Javier A484
Varela, Gonzalez A902
Varela, Raul P333
Varelas, Panayiotis A414
Varelas, Panayiotis P236
Varenne, Fran- §ois De W345
Varga, Paul A925
Varga, Daniel W. P550
Varga, Paul E445
Varga-Haszonits, Istvan E290
Vargas, Gilberto A A460
Vargas, Carlota A540
Vargas, Franklyn A670
Vargas, Diana P207
Vargas, Bolgen P454
Vargas, Nancy P519
Vargas, Michael M P646
Vargas, Francis E148
Varghese, George A68
Varghese, Jasmine A115
Varghese, Jasmine E38
Vargo, Alla A552
Vargo, Alla P324
Vari, Jamie A482
Varilek, James A. A624
Varin, Valerie A207
Varisco, Bridget P390
Varley, Elizabeth A61
Varma, Ravi A54
Varma, Vivek A779
Varma, Prasad A818
Varma, Gopal Das E102
Varma, Prasad E403
Varnado, Darryl P130
Varnado, Byron P329
Varner, Carol A54
Varner, Marc A937
Varney, Al A933
Varney, Mike P233
Varney, Michael D. W328
Varni, Sara A740
Varnum, Daniel P329
Varo, Susan A893
Varones, George A61
Varughese, Raj A692
Varvatos, John A702

Varvel, Eric W120
Varwig, Chris P605
Vasallo, Ralph A115
Vasallo, Ralph E38
Vascellaro, Jerome C. P102
Vascocu, Norman A449
Vascocu, Norman E220
Vasconcellos, Fabio A692
Vasilatos-Younken, Regina A828
Vasilatos-Younken, Regina P584
Vasiu, Peter P509
Vasos, Todd J. A272
Vasquez, Jaime A27
Vasquez, Janice A65
Vasquez, Gaddi A290
Vasquez, Hector A463
Vasquez, Florence A540
Vasquez, Ralph A686
Vasquez, Liliana A752
Vasquez, Bertha A887
Vasquez, Christann P82
Vasquez, Jaime P137
Vasquez, George P153
Vasquez, Juliana P174
Vasquez, Gregory P276
Vasquez, Ernest P387
Vasquez, Peter P428
Vasquez, Bob P605
Vassallo, Ralph R. P654
Vassalluzzo, Joseph S. (Joe) A620
Vassar, Tyler A120
Vassem, Timothy Van P455
Vassimon, Eduardo W205
Vaswani, Andrea A204
Vath, Richard R P209
Vats, Vikas E429
Vatulescu, Cristina P371
Vaughan, Michael A203
Vaughan, Michael A296
Vaughan, Dianna A423
Vaughan, Richard A546
Vaughan, Richard A696
Vaughan, Michael A850
Vaughan, Brent A895
Vaughan, Rob P112
Vaughan, Christine P198
Vaughan, Rick P253
Vaughan, Ben W80
Vaughan, Hayley E105
Vaughan, Emily E131
Vaughn, Tony D. A263
Vaughn, Ryan A405
Vaughn, Nooshin A447
Vaughn, Beth A466
Vaughn, Chad A524
Vaughn, Jack A762
Vaughn, David P107
Vaughn, Lorie P252
Vaughn, D Blayne P391
Vaughn, Jacqueline P428
Vaughn, Kathleen (Kathy) P434
Vaughn, Gregory R. (Greg) E40
Vaughn, Phil E81
Vaughn, Victor E394
Vaught, Jamie A449
Vaught, Turner E106
Vaught, Jamie E220
Vaughters, Ann A441
Vaupel, Mark D. A434
Vaupel, Autumn E47
Vavilala, Chandra P658
Vawter, Barrett A713
Vaysband, Seva P538
Vaytsman, Vadim E123
Vaz, Joao P532
Vazquez, Javier A391
Vazquez, Laura A559
Vazquez, Theresa A749
Vazquez, John A890
Vazquez, Anthony P443
Vazquez, Theresa E367
Veach, Steve A444
Veal, MIke A232
Veal, James P482
Vebber, Andrew A424

Vebber, Andrew E211
Vecchi, Mario P432
Vecchio, Jennifer A158
Ved, Kalpa A348
Ved, Kalpa E169
Vedovotto, Roberto W218
Vee, Kevin A203
Veer, Jeroen van der W200
Veeraghavachary, Srinivasan A216
Veeramachaneni, Ravindra P183
Veerni, Vandhana V P395
Vega, Olga De La A89
Vega, David A212
Vega, Venus A224
Vega, Alma A797
Vega, Elizabeth A827
Vega, Debbie P153
Vega, Yvette P423
Vega, Elizabeth P580
Vegas, Pablo A. A600
Vegh, Stephen A340
Vegh, Stephen E160
Veglia, Anthony P. P289
Vegliante, Paul C. P78
Vehr, Greg P625
Vehrs, Thomas P119
Veiel, Eric L. A799
Veintimilla, Pablo P287
Veirman, Geert De P572
Veit, David A706
Veksler, Angela D. A903
Vela, Amanda A804
Vela, Manuel R. (Manny) A811
Velasco, Maria Fernanda A658
Velasquez, Margaret A246
Velasquez, Angelica P250
Velasquez, Margaret E105
Velazquez, David M. (Dave) A304
Velde, Tamara Vande A168
Velder, Ronald P200
Veldhuizen, Norbert Van A135
Velez, Jorge A72
Velez, David A412
Velez, Patsy P164
Velez, Pablo P489
Velin, Tom P145
Velkey, Karen A446
Velkoff, Carole P644
Vella, Susan A126
Vella, Elizabeth A193
Vella, James G. (Jim) A359
Vella, Aimee A540
Vella, Antonio W155
Vellinga, David H. A226
Vellinga, David P117
Vellinga, David H. P150
Vellios, Thomas G. (Tom) E172
Veltmaat, Hans-Bernd A21
Veluvolu, Anil P670
Velver, Ron P200
Velasquez, Gustavo A202
Velasquez, Gustavo P136
Ven, Michael G Van De A773
Venable, Cheryl L. A319
Venable, Derek A381
Venable, Bryan A799
Venarchick, Paul P214
Vendemo, Shelly P117
Vendetti, Paul A723
Venditto, Michael A224
Vengco, Joel L. P73
Venherkar, Anil E290
Venhoek, Mark W366
Venhoff, Chris A884
Venhuizen, John S. A9
Venhuizen, John S. P4
Venkatachalam, Ramu A525
Venkatachalam, Kavitha E132
Venkatakrishnan, C.S. W58
Venkataraman, Viswanathan P484
Venkatesan, Mouli A876
Venkatesh, Kim A215
Venkatesh, Prasanna E143
Venkayya, Rajeev W381
Venn, Richard E. W85

COMBINED HOOVER'S HANDBOOK INDEX OF EXECUTIVES

A = AMERICAN BUSINESS
E = EMERGING COMPANIES
P = PRIVATE COMPANIES
W = WORLD BUSINESS

Vennam, Raj A255
VENOSTA, FRANCESCO W43
Venrooy, Maria Van P627
Venters, Patricia E223
Venti, Jane P558
Ventola, Tony P613
Ventola, Anthony P613
Ventre, Steve A195
Ventsam, Steve A509
Ventura, Lillian A324
Ventura, Alberto A480
Ventura, Joe A522
Ventura, Katie A833
Ventura, Alberto P270
Venturella, David E185
Venturi, Achille P56
Venturini, Francesco W153
Venturo, Dominic A884
Venugopalan, Ramakrishna A7
Venus, William A63
Venute, Stephen P2
Vera, Kurochkina P459
Veraldi, Veronica E433
Verbeek, Christoph A853
Verbeek, Christoph P612
Verberkmoes, Randy A939
Verbrugge, Joseph A A762
Vercammen, Victor A550
Verde, Edward W P184
Verdes, Marcelino Fernandez W6
Verdes, Marcelino Fernandez W183
Verdesca, Justin A112
Verdeschi, Margaret A137
Verdi, Joseph G A726
Verdi, Joseph G P453
Verdier, Damien W358
Verdile, Vincent P17
Verdone, Adrienne A325
Verdoorn, Ronald D. P494
Verduin, Patricia A218
Vereb, Russell A538
Verebelyi, Ernest R. (Ernie) E88
Verenna, Robin A718
Verenna, Robin E354
Vergara, Yanira A44
Vergara, Yanira E13
Verghese, Sunny G. W294
Vergine, Stephen A89
Verhagen, Amanda P76
Verhoff, Gary A339
Veri, Clive A224
Verinder, David P473
Verity, John R. A309
Verity, Cindy E319
Verker, Bruce P492
Verlinghieri, Ray A75
Verma, Pawan A359
Verma, Anuraag A390
Verma, Sarthak A442
Verma, Vivek W294
Vermeer, Kevin P258
Vermilye, David A806
Vermilye, David E398
Verna, Jonathan A933
Verner, Weston P392
Vernette, Townsend P72
Vernon, Zana A530
Vero, Bernadette P335
Veronneau, Marcel E45
Verrier, James R. A146
Verrios, Angela A686
Verschelden, Katie A748
Verslues, Ernie P337
Verst, Cynthia L. A474
Verstegen, Molly P329
Vertner, Arthur E442
Vertone, Susan P367
Vertucci, Bob A584
Vervalin, Paul P383

Vervlied, Michele A248
Vervlied, Michele E107
Verwer, Ben A123
Vesey, Joseph P. (Joe) A936
Vesey, Mary P546
Vespoli, Leila L. A350
Vespoli, Leila L P336
Vespoli, Leila L P411
Vespoli, L L P562
Vessels, Allen P180
Vestberg, Hans A889
Vester, Thomas A665
Vester, Thomas E334
Vetere, Jayne A654
Vetta, David J. (Dave) E156
Vetter, David R. (Dave) A809
Vetter, J D P279
Vetter, J D P280
Vetter, Hans-Jorg W231
Vetterick, Jason A25
Vetterick, Jason P14
Veum, Jonathan A364
Vezina, Maria P248
Veziris, Christina A651
Veziris, Christina E329
Vezuli, Ligerta A743
Via, Bill E16
Vial, Arnaud W313
Viale, Enrico W153
Vialle, Karen P540
Vian, Kathy A332
Viana, Valdir R P87
Vibert, Paul A119
Vicars, Don P664
Vice, Aresi
Vice, Charles A A462
Vicencio, Rachelle P208
Vicencio, Guillermo P419
Vicencio, Iris E57
Vicente, Marcos A220
Vichniac, Avi E290
Vicino, Kay A605
Vick, Christopher A580
Vick, Kathy P240
Vick, Stephen P496
Vick, Christopher E293
Vick, Tracy E349
Vickers, Andy A602
Vickers, Keeley P19
Vicki, Tomaso P287
Victor, Miles A713
Victoria, Farah P361
Victorino, Chris A540
Vidale, Mauro P534
Videka, Lynn A592
Videka, Lynn A711
Videka, Lynn P370
Videka, Lynn P444
Vido, Eileen A879
Viegas, Victor (Vic) E225
Vieira, Cory A54
Vieira, Thiago A470
Vielehr, Byron C. A352
Vielmetti, Steve A813
Vierula, Carmen P. W50
Vierzba, Christy P333
Vieten, Kevin A752
Vietor, Barbara E233
Viets, Robert A723
Viets, Hermann E28
Vietti, Danielle A313
Vietti, Danielle P200
Vig, Ravi P24
Vigano, Andrea A135
Vigar, Andy A559
Vigesaa, Claire P644
Viggiano, Laura P454
Vigil, Celia A72
Vigilante, Kevin A145
Vigo, Doris A88

Vigon, Carlos A176
Vihn, Daniel A538
Vij, Sandeep E86
Vijayakirthi, Emily P85
Vijayakumar, C P230
Vijayvargiya, Jugal K. W31
Vikara, Jerry A680
Vikram, Ashish A530
Vilakazi, Phinda W341
Vilardo, John A530
Vilarin, Luis A151
Villa, Marta A175
Villa, Helbert A543
Villa, Rembert de E140
Villafana, Carol A619
Villafana, Carol P393
Villalobos, Hilda P122
Villalonga, Ruth A571
Villaneda, Robert A104
Villanueva, Maritza A202
Villanueva, Kelly A405
Villanueva, Dayana A530
Villanueva, Rudy A798
Villanueva, Maritza P136
Villanueva, Jose P220
Villanueva, Gustavo Blanco W26
Villareal, Al A463
Villareal, David P168
Villareal, Roger E427
Villarreal, Lisa P587
Villarreal, Ramiro W91
Villars, Curtis A545
Villegas, Maria P642
Villeger, Nicolas A801
Villena, Christina A405
Villeneuve, Thomas E402
Viloria, Ron P162
Viltz, Simon A416
Vinall, David A105
Vinall, David E34
Vincent, Curtis A167
Vincent, Anton A376
Vincent, Simon A423
Vincent, Suzanne M A480
Vincent, Sherri P22
Vincent, Kelly P231
Vincent, Suzanne M P270
Vincent, Blane P461
Vincent, Tracy P483
Vincent, Mary Ann P518
Vincent, Nelson C. P625
Vincent, Jacques W128
Vincent, Yann W305
Vinci, Don A296
Vinci, Donald A296
Vinci, Francesco Saverio W252
Vinciquerra, Anthony A695
Vines, Brad A554
Vines, Michael A879
Vines, Robert E132
Vinet, Pascal A25
Vinet, Pascal P14
Vineyard, Tim P296
Vingerhoets, Cindy P184
Vining, Jeff A527
Vining, Alexis A741
Vining, Alexis E364
Vinitsky, Mark E433
Vinkler, David A571
Vinluan, Cynthia P628
Vinney, Les C. A164
Vinokur, Svetlana E149
Vinson, Ben P569
Vinson, Carroll D. E396
Viola, Mark A660
Viola, Mark P416
Viola, Mike E64
Violagis, Dean E99
Violi, Anthony A818
Violi, Anthony E403
Viotty, Michelle A540
Virago, Beverly P101
Virchaux, Dominique E248
Virella, Jose P265

Virgil, Marcia P332
Virta, Ronald F A902
Visco, Vincent P255
Visedpaitoon, Pong W95
Vishakhadatta, Diwakar P446
Visotski, Svetlana P325
Viswanathan, Ramesh A74
Vita, Celine A626
Vita, Bobelis P415
Vita, Giuseppe W407
Vitale, Richard H A107
Vitale, Domenick A367
Vitale, Robert V. A672
Vitale, Steven A888
Vitale, Steven E425
Vitalie, John A740
Vitek, Chris A289
Vitellas, Yianni A444
Vitelle, Richard K. (Rick) E58
Vitelli, Tom A462
Vitelli, Tom P256
Vitner, Stephanie P412
Vitt, Jim A86
Vitt, Jim E27
Vitto, Vincent E277
Vittoria, Ed A761
Vittorio, Michael N. A348
Vittorio, Michael N. E169
Vitulli, Christy E14
Vivaldi, Carlo W407
Vivaldi, Carlo W432
Vivas, Francisco J A747
Vivian, Formica A305
Vivian, Mike A910
Viviano, Jeffery A413
Viviano, Paul P559
Viviano, Jeffery E205
Vivier, Laurent W398
Vivona, Joseph F. P642
Vizag, Akw E143
Vizcarra, Shamara E319
Vlack, Valarie Van P552
Vlahos, Greg A761
Vlajic, Patty E80
Vlassis, Christine P573
Vlastelica, Pete A10
Vleck, Kathryn Van P189
Vnenchak, David A715
Vnuck, Steve A559
Vo, Phillip A71
Vo, Tri A722
Vo, Sue A801
Vodopivec, Larry A137
Voeke, Anne P329
Voelker, Joseph A778
Vogan, Rose A715
Vogel, Michael A658
Vogel, Richard L. A831
Vogel, Richard L. P601
Vogel, Roland W178
Vogel, David E77
Vogel, Eric E226
Vogelpohl, Joe A799
Vogelsang, Harold A. (Jay) P537
Vogl, Kristen P604
Vogt, Mary A414
Vogt, Mark A686
Vogt, Carol A798
Vogt, Mary P236
Vogt, Peter R. W276
Vohs, Erik A492
Voight, Grace P176
Voirand, Pascal A740
Voisin, Jean-Baptiste W241
Volandes, Angelo A642
Volandes, Angelo P407
Volino, Robert S. A268
Voliva, Richard L. A425
Volk, Christopher H. (Chris) A117
Volk, Vince A285
Volk, Jackie A872
Volk, Christopher H. (Chris) P61
Volkert, Michael A506
Volkert, Jacqueline A623
Volkert, Jacqueline E313

Volkmer, Mark A859
Voll, Brenda A341
Voll, Staci P547
Vollenweider, Emmett A484
Voller, Chris J P15
Vollmer, Greg A329
Vollmer, John E. P486
Vollmer, George E248
Voloch, Bill P662
Volpe, Jason A482
Volpe, Michele P429
Volpe, Rocco E85
Voltaire, Marie P135
Volynsky, Peter A452
Volz, Vince A272
Volz, Kim P176
Volz, Sheilagh P522
VonBerg, John A668
Vonderfecht, Dennis P428
Vong, Ann A266
Vong, Ann P182
Vongbunyong, Sumeth W95
Vongjitvuttikrai, Vallop W216
Vongvanich, Tevin W315
Vonmassenbach, Christian E138
Vonmuehlen, Constance A29
Vonwiller, Brett P364
Voorhees, Marc A392
Voorhies, Leah P270
Vopni, Scott K. A259
Vora, Sanjeev P125
Vorobyev, Vadim W310
Vorpahl, Larry L. A434
Vorpahl, Roberto Hetz W149
Vorsheck, John E267
Vortherms, Joseph Joe J A180
Vortherms, Joseph J. (Joe) A180
Vos, Glen De W31
Vosburg, Craig A544
Voser, Peter R. W3
Vosganian, Greg A7
Vosper, Donna A761
Vosper, Rod A761
Voss, Ryan A161
Vossoughi, John A460
Votaw, Jeff A220
Votek, Glenn A. A68
Votek, Glenn Alan A200
Voter, Eric P225
Vounatsos, Michel A133
Vouvalides, Alexander (Alex) E219
Vovos, Vassilis W208
Voyles, Robb L. A401
Voyles, Brent A. A831
Voyles, Janie P459
Voyles, David P497
Voyles, Paula P505
Voyles, Brent A. P601
Vradenburg, Daniel R. (Dan) P670
Vranich, Tracey P206
Vranken, Ross Van P639
Vranos, Michael W. E124
Vrcelj, Stevan W243
Vries, Loek De P458
Vrohidis, Ippocratis A3
Vroonland, David P333
Vruwink, Joe A727
Vruwink, Joe P453
Vu, John A571
Vu, Kevin P107
Vuckovich, Gail P199
Vuich, Richard A692
Vuncannon, Tony J A430
Vuolo, Lisa P631
Vuong, Sharon A893
Vazquez, Carlos J. A670
Vazquez, Mauricio Escobedo W26

W

Waak, Michelle A230
Waak, Michelle P154
Waccard, John A107
Wachowiak, Amy M A91

Wachowiak, Amy M P55
Wachowicz, Brian A363
Wachsman, Leslie P475
Wachtel, Jen A369
Wachtel, Steve A525
Wachtel, Andrew G A583
Wachter, Renée P641
Wackerhagen, George P356
Wacksman, Barry A469
Waclawski, Michael A140
Waclawski, Anthony A151
Waclawski, Janine A654
Wada, Isami W345
Waddell, Michael K. A343
Waddell, M. Keith A725
Waddell, Michael K. E163
Waddill, William E25
Wade, Ralph A145
Wade, Patrick A175
Wade, Betsy A226
Wade, Kevin A227
Wade, Susan A347
Wade, Scott A421
Wade, Heather A449
Wade, Donna A717
Wade, Anne A867
Wade, Todd A895
Wade, Jason A919
Wade, Pat P21
Wade, Brigitta P86
Wade, Sharon P138
Wade, Betsy P150
Wade, Joanne E P214
Wade, Deborah P405
Wade, Rusti P552
Wade, Kevin E90
Wade, Susan E167
Wade, Heather E221
Wade, Donna E351
Wade, Anne E418
Wadehra, Elaine A859
Wadhwa, Gaurav A686
Wadhwa, Shyam A738
Wadsworth, Kent A765
Wadsworth, Jeffrey P70
Waelde, Lisa P297
Waerum, Jesper A692
Wager, Todd K. P582
Wagers, Gary W. A116
Wagers, Gary W. E39
Waggoner, Brad P296
Waggoner, Douglas R. (Doug) E123
Waghorn, George P110
Waghray, Ajay A88
Wagler, Theresa E. A785
Wagman, Lawrence D P518
Wagner, Jason A69
Wagner, Elizabeth A112
Wagner, Jennifer A145
Wagner, Hank A158
Wagner, Jeff A161
Wagner, Janette A165
Wagner, Scott A228
Wagner, Lisa A233
Wagner, Stephen A277
Wagner, Darla A326
Wagner, Kevin A345
Wagner, Jim A367
Wagner, Andy A532
Wagner, Pat A533
Wagner, Eric R. A551
Wagner, Arthur A588
Wagner, Matthew P. (Matt) A638
Wagner, Paul A645
Wagner, Patricia K. (Patti) A753
Wagner, Mary A779
Wagner, Lucas A797
Wagner, Edward A831
Wagner, Matt A850
Wagner, Jack W. P6
Wagner, Eugene D Van P280
Wagner, Eric R. P321
Wagner, Harvey L P336
Wagner, Arthur P365
Wagner, Harvey L P394

Wagner, Harvey L P411
Wagner, Jack P491
Wagner, Jerry P498
Wagner, Monica P517
Wagner, Harvey L P562
Wagner, Michael P612
Wagner, Scott P675
Wagner, Gerhard W433
Wagner, Lisa E94
Wagner, Donald S. (Don) E116
Wagner, Kevin E166
Wagner, William R. E259
Wagner, Tom E318
Wagner, Matthew P. (Matt) E320
Wagner, David E453
Wagoner, Amy A1
Wagoner, Jeremy A879
Wagoner, Gale P508
Wagoner, Greg P656
Wagoner, Amy E1
Wagstaff, Craig C. A275
Wagstaff, Nathan V P516
Wahl, Douglas A574
Wahl, Bill A831
Wahl, Bill P601
Wahl, Theodore E203
Wahl, Peg E282
Wahlfeldt, Walter A482
Wahlin, Mary A108
Wahlman, Mark P403
Wahlroos, Bjorn W287
Wahlstrom, Pelle A684
Waid, Amber A630
Waidmann, Olivia P505
Waind, Mark P29
Wainwright, Brenda A337
Wainwright, Robbie A550
Wainwright, Robbie P319
Wainwright, Brenda E158
Wais, Marc A592
Wais, Marc P370
Wait, Mark P599
Waite, Stacey A559
Waitman, Ted E180
Waitz, Ian A. P314
Wajner, Matthew F. A332
Wajnrajch, Michael A657
Wajsgras, David C. A706
Wakabayashi, Takahiro W160
Wakabayashi, Tatsuo W262
Wakahara, Yasuyuki W34
Wakamura, Keith A182
Wakeen, Suzanne A651
Wakeen, Suzanne E329
Wakefiel, Peter D P161
Wakeman, David N A46
Wakerly, John A199
Wakita, Takeshi W127
Wakulchik, Grace P131
Walb, Terry P117
Walby, Dave A735
Walchirk, Mark S. A643
Walcott, Wanji A269
Wald, Leah P19
Waldbaum, Brian A417
Waldburger, Daniel A695
Waldburger, Dan A695
Walde, Van Der P32
Waldeck, Phil A686
Walden, Joshua M. (Josh) A460
Walden, Marni M. A889
Walden, Dawn P113
Walden, Jack E48
Waldman, Mitchell B. (Mitch) A446
Waldman, Tom A520
Waldman, Steve P611
Waldman, Stephen P611
Waldo, Terry P361
Waldo, Peggy E448
Waldoch, Timothy P211
Waldorf, Emily A164
Waldred, Linda P548
Waldrin, Michele P647
Waldron, Brad A160
Waldron, John A390

Waldron, John A431
Waldron, John A846
Waldron, Blain P148
Waldron, Jay P399
Waldron, Carolyn P514
Waldrop, Gabe A442
Walecki, Kurt A471
Walenga, Gail P337
Walesiewicz, Patricia A123
Waleski, Anne G. A536
Walia, Sandeep A538
Walia, Ash A779
Walje, Brigid A452
Walk, Belinda P104
Walke, Barbara P242
Walke, Barbara A P242
Walkenhorst, John P514
Walker, Mark A58
Walker, Sara A85
Walker, Marvonia A89
Walker, Clay A107
Walker, Jeanne A116
Walker, Trish A130
Walker, Michael A137
Walker, Lisa A151
Walker, John A167
Walker, Jason A167
Walker, Kevin A170
Walker, Chad A170
Walker, Andrew A188
Walker, Karen A198
Walker, Charles A203
Walker, Mark A205
Walker, David A222
Walker, Marlene A227
Walker, Terry A345
Walker, Sean N. A376
Walker, J Marvin A380
Walker, Kathryn A425
Walker, Kellye L. A446
Walker, Cody A449
Walker, Christopher A461
Walker, Amy A530
Walker, Myron A538
Walker, William A540
Walker, Cynthia L. A618
Walker, Pete A630
Walker, David M. (Dave) A648
Walker, Darren A654
Walker, Roberto A677
Walker, Steven G. A683
Walker, Sky A709
Walker, Robin A742
Walker, Kevin A769
Walker, Kevin A770
Walker, Scott A809
Walker, Fiona A833
Walker, Virginia A847
Walker, Bryan A858
Walker, Ben A866
Walker, James A902
Walker, Joseph C A929
Walker, Stephanie P58
Walker, Le Roy P64
Walker, Lynette P64
Walker, Patrcia P103
Walker, Karen P126
Walker, Robert L P218
Walker, Terry P259
Walker, Doug P262
Walker, Betty P276
Walker, Krystin P304
Walker, Kristen P311
Walker, Steve P330
Walker, George P335
Walker, Marsha P358
Walker, Jeanne P395
Walker, Sky P442
Walker, H. Fred P456
Walker, Randy P461
Walker, Brooks P477
Walker, Darren P477
Walker, Annette M P517
Walker, Alexis P610
Walker, Grace P617

COMBINED HOOVER'S HANDBOOK INDEX OF EXECUTIVES

```
A = AMERICAN BUSINESS
E = EMERGING COMPANIES
P = PRIVATE COMPANIES
W = WORLD BUSINESS
```

Walker, Robert P667
Walker, J. F. W212
Walker, Donald J. W244
Walker, Sara E26
Walker, Jeanne E39
Walker, Robert E73
Walker, Marlene E90
Walker, Daniel H. (Danny) E127
Walker, Daniel E153
Walker, Terry E166
Walker, Cody E221
Walker, Nico E278
Walker, David M. (Dave) E328
Walker, Kevin E380
Walker, Dale A. E386
Walker, Paul E416
Walker, Ben E418
Walker, William M. (Willy) E433
Walker, Joseph C E449
Walker-Vamos, Colleen P522
Walkup, Kevin A742
Wall, Roxanna A54
Wall, Tim A71
Wall, Preston A91
Wall, David J A165
Wall, Michael P A176
Wall, Daniel R. A308
Wall, Peter A373
Wall, Shane D. A438
Wall, Peter A753
Wall, David J P108
Wall, John P494
Wall, James P558
Wall, Richard W50
Wall, Kevin W58
Wall, Preston E29
Wallace, Grisel A108
Wallace, Frank A117
Wallace, Steve A140
Wallace, Jeff A167
Wallace, Marcus A179
Wallace, Diane A215
Wallace, Noel R. A217
Wallace, Mark K A245
Wallace, Mark E A253
Wallace, Shirley A267
Wallace, Akmar A284
Wallace, John A329
Wallace, Brent E. A462
Wallace, Henry D. G. A508
Wallace, John A662
Wallace, Matthew A692
Wallace, John A726
Wallace, Bruce E. A793
Wallace, Antoinette A835
Wallace, Madelyn A859
Wallace, Melissa A862
Wallace, Mark R. A870
Wallace, Robert T P25
Wallace, Jason S. P51
Wallace, Frank P61
Wallace, Bobby P71
Wallace, Jeffrey P117
Wallace, Brent E. P256
Wallace, Phillip O P285
Wallace, Paul P285
Wallace, Mark P304
Wallace, Mark A. P548
Wallace, Matthew P625
Wallace, Akmar E120
Wallace, Peter E359
Wallach, Russell A522
Wallach, Matthew E433
Wallenberg, Jacob W3
Wallenberg, Marcus W357
Wallenberg, Jacob W386
Wallenfelsz, Don A25
Wallenfelsz, Don P14
Wallenhaupt, Stephen L. P390

Wallenta, Craig A60
Waller, Kathy N. A215
Waller, Kathy A262
Waller, Cathy A682
Waller, Robert R P467
Waller, Nick E192
Walles, Rob A175
Walley, Pete P93
Wallfred, Teresa A232
Wallin, Joshua A137
Wallin, Ulrich W178
Wallin, Ulrich W382
Wallis, Julie A108
Wallis, James A465
Wallis-Lage, Cindy P85
Walljasper, William J. (Bill) A173
Walls, Robert H. A452
Walls, Kechette P392
Walls, LaMinda P610
Walmsley, Emma W171
Walner, Doug E386
Walno, Vicki A196
Walpert, Jason E99
Walrath, Teresa A538
Walsdorf, John A. (Jack) E152
Walser, Brett A850
Walsh, Jim A3
Walsh, Lambert A11
Walsh, Brian A36
Walsh, David A57
Walsh, Timothy A. A58
Walsh, Tim A89
Walsh, Mike A91
Walsh, Steven A126
Walsh, David A164
Walsh, John A166
Walsh, Bernadette A203
Walsh, Catherine A243
Walsh, Caitlin A390
Walsh, Andrea A412
Walsh, Matt A414
Walsh, Michael A452
Walsh, Joe A462
Walsh, Brian A482
Walsh, Kate A522
Walsh, William P. A588
Walsh, Timothy J. A641
Walsh, Wendy A695
Walsh, Amanda A741
Walsh, Marguerite A744
Walsh, Karen Bianchi A782
Walsh, Ian K. A821
Walsh, John L. A857
Walsh, Rich A887
Walsh, Ryan P35
Walsh, Kate E. P95
Walsh, Katie P123
Walsh, Kate P159
Walsh, Tim P187
Walsh, Joann P193
Walsh, Gerri P202
Walsh, Geraldine P202
Walsh, Andrea P233
Walsh, Matt P236
Walsh, Joe P256
Walsh, Jennifer P314
Walsh, Steve P315
Walsh, William P. P365
Walsh, Jay P389
Walsh, Vincent P404
Walsh, Timothy J. P407
Walsh, Karen Bianchi P525
Walsh, Matthew M. (Matt) P600
Walsh, Daniel P600
Walsh, Matthew P600
Walsh, Sean P600
Walsh, Daniel J. P600
Walsh, Matthew M P657
Walsh, Daniel J P657
Walsh, Paul S. W116
Walsh, Mike E29
Walsh, Robert B. E138
Walsh, Keith E147
Walsh, Daniel E243
Walsh, Amanda E364

Walsh, Joseph E431
Walsh, Kevin E433
Walstrom, Jan A476
Walta, Eric A715
Walter, Luc A66
Walter, Tim A203
Walter, John A250
Walter, Pati A325
Walter, Frank E. A413
Walter, Randall R A414
Walter, Glen A573
Walter, Lawrence A606
Walter, Michael A850
Walter, Robert D. (Bob) A937
Walter, Stephen R. P153
Walter, Stephen P210
Walter, Randall R P236
Walter, Stephen P266
Walter, Adam P319
Walter, Kevin P330
Walter, Dave P384
Walter, Kenneth E41
Walter, Mary E106
Walter, Frank E. E205
Walters, Cynthia A222
Walters, Kirk W. A650
Walters, Mary A727
Walters, Caroline A824
Walters, Matt P19
Walters, David P75
Walters, H Patrick P253
Walters, Brooke P362
Walters, Leigh P412
Walters, Mary P453
Walters, Norm P502
Walters, Caroline P562
Walters, Kelly S. P566
Walters, Tyler O. P652
Walters, Kirk W. E329
Walther, Leanna A6
Walther, Andrew A495
Walther, Andrew P282
Waltman, David A185
Waltman, Naomi A893
Waltman, Scott E407
Walton, Edward A61
Walton, John A89
Walton, Demetra A323
Walton, Karen A509
Walton, Lynell A621
Walton, Thomas W. H. (Tom) A637
Walton, Paul A654
Walton, Geoffrey A789
Walton, Dan A837
Walton, Jarrod P54
Walton, Lynell E312
Walts, Steven P429
Waltz, Mike A86
Waltz, Karen P235
Waltz, Mike E27
Wambold, Richard A813
Wambold, Christine P19
Wampler, Kevin S. A273
Wampler, Dan P412
Wamser, Chris A296
Wamsley, Cheryl P352
Wan, Kenneth A779
Wanblad, Duncan W28
Wanchik, Marry A108
Wanchun, Zheng W198
Wandeler, Roland A65
Wandell, Keith E A253
Wandell, Keith A277
Wander, John A137
Wander, Arden P625
Wandke, Simon W33
Wandschneider, Robin A224
Waner, Leo A813
Wang, Jimmy A137
Wang, Qinggang A151
Wang, Xiaoman A200
Wang, Pei A204
Wang, Bill A351
Wang, Xia A414
Wang, Gloria A432

Wang, Li A518
Wang, Spencer A587
Wang, Andy A728
Wang, Min A896
Wang, Peter P30
Wang, Ernest P123
Wang, George P127
Wang, Richard P173
Wang, WEI P173
Wang, Xia P236
Wang, Eileen P285
Wang, Su P371
Wang, Tom P399
Wang, Chin P540
Wang, Chenchen P612
Wang, William P655
Wang, Yidong W28
Wang, Leon W38
Wang, Chuanfu W82
Wang, Gregory K.H. W89
Wang, Chuan W98
Wang, Shi W104
Wang, Wilfred W165
Wang, Fengying W173
Wang, J.K. W380
Wang, Jihong E22
Wang, Wei-chung E110
Wang, David E179
Wang, Daniel E196
Wang, Gloria E216
Wangsness, Erik P7
Wangwattanapanich, Somchai W351
Wanland, Erik A175
Wanli, Lin W96
Wann, Robert A589
Wanta, Gregory T. A467
Wanzek, Kent W166
Wanzer, Carla A112
Warbinton, Craig A89
Warch, Steven A574
Warchut, Tony P405
Ward, Gary A93
Ward, Victor A107
Ward, Anita A170
Ward, Jason A224
Ward, Paul J. A227
Ward, Edward A227
Ward, Patrick J A247
Ward, David A343
Ward, Bill A349
Ward, Steven E. A413
Ward, Vicki A452
Ward, John M A524
Ward, Geoffrey A702
Ward, Thomas A761
Ward, Ron A796
Ward, Laysha L. A804
Ward, Peter P. A843
Ward, Susan A871
Ward, Brian A877
Ward, Kathy P125
Ward, Wendy P155
Ward, Betty Lou P162
Ward, Robert T P349
Ward, Melissa P390
Ward, Jennifer P423
Ward, Jim P437
Ward, Nicholas P448
Ward, Karen P546
Ward, Debra P548
Ward, Adam P594
Ward, Lisa P630
Ward, Keith P649
Ward, Pat P664
Ward, Greg C. W243
Ward, Douglas M E78
Ward, Paul J. E90
Ward, Edward E90
Ward, David E164
Ward, Steven E. E205
Ward, Adrian E319
Ward, Stew E387
Ward, Scott R. E395
Ward, Ron E397
Ward-Callan, Mary P572

Warden, Tom A293
Warden, Kathy J. A320
Warden, Kathy J. A608
Wardin, Kris P339
Wardlaw, Van M. A815
Wardlow, Kirk A855
Wardrup, James A19
Wardwell, Myra A107
Wardynski, Paula A596
Ware, Stacey A108
Ware, Brandon P409
Ware, Kinetra P430
Ware, Demetrius E433
Wareheim, Laura A332
Wareing, Peter A180
Wargo, Karla A108
Wariner, Clayton A859
Waring, Michael A182
Waring, Phillip A798
Waring, Stephen P496
Waring, Wendy P616
Warkoczeski, Larry P463
Warkomski, Denise A313
Warkomski, Denise P200
Warlow, Thomas P. E94
Warman, Chelsee A455
Warman, D. Scott N. A530
Warman, Scott A530
Warman, Chelsee E228
Warmbier, Kimberly (Kim) A259
Warminsky, Jeff E330
Warne, Jen A520
Warne, Peter H. W243
Warner, Jason A137
Warner, Jane A154
Warner, Joe A367
Warner, Jane A453
Warner, J A509
Warner, Tim R A510
Warner, Jason A550
Warner, Mark A605
Warner, Dan P166
Warner, Daniel P166
Warner, Donna P276
Warner, Tim R P290
Warner, John P420
Warner, Wendy P597
Warner, John P647
Warner, Richard C. E433
Warner, Michelle E433
Warnick, Lorin D. P159
Warrell, Kristen P441
Warren, Kathleen A119
Warren, Karmon A133
Warren, Jay A216
Warren, Eric A218
Warren, Kelcy L A295
Warren, Kenneth A309
Warren, Thomas A327
Warren, Dennis A405
Warren, Gary A479
Warren, Cindy A479
Warren, Laura A500
Warren, Celeste A554
Warren, Burney A581
Warren, Sandy A619
Warren, Tiffany R A626
Warren, V'Ella A880
Warren, Alice A884
Warren, Kristin A924
Warren, Kevin M. A933
Warren, Kelcy L P297
Warren, Sandy P393
Warren, Brian P423
Warren, David P597
Warren, V'Ella P640
Warren, Brian P. E98
Warren, Paul E123
Warren, Donnie E203
Warren, Burney E294
Warren, Galen E362
Warren, Miriam E450
Warrick, Joanna A336
Warrick, Betsy A472
Warrick, Joanna E157

Warrier, Ammu P174
Warsek, Gregory T A85
Warsek, Gregory T E27
Warsh, Kevin A871
Warshaw, Peter P286
Warshawsky, Ilka P131
Warsinske, Steven P483
Wartenbergh, Marcela A692
Warthen, Wayne B. E98
Wartman, Steven A P596
Warwick, John J. E58
Warzinski, Cheryl P55
Warznak, Robert A574
Waschow, Dan E184
Wascom, D. G. A309
Wasden, Mitch P633
Wasechek, Wayne E424
Waser, Eric H. A646
Waser, Eric H. E324
Washam, Daniel A885
Washburn, Dana P405
Washburn, Donald A. (Don) E14
Washburne, Tom A621
Washburne, Tom E311
Washek, Amy P482
Washer, Glenn E75
Washicko, Paul E58
Washington, Justina A139
Washington, Mike A175
Washington, Cynthia A296
Washington, Robin L. A385
Washington, Herbert A531
Washington, Lashondra A532
Washington, Alton J. P90
Washington, Justina P93
Washington, Donna P175
Washington, A. Eugene P187
Washington, Yvette P514
Washington, Adam P514
Washington, Marilyn P638
Washington, Roderick E105
Washington-warner, Charice A592
Washington-warner, Charice P370
Wasiak, Xavier A482
Wasielczyk, Michael A799
Wasik, Joe A329
Wasilewski, Raymond W. A316
Wasiuta, Robert P530
Wasmer, Steve A444
Wass, Adam P323
Wassel, Nabil P249
Wasser, Marilyn J A707
Wasser, Marilyn J. A708
Wasserman, Robert A36
Wasserman, Jack A451
Wasserman, Adrienne P94
Wassersug, Mark P A462
Wassmer, Michael J. A166
Wasson, Stewart A165
Wasson, Jim P415
Wasti, Rashid W422
Wastler, Ernst W167
Watanabe, Mauro A218
Watanabe, Yutaka W107
Watanabe, Yoshinori W127
Watanabe, Dai W227
Watanabe, Yoshiro W228
Watanabe, Shuichi W252
Watanabe, Shinjiro W252
Watanabe, Kenji W278
Watanabe, Kunio W286
Watanabe, Takao W392
Watari, Ryoji W293
Watchmaker, Kenneth A388
Waterfall, Marcy A540
Waterfield, Brett A528
Waterhouse, Danielle P285
Waterhouse, Deborah W171
Waterman, Josh A61
Waters, Eddie A58
Waters, Stephen M. A147
Waters, Andy D. A229
Waters, Scott A236
Waters, Jim A569
Waters, Geoffrey A704

Waters, Ron A741
Waters, Leteria A796
Waters, Glenn P70
Waters, Ron E364
Waters, Leteria E397
Waterson, Blake A260
Watford, Janis A219
Watford, Janis E87
Wathen, Brian E404
Watkin, Jared L. A5
Watkins, Charles E A296
Watkins, James A713
Watkins, James A760
Watkins, Brad A819
Watkins, Jennifer A882
Watkins, W Juan P85
Watkins, Thomas P179
Watkins, Jesse P193
Watkins, Ron P245
Watkins, Brad P549
Watkins, Ruth V. P597
Watkins, Mark P630
Watkins, Anthony P658
Watkins, Gretchen H. W1
Watkins, Kameshia E72
Watkins, James E374
Watne, Zachariah A376
Watriss, Whitney P497
Watsa, V.Prem W159
Watson, Jimmy A58
Watson, Bill A58
Watson, Tim A86
Watson, Deborah A107
Watson, Beth A108
Watson, Glenn A118
Watson, Joseph A160
Watson, Anthony A205
Watson, Wendy A A205
Watson, David N A220
Watson, Jim A224
Watson, David A240
Watson, Alanna A243
Watson, Brion A248
Watson, Lois A325
Watson, Traci A325
Watson, Peter A336
Watson, Randi A369
Watson, Katie L. A385
Watson, Ian A466
Watson, Lucas A471
Watson, Greg A548
Watson, Herman A574
Watson, Brandon A630
Watson, Jacci A749
Watson, Glenn P66
Watson, Marsha P93
Watson, Nancy P114
Watson, Anne P209
Watson, James P286
Watson, Veronica P326
Watson, George E P354
Watson, Jackie P363
Watson, Christopher P389
Watson, Robin P421
Watson, Harry P463
Watson, Leslyn P472
Watson, Bud P478
Watson, Amy E. P510
Watson, Dean P541
Watson, Crystal P586
Watson, James M. P594
Watson, Gordon W14
Watson, John W65
Watson, J. Howard W82
Watson, Tim E27
Watson, Brion E107
Watson, Bryan E131
Watson, Peter E157
Watson, Peter H. E171
Watson, Jacci E367
Watson, Bob E433
Watt, Graeme A. A99
Watt, Shannon A246
Watt, John H. A584
Watt, Stephen P595

Watt, Shannon E105
Watt, Brian R. E229
Watters, Lyle A360
Watters, Jim A447
Watters, Jill A722
Watters, Jim P247
Watters, James H. P456
Watterson, Andrew M A773
Watteville, Jacques de W55
Wattley, Mark A900
Watts, Phillip R. A267
Watts, Jeffery M. A315
Watts, Myles J. A317
Watts, Phil A320
Watts, Michael A391
Watts, Alan A423
Watts, James A807
Watts, Brianna A880
Watts, Karen P171
Watts, Tom P273
Watts, Richard P411
Watts, Christella P514
Watts, Charles P537
Watts, Brianna P640
Watts, Liz E46
Watts, Craig E144
Watts, Myles J. E146
Wattula, Andy E219
Waty, Elin W371
Watzinter, Johanna P597
Waugh, Scott A641
Waugh, Scott P407
Wavra, Laura A682
Wawrzyniak, Dore A492
Waxman, Jason A460
Waxman, Herbert S P19
Way, Alva A735
Way, John A. E339
Waycaster, C. Mitchell (Mitch) A717
Waycaster, C. Mitchell (Mitch) E351
Wayland, Joseph F. W106
Wayles, Doug A779
Wayling, Brian A462
Wayling, Brian P256
Waymack, Randy P376
Wayman, Brett E132
Wayne, Bo A850
Wayne, John C. P423
Wayne, Richard E305
Waynick, Randy P655
Weant, Paula A761
Weant, Jerry A. E60
Wear, Mark A170
Wear, Ralph A702
Weatherhead, Craig A315
Weatherhead, Jim A606
Weatherly, Lex A228
Weatherred, Michael A254
Weathers, Melanie A353
Weathers, Karen A885
Weathers, Will P201
Weathers, Melanie P204
Weatherwax, Michael A830
Weatherwax, Michael P593
Weaver, Jason A58
Weaver, Tracey A108
Weaver, Paul A185
Weaver, Gary A251
Weaver, Michelle A308
Weaver, Nicole A345
Weaver, Ken A520
Weaver, Jeff A569
Weaver, Susan A590
Weaver, Janine M A602
Weaver, Derrek A733
Weaver, Amy E. A739
Weaver, David H. A849
Weaver, Troy A850
Weaver, Jennifer A850
Weaver, Keith A934
Weaver, Amy P38
Weaver, Ron P281
Weaver, Tyler P399
Weaver, Carl P405
Weaver, Jeremy P439

COMBINED HOOVER'S HANDBOOK INDEX OF EXECUTIVES

```
A = AMERICAN BUSINESS
E = EMERGING COMPANIES
P = PRIVATE COMPANIES
W = WORLD BUSINESS
```

Weaver, Amanda P552
Weaver, Gail P675
Weaver, Paul E21
Weaver, Nicole E166
Webb, Ryan A23
Webb, Randy A74
Webb, Eileen A108
Webb, James R. A189
Webb, Thomas J. (Tom) A209
Webb, Patricia G. (Pat) A226
Webb, Thomas J. (Tom) A238
Webb, Mark O. A275
Webb, Cody A315
Webb, James A323
Webb, Sarah A326
Webb, Marva A356
Webb, Brian A442
Webb, Jan C. A456
Webb, Jan A520
Webb, Steve A530
Webb, Ian A544
Webb, Mary A574
Webb, John A616
Webb, Sandy A704
Webb, Mike A796
Webb, Robb A812
Webb, Joseph A833
Webb, Martin A933
Webb, Tammy P45
Webb, James P67
Webb, Jim P67
Webb, David P70
Webb, Donna P112
Webb, Patricia G. (Pat) P150
Webb, Aaron P193
Webb, Marie P193
Webb, Kim P282
Webb, Steven P372
Webb, Maryjo P489
Webb, Jan C. E228
Webb, Mike E397
Webber, Debbi A45
Webber, Jerome A89
Webber, Susanna A554
Webber, Kerry A606
Webber, Diane A784
Webber, Roland A835
Webber, Katey P146
Webber, Henry S. P600
Webber, Cheryl P612
Weber, Roger A25
Weber, Ron A25
Weber, Jennifer A53
Weber, Steven A85
Weber, Susan A163
Weber, Robert A346
Weber, Mike A368
Weber, Christopher T. (Chris) A401
Weber, Helen A405
Weber, David F A434
Weber, Bob A465
Weber, Scott A526
Weber, Jennifer A552
Weber, Cathi A567
Weber, Hubert A573
Weber, David A651
Weber, Roger P14
Weber, Ron P14
Weber, Peter P102
Weber, Jeff P103
Weber, Robert P157
Weber, Amy P265
Weber, Jennifer P324
Weber, Jeff P336
Weber, Julie P354
Weber, Joyce P529
Weber, Emily P626
Weber, Edythe P633
Weber, Jodi P678

Weber, Ulrich W133
Weber, Christophe W381
Weber, David M. E2
Weber, Steven E27
Weber, Susan E62
Weber, Robert E166
Weber, Phillip J. (Phil) E177
Weber, William E233
Weber, Walter E272
Weber, Cathi E284
Weber, Michael E316
Weber, Kathleen E317
Weber, David E329
Webster, Jay A63
Webster, Sabrina A492
Webster, Michele A778
Webster, Letitia A891
Webster, Keith P114
Webster, Kathleen P298
Webster, William M. P430
Webster, Kipp P556
Webster, Richard P604
Webster, Benita P625
Webster, Marshall W. P643
Webster, Kathy E81
Webster, Jule E358
Wechsler, Ron A823
Wechsler, Ron E405
Wechter, Zach A756
Weddington, Brian A112
Weddington, Sharon P419
Wedepohl, Eric A376
Wedge, Susan A465
Wedin, Robert J. (Rob) E58
Weed, Thaddeus G. (Tad) E84
Weekes, Cristina E72
Weekley, Daniel A275
Weekley, Kathy P30
Weeks, Wendell P. A240
Weeks, Richard A380
Weeks, Felicia A449
Weeks, Andrew M. A640
Weeks, Dan A859
Weeks, Susan P549
Weeks, Richard S. P660
Weeks, Felicia E221
Weel, Pascal A204
Weems, Charles A319
Weems, Mac A368
Weeshoff, Bill E218
Wegelin, Mark P31
Wegener, Hagy A179
Wegener, Paul A552
Wegener, Mildred P596
Wegener, Paul E275
Weglarz, Brian P31
Wegleitner, Edwin A108
Wegman, Jim P28
Wegman, Jill P157
Wegman, Thomas L. E46
Wegner, James P387
Wegner, Christoph W59
Wegner, Jeremy E76
Wegrzyn, Daniel A778
Wehe, Brad P29
Wehman, Erin A347
Wehman, Erin E168
Wehmann, James M. E144
Wehmer, Edward J. A925
Wehmer, Edward J. E445
Wehn, Steve E21
Wehner, David M. (Dave) A310
Wehner, Dominik W166
Wehr, Van A176
Wehring, Brad P469
Wehrly, Jennifer A345
Wehrly, Donald W. A534
Wehrly, Jennifer E165
Wei, Mary A284
Wei, Wang W12
Wei, Chris W40
Wei, Chen W110
Wei, Jiafu W118
Wei, Peter W123
Wei, C.C. W380

Wei, Mary E120
Wei, Frank E131
Weibelt, Daniel P590
Weiberg, Chris A621
Weiberg, Chris E312
Weichle, Scott A925
Weichle, Scott E445
Weideman, William H A624
Weidemoyer, Matt A137
Weidlich, Olaf A450
Weidlich, David A526
Weidman-Grunewald, Elaine W386
Weidner, Frank P432
Weidong, Chen W385
Weigel, Kelly E101
Weigley, David E. P7
Weigman, Mark A799
Weih, Lori P258
Weihe, Huang W227
Weihe, Huang W301
Weil, Robert J. A226
Weil, Robert J. A371
Weil, Julie A604
Weil, Robert J. P150
Weil, Robert J. P213
Weiland, Ed P471
Weiler, Joyce A491
Weiler, Ulrike A599
Weiler, Nathan P49
Weilinghoff, Andreas A289
Weill, Brendon P201
Weimer, Charles A347
Weimer, Gail A559
Weimer, Theodor W407
Weinand, Dieter W61
Weinbach, Lawrence A A269
Weinberg, Meryl A588
Weinberg, Meryl P365
Weinberg, John S. E138
Weiner, Jack P329
Weiner, Eli P392
Weiner, Edward G. P605
Weiner, Michael A. E372
Weinert, Robert S E35
Weinfurter, Daniel P174
Weingarden, Craig A222
Weingart, Tom A584
Weingart, Saul N P612
Weingartner, Jeffrey A340
Weingartner, Jeffrey E160
Weinick, Robin P447
Weinkle, Brian A574
Weinraub, Michelle P664
Weinstein, Larry A98
Weinstein, Laura A243
Weinstein, Roslyn A588
Weinstein, Craig A613
Weinstein, Larry A761
Weinstein, Michael Arthur P12
Weinstein, James P173
Weinstein, Nelson P293
Weinstein, Roslyn P365
Weinstein, Glen D. E239
Weinstock, Craig L A581
Weintraub, Jonathan P161
Weir, Walter P92
Weir, Daniela P125
Weir, David P368
Weir, Bob P383
Weir, Nicholas E102
Weir, Amanda E309
Weir, Matt E429
Weirick, Cecilia P209
Weis, Don A175
Weisberg, James P194
Weisblatt, Rick P54
Weise, Stuart A717
Weise, Lori P118
Weise, Stuart E351
Weisel, Thomas W. (Thom) A787
Weisenberg, Clay A922
Weisenberg, Clay P671
Weisenfeld, Paul P447
Weisenhorn, John A111
Weiser, Anna P559

Weishaar, Annette A160
Weishan, Dennis A727
Weishan, Dennis P453
Weishar, Evan A859
Weisickle, John A57
Weisickle, John P33
Weiskopff, Beth E81
Weisler, Dion J. A438
Weisman, Dan A747
Weismann, Burke A175
Weiss, Mark A56
Weiss, Larry A67
Weiss, Karl A173
Weiss, Justin A179
Weiss, Craig A232
Weiss, Jerry A364
Weiss, Maureen A507
Weiss, Greg A545
Weiss, Holly A549
Weiss, Richard A605
Weiss, Nick A831
Weiss, John P351
Weiss, Gary E. P386
Weiss, Jeff P461
Weiss, Philippe P486
Weiss, Nick P601
Weiss, Mark D P665
Weiss, David E. E23
Weiss, Elie E53
Weiss, Neil E110
Weiss, Richard R. E375
Weissbaum, Martha A723
Weissburg, Martin W420
Weisser, Hellmuth W248
Weissinger, Allison P177
Weissman, Gabriel A63
Weissman, Neil J. A551
Weissman, Michael A574
Weissman, Mark P130
Weissman, Neil J. P321
Weissman, Seth R. P547
Weissman, Paul P667
Weissmann, Josh P592
Weistra, Gerben E102
Weiszhaar, Barbara Barton A438
Weitgenant, David A349
Weitzel, Harry A299
Weitzman, Debbie A169
Weitzman, Kenneth A574
Weitzner, John S P459
Weksner, Ed A3
Welage, Lynda S. P634
Welber, Dave A853
Welber, Dave P612
Welborn, Jamie A569
Welborn, Jim P6
Welborn, Tom P344
Welborn, Thomas P345
Welborn, Ruth B. P551
Welborn, Marilyn R. E124
Welch, Marty A75
Welch, Jacqueline A364
Welch, J Phillip A380
Welch, John A446
Welch, Susan A828
Welch, Jerry A833
Welch, Jim P70
Welch, Shelly P133
Welch, Kevin P260
Welch, Patrick J P270
Welch, Patrick P270
Welch, H Ray P330
Welch, Kevin P359
Welch, Kip P417
Welch, Susan P584
Welch, Christopher A. (Chris) E112
Welch, Richard E126
Weldon, Alex A54
Weldon, William A251
Weldon, Gene A294
Weldon, Mary A329
Weldon, Michael A933
Weldon, Terry P198
Weldon, Aaron P203
Weldon, Dennis P326

Weldon, Marcus W284
Weldy, Dave P252
Welker, Kevin P P279
Welkie, Katherine A. (Katy) A462
Welkie, Katherine A. (Katy) P256
Welkley, Steve A933
Welkomer, Dalena A727
Welkomer, Dalena P453
Wellborn, W. Christopher (Chris) A569
Wellendorf, Don P303
Weller, Keith A325
Weller, Simon A380
Weller, Heiko A724
Weller, Matthew P273
Weller, Heiko P452
Welles, Scott A145
Welling, Brandon A222
Welling, John A647
Wellington, Glenn A137
Wellins, Chris P306
Wellisch, Alejandro A5
Wellman, Mark A315
Wellman, Arnold A871
Wells, Brooks A17
Wells, Martha K A89
Wells, Vernon A200
Wells, Cynthia A277
Wells, Gary A318
Wells, Scott R. A452
Wells, Dustin A464
Wells, Charles A478
Wells, David A587
Wells, Larry A606
Wells, Xiao A676
Wells, Michael K A676
Wells, Lisa A717
Wells, Robert A756
Wells, Warren A882
Wells, Tim A905
Wells, Brooks P9
Wells, Tammy P45
Wells, Charles P268
Wells, John P351
Wells, Jill P516
Wells, Janet P519
Wells, Richard P641
Wells, Mike W314
Wells, Stuart C. E144
Wells, Xiao E338
Wells, Lisa E351
Welsh, Robert A540
Welsh, Elise A780
Welsh, Bill A855
Welsh, Leston A882
Welsh, Deanne M A922
Welsh, Charles P330
Welsh, Richard P382
Welsh, Peter P531
Welsh, Amanda P648
Welsh, Deanne M P671
Welt, Philip S. A126
Welter, Ruth A376
Welters, Anthony A526
Welton, Isabelle W435
Welu, Todd P165
Welz, Edward A. (Ed) P367
Welzenbach, Mark A405
Wemmer, Dieter W24
Wempe, Debbie A168
Wen, Ling W102
Wenaas, Jeffrey K. (Jeff) P238
Wende, Will A176
Wendel, Jon S. A447
Wendel, Jon S. P247
Wendelboe, Steven A530
Wendelken, Roger P446
Wendell, Reid E105
Wender, Herbert A700
Wender, Joseph E237
Wendler, Kenneth A200
Wendt, Stephen C P184
Wendy, Warring P558
Wenerstrom, Stewart A132
Weng, Weibo A451
Weng, Kirsti A511

Weng, Kirsti P290
Wenger, E. Philip (Phil) A367
Wenger, Philip R. P573
Wenger, Stefan L. E360
Wengert, Amanda A224
Wengler, Frank A16
Wenhui, Qian W198
Wenig, Devin N. A287
Wenk, Martin W43
Wenkoff, Carman A272
Wenlong, Lou W12
Wenner, David E33
Wenning, Werner W61
Wenning, Werner W353
Wenstrom, Marlon A482
Wente, Lisa A759
Wente, Lisa P493
Wente, Tony P507
Wente, Susan P599
Wente, Heinz-Gerhard W117
Wenthur, Cary J E347
Wentling, Robert A409
Wentworth, Brian A5
Wentworth, Peter A222
Wentworth, Harold M. (Harry) A227
Wentworth, Steven D. A301
Wentworth, Steve A301
Wentworth, Kerry P389
Wentworth, Harold M. (Harry) E90
Wentz, Deanna P22
Wentz, Myron W. E423
Wentzel, Ladeana A437
Wenzel, Kathleen A86
Wenzel, Gregory G. (Greg) A145
Wenzel, Kathleen E27
Weppler, Rainer A849
Werbeckes, Jim A293
Werdegar, Stefan E412
Werft, Ronald C P472
Werkheiser, David E143
Werkhoven, Jim P387
Werle, Haley A200
Werley, Travis A838
Wermes, Eric A197
Werneck, Melissa A497
Werner, Frederick W. (Fred) A16
Werner, Gene A107
Werner, Todd S. A117
Werner, Tom A232
Werner, Chris A467
Werner, Melissa A491
Werner, Todd S. P61
Werner, Caroline C E248
Wernette, Terry P163
Wernick, Mark P22
Wernick, Joel P417
Wernikoff, Daniel A. (Dan) A471
Werpy, Dave A3
Werpy, Todd A. A77
Werra, Greg A606
Werrbach, John P22
Wersch, Wouter Van A374
Wersching, Patricia A559
Werth, Clinton P52
Werth, Dennis L. P374
Werth, Dennis E285
Werthauser, Judy E172
Wertheim, Ram D. A546
Werthman, Ronald P268
Wertman, Jessica P400
Wescoe, Nicole A921
Wescoe, David P350
Wescoe, Nicole P669
Wescombe, Gary E203
Wesley, Carla A50
Wesley, Rosalyn A63
Wesley, David A850
Wesley-Smith, Terence P628
Weslock, Kathleen A366
Weslow, Pat A774
Wesoff, Nancy P300
Wesolek, Lisa M. E112
Wesolek, Rick E265
Wesolowski, Karen P153
Wesolowski, Timothy M. (Tim) E366

Wessel, David P130
Wessel, Rick L. E171
Wessels, Philip W275
Wessler, Alan P337
Wessman, Cal A175
West, Phil A71
West, Ed A165
West, Hilda A207
West, Robert F. (Rob) A213
West, Wayne G. (Gil) A262
West, Gil A262
West, Roderick K. (Rod) A296
West, Robert A301
West, Jonathan A318
West, Gary A409
West, Brian A412
West, Lucia A444
West, Cliff A481
West, Chantel A492
West, Jayson A520
West, Jacqueline A575
West, Mindy K. A579
West, Lori A580
West, Jerret A587
West, William Corey A632
West, Richard A637
West, Tony A654
West, Rachel A664
West, James A682
West, Mark D. A711
West, Kelly A731
West, Shane A810
West, Tina A882
West, Steve A903
West, Buddy A905
West, Eric A933
West, Robert F. (Rob) P143
West, James P162
West, George P212
West, Sandy P277
West, Mary P329
West, David P340
West, Tom P390
West, James R P419
West, Mark D. P444
West, Jack P487
West, Karin P546
West, Mary Jo P607
West, Jeffrey P639
West, Stacey E106
West, Lori E293
West, Bradley (Brad) E332
West, Rachel E334
West, Brandy E374
West, Scott E429
West, Josh E433
West, Chris E443
Westad, Erik A301
Westad, Erik P196
Westapher, Bernard P404
Westbay, James A746
Westbrook, Larry A382
Westbrook, C Hunter A430
Westbrook, Bennett D. A736
Westbrook, Bennett D. P460
Westcott, David A353
Westcott, Justin A489
Westcott, Brian A850
Westcott, David P204
Westenberg, Rick A378
Westerbeke, Brian A512
Westerhold, Mary A346
Westerhold, Mary E166
Western, Keith A. A116
Western, Keith A. E39
Westervelt, Matthew A449
Westervelt, Karen S A827
Westervelt, Karen S P580
Westervelt, Matthew E221
Westfield, Michael A526
Westfield, Mike A526
Westin, Nicole A789
Westlake, Wayne P356
Westle, Marc B P343
Westlie, Trond - -. W129

Westlund, M. Randolph (Rand) A693
Westlund, Jessie P151
Westlund, M. Randolph (Rand) E341
Westman, David A105
Westman, Shelley A465
Westman, David A556
Westman, David P328
Westman, John P608
Westman, David E34
Westman, Don B. E399
Westmoreland, Rick A140
Westmoreland, Mary Beth E47
Westmoreland, Mary E47
Weston, Mike A198
Weston, Kathleen A361
Weston, Karl A717
Weston, Ivy P138
Weston, Marc A P173
Weston, Andrew P491
Weston, George G. W36
Weston, Galen G. W422
Weston, Alannah W422
Westphal, Carrie A554
Westra, Richard A252
Westrick, Thomas A374
Westrick, Karl J P307
Wet, Misty de A772
Wet, Misty de E383
Wetherell, Russell P277
Wetherington, Suzzane A98
Wetselaar, Maarten W334
Wettersten, Virginia P5
Wetzel, Larry A103
Wetzel, Kurt A112
Wetzel, Jaymie A574
Wetzel, Jonathan E172
Wetzel, Cindy L. E281
Wexler, Samantha A833
Wexler, Steve E366
Wexner, Leslie H. A500
Wexner, Abigail S A500
Wexner, Abigail S. P359
Weyerhaeuser, William T. A219
Weyerhaeuser, William T. E87
Weyland, Bill P605
Whalen, Ellie A112
Whalen, Douglas A155
Whalen, Edward A524
Whalen, Dan A739
Whalen, James W. A803
Whalen, Julie A921
Whalen, Chad P106
Whalen, Thomas V. P289
Whalen, Anna P299
Whalen, Douglas E54
Whalen, Chad E179
Whaley, Steven A647
Whaley, Alan P252
Whalley, Ken A388
Whang, Kyujung P592
Wharton, Charles A909
Wharton, Danny P115
Wharton, Charles E436
Wheat, William W. (Bill) A435
Wheat, Mary P399
Wheat, Douglas D. (Doug) E21
Wheatlake, Franklin C. A806
Wheatlake, Franklin C. E398
Wheatley, Chuck A695
Wheaton, Guy A596
Wheatstine, Valerie A872
Wheeler, Al A13
Wheeler, Mike A355
Wheeler, Michael J. A604
Wheeler, Scott A784
Wheeler, Robert H. A834
Wheeler, Paula A842
Wheeler, Monte A850
Wheeler, David A890
Wheeler, Penny Ann P26
Wheeler, Philip P331
Wheeler, Steven M. (Steve) P478
Wheeler, Peter P579
Wheeler, Laura P586
Wheeler, Lynette P608

COMBINED HOOVER'S HANDBOOK INDEX OF EXECUTIVES

```
A = AMERICAN BUSINESS
E = EMERGING COMPANIES
P = PRIVATE COMPANIES
W = WORLD BUSINESS
```

Wheeler, Kelsey P609
Wheeler, Bradley C. (Brad) P610
Wheeler, Brad P610
Wheeler, Scott E99
Wheeler, Chad E432
Wheeler-Fair, Martha P342
Whelan, Kellie A491
Whelan, Kathleen P541
Whelan, Michael P600
Whelan, John P610
Whelan, Lyndsey E123
Whelen, John K. W150
Whelton, Pamela Daley P502
Wherry, Robert P490
Whetstine, Michael J P279
Whetstone, Chesney A105
Whetstone, Hal P180
Whetstone, Jim P310
Whetstone, Chesney E34
Whewell, LuAnne A345
Whewell, LuAnne E166
Whichard, Betty M P634
Whiddon, Shelley A34
Whiddon, Jeremiah P52
Whiddon, Georgia P552
Whiitely, B Glen P162
Whipple, Andrew A482
Whipple, Bryan A844
Whipple, John P431
Whisler, J Steven A467
Whisler, Steven A467
Whisman, Jon A108
Whisperer, Shoe P108
Whitacre, Michael A327
Whitacre, Lisa A367
Whitaker, John A403
Whitaker, Maureen A701
Whitaker, Mitchell A891
Whitaker, Todd E225
Whitaker, Thomas A. (Tom) E370
Whitcher, Angela A520
Whitcomb, Rachel A804
Whitcutt, Peter W29
White, Miles D. A5
White, Brad A16
White, Teresa L. A19
White, Steve A21
White, Thomas A25
White, John A58
White, John A74
White, Amy A97
White, Wanda A108
White, Keith P A140
White, Terry A140
White, Brianna A150
White, Sylvia A165
White, Cris A A219
White, Antoine A219
White, Anthony A247
White, Robert A. A248
White, Bill A250
White, Tony A251
White, Jim A254
White, Bill A255
White, Nick A267
White, Elijah A309
White, Mary A346
White, Charles A353
White, Amy A368
White, Brett A376
White, Steve A405
White, Alan B. A421
White, Teresa A430
White, Bryan A451
White, James C. (Jim) A455
White, Katharyn A466
White, Ed A483
White, Barbara A498
White, Mike A512

White, George B. (Burt) A528
White, Shawn A528
White, Joseph W. A570
White, William S A578
White, Robert A592
White, Alison A595
White, Doug A598
White, Elizabeth V A605
White, Katherine A621
White, Kasi A651
White, J. Edward (Ed) A664
White, J. Harvey A664
White, Edward A665
White, Debbie A676
White, Andy A711
White, Megan A737
White, Garner A740
White, Brett A756
White, Lynn A796
White, Melissa A798
White, Suzanne A801
White, Clark A803
White, William A804
White, James A818
White, Debbie A829
White, Mark A833
White, Noel A855
White, Diana A866
White, Tyler A867
White, Wayne A877
White, Tom A882
White, Wendy A922
White, Cindy A922
White, Joseph A925
White, Patrick A933
White, Matthew P11
White, Thomas P14
White, Kim P45
White, Doug P45
White, Lisa P60
White, Rev. William W. P63
White, William W P65
White, Albert P122
White, Cooper P131
White, Inez P132
White, Joseph P135
White, Keith A. P140
White, Paul P140
White, Bonni L P174
White, Shannon P174
White, Tracy P174
White, Linda E P176
White, Kevin P187
White, Charles P204
White, Gregory P221
White, Joseph E P234
White, Bryan P249
White, Sandra P253
White, James P254
White, Joseph P300
White, Laura P314
White, David P327
White, Robert P370
White, Thomas D P391
White, Brad P395
White, Eric P399
White, Andy P444
White, Van Henri P454
White, Louise P489
White, Lori P505
White, Craig P544
White, Robert P577
White, Debbie P585
White, Winona P610
White, Carrie P625
White, Lawrence P627
White, Craig G. P634
White, Wendy P671
White, Cindy P671
White, Stephen W432
White, Dan E21
White, Antoine E87
White, Anthony E105
White, Chris E105
White, Robert A. E107

White, Richard D. E113
White, Randall W. E124
White, Craig M. E124
White, Duane E. E144
White, Ray E149
White, Mary E166
White, Andrew E189
White, Duane E205
White, James C. (Jim) E228
White, Katherine E312
White, Kasi E329
White, J. Edward (Ed) E333
White, J. Harvey E333
White, Edward E334
White, Debbie E338
White, Megan E361
White, Lynn E397
White, James E403
White, Diana E417
White, Tyler E418
White, Joseph E445
White-Bruton, Evelyn A856
White-Bruton, Evelyn P614
Whiteaker, Kim P662
Whited, Gary L. A373
Whited, Elizabeth F. (Beth) A863
Whitefield, Adam A940
Whitehead, Ken A518
Whitehead, Dane E. A533
Whitehead, Roy M. A903
Whitehead, H P130
Whitehead, David P229
Whitehead, Nigel W41
Whitehead, Jenifer E148
Whitehouse, Kirk A852
Whitehouse, Donna P489
Whitehurst, Bradford D. (Brad) A294
Whitehurst, Sally A341
Whitehurst, Jim P487
Whitehurst, Jay F. E93
Whitehurst, Julian E. (Jay) E296
Whiteing, David W114
Whitelaw, Gary W371
Whiteley, Dudley A376
Whiteley, Sherry A471
Whitely, B Glen P162
Whiteman, Charles H. A828
Whiteman, Jeffrey S. (Jeff) P195
Whiteman, Charles H. P584
Whitemore, James A586
Whiten, Torivia A108
Whitener, Pam P300
Whiteside, Hayes V. A678
Whiteside, Cathie A693
Whiteside, Cathy A693
Whiteside, S A693
Whiteside, Darwin P382
Whiteside, James P522
Whiteside, Cathie E341
Whiteside, Cathy E341
Whiteside, S E341
Whitfield, Charlene A275
Whitfield, Laura A294
Whitfield, Rob W424
Whitham, Rande A155
Whitham, Rande E54
Whiting, Jennifer A16
Whiting, Chris A379
Whiting, Steve A571
Whiting, Bill A831
Whiting, Autumn P102
Whiting, Bill P601
Whiting, Amanda P626
Whitley, David A782
Whitley, Russell A922
Whitley, Gary P361
Whitley, David P526
Whitley, Russell P671
Whitman, Reed H A153
Whitman, Robert A240
Whitman, Margaret C. (Meg) A420
Whitman, Terri A444
Whitman, John A555
Whitman, Cheryl A806
Whitman, Erika A859

Whitman, Debra P2
Whitman, Colton P147
Whitman, Roger P274
Whitman, Bill P541
Whitman, Reed H E52
Whitman, Robert E102
Whitman, Cheryl E399
Whitmer, Jeff A613
Whitmer, Tom A692
Whitmire, Larry P25
Whitmore, Martin A835
Whitmore, Colleen P130
Whitmyer, Laurie P420
Whitney, John A69
Whitney, Randy P74
Whitridge, John A538
Whitson, Linda A552
Whitson, Mark P185
Whitson, Linda P324
Whitt, Richard R. A536
Whitt, Jon E138
Whittaker, Gordon A574
Whittaker, Thomas F. (Tom) P260
Whittaker, Tom P261
Whittemore, Mark P403
Whittet, Jim A727
Whittet, Jim P453
Whittinghill, Kyle E170
Whittington, Lisa A436
Whittington, Ray P175
Whittle, Scott A462
Whittle, Scott P256
Whittle, John E178
Whittlinger, Keith A833
Whitton, R A750
Whitton, James A838
Whitwell, Rodney A786
Whitwell, Rodney E387
Whitwer, Derek A284
Whitwer, Derek E117
Whitworth, Luke A170
Whitworth, Gary L. P465
Wholesale, Lawrence P286
Whooley, Tom A224
Whorley, John F. (Jeff) A583
Whynot, Lori A882
Whyte, Mike A887
Wibbenmeyer, Nick E349
Wible, Brad E73
Wiborg, Brian A9
Wiborg, Brian P4
Wichman, Chris A327
Wichmann, Lisa A641
Wichmann, David S. A876
Wichmann, Lisa P407
Wichser, Michael A522
Wicinski, Tom A323
Wick, Molly P55
Wickens, Kim A171
Wickens, Brent A587
Wicker, Dennis A334
Wicker, Kirstin A449
Wicker, Cary A818
Wicker, Dennis E153
Wicker, Kirstin E221
Wicker, Cary E403
Wickham, Gregory I. (Greg) A253
Wickham, Charles L A574
Wickham, Robert A740
Wickham, Gregory I. (Greg) P169
Wickland, David E P150
Wickland, David E P354
Wicklander, Jeff P379
Wickman, Paul A702
Wickman, Brian A749
Wickman, Brian E367
Wicks, David A606
Widdicombe, Mark A567
Widdicombe, Mark E283
Widdows, Katie A402
Widdows, Katie E198
Wideman, Beverly A592
Wideman, Beverly P371
Widener, Jason A800
Wider, John J. P2

HOOVER'S HANDBOOK OF EMERGING COMPANIES 2020

Widerlite, Paula P40
Widing, Robert E. P116
Widler, Katie A538
Widmayer, Christopher E349
Widoe, Dale P396
Widuch, Paul A167
Wiebe, Robert L. A266
Wiebe, Robert L. P181
Wieber, Claudia A520
Wiede, John A559
Wiedeman, Bryce A842
Wiedemann, Herbert A824
Wiedemann, Herbert P561
Wiedemann, Clay E33
Wiedenfels, Gunnar A270
Wiederhorn, Valerie A91
Wiederhorn, Valerie E29
Wiederkehr, Michael A621
Wiederkehr, Bill E119
Wiederkehr, Michael E312
Wiedman, Mark K. A135
Wiefling, Guler A E102
Wiegand, Kathleen A90
Wiegand, Ken A145
Wiegand, Robert A628
Wiegandt, Jim A104
Wiegert, Cory A465
Wiegert, Michael A717
Wiegert, Michael E351
Wiehoff, John P. A728
Wieland, Robert A. P26
Wiele, Dana A715
Wielenga, Terilea A385
Wiemer, Frank W322
Wiemers, Kayla P596
Wiener, James S. (Jim) A111
Wiener, David A525
Wiener-Kronish, Jeanine P. P574
Wieringa, Christy A628
Wieringa, Christy P396
Wiernik, Karen A434
Wierschke, Janice A179
Wiertzema, Brian P343
Wiese, Aaron A448
Wiese, Jeremy A630
Wiese, Edward A. A799
Wiese, David A835
Wiese, Aaron P247
Wiese, Theresa E156
Wiesinger, Kathleen E319
Wiesner, Hagen W160
Wiessing, Theodore E. A810
Wieters, Laurie E106
Wietharn, Rick P668
Wietholter, Susan P560
Wigderson, Melissa A6
Wiggan, Tracy E149
Wiggans, Jerre P608
Wiggershaus, Tom A909
Wiggershaus, Tom E436
Wiggins, Bob E264
Wigginton, Andrea P422
Wiggs, Tammy A799
Wiggs, David H. P299
Wight, Bryan A379
Wight, Amy P650
Wight-Tally, Nancy A722
Wightman, Bernadette A198
Wightman, Macie P450
Wiginton, Brad A686
Wigle, Lorie A461
Wiglesworth, Janet A894
Wiglesworth, Janet P651
Wignall, Doug S. P231
Wijers, Hans W334
Wiker, Darren P248
Wikert, Lisa A325
Wikforss, MArten W420
Wiklund, Jens W377
Wikramanayake, Shemara W243
Wilbanks, Ann A325
Wilbanks, Cynthia H. A711
Wilbanks, Becky P55
Wilbanks, John F. P63
Wilbanks, Cynthia H. P444

Wilbanks, Johm P503
Wilbanks, John P503
Wilburn, Tom A198
Wilcher, Eric E131
Wilcox, Steve A16
Wilcox, Michael A115
Wilcox, Mike A137
Wilcox, Dustin A179
Wilcox, Greg A222
Wilcox, Kevin A332
Wilcox, Greg A386
Wilcox, Kevin A418
Wilcox, Jim A485
Wilcox, Darren A746
Wilcox, Mark A. A751
Wilcox, William H. (Bill) A811
Wilcox, Ella P333
Wilcox, Laura P343
Wilcox, Rob P353
Wilcox, Don P432
Wilcox, Ralph P638
Wilcox, Michael E38
Wilcox, Greg E188
Wilcox, Frank C E420
Wilcoxon, Nancy A326
Wilcoxson, Kristin P554
Wilczewska, Marta P702
Wilczynski, Donald E174
Wild, Sandra A413
Wild, Elizabeth P643
Wild, Sandra E205
Wilda, Christine P631
Wildberger, Karsten W143
Wilde, Malcolm A470
Wilde, Frederic de A661
Wildenthal, Kern P130
Wilder, Terry P157
Wildes, Kevin A569
Wilding, Deb A219
Wilding, Deb E87
Wildman, Neil A658
Wildrick, Edward A704
Wile, Jeff A779
Wileman, Linda A247
Wileman, Linda E105
Wilensky, Scott A932
Wiles, Sandy A606
Wiles, Rick A690
Wiles, Chris P75
Wiles, Paul M. P390
Wiley, Dorvan A760
Wiley, James (Rusty) P333
Wiley, Donald J P519
Wiley, Ronette P574
Wiley, Dorvan E374
Wilfert, Kelly P641
Wilfong, Philip E256
Wilford, Linda P243
Wilgenbusch, Scott A60
Wilhelm, Ryan A408
Wilhelm, Lance K P279
Wilhelm, Lura P514
Wilhelm, Edward W. (Ed) P567
Wilhelm, Harald W17
Wilhoite, Charles A. P399
Wilk, Thomas P578
Wilke, Jeffrey A. (Jeff) A42
Wilke, Brent A413
Wilke, Susan A512
Wilke, Brent E205
Wilkerson, Terrie A108
Wilkerson, Lee A420
Wilkerson, Drew A934
Wilkerson, Scott P508
Wilkes, Pamela A591
Wilkes, Pamela P369
Wilkin, Janine M. P579
Wilkins, Richard A22
Wilkins, Cliff A218
Wilkins, Craig A444
Wilkins, Chris C A846
Wilkins, David A867
Wilkins, Michael T. A867
Wilkins, Charles L. (Chad) A906
Wilkins, Richard P11

Wilkins, Benny P58
Wilkins, David P108
Wilkins, Jim P364
Wilkins, Karlyn P608
Wilkins, Carolyn W50
Wilkins, Horace E106
Wilkins, David E418
Wilkins, Charles L. (Chad) E435
Wilkinson, Jeff A63
Wilkinson, Kari A446
Wilkinson, Jason A466
Wilkinson, Colin A640
Wilkinson, Jonathan A799
Wilkinson, Gavin A859
Wilkinson, Vince A900
Wilkinson, Mark A934
Wilkinson, Christine K. P44
Wilkinson, Bruce P117
Wilkinson, Anne P173
Wilkinson, David P530
Wilkinson, William J P546
Wilkinson, Scott E231
Wilks, Matt A140
Wilkus, Malon E5
Will, Rick A349
Will, David A442
Will, Kristin A540
Will, Mark A797
Willard, Roger A16
Willard, Howard A. A41
Willard, Kathy A522
Willard, Lauren A641
Willard, Lauren P407
Willcoxon, Jennifer A682
Wille, Matt P354
Willemse, Norman A49
Willemsen, Marie A391
Willemsen, Eugene A654
Willemsen, Jane A. P267
Willensky, Scott M. A932
Willerson, James T P595
Willert, Greg A298
Willert, Greg E130
Willett, Steve W219
Willett, Robert E85
Willey, Stan A751
Willey, Darro P176
Willhoite, Nila P670
William, Aston A65
William, Bass A120
Williams, Julie A45
Williams, Anré A53
Williams, Julie F A56
Williams, Bill A60
Williams, Jeffrey E. (Jeff) A72
Williams, Gene A86
Williams, Xavier A89
Williams, Steve A89
Williams, Thomas A92
Williams, Valerie A107
Williams, Leilani A109
Williams, Bill A114
Williams, Carol A117
Williams, Mark A130
Williams, Candice A142
Williams, Shawn A155
Williams, Christopher A161
Williams, Lexie A181
Williams, Donna A. A197
Williams, Donald A199
Williams, Jason A202
Williams, Michael A205
Williams, Doug A212
Williams, Craig A215
Williams, Malcolm A217
Williams, Joe A224
Williams, Angela C A245
Williams, Ben A263
Williams, Benjamin A263
Williams, Roger A267
Williams, Janice L. A283
Williams, Weston A290
Williams, Randa D. A299
Williams, Marlene A320
Williams, John C. A321

Williams, John C. A322
Williams, Felicia A323
Williams, Denise A327
Williams, Dee A327
Williams, Jason A334
Williams, James R. A339
Williams, Brad A341
Williams, Karen A356
Williams, John C. A357
Williams, Todd R A414
Williams, Gary A440
Williams, Michael A444
Williams, Kristin A447
Williams, Kimberly A449
Williams, Travis A479
Williams, Philip A A485
Williams, Alan A491
Williams, Dale A492
Williams, R A498
Williams, Thomas A511
Williams, Dave A512
Williams, Holly A552
Williams, Adam A556
Williams, Robert A564
Williams, Clay C A581
Williams, Peter A606
Williams, Christina A608
Williams, Mark A613
Williams, Carol A. A616
Williams, Thomas L. (Tom) A640
Williams, Andy A654
Williams, Geisha J. A659
Williams, Andrew A659
Williams, Rick A676
Williams, Glenn A676
Williams, Debra A684
Williams, Donna A692
Williams, Greg A704
Williams, Stephanie A715
Williams, W. Mark A717
Williams, Scott A718
Williams, Ted A722
Williams, Tim A724
Williams, Grant A772
Williams, Rossann A779
Williams, Elizabeth A813
Williams, David A818
Williams, Lynn A850
Williams, Darren K. A865
Williams, Marlene A879
Williams, Brent A882
Williams, Dyfan A887
Williams, Lauren A890
Williams, James A895
Williams, Patrick A896
Williams, Daniel A902
Williams, Richard L. A915
Williams, Mark A919
Williams, Joseph A921
Williams, Jennifer A934
Williams, John D A938
Williams, Kevin P18
Williams, Julie P30
Williams, Julie F P33
Williams, Winifred P39
Williams, Carol P61
Williams, Robert D P66
Williams, Kenneth L P86
Williams, Michael P86
Williams, Kenneth L P86
Williams, Michael P86
Williams, Nicoletta P101
Williams, Kenneth L P104
Williams, Michael P104
Williams, Cleo P112
Williams, Jason P136
Williams, Sandra P168
Williams, Michael D. (Mike) P171
Williams, David A. P172
Williams, Lisa P173
Williams, Susan P177
Williams, Paul T P184
Williams, Jenell P209
Williams, Todd R P236
Williams, Derinda P246

COMBINED HOOVER'S HANDBOOK INDEX OF EXECUTIVES

A = AMERICAN BUSINESS
E = EMERGING COMPANIES
P = PRIVATE COMPANIES
W = WORLD BUSINESS

Williams, Kristin P247
Williams, Brodie P251
Williams, Avilla P254
Williams, David P258
Williams, Mike P258
Williams, Jack P262
Williams, Brandy P274
Williams, Thomas P290
Williams, Eric P300
Williams, Claire P303
Williams, Kenny P303
Williams, Henry P320
Williams, Adam P328
Williams, Robert P334
Williams, David W P376
Williams, William D P377
Williams, Betsy P379
Williams, Steven A P389
Williams, Brad P389
Williams, Chris P397
Williams, Denise P409
Williams, Greg P419
Williams, Aaron S. P447
Williams, Tom P448
Williams, Cindy P450
Williams, Kitty P450
Williams, Tim P452
Williams, A Greg P481
Williams, Christine P514
Williams, Eileen P515
Williams, Bonnie P516
Williams, Benjamin R P517
Williams, Christopher P540
Williams, Charles P541
Williams, Lori P548
Williams, Lacy H P552
Williams, Treby P591
Williams, Jovita P596
Williams, Joseph P616
Williams, Sheri P625
Williams, Gordon P629
Williams, Alison P632
Williams, Marlene P636
Williams, Calvin P638
Williams, John D P678
Williams, Gene E27
Williams, Bill E37
Williams, Candice E49
Williams, Shawn E54
Williams, Lexie E70
Williams, Bob E81
Williams, Janice L. E117
Williams, Dustin E123
Williams, Andrea E143
Williams, Jason E153
Williams, James R. E159
Williams, John C. E175
Williams, Kimberly E220
Williams, Michael J. E223
Williams, William E226
Williams, Bill E226
Williams, Patrick S. E229
Williams, Holly E276
Williams, Edward P. E281
Williams, Marsha C E286
Williams, Grayson E342
Williams, W. Mark E351
Williams, Scott E351
Williams, Timothy E366
Williams, Grant E383
Williams, David E403
Williams, Darren K. E416
Williams, Alan E430
Williams-Roll, Jacqueline A376
Williamson, Jen A34
Williamson, Steven A61
Williamson, Joe A63
Williamson, John A142
Williamson, Angela A165

Williamson, Keith H. A179
Williamson, Russell A227
Williamson, Tracey A596
Williamson, Christy A630
Williamson, Kemal A645
Williamson, James A782
Williamson, Scott H. A810
Williamson, Stephen A832
Williamson, Daniel E. (Dan) A939
Williamson, Anthony P383
Williamson, Robert P391
Williamson, James P526
Williamson, Ann P629
Williamson, J. David W85
Williamson, James W106
Williamson, John E49
Williamson, Russell E90
Williamson, Randall S. E232
Williamson, John B. E262
Willian, Craig E6
Willie, David P677
Williford, John E57
Willihnganz, Trent A599
Willihnganz, Shirley P629
Willihnganz, Trent E303
Willingham, Edward L. (Ed) A336
Willingham, Michael A578
Willingham, Phil A726
Willingham, Edward L. (Ed) E157
Willingham, Michael E289
Willinger, Jenny P486
Willis, Jeff A121
Willis, Jonathan A147
Willis, Richard T A228
Willis, Ken A319
Willis, Jack A442
Willis, Gina A465
Willis, Troy S A798
Willis, George A871
Willis, Jeremy P42
Willis, Velina P162
Willis, Margaret W187
Willis, Gary D. E14
Willis, Peter M. E76
Willis-Abner, Cassandra A847
Willis-Abner, Cassandra P606
Willmott, David A. P87
Willoughby, Dawn A207
Willoughby, Michele B. A264
Willoughby, Scott A608
Willoughby, Bob E244
Wills, Kevin G. A801
Wills, Julian B P498
Wills, Joseph M P602
Willson, Corey A3
Willson, Susan P536
Willy, Michael P266
Wilmore, Clare P508
Wilmot, Edward A56
Wilner, Brad A176
Wilsdon, Tim E102
Wilshaw, Robert K A649
Wilsher, Barbara A682
Wilson, Elizabeth A15
Wilson, Wayne A25
Wilson, Thomas J. A35
Wilson, Phil A54
Wilson, James A74
Wilson, Jason A85
Wilson, Doug A108
Wilson, Ron A130
Wilson, Roger A164
Wilson, David J. A169
Wilson, Michael A176
Wilson, Julia M. (Julie) A185
Wilson, Lacie A189
Wilson, Eliot A203
Wilson, Katie A210
Wilson, J. Michael A227
Wilson, James A227
Wilson, James D. (Jim) A245
Wilson, Floyd A246
Wilson, Christine A262
Wilson, Mike A296
Wilson, Dan A321

Wilson, Walter A325
Wilson, Rebekkah A352
Wilson, Alan A368
Wilson, Thomas A398
Wilson, Jay A418
Wilson, Spencer A438
Wilson, Andrew A449
Wilson, Timothy A449
Wilson, Mitch A449
Wilson, C Kevin A457
Wilson, Lynn A492
Wilson, Jennie A500
Wilson, Melissa A507
Wilson, Debora A536
Wilson, Debbie A538
Wilson, Charles A550
Wilson, Brad A565
Wilson, Ross A588
Wilson, Colleen A591
Wilson, Billy A599
Wilson, Judith A606
Wilson, Brent A627
Wilson, William A708
Wilson, Christine A741
Wilson, Ted A742
Wilson, Zilpha A760
Wilson, Brad A787
Wilson, Ira A797
Wilson, Alan A800
Wilson, Bill A818
Wilson, Donta L. A849
Wilson, Leon A850
Wilson, Rachel A865
Wilson, Jeff A867
Wilson, Betsy A870
Wilson, D. Ellen A876
Wilson, Tyner A877
Wilson, Lizabeth A. (Betsy) A880
Wilson, Ward A884
Wilson, Jake A884
Wilson, Don A887
Wilson, Patrick A903
Wilson, Jeff A915
Wilson, Mark A919
Wilson, Scott A928
Wilson, Malcolm A934
Wilson, Alex P5
Wilson, Elizabeth P7
Wilson, Wayne P14
Wilson, Nancy P38
Wilson, Carolyn P75
Wilson, Susan P133
Wilson, Elena P174
Wilson, Bob P179
Wilson, Ron P184
Wilson, Terrance E. P207
Wilson, Mark P219
Wilson, Thomas P222
Wilson, John P234
Wilson, Eric L. P238
Wilson, Kristin P244
Wilson, Selma P296
Wilson, Phil P301
Wilson, Keith A P307
Wilson, Mike P344
Wilson, John P349
Wilson, Ross P365
Wilson, Colleen P369
Wilson, San P376
Wilson, Charlene P421
Wilson, Daniel P425
Wilson, Lisa P443
Wilson, Matthew P449
Wilson, Mike P464
Wilson, Debbie P467
Wilson, Christine P511
Wilson, Nancy P511
Wilson, John P551
Wilson, Dan P583
Wilson, Tammy P590
Wilson, Carolyn S. P594
Wilson, Gordon P597
Wilson, Phillip P618
Wilson, Arnedra P637
Wilson, Lizabeth A. (Betsy) P640

Wilson, M. Roy P660
Wilson, Scott P673
Wilson, Mark A. W40
Wilson, Jimmy W69
Wilson, Nigel W233
Wilson, Jason E27
Wilson, J. Michael E90
Wilson, James E90
Wilson, James N. E96
Wilson, Floyd E105
Wilson, Kevin S. E210
Wilson, Andrew E220
Wilson, Timothy E220
Wilson, Mitch E221
Wilson, Edith E315
Wilson, Scott E349
Wilson, Christine E364
Wilson, Zilpha E374
Wilson, Wayne E374
Wilson, Bill E403
Wilson, Rachel E417
Wilson, Jeff E418
Wilson, Laurence E450
Wilson-Thompson, Kathleen A899
Wilston, Kathleen A531
Wilton, Keith A. A414
Wilton, Keith P255
Wilton, Keith A. E208
Wiltse, Peggy P343
Wiltshire, John A559
Wilus, Stephen A205
Wilwerding, Craig A308
Wilwerding, Dave P10
Wimes, Ed P92
Wimmer, Kelly A44
Wimmer, Kelly E13
Wims, Darryl A327
Winans, Kathy A877
Winborn, Steve A56
Winbush, Brandon P555
Winchek, J A528
Winchell, Richard Rhett E245
Winchester, Bob A105
Winchester, Jeffrey D A160
Winchester, Bob E34
Winchip, D. Scott A724
Winchip, D. Scott P452
Winckler, Georg W156
Wind, Edward S P382
Windele, Hanns P326
Windhaus, Donna P83
Windisch, Matt E245
Windley, John F. A769
Windley, John F. E380
Windram, Elizabeth A478
Windrow, Kimberly G. A910
Windsor, Bryan A171
Wine, Scott W. A669
Wineberger, Bruce P361
Winebrake, James J. P456
Winek, Chris A313
Winek, Chris E144
Wineland, Nora E235
Wineman, Scott A222
Wineman, Matthew A512
Wines, Lynne A115
Wines, Lynne E38
Winesett, Steve P127
Winfield, Sandy P209
Winfield, Ted P639
Winfree, Kersey P513
Winfrey, Alva P331
Winfrey, John P564
Wing, Mike A465
Wing, Bill P6
Wing, Nip Yun W100
Wingard, Brian W. A211
Wingard, Brian W. E82
Wingate, Angel P187
Wingenroth, Sharon A368
Wingerning, William M P78
Wingerson, Barbara A880
Wingerson, Barbara P640
Wingert, Bret A458
Wingerter, Joe A492

Wingerter, Joe P279
Wingerup, Per A893
Wingfield, Gena G. P45
Wingo, Pat A90
Wingo, Brett A198
Wingo, Jeff E131
Wingrning, William P78
Winick, Joseph P228
Winistorfer, Paul M. P652
Winkates, Scott A606
Winkelmeier, Stephan W62
Winkelried, John P599
Winker, Mark A859
Winkler, Barry A89
Winkler, Dana A804
WinklerPrins, Vince P570
Winlove-smith, Shannon A374
Winmill, Thomas B. E117
Winn, Kathy A35
Winn, Cathy A36
Winn, Kenneth V. A330
Winn, Share A559
Winn, Jason P220
Winn, Kenneth V. E152
Winn, Stephen T. (Steve) E346
Winningham, Rick E. E230
Winoker, Steven A374
Winokur, Barton J. P159
Winowiecki, Sue P353
Winskill, Debbie P540
Winslow, Alex A605
Winslow, Stephen P512
Winsor, Ned A871
Winstead, Kim A323
Winston, Wyman B A926
Winston, Wyman A926
Winsvold, Helge A581
Wintemute, Eric G. E18
Winter, Matthew A64
Winter, Kevin A145
Winter, Cindy A449
Winter, Katherine A460
Winter, Terra A867
Winter, Kris P636
Winter, Gert De W43
Winter, Jaap W319
Winter, Cindy E220
Winter, Terra E418
Winterbottom, Brad L. A911
Winterbottom, Brad L. E437
Winterer, Ed P138
Wintermyer, Janie P57
Winterroll, Christopher A686
Winters, Scott A45
Winters, Gene E436
Winters, Margaret E. P660
Winters, William T. (Bill) W364
Winters, Kathleen A. E290
Winterstein, Rhonda E3
Winton, James A247
Winton, James E105
Wipf, Todd V. A756
Wipf, Darin A823
Wipf, Darin E405
Wipfler, Gary A72
Wirahadiraksa, Ron H. W230
Wireman, Rich A677
Wirges, Kevin A69
Wirkman, Alan A845
Wirt, Ken A199
Wirth, Michael K. (Mike) A190
Wirth, Dave P48
Wirth, Suzanne P259
Wirth, Volker W231
Wirtz, Rolf W391
Wisadkosin, Yukontorn (Vickie) A360
Wisbar, Beverly A799
Wischer, James P106
Wisdom, Kimberlydawn A414
Wisdom, Kimberlydawn P236
Wisdom, Betty P333
Wise, Dean A138
Wise, Dean A157
Wise, Greg A245
Wise, Deanna L. A266

Wise, Steve A425
Wise, Allen A463
Wise, Angela A507
Wise, Lee A846
Wise, Dean P91
Wise, Bonnie P161
Wise, Sarah P194
Wise, Candy P223
Wise, Candace P223
Wise, Deanna L. P181
Wise, Elizabeth P289
Wise, Anne P554
Wise, Stephen E212
Wise, Michael E262
Wisecup, Reyne K. A315
Wiseman, Scott A46
Wiseman, Mark A135
Wiseman, Ken A695
Wiseman, Kim P112
Wiseman, Sheri P588
Wiseman, John W. E143
Wisenbaker, Randall C. A696
Wisenbaker, Jamie D P280
Wisener, Maureen P6
Wish, Dan A218
Wishart, Emily P455
Wishon, Gordon P44
Wisnewski, Nancy E210
Wisniewski, Alex Wisniewski Alex A108
Wisniewski, James A922
Wisniewski, James P671
Wisniewski, Dan E46
Wisniewski, Tony E122
Wisnoski, Kenneth (Ken) A79
Wisnoski, Mark A797
Wissink, Linda A25
Wissink, Linda P14
Wissmann, Karl P104
Wissmann, Jon P104
Wit, Harry de W166
Witcher, Mr Craig V A766
Witcher, Mr Craig V P500
Witcher, Norman E106
Witchko, Tracey A160
Witcombe, David A658
Witek, David A257
Witham, John A42
Withers, Mike A30
Withers, David A371
Withers, Mike P20
Withers, David P213
Witherspoon, Marisa A108
Witherspoon, Ivory A879
Withrow, Randy A664
Withrow, Sarah A925
Withrow, Randy E334
Withrow, Sarah E445
Witowski, Cindy P122
Witt, Tom A329
Witt, Todd A442
Witt, Leslie A471
Witt, Mary J. A717
Witt, Marshall A794
Witt, Kevin P375
Witt, Suann P396
Witt, Scott V P590
Witt, John W209
Witt, John R. W209
Witt, Mary J. E351
Witte, Blair A139
Witte, Ryan A925
Witte, Blair P93
Witte, Ryan E445
Wittebort, Ron P98
Wittekind, Beverly B. E127
Witten, Denise A718
Witten, Denise E354
Wittenberg, Joel R A487
Wittenberg, Stephen P72
Wittenburg, Stephen P72
Wittenstein, Robin P527
Witter, Jonathan W. A166
Witter, Marcia A356
Witter, Patrick A380
Witter, Brian A441
Witter, Frank W418

Witters, David A711
Witters, David P444
Witterschein, James A651
Witterschein, James E329
Wittgrove, Alan P332
Wittkop, Scott P318
Wittkop, Scott P319
Wittlinger, Todd P170
Wittman, Kurt A609
Wittman, Kurt P387
Wittmuss, Steve A316
Witts, Karen W219
Witynski, Michael A274
Witz, Bill — A376
Witz, Scott A393
Witzel, Leslie D A909
Witzel, Leslie A909
Witzel, Leslie D E436
Witzel, Leslie E436
Wixtead, James E. W106
Wlazlo, Michelle A647
Wlazlo, Michelle A804
WO, ROBERT A110
Wodark, Joe E429
Woeber, Andrew E72
Woehrle, Tom A149
Woelfel, Donna A791
Woelfel, Donna P535
Woelfer, W. Todd A834
Woeltjen, William P473
Woerner, Bruce A25
Woerner, Sangita A29
Woerner, John R. A60
Woerner, Bruce P14
Wofford, Susanne L. A592
Wofford, Susanne L. P370
Wohl, Richard H. A249
Wohl, Richard H. E108
Wohlgelernter, Beth P265
Wohlgemuth, Jay G. A698
Wohlhart, Nancy A571
Wohlrab, John A905
Wohn, James A166
Wojahn, Mark A545
Wojahn, Mark P317
Wojcik, Paulette A414
Wojcik, Paul A799
Wojcik, Paulette P236
Wojnar, T. J. A309
Wojnar, Bradley A337
Wojnar, Bradley E158
Wojtalewicz, Jeanette P21
Wojtowicz, Jean A345
Wojtowicz, Linda P611
Wolcott, Tom A651
Wolcott, Tom E329
Wolcowitz, Jeffrey P116
Wold, Lynn P258
Wold, Brianna P610
Wold, Kathleen P619
Woldt, Sheldon A605
Wolf, David A54
Wolf, Jeffrey A112
Wolf, Edward A500
Wolf, Mike A518
Wolf, Rose A559
Wolf, Matt A571
Wolf, Dale B. A571
Wolf, Duane A581
Wolf, Christopher G. A669
Wolf, Joseph B. A716
Wolf, Joseph P. A716
Wolf, Michael A906
Wolf, Karen A915
Wolf, Matthew P26
Wolf, Jim P476
Wolf, Reinhard W64
Wolf, Ute W158
Wolf, Michael E435
Wolfe, Blake A74
Wolfe, Debbie A257
Wolfe, Richard A355
Wolfe, Patrick A380
Wolfe, Lynn A583
Wolfe, Douglas A636

Wolfe, Douglas A637
Wolfe, Bernie A649
Wolfe, Joanne A835
Wolfe, Harriet M. A906
Wolfe, Stephen P160
Wolfe, Sam P556
Wolfe, Micaela P310
Wolfe, John P362
Wolfe, Douglas P403
Wolfe, Bethany P639
Wolfe, Anne E64
Wolfe, Harriet M. E434
Wolff, Johannes A6
Wolff, Lawrence A559
Wolff, Jennifer A709
Wolff, Drew A779
Wolff, Armand J P97
Wolff, Benjamin G. (Ben) E326
Wolff, Jennifer E348
Wolffis, Janet A329
Wolfgring, Alexander W60
Wolfle, Joan A145
Wolfram, Katie A498
Wolfram, Dan P618
Wolfrath, Steve A61
Wolfrom, Jennifer A46
Wolfson, Richard P639
Wolin, Edward P118
Wolinski, Jeffery A925
Wolinski, Jeffery E445
Wolitzer, Joel A200
Wolking, Christopher A. (Chris) A621
Wolking, Christopher A. (Chris) E311
Wolkoff, David A161
Wollan, Vegard P53
Wollberg, Johnny A301
Wollberg, Johnny P196
Wolle, Joerg W. W227
Wollenberg, Scott D. E286
Wollenhaupt, Daniel A509
Wollenzin, Susan P516
Wollman, Eric A227
Wollman, William J. (Bill) P202
Wollman, Eric E90
Wolma, John P423
Wolmart, Lisa A686
Wolpert, Alan A218
Wolske, Jeff A706
Wolstencroft, Tracy R. E207
Wolt, Dave P487
Woltanski, Laura E433
Wolterman, Daniel J. P324
Wolters, Janice A335
Wolters, Janice E155
Woltersdorf, Ken A893
Woltosz, Walter S. (Walt) E375
Woltosz, Virginia E. E375
Wolverton, David A829
Wolverton, David P585
Womack, Patty A266
Womack, Chris A382
Womack, Patty P182
Womack, Robert R P467
Womack, Mark P590
Womack, Marcus E30
Womble, Hill A755
Womble, Aaron P359
Womble, Hill E369
Womble, Dustin R. E412
Womersley, Beth P13
Wompey, John A359
Wondrasch, Michael A63
Wong, Dhobie A14
Wong, Robert A39
Wong, Alice A44
Wong, Christina A54
Wong, Gordon A112
Wong, Danny A112
Wong, Irwin A174
Wong, Rebecca A200
Wong, Winnie A218
Wong, Art A230
Wong, Robert A465
Wong, Wilfred A506
Wong, Stephen A510

COMBINED HOOVER'S HANDBOOK INDEX OF EXECUTIVES

A = AMERICAN BUSINESS
E = EMERGING COMPANIES
P = PRIVATE COMPANIES
W = WORLD BUSINESS

Wong, Yu-hin A530
Wong, Richard A574
Wong, Philip A676
Wong, John A676
Wong, Annie A692
Wong, Andy A692
Wong, Elwin A731
Wong, Belinda A779
Wong, Jennifer A880
Wong, Dhobie P6
Wong, Art P154
Wong, Lok P225
Wong, Stephen P290
Wong, Xx P377
Wong, John P612
Wong, Jennifer P640
Wong, Allan C. Y. W50
Wong, Jeanette W130
Wong, Peter T. S. W189
Wong, Alice E13
Wong, Irwin E68
Wong, Rick E196
Wong, Philip E338
Wong, John E338
Wong, Gregory E343
Wonnacott, David E126
Woo, Carolyn Y A600
Woo, Elizabeth A833
Woo, Meredith J. E. P442
Woo, Tracy P585
Woo, Melissa P636
Woo, Stephen E282
Woo, Deborah E423
Woo-Jong, Lee W237
Wood, Warren A46
Wood, Judith A86
Wood, Jonathan A167
Wood, William C. (Cliff) A171
WOOD, BRIAN A195
Wood, Dana A237
Wood, M Jay A309
Wood, Denise A323
Wood, Lauren A452
Wood, Laura A478
Wood, Jane A480
Wood, Elizabeth A514
Wood, Elizabeth A516
Wood, Lee A559
Wood, Sarah A596
Wood, Phoebe A674
Wood, Alex A690
Wood, Ben A730
Wood, Adam A768
Wood, Daniel A770
Wood, Matthew A856
Wood, Nola A870
Wood, Ken A891
Wood, Rick A891
Wood, Brian A895
Wood, Jason A899
Wood, Patrick A922
Wood, Dawn P60
Wood, Ronald P78
Wood, Erik P84
Wood, William P180
Wood, Kurt P185
Wood, Robert P202
Wood, Laura P268
Wood, Elizabeth P293
Wood, Jeff P412
Wood, Nancy P537
Wood, Matthew P614
Wood, Patrick P671
Wood, Adrian W353
Wood, Judith E27
Wood, Julie E185
Wood, John E207
Woodall, Jennifer A180
Woodall, James W. (Woody) A327

Woodall, Charles A740
Woodall, Charles P291
Woodall, Niki P624
Woodard, Jim A481
Woodard, Paul A530
Woodard, R. Bryan A784
Woodard, Beth P426
Woodard, Elizabeth P426
Woodard, Eric P497
Woodard, Troy E16
Woodburn, Scott A215
Woodburn, Charles W42
Woodbury, Eileen A452
Woodbury, Roy A491
Woodbury, Chip A888
Woodbury, Chip E425
Woodcock, Lori A469
Woodcock, John P59
Wooden, Sean A423
Wooden, Amy A647
Wooden, Maurice A930
Woodford, Buckner E245
Woodham, Roy A108
Woodhouse, Hope A854
Woodie, Joe P318
Woodland, Luann P76
Woodman, Clare A574
Woodrich, Debbie A219
Woodrich, Debbie E87
Woodring, Paula P469
Woodrow, Tracy A530
Woodruff, Steve A113
Woodruff, Seth A658
Woodruff, David P314
Woodruff, Steve E36
Woodrum, James A637
Woods, Don A87
Woods, Shelley A97
Woods, John F. A205
Woods, Teresa A246
Woods, J. Pat A301
Woods, J Pat A301
Woods, Darren W. A309
Woods, David A366
Woods, Mike A399
Woods, Marie A744
Woods, Chris A831
Woods, Don P50
Woods, Douglas E. (Doug) P185
Woods, Mike P223
Woods, Brian T P387
Woods, Randall P404
Woods, Christopher P531
Woods, Mike P577
Woods, Chris P601
Woods, Stephanie P639
Woods, Gregory A. E28
Woods, Stefani E73
Woods, Teresa E105
Woods, Dennis R. E418
Woodside, David B. A118
Woodside, David B. E40
Woodson, Bart A859
Woodson, Geraldine P60
Woodson, Nathaniel D P593
Woodson, Mindi E99
Woodson, Bret A E443
Woodward, Daniel A175
Woodward, David A353
Woodward, Jan A567
Woodward, Joan Kois A844
Woodward, David P204
Woodward, James L P332
Woodward, Rob E53
Woodward, Jan E283
Woodworth, Teresa A260
Woodworth, Leigh A799
Woody, Craig W. P146
Wool, Julius A588
Wool, Julius P365
Wooldridge, Keith A600
Wooldridge, Matthew P155
Woolery, John A798
Wooley, Mylowe P389
Woolf, Michael T. (Mike) E418

Woolfolk, James W P105
Woolley, Kenneth M. E141
Woolridge, Diane P343
Woolridge, Victor P631
Woolsey, Danielle A409
Woolsey, Christine P477
Woolson, Dan E222
Woolston, Kristina P125
Woolway, Paul V. A746
Woomer, Nicholas A204
Woon, Lau Hak W227
Woonton, David B. A183
Woonton, David B. E73
Wooten, Scott P63
Wooten, Karen P486
Wooten, M. Rhem E200
Worboys, Philip E230
Worcester, Hilary P340
Wordell, Doug P511
Work, Rick E171
Workley, Keila A262
Workman, Vince A206
Workman, Mike A765
Workman, Greg A863
Workman, Sue B. P116
Workman, Tamora P504
Workman, Donald W333
Worley, Andrew A120
Worley, Robert B. A449
Worley, Allan P523
Worley, Robert B. E220
Worman, Douglas M. (Doug) A210
Wormley, Mike P277
Worner, John R A723
Wornow, Scott M. P53
Worrall, Judy A369
Worrell, Donald A54
Worrell, Sally A155
Worrell, Robert G A863
Worrell, Larry P83
Worrell, Sally E54
Worsham, Todd A170
Worth, Denny A399
Worth, Denny P223
Worth, Greg P659
Worthington, Alice A142
Worthington, John A329
Worthington, Trich A449
Worthington, Joel A518
Worthington, Bob A552
Worthington, Bill P472
Worthington, Alice E49
Worthington, Trich E220
Worthington, Bob E276
Worthman, Cindy A533
Worthy, Steve A804
Wortley, Michael J. A187
Wortman, William P108
Wortmann-Kool, Corien M. W10
Worzel, Kenneth J. (Ken) A602
Woschenko, Christian J. E79
Wotring, Randall A. (Randy) A16
Wouda, Tito A376
Woychik, Eric E441
Wozniak, Rebecca A571
Wozniak, Greg P522
Wozniak, Kurt F. E88
Wrabel, David A121
Wrabetz, Joan A914
Wrang, William E. A906
Wrang, William E. E435
Wrappesenior, Tom A695
Wrassman, Owen (Joe) A726
Wrassman, Owen P453
Wray, Lucian A71
Wray, Christine R. A551
Wray, Joyce P259
Wray, Christine R. P321
Wray, Nathan E103
Wren, Christopher A200
Wren, John D. A626
Wresch, William P613
Wright, Will A16
Wright, Todd A16
Wright, Donald A49

Wright, Andrew A61
Wright, Winston A75
Wright, Kristen A95
Wright, Sean A108
Wright, Cooper A137
Wright, Frank H. A168
Wright, Chris A181
Wright, Lance A224
Wright, James A228
Wright, Peter A258
Wright, Jordan A266
Wright, Robert R. A308
Wright, Terry A320
Wright, Dennis A365
Wright, James A381
Wright, Christopher A391
Wright, Matt A408
Wright, Scott J. A447
Wright, Jeff A483
Wright, Margaret M A500
Wright, Ken A521
Wright, David A528
Wright, Tim A540
Wright, Greg A546
Wright, Lori A636
Wright, Terry A658
Wright, David A668
Wright, Robert C A702
Wright, Deanna A744
Wright, Soraya A804
Wright, Daniel A837
Wright, Dennis A859
Wright, Catherine A879
Wright, Clarice A922
Wright, Richard M. (Rick) A929
Wright, Rodney L P12
Wright, Craig P46
Wright, Victoria P116
Wright, Joseph P130
Wright, Nancy P177
Wright, Jordan P182
Wright, Mary P222
Wright, John P238
Wright, Roxanne P253
Wright, Lori A P274
Wright, Jamal P280
Wright, David H. (Dave) P299
Wright, Jamie P303
Wright, Alex P319
Wright, Rachel P350
Wright, Dale P368
Wright, Eric P375
Wright, Nancy P383
Wright, Adam P385
Wright, Lori P403
Wright, Douglas P429
Wright, Robert S P472
Wright, Donna P477
Wright, Judy P504
Wright, Kenneth M P563
Wright, Karensa P589
Wright, Daniel P618
Wright, Steve P642
Wright, Dion P649
Wright, Stacey P662
Wright, Clarice P671
Wright, A. W212
Wright, Timothy R. W389
Wright, Emory M. E9
Wright, William H. (Bill) E33
Wright, Bill E33
Wright, Chris E70
Wright, Joseph (Joe) E278
Wright, Weldon E284
Wright, Dickerson E309
Wright, Danyelle St E366
Wright, Murray H. E396
Wright, Tim E431
Wright, Richard M. (Rick) E449
Wright-Jones, Angela A224
Wrighton, Mark S. P600
Wrigley, Clark A644
Writt, Mark A175
Wroblowski, Peter W181
Wrona, Jennifer P477

Wroten, Paul A220
Wroten, Paul P149
Wrzalinski, Nancy A433
Wrzalinski, Nancy E217
Wu, Ernest A161
Wu, Douglas A390
Wu, Iris A460
Wu, Tracy A483
Wu, Ben A575
Wu, Shengpo (Samuel) A919
Wu, Michael P49
Wu, Tsung-Ching P53
Wu, Jiang P218
Wu, Wendy P472
Wu, Samuel P548
Wu, Yajun W239
Wu, Simone E80
Wuesthoff, Robert A479
Wujek, Christine A925
Wujek, Christine E445
Wulf, R. Gary E396
Wulfestieg, Brian A837
Wulff, John A177
Wulff, Henrik W290
Wuller, Lynn A203
Wunderlich, Xenia A161
Wurm, Greg A69
Wurm, David A376
Wurm, Judi A713
Wurman, Richard P220
Wurster, Sarah P431
Wurtz, Steven A651
Wurtz, Steven E329
Wurzburger, Ralph E433
Wurzer, Mitch A800
Wustefeld, Ed A559
Wutke, Steve P364
Wyant, Michael A170
Wyant, Jill S. A289
Wyant, Ashley A329
Wyatt, Thomas A198
Wyatt, E. Lee A361
Wyatt, Lee A361
Wyatt, Cheryl A364
Wyatt, John H. A. A778
Wyatt, Christa P189
Wyatt, Mark P509
Wyatt, Julia E407
Wyborg, Brian A9
Wyborg, Brian P4
Wyckoff, Beverly A277
Wyckoff, Sandra A281
Wyckoff, Kristin A325
Wyffels, Michael J. A693
Wyffels, Chad P511
Wyffels, Michael J. E341
Wykoff, Phyllis P337
Wyland, Marci A326
Wyles, Rick P357
Wylie, William A373
Wylie, Forrest E. E117
Wyllie, Robert A824
Wyllie, Robert P561
Wyman, Scott R A351
Wyman, Stephen A388
Wyman, Mark A924
Wyman, William P300
Wyman, Peter P393
Wyman, Matthew E77
Wynaendts, Alexander R. (Alex) W10
Wynia, Eric A618
Wynk, Kevin A500
Wynn, Stephen A. A930
Wynn, Karen P177
Wynn, Barry P501
Wynn, Jacklyn Mitchell P578
Wynn, Richard E226
Wynne, Susan P573
Wyrick, Cynthia A109
Wyrsch, Martha B. A753
Wyrsch, Martha B P549
Wyse, Christopher A493
Wyse, Kenneth L. (Ken) A692
Wyss, Andre A609
Wyss, Andre P391

Wyszkowski, Joni A749
Wyszkowski, Joni E367

X

Xi, Chuyu A428
Xia, Haijun W98
Xia, Howard E225
Xiangjun, Yao W72
Xiangqun, Zhong W72
Xiao, Harry A559
Xiao, Deming E288
Xiaobing, Chang W103
Xiaodong, Liu W72
Xiaolin, Yan W385
Xiaoqiu, Wang W336
Xiaoxuan, Lin W198
Xie, Sophia A284
Xie, Bing A820
Xie, Sophia E120
Xie, Ken E178
Xie, Michael E178
Xin, Xiao Li W103
Xing, Julie A518
Xiquan, Wang W198
Xiyong, Li W431
Xu, Betty A54
Xu, Kaili E131
Xubin, Huang W385
Xudong, Chen W234
Xue, Wang Zhi W103
Xulun, Ma W97
Xun, H A191

Y

Yabannavar, Vijay A554
Yabe, Nobuhiro W249
Yabuki, Jeffery W. A352
Yacob, Ezra Y. A301
Yacob, Desalegn P359
Yadavar, Ravi P678
Yadley, Sloan A704
Yaeger, Jackie P225
Yager, Jennifer A888
Yager, Jennifer E425
Yaggy, Lynne P291
Yagi, Makoto W215
Yagishita, Naomichi W143
Yagita, Masamichi W127
Yagley, Mike E59
Yahrling, Lisa A160
Yajima, Tsutomu W210
Yajima, Susumu W293
Yajnik, Sanjiv A166
Yako, Osamu A938
Yako, Osamu P678
Yakovlev, Vadim W169
Yakushinji, Hideomi W228
Yalamanchili, Lakshmi P496
Yalch, Diane A205
Yaldo, Zaid P47
Yale, Neha P74
Yalof, Stephen J. A761
Yamabe, Dayna P572
Yamada, Maureen P551
Yamada, Yasuhiro W51
Yamada, Yoshiomi W93
Yamada, Ryosuke W107
Yamada, Shoji W126
Yamada, Yuji W127
Yamada, Takashi W127
Yamada, Yoshihiko (Yoshi) W300
Yamada, Noboru W429
Yamaguchi, Hiroshi A19
Yamaguchi, Ikuhiro W221
Yamaguchi, Eiichiro W286
Yamaguchi, Hiroshi W394
Yamakawa, Mark P585
Yamakoshi, Koji W30
Yamamoto, Kazuo W191
Yamamoto, Ichiro W214

Yamamoto, Takashi W262
Yamanaka, Yasushi W132
Yamane, Yoshi W186
Yamane, Kenji W301
Yamaoka, Hiromi W51
Yamasaki, Takashi W228
Yamashina, Hiroko W298
Yamashita, Jadine A63
Yamashita, Akinori W11
Yamashita, Tadaie W40
Yamashita, Toshihiko W253
Yamashita, Mitsuhiko (Mike) W260
Yamashita, Yoshinori W324
Yamashita, Masashi W350
Yamatsuka, Jean A57
Yamatsuka, Jean P33
Yamauchi, Yasuhiro W283
Yamauchi, Masaki W430
Yamazaki, Yuji W374
Yamazoe, Shigeru W249
Yan, Lucy A64
Yan, Kelly A137
Yan, Bo A421
Yan, Helene A468
Yan, Yingli (Christine) A778
Yan, Nancy A818
Yan, Lihua P49
Yanagi, Hiroyuki W430
Yanagi, Jeff E326
Yanagisawa, David S. A504
Yanagisawa, David S. E251
Yanai, Tadashi W160
Yanaranop, Cholanat W351
Yancey, Terri A228
Yancey, Carol B. A379
Yancey, Stephen A379
Yancopoulos, George D. A710
Yancy, Luke A343
Yancy, Luke E164
Yandell, Candy E391
Yanfeng, Zhu W305
Yang, Irene A200
Yang, Yvonne A349
Yang, Taiyin A385
Yang, Peter A404
Yang, David A404
Yang, Kristie A676
Yang, Honggang P390
Yang, Sui W72
Yang, Amy W123
Yang, Elton W317
Yang, Shen W336
Yang, Thomas T. E59
Yang, Wenge E128
Yang, Peter E199
Yang, David E199
Yang, Kristie E338
Yanik, Sahin A266
Yanik, Sahin P182
Yanjiang, Li W96
Yanjun, Wang W72
Yankanich, Jackie A741
Yankanich, Jackie E364
Yankee, Colin A840
Yankevich, Alexei W169
Yankui, Mu W424
Yano, James A. (Jay) A781
Yano, Nancy P242
Yanok, Gregg A850
Yanshun, Chen W72
Yantis, Debbie A185
Yanzetich, Kevin E47
Yao, Felix A145
Yao, Fiona A284
Yao, Dong W98
Yao, Hiroshi W259
Yao, Howard E8
Yao, Fiona E120
Yao, Wenqing E226
Yao, Jay E290
Yap, Stella A135
Yap, Ronald P155
Yapp, Kelli A711
Yapp, John A742
Yapp, Kelli P444

Yarbrough, Mary A890
Yarbrough, Gerald P299
Yarbrough, Shelly P646
Yarde, Terence E143
Yardley, Scott A462
Yardley, William T P22
Yardley, Bill P22
Yardley, Scott P256
Yardley, William T. (Bill) P509
Yarimizu, Hiroshi W252
Yarlagadda, Choudhary A191
Yarobough, Martin P206
Yaros, Joseph A211
Yaros, Joseph E83
Yarrington, Patricia E. (Pat) A190
Yaryura, Ricardo P473
Yasaki, Glen A912
Yasseri, Amir A505
Yasuda, Daisuke A740
Yasuda, Masamichi (Mitch) W262
Yasui, Shinichi W400
Yatch, Emily A278
Yates, Robert A212
Yates, Robert A222
Yates, Kim A276
Yates, Lloyd M. A281
Yates, Brock A445
Yates, Beth A491
Yates, Dustin A747
Yates, W. Rufus A849
Yates, Richard P189
Yates, Vinson M. P395
Yates, A. David E447
Yau, Benjamin A419
Yaudes, Jason T. P35
Yazzie, Beverly P649
Ybarra, Francisco A45
Ybarra, Paco A203
Ye, Xiangdong W190
Yeager, Lori A160
Yeager, David A555
Yeager, Rande K. A622
Yeap, Geoffrey A695
Yearley, Douglas C. (Doug) A837
Yearous, Timothy A258
Yeater, Patrick A188
Yedla, Anupama P571
Yedvab, Lauren P374
Yee, Nancy A54
Yee, Tammy A54
Yee, James A85
Yee, Jessie A562
Yee, Michael A826
Yee, April A827
Yee, James E26
Yee, Michael E342
Yeghyayan, Silva A717
Yegneswaran, Pk A554
Yeh, Openmind W123
Yeh, Cheng E131
Yehiely, Fruma P389
Yehlen, Lorraine P564
Yeigh, Bjong Wolf A880
Yeigh, Bjong Wolf P640
Yeleswaram, Swamy E226
Yelicanin, Nicholas A881
Yelicanin, Nicholas E421
Yellen, Janet L. A322
Yellig, Laura P415
Yellin, Jason P555
Yellin, Jonathan D. E102
Yelverton, Richard A103
Yelverton, Greg A452
Yemin, Ezra Uzi A260
Yen, David A199
Yen, Andy A284
Yen, Andy E119
Yennie, Heather A448
Yennie, Heather P247
Yeo, Sally P246
Yeo, Sang-Deog (Eddie) W236
Yeoman, Justin P356
Yepes, Maria P299
Yerigan, Marna A340
Yerigan, Marna E161

COMBINED HOOVER'S HANDBOOK INDEX OF EXECUTIVES

A = AMERICAN BUSINESS
E = EMERGING COMPANIES
P = PRIVATE COMPANIES
W = WORLD BUSINESS

Yerkes, Nick A347
Yerkes, Nick E167
Yerkes, John B E266
Yesho, LaDawn D. A737
Yesho, LaDawn D. E361
Yeskie, Andrew P313
Yetemian, Michael A590
Yetto, Kristin A287
Yetton, Jason W424
Yeverino, Norma A170
Yezhkov, Sergey E133
Yi, Sang A939
Yi, Yue W72
Yi, Hao W385
Yi-bin, Chien W185
Yiannas, Frank A902
Yieh, Ellie A74
Yihye, Samer Haj W49
Yilin, Wang W301
Yim, Chang-Hee W311
Yimin, Lu W103
Yin, Cynthia A511
Yin, Paul P49
Yin, Cynthia P290
Ying, Song W72
Yingling, Nathaniel A325
Yio, Chris A740
Yiovanakos, John A204
Yip, Gordon A141
Ylonen, Paul A885
Yoakum, Jeffrey A89
Yocham, William P424
Yochum, Alice P114
Yocum, Deb P530
Yocum, Patricia R P537
Yoder, Lamont A117
Yoder, Ernest P47
Yoder, Lamont P61
Yoder, Katherine P171
Yoder, Cathy P519
Yoder, Kylie P610
Yogaratnam, Jeysen A480
Yohe, Erik A421
Yohe, Joseph A P570
Yoho, Franklin H. A281
Yokley, Jack A343
Yokley, Jack E164
Yokoo, Hiroshi W11
Yokouchi, Ryuzo W289
Yokoyama, Terunori W379
Yokum, Dan A132
Yoldas, Erol P101
Yon, Linda A909
Yon, Linda E436
Yoney, Dennis A722
Yoneyama, Yoshiteru W169
Yong, Tang W102
Yong, Li W110
Yong, Wei W336
Yong-soo, Huh W176
Yongliang, Wu W97
Yongqi, Zhao W227
Yoo, Tae A198
Yoo, Christie A431
Yoo, Lina A692
Yoo, Cheol Woo W193
Yoo, Christie E216
Yoon, Steve A156
Yoon, Sei Seung A695
Yoon, Jong Kyoo W217
Yoon, Dong-Jun W311
Yoor, Brian B. A5
York, Max A374
York, Greg A391
York, Johnny P96
York, John P599
York, Stephen E24
Yorks, Andrew A519
Yoshida, Hitoshi A565
Yoshida, Shinya W257
Yoshida, Yoshiyuki W282
Yoshida, Mamoru W301
Yoshida, Kazuo W349
Yoshida, Kenichiro W361
Yoshikawa, Randi A109
Yoshikawa, Matthew A833
Yoshikawa, Naotoshi W93
Yoshikawa, Masato W227
Yoshikawa, Tetsuya W266
Yoshimoto, Haruyuki W127
Yoshimura, Toshiharu W360
Yoshinaga, Yasuyuki W366
Yoshino, Takashi W360
Yoshioka, James P137
Yoshioka, Nobuyasu W51
Yost, Joseph P. A395
Yost, Kevin C. P668
Yoston, Jenifer P676
Yosu, Steve P214
You, Peter A204
You, Hai A686
Youatt, June P339
Youdeem, Gilda A104
Youkey, Jerry R. P430
Youmans, Adam A184
Youmei, Dong W72
Younes, George E319
Young, Val A3
Young, Robert H. A25
Young, James N A37
Young, Dennis A52
Young, Tom A54
Young, Ray G. A77
Young, Diane A89
Young, Robin A89
Young, Michael A107
Young, David A115
Young, Jackson A115
Young, Stephen A181
Young, David A184
Young, Brenda A191
Young, Ruben A218
Young, Jim A222
Young, Steven K. A281
Young, John A306
Young, Stacy A326
Young, Chris A327
Young, Steve A376
Young, Matthew A381
Young, Kevin A385
Young, Marlon A439
Young, Lesli C A440
Young, Jeremy A449
Young, Mark A449
Young, Monica A452
Young, Pete A476
Young, Christopher D. (Chris) A501
Young, Maureen A537
Young, Yvette A538
Young, Barbara A538
Young, Cynthia A571
Young, Steve A577
Young, Nate A593
Young, Renee A596
Young, C. Erik A644
Young, John D. A657
Young, Rita A713
Young, Tracie A719
Young, Dennis R. A742
Young, Wayne A784
Young, Mark R. A843
Young, Chris A891
Young, Joby A902
Young, Robert H. A908
Young, Mark R. A940
Young, Kevin P7
Young, Robert H. P14
Young, James N P27
Young, Lynn P114
Young, Christopher P140
Young, Mark P199
Young, Terrance P225
Young, Rebecca P227
Young, Tammy P233
Young, Zachary P274
Young, Carmen P338
Young, Joanna P339
Young, Sandra P344
Young, Dori P352
Young, Svetlana P402
Young, Bob P496
Young, Gary S. P563
Young, Randy P568
Young, Mary R P583
Young, Fred P588
Young, Michael P644
Young, James P652
Young, Nancy P655
Young, Theresay P656
Young, Jessica P657
Young, William L. W244
Young, David E38
Young, Jackson E38
Young, Stephen E70
Young, Terrence E89
Young, Steve E149
Young, Roberta E149
Young, Craig E215
Young, Jeremy E220
Young, Mark E220
Young, George E264
Young, Tracie E355
Young, Bryce E371
Young, Robert H. E436
Young, Jeff E440
Young-bong, Ha W176
Young-deuk, Lim W192
Young-ki, Son W176
Youngblood, Mike A550
Youngblood, Allison A717
Youngblood, Mike P319
Youngblood, Allison E351
Younger, Todd A925
Younger, Jon P537
Younger, Todd E445
Youngerman, Chuck A713
Younggren, Craig A491
Youngquist, Gene P82
Youngs, Michael P171
Yount, Dave P409
Youso, Steven R. A371
Youso, Steven R. P213
Youssef, Tarek A658
Youssef, Elie P122
Youssef, Matthew P335
Yovich, Mark A522
Yow, John A852
Yowan, David L E15
Ysteboe, Mark A502
Yu, Erix A74
Yu, Frank A249
Yu, Gwendolyn A574
Yu, Li A676
Yu, Gladys A692
Yu, Teb A746
Yu, Angel A779
Yu, Daniel A884
Yu, Nancy P333
Yu, Chun-mei P507
Yu, Yong W179
Yu, Xia W227
Yu, Seong W311
Yu, Frank E109
Yu, Li E338
Yuan, Carol A170
Yuan, Dana A695
Yuan, Bing W385
Yuan, Wei E290
Yuann, Susan E290
Yuanqing, Yang W234
Yudin, Alexander A581
Yue, Ian A564
Yue, Li W99
Yuejia, Sha W99
Yuen, Edmund A742
Yuen, Shelten G P227
Yuen, Wang Kai W96
Yuen, Loretta W299
Yuhas, George A. E72
Yuhong, Xie W110
Yuksel, Ozlem A740
Yule, Chris A54
Yultyev, Aleksandr P218
Yun, William Y. A363
Yun, Sun W72
Yunck, Kara P76
Yunoki, Osamu W160
Yupu, Wang W101
Yurgens, Igor W333
Yurich, Steve P. W256
Yuse, Richard R. (Rick) A706
Yusuf, Kareem A465
Yuzhuo, Zhang W102
Yvonne, Luttschwager P529
Yzaguirre, Joe P153
Yuce, Burcu Civelek W19
Yuksel, Alper Hakan W18

Z

Zaas, David P187
Zaballos, Peter E384
Zabaneh, Samir P234
Zabel, Matt A804
Zabicki, Katherina A641
Zabicki, Katherina P407
Zablocki, Edward P586
Zabriskie, Kathryn E91
Zaccariello, Giovanni A801
Zacconi, Riccardo A10
Zachan, Michael P. (Mike) E58
Zacharias, Elizabeth A511
Zacharias, Elizabeth P290
Zacharius, Sherrie P553
Zachary, Beth D. P6
Zachary, Jayton P302
Zachazewski, James A641
Zachazewski, James P407
Zack, Linda A444
Zack, Matthew E22
Zacur, Mark A833
Zadoks, Jeff A. A672
Zador, John A609
Zadrazil, Robert W407
Zaeske, Mark A. A439
Zafonte, Ross D. P574
Zagar, Frank A498
Zagzebski, Ken A18
Zahani, Nazrin A540
Zaharis, Chris P195
Zahedpour, Soheila A722
Zahka, Susan P220
Zahn, Chip P475
Zahner, Rick E185
Zahrt, Deb P49
Zaic, Daniel A149
Zaidman, Lily A654
Zaiter, Joe A704
Zajdel, Joseph A357
Zajdel, Joseph E175
Zajicek, Randall C. (Randy) A716
Zak, Jenal A222
Zakem, Jami E450
Zakhour, Lutfi A145
Zakian, Aram A114
Zakian, Aram E36
Zale, Kathleen A56
Zales, William A28
Zaleski, Ronald J. A751
Zalewski, Mark A726
Zalewski, Mark P453
Zallaps, Jeff A915
Zallie, James P. A457
Zalman, David A682
Zaluzney, Joseph B. A634
Zaman, Bill A900
Zambanini, Adam D. E409
Zambas, Becky A839
Zambataro, Joseph E86
Zamblera, Jerome A673
Zameczkowski, Anthony A587
Zammer, William P109
Zammit, Patrick A99

Zammit, Patrick A809
Zamora, Julius A859
Zamora, Marcela A890
Zamora, Ligia E427
Zamorano, Juan Pablo A218
Zamore, Neil A98
Zamorski, Thomas P237
Zampi, Jason A604
Zanardo, Fabrizio A692
Zanavich, W Marie P593
Zanayed, Juwana A623
Zanayed, Juwana E313
Zanco, Joseph B A426
Zanco, Joseph B. E212
Zander, Winfried W181
Zandvliet, Vincent A465
Zane, Kelly E172
Zanen, Nicolas A187
Zanen, Nicolas A188
Zanetich, Thomas N. P668
Zanetich, Tommy P668
Zanetton, Fausto A574
Zang, Linda P644
Zangari, Peter J. E290
Zanghi, Phyllis A150
Zanghi, Anna A544
Zangrilli, Janine A719
Zangrilli, Janine E355
Zanin, Ryan A312
Zank, Dennis W. A704
Zann, Greg A203
Zanni, Dave P5
ZANNINI, ALESSANDRO MASETTI W410
Zanolini, Annalena A109
Zanolli, Stephen A575
Zanten, Walter Van A668
Zapalac, Richard Rick A A180
Zapalac, Richard A. (Rick) A180
Zaparanick, Melissa A409
Zapin, Ross A762
Zappa, James (Jim) A194
Zaratzian, Dionne A488
Zarcone, Dominick P. (Nick) A524
Zarcufsky, Shana P405
Zardecki, James A248
Zardecki, James E107
Zardus, Craig A640
Zaretsky, Zev A749
Zaretsky, Zev E367
Zarian, Vladimir P137
Zarling, Kathy P467
Zarske, Samantha P285
Zaruba, Jeffrey A188
Zarubi, Kathy P478
Zasaretti, Loletta P465
Zaslav, David M. A270
Zaslavsky, Leah A243
Zastrow, Raymond A571
Zatina, Mary P75
Zatta, Jayson M. A908
Zatta, Jay A908
Zatta, Jayson M. E436
Zatta, Jay E436
Zauk, Adel M P519
Zauner, Alois P472
Zavaglia, Mary A727
Zavaglia, Mary P453
Zavala, Tony A246
Zavala, Elsa I. A249
Zavala, Veronica A900
Zavala, Donna P162
Zavala, Tony E105
Zavala, Elsa I. E108
Zavarella, Andrew A346
Zavarella, Andrew E166
Zavelovich, Lacey E132
Zawacki, Mark A458
Zayas, Ricardo A151
Zazon, Sue E. A444
Zazzarino, Carolyn A531
Zbell, Jennifer A906
Zbell, Jennifer E435
Zboray, Colleen P254
Zdrojeski, Christine A408

Zdunich, Amber P270
Zebian, Adam E330
Zebroski, Robin P439
Zebula, Charles E. (Chuck) A51
Zech, Gretchen A81
Zech, Kurt E245
Zechmeister, Michael P. A869
Zedeck, David A522
Zeev, Eti Ben W49
Zeevi, Gary P484
Zega, Ron A837
Zegal, Chris E433
Zehm, Laura P152
Zehr, Merle E3
Zeidel, Mark L. P79
Zeidler, Juergen A6
Zeiger, Vicki A51
Zeigler, Michael A565
Zeile, Arthur A581
Zeile, Arthur E294
Zeiler, Karen A571
Zeiler, Ann A605
Zeilor, Eric A798
Zeine, Elias P47
Zeinert, Bonnie A315
Zeitchick, Mark E250
Zeithaml, Carl P. P442
Zeitlin, Jide J. A801
Zeitz, Jochen A407
Zekoski, Joseph (Joe) A392
Zekraus, Edward A356
Zeldin, Marian A559
Zelermyer, Salo A887
Zeleszko, Tony A888
Zeleszko, Tony E425
Zelgart, David A3
Zelinske, John A559
Zell, Samuel A68
Zell, Lisa A194
Zell, Kristin A623
Zell, Lisa P133
Zell, Kristin E313
Zeller, Rick A161
Zeller, Luke A621
Zeller, Anthony A746
Zeller, Ken A850
Zeller, Pat P469
Zeller, James P596
Zeller, Luke E312
Zellman, David P524
Zellner, Jon A452
Zelnick, Strauss E387
Zemaitis, Kathleen A528
Zemanek, Kristin A518
Zember, Dennis J. A62
Zember, Dennis J. E20
Zemering, Christo A177
Zemke, Lisa A423
Zemkoski, Alex A246
Zemkoski, Alex E105
Zemlyak, James M. A787
Zen-Ruffinen, Bernard S. E248
Zendejas, Esperanza P102
Zender, Dale P410
Zeng, Qiang P543
Zenger, Mitch Null A199
Zenner, Jeanette A520
Zeno, Zoraida P466
Zens, Scot P173
Zente, Thomas A702
Zepeda, Carl P133
Zeppos, Nicholas S. P599
Zerbo, Joann A248
Zerbo, Joann E107
Zerbs, Michael W53
Zerhouni, Elias A A254
Zerio, Alex A544
Zernicke, Paul P383
Zetsche, Dieter W125
Zettel, John P57
Zetter, Bruce P558
Zettler, Casey A323
Zetwick, James (Jim) A595
Zeumer, Jim A690
Zevitas, Zachary P229

Zezzo, Anthony (Tony) E317
Zgombic, John A657
Zgonc, Kevin A329
Zha, Tao A319
Zhang, Lin A45
Zhang, Gene A126
Zhang, Cherry A139
Zhang, Guoqiang A151
Zhang, Frank A203
Zhang, Stella A203
Zhang, Helen A262
Zhang, Connell A289
Zhang, Ying A460
Zhang, Chet A483
Zhang, Stephen A559
Zhang, Jizhi A613
Zhang, Hongfei A713
Zhang, Steve P49
Zhang, Cherry P93
Zhang, Haizheng P314
Zhang, Richard P314
Zhang, Luxi P610
Zhang, Han P621
Zhang, Jianwei W73
Zhang, Xiaohua W98
Zhang, Guansong E179
Zhang, Daoping E290
Zhang, Helen E359
Zhao, Wenbiao A54
Zhao, Susan X P472
Zhao, Huan W12
Zhao, Qingchun W431
Zhao, Honggang W431
Zhao, Silvia E290
Zheng, Ru A149
Zheng, Zijian A896
Zheng, Baohua P475
Zhengzhang, Zhao W301
Zhenjiang, Li W12
Zhenming, Chang W108
Zhi, Huang A315
Zhi, Lin E257
Zhiqiang, He (George) W234
Zhiqing, Wang W354
Zhixin, Chen W336
Zhong, Xj E179
Zhou, Lily A198
Zhou, Ping P304
Zhou, Yongyi W165
Zhou, Hui W190
Zhou, Shawn E24
Zhu, Alex A108
Ziacik, Thomas A909
Ziacik, Thomas E436
Zickefoose, John Z P160
Zidar, Thomas P. (Tom) A925
Zidar, Thomas P. (Tom) E445
Ziebell, William F. A369
Ziecheck, Hal P349
Ziegler, Greg A195
Ziegler, Marie A693
Ziegler, Richard A P37
Ziegler, Andy P476
Ziegler, Marie E341
Zieglgansberger, Drew W92
ZIELINSKI, MIKE A3
Zielinski, Thomas C. A69
Zielinski, Miroslaw A661
Zielinski, Jeff A842
Zielinski, Bill A845
Ziemba, Lawrence M. (Larry) A662
Ziemba, Peter M. E447
Ziemianski, Karen P197
Zientara, David B P82
Zietlow, Paul A224
Zietlow, Donald P. (Don) P283
Zietlow, Steve P283
Ziffer, Jack A. P63
Zijderveld, Jan W408
Zijderveld, Jan W409
Zik, Eran W49
Zike, Nancy A346
Zike, Nancy E166
Zilbermann, Mark P556
Zilewicz, Eric A161

Zill, Michael A123
Zilvetti, George A544
Zilwa, Shane De E429
Ziman, Philip E316
Ziman, Richard S. E357
Zimmaro, Lisa P546
Zimmer, Anthony A37
Zimmer, Jeffrey J. A80
Zimmer, James A346
Zimmer, Tyler A375
Zimmer, Kris A. A776
Zimmer, Anthony P27
Zimmer, Tyler P215
Zimmer, Kris A. P512
Zimmer, Ing. Hans-Josef W151
Zimmer, James E166
Zimmerer, Maximilian W24
Zimmerli, Bert A451
Zimmerli, Bert R. A462
Zimmerli, Bert P249
Zimmerli, Bert R. P256
Zimmerman, James F A345
Zimmerman, Ron A449
Zimmerman, Michael R. A453
Zimmerman, Shawn A487
Zimmerman, Stanley A540
Zimmerman, Matt A552
Zimmerman, Scott A651
Zimmerman, Kent A715
Zimmerman, Christine A724
Zimmerman, Seth A804
Zimmerman, Matthew T. A834
Zimmerman, Jennifer P81
Zimmerman, Christopher (Chris) P97
Zimmerman, Kate P306
Zimmerman, Christine P452
Zimmerman, Gregory E E134
Zimmerman, Craig K. E136
Zimmerman, Julie E143
Zimmerman, James F E165
Zimmerman, Ron E221
Zimmerman, Matt E275
Zimmerman, Scott E329
Zimmerman, Timothy K. E386
Zimmermann, Deirdre A. P439
Zimmermann, Douglas E275
Zimmermann, Doug E275
Zimpfer, Matthew J. (Matt) A212
Zinchik, Alina A793
Zingariello, Filippo P496
Zinger, INA P129
Zingman, Barry P348
Zingoni, Maria Victoria W321
Ziniti, Joe A649
Zink, Mark A329
Zink, Daniel A552
Zink, Lauren P252
Zink, Daniel E276
Zinkan, Rob P610
Zinkin, Peter P60
Zinkula, Mark W233
Zinman, Jack E64
Zinn, Judy P101
Zinner, Michael J. P63
Zino, Jillian A692
Zins, Sebastien A740
Ziola, Andrew A630
Zionts, Paul P175
Zipf, Bruce G. A708
Zipparro, Vincent P356
Zitkus, Lester E197
Zito, Peter A590
Zito, Joseph A871
Zito-Volynets, Patricia P369
Zitterkopf, Brian A483
Zitting, Shaun A431
Zivelonghi, G. Larry A249
Zivelonghi, G. Larry E108
Zivley, Jill T E327
Ziyadeh, Omar P664
Zizzi, Michele A374
Zlaket, Mike P97
Zlatkis, Bella W343
Zmich, Kenneth W. P119
Zmoyro, Larisa P304

COMBINED HOOVER'S HANDBOOK INDEX OF EXECUTIVES

```
A = AMERICAN BUSINESS
E = EMERGING COMPANIES
P = PRIVATE COMPANIES
W = WORLD BUSINESS
```

Zobair, Talha A608
Zobrist, Sandra A161
Zoccoli, James G. (Zeke) E4
Zock, George J A432
Zockoll, Ken E143
Zoeller, Kathrin A596
Zogg, Jack A369
Zoghbi, Huda A710
Zohn, Patrick P141
Zoilo, John P131
Zoiss, Edward J. (Ed) A501
Zola, S. Robert (Bob) E78
Zolenas, Joseph A478
Zolenas, Joseph P268
Zoley, George C. E185
Zoller, Clifford A734
Zoller, Jeff A799
Zoller, Richard P334
Zoller, Edgar W62
Zollmann, Mary Ann P301
Zolnowski, David A530
Zongyan, Zhang W101
Zontos, Donna A287
Zonyk, Brent A606
Zook, Dennis R. A242
Zorn, Tom A176
ZORN, ELIZABETH P418
Zorn, Debbie P625
Zorn, Eric E356
Zorzi, Mia P630
Zou, Peter A364
Zou, Ed A632
Zoullas, Sophocles N. E117
Zoullas, Alexis P. E117
Zoullas, Alexis P. E118
Zubeck, Barbara P608
Zuber, Maria P314
Zuber, Steven P362
Zuberi, Faheem A440
Zubkov, Victor A. W309
Zubretsky, Joseph M. A570
Zubrickas, J. V. W212
Zucal, Jim P384
Zucaro, Aldo C. (Al) A622
Zucker, Keith P646
Zucker, Nehemia (Hemi) E240
Zuckerberg, Mark A310
Zuckerman, Jason A692
Zuehlke, Vonnie A804
Zuengler, Hugh A900
Zuhl, Colleen A. A834
Zuhlke, Dan A462
Zuhlke, Dan P256
Zuhlke, Eric P478
Zuhone, Laura A346
Zuhone, Laura E166
Zuiker, Joe E291
Zuk, Donna P75
Zukis, Katy A447
Zukowski, Andrew P448
Zulaica, Katya A204
Zulberti, Andrea A795
Zulli, Mark A893
Zuluaga, Patricia W144
Zulueta, Alfonso G. (Chito) A517
Zumbahlen, Zane A419
Zumwalt, LeAnne M. A257
Zundel, Shayne A746
Zuniga, Ramiro A179
Zuniga, Gaspar A480
Zuniga, Aamsa A703
Zuniga, Aamsa P439
Zupan, Leon W150
Zupko, Chris A929
Zupko, Chris E449
Zupo, Robert A872
Zurack, Marlene A588
Zurack, Marlene P365
Zuraitis, Marita A432
Zuraitis, Nancy P56
Zurek, Thomas M A628
Zurek, Thomas M P396
Zuro, Matthew A337
Zuro, Matthew E158
Zuschke, Stefan W77
Zussman, Corey P412
Zuziak, Jeffrey P496
Zvada, Robert A266
Zvada, Robert P181
Zwach, Jennifer A61
Zwang, Jonathan A701
Zwany, Abe A145
Zweier, George E. E53
Zwiebel, Rob A727
Zwiebel, Rob P453
Zydel, Brian A21
Zygiel, Kenneth A409
Zyl, Adriaan Van A100
Zyl, Adriaan Van P58
Zysk, Ralf A661
Zywicz, Margaret AE A349
Zuhlke, Oliver W61